YEARBOOK OF THE
UNITED NATIONS
1993

Volume 47

Yearbook of the United Nations, 1993

Volume 47   Sales No. E.94.I.1

Prepared by the Yearbook Section of the Department of Public Information, United Nations, New York. Although the *Yearbook* is based on official sources, it is not an official record.

Chief Editor: Yobert K. Shamapande.

Senior Editors: Kathryn Gordon, Christine B. Koerner.

Editors/Writers: Matthias Gueldner, Peter Jackson, Kikuko Maeyama, Melody C. Pfeiffer, Pio Schurti.

Contributing Editors/Writers: Dmitri Marchenkov, Juanita J. B. Phelan.

Copy Editors: Alison M. Koppelman, Janet E. Root.

Indexer: Elaine P. Adam.

Editorial Assistants: Lawri M. Moore, Nidia H. Morisset, Leonard M. Simon, Elizabeth Tabert.

Typesetter: Sunita Chabra.

YEARBOOK

OF THE
UNITED
NATIONS
1993

Volume 47

Department of Public Information
United Nations, New York

Martinus Nijhoff Publishers
DORDRECHT / BOSTON / LONDON

Published by Martinus Nijhoff Publishers
P.O. Box 163, 3300 AD Dordrecht, The Netherlands

Kluwer Academic Publishers incorporates the
publishing programmes of Martinus Nijhoff Publishers

Sold and distributed in the U.S.A. and Canada
by Kluwer Academic Publishers,
101 Philip Drive, Norwell, MA 02061, U.S.A.

In all other countries, sold and distributed
by Kluwer Academic Publishers Group,
P.O. Box 322, 3300 AH Dordrecht, The Netherlands

Yearbook of the United Nations, 1993
Vol. 47
ISBN: 0-7923-3077-3
ISSN: 0082-8521

UNITED NATIONS PUBLICATION
SALES NO. E.94.I.1

Printed in the United States of America

Foreword

T HE EVENTS OF 1993 DEMONSTRATED the compelling urgency for the United Nations to promote three underlying goals of its efforts: peace, development and democracy. They are interlocking and mutually reinforcing.

The United Nations peace operations in the field, most prominently in Cambodia, El Salvador, Somalia and the former Yugoslavia, ranged beyond the traditional notion and definition of peace-keeping, as they took on political, social, humanitarian and environmental dimensions. The concept of development also adopted an integrated approach; it was no longer merely a matter of economic policy and resources. Development meant political, social and cultural nation-building and took into account the educational and environmental imperatives of our time.

Democracy has re-emerged as another hallmark in the conduct of international affairs. Just as peace is a prerequisite to development, democracy is essential for sustainable development. State after State has found the immense value of popular participation in the development process, of democratization of national institutions and of the protection of the fundamental human rights of all citizens.

The globalization of international affairs presents the Organization with unique opportunities to take practical and urgent measures designed to advance the purposes and principles of the Charter. It also requires a profoundly renewed approach to information gathering and dissemination so as to engage the highest confidence of the international community in the United Nations. I trust that, as a faithful record of United Nations activities, this volume of the *Yearbook of the United Nations* will contribute significantly to a better knowledge and appreciation of the cooperative international endeavours to promote peace and construct a sustainable future for humanity.

Boutros BOUTROS-GHALI
Secretary-General
New York
October 1994

Contents

Part One: *Political and security questions*

Part Two: *Regional questions*

Part Three: *Economic and social questions*

Part Four: *Legal questions*

Part Five: *Administrative and budgetary questions*

Part Six: *Intergovernmental organizations related to the United Nations*

Appendices

Indexes

About the 1993 edition of the *Yearbook*

The *YEARBOOK OF THE UNITED NATIONS* stands as the single most comprehensive and up-to-date reference tool on the activities of the United Nations. The Department of Public Information of the United Nations remains committed to a timely annual publication of the *Yearbook* in order to ensure that the research community and the general public receive detailed and current accounts of the work of the United Nations. The efforts to ensure a timely publication of the *Yearbook*, however, pose the problem of having to rely on provisional documentation and other materials to prepare the relevant articles. As a result, all Security Council resolutions in the present volume are provisional, as the final texts were not available at the time of going to press.

Structure and scope of articles

The *Yearbook* is subject-oriented, dealing with political and security questions, regional questions, economic and social questions, legal questions, administrative and budgetary questions, and intergovernmental organizations related to the United Nations. Various chapters and topical headings present summaries of pertinent United Nations activities, including those of intergovernmental and expert bodies, major reports, Secretariat activities and, in selected cases, the views of States in written communications. The document symbols of all major reports cited appear in the REFERENCES, which are listed at the end of each chapter or subchapter and linked by numerical indicators to the text.

Activities of United Nations bodies. All resolutions, decisions and other major activities of the principal organs and, where applicable, those of subsidiary bodies are either reproduced or summarized in the respective articles. The texts of all resolutions and decisions of substantive nature adopted in 1993 by the General Assembly, the Security Council, the Economic and Social Council and the Trusteeship Council are reproduced or summarized under the relevant topic. These texts are followed by the procedural details giving date of adoption, meeting number and vote totals (in favour-against-abstaining); information on their approval by a sessional or subsidiary body prior to final adoption, approved amendments and committee reports; and a list of sponsors. Also given are the document symbols of any financial implications and relevant meeting numbers. Details are also provided of any recorded or roll-call vote on the resolution/decision as a whole.

Major reports. Most reports of the Secretary-General, in 1993, along with selected reports from other United Nations sources, such as seminars and working groups, are summarized briefly.

Secretariat activities. The operational activities of the United Nations for development and humanitarian assistance are described under the relevant topics. For major activities financed outside the United Nations regular budget, information is given, wherever available, on contributions and expenditures. Financial data are generally obtained from the audited accounts prepared for each fund and cover the 1993 calendar year unless otherwise specified.

Views of States. Written communications sent to the United Nations by Member States and circulated as documents of the principal organs have been summarized in selected cases, under the relevant topic. Substantive actions by the Security Council have been analysed and brief reviews of the Council's deliberations given, particularly in cases where an issue was taken up but no resolution was adopted.

Related organizations. The *Yearbook* also briefly describes the 1993 activities of the specialized agencies and other related organizations of the United Nations system.

Terminology

Formal titles of bodies, organizational units, conventions, declarations and officials are given in full on first mention in an article or sequence of articles. They are also used in resolution/decision texts, and in the SUBJECT INDEX under the key word of the title. Short titles may be used in subsequent references.

How to find information in the *Yearbook*

The 1993 edition, like the previous volumes, has been designed to enable the user to locate information on United Nations activities by the use of the table of contents, the SUBJECT INDEX and the INDEX OF RESOLUTIONS AND DECISIONS. The *Yearbook* also contains five appendices. APPENDIX I comprises a roster of Member States; APPENDIX II reproduces the Charter of the United Nations, including the Statute of the International Court of Justice; APPENDIX III gives the structure of the principal organs of the United Nations; APPENDIX IV provides the agenda for each session of the principal organs in 1993; and APPENDIX V gives the addresses of the United Nations information centres and services worldwide.

ABBREVIATIONS COMMONLY USED IN THE *YEARBOOK*

ACABQ	Advisory Committee on Administrative and Budgetary Questions
ACC	Administrative Committee on Coordination
ACPAQ	Advisory Committee on Post Adjustment Questions
ANC	African National Congress of South Africa
ASEAN	Association of South-East Asian Nations
CCAQ	Consultative Committee on Administrative Questions
CDP	Committee for Development Planning
CEDAW	Committee on the Elimination of Discrimination against Women
CERD	Committee on the Elimination of Racial Discrimination
CFA	Committee on Food Aid Policies and Programmes (WFP)
CILSS	Permanent Inter-State Committee on Drought Control in the Sahel
CPC	Committee for Programme and Coordination
CSDHA	Centre for Social Development and Humanitarian Affairs
DESD	Department of Economic and Social Development
DHA	Department of Humanitarian Affairs
DPI	Department of Public Information
EC	European Community
ECA	Economic Commission for Africa
ECDC	economic cooperation among developing countries
ECE	Economic Commission for Europe
ECLAC	Economic Commission for Latin America and the Caribbean
ECOWAS	Economic Community of West African States
EEC	European Economic Community
ESC	Economic and Social Council
ESCAP	Economic and Social Commission for Asia and the Pacific
ESCWA	Economic and Social Commission for Western Asia
FAO	Food and Agriculture Organization of the United Nations
GA	General Assembly
GATT	General Agreement on Tariffs and Trade
GDP	gross domestic product
GNP	gross national product
IAEA	International Atomic Energy Agency
ICAO	International Civil Aviation Organization
ICITO	Interim Commission for the International Trade Organization
ICJ	International Court of Justice
ICRC	International Committee of the Red Cross
ICSC	International Civil Service Commission
IDA	International Development Association
IFAD	International Fund for Agricultural Development
IFC	International Finance Corporation
ILC	International Law Commission
ILO	International Labour Organisation
IMF	International Monetary Fund
IMO	International Maritime Organization
INCB	International Narcotics Control Board
INSTRAW	International Research and Training Institute for the Advancement of Women
IPF	indicative planning figure (UNDP)
ITC	International Trade Centre (UNCTAD/GATT)
ITO	International Trade Organization
ITU	International Telecommunication Union
JAG	Joint Advisory Group on the International Trade Centre
JIU	Joint Inspection Unit
LDC	least developed country
NATO	North Atlantic Treaty Organization
NGO	non-governmental organization
NPT	Treaty on the Non-Proliferation of Nuclear Weapons
NSGT	Non-Self-Governing Territory
OAS	Organization of American States
OAU	Organization of African Unity
ODA	official development assistance
OECD	Organisation for Economic Cooperation and Development
ONUSAL	United Nations Observer Mission in El Salvador
OPEC	Organization of Petroleum Exporting Countries
PAC	Pan Africanist Congress of Azania
PLO	Palestine Liberation Organization
SC	Security Council
SDR	special drawing right
S-G	Secretary-General
SPC	Special Political Committee
TC	Trusteeship Council
TCDC	technical cooperation among developing countries
TDB	Trade and Development Board (UNCTAD)
TNC	transnational corporation
UN	United Nations
UNAVEM	United Nations Angola Verification Mission
UNCDF	United Nations Capital Development Fund
UNCED	United Nations Conference on Environment and Development
UNCHS	United Nations Centre for Human Settlements (Habitat)
UNCITRAL	United Nations Commission on International Trade Law
UNCTAD	United Nations Conference on Trade and Development
UNDCP	United Nations International Drug Control Programme
UNDOF	United Nations Disengagement Observer Force (Golan Heights)
UNDP	United Nations Development Programme
UNEP	United Nations Environment Programme
UNESCO	United Nations Educational, Scientific and Cultural Organization
UNFICYP	United Nations Peace-keeping Force in Cyprus
UNFPA	United Nations Population Fund
UNHCR	Office of the United Nations High Commissioner for Refugees
UNIC	United Nations Information Centre
UNICEF	United Nations Children's Fund
UNIDIR	United Nations Institute for Disarmament Research
UNIDO	United Nations Industrial Development Organization
UNIFIL	United Nations Interim Force in Lebanon
UNIKOM	United Nations Iraq-Kuwait Observation Mission
UNITAR	United Nations Institute for Training and Research
UNOSOM	United Nations Operation in Somalia
UNPROFOR	United Nations Protection Force
UNRFNRE	United Nations Revolving Fund for Natural Resources Exploration
UNRWA	United Nations Relief and Works Agency for Palestine Refugees in the Near East
UNSO	United Nations Sudano-Sahelian Office
UNTAC	United Nations Transitional Authority in Cambodia
UNU	United Nations University
UNV	United Nations Volunteers
UPU	Universal Postal Union
WFC	World Food Council
WFP	World Food Programme
WHO	World Health Organization
WIPO	World Intellectual Property Organization
WMO	World Meteorological Organization
WTO	World Tourism Organization
YUN	*Yearbook of the United Nations*

EXPLANATORY NOTE ON DOCUMENTS

References at the end of each article in Parts One to Five of this volume give the symbols of the main documents issued in 1993 on the topic, arranged in the order in which they are referred to in the text. The following is a guide to the principal document symbols:

A/- refers to documents of the General Assembly, numbered in separate series by session. Thus, A/48/- refers to documents issued for consideration at the forty-eighth session, beginning with A/48/1. Documents of special and emergency special sessions are identified as A/S- and A/ES-, followed by the session number.

A/C.- refers to documents of the Assembly's Main Committees, e.g. A/C.1/- is a document of the First Committee, A/C.6/-, a document of the Sixth Committee. A/BUR/- refers to documents of the General Committee. A/AC.- documents are those of the Assembly's ad hoc bodies and A/CN.-, of its commissions; e.g. A/AC.105/- identifies documents of the Assembly's Committee on the Peaceful Uses of Outer Space, A/CN.4/-, of its International Law Commission. Assembly resolutions and decisions since the thirty-first (1976) session have been identified by two arabic numerals: the first indicates the session of adoption; the second, the sequential number in the series. Resolutions are numbered consecutively from 1 at each session. Decisions of regular sessions are numbered consecutively, from 301 for those concerned with elections and appointments, and from 401 for all other decisions. Decisions of special and emergency special sessions are numbered consecutively, from 11 for those concerned with elections and appointments, and from 21 for all other decisions.

E/- refers to documents of the Economic and Social Council, numbered in separate series by year. Thus, E/1993/- refers to documents issued for consideration by the Council at its 1993 sessions, beginning with E/1993/1. E/AC.-, E/C.- and E/CN.-, followed by identifying numbers, refer to documents of the Council's subsidiary ad hoc bodies, committees and commissions. For example, E/1993/C.1/- and E/1993/C.2/- refer to documents of the Council's sessional committees, namely, its Economic and Social Committees; E/CN.5/- refers to documents of the Council's Commission for Social Development, E/C.7/-, to documents of its Committee on Natural Resources. E/ICEF/- documents are those of the United Nations Children's Fund (UNICEF). Symbols for the Council's resolutions and decisions, since 1978, consist of two arabic numerals: the first indicates the year of adoption and the second, the sequential number in the series. There are two series: one for resolutions, beginning with 1 (resolution 1993/1); and one for decisions, beginning with 201 (decision 1993/201).

S/- refers to documents of the Security Council. Its resolutions are identified by consecutive numbers followed by the year of adoption in parentheses, beginning with resolution 1(1946).

T/- refers to documents of the Trusteeship Council. Its resolutions are numbered consecutively, with the session at which they were adopted indicated by Roman numerals, e.g. resolution 2196(LX) of the sixtieth session. The Council's decisions are not numbered.

ST/-, followed by symbols representing the issuing department or office, refers to documents of the United Nations Secretariat.

Documents of certain bodies bear special symbols, including the following:

ACC/-	Administrative Committee on Coordination
CD/-	Conference on Disarmament
CERD/-	Committee on the Elimination of Racial Discrimination
DC/-	Disarmament Commission
DP/-	United Nations Development Programme
HS/-	Commission on Human Settlements
ITC/-	International Trade Centre
LOS/PCN/-	Preparatory Commission for the International Seabed Authority and for the International Tribunal for the Law of the Sea
TD/-	United Nations Conference on Trade and Development
UNEP/-	United Nations Environment Programme

Many documents of the regional commissions bear special symbols. These are sometimes preceded by the following:

E/ECA/-	Economic Commission for Africa
E/ECE/-	Economic Commission for Europe
E/ECLAC/-	Economic Commission for Latin America and the Caribbean
E/ESCAP/-	Economic and Social Commission for Asia and the Pacific
E/ESCWA/-	Economic and Social Commission for Western Asia

"L" in a symbol refers to documents of limited distribution, such as draft resolutions; "CONF." to documents of a conference; "INF." to those of general information. Summary records are designated by "SR.", verbatim records by "PV.", each followed by the meeting number.

United Nations sales publications each carry a sales number with the following components separated by periods: a capital letter indicating the language(s) of the publication; two arabic numerals indicating the year; a Roman numeral indicating the subject category; a capital letter indicating a subdivision of the category, if any; and an arabic numeral indicating the number of the publication within the category. Examples: E.93.II.A.2; E/F.R.93.II.E.7; E.93.X.1.

Report of the Secretary-General

Report of the Secretary-General on the work of the Organization

*Following is the Secretary-General's report on the work of the Organization, submitted to the General Assembly and dated 10 September 1993. The Assembly took note of it on 15 October (**decision 48/405**).*

CONTENTS

FIGURES

I. Introduction

1. A year ago the United Nations, its Member States and the peoples of the world recognized that a new opportunity had presented itself. The cold war being over, the United Nations could play the pivotal role in establishing world order and progress that had been assigned to it by the drafters of the Charter.

2. The past 12 months leave no doubt that the opportunity has been grasped in a positive way. The vast potential of the world Organization has been recognized and has begun to be employed in the establishment of a more stable world order: as a strengthened voice for the poorest countries, as deliverer of humanitarian relief, as guardian of human and minority rights, as rescuer of States in crisis and as an instrument for repairing a damaged global environment. In virtually every area, as the present report will show, there have been substantial achievements. But there have been serious set-backs and shortcomings as well. This mixed record is to be expected in view of the comprehensive agenda that we are facing, both in quantitative terms and in the light of its complexity.

3. Beyond the gains and losses inflicted by reality, however, troubling questions of will and purpose have been exposed. The pattern of the past 12 months displays three realities: the comprehensive nature of the global challenge, the indispensability of the United Nations and the gap that has been revealed as the demands of Member States on the Organization are not matched by the resources provided.

4. The comprehensive reality is most clearly revealed through three objectives: peace, development and democracy. They are interlocking and mutually reinforcing.

5. In mid-1992, in my report entitled "An Agenda for Peace", I discussed the need to view efforts for peace as a continuum over time. From

preventive diplomacy to peacemaking and peace-keeping, to post-conflict peace-building, the cycle continues through perpetual rounds. Increasingly we have learned that working for peace provides us with no place of rest.

6.   The past 12 months have demonstrated that peace operations involve interrelated functions. United Nations operations in the field, most prominently in Cambodia, El Salvador, Somalia and the former Yugoslavia, have had to range far beyond the accepted notion and definition of peace-keeping. Virtually every one of the departments and established functions of the United Nations may now be involved in operations for peace. The second generation of peace-keeping is certain to involve not only military but also political, economic, social, humanitarian and environmental dimensions, all in need of a unified and integrated approach.

7.   Development is now understood to involve many dimensions; it is no longer merely a matter of economic policy and resources. Political, social, educational and environmental factors must be part of an integrated approach to development. Without development on the widest scale, the young will be restless, resentful and unproductive. People will fight for resources, and creativity will be misdirected.

8.   A new, workable and widely agreed concept of development still eludes us. Until it is achieved, the United Nations will continue to face a sequence of conflicts.

9.   There can be no flowering of development without the parallel advance of another key concept: democratization. Peace is a prerequisite to development; democracy is essential if development is to succeed over the long term.

10.   The real development of a State must be based on the participation of its population; that requires human rights and democracy. To ensure such an achievement, democratization must not only take hold inside a State, but among States in the international community. And democracy within States can be fully sustained over time only if it is linked to expanding democratization among States and at all levels of the international system.

11.   Without peace, there can be no development and there can be no democracy. Without development, the basis for democracy will be lacking and societies will tend to fall into conflict. And without democracy, no sustainable development can occur; without such development, peace cannot long be maintained.

12.   And so it has become evident that three great concepts and priorities are interlinked, and they must be addressed at every level of human society. We can see in recent events the relationship between the individual, the State and the global society in which we all now participate. In the course of the modern era one or another of

these three has tended to be the primary focus, to the relative neglect of the others.

13.   At one time the individual was seen as having little need for State institutions. At other times the State has been exalted as the supreme object of human effort and sacrifice. And at still other times, the demise of the State has been predicted and an almost transcendental globalism has been promoted as the ultimate goal of life. We are fortunate today to see before us, in the theatre of history, a more integrated vision. The individual has been reaffirmed as the creative source of economic progress, political expression and artistic and intellectual achievement. States and their sovereignty are increasingly recognized as indispensable building-blocks of international order and problem-solving. Cooperative global integration is now an inescapable fact and requirement for all the world's peoples. This is anything but utopian; it is an effort to address compelling problems by practical methods, to produce the cooperative community that can manage global change.

14.   The globalization now taking place requires a profoundly renewed concept of the State. Between the isolated individual and the world there must be an intermediate element, an organized community that enables the individual to participate in the life of the world. This element is the State and its national sovereignty. They respond to the need of all human beings for identification. In a world both impersonal and fragmented, such a need is greater than it ever has been in history.

15.   Individuals find identity in nations. And nations should find identity in universalism. There is no international community if there are no nations. So the opposition between nationalism and globalization is to a large extent false.

16.   In Chapter I of the Charter of the United Nations the founders proclaimed the intention "to develop friendly relations among nations based on respect for the principle of equal rights . . . of peoples". This is the foundation of a well-ordered internationalism. National sovereignty is the art of rendering unequal power equal. Without State sovereignty, the very instrument of international cooperation might be destroyed and international organization might itself become impossible. States are not the only actors in the international arena; they must be part of regional associations and global organizations. Together they provide the framework for collective security and cooperative progress.

17.   Thus from every angle of vision—chronological, practical, functional, conceptual, individual and institutional—we come to one conclusion: humanity's project is now truly universal, and to cope with it we must fashion comprehensive and integral projects, policies and efforts.

18.   The character of the challenges and realities I have outlined here makes it clear that the world Organization—the United Nations—is indispensable. Only the United Nations has the universal character, the global convening power and the extensive networks which cover virtually every international function in the service of all peoples.

19.   As I have prepared this annual report on the work of the Organization, I have tried to do so in a way that reflects the comprehensive approach the times require. The sections proceed from the measures of coordination needed to strengthen the United Nations as an organization, to the development work of the Organization, to activities to strengthen societies against breakdown, to efforts to halt or contain conflict, to peace-keeping operations and peacemaking efforts, to building for a stable future of peace. In the new United Nations all these aspects must be coordinated to bring them into a coherent mission.

20.   I believe that this report provides a fair reflection of the work carried out by the various departments of the Secretariat and by other component parts of the United Nations system. If the work carried out in the economic and social sectors appears to be less focused than the work of the Organization in the fields of peace and security, this is, in my view, an inevitable consequence of the proliferation of intergovernmental bodies and organizations in the economic and social sectors and the lack of an effective coordinating mechanism. I invite further reflection on how that gap could be filled.

21.   It will be evident, from the detailed contents of each section of this report, that the reach of the international community at this time exceeds its grasp. United Nations Forces increasingly find themselves thrust into areas of conflict where major Powers are not willing to venture themselves and are reluctant to make the hard choices posed by a new era of challenges to peace. And the United Nations is struggling to keep a focus on development when the poorest countries no longer hold the same interest for the rich as they did in the previous decades of ideological competition.

22.   Yet, all too often, the eyes of the media are focused on some aspects of the Organization's work to the exclusion of others. As presented in the media, the work of the United Nations appears to centre around the multiple tasks of peace-keeping operations to the near exclusion of other activities. And as regards the media's concern with peace-keeping, the operations in Somalia and Bosnia and Herzegovina dominate reports. One of the aims of this annual report is to correct this distorted view of the Organization's work. Though activities for development may not be as glamorous as peace-keeping operations, they are just as important and, indeed, provide the foundations for global security and stability. Nor are some peace-keeping operations more important than others. The United Nations attaches equal importance to all conflicts.

23.   Global organizations, and especially the United Nations, are being called upon to do a growing share of the public's international work. But it must always be remembered that the Member States are the motive and supporting force of the world Organization. Clearly, the United Nations cannot resolve the major problems on the international agenda in the absence of the political will, sufficient support and continuing commitment which each particular endeavour requires.

24.   The achievements of the past year vastly outweigh the set-backs. Common concern has become more evident and effectively expressed. The readiness to rely upon the United Nations is heartening and gives reason for growing hope that the world Organization will fulfil its original purpose and, beyond that, prove able to adapt to the new challenges of this changing time in history. It is my hope that this annual report, by examining each area of action with a careful eye, will help to reveal the areas which require far greater effort by the Member States and by the United Nations system itself.

25.   Thus while recent accomplishments deserve great credit, they do not provide a sense of true satisfaction. The United Nations renaissance remains in question. The international community stands at a turning-point. There is an undeniable disparity between the vision and the reality. This must be faced squarely by the States Members of the world Organization and the peoples they represent. This report should serve as a stimulus to greater realism, engagement, effort and political creativity. All are essential if the present turning-point is to lead to a successful next stage in shaping the common future.

26.   This is the longest report of the Secretary-General to the General Assembly on the work of the Organization in many years. Yet it still does not do justice to the myriad activities undertaken by the United Nations in the course of the past year. The necessary reform of the Organization's Secretariat has been added to the multiplication of tasks and the emergence of new functions demanded by the Member States. This annual report attempts to reflect, in as factual and comprehensive a manner as possible, the scope and size of the tasks faced by the Organization in the previous year, yet a detailed catalogue of our work would require a report two or three times the size. In view of the growth in our responsibilities, a burden that we willingly accept, the annual report has grown in size and detail.

27.   My hope is that the report does justice to the men and women who have, in the course of

the year, given their time and effort in the service of the United Nations. The end of the cold war offers a valuable opportunity to revitalize the international civil service. In this connection, the General Assembly may wish to consider whether some personnel rules should be revised and whether the conditions of service should be improved to attract the best qualified candidates, particularly at the senior level, to serve in the Organization. I would like to see a system that rewards achievement while insisting on accountability for inadequate performance.

28.   By presenting a comprehensive overview of the work of the United Nations, I wish also to underscore the competence, dedication and industry of the staff of the Organization, who have continued to give of their best while their workload has increased substantially. I pay tribute to the men and women who strive to tackle some of the world's most intractable problems with energy and creativity, sometimes paying with their lives, and who seek to bring the world closer to the promise of our Charter.

II.   Coordinating a comprehensive strategy

"To be a centre for harmonizing the actions of nations in the attainment of these common ends."

Charter of the United Nations, Article 1, paragraph 4

A.   *Organs of the United Nations*

29.   The world is being changed by powerful forces that no State, or even group of States, has the capacity to manage by itself. The United Nations, as an Organization, is therefore embarking on a programme of far-reaching reform to enable it truly to become the instrument of world peace and development that its founders envisioned half a century ago. No organ of the United Nations can fail to be affected by this far-reaching reform process.

1.   General Assembly

30.   The General Assembly is playing an increasingly practical role in world activities. Its workload has remained consistently heavy over the past four sessions, with expanding activities in some areas. The total number of meetings held by the Assembly, its General Committee and Main Committees each year from the forty-fourth to the forty-seventh sessions has remained fairly constant: 436, 412, 418 and 420, respectively. However, the number of meetings held by working groups of the plenary and of the Main Committees during the same period showed a sharp increase. During the forty-fourth session, working groups met 52 times; during the forty-seventh session, they met 77 times. The number of informal meetings held by the Main Committees grew in even more dramatic proportions: from 193 during the forty-fourth session to 313 during the forty-seventh session.

31.   Although the number of resolutions adopted by the General Assembly during this period decreased, resolutions were increasingly adopted without a vote or by consensus. During the forty-seventh session, out of 295 resolutions, 75 per cent were adopted without a vote; by comparison, during the forty-fourth session, out of 336 resolutions, only 65 per cent were adopted without a vote (see figure 1).

32.   The expanding role of the United Nations in the area of peace-keeping was reflected in the activities of the General Assembly. The number of agenda items dealing with the financing of peace-keeping and other field operations more than doubled between the forty-fourth and forty-seventh sessions, from 6 to 14.

33.   From the forty-fourth to the forty-seventh session, the participation of heads of State and Government in the general debates of the General Assembly increased from 14 to 21 per cent. During that same period, the number of Members of the United Nations increased from 159 to 184.

34.   During the main part of its forty-seventh session, the General Assembly considered a wide variety of issues. The resolutions adopted concerned, *inter alia*, the convening of an international peace conference on Somalia, specific actions regarding the situation in Bosnia and Herzegovina, and follow-up action to the United Nations Conference on Environment and Development. The Assembly commended the Convention on the Prohibition of the Development, Production, Stockpiling and Use of Chemical Weapons and on Their Destruction, which has thus far been signed by 148 Member States. The General Assembly requested Member States to submit their views on a possible review of the membership of the Security Council. The Assembly also decided, as a first step in rationalizing its work, to reduce its Main Committees from seven to six.

35.   The work of the General Assembly could be further streamlined. It should be noted that many resolutions, particularly but not exclusively those affecting the economic and social areas, do not address policy issues, but are in the nature of work programme decisions (taking note of a report and requesting the Secretary-General to prepare another report). I suggest that in the interests of efficiency the resolution format be reserved for General Assembly actions that address policy matters and formulate recommendations for action by Member States and the international community. A simpler format could then be adopted for work-programme decisions in the economic and social areas. This system would also bring some order of priority to the agenda of the General Assembly. The agenda is also in need of some rationalization. For example, nine items on the agenda of the forty-seventh session were not discussed at all.

36. I should also like to suggest that, in view of the thousands of documents produced at the United Nations each year, Member States carefully review the need for every report. There are many documents requested by the General Assembly on a recurrent basis that add little or no useful information to the report of the previous year.

2. Security Council

37. In response to the new challenges to international peace and security that have come in the wake of the cold war, the Security Council has informally developed new working patterns even as calls have come for changes in its formal structure. In effect—in contrast to years past when sessions were clearly delineated in time and topic—the Council has found itself meeting almost continuously. During the period from 1 January 1992 to 31 August 1993, the Security Council held 359 sessions of consultations of the whole, totalling some 428 hours. In addition, the Council held 247 formal meetings, adopted 137 resolutions and issued 144 statements by the President (see figures 2 and 3). What has emerged is a pattern of operations akin to that of a task force dealing with situations as they arise, on an almost continuing basis.

38. As a result of these changes, the Security Council is now able to follow more closely, and in a more consistent manner than before, the variety of security threats around the world. But new problems have arisen too. It has become clear that immediate operations dealing urgently with crises around the world need to be supported by a more comprehensive understanding of the array of current challenges. I therefore favour the proposal that periodic sessions of the Council be held at the ministerial level. Informal consultations should be punctuated by more formal meetings in order both to inform, and to seek support from, the wider circle of Member States. And communications with other elements of the world Organization should be improved.

39. The Security Council is in the process of rationalizing its documentation and other procedures, while making its workings more transparent. In this regard, I welcome the decisions to make available to all Member States the tentative forecast of the programme of work of the Security Council for each month, and also to review the list of matters of which the Council is seized with a view to rationalizing it.

40. Pursuant to the request by the General Assembly in resolution 47/62 of 11 December 1992, I invited Member States to submit written comments on a possible review of the membership of the Security Council. Proposals warranting serious study are now on the table. The question of the Security Council's membership structure is of crucial importance, and I look forward to the issue being resolved by the time of the fiftieth anniversary of the Organization.

3. Economic and Social Council

41. The Economic and Social Council is perhaps the organ of the United Nations that received the least attention during the years of the cold war. With economic and social development firmly set as goals in their own right, but also viewed as necessary preconditions for lasting global peace and security, it seems clear that the Council must receive greater attention.

42. In my address to the Economic and Social Council at the high-level segment of its substantive session of 1993, at Geneva on 30 June, I stressed once again the importance of the Council. I also repeated a proposal that I first made last year: the Council should be invited to provide to the Security Council reports on situations in the economic and social areas which, in its opinion, constitute threats to international peace and security. I also recalled my suggestion that the Council introduce a flexible, high-level inter-sessional mechanism to respond in a timely way to new developments. I noted that these proposals had not received serious attention. I take this opportunity to reiterate them.

43. Following discussions during the high-level segment of the substantive session of 1992 of the Economic and Social Council, an ad hoc working group of the Council on enhancing international cooperation for development: the role of the United Nations was established by the President of the Council. Its aim was to complete consultations before the forty-seventh session of the General Assembly and thus to maintain the momentum of the discussions held during the high-level segment. I made available to the Assembly the position papers submitted by delegations or groups of delegations to the ad hoc working group, as well as a compendium of position papers prepared by the secretariat of the Economic and Social Council.

44. At the forty-seventh session, the President of the General Assembly established a second open-ended ad hoc working group of the plenary on agenda item 47 (Restructuring and revitalization of the United Nations in the economic, social and related fields) to continue discussions. The working group held meetings over a period of several months. Negotiations covered a number of significant issues, including the membership and composition of executive boards of United Nations programmes and funds and the financing of operational activities for development. The results of the group's work were officially presented to the President of the Assembly at a plenary meeting on 25 June 1993, immediately before the substantive session of 1993 of the Economic and Social Council. I am sorry to have to report that the

negotiations stalled, and that no action was taken at the meeting.

45.   At the substantive session of 1993 of the Economic and Social Council some progress was made towards reorienting the Council's work to the coordination of the United Nations system. At the high-level segment discussions devoted to the World Summit for Social Development, the contribution of the United Nations system to social development received considerable attention. Concern was expressed that the system should both be unified and function coherently. A number of participants expressed disappointment at the stalling of the talks aimed at restructuring the Economic and Social Council.

46.   I remain hopeful that the efforts and good will of Member States in pursuing the revitalization of the Economic and Social Council and the streamlining of the responsibilities of the General Assembly and the Council will come to fruition. This is a window of opportunity for the world community, a chance that may not recur. The process of revitalizing the work of the United Nations in the economic and social fields must be put back on track. I appeal to Member States to do all they can to that end.

47.   In the aftermath of the United Nations Conference on Environment and Development, held at Rio de Janeiro from 3 to 14 June 1992, it has become clear that Agenda 21 is the first international agreement expressing a global consensus and a political commitment at the highest levels to action on population, environment and economic advance, encompassed in a programme of sustainable development. The Conference challenged Governments to adopt long-term policies on matters of the environment and sustainable development that affect human well-being and survival. It further tested the willingness of nations to cooperate in developing global strategies for the sustainable use of resources.

48.   Following the Rio de Janeiro Conference, all United Nations agencies and bodies were required to contribute to system-wide efforts for the realization of sustainable development, and to support Governments in translating sustainable development policy into action. Agenda 21 was endorsed by the General Assembly at its forty-seventh session.

49.   The Commission on Sustainable Development held its first substantive session at Headquarters from 14 to 25 June 1993. Interest in the Commission has been amply demonstrated by the active way in which Governments have sought election to membership of the Commission, by the number of ministers who attended the high-level segment of its first session and by the approximately 700 non-governmental organizations that have obtained accreditation to it. The session

clearly revealed the strong determination of all parties involved, despite unfavourable prevailing economic and financial circumstances, to carry out the commitments made at the United Nations Conference on Environment and Development.

50.   This positive tone was echoed in the support expressed at the meeting of the Heads of Government of the Organisation for Economic Cooperation and Development (the "Tokyo Summit") in July 1993, both for the work of the Commission on Sustainable Development and for the other processes recommended by the Rio de Janeiro Conference.

51.   A new Inter-Agency Committee on Sustainable Development has been formed to ensure effective cooperation following the Rio de Janeiro Conference. The governing bodies of the various agencies and programmes have taken steps to reflect the decisions of the Conference in their work.

52.   The High-level Advisory Board on Sustainable Development provides advice to the Secretary-General and, through him, to the Commission on Sustainable Development and other relevant United Nations bodies. I have appointed its 21 members and expect the Board to hold its first meeting in September, just prior to the opening of the General Assembly. The follow-up work to the Rio de Janeiro Conference is discussed in section III of the present report.

4.   Trusteeship Council

53.   The Trusteeship Council, in accordance with Article 86 of the Charter, is composed of five Member States (China, France, the Russian Federation, the United Kingdom of Great Britain and Northern Ireland and the United States of America). Under the terms of Articles 83 and 87 of the Charter, the function of the Trusteeship Council is to assist the Security Council or the General Assembly in carrying out their responsibilities with respect to the International Trusteeship System. For more than 45 years, the Council has fulfilled its responsibilities, reviewing the situation in and dispatching regular visiting missions to Trust Territories. This year, Palau remains the only entity under the Trusteeship Agreement of 1947.

54.   At its sixtieth session in May 1993, the Trusteeship Council noted that the leadership of Palau wishes to end the trusteeship at an early date and had therefore decided to hold a plebiscite—the eighth—on the Compact of Free Association with the United States of America. The plebiscite, originally scheduled for July 1993, was postponed and is now scheduled, by Executive Order of the President of Palau, to take place on 9 November 1993.

5.   International Court of Justice

55.   The International Court of Justice at The Hague, one of the principal organs of the United

Nations under Article 7 of the Charter and, in accordance with Article 92, the principal judicial organ of the United Nations, has, in the past few years, experienced a clear increase in contentious cases as opposed to advisory opinions. In 1993, the Court had before it a record number of 12 cases, involving States from nearly every region of the world.

56.   In the reporting period, judgement has been given in two cases, and in a third case an Order indicating provisional measures of protection has been made in record time, and hearings have been held on the merits of two other cases. Voluminous written pleadings have been filed within the prescribed time-limits in the other cases.

57.   In September 1992, a Chamber of the Court, after considering some of the most extensive pleading, both written and oral, ever presented by Parties, gave Judgment in the case *Land, Island and Maritime Frontier Dispute (El Salvador/Honduras: Nicaragua intervening)*, in which the complex and varied issues in dispute would have amply justified up to eight separate cases. In its Judgment the Chamber drew the boundary line for each of six disputed sectors of the land boundary. It also decided on the legal situation of the islands in the Gulf of Fonseca, the legal rights to the waters of the Gulf of Fonseca, the waters outside the Gulf and the effect of the Judgment for the intervening State, Nicaragua.

58.   The full Court, at the end of March and beginning of April 1993, dealt with Bosnia and Herzegovina's request for the indication of provisional measures of protection at the same time that Bosnia and Herzegovina instituted proceedings against Yugoslavia (Serbia and Montenegro) in the case *Application of the Convention on the Prevention and Punishment of the Crime of Genocide (Bosnia and Herzegovina v. Yugoslavia (Serbia and Montenegro))*.

59.   As soon as possible after receiving the request and turning down a request for postponement, the Court held a hearing at which both Parties presented their observations. One week later, on 8 April 1993, the Court issued its Order, in which it called upon the Federal Republic of Yugoslavia (Serbia and Montenegro) "immediately [to] take all measures within its power to prevent commission of the crime of genocide". The Court also ordered that both Parties should ensure that no action is taken which might "aggravate or extend the existing dispute over the prevention or punishment of the crime of genocide, or render it more difficult of solution". In a further Order, the President of the Court fixed time-limits for the subsequent written procedure on the merits.

60.   The Court in late August 1993 held hearings on a second request from Bosnia and Herzegovina and a request from Yugoslavia for the indication of provisional measures in the same case.

61.   Hearings in the case *Maritime Delimitation in the Area between Greenland and Jan Mayen (Denmark v. Norway)* were held in January 1993. The Court delivered a Judgment on the merits on 14 June 1993, in which it observed that the continental shelf and fishery zones are two separate and conceptually distinct zones for delimitation purposes. It noted, however, that the task for the Court, under the law applicable to the delimitation of either zone, is to achieve an "equitable solution". The Court, in its Judgment, divided the area of the overlapping claims into three zones and drew the delimitation line in each of these zones.

62.   The day of the reading of the Judgment in this case was also the opening day of the hearings in the case *Territorial Dispute (Libyan Arab Jamahiriya/Chad)*, which the Libyan Arab Jamahiriya and Chad have presented to the Court by virtue of a special agreement. After five weeks of hearings, the Court is at present deliberating its decision in that case.

63.   New cases have kept the docket crowded. Cases on the Court's list during 1993, other than those referred to above, are:

(a)   *Aerial Incident of 3 July 1988 (Islamic Republic of Iran v. United States of America).*

(b)   *Certain Phosphate Lands in Nauru (Nauru v. Australia).*

(c)   *East Timor (Portugal v. Australia).*

(d)   *Maritime Delimitation between Guinea-Bissau and Senegal.*

(e)   *Maritime Delimitation and Territorial Questions between Qatar and Bahrain.*

(f)   *Questions of Interpretation and Application of the 1971 Montreal Convention arising from the Aerial Incident at Lockerbie (Libyan Arab Jamahiriya v. United Kingdom).*

(g)   *Questions of Interpretation and Application of the 1971 Montreal Convention arising from the Aerial Incident at Lockerbie (Libyan Arab Jamahiriya v. United States of America).*

(h)   *Oil Platforms (Islamic Republic of Iran v. United States of America).*

(i)   *Gabcikovo-Nagyamaros Project (Hungary/Slovakia).*

64.   The incidence of cases of considerable political as well as legal importance shows that the Court exists not only to settle questions of law, but is also an integral part of United Nations peace efforts. Seen in this context, the contentious and advisory jurisdictions of the Court are seen to be complementary. It is the role of the Court as an important component of the peacemaking apparatus of the United Nations as a whole that moved me to recommend, in "An Agenda for Peace", that the Secretary-General might be authorized to take advantage of the advisory competence of the Court.

65.   Under article 26, paragraph 1, of the Statute of the International Court of Justice, a seven-member Chamber for Environmental Matters has

been established. The members of the Chamber were elected by secret ballot to serve for an initial term of six months as at 6 August 1993.

66.   There is at present a tendency to proliferate the number of international tribunals: for example, there are proposals for various regional tribunals, and for tribunals to deal with environmental disputes, with human rights issues and with the law of the sea. It should be borne in mind that an essential feature of international law is that it is a single and universal system. Accordingly, if specialized tribunals are to be created, it may be necessary to establish a common system for referrals of questions of law to the principal judicial organ of the United Nations.

6.   Secretariat

67.   The Secretariat will continue to address the challenge of strengthening the Organization's ability to manage the 29 peace-keeping and other field missions. Action has already been taken to establish a clearer definition of the respective responsibilities of the Department of Political Affairs and the Department of Peace-keeping Operations with regard to these operations. The continuing effort during the coming year will involve enhancing planning activities through greater coordination among departments, improving budgetary planning and financial operations, invigorating structures for audit, investigation and programme evaluation, introducing a comprehensive staffing plan and ensuring the security and safety of staff in the field. Efforts will be made to develop more standardized, systematic, expeditious and cost-effective means of planning, launching, managing and terminating peace-keeping operations in a changing environment.

68.   Significant improvements have been made by the introduction of new computerized systems for field-related budget processing, accounting, procurement and inventory control; the enhanced delegation of administrative authority to the missions; the development of an integrated support service in the field to facilitate the interfacing of military and civilian components; and the establishment of new procedures for the staffing of field missions and field-related training.

69.   Given the extraordinary demands placed on the system by the large number of requests for the United Nations to establish and maintain peace-making and peace-keeping operations, and given the importance of deploying to the field experienced United Nations staff for key administrative positions in general administration, personnel, finance and procurement, the current shortage of experienced senior administrators familiar with United Nations policies and procedures available for assignment to these field missions will be addressed as a matter of priority.

70.   I paid a tribute, in my introduction to this annual report, to the staff of the United Nations.

No attempt to restructure the Secretariat will succeed unless it takes into account its most important asset, the staff. I am increasingly impressed by the dedication and professionalism of the Secretariat staff. In this period of expansion and restructuring, the commitment of staff members to the ideals of the United Nations, their willingness to work long hours under difficult conditions of service, and their flexibility to adapt to a variety of new conditions allow us to continue the day-to-day work of the Organization.

71.   In the course of the year, more than 1,200 members of the staff—both Professional and General Service employees—have volunteered to serve on United Nations peace missions. Such missions frequently entail a high degree of danger and stress. Many of the functions previously carried out by these staff members have had to be borne by employees remaining at Headquarters, who thus have had to carry an even greater burden. I take this opportunity to restate my commitment to the improvement of conditions of service for all of our staff members, particularly with respect to personal security, salaries and career development opportunities.

72.   Whether assigned to field missions or to other mandated programmes, the staff must be given the tools to make this an efficient and modern Organization. I am determined that training, which has been neglected in the past (when compared to other international organizations or national services), be given the place it deserves in management. The proposed programme budget for the next biennium reflects this concern. A comprehensive programme of management training, designed to develop leadership and managerial capacity within the Secretariat, has been launched with a series of management seminars for all director-level staff which will later be extended to other management levels.

73.   Improving and updating the skills of the Organization's staff is a significant step. Attracting talented and qualified candidates to join the Organization is another means of ensuring that it will be able to respond to the challenges of the 1990s. Although regular long-term recruitment has been suspended owing to the requirements of restructuring and streamlining, national competitive examinations have provided an excellent tool for selecting the best talent available in a given country for junior Professional positions. Nineteen countries will be asked to provide candidates for these examinations in 1993, compared with 12 in 1992. The filling of posts earmarked for these examinations has been exempted from the temporary suspension of recruitment.

74.   I intend to seek to improve the geographical distribution of posts and also to secure an input of fresh talent into the Organization. These are important considerations in the efficient management of the human resources of the United Nations.

Equally important, we must ensure that men and women can serve in conditions of equality.

75. A major effort is under way to advance the standing of women in the Organization, especially in senior-level positions. Although it is recognized that this is a long-term process, the policy is already producing tangible results. Guidelines on sexual harassment were issued during the past year as an important part of this general effort. It is also necessary to develop honourable and fair procedures to terminate the services of those staff members whose performance has failed to fulfil the promise of earlier years.

76. To train staff, to promote equality between men and women, and to select top-quality candidates from Member States are three key components of my efforts to increase the efficiency of the Organization. Yet if the conditions of service do not remain competitive, the Organization will lose some of its best elements.

77. During 1993, it became clear from work carried out by the Administrative Committee on Coordination that conditions of service of the United Nations are steadily deteriorating. They are losing their competitiveness in outside labour markets and *vis-à-vis* other international organizations. The General Assembly itself acknowledged that salary levels in a number of other international organizations outside the common system are higher than those of the United Nations. It is paradoxical that this should be happening at a time when many new demands are being placed on United Nations staff. At the request of the Committee, this concern is being brought to the attention of Member States and the International Civil Service Commission (ICSC). I have therefore decided to study with the Committee and ICSC ways to make compensation and conditions of service competitive. I hope that, as a result of these studies, the Administrative Committee on Coordination and ICSC will present specific recommendations to improve the conditions of service of the United Nations staff by the time of the next substantive consideration of these issues at the forty-ninth session of the General Assembly in 1994.

78. In this context, I must again stress the importance of a genuinely integrated, geographically balanced, independent international civil service of the highest calibre providing Member States with effective and integrated support. As part of my efforts to reinvigorate the international civil service, to preserve the integrity and independence of the staff, and to enhance career opportunities, I have been studying a new approach to higher echelon appointments. Taking into account the views of Member States as reflected in General Assembly resolution 47/212 B of 6 May 1993, I intend to make proposals about the senior structure

of the Organization during the forty-eighth session of the Assembly in the context of my submission on high-level posts in the proposed programme budget for the biennium 1994-1995.

79. In conjunction with streamlining in the administrative area, internal controls and audit mechanisms have been strengthened in 1993 as requested by Member States in different forums. Improvements involve better documentation of internal controls, follow-up on audit recommendations, whether external or internal, review of the staffing of the Division responsible for internal audits, and better planning of audit coverage. Improved internal controls will bring greater managerial accountability, which is crucial for more efficient organization.

80. In August 1993 I announced the creation of a new post of Assistant Secretary-General for Inspections and Investigations. The incumbent will head an independent Office for Inspections and Investigations that will incorporate various units dealing with audit, management advisory services, evaluation and monitoring, currently within the Department of Administration and Management. The new Assistant Secretary-General will report directly to me and will work closely with the Under-Secretary-General for Administration and Management. This appointment is the first step towards the establishment of a higher level post with broader audit, evaluation and investigation authority.

81. With the implementation of the Integrated Management Information System (IMIS), greater monitoring and audit capabilities will be available through electronic audit trails than ever before. IMIS is a major step in standardizing and rationalizing the management process in the Organization across duty stations. The Organization will be able, for the first time, to have access to timely, up-to-date and comprehensive information on its resources and their utilization. The use of IMIS by other programmes and organizations in the United Nations system could also promote greater transparency and compatibility of information across organizations, leading to standardization in administrative matters.

82. The heightened role of the United Nations as a focus for multilateral international dialogue has intensified the demand for conference services in the Secretariat. The enhanced activity of the Security Council and its subsidiary bodies, the establishment of a number of new intergovernmental or expert organs, and the increasing practice of holding formal meetings and informal consultations concurrently led to an increase of over 10 per cent in conference-servicing workloads in 1992 and to even higher projections for 1993. Despite the provisions of General Assembly resolution 41/213 of 19 December 1986 on limiting confer-

ence activities, the number of meetings, both those scheduled in the approved calendar of conferences and those unforeseen, has continued to increase.

83.   To the extent possible, the challenge has been met with measures to enhance productivity in conference services, mainly through the introduction of more advanced technology and coordination with substantive secretariats. The need to contain conference-servicing costs has, however, caused some interpretation and documentation services to be curtailed.

84.   Reliance on automation to increase individual productivity is not limited to conference services. Most areas of the Secretariat are undergoing significant changes in this respect. There is greater reliance on a global network of computers and telecommunications that are being upgraded.

85.   Together with the reform of management practice, steps are being taken to enhance the effectiveness of the economic and social sectors of the Organization. In my statement to the General Assembly on 2 November 1992, at the opening of the debate on the follow-up to the United Nations Conference on Environment and Development, I spoke of the need to rebuild "a unity of purpose for the economic, social and environmental sectors of the Organization" as one of the key objectives of my efforts.

86.   In furtherance of that objective, my aim has been to define the functions of the various parts of the Organization and to determine how those functions can most effectively be carried out by the Organization itself and within the United Nations system of specialized agencies and institutions. The core of my managerial strategy has been to secure a more rational distribution of responsibilities between Headquarters and the United Nations centres at Geneva, Nairobi and Vienna, as well as among global, regional and field structures. This should provide a clearer sense of purpose for each of the United Nations programmes and sharpen the substantive focus of each of the centres. Clear lines of responsibility in a simpler structure, together with steps to eliminate duplication and overlapping, will greatly improve coordination.

87.   Two broad principles govern my approach to the distribution of responsibilities between Headquarters and other parts of the economic and social structures of the Organization. The first is that responsibility for each sector or set of issues coming within the purview of the United Nations should, to the extent possible, be clearly assigned to, and the necessary critical mass for dealing with them concentrated in, a single unit or entity within the Secretariat, without duplication and as part of an organization-wide strategy. The second, related, requirement is that the provision of substantive support for central intergovernmental bodies should be regarded as a priority activity for all economic, social and environmental entities of the United Nations in their respective sectors, coordinated from Headquarters. Conversely, Headquarters capacities on cross-sectoral issues should be placed at the disposal, and help to orient the deliberations, not only of the central intergovernmental organs, but also of the governing and other intergovernmental bodies in each of the entities away from Headquarters.

88.   In proceeding to the second phase of restructuring on the basis of these guidelines, I took careful account of the experience gained in the first phase, which I initiated shortly after taking office early in 1992. A key element of that phase was the establishment in New York of a single Department of Economic and Social Development. I saw this as a first step, in order to create new synergies among the three pillars of Headquarters work: system-wide coordination and policy guidance, research, analysis and studies on important global economic and social issues, and technical cooperation activities in developing countries. This initial phase of the restructuring would prepare the ground for a second phase encompassing all of the economic and social sectors of the Organization.

89.   The process of restructuring the work, and often the offices, of over 1,000 people employed in the economic and social fields at Headquarters placed considerable demands on the staff. In the face of these challenges, the consolidated Department of Economic and Social Development was nevertheless able to bring about fruitful synergies between the operational staff on the one hand, and the research and analysis staff on the other, bringing fresh perspectives and new energy to a number of areas of work.

90.   In the light of this experience, and taking into account the work of a high-level panel of advisers and discussions in the General Assembly, I took steps in December 1992 that constitute a second phase of the reform effort in the economic and social sectors of the United Nations. These steps entailed the creation of three new departments focusing, respectively, on policy coordination and sustainable development, economic and social information and policy analysis, and development support and management services.

91.   As a result, the balance at Headquarters between Secretariat structures in the political, humanitarian, economic and social fields has improved. Organizational units now have clear and distinct terms of reference and clear lines of responsibility, and services to central intergovernmental bodies have been improved and integrated. In addition, there is now a greater capacity in terms of data and statistical support for national as well as international policy-making, and technical cooperation is more focused.

92. The redeployment to New York, in the Department for Policy Coordination and Sustainable Development, of the relevant functions and activities of the Centre for Social Development and Humanitarian Affairs at Vienna and the World Food Council secretariat in Rome should enhance the capacity of the United Nations for coherent policy development and provide more effective and better coordinated substantive support to central intergovernmental bodies. Overall, these measures will result in a more integrated approach to development.

93. The dispersion of different aspects of United Nations activities in the closely interrelated areas of trade, finance, investment, technology and services inevitably diluted the impact of these activities. The consolidation of these activities in the United Nations Conference on Trade and Development will eliminate these overlaps and create a broader base for enhancing the quality of substantive support provided to the United Nations Centre on Transnational Corporations and the Commission on Science and Technology for Development, as well as to the Trade and Development Board and its subsidiary bodies. In addition, the United Nations Centre for Human Settlements (Habitat) and the United Nations Environment Programme located at the United Nations Office at Nairobi have been placed under common management. This will facilitate synergies among the two programmes and result in some savings.

94. In 1993, the United Nations Office at Geneva has had to address and resolve a twin problem of substance and structure. A key priority has been to improve the management of the Office and its responsiveness to new demands, particularly in United Nations operational activities. Within the United Nations Office at Vienna, the United Nations International Drug Control Programme is responsible for confronting the crucial problems of crime and drugs. The United Nations Crime Prevention and Criminal Justice Programme, also within the United Nations Office at Vienna, has concentrated on direct support of Governments through technical cooperation activities and training. I take this opportunity to restate my commitment to maintaining Vienna as one of the principal United Nations centres.

95. The Administrative Committee on Coordination plays a crucial role in providing a sense of unity of purpose for the United Nations system as a whole. I have therefore paid particular attention to that Committee, of which I am Chairman. A thorough review of the workings of the Committee and its subsidiary structure was undertaken this year.

96. In the first instance, the functioning of the Administrative Committee on Coordination was reviewed and a series of guidelines agreed upon.

I intend to submit to the Committee for discussion any programme or proposal, of a general or system-wide nature, whose significance or content seem to me to require prior consultation with the agencies concerned and their subsequent cooperation in follow-up and implementation. I shall keep the Economic and Social Council fully apprised of the outcome of these consultations.

97. The executive heads, as members of the Administrative Committee on Coordination, for their part undertook to carry out the necessary consultations within the framework of the Committee when launching, on their own initiative, any operation—such as the organization of an international or world conference on a subject that involves the mandates and interests of a number of United Nations organizations—the implementation of which will require contributions by several or all of the members of the Committee. They also agreed to inform their deliberative organs of major impending initiatives within the United Nations system of particular relevance to their organizations or in which their organizations are expected to participate.

98. The complexity of the subsidiary structures of the Administrative Committee on Coordination has been greatly reduced. The new structures of the Committee are centred around two consultative committees—the Consultative Committee on Administrative Questions and the Consultative Committee on Programme and Operational Questions—and on the new Inter-Agency Committee on Sustainable Development. The new structures will provide a forum in which policy issues affecting system-wide aspects of the management of human and financial resources can be discussed in a coordinated fashion. They will also allow closer interaction between policies and operations. They reflect the importance of the concept of sustainable development as an integrating framework for the activities of the system.

99. I am convinced that the commitments I have outlined, together with the new spirit prevailing in the Administrative Committee on Coordination and the specific reforms which have been introduced, will greatly enhance inter-agency cooperation in support of development.

100. At the same time, I must remind Member States that they, too, have a responsibility to help to improve coordination within the system. These responsibilities must be exercised at two levels. First, at the level of the central intergovernmental bodies within the United Nations itself, Member States must develop system-wide strategies and policies and provide effective guidelines for the work of the secretariats represented in the Administrative Committee on Coordination. My earlier remarks on the reform of the Economic and Social Council are relevant in this context.

101.   Second, Member States must take coherent and consistent positions in the governing bodies of the various organizations. One glaring example of their failure to do so hitherto is the persistence of differences in the conditions of service adopted by Member States for the international staff serving in the Bretton Woods institutions on the one hand, and the rest of the system on the other. Further examples of divergent policy directives exist throughout the spectrum of substantive and operational issues before the various governing bodies. The Administrative Committee on Coordination stands ready to do its part to help to overcome these differences and to adopt mutually reinforcing policy stances throughout the system.

B.   *Interim offices*

102.   I undertook in my last annual report to focus attention on activities in the field and to bring greater unity to the United Nations presence at the country level. I have established interim offices in Armenia, Azerbaijan, Belarus, Georgia, Kazakhstan, Ukraine and Uzbekistan. My aim has been the creation of an integrated approach to the provision of the services that the United Nations system can offer, and the coordination of inter-agency activities in response to the requirements of Member States. Consultations on the establishment of integrated offices are currently under way in Cambodia, Eritrea and the Russian Federation.

103.   These measures are intended to facilitate access to the United Nations system for Member States, especially newly independent States and other States in transition, that wish to seek its assistance in various areas of activity. They are also intended to improve the capacity of the United Nations to respond appropriately to the specific socio-economic, environmental, political and humanitarian requirements of such countries.

104.   The interim offices have already begun to play an effective role in responding to the needs of their host Governments, both in development activities and in supporting the transition process that these countries are undergoing. The interim offices have facilitated the Organization's humanitarian and emergency relief activities. In those countries where I have been given a mandate to help to resolve actual or potential conflicts, the interim offices have been of great value as a channel of communication with the Government concerned and as an instrument for the dissemination of information about the United Nations.

105.   In all these activities, the interim offices have succeeded in strengthening the image of the United Nations as an integrated system whose component parts are able to work together, in support of host Governments, in response to the special and urgent requirements of countries in transition. This has been achieved with the full cooperation and assistance of the funds, programmes and offices of the United Nations system. The Administrative Committee on Coordination has welcomed my decision to work for a more unified field presence. The representatives of some of the specialized agencies, which are not yet taking part in these arrangements, have indicated a wish to be associated with them.

106.   In devising a new model for United Nations representation in those countries, it is not my intention to disturb or replace existing mechanisms for coordination. On the contrary, the intention is to build on what has already been achieved. I intend to apply to other countries, as needed, the approach that is evolving in the countries where interim offices have been established. My aim is to develop a more effective, unified United Nations presence at the country level.

C.   *Ensuring an adequate financial base*

107.   The conjunction of the persistent difficulties of a number of Member States in meeting their financial obligations and the unprecedented level of expenditures for mandated activities (see figure 4) is expected to cause major financial difficulties for the Organization by the autumn of 1993.

108.   The unprecedented growth in the demand for the services of the United Nations has stretched financial resources to the breaking-point. In January 1993, assessed contributions payable by Member States amounted, in rounded figures, to $1.6 billion for the regular budget. The cost of peace-keeping missions is expected to rise from $1.4 billion in 1992 to an estimated $3.6 billion by the end of 1993 (see figure 5).

109.   I must report with great concern and deep regret that, owing to the failure of many Member States to pay their assessed contributions in full and on time, the cash flow situation, with regard both to the regular budget and to United Nations peace-keeping operations, remains critical. As of 26 August 1993, only seven Member States had paid their assessed contributions to the regular budget and peace-keeping operations in full.

110.   If this pattern continues, the regular budget will need to borrow internally from other funds as from September 1993. Several peace-keeping operations have experienced severe cash shortages. In order to be able to respond to the needs of these operations, temporary advances have had to be made from the Peace-keeping Reserve Fund which was established by the General Assembly in resolution 47/217 of 23 December 1992. In order to meet its various other obligations, including the payment of salaries, the Organization had to resort to a variety of short-term measures such as borrowing from funds having available cash.

111.   The proposed programme budget for the biennium 1994-1995 will be considered by the

General Assembly at its forty-eighth session. It proposes a modest growth of 1 per cent in the level of resources, primarily in the areas of preventive diplomacy, peace operations, peace-building, human rights and the coordination of humanitarian assistance. This programme budget reflects the interest of Member States in strengthening these activities. It is my hope that all Member States will reach broad agreement and adopt this programme budget by consensus as they have done in the last several bienniums.

112. On 2 August 1993, with total cash reserves sufficient for less than two months of operations, I decided to send an urgent letter to the heads of State and Government of Security Council members and of all Member States with outstanding contributions, outlining the gravity of the financial situation. I stated that the financial situation was so precarious that it threatened the capacity of the Organization to finance new undertakings, and that even existing operations would be in jeopardy. On 26 August I told the Fifth Committee that the Organization's cash flow situation had become so serious that I had been compelled to take economy measures affecting conference services, including the servicing of the Security Council, the General Assembly and their committees and subsidiary bodies. Specifically, I made it clear that it would not be possible for meetings to be serviced, except in emergencies, during the evening, at night or during weekends. I also warned that, unless there was an improvement in the situation, further economy measures would have to follow.

113. At my request, the Ford Foundation convened an independent international advisory group of experts in September 1992 to examine the financing of the United Nations, with a view to creating a secure financial base for the Organization over the long term. The group met three times between September 1992 and January 1993 and published its report, entitled "Financing an Effective United Nations", in February 1993. The report is comprehensive and contains many valuable recommendations. I should like to take this opportunity of expressing my profound thanks and appreciation to the chairmen and members of the group for their work, and also to the Ford Foundation for sponsoring it. I have sent the report to Member States and am also transmitting it to the General Assembly for consideration at its forty-eighth session.

114. In spite of these unfavourable circumstances, indeed partly because of the strained cash situation, the Administration has pursued its efforts to enhance its productivity. The increased productivity of the United Nations during the past year is reflected in the remainder of this report.

D. *Preparing for the fiftieth anniversary*

115. The Preparatory Committee for the Fiftieth Anniversary of the United Nations, established by the General Assembly in decision 46/472 of 13 April 1992, held five meetings. Agreement was reached by consensus on a theme for the anniversary: "We the peoples of the United Nations . . . united for a better world". The Preparatory Committee also established a working group to prepare a solemn declaration for the observance.

116. To date, 13 Member States have notified me of the formation of national committees in support of this observance. I look forward to receiving confirmation from other Member States regarding their national committees. The fiftieth anniversary secretariat has been coordinating anniversary preparations and programme development within the system, with the support of non-governmental organizations and other partners. I regard the anniversary as a major milestone to be marked not only by celebration, but by programmes of serious reflection, education and communication.

III. Developing the global community

"To achieve international cooperation in solving international problems of an economic, social, cultural, or humanitarian character . . . "
Charter of the United Nations, Article 1, paragraph 3

117. The gap between the world's richest and poorest countries is widening, yet that shocking fact is more often than not greeted by indifference. The United Nations is the special voice of the world's poorest nations. No task is greater or more urgent than to impress upon the economically leading nations that the world cannot ultimately prosper if the poorest continue to suffer and decline.

118. The ideological contest of the cold war stimulated great super-Power interest in developing countries. The reasons were not always admirable, but poor countries could benefit from that interest. Today, we see that the world, in the wake of the cold war, recognizes the importance of competition; but the end of the cold war has ended the competition to bring development to the world.

119. The message from the United Nations has been clear: macroeconomic growth should not be pursued without due consideration for such aspects of human well-being as health, education, poverty levels, income levels and income distribution, and participation in the political process and in the market-place. In short, human development, in its social and economic dimensions, must be at the centre of all development efforts.

120. I intend to set out the United Nations approach to development in full in "An Agenda for Development", a preliminary report which will be submitted to the General Assembly at its forty-eighth session. An Agenda for Development will provide more than yet another development theory. As a practical document, it will set the guidelines for future United Nations action in the eco-

nomic and social fields. I look forward to a lively and fruitful discussion of the preliminary report during the forty-eighth session.

A. *Global development activities*

1. Secretariat departments at Headquarters

121. The Department for Policy Coordination and Sustainable Development provides substantive support for the central coordinating and policy-making functions vested in the Economic and Social Council in its high-level, coordination and operational activities segments and the Second and Third Committees of the General Assembly, the Commission on Sustainable Development, the Commission for Social Development, the Commission on the Status of Women and, pending the conclusion of the current intergovernmental review, the World Food Council. The Department serves, at the expert level, the High-level Advisory Board on Sustainable Development and, at the inter-secretariat level, the Inter-Agency Committee on Sustainable Development and other subsidiary bodies of the Administrative Committee on Coordination dealing with both operational and programme questions. The Department will coordinate the contributions of other Secretariat entities to the work of central intergovernmental bodies in the economic and social areas, but its aim is also to broaden the base and improve the quality of support by engaging all relevant parts of the economic and social sectors of the Organization.

122. The Department will assist me in ensuring the successful implementation of Agenda 21 and other major documents adopted at the United Nations Conference on Environment and Development. Considerable efforts will need to be made to ensure that sustainable development principles are adequately reflected in new or adjusted policies, in legislation, and in programme budgets and structures.

123. The redeployment to this Department of the relevant functions and activities of the Centre for Social Development and Humanitarian Affairs at Vienna and the World Food Council secretariat at Rome should enhance United Nations capacity for coherent policy development and provide more effective support for central intergovernmental bodies. It should, in general, help to promote a more integrated approach to development.

124. The Department, in addition to providing subject-specific policy reports, as required, for the relevant intergovernmental bodies, will assume primary responsibility for the preparation of an annual policy report of the Secretary-General focusing on a selected number of major policy issues calling for concerted international action. That report will draw on, and be coordinated with, the work of the Department for Economic and Social Information and Policy Analysis, the United Nations Conference on Trade and Development and other concerned entities.

125. I have also asked the Department for Policy Coordination and Sustainable Development to take on responsibility for coordinating the preparations for the World Summit for Social Development, to be held at Copenhagen in 1995. The Summit, which will coincide with the fiftieth anniversary of the Organization, is already the focus of much debate within the United Nations system, particularly within the Economic and Social Council. Preparatory studies for the Summit are under way on some of the major economic and social issues facing the international community. They include:

(*a*) Poverty and equity issues, both inter-State and intra-State;

(*b*) Unemployment, vulnerable groups and countries, and patterns of economic exclusion;

(*c*) Social security issues and safety nets;

(*d*) Migration and patterns of human and economic movement.

126. With respect to the advancement of women, my objective is to achieve a stronger and more unified programme. The relocation of the Division for the Advancement of Women within the Department for Policy Coordination and Sustainable Development will place its activities in the mainstream of the economic and social work of the Organization, and should assist in integrating gender issues into every aspect of our work on development. My proposal to merge the International Research and Training Institute for the Advancement of Women (INSTRAW) with the United Nations Development Fund for Women (UNIFEM) has been endorsed by the Economic and Social Council. It should give greater coherence to the policy, research and operational aspects of United Nations efforts for the advancement of women.

127. Taken together, these measures should help to focus preparations for the Fourth World Conference on Women, to be held in Beijing in 1995. Other preparatory work for that important global forum has involved support for national and regional preparations, the coordination of United Nations system participation, the involvement of non-governmental organizations, and efforts to heighten public awareness. The Secretary-General of the Conference, Gertrude Mongella, has already conducted missions to several States Members of the United Nations to promote the goals and objectives of the Conference, and to seek support for it at all levels.

128. The question of violence against women has continued to be of deep concern. A major step forward was the drafting of the draft Declaration on the Elimination of Violence against Women, which the Economic and Social Council, at its sub-

stantive session of 1993, urged the General Assembly to adopt. It is hoped that this work will be brought to a successful conclusion at the forty-eighth session of the Assembly.

* * *

129. The Department for Economic and Social Information and Policy Analysis has a central responsibility for maintaining and enhancing the quantitative information systems (population and statistics) of the United Nations. In addition, the Department is charged with servicing the substantive needs of the international community in the fields of economic and social policy and research. It thus provides the link between the various departments and organs at Headquarters and the regional commissions.

130. The Department also serves as the lead unit for economic and social information within the United Nations and provides statistical support to all parts of the Organization. In this regard, it will cooperate closely with the Bretton Woods institutions and other relevant organizations and will link its activities with the early-warning capabilities being developed in the political and humanitarian sectors of the Organization.

131. Since its inception in February 1993, the Department for Economic and Social Information and Policy Analysis has concentrated on the development and implementation of the 1993 System of National Accounts and on providing a new impetus for the collection of statistics on the environment. The Department has also undertaken considerable preparatory work for the International Conference on Population and Development, to be held at Cairo in September 1994, for which, together with the United Nations Population Fund, it is providing the secretariat. In addition, two reports were made available to the Economic and Social Council at its substantive session of 1993, namely, the *1993 Report on the World Social Situation* and the *World Economic Survey, 1993.* Those reports were the culmination of more than a year of intensive efforts. Their basic structure and approach were worked out under the authority of the head of the former Department of Economic and Social Development.

132. The Statistical Commission, and the Economic and Social Council at its substantive session of 1993, adopted the 1993 System of National Accounts, a basic tool for organizing and analysing economic statistics. With the adoption of the 1993 System, an international consensus was reached on an up-to-date and near-universal language for economic dialogue among countries and groups of countries. The adoption also marked the successful culmination of a 10-year effort by the Secretariat on the System of National Accounts, which was carried out in close collaboration with

the regional commissions, the International Monetary Fund, the World Bank, the Organisation for Economic Cooperation and Development, the European Community and many national experts.

133. Fresh impetus was given to work on environmental statistics. The development and implementation of integrated environmental and economic accounting will provide new tools for monitoring in this field. Further pioneering work on gender statistics continued, with a second issue of *The World's Women* in preparation. Priorities and an action plan were established from a global review of international statistical activities designed to improve international cooperation and statistical development with an enhanced regional dimension.

134. The work of the Secretariat in population aims to facilitate the work of the Economic and Social Council, through the Population Commission, in the formulation of policy recommendations, in the delivery of technical assistance and cooperation and in the substantive coordination of the activities of the United Nations system in the field of population.

135. The implications of the Single European Act for countries not members of the European Community, including the transitional economies and the developing countries, were explored in two issues of the *Journal of Development Planning*. Another issue of the same journal was devoted to examining the implications for developing countries of the economic, political and social transformations in central and eastern Europe.

136. Macroeconomic forecasts of the world economy for the period 1993-2001 and alternative policy simulations were prepared to serve as the basis for policy-oriented discussions at expert group meetings held at Ankara, Geneva and New York.

* * *

137. The Department for Development Support and Management Services is designed to sharpen the focus of United Nations technical assistance and enhance its impact on the priority needs of developing countries and countries in transition. The new Department's mandate is twofold. On the one hand, it will act as an executing agency for programmes and projects relating to institutional and human resource development in areas such as development planning, policies and infrastructure, public administration, private sector development and enterprise management, financial management and accounting, and natural resources and energy planning and management. On the other hand, the Department will be the focal point at United Nations Headquarters for the provision of management services and implementation functions for technical cooperation.

138. With effect from 1 January 1994, the Department will incorporate, as a semi-auton-

omous entity, the Office for Project Services, currently located within the United Nations Development Programme (UNDP). One consideration in making this change was the view, frequently voiced by Member States, that the current location of the Office within UNDP is incompatible with the primary purpose of UNDP as a central coordinating and funding mechanism. The change should also increase cost-effectiveness and eliminate duplication in the delivery of technical cooperation services by the United Nations. The incorporation of the Office for Project Services in the Secretariat also provides an opportunity for the redeployment, closer to the constituencies they are intended to serve, of relevant parts of the Organization's technical cooperation and advisory services.

139.   The Department for Development Support and Management Services has, since its creation in 1993, concentrated on the thematic and cross-sectoral aspects of its work. Special attention has been paid by the Department to the integration of its activities with the Organization's work in peace-keeping and humanitarian affairs. Ongoing activities in this area include support for election administration and reconstruction efforts in a number of countries, and work on the conversion of military infrastructure and industries to peaceful civilian use.

140.   The Department has taken part in the new UNDP support costs arrangements, and in discussions with the executing agencies and UNDP about how the system could be refined to make it more effective.

141.   The Department for Development Support and Management Services is also giving close attention to ensuring that it plays a dynamic role as an agent for technical cooperation, particularly in the context of national execution and the programme approach. It has intensified its efforts in institution-building and human resource development, with particular attention to the strengthening of institutions in developing countries. The Department is also implementing a multisectoral approach to technical cooperation and institution-building.

2.   United Nations Conference on Trade and Development

142.   In the area of international trade, the United Nations Conference on Trade and Development (UNCTAD) has focused on issues related to national transparent mechanisms in the context of the fight against protectionism. UNCTAD has also stressed the need for international support for the initiatives of developing countries, especially through improved market access and stronger financial flows. The link between the decreasing real price of primary commodities and the environment has been addressed in Agenda 21. Depressed commodity prices lead to overproduc-

tion to maintain foreign exchange income, a process which often leads in turn to environmental deterioration.

143.   The concept of comprehensive development has had a major impact on the work of UNCTAD. Whereas in the past proceedings were usually geared to the adoption of resolutions and decisions, the reforms adopted at the eighth session of UNCTAD, in February 1992, have led to an increasing role for negotiations. The pragmatic and non-confrontational approach implicit in those reforms has facilitated the search for convergence and consensus-building. On the other hand, unless opportunities for trade and development are enhanced, tensions will build up and confrontational approaches will once again come to the fore.

144.   The Special Committee on Preferences conducted an extensive exchange of views on the implementation of the generalized system of preferences and agreed to undertake a policy review of the system in 1995. Recent agreements reached by negotiations held under the auspices of UNCTAD include the International Sugar Agreement (March 1992), the Protocol extending the International Agreement on Olive Oil and Table Olives, 1986, with amendments (March 1993), and a new Convention on Maritime Liens and Mortgages (May 1993).

145.   UNCTAD has enhanced its capacity to address the new challenges and opportunities that have arisen for strengthening international cooperation for development. Furthermore, with the imminent transfer to UNCTAD from United Nations Headquarters of programmes relating to transnational corporations and science and technology for development, the UNCTAD secretariat will be well placed, through improved programme delivery, to enable the concerned commissions of the Economic and Social Council, as well as the competent UNCTAD intergovernmental bodies, to discharge their respective mandates more effectively.

3.   United Nations Environment Programme

146.   The new leadership of the United Nations Environment Programme (UNEP) has the responsibility of transforming its programme in recognition of Agenda 21 priorities. The seventeenth session of the Governing Council was held in May 1993. That was the first intergovernmental meeting to discuss Agenda 21 since its endorsement by the General Assembly at its forty-seventh session, and it provided an opportunity for Governments to agree on programmes and priorities affecting both the developing and the developed countries.

147.   In supporting the implementation of Agenda 21, the Governing Council called upon the Executive Director to make every effort to strengthen, orient and adjust, as appropriate, the activities, programmes and medium-term plan of UNEP to help achieve the objectives of Agenda 21.

After receiving and reviewing in detail the UNEP programme for the bienniums 1992-1993 and 1994-1995, the Council noted that the programme would require further development to incorporate changes required by the Rio de Janeiro Conference. The Governing Council reaffirmed that Agenda 21 must be implemented in close cooperation with the Commission on Sustainable Development, and requested the Executive Director to present to the Council at its next session her estimates of the costs to UNEP of the full implementation of those parts of Agenda 21 specifically recommended for the Programme's attention. The Council stressed that high priority should be given to the needs of developing countries.

148. UNEP provided technical cooperation in the field of environmental law and institutions to the Governments of 11 African, 10 Asian and Pacific and 3 Latin American and Caribbean countries. That work was conducted in cooperation with UNDP, the World Bank and regional organizations. In addition, national environmental plans and strategies were prepared in 14 developing countries in Africa, Asia and Latin America. Country studies on costs and benefits of environmental management and conservation of biodiversity were carried out in six countries with different biological profiles.

149. The international environmental information system of UNEP now brings together a total of 155 participating countries. About 25,000 queries were answered in 1992. The *INFOTERRA International Directory* contains over 6,000 sources of environmental information. Equipment and training were provided to 30 developing countries. The Global Resources Information Database (GRID) has now linked 30 affiliated centres around the world. This enables planners and scientists to access data, monitor trends and study the interactions between environmental variables using geographic information systems and data management computer techniques. The Global Environmental Monitoring System (GEMS) set up a regional environmental information network to promote the exchange of environmental information in support of strategies for collective preventive or remedial action on environmental issues. Regional surveys were conducted to identify environmental and natural resources information and information management requirements and activities in the African, Asian-Pacific and Latin American regions.

150. UNEP provided assistance, through joint undertakings with the regional commissions and the Food and Agriculture Organization of the United Nations, to seven countries for the formulation of national plans to combat desertification. Support was also provided, jointly with other organizations, to establish networks and mechanisms for mobilizing action for the implementation of the Plan of Action to Combat Desertification. Through the UNEP/UNDP joint venture, the United Nations Sahelian Office continued to assist Sudano-Sahelian countries to implement the Plan of Action and to bring together additional financial and technical assistance from other bodies. In addition, UNEP cooperated with regional and subregional organizations, such as the Southern Africa Development Community and the League of Arab States, to provide assistance through them to their member countries in the implementation of the Plan of Action.

151. UNEP is cooperating closely with African Governments, non-governmental organizations and development agencies in the implementation of the programme of the Conference of African Ministers on the Environment, in the area of energy and food security, and on measures to strengthen environmental machineries, the formulation of environmental action plans and programmes, and environmental training and public awareness. UNEP continues to emphasize in its outreach programme the topic of women and the environment.

152. UNEP is providing support for 24 projects under the Action Plan for the Environment in Latin America and the Caribbean, including the initial financing of the secretariat, located at the UNEP regional office for Latin America and the Caribbean. Those projects are being implemented in close association with Governments, the Economic Commission for Latin America and the Caribbean, regional offices of specialized agencies and other intergovernmental agencies and subregional organizations.

153. UNEP is also working closely with its partners UNDP and the World Bank to increase efficiency in the implementation of the Global Environment Facility (GEF). UNEP is strengthening its scientific inputs and servicing of the Science and Technology Advisory Panel; it is also taking an active part in the evaluation of GEF-funded projects and in discussions on the administration, legal framework and management of the next phase of GEF.

154. The range and variety of these programmes indicate the difficulty of acting coherently and comprehensively; clearly the level of integration which we seek and which the times demand has not yet been attained. A substantial effort has, however, been made and progress over the past year has been evident.

4. United Nations Centre for Human Settlements (Habitat)

155. The global housing crisis, which affects hundreds of millions of families in both rural and urban settlements, and the social, economic and environmental impact of the unprecedented pace of urbanization in the developing regions provide

the context of the work of the United Nations Centre for Human Settlements (Habitat).

156.   The main policy direction for the activities of the Centre derives from the Global Strategy for Shelter to the Year 2000, adopted by the General Assembly in December 1988. It has also been incorporated into the human settlements programme of Agenda 21. The Strategy encourages Governments to adopt policies that enable all the actors in the public and private sectors, including non-governmental organizations, community organizations and women's groups, to contribute to the process of improving shelter and human settlements conditions, and provide adequate mechanisms to monitor progress through quantitative and policy indicators.

157.   Similarly, the applied research and training activities of Habitat have focused on improving the capacity of Governments, especially at the local level, and low-income communities to face the challenges of human settlements management and development. Equally important is the identification of low-cost and environmentally sound technological options for human settlements infrastructure and services. Directly addressing the critical need to make an early contribution to the continuum of relief, rehabilitation and development activities of the United Nations system, Habitat has also played a notable role during the year in human settlements and rehabilitation efforts in Afghanistan and Cambodia.

158.   The decision by the General Assembly at its forty-seventh session to convene a second United Nations Conference on Human Settlements (Habitat II) in 1996 is a clear recognition of the need for new concerted action by the international community to address the issues of environmentally sustainable human settlements development in a rapidly urbanizing world. Habitat, which will provide the secretariat for the Conference, will have a major responsibility for the success of the Conference, in cooperation with Member States and the United Nations system.

B.   *Operational activities for development*

159.   Discussions on the reform of operational activities have been under way in the General Assembly and the Economic and Social Council since 1989. In 1992, in an important step forward, the General Assembly, in resolution 47/199, reaffirmed the need for reform in the field of development activities. It also stressed that development is a shared responsibility. The Assembly urged developed countries to increase their official development assistance, and emphasized that recipient Governments had the primary responsibility for coordinating, on the basis of national strategies and priorities, all types of external assistance. Resolution 47/199 also contained important guidelines on the role of the United Nations system in development. The country strategy note, introduced by the resolution, offers a major opportunity for coordinating the response of the entire United Nations system to the priorities of developing country Governments. The programme approach is another important feature of the resolution and will play a major role in securing logical and integrated donor responses to government development priorities at the sectoral and intersectoral levels. Under resolution 47/199, the United Nations is required to assist Governments to achieve self-reliance in managing their economic and social development.

1.   Technical cooperation programmes of the United Nations Secretariat

160.   In 1992, the then Department of Economic and Social Development had 918 technical cooperation projects under execution, with a total delivery of $141 million, against current year budget provisions of $185 million. The work programme of the Department consisted of giving advice and assistance to developing countries in national economic and social development planning, and providing expertise on energy policy, water resources projects, mineral resources, cartography, remote sensing and infrastructural work, public administration and finance, statistics, population policies, and transnational corporations, in addition to support services for other development agencies. The Department also participated in programmes relevant to the notion that political progress and economic development are inseparable and must be pursued simultaneously.

161.   A large-scale effort to assist in the national election held in Angola, in September 1992, focused on the coordination of foreign assistance and on logistical support. Other electoral missions were conducted in Albania, Ethiopia, Mali and Mozambique. Missions were also fielded to provide advice and assistance in preparing elections in El Salvador, Lesotho, Rwanda and Uganda. In this, the Department and, since December 1992, the Department for Development Support and Management Services worked closely with the Electoral Assistance Unit in the Department of Political Affairs.

162.   The Department of Economic and Social Development, with the cooperation of the Beijing Commission for Science and Technology, organized in Beijing, in October 1992, a seminar on urban information systems and their application to developing countries. The purpose of the seminar was to provide a forum for discussion and dissemination of current and improved techniques in this field.

163.   The Department provided secretariat services and technical background papers for the Sixth United Nations Conference on the Standardization of Geographical Names. In collabo-

ration with the Earth Observation Satellite Company and the International Society for Photogrammetry and Remote Sensing, the Department organized a two-week seminar on photogrammetry and remote sensing, to benefit developing countries.

164. I have followed with particularly close interest and concern the question of African development and the implementation of the United Nations New Agenda for the Development of Africa in the 1990s, adopted by the General Assembly in its resolution 46/151, as updated by the System-wide Plan of Action for African Economic Recovery and Development. The goals and activities of the New Agenda were central to the work programme of the Office of the Special Coordinator for Africa and the Least Developed Countries in 1992. To advise and assist me in this work I appointed a panel of high-level personalities. I took part myself in meetings of the panel, at Geneva in December 1992 and at Rome in May 1993. I am most grateful to the members of the panel for their valuable contribution, which is ongoing.

165. The Department of Economic and Social Development organized, in cooperation with IN-STRAW, an interregional workshop on women's role in the environment and sustainable development in September 1992 in Beijing. There were 120 participants and over 80 prototype project proposals were developed. The workshop was perceived as providing a key link between the Rio de Janeiro Conference and the Fourth World Conference on Women, to be held in 1995. The Department also organized, in cooperation with INSTRAW and the Economic and Social Commission for Asia and the Pacific, a regional workshop on training modules on women, water supply and sanitation, which was held in Thailand in September 1992, following a similar one held in the Gambia in 1991. The Department also responded to requests about developing national databases and reports for the 1995 Conference.

2. United Nations Children's Fund

166. In 1992, the United Nations Children's Fund (UNICEF) cooperated in programmes in over 130 countries. In addition, UNICEF expanded its programmes of support to central and eastern Europe and the republics of the former Soviet Union as mandated by the Executive Board. Programme expenditure totalled $744 million in 1992. Of that amount, 31 per cent was spent on child health, including the expanded programme on immunization and oral rehydration therapy; 22 per cent on emergency programmes; 15 per cent on planning, advocacy and prime support; 11 per cent on water supply and sanitation; 10 per cent on education, including young child development; 7 per cent on community development, women's programmes and children in especially difficult circumstances;

and 4 per cent on nutrition and household food security.

167. Overall UNICEF expenditure for 1992 was dominated by emergency assistance, owing partially to the situations in Angola, Iraq, Mozambique, Somalia, the Sudan and the former Yugoslavia. For the biennium 1992-1993, the estimated expenditure of UNICEF amounts to $1.8 billion. It is forecast that the total annual income of UNICEF will exceed $1 billion by 1995. Expenditure on emergency relief is expected to decrease, with a corresponding increase in expenditure on the development aspects of the work of UNICEF, including child health and nutrition, water supply and sanitation, education, community development, children in especially difficult circumstances and women-centred programmes.

168. The goals established by the international community for UNICEF include seven overarching goals and a number of supporting goals. The overarching goals include reduction of infant mortality by one third or to 50 per 1,000 live births, whichever is the lower; reduction of mortality among children under five years old by one third or to 70 per 1,000 live births; reduction of the maternal mortality rate by half by the year 2000; reduction of severe and moderate malnutrition among children under five by half by the year 2000; universal access to safe drinking water and to sanitary means of excreta disposal; universal access to basic education and completion of primary education by at least 80 per cent of children of primary school age by the year 2000; reduction of the adult illiteracy rate (the appropriate age group to be determined in each country) to at least half its 1990 level, with an emphasis on female literacy; and improved protection of children in especially difficult circumstances. Among the supporting goals, key items include eradication of polio by the year 2000; elimination of neonatal tetanus by 1995; elimination of guinea-worm disease by the year 2000; virtual elimination of iodine deficiency disorders and vitamin-A deficiency; and access by all pregnant women to basic maternal care.

169. Since the World Summit for Children in 1990, some 142 countries have embarked on national programmes of action, often developed with UNICEF support. The World Summit for Children captured the essence of UNICEF support and advocacy when it affirmed the principle of a "first call for children", which it defined as "a principle that the essential needs of children should be given high priority in the allocation of resources, in bad times as well as in good times, at national and international as well as at family levels". This was a logical consequence of the mandates given to the Organization in relation to the goals for children and development and the Convention on the Rights of the Child.

170. In June 1993, children addressed the World Conference on Human Rights at Vienna and demanded greater respect for the rights of children. A number of national programmes of action have been drawn up by developed countries. They include activities for their own children and commitments on assistance to children in developing countries. In developing countries, the national programmes of action have outlined strategies and priorities for budget allocations and provided a framework for the mobilization and coordination of development assistance.

3. United Nations Development Programme

171. The United Nations Development Programme (UNDP) is the largest provider of grant assistance for technical cooperation in the United Nations system. It serves over 170 developing countries and territories through its network of 124 field offices. UNDP coordinates operational activities for development for the United Nations system as a whole and works closely with the regional commissions, the Secretariat and the specialized agencies, and with the Bretton Woods institutions. At the country level, the head of each UNDP office is the Resident Representative, who is usually designated as the resident coordinator of the United Nations system's operational activities for development, and is also the local representative of several other United Nations organizations and programmes. Work has continued on the integration of 18 United Nations information centres with UNDP field offices, in such a way as to preserve the functional autonomy of the centres.

172. UNDP expenditure has increased considerably over the past 10 years (see figure 6). Over the past five years, UNDP has funded programmes and projects valued at around $7 billion. The resources of UNDP derive from voluntary contributions received from developed and developing countries alike. Those external resources support national programmes in which the major share is allocated by the countries themselves. In 1992, the largest share of spending was in Africa (39 per cent), followed by Asia and the Pacific (33 per cent), Latin America and the Caribbean (7 per cent), the Arab States (7 per cent) and Europe and the Commonwealth of Independent States (2 per cent). The remainder was spent on interregional and global programmes, for the support of national liberation movements, and in Caribbean and Pacific multi-island programmes. In each region, some 87 per cent of UNDP resources went to least developed countries (those with a gross national product per capita of less than $750 per year).

173. The bulk of UNDP-funded activities fall within the framework of country programmes through which UNDP and the recipient Government spell out the strategy for using UNDP resources effectively. Compared with earlier cycles, the country programmes approved for the fifth programming cycle are more focused on the priorities outlined in Governing Council decision 90/34, namely, poverty alleviation, management of development, environment and natural resources management, women in development, technical cooperation among developing countries and science and technology for development. Also emphasized are HIV/AIDS, education for all, and private sector development. UNDP is experienced in both long-term technical cooperation and emergency and transitional situations. The HIV/AIDS epidemic is a major natural disaster of planetary scope, with particularly devastating consequences for developing countries. Since 1987, UNDP has provided funds to some 30 countries for national HIV/AIDS-related programmes. While continuing to show concern for those infected, UNDP, in close cooperation with the World Health Organization (WHO), has stressed the importance of preventive measures for combating the pandemic.

174. In 1992 the number of projects aimed at fostering self-reliance through capacity-building for sustainable human development increased. Those projects included guiding the development process to reach the poor and alleviate poverty; protecting the environment and regenerating the resource base for future production; designing workable strategies, action plans and policy reforms; mobilizing financial resources, both public and private; and managing the aid process to help countries make the most of limited concessional resources. The aim of UNDP was to help countries develop economies that would achieve job-led growth and increase social equity and integration. Increased attention to human development has led to a greater recognition of the importance of the political, social, cultural, environmental and institutional aspects of development previously overshadowed by the focus on economic factors. There is now a growing acceptance that development cooperation must include measures to improve governance, judicial systems and social integration and other activities designed to remove obstacles to real participation. This was the theme of the *Human Development Report 1993*, which UNDP sponsored.

175. Developing countries sought specific UNDP support to apply the human development concept in national strategies. Since there is no blueprint for human development, each country has taken its own course, focusing on different issues and priorities. In each case, commitment is critical, from Governments and non-governmental sectors alike. Areas of concern for the national strategies have included the collection of data on development gaps and disparities, analysis, and building consensus between policy makers and

representatives of civil society, particularly between non-governmental organizations and the private sector. The aim is to offer multidisciplinary approaches to social justice in a sustainable manner.

176. The United Nations Conference on Environment and Development gave UNDP a particular mandate to support countries in their efforts to build capacity to implement Agenda 21. Together with the United Nations Environment Programme and the World Bank, UNDP manages the $1.3 billion Global Environment Facility (GEF), taking responsibility for capacity-building and targeted research projects, pre-investment activities, the GEF small grants programme for non-governmental organizations, and facilitating in-country coordination and dissemination of information.

177. Development activities are now clearly seen as helping to establish the conditions for peace. In the aftermath of conflict, developing countries are asking UNDP to assist them with the rehabilitation of war-torn areas, the return and resettlement of refugees and the demobilization and training of former soldiers. To create conditions likely to maintain peace, countries seek UNDP support for programmes to build their capacities to reconstitute the social fabric and to ensure that people can meet their basic needs.

178. At the same time, requests for assistance in fields relatively new for UNDP are being received as Governments seek to give people a say in the forces that shape their lives by increasing their participation in political processes. Support is increasingly sought to improve abilities to conduct elections, bring about democratization and ensure legal protection and human rights. In 1992 in Africa alone, UNDP contributed about $2 million to electoral assistance projects in eight countries that drew nearly $32 million in funds from the countries themselves and from bilateral donors. Countries turned to UNDP for assistance in these sensitive areas, showing their confidence in the objectivity, neutrality and effectiveness of UNDP.

179. UNDP has coordinated its activities with those of the multilateral financial institutions, including the Bretton Woods institutions and the regional development banks. The comparative advantages of UNDP include its field-based organization constantly in touch with local realities, its delivery of technical cooperation for capacity-building, and its effective and extensive cooperation with the specialized agencies. The collaboration includes joint activities at global and regional levels and the execution by multilateral financial institutions of UNDP-funded projects at inter-regional, regional and national levels.

180. UNDP cooperation with the International Monetary Fund (IMF) has focused on assisting developing countries to build their capacity for sound macroeconomic policy formulation and management and establishing necessary financial institutions. For the most part, IMF has acted as executing agency for UNDP-funded projects. In addition, there have been joint training programmes in macroeconomic adjustment and the design of structural adjustment programmes.

181. At the regional and global levels, many development issues require the mobilization of resources, expertise, research networks, forums for debate and media presentation on a massive scale. UNDP has worked with the World Bank and the donor community in many areas of global concern, including the Global Environment Facility, the Energy Sector Management Assistance Programme, the International Drinking Water Supply and Sanitation Decade, the Urban Management Programme, the Consultative Group on International Agricultural Research and the Onchocerciasis Control Programme. At the regional level, there are such joint activities as the African Capacity-building Initiative, the Social Dimensions of Adjustment and the National Long-term Perspective Studies.

182. In "An Agenda for Peace", I highlighted the role of regional organizations in peacemaking and preventive diplomacy. That role extends naturally across the spectrum of political, economic and social conflict. Long-term growth and political stability are mutually interdependent. This is recognized by the United Nations system in its inter-agency programmes, and in the work of UNDP.

183. UNDP cooperation with the African Development Bank covers a wide range of development issues, the Bank acting as executing agency for regional projects in such areas as support for women entrepreneurs, energy, and a feasibility study for the establishment of an African export-import bank. During the fourth programming cycle, UNDP-financed projects executed by the Bank amounted to $6 million.

184. UNDP cooperation with the Asian Development Bank covers almost all sectors, with particular focus on agriculture, forestry, fisheries, and natural resources. UNDP-financed projects executed by the Bank during the fourth programming cycle amounted to $21 million. The relationship is changing as a result of the growing trend towards national execution in the region, and as a result of the greater concentration of UNDP resources on fewer areas of activity.

185. For Latin America and the Caribbean, UNDP and the Inter-American Development Bank (IDB) have an agreement for cooperation and coordination that has led to successful co-financing and joint programming at the national level. Since it is clear that a modern economy without a modern society will not be viable, one aim of such joint

projects on human development and governance is to forestall conflict by supporting consensus-building and enhancing the responsiveness of government to civil society. A joint methodology for human development and social reform has been developed, based on consensus-building and the formulation of responsible long-term public policy. A new strategy for IDB lending to the social sector was debated at a major conference co-sponsored by UNDP and IDB, and was subsequently approved by the Bank's Governing Board.

186.   In the field of the environment, IDB and UNDP helped the countries of Latin America and the Caribbean to prepare a common agenda for the Rio de Janeiro Conference that was widely used in the discussions and negotiations. Given the region's strong capacity for policy analysis and also given small indicative planning figures, the role of UNDP has also been to provide seed money and to support Governments in managing loans from multilateral financial institutions.

187.   At a time when UNDP is being required to address both ongoing and new priorities in a growing number of recipient countries, it is disturbing to report that, after several years of annual increases, contributions to UNDP in 1992 fell to $1,073 million and in 1993 to an estimated $930 million (see figure 7). While I recognize that donor countries are under severe financial constraints, it is my hope that the levels of funding of UNDP will be restored, given the magnitude of the development challenge the world now faces.

4.   United Nations Population Fund

188.   The annual increase in the world's population reached a record level of 93 million. Rapid rates of population growth place a strain on economic growth and hence on development. Yet population growth can be greatly affected by development measures.

189.   The United Nations Population Fund (UNFPA) continues to promote the concept of family planning as a basic human right, based on the principle of informed and voluntary choice. According to the World Health Organization, some 910,000 conceptions occur every day. Half are unplanned. A quarter are unwanted. Some 1,370 women die every day from causes related to pregnancy or childbirth, most of them in developing countries. Thousands more nearly die. Many themselves are children. Many such tragic situations could be avoided if family planning and maternal health programmes were available.

190.   One encouraging development is that an increasing number of countries are now linking population issues to national development policies and priorities. To support those countries, UNFPA took steps to enhance strategic programming, promoted the provision of requisite technical assistance, and supported national capacity-building

for national execution and for coordination of population programme activities.

191.   In compliance with the requirements of General Assembly resolution 47/199, UNFPA strengthened its efforts to build national capacity to manage population programmes, with the aim of enabling countries to become self-reliant in population policy and execution. The core of the Fund's successor support-cost arrangements is high-level technical assistance to help Governments assume the management of UNFPA-funded programmes and projects. The principal UNFPA mechanism for providing technical support services is the country support team, consisting of a team leader and technical advisers; those teams are designed to support not only national execution and national capacity-building but also the decentralization of authority, another emphasis given by the Assembly in resolution 47/199.

192.   Low growth prospects, and indeed poor social integration policies, in many countries have increased migration from the underdeveloped to the developed world. There are today some 100 million international migrants, around 2 per cent of the world population. Of these, 17 million are refugees and a further 20 million have fled deteriorating economic and ecological conditions at home. This is causing strains in both the receiving countries—Europe alone received 15 million migrants between 1980 and 1992—and in the sending countries, strains which have resulted in a renewal of political and social tensions worldwide.

193.   UNFPA continues to pay particular attention to ensuring that gender issues are reflected in all aspects of development assistance, especially in capacity-building. Women and children are often the hardest-hit victims of conflict. In situations where no conflict exists, they are often denied their importance in social construction. For women to realize to the full their potential role as agents of change, they must be able to determine the frequency and timing of childbirth and must have equal access to education and jobs.

194.   The World Conference on Population and Development will be held at Cairo in September 1994. The second session of the Preparatory Committee for the Conference was successfully convened in New York in May 1993, and a third session is scheduled to take place in New York in April 1994. The regional commissions are preparing the ground for a conference which will take up the challenge of people-centred development.

5.   World Food Programme

195.   The World Food Programme (WFP), with total expenditure in 1992 of nearly $1.7 billion, is a major source of grant assistance for developing countries in the United Nations system. Of that amount, 65 per cent was for emergency relief, 29

per cent for development projects, and 6 per cent for programme support and administrative costs.

196. The balance between emergency and development assistance provided by WFP has altered considerably in the past three years, as the growing needs of victims of natural and man-made disasters have continued to dominate its work. Previously, emergency assistance accounted for no more than a third of the Programme's annual expenditure; in 1992, with active relief operations in 48 countries, WFP handled 60 per cent of all international relief food. Commitments for relief activities in 1992 were nearly 50 per cent higher than in 1991 and nearly three times as high as in 1990. For 1993, commitments for relief activities are expected to total $1.25 billion, down slightly from the 1992 record of $1.4 billion.

197. It is estimated that in 1992 some 42 million poor people in developing countries directly benefited from WFP food aid provided in support of development activities or as relief assistance. Of that number, some 27.5 million people, including 14.4 million refugees and displaced people, received WFP relief food in the course of the year.

198. As a result of the increase in relief food aid needs in 1992, WFP handled an all-time record of 5.2 million tons of food. The cost of transporting that food totalled more than $400 million. Three fifths of all shipments of WFP food for the year were for relief, both for short-term emergencies and for long-term refugees and displaced people, compared to one third in earlier years.

199. As conflict and civil strife continue to cause suffering throughout the world, WFP has encouraged international efforts to develop the principle of safe passage of relief food aid in war zones. In a number of countries, such as Afghanistan, Angola, Cambodia, Iraq, Liberia, Mozambique, Somalia, the Sudan and the former Yugoslavia, conflict has hampered efforts to deliver humanitarian relief. WFP staff are often exposed to personal risk in operations to deliver food to civilians trapped by fighting.

200. In 1992, the Committee on Food Aid Policies and Programmes endorsed a more extensive and systematic application of WFP assistance to support disaster prevention, preparedness, mitigation and rehabilitation measures, particularly in Africa. In several countries, including the Gambia, Malawi, Mozambique and Uganda, WFP responded to relief needs by providing food to an increasing number of beneficiaries through ongoing development projects. At the end of 1992, WFP was assisting 258 such projects, with total commitments valued at $3 billion. It is estimated that 15 million people received food through WFP-assisted development projects.

201. New WFP commitments for development projects in 1992 ($421 million, representing 1.1 million tons of food) were the lowest in value terms since 1978. This resulted from a continuing decline since 1988 in resources made available to WFP for development assistance and the need to bring commitments more into line with the expected future availability of resources. In 1993, commitments for future development projects are expected to decline further, to $300 million, representing 850,000 tons. Shipments to ongoing development projects in 1993 are expected to reach $470 million, representing 1.4 million tons, which is close to the average for the past four years.

6. United Nations International Drug Control Programme

202. The United Nations International Drug Control Programme coordinates all drug control activities within the United Nations system and acts as a point of reference for action taken by Governments. The Programme also supports technical cooperation activities which reflect its comparative advantage at the multilateral level. Its strategic priorities have been adapted to evolving drug-related trends, which are themselves driven by unprecedented developments in the political, economic and social fields. I am encouraged by the fact that, during the forty-eighth session of the General Assembly, four plenary meetings will be devoted to the issue of international cooperation against illicit drugs.

203. The United Nations International Drug Control Programme has indicated that the inter-agency meeting on international drug abuse control to be held in 1994 will focus on the theme of women, drug abuse and drug control.

C. *Regional development activities*

204. The regional commissions carry out important information-gathering and socio-economic analysis functions in their respective regions. They have been playing a major role in developing policy on economic integration and in clarifying economic, social, political and environmental issues relating to sustainable development. They thus provide a forum and a network for cooperation among their member States and between them and other States at the technical level. In addition, they are increasingly becoming providers of technical cooperation, especially in intersectoral areas and in areas where no other United Nations body has a comparative advantage.

205. In the restructuring process on which I have embarked I have emphasized the important contribution of the regional commissions. Steps have therefore been taken to strengthen the functions of the commissions and to increase their responsibilities. Those steps are designed to enhance the contribution of the commissions—as the regional arms of a single, integrated United Nations programme in the social and economic

field—to the global work of Headquarters departments.

206.   Regional commissions should function as the main centres within the United Nations system for general economic and social development in their respective regions. Decentralization should not, however, entail a fragmentation of the activities of the Secretariat; rather, it should promote complementarity and mutual reinforcement of activities and should contribute to the cohesiveness of the work of the United Nations.

1.   Economic Commission for Africa

207.   In 1993, the Economic Commission for Africa (ECA) intensified its search for durable solutions to the continent's problems and its efforts to put Africa on the path to sustained and sustainable development by articulating policy measures that respond to the needs of African countries in the social and economic fields.

208.   Among the principal activities undertaken by the ECA secretariat were the preparation for and convening of the Third African Population Conference, which was held at Dakar in December 1992. The Conference was convened in response to Economic and Social Council resolution 1991/93, in which the Council invited the regional commissions to convene conferences to review the experience gained in population policies and programmes in their regions as part of their contribution to the preparatory activities for the International Conference on Population and Development, to be held at Cairo in 1994.

209.   The ECA secretariat also contributed to the report of the Secretary-General on major issues and programme activities relating to social development to the Commission for Social Development at its thirty-third session, in February 1993. A progress report on preparatory activities for the International Year of the Family was also prepared for the inter-agency meeting on the Year held at Vienna in March 1993.

210.   During the seventh meeting of the Joint Intergovernmental Regional Committee on Human Settlements and Environment, which was held at Addis Ababa in March 1993, a report on the follow-up to the Rio de Janeiro Conference was presented. That report included preliminary proposals for strategies to implement Agenda 21 within the framework of the African Common Position on Environment and Development. The proposals related to the major African environmental and development concerns as expressed in the African Common Position. The comments of the Committee were brought to the attention of the ECA Conference of Ministers at its nineteenth meeting.

211.   The ECA secretariat continued its efforts to promote the objectives of the United Nations Decade of Disabled Persons (1983-1992) through the publication and circulation of the newsletter *Equal Time*, in which a number of activities undertaken by and for disabled persons were highlighted.

212.   With regard to the least developed, island and land-locked countries, ECA produced a *Survey of Economic and Social Conditions in the African Least Developed Countries (1991-1992)*. That study gives a detailed account of the structure of gross domestic product and the development of the major economic sectors (agriculture, manufacturing, mining), including an assessment of trade, balance of payments, debt and development finance flows and policies pursued in the African least developed, island and land-locked countries.

213.   The Executive Secretary of ECA participated in the meetings of the panel of high-level personalities on African development. ECA drafted for the panel a paper on the role of indigenous African non-governmental organizations, as part of a report on the role of non-governmental organizations in Africa's development prepared by the Department for Policy Coordination and Sustainable Development.

214.   The twenty-eighth session of the Economic Commission for Africa and nineteenth meeting of the Conference of Ministers responsible for economic development and planning, which was held in May 1993, devoted much attention to the challenges of Africa's development in the 1990s and beyond. It had before it the Commission's *Economic Report on Africa, 1993* and a number of technical studies prepared for its consideration.

215.   The Conference endorsed several strategic objectives as the key to Africa's development in the 1990s. It considered a study on financial resource mobilization for Africa's development, in which it was estimated that about $950 billion (in constant 1990 dollars) of external resources would be required to attain, between 1993 and 2005, the growth target set by the General Assembly in the United Nations New Agenda for the Development of Africa in the 1990s. In view of the gravity of Africa's external debt burden, well over 50 per cent of that amount would be consumed in servicing inherited external debt, unless steps bolder than conventional debt reduction initiatives are implemented.

216.   Other development issues addressed by the Conference included human development and the advancement of women in Africa, and preparations for the International Conference on Population and Development, the Fourth World Conference on Women, and the World Summit for Social Development. The Conference also addressed topics related to the implementation of Agenda 21, as well as trade and investment issues in Africa.

2. Economic Commission for Europe

217. The break-up of the Soviet Union and of Yugoslavia and the separation of the Czech and Slovak Republics led to the emergence of new States, and as a result the membership of the Economic Commission for Europe (ECE) has increased from 34 to 53, and includes former Soviet republics in Transcaucasia and Central Asia.

218. Not only the increase in the number of members poses new challenges to ECE: the very nature of the Commission has changed. Almost half the member States are now countries in transition, some of them clearly at the stage of developing countries. In its analytical work, the ECE secretariat now has to deal with 25 countries in transition which have replaced 8 centrally planned economies.

219. In accordance with the mandate drawn up by the Commission in 1990, ECE has launched a major programme of technical assistance to countries in transition. That programme could be considerably expanded in areas such as advisory services and training, provided the decentralization process now under way strengthens the resource base of ECE. Furthermore, given the number of United Nations programmes and bodies which provide technical assistance in the ECE region, a more coordinated approach is needed to ensure that the aid provided by the United Nations is coherent, well targeted and demand-driven. The interim office concept, described in section II.B above, was developed in response to that need.

220. Specific requests for assistance have been formulated by individual ECE countries. In response to General Assembly resolutions, the Commission invited all its subsidiary bodies to identify ways and means of contributing to international efforts to assist in the mitigation of the consequences of the Chernobyl nuclear disaster and in the reconstruction of Croatia. ECE involvement in the latter endeavour is in accordance with the original mandate of the Commission to assist in the reconstruction of war-devastated zones. A coherent United Nations strategy which ensures an integrated approach to the reconstruction and rehabilitation of war-ravaged areas in the ECE region should be prepared by competent United Nations programmes without delay.

221. The Commission, at its forty-eighth session, in April 1993, defined environment, transport, statistics, trade facilitation and economic analysis as its priority areas of activity. Those priorities were reflected in decisions adopted at that session on questions of environment and sustainable development, cooperation and sustainable development in the chemical industry and cooperation in the field of transport. The Commission also adopted a decision on activities designed to assist countries of the region in transition to a market economy and their integration with the European and global economy. ECE called for further economic cooperation in the Mediterranean region in the light of the Final Act of the Conference on Security and Cooperation in Europe, held at Helsinki in 1975.

222. The *Economic Survey of Europe in 1992-1993*, published by ECE, contains an in-depth analysis of the European transition countries; their output and demand; labour markets, prices and incomes; foreign trade and payments; macroeconomic policies; market reforms; and progress made in privatization. The *Survey* also includes a review of developments in central, eastern and south-eastern European countries, the countries of the former Yugoslavia and the former Soviet Union, and the Baltic republics, together with a discussion of Western responses to the transition in central and eastern Europe in aid and trade, analysing the financial flows and commitments of assistance, and East-West cooperation agreements and market access.

223. ECE continued to make useful contributions to global programmes of the United Nations. The Commission submitted to the Rio de Janeiro Conference a compendium of its conventions in the field of environmental protection. As a part of the preparations for the International Conference on Population and Development, ECE held a European Population Conference jointly with UNFPA and the Council of Europe in March 1993. At its forty-eighth session, the Commission decided to convene a high-level regional preparatory meeting for the Fourth World Conference on Women. It also endorsed work under way in socio-economic activities as a contribution to the World Summit for Social Development. Each year, more than 30 countries from outside the ECE region participate actively in the work of the Commission, and the results of its work are made available to the developing countries of other regions.

224. The intensive efforts of the ECE secretariat have resulted in further progress in strengthening cooperation and coordination with organizations and institutions such as the Commission of the European Communities, the Organisation for Economic Cooperation and Development, the European Bank for Reconstruction and Development and the Council of Europe.

3. Economic Commission for Latin America and the Caribbean

225. The Economic Commission for Latin America and the Caribbean (ECLAC), which includes the Latin American and Caribbean Institute for Economic and Social Planning (ILPES) and the Latin American Demographic Centre (CELADE), focused on the promotion of sustainable growth with equity. Two major publications

were produced and presented to the Commission at its twenty-fourth session, in April 1992, and were subsequently given wide distribution. The first publication, entitled *Social Equity and Changing Production Patterns: An Integrated Approach*, explores how the region's countries can advance simultaneously in sustainable growth with greater equity. It has been hailed by policy makers as an important conceptual contribution to development economics. The second publication was prepared jointly with UNESCO, under the title *Education and Knowledge: Basic Pillars of Changing Production Patterns with Social Equity*; it highlights the crucial importance of those topics for increasing levels of productivity and improved equity.

226. CELADE also helped to disseminate demographic knowledge among the Governments of the region by organizing the Meeting of Government Experts on Population and Development in Latin America and the Caribbean, which was held in Saint Lucia in October 1992.

227. The fourteenth and fifteenth meetings of the Presiding Officers of the Regional Conference on the Integration of Women into the Economic and Social Development of Latin America and the Caribbean were held in Curaçao in June 1992, and at Mexico City in October 1992.

228. With regard to the integration of women into the economic and social development of Latin America and the Caribbean, ECLAC undertook preparatory activities for the Fourth World Conference on Women. ECLAC has already begun activities related to the preparation of the new regional programme of action for women in Latin America and the Caribbean, 1995-2001, and is preparing a diagnosis of the status of women that substantively incorporates this question into the new ECLAC proposal on changing production patterns with social equity.

229. The Social Development Division concentrated its efforts on preparing technical documents for the Third Regional Conference on Poverty in Latin America and the Caribbean, held at Santiago in November 1992.

230. The Commission continues its permanent role in monitoring economic events in the region. The formal expression of its work is found in the *Preliminary Overview of the Economy of Latin America and the Caribbean*, published with up-to-date indicators in December of each year, and in the *Economic Survey of Latin America and the Caribbean* and the *Statistical Yearbook for Latin America and the Caribbean*. ECLAC also continues to be the main forum for economic and social affairs in the region, and the Latin American Centre for Economic and Social Documentation is strengthening information management in the region.

231. The Commission has undertaken numerous technical cooperation activities, at the request of member States, to assist Governments in the formulation and implementation of policies and plans for economic and social development within the overall strategy of changing production patterns with social equity.

232. ECLAC co-sponsored the Regional Preparatory Meeting for Latin America and the Caribbean (San José, January 1993) for the World Conference on Human Rights and provided technical support to several presidential forums, including the Meeting of Heads of State of Central America and Panama (Panama, December 1992), the Heads of State of the Rio Group (Buenos Aires, December 1992) and the third Ibero-American Summit of Heads of State and Government (San Salvador de Bahia, Brazil, July 1993).

4. Economic and Social Commission for Asia and the Pacific

233. On 9 April 1993, I was present when His Majesty King Bhumibol Adulyadej officially opened the new United Nations Conference Centre at Bangkok, where the Economic and Social Commission for Asia and the Pacific (ESCAP) has its offices.

234. Regional economic cooperation is gaining ever greater momentum in the ESCAP region. At the same time, subregional organizations are being revitalized and are focusing, in particular, on the development of infrastructure within their respective subregions. The newer forms of economic cooperation are transcending the deeply embedded constraints of the cold war; the States involved in the Viet Nam war, for example, are now entering into the mainstream of development efforts in the region.

235. Under the revised intergovernmental structure, the first session of the Committee for Regional Economic Cooperation was convened at Bangkok in October 1992, while the first session of its Steering Group was held at New Delhi in November 1992. The Steering Group considered and adopted an action programme for regional economic cooperation in trade and investment, which was submitted, through the Committee, to the Commission at its forty-ninth session.

236. The Fourth Asian and Pacific Population Conference was held in Bali in August 1992. The Conference, sponsored by ESCAP and UNFPA, considered and adopted the Bali Declaration on Population and Sustainable Development, which will serve as the basis for policy-making and programming.

237. The period since August 1992 has been one of transition for ESCAP from a sectoral to a thematic approach, in terms of both the Commission's subsidiary intergovernmental structure and its programmes. Considerable attention has been paid to evolving thematic subprogrammes on regional economic cooperation, poverty alleviation

through economic growth and social development, and environment and sustainable development in response to this shift in approach. During the same period, ESCAP activities have focused increasingly on the social dimensions of development. At the forty-ninth session of the Commission, in April 1993, 3 of the 10 resolutions adopted related to areas of social concern.

238. In December 1992, ESCAP convened the Meeting to Launch the Asian and Pacific Decade of Disabled Persons, 1993-2002, in Beijing. At that Meeting, the Proclamation on the Full Participation and Equality of People with Disabilities in the Asian and Pacific Region and the Agenda for Action for the Asian and Pacific Decade of Disabled Persons, 1993-2002, were considered and adopted.

239. The Special Body on Pacific Island Developing Countries held its first session at Bangkok in February 1993. The Special Body emphasized, *inter alia*, the importance of international trade and investment for the island economies and recommended the strengthening of finance, investment and trade links between them and the more dynamic economies of the ESCAP region. The secretariat has issued various research-oriented publications pertinent to the development of the Pacific island developing countries, including *Sustainable Agricultural Development Strategies in the Pacific Island Least Developed Countries: Issues and Policy Options* and *The Law of the Sea in the South Pacific: A Study on the Integration of Marine Affairs Activities within Government Concerns.*

240. A study of the theme topic ''Expansion of investment and intraregional trade as a vehicle for enhancing regional economic cooperation and development in Asia and the Pacific'', presented in part two of the *Economic and Social Survey of Asia and the Pacific, 1992*, assessed the contribution of the trade-investment nexus to the process of industrial restructuring in the ESCAP region.

241. Measures have been taken to reinforce the functional relationship between ESCAP and various United Nations organizations and bodies with a view to undertaking a coordinated approach to problem-solving and rendering assistance to the member States. In addition to meetings held in recent months by the various inter-agency mechanisms, including the Inter-agency Committee on Environment and Development in Asia and the Pacific, the Inter-agency Committee on Integrated Rural Development and the Inter-agency Task Force on Water for Asia and the Pacific, ESCAP has been seeking to develop greater linkages and cooperative frameworks with other regional bodies. In that context, special focus has been placed on strengthening the relationship between ESCAP and organizations such as the Association of South-East Asian Nations, the South Asian Association for Regional Cooperation, the South Pacific Forum secretariat, the Economic Coopera- tion Organization and the Asia-Pacific Economic Cooperation, as well as with financial institutions such as the Asian Development Bank.

5. Economic and Social Commission for Western Asia

242. In the post-cold-war era, as the world moves towards global economic management, and as conflict and cooperation battle for dominance, the challenges to the region of the Economic and Social Commission for Western Asia (ESCWA) increase in intensity and scope. The ESCWA region may also be considered a region in transition. It is at the crossroads between the politics and cultures of the East and the West, a region searching to assert the identity of its people, to protect its internal and external sovereignty, and to withstand internal and external pressures. A most serious challenge to the political stability of the region is the eruption of new forms of extremism. Political instability, uncertainty and unpredictability continue to plague the region and to exercise a preponderant influence on its peace, development and security prospects. These imminent challenges need to be tackled swiftly and surely.

243. The physical destruction and damage to the environment, the problems of returnees and pressures on the labour markets and the infrastructure, the instability in oil prices, the decline of recurrent financial transfers in aid and remittances, continued sanctions against Iraq and their adverse impact on neighbouring countries represent enormous challenges to the ESCWA region.

244. These crisis-related challenges come on top of long-standing structural imbalances, such as the income disparities between and within countries; the uneven distribution of energy resources at the regional level; inadequate energy supply, water shortages, desertification, and lack of food security and transport linkages in many rural and remote areas; vulnerability to fluctuations in oil prices; and external indebtedness.

245. In its desire to contribute to efforts to redress some of the worst physical and social ravages of the Gulf crisis, as well as man-made and natural disasters, the Commission at its sixteenth session, in September 1992, declared the period 1994-2003 a Reconstruction and Rehabilitation Decade for Western Asia. To streamline regional action, and in collaboration with the League of Arab States, ESCWA set up an inter-agency Joint Committee for Environment and Development in the Arab Region in April 1993. In addition, ESCWA is in the process of establishing a regional water council to coordinate activities for a more efficient use of scarce water resources. To that end, a regional inter-agency consultative mechanism was formed for water and environment which would serve as the nucleus for a regional administrative coordination committee.

246.   The secretariat participated in the formulation of a plan of action to combat desertification region-wide. The Second Amman Declaration on Population and Development of April 1993 is an instrument to promote regional cooperation and to assist member States in dealing with population issues and population movements. In the area of transport, ESCWA is heavily involved in activities related to the Transport and Communications Decade in Western Asia (1985-1994). To help bridge the widening technological gap, ESCWA focused on the formulation of policies and measures to increase the effectiveness of the technology factor in the investment process. To overcome the lack of timely, reliable and replicable statistics and data, ESCWA set up the Committee on Statistics as a subsidiary body of the Commission.

247.   In addition to preparing studies and convening intergovernmental and expert group meetings, ESCWA provided technical assistance and advisory services to member States to assist them in meeting challenges and formulating action-oriented policies. For example, the Commission convened an expert group meeting on the operation of enterprises under severe and fast-changing conditions. Other meetings were convened on the creation of indigenous entrepreneurship, especially to train returnees, and on unemployment as one of the major challenges facing society. Training activities were introduced as pilot projects to allow women to cope with their multiple roles and contribute to production. ESCWA also assisted in meeting the needs for rural energy through the introduction of biogas technology in selected countries of the region.

248.   Under the auspices of ESCWA, a multidisciplinary task force on the Palestinian people and the occupied Arab territories was set up to deal with socio-economic issues emanating from the Israeli occupation and the implications of a peace settlement for countries of the region. The task force will also provide technical assistance to the Palestinian people.

249.   The most important obstacles facing the Commission in fulfilling its mandate remain the uncertainty and political instability in the region, which have caused interruption in its activities and its relocation several times in the recent past. They have also contributed to the rifts among countries of the region and the set-backs in cooperation to which failures in the region's performance and inadequate rapport between member States and the secretariat are attributed. These in turn have caused a dwindling of extrabudgetary funding and a paucity of resources to address emerging needs and, consequently, inadequate regional coordination and harmonization in implementing projects of a regional scope.

D.   *Protection of human rights*

1.   Centre for Human Rights

250.   In the course of 1993, the activities of the Centre for Human Rights at Geneva underwent a significant expansion in the five main areas of its work: research, standard-setting and prevention of discrimination; implementation of international standards; special procedures; communications; and advisory services and information.

251.   On 1 January 1993, I appointed an Assistant Secretary-General to head the Centre for Human Rights, with responsibility for dealing exclusively with human rights issues, to report directly to me. The Assistant Secretary-General for Human Rights is responsible in particular for developing coherent policies and strengthening coordination in the field of human rights, and he serves as a focal point for United Nations relations with regional organizations on human rights matters.

252.   The World Conference on Human Rights, in June 1993, asked for an immediate increase in the Centre's resources from the regular budget. The Conference indicated clearly that those resources should support the work of the Centre in fulfilling its many urgent mandates, provide for the implementation of the fact-finding procedures of the Commission on Human Rights, ensure the functioning of the treaty bodies and provide sufficient resources to the advisory services programme to enable it to respond to requests by States for assistance. The Conference also called for increased contributions to the voluntary funds supporting advisory services and activities in favour of indigenous people and against racial discrimination. Those matters will be addressed in my budget proposals for the biennium 1994-1995.

2.   World Conference on Human Rights

253.   The World Conference on Human Rights, which was held at Vienna from 14 to 25 June 1993, was a turning-point in United Nations activities for the promotion and protection of human rights. The Conference was the culmination of three years of intense activity by all segments of the international community directed at reviewing past progress in the protection of human rights, identifying obstacles to further progress and charting the course of action for the coming years.

254.   The Vienna Conference and its preparatory process were worldwide, in terms both of the subjects dealt with and of participation. Three regional meetings, held at Tunis, San José and Bangkok, preceded the Conference, as did hundreds of other meetings around the world. Representatives from 172 States took part in the discussions at Vienna together with observers from 95 international organizations, human rights bodies and national human rights institutions and

from 840 non-governmental organizations. A high level of expertise, and a clear commitment to human rights on the part of the participants, contributed to the success of the debates. Long and careful exchanges of views revealed considerable common ground among the different participants. The Conference was therefore able to adopt by consensus a declaration and programme of action of historic proportions, but differences of opinion were also candidly stated.

255.   The Vienna Conference reaffirmed the universality of fundamental human rights and the principle that the human person is the central subject of human rights, should be the principal beneficiary and should participate actively in the realization of human rights. But the Conference did not deal with the question solely at a theoretical level: it also called for effective action to secure the human rights of every individual on a universal basis. The Conference also recognized the right to development as a human right and the mutually reinforcing interrelationship between democracy, development and respect for human rights, and the need to assist developing countries in their democratization process. It also clearly established the link between universality and equality, and stressed the need to eliminate all discrimination based on race and similar factors. The Conference provided substantive guidance for the United Nations in its future work in this area and called for world-wide action against discrimination and in favour of tolerance.

256.   There was also notable progress in two other areas. The Conference stressed that priority should be given to action to secure the full and equal enjoyment by women of all human rights: respect for women's rights must be integrated into the overall human rights programme and into development activities. Special attention must be given to protecting women and girl children from violence and other human rights violations which threaten them particularly. The Conference called for universal ratification of the Convention on the Elimination of All Forms of Discrimination against Women by the year 2000, and the drafting of an optional protocol to that Convention to permit individual complaints of violations of women's rights to be considered.

257.   The need to act effectively to protect the rights of children, including children in especially difficult circumstances and the girl child, was another step forward. All competent organs are being asked to review and monitor progress in protecting children's rights and the year 1995 has been set as the target for the universal ratification of the Convention on the Rights of the Child.

258.   Another important step forward was the recognition of the rights of persons with disabilities and of the need to take specific measures to protect vulnerable groups, including migrant workers, and to ensure that they participate in the search for solutions to their own problems. The human rights dimensions of extreme poverty and exclusion were also recognized, as was the need to deal not only with human rights violations but also with their causes. In this context the Conference called for national and international action on a priority basis to eliminate specific obstacles to the enjoyment of human rights.

259.   During this International Year of the World's Indigenous People, the Vienna Conference recognized the inherent dignity and unique contribution of indigenous people, reaffirmed the international community's commitment to their well-being, and reiterated the obligation of States to ensure respect for their rights.

260.   A key result of the Conference was the widespread acceptance of the need for cooperation between Governments, the United Nations, other international organizations, national human rights institutions and non-governmental organizations. An effective partnership involving all those actors is essential for the effective promotion and protection of human rights.

261.   The Vienna Conference recognized the increasingly important contribution non-governmental organizations can play in human rights activities, especially in relation to development and human rights. One of the most important achievements of the Conference was its success in harnessing the energies of hitherto-untapped grass-roots organizations, particularly from Africa, Asia and Latin America and the Caribbean.

262.   The importance of human rights to United Nations activities in the fields of peace-making, peace-keeping and preventive diplomacy, and in social and economic development, was also amply demonstrated by the Vienna Conference. The inclusion of the human rights dimension in the planning, implementation and evaluation of programmes and projects in those areas will be important to their success and to the promotion of human rights.

263.   Increased attention is to be given to implementing economic, social and cultural rights through, in particular, the drafting of optional protocols to the 1966 International Covenant on Economic, Social and Cultural Rights and the use of indicators.

264.   Education was repeatedly stressed as a crucial element in building future respect for human rights. By adopting a concrete and practical approach it should be possible for human rights to be included in teaching programmes in all countries, both in schools and in programmes for those who are not in school.

265.   The Vienna Conference reaffirmed that efforts to eradicate torture should be concentrated

on prevention, and called for the early adoption of an optional protocol to the 1984 Convention against Torture and Other Cruel, Inhuman or Degrading Treatment or Punishment to allow regular visits to places of detention. It also recommended that States should abrogate legislation leading to impunity for those responsible for torture.

266.   The role of the United Nations in the promotion and protection of human rights must be strengthened, renewed and revitalized if the promises of the Vienna Declaration and Programme of Action are to be kept. International coordination and cooperation were seen at Vienna as crucial for improving respect for human rights. United Nations bodies, specialized agencies, regional intergovernmental organizations and national human rights institutions all have important contributions to make in this overall coordinated approach.

267.   The Centre for Human Rights was identified as the focal point for global cooperation for human rights. The Conference called for an annual United Nations coordination meeting at a high level as one element in this approach. Close cooperation will also have to be established with other key actors.

268.   The Vienna Conference recognized that future progress would depend in large part on the availability of assistance to countries engaged in improving and strengthening their protection of human rights. An overall United Nations approach was called for, enabling States to strengthen democratic institutions and the rule of law, to protect minority rights and those of indigenous peoples, and to hold democratic elections. The programme of advisory services and technical assistance in the field of human rights has been given specific new and wide-ranging responsibilities in helping to improve respect for human rights.

269.   The United Nations must be able to respond rapidly and professionally to allegations of human rights violations and to service adequately the machinery set up for that purpose. We must at the same time seek ways of improving the operation and impact of those mechanisms.

270.   The Vienna Conference also proposed that United Nations activities in human rights be given greater focus by means of three decades for action: one relating to indigenous people, one for education and human rights and one against racism and racial discrimination. The General Assembly, in addition, has before it the Conference's proposal for a United Nations decade for human rights.

3.   Implementation of human rights conventions

271.   The Vienna Conference set universal ratification of the basic international human rights treaties as an important objective. In 1998 the follow-up review of the implementation of the

Vienna Declaration and Programme of Action will give special attention to the progress made towards universal ratification.

272.   As at 7 September 1993, the 1965 International Convention on the Elimination of All Forms of Racial Discrimination has been ratified by 137 States and the 1973 International Convention on the Suppression and Punishment of the Crime of Apartheid by 97 States. Of the two 1966 Human Rights Covenants, the International Covenant on Economic, Social and Cultural Rights has been ratified by 125 States and the International Covenant on Civil and Political Rights by 123 States. The 1979 Convention on the Elimination of All Forms of Discrimination against Women has been ratified by 126 States, and the 1989 Convention on the Rights of the Child by 146 States.

273.   The level of ratification of other conventions is most unsatisfactory, however. So far, only 76 States have ratified the 1984 Convention against Torture and Other Cruel, Inhuman or Degrading Treatment or Punishment; only 56 States have ratified the 1985 International Convention against Apartheid in Sports; only 2 States have ratified the 1990 International Convention on the Protection of the Rights of All Migrant Workers and Members of Their Families; and the Second Optional Protocol to the International Covenant on Civil and Political Rights, aiming at the abolition of the death penalty, adopted by the General Assembly on 15 December 1989, has been ratified by only 19 States.

274.   As Secretary-General of the United Nations, I strongly urge States to ratify all human rights treaties. To that end, I intend to open a dialogue with Member States to identify and to try to overcome the obstacles to ratification. I also believe that regional organizations have a positive role to play in making States more aware of this issue.

275.   The process of democratization cannot be separated from the protection of human rights. More precisely, the effective safeguarding of human rights is possible only in a democratic framework. It is therefore not possible to separate the United Nations promotion of human rights from the global trend towards democratization.

IV.   Expanding preventive diplomacy, humanitarian assistance and conflict resolution

". . . to take effective collective measures for the prevention and removal of threats to the peace, and for the suppression of acts of aggression or other breaches of the peace, and to bring about by peaceful means, and in conformity with the principles of justice and international law, adjustment or settlement of international disputes or situations which might lead to a breach of the peace;"

Charter of the United Nations, Article 1, paragraph 1

A. *Implementing an Agenda for Peace*

276. On 18 December 1992 the General Assembly, in its resolution 47/120, welcomed my report entitled "An Agenda for Peace" and encouraged me to pursue my efforts in preventive diplomacy. The Assembly also invited me to strengthen the capacity of the Secretariat for the collection of information and analysis to serve better the early-warning needs of the Organization. The informal open-ended working group established by the Assembly has continued to discuss other recommendations contained in my report, which has also been considered by the Special Committee on the Charter of the United Nations and on the Strengthening of the Role of the Organization and the Special Committee on Peacekeeping Operations.

277. The Security Council held monthly meetings between October 1992 and May 1993 to examine specific proposals made in "An Agenda for Peace". Eight statements by the President were issued as part of this process. On 15 June 1993, I submitted a report on the implementation of the recommendations contained in "An Agenda for Peace". An interdepartmental task force was also set up to propose further measures for implementing those recommendations.

278. In "An Agenda for Peace", I set out some definitions of the range of peace operations undertaken by the United Nations across the world. Preventive diplomacy is action to prevent disputes from arising between parties, to prevent existing disputes from escalating into conflicts and to limit the spread of the latter when they occur. Peacemaking is action to bring hostile parties to agreement, essentially through such peaceful means as those foreseen in Chapter VI of the Charter of the United Nations. Peace-keeping is the deployment of a United Nations presence in the field, hitherto with the consent of all the parties concerned, normally involving United Nations military or police personnel and frequently civilians also. Peacekeeping is a technique that expands the possibilities for both the prevention of conflict and the making of peace. The concept of peace enforcement should be added here. It involves peacekeeping activities which do not necessarily involve the consent of all the parties concerned. Peace enforcement is foreseen in Chapter VII of the Charter. Peace-building is action to identify and support structures which will tend to strengthen and solidify peace so as to avert a relapse into conflict. Preventive diplomacy seeks to resolve disputes before violence breaks out; peacemaking and peacekeeping, and sometimes peace enforcement, are required to halt conflicts and preserve peace once it is attained. If successful, they strengthen the opportunity for post-conflict peace-building, which can prevent the recurrence of violence among nations and peoples. In practice, the various steps of peace operations are intertwined and may be performed simultaneously and in parallel.

B. *Preventive diplomacy*

279. Once an elusive and undefined concept, preventive diplomacy is now becoming understood as a vital field for practical action. New forms of preventive diplomacy have evolved in the course of the past year; such diplomacy incorporates efforts designed to prevent the occurrence of armed conflict, such as fact-finding, good offices and goodwill missions, the dispatch of special envoys to tense areas, and efforts to bring parties to a potential conflict to the negotiating table. Today, the variety of challenges faced by the United Nations has led to a more intensive and creative use of such familiar techniques.

280. I find myself frequently engaged in preventive diplomacy. Because of the nature of this work, and the requirements of the parties, such diplomacy often takes place behind the scenes. When efforts fail, the results will be seen in public. When there is success, the story must often remain untold. Preventive diplomacy takes place continuously and can range from a brief telephone conversation to the movement of military units.

281. More than 100 missions of representation, fact-finding and goodwill offices to various countries were undertaken on my behalf. I have myself travelled extensively to extend good offices and represent the Organization throughout the world. A catalogue of all the missions undertaken by myself and on my behalf would be too long to include here. Suffice it to state that, between August 1992 and July 1993, I held high-level talks in 27 countries, visiting many of them more than once. Some examples of action taken during the past year will illustrate the nature of this field of endeavour and its new dimensions.

1. South Africa: observers

282. For the first time, civilian United Nations observers have been sent to a country with the consent of the Government, to assist the authorities of that country and the conflicting parties in what is purely a domestic matter: containing the level of violence. The country in question is South Africa. This is a significant breakthrough and could serve as a useful precedent in similar situations elsewhere.

283. The Security Council, in its resolution 772(1992), authorized me to deploy United Nations observers. I appointed Angela King Chief of the United Nations Observer Mission in South Africa; she took up her post on 23 September 1992. The observers, together with observers from other organizations, including the Organization of African Unity (OAU), the Commonwealth and the European Community, have worked in close cooper-

ation with the National Peace Committee, the National Peace Secretariat and the Commission of Inquiry regarding the Prevention of Public Violence and Intimidation to reduce tensions, contain demonstrations and stop clashes from getting out of control. There are now 49 United Nations observers in South Africa. After an initial mission undertaken on my behalf by Cyrus Vance, I designated two special envoys, Virendra Dayal and Tom Vraalsen, who visited South Africa. On the basis of their findings, I submitted on 22 December 1992 a second report on the question of South Africa, in which I noted that distinct progress had been made in implementing the recommendations set out in my report of 7 August 1992.

284. I have been in personal contact with President F. W. de Klerk, Chief Mangosuthu Buthelezi, Mr. Clarence Makwetu, Mr. Nelson Mandela and other South African leaders to assist in the strengthening of the structures set up under the National Peace Accord. I also addressed letters to leaders of the homelands. The decision to hold South Africa's first-ever free elections in accordance with the principles of universal suffrage opens the way for the country's transition to a democratic and non-racial society, an objective which has defined United Nations involvement in South Africa. The level of violence continues, however, to be a source of serious concern.

2. The former Yugoslav Republic of Macedonia

285. In the former Yugoslav Republic of Macedonia, for the first time ever in United Nations history, military units have been deployed as a measure of preventive diplomacy. The Security Council, in resolution 795(1992), authorized me to establish a presence of the United Nations Protection Force (UNPROFOR) in the former Yugoslav Republic of Macedonia, on the borders with Albania and the Federal Republic of Yugoslavia (Serbia and Montenegro). That act of preventive deployment was taken out of concern to avert a wider Balkan war. There are currently just under 1,000 peace-keepers in the region in addition to a small group of United Nations civilian police. At the same time, the United Nations is providing emergency relief assistance to the 900,000 persons displaced by the conflict. A consolidated appeal for $78 million has been launched for this humanitarian programme.

286. Under United Nations auspices, Greece and the former Yugoslav Republic of Macedonia are engaged in talks intended to reduce the tensions brought about by the recognition of the independence of the latter. The Co-Chairmen of the Steering Committee of the International Conference on the Former Yugoslavia have presented to the representatives of Greece and the former Yugoslav Republic of Macedonia a draft treaty prepared on the basis of extensive consultations with the two sides. Part A of the draft treaty includes a number of special provisions designed to promote friendly relations and to set up confidence-building measures, while parts B to E set out provisions for friendship and neighbourly cooperation appropriate to the interaction of two adjoining States establishing relations for the first time.

287. At the time of the deployment of UNPROFOR, the Government of the former Yugoslav Republic of Macedonia was gravely concerned about an external security threat. The presence of UNPROFOR and the admission to membership in the United Nations of the former Yugoslav Republic of Macedonia have contributed to alleviating those fears. In this connection, the strengthening of UNPROFOR under Security Council resolution 842(1993) is a welcome development.

288. On 18 June the Security Council, in resolution 845(1993), urged Greece and the former Yugoslav Republic of Macedonia to continue their efforts, under my auspices, to arrive at a speedy settlement of remaining issues between them. I have appointed Cyrus Vance to exercise good offices on my behalf.

3. Preventive humanitarian action

289. Frequently, situations of humanitarian need provide indications of impending conflict even before they develop into more serious threats to international peace and security. Early awareness of the root causes of conflict can allow appropriate preventive action to be taken. The provision of humanitarian assistance for such preventive purposes has made it possible to contain the impact of some emergencies. One such success has been the joint United Nations–Southern Africa Development Community drought emergency in southern Africa programme, under which comprehensive measures to mitigate the effects of the drought, minimize the potential population displacement and avert famine were put into place in 10 countries of the region.

290. Another type of preventive humanitarian action is the strengthening of the national capacity of disaster-prone countries. I fully support action taken to integrate disaster prevention and preparedness activities into the mainstream development projects of organizations of the United Nations system within the framework of the International Decade for Natural Disaster Reduction. For other emergencies that result from long-term economic deterioration, or slow-moving natural disasters such as drought, early humanitarian preventive action can save thousands of lives and millions of dollars in subsequent remedial action.

291. An inter-agency early-warning mechanism for examining possible situations of mass

population displacement is being managed by the Department of Humanitarian Affairs. One of its purposes is to assist in determining when preventive humanitarian action may be appropriate.

C. *Peace-keeping in a changing context*

292. Just as preventive diplomacy and conflict resolution, familiar responsibilities of the United Nations, have taken on new dimensions, so the term peace-keeping now stretches across a heretofore unimagined range of United Nations activities and responsibilities.

293. Peace-keeping is a United Nations invention. The concept is, however, not a static one, but is ever changing; in order to succeed, and to reflect the changing needs of the community of States, peace-keeping has to be reinvented every day. Each case in which United Nations peace-keepers are involved draws upon the fund of experience, imagination and professionalism of the Organization. It is not an exaggeration to state that today there are as many types of peace-keeping operations as there are types of conflict.

294. The task of peace-keeping, like that of peacemaking, is subject to an essential constraint: for peace-keeping to succeed, the parties to a conflict must have the necessary political will. Peace-keeping, even more than peacemaking, requires the adherence of the conflicting parties to the principle of peaceful resolution of conflicts, in other words, to the Charter itself.

295. Traditional assumptions relating to the upholding of agreements, the consent and cooperation of the parties and the minimum use of force have all been under challenge from recent developments in certain peace-keeping operations. United Nations peace-keepers have been sent to areas where there are no agreements, where Governments do not exist or have limited effective authority and where the consent and cooperation of the parties cannot be relied upon. All too frequently, their work is obstructed by well-armed irregular groups and warlords who defy both their national authorities, where these exist, and the international community.

296. Some 80,000 civilian and military personnel now serve in 17 United Nations peace-keeping operations across the world (see figures 8 and 9). If additional operations and troop reinforcements at present under consideration are implemented, the total could rise to 100,000 by the end of 1993. Today, peace-keepers perform a variety of complex tasks, such as protecting humanitarian aid convoys, supporting the supervision of elections and monitoring human rights, in addition to their basic responsibility of keeping apart the warring parties. Keeping the peace, therefore, is only a step in the process of the peaceful resolution of conflicts. It should not be confused with conflict resolution. Putting a halt to armed hostilities is not in itself a solution of the conflicts. It offers temporary respite from hostilities, while the crisis is being resolved in the political, humanitarian, economic and social spheres.

297. One key aspect of the new generation of United Nations peace-keeping operations is the role of public information in promoting understanding and generating support at both the national and the international level. That support can be built only on a clear understanding of why a particular mission has been sent to a specific area, and how the mission plans to accomplish its objectives. In the atmosphere of heightened tension in conflict areas, public information activities play a vital role in facilitating the mission's work by disseminating timely and objective information, and counteracting propaganda and misinformation. Effective public information activities can also be instrumental in generating and sustaining the support of the international community for the success of the missions. In the absence of information from the United Nations there may be misunderstandings of the United Nations mandate, which can give rise to unwarranted criticism of the Organization's activities.

298. In June 1992, I was able to report that Member States were keen to participate in peace-keeping operations and that military observers and infantry were invariably available. This is no longer generally the case. Difficulties which were previously encountered only when specialized logistic units were sought now arise also in the case of infantry and military as well as police observers.

299. To deal with the increased demand for peace-keeping operations and the consequent shortage of peace-keepers, several steps have been taken:

(a) I have invited Member States to designate qualified personnel for consideration for secondment to a peace-keeping operation;

(b) A special planning team has been set up with the task of defining standard components from which different types of peace-keeping operations might be put together. The team has briefed delegations on its work and Member States have been invited to enter into discussions with the Secretariat about the components of peace-keeping operations which they would, in principle, be ready to provide;

(c) I have accepted offers by Member States to make available peace-keeping personnel on loan;

(d) It has become necessary to use the services of contractors for support activities for field operations normally performed by United Nations staff.

300. The respective roles of the Department of Political Affairs and the Department of Peacekeeping Operations have, as indicated in section II above, been more clearly defined. The latter

Department now incorporates the Field Operations Division and is being strengthened. It will be responsible for providing Headquarters technical and administrative support for integrated operations in the field including, as appropriate, peace-keeping, peacemaking, electoral or humanitarian components. This restructuring will enhance the planning, coordination and reporting of peace-keeping operations and ensure better delivery of services to the various United Nations operations.

301.   A military planning cell has been formed within the Department of Peace-keeping Operations, with military staff on loan from Member States. A situation room, staffed by military officers, has been created to enable the competent Departments to maintain a continuous link with operations in Somalia and the former Yugoslavia. I am considering an integrated situation room which would cover United Nations peace-keeping worldwide in all its aspects.

302.   The growth in peace-keeping has profoundly affected the operations of the Organization (see figure 10). Every administrative entity in the Secretariat has been required to assign staff to one or more of the peace-keeping operations. As I reported in section II above, the staff members remaining have had to perform the tasks previously carried out by their absent colleagues. Demands have grown so much that it is now no longer possible to fill all the positions within the Secretariat or in the field with existing Secretariat staff, and substantial additional staff will be required, since staff on loan from Member States cannot be used to establish permanent structures.

303.   I am conscious of the mounting cost of peace-keeping and the burden this entails for Member States. I welcome, therefore, General Assembly resolution 47/217, by which the Assembly authorized a Peace-keeping Reserve Fund of $150 million, which, when fully funded, will enhance the Organization's ability to respond to new crises. I hope that the General Assembly will consider favourably, at its forty-eighth session, my proposal that it appropriate one third of the estimated cost of each new peace-keeping operation as soon as it is established by the Security Council. I have also asked the Assembly to encourage the inclusion of peace-keeping contributions in national defence budgets. I should like to restate here that, in accordance with the Charter and the relevant General Assembly resolutions, financing of peace-keeping is the collective responsibility of all Member States.

304.   One of the consequences of the delay in the payment of assessed contributions is that States contributing to peace operations are themselves reimbursed only after long delays. As a result, certain Member States have had to withdraw their contingents from peace-keeping operations.

305.   I have proposed the setting-up of a reserve, revolving stock of equipment to be drawn on for ongoing operations. The subsequent replenishment would be charged to the accounts of specific operations.

306.   The rapid rise in demand for peace-keeping operations, together with the expansion in their scope and nature, has highlighted the urgent need to develop and maintain uniform high standards for peace-keeping. Training manuals are now being prepared for troops, military observers and civilian police. The object is to create an international pool of peace-keeping personnel with comparable skills, knowledge, discipline and code of conduct, able to work together effectively at short notice.

307.   An issue to which I attach the greatest importance is the safety and security of peace-keeping personnel. As the United Nations takes on more complex and riskier mandates, the safety and security of United Nations troops and other personnel have become increasingly important. Since United Nations peace-keeping operations began, 949 peace-keepers have lost their lives. More than 550 have died in ongoing missions (see figure 11). At the request of the Security Council I have prepared a report on existing arrangements for the protection of United Nations forces and personnel and the adequacy of those arrangements. I take this opportunity to reaffirm my faith in the professionalism of United Nations peace-keeping forces and my appreciation of their courage. They have performed their difficult tasks admirably, often at the cost of life and limb, in a variety of difficult and often unfamiliar circumstances. The sacrifice of those who have lost their lives will not be forgotten by the international community.

D.   *New departures in peace operations*

308.   The past 12 months have shown that it is not possible to draw clear lines between the different aspects of today's peace operations. Each of the cases which follow will highlight one or more of the aspects of peace operations in all their diversity; in some, nearly every technique and activity available has to be employed across the board.

1.   Afghanistan

309.   The goal of establishing peace and stability in Afghanistan is still far from being achieved. The newly established Islamic State of Afghanistan has not yet, despite considerable efforts, succeeded in developing the political and security conditions necessary for the urgent tasks of reconstruction and rehabilitation and the return of refugees. My Personal Representative, Sotirios Mousouris, as head of the Office for the Coordination of Humanitarian Assistance to Afghanistan, is facilitating humanitarian assistance

to Afghanistan. He also, as head of the Office of the Secretary-General in Afghanistan and Pakistan, continues to monitor political developments there. It is my hope that the steps taken recently towards the implementation of the two peace accords reached over the past seven months will create the necessary conditions for a stable political process and the peaceful reconstruction and rehabilitation of the country.

310. The question of relations between Afghanistan and Tajikistan is crucial for peace and security in the region. I discuss this question in paragraphs 397 to 401 below.

2. Angola

311. The case of Angola illustrates the way in which United Nations peace-keepers have had to take on a multiplicity of roles. The United Nations Angola Verification Mission (UNAVEM II) had the responsibility of monitoring the cease-fire and demobilization arrangements in the country. In addition, UNAVEM II was entrusted with witnessing the balloting in the country's first multi-party elections after years of devastating civil war. The electoral component of UNAVEM II was approved by the Security Council on 24 March 1992, and its deployment began in April 1992. The registration and campaign processes were monitored by 98 international staff members in 5 regional headquarters and 18 provincial offices. During the period that followed, approximately 400 observers verified the process. In April 1992, a team of consultants provided substantive technical assistance and support to the electoral authorities, in close coordination with the European Community and the United States Agency for International Development. They contributed to the organization of a massive operation, involving a large number of planes and helicopters, for the transport of electoral material to areas of difficult access. Legislative elections and the first round of the presidential elections took place on 29 and 30 September 1992. Despite the Mission's assessment of the electoral process as fair, the results were not recognized by the National Union for the Total Independence of Angola (UNITA), which resumed hostilities, thereby precipitating a grave political and humanitarian crisis.

312. Since the resumption of hostilities, UNAVEM II has been engaged once more in peace-making activities in addition to its role of protecting access for relief assistance. I have been vigorously pressing the parties, in particular UNITA, to re-establish a cease-fire and to return as soon as possible to the peace process in order to achieve national reconciliation. Meanwhile, it should be made clear that the illegal occupation by UNITA of many localities is not acceptable to the international community.

313. The situation faced by Angola is now more tragic than ever. The humanitarian crisis is reaching unprecedented proportions and has been worsened by severe drought in the southern part of the country. Incidences of malnutrition and malnutrition-related diseases have increased, and medicine and medical supplies are frequently in short supply. It is estimated that drought, disease and civil war have severely disrupted the lives of at least 2 million Angolans, many of whom cannot be reached because of security constraints.

314. In May 1993, the Department of Humanitarian Affairs issued a consolidated inter-agency appeal for Angola, seeking $227 million in assistance for the one-year period ending in April 1994. At the conference of donors held at Geneva on 3 June, initial contributions of approximately $70 million were registered. The humanitarian crisis in Angola is at least as serious as that in Somalia; unfortunately the assistance programme in Angola has received much less financial support from the international community.

315. The United Nations has taken a number of measures to strengthen its humanitarian assistance capacity and better coordinate the efforts of all concerned, including the non-governmental organizations participating in the relief effort. The functions and responsibilities of my Special Representative for Angola have been expanded to cover all emergency relief operations arising out of the present situation. A humanitarian coordination assistance unit, headed by a senior official with extensive operational experience, and reporting directly to the Special Representative, has been set up at Luanda. Continuing hostilities have caused the suspension of the organized voluntary repatriation of Angolans from Zaire and Zambia. Repeated efforts since May 1993 to launch an emergency relief programme for conflict-affected areas have been thwarted by security incidents and difficult negotiations over the destinations and means of delivery of humanitarian assistance. As in many similar situations, the Government and UNITA have been called upon to observe international humanitarian law to allow for the provision of relief assistance.

316. The Angolan political and military situation has continued to deteriorate dangerously as fighting has intensified and as the mistrust which has inhibited significant political accommodation has deepened. The possible consequences, both for Angola and for regional security, are more and more worrying.

317. The Assembly of Heads of State and Government of the Organization of African Unity, meeting at Cairo in June 1993, called on UNITA to resume the peace talks with the Government as soon as possible with a view to establishing a definitive cease-fire and ensuring the full implementation of the Peace Accords for Angola. I took the opportunity of my participation in that

Assembly to consult extensively with President José Eduardo dos Santos and other African leaders on ways and means of advancing the peace process in Angola.

318.   Alioune Blondin Beye took over as my Special Representative from Margaret Anstee on 30 June 1993. I am most grateful to Ms. Anstee for her work. She accomplished much, in the most difficult circumstances.

319.   Since his arrival in Angola my Special Representative has been pursuing, at various levels, intensive consultations directed at resuming the peace talks under United Nations auspices with a view to the establishment of a cease-fire throughout the country and the full implementation of the Peace Accords. Those efforts have taken my Special Representative to Gabon, Namibia, Sao Tome and Principe, Zaire and Zimbabwe.

320.   In conformity with paragraph 1 of Security Council resolution 834(1993), I have reduced the size of UNAVEM II to its current strength of 43 international civilian staff members, 50 military observers, 18 police observers and 11 military paramedical personnel, as well as necessary local staff. The activities of the military and police components of the Mission, which are currently deployed in four locations in addition to Luanda, consist essentially of patrolling, assessing the military situation, carrying out liaison with military and civilian officials, assisting in the delivery of humanitarian assistance to the civilian population and participating in other humanitarian operations. Current staff and logistic resources are based on my assessment of the situation at the time Security Council resolution 834(1993) was adopted. However, additional administrative support will be required at short notice if there is an increase in operations.

3.   Armenia and Azerbaijan

321.   In October 1992 I sent a fact-finding mission to Armenia and Azerbaijan to report on the situation there regarding the conflicts over Nagorny Karabakh, an enclave within Azerbaijan. In March 1993, the conflict escalated further when the Kelbadzhar district of Azerbaijan, between Armenia and Nagorny Karabakh, was occupied. That development resulted in a sudden increase in the number of displaced persons in Azerbaijan.

322.   After the occupation of the Kelbadzhar district, the President of the Security Council made a statement on behalf of the Council, by which, *inter alia*, I was requested, in consultation with the Conference on Security and Cooperation in Europe (CSCE), to submit urgently a report to the Council regarding the situation on the ground. Following the submission of my report, the Security Council, on 30 April 1993, adopted resolution 822(1993), its first resolution on Nagorny Karabakh. Later in the year, following further

fighting and occupation of Azerbaijani territory, the Council in its resolution 853(1993) demanded the immediate cessation of all hostilities and the withdrawal of the occupying forces from Agdam and all other recently occupied areas of the Azerbaijani Republic.

323.   In the conflict relating to Nagorny Karabakh, the role of the United Nations is essentially one of support for the efforts of CSCE. A United Nations observer has participated regularly in the discussions of the Minsk Group of CSCE, which has drawn up a timetable setting out urgent steps to be taken for achieving the withdrawal of occupying forces from Kelbadzhar and a solution in Nagorny Karabakh, with appropriate verification and monitoring. I remain committed to supporting the efforts of CSCE.

324.   In December 1992, the Department of Humanitarian Affairs, after consulting United Nations humanitarian agencies, launched a joint appeal for humanitarian assistance to both Armenia and Azerbaijan in the amount of $12 million. Following further requests for assistance from the Governments of the two countries, inter-agency needs assessments were organized and humanitarian needs amounting to $22.5 million for Armenia and $12.5 million for Azerbaijan were reported. Those assessments were discussed at meetings of donors held at Geneva on 10 and 11 June 1993. The humanitarian programmes are being implemented by UNICEF, WFP, the Office of the United Nations High Commissioner for Refugees (UNHCR) and the World Health Organization (WHO), and cover the period from 1 July 1993 to 31 March 1994. UNHCR is providing assistance to some 50,000 persons displaced by the recent fighting. A further inter-agency needs assessment is being planned by the Department of Humanitarian Affairs to re-evaluate the humanitarian situation in Azerbaijan.

4.   Cyprus

325.   In March 1993, my Special Representative, Oscar Camilión, was recalled to the service of his Government after five years in the post. I wish to thank Mr. Camilión for all he has done to help bring lasting peace to Cyprus, notably his contribution to the Set of Ideas which remains the basis of my efforts to achieve a comprehensive political settlement of the conflict there. I appointed Joe Clark to succeed Mr. Camilión.

326.   Peace-keeping efforts in Cyprus have long been hampered by the inadequacy of financial resources. On 27 May 1993, the Security Council, in its resolution 831(1993), decided that with effect from the next extension of the mandate of the United Nations Peace-keeping Force in Cyprus (UNFICYP) on or before 15 June 1993, those costs of the Force which are not covered by voluntary contributions should be treated as expenses of

the Organization under Article 17, paragraph 2, of the Charter.

327. By its resolution 831(1993) the Security Council also endorsed the restructuring plan proposed in paragraphs 16 to 19 of my report of 30 March 1993, with the addition of a limited number of observers for reconnaissance and with a view to further restructuring the Force in the light of a comprehensive reassessment of UNFICYP at the time of the consideration of the Force's mandate in December 1993.

328. Also, in resolution 831(1993) the Security Council reaffirmed that the present status quo was not acceptable and expressed concern that the United Nations should not be entering into open-ended peace-keeping commitments. The restructuring of UNFICYP following successive reductions in strength has major implications for the two parties. Greater responsibility rests with them for ensuring that there is no increase in tension in Cyprus and that conditions can be maintained for a speedy overall agreement as envisaged by the Security Council. It is imperative that the two sides exercise maximum restraint and, in accordance with the package of confidence-building measures, extend without delay the 1989 unmanning agreement to all parts of the buffer zone where their forces remain in close proximity to each other. I urge both sides to take reciprocal measures to lower the tension, including mutual commitments, through UNFICYP, not to deploy along the cease-fire lines live ammunition or weapons (other than those which are hand-held), and to prohibit firing of weapons within sight or hearing of the buffer zone. It is also necessary for both sides to work together so that their own agencies can resume the humanitarian functions which, in its efforts to restore normal conditions, UNFICYP has assumed over the years.

329. In the aftermath of the 1974 hostilities in Cyprus, peace-building has been an integral part of United Nations efforts. The confidence-building measures I recommended to the Security Council in November 1992 include the rehabilitation of the fenced area of Varosha as a special area for bicommunal contact and commerce, a kind of free-trade zone in which both sides could trade goods and services. In addition, Nicosia International Airport would be opened for civilian passenger and cargo traffic under the administration of the United Nations in cooperation with the International Civil Aviation Organization. Both communities would have unrestricted use of the airport. Supported by my Special Representative, I am continuing my efforts to persuade the Turkish-Cypriot side to accept these proposals. In particular, I have held two rounds of talks in New York to bring the parties closer to agreement.

330. Some proposals for further confidence-building measures were also included in my report to the Security Council of 1 July 1993. They include cooperation on the short-term and the long-term water problem in Cyprus, cooperation on education to promote intercommunal harmony and friendship, joint cultural and sports events, meetings of political party leaders and of the Chambers of Commerce and Industry of both sides, expert cooperation in areas such as health and the environment, and cooperative arrangements on electricity. It should be emphasized, however, that confidence-building measures, beneficial though they may be, should not be substituted for an overall solution, nor can they be part of a step-by-step approach to such a solution. Their purpose is to serve as a catalyst in the negotiations leading to a comprehensive, overall solution to the question of Cyprus.

5. East Timor

331. Good offices efforts for a comprehensive and internationally acceptable solution to the question of East Timor are continuing. As indicated to the General Assembly at its forty-seventh session, the Foreign Ministers of Indonesia and Portugal, at my invitation, held informal consultations in New York on 26 September 1992. This was followed by two rounds of substantive discussions between the two Foreign Ministers under my auspices, the first in New York on 17 December 1992 and the second in Rome on 21 April 1993. A number of possible confidence-building measures, designed to create an atmosphere more propitious to addressing the core issues, were explored at those meetings. The discussions have continued in New York since April, at the Permanent Representative level. The next meeting between the two Foreign Ministers and myself will be held on 17 September in New York. My Personal Envoy, Amos Wako, was in Indonesia and East Timor from 3 to 9 April 1993. In May 1993 a United Nations observer attended the final stages of the trial at Dili, East Timor, of Xanana Gusmão, the detained leader of the pro-independence movement, the Frente Revolucionaria de Timor Leste Independente (FRETILIN).

6. Georgia

332. In August 1992, fighting broke out in Abkhazia, Georgia. Since then, hostilities between Georgian and Abkhaz troops, supported by irregular units from the northern Caucasus region, have resulted in hundreds of casualties and thousands of refugees and displaced persons. In September and October 1992, I dispatched two United Nations fact-finding missions to Georgia and Abkhazia in support of and pursuant to the Moscow agreement of 3 September. After the second mission, with Security Council endorsement, two United Nations personnel remained in Georgia to provide an initial United Nations presence, with

the tasks of maintaining continuing contact with all concerned, providing United Nations Headquarters with situation reports and acting as liaison.

333.   Early in 1993, the Department of Humanitarian Affairs organized a United Nations inter-agency mission which visited all parts of Georgia. A consolidated appeal in the amount of $21 million was issued at the end of March. The appeal covered the needs of the affected population in Abkhazia, in Government-controlled areas of Georgia and, to a small extent, in South Ossetia. The overall humanitarian needs of Georgia will shortly be re-evaluated in view of the changing situation and in consultation with United Nations humanitarian organizations.

334.   In view of the unabated fighting in Abkhazia at the beginning of May 1993, I appointed a Special Envoy, Edouard Brunner, to Georgia to revive the peace process; he undertook his first mission to the region from 20 to 31 May 1993. During that time, he also visited Stockholm, for consultations with the Chairman-in-Office of CSCE, and Moscow for discussions with the Foreign Minister of the Russian Federation. In pursuance of paragraph 2 of Security Council resolution 849(1993), I dispatched a planning team to the conflict area on 19 July 1993. The team returned to New York on 27 July 1993.

335.   A cease-fire agreement, mediated by the Personal Representative of the President of the Russian Federation, Boris Pastukhov, was signed on 27 July 1993 by the Georgian and Abkhaz sides. My Special Envoy arrived in the region on 28 July, four hours after the cease-fire had entered into force. He stayed in the region until 31 July and had discussions with both parties to the conflict, and with officials from the Russian Federation. He held further discussions with Mr. Pastukhov and others in Moscow on 3 August.

336.   I subsequently reported to the Security Council that I considered conditions to be right for the immediate deployment of United Nations observers to carry out functions envisaged in the cease-fire agreement. The readiness of the two parties to meet and talk with each other provides an opportunity that must not be missed. I have, accordingly, asked my Special Envoy to continue his efforts with a view to convening, before 15 September, a first round of negotiations under United Nations auspices, facilitated by the Russian Federation.

337.   The Security Council, in resolution 854(1993), approved the deployment of an advance team of up to 10 United Nations military observers to verify compliance with the cease-fire agreement. On 24 August 1993 the Security Council, in resolution 858(1993), decided to establish a United Nations Observer Mission in Georgia (UNOMIG), comprising up to 88 military observers.

7. Guatemala

338.   At the request of the Government of Guatemala and the Unidad Revolucionaria Nacional Guatemalteca, the United Nations has, since 1991, participated as an observer in negotiations directed at ending the longest war in Central America. The talks have been held in Mexico and focused throughout 1992 on the issue of human rights, the first of 11 items of the negotiation agenda. Both parties indicated their wish that the United Nations should verify the implementation of a future agreement on human rights. I made it clear that the United Nations stood ready to assist them in that area.

339.   In early 1993, with a view to facilitating final agreement on the human rights issue and speeding up the negotiation process, the parties agreed to consider, simultaneously with the human rights issue, a calendar for the discussion of all outstanding agenda items and the possibility of an early cease-fire verified by the United Nations. Colombia, Mexico, Spain and Venezuela constituted a "Group of Friends" to promote agreement between the parties. That objective has so far proved to be elusive, however.

340.   In recent months, on several occasions, the parties have expressed the wish that the format of the talks agreed in 1991 be altered, *inter alia*, to allow for a more prominent role by the United Nations in negotiations. I have stated that the United Nations is ready to continue its support for the negotiation process within a framework agreeable to both parties.

8. Haiti

341.   Haiti is one of the poorest countries in the world: two thirds of its population lives below the poverty line. Since the *coup d'état* of September 1991, a trade embargo and a halt to bilateral assistance have been imposed on Haiti.

342.   The search for a solution to the problems of Haiti has involved measures of diplomacy directed at nothing less than the restoration of freedom, democracy, just order and the potential for progress to an entire nation and State.

343.   On 11 December 1992, I appointed Dante Caputo as my Special Envoy for Haiti. His appointment was in pursuance of General Assembly resolution 47/20 A of 24 November 1992, in which I was requested to take the necessary measures to assist, in cooperation with the Organization of American States (OAS), in the solution of the Haitian crisis. On 13 January 1993, Mr. Caputo was also appointed Special Envoy of OAS. He promoted negotiations to reach a political solution involving the return of the legitimate President and the restoration of the democratic process. The General Assembly, by its resolution 47/20 B of 20 April 1993, mandated United Nations participation, jointly with OAS, in the Inter-

national Civilian Mission to Haiti. By March 1993, the Mission had already been deployed throughout Haiti and, on 3 June, I submitted the first report of the Mission to the General Assembly.

344.   On 16 June, by its resolution 841(1993), the Security Council imposed sanctions on Haiti. Following talks held on Governors Island, New York, agreement was reached on 3 July 1993 on various measures relating to the return of the democratically elected President.

345.   On 12 July and 13 August 1993 I reported to the Security Council on the Governors Island Agreement and the subsequent New York Pact, which provides for a six-month political truce and the resumption of the normal functioning of Parliament. In my report of 12 July, I recommended to the Council that the sanctions it had imposed by resolution 841(1993) should be suspended as soon as the Prime Minister of Haiti had taken office. In my report of 13 August, I referred to the letter addressed to me by the President of the Security Council on 15 July 1993, confirming the readiness of the members of the Council to suspend the measures imposed by resolution 841(1993) immediately after the ratification of the Prime Minister and his assumption of his functions in Haiti.

346.   The Prime Minister–designate of Haiti, Robert Malval, was ratified by the Senate on 18 August 1993 and by the Chamber of Deputies on 23 August. He subsequently won a vote of confidence on his programme in the Senate on 24 August and in the Chamber of Deputies on 25 August. The process of confirmation of the Prime Minister–designate had thus been completed. On 27 August, by its resolution 861(1993), the Security Council decided that the sanctions were suspended. The Council also stated that the suspension would be immediately terminated if I were to inform it that the Governors Island Agreement had not been implemented in good faith. Furthermore, the Council stood ready to lift the sanctions definitively once it was informed that the relevant provisions of the Agreement had been fully implemented.

347.   After being sworn in on 30 August, the Prime Minister travelled to Haiti the following day to assume his functions. Immediately after the return of President Aristide to Haiti on 30 October 1993, I shall report to the Security Council with a view to the sanctions being lifted definitively.

348.   The Governors Island Agreement includes provision for United Nations assistance for modernizing the armed forces of Haiti and establishing a new police force with the presence of United Nations personnel in these fields. In a report to the Security Council on 25 August 1993 I outlined my plans in this regard. On 31 August,

the Council, by its resolution 862(1993), approved the dispatch of an advance team to prepare for the possible deployment of the proposed United Nations Mission to Haiti.

349.   The "silent emergency" in Haiti has been a challenge for the humanitarian organizations of the United Nations system. The Organization of American States and the United Nations have made constant efforts to respond to the considerable humanitarian needs of the people. Central to this process has been the formulation of a joint United Nations/OAS comprehensive humanitarian plan of action in Haiti. The plan contains emergency programmes in the fields of health, nutrition and food aid, water supply and sanitation, and agriculture, as well as support services for those areas and education and other social services. The needs identified totalled $62.7 million.

350.   Haiti should now be set on the path to a stable democratic future in which all Haitians will fully enjoy human, civil and political rights. I trust that the international community will be generous and forthcoming in providing Haiti with the technical and financial assistance needed for the reconstruction of its economy and its institutions, as well as moral and political support to the Haitian people in their search for a just, peaceful and prosperous society.

351.   I wish here to place on record my gratitude for the support and assistance which I and the Special Envoy have received at all times since the beginning of the negotiating process, particularly during the negotiations at Governors Island, from the Governments of Canada, France, the United States of America and Venezuela, which formed a group of "Friends of the Secretary-General" for Haiti. Their invaluable support has been crucial to the successful completion of this stage of the process.

9.   India and Pakistan

352.   The United Nations Military Observer Group in India and Pakistan (UNMOGIP) has been monitoring the cease-fire in Jammu and Kashmir since 1949. In the Simla Agreement of 1972, the two countries affirmed their commitment to respecting the cease-fire line and to resolving the issue peacefully through negotiations. I have repeatedly urged both sides, in the context of preventive diplomacy, to find a peaceful solution to this difficult and complex problem. I have also expressed my readiness, should the two countries request it, to exert every possible effort to facilitate the search for a lasting solution.

10.   Iraq and Kuwait

353.   Another action was performed for the first time in history when the United Nations demarcated the boundary between two Member States, as part of its mandate to maintain inter-

national peace and security. The Security Council, in resolution 687(1991), demanded respect for the boundary agreed by Iraq and Kuwait in 1963, called upon me to assist in arranging demarcation of that boundary, and decided to take, as appropriate, all necessary measures to guarantee the inviolability of the boundary.

354.   On 2 May 1991, the United Nations Iraq-Kuwait Boundary Demarcation Commission was established to demarcate the international boundary under the formula agreed in 1963. Both Iraq and Kuwait unconditionally accepted the terms of reference of the Commission, which was called upon to perform a technical and not a political task. During its 11 sessions, the Commission examined many sources, such as maps, graphics, aerial photographs, diplomatic correspondence, notes and archival documents.

355.   That highly professional work has produced a precise, well-documented and verifiable demarcation of the entire boundary. It includes the offshore area from the khawrs to the eastern end of the Khawr Abd Allah. A complete set of coordinates was produced, and boundary markers will clearly display the course of the line. Satellite technology has enabled the Commission to position each marker with a margin of error of only 1.5 cm. This would have been unthinkable only a few years ago. Other countries are already looking at this precedent to demarcate their boundaries.

356.   The United Nations Iraq-Kuwait Observation Mission (UNIKOM) has continued to operate in the demilitarized zone established by the Security Council on both sides of the Iraq-Kuwait boundary; that zone has been realigned to conform to the border as demarcated. The area of operation of UNIKOM has been generally calm except for a tense situation last January, following a series of actions by Iraq. Subsequently, the Security Council decided on a phased strengthening of UNIKOM, in the first phase by a mechanized infantry battalion. Owing to the greatly increased commitments by Member States to United Nations peace-keeping operations elsewhere, the Council's decision remains unfulfilled.

357.   Because of the efforts of the Special Commission and the International Atomic Energy Agency (IAEA), Iraq's ability to pose a threat to its neighbours by producing or possessing weapons of mass destruction has been steadily diminishing. However, Iraq has yet to fulfil its commitment to provide the full, final and complete disclosure of all aspects of its programmes that is needed to assess adequately its capabilities and facilities. A secure environment can be assured only through long-term monitoring and verification of Iraq's unconditional obligation not to use, retain, possess, develop, construct or otherwise acquire items

prohibited under Security Council resolution 687(1991).

358.   Under resolution 687(1991), the disposal of nuclear-weapons-usable materials in Iraq is required. Early in 1992, IAEA assembled a multidisciplinary team, comprising experts from IAEA and representatives from the Special Commission and the Office of Legal Affairs, to implement that mandate. After lengthy negotiations a complex contract was concluded in late June 1993 with the Committee for International Relations of the Ministry of Atomic Energy (CIR-Minatom), a State entity of the Russian Federation, which provided for the removal and reprocessing of the materials and for the permanent storage of the resulting wastes.

359.   With regard to the suffering of the Iraqi civilian population, the United Nations has continued to make every effort to assist those most in need, often at great personal risk to relief workers. The inter-agency humanitarian assistance programme in Iraq has, from April 1991 to March 1993, brought relief aid to the Iraqi civilian population throughout the country. The programme was developed in response to Security Council resolution 688(1991), in which the Council recognized the pressing need for assistance, particularly to the 1.9 million Iraqis in the north and south of the country. To date, some $700 million has been raised through United Nations appeals to finance projects implemented by United Nations and non-governmental organizations. The humanitarian programmes in Iraq have been implemented within the framework of a series of memoranda of understanding which also provide for the deployment of the United Nations Guards Contingent in Iraq. The various phases of the programme share one goal, namely, a focus on meeting basic needs for food, water, medical drugs and equipment and shelter for Iraq's most vulnerable civilian population.

360.   The Legal Counsel was requested on 19 May 1993 by the Chairman of the Security Council Committee established under resolution 661(1990) to provide his opinion whether Iraq's frozen assets might be used as payment for the sale or supply to Iraq of medicine and health supplies, foodstuffs and materials and supplies for essential civilian needs approved by the Committee, within the scope of the pertinent Security Council resolutions, and, if so, under which conditions. The Legal Counsel responded by a letter dated 4 June 1993 to the Chairman of the Committee in which he reviewed the legal regime applicable to frozen Iraqi assets in the light of Security Council resolutions 661(1990), 687(1991), 706(1991), 712(1991) and 778(1992).

361.   At the end of June 1993, I met the Deputy Prime Minister of Iraq, Tariq Aziz; a fourth

round of talks between the United Nations Secretariat and the Government of Iraq was then held at United Nations Headquarters from 7 to 15 July 1993. The purpose was to reach an understanding on practical arrangements for the implementation of the scheme relating to the sale of Iraqi oil, provided for in Security Council resolutions 706(1991) and 712(1991), and in my report of 4 September 1991. Ten meetings were held during that round of talks. The delegation of the United Nations was led by the Under-Secretary-General for Legal Affairs and Legal Counsel, and the delegation of Iraq by Riyadh Al-Qaysi, Under-Secretary-General at the Ministry of Foreign Affairs. On 15 July 1993, the talks were suspended.

362.   I continued to facilitate the return of Kuwaiti property seized by Iraq in accordance with paragraph 15 of Security Council resolution 687(1991). I am pleased to report that, in carrying out this task, I received full cooperation from the Governments of Iraq and Kuwait.

363.   The Commission established to administer the United Nations Compensation Fund provided for in paragraph 18 of Security Council resolution 687(1991) has held four sessions since August 1992. The legal rules and procedures which govern the Commission's activities have been drawn up and approved. The first compensation commissioners have been appointed, and they will begin the examination and evaluation of the first category of claims in the next few months.

364.   It may be recalled that, in accordance with Security Council resolution 706(1991), the United Nations established an escrow account into which the proceeds of the sale of Iraqi petroleum and petroleum products, and voluntary contributions, were to be paid. As at 1 September 1993, approximately $195 million had been deposited in that account. The funds have been designated to pay for the costs of the Special Commission, the Compensation Fund, the return of all Kuwaiti property, the Boundary Commission and humanitarian activities in Iraq.

365.   Recently a new programme of humanitarian assistance for the period from 1 April 1993 to 31 March 1994 has been prepared to provide rehabilitation assistance designed to limit further deterioration of living conditions throughout Iraq. The aim is to facilitate self-sufficiency by promoting community-level projects. That programme includes specific project proposals from various United Nations organizations and programmes amounting to $489 million. The programme's current lack of funding jeopardizes the implementation of crucial rehabilitation activities, thereby prolonging the state of dependency and degradation of the living conditions of the Iraqi Kurds and the other vulnerable population groups in the country.

366.   On 1 September 1993 I met Deputy Prime Minister Tariq Aziz to urge Iraqi compliance across the range of outstanding issues.

11.   Lebanon

367.   In southern Lebanon, there has been an increase in hostilities between Israeli forces and armed elements that have proclaimed their resistance to Israeli occupation. The United Nations Interim Force in Lebanon (UNIFIL) has done its best to limit the conflict and to protect the inhabitants from its effects. In resolution 852(1993), the Security Council reaffirmed the mandate of UNIFIL as defined in its resolution 425(1978) and other relevant resolutions, which is to confirm the withdrawal of Israeli forces, restore international peace and security, and assist the Government of Lebanon in ensuring the return of its effective authority in the area. Although UNIFIL has not been able to make visible progress towards these objectives, its contribution to stability and the protection it is able to afford the population of the area remain important.

368.   The volatility of the situation manifested itself in a particularly grave escalation of hostilities in July 1993 when, in response to rocket attacks against northern Israel, the Israeli Defence Forces launched massive air strikes against southern Lebanon. The fighting caused the displacement of hundreds of thousands of civilians; dozens of Lebanese villages were destroyed or damaged; countless homes, schools, hospitals, roads and bridges were demolished. On 30 July 1993, in a letter to the President of the Security Council, I drew attention to the fact that the hostilities had severely affected the operations of UNIFIL, whose mandate had been extended by the Security Council two days earlier. The heavy bombardment of the UNIFIL area of operations by Israeli aircraft and artillery had, *inter alia*, hit the Nepalese battalion headquarters and positions in the Irish and Finnish battalion sectors. Fortunately, there were no serious casualties. After the cessation of hostilities, units of the Lebanese army were deployed in parts of the UNIFIL area of operation for the purpose of maintaining public order.

369.   In these circumstances, I requested the Under-Secretary-General for Humanitarian Affairs to act swiftly to coordinate the efforts of the United Nations system in the provision of emergency humanitarian assistance. A consolidated appeal for immediate assistance in the amount of $28.5 million was launched on 20 August. To start up urgent emergency work, advances of $5 million and $2 million from the Central Emergency Revolving Fund were made available to Habitat and WFP, respectively.

12.   Liberia

370.   In view of the ongoing conflict in Liberia and the continuing destruction and loss of life,

the Security Council, in its resolution 788(1992) of 19 November 1992, called upon all parties to the conflict in Liberia to respect and implement the cease-fire and the various accords of the peace process; decided, under Chapter VII of the Charter, that all States should, for the purposes of establishing peace and stability in Liberia, immediately implement a general and complete embargo on all deliveries of weapons and military equipment to Liberia, with the exception of weapons and military equipment destined for the sole use of the peace-keeping forces of the Economic Community of West African States (ECOWAS); and requested me to dispatch a Special Representative to Liberia to evaluate the situation.

371. In late 1992 and early 1993, my Special Representative, Trevor Gordon-Somers, visited Liberia and held extensive discussions there and in States members of ECOWAS. On the basis of his findings, I submitted a special report to the Security Council on 12 March 1993. The Council, in resolution 813(1993) of 26 March 1993, reaffirmed its belief that the Yamoussoukro IV Accord offered the best possible framework for a peaceful resolution of the conflict in Liberia and its support for increased humanitarian assistance to Liberia; demanded that the parties concerned refrain from any action that would impede or obstruct the delivery of humanitarian assistance; and called upon them to ensure the safety of all personnel involved in international humanitarian assistance.

372. After the discovery of the massacre of innocent displaced persons at Harbel on 6 June 1993, the Security Council on 9 June requested me to commence an investigation and warned that those found responsible would be held accountable for the serious violation of international humanitarian law. My Special Representative proceeded to Monrovia to conduct a thorough investigation into the incident. Preliminary action was taken by other United Nations officials on the spot. Since the first stage of the investigation, and after consultations, I have appointed a panel of inquiry, which is now undertaking a more comprehensive investigation of the massacre. As soon as the investigation is completed, I shall submit a full report to the Security Council.

373. During the protracted conflict in Liberia, the United Nations provided assistance to over 700,000 Liberian refugees in neighbouring countries, to 100,000 internally displaced Liberians and to some 100,000 destitute Sierra Leoneans who had sought refuge in Liberia. As a result of the emergency relief programme which has been carried out by the United Nations and its non-governmental organization partners since December 1990, severe malnutrition has been eliminated except in isolated pockets, and the health of the population has improved significantly. However, since the resumption of hostilities in August 1992, the humanitarian situation has deteriorated. Masses of people have been displaced and large areas of the country have become inaccessible to relief agencies.

374. The conflicting parties agreed, at Geneva, after a week of negotiations conducted under the joint auspices of ECOWAS, OAU and the United Nations, to restore peace to the country. The peace agreement, which was signed on 25 July 1993 at an ECOWAS summit meeting at Cotonou, Benin, calls on the ECOWAS Monitoring Group (ECOMOG) to continue its peace-keeping role in Liberia and on the United Nations to play a monitoring role through the establishment of an observer mission. The agreement also provides for the establishment of a broadly based central transitional government, to be replaced by a democratically elected body within seven months. Agreement was also reached on the provision of humanitarian relief to all Liberians in need through the most direct routes, which has facilitated the delivery of humanitarian assistance to the affected population. United Nations organizations have been asked to initiate the rapid voluntary repatriation and reintegration from neighbouring countries of the more than 700,000 refugees. The Department of Humanitarian Affairs is preparing an inter-agency consolidated appeal for Liberia.

375. The Security Council, in its resolution 856(1993) of 10 August 1993, decided to establish the United Nations Observer Mission in Liberia (UNOMIL) and approved the sending of an advance team of 30 military observers to participate in the work of the Joint Cease-fire Monitoring Committee.

13. Libyan Arab Jamahiriya

376. In an effort to prevent a dangerous deterioration of the situation regarding suspected Libyan involvement in the bombing of Pan Am flight 103 and UTA flight 772, and to facilitate the implementation of Security Council resolutions 731(1992) and 748(1992), I have remained in almost constant contact over the past seven months with the parties to the dispute and the League of Arab States. I met the Foreign Minister of the Libyan Arab Jamahiriya at Cairo in June 1993 and in New York in August in an attempt to resolve the dispute. I have on five occasions sent a personal envoy to Tripoli and intend to pursue every effort to facilitate a just settlement in accordance with the mandate given to me by the Security Council.

14. The Middle East

377. In the course of the past year, the plight of the Palestinian people living under occupation has not been alleviated. There has, moreover, been

a dramatic worsening of the human rights situation in the occupied territories. In a particularly grave incident, Israel deported over 400 Palestinian civilians to southern Lebanon in December 1992. The Security Council, in its resolution 799(1992), *inter alia* reaffirmed the applicability of the Fourth Geneva Convention to all the Palestinian territories occupied by Israel since 1967, including Jerusalem, demanded that Israel ensure the safe and immediate return to the occupied territories of all those deported, and requested me to send a representative to the area and to report to the Council. Conscious of the possible effect of that event on the fragile process of Arab-Israeli peace negotiations, and with a view to finding a solution, I dispatched several missions to the area, led respectively by the Under-Secretary-General for Political Affairs and my Special Political Adviser. I had a number of meetings and telephone conversations with leaders in the region and representatives of interested Governments. Regrettably, those efforts were not successful and, in my report to the Security Council of 25 January 1993, I recommended that the Council should take whatever measures were required to ensure that its unanimous decision was respected.

378. I have also been seriously alarmed by the reports of the rapid worsening of the socio-economic situation in the occupied territories. As the Palestinian economy is weak and highly dependent on that of Israel, the livelihood of the Palestinian communities suffered further damage when Israel closed off the occupied territories in March 1993. I have appealed to the international community to provide greater economic assistance to the occupied territories. In this connection, I have also reminded the major donors of the critical financial situation of the United Nations Relief and Works Agency for Palestine Refugees in the Near East.

379. Because of the long-standing commitment of the United Nations to a comprehensive, just and lasting settlement in the Middle East, based on Security Council resolutions 242(1967) and 338(1973), I welcomed the invitation extended in October 1992 by the co-sponsors of the Middle East peace process for the participation of the United Nations as a full extraregional participant in the multilateral working groups on environment, economic and regional development, water, refugees, arms control and regional security in the Middle East. Representatives of the United Nations attended and took an active part in the meetings of the working groups held in October/ November 1992 in Paris, The Hague and Ottawa and in April/May 1993 in Geneva, Rome, Oslo, Washington and Tokyo. In November 1992, I appointed Chinmaya Gharekhan as my Special Representative at the multilateral talks.

380. The United Nations Disengagement Observer Force (UNDOF) has continued to supervise the separation between the Israeli and Syrian forces, and the limitation of armaments and forces provided for in the disengagement agreement of 1974. With the cooperation of both sides, UNDOF has discharged its tasks effectively and its area of operation has been quiet.

381. The United Nations Truce Supervision Organization (UNTSO), which is the oldest existing peace-keeping operation, has continued to assist UNDOF and UNIFIL in carrying out their tasks and has maintained its presence in Egypt. During the last year, the personnel of UNTSO has been reduced by 25 per cent.

15. Mozambique

382. The signing in Rome of the General Peace Agreement between the Government of Mozambique and the Resistência Nacional Moçambicana (RENAMO) in October 1992 brought renewed hope to this war-torn country. The United Nations was called upon to play a central role in the implementation of various aspects of the Agreement. The mandate of the United Nations Operation in Mozambique (ONUMOZ) since its establishment in December 1992, as coordinated by my Special Representative, Aldo Ajello, is to monitor cease-fire arrangements and the demobilization of up to 100,000 soldiers from both sides, to fulfil political and electoral functions, to conduct a massive humanitarian operation and to organize mine clearance.

383. As part of the peace-building efforts in Mozambique, a meeting of donors was held at Maputo on 8 and 9 June 1993, under the joint chairmanship of the Government of Italy and the United Nations. The meeting, which followed the Donors Conference on Mozambique held in Rome on 15 and 16 December 1992 on the basis of article VII of the General Peace Agreement, reviewed the progress made in the implementation of the consolidated humanitarian assistance programme in Mozambique. That programme reflects a shift from the previous concentration on emergency relief; by focusing on the reintegration needs of refugees and displaced persons, leading to reconstruction and future development, it signals the end of a protracted emergency phase and the beginning of a return to normalcy. The humanitarian assistance programme encompasses support for the repatriation process, the demobilization of armed units, emergency relief, restoration of essential services and balance-of-payments and budget support. The programme will require $559.6 million for the period from May 1993 to April 1994. The repatriation and resettlement of 1.5 million Mozambicans, now living as refugees in neighbouring countries, will be the largest such operation undertaken in Africa under United Nations auspices.

384.   While donors have since announced new pledges totalling some $70 million, thereby increasing the total value of pledges to $520 million, against the programme's total requirements of $560 million, they have also expressed concern about delays related to the electoral process, demobilization and the work of certain commissions identified in the General Peace Agreement. The positive participation of all concerned parties in the implementation of the Agreement will contribute significantly to the strengthening of peace in Mozambique.

385.   In June 1993 I reported to the Security Council that the delays which had impeded the rapid deployment of the ONUMOZ military component had been overcome and that, by the beginning of May 1993, the five infantry battalions provided for in my operational plan had been fully deployed along the Beira, Tete, Limpopo and Nacala corridors and along national highway N1. Since then, the deployment of all contingents has been completed. At the end of August 1993 the total strength of the formed units, including support elements, was over 6,000.

386.   As envisaged, the operations of the contingents chiefly involve the conducting of motorized and air patrols along the corridors, establishing checkpoints and providing escorts for trains. United Nations troops have also escorted road convoys carrying relief food to populations in need in various regions, and transported equipment to assembly areas. In addition, they have carried out repair and reconnaissance of roads, both in populated locations and en route to assembly areas.

387.   The process of assembly and demobilization of Government and RENAMO forces scheduled to begin in mid-November 1992 has been delayed for several reasons, particularly the insistence of RENAMO on receiving financial support as a political party before participating in the work of the commissions and its insistence that 65 per cent of ONUMOZ troops be deployed before the assembly process begins.

388.   As at 25 August 1993, 303 of the authorized total number of 354 military observers had arrived in Mozambique. Assisted by troops from the contingents, the observers are now actively involved in the establishment and preparation of assembly areas, conducting inspections and investigations of cease-fire violation complaints.

389.   In late August 1993 I was able to report an important development, namely, the arrival at Maputo, after several postponements, of Mr. Afonso Dhlakama, President of RENAMO, and the start on 21 August of a series of meetings between him and the President of Mozambique, Mr. Joaquim Chissano. It is widely expected that the meetings will continue until some form of agreement has been reached on major outstanding is-

sues. The importance of this development cannot be overemphasized. Progress in many major areas of the peace process depends on the successful outcome of these discussions.

16.   Republic of Moldova

390.   After the signature of the disengagement agreement on 21 July 1992, and acting on a request from the President of the Republic of Moldova, I sent a second fact-finding mission to that country in late August 1992. The mission concluded that, despite the cessation of armed hostilities, prevailing conditions remained fragile.

391.   A major stumbling-block continues to be the question of the withdrawal of the Fourteenth Russian Army from the left bank of the Dniester. In a letter dated 2 October 1992 to the Secretary-General, the Minister for Foreign Affairs of the Republic of Moldova proposed the dispatch of United Nations observers, with the consent of the Russian Federation, to the negotiations between the two countries on the withdrawal of the Fourteenth Army. In my response of 5 January 1993, I offered to send a mission to meet the leaders of the Moldovan and Russian delegations to the negotiations and to discuss possible arrangements for the presence there of United Nations observers.

392.   In view of the establishment in the Republic of Moldova of an eight-member mission of the Conference on Security and Cooperation in Europe on 27 April 1993, an understanding has been reached with the Government that CSCE will take the leading role in the issue.

17.   Rwanda

393.   United Nations observers have been deployed to one side of a common border with the agreement of the two States involved, namely, Rwanda and Uganda. In my interim report to the Security Council on Rwanda, of 20 May 1993 following the mission of my representative, I proposed the establishment of a United Nations observer mission on the Ugandan side of the Rwanda-Uganda border. In recommending the deployment of United Nations observers, I noted that a decision to deploy observers to the border would highlight the international community's interest in peace and security in the area, could help to promote the negotiation process at Arusha and would encourage the parties actively to pursue their efforts for peace and national reconciliation in Rwanda.

394.   The Security Council, in its resolution 846(1993), taking note of the requests of the Governments of Rwanda and Uganda for the deployment of United Nations observers along their common border as a temporary confidence-building measure, decided to establish the United Nations Observer Mission Uganda-Rwanda (UNOMUR), with

the task of verifying that no military assistance is provided across the border between the two countries. At the same time, the United Nations is providing emergency relief assistance to the 900,000 persons displaced by the conflict. A consolidated appeal for $78 million has been launched for this humanitarian programme.

395.   The cease-fire agreement reached on 12 July 1992 was broken on 8 February 1993 but restored on 9 March. Two United Nations military experts were placed at the disposal of the Organization of African Unity, to provide it with technical assistance in the preparation of a submission to donors for the funding of an expanded Neutral Military Observer Group in Rwanda. That Group has been monitoring the cease-fire. The latest phase of the talks began in mid-March 1993 and has now been completed. A comprehensive peace agreement was signed at Arusha on 4 August 1993. The role of the United Republic of Tanzania, as facilitator in the negotiations, was important for their successful completion.

396.   Taking into account the communications received from the President of Rwanda and the Secretary-General of OAU and in pursuance of Security Council resolution 846(1993), I have sent a reconnaissance mission to Rwanda to examine the possible function of the neutral international force called for by the Government of Rwanda and the Rwandese Patriotic Front and to evaluate the human and financial resources that would be needed to carry them out. The findings of the mission, which will also hold consultations with OAU and the Government of the United Republic of Tanzania, will assist me in making recommendations to the Security Council regarding the United Nations contribution to the implementation of the Peace Agreement.

18.   Tajikistan

397.   During the summer of 1992, the number of armed clashes between various groups increased dramatically and by late August and early September 1992 fighting raged across southern Tajikistan. Concerned that events might lead to a wider regional conflict, I dispatched, in consultation with the Governments of Tajikistan and Uzbekistan, a fact-finding mission from 16 to 22 September 1992. It reported, *inter alia*, that the situation in Tajikistan was that of a civil war, and that since June 1992 more than 2,000 people had been killed and more than 200,000 had become refugees or displaced persons.

398.   I consequently dispatched a goodwill mission to Tajikistan and four neighbouring countries, from 3 to 14 November 1992, to assist and support regional peacemaking efforts. The mission also carried out a preliminary assessment of humanitarian needs and its report formed the basis of a preliminary appeal for $20 million to support

the humanitarian programmes of UNHCR, WFP and WHO. In the light of the mission's consultations with the various interlocutors in the region, I informed the Security Council on 21 December 1992 of my decision to establish a small, integrated United Nations unit at Dushanbe to monitor the situation on the ground and to provide liaison services. My decision was welcomed by the Government of Tajikistan.

399.   Early in 1993, I appointed, for a period of three months, a Special Envoy to Tajikistan, Ismat Kittani, whose mandate was to obtain agreement on a cease-fire with appropriate international monitoring, begin negotiations for a political solution, and enlist the help of neighbouring countries and others concerned in achieving those objectives. That appointment was welcomed by the Security Council.

400.   In May and June 1993, my Special Envoy visited the Islamic Republic of Iran, Kazakhstan, Kyrgyzstan, Pakistan, the Russian Federation, Tajikistan and Uzbekistan and, a few weeks later, Saudi Arabia for talks with their leaders. During that initial mission he was not able to complete his contacts and ascertain the positions of all parties concerned in accordance with his mandate. On 16 August 1993, I submitted a report to the Security Council summarizing the Special Envoy's findings, and expressed my concern about the escalating crisis on the Afghan-Tajik border. In a statement made by its President on 23 August 1993, the Security Council welcomed my proposal to extend the mandate of my Special Envoy until 31 October 1993 and to extend, by three months, the tenure of United Nations officials currently in Tajikistan.

401.   I have asked my Special Envoy to visit Kabul as soon as possible for discussions with government leaders regarding his mandate in Tajikistan and to ascertain the views and positions of the Tajik opposition leaders residing in Afghanistan. In addition, I requested him to undertake a second mission to Dushanbe and to visit other regional countries. Meanwhile, I have informed the Security Council of my concern about recent developments and my intention to monitor the situation closely. The Department of Humanitarian Affairs is carrying out an inter-agency re-evaluation of the humanitarian needs of Tajikistan.

19.   Western Sahara

402.   In April 1991, the Security Council decided, in resolution 690(1991), to establish a United Nations Mission for the Referendum in Western Sahara (MINURSO). The resolution provided for a referendum for self-determination to be organized by the United Nations in cooperation with the Organization of African Unity. The mission will consist of civilian, security and mili-

tary units functioning as an integrated operation. The civilian unit of MINURSO is expected to comprise approximately 275 international staff members, the security unit up to 300 police officers and the military unit approximately 1,700 military personnel, including observers and infantry and logistics battalions. Differences have arisen with respect to the criteria relating to voter eligibility. I have been in close contact with both parties, and I visited the area from 31 May to 4 June 1993, accompanied by my Special Representative, Sahabzada Yaqub-Khan, in order to urge the parties to accept a compromise solution with regard to the interpretation and application of those criteria.

403.   Notwithstanding difficulties in the preparation and organization of direct talks between the parties and other problems, mostly of a procedural nature, the delegations of Morocco and the Frente POLISARIO met from 17 to 19 July at Laayoune, in the presence of my Special Representative as United Nations observer. The dialogue was held in a positive spirit, marked by restraint and mutual respect. It is my earnest hope that the talks will be resumed soon as a follow-up to the Laayoune initiative, and that the referendum will take place before the end of the year.

20.   Zaire

404.   With respect to the situation in Zaire, I transmitted to the President of the Security Council, on 7 May 1993, a letter dated 24 March 1993 from Etienne Tshisekedi, the Prime Minister elected by the Sovereign National Conference, requesting the United Nations to appoint observers to safeguard respect for human rights; to assist in the preparation, monitoring and supervision of truly free and democratic elections; and to dispatch an evaluation mission to Shaba with a view to the provision of humanitarian assistance for people displaced within their own country. Mr. Tshisekedi also requested the dispatch of a United Nations intervention force to Zaire to restore law and order, peace and internal security, to ensure the protection of people and property, and to avert the possibility of a civil war. I also informed the President of the Security Council that I had met at Brussels on 23 April 1993 Monseigneur Laurent Monsengwo, President of the High Council of the Republic of Zaire, to discuss the deteriorating situation and the institutional stalemate in that country, and the possibility of a role for the United Nations.

405.   The humanitarian situation continues to be very serious, with the number of displaced persons reaching into the hundreds of thousands. Locally based United Nations and non-governmental organizations are doing their utmost to provide the necessary relief assistance. I decided to organize an inter-agency needs assessment mission in order to obtain a first-hand appreciation of the human-

itarian and related needs and to consult with all concerned on means of providing assistance to the affected population, in particular the displaced people. That mission did not take place because of reservations expressed by President Mobutu.

406.   During the OAU summit meeting at Cairo in July 1993, I had the opportunity to hold extensive discussions with President Mobutu. I then appointed my Special Envoy for Zaire, Lakhdar Brahimi, to undertake a goodwill mission, having as its principal objective the exploration of ways and means for the United Nations to assist in finding a solution to the current political situation. I have been assured by President Mobutu that my Special Envoy will have his full cooperation and the freedom to travel to any part of the country, as well as to meet with the opposition parties.

407.   My Special Envoy arrived in Zaire on 18 July. He met President Mobutu in Shaba and exchanged views with Prime Minister Faustin Birindwa and senior officials of his Government. He also met Etienne Tshisekedi, Monseigneur Monsengwo and leaders of the opposition parties. Mr. Brahimi was very well received by all his interlocutors and made every effort to encourage a dialogue among the parties, in order to put an end to the violence and facilitate national reconciliation.

408.   After the return of Mr. Brahimi to New York at the beginning of August 1993, I sent an inter-agency mission to Zaire to assess urgent humanitarian requirements, particularly in regions of concentration of internally displaced persons, and to identify ways of addressing those needs effectively. Besides the Kinshasa area, the mission is planning to visit the provinces of Shaba, North Kivu and West and East Kasai, and is expected to complete its work within three weeks. In the interim, I alerted the United Nations organizations concerned, and the donor community, to the need for an increased effort to alleviate the plight of the affected populations, particularly in the provinces of Shaba and Kivu.

E.   *Major comprehensive efforts*

409.   As the foregoing examples demonstrate, the range of responsibilities facing the new United Nations is not only vast but virtually open-ended, extending to almost every area of human activity.

410.   To cope with this revolutionary and novel situation, the United Nations must address its challenges in the most coherent and comprehensive way possible. Governments and private individuals must also realize that crises such as those just discussed transcend traditional boundaries of theory and practice. Food, water, land-mines, disease and death are inextricably intertwined with democratization, human rights and development. Efforts to deal with particular issues cannot succeed in the absence of a comprehensive vision of the whole.

411.   Four current cases will illustrate the comprehensive and challenging situations in which the United Nations is engaged: Cambodia, El Salvador, Somalia and the former Yugoslavia. They resemble each other in the all-encompassing nature of the tasks they demand, but each involves distinct and different factors.

1.   Cambodia

412.   The successful conduct of the recent election in Cambodia represents an affirmation of the important contribution United Nations peace-keeping operations can make to resolving complicated situations even in the face of serious obstacles. The mandate of the United Nations Transitional Authority in Cambodia (UNTAC), set out in the Paris Agreements, was one of the most complex and ambitious ever undertaken by a United Nations operation. It included aspects relating to human rights, the organization and conduct of free and fair general elections, military arrangements, civil administration, the maintenance of law and order, the repatriation and resettlement of the Cambodian refugees and displaced persons, and the rehabilitation of essential Cambodian infrastructures during the transitional period. At the same time it was planned as a peace-keeping operation in the time-honoured tradition, an operation based on the agreement and cooperation of the parties, relying on political authority and persuasion rather than on force.

413.   When one of the four Cambodian parties that had signed the Agreements and undertaken a range of obligations, the Party of Democratic Kampuchea, refused to honour its commitments, UNTAC was faced with grave difficulties. Indeed, that party, after its early refusal to implement Phase II of the cease-fire and to demobilize its troops under UNTAC supervision, progressively withdrew from the peace process, absenting itself from meetings of the Supreme National Council. Despite my continued efforts and those of my Special Representative, Yasushi Akashi, and of the Co-Chairmen of the Paris Conference and other concerned Governments to engage it in a dialogue, it eventually refused to participate in the election. I resolved nevertheless to go forward in implementing all aspects of the mandate of UNTAC to the maximum extent possible. I was determined not to allow the non-cooperation of one party to negate the unprecedented and far-reaching international efforts to restore peace to Cambodia.

414.   The Security Council consistently supported this course of action. While the cantonment of forces had to be suspended after some 55,000 of the approximately 200,000 troops belonging to the three factions cooperating in the peace process had been regrouped and cantoned, the 16,000-member military component of UNTAC redeployed itself to focus on providing security for voter registration and later for the election itself in all 21 provinces. With full deployment of its 21,000 military, police and civilian personnel achieved by mid-1992, UNTAC vigorously pursued its manifold tasks of promoting respect for human rights, contributing to the maintenance of law and order and exercising control and supervision of the activities of the existing administrative structures, especially in the five key areas of foreign affairs, national defence, finance, public security and information. An active education and information campaign was a vital aspect of those efforts.

415.   The successful repatriation of more than 360,000 refugees and displaced persons by 31 March 1993, exactly a year after the process began and in spite of major logistic and climatic impediments, was a testimony to the organizational capacity of UNTAC and the Office of the United Nations High Commissioner for Refugees, which served as the lead agency within an integrated effort, and to the faith that the returning Cambodians had in a future in their homeland.

416.   The Cambodian people at large repeatedly manifested their faith in the peace process and their courage and determination to build a stable future by first registering for and then massively voting in the election, which was held on schedule from 23 to 28 May 1993. Nearly 4.7 million people, or some 96 per cent of the estimated eligible population, registered to vote. A total of 4,267,192, representing nearly 90 per cent of the registered voters, cast their ballot. Despite concerns about disruption by the National Army of Democratic Kampuchea, and about earlier acts of intimidation attributed largely to another party, both the six-week election campaign, in which 20 political parties actively took part, and the polling itself proved to be remarkably peaceful and free of violent incidents. The UNTAC electoral staff, who were joined by more than 50,000 Cambodian electoral workers and 1,000 international polling station officers, were moved by the enthusiasm, patience and buoyant spirit manifested by the Cambodian voters everywhere during the election.

417.   On 10 June, after the verification and counting of the ballots had been completed, my Special Representative declared, with my authorization and on my behalf, that the election in Cambodia had been free and fair. The Security Council endorsed that determination on 15 June, and the results of the election have now been accepted by all the Cambodian parties. The newly elected Constituent Assembly held its inaugural meeting on 14 June to begin its task of drafting and adopting a new Constitution and establishing the new Government of Cambodia.

418.   Since then, the four Cambodian political parties that won seats in the election have agreed

to join in a joint interim administration, under the leadership of His Royal Highness Prince Norodom Sihanouk, for the remainder of the transitional period until the creation of the new Government in accordance with the Paris Agreements. I welcomed and supported this step as contributing to stability, national reconciliation and a smooth transition to the future Government of Cambodia.

419.   UNTAC will continue faithfully to fulfil its mandate for the remainder of the transitional period and will do its utmost to help the Cambodian people to consolidate their victory in this impressive feat of self-determination. I am convinced that the international community will not fail to continue to assist the people of Cambodia and their future Government in the arduous task of building a stable, peaceful and prosperous future.

420.   More than 20,000 United Nations troops began leaving Cambodia in August 1993, ending one of the largest operations in the history of the Organization. On 27 August 1993 the Security Council, in its resolution 860(1993), fixed the date of 15 November 1993 as the deadline for the withdrawal of the military component of UNTAC.

2. El Salvador

421.   El Salvador is another Member State where the United Nations is engaged in an operation of considerable complexity. The Organization mediated a series of peace agreements between the Government and the Frente Farabundo Martí para la Liberación Nacional (FMLN) and then assumed responsibility for assisting and verifying their implementation. The United Nations Observer Mission in El Salvador (ONUSAL), which was created for that purpose and is headed by my Special Representative Augusto Ramírez-Ocampo, comprises military observers, police officers, human rights experts and a variety of experts in other civilian disciplines. It will soon have added to it an Electoral Division to observe, at the request of the Government of El Salvador, the elections which are to be held in the spring of 1994 and which will mark the culmination of the peace process.

422.   The multidisciplinary nature of ONUSAL reflects the complexity of the peace agreements, which provided, even before a cease-fire came into effect, for United Nations monitoring of respect for human rights by both sides. A Commission of three distinguished non-Salvadorians was appointed to establish the truth about certain grave acts of violence committed during more than 10 years of bitter civil war. There was to be a cease-fire; the purification and progressive reduction of the armed forces; and the demobilization of FMLN and its legalization as a political party. The existing public security bodies were to be monitored by the United Nations and a new national civil police formed. The judicial system was to be reformed, as was the electoral system. A variety of amendments were to be made to the Constitution in order to ensure, in particular, that the Army and other security forces were fully under civilian control and that the Army would not be involved in police functions, such as the preservation of internal order, except in exceptional circumstances. Reforms were to take place in the economic and social spheres. In particular, land was to be provided for ex-combatants from both sides as they demobilized and for persons who during the war had taken over and worked land owned by others.

423.   It is to the credit of the Salvadorian people, in particular of the Government and FMLN, that it rapidly became clear that the peace process was irreversible. There have nevertheless been some set-backs in its implementation. The cease-fire was impeccably observed but there was an eight-month delay in the Government's implementation of the recommendations of the Ad Hoc Commission set up to purify the armed forces. Most seriously, the discovery of a substantial FMLN arms cache in Nicaragua on 23 May 1993 revealed that, despite repeated protestations to the contrary, FMLN had failed to declare and destroy all its arms, ammunition and other war *matériel*. During the following three months FMLN revealed to ONUSAL further arms caches inside and outside El Salvador, the contents of which were destroyed. That serious violation of the agreements put some strain on the peace process; I trust that this chapter is now closed.

424.   In recent months there have been delays in the formation and deployment of the new national civil police and a lack of progress in implementing the recommendations of the Commission on the Truth, which complemented the agreements and were intended to ensure that the conditions which permitted gross violations of human rights during the armed conflict would not recur. I firmly believe that implementation of those recommendations is necessary for national reconciliation.

425.   There have also been delays in putting into effect the complicated provisions of the peace agreements relating to land. There is an inescapable moral obligation to fulfil promises made to demobilized combatants of both sides.

426.   Like the delays in the formation of the national civil police, the delays in the land programme are due partly to lack of financial resources. My appeals for financial support from the international community have not so far produced all that is required. I believe that the Government has therefore an obligation to adjust its own expenditure priorities to ensure that critical elements in the peace process do not fail for want of finance; but it has to be acknowledged that this may prove difficult to reconcile with the eco-

nomic reform programme which is a condition of continuing support for El Salvador on the part of the international financial institutions.

427. The case of El Salvador is a prime example of the need for a fully integrated approach by the United Nations system as a whole to the requirements of peace-building in countries emerging from long years of armed conflict. A cease-fire and a successful election are not enough to claim success; that is only assured when the necessary political, economic and social measures have been taken to eradicate the underlying causes of the original conflict.

3. Somalia

428. Despite the best efforts of the international community to help Somalia with traditional peace-keeping and humanitarian assistance, the situation had become intolerable by the end of 1992. Somalia remained without a central Government, Mogadishu was divided by rival militia, and throughout the country a dozen or more factions were active.

429. Widespread looting of aid supplies, robbery, armed banditry and general lawlessness compounded the situation. Large sums of cash and relief aid were being extorted from donor organizations and the lives of their personnel were being put in danger. The result was that, while relief supplies were ready and in the pipeline, they were prevented from reaching Somalis dying of starvation. According to some estimates, as many as 3,000 persons a day were dying of starvation in Somalia, while warehouses remained stocked.

430. On 24 November 1992, I reported to the Security Council that I did not exclude the possibility that it might become necessary to review the basic premises and principles of the United Nations effort in Somalia. I also reported that traditional peace-keeping efforts were not yielding the desired results and that it might become necessary to resort to measures of peace-enforcement.

431. On 3 December 1992, the Security Council, by its resolution 794(1992), established a precedent in the history of the United Nations: it decided for the first time to intervene militarily for strictly humanitarian purposes. By that resolution the Council authorized the use of all necessary means to establish as soon as possible a secure environment for humanitarian relief operations in Somalia. Acting under Chapter VII of the Charter, the Council authorized the Secretary-General and the Member States concerned to make arrangements for the unified command and control of the forces involved, and called on all Member States that were in a position to do so to provide military forces and to make contributions in cash or in kind. The Council further decided that the United Nations Operation in Somalia (UNOSOM I) should proceed at my discretion in the light of my assessment of conditions on the ground.

432. In the first phase of the operation, the Unified Task Force, spearheaded by the United States of America, began arriving on 9 December 1992 to establish a secure environment for the unimpeded delivery of humanitarian assistance. I urged the Task Force command to take steps to disarm the factions involved in the fighting. In the course of five difficult months, the Task Force made progress in opening up access to more and more remote areas and in providing protection for the delivery of humanitarian assistance. Disarmament remains a major problem, but United Nations and non-governmental organizations were able to expand their relief activities in various parts of the country. As a result, there was a dramatic fall in malnutrition levels and in the number of deaths from starvation.

433. On 3 March 1993, I submitted to the Security Council my recommendations for effecting the transition from the Unified Task Force to UNOSOM II. I indicated that, since the adoption of Council resolution 794(1992), the Task Force had deployed approximately 37,000 troops, covering about 40 per cent of the country's territory. While the security situation had improved, incidents of violence continued to occur; I therefore concluded that UNOSOM II should be endowed with enforcement powers to enable it to establish a secure environment throughout Somalia.

434. On 26 March, in its resolution 814(1993), the Security Council, acting under Chapter VII of the Charter, set out the arrangements for the transition from the Unified Task Force to a new United Nations operation (UNOSOM II) under a changed mandate. Instead of a return to peace-keeping, as envisaged in its resolution 794(1992), the Council chose to set up an unprecedented operation involving, as necessary, enforcement action by the United Nations itself under the authority of the Security Council.

435. In this second phase, UNOSOM II is called upon to continue the restoration of peace, stability and law and order, to assist in the re-establishment of the Somali police force, to provide security and assistance in the repatriation of refugees and the resettlement of displaced persons; to assist in the development of a programme for the removal of mines throughout Somalia, to monitor the arms embargo and to facilitate disarmament; and to assist in the provision of relief and in the economic rehabilitation of Somalia. The accelerated deployment of all UNOSOM II contingents to meet the full requirement of 28,000 personnel, all ranks, as well as equipment, was encouraged by the Security Council. Member States were urged to contribute, on an emergency basis, military support and transportation, including armoured personnel carriers, tanks and attack helicopters, to enable UNOSOM II to confront and

deter armed attacks directed against it in carrying out its mandate. At 31 August 1993, the full target of 28,000 personnel had not been reached.

436.   After the transfer of military command to UNOSOM II on 4 May 1993, some of the political movements staged armed attacks against personnel of the operation, as a result of which 49 soldiers have lost their lives. Four journalists have also been killed, and about 160 UNOSOM personnel have been wounded.

437.   On 6 June 1993, the Security Council, by its resolution 837(1993), reaffirmed the authority of the Secretary-General to take all necessary measures against those responsible for the armed attacks and for publicly inciting them, including their arrest and detention for prosecution, trial and punishment. The Council also demanded that all Somali parties, including movements and factions, comply fully with their commitments. It re-emphasized the crucial importance of disarming them and of neutralizing radio broadcasting systems that contributed to the violence.

438.   In the course of the military action carried out by UNOSOM II forces since 12 June, great care has been taken to avoid civilian casualties. The President of the Security Council and I have both expressed deep regret and sorrow at the casualties which have occurred among innocent Somali civilians.

439.   One major task that lies ahead for UNOSOM II and for the Somali people is the implementation of the agreements signed at Addis Ababa in January and March 1993, which include specific provisions regarding a cease-fire, disarmament, demobilization and national reconciliation, as well as requests for United Nations assistance in enforcing them. Those agreements are Somali agreements, and the responsibility for their successful implementation lies with the Somali people. Under Chapter VII authority, UNOSOM II and my Special Representative in Somalia, Admiral Jonathan Howe, will be there to assist and facilitate.

440.   The importance of security both for the effective delivery of relief and for the transition to rehabilitation and reconstruction was fully recognized at the Third Coordination Meeting on Humanitarian Assistance for Somalia, held at Addis Ababa from 11 to 13 March 1993. Participants endorsed the United Nations relief and rehabilitation programme for 1993, which was developed in consultation with the Somalis. The meeting was attended by 190 Somalis, many of whom played an active role in the proceedings of the Conference on National Reconciliation in Somalia which I convened at Addis Ababa on 15 March 1993.

441.   At the Conference on National Reconciliation in Somalia, a two-year transitional period was set by the Somali participants for the re-establishment of a legitimate representative government. In choosing a target date of March 1995, Somalis have established for themselves a realistic time-frame in which to restore civil institutions, to pursue policies which will ensure economic recovery and to provide for their own security. It is my expectation that at the end of March 1995 the current phase in Somalia's history will have come to a successful conclusion and Somalia will have returned to normalcy.

442.   The United Nations is undertaking parallel efforts to put together a three-year, medium-term reconstruction and development plan for Somalia. United Nations development organizations, including UNDP and the World Bank, have been actively involved in this exercise, and arrangements have been made to integrate the efforts of Somalis into this plan. I trust that those efforts will enable the Somalis to rebuild a civil society in their country.

4.   The former Yugoslavia

443.   The tragic situation in the former Yugoslavia continues to drain the attention, resources and emotion of the international community. The Security Council is in session almost daily on this subject and, by the end of July 1993, had adopted 44 resolutions and issued 33 statements by the President on the various conflicts there. While the Council's wishes have been repeatedly flouted by the parties on the ground, I am encouraged by the fact that nations with vastly different interests have been able to respond collectively, again and again, with spontaneous and courageous initiatives, and that they have made valiant attempts to bring tranquillity to that troubled region.

444.   Since August 1993, the International Conference on the Former Yugoslavia has provided a permanent negotiating forum for seeking a political solution to all the problems of the former Yugoslavia. The Conference has a Steering Committee, now chaired by Lord Owen, representing the European Community, and Thorvald Stoltenberg, who in May replaced my Personal Envoy, Cyrus Vance, and who also serves as my Special Representative for the former Yugoslavia. I should like to place on record my gratitude for the tireless, selfless and dedicated efforts of Mr. Vance during the time that he served as my Personal Envoy. The Vance-Owen Plan for Bosnia and Herzegovina, and the Vance Plan for Croatia, still represent a basis for further political solutions to the conflicts in those Member States.

445.   Meanwhile the peace-keeping challenge both in Croatia and in Bosnia and Herzegovina has proved to be formidable. The original mandate of the United Nations Protection Force (UNPROFOR) was extended three times at my suggestion, on 21 February, 31 March and 30 June

1993. UNPROFOR now has almost 25,000 personnel—about 14,000 in Croatia, nearly 10,000 in Bosnia, and slightly under 1,000 in the former Yugoslav Republic of Macedonia. The experience of UNPROFOR in Bosnia and Herzegovina and, to a lesser extent, in Croatia has raised serious questions about the wisdom of deploying blue helmets in situations where the parties are unable or unwilling to honour commitments they enter into and where the peace-keepers themselves become targets of attack.

446.   In Croatia, the original United Nations peace plan remained unimplemented in crucial respects. Demilitarization of the United Nations Protected Areas never took place because of the resistance of local Serbian authorities, a resistance which was at times hardened by the threat, or fear, of attack by the Croatian Army. Consequently, the return of refugees and displaced persons, which can be effected only in secure circumstances, was repeatedly postponed, much to the dismay of all concerned. The mounting frustration of the Croatian Government with the lack of progress in recovering its sovereign territory led to three incursions against Serbs in sectors adjoining the area of deployment of UNPROFOR, and set the peace process back even further. At the time of writing the situation remains tense.

447.   In Bosnia and Herzegovina, the considerable peace-keeping and humanitarian effort of the international community has not brought an end to the brutal conflict, and the daily horrors inflicted on suffering civilians remain an affront to the world's conscience.

448.   The most visible and successful contribution of the international community in the former Yugoslavia is in the humanitarian sphere. The United Nations relief effort, headed by UNHCR, includes valuable contributions by UNICEF, the World Health Organization, the World Food Programme, and other organizations including the International Committee of the Red Cross, the International Organization for Migration and numerous non-governmental organizations.

449.   In March, the Office of the United Nations High Commissioner for Refugees reported that 3.8 million people were receiving assistance in the whole of the former Yugoslavia. In Bosnia and Herzegovina alone, some 2.28 million people, or half the original population, were benefiting from UNHCR assistance. UNPROFOR was able to facilitate the delivery of some 40,000 tons of humanitarian aid to over 800,000 besieged civilians, and to provide help for a huge number of displaced people in the area. Its presence was invaluable in helping to avert the mass starvation that many experts predicted would overtake Bosnia and Herzegovina during the past winter. The provision of relief has involved negotiation of access routes, coordination of airlifting supplies into Sarajevo, delivery of relief by road convoys, and the organization of air drops of relief supplies to areas under siege not accessible by road convoys.

450.   The conditions for the international community's humanitarian efforts have steadily deteriorated, however. In Bosnia and Herzegovina there is currently widespread fighting. Relief operations are obstructed, sabotaged or diverted for military purposes, while the personnel of UNPROFOR, UNHCR and other organizations are increasingly targeted deliberately by members of the armed forces of all parties. UNPROFOR has now suffered 548 casualties, including 51 fatalities, and the casualty rate has recently increased significantly. Meanwhile, the support of the international community for humanitarian operations is dwindling and the sums actually received fall far short of requirements.

451.   The role of the United Nations and other organizations in Bosnia and Herzegovina and the means at their disposal are therefore under serious challenge. It is obviously of paramount importance to sustain the humanitarian effort for as long as necessary but there is a real risk that, if the present downward spiral continues, it will be impossible for the Security Council to achieve its political objectives in Bosnia and Herzegovina. The ultimate consequences would be further large population displacements, which could have serious destabilizing effects on neighbouring countries and the region as a whole, and a humanitarian catastrophe.

452.   One of the most heinous aspects of the war in the former Yugoslavia is the massive and systematic violation of human rights, and the grave violations of humanitarian law, particularly in Bosnia and Herzegovina. The Special Rapporteur of the Commission on Human Rights has submitted several detailed reports on the situation, with recommendations. In his report of March 1993, he paid special attention to mounting evidence of war crimes.

453.   In August 1992, the Security Council reaffirmed the individual responsibility of those who committed or ordered the commission of grave breaches of the Geneva Conventions and violations of international humanitarian law in the former Yugoslavia. On 6 October 1992, the Council, in resolution 780(1992), requested me to appoint a Commission of Experts to reach conclusions on the evidence of grave breaches of the Geneva Conventions and other violations of international humanitarian law committed in the territory of the former Yugoslavia. A five-member Commission was established, which has held seven sessions since November 1992, compiled a computerized database, provided two interim reports

and conducted several field investigations. The Office of Legal Affairs has provided legal and administrative support services to the Commission.

454.   The initial findings of the Commission led the Security Council to conclude that an international tribunal should be established for the prosecution of persons responsible for serious violations of international humanitarian law committed in the territory of the former Yugoslavia since 1991. By its resolution 808(1993), the Council requested me to prepare a report on all aspects of this matter, including specific proposals for the establishment of such a tribunal. I submitted the report, including a draft Statute, on 3 May 1993, and it was approved in its entirety by the Security Council in resolution 827(1993) of 25 May 1993.

455.   The report and the Statute dealt with the constitutionally controversial question of the legal basis for the establishment of the Tribunal, the highly complex substantive legal issues regarding its competence, and the detailed procedural and organizational aspects of its work. The Statute is widely regarded as breaking new ground in the area of international criminal law.

F.   *Post-conflict peace-building*

456.   In "An Agenda for Peace", I stressed that a process of post-conflict peace-building was essential for preventing the recurrence of armed conflict between States. Despite the voluminous and very useful analysis and commentary which has emerged in the months since that report appeared, however, little attention has been given to this concept. Peace-building encompasses more than the reconstruction of the peace after the cessation of hostilities. Peace-building must be linked to the comprehensive development efforts of the United Nations, political, economic, social and cultural.

457.   The objective of peace-building is to involve hostile parties in mutually beneficial undertakings which not only contribute to economic and social development but also reinforce the confidence necessary for the creation of lasting peace. The reduction of hostile perceptions through educational exchanges and curriculum reform may also be essential to forestall the re-emergence of cultural and national tensions which could spark renewed hostilities. Such an approach can also play a vital role in building the peace in situations characterized by civil conflict.

458.   Peace-building begins with practical measures to restore the civil society, reinvigorate its economy, repair the land and restore its productivity, repatriate and resettle displaced people and refugees; it also entails reducing the levels of arms in society, as a component of the volatility that induces violence. These steps, taken in the context of comprehensive humanitarian efforts, are all essential to set the stage for sustainable social, political and economic development.

1.   Mine clearance

459.   Of all the tasks involved in setting a nation on a new road to peace and prosperity, perhaps none has the immediate urgency of mine clearance. Tens of millions of mines have been left in areas of conflict around the world. Although mine-clearance efforts may last for decades, the restoration of transport infrastructures, resettlement areas and agricultural land is often an early priority, and no attempt to restore a sense of community and security can succeed without effective land-mine removal.

460.   I have therefore launched a coordinated programme of action for mine clearance, involving the Department of Humanitarian Affairs, the Department of Peace-keeping Operations and other competent bodies. In Angola, Somalia and the former Yugoslavia, mine clearing is at present undertaken as part of peace-keeping and humanitarian efforts; a concerted drive to rid those countries of mine pollution must wait until the cessation of hostilities. In countries where major conflict has ceased or abated, mine clearance is under way and fighters are being disarmed, demobilized and aided in making the transition to productive peacetime work.

461.   In Afghanistan, at least 10 million mines were left behind after the recent war, and are now seriously hindering the restoration of normal life in many parts of the country. The Office for the Coordination of Humanitarian Assistance to Afghanistan is managing a mine-clearance programme involving the training and supervision of some 2,000 mine clearers fielded under the auspices of Afghan non-governmental organizations. If sufficient funding is made available by donors in a timely manner, it seems likely that the majority of the high priority cultivable land will be cleared by the end of 1997.

462.   Mine clearance progresses well in Cambodia, where some 1,400 mine clearers are now working. There are perhaps 5 million mines spread all over the eastern districts, and clearance is slow, especially in the flood plains and paddy-fields. Following the successful use of mine-detecting dogs in Afghanistan, a similar effort is under way in Cambodia, but it will be many years before this problem is finally resolved. It is therefore imperative that mine clearing should continue in Cambodia after the termination of UNTAC.

463.   A plan has been prepared for the clearance of an estimated 2 million mines in Mozambique. Funds have been raised, partly from the ONUMOZ budget and partly through a trust fund administered by UNDP. A mine-clearance training facility is to be a major part of the programme, since there too mine clearance will be a long-term operation.

2. Electoral assistance

464. During the year, I established an Electoral Assistance Unit in the Department of Political Affairs. Since the Unit became operational, it has provided electoral assistance to 36 Member States, including four cases where the requests were received before 1992 (Angola, Cambodia, Mali and Western Sahara). Of those 36 cases, 2 relate to organization and conduct, 4 to verification, 26 to technical assistance, 9 to coordination and support and 7 to follow-up and report. Twelve of those cases were a combination of technical assistance and one of the other categories. Of the Member States requesting assistance, 26 were from Africa, 4 from Eastern Europe, 4 from Latin America and 1 from Asia.

465. Member States seek electoral assistance from the United Nations essentially in four circumstances: when a country is undergoing a transition to democracy; when it is seeking to build a peaceful alternative to conflict; following decolonization; and in self-determination elections. In Eritrea and Western Sahara, for example, the United Nations has a long-term commitment to assisting in the design of the electoral and referendal systems. The case of Eritrea is an important illustration of this aspect of the Organization's activity.

466. Eritrea suffered more than 25 years of civil war, which ended in May 1991, and now benefits from overall political and security stability. In December 1991, the President of the Transitional Government of Ethiopia made the necessary arrangements with the Provisional Government of Eritrea to facilitate United Nations supervision of a referendum by which the people of Eritrea could determine their political future. On 19 May 1992, the Referendum Commission of Eritrea requested the United Nations to undertake the verification of the referendum. A technical team from the Electoral Assistance Unit visited Eritrea between 30 July and 8 August 1992 to gather information and submitted a report, on the basis of which I reported to the General Assembly, seeking a mandate to undertake a verification mission as requested. On 16 December 1992, the General Assembly, in its resolution 47/114, authorized the establishment of the United Nations Observer Mission to Verify the Referendum in Eritrea (UNOVER).

467. On 6 January 1993, I visited Eritrea to make a first-hand appraisal of the referendum process. UNOVER was inaugurated on 7 January 1993 and consisted of 21 international staff members supported by local personnel, headed by my Personal Representative, Samir Sanbar. They were joined by 85 observers during the referendum, which took place from 23 to 25 April 1993. The total budget of UNOVER was in the order of $2 million.

468. According to the Eritrean Referendum Commission, more than 98.5 per cent of the nearly 1.2 million registered voters voted in the referendum. Voting was overwhelmingly in favour of independence, which was declared on 27 April 1993. Soon after, Eritrea was admitted to membership in the United Nations and the Organization of African Unity.

469. In 1992, the Department of Humanitarian Affairs launched consolidated appeals for the region of the Horn of Africa. For Eritrea, the amount sought to meet emergency needs was $191 million, towards which the international community contributed resources in cash and in kind equivalent to $136 million. The results of any democratic electoral process must be supported by a fundamentally healthy society, economy and State if they are to be durable. The decades of warfare damaged or destroyed much of the physical infrastructure in Eritrea and, together with the drought in recent years, produced major relief needs; but the need is no longer for massive emergency relief but chiefly for major post-disaster rehabilitation and development. In July 1992, the United Nations and the Provisional Government of Eritrea launched a three-year programme for refugee reintegration and rehabilitation of resettlement areas, which requires $262 million and seeks to repatriate 500,000 Eritrean refugees from the Sudan. So far only $32.4 million has been pledged.

470. Not all the interventions of the United Nations in electoral observation have been large-scale missions such as UNAVEM II, UNTAC or UNOVER. Other approaches, involving the coordination and provision of logistic support to groups of international observers, have been effective. Malawi is a particularly interesting case. Coordination efforts began three months before the referendum date and included the deployment of observers during voter registration and the referendum campaign. The involvement of the United Nations was not limited to mere observation, however; on two occasions, I intervened to help secure the agreement of the parties to a change in the date of the elections and on the question of ballot boxes. The referendum confirmed the will of the Malawian people to move to a multi-party system, and the Government is now proceeding with the arrangements for parliamentary elections that will be fully supported by the United Nations.

G. *Disarmament*

471. Since my report on new dimensions of arms regulation and disarmament in the post-cold-war era, significant events have taken place in the international security environment, requiring new responses and renewed efforts by the international community to deal with them. The momentum created by the many positive breakthroughs of the past year must now be maintained.

472.   Most notable among such achievements is the recent decision of the Conference on Disarmament to give its Ad Hoc Committee on a Nuclear Test Ban a mandate to negotiate a treaty on a comprehensive nuclear test ban. That decision was made possible by the crucial commitment of nuclear-weapon States to a continuing moratorium on nuclear testing, and represents a culmination of the efforts of the international community to bring about progress in one of the most vital areas of international security. The year 1993 is the first in which no nuclear tests have been carried out since the moratoria of the 1960s.

473.   To be viable, a comprehensive nuclear-test-ban treaty should be universal, verifiable and of indefinite duration. Coupled with a renewed interest in the cessation of the production of fissionable material, a comprehensive nuclear test ban could help to halt the qualitative arms race and to prevent other countries from acquiring nuclear weapons. That would strengthen the nuclear non-proliferation regime, which has gained in significance as the number of nuclear weapons is being drastically reduced. Together, all these developments offer an incentive to the States parties to the Treaty on the Non-Proliferation of Nuclear Weapons to extend that Treaty in 1995 unconditionally and indefinitely.

474.   I am gratified by the fact that Belarus has recently ratified the Non-Proliferation Treaty, and I very much hope that Kazakhstan and Ukraine will follow that example. I have expressed my deep concern about the intention of the Democratic People's Republic of Korea to withdraw from the Treaty, and I am therefore encouraged by the fact that its Government has postponed a final decision on the matter and is engaged in negotiations with other interested parties, in particular the International Atomic Energy Agency.

475.   Global non-proliferation efforts can also be facilitated by the establishment of nuclear-weapon-free zones. The progress made towards the full entry into force of the Treaty of Tlatelolco is most welcome; in this context, regional initiatives such as those taken by Argentina and Brazil are commendable. I am also gratified by the advances made in the implementation of the Declaration on the Denuclearization of Africa. I extend my strongest support to the ongoing efforts to finalize the text of the treaty to establish formally a nuclear-weapon-free zone in that region.

476.   Another significant landmark in the prevention of the proliferation of weapons of mass destruction is the signature of the Convention on the Prohibition of the Development, Production, Stockpiling and Use of Chemical Weapons and on Their Destruction by some 148 States. The smooth establishment of the Preparatory Commission for the Organization on the Prohibition of Chemical Weapons augurs well for the effective and successful implementation of the Convention. Every effort must now be made to achieve universality at the earliest date.

477.   The establishment of the Register of Conventional Arms is another event of historic significance. In the current situation, where emphasis is placed on building confidence through increased openness and transparency in military matters, the Register has a unique potential. I am pleased that all major arms suppliers and recipient States have provided information to the Register in its first year of operation. The Register has proved to be a success.

478.   The importance of the Register becomes even clearer as we relate it to the question of excessive and destabilizing capabilities in conventional weapons. Although no substitute for actual arms reductions, the Register could help to make military behaviour more predictable and to reassure neighbouring States of each other's non-belligerent intentions. It could be particularly helpful in regions and subregions where there are potential hostilities, as it could lead to gradual reductions in armaments, while allowing the legitimate defence concerns of the parties involved to be considered. I would therefore strongly urge Member States to make use of the Register, together with other measures of confidence-building, particularly within regional and subregional frameworks. This is one way in which disarmament and arms control can contribute to the Organization's efforts in the fields of preventive diplomacy and peacemaking, and I have decided that this should become a priority task for the Office of Disarmament Affairs in the Department of Political Affairs.

479.   An issue closely related to non-proliferation efforts, and to which I attach great importance, is that of the transfer of dual-purpose technology. While it is essential for the international community to prevent the misuse of technology for military purposes, it would be unfair to obstruct legitimate development opportunities. To ensure that all countries, particularly developing countries, will enjoy the peaceful uses of science and technology, I call on the international community to seek agreement on control arrangements that will be universal and non-discriminatory.

H.   *The humanitarian imperative*

1.   Towards a coordinated United Nations response

480.   The international community has asked that more be done to strengthen the capacity of the United Nations to provide humanitarian assistance, through coordinated planning and implementation involving the Departments of Political Affairs, Peace-keeping Operations and

Humanitarian Affairs, and that humanitarian concerns should be reflected in fact-finding missions and in peace-keeping operations. I have therefore taken steps to ensure that essential collaboration takes place among those Departments and between them and all other United Nations organizations and bodies.

481. Humanitarian emergencies, by causing the mass exodus of people, may constitute threats to international peace and security, or aggravate existing threats; conversely, disturbances of the peace may give rise to humanitarian crises. I stress again that it is essential that the United Nations should develop the ability to link humanitarian action and protection of human rights with peacemaking, peace-keeping and peace-building. In formulating the response to humanitarian emergencies, we cannot ignore the infrastructural requirements of the societies in need. Rehabilitation and reconstruction must accompany emergency relief.

482. Because relief personnel frequently operate in areas of conflict or danger even prior to the deployment of United Nations forces, their security is of particular concern. The murder of United Nations staff members working in humanitarian programmes in Afghanistan and the Sudan this past year is a tragic reminder of the fragile status of the United Nations humanitarian presence in turbulent areas (see figure 12). Every effort is being made to ensure the safety of United Nations personnel, and I am also concerned about the security of the personnel of humanitarian non-governmental organizations who are assisting in the implementation of United Nations relief programmes. It is imperative that Governments and other parties to conflict respect their obligations under international law to ensure the secure access of relief personnel and supplies to the victims of humanitarian emergencies.

483. The United Nations system has continued to adapt, refine and strengthen its mechanisms to address new challenges. United Nations and other organizations, including non-governmental organizations, have had to increase their emergency humanitarian relief substantially, straining resources available for reconstruction and development efforts. The three principal United Nations organizations engaged in humanitarian assistance, UNICEF, WFP and UNHCR, increased their relief outlays from $278 million in 1989 to $1,287 million during 1992.

484. At the last meeting of the Administrative Committee on Coordination, I discussed extensively with the heads of organizations, funds and programmes the issues of coordination and effectiveness of United Nations humanitarian action. While many issues remain to be resolved, I believe that the organizations of the United Nations system are moving in the right direction to establish

mechanisms for greater coherence and increased rapidity in their response. One idea which I have encouraged relates to the immediate deployment, at the start of a crisis, of United Nations humanitarian emergency teams, which would draw on the capacities and expertise of the organizations of the system.

485. There is an Inter-Agency Standing Committee (IASC), composed of executive heads of organizations and chaired by the Under-Secretary-General for Humanitarian Affairs, which sets the direction on policy and coordination questions that shape the humanitarian response of the system. Arrangements have had to be made, however, to deal with issues that do not fall within the existing mandates of IASC member organizations, for example, the issue of internally displaced persons, whose numbers are growing at an alarming rate. Operational responsibility for programmes benefiting the internally displaced have been determined on the basis of the capacities of the organizations in the field. UNHCR, UNDP, UNICEF and WFP have all been addressing the various aspects of this problem.

486. As an integral part of the new arrangements for the prompt coordination of the international humanitarian response, the $50 million Central Emergency Revolving Fund has proved to be a useful instrument. Since its inception, $54 million has been advanced from the Fund to finance urgent humanitarian action in Afghanistan, Georgia, Iraq, Kenya, Lebanon, Mozambique, Somalia, Tajikistan and the former Yugoslavia; $20 million of the advances has been reimbursed, confirming the Fund's viability. I am at present considering how the scope and operations of the Fund could be broadened. Given the magnitude and range of emergency humanitarian crises, it may also be useful to consider expanding its resources.

487. Thus far in 1993, the new coordination arrangements under the Department of Humanitarian Affairs have helped to launch 17 inter-agency consolidated appeals for over $4 billion for relief and rehabilitation programmes in some 20 countries, involving assistance to more than 20 million affected people. Only a quarter of the resources appealed for were forthcoming, however, which has considerably hampered the effective implementation of humanitarian programmes. I have asked the Under-Secretary-General for Humanitarian Affairs to suggest ways in which international community support for those programmes could be further strengthened.

488. In northern Iraq, United Nations humanitarian efforts prevented another serious refugee crisis. For the Somalis, the spectre of starvation and disease has receded, and in Mozambique, too, the humanitarian situation seems hopeful. But in many other situations—in Afghanistan, Angola,

Bosnia and Herzegovina, Liberia and southern Sudan—human suffering continues to increase, and for many millions of refugees and displaced persons the situation remains desperate.

2. Disaster relief and mitigation

489. Apart from tragedies and crises caused by man's inhumanity to man, natural calamities, such as cyclones, drought, floods, earthquakes and volcanic eruptions, continue to take a heavy toll of human life and property. Indeed, the rapidly increasing rate of urbanization and the steady increase in world population mean that natural disasters are both more destructive and more costly than ever before. In 1991, natural disasters took more than 162,000 lives and caused damage to property estimated at $44 billion. Disaster mitigation, which should involve both preventive and preparedness measures, can effectively reduce the human toll and economic losses. Ensuring a more effective disaster management response system is yet one more challenge for the United Nations system and the international community.

490. From January 1992 to June 1993, the Department of Humanitarian Affairs coordinated the international response to more than 90 natural disasters, including earthquakes or floods in Egypt, Turkey, Indonesia, Kazakhstan and Pakistan. Coordination mechanisms such as search and rescue teams and on-site coordination of relief activities have been strengthened. The ultimate objective is to increase national and local capacities to deal with disasters. Efforts to prevent and mitigate disasters must begin at the grass-roots level if they are to be effective in minimizing the harm caused by natural disasters.

491. I am convinced that improved disaster management, especially through enhanced preventive action, benefiting from scientific and technological advances, can help to reduce substantially the impact of natural disasters and alleviate the sufferings of the victims. Indeed, the Scientific and Technical Committee on the International Decade for Natural Disaster Reduction, consisting of scientists and specialists from related disciplines, recommended holding a conference where their expertise could be transferred to policy makers in disaster-prone countries. The General Assembly endorsed that recommendation at its forty-sixth session, and I am confident that the World Conference on Natural Disaster Reduction will mobilize the more active involvement of international and national organizations in prevention, preparedness and mitigation activities. I look forward to the participation of all Member States in that Conference.

3. Relief operations

(a) *The Sudan*

492. The humanitarian situation caused by continuing conflict in southern Sudan is a matter of considerable concern. While much was done to ameliorate human suffering, the underlying problems remain, and they require greater humanitarian efforts.

493. A series of high-level initiatives have been taken to broaden and accelerate the delivery of relief assistance to conflict-affected areas. During a visit to the Sudan in September 1992 by the Under-Secretary-General for Humanitarian Affairs, agreement was reached with the Government on the principle of access to all people in need of assistance, and on specific air and river corridors for relief deliveries. Following "proximity talks" between the Government and three factions of the Sudanese People's Liberation Movement, conducted by the United Nations at Nairobi in December 1992, further agreements were reached on road, river and rail corridors, and on updated assessments of the location and condition of displaced populations. In January 1993, the United Nations sponsored talks between the Government and international non-governmental organizations which resulted in wide-ranging agreements designed to enhance the effectiveness of relief operations conducted by those organizations.

494. Despite various efforts, including those of Operation Lifeline Sudan, the humanitarian situation of the affected population remains precarious. I consequently appointed Vieri Traxler as Special Envoy for Humanitarian Affairs for the Sudan, to travel to the region to develop practical and verifiable measures to mitigate the human suffering in several parts of the country. The Government of the Sudan at first denied Mr. Traxler's mission access to the country but, after further contact, it has been accepted.

(b) *Kenya*

495. Early in 1993, Kenya faced major humanitarian challenges. They included requirements for drought relief and drought recovery, such as seeds, tools and veterinary aid, and assistance for refugees in Kenya, primarily from Somalia. It was also necessary to promote stability on both sides of the borders with Ethiopia and Somalia, and to help create the conditions for the return of refugees from Kenya to those countries. The Department of Humanitarian Affairs took the lead in coordinating the preparation of a consolidated inter-agency appeal for Kenya for a total of $192 million. As at 31 July, the nine United Nations organizations requesting funds had received $74.5 million, or 39 per cent of the amount requested.

496. It is clear that Kenya will continue to require substantial humanitarian assistance throughout the remainder of 1993 and in 1994, and that a consolidated inter-agency appeal will be necessary for 1994. Current crop assessments indicate the likelihood of a third consecutive year of lower

than normal harvests, primarily because of drought. UNHCR is preparing an appeal for the repatriation of refugees to Somalia from Kenya, a process which will extend well into 1994, as will the need for continued cross-border operations. Finally, special assistance efforts are now being considered to help Kenyans who have been internally displaced by violence in parts of the Rift Valley, Nyanza and Western provinces.

(c) *Ethiopia*

497. There continue to be significant relief needs in Ethiopia, but the overall emphasis has moved to rehabilitation efforts. In the course of 1993, the United Nations concentrated largely on providing humanitarian assistance to about 5 million people, mainly victims of drought, former soldiers and their families, several hundred thousand refugees from Somalia, returnees, and persons internally displaced. These numbers include an unabated influx of Sudanese refugees, as well as Kenyan and Djiboutian refugees and 400,000 to 500,000 Ethiopians who have returned over the past three years but who still have complex relief needs.

498. An especially noteworthy feature of the case of Ethiopia is the cross-mandate approach, under which those in need are assisted by competent United Nations organizations, the Government and others in a unified programme, regardless of their status (for example, returning refugees or internally displaced persons); the Emergency Preparation and Planning Group plays an important coordination role.

499. The consolidated inter-agency appeal for Ethiopia, launched in January 1993, sought $299.9 million to support such efforts. As at 31 July, $109.7 million had been received in donor contributions, or 36.6 per cent of the funds requested.

(d) *Drought emergency in southern Africa*

500. The drought emergency in southern Africa programme provides an example of the way in which the United Nations, in cooperation with Governments, regional organizations, international financial institutions and non-governmental organizations can meet the challenges of the humanitarian tasks that lie ahead. When 18 million lives were placed at risk by the worst drought to affect southern Africa in this century, that programme, a coordinated approach between the United Nations and a regional institution, the Southern Africa Development Community (SADC), was established as the cornerstone of a complex relief strategy involving assistance channelled through multilateral, bilateral and non-governmental organizations. Funding requirements amount to $858 million.

501. Tragedy was averted because the international community responded positively to the plight of southern Africa, and the Governments of the region made extraordinary efforts to mobilize large amounts of their own resources for food imports and the distribution of emergency aid. Although the unprecedented quantities of food aid they received placed a severe strain on the logistics capacity of individual countries, six of which are land-locked, the region demonstrated its capacity to deliver relief assistance to affected populations in a timely fashion.

502. The World Food Programme/SADC Logistics Advisory Centre was one of the collaborative mechanisms critical to the programme's success; it ensured well-coordinated utilization of ports and land and rail corridors. The Department of Humanitarian Affairs continues its collaboration with SADC to ensure that the emergency management capacity established under the programme is sustained. Of all the natural disasters affecting Africa, drought imposes the greatest toll in human suffering and economic costs.

(e) *Chernobyl*

503. Seven years have passed since the accident occurred at the Chernobyl nuclear power plant. I visited Ukraine recently and was greatly moved to see the continuing consequences of that disaster in the daily life of the population. Some sections of the populations of Belarus and the Russian Federation have also been affected.

504. My Coordinator of International Cooperation for Chernobyl has also visited the three affected States, including the exclusion zone around the encased reactor. After extensive consultations, a new approach has been formulated for the activities of the United Nations system in response to the Chernobyl accident, involving mitigation of its consequences through the implementation of specific projects to address priority needs in the affected areas. To be effective and credible, however, such activities require adequate funding, and thus depend on an appropriate response from the international donor community.

4. Office of the United Nations High Commissioner for Refugees

505. The world's refugee population now stands at a staggering 19 million, and the number of internally displaced persons is 25 million. Such is the magnitude of the problem the world faces in 1993. This is a particularly difficult challenge, and the human and material resources of the United Nations system have been stretched to the limit.

506. The Office of the United Nations High Commissioner for Refugees is carrying out a three-track strategy of prevention, preparedness and solutions. While responding to refugee situations in countries of asylum, the Office also turned its attention to countries of origin, seeking to prevent and contain refugee movements. UNHCR provided assistance not only to refugees, returnees

and displaced persons but also, in the case of the former Yugoslavia, to people affected by conflict or under a direct threat of expulsion, or subjected to the form of persecution now known as "ethnic cleansing". Invoking the human right to remain in one's country of origin, the Office of the High Commissioner sought to ensure that people were not forced to flee from their homes in the first place.

507. One of the highest priorities of UNHCR is to secure the protection of vulnerable groups in areas where peace-keeping operations have brought about a halt in military hostilities. UNHCR has given special attention to sexual violence against refugee women. Among the most odious practices to re-emerge on a large scale in recent conflicts is the use of rape and other forms of sexual violence as an instrument of systematic persecution and intimidation. UNHCR is attempting to achieve international consensus on concrete measures to prevent such practices.

508. UNHCR has also focused on refugee children. Persistent protection problems include military recruitment, detention, irregular adoption, denial of the right to education, and the situation of unaccompanied minors in the care of families not their own. The guidelines and considerations contained in the pamphlet entitled *Evacuation of Children from Conflict Areas*, published jointly by UNHCR and UNICEF in December 1992, illustrate the great potential for inter-agency cooperation in securing the protection of children's rights in the most difficult situations.

509. Among the most notable refugee problems of the past year, the situation in Afghanistan stands out. The end of the occupation by forces of the former Soviet Union, and the return of large parts of the country to relative stability, have made possible the return of large numbers of refugees from safe havens in Pakistan and elsewhere. Although continuing hostilities in parts of the country have deterred some refugees from returning, it is estimated that some 1.7 million Afghans have re-entered Afghanistan in the course of the past 18 months. The provision of assistance to those returnees is an important element in the emergency programmes being coordinated by the Office for the Coordination of Humanitarian Assistance to Afghanistan.

V. Conclusion: Strengthening the human foundation

". . . promoting and encouraging respect for human rights and for fundamental freedoms for all without distinction as to race, sex, language, or religion . . ."

Charter of the United Nations, Article 1, paragraph 3

510. This report has addressed an immense array of practical and urgent programmes and measures designed to carry forward the purposes and principles of the Charter. Underlying these practical efforts are broader endeavours which warrant our commitment over the long term so that we may construct a more enduringly just and advancing global society.

511. A year ago, I stated that a new opportunity had presented itself, that fulfilment of the Charter's original promise was once again achievable. That opportunity has been grasped. Responsibilities have been heaped upon the United Nations. The new activism has made it clear, however, that new levels of political will and intellectual creativity must be attained if wider engagement is to produce enduring achievement.

512. The events of the past 12 months should impress upon us the need for a new realism. The United Nations, by undertaking a range of problems as wide as the globe itself, must be expected to achieve successes but also to experience failure. The failures cannot be put to one side; they require continuing commitment. And successes cannot be regarded as permanent; every positive outcome is likely to be a starting-point for further effort. In a spirit of realism and new possibility, a synthesis of heretofore opposing concepts is conceivable: the United Nations as the instrument of the body of Member States, and the United Nations as more than the sum of its parts.

513. Only international action that emerges from the crucible of debate and decision in the General Assembly, the Security Council and the other organs of the United Nations carries with it the full authority of the world community. The United Nations is now understood to be humanity's best hope in the pursuit of peace, development and human rights.

514. Dedicated to the integrity and development of each individual, drawing legitimacy from all peoples, expressing the consensus of States, the United Nations Organization calls forth, through its universality and dedication to life's basic tasks, a greater potential than humanity has ever before conceived possible.

Boutros BOUTROS-GHALI
Secretary-General

FIGURE 1
> *General Assembly*: Number of resolutions adopted and agenda
> items, 1989-1993

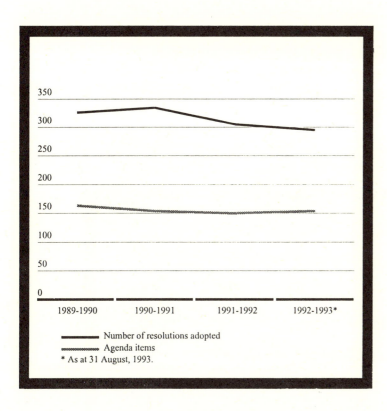

Number of resolutions adopted
Agenda items
* As at 31 August, 1993.

FIGURE 2
> *Security Council*: Number of formal meetings, resolutions adopted
> and statements by the President, 1988-1993

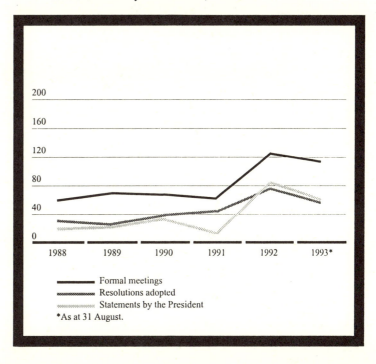

Formal meetings
Resolutions adopted
Statements by the President
*As at 31 August.

FIGURE 3

Security Council: Number of formal meetings and consultations
of the whole, 1988-1993

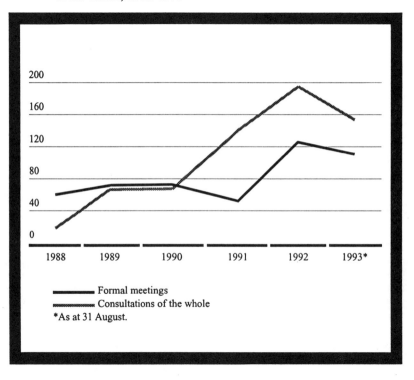

FIGURE 4

Estimated expenditures of the United Nations system by sector, 1992-1993,
all sources of funds*

(Millions of United States dollars)

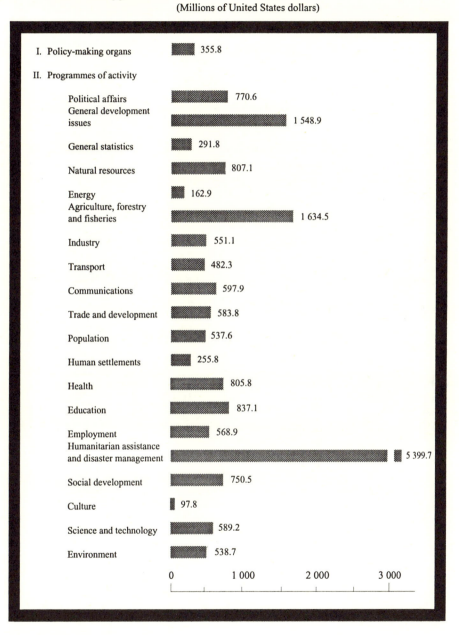

*Source: Report of the Administrative Committee on Coordination of 10 June 1993 (E/1993/84).

FIGURE 5

Summary of contributions: regular budget and peace-keeping,
as at 31 July, 1993

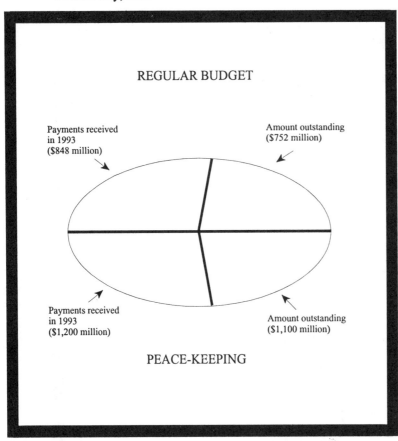

REGULAR BUDGET

Payments received
in 1993
($848 million)

Amount outstanding
($752 million)

Payments received
in 1993
($1,200 million)

Amount outstanding
($1,100 million)

PEACE-KEEPING

FIGURE 6

*Expenditures of funds and programmes administered by the
United Nations Development Programme, 1982-1992*
(Millions of United States dollars)

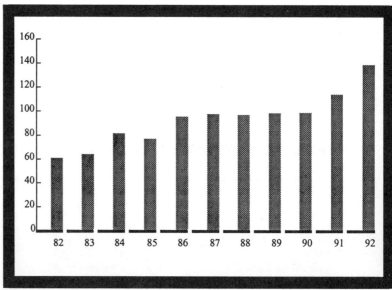

FIGURE 7

Core resources of the United Nations Development Programme, 1982-1992

(Millions of United States dollars)

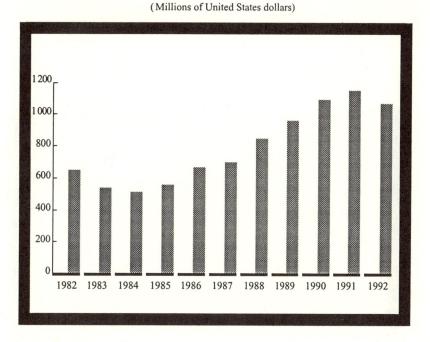

FIGURE 8

Peace-keeping operations as at 31 July 1993

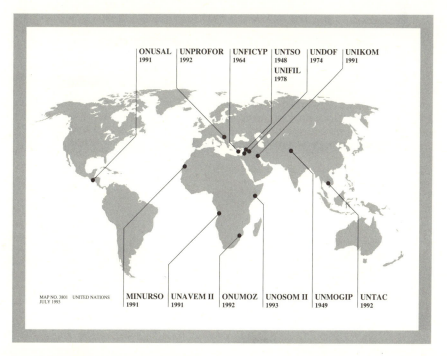

FIGURE 9

*Civilian and military personnel in peace-keeping operations
as at June 30, 1993*

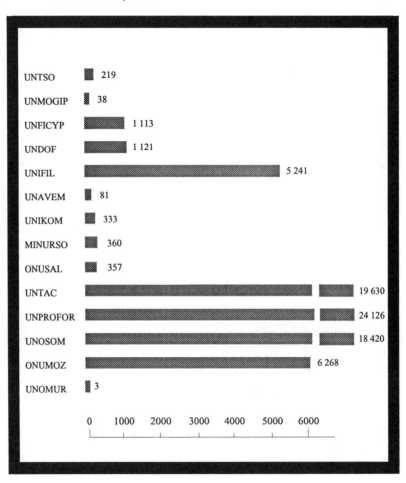

FIGURE 10
Internationally and locally recruited staff in peace-keeping missions

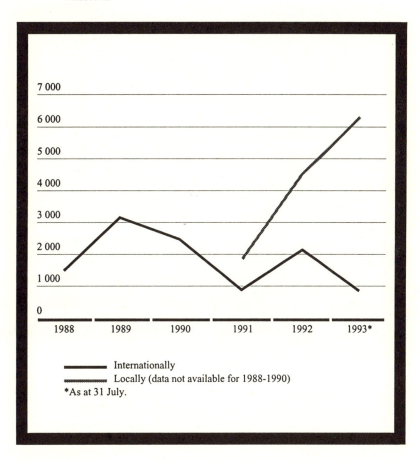

FIGURE 11
Total fatalities in peace-keeping operations since 1987

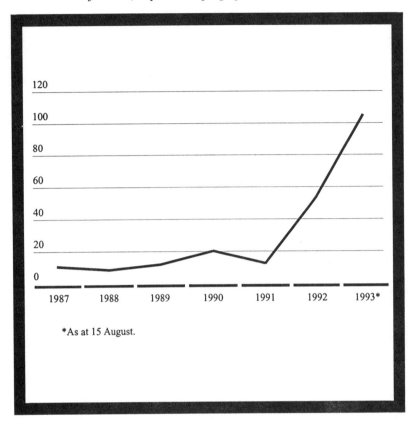

*As at 15 August.

FIGURE 12
Civilian fatalities in peace-keeping missions since 1989

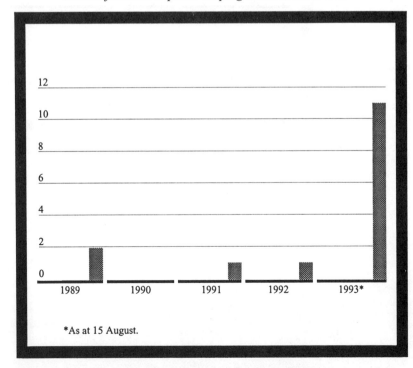

*As at 15 August.

PART ONE

Political and security questions

Chapter I

International peace and security

The United Nations intensified its activities in 1993 to safeguard international peace and security. A record number of 17 peace-keeping operations were deployed worldwide, involving nearly 80,000 military and civilian peace-keeping personnel under United Nations command. The Security Council established peace-keeping operations in Georgia, Liberia and Rwanda.

Demands increased for a new approach to United Nations peace-keeping operations, encompassing peace-enforcement and peace-building, as well as humanitarian and electoral responsibilities, as a result of mounting outbreaks of regional ethnic tensions, religious conflicts and secessionist pressures worldwide. Inter-State wars requiring the classical peace-keeping approach gave way to intra-State, ethnic and factional confrontations, necessitating the United Nations, in its settlement and relief operations, to deal with factions and religious and ethnic movements.

The Secretary-General stressed that the second generation of peace-keeping comprised not only military, but also political, economic, social, humanitarian and environmental dimensions, demanding a unified and integrated approach. Preventive diplomacy, peace-keeping, peace-making and even peace enforcement were intertwined instruments of one concept that strengthened the opportunity for post-conflict peace-building to prevent the recurrence of violence among nations and peoples.

At its resumed forty-seventh session, the General Assembly continued its consideration of the Secretary-General's 1992 "An Agenda for Peace" and adopted a seven-part resolution (47/120 B) dealing with preventive deployment and demilitarized zones, use of the International Court of Justice in the peaceful settlement of disputes, special economic problems arising from the implementation of preventive or enforcement measures, post-conflict peace-building, cooperation with regional arrangements and organizations, and safety of United Nations peace-keeping personnel.

On the basis of the report of the Special Committee on Peace-keeping Operations, the Assembly, by resolution 48/42, adopted a series of recommendations and conclusions on peace-keeping matters, addressing resources and finances, organization and effectiveness, issues arising from "An Agenda for Peace" and the status and safety of United Nations peace-keeping personnel. The Assembly also stressed the need to strengthen United Nations command and control capabilities in peace-keeping operations (48/43).

In September, the Security Council urged States and parties to a conflict to cooperate closely with the United Nations to ensure the security and safety of United Nations forces and personnel, and confirmed that attacks against such personnel would be considered interference with the exercise of the Council's responsibilities. The Council determined that the establishment of future operations would require the host country to take all appropriate steps to ensure the operation's security and safety (resolution 868(1993)).

In November, the Council intensified sanctions against the Libyan Arab Jamahiriya in order to ensure its compliance with two 1992 Council resolutions, requesting the surrender for trial of two Libyan nationals suspected in the 1988 bombing of Pan Am flight 103 over Lockerbie, Scotland, as well as cooperation with French authorities investigating the crash in 1989 of a Union de transports aériens flight in the Niger (883(1993)).

Maintenance of international security and strengthening of the international security system

---

Follow-up on "An Agenda for Peace"

The Security Council held monthly meetings between October 1992 and May 1993 to examine specific proposals contained in "An Agenda for Peace",[1] issued by the Secretary-General in June 1992.

The General Assembly, at the final meeting of its resumed forty-seventh session on 20 September 1993, adopted a seven-part resolution on the Secretary-General's wide-ranging strategy contained in "An Agenda for Peace", which was issued in response to a request emanating from the January 1992 Security Council summit of heads of State and Government.[2] By the resolution—the culmination of nine months of consultations in the Council and subsequent Assembly review—the Assembly decided to consider ways to improve cooperation among United Nations organs in order to strengthen the role of the Organization in promoting peace, and invited those organs to consider implementing preventive deployment and/or the establishment of demilitarized zones, with the objective of preventing conflict and promoting the peaceful settlement of disputes likely to endanger international peace and security. The Assembly encouraged States to consider making greater use of the International Court of Justice for the peaceful settlement of disputes. It decided to continue examining ways to implement Article 50 of the Charter of the United Nations, with a view to solving the special economic problems of other Member States when preventive or enforcement measures were decided on by the Security Council against a State. It emphasized that post-conflict peace-building should be carried out in accordance with the Charter, in particular the principles of sovereign equality, political independence and territorial integrity of States and non-intervention in matters within their domestic jurisdiction. It encouraged regional organizations, arrangements and agencies to consider closer cooperation and coordination with the United Nations to fulfil the purposes and principles of the Charter, and decided to consider further steps to enhance the status and safety of personnel in United Nations operations.

To the concepts of preventive diplomacy, peace-keeping, peacemaking and post-conflict peace-building as defined in the Agenda, the Secretary-General added, in his 1993 report on the work of the Organization,[3] peace enforcement, meaning peace-keeping activities foreseen in Chapter VII of the Charter and not necessarily involving the consent of all parties concerned. Peacemaking, peace-keeping and sometimes peace enforcement, which were intertwined and might be performed simultaneously and in parallel, were required to halt conflicts and preserve peace once it was attained; if successful, they strengthened the opportunity for post-conflict peace-building to prevent the recurrence of violence among nations and peoples.

New forms of preventive diplomacy had evolved; a variety of challenges had led to a more creative and intensive use of familiar techniques designed to prevent the occurrence of armed conflict, including fact-finding, good offices and goodwill missions, the dispatch of special envoys and efforts to bring parties to a potential conflict to the negotiating table.

More than 100 missions of representation, fact-finding and goodwill offices were undertaken to various countries on the Secretary-General's behalf; he had also travelled widely to extend good offices and represent the Organization throughout the world.

Just as preventive diplomacy and conflict resolution had taken on new dimensions, so peace-keeping stretched across a formerly unimagined range of activities and responsibilities, as recent developments challenged traditional assumptions relating to the upholding of agreements, the consent and cooperation of the parties and the minimum use of force.

The Secretary-General expressed regret that little attention had been given to the concept of post-conflict peace-building, which encompassed more than the reconstruction of peace after the cessation of hostilities—it had to be linked to comprehensive political, economic, social and cultural development efforts of the United Nations. He warned that humanitarian emergencies causing a mass exodus of people could threaten international peace and security or aggravate existing threats, just as disturbances of the peace could give rise to humanitarian crises. It was therefore essential to develop the ability to link humanitarian action and human rights protection to peacemaking, peace-keeping and peace-building.

In that context, the Secretary-General repeated his proposal, made in "An Agenda for Peace", that the Economic and Social Council, in accordance with Article 65 of the Charter, be invited to provide to the Security Council reports on economic and social situations threatening international peace and security.

Turning to the role of the International Court of Justice, he stressed that the incidence of cases of considerable political as well as legal importance showed that the Court was an integral part of the Organization's peace efforts. Therefore, he reiterated his recommendation that he be authorized to take advantage of the Court's advisory competence.

SECURITY COUNCIL ACTION (January-May)

In 1993, the Security Council held monthly meetings between January and May to examine specific proposals contained in "An Agenda for Peace". On 28 January, it considered cooperation between the United Nations and regional arrangements and organizations in the maintenance of international peace and security. Following consultations, the President made a statement on behalf of the Council members:[4]

Meeting number. SC 3166.

"The Security Council has continued its examination of the Secretary-General's report entitled 'An Agenda for Peace'.

"The Security Council notes with appreciation the views of the Secretary-General, as presented in paragraphs 63, 64 and 65 of his report, concerning cooperation with regional arrangements and organizations.

"Bearing in mind the relevant provisions of the United Nations Charter, the pertinent activities of the

General Assembly and the challenges to international peace and security in the new phase of international relations, the Security Council attaches great importance to the role of regional arrangements and organizations, and recognizes the need to coordinate their efforts with those of the United Nations in the maintenance of international peace and security.

"While reaffirming its primary responsibility for the maintenance of international peace and security and being aware of the variety of mandate, scope and composition of regional arrangements and organizations, the Security Council encourages and, where appropriate, supports such regional efforts as undertaken by regional arrangements and organizations within their respective areas of competence in accordance with the purposes and principles of the United Nations Charter.

"The Security Council therefore invites, within the framework of Chapter VIII of the Charter, regional arrangements and organizations to study, on a priority basis, the following:

—ways and means to strengthen their functions to maintain international peace and security within their areas of competence, paying due regard to the characteristics of their respective regions. Taking into account the matters of which the Security Council has been seized and in accordance with the United Nations Charter, they might consider, in particular, preventive diplomacy, including fact-finding, confidence-building, good offices and peace-building and, where appropriate, peace-keeping;

—ways and means to further improve coordination of their efforts with those of the United Nations. Being aware of the variety of mandate, scope and composition of the regional arrangements and organizations, the Council stresses that the forms of interaction of these arrangements and organizations with the United Nations should be flexible and adequate to each specific situation. These may include, in particular, exchange of information and consultations, with a view to enhancing the United Nations capability including monitoring and early-warning, with the Secretary-General or, where appropriate, his Special Representative, participating as observers in the sessions and the work of the General Assembly, secondment of officials to the United Nations Secretariat, making timely and specific requests for United Nations involvement, and a readiness to provide necessary resources.

"The Security Council requests the Secretary-General:

—to transmit this statement to those regional arrangements and organizations which have received a standing invitation to participate in the sessions and the work of the General Assembly as observers, and to other regional arrangements and organizations, with a view to promoting the aforementioned studies and encouraging the replies to the United Nations;

—to submit as soon as possible and preferably by the end of April 1993 to the Security Council a report concerning the replies from the regional arrangements and organizations.

"The Security Council invites the States which are members of regional arrangements and organizations to play a constructive role in the consideration by their respective arrangements or organizations of ways and means to improve coordination with the United Nations.

"In discharging its responsibilities, the Security Council will take into account the said replies as well as the specific nature of the issue and the characteristics of the region concerned. The Council considers it important to establish such forms of cooperation between the United Nations and the regional arrangements and organizations, in the area of maintaining peace and security, that are appropriate to each specific situation.

"The Security Council, noting the constructive relationship it has maintained with the League of Arab States, the European Community, the Organization of the Islamic Conference, the Organization of American States and the Organization of African Unity, supports the intention of the Secretary-General, as described in paragraph 27 of his report, to ask regional arrangements and organizations that have not yet sought observer status at the United Nations to do so.

"The Security Council notes the importance of the understanding reached at the Conference on Security and Cooperation in Europe to consider CSCE a regional arrangement in the sense of Chapter VIII of the United Nations Charter and of the further examination within the framework of CSCE of the practical implications of this understanding. The Council welcomes the role of CSCE, together with the European Community, in the implementation of action required to carry out the pertinent resolutions of the Council.

"The Security Council intends to continue its consideration of the Secretary-General's report, as indicated in the President's statement of 29 October 1992."

On 26 February, the Council addressed the relationship between humanitarian assistance and peacemaking, peace-keeping and peace-building. The President made the following statement on behalf of the Council members:[5]

Meeting number. SC 3178.

"The Security Council has continued its examination of the Secretary-General's report entitled 'An Agenda for Peace'.

"The Security Council welcomes the observations contained in 'An Agenda for Peace' concerning the question of humanitarian assistance and its relationship to peacemaking, peace-keeping and peace-building, in particular those contained in paragraphs 29, 40 and 56 to 59. It notes that in some particular circumstances there may be a close relationship between acute needs for humanitarian assistance and threats to international peace and security.

"In this respect, the Security Council notes the Secretary-General's assessment that the impartial provision of humanitarian assistance could be of critical importance in preventive diplomacy.

"Recalling its statement on fact-finding in connection with 'An Agenda for Peace', the Council recognizes the importance of humanitarian concerns in conflict situations, and thus recommends that the humanitarian dimension should be incorporated in the planning and dispatching of fact-finding missions.

It also recognizes the need to include this aspect in connection with information-gathering and analysis, and encourages Member States concerned to provide the Secretary-General and the Governments concerned with relevant humanitarian information.

"The Security Council notes with concern the incidence of humanitarian crises, including mass displacements of population, becoming or aggravating threats to international peace and security. In this connection, it is important to include humanitarian considerations and indicators within the context of early-warning information capacities as referred to in paragraphs 26 and 27 of 'An Agenda for Peace'. The Council emphasizes the role of the Department of Humanitarian Affairs in coordinating the activities of the various agencies and functional offices of the United Nations. It believes that this capacity should be utilized systematically at a pre-emergency phase to facilitate planning for action to assist Governments in averting crises that could affect international peace and security.

"The Security Council notes the ongoing and constructive collaboration between the United Nations and various regional arrangements and organizations, within their respective areas of competence, in identifying and addressing humanitarian emergencies, in order to solve crises in a manner appropriate to each specific situation. The Council also notes the important role which is being played by non-governmental organizations, in close cooperation with the United Nations, in the provision of humanitarian assistance in emergency situations around the world. The Council commends this cooperation and invites the Secretary-General further to explore ways in which this cooperation can be advanced in order to enhance the capacity of the United Nations to prevent and respond to emergency situations.

"The Council expresses concern about the increased incidence of deliberate obstruction of delivery of humanitarian relief and violence against humanitarian personnel, as well as misappropriation of humanitarian assistance, in many parts of the world, in particular in the former Yugoslavia, Iraq and Somalia where the Council has called for secure access to affected populations for the purpose of providing humanitarian assistance. The Council stresses the need for adequate protection of personnel involved in humanitarian operations, in accordance with relevant norms and principles of international law. The Council believes that this matter requires urgent attention.

"The Security Council believes that humanitarian assistance should help establish the basis for enhanced stability through rehabilitation and development. The Council thus notes the importance of adequate planning in the provision of humanitarian assistance in order to improve prospects for rapid improvement of the humanitarian situation. It also notes, however, that humanitarian considerations may become or continue to be relevant during periods in which the results of peacemaking and peace-keeping efforts are beginning to be consolidated. The Council thus recognizes the importance of ensuring a smooth transition from relief to development, and notes that the provision of coordinated humanitarian assistance is among the basic peace-building tools available to the Secretary-General. In particular, it fully endorses the Secretary-General's observations in paragraph 58 of 'An Agenda for Peace' regarding the problems of land-mines, and invites him to address this as a matter of special concern.

"The Security Council intends to continue its consideration of the Secretary-General's report, as indicated in the President's statement of 29 October 1992."

At a meeting on 31 March, the President again made a statement, after consideration of the safety of United Nations forces and personnel deployed in conditions of strife:[6]

Meeting number. SC 3190.

"The Security Council has continued its examination of the Secretary-General's report entitled 'An Agenda for Peace', including the problem identified in paragraphs 66-68—the safety of United Nations forces and personnel deployed in conditions of strife. The Council has considered this question with regard to persons deployed in connection with a Security Council mandate.

"The Security Council commends the Secretary-General for drawing attention to this problem, including the unconscionable increase in the number of fatalities and incidents of violence involving United Nations forces and personnel. The Council shares fully the Secretary-General's concerns.

"The Security Council recognizes that increasingly it has found it necessary, in discharging its responsibility for the maintenance of international peace and security, to deploy United Nations forces and personnel in situations of real danger. The Council greatly appreciates the courage and commitment of these dedicated people who accept considerable personal risk in order to implement the mandates of this Organization.

"The Security Council recalls that it has been necessary on a number of occasions to condemn incidents directed against United Nations forces and personnel. It deplores the fact that, despite its repeated calls, incidents of violence continue.

"The Council considers that attacks and other acts of violence, whether actual or threatened, including obstruction or detention of persons, against United Nations forces and personnel are wholly unacceptable and may require the Council to take further measures to ensure the safety and security of such forces and personnel.

"The Security Council reiterates its demand that States and other parties to various conflicts take all possible steps to ensure the safety and security of United Nations forces and personnel. It further demands that States act promptly and effectively to deter, prosecute and punish all those responsible for attacks and other acts of violence against such forces and personnel.

"The Security Council notes the particular difficulties and dangers that can arise when United Nations forces and personnel are deployed in situations where the State or States concerned are unable to exercise jurisdiction in order to ensure the safety and security of such forces and personnel, or where a State is unwilling to discharge its responsibilities in this regard. In such an eventuality, the Council may consider measures appropriate to the particular circumstances to ensure that persons responsible for attacks and other acts of violence against United Nations forces and personnel are held to account for their actions.

"The Security Council requests the Secretary-General to report as soon as possible on the existing arrangements for the protection of United Nations forces and personnel, and the adequacy thereof, taking into account, *inter alia*, relevant multilateral instruments and status of forces agreements concluded between the United Nations and host countries, as well as comments he may receive from Member States, and to make such recommendations as he considers appropriate for enhancing the safety and security of United Nations forces and personnel.

"The Security Council will consider the matter further in the light of the Secretary-General's report and of work done in the General Assembly and its subsidiary bodies, including, in particular, the Special Committee on Peace-keeping Operations established pursuant to General Assembly resolution 2006(XIX). In that regard, the Council recognizes the need for all relevant bodies of the Organization to take concerted action to enhance the safety and security of United Nations forces and personnel.

"The Security Council intends to continue its consideration of the Secretary-General's report entitled 'An Agenda for Peace', as indicated in the President's statement of 29 October 1992."

On 30 April, the Council focused on post-conflict peace-building. The President made the following statement on its behalf:[(7)]

Meeting number. SC 3207.

"Continuing its examination of the Secretary-General's report entitled 'An Agenda for Peace', the Security Council during the month of April 1993, emphasizing the importance of building strong foundations for peace in all countries and regions of the world, considered the subject of post-conflict peace-building.

"The Security Council supports the view that the United Nations, in order to meet its responsibilities in the context of international peace and security, should view its objectives in respect of economic and social cooperation and development with the same sense of responsibility and urgency as its commitments in the political and security areas.

"The Security Council stresses that, in examining the question of post-conflict peace-building, it wishes to highlight the importance and the urgency of the work of the United Nations in the field of development cooperation, without prejudice to the recognized priorities for the activities of the United Nations in that field as defined by the competent bodies.

"The Security Council took note of the Secretary-General's observation that, to be truly successful, peacemaking and peace-keeping operations 'must come to include comprehensive efforts to identify and support structures which will tend to consolidate peace and advance a sense of confidence and well-being among people'. It agreed that, in addition to the specific measures mentioned by the Secretary-General in paragraph 55 of his report 'An Agenda for Peace', activities such as disarming and demobilization of bel-

ligerent forces and their reintegration into society, electoral assistance, the restoration of national security through formation of national defence and police forces and mine-clearing, where appropriate and within the framework of comprehensive settlements of conflict situations, strengthen national political structures and enhance institutional and administrative capabilities and are important in restoring a sound basis for sustainable peace.

"The Security Council further agrees that, in the aftermath of an international conflict, peace-building may, *inter alia*, include measures and cooperative projects linking two or more countries in mutually beneficial undertakings which contribute not only to economic, social and cultural development but also enhance mutual understanding and confidence that are so fundamental to peace.

"In discharging its responsibilities in the prevention of breaches of peace and in the resolution of conflicts, the Security Council encourages coordinated action by other components of the United Nations system to remedy the underlying causes of threats to peace and security. The Council is convinced that the organizations and agencies of the United Nations system, in the development and implementation of their programmes, need to be constantly sensitive to the goal of strengthening international peace and security as envisaged in Article 1 of the Charter.

"The Security Council recognizes that post-conflict peace-building, in the context of overall efforts to build the foundations of peace, in order to be effective, also needs adequate financial resources. The Council, therefore, recognizes that it is important for Member States and financial and other United Nations bodies and agencies, as well as other organizations outside the United Nations system, to make all possible efforts to have adequate funding available for specific projects, such as the earliest possible return of refugees and displaced persons to their homes of origin, in post-conflict situations.

"The Security Council, as the organ having primary responsibility for the maintenance of international peace and security, fully recognizes, as stated in paragraph 59 of 'An Agenda for Peace', that social peace is as important as strategic or political peace and supports the Secretary-General's view that there is a new requirement for technical assistance for the purposes described in that paragraph.

"The Security Council intends to continue its consideration of the Secretary-General's report entitled 'An Agenda for Peace', as indicated in the President's statement of 29 October 1992."

On 28 May, the Council reviewed United Nations peace-keeping operations. After consultations, the President made the following statement:[(8)]

Meeting number. SC 3225.

"In accordance with its statement of 29 October 1992, the Security Council held a special meeting devoted to the Secretary-General's report entitled 'An Agenda for Peace'. This meeting concluded the present stage of the examination of this report by the Council. On this occasion, the Council wishes to express once again its gratitude to the Secretary-General for his report.

"The Security Council recommends that all States make participation in and support for international peace-keeping a part of their foreign and national security policy. It considers that United Nations peace-keeping operations should be conducted in accordance with the following operational principles consistent with the provisions of the United Nations Charter: a clear political goal with a precise mandate subject to periodic review and to change in its character or duration only by the Council itself; the consent of the Government and, where appropriate, the parties concerned, save in exceptional cases; support for a political process or for the peaceful settlement of the dispute; impartiality in implementing Security Council decisions; readiness of the Security Council to take appropriate measures against parties which do not observe its decisions; the right of the Security Council to authorize all means necessary for United Nations forces to carry out their mandate; and the inherent right of United Nations forces to take appropriate measures for self-defence. In this context, the Security Council emphasizes the need for the full cooperation of the parties concerned in implementing the mandates of peace-keeping operations, as well as relevant decisions of the Security Council, and stresses that peace-keeping operations should not be a substitute for a political settlement nor should they be expected to continue in perpetuity.

"The Security Council has studied thoroughly the recommendations of the Secretary-General contained in 'An Agenda for Peace'. It pays tribute to the valuable contributions made by the Special Committee on Peace-keeping Operations and other relevant bodies of the General Assembly. These discussions and consultations make it possible to formulate more clearly the common priorities of the Member States.

"In the context of the rapid growth in and new approaches to peace-keeping operations, the Security Council commends the initial measures taken by the Secretary-General to improve the capacity of the United Nations in this field. It believes that bold new steps are required and invites all Member States to make their views known to the Secretary-General and the Secretary-General to submit by September 1993 a further report addressed to all the Members of the United Nations containing specific new proposals for further enhancing these capabilities, including:

—the strengthening and consolidation of the peace-keeping and military structure of the Secretariat, including creation of a plans and current operations directorate reporting to the Under-Secretary-General for Peace-keeping Operations to facilitate planning and to enhance coordination;

—notification by Member States of specific forces or capabilities which, with the approval of their national authorities, they could make available on a case-by-case basis to the United Nations for the full spectrum of peace-keeping or humanitarian operations; in this context, the Council welcomes the Secretary-General's effort to ascertain the readiness and availability of Member States' forces or capabilities for peace-keeping operations and encourages Member States to cooperate in this effort;

—the feasibility of maintaining a limited revolving reserve of equipment commonly used in peace-keeping or humanitarian operations;

—elements for inclusion in national military or police training programmes for peace-keeping operations to prepare personnel for a United Nations peace-keeping role, including suggestions concerning the feasibility of conducting multinational peace-keeping exercises;

—refinement of standardized procedures to enable forces to work together more effectively;

—developing the non-military elements of peace-keeping operations.

"In view of the mounting cost and complexity of peace-keeping operations, the Security Council also requests the Secretary-General in his report to address measures designed to place them on a more solid and durable financial basis, taking into account where appropriate the Volcker-Ogata report [see PART FIVE, Chapter I] and addressing the necessary financial and managerial reforms, diversification of funding, and the need to ensure adequate resources for peace-keeping operations and maximum transparency and accountability in the use of resources. In this context, the Council recalls that, in accordance with the Charter and the relevant resolutions of the General Assembly, the financing of peace-keeping operations is the collective responsibility of all Member States. It calls upon all Member States to pay their assessed contributions in full and on time and encourages those States which can do so to make voluntary contributions.

"The Security Council expresses gratitude to the soldiers and civilians who have served or are serving in United Nations peace-keeping operations. It pays tribute to the courageous nationals of dozens of States who were killed or wounded while fulfilling their duty to the United Nations. It also strongly condemns attacks on United Nations peace-keepers and declares its determination to undertake more decisive efforts to ensure the security of United Nations personnel in the course of fulfilling their duties.

"In accordance with Chapter VI of the Charter, the Security Council notes the necessity to strengthen the United Nations potential for preventive diplomacy. It welcomes United Nations General Assembly resolution 47/120 A. It notes with satisfaction the increased use of fact-finding missions. It invites Member States to provide the Secretary-General with relevant detailed information on situations of tension and potential crisis. It invites the Secretary-General to consider appropriate measures for strengthening the Secretariat's capacity to collect and analyse information. The Security Council recognizes the importance of new approaches to prevention of conflicts, and supports preventive deployment, on a case-by-case basis, in zones of instability and potential crisis, the continuance of which is likely to endanger the maintenance of international peace and security.

"The Security Council underlines the close link which may exist, in many cases, between humanitarian assistance and peace-keeping operations and highly appreciates recent efforts by the Secretary-General aimed at further improvement of coordination among Member States and relevant agencies and organizations, including non-governmental organizations. It reiterates, in this context, its concern that humanitarian personnel should have unimpeded access to those in need.

"The Security Council reaffirms the importance it attaches to the role of regional arrangements and organizations and to coordination between their efforts and those of the United Nations in the maintenance of international peace and security. The Council welcomes the readiness of Member States, acting nationally or through regional organizations or arrangements, to cooperate with the United Nations and other Member States by providing their particular resources and capabilities for peace-keeping purposes. The Security Council, acting within the framework of Chapter VIII of the United Nations Charter, calls upon regional organizations and arrangements to consider ways and means of enhancing their contributions to the maintenance of peace and security. For its part the Security Council expresses its readiness to support and facilitate, taking into account specific circumstances, peace-keeping efforts undertaken in the framework of regional organizations and arrangements in accordance with Chapter VIII of the United Nations Charter. The Security Council looks forward to the report of the Secretary-General on cooperation between the United Nations and regional organizations.

"The Security Council draws attention to the increasing significance of post-conflict peace-building. The Council is convinced that in present circumstances peace-building is inseparably linked with the maintenance of peace.

"The Security Council stresses the value of high-level meetings of the Security Council and expresses its intention to convene such a meeting on the subject of peace-keeping in the near future."

Reports of the Secretary-General. In response to a 1992 resolution of the General Assembly,[9] the Secretary-General reported in June 1993[10] on the implementation of his recommendations in "An Agenda for Peace", relating to preventive diplomacy, including fact-finding missions, early-warning systems and confidence-building measures; peaceful settlement of disputes; humanitarian assistance; peace-keeping; peace-building; cooperation with regional arrangements and organizations; sanctions and special economic problems; and the safety of United Nations personnel.

Member States had voiced the desire to improve the United Nations ability to receive and analyse early signals on potential conflict situations. In particular, they wished to see: more timely and higher quality information made available to the Secretary-General; an improved capacity in the Secretariat to analyse diverse conflict sources; more effective action in response to potential or incipient conflicts; ready availability of trained Secretariat staff to undertake early-warning and conflict-resolution functions; and better coordination of those activities.

The Secretary-General estimated that during 1992-1993 more fact-finding missions would take place than in any previous biennium. Experience in that regard confirmed that early initiative, care-

ful preparation and coordination with regional organizations were necessary. The Secretary-General had issued a standing invitation to all Member States to make available to the United Nations information which might help forestall conflict. Initial steps for an early-warning mechanism had been taken, as the Department of Humanitarian Affairs had begun monthly consultations with other United Nations departments, agencies, organizations and observers to develop a mechanism providing advance warning of situations which might give rise to new flows of refugees and displaced persons. The Secretariat's training programmes for political affairs officers, including a training component in preventive diplomacy and early warning, were being improved.

Methods for peaceful settlement of conflicts were increasingly used, adapted to each specific situation. In the past year, the United Nations had dispatched special envoys or missions to the former Yugoslavia, several newly independent States of the former USSR, East Timor, Guatemala, Haiti, Israel, Liberia, the Libyan Arab Jamahiriya, Rwanda, Solomon Islands, Somalia and South Africa. A group of Member States, informally constituted as "Friends of the Secretary-General", played a helpful role in settling the long-standing conflict in El Salvador. Similar groups were formed for the situations in Afghanistan and Haiti, providing the Secretary-General with an informal forum for the exchange of ideas and with a source of diplomatic support from interested countries.

Since humanitarian assistance was closely connected to preventive diplomacy, early warning and the maintenance of international peace and security, the Secretary-General had taken measures to ensure the necessary coordination between the Departments of Political Affairs, Peace-keeping Operations and Humanitarian Affairs, as well as between all United Nations organizations. Training courses for humanitarian assistance were being developed, and steps were taken to develop a specific humanitarian dimension in the integrated early-warning approach.

In response to requests from Member States, the United Nations was taking on a wide array of responsibilities in helping to advance democratization, including electoral assistance. The new Secretariat unit created for that purpose had already handled 36 such requests.

In connection with the multidimensional and interdisciplinary concept of peace-building, the Secretary-General said the Security Council supported specific measures he had proposed and had added new elements to strengthen national political structures and institutional capabilities. The Council, stressing the importance and urgency of the Organization's work in development cooperation, encouraged coordinated action by other components of the United Nations system to remedy the underlying causes of threats to peace and security.

Significant progress had recently been made in strengthening cooperation between the United Nations and regional arrangements and organizations. Effective joint ventures included the association of the Organization of African Unity (OAU), the Organization of the Islamic Conference and the League of Arab States with the United Nations Operation in Somalia (see PART TWO, Chapter I); continuing progress by the United Nations and OAU in drafting a treaty on the denuclearization of Africa (see PART ONE, Chapter II); cooperation and division of labour with the Conference on Security and Cooperation in Europe in areas of actual or potential conflict, such as Georgia, Moldova, Nagorny Karabakh, Tajikistan and the former Yugoslav Republic of Macedonia; the setting in motion by the Secretary-General and the European Community (EC) of the International Conference on the Former Yugoslavia in 1992,[11] together with close cooperation in the field between the United Nations Protection Force (UNPROFOR) and the EC Monitoring Mission (see PART TWO, Chapter IV); cooperation with the Organization of American States to restore human rights and democracy in Haiti (see PART TWO, Chapter II); and the North Atlantic Treaty Organization's assistance to the United Nations in monitoring and enforcing the no-fly zone in the airspace of Bosnia and Herzegovina.

As demand had grown exponentially for the Organization's services in preventive diplomacy, peacemaking, peace-keeping, peace-building and humanitarian assistance, the Secretary-General observed in conclusion that Member States had not only discussed the ideas outlined in "An Agenda for Peace", but were putting some of them into practice, a notable example being the preventive deployment of UNPROFOR in the former Yugoslav Republic of Macedonia. He stressed the overriding importance of the full and timely provision by Member States of the resources needed to strengthen the Organization's capacity in the above realms.

Pursuant to the Security Council's request,[4] the Secretary-General submitted on 15 June a report, with five later addenda,[12] containing replies of seven intergovernmental organizations with standing invitations to participate as observers in the work of the General Assembly and of five other regional arrangements and organizations, regarding ways to strengthen their functions in the maintenance of international peace and security and to improve coordination of their efforts with those of the United Nations.

The General Assembly, on 20 September, adopted **resolution 47/120 B** without vote.

An Agenda for Peace

The General Assembly,

Recalling its resolution 47/120 A of 18 December 1992 entitled "An Agenda for Peace: preventive diplomacy and related matters",

Reaffirming its resolution 46/59 of 9 December 1991, the annex to which contains the Declaration on Fact-finding by the United Nations in the Field of the Maintenance of International Peace and Security,

Recalling also its resolution 46/182 of 19 December 1991 on the strengthening of the coordination of humanitarian emergency assistance of the United Nations,

Recalling further its resolution 47/71 of 14 December 1992 on the comprehensive review of the whole question of peace-keeping operations in all their aspects,

Emphasizing that, together with the Security Council and the Secretary-General, it has an important role in preventive diplomacy,

Recognizing that it has to work in close cooperation and coordination with the Security Council and the Secretary-General in accordance with the Charter of the United Nations and consistent with their respective mandates and responsibilities,

I

Role of the General Assembly

Recalling the relevant provisions of the Charter of the United Nations relating to the functions and powers of the General Assembly,

Recalling also the report of the Secretary-General entitled "An Agenda for Peace", which refers to the utilization of these functions and powers,

1. *Resolves* to make full and effective use of the functions and powers set out in Articles 10 and 14 of the Charter of the United Nations, in conformity with other relevant provisions of the Charter;

2. *Decides* to consider the use of existing or new machinery, including subsidiary organs under Article 22 of the Charter, to facilitate consideration of any situation coming within the scope of Article 14 of the Charter, with a view to recommending measures for the peaceful adjustment of such a situation;

3. *Also decides* to consider appropriate ways and means consistent with the Charter to improve cooperation among the competent United Nations organs in order to strengthen the role of the United Nations in the promotion of peace, including the possibility that the General Assembly receives reports, as appropriate, from the Secretary-General on matters related to the items on its agenda or on other matters within its competence;

II

Preventive deployment and demilitarized zones

Taking note of paragraphs 28 to 33 on preventive deployment and demilitarized zones contained in the report of the Secretary-General entitled "An Agenda for Peace", within the larger context of preventive diplomacy, as well as the views expressed on these issues by Member States,

Stressing that the implementation of any concepts and proposals on preventive deployment and demilitarized zones contained in "An Agenda for Peace" should be undertaken in accordance with the provisions of the Charter of the United Nations, in particular its purposes and principles, and other relevant principles of international law,

Welcoming the instances of effective use of United Nations preventive deployment and the establishment of demilitarized zones,

Stressing the importance of appropriate consultations with Member States and transparency in any decision-making concerning the undertaking of preventive deployment or the establishment of a demilitarized zone,

Recognizing that a United Nations preventive deployment or the establishment of demilitarized zones could promote the prevention or containment of conflicts, the continuance of which is likely to endanger the maintenance of international peace and security,

Emphasizing that respect for the principles of sovereignty, territorial integrity and political independence of States and non-intervention in matters which are essentially within the domestic jurisdiction of any State is crucial to any common endeavour to promote international peace and security,

Bearing in mind that, as each situation in which preventive deployment may be undertaken or a demilitarized zone established has its own special characteristics, it is of the utmost importance to make decisions on such measures on a case-by-case basis with due regard to all relevant factors and circumstances, including consultations with Member States,

Recognizing the need to preserve the impartiality of the United Nations when engaged in preventive deployment or in the establishment of demilitarized zones,

Recognizing also that preventive deployment and the establishment of demilitarized zones are evolving concepts,

1. *Acknowledges* the importance of considering, on a case-by-case basis, the use of preventive deployment and/or establishment of demilitarized zones as a means to prevent existing or potential disputes from escalating into conflicts and to promote efforts to achieve the peaceful settlement of such disputes, the continuance of which is likely to endanger the maintenance of international peace and security;

2. *Reaffirms* that a United Nations preventive deployment and/or the establishment of a demilitarized zone should be undertaken with the consent of and, in principle, on the basis of a request by the Member State or Member States involved, having taken into account the positions of other States concerned and all other relevant factors;

3. *Also reaffirms* that a United Nations preventive deployment and/or the establishment of a demilitarized zone should be undertaken in accordance with the provisions of the Charter of the United Nations, in particular its purposes and principles and other relevant principles of international law, also taking into account relevant General Assembly and Security Council resolutions;

4. *Invites* the competent organs of the United Nations, within their respective mandates, to consider implementing preventive deployment and/or the establishment of a demilitarized zone with the objective of preventing conflict and of promoting efforts to achieve the peaceful settlement of disputes, and to continue to examine practical, operational and financial aspects of such preventive deployment and demilitarized zones with a view to increasing their efficacy and effectiveness;

III

Use of the International Court of Justice in the peaceful settlement of disputes

Emphasizing the role of the International Court of Justice under the Charter of the United Nations in the peaceful settlement of disputes,

1. *Encourages* States to consider making greater use of the International Court of Justice for the peaceful settlement of disputes;

2. *Recommends* that States consider the possibility of accepting the jurisdiction of the International Court of Justice, including through the dispute settlement clauses of multilateral treaties;

3. *Notes* that the use of chambers of the International Court of Justice for dealing with particular cases submitted to the Court by the parties is a means of providing increased use of the Court for the peaceful settlement of disputes;

4. *Requests* States to consider making, if possible on a regular basis, contributions to the Trust Fund of the Secretary-General to assist States in resolving their disputes through the International Court of Justice, and invites the Secretary-General to report periodically on both the financial status and the utilization of the Fund;

5. *Recalls* that the General Assembly or the Security Council may request the International Court of Justice to give an advisory opinion on any legal question, and that other organs of the United Nations and specialized agencies, which may at any time be so authorized by the General Assembly, may also request advisory opinions of the Court on legal questions arising within the scope of their activities;

6. *Decides* to keep under examination all the recommendations of the Secretary-General concerning the International Court of Justice, including those related to the use of the advisory competence of the Court;

IV

Special economic problems arising from the implementation of preventive or enforcement measures

Recalling Article 50 of the Charter of the United Nations, which entitles States that find themselves confronted with special economic problems arising from the carrying out of preventive or enforcement measures taken by the Security Council against any other State to consult the Council with regard to a solution of those problems,

Recalling also the recommendation of the Secretary-General in his report entitled "An Agenda for Peace" that the Security Council devise a set of measures involving the financial institutions and other components of the United Nations system that can be put in place to insulate States from such difficulties and his view that such measures would be a matter of equity and a means of encouraging States to cooperate with decisions of the Council,

Recalling further the statement made on 30 December 1992 by the President of the Security Council, in which the Council expressed its determination to consider this matter further and invited the Secretary-General to consult with the heads of international financial institutions, other components of the United Nations system and

Member States of the United Nations, and to report to the Council as early as possible,

Recalling its resolution 47/120 A entitled "An Agenda for Peace: preventive diplomacy and related matters", in which it decided to continue early in 1993 its examination of other recommendations contained in the report of the Secretary-General entitled "An Agenda for Peace", including implementation of the provisions of Article 50 of the Charter, in conformity with the Charter and taking into account the relevant developments and practices in the competent organs of the United Nations,

Stressing the importance of economic and other measures not involving the use of armed forces in maintaining international peace and security, in accordance with Article 41 of the Charter,

Recalling Article 49 of the Charter, which requires the Members of the United Nations to join in affording mutual assistance in carrying out the measures decided upon by the Security Council,

Noting that the implementation of Article 50 of the Charter has been addressed recently in several forums, including the General Assembly and its subsidiary organs and the Security Council,

Recognizing that, in the conditions of economic interdependence that exist today, the implementation of preventive or enforcement measures under Chapter VII of the Charter against any State continues to create special economic problems for certain other States,

Recalling that Member States have engaged previously in consultations with bodies established by the Security Council regarding special economic problems confronted by them as a result of the implementation of preventive or enforcement measures against Iraq and the Federal Republic of Yugoslavia (Serbia and Montenegro),

Concerned that certain States continue to be confronted with adverse economic problems owing to the implementation of preventive and enforcement measures under Chapter VII of the Charter,

Recognizing the need for appropriate means to find solutions to these problems as soon as possible,

1. *Decides* to continue its examination of ways to implement Article 50 of the Charter of the United Nations, with a view to finding solutions to the special economic problems of other Member States when preventive or enforcement measures are decided upon by the Security Council against a State;

2. *Invites* the Security Council to consider what could be done within the United Nations system and involving international financial institutions with regard to solutions to the special economic problems of States arising from the carrying out of the measures imposed by the Council and to consider, *inter alia*, the following measures:

(a) Strengthening of the consultative process for studying, reporting on and suggesting solutions to the special economic problems, with a view to minimizing such economic problems through consultations with States adversely affected or, as appropriate, with States likely to be adversely affected as a result of their implementing the preventive or enforcement measures, as well as with the Secretary-General, the principal organs, programmes and agencies of the United Nations, and international financial institutions;

(b) Other measures, in consultation with Member States and, as appropriate, with international financial institutions, such as voluntary funds to provide assistance to States experiencing special economic problems arising from carrying out the measures imposed by the Security Council, additional credit lines, assistance for the promotion of exports of the affected countries, assistance for technical cooperation projects in such countries and/or assistance for the promotion of investment in the affected countries;

3. *Also invites* the committees of the Security Council and other bodies entrusted with the task of monitoring the implementation of preventive and enforcement measures to take into account, in discharging their mandates, the need to avoid unnecessary adverse consequences for other Member States, without prejudice to the effectiveness of such measures;

4. *Requests* the Secretary-General to report annually to the General Assembly on the implementation of Article 50 of the Charter;

V

Post-conflict peace-building

Noting that post-conflict peace-building is a new and evolving concept,

Recognizing the need for sustained cooperative efforts by the United Nations to deal with the underlying economic, social, cultural and humanitarian causes and effects of conflicts in order to promote a durable foundation for peace,

Recalling the provisions of Article 55 of the Charter of the United Nations,

Recognizing also that the concept of post-conflict peace-building is aimed at the creation of a new environment to forestall the recurrence of conflicts,

Bearing in mind that each situation in which post-conflict peace-building may be undertaken is unique and therefore should be considered on a case-by-case basis,

Bearing in mind also that post-conflict peace-building should complement efforts at peacemaking and peacekeeping in order to consolidate peace and advance a sense of confidence and well-being among people and States,

1. *Acknowledges* the usefulness of the proposals of the Secretary-General contained in paragraphs 55 to 59 of his report entitled "An Agenda for Peace", particularly in relation to the range of activities for post-conflict peace-building;

2. *Emphasizes* that post-conflict peace-building should be carried out in accordance with the Charter of the United Nations, in particular the principles of sovereign equality and political independence of States, territorial integrity, and non-intervention in matters that are essentially within the domestic jurisdiction of any State;

3. *Recalls* that each State has the right freely to choose and develop its political, social, economic and cultural systems;

4. *Stresses* that activities related to post-conflict peace-building should be carried out within a well-defined time-frame;

5. *Also stresses* that post-conflict peace-building be undertaken on the basis of agreements ending conflicts or reached after conflicts, or at the request of the Government or Governments concerned;

6. *Emphasizes* the need for measures to promote peace and cooperation among previously conflicting parties;

7. *Stresses* the need for coordinated action by relevant components of the United Nations system, including the contributions that the international financial institutions can make in the area of socio-economic development in post-conflict peace-building;

8. *Also stresses* the importance for post-conflict peace-building of contributions from diverse sources, including components of the United Nations system, regional organizations, Member States and non-governmental organizations;

9. *Requests* the Secretary-General to inform the General Assembly of requests relating to post-conflict peace-building by the Government or Governments concerned, or emanating from peace agreements ending conflicts or reached after conflicts by parties concerned;

10. *Affirms* its readiness to support, as appropriate, post-conflict peace-building;

VI
Cooperation with regional arrangements and organizations

Recognizing the importance of the role of regional organizations and arrangements in dealing with such matters relating to the maintenance of international peace and security as are appropriate for regional action, and the need to enhance, in this respect, cooperation between such organizations and arrangements and the United Nations,

Recalling Chapter VIII of the Charter of the United Nations and its acknowledgement of the role of regional arrangements and agencies in dealing with such matters relating to the maintenance of international peace and security as are appropriate for regional action, provided that such arrangements or agencies and their activities are consistent with the purposes and principles of the United Nations,

Taking into account the experience gained and the favourable results achieved by regional organizations in the peaceful settlement of disputes in different parts of the world,

1. *Recognizes* that regional organizations, arrangements and agencies can, in their fields of competence and in accordance with the Charter of the United Nations, make important contributions to the maintenance of international peace and security, preventive diplomacy, peacemaking, peace-keeping and post-conflict peace-building;

2. *Encourages* regional organizations, arrangements and agencies to consider, as appropriate, in their fields of competence, ways and means for promoting closer cooperation and coordination with the United Nations with the objective of contributing to the fulfilment of the purposes and principles of the Charter;

3. *Also encourages* the Secretary-General to continue his efforts at promoting cooperation between the United Nations and regional organizations, arrangements and agencies, in accordance with the Charter;

VII
Safety of personnel

Recalling its resolution 47/72 of 14 December 1992 on protection of peace-keeping personnel, and all other relevant resolutions,

Bearing in mind the concern expressed by the Secretary-General over the safety of United Nations personnel in his report entitled ''An Agenda for Peace'',

Also recalling the relevant resolutions of the Security Council,

Taking note with appreciation of the statement made on 31 March 1993 by the President of the Security Council on the protection of United Nations forces and personnel,

Noting with appreciation the work done by the Special Committee on Peace-keeping Operations on the issue of the status and safety of United Nations peace-keeping personnel,

Gravely concerned about the growing number of fatalities and injuries among United Nations peace-keeping and other personnel resulting from deliberate hostile actions in dangerous areas of deployment,

1. *Welcomes* the report of the Secretary-General on the security of United Nations operations;

2. *Decides* to consider further steps to enhance the status and safety of United Nations personnel involved in United Nations operations, taking into account the need for concerted action by all relevant bodies of the United Nations in this regard.

General Assembly resolution 47/120 B

20 September 1993   Meeting 112   Adopted without vote

Draft by President (A/47/L.65); agenda item 10.

Following adoption of the resolution, the Secretary-General said the text would strengthen the United Nations capacity to respond to a world in rapid transition. He was moving to implement all recommendations made on ''An Agenda for Peace'' by the various intergovernmental organs and bodies involved. He had set up an interdepartmental task force to work out practical measures in response to specific decisions by the Security Council and the Assembly.

The work of the United Nations in the social and economic fields was inseparable from its responsibility to promote international peace and security, the Secretary-General stated, adding that he intended to develop these linkages further in the forthcoming ''An Agenda for Development''. In the post-cold-war period, the world needed a new system for maintaining international peace and security; the resolution adopted was a step towards the realization of a new international consensus and framework for action in that respect. Therefore, he hoped that the implementation process would proceed vigorously.

Maintenance of international security

Pursuant to a 1992 resolution of the General Assembly,[13] the Secretary-General submitted in September 1993 a report[14] containing replies from Denmark (on behalf of EC) and the Dominican Republic in response to his note verbale of 6 April requesting Member States' views on further consideration of the maintenance of international security.

On 16 December, on the recommendation of the First (Disarmament and International Security) Committee, the General Assembly adopted **resolution 48/84 A** by recorded vote.

Maintenance of international security

The General Assembly,

Recalling its resolution 47/60 B of 9 December 1992 on maintenance of international security,

Recalling also its resolution 47/54 G of 8 April 1993, in which it, *inter alia*, decided that the First Committee of the General Assembly, in pursuing its efforts to respond to the new realities of international security, should continue to deal with questions of disarmament and related international security issues,

Welcoming the relaxation of global tensions and the emergence of a new spirit in relations among nations as a result of the end of the cold war and of bipolar confrontation,

Expressing its serious concern over new threats to international peace and security, the persistence of tensions in some regions and the emergence of new conflicts,

Recalling with appreciation the ideas and proposals of the Secretary-General aimed at the enhancement of the potential role of the United Nations in the area of preventive diplomacy, peacemaking, peace-keeping and post-conflict peace-building, as well as in multilateral disarmament, contained in his reports entitled "An Agenda for Peace" and "New dimensions of arms regulation and disarmament in the post-cold-war era",

Reaffirming the importance of multilateral mechanisms in the areas of disarmament and international peace and security,

Bearing in mind the crucial contribution that progress in the field of disarmament, arms control, non-proliferation, transparency in arms transfers and confidence-building measures can make to the maintenance of international peace and security,

Emphasizing that international peace and security must be seen in an integrated manner and that the efforts of the international community to build peace, justice, stability and security must encompass not only military matters, but also relevant political, economic, social, humanitarian, environmental and developmental aspects,

Noting with satisfaction the progress achieved at the Conference on Disarmament towards negotiations on a comprehensive nuclear-test-ban treaty,

Stressing the importance of global and regional approaches to disarmament, which should be pursued to promote regional and international peace and security,

Reaffirming the need to strengthen the mechanism for collective security provided for in the Charter of the United Nations,

Affirming its conviction that all Member States should endorse and support the role given by the Charter to the Security Council in the maintenance of international peace and security,

1. *Reaffirms* that, with the end of the cold war and of bipolar confrontation, the United Nations faces new tasks in the area of maintaining international peace and security;

2. *Recognizes* the need for effective, dynamic and flexible measures, in accordance with the Charter of the United Nations, to prevent and remove threats to peace and to suppress acts of aggression or other breaches of the peace, and in particular for measures to build, maintain or restore international peace and security;

3. *Emphasizes* its commitment to preventive diplomacy and the need to develop appropriate political mechanisms for the early solution of disputes and for the timely and peaceful resolution of any situation that might impair friendly relations among States, so as to preserve peace and strengthen international security;

4. *Stresses* the need for the full implementation of Security Council resolutions;

5. *Also recognizes* that it has an important role to play in helping to address situations that might lead to international friction or dispute, in close cooperation and coordination with the Security Council and the Secretary-General in accordance with the Charter;

6. *Stresses* the great importance of the role of regional arrangements and organizations and recognizes the need to coordinate their efforts with those of the United Nations in the maintenance of international peace and security;

7. *Urges* all States to strive for sustainable progress in the field of disarmament, arms control, non-proliferation, transparency in arms transfers and confidence-building measures, which can provide a crucial contribution to the maintenance of international peace and security;

8. *Further recognizes* the importance of humanitarian concerns in conflict situations, and welcomes the increasing role of the United Nations system in providing humanitarian assistance;

9. *Decides* to continue consideration of the question of maintenance of international security and invites Member States to provide their views on further consideration of this question;

10. *Also decides* to include in the provisional agenda of its forty-ninth session the item entitled "Maintenance of international security".

General Assembly resolution 48/84 A

16 December 1993   Meeting 81   84-0-83 (recorded vote)

Approved by First Committee (A/48/685) by recorded vote (67-0-75), 19 November (meeting 30); 38-nation draft (A/C.1/48/L.32); agenda item 80.
Sponsors: Australia, Austria, Belarus, Belgium, Bulgaria, Canada, Croatia, Czech Republic, Denmark, Finland, France, Georgia, Germany, Greece, Honduras, Hungary, Ireland, Italy, Japan, Kazakhstan, Kyrgyzstan, Luxembourg, Malta, Netherlands, New Zealand, Norway, Panama, Poland, Portugal, Romania, Russian Federation, Slovakia, Spain, Sweden, Tajikistan, the former Yugoslav Republic of Macedonia, United Kingdom, United States.
Meeting numbers. GA 48th session: 1st Committee 3-14, 18-24, 30; plenary 81.

Recorded vote in Assembly as follows:

In favour: Afghanistan, Albania, Andorra, Angola, Argentina, Armenia, Australia, Austria, Azerbaijan, Bahrain, Bangladesh, Belarus, Belgium, Belize, Bhutan, Bulgaria, Canada, Costa Rica, Croatia, Czech Republic, Denmark, Dominican Republic, Estonia, Fiji, Finland, France, Georgia, Germany, Greece, Guatemala, Honduras, Hungary, Iceland, Ireland, Israel, Italy, Japan, Kazakhstan, Kenya, Kuwait, Kyrgyzstan, Latvia, Liechtenstein, Lithuania, Luxembourg, Malawi, Maldives, Malta, Marshall Islands, Mauritius, Micronesia, Monaco, Mozambique, Nepal, Netherlands, New Zealand, Norway, Oman, Pakistan, Panama, Poland, Portugal, Qatar, Republic of Korea, Republic of Moldova, Romania, Russian Federation, Samoa, Saudi Arabia, Singapore, Slovakia, Slovenia, Solomon Islands, Spain, Swaziland, Sweden, the former Yugoslav Republic of Macedonia, Turkey, Turkmenistan, Ukraine, United Arab Emirates, United Kingdom, United States, Uruguay.
Against: None.
Abstaining: Algeria, Antigua and Barbuda, Bahamas, Barbados, Benin, Bolivia, Botswana, Brazil, Brunei Darussalam, Burkina Faso, Burundi, Cambodia, Cameroon, Cape Verde, Central African Republic, Chad, Chile,

China, Colombia, Comoros, Congo, Côte d'Ivoire, Cuba, Cyprus, Democratic People's Republic of Korea, Djibouti, Dominica, Ecuador, Egypt, Ethiopia, Gambia, Ghana, Grenada, Guinea, Guinea-Bissau, Guyana, Haiti, India, Indonesia, Iran, Iraq, Jamaica, Jordan, Lao People's Democratic Republic, Lebanon, Lesotho, Libyan Arab Jamahiriya, Madagascar, Malaysia, Mali, Mauritania, Mexico, Mongolia, Morocco, Myanmar, Namibia, Nicaragua, Niger, Nigeria, Papua New Guinea, Paraguay, Peru, Philippines, Rwanda, Saint Lucia, Saint Vincent and the Grenadines, Senegal, Sierra Leone, Sri Lanka, Sudan, Suriname, Syrian Arab Republic, Thailand, Togo, Trinidad and Tobago, Tunisia, Uganda, United Republic of Tanzania, Venezuela, Viet Nam, Yemen, Zambia, Zimbabwe.

By **resolution 48/11**, the Assembly, noting the idea of the Olympic Truce, urged Member States to abide by it and to pursue in conformity with the Charter the peaceful settlement of all international conflicts.

Implementation of the 1970 Declaration

In December 1993, the General Assembly reaffirmed the validity of its 1970 Declaration on the Strengthening of International Security[15] and urged States to take further immediate steps to promote and use the system of collective security as envisaged in the Charter.

The Secretary-General, in August 1993,[16] transmitted replies from five Member States to a 1992 Assembly invitation[17] to submit their views on the implementation of the Declaration.

GENERAL ASSEMBLY ACTION

On 16 December, on the recommendation of the First Committee, the General Assembly adopted **resolution 48/83** by recorded vote.

Review of the implementation of the Declaration on the Strengthening of International Security

The General Assembly,

Recalling its resolution 2734(XXV) of 16 December 1970 on the Declaration on the Strengthening of International Security, as well as all its previous resolutions on the review of the implementation of the Declaration,

Bearing in mind the final documents of the Tenth Conference of Heads of State or Government of Non-Aligned Countries, held at Jakarta from 1 to 6 September 1992,

Expressing its firm belief that disarmament, the relaxation of international tension, respect for international law and for the purposes and principles of the Charter of the United Nations, especially the principles of the sovereign equality of States and the peaceful settlement of disputes and the injunction to refrain from the use or threat of use of force in international relations, respect for the right to self-determination and national independence, economic and social development, the eradication of all forms of domination, and respect for basic human rights and fundamental freedoms, as well as the need for preserving the environment, are closely related and provide the basis for an enduring and stable universal peace and security,

Welcoming the recent positive changes in the international landscape, characterized by the end of the cold war, the relaxation of tensions on the global level and the emergence of a new spirit governing relations among nations,

Welcoming also the continuing dialogue between the major Powers, with its positive effects on world developments, and expressing its hope that these developments will lead to the renunciation of strategic doctrines based on the use of nuclear weapons and to the elimination of weapons of mass destruction, thereby making a real contribution to global security,

Expressing the hope that the positive trends that started in Europe, where a new system of security and cooperation is being built through the process of the Conference on Security and Cooperation in Europe, will succeed and be extended to the non-participating Mediterranean countries and encourage similar trends in other parts of the world,

Expressing its serious concern at the threat that could be posed to international peace and security by the resurgence of doctrines of racial superiority or exclusivity and the contemporary forms and manifestations of racism and xenophobia,

Stressing the need for the strengthening of international security through disarmament, particularly nuclear disarmament leading up to the elimination of all nuclear weapons, and restraints on the qualitative and quantitative escalation of the arms race,

Recognizing that peace and security are dependent on socio-economic factors as well as on political and military elements,

Recognizing also that the right and responsibility for making the world safe for all should be shared by all,

Stressing also that the United Nations is the fundamental instrument for regulating international relations and resolving global problems for the maintenance and effective promotion of peace and security, disarmament and social and economic development,

1. *Reaffirms* the continuing validity of the Declaration on the Strengthening of International Security, and calls upon all States to contribute effectively to its implementation;

2. *Also reaffirms* that all States must respect, in their international relations, the principles enshrined in the Charter of the United Nations;

3. *Emphasizes* that, until an enduring and stable universal peace based on a comprehensive, viable and readily implementable structure of international security is established, peace, the achievement of disarmament and the settlement of disputes by peaceful means continue to be the first and foremost task of the international community;

4. *Calls upon* all States to refrain from the use or threat of use of force, aggression, intervention, interference, all forms of terrorism, suppression, foreign occupation or measures of political and economic coercion that violate the sovereignty, territorial integrity, independence and security of other States, as well as the permanent sovereignty of peoples over their natural resources;

5. *Urges* all Governments to take immediate measures and to develop effective policies to prevent and combat all forms and manifestations of racism, xenophobia or related intolerance;

6. *Calls* for regional dialogues, where appropriate, to promote security and economic, environmental, social and cultural cooperation, taking into account the particular characteristics of each region;

7. *Stresses* the importance of global and regional approaches to disarmament, which should be pursued

simultaneously to promote regional and international peace and security;

8. *Reaffirms* the fundamental role of the United Nations in the maintenance of international peace and security, and expresses the hope that it will continue to address all threats to international peace and security in accordance with the Charter;

9. *Urges* all States to take further immediate steps aimed at promoting and using effectively the system of collective security as envisaged in the Charter, as well as halting effectively the arms race with the aim of achieving general and complete disarmament under effective international control;

10. *Also stresses* the urgent need for more equitable development of the world economy and for redressing the current asymmetry and inequality in economic and technological development between the developed and developing countries, which are basic prerequisites for the strengthening of international peace and security;

11. *Considers* that respect for and promotion of basic human rights and fundamental freedoms, as well as the recognition of the inalienable right of peoples to self-determination and independence, will strengthen international peace and security, and reaffirms the legitimacy of the struggle of peoples under foreign occupation and their inalienable right to self-determination and independence;

12. *Also reaffirms* that the democratization of international relations is an imperative necessity, and stresses its belief that the United Nations offers the best framework for the promotion of this goal;

13. *Invites* Member States to submit their views on the question of the implementation of the Declaration on the Strengthening of International Security, particularly in the light of recent positive developments in the global political and security climate, and requests the Secretary-General to submit a report to the General Assembly at its fiftieth session on the basis of the replies received;

14. *Decides* to include in the provisional agenda of its fiftieth session the item entitled ''Review of the implementation of the Declaration on the Strengthening of International Security''.

General Assembly resolution 48/83

16 December 1993   Meeting 81   122-1-45 (recorded vote)

Approved by First Committee (A/48/684) by recorded vote (100-1-41), 19 November (meeting 30); draft by Indonesia (for Non-Aligned Movement) and the former Yugoslav Republic of Macedonia (A/C.1/48/L.24); agenda item 79.

Meeting numbers. GA 48th session: 1st Committee 3-14, 18-23, 30; plenary 81.

Recorded vote in Assembly as follows:

In favour: Afghanistan, Algeria, Angola, Antigua and Barbuda, Azerbaijan, Bahamas, Bahrain, Bangladesh, Barbados, Belarus, Belize, Benin, Bhutan, Bolivia, Botswana, Brazil, Brunei Darussalam, Burkina Faso, Burundi, Cambodia, Cameroon, Cape Verde, Central African Republic, Chad, Chile, China, Colombia, Comoros, Congo, Costa Rica, Côte d'Ivoire, Cuba, Cyprus, Democratic People's Republic of Korea, Djibouti, Dominica, Dominican Republic, Ecuador, Egypt, Ethiopia, Fiji, Gabon, Gambia, Ghana, Grenada, Guatemala, Guinea, Guinea-Bissau, Guyana, Haiti, Honduras, India, Indonesia, Iran, Iraq, Jamaica, Jordan, Kenya, Kuwait, Kyrgyzstan, Lao People's Democratic Republic, Lebanon, Lesotho, Libyan Arab Jamahiriya, Madagascar, Malawi, Malaysia, Maldives, Mali, Marshall Islands, Mauritania, Mauritius, Mexico, Micronesia, Mongolia, Morocco, Mozambique, Myanmar, Namibia, Nepal, Nicaragua, Niger, Nigeria, Oman, Pakistan, Panama, Papua New Guinea, Paraguay, Peru, Philippines, Qatar, Rwanda, Saint Lucia, Saint Vincent and the Grenadines, Samoa, Saudi Arabia, Senegal, Seychelles, Sierra Leone, Singapore, Solomon Islands, Sri Lanka, Sudan, Suriname, Swaziland, Syrian Arab Republic, Tajikistan, Thailand, the former Yugoslav Republic of Macedonia, Togo, Trinidad and

Tobago, Tunisia, Uganda, Ukraine, United Arab Emirates, United Republic of Tanzania, Uruguay, Venezuela, Viet Nam, Yemen, Zambia, Zimbabwe.

Against: United States.

Abstaining: Albania, Andorra, Argentina, Armenia, Australia, Austria, Belgium, Bulgaria, Canada, Croatia, Czech Republic, Denmark, Estonia, Finland, France, Georgia, Germany, Greece, Hungary, Iceland, Ireland, Israel, Italy, Japan, Kazakhstan, Latvia, Liechtenstein, Lithuania, Luxembourg, Monaco, Netherlands, New Zealand, Norway, Poland, Portugal, Republic of Korea, Republic of Moldova, Romania, Russian Federation, Slovakia, Slovenia, Spain, Sweden, Turkey, United Kingdom.

Fiftieth anniversary of four nations' Declaration on general security

On 1 November 1993, the General Assembly commemorated the fiftieth anniversary of the Declaration of the Four Nations on General Security of 30 October 1943. The Declaration, issued by China, the USSR, the United Kingdom and the United States, recognized the necessity of establishing at the earliest practicable date a general international organization, based on the principle of the sovereign equality of all peace-loving States and open to membership by such States, for the maintenance of international peace and security.

GENERAL ASSEMBLY ACTION

On 19 October, the General Assembly adopted **resolution 48/6** without vote.

Commemoration of the fiftieth anniversary of the Declaration of the Four Nations on General Security

The General Assembly,

Recalling the adoption in Moscow on 30 October 1943 of the Declaration of the Four Nations on General Security, which, *inter alia*, called for the establishment at the earliest practicable date of a general international organization, based on the principle of the sovereign equality of all peace-loving States and open to membership by all such States, large or small, for the maintenance of international peace and security,

Decides to commemorate in its plenary meeting on 1 November 1993 the fiftieth anniversary of the Declaration of the Four Nations on General Security of 30 October 1943.

General Assembly resolution 48/6

19 October 1993   Meeting 32   Adopted without vote

Draft by Australia (A/48/L.7); agenda item 47.

The proposal to commemorate the Declaration was adopted unanimously by the Preparatory Committee for the Fiftieth Anniversary of the United Nations. The draft resolution was introduced by Australia as Chairman of the Committee.

Science and peace

The General Assembly's Fourth (Special Political and Decolonization) Committee considered the question of science and peace on 15 and 20 October 1993,[18] in accordance with a 1990 Assembly resolution.[19] On the Committee's recommendation, the Assembly, by **decision 48/419** of

10 December 1993, deferred consideration of the item until its 1994 session.

Introducing the draft decision in the Committee, Costa Rica, speaking also on behalf of El Salvador, Guatemala, Honduras, Nicaragua and Panama, said that since the report of the Secretary-General on activities by States and organizations in connection with the International Week of Peace, requested by the Assembly in 1990,[19] had not been submitted, the decision would defer consideration of the item until 1994 with a view to receiving that report. The importance of science as a factor for peace and the contributions that scientists could make to disarmament, peace, security, well-being and sustainable development could not be underestimated.

The Assembly had adopted a resolution on the topic in 1988,[20] in the framework of follow-up activities to the 1986 International Year of Peace.[21]

Regional aspects of international peace and security

Strengthening of security in the Mediterranean region

Pursuant to a General Assembly resolution of 1992,[22] the Secretary-General submitted in October 1993[23] a report on the strengthening of security and cooperation in the Mediterranean region, containing a summary of the debate on the question during the 1992 Assembly session. Also included were replies from six Governments submitted in response to his request of 24 March 1993 for their views.

The heads of Government of the countries of the Commonwealth (Limassol, Cyprus, 21-25 October)[24] adopted a communiqué reaffirming their support for continuing efforts to bring about regional consultations among Mediterranean States with a view to strengthening cooperation and resolving problems in the region. They noted that recent events in the region had underlined the linkage between Mediterranean security and security in Europe, as well as international peace and security. In that regard, they noted with interest the proposals for a Conference on Security and Cooperation in the Mediterranean and for the setting up of a Council for the Mediterranean as a forum for political, economic and social dialogue for the region.

GENERAL ASSEMBLY ACTION

On 16 December, the General Assembly, on the recommendation of the First Committee, adopted **resolution 48/81** without vote.

Strengthening of security and cooperation in the Mediterranean region

The General Assembly,

Recalling its relevant resolutions, including its resolution 47/58 of 9 December 1992,

Reaffirming the primary role of the Mediterranean countries in strengthening and promoting peace, security and cooperation in the Mediterranean region,

Recognizing the efforts realized so far and the determination of the Mediterranean countries to intensify the process of dialogue and consultations with a view to resolving the problems existing in the Mediterranean region and to eliminating the causes of tension and the consequent threat to peace and security,

Recognizing also the indivisible character of security in the Mediterranean and that the enhancement of cooperation among Mediterranean countries with a view to promoting the economic and social development of all peoples of the region will contribute significantly to stability, peace and security in the region,

Recognizing further that prospects for closer Euro-Mediterranean cooperation in all spheres can be enhanced by positive developments worldwide, particularly in Europe and in the Middle East,

Aware of the recent positive developments in the Middle East peace process,

Expressing its satisfaction at the growing awareness of the need for joint efforts by all Mediterranean countries so as to strengthen economic, social, cultural and environmental cooperation in the Mediterranean region,

Reaffirming the responsibility of all States to contribute to the stability and prosperity of the Mediterranean region and their commitment to respect the purposes and principles of the Charter of the United Nations, as well as the provisions of the Declaration on Principles of International Law concerning Friendly Relations and Cooperation among States in accordance with the Charter of the United Nations,

Expressing its concern at the persistent tension and continuing military activities in parts of the Mediterranean that hinder efforts to strengthen security and cooperation in the region,

Taking note of the report of the Secretary-General on this item,

1. *Reaffirms* that security in the Mediterranean is closely linked to European security as well as to international peace and security;

2. *Expresses its satisfaction* at the continuing efforts by Mediterranean countries to contribute actively to the elimination of all causes of tension in the region and to the promotion of just and lasting solutions to the persistent problems of the region through peaceful means, thus ensuring the withdrawal of foreign forces of occupation and respecting the sovereignty, independence and territorial integrity of all countries of the Mediterranean and the right of peoples to self-determination, and therefore calls for full adherence to the principles of non-interference, non-intervention, non-use of force or threat of use of force and the inadmissibility of the acquisition of territory by force, in accordance with the Charter and the relevant resolutions of the United Nations;

3. *Commends* the efforts by the Mediterranean countries in the continuation of initiatives and negotiations as well as the adoption of measures that will promote confidence- and security-building as well as disarmament in the Mediterranean region, and encourages them to pursue these efforts further;

4. *Recognizes* that the elimination of the economic and social disparities in levels of development as well as other obstacles in the Mediterranean area will contribute to

enhancing peace, security and cooperation among Mediterranean countries;

5. *Encourages* the Mediterranean countries to strengthen further their cooperation in facing the terrorist activities, which pose a serious threat to peace, security and stability in the region and therefore to the improvement of the current political, economic and social situation;

6. *Takes note* of the conclusions of the Tenth Conference of Heads of State or Government of Non-Aligned Countries, held at Jakarta in September 1992, concerning the Mediterranean;

7. *Takes note also* of the "Helsinki Document 1992—The Challenges of Change", adopted in July 1992, whereby the heads of State or Government of the States participating in the Conference on Security and Cooperation in Europe agreed, *inter alia*, to widen their cooperation and enlarge their dialogue with the non-participating Mediterranean States as a means to promote social and economic development, thereby enhancing stability in the region, in order to narrow the prosperity gap between Europe and its Mediterranean neighbours and protect the Mediterranean ecosystems;

8. *Takes note further* of the references concerning the Mediterranean region in paragraphs 37 and 38 of the communiqué adopted at the meeting of the heads of Government of the countries of the Commonwealth, held at Limassol, Cyprus, from 21 to 25 October 1993;

9. *Recalls* the decisions taken by the Second Ministerial Meeting of the Western Mediterranean Countries, held at Algiers in October 1991, and the decision concerning the forthcoming summit meeting of the Western Mediterranean countries to be held at Tunis;

10. *Recalls also* the final declaration adopted at the first regular session of the Presidential Council of the Arab Maghreb Union, held at Tunis in January 1990;

11. *Recalls further* the Declaration of the European Council of Ministers on relations between Europe and the Maghreb, issued at Lisbon on 25 June 1992, which underlines the views of the European Community and its member States on the principles and measures capable of strengthening stability and security and encouraging economic, social and cultural progress in the region;

12. *Takes note* of the final report of the international symposium on the future of the Mediterranean region, held at Tunis in November 1992;

13. *Notes* the seminar on the Mediterranean of the Conference on Security and Cooperation in Europe, held at Valletta in May 1993, as well as the two seminars held under the auspices of the Western European Union at Madrid in October 1992 and at Rome in March 1993, dealing respectively with security and cooperation in the Western Mediterranean and with the southern dimension of European security;

14. *Recalls* the conclusions and recommendations of the first Inter-Parliamentary Conference on Security and Cooperation in the Mediterranean, held at Malaga, Spain, in June 1992, which, *inter alia*, launched a pragmatic process of cooperation that would gradually gain in strength and coverage, generate a positive and irreversible momentum and facilitate the settlement of disputes;

15. *Encourages* the continued widespread support among Mediterranean countries for the convening of a conference on security and cooperation in the Mediterranean, as well as the ongoing regional consultations to create the appropriate conditions for its convening;

16. *Requests* the Secretary-General to submit a report on means to strengthen security and cooperation in the Mediterranean region;

17. *Decides* to include in the provisional agenda of its forty-ninth session the item entitled "Strengthening of security and cooperation in the Mediterranean region".

General Assembly resolution 48/81

16 December 1993   Meeting 81   Adopted without vote

Approved by First Committee (A/48/682) without vote, 18 November (meeting 29); 15-nation draft (A/C.1/48/L.43/Rev.1); agenda item 77.
Sponsors: Albania, Algeria, Croatia, Cyprus, Egypt, France, Greece, Italy, Libyan Arab Jamahiriya, Malta, Morocco, Portugal, Slovenia, Spain, Tunisia.
Meeting numbers. GA 48th session: 1st Committee 3-14, 18-24, 29; plenary 81.

South Atlantic zone of peace

The General Assembly in 1986[25] had declared the South Atlantic a zone of peace and cooperation and, in subsequent resolutions, reaffirmed the determination of States of the zone to enhance and accelerate their cooperation in political, economic, scientific, technical, cultural and other spheres.

In response to the latest such resolution, adopted in 1992,[26] the Secretary-General submitted in November 1993[27] a report containing the views of six Governments and 11 United Nations bodies on the implementation of the 1986 declaration.

The Ministerial Meeting of the Zone of Peace and Cooperation of the South Atlantic (New York, 5 October 1993) issued a Declaration,[28] which expressed hope that the zone would continue to be an active instrument for fostering human rights, fundamental freedoms, racial equality, justice and liberty as integral elements of peace, development and cooperation at national and regional levels. The Ministers stressed the importance for the region of attaining the objectives of the 1964 OAU Declaration on the Denuclearization of Africa[29] and the 1967 Treaty for the Prohibition of Nuclear Weapons in Latin America and the Caribbean (Treaty of Tlatelolco) and its Additional Protocols I and II. They welcomed the agreement reached between Namibia and South Africa setting February 1994 as the date for the transfer and reintegration of Walvis Bay and the offshore islands into Namibia, in accordance with a 1978 Security Council resolution.[30]

GENERAL ASSEMBLY ACTION

On 24 November, the General Assembly adopted **resolution 48/23** by recorded vote.

Zone of peace and cooperation of the South Atlantic

The General Assembly,

Recalling its resolution 41/11 of 27 October 1986, in which it solemnly declared the Atlantic Ocean, in the region situated between Africa and South America, the "Zone of peace and cooperation of the South Atlantic",

Recalling also its subsequent resolutions on the matter, including resolution 45/36 of 27 November 1990, in which it reaffirmed the determination of the States of the zone to enhance and accelerate their cooperation in the political, economic, scientific, technical, cultural and other spheres,

Reaffirming that the questions of peace and security and those of development are interrelated and inseparable, and considering that cooperation among all States, in particular those of the region, for peace and development is essential in promoting the objectives of the zone of peace and cooperation of the South Atlantic,

Aware of the importance that the States of the zone attach to the preservation of the region's environment, and recognizing the threat that pollution from any source poses to the marine and coastal environment, its ecological balance and its resources,

Noting the concern expressed on the use of fishing methods and practices that cause the over-exploitation of living marine resources, especially of highly migratory and straddling fish stocks, and that it has an adverse impact on the conservation and management of living resources of the marine environment, both within and beyond the exclusive economic zones,

1. *Reaffirms* the purpose and objective of the zone of peace and cooperation of the South Atlantic;

2. *Calls upon* all States to cooperate in the promotion of the objectives established in the declaration of the zone of peace and cooperation of the South Atlantic and to refrain from any action inconsistent with those objectives and with the Charter of the United Nations and relevant resolutions of the Organization, particularly action which may create or aggravate situations of tension and potential conflict in the region;

3. *Takes note* of the report submitted by the Secretary-General in accordance with its resolution 47/74 of 14 December 1992;

4. *Takes note also* of the Declaration of the Ministerial Meeting of the Zone of Peace and Cooperation of the South Atlantic which was held at United Nations Headquarters on 5 October 1993;

5. *Welcomes* the initiatives leading to the full entry into force of the Treaty for the Prohibition of Nuclear Weapons in Latin America and the Caribbean (Treaty of Tlatelolco), and stresses the relevance of such initiatives for the advancement of the objectives and principles of the zone of peace and cooperation of the South Atlantic;

6. *Notes with interest* the progress made in the drafting of a treaty on the establishment of a nuclear-weapon-free zone in Africa, and stresses the relevance of such a treaty to the advancement of the objectives of the zone of peace and cooperation of the South Atlantic;

7. *Notes* the proposal for negotiation among the South Atlantic countries of an appropriate instrument on marine protection as a complement to the United Nations Convention on the Law of the Sea and as a follow-up to the relevant parts of Agenda 21, particularly chapter 17, adopted by the United Nations Conference on Environment and Development, held at Rio de Janeiro in June 1992;

8. *Affirms* the importance of the South Atlantic to global maritime and commercial transactions and its determination to preserve the region for all activities protected by relevant international law, including the freedom of navigation on the high seas;

9. *Stresses* the importance for the zone of peace and cooperation of the South Atlantic of the results of the United Nations Conference on Environment and Development, particularly the principles of the Rio Declaration on Environment and Development and the programmes set forth in Agenda 21, as well as the United Nations Framework Convention on Climate Change and the Convention on Biological Diversity, in the conviction that their implementation will strengthen the basis for cooperation within the zone and for the benefit of the international community as a whole;

10. *Notes with interest* the hope expressed by the countries of the zone to welcome in the near future a united non-racial democratic South Africa into the community of South Atlantic States, and in that connection urges all parties concerned in South Africa to continue negotiations leading to the establishment of a united non-racial democratic South Africa;

11. *Expresses its appreciation* for the efforts of the international community, especially the recent adoption by the Security Council of resolutions aimed at achieving a permanent resolution of the conflicts in Angola and Liberia;

12. *Welcomes with appreciation* the humanitarian assistance thus far rendered to Angola and Liberia and urges the international community to continue to provide and also to increase such assistance;

13. *Welcomes* the agreement reached between the Governments of Namibia and South Africa setting 28 February 1994 as the date for the transfer and reintegration of Walvis Bay and the offshore islands to Namibia in accordance with Security Council resolution 432(1978) of 27 July 1978;

14. *Also welcomes* the initiative of the Government of Namibia to host a meeting of Ministers of Trade and Industry of States members of the zone at Windhoek on 25 and 26 November 1993;

15. *Further welcomes* the offer by Brazil to host at Rio de Janeiro, in the second half of 1994, the third meeting of high officials of the zone, simultaneously with the meeting of high officials in charge of sports and youth affairs;

16. *Requests* the relevant organizations, organs and bodies of the United Nations system to render all appropriate assistance which States of the zone may seek in their joint efforts to implement the declaration of the zone of peace and cooperation of the South Atlantic;

17. *Requests* the Secretary-General to keep the implementation of resolution 41/11 and subsequent resolutions on the matter under review and to submit a report to the General Assembly at its forty-ninth session, taking into account, *inter alia*, the views expressed by Member States;

18. *Decides* to include in the provisional agenda of its forty-ninth session the item entitled "Zone of peace and cooperation of the South Atlantic".

General Assembly resolution 48/23

24 November 1993   Meeting 63   103-1-1 (recorded vote)

17-nation draft (A/48/L.25), orally revised; agenda item 37.

Sponsors: Angola, Argentina, Benin, Brazil, Cameroon, Cape Verde, Côte d'Ivoire, Gabon, Ghana, Guinea, Guinea-Bissau, Namibia, Nigeria, Senegal, Sierra Leone, Togo, Uruguay.

Recorded vote in Assembly as follows:

In favour: Afghanistan, Algeria, Angola, Argentina, Armenia, Australia, Bahrain, Belarus, Belgium, Belize, Benin, Bhutan, Bolivia, Botswana, Brazil, Brunei Darussalam, Bulgaria, Burkina Faso, Cameroon, Canada, Cape Verde, Central African Republic, Chile, China, Colombia, Costa Rica, Côte d'Ivoire, Cuba, Cyprus, Czech Republic, Democratic People's Republic of Korea, Denmark, Djibouti, Ecuador, Ethiopia, Finland, France, Germany, Ghana, Greece, Guinea, Guinea-Bissau, Haiti, Hungary, Iceland, India, Indonesia, Iran, Iraq, Ireland, Israel, Italy, Jamaica, Japan, Jordan, Kazakhstan, Kenya, Kuwait, Libyan Arab Jamahiriya, Liechtenstein, Luxembourg, Malaysia, Mauritania, Mauritius, Mexico, Mongolia, Mozambique, Myanmar, Nepal, Netherlands, New Zealand, Nicaragua, Nigeria, Pakistan, Panama, Papua New Guinea, Philippines, Poland, Portugal, Republic of Korea, Russian Federation, Rwanda, Saint Lucia, Saint Vincent and the Grenadines, San Marino, Sierra Leone, Singapore, Spain, Sri Lanka, Suriname, Sweden, Syrian Arab Republic, Thailand, Togo, Tunisia, Turkey, Ukraine, United Arab Emirates, United Kingdom, Uruguay, Venezuela, Viet Nam, Yemen.

Against: United States.

Abstaining: Bahamas.*

*Later advised the Secretariat it had intended to vote in favour.

Explaining its negative vote in the Assembly, the United States asserted that, in view of the territorial claims of some States in the region, the resolution did not adequately protect the freedom of navigation and overflight or the right of passage through international straits and territorial seas, as established under international law.

REFERENCES

[1]YUN 1992, p. 35. [2]Ibid., p. 33. [3]A/48/1. [4]S/25184. [5]S/25344. [6]S/25493. [7]S/25696. [8]S/25859. [9]YUN 1992, p. 38, GA res. 47/120 A, 18 Dec. 1992. [10]A/47/965-S/25944. [11]YUN 1992, p. 327. [12]S/25996 & Corr.1 & Add.1-5. [13]YUN 1992, p. 41, GA res. 47/60 B, 9 Dec. 1992. [14]A/48/390. [15]YUN 1970, p. 105, GA res. 2734(XXV), 16 Dec. 1970. [16]A/48/316 & Add.1. [17]YUN 1992, p. 42, GA res. 47/60 A, 9 Dec. 1992. [18]A/48/650. [19]GA res. 45/70, 11 Dec. 1990. [20]YUN 1988, p. 32, GA res. 43/61, 6 Dec. 1988. [21]YUN 1986, p. 115. [22]YUN 1992, p. 50, GA res. 47/58, 9 Dec. 1992. [23]A/48/514. [24]A/48/564. [25]YUN 1986, p. 369, GA res. 41/11, 27 Oct. 1986. [26]YUN 1992, p. 51, GA res. 47/74, 14 Dec. 1992. [27]A/48/531. [28]A/48/581. [29]YUN 1964, p. 69. [30]YUN 1978, p. 915, SC res. 432(1978), 27 July 1978.

Review of peace-keeping operations

As at September 1993, a record number of some 80,000 civilian and military personnel served in 17 United Nations peace-keeping operations around the world.

Peace-keeping forces continued in 1993 to operate in Cyprus (see PART TWO, Chapter III), Lebanon and the Golan Heights between Israel and the Syrian Arab Republic, as did two long-standing military observer missions, the United Nations Truce Supervision Organization in the Middle East (see PART TWO, Chapter V) and the United Nations Military Observer Group in India and Pakistan. In Africa, the United Nations Angola Verification Mission, expanded in 1991, continued activities to verify the peace accords and demobilization arrangements between the Angolan Government and the guerrilla forces in the country, and the United Nations Operation in Mozam-

bique, set up in December 1992, monitored cease-fire and demobilization arrangements with the objective of fulfilling political, electoral and humanitarian functions, in addition to mine clearance (see PART TWO, Chapter I). The United Nations Mission for the Referendum in Western Sahara, created in 1991, was seized of verifying the cease-fire and cessation of hostilities in the disputed territory (see PART ONE, Chapter III).

The United Nations Iraq-Kuwait Observation Mission and the United Nations Transitional Authority in Cambodia continued to operate in 1993 under their respective mandates (see PART TWO, Chapter III), as did the United Nations Observer Mission in El Salvador (see PART TWO, Chapter II) and the United Nations Protection Force, deployed in 1992 in the territory of the former Yugoslavia (see PART TWO, Chapter IV).

In August 1993, the Security Council established the United Nations Observer Mission in Georgia to verify compliance with the cease-fire agreement, maintain contacts with both sides of the conflict and monitor the situation (see PART TWO, Chapter IV). In March, the Council set out arrangements for the transition from the Unified Task Force to a new United Nations Operation in Somalia to enforce the humanitarian and political objectives of the Organization in that country. In September, the Council set in motion the United Nations Observer Mission in Liberia to investigate cease-fire and human rights violations and observe the election process in that country devastated by protracted civil strife. The United Nations Assistance Mission to Rwanda became operative in October to monitor implementation of a peace agreement between the Government and the Rwandese Patriotic Front, succeeding the United Nations Observer Mission Uganda-Rwanda, established by the Council in June to ensure that no military assistance reached Rwanda through Uganda (see PART TWO, Chapter I).

The Council, in a presidential statement of 28 May,[1] recommended that all States participate in and support international peace-keeping as part of their foreign and national security policy. It considered that United Nations peace-keeping operations should be conducted with a clear political goal and a precise mandate subject to periodic review; the consent of the Government and, where appropriate, the parties concerned; support for a political process or for the peaceful settlement of the dispute; impartiality in implementing Council decisions; readiness of the Council to take measures against non-compliant parties; and enforcement rights for United Nations forces to carry out their mandate as well as their right to self-defence.

In a statement issued on 30 September following a meeting with the Secretary-General,[2] the

Ministers for Foreign Affairs of the five permanent Security Council members addressed a number of regional conflicts and pledged strong support to improve the efficiency of the United Nations and to revitalize its peace-keeping capabilities. They agreed to cooperate in strengthening those capabilities under the Council's authority, stressing the importance of improving budget procedures; modernizing command, control and communications; professionalizing and institutionalizing planning and civilian training functions; enhancing public affairs capabilities; and establishing a high degree of coordination among States willing to contribute troops and other assistance to United Nations peace operations. In view of the demands on the United Nations, they affirmed that new commitments should be weighed very carefully and made only after fundamental questions of mandate, its length, objectives, adequacy of force, availability of resources and risk to personnel were examined and satisfactorily resolved.

Reporting to the General Assembly on the work of the Organization,[3] the Secretary-General emphasized that peace-keeping now stretched across a formerly unimagined range of United Nations activities and responsibilities. Peace-keepers were sent to areas where there was no agreement, where Governments did not exist or exercised limited authority and where consent and cooperation of implicated parties could not be relied on. Frequently, their work was obstructed by well-armed irregular groups and warlords. They performed a variety of complex tasks, such as protecting humanitarian aid convoys, supervising elections and monitoring human rights, in addition to keeping apart warring parties. Keeping the peace, only a step in the process of peaceful resolution of conflicts, offered temporary respite from hostilities, while the crisis was being resolved in the political, humanitarian, economic and social spheres.

United Nations peace operations—most prominently in Cambodia, El Salvador, Somalia and the former Yugoslavia—involved interrelated functions and ranged far beyond the accepted notion and definition of peace-keeping, with virtually every department and established function of the United Nations engaged. This second generation of peace-keeping comprised not only military, but also political, economic, social, humanitarian and environmental dimensions, demanding a unified and integrated approach.

Referring to the United Nations engagement in South Africa, the Secretary-General said that, for the first time, civilian United Nations observers had been sent to a country with the consent of the Government to assist in a purely domestic matter, namely, containing the level of violence. In the former Yugoslav Republic of Macedonia, also for the first time ever in United Nations history, military units were deployed on the borders with Albania and the Federal Republic of Yugoslavia (Serbia and Montenegro) as a measure of preventive diplomacy.

In order to deal with the increased demand for peace-keeping operations and the consequent shortage of peace-keepers, the Secretary-General invited Member States to designate qualified personnel for consideration for secondment to a peace-keeping operation and accepted offers by States to make available such personnel on loan; he also set up a special planning team to define standard components from which different types of peace-keeping operations might be put together. A military planning cell with staff on loan from Member States had been formed within the Department of Peace-keeping Operations (DPKO). At Headquarters, a situation room, staffed by military officers, had been created to enable the competent departments to maintain a continuous link with operations in Somalia and the former Yugoslavia. The Secretary-General further considered setting up an integrated situation room for coverage of United Nations peace-keeping operations worldwide in all their aspects.

The Secretary-General noted with concern[4] that, as at 30 September 1993, the unpaid balance with regard to peace-keeping operations amounted to some $1.5 billion. Some operations were not fully solvent throughout the year, even after delaying payments to troop-contributing countries (see PART FIVE, Chapter I). Based on recommendations submitted by the Joint Inspection Unit, he suggested[5] that DPKO become the central or lead department in the Secretariat dealing with peace-keeping operations.

Report of the Special Committee. In 1993, the Special Committee on Peace-keeping Operations held six meetings in New York between 5 April and 19 May.[6] As a basis for discussion, it had before it an April report by the Secretary-General[7] containing further observations and suggestions on peace-keeping operations submitted by six Member States—Canada, Denmark (on behalf of the EC member States), Finland (on behalf of the Nordic countries), New Zealand, the Russian Federation and Yugoslavia (Serbia and Montenegro)—as requested by the Assembly in 1992,[8] and a draft working document prepared by its Bureau containing a list of items and elements for possible consideration by the Committee. An appendix, to the Committee's report contained draft elements for an international convention on the status and safety of the personnel of the United Nations force and associated civilian personnel.

Opening the meeting on 5 April, the Under-Secretary-General for Political Affairs suggested that the question of political conditions necessary for the success of peace-keeping operations, such as the conflicting parties' consent to the deployment of an operation and their continuing cooperation, merited the Committee's attention. He believed the Committee could play a very valuable role in reminding Member States and their legislative bodies of the importance, at a time of limited resources, to ensure that peace-keeping operations were set up only in conditions that were conducive to their success.

On 19 April, the Under-Secretary-General for Peace-keeping Operations referred to "An Agenda for Peace",[9] which suggested that stand-by arrangements for peace-keeping personnel be concluded between the United Nations and Member States. To that end, a special planning team had been set up with the task of defining standard components from which different types of peace-keeping operations might be put together. Training manuals were being prepared for troops, military observers and civilian police, and DPKO and the Field Operations Division were being gradually expanded to meet the increased peace-keeping demands. While appreciating the generosity of Member States which made available military personnel to DPKO free of charge, the Under-Secretary-General said it would be unrealistic for the Secretariat to continue depending on it and, in time, the United Nations would have to turn to Member States to fund additional posts.

To examine the substance of its mandate, the Special Committee established an open-ended working group, which submitted conclusions and recommendations for the Committee's approval and transmittal to the General Assembly. In those recommendations, the Committee encouraged Member States to develop, in cooperation with the Secretariat, arrangements for military, police and civilian personnel for participation in peace-keeping operations and to notify the Secretary-General of the existence and content of such arrangements on an ongoing basis. In view of the critical financial situation of the United Nations, it called on States to pay their assessed contributions in full and on time and encouraged those able to do so to make voluntary contributions.

The Committee suggested that the Security Council and the Secretary-General continue to analyse a given situation carefully before establishing a peace-keeping operation. A realistic mandate, with clear objectives and a time-frame for resolving the problem in a way conducive to furthering the political process, should be formulated in each case. To organize peace-keeping operations effectively and efficiently, the Committee urged the Secretary-General to initiate a comprehensive review of the role, tasks and functions of the various units of the Secretariat with a view to iden-

tifying the optimum Secretariat structure in that respect.

The Committee stressed that the conclusion of a status-of-forces agreement between the United Nations and a host State was of utmost importance when deploying peace-keeping operations and called on host States to give their fullest cooperation in that regard. It again requested the Secretary-General to consider establishing a training programme for key staff personnel of peace-keeping operations with a view to creating a pool of trained personnel with knowledge of the United Nations system and its working procedures. He was further requested to take concrete steps to improve the physical security of United Nations peace-keeping personnel in the field.

Report of the Secretary-General. Pursuant to a request of the Security Council, contained in the President's statement of 28 May 1993,[1] the Secretary-General submitted replies from 10 States and two intergovernmental organizations on improving the capacity of the United Nations for peace-keeping.[10]

GENERAL ASSEMBLY ACTION

On 10 December, on the recommendation of the Fourth Committee, the General Assembly adopted **resolution 48/42** without vote.

Comprehensive review of the whole question of peace-keeping operations in all their aspects
The General Assembly,

Recalling its resolution 2006(XIX) of 18 February 1965 and all other relevant resolutions,

Recalling in particular its resolutions 47/71 and 47/72 of 14 December 1992,

Welcoming the progress made by the Special Committee on Peace-keeping Operations during its recent sessions,

Convinced that peace-keeping operations constitute a considerable part of the efforts by the United Nations to maintain international peace and security and to enhance the effectiveness of the United Nations in this regard,

Recognizing that the peacemaking activities of the Secretary-General and of organs of the United Nations, which are actions to bring hostile parties to agreement essentially through peaceful means such as those foreseen in Chapter VI of the Charter of the United Nations, constitute an essential function of the United Nations and are among the important means for the prevention, containment and resolution of disputes, the continuance of which is likely to endanger the maintenance of international peace and security,

Emphasizing that respect for the principles of sovereignty, territorial integrity and political independence of States and non-intervention in matters which are essentially within the domestic jurisdiction of any States is crucial to any common endeavour to promote international peace and security,

Taking note of the statement by the President of the Security Council of 28 May 1993 and the recommendations contained therein,

Convinced that in order to ensure the effectiveness of peace-keeping operations it is necessary that they have precise and clearly defined mandates,

Taking into account that the increase in activities in the field of United Nations peace-keeping requires both increasing and better managed human, financial and material resources for the Organization,

Aware of the extremely difficult financial situation of the United Nations as described in the report of the Secretary-General and of the heavy burden on all the troop contributors, many of which are developing countries,

Taking note of the report of the Secretary-General on the work of the Organization, having examined the report of the Special Committee on Peace-keeping Operations, and being aware of the relevant parts of the report of the Joint Inspection Unit on staffing of the United Nations peace-keeping and related missions (civilian component),

1. *Welcomes* the report of the Special Committee on Peace-keeping Operations;

Resources

2. *Notes with appreciation* the initiative of the Secretary-General in establishing a stand-by forces planning team and looks forward to periodic reports on that initiative;

3. *Recommends* that contact between the Secretariat and Member States should be enhanced with a view to clarifying the military and civilian needs for United Nations peace-keeping operations and such capabilities of Member States as could be made available for those operations;

4. *Encourages* Member States, to the extent that their domestic arrangements permit, to develop, in cooperation with the Secretariat, arrangements for military, police and civilian personnel to participate in peace-keeping operations and to notify the Secretary-General of the existence and the modalities of such arrangements on an ongoing basis;

5. *Calls upon* the Secretary-General to develop a proposal for regularly updated data banks recording the type and availability of resources Member States could provide, as described in paragraph 4 above, as well as individuals with skills appropriate for civilian peace-keeping duties, and invites the Secretary-General to propose such other measures as he believes necessary to meet the urgent need for timely availability of personnel qualified to serve in the full spectrum of civilian peace-keeping capacities;

6. *Stresses* the need for the United Nations to be given the resources commensurate with its growing responsibilities in the area of peace-keeping, particularly with regard to the resources needed for the start-up phase of such operations;

7. *Takes note* of the recommendations of the Secretary-General concerning the timely provision of basic peace-keeping equipment, and suggests the development of a limited revolving reserve of such equipment within existing resources;

8. *Invites* the Secretary-General to consult in advance with Member States on their willingness to earmark certain equipment specified by the Secretary-General for immediate sale, loan or donation to the United Nations when required;

9. *Encourages* Member States to make available air- and sea-lift resources to the United Nations at the best available rates in accordance with the Financial Regulations and Rules of the United Nations;

10. *Requests* the Secretariat to develop guidelines concerning the disposition of United Nations equipment upon the termination of a peace-keeping operation;

Finances

11. *Recalls* that the financing of peace-keeping operations is the collective responsibility of all Member States in accordance with Article 17, paragraph 2, of the Charter of the United Nations, notes the report of the Secretary-General on improving the financial situation of the United Nations, reiterates its call upon all Member States to pay their assessed contributions in full and on time, and encourages States to make voluntary contributions in accordance with the Financial Regulations and Rules of the United Nations;

12. *Invites* the Secretary-General to review, as appropriate, the applicable United Nations financial and administrative regulations concerning peace-keeping operations, and to that end urges that steps be taken to strengthen lateral communication and the distribution of information within the Secretariat;

13. *Requests* that the Secretary-General improve the financial control mechanisms relative to peace-keeping by strengthening the system of audit and inspection, including external controls, stresses the need to ensure that appropriate accountability is maintained, and in that regard notes with appreciation recent steps to strengthen the capacity for independent oversight and investigation;

14. *Stresses* the need to delegate the appropriate degree of financial and administrative authority to Force Commanders or Special Representatives while ensuring that measures relating to responsibility and accountability are strengthened in order to increase the missions' capacity to adjust to new situations and specific requirements;

15. *Notes* that a number of military officers have been made available on loan on a non-reimbursable basis to the Secretariat at its request, and welcomes the efforts of the Secretary-General to implement financial arrangements, within existing resources, which would enable all Member States to contribute to such a system in the future and would ease the costs borne by Member States contributing those officers;

16. *Calls upon* the Secretariat to prepare comprehensive budget estimates for all new and ongoing peace-keeping operations in a timely fashion in order to allow for a thorough examination by the Advisory Committee on Administrative and Budgetary Questions and the General Assembly;

17. *Stresses also* the importance of reimbursing all outstanding dues of troop-contributing or other participating States without delay, and notes the report of the Secretary-General in that regard;

18. *Reaffirms* the competence of the General Assembly for the appropriation and apportionment of the costs of United Nations peace-keeping operations, and notes the importance for the Security Council to be aware of, *inter alia*, the availability of adequate physical and material resources and the cost implications before it establishes new peace-keeping operations;

19. *Considers* that the issue of supplementing diversified financial resources to the assessed contributions

should be studied further in all the appropriate United Nations forums;

20.   *Encourages* the consideration in the appropriate forums of further measures that could improve the financing of peace-keeping operations, including the feasibility of an improved billing system;

21.   *Requests* the Secretary-General to consult with Member States during his current review of the rates of reimbursement for depreciation of contingent-owned equipment deployed at the request of the United Nations;

22.   *Requests* the Secretariat to compile all the existing financial and administrative rules, regulations, practices and procedures relating to peace-keeping into a comprehensive document available to Member States;

23.   *Welcomes* the creation of the Peace-keeping Reserve Fund, notes the importance of adequate resources for peace-keeping start-up costs and that sufficient resources have not been made available for this purpose, stresses that the Fund should be supplied with the amount specified in its resolution 47/217 of 23 December 1992, thereby making the Fund operational as soon as possible, and emphasizes that the Fund should, in the future, serve as an essential source of funds for peace-keeping start-up costs;

Organization and effectiveness

24.   *Suggests* that the Security Council and the Secretary-General should continue to analyse a given situation very carefully before the establishment of a United Nations peace-keeping operation, that a realistic mandate, including clear objectives and a time-frame for the resolution of the problem, as appropriate, should be formulated in each case, conducive to the furtherance of the political process and that the Security Council should review periodically the effectiveness of current operations with a view to ensuring that they are consistent with the objectives and the mandates as approved by the Council, and affirms that no change in the mandate, character or duration of peace-keeping operations authorized by the Security Council is possible except through a specific decision of the Council;

25.   *Notes with appreciation* the steps taken by the Secretary-General to strengthen and reform those units of the Secretariat dealing with peace-keeping, as outlined in his report on the implementation of the recommendations contained in ''An Agenda for Peace'';

26.   *Stresses* the need for the Secretariat to deal effectively and efficiently with planning, launching, managing and providing administrative and logistics support to peace-keeping operations, and urges the Secretary-General, as the chief administrative officer of the Organization, in consultation with Member States, to initiate a comprehensive review of the role, tasks and functions, including civilian functions, of the various units of the Secretariat with a view to identifying the optimum Secretariat structure in that respect and to assuring the unity of command and control indispensable for successful peace-keeping by assigning executive responsibility for all aspects of a peace-keeping operation to the Department of Peace-keeping Operations of the Secretariat;

27.   *Also stresses* the importance of coordination of all aspects of the planning process in peace-keeping operations, and suggests that the emergency relief coordinator should be fully consulted in the overall planning of a peace-keeping operation when the mandate for such an operation contains a humanitarian component and in other cases should be consulted at an early stage when close coordination between humanitarian and peace-keeping activities is required;

28.   *Notes* the transfer of the Field Operations Division from the Department of Administration and Management to the Department of Peace-keeping Operations, and encourages the Secretary-General to continue his efforts to strengthen and make more effective the planning, management and administrative support for peace-keeping operations and the capability of the Secretariat for overall evaluation and analysis of peace-keeping operations from their initial stages to their conclusion;

29.   *Urges* the Secretary-General in his review of Secretariat capabilities to improve information flow and to enhance coordination and communication between United Nations Headquarters and field missions in order to manage peace-keeping operations effectively and inform Member States as appropriate;

30.   *Requests* the Secretary-General to keep Member States informed on organizational responsibilities of the various units of those Secretariat departments responsible for peace-keeping operations;

31.   *Invites* the Secretary-General to identify a focal point for contact by Member States seeking information on all facets, including operational, logistics and administrative matters, of ongoing and planned peace-keeping operations;

32.   *Also invites* the Secretary-General to continue arrangements and procedures for providing additional personnel on a short-term basis in order to ensure that the Secretariat can respond effectively and efficiently to fluctuations in its workload, particularly when new operations are planned and launched, and to keep the Member States informed of such procedures;

33.   *Once again invites* the Secretary-General to consider means whereby Special Representatives, Force Commanders and other key personnel of newly approved missions are identified and involved in the planning process at the earliest possible time;

34.   *Welcomes* the establishment in the Department of Peace-keeping Operations of a situation centre functioning twenty-four hours a day, seven days a week, which will be equipped with appropriately standardized communication and information management systems so as to enhance the management of all peace-keeping operations, and requests the Secretary-General to keep under review the efficiency and efficacy of the situation centre;

35.   *Also welcomes* the initiative of the Secretariat in establishing a logistics doctrine and procedures project charged with developing a set of guidelines of United Nations logistics doctrine and procedures in order to standardize logistics practices and procedures and thereby enhance the efficiency and effectiveness of logistics support to peace-keeping operations;

36.   *Requests* the Secretary-General to consider, in the ongoing restructuring of the Secretariat, the inclusion of a logistics planning capability in the Department of Peace-keeping Operations which would consider all aspects of support required for peace-keeping operations;

37.   *Stresses* that the conclusion of a status-of-forces agreement between the United Nations and a host State is of the utmost importance when deploying peace-keeping operations and calls upon host States to give

their fullest cooperation in that regard, and recommends that after the establishment of a peace-keeping operation by the Security Council the concerned Member States should cooperate fully with the operation in the implementation of its mandate;

38. *Also requests* the Secretary-General to include in the status-of-forces agreement between the United Nations and host States requirements for host States to treat United Nations peace-keeping forces at all times with full respect for the principles and relevant Articles of the Charter, for United Nations peace-keeping forces to respect local laws and regulations and for both parties to such an agreement to act at all times in accordance with the provisions of the status-of-forces agreement and the principles and relevant Articles of the Charter;

39. *Notes* the importance of concluding arrangements between the United Nations and troop contributors before deployment occurs and urges implementation of the agreements along the lines of the model agreement outlined in the report of the Secretary-General of 23 May 1991;

40. *Further requests* the Secretary-General to include, in the agreements to be concluded with States providing contingents, a clause by which those States would ensure that the members of their contingents serving in United Nations peace-keeping operations were fully acquainted with the principles and rules of relevant international law, in particular international humanitarian law and the purposes and principles of the Charter;

41. *Stresses* the importance of the institution of appropriate rules of engagement, on a case-by-case basis, for all United Nations peace-keeping operations;

42. *Also notes* the recent increase in the number of peace-keeping operations, and requests the Secretary-General to prepare a detailed report on operations that have significant difficulties in implementing their mandates by highlighting the root causes of such difficulties and suggesting possible measures to address them;

43. *Requests* the Secretary-General, once again, to report periodically to Member States on the performance of all peace-keeping operations;

44. *Welcomes* the increasingly frequent informal consultations between the Secretariat and contributing States, strongly recommends the continuation of such consultations on peace-keeping operations from their initial stages to their conclusion and strongly encourages the presence of the President of the Security Council and other members of the Council, as appropriate, at such consultations;

45. *Recognizes* that the training of peace-keeping personnel is primarily the responsibility of Member States;

46. *Also welcomes* the establishment of a focal point for peace-keeping training in the Department of Peacekeeping Operations, and recommends that the focal point act as the coordinating centre for the relationship between the United Nations and national and regional training facilities;

47. *Requests* the Secretary-General to review and improve arrangements for training civilian, police and military peace-keeping personnel, using the appropriate capabilities of Member States, regional organizations and arrangements, in accordance with their constitutional mandates and Chapter VIII of the Charter, and of non-governmental organizations and the Secretariat;

48. *Acknowledges* the increasing challenge of forging large and cohesive peace-keeping missions from many and diverse contingents, stresses the need for the effective training of civilian, police and military personnel before deployment, and in that regard urges the Secretary-General to develop, in consultation with Member States, official United Nations guidelines combined with performance goals for individuals and units, so that peace-keepers can be trained within a national framework in accordance with agreed-upon common standards, skills, practices and procedures;

49. *Also requests* the Secretary-General to develop and publish peace-keeping training guidelines, manuals and other relevant training material, including material for correspondence instruction, in order to assist Member States in preparing their civilian, police and military personnel for peace-keeping operations in a standardized and cost-effective manner;

50. *Further requests* the Secretary-General, in close consultation with Member States, to initiate, within resources which may be allocated for training purposes, a trial programme designed to train national peacekeeping trainers as a supplement to national training programmes, as well as to develop a proposal to strengthen the leadership cadre available for peacekeeping by training potential Force Commanders and senior military and civilian personnel for peace-keeping leadership and management duties;

51. *Recommends* that training for peace-keeping operations be included, as appropriate, in the training of those military, civilian and police personnel being sent on peace-keeping operations, and encourages Member States that have already developed such training to share information and experience with other Member States;

52. *Strongly recommends* that peace-keeping operations personnel be made generally aware of relevant local laws and customs of the host State and of the importance of respecting them;

53. *Encourages* troop contributors to consider arrangements between themselves for the loan and/or exchange of peace-keeping operations experts to enhance operational effectiveness through sharing of information and experience gained in peace-keeping operations;

54. *Once again requests* the Secretary-General to consider establishing a training programme for key staff personnel of peace-keeping operations with a view to creating a pool of trained personnel with knowledge of the United Nations system and its working procedures;

55. *Recognizes* that public information on peacekeeping operations, particularly an understanding of their mandates, is important, and calls for significant enhancement of the press and public information function for peace-keeping missions and in particular for rapid deployment at the start of a peace-keeping operation of a robust and professional media outreach programme in the area of operation commensurate with the scope and needs of the missions;

56. *Requests* the Secretary-General, in consultation with Member States, to establish guidelines for the public information function of peace-keeping operations;

57. *Requests* the Secretariat immediately to make all necessary arrangements for the reissue of *The Blue Helmets* in 1995;

58. *Also requests* the Secretariat to take the appropriate steps to record, in a dignified and yet simple man-

ner in a public area of the United Nations Headquarters, the names of those who have given their lives in the service of United Nations peace-keeping operations;

59. *Welcomes* the intention of the Secretariat to establish a memorial dedicated to those peace-keepers who have given their lives in the service of peace;

Issues arising from "An Agenda for Peace"

60. *Recalls* its resolutions 47/120 A of 18 December 1992 and 47/120 B of 20 September 1993, and takes note of the report of the Secretary-General on the implementation of the recommendations contained in "An Agenda for Peace", welcomes the efforts of the Secretary-General to take appropriate steps through preventive diplomacy and, recognizing the need for those steps to be based on timely and accurate knowledge of relevant facts, encourages him to strengthen the capability of the Secretariat to secure and analyse all relevant information from as wide a variety of sources as possible in accordance with the relevant provisions of the Charter, urges Member States to assist the Secretary-General in this regard, and requests the Secretary-General to keep the Member States regularly informed of such capabilities and mechanisms;

61. *Reaffirms* its resolution 47/120 B, in particular section II, entitled "Preventive deployment and demilitarized zones", and in this context recalls the importance of considering, on a case-by-case basis, the use of preventive deployment and/or the establishment of demilitarized zones as a means to prevent existing or potential disputes from escalating into conflicts and to promote efforts to achieve the peaceful settlement of such disputes, the continuance of which is likely to endanger the maintenance of international peace and security;

62. *Encourages*, in accordance with Chapter VIII of the Charter, the involvement of Member States through regional organizations and arrangements, as appropriate, in accordance with their respective areas of competence and the purposes and principles of the United Nations;

63. *Welcomes* efforts by the Secretary-General to develop, in consultation with Member States, a set of guidelines governing cooperation between the United Nations and regional organizations;

64. *Notes* the existing cooperation between the United Nations and regional organizations, in particular in the area of peace-keeping;

65. *Requests* the Secretary-General, in accordance with Chapter VIII of the Charter, to consider ways to provide advice and assistance, in a variety of forms such as advisory services, seminars and conferences, to regional organizations and arrangements in their respective areas of competence, so as to enhance their capacity to cooperate with the United Nations in the field of peace-keeping operations;

66. *Resolves* to continue consideration of these items;

Status and safety of United Nations
peace-keeping personnel

67. *Urges* all Member States in whose territory United Nations peace-keeping operations are conducted to provide, in accordance with relevant Articles of the Charter and other instruments, comprehensive support to all United Nations peace-keeping operations personnel in fulfilling their functions, as well as to take all necessary measures to ensure respect for and guarantee the safety and security of those personnel;

68. *Considers* that any State in whose territory a United Nations peace-keeping operation is conducted should act promptly to deter and prosecute all those responsible for attacks and other acts of violence against all personnel of United Nations peace-keeping operations;

69. *Notes* the particular difficulties and dangers that can arise when United Nations peace-keeping operations are conducted in situations where no authority exercises jurisdiction or discharges responsibilities with regard to ensuring the safety and security of United Nations personnel, and in such an eventuality agrees that measures appropriate to the particular circumstances and in accordance with the purposes and principles of the United Nations should be considered by the Security Council and other appropriate bodies of the United Nations;

70. *Emphasizes* the importance of all relevant information on conditions in the field of operations for the safety of United Nations peace-keepers, and invites the Secretariat to adopt measures to secure and analyse such information from as wide a variety of sources as possible for immediate transmission to field missions;

71. *Considers* that it is the responsibility of host countries to disseminate to their populations necessary information on the role of peace-keeping operations and the inviolability of the safety of peace-keepers, including the information the United Nations may make available for that purpose;

72. *Also considers* that host countries are required to provide all available information in a timely manner to the United Nations and the respective peace-keeping missions in the field on any potential dangers that might jeopardize the safety of the peace-keepers, and that that requirement should be clearly specified in the status-of-forces agreements;

73. *Urges* the Secretary-General to review the current arrangements of compensation for death, injury, disability or illness attributable to peace-keeping service with a view to developing equitable and appropriate arrangements, and to ensure expeditious reimbursement;

74. *Recognizes* that conditions in the field require practical steps aimed at enhancing the necessary operational, political and legal environment to deal effectively with the problem of the growing vulnerability of United Nations operations personnel deployed in the field;

75. *Requests* the Secretary-General to take concrete steps to improve the physical security of all United Nations peace-keeping personnel deployed in the field, including all aspects related to material, organizational, operational and other aspects of safety;

76. *Welcomes* the report of the Secretary-General on current measures and new proposals to ensure and enhance the security of United Nations operations and will consider what further steps might be taken to enhance their status and safety, taking into account the need for concerted action by all relevant bodies of the United Nations, and in that context welcomes Security Council resolution 868(1993) of 29 September 1993, in which connection the General Assembly:

(a) Will give consideration to promoting the elaboration of a declaration that would, *inter alia*, reaffirm the principles of international law and the obligations of

Member States concerning the status and safety of United Nations personnel;

(b) Calls upon the Security Council to include in mandates for the deployment of United Nations personnel specific provisions recalling the obligations of Member States and the expectations of the United Nations concerning the status and safety of United Nations personnel;

(c) Notes that a legally binding international instrument to reinforce the existing arrangements regarding the status and safety of United Nations personnel is being considered by the Sixth Committee;

* * *

77. *Recommends* that, should any of the proposals contained in the present resolution result in budgetary implications for the biennium 1994-1995, such additional costs should be accommodated within the appropriation level approved by the General Assembly for this biennium;

78. *Decides* that the Special Committee on Peace-keeping Operations, in accordance with its mandate, should continue its efforts for a comprehensive review of the whole question of peace-keeping operations in all their aspects;

79. *Requests* the Secretary-General to ensure that full conference services, including translation of official documents and simultaneous translation into all official languages, are provided to the Special Committee and its working group whenever they meet, normally for up to one month in April and May;

80. *Requests* the Special Committee to submit a report on its work to the General Assembly at its forty-ninth session;

81. *Invites* Member States to submit further observations and suggestions on peace-keeping operations to the Secretary-General by 1 March 1994, outlining practical proposals on specific items in order to allow for more detailed consideration by the Special Committee;

82. *Also requests* the Secretary-General to prepare, within existing resources, a compilation of the above-mentioned observations and suggestions and to submit it to the Special Committee by 30 March 1994;

83. *Decides* to include in the provisional agenda of its forty-ninth session the item entitled "Comprehensive review of the whole question of peace-keeping operations in all their aspects".

General Assembly resolution 48/42

10 December 1993   Meeting 75   Adopted without vote

Approved by Fourth Committee (A/48/648) without vote, 30 November (meeting 26); 7-nation draft (A/C.4/48/L.18), orally revised; agenda item 87.
Sponsors: Argentina, Canada, Egypt, Fiji, Japan, Nigeria, Poland.
Meeting numbers. GA 48th session: 4th Committee 21-26; plenary 81.

On the same date, the Assembly, also on the Fourth Committee's recommendation, adopted **resolution 48/43** without vote.

Strengthening United Nations command and control capabilities

The General Assembly,

Taking note of the report of the Special Committee on Peace-keeping Operations,

Taking into account the rapid growth in the number, size, complexity and cost of United Nations peace-keeping operations,

Noting the proposals put forward by the Secretary-General in the proposed programme budget for the biennium 1994-1995 for a strengthening of the peace-keeping capabilities in the Secretariat, as well as his initiative to establish a stand-by forces planning team,

Aware of the need to strengthen the capability of the United Nations to plan, conduct and coordinate its peace-keeping operations and of the need for extending and deepening ongoing consultations between the Secretary-General and troop-contributing States concerning specific peace-keeping operations and to involve more closely the members of the Security Council in such consultations,

1. *Stresses* the need to strengthen the capabilities of the Secretariat for the operational management, command and control of peace-keeping operations based on unity of instruction and clearly established lines of command in such operations, including a fully staffed and equipped situation centre covering all peace-keeping operations;

2. *Calls upon* the Secretary-General, in cooperation with the members of the Security Council, troop-contributing States and other interested Member States:

(a) To review thoroughly and take urgent steps to strengthen present arrangements for political direction, military command and control and to improve coordination with humanitarian and civilian aspects of peace-keeping operations, both at United Nations Headquarters and in the field;

(b) To strengthen existing arrangements for consultation and exchange of information at an early stage between the Secretary-General and troop-contributing countries and to hold such consultations in the presence of members of the Security Council, as appropriate, for the planning, management and coordination of peace-keeping operations;

(c) To report to Member States on the steps taken under subparagraphs *(a)* and *(b)* above, before the next session of the Special Committee on Peace-keeping Operations.

General Assembly resolution 48/43

10 December 1993   Meeting 75   Adopted without vote

Approved by Fourth Committee (A/48/648) without vote, 30 November (meeting 26); 21-nation draft (A/C.4/48/L.19); agenda item 87.
Sponsors: Argentina, Australia, Austria, Canada, Denmark, Fiji, Finland, France, Germany, Iceland, Ireland, Netherlands, New Zealand, Norway, Poland, Russian Federation, Sweden, Ukraine, United Kingdom, United States, Uruguay.
Meeting numbers. GA 48th session: 4th Committee 21-26; plenary 81.

Administrative and budgetary aspects of the financing of United Nations peace-keeping operations were dealt with in **resolution 48/227**. By **resolution 48/226**, the Assembly endorsed observations and recommendations of the Advisory Committee on Administrative and Budgetary Questions for funding by a support account for peace-keeping operations of posts in DPKO, the Field Operations Division, the Internal Audit Division and the Department of Administration and Management.

Security of United Nations operations

As the Organization took on more complex and riskier mandates, the Secretary-General said,[3] he attached greatest importance to the safety and security of peace-keeping personnel. Since the beginning of United Nations peace-keeping operations, 949 peace-keepers had lost their lives, more than 550 of them in ongoing operations. He stressed that their sacrifice would not be forgotten by the international community.

Because relief personnel frequently operated in areas of conflict or danger even prior to the deployment of United Nations forces, their security was of particular concern. The murder of staff members working in humanitarian programmes in Afghanistan and the Sudan in 1993 served as a tragic reminder of the fragile status of the United Nations humanitarian presence in turbulent areas. While every effort was being made to ensure the safety of United Nations personnel, the Secretary-General was also concerned about the security of personnel of non-governmental organizations (NGOs) assisting in United Nations relief programmes. It was imperative that Governments and other parties to conflict respected their obligations under international law to ensure secure access of relief personnel and supplies to the victims of humanitarian emergencies.

Report of the Secretary-General. As requested by the Security Council in March,[11] the Secretary-General submitted in August a report[12] on the security of United Nations operations, containing information on existing arrangements and recommendations for enhancing the safety of United Nations forces and personnel. While United Nations forces had means of protection and were authorized to use their weapons in self-defence, they often included sizeable civilian components or operated side by side with unarmed civilian personnel and military observers. Thus, many categories of United Nations personnel were at risk.

The Secretary-General stressed that the primary responsibility for the safety of United Nations personnel and their dependants rested with the host Government of the respective United Nations operation, flowing from every Government's inherent function of maintaining order and protecting persons and property within its jurisdiction. The risk to United Nations personnel was particularly acute in times of civil disorder and domestic strife when the capacity of host Governments to provide protection might be greatly diminished. To meet such crises better, a set of rules and procedures was instituted in 1980[13] on an inter-agency basis and revised in 1991. Under those arrangements, the responsibility for coordinating all security matters rested with the Secretary-General, who had appointed a United Nations Security Coordinator—currently the Under-Secretary-General for Administration and Management—to act on his behalf. Each United Nations organi-

zation had appointed an official responsible for liaison with the Security Coordinator. In the field, a senior United Nations official was appointed in each country to serve as designated official for security, with overall and special responsibility for the security and protection of the organization's personnel there and directly accountable to the Secretary-General.

The primary tool for security preparedness at any duty station was a country-specific security plan. Written in conformity with established procedures and subject to approval of the Security Coordinator, it defined the responsibilities of each person at the respective duty station, actions to be taken and the sequence to be followed. Under the current arrangements, the Organization's response to security threats was divided into five phases: phase one was precautionary, with travel to the area requiring prior clearance by the designated official; in phase two, all personnel and their dependants were restricted to their homes unless otherwise instructed and all movement was severely restricted, requiring specific authorization by the designated official; in phase three, personnel and their dependants could be concentrated at safe sites or relocated to other parts of the country, with the relocation of dependants and non-essential personnel outside the country; phase four meant the suspension of programmes and evacuation of personnel not directly concerned with emergency or humanitarian relief operations or security matters; during phase five, all personnel were evacuated except those required for Security Council–mandated activities related to the maintenance of international peace and security. Those security arrangements covered all except locally recruited personnel, who were normally not evacuated unless their security was endangered as a direct consequence of their United Nations employment.

It was apparent, the Secretary-General stated, that the above security system, oriented towards civilian staff engaged in normal peacetime activity, could not accommodate peace-keeping operations in situations where other activities had to be suspended. Peace-keeping personnel remained therefore under the exclusive jurisdiction of their chief of mission. There was, however, a considerable overlap, and the chief of a peace-keeping mission might be appointed designated security official. When that was not the case, the peace-keeping operation maintained close coordination and cooperation with the designated official and would normally take all necessary action to the extent compatible with the operation's continued functioning. All peace-keeping operations had contingency plans for their suspension and evacuation, if unavoidable. Existing arrangements for the protection of peace-keeping personnel were reflected in the model status-of-force agreement, annexed to a 1990 report of the Secretary-General,[14] which embodied relevant principles of international law.

Peace-keeping forces were armed and authorized to use their weapons in self-defence. Though occasionally compelled to exercise that right and inflicting casualties doing so, their effective functioning was based on cooperation and consent. United Nations peace-keeping forces had always shown the greatest possible restraint in order to avoid involvement in a cycle of violence with any one party. Instead, they sought to contain whatever disputes arose and to resolve them politically so as to preserve their role as a third party above the conflict.

According to the Secretary-General, developments in the preceding year highlighted gaps in the existing system and the need for its strengthening, mainly concerning conditions of operation and the acceptable risk level. In fulfilling responsibilities entrusted to them by Member States, United Nations personnel were increasingly required to perform in extremely hazardous conditions where decisions regarding their safety assumed an immediacy not encountered in the past, particularly in areas where government authority was inadequately exercised or lacking altogether. Whereas in the past personnel were assured protection by virtue of their association with the United Nations, now they were often exposed to risk precisely because of it. Moreover, actions by the United Nations in one part of the globe could generate threats to its personnel in another. As a result, casualties had mounted: in 1992, on average one staff member was killed every month; that rate had doubled in 1993. Military personnel suffered 51 fatal casualties in all of 1992 and 97 in the first half of 1993.

The establishment of multidimensional operations involving military operations, humanitarian assistance, electoral assistance, human rights monitoring and development projects brought to light further gaps in the existing security system. The urgency of humanitarian needs often necessitated the deployment of personnel for the implementation of relief programmes, even before United Nations forces were deployed and before agreement on a precise legal framework governing the operation could be obtained. Such situations often invited great insecurity for those providing assistance; the hijacking of goods and equipment with concomitant serious implications for personnel safety was frequent, and so far no sufficient protection measures had been defined.

The tens of thousands of soldiers serving under United Nations command and an increasing number of civilian personnel of NGOs, on which the Organization had come to rely on to an un-

precedented extent, ran the same or similar risks and also required protection.

Finally, the new feature of the Security Council using its enforcement powers under Chapter VII of the Charter led to the establishment of operations that were not based on consent and cooperation and might face outright opposition. In such cases, it would be prudent to provide reserves to reinforce an operation quickly if required.

With regard to the overall security of United Nations personnel, the Secretary-General said security matters would become an integral part of the planning of new operations. Priority would be given to the improvement and standardization of communications and to the training of staff in security matters. Expert staff would be recruited to assist the Security Coordinator at Headquarters and the designated officials in the field. Arrangements would be made, through the situation room being established by DPKO, to ensure that security staff could be reached at all times. An area of concern was the need for information on and analysis of possible risks, and for technical expertise with regard to air safety, criminal investigation, forensics, ballistics and pathology. The Secretary-General noted that the measures outlined entailed additional expenditures, but were essential for the discharge of the Organization's responsibility for the safety of its personnel; he trusted that Member States would provide the necessary means.

In the long term, he proposed to consider elaborating a new international instrument to codify and develop further international law relating to the security and safety of United Nations forces and personnel. The adoption of such an instrument, as suggested by New Zealand in April,[15] would make possible the consolidation in a single document of the set of principles and obligations contained in current multilateral and bilateral treaties and provide an opportunity to codify and develop customary international law as reflected in recent United Nations and State practice.

For more immediate action, a short-term strategy should be implemented, under which the Security Council, when setting up a new operation, would consider including in the relevant resolution the necessary security conditions, including: application to the operation of the provisions of the 1946 Convention on the Privileges and Immunities of the United Nations;[16] confirmation that the host Government was obliged to take all necessary measures to ensure the safety of the United Nations operation and personnel; clarification to the effect that security arrangements undertaken by the host Government extended to contractors and NGOs involved in an operation; a timetable for concluding an agreement on the status of the operation in the host country or countries; a statement reaffirming that attacks and use of force against United Nations personnel were considered interference with the exercise of the Council's responsibilities and might require appropriate measures; and a statement indicating that failure by the host State to meet its obligations with regard to the safety of an operation and its personnel might result in the Council considering measures to ensure such security.

SECURITY COUNCIL ACTION

The Security Council convened on 29 September to consider, on the basis of the Secretary-General's report, the security of United Nations operations. The President drew the Council's attention to a letter of 13 September from New Zealand,[17] proposing certain Security Council action on resolutions establishing peace-keeping operations. After statements, the Council unanimously adopted **resolution 868(1993)**.

The Security Council,

Recalling the statement made by the President of the Council, on behalf of the Council, on 31 March 1993 in connection with the Council's consideration of the item entitled "An agenda for peace: preventive diplomacy, peacemaking and peace-keeping",

Having considered the report of the Secretary-General of 27 August 1993 on the security of United Nations operations,

Recalling the provisions of the Charter concerning privileges and immunities, and the Convention on the Privileges and Immunities of the United Nations, as applicable to United Nations operations and persons engaged in such operations,

Expressing grave concern at the increasing number of attacks and use of force against persons engaged in United Nations operations and resolutely condemning all such actions,

Welcoming the initiatives being taken in the General Assembly to consider the elaboration of new instruments relating to the security and safety of United Nations forces and personnel, and noting the Secretary-General's proposals in this regard,

1. *Welcomes* the report of the Secretary-General of 27 August 1993 on the security of United Nations operations;

2. *Encourages* the Secretary-General to take forward those measures proposed in his report falling within his responsibilities with a view, in particular, to ensuring that security matters are an integral part of the planning for an operation and that any such precautions extend to all persons engaged in the operation;

3. *Urges* States and parties to a conflict to cooperate closely with the United Nations to ensure the security and safety of United Nations forces and personnel;

4. *Confirms* that attacks and use of force against persons engaged in a United Nations operation authorized by the Security Council will be considered interference with the exercise of the responsibilities of the Council and may require the Council to consider measures it deems appropriate;

5. *Confirms also* that if, in the Council's view, the host country is unable or unwilling to meet its obligations with regard to the safety and security of a United Nations operation and personnel engaged in the operation, the Council will consider what steps should be taken appropriate to the situation;

6. *Determines* that, when considering the establishment of future United Nations operations authorized by the Council, the Security Council will require *inter alia:*

(a) That the host country take all appropriate steps to ensure the security and safety of the operation and personnel engaged in the operation;

(b) That the security and safety arrangements undertaken by the host country extend to all persons engaged in the operation;

(c) That an agreement on the status of the operation, and all personnel engaged in the operation in the host country be negotiated expeditiously and should come into force as near as possible to the outset of the operation;

7. *Requests* the Secretary-General when recommending the establishment or renewal of a United Nations operation by the Security Council to take into account the provisions of the present resolution;

8. *Decides* to remain seized of the matter.

Security Council resolution 868(1993)

29 September 1993   Meeting 3283   Adopted unanimously

Draft prepared in consultations among Council members (S/26499).

GENERAL ASSEMBLY ACTION

In December, in **resolution 48/37**, the General Assembly decided to establish an Ad Hoc Committee open to all Member States to elaborate an international convention dealing with the safety and security of United Nations and associated personnel, with particular reference to responsibility for attacks on such personnel.

REFERENCES

[1]S/25859. [2]S/26517. [3]A/48/1. [4]A/48/503 & Add.1. [5]A/48/421/Add.1. [6]A/48/173. [7]A/AC.121/40 & Add.1,2. [8]YUN 1992, p. 45, GA res. 47/71, 14 Dec. 1992. [9]Ibid., p. 35. [10]A/48/403-S/26450/Add.1 & Corr.1 & Add.2. [11]S/25493. [12]A/48/349-S/26358. [13]YUN 1980, p. 180. [14]A/45/594. [15]S/25667. [16]YUN 1946-47, p. 100, GA res. 22 A (I), annex, 13 Feb. 1946. [17]S/26444.

Aerial incidents and the Libyan Arab Jamahiriya

In November 1993, the Security Council intensified sanctions under the air and arms embargo imposed in 1992 on the Libyan Arab Jamahiriya in key oil- and technology-related fields and by freezing Libyan financial funds abroad, in order to ensure compliance by the Jamahiriya with Council resolutions 731(1992)[1] and 748(1992).[2] Those resolutions had requested the surrender for trial in the United Kingdom or the United States of two Libyan nationals, Abdelbaset Ali Mohamed Al Megrahi and Al Amin Khalifa Fhima, suspects in the 1988 bombing of Pan Am flight 103 over Lockerbie in southern Scotland, and cooperation with French judicial authorities investigating the crash after the bombing in 1989 of Union de transports aériens (UTA) flight 772 over the Ténéré desert in the Niger. The Council expressed readiness to suspend those measures immediately if the Libyan Government ensured the appearance before the appropriate courts of those charged with bombing the Pan Am airliner and satisfied the French judicial authorities with respect to the bombing case of UTA 772.

Communications (April-October). Algeria, the Libyan Arab Jamahiriya, Mauritania, Morocco and Tunisia (the Arab Maghreb Union), in an 8 April 1993 letter to the President of the Security Council,[3] urged the Council to reconsider its resolutions so that the embargo and restrictions imposed on the Libyan Arab Jamahiriya could be lifted, with a view to ending the suffering and eliminating the risks inherent in the continued application or strengthening of sanctions. The Libyan Arab Jamahiriya, in July[4] and October,[5] reported to the Secretary-General on the negative impact and damage resulting from the implementation of resolution 748(1992) in the humanitarian, economic and aviation sectors.

By a tripartite declaration of 13 August,[6] France, the United Kingdom and the United States stated that, after 16 months since the imposition of sanctions for failure to comply with the demands set forth in resolution 731(1992), the Council found the Libyan Arab Jamahiriya for the fourth time in defiance of the will of the international community. The three countries observed with diminishing patience that the envoys of the Secretary-General to Tripoli repeatedly returned empty-handed and without indications of Libyan compliance, although with many assurances of its cooperation. After having waited the four months requested by the Secretary-General of the League of Arab States, who wished to serve as an intermediary between the international community and the Libyans, the three States asked the Secretary-General to take the necessary steps to achieve full compliance by the Libyan Government within 40 to 45 days. If it failed to do so by 1 October, including the transfer to United Kingdom or United States jurisdiction of the Lockerbie suspects and compliance with French judicial requests, the three Governments would table a resolution strengthening the sanctions in key oil-related, financial and technological areas. Full implementation by the Libyan Arab Jamahiriya of resolutions 731(1992) and 748(1992) would result in lifting the sanctions.

Refuting the tripartite declaration, the Libyan Arab Jamahiriya affirmed on 14 August[7] that it had fully complied with resolution 731(1992) in all its aspects, having informed the Secretary-General of all the measures undertaken to implement the resolution and to cooperate with him and his envoys. It said it had acceded to the request for cooperation with the United Kingdom with regard to organizations accused of terrorism, for which the United Kingdom had expressed official satisfaction. It had also expressed complete readiness to cooperate with French justice and acknowledged the need for the two suspects to be brought to trial, stating that it was prepared to discuss the venue for a just and fair trial.

On 11 September,[8] the Libyan Arab Jamahiriya contended again that it had implemented all provisions of resolution 731(1992), except for a single point relating to the venue of trial, which it intended to resolve through negotiations. In an enclosed memorandum outlining its legal position on the matter, it stressed that it had requested the Secretary-General to dispatch a technical mission to verify its compliance. Although interpreting the lack of response to that offer as meaning that the Council was persuaded that it had carried out all measures called for, the Libyan Arab Jamahiriya renewed its invitation promptly to dispatch a mission. An extradition of its nationals, however, would violate Article 2 of the Charter, which established the principle of non-intervention in the domestic jurisdiction of Member States; also, there was no agreement between the parties concerned governing rules of extradition. Therefore, it remained for the two suspects to decide whether they would present themselves to the jurisdiction of either the United Kingdom or the United States. Meanwhile, the intense media campaigns, the hostility against the two suspects and official declarations to the effect that they were guilty dissipated any hope of a just and fair trial.

In further letters of 29 September and 1 October,[9] the Libyan Arab Jamahiriya said it was no longer opposed to the suspects going to trial and encouraged them to do so. It also assured the Secretary-General of its full willingness to cooperate with the French authorities in their investigation.

Addressing the situation on 7 October before the General Assembly, the Jamahiriya reiterated its readiness to respond to resolution 731(1992), including cooperating with the Secretary-General to ensure success of the mission entrusted to him by that resolution. It again condemned international terrorism and declared that it had severed relations with all organizations and entitites suspected of being involved in terrorist acts. It would not allow its territory, institutions or citizens to be used for terrorist acts and would severely punish those guilty of terrorist activities.

In a statement of 13 October,[10] the Arab Lawyers' Union said the Lockerbie case had been transformed from a legal matter into a political dispute with the threat of the use of force and pressure. It urged the United Nations, international parties and local organizations to remove all obstacles to keeping the matter within a legal framework, so that the two suspects could be given a fair trial after due legal process and thorough investigations.

The Libyan Arab Jamahiriya informed the Secretary-General[11] of a meeting on 8 and 9 October between the two suspects and their legal advisers, during which the suspects confirmed their innocence and their willingness to stand a fair trial after due process of law.

SECURITY COUNCIL ACTION

After consultations held on 8 April, 13 August and 10 December 1993 in connection with the sanctions imposed on the Libyan Arab Jamahiriya under resolution 748(1992),[2] the President of the Security Council made the following identical statement on behalf of the Council members:[12]

"The members of the Security Council held informal consultations on 8 April [13 August] [10 December] 1993 pursuant to paragraph 13 of resolution 748(1992), by which the Council decided to review every 120 days or sooner, should the situation so require, the measures imposed by paragraphs 3 to 7 against the Libyan Arab Jamahiriya.

"After hearing all the opinions expressed in the course of consultations, the President of the Council concluded that there was no agreement that the necessary conditions existed for modification of the measures of sanctions established in paragraphs 3 to 7 of resolution 748(1992)."

The Council convened on 11 November to consider charges of December 1991 by France, the United Kingdom and the United States[13] that nationals and possibly officials of the Libyan Arab Jamahiriya were involved in the two aerial incidents, as well as demands for judicial steps.

At their request, Egypt, the Libyan Arab Jamahiriya and the Sudan were invited to participate in the discussion without the right to vote, in accordance with rule 37[a] of the Council's provisional rules of procedure.

Opening the discussion, the Jamahiriya stated that the matter considered by the Council was not one threatening international peace and security. It had fully responded to resolution 731(1992),[1] and the only remaining problem arose from the demand by the United Kingdom and the United States that the two suspects be extradited and from the legal wrangle over which country had the competence to try them. That question was definitively settled by the provisions of the 1971 Montreal Convention for the Suppression of Unlawful Acts against the Safety of Civil Aviation,[14] to which all three States were parties and which stipulated jurisdiction re-

garding the trial to the Libyan Arab Jamahiriya. No bilateral treaty or convention regulating extradition existed between the Jamahiriya and the United Kingdom or the United States.

Accordingly, the Jamahiriya had appointed a judge to investigate the matter and he started his preliminary investigation by placing the two suspects under preventive custody. The United Kingdom and the United States were notified and requested to cooperate with the Libyan judicial authorities either by allowing access to their records of investigation or by arranging a date for carrying out the necessary investigation. However, they refused to cooperate and submit the case to arbitration, as foreseen by the Montreal Convention. As a result, the Jamahiriya had taken the question of the Convention's applicability before the International Court of Justice, where it was still pending (see PART FOUR, Chapter I).

It had further proposed to request the Court to ascertain the validity of the accusation against the two Libyan nationals and suggested that they be surrendered to the office of the United Nations Development Programme at Tripoli for investigation. It also proposed that the Secretary-General form a legal committee composed of neutral judges to conduct a comprehensive investigation. The Jamahiriya declared that, if the Secretary-General concluded that the accusations were justified, it would not object to extraditing the two suspects under the Secretary-General's personal supervision to a third party, provided that they not be surrendered to any other party.

As for the French demands, the Jamahiriya did not regard them counter to Libyan law. Intensive contacts between the judicial authorities of both countries were held in order to reach a determination of responsibility for the explosion of UTA flight 772. After the French investigative judge had seen the minutes of the investigation by the Libyan judge, it was agreed that he would continue his investigation in the Jamahiriya.

Summing up its position, the Libyan Arab Jamahiriya said that the draft resolution before the Council repeated the same legal mistake of resolutions 731(1992) and 748(1992) in linking the Jamahiriya to international terrorism based on suspicions created by intelligence agencies, thereby making an a priori judgement not substantiated by any evidence.

Following further statements, the Council adopted **resolution 883(1993)**.

[a]Rule 37 of the Council's provisional rules of procedure states: "Any Member of the United Nations which is not a member of the Security Council may be invited, as the result of a decision of the Security Council, to participate, without vote, in the discussion of any question brought before the Security Council when the Security Council considers that the interests of that Member are specially affected, or when a Member brings a matter to the attention of the Security Council in accordance with Article 35(1) of the Charter."

The Security Council,

Reaffirming its resolutions 731(1992) of 21 January 1992 and 748(1992) of 31 March 1992,

Deeply concerned that after more than twenty months the Libyan Government has not fully complied with these resolutions,

Determined to eliminate international terrorism,

Convinced that those responsible for acts of international terrorism must be brought to justice,

Convinced also that the suppression of acts of international terrorism, including those in which States are directly or indirectly involved, is essential for the maintenance of international peace and security,

Determining, in this context, that the continued failure by the Libyan Government to demonstrate by concrete actions its renunciation of terrorism, and in particular its continued failure to respond fully and effectively to the requests and decisions in resolutions 731(1992) and 748(1992), constitute a threat to international peace and security,

Taking note of the letters to the Secretary-General dated 29 September and 1 October 1993 from the Secretary of the General People's Committee for Foreign Liaison and International Cooperation of Libya and his speech in the general debate at the forty-eighth session of the General Assembly in which Libya stated its intention to encourage those charged with the bombing of Pan Am 103 to appear for trial in Scotland and its willingness to cooperate with the competent French authorities in the case of the bombing of UTA 772,

Expressing its gratitude to the Secretary-General for the efforts he has made pursuant to paragraph 4 of resolution 731(1992),

Recalling the right of States, under Article 50 of the Charter, to consult the Security Council where they find themselves confronted with special economic problems arising from the carrying out of preventive or enforcement measures,

Acting under Chapter VII of the Charter,

1. *Demands* once again that the Libyan Government comply without any further delay with resolutions 731(1992) and 748(1992);

2. *Decides,* in order to secure compliance by the Libyan Government with the decisions of the Council, to take the following measures, which shall come into force at 0001 EST on 1 December 1993 unless the Secretary-General has reported to the Council in the terms set out in paragraph 16 below;

3. *Decides* that all States in which there are funds or other financial resources (including funds derived or generated from property) owned or controlled, directly or indirectly, by:

(a) the Government or public authorities of Libya, or

(b) any Libyan undertaking,

shall freeze such funds and financial resources and ensure that neither they nor any other funds and financial resources are made available, by their nationals or by any persons within their territory, directly or indirectly, to or for the benefit of the Government or public authorities of Libya or any Libyan undertaking, which for the purposes of this paragraph means any commercial, industrial or public utility undertaking which is owned or controlled, directly or indirectly, by

(i) the Government or public authorities of Libya,

(ii) any entity, wherever located or organized, owned or controlled by (i), or

(iii) any person identified by States as acting on behalf of (i) or (ii) for the purposes of this resolution;

4. *Further decides* that the measures imposed by paragraph 3 above do not apply to funds or other financial resources derived from the sale or supply of any petroleum or petroleum products, including natural gas and natural gas products, or agricultural products or commodities, originating in Libya and exported therefrom after the time specified in paragraph 2 above, provided that any such funds are paid into separate bank accounts exclusively for these funds;

5. *Decides* that all States shall prohibit any provision to Libya by their nationals or from their territory of the items listed in the annex to this resolution, as well as the provision of any types of equipment, supplies and grants of licensing arrangements for the manufacture or maintenance of such items;

6. *Further decides* that, in order to make fully effective the provisions of resolution 748(1992), all States shall:

(a) require the immediate and complete closure of all Libyan Arab Airlines offices within their territories;

(b) prohibit any commercial transactions with Libyan Arab Airlines by their nationals or from their territory, including the honouring or endorsement of any tickets or other documents issued by that airline;

(c) prohibit, by their nationals or from their territory, the entering into or renewal of arrangements for:

(i) the making available, for operation within Libya, of any aircraft or aircraft components, or

(ii) the provision of engineering or maintenance servicing of any aircraft or aircraft components within Libya;

(d) prohibit, by their nationals or from their territory, the supply of any materials destined for the construction, improvement or maintenance of Libyan civilian or military airfields and associated facilities and equipment, or of any engineering or other services or components destined for the maintenance of any Libyan civil or military airfields or associated facilities and equipment, except emergency equipment and equipment and services directly related to civilian air traffic control;

(e) prohibit, by their nationals or from their territory, any provision of advice, assistance or training to Libyan pilots, flight engineers, or aircraft and ground maintenance personnel associated with the operation of aircraft and airfields within Libya;

(f) prohibit, by their nationals or from their territory, any renewal of any direct insurance for Libyan aircraft;

7. *Confirms* that the decision taken in resolution 748(1992) that all States shall significantly reduce the level of the staff at Libyan diplomatic missions and consular posts includes all missions and posts established since that decision or after the coming into force of this resolution;

8. *Decides* that all States, and the Government of Libya, shall take the necessary measures to ensure that no claim shall lie at the instance of the Government or public authorities of Libya, or of any Libyan national, or of any Libyan undertaking as defined in paragraph 3 of this resolution, or of any person claiming through or for the benefit of any such person or undertaking, in connection with any contract or other transaction or commercial operation where its performance was af-

fected by reason of the measures imposed by or pursuant to this resolution or related resolutions;

9. *Instructs* the Committee established by resolution 748(1992) to draw up expeditiously guidelines for the implementation of paragraphs 3 to 7 of this resolution, and to amend and supplement, as appropriate, the guidelines for the implementation of resolution 748(1992), especially its paragraph 5 *(a)*;

10. *Entrusts* the Committee established by resolution 748(1992) with the task of examining possible requests for assistance under the provisions of Article 50 of the Charter of the United Nations and making recommendations to the President of the Security Council for appropriate action;

11. *Affirms* that nothing in this resolution affects Libya's duty scrupulously to adhere to all of its obligations concerning servicing and repayment of its foreign debt;

12. *Calls upon* all States, including States not Members of the United Nations, and all international organizations to act strictly in accordance with the provisions of the present resolution, notwithstanding the existence of any rights or obligations conferred or imposed by any international agreement or any contract entered into or any licence or permit granted prior to the effective time of this resolution;

13. *Requests* all States to report to the Secretary-General by 15 January 1994 on the measures they have instituted for meeting the obligations set out in paragraphs 3 to 7 above;

14. *Invites* the Secretary-General to continue his role as set out in paragraph 4 of resolution 731(1992);

15. *Calls again upon* all Member States individually and collectively to encourage the Libyan Government to respond fully and effectively to the requests and decisions in resolutions 731(1992) and 748(1992);

16. *Expresses its readiness* to review the measures set forth above and in resolution 748(1992) with a view to suspending them immediately if the Secretary-General reports to the Council that the Libyan Government has ensured the appearance of those charged with the bombing of Pan Am 103 for trial before the appropriate United Kingdom or United States court and has satisfied the French judicial authorities with respect to the bombing of UTA 772, and with a view to lifting them immediately when Libya complies fully with the requests and decisions in resolutions 731(1992) and 748(1992); and requests the Secretary-General, within 90 days of such suspension, to report to the Council on Libya's compliance with the remaining provisions of its resolutions 731(1992) and 748(1992) and, in the case of non-compliance, expresses its resolve to terminate immediately the suspension of these measures;

17. *Decides* to remain seized of the matter.

ANNEX

The following are the items referred to in paragraph 5 of this resolution:

I. Pumps of medium or large capacity whose capacity is equal to or larger than 350 cubic metres per hour and drivers (gas turbines and electric motors) designed for use in the transportation of crude oil and natural gas

II. Equipment designed for use in crude oil export terminals:
— Loading buoys or single point moorings (spm)
— Flexible hoses for connection between underwater manifolds (plem) and single point mooring and floating loading hoses of large sizes (from 12" to 16")
— Anchor chains

III. Equipment not specially designed for use in crude oil export terminals but which because of their large capacity can be used for this purpose:
— Loading pumps of large capacity (4,000 m^3/h) and small head (10 bars)
— Boosting pumps within the same range of flow rates
— Inline pipe line inspection tools and cleaning devices (i.e. pigging tools) (16" and above)
— Metering equipment of large capacity (1,000 m^3/h and above)

IV. Refinery equipment:
— Boilers meeting American Society of Mechanical Engineers 1 standards
— Furnaces meeting American Society of Mechanical Engineers 8 standards
— Fractionation columns meeting American Society of Mechanical Engineers 8 standards
— Pumps meeting American Petroleum Institute 610 standards
— Catalytic reactors meeting American Society of Mechanical Engineers 8 standards
— Prepared catalysts, including the following:
  Catalysts containing platinum
  Catalysts containing molybdenum

V. Spare parts destined for the items in I to IV above.

Security Council resolution 883(1993)

11 November 1993   Meeting 3312   11-0-4

3-nation draft (S/26701).
Sponsors: France, United Kingdom, United States.

Vote in Council as follows:
In favour: Brazil, Cape Verde, France, Hungary, Japan, New Zealand, Russian Federation, Spain, United Kingdom, United States, Venezuela.
Against: None.
Abstaining: China, Djibouti, Morocco, Pakistan.

After the vote, the United Kingdom and the United States said that, nearly two years after adoption of resolution 731(1992), the Libyan Government had refused to heed it and had spared no effort to break the Council's resolve and compromise the will of the international community. Such failure left no other alternative to further sanctions. The United Kingdom went on to say that the resolution's provision to lift sanctions immediately should the Jamahiriya comply with the two 1992 resolutions proved that the sanctions were not intended to punish, but to bring the Jamahiriya to compliance.

France stated that it, the United Kingdom and the United States had decided to give the Libyan Arab Jamahiriya a final chance to prove its good will by complying with its obligations before 1 October 1993; unfortunately, the Jamahiriya's continued delaying tactics, obstruction and contradictory positions closed the door to any solution.

REFERENCES

[1]YUN 1992, p. 53, SC res. 731(1992), 21 Jan. 1992. [2]Ibid., p. 55, SC res. 748(1992), 31 Mar. 1992. [3]S/25559. [4]S/26139. [5]S/26654. [6]A/48/314-S/26304. [7]S/26313. [8]S/26500. [9]S/26523. [10]S/26604. [11]S/26629. [12]S/25554, S/26303, S/26861. [13]YUN 1992, p. 52. [14]YUN 1971, p. 739.

Chapter II

Disarmament

During 1993, in spite of widespread strife and militant nationalism, further progress was made towards disarmament, particularly with respect to weapons of mass destruction. Achievements in that area included: progress towards nuclear disarmament by the Russian Federation and the United States; the wider observance of a de facto moratorium on nuclear testing and the collective decision of the Conference on Disarmament to commence substantive negotiations, early in 1994, aimed at concluding a comprehensive nuclear-test ban; widening acceptance of the nuclear non-proliferation regime and ever-increasing support for the 1968 Treaty on the Non-Proliferation of Nuclear Weapons; and the opening of the process of signature and ratification of the Convention on the Prohibition of the Development, Production, Stockpiling and Use of Chemical Weapons and on Their Destruction.

Nuclear disarmament negotiations between the Russian Federation and the United States continued to gain momentum with the signing in Moscow on 3 January, by President George Bush of the United States and President Boris Yeltsin of the Russian Federation, of the Treaty on Further Reduction and Limitation of Strategic Offensive Arms.

The Conference on Disarmament, a 39-nation multilateral negotiating body, mandated its Ad Hoc Committee on a Nuclear Test Ban to negotiate a comprehensive test-ban treaty. By the end of the year, a draft mandate was ready for consideration by the Conference, which was to reconvene in January 1994. In December, the General Assembly urged the Conference to proceed intensively, as a priority task, with its negotiation of such a treaty (resolution 48/70).

The Disarmament Commission, a deliberative body composed of all United Nations Member States, dealt with nuclear disarmament in the framework of international peace and security, with the objective of eliminating nuclear weapons; regional disarmament within the context of global security; and the role of science and technology in international security, disarmament and related fields. The Commission succeeded in adopting by consensus guidelines and recommendations for regional approaches to disarmament within the context of global security, which were subsequently endorsed by the General Assembly (48/77 A).

As part of the process of restructuring the United Nations Secretariat, the Office for Disarmament Affairs became the Centre for Disarmament Affairs within the Department for Political Affairs.

UN role in disarmament

UN machinery

In 1993, United Nations disarmament efforts continued mainly through the General Assembly and its First (Disarmament and International Security) Committee, the Disarmament Commission (a subsidiary body of the Assembly) and the Conference on Disarmament (a multilateral negotiating forum at Geneva).

The existing disarmament machinery, which was agreed on at the Assembly's tenth special session in 1978,[1] its first special session devoted to disarmament, remained essentially the same. However, in response to the Secretary-General's 1992 suggestion[2] that the disarmament machinery, created during the cold war, should be reassessed in order to meet the new realities and priorities, the existing disarmament machinery was examined by Member States (see below).

Report of the Secretary-General. In accordance with a 1992 General Assembly request,[3] the Secretary-General submitted, in a February report with later addenda,[4] the views of 33 Member States on his 1992 report in which he suggested that the existing disarmament machinery be reassessed.[2]

Conference on Disarmament consideration. Also in accordance with the Assembly's 1992 decision,[3] the Conference on Disarmament issued its views, in February,[5] on the Secretary-General's 1992 report. The Conference stated that, together with unilateral measures and bilateral and regional agreements, disarmament needed more and more a multilateral approach and was a collective responsibility; thus the Conference had an increased role to play. It decided to intensify its consultations on its improved and effective functioning, including its decision to carry out consultations on the issues of its membership and agenda. It was the sense of the Conference that it could best serve the international community by preserving its role as the sole multilateral global negotiating body on disarmament.

In another February report,[6] the Conference discussed the status of the ongoing review of its agenda, composition and methods of work.

First Committee action. Pursuant to a 1992 Assembly decision,[3] the First Committee met from 8 to 12 March 1993 to reassess the multi-lateral arms-control and disarmament machinery. It examined the respective roles and interrelationship of the First Committee, the Disarmament Commission and the Conference on Disarmament, as well as the role of the Office for Disarmament Affairs. Member States expressed their concern that the Office should be strengthened to allow it to perform its mandated tasks.

GENERAL ASSEMBLY ACTION

On 8 April, the General Assembly, on the recommendation of the First Committee, adopted **resolution 47/54 G** without vote.

Review of the implementation of the recommendations and decisions adopted by the General Assembly at its tenth special session

The General Assembly,

Recalling its decision 47/422 of 9 December 1992, by which it decided to reconvene meetings of the First Committee from 8 to 12 March 1993 in order to reassess the multilateral arms control and disarmament machinery, in particular the respective roles of the First Committee, the Disarmament Commission and the Conference on Disarmament and their interrelationship, as well as the role of the Office for Disarmament Affairs of the Secretariat, including ways and means to enhance the functioning and efficiency of the said machinery, bearing in mind the competence of the Security Council in those matters,

Taking note of the report of the Secretary-General entitled "New dimensions of arms regulation and disarmament in the post-cold-war era",[a]

Taking note also of the views of Member States on that report,

Taking note further of the report of the Conference on Disarmament on its consideration of the report of the Secretary-General, as well as its report on the ongoing review of the agenda, composition and methods of work of the Conference,

Recalling the Final Document of the Tenth Special Session of the General Assembly, the first special session devoted to disarmament,

Having considered the views expressed by Member States at the resumed session of the First Committee on these questions,

Conscious that the new international situation has enhanced the prospects for disarmament and arms regulation, which is conducive to further multilateral efforts in disarmament,

Stressing the need for the multilateral arms control and disarmament machinery to respond to the new international situation,

Noting that a review is being undertaken regarding the allocation of agenda items to the Main Committees of the General Assembly,

Noting also the continuing review of the role and resources of the Office for Disarmament Affairs in order to strengthen its effective functioning,

Welcoming the Secretary-General's statement of 9 March 1993 that the Secretariat's capabilities are being strengthened to enable it to discharge its responsibilities effectively in the field of disarmament,

Desiring to enhance the effective functioning of the present multilateral disarmament machinery,

1. *Decides* that the First Committee of the General Assembly, in pursuing its efforts to respond to the new realities of international security, should continue to deal with the questions of disarmament and related international security issues;

2. *Requests* the Chairman of the First Committee to continue his consultations on the further rationalization of the work and the effective functioning of the Committee, taking into account all the views and proposals presented to the Committee, including those related to the thematic clustering of agenda items;

3. *Reaffirms* the role of the Disarmament Commission as a specialized deliberative body within the United Nations disarmament machinery, and notes the progress achieved in its ongoing process of reform;

4. *Recommends* that every effort be made to continue to enhance the working methods of the Disarmament Commission so as to enable it to give focused consideration to a limited number of priority issues in the field of disarmament, and to that end welcomes the decision of the Commission to move its agenda towards a three-item phased approach;

5. *Notes* the fact that the Conference on Disarmament, as the single global disarmament negotiating forum, is a body of limited composition taking its decisions on the basis of consensus and maintains its special status in relationship with the United Nations disarmament machinery;

6. *Welcomes* the fact that the Conference on Disarmament, in addition to the review of its composition, has also intensified the review of its agenda and methods of work, with a view to reaching prompt decisions on these questions;

7. *Encourages* the Conference on Disarmament to reach early agreement on the expansion of its membership;

8. *Stresses* the importance of further enhancing the dialogue and cooperation among the First Committee, the Disarmament Commission and the Conference on Disarmament;

9. *Urges* the Secretary-General to take concrete steps to strengthen the Office for Disarmament Affairs in order to ensure that it has the necessary means and resources to carry out its mandated tasks;

10. *Requests* the Secretary-General to report on those steps to the General Assembly at its forty-eighth session;

11. *Decides* to review these questions at its forty-eighth session.

---

[a]A/C.1/47/7.

General Assembly resolution 47/54 G

8 April 1993   Meeting 98   Adopted without vote

Approved by First Committee (A/47/693/Add.1) without vote, 12 March (meeting 44); draft by Chairman (A/C.1/47/L.56), orally revised, and orally amended by Pakistan; agenda item 63.

Meeting numbers. GA 47th session: 1st Committee 41, 42, 44; plenary 98.

Report of the Secretary-General. As requested by the Assembly, the Secretary-General submitted a report in September on steps being taken to strengthen the Office for Disarmament Affairs.[7] His proposals included renaming the Office the Centre for Disarmament Affairs, to be headed by a Director, allocating additional human resources, and appropriating financial resources for the acquisition of office automation equipment.

Work of the First Committee

In November 1993, the First Committee devoted two meetings to discussing the further rationalization of its work and reform of its agenda, a subject that was included in the Assembly's agenda at the request of the European Community (EC).[8] Proposals concerning rationalization emphasized: more detailed and focused discussion of specific agenda items; reducing the number of draft resolutions; and the relationship between disarmament and security items. Proposals concerning reform of the agenda involved rearranging the agenda along thematic lines and clustering items under a limited number of "head items".

GENERAL ASSEMBLY ACTION

On 16 December, the General Assembly, on the recommendation of the First Committee, adopted **resolution 48/87** without vote.

Rationalization of the work of the Disarmament and International Security Committee (First Committee)

The General Assembly,

Recalling its resolution 47/54 G of 8 April 1993, particularly paragraph 2 thereof, in which the Chairman of the First Committee was requested to continue his consultations on the further rationalization of the work and the effective functioning of the Committee, taking into account all the views and proposals presented to the Committee, including those related to the thematic clustering of agenda items,

Recalling also the ongoing efforts of the General Assembly aimed at revitalizing its work, and recalling further its resolution 47/233 of 17 August 1993,

Mindful that the United Nations has a central role and responsibility in the sphere of disarmament and international security,

Recalling the Final Document of the Tenth Special Session of the General Assembly, the first special session devoted to disarmament, and the objectives and priorities set out therein, as well as the progress achieved in arms control and disarmament towards these ends,

Encouraged by the changed political climate in the post-cold-war era, which is conducive to further bilateral, regional and multilateral efforts in disarmament, and aware of the consequent need to adjust the work of the United Nations, including that concerned with disarmament and international security,

Desiring to enhance the effective functioning of the disarmament machinery of the United Nations,

Conscious of the need to improve the interrelationship between disarmament and arms regulation issues and the broader international security context,

Encouraged by the efforts undertaken by the Secretary-General to strengthen the Secretariat's capabilities to enable it to discharge its tasks effectively,

1. *Decides* to enhance the effectiveness of the First Committee by:

   (a) Addressing in a more systematic manner the issues of disarmament and related matters of international security;

   (b) Streamlining its functioning and, as a first step towards that end, encouraging more detailed and focused discussion of the specific agenda items;

   (c) Reviewing annually the time and resources allotted for its work;

2. *Decides also*, in relation to the restructuring and reorganization of the annual agenda of the First Committee, to adopt, in order to promote more detailed and focused discussions, a thematic approach whereby items presented by Member States are clustered in broad topic areas, such as:

   (a) Nuclear weapons;

   (b) Other weapons of mass destruction;

   (c) Conventional weapons;

   (d) Regional disarmament and security;

   (e) Confidence-building measures, including transparency in armaments;

   (f) Outer space (disarmament aspects);

   (g) Disarmament machinery;

   (h) Other disarmament measures;

   (i) International security;

   (j) Related matters of disarmament and international security;

3. *Requests* the Chairman of the First Committee to continue consultations on the further rationalization of the work of the Committee in terms of improving its effective functioning, taking into account relevant resolutions adopted by the Committee, as well as views and proposals presented to it on this issue;

4. *Urges* the Secretary-General to provide the appropriate means and adequate resources to the Office for Disarmament Affairs of the Secretariat in order to ensure that it can carry out its mandated tasks, in particular those relating to deliberation and negotiation, taking into account existing resource constraints, and to report thereon to the General Assembly at its forty-ninth session;

5. *Decides* to review the question of further rationalization and improvement of the work of the First Committee at its forty-ninth session.

General Assembly resolution 48/87

16 December 1993   Meeting 81   Adopted without vote

Approved by First Committee (A/48/688) without vote, 19 November (meeting 31); draft by Chairman (A/C.1/48/L.51); agenda item 156.

Meeting numbers. GA 48th session: 1st Committee 16, 17, 31; plenary 81.

Disarmament Commission

The Disarmament Commission, composed of all United Nations Member States, held eight plenary meetings at its 1993 session (New York, 19 April–10 May).[9] It also held an organizational session on 23 March and 14 April to elect its officers and adopt the provisional agenda for its 1993 session. At a further organizational session on 9 and 14 December, it decided to schedule its items on nuclear disarmament and on the role of science and technology for conclusion in 1994 and inscribed on the agenda a new item on international arms transfers.

The Commission's 1993 agenda included items on nuclear disarmament in the framework of international peace and security, with the objective of eliminating nuclear weapons; regional disarmament within the context of global security; and the role of science and technology in international security, disarmament and related fields. All of those items were carried over from the 1992 session.[2]

Three working groups were established to deal with the agenda items. Working Group I, dealing with nuclear disarmament, adopted an outline of guidelines and recommendations for consideration in 1994, which was annexed to the Commission's report. Working Group II succeeded in adopting by consensus a text on guidelines and recommendations for regional approaches to disarmament within the context of global security, thereby completing its consideration of the item. That text was also annexed to the Commission's report. Although Working Group III was able to draft guidelines on almost all aspects of the role of science and technology, differences of opinion remained on a number of issues. Consequently, it was decided to allow another year for completion of the item.

GENERAL ASSEMBLY ACTION

On 16 December, the General Assembly, on the recommendation of the First Committee, adopted **resolution 48/77 A** without vote.

Report of the Disarmament Commission
The General Assembly,

Having considered the annual report of the Disarmament Commission,

Recalling its resolutions 47/54 A of 9 December 1992 and 47/54 G of 8 April 1993,

Recalling also the proposal to include a new item in the agenda of the Disarmament Commission entitled "General guidelines for non-proliferation, with special emphasis on weapons of mass destruction",

Considering the role that the Disarmament Commission has been called upon to play and the contribution that it should make in examining and submitting recommendations on various problems in the field of disarmament and in the promotion of the implementation of the relevant decisions of the tenth special session of the General Assembly,

1. *Takes note* of the annual report of the Disarmament Commission;

2. *Commends* the Disarmament Commission for its adoption by consensus, at its 1993 substantive session, of a set of guidelines and recommendations for regional approaches to disarmament within the context of global security, which were recommended to the General Assembly for consideration, pursuant to the adopted "Ways and means to enhance the functioning of the Disarmament Commission";[a]

3. *Endorses* the guidelines and recommendations for regional approaches to disarmament within the context of global security as adopted by the Disarmament Commission;

4. *Notes with satisfaction* that the Disarmament Commission has made significant progress in achieving agreement on guidelines and recommendations under its agenda item entitled "The role of science and technology in the context of international security, disarmament and other related fields", consideration of which is to be concluded in 1994;

5. *Notes* the continuing consideration by the Disarmament Commission of its agenda item entitled "Process of nuclear disarmament in the framework of international peace and security, with the objective of the elimination of nuclear weapons", which is to be concluded in 1994;

6. *Reaffirms* the importance of further enhancing the dialogue and cooperation among the First Committee, the Disarmament Commission and the Conference on Disarmament;

7. *Recommends* that the Conference on Disarmament consider, within its competence, the guidelines and recommendations for regional approaches to disarmament within the context of global security;

8. *Reaffirms also* the role of the Disarmament Commission as the specialized, deliberative body within the United Nations multilateral disarmament machinery that allows for in-depth deliberations on specific disarmament issues, leading to the submission of concrete recommendations on those issues;

9. *Encourages* the Disarmament Commission to continue to make every effort to enhance its working methods so as to enable it to give focused consideration to a limited number of priority issues in the field of disarmament, bearing in mind the decision it has taken to move its agenda towards a three-item phased approach;

10. *Requests* the Disarmament Commission to continue its work in accordance with its mandate, as set forth in paragraph 118 of the Final Document of the Tenth Special Session of the General Assembly, and with paragraph 3 of resolution 37/78 H of 9 December 1982, and to that end to make every effort to achieve specific recommendations on the items on its agenda, taking into account the adopted "Ways and means to enhance the functioning of the Disarmament Commission";

11. *Notes* that the Disarmament Commission, at its 1993 organizational session, adopted the following items for consideration and conclusion at its 1994 substantive session:

(1) Process of nuclear disarmament in the framework of international peace and security, with the objective of the elimination of nuclear weapons;

(2) The role of science and technology in the context of international security, disarmament and other related fields;

12. *Notes also* that the Disarmament Commission, at its 1993 organizational session, included in the agenda of its 1994 substantive session an item entitled "International arms transfers, with particular reference to resolution 46/36 H of 6 December 1991";

---

[a]A/CN.10/137.

13. *Also requests* the Disarmament Commission to meet for a period not exceeding four weeks during 1994 and to submit a substantive report to the General Assembly at its forty-ninth session;

14. *Requests* the Secretary-General to transmit to the Disarmament Commission the annual report of the Conference on Disarmament, together with all the official records of the forty-eighth session of the General Assembly relating to disarmament matters, and to render all assistance that the Commission may require for implementing the present resolution;

15. *Also requests* the Secretary-General to ensure full provision to the Commission and its subsidiary bodies of interpretation and translation facilities in the official languages and to assign, as a matter of priority, all the necessary resources and services to that end;

16. *Decides* to include in the provisional agenda of its forty-ninth session the item entitled "Report of the Disarmament Commission".

General Assembly resolution 48/77 A

16 December 1993   Meeting 81   Adopted without vote

Approved by First Committee (A/48/678) by recorded vote (139-0-1), 18 November (meeting 29); 12-nation draft (A/C.1/48/L.3/Rev.1); agenda item 73 *(a)*.

Sponsors: Benin, Brazil, Bulgaria, Canada, Czech Republic, Ecuador, Germany, Ireland, Mauritius, Mongolia, Republic of Korea, Ukraine.

Meeting numbers. GA 48th session: 1st Committee 3-14, 29; plenary 81.

Conference on Disarmament

The Conference on Disarmament, a multilateral negotiating body, met three times in 1993 at Geneva (19 January–26 March, 10 May–25 June and 26 July–3 September); 37 members participated.[10] During 30 formal plenary meetings and 10 informal meetings, it considered a nuclear test ban; cessation of the nuclear-arms race and nuclear disarmament; prevention of nuclear war; prevention of an arms race in outer space; effective international arrangements to assure non-nuclear-weapon States against the use or threat of use of nuclear weapons; new types of weapons of mass destruction and new systems of such weapons; radiological weapons; a comprehensive programme of disarmament; and transparency in armaments.

The Conference agreed to begin work immediately on a nuclear test ban, prevention of an arms race in outer space, effective international arrangements to assure non-nuclear-weapon States against the use or threat of use of nuclear weapons, and transparency in armaments, and established ad hoc committees for each item. Interested members continued their ongoing open-ended informal consultations on non-proliferation in all its aspects. Two Special Coordinators were appointed to conduct consultations on the issues of membership and agenda. Following discussions, the Special Coordinator for the expansion of membership submitted in August a list of countries that would form the recommended composition of the Conference following expansion.[11] The Conference discussed the Special Coordinator's report but was unable to reach a conclusion on the matter. The Special Coordinator for the agenda reported that it had been agreed to continue consultations in 1994.

GENERAL ASSEMBLY ACTION

On 16 December, the General Assembly, on the recommendation of the First Committee, adopted **resolution 48/77 B** without vote.

Report of the Conference on Disarmament
The General Assembly,

Having considered the report of the Conference on Disarmament,

Convinced that the Conference on Disarmament, as the single multilateral disarmament negotiating forum of the international community, has the primary role in substantive negotiations on priority questions of disarmament,

Considering, in this respect, that the present international climate should give additional impetus to multilateral negotiations with the aim of reaching concrete agreements,

Taking note of the decision of the Conference on Disarmament to give to its Ad Hoc Committee on a Nuclear Test Ban a mandate to negotiate such a ban,

Noting with satisfaction the results achieved so far on the subject of improved and effective functioning of the Conference on Disarmament, as well as the decision to carry out inter-sessional consultations with a view to achieving consensus on the issue of its membership during the inter-sessional period, and the decision to continue consultations on the issue of the agenda at its 1994 session,

1. *Reaffirms* the role of the Conference on Disarmament as the single multilateral disarmament negotiating forum of the international community;

2. *Welcomes* the determination of the Conference on Disarmament to fulfil that role in the light of the evolving international situation with a view to making early substantive progress on priority items of its agenda;

3. *Also welcomes* the decision of the Conference on Disarmament to give to its Ad Hoc Committee on a Nuclear Test Ban a mandate to negotiate such a ban;

4. *Urges* the Conference on Disarmament to reach a consensus that would result in the expansion of its membership before the start of its 1994 session;

5. *Encourages* the ongoing review of the agenda, membership and methods of work of the Conference on Disarmament;

6. *Requests* the Secretary-General to ensure the provision to the Conference on Disarmament of additional administrative, substantive and conference support services for its negotiations;

7. *Requests* the Conference on Disarmament to submit a report on its work to the General Assembly at its forty-ninth session;

8. *Decides* to include in the provisional agenda of its forty-ninth session the item entitled "Report of the Conference on Disarmament".

General Assembly resolution 48/77 B

16 December 1993   Meeting 81   Adopted without vote

Approved by First Committee (A/48/678) without vote, 19 November (meeting 30); 2-nation draft (A/C.1/48/L.41); agenda item 73 *(b)*.

Sponsors: Czech Republic, Egypt.

Financial implications. 5th Committee, A/48/759; S-G, A/C.1/48/L.55, A/C.5/48/34.

Meeting numbers. GA 48th session: 1st Committee 3-14, 23, 30; 5th Committee 38; plenary 81.

Disarmament agreements

Parties and signatories

In October 1993, the Secretary-General submitted to the General Assembly his annual report on the status of multilateral disarmament agreements,[12] based on information received from the depositaries of those instruments. It listed the parties to and signatories of those agreements as at 31 July 1993.

As at 31 December 1993, the following numbers of States had become parties to the multilateral agreements covered in the Secretary-General's report (listed in chronological order, with the years in which they were initially signed or opened for signature).[13]

(Geneva) Protocol for the Prohibition of the Use in War of Asphyxiating, Poisonous or Other Gases, and of Bacteriological Methods of Warfare (1925): 130 parties
The Antarctic Treaty (1959): 42 parties
Treaty Banning Nuclear Weapon Tests in the Atmosphere, in Outer Space and under Water (1963): 122 parties
Treaty on Principles Governing the Activities of States in the Exploration and Use of Outer Space, including the Moon and Other Celestial Bodies (1967):[14] 93 parties
Treaty for the Prohibition of Nuclear Weapons in Latin America and the Caribbean (Treaty of Tlatelolco) (1967): 33 parties
Treaty on the Non-Proliferation of Nuclear Weapons (1968):[15] 162 parties
Treaty on the Prohibition of the Emplacement of Nuclear Weapons and Other Weapons of Mass Destruction on the Seabed and the Ocean Floor and in the Subsoil Thereof (1971):[16] 89 parties
Convention on the Prohibition of the Development, Production and Stockpiling of Bacteriological (Biological) and Toxin Weapons and on Their Destruction (1972):[17] 130 parties
Convention on the Prohibition of Military or Any Other Hostile Use of Environmental Modification Techniques (1977):[18] 62 parties
Agreement Governing the Activities of States on the Moon and Other Celestial Bodies (1979):[19] 9 parties
Convention on Prohibitions or Restrictions on the Use of Certain Conventional Weapons Which May Be Deemed to Be Excessively Injurious or to Have Indiscriminate Effects (1981): 41 parties
South Pacific Nuclear Free Zone Treaty (Treaty of Rarotonga) (1985): 13 parties
Treaty on Conventional Armed Forces in Europe (1990): 30 parties
Treaty on Open Skies (1992): 11 parties
Convention on the Prohibition of the Development, Production, Stockpiling and Use of Chemical Weapons and on Their Destruction (1993): 4 parties

REFERENCES

[1]YUN 1978, p. 17. [2]YUN 1992, p. 60. [3]Ibid., GA dec. 47/422, 9 Dec. 1992. [4]A/47/887 & Corr.1 & Add.1-6. [5]CD/1183. [6]CD/1184. [7]A/48/358. [8]A/48/194. [9]A/48/42. [10]A/48/27. [11]CD/1214. [12]A/48/388. [13]*The United Nations Disarmament Yearbook*, vol. 18, *1993*, Sales No. E.94.IX.1. [14]YUN 1966, p. 41, GA res. 2222(XXI), annex, 19 Dec. 1966. [15]YUN 1968, p. 17, GA res. 2373(XXII), annex, 12 June 1968. [16]YUN 1970, p. 18, GA res. 2660(XXV), annex, 7 Dec. 1970. [17]YUN 1971, p. 19, GA res. 2826(XXVI), annex, 16 Dec. 1971. [18]YUN 1976, p. 45, GA res. 31/72, annex, 10 Dec. 1976. [19]YUN 1979, p. 111, GA res. 34/68, annex, 5 Dec. 1979.

Major trends and developments

Non-proliferation

In 1993, non-proliferation continued to be one of the most prominent disarmament issues at the bilateral, regional and global levels. As the threat of nuclear confrontation diminished with the end of the cold war, the proliferation of weapons of mass destruction and the transfer of military technology emerged as the dominant challenge to international security. A number of international treaties and several control mechanisms imposed non-proliferation regimes with respect to various categories of weapons and weapons systems—biological, chemical and conventional. Issues related to the implementation or broadening of those regimes and to the transfer of technology were the focus of attention in different disarmament forums throughout the year.

Non-Proliferation Treaty

Signatures and accessions

In 1993, the Czech Republic and Slovakia succeeded to the 1968 Treaty on the Non-Proliferation of Nuclear Weapons (NPT)[1] and Armenia, Belarus, Guyana, Mauritania and Saint Kitts and Nevis acceded to it, bringing the number of States parties to 162 at the end of the year.[2]

Communications. On 12 March 1993,[3] the Democratic People's Republic of Korea informed the President of the Security Council that it had decided to withdraw from NPT, in accordance with paragraph 1 of article X of the Treaty, following controversy over inspections of its nuclear facilities conducted by the International Atomic Energy Agency (IAEA). (For details, see PART TWO, Chapter III.)

During March, April and May, a number of States issued statements on the decision taken by the Democratic People's Republic of Korea: Bulgaria,[4] Costa Rica,[5] Croatia,[6] the Czech Republic,[7] Honduras,[8] Mexico,[9] Nicaragua,[10] Norway,[11] Panama[12] and Paraguay.[13] The Russian Federation, the United Kingdom and the United States issued a joint statement on the subject.[14]

Preparations for the
1995 review Conference on NPT

Following the entry into force on 5 March 1970 of NPT, quinquennial review conferences were held in 1975,[15] 1980,[16] 1985[17] and 1990,[18] as called for under article VIII, paragraph 3, of the Treaty.

The Preparatory Committee for the 1995 Conference of the Parties to NPT, which would review the Treaty's operation and decide on its extension, held its first session in New York from 10 to 14 May 1993.[19] The States parties to NPT had formed the Committee in 1992.[20]

The Committee decided to hold the Conference in New York from 17 April to 12 May 1995 and to hold two of its own sessions in 1994 and one in 1995.

The Committee deferred decisions with regard to its own decision-making and to participation in its meetings. It held preliminary discussions and decided to defer decisions on the Conference's draft rules of procedure, agenda, final document(s) and background documentation.

GENERAL ASSEMBLY ACTION

On 16 December, the General Assembly, on the recommendation of the First Committee, adopted **resolution 48/75 C** by recorded vote.

General and complete disarmament

The General Assembly,

Aware of its role in the field of disarmament,

Aware also of the interest of the international community in continuing and intensifying consideration of the question of the non-proliferation of weapons of mass destruction and of vehicles for their delivery in all its aspects,

1. *Requests* the Secretary-General to prepare a short report containing a brief description of the question of the non-proliferation of weapons of mass destruction and of vehicles for their delivery in all its aspects and to transmit it, no later than 1 May 1994, to a representative intergovernmental group of experts for its consideration and suggestions regarding further study of the question by the international community in various multilateral disarmament forums;

2. *Also requests* the Secretary-General to submit his report, together with the suggestions of the representative intergovenmental group of experts, to the General Assembly at its forty-ninth session;

3. *Decides* to include in the provisional agenda of its forty-ninth session an item entitled ''Non-proliferation of weapons of mass destruction and of vehicles for their delivery in all its aspects''.

General Assembly resolution 48/75 C

16 December 1993   Meeting 81   114-6-45 (recorded vote)

Approved by First Committee (A/48/676) by recorded vote (94-5-39), 12 November (meeting 25); 3-nation draft (A/C.1/48/L.10); agenda item 71.
Sponsors: Bolivia, Mexico, Rwanda.
Meeting numbers. GA 48th session: 1st Committee 3-14, 21, 25; plenary 81.

Recorded vote in Assembly as follows:

In favour: Afghanistan, Algeria, Antigua and Barbuda, Australia, Bahamas, Bahrain, Bangladesh, Barbados, Belize, Benin, Bhutan, Bolivia, Bo- tswana, Brazil, Brunei Darussalam, Burkina Faso, Burundi, Cambodia, Cameroon, Canada, Cape Verde, Central African Republic, Chad, Chile, China, Colombia, Comoros, Congo, Costa Rica, Côte d'Ivoire, Cuba, Democratic People's Republic of Korea, Djibouti, Dominica, Dominican Republic, Ecuador, Egypt, Ethiopia, Fiji, Gabon, Gambia, Ghana, Grenada, Guatemala, Guinea, Guinea-Bissau, Guyana, Haiti, Honduras, India, Indonesia, Iran, Iraq, Jamaica, Jordan, Kenya, Lao People's Democratic Republic, Lebanon, Lesotho, Libyan Arab Jamahiriya, Madagascar, Malawi, Malaysia, Maldives, Mali, Mauritania, Mauritius, Mexico, Mongolia, Morocco, Myanmar, Namibia, Nepal, New Zealand, Nicaragua, Niger, Nigeria, Oman, Pakistan, Panama, Papua New Guinea, Paraguay, Peru, Philippines, Qatar, Rwanda, Saint Lucia, Saint Vincent and the Grenadines, Samoa, Saudi Arabia, Senegal, Seychelles, Sierra Leone, Singapore, Solomon Islands, Sri Lanka, Sudan, Suriname, Swaziland, Syrian Arab Republic, Thailand, the former Yugoslav Republic of Macedonia, Togo, Trinidad and Tobago, Tunisia, Uganda, United Arab Emirates, United Republic of Tanzania, Uruguay, Venezuela, Viet Nam, Yemen, Zambia, Zimbabwe.

Against: France, Israel, Monaco, Russian Federation, United Kingdom, United States.

Abstaining: Albania, Andorra, Argentina, Armenia, Austria, Belarus, Belgium, Bulgaria, Croatia, Cyprus, Czech Republic, Denmark, Estonia, Finland, Georgia, Germany, Greece, Hungary, Iceland, Ireland, Italy, Japan, Kazakhstan, Kyrgyzstan, Latvia, Liechtenstein, Lithuania, Luxembourg, Malta, Marshall Islands, Micronesia, Netherlands, Norway, Poland, Portugal, Republic of Korea, Republic of Moldova, Romania, Slovakia, Slovenia, Spain, Sweden, Tajikistan, Turkey, Ukraine.

IAEA safeguards

Steps continued to be taken in 1993 to strengthen the IAEA safeguards system—the cornerstone of NPT and of the whole non-proliferation regime. In December, the IAEA Board of Governors approved a programme by which a more effective and efficient safeguards system would be implemented prior to the 1995 NPT review Conference. Key elements of the programme entailed the achievement of greater transparency at all levels of the system and the accessibility necessary to verify information provided by States. In addition, the Board reaffirmed the Agency's right to perform special inspections when there was reason to believe that installations or material which should have been declared had not been so declared. Safeguards agreements between IAEA and the following parties to NPT entered into force in 1993: Latvia, Solomon Islands and Tonga.

Country situations

On 1 April,[21] the IAEA Board of Governors adopted a resolution, by which it found the Democratic People's Republic of Korea in non-compliance with its obligations under its safeguards agreement with IAEA. It decided to report such non-compliance, if not remedied, to all IAEA members and to the Security Council and the General Assembly. (For details, see PART TWO, Chapter III.)

The Secretary-General transmitted to the Security Council on 1 December[22] a joint report describing talks between the United Nations Special Commission (UNSCOM) and IAEA, for the one part, and the Government of Iraq, for the other (New York, 15-30 November). UNSCOM and IAEA welcomed Iraq's formal acceptance in November[23]—welcomed by the Council in December[24]—of the obligations under a 1991 Council resolution,[25] enabling UNSCOM to initiate immediately full-scale monitoring and verification. In another December report transmitted by the Secretary-General to the Council,[26] the Executive Chairman of UNSCOM described developments in Iraq and UNSCOM's activities there from 14 June to 14 December 1993. (For details, see PART TWO, Chapter III.)

IAEA continued to carry out safeguards missions in South Africa. However, a new dimension was added when F. W. de Klerk, President of South Africa, declared on 24 March[27] that South Africa had, in the past, developed a limited nuclear deterrent capability and had completed six nuclear fission devices, but that it had voluntarily dismantled and destroyed all of them before acceding to NPT in 1991. He further stated that South Africa had never conducted a clandestine nuclear test and that at no time had it acquired nuclear weapons technology or materials from another country, nor had it provided any to another country, nor had it cooperated with another country in that regard. IAEA was invited, on the basis of the safeguards agreement, to verify that the programme had in fact been terminated and that all nuclear material had been placed under safeguards.

Other weapons of mass destruction

Chemical weapons

The Convention on the Prohibition of the Development, Production, Stockpiling and Use of Chemical Weapons and on Their Destruction, adopted by the Conference on Disarmament in 1992,[28] was opened for signature in Paris on 13 January 1993. By the end of the year, 154 States had signed and 4 States had ratified the Convention.[2]

In response to a 1992 General Assembly request,[29] the Secretary-General reported, in his capacity as depositary, on the status of the Convention as at 15 August.[30]

During the year, the Preparatory Commission for the Organization for the Prohibition of Chemical Weapons, established in 1992 to prepare for the Convention's implementation,[28] worked, with the assistance of the Provisional Technical Secretariat, an arm of the organization, on implementation procedures. A priority was the development, in cooperation with member States, of the mechanisms required to verify compliance; training modules for future inspectors were being prepared and training programmes were launched by a number of member States. The Provisional Technical Secretariat also assisted members to establish national authorities and prepare national databases.

Bacteriological (biological) weapons

Further strengthening of the Convention on the Prohibition of the Development, Production and Stockpiling of Bacteriological (Biological) and Toxin Weapons and on Their Destruction[31] was carried out on the basis of the Final Declaration of the Third (1991) Review Conference of the Parties to the Convention[32] in which the States parties agreed to expand the confidence-building measures they had agreed to at the Second (1986) Review Conference.[33] Among measures decided on was the requirement that parties declare what legislation and other regulations they had enacted to implement the Convention's provisions and to control the export or import of pathogenic microorganisms. At the end of 1993, 40 States parties had submitted reports to the United Nations, including information concerning their export and import of certain biological weapons–related materials.

In addition, the Ad Hoc Group of Governmental Experts to Identify and Examine Potential Verification Measures from a Scientific and Technical Standpoint (Geneva, 24 May–4 June and 13-24 September), established by the Third Review Conference, finalized its deliberations and submitted a report to the States parties.[34] The Group identified, examined and evaluated 21 potential measures, which were categorized as off-site (information monitoring, data exchange, remote sensing and inspections) and on-site (exchange visits, inspections and continuous monitoring). The Group concluded that the potential verification measures could be useful in enhancing confidence, through increased transparency, and that States parties were fulfilling their obligations, thereby strengthening the Convention.

GENERAL ASSEMBLY ACTION

On 16 December, the General Assembly, on the recommendation of the First Committee, adopted **resolution 48/65** without vote.

Convention on the Prohibition of the Development, Production and Stockpiling of Bacteriological (Biological) and Toxin Weapons and on Their Destruction

The General Assembly,

Recalling, in particular, its previous resolutions relating to the complete and effective prohibition of bacteriological (biological) and toxin weapons and to their destruction,

Recalling also its resolution 46/35 A, adopted without a vote on 6 December 1991, in which it welcomed, *inter alia,* the establishment, proceeding from the recommendations of the Third Review Conference of the Parties to the Convention on the Prohibition of the Development, Production and Stockpiling of Bacteriological (Biological) and Toxin Weapons and on Their Destruction, of an ad hoc group of governmental experts open to all States parties to identify and examine potential verification measures from a scientific and technical standpoint,

Noting with satisfaction that there are more than a hundred and thirty States parties to the Convention on the

Prohibition of the Development, Production and Stock-piling of Bacteriological (Biological) and Toxin Weapons and on Their Destruction, including all the permanent members of the Security Council,

Recalling its call upon all States parties to the Convention to participate in the implementation of the recommendations of the Third Review Conference, including the exchange of information and data agreed to in the Final Declaration of the Third Review Conference, and to provide such information and data in conformity with standardized procedure to the Secretary-General on an annual basis and no later than 15 April,

Recalling also the provisions of the Convention related to scientific and technological cooperation and the related provisions of the Final Document of the Third Review Conference and the final report of the Ad Hoc Group of Governmental Experts to Identify and Examine Potential Verification Measures from a Scientific and Technical Standpoint,

1. *Notes with satisfaction* that the Ad Hoc Group of Governmental Experts to Identify and Examine Potential Verification Measures from a Scientific and Technical Standpoint completed its work on 24 September 1993;

2. *Commends* to all States parties the final report of the Ad Hoc Group of Governmental Experts, agreed to by consensus at its last meeting at Geneva on 24 September 1993;

3. *Requests* the Secretary-General to render the necessary assistance to the depositary Powers of the Convention on the Prohibition of the Development, Production and Stockpiling of Bacteriological (Biological) and Toxin Weapons and on Their Destruction and to provide such services as may be required for the convening of a special conference should the depositary Powers be requested by a majority of States parties to convene such a conference in order to consider the final report of the Ad Hoc Group of Governmental Experts;

4. *Welcomes* the information and data provided to date and reiterates its call upon all States parties to the Convention to participate in the exchange of information and data agreed to in the Final Declaration of the Third Review Conference;

5. *Also requests* the Secretary-General to render the necessary assistance and to provide such services as may be required for the implementation of the decisions and recommendations of the Third Review Conference of the Parties to the Convention on the Prohibition of the Development, Production and Stockpiling of Bacteriological (Biological) and Toxin Weapons and on Their Destruction;

6. *Calls upon* all signatory States that have not yet ratified the Convention to do so without delay, and also calls upon those other States that have not signed the Convention to become parties thereto at an early date, thus contributing to the achievement of universal adherence to the Convention.

General Assembly resolution 48/65

16 December 1993					Meeting 81					Adopted without vote

Approved by First Committee (A/48/666) without vote, 12 November (meeting 25); 47-nation draft (A/C.1/48/L.33); agenda item 61.
Sponsors: Argentina, Australia, Austria, Belarus, Belgium, Brazil, Bulgaria, Canada, Chile, Costa Rica, Croatia, Cuba, Czech Republic, Denmark, Finland, France, Germany, Greece, Honduras, Hungary, Iran, Ireland, Italy, Japan, Luxembourg, Malta, Netherlands, New Zealand, Nigeria, Norway, Panama, Peru, Philippines, Poland, Portugal, Republic of Korea, Romania,

Russian Federation, Slovakia, Slovenia, Spain, Sweden, the former Yugoslav Republic of Macedonia, Turkey, Ukraine, United Kingdom, United States.
Meeting numbers. GA 48th session: 1st Committee 3-14, 19, 20, 25, 30; plenary 81.

Strengthening the security of non-nuclear-weapon States

On 21 January,[35] the Conference on Disarmament re-established its Ad Hoc Committee on Effective International Arrangements to Assure Non-Nuclear-Weapon States against the Use or Threat of Use of Nuclear Weapons, also known as negative security assurances. The Ad Hoc Committee held meetings between 5 March and 24 August.

In its conclusions and recommendations,[36] the Ad Hoc Committee noted that the complex nature of the issues involved and differing perceptions of security interests continued to impede work on the substance of effective arrangements and the search for a common formula. Recognizing the importance of the question and feeling that, in the light of recent transformations in the international political climate and other positive developments, there was a need to step up efforts to agree on a common approach and to proceed to negotiations with a view to reaching agreement as soon as possible, the Committee recommended that it be re-established at the beginning of the 1994 session of the Conference.

GENERAL ASSEMBLY ACTION

On 16 December, the General Assembly, on the recommendation of the First Committee, adopted **resolution 48/73** by recorded vote.

Conclusion of effective international arrangements to assure non-nuclear-weapon States against the use or threat of use of nuclear weapons

The General Assembly,

Bearing in mind the need to allay the legitimate concern of the States of the world with regard to ensuring lasting security for their peoples,

Convinced that nuclear weapons pose the greatest threat to mankind and to the survival of civilization,

Welcoming the progress achieved in recent years in both nuclear and conventional disarmament,

Noting that, despite recent progress in the field of nuclear disarmament, further efforts are necessary towards the achievement of the goal of general and complete disarmament under effective international control,

Also convinced that nuclear disarmament and the complete elimination of nuclear weapons are essential to remove the danger of nuclear war,

Determined strictly to abide by the relevant provisions of the Charter of the United Nations on the non-use of force or threat of force,

Recognizing that the independence, territorial integrity and sovereignty of non-nuclear-weapon States need to be safeguarded against the use or threat of use of force, including the use or threat of use of nuclear weapons,

Considering that, until nuclear disarmament is achieved on a universal basis, it is imperative for the international community to develop effective measures and arrangements to ensure the security of non-nuclear-weapon States against the use or threat of use of nuclear weapons from any quarter,

Recognizing also that effective measures and arrangements to assure the non-nuclear-weapon States against the use or threat of use of nuclear weapons can contribute positively to the prevention of the spread of nuclear weapons,

Bearing in mind paragraph 59 of the Final Document of the Tenth Special Session of the General Assembly, the first special session devoted to disarmament, in which it urged the nuclear-weapon States to pursue efforts to conclude, as appropriate, effective arrangements to assure non-nuclear-weapon States against the use or threat of use of nuclear weapons, and desirous of promoting the implementation of the relevant provisions of the Final Document,

Recalling the relevant parts of the special report of the Committee on Disarmament,[a] submitted to the General Assembly at its twelfth special session, the second special session devoted to disarmament, and of the special report of the Conference on Disarmament submitted to the Assembly at its fifteenth special session, the third special session devoted to disarmament, as well as of the report of the Conference on its 1992 session,

Recalling also paragraph 12 of the Declaration of the 1980s as the Second Disarmament Decade, contained in the annex to its resolution 35/46 of 3 December 1980, which states, *inter alia*, that all efforts should be exerted by the Committee on Disarmament urgently to negotiate with a view to reaching agreement on effective international arrangements to assure non-nuclear-weapon States against the use or threat of use of nuclear weapons,

Noting the in-depth negotiations undertaken in the Conference on Disarmament and its Ad Hoc Committee on Effective International Arrangements to Assure Non-Nuclear-Weapon States against the Use or Threat of Use of Nuclear Weapons, with a view to reaching agreement on this item,

Taking note of the proposals submitted under that item in the Conference on Disarmament, including the drafts of an international convention,

Taking note also of the decision adopted by the Tenth Conference of Heads of State or Government of Non-Aligned Countries, held at Jakarta in September 1992,[b] as well as the relevant recommendations of the Organization of the Islamic Conference reiterated in the Final Communiqué of the Twentieth Islamic Conference of Foreign Ministers, held at Istanbul in August 1991,[c] calling upon the Conference on Disarmament to reach an urgent agreement on an international convention to assure non-nuclear-weapon States against the use or threat of use of nuclear weapons,

Taking note further of the unilateral declarations made by all nuclear-weapon States on their policies of non-use or non-threat of use of nuclear weapons against non-nuclear-weapon States,

Noting the support expressed in the Conference on Disarmament and in the General Assembly for the elaboration of an international convention to assure non-nuclear-weapon States against the use or threat of use of nuclear weapons, as well as the difficulties pointed out in evolving a common approach acceptable to all,

Noting also the greater willingness to overcome the difficulties encountered in previous years,

Recalling its relevant resolutions adopted in previous years, in particular resolutions 45/54 of 4 December 1990, 46/32 of 6 December 1991 and 47/50 of 9 December 1992,

1. *Reaffirms* the urgent need to reach an early agreement on effective international arrangements to assure non-nuclear-weapon States against the use or threat of use of nuclear weapons;

2. *Notes with satisfaction* that in the Conference on Disarmament there is no objection, in principle, to the idea of an international convention to assure non-nuclear-weapon States against the use or threat of use of nuclear weapons, although the difficulties as regards evolving a common approach acceptable to all have also been pointed out;

3. *Appeals* to all States, especially the nuclear-weapon States, to work actively towards an early agreement on a common approach and, in particular, on a common formula that could be included in an international instrument of a legally binding character;

4. *Recommends* that further intensive efforts should be devoted to the search for such a common approach or common formula and that the various alternative approaches, including, in particular, those considered in the Conference on Disarmament, should be further explored in order to overcome the difficulties;

5. *Recommends also* that the Conference on Disarmament should actively continue intensive negotiations with a view to reaching early agreement and concluding effective international arrangements to assure non-nuclear-weapon States against the use or threat of use of nuclear weapons, taking into account the widespread support for the conclusion of an international convention and giving consideration to any other proposals designed to secure the same objective;

6. *Decides* to include in the provisional agenda of its forty-ninth session the item entitled ''Conclusion of effective international arrangements to assure non-nuclear-weapon States against the use or threat of use of nuclear weapons''.

---

[a]The Committee on Disarmament was redesignated the Conference on Disarmament as from 7 February 1984.

[b]A/47/675-S/24816.

[c]A/46/486-S/23055.

General Assembly resolution 48/73

16 December 1993   Meeting 81   166-0-4 (recorded vote)

Approved by First Committee (A/48/674) by recorded vote (142-0-3), 16 November (meeting 27); 12-nation draft (A/C.1/48/L.37); agenda item 69.

Sponsors: Bangladesh, Colombia, Costa Rica, Democratic People's Republic of Korea, Iran, Madagascar, Nepal, Pakistan, Panama, Sri Lanka, Sudan, Viet Nam.

Meeting numbers. GA 48th session: 1st Committee 3-14, 27; plenary 81.

Recorded vote in Assembly as follows:

In favour: Afghanistan, Albania, Algeria, Andorra, Angola, Antigua and Barbuda, Argentina, Armenia, Australia, Austria, Azerbaijan, Bahamas, Bahrain, Bangladesh, Barbados, Belarus, Belgium, Belize, Benin, Bhutan, Bolivia, Botswana, Brazil, Brunei Darussalam, Bulgaria, Burkina Faso, Burundi, Cambodia, Cameroon, Canada, Cape Verde, Central African Republic, Chad, Chile, China, Colombia, Comoros, Congo, Costa Rica, Côte d'Ivoire, Croatia, Cuba, Cyprus, Czech Republic, Democratic People's Republic of Korea, Denmark, Djibouti, Dominica, Dominican Republic, Ecuador, Egypt, Estonia, Ethiopia, Fiji, Finland, Gabon, Gambia, Georgia, Germany, Ghana, Greece, Grenada, Guatemala, Guinea, Guinea-Bissau, Guyana, Haiti, Honduras, Hungary, Iceland, India, Indonesia, Iran, Iraq, Ireland, Israel, Italy, Jamaica, Japan, Jordan, Kazakhstan, Kenya, Kuwait, Kyrgyzstan, Lao People's Democratic Republic, Latvia, Lebanon, Lesotho, Libyan Arab Jamaniriya, Liechtenstein, Lithuania, Luxembourg, Madagascar, Malawi, Malaysia, Maldives, Mali, Malta, Marshall Islands, Mauritania, Mauritius, Mexico, Micronesia, Mongolia, Morocco, Mozambique, Myanmar, Namibia, Nepal, Netherlands, New Zealand, Nicaragua, Niger, Nigeria, Norway, Oman, Pakistan, Panama, Papua New Guinea, Paraguay, Peru, Philippines, Poland, Portugal, Qatar, Republic of Korea, Republic of Moldova, Romania, Russian Federation, Rwanda, Saint Lucia, Saint Vincent and the Grenadines, Samoa, Saudi Arabia, Senegal, Seychelles, Sierra Leone, Singapore, Slovakia, Slovenia, Solomon Islands, Spain, Sri Lanka, Sudan, Suriname, Swaziland, Sweden, Syrian Arab Republic, Tajikistan, Thailand, the former Yugoslav Republic of Macedonia, Togo, Trinidad and Tobago, Tunisia, Turkey, Turkmenistan, Uganda, Ukraine, United Arab Emirates, United Republic of Tanzania, Uruguay, Venezuela, Viet Nam, Yemen, Zambia, Zimbabwe.

Against: None.

Abstaining: France, Monaco, United Kingdom, United States.

Nuclear-arms limitation and disarmament

Comprehensive test-ban treaty

Conference on Disarmament consideration. The Ad Hoc Committee on a Nuclear Test Ban of the Conference on Disarmament held 19 meetings between 18 February and 24 August. On 10 August,[37] the Conference gave the Ad Hoc Committee a mandate to negotiate a comprehensive nuclear-test-ban treaty and requested the Chairman to conduct consultations in the inter-sessional period—between 3 September 1993 and 17 January 1994—on the specific mandate for, and the organization of, the negotiation. On the basis of that action, the Ad Hoc Committee's Chairman initiated consultations on adopting specific wording for a negotiating mandate and on organizing the negotiations to begin in January 1994.

The Ad Hoc Committee also discussed a draft comprehensive test-ban treaty proposed by Sweden in June,[38] for which verification protocols were yet to be prepared. It devoted considerable attention to questions related to verification, a crucial element of the future treaty. It was generally recognized that in order to ensure compliance with a future test ban, an effective, internationally applicable verification system would be required. Documents related to verification were submitted by Canada.[39] Some of the issues discussed during the session were: the substantial role that a global seismic monitoring network would have, especially in underground testing; the possible use of additional non-seismic verification technologies to detect nuclear tests in various environments, including in relation to evasion, and the possible use of such techniques to detect pre-testing preparations; the costs of a future verification system *vis-à-vis* its capabilities; the implementing agency, its powers, functions and costs; the close interrelationship between applicable verification techniques and the scope of obligations under the treaty; and a possible mix of national and international means of verification, taking into account cost effectiveness.

On 3 September,[35] the Conference adopted the report of the Ad Hoc Committee.[40] Following the conclusion of the Conference's 1993 session in September, further documents related to

a test ban were circulated. On 29 November, Mexico, as Coordinator of the Group of 21 neutral and non-aligned States (Algeria, Argentina, Brazil, Cuba, Egypt, Ethiopia, India, Indonesia, Iran, Kenya, Mexico, Morocco, Myanmar, Nigeria, Pakistan, Peru, Sri Lanka, Sweden, Venezuela, Yugoslavia, Zaire), submitted a working paper on the conclusion of a comprehensive nuclear-test-ban treaty.[41] Sweden, on 6 December, submitted a revised draft comprehensive nuclear-test-ban treaty, incorporating several additional articles and a protocol on verification.[42] On 9 December, during the inter-sessional consultations, Australia introduced a draft structural outline for a comprehensive nuclear-test-ban treaty.[43]

The Ad Hoc Group of Scientific Experts to Consider International Cooperative Measures to Detect and Identify Seismic Events held two sessions at Geneva in 1993 (thirty-fifth, 15-26 February; thirty-sixth, 26 July–6 August). The Group had completed a comprehensive seismological evaluation of its second technical test, a large-scale international experiment on the exchange and analysis of seismic data (GSETT-2) conducted in 1991,[44] a summary of which was annexed to a February progress report.[45] Later in the year, the Ad Hoc Group continued its reassessment of the concept of a global system for exchanging seismic data and discussed plans for developing, testing and evaluating an experimental international seismic monitoring system (GSETT-3). A summary of the GSETT-3 exercise and a costs analysis were annexed to the Group's August progress report.[46]

Note by the Secretary-General. By a May note with later addenda,[47] prepared in response to a 1987 General Assembly request,[48] the Secretary-General transmitted three quarterly reports (October-December 1992, January-March and April-June 1993) from Australia, which indicated that no underground nuclear explosions had been detected.

Moratoriums on testing

During the year, there were developments on moratoriums on testing, pending the achievement of a comprehensive test-ban treaty, which were closely connected with the unilateral moratoriums that had been declared or extended by three nuclear-weapon States—France, the Russian Federation and the United States—in 1992.[49]

On 2 July 1993,[50] President William Clinton of the United States announced his decision to extend the 1992 United States moratorium on nuclear testing, at least until the end of September 1994, as long as no other nation tested, and called on the other nuclear Powers to do the same. If those nations were to join the United States in observing the moratorium, the President said, the five nuclear Powers would be in the strongest possible position to negotiate a comprehensive nuclear-test ban and to discourage other nations from developing their own nuclear arsenals. If, however, the moratorium was broken by another nation, approval would be sought from the United States Congress for additional tests.

In a 5 October statement,[51] China informed the Secretary-General that it had conducted an underground nuclear test. It stated that it possessed a small number of nuclear weapons entirely for the purpose of self-defence and that it stood for the complete prohibition and thorough destruction of nuclear weapons and for a comprehensive nuclear-test ban. China believed that a comprehensive test-ban treaty would have positive significance and it would take an active part in the negotiating process. After the treaty had been concluded and had come into effect, China would abide by it and carry out no more nuclear tests. Several States, either at the time the text was announced or later in the First Committee, voiced disappointment that China had resumed nuclear testing. On 21 October,[52] the Russian Federation, expressing deep regret over China's action, declared its intention to continue to adhere to the nuclear-testing moratorium, of which it had been the initiator, while retaining the right to reconsider its decision in the event of further unfavourable developments in the nuclear-testing area. Also in October,[53] Mexico lamented the resumption of nuclear testing by China as a step backwards and called on other nuclear-weapon States to continue to observe their unilateral moratoriums.

GENERAL ASSEMBLY ACTION

On 16 December, the General Assembly, on the recommendation of the First Committee, adopted **resolution 48/70** without vote.

Comprehensive test-ban treaty

The General Assembly,

Recalling that a comprehensive nuclear-test ban is one of the priority objectives of the international community in the field of disarmament and non-proliferation,

Convinced that the most effective way to achieve an end to nuclear testing is through the conclusion of a multilaterally and effectively verifiable comprehensive test-ban treaty that will attract the adherence of all States and will contribute to the prevention of the proliferation of nuclear weapons in all its aspects, to the process of nuclear disarmament and therefore to the enhancement of international peace and security,

Convinced also that the exercise of utmost restraint in respect of nuclear testing would be consistent with the objective of an international negotiation of a comprehensive test ban,

Noting the aspirations expressed by the parties to the 1963 Treaty Banning Nuclear Weapon Tests in the Atmosphere, in Outer Space and under Water to seek to achieve the discontinuance of all test explosions of nuclear weapons for all time, which are recalled in the preamble to the 1968 Treaty on the Non-Proliferation of Nuclear Weapons,

Welcoming the willingness of all nuclear-weapon States as well as the rest of the international community to pursue the multilateral negotiation of a comprehensive test-ban treaty,

Noting with satisfaction the initiation in 1993 by the Conference on Disarmament of work under item 1 of its agenda, entitled "Nuclear test ban", and the programme of substantive work subsequently undertaken within its Ad Hoc Committee on a Nuclear Test Ban,

Noting also the ongoing activity of the Ad Hoc Group of Scientific Experts to Consider International Cooperative Measures to Detect and Identify Seismic Events,

1. *Welcomes* the decision taken by the Conference on Disarmament on 10 August 1993 to give its Ad Hoc Committee on a Nuclear Test Ban a mandate to negotiate a universal and internationally and effectively verifiable comprehensive test-ban treaty, and fully endorses the contents of that decision;

2. *Calls upon* participants in the Conference on Disarmament to approach the inter-sessional consultations mandated by that decision in a positive and constructive light;

3. *Urges* the Conference on Disarmament at the commencement of its 1994 session to re-establish, with an appropriate negotiating mandate, the Ad Hoc Committee on its agenda item entitled "Nuclear test ban";

4. *Calls upon* all States to support the multilateral negotiations in the Conference on Disarmament for a comprehensive test-ban treaty;

5. *Also urges* the Conference on Disarmament to proceed intensively, as a priority task, in its negotiation of such a universal and internationally and effectively verifiable treaty;

6. *Requests* the Secretary-General to ensure the provision to the Conference on Disarmament of additional administrative, substantive and conference support services for these negotiations;

7. *Decides* to include in the provisional agenda of its forty-ninth session an item entitled "Comprehensive test-ban treaty".

General Assembly resolution 48/70

16 December 1993   Meeting 81   Adopted without vote

Approved by First Committee (A/48/671) without vote, 19 November (meeting 30); 157-nation draft (A/C.1/48/L.40); agenda item 66.

Sponsors: Afghanistan, Albania, Algeria, Angola, Antigua and Barbuda, Argentina, Armenia, Australia, Austria, Azerbaijan, Bahamas, Bangladesh, Barbados, Belarus, Belize, Belgium, Benin, Bhutan, Bolivia, Bosnia and Herzegovina, Botswana, Brazil, Brunei Darussalam, Bulgaria, Burundi, Cambodia, Cameroon, Canada, Cape Verde, Central African Republic, Chad, Chile, Colombia, Comoros, Congo, Costa Rica, Croatia, Cuba, Cyprus, Czech Republic, Denmark, Dominican Republic, Ecuador, Egypt, El Salvador, Estonia, Ethiopia, Fiji, Finland, Gabon, Gambia, Georgia, Germany, Ghana, Greece, Grenada, Guatemala, Guinea, Guinea-Bissau, Guyana, Haiti, Honduras, Hungary, Iceland, India, Indonesia, Iran, Ireland, Italy, Jamaica, Japan, Jordan, Kazakhstan, Kenya, Kuwait, Kyrgyzstan, Lao People's Democratic Republic, Latvia, Lebanon, Lesotho, Liberia, Liechtenstein, Lithuania, Luxembourg, Madagascar, Malawi, Malaysia, Maldives, Mali, Malta, Marshall Islands, Mauritania, Mauritius, Mexico, Micronesia, Mongolia, Mozambique, Myanmar, Namibia, Nepal, Netherlands, New Zealand, Nicaragua, Niger, Nigeria, Norway, Pakistan, Panama, Papua New Guinea, Paraguay, Peru, Philippines, Poland, Portugal, Republic of Korea, Republic of Moldova, Romania, Russian Federation, Rwanda, Saint Kitts and Nevis, Saint Lucia, Saint Vincent and the Grenadines, Samoa, San Marino, Sao Tome and Principe, Senegal, Seychelles, Sierra Leone, Singapore, Slovakia, Slovenia, Solomon Islands, Spain, Sri Lanka, Sudan, Suriname, Swaziland, Sweden, Tajikistan, Thailand, the former Yugoslav Republic of Macedonia, Togo, Trinidad and Tobago, Tunisia, Turkey, Turkmenistan, Uganda,

Ukraine, United Republic of Tanzania, United States, Uruguay, Vanuatu, Venezuela, Viet Nam, Zaire, Zambia, Zimbabwe.
Financial implications. 5th Committee, A/48/759; S-G, A/C.1/48/L.55, A/C.5/48/34.
Meeting numbers. GA 48th session: 1st Committee 3-14, 21, 30; 5th Committee 38; plenary 81.

Follow-up to the Amendment Conference of States parties to the partial test-ban Treaty

On 5 August,[54] Ali Alatas, Minister for Foreign Affairs of Indonesia and President of the 1991 Amendment Conference[55] of the States Parties to the Treaty Banning Nuclear Weapon Tests in the Atmosphere, in Outer Space and under Water (1963)[56] (also known as the partial test-ban Treaty), recalling that the Conference had empowered its President to consult with the States parties on possibly resuming the Conference's work, indicated that he would, in August, convene a special meeting of the States parties to examine the feasibility of reconvening the Conference later in 1993.

On 9 August,[57] the United States indicated that it looked favourably on the Conference on Disarmament as the forum for negotiating a comprehensive test-ban treaty. Global support for such a treaty would be more difficult to secure if the Conference—the recognized multilateral arms-control negotiating body—were excluded. The United States held that the Amendment Conference would not be the most effective forum in which to achieve a comprehensive test-ban treaty, because China and France were not parties to the partial test-ban Treaty and because of the risk of opening the Treaty for other amendments. At some point there might be other helpful steps the parties to the Treaty could take to move the international community to join a comprehensive test-ban treaty.

At the special meeting of the States parties to the partial test-ban Treaty held on 10 August,[58] there was consensus that the work on a comprehensive test ban in the different forums, and especially the Amendment Conference and the Conference on Disarmament, should be mutually supportive and complementary. There was also broad agreement that the President of the Amendment Conference should continue his consultations with the States parties as well as with States not parties to the Treaty and should hold another special meeting early in 1994 in order to review developments, assess the situation and examine the feasibility of resuming the Amendment Conference's work later that year.

GENERAL ASSEMBLY ACTION

On 16 December, the General Assembly, on the recommendation of the First Committee, adopted **resolution 48/69** by recorded vote.

Amendment of the Treaty Banning Nuclear Weapon Tests in the Atmosphere, in Outer Space and under Water

The General Assembly,

Recalling its resolutions 44/106 of 15 December 1989,

45/50 of 4 December 1990, 46/28 of 6 December 1991 and 47/46 of 9 December 1992,

Reiterating its conviction that a comprehensive nuclear-test-ban treaty is the highest-priority measure for the cessation of the nuclear-arms race and for the achievement of the objective of nuclear disarmament,

Recalling the central role of the United Nations in the field of nuclear disarmament and in particular in the cessation of all nuclear-test explosions, as well as the persistent efforts of non-governmental organizations in the achievement of a comprehensive nuclear-test-ban treaty,

Conscious of the growing environmental concerns throughout the world and of the past and potential negative effects of nuclear testing on the environment,

Recalling its resolution 1910(XVIII) of 27 November 1963, in which it noted with approval the Treaty Banning Nuclear Weapon Tests in the Atmosphere, in Outer Space and under Water, signed on 5 August 1963, and requested the Conference of the Eighteen-Nation Committee on Disarmament[a] to continue with a sense of urgency its negotiations to achieve the objectives set forth in the preamble to the Treaty,

Recalling also that more than one third of the parties to the Treaty requested the depositary Governments to convene a conference to consider an amendment that would convert the Treaty into a comprehensive test-ban treaty,

Recalling further that a substantive session of the Amendment Conference of the States Parties to the Treaty Banning Nuclear Weapon Tests in the Atmosphere, in Outer Space and under Water was held in New York from 7 to 18 January 1991,

Reiterating its conviction that the Amendment Conference will facilitate the attainment of the objectives set forth in the Treaty and thus serve to strengthen it,

Noting with satisfaction the unilateral nuclear-test moratoria announced by several nuclear-weapon States,

Welcoming the decision of the Conference on Disarmament to give its Ad Hoc Committee on a Nuclear Test Ban a mandate to negotiate a comprehensive test ban,

Recalling its recommendation that arrangements be made to ensure that intensive efforts continue, under the auspices of the Amendment Conference, until a comprehensive nuclear-test-ban treaty is achieved, and its call that all parties participate in, and contribute to the success of, the Amendment Conference,

Recalling also the decision adopted by the Amendment Conference to the effect that, since further work needed to be undertaken on certain aspects of a comprehensive test-ban treaty, especially those with regard to verification of compliance and possible sanctions against non-compliance, the President of the Conference should conduct consultations with a view to achieving progress on those issues and to resuming the work of the Conference at an appropriate time,

Welcoming also the ongoing consultations being conducted by the President of the Amendment Conference,

1. *Takes note* of the concluding statement made by the President of the Amendment Conference of the States Parties to the Treaty Banning Nuclear Weapon Tests in the Atmosphere, in Outer Space and under Water at the special meeting of the States parties held on 10 August 1993, in which broad agreement was found for:

---

[a]Redesignated the Conference on Disarmament as from 7 February 1984.

(a) Pursuing work for a comprehensive test ban in the Amendment Conference and the Conference on Disarmament in a mutually supportive and mutually complementary manner;

(b) Holding another special meeting early in 1994 to review developments and assess the situation regarding a comprehensive test ban and to examine the feasibility of resuming the work of the Amendment Conference later that year;

(c) Promoting universality of a comprehensive test ban by having the President of the Amendment Conference liaise closely with the Conference on Disarmament and the five nuclear-weapon States;

2. *Recommends* that arrangements be made to ensure the fullest possible participation of non-governmental organizations in the Amendment Conference;

3. *Reiterates its conviction* that, pending the conclusion of a comprehensive nuclear-test-ban treaty, the nuclear-weapon States should suspend all nuclear-test explosions through an agreed moratorium or unilateral moratoria;

4. *Decides* to include in the provisional agenda of its forty-ninth session the item entitled "Amendment of the Treaty Banning Nuclear Weapon Tests in the Atmosphere, in Outer Space and under Water".

General Assembly resolution 48/69

16 December 1993   Meeting 81   118-3-45 (recorded vote)

Approved by First Committee (A/48/670) by recorded vote (99-3-40), 16 November (meeting 27); 26-nation draft (A/C.1/48/L.9); agenda item 65.
Sponsors: Bolivia, Brunei Darussalam, Chile, Colombia, Costa Rica, Ecuador, Gabon, India, Indonesia, Iran, Kazakhstan, Malaysia, Mexico, Mongolia, Nepal, Nigeria, Peru, Philippines, Rwanda, Senegal, Singapore, Sri Lanka, Sudan, Thailand, United Republic of Tanzania, Venezuela.
Meeting numbers. GA 48th session: 1st Committee 3-14, 21, 27; plenary 81.

Recorded vote in Assembly as follows:

In favour: Afghanistan, Algeria, Angola, Antigua and Barbuda, Azerbaijan, Bahamas, Bahrain, Bangladesh, Barbados, Belarus, Belize, Benin, Bhutan, Bolivia, Botswana, Brazil, Brunei Darussalam, Burkina Faso, Burundi, Cambodia, Cameroon, Cape Verde, Central African Republic, Chad, Chile, Colombia, Comoros, Congo, Costa Rica, Côte d'Ivoire, Cuba, Cyprus, Democratic People's Republic of Korea, Djibouti, Dominica, Dominican Republic, Ecuador, Egypt, Ethiopia, Fiji, Gabon, Gambia, Ghana, Grenada, Guatemala, Guinea, Guinea-Bissau, Guyana, Haiti, Honduras, India, Indonesia, Iran, Iraq, Jamaica, Jordan, Kazakhstan, Kenya, Kuwait, Kyrgyzstan, Lao People's Democratic Republic, Lebanon, Lesotho, Libyan Arab Jamahiriya, Madagascar, Malawi, Malaysia, Maldives, Mali, Mauritania, Mauritius, Mexico, Mongolia, Morocco, Mozambique, Myanmar, Namibia, Nepal, Nicaragua, Niger, Nigeria, Oman, Pakistan, Panama, Papua New Guinea, Paraguay, Peru, Philippines, Qatar, Rwanda, Saint Lucia, Saint Vincent and the Grenadines, Samoa, Saudi Arabia, Seychelles, Sierra Leone, Singapore, Solomon Islands, Sri Lanka, Sudan, Suriname, Swaziland, Syrian Arab Republic, Thailand, the former Yugoslav Republic of Macedonia, Togo, Trinidad and Tobago, Tunisia, Uganda, Ukraine, United Arab Emirates, United Republic of Tanzania, Uruguay, Venezuela, Viet Nam, Yemen, Zambia, Zimbabwe.

Against: Israel, United Kingdom, United States.

Abstaining: Albania, Andorra, Argentina, Armenia, Australia, Austria, Belgium, Bulgaria, Canada, Croatia, Czech Republic, Denmark, Estonia, Finland, Georgia, Germany, Greece, Hungary, Iceland, Ireland, Italy, Japan, Latvia, Liechtenstein, Lithuania, Luxembourg, Malta, Marshall Islands, Micronesia, Netherlands, New Zealand, Norway, Poland, Portugal, Republic of Korea, Republic of Moldova, Romania, Russian Federation, Senegal, Slovakia, Slovenia, Spain, Sweden, Tajikistan, Turkey.

Issues related to START

A major development in the nuclear field in 1993 was the signing, on 3 January, of the Treaty on Further Reduction and Limitation of Strategic Offensive Arms (START II) by President George Bush of the United States and President Boris Yeltsin of the Russian Federation.[59]

The entry into force of START II was conditional upon the entry into force of the 1991 START I Treaty[60] and the 1992 Protocol thereto, known as the Lisbon Protocol,[61] under which Belarus, Kazakhstan, the Russian Federation and Ukraine assumed the obligations of the former USSR under the Treaty.

In connection with START I, an agreement was signed on 3 September 1993 between the Russian Federation and Ukraine concerning the dismantling and destruction of nuclear weapons deployed in Ukraine.[62] One article of that agreement provided for the recycling of nuclear warheads and attached to the agreement was a statement of basic principles for the recycling of nuclear warheads from strategic nuclear forces deployed in Ukraine.

By the end of the year, all of the States concerned had ratified START I and the Lisbon Protocol—Kazakhstan, the Russian Federation and the United States in 1992,[49] Belarus on 4 February 1993[63] and Ukraine, by a parliamentary resolution, on 18 November.[64] Owing to the late date of Ukraine's ratification and to a number of reservations that accompanied it, no further action was taken on START II during 1993. On 25 November,[65] the Russian Federation stated that it considered that Ukraine's resolution and the reservations contained therein subverted the objectives of START I. Efforts to address Ukraine's reservations continued during December.

GENERAL ASSEMBLY ACTION

On 16 December, the General Assembly, on the recommendation of the First Committee, adopted **resolution 48/75 B** without vote.

Bilateral nuclear-arms negotiations and nuclear disarmament

The General Assembly,

Recalling its previous relevant resolutions,

Recognizing the fundamental changes that have taken place with respect to international security, which have permitted agreements on deep reductions in the nuclear armaments of the States possessing the largest inventories of such weapons,

Mindful that it is the responsibility and obligation of all States to contribute to the process of the relaxation of international tension and to the strengthening of international peace and security,

Stressing the importance of strengthening international peace and security through disarmament,

Emphasizing that nuclear disarmament remains one of the principal tasks of our times,

Stressing also that it is the responsibility of all States to adopt and implement measures towards the attainment of general and complete disarmament under effective international control,

Appreciating a number of positive developments in the field of nuclear disarmament, in particular the treaty that was concluded on 8 December 1987 between the former Union of Soviet Socialist Republics and the

United States of America on the elimination of their intermediate-range and shorter-range missiles, and the treaties on the reduction and limitation of strategic offensive arms,

Noting that there are still significant nuclear arsenals and that the primary responsibility for nuclear disarmament, with the objective of the elimination of nuclear weapons, rests with the nuclear-weapon States, in particular those which possess the largest stockpiles,

Welcoming the steps that have already been taken by those States to begin the process of reducing the number of nuclear weapons and removing such weapons from a deployed status,

Noting also the new climate of relations between the United States of America and the States of the former Soviet Union, which permits them to intensify their cooperative efforts to ensure the safety, security and environmentally sound destruction of nuclear weapons,

Urging the further intensification of such efforts to accelerate the implementation of agreements and unilateral decisions relating to nuclear-arms reduction,

Welcoming also the reductions made by other nuclear-weapon States in some of their nuclear-weapon programmes, and encouraging all nuclear-weapon States to consider appropriate measures relating to nuclear disarmament,

Affirming that bilateral and multilateral negotiations on nuclear disarmament should facilitate and complement each other,

1. *Welcomes* the actions taken towards the ratification of the Treaty on the Reduction and Limitation of Strategic Offensive Arms signed in Moscow on 31 July 1991 by the former Union of Soviet Socialist Republics and the United States of America and the protocol to that Treaty signed at Lisbon on 23 May 1992 by the four parties thereto, and urges the parties to take the necessary steps to ensure its entry into force at the earliest possible date;

2. *Also welcomes* the signing of the Treaty between the Russian Federation and the United States of America on the Further Reduction and Limitation of Strategic Offensive Arms, in Moscow on 3 January 1993, and urges the parties to take the steps necessary to bring that Treaty into force at the earliest possible date;

3. *Expresses its satisfaction* at the continuing implementation of the treaty between the former Union of Soviet Socialist Republics and the United States of America on the elimination of their intermediate-range and shorter-range missiles, in particular at the completion by the parties of the destruction of all their declared missiles subject to elimination under the treaty;

4. *Encourages* the United States of America, the Russian Federation, Belarus, Kazakhstan and Ukraine to continue their cooperative efforts aimed at eliminating nuclear weapons and strategic offensive arms on the basis of existing agreements, and welcomes the contributions that other States are making to such cooperation as well;

5. *Further encourages and supports* the Russian Federation and the United States of America in their efforts to reduce their nuclear armaments and to continue to give those efforts the highest priority in order to contribute to the objective of the elimination of nuclear weapons;

6. *Invites* the Russian Federation and the United States of America to keep other States Members of the United Nations duly informed of progress in their discussions and in the implementation of their strategic offensive arms agreements and unilateral decisions.

General Assembly resolution 48/75 B

16 December 1993   Meeting 81   Adopted without vote

Approved by First Committee (A/48/676) without vote, 16 November (meeting 27); draft by Australia, Bolivia, Finland, France, Honduras, Indonesia (for Non-Aligned Movement), Italy, Japan, Marshall Islands, New Zealand, Norway, Paraguay, Portugal, Russian Federation, Sweden, the former Yugoslav Republic of Macedonia, United Kingdom and United States (A/C.1/48/L.8/Rev.2); agenda item 71.
Meeting numbers. GA 48th session: 1st Committee 3-14, 23, 27; plenary 81.

Prohibition of the production of fissile material

Another major development in the nuclear field was the adoption by the General Assembly of a resolution recommending the negotiation of a treaty banning the production of fissile material for nuclear weapons or other nuclear explosive devices.

GENERAL ASSEMBLY ACTION

On 16 December, the General Assembly, on the recommendation of the First Committee, adopted **resolution 48/75 L** without vote.

Prohibition of the production of fissile material for nuclear weapons or other nuclear explosive devices
The General Assembly,

Welcoming the significant progress in reducing nuclear-weapon arsenals as evidenced by the substantive bilateral agreements between the Russian Federation and the United States of America and their respective unilateral undertakings regarding the disposition of fissile material,

Welcoming also the initiative of the United States of America concerning a multilateral, internationally and effectively verifiable treaty on the prohibition of the production of fissile material for nuclear weapons or other nuclear explosive devices,

Welcoming further the decision taken by the Conference on Disarmament on 10 August 1993 to give its Ad Hoc Committee on a Nuclear Test Ban a mandate to negotiate a universal and internationally and effectively verifiable comprehensive nuclear test-ban treaty, and fully endorsing the contents of that decision,

Convinced that a non-discriminatory, multilateral and internationally and effectively verifiable treaty banning the production of fissile material for nuclear weapons or other nuclear explosive devices would be a significant contribution to nuclear non-proliferation in all its aspects,

1. *Recommends* the negotiation in the most appropriate international forum of a non-discriminatory, multilateral and internationally and effectively verifiable treaty banning the production of fissile material for nuclear weapons or other nuclear explosive devices;

2. *Requests* the International Atomic Energy Agency to provide assistance for examination of verification arrangements for such a treaty as required;

3. *Calls upon* all States to demonstrate their commitment to the objectives of a non-discriminatory, multilateral and internationally and effectively verifiable treaty banning the production of fissile material for nuclear weapons or other nuclear explosive devices;

4. *Decides* to include in the provisional agenda of its forty-ninth session an item entitled ''Prohibition of the production of fissile material for nuclear weapons or other nuclear explosive devices''.

General Assembly resolution 48/75 L

16 December 1993   Meeting 81   Adopted without vote

Approved by First Committee (A/48/676) without vote, 16 November (meeting 27); 30-nation draft (A/C.1/48/L.44/Rev.1); agenda item 71 *(c)*.

Sponsors: Australia, Austria, Belarus, Belgium, Bulgaria, Cameroon, Canada, Denmark, Finland, Germany, Greece, Hungary, India, Ireland, Italy, Japan, Latvia, Luxembourg, Netherlands, New Zealand, Norway, Panama, Philippines, Poland, Portugal, Spain, Sweden, the former Yugoslav Republic of Macedonia, United States, Uruguay.

Meeting numbers. GA 48th session: 1st Committee 3-14, 24, 27; plenary 81.

Nuclear-weapon-free zones and zones of peace

Africa

Report of the Secretary-General. As requested by the General Assembly in 1992,[66] the Secretary-General submitted in October 1993[67] a report on the implementation of the Declaration on the Denuclearization of Africa, adopted by the Organization of African Unity (OAU) in 1964.[68] The report contained the text of a resolution on the subject adopted by the IAEA General Conference on 1 October and a report by the IAEA Director General on the Agency's verification activities in South Africa, in which he stated that in April an IAEA team in South Africa had found that the dismantling and destruction of weapons components and the destruction of technical documentation were nearly complete. Further, the team found no indication that there remained any sensitive components of the nuclear-weapons programme that had not been either rendered useless or converted to commercial non-nuclear applications or peaceful nuclear usage.

Expert group meeting. In response to a 1992 General Assembly request,[66] the Secretary-General, in October 1993,[69] submitted the report of the Third Meeting of the Group of Experts to Draw up a Draft Treaty or Convention on the Denuclearization of Africa (Harare, Zimbabwe, 5-8 April), organized by the United Nations in cooperation with OAU. Attached to the Group's report was the draft text of an African nuclear-weapon-free zone treaty, together with four annexes and three protocols. The Group requested the Secretary-General to convene a further meeting in order to finalize the drafting of a treaty.

GENERAL ASSEMBLY ACTION

On 16 December, the General Assembly, on the recommendation of the First Committee, adopted **resolution 48/86** without vote.

Establishment of a nuclear-weapon-free zone in Africa

The General Assembly,

Bearing in mind the Declaration on the Denuclearization of Africa adopted by the Assembly of Heads of State and Government of the Organization of African Unity

at its first ordinary session, held at Cairo in July 1964, in which they solemnly declare their readiness to undertake, through an international agreement to be concluded under United Nations auspices, not to manufacture or acquire control of atomic weapons,

Recalling its resolutions 1652(XVI) of 24 November 1961 and 47/76 of 15 December 1992, its earliest and latest on the subject, as well as all its previous resolutions on the implementation of the Declaration on the Denuclearization of Africa,

Desirous of ensuring the implementation of the provisions of paragraphs 60 to 63 of the Final Document of the Tenth Special Session of the General Assembly,

Calling upon all States to consider and respect the continent of Africa and its surrounding areas as a nuclear-weapon-free zone,

Bearing in mind the provisions of resolutions CM/Res.1342(LIV) and CM/Res.1395(LVI)Rev.1 on the implementation of the Declaration on the Denuclearization of Africa adopted by the Council of Ministers of the Organization of African Unity at its fifty-fourth and fifty-sixth ordinary sessions, held at Abuja in May and June 1991 and at Dakar in June 1992, respectively,

Noting that the Government of South Africa acceded to the Treaty on the Non-Proliferation of Nuclear Weapons on 10 July 1991 and that it concluded a safeguards agreement with the International Atomic Energy Agency, which entered into force on 16 September 1991, and committed itself to early and full implementation of that agreement,

Noting also the announcement by South Africa that it had voluntarily abandoned its nuclear deterrent capability before accession to the Treaty on the Non-Proliferation of Nuclear Weapons, and of its standing invitation to the Agency to inspect past nuclear-weapon-programme activities and facilities and to verify its disclosure,

Recalling resolution GC(XXXVII)/RES/625 on an African nuclear-weapon-free zone, adopted on 1 October 1993 by the General Conference of the Agency,

Stressing that the full disclosure of South Africa's nuclear installations and materials is essential to the peace and security of the region and to the success of the commendable efforts exerted by the African States towards the establishment of a nuclear-weapon-free zone in Africa,

Welcoming the progress made at the Third Meeting of the Group of Experts to Draw up a Draft Treaty or Convention on the Denuclearization of Africa, which was organized by the United Nations in cooperation with the Organization of African Unity and held at Harare from 5 to 8 April 1993,

1. *Takes note* of the report of the Third Meeting of the Group of Experts to Draw up a Draft Treaty or Convention on the Denuclearization of Africa;

2. *Reaffirms* that the implementation of the Declaration on the Denuclearization of Africa adopted by the Assembly of Heads of State and Government of the Organization of African Unity would be an important measure to prevent the proliferation of nuclear weapons and to promote international peace and security;

3. *Strongly renews its call* upon all States to consider and respect the continent of Africa and its surrounding areas as a nuclear-weapon-free zone;

4. *Takes note* of the report of the Director General of the International Atomic Energy Agency on the Agency's verification activities in South Africa;

5. *Calls upon* South Africa to continue to comply fully with the implementation of its safeguards agreement with the International Atomic Energy Agency;

6. *Commends* the Secretary-General for the diligence with which he has rendered effective assistance to the Organization of African Unity in organizing the meetings of the above-mentioned Group of Experts;

7. *Requests* the Secretary-General, in consultation with the Organization of African Unity, to take appropriate action to enable the Group of Experts designated by the United Nations in cooperation with the Organization of African Unity to meet during 1994 at Windhoek and Addis Ababa, in order to finalize the drafting of a treaty on a nuclear-weapon-free zone in Africa, and to submit the text of the treaty to the General Assembly at its forty-ninth session under an agenda item entitled ''Final text of a treaty on an African nuclear-weapon-free zone'';

8. *Also requests* the Secretary-General to report to the General Assembly at its forty-ninth session on the progress made by the Director General of the International Atomic Energy Agency in ensuring the full implementation of the safeguards agreement with South Africa.

General Assembly resolution 48/86

16 December 1993   Meeting 81   Adopted without vote

Approved by First Committee (A/48/687) without vote, 19 November (meeting 30); draft by Algeria, for African Group (A/C.1/48/L.19); agenda item 82.
Financial implications. 5th Committee, A/48/760; S-G, A/C.1/48/L.53, A/C.5/48/33.
Meeting numbers. GA 48th session: 1st Committee 3-14, 21, 30; 5th Committee 38; plenary 81.

Latin America

At the regional level, the process of consolidation of the regime established by the 1967 Treaty for the Prohibition of Nuclear Weapons in Latin America and the Caribbean (Treaty of Tlatelolco) through amendments adopted in 1992[70] continued. Mexico was the first State to deposit its instrument of ratification. In 1993, Dominica became party to the Treaty, bringing the total number of parties to 33 at 31 December.

GENERAL ASSEMBLY ACTION

On 16 December, the General Assembly, on the recommendation of the First Committee, adopted **resolution 48/85** without vote.

Consolidation of the regime established by the Treaty for the Prohibition of Nuclear Weapons in Latin America and the Caribbean (Treaty of Tlatelolco)

The General Assembly,

Recalling that in its resolution 1911(XVIII) of 27 November 1963 it expressed the hope that the States of Latin America would take appropriate measures to conclude a treaty that would prohibit nuclear weapons in Latin America,

Recalling also that in the same resolution it voiced its confidence that, once such a treaty was concluded, all States, and particularly the nuclear-weapon States, would lend it their full cooperation for the effective realization of its peaceful aims,

Considering that in its resolution 2028(XX) of 19 November 1965 it established the principle of an acceptable balance of mutual responsibilities and obligations between nuclear-weapon States and those which do not possess such weapons,

Recalling that the Treaty for the Prohibition of Nuclear Weapons in Latin America and the Caribbean (Treaty of Tlatelolco) was opened for signature at Mexico City on 14 February 1967,

Recalling also that in its preamble the Treaty of Tlatelolco states that military denuclearized zones are not an end in themselves but rather a means for achieving general and complete disarmament at a later stage,

Recalling further that in its resolution 2286(XXII) of 5 December 1967 it welcomed with special satisfaction the Treaty of Tlatelolco as an event of historic significance in the efforts to prevent the proliferation of nuclear weapons and to promote international peace and security,

Bearing in mind that the Treaty of Tlatelolco is open for signature to all the sovereign States of Latin America and the Caribbean and that it contains two additional protocols that are open for signature, respectively, to the States that *de jure* or de facto are internationally responsible for territories located within the zone of application of the Treaty and to the nuclear-weapon States,

Bearing in mind also that, with the adherence in 1993 of Dominica, the Treaty of Tlatelolco is in force for twenty-five sovereign States of the region,

Recalling that since 1992 Additional Protocol I has been in force for all the States that *de jure* or de facto are internationally responsible for territories located within the zone of application of the Treaty,

Recalling also that since 1974 Additional Protocol II has been in force for the five nuclear-weapon States,

Mindful that international conditions are more propitious for the consolidation of the regime established by the Treaty of Tlatelolco,

Recalling further that in 1992 the General Conference of the Agency for the Prohibition of Nuclear Weapons in Latin America and the Caribbean approved and opened for signature a set of amendments to the Treaty of Tlatelolco, submitted jointly by Argentina, Brazil, Chile and Mexico, with the aim of enabling the full entry into force of that instrument,

Noting with satisfaction the holding of the thirteenth regular session of the General Conference at Mexico City on 27 and 28 May 1993,

Noting that the Government of Cuba has declared that, in pursuit of regional unity, it would be ready to sign the Treaty of Tlatelolco once all the States of the region have assumed the undertakings of that Treaty,

Taking into account the declaration presented by the delegation of Brazil at the aforementioned session of the General Conference in which it was stated that the full entry into force of the Treaty of Tlatelolco for Argentina, Brazil and Chile was imminent,

Also noting with satisfaction that on 1 September 1993 the Government of Mexico made that country the first State to deposit its instrument of ratification of the amendments to articles 14, 15, 16, 19 and 20 of the Treaty of Tlatelolco approved by the General Conference on 26 August 1992 in its resolution 290(VII),

1. *Welcomes* the concrete steps taken by several countries of the region during the past year for the consolidation of the regime of military denuclearization estab-

lished by the Treaty for the Prohibition of Nuclear Weapons in Latin America and the Caribbean (Treaty of Tlatelolco);

2. *Notes with satisfaction* the joint declaration by the Governments of Argentina, Brazil and Chile to the effect that the entry into force of the Treaty of Tlatelolco for those countries is imminent;

3. *Urges* the countries of the region that have not yet done so to deposit their instruments of ratification of the amendments to the Treaty of Tlatelolco approved by the General Conference of the Agency on the Prohibition of Nuclear Weapons in Latin America and the Caribbean in its resolutions 267(E-V) of 3 July 1990, 268(XII) of 10 May 1991 and 290(VII) of 26 August 1992;

4. *Decides* to include in the provisional agenda of its forty-ninth session the item entitled "Consolidation of the regime established by the Treaty for the Prohibition of Nuclear Weapons in Latin America and the Caribbean (Treaty of Tlatelolco)".

General Assembly resolution 48/85

16 December 1993   Meeting 81   Adopted without vote

Approved by First Committee (A/48/686) without vote, 12 November (meeting 25); 26-nation draft (A/C.1/48/L.21); agenda item 81.

Sponsors: Argentina, Bahamas, Barbados, Bolivia, Brazil, Chile, Colombia, Costa Rica, Dominica, Dominican Republic, Ecuador, El Salvador, Guatemala, Haiti, Honduras, Jamaica, Mexico, Nicaragua, Panama, Paraguay, Peru, Philippines, Suriname, Trinidad and Tobago, Uruguay, Venezuela.

Meeting numbers. GA 48th session: 1st Committee 3-14, 23, 25; plenary 81.

Middle East

As requested by the General Assembly in 1992,[71] the Secretary-General submitted in October 1993 a report[72] describing major international developments bearing on the establishment of a nuclear-weapon-free zone in the Middle East and the attitudes of States in the region on such a zone and related questions. He noted that, as of May, the United Nations was invited to participate in the work of the Middle East Multilateral Working Group on Arms Control and Regional Security and that the prospects for establishing a nuclear-weapon-free zone in the Middle East were somewhat more promising than a few years earlier.

GENERAL ASSEMBLY ACTION

On 16 December, the General Assembly, on the recommendation of the First Committee, adopted **resolution 48/71** without vote.

Establishment of a nuclear-weapon-free zone in the region of the Middle East

The General Assembly,

Recalling its resolutions 3263(XXIX) of 9 December 1974, 3474(XXX) of 11 December 1975, 31/71 of 10 December 1976, 32/82 of 12 December 1977, 33/64 of 14 December 1978, 34/77 of 11 December 1979, 35/147 of 12 December 1980, 36/87 of 9 December 1981, 37/75 of 9 December 1982, 38/64 of 15 December 1983, 39/54 of 12 December 1984, 40/82 of 12 December 1985, 41/48 of 3 December 1986, 42/28 of 30 November 1987, 43/65 of 7 December 1988, 44/108 of 15 December 1989, 45/52 of 4 December 1990, 46/30 of 6 December 1991 and 47/48 of 9 December 1992 on the establishment of a nuclear-weapon-free zone in the region of the Middle East,

Recalling also the recommendations for the establishment of such a zone in the Middle East consistent with paragraphs 60 to 63, and in particular paragraph 63 *(d)*, of the Final Document of the Tenth Special Session of the General Assembly,

Emphasizing the basic provisions of the above-mentioned resolutions, which call upon all parties directly concerned to consider taking the practical and urgent steps required for the implementation of the proposal to establish a nuclear-weapon-free zone in the region of the Middle East and, pending and during the establishment of such a zone, to declare solemnly that they will refrain, on a reciprocal basis, from producing, acquiring or in any other way possessing nuclear weapons and nuclear explosive devices and from permitting the stationing of nuclear weapons on their territory by any third party, to agree to place all their nuclear facilities under International Atomic Energy Agency safeguards and to declare their support for the establishment of the zone and to deposit such declarations with the Security Council for consideration, as appropriate,

Reaffirming the inalienable right of all States to acquire and develop nuclear energy for peaceful purposes,

Emphasizing also the need for appropriate measures on the question of the prohibition of military attacks on nuclear facilities,

Bearing in mind the consensus reached by the General Assembly at its thirty-fifth session that the establishment of a nuclear-weapon-free zone in the region of the Middle East would greatly enhance international peace and security,

Desirous of building on that consensus so that substantial progress can be made towards establishing a nuclear-weapon-free zone in the region of the Middle East,

Welcoming all initiatives leading to general and complete disarmament, including in the region of the Middle East, and in particular on the establishment therein of a zone free of weapons of mass destruction, including nuclear weapons,

Emphasizing the essential role of the United Nations in the establishment of a nuclear-weapon-free zone in the region of the Middle East,

Having examined the report of the Secretary-General on the implementation of resolution 47/48,

1. *Urges* all parties directly concerned seriously to consider taking the practical and urgent steps required for the implementation of the proposal to establish a nuclear-weapon-free zone in the region of the Middle East in accordance with the relevant resolutions of the General Assembly, and, as a means of promoting this objective, invites the countries concerned to adhere to the Treaty on the Non-Proliferation of Nuclear Weapons;

2. *Calls upon* all countries of the region that have not done so, pending the establishment of the zone, to agree to place all their nuclear activities under International Atomic Energy Agency safeguards;

3. *Takes note* of resolution GC(XXXVII)/RES/627, adopted on 1 October 1993 by the General Conference of the International Atomic Energy Agency at its thirty-seventh regular session, concerning the application of Agency safeguards in the Middle East;

4. *Invites* all countries of the region, pending the establishment of a nuclear-weapon-free zone in the region of the Middle East, to declare their support for establishing such a zone, consistent with paragraph 63 *(d)* of the Final Document of the Tenth Special Session of the General Assembly, and to deposit those declarations with the Security Council;

5. *Also invites* those countries, pending the establishment of the zone, not to develop, produce, test or otherwise acquire nuclear weapons or permit the stationing on their territories, or territories under their control, of nuclear weapons or nuclear explosive devices;

6. *Invites* the nuclear-weapon States and all other States to render their assistance in the establishment of the zone and at the same time to refrain from any action that runs counter to both the letter and the spirit of the present resolution;

7. *Takes note* of the report of the Secretary-General;

8. *Invites* all parties to consider the appropriate means that may contribute towards the goal of general and complete disarmament and the establishment of a zone free of weapons of mass destruction in the region of the Middle East;

9. *Requests* the Secretary-General to continue to pursue consultations with the States of the region and other concerned States, in accordance with paragraph 7 of resolution 46/30 and taking into account the evolving situation in the region, and to seek from those States their views on the measures outlined in chapters III and IV of the study annexed to his report or other relevant measures, in order to move towards the establishment of a nuclear-weapon-free zone in the region of the Middle East;

10. *Also requests* the Secretary-General to submit to the General Assembly at its forty-ninth session a report on the implementation of the present resolution;

11. *Decides* to include in the provisional agenda of its forty-ninth session the item entitled "Establishment of a nuclear-weapon-free zone in the region of the Middle East".

General Assembly resolution 48/71

16 December 1993   Meeting 81   Adopted without vote

Approved by First Committee (A/48/672) without vote, 15 November (meeting 26); 3-nation draft (A/C.1/48/L.35); agenda item 67.
Sponsors: Egypt, Honduras, Philippines.
Meeting numbers. GA 48th session: 1st Committee 3-14, 23, 26; plenary 81.

Israeli nuclear armament

In response to a 1992 General Assembly request,[73] the Secretary-General submitted in October 1993 a report[74] containing the text of a resolution adopted on 1 October 1993 by the IAEA General Conference on the application of IAEA safeguards in the Middle East.

GENERAL ASSEMBLY ACTION

On 16 December, the General Assembly, on the recommendation of the First Committee, adopted **resolution 48/78** by recorded vote.

Israeli nuclear armament

The General Assembly,

Bearing in mind relevant United Nations resolutions,
Taking note of relevant resolutions adopted by the General Conference of the International Atomic Energy

Agency, the latest of which is GC(XXXVII)/RES/627 of 1 October 1993,

Aware of the recent positive developments in the Middle East peace process,

1. *Calls upon* Israel to renounce possession of nuclear weapons and to accede to the Treaty on the Non-Proliferation of Nuclear Weapons;

2. *Calls upon* the States of the region to place all their nuclear facilities under International Atomic Energy Agency safeguards;

3. *Requests* the Secretary-General to report to the General Assembly on the implementation of the present resolution;

4. *Decides* to include in the provisional agenda of its forty-ninth session the item entitled "Israeli nuclear armament".

General Assembly resolution 48/78

16 December 1993   Meeting 81   53-45-65 (recorded vote)

Approved by First Committee (A/48/679) by recorded vote (55-39-47), 16 November (meeting 27); 18-nation draft (A/C.1/48/L.48); agenda item 74.
Sponsors: Bahrain, Djibouti, Egypt, Iraq, Jordan, Kuwait, Lebanon, Libyan Arab Jamahiriya, Malaysia, Mauritania, Morocco, Oman, Qatar, Saudi Arabia, Sudan, Tunisia, United Arab Emirates, Yemen.
Meeting numbers. GA 48th session: 1st Committee 3-14, 24, 27; plenary 81.

Recorded vote in Assembly as follows:

In favour: Afghanistan, Algeria, Azerbaijan, Bahrain, Bangladesh, Bhutan, Botswana, Brunei Darussalam, Burkina Faso, Chad, China, Colombia, Comoros, Cuba, Democratic People's Republic of Korea, Djibouti, Egypt, Guinea, Indonesia, Iran, Iraq, Jordan, Kuwait, Lebanon, Libyan Arab Jamahiriya, Madagascar, Malaysia, Maldives, Mali, Mauritania, Morocco, Mozambique, Namibia, Niger, Oman, Pakistan, Philippines, Qatar, Saudi Arabia, Senegal, Sierra Leone, Sri Lanka, Sudan, Syrian Arab Republic, Thailand, Tunisia, Uganda, United Arab Emirates, United Republic of Tanzania, Venezuela, Viet Nam, Yemen, Zimbabwe.

Against: Andorra, Armenia, Austria, Belgium, Bulgaria, Canada, Croatia, Czech Republic, Denmark, Estonia, Fiji, Finland, France, Georgia, Germany, Greece, Hungary, Iceland, Ireland, Israel, Italy, Japan, Kenya, Latvia, Liechtenstein, Lithuania, Luxembourg, Malta, Marshall Islands, Micronesia, Monaco, Netherlands, Norway, Poland, Portugal, Republic of Moldova, Romania, Samoa, Slovakia, Slovenia, Solomon Islands, Spain, Sweden, United Kingdom, United States.

Abstaining: Albania, Angola, Antigua and Barbuda, Argentina, Australia, Bahamas, Barbados, Belarus, Belize, Benin, Bolivia, Brazil, Cambodia, Cameroon, Central African Republic, Chile, Costa Rica, Côte d'Ivoire, Cyprus, Dominica, Dominican Republic, Ecuador, Ethiopia, Gabon, Gambia, Ghana, Grenada, Guatemala, Guyana, Haiti, Honduras, India, Jamaica, Kazakhstan, Kyrgyzstan, Lesotho, Malawi, Mauritius, Mexico, Mongolia, Myanmar, Nepal, New Zealand, Nicaragua, Nigeria, Panama, Papua New Guinea, Paraguay, Peru, Republic of Korea, Russian Federation, Rwanda, Saint Lucia, Saint Vincent and the Grenadines, Singapore, Suriname, Swaziland, Tajikistan, the former Yugoslav Republic of Macedonia, Togo, Trinidad and Tobago, Turkey, Ukraine, Uruguay, Zambia.

South Asia

Pursuant to a 1992 General Assembly request,[75] the Secretary-General submitted in July 1993 a report[76] summarizing the views of one Government (United Kingdom) on the establishment of a nuclear-weapon-free zone in South Asia.

GENERAL ASSEMBLY ACTION

On 16 December, the General Assembly, on the recommendation of the First Committee, adopted **resolution 48/72** by recorded vote.

Establishment of a nuclear-weapon-free zone in South Asia

The General Assembly,

Recalling its resolutions 3265 B (XXIX) of 9 December 1974, 3476 B (XXX) of 11 December 1975, 31/73 of 10 December 1976, 32/83 of 12 December 1977, 33/65 of 14 December 1978, 34/78 of 11 December 1979, 35/148 of 12 December 1980, 36/88 of 9 December 1981, 37/76 of 9 December 1982, 38/65 of 15 December 1983, 39/55 of 12 December 1984, 40/83 of 12 December 1985, 41/49 of 3 December 1986, 42/29 of 30 November 1987, 43/66 of 7 December 1988, 44/109 of 15 December 1989, 45/53 of 4 December 1990, 46/31 of 6 December 1991 and 47/49 of 9 December 1992 concerning the establishment of a nuclear-weapon-free zone in South Asia,

Reiterating its conviction that the establishment of nuclear-weapon-free zones in various regions of the world is one of the measures that can contribute effectively to the objectives of non-proliferation of nuclear weapons and general and complete disarmament,

Believing that the establishment of a nuclear-weapon-free zone in South Asia, as in other regions, will assist in the strengthening of the security of the States of the region against the use or threat of use of nuclear weapons,

Taking note with appreciation of the declarations issued at the highest level by the Governments of South Asian States that are developing their peaceful nuclear programmes, reaffirming their undertaking not to acquire or manufacture nuclear weapons and to devote their nuclear programmes exclusively to the economic and social advancement of their peoples,

Welcoming the recent proposal for the conclusion of a bilateral or regional nuclear-test-ban agreement in South Asia,

Taking note of the proposal to convene, under the auspices of the United Nations, a conference on nuclear non-proliferation in South Asia as soon as possible, with the participation of the regional and other concerned States,

Taking note also of the proposal to hold consultations among five nations with a view to ensuring nuclear non-proliferation in the region,

Considering that the eventual participation of other States, as appropriate, in this process could be useful,

Bearing in mind the provisions of paragraphs 60 to 63 of the Final Document of the Tenth Special Session of the General Assembly regarding the establishment of nuclear-weapon-free zones, including in the region of South Asia,

Taking note of the report of the Secretary-General,

1. *Reaffirms its endorsement*, in principle, of the concept of a nuclear-weapon-free zone in South Asia;

2. *Urges once again* the States of South Asia to continue to make all possible efforts to establish a nuclear-weapon-free zone in South Asia and to refrain, in the meantime, from any action contrary to that objective;

3. *Welcomes* the support of all the five nuclear-weapon States for this proposal, and calls upon them to extend the necessary cooperation in the efforts to establish a nuclear-weapon-free zone in South Asia;

4. *Requests* the Secretary-General to communicate with the States of the region and other concerned States in order to ascertain their views on the issue and to promote consultations among them with a view to exploring the best possibilities of furthering the efforts for the establishment of a nuclear-weapon-free zone in South Asia;

5. *Also requests* the Secretary-General to report on the subject to the General Assembly at its forty-ninth session;

6. *Decides* to include in the provisional agenda of its forty-ninth session the item entitled ''Establishment of a nuclear-weapon-free zone in South Asia''.

General Assembly resolution 48/72
16 December 1993   Meeting 81   153-3-12 (recorded vote)

Approved by First Committee (A/48/673) by recorded vote (125-3-12), 12 November (meeting 25); 3-nation draft (A/C.1/48/L.39); agenda item 68.
Sponsors: Bangladesh, Pakistan, Philippines.
Meeting numbers. GA 48th session: 1st Committee 3-14, 25; plenary 81.

Recorded vote in Assembly as follows:

In favour: Afghanistan, Albania, Andorra, Angola, Antigua and Barbuda, Argentina, Armenia, Australia, Austria, Azerbaijan, Bahamas, Bahrain, Bangladesh, Barbados, Belarus, Belgium, Belize, Benin, Bolivia, Botswana, Brunei Darussalam, Bulgaria, Burkina Faso, Burundi, Cambodia, Cameroon, Canada, Cape Verde, Central African Republic, Chad, Chile, China, Colombia, Comoros, Congo, Costa Rica, Côte d'Ivoire, Croatia, Czech Republic, Denmark, Djibouti, Dominica, Dominican Republic, Ecuador, Egypt, Estonia, Fiji, Finland, France, Gabon, Gambia, Georgia, Germany, Ghana, Greece, Grenada, Guatemala, Guinea, Guinea-Bissau, Guyana, Haiti, Honduras, Hungary, Iceland, Iran, Iraq, Ireland, Israel, Italy, Jamaica, Japan, Jordan, Kazakhstan, Kenya, Kuwait, Kyrgyzstan, Latvia, Lebanon, Lesotho, Libyan Arab Jamahiriya, Liechtenstein, Lithuania, Luxembourg, Malawi, Malaysia, Maldives, Mali, Malta, Marshall Islands, Mauritania, Mexico, Micronesia, Monaco, Mongolia, Morocco, Mozambique, Namibia, Nepal, Netherlands, New Zealand, Nicaragua, Niger, Nigeria, Norway, Oman, Pakistan, Panama, Papua New Guinea, Paraguay, Peru, Philippines, Poland, Portugal, Qatar, Republic of Korea, Republic of Moldova, Romania, Russian Federation, Rwanda, Saint Lucia, Saint Vincent and the Grenadines, Samoa, Saudi Arabia, Senegal, Sierra Leone, Singapore, Slovakia, Slovenia, Solomon Islands, Spain, Sri Lanka, Sudan, Suriname, Swaziland, Sweden, Tajikistan, Thailand, the former Yugoslav Republic of Macedonia, Togo, Trinidad and Tobago, Tunisia, Turkey, Turkmenistan, Uganda, Ukraine, United Arab Emirates, United Kingdom, United Republic of Tanzania, United States, Uruguay, Venezuela, Zambia, Zimbabwe.
Against: Bhutan, India, Mauritius.
Abstaining: Algeria, Brazil, Cuba, Cyprus, Democratic People's Republic of Korea, Ethiopia, Indonesia, Lao People's Democratic Republic, Madagascar, Myanmar, Seychelles, Viet Nam.

Declaration of the Indian Ocean as a Zone of Peace

At its 1993 session (New York, 21 June–2 July),[77] the Ad Hoc Committee on the Indian Ocean considered new alternative approaches to achieving the goals contained in the 1971 Declaration of the Indian Ocean as a Zone of Peace.[78]

The Committee dealt mainly with the implementation of a 1992 General Assembly resolution[79] by which it was asked to consider new alternative approaches and to address the complex ramifications of the issues involved and differing perceptions on those issues, as well as its future role. The Chairman's summary of the discussion, annexed to the Committee's report, focused on: the changing international situation and its impact on the Indian Ocean as a zone of peace; ramifications of the issues involved and differing perceptions on those issues; new alternative approaches; and the future role of the Ad Hoc Committee.

The Committee recommended that it continue to consider new alternative approaches, building on the deliberations at its 1993 session, with a view to reaching early agreement to give new impetus to the process of strengthening cooperation and ensuring peace, security and stability in the Indian Ocean region. In that context, it recommended that the Assembly invite the views of

Member States, including views on the new alternative approaches discussed at its 1993 session.

On 16 December, the General Assembly, on the recommendation of the First Committee, adopted **resolution 48/82** by recorded vote.

Implementation of the Declaration of the Indian Ocean as a Zone of Peace

The General Assembly,

Recalling the Declaration of the Indian Ocean as a Zone of Peace, contained in its resolution 2832(XXVI) of 16 December 1971, and recalling also its resolution 47/59 of 9 December 1992 and other relevant resolutions,

Recalling also the report on the Meeting of the Littoral and Hinterland States of the Indian Ocean held in July 1979,

Recalling further paragraphs 15 and 16 of chapter III of the Final Document adopted by the Tenth Conference of Heads of State or Government of Non-Aligned Countries, held at Jakarta in September 1992,

Noting that great-Power rivalry is being replaced by a new and welcome phase of confidence, trust and cooperation, and that the improved international political environment following the end of the cold war has created favourable opportunities to renew comprehensive multilateral and regional efforts towards the realization of the goals of peace, security and stability in the Indian Ocean region,

Welcoming the positive developments in international political relations, which offer opportunities for enhancing peace, security and cooperation and which have been reflected in the work of the Ad Hoc Committee on the Indian Ocean,

Reaffirming the importance of the freedom of navigation in the high seas, including in the Indian Ocean, in accordance with the United Nations Convention on the Law of the Sea,

Convinced that the Ad Hoc Committee should continue its consideration of new alternative approaches,

Emphasizing the need for the permanent members of the Security Council and the major maritime users of the Indian Ocean to cooperate with and participate in the work of the Ad Hoc Committee, particularly at a time when the Committee is actively engaged in the task of developing new alternative approaches,

1. *Takes note* of the report of the Ad Hoc Committee on the Indian Ocean;

2. *Requests* the Ad Hoc Committee to continue consideration of new alternative approaches building upon its deliberations at the session held in 1993, with a view to reaching early agreement to give new impetus to the process of strengthening cooperation and ensuring peace, security and stability in the Indian Ocean region;

3. *Calls upon* the permanent members of the Security Council and the major maritime users of the Indian Ocean to participate in the work of the Ad Hoc Committee;

4. *Invites* Member States to submit to the Secretary-General, by 31 May 1994, their views on new alternative approaches, including those discussed at the 1993 session of the Ad Hoc Committee and contained in its report to the General Assembly;

5. *Requests* the Secretary-General to submit, by 30 June 1994, a report based on replies received from Member States;

6. *Requests* the Ad Hoc Committee to hold a session during 1994, of a duration of not more than five working days;

7. *Also requests* the Ad Hoc Committee to submit to the General Assembly at its forty-ninth session a comprehensive report on the implementation of the present resolution;

8. *Requests* the Secretary-General to continue to render all necessary assistance to the Ad Hoc Committee, including the provision of summary records;

9. *Decides* to include in the provisional agenda of its forty-ninth session the item entitled ''Implementation of the Declaration of the Indian Ocean as a Zone of Peace''.

General Assembly resolution 48/82

16 December 1993   Meeting 81   130-4-36 (recorded vote)

Approved by First Committee (A/48/683) by recorded vote (110-3-32), 16 November (meeting 27); draft by Panama, Philippines, and Sri Lanka (for Non-Aligned Movement) (A/C.1/48/L.15); agenda item 78.
Meeting numbers. GA 48th session: 1st Committee 3-14, 22, 27; plenary 81.

Recorded vote in Assembly as follows:

In favour: Afghanistan, Algeria, Angola, Antigua and Barbuda, Argentina, Armenia, Australia, Azerbaijan, Bahamas, Bahrain, Bangladesh, Barbados, Belarus, Belize, Benin, Bhutan, Bolivia, Botswana, Brazil, Brunei Darussalam, Burkina Faso, Burundi, Cambodia, Cameroon, Canada, Cape Verde, Central African Republic, Chad, Chile, China, Colombia, Comoros, Congo, Costa Rica, Côte d'Ivoire, Cuba, Cyprus, Democratic People's Republic of Korea, Djibouti, Dominica, Dominican Republic, Ecuador, Egypt, Ethiopia, Fiji, Gabon, Gambia, Ghana, Grenada, Guatemala, Guinea, Guinea-Bissau, Guyana, Haiti, Honduras, India, Indonesia, Iran, Iraq, Jamaica, Japan, Jordan, Kazakhstan, Kenya, Kuwait, Kyrgyzstan, Lao People's Democratic Republic, Lebanon, Lesotho, Libyan Arab Jamahiriya, Madagascar, Malawi, Malaysia, Maldives, Mali, Marshall Islands, Mauritania, Mauritius, Mexico, Micronesia, Mongolia, Morocco, Mozambique, Myanmar, Namibia, Nepal, New Zealand, Nicaragua, Niger, Nigeria, Oman, Pakistan, Panama, Papua New Guinea, Paraguay, Peru, Philippines, Qatar, Russian Federation, Rwanda, Saint Lucia, Saint Vincent and the Grenadines, Samoa, Saudi Arabia, Senegal, Seychelles, Sierra Leone, Singapore, Solomon Islands, Sri Lanka, Sudan, Suriname, Swaziland, Syrian Arab Republic, Tajikistan, Thailand, Togo, Trinidad and Tobago, Tunisia, Turkmenistan, Uganda, Ukraine, United Arab Emirates, United Republic of Tanzania, Uruguay, Venezuela, Viet Nam, Yemen, Zambia, Zimbabwe.
Against: France, Monaco, United Kingdom, United States.
Abstaining: Albania, Andorra, Austria, Belgium, Bulgaria, Croatia, Czech Republic, Denmark, Estonia, Finland, Georgia, Germany, Greece, Hungary, Iceland, Ireland, Israel, Italy, Latvia, Liechtenstein, Lithuania, Luxembourg, Malta, Netherlands, Norway, Poland, Portugal, Republic of Korea, Republic of Moldova, Romania, Slovakia, Slovenia, Spain, Sweden, the former Yugoslav Republic of Macedonia, Turkey.

Other nuclear and related issues

The United Nations disarmament forums considered several less prominent nuclear and related issues that had been on their agendas for a number of years.

Disarmament Commission consideration. The Commission again discussed the item ''Process of nuclear disarmament in the framework of international peace and security, with the objective of the elimination of nuclear weapons'', which it had first considered in 1991.[60] The Commission entrusted Working Group I with the item but, in view of the Commission's decision to postpone conclusion of the item to 1994, the Group held only five meetings between 22 April and 6 May. The Group had before it new working papers submitted by Australia,[80] the Russian Federation[81] and South Africa.[82] On the basis of the four subjects agreed on in 1992,[83] the Chairman proposed the following general outline for guidelines and recommendations for nuclear disarmament: a general overview concerning the relationship between the process of nuclear disarmament and international peace and security and a review and assessment of recent developments in the process of nuclear disarmament; mechanisms for nuclear disarmament; the role of the United Nations system; and conditions and measures required for strengthening the process of nuclear disarmament. The general outline was annexed to the Commission's report.[84]

Conference on Disarmament consideration.
In view of the agreement by members of the Conference to focus on four agenda items in 1993, the Conference dealt with a number of items only in plenary meetings (see below, under ''Disarmament machinery''). It decided not to establish ad hoc committees on the cessation of the nuclear-arms race and nuclear disarmament and on prevention of nuclear war, including all related matters. In addition, in the context of the item ''New types of weapons of mass destruction and new systems of such weapons; radiological weapons'', it did not establish its traditional ad hoc committee on radiological weapons.

GENERAL ASSEMBLY ACTION

On 16 December, the General Assembly, on the recommendation of the First Committee, adopted **resolution 48/61** without vote.

Prohibition of the development and manufacture of new types of weapons of mass destruction and new systems of such weapons: report of the Conference on Disarmament

The General Assembly,

Recalling its previous resolutions on the prohibition of the development and manufacture of new types of weapons of mass destruction and new systems of such weapons,

Taking note of paragraph 77 of the Final Document of the Tenth Special Session of the General Assembly,

Determined to prevent the emergence of new types of weapons of mass destruction that have characteristics comparable in destructive effect to those of weapons of mass destruction identified in the definition of weapons of mass destruction adopted by the United Nations in 1948,

Noting that in the course of its 1992 and 1993 sessions the Conference on Disarmament considered the item entitled ''New types of weapons of mass destruction and new systems of such weapons: radiological weapons'',

Taking into account the sections of the reports of the Conference on Disarmament relating to this question,

1. *Reaffirms* that effective measures should be taken to prevent the emergence of new types of weapons of mass destruction;

2. *Requests* the Conference on Disarmament, in the light of its existing priorities, to keep under review, with expert assistance, as appropriate, the questions of the prohibition of the development and manufacture of new types of weapons of mass destruction and new systems of such weapons with a view to making, when necessary, recommendations on undertaking specific negotiations on the identified types of such weapons;

3. *Calls upon* all States, immediately following the recommendation of the Conference on Disarmament, to give favourable consideration to those recommendations;

4. *Requests* the Secretary-General to transmit to the Conference on Disarmament all documents relating to the consideration of this item by the General Assembly at its forty-eighth session;

5. *Requests* the Conference on Disarmament to continue the practice of reporting the results of its consideration of these questions in its annual report to the General Assembly;

6. *Decides* to include in the provisional agenda of its fifty-first session the item entitled ''Prohibition of the development and manufacture of new types of weapons of mass destruction and new systems of such weapons: report of the Conference on Disarmament''.

General Assembly resolution 48/61

16 December 1993   Meeting 81   Adopted without vote

Approved by First Committee (A/48/662) without vote, 12 November (meeting 25); 23-nation draft (A/C.1/48/L.16); agenda item 57.

Sponsors: Afghanistan, Austria, Belarus, Belgium, Bolivia, Canada, Costa Rica, Czech Republic, Denmark, Greece, India, Italy, Kazakhstan, Lao People's Democratic Republic, Mongolia, Netherlands, Philippines, Russian Federation, Slovakia, the former Yugoslav Republic of Macedonia, Ukraine, United Kingdom, Viet Nam.

Meeting numbers. GA 48th session: 1st Committee 3-14, 19, 25; plenary 81.

Also on 16 December and on the recommendation of the First Committee, the Assembly adopted **resolution 48/76 B** by recorded vote.

Convention on the Prohibition of the Use of Nuclear Weapons

The General Assembly,

Convinced that the use of nuclear weapons poses the most serious threat to the survival of mankind,

Convinced also that a multilateral agreement prohibiting the use or threat of use of nuclear weapons should strengthen international security and contribute to the climate for negotiations leading to the ultimate elimination of nuclear weapons,

Welcoming the Treaty between the Russian Federation and the United States of America on Further Reduction and Limitation of Strategic Offensive Arms, signed in Moscow on 3 January 1993, aimed at reducing the strategic arsenals to an aggregate level not to exceed 3,500 deployed strategic warheads for each side no later than the year 2003,

Conscious that the recent steps taken by the Russian Federation and the United States of America towards a reduction of their nuclear weapons and the improvement in the international climate can contribute towards the goal of complete elimination of nuclear weapons,

Recalling that, in paragraph 58 of the Final Document of the Tenth Special Session of the General Assembly, it is stated that all States should actively participate in efforts to bring about conditions in international relations among States in which a code of peaceful conduct of nations in international affairs could be agreed upon and that would preclude the use or threat of use of nuclear weapons,

Reaffirming that any use of nuclear weapons would be a violation of the Charter of the United Nations and a crime against humanity, as declared in its resolutions 1653(XVI) of 24 November 1961, 33/71 B of 14 December 1978, 34/83 G of 11 December 1979, 35/152 D of 12 December 1980 and 36/92 I of 9 December 1981,

Stressing that an international convention would be a step towards the complete elimination of nuclear weapons leading to general and complete disarmament under strict and effective international control,

Noting with regret that the Conference on Disarmament, during its 1993 session, was unable to undertake negotiations on this subject,

1. *Reiterates its request* to the Conference on Disarmament to commence negotiations, as a matter of priority, in order to reach agreement on an international convention prohibiting the use or threat of use of nuclear weapons under any circumstances, taking as a possible basis the draft Convention on the Prohibition of the Use of Nuclear Weapons annexed to the present resolution;

2. *Requests* the Conference on Disarmament to report to the General Assembly on the results of those negotiations.

ANNEX
Draft Convention on the Prohibition of the Use of Nuclear Weapons

The States Parties to this Convention,

Alarmed by the threat to the very survival of mankind posed by the existence of nuclear weapons,

Convinced that any use of nuclear weapons constitutes a violation of the Charter of the United Nations and a crime against humanity,

Convinced also that this Convention would be a step towards the complete elimination of nuclear weapons leading to general and complete disarmament under strict and effective international control,

Determined to continue negotiations for the achievement of this goal,

Have agreed as follows:

Article 1

The States Parties to this Convention solemnly undertake not to use or threaten to use nuclear weapons under any circumstances.

Article 2

This Convention shall be of unlimited duration.

Article 3

1. This Convention shall be open to all States for signature. Any State that does not sign the Convention before its entry into force in accordance with paragraph 3 of this article may accede to it at any time.

2. This Convention shall be subject to ratification by signatory States. Instruments of ratification or accession shall be deposited with the Secretary-General of the United Nations.

3. This Convention shall enter into force on the deposit of instruments of ratification by twenty-five Governments, including the Governments of the five nuclear-weapon States, in accordance with paragraph 2 of this article.

4. For States whose instruments of ratification or accession are deposited after the entry into force of the Convention, it shall enter into force on the date of the deposit of their instruments of ratification or accession.

5. The depositary shall promptly inform all signatory and acceding States of the date of each signature, the date of deposit of each instrument of ratification or accession and the date of the entry into force of this Convention, as well as of the receipt of other notices.

6. This Convention shall be registered by the depositary in accordance with Article 102 of the Charter of the United Nations.

Article 4

This Convention, of which the Arabic, Chinese, English, French, Russian and Spanish texts are equally authentic, shall be deposited with the Secretary-General of the United Nations, who shall send duly certified copies thereof to the Government of the signatory and acceding States.

IN WITNESS WHEREOF, the undersigned, being duly authorized thereto by their respective Governments, have signed this Convention, opened for signature at _____ on the _____ day of _____ one thousand nine hundred and _____.

General Assembly resolution 48/76 B

16 December 1993   Meeting 81   120-23-24 (recorded vote)

Approved by First Committee (A/48/677) by recorded vote (102-21-23), 16 November (meeting 27); 20-nation draft (A/C.1/48/L.13/Rev.2); agenda item 72 *(b)*.

Sponsors: Algeria, Bangladesh, Bhutan, Bolivia, Colombia, Costa Rica, Democratic People's Republic of Korea, Ecuador, Egypt, Ethiopia, Haiti, Honduras, India, Indonesia, Lao People's Democratic Republic, Madagascar, Malaysia, Mexico, Sudan, Viet Nam.

Meeting numbers. GA 48th session: 1st Committee 3-14, 22, 27; plenary 81.

Recorded vote in Assembly as follows:

In favour: Afghanistan, Algeria, Angola, Antigua and Barbuda, Bahamas, Bahrain, Bangladesh, Barbados, Belarus, Belize, Benin, Bhutan, Bolivia, Botswana, Brazil, Brunei Darussalam, Burkina Faso, Burundi, Cambodia, Cameroon, Cape Verde, Central African Republic, Chad, Chile, China, Colombia, Comoros, Congo, Costa Rica, Côte d'Ivoire, Cuba, Cyprus, Democratic People's Republic of Korea, Djibouti, Dominica, Dominican Republic, Ecuador, Egypt, Ethiopia, Fiji, Gabon, Gambia, Ghana, Grenada, Guatemala, Guinea, Guinea-Bissau, Guyana, Haiti, Honduras, India, Indonesia, Iran, Iraq, Jamaica, Jordan, Kazakhstan, Kenya, Kuwait, Kyrgyzstan, Lao People's Democratic Republic, Lebanon, Lesotho, Libyan Arab Jamahiriya, Madagascar, Malawi, Malaysia, Maldives, Mali, Mauritania, Mauritius, Mexico, Micronesia, Mongolia, Morocco, Mozambique, Myanmar, Namibia, Nepal, Nicaragua, Niger, Nigeria, Oman, Pakistan, Panama, Papua New Guinea, Paraguay, Peru, Philippines, Qatar, Rwanda, Saint Lucia, Saint Vincent and the Grenadines, Samoa, Saudi Arabia, Senegal, Seychelles, Sierra Leone, Singapore, Solomon Islands, Sri Lanka, Sudan, Suriname, Swaziland, Syrian Arab Republic, Tajikistan, Thailand, Togo, Trinidad and Tobago, Tunisia, Uganda, Ukraine, United Arab Emirates, United Republic of Tanzania, Uruguay, Venezuela, Viet Nam, Yemen, Zambia, Zimbabwe.

Against: Andorra, Belgium, Bulgaria, Canada, Czech Republic, Denmark, Finland, France, Germany, Hungary, Iceland, Italy, Luxembourg, Monaco, Netherlands, Norway, Poland, Portugal, Slovakia, Spain, Turkey, United Kingdom, United States.

Abstaining: Albania, Argentina, Armenia, Australia, Austria, Estonia, Georgia, Greece, Ireland, Israel, Japan, Latvia, Liechtenstein, Lithuania, Malta, Marshall Islands, New Zealand, Republic of Korea, Republic of Moldova, Romania, Russian Federation, Slovenia, Sweden, the former Yugoslav Republic of Macedonia.

On the same date, the Assembly, also on the recommendation of the First Committee, adopted **resolution 48/75 D** without vote.

Prohibition of the dumping of radioactive wastes

The General Assembly,

Bearing in mind resolutions CM/Res.1153(XLVIII) of 1988 and CM/Res.1225(L) of 1989, adopted by the Council of Ministers of the Organization of African

Unity, concerning the dumping of nuclear and industrial wastes in Africa,

Welcoming resolution GC(XXXIII)/RES/509 on the dumping of nuclear wastes, adopted on 29 September 1989 by the General Conference of the International Atomic Energy Agency at its thirty-third regular session,

Welcoming also resolution GC(XXXIV)/RES/530 establishing a Code of Practice on the International Transboundary Movement of Radioactive Waste, adopted on 21 September 1990 by the General Conference of the International Atomic Energy Agency at its thirty-fourth regular session,

Considering its resolution 2602 C (XXIV) of 16 December 1969, in which it requested the Conference of the Committee on Disarmament, *inter alia*, to consider effective methods of control against the use of radiological methods of warfare,

Recalling resolution CM/Res.1356(LIV) of 1991, adopted by the Council of Ministers of the Organization of African Unity, on the Bamako Convention on the Ban on the Import of Hazardous Wastes into Africa and on the Control of Their Transboundary Movements within Africa,

Aware of the potential hazards underlying any use of radioactive wastes that would constitute radiological warfare and its implications for regional and international security, in particular for the security of developing countries,

Recalling also its resolutions 43/75 Q of 7 December 1988, 44/116 R of 15 December 1989, 45/58 K of 4 December 1990, 46/36 K of 6 December 1991 and 47/52 D of 9 December 1992,

Desirous of promoting the implementation of paragraph 76 of the Final Document of the Tenth Special Session of the General Assembly,

1. *Takes note* of the part of the report of the Conference on Disarmament relating to a future convention on the prohibition of radiological weapons;

2. *Expresses grave concern* regarding any use of nuclear wastes that would constitute radiological warfare and have grave implications for the national security of all States;

3. *Calls upon* all States to take appropriate measures with a view to preventing any dumping of nuclear or radioactive wastes that would infringe upon the sovereignty of States;

4. *Requests* the Conference on Disarmament to take into account, in the negotiations for a convention on the prohibition of radiological weapons, radioactive wastes as part of the scope of such a convention;

5. *Also requests* the Conference on Disarmament to intensify efforts towards an early conclusion of such a convention and to include in its report to the General Assembly at its forty-ninth session the progress recorded in the negotiations on this subject;

6. *Takes note* of resolution CM/Res.1356(LIV) of 1991, adopted by the Council of Ministers of the Organization of African Unity, on the Bamako Convention on the Ban on the Import of Hazardous Wastes into Africa and on the Control of Their Transboundary Movements within Africa;

7. *Expresses the hope* that the effective implementation of the International Atomic Energy Agency Code of Practice on the International Transboundary Movement of Radioactive Waste will enhance the protection of all States from the dumping of radioactive wastes on their territories;

8. *Requests* the International Atomic Energy Agency to continue keeping the subject under active review, including the desirability of concluding a legally binding instrument in this field;

9. *Decides* to include in the provisional agenda of its forty-ninth session the item entitled "Prohibition of the dumping of radioactive wastes".

General Assembly resolution 48/75 D

16 December 1993   Meeting 81   Adopted without vote

Approved by First Committee (A/48/676) without vote, 15 November (meeting 26); draft by Algeria (for African Group), Bolivia and Haiti (A/C.1/48/L.17); agenda item 71 *(d)*.

Meeting numbers. GA 48th session: 1st Committee 3-14, 21, 26; plenary 81.

Transparency and the arms Register

In the area of transparency—the systematic provision of information under formal or informal international arrangements—an important development took place in 1993 with the issuance of the first report of the Secretary-General on the United Nations Register of Conventional Arms (see below),[85] established in accordance with a 1991 General Assembly request.[86] The report presented official governmental data on arms transfers in seven major categories of what were considered to be the most destabilizing weapons systems. With almost all of the major exporters having reported to the Register, it was estimated that most of the world's trade in major conventional arms in 1992 was known. Despite the fact that several known major arms-recipient States—particularly in the Middle East and Asia—did not report, the data in the Register accounted for approximately two thirds of all imports.

Conference on Disarmament consideration. On 21 January 1993,[35] the Conference on Disarmament established an Ad Hoc Committee on Transparency in Armaments, which held 15 meetings between 19 March and 23 August.[87] In 1991,[86] the General Assembly had called on the Conference to address the interrelated aspects of the excessive and destabilizing accumulation of arms, including military holdings and procurement through national production, and to elaborate universal and non-discriminatory practical means to increase openness and transparency. The Conference was also asked to address the problems and the elaboration of practical means to increase openness and transparency related to the transfer of high technology with military applications and to weapons of mass destruction, in accordance with existing legal instruments.

Many suggestions and working papers were presented on a wide variety of topics, several of them containing concrete proposals for practical measures to increase openness and transparency. Although agreement was not reached on any of them, it was felt that many of the issues contained therein were useful for future consideration and work with a view to promoting trust, confidence-building and stability. At the conclusion of its work, the Ad Hoc Committee recommended that it be re-established at the beginning of the Conference's 1994 session.

Register of Conventional Arms

In accordance with a 1992 General Assembly request,[88] the Secretary-General issued in October 1993[85] the first report on the United Nations Register of Conventional Arms. He provided information received from 83 Member States on their national arms import and export policies, legislation and administrative procedures. Of those States, 33 provided background information on military holdings, procurement through national production and relevant policies. Annexed to the report was a list of the seven major arms categories used for reporting to the Register—battle tanks, armoured combat vehicles, large-calibre artillery systems, combat aircraft, attack helicopters, warships, and missiles and missile launchers—and their definitions.

On 16 December, the General Assembly, on the recommendation of the First Committee, adopted **resolution 48/75 E** without vote.

Transparency in armaments
The General Assembly,

Recalling its resolutions 46/36 L of 9 December 1991 and 47/52 L of 15 December 1992,

Continuing to take the view that an enhanced level of transparency in armaments contributes greatly to confidence-building and security among States and that the establishment of the Register of Conventional Arms constitutes an important step forward in the promotion of transparency in military matters,

Welcoming the report of the Secretary-General on the first year of operation of the Register of Conventional Arms,

Encouraged by the response of Member States to the request contained in paragraphs 9 and 10 of its resolution 46/36 L to provide data on their imports and exports of arms, as well as available background information regarding their military holdings, procurement through national production and relevant policies,

Welcoming also the work of the Conference on Disarmament under the item of its agenda entitled "Transparency in armaments",

Welcoming further the organization by Member States of initiatives and seminars intended to promote transparency in military matters through a widespread reporting of data to the Register of Conventional Arms,

1. *Reaffirms its determination* to ensure the effective operation of the Register of Conventional Arms as provided for in paragraphs 7, 9 and 10 of its resolution 46/36 L;

2. *Calls upon* all Member States to provide the requested data and information for the Register to the Secretary-General by 30 April annually;

3. *Reaffirms its request* to the Secretary-General to prepare a report, with the assistance of a group of governmental experts to be convened in 1994 on the basis of equitable geographical representation, on the continu-

ing operation of the Register and its further development, taking into account the work of the Conference on Disarmament and the views expressed by Member States, so that a decision may be taken by the General Assembly at its forty-ninth session;

4. *Requests* the Secretary-General to ensure that sufficient resources are made available for the United Nations Secretariat to operate and maintain the Register;

5. *Encourages* the Conference on Disarmament to continue its work undertaken in response to the requests contained in paragraphs 12 to 15 of resolution 46/36 L;

6. *Reiterates its call* upon all Member States to cooperate at a regional and subregional level, taking fully into account the specific conditions prevailing in the region or subregion, with a view to enhancing and coordinating international efforts aimed at increased openness and transparency in armaments;

7. *Also requests* the Secretary-General to report to the General Assembly at its forty-ninth session on progress made in implementing the present resolution;

8. *Decides* to include in the provisional agenda of its forty-ninth session the item entitled "Transparency in armaments".

General Assembly resolution 48/75 E
16 December 1993   Meeting 81   Adopted without vote

Approved by First Committee (A/48/676) without vote, 11 November (meeting 24); 64-nation draft (A/C.1/48/L.18); agenda item 71 (g).
Sponsors: Albania, Angola, Argentina, Australia, Austria, Belarus, Belgium, Bolivia, Brazil, Bulgaria, Canada, Cape Verde, Central African Republic, Chile, Costa Rica, Czech Republic, Denmark, Estonia, Finland, France, Germany, Greece, Guinea, Haiti, Hungary, Iceland, Ireland, Italy, Japan, Kazakhstan, Latvia, Lesotho, Lithuania, Luxembourg, Malaysia, Mali, Malta, Nepal, Netherlands, New Zealand, Nicaragua, Norway, Panama, Peru, Poland, Portugal, Republic of Korea, Republic of Moldova, Romania, Russian Federation, Senegal, Singapore, Slovakia, Slovenia, Spain, Suriname, Swaziland, Sweden, the former Yugoslav Republic of Macedonia, Turkey, Ukraine, United Kingdom, United States, Venezuela.
Meeting numbers. GA 48th session: 1st Committee 3-14, 20, 24; plenary 81.

Other transparency issues and verification

Transparency of military expenditures

In an August report with later addenda,[89] the Secretary-General presented information received from 33 Member States on their military expenditures, as requested by the General Assembly in 1985.[90]

On 16 December, the General Assembly, on the recommendation of the First Committee, adopted **resolution 48/62** without vote.

Reduction of military budgets: transparency of military expenditures
The General Assembly,

Recalling its resolutions 35/142 B of 12 December 1980, which introduced the United Nations system for the standardized reporting of military expenditures, 46/25 of 6 December 1991 and 47/54 B of 9 December 1992, dealing with the guidelines and recommendations for objective information on military matters,

Noting that since then national reports on military expenditures have voluntarily been submitted by a number of Member States belonging to different geographic regions,

Expressing its appreciation to the Secretary-General for providing Member States with the reports on military expenditures,

Welcoming the decision of the States participating in the Conference on Security and Cooperation in Europe, as contained in the Vienna Document 1990 of the negotiations on confidence- and security-building measures, to exchange information annually on their military budgets, on the basis of the categories of the United Nations standardized reporting system,

Welcoming also the recent progress achieved in arms limitations and disarmament, which, in the long term, will lead to significant reductions in military expenditures,

Convinced that the end of the East-West confrontation and the resulting improvement of international relations form a sound basis for promoting further openness and transparency on all military matters,

Emphasizing that an increased flow and exchange of information on military expenditures will contribute to the predictability of military activities, thus strengthening international peace and security on a global and regional level,

Recalling that the guidelines and recommendations for objective information on military matters stated that the United Nations system for the standardized reporting of military expenditures should continue in operation and could be further improved,

1. *Calls upon* all Member States to participate in the United Nations system for the standardized reporting of military expenditures as adopted by the General Assembly;

2. *Requests* the Secretary-General to seek the views of Member States on ways and means to strengthen, and to broaden participation in, the United Nations system for the standardized reporting of military expenditures and to submit a report on the subject to the General Assembly at its forty-ninth session;

3. *Decides* to include in the provisional agenda of its forty-ninth session the item entitled "Transparency of military expenditures".

General Assembly resolution 48/62

16 December 1993   Meeting 81   Adopted without vote

Approved by First Committee (A/48/663) without vote, 11 November (meeting 24); 35-nation draft (A/C.1/48/L.2/Rev.1); agenda item 58.
Sponsors: Austria, Belarus, Belgium, Brazil, Bulgaria, Canada, Costa Rica, Denmark, Finland, France, Germany, Greece, Haiti, Hungary, Ireland, Italy, Japan, Latvia, Lesotho, Lithuania, Luxembourg, Malta, Netherlands, Norway, Panama, Poland, Portugal, Romania, Slovakia, Spain, Sweden, the former Yugoslav Republic of Macedonia, Turkey, United Kingdom, United States.
Meeting numbers. GA 48th session: 1st Committee 3-14, 19, 24; plenary 81.

Verification

As requested by the General Assembly in 1992,[91] the Secretary-General submitted a July report with a later addendum[92] containing the views of two Member States (Bulgaria and Canada) on actions that might be taken to implement the recommendations made in a 1990 study on the United Nations role in verification[93] and on other aspects of verification. (For information on the 1993 activities of the Ad Hoc Group of Governmental Experts to Identify and Examine Potential Verification Measures from a Scientific and Technical Standpoint, see above, under "Non-proliferation".)

On 16 December, the General Assembly, on the recommendation of the First Committee, adopted **resolution 48/68** by recorded vote.

Verification in all its aspects, including the role of the United Nations in the field of verification

The General Assembly,

Recalling its resolutions 40/152 O of 16 December 1985, 41/86 Q of 4 December 1986, 42/42 F of 30 November 1987, 43/81 B of 7 December 1988, 45/65 of 4 December 1990 and 47/45 of 9 December 1992,

Stressing that the critical importance of verification of and compliance with arms limitation and disarmament agreements is universally recognized and that the issue of verification is a matter of concern to all nations,

Recognizing that the United Nations, in accordance with its role and responsibilities established under the Charter, can make a significant contribution in the field of verification, in particular of multilateral agreements, and taking into consideration its specific experience,

Affirming its continued support for the sixteen principles of verification drawn up by the Disarmament Commission,

Noting that recent developments in international relations continue to underscore the importance of effective verification of existing and future agreements to limit or eliminate arms, and that some of these developments have significant effects on the role of the United Nations in the field of verification, which require careful and ongoing examination,

Taking note of the report of the Secretary-General pursuant to the statement of 31 January 1992 adopted at the conclusion of the first meeting held by the Security Council at the level of Heads of State and Government,

Taking note also of the report of the Secretary-General on the occasion of Disarmament Week,

Welcoming the final report, adopted by consensus, of the Ad Hoc Group of Governmental Experts open to all States parties to the Convention on the Prohibition of the Development, Production and Stockpiling of Bacteriological (Biological) and Toxin Weapons and on Their Destruction, submitted in accordance with its mandate to identify and examine potential verification measures from a scientific and technical standpoint,

Welcoming also the conclusion of the Convention on the Prohibition of the Development, Production, Stockpiling and Use of Chemical Weapons and on Their Destruction, which contains an unprecedented regime of verification, and the ongoing work to bring this Convention into force,

Recalling that in its resolution 47/45 it requested the Secretary-General, as a follow-up to the 1990 study on the role of the United Nations in the field of verification and in view of significant developments in international relations since that study, to seek the views of Member States on:

(a) Additional actions that might be taken to implement the recommendations contained in the study;

(b) How the verification of arms limitation and disarmament agreements could facilitate United Nations activities with respect to preventive diplomacy, peacemaking, peace-keeping and post-conflict peace-building;

(c) Additional actions with respect to the role of the United Nations in the field of verification, including further studies by the United Nations on this subject;

and to report to the General Assembly at its forty-eighth session on the subject,

1. *Takes note* of the report of the Secretary-General containing the views of Member States;

2. *Requests* the Secretary-General, as a further follow-up to the study on the role of the United Nations in the field of verification and in view of significant developments in international relations since that study, to undertake with the assistance of a group of qualified governmental experts, an in-depth study that would:

(*a*) Examine the lessons from recent United Nations verification experiences, as well as other relevant international developments, for future activities by the United Nations and by the Conference on Disarmament in the field of verification in all its aspects, taking into consideration its specific experience, and with particular attention to the ways verification can facilitate United Nations activities with respect to confidence-building and conflict management and disarmament;

(*b*) Explore the further development of guidelines and principles for the involvement of the United Nations in verification;

(*c*) Review the conclusions of the 1990 study group with particular attention to the ways that the United Nations might facilitate verification through relevant procedures, processes and bodies for acquiring, integrating and analysing verification information from a variety of sources;

3. *Also requests* the Secretary-General to submit a report on the subject to the General Assembly at its fiftieth session;

4. *Decides* to include in the provisional agenda of its fiftieth session the item entitled "Verification in all its aspects, including the role of the United Nations in the field of verification".

General Assembly resolution 48/68

16 December 1993   Meeting 81   145-0-22 (recorded vote)

Approved by First Committee (A/48/669) by recorded vote (127-0-19), 19 November (meeting 30); 23-nation draft (A/C.1/48/L.45/Rev.1), orally revised; agenda item 64.
Sponsors: Armenia, Australia, Austria, Brazil, Bulgaria, Cameroon, Canada, Costa Rica, Czech Republic, Finland, Hungary, India, Kenya, Mexico, New Zealand, Nigeria, Panama, Republic of Korea, Russian Federation, Singapore, Slovakia, Thailand, the former Yugoslav Republic of Macedonia.
Meeting numbers. GA 48th session: 1st Committee 3-14, 28, 30; plenary 81.

Recorded vote in Assembly as follows:

In favour: Afghanistan, Albania, Algeria, Antigua and Barbuda, Argentina, Armenia, Australia, Austria, Azerbaijan, Bahamas, Bahrain, Bangladesh, Barbados, Belarus, Belize, Benin, Bhutan, Bolivia, Botswana, Brazil, Brunei Darussalam, Bulgaria, Burkina Faso, Burundi, Cambodia, Cameroon, Canada, Cape Verde, Central African Republic, Chad, Chile, China, Colombia, Comoros, Congo, Costa Rica, Côte d'Ivoire, Croatia, Cuba, Cyprus, Czech Republic, Democratic People's Republic of Korea, Djibouti, Dominica, Dominican Republic, Ecuador, Egypt, Estonia, Ethiopia, Fiji, Finland, Gabon, Gambia, Ghana, Grenada, Guatemala, Guinea, Guinea-Bissau, Guyana, Haiti, Hungary, India, Indonesia, Iran, Iraq, Jamaica, Jordan, Kazakhstan, Kenya, Kyrgyzstan, Lao People's Democratic Republic, Latvia, Lebanon, Lesotho, Libyan Arab Jamahiriya, Lithuania, Madagascar, Malawi, Malaysia, Maldives, Mali, Marshall Islands, Mauritania, Mauritius, Mexico, Micronesia, Mongolia, Morocco, Mozambique, Myanmar, Namibia, Nepal, New Zealand, Nicaragua, Niger, Nigeria, Oman, Pakistan, Panama, Papua New Guinea, Paraguay, Peru, Philippines, Poland, Qatar, Republic of Korea, Republic of Moldova, Romania, Russian Federation, Rwanda, Saint Lucia, Saint Vincent and the Grenadines, Samoa, Saudi Arabia, Senegal, Seychelles, Sierra Leone, Singapore, Slovakia, Slovenia, Solomon Islands, Sri Lanka, Sudan, Suriname, Swaziland, Sweden, Syrian Arab Republic, Tajikistan, Thailand, the former Yugoslav Republic of Macedonia, Togo, Trinidad and Tobago, Tunisia, Turkey, Turkmenistan, Uganda, Ukraine, United Arab Emirates, United Republic of Tanzania, Uruguay, Venezuela, Viet Nam, Yemen, Zambia, Zimbabwe.

Against: None.

Abstaining: Andorra, Belgium, Denmark, France, Georgia, Germany, Greece, Iceland, Ireland, Israel, Italy, Japan, Liechtenstein, Luxembourg, Malta, Monaco, Netherlands, Norway, Portugal, Spain, United Kingdom, United States.

Before the Committee approved the draft text as a whole, it adopted paragraph 2 by a recorded vote of 120 to 7, with 14 abstentions. A recorded vote on that paragraph was also requested in the Assembly, where it was adopted by 140 to 8, with 17 abstentions.

Compliance

On 16 December, the General Assembly, on the recommendation of the First Committee, adopted **resolution 48/63** without vote.

Compliance with arms limitation and disarmament agreements

The General Assembly,

Recalling its resolution 46/26 of 6 December 1991 and other relevant resolutions on the question,

Recognizing the abiding concern of all Member States for maintaining respect for rights and obligations arising from treaties and other sources of international law,

Convinced that observance of the Charter of the United Nations, relevant treaties and other sources of international law is essential for the strengthening of international security,

Mindful, in particular, of the fundamental importance of full implementation and strict observance of agreements and other obligations on arms limitation and disarmament if individual nations and the international community are to derive enhanced security from them,

Stressing that any violation of such agreements and other obligations not only adversely affects the security of States parties but can also create security risks for other States relying on the constraints and commitments stipulated in those agreements and other obligations,

Stressing also that any weakening of confidence in such agreements and other obligations diminishes their contribution to global or regional stability and to further disarmament and arms limitation efforts and undermines the credibility and effectiveness of the international legal system,

Recognizing, in this context, that full compliance by parties with existing agreements and the resolving of compliance concerns effectively can, *inter alia*, facilitate the conclusion of additional arms limitation and disarmament agreements,

Believing that compliance with arms limitation and disarmament agreements by States parties is a matter of interest and concern to all members of the international community, and noting the role that the United Nations has played and should continue to play in that regard,

Convinced that resolution of non-compliance questions that have arisen with regard to arms limitation and disarmament obligations would contribute to better relations among States and the strengthening of world peace and security,

Welcoming the universal recognition of the critical importance of the question of compliance with and verification of arms limitation and disarmament agreements and other obligations,

1. *Urges* all States parties to arms limitation and disarmament agreements to implement and comply with

the entirety of the spirit and provisions of such agreements;

2. *Calls upon* all Member States to give serious consideration to the implications that non-compliance with arms limitation and disarmament obligations has for international security and stability, as well as for the prospects for further progress in the field of disarmament;

3. *Also calls upon* all Member States to support efforts aimed at the resolution of non-compliance questions, with a view to encouraging strict observance by all parties of the provisions of arms limitation and disarmament agreements and maintaining or restoring the integrity of such agreements;

4. *Welcomes* the role that the United Nations has played in restoring the integrity of certain arms limitation and disarmament agreements and in the removal of threats to peace;

5. *Requests* the Secretary-General to continue to provide assistance that may be necessary in restoring and protecting the integrity of arms limitation and disarmament agreements;

6. *Encourages* efforts by States parties to develop additional cooperative measures, as appropriate, that can increase confidence in compliance with existing arms limitation and disarmament obligations and reduce the possibility of misinterpretation and misunderstanding;

7. *Notes* the contribution that verification experiments and research can make and already have made in confirming and improving verification procedures for arms limitation and disarmament agreements under study or negotiation, thereby providing an opportunity, from the time that such agreements enter into force, for enhancing confidence in the effectiveness of verification procedures as a basis for determining compliance;

8. *Decides* to include in the provisional agenda of its fiftieth session an item entitled "Compliance with arms limitation and disarmament obligations".

General Assembly resolution 48/63

16 December 1993   Meeting 81   Adopted without vote

Approved by First Committee (A/48/664) without vote, 15 November (meeting 26); 55-nation draft (A/C.1/48/L.47); agenda item 59.
Sponsors: Argentina, Australia, Austria, Belarus, Belgium, Belize, Bulgaria, Cameroon, Canada, Chile, Costa Rica, Czech Republic, Denmark, El Salvador, Estonia, Finland, France, Gambia, Germany, Ghana, Greece, Grenada, Honduras, Hungary, Iceland, Ireland, Italy, Japan, Latvia, Liberia, Lithuania, Luxembourg, Netherlands, New Zealand, Norway, Panama, Peru, Poland, Portugal, Republic of Korea, Romania, Russian Federation, Rwanda, Saint Lucia, Senegal, Sierra Leone, Slovakia, Spain, Sweden, Thailand, the former Yugoslav Republic of Macedonia, Togo, Turkey, United Kingdom, United States.
Meeting numbers. GA 48th session: 1st Committee 3-14, 23, 26; plenary 81.

Regional disarmament

At the regional level, a number of initiatives were taken in 1993 to seek the adoption of arms limitation and disarmament measures, as well as of confidence-building measures.

Disarmament Commission consideration. The Disarmament Commission's working group on a regional approach to disarmament within the context of global security considered the subject between 21 April and 7 May 1993 under the following topics: relationship between regional disarmament and global security and arms limitation and disarmament; principles and guidelines;

ways and means; machineries and modalities; and role of the United Nations. It agreed to concentrate on the last three topics, given the fact that the first two had been the focus of attention in 1992.[94] In addition to documents submitted by members at previous sessions, three new documents were submitted by South Africa.[95] Following intensive deliberations, the working group adopted guidelines and recommendations for regional approaches to disarmament within the context of global security, which was annexed to the Commission's report.[84]

Report of the Secretary-General. In response to a 1992 General Assembly decision,[96] the Secretary-General submitted a report presenting the views of three Member States (Belarus, Namibia and New Zealand) on conventional disarmament on a regional scale.[97]

GENERAL ASSEMBLY ACTION

On 16 December, the General Assembly, on the recommendation of the First Committee, adopted **resolution 48/75 G** without vote.

Regional disarmament

The General Assembly,

Recalling its resolutions 47/52 G and 47/52 J of 9 December 1992,

Affirming the abiding commitment of all States to the purposes and principles enshrined in the Charter of the United Nations and to international law in the conduct of their international relations,

Believing that the efforts of the international community to move towards the ideal of general and complete disarmament are guided by the inherent human desire for genuine peace and security, the elimination of the danger of war and the release of economic, intellectual and other resources for peaceful pursuits,

Noting that regional arrangements for disarmament and arms limitation may free resources of participating States for peaceful purposes, *inter alia*, the promotion of their economic and social development,

Reaffirming its firm conviction that the regional approach to disarmament is essential to strengthening international peace and security at the regional and global levels,

Welcoming the initiatives towards disarmament, nuclear non-proliferation and security undertaken by some countries at the regional level,

Noting with satisfaction the important progress made in various regions of the world through the adoption of arms limitation, peace, security and cooperation agreements, including those related to the prohibition of weapons of mass destruction, and encouraging States in the regions concerned to continue implementing those agreements,

Convinced that endeavours by countries to promote regional disarmament, taking into account the specific characteristics of each region and in accordance with the principle of undiminished security at the lowest level of armaments for all the participating States, would enhance the security of all States and would thus contribute to international peace and security,

Recognizing the useful role played by the United Nations regional centres,

Taking note of the report of the Disarmament Commission, containing the text, adopted by the Commission at its 1993 substantive session, of the guidelines and recommendations for regional approaches to disarmament within the context of global security,

Expressing its appreciation for the work accomplished by the Disarmament Commission in finalizing the text of those guidelines and recommendations,

1. *Endorses* the guidelines and recommendations for regional approaches to disarmament within the context of global security adopted by the Disarmament Commission at its 1993 substantive session, and recommends them to all Member States for implementation;

2. *Affirms* that global and regional approaches to disarmament complement each other and should therefore be pursued simultaneously to promote regional and international peace and security;

3. *Affirms also* that multifaceted cooperation among States of a region, especially encompassing the political, economic, social and cultural fields, can be conducive to the strengthening of regional security and stability;

4. *Encourages* States to reach, wherever possible, freely concluded agreements at the regional level on confidence- and security-building measures, disarmament and arms limitations, arrangements to prevent the proliferation in all its aspects of nuclear weapons and other weapons of mass destruction, zones of peace and zones free of nuclear weapons and other weapons of mass destruction, as well as consultative and cooperative arrangements;

5. *Supports and encourages* efforts aimed at promoting confidence-building measures at the regional level in order to ease regional tensions and to further disarmament and nuclear non-proliferation measures at the regional level;

6. *Also encourages* States to address, in regional arrangements for disarmament and arms limitations, the question of the accumulation of conventional weapons beyond the legitimate self-defence requirements of States;

7. *Encourages* States of a region to examine the possibility of creating, on their own initiative, regional mechanisms and/or institutions for the establishment of measures in the framework of an effort of regional disarmament or for the prevention and peaceful settlement of disputes and conflicts with the assistance, if requested, of the United Nations;

8. *Invites* Member States and regions to bring to the attention of the General Assembly results achieved on regional disarmament, and requests the Secretary-General to submit a report to the Assembly at its forty-ninth session on the basis of the replies received;

9. *Decides* to include in the provisional agenda of its forty-ninth session the item entitled ''Regional disarmament''.

General Assembly resolution 48/75 G

16 December 1993   Meeting 81   Adopted without vote

Approved by First Committee (A/48/676) without vote, 18 November (meeting 28); 40-nation draft (A/C.1/48/L.28); agenda item 71 *(f)*.

Sponsors: Australia, Austria, Belgium, Bulgaria, Canada, Cape Verde, Costa Rica, Czech Republic, Denmark, Finland, France, Germany, Greece, Haiti, Hungary, Indonesia, Ireland, Italy, Japan, Latvia, Lithuania, Luxembourg, Malta, Netherlands, New Zealand, Nicaragua, Norway, Panama, Peru, Po-

land, Portugal, Romania, Slovakia, Slovenia, Spain, Sweden, the former Yugoslav Republic of Macedonia, Turkey, United Kingdom, United States. *Meeting numbers.* GA 48th session: 1st Committee 3-14, 23, 28; plenary 81.

Also on 16 December, the Assembly, on the recommendation of the First Committee, adopted **resolution 48/75 I** by recorded vote.

Regional disarmament
The General Assembly,

Recalling its resolutions 45/58 P of 4 December 1990, 46/36 I of 6 December 1991 and 47/52 J of 9 December 1992,

Believing that the efforts of the international community to move towards the ideal of general and complete disarmament are guided by the inherent human desire for genuine peace and security, the elimination of the danger of war and the release of economic, intellectual and other resources for peaceful pursuits,

Affirming the abiding commitment of all States to the purposes and principles enshrined in the Charter of the United Nations in the conduct of their international relations,

Noting that essential guidelines for progress towards general and complete disarmament were adopted at the tenth special session of the General Assembly,

Taking note of the guidelines and recommendations for regional approaches to disarmament within the context of global security adopted by the Disarmament Commission at its 1993 substantive session,

Welcoming the prospects of genuine progress in the field of disarmament engendered in recent years as a result of negotiations between the two super-Powers,

Taking note also of the recent proposals for disarmament and nuclear non-proliferation at the regional and subregional levels,

Recognizing the importance of confidence-building measures for regional and international peace and security,

Convinced that endeavours by countries to promote regional disarmament, taking into account the specific characteristics of each region and in accordance with the principle of undiminished security at the lowest level of armaments, would enhance the security of smaller States and would thus contribute to international peace and security by reducing the risk of regional conflicts,

1. *Stresses* that sustained efforts are needed, within the framework of the Conference on Disarmament and under the umbrella of the United Nations, to make progress on the entire range of disarmament issues;

2. *Affirms* that global and regional approaches to disarmament complement each other and should therefore be pursued simultaneously to promote regional and international peace and security;

3. *Calls upon* States to conclude agreements, wherever possible, for nuclear non-proliferation, disarmament and confidence-building measures at regional and subregional levels;

4. *Welcomes* the initiatives towards disarmament, nuclear non-proliferation and security undertaken by some countries at the regional and subregional levels;

5. *Supports and encourages* efforts aimed at promoting confidence-building measures at regional and subregional levels in order to ease regional tensions and to further disarmament and nuclear non-proliferation measures at regional and subregional levels;

6. *Decides* to include in the provisional agenda of its forty-ninth session the item entitled "Regional disarmament".

General Assembly resolution 48/75 I

16 December 1993   Meeting 81   170-0-1 (recorded vote)

Approved by First Committee (A/48/676) by recorded vote (139-0-1), 18 November (meeting 28); 60-nation draft (A/C.1/48/L.36); agenda item 71 (f).

Sponsors: Albania, Armenia, Austria, Belgium, Benin, Bolivia, Bosnia and Herzegovina, Cameroon, Canada, Cape Verde, Central African Republic, Chile, Colombia, Costa Rica, Côte d'Ivoire, Czech Republic, Ecuador, Egypt, Gabon, Ghana, Guinea, Haiti, Honduras, Italy, Lesotho, Madagascar, Mali, Malta, Marshall Islands, Mauritania, Micronesia, Nepal, Netherlands, New Zealand, Nicaragua, Niger, Pakistan, Panama, Papua New Guinea, Poland, Rwanda, Saudi Arabia, Senegal, Sierra Leone, Sri Lanka, Sudan, Suriname, Swaziland, the former Yugoslav Republic of Macedonia, Togo, Tunisia, Turkey, Turkmenistan, Ukraine, United Kingdom, United States, Vanuatu, Venezuela, Zambia, Zimbabwe.

Meeting numbers. GA 48th session: 1st Committee 3-14, 28; plenary 81.

Recorded vote in Assembly as follows:

In favour: Afghanistan, Albania, Algeria, Andorra, Angola, Antigua and Barbuda, Argentina, Armenia, Australia, Austria, Azerbaijan, Bahamas, Bahrain, Bangladesh, Barbados, Belarus, Belgium, Belize, Benin, Bhutan, Bolivia, Bosnia and Herzegovina, Botswana, Brazil, Brunei Darussalam, Bulgaria, Burkina Faso, Burundi, Cambodia, Cameroon, Canada, Cape Verde, Central African Republic, Chad, Chile, China, Colombia, Comoros, Congo, Costa Rica, Côte d'Ivoire, Croatia, Cuba, Cyprus, Czech Republic, Democratic People's Republic of Korea, Denmark, Djibouti, Dominica, Dominican Republic, Ecuador, Egypt, Estonia, Ethiopia, Fiji, Finland, France, Gabon, Gambia, Georgia, Germany, Ghana, Greece, Grenada, Guatemala, Guinea, Guinea-Bissau, Guyana, Haiti, Honduras, Hungary, Iceland, Indonesia, Iran, Iraq, Ireland, Israel, Italy, Jamaica, Japan, Jordan, Kazakhstan, Kenya, Kuwait, Kyrgyzstan, Lao People's Democratic Republic, Latvia, Lebanon, Lesotho, Libyan Arab Jamahiriya, Liechtenstein, Lithuania, Luxembourg, Madagascar, Malawi, Malaysia, Maldives, Mali, Malta, Marshall Islands, Mauritania, Mauritius, Mexico, Micronesia, Monaco, Mongolia, Morocco, Mozambique, Myanmar, Namibia, Nepal, Netherlands, New Zealand, Nicaragua, Niger, Nigeria, Norway, Oman, Pakistan, Panama, Papua New Guinea, Paraguay, Peru, Philippines, Poland, Portugal, Qatar, Republic of Korea, Republic of Moldova, Romania, Russian Federation, Rwanda, Saint Lucia, Saint Vincent and the Grenadines, Samoa, Saudi Arabia, Senegal, Seychelles, Sierra Leone, Singapore, Slovakia, Slovenia, Solomon Islands, Spain, Sri Lanka, Sudan, Suriname, Swaziland, Sweden, Syrian Arab Republic, Tajikistan, Thailand, the former Yugoslav Republic of Macedonia, Togo, Trinidad and Tobago, Tunisia, Turkey, Turkmenistan, Uganda, Ukraine, United Arab Emirates, United Kingdom, United Republic of Tanzania, United States, Uruguay, Venezuela, Viet Nam, Yemen, Zambia, Zimbabwe.

Against: None.

Abstaining: India.

On the same date, the Assembly, also on the recommendation of the First Committee, adopted **resolution 48/75 J** by recorded vote.

Conventional arms control at the regional and subregional levels

The General Assembly,

Recognizing the crucial role of conventional arms control in promoting regional and international peace and security,

Convinced that conventional arms control needs to be pursued primarily in the regional and subregional contexts since most threats to peace and security in the post-cold-war era arise mainly among States located in the same region or subregion,

Aware that the preservation of a balance in the defence capabilities of States at the lowest level of armaments would contribute to peace and stability and should be a prime objective of conventional arms control,

Desirous of promoting agreements to strengthen regional peace and security at the lowest possible level of armaments and military forces,

Believing that militarily significant States, and States with larger military capabilities, have a special responsibility in promoting such agreements for regional security,

Believing also that one of the principal objectives of conventional arms control should be to prevent the possibility of military attack launched by surprise,

1. *Decides* to give urgent consideration to the issues involved in conventional arms control at the regional and subregional levels;

2. *Requests* the Conference on Disarmament, as a first step, to consider the formulation of principles that can serve as a framework for regional agreements on conventional arms control, and looks forward to a report of the Conference on this subject;

3. *Decides* to include in the provisional agenda of its forty-ninth session an item entitled "Conventional arms control at the regional and subregional levels".

General Assembly resolution 48/75 J

16 December 1993   Meeting 81   156-0-11 (recorded vote)

Approved by First Committee (A/48/676) by recorded vote (123-0-15), 18 November (meeting 28); 5-nation draft (A/C.1/48/L.38/Rev.1); agenda item 71 (i).

Sponsors: Haiti, Pakistan, Panama, Swaziland, United Kingdom.

Meeting numbers. GA 48th session: 1st Committee 3-14, 28; plenary 81.

Recorded vote in Assembly as follows:

In favour: Afghanistan, Albania, Algeria, Andorra, Angola, Antigua and Barbuda, Argentina, Armenia, Austria, Azerbaijan, Bahamas, Bahrain, Bangladesh, Barbados, Belarus, Belgium, Belize, Benin, Bhutan, Bolivia, Botswana, Brunei Darussalam, Bulgaria, Burkina Faso, Burundi, Cambodia, Cameroon, Canada, Cape Verde, Central African Republic, Chad, Chile, China, Comoros, Congo, Costa Rica, Côte d'Ivoire, Croatia, Cyprus, Czech Republic, Democratic People's Republic of Korea, Denmark, Djibouti, Dominica, Dominican Republic, Egypt, Estonia, Ethiopia, Fiji, Finland, France, Gabon, Gambia, Georgia, Germany, Ghana, Greece, Grenada, Guatemala, Guinea, Guinea-Bissau, Guyana, Haiti, Honduras, Hungary, Iceland, Indonesia, Iran, Iraq, Ireland, Israel, Italy, Jamaica, Jordan, Kazakhstan, Kenya, Kuwait, Kyrgyzstan, Lao People's Democratic Republic, Latvia, Lebanon, Lesotho, Liechtenstein, Lithuania, Luxembourg, Madagascar, Malawi, Malaysia, Maldives, Mali, Malta, Marshall Islands, Mauritania, Mauritius, Micronesia, Monaco, Mongolia, Morocco, Mozambique, Myanmar, Namibia, Nepal, Netherlands, New Zealand, Nicaragua, Niger, Norway, Oman, Pakistan, Panama, Papua New Guinea, Paraguay, Philippines, Poland, Portugal, Qatar, Republic of Korea, Republic of Moldova, Romania, Russian Federation, Rwanda, Saint Lucia, Saint Vincent and the Grenadines, Samoa, Saudi Arabia, Senegal, Seychelles, Sierra Leone, Slovakia, Slovenia, Solomon Islands, Spain, Sri Lanka, Sudan, Suriname, Swaziland, Sweden, Syrian Arab Republic, Tajikistan, Thailand, the former Yugoslav Republic of Macedonia, Togo, Trinidad and Tobago, Tunisia, Turkey, Turkmenistan, Uganda, Ukraine, United Arab Emirates, United Kingdom, United States, Uruguay, Venezuela, Yemen, Zambia, Zimbabwe.

Against: None.

Abstaining: Australia, Brazil, Colombia, Cuba, Ecuador, India, Japan, Mexico, Peru, Singapore, Viet Nam.

Africa

Pursuant to a 1992 General Assembly request,[98] the Secretary-General submitted in October 1993 a report on regional confidence-building measures,[99] which focused on the programme of work of the Standing Advisory Committee on Security Questions in Central Africa, established by him in 1992.[100] The Committee's second meeting (Bujumbura, Burundi) was held at the expert level from 8 to 10 March and at the ministerial level on 11 and 12 March. The third meeting (Libreville, Gabon) was held at the expert level from 30 August to 1 September and at the ministerial level on 2 and 3 September. The Committee adopted a non-aggression pact between the States members of the Economic Community of Central African States and decided to submit it for signature by the heads of State and/or Government of the subregion. It mandated its officers to play a more active political role and to undertake visits of solidarity and sympathy to countries engaged in conflict. Pending the establishment of a system to manage crises and conflicts in the subregion, the Committee recommended the adoption of a number of transitional measures relating to policy, legislation and administration.

GENERAL ASSEMBLY ACTION

On 16 December, the General Assembly, on the recommendation of the First Committee, adopted **resolution 48/76 A** by recorded vote.

Regional confidence-building measures

The General Assembly,

Recalling the purposes and principles of the United Nations and its primary responsibility for the maintenance of international peace and security in accordance with the Charter of the United Nations,

Bearing in mind the guidelines for general and complete disarmament adopted at its tenth special session, the first special session devoted to disarmament,

Recalling also its resolutions 43/78 H and 43/85 of 7 December 1988, 44/21 of 15 November 1989, 45/58 M of 4 December 1990, 46/37 B of 6 December 1991 and 47/53 F of 15 December 1992,

Considering the importance and effectiveness of confidence-building measures taken at the initiative and with the participation of all States concerned and taking into account the specific characteristics of each region, in that they can contribute to regional disarmament and to international security, in accordance with the principles of the Charter,

Convinced that the resources released by disarmament, including regional disarmament, can be devoted to economic and social development and to the protection of the environment for the benefit of all peoples, in particular those of the developing countries,

Bearing in mind the establishment by the Secretary-General on 28 May 1992 of the Standing Advisory Committee on Security Questions in Central Africa, the purpose of which is to encourage arms limitation, disarmament, non-proliferation and development in the subregion,

1. *Takes note* of the report of the Secretary-General on regional confidence-building measures, which deals chiefly with the meetings of the Standing Advisory Committee on Security Questions in Central Africa, held at Bujumbura in March 1993 and at Libreville in August and September 1993;

2. *Reaffirms its support* for efforts aimed at promoting confidence-building measures at the regional and subregional levels in order to ease regional tensions and to further disarmament, non-proliferation and the peaceful settlement of disputes in Central Africa;

3. *Also reaffirms its support* for the programme of work of the Standing Advisory Committee adopted at the organizational meeting held at Yaoundé in 1992;

4. *Welcomes* the results of the meetings of the Standing Advisory Committee held at Bujumbura and at Libreville, particularly the adoption of the non-

aggression pact between the States members of the Economic Community of Central African States, a pact that is likely to contribute to the prevention of conflicts and to confidence-building in the subregion;

5. *Takes note* of the readiness of the States members of the Economic Community of Central African States to reduce the military forces, equipment and budgets in the subregion and to carry out a study on that subject;

6. *Requests* the Secretary-General to continue to provide assistance to the Central African States in implementing the programme of work of the Standing Advisory Committee;

7. *Also requests* the Secretary-General to submit to the General Assembly at its forty-ninth session a report on the implementation of the present resolution;

8. *Decides* to include in the provisional agenda of its forty-ninth session the item entitled ''Regional confidence-building measures''.

General Assembly resolution 48/76 A

16 December 1993   Meeting 81   168-1-2 (recorded vote)

Approved by First Committee (A/48/677) by recorded vote (141-1-1), 19 November (meeting 30); 12-nation draft (A/C.1/48/L.6); agenda item 72 (e).
Sponsors: Angola, Burundi, Cameroon, Central African Republic, Chad, Congo, Democratic People's Republic of Korea, Equatorial Guinea, Gabon, Rwanda, Sao Tome and Principe, Zaire.
Financial implications. 5th Committee, A/48/758; S-G, A/C.1/48/L.52, A/C.5/48/32.
Meeting numbers. GA 48th session: 1st Committee 3-14, 20, 30; 5th Committee 38; plenary 81.

Recorded vote in Assembly as follows:

In favour: Afghanistan, Albania, Algeria, Andorra, Angola, Antigua and Barbuda, Argentina, Armenia, Australia, Austria, Azerbaijan, Bahamas, Bahrain, Bangladesh, Barbados, Belarus, Belgium, Belize, Benin, Bhutan, Bolivia, Bosnia and Herzegovina, Botswana, Brazil, Brunei Darussalam, Bulgaria, Burkina Faso, Burundi, Cambodia, Cameroon, Canada, Cape Verde, Central African Republic, Chad, Chile, China, Colombia, Comoros, Congo, Costa Rica, Côte d'Ivoire, Croatia, Cuba, Cyprus, Czech Republic, Democratic People's Republic of Korea, Denmark, Djibouti, Dominica, Dominican Republic, Ecuador, Egypt, Estonia, Ethiopia, Fiji, Finland, France, Gabon, Gambia, Germany, Ghana, Greece, Grenada, Guatemala, Guinea, Guinea-Bissau, Guyana, Haiti, Honduras, Hungary, Iceland, India, Indonesia, Iran, Iraq, Ireland, Israel, Italy, Jamaica, Japan, Jordan, Kazakhstan, Kenya, Kuwait, Kyrgyzstan, Lao People's Democratic Republic, Latvia, Lebanon, Lesotho, Libyan Arab Jamahiriya, Liechtenstein, Lithuania, Luxembourg, Madagascar, Malawi, Malaysia, Maldives, Mali, Malta, Marshall Islands, Mauritania, Mauritius, Mexico, Micronesia, Monaco, Mongolia, Morocco, Mozambique, Myanmar, Namibia, Nepal, Netherlands, New Zealand, Nicaragua, Niger, Nigeria, Norway, Oman, Pakistan, Panama, Papua New Guinea, Paraguay, Peru, Philippines, Poland, Portugal, Qatar, Republic of Korea, Republic of Moldova, Romania, Russian Federation, Rwanda, Saint Lucia, Saint Vincent and the Grenadines, Samoa, Saudi Arabia, Senegal, Seychelles, Sierra Leone, Singapore, Slovakia, Slovenia, Solomon Islands, Spain, Sri Lanka, Sudan, Suriname, Swaziland, Sweden, Syrian Arab Republic, Tajikistan, Thailand, the former Yugoslav Republic of Macedonia, Togo, Trinidad and Tobago, Tunisia, Turkey, Turkmenistan, Uganda, Ukraine, United Arab Emirates, United Republic of Tanzania, Uruguay, Venezuela, Viet Nam, Yemen, Zambia, Zimbabwe.
Against: United States.
Abstaining: Georgia, United Kingdom.

Conventional weapons and advanced technologies

Questions related to conventional weapons and armed forces and to military technology continued to be addressed in different disarmament forums. Most States referred to conventional disarmament in the context of regional disarmament, confidence-building measures (including transparency), and exports and imports of conventional weapons and science and technology. With the conclusion of a number of agreements on significant reductions of nuclear weapons, there had been growing concern over the fact that conventional weapons were increasingly used in areas of tension. Although some progress had been made at the regional level in the reduction of conventional weapons, there was no discernible progress at the global level. Over the last several years, the efforts of the international community had come to focus on ways to regulate exports and imports of arms, including efforts to reduce illicit traffic, and especially to regulate the transfer of high technology with military applications. In addition to those issues, the economic repercussions of efforts to reduce or regulate conventional arms had attracted the attention of the international community.

International arms transfers

As requested by the General Assembly in 1992,[101] the Secretary-General submitted the reply received from one Member State (Colombia) on its national legislation and regulations on the authorization of arms transfers and prevention of the illicit arms trade.[102] Colombia's reply included a statistical table of arms destined for illicit and destabilizing activities that had been confiscated by the military forces and national police.

GENERAL ASSEMBLY ACTION

On 16 December, the General Assembly, on the recommendation of the First Committee, adopted **resolution 48/75 F** without vote.

International arms transfers

The General Assembly,

Recalling its resolutions 43/75 I of 7 December 1988, 46/36 H of 6 December 1991 and 47/54 A of 9 December 1992, and its decisions 45/415 of 4 December 1990 and 47/419 of 9 December 1992,

Realizing the urgent need to resolve underlying conflicts, to diminish tensions and to accelerate efforts towards general and complete disarmament with a view to maintaining regional and international peace and security in a world free from the scourge of war and the burden of armaments,

Reaffirming the role of the United Nations in the field of disarmament and the commitment of Member States to take concrete steps in order to strengthen that role,

Recognizing that, in the context of international arms transfers, the illicit arms traffic is a disturbing, dangerous and increasingly common phenomenon, and that, with the technical sophistication and destructive capability of conventional weapons, the destabilizing effects of the illicit arms traffic increase,

Considering that, in the context of international arms transfers, the illicit arms traffic, by its clandestine nature, defies transparency and until now has escaped inclusion within the Register of Conventional Arms,

Realizing that arms obtained through the illicit arms traffic are most likely to be used for violent purposes, and that even small arms so obtained, directly or indirectly, by underground organizations such as merce-

nary groups can pose a threat to the security and political stability of the States affected,

Stressing that effective control over the imports and exports of conventional weapons falls under the responsibility of Member States,

1. *Takes note* of the report of the Secretary-General;

2. *Calls upon* all Member States to give priority to eradicating the illicit arms traffic associated with destabilizing activities, such as terrorism, drug trafficking and common criminal acts, and to take immediate action towards this end;

3. *Urges* Member States to monitor arms transfers effectively and to strengthen or adopt strict measures in an effort to prevent arms from falling into the hands of parties engaged in the illicit arms traffic;

4. *Notes* that the Disarmament Commission, at its organizational session in 1993, included the question of international arms transfers, with particular reference to General Assembly resolution 46/36 H, in the agenda of its substantive session in 1994, and requests the Commission to report thereon to the Assembly at its forty-ninth session;

5. *Decides* to include in the provisional agenda of its forty-ninth session an item entitled "International illicit arms traffic".

General Assembly resolution 48/75 F

16 December 1993   Meeting 81   Adopted without vote

Approved by First Committee (A/48/676) by recorded vote (143-0-1), 18 November (meeting 28); 24-nation draft (A/C.1/48/L.27/Rev.1); agenda item 71 *(h)*.

Sponsors: Australia, Belarus, Bolivia, Brazil, Chile, Colombia, Costa Rica, Czech Republic, Dominican Republic, Ecuador, Guatemala, Haiti, Honduras, India, Jamaica, Malaysia, Mexico, New Zealand, Panama, Peru, Philippines, Slovakia, Sri Lanka, Turkey.

Meeting numbers. GA 48th session: 1st Committee 3-14, 21, 28; plenary 81.

Also on 16 December, the Assembly, on the recommendation of the First Committee, adopted **resolution 48/75 H** by recorded vote.

Measures to curb the illicit transfer and use of conventional arms

The General Assembly,

Recalling its resolution 46/36 H of 6 December 1991 and its decision 47/419 of 9 December 1992 on international arms transfers,

Considering that the availability of massive quantities of conventional weapons is a contributory factor to armed conflicts around the world,

Stressing the need for measures that curb the illicit transfer and use of conventional weapons,

Recognizing that the excessive quantity of conventional weapons in a number of countries constitutes a source of destabilization of their national and their regional security,

Convinced that peace and security are imperatives for economic development and reconstruction,

1. *Invites* Member States to take appropriate enforcement measures directed at ending the illegal export of conventional weapons from their territories;

2. *Requests* the Secretary-General to seek the views of Governments on effective ways and means of collecting weapons illegally distributed in countries, in the event that such countries so request, and to submit a report to the General Assembly at its forty-ninth session.

General Assembly resolution 48/75 H
16 December 1993   Meeting 81   146-0-22 (recorded vote)

Approved by First Committee (A/48/676) by recorded vote (108-0-33), 19 November (meeting 30); draft by Afghanistan (A/C.1/48/L.31/Rev.2), amended by Cuba (A/C.1/48/L.56); agenda item 71 *(h)*.
Meeting numbers. GA 48th session: 1st Committee 3-14, 23, 30; plenary 81.

Recorded vote in Assembly as follows:

In favour: Afghanistan, Algeria, Andorra, Angola, Antigua and Barbuda, Argentina, Armenia, Australia, Austria, Azerbaijan, Bahamas, Bahrain, Bangladesh, Barbados, Belarus, Belgium, Belize, Benin, Bhutan, Bolivia, Botswana, Brunei Darussalam, Bulgaria, Burkina Faso, Burundi, Cambodia, Cameroon, Cape Verde, Central African Republic, Chad, China, Comoros, Congo, Côte d'Ivoire, Croatia, Cuba, Cyprus, Democratic People's Republic of Korea, Denmark, Djibouti, Dominica, Dominican Republic, Estonia, Ethiopia, Fiji, France, Gabon, Gambia, Germany, Ghana, Greece, Grenada, Guatemala, Guinea, Guinea-Bissau, Guyana, Haiti, Honduras, Hungary, Iceland, India, Indonesia, Iran, Iraq, Ireland, Israel, Italy, Japan, Jordan, Kazakhstan, Kenya, Kuwait, Kyrgyzstan, Lao People's Democratic Republic, Lebanon, Lesotho, Libyan Arab Jamahiriya, Liechtenstein, Luxembourg, Madagascar, Malawi, Maldives, Mali, Malta, Marshall Islands, Mauritania, Mauritius, Micronesia, Monaco, Mongolia, Morocco, Mozambique, Myanmar, Namibia, Nepal, Netherlands, New Zealand, Nicaragua, Niger, Nigeria, Norway, Oman, Pakistan, Panama, Papua New Guinea, Paraguay, Peru, Philippines, Poland, Portugal, Qatar, Republic of Korea, Romania, Russian Federation, Rwanda, Saint Lucia, Saint Vincent and the Grenadines, Samoa, Saudi Arabia, Senegal, Seychelles, Sierra Leone, Singapore, Slovenia, Solomon Islands, Spain, Sri Lanka, Sudan, Suriname, Swaziland, Syrian Arab Republic, Tajikistan, Thailand, the former Yugoslav Republic of Macedonia, Togo, Trinidad and Tobago, Tunisia, Turkey, Ukraine, United Arab Emirates, United Kingdom, Uruguay, Venezuela, Viet Nam, Yemen, Zambia.

Against: None.

Abstaining: Brazil, Canada, Chile, Colombia, Costa Rica, Czech Republic, Ecuador, Egypt, Finland, Georgia, Jamaica, Latvia, Lithuania, Malaysia, Mexico, Republic of Moldova, Slovakia, Sweden, Uganda, United Republic of Tanzania, United States,* Zimbabwe.

*Later advised the Secretariat it had intended to vote in favour.

Before approval of the draft text in the First Committee, Cuba introduced amendments[105] to the fourth preambular paragraph and paragraph 2. The first amendment was adopted by a recorded vote of 105 to 1, with 34 abstentions, and the second by 100 to 1, with 40 abstentions.

Science and technology

In 1993, differences of view persisted concerning the role of science and technology in the context of international security. Most industrialized countries maintained that there was a need to strengthen the existing control regimes regarding the transfer of science and technology that could be used for military purposes, while most developing countries considered that such regimes were discriminatory and adversely affected their economic development. Mention was also made of the danger of the possible dissemination of knowledge regarding weapons of mass destruction and their means of delivery.

Reports of the Secretary-General. As requested by the General Assembly in 1992,[103] the Secretary-General continued to follow scientific and technological developments in order to assess emerging new technologies. In a September report,[104] he stated that between 1991 and 1993 detailed discussion had taken place in the Disarmament Commission on scientific and technological developments and their impact on international security and that further deliberations would be

conducted in 1994 with a view to concluding the item. As the item was still under consideration, it was premature for any further action to be taken. He pointed out that his report on the relationship between disarmament and development[105] covered certain considerations that showed how scientific and technological developments had an impact on international security (see below, under "Economic aspects of disarmament").

Disarmament Commission consideration. The Disarmament Commission established a working group to deal with the role of science and technology in the context of international security, disarmament and other related fields. The group held six meetings between 21 April and 8 May in addition to informal consultations. On 27 April, the group established a drafting group which held 13 meetings.

The working group based its deliberations on a working paper presented by the Chairman, prepared on the basis of a text contained in the report of the corresponding working group of 1992,[106] and on working papers submitted during the 1993 session. As at its 1992 session, the group concentrated on scientific and technological developments and their impact on international security; science and technology for disarmament; the transfer of high technology with military applications; the role of science and technology in other related fields; and the role of the United Nations. New papers were submitted by Australia,[107] Brazil and Canada,[108] and Cuba.[109] Although the group made progress in reconciling differences on a large number of issues, differences of opinion remained. It thereof recommended that the debate be continued at the 1994 session. That recommendation was made on the understanding that the Chairman's working paper, as annexed to the Commission's report,[84] could serve as a basis for further work.

GENERAL ASSEMBLY ACTION

On 16 December, the General Assembly, on the recommendation of the First Committee, adopted **resolution 48/66** by recorded vote.

Scientific and technological developments and their impact on international security

The General Assembly,

Recalling that at its tenth special session, the first special session devoted to disarmament, it unanimously stressed the importance of both qualitative and quantitative measures in the process of disarmament,

Recognizing that scientific and technological developments can have both civilian and military applications and that progress in science and technology for civilian applications needs to be maintained and encouraged,

Noting with concern the potential in technological advances for application to military purposes, which could lead to more sophisticated weapons and new weapon systems,

Stressing the interests of the international community in the subject and the need to follow closely the scientific and technological developments that may have a negative impact on the security environment and on the process of arms limitation and disarmament, and to channel scientific and technological developments for beneficial purposes,

Emphasizing that the proposal contained in its resolution 43/77 A of 7 December 1988 is without prejudice to research and development efforts being undertaken for peaceful purposes,

Noting the results of the United Nations Conference on New Trends in Science and Technology: Implications for International Peace and Security, held at Sendai, Japan, in April 1990,[a] and recognizing, in this regard, the need for the scientific and policy communities to work together in dealing with the complex implications of technological change,

1. *Takes note* of the report of the Secretary-General entitled "Scientific and technological developments and their impact on international security";[a]

2. *Takes note also* of the interim report of the Secretary-General submitted in pursuance of its resolution 45/60 of 4 December 1990;

3. *Fully agrees* that:

(a) The international community needs to position itself better to follow the nature and direction of technological change;

(b) The United Nations can serve as a catalyst and a clearing-house for ideas to this purpose;

4. *Calls upon* the Disarmament Commission to conclude its work on the agenda item entitled "The role of science and technology in the context of international security, disarmament and other related fields" and to submit to the General Assembly its recommendations in this regard;

5. *Requests* the Secretary-General to continue to follow scientific and technological developments in order to make an assessment of emerging new technologies and to submit to the General Assembly at its forty-ninth session a framework for technology assessment guided, *inter alia*, by the criteria suggested in his report;

6. *Decides* to include in the provisional agenda of its forty-ninth session the item entitled "Scientific and technological developments and their impact on international security".

---

[a] A/45/568.

General Assembly resolution 48/66

16 December 1993   Meeting 81   126-4-35 (recorded vote)

Approved by First Committee (A/48/667) by recorded vote (104-4-29), 15 November (meeting 26); 11-nation draft (A/C.1/48/L.22); agenda item 62.

Sponsors: Belarus, Bhutan, Bolivia, Costa Rica, Honduras, India, Indonesia, Nigeria, Panama, Sri Lanka, Venezuela.

Meeting numbers. GA 48th session: 1st Committee 3-14, 23, 26; plenary 81.

Recorded vote in Assembly as follows:

In favour: Afghanistan, Algeria, Antigua and Barbuda, Armenia, Australia, Azerbaijan, Bahamas, Bahrain, Bangladesh, Barbados, Belarus, Belize, Benin, Bhutan, Bolivia, Botswana, Brazil, Brunei Darussalam, Burkina Faso, Burundi, Cambodia, Cameroon, Cape Verde, Central African Republic, Chad, Chile, China, Colombia, Comoros, Congo, Costa Rica, Côte d'Ivoire, Cuba, Cyprus, Democratic People's Republic of Korea, Djibouti, Dominica, Dominican Republic, Ecuador, Egypt, Estonia, Ethiopia, Fiji, Gabon, Gambia, Ghana, Grenada, Guatemala, Guinea, Guinea-Bissau, Guyana, Haiti, Hungary, India, Indonesia, Iran, Iraq, Ireland, Jamaica, Jordan, Kazakhstan, Kenya, Kuwait, Kyrgyzstan, Lao People's Democratic Republic, Lebanon, Lesotho, Libyan Arab Jamahiriya, Madagascar, Malawi, Malaysia, Maldives, Mali, Marshall Islands, Mauritania, Mauritius, Mexico, Micronesia, Mongolia, Morocco, Mozambique, Myanmar, Namibia, Nepal, New Zealand, Nicaragua, Niger, Nigeria, Oman, Pakistan, Panama, Papua New Guinea, Paraguay, Peru, Philippines, Qatar, Republic of Korea, Rwanda, Saint Lucia, Saint Vincent and the Grenadines, Samoa, Saudi Arabia, Senegal, Seychelles, Sierra Leone, Singapore, Solomon Islands, Sri Lanka, Sudan, Suriname, Swaziland, Syrian Arab Republic, Thailand, Togo, Trinidad and Tobago, Tunisia, Uganda, Ukraine, United Arab Emirates, United Republic of Tanzania, Uruguay, Venezuela, Viet Nam, Yemen, Zambia, Zimbabwe.

Against: France, Israel, Monaco, United Kingdom.

Abstaining: Andorra, Argentina, Austria, Belgium, Bulgaria, Canada, Croatia, Czech Republic, Denmark, Finland, Germany, Greece, Iceland, Italy, Japan, Latvia, Liechtenstein, Lithuania, Luxembourg, Malta, Netherlands, Norway, Poland, Portugal, Republic of Moldova, Romania, Russian Federation, Slovakia, Slovenia, Spain, Sweden, Tajikistan, the former Yugoslav Republic of Macedonia, Turkey, United States.*

*Later advised the Secretariat it had intended to vote against.

Also on 16 December, the Assembly, on the recommendation of the First Committee, adopted **resolution 48/67** by recorded vote.

The role of science and technology in the context of international security, disarmament and other related fields

The General Assembly,

Recalling its resolution 47/44 of 9 December 1992,

Taking note of the report of the Disarmament Commission on its 1993 substantive session, in particular on the work of Working Group III on agenda item 6, entitled "The role of science and technology in the context of international security, disarmament and other related fields",

Taking note also of the report of the Secretary-General of 28 September 1993 on scientific and technological developments and their impact on international security,

Recognizing that science and technology *per se* are deemed to be neutral, that scientific and technological developments can have both civilian and military applications and that progress in science and technology for civilian applications needs to be maintained and encouraged,

Noting that qualitative improvements in science and technology with military applications have implications for international security and that States, in this regard, should assess carefully the impact of the use of science and technology on international security,

Recognizing also that progress in the application of science and technology contributes substantially to the implementation of arms control and disarmament agreements, *inter alia*, in the fields of weapons disposal, military conversion and verification,

Recalling that norms and guidelines for the transfer of high technology with military applications should take into account legitimate requirements for the maintenance of international peace and security, while ensuring that they do not deny access to high-technology products, services and know-how for peaceful purposes,

Emphasizing that commitment to, and the fulfilment of, comprehensive and balanced objectives of non-proliferation in all its aspects pertaining to the acquisition or transfer of high technology relevant to weapons of mass destruction are essential for the maintenance of international security and international cooperation and for the promotion of transfers of such technology for peaceful purposes,

Noting the interest of the international community in cooperation in the fields of disarmament-related science and technology and the transfer of high technology with military applications,

Mindful that international cooperation should be encouraged with respect to the production of disarmament-related technical equipment with the purpose, *inter alia*, of reducing the costs of implementing arms limitation and disarmament agreements,

1. *Calls upon* the Disarmament Commission to conclude its work on the agenda item entitled "The role of science and technology in the context of international security, disarmament and other related fields" in 1994 and to submit as soon as possible specific recommendations on this matter to the General Assembly;

2. *Requests* the Conference on Disarmament to pursue constructively, in response to General Assembly resolution 46/36 L of 9 December 1991, its work on the agenda item entitled "Transparency in armaments", which includes consideration of the elaboration of practical means to increase openness and transparency related to the transfer of high technology with military applications;

3. *Invites* Member States to undertake additional efforts to apply science and technology for disarmament-related purposes and to make disarmament-related technologies available to interested States;

4. *Also invites* Member States to widen multilateral dialogue, bearing in mind the proposal for seeking universally acceptable norms or guidelines that would regulate international transfers of high technology with military applications;

5. *Encourages* the United Nations to contribute, within existing mandates, to promoting the application of science and technology for peaceful purposes;

6. *Decides* to include in the provisional agenda of its forty-ninth session the item entitled "The role of science and technology in the context of international security, disarmament and other related fields".

General Assembly resolution 48/67

16 December 1993   Meeting 81   161-0-5 (recorded vote)

Approved by First Committee (A/48/668) by recorded vote (133-0-3), 15 November (meeting 26); 33-nation draft (A/C.1/48/L.30); agenda item 63.

Sponsors: Argentina, Australia, Austria, Brazil, Bolivia, Bulgaria, Canada, Chile, Costa Rica, Czech Republic, Denmark, Ecuador, Finland, Germany, Greece, Honduras, Hungary, Ireland, Japan, Luxembourg, Nepal, New Zealand, Norway, Panama, Portugal, Republic of Korea, Romania, Russian Federation, Slovakia, Slovenia, Sweden, the former Yugoslav Republic of Macedonia, Uruguay.

Meeting numbers. GA 48th session: 1st Committee 3-14, 23, 26; plenary 81.

Recorded vote in Assembly as follows:

In favour: Afghanistan, Albania, Algeria, Antigua and Barbuda, Argentina, Armenia, Australia, Austria, Azerbaijan, Bahamas, Bahrain, Bangladesh, Barbados, Belarus, Belgium, Belize, Benin, Bhutan, Bolivia, Botswana, Brazil, Brunei Darussalam, Bulgaria, Burkina Faso, Burundi, Cambodia, Cameroon, Canada, Cape Verde, Central African Republic, Chad, Chile, China, Colombia, Comoros, Congo, Costa Rica, Côte d'Ivoire, Croatia, Cuba, Cyprus, Czech Republic, Democratic People's Republic of Korea, Denmark, Djibouti, Dominica, Dominican Republic, Ecuador, Egypt, Estonia, Ethiopia, Fiji, Finland, Gabon, Gambia, Germany, Ghana, Greece, Grenada, Guatemala, Guinea, Guinea-Bissau, Guyana, Haiti, Hungary, Iceland, India, Indonesia, Iraq, Ireland, Israel, Italy, Jamaica, Japan, Jordan, Kazakhstan, Kenya, Kuwait, Kyrgyzstan, Lao People's Democratic Republic, Latvia, Lebanon, Lesotho, Libyan Arab Jamahiriya, Liechtenstein, Lithuania, Luxembourg, Madagascar, Malawi, Malaysia, Maldives, Mali, Malta, Marshall Islands, Mauritania, Mauritius, Mexico, Micronesia, Mongolia, Morocco, Mozambique, Myanmar, Namibia, Nepal, Netherlands, New Zealand, Nicaragua, Niger, Nigeria, Norway, Oman, Pakistan, Panama, Papua New Guinea, Paraguay, Peru, Philippines, Poland, Portugal, Qatar, Republic of Korea, Republic of Moldova, Romania, Russian Federation, Rwanda, Saint Lucia, Saint Vincent and the Grenadines, Samoa, Saudi Arabia, Senegal, Seychelles, Sierra Leone, Singapore, Slovakia, Slovenia, Solomon Islands, Spain, Sri Lanka, Sudan, Suriname, Swaziland, Sweden, Syrian Arab Republic, Tajikistan, Thailand, the former Yugoslav Republic of Macedonia, Togo, Trinidad and Tobago, Tunisia, Turkey, Turkmenistan, Uganda, Ukraine, United Arab Emirates, United Republic of Tanzania, Uruguay, Venezuela, Viet Nam, Yemen, Zambia, Zimbabwe.

Against: None.

Abstaining: Andorra, France, Monaco, United Kingdom, United States.

Convention on excessively injurious conventional weapons and its Protocols

Throughout 1993, there was renewed interest, in different international forums, in questions related to the prohibition of certain conventional weapons considered to be excessively injurious, especially anti-personnel mines. While the Convention on Prohibitions or Restrictions on the Use of Certain Conventional Weapons Which May Be Deemed to Be Excessively Injurious or to Have Indiscriminate Effects and its three Protocols (dealing with non-detectable fragments; mines, booby traps and other devices; and incendiary weapons) had been kept under review with regard to the status of adherence ever since its conclusion in 1980,[110] the question of broadening its scope, either by amending its Protocols or adopting additional protocols, had gained momentum in the last few years, as concerns had grown over the enormous quantity of mines sown on the territory of many countries and the consequent suffering of civilians, not only in time of war but also after the cessation of hostilities. During the year, three related subjects were discussed: the Convention and its Protocol II (on mines); a moratorium on the export of anti-personnel mines; and assistance in mine clearance.

Status of the Convention

Pursuant to a 1992 General Assembly request,[111] the Secretary-General submitted in October 1993 a report on the status of the Convention and its Protocols during the period 1 September 1989 to 31 August 1993.[112]

The number of States parties to the Convention stood at 41, as at 31 December 1993.[113] During 1993, Latvia acceded to the Convention, Bosnia and Herzegovina, Croatia, the Czech Republic and Slovakia succeeded to it and New Zealand and Spain ratified it. The Convention and Protocols entered into force in 1983.[114]

Review conference

In October,[112] the Secretary-General reported that, on 9 February, France had requested him to convene, in conformity with article 8, paragraph 3, of the Convention, a conference to review the Convention and its Protocols, with priority to be given to anti-personnel mines. That request was transmitted to the parties to the Convention.

GENERAL ASSEMBLY ACTION

On 16 December, the General Assembly, on the recommendation of the First Committee, adopted **resolution 48/79** by recorded vote.

Convention on Prohibitions or Restrictions on the Use of Certain Conventional Weapons Which May Be Deemed to Be Excessively Injurious or to Have Indiscriminate Effects

The General Assembly,

Recalling its resolutions 32/152 of 19 December 1977, 35/153 of 12 December 1980, 36/93 of 9 December 1981, 37/79 of 9 December 1982, 38/66 of 15 December 1983, 39/56 of 12 December 1984, 40/84 of 12 December 1985, 41/50 of 3 December 1986, 42/30 of 30 November 1987, 43/67 of 7 December 1988, 45/64 of 4 December 1990, 46/40 of 6 December 1991 and 47/56 of 9 December 1992,

Recalling with satisfaction the adoption, on 10 October 1980, of the Convention on Prohibitions or Restrictions on the Use of Certain Conventional Weapons Which May Be Deemed to Be Excessively Injurious or to Have Indiscriminate Effects, together with the Protocol on Non-Detectable Fragments (Protocol I), the Protocol on Prohibitions or Restrictions on the Use of Mines, Booby Traps and Other Devices (Protocol II) and the Protocol on Prohibitions or Restrictions on the Use of Incendiary Weapons (Protocol III),

Recalling also the role played by the International Committee of the Red Cross in the elaboration of the Convention and the Protocols annexed thereto,

Noting with satisfaction that, the conditions set forth in article 5 of the Convention having been met, the Convention and the three Protocols annexed thereto entered into force on 2 December 1983,

Recalling further the commitment by the States that are parties to the Convention and the Protocols annexed thereto to respect the objectives and the provisions thereof, especially those set forth in the ninth preambular paragraph of the Convention, relating to the wish to prohibit or restrict further the use of certain conventional weapons, and believing that the positive results achieved in this area may facilitate the main talks on disarmament with a view to putting an end to the production, stockpiling and proliferation of such weapons,

Noting that, in conformity with article 8 of the Convention, conferences may be convened to examine amendments to the Convention or to any of the Protocols thereto, to examine additional protocols concerning other categories of conventional weapons not covered by the existing Protocols or to review the scope and application of the Convention and the Protocols annexed thereto and to examine any proposed amendments or additional protocols,

Noting with satisfaction that a State party has asked the Secretary-General of the United Nations to convene, in conformity with article 8, paragraph 3, of the Convention, a conference to review the Convention and the Protocols annexed thereto, giving priority to the question of anti-personnel land mines,

Noting also that international meetings have discussed possible restrictions on the use of other weapon categories presently not covered by the Convention and the Protocols annexed thereto,

Reaffirming its conviction that a general and verifiable agreement on prohibitions or restrictions on the use of certain conventional weapons would significantly reduce the suffering of civilians and combatants,

Being desirous of reinforcing international cooperation in the area of prohibitions or restrictions on the use of certain conventional weapons, and particularly for the removal of minefields, mines and booby traps,

Recalling in this respect its resolution 48/7 of 19 October 1993 on assistance in mine clearance,

1. *Registers its satisfaction* with the report of the Secretary-General;

2. *Notes with satisfaction* that additional States have signed, ratified or accepted the Convention on Prohibitions or Restrictions on the Use of Certain Conventional Weapons Which May Be Deemed to Be Excessively Injurious or to Have Indiscriminate Effects, which was opened for signature in New York on 10 April 1981, or have acceded to the Convention;

3. *Urgently calls upon* all States that have not yet done so to take all measures to become parties, as soon as possible, to the Convention and upon successor States to take appropriate measures so that ultimately access to this instrument will be universal;

4. *Calls upon* the Secretary-General of the United Nations, in his capacity as Depositary of the Convention and the three Protocols annexed thereto, to inform it periodically of accessions to the Convention and the Protocols;

5. *Welcomes* the request to the Secretary-General to convene at an appropriate time, if possible in 1994, in accordance with article 8, paragraph 3, of the Convention, a conference to review the Convention;

6. *Encourages* the States parties to request the Secretary-General to establish as soon as possible a group of governmental experts to prepare the review conference and to furnish needed assistance and assure services, including the preparation of analytical reports that the review conference and the group of experts might need;

7. *Calls upon* the maximum number of States to attend the conference, to which the States parties may invite interested non-governmental organizations, in particular the International Committee of the Red Cross;

8. *Decides* to include in the provisional agenda of its forty-ninth session the item entitled ''Convention on Prohibitions or Restrictions on the Use of Certain Conventional Weapons Which May Be Deemed to Be Excessively Injurious or to Have Indiscriminate Effects''.

General Assembly resolution 48/79

16 December 1993   Meeting 81   162-0-3 (recorded vote)

Approved by First Committee (A/48/680) by recorded vote (140-0-2), 19 November (meeting 30); 23-nation draft (A/C.1/48/L.34/Rev.1), amended by Mexico (A/C.1/48/L.49/Rev.1); agenda item 75.

Sponsors: Afghanistan, Australia, Austria, Bolivia, Canada, Costa Rica, Cuba, Democratic People's Republic of Korea, Ecuador, Finland, Honduras, Iceland, Ireland, Lao People's Democratic Republic, Latvia, Liechtenstein, Lithuania, Mongolia, Netherlands, New Zealand, Nicaragua, Sweden, the former Yugoslav Republic of Macedonia.

Meeting numbers. GA 48th session: 1st Committee 3-14, 22, 30; plenary 81.

Recorded vote in Assembly as follows:

In favour: Afghanistan, Albania, Algeria, Andorra, Angola, Antigua and Barbuda, Argentina, Armenia, Australia, Austria, Azerbaijan, Bahamas, Bahrain, Bangladesh, Barbados, Belarus, Belgium, Belize, Benin, Bhutan, Bolivia, Botswana, Brazil, Brunei Darussalam, Bulgaria, Burundi, Cambodia, Cameroon, Canada, Cape Verde, Central African Republic, Chad, Chile, Colombia, Comoros, Congo, Costa Rica, Côte d'Ivoire, Croatia, Cuba, Cyprus, Czech Republic, Democratic People's Republic of Korea, Denmark, Djibouti, Dominica, Dominican Republic, Ecuador, Egypt, Estonia, Ethiopia, Finland, France, Gabon, Germany, Ghana, Greece, Grenada, Guinea, Guinea-Bissau, Guyana, Haiti, Honduras, Hungary, Iceland, India, Indonesia, Iran, Iraq, Ireland, Israel, Italy, Jamaica, Japan, Jordan, Kazakhstan, Kenya, Kuwait, Kyrgyzstan, Lao People's Democratic Republic, Latvia, Lebanon, Lesotho, Libyan Arab Jamahiriya, Liechtenstein, Lithuania, Luxembourg, Madagascar, Malawi, Malaysia, Maldives, Mali, Malta, Marshall Islands, Mauritania, Mauritius, Micronesia, Mexico, Monaco, Mongolia,

Morocco, Mozambique, Myanmar, Namibia, Nepal, Netherlands, New Zealand, Nicaragua, Niger, Nigeria, Norway, Oman, Pakistan, Panama, Papua New Guinea, Paraguay, Peru, Philippines, Poland, Portugal, Qatar, Republic of Korea, Republic of Moldova, Romania, Rwanda, Saint Lucia, Saint Vincent and the Grenadines, Samoa, Saudi Arabia, Senegal, Seychelles, Sierra Leone, Singapore, Slovakia, Slovenia, Solomon Islands, Spain, Sri Lanka, Sudan, Suriname, Swaziland, Sweden, Syrian Arab Republic, Tajikistan, Thailand, the former Yugoslav Republic of Macedonia, Togo, Trinidad and Tobago, Tunisia, Turkey, Turkmenistan, Uganda, Ukraine, United Arab Emirates, United Kingdom, United Republic of Tanzania, Uruguay, Venezuela, Viet Nam, Yemen, Zambia, Zimbabwe.
Against: None.
Abstaining: Georgia, Russian Federation, United States.

In the First Committee, Mexico submitted an amendment to the fifth preambular paragraph of the draft resolution. The Committee adopted it by a recorded vote of 52 to 24, with 32 abstentions. The amended paragraph was then adopted by a recorded vote of 57 to 4, with 55 abstentions.

A recorded vote on the fifth preambular paragraph was also requested in the Assembly. The paragraph was retained by 85 votes to 2, with 62 abstentions.

Land-mines

In February,[115] the President of the Security Council, in the context of the Council's consideration of the Secretary-General's 1992 report "An Agenda for Peace",[116] asked the Secretary-General to address the problem of land-mines as a matter of special concern.

In June,[117] the Secretary-General reported that he had instituted a coordinated programme of action for demining involving the United Nations Department of Humanitarian Affairs, the Department of Peace-keeping Operations and others. Considerable progress was being made.

In view of the seriousness of the situation, the 12 EC members requested in August[118] that an item entitled "Assistance in mine clearance" be inscribed on the agenda of the General Assembly's forty-eighth (1993) session. They stressed their conviction that a comprehensive programme of assistance in mine clearance which took into account all the aspects of economic and social reconstruction must be contemplated on a priority basis.

Symposium. The International Committee of the Red Cross organized a symposium on anti-personnel mines (Montreux, Switzerland, 21-23 April 1993) in the course of which a number of governmental and non-governmental experts addressed the humanitarian concerns raised by the use of such mines. The symposium concluded that there was a need to develop a coordinated strategy to tackle the medical, commercial, legal, technical, socio-economic and data-related aspects of the entire problem with a view to alleviating the sufferings of mine victims.

GENERAL ASSEMBLY ACTION

On 19 October, the General Assembly adopted **resolution 48/7** without vote.

Assistance in mine clearance

The General Assembly,

Gravely alarmed by the increasing presence of mines and other unexploded devices resulting from armed conflicts,

Dismayed by the high number of victims of mines, especially among civilian populations, and taking note in this context of resolution 1993/83 of the Commission on Human Rights of 10 March 1993, on the effects of armed conflicts on children's lives,

Gravely concerned by the serious humanitarian, social, economic and ecological disruption which can be caused by the failure to remove mines and other unexploded devices,

Bearing in mind the serious threat which mines and other unexploded devices pose to the safety, the health and the lives of personnel participating in humanitarian, peace-keeping and rehabilitation operations,

Aware that mines constitute an obstacle to reconstruction and economic development as well as to the restoration of normal social conditions,

Considering that, in addition to the responsibilities incumbent upon States, there is scope for the United Nations to strengthen its contribution to the solution of problems relating to mine clearance,

Taking note with interest, in this regard, of the recommendations made by the Secretary-General in paragraph 58 of his report of 17 June 1992 entitled "An Agenda for Peace", as well as in his report of 15 June 1993,

Recalling its resolution 47/120 B of 20 September 1993 on the "Agenda for Peace",

Taking note of the statement made by the President of the Security Council on 26 February 1993,

Recalling also its resolution 47/56 of 9 December 1992 on the Convention on Prohibitions or Restrictions on the Use of Certain Conventional Weapons Which May Be Deemed to Be Excessively Injurious or to Have Indiscriminate Effects, and in particular on the Protocol on Prohibitions or Restrictions on the Use of Mines, Booby Traps and Other Devices (Protocol II),

Noting with interest, in this regard, the convening by the Secretary-General of a review conference to amend the above-mentioned Convention and in particular its Protocol II,

Noting with satisfaction the inclusion in the mandate of several peace-keeping operations of provisions relating to mine clearance,

Commending the activities already undertaken by the United Nations system, the International Committee of the Red Cross and non-governmental organizations to address the solution of problems relating to the presence of mines,

Welcoming the establishment, within the Secretariat, of a coordinated mine-clearance programme,

1. *Deplores* the adverse consequences which can be caused by the failure to remove mines and other unexploded devices remaining in place after armed conflicts, and considers it a matter of urgency to correct the situation;

2. *Stresses* the importance of coordination by the United Nations of activities, including those by regional organizations, related to mine clearance, in particular those activities relating to information and training with a view to improving the effectiveness of activities in the field;

3. *Invites* all relevant programmes and bodies, multilateral or national, to include, in a coordinated manner, activities related to mine clearance in their humanitarian, social and economic assistance activities;

4. *Requests* the Secretary-General to submit to the General Assembly, before its forty-ninth session, a comprehensive report on the problems caused by the increasing presence of mines and other unexploded devices resulting from armed conflicts and on the manner in which the United Nations contribution to the solution of problems relating to mine clearance could be strengthened;

5. *Also requests* the Secretary-General to include in his report consideration of the financial aspects of activities related to mine clearance and, in this context, of the advisability of establishing a voluntary trust fund to finance, in particular, information and training programmes relating to mine clearance and to facilitate the launching of mine-clearance operations;

6. *Urges* all Member States to extend full assistance and cooperation to the Secretary-General in this respect and to provide him with any information and data which could be useful in drawing up the above-mentioned report;

7. *Decides* to include in the provisional agenda of its forty-ninth session the item entitled ''Assistance in mine clearance''.

General Assembly resolution 48/7

19 October 1993   Meeting 32   Adopted without vote

88-nation draft (A/48/L.5 & Add.1); agenda item 155.

Sponsors: Afghanistan, Albania, Andorra, Angola, Antigua and Barbuda, Argentina, Armenia, Australia, Austria, Bangladesh, Barbados, Belgium, Benin, Bosnia and Herzegovina, Bulgaria, Cambodia, Cameroon, Canada, Cape Verde, Costa Rica, Croatia, Czech Republic, Denmark, Djibouti, Dominican Republic, Egypt, El Salvador, Estonia, Finland, France, Gabon, Germany, Greece, Grenada, Guatemala, Guinea, Honduras, Hungary, Iceland, India, Ireland, Italy, Japan, Kazakhstan, Kuwait, Latvia, Lesotho, Liechtenstein, Lithuania, Luxembourg, Malawi, Malaysia, Malta, Mauritius, Monaco, Mongolia, Mozambique, Nepal, Netherlands, New Zealand, Nicaragua, Nigeria, Norway, Pakistan, Panama, Poland, Portugal, Republic of Korea, Republic of Moldova, Romania, Russian Federation, Rwanda, Saint Lucia, San Marino, Sierra Leone, Singapore, Slovakia, Spain, Sri Lanka, Sudan, Sweden, Thailand, Togo, Tunisia, Ukraine, United Kingdom, United Republic of Tanzania, United States.

On 16 December, the Assembly, on the recommendation of the First Committee, adopted **resolution 48/75 K** without vote.

Moratorium on the export of anti-personnel land-mines

The General Assembly,

Noting that there are as many as 85 million uncleared land-mines throughout the world, particularly in rural areas,

Expressing deep concern that such mines kill or maim hundreds of people each week, mostly unarmed civilians, obstruct economic development and have other severe consequences, which include inhibiting the repatriation of refugees and the return of internally displaced persons,

Recalling with satisfaction its resolution 48/7 of 19 October 1993, by which it, *inter alia*, requested the Secretary-General to submit a comprehensive report on the problems caused by mines and other unexploded devices,

Convinced that a moratorium by States exporting anti-personnel land-mines that pose grave dangers to civilian populations would reduce substantially the human and economic costs resulting from the use of such devices and would complement the aforementioned initiative,

Noting with satisfaction that several States have already declared moratoriums on the export, transfer or purchase of anti-personnel land-mines and related devices,

1. *Calls upon* States to agree to a moratorium on the export of anti-personnel land-mines that pose grave dangers to civilian populations;

2. *Urges* States to implement such a moratorium;

3. *Requests* the Secretary-General to prepare a report concerning progress on this initiative, including possible recommendations regarding further appropriate measures to limit the export of anti-personnel land-mines, and to submit it to the General Assembly at its forty-ninth session under the item entitled ''General and complete disarmament''.

General Assembly resolution 48/75 K

16 December 1993   Meeting 81   Adopted without vote

Approved by First Committee (A/48/676) without vote, 18 November (meeting 28); 66-nation draft (A/C.1/48/L.42); agenda item 71.

Sponsors: Afghanistan, Argentina, Austria, Azerbaijan, Bangladesh, Belgium, Belize, Bulgaria, Cambodia, Cameroon, Canada, Chad, Costa Rica, Côte d'Ivoire, Croatia, Cyprus, Czech Republic, Denmark, El Salvador, Ethiopia, Finland, France, Greece, Guatemala, Guyana, Honduras, Hungary, Iceland, Ireland, Israel, Japan, Kuwait, Kyrgyzstan, Latvia, Lebanon, Lesotho, Liberia, Luxembourg, Madagascar, Malawi, Maldives, Malta, Marshall Islands, Micronesia, Mongolia, Mozambique, Namibia, Netherlands, New Zealand, Nicaragua, Nigeria, Norway, Panama, Philippines, Poland, Portugal, Romania, Rwanda, Senegal, Sierra Leone, Slovakia, Slovenia, Sweden, the former Yugoslav Republic of Macedonia, Togo, United States.

Meeting numbers. GA 48th session: 1st Committee 3-14, 24, 28; plenary 81.

Economic aspects of disarmament

Disarmament and development

As requested by the General Assembly in 1992,[119] the Secretary-General in September 1993[105] reported on action taken with regard to the relationship between disarmament and development, particularly the implementation of priorities for the period 1990-1993, as determined by a high-level intra-Secretariat task force in 1990.[120] The task force had been established pursuant to the Final Document adopted at the 1987 International Conference on the Relationship between Disarmament and Development.[121]

Activities described by the Secretary-General included the Conference on International Cooperation to Promote Conversion from Military to Civilian Industry (Hong Kong, 7-10 July) and consideration of the matter in 1993 by the Disarmament Commission.[84] He noted that the Commission recommended that every effort be made to apply scientific and technological resources, dedicated to military ends, to related activities in other fields, such as economic and social development, conversion, protection of the environment and other peaceful purposes. In addition, he had requested the United Nations Conference on Trade and Development to coordinate the establishment of an interdepartmental task force on conversion and to prepare a preliminary proposal for its organization and programme of work.

On 30 July, the Economic and Social Council adopted **resolution 1993/70** on the scientific and technological aspects of the conversion of military capacity for civilian use and sustainable development.

GENERAL ASSEMBLY ACTION

On 16 December, the General Assembly, on the recommendation of the First Committee, adopted **resolution 48/75 A** without vote.

Relationship between disarmament and development

The General Assembly,

Recalling the provisions of the Final Document of the Tenth Special Session of the General Assembly concerning the relationship between disarmament and development,

Recalling also the adoption on 11 September 1987 of the Final Document of the International Conference on the Relationship between Disarmament and Development,

Recalling further its resolution 47/52 F of 9 December 1992,

Bearing in mind the final documents of the Tenth Conference of Heads of State or Government of Non-Aligned Countries, held at Jakarta in September 1992,

Stressing the growing importance of the symbiotic relationship between disarmament and development in current international relations,

1. *Welcomes* the report of the Secretary-General and actions undertaken in accordance with the Final Document of the International Conference on the Relationship between Disarmament and Development;

2. *Requests* the Secretary-General to continue to take action, through appropriate organs and within available resources, for the implementation of the action programme adopted at the International Conference;

3. *Also requests* the Secretary-General to submit a report to the General Assembly at its forty-ninth session;

4. *Decides* to include in the provisional agenda of its forty-ninth session the item entitled "Relationship between disarmament and development".

General Assembly resolution 48/75 A

16 December 1993   Meeting 81   Adopted without vote

Approved by First Committee (A/48/676) without vote, 15 November (meeting 26); draft by Bolivia, Haiti, Indonesia (for Non-Aligned Movement) and the former Yugoslav Republic of Macedonia (A/C.1/48/L.7/Rev.1); agenda item 71 *(e)*.

Meeting numbers. GA 48th session: 1st Committee 3-14, 23, 26; plenary 81.

Prevention of an arms race in outer space

In 1993, positive developments in international relations caused differences of view to be less pronounced between the majority of States, on the one hand, and a small group of States, on the other, regarding the appropriateness of multilateral negotiations on preventing an arms race in outer space. In all forums dealing with the question, concern continued to be expressed about the danger of the militarization of outer space and the impor-

tance and urgency of preventing an arms race in that environment.

Conference on Disarmament consideration. In 1993, the Conference on Disarmament[35] re-established its Ad Hoc Committee on the Prevention of an Arms Race in Outer Space, which held 17 meetings between 16 February and 18 August.[122] The Committee adopted the same programme of work as in 1992,[123] which included the examination and identification of relevant issues; existing agreements; and existing proposals and future initiatives relating to the subject.

The Committee Chairman appointed friends of the Chairman, who held open-ended consultations on confidence-building measures in outer space and terminology and other relevant legal aspects related to the prevention of an arms race in outer space. In addition, the Committee benefited from scientific and technical contributions by experts from various delegations.

The Committee gave considerable attention to the question of confidence-building measures and the importance of transparency in outer space activities, which was discussed in conjunction with the possible formulation of a new mandate for the Committee. A number of Western and Eastern European delegations, as well as several members of the Group of 21, shared and supported the Chairman's view that the Ad Hoc Committee should be given a mandate to negotiate confidence-building measures. The majority of delegations, while agreeing that the Committee should be given such a mandate, emphasized that it should not be narrow but should encompass all relevant aspects of the prevention of an arms race in outer space. There was wide agreement that the conclusion of an international agreement, or agreements, to prevent an arms race in outer space remained the fundamental task of the Committee, and that concrete proposals on confidence-building measures could form an integral part of such agreements. It was recommended that the Conference on Disarmament re-establish the Ad Hoc Committee with an appropriate mandate at the beginning of the 1994 session, taking into account the work undertaken since 1985.

GENERAL ASSEMBLY ACTION

On 16 December, the General Assembly, on the recommendation of the First Committee, adopted **resolution 48/74 A** by recorded vote.

Prevention of an arms race in outer space

The General Assembly,

Recognizing the common interest of all mankind in the exploration and use of outer space for peaceful purposes,

Reaffirming the will of all States that the exploration and use of outer space, including the Moon and other celestial bodies, shall be for peaceful purposes, shall be carried out for the benefit and in the interest of all countries, irrespective of their degree of economic or scientific development, and shall be the province of all mankind,

Reaffirming also provisions of articles III and IV of the Treaty on Principles Governing the Activities of States in the Exploration and Use of Outer Space, including the Moon and Other Celestial Bodies,

Recalling the obligation of all States to observe the provisions of the Charter of the United Nations regarding the use or threat of use of force in their international relations, including in their space activities,

Reaffirming further paragraph 80 of the Final Document of the Tenth Special Session of the General Assembly, in which it is stated that in order to prevent an arms race in outer space further measures should be taken and appropriate international negotiations held in accordance with the spirit of the Treaty,

Recalling also its previous resolutions on this question and the Final Document adopted by the Tenth Conference of Heads of State or Government of Non-Aligned Countries, held at Jakarta in September 1992, and taking note of the proposals submitted to the General Assembly at its tenth special session and at its regular sessions, and of the recommendations made to the competent organs of the United Nations and to the Conference on Disarmament,

Recognizing the grave danger for international peace and security of an arms race in outer space and of developments contributing to it,

Emphasizing the paramount importance of strict compliance with existing arms limitation and disarmament agreements relevant to outer space, including bilateral agreements, and with the existing legal regime concerning the use of outer space,

Considering that wide participation in the legal regime applicable to outer space could contribute to enhancing its effectiveness,

Noting that bilateral negotiations, begun in 1985 between the Union of Soviet Socialist Republics and the United States of America, were conducted with the declared objective of working out effective agreements aimed, *inter alia*, at preventing an arms race in outer space,

Welcoming the re-establishment of the Ad Hoc Committee on the Prevention of an Arms Race in Outer Space at the 1993 session of the Conference on Disarmament, in the exercise of the negotiating responsibilities of this sole multilateral body on disarmament, to continue to examine and identify, through substantive and general consideration, issues relevant to the prevention of an arms race in outer space,

Noting also that the Ad Hoc Committee on the Prevention of an Arms Race in Outer Space, taking into account its previous efforts since its establishment in 1985 and seeking to enhance its functioning in qualitative terms, continued the examination and identification of various issues, existing agreements and existing proposals, as well as future initiatives relevant to the prevention of an arms race in outer space, and that this contributed to a better understanding of a number of problems and to a clearer perception of the various positions,

Emphasizing the mutually complementary nature of bilateral and multilateral efforts in the field of preventing an arms race in outer space, and hoping that concrete results will emerge from those efforts as soon as possible,

Convinced that further measures should be examined in the search for effective and verifiable bilateral and multilateral agreements in order to prevent an arms race in outer space,

Stressing that the growing use of outer space increases the need for greater transparency and better information on the part of the international community,

Recalling in this context its previous resolutions, in particular resolutions 45/55 B of 4 December 1990 and 47/51 of 9 December 1992, in which, *inter alia*, it reaffirmed the importance of confidence-building measures as means conducive to ensuring the attainment of the objective of the prevention of an arms race in outer space,

Conscious of the benefits of confidence- and security-building measures in the military field,

Recognizing that there was wide agreement in the Ad Hoc Committee that the conclusion of an international agreement or agreements to prevent an arms race in outer space remained the fundamental task of the Committee and that the concrete proposals on confidence-building measures could form an integral part of such agreements,

1. *Reaffirms* the importance and urgency of preventing an arms race in outer space and the readiness of all States to contribute to that common objective, in conformity with the provisions of the Treaty on Principles Governing the Activities of States in the Exploration and Use of Outer Space, including the Moon and Other Celestial Bodies;

2. *Reaffirms its recognition*, as stated in the report of the Ad Hoc Committee on the Prevention of an Arms Race in Outer Space, that the legal regime applicable to outer space by itself does not guarantee the prevention of an arms race in outer space, that this legal regime plays a significant role in the prevention of an arms race in that environment, that there is a need to consolidate and reinforce that regime and enhance its effectiveness, and that it is important strictly to comply with existing agreements, both bilateral and multilateral;

3. *Emphasizes* the necessity of further measures with appropriate and effective provisions for verification to prevent an arms race in outer space;

4. *Calls upon* all States, in particular those with major space capabilities, to contribute actively to the objective of the peaceful use of outer space and of the prevention of an arms race in outer space and to refrain from actions contrary to that objective and to the relevant existing treaties in the interest of maintaining international peace and security and promoting international cooperation;

5. *Reiterates* that the Conference on Disarmament, as the single multilateral disarmament negotiating forum, has the primary role in the negotiation of a multilateral agreement or agreements, as appropriate, on the prevention of an arms race in outer space in all its aspects;

6. *Requests* the Conference on Disarmament to consider as a matter of priority the question of preventing an arms race in outer space;

7. *Also requests* the Conference on Disarmament to intensify its consideration of the question of the prevention of an arms race in outer space in all its aspects, building upon areas of convergence and taking into ac-

count relevant proposals and initiatives, including those presented in the Ad Hoc Committee at the 1993 session of the Conference and at the forty-eighth session of the General Assembly;

8. *Further requests* the Conference on Disarmament to re-establish an ad hoc committee with an adequate mandate at the beginning of its 1994 session and to continue building upon areas of convergence, taking into account the work undertaken since 1985, with a view to undertaking negotiations for the conclusion of an agreement or agreements, as appropriate, to prevent an arms race in outer space in all its aspects;

9. *Recognizes*, in this respect, the growing convergence of views on the elaboration of measures designed to strengthen transparency, confidence and security in the peaceful uses of outer space;

10. *Urges* the Russian Federation and the United States of America to resume their bilateral negotiations with a view to reaching early agreement for preventing an arms race in outer space, and to advise the Conference on Disarmament periodically of the progress of their bilateral sessions so as to facilitate its work;

11. *Decides* to include in the provisional agenda of its forty-ninth session the item entitled "Prevention of an arms race in outer space".

General Assembly resolution 48/74 A

16 December 1993   Meeting 81   169-0-1 (recorded vote)

Approved by First Committee (A/48/675) by recorded vote (136-0-2), 18 November (meeting 29); 23-nation draft (A/C.1/48/L.5/Rev.1); agenda item 70.

Sponsors: Algeria, Australia, Bolivia, Brazil, China, Democratic People's Republic of Korea, Egypt, Ethiopia, India, Indonesia, Iran, Ireland, Kazakhstan, Mexico, Myanmar, Nigeria, Panama, Romania, Sri Lanka, Sudan, Ukraine, Venezuela, Viet Nam.

Meeting numbers. GA 48th session: 1st Committee 3-14, 23, 29; plenary 81.

Recorded vote in Assembly as follows:

In favour: Afghanistan, Albania, Algeria, Andorra, Angola, Antigua and Barbuda, Argentina, Armenia, Australia, Austria, Azerbaijan, Bahamas, Bahrain, Bangladesh, Barbados, Belarus, Belgium, Belize, Benin, Bhutan, Bolivia, Botswana, Brazil, Brunei Darussalam, Bulgaria, Burkina Faso, Burundi, Cambodia, Cameroon, Canada, Cape Verde, Central African Republic, Chad, Chile, China, Colombia, Comoros, Congo, Costa Rica, Côte d'Ivoire, Croatia, Cuba, Cyprus, Czech Republic, Democratic People's Republic of Korea, Denmark, Djibouti, Dominica, Dominican Republic, Ecuador, Egypt, Estonia, Ethiopia, Fiji, Finland, France, Gabon, Gambia, Georgia, Germany, Ghana, Greece, Grenada, Guatemala, Guinea, Guinea-Bissau, Guyana, Haiti, Honduras, Hungary, Iceland, India, Indonesia, Iran, Iraq, Ireland, Israel, Italy, Jamaica, Japan, Jordan, Kazakhstan, Kenya, Kuwait, Kyrgyzstan, Lao People's Democratic Republic, Latvia, Lebanon, Lesotho, Libyan Arab Jamahiriya, Liechtenstein, Lithuania, Luxembourg, Madagascar, Malawi, Malaysia, Maldives, Mali, Malta, Marshall Islands, Mauritania, Mauritius, Mexico, Micronesia, Monaco, Mongolia, Morocco, Mozambique, Myanmar, Namibia, Nepal, Netherlands, New Zealand, Nicaragua, Niger, Nigeria, Norway, Oman, Pakistan, Panama, Papua New Guinea, Paraguay, Peru, Philippines, Poland, Portugal, Qatar, Republic of Korea, Republic of Moldova, Romania, Russian Federation, Rwanda, Saint Lucia, Saint Vincent and the Grenadines, Samoa, Saudi Arabia, Senegal, Seychelles, Sierra Leone, Singapore, Slovakia, Slovenia, Solomon Islands, Spain, Sri Lanka, Sudan, Suriname, Swaziland, Sweden, Syrian Arab Republic, Tajikistan, Thailand, the former Yugoslav Republic of Macedonia, Togo, Trinidad and Tobago, Tunisia, Turkey, Turkmenistan, Uganda, Ukraine, United Arab Emirates, United Kingdom, United Republic of Tanzania, Uruguay, Venezuela, Viet Nam, Yemen, Zambia, Zimbabwe.

Against: None.

Abstaining: United States.

Before adopting the text as a whole, the Committee retained paragraphs 8 and 10 by recorded votes of 110 to 1, with 22 abstentions, and 95 to none, with 35 abstentions, respectively. The eigh-

teenth preambular paragraph was retained by a recorded vote of 102 to none, with 32 abstentions.

Similarly, the Assembly retained paragraphs 8 and 10 by recorded votes of 138 to 1, with 30 abstentions, and 118 to none, with 47 abstentions, respectively, and the eighteenth preambular paragraph by 129 to none, with 40 abstentions.

Confidence-building measures in outer space

As requested by the General Assembly in 1990,[124] the Secretary-General, by an October 1993 report, submitted a study on the application of confidence-building measures in outer space, prepared by a group of governmental experts.[125] The group prepared the report between July 1991 and July 1993, during which time it held four sessions in New York (29 July–2 August 1991, 23-27 March 1992, and 1-12 March and 6-16 July 1993). The experts examined specific aspects of the application of different confidence-building measures in outer space, including the different technologies available, and possibilities for defining appropriate mechanisms of international cooperation in specific areas of interest. They considered the current uses of outer space and emerging trends, with special emphasis on the technical problems involved, and described global multilateral and bilateral agreements concerning military and peaceful aspects of the exploration and uses of outer space.

Among other things, the group recommended that all States parties observe the provisions of the 1966 Treaty on Principles Governing the Activities of States in the Exploration and Use of Outer Space, including the Moon and Other Celestial Bodies;[126] that bilateral and multilateral mechanisms should continue to play an important role in considering and elaborating confidence-building measures in the context of preventing an arms race in outer space; and that institutional mechanisms to encourage international cooperation among States regarding space technology should be evaluated.

GENERAL ASSEMBLY ACTION

On 16 December, the General Assembly, on the recommendation of the First Committee, adopted **resolution 48/74 B** without vote.

Study on the application of confidence-building measures in outer space

The General Assembly,

Recalling its resolution 45/55 B of 4 December 1990, in which it requested the Secretary-General to carry out, with the assistance of government experts, a study on the specific aspects related to the application of different confidence-building measures in outer space, including the different technologies available, and possibilities for defining appropriate mechanisms of international cooperation in specific areas of interest,

1. *Takes note* of the report of the Secretary-General, the annex to which contains the study on the application of confidence-building measures in outer space;

2. *Requests* the Secretary-General to arrange for the reproduction of the study as a United Nations publication and to give it the widest possible distribution;

3. *Commends* the study to the attention of all Member States.

General Assembly resolution 48/74 B

16 December 1993   Meeting 81   Adopted without vote

Approved by First Committee (A/48/675) without vote, 11 November (meeting 24); 2-nation draft (A/C.1/48/L.12); agenda item 70.
Sponsors: Argentina, Bolivia.
Meeting numbers. GA 48th session: 1st Committee 3-14, 24; plenary 81.

REFERENCES

[1]YUN 1968, p. 17, GA res. 2373(XXII), annex, 12 June 1968. [2]*The United Nations Disarmament Yearbook*, vol. 18, *1993*, Sales No. E.94.IX.1. [3]S/25405. [4]A/48/135-S/25581. [5]A/48/119-S/25439. [6]A/48/154-S/25614. [7]A/48/166-S/25767. [8]A/48/179-S/25853. [9]A/48/115-S/25419. [10]A/48/190-S/25890. [11]A/48/157-S/25665. [12]A/48/165-S/25762. [13]A/48/160-S/25734 & Corr.1. [14]CD/1195. [15]YUN 1975, p. 27. [16]YUN 1980, p. 51. [17]YUN 1985, p. 56. [18]NPT/CONF.IV.45/I. [19]NPT/CONF.1995/PC.I/2. [20]YUN 1992, p. 67. [21]A/48/133-S/25556. [22]S/26825. [23]S/26811. [24]S/26841. [25]YUN 1991, p. 194, SC res. 715(1991), 11 Oct. 1991. [26]S/26910. [27]A/48/126. [28]YUN 1992, p. 65. [29]Ibid., p. 66, GA res. 47/39, 30 Nov. 1992. [30]A/48/311. [31]YUN 1971, p. 19, GA res. 2826(XXVI), annex, 16 Dec. 1971. [32]YUN 1991, p. 52. [33]YUN 1986, p. 64. [34]BWC/CONF.III/VEREX/9 & Corr.1. [35]A/48/27. [36]CD/1219. [37]CD/1212. [38]CD/1202. [39]CD/1199, CD/1201. [40]CD/1220. [41]CD/1231. [42]CD/1232. [43]CD/1235 & Corr.1. [44]YUN 1991, p. 39. [45]CD/1185. [46]CD/1211. [47]A/48/171 & Add.1,2. [48]YUN 1987, p. 54, GA res. 42/38 C, 30 Nov. 1987. [49]YUN 1992, p. 80. [50]CD/1205. [51]A/C.1/48/3. [52]A/C.1/48/6. [53]A/C.1/48/4. [54]A/48/297. [55]YUN 1991, p. 38. [56]YUN 1963, p. 137. [57]*Disarmament: A Periodic Review by the United Nations*, vol. XVI, No. 2 (1993). [58]A/48/381. [59]CD/1194. [60]YUN 1991, p. 34. [61]YUN 1992, p. 79. [62]CD/1225. [63]A/48/86. [64]A/48/620-S/26770. [65]A/48/658-S/26803. [66]YUN 1992, p. 88, GA res. 47/76, 15 Dec. 1992. [67]A/48/339. [68]YUN 1964, p. 69. [69]A/48/371. [70]YUN 1992, p. 89. [71]Ibid., p. 90, GA res. 47/48, 9 Dec. 1992. [72]A/48/399. [73]YUN 1992, p. 91, GA res. 47/55, 9 Dec. 1992. [74]A/48/494. [75]YUN 1992, p. 92, GA res. 47/49, 9 Dec. 1992. [76]A/48/256. [77]A/48/29. [78]YUN 1971, p. 34, GA res. 2832(XXVI), 16 Dec. 1971. [79]YUN 1992, p. 93, GA res. 47/59, 9 Dec. 1992. [80]A/CN.10/178. [81]A/CN.10/180. [82]A/CN.10/179. [83]YUN 1992, p. 82. [84]A/48/42. [85]A/48/344 & Corr.1 & Add.1,2. [86]YUN 1991, p. 58, GA res. 46/36 L, annex, 9 Dec. 1991. [87]CD/1218. [88]YUN 1992, p. 75, GA res. 47/52 L, 15 Dec. 1992. [89]A/48/271 & Add. 1,2. [90]YUN 1985, p. 84, GA res. 40/91 B, 12 Dec. 1985. [91]YUN 1992, p. 79, GA res. 47/45, 9 Dec. 1992. [92]A/48/227 & Add.1. [93]A/45/372 & Corr.1. [94]YUN 1992, p. 70. [95]A/CN.10/179, A/CN.10/181, A/CN.10/182. [96]YUN 1992, p. 96, GA dec. 47/420, 9 Dec. 1992. [97]A/48/228. [98]YUN 1992, p. 72, GA res. 47/53 F, 15 Dec. 1992. [99]A/48/412. [100]YUN 1992, p. 72. [101]Ibid., p. 94, GA dec. 47/419, 9 Dec. 1992. [102]A/48/324. [103]YUN 1992, p. 95, GA res. 47/43, 9 Dec. 1992. [104]A/48/360. [105]A/48/400. [106]YUN 1992, p. 95. [107]A/CN.10/177. [108]A/CN.10/176. [109]A/CN.10/175. [110]YUN 1980, p. 76. [111]YUN 1992, p. 97, GA res. 47/56, 9 Dec. 1992. [112]A/48/389. [113]*Multilateral Treaties Deposited with the Secretary-General: Status as at 31 December 1993* (ST/LEG/SER.E/12), Sales No. E.94.V.11. [114]YUN 1983, p. 66. [115]S/25344. [116]YUN 1992, p. 35. [117]A/47/965-S/25944. [118]A/48/193. [119]YUN 1992, p. 100, GA res. 47/52 F, 9 Dec. 1992. [120]A/45/592. [121]YUN 1987, p. 82. [122]CD/1217. [123]YUN 1992, p. 98. [124]GA res. 45/55 B, 4 Dec. 1990. [125]A/48/305 & Corr.1. [126]YUN 1966, p. 41, GA res. 2222(XXI), annex, 19 Dec. 1966.

Information and studies

Disarmament Information Programme

As requested by the General Assembly in 1992,[1] the Secretary-General submitted in August 1993 a report on activities carried out under the United Nations Disarmament Information Programme.[2] Annexed to the report was a summary of the status of the Voluntary Trust Fund for the Programme as at 30 June 1993.

A symposium on transparency in armaments for the Mediterranean region was held (Florence, Italy, 29 March–1 April), in cooperation with the Forum on the Problems of Peace and War, to explore the concepts of openness and transparency as they applied to the pursuit of peace, security and disarmament. A conference on disarmament issues (Kyoto, Japan, 13-16 April), organized in cooperation with Japan, reviewed national security trends in the post-cold-war era and studied the challenges to disarmament in an increasingly interdependent world. A symposium on regional approaches to confidence- and security-building measures (Graz, Austria, 2-4 June) examined the challenges that confront States in implementing confidence-building concepts and the evolution of confidence-building methodology in Africa, Asia and the Pacific, Europe and Latin America. A symposium on security, disarmament and confidence-building in the context of the Commonwealth of Independent States (CIS) (Kiev, Ukraine, 27-30 September) focused on clarifying the security concerns of various CIS member States and exploring ways in which the newly independent States could be assisted to promote stability and cooperation in specific areas of concern.

The Centre for Disarmament Affairs (CDA) continued to produce and disseminate publications on disarmament. The Department of Public Information (DPI) produced radio and video programmes on disarmament for world-wide dissemination and included the subject in guided tours, lectures, press conferences, seminars and meetings. It also issued a press kit and documents and other information materials. United Nations information centres helped to provide press coverage and media support for workshops and seminars organized by CDA. In 1993, CDA maintained its involvement in a joint project with the International Association of University Presidents to develop prototype courses in arms control, disarmament and security for use at the undergraduate level and in professional schools worldwide.

As to special events, CDA supported an international non-governmental organization (NGO) conference (New York, 20-23 April), sponsored by the NGO Committee on Disarmament (New York) and the Special NGO Committee on Disarmament (Geneva), which had as its theme new realities: disarmament, peace-building and global security. Disarmament Week in 1993 was observed in New York and Geneva from 25 to 29 October. At a special meeting of the First Committee held on 29 October to commemorate the Week, opening statements were made by the Committee Chairman, the General Assembly President and the Under-Secretary-General for Political Affairs. A symposium, held from 26 to 28 October under the auspices of DPI, CDA and the NGO Committee on Disarmament, discussed prospects for achieving a comprehensive test-ban treaty and a ban on the production of weapons-grade fissionable material, and for preventing the proliferation of weapons of mass destruction; the United Nations Register of Conventional Arms and the discussion of transparency in armaments in the Conference on Disarmament; and progress towards a nuclear-weapon-free zone in Africa and confidence-building measures in Central Africa. (See below for a description of the 1993 activities of the disarmament fellowship, training and advisory services programme.)

In his annual report to the Assembly on the work of the Advisory Board on Disarmament Matters (see below),[3] the Secretary-General noted that the Board was informed that, in carrying out the activities of the Programme, CDA had continued to promote priorities such as non-proliferation, regional approaches to disarmament, openness and transparency and other confidence-building measures.

Financing

The Eleventh United Nations Pledging Conference for the United Nations Disarmament Information Programme was held in New York on 29 October, with 49 delegations participating.[4]

Either during the Conference or at other times during the year, the following pledges were announced for the Programme:[5] Austria ($10,000), Cyprus ($1,000), Greece ($5,000), Indonesia ($5,000), Italy ($12,698), Mexico ($2,500), New Zealand ($3,315), Pakistan ($4,515), Republic of Korea ($5,000); for the African regional centre: Algeria ($5,482), France ($8,850), Italy ($12,698), Norway ($9,400); for the Latin American and Caribbean regional centre: Chile ($1,000), Italy ($12,698), Mexico ($2,500), Norway ($9,400), Spain ($5,158); for the Asian and Pacific regional

centre: China ($10,000), Italy ($12,698), Nepal ($7,000), New Zealand ($5,525), Norway ($9,400), Pakistan ($4,515), Republic of Korea ($4,000), Sri Lanka ($2,500). Finland pledged $8,696, subject to parliamentary approval, half of which was earmarked for activities related to the United Nations Register of Conventional Arms and the other half to those related to the 1980 Convention on Prohibitions or Restrictions on the Use of Certain Conventional Weapons Which May Be Deemed to Be Excessively Injurious or to Have Indiscriminate Effects.[6] Italy pledged $31,746 for the Trust Fund for Global and Regional Disarmament Activities and Norway $2,800 for publishing activities.

GENERAL ASSEMBLY ACTION

On 16 December, the General Assembly, on the recommendation of the First Committee, adopted **resolution 48/76 D** without vote.

United Nations Disarmament Information Programme
The General Assembly,

Recalling its decision taken in 1982 at its twelfth special session, the second special session devoted to disarmament, by which the World Disarmament Campaign was launched,

Bearing in mind its various resolutions on the subject, including resolution 47/53 D of 9 December 1992 in which it decided, *inter alia,* that the World Disarmament Campaign should be known thereafter as the "United Nations Disarmament Information Programme" and the World Disarmament Campaign Voluntary Trust Fund as the "Voluntary Trust Fund for the United Nations Disarmament Information Programme",

Having examined the reports of the Secretary-General of 24 August 1993 on the United Nations Disarmament Information Programme, and of 22 September 1993 on the Advisory Board on Disarmament Matters relating to the implementation of the Disarmament Information Programme, as well as the Final Act of the Eleventh United Nations Pledging Conference for the Programme, held on 29 October 1993,

Noting with appreciation the contributions that Member States have already made to the Programme,

1. *Welcomes* the report of the Secretary-General of 24 August 1993 on the United Nations Disarmament Information Programme;

2. *Commends* the Secretary-General for his efforts to make effective use of the resources available to him in disseminating as widely as possible information on arms limitation and disarmament to elected officials, the media, non-governmental organizations, educational communities and research institutes, and in carrying out an active seminar and conference programme;

3. *Notes with appreciation* the contributions to the efforts of the Programme by the United Nations information centres and the regional centres for disarmament;

4. *Recommends* that the Programme should further focus its efforts:

(a) To inform, to educate and to generate public understanding of the importance of and support for multilateral action, including action by the United Nations and the Conference on Disarmament, in the field of arms limitation and disarmament, in a factual, balanced and objective manner;

(b) To facilitate unimpeded access to and an exchange of information on ideas between the public sector and public interest groups and organizations, and to provide an independent source of balanced and factual information that takes into account a range of views to help further an informed debate on arms limitation, disarmament and security;

(c) To organize meetings to facilitate exchanges of views and information between governmental and non-governmental sectors and between governmental and other experts in order to facilitate the search for common ground;

5. *Invites* all Member States to contribute to the Voluntary Trust Fund for the United Nations Disarmament Information Programme;

6. *Commends* the Secretary-General for supporting the efforts of universities, other academic institutions and non-governmental organizations active in the educational field in widening the world-wide availability of disarmament education, and invites him to continue to support and cooperate, without cost to the regular budget of the United Nations, with educational institutions and non-governmental organizations engaged in such efforts;

7. *Decides* that at its forty-ninth session there should be a twelfth United Nations Pledging Conference for the United Nations Disarmament Information Programme, and expresses the hope that on that occasion all those Member States which have not yet announced any voluntary contributions will do so, bearing in mind the objectives of the Third Disarmament Decade and the need to ensure its success;

8. *Requests* the Secretary-General to submit to the General Assembly at its forty-ninth session a report covering both the implementation of the activities of the Programme by the United Nations system during 1994 and the activities of the Programme contemplated by the system for 1995;

9. *Also decides* to include in the provisional agenda of its forty-ninth session the item entitled "United Nations Disarmament Information Programme".

General Assembly resolution 48/76 D

16 December 1993   Meeting 81   Adopted without vote

Approved by First Committee (A/48/677) without vote, 11 November (meeting 24); 12-nation draft (A/C.1/48/L.20); agenda item 72 *(c)*.

Sponsors: Bangladesh, Bolivia, Costa Rica, Honduras, Indonesia, Iran, Mexico, Myanmar, Philippines, Sri Lanka, Ukraine, Venezuela.

Meeting numbers. GA 48th session: 1st Committee 3-14, 23, 24; plenary 81.

Regional centres for peace and disarmament

In response to a 1992 General Assembly request,[7] the Secretary-General reported in September 1993[8] on the activities of the three regional centres for peace and disarmament covering Africa, Asia and the Pacific and Latin America and the Caribbean for the period August 1992 to July 1993. He noted that during the period under review the financial situation of the centres remained precarious owing to a continued decline in voluntary contributions to their respective trust funds. The centres' programmes had been adjusted accordingly, resulting in drastically curtailed activities.

The United Nations Regional Centre for Peace and Disarmament in Africa, established at Lomé, Togo, in 1986,[9] continued to focus on disseminating information relating to disarmament, peace and security, organizing seminars and conferences and undertaking studies. In cooperation with the Government of Namibia and the Friedrich Ebert Foundation Namibia Office, the Centre organized an international seminar (Windhoek, 24-26 February) which dealt with confidence- and security-building measures in southern Africa. The Centre also provided support to two meetings of the Standing Advisory Committee on Security Questions in Central Africa (Bujumbura, Burundi, 8-12 March, and Libreville, Gabon, 30 August–3 September). It continued to publish its quarterly newsletter, *African Peace Bulletin*.

The United Nations Regional Centre for Peace, Disarmament and Development in Latin America and the Caribbean was established on 1 January 1987 and inaugurated at Lima, Peru, on 9 October of that year.[10] Despite financial constraints, the Centre continued to expand its contacts and cooperation with governmental and non-governmental organizations, research centres, academic institutions and other United Nations bodies. As part of its programme for promoting awareness of regional security issues, the Centre held a workshop at Lima on 1 October 1992 on military expenditures in South America and their relation to overall government expenditures in general and to social expenditures in particular. In cooperation with CDA, the Centre organized a seminar on arms proliferation and confidence- and security-building measures in Latin America and the Caribbean (Asunción, Paraguay, 18-20 January 1993). In June, it held a workshop on hemispheric strategic issues for scholars, retired military officers and diplomats and also the third annual seminar for the members of the Association of Military Attachés accredited in Peru. The Centre also provided assistance to Chile in organizing a workshop on chemical weapons (Santiago, 9 and 10 September), and to Ecuador and its Diplomatic Academy in organizing a seminar on disarmament and security in Latin America (Quito, 15-17 September). The Centre published its quarterly newsletter, *Boletín*, and its reference library continued to serve as a resource centre for students and researchers on issues of peace, security, disarmament and development in the region.

The United Nations Regional Centre for Peace and Disarmament in Asia and the Pacific, inaugurated on 30 January 1989 at Kathmandu, Nepal, organized two major regional meetings in

1993. One, the fourth in the series (Kathmandu, 1-3 February), focused on national security and confidence-building in the region, and the second (Kyoto, 13-16 April), held in cooperation with the Government of Japan, centred on national security in an interdependent world. In conjunction with the latter meeting, the Centre cooperated with local authorities in organizing 3 one-day seminars on: early warning, preventive diplomacy and disarmament (Kyoto); new disarmament agenda and international security in the interdependent world (Nagasaki); and building on dialogue and searching for common security in Asia and the Pacific (Hiroshima). The Centre's activities also included disseminating information on disarmament and answering inquiries from the general public, students and NGOs.

GENERAL ASSEMBLY ACTION

On 16 December, the General Assembly, on the recommendation of the First Committee, adopted **resolution 48/76 E** without vote.

United Nations Regional Centre for Peace and Disarmament in Africa, United Nations Regional Centre for Peace and Disarmament in Asia and the Pacific and United Nations Regional Centre for Peace, Disarmament and Development in Latin America and the Caribbean
The General Assembly,

Recalling its resolutions 40/151 G of 16 December 1985, 41/60 D of 3 December 1986, 42/39 J of 30 November 1987 and 43/76 D of 7 December 1988 on the United Nations Regional Centre for Peace and Disarmament in Africa, 41/60 J of 3 December 1986, 42/39 K of 30 November 1987 and 43/76 H of 7 December 1988 on the United Nations Regional Centre for Peace, Disarmament and Development in Latin America and the Caribbean, 42/39 D of 30 November 1987 and 43/76 G of 7 December 1988 on the United Nations Regional Centre for Peace and Disarmament in Asia, 44/117 F of 15 December 1989, 45/59 E of 4 December 1990 and 46/37 F of 9 December 1991 and its decision 47/421 of 9 December 1992 on the United Nations Regional Centre for Peace and Disarmament in Africa, the United Nations Regional Centre for Peace and Disarmament in Asia and the Pacific and the United Nations Regional Centre for Peace, Disarmament and Development in Latin America and the Caribbean,

Reaffirming its resolutions 46/36 F of 6 December 1991 and 47/52 G of 9 December 1992 on regional disarmament, including confidence-building measures,

Mindful of the provisions of Article 11, paragraph 1, of the Charter of the United Nations stipulating that a function of the General Assembly is to consider the general principles of cooperation in the maintenance of international peace and security, including the principles governing disarmament and arms limitation,

Bearing in mind that the changed international environment has created new opportunities for the pursuit of disarmament, as well as posed new challenges,

Taking note of the report of the Secretary-General containing the steps taken to strengthen the Office for Disarmament Affairs of the Secretariat,

Convinced that the initiatives and activities mutually agreed upon by Member States of the respective regions aimed at fostering confidence, as well as the implementation and coordination of regional activities under the United Nations Disarmament Information Programme, would encourage and facilitate the development of effective measures of confidence-building, arms limitation and disarmament in these regions,

Welcoming the programme of activities carried out by the regional centres, which have contributed substantially to understanding and cooperation among the States in each particular region and have thereby strengthened the role assigned to each regional centre in the areas of peace, disarmament and development,

Taking note of the views on the regional centres contained in the report of the Secretary-General on the Advisory Board on Disarmament Matters,

Recognizing the need to provide the regional centres with financial viability and stability so as to facilitate the effective planning and implementation of their respective programmes of activities,

Expressing its gratitude to the Member States and international governmental and non-governmental organizations and foundations that have contributed to the trust funds of the three regional centres,

1. *Commends* the activities being carried out by the regional centres in identifying and broadening the understanding of pressing disarmament and security issues and exploring optimum solutions under given specific conditions prevailing in each region, in accordance with their mandates;

2. *Encourages* the regional centres to continue intensifying their efforts in promoting cooperation among the States in their respective regions to facilitate the development of effective measures of confidence-building, arms limitation and disarmament, with a view to strengthening peace and security;

3. *Also encourages* further use of the potential of the regional centres to maintain the increased interest in and momentum for revitalization of the Organization to meet the challenges of a new phase of international relations in order to fulfil the purposes and principles of the Charter of the United Nations related to peace, disarmament and development, taking into account the guidelines and recommendations for regional approaches to disarmament within the context of global security as adopted by the Disarmament Commission at its 1993 substantive session;

4. *Appeals once again* to Member States, as well as to international governmental and non-governmental organizations and foundations, to make voluntary contributions in order to strengthen the programmes of activities of the regional centres and their effective implementation;

5. *Requests* the Secretary-General to continue to provide all necessary support to the regional centres in carrying out their programmes of activities;

6. *Also requests* the Secretary-General to report to the General Assembly at its forty-ninth session on the implementation of the present resolution;

7. *Decides* to include in the provisional agenda of its forty-ninth session the item entitled "United Nations Regional Centre for Peace and Disarmament in Africa, United Nations Regional Centre for Peace and Disarmament in Asia and the Pacific and United Nations

Regional Centre for Peace, Disarmament and Development in Latin America and the Caribbean''.

General Assembly resolution 48/76 E

16 December 1993   Meeting 81   Adopted without vote

Approved by First Committee (A/48/677) without vote, 11 November (meeting 24); draft by Algeria (for African Group), Bangladesh, China, Costa Rica, Democratic People's Republic of Korea, Dominican Republic (for Latin American and Caribbean Group), Honduras, Indonesia, Iran, Kyrgyzstan, Lao People's Democratic Republic, Malaysia, Mongolia, Myanmar, Nepal, Pakistan, Panama, Philippines, Singapore, Sri Lanka, Thailand and Viet Nam (A/C.1/48/L.29); agenda item 72 *(f)*.

Meeting numbers. GA 48th session: 1st Committee 3-14, 22, 24; plenary 81.

Disarmament studies and research

Advisory Board on Disarmament Matters

The Advisory Board on Disarmament Matters (New York, 28 June–2 July)[3] discussed current developments and trends in international affairs and their bearing on the role of the United Nations in international security and disarmament. The main issues discussed were the maintenance of peace, non-proliferation, conventional armament/disarmament and multilateral disarmament machinery. The Board expressed strong concern over the difficult financial situation of the three regional centres (see above).

In its capacity as the Board of Trustees of the United Nations Institute for Disarmament Research (UNIDIR), the Advisory Board considered and approved the report of the UNIDIR Director on the Institute's 1992-1993 activities (see below) and the proposed research programme and annual budget for 1994. It recommended a subvention from the United Nations regular budget of $220,000 for 1994 to assure the independence and financial viability of the Institute. In November,[11] the Secretary-General transmitted the Board's recommendation, which was supported by the Advisory Committee on Administrative and Budgetary Questions, to the General Assembly.

By **resolution 48/230, section VIII**, of 23 December, the Assembly approved the subvention.

UN Institute for Disarmament Research

In August,[12] the Secretary-General transmitted to the General Assembly the UNIDIR Director's report covering the period July 1992 to June 1993, which described UNIDIR's completed and ongoing research projects. Publication of the UNIDIR *Newsletter* continued, as did the fellowship programme enabling scholars from developing countries to undertake research on disarmament. UNIDIR also continued to publish studies on national concepts of security and to update its computerized information and documentation database service. Among its research projects were disarmament problems related to outer space; confidence-building measures for maritime security; economic aspects of disarmament; chemical weapons; and START implementation problems and nuclear non-proliferation efforts.

Disarmament studies programme

In 1993, a study on the application of confidence-building measures in outer space was completed and another, on verification in all its aspects including the role of the United Nations, was initiated.

With the assistance of a group of governmental experts, the Secretary-General carried out a study on the specific aspects related to the application of different confidence-building measures in outer space, including the different technologies available, and possibilities for defining appropriate mechanisms of international cooperation in specific areas of interest.[13] (For details, see above, under ''Prevention of an arms race in outer space''.)

On 16 December, the General Assembly, in **resolution 48/68**, requested the Secretary-General to undertake, with the assistance of a group of qualified governmental experts, an in-depth study on verification (see above, under ''Transparency and the arms register'').

Disarmament fellowship, training and advisory services programme

In October,[14] the Secretary-General submitted his annual report on the United Nations disarmament fellowship, training and advisory services programme, stating that the emergence of new issues in the field of arms limitation, disarmament and security had led to a corresponding broadening in the focus of the content of the programme. In that context, the programme of lectures was revised to include such topics as regional approaches to disarmament, non-proliferation issues, openness and transparency, preventive diplomacy, conflict resolution, United Nations peace-keeping operations, international humanitarian law in armed conflicts and human dimensions of international security. The 1993 programme of studies, which began on 9 August at Geneva and ended on 29 October in New York, included a series of lectures; speaking, drafting and simulation exercises; preparation of individual research papers; attending the Conference on Disarmament and the General Assembly; study visits to IAEA headquarters at Vienna; and, at the invitation of the States concerned, visits to offices and institutions in Finland, Germany, Japan and Sweden.

GENERAL ASSEMBLY ACTION

On 16 December, the General Assembly, on the recommendation of the First Committee, adopted **resolution 48/76 C** without vote.

United Nations disarmament fellowship, training and advisory services programme

The General Assembly,

Having considered the report of the Secretary-General on the United Nations disarmament fellowship, training and advisory services programme,

Recalling its decision, contained in paragraph 108 of the Final Document of the Tenth Special Session of the General Assembly, the first special session devoted to disarmament, to establish a programme of fellowships on disarmament, as well as its decisions contained in annex IV to the Concluding Document of the Twelfth Special Session of the General Assembly, the second special session devoted to disarmament, in which it decided, *inter alia*, to continue the programme,

Noting with satisfaction that the programme has already trained an appreciable number of public officials selected from geographical regions represented in the United Nations system, most of whom are now in positions of responsibility in the field of disarmament affairs in their respective countries or Governments,

Recalling also its resolutions 37/100 G of 13 December 1982, 38/73 C of 15 December 1983, 39/63 B of 12 December 1984, 40/151 H of 16 December 1985, 41/60 H of 3 December 1986, 42/39 I of 30 November 1987, 43/76 F of 7 December 1988, 44/117 E of 15 December 1989, 45/59 A of 4 December 1990, 46/37 E of 6 December 1991 and 47/53 A of 9 December 1992,

Noting also with satisfaction that the programme, as designed, has enabled an increased number of public officials, particularly from the developing countries, to acquire more expertise in the sphere of disarmament,

Believing that the forms of assistance available to Member States, particularly to developing countries, under the programme will enhance the capabilities of their officials to follow ongoing deliberations and negotiations on disarmament, both bilateral and multilateral,

1. *Reaffirms* its decisions contained in annex IV to the Concluding Document of the Twelfth Special Session of the General Assembly and the report of the Secretary-General approved by resolution 33/71 E of 14 December 1978;

2. *Expresses its appreciation* to the Governments of Finland, Germany, Japan and Sweden for inviting the 1993 fellows to study selected activities in the field of disarmament, thereby contributing to the fulfilment of the overall objectives of the programme;

3. *Notes with satisfaction* that, within the framework of the programme, the Office for Disarmament Affairs of the Secretariat organizes regional disarmament workshops for Africa, Asia and the Pacific, and Latin America and the Caribbean;

4. *Commends* the Secretary-General for the diligence with which the programme has continued to be carried out;

5. *Requests* the Secretary-General to continue the implementation of the Geneva-based programme within existing resources and to report thereon to the General Assembly at its forty-ninth session.

General Assembly resolution 48/76 C

16 December 1993   Meeting 81   Adopted without vote

Approved by First Committee (A/48/677) without vote, 11 November (meeting 24); 48-nation draft (A/C.1/48/L.14); agenda item 72 *(a)*.

Sponsors: Algeria, Argentina, Benin, Bolivia, Bulgaria, Cameroon, Canada, China, Costa Rica, Cuba, Czech Republic, Democratic People's Republic of Korea, Finland, France, Germany, Ghana, Greece, Hungary, Indonesia, Iran, Jamaica, Japan, Kenya, Liberia, Mali, Mongolia, Myanmar, Namibia, Nepal, New Zealand, Nicaragua, Nigeria, Pakistan, Panama, Philippines, Russian Federation, Senegal, Slovakia, Sweden, the former Yugoslav Republic of Macedonia, Togo, Trinidad and Tobago, Uganda, United Republic of Tanzania, United States, Venezuela, Viet Nam, Zimbabwe.

Meeting numbers. GA 48th session: 1st Committee 3-14, 20, 24; plenary 81.

Education and information for disarmament

Pursuant to a 1991 General Assembly resolution,[15] the Secretary-General, in a September report with a later addendum,[16] submitted the replies of seven Governments, one specialized agency and six NGOs to his request for information on their activities with regard to disarmament education.

GENERAL ASSEMBLY ACTION

On 16 December, the General Assembly, on the recommendation of the First Committee, adopted **resolution 48/64** without vote.

Education and information for disarmament
The General Assembly,

Recalling its resolutions 44/123 of 15 December 1989 and 46/27 of 6 December 1991,

Taking into account the Final Document of the Tenth Special Session of the General Assembly, in particular paragraph 106 thereof, in which the Assembly urged Governments and international governmental and non-governmental organizations to take steps to develop programmes of education for disarmament and peace studies at all levels,

Considering that paragraphs 99, 100 and 101 of the Final Document provide for the mechanisms of a programme to mobilize world public opinion to promote disarmament, including the dissemination of information and publicity to complement the educational work,

Also considering that the United Nations Disarmament Information Programme plays an important role in complementing the educational and information efforts for disarmament carried out by Member States within their own educational and cultural development systems,

Recognizing that the important changes that have taken place in the world aimed at promoting freedom, democracy, respect for and enjoyment of human rights, disarmament and social development contribute to the achievement of positive results in the promotion of education and information for disarmament,

Noting with satisfaction the efforts that the educational community is making in the preparation of curricula and activities to promote education for disarmament and peace, as a means of contributing to the implementation of resolutions 44/123 and 46/27,

1. *Expresses its appreciation* to the Secretary-General for his reports submitted pursuant to resolutions 44/123 and 46/27;

2. *Also expresses its appreciation* for the valuable information submitted by Member States, international governmental and non-governmental organizations and educational institutions for peace and disarmament and contained in the reports;

3. *Reaffirms* that, in order to achieve positive results, it is indispensable to carry out educational and advisory programmes that promote peace and disarmament at all levels and are aimed at changing basic attitudes with respect to aggression, violence, armaments and war, and that support regional and international measures geared to peace, security and cooperation;

4. *Reiterates* that the efforts of Member States, international governmental and non-governmental organi-

zations and educational institutions for peace and dis-armament, in the promotion of activities under the United Nations Disarmament Information Programme, will strengthen not only education and information for disarmament, as described in the second and third preambular paragraphs above, but also the arms reduc-tion and disarmament processes or agreements that are being carried out at the regional and international levels;

5. *Invites* Member States and international govern-mental and non-governmental organizations and educa-tional institutions for peace and disarmament to redou-ble their efforts to respond to the appeal made in paragraph 106 of the Final Document of the Tenth Spe-cial Session of the General Assembly and to submit to the Secretary-General a report on their activities in this regard;

6. *Requests* the Secretary-General to submit to the General Assembly at its fiftieth session, under the item entitled ''Education and information for disarmament'' and from within existing resources, the reports requested in paragraph 5 above.

General Assembly resolution 48/64

16 December 1993   Meeting 81   Adopted without vote

Approved by First Committee (A/48/665) without vote, 11 November (meet-ing 24); 51-nation draft (A/C.1/48/L.1); agenda item 60.

Sponsors: Angola, Antigua and Barbuda, Austria, Belgium, Benin, Bolivia, Brazil, Cameroon, Canada, Chile, Colombia, Congo, Costa Rica, Côte d'Ivoire, Dominican Republic, Ecuador, El Salvador, Guatemala, Guinea-Bissau, Honduras, India, Indonesia, Ireland, Kenya, Kuwait, Malaysia, Mar-shall Islands, Mauritius, Monaco, Mongolia, New Zealand, Nicaragua, Ni-geria, Pakistan, Panama, Paraguay, Peru, Philippines, Russian Federation, Sierra Leone, Slovakia, Spain, Suriname, Thailand, the former Yugoslav Republic of Macedonia, Togo, Trinidad and Tobago, Tunisia, Ukraine, Uru-guay, Venezuela.

Meeting numbers. GA 48th session: 1st Committee 3-14, 18, 24; plenary 81.

REFERENCES

[1]YUN 1992, p. 104, GA res. 47/53 D, 9 Dec. 1992. [2]A/48/326. [3]A/48/325. [4]A/CONF.170/1. [5]A/CONF.170/2. [6]YUN 1980, p. 76. [7]YUN 1992, p. 105, GA dec. 47/421, 9 Dec. 1992. [8]A/48/346. [9]YUN 1986, p. 85. [10]YUN 1987, p. 88. [11]A/C.5/48/16. [12]A/48/270. [13]A/48/305 & Corr.1. [14]A/48/469. [15]YUN 1991, p. 70, GA res. 46/27, 6 Dec. 1991. [16]A/48/366 & Add.1.

Chapter III

Trusteeship and decolonization

In 1993, the United Nations continued its efforts to eliminate colonialism. The General Assembly's Special Committee on the Situation with regard to the Implementation of the Declaration on the Granting of Independence to Colonial Countries and Peoples (Committee on colonial countries) held its annual session in New York (10 February–28 May and 7 July–12 August) to consider various aspects of the implementation of the 1960 Declaration. The Committee examined decolonization in general as well as the situation of individual Non-Self-Governing Territories.

The Trusteeship Council, composed of China, France, the Russian Federation, the United Kingdom and the United States, held its sixtieth session in New York from 12 to 17 May and on 1 November 1993, with its final meeting in January 1994.

The Council continued to supervise, on behalf of the Security Council, the one remaining Trust Territory under the International Trusteeship System—Palau, Trust Territory of the Pacific Islands—a strategic territory administered by the United States.

1960 Declaration on colonial countries

Decade for the Eradication of Colonialism

As called for in the plan of action adopted by the General Assembly in 1991[1] for the International Decade for the Eradication of Colonialism (1990-2000), which the Assembly had declared in 1988,[2] the Committee on colonial countries organized a seminar in the Pacific region (Port Moresby, Papua New Guinea, 8-10 June 1993) to review political, economic and social conditions in the small island Non-Self-Governing Territories (NSGTs). Political questions addressed were self-determination and the future political status of NSGTs. A broad range of economic and social questions were considered, including: development and its impact on self-determination; problems of small, structurally open economies; food production; tourism development; drug trafficking and money laundering; development of financial

management expertise; human resources development; the role of specialized agencies and international and regional organizations in economic and social development; environmental issues; women in development; and access to information. It also considered regional cooperation in the preservation and protection of marine resources from over-exploitation; disaster preparedness and relief; sea and air transport; higher education; research and development; and regional pooling arrangements for sharing special skills and expertise. On 10 June, the seminar adopted a summary of its discussions and recommendations.[3] The guidelines and rules of procedure for the seminar were contained in a separate report to the Committee on colonial countries.[4]

On 14 July,[5] the Committee's Working Group recommended that the summary of discussions of the seminar be taken into account when considering the situation in NSGTs of the Pacific region. Noting that the plan of action provided for holding seminars in the Caribbean and Pacific regions alternately, the Working Group recommended that the Committee organize a seminar in 1994 in New York for all Trust and Non-Self-Governing Territories, irrespective of their location, with the view to providing an opportunity to carry out a mid-term review of the plan of action. The Group further recommended that the Committee invite United Nations organs, agencies and institutions to apprise the Secretary-General of actions taken to implement the 1991 Assembly resolution relating to the plan of action and report to the Assembly in 1994.

The Committee approved those recommendations on 27 July.[6]

Committee on colonial countries

The Committee on colonial countries held its 1993 session in two parts, with a total of 17 meetings, from 10 February to 28 May and from 7 July to 12 August in New York.[6] It considered the report of its Working Group,[5] the report of an open-ended working group on improving the efficiency of the Committee's work,[7] and four reports of the Subcommittee on Small Territories, Petitions, Information and Assistance on: the dissemination of information on decolonization,[8] Pitcairn,[9] St. Helena[10] and 10 other small Territories.[11]

Implementation of the Declaration

On 10 December 1993, the General Assembly adopted **resolution 48/52** by recorded vote.

Implementation of the Declaration on the Granting of Independence to Colonial Countries and Peoples

The General Assembly,

Having examined the report of the Special Committee on the Situation with regard to the Implementation of the Declaration on the Granting of Independence to Colonial Countries and Peoples,

Recalling its resolution 1514(XV) of 14 December 1960, containing the Declaration on the Granting of Independence to Colonial Countries and Peoples, and all its previous resolutions concerning the implementation of the Declaration, most recently resolution 47/23 of 25 November 1992, as well as the relevant resolutions of the Security Council,

Recognizing that the eradication of colonialism is one of the priorities of the Organization for the decade that began in 1990,

Deeply conscious of the need to take, speedily, measures to eliminate the last vestiges of colonialism by the year 2000, as called for in its resolution 43/47 of 22 November 1988,

Reiterating its conviction of the need for the elimination of colonialism, as well as of the need for the total eradication of racial discrimination and violations of basic human rights,

Conscious that the success of national liberation struggles and the resultant international situation have provided the international community with a unique opportunity to make a decisive contribution towards the elimination of colonialism in all its forms and manifestations,

Noting with satisfaction the achievements of the Special Committee in contributing to the effective and complete implementation of the Declaration and other relevant resolutions of the United Nations on decolonization,

Stressing the importance of the participation of the administering Powers in the work of the Special Committee,

Also noting with satisfaction the cooperation and active participation of some administering Powers in the work of the Special Committee, as well as their continued readiness to receive United Nations visiting missions in the Territories under their administration,

Noting with concern the negative impact which the nonparticipation of certain administering Powers has had on the work of the Special Committee, depriving it of an important source of information on the Territories under their administration,

Aware of the pressing need of newly independent and emerging States for assistance from the United Nations and its system of organizations in the economic, social and other fields,

Aware also of the pressing need of the remaining Non-Self-Governing Territories, including particularly the small island Territories, for economic, social and other assistance from the United Nations and the organizations within its system,

1. *Reaffirms* its resolution 1514(XV) and all other resolutions on decolonization, including its resolution 43/47, in which it declared the decade that began in 1990 as the International Decade for the Eradication of Colonialism, and calls upon the administering Powers, in accordance with those resolutions, to take all necessary steps to enable the peoples of the Territories concerned to exercise fully as soon as possible their right to self-determination and independence;

2. *Affirms once again* that the continuation of colonialism in any form or manifestation—including racism and economic exploitation—is incompatible with the Charter of the United Nations, the Universal Declaration of Human Rights and the Declaration on the Granting of Independence to Colonial Countries and Peoples;

3. *Reaffirms its determination* to continue to take all steps necessary to bring about the complete and speedy eradication of colonialism and the faithful observance by all States of the relevant provisions of the Charter, the Declaration on the Granting of Independence to Colonial Countries and Peoples and the Universal Declaration of Human Rights;

4. *Affirms once again its support* for the aspirations of the peoples under colonial rule to exercise their right to self-determination and independence;

5. *Approves* the report of the Special Committee on the Situation with regard to the Implementation of the Declaration on the Granting of Independence to Colonial Countries and Peoples covering its work during 1993, including the programme of work envisaged for 1994;

6. *Calls upon* all States, in particular the administering Powers, as well as the specialized agencies and other organizations of the United Nations system, to give effect within their respective spheres of competence to the recommendations of the Special Committee for the implementation of the Declaration and other relevant resolutions of the United Nations;

7. *Calls upon* the administering Powers to ensure that no activity of foreign economic and other interests in the Non-Self-Governing Territories under their administration hinders the peoples of those Territories from exercising their right to self-determination and independence;

8. *Calls upon* the administering Powers to terminate military activities in the Territories under their administration and to eliminate military bases there in compliance with the relevant resolutions of the General Assembly, and urges them not to involve those Territories in any offensive acts or interference against other States;

9. *Urges* all States, directly and through their action in the specialized agencies and other organizations of the United Nations system, to provide moral and material assistance to the peoples of colonial Territories, and requests that the administering Powers, in consultation with the Governments of the Territories under their administration, take steps to enlist and make effective use of all possible assistance, on both a bilateral and a multilateral basis, in the strengthening of the economies of those Territories;

10. *Requests* the Special Committee to continue to seek suitable means for the immediate and full implementation of the Declaration and to carry out those actions approved by the General Assembly regarding the International Decade for the Eradication of Colonialism in all Territories that have not yet exercised their right to self-determination and independence, and in particular:

(a) To formulate specific proposals for the elimination of the remaining manifestations of colonialism and

to report thereon to the General Assembly at its forty-ninth session;

(b) To make concrete suggestions which could assist the Security Council in considering appropriate measures under the Charter with regard to developments in colonial Territories that are likely to threaten international peace and security;

(c) To continue to examine the implementation by Member States of resolution 1514(XV) and other relevant resolutions on decolonization;

(d) To continue to pay special attention to the small Territories, in particular through the dispatch of regular visiting missions, and to recommend to the General Assembly the most suitable steps to be taken to enable the populations of those Territories to exercise their right to self-determination and independence;

(e) To take all necessary steps to enlist world-wide support among Governments, as well as national and international organizations, for the achievement of the objectives of the Declaration and the implementation of the relevant resolutions of the United Nations;

11. *Also calls upon* the administering Powers to continue to cooperate with the Special Committee in the discharge of its mandate and to receive visiting missions to the Territories to secure first-hand information and ascertain the wishes and aspirations of their inhabitants;

12. *Further calls upon* the administering Powers that have not participated in the work of the Special Committee to do so at its 1994 session;

13. *Requests* the Secretary-General, the specialized agencies and other organizations of the United Nations system to provide economic, social and other assistance to the Non-Self-Governing Territories and to continue to do so, as appropriate, after they exercise their right to self-determination and independence;

14. *Requests* the Secretary-General to provide the Special Committee with the facilities and services required for the implementation of the present resolution, as well as of the other resolutions and decisions on decolonization adopted by the General Assembly and the Special Committee.

General Assembly resolution 48/52

10 December 1993   Meeting 75   139-2-19 (recorded vote)

11-nation draft (A/48/L.38 & Add.1); agenda item 18.
Sponsors: Fiji, Grenada, India, Micronesia, Namibia, Papua New Guinea, Sierra Leone, Solomon Islands, Swaziland, United Republic of Tanzania, Zimbabwe.
Meeting numbers. GA 48th session: plenary 70, 75.

Recorded vote in Assembly as follows:

In favour: Afghanistan, Algeria, Angola, Antigua and Barbuda, Argentina, Armenia, Australia, Austria, Azerbaijan, Bahamas, Bahrain, Bangladesh, Barbados, Belarus, Benin, Bhutan, Bolivia, Botswana, Brazil, Brunei Darussalam, Burkina Faso, Cambodia, Cameroon, Cape Verde, Central African Republic, Chad, Chile, China, Colombia, Comoros, Congo, Costa Rica, Côte d'Ivoire, Cuba, Cyprus, Czech Republic, Democratic People's Republic of Korea, Denmark, Djibouti, Dominica, Dominican Republic, Ecuador, Egypt, El Salvador, Ethiopia, Fiji, Gabon, Gambia, Ghana, Greece, Grenada, Guatemala, Guinea, Guinea-Bissau, Guyana, Haiti, Honduras, Iceland, India, Indonesia, Iran, Iraq, Ireland, Jamaica, Japan, Jordan, Kazakhstan, Kenya, Kuwait, Lao People's Democratic Republic, Latvia, Lesotho, Libyan Arab Jamahiriya, Liechtenstein, Lithuania, Madagascar, Malawi, Malaysia, Maldives, Mali, Malta, Marshall Islands, Mauritania, Mauritius, Mexico, Micronesia, Mongolia, Morocco, Mozambique, Myanmar, Namibia, Nepal, New Zealand, Nicaragua, Niger, Nigeria, Norway, Oman, Pakistan, Panama, Papua New Guinea, Paraguay, Peru, Philippines, Poland, Portugal, Qatar, Republic of Korea, Russian Federation, Rwanda, Saint Lucia, Saint Vincent and the Grenadines, Samoa, Saudi Arabia, Senegal, Sierra Leone, Singapore, Spain, Sri Lanka, Sudan, Suriname, Swaziland, Sweden, Syrian Arab Republic, Thailand, the former Yugoslav Republic of Macedonia, Togo, Trinidad and Tobago, Tunisia,

Uganda, Ukraine, United Arab Emirates, United Republic of Tanzania, Uruguay, Venezuela, Viet Nam, Yemen, Zaire, Zimbabwe.
Against: United Kingdom, United States.
Abstaining: Belgium, Belize, Bulgaria, Canada, Estonia, Finland, France, Georgia, Germany, Hungary, Israel, Italy, Luxembourg, Netherlands, Republic of Moldova, Romania, Slovakia, Slovenia, Turkey.

Implementation by international organizations

Report of the Secretary-General. As requested by the General Assembly in 1992,[12] the Secretary-General submitted in June 1993 a report with later addenda,[13] containing summaries of information provided by eight specialized agencies, three United Nations bodies and one regional commission on action taken to implement the Declaration.[14]

Report of the President of the Economic and Social Council. As requested by the Economic and Social Council[15] and the General Assembly[12] in 1992, the President of the Council, in July 1993,[16] described assistance programmes and technical cooperation projects extended to Trust and Non-Self-Governing Territories by specialized agencies and other United Nations organizations, and reported on his ongoing consultations on the implementation of the Declaration with the Chairmen of the Committee on colonial countries and the Special Committee against Apartheid. The President appealed to the agencies and other organizations concerned to increase assistance to the Territories and suggested that they explore additional ways of coordination. He provided information on his 1992 consultations with the Chairman of the Special Committee against Apartheid regarding developments in South Africa and gave an account of action taken by the General Assembly and the Special Committee during that period. In conclusion, he stated that he would continue to maintain close contact with the two Chairmen.

ECONOMIC AND SOCIAL COUNCIL ACTION

On 29 July 1993, the Economic and Social Council adopted **resolution 1993/55** by roll-call vote.

Implementation of the Declaration on the Granting of Independence to Colonial Countries and Peoples by the specialized agencies and the international institutions associated with the United Nations

The Economic and Social Council,

Having examined the report of the Secretary-General and the report of the President of the Economic and Social Council on consultations held with the Chairman of the Special Committee on the Situation with regard to the Implementation of the Declaration on the Granting of Independence to Colonial Countries and Peoples and the Chairman of the Special Committee against Apartheid,

Having heard the statement by the Chairman of the Special Committee on the Situation with regard to the Implementation of the Declaration on the Granting of Independence to Colonial Countries and Peoples,

Recalling General Assembly resolution 1514(XV) of 14 December 1960, containing the Declaration on the

Granting of Independence to Colonial Countries and Peoples, and all other resolutions adopted by United Nations bodies on the subject, in particular Economic and Social Council resolution 1992/59 of 31 July 1992,

Reaffirming the responsibility of the specialized agencies and other organizations of the United Nations system to take all effective measures, within their respective spheres of competence, to assist in the full and speedy implementation of the Declaration and other relevant resolutions of the United Nations bodies,

Recalling General Assembly resolution S-16/1 of 14 December 1989, the annex to which contains the Declaration on Apartheid and its Destructive Consequences in Southern Africa,

Recognizing the responsibility of the United Nations and the international community, as envisaged in the Declaration, to help the South African people in their legitimate struggle for the total elimination of apartheid through peaceful means,

Concerned that the objectives of the Charter of the United Nations and the Declaration on the Granting of Independence to Colonial Countries and Peoples have not been fully achieved,

Bearing in mind the extremely fragile economies of the small island Non-Self-Governing Territories and their vulnerability to natural disasters, such as hurricanes, cyclones and sea-level rise, recalling relevant General Assembly resolutions and taking note, in particular, of Assembly resolution 47/189 of 22 December 1992,

Stressing that, because the development options of small island Non-Self-Governing Territories are limited, there are special challenges to planning for and implementing sustainable development, and that those Territories will be constrained in meeting the challenges without the cooperation and assistance of the specialized agencies and other organizations of the United Nations system,

Also bearing in mind the conclusions and recommendations of the Meeting of Governmental Experts of Island Developing Countries and Donor Countries and Organizations, held in New York from 25 to 29 June 1990,[a]

Taking note of General Assembly resolution 47/22 of 25 November 1992 on cooperation and coordination of specialized agencies and the international institutions associated with the United Nations in their assistance to Non-Self-Governing Territories,

Noting with appreciation that assistance has continued to be extended to refugees from southern Africa through the Office of the United Nations High Commissioner for Refugees,

1. *Takes note* of the report of the President of the Economic and Social Council, and endorses the conclusions and suggestions contained therein;

2. *Also takes note* of the report of the Secretary-General;

3. *Reaffirms* that the recognition by the General Assembly, the Security Council and other United Nations organs of the legitimacy of the aspiration of peoples of Non-Self-Governing Territories to exercise their right to self-determination and independence entails, as a corollary, the extension by the organizations of the United Nations system of all the moral and material assistance necessary to those peoples;

4. *Expresses its appreciation* to those specialized agencies and other organizations of the United Nations system that have continued to cooperate in varying forms and degrees with the United Nations and the regional organizations concerned in the implementation of the Declaration on the Granting of Independence to Colonial Countries and Peoples and other relevant resolutions of United Nations bodies, and urges all the specialized agencies and other organizations of the United Nations system to contribute to the full and speedy implementation of the relevant provisions of those resolutions;

5. *Recommends* that all States intensify their efforts in the specialized agencies and other organizations of the United Nations system to ensure the full and effective implementation of the Declaration and other related resolutions of the United Nations system;

6. *Requests* the specialized agencies and the international institutions associated with the United Nations, as well as regional organizations, to strengthen existing measures of support and formulate additional appropriate programmes of assistance to the remaining Trust and Non-Self-Governing Territories within the framework of their respective mandates in order to accelerate progress in the economic and social sectors of those Territories;

7. *Also requests* the specialized agencies and other organizations of the United Nations system, in formulating their assistance programmes, to take due account of the text entitled "Challenges and opportunities: a strategic framework", which was adopted unanimously by the Meeting of Governmental Experts of Island Developing Countries and Donor Countries and Organizations;

8. *Urges* the specialized agencies and other organizations of the United Nations system to formulate programmes that will support the sustainable development of small island Non-Self-Governing Territories, and to adopt measures that will enable those Territories to cope effectively, creatively and in a sustainable manner with environmental changes and to mitigate the impact on and reduce the threats posed to marine and coastal resources;

9. *Welcomes* the continued initiative exercised by the United Nations Development Programme in maintaining close liaison among the specialized agencies and other organizations of the United Nations system and in coordinating the activities of the specialized agencies in extending effective assistance to the peoples of colonial Territories, and calls upon the specialized agencies and other organizations of the United Nations system, as a matter of urgency, to contribute generously to the relief, rehabilitation and reconstruction efforts in the Non-Self-Governing Territories affected by natural disasters;

10. *Urges* the administering Powers concerned to facilitate the participation of the representatives of the Governments of Trust and Non-Self-Governing Territories in the relevant meetings and conferences of the agencies and organizations so that the Territories may draw the maximum benefits from the related activities of the specialized agencies and other organizations of the United Nations system;

11. *Urges* the governing bodies of those specialized agencies and other organizations of the United Nations system that have not already done so to include in the agenda of their regular sessions a separate item on the progress made and action to be taken by their organi-

---

[a]A/CONF.147/5.

zations in the implementation of the Declaration and other relevant resolutions of United Nations bodies;

12. *Urges* the executive heads of the specialized agencies and other organizations of the United Nations system to formulate, with the active cooperation of the regional organizations concerned, concrete proposals for the full implementation of the relevant United Nations resolutions and to submit the proposals as a matter of priority to their governing and legislative organs;

13. *Appeals* to the specialized agencies and other organizations of the United Nations system to increase humanitarian and legal assistance for the victims of apartheid, returning refugees and exiles and released political prisoners;

14. *Draws the attention* of the Special Committee on the Situation with regard to the Implementation of the Declaration on the Granting of Independence to Colonial Countries and Peoples to the present resolution and to the discussion held on the subject at the substantive session of 1993 of the Economic and Social Council;

15. *Requests* the President of the Economic and Social Council to continue to maintain close contact on these matters with the Chairman of the Special Committee on the Situation with regard to the Implementation of the Declaration on the Granting of Independence to Colonial Countries and Peoples and to report thereon to the Council;

16. *Also requests* the President of the Council to maintain contact with the Chairman of the Special Committee against Apartheid, which is the focal point for the international campaign against apartheid, and to report thereon to the Council as appropriate;

17. *Requests* the Secretary-General to follow the implementation of the present resolution, paying particular attention to cooperation and integration arrangements for maximizing the efficiency of the assistance activities undertaken by various organizations of the United Nations system, and to report thereon to the Council at its substantive session of 1994;

18. *Decides* to keep these questions under continuous review.

Economic and Social Council resolution 1993/55

29 July 1993   Meeting 45   28-12-8 (roll-call vote)

13-nation draft (E/1993/L.37); agenda item 4 *(b)*.
Sponsors: Algeria, Angola, Benin, China, Cuba, Guinea, Malaysia, Namibia, Nigeria, Papua New Guinea, Suriname, Trinidad and Tobago, United Republic of Tanzania.
Meeting numbers. ESC 41, 43, 45.

Roll-call vote in Council as follows:

In favour: Angola, Argentina, Bahamas, Bangladesh, Benin, Bhutan, Botswana, Brazil, Chile, China, Colombia, Cuba, Guinea, India, Kuwait, Madagascar, Malaysia, Mexico, Morocco, Nigeria, Peru, Philippines, Sri Lanka, Suriname, Swaziland, Syrian Arab Republic, Togo, Trinidad and Tobago.
Against: Austria, Belgium, Canada, Denmark, France, Germany, Italy, Japan, Norway, Romania, United Kingdom, United States.
Abstaining: Australia, Belarus, Poland, Republic of Korea, Russian Federation, Spain, Turkey, Ukraine.

GENERAL ASSEMBLY ACTION

On 10 December 1993, the General Assembly, on the recommendation of the Fourth (Special Political and Decolonization) Committee, adopted **resolution 48/47** by recorded vote.

Implementation of the Declaration on the Granting of Independence to Colonial Countries and Peoples by the specialized agencies and the international institutions associated with the United Nations

The General Assembly,

Having considered the item entitled "Implementation of the Declaration on the Granting of Independence to Colonial Countries and Peoples by the specialized agencies and the international institutions associated with the United Nations",

Having also considered the report of the Secretary-General on the item and that of the Chairman of the Special Committee on the Situation with regard to the Implementation of the Declaration on the Granting of Independence to Colonial Countries and Peoples,

Having examined the chapter of the report of the Special Committee on the Situation with regard to the Implementation of the Declaration on the Granting of Independence to Colonial Countries and Peoples relating to the item,

Recalling its resolution 1514(XV) of 14 December 1960, containing the Declaration on the Granting of Independence to Colonial Countries and Peoples, and resolution 1541(XV) of 15 December 1960, as well as all its other resolutions on this subject, including, in particular, resolution 46/181 of 19 December 1991, endorsing the plan of action for the International Decade for the Eradication of Colonialism,

Recalling also its resolution S-16/1 of 14 December 1989, the annex to which contains the Declaration on Apartheid and its Destructive Consequences in Southern Africa,

Bearing in mind the relevant provisions of the final documents of the successive Conferences of Heads of State or Government of Non-Aligned Countries and of the resolutions adopted by the Assembly of Heads of State and Government of the Organization of African Unity, the South Pacific Forum and the Caribbean Community,

Welcoming the announcement that the first democratic elections in South Africa will be held on 27 April 1994, and expressing the hope that these elections will lead to the establishment of a united, democratic and non-racial South Africa,

Concerned that the objectives of the Charter of the United Nations and the Declaration on the Granting of Independence to Colonial Countries and Peoples have not been fully achieved,

Noting that the large majority of the remaining Non-Self-Governing Territories are small island Territories,

Recalling its resolution 43/189 of 20 December 1988, concerning specific measures in favour of island developing countries,

Bearing in mind the conclusions and recommendations of the Meeting of Governmental Experts of Island Developing Countries and Donor Countries and Organizations, held in New York in June 1990,

Recalling relevant resolutions of the Caribbean Development and Cooperation Committee concerning the access of Non-Self-Governing Territories to programmes of the United Nations system,

Noting the assistance extended thus far to Non-Self-Governing Territories by certain specialized agencies and other organizations of the United Nations system, in particular the United Nations Development Programme, and considering that such assistance should be expanded further, commensurate with the pressing needs of the peoples concerned for external assistance,

Stressing that, because the development options of small island Non-Self-Governing Territories are limited, there are special challenges to planning for and implementing sustainable development and that those Territories will be constrained in meeting the challenges without the cooperation and assistance of the specialized agencies and other organizations of the United Nations system,

Stressing the importance of securing necessary resources for funding expanded assistance programmes for the peoples concerned and the need to enlist the support of all major funding institutions within the United Nations system in that regard,

Noting with concern the continuing effects of the acts of aggression and destabilization that were committed by South Africa against neighbouring independent African States,

Reaffirming the responsibility of the specialized agencies and other organizations of the United Nations system to take all the necessary measures, within their respective spheres of competence, to ensure the full implementation, without further delay, of General Assembly resolution 1514(XV) and other relevant resolutions of the United Nations, particularly those relating to the extension of assistance to the peoples of the Non-Self-Governing Territories,

Expressing its appreciation to the Organization of African Unity, the South Pacific Forum and the Caribbean Community, as well as other regional organizations, for the continued cooperation and assistance they have extended to the specialized agencies and other organizations of the United Nations system in this regard,

Expressing its conviction that closer contacts and consultations between and among the specialized agencies and other organizations of the United Nations system and regional organizations help to facilitate the effective formulation of assistance programmes to the peoples concerned,

Mindful of the imperative need to keep under continuous review the activities of the specialized agencies and other organizations of the United Nations system in the implementation of the various United Nations decisions relating to decolonization,

Bearing in mind the extremely fragile economies of the Non-Self-Governing small island Territories and their vulnerability to natural disasters, such as hurricanes, cyclones and sea-level rise, and recalling its relevant resolutions, in particular resolution 47/189 of 22 December 1992,

Recalling its resolution 47/22 of 25 November 1992 on cooperation and coordination of the specialized agencies and the international institutions associated with the United Nations in their assistance to Non-Self-Governing Territories,

1. *Takes note* of the report of the Chairman of the Special Committee on the Situation with regard to the Implementation of the Declaration on the Granting of Independence to Colonial Countries and Peoples on his consultations with the President of the Economic and Social Council and endorses the observations and suggestions arising therefrom;

2. *Recommends* that all States intensify their efforts in the specialized agencies and other organizations of the United Nations system to ensure the full and effective implementation of the Declaration on the Granting of Independence to Colonial Countries and Peoples and other relevant resolutions of the United Nations;

3. *Reaffirms* that the specialized agencies and other organizations and institutions of the United Nations system should continue to be guided by the relevant resolutions of the United Nations in their efforts to contribute to the full implementation, without further delay, of the Declaration on the Granting of Independence to Colonial Countries and Peoples and all other relevant General Assembly resolutions;

4. *Reaffirms also* that the recognition by the General Assembly, the Security Council and other United Nations organs of the legitimacy of the aspiration of the peoples of Non-Self-Governing Territories to exercise their right to self-determination and independence entails, as a corollary, the extension of all necessary moral and material assistance to those peoples;

5. *Expresses its appreciation* to those specialized agencies and other organizations of the United Nations system that have continued to cooperate with the United Nations and the regional and subregional organizations in the implementation of General Assembly resolution 1514(XV) and other relevant resolutions of the United Nations, and urges all the specialized agencies and other organizations of the United Nations system to accelerate the full and speedy implementation of the relevant provisions of those resolutions;

6. *Requests* the specialized agencies and other organizations of the United Nations system, as well as international and regional organizations, to examine and review conditions in each Territory so as to take appropriate measures to accelerate progress in the economic and social sectors of the Territories;

7. *Also requests* the specialized agencies and the international institutions associated with the United Nations, as well as regional organizations, to strengthen existing measures of support and formulate additional appropriate programmes of assistance to the remaining Trust and Non-Self-Governing Territories, within the framework of their respective mandates, in order to accelerate progress in the economic and social sectors of those Territories;

8. *Further requests* the specialized agencies and other organizations of the United Nations system, in formulating their assistance programmes, to take due account of the conclusions and recommendations, entitled ''Challenges and opportunities: a strategic framework'', of the Meeting of Governmental Experts of Island Developing Countries and Donor Countries and Organizations;

9. *Urges* the specialized agencies and other organizations of the United Nations system to formulate programmes that will support the sustainable development of small island Non-Self-Governing Territories and adopt measures that will enable those Territories to cope effectively, creatively and sustainably with environmental changes and to mitigate impacts and reduce the threats posed to marine and coastal resources;

10. *Urges* the executive heads of the specialized agencies and other organizations of the United Nations system to formulate, with the active cooperation of the regional organizations concerned, concrete proposals for the full implementation of the relevant resolutions of the

United Nations and to submit the proposals as a matter of priority to their governing and legislative organs;

11. *Recommends* that the executive heads of the World Bank and the International Monetary Fund should draw the attention of their governing bodies to the present resolution and consider introducing flexible procedures to prepare specific programmes for the peoples of the Trust and Non-Self-Governing Territories;

12. *Urges* the specialized agencies and other organizations of the United Nations system that have not already done so to include in the agenda of the regular meetings of their governing bodies a separate item on the progress they have made in the implementation of General Assembly resolution 1514(XV) and other relevant resolutions of the United Nations;

13. *Welcomes* the continued initiative exercised by the United Nations Development Programme in maintaining close liaison among the specialized agencies and other organizations of the United Nations system and in coordinating the activities of the agencies in extending effective assistance to the peoples of Non-Self-Governing Territories, and calls upon the specialized agencies and other organizations of the United Nations system, as a matter of urgency, to contribute generously to the relief, rehabilitation and reconstruction efforts in those Non-Self-Governing Territories affected by natural disasters;

14. *Urges* the administering Powers concerned to facilitate the participation of the representatives of the Governments of Trust and Non-Self-Governing Territories in the relevant meetings and conferences of the agencies and organizations so that the Territories may draw the maximum benefits from the related activities of the specialized agencies and other organizations of the United Nations system;

15. *Appeals* to the specialized agencies and other organizations of the United Nations system to increase humanitarian and legal assistance to the victims of apartheid;

16. *Urges* the specialized agencies and other organizations of the United Nations system to increase their support for the forces working for the transformation of South Africa into a united, democratic and non-racial society, on the basis of the pertinent provisions of the Programme of Action contained in the Declaration on Apartheid and its Destructive Consequences in Southern Africa;

17. *Appeals* to the specialized agencies and the organizations of the United Nations system to render all possible assistance to the front-line and neighbouring States to enable them to rebuild their economies, which were adversely affected by acts of aggression and destabilization by South Africa;

18. *Recommends* that all Governments intensify their efforts in the specialized agencies and other organizations of the United Nations system of which they are members to ensure the full and effective implementation of General Assembly resolution 1514(XV) and other relevant resolutions of the United Nations and, in that connection, accord priority to the question of providing assistance on an emergency basis to the peoples of the Trust and Non-Self-Governing Territories;

19. *Requests* the Secretary-General to continue to assist the specialized agencies and other organizations of the United Nations system in working out appropriate measures for implementing the relevant resolutions of the United Nations and to prepare for submission to the relevant bodies, with the assistance of those agencies and organizations, a report on the action taken in implementation of the relevant resolutions, including the present resolution, since the circulation of his previous report;

20. *Commends* the Economic and Social Council for its debate and its resolution 1993/55 of 29 July 1993 on this issue and requests it to continue to consider, in consultation with the Special Committee on the Situation with regard to the Implementation of the Declaration on the Granting of Independence to Colonial Countries and Peoples, appropriate measures for coordination of the policies and activities of the specialized agencies and other organizations of the United Nations system in implementing the relevant resolutions of the General Assembly;

21. *Requests* the specialized agencies to report periodically to the Secretary-General on the implementation of the present resolution;

22. *Requests* the Secretary-General to transmit the present resolution to the governing bodies of the appropriate specialized agencies and international institutions associated with the United Nations so that those bodies take the necessary measures to implement the resolution, and also requests the Secretary-General to report to the General Assembly at its forty-ninth session on the implementation of the present resolution;

23. *Requests* the Special Committee to continue to examine the question and to report thereon to the General Assembly at its forty-ninth session.

General Assembly resolution 48/47

10 December 1993   Meeting 75   113-5-43 (recorded vote)

Approved by Fourth Committee (A/48/654) by recorded vote (90-6-33), 29 October (meeting 12); draft by Committee on colonial countries (A/48/23), amended by Papua New Guinea, for Committee on colonial countries (A/C.4/48/L.13); agenda items 118 & 12.

Meeting numbers. GA 48th session: 4th Committee 2-6, 11, 12; plenary 75.

Recorded vote in Assembly as follows:

In favour: Afghanistan, Algeria, Angola, Antigua and Barbuda, Bahamas, Bahrain, Bangladesh, Barbados, Belize, Benin, Bhutan, Bolivia, Botswana, Brazil, Brunei Darussalam, Burkina Faso, Cambodia, Cameroon, Cape Verde, Central African Republic, Chad, Chile, China, Colombia, Comoros, Congo, Costa Rica, Côte d'Ivoire, Cuba, Cyprus, Democratic People's Republic of Korea, Djibouti, Dominica, Dominican Republic, Ecuador, Egypt, El Salvador, Ethiopia, Fiji, Gabon, Gambia, Ghana, Grenada, Guatemala, Guinea, Guinea-Bissau, Guyana, Haiti, Honduras, India, Indonesia, Iran, Iraq, Jamaica, Jordan, Kenya, Kuwait, Lao People's Democratic Republic, Lesotho, Libyan Arab Jamahiriya, Madagascar, Malawi, Malaysia, Maldives, Mali, Marshall Islands, Mauritania, Mauritius, Mexico, Micronesia, Mongolia, Morocco, Mozambique, Myanmar, Namibia, Nepal, New Zealand, Nicaragua, Niger, Nigeria, Oman, Pakistan, Panama, Papua New Guinea, Peru, Philippines, Qatar, Republic of Korea, Rwanda, Saint Lucia, Saint Vincent and the Grenadines, Samoa, Saudi Arabia, Senegal, Sierra Leone, Singapore, Sri Lanka, Sudan, Suriname, Swaziland, Syrian Arab Republic, Thailand, Togo, Trinidad and Tobago, Tunisia, Uganda, United Arab Emirates, United Republic of Tanzania, Venezuela, Viet Nam, Yemen, Zaire, Zimbabwe.

Against: France, Netherlands, Russian Federation, United Kingdom, United States.

Abstaining: Argentina, Armenia, Australia, Austria, Azerbaijan, Belarus, Belgium, Bulgaria, Canada, Czech Republic, Denmark, Estonia, Finland, Georgia, Germany, Greece, Hungary, Iceland, Ireland, Israel, Italy, Japan, Kazakhstan, Latvia, Liechtenstein, Lithuania, Luxembourg, Malta, Norway, Paraguay, Poland, Portugal, Republic of Moldova, Romania, San Marino, Slovakia, Slovenia, Spain, Sweden, the former Yugoslav Republic of Macedonia, Turkey, Ukraine, Uruguay.

Foreign interests impeding implementation of the Declaration

The Committee on colonial countries again considered foreign economic and other interests which impeded implementation of the 1960 Declaration. It had before it working papers prepared by the Secretariat describing economic conditions and foreign activities in Anguilla,[17] Bermuda,[18] the Cayman Islands,[19] Montserrat,[20] the Turks and Caicos Islands[21] and the United States Virgin Islands.[22]

GENERAL ASSEMBLY ACTION

On 10 December 1993, the General Assembly, on the recommendation of the Fourth Committee, adopted **resolution 48/46** by recorded vote.

Activities of foreign economic and other interests which impede the implementation of the Declaration on the Granting of Independence to Colonial Countries and Peoples in Territories under colonial domination

The General Assembly,

Having considered the item entitled "Activities of foreign economic and other interests which impede the implementation of the Declaration on the Granting of Independence to Colonial Countries and Peoples in Territories under colonial domination",

Having examined the chapter of the report of the Special Committee on the Situation with regard to the Implementation of the Declaration on the Granting of Independence to Colonial Countries and Peoples relating to the item,

Recalling its resolution 1514(XV) of 14 December 1960, containing the Declaration on the Granting of Independence to Colonial Countries and Peoples, as well as all its other resolutions on this subject, including, in particular, resolution 46/181 of 19 December 1991, endorsing the plan of action for the International Decade for the Eradication of Colonialism,

Reaffirming the solemn obligation of the administering Powers under the Charter of the United Nations to promote the political, economic, social and educational advancement of the inhabitants of the Territories under their administration and to protect the human and natural resources of those Territories against abuses,

Reaffirming also that any economic or other activity that constitutes an obstacle to the implementation of the Declaration on the Granting of Independence to Colonial Countries and Peoples and obstructs efforts aimed at the elimination of colonialism, apartheid and racial discrimination is a direct violation of the rights of the inhabitants and of the principles of the Charter and all relevant resolutions of the United Nations,

Reaffirming further that the natural resources are the heritage of the indigenous populations of the colonial and Non-Self-Governing Territories,

Concerned about the activities of those foreign economic, financial and other interests that exploit the natural and human resources of the Non-Self-Governing Territories to the detriment of the interests of the inhabitants of those Territories and deprive them of their right to control the wealth of their countries,

Bearing in mind the relevant provisions of the final documents of the successive Conferences of Heads of State or Government of Non-Aligned Countries and of the resolutions adopted by the Assembly of Heads of State

and Government of the Organization of African Unity, the South Pacific Forum and the Caribbean Community,

Recognizing the crucial and decisive role that the imposition of international sanctions played in applying the necessary pressure on the South African regime to undertake significant measures towards the eradication of apartheid,

1. *Reaffirms* the inalienable right of the peoples of colonial and Non-Self-Governing Territories to self-determination and independence and to the enjoyment of the natural resources of their Territories, as well as their right to dispose of those resources in their best interests;

2. *Reiterates* that any administering Power that deprives the colonial peoples of Non-Self-Governing Territories of the exercise of their legitimate rights over their natural resources, or subordinates the rights and interests of those peoples to foreign economic and financial interests, violates the solemn obligations it has assumed under the Charter of the United Nations;

3. *Reaffirms its concern* over the activities of those foreign economic, financial and other interests which continue to exploit the natural resources that are the heritage of the indigenous populations of the colonial and Non-Self-Governing Territories in the Caribbean, the Pacific and other regions, as well as their human resources, to the detriment of their interests, thus depriving them of their right to control the resources of their Territories and impeding the realization by those peoples of their legitimate aspirations for self-determination and independence;

4. *Condemns* those activities of foreign economic and other interests in the colonial and Non-Self-Governing Territories which are impeding the implementation of the Declaration on the Granting of Independence to Colonial Countries and Peoples, contained in General Assembly resolution 1514(XV), and the efforts to eliminate colonialism and racial discrimination;

5. *Calls once again upon* all Governments that have not yet done so to take, in accordance with the relevant provisions of General Assembly resolution 2621(XXV) of 12 October 1970, legislative, administrative or other measures in respect of their nationals and the bodies corporate under their jurisdiction that own and operate enterprises in colonial and Non-Self-Governing Territories that are detrimental to the interests of the inhabitants of those Territories, in order to put an end to such enterprises and to prevent new investments that run counter to the interests of the inhabitants of those Territories;

6. *Reiterates* that the exploitation and plundering of the marine and other natural resources of colonial and Non-Self-Governing Territories by foreign economic interests, in violation of the relevant resolutions of the United Nations, is a threat to the integrity and prosperity of those Territories;

7. *Invites* all Governments and organizations of the United Nations system to take all possible measures to ensure that the permanent sovereignty of the peoples of colonial and Non-Self-Governing Territories over their natural resources is fully respected and safeguarded;

8. *Urges* the administering Powers concerned to take effective measures to safeguard and guarantee the inalienable right of the peoples of the colonial and Non-Self-Governing Territories to their natural resources and to establish and maintain control over the future devel-

opment of those resources, and requests the administering Powers to take all necessary steps to protect the property rights of the peoples of those Territories;

9. *Calls upon* the administering Powers concerned to ensure that no discriminatory and unjust wage systems or working conditions prevail in the Territories under their administration and to apply in each Territory a uniform system of wages to all the inhabitants without any discrimination;

10. *Requests* the Secretary-General to continue, through all means at his disposal, to inform world public opinion of those activities of foreign economic and other interests which impede the implementation of the Declaration on the Granting of Independence to Colonial Countries and Peoples;

11. *Appeals* to mass media, trade unions and non-governmental organizations, as well as individuals, to continue their efforts for the full implementation of the Declaration on the Granting of Independence to Colonial Countries and Peoples;

12. *Decides* to continue to monitor closely the situation in the colonial and Non-Self-Governing Territories so as to ensure that all economic activities in those Territories are aimed at strengthening and diversifying their economies in the interest of the indigenous peoples and at promoting the economic and financial viability of those Territories, in order to facilitate and accelerate the exercise by the peoples of those Territories of their right to self-determination and independence;

13. *Requests* the Special Committee on the Situation with regard to the Implementation of the Declaration on the Granting of Independence to Colonial Countries and Peoples to continue to examine this question and to report thereon to the General Assembly at its forty-ninth session.

General Assembly resolution 48/46

10 December 1993   Meeting 75   111-43-3 (recorded vote)

Approved by Fourth Committee (A/48/653) by recorded vote (89-35-3), 29 October (meeting 12); draft by Committee on colonial countries (A/48/23), amended by Papua New Guinea, for Committee on colonial countries (A/C.4/48/L.11); agenda items 117 & 18.
Meeting numbers. GA 48th session: 4th Committee 2-6, 11, 12; plenary 75.

Recorded vote in Assembly as follows:

In favour: Afghanistan, Algeria, Angola, Antigua and Barbuda, Bahamas, Bahrain, Bangladesh, Barbados, Benin, Bhutan, Bolivia, Botswana, Brazil, Brunei Darussalam, Burkina Faso, Cameroon, Cape Verde, Central African Republic, Chad, Chile, China, Colombia, Comoros, Congo, Costa Rica, Côte d'Ivoire, Cuba, Cyprus, Democratic People's Republic of Korea, Djibouti, Dominica, Dominican Republic, Ecuador, Egypt, El Salvador, Ethiopia, Fiji, Gabon, Gambia, Ghana, Grenada, Guatemala, Guinea, Guinea-Bissau, Guyana, Haiti, Honduras, India, Indonesia, Iran, Iraq, Jamaica, Jordan, Kenya, Kuwait, Lao People's Democratic Republic, Lesotho, Libyan Arab Jamahiriya, Madagascar, Malawi, Malaysia, Maldives, Mali, Marshall Islands, Mauritania, Mauritius, Mexico, Micronesia, Mongolia, Morocco, Mozambique, Myanmar, Namibia, Nepal, Nicaragua, Niger, Nigeria, Oman, Pakistan, Papua New Guinea, Peru, Philippines, Qatar, Republic of Korea, Rwanda, Saint Lucia, Saint Vincent and the Grenadines, Samoa, Saudi Arabia, Senegal, Sierra Leone, Singapore, Sri Lanka, Sudan, Suriname, Swaziland, Syrian Arab Republic, Thailand, the former Yugoslav Republic of Macedonia, Togo, Trinidad and Tobago, Tunisia, Uganda, United Arab Emirates, United Republic of Tanzania, Uruguay, Venezuela, Viet Nam, Yemen, Zaire, Zimbabwe.

Against: Armenia, Australia, Austria, Belgium, Bulgaria, Canada, Czech Republic, Denmark, Estonia, Finland, France, Georgia, Germany, Greece, Hungary, Iceland, Ireland, Israel, Italy, Japan, Latvia, Liechtenstein, Lithuania, Luxembourg, Malta, Netherlands, New Zealand, Norway, Panama, Poland, Portugal, Republic of Moldova, Romania, Russian Federation, San Marino, Slovakia, Slovenia, Spain, Sweden, Turkey, Ukraine, United Kingdom, United States.

Abstaining: Argentina, Belize, Paraguay.

Military activities and arrangements in colonial countries

The Committee on colonial countries in 1993 again considered military activities by colonial Powers in Territories under their administration which might impede the implementation of the 1960 Declaration. It had before it working papers prepared by the Secretariat on military activities and arrangements in Bermuda,[23] Guam[24] and the United States Virgin Islands.[25]

The Committee decided to change the title of the item to "Military activities and arrangements by colonial Powers in Territories under their administration".

GENERAL ASSEMBLY ACTION

In December 1993, the General Assembly adopted **decision 48/421** by recorded vote.

Military activities and arrangements by colonial Powers in Territories under their administration

At its 75th plenary meeting, on 10 December 1993, the General Assembly, on the recommendation of the Special Political and Decolonization Committee (Fourth Committee), adopted the following text:

"1. The General Assembly, having considered the chapter of the report of the Special Committee on the Situation with regard to the Implementation of the Declaration on the Granting of Independence to Colonial Countries and Peoples relating to an item on the agenda of the Special Committee entitled 'Military activities and arrangements by colonial Powers in Territories under their administration', and recalling its resolution 1514(XV) of 14 December 1960 and all other relevant resolutions and decisions of the United Nations relating to military activities in colonial and Non-Self-Governing Territories, reaffirms its strong conviction that military bases and installations in the Territories concerned could constitute an obstacle to the exercise by the people of those Territories of their right to self-determination, and reiterates its strong views that existing bases and installations, which are impeding the implementation of the Declaration on the Granting of Independence to Colonial Countries and Peoples, should be withdrawn.

"2. Aware of the presence of such bases and installations in some of those Territories, the General Assembly urges the administering Powers concerned to continue to take all necessary measures not to involve those Territories in any offensive acts or interference against other States.

"3. The General Assembly reiterates its concern that military activities and arrangements by colonial Powers in Territories under their administration might run counter to the rights and interests of the colonial peoples concerned, especially their right to self-determination and independence. The Assembly once again calls upon the administering Powers concerned to terminate such activities and to eliminate such military bases in compliance with its relevant resolutions.

"4. The General Assembly reiterates that the colonial and Non-Self-Governing Territories and areas adjacent thereto should not be used for nuclear testing, dumping of nuclear wastes or deployment of nuclear and other weapons of mass destruction.

"5.   The General Assembly deplores the continued alienation of land in colonial and Non-Self-Governing Territories, particularly in the small island Territories of the Pacific and Caribbean regions, for military installations. The large-scale utilization of the local resources for this purpose could adversely affect the economic development of the Territories concerned.

"6.   The General Assembly requests the Secretary-General to continue to inform world public opinion of those military activities and arrangements in colonial and Non-Self-Governing Territories which constitute an obstacle to the implementation of the Declaration on the Granting of Independence to Colonial Countries and Peoples.

"7.   The General Assembly requests the Special Committee on the Situation with regard to the Implementation of the Declaration on the Granting of Independence to Colonial Countries and Peoples to continue to examine this question and to report thereon to the Assembly at its forty-ninth session."

General Assembly decision 48/421

112-42-3 (recorded vote)

Approved by Fourth Committee (A/48/653) by recorded vote (92-34-3), 29 October (meeting 12); draft by Committee on colonial countries (A/48/23), amended by Papua New Guinea, for Committee on colonial countries (A/C.4/48/L.12); agenda items 117 & 18.

Meeting numbers. GA 48th session: 4th Committee 2-6, 11, 12; plenary 75.

Recorded vote in Assembly as follows:

In favour: Afghanistan, Algeria, Angola, Antigua and Barbuda, Bahamas, Bahrain, Bangladesh, Barbados, Benin, Bhutan, Bolivia, Botswana, Brazil, Brunei Darussalam, Burkina Faso, Cameroon, Cape Verde, Central African Republic, Chad, Chile, China, Colombia, Comoros, Congo, Costa Rica, Côte d'Ivoire, Cuba, Cyprus, Democratic People's Republic of Korea, Djibouti, Dominica, Dominican Republic, Ecuador, Egypt, El Salvador, Ethiopia, Fiji, Gabon, Gambia, Ghana, Grenada, Guatemala, Guinea, Guinea-Bissau, Guyana, Haiti, Honduras, India, Indonesia, Iran, Iraq, Jamaica, Jordan, Kenya, Kuwait, Lao People's Democratic Republic, Lesotho, Libyan Arab Jamahiriya, Madagascar, Malawi, Malaysia, Maldives, Mali, Marshall Islands, Mauritania, Mauritius, Mexico, Micronesia, Mongolia, Morocco, Mozambique, Myanmar, Namibia, Nepal, Nicaragua, Niger, Nigeria, Oman, Pakistan, Panama, Papua New Guinea, Peru, Philippines, Qatar, Republic of Korea, Rwanda, Saint Lucia, Saint Vincent and the Grenadines, Samoa, Saudi Arabia, Senegal, Sierra Leone, Singapore, Sri Lanka, Sudan, Suriname, Swaziland, Syrian Arab Republic, Thailand, the former Yugoslav Republic of Macedonia, Togo, Trinidad and Tobago, Tunisia, Uganda, United Arab Emirates, United Republic of Tanzania, Uruguay, Venezuela, Viet Nam, Yemen, Zaire, Zimbabwe.

Against: Armenia, Australia, Austria, Belgium, Bulgaria, Canada, Czech Republic, Denmark, Estonia, Finland, France, Georgia, Germany, Greece, Hungary, Iceland, Ireland, Israel, Italy, Japan, Latvia, Liechtenstein, Lithuania, Luxembourg, Malta, Netherlands, New Zealand, Norway, Poland, Portugal, Republic of Moldova, Romania, Russian Federation, San Marino, Slovakia, Slovenia, Spain, Sweden, Turkey, Ukraine, United Kingdom, United States.

Abstaining: Argentina, Belize, Paraguay.

Information dissemination

In July, the Committee on colonial countries adopted recommendations for the dissemination of information on decolonization, based on a report of its Subcommittee on Small Territories, Petitions, Information and Assistance,[8] which related to consultations with the representatives of the United Nations Department of Public Information (DPI) and Department of Political Affairs, and to the Week of Solidarity with the Peoples of All Colonial Territories, as well as Those

in South Africa, Fighting for Freedom, Independence and Human Rights (24-28 May).

Among the recommendations were that DPI continue intensifying its publicity of decolonization; that it produce new visual material on problems of decolonization; that it provide feedback from United Nations information centres; that it utilize materials pertaining to the participation of United Nations organizations and agencies in the decolonization process and distribute those materials through the information centres; and that it increase, in cooperation with the Department of Political Affairs, its speaking engagements at universities and intensify cooperation with non-governmental organizations.

GENERAL ASSEMBLY ACTION

On 10 December, the General Assembly adopted **resolution 48/53** by recorded vote.

Dissemination of information on decolonization

The General Assembly,

Having examined the chapter of the report of the Special Committee on the Situation with regard to the Implementation of the Declaration on the Granting of Independence to Colonial Countries and Peoples relating to the dissemination of information on decolonization and publicity for the work of the United Nations in the field of decolonization,

Recalling its resolution 1514(XV) of 14 December 1960, containing the Declaration on the Granting of Independence to Colonial Countries and Peoples, and other resolutions and decisions of the United Nations concerning the dissemination of information on decolonization, in particular General Assembly resolution 47/24 of 25 November 1992,

Reiterating the importance of publicity as an instrument for furthering the aims of the Declaration, and mindful of the role of world public opinion in effectively assisting the peoples of the colonial Territories to achieve self-determination and independence,

Aware of the importance of non-governmental organizations in the dissemination of information on decolonization,

1.   *Approves* the chapter of the report of the Special Committee on the Situation with regard to the Implementation of the Declaration on the Granting of Independence to Colonial Countries and Peoples relating to the dissemination of information on decolonization and publicity for the work of the United Nations in the field of decolonization;

2.   *Considers it important* for the United Nations to continue to play an active role in the process of decolonization and to intensify its efforts to ensure the widest possible dissemination of information on decolonization, with a view to further mobilizing international public opinion in support of complete decolonization by the year 2000;

3.   *Requests* the Secretary-General, taking into account the suggestions of the Special Committee, to continue to take concrete measures through all the media at his disposal, including publications, radio and television, to give widespread and continuous publicity to the work

of the United Nations in the field of decolonization and, *inter alia:*

(a) To continue, in consultation with the Special Committee, to collect, prepare and disseminate basic material, studies and articles relating to the problems of decolonization and, in particular, to continue to publish the periodical *Objective: Justice* and other publications, special articles and studies, including the *Decolonization* series, and to increase the information on all the Territories under consideration by the Special Committee, selecting appropriate material for wider dissemination by reprints in various languages;

(b) To seek the full cooperation of the administering Powers in the discharge of the tasks referred to above;

(c) To intensify the decolonization-oriented activities of all United Nations information centres;

(d) To maintain a working relationship with the appropriate regional and intergovernmental organizations, particularly in Africa and the Pacific and Caribbean regions, by holding periodic consultations and exchanging information;

(e) To solicit, in consultation with United Nations information centres, assistance in the dissemination of information on decolonization from non-governmental organizations;

(f) To continue to produce comprehensive press releases for all meetings of the Special Committee and its subsidiary bodies;

(g) To ensure that the necessary facilities and services to that end are made available;

(h) To report to the Special Committee on measures taken in the implementation of the present resolution;

4. *Requests* all States, in particular the administering Powers, as well as the specialized agencies and other organizations of the United Nations system and non-governmental organizations with a special interest in decolonization, to undertake or intensify, in cooperation with the Secretary-General and within their respective spheres of competence, the large-scale dissemination of information referred to in paragraph 2 above;

5. *Requests* the Special Committee to follow the implementation of the present resolution and to report thereon to the General Assembly at its forty-ninth session.

General Assembly resolution 48/53

10 December 1993   Meeting 75   141-2-18 (recorded vote)

12-nation draft (A/48/L.39 & Add.1); agenda item 18.
Sponsors: Fiji, Grenada, India, Madagascar, Micronesia, Namibia, Papua New Guinea, Sierra Leone, Solomon Islands, Swaziland, United Republic of Tanzania, Zimbabwe.
Meeting numbers. GA 48th session: plenary 70, 75.

Recorded vote in Assembly as follows:

In favour: Afghanistan, Algeria, Angola, Antigua and Barbuda, Argentina, Armenia, Australia, Austria, Azerbaijan, Bahamas, Bahrain, Bangladesh, Barbados, Belarus, Belize, Benin, Bhutan, Bolivia, Bosnia and Herzegovina, Botswana, Brazil, Brunei Darussalam, Burkina Faso, Cambodia, Cameroon, Cape Verde, Central African Republic, Chad, Chile, China, Colombia, Comoros, Congo, Costa Rica, Côte d'Ivoire, Cuba, Cyprus, Democratic People's Republic of Korea, Denmark, Djibouti, Dominica, Dominican Republic, Ecuador, Egypt, El Salvador, Ethiopia, Fiji, Gabon, Gambia, Georgia, Ghana, Greece, Grenada, Guatemala, Guinea, Guinea-Bissau, Guyana, Haiti, Honduras, Iceland, India, Indonesia, Iran, Iraq, Ireland, Jamaica, Japan, Jordan, Kazakhstan, Kenya, Kuwait, Lao People's Democratic Republic, Latvia, Lesotho, Libyan Arab Jamahiriya, Liechtenstein, Lithuania, Madagascar, Malawi, Malaysia, Maldives, Mali, Malta, Marshall Islands, Mauritania, Mauritius, Mexico, Micronesia, Mongolia, Morocco, Mozambique, Myanmar, Namibia, Nepal, New Zealand, Nicaragua, Niger, Nigeria, Norway, Oman, Pakistan, Panama, Papua New Guinea, Paraguay, Peru, Philippines, Portugal, Qatar, Republic of Korea, Russian Federation, Rwanda, Saint Lucia, Saint Vincent and the Grenadines,

Samoa, Saudi Arabia, Senegal, Sierra Leone, Singapore, Spain, Sri Lanka, Sudan, Suriname, Swaziland, Sweden, Syrian Arab Republic, Thailand, the former Yugoslav Republic of Macedonia, Togo, Trinidad and Tobago, Tunisia, Turkey, Uganda, Ukraine, United Arab Emirates, United Republic of Tanzania, Uruguay, Venezuela, Viet Nam, Yemen, Zaire, Zimbabwe.
Against: United Kingdom, United States.
Abstaining: Belgium, Bulgaria, Canada, Czech Republic, Estonia, Finland, France, Germany, Hungary, Israel, Italy, Luxembourg, Netherlands, Poland, Republic of Moldova, Romania, Slovakia, Slovenia.

New Caledonia

The Committee on colonial countries had before it a working paper prepared by the Secretariat on recent political developments and economic, social and educational conditions in New Caledonia.[26]

According to the Committee to Monitor the Matignon Accords (Paris, 2-4 February 1993), overall progress had been made but more was needed in education, nickel mining—the most important sector of the economy—and regional links. The Accords, adopted in 1988,[27] called for a self-determination referendum to be held in 1998, following a 10-year period of development aimed at effecting more equitable economic distribution between indigenous Melanesians, known as Kanaks, who comprised about 45 per cent of the population, and persons of European origin, mainly French.

GENERAL ASSEMBLY ACTION

On 10 December 1993, the General Assembly, on the recommendation of the Fourth Committee, adopted **resolution 48/50** without vote.

Question of New Caledonia

The General Assembly,

Having considered the question of New Caledonia,

Having examined the chapter of the report of the Special Committee on the Situation with regard to the Implementation of the Declaration on the Granting of Independence to Colonial Countries and Peoples relating to New Caledonia,

Reaffirming the right of peoples to self-determination as enshrined in the Charter of the United Nations,

Recalling its resolutions 1514(XV) of 14 December 1960 and 1541(XV) of 15 December 1960,

Noting the importance of the positive measures being pursued in New Caledonia by the French authorities, in cooperation with all sectors of the population, to promote political, economic and social development in the Territory, including measures in the area of environmental protection and action with respect to drug abuse and trafficking, in order to provide a framework for its peaceful progress to self-determination,

Noting also, in this context, the importance of equitable economic and social development, as well as continued dialogue among the parties involved in New Caledonia in the preparation of the act of self-determination of New Caledonia,

Welcoming the positive outcome of the mid-term review of the Matignon Accords in February 1993 and the continuing support for the process by the new French Government,

Noting the holding of the Pacific Regional Seminar at Port Moresby from 8 to 10 June 1993 to examine the political, economic and social situation in small island Non-Self Governing Territories,

Noting with satisfaction the intensification of contacts between New Caledonia and neighbouring countries of the South Pacific region,

1. *Approves* the chapter of the report of the Special Committee on the Situation with regard to the Implementation of the Declaration on the Granting of Independence to Colonial Countries and Peoples relating to New Caledonia;

2. *Urges* all the parties involved, in the interest of all the people of New Caledonia and building on the positive outcome of the mid-term review of the Matignon Accords, to maintain their dialogue in a spirit of harmony;

3. *Invites* all the parties involved to continue promoting a framework for the peaceful progress of the Territory towards an act of self-determination in which all options are open and which would safeguard the rights of all New Caledonians according to the letter and the spirit of the Matignon Accords, which are based on the principle that it is for the populations of New Caledonia to choose how to control their destiny;

4. *Welcomes* recent and impending measures to strengthen and diversify the New Caledonian economy in all fields;

5. *Also welcomes* the call by the parties to the Matignon Accords for greater progress in housing, employment, training, education and health care in New Caledonia;

6. *Commends* the decision to establish a Melanesian cultural centre as a contribution to preserving the indigenous culture of New Caledonia;

7. *Notes* the recent positive initiatives aimed at protecting New Caledonia's natural environment, notably the "Zonéco" operation designed to map and evaluate marine resources within the economic zone of New Caledonia;

8. *Acknowledges* the close links between New Caledonia and the peoples of the South Pacific and the positive actions being taken by the French authorities to facilitate the further development of those links, including the development of closer relations with the member countries of the South Pacific Forum;

9. *Welcomes in particular*, in this regard, recent high-level visits to New Caledonia by delegations from countries of the Pacific region;

10. *Requests* the Special Committee to continue the examination of this question at its next session and to report thereon to the General Assembly at its forty-ninth ssion.

General Assembly resolution 48/50

10 December 1993   Meeting 75   Adopted without vote

Approved by Fourth Committee (A/48/656) without objection, 29 October (meeting 13); draft by Committee on colonial countries (A/48/23); agenda item 18.

Meeting numbers. GA 48th session: 4th Committee 2-8, 12, 13; plenary 75.

Puerto Rico

In May 1993, the Committee on colonial countries endorsed the recommendation of its open-ended working group[7] that the Committee defer until 1994 consideration of its decision of 15 August 1991,[28] by which it deplored the fact that the United States Congress had not adopted a legal framework for holding a referendum to enable the people of Puerto Rico to determine their political future. In accordance with the group's suggestion that it give due consideration to requests for hearings, the Committee heard 30 representatives of organizations from Puerto Rico in July.

REFERENCES

[1]YUN 1991, p. 777, GA res. 46/181, 19 Dec. 1991. [2]YUN 1988, p. 734, GA res. 43/47, 22 Nov. 1988. [3]A/AC.109/1159. [4]A/AC.109/1140. [5]A/AC.109/L.1804. [6]A/48/23. [7]A/AC.109/L.1795. [8]A/AC.109/L.1797. [9]A/AC.109/L.1799. [10]A/AC.109/L.1800. [11]A/AC.109/L.1796. [12]YUN 1992, p. 950, GA res. 47/16, 16 Nov. 1992. [13]A/48/224 & Corr.1 & Add.1-3. [14]YUN 1960, p. 49, GA res. 1514(XV), 14 Dec. 1960. [15]YUN 1992, p. 948, ESC res. 1992/59, 31 July 1992. [16]E/1993/98. [17]A/AC.109/1158. [18]A/AC.109/1153. [19]A/AC.109/1157. [20]A/AC.109/1156. [21]A/AC.109/1161. [22]A/AC.109/1155. [23]A/AC.109/1144. [24]A/AC.109/1149. [25]A/AC.109/1151. [26]A/AC.109/1170. [27]YUN 1988, p. 742. [28]YUN 1991, p. 790.

Other general questions

Scholarships

As requested by the General Assembly in 1992,[1] the Secretary-General reported in September 1993 on offers made by Member States of study and training facilities for inhabitants of NSGTs.[2] Four States informed the Secretary-General of scholarships between 1 October 1992 and 30 September 1993. Australia granted to students from New Caledonia 12 training awards for English language and technical or vocational training, and another 12 awards to attend Australian institutions of higher education; in addition, it gave academic assistance to two students from Tokelau and offered a variety of training awards to Palau. Barbados awarded 20 scholarships to nationals from NSGTs, New Zealand gave support to students from Tokelau, and the United Kingdom offered 124 scholarships to students from British NSGTs. Between 1 October 1992 and 30 September 1993, the Secretariat received requests from 54 students for information on the availability of scholarships. None were inhabitants of NSGTs.

GENERAL ASSEMBLY ACTION

On 10 December, the General Assembly, on the recommendation of the Fourth Committee, adopted **resolution 48/48** without vote.

Offers by Member States of study and training facilities for inhabitants of Non-Self-Governing Territories

The General Assembly,

Recalling its resolution 47/17 of 16 November 1992,

Having examined the report of the Secretary-General on offers by Member States of study and training facilities for inhabitants of Non-Self-Governing Territories, prepared pursuant to General Assembly resolution 845(IX) of 22 November 1954,

Conscious of the importance of promoting the educational advancement of the inhabitants of Non-Self-Governing Territories,

Strongly convinced that the continuation and expansion of offers of scholarships is essential in order to meet the increasing need of students from Non-Self-Governing Territories for educational and training assistance, and considering that students in those Territories should be encouraged to avail themselves of such offers,

1. *Takes note* of the report of the Secretary-General;

2. *Expresses its appreciation* to those Member States that have made scholarships available to the inhabitants of Non-Self-Governing Territories;

3. *Invites* all States to make or continue to make generous offers of study and training facilities to the inhabitants of those Territories that have not yet attained self-government or independence and, wherever possible, to provide travel funds to prospective students;

4. *Urges* the administering Powers to take effective measures to ensure the widespread and continuous dissemination in the Territories under their administration of information relating to offers of study and training facilities made by States and to provide all the necessary facilities to enable students to avail themselves of such offers;

5. *Requests* the Secretary-General to report to the General Assembly at its forty-ninth session on the implementation of the present resolution;

6. *Draws the attention* of the Special Committee on the Situation with regard to the Implementation of the Declaration on the Granting of Independence to Colonial Countries and Peoples to the present resolution.

General Assembly resolution 48/48

10 December 1993   Meeting 75   Adopted without vote

Approved by Fourth Committee (A/48/655) without objection, 29 October (meeting 12); 34-nation draft (A/C.4/48/L.5); agenda item 119.

Sponsors: Algeria, Antigua and Barbuda, Argentina, Australia, Barbados, Brazil, Bulgaria, China, Costa Rica, Cuba, Guinea, Guyana, India, Indonesia, Iran, Madagascar, Mali, New Zealand, Nicaragua, Nigeria, Pakistan, Panama, Papua New Guinea, Philippines, Samoa, Singapore, Sri Lanka, Sudan, Sweden, Thailand, Trinidad and Tobago, Tunisia, United Republic of Tanzania, Vanuatu.

Meeting numbers. GA 48th session: 4th Committee 2-7, 12; plenary 75.

Information to the United Nations

States responsible for the administration of NSGTs continued to inform the Secretary-General of the economic, social and educational conditions in the Territories, under the terms of Article 73 *e* of the United Nations Charter. In reports to the Committee on colonial countries[3] and the General Assembly,[4] the Secretary-General listed the date of receipt of the information provided by the administering Powers and the period covered

by their reports. In 1993, he had received information with respect to the following NSGTs:

New Zealand: Tokelau

United Kingdom: Anguilla, Bermuda, British Virgin Islands, Falkland Islands (Malvinas), Gibraltar, Montserrat, Pitcairn, St. Helena, Turks and Caicos Islands

United States: American Samoa, Guam, United States Virgin Islands

GENERAL ASSEMBLY ACTION

On 10 December, the General Assembly, on the recommendation of the Fourth Committee, adopted **resolution 48/45** by recorded vote.

Information from Non-Self-Governing Territories transmitted under Article 73 *e* of the Charter of the United Nations

The General Assembly,

Having examined the chapter of the report of the Special Committee on the Situation with regard to the Implementation of the Declaration on the Granting of Independence to Colonial Countries and Peoples relating to the information from Non-Self-Governing Territories transmitted under Article 73 *e* of the Charter of the United Nations and the action taken by the Special Committee in respect of that information,

Having also examined the report of the Secretary-General on the item,

Recalling its resolution 1970(XVIII) of 16 December 1963, in which it requested the Special Committee to study the information transmitted to the Secretary-General in accordance with Article 73 *e* of the Charter and to take such information fully into account in examining the situation with regard to the implementation of the Declaration on the Granting of Independence to Colonial Countries and Peoples, contained in General Assembly resolution 1514(XV) of 14 December 1960,

Recalling also its resolution 47/14 of 16 November 1992, in which it requested the Special Committee to continue to discharge the functions entrusted to it under resolution 1970(XVIII),

Stressing the importance of timely transmission by the administering Powers of adequate information under Article 73 *e* of the Charter, in particular in relation to the preparation by the Secretariat of the working papers on the Territories concerned,

1. *Approves* the chapter of the report of the Special Committee on the Situation with regard to the Implementation of the Declaration on the Granting of Independence to Colonial Countries and Peoples relating to the information from Non-Self-Governing Territories transmitted under Article 73 *e* of the Charter of the United Nations;

2. *Reaffirms* that, in the absence of a decision by the General Assembly itself that a Non-Self-Governing Territory has attained a full measure of self-government in terms of Chapter XI of the Charter, the administering Power concerned should continue to transmit information under Article 73 *e* of the Charter with respect to that Territory;

3. *Requests* the administering Powers concerned to transmit or continue to transmit to the Secretary-General the information prescribed in Article 73 *e* of the Charter, as well as the fullest possible information

on political and constitutional developments in the Territories concerned, within a maximum period of six months following the expiration of the administrative year in those Territories;

4. *Requests* the Secretary-General to continue to ensure that adequate information is drawn from all available published sources in connection with the preparation of the working papers relating to the Territories concerned;

5. *Requests* the Special Committee to continue to discharge the functions entrusted to it under General Assembly resolution 1970(XVIII), in accordance with established procedures, and to report thereon to the Assembly at its forty-ninth session.

General Assembly resolution 48/45

10 December 1993   Meeting 75   159-0-3 (recorded vote)

Approved by Fourth Committee (A/48/652) by recorded vote (122-0-3), 29 October (meeting 12); draft by Committee on colonial countries (A/48/23); agenda item 116.

Meeting numbers. GA 48th session: 4th Committee 2-6, 12; plenary 75.

Recorded vote in Assembly as follows:

In favour: Afghanistan, Algeria, Angola, Antigua and Barbuda, Argentina, Armenia, Australia, Austria, Azerbaijan, Bahamas, Bahrain, Bangladesh, Barbados, Belarus, Belgium, Belize, Benin, Bhutan, Bolivia, Bosnia and Herzegovina, Botswana, Brazil, Brunei Darussalam, Bulgaria, Burkina Faso, Cambodia, Cameroon, Canada, Cape Verde, Central African Republic, Chad, Chile, China, Colombia, Comoros, Congo, Costa Rica, Côte d'Ivoire, Cuba, Cyprus, Czech Republic, Democratic People's Republic of Korea, Denmark, Djibouti, Dominica, Dominican Republic, Ecuador, Egypt, El Salvador, Estonia, Ethiopia, Fiji, Finland, Gabon, Gambia, Georgia, Germany, Ghana, Greece, Grenada, Guatemala, Guinea-Bissau, Guyana, Haiti, Honduras, Hungary, Iceland, India, Indonesia, Iran, Iraq, Ireland, Israel, Italy, Jamaica, Japan, Jordan, Kazakhstan, Kenya, Kuwait, Lao People's Democratic Republic, Latvia, Lesotho, Libyan Arab Jamahiriya, Liechtenstein, Lithuania, Luxembourg, Madagascar, Malawi, Malaysia, Maldives, Mali, Malta, Marshall Islands, Mauritania, Mauritius, Mexico, Micronesia, Mongolia, Morocco, Mozambique, Myanmar, Namibia, Nepal, Netherlands, New Zealand, Nicaragua, Niger, Nigeria, Norway, Oman, Pakistan, Panama, Papua New Guinea, Paraguay, Peru, Philippines, Poland, Portugal, Qatar, Republic of Korea, Republic of Moldova, Romania, Russian Federation, Rwanda, Saint Lucia, Saint Vincent and the Grenadines, Samoa, San Marino, Saudi Arabia, Senegal, Sierra Leone, Singapore, Slovakia, Slovenia, Spain, Sri Lanka, Sudan, Suriname, Swaziland, Sweden, Syrian Arab Republic, Thailand, the former Yugoslav Republic of Macedonia, Togo, Trinidad and Tobago, Tunisia, Turkey, Turkmenistan, Uganda, Ukraine, United Arab Emirates, United Republic of Tanzania, Uruguay, Venezuela, Viet Nam, Yemen, Zaire, Zimbabwe.

Against: None.

Abstaining: France, United Kingdom, United States.

Visiting missions

The Chairman of the Committee on colonial countries, as requested by the Committee in 1992,[5] held consultations with representatives of administering Powers on the question of sending visiting missions to NSGTs. In July 1993,[6] he reported that some NSGTs had expressed their willingness to receive United Nations visiting missions. He drew the attention of the administering Powers to the efforts of the Committee to improve its efficiency and methods of work in fulfilling its mandate. Regarding the dispatch of visiting missions, he pointed out that in most cases further efforts by the Committee were required before the full cooperation of the administering Powers could be restored.

The Chairman took note of a May letter from New Zealand[7] inviting the Committee to send a visiting mission to Tokelau in 1994.

On 12 July,[8] the Committee adopted a resolution, stressing the need to dispatch periodic missions to NSGTs to facilitate full implementation of the 1960 Declaration,[9] calling on the administering Powers to continue to cooperate by receiving United Nations missions in Territories under their administration and to participate in the work of the Committee, and requesting its Chairman to continue consulting with those Powers and to report as appropriate.

REFERENCES

[1]YUN 1992, p. 959, GA res. 47/17, 16 Nov. 1992. [2]A/48/443. [3]A/AC.109/1160. [4]A/48/436. [5]YUN 1992, p. 961. [6]A/AC.109/L.1801. [7]A/AC.109/1162. [8]A/AC.109/1166. [9]YUN 1960, p. 49, GA res. 1514(XV), 14 Dec. 1960.

Other colonial Territories

East Timor

The Committee on colonial countries, in July 1993, considered a working paper prepared by the Secretariat on political developments, the human rights situation, economic and social conditions and other developments in East Timor.[1] The paper also described United Nations consideration of the situation. The Committee heard statements by, among others, Portugal, as the administering Power, and 21 petitioners.

In a letter to the Committee Chairman,[2] Indonesia reiterated that any consideration of the so-called question of East Timor was inappropriate and constituted unacceptable interference in matters within the domestic jurisdiction of a sovereign Member State. The process of decolonization had been carried out in conformity with the Charter of the United Nations and General Assembly resolutions, and East Timor's integration into Indonesia was formalized in 1976; it had rights and obligations equal to those of the other provinces. Indonesia, therefore, strongly objected to the participation of petitioners in the Committee's deliberations.

Acting on a proposal of its Chairman, the Committee decided to continue consideration of the item at its 1994 session, subject to any directives by the General Assembly.

In September,[3] the Secretary-General updated his 1992 progress report[4] regarding a comprehensive solution to the question of East Timor. The Foreign Ministers of Indonesia and Portugal had held substantive discussions in December 1992 (New York), and April (Rome) and September (New York) 1993. United Nations officials had also had contacts with various East Timorese groups and prominent individuals.

The Secretary-General stated that it had proved difficult to make progress owing to the wide difference in the positions of the two sides, but he was moderately encouraged and planned to hold another round of discussions with the two Foreign Ministers in May 1994 at Geneva. The improvement of the conditions in East Timor, especially of the human rights situation there (see PART THREE, Chapter X), was *sine qua non* to progress in the talks.

Falkland Islands (Malvinas)

The Committee on colonial countries considered the question of the Falkland Islands (Malvinas) on 14 July 1993. The United Kingdom, the administering Power, did not participate in consideration of the item. The Committee acceded to a request from Argentina to participate. It had before it a working paper,[5] prepared by the Secretariat, which outlined political developments and economic, social and educational conditions and described the Constitution and Government of the islands and consideration of the question by the United Nations and other intergovernmental organizations.

The Committee adopted a resolution,[6] requesting Argentina and the United Kingdom to consolidate the process of dialogue and cooperation by resuming negotiations to find a peaceful solution to the sovereignty dispute relating to the islands, and reiterating its support for the mission of good offices of the Secretary-General in assisting the parties.

GENERAL ASSEMBLY ACTION

On 16 November, the General Assembly, by **decision 48/408,** deferred consideration of the Falkland Islands (Malvinas) and included it in the provisional agenda of its 1994 session.

Western Sahara

In 1993, efforts continued towards organizing a United Nations–supervised referendum for self-determination of the people of Western Sahara, in accordance with a settlement plan approved by the Security Council in 1991.[7] The Secretary-General continued exercising his good offices, in close cooperation with the Chairman of the Organization of African Unity (OAU), to settle the differences between the two parties concerned—the Government of Morocco and the Frente Popular para la Liberación de Saguia el-Hamra y de Río de Oro (Frente POLISARIO). In order to resolve the outstanding issues—related mainly to the basic question of the establishment of the electorate eligible to participate in the referendum—the Secretary-General put forward a compromise proposal.

During consultations in November 1993, both sides confirmed their intention to proceed expeditiously with the initial stage of the registration of voters, in cooperation with the United Nations Mission for the Referendum in Western Sahara (MINURSO). Accordingly, in late November, the revised lists of the 1974 census, together with a supplement listing additional persons expected to reach 18 years of age by 31 December 1993, were made accessible at 10 different locations at Laayoune and several places in the El-Aiun refugee camp in the Tindouf area. Beginning in December, application forms for preliminary registration of potential participants in the referendum were distributed. In May 1993, Erik Jensen of Malaysia was appointed Chairman of the Identification Commission, responsible for establishing the final list of Saharans qualified to participate in the voting.

MINURSO continued monitoring and verifying the cease-fire in effect since September 1991. For the period between 1 January and 31 October 1993, 23 cease-fire violations—which were of a non-violent nature and did not result in casualties—were reported.

As at 1 November, the military component of MINURSO totalled 324 personnel, comprising 226 military observers and 98 military support personnel. Brigadier-General André Van Baelen of Belgium continued to serve as Force Commander. His tour of duty was renewed on 1 October for an additional one-year period.

MINURSO's Security Unit—responsible for maintaining order in and around the identification and registration offices—was composed of a first contingent of 26 police officers, including the Police Commissioner, Colonel Jürgen Friedrich Reimann of Germany, who assumed his functions in early June. Current activities of the police officers were complementary to the work of the Identification Commission and included coordination of logistics and technical and physical support.

Report of the Secretary-General (January). In January 1993,[8] the Secretary-General described the military and financial aspects of MINURSO, events in the mission area having a bearing on MINURSO's activities, and developments since his previous report to the Security Council in August 1992.[9] He stated that, notwithstanding prior acceptance of the general provisions of the settlement plan,[10] approved by the Council in April 1991,[7] important disagreements persisted between the parties regarding fundamental issues. Annexed to the report were an interpretation by the parties of the criteria for eligibility to vote in a United Nations–organized referendum, in accordance with the plan for implementation of the settlement proposals, and other instructions relating to evidence that individuals were required to furnish for participation in the referendum.

The Secretary-General presented three broad options for resolving the differences, namely: continuation and intensification of talks; immediate implementation of the settlement plan; and adoption of an alternative approach. He said he awaited guidance from the Council by way of a resolution.

SECURITY COUNCIL ACTION

On 2 March 1993, the Security Council unanimously adopted **resolution 809(1993)**.

The Security Council,

Reaffirming its resolutions 621(1988) of 20 September 1988, 658(1990) of 27 June 1990, 690(1991) of 29 April 1991 and 725(1991) of 31 December 1991,

Recalling that in conformity with the settlement plan regarding the question of Western Sahara, as adopted by resolutions 658(1990) and 690(1991), it was for the Secretary-General to determine the instructions for the review of the applications for participation in the referendum, and that the Council welcomed in its resolution 725(1991) the report of the Secretary-General dated 19 December 1991,

Having considered the report of the Secretary-General on the situation concerning Western Sahara,

Concerned by the difficulties and delays encountered in the implementation of the settlement plan regarding the question of Western Sahara and in particular the persistent divergences between the two parties on the interpretation and application of the criteria for voter eligibility set out by the Secretary-General in his report dated 19 December 1991,

Determined that the settlement plan regarding the question of Western Sahara be implemented without further delay in order to achieve a just and lasting solution,

Stressing the desirability of ensuring the full cooperation of both parties for the implementation of the settlement plan,

1. *Welcomes* the report of the Secretary-General on the situation concerning Western Sahara;

2. *Invites* the Secretary-General and his Special Representative to intensify their efforts, with the parties, in order to resolve the issues identified in his report, in particular those relating to the interpretation and application of the criteria for voter eligibility;

3. *Invites further* the Secretary-General to make the necessary preparations for the organization of the referendum of self-determination of the people of Western Sahara and to consult accordingly with the parties for the purpose of commencing voter registration on a prompt basis starting with the updated lists of the 1974 census;

4. *Invites also* the Secretary-General to report to the Council as soon as possible and not later than May 1993 on the outcome of his efforts, on the cooperation of the parties and on the prospects and modalities for the holding of the referendum on a free and fair basis with a view that this take place by the end of the current year at the latest, and requests the Secretary-General to include in this report proposals for the necessary adjustments to the present role and strength of the United Nations Mission for the Referendum in Western Sahara;

5. *Urges* the two parties to cooperate fully with the Secretary-General in implementing the settlement plan which has been accepted by them and approved by the Council in its resolutions 658(1990) and 690(1991), and in resolving the issues identified in the Secretary-General's recent report, in particular those relating to the interpretation and application of the criteria for voter eligibility;

6. *Decides* to remain actively seized of the matter.

Security Council resolution 809(1993)

2 March 1993   Meeting 3179   Adopted unanimously

Draft prepared in consultations among Council members (S/25340).

Reports of the Secretary-General (May-November). In May,[11] the Secretary-General submitted an interim status report, informing the Security Council of his decision to visit the mission area in June, in pursuance of the Council's call in March for an intensification of efforts in order to resolve outstanding issues, particularly those relating to the interpretation and application of the criteria for voter eligibility.

In accordance with the Council's request to the Secretary-General to make the necessary preparations for organization of the referendum and to consult with the parties regarding an early registration of voters, starting with the updated lists of the 1974 census, discussions were held in March and April with the parties, which confirmed their desire to proceed promptly with the registration and to cooperate with MINURSO in so doing. They also agreed to the participation of tribal chiefs, as well as observers from either side, in the registration process. Both parties showed a desire to move towards an early referendum, although the Frente POLISARIO maintained reservations concerning the eligibility of applicants to vote.

In the light of the consultations, it was decided to establish an identification commission to begin voter registration and draw up plans, including resource requirements, for expanding the identification process to include all potentially eligible voters. In view of the above, the Secretary-General postponed publication of the report requested of him by the Council.

On 28 May,[12] the President of the Council informed the Secretary-General that the Council members understood the reasons for such postponement. They welcomed his decision to visit the region, as well as the establishment of an identification commission.

The Secretary-General reported in July[13] that he had met with officials of both sides during his visit to the mission area with his Special Representative from 31 May to 4 June. The aim of the visit was to urge the parties to accept a compromise solution regarding the interpretation and application of the criteria for voter eligibility. The compromise proposal was annexed to the report, as were the terms of reference of the Identification Commission and general regulations for the organization and conduct of the referendum.

Despite initial reservations concerning tribal links with the Territory that it felt were unduly restrictive, Morocco acquiesced to the compromise. The Frente POLISARIO proposed amendments to provisions relating to tribal links and the composition of the teams of tribal chiefs invited to testify, which it considered unduly permissive. The Secretary-General stated that the Identification Commission in June had begun with both parties to establish procedures for identification and registration of voters.

By a letter of 4 August,[14] the President of the Council stated that the Council members supported the Secretary-General's efforts and noted that the Identification Commission had started preparatory work. They welcomed the parties' commitment to implement the peace plan.

In November,[15] the Secretary-General provided an update of the situation, including the military aspects of MINURSO and its civil police component. He stated that although the Frente POLISARIO had accepted the criteria for voter eligibility, it maintained substantial reservations on the interpretation and application of the criteria and requested amendments. Morocco, on the other hand, rejected any modification of the compromise text in its current form. Both parties agreed that membership of a Saharan subfraction existing in the Territory was a prerequisite to voter eligibility; however, they disagreed over which tribes or tribal units had a clearly established connection with or were existing in the Territory. Morocco held the view that members of all subfractions of a given Saharan tribe should be considered for participation in the referendum, including those not represented in the 1974 census. The Frente POLISARIO contended that, unless the vast majority of the members of a subfraction had been counted in the 1974 census, that subfraction should not be considered as existing in the Territory and its members, other than those already counted, should not be eligible. As a compromise, the Secretary-General proposed that the potential electorate encompass members of all the Saharan tribal subfractions, but only those represented in the 1974 census, regardless of the number of individuals from those subfractions who were counted in 1974. The Frente POLISARIO, however, did not agree with that proposal, as it remained concerned about the possible inclusion of members of some tribal units which it did not consider as existing in the Territory.

In view of the remaining difficulties, the Secretary-General said, it was not possible to hold the referendum by the end of 1993. He stressed that acceptance by both parties of his role as guarantor of an objective and impartial referen-

dum was central to the issue. On the assumption that the remaining difficulties were settled and progress was made in the initial stages of the registration process, he hoped to be able to report early in 1994 on the prospects and modalities of the referendum, together with a timetable and recommendations for necessary adjustments with regard to MINURSO's strength, with a view to holding the referendum in mid-1994.

On 6 December,[16] the President of the Council informed the Secretary-General that the Council members supported his compromise proposal and reaffirmed his role as guarantor of an objective and impartial referendum. They expected any difficulties with the compromise to be resolved by early 1994.

In September 1993,[17] the Secretary-General, as requested by the General Assembly in 1992,[18] reported on the situation in Western Sahara and described the activities he had undertaken since 3 October 1992. In close cooperation with the Chairman of OAU, he continued to exercise his good offices with the parties. He recalled that, pending fulfilment of the conditions necessary for the commencement of the transitional period in accordance with the timetable and plan of action set out in his April 1991 report, MINURSO's military mandate remained restricted to monitoring and verifying the cease-fire in effect since September 1991. There were no breaches of the cease-fire resulting in casualties on either side and violations were of a non-violent nature.

The basic question of the establishment of the electorate largely accounted for the differences of view of the parties concerned. In order to resolve the outstanding issues and prepare for the holding of the referendum, the Secretary-General and his Special Representative were continuing their efforts through regular contacts with the parties and with government officials of the neighbouring countries.

Consideration by the Committee on colonial countries. In July,[19] the Committee on colonial countries heard the views of a representative of the Frente POLISARIO and considered a working paper prepared by the Secretariat containing information on developments in Western Sahara.[20] The paper presented an overview of the General Assembly's consideration of the question in 1992, of the Secretary-General's good offices, and of political and other developments from September 1992 to July 1993.

GENERAL ASSEMBLY ACTION

On 10 December, the General Assembly, on the recommendation of the Fourth Committee, adopted **resolution 48/49** without vote.

Question of Western Sahara

The General Assembly,

Having considered the question of Western Sahara,

Reaffirming the inalienable right of all peoples to self-determination and independence, in accordance with the principles set forth in the Charter of the United Nations and in General Assembly resolution 1514(XV) of 14 December 1960, containing the Declaration on the Granting of Independence to Colonial Countries and Peoples,

Recalling its resolution 47/25 of 25 November 1992,

Recalling also the agreement in principle given on 30 August 1988 by the Kingdom of Morocco and the Frente Popular para la Liberación de Saguia el-Hamra y de Río de Oro to the proposals of the Secretary-General of the United Nations and the current Chairman of the Assembly of Heads of State and Government of the Organization of African Unity in the context of their joint mission of good offices,

Recalling further Security Council resolutions 621(1988) of 20 September 1988, 658(1990) of 27 June 1990, 690(1991) of 29 April 1991 and 725(1991) of 31 December 1991 relating to the question of Western Sahara,

Recalling with satisfaction the entry into force of the cease-fire in Western Sahara on 6 September 1991, in accordance with the proposal of the Secretary-General accepted by the two parties,

Noting the adoption by the Security Council on 2 March 1993 of resolution 809(1993),

Taking note of the letter dated 4 August 1993 from the President of the Security Council addressed to the Secretary-General,

Considering that the holding of talks between the two parties at Laayoune from 17 to 19 July 1993 is a positive development,

Having examined the relevant chapter of the report of the Special Committee on the Situation with regard to the Implementation of the Declaration on the Granting of Independence to Colonial Countries and Peoples,

Having also examined the report of the Secretary-General,

1. *Takes note with appreciation* of the report of the Secretary-General;

2. *Pays tribute* to the Secretary-General and to his Special Representative for their action with a view to settling the question of Western Sahara by the implementation of the settlement plan;

3. *Reiterates its support* for further efforts of the Secretary-General for the organization and supervision by the United Nations, in cooperation with the Organization of African Unity, of a referendum for self-determination of the people of Western Sahara, in conformity with Security Council resolutions 658(1990) and 690(1991) in which the Council adopted the settlement plan for Western Sahara;

4. *Endorses* the contents of the letter dated 4 August 1993 from the President of the Security Council to the Secretary-General, in which the members of the Council, *inter alia*, fully supported the efforts of the Secretary-General to make swift progress on the preparations for holding a referendum in accordance with Council resolution 809(1993), noted that the Identification Commission had begun its preparatory work, welcomed the reaffirmation by the two parties of their commitment to the implementation of the peace plan in its entirety, in particular their encouraging responses to the compromise proposal of the Secretary-General concerning the interpretation and application of the criteria, and shared his hope that direct talks between the two parties will soon resume;

5. *Requests* the Special Committee on the Situation with regard to the Implementation of the Declaration on the Granting of Independence to Colonial Countries and Peoples to continue to consider the situation in Western Sahara, bearing in mind the ongoing referendum process, and to report thereon to the General Assembly at its forty-ninth session;

6. *Invites* the Secretary-General to submit to the General Assembly at its forty-ninth session a report on the implementation of the present resolution.

General Assembly resolution 48/49

10 December 1993   Meeting 75   Adopted without vote

Approved by Fourth Committee (A/48/656) without vote, 29 October (meeting 12); draft by Chairman (A/C.4/48/L.4); agenda item 18.
Meeting numbers. GA 48th session: 4th Committee 2-8, 12; plenary 75.

Financing of MINURSO

In April 1993, the General Assembly, on the recommendation of the Fifth (Administrative and Budgetary) Committee, adopted **decision 47/451 B** without vote.

At its 98th plenary meeting, on 8 April 1993, the General Assembly, on the recommendation of the Fifth Committee, decided, in the light of Security Council resolution 809(1993) of 2 March 1993 and in particular of the activities enumerated in paragraphs 2 and 3 of that resolution, to authorize the Secretary-General to enter into commitments in an amount not exceeding 3,499,700 United States dollars gross (3,319,400 dollars net) per month for the period from 1 March to 30 June 1993, subject to the concurrence of the Advisory Committee on Administrative and Budgetary Questions. Those resources should be utilized from the unencumbered balance of the appropriation provided for the United Nations Mission for the Referendum in Western Sahara.

General Assembly decision 47/451 B

Adopted without vote

Approved by Fifth Committee (A/47/796/Add.1) without vote, 19 March (meeting 57); oral proposal by Chairman; agenda item 121.
Meeting numbers. GA 47th session: 5th Committee 55, 57; plenary 98.

Reporting on 19 March on the informal consultations with regard to the financing of MINURSO, Belgium said the Fifth Committee would not be able to consider the Secretary-General's December 1992 report on the subject,[21] in view of the Security Council's March 1993 resolution concerning implementation of the settlement plan for Western Sahara. Activities required under that resolution, for which additional resources had to be allocated, were the following: intensified efforts by the Secretary-General to conduct several rounds of talks with the parties and neighbouring countries, and preparations for the referendum, specifically the establishment of the Identification Commission. The Commission would conduct research in order to review the 1974 census carefully, arrange for a revised list to be published in the Territory and in other places where a number of Western Saharans were known to be living, and publish instructions on how Western Saharans could apply in writing.

In September 1993, the Assembly adopted **decision 47/451 C** without vote.

At its 110th plenary meeting, on 14 September 1993, the General Assembly, on the recommendation of the Fifth Committee, decided:

(a) To utilize an amount not exceeding 6,525,380 United States dollars gross (6,181,980 dollars net) for the maintenance of the United Nations Mission for the Referendum in Western Sahara for the period from 1 July to 31 August 1993 from the unencumbered balance of the appropriation provided for the Mission;

(b) To authorize the Secretary-General to enter into commitments in an amount not exceeding 3,204,600 dollars gross (3,028,200 dollars net) per month for the period from 1 September to 31 December 1993, subject to the concurrence of the Advisory Committee on Administrative and Budgetary Questions, and that that amount be provided from the unencumbered balance of the appropriation provided for the Mission.

General Assembly decision 47/451 C

Adopted without vote

Approved by Fifth Committee (A/47/796/Add.2) without vote, 3 September (meeting 74); draft by Chairman (A/C.5/47/L.48); agenda item 121.
Meeting numbers. GA 47th session: 5th Committee 73, 74; plenary 110.

On 1 October, the United Nations Controller sought the concurrence of the Advisory Committee on Administrative and Budgetary Questions (ACABQ) to enter into further commitments on a monthly basis in an amount not exceeding $3,204,600 gross ($3,028,200 net) for the maintenance of MINURSO from 1 September to 31 December 1993. The Chairman of ACABQ, in a letter of 22 October to the Secretary-General, concurred in the entering into further commitments for those four months in an amount not exceeding $3 million gross per month, to be provided from the unencumbered balance of the appropriation provided for MINURSO.

Report of the Secretary-General. In a December report to the Fifth Committee on the financing of United Nations peace-keeping operations,[22] the Secretary-General presented a revised apportionment for MINURSO totalling $12,000,000 gross ($11,294,000 net) for the period from 1 September to 31 December 1993, and a cost estimate of $12,782,000 gross ($12,086,000 net) for the period from 1 January to 30 April 1994.

ACABQ recommendations. Also in December,[23] ACABQ recommended that the Assembly authorize the Secretary-General to enter into commitments up to $12.8 million gross ($12.1 million net) from the unencumbered balance of the appropriation for MINURSO, for the period from 1 January to 30 April 1994. No assessment was currently necessary, the Committee added.

GENERAL ASSEMBLY ACTION (December)

Concurring with the observations of ACABQ, the General Assembly, by **decision 48/467** of 23 December 1993, authorized the Secretary-General, on an exceptional basis, to enter into commitments up to $9,586,500 gross ($9,064,500 net) from the unencumbered balance of the appropriation for MINURSO, for the period from 1 January to 31 March 1994.

Island Territories

The Committee on colonial countries considered the following 12 island Territories and had before it working papers prepared by the Secretariat describing their constitutional and political developments and economic and social conditions: American Samoa,[24] Anguilla,[25] Bermuda,[26] British Virgin Islands,[27] Cayman Islands,[28] Guam,[29] Montserrat,[30] Pitcairn,[31] St. Helena,[32] Tokelau,[33] Turks and Caicos Islands[34] and United States Virgin Islands.[35] In view of Palau's intention to hold a plebiscite on 27 July 1993 regarding the Compact of Free Association (see below), the Committee's open-ended working group recommended that the Committee suspend consideration of the Trust Territory of the Pacific Islands until 1994.[36]

The Committee allocated the item to its Subcommittee on Small Territories, Petitions, Information and Assistance[37] for preliminary consideration and subsequently took up the item between 28 May and 27 July.[19] It adopted a consolidated draft resolution, the first part of which dealt with 10 island Territories in general and the second with specific conditions in those same 10 Territories; it also recommended two draft decisions to the General Assembly, one on Pitcairn and the other on St. Helena (see below).

GENERAL ASSEMBLY ACTION

On 10 December, the General Assembly, on the recommendation of the Fourth Committee, adopted **resolutions 48/51 A and B** without vote.

Questions of American Samoa, Anguilla, Bermuda, the British Virgin Islands, the Cayman Islands, Guam, Montserrat, Tokelau, the Turks and Caicos Islands and the United States Virgin Islands

A
General

The General Assembly,

Having considered the questions of American Samoa, Anguilla, Bermuda, the British Virgin Islands, the Cayman Islands, Guam, Montserrat, Tokelau, the Turks and Caicos Islands and the United States Virgin Islands,

Having examined the relevant chapter of the report of the Special Committee on the Situation with regard to

the Implementation of the Declaration on the Granting of Independence to Colonial Countries and Peoples,

Recalling its resolution 1514(XV) of 14 December 1960,
containing the Declaration on the Granting of Independence to Colonial Countries and Peoples, and all resolutions and decisions of the United Nations relating to
those Territories, including, in particular, those resolutions adopted by the General Assembly at its forty-
seventh session on the individual Territories covered by
the present resolution,

Recalling also its resolution 1541(XV) of 15 December
1960, containing the principles which should guide
Member States in determining whether or not an obligation exists to transmit the information called for under
Article 73 *e* of the Charter of the United Nations,

Conscious of the need to ensure the full and speedy implementation of the Declaration in respect of those Territories, in view of the target set by the United Nations
to eradicate colonialism by the year 2000,

Aware of the special circumstances of the geographical
location and economic conditions of each Territory, and
bearing in mind the necessity of promoting economic
stability and diversifying and strengthening further the
economies of the respective Territories as a matter of
priority,

Taking note of the report of the Pacific Regional Seminar to Review the Political, Economic and Social Conditions in the Small Island Non-Self-Governing Territories, held at Port Moresby from 8 to 10 June 1993,
and the information provided at the Seminar by the
Lieutenant-Governor of American Samoa and other
participants,

Conscious of the particular vulnerability of the small
Territories to natural disasters and environmental degradation,

Aware also of the usefulness both to the Territories and
to the Special Committee of the participation of
representatives of the Non-Self-Governing Territories in
the work of the Special Committee,

Mindful that United Nations visiting missions provide
a means of ascertaining the situation in the small Territories, and considering that the possibility of sending
further visiting missions to those Territories at an appropriate time and in consultation with the administering Powers should be kept under review,

Noting with appreciation the contribution to the development of some Territories by specialized agencies and
other organizations of the United Nations system, in
particular the United Nations Development Programme, as well as regional institutions such as the
Caribbean Development Bank,

Bearing in mind the fragile economy of the small Territories and their vulnerability to natural disasters and
environmental degradation, and recalling General Assembly resolutions and the recommendations of the
Meeting of Governmental Experts of Island Developing Countries and Donor Countries and Organizations,
held in New York in June 1990,

Recalling the conclusions and recommendations of the
Regional Seminar to Review the Special Development
Needs of Island Territories, held in connection with the
plan of action of the International Decade for the Eradication of Colonialism, at St. George's from 17 to 19 June
1992, as well as the position taken by the territorial
Governments contained in the report of the Seminar,

1. *Takes note* of the chapter of the report of the Special Committee on the Situation with regard to the Implementation of the Declaration on the Granting of Independence to Colonial Countries and Peoples relating
to American Samoa, Anguilla, Bermuda, the British
Virgin Islands, the Cayman Islands, Guam, Montserrat, Tokelau, the Turks and Caicos Islands and the
United States Virgin Islands;

2. *Reaffirms* the inalienable right of the people of
those Territories to self-determination and independence
in conformity with the Charter of the United Nations
and General Assembly resolution 1514(XV), containing the Declaration on the Granting of Independence
to Colonial Countries and Peoples;

3. *Reaffirms also* that it is ultimately for the people
of those Territories themselves to determine freely their
future political status in accordance with the relevant
provisions of the Charter, the Declaration and the relevant resolutions of the General Assembly and in that
connection calls upon the administering Powers, in
cooperation with the territorial Governments, to facilitate programmes of political education in order to foster an awareness among the people of the possibilities
open to them in the exercise of their right to self-
determination, in conformity with the legitimate political status options clearly defined in Assembly resolution 1541(XV);

4. *Reiterates* that it is the responsibility of the administering Powers to create such conditions in the Territories as will enable their peoples to exercise freely and
without interference their inalienable right to self-
determination and independence;

5. *Requests* the administering Powers to encourage
and facilitate the participation of elected representatives
of the Non-Self-Governing Territories under their administration and other appropriate authorities or personalities duly mandated by those representatives in the
work of the Special Committee, its Working Group and
its Subcommittee on Small Territories, Petitions, Information and Assistance, as well as in the work of its
seminars;

6. *Reiterates the view* that factors such as territorial size,
geographical location, size of population and limited natural resources should in no way serve as a pretext to
delay the speedy exercise by the peoples of those Territories of their inalienable right to self-determination;

7. *Reaffirms* the responsibility of the administering
Powers under the Charter to promote the economic and
social development and to preserve the cultural identity of those Territories, and recommends that priority
should continue to be given, in consultation with the
territorial Governments concerned, to the strengthening and diversification of their respective economies;

8. *Urges* the administering Powers, in cooperation
with the territorial Governments concerned, to take or
continue to take effective measures to safeguard and
guarantee the inalienable right of the peoples of those
Territories to own, develop or dispose of the natural
resources of those Territories, including marine
resources, and to establish and maintain control over
the future development of those resources;

9. *Also urges* the administering Powers to take all
necessary measures to protect and conserve the environment of the Territories under their administration
against any environmental degradation, and requests

the specialized agencies concerned to continue to monitor environmental conditions in those Territories;

10. *Calls upon* the administering Powers to continue to take all necessary measures, in cooperation with the respective territorial Governments, to counter problems related to drug trafficking;

11. *Urges* the administering Powers to foster or continue to foster close relations between the Territories and other island communities in their respective regions and to promote cooperation between the respective territorial Governments and regional institutions, as well as the specialized agencies and other organizations of the United Nations system;

12. *Also urges* the administering Powers to cooperate or continue to cooperate with the Special Committee in its work by providing timely and up-to-date information for each Territory under their administration, in accordance with Article 73 *e* of the Charter, and by facilitating the dispatch of visiting missions to secure firsthand information thereon and to ascertain the wishes and aspirations of the inhabitants;

13. *Appeals* to the administering Powers to continue or to resume their participation in future meetings and activities of the Special Committee and to ensure the participation in the work of the Special Committee of representatives of the Non-Self-Governing Territories;

14. *Urges* Member States to contribute to the efforts of the United Nations to achieve the eradication of colonialism by the year 2000, and calls upon them to continue to give their full support to the action of the Special Committee towards the attainment of that objective;

15. *Invites* the specialized agencies and other organizations of the United Nations system to initiate or to continue to take all necessary measures to accelerate progress in the social and economic life of the Territories;

16. *Requests* the specialized agencies and other organizations of the United Nations system, in formulating their assistance programmes, to take due account of the text entitled ''Challenges and opportunities: a strategic framework'', which was adopted unanimously by the Meeting of Governmental Experts of Island Developing Countries and Donor Countries and Organizations;

17. *Requests* the Special Committee to continue the examination of the question of the small Territories and to recommend to the General Assembly the most suitable steps to be taken to enable the populations of those Territories to exercise their right to self-determination and independence, and to report thereon to the Assembly at its forty-ninth session.

B
Individual Territories

I. *American Samoa*

The General Assembly,

Referring to resolution A above,

Noting that efforts are currently aimed at increasing the production of food crops for local consumption,

Noting also the announcement by the Governor that his administration was planning to lay off over one thousand public employees, including some four hundred permanent career civil servants,

Noting further that American Samoa is the only United States of America Territory in which employers are allowed to pay workers less than the mainland minimum wage,

Aware that one third of the population is dependent on village-based water systems which often lack basic sanitary conditions,

Noting the devastation caused by hurricane Val in December 1991 and the recovery efforts of the territorial Government in conjunction with the administering Power and the international community,

Recalling the dispatch in 1981 of a United Nations visiting mission to the Territory,

1. *Calls upon* the administering Power, in cooperation with relevant regional and international institutions, to assist the Territory in increasing its agricultural output;

2. *Also calls upon* the administering Power, in cooperation with the territorial Government, to continue to promote the economic and social development of the Territory in order to reduce its heavy economic and financial dependence on the United States of America;

3. *Requests* additional information from the elected representatives of American Samoa, the administering Power and/or other sources to enable the Special Committee on the Situation with regard to the Implementation of the Declaration on the Granting of Independence to Colonial Countries and Peoples to determine its future course of action on the question of American Samoa, and in this connection expresses its firm conviction that a visiting mission at this stage would provide an effective means of obtaining information on developments in the Territory and ascertaining the views of the people of American Samoa with regard to their future status.

II. *Anguilla*

The General Assembly,

Referring to resolution A above,

Having heard the statement of the representative of the United Kingdom of Great Britain and Northern Ireland, as the administering Power,

Noting the decision of the administering Power to effect a policy change aimed at enhancing its relations with its Caribbean dependent Territories,

Aware that the educational system in Anguilla is facing severe problems, including overcrowding and insufficient equipment and supplies in the schools, as well as a high percentage of untrained teachers and the loss of teachers to the private sector and to other parts of the civil service,

Aware also of the inability of Anguilla's educational system to alleviate the problem of scarcity of skilled national personnel, particularly in the fields of economic management and tourism, and that educational reform is of paramount importance to the achievement of the long-term economic goals of the Territory,

Noting that the territorial Government is placing great emphasis on manpower development and training,

Also noting that the Government's Public Sector Investment Programme for 1991-1995 is expected to be financed by external donors through grants and concessional loans,

Aware that the exploitation of deep-sea resources would help to reduce the risk of depleting the Territory's own fishing resources as a result of overfishing,

Recalling the dispatch of a United Nations visiting mission to the Territory in 1984,

1. *Notes* the efforts of the administering Power aimed at improving its relations with its dependent Territories of the Caribbean;

2. *Requests* the administering Power, in considering, adopting and/or implementing policy decisions likely to affect its dependent Territories, to continue to grant the highest attention to the interests, needs and wishes of the territorial Government and the people of Anguilla;

3. *Calls upon* national, regional and international institutions specializing in the field of education to grant Anguilla funds and equipment and to make available to the Territory teacher training courses, to enable it to overcome its educational problems;

4. *Calls upon* all countries, institutions and organizations endowed with expertise in manpower training to grant Anguilla assistance in this field;

5. *Invites* the international donor community to contribute generously to the Government's Public Sector Investment Programme for 1991-1995 and to grant the Territory all possible assistance to enable it to reach the main development objectives established by the Executive Council of the Territory;

6. *Requests* all countries and organizations with deep-sea fishing experience to facilitate the acquisition by the fishing sector of the Territory of larger boats and ad hoc fishing equipment and to provide the Territory's fishermen with deep-sea fishing training programmes;

7. *Notes* that a period of nine years has elapsed since a United Nations mission visited Anguilla, and calls upon the administering Power to facilitate the dispatch of a further visiting mission to the Territory.

III. *Bermuda*

The General Assembly,

Referring to resolution A above,

Having heard the statement of the representative of the United Kingdom of Great Britain and Northern Ireland, as the administering Power,

Noting the negative effects of the world recession on the economy of Bermuda,

Noting also the recent review of the criminal justice system in the Territory,

Noting with concern the incidence of crime in the secondary schools, and noting also the planned restructuring of the public school system,

Reaffirming its strong conviction that the presence of military bases and installations in the Territory could, in certain circumstances, constitute an obstacle to the implementation of the Declaration on the Granting of Independence to Colonial Countries and Peoples,

Noting that the Territory has never been visited by a United Nations visiting mission,

1. *Reaffirms its view* that it is ultimately for the people of Bermuda to decide their own future;

2. *Requests* the administering Power to assist the territorial Government in its efforts to mitigate the effects of the world recession, particularly in the domains of tourism and international business;

3. *Calls upon* the administering Power to ensure that the criminal justice system is fair to all inhabitants of the Territory;

4. *Also calls upon* the administering Power to ensure that the planned restructuring of the public school system is not prejudicial to the economically less advantaged sectors of the population;

5. *Further calls upon* the administering Power to ensure that the presence of military bases and installations in the Territory would not constitute an obstacle to the implementation of the Declaration on the Granting of Independence to Colonial Countries and Peoples nor hinder the population from exercising its right to self-determination and independence in conformity with the purposes and principles of the Charter of the United Nations;

6. *Again calls upon* the administering Power to facilitate the dispatch of a United Nations visiting mission to the Territory.

IV. *British Virgin Islands*

The General Assembly,

Referring to resolution A above,

Having heard the statement of the representative of the United Kingdom of Great Britain and Northern Ireland, as the administering Power,

Noting the request of the Territory for a review of its Constitution,

Also noting the statements made by the Chief Minister, the Leader of the Opposition and members of the public of the Territory concerning the review by the administering Power of its policy towards, and management of, its Caribbean dependent Territories,

Aware of the impact of the world economic recession on the economy of the British Virgin Islands,

Noting the measures taken by the territorial Government to develop the agricultural, industrial, educational and communications sectors,

Noting also the desire of the Territory for membership in the Food and Agriculture Organization of the United Nations,

Noting further that, according to the Caribbean Development Bank, the Territory's unmet manpower requirements continue to be a critical constraint to its economic growth,

Recognizing the measures being taken by the territorial Government to prevent drug trafficking and money laundering,

1. *Requests* the administering Power to take into account any views or wishes which may be expressed by the territorial Government and the people of the Territory in connection with the constitutional review;

2. *Also requests* the administering Power, in implementing its review of policy towards, and management of, its Caribbean dependent Territories, to give the highest consideration to the opinions expressed by the Government and the people of the Territory;

3. *Further requests* the administering Power and all financial institutions to grant the Territory economic assistance, including concessionary funding, to enable it to mitigate the effects of the world economic recession and to pursue its development programmes;

4. *Reiterates its call* upon the administering Power to facilitate the admission of the Territory to associate membership in the Food and Agriculture Organization of the United Nations, as well as its participation in other regional and international organizations;

5. *Calls upon* the United Nations Development Programme to continue its technical assistance to the British Virgin Islands, bearing in mind the vulnerability of the Territory to external economic factors and the scarcity of skilled workers in the Territory;

6. *Calls upon* all countries and organizations with expertise in the development of skilled labour to grant the territorial Government every assistance in the implementation of its educational and manpower training programmes;

7. *Notes with satisfaction* the measures being taken by the territorial Government to prevent drug trafficking and money laundering, and urges the administering Power to continue its assistance to the Territory in those endeavours;

8. *Notes with regret* that a period of seventeen years has elapsed since a United Nations mission visited the Territory and appeals to the administering Power to facilitate the dispatch of such a mission.

V. Cayman Islands

The General Assembly,

Referring to resolution A above,

Having heard the statement of the representative of the United Kingdom of Great Britain and Northern Ireland, as the administering Power,

Noting the action taken by the territorial Government to implement its localization programme to promote increased participation of the local population in the decision-making process in the Cayman Islands,

Also noting that an increased proportion of the labour force of the Territory consists of expatriates and that there is a need for the training of nationals in the technical, vocational, managerial and professional fields,

Aware that the general election of November 1992 in the Territory resulted in the naming of a new Government,

Conscious of the economic priorities recommended by the new territorial Government, namely, to reduce spending, balance the budget, slow down growth to manageable levels and increase tourism,

Noting the Territory's dependence on imported agricultural provisions,

Noting with concern the vulnerability of the Territory to drug trafficking and related activities,

Noting with satisfaction the efforts of the territorial Government, the Governments of other countries of the region and the United Kingdom of Great Britain and Northern Ireland, as the administering Power, to prevent and repress illicit activities such as money laundering, funds smuggling, false invoicing and other related frauds, as well as the use of and trafficking in illegal drugs,

Recalling the dispatch in 1977 of a United Nations visiting mission to the Territory,

1. *Notes* the change of Government in the Territory as a result of the election of November 1992;

2. *Notes also* that, according to election officials, more than 90 per cent of the Territory's registered voters participated in that election;

3. *Urges* the administering Power, in consultation with the territorial Government, to continue to facilitate the expansion of the current programme of securing employment for the local population, in particular at the decision-making level;

4. *Requests* the administering Power to assist the new territorial Government in acquiring all required expertise to enable it to achieve its economic aims;

5. *Calls upon* the administering Power, in consultation with the territorial Government, to continue to promote the agricultural development of the Cayman Islands;

6. *Requests* the specialized agencies and other organizations of the United Nations system to continue to increase their programmes of assistance to the Territory with a view to strengthening, developing and diversifying its economy;

7. *Also calls upon* the administering Power to continue to take all necessary measures, in cooperation with the territorial Government, to counter problems related to money laundering, funds smuggling and other related crimes, as well as drug trafficking;

8. *Notes* the importance of sending United Nations visiting missions to the Non-Self-Governing Territories and the fact that a period of sixteen years has elapsed since the last mission was dispatched to the Territory.

VI. Guam

The General Assembly,

Referring to resolution A above,

Noting that pursuant to the request of the Government of Guam and the recommendation of the independent Base Relocation and Closure Commission of the administering Power, the administering Power has approved of the closure of aviation activities at the Naval Air Station Agana,

Aware that large tracts of land in the Territory continue to be reserved for the use of the Department of Defense of the administering Power,

Cognizant that the administering Power has undertaken a programme of transferring surplus federal land to the Government of Guam,

Cognizant also of the potential for diversifying and developing the economy of Guam through commercial fishing and agriculture,

Conscious that immigration into the Territory has resulted in the indigenous Chamorros becoming a minority in their homeland and that, in 1990, 50 per cent of the residents were not born in the Territory,

Mindful that discussions between the Guam Commission on Self-Determination and the executive branch of the administering Power on the draft Guam Commonwealth Act concluded at the end of the previous administration of the administering Power, and that the Guam Commission on Self-Determination has requested the new Administration to appoint a special representative of the President to lead the administering Power's review of the Guam Commonwealth Act,

Recalling that in referendums held in Guam in 1987 the people of Guam endorsed a draft Commonwealth Act that, upon expeditious enactment by the Congress of the United States of America, would reaffirm the right of the people of Guam to draft their own constitution and to govern themselves,

Recalling also the dispatch in 1979 of a United Nations visiting mission to the Territory,

1. *Calls upon* the administering Power to continue to ensure that the presence of military bases and installations in the Territory does not constitute an obstacle to the implementation of the Declaration on the Granting of Independence to Colonial Countries and Peoples nor hinder the population of the Territory from exercising its right to self-determination, including independence, in conformity with the purposes and principles of the Charter of the United Nations;

2. *Also calls upon* the administering Power, in cooperation with the territorial Government, to continue to expedite the transfer of land to the people of the Territory and to take the necessary steps to safeguard their property rights;

3. *Notes* that discussions held since 1988 between the Government of the United States of America and the Guam Commission on Self-Determination have resulted

in qualified agreements on the provisions of the Guam Commonwealth Act, including agreements to disagree on several substantive portions of the Guam proposal, and that the new Administration of the administering Power has been requested by Guam to conduct expeditiously its review of the Guam Commonwealth Act in concert with the Guam Commission on Self-Determination;

4. *Requests* the administering Power to take all necessary measures to respond to the concerns of the territorial Government with regard to the immigration issue;

5. *Reiterates its request* to the administering Power to continue to recognize and respect the cultural and ethnic identity of the Chamorro people, the indigenous inhabitants of Guam;

6. *Urges* the administering Power to continue to support appropriate measures by the territorial Government aimed at promoting growth in commercial fishing and agriculture;

7. *Notes* that a period of fourteen years has elapsed since a United Nations mission visited the Territory, and again calls upon the administering Power to facilitate the dispatch of such a mission.

VII.   *Montserrat*

The General Assembly,

Referring to resolution A above,

Having heard the statement of the representative of the United Kingdom of Great Britain and Northern Ireland, as the administering Power,

Aware of the decision of the administering Power to implement a policy change aimed at establishing better dialogue, coordination and cooperation between itself and its Caribbean dependent Territories,

Noting the position of the territorial Government that while independence is both desirable and inevitable, it should be preceded by economic and financial viability sufficient to sustain Montserrat as an independent State,

Expressing concern at the high incidence of drug trafficking and money laundering in the Territory,

Taking into account the membership of Montserrat in regional and international bodies and the outstanding request of the Territory for readmission to associate membership in the United Nations Educational, Scientific and Cultural Organization,

Aware of the Government's policy to continue to train and develop local human resources,

Recalling that the last United Nations visiting mission to the Territory took place in 1982,

1. *Calls upon* the administering Power to consider all suggestions made by the Territories concerned within the framework of its review of policy and management of the Caribbean dependent Territories, as well as in the context of any future policy changes affecting them;

2. *Requests* the administering Power to work towards promoting the economic and social development of the Territory with a view to its attaining self-determination and independence;

3. *Notes* the territorial Government's expressed preference for independence within a political union with the Organization of Eastern Caribbean States;

4. *Requests* the administering Power, competent regional and international organizations, as well as countries in a position to do so, to grant the Government

of Montserrat every assistance it requires to achieve its stated goal of improving the efficiency and productivity of the public service through training at all levels;

5. *Reiterates its call* upon the administering Power, in cooperation with the territorial Government, to take, as a matter of urgency, the necessary steps to facilitate the readmission of Montserrat as an associate member of the United Nations Educational, Scientific and Cultural Organization;

6. *Urges* the specialized agencies and other organizations of the United Nations system, as well as regional and other multilateral financial institutions, to continue to expand their assistance to the Territory in the strengthening, development and diversification of its economy in accordance with its medium-term and long-term development plans;

7. *Urges* the administering Power to continue its assistance to the Territory in the prevention of drug trafficking and money laundering;

8. *Notes with regret* that a period of eleven years has elapsed since a United Nations mission visited the Territory, and calls upon the administering Power to facilitate the dispatch of such a mission.

VIII.   *Tokelau*

The General Assembly,

Referring to resolution A above,

Having heard the statement of the representative of New Zealand, the administering Power,

Noting the continuing devolution of power to the local authority, the General *Fono* (Council), and mindful that the cultural heritage and traditions of the people of Tokelau should be taken fully into account in the evolution of the political institutions of Tokelau,

Noting also the continuing commitment of New Zealand to assist Tokelau in attaining a greater degree of self-government and economic self-sufficiency, and its stated intention to be guided in this regard by the wishes of the Tokelauan people,

Taking note of the plans to transfer the Office for Tokelau Affairs from Apia to Tokelau,

Noting the Territory's continuing efforts to strengthen the role of its local institutions and to assume more responsibility for its own affairs, while reaffirming its desire to retain its special relationship with New Zealand,

Noting also the endeavours of Tokelau to develop its marine and other resources and its efforts to diversify the income-earning ability of its population,

Noting further the concern of the people of the Territory regarding the serious consequences of changes in climatic patterns on the future of Tokelau,

Noting with appreciation the assistance extended to Tokelau by the administering Power, other Member States and specialized agencies, in particular the United Nations Development Programme and its setting up of a third country programme for Tokelau for the period 1992-1996,

1. *Encourages* the Government of New Zealand, the administering Power, to continue to respect fully the wishes of the people of Tokelau in carrying out the political and economic development of the Territory in such a way as to preserve their social, cultural and traditional heritage and to seek solutions which would meet the unique future needs of Tokelau;

2. *Notes with satisfaction* the agreement to continue the process of transferring to Tokelau the responsibility for administration of the Territory, and the decision by Tokelau to establish a Council of *Faipule* (joint chairmen of the General *Fono*) to provide ongoing government for the Territory between sessions of the General *Fono*;

3. *Requests* the administering Power to take all necessary measures to facilitate the exercise by the Territory of its political and administrative functions, and in this regard takes note of the plans to transfer the Office for Tokelau Affairs from Apia to Tokelau;

4. *Invites* all governmental and non-governmental organizations, financial institutions, Member States and specialized agencies to grant or continue to grant Tokelau special emergency economic assistance to mitigate the effects of cyclonic storms and to enable the Territory to meet its medium- and long-term reconstruction and rehabilitation requirements and address the issues of changes in climatic patterns;

5. *Welcomes* the invitation of the administering Power to the Special Committee on the Situation with regard to the Implementation of the Declaration on the Granting of Independence to Colonial Countries and Peoples to dispatch a visiting mission to Tokelau in 1994.

IX. *Turks and Caicos Islands*
The General Assembly,
Referring to resolution A above,
Having heard the statement of the representative of the United Kingdom of Great Britain and Northern Ireland, as the administering Power,
Noting the different views expressed by the elected representatives of the Turks and Caicos Islands on the question of the future status of the Territory,
Aware of the decision of the administering Power to implement a policy change aimed at establishing better dialogue, coordination and cooperation between itself and its Caribbean dependent Territories,
Noting the territorial Government's commitment to reform the public service to achieve greater efficiency and to implement its policy of localization of employment,
Noting the Government's expressed need for development assistance to achieve its stated goal of economic independence by the year 1996,
Noting also the Government's decision to establish an investment bank in order to attract substantial investments worldwide for much-needed projects,
Noting further that 90 per cent of the food consumed in the Territory is imported and that the Government has exerted efforts to improve the agricultural and fisheries sectors,
Noting the number of unqualified teachers and the number of expatriate staff in the educational system of the Territory,
Noting with interest the statement made and the information provided by an elected member of the Territory's Legislative Council in March 1993 to the Subcommittee on Small Territories, Petitions, Information and Assistance of the Special Committee on the Situation with regard to the Implementation of the Declaration on the Granting of Independence to Colonial Countries and Peoples on the overall political, economic and social situation in the Turks and Caicos Islands,
1. *Reiterates* that it is ultimately for the people of the Territory themselves to determine their own future

through the exercise of their right to self-determination, including independence;

2. *Invites* the administering Power, in implementing policy changes concerning its dependent Territories, to continue to take fully into account the wishes and interests of the Government and people of the Turks and Caicos Islands;

3. *Calls upon* the territorial Government to continue to promote alternative employment opportunities for those civil servants whose employment will be terminated as a result of the public service reform and the planned reduction of employees in the service;

4. *Also calls upon* the territorial Government to ensure that the employment of expatriates in the Territory's labour force is not prejudicial to the recruitment of suitably qualified and available islanders;

5. *Calls upon* the specialized agencies and other institutions of the United Nations system to explore concrete ways of assisting the Turks and Caicos Government to reach its stated goal of achieving economic independence by 1996;

6. *Notes with satisfaction* the increase in aid, particularly financial assistance, granted to the territorial Government by the Government of the United Kingdom of Great Britain and Northern Ireland, and invites that Government to maintain this level of assistance;

7. *Calls upon* all national, regional, interregional and international financial institutions, including the International Monetary Fund and the World Bank, to take all necessary steps to assist the Government of the Turks and Caicos Islands in the establishment and/or operation of its investment bank;

8. *Urges* the administering Power and the relevant regional and international organizations to assist the territorial Government in increasing the efficiency of the agricultural and fisheries sectors;

9. *Also urges* the administering Power and the relevant regional and international organizations to support the efforts of the territorial Government to address the problem of environmental pollution and degradation;

10. *Calls upon* all countries and organizations with experience in the training of teachers to extend generous assistance to the Territory in this field, with particular emphasis on the training of its nationals;

11. *Draws the attention* of the administering Power to the statement made and the information provided in March 1993 to the Subcommittee on Small Territories, Petitions, Information and Assistance of the Special Committee on the Situation with regard to the Implementation of the Declaration on the Granting of Independence to Colonial Countries and Peoples by an elected member of the Territory's Legislative Council on the political, economic and social situation in the Territory;

12. *Notes with regret* that a period of thirteen years has elapsed since a United Nations mission visited the Territory, and appeals to the administering Power to facilitate the dispatch of such a mission.

X. *United States Virgin Islands*
The General Assembly,
Referring to resolution A above,
Noting that a referendum on political status in the Territory was held on 11 October 1993,

Noting also the concerns expressed in the Territory on the issues of residency requirements for voter eligibility and the availability to all voters of full information on the political options offered to them in the referendum and the implications of these options,

Noting further that the Governor, in his state of the Territory address in January 1993, mentioned the necessity of diversifying the Territory's economy further,

Aware that the insurance crisis in the United States Virgin Islands affects home-owners and has an adverse impact on the Territory's real estate market,

Noting that the question of the transfer of Water Island to the Territory is still under consideration,

Noting also the steps taken by the territorial authorities to acquire the St. Thomas Harbour, including the West Indian Company,

Noting further the continuing interest of the territorial Government in seeking associate membership in the Organization of Eastern Caribbean States and observer status in the Caribbean Community, and its inability, for financial reasons, to participate in the Food and Agriculture Organization of the United Nations and the World Health Organization,

Recalling the dispatch in 1977 of a United Nations visiting mission to the Territory and the request by the territorial Government for the dispatch of a United Nations mission to the Territory to observe the referendum process,

1. *Notes* the consultative character of the referendum which was held on 11 October 1993;

2. *Notes also* the concerns raised in the Territory, prior to the referendum, on the questions of residency requirements and the availability of information on this political process;

3. *Requests* the administering Power to assist the territorial Government in its efforts to attract light manufacturing and other enterprises to the Territory in order to diversify its economy;

4. *Invites* the administering Power, as a matter of urgency, to facilitate the transfer of Water Island to the territorial Government;

5. *Reiterates its request* to the administering Power to facilitate as appropriate the participation of the Territory in the Organization of Eastern Caribbean States and the Caribbean Community, as well as in various international and regional organizations, including the Caribbean Group for Cooperation in Economic Development of the World Bank, in accordance with the policy of the administering Power and the terms of reference of such organizations;

6. *Calls upon* the administering Power to respond favourably to the request of the territorial Government for the dispatch of a United Nations visiting and observer mission to the Territory.

General Assembly resolutions 48/51 A and B

10 December 1993   Meeting 75   Adopted without vote

Approved by Fourth Committee (A/48/656) without objection, 29 October (meeting 13); draft by Committee on colonial countries (A/48/23), amended by United States (draft res. A by A/C.4/48/L.7 (orally revised); draft res. B by A/C.4/48/L.8, L.9 & L.10); agenda item 18.
Meeting numbers. GA 48th session: 4th Committee 2-8, 13; plenary 75.

In the Fourth Committee, the United States introduced an amendment to paragraph 1 of resolution 48/51 A, which the Committee approved by a recorded vote of 57 to 11, with 41 abstentions,[38] and a series of amendments to resolution 48/51 B, which the Committee approved by recorded votes as follows: an amendment to delete paragraphs 2, 3 and 4 of section I by 48 to 1, with 62 abstentions, 52 to none, with 58 abstentions, and 46 to none, with 64 abstentions, respectively;[39] an amendment to replace the second preambular paragraph of section VI by 62 to none, with 48 abstentions;[40] and an amendment to delete paragraphs 4 and 6 of section X by 50 to none, with 58 abstentions, and 47 to none, with 64 abstentions, respectively.[41]

Gibraltar

In July 1993,[19] the Committee on colonial countries considered the question of Gibraltar. It had before it a working paper by the Secretariat containing information on developments in the Territory, as well as economic, social and educational conditions there.[42]

The Committee decided to continue its consideration of the question in 1994, subject to any directives by the General Assembly, and, in order to facilitate consideration by the Fourth Committee, to transmit the relevant documentation to the Assembly.

GENERAL ASSEMBLY ACTION

In December 1993, the General Assembly adopted **decision 48/422** without vote.

Question of Gibraltar

At its 75th plenary meeting, on 10 December 1993, the General Assembly, on the recommendation of the Special Political and Decolonization Committee (Fourth Committee), adopted the following text as representing the consensus of the members of the Assembly:

"The General Assembly, recalling its decision 47/411 of 25 November 1992 and recalling at the same time that the statement agreed to by the Governments of Spain and the United Kingdom of Great Britain and Northern Ireland at Brussels on 27 November 1984 stipulates, *inter alia*, the following:

'The establishment of a negotiating process aimed at overcoming all the differences between them over Gibraltar and at promoting cooperation on a mutually beneficial basis on economic, cultural, touristic, aviation, military and environmental matters. Both sides accept that the issues of sovereignty will be discussed in that process. The British Government will fully maintain its commitment to honour the wishes of the people of Gibraltar as set out in the preamble of the 1969 Constitution',

takes note of the fact that, as part of this process, the Ministers for Foreign Affairs of Spain and of the United Kingdom of Great Britain and Northern Ireland have held annual meetings alternately in each capital, the most recent of which took place at Madrid on 1 March 1993, and urges both Governments to continue their negotiations with the object of reaching a definitive solution to the problem of Gibraltar in the light of relevant resolutions of the General Assembly and in the spirit of the Charter of the United Nations.''

General Assembly decision 48/422

Adopted without vote

Approved by Fourth Committee (A/48/656) without objection, 29 October (meeting 13); draft by Chairman (A/C.4/48/L.6); agenda item 18.
Meeting numbers. GA 48th session: 4th Committee 2-8, 12, 13; plenary 75.

Pitcairn

The Subcommittee on Small Territories, Petitions, Information and Assistance,[43] noting with regret that the United Kingdom, the administering Power, did not participate in its deliberations on Pitcairn, appealed to it to reconsider its position and resume its participation in the Committee on colonial countries.

GENERAL ASSEMBLY ACTION

In December 1993, the General Assembly adopted **decision 48/423** without vote.

Question of Pitcairn

At its 75th plenary meeting, on 10 December 1993, the General Assembly, on the recommendation of the Special Political and Decolonization Committee (Fourth Committee), adopted the following text as representing the consensus of the members of the Assembly:

''The General Assembly, having examined the situation in Pitcairn, reaffirms the inalienable right of the people of Pitcairn to self-determination in conformity with the Declaration on the Granting of Independence to Colonial Countries and Peoples, contained in Assembly resolution 1514(XV) of 14 December 1960, which fully applies to the Territory. The Assembly also reaffirms the responsibility of the administering Power to promote the economic and social development of the Territory. The Assembly urges the administering Power to continue to respect the very individual lifestyle that the people of the Territory have chosen and to preserve, promote and protect it. The Assembly requests the Special Committee on the Situation with regard to the Implementation of the Declaration on the Granting of Independence to Colonial Countries and Peoples to continue to examine the question of Pitcairn at its next session and to report thereon to the Assembly at its forty-ninth session.''

General Assembly decision 48/423

Adopted without vote

Approved by Fourth Committee (A/48/656) without objection, 29 October (meeting 13); draft by Committee on colonial countries (A/48/23); agenda item 18.
Meeting numbers. GA 48th session: 4th Committee 2-8, 12, 13; plenary 75.

St. Helena

The Subcommittee on Small Territories, Petitions, Information and Assistance,[44] noting with regret that the United Kingdom, the administering Power, did not participate in its deliberations on St. Helena, appealed to it to reconsider its position and resume its participation in the Committee on colonial countries.

GENERAL ASSEMBLY ACTION

In December 1993, the General Assembly adopted **decision 48/424** by recorded vote.

Question of St. Helena

At its 75th plenary meeting, on 10 December 1993, the General Assembly, on the recommendation of the Special Political and Decolonization Committee (Fourth Committee), adopted the following text:

''1.   The General Assembly, having examined the question of St. Helena, reaffirms the inalienable right of the people of St. Helena to self-determination and independence in conformity with the Declaration on the Granting of Independence to Colonial Countries and Peoples, contained in Assembly resolution 1514(XV) of 14 December 1960. The Assembly urges the administering Power, in consultation with the Legislative Council and other representatives of the people of St. Helena, to continue to take all necessary steps to ensure the speedy implementation of the Declaration in respect of the Territory, and in that connection reaffirms the importance of promoting an awareness among the people of St. Helena of the possibilities open to them in the exercise of their right to self-determination.

''2.   The General Assembly reaffirms the responsibility of the administering Power to promote the economic and social development of the Territory and calls upon the administering Power to continue, in cooperation with the territorial Government, to strengthen the economy, to encourage local initiative and enterprise and to increase its assistance to diversification programmes with the aim of improving the general welfare of the community, including the employment situation in the Territory.

''3.   The General Assembly urges the administering Power, in cooperation with the territorial Government, to continue to take effective measures to safeguard and guarantee the inalienable right of the people of St. Helena to own and dispose of the natural resources of the Territory, including marine resources, and to establish and maintain control over the future development of those resources.

''4.   The General Assembly reaffirms that continued development assistance from the administering Power, together with any assistance that the international community might be able to provide, constitutes an important means of developing the economic potential of the Territory and of enhancing the capacity of its people to realize fully the goals set forth in the relevant provisions of the Charter of the United Nations. The Assembly, in that connection, welcomes the assistance rendered by the United Nations Development Programme and invites other organizations of the United Nations system to assist in the development of the Territory.

''5.   The continued presence of military facilities in the Territory prompts the General Assembly, on the basis of previous United Nations resolutions and decisions concerning military bases and installations in colonial and Non-Self-Governing Territories, to urge the administering Power to take measures to avoid the involvement of the Territory in offensive acts or interference against neighbouring States.

''6.   The General Assembly considers that the possibility of dispatching a United Nations visiting mission to St. Helena at an appropriate time should be kept under review, and requests the Special Committee on the Situation with regard to the Implementation of the Declaration on the Granting of Independence to Colonial Countries and Peoples to continue to examine the question of St. Helena at its next session and to report thereon to the Assembly at its forty-ninth session.''

General Assembly decision 48/424

101-2-51 (recorded vote)

Approved by Fourth Committee (A/48/656) by recorded vote (79-2-43), 29 October (meeting 13); draft by Committee on colonial countries (A/48/23); agenda item 18.

Meeting numbers. GA 48th session: 4th Committee 2-8, 12, 13; plenary 75.

Recorded vote in Assembly as follows:

In favour: Afghanistan, Algeria, Angola, Antigua and Barbuda, Argentina, Bahamas, Bahrain, Bangladesh, Barbados, Benin, Bhutan, Bolivia, Brazil, Brunei Darussalam, Burkina Faso, Cambodia, Cape Verde, Chad, Chile, China, Colombia, Congo, Costa Rica, Côte d'Ivoire, Cuba, Cyprus, Democratic People's Republic of Korea, Dominica, Dominican Republic, Ecuador, Egypt, El Salvador, Ethiopia, Fiji, Gabon, Gambia, Ghana, Grenada, Guatemala, Guinea, Guinea-Bissau, Guyana, Haiti, Honduras, India, Indonesia, Iran, Iraq, Jamaica, Jordan, Kenya, Kuwait, Lao People's Democratic Republic, Libyan Arab Jamahiriya, Madagascar, Malawi, Malaysia, Maldives, Mali, Marshall Islands, Mauritania, Mauritius, Mexico, Mongolia, Myanmar, Namibia, Nepal, Nicaragua, Niger, Nigeria, Oman, Pakistan, Papua New Guinea, Paraguay, Peru, Philippines, Qatar, Republic of Korea, Rwanda, Saint Lucia, Saint Vincent and the Grenadines, Samoa, Saudi Arabia, Sierra Leone, Singapore, Sri Lanka, Sudan, Suriname, Syrian Arab Republic, Thailand, Togo, Trinidad and Tobago, Tunisia, United Arab Emirates, United Republic of Tanzania, Uruguay, Venezuela, Viet Nam, Yemen, Zaire, Zimbabwe.

Against: United Kingdom, United States.

Abstaining: Armenia, Australia, Austria, Azerbaijan, Belarus, Belgium, Belize, Bulgaria, Cameroon, Canada, Central African Republic, Czech Republic, Denmark, Djibouti, Estonia, Finland, France, Georgia, Germany, Greece, Hungary, Iceland, Ireland, Israel, Italy, Japan, Kazakhstan, Latvia, Liechtenstein, Lithuania, Luxembourg, Malta, Micronesia, Netherlands, New Zealand, Norway, Panama, Poland, Portugal, Republic of Moldova, Romania, Russian Federation, San Marino, Senegal, Slovakia, Slovenia, Spain, Sweden, the former Yugoslav Republic of Macedonia, Turkey, Ukraine.

REFERENCES

[1]A/AC.109/1154. [2]A/AC.109/1167. [3]A/48/418. [4]A/47/435. [5]A/AC.109/1168 & Corr.1. [6]A/AC.109/1169. [7]YUN 1991, p. 794, SC res. 690(1991), 29 Apr. 1991. [8]S/25170. [9]YUN 1992, p. 962. [10]YUN 1991, p. 793. [11]S/25818. [12]S/25861. [13]S/26185. [14]S/26239. [15]S/26797. [16]S/26848. [17]A/48/426. [18]YUN 1992, p. 963, GA res. 47/25, 25 Nov. 1992. [19]A/48/23. [20]A/AC.109/1163. [21]A/47/743. [22]A/C.5/48/40. [23]A/48/773. [24]A/AC.109/1145. [25]A/AC.109/1141. [26]A/AC.109/1143. [27]A/AC.109/1142. [28]A/AC.109/1138. [29]A/AC.109/1148. [30]A/AC.109/1137. [31]A/AC.109/1146. [32]A/AC.109/1152. [33]A/AC.109/1147. [34]A/AC.109/1139. [35]A/AC.109/1150. [36]A/AC.109/L.1795. [37]A/AC.109/L.1796. [38]A/C.4/48/L.7. [39]A/C.4/48/L.8. [40]A/C.4/48/L.9. [41]A/C.4/48/L.10. [42]A/AC.109/1164. [43]A/AC.109/L.1799. [44]A/AC.109/L.1800.

International Trusteeship System

Trust Territory of the Pacific Islands

In 1993, Palau was the last remaining entity of the Trust Territory of the Pacific Islands under the 1947 Trusteeship Agreement,[1] which had designated the United States as the Administering Authority of the Territory. The Security Council, in December 1990,[2] had determined that, in view of the entry into force of new status agreements between the United States and the other three entities of the Trust Territory—the Marshall Islands, the Federated States of Micronesia and the Northern Mariana Islands[3]—the objectives

of the Trusteeship Agreement had been fully attained and the applicability of the Agreement to them had terminated.

Palau, located in the Western Caroline Islands, is composed of many islands with a total land area of 492 square kilometres. The estimated 1993 population was 16,642, two thirds of whom lived in the capital, consisting of Koror and several adjacent islands.

In a working paper submitted to the Trusteeship Council in May 1993,[4] the Secretariat described conditions in the Trust Territory, covering political, economic, social and educational developments.

Constitutional and political status of Palau

The Palau National Congress (*Olbiil Era Kelulau*) had linked its approval of a plebiscite to a favourable United States response to requests submitted to the United States on 25 March 1993 by the President of Palau for certain modifications and assurances related to the proposed Compact of Free Association. Following meetings which began on 2 April between President Kuniwo Nakamura of Palau and the former United States Assistant Secretary of State, a letter was sent on 6 May to the President of Palau containing assurances concerning United States intentions with respect to the implementation of the Compact.

The Compact would recognize Palau as fully self-governing, while the United States would remain responsible for its defence. However, because the Compact would conflict with the non-nuclear provisions of Palau's Constitution, local courts had ruled that it would need to be approved by 75 per cent of the voters—the same margin required for a constitutional amendment. In none of the seven plebiscites (February 1983, September 1984, February and December 1986, June and August 1987 and February 1990) was the required 75 per cent vote obtained.

On 29 October 1993, the Supreme Court of Palau delivered final adjudication upholding the validity of a 1992 constitutional referendum,[5] which reduced the votes required to approve the Compact from 75 per cent to a simple majority of 51 per cent.

Trusteeship Council consideration. In April,[6] the Secretary-General forwarded to the Security Council and the Trusteeship Council a report by the United States on the administration of the Trust Territory for the year ending 30 September 1992.[7]

On 17 May 1993, the Trusteeship Council adopted the conclusions and recommendations prepared by its Drafting Committee (China, France, Russian Federation, United Kingdom). Taking note of a 1990 Security Council resolution on the Trust Territory,[2] the Council expressed the hope that the people of Palau would be able to exercise freely their right to self-determination and that it would be possible to terminate the Trusteeship Agreement.

The Council noted with satisfaction recent economic, social and educational improvements in the Trust Territory and hoped that further progress would continue to be made. It also noted with satisfaction the Administering Authority's assurances that it would continue to fulfil its responsibilities under the Charter of the United Nations and the Trusteeship Agreement, and further noted that it had no plans to establish military bases in Palau.

The Council heard two petitioners on various issues concerning conditions in the Trust Territory and considered four communications and one written petition.

Visiting mission

On 13 May 1993,[8] the United States informed the President of the Trusteeship Council of Palau's intention to hold a plebiscite on the Compact of Free Association, which it said was likely to occur on 27 July. The United States invited the Council to send a visiting mission to observe the plebiscite.

On 9 September,[9] the United States informed the Council President that on 6 August the President of Palau had issued Executive Order No. 124, which decreed that Palau would hold a plebiscite regarding the Compact on 9 November. Referring to the Council's resolution of 17 May (see below) and its letter of 13 May, the United States invited the Council to send a mission to observe the plebiscite.

TRUSTEESHIP COUNCIL ACTION

On 17 May, the Trusteeship Council adopted **resolution 2196(LX)** without vote.

Arrangements for the dispatch of a visiting mission to observe the plebiscite in Palau, Trust Territory of the Pacific Islands, July 1993

The Trusteeship Council,

Aware of the plebiscite scheduled for 27 July 1993 in Palau, Trust Territory of the Pacific Islands, on the Compact of Free Association with the United States of America,

Having been invited by the Administering Authority to dispatch a mission to observe the plebiscite,

Considering that it would be desirable to include in such a mission representatives of countries of the region that are not members of the Trusteeship Council,

1. *Decides* to send to Palau a visiting mission to begin on or about 20 July 1993 and to end as soon as practicable after the declaration of the results of the plebiscite;

2. *Further decides* that the Visiting Mission to Palau should be composed of four members of the Trusteeship Council—China, France, the Russian Federation and the United Kingdom of Great Britain and North-

ern Ireland—and two representatives of countries of the region that are not members of the Council, to be determined through further consultations;

3. *Directs* the Visiting Mission to observe the plebiscite, specifically the polling arrangements, the casting of votes, the closure of voting, the counting of ballots and the declaration of results;

4. *Requests* the Visiting Mission to submit to the Trusteeship Council as soon as practicable a report on its observation of the plebiscite, containing such conclusions and recommendations as it may wish to make;

5. *Requests* the Secretary-General to provide the necessary staff and facilities to assist the Visiting Mission in the performance of its functions.

Trusteeship Council resolution 2196(LX)

17 May 1993   Meeting 1701   Adopted without vote

4-nation draft (T/L.1286); agenda item 13.
Sponsors: China, France, Russian Federation, United Kingdom.
Financial implications. S-G, T/L.1287.

On 1 November, the Council adopted **resolution 2197(LX)** without vote.

Arrangements for the dispatch of a visiting mission to observe the plebiscite in Palau, Trust Territory of the Pacific Islands, November 1993

The Trusteeship Council,

Aware of the plebiscite scheduled for 9 November 1993 in Palau, Trust Territory of the Pacific Islands, on the Compact of Free Association with the United States of America,

Having been invited by the Administering Authority to dispatch a mission to observe the plebiscite,

Considering that it would be desirable to include in such a mission representatives of countries of the region that are not members of the Trusteeship Council,

1. *Decides* to send to Palau a visiting mission to begin on or about 2 November 1993 and to end as soon as practicable after the declaration of the results of the plebiscite:

2. *Further decides* that the Visiting Mission to Palau should be composed of six members, the members to be representatives of China, France, the Marshall Islands, the Russian Federation, Samoa and the United Kingdom of Great Britain and Northern Ireland;

3. *Directs* the Visiting Mission to observe the plebiscite, specifically the polling arrangements, the casting of votes, the closure of voting, the counting of ballots and the declaration of results;

4. *Requests* the Visiting Mission to submit to the Trusteeship Council, as soon as practicable, a report on its observation of the plebiscite, containing such conclusions and recommendations as it may wish to make;

5. *Requests* the Secretary-General to provide the necessary staff and facilities to assist the Visiting Mission in the performance of its functions.

Trusteeship Council resolution 2197(LX)

1 November 1993   Meeting 1702   Adopted without vote

4-nation draft (T/L.1288); agenda item 14.
Sponsors: China, France, Russian Federation, United Kingdom.
Financial implications. S-G, T/L.1289.

Report of the visiting mission. The 1993 Visiting Mission[10] was composed of four Council members—one representative each from China, France, the Russian Federation and the United Kingdom—and two representatives of countries of the region that were not Council members—the Marshall Islands and Samoa. The visit in Palau took place from 5 to 12 November.

The Mission concluded that the plebiscite held on 9 November was conducted fairly and reflected the wishes of the people of Palau; of a total of 7,608 valid votes cast, 5,193 or 68.26 per cent were in favour of the Compact.

Other aspects of the International Trusteeship System

Fellowships and scholarships

Under a scholarship programme launched by the General Assembly in 1952,[11] 11 Member States had in past years made scholarships available for students from Trust Territories: Czechoslovakia, Hungary, Indonesia, Italy, Mexico, Pakistan, the Philippines, Poland, Tunisia, the Russian Federation and Yugoslavia. In a report to the Trusteeship Council covering the period 16 May 1992 to 7 May 1993,[12] the Secretary-General stated that he had requested up-to-date information on scholarships for students from the Trust Territory of the Pacific Islands, but had received no response. On 13 May,[13] the Council took note of the report.

Information dissemination

The Department of Public Information (DPI) in 1993 continued to disseminate information on the United Nations and the International Trusteeship System in the Trust Territory of the Pacific Islands. The Secretary-General described those activities in a report covering the period from 1 May 1992 to 30 April 1993.[14] Annexed to the report was a detailed list of information materials distributed during that period. DPI and the United Nations information centres, primarily the Centre at Tokyo, disseminated information to the Trust Territory on the aims and objectives of the International Trusteeship System and of the United Nations. DPI mailed directly to 97 recipients in the Trust Territory documents of the Trusteeship Council and taped radio, video and film programmes. It also produced and transmitted press releases and publications covering the issue of the Trust Territory. Regarding feedback, DPI sent out a second series of questionnaires to the 97 direct-mail recipients. The first questionnaire was sent in 1992.[15]

On 14 May, the President of the Trusteeship Council announced that, following consultations between the secretariats of the Council and DPI, the staff servicing the next visiting mission to the Territory would also carry out functions on behalf of DPI while in the Territory.

On the same date, the Council took note of the Secretary-General's report.

REFERENCES

[1]YUN 1946-47, p. 398. [2]SC res. 683(1990), 22 Dec. 1990. [3]YUN 1986, p. 917. [4]T/L.1284. [5]YUN 1992, p. 973. [6]S/25633. [7]T/1969. [8]T/1974. [9]T/1975. [10]T/1978. [11]YUN 1951, p. 788, GA res. 557(VI), 18 Jan. 1952. [12]T/1971. [13]S/1994/346. [14]T/1972. [15]YUN 1992, p. 975.

Chapter IV

Peaceful uses of outer space

During 1993, the Committee on the Peaceful Uses of Outer Space (Committee on outer space) and its Scientific and Technical and Legal Subcommittees again considered matters relating to international cooperation in the peaceful uses of outer space. The Committee, at its thirty-sixth session (New York, 7-18 June), agreed, as a follow-up to the 1992 United Nations Conference on Environment and Development, to promote international cooperation in the application of space technologies for environmental monitoring and sustainable development. It recommended the convening of a third United Nations Conference on the Exploration and Peaceful Uses of Outer Space, possibly in 1995.

The General Assembly, in December, endorsed the Committee's recommendations and the United Nations Programme on Space Applications for 1994 (resolution 48/39). The Assembly also welcomed the Secretary-General's report on international cooperation in space activities for enhancing security in the post-cold-war era and called on the competent bodies to take into account its contents.

Science, technology and law

Space science and technology

The Scientific and Technical Subcommittee of the Committee on outer space held its thirtieth session in 1993 (New York, 16-26 February).[1] It continued to consider the United Nations Programme on Space Applications, coordination of space activities within the United Nations system and implementation of the recommendations of the Second (1982) United Nations Conference on the Exploration and Peaceful Uses of Outer Space (UNISPACE-82).[2] The Subcommittee also considered matters related to remote sensing of the Earth by satellites, particularly its applications for developing countries; the use of nuclear power sources in outer space; questions relating to space transportation systems and their implications for future activities in space; the physical nature and technical attributes of the geostationary orbit; progress in national and international space activities related to the Earth environment; matters

relating to life sciences, including space medicine; and issues concerning planetary exploration and astronomy.

In accordance with a 1992 General Assembly resolution,[3] the Subcommittee reconvened the Working Group of the Whole to Evaluate the Implementation of the Recommendations of UNISPACE-82.

During the Subcommittee's session, the Committee on Space Research (COSPAR) of the International Council of Scientific Unions and the International Astronautical Federation (IAF), in response to a 1992 Assembly request,[3] organized a symposium (16 and 17 February 1993) on the subject "Space-based communications: global systems and new services",[4] selected by the Subcommittee for special attention. France made a special presentation to the Subcommittee on the issue of space debris.

The Subcommittee's recommendations were acted on by the Committee on outer space in June.[5]

Implementation of the recommendations of the 1982 Conference on outer space

In 1993, the Scientific and Technical Subcommittee, noting that the General Assembly in 1992[3] had again emphasized the urgency and importance of implementing fully the recommendations of UNISPACE-82, endorsed by the Assembly in 1982,[6] reconvened the Working Group of the Whole to Evaluate the Implementation of the Recommendations of UNISPACE-82, which held three meetings between 18 and 25 February 1993.

In the report on its seventh session, annexed to the Subcommittee's report,[1] the Working Group made recommendations that were endorsed by the Subcommittee and by the Assembly in **resolution 48/39**. Among the recommendations were that: the organization of seminars and workshops on advanced applications of space science and technology should continue so that the recent advances in space technologies and applications for development could be brought to the attention of planners, administrators and decision-makers in developing countries; the emphasis of the United Nations Programme on Space Applications should continue to be on long-term, project-oriented, on-the-job training in space technology and specific applications areas; Member States and international organizations should make offers for long-term training and every effort should be made to increase the number of fellowships and encourage full utilization of those available; Member States should introduce or improve space science, technology and applications curricula in their educational institutions; the United Nations should continue to arrange for funding and other support for the establishment and operation in developing countries of regional centres for space science and technology education; particularly those States with major space and space-related capabilities and international organizations should continue to inform the Secretary-General about activities that were or could be the subject of greater international cooperation, with special emphasis on the needs of developing countries; extensive regional cooperation should be encouraged, particularly among developing countries; to assist developing countries, the United Nations should strengthen its cooperation with governmental and non-governmental organizations (NGOs) and other international and regional bodies specializing in space activities; countries with relevant capabilities should be encouraged to provide developing countries with technical and financial assistance for developing low-cost community receivers and power sources for communication satellites; and satellite-operating States should ensure the availability of data on a continued basis and in a form compatible with current systems.

The Working Group recommended specific studies on the use of low Earth-orbiting communications satellites, forest resources management, space applications for sustainable development, and satellite-based radio broadcasting services. It also recommended that the United Nations continue to assist in the preparation of integrated national action plans for initiating, strengthening or reorienting space applications programmes.

It identified a number of priority areas to promote the applications of space science and technology for development, including stimulation of indigenous nuclei and an autonomous technological base in space technology in developing countries, greater exchange of space applications experience, and funding for the United Nations Programme on Space Applications. The Group also recommended that the Committee on outer space at its 1993 session address the question of convening a third UNISPACE conference (see below).

In response to a 1992 General Assembly request,[3] the Secretary-General, in October 1993,[7] provided information on progress made in implementing the recommendations of UNISPACE-82. The report reflected the work of the Committee on outer space and its subsidiary bodies in 1993.

The Secretariat, responding to 1992 requests of the Working Group of the Whole, submitted to the Scientific and Technical Subcommittee studies on the applications of space technology for ocean resources development[8] and for remote and rural communications and broadcasting,[9] and a report on the activities of Member States in the context of international cooperation.[10]

The Committee on outer space, in endorsing the recommendations of the Working Group, noted its concern over the continuing inadequacy of budgetary allocations to implement UNISPACE-82 recommendations. It noted the recommendations and actions of the Assembly's Special Political Committee in 1992 concerning the provision of adequate budgetary allocations,[11] and expressed the hope that those actions would be reflected in adequate allocations for the Programme on Space Applications in the 1994-1995 programme budget.

The Committee noted that the Secretariat continued to strengthen cooperation through regional workshops and training courses, technical assistance and the establishment of regional centres for space science and technology education. It expressed appreciation to France and Germany for providing experts for an evaluation mission to potential host countries for a centre in Africa. It also noted the contributions of other international organizations towards implementing UNISPACE-82 recommendations.

The Committee recognized the contribution of the Second Space Conference of the Americas (Santiago, Chile, 26-30 April) and the Santiago Declaration, annexed to the Committee's report, and that of the Asia-Pacific Workshop on Multilateral Cooperation in Space Technology and Applications (Beijing, China, 30 November-5 December 1992) in promoting international cooperation in outer space.

UN Programme on Space Applications

In accordance with its 1982 mandate,[6] the United Nations Programme on Space Applications focused on developing indigenous capability in space science and technology; providing fellowships for in-depth training and technical advisory services to Member States; organizing regional and international training courses, conferences and meetings; assisting in the development of information systems; and promoting greater cooperation in space science and technology.

In a December 1993 report to the Scientific and Technical Subcommittee,[12] the United Nations Expert on Space Applications stated that the Programme continued to help developing countries build up indigenous capability through the establishment and operation of centres for space science and technology education at the regional level.[13] The activities of the centres would allow the introduction of space science and technology into existing education curricula and contribute to countries' development programmes. They would also contribute to the sustainable development of natural resources, provide a supplementary input for biodiversity conservation and related environmental programmes and improve the development of the national technological base, including that of the telecommunications industry.

The Programme received 19 long-term fellowship offers for 1993-1994: 10 from Brazil in research and applications in remote sensing; 4 from China in geodesy, photogrammetry and remote sensing; and 5 from the European Space Agency (ESA) in space antennae and propagation, communications systems, satellite meteorology, and remote-sensing information and instrumentation.

The Programme, under projects jointly sponsored with ESA, continued to provide remote-sensing data to scientists in Guinea, Morocco, Nigeria and Tunisia through two ESA ground-receiving stations at Maspalomas, Spain, and Fucino, Italy. It would also train those scientists at ESA facilities in Frascati, Italy, in the use of European Remote Sensing Satellite (ERS-1) data in relevant application projects in their countries.

The Programme continued to promote cooperation among the countries covered by the Cotopaxi station in Ecuador. It conducted a mission in March to Colombia, Ecuador, Peru and Venezuela to review the possibilities and modalities of operating the station within a regional framework and to evaluate its current status. The mission recommended that the Governments within the Andean Group (Bolivia, Chile, Colombia, Ecuador, Peru, Venezuela) establish a working group to strengthen the use of data available at the station, determine and advise on technical upgrades, and guarantee the continuous operation of the station and maintenance of a regional data archive.

In 1993, the Programme conducted three training courses, four workshops and two regional conferences. In cooperation with ESA, it sponsored a training course for African francophone countries on applications of ERS-1 data for natural resources, renewable energy and the environment (Frascati, 19-30 April).[14] The course, with 24 participants, examined the physical theory of active and passive remote sensing and presented an overall view of remote sensing in the electromagnetic spectrum.

The third United Nations training course on remote-sensing education for 26 educators from developing countries (Stockholm and Kiruna, 3 May–4 June)[15] was organized in cooperation with Sweden and hosted by the University of Stockholm and the Swedish Space Corporation.

A United Nations workshop on space communications for development (Athens, 10-12 May),[16] organized in cooperation with Greece as a contribution to International Space Year (1992) (ISY) activities, was attended by 47 experts from 22 Member States of the Mediterranean and adjacent areas. The workshop addressed the current state and future trends of satellite communication technologies and their contributions to economic and social development.

A United Nations/Indonesia regional conference on space science and technology for sustainable development (Bandung, 17-21 May),[17] hosted by the Indonesian ISY Committee, concluded that countries in the region should give the highest priority to human resources and infrastructure development for effective use of space technology in their social and economic development programmes, particularly through the planned centres for space science and technology education. The conference, attended by 182 experts and scientists, identified a number of programmes of primary interest to the region.

A United Nations/ESA workshop on applications of space techniques to prevent and combat natural disasters, organized in cooperation with Mexico and the Economic Commission for Latin America and the Caribbean (Mexico City, 27-30 September),[18] exposed 69 experts from 19 countries to the use of space technology for natural disaster prevention or mitigation and addressed the development of databases and the Geographic Information System. The workshop agreed that a network of focal points should be established to disseminate information and provide emergency services through communication with the international relief community.

The fifth United Nations/Carl Duisberg Gesellschaft/ESA training course on remote-sensing applications to geological sciences: the planning and management of the environment, natural resources and physical infrastructure was organized in cooperation with Germany through the Carl Duisberg Gesellschaft and hosted by the International Centre for Integrated Mountain Development (Kathmandu, Nepal, 10 October–6 November).[19] The third United Nations/ESA workshop on basic space science, organized in cooperation with Nigeria and hosted by the National Agency for Science and Engineering Infrastructure, University of Nigeria, Nsukka, and Obafemi Awolowo University, Ile-Ife, was held at Lagos (18-22 October).[20]

A United Nations/IAF workshop on organizing space activities in developing countries (Graz, Austria, 15-17 October)[21] was co-sponsored by the Commission of the European Communities and ESA and hosted by the Austrian Space Agency on behalf of the Government of Austria. A United

Nations regional conference on space technology for sustainable development in Africa, organized with the assistance of Senegal and the United Nations Development Programme Office at Dakar (Dakar, 25-29 October),[22] focused on national participation in developing and utilizing environmental information systems and space technology in the social and economic development of Africa; investment in comunications research, development and growth; privatization and commercialization; and promoting cooperation and development of indigenous capability.

The Programme also assisted Chile in planning and organizing the Second Space Conference of the Americas (Santiago, 26-30 April) and would provide support to follow up its recommendations. It would also assist the Republic of Korea in organizing an Asia-Pacific workshop on satellite communications, to be held in 1994.

The Programme conducted a survey to evaluate the effectiveness of its 1990 activities. As a result of United Nations ISY activities, the Programme was consulting with appropriate entities on providing basic space-related education to youth on a global basis, particularly through elementary and secondary school programmes.

The General Assembly in 1992 had approved appropriations of $443,200 under the regular United Nations budget for implementing Programme activities in 1994-1995. In addition, the Programme received voluntary contributions in cash and kind from Member States, governmental organizations and NGOs.

Both the Scientific and Technical Subcommittee and the Committee on outer space expressed concern over the limited financial resources available for carrying out the Programme and appealed for further voluntary contributions.

The Assembly, in **resolution 48/39**, endorsed the Programme for 1994, as proposed by the Expert on Space Applications.[23]

Remote sensing of the Earth by satellites

The Scientific and Technical Subcommittee,[1] in accordance with a 1992 General Assembly resolution,[3] continued consideration of matters relating to remote sensing of the Earth by satellites. It reviewed national and cooperative programmes in remote sensing and received information on national programmes in developed and developing countries and international programmes based on bilateral, regional and international cooperation, including technical cooperation to developing countries.

The Subcommittee noted the continuing programmes for remote-sensing satellites of China, France, India, Japan, the Russian Federation, the United States and ESA and the planned systems of Brazil and Canada. It noted the recent launch-

ings of ERS-1, the Japanese Earth Resources Satellite and the Indian Remote Sensing and Marine Observation Satellite. The Subcommittee also noted the remote-sensing activities of the Food and Agriculture Organization of the United Nations in the area of renewable natural resources, including land-cover mapping and geographic information systems; those of the United Nations Educational, Scientific and Cultural Organization (UNESCO) in establishing satellite data centres; those of the World Meteorological Organization in weather forecasting and storm warning; and those of the International Society for Photogrammetry and Remote Sensing in promoting international cooperation in remote sensing and image processing.

The Subcommittee reiterated that remote-sensing activities should take into account the need to provide appropriate and non-discriminatory assistance to developing countries. It emphasized the importance of making remote-sensing data and analysed information openly available, affordable and timely, and recognized the need for free access to data from meteorological satellites.

The Subcommittee suggested that international cooperation in remote sensing should be encouraged through coordination of the operations of ground stations and regular meetings of satellite operators and users. It noted the importance of compatibility and complementarity of existing and future systems and the importance, particularly for developing countries, of sharing experiences and technologies, of cooperation through remote-sensing centres and of work on collaborative projects.

The Committee on outer space recognized the importance of international efforts to ensure the continuity, compatibility and complementarity of remote-sensing systems and to promote cooperation through regular meetings of satellite and ground-station operators and users. It encouraged countries and agencies to continue the free distribution of meteorological information.

Nuclear power sources in outer space

The Scientific and Technical Subcommittee, in response to a 1992 General Assembly request,[3] reconvened its Working Group on the Use of Nuclear Power Sources in Outer Space. The Group held its tenth session from 22 to 25 February 1993. Its report was annexed to the Subcommittee's report.[1]

The Working Group considered questions relating to a possible revision of the Principles Relevant to the Use of Nuclear Power Sources in Outer Space, adopted by the Assembly in 1992.[24] It considered a further definition of terms, expanding the scope of the Principles, criteria for acceptable risk, risk assessment, applicability of fundamental nuclear safety principles, adoption of a safety culture, the effect of space debris on the safety of nuclear power sources, and application of the relevant recommendations of the International Atomic Energy Agency (IAEA) and the International Commission on Radiological Protection.

The Subcommittee agreed that Member States should continue to report regularly to the Secretary-General on national and international research concerning the safety of nuclear-powered satellites, that further studies should be conducted on the problem of collision of nuclear-powered sources with space debris, and that it should be informed of the results. It noted papers by the Russian Federation and the United Kingdom on safety aspects of nuclear power sources in space and by Pakistan on risks and radiological consequences of debris collisions with nuclear power sources in space.

The Committee on outer space endorsed the Subcommittee's recommendations and recommended that it reconvene the Working Group to consider further a possible revision of the Principles.

Legal aspects of the revision of the Principles were considered by the Legal Subcommittee (see below).

Space transportation

The Scientific and Technical Subcommittee reviewed national and international cooperative programmes in space transportation systems, including expendable launchers, reusable space shuttles and space stations. It noted progress in the various programmes of Canada, China, India, Japan, the Russian Federation, Ukraine, the United Kingdom, the United States and ESA. It also noted developments in low-cost microsatellite technology and applications and stressed the importance of international cooperation in space transportation to provide all countries with access to the benefits of space science and technology.

The Committee on outer space endorsed the Subcommittee's recommendation that it continue consideration of the item at its next session.

Technical aspects of the geostationary orbit

The Scientific and Technical Subcommittee examined the utilization and applications of the geostationary orbit—in which communications and other satellites are positioned some 36,000 kilometres above the equator. It reviewed national and international cooperative programmes in satellite communications, including technological progress to make such communications more accessible and affordable and increase the communications capacity of the geostationary orbit and the electromagnetic spectrum. It noted the growing use of satellite systems for telecommunications,

television broadcasting, data networks, environmental data relay, mobile communications, disaster warning and relief, telemedicine and other communication functions, as well as studies and research on the use of multiple, low-orbiting communication satellites.

As in previous years, some delegations advocated avoiding saturation of the geostationary orbit and a special regime to ensure equitable access, particularly by developing countries, in particular taking into account the characteristics of the equatorial countries. Others suggested that efforts be made to minimize the generation of space debris by moving satellites before the end of their useful lives into disposal orbits beyond the geostationary orbit.

The Subcommittee recommended that countries participate in the Space System for Tracking Ships in Distress/Search and Rescue Satellite Tracking System.

The Committee on outer space expressed appreciation to the International Telecommunication Union (ITU) for its thirty-second annual progress report on telecommunications and the peaceful uses of outer space.[25] Some delegations stressed the important technical scope of the work of ITU, while drawing attention to the competence of the Committee in preparing policy decisions relating to the geostationary orbit.

Legal aspects of the geostationary orbit were considered by the Legal Subcommittee (see below).

Space and Earth environment

In 1992,[3] the General Assembly had recommended that more attention be paid to all aspects of the protection and preservation of the outer space environment, especially those affecting the Earth environment, as well as the problem of space debris, and had called for continued national research and development of improved technology to monitor space debris. In response to the Assembly's request, Austria, Germany, Pakistan, Sweden and the United Kingdom provided information to the Scientific and Technical Subcommittee on their research on space debris.[26]

The Subcommittee agreed that information on national research should continue to be provided to it and that there was a need for further research, for the development of improved monitoring technology and for compiling and disseminating data on space debris. It noted the importance of international cooperation in addressing those issues. It also noted a proposal of Poland that COSPAR prepare a report on the protection and preservation of outer space, especially activities potentially affecting the Earth environment.

The Committee on outer space agreed that, beginning in 1994, the Scientific and Technical Subcommittee would consider scientific research, including studies, mathematical modelling and the characterization of the space debris environment, under a new agenda item on space debris. It noted the importance of satellite remote sensing for monitoring the Earth's environment, particularly for studying and monitoring global change.

Following an invitation by the Committee on outer space in 1992, the Secretary-General submitted in May 1993 a report[27] on the Committee's role in implementing the recommendations of the 1992 United Nations Conference on Environment and Development (UNCED).[28] The report identified, for applications of satellite remote-sensing technology for environmental protection and development, eight areas related to Agenda 21 programmes: protection of the atmosphere; integrated planning and management of land resources; combating deforestation; combating desertification and drought; sustainable agriculture and rural development; protection of oceans, coastal areas and marine resources; protection, development and management of freshwater resources; and science for sustainable development.

The report outlined the activities of the Committee and the Office for Outer Space Affairs relevant to the application of space technology for implementing Agenda 21, particularly those of the United Nations Programme on Space Applications.

Among the report's recommendations were that the Office for Outer Space Affairs and the Committee keep the Commission on Sustainable Development, which was primarily responsible for coordinating activities to implement Agenda 21, informed of developments in space technology and its applications, and that the Committee consider further action it could take in developing international policy to protect the space environment. Suggestions were also made for action by Member States.

The Committee agreed that it could make an important contribution to implementing the recommendations of UNCED by promoting international cooperation in the applications of space technologies for environmental monitoring and sustainable development. It noted that the Programme on Space Applications could assist developing countries in strengthening their capabilities in related space technologies and applications through education, training and technical advisory activities.

The Committee requested the Scientific and Technical Subcommittee to review the Secretary-General's report in 1994 and to consider how the Committee could best promote the use of space technology for environmental monitoring and sustainable development. It requested the Secretariat

to provide the Subcommittee with updated information on the implementation of Agenda 21 by the United Nations system and on the related activities of the Programme on Space Applications, with suggestions for expanding those activities.

The Subcommittee also considered progress in the geosphere-biosphere (global change) programme and its importance for examining the future habitability of the planet and managing its natural resources. It noted the contributions of satellite remote sensing for environmental monitoring, planning sustainable development, water resource development, monitoring crop conditions and predicting and assessing drought; the contribution of meteorological and atmospheric research satellites for studying global climate change, the greenhouse effect, the ozone layer and other global environmental processes; and the need for further space research on climate change, weather patterns, vegetation distribution, storm and flood risk and other environmental factors. The Subcommittee recommended that States participate in international cooperation activities of existing and planned satellite systems for environmental monitoring.

Spin-off benefits of space technology

In accordance with a 1992 General Assembly request,[3] the Committee on outer space reviewed the status of spin-off benefits of space technology. It agreed that spin-offs were yielding substantial benefits by providing new techniques for industrial measurement and control, image and data processing, medical techniques, computer systems, robotics, special materials and chemicals, water treatment and refrigeration.

The Committee also agreed on the need to strengthen and enhance international cooperation by improving access to spin-off benefits for all countries and by giving attention to those which addressed the needs of developing countries. It recommended that the Programme on Space Applications include the promotion of spin-off benefits in its training courses, seminars or expert meetings.

Coordination in the UN system

The fifteenth Ad Hoc Inter-Agency Meeting on Outer Space Activities, convened by the Administrative Committee on Coordination (Geneva, 11-13 October),[29] reviewed progress in the implementation of UNISPACE-82 recommendations, discussed plans and programmes requiring coordination, exchanged views on activities in the practical applications of space technology and related areas, and reviewed cooperation within the United Nations system in remote sensing and coordination of follow-up to ISY. The Meeting agreed that remote-sensing and Geographic Information System technologies should be linked to enhance the scope, accuracy and cost benefits of remote-sensing applications, and on the formatting of satellite data by the proposed satellite data centres of UNESCO.

The Committee on outer space and its Scientific and Technical Subcommittee noted that the General Assembly, in 1992,[3] had reaffirmed that all United Nations organs and organizations and other intergovernmental bodies working in the field of outer space or on space-related matters should cooperate in implementing the recommendations of UNISPACE-82.

Following consideration of the report of the 1992 Inter-Agency Meeting,[30] the Subcommittee noted the progress achieved in coordinating United Nations space activities. It expressed appreciation for the report of the Secretary-General on coordination of space activities within the United Nations system,[31] which described major activities and programmes planned for 1993, 1994 and future years in remote sensing, communications, meteorology, hydrology, space science, maritime communications and air navigation, and other activities in space science and technology and its applications.

In December 1993,[32] the Secretary-General submitted his annual report outlining major United Nations system space activities and programmes planned for 1994, 1995 and future years.

The Committee on outer space noted that the Scientific and Technical Subcommittee had stressed the necessity of ensuring continuous and effective consultations and coordination in outer space activities. It found the reports submitted by the specialized agencies and other international organizations helpful in enabling it and its subsidiary bodies to fulfil their role as a focal point for international cooperation, especially in the practical applications of space science and technology in developing countries.

The Committee also noted that, as part of the restructuring of the United Nations Secretariat (see PART FIVE, Chapter II), the Office for Outer Space Affairs would be relocated to the United Nations Office at Vienna and would be responsible for servicing the Committee, its Subcommittees and their subsidiary bodies. The Office would continue to cooperate with the Office of Legal Affairs.

Convening of a third UNISPACE conference

The General Assembly in 1992[3] had endorsed the recommendation of the Committee on outer space that the Committee discuss the possibility of holding a third UNISPACE conference. The Scientific and Technical Subcommittee, at its 1993 session, endorsed the recommendation of its Working Group of the Whole to Evaluate the Implementation of the Recommendations of UNISPACE-82 that the Committee discuss the con-

vening of such a conference. The Working Group had also noted the suggestions that it could serve as the preparatory committee for the conference and that the conference could take place in 1995.

The Committee requested the Subcommittee to discuss the subject in 1994 so as to enable it to arrive at an early conclusion on the matter. The Committee noted the importance of defining sharply focused objectives for the conference, and that the goals of such a conference might also be achieved through other means, including intensification of work within the Committee. It also requested the Subcommittee to consider the organizational and funding details, and noted India's proposal to host the conference.

Other questions

The Committee on outer space and its Scientific and Technical Subcommittee considered various other space-related questions, including life sciences, space medicine and matters relating to planetary exploration and astronomy. The Committee noted the variety of space activities being undertaken in those areas and encouraged further cooperation, especially efforts to increase the participation of developing countries. It also noted the report[27] on the role it could play in relation to the decisions and recommendations of UNCED (see above).

In the area of life sciences, the Subcommittee noted the important advances in medical knowledge resulting from studies of human and animal physiology under microgravity conditions, the growing promise of space technology applications in public health, the role of satellite communications in providing expert medical advice to distant areas, and the contribution of space biotechnology to improved health care. It encouraged further research and exchange of information on those applications, and recommended promoting international cooperation so that all countries could benefit from those advances.

In the area of planetary exploration, the Subcommittee noted the several missions in progress and plans for comprehensive investigations of Mars and Saturn and its moons. It stressed the need further to enhance international cooperation in that area. The Subcommittee noted that the use of spacecraft for astronomical observations had greatly advanced knowledge of the universe and that planned activities would open further realms of the universe to detailed observation.

The Subcommittee welcomed the annual reports of various organizations in and outside the United Nations system[33] and the report of ITU on telecommunications and the peaceful uses of outer space.[25] It expressed appreciation to COSPAR and IAF for their report on progress in space science, technology and applications in 1992.[34]

The Committee expressed appreciation to those organizations that had submitted reports and requested that it continue to be kept informed. It also noted the participation in its work and that of its Subcommittees by various organizations.

It recommended that the Secretariat invite Member States to submit annual reports on their space activities, including space programmes, spin-off benefits of space activities and other topics. The Secretariat in December[35] submitted such information from eight Member States.

Follow-up to International Space Year

The Scientific and Technical Subcommittee noted that the international programmes for ISY, which was endorsed by the General Assembly in 1989[36] and celebrated in 1992,[37] had made important contributions to international cooperation, particularly in the use of space technology for studying and monitoring the environment, and urged that other countries be encouraged to participate in those activities. It requested the Secretariat to continue to promote international cooperation initiated during ISY and to keep it informed of further developments.

The Committee on outer space agreed that one way to broaden and deepen international cooperation in outer space was through international and regional endeavours such as ISY. It noted that the United Nations Programme on Space Applications was continuing its collaboration with ESA in a follow-up to the United Nations/ESA ISY activity on the use of remote-sensing data being provided by ESA to African countries covered by the receiving stations at Maspalomas and Fucino.

Space activities
in the post-cold-war era

The Secretary-General, in a July 1993 report[38] to the General Assembly, presented his views on international cooperation in space activities for enhancing security in the post-cold-war era. He stated that the end of the cold war and subsequent changes in the international security environment had raised new possibilities for utilizing space technology to promote international peace, security and stability. In the light of the new political environment and the rapid advancement and widespread use of space technology for economic and social services, the international community should ensure that that technology was used to promote security in all its forms.

He suggested that the United Nations and its specialized agencies should develop new policies and programmes for the innovative use of space technologies; international cooperation should be expanded by revitalizing existing mechanisms and developing new ones; and new initiatives should be taken to ensure access of all countries to the benefits of space activities. He contended that the security benefits to the international community from greater cooperative utilization of space technology were many, and that the United Nations should ensure that the improved technologies benefited all people, either through existing organizations or through the establishment of new ones.

The Secretary-General outlined the post-cold-war challenges, including the conversion of military technology, commercialization and proliferation, environmental protection and the new role of the United Nations. He made recommendations for enhancing security through space technology in the areas of international space policy, arms control and disarmament, scientific and technical cooperation, and the commercialization of space activities, and proposed new approaches to space and security through confidence-building and improving access to space technology.

According to the Secretary-General, the report represented a blueprint for integrating space technology more fully into the mechanisms for preserving and enhancing international security. He called for open discussion to determine the best methods for implementing the recommendations in the report.

The General Assembly, in **resolution 48/39**, welcomed the report. In **resolution 48/74 B**, it noted the study submitted by the Secretary-General on the application of confidence-building measures in outer space.[39] Prevention of an arms race in outer space was the subject of **resolution 48/74 A**.

Space law

The Legal Subcommittee of the Committee on outer space, at its thirty-second session (New York, 22 March–8 April 1993),[40] considered questions relating to an early review and possible revision of the Principles Relevant to the Use of Nuclear Power Sources in Outer Space; matters relating to the definition and delimitation of outer space and to the character and utilization of the geostationary orbit; and legal aspects related to the application of the principle that the exploration and utilization of outer space should be carried out for the benefit of and in the interests of all States.

The Committee on outer space took note with appreciation of the Subcommittee's report on its 1993 session.[5]

Legal aspects of nuclear
power sources in outer space

The Legal Subcommittee re-established its working group to consider the revision of the Principles Relevant to the Use of Nuclear Power Sources in Outer Space, adopted by the General Assembly in 1992.[24] The group considered that revision of the substantive provisions of the Principles should be based on possible scientific and technical developments and decided to await the input of the Scientific and Technical Subcommittee in that respect. Some delegations were of the view that sufficient time had not elapsed since adoption of the Principles to allow for a meaningful assessment of their operation, while others considered that concerns relating to the Principles should be freely expressed and recorded. Questions relating to Principle 4, on safety assessment, were also raised.

The Committee on outer space agreed that the Principles should be implemented and reviewed to determine whether revision was necessary. It also agreed that the need for revision should be considered by the Scientific and Technical Subcommittee in the light of changing technology before any actual revision was undertaken by the Legal Subcommittee or the Committee.

Legal aspects of the geostationary orbit and definition of outer space

The Legal Subcommittee, through a working group, continued consideration of matters relating to the definition and delimitation of outer space and to the character and utilization of the geostationary orbit, including ways to ensure its rational and equitable use without prejudice to the role of ITU. In addition to working papers submitted at previous sessions, the Subcommittee had before it a working paper presented by Colombia on the geostationary satellite orbit.

The Committee on outer space noted that a working paper on the legal regime for aerospace objects had been submitted by the Russian Federation and a draft questionnaire, based on an informal paper by the Chairman of the working group, had been discussed and would be forwarded for comments to Member States, the International Civil Aviation Organization and the Scientific and Technical Subcommittee. The Committee agreed that those documents, among others, could form a suitable basis for further discussion. It noted the deliberations of the Legal Subcommittee and the exchange of views on the geostationary orbit, based on Colombia's paper. The Committee recognized that space debris in the geostationary and lower orbits was cause for concern.

Exploration of outer space

The Legal Subcommittee re-established its working group to consider the legal aspects related to the application of the principle that the exploration and utilization of outer space should be carried out for the benefit of all States, taking into

particular account the needs of developing countries. The group based its discussion on a working paper on principles regarding international cooperation in the exploration and utilization of outer space for peaceful purposes, submitted by Argentina, Brazil, Chile, Colombia, Mexico, Nigeria, Pakistan, the Philippines, Uruguay and Venezuela.

The Committee on outer space noted the constructive work carried out by the Subcommittee and the working group, the discussion based on the working paper and the positive responses of its co-sponsors to comments by other delegations, which would be taken into account in future discussions.

GENERAL ASSEMBLY ACTION

On 10 December, the General Assembly, on the recommendation of the Fourth (Special Political and Decolonization) Committee, adopted **resolution 48/39** without vote.

International cooperation in the peaceful uses of outer space

The General Assembly,

Recalling its resolution 47/67 of 14 December 1992,

Deeply convinced of the common interest of mankind in promoting the exploration and use of outer space for peaceful purposes and in continuing efforts to extend to all States the benefits derived therefrom, and also of the importance of international cooperation in this field, for which the United Nations should continue to provide a focal point,

Reaffirming the importance of international cooperation in developing the rule of law, including the relevant norms of space law and their important role in international cooperation for the exploration and use of outer space for peaceful purposes,

Concerned about the possibility of an arms race in outer space,

Recognizing that all States, in particular those with major space capabilities, should contribute actively to the goal of preventing an arms race in outer space as an essential condition for the promotion of international cooperation in the exploration and use of outer space for peaceful purposes,

Considering that space debris is an issue of concern to all nations,

Noting the progress achieved in the further development of peaceful space exploration and application as well as in various national and cooperative space projects, which contribute to international cooperation, and the importance of further international cooperation in this field,

Taking note of the report of the Secretary-General on implementation of the recommendations of the Second United Nations Conference on the Exploration and Peaceful Uses of Outer Space,

Having considered the report of the Committee on the Peaceful Uses of Outer Space on the work of its thirty-sixth session,

1. *Endorses* the report of the Committee on the Peaceful Uses of Outer Space;

2. *Invites* States that have not yet become parties to the international treaties governing the uses of outer space to give consideration to ratifying or acceding to those treaties;

3. *Notes* that, at its thirty-second session, the Legal Subcommittee of the Committee on the Peaceful Uses of Outer Space, in its working groups, continued its work as mandated by the General Assembly in its resolution 47/67;

4. *Endorses* the recommendations of the Committee that the Legal Subcommittee, at its thirty-third session, taking into account the concerns of all countries, particularly those of developing countries, should:

(*a*) Continue, through its working group, its consideration of the question of early review and possible revision of the Principles Relevant to the Use of Nuclear Power Sources in Outer Space;

(*b*) Continue, through its working group, its consideration of matters relating to the definition and delimitation of outer space and to the character and utilization of the geostationary orbit, including consideration of ways and means to ensure the rational and equitable use of the geostationary orbit without prejudice to the role of the International Telecommunication Union;

(*c*) Continue, through its working group, its consideration of the legal aspects related to the application of the principle that the exploration and utilization of outer space should be carried out for the benefit and in the interests of all States, taking into particular account the needs of developing countries;

5. *Notes* that deliberations on the question of the geostationary orbit have been undertaken by the Legal Subcommittee, as reflected in its report, on the basis of recent proposals which might provide a new and enhanced basis for future work;

6. *Endorses* the recommendations and agreements concerning the organization of work in the Legal Subcommittee;

7. *Notes* that the Scientific and Technical Subcommittee of the Committee on the Peaceful Uses of Outer Space, at its thirtieth session, continued its work as mandated by the General Assembly in its resolution 47/67;

8. *Welcomes* the decision of the Committee to consider the matter of space debris, and in this regard endorses the recommendation of the Committee that a new item, entitled "Space debris", should be added to the agenda of the Scientific and Technical Subcommittee beginning with its next session;

9. *Endorses* the agreement of the Committee that, under this item, the Scientific and Technical Subcommittee would consider scientific research relating to space debris, including relevant studies, mathematical modelling and other analytical work on the characterization of the space debris environment;

10. *Also endorses* the recommendations of the Committee that the Scientific and Technical Subcommittee, at its thirty-first session, taking into account the concerns of all countries, particularly those of developing countries, should:

(*a*) Consider the following items on a priority basis:

(i) United Nations Programme on Space Applications and the coordination of space activities within the United Nations system;

(ii) Implementation of the recommendations of the Second United Nations Conference on the Exploration and Peaceful Uses of Outer Space;

(iii) Matters relating to remote sensing of the Earth by satellites, including, *inter alia*, applications for developing countries;

(iv) Use of nuclear power sources in outer space;

(*b*) Consider the following items:

(i) Space debris;

(ii) Questions relating to space transportation systems and their implications for future activities in space;

(iii) Examination of the physical nature and technical attributes of the geostationary orbit and its utilization and applications, including, *inter alia*, in the field of space communications, as well as other questions relating to space communications developments, taking particular account of the needs and interests of developing countries;

(iv) Matters relating to life sciences, including space medicine;

(v) Progress in national and international space activities related to the Earth's environment, in particular progress in the geosphere-biosphere (global change) programme;

(vi) Matters relating to planetary exploration;

(vii) Matters relating to astronomy;

(viii) The theme fixed for special attention at the 1994 session of the Scientific and Technical Subcommittee: "Space applications for disaster prevention, warning, mitigation and relief"; the Committee on Space Research and the International Astronautical Federation, in liaison with Member States, should be invited to arrange a symposium, with as wide a participation as possible, to be held during the first week of the Subcommittee's session, to complement discussions within the Subcommittee on the special theme;

11. *Considers*, in the context of paragraph 10 (*a*) (ii) above, that it is particularly urgent to implement the following recommendations:

(*a*) All countries should have the opportunity to use the techniques resulting from medical studies in space;

(*b*) Data banks at the national and regional levels should be strengthened and expanded and an international space information service should be established to function as a centre of coordination;

(*c*) The United Nations should support the creation of adequate training centres at the regional level, linked, whenever possible, to institutions implementing space programmes; necessary funding for the development of such centres should be made available through financial institutions;

(*d*) The United Nations should organize a fellowship programme through which selected graduates or postgraduates from developing countries should get in-depth, long-term exposure to space technology or applications; it would also be desirable to encourage the availability of opportunities for such exposure on other bilateral or multilateral bases outside the United Nations system;

12. *Endorses* the recommendation of the Committee that the Scientific and Technical Subcommittee should reconvene, at its thirty-first session, the Working Group of the Whole to Evaluate the Implementation of the Recommendations of the Second United Nations Conference on the Exploration and Peaceful Uses of Outer Space, to continue its work;

13. *Also endorses* the recommendations of the Working Group of the Whole of the Scientific and Technical Subcommittee, as endorsed by the Committee and as contained in the report of the Working Group of the Whole;

14. *Decides* that, during the thirty-first session of the Scientific and Technical Subcommittee, the Working Group on the Use of Nuclear Power Sources in Outer Space should be reconvened, and invites Member States to report to the Secretary-General on a regular basis with regard to national and international research concerning the safety of nuclear-powered satellites;

15. *Endorses* the United Nations Programme on Space Applications for 1994, as proposed to the Committee by the Expert on Space Applications;

16. *Emphasizes* the urgency and importance of implementing fully the recommendations of the Second United Nations Conference on the Exploration and Peaceful Uses of Outer Space;

17. *Reaffirms its approval* of the recommendation of the Conference regarding the establishment and strengthening of regional mechanisms of cooperation and their promotion and creation through the United Nations system;

18. *Expresses its appreciation* to all Governments that have made or expressed their intention to make contributions towards carrying out the recommendations of the Conference;

19. *Invites* all Governments to take effective action for the implementation of the recommendations of the Conference;

20. *Requests* all organs, organizations and bodies of the United Nations system and other intergovernmental organizations working in the field of outer space or on space-related matters to cooperate in the implementation of the recommendations of the Conference;

21. *Invites* the Secretary-General to report to the General Assembly at its forty-ninth session on the implementation of the recommendations of the Conference;

22. *Notes* that, pursuant to the request of the General Assembly contained in paragraph 20 of its resolution 47/67, the Committee discussed the possibility of holding a third United Nations Conference on the Exploration and Peaceful Uses of Outer Space in the future, and requests the Scientific and Technical Subcommittee to continue these discussions at its thirty-first session with a view to promoting an early conclusion on the matter by the Committee;

23. *Agrees* that the most important step is to define a set of sharply focused objectives for such a conference and that details such as organization, venue, timing and funding should also be considered;

24. *Notes* that the goals set for such a conference might also be achieved through other means, including intensification of work within the Committee;

25. *Recognizes* the contribution of the Second Space Conference of the Americas, held at Santiago in 1993, and the Asia-Pacific Workshop on Multilateral Cooperation in Space Technology and Applications, held at Beijing in 1992, towards promoting regional cooperation in space activities, as well as the meetings mentioned in paragraph 13 of the report of the Secretary-General on the implementation of the recommendations of the Second United Nations Conference on the Exploration and Peaceful Uses of Outer Space, and calls upon the regional commissions to support these initiatives;

26. *Recommends* that more attention be paid to all aspects related to the protection and the preservation of the outer space environment, especially those potentially affecting the Earth's environment;

27. *Considers* that it is essential that Member States pay more attention to the problem of collisions of space objects, including nuclear power sources, with space debris, and other aspects of space debris, calls for the continuation of national research on this question, for the development of improved technology for the monitoring of space debris and for the compilation and dissemination of data on space debris, and also considers that, to the extent possible, information thereon should be provided to the Scientific and Technical Subcommittee;

28. *Takes note with interest* of the analytical report prepared by the Secretariat on the role that the Committee could play in view of the decisions and recommendations of the United Nations Conference on Environment and Development and agrees that it could make an important contribution to the Committee's future work in this area;

29. *Requests* the Scientific and Technical Subcommittee to review the report at its next session and consider further how the Committee might best promote the effective use of space technology, on the basis of international cooperation, for environmental monitoring and sustainable development;

30. *Requests* the Secretariat to provide the Scientific and Technical Subcommittee with updated information on the implementation of Agenda 21 by the United Nations system, with information on activities of the United Nations Programme on Space Applications related to environment and development, and with suggestions as to how the activities of the Programme on Space Applications in this area might be expanded;

31. *Recommends* that permanent observer status to the Committee be granted to the Association of Space Explorers, on the understanding that, in accordance with the agreement of the Committee at its thirty-third session concerning observer status for non-governmental organizations, the Association would apply for consultative status with the Economic and Social Council;

32. *Notes* that, in accordance with the decisions of the General Assembly and of the Secretary-General, the Office for Outer Space Affairs has been relocated to the United Nations Office at Vienna and that, as part of that restructuring, the Office for Outer Space Affairs will be responsible for servicing the Committee, the Scientific and Technical Subcommittee and the Legal Subcommittee and their subsidiary bodies;

33. *Endorses* the agreement of the Committee that the meetings of the Committee and of the Scientific and Technical Subcommittee should be held at Vienna in accordance with the headquarters rule contained in General Assembly resolution 40/243 of 18 December 1985, that the thirty-third session of the Legal Subcommittee should be held at Vienna and that the venue for its subsequent meetings should be reviewed in the light of the 1994 session;

34. *Urges* all States, in particular those with major space capabilities, to contribute actively to the goal of preventing an arms race in outer space as an essential condition for the promotion of international cooperation in the exploration and uses of outer space for peaceful purposes;

35. *Emphasizes* the need to increase the benefits of space technology and its applications and to contribute to an orderly growth of space activities favourable to the socio-economic advancement of humanity, in particular that of the people of the developing countries;

36. *Takes note* of the views expressed during the thirty-sixth session of the Committee and during the forty-eighth session of the General Assembly concerning ways and means of maintaining outer space for peaceful purposes;

37. *Requests* the Committee to continue to consider, as a matter of priority, ways and means of maintaining outer space for peaceful purposes and to report thereon to the General Assembly at its forty-ninth session;

38. *Also requests* the Committee to continue to consider, at its thirty-seventh session, its agenda item entitled ''Spin-off benefits of space technology: review of current status'';

39. *Requests* the specialized agencies and other international organizations to continue and, where appropriate, enhance their cooperation with the Committee and to provide it with progress reports on their work relating to the peaceful uses of outer space;

40. *Welcomes* the report of the Secretary-General on international cooperation in space activities for enhancing security in the post-cold-war era and calls upon the competent bodies to take into account its contents;

41. *Requests* the Committee to continue its work, in accordance with the present resolution, to consider, as appropriate, new projects in outer space activities and to submit a report to the General Assembly at its forty-ninth session, including its views on which subjects should be studied in the future.

General Assembly resolution 48/39

10 December 1993   Meeting 75   Adopted without vote

Approved by Fourth Committee (A/48/645) without vote, 11 November (meeting 17); draft by Austria, for Fourth Committee Working Group on cooperation in outer space (A/C.4/48/L.16), orally amended by France and Mexico; agenda item 84.
Meeting numbers. GA 48th session: 4th Committee 2, 15-17; plenary 75.

REFERENCES
[1]A/AC.105/543. [2]YUN 1982, p. 162. [3]YUN 1992, p. 119, GA res. 47/67, 14 Dec. 1992. [4]A/AC.105/546. [5]A/48/20. [6]YUN 1982, p. 163, GA res. 37/90, 10 Dec. 1982.

[7]A/48/365 & Corr.1. [8]A/AC.105/535. [9]A/AC.105/536. [10]A/AC.105/523 & Add.1. [11]YUN 1992, p. 112. [12]A/AC.105/555. [13]A/AC.105/534. [14]A/AC.105/556. [15]A/AC.105/552. [16]A/AC.105/553. [17]A/AC.105/557. [18]A/AC.105/558. [19]A/AC.105/561. [20]A/AC.105/560. [21]A/AC.105/559. [22]A/AC.105/562. [23]A/AC.105/533. [24]YUN 1992, p. 116, GA res. 47/68, 14 Dec. 1992. [25]A/AC.105/549. [26]A/AC.105/542 & Add.1, 2. [27]A/AC.105/547. [28]YUN 1992, p. 670. [29]A/AC.105/554. [30]YUN 1992, p. 115. [31]A/AC.105/524. [32]A/AC.105/551. [33]A/AC.105/537-541, 550. [34]A/AC.105/522. [35]A/AC.105/567. [36]GA res. 44/46, 8 Dec. 1989. [37]YUN 1992, p. 110. [38]A/48/221. [39]A/48/305 & Corr.1. [40]A/AC.105/544.

Spacecraft launchings

During 1993, eight countries (Australia, Brazil, China, Germany, India, Japan, Russian Federation, United States) and ESA provided information to the United Nations on the launchings of objects into orbit or beyond,[1] in accordance with a 1961 General Assembly resolution[2] and article IV of the Convention on Registration of Objects Launched into Outer Space,[3] which entered into force in 1976.

Convention on registration of launchings

As at 31 December 1993, there were 38 States parties to the Convention on registration. During the year, Argentina, the Czech Republic and Slovakia became parties to the Convention, following the dissolution of Czechoslovakia on 31 December 1992. In 1979, ESA had declared its acceptance of the rights and obligations of the Convention.

REFERENCES
[1]ST/SG/SER.E/258-270, A/AC.105/INF/397. [2]YUN 1961, p. 35, GA res. 1721 B (XVI), 20 Dec. 1961. [3]YUN 1974, p. 63, GA res. 3235(XXIX), annex, 12 Nov. 1974.

Chapter V

Other political questions

In 1993, issues relating to information, effects of atomic radiation and Antarctica continued to be on the General Assembly's agenda. The Assembly adopted resolutions on promotion of communication and the free flow of information (resolution 48/44 A) and on United Nations public information activities (48/44 B). It requested the United Nations Scientific Committee on the Effects of Atomic Radiation to continue its work on the levels, effects and risks of ionizing radiation from all sources (48/38). The Assembly reaffirmed the need to promote further public awareness of Antarctica's importance to the ecosystem, encouraged the Antarctic Treaty Consultative Parties to increase cooperation with a view to reducing the number of scientific stations on that continent, and urged the international community to ensure protection of the Antarctic environment (48/80).

Six States were admitted to United Nations membership, bringing the total number to 184. One Member State—the Czech and Slovak Federal Republic—ceased to exist on 31 December 1992, while a new State was admitted under the provisional name of the former Yugoslav Republic of Macedonia. Yugoslavia (Serbia and Montenegro) was barred from participating in the work of the Economic and Social Council pending its admission to United Nations membership (47/229).

Information

The public information activities of the United Nations continued to focus on publicizing the Organization's work and goals and enhancing the information and communication capabilities of developing countries. Those activities were carried out by the Department of Public Information (DPI) of the Secretariat, the United Nations Educational, Scientific and Cultural Organization (UNESCO) and the Joint United Nations Information Committee (JUNIC).

Information policies and activities were reviewed at the fifteenth session of the General Assembly's Committee on Information (New York, 10-28 May 1993).[1] Its recommendations were considered by the Fourth (Special Political and Decolonization) Committee in October and

November and acted on by the Assembly in December. Also in December, the Assembly, by **decision 48/318**, appointed Gabon and Israel as members of the Committee on Information, thereby increasing its membership from 81 to 83 (see APPENDIX III).

The Committee had before it six reports submitted by the Secretary-General in response to a 1992 General Assembly resolution.[2] A report on ways and means of furthering the development of communication infrastructures and capabilities in developing countries[3] reproduced the observations and suggestions of 13 Member States, as at 12 May 1993, on the subject. Other reports reviewed implementation of a system-wide information programme for the 1992 United Nations Conference on Environment and Development (UNCED),[4] outlined United Nations publications policy[5] and continuous and major publications of DPI,[6] and described the allocation of resources to United Nations information centres (UNICs)[7] and their integration with other United Nations offices.[8] Another report, dealing with the enhancing and reactivation of UNICs and the establishment of new ones,[9] was submitted pursuant to a decision taken by the Bureau of the Committee on 10 February. The Committee also considered a report of the Secretary-General on JUNIC activities,[10] presented in response to a 1991 Assembly request.[11]

Mass communication

At its 1993 session, the Committee on Information discussed the establishment of a new, more just and more effective world information and communication order, examined United Nations public information policies and activities, and evaluated the progress achieved by the United Nations system in information and communications.

UNESCO activities. In 1993, UNESCO continued to promote the free flow of information and to develop communication through its International Programme for the Development of Communication (IPDC), the General Information Programme and the Intergovernmental Informatics Programme. In accordance with a resolution of its 1991 General Conference, UNESCO began to develop a coherent approach to its information activities through cooperation and closer coordination among those programmes.

A meeting of African communications experts (Yaoundé, Cameroon, 17-19 March), organized by IPDC, discussed the situation of the mass media in Africa and issues related to the preparation of projects, their priorities and funding. UNESCO sponsored a national seminar on improving press pluralism in Mali and an awareness-raising seminar on problems of professional ethics in Cameroon and co-sponsored a workshop on the acquired immunodeficiency syndrome for 24 African radio and television producers. It provided financial assistance for training 30 press photographers from South Africa, as well as for a programme in management techniques for 25 publishers of the private African press and a course in electronic page-setting and media management for eight women journalists and editors from China. The fifth IPDC/UNESCO Prize for rural communication was awarded in October to the Collège de l'Air of Mauritius for its media campaign to increase awareness of health problems associated with stress.

The General Conference of UNESCO, at its twenty-seventh session (Paris, 25 October–16 November 1993), in a resolution on communication, information and informatics in the service of humanity, invited the Director-General to promote a better balanced dissemination of information, support programme exchange and foster the broadcasting in industrialized countries of radio and television programmes produced in developing countries; to strengthen communication capacities in developing countries by expanding IPDC's activities, provide training for communication professionals and technicians, especially for women producers, and foster the development of communication infrastructures in rural and disadvantaged suburban areas; to encourage member States to adopt information policies and promote regional cooperation in the development of and access to specialized information services; to strengthen regional informatics networks and the training of informatics specialists; and to develop further the INFORMAFRICA programme aimed at introducing informatics into education systems in Africa. By two other resolutions, the General Conference invited the Director-General to mobilize extrabudgetary resources for communication activities for the benefit of women and to promote the establishment of a network of schools of journalism associated with UNESCO.

During 1993, IPDC continued activities aimed at channelling international cooperation and funding to support the development of media infrastructure in developing countries. The Bureau of the IPDC Intergovernmental Council (Paris, 19-28 April) earmarked a supplementary $1,230,000 to finance projects approved in 1992 and $20,000 to cover the urgent needs of students with IPDC scholarships in the former USSR. It also pre-selected 58 out of the 102 projects received for submission to the Intergovernmental Council, including several private projects as well as projects for Central European countries.

Under a joint IPDC/Republic of Korea training programme, 15 scholarships for further training in television were awarded to specialists from developing countries and Eastern Europe; 10 more were awarded to African nationals under the IPDC/Nigeria programme.

During 1992-1993,[12] 46 projects amounting to $6,837,718 were financed under the IPDC Special Account and funds-in-trust arrangements. That total included 15 projects ($3,549,466) for Africa, 14 ($1,914,252) for Asia and the Pacific, 11 ($611,000) for Latin America and the Caribbean, 3 ($500,000) for the Arab States, 1 ($113,000) for Europe and 2 interregional projects ($150,000). In 1993, a total of $1,433,000 in pledged or received contributions was allocated to the Special Account and $2,944,600 to funds-in-trust; in addition, Germany and the Netherlands pledged or contributed DM 150,000 and 400,000 guilders, respectively, to the Special Account.

Projects financed in 1993 dealt with the publication of a women's magazine in Mozambique; improved radio coverage of the capital of Mauritania; newspaper and journal development in Gabon, Ghana, Kiribati and Samoa; television programmes on cultural heritage in Belize; refurbishing radio broadcasting facilities in Grenada; establishment of an educational media unit in Saint Kitts and Nevis; development of a computer system for the Information Service of Jamaica; human resources development in State television of Uruguay; and assistance to rehabilitate broadcasting in Uganda.

At its fourteenth session (Paris, 5-8 October),[13] the IPDC Intergovernmental Council approved 60 projects amounting to $2.2 million, excluding funds-in-trust arrangements. Of the total, 3 projects were interregional, 13 regional, 26 national and 18 for the least developed countries.

GENERAL ASSEMBLY ACTION

On 10 December, the Assembly, on the recommendation of the Fourth Committee, adopted **resolution 48/44 A** without vote.

Information in the service of humanity
The General Assembly,

Taking note of the comprehensive and important report of the Committee on Information,

Also taking note of the report of the Secretary-General on questions relating to information,

Urges all countries, organizations of the United Nations system as a whole and all others concerned, reaffirming their commitment to the principles of the Charter of the United Nations and to the principles of freedom of the press and freedom of information, as well as to those of the independence, pluralism and diversity of the media, deeply concerned by the disparities existing between developed and developing countries and the consequences of every kind arising from those disparities that affect the capability of the public, private or other media and individuals in developing countries to disseminate information and communicate their views and their cultural and ethical values through endogenous cultural production, as well as to ensure the diversity of sources and their free access to information, and recognizing the call in this context for what in the United Nations and at various international forums has been termed "a new world information and communication order, seen as an evolving and continuous process":

(a) To cooperate and interact with a view to reducing existing disparities in information flows at all levels by increasing assistance for the development of communication infrastructures and capabilities in developing countries, with due regard for their needs and the priorities attached to such areas by those countries, and in order to enable them and the public, private or other media in developing countries to develop their own information and communication policies freely and independently and increase the participation of media and individuals in the communication process, and to ensure a free flow of information at all levels;

(b) To ensure for journalists the free and effective performance of their professional tasks and condemn resolutely all attacks against them;

(c) To provide support for the continuation and strengthening of practical training programmes for broadcasters and journalists from public, private and other media in developing countries;

(d) To enhance regional efforts and cooperation among developing countries, as well as cooperation between developed and developing countries, to strengthen communication capacities and to improve the media infrastructure and communication technology in the developing countries, especially in the areas of training and dissemination of information;

(e) To aim, in addition to bilateral cooperation, at providing all possible support and assistance to the developing countries and their media, public, private or other, with due regard to their interests and needs in the field of information and to action already taken within the United Nations system, including:

(i) The development of the human and technical resources that are indispensable for the improvement of information and communication systems in developing countries and support for the continuation and strengthening of practical training programmes, such as those already operating under both public and private auspices throughout the developing world;

(ii) The creation of conditions that will enable developing countries and their media, public, private or other, to have, by using their national and regional resources, the communication technology suited to their national needs, as well as the necessary programme material, especially for radio and television broadcasting;

(iii) Assistance in establishing and promoting telecommunication links at the subregional, regional and interregional levels, especially among developing countries;

(iv) The facilitation, as appropriate, of access by the developing countries to advanced communication technology available on the open market;

(f) To provide full support for the International Programme for the Development of Communication of the United Nations Educational, Scientific and Cultural Organization, which should support both public and private media.

General Assembly resolution 48/44 A

10 December 1993   Meeting 75   Adopted without vote

Approved by Fourth Committee (A/48/649) without vote, 15 November (meeting 18); draft by Committee on Information (A/48/21); agenda item 88.
Meeting numbers. GA 48th session: 4th Committee 8-14, 17, 18; plenary 75.

Promotion of press freedom

The UNESCO General Conference again invited the Director-General to promote press freedom and independent and pluralistic media, while the IPDC Intergovernmental Council decided that IPDC's orientation regarding freedom of the press and the pluralism and independence of the media must become a priority concern. UNESCO fielded a high-level mission to Kazakhstan to help develop legislation promoting press freedom and media pluralism and began, in cooperation with DPI, preparations for a seminar on promoting independent and pluralistic media in Latin America and the Caribbean, to be held in 1994. In addition, IPDC co-sponsored the establishment of an early-warning network to combat infringements of press freedom.

Pursuant to a 1992 General Assembly resolution,[2] the Secretariat, by an April 1993 note,[14] transmitted to the Economic and Social Council a 1991 resolution of the General Conference[15] calling for the promotion of press freedom in the world.

ECONOMIC AND SOCIAL COUNCIL ACTION

On 29 July, the Economic and Social Council adopted **resolution 1993/54** without vote.

Promotion of press freedom in the world

The Economic and Social Council,

Having examined the note by the Secretariat,

Taking cognizance of resolution 4.3 of 6 November 1991 of the General Conference of the United Nations Educational, Scientific and Cultural Organization, contained in the annex to that note,

Taking note of General Assembly resolution 47/73 B of 14 December 1992, in which the Assembly decided, on procedural grounds, to refer the resolution mentioned above to the Economic and Social Council for consideration,

Recommends that the General Assembly declare 3 May World Press Freedom Day.

Economic and Social Council resolution 1993/54

29 July 1993   Meeting 45   Adopted without vote

7-nation draft (E/1993/L.30), orally revised following informal consultations; agenda item 4.
Sponsors: Benin, France, Germany, Mauritius, Namibia, Poland, Slovakia.
Meeting numbers. ESC 31, 41, 45.

By **decision 48/432** of 20 December, the General Assembly declared 3 May World Press Freedom Day.

UN public information

DPI activities

In response to a 1992 General Assembly resolution,[2] the Secretary-General submitted in October 1993 a report on questions relating to information,[16] which focused on activities of DPI.

The report stated that DPI continued in 1993 to disseminate information about United Nations activities pertaining to peace-keeping and peacemaking. It provided advice and technical support to peace-keeping missions, issued periodic updates on peace-keeping operations and produced new ad hoc radio programmes on the situation in Somalia and in the former Yugoslavia, as well as features on the situation in Haiti and on activities concerning Iraq's weapons capabilities. DPI also prepared a variety of printed and audiovisual materials at the request of the United Nations Observer Mission to Verify the Referendum in Eritrea and provided on-the-spot coverage of the referendum. Among other materials produced by DPI were a television news story on Cambodia, a documentary on the peace process in Central America, and an educational video and a teaching manual on United Nations peace-keeping and peacemaking activities in English, French and Spanish.

Activities under the United Nations Disarmament Information Programme included a press kit on the Secretary-General's report on new dimensions of arms regulation and disarmament in the post-cold-war era (see PART ONE, Chapter II) and several features, documentaries and radio and video programmes on disarmament-related issues, as well as the preparation of a two-day symposium in New York in the context of Disarmament Week.

DPI also pursued activities within the framework of the International Decade for the Eradication of Colonialism (1990-2000) (see PART ONE, Chapter III) and disseminated information on the advancement of the status of women and their role in society through feature articles on women and poverty and women in public life, the weekly radio series entitled "Women" and bimonthly programmes in Arabic, French and Spanish, four video segments on women's issues and a programme on the rights of women in the development process. It continued to develop a public information strategy for the Fourth World Conference on Women (1995) (see PART THREE, Chapter XIII) and held a panel discussion on violence against women (New York, 4 March).

During the reporting period, DPI received almost 4,000 requests for information on human rights and distributed some 273,000 copies of its human rights publications in bulk and more than 500,000 copies by request. They included reprints and new language versions of various human rights instruments, the biennial *Objective: Justice*, and numerous pamphlets, booklets, feature articles and brochures. DPI provided extensive coverage of the World Conference on Human Rights (Vienna, 14-25 June) (see PART THREE, Chapter X) and organized an encounter for journalists on the main issues before the Conference. It also publicized the International Year of the World's Indigenous People (1993), (see PART THREE, Chapter X) and prepared an exhibition on indigenous people and the modern world, held in New York in November/December 1993.

As to activities relating to economic and social development, DPI organized the press launch of the *World Economic Survey 1993* and promoted the *Report on the World Social Situation 1993*; produced, among other materials, a press kit and a radio documentary on disability-related issues, in connection with the end of the Decade of Disabled Persons (1983-1992); and prepared an information programme for the Year of the Family (1994), including a radio programme on women and the family and materials for the Year's launch by non-governmental organizations (NGOs) in Malta in November/December. The Department helped prepare an information programme for the International Decade for Natural Disaster Reduction (1990-2000) and a public information campaign for the World Conference on Natural Disaster Reduction, to be held in Japan in 1994 (see PART THREE, Chapter III). DPI also sponsored the 1993 annual NGO conference, on social development (New York, 8-10 September), and was preparing information programmes for the World Summit for Social Development and the Ninth United Nations Congress on the Prevention of Crime and the Treatment of Offenders, both to be held in 1995 (see PART THREE, Chapter XII).

Activities on environment and development included an information programme as a follow-up to UNCED and media campaigns for the first session of the Commission on Sustainable Development (New York, 14-25 June) and for the Conference on Straddling Fish Stocks and Highly Migratory Fish Stocks (New York, 12-30 July). DPI also planned an information campaign for the 1994 Global Conference on the Sustainable Development of Small Island Developing States (see PART THREE, Chapter I) and for negotiations for a Convention on Desertification.

DPI pursued its activities pertaining to African economic recovery and development, based on the United Nations New Agenda for the Development of Africa in the 1990s, adopted in 1991,[17] through continued publication of its quarterly periodical *Africa Recovery* and production of briefing papers on the peace-keeping and humanitarian operations in Somalia and Mozambique, food security on the continent and the prevention of famine in southern Africa. The Department also produced a brochure on external debt and African development and held a briefing on the subject (Washington, D.C., 15 April) for United States congressional aides and administration officials.

As part of its programme on the question of Palestine, mandated by the Assembly in 1992,[18] DPI sponsored an encounter for European journalists on the question of promoting a culture for peace in the Middle East (London, 9-11 June) and began preparations for a fact-finding mission for journalists to that region. In addition, a radio documentary on the question of international protection for the Palestinian people was produced and distributed worldwide.

In 1993, DPI extended its services to public access databases, such as Federal News in Washington, D.C., and Agora in Italy. It continued to issue its annual directory of associated NGOs and began preparing two new directories to classify them by country and by their speciality and/or field of interest. The United Nations/International Public Relations Association Award for outstanding public relations campaigns addressing priority United Nations issues was established, and the 1992 Award and honourable mentions were presented, respectively, for programmes aimed at raising the status of women in India, expanding community-based health care in Africa and increasing awareness of environment/development issues in the United States. DPI's annual training programme for broadcasters and journalists from developing countries was held (New York, 14 September–22 October); since 1981, 224 participants from more than 120 countries had been trained under the programme. DPI also continued its cooperation with the News Agencies Pool of Non-Aligned Countries and other news agencies of and in developing countries by providing them with daily news items on a variety of issues.

The Secretary-General's report also described DPI activities in connection with international efforts against drug abuse and illicit drug trafficking (see PART THREE, Chapter XVI) and against apartheid, as well as United Nations publications during 1993, including the *UN Chronicle* and the *Yearbook of the United Nations*. It noted that publication of *Development Forum* had ceased by 31 December 1992 for financial reasons, and that an option of merging the United Nations *Development Business* and the World Bank's *International Business Opportunities* was being considered.

UN information centres

In the interest of improved productivity and economies of scale, as well as in order to present a unified United Nations image, the Secretary-General decided in March 1992[19] that, wherever feasible, the operations of UNICs should be integrated with those of field offices of the United Nations Development Programme (UNDP). In March 1993,[8] he reported on the integration of UNICs with other United Nations offices, while maintaining the centres' functional autonomy and ensuring that they were fully operational. A 1990 agreement between UNDP and DPI formed the basis for further cooperation in that regard.

At the time of the report, 18 UNICs were headed by a UNDP resident representative who served concurrently as full-time centre director. The director reported to DPI on every aspect of the work connected with the centre, including administration, budget and staffing, all of which remained independent from UNDP.

In addition to financial advantages, the integration of offices was expected to have qualitative benefits arising from closer interaction and increased cooperation. For instance, it was recommended that a schedule of events for the year be established, identifying priority themes, selecting target audiences, coordinating promotional efforts and seeking the cooperation of local institutions and organizations. The offices were requested to identify one information staff member to serve as the focal point in dealings with national institutions and organizations.

Most of the integrated UNICs shared common office premises with UNDP. Where there were separate premises, as was the case with six UNICs, the UNDP resident representative was requested to explore the feasibility of common premises at a future date.

Concluding, the Secretary-General stated that the experience would be evaluated after a trial period of one year, during which time the terms of integration would be refined. In the meantime, DPI and UNDP regularly reviewed the integration and ensured maximum collaboration.

On 10 December, by **decision 48/418**, the Assembly requested the Committee on Information to consider on a priority basis, at its 1994 session, recent initiatives regarding the creation of new UNICs and to make a recommendation on the matter, bearing in mind the need for improved criteria for the establishment of centres.

In **resolution 48/44 B**, the Assembly requested the Secretary-General to report to the Committee in 1994 on the results of the current trial of integrating 18 UNICs with UNDP field offices, for the purpose of evaluating the need for any subsequent integration. The report should also contain the host countries' views, bearing in mind Member States' concerns that integration could adversely affect the centres' functions in developing countries.

In **resolution 48/209**, the Assembly reaffirmed that field office activities related to public information should follow the relevant provisions of the Assembly, particularly **resolution 48/44 B**. The Assembly also affirmed the need to increase the number of common premises, in cooperation with host Governments, in a way that increased efficiency but did not increase costs.

Resource allocation to UNICs

In an April 1993 report on allocation of resources to and strengthening of UNICs,[7] the Secretary-General noted DPI's efforts to enhance the centres' electronic communications capabilities and provide training for staff. However, its limited resources seriously curtailed the centres' ability to expand public information activities; therefore, they had to rely more and more on the cooperation of Governments, NGOs and local interest groups. The centres' overall situation continued to be critical, as DPI had to absorb an increasing amount of extrabudgetary funds not forthcoming from a number of host Governments.

A means of redressing differences in the allocation of resources to all centres was, in the Secretary-General's view, effective support from every host Government on an assured and continuing basis. Equally important and an essential prerequisite for the establishment of new centres and information components, as well as for the enhancement of existing ones, must be General Assembly approval and provision of additional staffing and financial resources.

Taking note of the report, the Assembly, in **resolution 48/44 B**, called on the Secretary-General to study ways to rationalize and effect equitable disbursement of resources to all UNICs and to report thereon to the Committee on Information in 1994.

UN interim offices in new Member States

In response to a 1992 General Assembly request,[20] the Secretary-General reported in March 1993[21] on the establishment of United Nations interim offices in Armenia, Azerbaijan, Belarus, Georgia, Kazakhstan, Ukraine and Uzbekistan to facilitate dialogue between the Organization and its programmes and the new Member States.

The report summarized objectives and functions of the interim offices and described related administrative and financial arrangements and budget requirements. Total costs for 1992-1993 were estimated at $4,149,100 gross, of which

$2,008,400 was to be financed by UNDP, $1,822,900 from the United Nations regular budget and $317,800 by host Governments. On the basis of those estimates, the Secretary-General requested an additional net appropriation of $1,244,400 under the Organization's programme budget for 1992-1993.

The Advisory Committee on Administrative and Budgetary Questions (ACABQ), also in March,[22] noted that the relevant intergovernmental bodies had yet to decide on financing the interim offices and that it had no mandate to recommend funding from the regular budget. It recommended that the existing arrangements be considered provisional and exceptional, pending a policy decision by the Assembly.

By **decision 47/469** of 6 May, the Assembly, on the recommendation of the Fifth (Administrative and Budgetary) Committee, endorsed ACABQ's observations and requested the Secretary-General to ensure that his proposals relating to the interim offices complied with its resolutions pertaining to operational activities and dissemination of information. It took note of the provisional and exceptional arrangements in place and stressed that they could continue until its policy decision on the matter at its forty-eighth session.

Coordination in the UN system

The inter-agency Joint United Nations Information Committee, which coordinates information activities in the United Nations system, held its nineteenth session in 1993 (London, 20-22 July).[23] Its discussions focused on the programme and funding of the United Nations Non-Governmental Liaison Service, the question of a system-wide publication on development issues, participation in international exhibits and project proposals for inter-agency information programmes on upcoming events, such as the Global Conference on the Sustainable Development of Small Island Developing States, the International Conference on Population and Development and the World Conference on Natural Disaster Reduction, all scheduled for 1994, as well as the observance of the United Nations fiftieth anniversary, the Fourth World Conference on Women and the World Summit for Social Development, both to be held in 1995.

JUNIC also considered proposed activities for the 1993 International Year of the World's Indigenous People, the 1994 International Year of the Family and the launching of World Day for Water (22 March). It reviewed inter-agency cooperation in audiovisual productions, discussed the use of computer technology in the field of information and examined its cooperation with United Nations information centres and services. The Committee noted that *Agenda IV* of the *Agenda for a Small*

Planet series of television documentaries was never completed for lack of financial support, and decided to postpone implementation of *Agenda V* until sufficient start-up funds could be raised.

GENERAL ASSEMBLY ACTION

On 10 December, the General Assembly, on the recommendation of the Fourth Committee, adopted **resolution 48/44 B** without vote.

United Nations public information policies and activities

The General Assembly,

Reaffirming its primary role in elaborating, coordinating and harmonizing United Nations policies and activities in the field of information,

Also reaffirming that the Secretary-General should ensure that the activities of the Department of Public Information of the Secretariat, as the focal point of the public information tasks of the United Nations, are strengthened and improved, keeping in view the purposes and principles of the Charter of the United Nations, the priority areas defined by the General Assembly and the recommendations of the Committee on Information,

Taking note of all reports of the Secretary-General submitted to the Committee on Information at its fifteenth session,

1. *Decides* to consolidate the role of the Committee on Information as its main subsidiary body mandated to make recommendations relating to the work of the Department of Public Information of the Secretariat;

2. *Calls upon* the Secretary-General, in respect of United Nations public information policies and activities, to implement the following recommendations in accordance with relevant United Nations resolutions and in this regard to ensure that the Department of Public Information:

(a) Continues to disseminate information about the activities of the United Nations in coordination with the information services of other relevant agencies in accordance with the United Nations medium-term plan, the programme budget and their relevant revisions, pertaining, *inter alia*, to:

(i)   International peace and security;

(ii)   Disarmament;

(iii) Peace-keeping operations and peacemaking;

(iv)   Decolonization and the situation in the Non-Self-Governing Territories in the light of the International Decade for the Eradication of Colonialism;

(v)   The promotion and protection of human rights and in that context the 1993 World Conference on Human Rights, held at Vienna from 14 to 25 June 1993;

(vi)   The elimination of all forms of racial discrimination;

(vii) The advancement of the status of women and their role in society;

(viii) The promotion of the Convention on the Rights of the Child;

(ix)   Problems of economic and social development, as well as international economic cooperation aimed at resolving external debt problems;

(x)   The least developed countries;

(xi)   The environment and development;

(xii) The elimination of foreign occupation;

(xiii) The campaign against terrorism in all its forms in accordance with General Assembly resolution 40/61 of 9 December 1985;

(xiv) International efforts against drug abuse and illicit drug trafficking;

(xv)   Crime prevention and criminal justice;

(xvi) Support for the United Nations New Agenda for the Development of Africa in the 1990s and for the tremendous efforts of the African countries aimed at recovery and development, as well as the positive response by the international community to alleviate the serious economic situation prevailing in Africa;

(xvii) International efforts towards the total eradication of apartheid and support for the establishment of a united, non-racial and democratic South Africa and, where necessary, the role of the United Nations in this context;

(xviii) United Nations activities pertaining to the situation in the Middle East and the question of Palestine in particular, also including current developments in that region and the ongoing peace process;

(b) Provides the necessary level of information support for the activities of the United Nations in situations requiring immediate and special response;

(c) Continues its efforts at promoting an informed understanding of the work and purposes of the United Nations system among the peoples of the world and at strengthening the positive image of the system as a whole;

(d) Continues its briefings, assistance and orientation programmes for broadcasters, journalists and other media professionals from developing countries focused on United Nations–related issues;

(e) Provides, on the basis of its activities, information to the United Nations Educational, Scientific and Cultural Organization about new forms of cooperation, at the regional and subregional levels, for the training of media professionals and for the improvement of the information and communication infrastructures of developing countries;

(f) Continues its policies of cooperation with all agencies of the United Nations system, in particular with the United Nations Educational, Scientific and Cultural Organization;

(g) Continues its policies of cooperation with the news agencies in and of the developing countries, in particular the News Agencies Pool of Non-Aligned Countries;

3. *Welcomes* the decision by the Department of Public Information to establish a task force to look into the allocation of office space to the media at United Nations Headquarters;

4. *Takes note* of the report of the Secretary-General regarding the continuous and major publications of the Department of Public Information, and urges all efforts to ensure timely production and dissemination of its major publications, in particular the *UN Chronicle*, the *Yearbook of the United Nations* and *Africa Recovery*, maintaining consistent editorial independence and accuracy and taking necessary measures to ensure that its output contains adequate, objective and equitable information about issues before the Organization, reflecting divergent opinions wherever they occur;

5. *Expresses regret* at the circumstances leading to the discontinuation of *Development Forum* and encourages the Secretary-General to suggest ways and means to revive this publication, which has continued to receive a mandate of the General Assembly, and to report thereon to the Committee on Information;

6. *Requests* the management of the Department of Public Information to review the Department's publications and proposals for publications to ensure that all publications fulfil an identifiable need, that they do not duplicate other publications inside or outside the United Nations system and that they are produced in a cost-effective manner, and to report to the Committee on Information at its sixteenth substantive session, in 1994;

7. *Reaffirms* the importance attached by Member States to the role of United Nations information centres in effectively and comprehensively disseminating information about United Nations activities and the optimization of the resources allocated to the Department of Public Information;

8. *Requests* the Secretary-General to report to the Committee on Information at its sixteenth session for the purpose of evaluating the need for any subsequent integration, the results of the current trial of integrating eighteen United Nations information centres with field offices of the United Nations Development Programme, as mentioned in the report of the Secretary-General, as well as the views of the host countries, bearing in mind the concerns of Member States that the integration of the United Nations information centres with the United Nations offices could adversely affect their functions in the developing countries;

9. *Reaffirms* the role of the General Assembly in relation to the opening of new United Nations information centres, and invites the Secretary-General, as well, to make such recommendations as he may judge necessary regarding the establishment and location of these centres;

10. *Requests* the Secretary-General to ensure that his proposals relating to the structure, functions and activities of the seven United Nations interim offices in Armenia, Azerbaijan, Belarus, Georgia, Kazakhstan, Ukraine and Uzbekistan fully comply with the mandates of the relevant General Assembly resolutions pertaining to operational activities and dissemination of information, taking into account the observations and recommendations in the report of the Advisory Committee on Administrative and Budgetary Questions, General Assembly decision 47/469 of 6 May 1993 and relevant Assembly resolutions, especially resolution 47/199 of 22 December 1992;

11. *Takes note* of the report of the Secretary-General regarding the allocation of resources to the United Nations information centres in 1992 and would appreciate information on the status of the relevant General Assembly resolutions, as well as a detailed breakdown of resource deployment between centres, and, while welcoming the action by some Governments with regard to the financial and material support for United Nations information centres in their respective capitals, calls upon the Secretary-General to study ways and means to rationalize and effect equitable disbursement of available resources to all United Nations information centres and to report thereon to the Committee on Information at its sixteenth substantive session;

12. *Notes* the substantial contribution by the Government of Poland and requests the Secretary-General to continue to consult with the Polish authorities, with a view to finalizing arrangements for a United Nations information component at Warsaw;

13. *Also takes note* of the report of the Secretary-General regarding the enhancing, reactivation and establishment of United Nations information centres, and again calls upon the Secretary-General to implement fully and expeditiously the recommendation contained in paragraph 10 of its resolution 47/73 B of 14 December 1992 regarding the establishment of an information centre at Sana'a, the reactivation of the information centre at Tehran, the enhancement of the information centres at Bujumbura, at Dar es Salaam, United Republic of Tanzania, and at Dhaka, and to submit the implementation report to the Committee on Information at its sixteenth substantive session;

14. *Calls upon* the Secretary-General to submit a report on the implementation of the aforementioned recommendation to the Committee on Information at its sixteenth session;

15. *Welcomes* the report of the Secretary-General, and encourages continued enhanced cooperation between the Department of Public Information and the University for Peace in Costa Rica as a focal point for promoting United Nations activities and disseminating United Nations information materials;

16. *Takes note* of the requests by Bulgaria, Gabon, Haiti and Slovakia for information components;

17. *Expresses full support* for the wide and prompt coverage of United Nations activities through a continuation of United Nations press releases;

18. *Calls upon* the Secretary-General to enhance the efficiency of regional radio units in the Department of Public Information;

19. *Also calls upon* the Secretary-General to make every effort to create conditions more conducive to achieving parity in the press coverage of meetings in English and French by appropriate utilization of existing equipment;

20. *Takes note* of the recommendations and observations by Member States contained in the report of the Secretary-General and invites Member States that wish to do so to submit their observations and suggestions to the Secretary-General by 1 January 1994 on ways and means of furthering the development of communication infrastructures and capabilities in developing countries, with a view to consolidating recent experience in the field of international cooperation aimed at enabling them to develop their own information and communication capacities freely and independently, and requests the Secretary-General to report thereon to the Committee on Information at its sixteenth session;

21. *Recommends*, in order to facilitate continued contact between the Department of Public Information and the Committee on Information between sessions, that the Bureau of the Committee on Information, together with representatives of each regional group, the Group of Seventy-seven and China, in close contact with members of the Committee, should meet, as required, and consult at periodic intervals with representatives of the Department;

22. *Supports* decision 5 of the Preparatory Committee for the World Summit for Social Development, requesting the Secretary-General to develop and launch,

on a priority basis, in cooperation with relevant specialized agencies, funds and programmes, a specific programme of public information on the core issues of the Summit as well as on its objectives;

23. *Also supports* the decision of the Preparatory Committee for the International Conference on Population and Development, to be held at Cairo in 1994, requesting the Secretary-General, in cooperation with competent United Nations bodies and specialized agencies, to develop and launch, on a priority basis, a coordinated public information programme;

24. *Takes note* of the request by Belarus and Ukraine to consider the development and implementation of a system-wide programme for the tenth anniversary in 1996 of the Chernobyl disaster;

25. *Requests* the Secretary-General to report to the Committee on Information at its sixteenth session and to the General Assembly at its forty-ninth session on the activities of the Department of Public Information and on the implementation of the recommendations contained in the present resolution;

26. *Decides* that the next session of the Committee on Information should last twelve working days and invites the Bureau of the Committee to explore ways and means of making optimum use of the Committee's time;

27. *Requests* the Committee on Information to report to the General Assembly at its forty-ninth session;

28. *Decides* to include in the provisional agenda of its forty-ninth session the item entitled "Questions relating to information".

General Assembly resolution 48/44 B

10 December 1993   Meeting 75   Adopted without vote

Approved by Fourth Committee (A/48/649) without vote, 15 November (meeting 18); draft by Committee on Information (A/48/21); agenda item 88.
Financial implications. S-G, A/C.4/48/L.15.
Meeting numbers. GA 48th session: 4th Committee 8-14, 17, 18; plenary 75.

REFERENCES

[1]A/48/21. [2]YUN 1992, p. 127, GA res. 47/73 B, 14 Dec. 1992. [3]A/AC.198/1993/2 & Add.1. [4]A/AC.198/1993/3. [5]A/AC.198/1993/4. [6]A/AC.198/1993/5. [7]A/AC.198/1993/6. [8]A/AC.198/1993/7. [9]A/AC.198/1993/9. [10]A/AC.198/1993/8. [11]YUN 1991, p. 84, GA res. 46/73 B, 11 Dec. 1991. [12]27 C/108. [13]CII/MD/5. [14]E/1993/58. [15]YUN 1991, p. 82. [16]A/48/407. [17]YUN 1991, p. 402, GA res. 46/151, annex, sect. II, 18 Dec. 1991. [18]YUN 1992, p. 403, GA res. 47/64 C, 11 Dec. 1992. [19]Ibid., p. 126. [20]YUN 1992, p. 126, GA res. 47/219, sect. XVIII, 23 Dec. 1992. [21]A/C.5/47/89. [22]A/47/7/Add.16. [23]ACC/1993/20.

Radiation effects

The United Nations Scientific Committee on the Effects of Atomic Radiation held its forty-second session at Vienna (17-28 May 1993). In September, the Committee submitted to the General Assembly its eleventh comprehensive report on the sources and effects of ionizing radiation for the period 1989-1993,[1] later issued with scientific annexes as a United Nations publication.[2]

The report focused on natural, medical, occupational and man-made radiation exposures, including those from nuclear explosions and major accidents and from the production of nuclear weapons and nuclear power; radiobiological and epidemiological studies; deterministic effects of radiation on the developing human brain and in children; radiation-induced cancer; hereditary effects of radiation; and perception of radiation risks.

The report presented collective doses of radiation from natural and man-made sources. The Committee concluded that improved procedures had generally decreased radiation exposures. Its estimates indicated that, contrary to the general belief, radiation was a weak carcinogen, accounting for only some 4 per cent of deaths caused by cancer, and that most of that radiation came from natural sources.

GENERAL ASSEMBLY ACTION

On 10 December, the General Assembly, on the recommendation of the Fourth Committee, adopted **resolution 48/38** without vote.

Effects of atomic radiation

The General Assembly,

Recalling its resolution 913(X) of 3 December 1955, in which it established the United Nations Scientific Committee on the Effects of Atomic Radiation, and its subsequent resolutions on the subject, including resolution 47/66 of 14 December 1992, in which, *inter alia,* it requested the Scientific Committee to continue its work,

Taking note with appreciation of the report of the United Nations Scientific Committee on the Effects of Atomic Radiation,

Reaffirming the desirability of the Scientific Committee continuing its work,

Concerned about the potentially harmful effects on present and future generations resulting from the levels of radiation to which man is exposed,

Conscious of the continued need to examine and compile information about atomic and ionizing radiation and to analyse its effects on man and the environment,

1. *Commends* the United Nations Scientific Committee on the Effects of Atomic Radiation for the valuable contribution it has been making in the course of the past thirty-eight years, since its inception, to wider knowledge and understanding of the levels, effects and risks of atomic radiation and for fulfilling its original mandate with scientific authority and independence of judgement;

2. *Notes with satisfaction* the completion in 1993 of the eleventh comprehensive report of the Scientific Committee entitled *Sources and Effects of Ionizing Radiation,* thereby providing to the scientific and world community its latest evaluations of the sources and effects of ionizing radiation;

3. *Requests* the Scientific Committee to continue its work, including its important activities to increase knowledge of the levels, effects and risks of ionizing radiation from all sources;

4. *Endorses* the intentions and plans of the Scientific Committee for its future activities of scientific review and assessment on behalf of the General Assembly;

5. *Also requests* the Scientific Committee to continue at its next session the review of the important problems in the field of radiation and to report thereon to the General Assembly at its forty-ninth session;

6. *Requests* the United Nations Environment Programme to continue providing support for the effective conduct of the work of the Scientific Committee and for the dissemination of its findings to the General Assembly, the scientific community and the public;

7. *Expresses its appreciation* for the assistance rendered to the Scientific Committee by Member States, the specialized agencies, the International Atomic Energy Agency and non-governmental organizations, and invites them to increase their cooperation in this field;

8. *Invites* Member States, the organizations of the United Nations system and non-governmental organizations concerned to provide further relevant data about doses, effects and risks from various sources of radiation, which would greatly help in the preparation of future reports of the Scientific Committee to the General Assembly.

General Assembly resolution 48/38

10 December 1993   Meeting 75   Adopted without vote

Approved by Fourth Committee (A/48/644) without vote, 20 October (meeting 7); 35-nation draft (A/C.4/48/L.2); agenda item 83.

Sponsors: Argentina, Australia, Austria, Azerbaijan, Belarus, Belgium, Canada, China, Costa Rica, Czech Republic, Denmark, France, Germany, Greece, India, Indonesia, Ireland, Italy, Japan, Lithuania, Luxembourg, Netherlands, New Zealand, Pakistan, Poland, Portugal, Republic of Korea, Russian Federation, Slovakia, Spain, Sweden, Ukraine, United Kingdom, United States, Uruguay.

Meeting numbers. GA 48th session: 4th Committee 5-7; plenary 75.

REFERENCES

[1]A/48/46. [2]*Sources and Effects of Ionizing Radiation*, Sales No. E.94.IX.2.

Antarctica

Pursuant to a 1992 General Assembly resolution,[1] the Secretary-General submitted in October 1993 a report[2] evaluating the response to the Assembly's call on the 1959 Antarctic Treaty Consultative Parties to deposit with him information covering all aspects of Antarctica.

On 19 August 1993, Italy, on behalf of the States parties to the Treaty (*Argentina, Australia,* Austria, *Belgium, Brazil,* Bulgaria, Canada, *Chile, China,* Colombia, Cuba, Czech Republic, Democratic People's Republic of Korea, Denmark, *Ecuador, Finland, France, Germany,* Greece, Hungary, *India, Italy, Japan, Netherlands, New Zealand, Norway,* Papua New Guinea, *Peru, Poland, Republic of Korea,* Romania, *Russian Federation,* Slovakia, *South Africa, Spain, Sweden,* Switzerland, Ukraine, *United Kingdom, United States, Uruguay* (italic indicates consultative status)), transmitted to the Secretary-General the final report of the Seventeenth Antarctic Treaty Consultative Meeting (Venice, 11-20 November 1992), containing detailed information about different aspects of Antarctica.

The Meeting reviewed reports from a number of international bodies—such as the Commission for the Conservation of Antarctic Marine Living Resources, the Scientific Committee on Antarctic Research (SCAR), the Council of the Managers of National Antarctic Programmes, the World Meteorological Organization, the International Hydrographic Organization and the Antarctic and Southern Ocean Coalition—and from the depository Government of the Convention for the Conservation of Antarctic Seals. It emphasized the importance of promoting inspections under the Antarctic Treaty as a means of monitoring activities in Antarctica and exchanging information. It adopted recommendations concerning proposed management plans for some specially protected areas and examined environmental monitoring issues, including the report of the First Meeting of Experts on Environmental Monitoring in Antarctica (Buenos Aires, Argentina, 1-4 June 1992).

The Meeting noted that Spain had ratified the Treaty's Protocol on Environmental Protection and that other parties were expected to do so, and considered the establishment of the Committee for Environmental Protection foreseen in the Protocol, following its entry into force. Consensus was reached that a secretariat should be set up to assist both the Meeting and the Committee in performing their functions. The Meeting also analysed recommendations regarding tourism and non-governmental activities and pertinent regulations contained in the Protocol and its annexes.

The Meeting recommended that Governments adopt emission standards for the combustion of fossil fuels and incineration of waste to contain contamination of the Antarctic environment, and that they seek advice from SCAR on the types of long-term programmes necessary to verify that tourism, scientific research and other human activities did not have significant adverse effects on birds, seals and plants. In addition, the Meeting acknowledged continuing ozone depletion and a rise in ultraviolet radiation that could have adverse effects on the Antarctic marine ecosystem, and agreed that that information should be made known to the parties to the 1987 Montreal Protocol on Substances that Deplete the Ozone Layer.[3]

Other matters discussed included Antarctic meteorology and telecommunications, marine hydrometeorological services to navigation in the Southern Ocean, cooperation in hydrographic surveying and charting of Antarctic water, air safety in Antarctica, international scientific and logistic cooperation and questions related to the exercise of jurisdiction in Antarctica.

Concluding his report, the Secretary-General noted continuing progress in international cooperation on Antarctica and a trend to move the Antarctic Treaty system towards increased environment-related action. International cooperation in scientific research and environmental priorities given by that system, he said, served as a guarantee for the preservation of the continent as a zone of peace and cooperation.

Antarctica and the environment

In October 1993,[4] in response to a 1992 General Assembly resolution,[1] the Secretary-General reported on the state of the environment in Antarctica. The report, which took into account information from Member States, United Nations bodies and intergovernmental and non-governmental organizations, considered Antarctica's influence on the global environmental system and questions relating to scientific research and protection of the Antarctic environment.

The report indicated that the most important among global change effects in the polar regions were man-induced ozone depletion and the "greenhouse effect", which might result in sea-ice and ice-sheet melting and a consequent global sealevel rise. It further noted a programme of global change research in the Antarctic, developed by SCAR, and summarized the objectives, current status and future plans of its six core projects, dealing with the continent's sea-ice zone interactions and feedbacks within the global geosphere-biosphere system; global palaeo-environmental records from the Antarctic ice sheet and marine and land sediments; mass balance of the ice sheet and sealevel; Antarctica's stratospheric ozone, tropospheric chemistry and the effect of ultraviolet radiation on the biosphere; the role of the Antarctic in biogeochemical cycles and exchanges, its atmosphere and ocean; and environmental monitoring and detection of global change in Antarctica.

In conclusion, the Secretary-General said interdependence between human activities and the state of the environment increased the importance of effective actions aimed at establishing harmonious relations between nature and man, and, in that context, the significance of scientific research of the Antarctic ecosystems, given the continent's paramount value in the global environment.

GENERAL ASSEMBLY ACTION

On 16 December, the General Assembly, on the recommendation of the First (Disarmament and International Security) Committee, adopted **resolution 48/80** by roll-call vote.

Question of Antarctica

The General Assembly,

Having considered the item entitled "Question of Antarctica",

Recalling its resolutions 38/77 of 15 December 1983, 39/152 of 17 December 1984, 40/156 A and B of 16 December 1985, 41/88 A and B of 4 December 1986, 42/46 A and B of 30 November 1987, 43/83 A and B of 7 December 1988, 44/124 A and B of 15 December 1989, 45/78 A and B of 12 December 1990, 46/41 A and B of 6 December 1991 and 47/57 of 9 December 1992,

Recalling also the relevant paragraphs of the final documents adopted by the second meeting of States of the Zone of Peace and Cooperation of the South Atlantic, held at Abuja in June 1990, the Twentieth Islamic Conference of Foreign Ministers, held at Istanbul in August 1991, the meeting of the Commonwealth Heads of Government, held at Harare in October 1991, and the Tenth Conference of Heads of State or Government of Non-Aligned Countries, held at Jakarta in September 1992,

Taking into account the debates on this item held since its thirty-eighth session,

Reaffirming the principle that the international community is entitled to information covering all aspects of Antarctica and that the United Nations should be made the repository for all such information in accordance with General Assembly resolutions 41/88 A, 42/46 B, 43/83 A, 44/124 B, 45/78 A, 46/41 A and 47/57,

Welcoming the decision of the Antarctic Treaty Consultative Parties to submit to the Secretary-General the final report of the Seventeenth Antarctic Treaty Consultative Meeting, which took place at Venice, Italy, from 11 to 20 November 1992,

Conscious of the particular significance of Antarctica to the international community in terms, *inter alia*, of international peace and security, environment, its effects on global climate conditions, economy and scientific research,

Conscious also of the interrelationship between Antarctica and the physical, chemical and biological processes that regulate the total Earth system,

Welcoming the increasing recognition of the significant impact that Antarctica exerts on the global environment and ecosystems,

Welcoming also the recognition by the United Nations Conference on Environment and Development of the value of Antarctica as an area for the conduct of scientific research, in particular research essential to understanding the global environment,

Welcoming further the increasing support, including by some Antarctic Treaty Consultative Parties, for the establishment of Antarctica as a nature reserve or world park to ensure the protection and conservation of its environment and its dependent and associated ecosystems for the benefit of all mankind,

Welcoming the ongoing trend in acknowledging the need for internationally coordinated scientific research stations in Antarctica in order to minimize unnecessary duplication and logistical support facilities,

Welcoming also the increasing awareness of an interest in Antarctica shown by the international community, and convinced of the advantages to the whole of mankind of a better knowledge of Antarctica,

Reaffirming that the management and use of Antarctica should be conducted in accordance with the purposes and principles of the Charter of the United Nations and in the interest of maintaining international peace and security and of promoting international cooperation for the benefit of mankind as a whole,

Convinced of the need for concerted international cooperation in order to protect and safeguard Antarctica and its dependent ecosystems from external environmental disturbances for future generations,

1. *Takes note* of the report of the Secretary-General on the report of the Seventeenth Antarctic Treaty Consultative Meeting;

2. *Welcomes* the report of the Secretary-General on the state of the environment in Antarctica, and requests the Secretary-General to explore the possibilities of publishing, as official documents of the United Nations, extracts of data received from the various organizations in the preparation of future annual reports, within existing resources;

3. *Reiterates*—while noting the cooperation of some United Nations specialized agencies and programmes at the Seventeenth Antarctic Treaty Consultative Meeting—the need for the Secretary-General or his representative to be invited to the meetings of the Antarctic Treaty Consultative Parties;

4. *Encourages*—while welcoming the decision of the Antarctic Treaty Consultative Parties to provide information regarding the Seventeenth Antarctic Treaty Consultative Meeting—the Parties to provide to the Secretary-General, on a continuing basis, more information and documents covering all aspects of Antarctica, and requests the Secretary-General to submit a report on his evaluations thereof to the General Assembly at its forty-ninth session;

5. *Welcomes* the commitment made by the Antarctic Treaty Consultative Parties under chapter 17 of Agenda 21, adopted by the United Nations Conference on Environment and Development, as provided for in article III of the Antarctic Treaty, to continue:

(*a*) To ensure that data and information resulting from scientific research activities conducted in Antarctica are freely available to the international community;

(*b*) To enhance access of the international scientific community and specialized agencies of the United Nations to such data and information, including the encouragement of periodic seminars and symposia;

6. *Urges* the Antarctic Treaty Consultative Parties to build on the agreements achieved at the United Nations Conference on Environment and Development, particularly as noted in paragraph 5 above, and in this connection actively to consider the possibility of organizing an annual seminar/symposium covering issues relating to the environment, commencing in 1994, with international participation as wide as possible, including that of international organizations such as the United Nations;

7. *Also urges* the Antarctic Treaty Consultative Parties to establish monitoring and implementation mechanisms to ensure compliance with the provisions of the 1991 Madrid Protocol on Environmental Protection;

8. *Reiterates its call*, in welcoming the ban on prospecting and mining in and around Antarctica for the next fifty years by Antarctic Treaty Consultative Parties in accordance with the Madrid Protocol, for the ban to be made permanent;

9. *Also reiterates its call* that any move at drawing up an international convention to establish a nature reserve or world park in Antarctica and its dependent and associated ecosystems must be negotiated with the full participation of the international community;

10. *Reaffirms*, while welcoming the concrete steps taken by the Secretariat through the publication on Antarctica by the Department of Public Information, the need to promote further public awareness of the importance of Antarctica to the ecosystem, and in this regard requests the Secretary-General to continue to provide relevant materials on Antarctica through the Department of Public Information within existing resources;

11. *Encourages* the Antarctic Treaty Consultative Parties to increase the level of cooperation and collaboration with a view to reducing the number of scientific stations in Antarctica and to handle tourism effectively through transparent environmental impact assessment studies;

12. *Urges* the international community to ensure that all activities in Antarctica are carried out exclusively for the purpose of peaceful scientific investigation and that all such activities will ensure the maintenance of international peace and security and the protection of the Antarctic environment and are for the benefit of all mankind;

13. *Urges* all States Members of the United Nations to cooperate with the Secretary-General on matters pertaining to Antarctica;

14. *Decides* to include in the provisional agenda of its forty-ninth session the item entitled "Question of Antarctica".

General Assembly resolution 48/80

16 December 1993   Meeting 81   96-0-7 (roll-call vote)

Approved by First Committee (A/48/681) by roll-call vote (71-0-6), 24 November (meeting 33); 36-nation draft (A/C.1/48/L.57); agenda item 76.

Sponsors: Angola, Antigua and Barbuda, Bangladesh, Belize, Benin, Bhutan, Central African Republic, Chad, Ghana, Guinea, Guinea-Bissau, Honduras, Indonesia, Iran, Kenya, Lesotho, Libyan Arab Jamahiriya, Malaysia, Mauritania, Mauritius, Namibia, Nepal, Nigeria, Oman, Philippines, Rwanda, Senegal, Sierra Leone, Sri Lanka, Sudan, Swaziland, Uganda, United Republic of Tanzania, Yemen, Zambia, Zimbabwe.

Meeting numbers. GA 48th session: 1st Committee 32, 33; plenary 81.

Roll-call vote in Assembly as follows:

In favour: Afghanistan, Algeria, Angola, Antigua and Barbuda, Azerbaijan, Bahamas, Bahrain, Bangladesh, Barbados, Belize, Benin, Bhutan, Bolivia, Botswana, Brunei Darussalam, Burkina Faso, Burundi, Cameroon, Cape Verde, Central African Republic, Chad, Comoros, Congo, Costa Rica, Cyprus, Djibouti, Dominica, Egypt, Ethiopia, Fiji, Gambia, Ghana, Grenada, Guinea, Guinea-Bissau, Guyana, Haiti, Honduras, Indonesia, Iran, Iraq, Jamaica, Jordan, Kenya, Kuwait, Lao People's Democratic Republic, Lebanon, Lesotho, Libyan Arab Jamahiriya, Madagascar, Malawi, Malaysia, Maldives, Mali, Mauritania, Mauritius, Mexico, Mongolia, Morocco, Mozambique, Myanmar, Namibia, Nepal, Nicaragua, Niger, Nigeria, Oman, Pakistan, Panama, Philippines, Qatar, Rwanda, Saint Lucia, Saint Vincent and the Grenadines, Saudi Arabia, Senegal, Seychelles, Sierra Leone, Singapore, Sri Lanka, Sudan, Suriname, Swaziland, Syrian Arab Republic, Thailand, the former Yugoslav Republic of Macedonia, Togo, Trinidad and Tobago, Tunisia, Uganda, United Arab Emirates, United Republic of Tanzania, Viet Nam, Yemen, Zambia, Zimbabwe.

Against: None.

Abstaining: Gabon, Ireland, Liechtenstein, Malta, Portugal, Turkey, Venezuela.

During the vote in the Assembly, the following 66 States announced that they were not participating: Andorra, Argentina, Armenia, Australia, Austria, Belarus, Belgium, Brazil, Bulgaria, Cambodia, Canada, Chile, China, Colombia, Côte d'Ivoire, Croatia, Cuba, Czech Republic, Democratic People's Republic of Korea, Denmark, Dominican Republic, Ecuador, Estonia, Finland, France, Georgia, Germany, Greece, Guatemala, Hungary, Iceland, India, Israel, Italy, Japan, Kazakhstan, Kyrgyzstan, Latvia, Lithuania, Luxembourg, Marshall Islands, Micronesia, Monaco, Netherlands, New Zealand, Norway, Papua New Guinea, Paraguay, Peru, Poland, Republic of Korea, Republic of Moldova, Romania, Russian Federation, Samoa, Slovakia, Slovenia, Solo-

mon Islands, Spain, Sweden, Tajikistan, Turkmenistan, Ukraine, United Kingdom, United
States, Uruguay.

In the Committee, 48 States made a similar announcement.

REFERENCES
[1]YUN 1992, p. 131, GA res. 47/57, 9 Dec. 1992. [2]A/48/482.
[3]YUN 1987, p. 686. [4]A/48/449.

Institutional questions

Admission to UN membership

During 1993, six States—Andorra, the Czech
Republic, Eritrea, Monaco, the Slovak Republic
and the former Yugoslav Republic of
Macedonia—were admitted to the United Nations, bringing the total membership of the Organization to 184.

The Security Council recommended the Czech
Republic[1] and the Slovak Republic[2] for mem-
bership on 8 January. On 19 January, the General
Assembly admitted them to the United Nations.

Acting on the application of the Czech Republic,[3] the Council adopted **resolution 801(1993)**
without vote.

The Security Council,
Having examined the application of the Czech Repub-
lic for admission to the United Nations,
Recommends to the General Assembly that the Czech
Republic be admitted to membership in the United
Nations.

Security Council resolution 801(1993)
8 January 1993   Meeting 3158   Adopted without vote
Draft by Committee on the Admission of New Members (S/25067).

The Assembly adopted **resolution 47/221** by
acclamation.

Admission of the Czech Republic to membership
in the United Nations
The General Assembly,
Having received the recommendation of the Security
Council of 8 January 1993 that the Czech Republic
should be admitted to membership in the United
Nations,
Having considered the application for membership of the
Czech Republic,
Decides to admit the Czech Republic to membership
in the United Nations.

General Assembly resolution 47/221
19 January 1993   Meeting 95   Adopted by acclamation

97-nation draft (A/47/L.52 & Add.1); agenda item 19.
Sponsors: Afghanistan, Albania, Algeria, Argentina, Armenia, Australia, Austria, Azerbaijan, Bahamas, Belarus, Belgium, Belize, Benin, Bhutan, Bosnia and Herzegovina, Brazil, Bulgaria, Canada, Cape Verde, Chile, China,
Colombia, Congo, Costa Rica, Croatia, Cyprus, Democratic People's
Republic of Korea, Denmark, Djibouti, Ecuador, Egypt, El Salvador, Estonia, Fiji, Finland, France, Germany, Greece, Guatemala, Hungary, Iceland,

India, Indonesia, Iran, Ireland, Israel, Italy, Japan, Jordan, Kazakhstan,
Kuwait, Kyrgyzstan, Latvia, Lebanon, Lesotho, Lithuania, Luxembourg,
Madagascar, Maldives, Malta, Marshall Islands, Mexico, Micronesia, Mongolia, Morocco, Mozambique, Nepal, Netherlands, New Zealand, Nicaragua, Norway, Oman, Pakistan, Panama, Paraguay, Philippines, Poland, Portugal, Republic of Korea, Republic of Moldova, Romania, Russian
Federation, Samoa, Singapore, Slovenia, Spain, Sri Lanka, Suriname,
Sweden, Tunisia, Turkey, Ukraine, United Kingdom, United Republic of Tanzania, Vanuatu, Venezuela, Yemen.

The Council considered the application of the
Slovak Republic[4] and adopted **resolution
800(1993)** without vote.

The Security Council,
Having examined the application of the Slovak Repub-
lic for admission to the United Nations,
Recommends to the General Assembly that the Slovak
Republic be admitted to membership in the United
Nations.

Security Council resolution 800(1993)
8 January 1993   Meeting 3157   Adopted without vote
Draft by Committee on the Admission of New Members (S/25066).

The Assembly adopted **resolution 47/222** by
acclamation.

Admission of the Slovak Republic to membership
in the United Nations
The General Assembly,
Having received the recommendation of the Security
Council of 8 January 1993 that the Slovak Republic
should be admitted to membership in the United
Nations,
Having considered the application for membership of the
Slovak Republic,
Decides to admit the Slovak Republic to membership
in the United Nations.

General Assembly resolution 47/222
19 January 1993   Meeting 95   Adopted by acclamation

98-nation draft (A/47/L.53 & Add.1); agenda item 19.
Sponsors: Afghanistan, Albania, Algeria, Argentina, Armenia, Australia, Aus-
tria, Azerbaijan, Bahamas, Belarus, Belgium, Belize, Benin, Bhutan, Bos-
nia and Herzegovina, Brazil, Bulgaria, Canada, Cape Verde, Chile, China,
Colombia, Congo, Costa Rica, Croatia, Cyprus, Czech Republic,
Democratic People's Republic of Korea, Denmark, Djibouti, Ecuador, Egypt,
El Salvador, Estonia, Fiji, Finland, France, Germany, Greece, Guatemala,
Hungary, Iceland, India, Indonesia, Iran, Ireland, Israel, Italy, Japan, Jor-
dan, Kazakhstan, Kuwait, Kyrgyzstan, Latvia, Lebanon, Lesotho, Lithua-
nia, Luxembourg, Madagascar, Maldives, Malta, Marshall Islands, Mex-
ico, Micronesia, Mongolia, Morocco, Mozambique, Nepal, Netherlands,
New Zealand, Nicaragua, Norway, Oman, Pakistan, Panama, Paraguay,
Philippines, Poland, Portugal, Republic of Korea, Republic of Moldova,
Romania, Russian Federation, Samoa, Singapore, Slovenia, Spain, Sri
Lanka, Suriname, Sweden, Tunisia, Turkey, Ukraine, United Kingdom, United
Republic of Tanzania, Vanuatu, Venezuela, Yemen.

On 26 May, the Security Council recommended
Eritrea[5] and Monaco.[6] Their membership was
granted by the Assembly on 28 May.

Upon consideration of Eritrea's application,[7]
the Council adopted **resolution 828(1993)** without vote.

The Security Council,
Having examined the application of Eritrea for admission to the United Nations,
Recommends to the General Assembly that Eritrea be
admitted to membership in the United Nations.

Security Council resolution 828(1993)

26 May 1993   Meeting 3218   Adopted without vote

Draft by Committee on the Admission of New Members (S/25841).

The Assembly adopted **resolution 47/230** by acclamation.

Admission of Eritrea to membership in the United Nations

The General Assembly,

Having received the recommendation of the Security Council of 26 May 1993 that Eritrea should be admitted to membership in the United Nations,

Having considered the application for membership of Eritrea,

Decides to admit Eritrea to membership in the United Nations.

General Assembly resolution 47/230

28 May 1993   Meeting 104   Adopted by acclamation

92-nation draft (A/47/L.61 & Add.1); agenda item 19.

Sponsors: Algeria, Argentina, Australia, Austria, Bahamas, Bahrain, Belgium, Bhutan, Brazil, Canada, Cape Verde, Chile, China, Colombia, Costa Rica, Cyprus, Czech Republic, Democratic People's Republic of Korea, Denmark, Djibouti, Egypt, El Salvador, Estonia, Finland, France, Gabon, Germany, Greece, Guatemala, Guinea, India, Indonesia, Iran, Ireland, Israel, Italy, Japan, Jordan, Kenya, Kuwait, Latvia, Lebanon, Lesotho, Libyan Arab Jamahiriya, Liechtenstein, Lithuania, Luxembourg, Madagascar, Malawi, Malaysia, Maldives, Mali, Malta, Mauritius, Mexico, Morocco, Myanmar, Namibia, Netherlands, New Zealand, Nicaragua, Nigeria, Norway, Oman, Panama, Philippines, Poland, Portugal, Qatar, Republic of Korea, Romania, Russian Federation, Saudi Arabia, Senegal, Singapore, Slovenia, Spain, Sudan, Suriname, Sweden, Syrian Arab Republic, Thailand, Tunisia, Turkey, Uganda, United Arab Emirates, United Kingdom, United Republic of Tanzania, United States, Uruguay, Venezuela, Yemen.

The Council considered Monaco's application[8] and adopted **resolution 829(1993)** without vote.

The Security Council,

Having examined the application of the Principality of Monaco for admission to the United Nations,

Recommends to the General Assembly that the Principality of Monaco be admitted to membership in the United Nations.

Security Council resolution 829(1993)

26 May 1993   Meeting 3219   Adopted without vote

Draft by Committee on the Admission of New Members (S/25842).

The Assembly adopted **resolution 47/231** by acclamation.

Admission of the Principality of Monaco to membership in the United Nations

The General Assembly,

Having received the recommendation of the Security Council of 26 May 1993 that the Principality of Monaco should be admitted to membership in the United Nations,

Having considered the application for membership of the Principality of Monaco,

Decides to admit the Principality of Monaco to membership in the United Nations.

General Assembly resolution 47/231

28 May 1993   Meeting 104   Adopted by acclamation

74-nation draft (A/47/L.62 & Add.1); agenda item 19.

Sponsors: Argentina, Australia, Austria, Bahamas, Bahrain, Belgium, Bhutan, Brazil, Bulgaria, Canada, China, Colombia, Costa Rica, Cyprus, Czech

Republic, Denmark, Djibouti, El Salvador, Estonia, Finland, France, Gabon, Germany, Greece, Guatemala, Hungary, India, Indonesia, Ireland, Israel, Italy, Japan, Jordan, Kuwait, Latvia, Lebanon, Liechtenstein, Lithuania, Luxembourg, Madagascar, Maldives, Mali, Malta, Mexico, Morocco, Myanmar, Namibia, Netherlands, New Zealand, Nicaragua, Norway, Oman, Panama, Philippines, Poland, Portugal, Qatar, Romania, Russian Federation, Senegal, Singapore, Slovenia, Spain, Suriname, Sweden, Thailand, Turkey, United Arab Emirates, United Kingdom, United Republic of Tanzania, United States, Uruguay, Venezuela, Yemen.

On 8 July,[9] the Council recommended the granting of United Nations membership to Andorra. The Assembly endorsed the recommendation on 28 July.

Acting on Andorra's application,[10] the Council adopted **resolution 848(1993)** without vote.

The Security Council,

Having examined the application of the Principality of Andorra for admission to the United Nations,

Recommends to the General Assembly that the Principality of Andorra be admitted to membership in the United Nations.

Security Council resolution 848(1993)

8 July 1993   Meeting 3251   Adopted without vote

Draft by Committee on the Admission of New Members (S/26051).

The Assembly adopted **resolution 47/232** by acclamation.

Admission of the Principality of Andorra to membership in the United Nations

The General Assembly,

Having received the recommendation of the Security Council of 8 July 1993 that the Principality of Andorra should be admitted to membership in the United Nations,

Having considered the application for membership of the Principality of Andorra,

Decides to admit the Principality of Andorra to membership in the United Nations.

General Assembly resolution 47/232

28 July 1993   Meeting 108   Adopted by acclamation

39-nation draft (A/47/L.63 & Add.1); agenda item 19.

Sponsors: Albania, Australia, Austria, Belgium, Bulgaria, China, Croatia, Cyprus, Djibouti, Egypt, El Salvador, Finland, France, Greece, Guatemala, Iceland, Ireland, Israel, Liechtenstein, Lithuania, Luxembourg, Malta, Mexico, Morocco, Nicaragua, Norway, Panama, Philippines, Poland, Portugal, Romania, Senegal, Singapore, Slovenia, Spain, Sweden, Thailand, Turkey, United Kingdom.

The former Yugoslav Republic of Macedonia

In January 1993, the Secretary-General circulated to the General Assembly and the Security Council an application of the former Yugoslav Republic of Macedonia[11] for admission to the United Nations. The application was made in July 1992 and was followed by informal consultations of the Council President.

In March 1993,[12] the Republic expressed willingness to continue cooperating with the Co-Chairmen of the Steering Committee of the International Conference on the Former Yugoslavia to settle the difference that had arisen over the country's name and to promote confidence-building measures with Greece, on the understanding that that in no way affected the process of the Republic's admission to United Nations membership. It pointed out, however, that it would not accept "the former Yugoslav Republic of Macedonia" as the name of the country.

In April,[13] the Republic informed the Council that it would submit to the Co-Chairmen of the Steering Committee proposals for promotion of confidence-building measures with Greece. Greece, also in April,[14] agreed to admitting the new State to the Organization under a provisional name, but objected to using the flag bearing the Sun of Vergina as the symbol of the Republic.

SECURITY COUNCIL ACTION (April)

On 7 April, acting on the Republic's application, the Security Council adopted **resolution 817(1993)** without vote.

The Security Council,

Having examined the application for admission to the United Nations contained in document A/47/876-S/25147,

Noting that the applicant fulfils the criteria for membership in the United Nations laid down in Article 4 of the Charter,

Noting, however, that a difference has arisen over the name of the State, which needs to be resolved in the interest of the maintenance of peaceful and good-neighbourly relations in the region,

Welcoming the readiness of the Co-Chairmen of the Steering Committee of the International Conference on the Former Yugoslavia, at the request of the Secretary-General, to use their good offices to settle the above-mentioned difference and to promote confidence-building measures among the parties,

Taking note of the contents of the letters received from the parties,

1. *Urges* the parties to continue to cooperate with the Co-Chairmen of the Steering Committee of the International Conference on the Former Yugoslavia in order to arrive at a speedy settlement of their difference;

2. *Recommends* to the General Assembly that the State whose application is contained in document A/47/876-S/25147 be admitted to membership in the United Nations, this State being provisionally referred to for all purposes within the United Nations as "the former Yugoslav Republic of Macedonia" pending settlement of the difference that has arisen over the name of the State;

3. *Requests* the Secretary-General to report to the Council on the outcome of the initiative taken by the Co-Chairmen of the Steering Committee of the International Conference on the Former Yugoslavia.

Security Council resolution 817(1993)

7 April 1993   Meeting 3196   Adopted without vote

Draft by Committee on the Admission of New Members (S/25544).

Following the adoption of the resolution, the Council President made a statement on behalf of the members:[15]

"The Security Council has just recommended that the State whose application is in document S/25147

be admitted to membership in the United Nations. It is with great pleasure that, on behalf of the members of the Council, I congratulate the State concerned on this historic occasion. The members of the Council look forward to its early admission to the United Nations.

"The Council welcomes the initiative taken by the Co-Chairmen of the Steering Committee of the International Conference on the Former Yugoslavia, at the request of the Secretary-General, in order to set up a mechanism to settle the difference which has arisen over the name of the State, and to promote confidence-building measures among the two parties. The Council attaches the highest importance to implementing as soon as possible the confidence-building measures referred to in the resolution which has just been adopted. The Council expresses the hope that the initiative of the Co-Chairmen will be pursued expeditiously, that both sides will fully cooperate with the Co-Chairmen, that both sides, and all others concerned, will avoid taking steps that would render a solution more difficult, and that both will accept and implement the outcome. A mutually acceptable solution to these matters would be a major contribution to the maintenance of peaceful and good-neighbourly relations in the region.

"The Council is clear that the reference in the resolution that has just been adopted to 'the former Yugoslav Republic' carries no implication whatsoever that the State concerned has any connection with the Federal Republic of Yugoslavia (Serbia and Montenegro). It merely reflects the historic fact that the State recommended for admission to the United Nations in the present resolution was in the past a republic of the former Socialist Federal Republic of Yugoslavia.''

GENERAL ASSEMBLY ACTION

On 8 April, having considered the Council's recommendation,[16] the General Assembly adopted **resolution 47/225** by acclamation.

Admission of the State whose application is contained in document A/47/876-S/25147 to membership in the United Nations

The General Assembly,

Having received the recommendation of the Security Council of 7 April 1993 that the State whose application is contained in document A/47/876-S/25147 should be admitted to membership in the United Nations,

Having considered the application for membership contained in document A/47/876-S/25147,

Decides to admit the State whose application is contained in document A/47/876-S/25147 to membership in the United Nations, this State being provisionally referred to for all purposes within the United Nations as "the former Yugoslav Republic of Macedonia" pending settlement of the difference that has arisen over the name of the State.

General Assembly resolution 47/225

8 April 1993   Meeting 98   Adopted by acclamation

65-nation draft (A/47/L.54 & Add.1); agenda item 19.

Sponsors: Argentina, Australia, Austria, Belgium, Bhutan, Bosnia and Herzegovina, Brazil, Bulgaria, Canada, China, Colombia, Croatia, Cyprus, Czech Republic, Denmark, Djibouti, Ecuador, Egypt, Finland, France, Germany, Greece, Guatemala, Hungary, Iceland, India, Iran, Ireland, Israel, Italy, Jordan, Kuwait, Latvia, Liechtenstein, Lithuania, Luxembourg, Malaysia,

Malta, Mexico, Morocco, Nepal, Netherlands, New Zealand, Nicaragua, Norway, Oman, Pakistan, Philippines, Poland, Portugal, Republic of Moldova, Romania, Russian Federation, Slovakia, Slovenia, Spain, Suriname, Sweden, Tunisia, Turkey, United Arab Emirates, United Kingdom, United States, Uruguay, Venezuela.

Report of the Secretary-General (May). Pursuant to the Council's 7 April resolution, the Secretary-General reported in May[17] that, following extensive consultations with the parties, the Co-Chairmen of the Steering Committee had submitted to them a draft Treaty Confirming the Existing Frontier and Establishing Measures for Confidence Building, Friendship and Neighbourly Cooperation. The proposed Treaty (which was annexed to the report) represented a fair balance of both parties' claims and aspirations and included special provisions to promote friendly relations and to constitute confidence-building measures, as well as provisions for friendship and neighbourly cooperation.

With regard to the name to be used by the former Yugoslav Republic of Macedonia, Greece stated that it should not include the word "Macedonia" but indicated that, if that term were to be included, the name "Slavomacedonia" could be envisaged. The other side preferred "The Republic of Macedonia" to be used for all purposes but was prepared to discuss the modalities of the use of a name for international purposes only. Taking into account those positions, the Co-Chairmen proposed the name "The Republic of Nova Makedonija" for all official purposes, both domestic and international.

Communications. On 27 May,[18] Greece, without objecting to the draft Treaty in general, said it had difficulties with the name "Nova Makedonija" and considered that further efforts should be deployed to resolve the issue, including possible direct talks under the Secretary-General's auspices.

On 29 May,[19] the former Yugoslav Republic of Macedonia proposed an amendment to article 8 of the draft Treaty (concerning human rights) and raised specific objections in connection with articles 5 (on the use of the name of the Republic of Nova Makedonija for all official purposes) and 7 (on the use of symbols, names, flags, monuments or emblems), which it considered to be drafted in a wide and inprecise manner. Another objection related to the necessity to stipulate Macedonian and Greek (apart from English) as the languages of the two parties that were to sign an international agreement. The Republic found it indispensable for negotiations to continue, including possible bilateral talks. It emphasized that its constitutional name, "The Republic of Macedonia", did not imply territorial aspirations and that therefore no other proposals were necessary.

On 7 June,[20] Albania objected to "Slavo-Macedonia" as a possible name of the former Yugoslav Republic of Macedonia, saying that it ignored the existence of the Albanian community in that country.

SECURITY COUNCIL ACTION (June)

On 18 June, the Security Council adopted **resolution 845(1993)** unanimously.

The Security Council,

Recalling its resolution 817(1993) of 7 April 1993, in which it urged Greece and the former Yugoslav Republic of Macedonia to continue to cooperate with the Co-Chairmen of the Steering Committee of the International Conference on the Former Yugoslavia in order to arrive at a speedy settlement of their difference,

Having considered the report of the Secretary-General submitted pursuant to resolution 817(1993), together with the statement of the Government of Greece and the letter of the President of the former Yugoslav Republic of Macedonia dated 27 and 29 May 1993, respectively,

1. *Expresses its appreciation* to the Co-Chairmen of the Steering Committee of the International Conference on the Former Yugoslavia for their efforts and commends to the parties as a sound basis for the settlement of their difference the proposals set forth in annex V to the report of the Secretary-General;

2. *Urges* the parties to continue their efforts under the auspices of the Secretary-General to arrive at a speedy settlement of the remaining issues between them;

3. *Requests* the Secretary-General to keep the Council informed on the progress of these further efforts, the objective of which is to resolve the difference between the two parties before the commencement of the forty-eighth session of the General Assembly, and to report to the Council on their outcome in good time, and decides to resume consideration of the matter in the light of the report.

Security Council resolution 845(1993)
18 June 1993   Meeting 3243   Adopted unanimously
Draft prepared in consultations among Council members (S/25968).

On 13 July,[21] the Secretary-General informed the Council that Cyrus Vance, the former Co-Chairman of the Steering Committee, had accepted the request to continue his good offices, beginning on 1 August, to help the parties reach agreement. The Council welcomed that information on 15 July.[22]

Report of the Secretary-General (September) and further developments. In response to the Council's June resolution, the Secretary-General reported in September[23] that both parties, at their meeting in New York on 23 August under Mr. Vance's auspices, agreed to commence direct discussions in Mr. Vance's presence in New York on 28 September. Pending the opening of the discussions, they reserved their positions as stated earlier.

In a statement following the 28 September meeting, Mr. Vance said the parties agreed to defer further direct talks until after the 10 October elections in Greece.

Following the elections and the installation of a new Government, Greece addressed a letter to the Secretary-General regarding the matter. In his reply of 8 November, the Secretary-General noted that a solution would require both parties to demonstrate the necessary political will, mutual respect and a spirit of compromise. He expressed readiness to assist the two countries in their efforts to reach a speedy settlement. Following the exchange of letters, Mr. Vance maintained contact with the parties with a view to determining steps which might lead to progress towards a settlement.

Yugoslavia and UN membership

In 1993, the Security Council again considered the question of membership of the Federal Republic of Yugoslavia (Serbia and Montenegro) in the United Nations, further to a 1992 General Assembly resolution[(24)] barring it from participating in the Assembly's work.

On 28 April, the Council adopted **resolution 821(1993)**.

The Security Council,

Reaffirming its resolution 713(1991) of 25 September 1991 and all subsequent relevant resolutions,

Considering that the State formerly known as the Socialist Federal Republic of Yugoslavia has ceased to exist,

Recalling resolution 757(1992) of 30 May 1992 which noted that "the claim by the Federal Republic of Yugoslavia (Serbia and Montenegro) to continue automatically the membership of the former Socialist Federal Republic of Yugoslavia in the United Nations has not been generally accepted",

Recalling also its resolution 777(1992) of 19 September 1992, in which it recommended to the General Assembly that it decide that the Federal Republic of Yugoslavia (Serbia and Montenegro) should apply for membership in the United Nations and that it shall not participate in the work of the General Assembly,

Recalling further that the General Assembly by resolution 47/1 of 22 September 1992, having received the recommendation of the Security Council of 19 September 1992, considered that the Federal Republic of Yugoslavia (Serbia and Montenegro) could not continue automatically the membership of the former Socialist Federal Republic of Yugoslavia in the United Nations, and therefore decided that the Federal Republic of Yugoslavia (Serbia and Montenegro) should apply for membership in the United Nations and that it shall not participate in the work of the General Assembly,

Recalling further that in its resolution 777(1992) the Council decided to consider the matter again before the end of the main part of the forty-seventh session of the General Assembly, and that in December 1992 the members of the Council agreed to keep the subject-matter of resolution 777(1992) under continuous review and to consider it again at a later date,

Reaffirms that the Federal Republic of Yugoslavia (Serbia and Montenegro) cannot continue automatically the membership of the former Socialist Federal Republic of Yugoslavia in the United Nations, and therefore recommends to the General Assembly that, further to the decisions taken in resolution 47/1, it decide that the Federal Republic of Yugoslavia (Serbia and Montenegro) shall not participate in the work of the Economic and Social Council;

Decides to consider the matter again before the end of the forty-seventh session of the General Assembly.

Security Council resolution 821(1993)

28 April 1993   Meeting 3204   13-0-2

4-nation draft (S/25675), orally revised.
Sponsors: France, Spain, United Kingdom, United States.

Vote in Council as follows:

In favour: Brazil, Cape Verde, Djibouti, France, Hungary, Japan, Morocco, New Zealand, Pakistan, Spain, United Kingdom, United States, Venezuela.
Against: None.
Abstaining: China, Russian Federation.

Explaining its abstention, China said that all the Republics of the former Yugoslavia should take their own seats in the United Nations and no Republic should be excluded lightly; in its opinion, the resolution was a transitory arrangement. The Russian Federation was against any further steps, in addition to the action taken in 1992, to keep Belgrade outside international organizations.

GENERAL ASSEMBLY ACTION

On 29 April, the Assembly adopted **resolution 47/229** by roll-call vote.

Recommendation of the Security Council of 28 April 1993

The General Assembly,

Recalling its resolution 47/1 of 22 September 1992,

Having received the recommendation made by the Security Council in its resolution 821(1993) of 28 April 1993 that, further to the decisions taken in resolution 47/1, the Federal Republic of Yugoslavia (Serbia and Montenegro) shall not participate in the work of the Economic and Social Council,

1. *Decides* that the Federal Republic of Yugoslavia (Serbia and Montenegro) shall not participate in the work of the Economic and Social Council;

2. *Takes note* of the intention of the Security Council to consider the matter again before the end of the forty-seventh session of the General Assembly.

General Assembly resolution 47/229

29 April 1993   Meeting 101   107-0-11 (roll-call vote)

49-nation draft (A/47/L.57 & Add.1); agenda item 8.
Sponsors: Afghanistan, Albania, Algeria, Australia, Austria, Bahrain, Bangladesh, Belgium, Bosnia and Herzegovina, Canada, Comoros, Croatia, Denmark, Djibouti, Egypt, Estonia, Finland, France, Germany, Greece, Iceland, Iran, Ireland, Italy, Kuwait, Latvia, Liechtenstein, Lithuania, Luxembourg, Malaysia, Malta, Morocco, Netherlands, Norway, Oman, Pakistan, Portugal, Qatar, Republic of Moldova, San Marino, Senegal, Slovenia, Spain, Sweden, Tunisia, Turkey, United Arab Emirates, United Kingdom, United States.

Roll-call vote in Assembly as follows:

In favour: Afghanistan, Albania, Algeria, Antigua and Barbuda, Argentina, Australia, Austria, Bahamas, Bahrain, Bangladesh, Barbados, Belarus, Belgium, Belize, Bhutan, Bolivia, Bosnia and Herzegovina, Botswana, Brazil, Brunei Darussalam, Bulgaria, Burundi, Canada, Cape Verde, Chile, Colombia, Costa Rica, Croatia, Cyprus, Czech Republic, Denmark, Djibouti, Ecuador, Egypt, Estonia, Fiji, Finland, France, Gabon, Germany, Greece, Guyana, Haiti, Honduras, Hungary, Iceland, Indonesia, Iran, Ireland, Israel, Italy, Jamaica, Japan, Jordan, Kuwait, Latvia, Lebanon, Libyan Arab Jamahiriya, Liechtenstein, Lithuania, Luxembourg, Malaysia, Maldives, Malta, Marshall Islands, Mauritius, Micronesia, Mongolia, Morocco, Nepal, Netherlands, New Zealand, Nicaragua, Norway, Oman, Pakistan, Panama, Paraguay, Peru, Philippines, Poland, Portugal, Qatar, Republic of Korea,

Republic of Moldova, Romania, Rwanda, Samoa, San Marino, Senegal, Singapore, Slovakia, Slovenia, Solomon Islands, Spain, Suriname, Swaziland, Sweden, Trinidad and Tobago, Tunisia, Turkey, Ukraine, United Arab Emirates, United Kingdom, United States, Uruguay, Venezuela.
Against: None.
Abstaining: Cameroon, China, India, Iraq, Kenya, Lesotho, Mexico, Myanmar, Russian Federation, Sri Lanka, Zimbabwe.

Introducing the draft on behalf of the sponsors, Denmark said it was necessitated by continued disregard of the Federal Republic of Yugoslavia (Serbia and Montenegro) for the resolve of the international community. It expressed the hope that the Assembly's decision would open the eyes of the authorities in Belgrade and thus obviate the need for further Security Council and Assembly action.

In a statement of 30 April,[25] Yugoslavia expressed deep regret at the adoption of the resolution, which it called an incredulous example of exerting pressure on Yugoslavia to stop the civil war in Bosnia and Herzegovina to which it was not a party. The decision to deny it the right to participate in the work of the Economic and Social Council would affect negatively cooperation with neighbouring countries and the region as a whole in providing humanitarian assistance, securing basic human rights, combating illicit drug trafficking, crime prevention and assistance to vulnerable groups.

On 17 September,[26] the Security Council President informed the President of the Assembly that the Council members agreed to keep the subject-matter of the 28 April resolution under continuous review and to consider it again at a later date.

Institutional machinery

Security Council

In 1993, the Security Council held 171 meetings and adopted 93 resolutions.

Agenda

The Security Council considered 42 agenda items during 1993. It continued the practice of adopting at each meeting the agenda for that meeting. (For list of agenda items, see APPENDIX IV.)

On 20 September,[27] the Secretary-General notified the General Assembly, in accordance with Article 12, paragraph 2, of the Charter of the United Nations, of 44 matters relative to the maintenance of international peace and security that the Council had discussed since his previous annual notification.[28] He listed 172 other matters not discussed during the period but of which the Council remained seized.

On 16 November,[29] the Secretary-General notified the Assembly of a matter with which the Council had ceased to deal (concerning the destruction of the diplomatic mission of Venezuela in Tripoli, Libyan Arab Jamahiriya, on 2 April

1992)[30] and of two matters subsumed under a new item, of which the Council remained seized.

By **decision 48/409 A** of 17 November, the Assembly took note of those matters.

On 10 December,[31] the Secretary-General notified the Assembly of the Council's decision[32] to remove 76 items from the list of matters of which it remained seized. The Assembly took note of those matters by **decision 48/409 B** of 21 December.

Documentation

In June,[33] July[34] and August,[35] the Council agreed on changes concerning its documentation. It decided, among other things, to adopt the draft annual report to the General Assembly at a public meeting and issue it for limited distribution; to publish Council documents and presidential statements in annual series, as of 1 January 1994; to include a chronological listing of presidential statements, with relevant agenda items, in annual reports starting with the report for 1992/93; to make tentative forecasts of the Council's programme of work for each month available to Member States for information; and to ensure the timely submission of the annual report for consideration by the Assembly during the main part of its regular session. The Council further agreed to keep under due consideration the question of establishing new ways to provide information to States not members of the Council.

Report for 1991/92

At a private meeting on 26 May 1993, the Security Council unanimously adopted its report covering the period from 16 June 1991 to 15 June 1992.[36] The General Assembly took note of the report by **decision 47/470** of 22 June 1993.

Report for 1992/93

On 19 October, the Council unanimously adopted its report covering the period from 16 June 1992 to 15 June 1993.[37] The General Assembly took note of it by **decision 48/407** of 28 October.

Membership

In 1993, the Secretary-General reported to the General Assembly on the question of equitable representation on and increase in the membership of the Security Council, in response to a 1992 Assembly request.[38] The report[39] contained comments received from 76 Member States as at 30 November 1993.

The item was first considered by the Assembly in 1979,[40] when it was introduced on the grounds that United Nations membership had grown to 152, compared to 113 in 1963, when the Council membership was increased from 11 to 15.[41]

On 3 December, the General Assembly adopted **resolution 48/26** by consensus.

Question of equitable representation on and increase in the membership of the Security Council

The General Assembly,

Recalling its resolution 47/62 of 11 December 1992,

Noting with appreciation the report of the Secretary-General which reflected the views of a number of Member States on the agenda item entitled "Question of equitable representation on and increase in the membership of the Security Council",

Recalling also the relevant provisions of the Charter of the United Nations, especially Article 23,

Recalling further that the Members confer on the Security Council primary responsibility for the maintenance of international peace and security and agree that in carrying out its duties under this responsibility the Security Council acts on their behalf,

Recognizing the need to review the membership of the Security Council and related matters in view of the substantial increase in the membership of the United Nations, especially of developing countries, as well as the changes in international relations,

Bearing in mind the need to continue to enhance the efficiency of the Security Council,

Reaffirming the principle of the sovereign equality of all Members of the United Nations,

Acting in accordance with the purposes and principles of the Charter,

Mindful of the importance of reaching general agreement,

1. *Decides* to establish an Open-ended Working Group to consider all aspects of the question of increase in the membership of the Security Council, and other matters related to the Security Council;

2. *Requests* the Open-ended Working Group to submit a report on the progress of its work to the General Assembly before the end of its forty-eighth session;

3. *Decides* to include in the provisional agenda of its forty-ninth session an item entitled "Question of equitable representation on and increase in the membership of the Security Council and related matters".

General Assembly resolution 48/26

3 December 1993   Meeting 69   Adopted by consensus

Draft by President (A/48/L.28); agenda item 33.
Financial implications. 5th Committee, A/48/710; S-G, A/C.5/48/38.
Meeting numbers. GA 48th session: 5th Committee 27; plenary 61, 62, 64, 69.

General Assembly

The General Assembly met in two sessions during 1993, to resume and conclude its forty-seventh (1992) regular session and to hold the main part of its forty-eighth session. The forty-seventh session resumed on 19 January, 11 February, 16 March, 8, 15, 20 and 29 April, 6, 10 and 28 May, 15 and 22 June, 28 July, 17 August and 14, 15 and 20 September.

The forty-eighth session opened on 21 September and continued until its suspension on 23 December.

Representatives' credentials

At its first meeting on 14 October 1993,[42] the Credentials Committee examined a memorandum from the Secretary-General indicating that, as at 13 October, credentials of representatives to the General Assembly's forty-eighth session had been submitted by 118 Member States. The Legal Counsel explained that the memorandum related solely to Member States which had submitted formal credentials. The Counsel further explained that, subsequent to the memorandum, credentials in due form had been received in respect of the representatives of China. Noting that, in addition to credentials signed by the head of State of Zaire, another communication had been received containing a list of purported representatives of Zaire but not signed by the head of State or issued in his name, the Counsel explained that only the credentials signed by the head of State were to be regarded as formally correct.

Austria stated that acceptance of Zaire's credentials in no way implied its acceptance of that country's Government, formed without the approval of the High Council of the Republic and therefore outside the transition process defined by the sovereign national conference. It said its position was analogous to that of the European Community. The United States associated itself with Austria's disclaimer.

On 15 December, at its second meeting,[43] the Committee examined a further memorandum from the Secretary-General, reporting that, since the first meeting, formal credentials had been received from 42 other Member States. In addition, information concerning the appointment of their representatives to the forty-eighth session had been communicated to the Secretary-General by 20 Member States, by means of a facsimile communication, letter or note verbale. The Committee Chairman proposed that the Committee accept the credentials of all those Member States, including those that had communicated by facsimile, letter or note verbale, on the understanding that the latter would submit formal credentials as soon as possible.

At each meeting, the Committee, acting without vote on an oral proposal by its Chairman, adopted a resolution by which it accepted the credentials received. The Committee also recommended to the Assembly two draft resolutions. On 29 October and 21 December, the Assembly, by **resolutions 48/13 A and B**, respectively, approved the first[42] and second[43] reports of the Credentials Committee.

Before resolution 48/13 A was adopted, Iran expressed reservations regarding the credentials of Israel and dissociated itself from the parts of the Committee's report referring to their approval.

The Libyan Arab Jamahiriya stated that its approval of the report did not mean recognition of Israel's credentials.

Organization of the 1993 session

On 24 September 1993, by **decision 48/401**, the General Assembly, on the recommendation of the General Committee as set forth in its first report,[44] adopted a number of provisions concerning the organization of the forty-eighth session.

The Committee's recommendations concerned rationalization of the Assembly's work; the closing date of the session; the schedule of meetings; the general debate; explanations of vote, right of reply, points of order and length of statements; meeting records; concluding statements; resolutions; documentation; questions related to the programme budget; observances and commemorative meetings; special conferences; and meetings of subsidiary organs.

Subsidiary organs

By **decision 48/403 A** of 24 September, on the recommendation of the General Committee,[44] the General Assembly authorized the following subsidiary organs to hold meetings during its 1993 session: Advisory Committee on the United Nations Educational and Training Programme for Southern Africa; Committee for Programme and Coordination; Committee of Trustees of the United Nations Trust Fund for South Africa; Committee on Conferences; Committee on Relations with the Host Country; Committee on the Exercise of the Inalienable Rights of the Palestinian People; Executive Board of the United Nations Children's Fund; Intergovernmental Group to Monitor the Supply and Shipping of Oil and Petroleum Products to South Africa; Preparatory Committee for the Fiftieth Anniversary of the United Nations; Special Committee against Apartheid; Special Committee to Select the Winners of the United Nations Human Rights Prize; and Working Group on the Financing of the United Nations Relief and Works Agency for Palestine Refugees in the Near East.

On 29 November, by **decision 48/403 B**, the Assembly, acting on the recommendation of the Committee on Conferences,[45] also authorized meetings of the Governing Council of UNDP.

Agenda

At its resumed forty-seventh session, on 19 January 1993, the General Assembly, on the Secretary-General's proposals, included in the agenda sub-items on the election of a member of the Governing Council of the United Nations Environment Programme (UNEP) and of a member of the United Nations Commission on International Trade Law[46] and reopened consideration of the items on the appointment of members of ACABQ;[47] implementation of the Declaration on the Granting of Independence to Colonial Countries and Peoples; effects of atomic radiation; international cooperation in the peaceful uses of outer space; questions relating to information; and the report of the Special Committee on the Charter of the United Nations and on the Strengthening of the Role of the Organization[48] (**decision 47/402 B**).

By the same decision, on 11 February, the Assembly, also on the Secretary-General's proposals, included an item on financing of the United Nations Operation in Mozambique[49] and a sub-item on the election of a member of the International Court of Justice;[50] on 16 March, it deleted the item on financing of the United Nations Observer Group in Central America from the provisional agenda of its forty-eighth session; on 8 April, on the recommendation of the General Committee,[51] it included in the agenda of its forty-seventh session a sub-item on the appointment of members and alternate members of the United Nations Staff Pension Committee and an item on emergency assistance to Cuba.

On 28 May, the Assembly, on the Secretary-General's proposal,[52] included in the agenda items on the election of judges and financing of the International Tribunal for the Prosecution of Persons Responsible for Serious Violations of International Humanitarian Law Committed in the Territory of the Former Yugoslavia since 1991 (**decision 47/402 C**). By the same decision, on 15 June, also on the Secretary-General's proposals, it included a sub-item on confirmation of the appointment of the Administrator of UNDP[53] and reopened consideration of the sub-items on the appointment of members of the Committee on Contributions[54] and of members and alternate members of the United Nations Staff Pension Committee;[55] on 22 June, on the Secretary-General's proposal,[56] it included an item on financing of the United Nations Peace-keeping Force in Cyprus.

By **decision 47/402 D** of 20 September, the Assembly, at the request of the President of the Economic and Social Council,[57] reopened consideration of the item on the report of the Council and the sub-item on questions relating to the world social situation and to youth, ageing, disabled persons and the family.

By **decision 48/402 A**, acting on recommendations of the General Committee,[58] the Assembly, on 24 September and 8, 15 and 25 October, adopted the agenda of its forty-eighth session,[59] and allocated the items to the appropriate Main Committees.[60] Also on the General Committee's recommendations, it included items on financing of the United Nations Observer Mission Uganda-Rwanda, of the United Nations Mission in Haiti and of the United Nations Observer Mission in Liberia; building a peaceful and better world through sport; personnel questions; and economic assistance to States affected by the implementation of the Security Council resolutions imposing sanctions against the Federal Republic of Yugoslavia (Serbia and Montenegro).

By **decision 48/402 B**, on further recommendations of the General Committee,[61] the Assembly, on 2, 4 and 17 November, included items on the situation in Burundi; emergency assistance for the socio-economic rehabilitation of Rwanda; the necessity of adopting effective measures for promoting and protecting the rights of children throughout the world who were victims of especially difficult circumstances, including armed conflicts; financing of the United Nations Assistance Mission for Rwanda; financing of the United Nations Military Liaison Team in Cambodia; and emergency action to combat locust infestation in Africa.

On 10 December, on the recommendation of the Fourth Committee,[62] the Assembly, by **decision 48/402 C**, amended item 117 to read "Activities of foreign economic and other interests which impede the implementation of the Declaration on the Granting of Independence to Colonial Countries and Peoples in Territories under colonial domination". By the same decision, on 14 December, it reopened consideration of the item on commemoration of the fiftieth anniversary of the United Nations in 1995, on Australia's request.[63]

On 23 December, by **decision 48/484**, the Assembly retained 46 items or sub-items on the agenda of its forty-eighth session.

1994 agenda

By **decision 48/402 A**, the Assembly, on 24 September, on the General Committee's recommendation,[44] included in the provisional agenda of the forty-ninth (1994) session the questions of the Malagasy islands of Glorieuses, Juan de Nova, Europa and Bassas da India, and of East Timor.

The Assembly further included in the provisional agenda of its 1994 session the following items, consideration of which was deferred in 1993: question of the Falkland Islands (Malvinas) (**decision 48/408** of 16 November); science and peace (**decision 48/419** of 10 December); question of the composition of the relevant organs of the United Nations (**decision 48/420** of 10 December); Declaration of the Assembly of Heads of State and Government of the Organization of African Unity on the aerial and naval military attack against the Libyan Arab Jamahiriya by the United States Administration in April 1986 (**decision 48/435** of 20 December); armed Israeli aggression against the

Iraqi nuclear installations and its grave consequences for the established international system concerning the peaceful uses of nuclear energy, the non-proliferation of nuclear weapons and international peace and security (**decision 48/436** of 20 December); launching of global negotiations on international economic cooperation for development (**decision 48/437** of 20 December); and implementation of resolutions of the United Nations (**decision 48/438** of 20 December).

Revitalization of the General Assembly

On 17 August 1993, the General Assembly adopted without vote **resolution 47/233**.

Revitalization of the work of the General Assembly

The General Assembly,

Recalling its resolutions 2837(XXVI) of 17 December 1971, 33/138 of 19 December 1978, 39/88 of 13 December 1984, 45/45 of 28 November 1990, 46/77 of 12 December 1991, 46/140 of 17 December 1991 and 46/220 of 20 December 1991,

Conscious of the increasingly important role of the United Nations in fulfilling the purposes set forth in Article 1 of the Charter of the United Nations,

Recalling that the Organization is based on the principle of the sovereign equality of all its Members,

Recognizing in this regard that the General Assembly is the only principal organ of the United Nations consisting of all the Members of the United Nations in which each Member State has equal opportunity to participate in the decision-making process,

Emphasizing the importance of the functions and powers of the General Assembly in any questions or any matters within the scope of the Charter, in accordance with the relevant provisions of the Charter,

Desiring to undertake efforts to enhance the capacity of the General Assembly to fulfil the role envisaged for it under the Charter and increase its effectiveness in the interest of strengthening the overall work of the Organization,

Underlining that the revitalization of the General Assembly should be addressed in a comprehensive manner,

Recognizing in this regard the need, as a first step, to rationalize the Committee structure of the General Assembly to respond better to the requirements of the new phase of international relations,

Recognizing also the importance of the reports of the Security Council and other principal organs of the United Nations to the General Assembly and of their substantive and in-depth consideration by the Assembly,

1. *Decides* that the Main Committees of the General Assembly shall be as follows:

(*a*) Disarmament and International Security Committee (First Committee);

(*b*) Special Political and Decolonization Committee (Fourth Committee);

(*c*) Economic and Financial Committee (Second Committee);

(*d*) Social, Humanitarian and Cultural Committee (Third Committee);

(*e*) Administrative and Budgetary Committee (Fifth Committee);

(f) Legal Committee (Sixth Committee);

2. *Also decides* to amend the rules of procedure of the General Assembly as set forth in the annex to the present resolution;

3. *Further decides* that, as an interim measure and pending a decision on the pattern of election of the six Chairmen of the Main Committees, the six Chairmen of the Main Committees at the forty-eighth session shall be elected as follows:

Two representatives from African States;

One representative from an Asian State;

One representative from an Eastern European State;

One representative from a Latin American or Caribbean State;

One representative from a Western European or other State;

4. *Recommends* that, pending further consideration of the revitalization process, the agenda items at present allocated to the Special Political Committee and to the Fourth Committee be allocated at the forty-eighth session to the new Special Political and Decolonization Committee;

5. *Encourages* Member States to participate actively in a substantive and in-depth discussion on, and consideration of, the reports of the Security Council and other principal organs of the United Nations, in order to fulfil the relevant provisions of the Charter of the United Nations;

6. *Decides* to continue consideration of the revitalization process of the General Assembly at its forty-eighth session in a comprehensive manner in an informal open-ended working group, which will make proposals as appropriate on questions relating to, *inter alia*, the rationalization of the agenda, the reports of the other principal organs of the United Nations in accordance with the Charter and the reports requested of the Secretary-General;

7. *Decides* to include in the provisional agenda of its forty-eighth session the item entitled "Revitalization of the work of the General Assembly".

ANNEX

Rule 31 shall read as follows:

"The General Assembly shall elect a President and twenty-one Vice-Presidents, who shall hold office until the close of the session at which they are elected. The Vice-Presidents shall be elected, after the election of the Chairmen of the six Main Committees referred to in rule 98, in such a way as to ensure the representative character of the General Committee."

The first sentence of rule 38 shall read as follows:

"The General Committee shall comprise the President of the General Assembly, who shall preside, the twenty-one Vice-Presidents and the Chairmen of the six Main Committees."

Rule 98 is amended according to paragraph 1 of the present resolution.

General Assembly resolution 47/233

17 August 1993   Meeting 109   Adopted without vote

Draft by President (A/47/L.64); agenda item 31.

Speaking on behalf of the Asian Group, Fiji said it was not happy with the interim solution because the reduction in the number of the Main Committees resulted in an inequitable allocation of posts, with the Group losing a second chairmanship; however, it supported the resolution on the understanding that the interim arrangement not be construed as a legal basis for future decisions and was applicable only to the forty-eighth session.

Commemoration of the fiftieth anniversary of the United Nations in 1995

In 1993, the Preparatory Committee for the Fiftieth Anniversary of the United Nations, established by the General Assembly in 1992,[64] agreed on organizing principles for the commemoration and chose the theme of the fiftieth anniversary, namely, "We the Peoples of the United Nations . . . United for a Better World". An open-ended drafting group, established to prepare a solemn declaration marking the observance of the anniversary in 1995, discussed the conceptual framework for the declaration at its first meeting on 22 June 1993. The Committee also agreed to encourage the participation of NGOs in commemorative events, at both the national and global levels. The Committee further requested that its secretariat be assured adequate staff and related resources. The General Assembly endorsed that request by **resolution 48/215**.

Activities within the United Nations system were coordinated through the Administrative Committee on Coordination. The secretariat prepared a paper on the status of the commemorative programme and compiled a list of proposed events and activities, divided into three categories: communication/education projects to promote awareness of the United Nations history, structure and functions, to increase grass-roots support of the Organization and to highlight issues on its agenda; commemorative projects to review its past achievements with a view to promoting its future; and celebratory events. Thirteen Member States informed the Secretary-General that they had established national committees for the anniversary and 14 others expressed their intention to do so. A Fiftieth Anniversary Committee was established by the city of San Francisco, United States, where the Charter of the Organization had been signed. As commemorative programmes and events could not be financed from the regular budget, the Secretary-General set up a Trust Fund for the Fiftieth Anniversary Celebrations and urged Member States to support the initiative. A Foundation for the Fiftieth Anniversary was created to allow contributions from corporations, foundations and individuals.

The Committee adopted unanimously a proposal to commemorate the fiftieth anniversary of the Declaration of the Four Nations on General Security. The General Assembly acted on the proposal by adopting **resolution 48/6**.

By **decision 48/406** of 19 October, the Assembly, having considered the Preparatory Committee's report,[65] took note of its activities and decided that it should continue its work.

REFERENCES

[1]A/47/863. [2]A/47/864. [3]A/47/851-S/25045. [4]A/47/852-S/25046. [5]A/47/953. [6]A/47/954. [7]A/47/948-S/25793. [8]A/47/950-S/25796. [9]A/47/976. [10]A/47/973-S/26039. [11]A/47/876-S/25147. [12]S/25541. [13]S/25542. [14]S/25543. [15]S/25545. [16]A/47/923. [17]S/25855. [18]S/25855/Add.1. [19]S/25855/Add.2. [20]S/25892. [21]S/26088. [22]S/26089. [23]S/26483. [24]YUN 1992, p. 139, GA res. 47/1, 22 Sep. 1992. [25]A/47/936-S/25707. [26]S/26466. [27]A/48/411. [28]YUN 1992, p. 140. [29]A/48/411/Add.1. [30]YUN 1992, p. 57. [31]A/48/411/Add.2. [32]S/26812. [33]S/26015. [34]S/26176. [35]S/26389. [36]A/47/2. [37]A/48/2. [38]YUN 1992, p. 140, GA res. 47/62, 11 Dec. 1992. [39]A/48/264 & Add.1,2 & Add.2/Corr.1 & Add.3-5. [40]YUN 1979, p. 435. [41]YUN 1963, p. 87, GA res. 1991 A (XVIII), 17 Dec. 1963. [42]A/48/512. [43]A/48/512/Add.1. [44]A/48/250. [45]A/48/417/Add.1. [46]A/47/860. [47]A/47/101/Add.2. [48]A/47/861. [49]A/47/881. [50]A/47/884. [51]A/47/250/Add.6. [52]A/47/955. [53]A/47/961. [54]A/47/102/Add.2. [55]A/47/907/Add.2. [56]A/47/966. [57]A/47/1011. [58]A/48/250 & Add.1-4. [59]A/48/251 & Add.1-6. [60]A/48/252 & Add.1-6. [61]A/48/250/Add.5-7. [62]A/48/653. [63]A/48/749. [64]YUN 1992, p. 142, GA dec. 46/472, 13 Apr. 1992. [65]A/48/48.

Cooperation with other organizations

League of Arab States

In response to a 1992 General Assembly resolution,[1] the Secretary-General submitted in October 1993 a report[2] on cooperation between the United Nations and the League of Arab States.

According to the report, the secretariats of both organizations and the Office of the Permanent Observer for the League of Arab States to the United Nations continued to maintain close contact on matters of mutual concern. The report reviewed follow-up action on proposals agreed to at previous meetings and summarized the activities of 25 United Nations bodies and organizations, which cooperated with the League in six sectoral areas—international peace and security; food and agriculture; labour, trade, industry and environment; social affairs; education, science, culture and information; and communications—in accordance with a decision taken at a joint meeting at Geneva in July 1990.[3]

Following a coordinating meeting of their secretariats (New York, 10 and 11 May 1993), the two organizations held a general meeting (Geneva, 30 and 31 August) to commemorate the tenth anniversary of the first general meeting of cooperation between them.[4] The general meeting, preceded by a meeting of experts on 26 and 27 August, reviewed and appraised the progress of cooperation, established priority areas and agreed

on a framework for cooperation, including international peace and security; economic, financial and technical cooperation for development; natural resources and environment; food and agriculture; transport and communications; trade and development; atomic energy; finance; and social affairs. The meeting agreed to establish standing sectoral committees to review annually and monitor the implementation of mutual agreements and the progress of joint activities and to identify new areas of cooperation.

GENERAL ASSEMBLY ACTION

On 22 November, the General Assembly adopted **resolution 48/21** without vote.

Cooperation between the United Nations and the League of Arab States

The General Assembly,

Recalling its previous resolutions on the promotion of cooperation between the United Nations and the League of Arab States,

Having considered the report of the Secretary-General on cooperation between the United Nations and the League of Arab States,

Recalling also the decision of the Council of the League of Arab States that it considers the League as a regional organization within the meaning of Chapter VIII of the Charter of the United Nations,

Noting the desire of the League of Arab States to consolidate and develop the existing ties with the United Nations in the political, economic, social, humanitarian, cultural and administrative fields,

Taking into account the report of the Secretary-General entitled "An Agenda for Peace", in particular section VII, concerning cooperation with regional arrangements and organizations,

Convinced that the maintenance and further strengthening of cooperation between the United Nations system and the League of Arab States contribute to the promotion of the purposes and principles of the United Nations,

Also convinced of the need for more efficient and coordinated utilization of available economic and financial resources to promote common objectives of the two organizations,

Recognizing the need for closer cooperation between the United Nations system and the League of Arab States and its specialized organizations in realizing the goals and objectives of both organizations,

Welcoming the general meeting between the representatives of the secretariats of the United Nations system and the General Secretariat of the League of Arab States and its specialized institutions, held at Geneva on 30 and 31 August 1993, in commemoration of the tenth anniversary of the first meeting of cooperation between the two organizations,

1. *Takes note with satisfaction* of the report of the Secretary-General;

2. *Commends* the continued efforts of the League of Arab States to promote multilateral cooperation among Arab States, and requests the United Nations system to continue to lend its support;

3. *Takes note* of the conclusions and recommendations adopted at the general meeting on cooperation between the representatives of the secretariats of the United Nations system and the General Secretariat of the League of Arab States and its specialized organizations;

4. *Expresses its appreciation* to the Secretary-General for the follow-up action taken by him to implement the proposals adopted at the meetings between the representatives of the secretariats of the United Nations and other organizations of the United Nations system and the General Secretariat of the League of Arab States and its specialized organizations, held at Tunis in 1983, at Amman in 1985 and at Geneva in 1988 and 1993;

5. *Also expresses its appreciation* to the organizational entities of the United Nations system and the League of Arab States and its specialized organizations for their contributions leading to the success of the general meeting on cooperation between the two organizations;

6. *Requests* the Secretariat of the United Nations and the General Secretariat of the League of Arab States, within their respective fields of competence, to intensify further their cooperation towards the realization of the purposes and principles of the Charter of the United Nations, the strengthening of international peace and security, economic development, disarmament, decolonization, self-determination and the eradication of all forms of racism and racial discrimination;

7. *Requests* the Secretary-General to continue his efforts to strengthen cooperation and coordination between the United Nations and other organizations and agencies of the United Nations system and the League of Arab States and its specialized organizations in order to enhance their capacity to serve the mutual interests of the two organizations in the political, economic, social, humanitarian, cultural and administrative fields;

8. *Also requests* the Secretary-General to continue to coordinate the follow-up action to facilitate the implementation of the proposals of a multilateral nature adopted at the Tunis meeting in 1983 and to take appropriate action regarding the proposals adopted at previous meetings, including the following:

(a) Promotion of contacts and consultations between the counterpart programmes of the United Nations system;

(b) Setting up joint sectoral inter-agency working groups;

9. *Calls upon* the specialized agencies and other organizations and programmes of the United Nations system:

(a) To continue to cooperate with the Secretary-General and among themselves, as well as with the League of Arab States and its specialized organizations, in the follow-up of multilateral proposals aimed at strengthening and expanding cooperation in all fields between the United Nations system and the League of Arab States and its specialized organizations;

(b) To maintain and increase contacts and improve the mechanism of consultation with the counterpart programmes, organizations and agencies concerned regarding projects and programmes, in order to facilitate their implementation;

(c) To associate whenever possible with organizations and institutions of the League of Arab States in the execution and implementation of development projects in the Arab region;

(d) To inform the Secretary-General, not later than 15 May 1994, of the progress of their cooperation with the League of Arab States and its specialized organizations, in particular the follow-up action taken on the multilateral and bilateral proposals adopted at the previous meetings between the two organizations;

10. *Decides* that, in order to intensify cooperation and for the purpose of review and appraisal of progress as well as to prepare comprehensive periodic reports, a general meeting between the United Nations system and the League of Arab States should take place once every two years, and inter-agency sectoral meetings should be organized annually on areas of priority and wide importance in the development of the Arab States;

11. *Recommends* that the next general meeting on cooperation between the representatives of the secretariats of the United Nations system and the General Secretariat of the League of Arab States and its specialized organizations be held during 1995;

12. *Requests* the Secretary-General of the United Nations, in cooperation with the Secretary-General of the League of Arab States, to encourage periodic consultation between representatives of the Secretariat of the United Nations and the General Secretariat of the League of Arab States to review and strengthen coordination mechanisms with a view to accelerating implementation and follow-up action of multilateral projects, proposals and recommendations adopted at the meetings between the two organizations;

13. *Also requests* the Secretary-General to submit to the General Assembly at its forty-ninth session a progress report on the implementation of the present resolution;

14. *Decides* to include in the provisional agenda of its forty-ninth session the item entitled "Cooperation between the United Nations and the League of Arab States".

General Assembly resolution 48/21

22 November 1993   Meeting 60   Adopted without vote

18-nation draft (A/48/L.26); agenda item 27.

Sponsors: Algeria, Bahrain, Djibouti, Egypt, Iraq, Jordan, Kuwait, Lebanon, Libyan Arab Jamahiriya, Mauritania, Morocco, Oman, Qatar, Saudi Arabia, Sudan, Tunisia, United Arab Emirates, Yemen.

Organization of the Islamic Conference

Pursuant to a 1992 General Assembly resolution,[5] the Secretary-General submitted in September 1993 a report[6] on cooperation between the United Nations and the Organization of the Islamic Conference (OIC). He reported that, during the year, the United Nations Department of Political Affairs had held regular consultations with the General Secretariat of OIC and the Office of the Permanent Observer for OIC to the United Nations, and that representatives of OIC had participated in meetings of the Security Council and the Assembly. On 15 May, the Secretaries-General of the two organizations met in New York to discuss matters of common interest.

The report further described follow-up action in nine priority areas of cooperation: development of science and technology; development of trade; technical cooperation among Islamic countries; assistance to refugees; food security and agriculture;

education and eradication of illiteracy; investment mechanisms and joint ventures; human resources development; and environment. It summarized the activities of six United Nations organizations and agencies serving as focal points for the priority areas and of 20 other United Nations bodies which cooperated with OIC in the field of economic, social and cultural development.

The Secretary-General further reported on a sectoral meeting on science and technology with special emphasis on environment (Dhaka, Bangladesh, 19-22 December 1992), held by the two organizations in response to a 1991 Assembly resolution.[7] The meeting identified strategic objectives and areas of cooperation in science and technology for development and in environment and development, and requested the Islamic Foundation for Science, Technology and Development and UNEP, as focal points, to work out a programme of action in those fields. UNDP was asked to provide the necessary consultancy support to the focal points in drafting a medium-term plan of cooperation.

GENERAL ASSEMBLY ACTION

On 24 November, the General Assembly adopted **resolution 48/24** without vote.

Cooperation between the United Nations and the Organization of the Islamic Conference

The General Assembly,

Having considered the report of the Secretary-General on cooperation between the United Nations and the Organization of the Islamic Conference,

Taking into account the desire of both organizations to cooperate more closely in their common search for solutions to global problems, such as questions relating to international peace and security, disarmament, self-determination, decolonization, fundamental human rights and economic and technical development,

Recalling the Articles of the Charter of the United Nations that encourage activities through regional cooperation for the promotion of the purposes and principles of the United Nations,

Noting the strengthening of cooperation between the specialized agencies and other organizations of the United Nations system and the Organization of the Islamic Conference and its specialized institutions,

Noting also the encouraging progress made in the seven priority areas of cooperation as well as in the identification of other areas of cooperation,

Convinced that the strengthening of cooperation between the United Nations and other organizations of the United Nations system and the Organization of the Islamic Conference contributes to the promotion of the purposes and principles of the United Nations,

Noting with appreciation the determination of both organizations to strengthen further the existing cooperation by developing specific proposals in the designated priority areas of cooperation,

Recognizing the ongoing need for closer cooperation between the specialized agencies and other organizations of the United Nations system and the Organization of

the Islamic Conference and its specialized institutions in the implementation of the proposals adopted at the coordination meeting of the focal points of the lead agencies of the two organizations,

Taking into account the sectoral meeting between the organizations and agencies of the United Nations system and the Organization of the Islamic Conference and its specialized institutions on science and technology with special emphasis on environment, held at Dhaka from 19 to 22 December 1992,

Recalling its resolutions 37/4 of 22 October 1982, 38/4 of 28 October 1983, 39/7 of 8 November 1984, 40/4 of 25 October 1985, 41/3 of 16 October 1986, 42/4 of 15 October 1987, 43/2 of 17 October 1988, 44/8 of 18 October 1989, 45/9 of 25 October 1990, 46/13 of 28 October 1991 and 47/18 of 23 November 1992,

1. *Takes note with satisfaction* of the report of the Secretary-General;

2. *Recalls* the conclusions and recommendations of the sectoral meetings, especially the sectoral meeting on science and technology with special emphasis on environment;

3. *Notes with satisfaction* the active participation of the Organization of the Islamic Conference in the work of the United Nations towards the realization of the purposes and principles of the Charter of the United Nations;

4. *Requests* the United Nations and the Organization of the Islamic Conference to continue cooperation in their common search for solutions to global problems, such as questions relating to international peace and security, disarmament, self-determination, decolonization, fundamental human rights and economic and technical development;

5. *Encourages* the specialized agencies and other organizations of the United Nations system to continue to expand their cooperation with the Organization of the Islamic Conference, particularly by negotiating cooperation agreements, and invites them to multiply the contacts and meetings of the focal points for cooperation in priority areas of interest to the United Nations and the Organization of the Islamic Conference;

6. *Recommends* that a general meeting between representatives of the secretariats of the United Nations system and the Organization of the Islamic Conference and its specialized institutions be organized at Geneva in May 1994;

7. *Urges* the organizations of the United Nations system, especially the lead agencies, to provide increased technical and other forms of assistance to the Organization of the Islamic Conference and its specialized institutions in order to enhance cooperation;

8. *Expresses its appreciation* to the Secretary-General for his continued efforts to strengthen cooperation and coordination between the United Nations and other organizations of the United Nations system and the Organization of the Islamic Conference to serve the mutual interests of the two organizations in the political, economic, social and cultural fields;

9. *Requests* the United Nations and the Organization of the Islamic Conference to hold consultations on a regular basis between representatives of the Secretariat of the United Nations and the General Secretariat of the Organization of the Islamic Conference focusing on the implementation of programmes, projects and follow-up action;

10. *Requests* the Secretary-General of the United Nations, in cooperation with the Secretary-General of the Organization of the Islamic Conference, to continue encouraging the convening of sectoral meetings in the priority areas of cooperation, as recommended by the previous meetings between the two organizations, including follow-up to the sectoral meetings;

11. *Also expresses its appreciation* for the efforts of the Secretary-General in the promotion of cooperation between the United Nations and the Organization of the Islamic Conference, and expresses the hope that he will continue to strengthen the mechanisms of coordination between the two organizations;

12. *Also requests* the Secretary-General to report to the General Assembly at its forty-ninth session on the state of cooperation between the United Nations and the Organization of the Islamic Conference;

13. *Decides* to include in the provisional agenda of its forty-ninth session the item entitled "Cooperation between the United Nations and the Organization of the Islamic Conference".

General Assembly resolution 48/24

24 November 1993   Meeting 63   Adopted without vote

Draft by Pakistan (A/48/L.27); agenda item 29.
Meeting numbers. GA 48th session: plenary 60, 63.

Observer status for the Conference on Security and Cooperation in Europe

In September 1993,[8] 44 participating States of the Conference on Security and Cooperation in Europe (CSCE) requested that an item on its observer status in the General Assembly be included in the agenda of the forty-eighth session. The accompanying explanatory memorandum stated that, as CSCE was discussing ways to strengthen its functions in maintaining international peace and security and its role in preventive diplomacy and peace-keeping, the Council of CSCE, at its December 1992 meeting (Stockholm, Sweden), decided that the relationship between the United Nations and CSCE should be developed further and requested the Committee of Senior Officials to examine the practical implications of the understanding that CSCE was a regional arrangement in the sense of Chapter VIII of the Charter of the United Nations. The Committee's Chairman-in-Office was asked to establish regular contacts with the Secretary-General to ensure that the United Nations and CSCE participating States were kept informed of relevant activities, especially in early warning, conflict prevention, management and resolution of conflicts, and the promotion of democratic values and human rights.

GENERAL ASSEMBLY ACTION

On 13 October, the Assembly adopted **resolution 48/5** without vote.

Observer status for the Conference on Security and Cooperation in Europe in the General Assembly

The General Assembly,

Noting the desire of the Conference on Security and Cooperation in Europe to intensify its cooperation with the United Nations,

1. *Decides* to invite the Conference on Security and Cooperation in Europe to participate in the sessions and the work of the General Assembly in the capacity of observer;

2. *Requests* the Secretary-General to take the necessary action to implement the present resolution.

General Assembly resolution 48/5

13 October 1993   Meeting 29   Adopted without vote

48-nation draft (A/48/L.6 & Add.1); agenda item 158.
Sponsors: Albania, Armenia, Austria, Azerbaijan, Belarus, Belgium, Bosnia and Herzegovina, Bulgaria, Canada, Croatia, Cyprus, Czech Republic, Denmark, Estonia, Finland, France, Georgia, Germany, Greece, Hungary, Iceland, Ireland, Italy, Kazakhstan, Kyrgyzstan, Latvia, Liechtenstein, Lithuania, Luxembourg, Malta, Netherlands, Norway, Poland, Portugal, Republic of Moldova, Romania, Russian Federation, San Marino, Slovakia, Slovenia, Spain, Sweden, Tajikistan, Turkey, Ukraine, United Kingdom, United States, Uzbekistan.

Observer status for the Economic Cooperation Organization

In April 1993,[9] members of the Economic Cooperation Organization—Afghanistan, Azerbaijan, Iran, Kazakhstan, Kyrgyzstan, Pakistan, Tajikistan, Turkey, Turkmenistan and Uzbekistan—requested the inclusion in the agenda of the General Assembly's forty-eighth session of an item on its observer status in the Assembly. According to the accompanying explanatory memorandum, the Economic Cooperation Organization was established in 1990 as the successor to the Regional Cooperation for Development Organization. Its objectives were to expand trade among member States by providing free access to each other's markets, to promote conditions for sustained economic growth in each member State, to consolidate cultural affinities and spiritual and fraternal ties among them, to contribute to the growth of world trade and to strive to remove trading policies resulting in adverse terms of trade for the developing countries.

GENERAL ASSEMBLY ACTION

On 13 October, the General Assembly adopted **resolution 48/2** by consensus.

Observer status for the Economic Cooperation Organization in the General Assembly

The General Assembly,

Noting the desire of the Economic Cooperation Organization for cooperation between the United Nations and the Economic Cooperation Organization,

1. *Decides* to invite the Economic Cooperation Organization to participate in the sessions and the work of the General Assembly in the capacity of observer;

2. *Requests* the Secretary-General to take the necessary action to implement the present resolution.

General Assembly resolution 48/2

13 October 1993   Meeting 29   Adopted by consensus

11-nation draft (A/48/L.1); agenda item 150.
Sponsors: Afghanistan, Azerbaijan, Iran, Kazakhstan, Kyrgyzstan, Pakistan, Senegal, Tajikistan, Turkey, Turkmenistan, Uzbekistan.

Observer status for the Latin American Parliament

In August 1993,[10] 13 Latin American and Caribbean States requested that an item on observer status for the Latin American Parliament in the General Assembly be included in the agenda of the forty-eighth session. The Parliament, established in 1964 at Lima, Peru, and institutionalized by the Lima Treaty of 1987, had been ratified by 11 States. The accompanying explanatory memorandum stated that the Parliament, headquartered since 1990 at São Paulo, Brazil, served to promote socio-economic development and integration of Latin America and its peoples, to channel and support their demands in the international arena, to strengthen Latin America's parliaments and to guarantee the constitutional and democratic life of States.

GENERAL ASSEMBLY ACTION

On 13 October, the General Assembly adopted **resolution 48/4** without vote.

Observer status for the Latin American Parliament in the General Assembly

The General Assembly,

Noting the desire of the Latin American Parliament for increased cooperation with the United Nations,

1. *Decides* to invite the Latin American Parliament to participate in the sessions and the work of the General Assembly in the capacity of observer;

2. *Requests* the Secretary-General to take the necessary action to implement the present resolution.

General Assembly resolution 48/4

13 October 1993   Meeting 29   Adopted without vote

20-nation draft (A/48/L.3 & Add.1); agenda item 157.
Sponsors: Argentina, Bolivia, Brazil, Chile, Colombia, Costa Rica, Cuba, Dominican Republic, Ecuador, El Salvador, Guatemala, Mexico, Nicaragua, Panama, Paraguay, Peru, Portugal, Spain, Uruguay, Venezuela.

Observer status for the Permanent Court of Arbitration

In July 1993,[11] 37 States parties to either or both of the 1899 and 1907 Hague Conventions for the Pacific Settlement of International Disputes requested the inclusion in the agenda of the General Assembly's forty-eighth session of an item on observer status in the Assembly for the Permanent Court of Arbitration, created in 1899 at The Hague, Netherlands, and dedicated to resolving disputes between States. The accompanying explanatory memorandum said observer status would enable the Court to participate more actively in the United Nations Decade of International Law (1990-1999), to supplement the functions of the International Court of Justice and to intensify its cooperation with the United Nations in all appropriate fields.

GENERAL ASSEMBLY ACTION

On 13 October, the Assembly adopted **resolution 48/3** without vote.

Observer status for the Permanent Court of Arbitration in the General Assembly

The General Assembly,

Noting the desire of the Permanent Court of Arbitration to intensify its cooperation with the United Nations,

1. *Decides* to invite the Permanent Court of Arbitration to participate in the sessions and the work of the General Assembly in the capacity of observer;

2. *Requests* the Secretary-General to take the necessary action to implement the present resolution.

General Assembly resolution 48/3

13 October 1993   Meeting 29   Adopted without vote

58-nation draft (A/48/L.4 & Add.1); agenda item 153.
Sponsors: Albania, Argentina, Australia, Austria, Belarus, Belgium, Bulgaria, Burkina Faso, Cambodia, Cameroon, Canada, China, Colombia, Cuba, Cyprus, Czech Republic, Denmark, Dominican Republic, Egypt, Finland, France, Germany, Greece, Hungary, Iceland, Iran, Iraq, Israel, Italy, Jordan, Kyrgyzstan, Luxembourg, Malta, Mauritius, Netherlands, New Zealand, Nigeria, Norway, Panama, Paraguay, Peru, Poland, Portugal, Romania, Russian Federation, Senegal, Spain, Sri Lanka, Sudan, Suriname, Swaziland, Sweden, Thailand, Turkey, Uganda, Ukraine, United Kingdom, United States.

Other organizations

At the request of the host Governments of several intergovernmental conferences in 1993, the main documents of those meetings were transmitted to the Secretary-General for circulation as documents of the General Assembly, the Security Council or both, as follows:

—forty-sixth,[12] forty-seventh[13] and forty-eighth[14] sessions (Riyadh, Saudi Arabia, 4 and 5 April, 7 and 8 June, 5 and 6 September) of the Ministerial Council of the Gulf Cooperation Council and fourteenth session of its Supreme Council (Riyadh, 20-22 December);[15]

—Eighty-ninth (New Delhi, India, 9-17 April)[16] and Ninetieth (Canberra, Australia, 13-18 September)[17] Inter-Parliamentary Conferences;

—Twenty-first Islamic Conference of Foreign Ministers (Karachi, Pakistan, 25-29 April);[18]

—fifty-eighth session of the Council of Ministers of the Organization of African Unity (Cairo, Egypt, 21-26 June) and twenty-ninth session of its Assembly of Heads of State and Government (Cairo, 28-30 June);[19]

—special meeting of the Council of Ministers of the Economic Cooperation Organization (Istanbul, Turkey, 5-7 July);[20]

—Fourteenth Conference of Heads of Government of the Caribbean Community (Nassau, Bahamas, 5-8 July);[21]

—Third Ibero-American Summit (Salvador, Brazil, 15 and 16 July);[22]

—Twenty-sixth Ministerial Meeting of the Association of South-East Asian Nations (Singapore, 23 and 24 July);[23]

—Twenty-fourth South Pacific Forum (Nauru, 10 and 11 August);[24]

—meeting of heads of State and Government of the member States of the Council of Europe (Vienna, 8 and 9 October);[25]

—meeting of the Commonwealth heads of Government (Limassol, Cyprus, 21-25 October);[26]

—fourth meeting of the CSCE Council (Rome, Italy, 30 November and 1 December).[27]

REFERENCES

[1]YUN 1992, p. 142, GA res. 47/12, 29 Oct. 1992. [2]A/48/468 & Add.1. [3]A/45/481/Add.1. [4]YUN 1983, p. 394. [5]YUN 1992, p. 145, GA res. 47/18, 23 Nov. 1992. [6]A/48/422 & Add.1. [7]YUN 1991, p. 103, GA res. 46/13, 28 Oct. 1991. [8]A/48/231. [9]A/48/141. [10]A/48/195 & Add.1,2. [11]A/48/145 & Add.1,2. [12]A/48/140-S/25597. [13]A/48/205-S/25923. [14]A/48/379-S/26411. [15]A/49/96-S/26926. [16]A/48/222. [17]A/48/637. [18]A/48/396-S/26440. [19]A/48/322. [20]A/48/337. [21]A/48/309. [22]A/48/291-S/26242. [23]A/48/294-S/26247. [24]A/48/359. [25]A/48/496. [26]A/48/564. [27]S/26843.

PART TWO

Regional questions

Chapter I

Africa

During 1993, the United Nations intensified its efforts to assist the transformation of South Africa into a united, democratic and non-racial society and the eradication of the legacies of the apartheid system. Those ambitions, however, were constantly threatened by a hostile climate of political and ethnic mistrust and the unprecedented escalation of violence, resulting in much loss of innocent lives. The assassination, on 10 April, of Chris Hani, General Secretary of the South African Communist Party, caused widespread unrest. The Security Council condemned that assassination. The General Assembly urged the South African authorities to halt such violence and to protect all South Africans while bringing to justice those responsible (resolution 48/159 A). The Economic and Social Council demanded the release of any political prisoners and detainees and appealed to the international community to support the critical process under way (1993/13).

The South African Parliament established the Transitional Executive Council to oversee the transition to a democratic order. The Assembly lifted all economic sanctions imposed against South Africa, including the oil embargo. As a result, South Africa's political and economic isolation continued to lessen, as more States established or resumed diplomatic, trade and other ties with it, in recognition of the country's achievements towards democracy.

The Security Council increased the number of observers of the United Nations Observer Mission in South Africa to serve as a nucleus for the anticipated United Nations role in the upcoming electoral process.

The United Nations continued to face severe challenges elsewhere in Africa. Peace negotiations resumed in Angola, prompting the Security Council to extend the mandate of the second United Nations Angola Verification Mission through March 1994. The Council established the United Nations Observer Mission in Liberia to monitor the implementation of a peace agreement signed by the protagonists in the civil war there. It renewed for six months the mandate of the United Nations Operation in Mozambique to monitor the implementation of the General Peace Agreement between the Government and its main rival, the Resistência Nacional Moçambicana. The situation in Rwanda continued to deteriorate and was monitored by two new missions, namely, the United Nations Observer Mission Uganda-Rwanda, established to verify that no

military assistance reached Rwanda from Ugandan territory, and the United Nations Assistance Mission for Rwanda, created to assist in implementing the peace agreement signed between the Government and the Rwandese Patriotic Front.

The Security Council established the second United Nations Operation in Somalia, which took over the responsibilities of the Unified Task Force led by the United States. The Council subsequently extended that Operation's mandate through May 1994. Despite a cease-fire agreement signed by the Somali political factions, the security situation in that country remained tense and was characterized by repeated attacks against the United Nations and United States forces.

The Security Council also considered the situation in Burundi, following the October *coup d'état* that resulted in the assassination of the President. The General Assembly demanded the immediate restoration of the constitutional Government and requested the international community to provide emergency humanitarian assistance to the people of Burundi.

Based on the results of the referendum verified by the United Nations Observer Mission, Eritrea declared independence in April and was admitted to United Nations membership in May.

The Secretary-General continued to exercise his good offices towards finding a solution to the question of the island of Mayotte. The Assembly reaffirmed the sovereignty of the Comoros over the island and urged France to accelerate negotiations with a view to ensuring the return of the island to the Comoros.

In October, organizations of the United Nations system and the Organization of African Unity (OAU) adopted recommendations for a new joint action programme. The Assembly urged the United Nations to continue to support OAU in its efforts to promote a peaceful settlement of disputes and conflicts, and to collaborate with it in implementing the United Nations New Agenda for the Development of Africa in the 1990s.

South Africa and apartheid

Important developments continued to take place in South Africa in 1993 as the country progressed towards the complete elimination of apartheid and implementation of transitional arrangements for the establishment of a non-racial democratic society. In March, discussions in preparation for multi-party talks began among 26 political formations. In April, agreement was reached on the establishment of a Plenary, a Multi-Party Negotiating Council (MPNC) and a Planning Committee as the structure for the multi-party negotiation process. In July, MPNC adopted binding constitutional principles for a democratic Government. It was decided that non-racial elections for a constitutional assembly would be held on 27 April 1994. In September, the South African Parliament established a Transitional Executive Council (TEC) to oversee the preparation for and transition to a democratic order in South Africa. Bills were also passed setting up independent media and electoral commissions and an independent broadcasting authority.

In November, the leaders of 20 political parties of the multi-party negotiating framework endorsed an interim constitution for the transitional period and the electoral bill agreed on by MPNC. They confirmed the election date of 27 April 1994 and adopted transitional agreements, allowing for TEC and other commissions to become operational. In December, Parliament restored South African citizenship to an estimated 10 million people in the four nominally independent homelands of Bophuthatswana, Ciskei, Transkei and Venda. It also adopted the interim constitution and electoral bill.

Throughout 1993, unprecedented political violence threatened the negotiation process and the transition to democracy, culminating in the assassination in April of Chris Hani, General Secretary of the South African Communist Party (SACP). That crime caused widespread unrest, attracted international attention and was subsequently condemned by the Security Council. The General Assembly, in December, urged the South African authorities to bring such violence to an end and to protect all South Africans, while bringing to justice those responsible and protecting and promoting the democratic process (resolution 48/159 A). The Assembly and the Economic and Social Council demanded the immediate release of remaining political prisoners.

The Security Council authorized an increase in the number of observers of the United Nations Observer Mission in South Africa (UNOMSA)—bringing the total complement to 100. That group served as a nucleus for the anticipated United Nations role in the electoral process in South Africa. The Secretary-General proposed the expansion of UNOMSA's mandate to observe all aspects and stages of the upcoming electoral process. In December, he appointed Lakhdar Brahimi as his Special Representative for South Africa.

Following an appeal by Nelson Mandela, President of the African National Congress (ANC), and a recommendation of OAU, the General Assembly, in October, lifted with immediate effect all economic sanctions imposed on South Africa and decided to lift the oil embargo as of the date when TEC became operational (48/1). Since TEC met formally for the first time on 7 December, that became the effective date for the lifting of the oil embargo. Meanwhile, South Africa's political and economic isolation continued to lessen as more States established diplomatic ties with Pretoria, resumed trade and lifted sanctions in recognition of the country's achievements towards establishing a non-racial democracy.

Activities of the Special Committee against Apartheid. In its annual report covering the period October 1992 to October 1993,[1] the Special Committee against Apartheid reviewed the political, socio-economic, military and other developments in and relating to South Africa, including the international response to the elimination of apartheid and establishment of a united, non-racial South Africa based on a democratically negotiated and agreed constitution. The Committee reviewed those developments in accordance with its mandate and guidelines set out by the General Assembly in 1989.[2] It also facilitated a peaceful and stable transition in South Africa by promoting international assistance to enable South Africans to overcome the negative consequences of apartheid.

In order to reflect the emerging political reforms in South Africa, the Committee requested the General Assembly in September[3] to change the wording of the agenda item from ''Policies of apartheid of the Government of South Africa'' to ''Elimination of apartheid and establishment of a united, democratic and non-racial South Africa''. The Assembly, by **decision 48/402 A** of 24 September, approved that request (see PART ONE, Chapter V).

During the period under review, the Special Committee focused on the continuing political violence in South Africa; the creation of an atmosphere of political tolerance; the grave socio-economic inequalities; the urgent need for human resource development assistance for the disadvantaged sectors of the population; and ensuring that the international community continued to support the vulnerable and critical process under way in the country.

The Committee was encouraged by the transformation of the international anti-apartheid movement into a pro-democratic campaign for a new South Africa. It emphasized the vital importance of the support of non-governmental organizations (NGOs) worldwide during the transition period and called on the international community to support the ongoing democratic process. It welcomed the setting of the date for South Africa's first non-racial elections and emphasized the need to end the senseless violence that threatened to disrupt the peaceful political change. The Committee sent a mission to South Africa (1-11 March), which held consultations with high-ranking representatives of major parties and with a wide range of civic, religious, business, labour and media leaders to obtain first-hand understanding of the political factors influencing the transitional process. In its report,[4] the mission recommended the expansion of the number and mandate of the United Nations observers, that the United Nations examine the requirements relating to the functions and capabilities of international electoral monitors in South Africa, and that their deployment should begin several months in advance of the elections. The mission also recommended that UNOMSA become a ''United Nations Transition Mission in South Africa'' with a view to promoting and assisting the multi-party negotiations, the work of the National Peace Accord structure and the monitoring of the elections process. It further recommended that the international community assist in voter education, that the United Nations start planning programmes of socio-economic assistance, and that a resource mobilization conference be convened.

The Committee decided on 17 February to discontinue the registers set up to discourage sports and enforce a cultural boycott of South Africa.

It co-sponsored an International Conference on Southern Africa: Making Hope a Reality (London, 14 and 15 June), organized by the British Anti-Apartheid Movement. In its Declaration,[5] the Conference urged support for the democratic transformation of South Africa, and that the international community ensure that the people of South Africa exercised their democratic rights in the country's first-ever one person, one vote elections, and that those elections were free and fair.

The Committee also co-sponsored, with the Institute for a Democratic Alternative for South Africa (IDASA) and the Institute for Multi-Party Democracy, the Symposium on Political Tolerance in South Africa: Role of Opinion-Makers and Media (Cape Town, 30 July–1 August), its first event ever organized inside South Africa. The Symposium was attended by representatives of a broad spectrum of South African opinion-makers, media experts, academics, political scientists, trade unionists and international observers. It agreed that the United Nations should share its resources with the South African media on issues relating to the transition and the role of the media.

The Special Committee also cooperated in organizing the joint North American/European NGO consultation (Geneva, 30 and 31 August), involving South African NGOs and United Nations agencies, on the social and development needs in rural and township communities in South Africa and the role of international NGOs in helping them meet those needs. Participants reached an understanding on cooperation between international and South African NGOs in developing and implementing projects at the grass-roots level.

As in previous years, the Special Committee observed the International Day for the Elimination of Racial Discrimination (22 March). On that occasion, the Minister for Foreign Affairs of South Africa sent a message to the Secretary-General,[6] expressing his Government's commitment to and solidarity with the Day's objectives. The Committee also observed the International Day of Solidarity with the Struggling People of South Africa (16 June), the International Day of Solidarity with the Struggle of Women in South Africa (9 August) and the Day of Solidarity with South African Political Prisoners (11 October).

In its conclusions and recommendations, the Special Committee stated that the current negotiating framework, which brought together 26 parties, was a milestone in South African history. It was all the more significant since the negotiations were not disrupted despite frequent cases of violence and intimidation.

The Committee noted that, with the economy facing an unprecedented recession and society threatened by the disintegration and collapse of all social norms, it was clear that unless a credible, representative, legitimate and democratically elected Government was established soon, South Africa's problems could not be effectively addressed. Thus, the United Nations needed to examine immediately the functions and requirements of international electoral monitors for their early deployment. It was also essential to maintain effective coordination with the Independent Electoral Commission (IEC), the National Peace Accord structure and the international observers already deployed. The Committee recommended that the General Assembly reaffirm the objectives envisaged in the 1989 Declaration on Apartheid and its Destructive Consequences in Southern Africa,[2] and the international community's determination to support the South African people in achieving a speedy and peaceful transition to a non-racial and democratic society; request that mandatory measures imposed by the Security Council remain in effect; and urge Member States to respect them until they were lifted by the Council. It also recommended that the Assembly urge those parties that had suspended their participation in the multi-party negotiations to return to that framework until its successful conclusion.

Among other recommendations, the Special Committee requested that the Assembly urge the

South African authorities to exercise fully and impartially their responsibility to end the violence, protect the lives and property of all South Africans, and promote their right to participate in the democratic process, including the rights to demonstrate peacefully, to organize political rallies, to run for election and to participate in the elections without intimidation. The Assembly was also urged to call on the signatories to the National Peace Accord to recommit themselves to the process of peaceful change by fully implementing its provisions; to recommend the immediate expansion of the number of observers and their mandate to enable them to function as international election monitors in close cooperation with IEC; and to appeal to the international community to maintain its humanitarian, legal and financial assistance to the victims of apartheid, in particular to the returning refugees and exiles and released political prisoners.

GENERAL ASSEMBLY ACTION

On 20 December 1993, the General Assembly adopted **resolution 48/159 B** without vote.

Programme of work of the Special Committee against Apartheid

The General Assembly,

Having considered the report of the Special Committee against Apartheid,

Recognizing the important role that the Special Committee has held in mobilizing international support for the elimination of apartheid and in promoting an international consensus on this critical issue, as reflected in the adoption by consensus on 14 December 1989 of the Declaration on Apartheid and its Destructive Consequences in Southern Africa, in General Assembly decision 45/457 B of 13 September 1991 and in Assembly resolutions 45/176 A of 19 December 1990, 46/79 A of 13 December 1991 and 47/116 A and B of 18 December 1992,

1. *Takes note with appreciation* of the report of the Special Committee against Apartheid on its work, under its mandate, in support of the peaceful elimination of apartheid through the process of a negotiated transition of South Africa to a democratic, non-racial society;

2. *Also takes note with appreciation* of the report of the Chairman of the Special Committee on his mission, together with a delegation of the Committee, to South Africa from 1 to 11 March 1993;

3. *Commends* the Special Committee for organizing, together with the Institute for a Democratic Alternative for South Africa and the Institute for Multi-Party Democracy, the Symposium on Political Tolerance in South Africa: Role of Opinion-Makers and Media, which was held at Cape Town from 30 July to 1 August 1993;

4. *Authorizes* the Special Committee, until the completion of its mandate following the establishment of a democratically elected non-racial Government in South Africa:

(a) To follow closely developments in South Africa;

(b) To continue to facilitate a peaceful and stable transition in South Africa by promoting international assistance in helping South Africans to overcome the negative social and economic consequences of the policies of apartheid;

(c) To maintain contacts with academic institutions and the labour, business and civic communities, including community-based and other non-governmental organizations in South Africa;

(d) To consult with the parties participating in the political process, with legitimate non-racial structures and with a democratically elected non-racial Government with a view to facilitating the resumption of the participation of South Africa in the work of the General Assembly;

(e) To submit, as soon as possible following the establishment of a democratically elected non-racial Government, a final report to the General Assembly;

(f) To undertake other relevant activities aimed at supporting the political process of peaceful change until a democratically elected non-racial Government has been established in South Africa;

5. *Expresses its appreciation* for the cooperation extended to the Special Committee by Governments, intergovernmental and non-governmental organizations and relevant components of the United Nations system, and invites them to continue their cooperation;

6. *Decides* that the special allocation of 240,000 United States dollars to the Special Committee for 1994 from the regular budget of the United Nations should be used towards the cost of special projects aimed at promoting the process towards the elimination of apartheid through the establishment of a democratically elected and non-racial Government in South Africa;

7. *Also decides* to continue to authorize adequate financial provision in the regular budget of the United Nations to enable the African National Congress of South Africa and the Pan Africanist Congress of Azania to maintain offices in New York so that they may participate effectively in the deliberations of the Special Committee and in deliberations relating to the situation in South Africa in other relevant United Nations bodies, on the understanding that such grants will continue until the situation of the two organizations as political parties has been regularized.

General Assembly resolution 48/159 B

20 December 1993   Meeting 85   Adopted without vote

Draft by Nigeria (A/48/L.30); agenda item 38.
Financial implications. 5th Committee, A/48/788; S-G, A/C.5/48/59.
Meeting numbers. GA 48th session: 5th Committee 43; plenary 72, 76-80, 85.

Progress report of the Secretary-General. In response to a 1992 General Assembly resolution,[7] the Secretary-General in December 1993 presented a fourth progress report[8] on the implementation of the 1989 Declaration on Apartheid and its Destructive Consequences in Southern Africa.[2] The report, which analysed the progress made towards dismantling apartheid since September 1992, was based on written submissions by the Government of South Africa, participants in the multi-party negotiating process, and movements and other organizations, supplemented by official statements and press releases. It dealt with factors conducive to enhancing a negotiated settlement to end apartheid, relevant socio-economic factors, and arrangements and modalities for the transition to a new democratic order, and reviewed international action with regard to South Africa.

The Secretary-General observed that the resumption, after a 10-month suspension, of multi-party negotiations in April, with broader representation than the preceding Convention for a Democratic South Africa (CODESA), was a welcome development. It resulted in significant breakthroughs, including agreement on a date in April 1994 for South Africa's first non-racial and democratic elections. That was followed by enactment into law of most of the principal provisions of the transitional arrangements, including TEC, IEC, an Independent Media Commission, (IMC), an Independent Broadcasting Authority (IBA) and an interim constitution. However, violence continued to pose a major threat to the peace process, and breaking the cycle of violence required the cooperation of the Government and of all parties in South Africa.

The Secretary-General met in New York with the South African President, F. W. de Klerk, and Nelson Mandela, President of ANC, on 23 and 29 September, respectively. He also met with Clarence Makwetu, President of the Pan Africanist Congress of Azania (PAC), Chief Mangosuthu Buthelezi, President of the Inkatha Freedom Party (IFP), and Foreign Minister Roelof Botha. During his meeting with Chief Buthelezi, he stressed the importance accorded by the international community to the multi-party negotiations and the formation of TEC. He stated that participation by all parties, including the Freedom Alliance—a new political grouping consisting of the Bophuthatswana and Ciskei homelands, IFP and the Afrikaner Volksfront (Afrikaner People's Front)—was essential to the establishment of a democratic, non-racial and united South Africa, and to ensuring that their views were reflected in the interim constitution. The Secretary-General further met with John Hall and Antonie Gildenhuys, respectively the chairman of the National Peace Committee and the head of its secretariat, to discuss strengthening and broadening the peace structures to defuse violence and to make them more representative of the population.

In its submission to the Secretary-General, ANC averred that the continued application of certain security legislation was hampering free and peaceful political activity in the country, especially in the so-called Bantustans. Therefore, it urged that the leaders of Bophuthatswana, Ciskei and KwaZulu be prevailed upon to allow free political activity in the areas under their control, in order to eliminate the "no-go" areas where ANC leaders

and activists engaged in legitimate political activity continued to be routinely attacked and even assassinated. PAC stated that the Government had not yet repealed all legislation impeding free political activity, and submitted a list of 10 such inhibiting laws, among them the Internal Security Act, which allowed for the arrest of political opponents and denial of access to a speedy trial, legal representation and visits from family members, and the Post Office Act, which allowed for interference with the mail of political opponents.

Among other initiatives was the organization by the United Nations and the Commonwealth secretariat of an international donors' conference, scheduled for June 1994, to mobilize international support for addressing the human resource development needs of a post-apartheid South Africa.

In conclusion, the Secretary-General urged all parties in South Africa to cooperate in implementing the transitional arrangements for the early establishment of a non-racial and democratic society. He assured them of his continued assistance in facilitating the success of the transitional process.

Multi-party negotiations and political developments

Following a 10-month deadlock, delegations from 26 political formations in South Africa met on 5 and 6 March 1993 for a multi-party planning conference to review earlier agreements and prepare for multi-party talks. It was the most representative gathering of political leaders in South African history and included parties such as PAC and the Conservative Party (CP) that had not participated in the 1991[9] or 1992[10] Convention for a Democratic South Africa (CODESA I and II). As communicated by South Africa's Permanent Representative to the United Nations on 9 March,[11] participants at the conference, with the exception of CP, committed themselves to resuming the multi-party constitutional negotiations within a month and to reconvening the multi-party forum not later than 5 April. Negotiations resumed on 1 April, but without the participation of the Azanian People's Organization and the Afrikaanse Weerstandsbeweging (AWB), also known as the Afrikaner Resistance Movement. It was agreed to establish a Plenary, MPNC and a Planning Committee as the structure for the multi-party negotiating process. MPNC appointed seven technical committees, on constitutional issues, fundamental rights during the transition period, TEC, IEC, IMC, IBA, repeal or amendment of legislation impeding free political activity and of discriminatory legislation, and violence. To facilitate the negotiation process, an understanding was reached on the use of "sufficient consensus" as a decision-making mechanism, by which dissenting parties would not block decisions agreed on by a majority.

Important issues discussed included interim constitutional provisions; the powers of the central Government; the degree of devolution of powers to regional and local governments and the exercise of residual powers; the extent and mandatory character of principles for the future constitution to be agreed on in advance of elections, including regional boundaries; the justiciability of disputes regarding the elections; reincorporation of the homelands; and the control of the security forces and maintenance of law and order. Also discussed was the question of integrating all armed formations, including the South African Defence Force (SADF), military wings of liberation movements and homeland armies, into a national defence force.

With regard to regional boundaries, a Commission on the Demarcation/Delimitation of Regions was given the task of making recommendations to MPNC. In the course of the negotiations, a demand was made for a separate Afrikaner State to be provided for in the constitution. Discussions also continued regarding the reincorporation of the 10 ethnically based homelands into a united South Africa, viewed as essential for their own development and as a prerequisite for a united, democratic and non-racial South Africa. However, most homeland leaders opposed the suggestion for an early reincorporation of their territories.

On 2 July, MPNC adopted by consensus a set of binding constitutional principles for a democratic Government, including provisions for a strong central Government, while accommodating regional diversity, a bill of fundamental human rights and an independent judiciary. The justiciability of constitutional principles would be ensured by a constitutional court. A decision was also taken by "sufficient consensus" for non-racial democratic elections to a constitutional assembly to be held on 27 April 1994. However, IFP, the KwaZulu Government and CP were among seven parties that opposed setting a date at that stage. On 23 September, the South African Parliament passed a bill, by a vote of 211 to 36, establishing TEC to oversee preparation for and transition to a democratic order, including the conduct of free and fair elections to the constituent assembly and the establishment of legislative and executive structures at all levels of government (see also below, under "Transition to democracy"). TEC was to have seven subcouncils: regional and local government and traditional authorities; law and order, stability and security; defence; intelligence; finance; foreign affairs; and the status of women. Bills were also passed enabling IMC, IEC and IBA to be set up.

In a statement made on 20 July, the Special Committee against Apartheid expressed concern over the possible withdrawal of CP and IFP from the multi-party negotiations and the view that the active participation of all parties was crucial in building on the significant consensus already achieved on essential constitutional principles.

On 24 September, Mr. Mandela told the Special Committee that TEC would mark the first-ever participation by the majority of the South African people at governmental levels in the process of determining the destiny of their country. Although a democratic Government was not yet elected, TEC would provide the appropriate mechanism for interaction with the international community.

The Secretary-General reported[8] the announced withdrawal, on 7 October, of the homelands of Bophuthatswana and Ciskei from the multi-party negotiating process, and the announcement that the Concerned South Africans Group had been disbanded and replaced by the new Freedom Alliance, which declared that it would henceforth discuss outstanding issues only through a joint negotiating team. IFP proposed a constitutional convention of leaders to draft a final constitution, which could provide for the establishment of a federation of states and which could be approved by a national referendum. ANC stated that, while it was continuing bilateral discussions with the Freedom Alliance, no organization should hold the country to ransom or derail the process in any way.

On 18 November, at a meeting of the Plenary of the multi-party negotiating process, the leaders of 20 political parties endorsed a constitution for the transitional period and an electoral bill agreed on by MPNC. The Plenary further confirmed the election date and adopted transitional agreements, allowing for TEC, IMC, IEC and IBA to become operational. TEC was to succeed MPNC. The Afrikaner Volksunie, or Afrikaner People's Union, voted against the transitional agreements, while IFP and other members of the Freedom Alliance did not participate in the session.

On 15 December, the Parliament voted to restore citizenship to an estimated 10 million people in the four nominally independent homelands of Bophuthatswana, Ciskei, Transkei and Venda. On 22 December, it adopted an Interim Constitution and Electoral Bill, endorsed on 18 November by 20 political parties at MPNC by a vote of 237 in favour to 46 against.

Among other political developments, the South African Government and PAC resumed bilateral talks, focusing mainly on the cessation of the armed struggle. At a bilateral meeting held from 9 to 12 February, the Government and ANC agreed on the holding of elections within a year for a constituent assembly that would draft and adopt a new constitution and, simultaneously, serve as an interim parliament. It was also agreed that parties receiving a certain minimum percentage of votes would be entitled to participate in a coalition cabinet and that such an "interim government of national unity" would serve for five years. New elections would then take place under a new constitution. Discussions were also held with regard to TEC and its role in overseeing the conduct of security forces, the media and electoral mechanisms.

Political violence

Political violence and economic crime reached unprecedented levels in 1993, taking a high toll in human lives and destruction of property, and spreading fear and anguish throughout the country. The Human Rights Commission of South Africa underlined the fact that violent incidents increased markedly each time progress was achieved in the multi-party negotiations. Following the 2 July announcement of the date for elections to a constitutional assembly, 605 deaths were recorded. According to the Commission, 2,768 people died in political violence between June and November, an increase of 46 per cent over the same period in 1992. The regions of the East Rand and Natal together accounted for approximately 90 per cent of the death toll, with 1,299 such fatalities in the East Rand. While much of South Africa's violence was rooted in the legacies of the apartheid system, human rights observers noted that recent violence also included fighting for political domination, struggle for scarce economic resources, ethnic and racial hatred, criminal gangs exploiting the political instability and revenge killers settling old scores.

The Secretary-General observed[8] fluctuations in the pattern and frequency of violence, but with no change in its negative effects on society, a peaceful transition and stable development. Township, squatter, rural and urban communities suffered greatly from attacks by criminal vigilante and other groups and persons alleged to be members of covert security forces. In the first nine months of 1993, deaths due to political violence totalled 3,049, an increase of 10 per cent over the corresponding period in 1992.

Political violence within black communities abated somewhat in the first half of the year, resulting in 1,387 deaths, with Natal accounting for the largest number of casualties (774 deaths). However, the unprecedented violence in July in the East Rand resulted in 605 deaths, up from a monthly average of 231 deaths, while some 554 deaths were reported in August.

There was a marked increase in attacks against civilian whites, with 34 being killed during the first half of the year. The number of media reporters attacked or killed also increased, and at least 130 policemen were killed in the first seven months of 1993. There was also a rise in right-wing violence.

On 25 June, armed right-wingers, many of them members of AWB, forcibly broke into and occupied Johannesburg's World Trade Centre, where multi-party negotiations were taking place. On 13 December, in an attack in Randfontein, men in camouflage uniform forced two cars off the road and shot their black occupants, killing three people and injuring four others.

In a raid conducted during the night of 8 October, SADF soldiers shot dead five young people sleeping in a house at Umtata in Transkei. SADF claimed that the house served as a base for PAC's military wing. Police later admitted that forensic tests had been unable to link the weapons found in the house with any crimes. UNOMSA, together with the observer missions of the Commonwealth and OAU, condemned the raid, which had been authorized at the highest levels of government.

On 10 April, Chris Hani, General Secretary of SACP, was assassinated, an incident that caused widespread unrest and attracted international attention. Janusz Jakob Walus, a Polish immigrant and member of AWB and CP, and Clive Derby-Lewis, a former member of the President's Council, were convicted and sentenced to death.

SECURITY COUNCIL ACTION (April)

Following consultations held on 12 April on the question of South Africa, the President of the Security Council made the following statement on behalf of its members:[12]

Meeting number. SC 3197.

"The assassination of Chris Hani, a member of ANC's National Executive Committee and the Secretary-General of the South African Communist Party, is a deplorable and troubling event. This brutal murder saddens all who are working for peace, democracy and justice in South Africa. Mr. Hani's murder further underscores the urgent need to end violence in the country and to push ahead with the negotiations which will create a united, non-racial and democratic South Africa.

"Chris Hani actively supported these negotiations and only last week called for an end to violence so the negotiations could proceed in a climate of peace and stability. In this regard, the Security Council welcomes the announcements by all those who have reaffirmed their commitment to the negotiating process, including ANC, the South African Communist Party and the Congress of South African Trade Unions. Negotiations leading to non-racial democracy must not be held hostage by the perpetrators of violence.

"The Security Council states its determination to remain supportive of efforts to facilitate this peaceful transition to a non-racial democracy for the benefit of all South Africans."

Further developments. The Commission of Inquiry regarding the Prevention of Public Violence and Intimidation (Goldstone Commission) continued to play a major role in investigating the behaviour of security forces of the various parties in the ongoing political violence and in specific incidents. It conducted inquests into political assassinations and probes into the smuggling of arms into the country, the school crisis, activities of the Azanian People's Liberation Army (APLA)—the military wing of PAC—and the KwaZulu police, the alleged involvement of SADF's military intelligence in fomenting conflict, police actions during the AWB raid on the Johannesburg World Trade Centre in June and the violence in the East Rand since July. To assist its investigations, the Goldstone Commission established the Institute for the Study of Public Violence, which received financial and technical support from Norway. In its report on the raid on the World Trade Centre, the Commission concluded that the police were guilty of dereliction of duty by not organizing a strong and visible show of force during the assault, which was anything but spontaneous.

South Africa transmitted on 30 March[13] the Goldstone Commission's report on the activities of APLA. According to information placed before the Commission, APLA's policy was to kill policemen, white farmers in rural areas and whites in general, whom it referred to as settlers. Statistics were given of 15 attacks on policemen, 13 on farmhouses, 3 on houses in the town of Fickburg, attacks on the Golf Club at King William's Town, and attacks on restaurants in Cape Town and Queenstown. According to the South African Police (SAP), 16 people were killed in alleged APLA assaults. Asserting that APLA used Transkei as a springboard for attacks into South Africa, the Commission recommended that perpetrators of violence be prosecuted in terms of the common law, and requested the international community to withhold assistance to APLA and to exert pressure on PAC to cease condoning and supporting violence and to join other political groups in their search for a negotiated settlement.

The Government identified a number of problem areas where improvements could be made to implement better the National Peace Accord and reduce violence: the open hostility between ANC and IFP; the use by political groups of local dispute-resolution committees as political platforms; the lack of objectivity of such committees' chairmen; and extending to the other Peace Accord signatories the code of conduct currently only applicable to and binding on SAP. The Government stated that coordination between SAP, the National Peace Committee secretariat and the international observers resulted in the defusing of many potentially violent situations.

As part of its proposals for creating conditions to eliminate violence, the multi-party negotiating process, on 22 June, proposed the establishment of an independent, national, multi-party peace-keeping force. While the idea was supported in principle by the Government, ANC and IFP, they differed on its form and authority. In addition, in the legislation adopted by the South African Parliament on the establishment of TEC, provisions were made for the creation of a national peace-keeping force, comprising members of all armed forces. On 23 June, a meeting between Mr. Mandela and Chief Buthelezi was held under the chairmanship of Archbishop Desmond Tutu and Bishop Stanley Mogoba. The two leaders issued a joint statement expressing their determination to end the violence and promote national reconciliation, and to hold joint peace rallies. They also called for the strengthening of the National Peace Accord.

On 2 September, addressing a rally in commemoration of Peace Day, the two leaders urged the gathering to put an end to violence.

SECURITY COUNCIL ACTION (August)

Following consultations held on 24 August on the political violence in South Africa, the President of the Security Council made the following statement on behalf of its members:[14]

Meeting number. SC 3267.

"The Security Council deplores the recent upsurge in violence and discord in South Africa, especially in the East Rand. This violence—terrible in its human toll—is even more tragic as the country proceeds on the path to a democratic, non-racial and united South Africa and a new, more promising future for all its citizens.

"The Council recalls its statement in resolution 765(1992) that it is the responsibility of the South African authorities to take all necessary measures to stop immediately the violence and protect the life and property of all South Africans. The Council affirms that all parties in South Africa must assist the Government in preventing opponents of democracy from using violence to threaten the country's democratic transition. In this regard, the Council notes the proposal for a national peace force to restore and maintain order in volatile areas. Any such force should be genuinely representative of South African society and its major political bodies. Just as importantly, it must have the confidence, support and cooperation of the people of South Africa. The Council also welcomes efforts by the leaders of the African National Congress and the Inkatha Freedom Party to convince their followers to avoid further violence. The Council urges all of South Africa's leaders to work jointly to prevent violence in the election period ahead.

"The Security Council commends the international community, including the Organization of African Unity, the European Community and the Commonwealth, for playing a constructive role in helping to curb the violence in South Africa. The United Nations Peace Monitors, under the able supervision of the chief of the United Nations Observer Mission in South Africa, have made a difference. People are alive today because of the tireless and courageous efforts of these and other international peace monitors. Yet far too many are dying. The world community must continue to signal firmly that it will not allow the violence to derail South Africa's political transition.

"The Council emphasizes the key role of the multi-party negotiating process in securing the transition to a democratic, non-racial and united South Africa. It urges the parties to reaffirm their commitment to the multi-party negotiating process, to redouble their efforts to reach consensus on the transitional arrangements and constitutional issues still outstanding and to proceed to elections as planned in the coming year.

"The Security Council reaffirms its determination to remain supportive of efforts to facilitate the peaceful transition to a non-racial democracy for the benefit of all South Africans. The Council is following developments in South Africa closely and will remain seized of the matter."

International efforts for a united, non-racial and democratic South Africa

Developments in South Africa remained the focus of attention of the international community, which continued to monitor those developments closely and welcomed the resumption of multi-party negotiations in March and subsequent understandings and agreements reached.

On 15 October, the 1993 Nobel Peace Prize was awarded jointly to Mr. Mandela and President de Klerk for their work towards the peaceful termination of the apartheid regime and for laying the foundations for a new South Africa. In announcing the award, the Nobel Committee stated that their constructive policy of peace and reconciliation also pointed the way to a peaceful resolution of similar conflicts elsewhere in the world.

The United Nations, with the sponsorship and funding of the Nordic countries (Denmark, Finland, Iceland, Norway and Sweden) and the Friedrich Ebert Foundation of Germany, held an International Seminar on Confidence- and Security-building Measures in Southern Africa (Windhoek, Namibia, 24-26 February). The Seminar brought together high-ranking experts from military, political, government-related and academic areas in the countries of southern Africa, including South Africa. It concluded that most major security problems in the region bore an internal and domestic character, albeit with potentially dangerous implications for neighbouring States. There was a need to give innovative consideration to confidence- and security-building measures of domestic applicability in the military sphere.

In February, the International Labour Organisation (ILO) dispatched an interdisciplinary planning mission to assess the needs for technical cooperation and assistance, and met with representatives of South African employers' and employees' organizations. The findings of the mission were to be used to design a programme of action for implementation in priority areas, such as employment creation, human resource development, economic policy, worker education and training, and reform of labour legislation. ILO also assisted and participated in training workshops for non-racial civil organizations.

GENERAL ASSEMBLY ACTION

The General Assembly on 24 September decided that the item on the elimination of apartheid and establishment of a united, democratic and non-racial South Africa would be considered directly in plenary meeting, on the understanding that representatives of OAU and of national liberation movements recognized by it would be permitted to participate and that organizations and individuals with special interest in the item would be heard by the Fourth (Special Political and Decolonization) Committee.

In accordance with that decision, the Fourth Committee on 8 and 9 November[15] heard 10 persons representing the following organizations: PAC, ANC, the Interfaith Center on Corporate Responsibility, the Lawyers' Committee for Civil Rights Under Law, the International Confederation of Free Trade Unions, the NGO Committee on Southern Africa, the National Democratic Institute for International Affairs, the City of London Anti-Apartheid Group, the American Committee on Africa, and IFP. By **decision 48/425** of 13 December, the Assembly took note of the Committee's report.

On 20 December, the Assembly adopted **resolution 48/159 A** without vote.

International efforts towards the total eradication of apartheid and support for the establishment of a united, non-racial and democratic South Africa

The General Assembly,

Recalling the Declaration on Apartheid and its Destructive Consequences in Southern Africa, set forth in the annex to its resolution S-16/1, adopted by consensus on 14 December 1989,

Also recalling its resolution 48/1 of 8 October 1993 on the lifting of sanctions against South Africa,

Further recalling the initiative of the Organization of African Unity to place before the Security Council the question of violence in South Africa,

Recalling with satisfaction Security Council resolutions 765(1992) of 16 July 1992, and 772(1992) of 17 August 1992, in which the Council authorized the deployment of the United Nations Observer Mission in South Africa and invited the deployment there of observers from the Organization of African Unity, the Commonwealth and the European Community,

Welcoming the statement of the extraordinary session with Ministers for Foreign Affairs of the Ad Hoc Committee on Southern Africa of the Organization of African Unity, held in New York on 29 September 1993,

Taking note of the report of the Special Committee against Apartheid and of the report of the Chairman of the Special Committee against Apartheid on his mission to South Africa, as well as of the report of the Secretary-General on the coordinated approach by the United Nations system on questions relating to South Africa and the fourth progress report of the Secretary-General on the implementation of the Declaration on Apartheid,

Recognizing the responsibility of the United Nations and the international community, as envisaged in the Declaration on Apartheid, to help the South African people in their legitimate struggle for the total elimination of apartheid through peaceful means,

Noting the agreements reached within the framework of the resumed multi-party negotiations on holding elections on 27 April 1994, and on the establishment of the Transitional Executive Council, the Independent Electoral Commission, the Independent Media Commission and the Independent Broadcasting Authority,

Also noting the endorsement by the parties in the multi-party negotiations of the Constitution for the Transitional Period and the Electoral Bill,

Gravely concerned that continued and escalating violence threatens to undermine the process of peaceful change, through negotiated agreements, to a united, non-racial and democratic South Africa,

Bearing in mind the need to strengthen and reinforce all mechanisms set up to prevent violence in South Africa, and emphasizing the need for all parties to cooperate in combating violence and to exercise restraint,

Encouraging the efforts of all parties, including ongoing talks among them, aimed at establishing arrangements for the transition to a democratic order,

Noting with concern the remaining effects of the acts of destabilization that were committed by South Africa against the neighbouring African States,

1. *Welcomes* the agreements reached within the framework of the multi-party negotiations on holding elections on 27 April 1994, on the establishment of the Transitional Executive Council, the Independent Electoral Commission, the Independent Media Commission and the Independent Broadcasting Authority, and on the Constitution for the Transitional Period, as well as the Electoral Bill;

2. *Strongly urges* the South African authorities to exercise fully and impartially the primary responsibility of government to bring to an end the ongoing violence, to protect the lives, security and property of all South Africans in all of South Africa and to promote and protect their right to participate in the democratic process, including the right to demonstrate peacefully in public, to organize and participate in political rallies in all parts of South Africa and to run for election and participate in the elections without intimidation;

3. *Calls upon* the South African authorities in this context to bring to justice those responsible for acts of violence, to take the necessary measures for the peaceful reincorporation of the "homelands" into South Africa and to ensure that the populations in those territories can freely participate in the elections and that all political parties will be able to run election campaigns there free of intimidation;

4. *Calls upon* all parties to refrain from acts of violence and to do their utmost to combat violence;

5. *Urgently calls upon* all signatories to the National Peace Accord to recommit themselves to the process of peaceful change by fully and effectively implementing its provisions, and by cooperating with each other to that end;

6. *Calls upon* all other parties to contribute to the achievement of the aims of the National Peace Accord;

7. *Commends* the Secretary-General for those measures taken to address areas of concern noted in his reports and particularly to assist in strengthening the structures set up under the National Peace Accord, including the deployment of United Nations observers in South Africa, and expresses its appreciation for the activities carried out by the United Nations Observer Mission in South Africa;

8. *Supports* the recommendation of the Secretary-General for the additional deployment of observers in South Africa to further the purposes of the National Peace Accord, and urges him to continue to address all the areas of concern noted in his report which fall within the purview of the United Nations;

9. *Welcomes* the continuing role of the observers of the Organization of African Unity, the Commonwealth and the European Union[a] deployed in South Africa;

10. *Urges* all parties in South Africa, including those which did not participate fully in the multi-party talks, to respect agreements reached during the negotiations, to recommit themselves to democratic principles, to take part in the elections and to resolve outstanding issues by peaceful means only;

11. *Calls upon* all Governments to observe fully the mandatory arms embargo imposed by the Security Council, requests the Council to continue to monitor effectively the strict implementation of that embargo, and urges States to adhere to the provisions of other Council resolutions on the import of arms from South Africa and the export of equipment and technology destined for military purposes in that country;

12. *Demands* the immediate release of remaining political prisoners;

13. *Appeals* to the international community to increase humanitarian and legal assistance to the victims of apartheid, to the returning refugees and exiles and to released political prisoners;

14. *Calls upon* the international community to continue to assist disadvantaged South African democratic anti-apartheid organizations and individuals in the academic, scientific and cultural fields;

15. *Also calls upon* the international community to assist the non-racial sports bodies in South Africa in redressing the continuing structural inequalities in sports in that country;

16. *Strongly urges* the international community, following the adoption of resolution 48/1 on 8 October 1993, to respond to the appeal by the people of South Africa for assistance in the economic reconstruction of their country and to ensure that the new South Africa begins its existence on a firm economic base;

17. *Appeals* to the international community to render all possible assistance to States neighbouring South Africa to enable them to recover from the effects of past acts of destabilization and to contribute to the stability and prosperity of the subregion;

---

[a]As from 1 November 1993, when the Treaty on European Union came into effect, the European Community became the European Union.

18. *Calls upon* the Secretary-General to respond promptly and positively to a request for electoral assistance from the transitional authorities in South Africa, bearing in mind that the elections are set for 27 April 1994;

19. *Requests* the Secretary-General to accelerate planning for a United Nations role in the election process, in consultation with the Security Council and in coordination with the observer missions of the Organization of African Unity, the Commonwealth and the European Union;

20. *Also requests* the Secretary-General to take the necessary measures for the initiation and coordination among the United Nations and its agencies of detailed planning for programmes of socio-economic assistance, particularly in the areas of human resource development, employment, health and housing, and to ensure also that those programmes are coordinated with other international agencies and with legitimate non-racial structures in South Africa;

21. *Commends* the Secretary-General of the United Nations and the Secretary-General of the Commonwealth for their initiative to start planning for an international donors' conference on human resource development for post-apartheid South Africa, to take place following the election of a non-racial and democratic Government;

22. *Calls upon* the international community to continue to exercise vigilance with respect to developments in South Africa to ensure that the common objective of the people of South Africa and the international community is achieved, without deviation or obstruction, by the establishment of a united, non-racial and democratic South Africa.

General Assembly resolution 48/159 A

20 December 1993   Meeting 85   Adopted without vote

Draft by Nigeria (A/48/L.29); agenda item 38.
Financial implications. 5th Committee, A/48/788; S-G, A/C.5/48/59.
Meeting numbers. GA 48th session: 5th Committee 43; plenary 72, 76-80, 85.

Transition to democracy

On 2 July, the plenary of the multi-party negotiating process adopted by consensus 27 constitutional principles which, along with a bill of fundamental human rights, would be included in both the interim constitution and the final constitution to be adopted by an elected constituent assembly or an interim parliament. The principles were intended to provide for a strong central Government while accommodating regional diversity in the country.[16]

Under the Transitional Constitution, the national Parliament would consist of a 400-member National Assembly, elected on the basis of proportional representation, and a 90-member Senate, to be elected by nine provincial legislatures. The National Assembly would elect the President. The full Parliament would serve both as an interim parliament and as a constituent assembly and would draw up the final constitution within two years. The homelands would be abolished and the country divided into nine provinces, each with an elected provincial legislature to administer education, health, police and other services at the provincial level, as well as to elect the representatives for the 10 seats allocated to each province in the national Parliament's Senate. The interim constitution further guaranteed fundamental rights, including: equality of race and gender; freedom of speech, assembly and movement; the right to vote and to a fair trial; prohibition of torture and cruel or inhuman punishment; and the right of those dispossessed of land under apartheid legislation to seek restitution. It also limited the President's power to declare a state of emergency.

It was envisaged that the transition to a new democratic order would commence with the establishment and functioning of TEC, which was to include one member from each of the parties represented in the multi-party negotiating process. The State President would be an Executive President chosen by the governing party. The Cabinet, based on the principle of proportional representation, was to be composed of those political parties obtaining 5 per cent or more of the electoral vote. The State President and the Cabinet would keep TEC informed of any proposed legislation, decisions and intended actions, and, if 75 per cent of its members so decided, it could stop legislation or reverse a government decision. TEC was entitled to request documents and information and could conduct investigations and delegate powers to its subcouncils. The President must consult TEC before declaring a state of emergency or "unrest areas" in the country. TEC could reverse such a decision, if 80 per cent of its members so decided.

The future Constitutional Court of South Africa would have final and binding jurisdiction over the interpretation, protection and enforcement of the interim constitution.

Meanwhile, the structures established under the National Peace Accord were all functioning at the national, regional and local levels, with the number of peace committees rising from 50 to about 200 in the second half of 1993. Their performance was, however, far from uniform due to lack of agreement between political parties on measures to be taken or failure to implement decisions. Most peace committees suffered from budgetary and human resource constraints, as well as the absence of political commitment of major players, including the police and security forces.

SECURITY COUNCIL ACTION

Following consultations held on 23 November, at which South Africa was invited to participate under rule 37[a] of the Security Council's provisional rules

[a]Rule 37 of the Council's provisional rules of procedure states: "Any Member of the United Nations which is not a member of the Security Council may be invited, as the result of a decision of the Security Council, to participate, without vote, in the discussion of any question brought before the Security Council when the Security Council considers that the interests of that Member are specially affected, or when a Member brings a matter to the attention of the Security Council in accordance with Article 35(1) of the Charter."

of procedure, the President of the Council made a statement on behalf of its members:[17]

Meeting number. SC 3318.

"The Security Council welcomes the successful completion of the multi-party negotiating process in South Africa, and the conclusion of agreements reached therein on an interim constitution and electoral bill. These agreements constitute a historic step forward in establishing a democratic, non-racial and united South Africa.

"The Security Council looks forward to the elections to be held in South Africa in April 1994. It urges all parties in South Africa, including those which did not participate fully in the multi-party talks, to respect agreements reached during the negotiations, to recommit themselves to democratic principles, to take part in the elections and to resolve outstanding issues by peaceful means only.

"The Security Council reiterates its determination to continue to support the process of peaceful democratic change in South Africa for the benefit of all South Africans. The Security Council commends once again the work being done by the Secretary-General and the United Nations Observer Mission in South Africa in assisting that process. It invites the Secretary-General to accelerate contingency planning for a possible United Nations role in the election process, including coordination with the observer missions of the Organization of African Unity, European Community and Commonwealth, to enable expeditious consideration of a request to the United Nations for such assistance. In this connection, the Council urges early establishment of the Transitional Executive Council and the Independent Electoral Commission.

"The Security Council considers that South Africa's transition to democracy must be underpinned by economic and social reconstruction and development, and calls on the international community to assist in this regard."

Report of the Secretary-General. The Secretary-General reported[18] that, pursuant to Security Council resolutions of July[19] and August[20] 1992, and taking into account the progress achieved in the peace process, he had advised the President of the Council on 13 December[21] of his intention to appoint Lakhdar Brahimi, former Minister for Foreign Affairs of Algeria, as his Special Representative for South Africa. His tasks were to assist in implementing relevant Council resolutions and decisions and to coordinate the activities of other international observers, as requested by TEC. On 16 December,[22] the Council President indicated the Council's agreement to that proposal.

The Special Representative visited South Africa and met in Cape Town with President de Klerk and Foreign Minister Roelof F. Botha on 17 and 23 December, respectively. The President welcomed national and international assistance in voter education. Both the President and the Foreign Minister stressed that the most difficult problem facing the transition process was political vio-

lence and intimidation. They noted that UNOMSA had assisted in curbing such violence and in encouraging dialogue and tolerance. In the process, the United Nations had succeeded in establishing its credibility among the South African population. They underlined the historical importance of the elections and the need for them to be free, fair and legitimate. The Minister expressed the hope that the United Nations would allocate resources to provide for the largest possible number of observers needed during the elections.

At a meeting in Johannesburg on 18 December, the ANC President, Mr. Mandela, stated that he and President de Klerk were coordinating efforts to bring the members of the Freedom Alliance into the peace process. He noted that the groups which had the potential to disrupt the electoral process were those that enjoyed support within the military police and security forces as well as within the bureaucracy. He stressed the importance of maintaining lines of communication with the Freedom Alliance and urged the Special Representative to meet with its members during his visit. He called for a strong United Nations presence during the electoral process to ensure that the elections were free and fair.

On 17 December, the Special Representative met in Cape Town with Archbishop Desmond Tutu and Justice Richard Goldstone, Chairman of the Goldstone Commission. Archbishop Tutu, who had recently held discussions with Chief Buthelezi, Mr. Mandela and other leaders, was optimistic that the transitional arrangements would succeed, despite the decision of the Freedom Alliance not to participate in the electoral process and violence in the East Rand and Natal/KwaZulu.

The Special Representative held talks on 18 December with Legwaila J. Legwaila, head of the OAU Observer Mission in South Africa, and a team of the Commonwealth Observer Mission on strengthening and broadening cooperation between them and UNOMSA in connection with the electoral process.

On 22 December, Mr. Brahimi held talks in Johannesburg with John Hall and Antonie Gildenhuys, chairman of the National Peace Committee and head of its secretariat, respectively. Discussing the role that the two bodies would play in the electoral process and their cooperation with UNOMSA, Mr. Gildenhuys informed the Special Representative that the various local and regional peace committees would continue to be involved in promoting peace, but would not observe the electoral process.

The Special Representative also discussed arrangements for the elections and the United Nations role in them with Zach de Beer, leader of the Democratic Party, Thabo Mbeki, Chairman of ANC, Benny Alexander, Secretary-General of PAC, and other officials, as well as with representatives of the transitional institutions.

On 28 July, the Economic and Social Council adopted **resolution 1993/45** on monitoring the transition to democracy in South Africa.

UN Observer Mission in South Africa

UNOMSA, which was established by the Security Council in August 1992[20] and which initially deployed 50 observers to South Africa,[23] was expanded in 1993 in its scope of operations and strengthened in personnel.

Responding to the Secretary-General's requests of December 1992[24] and September 1993,[25] the Security Council authorized an increase in the number of UNOMSA observers—10 in February[26] and 40 in September,[27] for a total complement of 100—to serve as a nucleus for the anticipated United Nations role in the electoral process in South Africa.

The Secretary-General reported in November[28] that the additional observers would supplement those already serving the local peace committees, whose numbers had risen from 23 to 120 in less than a year, and would be deployed as follows: two teams each at the Western, Northern and Eastern Capes; Western, Northern, Far Northern and Eastern Transvaals; and Border/Ciskei and Orange Free State; and seven each at Durban and Johannesburg.

UNOMSA continued to carry out its tasks in all regions and at all levels. Its Chief of Mission, Angela King, held meetings with a cross-section of political, church and community leaders to discuss the peace process, the question of political violence and developments in the multi-party negotiations. UNOMSA observers worked closely with organizers and the security forces to ensure that demonstrations, marches, rallies, funerals and other mass actions were adequately planned and that the Goldstone Commission guidelines for marches and political gatherings were complied with. Observers held 832 informal bilateral meetings and acted as channels of communication between international observer missions, government officials, security forces, political parties and NGOs actively involved in the peace process. In total, its observers attended well over 9,000 meetings and events throughout the country in the 15 months since its deployment.

The Secretary-General proposed that UNOMSA's mandate be expanded to include the observation of the April 1994 elections. Under the proposed expanded mandate, UNOMSA would be required to: observe the actions of IEC and its organs in all aspects and stages of the electoral process, verifying their compatibility with the conduct of a free and fair election under IEC and Electoral Acts; observe the extent of freedom of organization, move-

ment, assembly and expression during the electoral campaign and ascertain the adequacy of the measures taken to ensure that political parties and alliances enjoyed those freedoms without hindrance or intimidation; monitor compliance of the security forces with the requirements of the relevant TEC laws and decisions; and verify the satisfactory implementation of the disposition of the IMC and IBA Acts. UNOMSA would also verify adequate voter education, the proper exercise of voting rights, that voting was free of intimidation, that there was free access to voting stations and secrecy of vote, the proper transport and custody of the ballots, security of the vote count and timely announcement of the results. The Mission would coordinate the activities of the international electoral observers and establish effective cooperation with national and foreign NGOs monitoring the electoral process. It would report complaints, irregularities and interferences to the electoral authorities for remedial action. It would also play a more proactive role in the socio-economic reconstruction and development of the country.

At its first meeting on 7 December, TEC endorsed a resolution adopted the previous day by MPNC requesting the United Nations to provide a sufficient number of international observers to monitor the electoral process and to coordinate the activities of other international observers provided by OAU, the European Union and the Commonwealth as well as those provided by individual Governments. Accordingly, the Secretary-General dispatched a survey team to South Africa on 9 December to assess the electoral assistance needs.

UNOMSA financing

In a November report[28] to the General Assembly's Fifth (Administrative and Budgetary) Committee, the Secretary-General estimated UNOMSA's costs for the period from mid-September 1992 to 31 December 1993 at $13,106,100 against an appropriation of $13,044,900. The additional requirement of $61,200 would be reflected in the second performance report of the programme budget for the biennium 1992-1993. An amount of $8,994,100 would be required under the proposed budget for the 1994-1995 biennium to cover the costs of UNOMSA up to 31 July 1994, excluding provisions for staff assessment in the amount of $1,324,300. Should decisions be made concerning specific additional electoral requirements or extension of the Mission beyond 31 July 1994, he would seek the concurrence of the Advisory Committee on Administrative and Budgetary Questions (ACABQ) to enter into related commitments under Assembly **resolution 48/229** on unforeseen and extraordinary expenses for 1994-1995.

ACABQ communicated in December[29] that it had no objection to those proposals.

By **resolution 48/230, section I,** of 23 December, the Assembly endorsed ACABQ's recommendations, concurring in particular with the one concerning the Committee's concurrence to enter into related commitments under **resolution 48/229.** The Assembly requested the Secretary-General, in administering the appropriation, to take full account of ACABQ's recommendations to seek the Government's assistance in procuring office space with minimum charge and to make every reasonable effort to acquire services and materials from local area sources.

Other aspects

Political prisoners and exiles

In 1992, 192 political prisoners had been released as part of the Record of Understanding agreed to by the South African Government and ANC on 26 September of that year. However, at the end of September 1993, 46 persons remained listed as political prisoners by the Human Rights Commission of South Africa. During the first half of 1993, 281 cases of detention without trial were reported under South Africa's Public Safety Act of 1953 and section 29 of the Internal Security Act.

ANC said that despite the Government's undertaking to release all the remaining political prisoners, a number of them were still in jail. Statistics of research groups indicated that the monthly average number of people detained without trial was higher during 1993 than in 1992. According to the South African Institute of Race Relations, detention without trial was used during 1993 against dozens of people.

The Human Rights Commission of South Africa reported that during the first half of the year, 84 political trials were concluded in which 145 persons out of 824 accused were convicted. From October 1992 to October 1993, representatives of the International Committee of the Red Cross (ICRC) made over 500 visits to detainees in some 300 police stations and prisons.

PAC reported that, on 25 May, the Government had arrested over 100 of its leaders and members. However, no serious charge was brought against any PAC member.

Significant progress continued with regard to political exiles. The Office of the United Nations High Commissioner for Refugees (UNHCR) indicated that, by the end of May, 10,957 South African refugees and exiles had registered for voluntary repatriation. The Government cleared some 10,730 for return and 6,604 returned to South Africa under UNHCR auspices. Member States and regional and other organizations contributed over $27 million to the repatriation and reintegration effort, including small-scale income-generating training programmes for returnees.

Women and children under apartheid

Responding to a 1992 Economic and Social Council request,[30] the Secretary-General submitted to the Commission on the Status of Women in January 1993 a report[31] on women and children living under apartheid. The report, which updated information contained in his 1991 report,[32] examined the legal, social and economic situation of women in South Africa and action taken to assist them.

The report indicated that, on 29 January, the Government of South Africa signed a number of international treaties relating to women and children, including the Convention on the Political Rights of Women,[33] the Convention on the Nationality of Married Women,[34] the Convention on the Elimination of All Forms of Discrimination against Women,[35] the Convention against Torture and Other Cruel, Inhuman or Degrading Treatment or Punishment[36] and the Convention on the Rights of the Child;[37] it also acceded to the Convention on Consent to Marriage, Minimum Age for Marriage and Registration of Marriage.[38]

In the economic and social spheres, women in South Africa continued to be subject to race and gender discrimination and were further disadvantaged by living in a male-dominated and patriarchal society. Apartheid had confined the majority of women to impoverished homelands, with limited opportunities for employment and income-generating activities. Those in urban areas tended to be concentrated in unskilled and semi-skilled positions in the informal sector, and were exploited in terms of salary and working conditions. Data also indicated that black women were concentrated in the service sector, mainly as domestic assistants, nurses and teachers, and constituted a negligible proportion of the black workers in managerial and professional jobs.

As the Government devoted 35 per cent of its overall education expenditure to the minority white children, the crisis of black education reached alarming proportions. An estimated 1.5 million children of school-going age were not attending school. The crisis was exacerbated by a severe shortage of basic materials and qualified teachers. Announced government reforms for semi-private status for white schools were denounced as a new attempt at segregation. Children were also exploited as agricultural labourers and in the informal sector in the urban areas and townships.

Poverty affected the majority of South African families. As many as 2.5 million people could not afford basic nutritional needs. Infant mortality rates were rising as nutritional problems worsened. It was estimated that only 8 per cent of the rural black population were self-sufficient, while the majority relied on remittances from relatives working in the cities.

United Nations organs undertook several activities to assist women and children living under apartheid, including the Centre against Apartheid, the United Nations Development Fund for Women, the United Nations Population Fund, the United Nations Children's Fund (UNICEF) and ILO.

ECONOMIC AND SOCIAL COUNCIL ACTION

On 27 July, on the recommendation of its Social Committee, the Economic and Social Council adopted **resolution 1993/13** without vote.

Women and children under apartheid

The Economic and Social Council,

Recalling its resolution 1992/15 of 30 July 1992,

Reaffirming the provisions of the Declaration on Apartheid and its Destructive Consequences in Southern Africa, contained in the annex to General Assembly resolution S-16/1 of 14 December 1989,

Taking note of General Assembly resolution 47/95 of 16 December 1992,

Alarmed by the grave socio-economic deprivation to which the majority of the people, especially the women and children, are subjected as a direct consequence of apartheid,

Deeply concerned about the politically motivated violence that has to date claimed thousands of lives and left hundreds of thousands of people homeless, the majority of whom are women and children, especially in Natal and Transvaal provinces,

Noting the positive changes initiated by the South African authorities aimed at dismantling apartheid, which were the result of the relentless struggle waged by the people of South Africa as well as of the pressure exerted by the international community,

Welcoming the progress made by the Convention for a Democratic South Africa, and encouraging the multi-party forum to discuss and debate the political dispensation and future of a democratic, non-racial, non-sexist South Africa,

Concerned at the fact that women are not integrated in the ongoing attempts to resolve the problems of South Africa by peaceful means, as envisaged in the Declaration on Apartheid, and stressing the need to ensure their full participation in that process by, *inter alia*, directly involving the gender advisory committee in the multi-party forum,

Taking note of the report of the Secretary-General on women and children living under apartheid, in which it is mentioned that the Government of South Africa signed on 29 January 1993 a number of conventions aimed at promoting and implementing fundamental rights and freedoms without distinction as to sex, namely, the Convention on the Political Rights of Women, the Convention on the Nationality of Married Women, the Convention on the Elimination of All Forms of Discrimination against Women, the Convention against Torture and Other Cruel, Inhuman or Degrading Treatment or Punishment and the Convention on the Rights of the Child,

Noting the subsequent release by the Government of South Africa of the draft bill on the promotion of equal opportunities and concerned that it failed to deal with questions of substantive sexism that are integral to the problems of poverty, ignorance and disempowerment,

Convinced that the present legal system requires structural changes to be relevant to a new and just South Africa and that the draft bill should represent the views and experiences of those most affected by it,

Recognizing that the equality of women and men cannot be achieved without the success of the struggle towards a united, non-racist, non-sexist and democratic South Africa,

Commending the role played by the United Nations, particularly the Centre against Apartheid and the Division for the Advancement of Women of the Centre for Social Development and Humanitarian Affairs of the Secretariat, in helping South African women to participate fully in the process of establishing a non-racist, non-sexist democracy in South Africa,

1. *Commends* those women both inside and outside South Africa who have resisted oppression and have remained steadfast in their opposition to apartheid;

2. *Demands* the immediate and unconditional release of any political prisoners and detainees, among whom are women and children, in accordance with the undertaking of the South African authorities;

3. *Urges* those involved in the multi-party forum to place high on their agenda issues concerning women, such as freedom, justice and equality, development and the environment;

4. *Appeals* to all countries and United Nations bodies, in conformity with General Assembly resolution 46/79 A of 13 December 1991 and in consultation with liberation movements, to increase their support for educational, health, vocational training and employment opportunities for women and children living under apartheid;

5. *Requests* the Centre against Apartheid to widen and strengthen its cooperation with the Division for the Advancement of Women of the Centre for Social Development and Humanitarian Affairs of the Secretariat, with a view to creating specific programmes of assistance to South African women to enable them to participate fully in the process of transition of their country towards a non-racist democracy;

6. *Appeals* to the international community to give its full and concerted support to the vulnerable and critical process now under way in South Africa through a phased application of appropriate pressures on the South African authorities, as warranted by developments, and to provide assistance to the opponents of apartheid and the disadvantaged sectors of society in order to ensure the rapid and peaceful attainment of the objectives of the Declaration on Apartheid and its Destructive Consequences in Southern Africa;

7. *Requests* the international community to provide financial, material and human resources to South African women towards the establishment of special programmes and projects geared to women's integration and advancement at the present time and in post-apartheid South Africa;

8. *Calls upon* the Secretary-General to consolidate the United Nations observer mission already deployed in South Africa to monitor and report on the unprecedented proportion of incidents of political and domestic violence directed against women and children from a variety of sources;

9. *Decides* that the Commission on the Status of Women should remain seized of the question of women and children living under apartheid;

10. *Requests* the Secretary-General to submit to the Commission at its thirty-eighth session a report on the implementation of the present resolution.

Economic and Social Council resolution 1993/13

27 July 1993   Meeting 43   Adopted without vote

Approved by Social Committee (E/1993/105) without vote, 12 July (meeting 6); draft by Commission on women (E/1993/27); agenda item 19.

Economic and social conditions

As the structures of apartheid were being dismantled and new agreements reached for their replacement, all major groupings in South Africa called for social reconstruction to eliminate the economic, social and political consequences of apartheid. Progress was made in addressing the critical needs in the socio-economic sectors, through the establishment of national forums in the areas of housing, electrification, local governments, drought, education and training.

In 1993, there were signs that the country was emerging from the longest recession it had suffered in the twentieth century. The gross domestic product (GDP) grew by 1.4 per cent in the first quarter and by 5.1 per cent in the second. The recession had severely affected employment, and was marked by a further decline in investment because of depressed demand and political uncertainties. The 1992/93 budget deficit reached 8.6 per cent, with revenues lower than expected because of the recession and higher expenditures, mainly on drought relief. With a generally declining inflation rate, the South Africa Reserve Bank cut the discount rate in February to 13 per cent, compared to 16 per cent in March 1992. The current account surplus continued to decline, to 700 million rand (R) during the first quarter of 1993, reflecting an increase in the price and volume of non-agricultural exports. The country recorded a capital outflow of R 3.7 billion during the first quarter, while gold and foreign reserves declined to R 9.5 billion in March 1993 from R 13.2 billion in August 1992.

The budget presented in March 1993 projected a decline in the deficit to 6.8 per cent of GDP. It also earmarked increases of 8 per cent in social expenditures, 12 per cent for education and 28 per cent for housing and related services. In March, the Minister of Finance presented a long-term restructuring programme for the South African economy. The programme recommended measures to improve growth, but recognized that, to improve the living standards of the poor, additional measures would be necessary to address the disparities in the socio-economic sectors. In May, the World Bank, in a paper entitled "An economic perspective of South Africa", recommended a

number of measures to maximize employment growth and reduce income differences.

In the area of housing, conditions for blacks deteriorated, with squatters in the Johannesburg area having quadrupled to 400,000 since 1990. To alleviate that situation, the Independent Development Trust, a leading development group, aimed to provide 110,000 residential sites to homeless families before the end of 1993 through its capital subsidy scheme. Special funds were allocated for the construction of primary health care clinics, of which 73 were completed, 50 were under construction and 28 were in the planning phase. Nevertheless, the provision of health care remained inequitable and inefficient.

On 26 January, the Minister of National Education released an education renewal strategy, envisaging compulsory education for at least nine years, equal spending per head across racial categories, the creation of a single department supervising all education, recognition of diversity and a new system to promote national unity. Following widespread disruption in schooling due to mass action by students and teachers, President de Klerk and Mr. Mandela reached agreement on the setting up of an education negotiating forum. In August, a National Education Training Forum was launched to create a single non-racial education system.

In terms of land distribution, the Advisory Commission on Land Allocation was established to deal with the task of restoring land to dispossessed communities and peoples, by acting as an advisory body on land claims.

In the area of trade and finance, the Johannesburg Chamber of Commerce and Industry adopted a three-pronged approach, aimed at re-establishing and expanding trade relations with traditional partners, mainly the United Kingdom and other Western European countries; creating new markets in the economically buoyant regions of the Pacific Rim; and expanding and creating links with African countries. The number of trade missions visiting South Africa soared to 160 in 1992, with a bigger increase expected for 1993.

South African exports in the first six months of 1993, totalling R 3.69 billion, were 11 per cent higher than those recorded for the same 1992 period, while imports, totalling R 2.76 billion, were up by 14 per cent.

Relations with South Africa

South Africa continued to emerge from its political and economic isolation in 1993 as more States established diplomatic ties with Pretoria, resumed trade and lifted sanctions in recognition of the country's achievements towards establishing a non-racial, democratic order.

Albania, the Central African Republic, the Congo, Gabon, Morocco, Norway, Qatar and the Republic of Korea established diplomatic relations with South Africa during the year. Agreements were concluded on the opening of representative offices in Oman, Jordan and Zambia, while consular relations were established with Greece and Turkey. In May, South Africa opened a representative office in Angola.

Economic relations

Lifting of sanctions

Addressing the Special Committee against Apartheid on 24 September, ANC President Mandela said the time had come for the international community to lift all economic sanctions against South Africa in response to the historic advances achieved towards democracy, so as to give added impetus to that process and to strengthen the forces of democratic change towards stability and social progress. PAC, on the other hand, called for existing sanctions to remain in effect until a new constitution was in place ensuring election of a new Government.

Following Mr. Mandela's appeal, the OAU Ad Hoc Committee on Southern Africa, meeting in extraordinary ministerial session on 29 September in New York, issued a statement[39] supporting the lifting of sanctions, except those relating to the arms embargo and nuclear matters. The Committee urged that the oil embargo be lifted after the establishment and commencement of the work of TEC.

On 24 September, the Secretary-General of the Commonwealth announced the immediate lifting of all trade, investment and financial sanctions. Several Governments, including those of Australia, Canada, India and the United States, announced similar steps. Norway had announced on 15 March the lifting of sanctions, excluding the Assembly's oil embargo and the mandatory arms embargo imposed by the Security Council in 1977.[40]

GENERAL ASSEMBLY ACTION

On 8 October, the General Assembly adopted **resolution 48/1** by consensus.

Lifting of sanctions against South Africa
The General Assembly,
Bearing in mind the objectives of the Declaration on Apartheid and its Destructive Consequences in Southern Africa, adopted by consensus on 14 December 1989,
Noting that the transition to democracy has now been enshrined in the law of South Africa,
1. *Decides* that all provisions adopted by the General Assembly relating to prohibitions or restrictions on economic relations with South Africa and its nationals, whether corporate or natural, including the areas of trade, investment, finance, travel and transportation, shall cease to have effect as of the date of the adoption of the present resolution, and requests all States to take appropriate measures within their jurisdiction to lift the restrictions and prohibitions they had imposed to implement the previous resolutions and decisions of the General Assembly;
2. *Also decides* that all provisions adopted by the General Assembly relating to the imposition of an embargo on the supply of petroleum and petroleum products to South Africa, and on investment in the petroleum industry there, shall cease to have effect as of the date that the Transitional Executive Council becomes operational, and requests all States to take appropriate measures within their jurisdiction to lift any restrictions or prohibitions they had imposed to implement previous resolutions and decisions of the General Assembly in this respect.

General Assembly resolution 48/1
8 October 1993   Meeting 22   Adopted by consensus
Draft by Nigeria (A/48/L.2); agenda item 38.

Monitoring of the oil embargo

The Intergovernmental Group to Monitor the Supply and Shipping of Oil and Petroleum Products to South Africa continued to investigate alleged violations and port calls in South Africa of ships capable of carrying oil and petroleum products. The Group maintained contact with Governments, intergovernmental organizations, NGOs and the shipping industry, following up cases of alleged violations.

During 1993, the Group queried 71 cases of alleged violations that occurred mainly during 1992 and collected information on 198 additional cases involving 149 ships of oil-shipping States.

Since 1987, the Group had removed a number of cases of alleged violations from further consideration, using the following criteria: when the certificate of discharge confirmed the delivery of oil to ports other than those in South Africa; when there was no oil-loading facility in the port concerned; and when it was certified that the ship in question was not capable of transporting oil or petroleum products. During 1993, the Group removed 22 such cases from further consideration after receiving information from Governments. Four annexes to the Group's annual report to the Assembly, issued in November,[41] contained a list of ships and companies reportedly involved in supplying oil to South Africa between 1987 and 1992; a summary of cases of alleged violations reported and investigated in 1993; and surveys of unclarified tanker calls at South African ports reported in 1991 and 1992, and in 1993.

The Group concluded that changes in South Africa were sufficiently profound and irreversible to warrant the lifting of the oil embargo, and endorsed the OAU decision that the embargo should be lifted after the establishment and commencement of work of TEC. It recommended to the

General Assembly that its mandate be terminated when TEC became operational.

By letters of 7 December, the Chairman of the Group,[42] the Chairman of the Special Committee against Apartheid[43] and the Permanent Representative of South Africa[44] informed the President of the Assembly that TEC had convened that day for its first formal meeting.

GENERAL ASSEMBLY ACTION

On 20 December, the General Assembly adopted **resolution 48/159 C** without vote.

Work of the Intergovernmental Group to Monitor the Supply and Shipping of Oil and Petroleum Products to South Africa

The General Assembly,

Having considered the report of the Intergovernmental Group to Monitor the Supply and Shipping of Oil and Petroleum Products to South Africa,

Recalling its resolutions 47/116 D of 18 December 1992 and 48/1 of 8 October 1993,

Welcoming the establishment of the Transitional Executive Council in South Africa,

1. *Takes note with appreciation* of the report of the Intergovernmental Group to Monitor the Supply and Shipping of Oil and Petroleum Products and endorses its recommendations;

2. *Decides* to terminate the mandate of the Intergovernmental Group as of the date of the adoption of the present resolution;

3. *Requests* the Secretary-General to issue by 30 January 1994, as addenda to the report of the Intergovernmental Group, the responses of States to requests addressed to them regarding the cases contained in the annexes to that report.

General Assembly resolution 48/159 C

20 December 1993   Meeting 85   Adopted without vote

10-nation draft (A/48/L.31/Rev.1 & Add.1); agenda item 38.
Sponsors: Algeria, Costa Rica, Cuba, Indonesia, Kuwait, New Zealand, Nicaragua, Nigeria, Ukraine, United Republic of Tanzania.
Financial implications. 5th Committee, A/48/788; S-G, A/C.5/48/59.
Meeting numbers. GA 48th session: 5th Committee 43; plenary 72, 76-80, 85.

Transnational corporations

In a March 1993 report to the Commission on Transnational Corporations (TNCs),[45] the Secretary-General examined the economy of South Africa in the context of the world recession and the economic measures necessary to encourage long-term inward foreign investments by TNCs. In an addendum to the report, the Secretary-General updated the list of TNCs with equity interests of more than 10 per cent in South Africa and those which had divested. It also contained the Code of Conduct for Multinational Companies Investing in South Africa and the Platform of Guiding Principles for Foreign Investors, formulated by the Congress of South African Trade Unions in conjunction with ANC.

By **resolution 1993/49**, the Economic and Social Council invited TNCs to give their full support to the demise of apartheid and to take appropriate measures regarding the vulnerable and critical process currently under way in South Africa. It requested the Secretary-General to continue examining possible contributions of TNCs to a united, non-racial and democratic South Africa in the economic and social fields, taking into account the special need for development of human resources, particularly the training of black South African entrepreneurs, and for employment, housing and health.

The Commission on Transnational Corporations, at its nineteenth session (Geneva, 5-15 April),[46] reiterated the urgent need for the removal of the remaining obstacles to the creation of an atmosphere conducive to constitutional negotiations in South Africa. It invited Governments, entrepreneurs and enterprises, including TNCs, to give their full support to the end of apartheid.

Military and nuclear aspects

South Africa reduced its 1993/94 defence budget to R 9.3 billion from R 9.7 billion in 1992/93, a decrease of 3.8 per cent. However, the South African Parliament was informed that SADF had a R 4.38 billion budget for its secret special defence account, an appropriation that was sharply criticized by ANC and PAC as undermining the transition to democracy and fomenting the violence.

In spite of protests and appeals, Switzerland announced on 1 June its approval for the export of 60 Pilatus PC-70 military trainer aircraft to the South African Air Force, stating that the technical changes made by its manufacturer would make it impossible to convert the aircraft for combat use.

The South African Arms Corporation (ARMSCOR) held a six-day armaments fair, the Defence Exposition of South Africa (Nasrec, 16-22 November 1992), with more than 150 South African companies participating. The Special Committee against Apartheid called on all Governments and other institutions not to support the exhibition.

As regards South Africa's long-suspected nuclear programme, President de Klerk confirmed on 24 March that over a 15-year period South Africa had built six nuclear fission devices and had been working on a seventh, when it decided, in 1989, to dismantle its arsenal so as to accede to the 1968 Treaty on the Non-Proliferation of Nuclear Weapons,[47] and sign an international safeguards agreement with the International Atomic Energy Agency (IAEA), which it did in 1991.[48] He stated that at no time did South Africa acquire nuclear-weapon technology or material from another country, nor had it provided any to or cooperated with any third country in that regard.

In September,[49] the Director General of IAEA reported on implementation of the safeguards agreement and the Agency's assessment of South Africa's nuclear-weapon programme. The Agency reported that it had found no indication that there remained any sensitive components of the nuclear-weapon programme that had not been either rendered useless or converted to commercial non-nuclear applications or peaceful nuclear usage.

On 1 October,[50] the General Conference of IAEA took note of South Africa's announcement concerning the voluntary abandonment of its nuclear deterrent capability and its invitation to IAEA to inspect past nuclear-weapon programme activities and facilities and to verify its full disclosure. It requested South Africa to continue its stated policy of full transparency.

Aid programmes and inter-agency cooperation

In an October 1993 report,[51] submitted in response to a 1992 General Assembly request,[7] the Secretary-General outlined the coordinated approach of 16 United Nations bodies and 13 specialized agencies to facilitate the peaceful elimination of apartheid and the transition of South Africa to a non-racial and democratic society as envisaged by the Assembly in 1989.[2] Guidelines for a coordinated United Nations approach to questions relating to South Africa had been adopted by the Administrative Committee on Coordination in 1991.[52]

The Secretariat's Centre against Apartheid was involved in organizing the Symposium on Political Tolerance in South Africa: Role of Opinion-Makers and the Media (Cape Town, 30 July–1 August), as well as the Joint North American/European NGO Consultation (Geneva, 30 and 31 August). The Centre for Human Rights invited 11 South Africans representing a wide cross-section of society to participate in its fellowship programme and to attend the annual study session of the International Institute of Human Rights (Strasbourg, France). The Department of Public Information (DPI) provided television, radio and photographic coverage of meetings and events sponsored by the Special Committee against Apartheid. It issued a background article in January in *UN Focus* on recent developments in the issue of apartheid in South Africa, as well as 76 press releases in English and 21 in French, which were distributed to 67 United Nations information centres (UNICs). Articles on the topic were also published in four editions of the *UN Chronicle*. The DPI Radio Section's Anti-Apartheid Programmes Section produced 89 radio programmes in the first four months of 1993 in Arabic, Bangla, Chinese, Dutch, English, French, Kiswahili and Spanish and distributed them to local radio stations through UNICs. Regular weekly broadcast slots

were secured for "One South Africa" and "Southern Africa Review" by the Harare UNIC on Zimbabwe Broadcasting Corporation, and by the Cairo UNIC on Cairo Radio Overseas Service.

The United Nations Development Programme (UNDP) was preparing a project for technical assistance in public service reform and conducted an assessment of NGOs in South Africa as a basis for providing assistance for human development and capacity-building. It was also providing support to the core group responsible for organizing a donors' conference to mobilize resources for South Africa.

UNICEF launched a national advocacy and social mobilization drive (Johannesburg, 14-18 June) and assisted in organizing a conference on food security, hosted by the National Consultative Forum on Drought; activities relating to the celebration of the Day of the African Child; and a situation analysis dissemination conference. The United Nations University held a seminar in July, financed by the International Development Research Centre of Canada, on industrial policy in post-apartheid South Africa.

The Economic Commission for Africa jointly organized with the African Institute of South Africa a workshop at Johannesburg in August entitled "Towards a Development Strategy for South Africa", attended by international and South African experts in the field. It debated the theoretical underpinnings of and options for development in a post-apartheid South Africa.

An ILO planning mission to South Africa met in February with a wide range of trade unionists, employer organizations and liberation movements and determined priority technical cooperation needs in the transition to democracy. Those priorities included employment creation, human resource development, economic policy formulation, worker education and labour law reform. ILO assisted in organizing a workshop on labour relations in the public sector (Johannesburg, 20 and 21 April) and participated in a conference on labour law in the rural sector (Stellenbosch, 13 and 14 May) and a conference on workers' rights (Cape Town, 18 and 19 June).

The United Nations Educational, Scientific and Cultural Organization (UNESCO) established a special programme for South Africa in May in support of a democratic, united and non-racial society. Through its regular programme, UNESCO granted fellowships for university studies and provided technical advice and material assistance to education officers and departments of ANC and PAC, as well as joint assistance with UNDP for the setting up of ANC and PAC education centres in the United Republic of Tanzania. In June, 20 South African trainees completed a three-year course for secondary schoolteachers at Tanzania's Mkwaja Teacher Training Institute.

A World Health Organization mission to South Africa in February covered four major areas: the general functioning of the national immunization programme as a part of primary health care activities and a basis for polio eradication; the surveillance system for vaccine-preventable diseases; diagnostic virology activities; and production and control of the Expanded Programme of Immunization vaccines. A follow-up visit in September carried out further analysis of the vaccine production situation.

The Assembly, by **resolution 48/159 A**, called on the international community to assist disadvantaged South African democratic anti-apartheid organizations and individuals in the academic, scientific and cultural fields.

UN Trust Fund for South Africa

Five grants totalling $1,880,000 were made in 1993 from the United Nations Trust Fund for South Africa, established in 1965[53] to provide legal, relief and educational assistance to persons persecuted under the country's repressive and discriminatory legislation, as well as relief to South African refugees.

According to an October 1993 report of the Secretary-General,[54] the Fund had received, since his October 1992 report,[55] $2,188,955 in voluntary contributions from 25 Member States. Total income of the Fund since its inception, including interest, was $50,298,190, and the total amount of grants was $47,850,974, including those approved in 1993. Pledges from 15 Governments totalling $82,357 were outstanding.

In accordance with a 1992 General Assembly resolution,[56] the Fund's Committee of Trustees provided assistance for the reintegration of former political prisoners and newly released prisoners into South African society, as well as assistance to voluntary agencies inside South Africa to alleviate the adverse effects of the apartheid legacy and to encourage increased public confidence in the rule of law. The Committee supported the involvement of the international community and the United Nations in support of the multi-party negotiating process, human rights and democracy in South Africa.

GENERAL ASSEMBLY ACTION

On 20 December, the General Assembly adopted **resolution 48/159 D** without vote.

United Nations Trust Fund for South Africa

The General Assembly,

Recalling its resolutions on the United Nations Trust Fund for South Africa, in particular resolution 47/116 C of 18 December 1992,

Having considered the report of the Secretary-General on the United Nations Trust Fund for South Africa, to which is annexed the report of the Committee of Trustees of the Trust Fund,

Taking note of its resolution 46/79 F, adopted without a vote on 13 December 1991, in particular paragraph 3, relating to assistance by the Trust Fund for work in the legal field,

Welcoming the agreements reached within the framework of the resumed multi-party negotiations and approved by Parliament to hold elections in 1994 on the basis of universal suffrage and to establish a Transitional Executive Council, as well as legislative and other measures adopted to promote free political activity in the run-up to free and fair elections,

Recognizing the work being carried out by broad-based, impartial voluntary organizations inside South Africa in providing legal and humanitarian assistance to victims of apartheid and racial discrimination, and noting with satisfaction the working relationship that the Trust Fund has established with those South African organizations,

Concerned about continued political violence and the dangers it represents for the democratic process and for the country at large,

Convinced that the time is nearing when South African authorities, within new, non-racial and democratic structures, will take responsibility for matters which have been within the mandate of the Trust Fund,

1. *Endorses* the report of the Secretary-General on the United Nations Trust Fund for South Africa;

2. *Supports* continued humanitarian, legal and educational assistance by the international community towards alleviating the plight of victims of apartheid in South Africa and towards facilitating the reintegration of released political prisoners and returning exiles into South African society;

3. *Endorses* the decision of the Trust Fund to channel its assistance through appropriate non-governmental organizations inside South Africa;

4. *Expresses its appreciation* to the Governments, organizations and individuals that have contributed to the Trust Fund and to the voluntary agencies engaged in rendering humanitarian and legal assistance to the victims of apartheid in South Africa;

5. *Expresses its conviction* that the Trust Fund has an important role to play during the final stage of the elimination of apartheid by assisting efforts in the legal field aimed at ensuring effective implementation of legislation repealing major apartheid laws, redressing the continuing adverse effects of those laws and encouraging increased public confidence in the role of law, and, therefore, appeals for generous contributions to the Fund;

6. *Commends* the Secretary-General and the Committee of Trustees of the Trust Fund for their persistent and worthy efforts throughout the years to promote humanitarian and legal assistance to the victims of apartheid and racial discrimination.

General Assembly resolution 48/159 D

20 December 1993   Meeting 85   Adopted without vote

34-nation draft (A/48/L.36 & Add.1); agenda item 38.

Sponsors: Angola, Argentina, Australia, Austria, Benin, Brazil, Canada, Chile, China, Costa Rica, Finland, France, Germany, Greece, Iceland, India, Ireland, Japan, Libyan Arab Jamahiriya, Malaysia, Morocco, Namibia, Nepal, New Zealand, Nigeria, Pakistan, Panama, Spain, Sweden, Turkey, Ukraine, United Republic of Tanzania, Zambia, Zimbabwe.

Meeting numbers. GA 48th session: plenary 72, 76-80, 85.

UN Educational and Training
Programme for Southern Africa

Scholarship awards under the United Nations Educational and Training Programme for Southern Africa reached 2,553 in 1992/93, compared to 2,108 in 1991/92, according to a report of the Secretary-General covering the period between 1 September 1992 and 31 August 1993.[57] The Programme was administered by the Secretary-General in consultation with an Advisory Committee and financed from a Trust Fund made up of voluntary contributions from States, organizations and individuals. Scholarship assistance was granted to 2,459 students from South Africa and to 94 students from Namibia who had enrolled prior to 31 December 1992. New awards were granted only to disadvantaged South Africans.

During the period, a total of $3,279,817 in contributions was received from 23 countries. In addition, pledges for 1993 from 14 States amounting to $759,345 were outstanding. The 1993 contributions and pledges, totalling $4,039,162, represented a decrease of $1,384,123 from the previous year.

The Advisory Committee on the Programme held three meetings to consider several aspects relating to the Programme's development in the light of the changing circumstances in South Africa. It noted the need for intensive educational and training assistance to disadvantaged South Africans to facilitate the country's transition.

The Programme initiated several new projects in cooperation with a broader network of scholarship agencies, educational institutions and NGOs, particularly inside South Africa. In its work plan for 1993-1994, it allocated $2.4 million, or 64 per cent of its total budget, for new awards to projects inside the country, 10.5 per cent in other low-cost countries and 19.5 per cent in high-cost countries. Currently, 84 per cent of its students were placed in South Africa and other low-cost countries, while 16 per cent were pursuing their studies in high-cost countries in short-term specialized courses. The Programme was mounting a major co-sponsorship training programme with *technikons* in South Africa, which would absorb a greater percentage of its resources in the near future. Training and placement of mid- and high-level cadres in key sectors of science and technology were considered a crucial requirement for sustained growth and development in South Africa.

In accordance with a 1992 Assembly resolution,[58] co-sponsorship and other arrangements inside South Africa were consolidated and expanded with a number of universities, *technikons* and NGOs. As the Programme shifted the focus of its educational and training activities to South Africa, particular attention was given to distance programmes with a view to enhancing institution-building and to filling South Africa's human resource needs during the transition period and beyond. Some graduate studies were primarily carried out abroad in programmes involving tuition waivers, graduate assistantships and other cost-sharing arrangements. The Programme's administrative costs were maintained at a minimum through group arrangements with educational institutions in South Africa.

In conclusion, the Secretary-General stated that it was increasingly recognized that a large trained cadre of black South Africans, especially at the high- and mid-management levels in education, science, technology and other priority areas, would play an important role in the country's economic and social development. He appealed for generous financial and other support to the Programme.

GENERAL ASSEMBLY ACTION

On 20 December, the General Assembly adopted **resolution 48/160** without vote.

United Nations Educational and Training Programme for Southern Africa

The General Assembly,

Recalling its resolutions on the United Nations Educational and Training Programme for Southern Africa, in particular resolution 47/117 of 18 December 1992,

Having considered the report of the Secretary-General containing an account of the work of the Advisory Committee on the United Nations Educational and Training Programme for Southern Africa and the administration of the Programme for the period from 1 September 1992 to 31 August 1993,

Noting with satisfaction that the recommendations of the evaluation of the Programme undertaken in 1989 as endorsed by the Advisory Committee continued to be implemented,

Recognizing the valuable assistance rendered by the Programme to the peoples of South Africa and Namibia,

Emphasizing the need for assistance to the people of South Africa particularly in the field of education during the transitional period,

Fully recognizing the need to provide continuing educational opportunities and counselling to students from South Africa in a wide variety of professional, cultural and linguistic disciplines, as well as opportunities for vocational and technical training and for advanced studies at graduate and postgraduate levels in priority fields of study, as often as possible at educational and training institutions within South Africa,

Noting that, in order to address the priority needs of disadvantaged South Africans, the Programme is continuing to allocate a higher proportion of resources for the purpose of institution-building in South Africa, in particular by strengthening the historically black and other institutions of higher learning, especially the *technikons*, through specialized training courses with built-in employability of graduates,

1. *Endorses* the report of the Secretary-General on the United Nations Educational and Training Programme for Southern Africa;

2. *Commends* the Secretary-General and the Advisory Committee on the United Nations Educational and Training Programme for Southern Africa for their efforts to adjust the Programme so that it can best help meet the needs evolving from changing circumstances in South Africa, to promote generous contributions to the Programme and to enhance cooperation with governmental, intergovernmental and non-governmental agencies involved in educational and technical assistance to South Africa;

3. *Also endorses* the Programme activities aimed at contributing to South Africa's human resources needs, especially during the transition period, by:

(a) Supporting co-sponsored projects with *technikons* and the historically black and other universities;

(b) Strengthening the institutional, technical and financial capacity as well as the decision-making of non-governmental organizations, community-based organizations and educational institutions that serve the needs and interests of disadvantaged South Africans;

(c) Engaging educational institutions, non-governmental organizations and the private sector in South Africa in co-sponsorship arrangements and job placement of graduates;

4. *Welcomes* the fact that educational and training activities of the Programme inside South Africa have expanded, and the Programme's close cooperation with South African non-governmental organizations, universities and *technikons*;

5. *Calls upon* non-governmental educational institutions, private organizations and individuals concerned to assist the Programme by entering into cost-sharing and other arrangements with it and by facilitating the returnability and job placement of its graduates;

6. *Appeals* to Governments, intergovernmental and non-governmental organizations, international professional associations and individuals to assist, within their areas of activity and influence inside South Africa, graduates of the Programme in obtaining access to job opportunities so that they can effectively contribute their professional competence and expertise towards the political, economic and social development of South Africa during the period of transition and beyond;

7. *Considers* that the activities of the Programme, under changing circumstances, should be planned in such a manner as to ensure that commitments made with regard to educational and training assistance to disadvantaged South Africans can be fully met;

8. *Requests* the Secretary-General to include the United Nations Educational and Training Programme for Southern Africa in the annual United Nations Pledging Conference for Development Activities;

9. *Expresses its appreciation* to all those who have supported the Programme by providing contributions, scholarships or places in their educational institutions;

10. *Appeals* to all States, institutions, organizations and individuals to offer such financial and other assistance to the Programme so as to enable it to carry out its programmed activities.

General Assembly resolution 48/160

20 December 1993   Meeting 85   Adopted without vote

33-nation draft (A/48/L.37 & Add.1); agenda item 39.

Sponsors: Angola, Argentina, Australia, Austria, Belgium, Benin, Brazil, Costa Rica, Finland, France, Germany, Greece, Guyana, Iceland, India, Ireland, Japan, Madagascar, Malaysia, Myanmar, Nepal, Netherlands, New Zealand, Nigeria, Norway, Portugal, Spain, Thailand, Turkey, Ukraine, United Republic of Tanzania, Zambia, Zimbabwe.

Meeting numbers. GA 48th session: plenary 76-80, 85.

REFERENCES

[1]A/48/22. [2]GA res. S-16/1, annex, 14 Dec. 1989. [3]A/48/419. [4]A/48/202-S/25895. [5]A/48/255-S/26048. [6]A/48/118. [7]YUN 1992, p. 162, GA res. 47/116 A, 18 Dec. 1992. [8]A/48/691. [9]YUN 1991, p. 108. [10]YUN 1992, p. 154. [11]A/48/114-S/25406. [12]S/25578. [13]A/48/122-S/25494. [14]S/26347. [15]A/48/657. [16]A/48/285-S/26198. [17]S/26785. [18]A/48/845-S/1994/16 & Add.1. [19]YUN 1992, p. 158, SC res. 765(1992), 16 July 1992. [20]Ibid., p. 160, SC res. 772(1992), 17 Aug. 1992. [21]S/26883. [22]S/26884. [23]YUN 1992, p. 164. [24]Ibid., p. 161. [25]S/26558. [26]S/25315. [27]S/26559. [28]A/C.5/48/28. [29]A/48/745. [30]YUN 1992, p. 165, ESC res. 1992/15, 30 July 1992. [31]E/CN.6/1993/11. [32]YUN 1991, p. 122. [33]YUN 1952, p. 484, GA res. 640(VII), annex, 20 Dec. 1952. [34]YUN 1956, p.241, GA res. 1040(XI), annex, 29 Jan. 1957. [35]YUN 1979, p. 895, GA res. 34/180, annex, 18 Dec. 1979. [36]YUN 1984, p. 813, GA res. 39/46, annex, 10 Dec. 1984. [37]GA res. 44/25, annex, 20 Nov. 1989. [38]YUN 1962, p. 330, GA res. 1763 A (XVII), annex, 7 Nov. 1962. [39]A/48/461-S/26514. [40]YUN 1977, p. 161, SC res. 418(1977), 4 Nov. 1977. [41]A/48/43-S/26789. [42]A/48/747. [43]A/48/744. [44]A/48/748. [45]E/C.10/1993/13 & Add.1. [46]E/1993/30. [47]YUN 1968, p. 17, GA res. 2373(XXII), annex, 12 June 1968. [48]YUN 1991, p. 119. [49]GC(XXXVII)/107S. [50]GC(XXXVII)/RES/625. [51]A/48/467 & Add.1. [52]YUN 1991, p. 109. [53]YUN 1965, p. 115, GA res. 2054 B (XX), 15 Dec. 1965. [54]A/48/523. [55]YUN 1992, p. 174. [56]Ibid., p. 175, GA res. 47/116 C, 18 Dec. 1992. [57]A/48/524. [58]YUN 1992, p. 176, GA res. 47/117, 18 Dec. 1992.

Other States

Angola

The armed conflict between the Government of Angola and the National Union for the Total Independence of Angola (UNITA) escalated during 1993, following an outbreak of fighting in late 1992 as a result of UNITA's refusal to accept the validity of the 1992 multi-party elections.[1] Peace negotiations resumed twice and resulted in the drafting of a Memorandum of Understanding and adoption of several specific principles on the re-establishment of the cease-fire and the formation of the Angolan armed forces. The Security Council extended the mandate of the second United Nations Angola Verification Mission (UNAVEM II), established in 1991,[2] six times, until 16 March 1994. In June, an international appeal was launched for emergency humanitarian assistance to the Angolan population.

Communication and report of the Secretary-General (January). On 8 January 1993,[3] the Secretary-General informed the Security Council that the situation in Angola had deteriorated since the beginning of the year, with heavy fighting in at least 10 provincial capitals and other population centres. The Government was unable to re-establish its administration in many rural areas, and the majority of municipalities remained in UNITA's hands. The Secretary-General's Special Representative for Angola and Chief of UNAVEM II, Margaret Joan Anstee, in an effort to restore the cease-fire and relaunch the dialogue begun in 1992, obtained the agreement of both sides to a meeting of military leaders. The Secretary-General recommended that the Council endorse her efforts and appeal to the two sides to meet as early as possible.

In a 21 January report,[4] submitted in response to a 1992 Council request,[5] the Secretary-General described the political and military developments in Angola and outlined the role and situation of UNAVEM II. He stated that, although the Angolan President, José Eduardo dos Santos, and the President of UNITA, Jonas Malheiro Savimbi, continued to reiterate their commitment to peace and resumed negotiations, fierce armed clashes broke out on 3 January in the city of Lubango and spread quickly throughout the country, effectively returning Angola to civil war. The military meeting, scheduled for 16 and 17 January, was suspended after UNITA insisted that political talks should take place at the same time. On 19 January, the Government of Angola accepted UNITA's proposal for a political-military meeting at Addis Ababa, Ethiopia. The Secretary-General noted that there were reports of foreign interference in the conflict, in violation of the 1991 Peace Accords.[6] In a 21 January letter[7] to the Secretary-General, the President of Angola requested that the Security Council extend and update UNAVEM's mandate, in the light of the escalating military action, to reinforce its presence in Angola and to ensure full implementation of the Peace Accords.

The Secretary-General said UNAVEM II played a mediating role following post-election developments, facilitating negotiations between the Government and UNITA, including between military commanders in combat. At the same time, its original mandate had become less relevant with the collapse of joint monitoring mechanisms, and the deteriorating security situation made it impossible to restore the Mission to full strength. By 20 January, its military and police observers had been reduced from 350 and 126 to 247 and 87, respectively, and civilian observers to nine. Of 67 UNAVEM locations, 45 had to be evacuated due to extensive fighting, with an estimated loss of some $5.2 million in abandoned, damaged or looted equipment. In addition, United Nations personnel were subjected to harassment and physical abuse. As a result, the Mission could no longer monitor the course of events adequately; however, it continued to assist in the evacuation efforts of ICRC, foreign consulates and NGOs. Following the return of Major-General Edward U. Unimna of Nigeria to na-

tional service on 14 December 1992, Brigadier-General Michael Nyambuya of Zimbabwe acted as Chief Military Observer.

The Secretary-General noted that his Special Representative had submitted to the two parties on 24 December 1992 a discussion paper on the future mandate of an enlarged UNAVEM. He recommended that the Security Council renew the mandate of his Special Representative, but confine the deployment of UNAVEM II, with reduced staff, to the capital city of Luanda, while maintaining sufficient equipment to permit subsequent expeditious redeployment to regional centres when feasible. The Secretary-General also recommended 30 April 1993 as the deadline for the Mission's withdrawal, should the two parties fail to agree on a cease-fire and resume negotiations.

Monthly cost estimates for the extension of UNAVEM II were provided in an addendum to the report.

SECURITY COUNCIL ACTION (January)

The Security Council met on 29 January to consider the situation in Angola, in accordance with the understanding reached in its prior consultations and in response to Angola's request.[8] Angola, Cuba, Guinea-Bissau, Mozambique, Namibia, Nigeria, Portugal, Zaire and Zimbabwe were invited to participate in the discussion, in accordance with the Charter of the United Nations and rule 37ᵃ of the Council's provisional rules of procedure.

The Council adopted **resolution 804(1993)** unanimously.

The Security Council,

Reaffirming its resolutions 696(1991) of 30 May 1991, 747(1992) of 24 March 1992, 785(1992) of 30 October 1992 and 793(1992) of 30 November 1992,

Having considered the further report of the Secretary-General dated 21 January 1993,

Having considered also the request submitted to the Secretary-General by the Government of Angola in its letter dated 21 January 1993,

Gravely disturbed by the recent outbreak of heavy fighting in many parts of Angola and the further deterioration of the already dangerous political and military situation in that country,

Gravely concerned at the continuing non-implementation of the major provisions of the "Acordos de Paz para Angola",

Concerned at the recent absence of dialogue between the Government of Angola and UNITA, and welcoming the meeting between them under United Nations auspices in Addis Ababa to discuss the cease-fire and political matters,

Also concerned at the outrageous harassment and physical abuse to which UNAVEM II personnel have been subjected, and the looting and destruction of United Nations property, as described in the above-mentioned report of the Secretary-General,

Further concerned at reports of foreign support for and involvement in military actions in Angola,

Regretting that the deteriorating situation has made it increasingly difficult for UNAVEM II to carry out its mandate,

Recalling that democratic elections were held on 29 and 30 September 1992, which the Special Representative of the Secretary-General certified as being generally free and fair, and that steps have been taken to set up a Government of National Unity which would reflect the results of the legislative elections, and deeply regretting the failure of UNITA to take part in the political institutions thus established,

Reaffirming its commitment to preserve the unity and territorial integrity of Angola,

Recognizing that the Angolans themselves bear ultimate responsibility for the restoration of peace and national reconciliation of their country,

Reiterating its support for the efforts of the Secretary-General and his Special Representative aimed at resolving the present crisis and resuming the political process, in particular through the completion of the electoral process,

1. *Notes with appreciation* the above-mentioned report of the Secretary-General;

2. *Strongly condemns* the persistent violations of the main provisions of the "Acordos de Paz", in particular the initial rejection by UNITA of the election results, its withdrawal from the new Angolan armed forces, its seizure by force of provincial capitals and municipalities and the resumption of hostilities;

3. *Demands* that the two parties cease fire immediately, restore at their meeting in Addis Ababa continued and meaningful dialogue, and agree on a clear timetable for the full implementation of the "Acordos de Paz", in particular with regard to confinement of their troops and collection of their weapons, demobilization and formation of the unified national armed forces, effective restoration of the Government administration throughout the country, the completion of the electoral process and the free circulation of people and goods;

4. *Supports* fully the Secretary-General and his Special Representative in their continuing efforts to restore the peace process and to carry out the mandate of UNAVEM II under extremely difficult conditions;

5. *Urges* once again the two parties, and in particular UNITA, to produce early evidence of their adherence to, and fulfilment without exception of, the "Acordos de Paz";

6. *Appeals* strongly to the Government of Angola and UNITA to confirm as soon as possible to the Secretary-General that real progress has been made towards implementation of the "Acordos de Paz";

7. *Appeals* to all Member States to render economic and technical assistance to the Government of Angola for reconstruction and development of the country;

8. *Calls upon* all Member States to support all those concerned in their efforts for the implementation of the "Acordos de Paz";

9. *Urges* all Member States to take all necessary steps to stop immediately and effectively any direct or indirect military or paramilitary interference from their territories and to respect scrupulously the provisions of the

"Acordos de Paz" concerning the cessation of supply of lethal material to any Angolan party;

10. *Strongly condemns* violations of international humanitarian law, in particular the attacks against the civilian population, including the extensive killings carried out by armed civilians, and calls upon both parties to abide by their obligations thereunder and the appropriate provisions of the "Acordos de Paz";

11. *Demands* that UNITA immediately release foreign nationals taken hostage;

12. *Strongly condemns* attacks against UNAVEM II personnel in Angola, and demands that the Government and UNITA take all necessary measures to ensure their safety and security;

13. *Expresses* its condolences to the family of the UNAVEM II police observer who lost his life;

14. *Approves* the recommendation of the Secretary-General to maintain a Special Representative for Angola based in Luanda, with the necessary civilian, military and police staff with the mandate as described in paragraph 29 of the report of the Secretary-General;

15. *Decides* to extend the mandate of UNAVEM II for a period of three months until 30 April 1993, with the proviso that, as a provisional measure based on security considerations, the Secretary-General is authorized to concentrate UNAVEM II deployment in Luanda, and at his discretion in other provincial locations, with the levels of equipment and personnel he deems appropriate to be retained in order to allow the subsequent expeditious redeployment of UNAVEM II as soon as this becomes feasible, with a view to the resumption of its functions in accordance with the "Acordos de Paz" and previous resolutions on this matter;

16. *Requests* the Secretary-General to submit to it as soon as the situation warrants, and in any case before 30 April 1993, a report on the situation in Angola together with his recommendations for the further role of the United Nations in the peace process, and in the meantime to keep the Council regularly informed;

17. *Stresses* its readiness to take action promptly, at any time within the period of the mandate authorized by this resolution, on the recommendation of the Secretary-General, to expand substantially the United Nations presence in Angola in the event of significant progress in the peace process;

18. *Reiterates* its readiness to consider all appropriate measures under the Charter of the United Nations to secure implementation of the "Acordos de Paz";

19. *Decides* to remain seized of the matter.

Security Council resolution 804(1993)

29 January 1993   Meeting 3168   Adopted unanimously

Draft prepared in consultations among Council members (S/25187).

Further developments (January-March). A high-level meeting between the Government of Angola and UNITA was held at Addis Ababa from 27 to 30 January, to consider the re-establishment of the cease-fire, conclusion of the implementation of the Peace Accords, the role of the United Nations in the peace process and the release of prisoners. Although no agreement on a cease-fire was reached, the parties agreed on some issues and to discuss outstanding ones. A second meeting, scheduled initially for 10 February at Addis Ababa, was postponed at UNITA's request until 26 February. On 23 February, the States observers to the Peace Accords (Portugal, the Russian Federation and the United States), meeting at Lisbon, Portugal, in preparation for the second meeting, called on the parties to the conflict to respond immediately to the appeals for truce launched by ICRC and the United Nations, pending agreement on a cease-fire, and to facilitate the provision of urgent humanitarian assistance. The meeting was cancelled following UNITA's request for a further delay of unspecified duration. The Special Representative regretted the cancellation of the meeting, since it was crucial for obtaining a cease-fire agreement. The observer States also issued a statement deploring the outcome.

In the meantime, civil war continued throughout most of the country. On 7 March, UNITA declared full control of Huambo, Angola's second largest city, following a battle which lasted for almost two months and cost more than 10,000 lives. On 8 March,[9] Angola appealed to the Security Council to condemn the aggressor and violator of the Peace Accords, to release Angola from compliance with the provision of the Accords concerning arms supplies, in acknowledgement of its right to recourse to Article 51 of the Charter, and to adopt international sanctions against UNITA.

In an oral report to the Council on 11 March, the Special Representative outlined several options for UNAVEM II, including the deployment of a major peace-keeping force, and emphasized that it was essential to review the Mission's mandate and make it more relevant to the changed circumstances.

UNAVEM personnel continued to be exposed to threats, intimidation and physical attacks; a military observer from Jordan was kidnapped at Cabinda on 23 February, and a police observer was wounded during a 6 March attack on the UNAVEM camp there.

In a 22 February letter[10] to the Security Council President, the Secretary-General announced his intention to appoint Major-General Chris Abutu Garuba of Nigeria as Chief Military Observer of UNAVEM II. On 26 February,[11] the President informed the Secretary-General of the Council's agreement.

SECURITY COUNCIL ACTION (March)

The Security Council considered further developments in Angola on 12 March. At its request, Angola was invited to participate in the discussion, in accordance with the Charter and rule 37ᵃ of the Council's provisional rules of procedure.

The Council adopted **resolution 811(1993)** unanimously.

The Security Council,

Reaffirming its resolutions 696(1991) of 30 May 1991, 747(1992) of 24 March 1992, 785(1992) of 30 October 1992, 793(1992) of 30 November 1992 and 804(1993) of 29 January 1993,

Gravely disturbed by the recent outbreak of heavy fighting in many parts of Angola, the large number of casualties and massive loss of human life which have ensued and the further deterioration of the already dangerous political and military situation, bringing the country to the verge of the resumption of civil war,

Gravely concerned at the persistent violations by UNITA of the major provisions of the "Acordos de Paz para Angola",

Further concerned at reports that military support and equipment continue to flow in contravention of the "Acordos de Paz",

Noting with particular concern that a humanitarian tragedy of grave proportions is developing in Angola and the need, therefore, for increased international humanitarian assistance,

Deeply regretting that the second meeting between the delegations of the Government of Angola and UNITA, which had been scheduled to be held on 26 February 1993 in Addis Ababa under the auspices of the United Nations, did not take place because of the failure by UNITA to fulfil its commitment to send a delegation to Addis Ababa,

Noting with satisfaction the readiness displayed by the Government of Angola to participate in the Addis Ababa meeting,

Reaffirming its commitment to preserve the unity and territorial integrity of Angola,

Welcoming and supporting the efforts of the Secretary-General and his Special Representative aimed at resolving the present crisis through negotiations,

1. *Strongly condemns* the persistent violations by UNITA of the major provisions of the "Acordos de Paz", in particular the continued rejection by UNITA of the results of the elections held on 29 and 30 September 1992 which the Special Representative of the Secretary-General determined as generally free and fair, its failure to take part in the political institutions established on the basis of those elections, its failure to engage in meaningful negotiations with the Government of Angola, its withdrawal from the new Angolan armed forces, its seizure by force of provincial capitals and municipalities and the resumption of hostilities;

2. *Demands* that UNITA accept unreservedly the results of the democratic elections of 1992 and abide fully by the "Acordos de Paz", and further demands that the two parties, particularly UNITA, produce early evidence, not later than 30 March 1993, that real progress has been made towards the implementation of the "Acordos de Paz";

3. *Strongly demands* an immediate cease-fire throughout the country, and further demands the resumption without delay and without preconditions of a continued and meaningful dialogue under United Nations auspices so that a clear timetable for the completion of the implementation of the "Acordos de Paz" may be established;

4. *Reaffirms* that it will hold responsible any party which refuses to take part in such a dialogue, thereby jeopardizing the entire process, and will consider all ap-

propriate measures under the Charter of the United Nations to advance the implementation of the "Acordos de Paz";

5. *Strongly condemns* verbal and physical attacks against the Special Representative of the Secretary-General and UNAVEM II personnel in Angola, and demands that these attacks cease forthwith and that the Government of Angola and UNITA take all necessary measures to ensure their safety and security;

6. *Condemns* the kidnapping of a UNAVEM II military observer in Cabinda on 23 February 1993 and demands that he be released unharmed and unconditionally and without further delay;

7. *Supports fully* the Secretary-General and his Special Representative in their continuing efforts to restore the peace process and to carry out the mandate of UNAVEM II under extremely difficult conditions;

8. *Invites* the Secretary-General to seek to organize a meeting between the Government of Angola and UNITA at the highest possible level with a view to securing the full implementation of the "Acordos de Paz", this meeting to take place in good time before 30 April 1993 and to consider also the future role of the United Nations in Angola, and encourages the parties to respond positively;

9. *Requests* the Secretary-General, pending the submission of the report referred to in paragraph 16 of resolution 804(1993), to present as soon as possible a progress report on the efforts for the resumption of the talks between the two parties in Angola at all appropriate levels;

10. *Calls on* all Member States, United Nations agencies and non-governmental organizations to accord or increase humanitarian relief assistance to Angola and encourages the Special Representative of the Secretary-General, with the resources at her disposal, to coordinate the provision of humanitarian assistance to the civilian population in need;

11. *Strongly appeals* to both parties strictly to abide by applicable rules of international humanitarian law, including unimpeded access for humanitarian assistance to the civilian population in need;

12. *Appeals once again* to all Member States to render economic, material and technical assistance to the Government of Angola for the reconstruction and development of the country;

13. *Looks forward* to the report of the Secretary-General referred to in paragraph 16 of resolution 804(1993) on the situation in Angola together with his recommendations for the further role of the United Nations in the peace process;

14. *Decides* to remain seized of the matter.

Security Council resolution 811(1993)

12 March 1993   Meeting 3182   Adopted unanimously

Draft prepared in consultations among Council members (S/25399).

Further developments (March/April). Following bilateral talks between the United States and UNITA at Abidjan, Côte d'Ivoire, from 25 to 29 March and subsequent consultations of the Special Representative with both parties to the conflict, direct talks resumed at Abidjan on 12 April under the auspices of the United Nations. The agenda of the meeting included arrangements for

a cease-fire, completion of the Peace Accords, national reconciliation, release of prisoners and humanitarian assistance, as well as guarantees for the security of people and property, freedom of the press, definition of the powers of provincial administration and the question of the future role of the United Nations in the peace process. Efforts concentrated on preparing a Protocol of Abidjan which, once signed, would immediately lead to a cease-fire and provide the basis for its implementation. The draft Protocol also provided for an expanded United Nations peace-keeping presence.

As hostilities in Angola continued, efforts to deliver humanitarian assistance to both Government- and UNITA-controlled areas met with increasing difficulties. On three separate occasions, United Nations aircraft came under fire, and a UNAVEM helicopter was damaged by stray bullets while evacuating refugees. On 26 April, an aircraft of the World Food Programme (WFP) was hit and made a crash landing short of the runway, which led to the death of the flight navigator and injuries to the seven other crew members. On the positive side, the military observer kidnapped on 23 February was released on 15 March. On 2 April, the southern African frontline States—a subregional group that included Angola—declared that the Angolan Government had a legitimate right to use all means to defend its sovereignty and territorial integrity and appealed to the international community to provide assistance to the Government.

An oral report on the developments in Angola was presented to the Security Council on 22 April. On 29 April,[(12)] the Secretary-General apprised the Council of the progress of the talks, which were expected to continue beyond 30 April, and recommended extending the existing mandate of UNAVEM II for an interim period of 31 days, until 31 May. He noted that the current strength of the Mission consisted of 75 military observers, 30 police officers, 49 international civilian staff, 12 paramedics and 70 local staff, which corresponded roughly to the wider deployment option envisaged in **resolution 804(1993)**.

SECURITY COUNCIL ACTION (April)

The Council met on 30 April, with Angola participating under rule 37[a] of the provisional rules of procedure, and adopted **resolution 823(1993)** unanimously.

The Security Council,

Reaffirming its resolutions 696(1991) of 30 May 1991, 747(1992) of 24 March 1992, 785(1992) of 30 October 1992, 793(1992) of 30 November 1992, 804(1993) of 29 January 1993 and 811(1993) of 12 March 1993,

Recalling its resolution 804(1993), in particular its paragraph 15, by which it decided to extend the mandate of UNAVEM II for a period of three months until 30 April 1993,

Extending its support to the current and ongoing peace talks in Abidjan between the Government of Angola and UNITA under United Nations auspices and chairmanship and expressing the hope that those talks will result in an immediate cease-fire and in the full implementation of the "Acordos de Paz",

Gravely concerned at the continuing attacks against international humanitarian flights operating in Angola, in particular the recent shooting down of a World Food Programme aircraft,

Taking into account the letter dated 29 April 1993 from the Secretary-General addressed to the President of the Security Council,

1. *Decides* to extend the existing mandate of UNAVEM II until 31 May 1993;

2. *Requests* the Secretary-General to submit to it as soon as the situation warrants, and in any case before 31 May 1993, a report on the situation in Angola with his recommendations for the further role of the United Nations in the peace process and in the meantime to keep the Council regularly informed;

3. *Stresses* its readiness to take action promptly, at any time within the period of the mandate authorized by this resolution, on the recommendation of the Secretary-General, to expand substantially the United Nations presence in Angola in the event of significant progress in the peace process;

4. *Condemns* the attacks against international humanitarian flights operating in Angola and demands that these attacks cease forthwith and that both parties, in particular UNITA, take all necessary measures to ensure the safety of these flights as well as the security of UNAVEM II personnel;

5. *Decides* to remain seized of the matter.

Security Council resolution 823(1993)
30 April 1993   Meeting 3206   Adopted unanimously
Draft prepared in consultations among Council members (S/25694).

Communication and reports of the Secretary-General (May).

In a 25 May report,[13] the Secretary-General described political and military developments and humanitarian assistance efforts in Angola since his January report. He stated that fighting throughout the country had intensified, with UNITA occupying an estimated 75 per cent of the territory. The direct talks between the Government and UNITA that led to the drafting of the Abidjan Protocol and its Memorandum of Understanding had to be suspended on 21 May due to UNITA's insistence on absolute parity in the simultaneous movement and quartering of government and UNITA troops, rather than just UNITA troops, as drafted in the Memorandum.

By a 27 May letter[14] to the Security Council President, the Secretary-General announced his intention to release Ms. Anstee, at her request, from her responsibilities as his Special Representative for Angola, and to appoint Alioune Blondin Beye of Mali to the post, effective 28 June. As stated in a 4 June letter[15] of the President, the Council members welcomed Mr. Beye's appointment.

As the war continued, the emerging humanitarian disaster was further aggravated by the recent drought in southern Africa, the Secretary-General said. According to WFP estimates, nearly 2 million Angolans were suffering from hunger, drought and disease, with at least 1,000 people dying daily. Activities of the United Nations humanitarian assistance coordination unit, set up in Luanda in late April, were supported by UNAVEM II, which coordinated security clearance for land and air transportation, provided communications services and its aircraft for humanitarian operations, and accompanied humanitarian flights and land convoys. Their efforts resulted in the transfer of nearly 6,000 refugees, mostly women and children, from Huambo and the delivery of some 350 tons of food and medical supplies to Caimbambo. The Special Representative proposed an emergency one-month plan for the delivery of humanitarian aid through land and air corridors to be mutually agreed on. An international appeal to fund the Emergency Humanitarian Programme, covering the period from 1 May 1993 to 30 April 1994, with a total funding requirement of $226 million was planned. The Secretary-General pointed to increasing reports of human rights violations and other atrocities against civilians, committed by both parties to the conflict, and urged them to respect their responsibilities under international humanitarian law.

He further reported that 18 UNAVEM locations had been evacuated since January, leaving only four outside Luanda, and that the losses since UN-AVEM's first withdrawal in late 1992 totalled $6.7 million. Noting that, apart from assisting in the delivery of humanitarian aid, the Mission's military and police components concentrated on patrolling and providing liaison with local military and civilian officials and other confidence-building measures, the Secretary-General recommended a further interim extension of UNAVEM II, on a reduced basis, from 1 June to 31 July, to provide good offices and mediation aimed at restoring a cease-fire and reinstating the peace process. He also recommended increasing resources for coordination of humanitarian assistance, including protection of the relief personnel and supervision of aid distribution.

The cost of the two-month extension was estimated at $3,659,000.

SECURITY COUNCIL ACTION (June)

The Security Council considered the Secretary-General's report on 1 June. Angola and Portugal were invited to participate in the discussion under rule 37[a] of the Council's provisional rules of procedure.

Resolution 834(1993) was adopted unanimously.

The Security Council,

Reaffirming its resolutions 696(1991) of 30 May 1991, 747(1992) of 24 March 1992, 785(1992) of 30 October 1992, 793(1992) of 30 November 1992, 804(1993) of 29 January 1993, 811(1993) of 12 March 1993 and 823(1993) of 30 April 1993,

Having considered the further report of the Secretary-General dated 25 May 1993,

Expressing grave concern at the deterioration of the political and military situation, and noting with consternation the further deterioration of an already grave humanitarian situation,

Gravely concerned at the failure of the talks between the Government of Angola and UNITA held in Abidjan under the auspices of the United Nations and the chairmanship of the Special Representative of the Secretary-General with participation of the representatives of the three observer States to the Angolan peace process— Portugal, the Russian Federation and the United States of America—and in particular at the failure to establish a cease-fire,

Welcoming and supporting the efforts of the Secretary-General and his Special Representative aimed at the earliest resolution of the Angolan crisis through negotiations,

Emphasizing the importance of a continued and effective United Nations presence in Angola, with a view to fostering the peace process and advancing the implementation of the "Acordos de Paz",

Reaffirming its commitment to preserve the unity and territorial integrity of Angola,

1. *Decides* to extend the existing mandate of the United Nations Angola Verification Mission (UNAVEM II) for a period of forty-five days until 15 July 1993 in accordance with the recommendations contained in paragraphs 36 and 37 of the Secretary-General's report;

2. *Stresses* the importance of the functions of good offices and mediation by UNAVEM II and the Special Representative, with the goal of restoring a cease-fire and reinstating the peace process for the full implementation of the "Acordos de Paz";

3. *Reiterates its demand* that UNITA accept unreservedly the results of the democratic elections of 1992 and abide fully by the "Acordos de Paz";

4. *Condemns* UNITA for its actions and armed attacks, which have resulted in increased hostilities and which endanger the peace process, and demands that it immediately cease such actions and armed attacks;

5. *Welcomes* the disposition of the Government of Angola to reach a peaceful settlement of the conflict in conformity with the "Acordos de Paz" and pertinent Security Council resolutions, deeply regrets UNITA's refusal at the talks to agree to the withdrawal of its troops from the locations which it has occupied since the resumption of the hostilities, and demands that it do so;

6. *Affirms* that such occupation is a grave violation of the "Acordos de Paz";

7. *Strongly appeals* to the two parties, and in particular to UNITA, to reinitiate as soon as possible the interrupted peace talks under United Nations auspices with a view to the earliest establishment of a cease-fire throughout the country and the full implementation of the "Acordos de Paz", further undertakings between the two parties, and relevant resolutions of the Security

Council, due account being taken of what was achieved during the discussion of the Abidjan draft protocol;

8. *Holds* UNITA responsible for the breakdown of the talks and for thereby jeopardizing the peace process, and reaffirms that it will consider all appropriate measures under the Charter of the United Nations to advance the implementation of the "Acordos de Paz";

9. *Supports fully* the continuing efforts of the Secretary-General and his Special Representative aimed at restoring the peace process and at carrying out the mandate of UNAVEM II under extremely difficult conditions;

10. *Calls on* all States to refrain from any action which directly or indirectly could jeopardize the implementation of the "Acordos de Paz", and urges all States to refrain from providing any form of direct or indirect military assistance or other support to UNITA inconsistent with the peace process;

11. *Welcomes* the steps taken by the Secretary-General to strengthen the humanitarian activities being undertaken by the United Nations system in Angola under the overall coordination of the Special Representative, including the preparation of the United Nations humanitarian assistance plan for Angola, and strongly appeals to the Government of Angola and to UNITA to cooperate fully with the Secretary-General's efforts in this field;

12. *Calls on* all Member States, United Nations agencies and non-governmental organizations to respond swiftly and generously to the Secretary-General's appeal in implementation of the above-mentioned plan and to accord or increase humanitarian relief assistance to Angola, and encourages the Special Representative of the Secretary-General to continue to coordinate the provision of humanitarian assistance;

13. *Reiterates* its appeal to both parties strictly to abide by applicable rules of international humanitarian law, including to guarantee unimpeded access for humanitarian assistance to the civilian population in need, and commends in particular the efforts of the Secretary-General and his Special Representative to establish agreed humanitarian relief corridors;

14. *Reiterates* its appeal to both parties to take all necessary measures to ensure the security and the safety of the personnel involved in humanitarian relief operations;

15. *Requests* the Secretary-General to submit to it as soon as the situation warrants, and in any case before 15 July 1993, a report on the situation in Angola with his recommendation for the further role of the United Nations in the peace process and, in the meantime, to keep the Council regularly informed of developments;

16. *Reiterates* its readiness to take action promptly, at any time within the period of the mandate authorized by this resolution, on the recommendation of the Secretary-General to expand substantially the United Nations presence in Angola in the event of significant progress in the peace process;

17. *Decides* to remain seized of the matter.

Security Council resolution 834(1993)

1 June 1993   Meeting 3226   Adopted unanimously

Draft prepared in consultations among Council members (S/25857).

On 8 June, following consultations with Council members, the President, on behalf of the Council, made the following statement:[16]'

Meeting number. SC 3232.

"The Security Council received with grave concern and shock the report of the Secretary-General on the attack by UNITA forces, on 27 May 1993, between Quipungo and Matala, against a train carrying civilians, which resulted in the death of 225 persons, including women and children, and several hundred wounded.

"The Security Council strongly condemns this action by UNITA, which is a clear violation of Security Council resolutions and of international humanitarian law, and it reiterates its demand that UNITA immediately cease its armed attacks. The Security Council expresses its condemnation of such criminal attacks and it stresses that those responsible must be held accountable. The Security Council urges UNITA leaders to make sure that its forces abide by the rules of international humanitarian law.

"The Security Council emphasizes once again the imperative need for an immediate cease-fire throughout the country and it reiterates its appeal to the two parties, in particular UNITA, to reinitiate the interrupted peace talks with a view to the full implementation of the Acordos de Paz.''

Communications (June/July). On 14 June,[17] the observer States communicated to the Security Council a statement issued at their 8 June meeting in Washington, D.C., reaffirming that the key principles of the Peace Accords and additional principles of the draft Abidjan Protocol's Memorandum of Understanding remained the basis for a peaceful settlement in Angola. They expressed their readiness to reactivate the monitoring and guarantee mechanisms of the Peace Accords, support the reinforcement of the United Nations role once agreement was reached, and ensure the delivery of humanitarian assistance throughout Angola. On 9 July,[18] they transmitted a statement issued at their 8 July meeting in Moscow, calling for an immediate cessation of hostilities and strongly urging UNITA to end its threats and intimidation against United Nations personnel and other participants in the peace process and to refrain from direct actions or threats against citizens or installations of third countries. Recognizing the right of the Angolan Government to self-defence, the observer States stressed the need to exercise restraint so as not to aggravate the situation. They also discussed additional measures to resolve the crisis, including an arms embargo against UNITA.

On 13 July,[19] Uganda communicated to the Council the Declaration on Angola, adopted by the OAU Assembly of Heads of State and Government at its twenty-ninth ordinary session (Cairo, Egypt, 28-30 June), calling on UNITA to resume peace talks with the Government, with a view to establishing a cease-fire and ensuring the full implementation of the Peace Accords. Condemning UNITA for repeated massacres of civilians and destruction of social infrastructures, the Assembly recommended that the Security Council impose sanctions against UNITA and neutralize its activities. It called on neighbouring countries not to allow the use of their territories as a springboard for military action by UNITA. By a letter of 14 July,[20] Uganda transmitted a resolution on the situation in Angola, adopted by the OAU Council of Ministers at its fifty-eighth ordinary session (Cairo, 21-26 June). The Ministers demanded that UNITA refrain from military actions and withdraw its troops from the occupied areas, and appealed to African States to end support to UNITA's military wing.

Report of the Secretary-General (July). In a 12 July report,[21] submitted pursuant to **resolution 834(1993)**, the Secretary-General said that the political and military situation in Angola continued to deteriorate as fighting intensified and mistrust deepened. UNITA increased efforts to seize additional territory and intensified attacks, aimed at causing serious economic losses to the Government. For its part, the Government reintroduced military conscription and the National Assembly on 17 June empowered it to use any means to confront the UNITA offensive. In a particularly serious incident, UNITA ambushed a train between Quipungo and Matala on 27 May, resulting in the deaths of some 300 people and hundreds of wounded. At meetings with the Special Representative on 5 and 8 July, respectively, both President dos Santos and Dr. Savimbi expressed readiness to resume peace talks and facilitate relief operations. Dr. Savimbi also stressed the need for the United Nations to assume a mediation role.

The Secretary-General also reported on efforts of United Nations organizations to provide humanitarian assistance to Angola and said that an estimated $70 million was received in response to the United Nations Consolidated Appeal for Angola, presented at a donors' conference at Geneva on 3 June (see PART THREE, Chapter III). WFP and UNICEF delivered food, medicines, vegetable oil and blankets under the one-month emergency relief plan, before its suspension at the end of June. The Secretary-General noted a declaration adopted on 24 June by the World Conference on Human Rights, urging the Security Council to take steps towards reaching a cease-fire and restoring peace in Angola, and calling for immediate humanitarian assistance (see PART THREE, Chapter X).

The Secretary-General reported that the Chief Military Observer appointed in June (see above) assumed command of UNAVEM II on 9 July. He had reduced the size of the Mission to 50 military and 18 police observers, 43 international civilian staff and 11 military paramedics, as well as necessary local staff. Its activities focused on patrolling, assessing the military situation, providing liaison between military and civilian officials and participating in humanitarian operations. The Secretary-General concluded that UNAVEM II had become an essential factor in advancing the peace process and an indispensable channel for communication between the parties; he recommended extension of its mandate for three months, from 16 July to 15 October. The total cost of a two-month extension until 15 September was estimated at $4,307,600.

SECURITY COUNCIL ACTION (July)

The Security Council met on 15 July to consider the situation in Angola. Angola, Egypt, Namibia, Portugal, the United Republic of Tanzania, Zambia and Zimbabwe were invited to participate in the discussion under rule 37ª of the Council's provisional rules of procedure.

The Council adopted **resolution 851(1993)** unanimously.

The Security Council,

Reaffirming its resolutions 696(1991) of 30 May 1991, 747(1992) of 24 March 1992, 785(1992) of 30 October 1992, 793(1992) of 30 November 1992, 804(1993) of 29 January 1993, 811(1993) of 12 March 1993, 823(1993) of 30 April 1993 and 834(1993) of 1 June 1993,

Having considered the further report of the Secretary-General dated 12 July 1993,

Recalling the statement made by the President of the Security Council on 8 June 1993,

Welcoming the Declaration on the Situation in Angola adopted by the Assembly of Heads of State and Government of the Organization of African Unity (OAU) at its twenty-ninth ordinary session, and the resolution on the situation in Angola adopted by the Council of Ministers of OAU at its fifty-eighth ordinary session,

Welcoming also the joint statement issued in Moscow on 8 July 1993 by the representatives of Portugal, the Russian Federation and the United States of America, the three observer States to the Angolan peace process,

Noting the Special Declaration on Angola adopted by the World Conference on Human Rights in Vienna,

Expressing grave concern at the deterioration of the political and military situation, and noting with consternation the further deterioration of an already grave humanitarian situation,

Deeply concerned that the peace talks remain suspended and that a cease-fire has not been established,

Welcoming and supporting the efforts of the Secretary-General and his Special Representative aimed at the earliest resolution of the Angolan crisis through negotiations,

Emphasizing the importance of a continued and effective United Nations presence in Angola with a view to fostering the peace process and advancing the implementation of the "Acordos de Paz",

Reaffirming its commitment to preserve the unity and territorial integrity of Angola,

1. *Welcomes* the further report of the Secretary-General dated 12 July 1993 and decides to extend the existing mandate of the United Nations Angola Verification Mission (UNAVEM II) for a period of two months until 15 September 1993;

2. *Reiterates* its readiness to consider taking action promptly, at any time within the period of the mandate authorized by this resolution, on the recommendation of the Secretary-General to expand substantially the United Nations presence in Angola in the event of significant progress in the peace process;

3. *Stresses* the importance of the functions of good offices and mediation by UNAVEM II and the Special Representative, with the goal of restoring a cease-fire and reinstating the peace process for the full implementation of the "Acordos de Paz";

4. *Reiterates its demand* that UNITA accept unreservedly the results of the democratic elections of 1992 and abide fully by the "Acordos de Paz";

5. *Condemns* UNITA for continuing military actions, which are resulting in increased suffering to the civilian population of Angola and damage to the Angolan economy and again demands that UNITA immediately cease such actions;

6. *Also condemns* UNITA's repeated attempts to seize additional territory and its failure to withdraw its troops from the locations which it has occupied since the resumption of the hostilities, and demands once again that it immediately do so and agree without delay to return its troops to United Nations–monitored areas as a transitional measure pending full implementation of the "Acordos de Paz";

7. *Reaffirms* that such occupation is a grave violation of the "Acordos de Paz" and is incompatible with the goal of peace through agreements and reconciliation;

8. *Stresses* the fundamental need to reinitiate without delay the peace talks under United Nations auspices with a view to the immediate establishment of a cease-fire throughout the country and the full implementation of the "Acordos de Paz" and relevant resolutions of the Security Council;

9. *Takes note* of statements by UNITA that it is prepared to resume peace negotiations and demands that UNITA act accordingly;

10. *Welcomes* the continued disposition of the Government of Angola to reach a peaceful settlement of the conflict in conformity with the "Acordos de Paz" and relevant resolutions of the Security Council;

11. *Urges* all States to refrain from any action which directly or indirectly could jeopardize the implementation of the "Acordos de Paz", especially from providing any form of direct or indirect military assistance to UNITA, or any other support to UNITA inconsistent with the peace process;

12. *Expresses its readiness* to consider the imposition of measures under the Charter of the United Nations, including a mandatory embargo on the sale or supply to UNITA of arms and related matériel and other military assistance, to prevent UNITA from pursuing its military actions, unless by 15 September 1993 the Secretary-General has reported that an effective cease-fire has been established and that agreement has been reached on the full implementation of the "Acordos de Paz" and relevant resolutions of the Security Council;

13. *Recognizes* the legitimate rights of the Government of Angola and in this regard welcomes the provision of assistance to the Government of Angola in support of the democratic process;

14. *Welcomes* the steps taken by the Secretary-General to implement the emergency humanitarian assistance plan;

15. *Takes note* of statements by UNITA that it will cooperate in ensuring the unimpeded delivery of humanitarian assistance to all Angolans and demands that UNITA act accordingly;

16. *Calls upon* all Member States, United Nations agencies and non-governmental organizations to respond swiftly and generously to the Secretary-General's appeal in implementation of the above-mentioned plan and to accord or increase humanitarian relief assistance to Angola, and encourages the Special Representative of the Secretary-General to continue to coordinate the provision of humanitarian assistance;

17. *Demands* that UNITA continue to extend its cooperation in ensuring the immediate evacuation of foreign nationals and their family members from Huambo and other locations occupied by UNITA;

18. *Reiterates* its strong condemnation of the attack by UNITA forces, on 27 May 1993, against a train carrying civilians, and reaffirms that such criminal attacks are clear violations of international humanitarian law;

19. *Reiterates also* its appeal to both parties strictly to abide by applicable rules of international humanitarian law, including to guarantee unimpeded access for humanitarian assistance to the civilian population in need, and commends in particular the efforts of the Secretary-General and his Special Representative to establish agreed humanitarian relief corridors;

20. *Reiterates* its appeal to both parties to take all necessary measures to ensure the security and safety of UNAVEM II personnel as well as of the personnel involved in humanitarian relief operations;

21. *Requests* the Secretary-General to submit to it as soon as the situation warrants, and in any case before 15 September 1993, a report on the situation in Angola with his recommendation for the further role of the United Nations in the peace process and, in the meantime, to keep the Council regularly informed of developments;

22. *Requests also* the Secretary-General to submit as soon as possible the budgetary implications of bringing UNAVEM II up to its full strength as mandated in resolution 696(1991) of 30 May 1991;

23. *Decides* to remain seized of the matter.

Security Council resolution 851(1993)

15 July 1993   Meeting 3254   Adopted unanimously

Draft prepared in consultations among Council members (S/26080).

In a 10 September statement,[22] issued at a meeting at Lisbon, the observer States, noting with concern the intensification of the war in Angola, recommended that the Security Council propose measures to undercut UNITA's ability to pursue war and make it resume negotiations. They gave special attention to the tragic humanitarian situation in Angola and demanded the immediate release of all foreigners held captive by UNITA.

Report of the Secretary-General (September). The Secretary-General reported on 13 September[23] that the Angolan Government had launched a counter-offensive in early August and succeeded in broadening its area of control. On 11 August, Dr. Savimbi proposed an immediate cease-fire without preconditions, which was communicated to the Security Council President and the Special Representative on 13 and 20 August, respectively. However, while reiterating its readiness to resume dialogue, the Government of Angola asserted that the proposal could not be considered seriously since it had not been communicated to it officially. Subsequent efforts by the Special Representative to discuss the proposal with Dr. Savimbi were to no avail, due to ongoing hostilities at Huambo.

The Special Representative continued to maintain regular contacts with the Government and the three observer States, as well as with UNITA, and held intensive consultations in the Congo, Gabon, Namibia, Sao Tome and Principe, Zaire, Zambia and Zimbabwe, which led to initiatives to hold a high-level meeting between the parties to the conflict either in Gabon or in Sao Tome and Principe. In a 3 September communiqué, UNITA expressed readiness to meet with the Presidents of Sao Tome and Principe and of Portugal and reiterated its offer to suspend military hostilities immediately. On 4 September, the Government stated that a cease-fire should be established in accordance with the Peace Accords and relevant Security Council resolutions and that UNITA's offer was not made within such a context. On 9 September, UNITA announced that Dr. Savimbi was not included in its delegation due to the security situation at Huambo.

The report noted that, with the further intensification of the fighting, the humanitarian situation had worsened dramatically. Food and other emergency assistance were provided under a relief programme to the areas considered secure. On 7 July, agreement was reached between the Government of Angola, UNITA and the United Nations to resume the emergency relief plan suspended in June. On 15 July, relief flights were resumed to agreed locations in combat zones for an initial period of 10 days. On 29 July, the Government approved a twofold plan covering emergency assistance to areas of active conflict and to those outside conflict but still considered unsafe. On 3 September, UNITA agreed to the proposed plan.

The Secretary-General recommended restoring the level of UNAVEM's international civilian staff to at least 59 and extending its mandate for a further three months. The total cost of the extension was estimated at some $7.2 million.

SECURITY COUNCIL ACTION (September)

On 15 September, the Security Council considered the Secretary-General's report, with Angola, Egypt, Nigeria and Portugal participating in the discussion under rule 37[a] of the Council's provisional rules of procedure. The Council adopted **resolution 864(1993)** unanimously.

The Security Council,

Reaffirming its resolutions 696(1991) of 30 May 1991, 747(1992) of 24 March 1992, 785(1992) of 30 October 1992, 793(1992) of 30 November 1992, 804(1993) of 29 January 1993, 811(1993) of 12 March 1993, 823(1993) of 30 April 1993, 834(1993) of 1 June 1993 and 851(1993) of 15 July 1993,

Having considered the report of the Secretary-General dated 13 September 1993,

Expressing grave concern at the continuing deterioration of the political and military situation, and noting with consternation the further deterioration of an already grave humanitarian situation,

Deeply concerned that, despite its previous resolutions and the efforts undertaken by the Secretary-General and his Special Representative, the peace talks remain suspended and a cease-fire has not been established,

Welcoming the joint statement issued in Lisbon on 10 September 1993 by the representatives of Portugal, the Russian Federation and the United States of America, the three observer States to the Angolan peace process,

Welcoming also and supporting to that end the efforts of the Secretary-General and his Special Representative aimed at the earliest resolution of the Angolan crisis through negotiations, and stressing the importance it attaches thereto,

Welcoming further the efforts of the Ad Hoc Committee on Southern Africa of the Organization of African Unity (OAU) and of heads of State of neighbouring countries to facilitate the resumption of the peace process in Angola,

Emphasizing the importance of a continued and effective United Nations presence in Angola with a view to fostering the peace process and advancing the full implementation of the "Acordos de Paz",

Reaffirming its commitment to preserve the unity and territorial integrity of Angola,

A

1.   *Welcomes* the report of the Secretary-General dated 13 September 1993 and decides to extend the existing mandate of the United Nations Angola Verification Mission (UNAVEM II) for a period of three months until 15 December 1993;

2.   *Reiterates its readiness* to consider taking action promptly, at any time within the period of the mandate authorized by this resolution, on the recommendation of the Secretary-General, to expand substantially the United Nations presence in Angola in the event of significant progress in the peace process;

3.   *Reaffirms* the importance of the functions of good offices and mediation by UNAVEM II and the Special Representative, with the goal of restoring a cease-fire and reinstating the peace process for the full implementation of the "Acordos de Paz";

4.   *Welcomes* the continued disposition of the Government of Angola to reach a peaceful settlement of the conflict in conformity with the "Acordos de Paz" and relevant resolutions of the Security Council;

5.   *Reaffirms its recognition* of the legitimate rights of the Government of Angola and in this regard welcomes the provision of assistance to the Government of Angola in support of the democratic process;

6.   *Reiterates once again its demand* that UNITA accept unreservedly the results of the democratic elections of 30

September 1992 and abide fully by the "Acordos de Paz";

7.   *Condemns* UNITA for continuing military actions, which are resulting in increased suffering to the civilian population of Angola and damage to the Angolan economy and again demands that UNITA immediately cease such actions;

8.   *Also condemns* UNITA's repeated attempts to seize additional territory and its failure to withdraw its troops from the locations which it has occupied since the resumption of the hostilities, and demands once again that it immediately do so and agree without delay to return its troops to United Nations–monitored areas as a transitional measure pending full implementation of the "Acordos de Paz";

9.   *Reaffirms* that such occupation is a grave violation of the "Acordos de Paz" and is incompatible with the goal of peace through agreements and reconciliation;

10. *Stresses once again* the fundamental need to reinitiate without delay the peace talks under United Nations auspices with a view to the immediate establishment of a cease-fire throughout the country and the full implementation of the "Acordos de Paz" and resolutions of the Security Council;

11. *Takes note* of statements by UNITA that it is prepared to resume peace negotiations and demands that UNITA act accordingly;

12. *Welcomes* the further steps taken by the Secretary-General to implement the emergency humanitarian assistance plan;

13. *Strongly condemns* the repeated attacks carried out by UNITA against United Nations personnel working to provide humanitarian assistance and reaffirms that such attacks are clear violations of international humanitarian law;

14. *Takes note* of statements by UNITA that it will cooperate in ensuring the unimpeded delivery of humanitarian assistance to all Angolans and demands that UNITA act accordingly;

15. *Reiterates its appeal* to both parties to take all necessary measures to ensure the security and safety of UNAVEM II personnel as well as of the personnel involved in humanitarian relief operations, and strictly to abide by applicable rules of international humanitarian law;

16. *Demands* that UNITA proceed immediately to the release of all foreign citizens held against their will and to abstain from any action which might cause damage to foreign property;

B

Strongly condemning UNITA and holding its leadership responsible for not having taken the necessary measures to comply with the demands made by the Council in its previous resolutions,

Determined to ensure respect for its resolutions and the full implementation of the "Acordos de Paz",

Urging all States to refrain from providing any form of direct or indirect assistance, support or encouragement to UNITA,

Determining that, as a result of UNITA's military actions, the situation in Angola constitutes a threat to international peace and security,

Acting under Chapter VII of the Charter of the United Nations,

17. *Decides* that the provisions set forth in paragraphs 19 to 25 below shall come into force ten days after the date of adoption of the present resolution unless the Secretary-General notifies the Council that an effective cease-fire has been established and that agreement has been reached on the implementation of the "Acordos de Paz" and relevant resolutions of the Security Council;

18. *Decides further* that if, at any time after the submission of the above-mentioned report of the Secretary-General, the Secretary-General reports to the Council that UNITA has broken the cease-fire or ceased to participate constructively in the implementation of the "Acordos de Paz" and the relevant resolutions of the Security Council, the provisions set forth in paragraphs 19 to 25 below shall come into force immediately;

19. *Decides*, with a view to prohibiting all sale or supply to UNITA of arms and related *matériel* and military assistance, as well as petroleum and petroleum products, that all States shall prevent the sale or supply, by their nationals or from their territories or using their flag vessels or aircraft, of arms and related *matériel* of all types, including weapons and ammunition, military vehicles and equipment and spare parts for the aforementioned, as well as of petroleum and petroleum products, whether or not originating in their territory, to the territory of Angola other than through named points of entry on a list to be supplied by the Government of Angola to the Secretary-General, who shall promptly notify the Member States of the United Nations;

20. *Calls upon* all States, and all international organizations, to act strictly in accordance with the provisions of the present resolution, notwithstanding the existence of any rights or obligations conferred or imposed by any international agreement or any contract entered into or any licence or permit granted prior to the date of adoption of this resolution;

21. *Calls upon* States to bring proceedings against persons and entities violating the measures imposed by this resolution and to impose appropriate penalties;

22. *Decides* to establish, in accordance with rule 28 of its provisional rules of procedure, a Committee of the Security Council consisting of all the members of the Council to undertake the following tasks and to report on its work to the Council with its observations and recommendations:

(a) To examine the reports submitted pursuant to paragraph 24 below;

(b) To seek from all States further information regarding the action taken by them with a view to effectively implementing the measures imposed by paragraph 19 above;

(c) To consider information brought to its attention by States concerning violations of the measures imposed by paragraph 19 above and to recommend appropriate measures in response thereto;

(d) To make periodic reports to the Security Council on information submitted to it regarding alleged violations of the measures imposed by paragraph 19 above, identifying where possible persons or entities, including vessels, reported to be engaged in such violations;

(e) To promulgate guidelines that may be necessary to facilitate the implementation of the measures imposed by paragraph 19 above;

23. *Calls upon* all States to cooperate fully with the Committee established by paragraph 22 above in the fulfilment of its tasks, including supplying such infor-

mation as may be sought by the Committee in pursuance of the present resolution;

24. *Requests* all States to report to the Secretary-General by 15 October 1993 on the measures they have adopted in order to meet the obligations set out in paragraph 19 above;

25. *Requests* the Secretary-General to provide all necessary assistance to the Committee established by paragraph 22 above and to make the necessary arrangements in the Secretariat for this purpose;

26. *Expresses its readiness* to consider the imposition of further measures under the Charter of the United Nations, including, *inter alia*, trade measures against UNITA and restrictions on the travel of UNITA personnel, unless by 1 November 1993 the Secretary-General has reported that an effective cease-fire has been established and that agreement has been reached on the full implementation of the "Acordos de Paz" and relevant resolutions of the Security Council;

C

27. *Expresses also its readiness* to review the measures in the present resolution if the Secretary-General reports to the Council that an effective cease-fire has been established and that substantial progress has been achieved towards the full implementation of the "Acordos de Paz" and relevant resolutions of the Security Council;

28. *Requests* the Secretary-General to submit to it as soon as the situation warrants, and in any case in good time before 1 November 1993 and again before 15 December 1993, a report on the situation in Angola and the implementation of this resolution, with his recommendation for the further role of the United Nations in the peace process and, in the meantime, to keep the Council regularly informed of developments;

29. *Decides* to remain seized of the matter.

Security Council resolution 864(1993)

15 September 1993   Meeting 3277   Adopted unanimously

Draft prepared in consultations among Council members (S/26445).

Report of the Secretary-General (October). On 27 October,[24] the Secretary-General reported to the Security Council that UNITA, at a meeting with his Special Representative at Abidjan on 14 and 15 September, proposed a unilateral declaration of a cease-fire throughout Angola, effective 20 September, and called for immediate discussions of a number of political and military issues. The proposal, however, included no references to the legal framework for the peace process, acceptance of the 1992 election results, or a bilateral cease-fire agreement between the parties. The report noted that the Angolan Government had, on 22 September, announced its peace plan,[25] which included principles for the resolution of the post-electoral crisis, such as UNITA's withdrawal from the occupied areas, followed by a cease-fire; unimpeded access for humanitarian aid and immediate evacuation of the wounded, sick and foreigners after the establishment of the cease-fire; complete acceptance of the validity of the Peace Accords and the election results; and respect for the legislation produced by the institutions resulting from the elections. In a 6 October communiqué, UNITA reaffirmed the validity of the Peace Accords and its acceptance of the election results, although holding them fraudulent, and considered the Abidjan Protocol as a serious basis for negotiations. It also stated that institutions resulting from the elections should reflect the current position of UNITA and other opposition forces. It pledged to maintain the unilateral cease-fire and requested the Special Representative to announce a date for the resumption of negotiations. On 25 October, the two sides began exploratory talks at Lusaka, Zambia.

Although the intensity of military operations generally decreased, specific activities were reported in various parts of the country, including troop movements, attacks, ambushes and shelling. The Secretary-General noted that UNAVEM II at its current level could not provide nationwide coverage to verify those reports. As the humanitarian situation worsened, the programme of emergency assistance was expanded. Food deliveries by WFP and NGOs increased to more than 8,800 tons in September, while UNICEF initiated its second 90-day plan providing aid in primary health care, vaccination and diarrhoeal disease control, nutrition, relief and survival assistance, water and sanitation, household food security and education.

In view of the ongoing political talks, the Secretary-General recommended that the Security Council postpone action to impose further measures against UNITA until 1 December. He also recommended increasing the number of UNAVEM II military observers to 175, police observers to 60 and military paramedics to 14, to be deployed in the event of a political breakthrough. Cost estimates of the Mission's enlargement for a six-month period were set at $14,194,000.

SECURITY COUNCIL ACTION (November)

The Security Council met on 1 November to consider the Secretary-General's report. Angola participated in the discussion under rule 37ª of the Council's provisional rules of procedure.

Following consultations, the President, on behalf of the Council, made the following statement:[26]

Meeting number. SC 3302.

"The Security Council has considered the Secretary-General's report of 27 October 1993 submitted in response to operative paragraph 28 of resolution 864(1993). It notes the exploratory talks in Lusaka, Zambia, under the auspices of the United Nations, to which both the Government of Angola and UNITA have sent delegations. It affirms its complete support for the Secretary-General and his Special Representative in their efforts aimed at the earliest resolution of the Angolan crisis through negotiations within the framework of the 'Acordos de Paz' and

Security Council resolutions. It calls upon the Angolan parties to cooperate fully with the Secretary-General and his Special Representative to this end.

"The Security Council notes recent actions taken by both parties, including the lessening of hostilities, and considers it essential that the two parties take the necessary steps to resume direct negotiations towards a peaceful settlement and agree without delay on the modalities for an effective cease-fire in accordance with Security Council resolutions.

"The Security Council notes UNITA's communiqué of 6 October referred to in paragraph 11 of the Secretary-General's report. It expresses its concern that the Secretary-General has reported that not enough progress has yet been made towards the full implementation of the 'Acordos de Paz' and relevant resolutions of the Council. It demands that UNITA take the necessary steps to comply with its previous resolutions. It expresses its readiness to consider the immediate imposition of further measures under the Charter of the United Nations, including *inter alia* trade measures against UNITA and restrictions on the travel of UNITA personnel, at any time that it observes that UNITA is not cooperating in good faith to make the cease-fire effective and implement the 'Acordos de Paz' and relevant resolutions of the Security Council, or upon a report from the Secretary-General to that effect.

"The Security Council expresses its grave concern at the serious deterioration in the humanitarian situation in Angola. It is encouraged however by the Secretary-General's report that the United Nations system, working with humanitarian agencies, has now been able significantly to increase the rate of delivery of relief aid to all parts of the country. It welcomes the resumption of humanitarian relief deliveries to the cities of Cuito and Huambo. It calls upon the parties to cooperate fully in ensuring the unimpeded delivery of humanitarian assistance to all Angolans throughout the country, to take all necessary measures to ensure the security and safety of United Nations and other personnel involved in humanitarian relief operations, and strictly to abide by applicable rules of international humanitarian law. It commends the international community for its generous provision of relief aid and calls upon the international community to make available further relief aid rapidly to meet the growing need.

"The Security Council shares the Secretary-General's view that UNAVEM II should be able to respond rapidly to any progress which might be achieved in the peace process. It encourages the Secretary-General to carry out urgent contingency planning for the possible augmentation of the existing strength of the military, police and medical components of UNAVEM II for deployment in the event of significant progress in the peace process, including contacting potential troop contributors. It stands ready to take decisions in the matter at any time within the period of the mandate authorized by resolution 864(1993).

"The Security Council again expresses its strongest appeal that both sides, in particular UNITA, undertake to commit themselves to the peace process that will lead to a comprehensive settlement in Angola on the basis of the 'Acordos de Paz'.

"The Security Council will remain actively seized of the matter and will review the position again with regard to further measures at the latest on 15 December in the context of its consideration of the report that the Secretary-General is due to make by that date pursuant to its resolution 864(1993).''

Report of the Secretary-General (December). The Secretary-General reported on 14 December[27] that UNITA had clarified its position stated in the 6 October communiqué, as requested by the Angolan Government, and accepted the principle of immediate withdrawal of its troops to United Nations–monitored areas, pending full implementation of the Peace Accords. Responding to the Special Representative's request, the Angolan Government said it could not observe a unilateral cessation of hostilities because UNITA had launched a number of offensives and would consider the principle of withdrawal of UNITA troops only within the framework of a bilateral cease-fire. The Special Representative nevertheless emphasized that the Government should ensure a pause in military operations during the peace talks.

The talks began at Lusaka on 15 November and concluded on 10 December with the adoption of general and specific principles on the re-establishment of the cease-fire and on completing the formation of the Angolan armed forces, as well as implementation arrangements. The Secretary-General noted that there were unconfirmed reports of the violation of the arms embargo against UNITA, which came into force on 26 September, as well as of troop movements, attacks, ambushes, mine-laying and shelling. Although the ability of UNAVEM II to evaluate the military situation remained limited, the military observers confirmed that the Government had enlarged the area of the country under its control. Contingency planning was initiated for the possible augmentation of the Mission's strength in the event of progress in the Lusaka talks, and projections for the involvement of the United Nations in the implementation of agreements under discussion were drawn up.

The report assessed the humanitarian situation in the coastal areas, non-intensive conflict areas and those until recently known as intensive conflict areas. It noted the cooperation of the Government and UNITA in facilitating the provision of humanitarian assistance. The emergency programmes, however, faced serious financial difficulties, which prompted preparation of a revised inter-agency appeal to the donor community.

In conclusion, the Secretary-General again recommended postponing further additional measures against UNITA and extending the mandate of UNAVEM II for three months. He stated that both parties insisted on an increase in United Nations involvement to verify and monitor the withdrawal and quartering of UNITA's troops; collect, store and guard UNITA's armaments; oversee the disarming of civilians; and verify the for-

mation of the Angolan armed forces and the police, as well as the extension of State administration throughout Angola. The cost of the three-month extension was estimated at $6,455,000.

SECURITY COUNCIL ACTION (December)

On 15 December, the Security Council considered the Secretary-General's report, with Angola participating in the discussion under rule 37ᵃ of the Council's provisional rules of procedure. The Council adopted **resolution 890(1993)** unanimously.

The Security Council,

Reaffirming its resolutions 696(1991) of 30 May 1991, 747(1992) of 24 March 1992, 785(1992) of 30 October 1992, 793(1992) of 30 November 1992, 804(1993) of 29 January 1993, 811(1993) of 12 March 1993, 823(1993) of 30 April 1993, 834(1993) of 1 June 1993, 851(1993) of 15 July 1993 and 864(1993) of 15 September 1993,

Recalling the statement made by the President of the Security Council on 1 November 1993,

Having considered the report of the Secretary-General dated 13 December 1993,

Reiterating the importance it attaches to the full implementation of the ''Acordos de Paz'' and relevant Security Council resolutions,

Welcoming the resumption of direct negotiations in Lusaka under the auspices of the United Nations, and the ongoing efforts of the Government of Angola and UNITA to reach a negotiated settlement,

Commending the efforts of the Secretary-General and his Special Representative aimed at the earliest resolution of the Angolan crisis through negotiations within the framework of the ''Acordos de Paz'' and relevant Security Council resolutions,

Taking note of actions taken by both parties, including the lessening of hostilities, but deeply concerned that an effective cease-fire has not yet been established,

Stressing the importance it attaches to UNITA's acceptance without reservations, as requested by the Security Council, of the results of the democratic elections of 30 September 1992 held under United Nations supervision and to their abiding fully by the ''Acordos de Paz'' and relevant Security Council resolutions,

Deeply concerned also about the continued grave humanitarian situation,

Reaffirming its commitment to preserve the unity and territorial integrity of Angola,

1. *Welcomes* the report of the Secretary-General dated 13 December 1993;

2. *Stresses* again the importance it places on a peaceful resolution of the conflict in Angola in conformity with the ''Acordos de Paz'' and relevant resolutions of the Security Council, and urges both parties to continue to demonstrate flexibility in the negotiations and a commitment to peace;

3. *Decides* to extend the existing mandate of the United Nations Angola Verification Mission (UNAVEM II) until 16 March 1994;

4. *Reaffirms* its willingness as necessary to review the existing mandate of UNAVEM II to determine whether it is able to carry out effectively its mission, taking ac-

count of any progress achieved towards the early establishment of peace in the country;

5. *Reaffirms* the importance of the functions of good offices and mediation of the Secretary-General and his Special Representative and UNAVEM II, with the goal of restoring a cease-fire and reinstating the peace process for the full implementation of the "Acordos de Paz" and relevant Security Council resolutions;

6. *Calls upon* both parties to honour the commitments already made by them at the talks in Lusaka, urges them to exercise their maximum restraint and to stop immediately all military actions in order to prevent further suffering on the part of the civilian population of Angola and damage to Angola's economy, and further urges them to agree on the modalities for and establishment of an effective and sustainable cease-fire in accordance with relevant Security Council resolutions and to conclude a peaceful settlement as soon as possible;

7. *Requests* the Secretary-General to inform the Council as soon as an effective cease-fire is established and in any case by 1 February 1994 on progress made by the parties in the Lusaka talks, including a report on progress achieved in furthering the peace process, establishing an effective cease-fire, and implementing relevant Security Council resolutions and the "Acordos de Paz";

8. *Takes note* of the steps taken by the Secretary-General to initiate contingency planning for the possible augmentation of the existing components of UNAVEM II for deployment in the event of significant progress in the peace process, and requests him to inform the Council periodically in this regard;

9. *Reiterates* its readiness, in the event of the achievement of an effective and sustainable cease-fire, to consider promptly any recommendations by the Secretary-General on the basis of that contingency planning;

10. *Reaffirms further* the need for unimpeded delivery of humanitarian assistance to all civilian populations in need;

11. *Welcomes also* the actions taken by the Secretary-General to implement the emergency humanitarian assistance plan;

12. *Commends* those Member States, United Nations agencies and non-governmental organizations that have already contributed to the relief efforts and strongly appeals to all Member States, United Nations agencies and non-governmental organizations to provide rapidly further assistance to Angola to meet the growing humanitarian needs;

13. *Reaffirms* the obligation of all States to implement fully the provisions of paragraph 19 of resolution 864(1993);

14. *Decides* in view of the direct negotiations under way between the parties not to impose at present the additional measures against UNITA contained in paragraph 26 of resolution 864(1993), but reiterates its readiness to consider at any time further steps, in the light, *inter alia*, of a recommendation of the Secretary-General, either to impose such additional measures or to review those in effect;

15. *Decides* to remain seized of the matter.

Security Council resolution 890(1993)

15 December 1993   Meeting 3323   Adopted unanimously

Draft prepared in consultations among Council members (S/26877).

Further developments (December). In a note to the Security Council,[28] the Secretary-General listed replies received from 18 Member States, as at 17 December, concerning their implementation of measures imposed against UNITA in response to **resolution 864(1993)**.

The Lusaka talks, interrupted on 13 December to investigate an alleged attempt on Dr. Savimbi's life, resumed on 21 December and were suspended on 23 December until 5 January 1994. The military situation in December was marked by an intensification of hostilities and military preparations. At the same time, significant progress was made with regard to access to areas of extreme need, as both sides agreed to increased use of two land corridors and to the opening of an airport for humanitarian air operations.

Financing of UNAVEM II

On 19 March, the Assembly's Fifth Committee, on a proposal of its Chairman and in view of the changes in the operational plan of UNAVEM II and the need to revise the Secretary-General's December 1992 report on its financing,[29] recommended that, as an ad hoc measure to provide for the Mission's continued maintenance, the Assembly authorize the Secretary-General to enter into commitments up to $3.5 million gross ($3.4 million net) per month for the period 1 March to 30 April, subject to the concurrence of ACABQ. That amount was to be apportioned among Member States in accordance with the scheme set out in **resolution 47/224 A** on the financing of the United Nations Operation in Mozambique. The Committee further recommended that the Assembly request the Secretary-General to review current procedures for the planning of peace-keeping operations to make them more cost-effective.

The Assembly endorsed the Committee's recommendations in **decision 47/450 B** of 8 April 1993.

In a March 1993 report on the financing of UNAVEM II,[30] the Secretary-General said outstanding assessments due from Member States for the period since the Mission's inception up to 28 February 1993 totalled $33,160,200. An additional appropriation of $1,260,400 was required for the period from 1 January to 31 October 1992, while the unencumbered balance for the period from 1 November 1992 to 28 February 1993 amounted to $3,804,100 gross ($3,491,900 net). The cost from 1 March to 30 April was estimated at $5,322,500 gross ($5,124,300 net), with a total of $25,516,800 gross ($24,590,000 net) for the period from 1 November 1992 to 30 April 1993. That amount reflected a net additional requirement of $1,632,400 for that period. In view of an operating deficit of $26,476,300 in the Mission's special account and of $15.9 million loaned to it from the

Peace-keeping Reserve Fund, the Secretary-General recommended retaining the unencumbered balance in the account pending receipt of outstanding assessed contributions. He further set out financial requirements for UNAVEM II operations up to and after 30 April. Annexed to the report was supplementary information on cost estimates and proposed staffing requirements.

In April,[31] ACABQ concurred with the Secretary-General's proposals.

GENERAL ASSEMBLY ACTION (September)

In September, the General Assembly adopted **decision 47/450 C** without vote.

At its 110th plenary meeting, on 14 September 1993, the General Assembly, on the recommendation of the Fifth Committee, decided:

(a) To appropriate the amount of 25,258,800 United States dollars gross (24,218,000 dollars net) authorized and apportioned under the terms of its decision 47/450 A of 22 December 1992 for the period ending 28 February 1993;

(b) To appropriate the amount of 1,518,400 dollars gross (1,632,400 dollars net) for the maintenance of the United Nations Angola Verification Mission for the period from 1 March to 30 April 1993, and that there shall be set off against the apportionment thereof among Member States, in accordance with the scheme set out in its resolution 47/224 A of 16 March 1993, their respective share in an equal amount from the total unencumbered balance of appropriations for the prior periods;

(c) To appropriate the amount of 9,830,950 dollars gross (9,466,050 dollars net), consisting of:

 (i) The amount of 5,948,650 dollars gross (5,723,950 dollars net) authorized by the Advisory Committee on Administrative and Budgetary Questions for the period from 1 May to 15 July 1993;

 (ii) The amount of 3,882,300 dollars gross (3,742,100 dollars net) requested by the Secretary-General for the period from 16 July to 15 September 1993;

(d) To apportion the amount indicated in subparagraph *(c)* above among Member States in accordance with paragraphs 12 and 15 of its resolution 47/210 B of 14 September 1993;

(e) To authorize the Secretary-General to enter into commitments up to the amount of 1,942,000 dollars gross (1,871,900 dollars net) per month for the continued maintenance of the United Nations Angola Verification Mission after 15 September 1993 for a period of three months, subject to the concurrence of the Advisory Committee on Administrative and Budgetary Questions, should the Security Council decide to extend the mandate of the Verification Mission beyond 15 September 1993. As an ad hoc arrangement, the amount decided upon by the Advisory Committee shall be apportioned among Member States in accordance with the scheme set out in General Assembly resolution 47/210 B.

General Assembly decision 47/450 C

Adopted without vote

Approved by Fifth Committee (A/47/795/Add.2) without vote, 3 September (meeting 74); draft by Chairman (A/C.5/47/L.47), orally revised; agenda item 117.
Meeting numbers. GA 47th session: 5th Committee 72-74; plenary 110.

Report of the Secretary-General (December). In a December report[32] to the Fifth Committee, the Secretary-General noted that ACABQ had, on 21 October, concurred in an amount not exceeding $5.5 million gross for the three-month period ending 15 December. He estimated the cost of maintaining UNAVEM II beyond that date at $22,560,000 gross ($21,338,400 net) for the next 12-month period, at a monthly rate of $1,880,000 gross ($1,778,200 net), including the amount of $8,460,000 gross ($8,001,900 net) required for the period from 16 December to 30 April 1994.

In December ACABQ recommended that the General Assembly authorize further commitment up to $6.8 million gross (6.4 million net) for the period 16 December to 31 March 1994.[33]

As at 30 November, outstanding assessed contributions due from Member States totalled $29,378,680, with an operating deficit in the Mission's special account running at $27,305,600. The unencumbered balance for the period from 1 March to 15 September 1993 amounted to $90,100 gross ($126,100 net).

GENERAL ASSEMBLY ACTION (December)

On 23 December, the General Assembly, on the recommendation of the Fifth Committee, adopted **decision 48/465**.

Financing of the United Nations Angola Verification Mission II

At its 87th plenary meeting, on 23 December 1993, the General Assembly, on the recommendation of the Fifth Committee, in accordance with the framework set out in its resolution 48/227 of 23 December 1993, having considered the report of the Secretary-General on the financing of seventeen peace-keeping operations and the related reports of the Advisory Committee on Administrative and Budgetary Questions, and concurring with the observations of the Advisory Committee:

(a) Authorized the Secretary-General, on an exceptional basis, to enter into commitments up to the amount of 6.8 million United States dollars gross (6.4 million dollars net) for the United Nations Angola Verification Mission II for the period from 16 December 1993 to 31 March 1994;

(b) Decided at that time to apportion, as an ad hoc arrangement, the amount of 6,478,800 dollars gross (6,097,700 dollars net) among Member States in accordance with the composition of groups set out in paragraphs 3 and 4 of Assembly resolution 43/232 of 1 March 1989, as adjusted by the Assembly in its resolutions 44/192 B of 21 December 1989, 45/269 of 27 August 1991, 46/198 A of 20 December 1991 and 47/218 A of 23 December 1992 and its decision 48/472 of 23 December 1993, and taking into account the scale of assessments for the years 1992, 1993 and 1994 as set out in Assembly resolutions 46/221 A of 20 December 1991 and 48/223 A of 23 December 1993 and its decision 47/456 of 23 December 1992;

(c) Also decided that, in accordance with the provisions of its resolution 973(X) of 15 December 1955, there should be set off against the apportionment among

Member States, as provided for in subparagraph *(b)* above, their respective share in the Tax Equalization Fund of the estimated staff assessment income of 381,100 dollars for the period from 16 December 1993 to 31 March 1994.

General Assembly decision 48/465

Adopted without vote

Approved by Fifth Committee (A/48/814) without vote, 22 December (meeting 46); draft by Chairman (A/C.5/48/L.17); agenda item 131.
Meeting numbers. GA 48th session: 5th Committee 44, 46; plenary 87.

Burundi

On 10 July 1993, Melchior Ndadaye was installed as President of Burundi, following the 1 June Presidential elections in that country, and a National Assembly set up as a result of legislative elections of 29 June, effectively indicating the beginning of Burundi's transition to democracy. On 22 October,[34] however, the Permanent Representative of Burundi to the United Nations informed the Security Council of a military coup d'état that occurred on the night of 20-21 October resulting in the assassination of the President and a number of other political leaders. In a statement issued on 23 October at Addis Ababa, the Secretary-General condemned the coup d'état and expressed concern over the situation in Burundi. He asked Under-Secretary-General James O. C. Jonah to travel there immediately as his Special Envoy to facilitate the return of the country to constitutional rule.

By a letter of 25 October,[35] Burundi requested an urgent meeting of the Security Council to consider the situation. Similar requests were received from Cape Verde, Djibouti and Morocco[36] and from Zimbabwe.[37]

SECURITY COUNCIL ACTION (October)

The Council considered the situation in Burundi on 25 October. Burundi, Egypt, Mali and Zimbabwe were invited to participate in the discussion under rule 37ª of the Council's provisional rules of procedure.

On the same date, following consultations, the President, on behalf of the Council, made the following statement:[38]

Meeting number. SC 3297.

"The Security Council expresses its grave concern at and condemnation of the military coup of 21 October 1993 against the democratically elected Government of Burundi.

"The Security Council deeply regrets and strongly condemns the acts of violence and the loss of life which have been caused by the perpetrators of the military coup. It demands that they desist forthwith from taking any action which would exacerbate tension and plunge the country into more violence and bloodshed, which could have serious implications for peace and stability in the region.

"The Security Council demands that the perpetrators of the military coup cease all acts of violence, reveal the whereabouts and fate of Government officials, release all prisoners, return to their barracks and put an immediate end to their illegal act, with a view to the immediate reinstitution of democracy and constitutional rule in Burundi.

"The Security Council pays tribute to the deceased President of Burundi, His Excellency Mr. Melchior Ndadayem, and members of his Government for their supreme sacrifice for democracy. Those responsible for their violent deaths and other acts of violence should be brought to justice.

"The Security Council requests the Secretary-General to monitor and follow closely the situation in Burundi, in close association with the Organization of African Unity (OAU), and report to the Security Council thereon urgently. In this context, it takes note with appreciation of the dispatch by the Secretary-General of a Special Envoy to Burundi.

"The Council will remain seized of the matter."

Further developments (October/November). The Special Envoy arrived in Bujumbura, Burundi, on 27 October and reported that the military had returned to barracks while surviving members of the Government had taken refuge in the French Embassy compound; neither side was exercising authority in the country. He held three meetings with Prime Minister Sylvie Kinigi and several members of the Government, who maintained that the coup d'état was continuing and called for the complete disbandment of the army and the deployment of a large international force. At a subsequent meeting with the army command, the Special Envoy was informed that the army assumed no responsibility for governing the country and was ready to respond to decisions of the Government through the Minister of Defence. The commander asserted that the coup had been carried out by a small military group and that the majority of the army remained loyal to the Government. It rejected the deployment of an outside force. Both sides supported the proposal to appoint a Special Representative of the Secretary-General for Burundi. The Special Envoy also met with members of the opposition, representatives of the African Group (Egypt, Rwanda and Zaire), the European Community and the United States, all of whom urged him to ensure that the Government assumed its authority. On 29 October, the Government re-established its authority, but continued to operate from the French Embassy compound. The Special Envoy briefed the Security Council on 1 November on the situation in Burundi.

By a 27 October letter,[39] Burundi requested the General Assembly to include an item on the situation in Burundi in the agenda of its forty-eighth session and to consider it in plenary. The explanatory memorandum accompanying the letter stated that the continuing violence had resulted in some 300,000 refugees and displaced persons and was bringing the country to the verge of civil war, and that the Assembly should request the intervention of the international community to restore the functioning of democratic institutions and provide emergency humanitarian assistance.

A Regional Summit on the situation in Burundi (Kigali, Rwanda, 28 October), convened by the President of Rwanda, requested the Secretary-General, in consultation with the Secretary-General of OAU, to establish an international force for confidence-building and stabilization of the situation, to be composed essentially of troops from African countries chosen in consultation with the Government of Burundi. The Summit urged the Burundi military personnel to return to their barracks and appealed to the international community to provide assistance to the proposed international force as well as emergency assistance to the Burundi refugees and displaced persons. The communiqué issued at the Summit was transmitted to the Security Council[40] and to the Secretary-General on 1 November.[41]

By a letter of 2 November,[42] the Secretary-General apprised the Security Council of developments in Burundi and announced his intention to hold consultations with the OAU Secretary-General and to appoint a Special Representative for Burundi.

GENERAL ASSEMBLY ACTION

On 3 November, the General Assembly adopted without vote **resolution 48/17**.

The situation in Burundi

The General Assembly,

Having considered the item entitled "The situation in Burundi",

Deeply concerned by the military *coup d'état* which took place in Burundi on 21 October 1993,

Shocked by the cowardly assassination of the President of the Republic and other political leaders,

Seriously disturbed by the tragic consequences of the *coup d'état* which is plunging Burundi into violence, thus causing loss of life and mass displacement of the population with considerable regional repercussions,

1. *Unreservedly condemns* the *coup* which has caused an abrupt and violent interruption of the democratic process initiated in Burundi;

2. *Demands* that the perpetrators of the putsch lay down their arms and return to their barracks;

3. *Also demands* the immediate restoration of democracy and the constitutional regime;

4. *Supports* the efforts being made by the Secretary-General, by the Organization of African Unity and by the countries of the region to promote a return to constitutional order and the protection of democratic institutions in Burundi;

5. *Commends* the Secretary-General for having sent a special envoy to Burundi;

6. *Requests* the States Members of the United Nations, international organizations, intergovernmental organizations and non-governmental organizations to provide emergency humanitarian assistance and/or any other assistance to the people of Burundi;

7. *Decides* to remain seized of the matter until a solution to the crisis is found.

General Assembly resolution 48/17

3 November 1993   Meeting 48   Adopted without vote

3-nation draft (A/48/L.16 & Add.1), orally revised; agenda item 170.
Sponsors: Algeria, Burundi, Haiti.

Appointment of the Special Representative. On 4 November,[43] the Secretary-General informed the Security Council of his decision to appoint a Special Representative for Burundi. On 16 November,[44] the Secretary-General announced that Mr. Maxime Zollner, his original appointee, was not available to take up the position and that Ahmedou Ould Abdallah, United Nations Special Coordinator for Africa and the Least Developed Countries, was appointed to that post with immediate effect. On 19 November,[45] the Security Council President informed the Secretary-General that the Council members took note of that information.

SECURITY COUNCIL ACTION (November)

At Burundi's request,[46] the Security Council met on 16 November to consider the situation in that country. Burundi and Rwanda participated in the discussion under rule 37a of the Council's provisional rules of procedure.

On the same date, the President, on behalf of the Council, made the following statement:[47]

Meeting number. SC 3316.

"The Security Council continues to follow with deep concern the developments in Burundi, which have threatened that country's nascent democracy, and caused widespread violence and bloodshed.

"The Security Council reiterates its condemnation of the abrupt and violent interruption of the democratic process initiated in Burundi and demands the immediate cessation of acts of violence.

"The Security Council warmly commends the Prime Minister and the other members of the Government of Burundi for their courage, and the spirit of reconciliation they have demonstrated at this very difficult moment.

"The Security Council is alarmed at the grave humanitarian consequences of this tragedy, which has resulted in the movement of over 700,000 refugees into neighbouring countries and an increasing number of internally displaced persons throughout the country. The Council appeals to all States, international agencies and other humanitarian organizations to provide prompt humanitarian assistance to the affected civilian population in Burundi and neighbouring countries.

"The Security Council notes with satisfaction the immediate response of the Secretary-General to this situation by the dispatch of a Special Envoy on a good offices mission to facilitate the return of the country to constitutional rule, and welcomes the appointment by the Secretary-General of a Special Representative for Burundi. The Security Council also welcomes the efforts of the Organization of African Unity (OAU) to assist the Government of Burundi in its efforts to restore democratic institutions, rebuild confidence and stabilize the situation.

"The Security Council expresses gratitude to the States which provided shelter in their diplomatic compounds to the members of the Government of Burundi and also expresses its gratitude for the technical assistance provided by those countries to ensure the security and safety of the members of the Government.

"The Security Council encourages the Secretary-General to continue using his good offices through his Special Representative and to consider dispatching in his support as soon as possible a small United Nations team, within existing resources, to Burundi for fact-finding and advice with a view to facilitating the efforts of the Government of Burundi and the OAU.

"The Security Council requests the Secretary-General to keep it informed as appropriate on the situation and the progress of the United Nations good offices mission. It also requests the Secretary-General to report, at the earliest, with recommendations on the possible establishment of a voluntary fund to assist in the dispatch of an OAU mission as announced by the Secretary-General of the OAU.

"The Council will remain seized of the matter."

Comorian island of Mayotte

The question of Mayotte—one of a group of four islands in the Indian Ocean Comoro Archipelago—remained on the General Assembly's agenda in 1993. The Islamic Federal Republic of the Comoros acceded to independence on 6 July 1975, following a referendum in 1974. France, the former colonial Power, had since continued to administer the island of Mayotte.

Report of the Secretary-General. In an October 1993 report,[(48)] the Secretary-General described his note verbale to the Comoros and France, drawing their attention to a 1992 General Assembly resolution on the question of Mayotte[(49)] and inviting them to provide him with any pertinent information. A similar letter was sent to the Secretary-General of OAU. Under the 1992 resolution, the Assembly requested the United Nations Secretary-General to make available his good offices in the search for a negotiated solution to the problem.

France, in its response, pointed out that Mayotte's special status acquired under the December 1976 law proclaiming Mayotte a territorial collectivity of the French Republic did not bar any further development. France was willing to seek conditions for a solution to the problem, on the basis of respect for its domestic laws and international law, and to promote such a just and lasting solution in conformity with its Constitution and the wishes of the peoples concerned. Accordingly, a constructive dialogue was continually taking

place at the highest level with the Comoros, as shown by regular visits of the Comorian President to France.

The Comoros said the United Nations recognized the independence of the Comorian State—comprising the four islands of Grande Comore, Anjouan, Mohéli and Mayotte—and considered it as a single entity. Notwithstanding resolutions to that effect by the United Nations and other organizations, including OAU and the Organization of the Islamic Conference, France continued to maintain its military and administrative presence on Mayotte, on the grounds that a two-thirds majority of the island's population voted against independence. Under agreements reached between the two parties, however, France had undertaken to respect the Comoros' unity and territorial integrity and to announce the referendum results on a global basis, although considering them island by island.

In 1989, all the country's political organizations reaffirmed unanimously that Mayotte belonged to the Islamic Federal Republic of the Comoros and called for its reincorporation into that nation. Despite international support and solidarity in that matter, the situation hardly evolved, prompting the Comoros to call again on the Secretary-General to continue his mediating role by bringing the two parties together in the search for a just and fair settlement.

The OAU Secretary-General quoted a resolution adopted by the Assembly of Heads of State and Government of OAU at its twenty-ninth session (Cairo, 28-30 June 1993), reaffirming the sovereignty of the Comoros over the island of Mayotte and appealing to the French Government to accede to the legitimate claims of the Government of the Comoros. The resolution also appealed to all OAU member States and the international community to reject any consultations regarding the international legal status of the island and condemn any initiative by France to make the Comorian island of Mayotte participate in activities as an entity different from the Federal Islamic Republic of the Comoros. It charged the OAU Secretary-General to resume dialogue with France for a rapid settlement of the Comorian issue and to consider the possibility of convening a tripartite conference on the issue.

GENERAL ASSEMBLY ACTION

On 13 December, the General Assembly adopted **resolution 48/56** by recorded vote.

Question of the Comorian island of Mayotte
The General Assembly,

Recalling its resolutions 1514(XV) of 14 December 1960, containing the Declaration on the Granting of Independence to Colonial Countries and Peoples, and

2621(XXV) of 12 October 1970, containing the programme of action for the full implementation of the
Declaration,

Recalling also its previous resolutions, in particular resolutions 3161(XXVIII) of 14 December 1973,
3291(XXIX) of 13 December 1974, 31/4 of 21 October
1976, 32/7 of 1 November 1977, 34/69 of 6 December
1979, 35/43 of 28 November 1980, 36/105 of 10 December 1981, 37/65 of 3 December 1982, 38/13 of 21 November 1983, 39/48 of 11 December 1984, 40/62 of 9 December 1985, 41/30 of 3 November 1986, 42/17 of 11
November 1987, 43/14 of 26 October 1988, 44/9 of 18
October 1989, 45/11 of 1 November 1990, 46/9 of 16 October 1991 and 47/9 of 27 October 1992, in which, *inter
alia*, it affirmed the unity and territorial integrity of the
Comoros,

Recalling, in particular, its resolution 3385(XXX) of
12 November 1975 on the admission of the Comoros to
membership in the United Nations, in which it
reaffirmed the necessity of respecting the unity and territorial integrity of the Comoro Archipelago, composed
of the islands of Anjouan, Grande-Comore, Mayotte and
Mohéli,

Recalling further that, in accordance with the agreements
between the Comoros and France, signed on 15 June
1973, concerning the accession of the Comoros to independence, the results of the referendum of 22 December 1974 were to be considered on a global basis and
not island by island,

Convinced that a just and lasting solution to the question of Mayotte is to be found in respect for the sovereignty, unity and territorial integrity of the Comoro Archipelago,

Convinced also that a speedy solution of the problem is
essential for the preservation of the peace and security
which prevail in the region,

Bearing in mind the wish expressed by the President of
the French Republic to seek actively a just solution to
that problem,

Noting the repeated wish of the Government of the
Comoros to initiate as soon as possible a frank and serious dialogue with the French Government with a view
to accelerating the return of the Comorian island of
Mayotte to the Islamic Federal Republic of the Comoros,

Taking note of the report of the Secretary-General,

Bearing in mind also the decisions of the Organization
of African Unity, the Movement of Non-Aligned Countries and the Organization of the Islamic Conference
on this question,

1. *Reaffirms* the sovereignty of the Islamic Federal
Republic of the Comoros over the island of Mayotte;

2. *Invites* the Government of France to honour the
commitments entered into prior to the referendum on
the self-determination of the Comoro Archipelago of 22
December 1974 concerning respect for the unity and territorial integrity of the Comoros;

3. *Calls for* the translation into practice of the wish
expressed by the President of the French Republic to
seek actively a just solution to the question of Mayotte;

4. *Urges* the Government of France to accelerate the
process of negotiations with the Government of the
Comoros with a view to ensuring the effective and
prompt return of the island of Mayotte to the Comoros;

5. *Requests* the Secretary-General of the United Nations to maintain continuous contact with the Secretary-
General of the Organization of African Unity with regard to this problem and to make available his good
offices in the search for a peaceful negotiated solution
to the problem;

6. *Also requests* the Secretary-General to report on this
matter to the General Assembly at its forty-ninth session;

7. *Decides* to include in the provisional agenda of its
forty-ninth session the item entitled "Question of the
Comorian island of Mayotte".

General Assembly resolution 48/56

13 December 1993   Meeting 76   91-2-36 (recorded vote)

24-nation draft (A/48/L.48); agenda item 25.
Sponsors: Algeria, Bahrain, Benin, Burkina Faso, Comoros, Cuba, Gambia,
Guinea, Guinea-Bissau, Libyan Arab Jamahiriya, Kenya, Lesotho, Madagas-
car, Morocco, Oman, Pakistan, Qatar, Senegal, Sierra Leone, Sudan, United
Arab Emirates, United Republic of Tanzania, Yemen, Zambia.

Recorded vote in Assembly as follows:

In favour: Algeria, Angola, Antigua and Barbuda, Argentina, Australia,
Bahamas, Bahrain, Bangladesh, Barbados, Belarus, Benin, Bolivia, Bo-
tswana, Brazil, Brunei Darussalam, Burkina Faso, Cambodia, Cameroon,
Chad, China, Comoros, Cuba, Democratic People's Republic of Korea,
Djibouti, Dominican Republic, Ecuador, El Salvador, Ethiopia, Fiji, Finland,
Ghana, Grenada, Guinea, Guinea-Bissau, Guyana, Haiti, Honduras, India,
Indonesia, Iran, Iraq, Jordan, Kazakhstan, Kenya, Kuwait, Lao People's
Democratic Republic, Lesotho, Libyan Arab Jamahiriya, Madagascar,
Malawi, Malaysia, Maldives, Marshall Islands, Mauritania, Mexico, Mon-
golia, Mozambique, Myanmar, Nepal, New Zealand, Nicaragua, Nigeria,
Oman, Pakistan, Panama, Papua New Guinea, Paraguay, Peru, Philippines,
Qatar, Rwanda, Samoa, Saudi Arabia, Senegal, Sierra Leone, Singapore,
Sri Lanka, Suriname, Sweden, Syrian Arab Republic, Thailand, Togo, Tur-
key, Ukraine, United Arab Emirates, United Republic of Tanzania, Venezuela,
Viet Nam, Yemen, Zambia, Zimbabwe.

Against: France, Monaco.

Abstaining: Andorra, Armenia, Austria, Belgium, Burundi,* Canada, Croatia, Cyprus, Czech Republic, Denmark, Germany, Greece, Hungary, Iceland, Ireland, Israel, Italy, Japan, Liechtenstein, Luxembourg, Malta,
Micronesia, Netherlands, Norway, Poland, Portugal, Republic of Korea,
Romania, Russian Federation, Saint Lucia, Saint Vincent and the Grenadines, San Marino, Slovak Republic, Spain, United Kingdom, United States.

*Later advised the Secretariat it intended to vote in favour.

Eritrea

The right of the Eritrean people to determine
their political future by an internationally super-
vised referendum was formally recognized in July
1991 by the Conference on Peace and Democracy
(Addis Ababa). In 1992, at the invitation of the
Referendum Commissioner of Eritrea, the
General Assembly established the United Nations
Observer Mission to Verify the Referendum in
Eritrea (UNOVER).[50]

Following his visit to Eritrea on 6 January 1993,
the Secretary-General appointed Samir Sanbar
as his Special Representative and the Chief of
UNOVER, headquartered at Asmara. The Mission
also had regional offices at Asmara, Keren and
Mendefera. At its maximum strength, UNOVER
consisted of 21 international staff and 86 observers,
including 57 from 35 countries, deployed in 45
teams in the three regions.

The referendum was held from 23 to 25 April
and was observed, in addition to UNOVER, by
several organizations such as OAU and the League
of Arab States. The results of the referendum
showed that the majority of Eritreans (99.8 per
cent in a turnout of 98.5 per cent) voted in favour

of independence. On 27 April, the Provisional Government declared Eritrea as an independent and sovereign State.

In its application for admission to membership of the United Nations,[51] Eritrea said that the peaceful and democratic resolution of its case through the referendum would consolidate peace and stability and contribute to cooperation and progress in the subregion and thus on the African continent, and underlined Eritrea's active engagement in the peaceful resolution of conflicts in the Horn of Africa.

On 28 May, by **resolution 47/230**, the General Assembly admitted Eritrea to membership in the United Nations, as recommended by the Security Council in its **resolution 828(1993)** of 26 May (see PART ONE, Chapter V).

Speaking before the Assembly, the Eritrea representative thanked the Secretary-General and Member States for supporting the referendum and its membership in the Organization, and expressed the hope that the United Nations would play an active role in supporting reconstruction of that country devastated by 30 years of war.

The referendum process and activities of UNOVER were described in the Secretary-General's August report[52] to the General Assembly. In a letter dated 23 November,[53] the Permanent Mission of Eritrea to the United Nations updated the information contained in the Secretary-General's report. By **decision 48/430** of 20 December, the Assembly took note of the Secretary-General's report.

Liberia

Efforts of the United Nations and the Economic Community of West African States (ECOWAS) to end the three-year civil war in Liberia culminated in the signing of the Cotonou Peace Agreement in July 1993, providing for a cease-fire, the cessation of hostilities, disarmament and demobilization of the warring factions, the establishment of a transitional government and the holding of national elections in 1994. The war—whose main protagonists were the National Patriotic Front of Liberia (NPFL) of Charles Taylor and the United Liberation Movement of Liberia for Democracy (ULIMO), led by Alhaji Kromah and inspired by the memory of the former President of Liberia killed in that war—began with the complete breakdown of law and order and civil authority that accompanied the overthrow in 1990 of the regime headed by President Samuel Doe.

Earlier initiatives for a peaceful settlement of the conflict included the creation of an ECOWAS Cease-Fire Monitoring Group (ECOMOG) in 1990 and agreement reached at the fourth Yamoussoukro (Côte d'Ivoire) meeting in October 1991

and known as the Yamoussoukro IV Accord or the Yamoussoukro IV Agreement. The implementation of the 1993 Peace Accord was to be monitored by an expanded ECOMOG and a United Nations Observer Mission in Liberia. Major-General Daniel Opande of Kenya was appointed the Chief Military Observer for UNOMIL.

Report of the Secretary-General (March). In a March report[54] submitted in response to a 1992 Security Council request,[55] the Secretary-General said that his Special Representative for Liberia visited Benin, Burkina Faso, Côte d'Ivoire, the Gambia, Guinea, Nigeria, Senegal and Sierra Leone as well as Liberia between November 1992 and February 1993 to meet with senior government officials and the parties to the conflict. They emphasized the need for continued support by the international community for the peace efforts of ECOWAS. President Nicephore Soglo of Benin, the current Chairman of ECOWAS, stressed that there was a clear role for the United Nations in monitoring a cease-fire, encampment, disarmament, demobilization and the organization of free and fair elections. In Liberia, the Special Representative held extensive consultations with all parties to the conflict, including NGOs, civic, religious and voluntary associations. The NPFL leader, Charles Taylor, expressed his willingness to agree to a cease-fire and talks with other parties leading to elections as long as the United Nations were fully involved in the process. Questions related to national reconciliation and the organization of elections were also discussed, including the repatriation of refugees and establishment of conditions that would allow for an agreement on a unified administration, freedom of movement, disarmament and encampment as essential factors for free and fair elections.

Meanwhile, the fighting which resumed in October 1992 continued. The country remained partitioned, with the Interim Government of National Unity, headed by President Amos Sawyer, administering the province of Monrovia and its environs, while NPFL controlled 10 counties and ULIMO two. War-related casualties were estimated at 150,000, while Liberian refugees numbered between 600,000 and 700,000, mainly in Côte d'Ivoire, Guinea and Sierra Leone. The President of the Interim Government, Amos Sawyer, supported the call by ECOWAS for a greater United Nations involvement in the peace process under the Yamoussoukro IV Accord and expressed his readiness for genuine dialogue to expedite a settlement.

The Secretary-General noted that the United Nations emergency relief and humanitarian programmes in Liberia experienced a funding gap of $57 million in priority areas such as food aid, health, water and sanitation, agriculture and assistance to displaced persons and refugees, former combatants and children. He also pointed to the need to initiate steps towards a comprehensive programme for the post-war reconstruction and development in that country (see PART THREE, Chapter III).

The Secretary-General recommended that the Security Council expand cooperation between the United Nations and ECOWAS and consider enlarging the scope of sanctions under Chapter VII of the Charter. He expressed his readiness to assist ECOWAS in monitoring the sanctions and in convening a meeting of the Interim Government and the warring factions.

SECURITY COUNCIL ACTION (March and June)

On 26 March, the Security Council considered the Secretary-General's report, with Liberia participating without the right to vote under rule 37ª of the Council's provisional rules of procedure, and adopted unanimously **resolution 813(1993)**, as orally revised.

The Security Council,

Having considered the report of the Secretary-General on the question of Liberia,

Recalling its resolution 788(1992) of 19 November 1992,

Further recalling the statements by the President of the Council on its behalf on 22 January 1991 and 7 May 1992 on the situation in Liberia,

Reaffirming its belief that the Yamoussoukro IV Accord of 30 October 1991 offers the best possible framework for a peaceful resolution of the Liberian conflict by creating the necessary climate and conditions for free and fair elections in Liberia,

Deploring that parties to the conflict in Liberia have not respected or implemented the various accords to date, especially the Yamoussoukro IV Accord,

Noting that the continuing breach of earlier accords hinders the creation of a climate and conditions conducive to the holding of free and fair elections in accordance with the Yamoussoukro IV Accord,

Recognizing the need for increased humanitarian assistance,

Welcoming the continued commitment of the Economic Community of West African States (ECOWAS) to and the efforts towards a peaceful resolution of the Liberian conflict,

Further welcoming the endorsement and support by the Organization of African Unity (OAU) of these efforts,

Recalling the provisions of Chapter VIII of the Charter of the United Nations,

Determining that the deterioration of the situation in Liberia constitutes a threat to international peace and security, particularly in this region of West Africa,

1. *Approves* the report of the Secretary-General on the question of Liberia;

2. *Commends* ECOWAS for its efforts to restore peace, security and stability in Liberia;

3. *Commends* the OAU for its efforts in support of the peace process in Liberia;

4. *Reaffirms* its belief that the Yamoussoukro IV Accord offers the best possible framework for a peaceful

resolution of the Liberian conflict by creating the necessary conditions for free and fair elections in Liberia, and encourages ECOWAS to continue its efforts to assist in the peaceful implementation of this Accord;

5. *Condemns* the violation of the cease-fire of 28 November 1990 by any party to the conflict;

6. *Condemns* the continuing armed attacks against the peace-keeping forces of ECOWAS in Liberia by one of the parties to the conflict;

7. *Reiterates its call upon* all parties to respect and implement the cease-fire and the various accords of the peace process, including the Yamoussoukro IV Accord of 30 October 1991, and the Final Communiqué of the Informal Consultative Group Meeting of the ECOWAS Committee of Five in Liberia, issued at Geneva on 7 April 1992, to which they themselves have agreed;

8. *Welcomes* the Secretary-General's appointment of Mr. Trevor Gordon-Somers as his Special Representative for Liberia;

9. *Calls upon* all States strictly to abide by and comply with the general and complete embargo on all deliveries of weapons and military equipment to Liberia imposed by resolution 788(1992) under Chapter VII of the United Nations Charter;

10. *Demands* that all parties fully cooperate with the Secretary-General of the United Nations and ECOWAS with a view to ensuring the full and prompt implementation of the Yamoussoukro IV Accord of 30 October 1991;

11. *Declares* its readiness to consider appropriate measures in support of ECOWAS if any party is unwilling to cooperate in implementation of the provisions of the Yamoussoukro Accords, in particular the encampment and disarmament provisions;

12. *Reiterates its call on* Member States to exercise self-restraint in their relations with all parties to the Liberian conflict, in particular to refrain from providing any military assistance to any of the parties and also to refrain from taking any action that would be inimical to the peace process;

13. *Reaffirms* that the embargo imposed by resolution 788(1992) shall not apply to weapons, military equipment and military assistance destined for the sole use of the peace-keeping forces of ECOWAS in Liberia;

14. *Further commends* the efforts of Member States, the United Nations system and humanitarian organizations in providing humanitarian assistance to the victims of the conflict in Liberia, and in this regard reaffirms its support for increased humanitarian assistance;

15. *Demands* that the parties concerned refrain from any action that will impede or obstruct the delivery of humanitarian assistance and calls upon them to ensure the safety of all personnel involved in international humanitarian assistance;

16. *Reiterates its call upon* all parties to the conflict and all others concerned to respect strictly the provisions of international humanitarian law;

17. *Requests* the Secretary-General, in consultation with ECOWAS, to consider the possibility of convening a meeting of the President of the Interim Government of National Unity and the warring factions, after thorough and detailed groundwork, to restate their commitment to the implementation of the Yamoussoukro IV Accord within an agreed timetable;

18. *Requests* the Secretary-General to discuss with ECOWAS and the parties concerned the contribution

which the United Nations could make in support of the implementation of the Yamoussoukro IV Accord, including the deployment of United Nations observers;

19. *Requests* the Secretary-General to submit a report on the implementation of this resolution as soon as possible;

20. *Decides* to remain seized of the matter.

Security Council resolution 813(1993)

26 March 1993   Meeting 3187   Adopted unanimously

Draft prepared in consultations among Council members (S/25469), orally revised.

On 9 June, having received an 8 June communication from Liberia[56] on the massacre of civilians in the Harbel area and following consultations with the Council members, the President, on behalf of the Council, made the following statement:[57]

Meeting number. SC 3233.

"The Security Council is shocked and saddened by the senseless killing of innocent civilians which occurred near Harbel, Liberia, on the morning of 6 June 1993. It strongly condemns this massacre of innocent displaced persons, including women and children, which comes at a time when the Secretary-General's Special Representative is working diligently, in furtherance of the efforts of the Economic Community of West African States (ECOWAS), on the basis of the Yamoussoukro IV Accord, to arrange a meeting of the warring factions in order to bring the three-year civil war to a peaceful end.

"The Security Council urges all parties to the conflict to respect the rights of the civilian population and take all necessary measures to secure their safety.

"The Security Council requests the Secretary-General to commence immediately a thorough and full investigation of the massacre, including any allegations as to the perpetrators whoever they may be, and report to it as soon as possible. It warns that those found responsible for such serious violations of international humanitarian law will be held accountable for such crimes and demands that the leaders of any faction responsible for such acts effectively control their forces and take decisive steps to ensure that such deplorable tragedies do not happen again.

"The Council remains firmly supportive of the efforts of ECOWAS and the Secretary-General to bring peace to Liberia. It urges all Liberian factions and regional leaders to give their full cooperation to current efforts by Special Representative Trevor Gordon-Somers to assist in the implementation of the Yamoussoukro IV Accord calling, *inter alia*, for a cease-fire, encampment, disarmament and democratic elections."

By a 4 August letter,[58] the Secretary-General informed the Security Council of his decision to appoint a three-expert Panel of Inquiry to investigate the Harbel massacre.

Communication and report of the Secretary-General (August). In August, the Secretary-General reported[59] to the Security Council that peace talks between the Interim Government,

NPFL and ULIMO were held at Geneva from 10 to 17 July. A final agreement on the framework settlement between the parties to the conflict was signed on 25 July following the ECOWAS Summit meeting (Cotonou, Benin, 22-24 July). The Agreement provided for a cease-fire and the cessation of hostilities on 1 August; ECOMOG and the United Nations Observer Mission to supervise and monitor implementation of the Agreement; establishment of a Joint Cease-fire and Monitoring Committee; and expansion of ECOMOG. It also provided for the structure and mandate of a national transitional government for a seven-month transition period, comprising legislative, executive and judicial branches; modalities for general and presidential elections, including the establishment of an Electoral Commission; as well as modalities for disarmament, demobilization, encampment and peace enforcement, the release of prisoners-of-war, repatriation of refugees, humanitarian assistance and general amnesty.

A Memorandum of Understanding was also signed providing for United Nations' assistance in demobilizing soldiers. The Secretary-General announced his intention to dispatch an advance United Nations team of 30 military observers and a technical team to prepare for the establishment of an observer mission. He noted that ECOWAS had requested the United Nations to set up a trust fund to facilitate the implementation of the Agreement and that arrangements were being made for the expansion of humanitarian assistance activities throughout Liberia.

The text of the Cotonou Agreement was communicated to the Security Council on 6 August.[60]

SECURITY COUNCIL ACTION (August)

The Security Council met on 10 August to consider the situation in Liberia. Benin, Egypt, Liberia and Nigeria were invited to participate in the discussion under rule 37ª of the Council's provisional rules of procedure.

On the same date, the Council adopted **resolution 856(1993)** unanimously.

The Security Council,

Recalling its resolution 813(1993) of 26 March 1993,

Welcoming the signing under the auspices of ECOWAS, on 25 July 1993, at Cotonou, Benin, of a Peace Agreement between the Interim Government of National Unity of Liberia (IGNU), the National Patriotic Front of Liberia (NPFL) and the United Liberation Movement for Democracy (ULIMO),

Considering that the signing of the Peace Agreement constitutes a major achievement and an important contribution to the restoration of peace and security in Liberia and in this region of West Africa, and creates the opportunity to bring an end to the conflict,

Taking note of the report of the Secretary-General dated 3 August 1993,

1. *Welcomes* the decision of the Secretary-General to send a technical team to Liberia to gather and evaluate information relevant to the proposed establishment of a United Nations Observer Mission in Liberia (UNOMIL);

2. *Approves* the dispatch to Liberia as soon as possible of an advance team of thirty military observers to participate in the work of the Joint Cease-fire Monitoring Committee, including in particular to monitor, investigate and report cease-fire violations in conjunction with the said Committee, the mandate of said team to expire within three months;

3. *Looks forward* to the report of the Secretary-General on the proposed establishment of UNOMIL, including in particular a detailed estimate of the cost and scope of this operation, a time-frame for its implementation, the projected conclusion of this operation, how to ensure coordination between UNOMIL and the peace-keeping forces of ECOWAS and their respective roles and responsibilities;

4. *Calls upon* all parties to the conflict to respect and implement the cease-fire provided for in the Peace Agreement and to cooperate fully with the advance mission and ensure the safety of all United Nations personnel and all other peace-keeping and humanitarian personnel within Liberia;

5. *Urges* the conclusion at the earliest possible stage of a status of mission agreement;

6. *Commends* ECOWAS for its efforts to restore peace, security and stability in Liberia;

7. *Commends* the Organization of African Unity (OAU) for its efforts in support of the peace process in Liberia;

8. *Decides* to remain actively seized of this matter.

Security Council resolution 856(1993)

10 August 1993   Meeting 3263   Adopted unanimously

Draft prepared in consultations among Council members (S/26259).

On 27 August,[61] the Council President informed the Secretary-General that the Council would support the establishment of a United Nations voluntary trust fund for Liberia to finance the implementation of the Cotonou Accord, including deployment of ECOMOG peace-keeping troops, demobilization of combatants, elections and humanitarian assistance.

Report of the Secretary-General (September). In a September report,[62] the Secretary-General proposed the structure and concept of operations of the United Nations Observer Mission in Liberia (UNOMIL), paying particular attention to the division of functions between UNOMIL and ECOMOG. He also described preparations for its deployment and recommended that the Security Council approve the establishment and deployment of UNOMIL as set out in the report. The Secretary-General reported that members of the Council of State of the Liberia National Transitional Government were selected on 17 August and that the newly established Joint Cease-fire Monitoring Committee, which was to be replaced by a Violations Committee upon the full deployment of ECOMOG and UNOMIL, had addressed

eight alleged violations of the cease-fire to date. The report further outlined arrangements for humanitarian and development assistance, pointing in particular to the related problem of land mines, and discussed modalities for the United Nations verification of the elections process.

The Secretary-General stated that the United Nations would work with the Transitional Government, other agencies and organizations and NGOs to develop a comprehensive cantonment, disarmament and demobilization programme. He urged Member States to support the peace process by contributing to its trust fund for Liberia.

Staffing requirements for the Mission were provided in an addendum to the report. The total cost for a seven-month period was estimated at $42.6 million gross, to be borne by Member States.

SECURITY COUNCIL ACTION (September)

On 22 September, the Security Council considered the Secretary-General's report, with Liberia participating in the discussion under rule 37[a] of the Council's provisional rules of procedure, and adopted unanimously **resolution 866(1993)**.

The Security Council,

Recalling its resolutions 813(1993) of 26 March 1993 and 856(1993) of 10 August 1993,

Having considered the report of the Secretary-General dated 9 September 1993 on the proposed establishment of the United Nations Observer Mission in Liberia (UNOMIL),

Noting that the Peace Agreement signed by the three Liberian parties in Cotonou on 25 July 1993 calls on the United Nations and the Military Observer Group (ECOMOG) of the Economic Community of West African States (ECOWAS) to assist in the implementation of the Agreement,

Emphasizing as noted in the Secretary-General's report of 4 August 1993, that the Peace Agreement assigns ECOMOG the primary responsibility of supervising the implementation of the military provisions of the Agreement and envisages that the United Nations role shall be to monitor and verify this process,

Noting that this would be the first peace-keeping mission undertaken by the United Nations in cooperation with a peace-keeping mission already set up by another organization, in this case ECOWAS,

Recognizing that United Nations involvement would contribute significantly to the effective implementation of the Peace Agreement and would serve to underline the international community's commitment to conflict resolution in Liberia,

Commending ECOWAS for its continuing efforts to restore peace, security and stability in Liberia,

Commending also the efforts of the Organization of African Unity in support of the peace process in Liberia,

Stressing the importance of full cooperation and close coordination between UNOMIL and ECOMOG in the implementation of their respective mandates,

Taking note of the deployment of an advance team of United Nations military observers to Liberia as authorized under resolution 856(1993),

Welcoming the establishment of the Joint Cease-fire Monitoring Committee (JCMC) composed of the three Liberian parties, ECOMOG and the United Nations,

Welcoming also the formation in Cotonou on 27 August 1993 of the five-member Council of States representing all three Liberian parties, which, in accordance with the Peace Agreement, shall be installed concomitantly with the commencement of the disarmament process and shall be responsible for the day-to-day operation of the transitional government,

Noting that the Peace Agreement calls for legislative and presidential elections to take place approximately seven months after the signing of the Peace Agreement,

1. *Welcomes* the report of the Secretary-General dated 9 September 1993 on the proposed establishment of UNOMIL;

2. *Decides* to establish UNOMIL under its authority and under the direction of the Secretary-General through his Special Representative for a period of seven months, subject to the proviso that it will continue beyond 16 December 1993 only upon a review by the Council based on a report from the Secretary-General on whether or not substantive progress has been made towards the implementation of the Peace Agreement and other measures aimed at establishing a lasting peace;

3. *Decides* that UNOMIL shall comprise military observers as well as medical, engineering, communications, transportation and electoral components, in the numbers indicated in the Secretary-General's report, together with minimal staff necessary to support it, and shall have the following mandate:

(a) To receive and investigate all reports on alleged incidents of violations of the cease-fire agreement and, if the violation cannot be corrected, to report its findings to the Violations Committee established pursuant to the Peace Agreement and to the Secretary-General;

(b) To monitor compliance with other elements of the Peace Agreement, including at points on Liberia's borders with Sierra Leone and other neighbouring countries, and to verify its impartial application, and in particular to assist in the monitoring of compliance with the embargo on delivery of arms and military equipment to Liberia and the cantonment, disarmament and demobilization of combatants;

(c) To observe and verify the election process, including the legislative and presidential elections to be held in accordance with the provisions of the Peace Agreement;

(d) To assist, as appropriate, in the coordination of humanitarian assistance activities in the field in conjunction with the existing United Nations humanitarian relief operation;

(e) To develop a plan and assess financial requirements for the demobilization of combatants;

(f) To report on any major violations of international humanitarian law to the Secretary-General;

(g) To train ECOMOG engineers in mine clearance and, in cooperation with ECOMOG, coordinate the identification of mines and assist in the clearance of mines and unexploded bombs;

(h) Without participation in enforcement operations, to coordinate with ECOMOG in the discharge of ECOMOG's separate responsibilities both formally, through the Violations Committee, and informally;

4. *Welcomes* the Secretary-General's intention to conclude with the Chairman of ECOWAS an agreement defining, before deployment of UNOMIL, the roles and responsibilities of UNOMIL and ECOWAS in the implementation of the Peace Agreement, in accordance with the concept of operations outlined in Chapter IV of the Secretary-General's report, and requests the Secretary-General to keep the Council informed on the progress and outcome of the negotiations leading thereto;

5. *Encourages* African States to provide the additional troops requested from them by ECOWAS for ECOMOG;

6. *Welcomes* the steps taken by the Secretary-General to establish a Trust Fund, which would facilitate the sending of reinforcements by African States to ECOMOG, assist in supporting troops of participating ECOMOG countries and also assist in mine-clearing, humanitarian and development activities, as well as the electoral process, and calls on Member States to support the peace process in Liberia by contributing to the Trust Fund;

7. *Urges* the Liberian parties to commence the encampment, disarmament and demobilization process without delay;

8. *Welcomes* the decision to establish the transitional government and urges also the Liberian parties to begin the exercise of that government's responsibilities concomitantly with the process described in paragraph 7 above and consistent with the Peace Agreement;

9. *Calls on* the transitional government to conclude expeditiously, and no later than 60 days after its installation, a Status of Mission Agreement with the United Nations to facilitate the full deployment of UNOMIL;

10. *Urges* the Liberian parties to finalize the composition of the Elections Commission so that it can promptly undertake the necessary preparations for legislative and presidential elections by March 1994, at the latest, in accordance with the timetable foreseen in the Peace Agreement;

11. *Calls on* the Liberian parties to cooperate fully in the safe delivery of humanitarian assistance to all parts of the country by the most direct routes, in accordance with the Peace Agreement;

12. *Welcomes* ECOMOG's stated commitment to ensure the safety of UNOMIL observers and civilian staff and urges the Liberian parties to take all necessary measures to ensure the security and safety of UNOMIL personnel, as well as of the personnel involved in relief operations, and strictly to abide by applicable rules of international humanitarian law;

13. *Requests* the Secretary-General to submit progress reports to the Council on the implementation of the present resolution by 16 December 1993 and by 16 February 1994;

14. *Decides* to remain actively seized of the matter.

Security Council resolution 866(1993)

22 September 1993   Meeting 3281   Adopted unanimously

Draft prepared in consultations among Council members (S/26477), orally revised.

On 27 September,[63] the Secretary-General announced his intention to appoint Major-General Daniel Ishmael Opande of Kenya as the Chief Military Observer of UNOMIL. As stated in a 4 October letter[64] from the Security Council President, the Council members agreed to the proposed appointment. On the same date,[65] the

Secretary-General proposed that the military elements of UNOMIL be composed of personnel from Austria, Bangladesh, China, Ecuador, Egypt, Guinea-Bissau, Jordan, Kenya, Malaysia, Slovakia and Uruguay; subsequently added to that list were the Czech Republic, Hungary and Pakistan[66] and India.[67] On 8 October,[68] 19 November[69] and 8 December,[70] the Council President communicated to the Secretary-General its members' agreement with those proposals.

Report of the Secretary-General (December). In a December report,[71] the Secretary-General said that the Liberian parties had selected the five members of the Council of State and had chosen its chairman and vice-chairman. In addition, 13 out of 17 cabinet posts in the Transitional Government were distributed among the parties and agreement was reached on the composition of the Elections Commission, members of the Supreme Court and the Speaker of the Legislature. UNOMIL's deployment began as scheduled, while the United Nations and ECOWAS agreed on the respective roles and responsibilities of UNOMIL and ECOMOG. The Joint Cease-fire Monitoring Committee had resolved 59 out of 99 alleged cease-fire violations and was investigating 25 others. Initial steps were taken to commence the disarmament and demobilization campaign, which was conditioned on the expansion of ECOMOG. The Trust Fund for the Implementation of the Cotonou Accord on Liberia, established on 23 September, had received a single pledge of $19.83 million to meet the costs of expansion and a $1 million contribution for humanitarian activities; however, as no pledges had been made for disarmament and demobilization, the immediate needs of that campaign had to be met from the UNOMIL budget.

The report noted that recent efforts to improve coordination of humanitarian activities between the United Nations and NGOs were yielding positive results and that food and other essential assistance were reaching the most vulnerable groups; however, shortfalls remained in the quantities of assistance delivered. At the same time, UNHCR had launched an appeal for funding to facilitate repatriation and held a regional meeting in October to assess requirements for setting up transit and reception centres. Also in October, a joint mission of the United Nations and the International Foundation for an Election System assessed the requirements for holding elections and found that the timetable provided for in the Peace Agreement, although optimistic, was unlikely to be met and that elections could possibly be held by May 1994.

The Secretary-General also stated that reported human rights abuses, particularly recent reports of alleged killings in the Upper Lofa region resulting from ethnic animosities, prompted his Special Representative to request a Human Rights Officer for his team in Monrovia.

As stated in a 16 December letter[72] of the Security Council President, the Council members took note of the Secretary-General's report and requested a further report on the situation in Liberia by 16 February 1994. They also urged Member States to contribute generously to the Trust Fund.

Financing of UNOMIL

In November,[73] the Secretary-General informed the General Assembly that ACABQ had, on 20 September, authorized him to enter into commitments not exceeding $3.3 million under a 1991 Assembly resolution on unforeseen and extraordinary expenses,[74] to finance UNOMIL activities for a period of three months, including $164,700 for the technical survey mission to Liberia. The total cost of maintaining UNOMIL for the period from 22 September 1993 to 21 April 1994 was estimated at $43,509,200 gross ($42,603,800 net), while the cost estimate for its liquidation, projected to be completed by 30 June 1994, amounted to $3,512,200 gross ($3,347,800 net). Subsequently, estimates for the seven-month period were revised down to $40,318,000 gross ($39,560,800 net).[32]

In December,[75] ACABQ recommended that the Assembly authorize a further commitment and assessment of that amount.

GENERAL ASSEMBLY ACTION

In December, the General Assembly adopted **decision 48/478** without vote.

Financing of the United Nations Observer Mission in Liberia

At its 87th plenary meeting, on 23 December 1993, the General Assembly, on the recommendation of the Fifth Committee, and in accordance with the framework set out in its resolution 48/227 of 23 December 1993, having considered the report of the Secretary-General on the financing of seventeen peace-keeping operations and the related reports of the Advisory Committee on Administrative and Budgetary Questions, and concurring with the observations of the Advisory Committee:

(a) Authorized the Secretary-General, on an exceptional basis, to enter into total commitments up to the amount of 40,318,000 United States dollars gross (39,560,800 dollars net), inclusive of the amount authorized by the Advisory Committee in accordance with Assembly resolution 46/187 of 20 December 1991, for the United Nations Observer Mission in Liberia for the period from 22 September 1993 to 21 April 1994, and requested him to establish a special account for the Observer Mission;

(b) Decided to apportion, as an ad hoc arrangement, the amount indicated in subparagraph (a) above among Member States in accordance with the composition of groups set out in paragraphs 3 and 4 of Assembly resolution 43/232 of 1 March 1989, as adjusted by the Assembly in its resolutions 44/192 B of 21 December 1989,

45/269 of 27 August 1991, 46/198 A of 20 December 1991 and 47/218 A of 23 December 1992 and its decision 48/472 of 23 December 1993, and taking into account the scale of assessments for the years 1992, 1993 and 1994 as set out in Assembly resolutions 46/221 A of 20 December 1991 and 48/223 A of 23 December 1993 and its decision 47/456 of 23 December 1992;

(c) Also decided that, in accordance with the provisions of its resolution 973(X) of 15 December 1955, there should be set off against the apportionment among Member States, as provided for in subparagraph *(b)* above, their respective share in the Tax Equalization Fund of the estimated staff assessment income of 757,200 dollars for the period from 22 September 1993 to 21 April 1994.

General Assembly decision 48/478

Adopted without vote

Approved by Fifth Committee (A/48/827) without vote, 22 December (meeting 46); draft by Chairman (A/C.5/48/L.29); agenda item 166.
Meeting numbers. GA 48th session: 5th Committee 44, 46; plenary 87.

Mozambique

During 1993, United Nations activities in Mozambique were geared towards the implementation of the General Peace Agreement, signed in October 1992[76] between the Government of Mozambique and the Resistência Nacional Moçambicana (RENAMO) and monitored by the United Nations Operation in Mozambique (ONUMOZ), established in December 1992.[77] Despite delays and difficulties, progress was made in implementing the Peace Agreement and action taken to address the humanitarian situation. In November, the Security Council renewed the mandate of ONUMOZ for a further six months.

Report of the Secretary-General (April). In an April report[78] to the Security Council, the Secretary-General said that RENAMO considered a substantial United Nations military presence in Mozambique as a condition for the cantonment and demobilization of its troops, thus giving the ONUMOZ role a broader interpretation than originally intended, whereas the Government asked for a wider deployment of ONUMOZ forces so that the movements of RENAMO and government troops could be monitored equally. By mid-March, following the delayed approval by both parties of the initial list of troop-contributing countries, some 154 military observers from 12 States were deployed at three regional headquarters (Nampula, Beira and Matola) and in Maputo, the capital. Inspections of the deployment areas and assessments of resource requirements were completed also in March. The bulk of forces were expected to arrive in April, and full deployment completed in May. At the same time, the absence of a status-of-forces agreement restricted the Operation's freedom of movement and, along with certain administrative and logistical problems, affected its effectiveness.

Little progress was made in implementing the provisions of the General Peace Agreement dealing with the separation and demobilization of forces, due to the failure of the parties to provide ONUMOZ with necessary information, the unsuitability of the designated troop assembly locations and the linking by RENAMO of the demobilization of its troops to the deployment of United Nations forces. A United Nations technical unit was set up to assist with the demobilization programme, while WFP and UNICEF provided food and other assistance.

The Secretary-General further described activities of the four commissions established in November 1992 under the General Peace Agreement. He noted that the Supervisory and Monitoring Commission had adopted rules governing the work of the entire monitoring machinery, while its subsidiary Cease-fire Commission set up a plan to clear an estimated 2 million mines, including the creation of a mine-clearing school. Two other subsidiary bodies—the Reintegration Commission and the Joint Commission for the Formation of the Mozambican Defence Force—were at the initial stage of their work. At the same time, the establishment of national commissions stipulated in the Agreement—the National Police Affairs Commission, the National Information Commission, the National Elections Commission and the National Commission for Administrative Questions—was delayed. As a result, the timetable for holding the elections in October 1993 was seriously in question.

The United Nations Office for Humanitarian Assistance Coordination, integrated with ONUMOZ, was preparing a consolidated humanitarian assistance programme for 1993-1994, while the Secretariat's Department of Humanitarian Affairs set up a United Nations Trust Fund for Humanitarian Assistance to Mozambique. There were an estimated 3 million to 4 million displaced persons within Mozambique and some 1.5 million refugees receiving assistance in neighbouring countries.

The Special Representative for Mozambique, appointed in 1992,[79] maintained regular contacts with both parties to the Agreement. On 31 March, the Secretary-General reviewed in detail various aspects of the peace process at his meeting with the Foreign Minister. He noted the difficulties in implementing the peace process and underlined the importance of completing all arrangements for the successful implementation of the Agreement without further delay. He stated that although a draft electoral law had been circulated, it was unlikely that the elections could be held in October as scheduled and he undertook to continue discussions on new dates. He also indicated that President Joaquim Chissano and

Alfonso Dhlakama, the President of RENAMO, had agreed to meet to discuss outstanding problems.

SECURITY COUNCIL ACTION (April)

The Security Council met on 14 April to consider the Secretary-General's report. Mozambique and Portugal were invited to participate in accordance with rule 37ª of the Council's provisional rules of procedure.

The Council adopted unanimously **resolution 818(1993)**.

The Security Council,

Reaffirming its resolutions 782(1992) of 13 October 1992 and 797(1992) of 16 December 1992,

Having considered the report of the Secretary-General dated 2 April 1993,

Welcoming the efforts of the Secretary-General to implement fully the mandate entrusted to the United Nations Operation in Mozambique (ONUMOZ),

Reiterating the importance it attaches to the General Peace Agreement for Mozambique and to the timely fulfilment by all parties in good faith of the obligations contained therein,

Seriously concerned at delays in the implementation of major aspects of the Agreement,

Noting the efforts of the Government of Mozambique and the Resistência Nacional Moçambicana (RENAMO) to maintain the cease-fire,

1. *Notes with appreciation* the report of the Secretary-General dated 2 April 1993 and the recommendations contained therein;

2. *Calls upon* the Government of Mozambique and RENAMO to cooperate fully with the Secretary-General and his Special Representative in the full and timely implementation of the mandate of ONUMOZ;

3. *Stresses* its concern about the delays and difficulties which are seriously affecting the timetable for implementation of the peace process envisaged in the Agreement and in the report of the Secretary-General containing the operational plan for ONUMOZ;

4. *Urges* the Government of Mozambique and RENAMO to take urgent and determined steps to comply with the commitments they entered into within the framework of the above-mentioned Agreement, in particular with respect to the concentration, assembly and demobilization of their armed troops and the formation of the new unified armed forces;

5. *Further urges* the Government of Mozambique and RENAMO, in this context, to initiate the training of the first elements of the new Mozambican Defence Force as soon as possible, and calls upon the countries which have offered assistance to cooperate in this respect, with a view to the earliest possible completion of the arrangements for such training;

6. *Welcomes* the initiatives and readiness of both parties to convene as soon as possible a meeting between the President of the Republic of Mozambique and the President of RENAMO, in order to address major issues pertaining to peace in Mozambique;

7. *Strongly appeals* to RENAMO to ensure the effective and uninterrupted functioning of the joint commissions and monitoring mechanisms;

8. *Strongly appeals also* to both the Government of Mozambique and RENAMO to allow timely investigation of all cease-fire violations and to ensure the freedom of movement of people and goods as foreseen in the Agreement;

9. *Welcomes* the Secretary-General's intention to ensure prompt deployment of ONUMOZ military contingents, and calls upon troop-contributing countries to expedite the dispatch of their troops earmarked for service in ONUMOZ;

10. *Strongly urges* the Government of Mozambique and RENAMO to finalize, in consultation with the Secretary-General, the precise timetable for the full implementation of the provisions of the General Peace Agreement, including the separation, concentration and demobilization of forces, as well as for the elections;

11. *Stresses* the importance it attaches to the early signature of the status-of-forces agreement between the Government of Mozambique and the United Nations to facilitate the free, efficient and effective operation of ONUMOZ;

12. *Strongly urges* both sides to guarantee ONUMOZ's freedom of movement and verification capabilities pursuant to the commitments made under the General Peace Agreement;

13. *Appreciates* the assistance and pledges made by Member States in support of the peace process, and encourages the donor community to provide appropriate and prompt assistance for the implementation of major aspects of the Agreement;

14. *Requests* the Secretary-General to keep the Security Council informed of developments regarding the full implementation of the provisions of the General Peace Agreement, including on progress in the consultations with the Government of Mozambique and RENAMO concerning the finalization of the precise timetable for separation, concentration and demobilization of forces, as well as for the elections, and to submit a further report to the Council by 30 June 1993;

15. *Expresses* its confidence in the Secretary-General's Special Representative and its appreciation for the work he has done to date in coordinating all aspects of the Agreement;

16. *Decides* to remain seized of the matter.

Security Council resolution 818(1993)

14 April 1993   Meeting 3198   Adopted unanimously

Draft prepared in consultations among Council members (S/25591), orally revised.

Report of the Secretary-General (June). In June,[80] the Secretary-General reported that the main military components of ONUMOZ, with a total strength of some 6,100 personnel, had been fully deployed by the beginning of May and that the withdrawal of foreign troops had been completed. He indicated the need to bring the strength of the Operation's military component to the levels originally envisaged, and regretted that the deadlines for the cantonment of government and RENAMO troops had not been met. In the meantime, the Cease-fire Commission approved 13 areas for the assembly of troops, out of 49 envisaged in the Agreement, 6 of which (3 each for the Government and RENAMO) were declared ready by ONUMOZ. Since mid-April, ONUMOZ had also been involved in registering and resettling some 16,000 government soldiers along with their dependants, demobilized prior to the Agreement. ONUMOZ activities were facilitated by the status-of-forces agreement between the Government and the United Nations, signed in New York on 14 May.

The work of the monitoring commissions was temporarily suspended when RENAMO withdrew its delegation, but was resumed at the end of May. The Joint Commission for the Formation of the Mozambican Defence Force, however, was expected to start work in July. In addition, the President of Mozambique appointed members of the National Information Commission and Police Affairs Commission.

A new timetable for implementing the General Peace Agreement was proposed to the parties; it called for demobilization to begin on 1 July, the training of soldiers for and the formation of the new Mozambican Defence Force (FADM) by 1 September, approval of the electoral law by the end of July and the holding of elections in September/October 1994.

The report said that $19 million was available for the demining of priority roads, a nationwide mine survey, establishment of a mine-clearing training facility and a mine-awareness programme. A consolidated humanitarian assistance programme for 1993-1994 was presented to a donors' meeting held at Maputo on 8 and 9 June. The programme projected the resettlement of some 4 million displaced persons, 1.5 million refugees and 370,000 demobilized soldiers and their dependants. Its funding requirement from May 1993 to April 1994 was estimated at $559.6 million, of which $450 million had been pledged in December 1992 and an additional $70 million at the June meeting. On 12 June, UNHCR organized the start of the voluntary return of some 250,000 Mozambican refugees from Zimbabwe.

To accelerate the peace process, the Secretary-General said that he was ready to accede, with the consent of the Security Council, to the request that ONUMOZ assume chairmanship of the Joint Commission for the Formation of FADM.

SECURITY COUNCIL ACTION (July)

On 9 July, the Security Council considered the Secretary-General's report, with Mozambique participating in the discussion under rule 37ª of the Council's provisional rules of procedure. The Council adopted unanimously **resolution 850(1993)**.

The Security Council,

Reaffirming its resolutions 782(1992) of 13 October 1992, 797(1992) of 16 December 1992 and 818(1993) of 14 April 1993,

Having considered the report of the Secretary-General dated 30 June 1993,

Reiterating the importance it attaches to the General Peace Agreement for Mozambique and to the timely fulfilment by all parties in good faith of obligations contained therein,

Seriously concerned that the delays in the implementation of major aspects of the General Peace Agreement have not been entirely overcome,

Encouraged by the efforts of the Government of Mozambique and the Resistência Nacional Moçambicana (RENAMO) to maintain the cease-fire,

Noting with satisfaction the signature of the Status-of-Forces Agreement between the Government of Mozambique and the United Nations, and the full deployment of all the main infantry battalions of ONUMOZ,

Noting also with satisfaction the successful completion of the withdrawal of Zimbabwean and Malawian troops as provided for in the General Peace Agreement,

1. *Approves* the report of the Secretary-General dated 30 June 1993;

2. *Pays tribute* to the Special Representative of the Secretary-General, to the Force Commander of ONUMOZ, and to the military and civilian personnel of ONUMOZ who are tackling with determination and dedication the difficult task of helping the people of Mozambique to achieve lasting peace and democracy in their country;

3. *Welcomes* the progress made to date in the implementation of the provisions of the General Peace Agreement but stresses its concern that the delays previously reported to the Security Council have not been entirely overcome, in particular with respect to the assembly and demobilization of forces, the formation of the new unified armed forces, and finalizing the arrangements for the elections;

4. *Underlines* in this respect the importance it attaches to the holding of the elections no later than October 1994;

5. *Welcomes* the agreement of the parties to the convening of a meeting between the President of the Republic of Mozambique and the President of RENAMO in Maputo on 17 July 1993 to address major issues pertaining to the implementation of the General Peace Agreement;

6. *Invites* the Government of Mozambique and RENAMO to cooperate fully with the Secretary-General and his Special Representative in their efforts to promote a resolution of these difficulties and to agree without delay to the revised timetable for the implementation of the provisions of the General Peace Agreement on the basis of the general parameters described in paragraphs 21-23 of the report of the Secretary-General;

7. *Urges* the Government of Mozambique and RENAMO to begin, as a matter of urgency, the assembly and demobilization of their forces without waiting for all assembly areas to become operational;

8. *Further urges* RENAMO to dispatch without further delay its military personnel to the military centre in Nyanga (Zimbabwe) for training, together with military personnel of the Government of Mozambique, as the first elements of the new Mozambican Defence Force;

9. *Approves* the recommendation of the Secretary-General that ONUMOZ should chair the Joint Commission for the Formation of the Mozambican Defence Force, on the strict understanding that this would not

entail any obligation on the part of the United Nations for training or establishing the new armed forces, and encourages RENAMO to participate fully in the work of the Commission;

10. *Stresses* the importance of the early establishment of the Commission of State Administration, and the application throughout the country of the provisions of the General Peace Agreement concerning public administration;

11. *Notes with appreciation* the assistance and pledges made by Member States in support of the peace process, and encourages donors to provide appropriate and prompt assistance for the implementation of major aspects of the General Peace Agreement;

12. *Also notes with appreciation* the contribution from the Government of Italy to the Trust Fund described in paragraph 12 of the report of the Secretary-General, and welcomes the intention of a number of other Member States to contribute;

13. *Requests* the Secretary-General to keep the Security Council informed of developments regarding the full implementation of the provisions of the General Peace Agreement and to submit a report to the Security Council by 18 August 1993 on the outcome of the discussions on the revised timetable, including for the assembly and demobilization of forces and the formation of the new unified armed forces;

14. *Decides* to remain seized of the matter.

Security Council resolution 850(1993)

9 July 1993   Meeting 3253   Adopted unanimously

Draft prepared in consultations among Council members (S/26055), orally revised.

Report of the Secretary-General (August/September).

In August,[81] the Secretary-General reported that progress continued towards the full deployment of ONUMOZ military units, whose total strength stood at 6,004 at the end of the month, while the number of military observers was at 303 of the authorized 354. Regarding the assembly of troops, the Cease-fire Commission approved 34 assembly areas (26 for the Government and 8 for RENAMO), and military observers were deployed in 18 of them. However, RENAMO refused to begin demobilization of its troops until the question of administrative control over RENAMO-held areas was resolved.

Following the first formal meeting of the Joint Commission for the Formation of FADM on 22 July, at which assistance programmes offered by France, Portugal and the United Kingdom were approved, 100 officers (50 from each party) were sent to the training facility at Nyanga, Zimbabwe, and an additional 440 officers were expected to be dispatched at the beginning of September. On 13 August, the Joint Commission approved the timetable for the formation of FADM, the structure of its high command and the rules and criteria for the instructors to be trained at Nyanga.

The multi-party consultative conference on the draft electoral law resumed on 2 August. However, those talks broke down due to disagreement on the composition of the National Electoral Commission. Other developments included the establishment of the National Commission for State Administration; approval by the Commission for Reintegration of key programmes for demobilized soldiers in the areas of training and labour-intensive employment, and an information programme for soldiers in the assembly areas. However, agreement was still not reached on the revised timetable for implementation of the Peace Agreement, calling for the beginning of the demobilization of troops in October.

The report indicated continued deliveries of food to many regions, including RENAMO areas, and the expansion of humanitarian assistance to include health, water, agricultural inputs and education. The number of returnees to Mozambique stood at some 326,000, and an agreement was signed with Swaziland to begin the repatriation of some 24,000 refugees.

In a September addendum to his report,[82] the Secretary-General informed the Council that direct talks between President Chissano and Mr. Dhlakama of RENAMO, begun at Maputo on 23 August, had resulted in the signing of a final document on 3 September,[83] containing agreements on territorial administration and the national police. They agreed to integrate all areas under RENAMO control into the State administration and to request the United Nations to monitor all police activities as well as the rights and liberties of citizens, and to provide technical support to the Police Commission. The Government also indicated that it would seek international support in reorganizing its Rapid Intervention Police. Among other issues discussed were the impartiality of the press and economic assistance to RENAMO.

The Secretary-General announced his intention to dispatch an expert team to Mozambique to assess requirements for the ONUMOZ police contingent and, pending the team's findings, to begin preparations for the deployment of the 128 police observers authorized by the Council in December 1992.[77]

SECURITY COUNCIL ACTION (September and October)

The Security Council met on 13 September to consider the Secretary-General's report. Mozambique was invited to participate in the discussion under rule 37[a] of the Council's provisional rules of procedure.

The Council unanimously adopted **resolution 863(1993)**.

The Security Council,

Reaffirming its resolutions 782(1992) of 13 October 1992, 797(1992) of 16 December 1992, 818(1993) of 14 April 1993 and 850(1993) of 9 July 1993,

Having considered the report of the Secretary-General dated 30 August 1993,

Reiterating the importance it attaches to the General Peace Agreement for Mozambique and to the timely fulfilment in good faith by all parties of the obligations contained therein,

Commending the efforts of the Secretary-General, his Special Representative and the personnel of the United Nations Operation in Mozambique (ONUMOZ) to implement fully the mandate entrusted to the Mission and to carry it out to a successful conclusion,

Commending also the role played by the Organization of African Unity, through the Special Representative of its Secretary-General, in the implementation of the General Peace Agreement,

Noting with satisfaction the recent positive developments in the Mozambican peace process, especially the direct talks in Maputo between the President of Mozambique, Mr. Joaquim Chissano, and Mr. Afonso Dhlakama, President of the Resistência Nacional Moçambicana (RENAMO), which led to the agreements signed on 3 September 1993,

Noting also with satisfaction the full deployment of the military component of ONUMOZ, and the progress made in the establishment by ONUMOZ of assembly areas,

Stressing the unacceptability of attempts to attach conditions to the peace process, in particular to the assembly and demobilization of troops, or to gain more time or further concessions,

Expressing concern at the continuing delays in the implementation of major aspects of the General Peace Agreement as well as at cases of violations of the cease-fire,

1. *Welcomes* the report of the Secretary-General dated 30 August 1993;

2. *Emphasizes* the need to respect fully all the provisions of the General Peace Agreement, in particular those concerning the cease-fire and the movement of troops;

3. *Reaffirms* the importance it attaches to the holding of elections no later than October 1994;

4. *Strongly urges* the Government of Mozambique and RENAMO to agree with, and to apply, without further postponement, the revised timetable for the implementation of all provisions of the General Peace Agreement as described in paragraphs 29 to 31 of the Secretary-General's report, and appeals to the parties to cooperate fully with the Special Representative of the Secretary-General in this regard;

5. *Stresses* once again the urgent need for the early initiation of the process of assembly and demobilization of troops, and its continuation, in accordance with the revised timetable without preconditions;

6. *Urges* RENAMO to join the Government of Mozambique in authorizing immediate assembly of forces, and equally urges that both the Government of Mozambique and F.. IAMO immediately thereupon begin demobilization;

7. *Welcomes* the progress made by the Joint Commission for the Formation of the Mozambican Defence Force, in particular in relation to the training of instructors at Nyanga, and also the progress on mine-clearing;

8. *Deplores* the lack of progress in the multi-party consultative conference and urges RENAMO and other political parties to join with the Government of Mozambique in quickly agreeing on an election law, which should include provision for an effective national election commission;

9. *Calls on* the Government of Mozambique and RENAMO to make operational without further delay the National Commission for Administration, the National Information Commission and the Police Affairs Commission;

10. *Commends* the agreements reached in the Maputo talks between the Government of Mozambique and RENAMO on the reintegration into the State administration of all areas now under the control of RENAMO as well as on the request for monitoring by the United Nations of all police activities in Mozambique and on undertaking additional tasks, as set out in document S/26385/Add.1;

11. *Requests* the Secretary-General to examine expeditiously the proposal by the Government of Mozambique and RENAMO for United Nations monitoring of police activities in the country, as set out in document S/26385/Add.1, and welcomes his intention to send a survey team of experts in connection with the proposed United Nations police contingent, and to report thereon to the Council;

12. *Urges* the Government of Mozambique and RENAMO to ensure that the momentum towards implementing the General Peace Agreement in full is maintained so that a just and lasting peace in Mozambique can be established, and to this end encourages the President of Mozambique and the President of RENAMO to continue their direct talks;

13. *Encourages* the international community to provide appropriate and prompt assistance for the implementation of the humanitarian programme carried out in the framework of the General Peace Agreement, and urges the Government of Mozambique and RENAMO to continue to facilitate unimpeded access of humanitarian assistance to the civilian population in need;

14. *Requests* the Secretary-General to keep the Security Council informed of developments regarding the implementation of the provisions of the General Peace Agreement and to submit a report on the matter to the Security Council in good time before 31 October 1993;

15. *Decides* to remain actively seized of the matter.

Security Council resolution 863(1993)

13 September 1993   Meeting 3274   Adopted unanimously

Draft prepared in consultations among Council members (S/26426), orally revised.

The Council considered the situation in Mozambique again on 29 October, with Mozambique participating under rule 37.[a] It adopted **resolution 879(1993)** unanimously.

The Security Council,

Reaffirming its resolutions 782(1992) of 13 October 1992, 797(1992) of 16 December 1992, 818(1993) of 14 April 1993, 850(1993) of 9 July 1993 and 863(1993) of 13 September 1993,

Reiterating the importance it attaches to the General Peace Agreement for Mozambique and to the timely fulfilment by all parties in good faith of obligations contained therein,

1. *Decides*, pending examination of the report of the Secretary-General due under resolution 863(1993), to extend ONUMOZ's mandate for an interim period terminating on 5 November 1993;

2. *Decides* to remain actively seized of the matter.

Security Council resolution 879(1993)

29 October 1993   Meeting 3300   Adopted unanimously

Draft prepared in consultations among Council members (S/26664).

Report of the Secretary-General (November). In November,[84] the Secretary-General reported that he had visited Mozambique from 17 to 20 October and met with President Chissano and Mr. Dhlakama, as well as leaders of other political parties and representatives of the international community. During that visit, a number of agreements were reached between the Government and RENAMO, covering, *inter alia*, the assembly and demobilization of RENAMO and government troops and the simultaneous disarmament of paramilitary forces, militia and irregular troops; the composition of the National Elections Commission and the system and timetable for finalizing the electoral law; the chairmanship of the national commissions for administration, police affairs and information; creation of local bodies to monitor police activities; and guidelines for the Cease-fire Commission related to the movement of troops after signature of the peace agreement. The multi-party conference on the draft electoral law, which had broken down in August, was dissolved on 17 September. Further negotiations failed to resolve the stalemate and the Government declared its intention to finalize the draft law through bilateral consultations. The parties also agreed that the law would be examined by technical multi-party meetings. Further adjustments were made to the timetable for the peace process, with regard to voter registration scheduled for April-June 1994, the electoral campaign in September and elections in October, as well as to the training and formation of FADM, which was to become operational by September 1994.

On 22 October 1993, the Supervisory and Monitoring Commission approved the new dates for the assembly and demobilization of troops, beginning in November 1993 and January 1994, respectively. All troops were to be demobilized by May 1994. There were 36 assembly areas approved by the Cease-fire Commission (26 for the Government and 10 for RENAMO), with military observers deployed in 23 of them.

As for ONUMOZ activities, the Secretary-General confirmed his intention to proceed with the deployment of the initial police contingent and to deploy an infantry unit in Zambezia Province, due to a recent increase in incidents of banditry along the main routes. He also indicated an increased demand for ONUMOZ air transport.

The Joint Commission for the Formation of FADM decided on the staffing table and structure of its High Command and General Staff, as well as on its uniform and rules of military discipline, while the Commission for Reintegration approved two programmes for demobilized soldiers, dealing with assistance in farming and in training. The Cease-fire Commission had reviewed 59 complaints of alleged violations since June, while guidelines governing the movement of troops, prepared by ONUMOZ, were signed by both parties on 23 October.

On 15 October, a tripartite agreement was signed between the respective Governments and UNHCR on repatriation of some 250,000 Mozambican refugees from South Africa. At the same time, some 400,000 refugees and 1.2 million internally displaced persons were estimated to have returned to their home areas. The first pilot project in mine-clearing was expanded with five additional teams, and a second mine-clearing operation was launched. Another project, aimed at training 1,500 deminers, was at an advanced stage of preparation.

The Secretary-General noted that the trust fund to finance RENAMO's participation in administrative structures and to ensure the transformation of RENAMO into a political party had fallen short of the estimated requirements of $10 million. He proposed establishing complementary funding mechanisms for that purpose and indicated that it might also be necessary to set up a separate trust fund for other political parties, following the approval of the electoral law and establishment of the Elections Commission. In conclusion, the Secretary-General recommended that the Security Council extend the mandate of ONUMOZ until October 1994.

An addendum to the report provided cost estimates related to the deployment of 128 police observers and to additional requirements for transport and air operations, amounting to some $6,480,000 for the period from 1 November 1993 to 30 April 1994 and some $1,405,000 per month thereafter.

SECURITY COUNCIL ACTION (November)

On 5 November, the Security Council considered the Secretary-General's report, with Mozambique participating in the discussion under rule 37.[a] It adopted **resolution 882(1993)** unanimously.

The Security Council,

Reaffirming its resolution 782(1992) of 13 October 1992 and all subsequent resolutions,

Having considered the report of the Secretary-General on the United Nations Operation in Mozambique (ONUMOZ) dated 1 November 1993,

Reiterating the importance it attaches to the General Peace Agreement for Mozambique and to the timely fulfilment in good faith by all parties of the obligations contained therein,

Commending the efforts of the Secretary-General, his Special Representative and the personnel of ONUMOZ to implement the mandate fully,

Reaffirming its conviction that the resolution of conflict in Mozambique would contribute to peace and stability in the region,

Emphasizing with satisfaction the recent positive developments in the Mozambican peace process, including the direct talks between the President of Mozambique, Mr. Joaquim Chissano, and the President of the Resistência Nacional Moçambicana (RENAMO), Mr. Afonso Dhlakama, and the agreements reached on 3 September 1993,

Stressing with mounting concern the continuing delays in the implementation of the General Peace Agreement which both parties signed,

Stressing once again the unacceptability of attempts to gain more time or further concessions, or to attach new conditions to the peace process, and urging strongly the parties not to raise any further issues which might jeopardize the implementation of the General Peace Agreement, particularly in light of the commitments entered into during the Secretary-General's recent visit to Mozambique,

1. *Welcomes* the report of the Secretary-General;

2. *Commends* the agreements that were reached between President Chissano and Mr. Dhlakama during the visit of the Secretary-General to Maputo on outstanding issues that were impeding the peace process;

3. *Reaffirms* the vital importance it attaches to the holding of elections no later than October 1994;

4. *Welcomes* the approval by the Mozambican parties of the revised timetable for the implementation of the General Peace Agreement, and urges the parties to adhere to it without any delay;

5. *Urges* the Mozambican parties to commence assembly of troops in November 1993 and to initiate demobilization by January 1994 with a view to ensuring the completion of the demobilization process by May 1994 on the basis of the revised timetable;

6. *Takes note* of the progress made with regard to the formation of the new Mozambican Defence Forces, particularly the commencement of full-scale training in Nyanga (Zimbabwe) of troops from the Government and RENAMO for the new national army;

7. *Welcomes* the approval of the guidelines for the Cease-fire Commission governing the movement of troops after signature of the General Peace Agreement, and urges the parties to adhere to the guidelines and to cooperate with ONUMOZ in the efforts to enforce them;

8. *Underlines* the need to make immediately operational the National Commission for Administration, the National Police Affairs Commission and the Commission for Information following the agreements reached recently on their chairmanship;

9. *Authorizes* the Secretary-General to proceed with the selection and deployment of the 128 United Nations police observers approved by resolution 797(1992) of 16 December 1992 with a view to deploying the observers as soon as possible;

10. *Underscores* the importance of the parties making progress on achieving agreed political goals, specifically,

the approval of an electoral law and establishment of an electoral commission by 30 November 1993 and the beginning of the concentration of troops in the assembly areas, demobilization of 50 per cent of troops by 31 March 1994, sufficient progress to meet complete demobilization by 31 May 1994, and accelerated progress in training and integrating forces in the new Mozambican Defence Forces so that the process is complete by August 1994;

11. *Calls on* the Government of Mozambique and RENAMO to build on the progress which has been achieved and to respect fully all the provisions of the General Peace Agreement, in particular those concerning the cease-fire and the movement of troops;

12. *Decides* to renew the mandate of ONUMOZ for a period of six months, subject to the proviso that the Security Council will review the status of the mandate of ONUMOZ within 90 days based on a report by the Secretary-General as described in paragraph 13;

13. *Requests* the Secretary-General to report by 31 January 1994 and every three months thereafter on whether the parties have made sufficient and tangible progress towards implementing the General Peace Agreement and meeting the timetable laid out in paragraphs 3 and 10, and also to report on the situation concerning the implementation of the mandate of ONUMOZ, taking into consideration the need to achieve cost savings to the greatest extent possible, while remaining mindful of the importance of an effective discharge of its mandate;

14. *Appeals* to the international community to provide the necessary financial assistance to facilitate the implementation of the General Peace Agreement;

15. *Appeals* to the international community to make voluntary financial contributions to the Trust Fund to be set up to support electoral activities of the political parties upon the approval of the electoral law;

16. *Reiterates* its encouragement to the international community to provide appropriate and prompt assistance for the implementation of the humanitarian programme carried out in the framework of the General Peace Agreement, and urges the Government of Mozambique and RENAMO to facilitate unimpeded access to humanitarian assistance to the civilian population in need;

17. *Calls on* all parties to cooperate with the United Nations High Commissioner for Refugees and other humanitarian agencies operating in Mozambique to facilitate the speedy repatriation and resettlement of refugees and displaced persons;

18. *Decides* to remain actively seized of the matter.

Security Council resolution 882(1993)

5 November 1993   Meeting 3305   Adopted unanimously

Draft prepared in consultations among Council members (S/26694), orally revised.

Further developments (November/December). Following the ratification by the Supervisory and Monitoring Commission of a declaration regarding the opening of assembly areas, troop cantonment formally commenced on 30 November and 35 assembly areas were open by 20 December. By the same date, the training of 540 instructors for FADM had been completed at

Nyanga. In November, the national commissions for administration, police affairs and information were appointed. On 9 December, the Mozambican National Assembly approved the Electoral Law, following agreement reached between the parties on 26 November. Also in December, the Cease-fire Commission approved a national mine-clearance plan and the Supervisory and Monitoring Commission decided to reactivate the Humanitarian Assistance Committee. The consolidated humanitarian assistance programme, updated in November, projected the funding requirement at $609.7 million, up by $50 million from an earlier estimate.

Composition of ONUMOZ

In January,[85] the Secretary-General sought and received from the Security Council agreement to his proposal that the ONUMOZ military elements be composed of contingents from Argentina, Bangladesh, Brazil, Cape Verde, Egypt, Italy, Malaysia, Sweden and Uruguay. Subsequently added to that list were Botswana, Canada, Guinea-Bissau, Hungary, India, Spain and Zambia in February;[86] the Czech Republic, Portugal and the Russian Federation in March;[87] China and Japan in April;[88] the Congo and the Netherlands in June;[89] the United States in August;[90] and Australia and New Zealand in December.[91]

On 10 February,[92] the Secretary-General announced his intention to appoint Major-General Lélio Gonçalves Rodrigues da Silva of Brazil as the Force Commander of ONUMOZ. The Council agreed to that proposal on 12 February.[93]

Financing of ONUMOZ

Report of the Secretary-General (February). In February,[94] the Secretary-General requested the inclusion of an item on the financing of ONUMOZ in the agenda of the General Assembly's resumed forty-seventh session. Later that month, he submitted a report,[95] which included information on initial commitments for the Operation, cost estimates from 15 October 1992 to 31 October 1993, the status of voluntary contributions and the financial administration of the Operation. He stated that ACABQ had authorized him to enter into commitments not exceeding $9.5 million, including the pre-implementation costs, to meet the immediate operational requirements of ONUMOZ. He further estimated the total cost of the Operation for the period from 15 October 1992 to 31 October 1993 at $264,090,700 gross ($259,712,000 net).

ACABQ recommendations. ACABQ in February[96] noted that the previously authorized commitment had been fully obligated and that substantial funds were urgently required to ensure the deployment of military and civilian personnel. It recommended that the Assembly appropriate and assess a lump sum amount of $140 million for the period from 15 October 1992 to 30 June 1993. ACABQ requested revised and detailed cost estimates for that period by 1 July. It also recommended that the Secretary-General take urgent measures to make peace-keeping operations more cost-effective.

GENERAL ASSEMBLY ACTION (March)

On 16 March, the General Assembly, on the recommendation of the Fifth Committee, adopted **resolutions 47/224 A and B** without vote.

Financing of the United Nations Operation in Mozambique

A

The General Assembly,

Having considered the report of the Secretary-General on the financing of the United Nations Operation in Mozambique and the related report of the Advisory Committee on Administrative and Budgetary Questions,

Bearing in mind Security Council resolution 782(1992) of 13 October 1992,

Bearing in mind also Security Council resolution 797(1992) of 16 December 1992, by which the Council, *inter alia*, decided to establish under its authority a United Nations Operation in Mozambique for a period until 31 October 1993,

Recognizing that the costs of the Operation in Mozambique are expenses of the Organization to be borne by Member States in accordance with Article 17, paragraph 2, of the Charter of the United Nations,

Recognizing also that, in order to meet the expenditures caused by the Operation in Mozambique, a different procedure is required from the one applied to meet expenditures of the regular budget of the United Nations,

Taking into account the fact that the economically more developed countries are in a position to make relatively larger contributions and that the economically less developed countries have a relatively limited capacity to contribute towards such an operation,

Bearing in mind the special responsibilities of the States permanent members of the Security Council, as indicated in General Assembly resolution 1874(S-IV) of 27 June 1963, in the financing of such operations,

Mindful of the fact that it is essential to provide the Operation in Mozambique with the necessary financial resources to enable it to fulfil its responsibilities under the relevant resolutions of the Security Council,

1. *Expresses concern* over the delays in launching and in the submission of the financing proposal for the United Nations Operation in Mozambique;

2. *Regrets* that the report of the Secretary-General did not provide full and detailed information on the cost estimates of the operation;

3. *Endorses* the observations and recommendations contained in the report of the Advisory Committee on Administrative and Budgetary Questions;

4. *Urges* all Member States to make every possible effort to ensure payment of their assessed contributions to the Operation in Mozambique in full and on time;

5. *Notes* that, pursuant to Security Council resolution 797(1992), the Secretary-General is requested to submit a further report to the Council by 31 March 1993;

6. *Decides,* at this stage to appropriate, in accordance with the recommendation contained in paragraph 14 of the report of the Advisory Committee, a lump sum amount of 140 million United States dollars, inclusive of the amount of 9.5 million dollars authorized with the prior concurrence of the Advisory Committee, for the period from 15 October 1992 to 30 June 1993, inclusive, and requests the Secretary-General to establish a special account for the United Nations Operation in Mozambique in accordance with paragraph 34 of his report;

7. *Decides also,* as an ad hoc arrangement, to apportion the amount of 140 million dollars for the period from 15 October 1992 to 30 June 1993 among Member States in accordance with the composition of groups set out in paragraphs 3 and 4 of General Assembly resolution 43/232 of 1 March 1989, as adjusted by the Assembly in its resolutions 44/192 B of 21 December 1989, 45/269 of 27 August 1991, 46/198 A of 20 December 1991 and 47/218 of 23 December 1992, and taking into account the scale of assessments for the years 1992, 1993 and 1994;

8. *Decides further* to establish the contributions of the Czech Republic and Slovakia to the Operation in Mozambique in accordance with the rates of assessment to be adopted by the General Assembly for these Member States at its forty-eighth session;

9. *Invites* the new Member States mentioned in paragraph 8 above to make advance payments against their assessed contributions, to be determined;

10. *Requests* the Secretary-General to submit as soon as possible but no later than 1 July 1993 revised and detailed cost estimates for the Operation in Mozambique for the entire mandate period, taking into account any possible adjustments in the operational plan and related decisions of the Security Council, and the financial performance of the Operation in Mozambique during the start-up period;

11. *Invites* voluntary contributions to the Operation in Mozambique in cash and in the form of services and supplies acceptable to the Secretary-General, to be administered, as appropriate, in accordance with the procedure established by the General Assembly in its resolutions 43/230 of 21 December 1988, 44/192 A of 21 December 1989 and 45/258 of 3 May 1991;

12. *Requests* the Secretary-General to take all necessary action to ensure that all United Nations activities related to the Operation in Mozambique are administered under the authority of his interim Special Representative in a coordinated fashion with a maximum of efficiency and economy and in accordance with the relevant mandate, and to include information on the arrangement made in this regard in his report on the financial performance of the Operation in Mozambique;

13. *Decides* to include in the provisional agenda of its forty-eighth session the item entitled "Financing of the United Nations Operation in Mozambique".

B

The General Assembly

1. *Requests* the Secretary-General to take the necessary measures to ensure a more effective planning of peace-keeping operations and to undertake an urgent review of the current procedures to enable the proper and timely launching of such missions in a cost-effective and efficient manner, and to report on his efforts to the General Assembly at its current session;

2. *Also requests* the Secretary-General to continue to improve the format, contents and transparency of information contained in the cost estimates for peace-keeping operations, in accordance with the relevant recommendations of the Advisory Committee on Administrative and Budgetary Questions as approved by the General Assembly.

General Assembly resolutions 47/224 A and B

16 March 1993   Meeting 97   Adopted without vote

Approved by Fifth Committee (A/47/906) without vote, 10 March (meeting 55); draft by Chairman (A/C.5/47/L.32); agenda item 153.
Meeting numbers. GA 47th session: 5th Committee 54, 55; plenary 97.

Report of the Secretary-General (June). In a June report on the financing of ONUMOZ,[97] the Secretary-General provided information on its financial performance up to 30 June 1993 and revised cost estimates for the entire mandate period, as well as for the period from 1 November 1993 to 31 October 1994. He reported that outstanding assessments due from Member States totalled $87,894,122 as at 15 June, while the unencumbered balance for the period from 15 October 1992 to 30 June 1993 amounted to $46,867,300 gross ($47,870,400 net). The Operation's cost from 1 July to 31 October 1993 was estimated at $113,477,700 gross ($111,885,100 net), providing for a total of 354 military observers, 6,625 military contingent personnel, 355 civilian personnel and 506 local staff. The cost estimate for the entire mandate period from 15 October 1992 to 31 October 1993, including the unencumbered balance, was revised down to $206,610,400 gross ($204,014,700 net). The report also provided the monthly cost of maintaining ONUMOZ from 1 November 1993 to 31 October 1994, estimated at $25,823,408 gross ($25,261,600 net).

In July,[98] ACABQ made a downward revision of the cost estimates from 1 July to 31 October 1993 to $110,810,700 gross ($109,218,100 net) and recommended for that period the amount of $54 million gross to be appropriated and assessed and the commitment authority of $20 million gross per month for the period beyond 31 October.

GENERAL ASSEMBLY ACTION (September)

On 14 September, the General Assembly, on the recommendation of the Fifth Committee, adopted **resolution 47/224 C** without vote.

The General Assembly,

Having considered the report of the Secretary-General on the financing of the United Nations Operation in Mozambique and the related report of the Advisory Committee on Administrative and Budgetary Questions,

Bearing in mind Security Council resolution 797(1992) of 16 December 1992, by which the Council established the United Nations Operation in Mozambique for a period until 31 October 1993,

Reaffirming that the costs of the Operation in Mozambique are expenses of the Organization to be borne by Member States in accordance with Article 17, paragraph 2, of the Charter of the United Nations,

Recalling its previous decision regarding the fact that, in order to meet the expenditures caused by the Operation in Mozambique, a different procedure is required from the one applied to meet expenditures of the regular budget of the United Nations,

Taking into account the fact that the economically more developed countries are in a position to make relatively larger contributions and that the economically less developed countries have a relatively limited capacity to contribute towards such an operation,

Bearing in mind the special responsibilities of the States permanent members of the Security Council, as indicated in General Assembly resolution 1874(S-IV) of 27 June 1963, in the financing of such operations,

Mindful of the fact that it is essential to provide the Operation in Mozambique with the necessary financial resources to enable it to fulfil its responsibilities under the relevant resolutions of the Security Council,

Expressing concern about the deteriorating financial situation with regard to peace-keeping activities owing to overdue payments by Member States of their assessments, particularly Member States in arrears,

Expressing deep concern about the adverse effect that the deteriorating financial situation has on reimbursement to troop contributors, placing an additional burden on these countries and putting at risk the continuing supply of troops to the Operation in Mozambique and, consequently, the success of the Operation,

1. *Endorses* the observations and recommendations contained in the report of the Advisory Committee on Administrative and Budgetary Questions, subject to the terms of the present resolution;

2. *Urges* all Member States to make every possible effort to ensure payment of their assessed contributions to the United Nations Operation in Mozambique in full and on time;

3. *Requests* the Secretary-General to explore all possibilities in order to ensure prompt reimbursement to troop-contributing countries;

4. *Decides* to appropriate to the Special Account for the United Nations Operation in Mozambique a total amount of 54 million United States dollars gross (52,785,200 dollars net) for the Operation in Mozambique for the period from 1 July to 31 October 1993;

5. *Decides also,* as an ad hoc arrangement, to apportion the amount of 54 million dollars gross (52,785,200 dollars net) for the period from 1 July to 31 October 1993 among Member States in accordance with the composition of groups set out in paragraphs 3 and 4 of General Assembly resolution 43/232 of 1 March 1989, as adjusted by the Assembly in its resolutions 44/192 B of 21 December 1989, 45/269 of 27 August 1991, 46/198 A of 20 December 1991 and 47/218 A of 23 December 1992, and taking into account the scale of assessments set out in Assembly resolution 46/221 A of 20 December 1991 and Assembly decision 47/456 of 23 December 1992;

6. *Decides further* that, in accordance with the provisions of its resolution 973(X) of 15 December 1955, there shall be set off against the apportionment among Member States, as provided for in paragraph 5 above, their respective share in the Tax Equalization Fund of the es-timated staff assessment income of 1,214,800 dollars for the period from 1 July to 31 October 1993 approved for the Operation in Mozambique;

7. *Authorizes* the Secretary-General to enter into commitments for the Operation in Mozambique at a rate not to exceed 20 million dollars gross (19,439,000 dollars net) per month, should the Security Council decide to extend the mandate of the Operation beyond 31 October 1993, subject to obtaining the prior concurrence of the Advisory Committee for the actual level of commitments to be entered into for the period from 1 November 1993 to 28 February 1994, and, in this regard, requests the Secretary-General to submit, no later than 8 February 1994, budget proposals, including revised estimates for the period the Council might have decided to continue the mandate of the Operation beyond 31 October 1993, as well as budget proposals for the subsequent period of six months;

8. *Decides* to establish the contributions of Andorra, the Czech Republic, Eritrea, the former Yugoslav Republic of Macedonia, Monaco and Slovakia to the Operation in Mozambique in accordance with the rates of assessment to be adopted by the General Assembly for those Member States at its forty-eighth session;

9. *Invites* the new Member States listed in paragraph 8 above to make payments against their assessed contributions, to be determined;

10. *Invites* voluntary contributions to the Operation in Mozambique in cash and in the form of services and supplies acceptable to the Secretary-General, to be administered, as appropriate, in accordance with the procedure established by the General Assembly in its resolutions 43/230 of 21 December 1988, 44/192 A of 21 December 1989 and 45/258 of 3 May 1991;

11. *Requests* the Secretary-General to take all necessary action to ensure that all United Nations activities related to the Operation in Mozambique are administered under the authority of his Special Representative in a coordinated fashion with a maximum of efficiency and economy and in accordance with the relevant mandate, and to include information on the arrangements made in this regard in his report on the financing of the Operation.

General Assembly resolution 47/224 C

14 September 1993   Meeting 110   Adopted without vote

Approved by Fifth Committee (A/47/906/Add.1) without vote, 3 September (meeting 74); draft by Chairman (A/C.5/47/L.44); agenda item 153.
Meeting numbers. GA 47th session: 5th Committee 68, 69, 72, 74; plenary 110.

Report of the Secretary-General (December). In December,[32] the Secretary-General requested authorization to enter into revised commitments of $86,842,000 gross ($85,492,700 net) for the period from 1 November 1993 to 28 February 1994, based on additional requirements for the deployment of civilian police and an increase in air operations. He also provided cost estimates of maintaining ONUMOZ from 1 November 1993 to 30 April 1994, amounting to $131,103,000 gross ($129,078,000 net).

ACABQ concurred with the request for revised commitment authority and recommended a further authorization of $20 million for the six-month period ending 30 April 1994, in addition to $80 million authorized in September.[99]

As at 31 December 1993, outstanding assessed contributions due from Member States totalled $81,319,883, while the unencumbered balance for the period from 1 July to 31 October amounted to $21,527,100 gross ($21,212,300 net). The revised cost for ONUMOZ from 1 November 1993 to 30 April 1994 was estimated at $163,409,500 gross ($161,072,800 net).

GENERAL ASSEMBLY ACTION (December)

In December, the General Assembly adopted **decision 48/473** without vote.

Financing of the United Nations Operation in Mozambique

At its 87th plenary meeting, on 23 December 1993, the General Assembly, on the recommendation of the Fifth Committee, in accordance with the framework set out in its resolution 48/227 of 23 December 1993, having considered the report of the Secretary-General on the financing of seventeen peace-keeping operations and the related reports of the Advisory Committee on Administrative and Budgetary Questions, and concurring with the observations of the Advisory Committee:

(a) Authorized the Secretary-General, on an exceptional basis, to enter into total commitments up to the amount of 82,308,700 United States dollars gross (80 million dollars net), inclusive of the authorization provided under Assembly resolution 47/224 C of 14 September 1993, for the United Nations Operation in Mozambique for the period from 1 November 1993 to 28 February 1994;

(b) Decided at that time to apportion, as an ad hoc arrangement, the amount of 61,731,500 dollars gross (60 million dollars net) among Member States in accordance with the composition of groups set out in paragraphs 3 and 4 of Assembly resolution 43/232 of 1 March 1989, as adjusted by the Assembly in its resolutions 44/192 B of 21 December 1989, 45/269 of 27 August 1991, 46/198 A of 20 December 1991 and 47/218 A of 23 December 1992 and its decision 48/472 of 23 December 1993, and taking into account the scale of assessments for the years 1992, 1993 and 1994 as set out in Assembly resolutions 46/221 A of 20 December 1991 and 48/223 A of 23 December 1993 and its decision 47/456 of 23 December 1992;

(c) Also decided that, in accordance with the provisions of its resolution 973(X) of 15 December 1955, there should be set off against the apportionment among Member States, as provided for in subparagraph *(b)* above, their respective share in the Tax Equalization Fund of the estimated staff assessment income of 1,731,500 dollars for the period from 1 November 1993 to 28 February 1994;

(d) Further decided that, in view of the expiration of the commitment authority on 28 February 1994, priority should be given to the cost estimates for the Operation in the consideration by the General Assembly of peace-keeping budgets.

General Assembly decision 48/473

Adopted without vote

Approved by Fifth Committee (A/48/821) without vote, 22 December (meeting 46); draft by Chairman (A/C.5/48/L.24); agenda item 149.
Meeting numbers. GA 48th session: 5th Committee 44, 46; plenary 87.

The situation concerning Rwanda

The armed conflict between the Government of Rwanda and the Rwandese Patriotic Front (RPF), which originally broke out in October 1990, resumed on 8 February 1993 in violation of the Cease-fire Agreement signed in July 1992 at Arusha, United Republic of Tanzania. In June, the Security Council established the United Nations Observer Mission Uganda-Rwanda to verify that no military assistance reached Rwanda across their common border. In October, the Council established the United Nations Assistance Mission for Rwanda to assist in implementing the peace agreement signed by the parties in August.

Communications (February/March). On 22 February,[100] Rwanda informed the Security Council of the resumption of hostilities in the northern part of the country by RPF, composed essentially of Rwandese refugees in Uganda, and requested the deployment of United Nations military observers on both sides of the frontier between the two countries to ensure that no military assistance reached Rwandese territory from Uganda. Uganda made a similar request, also on 22 February.[101]

On 4 March,[102] Rwanda requested an immediate meeting of the Security Council to consider ways to end the fighting and ensure the observance of the 1992 Cease-fire Agreement and implementation of declarations of cease-fire, issued by RPF and the Government on 21 and 22 February. It requested that an international force supervise the zone along the front line between the positions occupied prior to the violation of the cease-fire. Also on 4 March,[103] a similar request for a meeting of the Council was received from France.

A joint communiqué issued at the end of a high-level meeting between the Government and RPF (Dar es Salaam, United Republic of Tanzania, 5-7 March) was transmitted to the Council.[104] The two parties agreed on the cessation of hostilities as of 9 March, the resumption of the Arusha peace negotiations on 15 March, the withdrawal of their troops to positions identified by the OAU Neutral Military Observer Group (NMOG) and by the 1992 Cease-fire Agreement, and the withdrawal of foreign troops, to be replaced by an international humanitarian force of the United Nations and OAU. The parties called for increased relief assistance to persons displaced by the conflict and undertook to facilitate the delivery of relief supplies and the return of displaced persons.

Following consultations of the Security Council on 24 February, the Secretary-General sent a goodwill mission to Rwanda and Uganda, which held consultations with the Rwandese Government from 4 to 9 March. An oral report on the mission's activities was presented to the Council.

The Security Council met on 12 March to consider the situation concerning Rwanda. Rwanda was invited to participate in accordance with rule 37[a] of the Council's provisional rules of procedure.

The Council adopted **resolution 812(1993)** unanimously.

The Security Council,

Taking note of the request contained in the letter of the Chargé d'affaires a.i. of Rwanda dated 4 March 1993,

Also taking note of the letters of the Permanent Representative of Rwanda and of the Permanent Representative of Uganda dated 22 February 1993 in which the Governments of both these countries called for the deployment of United Nations observers along their common border,

Gravely concerned by the fighting in Rwanda and its consequences regarding international peace and security,

Alarmed by the humanitarian consequences of the latest resumption of the fighting in Rwanda, in particular the increasing number of refugees and displaced persons, and by the threats to the civilian populations,

Stressing the need for a negotiated political solution, in the framework of the agreements signed by the parties in Arusha, in order to put an end to the conflict in Rwanda,

Paying tribute to the efforts of the Organization of African Unity (OAU), in order to promote such a political solution,

Taking note of the statements by the Government of Rwanda and the Rwandese Patriotic Front (RPF) by which the Rwandese armed forces would remain in their current positions, the army of RPF would pull back to the positions it occupied before 7 February 1993 and the buffer zone between the forces would be considered as a neutral demilitarized zone used to monitor the implementation of the cease-fire by an international force,

Welcoming the joint communiqué issued in Dar es Salaam on 7 March 1993 by the Government of Rwanda and RPF, concerning in particular the modalities of the cease-fire which should be effective on 9 March 1993 and on the situation of displaced persons,

Welcoming the decision of the Secretary-General to send a goodwill mission to the region and having heard a first oral report on the mission,

Determined that the United Nations, in consultation with OAU, and in support of its ongoing efforts, should consider how a United Nations contribution might assist the process towards a political settlement in Rwanda, in particular by preventing the resumption of fighting and by monitoring the cease-fire,

1. *Calls upon* the Government of Rwanda and RPF to respect the cease-fire which took effect on 9 March 1993, to allow the delivery of humanitarian supplies and the return of displaced persons, to fulfil the obligations they have accepted in the agreements they have signed and to implement the commitments they have undertaken in their above-mentioned statements and joint communiqué;

2. *Invites* the Secretary-General to examine in consultation with OAU the contribution that the United Nations, in support of OAU's efforts, could bring to strengthen the peace process in Rwanda, in particular through the possible establishment of an international force under the aegis of OAU and the United Nations,

entrusted *inter alia* with the protection of, and humanitarian assistance to, the civilian population and the support of the OAU force for the monitoring of the cease-fire, and to report most urgently on the matter;

3. *Also invites* the Secretary-General to examine the request by Rwanda and Uganda for the deployment of observers at the border between these two countries;

4. *Expresses* its readiness to examine without delay the recommendations that the Secretary-General could submit in this regard;

5. *Invites* the Secretary-General to coordinate closely his efforts with those of OAU;

6. *Calls upon* the Government of Rwanda and RPF to cooperate fully with the efforts of the United Nations and OAU;

7. *Urges* the Government of Rwanda and RPF to resume the negotiations on 15 March 1993 as agreed, in order to resolve the pending questions with a view to signing a peace agreement at the beginning of April 1993 at the latest;

8. *Urges* both parties strictly to respect the rules of international humanitarian law;

9. *Urges* all States to refrain from any action that could increase the tension in Rwanda and jeopardize respect for the cease-fire;

10. *Decides* to remain actively seized of the matter.

Security Council resolution 812(1993)

12 March 1993   Meeting 3183   Adopted unanimously

Draft prepared in consultations among Council members (S/25400).

Communications (April-June). On 8 April,[105] the Secretary-General informed the Council of his decision to strengthen the goodwill mission, which had visited Ethiopia, Rwanda, Uganda and the United Republic of Tanzania from 4 to 19 March, by adding three military advisers. The Council welcomed that decision on 13 April.[106]

On 18 May,[107] Uganda reiterated its agreement with the deployment of a monitoring team on its territory, but expected the Security Council to reflect an earlier agreement that a neutral observer or peace-keeping force would be deployed in the buffer zone between the conflicting forces inside Rwanda. On 14 June,[108] Rwanda communicated to the Council a joint request of the Government and RPF for the deployment, following the signing of a peace agreement between the parties, of a neutral international force in that country to assist in its implementation.

Interim report of the Secretary-General (May). In May,[109] the Secretary-General reported to the Council that peace talks between the parties had resumed at Arusha on 16 March, with the United Republic of Tanzania acting as facilitator. The negotiations focused on the composition and size of the new army, arrangements related to security services, demobilization, international assistance and the establishment of an international neutral force. Discussions also centred on amendments to the Constitution, the duration of the transitional period and questions relating to refugees and displaced persons.

The report noted that the United Nations had assisted OAU in preparing a funding proposal for the expansion of NMOG. It also outlined the findings of the technical mission that visited Rwanda and Uganda from 2 to 6 April to assess the requirements for the deployment of a United Nations Observer Mission Uganda-Rwanda (UNOMUR). The Secretary-General described the structure, concept of operations, phases of deployment and staffing requirements of UNOMUR. He recommended that the Security Council authorize the establishment of the Mission on the Uganda side of the border for an initial period of up to six months. The total cost for that period was estimated at $8,529,000.

SECURITY COUNCIL ACTION (June)

On 22 June, the Security Council considered the Secretary-General's report, with Rwanda participating in the discussion under rule 37ª of the provisional rules of procedure. It adopted **resolution 846(1993)** unanimously.

The Security Council,

Reaffirming its resolution 812(1993) of 12 March 1993,

Taking note of the interim report of the Secretary-General dated 20 May 1993,

Also taking note of the requests of the Governments of Rwanda and Uganda for the deployment of United Nations observers along their common border as a temporary confidence-building measure,

Emphasizing the need to prevent the resumption of fighting in Rwanda that could have adverse consequences on the situation in Rwanda and on international peace and security,

Stressing the need for a negotiated political solution, in the framework of the agreements to be signed by the parties in Arusha, in order to put an end to the conflict in Rwanda,

Paying tribute to the efforts of the Organization of African Unity (OAU) and the Government of the United Republic of Tanzania to promote such a political solution,

Taking note of the joint request of the Government of Rwanda and the Rwandese Patriotic Front (RPF) concerning the establishment of a neutral international force in Rwanda,

Stressing the importance of the ongoing negotiations in Arusha between the Government of Rwanda and RPF, and expressing its readiness to consider assistance to OAU in the implementation of the agreements as soon as they are signed,

1. *Welcomes with appreciation* the report of the Secretary-General;

2. *Decides* to establish the United Nations Observer Mission Uganda-Rwanda (UNOMUR) that will be deployed on the Ugandan side of the border, for an initial period of six months, as set out in the report of the Secretary-General, and subject to review every six months;

3. *Decides* that UNOMUR shall monitor the Uganda/Rwanda border to verify that no military assistance reaches Rwanda, focus being put primarily in this regard on transit or transport, by roads or tracks which could accommodate vehicles, of lethal weapons and ammunition across the border, as well as any other material which could be of military use;

4. *Requests* the Secretary-General to conclude with the Government of Uganda, before the full deployment of UNOMUR, a status of mission agreement including the safety, cooperation and support the Government of Uganda will provide to UNOMUR;

5. *Approves* the dispatching of an advance party within fifteen days of the adoption of this resolution or as soon as possible after the conclusion of the status of mission agreement and the full deployment within thirty days of the arrival of the advance party;

6. *Urges* the Government of Rwanda and RPF strictly to respect the rules of international humanitarian law;

7. *Further urges* the Government of Rwanda and RPF to refrain from any action that could contribute to tension;

8. *Welcomes* the decision of the Secretary-General to support the peace efforts of the OAU by putting two military experts at its disposal with a view to assisting the Neutral Military Observer Group (NMOG), in particular through logistic expertise to help expedite deployment of the enlarged NMOG to Rwanda;

9. *Urges* the Government of Rwanda and RPF to conclude quickly a comprehensive peace agreement;

10. *Requests* the Secretary-General to report to the Council on the results of the Arusha peace talks;

11. *Further requests* the Secretary-General to report on the contribution the United Nations could make to assist OAU in the implementation of the above-mentioned agreement and to begin contingency planning in the event that the Council decides such a contribution is needed;

12. *Also requests* the Secretary-General to report to the Council on the implementation of the present resolution within sixty days of the deployment of UNOMUR;

13. *Decides* to remain actively seized of the matter.

Security Council resolution 846(1993)
22 June 1993   Meeting 3244   Adopted unanimously
Draft prepared in consultations among Council members (S/25981).

On 29 June,[110] the Secretary-General announced his intention to appoint Brigadier-General Romeo A. Dallaire of Canada as the Chief Military Observer of UNOMUR and proposed that the Mission be composed of military observers from Bangladesh, Botswana, Brazil, Canada, Fiji, Hungary, the Netherlands, Senegal, Slovakia and Zimbabwe. The Security Council agreed to those proposals on 30 June.[111]

Further report of the Secretary-General (August). In August,[112] the Secretary-General reported that the Government of Rwanda and RPF had signed a peace agreement at Arusha on 4 August, following the conclusion of the peace talks. They agreed that the war had come to an end and that they would promote national reconciliation. The agreement incorporated six protocols: the 1992 Cease-fire Agreement and protocols on the rule of law, power-sharing, repatriation of refugees and resettlement of displaced persons, integration of the armed forces and issues related to the appointment of the Prime Minister and the transitional period, which was set at 22 months. The Secretary-General indicated that NMOG had been replaced by NMOG II as of 3 August, pending the deployment of an international force. He dispatched a reconnaissance mission to Rwanda on 19 August to assess the human and financial requirements for establishing such a force.

SECURITY COUNCIL ACTION (September)

On 10 September, the President, on behalf of the Council, made the following statement:[(113)]

Meeting number. SC 3273.

"The Security Council welcomes the peace agreement concluded by the Government of Rwanda and the Rwandese Patriotic Front at Arusha on 4 August 1993. The Council is aware of the hopes the Rwandese parties entertain that the international community will lend its assistance in the implementation of the agreement. It has also taken note of the importance they attach to 10 September 1993, the date that is to mark the establishment of transitional institutions.

"The Security Council welcomes in this regard the decision taken by the Secretary-General to send a reconnaissance mission to Rwanda. The Council hopes to have the report of the Secretary-General based on the recommendations of the reconnaissance mission in the next few days so that it can consider the contribution the United Nations could make to facilitate the implementation of the Arusha peace agreement.

"The Security Council urges the Government of Rwanda and the Rwandese Patriotic Front to continue to honour the Arusha agreements in accordance with their commitments. It further urges them to continue to cooperate with the Neutral Military Observer Group, whose mandate the Secretary-General of OAU has decided to extend on an interim basis."

Report of the Secretary-General (September). In a September report,[(114)] the Secretary-General stated that the reconnaissance mission visited Rwanda, the United Republic of Tanzania and Ethiopia between 19 August and 3 September. On the basis of its observations and recommendations, he outlined the United Nations contribution to the establishment of a peace-keeping mission to Rwanda, as provided for in the Arusha Peace Agreement. The Mission would assist in ensuring the security of the capital, Kigali; monitor the cease-fire, including demobilization and the establishment of a demilitarized zone, and the security situation during the transitional period; and assist with mine clearance. It would incorporate

NMOG II forces, have under its command UNOMUR military observers, and operate in five sectors, with headquarters at Kigali. The report set out the concept of operations, proposed structure and deployment schedule of the new Mission, as well as functions and staffing requirements of its military, civilian police and administrative components. He proposed that the military personnel be deployed progressively and that the operation be conducted in four phases.

The Secretary-General also proposed that the Mission's activities be coordinated with humanitarian assistance to Rwanda. Humanitarian programmes were envisaged for the repatriation and reintegration of refugees, the resettlement of displaced persons, assistance to demobilized soldiers, mine clearance and reconstruction. In February, UNDP adopted a programme on Rwanda, and a consolidated appeal was launched in April to meet the emergency needs of displaced persons. The report noted that, while some 600,000 people had returned to their homes, an estimated 300,000 remained displaced and continued to rely on emergency assistance, and that some $100 million had been contributed to that programme since January.

The Secretary-General recommended that the Security Council authorize the establishment of a United Nations Assistance Mission for Rwanda (UNAMIR), led by a Special Representative, and urge Member States to support the United Nations aid effort there. Cost estimates for a six-month period were estimated at $62.6 million.

SECURITY COUNCIL ACTION (October)

The Security Council met on 5 October to consider the Secretary-General's report. Rwanda was invited to participate under rule 37ª of the provisional rules of procedure.

The Council adopted **resolution 872(1993)** unanimously.

The Security Council,

Reaffirming its resolutions 812(1993) of 12 March 1993 and 846(1993) of 22 June 1993,

Reaffirming also its resolution 868(1993) of 29 September 1993 on the security of United Nations operations,

Having considered the report of the Secretary-General of 24 September 1993,

Welcoming the signing of the Arusha Peace Agreement (including its Protocols) on 4 August 1993 and urging the parties to continue to comply fully with it,

Noting the conclusion of the Secretary-General that in order to enable the United Nations to carry out its mandate successfully and effectively the full cooperation of the parties with one another and with the Organization is required,

Stressing the urgency of the deployment of an international neutral force in Rwanda, as underlined both by the Government of the Republic of Rwanda and by the

Rwandese Patriotic Front and as reaffirmed by their joint delegation in New York,

Paying tribute to the role played by the Organization of African Unity (OAU) and by the Government of the United Republic of Tanzania in the conclusion of the Arusha Peace Agreement,

Resolved that the United Nations should, at the request of the parties and under peaceful conditions with the full cooperation of all the parties, make its full contribution to the implementation of the Arusha Peace Agreement,

1. *Welcomes* the report of the Secretary-General;

2. *Decides* to establish a peace-keeping operation under the name "United Nations Assistance Mission for Rwanda" (UNAMIR) for a period of six months subject to the proviso that it will be extended beyond the initial ninety days only upon a review by the Council based on a report from the Secretary-General as to whether or not substantive progress has been made towards the implementation of the Arusha Peace Agreement;

3. *Decides* that, drawing from the Secretary-General's recommendations, UNAMIR shall have the following mandate:

(a) To contribute to the security of the city of Kigali *inter alia* within a weapons-secure area established by the parties in and around the city;

(b) To monitor observance of the cease-fire agreement, which calls for the establishment of cantonment and assembly zones and the demarcation of the new demilitarized zone and other demilitarization procedures;

(c) To monitor the security situation during the final period of the transitional government's mandate, leading up to the elections;

(d) To assist with mine clearance, primarily through training programmes;

(e) To investigate at the request of the parties or on its own initiative instances of alleged non-compliance with the provisions of the Arusha Peace Agreement relating to the integration of the armed forces, and pursue any such instances with the parties responsible and report thereon as appropriate to the Secretary-General;

(f) To monitor the process of repatriation of Rwandese refugees and resettlement of displaced persons to verify that it is carried out in a safe and orderly manner;

(g) To assist in the coordination of humanitarian assistance activities in conjunction with relief operations;

(h) To investigate and report on incidents regarding the activities of the gendarmerie and police;

4. *Approves* the Secretary-General's proposal that the United Nations Observer Mission Uganda-Rwanda (UNOMUR) established by resolution 846(1993) should be integrated within UNAMIR;

5. *Welcomes* the efforts and the cooperation of OAU in helping to implement the Arusha Peace Agreement, in particular the integration of the Neutral Military Observer Group (NMOG II) within UNAMIR;

6. *Further approves* the Secretary-General's proposal that the deployment and withdrawal of UNAMIR should be carried out in stages and notes in this connection that UNAMIR's mandate, if extended, is expected to terminate following national elections and the installation of a new Government in Rwanda, events which are scheduled to occur by October 1995, but no later than December 1995;

7. *Authorizes* the Secretary-General, in this context, to deploy the first contingent, at the level specified by the Secretary-General's report, to Kigali for an initial period of six months, in the shortest possible time, which, when fully in place, will permit the establishment of the transitional institutions and implementation of the other relevant provisions of the Arusha Peace Agreement;

8. *Invites* the Secretary-General, in the context of the report referred to in paragraph 2 above, also to report on the progress of UNAMIR following its initial deployment, and resolves to review as appropriate, on the basis of that report and as part of the review referred to in paragraph 2 above, the requirement for further deployments in the scale and composition recommended by the Secretary-General in his report;

9. *Invites* the Secretary-General to consider ways of reducing the total maximum strength of UNAMIR, in particular through phased deployment without thereby affecting the capacity of UNAMIR to carry out its mandate, and requests the Secretary-General in planning and executing the phased deployment of UNAMIR to seek economies and to report regularly on what is achieved in this regard;

10. *Welcomes* the intention of the Secretary-General to appoint a Special Representative who would lead UNAMIR in the field and exercise authority over all its elements;

11. *Urges* the parties to implement the Arusha Peace Agreement in good faith;

12. *Also requests* the Secretary-General to conclude expeditiously an agreement on the status of the operation, and all personnel engaged in the operation in Rwanda, to come into force as near as possible to the outset of the operation and no later than thirty days after the adoption of this resolution;

13. *Demands* that the parties take all appropriate steps to ensure the security and safety of the operation and personnel engaged in the operation;

14. *Urges* Member States, United Nations agencies and non-governmental organizations to provide and intensify their economic, financial and humanitarian assistance in favour of the Rwandese population and of the democratization process in Rwanda;

15. *Decides* to remain actively seized of the matter.

Security Council resolution 872(1993)

5 October 1993   Meeting 3288   Adopted unanimously

Draft prepared in consultations among Council members (S/26519).

On 8 November,[115] the Secretary-General informed the Council of his decision to appoint Jacques-Roger Booh-Booh of Cameroon as his Special Representative for Rwanda, with immediate effect. As stated in a 12 November letter[116] of the Council President, its members took note of that information. On 12 October,[117] the Secretary-General announced his intention to appoint Brigadier-General Romeo A. Dallaire of Canada, the Chief Military Observer of UNOMUR, as the Force Commander of UNAMIR. The Council agreed to that proposal on 18 October.[118]

In November,[119] the Secretary-General sought and received agreement of the Security Council to his proposal that UNAMIR's military elements be composed of personnel from Bangladesh, Belgium, Canada, Ecuador, Egypt, Fiji, Ghana, Malawi, Senegal, Togo, Tunisia, the United Republic of Tanzania and Uruguay; added to that list in December were Argentina, Austria, the Congo, Mali, Nigeria, Pakistan, the Russian Federation and Zimbabwe[120] and Romania.[121]

Reports of the Secretary-General (October and December). In October,[122] the Secretary-General reported that, following the conclusion of a status-of-mission agreement with the Government of Uganda on 16 August, UNOMUR had been fully deployed and had reached its authorized strength.

In a second report, submitted in December,[123] he said that UNOMUR had established its headquarters at Kabale, Uganda, and set up five observation posts in two sectors along the border, which was monitored through mobile patrols, to be enhanced with airborne coverage. He stated that consultations had been held with the Government of Uganda on integrating the Mission into UNAMIR, without prejudice to UNOMUR's mandate and the status-of-mission agreement. The total cost of UNOMUR for the period from 22 June to 21 December was estimated at $4,392,900 gross ($4,308,000 net). The Secretary-General recommended that UNOMUR's mandate be extended for a period of six months.

SECURITY COUNCIL ACTION (December)

On 20 December, the Security Council considered the Secretary-General's December report on UNOMUR, with Rwanda and Uganda participating in the discussion under rule 37ᵃ of the Council's provisional rules of procedure. The Council adopted **resolution 891(1993)** unanimously.

The Security Council,

Reaffirming its resolutions 812(1993) of 12 March 1993 and 846(1993) of 22 June 1993,

Recalling its resolution 872(1993) of 5 October 1993 establishing the United Nations Assistance Mission for Rwanda (UNAMIR),

Having examined the Secretary-General's report dated 15 December 1993,

Welcoming the substantial results obtained by the deployment of the United Nations Observer Mission Uganda-Rwanda (UNOMUR),

Endorsing the Secretary-General's view, shared by the Governments of Uganda and Rwanda, that UNOMUR has been a factor of stability in the area and that it is playing a useful role as a confidence-building mechanism,

1. *Welcomes* the Secretary-General's report;

2. *Decides* to extend the mandate of UNOMUR for a period of six months, as envisaged in Security Council resolution 846(1993);

3. *Notes* that the integration of UNOMUR within UNAMIR is purely administrative in nature and that it will in no way affect the mandate of UNOMUR as set out in resolution 846(1993);

4. *Expresses its appreciation* to the Government of Uganda for its cooperation and support for UNOMUR;

5. *Underlines* the importance of civilian and military authorities in the mission area continuing to have a cooperative attitude;

6. *Decides* to remain seized of the matter.

Security Council resolution 891(1993)
20 December 1993   Meeting 3324   Adopted unanimously
Draft prepared in consultations among Council members (S/26888).

Report of the Secretary-General (December). In a December report on UNAMIR,[124] the Secretary-General said his Special Representative arrived in Kigali on 23 November and took initiatives to defuse tension resulting from a series of violent incidents in November/December, including the convening of a meeting at Kinihira, Rwanda, at which the two parties agreed to set up a broad-based transitional Government before 31 December. He indicated that, as at 27 December, UNAMIR had been deployed to the strength of 1,260 military personnel, including the 81 UNOMUR observers. The withdrawal of foreign troops was completed by 15 December; however, the security situation in the demilitarized zone and the north-west of the country remained unstable. In addition, the humanitarian situation in the south was aggravated by the influx of some 375,000 Burundese refugees to Rwanda, following the October *coup d'état* in Burundi (see above, under ''Burundi''). According to UNHCR, $52 million was required to meet their emergency needs.

In the light of those developments, the Secretary-General noted an urgent need to proceed with the second phase of UNAMIR's deployment and recommended that the Security Council agree on the continued implementation of the Mission's mandate. With respect to the Council's request to reduce the maximum strength of UNAMIR, he said that, while seeking economies through the phased deployment and withdrawal of UNAMIR personnel, he considered a reduction in resource levels, at the current time, would negatively affect the performance and credibility of UNAMIR.

Financing of UNOMUR

In a November report to the General Assembly on the financing of UNOMUR,[125] the Secretary-General stated that ACABQ had authorized him to enter into commitments not exceeding $6 million for the period from 22 June to 31 October. He estimated the total cost of the Mission from 22 June to 21 December at $4,392,900 gross ($4,308,000 net). In December,[32] he indicated that for the period beyond 21 December, costs related to the administrative integration of UNOMUR into UNAMIR would be included in UNAMIR's cost estimates.

ACABQ, also in December,[126] recommended that the General Assembly take no further action on the financing of UNOMUR, pending its consideration of the report on the financing of UNAMIR. By **decision 48/476** of 23 December, the Assembly endorsed that recommendation.

Financing of UNAMIR

Reporting in December on the financing of UNAMIR,[32] the Secretary-General stated that ACABQ had authorized him to enter into commitments not exceeding $4.6 million from 5 October to 30 November. He estimated the total cost from 5 October 1993 to 4 April 1994 at $51,120,000 gross ($50,478,000 net). That estimate included the authorized commitments, costs of integrating NMOG II and UNOMUR and of maintaining UNOMUR's mandate, and requirements for the deployment of 331 military observers, 1,420 troops, 60 civilian police and 112 international and 68 local civilian staff.

ACABQ, also in December,[127] recommended a further authorization of up to $46.5 million gross ($45.9 million net).

GENERAL ASSEMBLY ACTION

In December, the General Assembly adopted **decision 48/479** without vote.

Financing of the United Nations Assistance Mission for Rwanda

At its 87th plenary meeting, on 23 December 1993, the General Assembly, on the recommendation of the Fifth Committee, in accordance with the framework set out in its resolution 48/227 of 23 December 1993, having considered the report of the Secretary-General on the financing of seventeen peace-keeping operations and the related reports of the Advisory Committee on Administrative and Budgetary Questions, and concurring with the observations of the Advisory Committee:

(*a*)　Noted that the integration of the United Nations Observer Mission Uganda-Rwanda within the United Nations Assistance Mission for Rwanda was purely administrative in nature and that it would in no way affect the mandate of the Observer Mission as set out in Security Council resolution 846(1993) of 22 June 1993;

(*b*)　Authorized the Secretary-General, on an exceptional basis, to enter into total commitments up to the amount of 51,120,000 United States dollars gross (50,478,000 dollars net), inclusive of the amount authorized by the Advisory Committee in accordance with Assembly resolution 46/187 of 20 December 1991, for the United Nations Assistance Mission for Rwanda for the period from 5 October 1993 to 4 April 1994, and requested him to establish a special account for the Assistance Mission;

(*c*)　Decided to apportion, as an ad hoc arrangement, the amount indicated in subparagraph (*b*) above among Member States in accordance with the composition of groups set out in paragraphs 3 and 4 of Assembly resolution 43/232 of 1 March 1989, as adjusted by the Assembly in its resolutions 44/192 B of 21 December 1989, 45/269 of 27 August 1991, 46/198 A of 20 December 1991

and 47/218 A of 23 December 1992 and its decision 48/472 of 23 December 1993, and taking into account the scale of assessments for the years 1992, 1993 and 1994 as set out in Assembly resolutions 46/221 A of 20 December 1991 and 48/223 A of 23 December 1993 and its decisions 47/456 of 23 December 1992;

(*d*)　Also decided that, in accordance with the provisions of its resolution 973(X) of 15 December 1955, there should be set off against the apportionment among Member States, as provided for in subparagraph (*c*) above, their respective share in the Tax Equalization Fund of the estimated staff assessment income of 642,000 dollars for the period from 5 October 1993 to 4 April 1994.

General Assembly decision 48/479

Adopted without vote

Approved by Fifth Committee (A/48/828) without vote, 22 December (meeting 46); draft by Chairman (A/C.5/48/L.30); agenda item 173.
Meeting numbers. GA 48th session: 5th Committee 44, 46; plenary 87.

Somalia

During 1993, the United Nations continued efforts to end the clan-based civil war in Somalia, which broke out after the ousting of President Mohammed Siad Barre—Somalia's leader for 21 years—in January 1991. On 26 March, the Security Council expanded the size and mandate of the United Nations Operation in Somalia (UNOSOM), established in April 1992.[128] UNOSOM II took over responsibilities of the Unified Task Force (UNITAF), led by the United States and dispatched to Somalia in December 1992 to establish a secure environment for humanitarian relief operations in that country, in accordance with a December 1992 resolution of the Security Council.[129] In February 1993, Lieutenant-General Cevik Bir of Turkey was appointed the Force Commander of UNOSOM II. Activities of UNITAF and UNOSOM II ensured the provision of emergency assistance which averted the mass starvation threatening almost 4.5 million of the 6 million Somalis. Efforts were also made to facilitate the return of some 1.7 million Somalis displaced by the conflict, including more than 1 million refugees in neighbouring countries (see PART THREE, Chapter XV).

In March 1993, the Somali political factions signed the Addis Ababa agreement on the cessation of hostilities and transitional mechanisms for re-establishing civil authority. The security situation in the capital city of Mogadishu and surrounding area remained tense, however, as General Mohamed Farah Aidid, Chairman of the United Somali Congress/Somali National Alliance (USC/SNA), demanded the revision of the agreement. His militia attacked UNOSOM II and UNITAF forces on 5 June and 3 October, causing significant loss of life and prompting the Special Representative of the Secretary-General for Somalia, Admiral Jonathan Howe, to call for his arrest and detention. On 6 June, the Security Council condemned hostile actions against UNOSOM II and, on 16 November, established a Commission of Inquiry to investigate them. On 18 November, the Council extended the mandate of UNOSOM II until 31 May 1994.

Reports of the Secretary-General (January and March). In a progress report on the situation in Somalia,[(130)] submitted to the Security Council in January, the Secretary-General said that the informal preparatory meeting for a conference of national reconciliation and unity on Somalia (Addis Ababa, 4-15 January) agreed on an immediate and binding cease-fire throughout the country and its monitoring, the cessation of hostile propaganda, disarmament and the release of prisoners-of-war. A General Agreement, supplemented by an agreement on implementing the cease-fire and on modalities of disarmament, was signed on 8 January. The meeting also agreed to set up an ad hoc committee to consider the criteria for participation in the conference, its agenda and other pending issues, and to convene the conference at Addis Ababa on 15 March. However, the first meeting of the ad hoc committee, held on 22 January at Addis Ababa, was suspended to consider an unconfirmed allegation by SNA that the Somali National Front (SNF) had violated the cease-fire agreement of 15 January.

In terms of the security situation, the Secretary-General noted that the United States had reported in January[(131)] that UNITAF forces continued to expand security operations at Mogadishu and other major relief centres as well as in the countryside, and that their strength totalled 21,000 military personnel from the United States and 9,995 from other countries, including Belgium, Botswana, Canada, Egypt, France, Germany, Italy, Kuwait, Morocco, New Zealand, Saudi Arabia, Turkey and the United Kingdom.

He described preparations for the transition from UNITAF operations to UNOSOM II, including plans for deploying troops to northern Somalia and proposals for mine clearance. As part of those preparations, it was decided to authorize the deployment of an additional 30 officers to UNOSOM headquarters and 250 soldiers from Pakistan. The current strength of UNOSOM totalled 634 all ranks, including 50 military observers. However, further deployment was put on hold pending assessment of conditions on the ground.

Noting that the security situation, although generally improved, was still characterized by occasional outbreaks of inter-clan fighting in certain areas and posed a threat to relief workers and military personnel, the Secretary-General announced his decision to send an expert team to Somalia to prepare for the establishment of a neutral police force. He said that there was greater security and efficiency at the port of Mogadishu and the main airport, enabling the delivery of food and other supplies to more remote areas in the country.

The Secretary-General pointed to a marked increase in humanitarian assistance to Somalia and summarized related activities of several United Nations specialized agencies. He noted the establishment of Humanitarian Operations Centres (HOCs) in six Somalian cities in addition to Mogadishu, as well as the preparation of a Relief and Rehabilitation Programme for Somalia for 1993 (see PART THREE, Chapter III).

In March,[(132)] the Secretary-General reported that the Ad Hoc Committee on the National Reconciliation Conference had met on 23 and 27 February and adopted a report on participation in the conference, with SNA's reservations regarding the criteria, as well as its draft agenda and decision-making procedures. In the meantime, the Special Representative for Somalia and other senior United Nations officials, in cooperation with regional organizations, the League of Arab States (LAS), OAU and the Organization of the Islamic Conference (OIC), continued to promote national reconciliation and to enhance Somalia's capability to govern itself, and held consultations with Somali elders, leaders, warring factions and women's professional groups on ways to establish a broad-based Government.

In describing UNOSOM's activities, the Secretary-General stated that the Operation's strength had risen to 715 all ranks, while that of UNITAF totalled 37,000 troops deployed in southern and central Somalia. Although all areas were declared stable or relatively stable by the UNITAF Commander, incidents of fighting or rioting had been recently reported from Kismayo and Mogadishu, and UNITAF forces continued to be the target of sniper fire and harassment. A number of disarmament forays were carried out on a limited scale, and an auxiliary force of former police officers was being constituted at Mogadishu to oversee road traffic control and protect feeding centres, pending the establishment of a national civilian police.

The Secretary-General summarized the proposed modalities for the transition of operations in Somalia from UNITAF to UNOSOM II, stating that the Operation's new mandate should cover the whole territory of Somalia including disarmament. He recommended that it be endowed with enforcement powers under Chapter VII of the Charter. The formal date of transfer of command from UNITAF to UNOSOM II was set as 1 May 1993 and would be the first operation of its kind authorized by the international community. He also outlined the cease-fire and disarmament concepts and the military concept of operations designed to facilitate implementation of the Addis Ababa agreements, including the four phases of deployment and rules of engagement. The overall operations required 20,000 military personnel and 8,000 logistical support staff as well as some 2,800 civilian staff. An expanded public information campaign was also required to support the execution of the mandate and to strengthen the peace process. In that regard, the Secretariat's Department of Public Information had entered into an agreement with Radio Cairo to translate and broadcast in Somalia United Nations-produced material.

With regard to humanitarian assistance, the Secretary-General stated that the major challenges in 1993 were to facilitate the return of refugees and displaced persons, provide jobs for the millions of unemployed Somalis, reinstate national institutions and civil administration, re-establish education facilities and set up integrated programmes for mine clearance and mine awareness. Under the assistance programme, 10 core groups were formed to assess needs and devise projects in the priority sectors such as health, water, food, security, nutrition, sanitation, employment, administrative rehabilitation, police forces and agriculture and livestock.

The Secretary-General concluded that a secure environment had not yet been established and was a matter of grave concern especially in the northeast and north-west of Somalia and along the Kenyan-Somali border where no troops were deployed. He recommended that troop deployment under UNOSOM II be at the discretion of the Secretary-General, his Special Representative and the Force Commander and not be subject to the agreement of any local faction leaders.

An addendum to the report provided cost estimates of UNOSOM II for a 12-month period, totalling $1,550 million, excluding the unencumbered balance from UNOSOM, estimated at some $70 million. The cost for the first six months, amounting to some $856.4 million and including $189.5 million for start-up costs, was provided in a further addendum to the report.

On 5 March, the Secretary-General announced the appointment of Admiral Jonathan Trumbull Howe (United States) as his Special Representative for Somalia, effective 9 March, to replace Ambassador Ismat Kittani (Iraq).

The Third Coordination Meeting on Humanitarian Assistance for Somalia (Addis Ababa, 11-13 March), attended by representatives of Governments, United Nations agencies, regional and intergovernmental organizations and NGOs as well as 190 Somali political leaders, community elders and representatives of women's organizations and indigenous NGOs, adopted the 1993 relief and rehabilitation programme with a funding requirement of $160 million. Subsequently, the Conference on National Reconciliation for Somalia was

convened at Addis Ababa on 15 March, with the participation of 250 representatives of political movements, civic and non-governmental organizations, elders and eminent persons as well as community, religious and women's groups.

SECURITY COUNCIL ACTION (March)

The Security Council met on 26 March to consider the second report of the Secretary-General. Somalia was invited to participate in accordance with rule 37[a] of the Council's provisional rules of procedure.

On the same date, the Council adopted unanimously **resolution 814(1993)**.

The Security Council,

Reaffirming its resolutions 733(1992) of 23 January 1992, 746(1992) of 17 March 1992, 751(1992) of 24 April 1992, 767(1992) of 27 July 1992, 775(1992) of 28 August 1992 and 794(1992) of 3 December 1992,

Bearing in mind General Assembly resolution 47/167 of 18 December 1992,

Commending the efforts of Member States acting pursuant to resolution 794(1992) to establish a secure environment for humanitarian relief operations in Somalia,

Acknowledging the need for a prompt, smooth and phased transition from the Unified Task Force (UNITAF) to the expanded United Nations Operation in Somalia (UNOSOM II),

Regretting the continuing incidents of violence in Somalia and the threat they pose to the reconciliation process,

Deploring the acts of violence against persons engaging in humanitarian efforts on behalf of the United Nations, States, and non-governmental organizations,

Noting with deep regret and concern the continuing reports of widespread violations of international humanitarian law and the general absence of the rule of law in Somalia,

Recognizing that the people of Somalia bear the ultimate responsibility for national reconciliation and reconstruction of their own country,

Acknowledging the fundamental importance of a comprehensive and effective programme for disarming Somali parties, including movements and factions,

Noting the need for continued humanitarian relief assistance and for the rehabilitation of Somalia's political institutions and economy,

Concerned that the crippling famine and drought in Somalia, compounded by the civil strife, have caused massive destruction to the means of production and the natural and human resources of that country,

Expressing its appreciation to the Organization of African Unity, the League of Arab States, the Organization of the Islamic Conference and the Non-Aligned Movement for their cooperation with, and support of, the efforts of the United Nations in Somalia,

Further expressing its appreciation to all Member States which have made contributions to the Fund established pursuant to paragraph 11 of resolution 794(1992) and to all those who have provided humanitarian assistance to Somalia,

Commending the efforts, in difficult circumstances, of the initial United Nations Operation in Somalia (UNOSOM) established pursuant to resolution 751(1992),

Expressing its appreciation for the invaluable assistance the neighbouring countries have been providing to the international community in its efforts to restore peace and security in Somalia and to host large numbers of refugees displaced by the conflict and taking note of the difficulties caused to them due to the presence of refugees in their territories,

Convinced that the restoration of law and order throughout Somalia would contribute to humanitarian relief operations, reconciliation and political settlement, as well as to the rehabilitation of Somalia's political institutions and economy,

Convinced also of the need for broad-based consultations and deliberations to achieve reconciliation, agreement on the setting up of transitional government institutions and consensus on basic principles and steps leading to the establishment of representative democratic institutions,

Recognizing that the re-establishment of local and regional administrative institutions is essential to the restoration of domestic tranquillity,

Encouraging the Secretary-General and his Special Representative to continue and intensify their work at the national, regional and local levels, including and encouraging broad participation by all sectors of Somali society, to promote the process of political settlement and national reconciliation and to assist the people of Somalia in rehabilitating their political institutions and economy,

Expressing its readiness to assist the people of Somalia, as appropriate, on a local, regional or national level, to participate in free and fair elections, with a view towards achieving and implementing a political settlement,

Welcoming the progress made at the United Nations-sponsored Informal Preparatory Meeting on Somali Political Reconciliation in Addis Ababa from 4 to 15 January 1993, in particular the conclusion at that meeting of three agreements by the Somali parties, including movements and factions, and welcoming also any progress made at the Conference on National Reconciliation which began in Addis Ababa on 15 March 1993,

Emphasizing the need for the Somali people, including movements and factions, to show the political will to achieve security, reconciliation and peace,

Noting the reports of States concerned of 17 December 1992 and 19 January 1993 and of the Secretary-General of 19 December 1992 and 26 January 1993 on the implementation of resolution 794(1992),

Having examined the report of the Secretary-General of 3 March 1993,

Welcoming the intention of the Secretary-General to seek maximum economy and efficiency and to keep the size of the United Nations presence, both military and civilian, to the minimum necessary to fulfil its mandate,

Determining that the situation in Somalia continues to threaten peace and security in the region,

A

1. *Approves* the report of the Secretary-General of 3 March 1993;

2. *Expresses its appreciation* to the Secretary-General for convening the Conference on National Reconciliation for Somalia in accordance with the agreements reached during the Informal Preparatory Meeting on Somali Political Reconciliation in Addis Ababa in January 1993 and for the progress achieved towards political reconciliation in Somalia, and also for his efforts to ensure that, as appropriate, all Somalis, including movements, factions, community leaders, women, professionals, intellectuals, elders and other representative groups are suitably represented at such conferences;

3. *Welcomes* the convening of the Third United Nations Coordination Meeting for Humanitarian Assistance for Somalia in Addis Ababa from 11 to 13 March 1993 and the willingness expressed by Governments through this process to contribute to relief and rehabilitation efforts in Somalia, where and when possible;

4. *Requests* the Secretary-General, through his Special Representative, and with assistance, as appropriate, from all relevant United Nations entities, offices and specialized agencies, to provide humanitarian and other assistance to the people of Somalia in rehabilitating their political institutions and economy and promoting political settlement and national reconciliation, in accordance with the recommendations contained in his report of 3 March 1993, including in particular:

(a) To assist in the provision of relief and in the economic rehabilitation of Somalia, based on an assessment of clear, prioritized needs, and taking into account, as appropriate, the 1993 Relief and Rehabilitation Programme for Somalia prepared by the United Nations Department of Humanitarian Affairs;

(b) To assist in the repatriation of refugees and displaced persons within Somalia;

(c) To assist the people of Somalia to promote and advance political reconciliation, through broad participation by all sectors of Somali society, and the re-establishment of national and regional institutions and civil administration in the entire country;

(d) To assist in the re-establishment of Somali police, as appropriate at the local, regional or national level, to assist in the restoration and maintenance of peace, stability and law and order, including in the investigation and facilitating the prosecution of serious violations of international humanitarian law;

(e) To assist the people of Somalia in the development of a coherent and integrated programme for the removal of mines throughout Somalia;

(f) To develop appropriate public information activities in support of the United Nations activities in Somalia;

(g) To create conditions under which Somali civil society may have a role, at every level, in the process of political reconciliation and in the formulation and realization of rehabilitation and reconstruction programmes;

B

Acting under Chapter VII of the Charter of the United Nations,

5. *Decides* to expand the size of the UNOSOM force and its mandate in accordance with the recommendations contained in paragraphs 56-88 of the report of the Secretary-General of 3 March 1993, and the provisions of this resolution;

6. *Authorizes* the mandate for the expanded UNOSOM (UNOSOM II) for an initial period through 31 October 1993, unless previously renewed by the Security Council;

7. *Emphasizes* the crucial importance of disarmament and the urgent need to build on the efforts of UNITAF in accordance with paragraphs 56-69 of the report of the Secretary-General of 3 March 1993;

8. *Demands* that all Somali parties, including movements and factions, comply fully with the commitments they have undertaken in the agreements they concluded at the Informal Preparatory Meeting on Somali Political Reconciliation in Addis Ababa, and in particular with their Agreement on Implementing the Cease-fire and on Modalities of Disarmament;

9. *Further demands* that all Somali parties, including movements and factions, take all measures to ensure the safety of the personnel of the United Nations and its agencies as well as the staff of the International Committee of the Red Cross (ICRC), intergovernmental organizations and non-governmental organizations engaged in providing humanitarian and other assistance to the people of Somalia in rehabilitating their political institutions and economy and promoting political settlement and national reconciliation;

10. *Requests* the Secretary-General to support from within Somalia the implementation of the arms embargo established by resolution 733(1992), utilizing as available and appropriate the UNOSOM II forces authorized by this resolution, and to report on this subject, with any recommendations regarding more effective measures if necessary, to the Security Council;

11. *Calls upon* all States, in particular neighbouring States, to cooperate in the implementation of the arms embargo established by resolution 733(1992);

12. *Requests* the Secretary-General to provide security, as appropriate, to assist in the repatriation of refugees and the assisted resettlement of displaced persons, utilizing UNOSOM II forces, paying particular attention to those areas where major instability continues to threaten peace and security in the region;

13. *Reiterates its demand* that all Somali parties, including movements and factions, immediately cease and desist from all breaches of international humanitarian law and reaffirms that those responsible for such acts be held individually accountable;

14. *Requests* the Secretary-General, through his Special Representative, to direct the Force Commander of UNOSOM II to assume responsibility for the consolidation, expansion and maintenance of a secure environment throughout Somalia, taking account of the particular circumstances in each locality, on an expedited basis in accordance with the recommendations contained in his report of 3 March 1993, and in this regard to organize a prompt, smooth and phased transition from UNITAF to UNOSOM II;

C

15. *Requests* the Secretary-General to maintain the fund established pursuant to resolution 794(1992) for the additional purpose of receiving contributions for maintenance of UNOSOM II forces following the departure of UNITAF forces and for the establishment of Somali police, and calls on Member States to make contributions to this fund, in addition to their assessed contributions;

16. *Expresses appreciation* to the United Nations agencies, intergovernmental and non-governmental organizations and the ICRC for their contributions and assistance and requests the Secretary-General to ask them to continue to extend financial, material and technical support to the Somali people in all regions of the country;

17. *Requests* the Secretary-General to seek, as appropriate, pledges and contributions from States and others to assist in financing the rehabilitation of the political institutions and economy of Somalia;

18. *Requests* the Secretary-General to keep the Security Council fully informed on action taken to implement the present resolution, in particular to submit as soon as possible a report to the Council containing recommendations for establishment of Somali police forces and thereafter to report no later than every ninety days on the progress achieved in accomplishing the objectives set out in the present resolution;

19. *Decides* to conduct a formal review of the progress towards accomplishing the purposes of the present resolution no later than 31 October 1993;

20. *Decides* to remain actively seized of the matter.

Security Council resolution 814(1993)

26 March 1993   Meeting 3188   Adopted unanimously

Draft prepared in consultations among Council members (S/25472), orally revised.

Further developments (March-June). On 27 March, the Somali political leaders attending the National Reconciliation Conference in Addis Ababa signed a comprehensive agreement covering disarmament and security issues, reconstruction and rehabilitation, restoration of property and the peaceful settlement of disputes and the establishment of transitional mechanisms. The Agreement provided for the creation of the Transitional National Council (TNC) and the Transitional Drafting Committee to prepare a transitional charter for Somalia, and for the establishment of central administrative departments and regional and district councils. The agreement was adopted on 28 March at Addis Ababa. In a statement of 29 March, the Secretary-General urged the Somali political leaders to work out arrangements for implementing the agreement.

The Transitional Drafting Committee, meeting at Mogadishu from 15 to 20 April and from 26 May to 4 June, considered six chapters for the draft transitional charter, including general principles, functions and powers of TNC, central administrative departments, regional administration, judiciary and transitional rules. The Committee set up a working group to finalize the text of the Transitional Charter, but its work had to be suspended on 5 June due to the outbreak of violence in the capital. The Committee on the Peaceful Settlement of Disputes held three sessions (Addis Ababa, 19-21 March; Mogadishu, 15-21 April and 25 May–4 June) to draft guidelines relating to compensation and procedures for the settlement of property claims. The Cease-fire and Disarmament Committee met several times between 7 March and 25 May to investigate incidents of cease-fire violations. It agreed on penalties to be applied for violating the cease-fire. It also completed the delineation of regions to be disarmed simultaneously and extended the disarmament process to cover small weapons in the hands of civilians.

Following the transfer of military command from UNITAF to UNOSOM II on 4 May, the nine UNITAF humanitarian relief sectors were realigned into four UNOSOM areas of responsibility, including Kismayo, Baidoa, Merca-Mogadishu and Belet Weyne-Jalalasi. From March to May, UNOSOM II assisted in organizing a regional reconciliation conference at Boroma in the northwest and a Mogadishu conference on Galkayo and central regions. In the meantime, UNITAF continued to confiscate weapons, recovering during March and April alone some 150 handguns, more than 750 rifles, 400 heavy weapons such as machine-guns, rocket launchers and mortars, nearly 50 armoured vehicles, more than 400 artillery pieces, almost 700 other weapons and close to 79,000 items of ordnance. On 6 and 7 May, UNOSOM forces repelled an attack on Kismayo as inter-clan fighting resumed for the control of that city. The Operation was also the target of increasingly hostile propaganda from Radio Mogadishu, controlled by USC/SNA. Hostile actions against UNOSOM forces culminated in the killing of 24 Pakistani soldiers in Mogadishu on 5 June.

SECURITY COUNCIL ACTION (June)

On 6 June, the Security Council, meeting at the requests of Italy[133] and Pakistan,[134] adopted **resolution 837(1993)** unanimously.

The Security Council,

Reaffirming its resolutions 733(1992) of 23 January 1992, 746(1992) of 17 March 1992, 751(1992) of 24 April 1992, 767(1992) of 27 July 1992, 775(1992) of 28 August 1992, 794(1992) of 3 December 1992 and 814(1993) of 26 March 1993,

Bearing in mind General Assembly resolution 47/167 of 18 December 1992,

Gravely alarmed at the premeditated armed attacks launched by forces apparently belonging to the United Somali Congress (USC/SNA) against the personnel of the United Nations Operation in Somalia (UNOSOM II) on 5 June 1993,

Strongly condemning such actions, which directly undermine international efforts aimed at the restoration of peace and normalcy in Somalia,

Expressing outrage at the loss of life as a result of these criminal attacks,

Reaffirming its commitment to assist the people of Somalia in re-establishing conditions of normal life,

Stressing that the international community is involved in Somalia in order to help the people of Somalia who have suffered untold miseries due to years of civil strife in that country,

Acknowledging the fundamental importance of completing the comprehensive and effective programme for disarming all Somali parties, including movements and factions,

Convinced that the restoration of law and order throughout Somalia would contribute to humanitarian relief operations, reconciliation and political settlement,

as well as to the rehabilitation of Somalia's political institutions and economy,

Condemning strongly the use of radio broadcasts, in particular by the USC/SNA, to incite attacks against United Nations personnel,

Recalling the statement made by its President on 31 March 1993 concerning the safety of United Nations forces and personnel deployed in conditions of strife and committed to consider promptly measures appropriate to the particular circumstances to ensure that persons responsible for attacks and other acts of violence against United Nations forces and personnel are held to account for their actions,

Taking note of the information provided to the Council by the Secretary-General on 6 June 1993,

Determining that the situation in Somalia continues to threaten peace and security in the region,

Acting under Chapter VII of the Charter of the United Nations,

1. *Strongly condemns* the unprovoked armed attacks against the personnel of UNOSOM II on 5 June 1993, which appear to have been part of a calculated and premeditated series of cease-fire violations to prevent by intimidation UNOSOM II from carrying out its mandate as provided for in resolution 814(1993);

2. *Expresses* its condolences to the Government and people of Pakistan and the families of the UNOSOM II personnel who have lost their lives;

3. *Re-emphasizes* the crucial importance of the early implementation of the disarmament of all Somali parties, including movements and factions, in accordance with paragraphs 56-69 of the report of the Secretary-General of 3 March 1993, and of neutralizing radio broadcasting systems that contribute to the violence and attacks directed against UNOSOM II;

4. *Demands once again* that all Somali parties, including movements and factions, comply fully with the commitments they have undertaken in the agreements they concluded at the informal Preparatory Meeting on Somali Political Reconciliation in Addis Ababa, and in particular with their Agreement on Implementing the Cease-fire and on Modalities of Disarmament;

5. *Reaffirms* that the Secretary-General is authorized under resolution 814(1993) to take all necessary measures against all those responsible for the armed attacks referred to in paragraph 1 above, including against those responsible for publicly inciting such attacks, to establish the effective authority of UNOSOM II throughout Somalia, including to secure the investigation of their actions and their arrest and detention for prosecution, trial and punishment;

6. *Requests* the Secretary-General urgently to inquire into the incident, with particular emphasis on the role of those factional leaders involved;

7. *Encourages* the rapid and accelerated deployment of all UNOSOM II contingents to meet the full requirements of 28,000 men, all ranks, as well as equipment, as indicated in the Secretary-General's report of 3 March 1993;

8. *Urges* Member States to contribute, on an emergency basis, military support and transportation, including armoured personnel carriers, tanks and attack helicopters, to provide UNOSOM II the capability appropriately to confront and deter armed attacks directed against it in the accomplishment of its mandate;

9. *Further requests* the Secretary-General to submit a report to the Council on the implementation of the present resolution, if possible within seven days from the date of its adoption;

10. *Decides* to remain actively seized of the matter.

Security Council resolution 837(1993)

6 June 1993   Meeting 3229   Adopted unanimously

Draft prepared in consultations among Council members (S/25889).

Further report of the Secretary-General (August). In August,[135] the Secretary-General reported that UNOSOM II's strength had been built up to the level of more than 20,000 military personnel from 27 countries, with an additional 8,000 personnel from 8 other States expected to arrive in August/September. The Operation was supported by the United States Quick Reaction Force of 1,167 all ranks. However, the deployment of UNOSOM II forces was delayed due to administrative, logistical and financial difficulties. Those delays and the recalcitrance of certain elements in the country hindered UNOSOM's capacity to extend its operations through the country and to help towards recovery. As at 31 July, UNOSOM casualties were 39 military and 6 civilian fatalities and 160 wounded.

Under the disarmament programme, aimed primarily at the militias and their heavy weapons, cooperative and voluntary disarmament was negotiated in several parts of Somalia. UNOSOM contingents removed mines from the roads in their areas of responsibility, while European and North American countries were financing mine clearance in the north-west. The Operation continued to support the Somali police force, assisted in developing mechanisms for selecting judges and magistrates at Mogadishu and encouraged the development of judicial and penal systems in other areas. It also provided resources for the prison population in that city, and encouraged the development of judicial and penal systems in other areas. It assisted in establishing the district councils envisaged in the Addis Ababa agreement, 21 of which had been created in 7 regions by 31 July. On 6 August, 152 elders representing more than 20 clans of the Juba region signed the Jubaland peace agreement at a regional peace conference at Kismayo, convened by UNOSOM II, committing themselves to ending all hostilities among their clans. The Secretary-General indicated that the overall situation in Somalia had stabilized and that significant gains were made in reducing banditry and fostering the goodwill of the local population.

The United Nations relief and rehabilitation programmes throughout the country resulted in the eradication of starvation, improved nutrition and massive immunization programmes for children, the reopening of schools and plans to begin vocational and teacher training, excellent prospects for the coming harvest, facilitation of livestock exports and an increase in trade. At Mogadishu, however, humanitarian programmes were suspended following the 5 June attack and subsequent relocation of many relief workers to Nairobi. The report also pointed to the shortage of funds for the 1993 Programme, as only $16 million had been pledged by 27 July. Urgent action was required to ensure continuing emergency relief operations, the resettlement of refugees and displaced persons, reinvigoration of agriculture and livestock and fisheries, revitalization of social services and resuscitation of commerce and trade, said the Secretary-General. Meanwhile, consultations were initiated with the World Bank on Somalia's long-term reconstruction and recovery.

The public information campaign in support of UNOSOM activities included broadcasting on Radio Maanta and distributing the *Maanta* newspaper in the Somali and English languages. The report noted that Radio Mogadishu had been neutralized during a disarmament operation on 12 June.

In conclusion, the Secretary-General underlined the transformation in the overall situation in Somalia and pointed to the strong support from OAU, LAS and OIC for the United Nations' role in that country's peace process. He stated that some faction leaders hostile to UNOSOM's disarmament efforts, in particular General Aidid, carried primary responsibility for incidents of violence and the loss of life, and that unless disarmament was fully implemented, the Operation could not be expected to fulfil other aspects of its mandate. He recommended the assignment of an additional brigade to extend UNOSOM's activities and drew the Security Council's attention to the need for ensuring clear subordination in the chain of command and control over UNOSOM II to avoid complications in the future.

An annex to the report provided a proposed UNOSOM strategy regarding the re-establishment of the police, judicial and penal systems in Somalia. The strategy envisaged the creation of a neutral three-tier (national, regional and district) police force of 10,000 by December 1994; establishment of an interim three-tier judicial system by 31 October 1993, to be replaced by a permanent one by 31 March 1995; renovation or re-establishment of prison facilities, to be managed by the Custodial Corps and monitored by ICRC, United Nations agencies and NGOs; and establishment of an Office of Human Rights to investigate and facilitate prosecution of violations of international humanitarian law (see also PART THREE, Chapter X). The one-year cost of maintaining the Office was estimated at $2,322,000, while the total cost of re-establishing the police, judicial and penal systems amounted to $45,130,000.

On 27 August,[136] the Security Council President informed the Secretary-General that the Council members had taken note of his report.

SECURITY COUNCIL ACTION (September)

On 22 September, the Security Council considered the Secretary-General's report, with Somalia participating in the discussion under rule 37ª of the Council's provisional rules of procedure, and adopted unanimously **resolution 865(1993)**.

The Security Council,

Reaffirming its resolutions 733(1992) of 23 January 1992, 746(1992) of 17 March 1992, 751(1992) of 24 April 1992, 767(1992) of 27 July 1992, 755(1992) of 28 August 1992, 794(1992) of 3 December 1992, 814(1993) of 26 March 1993 and 837(1993) of 6 June 1993,

Having considered the report of the Secretary-General of 17 August 1993,

Stressing the importance of continuing the peace process initiated by the Addis Ababa agreement and in this connection welcoming the efforts of African countries, the Organization of African Unity, in particular its Horn of Africa Standing Committee, the League of Arab States and the Organization of the Islamic Conference, in cooperation with and in support of the United Nations, to promote national reconciliation in Somalia,

Stressing the commitment of the international community to help Somalia regain a normal, peaceful life, while recognizing that the people of Somalia bear the ultimate responsibility for national reconciliation and reconstruction of their own country,

Expressing its appreciation for the improvements in the overall situation, which have been achieved by the United Nations Operation in Somalia (UNOSOM II), in particular, eradication of starvation, establishment of a large number of district councils, opening of schools and resumption by the Somali people in most areas of the country of their normal lives,

Recognizing the continuing need for broadbased consultations and consensus on basic principles to achieve national reconciliation and the establishment of democratic institutions,

Calling upon all Somali parties, including movements and factions, to show the political will to achieve reconciliation, peace and security,

Recognizing that the highest priority for UNOSOM II is to assist the people of Somalia in the furtherance of the national reconciliation process and to promote and advance the re-establishment of regional and national institutions and civil administration in the entire country, as set out in resolution 814(1993),

Noting with great concern, despite the improvements in the overall situation in Somalia, continuing reports of violence in Mogadishu and the absence of law enforcement and judicial authorities and institutions in the country as a whole, and recalling the request to the Secretary-General in resolution 814(1993) to assist in the re-establishment of the Somali police and the restoration and maintenance of peace, stability, and law and order,

Convinced that the re-establishment of the Somali police, and judicial and penal systems, is critical for the restoration of security and stability in the country,

Gravely concerned at the continuation of armed attacks against the personnel of UNOSOM II, and recalling its resolution 814(1993) which emphasized the fundamental importance of a comprehensive and effective programme for disarming Somali parties, including movements and factions,

A

1. *Welcomes* the reports by the Secretary-General and his Special Representative on the progress achieved in accomplishing the objectives set out in resolution 814(1993);

2. *Commends* the Secretary-General, his Special Representative, and all the personnel of UNOSOM II, for their achievements in greatly improving the conditions of the Somali people and beginning the process of nation-building apparent in the restoration in much of the country of stable and secure conditions in stark contrast with the prior suffering caused by inter-clan conflict;

3. *Condemns* all attacks on UNOSOM II personnel and reaffirms that those who have committed or have ordered the commission of such criminal acts will be held individually responsible for them;

4. *Affirms* the importance it attaches to the successful fulfilment on an urgent and accelerated basis of UNOSOM II's objectives of facilitation of humanitarian assistance and the restoration of law and order, and of national reconciliation in a free, democratic and sovereign Somalia, so that it can complete its mission by March 1995;

5. *Requests,* in that context, the Secretary-General to direct the urgent preparation of a detailed plan with concrete steps setting out UNOSOM II's future concerted strategy with regard to its humanitarian, political and security activities and to report thereon to the Council as soon as possible;

6. *Urges* the Secretary-General to re-double his efforts at the local, regional and national levels, including encouraging broad participation by all sectors of Somali society, to continue the process of national reconciliation and political settlement, and to assist the people of Somalia in rehabilitating their political institutions and economy;

7. *Calls on* all Member States to assist, in all ways possible, including the urgent full staffing of UNOSOM II civil positions, the Secretary-General, in conjunction with regional organizations, in his efforts to reconcile the parties and rebuild Somali political institutions;

8. *Invites* the Secretary-General to consult the countries of the region and regional organizations concerned on means of further reinvigorating the reconciliation process;

B

9. *Approves* the recommendations of the Secretary-General contained in annex I to his report of 17 August 1993 relating to the re-establishment of the Somali police, judicial and penal systems in accordance with resolution 814(1993) and requests the Secretary-General to take the necessary steps on an urgent and accelerated basis to implement them;

10. *Welcomes* the Secretary-General's intention to convene at the earliest possible date a meeting of Member States interested in supporting UNOSOM II in the re-establishment of the police, judicial and penal systems,

for the purpose of determining specific requirements and identifying specific sources of support;

11. *Further requests* the Secretary-General to undertake actively and as a matter of great urgency an international recruiting programme for staffing the UNOSOM II Justice Division with police, judicial and penal system specialists;

12. *Welcomes* the Secretary-General's intention to maintain and utilize the fund established pursuant to resolution 794(1992) and maintained in resolution 814(1993) for the additional purpose of receiving contributions for the re-establishment of the Somali judicial and penal systems in addition to the establishment of the Somali police, other than for the cost of international staff;

13. *Urges* Member States, on an urgent basis, to contribute to that fund or otherwise to provide assistance for the re-establishment of the Somali police, judicial and penal systems, including personnel, financial support, equipment and training to help attain the objectives outlined in annex I to the Secretary-General's report;

14. *Encourages* the Secretary-General to take the necessary steps to ensure continuation of the current police, judicial and penal programme from October to the end of December 1993 until additional funding from Member States is forthcoming, and to make recommendations as appropriate to the General Assembly;

15. *Requests* the Secretary-General to keep the Council fully informed on a regular basis on the implementation of this resolution;

16. *Decides* to remain actively seized of the matter.

Security Council resolution 865(1993)

22 September 1993   Meeting 3280   Adopted unanimously

Draft prepared in consultations among Council members (S/26476), orally revised.

On 1 October,[137] the Secretary-General informed the Council that Mr. Mohamed Ibrahim Egal, the "President" of "Somaliland" in the north-west of the country, had demanded the withdrawal of United Nations troops from that region by 2 October. Mr. Egal also asked the Special Representative to inform him about the United Nations plans for the region in the political and economic areas. In view of security concerns for the UNOSOM personnel, the Secretary-General sought the Council's guidance on that matter.

On the same date,[138] the Council expressed confidence that necessary precautions would be taken for the safety and protection of United Nations personnel deployed in north-west Somalia and the hope that UNOSOM II would be able to continue its work in that region, using all peaceful means for the benefit of the local population.

By a 28 October letter,[139] the Secretary-General apprised the Council of his recent visit to Somalia and discussions with the heads of State and Government and other high-level officials interested in supporting the United Nations involvement in that country. Pending the submission of

his report on the situation in Somalia, he requested the extension of UNOSOM II until 18 November.

SECURITY COUNCIL ACTION (October)

On 29 October, the Council adopted **resolution 878(1993)** unanimously.

The Security Council,

Reaffirming its resolutions 733(1992) of 23 January 1992, 746(1992) of 17 March 1992, 751(1992) of 24 April 1992, 767(1992) of 27 July 1992, 775(1992) of 28 August 1992, 794(1992) of 3 December 1992, 814(1993) of 26 March 1993, 837(1993) of 6 June 1993 and 865(1993) of 22 September 1993,

Having considered the letter of the Secretary-General of 28 October 1993,

Stressing the need for all the parties in Somalia to exercise maximum restraint and to work towards national reconciliation,

Expressing once again its commitment to a future concerted strategy for UNOSOM II in Somalia and, in that context, to undertake an in-depth consideration of its humanitarian, political and security activities on the basis of the concrete suggestions to be submitted by the Secretary-General as requested in resolution 865(1993),

Acting under Chapter VII of the Charter of the United Nations,

1. *Decides* to extend UNOSOM II's mandate for an interim period terminating on 18 November 1993;

2. *Requests* the Secretary-General, in his report to the Security Council concerning the further extension of UNOSOM II's mandate which should be submitted in good time before 18 November 1993, to report also on recent developments in Somalia in order to enable the Council to take appropriate decisions;

3. *Decides* to remain actively seized of the matter.

Security Council resolution 878(1993)

29 October 1993   Meeting 3299   Adopted unanimously

Draft prepared in consultations among Council members (S/26660).

Further report of the Secretary-General (November). In a November report,[140] describing the general situation in Somalia and events affecting UNOSOM II, the Secretary-General said that to date 39 district and 6 regional councils had been established and 651 councillors had participated in training programmes on leadership, management and development. UNOSOM II facilitated the reconciliation between competing wings of the Somali Salvation Democratic Front (SSDF) in the northeast and central regions and worked towards reconciling clans in the north-west and Gedo region. It supported an all-Somali peace conference from 30 September to 1 October, attended by 600 delegates, and a reconciliation conference for Hawiye sub-clans from 14 to 16 October. The authorities in north-west Somalia did not pursue their demand for United Nations withdrawal and the Special Representative clarified the issue further during his visit to the region on 6 November.

The Operation funded the expansion of the police force by 5,000 people, including 3,000 at

Mogadishu and 2,000 in other regions, while police experts from Canada, Italy and the United Kingdom formulated relevant assistance programmes for their Governments to implement. The United States pledged $6 million for the re-establishment of the Somali judicial and penal systems, $2 million for the police and up to $25 million-worth of equipment; a $1 million contribution was also received from Norway.

The security situation remained tense even after the 9 October unilateral cessation of hostilities by USC/SNA, with major factions reportedly rearming in anticipation of a return to fighting. Limited success was achieved in disarming militia in the north-east and central regions, as well as in cantonment of heavy weapons in Gardo. Disarmament and demobilization progressed in the north-west, but on a lesser scale in other areas under United Nations control. A Mogadishu peace conference on 1 and 2 October, attended by 12 of the 15 political factions and representatives from all segments of Somali society, condemned the violence against UNOSOM II and called for the simultaneous disarmament of all militias throughout the country. The report also underscored the importance of demobilization, training and rehabilitation, especially of the young militiamen, as well as of mine clearance, which had been limited so far by the lack of trained staff, security and funds.

UNOSOM II's strength reached 29,284 all ranks from 29 countries, with additional battalions expected from Egypt and Pakistan. They were supported by some 17,700 troops of the United States Joint Task Force. However, its operations were seriously affected by violent incidents that occurred at Mogadishu between 5 June and 3 October. On 12 July, in the aftermath of military action to neutralize USC/SNA command and control capability, four journalists were murdered by Somali civilians. Four United States soldiers serving with UNOSOM II were killed on 8 August. On 5 September, 7 Nigerian soldiers were killed, 10 wounded and 1 held prisoner, but released on 14 October. One Pakistani soldier was killed and two Pakistani and three United States soldiers wounded in an ambush on 9 September; on 15 September, two Italian soldiers were killed by snipers.

On 3 October, during an operation launched by the United States forces to capture a number of key aides to General Aidid suspected of complicity in attacks against UNOSOM II, two helicopters were shot down, 18 United States soldiers killed and 75 wounded. One helicopter pilot was captured but subsequently released on 14 October. Following the attack, the United States reinforced its Quick Reaction Force and announced its intention to withdraw its combat troops from Somalia by 31 March 1994. Similar decisions had been announced earlier by Belgium, France and Sweden.

During his visit to the region, the Secretary-General met on 14 October at Cairo with President Hosni Mubarak of Egypt and the Secretaries-General of OAU, LAS and OIC. They expressed concern over the consequences of the United States withdrawal from Somalia, reaffirmed their commitment to advancing the process of reconciliation in that country and called for the establishment of a trust fund for the rehabilitation and reconstruction of Somalia. The Secretary-General also discussed the situation in Somalia with the Presidents of Djibouti, Ethiopia and Kenya and held talks with UNOSOM military and civilian officials and Somali leaders at Mogadishu and Baidoa.

In the meantime, humanitarian assistance continued to reach all parts of Somalia. A draft framework for planning the long-term reconstruction and recovery was prepared by donors, United Nations agencies and NGOs in coordination with the World Bank, and reviewed at their third informal meeting in Paris on 22 October. Agreement was reached among humanitarian agencies to coordinate efforts to resettle some 1.7 million Somalis displaced by the war and famine. The Fourth Coordination Meeting on Humanitarian Assistance for Somalia was convened at Addis Ababa from 29 November to 1 December. The meeting adopted the Addis Ababa Declaration, which outlined a regional strategy for resource mobilization and allocation and project development, as well as principles for its implementation.

The Secretary-General stated that the overwhelming majority of the Somali people wanted the United Nations to continue supporting the reconciliation and rehabilitation process in their country. He recommended that the Security Council renew the existing mandate of UNOSOM II until 31 March 1994, while proposing other options to the Operation's mandate which future circumstances might oblige the Council to consider.

SECURITY COUNCIL ACTION (November)

The Security Council met on 18 November to consider the Secretary-General's report. Ethiopia and Somalia were invited to participate under rule 37ª of the Council's provisional rules of procedure.

On the same date, the Council adopted **resolution 886(1993)** unanimously.

The Security Council,

Reaffirming its resolutions 733(1992) of 23 January 1992 and all subsequent relevant resolutions,

Having considered the report of the Secretary-General of 12 November 1993,

Noting the significant improvement in the situation in most areas of Somalia achieved by the United Nations Operation in Somalia (UNOSOM II) as described in that report,

Noting also paragraph 72 of the report of the Secretary-General,

Recognizing that the people of Somalia bear the ultimate responsibility for national reconciliation and reconstruction of their own country,

Stressing the commitment of the international community to continue helping Somalia in its efforts to accelerate the process of national reconstruction and to promote stability, rehabilitation and political reconciliation and to regain a normal, peaceful life,

Recalling that the highest priority of UNOSOM II continues to be to support the efforts of the Somali people in promoting the process of national reconciliation and the establishment of democratic institutions,

Affirming that the General Agreement signed in Addis Ababa on 8 January 1993 and the Addis Ababa Agreement of the First Session of the Conference on National Reconciliation in Somalia signed on 27 March 1993, establish a sound basis for resolution of the problems in Somalia,

Emphasizing also, in this context, the crucial importance of disarmament in achieving lasting peace and stability throughout Somalia,

Condemning the continuing acts of violence and armed attacks against persons engaged in humanitarian and peace-keeping efforts and paying tribute to those troops and humanitarian personnel of several countries who have been killed or injured while serving in Somalia,

Determining that the situation in Somalia continues to threaten peace and security in the region,

1. _Welcomes_ the report of the Secretary-General;

2. _Commends_ the Secretary-General, his Special Representative and the personnel of UNOSOM II for their achievements in improving the conditions of the Somali people and in promoting the process of national reconciliation and reconstruction of the country;

3. _Decides,_ acting under Chapter VII of the Charter of the United Nations, to renew the mandate of UNOSOM II for an additional period expiring on 31 May 1994;

4. _Requests_ the Secretary-General to report to the Security Council by 15 January 1994, or at any time before that if the situation warrants, on the progress made in achieving national reconciliation by the Somali people and that made in the attainment of political, security and humanitarian goals, and further requests the Secretary-General, as part of that report, to provide an updated plan setting out UNOSOM II's future concerted strategy with regard to its humanitarian, political and security activities;

5. _Decides_ to undertake a fundamental review of the mandate of UNOSOM II by 1 February 1994 in light of the report of the Secretary-General and his updated plan;

6. _Urges_ all parties in Somalia, including movements and factions, to accelerate their efforts to achieve political reconciliation, peace and security, and immediately to abide by the cease-fire and disarmament agreements reached in Addis Ababa, particularly the immediate cantonment of all heavy weapons;

7. _Underscores_ the importance of the Somali people attaining specific goals in the context of political reconciliation, in particular the early establishment and effective functioning of all district and regional councils and an interim national authority;

8. _Stresses_ in this regard the importance it attaches to the accelerated implementation by the Somali people, with the assistance of the United Nations and donor countries, of the recommendations contained in annex I of the Secretary-General's report of 17 August 1993 and

endorsed by the Security Council in its resolution 865(1993), and in particular the establishment of an operational police, penal and judiciary system at the regional and district level as soon as feasible;

9. _Reminds_ all parties in Somalia, including movements and factions, that continued United Nations involvement in Somalia depends on their active cooperation and tangible progress towards a political settlement;

10. _Welcomes and supports_ the ongoing diplomatic efforts being made by Member States and international organizations, in particular those in the region, to assist United Nations efforts to bring all parties in Somalia, including movements and factions, to the negotiating table;

11. _Reaffirms_ the obligations of States to implement fully the embargo on all deliveries of weapons and military equipment to Somalia imposed by paragraph 5 of resolution 733(1992);

12. _Expresses concern_ at the destabilizing effects of cross-border arms flows in the region, affirms the importance it attaches to the security of the countries neighbouring Somalia and calls for the cessation of such arms flows;

13. _Welcomes_ the fourth Coordination Meeting on Humanitarian Assistance for Somalia to be convened in Addis Ababa from 29 November to 1 December 1993;

14. _Emphasizes_ the relationship between national rehabilitation and progress in the process of national reconciliation in Somalia, and encourages donor countries to make contributions to Somalia's rehabilitation as demonstrable political progress occurs, and in particular to contribute urgently to rehabilitation projects in those regions where progress on political reconciliation and security has been made;

15. _Expresses its appreciation_ to those Member States which have contributed to or provided logistical or other assistance to UNOSOM II or offered to do so, and encourages those who are in a position to do so to contribute, on an urgent basis, troops, equipment, financial and logistical support to enhance UNOSOM II's capability to carry out its mandate and to ensure the safety of the personnel;

16. _Requests_ the Secretary-General to ask the Somalia Trust Fund Committee to review claims and make payments on an urgent basis and urges Member States to make funds available directly or through the Somalia Trust Fund for priority projects, including the re-establishment of the Somali police and demining, on an urgent basis;

17. _Decides_ to remain actively seized of the matter.

Security Council resolution 886(1993)

18 November 1993   Meeting 3317   Adopted unanimously

Draft prepared in consultations among Council members (S/26767).

Further developments (December). Progress in political reconciliation and reconstruction in Somalia continued to be impeded by SNA's rejection of all political initiatives undertaken by UNOSOM II and by deep divisions between the two main factional alliances—the Group of 12 and SNA. At their Addis Ababa meeting from 2 to 11 December, they failed to arrive at any agreement. SNA insisted that the United Nations had no role to play in national reconciliation, preferring that to be done by regional Powers, whereas the Group of 12 felt that UNOSOM II should remain in Somalia and play a key role in the political process. Sharp differences also arose over the status and mandate of regional and district councils and SNA's demand that the Addis Ababa agreement be revised. In December, the Group of 12 issued an interim plan calling for the establishment of a contact group to discuss with SNA implementation of the Addis Ababa agreement. Other initiatives were also undertaken to achieve a general reconciliation at Garowe in the north-east, Bula-Haji in the Lower Juba, Bardhera in the Gedo region and Mogadishu.

In the meantime, Somali factions, except USC/SNA, expressed their intention to work towards the rapid establishment of TNC. By the end of the year, a total of 53 district and 8 regional councils had been set up, and efforts were made to establish councils in the 15 districts of the greater Mogadishu area; on 6 December, a district council was certified in North Mogadishu. Progress was achieved in re-establishing the police and justice systems as 107 district police stations and 2 prisons were reopened and 16 district and 6 regional courts as well as 6 courts of appeal began to function, including one of each at Mogadishu.

However, the security situation was characterized by an increase in banditry in parts of the countryside and especially in Mogadishu, as well as by outbreaks of localized inter-clan fighting. Voluntary disarmament was stalled as the Somali factions failed to honour their commitments under the Addis Ababa agreement, and there were reports of rearmament and build-up of troops in certain areas. The lack of security also prevented the provision of professional assistance in mine clearing in some areas. At the same time, the withdrawal by several Governments of their military contingents in December reduced UNOSOM II's strength.

As malnutrition levels began to rise again in parts of the country, efforts were increased to provide emergency food relief and medical treatment. Assistance was extended to flood victims in the north-east, to Ethiopian refugees at Mogadishu, to the disabled, orphans and schoolchildren and to returnees in the Juba valley. More than 3,000 refugees and displaced persons were estimated to have returned to their homes since October from camps in Kenya, Kismayo and Mogadishu.

Investigation of the 5 June attack

In response to the 6 June resolution of the Security Council, the Secretary-General in July[141] provided detailed information on the 5 June attack against UNOSOM forces and on efforts to disarm South Mogadishu and the headquarters of General Aidid and neutralize broadcasting systems inciting violence. He stated that, on 8 June, his Special Representative had addressed letters to General Aidid and Chairmen of 11 other political factions, seeking their cooperation in the disarmament programme and in the reconstruction of the country. On 12 June, UNOSOM II began the first phase of its disarmament programme in South Mogadishu. From 12 to 14 June, it took military action to disable or destroy ordnance, weapons and equipment and to neutralize Radio Mogadishu. Citizens were called upon to turn in their arms peacefully and to help identify clandestine arms caches. The second phase of the programme was carried out from 17 to 25 June, during which General Aidid's headquarters area was searched and disarmed. The Secretary-General indicated that there was increasing evidence that General Aidid deliberately and personally directed the use of women and children for attacks on UNOSOM II and that he had directed his militia to shoot into the civilian crowd on 13 June. Military casualties from 5 June to date were 29 Pakistani and Moroccan soldiers killed and 88 Moroccan, Pakistani and United States soldiers wounded. In the light of the 5 June attack on Pakistani troops and subsequent attacks on UNOSOM II by the USC/SNA militia, the Special Representative, on 17 June, publicly called for the arrest and detention of General Mohamed Aidid.

In August, the Secretary-General reported[142] that an independent expert, Professor Tom Farer of the American University in Washington, had conducted on his behalf an investigation into the 5 June attack and concluded that General Aidid's complicity in the attack was supported by clear and convincing evidence and that the attack itself was a violation of international humanitarian law. There was also sufficient evidence to make out a *prima facie* case that the subsequent attack on 13 June was designed by persons associated with SNA.

SECURITY COUNCIL ACTION

On 16 November, the Security Council considered the two reports of the Secretary-General, with Somalia participating in the discussion under rule 37[a] of the Council's provisional rules of procedure, and adopted unanimously **resolution 885(1993)**.

The Security Council,

Reaffirming resolutions 733(1992), 746(1992), 751(1992), 767(1992), 775(1992), 794(1992), 814(1993), 837(1993), 865(1993) and 878(1993),

Also reaffirming resolution 868(1993) on the need to ensure the safety and protection of United Nations personnel,

Recognizing the critical need for broad-based consultations among all parties and consensus on basic principles to achieve national reconciliation and the establishment of democratic institutions in Somalia,

Stressing that the people of Somalia bear the ultimate responsibility for achieving these objectives and in this context noting in particular resolution 837(1993) which condemned the 5 June 1993 attack on UNOSOM II personnel and called for an investigation,

Noting further proposals made by Member States, in particular from the Organization of African Unity (OAU), including those in document S/26627, which recommended the establishment of an impartial Commission of Inquiry to investigate armed attacks on UNOSOM II,

Having received and considered the reports of the Secretary-General on the implementation of resolution 837(1993),

1. *Authorizes* the establishment of a Commission of Inquiry, in further implementation of resolutions 814(1993) and 837(1993), to investigate armed attacks on UNOSOM II personnel which led to casualties among them;

2. *Requests* the Secretary-General, having conveyed his views to the Security Council, to appoint the Commission at the earliest possible time, and to report to the Council on the establishment of the Commission;

3. *Directs* the Commission to determine procedures for carrying out its investigation taking into account standard United Nations procedures;

4. *Notes* that members of the Commission will have the status of experts on mission within the meaning of the Convention on the Privileges and Immunities of the United Nations, which shall apply to the Commission;

5. *Urges* the Secretary-General to provide the Commission with all assistance necessary to facilitate its work;

6. *Calls on* all parties in Somalia fully to cooperate with the Commission;

7. *Requests* the Commission to report its findings through the Secretary-General to the Security Council as soon as possible, taking into consideration the need for a thorough inquiry;

8. *Requests* that the Secretary-General, under his authority in resolutions 814(1993) and 837(1993), pending completion of the report of the Commission, suspend arrest actions against those individuals who might be implicated but are not currently detained pursuant to resolution 837(1993), and make appropriate provision to deal with the situation of those already detained under the provisions of resolution 837(1993);

9. *Decides* to remain seized of this matter.

Security Council resolution 885(1993)
16 November 1993   Meeting 3315   Adopted unanimously
Draft by United States (S/26750), orally revised.

On 23 November,[143] the Secretary-General communicated to the Council the composition of the three-person Commission of Inquiry and his decision to establish a separate secretariat to assist it. On 30 November,[144] the Council welcomed that decision and took note of the Commission's composition.

Composition of UNOSOM II

On 16 February,[145] the Secretary-General obtained the agreement of the members of the Security Council to his proposal [146] to appoint Lieutenant-General Cevik Bir of Turkey as Force Commander of UNOSOM II. In April,[147] the Secretary-General sought and received the Council's approval that UNOSOM II be composed of contingents from Argentina, Australia, Bangladesh, Belgium, Botswana, Egypt, France, Germany, Greece, Hungary, India, Indonesia, Ireland, Italy, Jordan, Malaysia, Morocco, New Zealand, Nigeria, Norway, Pakistan, Republic of Korea, Romania, Saudi

Arabia, Sweden, Tunisia, Turkey, United Arab Emirates, United States and Zimbabwe. The addition of Namibia, Uganda and Zambia[148] to these troop-contributing countries, as he later proposed, was also agreed to by members of the Council.

Financing of UNOSOM II

In a March report on the financing of UNOSOM II,[149] the Secretary-General estimated the Operation's cost for May and June 1993 at $397.2 million gross ($396.0 million net), including start-up costs of $186.3 million and operational costs of $210.9 million gross ($209.7 million net). He also noted that, as at 28 March, outstanding assessed contributions due from Member States for UNOSOM totalled $58.9 million and that the unencumbered balance amounted to $70 million. The Secretary-General recommended that the special account established for UNOSOM should continue to be used for UNOSOM II and requested that the General Assembly approve an additional appropriation to cover the requirements of UNOSOM II for that period.

In April, ACABQ, in an oral report to the Fifth Committee, recommended that the Assembly appropriate and assess the sum of $300 million for the two-month period.

GENERAL ASSEMBLY ACTION (April)

On 15 April, the General Assembly, on the report of its Fifth Committee, adopted **resolution 47/41 B** without vote.

The General Assembly,

Having considered the report of the Secretary-General on the financing of the initial phase of the expanded size and mandate of the United Nations Operation in Somalia and the related oral report of the Advisory Committee on Administrative and Budgetary Questions,

Bearing in mind Security Council resolution 751(1992) of 24 April 1992, by which the Council established the United Nations Operation in Somalia, and Council resolution 814(1993) of 26 March 1993, by which the Council expanded the size of the United Nations Operation in Somalia and authorized the mandate for the expanded Operation (United Nations Operation in Somalia II) for an initial period through 31 October 1993,

Bearing in mind also Security Council resolution 794(1992) of 3 December 1992,

Expressing its appreciation to those countries that participated in, and made contributions to, the Unified Task Force in Somalia,

Recalling its resolution 47/41 A of 1 December 1992 on the financing of the United Nations Operation in Somalia,

Recalling also its responsibility in considering and approving the budget of the Organization in accordance with Article 17, paragraph 1, of the Charter of the United Nations,

Recognizing that the costs of the United Nations Operation in Somalia II are expenses of the Organization to be borne by Member States in accordance with Article 17, paragraph 2, of the Charter,

Recognizing also that, in order to meet the expenditures caused by the deployment of the Operation in Somalia II, a different procedure is required from the one applied to meet expenditures of the regular budget of the United Nations,

Taking into account the fact that the economically more developed countries are in a position to make relatively larger contributions and that the economically less developed countries have a relatively limited capacity to contribute towards such an operation,

Bearing in mind the special responsibilities of the States permanent members of the Security Council, as indicated in General Assembly resolution 1874(S-IV) of 27 June 1963, in the financing of such operations,

Mindful of the fact that it is essential to provide the expanded Operation with the required resources to enable it to fulfil its responsibilities under the relevant resolutions of the Security Council,

Expressing concern about the financial situation of the Organization, in particular the fact that its reserves, including the Peace-keeping Reserve Fund, are almost depleted owing to the late payment of contributions by Member States,

1. *Endorses* the observations and recommendations made in the oral report of the Advisory Committee on Administrative and Budgetary Questions;

2. *Reiterates* the concern it had expressed, in considering other peace-keeping budget estimates, about the lack of detailed budgetary information in the report of the Secretary-General, and regrets that the figures presented do not have enough justification and will need to be adjusted in the detailed budget estimates to be submitted not later than 15 June 1993;

3. *Urges* all Member States to ensure payment of their assessed contributions to the United Nations Operation in Somalia II promptly and in full;

4. *Decides* to continue to use the Special Account for the United Nations Operation in Somalia, established in accordance with General Assembly resolution 47/41 A, for the Operation in Somalia II;

5. *Decides also*, as an exceptional measure, pending submission of detailed budget estimates for the Operation in Somalia II and the performance report on the United Nations Operation in Somalia by the Secretary-General, to appropriate to the Special Account an amount of 300 million United States dollars for the Operation in Somalia II for the period from 1 May to 30 June 1993, and notes that this appropriation takes into account the unencumbered balance of appropriation remaining in the Special Account;

6. *Decides further* to take into account the amount of 300 million dollars appropriated in paragraph 5 above against the full assessments to be levied on Member States upon the approval of the total cost estimates of the Operation in Somalia II;

7. *Decides*, as an ad hoc arrangement, to assess the amount of 300 million dollars for the period from 1 May to 30 June 1993 and to apportion that amount among Member States in accordance with the composition of groups set out in paragraphs 3 and 4 of General Assembly resolution 43/232 of 1 March 1989, as adjusted by the Assembly in its resolutions 44/192 B of 21 December 1989, 45/269 of 27 August 1991 and 46/198 A of 20 December 1991, and taking into account the scale of assessments set out in Assembly resolution 46/221 A of 20 December 1991 and the rates of assessment adopted by Assembly decision 47/456 of 23 December 1992;

8. *Decides also* that, in accordance with the provisions of its resolution 973(X) of 15 December 1955, there shall be set off against the apportionment among Member States their respective share in the Tax Equalization Fund of the estimated staff assessment income for the period from 1 May to 31 October 1993 in the context of the detailed budget estimates to be submitted not later than 15 June 1993;

9. *Decides further* to establish the contributions of the Czech Republic, the Slovak Republic and the former Yugoslav Republic of Macedonia to the Operation in Somalia II in accordance with the rates of assessment to be adopted by the General Assembly for those Member States at its forty-eighth session;

10. *Invites* the new Member States mentioned in paragraph 9 above to make advance payments against their assessed contributions, to be determined;

11. *Requests* the Secretary-General to submit as soon as possible but not later than 15 June 1993 detailed cost estimates for the Operation in Somalia II for the entire mandate period through 31 October 1993, taking into account the views and observations of Member States in the Fifth Committee, and to report at that time on the actual expenditure for the Operation;

12 *Invites* voluntary contributions to the Operation in Somalia II in cash and in the form of services and supplies acceptable to the Secretary-General, to be administered, as appropriate, in accordance with the procedure established by the General Assembly in its resolutions 43/230 of 21 December 1988, 44/192 A of 21 December 1989 and 45/258 of 3 May 1991;

13. *Invites* Member States to make voluntary contributions to the fund established pursuant to Security Council resolution 794(1992) in accordance with paragraph 15 of Council resolution 814(1993);

14. *Requests* the Secretary-General to take all necessary action to ensure that all United Nations activities related the Operation in Somalia II are administered under the authority of his Special Representative in a coordinated fashion with a maximum of efficiency and economy and in accordance with the relevant mandates.

General Assembly resolution 47/41 B

15 April 1993   Meeting 99   Adopted without vote

Approved by Fifth Committee (A/47/734/Add.1) without vote, 8 April (meeting 64); draft by Chairman (A/C.5/47/L.37), orally amended by Austria; agenda item 145.
Meeting numbers. GA 47th session: 5th Committee 63, 64; plenary 99.

Report of the Secretary-General (June). In June,[150] the Secretary-General reported that, as at 15 June, outstanding assessed contributions due from Member States totalled $51,711,057 for UNOSOM and $255,734,591 for UNOSOM II. The Trust Fund for Somalia, established by the Secretary-General, received some $106 million in voluntary contributions. Full reimbursement to the troop-contributing countries for UNOSOM was made through the period ending 30 April 1993.

The report indicated an unencumbered balance of $66,201,100 gross ($64,981,100 net) left from UNOSOM as at 30 April, and estimated the cost of UNOSOM II for the period from 1 May to 31 October at $615,934,000 gross ($610,852,000 net). An additional appropriation of $249,732,900 gross

($245,870,900 net) was required for that period. Cost estimates from 1 November 1993 to 31 October 1994 amounted to $82,700,000 gross ($81,382,500 net).

In July,[151] ACABQ was informed that the estimates had been revised down by $36 million. It recommended that the General Assembly appropriate and assess an additional $190 million from 1 May to 31 October, bringing the total estimated cost for that period to $556 million.

GENERAL ASSEMBLY ACTION (September)

On 14 September, the General Assembly, on the recommendation of its Fifth Committee, adopted **resolution 47/41 C** without vote.

The General Assembly,

Having considered the report of the Secretary-General on the financing of the initial phase of the expanded size and mandate of the United Nations Operation in Somalia and the related report of the Advisory Committee on Administrative and Budgetary Questions,

Bearing in mind Security Council resolution 751(1992) of 24 April 1992, by which the Council established the United Nations Operation in Somalia,

Bearing in mind also Security Council resolution 814(1993) of 26 March 1993, by which the Council expanded the size of the United Nations Operation in Somalia and authorized the mandate for the expanded Operation (United Nations Operation in Somalia II) for an initial period through 31 October 1993, and Council resolution 837(1993) of 6 June 1993, by which the Council reaffirmed that the Secretary-General was authorized under resolution 814(1993) to take all necessary measures against all those responsible for the armed attacks and to establish the effective authority of the Operation in Somalia II throughout Somalia, including to secure the investigation of their actions and their arrest and detention for prosecution, trial and punishment,

Recalling Security Council resolution 794(1992) of 3 December 1992,

Expressing its appreciation to those countries which participated in, and made contributions to, the Unified Task Force in Somalia,

Reaffirming that the costs of the Operation in Somalia II are expenses of the Organization to be borne by Member States in accordance with Article 17, paragraph 2, of the Charter of the United Nations,

Recalling its previous decision regarding the fact that, in order to meet the expenditures caused by the Operation in Somalia II, a different procedure is required from the one applied to meet expenditures of the regular budget of the United Nations,

Taking into account the fact that the economically more developed countries are in a position to make relatively larger contributions and that the economically less developed countries have a relatively limited capacity to contribute towards such an operation,

Bearing in mind the special responsibilities of the States permanent members of the Security Council, as indicated in General Assembly resolution 1874(S-IV) of 27 June 1963, in the financing of such operations,

Mindful of the fact that it is essential to provide the Operation in Somalia II with the required resources to ena-

ble it to fulfil its responsibilities under the relevant resolutions of the Security Council,

Expressing concern about the financial situation with regard to the activities of the Operation in Somalia II owing to overdue payments by Member States of their assessments, particularly Member States in arrears,

Also expressing concern about the delays in submission of budget documents until well into the financial period of the Operation in Somalia II, which have contributed to the financial difficulties of the Operation,

Expressing deep concern about the adverse effect that the deteriorating financial situation has on reimbursement to troop contributors, placing an additional burden on these countries and putting at risk the continuing supply of troops to the Operation in Somalia II and, consequently, the success of the Operation,

1. *Endorses* the observations and recommendations contained in the report of the Advisory Committee on Administrative and Budgetary Questions, subject to the terms of the present resolution;

2. *Requests* the Secretary-General to take all necessary action to ensure that the United Nations Operation in Somalia II is administered with a maximum of efficiency and economy, to improve management, and to include in his report on the item to the General Assembly information on steps taken in this regard;

3. *Regrets* the absence of any reimbursements to countries contributing troops to the Operation in Somalia II and requests the Secretary-General to undertake all efforts to ensure that such reimbursements are expedited;

4. *Urges* all Member States to ensure payment of their assessed contributions to the Operation in Somalia II promptly and in full;

5. *Decides* to appropriate an amount of 256,201,100 United States dollars gross (251,119,100 dollars net) for the Operation in Somalia II for the period from 1 May to 31 October 1993, in addition to the 300 million dollars already appropriated in accordance with General Assembly resolution 47/41 B of 15 April 1993;

6. *Decides also,* as an ad hoc arrangement, to apportion the amount of 256,201,100 dollars gross (251,119,100 dollars net) for the period from 1 May to 31 October 1993 among Member States in accordance with the composition of groups set out in paragraphs 3 and 4 of General Assembly resolution 43/232 of 1 March 1989, as adjusted by the Assembly in its resolutions 44/192 B of 21 December 1989, 45/269 of 27 August 1991, 46/198 A of 20 December 1991 and 47/218 A of 23 December 1992, and taking into account the scale of assessments set out in Assembly resolution 46/221 A of 20 December 1991 and Assembly decision 47/456 of 23 December 1992;

7. *Decides further* that there shall be set off against the apportionment among Member States, as provided in paragraph 6 above, their respective share in the unencumbered balance of 66,201,100 dollars gross (64,981,100 dollars net) for the period from 1 May 1992 to 30 April 1993;

8. *Decides* that, in accordance with the provisions of its resolution 973(X) of 15 December 1955, there shall be set off against the apportionment among Member States, as provided for in paragraph 6 above, their respective share in the Tax Equalization Fund of the remaining estimated staff assessment income of 5,082,000 dollars for the period from 1 May to 31 October 1993 approved for the Operation in Somalia II;

9. *Authorizes* the Secretary-General to enter into commitments for the Operation in Somalia II at a rate not

to exceed 82.7 million dollars gross (81,380,000 dollars net) per month for the period from 1 November 1993 to 28 February 1994, should the Security Council decide to continue the Operation beyond 31 October 1993, subject to obtaining the prior concurrence of the Advisory Committee, the said amount to be apportioned among Member States in accordance with the scheme set out in the present resolution;

10. *Requests*, in this regard, the Secretary-General to submit to the General Assembly, no later than 8 February 1994, budget proposals, including revised estimates for the period the Security Council might have decided to continue the mandate of the Operation in Somalia II beyond 31 October 1993, as well as budget proposals for the subsequent period of six months;

11. *Decides* to establish the contributions of Andorra, Eritrea and Monaco to the Operation in Somalia II in accordance with the rates of assessment to be adopted by the General Assembly for these Member States at its forty-eighth session;

12. *Invites* the new Member States mentioned in paragraph 11 above to make advance payments against their assessed contributions, to be determined;

13. *Invites* voluntary contributions to the Operation in Somalia II in cash and in the form of services and supplies acceptable to the Secretary-General, to be administered, as appropriate, in accordance with the procedure established by the General Assembly in its resolutions 43/230 of 21 December 1988, 44/192 A of 21 December 1989 and 45/258 of 3 May 1991;

14. *Invites* Member States to make voluntary contributions to the fund established pursuant to Security Council resolution 794(1992) in accordance with paragraph 15 of Council resolution 814(1993).

General Assembly resolution 47/41 C

14 September 1993   Meeting 110   Adopted without vote

Approved by Fifth Committee (A/47/734/Add.2 & Add.2/Corr.1) without vote, 3 September (meeting 74); draft by Rapporteur (A/C.5/47/L.43); agenda item 145.
Meeting numbers. GA 47th session: 5th Committee 68, 69, 72, 74; plenary 110.

Report of the Secretary-General (December). Reporting in December on the financing of UNOSOM II,[32] the Secretary-General estimated the revised costs for the period from 1 November 1993 to 30 April 1994 at $475,950,000 gross ($473,600,000 net), including the amount authorized in September, which incorporated increased requirements for public information programmes, rental of vehicles and contractual services.

Also in December,[152] ACABQ recommended an additional authorization of $49,200,000 for the period 1 November 1993 to 31 March 1994, bringing total authorized commitments for that period to $380,000,000 and that the amount of $280,000,000 be assessed.

As at 31 December 1993, outstanding assessed contributions due from Member States totalled $15,535,889 for UNOSOM and $82,896,979 for UNOSOM II, while the unencumbered balance for UNOSOM II from 1 May to 31 October amounted to $56,027,000 gross ($53,018,000 net). At the end of December, full reimbursement to the troop-

contributing States was complete for the period ending 31 October 1993.

In December, the General Assembly adopted **decision 48/471** without vote.

Financing of the United Nations Operation in Somalia II

At its 87th plenary meeting, on 23 December 1993, the General Assembly, on the recommendation of the Fifth Committee, in accordance with the framework set out in its resolution 48/227 of 23 December 1993, having considered the report of the Secretary-General on the financing of seventeen peace-keeping operations and the related reports of the Advisory Committee on Administrative and Budgetary Questions, and concurring with the observations of the Advisory Committee:

(*a*) Authorized the Secretary-General, on an exceptional basis, to enter into total commitments up to the amount of 302,869,200 United States dollars gross (300 million dollars net), inclusive of the authorization provided under General Assembly resolution 47/41 C of 14 September 1993, for the United Nations Operation in Somalia II for the period from 1 November 1993 to 28 February 1994;

(*b*) Decided at that time to apportion, as an ad hoc arrangement, the amount of 126,195,500 dollars gross (125 million dollars net) among Member States in accordance with the composition of groups set out in paragraphs 3 and 4 of Assembly resolution 43/232 of 1 March 1989, as adjusted by the Assembly in its resolutions 44/192 B of 21 December 1989, 45/269 of 27 August 1991, 46/198 A of 20 December 1991 and 47/218 A of 23 December 1992 and its decision 48/472 of 23 December 1993, and taking into account the scale of assessments for the years 1992, 1993 and 1994 as set out in Assembly resolutions 46/221 A of 20 December 1991 and 48/223 A of 23 December 1993 and its decision 47/456 of 23 December 1992;

(*c*) Also decided that, in accordance with the provisions of its resolution 973(X) of 15 December 1955, there should be set off against the apportionment among Member States, as provided for in subparagraph (*b*) above, their respective share in the Tax Equalization Fund of the estimated staff assessment income of 1,195,500 dollars for the period from 1 November 1993 to 28 February 1994;

(*d*) Further decided that, in view of the expiration of the commitment authority on 28 February 1994, priority should be given to the cost estimates for the Operation in the consideration by the General Assembly of peace-keeping budgets.

General Assembly decision 48/471

Adopted without vote

Approved by Fifth Committee (A/48/820) without vote, 22 December (meeting 46); draft by Chairman (A/C.5/48/L.23); agenda item 137.
Meeting numbers. GA 48th session: 5th Committee 44, 46; plenary 87.

REFERENCES

[1]YUN 1992, p. 178. [2]YUN 1991, p. 127, SC res. 696(1991), 30 May 1991. [3]S/25076. [4]S/25140 & Add.1. [5]YUN 1992, p. 184, SC res. 793(1992), 30 Nov. 1992. [6]YUN 1991, p. 127. [7]S/25155. [8]S/25161. [9]S/25390. [10]S/25342. [11]S/25343. [12]S/25690. [13]S/25840 & Add.1. [14]S/25882. [15]S/25883. [16]S/25899. [17]S/25967. [18]S/26064. [19]S/26076. [20]S/26081. [21]S/26060 & Add.1,2. [22]S/26448. [23]S/26434 & Add.1. [24]S/26644 & Add.1 & Add.1/Corr.1. [25]S/26492. [26]S/26677. [27]S/26872 & Add.1. [28]S/26702 & Add.1. [29]YUN 1992, p. 187.

(30)A/47/744/Add.1. (31)A/47/925. (32)A/C.5/48/40. (33)A/48/771. (34)S/26628. (35)S/26626. (36)S/26625. (37)S/26630. (38)S/26631. (39)A/48/240. (40)S/26676. (41)A/48/567. (42)S/26745. (43)S/26708. (44)S/26775. (45)S/26776. (46)S/26703. (47)S/26757. (48)A/48/447. (49)YUN 1992, p. 188, GA res. 47/9, 27 Oct. 1992. (50)Ibid., p. 190, GA res. 47/114, 16 Dec. 1992. (51)A/47/948-S/25793. (52)A/48/283. (53)A/48/643. (54)S/25402. (55)YUN 1992, p. 192, SC res. 788(1992), 19 Nov. 1992. (56)S/25919. (57)S/25918. (58)S/26265. (59)S/26200. (60)S/26272. (61)S/26376. (62)S/26422 & Add.1 & Add.1/Corr.1. (63)S/26532. (64)S/26533. (65)S/26554. (66)S/26778. (67)S/26857. (68)S/26555. (69)S/26779. (70)S/26858. (71)S/26868. (72)S/26886. (73)A/48/592. (74)YUN 1991, p. 869, GA res. 46/187, 20 Dec. 1991. (75)A/48/784. (76)YUN 1992, p. 193. (77)Ibid., p. 197, SC res. 797(1992), 16 Dec. 1992. (78)S/25518. (79)YUN 1992, p. 194. (80)S/26034. (81)S/26385. (82)S/26385/Add.1. (83)S/26432. (84)S/26666 & Add.1. (85)S/25121, S/25122. (86)S/25211, S/25212. (87)S/25368, S/25369. (88)S/25655, S/25656. (89)S/25964, S/25965. (90)S/26291, S/26292. (91)S/26920, S/26921. (92)S/25285. (93)S/25286. (94)A/47/881. (95)A/47/881/Add.1. (96)A/47/896. (97)A/47/969 & Corr.1. (98)A/47/985. (99)A/48/779. (100)S/25355. (101)S/25356. (102)S/25363. (103)S/25371. (104)S/25385. (105)S/25561. (106)S/25592. (107)S/25797. (108)S/25951. (109)S/25810 & Add.1. (110)S/26019. (111)S/26020. (112)S/26350. (113)S/26425. (114)S/26488 & Add.1. (115)S/26730. (116)S/26731. (117)S/26593. (118)S/26594. (119)S/26699, S/26700. (120)S/26850, S/26851. (121)S/1994/9, S/1994/10. (122)S/26618. (123)S/26878. (124)S/26927. (125)A/48/636. (126)A/48/782. (127)A/48/785. (128)YUN 1992, p. 202, SC res. 751(1992), 24 Apr. 1992. (129)Ibid., p. 209, SC res. 794(1992), 3 Dec. 1992. (130)S/25168. (131)S/25126. (132)S/25354 & Add.1,2. (133)S/25887. (134)S/25888. (135)S/26317. (136)S/26375. (137)S/26526. (138)S/26527. (139)S/26663. (140)S/26738. (141)S/26022. (142)S/26351. (143)S/26823. (144)S/26824. (145)S/25296. (146)S/25295. (147)S/25532, S/25533. (148)S/25673, S/25674. (149)A/47/916. (150)A/47/916/Add.1. (151)A/47/984. (152)A/48/777.

Cooperation between OAU and the UN system

Cooperation between the United Nations and the Organization of African Unity was described by the Secretary-General, pursuant to a 1992 General Assembly resolution,[1] in an October 1993 report.[2] In 1992, the Assembly had called on the Secretaries-General of both organizations to work closely, in particular regarding the follow-up to and review of implementation of the United Nations New Agenda for the Development of Africa in the 1990s.[3]

The report gave an overview of consultations and exchange of information between the two organizations and of cooperation in the field of economic and social development as well as in other areas.

A meeting was held between the secretariats of the United Nations system and OAU (New York, 8-10 September 1993) to evaluate progress achieved in implementing the proposals and recommendations for cooperation agreed on in 1991 and 1992, and to adopt new joint action.

The meeting agreed on follow-up arrangements within the United Nations to ensure implementa-

tion of OAU resolutions and recommendations, particularly those on the acquired immunodeficiency syndrome (AIDS) epidemic and the African Regional Food and Nutrition Strategy, adopted at the twenty-ninth ordinary session of the OAU Assembly of Heads of State and Government (Cairo, 28-30 June).[4] The meeting called for cooperation in popularizing the 1991 Treaty establishing the African Economic Community;[5] enhancing regional cooperation and integration; and coordinating the programmes of the two organizations. United Nations agencies were called upon to assist OAU in preparing the protocols of the Economic Community and in examining the implications of the Treaty on the free movement of persons within the Economic Community, particularly refugees and displaced persons; and to intensify cooperation with the OAU Labour Commission.

With regard to conflict prevention, management and resolution, the meeting recommended supplementing the updated 1990 Cooperation Agreement between the United Nations and OAU with an agreement on conflict management and resolution. It also recommended that the United Nations assist OAU in establishing an early warning system; developing its capacity for confidence building among its member States; developing joint training programmes on the settlement of disputes; and supporting the African Commission on Human and Peoples' Rights. It recommended that the two organizations engage in regular joint peacemaking and peace-keeping activities in Africa and cooperate in post-conflict peace-building.

The meeting adopted other recommendations on the exchange of information and training, technical assistance and electoral observation and cooperation in monitoring democratic change and election monitoring in Africa. It identified priorities for implementing Agenda 21, adopted by the 1992 United Nations Conference on Environment and Development,[6] including the establishment of an OAU ad hoc expert group to prepare a document on Africa's inputs to the proposed international convention to combat desertification; technical and financial assistance to OAU; and measures to organize the follow-up to and mobilize resources for the implementation of Agenda 21 and related agreements.

The meeting discussed areas of cooperation between OAU and the United Nations in implementing the Consensus of Dakar, adopted by the 1992 International Conference on Assistance to African Children.[7]

With regard to the implementation of the New Agenda, the meeting welcomed the establishment by the United Nations Secretary-General of the Panel of High-level Personalities and stressed the need for additional resources to support economic development in Africa. It emphasized that resources intended for long-term development should not be used for emergency situations and that bilateral and multilateral financial assistance should be directed to the sectors identified in the New Agenda. The meeting called for improvement of the international economic environment to facilitate Africa's economic recovery and development and to address the questions of external debt, resources flows, commodities, market access and terms of trade.

GENERAL ASSEMBLY ACTION

On 29 November, the General Assembly adopted **resolution 48/25** without vote.

Cooperation between the United Nations and the Organization of African Unity

The General Assembly,

Having considered the report of the Secretary-General on cooperation between the United Nations and the Organization of African Unity,

Recalling the agreement of 15 November 1965 on cooperation between the United Nations and the Organization of African Unity as updated and signed on 9 October 1990 by the Secretaries-General of the two organizations,

Recalling also its resolutions on the enhancement of cooperation between the United Nations and the Organization of African Unity, in particular resolutions 43/12 of 25 October 1988, 43/27 of 18 November 1988, 44/17 of 1 November 1989, 45/13 of 7 November 1990, 46/20 of 26 November 1991 and 47/148 of 18 December 1992,

Recalling further that in its resolutions 46/20 and 47/148 it, *inter alia*, urged the Secretary-General of the United Nations and the relevant agencies of the United Nations system to extend their support for the establishment of an African economic community,

Taking note of the resolutions, decisions and declarations on democratization, conflict resolution and economic integration adopted by the Council of Ministers of the Organization of African Unity at its fifty-eighth ordinary session, held at Cairo from 21 to 26 June 1993, and by the Assembly of Heads of State and Government of that organization at its twenty-ninth ordinary session, held at Cairo from 28 to 30 June 1993,

Considering the important statement made by the representative of the current Chairman of the Assembly of Heads of State and Government of the Organization of African Unity before the General Assembly on 28 September 1993,

Mindful of the need for continued and closer cooperation between the United Nations and the specialized agencies and the Organization of African Unity, in particular in the political, economic, social, technical, cultural and administrative fields,

Noting the establishment by the Assembly of Heads of State and Government of the Organization of African Unity in June 1993 of a mechanism for the prevention, management and resolution of conflicts in Africa,

Also noting the efforts of the Organization of African Unity, and the support and assistance of the United Nations, to promote the peaceful settlement of disputes and conflicts in Africa and the harmonious continuation of the process of democratization,

Deeply concerned that, despite the policies of reform being implemented by most African countries, their economic situation remains critical and African recovery and development continue to be severely hindered by the persistence of lower level commodity prices, the heavy debt burden and the paucity of funding possibilities, as well as by the effects of the devastating drought affecting certain regions of the continent,

Aware of the efforts under way by the Organization of African Unity and its member States in the area of economic integration and, in particular, of the adoption by the Assembly of Heads of State and Government of that organization on 3 June 1991 at Abuja of the Treaty establishing the African Economic Community,

Deeply concerned also about the gravity of the situation of refugees and displaced persons in Africa and the urgent need for increased international assistance to help refugees and, subsequently, African countries of asylum,

Acknowledging the assistance already rendered by the international community, particularly to refugees, displaced persons and African countries of asylum,

Taking note of the report of the Secretary-General on the meeting between the representatives of the secretariats of the United Nations system and the General Secretariat of the Organization of African Unity, held at United Nations Headquarters from 8 to 10 September 1993,

1. *Takes note* of the report of the Secretary-General on cooperation between the United Nations and the Organization of African Unity and of his efforts to strengthen that cooperation and to implement the relevant resolutions;

2. *Takes note also* of the conclusions contained in the report of the Secretary-General on the meeting between the representatives of the secretariats of the United Nations system and the General Secretariat of the Organization of African Unity;

3. *Notes with appreciation* the continued and increasing participation of the Organization of African Unity in the work of the United Nations and the specialized agencies and its constructive contribution to that work;

4. *Calls upon* the United Nations organs, in particular the Security Council and the Economic and Social Council, to continue to involve the Organization of African Unity closely in all their activities concerning Africa;

5. *Commends* the establishment by the Assembly of Heads of State and Government of the Organization of African Unity in June 1993 of a mechanism for the prevention, management and resolution of conflicts in Africa;

6. *Commends* the United Nations and the Organization of African Unity for their ongoing cooperative activities in the resolution of conflicts in Africa, and stresses the need to enhance and strengthen the existing pattern of exchange of information and consultations, especially in the area of monitoring and early warning of conflict situations;

7. *Calls upon* the United Nations to coordinate its efforts and to cooperate with the Organization of African Unity in the context of the pacific settlement of disputes and the maintenance of international peace and security in Africa, as provided for under Chapter VIII of the Charter of the United Nations;

8. *Notes with appreciation* the assistance provided by the United Nations and its agencies to African countries in the context of the democratization process;

9. *Urges* the United Nations and its Member States to continue to provide assistance, as appropriate, to the Organization of African Unity, should the latter decide to launch a peace-keeping operation;

10. *Urges* the United Nations to continue to support the Organization of African Unity in its efforts to promote the peaceful settlement of disputes and conflicts and peacefully to manage change in Africa;

11. *Urges* all Member States and regional and international organizations, in particular those of the United Nations system, as well as non-governmental organizations, to provide the necessary and appropriate economic, financial and technical assistance to refugees and displaced persons, as well as to African countries of asylum, taking into account recent disquieting developments in this respect;

12. *Commends* the continued efforts of the Organization of African Unity to promote multilateral cooperation and economic integration among African States, and requests United Nations agencies to continue to support those efforts;

13. *Stresses* that the economic, technical and development assistance provided to Africa by the organizations of the United Nations system must continue, and emphasizes the current need for those organizations to accord priority to Africa in this field;

14. *Urges* the Secretary-General and Member States, regional and international organizations, non-governmental organizations and relevant agencies of the United Nations system to extend their support to the establishment of the African Economic Community and to assist in economic integration and cooperation;

15. *Requests* the Secretary-General to continue to support the efforts of the Secretary-General of the Organization of African Unity with a view to holding sectoral meetings on the priority areas of cooperation, particularly the establishment of the African Economic Community and the strengthening of the African regional and subregional organizations;

16. *Requests* the agencies of the United Nations system working in Africa to include in their programme at the national and regional levels the activities which will enhance regional cooperation in their respective areas and to facilitate the realization of the objectives of the Treaty establishing the African Economic Community;

17. *Calls upon* United Nations agencies to make an effort to coordinate their regional programmes in Africa in order to create inter-linkages among them and to ensure harmonization of their programmes with those of the African regional and subregional economic organizations;

18. *Emphasizes* the urgency of the need to adopt appropriate measures to ensure the implementation of the United Nations New Agenda for the Development of Africa in the 1990s, in particular in the areas of resource flows, debt relief and diversification of African economies;

19. *Calls upon* the Secretary-General to work in close coordination and cooperation with the Secretary-General of the Organization of African Unity, in particular on follow-up to review and evaluate the implementation of the United Nations New Agenda for the Development of Africa in the 1990s;

20. *Endorses* the agreement reached between the organizations of the United Nations system and the Organization of African Unity on the convening of a meeting between the secretariats of those organizations, to be held in 1994 at Addis Ababa, to review and evaluate the progress made in implementing the proposals and recommendations agreed upon in September 1993 on cooperation between them in 1993-1994 and to adopt new and effective joint action;

21. *Calls upon* the relevant organs of the United Nations to ensure the effective, fair and equitable representation of Africa at senior and policy levels at their respective headquarters and in their regional field operations;

22. *Requests* the Secretary-General to continue to ensure that the United Nations information network continues to disseminate information so as to increase public awareness of the situation prevailing in southern Africa, as well as of the social and economic problems and needs of African States and of their regional and subregional institutions;

23. *Also requests* the Secretary-General to report to the General Assembly at its forty-ninth session on the implementation of the present resolution and on the development of cooperation between the Organization of African Unity and organizations of the United Nations system.

General Assembly resolution 48/25

29 November 1993   Meeting 65   Adopted without vote

Draft by Algeria (A/48/L.23/Rev.1); agenda item 43.
Meeting numbers. GA 48th session: plenary 60, 65.

REFERENCES

(1)YUN 1992, p. 215, GA res. 47/148, 18 Dec. 1992. (2)A/48/475 & Add.1. (3)YUN 1991, p. 402, GA res. 46/151, annex, sect. II, 18 Dec. 1991. (4)A/48/322. (5)YUN 1992, p. 215. (6)Ibid., p. 670. (7)Ibid., p. 883.

Chapter II

Americas

The General Assembly in 1993 commended the sustained efforts of the Governments of Costa Rica, El Salvador, Guatemala, Honduras, Nicaragua and Panama to consolidate peace and economic growth throughout Central America. The United Nations system maintained its support for those efforts in the form of technical, humanitarian and other assistance within country programmes or regional frameworks.

The Secretary-General continued to play a key role in the peace process in El Salvador, assisting the Government and Frente Farabundo Martí para la Liberación Nacional in every way possible to complete implementation of their 1992 Peace Agreement and supplementary accords. The United Nations Observer Mission in El Salvador, charged with verifying the parties' compliance with the Agreement, was additionally charged by the Security Council in 1993 with the observance of the Salvadorian electoral process, officially begun in November and expected to conclude in general elections in March 1994. To that end, the Council extended the Mission's mandate until 31 May 1994.

Through the efforts of the Special Envoy for Haiti of the Secretaries-General of the United Nations and the Organization of American States, the Governors Island Agreement and the New York Pact were concluded, providing for measures aimed at restoring constitutional order in Haiti and for the return of its duly elected President, Jean-Bertrand Aristide, on 30 October 1993. As part of the Agreement, the Security Council established the United Nations Mission in Haiti, whose deployment was prevented, however, by the military authorities and other elements opposed to President Aristide's return. The incident drew the condemnation of the Council and the Assembly, which asserted that the Governors Island Agreement remained the only valid basis for resolving the Haitian crisis. None the less, the Special Envoy maintained contact with all the parties in order to put the political dialogue back on track and arrive at a negotiated settlement.

The Secretary-General, in the exercise of his good offices, remained involved in the peace process to settle the civil conflict in Guatemala. In December, the Assembly reiterated the importance of resuming negotiations between the Government and Unidad Revolucionaria Nacional Guatemalteca, bearing in mind the progress and agreements achieved up to May 1993.

In other actions relating to Latin America and the Caribbean as a whole, the Assembly granted observer status to the Latin American Parliament in the Assembly and urged the broadening of cooperation between the United Nations and the Latin American Economic System (see PART ONE, Chapter V, and PART TWO, Chapter VI).

Central America situation

The Governments of Costa Rica, El Salvador, Guatemala, Honduras, Nicaragua and Panama continued efforts in 1993 to achieve peace, consolidation of democracy and development throughout all of Central America. In June, their Presidents met at Guatemala City to reaffirm their commitment to those purposes. By the Joint Declaration adopted at that meeting, they acknowledged the need to continue improving the underpinnings of existing democratic and constitutional systems throughout the subregion and reiterated their determination to promote dialogue, coordination and consensus; they accordingly welcomed the peaceful settlement of the recent political crisis in Guatemala (see below, under ''Guatemala situation'').

At an August meeting at San Salvador, El Salvador, the Presidents, considering that peace in Central America was indivisible and that any development disrupting it had repercussions throughout the subregion, adopted a Declaration on the Situation in Nicaragua (see below, under ''Nicaragua'').

In the Guatemala Declaration, adopted at the conclusion of their fourteenth summit meeting (Guatemala City, 27-29 October), the Presidents called for an international conference on peace and development in Central America for the purpose of assessing the status of the subregion's peace process, cooperation and requirements for technical assistance and financing.

The General Assembly, in December, adopted a resolution on the overall situation in Central America (see below). By other resolutions, it requested the United Nations system to continue to implement the humanitarian programmes for the uprooted populations of the subregion within the framework of the International Conference on

Central American Refugees (resolution 48/117); it also urged all States and the United Nations system to step up support for the 1988 Special Plan of Economic Cooperation for Central America with a view to preventing a reversal of achievements in the subregion and building peace through integrated and sustained development (48/199).

Report of the Secretary-General. In response to a General Assembly request of 1992,[1] the Secretary-General submitted a report on 11 November 1993 reviewing the situation in Central America.[2] He noted that the goals of peace, democratization, reconciliation, development and justice, set out by the Central American Presidents in 1986[3] and 1987[4] and to which they had renewed their commitment at all presidential summit meetings since, had materialized in several areas.

The events leading to the election of a President in Guatemala on 6 June and the ongoing democratic electoral processes in Costa Rica, El Salvador, Honduras and Panama, as well as the rise of issue-oriented organizations, such as those that had begun pressing for government protection of human rights, testified to improved prospects for the continued strengthening of democratic institutions and to the growing assertiveness of civil society. The settlement of the conflicts in Nicaragua and El Salvador had allowed thousands of refugees and displaced persons to return to their homes. The improved political climate and ongoing macroeconomic reforms had increased business confidence within the subregion. The transition from confrontation to consensus in intergovernmental relations had engendered cooperation on a large number of issues and rekindled the thrust towards regional integration, with results particularly in trade.

However, as the Central American Presidents acknowledged in the Guatemala Declaration, there was still a long way to go to reach the goals of Central America's transformation. The civil conflict in Guatemala, the longest lasting one in the subregion, had yet to be settled. Many of the structural causes of the acute crisis of the 1980s persisted. Extreme poverty was growing and social disparities remained a source of tension. The state of health care, housing, education and employment were a continuing cause for concern. Drug trafficking and environmental degradation had emerged as new challenges.

Economic policies essential for macroeconomic stabilization had often been stymied by deteriorating social conditions and a diminished government ability to take remedial action, further straining the political process. The difficulties of simultaneously adjusting the economy, correcting social inequalities and easing political tensions had become

particularly obvious in Nicaragua, still grappling with the legacy of a decade of civil war. Similar difficulties faced El Salvador, which was contending with stabilizing its economy and meeting the financial burdens of its 1992 Peace Agreement[5] and supplementary accords.

By the Panama Declaration that concluded their thirteenth summit meeting (Panama City, 9-11 December 1992),[6] the Central American Presidents underscored the imperative to ensure the continuous improvement of genuine democratic, pluralistic and participatory processes. They recognized that the primary challenges confronting Central America were the improvement of democracy, the consolidation of peace, access to international markets on equitable conditions and sustainable development with social justice—challenges that called for an institutional framework for integrated subregional development, with the agricultural sector as the linchpin of economic revitalization. Therefore, as decided at that meeting, the Central American Integration System, provided for by the 1991 Tegucigalpa Protocol,[7] was formally established on 1 February 1993; its headquarters at San Salvador were inaugurated on 27 October. Since the System's inception, its secretariat had been fostering coordination among its constituent agencies and assisting the Presidents' good-offices mission to Nicaragua.

At their fourteenth summit, the Presidents signed a protocol updating the 1960 General Treaty on Central American Economic Integration[8] with the aim of promoting a voluntary and gradual process towards a Central American economic union.

Throughout 1993, meetings among the Central American Presidents continued to prove an effective format for high-level regional decision-making. In addition to the fourteenth (regular) summit meeting, the Presidents met in special summit (Belize, 19-21 February) to coordinate regional efforts against drug trafficking. They held two ad hoc meetings (El Salvador, 1 June; Guatemala, 17 June) to address the Guatemalan crisis which arose in late May, and held a third one (El Salvador, 27 August) to offer their good offices to facilitate national reconciliation in Nicaragua.

The Central American countries continued to enlist the international community's cooperation through various mechanisms. At a meeting early in the year (Caracas, Venezuela, 12 February), their Presidents and those of the Group of Three cooperating countries (Colombia, Mexico and Venezuela) adopted the Caracas Commitment, establishing a new framework for cooperation, as well as the Caracas Statement, renewing their commitment to the creation of a free-trade zone. At their ninth ministerial meeting (San Salvador,

22 and 23 February), the Central American countries and the European Community (EC) signed the San Salvador Agreement on further cooperation between them. At a special session of the Partnership for Democracy and Development in Central America (Tokyo, 15 and 16 March), the 30 participating countries shared the view that, to consolidate the Central American peace process, democratic and economic development must proceed in tandem, and assistance to both must be well balanced.

The World Bank, the International Monetary Fund and the Inter-American Development Bank endeavoured to promote structured dialogue between the international donor community and the Central American countries. The first meeting of the Regional Consultative Group for Central America (Brussels, March), coordinated by the Inter-American Development Bank, discussed regional technical cooperation in energy, human resources, the environment, and science and technology. Meetings of national consultative groups were held under World Bank auspices (Paris, April). A meeting on El Salvador reviewed the first year's implementation of the National Reconstruction Plan and received pledges from donor countries amounting to $800 million, while a meeting on Nicaragua evaluated the national reconciliation process and received pledges totalling some $750 million. At an informal meeting organized by the World Bank (Washington, D. C., September) at Guatemala's request, donors offered financial support to meet a $150-million short-term need.

In cooperation with the Central American Governments, the Organization of American States (OAS) played a prominent part in efforts that successfully reinstated democratic institutions in Guatemala, suspended on 25 May by the then President, Jorge Antonio Serrano Elías. In connection with developments disrupting national reconciliation in Nicaragua in late August and early September, the OAS Permanent Council met in special session on 3 September to affirm support for President Violeta Barrios de Chamorro and for the good offices of the other Central American Presidents on Nicaragua's behalf.

The Secretary-General stated that the United Nations had continued to support the efforts of the Central American Governments to consolidate peace, democracy and development. He had exercised his own good offices to advance the implementation of the Salvadorian Peace Agreement, highlighting what had been achieved and what remained to be done (see below, under "El Salvador situation"), and to assist in the search for a negotiated settlement of the Guatemala conflict (see below, under "Guatemala situation"). United Nations operational activities remained in place within national programmes and subregional

frameworks, such as the Special Plan of Economic Cooperation for Central America and the International Conference on Central American Refugees (see PART THREE, Chapters II and XV, respectively).

Referring to further prospects, the Secretary-General pointed to the three assets that had helped Central America emerge from the difficult decade of the 1980s: a dynamic institutional framework; a comprehensive agenda of social, economic and other reforms; and an active partnership with the international community through several cooperation mechanisms, including the United Nations itself. Together they constituted a powerful instrument to address the challenges of further democratization, improved social justice and economic growth. A key to success, he stated, would be the sustained dedication and sense of urgency that were mustered in addressing the challenges of civil war and regional tensions. He called on the international community to remain a prominent contributor, not by directing or substituting regional efforts but by supporting Central America's own commitment. The Secretary-General affirmed his readiness, within the mandate entrusted to him by the General Assembly, to play an active part in that endeavour.

GENERAL ASSEMBLY ACTION

On 20 December, the General Assembly adopted without vote **resolution 48/161**.

The situation in Central America: procedures for the establishment of a firm and lasting peace and progress in fashioning a region of peace, freedom, democracy and development

The General Assembly,

Recalling the relevant resolutions of the Security Council and its own resolutions, particularly resolution 47/118 of 18 December 1992, in which it recognized that there remained in Central America major obstacles to the full exercise of peace, freedom, democracy and development and the need for a global frame of reference that would enable the international community to channel support to the efforts of the Central American Governments, as well as the desirability of increasing support by providing resources for the consolidation of the objectives set, in order to prevent the region's material limitations from diminishing or reversing the progress made,

Recognizing the importance and validity of the commitments assumed by the Central American Presidents in the "Procedures for the establishment of a firm and lasting peace in Central America", adopted at the Esquipulas II summit meeting on 7 August 1987, and the agreements adopted at their subsequent summit meetings, especially the commitments undertaken at the fourteenth summit meeting, held at Guatemala City from 27 to 29 October 1993, which established a framework of priorities for the consolidation of peace and human development in Central America based on democratic participation and the identification of fundamentally new courses of action which call for a new strategy reflecting the concept of integrated and sustained human development,

Aware of the importance of supporting the efforts of the Central American peoples and Governments for the consolidation of a firm and lasting peace in Central America, and bearing in mind that the Central American Integration System constitutes the institutional framework for subregional integration through which integrated development can be promoted in an effective, orderly and coherent manner,

Convinced of the hopes that inspire the peoples of Central America to achieve peace, reconciliation, development and social justice, as well as the commitment to settle their differences by means of dialogue, negotiation and respect for the legitimate interests of all States, in accordance with their own decision and their own historical experience while fully respecting the principles of self-determination and non-intervention,

Recognizing the importance of the peace-keeping operations that have been carried out in Central America pursuant to the decisions of the Security Council and with the support of the Secretary-General,

Recognizing also the need to preserve and enhance the results obtained by means of new and innovative initiatives,

Reaffirming the belief that there can be no peace in Central America without development or democracy, which are essential for transforming the region and realizing the hope of the Central American peoples and Governments that Central America may become a region of peace, freedom, democracy and development,

Emphasizing the important role of international cooperation in helping to implement the decisions adopted at the summit meetings of Central American Presidents in order to consolidate peace with human development and social justice,

Stressing the importance of honouring the commitments to accelerate the establishment of a new model of regional security in Central America as established in the Tegucigalpa Protocol of 13 December 1991, which established the Central American Integration System, and bearing in mind the institutional changes that have taken place in the armed forces in Central America,

Noting with concern the recent acts of violence, with possible political motives, in El Salvador which may, if measures to halt them are not taken, jeopardize the peace process initiated under the Peace Agreement signed at Mexico City by the Government of El Salvador and the Frente Farabundo Martí para la Liberación Nacional on 16 January 1992,

Noting with interest the steps taken by both the Government of El Salvador and the Frente Farabundo Martí with the Secretary-General and officials of countries that support the peace process, as well as the initial measures adopted by the Government of El Salvador and the decision of the Secretary-General to have the Human Rights Division of the United Nations Observer Mission in El Salvador collaborate with the competent authorities in conducting immediately a full, impartial and reliable investigation of illegal armed groups, which would result in the determination of responsibility for the acts of violence that could reverse and obstruct the implementation of the Peace Agreement,

Convinced of the importance of achieving a negotiated political solution to the situation in Guatemala and of resuming the talks between the Unidad Revolucionaria Nacional Guatemalteca and the Government of Guatemala in order to end the internal armed confrontation in the shortest possible time and to bring about national reconciliation and full respect for human rights, in keeping with the wishes of the Guatemalan people,

Noting with satisfaction that the obstacles that led to the recent institutional crisis between the legislative and the executive branches in Guatemala have been overcome,

Bearing in mind the efforts made by the Government of Nicaragua to promote a broad national dialogue as the best way to consolidate peace, national reconciliation, democracy and development in that country,

Welcoming the adoption of resolution 48/8 of 22 October 1993, entitled "International assistance for the rehabilitation and reconstruction of Nicaragua: aftermath of the war and natural disasters", in which it recognized the exceptional circumstances prevailing in Nicaragua,

Recognizing that the consolidation of peace in Nicaragua is a key factor in the Central American peace process, as well as the urgent need for the international community and the United Nations system to continue providing Nicaragua with the support it needs to continue promoting its economic and social rehabilitation and reconstruction in order to strengthen democracy and overcome the aftermath of war and recent natural disasters,

Recognizing also the valuable and effective contribution of the United Nations and of various governmental and non-governmental mechanisms to the process of democratization, pacification and development in Central America, and the importance for the gradual transformation of Central America into a region of peace, freedom, democracy and development of both the political dialogue and the economic cooperation set in motion by the ministerial conference between the European Community and the Central American countries and the joint initiative of the industrialized countries (Group of Twenty-four) and the group of cooperating countries (Group of Three) through the Partnership for Democracy and Development in Central America,

Bearing in mind that the process established by the International Conference on Central American Refugees will be completed in May 1994 and that the United Nations Development Programme has assumed the role of lead agency in completing unfinished programmes, and bearing in mind as well the eventual depletion of the Special Plan of Economic Cooperation for Central America, through which both the United Nations system and the international community, and especially the cooperating countries, have supported the Central American peace process,

Noting with concern that events have occurred in Central America that may hinder the consolidation of a firm and lasting peace,

Aware that Central America is facing a difficult transition period requiring every effort of the Governments and the various sectors of the Central American countries, as well as support from the international community, in overcoming the underlying structural causes that gave rise to the crisis in the region,

Taking note of the report of the Secretary-General of 11 November 1993 on the situation in Central America,

Bearing in mind the initiative of the Central American Presidents to convene an international conference on peace and development in Central America, contained in the Guatemala Declaration adopted at their fourteenth summit meeting on 29 October 1993,

1. *Commends* the efforts of the Central American peoples and Governments to consolidate peace by implementing the agreements adopted at summit meetings since 1987, urges them to continue with their efforts to consolidate a firm and lasting peace in Central America, and requests the Secretary-General to continue to afford the fullest possible support for the initiatives and efforts of the Central American Governments;

2. *Supports* the decision of the Central American Presidents to declare Central America a region of peace, freedom, democracy and development, as set out in the Tegucigalpa Protocol, and encourages the initiatives of the Central American countries to consolidate Governments which base their development on democracy, peace, cooperation and full respect for human rights;

3. *Takes note* of the Guatemala Declaration adopted on 29 October 1993 by the Central American Presidents at their fourteenth summit meeting, and shares the view that an opportunity exists in Central America to translate into reality the relation of interdependence between peace and development, which would constitute an historic achievement and a frame of reference useful in the settlement of disputes and the consolidation of peace and democracy through integrated and sustained development;

4. *Welcomes with satisfaction* the efforts of the Central American countries to promote economic growth within a context of human development, as well as the progress achieved in strengthening democracy in the region, as amply demonstrated by the elections to be held shortly in Costa Rica, El Salvador, Honduras and Panama;

5. *Emphasizes* the functioning of the Central American Integration System since 1 February 1993 and the registry of the Tegucigalpa Protocol with the United Nations Secretariat, expresses its full support for the efforts made by the Central Americans to stimulate and broaden the integration process in the context of the Central American Integration System, and calls on Member States and international organizations to provide effective cooperation to Central America so that it may promote and strengthen sustained subregional integration and achieve its fundamental goal;

6. *Welcomes with interest* the proposals to establish a new model of regional security based on a reasonable balance of forces, the pre-eminence of civilian authority, the eradication of extreme poverty, the promotion of sustained development, protection of the environment and the elimination of violence, corruption, terrorism and trafficking in drugs and weapons;

7. *Calls upon* the international community and the United Nations system to expand their technical and financial support for the professionalization of the police forces of the Central American countries in order to safeguard democratic institutions;

8. *Reiterates its appreciation* for the effective and timely participation of the Secretary-General and his representatives and encourages them to continue to take all necessary steps to contribute to the successful implementation of all the commitments subscribed to by the parties to the Peace Agreement in El Salvador, including efforts to mobilize the necessary resources for the reconstruction and development of the country, which are indispensable to the consolidation of peace and democracy there;

9. *Reiterates its appreciation also* to the Governments of Colombia, Mexico, Spain and Venezuela, which make up the Group of Friends of the Secretary-General, as well as to the Government of the United States of America and other interested Governments, for their constant support and contribution to the efforts to implement the Peace Agreement, and urges them to continue to lend their support until the full implementation of the agreements, which reflect the will and aspirations of the Salvadorian people, is brought about;

10. *Notes with concern* the acts of violence that have occurred in recent months in El Salvador, which could indicate the resurgence of illegal armed groups, as well as the delay in the implementation of specific provisions of the Peace Agreement, and in this regard highlights the importance of complying with the agreement between the Government of El Salvador and the Frente Farabundo Martí para la Liberación Nacional concerning the need to accelerate the implementation of the provisions of the Peace Agreement, urging all political forces to cooperate to this end;

11. *Calls upon* the Government of El Salvador and all other institutions involved in the electoral process to adopt the necessary measures to ensure that the elections to be held in March 1994 be free, representative and irreproachable, as they constitute an essential element in the peace process;

12. *Reiterates* the importance of resuming, in the shortest possible time, the negotiations between the Government of Guatemala and the Unidad Revolucionaria Nacional Guatemalteca, bearing in mind the progress and agreements achieved up to May 1993, expresses its appreciation to the Secretary-General and his representative for their participation in the peace process in Guatemala, and requests him to continue supporting that process;

13. *Takes note* in this context of the Peace Plan of the President of Guatemala;

14. *Expresses its appreciation* to the international community and encourages it to continue providing the necessary assistance for the people of Guatemala to achieve, in the shortest possible time, its aspirations of peace, national reconciliation, democracy and development;

15. *Calls upon* all political groups in Nicaragua to pursue, by means of the national dialogue promoted by the Government, their efforts to conclude agreements for the consolidation of the democratic process, reconstruction and national reconciliation;

16. *Supports* the efforts that the Government of Nicaragua is making to consolidate peace, and endorses the provision concerning exceptional circumstances so that the international community and funding agencies may provide their support for rehabilitation, economic and social reconstruction and the strengthening of reconciliation and democracy in that country;

17. *Welcomes with interest* the initiative by the Government of Nicaragua concerning the establishment of an active group of friendly countries to play a particularly important role in supporting the reactivation of the economic and social development of the country, which will facilitate the strengthening of its institutional and democratic structures, and requests the Secretary-General to give his full support to that initiative;

18. *Stresses* the importance of the political dialogue and economic cooperation between the European Community and its member States and the Central American countries within the ministerial conference in sup-

port of the efforts of the Central American countries in their quest for peace, consolidation of democracy and sustained development;

19. *Stresses also* the importance of the joint initiative of the industrialized countries (Group of Twenty-four) and the group of cooperating countries (Group of Three), through the Partnership for Democracy and Development in Central America;

20. *Requests* the Secretary-General to provide the Central American countries with all possible assistance for the consolidation of peace in the region;

21. *Requests* the agencies of the United Nations system, especially the United Nations Development Programme, and the international institutions to consider providing the necessary resources to establish new and up-to-date regional programmes through arrangements to be defined jointly by the Central American countries and the cooperation community as part of the new development strategy, given the need to anticipate the eventual depletion of resources from the Special Plan of Economic Cooperation for Central America and to prevent any reversal of the achievements in Central America thus far and consolidate peace in the region through comprehensive and sustained development;

22. *Recognizes* the importance of the programmes undertaken in the context of the Special Plan of Economic Cooperation for Central America to strengthen democratic institutions and modernize State infrastructure, telecommunications, agricultural development, environmental protection and human development;

23. *Expresses its appreciation* to the United Nations High Commissioner for Refugees for carrying out her mandate under the International Conference on Central American Refugees, and supports the United Nations Development Programme as it completes the unfinished programmes within a comprehensive and sustained concept of development with a human face;

24. *Notes with interest* the proposal to convene an international conference for peace and development in Central America, the primary objectives of which would be to assess the status of the peace process, cooperation and technical assistance needs and the financing required for the region to become one of peace, freedom, democracy and development, and in this context expresses its satisfaction at the holding of an international technical meeting on Central America at United Nations Headquarters on 16 November 1993, with the participation of Ministers for Foreign Affairs of Central America and representatives of cooperating countries and international institutions;

25. *Decides* to include in the provisional agenda of its forty-ninth session the item entitled "The situation in Central America: procedures for the establishment of a firm and lasting peace and progress in fashioning a region of peace, freedom, democracy and development";

26. *Requests* the Secretary-General to submit a report to the General Assembly at its forty-ninth session on the implementation of the present resolution.

General Assembly resolution 48/161

20 December 1992   Meeting 85   Adopted without vote

37-nation draft (A/48/L.21/Rev.1); agenda item 40.
Sponsors: Antigua and Barbuda, Argentina, Belgium, Bolivia, Brazil, Canada, Chile, Colombia, Costa Rica, Denmark, Ecuador, El Salvador, France, Germany, Greece, Guatemala, Honduras, Ireland, Italy, Luxembourg, Mexico,

Netherlands, Nicaragua, Norway, Panama, Paraguay, Peru, Portugal, Russian Federation, Spain, Suriname, Sweden, Trinidad and Tobago, United Kingdom, United States, Uruguay, Venezuela.
Financial implications: 5th Committee, A/48/789; S-G, A/C.5/48/50.
Meeting numbers. GA 48th session: 5th Committee 43; plenary 57, 85.

El Salvador situation

Implementation of the 1992 Peace Agreement[5] and other subsequent supplementary agreements between the Government of El Salvador and the Frente Farabundo Marti para la Liberación Nacional (FMLN) continued throughout 1993. In this regard, the Secretary-General was able to confirm two major accomplishments: compliance by the Government with the recommendations of the Ad Hoc Commission on the Purification of the Armed Forces by 30 June 1993; and, with the destruction by 18 August of virtually all FMLN weapons inventoried in 1992 following the formal cease-fire date[9] and those declared in 1993, the effective dismantling of FMLN's military structure.

On the other hand, considerable delays continued to hamper the implementation of other key provisions of the Agreement, notably the recovery from private hands of assault weapons, the programmes for the reintegration of demobilized combatants into productive civilian life and the establishment of the National Civil Police (PNC). Certain other police and public security provisions remained to be complied with. The human rights situation gave cause for concern in view of recent cases of executions, death-squad style. Above all, the critical issue of financing necessary to implement the Agreement remained unresolved.

Implementation of the recommendations of the Commission on the Truth, released in March, had given rise to controversy and remained outstanding. Five days after the report's release, a general amnesty came into force. The Minister for Foreign Affairs of El Salvador, by a note of 16 April[10] to the Foreign Ministers of countries with which El Salvador had diplomatic relations, explained the event in the context of his country's efforts to foster genuine national reconciliation. He asserted that, to eradicate the hatred, bitterness and confrontation which marked the 12-year armed conflict, the Salvadorian Legislative Assembly, by Decree No. 486 of 20 March, adopted the "General Amnesty Act for the Consolidation of Peace", granting full, complete and unconditional amnesty to all persons who in any way had participated in criminal acts committed before 1 January 1992, whether they involved political crimes, related common crimes or common crimes committed by at least 20 persons.

The Secretary-General expressed concern at the haste with which the amnesty was approved, namely, by simple majority in the Legislative Assembly, commenting that it would have been preferable if the amnesty had been promulgated by a broad degree of national consensus.

Despite the outstanding commitments, the electoral process began in November. At the request of the Salvadorian Government and on the recommendation of the Secretary-General, the Security Council enlarged the mandate of the United Nations Observer Mission in El Salvador (ONUSAL) to include the observation of the electoral process.

The General Assembly, in addition to providing for the continued financing of ONUSAL, adopted **resolution 48/203**, calling on the signatories to the Peace Agreement to expedite the implementation of outstanding commitments under that Agreement, in order to guarantee fully the building of peace in El Salvador and hence to encourage the international community to increase the level of financial resources accorded to priority projects for reconstruction, development and the strengthening of democratic institutions in El Salvador.

Ad Hoc Commission on the Purification of the Armed Forces

Communication (January). On 7 January 1993,[11] the Secretary-General reported to the Security Council, through its President, on the latest developments relating to the implementation of the recommendations of the Ad Hoc Commission on the Purification of the Armed Forces of El Salvador. The Government had expressed reservations in 1992[12] on the time-frame specified for implementation.

The Secretary-General recalled that the arrangements formally ending the armed conflict in El Salvador on 15 December 1992[13] included agreement by that country's President, Alfredo F. Cristiani, to complete implementation, within a specified time-frame, of the recommendations of the Ad Hoc Commission concerning all the officers named in its report. The President punctually communicated that he had adopted appropriate administrative decisions, to take effect on 1 January 1993 and to be made known the preceding day at the latest. The officers in question numbered 103, one of whom was no longer serving in the Armed Forces (FAES). Of the remaining 102 officers, 76 had been recommended for discharge and 26 for transfer to other functions.

The Secretary-General stated that President Cristiani informed him on 1 January of measures adopted in respect of 94 of the officers, as follows: *(a)* 25 had been transferred to other functions; *(b)* 4 had been discharged for disciplinary reasons (among them the twenty-sixth officer recommended for transfer to other functions); *(c)* 19 had been discharged for administrative reasons; *(d)* 38 had been placed on leave with pay pending completion of the legal formalities for their retirement, which would take place within a period not to exceed six months; *(e)* 7 had been appointed as military attachés to Salvadorian embassies abroad; and *(f)* 1 had been permitted for personal reasons to remain in active service until his retirement on 1 March. Administrative decisions regarding the other 8 officers would be deferred during "the period of transition", understood to mean during the remainder of President Cristiani's presidency.

Having studied the information and verified that the names in the accompanying administrative orders relating to categories *(a)* to *(e)* corresponded with those in the Commission report, the Secretary-General concluded that the measures relating to categories *(a)* to *(c)* were in full compliance with the Commission recommendations; those relating to categories *(d)* and *(f)*, although complying only broadly, could be accepted as satisfactory. The measure adopted for category *(e)* was not in compliance with the recommendation for the discharge of the seven officers, nor was the deferral of decisions on the remaining eight; the Secretary-General asked President Cristiani to take early action to regularize the position of those 15 officers.

SECURITY COUNCIL ACTION

The Security Council met on 9 February 1993. Before it were the Secretary-General's latest 1992 report on ONUSAL[13] and his communication of 7 January 1993. After consultations among Council members, the President made the following statement[14] on behalf of the Council in connection with its consideration of the item entitled "Central America: efforts towards peace":

Meeting number. SC 3172.

"The Security Council welcomes with satisfaction the important progress made thus far towards the full implementation of the Peace Agreement for El Salvador and the cooperation shown by the parties to this end. The Security Council takes note of the report of the Secretary-General dated 23 December 1992 in which he indicates that the armed conflict between the Government of El Salvador and the Frente Farabundo Martí para la Liberación Nacional (FMLN) was brought formally to an end on 15 December 1992. The Council emphasizes this event, which puts an end to more than 10 years of armed conflict.

"However, the Security Council expresses concern at the observations made by the Secretary-General in his letter dated 7 January 1993 addressed to the President of the Security Council, by which he reported on the situation with regard to the implementation of the recommendations of the Ad Hoc Commission concerning the purification of the armed forces of El Salvador and, basically, at the fact that those recommendations have yet to be fully complied with despite prior assurance by the Government of El Salvador. The Security Council also expresses concern at the indication in the letter dated 29 January 1993 from the Secretary-General addressed to the President of the Security Council that FMLN, despite prior assurances, did not complete the destruction of its weapons by the agreed deadline and that it is therefore not yet in full compliance with its undertakings under the Peace Agreement.

"In this connection, the Security Council emphasizes the solemn nature of the undertakings made by each of the parties when they signed the Peace Agreement and reaffirms the obligation of the parties to comply fully and in a timely fashion with those undertakings.

"The Council welcomes with satisfaction the decision of the Government of El Salvador to request the United Nations to verify the forthcoming general elections and the intention of the Secretary-General, communicated in his letter dated 26 January 1993 to the President of the Security Council to recommend to the Security Council that it accede to this request.

"The Security Council strongly urges the parties to persist in their determination to complete the process of bringing peace and national reconciliation to El Salvador and to continue cooperating with the Secretary-General in the efforts that he is making to ensure that the Peace Agreement is implemented fully. To that end, the Council will follow closely the progress and results of those efforts."

(For the statement's references to FMLN armaments and the Salvadorian electoral process, see below under those topics.)

Communications (April-July). On 2 April,[15] the Secretary-General informed the Security Council President that the President's plan for the 15 officers had been conveyed to him during a visit from the Minister of the Presidency of El Salvador. In order to take account of the Secretary-General's comments, the plan was revised to provide that, by 30 June at the latest, all 15 officers would be placed on leave with pay pending completion of the procedures for their retirement, to take place no later than 31 December; they would not perform any official functions while on leave.

The Secretary-General confirmed on 7 July[16] that, as verified by ONUSAL, the 15 officers had been placed on leave with pay by a General Order of 30 June of the FAES High Command. On 13 July,[17] the Council acknowledged the information that the Government was finally in compliance with the Commission's recommendations, describing the Government's actions as a significant achievement in the consolidation of the peace process in El Salvador.

Commission on the Truth

The Commission on the Truth, established in accordance with the 1991 Mexico Agreements[18] and formally constituted by the Secretary-General in 1992,[19] presented its report on 15 March 1993 on its investigation of the serious acts of violence perpetrated during the 12-year armed conflict in El Salvador and whose impact on society demanded that the public know the truth. The Secretary-General transmitted the report to the Security Council on 29 March.[20]

The report reproduced excerpts of the Commission's mandate as set forth in the Mexico Agreements, defined the legal norms applicable to its task, outlined the methodology used, and gave a chronology of the violence, as well as an overview of the cases and patterns of violence perpetrated. The Commission registered more than 22,000 complaints of serious acts of violence perpetrated between January 1980 and July 1991, involving extrajudicial executions (over 60 per cent), enforced disappearances (over 25 per cent) and torture (over 20 per cent). Some 30 cases examined were illustrative of violence by State agents, massacres of peasants by FAES, death-squad assassinations, violence by FMLN and murders of judges.

The Commission made some 40 recommendations grouped into four categories: (1) recommendations arising directly from the Commission's investigations, relating to specific persons (whose dismissal from either FAES or the civil service, or disqualification from holding public office, were called for) and to the reform of the judicial system; (2) recommendations for the eradication of structural causes directly linked to the acts investigated, for the investigation of illegal groups and for the reform of FAES and public security arrangements; (3) recommendations for institutional reforms in respect of the administration of justice, the protection of human rights (including some 19 recommendations already made by ONUSAL's Human Rights Division) and the new PNC; and (4) recommendations for national reconciliation, including material and moral compensation, for the creation of a forum for truth and reconciliation and for international follow-up.

The annexes to the report were published separately in two volumes. They consisted of, among other documents, texts of the Mexico Peace Agreements, the forensic and photographic reports of the 1981 massacre of peasants at El Mozote, statistical analysis of testimony received by the Commission; and lists of victims submitted to the Commission, of disappeared persons compiled by the United Nations, and of FAES and FMLN members killed in the armed conflict.

(For other aspects of the human rights situation in El Salvador, see PART THREE, Chapter X.)

SECURITY COUNCIL ACTION

The Security Council met on 18 March and, following consultations with Council members, the President was authorized to make the following statement[21] on behalf of the Council:

Meeting number. SC 3185.

"The Security Council welcomes the recent efforts to apply fully the peace accords in El Salvador and acknowledges the sense of responsibility and cooperation demonstrated by the Government of El Salvador and the Frente Farabundo Martí para la Liberación Nacional to reach this objective.

"In this context, the Security Council welcomes the submission of the report of the Commission on the Truth and of its recommendations intended to prevent the repetition of the acts of violence committed during the twelve years of armed confrontation, as well as to create confidence in the positive changes caused by the peace process and stimulate national reconciliation.

"The Security Council underlines the need for the parties, in accordance with the peace accords, to comply with the recommendations contained in the report of the Commission on the Truth, as well as all other obligations which remain to be implemented. In addition, it calls upon Salvadorian society to continue acting with the responsibility which it has demonstrated throughout this process, in order to contribute to the consolidation of internal peace and the maintenance of a genuine and lasting atmosphere of national harmony.

"The Security Council invites the Secretary-General to keep it informed regarding the implementation of the parties' pending commitments and reiterates that it will continue to follow closely the evolution of the peace process in El Salvador and stands ready to assist the parties as appropriate to achieve the successful completion of that process."

Reports of the Secretary-General (May and October). In his 21 May 1993 report[22] on the activities of ONUSAL and developments in the overall implementation of the Peace Agreement (see below, under "UN Observer Mission in El Salvador"), the Secretary-General observed that the recommendations of the Commission on the Truth required a wide range of administrative, legislative and constitutional measures to be undertaken by: the Government; the Legislative Assembly, which would have to adopt new laws, amend existing ones and ratify constitutional amendments to allow implementation; FMLN; and certain individuals and institutions.

He reported that the Government and a number of institutions expressed serious reservations as to the applicability of some of the recommendations. President Cristiani, in a public statement and in a letter to the Secretary-General, stated his willingness to comply with those recommendations that fell within his competence, were consistent with the Salvadorian Constitution, were in harmony with the Peace Agreement and contributed to national reconciliation. At the same time, however, government spokesmen accused the Commission of exceeding its mandate, in particular of having assumed judicial functions. The FMLN Coordinator-General, Schafik Jorge Handal, accepted the recommendations in their entirety and would implement them provided the Government did likewise.

In the light of that reaction, the Secretary-General asked the United Nations to make a detailed analysis of the recommendations, examine whether any fell outside the Commission's mandate or was incompatible with the Constitution and identify what action was required by whom and within what time-frame. The resultant analysis, set out in an addendum to his report,[23] was conveyed on 20 May to the Government, FMLN and the Coordinator of the National Commission for the Consolidation of Peace (COPAZ),[9] with a request for information by 20 June on action taken or planned to implement the recommendations.

The analysis found that only one of the recommendations—that calling for the disqualification by law of specific persons from holding public office—could not be implemented, since it was at variance with fundamental provisions of the Constitution and in conflict with the recommendation on the ratification of international human rights instruments under which citizens could not be deprived of their political rights in the manner recommended by the Commission.

In a progress report of 14 October,[24] the Secretary-General outlined the positions of the Government, FMLN and COPAZ on the recommendations, following communication exchanges between them and the United Nations. For FMLN, while disqualification by law from holding office appeared impossible, it would be ready to accept a procedure of "self-disqualification" by the FMLN members named, provided the government officials and FAES officers named did likewise. COPAZ reported having taken specific action with respect to the recommendations for reforming the judicial system and FAES (revision of military legislation and curricula); on the issue of the relationship between FAES and paramilitary or illegal groups; and for ensuring the civilian character of PNC.

The Government confirmed on 13 July that it would be in a position to implement all of the recommendations, except for (a) those involving dismissal from the civil service and disqualification from holding public office; (b) those implying constitutional reforms; and (c) those which would have to be implemented by the judiciary through the Supreme Court of Justice. COPAZ seemed to indicate the existence of a consensus that the recommendations involving dismissals from civil service, including FAES, and disqualification from holding public office, should not be implemented—a position on which FMLN raised doubts. Since constitutional reform required ratification by two successive legislatures, it was imperative that action on the relevant recommendations be initiated during the current Legislative Assembly, otherwise the earliest time in which they could be implemented would be 1997. The Commission stressed that the Government's undertaking to implement its recommendations meant that it must take action to ensure that the recommendations to be implemented by the judiciary through the Supreme Court of Justice were put into practice by the appropriate State machinery.

Annexed to the progress report was an item-by-item description of the status of implementation of the recommendations. Under the item on the investigation of illegal groups, it was noted that recent cases of arbitrary executions had given ground for concern that such groups were operating, whose methods seemed to repeat behavioural patterns that had prevailed in the past.

Illegal armed groups

The Secretary-General informed the Security Council President on 3 November 1993[25] of the execution, death-squad style, of a leader of FMLN on 25 October, followed five days later by the murder of another leading member. He said the murders called for a vigorous investigation and confirmed the need for immediate implementation of the recommendation of the Commission on the Truth for a thorough investigation of private armed groups. Accordingly, he had asked the Director of the Human Rights Division of ONUSAL, with supplementary expert assistance, to work with those concerned to assist the Salvadorian Government in those investigations, in which the National Counsel for the Defence of Human Rights, created under the Peace Agreement, could also play an important role.

SECURITY COUNCIL ACTION (November)

In the light of the Secretary-General's letter, the Security Council met on 5 November. After consultations among Council members, the President made the following statement[26] on behalf of the Council:

Meeting number. SC 3306.

"The Security Council has learned with shock and concern of the violent deaths in recent days in El Salvador of two leaders and other members of the Frente Farabundo Martí para la Liberación Nacional (FMLN), as well as one member of the Alianza Republicana Nacionalista (ARENA) party. It notes, in this respect, that the Human Rights Division of the United Nations Observer Mission in El Salvador (ONUSAL) has referred in its last two reports to what appears to be a pattern of politically motivated murders, a development all the more serious in the light of the upcoming electoral process. The Council insists that this violence has to stop.

"The Security Council deems it essential that the authorities of El Salvador take all necessary measures so that those responsible for the killings be promptly brought to justice, with a view to preventing such events from occurring in the future. It welcomes the technical cooperation that Member States are extending to the competent Salvadorian authorities, at their

request, in order to assist them in the investigation of these criminal acts.

"The Security Council notes with particular concern that the Secretary-General, in his report on the implementation of the recommendations of the Commission on the Truth, underscored the significance of cases of killings over the past few months that seemed to follow patterns that could indicate a resurgence of illegal armed groups, whose activities had diminished following the signature of the peace accords in January 1992.

"In this regard, the Council takes note, with approval, of the Secretary-General's decision, as reported in his letter to the President of the Council, to direct the Human Rights Division of ONUSAL to work with the El Salvador Human Rights Prosecutor in order to assist the Government of El Salvador in implementing the recommendation of the Commission on the Truth that a thorough investigation of illegal armed groups be undertaken immediately.

"The Security Council further underlines the importance of full and timely implementation of all the provisions of the peace accords. It remains concerned about delays occurring in several instances, namely, the phasing out of the National Police and full deployment of the National Civil Police, the implementation of the recommendations of the Commission on the Truth and the transfer of lands and other reintegration programmes, which are essential for the development of a solid framework and a new climate for the respect of human rights in El Salvador.

"The Security Council also calls upon all parties to continue their efforts to make the March 1994 elections representative and successful. It recognizes the progress that has been made in registering thousands of voters but, taking into account the delays and problems reported by the Secretary-General, calls upon the Government and all concerned to ensure that all qualified voters who have applied will receive the necessary documents in time to vote. It welcomes the steps taken by the Secretary-General to assist in this process through the Electoral Division of ONUSAL.

"The Security Council welcomes the agreement reached between the Government and FMLN on the need to speed up the implementation of the provisions of the peace accords and, accordingly, urges all parties concerned to accelerate the fulfilment of their commitments under those accords before the electoral campaign gets under way. It expects ONUSAL to be allowed fully to carry out its verification mandate unimpeded. The Council will continue to follow developments in El Salvador with close attention."

Communications. The Secretary-General, in a follow-up letter of 7 December[27] to the Security Council President, stated that he had dispatched a mission headed by Under-Secretary-General Marrack Goulding to El Salvador, from 8 to 15 November, which negotiated an agreed set of principles for the establishment of a two-member Joint Group for the investigation of what could be politically motivated illegal armed groups. The principles, annexed to the letter, defined the Joint Group's membership, faculties (including organizing a technical team of Salvadorian and foreign investigators of renowned competence, impartiality and respect for human rights) and the impartial and non-political framework for the conduct of its functions.

The Joint Group was to be established on 8 December with a six-month mandate, at the end of which it would submit a public report to the President of El Salvador and to the United Nations Secretary-General. José Leandro Echevarría and Juan Jerónomo Castillo, two independent Salvadorian lawyers of long-standing prestige, were subsequently nominated, as prescribed, by the President, with the approval of the National Counsel for the Defence of Human Rights and the Director of the Human Rights Division of ONUSAL.

In stating its support for the agreed principles on 10 December,[28] the Security Council stressed the utmost importance of taking all measures to facilitate the task of the Joint Group and called for the full cooperation of all the parties.

FMLN armaments

Communications (January and June). On 29 January 1993,[29] the Secretary-General reported to the Security Council President on the status of the destruction of arms and equipment which, in accordance with the provisions of the Peace Agreement, FMLN had inventoried and collected at designated centres and placed under ONUSAL supervision. FMLN was to have completed their destruction on 15 December 1992, except for those categories of weapons which for technical reasons would take longer to destroy. Because of the Government's delay in complying with its own commitments under the Agreement, FMLN suspended the destruction process towards the end of December.

Following repeated ONUSAL requests and a warning that alternative ways to ensure compliance would have to be put into effect, FMLN resumed the process on 22 January 1993. Despite prior assurances, the agreed completion date of 29 January was not met. In his statement of 9 February,[14] the Council President expressed the Council's concern over FMLN's failure to comply fully with this particular undertaking.

In an unexpected development relating to FMLN armaments, the Secretary-General, on 8 June,[30] confirmed that, as Council members had been advised at informal consultations on 1 June, an explosion in an automobile repair shop at Managua, Nicaragua, on 23 May had led to the discovery of a cache of surface-to-air missiles, large quantities of ammunition, military weapons and plastic and other explosives. Also found were a number of documents, including over 300 passports of various nationalities. Evidence linked the

cache to Fuerzas Populares de Liberación (FPL), an FMLN constituent group, which promptly acknowledged responsibility for the existence of the cache, but denied any intention of reverting to the use of arms as an instrument of political pressure.

The Secretary-General's Special Representative in El Salvador and several ONUSAL members travelled to Managua to join an investigation launched by the Government of Nicaragua that uncovered the existence in the country of other clandestine deposits of weapons. ONUSAL specialists were working with a Nicaraguan team on the inventory and disposal of those weapons. FMLN was also cooperating in the search and destruction of other possible weapons caches. It moreover agreed to destroy its sophisticated weapons under ONUSAL custody on 4 June, previously to be destroyed at the end of that month, to coincide with the Salvadorian Government's compliance with recommendations relating to the post-conflict purification of FAES.

The Secretary-General stressed that the maintenance of clandestine arms deposits by FMLN and their exclusion from the final weapons inventory it had presented to ONUSAL raised serious questions of confidence and trust. He added that the peace process could be jeopardized if such damaging incidents as the one of 23 May should again occur.

SECURITY COUNCIL ACTION

On 11 June, after Security Council consultations on the incident, the President was authorized to make the following statement[31] on behalf of the Council:

Meeting number. SC 3236.

"The Security Council takes note with concern of the Secretary-General's letter of 8 June 1993 regarding the existence in Nicaragua of a weapons cache belonging to the Frente Farabundo Martí para la Liberación Nacional (FMLN), discovered on 23 May 1993.

"The Security Council considers that the maintenance of clandestine arms deposits is the most serious violation to date of the commitments assumed under the Peace Agreement signed at Mexico City on 16 January 1992 and agrees with the Secretary-General that this is a cause of serious concern.

"The Security Council reiterates its demand that the Peace Agreement be complied with fully and promptly. In this context, the Council again urges FMLN to comply fully with its obligation to provide a complete inventory of its arms and munitions both inside and outside El Salvador and surrender them in accordance with the provisions of the Peace Agreement, and to continue to cooperate in this regard with the United Nations Observer Mission in El Salvador (ONUSAL).

"The Security Council takes note with satisfaction of the cooperation of the Government of Nicaragua in itemizing and disposing of the war *matériel* found.

"The Security Council expects that the parties to the Peace Agreement will continue their efforts to complete the peace process and achieve national reconciliation in El Salvador."

Report of the Secretary-General (June). In a report of 29 June,[32] the Secretary-General brought the Security Council up to date on action taken in the aftermath of the Managua explosion, as described in communications annexed to the report.

He reminded the FMLN Coordinator-General on 12 June that FMLN had been legalized as a political party based on ONUSAL's confirmation that all items in the weapons inventory presented to it by FMLN had been accounted for and were being destroyed; therefore, the deliberate attempt to mislead him placed his credibility in doubt. The Coordinator-General responded on 16 June that, notwithstanding the existence of undeclared war *matériel*—held as a last negotiating card to guarantee peace and the conclusion of the agreements—FMLN had at no time considered resuming its armed struggle and reaffirmed its commitment to the peace process. FMLN had no armed groups under its command and was considering how best to collect the arms that might have been concealed.

The Coordinator-General transmitted an apology of 11 June from FPL, which explained that concealment of its arms stemmed from its profound distrust of FAES, exacerbated by the Government's delays and failure to meet its commitments under the peace accords. In line with FMLN's new status as a political party, FPL had decided to hand over all of its caches to the Nicaraguan Government and to ONUSAL and had taken steps to rid itself of all arms. Once the weapons in Nicaragua had been destroyed, it would notify ONUSAL of the location of its remaining caches in El Salvador.

Accordingly, FPL later reported to the Secretary-General's Special Representative that it had assigned a liaison officer to draw up with ONUSAL a plan for the location and destruction, by 4 August, of the remaining arms caches. On 19 June, the Coordinator-General pledged FMLN's cooperation with ONUSAL in the execution of the plan by that deadline. At the same time he expressed concern over the Government's delays and non-compliance with the accords, stressing the need for specific time-limits for the implementation of outstanding commitments, as well as for renewed direct communication between the Government and FMLN.

Meanwhile, the investigations in Nicaragua determined the existence of 16 "safe houses", including the site of the 23 May explosion, for the storage of arms and documents. Five contained some

1,240 rifles, 2,025 kilogrammes of explosives, 1.4 million rounds of ammunition, 1,300 mortar grenades, 3,970 assorted grenades, 350 rockets, 35,700 detonators, 42 machine-guns and 19 surface-to-air missiles. Two other FMLN constituent groups would be transferring their arms holdings to ONUSAL for destruction; a third had earlier handed over holdings of two to three tons. Nicaragua continued to inquire into the possible involvement of parties foreign to El Salvador.

President Cristiani, on 11 June, stated that FMLN's conduct, which he described as a violation not only of its commitments but also of the constitutional provision prohibiting the existence of armed groups, could be a reason to disband FMLN as a political party. He asked that the 1992 certification by ONUSAL of complete FMLN disarmament[13] be held in abeyance until FMLN had surrendered all its war-related *matériel*. He demanded that FMLN demobilize the armed groups constituted by its members or sympathizers, or declare the severance of its links with such groups. He was of the view that the gravity of the breach warranted a Council resolution.

The Secretary-General noted that the right of FMLN to retain its status as a political party in the circumstances had also been questioned in other quarters and its cancellation or suspension intimated. On 14 June, the Supreme Electoral Tribunal, which had granted that status, requested a full report from ONUSAL.

ONUSAL investigations into the possibility, advanced by FMLN, that some of its ex-combatants might belong to groups of delinquents, confirmed the existence of fully autonomous armed bands of from 20 to 50 members, composed of FMLN and FAES ex-combatants and civilians whose behaviour was criminal but non-political. ONUSAL found neither direct relationship between those bands and the recently discovered arms caches nor evidence of armed groups under FMLN command.

In the Secretary-General's view, the transformation of FMLN into a political party was at the core of the peace accords. Thus, cancellation or suspension of that status could jeopardize all that had been achieved. He said it was a credit to the parties that they did not allow the incident to derail the peace process.

Communications (June and July). Nicaragua, on 22 June,[33] informed the Secretary-General of the findings of its investigation, confirming that the arms found in 15 "safe houses" had been inventoried and promptly destroyed in collaboration with ONUSAL. In accordance with its security commitments under the 1987 Esquipulas II Agreement,[34] and the corresponding provisions of its Penal Code, Nicaragua had instituted criminal proceedings against the persons linked to the concealed weapons.

On 12 July,[35] the Security Council President, in taking note of the June report of the Secretary-General,[32] agreed with the assessment that cancellation or suspension of FMLN's status as a political party could deal a severe blow to the peace process. The President further welcomed Nicaragua's 22 June letter, saying he expected that country to comply with its international obligations to prevent the use of its territory for the illegal storage or transshipment of arms and other war *matériel* and to investigate fully all such deposits discovered in Nicaragua, including possible links to international terrorism.

Report of the Secretary-General (August). In a follow-up report of 30 August,[36] the Secretary-General stated that only 85 per cent of the recently discovered FMLN arms caches had been destroyed by the 4 August deadline. Apart from delays due to, among other causes, logistical and operational difficulties of dealing with the widely dispersed small caches in El Salvador, Honduras and Nicaragua and of coordinating with national authorities, a fifth FMLN group presented a new list of clandestine arms only the day preceding the deadline.

However, the overall process of verification and destruction of FMLN weapons and equipment as mandated by the Peace Agreement was finally completed on 18 August. The process involved two distinct phases. The first covered the period from the cease-fire on 1 February 1992 until the accidental explosion on 23 May 1993. Weapons verified and destroyed during that period included those that had been turned in at 15 ONUSAL verification centres in El Salvador by 15 December 1992 and those voluntarily declared later; those two groups represented about 70 per cent of the total FMLN arms verified.

During the second phase, from 23 May to 18 August, the weapons verified and destroyed were those discovered in the aftermath of the 23 May explosion and those declared by FMLN in compliance with its renewed commitment to disclose all of its remaining weapons, representing 20 per cent and 10 per cent of total holdings, respectively.

In sum, the weapons identified in the complete FMLN arms and munitions inventory included: 10,230 arms (9,851 individual and 379 support weapons); 4,032,606 rounds of ammunition, 140 rockets and 9,228 grenades; 5,107 kilogrammes of explosives; 63 pieces of communications equipment; and 74 surface-to-air missiles. The arms caches declared by the five FMLN constituent groups numbered 128, of which 109 were in El Salvador, 14 in Nicaragua and 5 in Honduras. In addition, FAES press bulletins throughout the war indicated the capture of more than 4,000 individual weapons (7,000 according to unofficial figures), 270 support weapons, some 4.5 million rounds of ammunition and 31 surface-to-air missiles.

The Secretary-General concluded that, by all available indications, FMLN's military structure had been effectively dismantled and its former combatants demobilized and reintegrated, within a framework of full legality, into the civil, institutional and political life of El Salvador. The apprehensions raised by the discovery of the large quantities of undeclared FMLN weapons appeared to have been surmounted. He added that, because of the irregular nature of the 12-year war and the sense of insecurity inherent to a post-war period, an unknown number of weapons and remnants of war-related *matériel* were likely to remain for some time in the hands of individuals or groups, including criminal ones. As FMLN announced, such cases should be dealt with according to the laws of the country in which they were found.

Electoral process

On 26 January 1993,[37] the Secretary-General informed the President of the Security Council of a formal request from the Government of El Salvador that the United Nations verify the general elections, scheduled for March 1994, and of his intention to recommend acceptance. The Council President welcomed that development in a 9 February statement.[14]

On the basis of the report of the Secretary-General below, the Council, by **resolution 832 (1993)**, enlarged the ONUSAL mandate to include the observation of the electoral process and asked him to take the necessary action to that effect.

Reports of the Secretary-General (May and October). In a 21 May report[22] on the activities of ONUSAL (see below, under "UN Observer Mission in El Salvador"), the Secretary-General stated that, as a follow-up to his recommendation that the request for United Nations observation of the electoral process be accepted, a technical mission visited El Salvador from 18 to 28 April in order to define the terms of reference, concept of operations and financial implications of expanding the ONUSAL mandate to include that function. As a result of its meetings with the Supreme Electoral Tribunal, COPAZ and the political parties, the mission identified several areas of concern and made recommendations for improvement.

The concerns revolved around serious inadequacies of the existing electoral roll and the obstacles to the timely issue of electoral documents. Foremost among them were: the inclusion of a large number of names belonging to expatriates or deceased persons and insufficient controls at the national level to prevent double registration, both of which could result in multiple voting; discrepancies between the names in the rolls and those on electoral cards, and/or holders of valid electoral cards whose names were not in the rolls; non-inclusion of about a third of the total number of

potential voters due to problems in the registration process; and the failure of the campaign
launched by the Supreme Electoral Tribunal to
produce significant results, although registration
requests more than tripled during the campaign.

The additional terms of reference of an expanded
ONUSAL would be to observe the electoral process
before, during and after the elections. Specifically,
it would verify that: measures taken by the electoral authorities were impartial and consistent with
free and fair elections; steps were taken to include
all qualified voters in the electoral roster; mechanisms to prevent multiple voting were set up; freedom
of expression, organization, movement and assembly
were respected; and voters were sufficiently informed
of the mechanisms for participating in the election.
ONUSAL would also examine, analyse and assess
any objections to the electoral process or attempts
to de-legitimize it and, as required, convey such
information to the Supreme Electoral Tribunal; inform the Tribunal of complaints of irregularities
in electoral advertising or of interference with the
electoral process; post observers at every polling site
on election day to ensure full respect for the right
to vote; and assist the Chief of Mission in preparing periodic reports to the Secretary-General, who
in turn would inform the Tribunal and report to
the Security Council.

The Secretary-General thus recommended that
an Electoral Division be established as part of
ONUSAL, to carry out its work in five stages. It
would devote the first stage (1-30 June) to organizational activities at the central and regional levels;
the second (1 July–15 December) to verifying voter
registration and monitoring political activities; the
third (16 December 1993–14 March 1994) to observing the electoral campaigns; and the fourth (15-31
March 1994) to observing the elections, vote counting
and announcement of results. If the first round did
not yield a definitive result, the Division would observe, during a fifth and final stage (1-30 April),
a second round of elections for the presidency.

An addendum to the report, dated 24 May,[38]
set out the personnel requirements for the additional responsibilities: 38 international staff, including administrative support staff, and 7 locally
recruited staff; and 900 electoral observers during
the polling, 320 from existing ONUSAL personnel,
330 from the United Nations Development Programme (UNDP), other United Nations agency
personnel in El Salvador and volunteers from
selected non-governmental organizations (NGOs),
and 250 from the United Nations Secretariat
and/or Member States. Also required were
premises, transport operations, communication
and miscellaneous equipment, supplies and services, and public information programmes. Additional costs involved were estimated at $7 million
for the 11-month period from 1 June 1993 to 30

April 1994, a breakdown of which was annexed to
the addendum. The additional costs would be considered an expense to the Organization, to be
borne by Member States in accordance with Article 17 of the Charter of the United Nations.

In the first of a series of periodic reports on the
activities of the Electoral Division of ONUSAL,
dated 20 October 1993,[39] the Secretary-General
confirmed that the institutional framework for the
electoral process had been established. The Supreme Electoral Tribunal had set up offices in all
of the country's departments and municipalities.
To supervise their work, a Board of Vigilance composed of representatives of all political parties was
established. In December,[40] departmental election boards were set up with authority to monitor
elections, report violations of electoral legislation,
deliver election material to municipal boards and
collect ballots. The board chairmen were elected
from four political parties, including FMLN.

As scheduled, four elections were to be held
simultaneously on 20 March 1994: presidential
elections, to be followed, if necessary, with a second round within the next 30 days; parliamentary
elections for 84 seats in the National Assembly,
based on proportional representation; municipal
elections in 262 mayoral districts on the basis of
a simple majority; and elections for 20 deputies
to the Central American Parliament,[3] treated as
a single national district and based on proportional
representation.

At reporting time, there were 12 competing political parties, including FMLN, and five presidential candidates. Access to the media, as regulated
by the Electoral Law, was available to all parties,
with space and time allocated according to Electoral Tribunal rules. Private communication enterprises were obliged to provide services to all parties on an equal basis.

Problems limiting voter registration persisted,
as illustrated by a joint ONUSAL/UNDP study,
which found that 27 per cent of Salvadorians of
voting age, or some 700,000 persons, had no electoral cards. This was due in large measure to deficiencies in the mechanism for issuing such cards.
In addition, Electoral Tribunal personnel were not
adequately trained, transport for the mobile registration teams was limited and public information
campaigns were marked by many shortcomings.

Between 1 July and 19 November, however,
registration requests reached 787,834, reflecting
a high degree of citizen mobilization. These were
requests for new registration (469,098), changes
(85,560) and reinstatement (229,800).

UN Observer Mission in El Salvador

The mandate of the United Nations Observer
Mission in El Salvador was extended twice in 1993:
on 27 May, when it was also enlarged, and on 30

November. The extensions, for periods ending, respectively, on 30 November 1993 and on 31 May 1994, were based on the Secretary-General's reports on all operational aspects of ONUSAL before the expiry of each mandate period.

Established by the Security Council in May 1991[41] to monitor all agreements concluded between the Government of El Salvador and FMLN, ONUSAL, in its initial phase as an integrated peace-keeping operation, was mandated to verify compliance by the parties with the 1990 San José Agreement on Human Rights.[42] As enlarged in 1992,[43] its mandate included verification and monitoring of the implementation of the 1992 Peace Agreement,[5] in particular the cessation of the armed conflict and the establishment of PNC; as enlarged in 1993, it included observance of the electoral process (see above).

Report of the Secretary-General (May). On 21 May 1993,[22] the Secretary-General submitted a report covering all aspects of ONUSAL operations. These included military and public security matters; human rights and the administration of justice; the report of the Commission on the Truth; economic and social matters, in particular the land-transfer programme; the status of FMLN as a political party; the restoration of public administration in the former zones of conflict; and the electoral system. In addition, the Secretary-General commented on the financial requirements of implementing the Salvadorian peace accords.

The Secretary-General described the status of the implementation of those provisions of the peace accords that were outstanding as at the formal end of the armed conflict in December 1992.[13] As verified by the Military Division of ONUSAL, the demobilization of FMLN combatants had been completed. FMLN resumed destruction of its existing weapons (65 per cent of inventory), finally destroying most of them—by 11 February those collected at designated points within El Salvador, and by 1 April those in deposits outside the country; the exceptions were those reported lost or stolen (3.5 per cent) and a small number of sophisticated weapons, whose destruction FMLN had scheduled to coincide with full government compliance with the recommendations of the Ad Hoc Commission on the Purification of the Armed Forces. FAES troop reduction had been accelerated and completed on 31 March 1993, instead of January 1994 as previously scheduled, with reductions reaching 54.4 per cent, rather than the planned 50.2 per cent. The new armed forces reserve system had been introduced and 14 recruitment and reserve centres had been set up. The recovery of weapons from private hands had failed to meet the latest deadline of 31 March, with only 40 per cent of inventory recovered and an even smaller percentage verified by ONUSAL.

The Police Division of ONUSAL continued to monitor and assist the National Police pending full deployment of the new PNC; to supervise and support the Auxiliary Transitory Police in maintaining public order and security in the former zones of conflict; to assist in locating illegal arms caches; and to support the Human Rights Division, conducting special inquiries when required.

By the end of the year, PNC candidates at the National Public Security Academy were expected to number 5,500 and graduates to number some 3,000. The 10 former Treasury Police and National Guardsmen transferred to the National Police and accepted as PNC candidates by the Academic Council in 1992,[44] in contravention of the Peace Agreement, remained the subject of ONUSAL discussions with the Government. After four months of training abroad, those candidates joined PNC as provisional commands. ONUSAL eventually recommended that their admission be treated as an exceptional circumstance to keep it from being regarded as constituting a precedent. Since January 1993, the monitoring of the Academy's functioning had been strengthened through the presence of an ONUSAL observer in the Academic Council. The gradual phasing out of the National Police, as stipulated by the Agreement, had not begun, despite the replacement of 3 out of 14 of its departments by PNC. Moreover, the National Police training school remained in existence, as did certain police structures, notably the Customs Police, whose continued existence was incompatible with the newly established PNC Finance Division. Although PNC was open to candidates from the National Police, ONUSAL, in monitoring the entrance examinations for the Academy, ascertained that included in the last examinations were a number of former members of the National Police who had left four to six years earlier—many for disciplinary reasons—but who rejoined once the Peace Agreement was signed.

The Human Rights Division continued to discharge its work in relation to the 1990 San José Agreement on Human Rights,[42] recording facts and assisting Salvadorians in the search for remedies to persistent human rights violations. It held discussions with the Government on its findings and proposals for implementing its recommendations. It actively supported the National Counsel for the Defence of Human Rights and strengthened its relations with relevant NGOs. In the context of the recommendation of the Commission on the Truth for the investigation of illegal armed groups (see above, under "Commission on the Truth"), the Division was to provide the list of cases of recent arbitrary executions requiring special investigation to the Minister of the Presidency, the Minister of Justice and the Criminal Investigation Commission.[24]

The work of the Human Rights Division was the subject of a separate series of reports. Those pertaining to the human rights situation in 1993 were issued as follows: one report (the sixth) covered the eight-month period from 1 July 1992 to 31 January 1993;[45] the following three reports (the seventh, eighth and ninth) covered the periods 1 February to 30 April,[46] 1 May to 31 July,[47] and 1 August to 31 October[48] (see also PART THREE, Chapter X). The eighth report noted definite improvements but also serious violations, especially of the right to life, and that politically motivated human rights violations had become more open and rendered more serious in the light of the forthcoming electoral process.

With respect to social and economic issues, the Secretary-General noted that implementation of the land-transfer programme was slow and fraught with problems. Under the programme, up to 237,000 mz (manzana: 1 mz = 0.7 hectare) were to be transferred in three phases to a maximum of 47,500 people, including ex-combatants of both sides and landholders (people who had occupied land without title during the conflict). The land-transfer proposal, made by the Secretary-General and accepted separately by the Government and FMLN in 1992,[49] was set out in detail in an addendum to the current report.[50] It was a supplement to the Peace Agreement and deemed an integral part of it.

During the first phase, scheduled from October 1992 to January 1993, 15,400 people were to receive 77,000 mz, with priority to demobilized FMLN combatants, who would be given all available land not legally transferred to landholders. By the reporting date, some 45,000 mz (made up of 36 State and 196 private properties) had been acquired and earmarked for 10,000 FMLN ex-combatants and landholders; issuance of most of the titles were awaiting completion of legal formalities. The second phase started in February when EC funds became available for the purchase of 20,000 mz for 4,000 recipients. EC required that FMLN and FAES equally benefit from its assistance. Thus far, 11 properties totalling 1,400 mz had been registered and transferred to over 600 FAES ex-combatants. The third phase would parcel out 140,500 mz to some 28,100 recipients, for which neither the land nor the estimated $85 million required was currently available.

The programme suffered a number of delays that had generated tension. This was true in the case of loans for agricultural activities. The Government had agreed to grant credit to landholders who had negotiated acquisition of land they occupied, but not to about 80 per cent of those who had not. In addition, original contracts for land legalization did not conform to the accords and had to be changed. The number of land-

holders was likely to be significantly higher than the ceiling of 25,000 stipulated in the Agreement. Besides rejecting some of the plots identified as not meeting expectations, FMLN had had difficulty submitting the names and identification numbers of designated recipients; thus, after six months into the programme, lists had yet to be presented for 97 of the 196 properties already negotiated for.

Under existing laws, moreover, land transfer through the Lands Bank involved 17 stages of time-consuming steps. The Government was endeavouring to accelerate the process in cooperation with ONUSAL and FMLN, and with the United States Agency for International Development and EC (the donors). Despite several ONUSAL requests, the Government had not provided information relating to FAES, in particular on its negotiations with the Lands Bank. Consequently, ONUSAL had been unable either to verify beneficiary lists or to observe the negotiations in the buying and selling of land and in the determination of the number of beneficiaries, as it had done in the case of FMLN.

The Secretary-General noted with concern the relocation, by the Government and FMLN, of landholders occupying land whose rightful owners were not willing to sell. This was contrary to the 1992 agreed land-transfer proposal, which provided that such landholders would be relocated last, based on the Peace Agreement's stipulation that combatants of either side were to have priority and be given land as they demobilized, from which they were not to be evicted until a solution was found to relocate them. However, pressures were brought to bear on the Government by landowners wanting to repossess their land and on FMLN by those occupying land not available for purchase, as that precluded their access to credit for housing and agricultural production. Moreover, some FMLN ex-combatants had been unwilling to accept State lands offered by the Government in the expectation of getting private land closer to where their families lived.

On 22 February, government, business and labour representatives signed a landmark agreement at the Forum for Economic and Social Consultation, recognizing for the first time the right of labour to associate and establishing the principle of a tripartite mechanism for dealing with labour conflicts. On 14 April, the Forum created a commission to examine 29 International Labour Organisation conventions proposed by labour for ratification.

Under the National Reconstruction Plan, government programmes for the reintegration of some 11,000 FMLN ex-combatants, including the war-disabled, were under way. A UNDP-coordinated agricultural training programme and the distribution of agricultural tools and household goods were completed by the end of April. The programme for industrial and services training was expected to continue up to August. As to credit for small business ventures and agricultural activities, the Government and FMLN set the interest rate at 14 per cent. Programmes for the war-disabled had met with difficulties stemming from the failure of both sides to agree on provisions for long-term rehabilitation. The functioning of the Fund for the Protection of the Wounded and War-disabled, created by Decree No. 416 of 13 December 1992, was dependent on the Government's making its initial financial contribution on 22 June. EC would contribute some $46,000 upon registration of the Fund's potential beneficiaries.

ONUSAL had had no access to the implementation of programmes for FAES reintegration, including the payment of compensation to demobilized troops. On 4 February, agreement was reached on a reintegration programme for former FMLN officers and medium-rank commanders, covering a maximum of 600 and providing for training, subsistence allowance, credit for production ventures and housing. UNDP began to administer the training and technical assistance part of the programme in April, to be completed by June.

FMLN had begun reorganizing according to its full legal status as a political party, granted by the Supreme Electoral Tribunal of El Salvador in 1992.[(13)] It had replaced its five-member General Command with a 15-member national committee, appointed a Coordinator-General with authority to represent the party, set up offices in municipalities throughout El Salvador and held meetings for the recruitment of new membership. Draft legislation providing security for its leadership had been approved by COPAZ and was before the Legislative Assembly for consideration. The Government, by making available four radio frequencies (one AM and three FM), had partially implemented its agreement of 1992 to assign a series of radio and television frequencies by 15 January 1993.

Of special significance was the fact that public administration in the former zones of conflict had been fully restored. Most of the mayors and judges had returned to their jurisdictions. By mid-April, the mayors had organized town meetings for the purpose of identifying community reconstruction projects.

The groundwork had been laid for expanding the ONUSAL mandate to include the observation of the electoral process, for which the Secretary-General recommended that an Electoral Division be established as part of ONUSAL (see above, under "Electoral process").

The long-delayed implementation of the recommendations of the Ad Hoc Commission on the Purification of the Armed Forces was on its way to completion (see above, under "Ad Hoc Commission on the Purification of FAES"), but the recommendations of the Commission on the Truth remained outstanding (see above, under "Commission on the Truth"). The release of the Commission report was shortly followed by a general amnesty, approved by simple majority in the Legislative Assembly. The Secretary-General expressed concern at the haste of that step, stating it would have been preferable if the amnesty had been promulgated by a broad degree of national consensus.

The successful conclusion of the Salvadorian peace process, the Secretary-General stressed, could be achieved only if the necessary financing was forthcoming. He further stressed that, while urgent response was required from the international donor community and the Government, it was the Government's responsibility to define fiscal policies and set public expenditure priorities to enable it to fulfil its commitment to implement the Peace Agreement fully.

In the light of the foregoing, the Secretary-General recommended to the Security Council that it renew the mandate of ONUSAL until 30 November 1993 and that it authorize the addition to it of an Electoral Division to observe the 1994 elections.

SECURITY COUNCIL ACTION

The Security Council met on 27 May to consider the Secretary-General's report, together with its addenda, following which it unanimously adopted **resolution 832(1993)**.

The Security Council,
Recalling its resolution 637(1989) of 27 July 1989,
Recalling also its resolutions 693(1991) of 20 May 1991, 714(1991) of 30 September 1991, 729(1992) of 14 January 1992, 784(1992) of 30 October 1992 and 791(1992) of 30 November 1992,
Having studied the report of the Secretary-General,
Noting with appreciation the continuing efforts of the Secretary-General to support the full implementation of the agreements signed by the Government of El Salvador and the Frente Farabundo Martí para la Liberación Nacional to re-establish peace and promote reconciliation in El Salvador,
Welcoming the observation by the Secretary-General that sixteen months after the cease-fire the peace process in El Salvador has advanced significantly and is on course, and that significant progress has also been made towards other principal objectives of the Peace Agreement,
Emphasizing that determined efforts are required of both parties to ensure that the remaining problems do not become obstacles to the continuing fulfilment of their undertakings,
Noting that the Government of El Salvador has requested the United Nations to verify the next general elections scheduled to be held in March 1994 and that

the Secretary-General has recommended that this request be accepted,

Stressing the necessity, in this as in other peace-keeping operations, to continue to monitor expenditures carefully during this period of increasing demands on peace-keeping resources,

1. *Approves* the report of the Secretary-General;

2. *Welcomes* the continuing adaptation by the Secretary-General of the activities and strength of the United Nations Observer Mission in El Salvador, taking into account progress made in implementing the peace process;

3. *Decides*, on the basis of the Secretary-General's report and in accordance with the provisions of resolution 693(1991), to enlarge the mandate of the United Nations Observer Mission in El Salvador, to include the observation of the electoral process due to conclude with the general elections in El Salvador in March 1994, and requests the Secretary-General to take the necessary measures to this effect;

4. *Also decides* that the mandate of the Observer Mission, enlarged in accordance with this resolution, will be extended until 30 November 1993 and that it will be reviewed at that time on the basis of recommendations to be presented by the Secretary-General;

5. *Endorses* the view of the Secretary-General, contained in his letter of 26 January 1993 to the President of the Security Council, that the general elections of March 1994 should constitute the logical culmination of the entire peace process in El Salvador;

6. *Urges* the Government of El Salvador and the Frente Farabundo Martí para la Liberación Nacional to respect and implement fully all the commitments they assumed under the Peace Agreement, including, *inter alia*, those related to the transfer of lands, the reinsertion into civilian society of ex-combatants and war-wounded, the deployment of the National Civil Police and the phasing out of the National Police, and the recommendations of the Ad Hoc Commission on the Purification of the Armed Forces and the Commission on the Truth;

7. *Reaffirms its support* for the Secretary-General's use of his good offices in the El Salvador peace process;

8. *Calls upon* both parties to cooperate fully with the Secretary-General's Special Representative and the United Nations Observer Mission in El Salvador in their task of assisting and verifying the parties' implementation of their commitments and requests the parties to continue to exercise utmost moderation and restraint, especially in the former zones of conflict, in order to promote the process of national reconciliation;

9. *Urges* all States, as well as the international institutions in the fields of development and finance, to contribute generously in support of the execution of the Peace Agreement and the consolidation of peace in El Salvador;

10. *Requests* the Secretary-General to keep the Security Council fully informed of further developments in the El Salvador peace process and to report on the operations of the United Nations Observer Mission in El Salvador, at the latest before the expiry of the new mandate period;

11. *Decides* to remain seized of the matter.

Security Council resolution 832(1993)

27 May 1993   Meeting 3223   Adopted unanimously

Draft prepared in consultations among Council members (S/25851).

Report of the Secretary-General (November). On 23 November 1993,[51] the Secretary-General submitted a second report describing the overall activities of ONUSAL during the period 22 May to 20 November. According to the report, ONUSAL held a series of meetings separately with the Government and FMLN in late August, in an effort to find ways of tackling the serious delays hindering the full implementation of the key aspects of the 1992 Peace Agreement. At their meeting with ONUSAL on 8 September, the parties agreed "to sweep the table clean" of all outstanding commitments before the start of the electoral campaign on 20 November.

During the reporting period, ONUSAL's Military Division was concerned mainly with activities resulting from the 23 May explosion at Managua of an arsenal belonging to an FMLN constituent group that led to the declaration of the existence of 128 widely dispersed FMLN arms caches: 109 in El Salvador, 14 in Nicaragua and 5 in Honduras (see above, under "FMLN armaments"). ONUSAL, in cooperation with FMLN and the national authorities involved, completed verification and destruction of the caches in August.

Development of plans to reduce the officer strength of FAES was in progress. However, the reintegration programmes, notably land transfer and training, for FAES and FMLN troops already demobilized had been so delayed that only a small percentage had benefited. Payment to them of one year's wages in compensation, as stipulated by the Agreement, had not begun. The new State Intelligence Agency had been created, but it was not clear that the conduct of intelligence activities fully complied with the doctrinal principles set forth in the Agreement and with the reformed Constitution. The Government had yet to clarify the ultimate disposition of the files on individuals maintained by the disbanded National Intelligence Department; instead of being destroyed or transferred to the new Agency, those files were currently with the FAES Joint Chiefs of Staff.

The recovery of privately held arms could not be fully implemented until two laws governing the use of arms by individuals and by security institutions were enacted; one draft law was near enactment but the other had to be submitted to the Legislative Assembly. Despite contractual difficulties, the mine-clearance programme, coordinated by the Military Division and covering 425 minefields, was expected to be completed by the end of the year.

A number of unresolved problems related to the police and public security provisions of the Agreement and complementary accords, notably, the fulfilment of entrance requirements to the National Public Security Academy, which was open to candidates as follows: 20 per cent from FMLN,

20 per cent from the National Police and 60 per cent from civilians who did not take part in the armed conflict. To verify that former members of the National Guard and Treasury Police (former public security bodies) and the elite battalions (immediate reaction infantry battalions) had not also been admitted as civilians, ONUSAL asked the Government for personnel lists of those entities prior to their dissolution and demobilization. It further asked for documentation to verify fulfilment of the special entrance requirements and functional limitations applicable to former members of the Criminal Investigation Commission and Special Antinarcotics Unit who were being considered for PNC, or had already been admitted to it. As to the ongoing use of FAES for public security duties, the Government had not yet reported to the Legislative Assembly that the exceptional circumstances permitting such use existed.

ONUSAL continued to press the Government to accelerate the phasing out of the National Police in line with the rate of PNC deployment. The two-stage plan recently presented would extend the process from October 1993 to October 1994.

Regarding economic and social matters, the land-transfer programme continued to suffer delays from technical, financial and legal difficulties. Chief among these was the inability of FMLN to satisfy the Government's requirement that all beneficiaries on its lists be verified. None the less, at the Secretary-General's behest, the Government agreed on 17 November to accept the FMLN lists for 120 private properties and 50 State properties already negotiated for, giving 12,000 beneficiaries access to credit for agricultural production by year's end. In addition, a German-financed project for the construction of 2,000 houses for FMLN ex-combatants was inaugurated in eight departments at the end of October.

Discussions in the Forum for Economic and Social Consultation resulted in the lifting of restrictions on unionization of rural workers. To institutionalize consultation on labour issues, the Government, business and labour agreed to the creation of a Labour Council within the Ministry of Labour.

In keeping with its new status as a political party, FMLN held a national convention on 5 September to choose its candidates for the 1994 elections. Besides the previously assigned AM and FM radio frequencies, the Government additionally assigned for FMLN use one short-wave and two television frequencies and exempted from tax all vehicles imported for the use of its leadership. Under a law of 17 June providing protection to individuals subject to special security, FMLN bodyguards were incorporated into PNC as supernumeraries.

The first stage of the electoral process was completed. The second was still in progress; by 19 November, the Supreme Electoral Tribunal had received 787,834 registration forms, and the following day the campaign began.

It was of great concern to the Secretary-General that the campaign should have begun when key elements of the accords remained only partially implemented and when there were signs that some ugly features of El Salvador's past had reappeared, such as the possible re-emergence of death squads noted by the Human Rights Division reports and the October murders of two FMLN leaders. He said ONUSAL reports on public security matters gave the impression of a lack of commitment, at some levels of Government, to the objective of the Peace Agreement, as reflected in the denial to PNC of the necessary logistical and technical resources, the incorporation into it of military personnel, the prolongation of the existence of the National Police, and the denial to ONUSAL of information it required for verification purposes. Severe delays in implementing the reintegration programmes for ex-combatants had given rise to tension that could become a source of instability.

The Secretary-General thus called for more financing, technical assistance and political will from the parties. In addition, he had asked his Special Representative to obtain the Government's and FMLN's agreement to a new timetable setting the firmest possible dates for completing implementation of the most important outstanding points in the Peace Agreement. In this connection, a significant step was taken on 5 November when, in response to the Special Representative's initiative, six of the seven presidential candidates signed a statement solemnly committing themselves to maintain the constructive evolution of the peace process and to implement all the obligations contained in the Peace Agreement, and rejecting any politically motivated violence or intimidation.

In view of the clear necessity for ONUSAL to continue to carry out its verification and good-offices functions through the forthcoming elections and inauguration of the newly elected President on 1 June 1994, the Secretary-General recommended that the Security Council extend ONUSAL's mandate for a further period of six months, until 31 May 1994.

SECURITY COUNCIL ACTION

The Security Council, having considered the Secretary-General's report, unanimously adopted **resolution 888(1993)** on 30 November.

The Security Council,
Recalling its resolution 637(1989) of 27 July 1989,
Recalling also its resolutions 693(1991) of 20 May 1991, 714(1991) of 30 September 1991, 729(1992) of 14 January 1992, 784(1992) of 30 October 1992, 791(1992) of 30 November 1992 and 832(1993) of 27 May 1993,

Recalling also its presidential statements of 18 March 1993, 11 June 1993 and 5 November 1993,

Having studied the report of the Secretary-General of 23 November 1993,

Noting with appreciation the continuing efforts of the Secretary-General to support the full and timely implementation of the agreements signed by the Government of El Salvador and the Frente Farabundo Martí para la Liberación Nacional to maintain and consolidate peace and promote reconciliation in El Salvador,

Welcoming the Secretary-General's observation that the peace process in El Salvador has advanced, and that significant progress has been made towards other objectives of the Peace Agreement,

Concerned at the continuing problems and delays in implementing several important components of the Peace Agreement, including *inter alia* those related to the transfer of lands, the reintegration into civilian society of ex-combatants and war-disabled, the deployment of the National Civil Police and the phasing out of the National Police, and the recommendations of the Commission on the Truth,

Noting with concern the recent acts of violence in El Salvador, which may indicate renewed activity by illegal armed groups, and could, if unchecked, negatively affect the peace process in El Salvador including the elections scheduled for March 1994,

Welcoming in this regard the efforts of the Secretary-General in cooperation with the Government of El Salvador towards the establishment of a mechanism to investigate illegal armed groups and their possible connection with renewed political violence,

Noting also with concern the seemingly politically motivated murders of members of the different political parties, including the Frente Farabundo Martí para la Liberación Nacional and the Alianza Republicana Nacionalista,

Noting that El Salvador has entered a critical phase in the peace process and that political parties have just begun a campaign for the elections to be held in March 1994, which should take place in a peaceful environment,

Stressing the importance of free and fair elections as an essential element of the entire peace process in El Salvador,

Noting recent progress in voter registration and stressing the importance that all registered voters be issued relevant credentials so as to enable broad participation in the elections,

Welcoming the commitment of the presidential candidates to peace and stability in El Salvador of 5 November 1993, as referred to in paragraph 92 of the report of the Secretary-General,

Welcoming also the recent announcement by the Government of El Salvador to expedite the implementation of the land-transfer programme,

Welcoming also the work of the United Nations Observer Mission in El Salvador (ONUSAL) and noting its vital importance to the entire peace and reconciliation process in El Salvador,

Reiterating the necessity, in this as in all peace-keeping operations, to continue to monitor expenditures carefully during this period of increasing demands on peace-keeping resources,

1. *Welcomes* the report of the Secretary-General of 23 November 1993;

2. *Condemns* recent acts of violence in El Salvador;

3. *Expresses concern* that important elements of the Peace Agreement remain only partially implemented;

4. *Urges* the Government of El Salvador and the Frente Farabundo Martí para la Liberación Nacional to make determined efforts to prevent political violence and accelerate compliance with their commitments under the Peace Accords;

5. *Reaffirms* its support for the Secretary-General's use of his good offices in the El Salvador peace process;

6. *Reaffirms also* its support, in this context, for the efforts of the Secretary-General, in cooperation with the Government of El Salvador, aimed at the immediate launching of an impartial, independent and credible investigation into illegal armed groups, and urges all sectors of society in El Salvador to cooperate in such an investigation;

7. *Calls upon* all parties concerned to cooperate fully with the Secretary-General's Special Representative and ONUSAL in their task of verifying the parties' implementation of their commitments and urges them to complete such implementation within the framework of the agreed calendar and the new timetable proposed by ONUSAL;

8. *Stresses* the need to ensure that the police and public security provisions of the Peace Agreement are scrupulously observed, with full ONUSAL verification, and that necessary steps are taken to complete the recovery of all weapons held by private individuals, in contravention of the Peace Agreement;

9. *Urges* the Government of El Salvador and the Frente Farabundo Martí para la Liberación Nacional to remove all obstacles facing implementation of the land-transfer programme and stresses the need to accelerate reintegration programmes for ex-combatants of both sides in conformity with the Peace Agreement;

10. *Reaffirms* the need for full and timely implementation of the recommendations of the Commission on the Truth;

11. *Calls upon* the relevant authorities in El Salvador to take all necessary measures to ensure that the elections to be held in March 1994 be free and fair and requests the Secretary-General to continue to provide assistance in this regard;

12. *Urges* all States, as well as the international institutions engaged in the fields of development and finance, to contribute promptly and generously in support of the implementation of all aspects of the Peace Agreement;

13. *Decides* to extend the mandate of ONUSAL until 31 May 1994;

14. *Requests* the Secretary-General to keep the Security Council fully informed of further developments in the El Salvador peace process;

15. *Requests* the Secretary-General to report by 1 May 1994 on the operations of ONUSAL so that the Council may review the Mission's size and scope for the period after 31 May 1994, taking into account the Secretary-General's relevant recommendations for the fulfilment and completion of its mandate;

16. *Decides* to remain seized of the matter.

Security Council resolution 888(1993)

30 November 1993   Meeting 3321   Adopted unanimously

Draft prepared in consultations among Council members (S/26820).

Composition

In 1993, the Secretary-General appointed Augusto Ramírez-Ocampo as his Special Representative and ONUSAL's Chief of Mission with effect from 1 April,[52] succeeding Iqbal Riza, who had served in that capacity until 6 March. That decision was conveyed to the Security Council President on 18 March, which the Council welcomed four days later.[53] Brigadier-General Victor Suanzes Pardo, Chief of the Military Division, served as Interim Chief of Mission until the arrival of the new Special Representative on 14 April.[22].

The Military Division, composed of 74 military observers in May,[22] began to be phased out on 1 June, the same date on which the Electoral Division started to be phased in. By 1 November, the strength of ONUSAL stood at 31 military observers, contributed by Brazil, Canada, Colombia, Ecuador, India, Ireland, Spain, Sweden and Venezuela. There were also seven medical officers from Argentina.[51] The reduced Division was restructured and redeployed in two regional offices in the eastern and western parts of El Salvador, from which they patrolled the former zones of conflict.

Also by 1 November, ONUSAL had 277 police observers contributed by Austria, Brazil, Chile, Colombia, France, Guyana, Italy, Mexico, Norway, Spain and Sweden; 19 of them were seconded to the Human Rights Division.

Financing

On 2 March 1993,[54] the Advisory Committee on Administrative and Budgetary Questions (ACABQ) considered the Secretary-General's 1992 report[13] on the financing of ONUSAL from 1 December 1992 to 31 May 1993, as well as on the budget performance for the preceding periods from 1 January to 31 October and from 1 to 30 November 1992. The General Assembly had decided in 1992 on measures for the continued maintenance of ONUSAL until 28 February 1993,[55] pending ACABQ's consideration of that report.

Representatives of the Secretary-General updated the information to 31 December 1992, as follows: the outstanding assessments for ONUSAL amounted to $11,593,125; with the merger of the special accounts for the United Nations Observer Group in Central America (ONUCA) and ONUSAL, the ONUCA/ONUSAL Special Account showed a combined miscellaneous and interest income of $4,591,654, recommended for retention, and a net operating deficit of $6,736,160, reduced to $2,146,153 as at 31 January 1993.

ONUSAL expenditures from 1 January to 30 November 1992, as at 31 December 1992, amounted to $36,408,900 gross ($34,589,800 net), against an apportionment of $39 million gross ($37 million net), resulting in savings of $2,591,100 gross ($2,410,200 net). As to expenditures for the period 1 December 1992 to 31 May 1993, estimates were reduced to $18.1 million gross ($16.7 million net),

due to downward adjustments for major expenditures, including reductions of military personnel and delays in the recruitment of civilian police. Owing to possible additional reductions in respect of other items of expenditure that the Secretary-General was asked to review (subsistence allowance, salaries and staff costs, the number of administrative staff and the grades of senior staff, consultant fees, premises and accommodation), ACABQ recommended that the Assembly appropriate $17.2 million gross ($16 million net) for ONUSAL for the period 1 December 1992 to 31 May 1993.

ACABQ saw no need to retain the $4.6 million in the ONUCA/ONUSAL Special Account and recommended that the amount be credited to Member States against assessments for ONUSAL. Since the $8,045,600 gross ($7,514,200 net) authorized for commitment and apportioned by the Assembly in 1992 for the period ending 28 February 1993 had already been fully assessed, what remained to be assessed on Member States for the current mandate period, after crediting the combined income, was $4.6 million gross ($3.9 million net).

As to the period after 31 May 1993, ACABQ recommended that the Secretary-General be given commitment authority in the amount of $2.9 million gross ($2.7 million net) per month for the period of the extension, with prior ACABQ concurrence. Should ONUSAL's mandate be extended, ACABQ asked the Secretary-General to submit cost estimates for the extension period, together with a detailed performance report for the current mandate period, not later than 1 July.

GENERAL ASSEMBLY ACTION (March)

Acting on the recommendation of the Fifth (Administrative and Budgetary) Committee, the General Assembly adopted **resolution 47/223** without vote on 16 March 1993.

Financing of the United Nations Observer Group in Central America and the United Nations Observer Mission in El Salvador

The General Assembly,

Having considered the reports of the Secretary-General on the financing of the United Nations Observer Group in Central America and the United Nations Observer Mission in El Salvador, as well as the related report of the Advisory Committee on Administrative and Budgetary Questions,

Bearing in mind Security Council resolution 644(1989) of 7 November 1989, by which the Council established the United Nations Observer Group in Central America, and Council resolution 730(1992) of 16 January 1992, by which the Council terminated the mandate of the Group,

Bearing in mind also Security Council resolution 693(1991) of 20 May 1991, by which the Council established the United Nations Observer Mission in El Salvador, and Council resolution 729(1992) of 14 January 1992, by which the Council decided to extend and enlarge the mandate of the Mission, as well as the subsequent resolutions by which the Council extended the mandate of the Mission, the latest of which was resolution 791(1992) of 30 November 1992,

Recalling its resolution 46/240 of 22 May 1992, wherein it decided, in principle, that the special accounts for the United Nations Observer Group in Central America and the United Nations Observer Mission in El Salvador should be merged,

Noting the current status of the combined Special Account for the United Nations Observer Group in Central America and the United Nations Observer Mission in El Salvador,

Reaffirming that the costs of the United Nations Observer Mission in El Salvador are expenses of the Organization to be borne by Member States in accordance with Article 17, paragraph 2, of the Charter of the United Nations,

Reaffirming also that, in order to meet the expenditures caused by the United Nations Observer Mission in El Salvador, a different procedure is required from the one applied to meet expenditures of the regular budget of the United Nations,

Taking into account the fact that the economically more developed countries are in a position to make relatively larger contributions and that the economically less developed countries have a relatively limited capacity to contribute towards such an operation,

Bearing in mind the special responsibilities of the States permanent members of the Security Council, as indicated in General Assembly resolution 1874(S-IV) of 27 June 1963, in the financing of such operations,

Mindful of the fact that it is essential to provide the United Nations Observer Mission in El Salvador with the necessary financial resources to enable it to fulfil its responsibilities under the relevant resolutions of the Security Council,

1. *Takes note* of the observations and recommendations contained in the report of the Advisory Committee on Administrative and Budgetary Questions;

2. *Endorses* the observations and recommendations contained in the report of the Advisory Committee regarding economy measures, and urges the Secretary-General to implement them immediately;

3. *Takes note* of the outstanding assessments and the net operating deficit of the combined Special Account for the United Nations Observer Group in Central America and the United Nations Observer Mission in El Salvador;

4. *Urges* all Member States to expedite payments of their assessed contributions to the Special Account in full and on time;

5. *Decides*, at this stage, to appropriate to the Special Account, in accordance with the recommendation contained in paragraph 29 of the report of the Advisory Committee, for the operation of the United Nations Observer Mission in El Salvador for the period from 1 December 1992 to 31 May 1993, an amount of 17.2 million United States dollars gross (16 million dollars net), inclusive of the amount of 8,045,600 dollars gross (7,514,200 dollars net) authorized and apportioned in accordance with its decision 47/452 of 22 December 1992;

6. *Decides also*, as an ad hoc arrangement, to apportion the remaining amount of 9,154,400 dollars gross (8,485,800 dollars net) for the period from 1 December 1992 to 31 May 1993 among Member States in accordance with the composition of the groups set out in paragraphs 3 and 4 of General Assembly resolution 43/232 of 1 March 1989, as adjusted by the Assembly in its resolutions 44/192 B of 21 December 1989, 45/269 of 27 August 1991, 46/198 A of 20 December 1991 and 47/218 of 23 December 1992, and taking into account the scale of assessments for the years 1992, 1993 and 1994;

7. *Decides further* that, in accordance with the provisions of its resolution 973(X) of 15 December 1955, there shall be set off against the apportionment among Member States, as provided for in paragraph 6 above, their respective share in the Tax Equalization Fund of the remaining estimated staff assessment income of 668,600 dollars for the period from 1 December 1992 to 31 May 1993 approved for the United Nations Observer Mission in El Salvador;

8. *Decides* that there shall be set off against the apportionment among Member States, as provided for in paragraph 6 above, their respective share in the combined miscellaneous and interest income of 4.6 million dollars in the Special Account for the period from 1 December 1992 to 31 May 1993;

9. *Decides also* that the remaining unencumbered balance of the United Nations Observer Group in Central America shall be credited to Member States against their assessed contributions for the next mandate period of the United Nations Observer Mission in El Salvador, should the Security Council decide to renew the mandate of the Mission beyond 31 May 1993, or shall be made available to be set off against the assessed contributions of Member States for other United Nations peace-keeping operations, in accordance with the Financial Regulations and Rules of the United Nations, in the event that the Council decides not to renew the mandate of the Mission beyond 31 May 1993;

10. *Authorizes* the Secretary-General to enter into commitments for the operation of the United Nations Observer Mission in El Salvador at a rate not to exceed 2.9 million dollars gross (2.7 million dollars net) per month for the period beginning 1 June 1993, should the Security Council decide to continue the Mission beyond 31 May 1993, subject to obtaining the prior concurrence of the Advisory Committee for the actual level of commitments to be entered into for the period beyond 31 May 1993, the said amount to be apportioned among Member States in accordance with the scheme set out in the present resolution;

11. *Decides* to establish the contributions of the Czech Republic and Slovakia to the United Nations Observer Mission in El Salvador in accordance with the rates of assessment to be adopted by the General Assembly for these Member States at its forty-eighth session;

12. *Invites* the new Member States mentioned in paragraph 11 above to make advance payments against their assessed contributions, to be determined;

13. *Invites* voluntary contributions to the United Nations Observer Mission in El Salvador in cash and in the form of services and supplies acceptable to the Secretary-General, to be administered, as appropriate, in accordance with the procedure established by the General Assembly in its resolutions 43/230 of 21 December 1988, 44/192 A of 21 December 1989 and 45/258 of 3 May 1991;

14. *Requests* the Secretary-General to take all necessary action to ensure that all United Nations activities related to the United Nations Observer Mission in El Salvador are administered with a maximum of efficiency and economy and in accordance with the relevant mandate, and to include information on the arrangements in this regard in his report on the financial performance of the Mission;

15. *Decides* that future reports on the status of contributions and financial statements prepared by the Secretariat shall provide combined information for the United Nations Observer Group in Central America and the United Nations Observer Mission in El Salvador;

16. *Decides also* to include in the provisional agenda of its forty-eighth session the item entitled "Financing of the United Nations Observer Mission in El Salvador".

General Assembly resolution 47/223

16 March 1993   Meeting 97   Adopted without vote

Approved by Fifth Committee (A/47/797/Add.1) without vote, 12 March (meeting 56); draft by Chairman following informal consultations (A/C.5/47/L.33); agenda items 119 & 122.
Meeting numbers. GA 47th session: 5th Committee 55, 56; plenary 97.

Reports of the Secretary-General and ACABQ (July). By a report of 8 July 1993,[56] the Secretary-General set out the costs of operating ONUSAL in the light of the enlargement and extension of its mandate from 1 June to 30 November 1993, as well as of his request for a further mandate renewal from 1 December 1993 up to 30 April 1994, to enable ONUSAL to complete the verification of the Salvadorian elections and for a transition period immediately thereafter.

For the current mandate period from 1 June to 30 November, the total cost of ONUSAL was estimated at $20,248,300 gross ($18,341,900 net); for the period from 1 December 1993 to 30 April 1994, the total cost was estimated at $20,239,500 gross ($18,474,900 net). The Secretary-General requested appropriation of the first amount and apportionment thereof. In that connection, he said it would be prudent for continuing authorization to exist for ONUSAL, as well as for other peacekeeping operations. In the event that the Council decided to continue ONUSAL beyond 30 November 1993, he requested that provision be made for the second amount, either by appropriation or commitment authorization, together with apportionment thereof.

The cost for the liquidation phase, projected to take three months, was estimated at $3,219,100 gross ($3,015,100 net). A full report on the disposition of the ONUSAL assets would be submitted to the General Assembly through ACABQ. In connection with that phase, the Secretary-General requested that the Assembly extend to ONUSAL the special arrangements regarding the application of regulations 4.3 and 4.4 under article IV of the Financial Regulations of the United Nations, as it did to the United Nations Transition Assistance

Group in 1991.[57] That would allow retention of appropriations required in respect of obligations owed to Governments providing troops and/or logistic support beyond the period stipulated under those regulations.

The ONUCA/ONUSAL Special Account showed an unencumbered balance of $14,835,505 ($829,032 for ONUSAL and $14,006,473 for ONUCA). However, assessed contributions amounting to $22,404,703 ($10,212,215 for ONUSAL and $12,192,488 for ONUCA) remained outstanding as at 31 May 1993, resulting in an operating deficit of $7,569,198. Loans totalling $5 million were made to the Special Account from the Peace-keeping Reserve Fund in order to meet cash requirements. Hence, the Secretary-General recommended that no action be taken as to the unutilized ONUCA balance of $1,813,985 and that it be retained in the ONUCA/ONUSAL Special Account.

Having reviewed the expenditure items and identified areas where savings could be achieved, ACABQ[58] recommended that the Assembly appropriate $18 million gross for 1 June to 30 November 1993; that, as decided by the Assembly in March, the unutilized ONUCA balance be credited to Member States against their assessments of $18 million gross for ONUSAL for the same period, thus reducing that amount to $16,186,015 gross; and that, should the Security Council extend ONUSAL beyond 30 November 1993, the Secretary-General should submit revised cost estimates for that extension and for ONUSAL's liquidation, based on a detailed performance report for the current mandate period and taking account of ACABQ's observations.

ACABQ concurred, on an exceptional basis, with the request relating to the application of the financial regulations mentioned above, but recommended that the Secretary-General enhance his communication with troop-contributing States to bring about the timely submission of their claims and relevant information.

GENERAL ASSEMBLY ACTION (September)

On 14 September 1993, on the recommendation of the Fifth Committee, the General Assembly adopted **resolution 47/234** without vote.

Financing of the United Nations Observer Mission in El Salvador

The General Assembly,

Having considered the report of the Secretary-General on the financing of the United Nations Observer Mission in El Salvador and the related report of the Advisory Committee on Administrative and Budgetary Questions,

Bearing in mind Security Council resolution 693(1991) of 20 May 1991, by which the Council established the United Nations Observer Mission in El Salvador, and Council resolution 729(1992) of 14 January 1992, by which the Council decided to extend and enlarge the mandate of the Observer Mission, as well as the subsequent resolutions by which the Council extended the mandate of the Mission, the latest of which was resolution 832(1993) of 27 May 1993,

Recalling its resolution 46/240 of 22 May 1992, in which it decided, in principle, that the special accounts for the United Nations Observer Mission in El Salvador and the United Nations Observer Group in Central America should be merged,

Noting the current status of the combined Special Account for the United Nations Observer Mission in El Salvador and the United Nations Observer Group in Central America,

Reaffirming that the costs of the Observer Mission are expenses of the Organization to be borne by Member States in accordance with Article 17, paragraph 2, of the Charter of the United Nations,

Recalling its previous decisions regarding the fact that, in order to meet the expenditures caused by the Observer Mission, a different procedure is required from the one applied to meet expenditures of the regular budget of the United Nations,

Taking into account the fact that the economically more developed countries are in a position to make relatively larger contributions and that the economically less developed countries have a relatively limited capacity to contribute towards such an operation,

Bearing in mind the special responsibilities of the States permanent members of the Security Council, as indicated in General Assembly resolution 1874(S-IV) of 27 June 1963, in the financing of such operations,

Mindful of the fact that it is essential to provide the Observer Mission with the necessary financial resources to enable it to fulfil its responsibilities under the relevant resolutions of the Security Council,

Expressing concern about the financial situation with regard to the Observer Mission owing to overdue payment by Member States of their assessments, particularly Member States in arrears,

Also expressing concern about the delays in submission of budget documents until well into the financial period of the Observer Mission, which have contributed to the financing difficulties of the Mission,

1. *Endorses* the observations and recommendations contained in the report of the Advisory Committee on Administrative and Budgetary Questions, subject to the terms of the present resolution, and approves on an exceptional basis the special arrangements for the United Nations Observer Mission in El Salvador with regard to the application of article IV of the Financial Regulations of the United Nations, whereby appropriations required in respect of obligations owed to Governments providing contingents and/or logistic support to the Observer Mission shall be retained beyond the period stipulated under financial regulations 4.3 and 4.4, as set out in the annex to the present resolution;

2. *Requests* the Secretary-General to take all necessary action to ensure that the Observer Mission is administered with a maximum of efficiency and economy, to improve management, and to include in his report on this item to the General Assembly information on the steps taken in this regard;

3. *Takes note* of the outstanding assessments and the net operating deficit of the Special Account for the United Nations Observer Mission in El Salvador and the United Nations Observer Group in Central America;

4. *Urges* all Member States to expedite payments of their assessed contributions to the Special Account promptly and in full;

5. *Decides* to appropriate to the Special Account, in accordance with the recommendation contained in paragraph 40 of the report of the Advisory Committee, for the operation of the Observer Mission for the period from 1 June to 30 November 1993, an amount of 18 million United States dollars gross (16,324,000 dollars net);

6. *Decides also*, as an ad hoc arrangement, to apportion the amount of 18 million dollars gross (16,324,000 dollars net) for the above-mentioned period among Member States in accordance with the composition of the groups set out in paragraphs 3 and 4 of General Assembly resolution 43/232 of 1 March 1989, as adjusted by the Assembly in its resolutions 44/192 B of 21 December 1989, 45/267 of 21 June 1991, 46/198 A of 20 December 1991 and 47/218 A of 23 December 1992, and taking into account the scale of assessments set out in Assembly resolution 46/221 A of 20 December 1991 and Assembly decision 47/456 of 23 December 1992;

7. *Decides further* that, in accordance with the provisions of its resolution 973(X) of 15 December 1955, there shall be set off against the apportionment among Member States, as provided for in paragraph 6 above, their respective share in the Tax Equalization Fund of the estimated staff assessment income of 1,676,000 dollars for the period from 1 June to 30 November 1993 approved for the Observer Mission;

8. *Reiterates* its decision in paragraph 9 of its resolution 47/223 of 16 March 1993;

9. *Notes* that, in the light of the termination of the mandate of the United Nations Observer Group in Central America as at 17 January 1992, the net estimated costs of the Observer Group will be revised to reflect a final recorded expenditure and that the financial obligations of Member States to the Group will be adjusted accordingly;

10. *Decides* that the remaining unencumbered balance of the Observer Group after the revision of the net estimated costs as mentioned above shall be first applied as credits to Member States against their assessed contributions for the current mandate period of the Observer Mission in accordance with the provisions of paragraph 9 of its resolution 47/223, on the understanding that:

(a) Those Member States whose payments to the Observer Group are lower than their adjusted obligations shall pay their remaining outstanding assessed contributions to the Group;

(b) Those Member States whose payments to the Observer Group exceed their adjusted obligations shall be credited in full with the difference;

11. *Requests* the Secretary-General to provide the General Assembly with the recorded expenditure of the Observer Group in order to assist it in its decision on the adjustment of the financial obligations of Member States as noted in paragraph 9 above;

12. *Decides* that there shall be set off against the apportionment among Member States, as provided in paragraph 6 above, their respective share in the unutilized balance of 1,813,985 dollars in the Special Account for the period from 1 June to 30 November 1993;

13. *Authorizes* the Secretary-General to enter into commitments for the operation of the Observer Mission at a rate not to exceed 3 million dollars gross (2,720,000 dollars net) per month for the period from 1 December 1993 to 31 March 1994, should the Security Council decide to continue the Mission beyond 30 November 1993, subject to obtaining the prior concurrence of the Advisory Committee for the actual level of commitments to be entered into for the period beyond 30 November 1993, the said amount to be apportioned among Member States in accordance with the scheme set out in the present resolution;

14. *Requests* the Advisory Committee to report to the General Assembly at its forty-eighth session on action taken with regard to paragraph 13 above;

15. *Requests*, in this regard, the Secretary-General to submit to the General Assembly, no later than 8 February 1994, budget proposals, including revised estimates for the period the Security Council might have decided to continue the mandate of the Observer Mission beyond 30 November 1993;

16. *Decides* to establish the contributions of Andorra, the Czech Republic, Eritrea, the former Yugoslav Republic of Macedonia, Monaco and Slovakia to the Observer Mission in accordance with the rates of assessment to be adopted by the General Assembly for these Member States at its forty-eighth session;

17. *Invites* the new Member States listed in paragraph 16 above to make advance payments against their assessed contributions, to be determined;

18. *Invites* voluntary contributions to the Observer Mission in cash and in the form of services and supplies acceptable to the Secretary-General, to be administered, as appropriate, in accordance with the procedure established by the General Assembly in its resolutions 43/230 of 21 December 1988, 44/192 A of 21 December 1989 and 45/258 of 3 May 1991.

ANNEX
Special arrangements with regard to the application of article IV of the Financial Regulations of the United Nations

1. At the end of the twelve-month period provided in regulation 4.3, any unliquidated obligations of the financial period in question relating to goods supplied and services rendered by Governments for which claims have been received or which are covered by established reimbursement rates shall be transferred to accounts payable; such accounts payable shall remain recorded in the Special Account until payment is effected.

2. *(a)* Any other unliquidated obligations of the financial period in question owed to Governments for goods supplied and services rendered, as well as other obligations owed to Governments, for which required claims have not yet been received shall remain valid for an additional period of four years following the end of the twelve-month period provided for in regulation 4.3;

(b) Claims received during this four-year period shall be treated as provided under paragraph 1 of the present annex, if appropriate;

(c) At the end of the additional four-year period any unliquidated obligations shall be cancelled and the then remaining balance of any appropriations retained therefor shall be surrendered.

General Assembly resolution 47/234

14 September 1993   Meeting 110   Adopted without vote

Approved by Fifth Committee (A/47/797/Add.2) without vote, 7 September (meeting 75); draft by Chairman (A/C.5/47/L.40), orally revised; agenda item 122.
Meeting numbers. GA 47th session: 5th Committee 68, 69, 72, 75; plenary 110.

Reports of the Secretary-General and ACABQ (December). Following the extension of ONUSAL's mandate for the period from 1 December 1993 to 31 May 1994, the Secretary-General, in a report submitted to the General Assembly on 9 December 1993[59] on the financing of 17 peace-keeping operations, including ONUSAL, estimated that the cost of maintaining ONUSAL for five months, from 1 December 1993 to 30 April 1994, would amount to $18,137,400 gross ($16,475,500 net), appropriation and apportionment for which he requested. That figure was inclusive of the commitment of $12 million gross ($10,880,000 net) authorized by the Assembly resolution above for the four-month period from 1 December 1993 to 31 March 1994. An apportionment of the amount by major line-items of expenditure was provided, as was the revised apportionment for the preceding six-month period ending 30 November 1993 for comparison purposes.

ACABQ observed on 17 December[60] that it would be examining the detailed performance report of ONUSAL in February 1994 and that the current Assembly authorization of $12 million covered the period up to 31 March 1994; it therefore recommended that, currently, the amount of $12 million gross ($10,880,000 net) be maintained and assessed. It further pointed out[61] that the cost estimates as presented in no way constituted the ''normal'' performance/financing reports submitted by the Secretary-General. His explanations notwithstanding, ACABQ expressed its serious concern over the manner of presentation, noting that it represented a lack of budgetary discipline and eroded the role of the General Assembly. It added that its recommendation for ONUSAL, as for the other 16 peace-keeping operations, was for commitment authority rather than appropriation in view of the fact that the relevant budgets had not been considered and approved.

As requested by ACABQ, the Secretary-General subsequently submitted a separate report on ONUSAL financing, containing essentially the same information as above, but in the standard form of presentation.[62]

GENERAL ASSEMBLY ACTION (December)

The General Assembly, in December, adopted **decision 48/468** without vote.

Financing of the United Nations Observer Mission in El Salvador

At its 87th plenary meeting, on 23 December 1993, the General Assembly, on the recommendation of the

Fifth Committee, in accordance with the framework set out in its resolution 48/227 of 23 December 1993, having considered the report of the Secretary-General on the financing of seventeeen peace-keeping operations and the related reports of the Advisory Committee on Administrative and Budgetary Questions, and concurring with the observations of the Advisory Committee:

(a) Authorized the Secretary-General, on an exceptional basis, to enter into commitments up to the amount of 8,823,500 United States dollars gross (8 million dollars net) for the United Nations Observer Mission in El Salvador for the period from 1 December 1993 to 28 February 1994;

(b) Decided at that time to apportion, as an ad hoc arrangement, the amount of 5,382,300 dollars gross (4,880,000 dollars net) among Member States in accordance with the composition of groups set out in paragraphs 3 and 4 of Assembly resolution 43/232 of 1 March 1989, as adjusted by the Assembly in its resolutions 44/192 B of 21 December 1989, 45/269 of 27 August 1991, 46/198 A of 20 December 1991 and 47/218 A of 23 December 1992 and its decision 48/472 of 23 December 1993, and taking into account the scale of assessments for the years 1992, 1993 and 1994 as set out in Assembly resolutions 46/221 A of 20 December 1991 and 48/223 A of 23 December 1993 and its decision 47/456 of 23 December 1992;

(c) Also decided that, in accordance with the provisions of its resolution 973(X) of 15 December 1955, there should be set off against the apportionment among Member States, as provided for in subparagraph *(b)* above, their respective share in the Tax Equalization Fund of the estimated staff assessment income of 502,300 dollars for the period from 1 December 1993 to 28 February 1994;

(d) Further decided that, in view of the expiration of the commitment authority on 28 February 1994, priority should be given to the cost estimates for the Observer Mission in the consideration by the General Assembly of peace-keeping budgets.

General Assembly decision 48/468

Adopted without vote

Approved by Fifth Committee (A/48/817) without vote, 22 December (meeting 46); draft by Chairman (A/C.5/48/L.20); agenda item 134.
Meeting numbers. GA 48th session: 5th Committee 44, 46; plenary 87.

Also on 23 December, the Assembly, by **decision 48/484**, decided that the item on the financing of ONUSAL remained for consideration during its forty-eighth session.

Guatemala situation

The President of Guatemala, Jorge Antonio Serrano Elías, personally delivered to the Secretary-General on 19 January 1993 a document containing a government proposal to the Unidad Revolucionaria Nacional Guatemalteca (URNG) for the immediate signing of an agreement on a firm and lasting peace in the country. A copy was transmitted to the Secretary-General by the Permanent Representative of Guatemala to the United Nations on the same day.[63]

The proposal, reported as having received the broadest possible support of the Guatemalan people, called for the signing of a peace agreement

to end the country's internal armed conflict within a period not exceeding 90 days from the signing also of a human rights agreement that included provisions for immediate verification. In the event that agreement was not reached, the proposal called for the declaration of a definitive cease-fire at the end of the 90-day period and the temporary concentration of URNG's armed contingents at government-designated locations until a peace agreement was negotiated and procedures were established for their disarmament, demobilization and integration into the legal and institutional life of Guatemala. It was further proposed that the Secretary-General be requested to draw up the appropriate procedures.

The Minister for Foreign Affairs of Guatemala, on 19 February,[64] stated his understanding that the Secretary-General had reported orally on the proposal to the Security Council on 22 January and had expressed readiness to initiate steps for the establishment of a machinery to verify compliance with any agreement reached on human rights. In that connection, the Minister reiterated the request that the Secretary-General draw up the procedures needed to set the peace process in motion.

On 27 May,[65] however, EC issued a statement expressing concern over President Serrano's decision to break off constitutional order, in particular to dissolve Parliament and the Supreme Court. It urged the immediate re-establishment of those democratic institutions, saying they were fundamental to a successful conclusion of the peace process and the full observance of human rights. The subsequent return to constitutional order in Guatemala through legal and peaceful means was welcomed on 7 June[66] by EC, which expressed support for the new constitutional President, Ramiro de León Carpio.

The Presidents of Costa Rica, El Salvador, Guatemala, Honduras, Nicaragua and Panama, at their meeting at Guatemala City on 17 June[67] to reaffirm their commitment to the strengthening of peace and democratic development of Central America, signed a Joint Declaration by which, among other things, they hailed the peaceful settlement of the recent political crisis in Guatemala, warmly welcomed an OAS resolution adopted on 8 June on the restoration of democracy in that country, and expressed their gratitude for the determination of all Guatemalan society, which fought resolutely to re-establish constitutional order.

In **resolution 48/161**, the General Assembly reiterated the importance of resuming the negotiations between the Government of Guatemala and URNG, bearing in mind the agreements achieved up to May 1993. It expressed appreciation to the Secretary-General and his representative for their participation in the Guatemalan peace process and, in that context, took note of the peace plan of Guatemala's President.

Nicaragua

On 27 August 1993, the Presidents of Costa Rica, El Salvador, Guatemala, Honduras, Nicaragua and Panama, meeting at San Salvador,[68] adopted a Declaration on the Situation in Nicaragua, by which they reaffirmed that peace in Central America was indivisible and that any development disrupting it had repercussions throughout the subregion. They condemned any act of violence and terrorism that threatened the lives and personal safety of Nicaraguans or the security of the State and the stability of the lawfully constituted Government; expressed solidarity with and support for President Violeta Barrios de Chamorro; appealed to all sectors of Nicaraguan society to assume their share of responsibility in building their country's future; supported the early implementation of the Agreement concluded on 21 August between the Government, Unión Nacional Opositora and Frente Sandinista de Liberación Nacional, so that the obstacles impeding the institutional, economic and social normalization of Nicaragua might be removed; urged the subregion's Foreign Ministers to use their good offices to bring about national agreement in Nicaragua; and appealed for the international community's cooperation.

In **resolution 48/161**, the General Assembly supported the Nicaraguan Government's efforts to consolidate peace. In **resolution 48/8**, it encouraged Nicaragua to continue its efforts aimed at reconstruction and national reconciliation and called on the Secretary-General to provide, at the request of the Government, all possible assistance to support the consolidation of peace in, among other areas, the settlement of displaced and demobilized persons and refugees, land ownership and land tenure in rural areas, direct care for war victims, mine clearance and, in general, a process of sustained economic and social recovery and development that would render the peace and democracy achieved irreversible.

REFERENCES

(1)YUN 1992, p. 218, GA res. 47/118, 18 Dec. 1992. (2)A/48/586. (3)YUN 1986, p. 177. (4)YUN 1987, p. 188. (5)YUN 1992, p. 222. (6)A/47/897. (7)YUN 1991, p. 141. (8)YUN 1960, p. 315. (9)YUN 1992, p. 226. (10)A/47/946-S/25754. (11)S/25078. (12)YUN 1992, p. 228. (13)Ibid., p. 230. (14)S/25257. (15)S/25516. (16)S/26052. (17)S/26077. (18)YUN 1991, p. 147. (19)YUN 1992, p. 231. (20)S/25500. (21)S/25427. (22)S/25812. (23)S/25812/Add.3. (24)S/26581. (25)S/26689. (26)S/26695. (27)S/26865. (28)S/26866. (29)S/25200. (30)S/25901. (31)S/25929. (32)S/26005. (33)A/47/970-S/26008. (34)YUN 1987, p. 188. (35)S/26071. (36)S/26371. (37)S/25241. (38)S/25812/Add.1. (39)S/26606. (40)S/1994/179. (41)YUN 1991, p. 149, SC res. 693(1991), 20 May 1991. (42)A/44/971-S/21541. (43)YUN 1992, p. 223, SC res. 729(1992), 14 Jan. 1992. (44)Ibid., p. 229. (45)A/47/912-S/25521. (46)A/47/968-S/26033. (47)A/47/1012-S/26416 & Add.1. (48)A/49/59-S/1994/47. (49)YUN 1992, p. 227. (50)S/25812/Add.2. (51)S/26790. (52)S/25451. (53)S/25452. (54)A/47/900. (55)YUN 1992, p. 230, GA dec. 47/452, 22 Dec. 1992. (56)A/47/751/Add.1. (57)YUN 1991, p. 135, GA res. 45/265, 17 May 1991. (58)A/47/983. (59)A/C.5/48/40. (60)A/48/774. (61)A/48/778. (62)A/48/842 & Corr.1. (63)A/47/873-S/25134. (64)A/47/895-S/25326. (65)A/47/956. (66)A/47/963. (67)A/47/971. (68)A/47/1009-S/26397.

The Caribbean

Cuba–United States

Cuba continued in 1993 to protest to the Security Council against terrorist acts perpetrated against Cuba or Cuban juridical persons in which the United States was involved, either by commission or omission.

On 4 February,[1] it drew attention to the hijacking and diversion to the United States, on the morning of 29 December 1992, of a Cuban AN-28 aircraft bearing registration number CUT-110 and belonging to Aerocaribbean. Cuba asserted that the gravity of that air piracy—clearly defined as an act of terrorism condemnable by the international community—was compounded by the favourable reception, preferential treatment and attention lavished with fanfare on the hijackers at Miami International Airport, Florida, by United States authorities.

Cuba objected to the failure of the United States to take legal action against the perpetrators, who remained at large, having been admitted "on their own recognizance" into the United States.

United States embargo against Cuba

In accordance with its decision of 1992,[2] the General Assembly included in its 1993 agenda an item on the necessity of ending the economic, commercial and financial embargo imposed by the United States against Cuba.

To bolster the need for ending that embargo, imposed more than 30 years earlier, Cuba transmitted to the Secretary-General several documents during the second half of the year. One was a study by an expert group giving what it described as the historical truth behind the embargo,[3] justified by reason of Cuba's nationalization of properties belonging to United States companies but, in truth, imposed and strengthened to coerce Cuba into changing its political and economic system according to United States wishes; and underscoring the refusal of the United States to respond to repeated Cuban proposals for negotiations on the nationalization dispute. Another study, undertaken by Cuban experts,[4] calculated the economic and social cost to Cuba of the embargo at $40.8 billion and detailed its negative impact on the Cuban population.

Also transmitted were 16 communications from NGOs and individuals[5] urging the Assembly to call for an end to the economic blockade, as well as a letter citing specific examples[6] that proved false the United States assertion that the economic blockade redirected the flow of convertible currencies that Cuba might otherwise have used to suppress its own population and support insurgencies abroad.

Report of the Secretary-General. As called for by the General Assembly in 1992,[2] the Secretary-General submitted to it a report of 28 September 1993, with a later addendum,[7] reproducing the replies from 32 States to his request for information on steps taken or envisaged to repeal or invalidate any of their laws whose extraterritorial effects affected the sovereignty of other States. The report also noted that over 120 NGOs had urged the Secretary-General promptly to implement the Assembly's 1992 resolution on the subject.[8]

GENERAL ASSEMBLY ACTION

On 3 November, the General Assembly adopted **resolution 48/16** by recorded vote.

Necessity of ending the economic, commercial and financial embargo imposed by the United States of America against Cuba

The General Assembly,

Determined to encourage strict compliance with the purposes and principles enshrined in the Charter of the United Nations,

Reaffirming, among other principles, the sovereign equality of States, non-intervention and non-interference in their internal affairs and freedom of trade and international navigation, which are also enshrined in many international legal instruments,

Taking note of the statement of the heads of State and Government at the third Ibero-American Summit, held at Salvador, Brazil, on 15 and 16 July 1993, concerning the need to eliminate the unilateral application of economic and trade measures by one State against another for political purposes,

Concerned about the continued promulgation and application by Member States of laws and regulations whose extraterritorial effects affect the sovereignty of other States and the legitimate interests of entities or persons under their jurisdiction, as well as the freedom of trade and navigation,

Recalling its resolution 47/19 of 24 November 1992,

Having learned that, since the adoption of resolution 47/19, further measures of that nature aimed at strengthening and extending the economic, commercial and financial embargo against Cuba have been promulgated and applied, and concerned about the adverse effects of those measures on the Cuban population,

1. *Takes note* of the report of the Secretary-General on the implementation of resolution 47/19;

2. *Reiterates its call* to all States to refrain from promulgating and applying laws and measures of the kind referred to in the preamble to the present resolution in conformity with their obligations under the Charter of the United Nations and international law which, *inter alia,* reaffirm the freedom of trade and navigation;

3. *Once again urges* States that have and continue to apply such laws and measures to take the necessary steps to repeal or invalidate them as soon as possible in accordance with their legal regime;

4. *Requests* the Secretary-General, in consultation with the appropriate organs and agencies of the United Nations system, to prepare a report on the implementation of the present resolution in the light of the purposes and principles of the Charter and international law, and to submit it to the General Assembly at its forty-ninth session;

5. *Decides* to include in the provisional agenda of its forty-ninth session the item entitled ''Necessity of ending the economic, commercial and financial embargo imposed by the United States of America against Cuba''.

General Assembly resolution 48/16

3 November 1993   Meeting 48   88-4-57 (recorded vote)

Draft by Cuba (A/48/L.14/Rev.1); agenda item 30.

Recorded vote in Assembly as follows:

In favour: Afghanistan, Algeria, Andorra, Angola, Australia, Austria, Azerbaijan, Bahamas, Barbados, Belgium, Belize, Benin, Bolivia, Brazil, Burkina Faso, Burundi, Cambodia, Cameroon, Cape Verde, Central African Republic, Chile, China, Colombia, Comoros, Congo, Costa Rica, Cuba, Democratic People's Republic of Korea, Dominica, Dominican Republic, Ecuador, France, Ghana, Greece, Guatemala, Guinea, Guinea-Bissau, Guyana, Haiti, Honduras, India, Indonesia, Iran, Iraq, Jamaica, Jordan, Kenya, Lao People's Democratic Republic, Lesotho, Libyan Arab Jamahiriya, Liechtenstein, Madagascar, Malaysia, Mali, Mauritania, Mexico, Monaco, Myanmar, Namibia, New Zealand, Niger,* Nigeria, Norway, Pakistan, Papua New Guinea, Peru, Philippines, Saint Kitts and Nevis, Saint Lucia, Saint Vincent and the Grenadines, San Marino, Spain, Sudan, Sweden, Syrian Arab Republic, Togo, Trinidad and Tobago, Tunisia, Uganda, United Republic of Tanzania, Uruguay, Vanuatu, Venezuela, Viet Nam, Yemen, Zaire, Zambia, Zimbabwe.

Against: Albania, Israel, Paraguay, United States.

Abstaining: Antigua and Barbuda, Argentina, Armenia, Bangladesh, Belarus, Bhutan, Botswana, Brunei Darussalam, Bulgaria, Canada, Chad, Côte d'Ivoire, Cyprus, Czech Republic, Denmark, Estonia, Ethiopia, Fiji, Finland, Germany, Hungary, Iceland, Ireland, Italy, Japan, Kazakhstan, Kuwait, Latvia, Luxembourg, Malawi, Maldives, Malta, Marshall Islands, Micronesia, Mozambique, Nepal, Netherlands, Nicaragua, Panama, Poland, Portugal, Republic of Korea, Republic of Moldova, Romania, Russian Federation, Rwanda, Samoa, Singapore, Slovakia, Slovenia, Sri Lanka, Suriname, Thailand, Macedonia, Turkey, Ukraine, United Kingdom.

*Later advised the Secretariat it had intended to abstain.

Explaining its vote, the United States said it had a political and economic right to exclude as trading partners those who violated fundamental human rights and demonstrated little respect for human dignity and the worth of the individual. It maintained its comprehensive economic embargo against Cuba in order to continue pressuring the regime to restore freedom and democracy.

Haiti

In 1993, intensive efforts were mounted by the Special Envoy for Haiti of the Secretaries-General of the United Nations and the Organization of American States, Dante Caputo (Argentina), in order to restore constitutional order to Haiti and the return of its democratically elected President,

Jean-Bertrand Aristide, who remained in exile in the United States. Through those efforts, the Governors Island Agreement and the New York Pact were concluded, the first by President Aristide and the Commander-in-Chief of the Armed Forces of Haiti, General Raoul Cédras, and the second by the political parties represented in the Haitian Parliament. Both documents embodied a series of undertakings whose implementation would make possible the return of President Aristide to Haiti on 30 October.

As part of the Agreement, the Security Council established and authorized the dispatch to Haiti of the United Nations Mission in Haiti (UNMIH) (resolutions 862(1993) and 867(1993)), which was prevented by the Haitian military authorities, together with the police, from entering the country on 11 October, in serious breach of the Agreement. Consequently, the sanctions imposed against Haiti by the Council in mid-June, shortly before the Agreement was signed (841(1993)), and suspended in August when certain measures in the Agreement were implemented (861(1993)), were promptly reimposed in October (873(1993)) and thereafter strengthened (875(1993)).

The joint United Nations/OAS International Civilian Mission in Haiti (MICIVIH), in operation in the country since February and whose United Nations component had been authorized by the Assembly in April to verify compliance with Haiti's human rights obligations, was withdrawn immediately following the prevention of UNMIH's emplacement, amidst mounting demonstrations and threats against the two missions and President Aristide's return.

SECURITY COUNCIL ACTION (October)

The Security Council met on 30 October 1993, the date on which the President of Haiti was to have returned to his country pursuant to the Governors Island Agreement. In connection with its consideration of the item "The question concerning Haiti", the President made the following statement[9] on behalf of the Council:

Meeting number. SC 3301.

"The Security Council continues to insist on full and unconditional compliance with the Governors Island Agreement and the early return of President Aristide and full democracy to Haiti, in accordance with relevant resolutions and statements by the President of the Council. It reaffirms that the Governors Island Agreement remains fully in force as the only valid framework for the solution of the crisis in Haiti which continues to threaten peace and security in the region.

"The Security Council is deeply concerned by the suffering of the Haitian people which results directly from the refusal by the military authorities to comply with the Governors Island process.

"The Security Council stresses that the signatories to the Governors Island Agreement remain obligated to comply in full with its provisions. The Security Council condemns the fact that General Cédras and the military authorities have not so far fulfilled their obligations under that Agreement. It moreover deplores the fact that the Haitian military leaders have fostered and perpetuated in Haiti a political and security environment which prevents the President's return to Haiti as provided for in paragraph 9 of the Governors Island Agreement.

"The Security Council expresses its support for the invitation by the Special Envoy of the Secretaries-General of the United Nations and the Organization of American States to all parties to meet next week solely to resolve the remaining obstacles to full implementation of the Governors Island Agreement. Further, it reaffirms its determination to maintain and effectively enforce sanctions on Haiti until the commitments made on Governors Island are honoured, and to consider strengthening them, in accordance with its resolutions 873(1993) and 875(1993) and its Presidential statement of 25 October 1993, if the military authorities continue to interrupt the democratic transition. In this regard, it requests the Secretary-General to report urgently to the Council."

Report and communication (November). The Secretary-General, on 12 November,[10] described events following the withdrawal of the two missions.

Prime Minister Robert Malval and General Cédras met on 23 October but failed to produce an agreement. Also on that date, a "Crisis Committee", composed of parliamentarians opposed to President Aristide and led by the President of the Chamber of Deputies, proposed an 11-point compromise calling for, among other things, simultaneous and immediate enactment of legislation on a broad amnesty and separation of the police from the military, the expansion of the Government and the elaboration by the Government of a protocol governing international missions to Haiti. Unable to constitute a quorum by 27 October, Parliament could not consider the proposals.

On 26 October, a parliamentary bloc called Front national pour le changement et la démocratie (FNCD), supporting President Aristide, offered its own eight-point compromise. President Aristide addressed the General Assembly on 28 October, asking for a total blockade of Haiti and calling for the departure of General Cédras, the Armed Forces High Command and General Staff, as well as the Police Chief, Colonel Michel François, and his allies; upon their departure, he would summon Parliament to vote on the police and amnesty bills. Lastly, he invited the Prime Minister and his Cabinet not to resign, in solidarity with the people.

On 29 October, the Special Envoy invited President Aristide and his Government, the President of the Chamber of Deputies, the President of the Senate and General Cédras to a meeting. Following several exchanges of correspondence clarifying certain conditions from the parties, a further exchange took place with the Special Envoy explaining that the Agreement remained valid and that the sequence of events which it envisaged could not be modified unilaterally.

The meeting took place on 5 November at Port-au-Prince. Present were the entire Government, assisted by two of President Aristide's advisers; the Senate President, accompanied by two FNCD senators; the President of the Chamber of Deputies, a member of the opposition, accompanied by two FNCD senators and an opposition deputy; and the international community, represented by the four Friends of the Secretary-General (Canada, France, United States, Venezuela) and the United Nations. The seats reserved for the military remained empty. Less than an hour into the meeting, a letter of 4 November from General Cédras was delivered to the Special Envoy, criticizing the planning of the meeting in the absence of the signatories to the Agreement and the use of foreign civilians to provide internal security. The meeting was thus adjourned with the participants' agreement.

In a statement to the press, the Special Envoy described as regrettable the absence of the military authorities—the party responsible for prolonging the crisis in Haiti and for the reimposition of the sanctions. He pointed out again that the basis for any settlement of the Haitian crisis was the Agreement, in the context of which he reaffirmed the international community's determination to persevere in the search for a negotiated settlement.

On 12 November,[11] Haiti informed the Security Council of a meeting between President Aristide and a government delegation in Washington, D.C., from 9 to 11 November. Several resolutions were adopted, some of which affirmed that: the Government of Prime Minister Malval remained in power with the absolute confidence of the President of the Republic; the Prime Minister's mandate was consistent with, *inter alia*, the Constitution and the Governors Island Agreement; and the Agreement remained the sole framework for resolving the Haitian crisis.

Other resolutions called on the Haitian military to honour its commitments under the Agreement, requested the international community to ensure the immediate return of MICIVIH and UNMIH to Haiti, and called on the Cabinet Ministers to rally all democratic forces willing to strive for the Agreement's implementation and the establishment of the rule of law in Haiti. By a final resolution, the President decided to implement an urgent economic and social programme to alleviate the suffering of the Haitian people.

SECURITY COUNCIL ACTION (November)

At a meeting of the Security Council on 15 November, the President made the following statement[12] on behalf of the Council:

Meeting number. SC 3314.

"The Security Council takes note of the report of the Secretary-General on the question concerning Haiti and the letter dated 12 November 1993 from the Permanent Representative of Haiti to the United Nations.

"The Security Council commends the efforts of the Special Envoy of the Secretaries-General of the United Nations and the Organization of American States, Mr. Dante Caputo, takes note of his oral report made to the Council on 12 November 1993 and confirms its full support for his continued active diplomacy for resolving the crisis in Haiti.

"The Security Council condemns the military authorities in Port-au-Prince for failing to comply fully with the Governors Island Agreement and in particular with points 7, 8 and 9. It reaffirms that this Agreement constitutes the only valid framework for resolving the crisis in Haiti, which continues to threaten peace and security in the region.

"The Security Council also reaffirms its support for the democratically elected President, Mr. Jean-Bertrand Aristide, and for the legitimate Government of Mr. Robert Malval. It recalls that it holds the military authorities responsible for the security of the members of this Government and for the security of the United Nations and Organization of American States personnel in Haiti.

"The Security Council is deeply concerned by the plight of the Haitian people. It reaffirms that the military authorities in Haiti are fully responsible for this suffering which directly results from their non-compliance with their public commitments to the Governors Island Agreement. The Council expresses its determination to minimize the impact of the present situation on the most vulnerable groups and calls upon Member States to continue, and to intensify, their humanitarian assistance to the people of Haiti. The Security Council welcomes in this regard the decision of the Secretary-General to dispatch a team of additional humanitarian personnel to Haiti.

"The Security Council encourages the Secretary-General, in consultation with the Secretary-General of the Organization of American States, to work for the earliest possible return of the International Civilian Mission in Haiti (MICIVIH). The Security Council requests the Secretary-General to continue planning for additional measures including for an appropriate United Nations Mission in Haiti (UNMIH) to be deployed as conditions permit, consistent with the Governors Island Agreement.

"The Security Council stresses that the sanctions contained in resolutions 841(1993), 873(1993) and 875(1993) will remain in force until the objectives of the Governors Island Agreement are fulfilled, including the departure of the Commander-in-Chief of the Haitian Armed Forces, the creation of a new police force permitting the restoration of constitutional order to Haiti and the return of the democratically elected President.

"The Security Council reaffirms its determination, expressed in the above-mentioned resolutions, to ensure the full and effective enforcement of current sanctions. It welcomes measures taken to this effect by States on a national basis in accordance with the Charter of the United Nations and relevant Security Council resolutions. In this regard, the Council is prepared to consider additional mechanisms and practical measures to help verify the full compliance with the decisions of the Security Council.

"The Security Council reaffirms its determination to consider strengthening the measures regarding Haiti in accordance with its resolutions 873(1993) and 875(1993) and its presidential statements of 25 October 1993 and of 30 October 1993 if the military authorities continue to obstruct full compliance with the Governors Island Agreement, thus preventing the restoration of lawful order and democracy in Haiti."

GENERAL ASSEMBLY ACTION (December)

On 6 December 1993, the General Assembly adopted without vote **resolution 48/27**.

The situation of democracy and human rights in Haiti

The General Assembly,

Having considered anew the question entitled "The situation of democracy and human rights in Haiti",

Recalling its resolutions 46/7 of 11 October 1991 and 46/138 of 17 December 1991, 47/20 A of 24 November 1992 and 47/20 B of 20 April 1993, as well as the resolutions and decisions adopted on the question by the Economic and Social Council, the Commission on Human Rights and other international forums,

Recalling also Security Council resolutions 841(1993) of 16 June 1993, 861(1993) of 27 August 1993, 862(1993) of 31 August 1993, 867(1993) of 23 September 1993, 873(1993) of 13 October 1993 and 875(1993) of 16 October 1993,

Taking note with satisfaction of resolutions MRE/RES.1/91, MRE/RES.2/91, MRE/RES.3/92 and MRE/RES.5/93, adopted on 3 and 8 October 1991, 17 May 1992 and 5 June 1993, respectively, by the Ministers for Foreign Affairs of the member countries of the Organization of American States, as well as resolutions CP/RES.594(923/92) of 10 November 1992 and CP/SA.968/93 of 18 October 1993, adopted by the Permanent Council of the Organization of American States,

Taking note of the Governors Island Agreement signed on 3 July 1993 and the New York Pact signed on 16 July 1993,

Noting that, in spite of the efforts of the international community, President Jean-Bertrand Aristide has not been returned to power and democratic order has not been re-established in Haiti in accordance with the terms of the Governors Island Agreement,

Gravely alarmed by the persistence and worsening of flagrant violations of human rights, in particular summary and arbitrary executions, involuntary disappearances, torture and rape, and arbitrary arrests and detention, as well as the refusal to recognize freedom of expression, assembly and association,

Deeply concerned by the multiplication of acts of violence and intimidation against the Government of Haiti, in particular the assassination of the Minister of Justice,

François Guy Malary, which have contributed to the withdrawal of the International Civilian Mission to Haiti,

Deeply disturbed by the obstacles which continue to oppose deployment of the United Nations Mission in Haiti, sent under Security Council resolution 867(1993), and also by the fact that the Haitian armed forces have failed in their responsibility to permit the Mission to start its work,

Recognizing the importance of the measures adopted by the Security Council with a view to reaching a settlement of the Haitian crisis,

Welcoming the efforts of the Special Envoy of the Secretary-General of the United Nations and the Secretary-General of the Organization of American States,

Taking into account its resolution 47/11 of 29 October 1992 on cooperation between the United Nations and the Organization of American States,

Having regard to the report of the Secretary-General dated 13 October 1993 informing the Security Council that the military authorities of Haiti, including the metropolitan police of Port-au-Prince, have not complied with the Governors Island Agreement, and also the reports submitted by the International Civilian Mission to Haiti on 25 October and 18 November 1993 and the report submitted by the Special Rapporteur of the Commission on Human Rights on the situation of human rights in Haiti on 10 November 1993,

Taking note of the proposals for a solution to the crisis in Haiti presented by President Aristide before the General Assembly,

Recalling that the aim of the international community remains the prompt re-establishment of democracy in Haiti and the return of President Aristide, the complete return of human rights and fundamental freedoms and the promotion of social and economic development in Haiti,

Considering that it is urgent to arrive as soon as possible at a definitive settlement of the Haitian crisis in accordance with the Charter of the United Nations and international law,

1. *Strongly condemns again* the attempt to replace unlawfully the constitutional President of Haiti, the employment of violence and military coercion and the violation of human rights in that country;

2. *Condemns* all attempts to delay or prevent the immediate reinstatement of President Jean-Bertrand Aristide as the constitutional President of Haiti;

3. *Declares again* to be unacceptable any entity arising from this unlawful situation, and demands the return of President Aristide, as well as full implementation of the National Constitution and, consequently, complete respect for human rights in Haiti;

4. *Supports energetically* the process of political dialogue carried out under the auspices of the Special Envoy of the Secretary-General of the United Nations and the Secretary-General of the Organization of American States in order to resolve the political crisis in Haiti;

5. *Asserts* that the Governors Island Agreement continues to be the only valid framework for resolving the crisis in Haiti;

6. *Asserts once again* that the solution of the Haitian crisis must take into account resolutions MRE/RES.2/91, MRE/RES.3/92 and CP/RES.594(923/92) of the Organization of American States;

7. *Takes note of* the report of the Secretary-General;

8. *Requests* the Secretary-General, acting in consultation with the Secretary-General of the Organization of American States, to do his utmost to bring back the International Civilian Mission to Haiti as rapidly as possible;

9. *Encourages* the Secretary-General to pursue the efforts for deploying the United Nations Mission in Haiti in accordance with the Governors Island Agreement;

10. *Recalls* the obligation of all Member States to comply fully and effectively with the measures adopted by the Security Council in its resolutions 841(1993) and 875(1993);

11. *Encourages* the States Members of the United Nations to offer their support anew, within the framework of the Charter of the United Nations and international law, by adopting measures consistent with resolutions MRE/RES.2/91, MRE/RES.3/92 and CP/RES.594 (923/92) of the Organization of American States, acting in particular on strengthening representative democracy, constitutional order and the trade embargo against Haiti;

12. *Expresses its profound concern* for the fate of the Haitian people, and reasserts that the Haitian military authorities are fully responsible for the suffering resulting directly from their disrespect for the Haitian Constitution and for their public commitments to the Governors Island Agreement;

13. *Confirms once again* that the international community intends to increase technical, economic and financial cooperation when constitutional order has been established in Haiti, by supporting implementation of economic and social development and in order to strengthen the institutions upon which it is incumbent to dispense justice and guarantee democracy, political stability and economic development;

14. *Affirms its support* for the constitutional President of Haiti, Jean-Bertrand Aristide, and his Prime Minister;

15. *Requests* the Secretary-General to submit to the General Assembly by mid-February 1994, during a resumption of its forty-eighth session, a report on the implementation of the present resolution;

16. *Decides* to remain seized of this matter until a solution to the situation is found.

General Assembly resolution 48/27

6 December 1993   Meeting 70   Adopted without vote

32-nation draft (A/48/L.35/Rev.1), orally revised; agenda item 31.

Sponsors: Antigua and Barbuda, Argentina, Bahamas, Barbados, Belize, Bolivia, Brazil, Chile, Colombia, Costa Rica, Cuba, Dominica, Dominican Republic, Ecuador, El Salvador, Grenada, Guatemala, Guyana, Haiti, Honduras, Jamaica, Mexico, Nicaragua, Panama, Paraguay, Peru, Saint Lucia, Saint Vincent and the Grenadines, Suriname, Trinidad and Tobago, Uruguay, Venezuela.

Meeting numbers. GA 48th session: plenary 69, 70.

On 23 December, by **decision 48/484**, the Assembly retained the agenda item on the situation of democracy and human rights in Haiti for consideration during the forty-eighth session.

(For the report of the Special Rapporteur of the Commission on Human Rights on the situation of human rights in Haiti, see PART THREE, Chapter X.)

International Civilian Mission in Haiti

As requested by the General Assembly in 1992,[13] the Secretary-General submitted a report, dated 24 March 1993,[14] stating that, on 8 January, President Aristide made the following requests: deployment by the United Nations and OAS of an international civilian mission in Haiti to monitor respect for human rights and the elimination of all forms of violence; establishment of dialogue among the Haitian parties for the purpose of reaching agreement on the appointment by the President of a Prime Minister to lead a Government of national concord aimed at the full restoration of democratic order, on the reform of Haitian institutions (the judicial system, armed forces and police) and on international assistance for national reconstruction; and a system of guarantees to ensure a lasting solution.

The report noted that the Special Envoy for Haiti, in a series of consultations undertaken since his appointment in December 1992[15] to help resolve the Haitian crisis, sought to achieve agreement on three main issues: the return of President Aristide to Haiti, the appointment of a Prime Minister to head a Government of national concord, and the question of amnesty. As a result of his recent meetings with the Commander-in-Chief of the Armed Forces and the Prime Minister of the de facto Government, Marc Bazin, the Special Envoy obtained from both acceptance in principle of the proposed mission, as well as of the proposed dialogue among the Haitian parties.

Accordingly, the Secretary-General dispatched an advance team, together with a survey group, to Haiti on 13 February to make the necessary preparations for the deployment of the United Nations component of the mission. A three-member human rights team also visited Haiti, from 15 to 22 February, to determine how the mission's tasks should be undertaken. As determined by the Secretary-General and OAS, with President Aristide's agreement, the mission, to be called the International Civilian Mission in Haiti, would be integrated under one Head of Mission, to be appointed jointly by the Secretaries-General of the United Nations and OAS, under whom would be a Director for Human Rights, and an integrated structure down to the level of Local Office Coordinator.

An annex to the report contained a series of recommendations for the deployment of the Mission, the modalities of its operation and requirements in terms of personnel and financial resources. Its initial task would be to verify Haiti's compliance with its human rights obligations, as laid down in the Haitian Constitution and in international human rights instruments to which Haiti was a party, and make recommendations as appropriate, so that a climate conducive to the restoration of constitutional authority might be created. It was to devote special attention to respect for the right to life and integrity and security of person, and to freedom of expression and association.

GENERAL ASSEMBLY ACTION

In addition to the Secretary-General's report, the General Assembly had before it three declarations adopted by the Permanent Council of OAS on 13 January, 11 February and 5 March. The first considered that the partial elections to the Haitian Parliament held by the de facto Government in January were illegitimate; the second trusted that MICIVIH would have the agreed safeguards for the performance of its functions; and the third condemned the recent acts of organized violence and serious human rights violations in Haiti.

Having taken note of those documents, the Assembly adopted **resolution 47/20 B** without vote on 20 April.

The situation of democracy and human rights in Haiti

The General Assembly,

Having considered further the item entitled "The situation of democracy and human rights in Haiti",

Recalling its resolutions 46/7 of 11 October 1991, 46/138 of 17 December 1991, 47/20 A of 24 November 1992 and 47/143 of 18 December 1992, as well as the relevant resolutions and decisions of the Economic and Social Council and the Commission on Human Rights, in particular Commission on Human Rights resolution 1993/68 of 10 March 1993,

Welcoming resolutions MRE/RES.1/91, MRE/RES.2/91, MRE/RES.3/92 and MRE/RES.4/92 adopted on 3 and 8 October 1991, 17 May 1992 and 13 December 1992, respectively, by the Ministers for Foreign Affairs of the member countries of the Organization of American States,

Also welcoming resolution CP/RES.594(923/92) and declarations CP/DEC.8(927/93), CP/DEC.9(931/93) and CP/DEC.10(934/93) adopted by the Permanent Council of the Organization of American States on 10 November 1992, and 13 January, 11 February and 5 March 1993, respectively,

Deploring the fact that, despite the efforts of the international community, the legitimate government of President Jean-Bertrand Aristide has not been re-established and that violent denial of human rights and civil and political liberties continues in Haiti,

Reiterating that the goal of the international community remains the early restoration of democracy in Haiti and the return of President Aristide, the full observance of human rights and fundamental freedoms, and the promotion of social and economic development in Haiti,

Strongly supportive of the continuing leadership by the Secretary-General of the United Nations and the Secretary-General of the Organization of American States of the efforts of the international community to reach a political solution to the Haitian crisis,

Noting with satisfaction the designation by the Secretary-General of the United Nations of a Special Envoy for Haiti and the designation by the Secretary-General of the Organization of American States of the same Special Envoy,

Welcoming the agreement which has made possible the deployment of the International Civilian Mission to Haiti by the United Nations and the Organization of American States, as described in the letter dated 8 January 1993 to the Secretary-General from President Aristide, which is contained in annex I to the report of the Secretary-General,

Convinced that the work of the Mission can contribute to the full observance of human rights and create a climate propitious to the restoration of the constitutional authority,

Expressing its agreement with declaration CP/DEC.8(927/93) of the Permanent Council of the Organization of American States that the partial elections to Parliament held by the de facto government in January 1993 would be illegitimate,

Taking note of the report of the Secretary-General on the situation of democracy and human rights in Haiti and the recommendations contained therein,

1. *Approves* the report of the Secretary-General and the recommendations contained therein for United Nations participation, jointly with the Organization of American States, in the International Civilian Mission to Haiti, with the initial task of verifying compliance with Haiti's international human rights obligations, with a view to making recommendations thereon, in order to assist in the establishment of a climate of freedom and tolerance propitious to the re-establishment of democracy in Haiti;

2. *Decides* to authorize the deployment without delay of the United Nations participation in the International Civilian Mission to Haiti and requests the Secretary-General to take the steps necessary to expedite and strengthen its presence in Haiti;

3. *Expresses its full support* for the International Civilian Mission to Haiti and urges that all parties afford it timely, complete and effective cooperation;

4. *Reiterates* the need for an early return of President Aristide to resume his constitutional functions as President, as the means to restore without further delay the democratic process in Haiti;

5. *Strongly supports* the process of political dialogue under the auspices of the Special Envoy with a view to resolving the political crisis in Haiti;

6. *Considers* that any modifications regarding the economic measures recommended by the ad hoc meeting of the Ministers for Foreign Affairs of the member countries of the Organization of American States should be considered according to progress in the observance of human rights and in the solution of the political crisis leading to the restoration of President Jean-Bertrand Aristide;

7. *Reiterates* that any entity resulting from actions of the de facto regime, including the partial elections to Parliament in January 1993, is illegitimate;

8. *Reaffirms once again* the commitment of the international community to an increase in technical, economic and financial cooperation when constitutional order is restored in Haiti, as a support for its economic and social development efforts and in order to strengthen its institutions responsible for dispensing justice and guaranteeing democracy, political stability and economic development;

9. *Requests* the Secretary-General to make regular reports to the General Assembly on the work of the International Civilian Mission to Haiti, and in particular to report no later than September 1993 on the outcome of the comprehensive review referred to in paragraph 95 of annex III to his report;

10. *Decides* to keep open the consideration of this item until a solution to the situation is found.

General Assembly resolution 47/20 B
20 April 1993   Meeting 100   Adopted without vote

15-nation draft (A/47/L.56 & Add.1); agenda item 22.
Sponsors: Belgium, Belize, Canada, Denmark, France, Germany, Greece, Ireland, Italy, Luxembourg, Netherlands, Portugal, Spain, United Kingdom, United States.
Financial implications: ACABQ, A/47/7/Add.17; 5th Committee, A/47/930; S-G, A/C.5/47/93.
Meeting numbers. GA 47th session: 5th Committee 65; plenary 100.

MICIVIH reports. As requested by the General Assembly, the Secretary-General transmitted to it the Mission's periodic reports on the situation of democracy and human rights in Haiti, which were also transmitted to OAS by the Special Envoy. The first of these was an interim report dated 3 June 1993,[16] covering the period 9 February to 31 May.

The most serious and greatest incidence of human rights violations observed by the Mission included: violations of the right to physical integrity and individual security, intended primarily to restrict or prohibit freedom of expression, of assembly and of peaceful association; abridgement of the freedom of the press, by the continued closure of radio stations and by subjecting journalists and reporters to threats, intimidation, harassment, assault and sometimes detention; systematic beatings and torture; deaths in detention following torture; enforced disappearances, several cases of which the Mission was investigating; and arbitrary executions, perpetrated by "zenglendos" (criminal recruits operating at night in the slums and working-class districts), paramilitary groups, bands of delinquents or State agents.

The report cited cases for each of the foregoing categories of violations, which the Mission had communicated to local or departmental authorities, or, for the most serious cases, to the High Command of the Haitian Armed Forces. Written replies had yet to be received, but the High Command had orally informed the Mission that it had taken measures against perpetrators within the army's ranks.

The report observed that the Mission's presence had encouraged some Haitians to exercise their right to free expression and association and had taken the Haitian police and their auxiliaries somewhat by surprise, but had not led them to abandon their repressive practices. With political negotiations deadlocked, the Armed Forces had adopted a more aggressive attitude to prevent or reduce contact between the Mission and the population.

A second report, transmitted on 25 October,[17] covered the Mission's activities from 1 June to 31 August. The Mission gave wide publicity to its presence and mandate by establishing contacts with local associations, churches and the Haitian authorities, by using radio and television spots, and by distributing information on its purposes and objectives in French and Creole. It intensified its information-gathering, visited prisons and other detention sites, notified local and judicial authorities about cases of concern, submitting recommendations as necessary; and arranged access to legal representation and/or medical treatment for victims. It maintained a dissuasive presence whenever it was feared that violations might occur, such as at peaceful gatherings or demonstrations.

The report gave a full analysis of the human rights situation during the reporting period, based on information gathered on violations of the rights to life, personal integrity and security, and freedom of expression and association. Among the violation cases cited were several assassinations, notably the killings at Port-au-Prince, outside City Hall, at the time of the reinvestiture of the elected mayor on 8 September and the assassinations of Antoine Izméry, a prominent supporter of President Aristide and co-founder of the Joint Committee for the Emergence of the Truth, and of Jean-Claude Maturin near the Church of Sacré-Coeur on 11 September. Thirty cases of enforced disappearance in the capital alone were reported, as were several hundred cases of arbitrary arrests, illegal detention and torture throughout the country. The victims were usually members of political groups or organizations, individual activists or their relatives, or supporters of President Aristide. Many people who had had contact with the Mission became targets of threats by the military.

Apart from the military's clear refusal to permit public demonstrations in support of President Aristide's return, the report stated that the September assassinations appeared to have succeeded in creating a climate of fear in which no such demonstrations were attempted. On the other hand, hostile groups of demonstrators were able to invade the Ministry of Finance on two occasions and to disrupt the investiture of the new Minister for Foreign Affairs. Moreover, a large gathering of self-styled Duvalierists was permitted in central Port-au-Prince on 22 September.

An addendum to the report, transmitted on 18 November,[18] covered the period 1 September to 15/16 October, when the Mission evacuated Haiti for security reasons. The report noted many cases of arbitrary arrests, illegal detention and torture linked to attempts at exercising the right to freedom of expression, mostly of support for President Aristide. It also noted over 60 killings or suspect deaths in Port-au-Prince during September, including targeted assassinations of local political activists by paramilitary groups linked to the Armed Forces.

The Mission's investigation into the assassination of Antoine Izméry found that the perpetrators included an Armed Forces member and several "attachés" (civilian auxiliaries of the army) and concluded that the assassination could have been carried out only with the complicity, if not the direct participation, of high-ranking army members.

National political leaders were also targeted, among them the Minister of Justice, gunned down on 14 October. Groups hostile to the constitutional Government were not only permitted but also encouraged to engage in intimidatory demonstrations, which began to mount throughout Haiti as the date agreed upon for President Aristide's return drew near. Parades were staged on 30 September to celebrate the anniversary of the coup. The recruitment of attachés increased as did the distribution of arms to them; in some places, their presence led to a virtual curfew.

Among the demonstrations' demands were the withdrawal from Haiti of the Special Envoy of the Secretaries-General of the United Nations and OAS and of MICIVIH. Mission observers were increasingly subjected to threats, at times with loaded weapons, from the military and the attachés. On 12 October, about 300 men, some with batons, surrounded the Mission office at Hinche, shouting slogans and tearing down a human rights education banner, after which they proceeded to a Mission residence where they assaulted a local employee and smashed the windows of a Mission vehicle.

Composition

As at 15 September 1993,[17] MICIVIH had 204 human rights observers (against the planned 280) and other substantive professional personnel (97 OAS, 107 United Nations) and 28 international (3 OAS, 25 United Nations) administrative staff deployed in 13 offices set up in the main towns of each of Haiti's nine departments. More than 45 nationalities were represented.

MICIVIH was headquartered at Port-au-Prince, organized into the Office of the Executive Director (media, operations, administration) and the Human Rights Division (Director's Office, investigation and research, legal and human rights departments).

Financing

To finance the initial requirements of MICIVIH, including the Office of the Special Envoy, the advance team, survey group and human rights experts, the Secretary-General sought and received in February 1993[19] the concurrence of ACABQ to enter into commitments of up to $1 million under the terms of a 1991 General Assembly resolution[20] on the 1992-1993 unforeseen and extraordinary expenses. Meanwhile, in discussions between the United Nations and OAS on how costs should be divided between them, it was agreed that each organization would be responsible for the personnel costs of international staff serving in its component.

Requirements for 1993—inclusive of the $1 million commitment authority for initial requirements—were estimated at $23,694,900 net. Of the total, $18,083,200 related to personnel costs (salaries, fees, travel and related allowances) and $5,611,700 to operational costs (such as premises, vehicles, furniture, communications equipment).

Pending agreement with OAS on a comprehensive cost-sharing formula, the Secretary-General requested the Assembly to appropriate $19,112,600 (exclusive of $2,925,000 for staff assessment), which was equivalent to the full costs of the international staff of the United Nations component, plus 35 per cent of the estimated costs of the local personnel, goods and services required to support the joint mission. On the recommendation of ACABQ,[21] the Secretary-General was authorized further commitments of up to $18,112,600 over the previously authorized $1 million.

According to a 29 November report of the Secretary-General,[22] the financial performance for February to 31 December 1993 indicated $13,183,500 in total estimated requirements against the initial commitment authority (interim funding) of $19,112,600, resulting in an estimated net balance of $5,929,100. However, the second performance report under section 2 of the 1992-1993 programme budget would reflect an increase of $13,183,500 relating to MICIVIH, or $5,929,100 less than the total commitment authority for the biennium.

MICIVIH operations had been suspended since 15 October 1993. Except for a small core group remaining in Haiti, international and local staff had been evacuated to Santo Domingo, Dominican Republic. To some extent, this interim status had affected budgetary requirements. For budgetary purposes, the assumption was that normal operations would resume in Haiti in December.

Cost estimates for the three-month period from 1 January to 31 March 1994 totalled $5,936,400, for which an additional appropriation would be required under the relevant section of the 1994-1995 programme budget.

A Trust Fund for Haiti, set up to help meet United Nations costs, had received $1 million from Japan. Approximately $500,000 would be expended in 1993 for consultant fees and operating costs.

The report also stated that the General Secretariat of OAS and the United Nations signed a memorandum of understanding on 6 May assigning responsibilities and costs between the two organizations. Among other provisions, the memorandum confirmed that MICIVIH senior officials would be provided as follows: the Special

Envoy (United Nations), the Executive Director (OAS) and the Human Rights Director (United Nations). It specified how the other categories of staff were to be apportioned, spelt out the modalities for the procurement of goods and services, as well as for administration, assigning the recruitment and payment of local staff to the United Nations, and the procurement and costs of all office accommodations, utilities and commercial communications to OAS. A final agreement on the practical applications of a comprehensive cost-sharing formula was under negotiation.

In the view of ACABQ,[23] the events that had taken place in Haiti since 15 October would affect MICIVIH operations for 1 January to 31 March 1994. Given the current circumstances, it was doubtful that all of the 188 international staff would be deployed, or that consultants would be required during that period. Implementation of public information and human rights education also assumed normal operations, which were currently questionable.

Accordingly, ACABQ recommended approval of only $4 million. Should MICIVIH continue beyond 31 March 1994, or if developments between January and March should call for additional resources, the Secretary-General could seek ACABQ's concurrence to enter into related commitments under the terms of an Assembly resolution to be adopted on unforeseen and extraordinary expenses for 1994-1995. The Fifth Committee, in its consideration of the proposed 1994-1995 programme budget on 19 December,[24] endorsed those recommendations for Assembly approval.

By **section IV of resolution 48/230** of 23 December, on special subjects relating to the proposed 1994-1995 programme budget, the Assembly endorsed the ACABQ recommendations, approved $4 million for the period 1 January to 31 March 1994 and authorized the Secretary-General, should the Mission continue beyond 31 March, to seek ACABQ concurrence to enter into related commitments as recommended.

Sanctions

Haiti, on 7 June 1993,[25] drew the attention of the President of the Security Council to the fact that, despite the international community's efforts during the past 20 months to bring about a reversal of the situation in Haiti and restore the legitimate Government, constitutional order had not been re-established as the de facto authorities continued obstructing all initiatives that had been proposed. Consequently, Haiti requested that the Council make universal and mandatory the sanctions against the de facto authorities adopted at the Ad Hoc Meeting of Ministers for Foreign Affairs of OAS, giving priority to the embargo on petroleum products and arms and munitions.

The Secretary-General, in July,[26] confirmed that the Council had further been informed, in informal consultations on 11 June, that the de facto authorities had not displayed the required political will to reach a negotiated solution to the Haitian crisis, despite efforts exerted since mid-December 1992 by his Special Envoy and OAS to establish dialogue between those authorities and Haiti's constitutional Government. The Secretary-General also mentioned to the Council his belief that, in the absence of stronger pressures by the international community, prospects for a swift and peaceful solution would be in jeopardy. The Special Envoy had also drawn the de facto regime's attention to the fact that sanctions, currently under consideration by the Council, would enter into force on 23 June unless the results of his negotiations enabled the Secretary-General to report that sanctions were not warranted.

SECURITY COUNCIL ACTION (June)

The Security Council convened on 16 June in response to Haiti's request. It had before it, in addition to that request, a letter of 14 June from Cuba[27] asserting that the question at hand did not fall within the purview of the Council, whose primary responsibility under the Charter was the maintenance of international peace and security.

At their request, the Council invited the Bahamas, Canada and Haiti to participate in the discussion without the right to vote, in accordance with the relevant provisions of the Charter and rule 37[a] of the Council's provisional rules of procedure.

The Council unanimously adopted **resolution 841(1993)**.

The Security Council,

Having received a letter from the Permanent Representative of Haiti to the President of the Council dated 7 June 1993 requesting that the Council make universal and mandatory the trade embargo on Haiti recommended by the Organization of American States,

Having also heard a report of the Secretary-General on 10 June 1993 regarding the crisis in Haiti,

Noting resolutions MRE/RES.1/91, MRE/RES.2/91, MRE/RES.3/92 and MRE/RES.4/92 adopted by the Foreign Ministers of the Organization of American States, and resolution CP/RES.594(923/92) and declarations CP/DEC.8(927/93), CP/DEC.9(931/93) and CP/DEC.10(934/93) adopted by the Permanent Council of the Organization of American States,

Noting in particular resolution MRE/RES.5/93 adopted by the Foreign Ministers of the Organization of American States in Managua, Nicaragua, on 6 June 1993,

[a]Rule 37 of the Council's provisional rules of procedure states: "Any Member of the United Nations which is not a member of the Security Council may be invited, as the result of a decision of the Security Council, to participate, without vote, in the discussion of any question brought before the Security Council when the Security Council considers that the interests of that Member are specially affected, or when a Member brings a matter to the attention of the Security Council in accordance with Article 35(1) of the Charter."

Recalling General Assembly resolutions 46/7 of 11 October 1991, 46/138 of 17 December 1991, 47/20 A of 24 November 1992, 47/143 of 18 December 1992 and 47/20 B of 23 April 1993,

Strongly supportive of the continuing leadership by the Secretary-General of the United Nations and the Secretary-General of the Organization of American States and of the efforts of the international community to reach a political solution to the crisis in Haiti,

Commending the efforts undertaken by the Special Envoy for Haiti of the United Nations and Organization of American States Secretaries-General, Mr. Dante Caputo, to establish a political dialogue with the Haitian parties with a view to resolving the crisis in Haiti,

Recognizing the urgent need for an early, comprehensive and peaceful settlement of the crisis in Haiti in accordance with the provisions of the Charter of the United Nations and international law,

Also recalling the statement of 26 February 1993, in which the Council noted with concern the incidence of humanitarian crises, including mass displacements of population, becoming or aggravating threats to international peace and security,

Deploring the fact that, despite the efforts of the international community, the legitimate Government of President Jean-Bertrand Aristide has not been reinstated,

Concerned that the persistence of this situation contributes to a climate of fear of persecution and economic dislocation which could increase the number of Haitians seeking refuge in neighbouring Member States, and convinced that a reversal of this situation is needed to prevent its negative repercussions on the region,

Recalling, in this respect, the provisions of Chapter VIII of the Charter of the United Nations, and stressing the need for effective cooperation between regional organizations and the United Nations,

Considering that the above-mentioned request of the Permanent Representative of Haiti, made within the context of the related actions previously taken by the Organization of American States and by the General Assembly of the United Nations, defines a unique and exceptional situation warranting extraordinary measures by the Security Council in support of the efforts undertaken within the framework of the Organization of American States,

Determining that, in these unique and exceptional circumstances, the continuation of this situation threatens international peace and security in the region,

Acting, therefore, under Chapter VII of the Charter of the United Nations,

1. *Affirms* that the solution of the crisis in Haiti should take into account the above-mentioned resolutions of the Organization of American States and of the General Assembly of the United Nations;

2. *Welcomes* the request of the General Assembly that the Secretary-General take the necessary measures in order to assist, in cooperation with the Organization of American States, in the solution of the crisis in Haiti;

3. *Decides* that the provisions set forth in paragraphs 5 to 14 below, which are consistent with the trade embargo recommended by the Organization of American States, shall come into force at 0001 EST on 23 June 1993 unless the Secretary-General, having regard to the views of the Secretary-General of the Organization of American States, has reported to the Council that, in the light of the results of the negotiations conducted by the Special Envoy for Haiti of the United Nations and Organization of American States Secretaries-General, the imposition of such measures is not warranted at that time;

4. *Decides* that if, at any time after the submission of the above-mentioned report of the Secretary-General, the Secretary-General, having regard to the views of the Secretary-General of the Organization of American States, reports to the Council that the de facto authorities in Haiti have failed to comply in good faith with their undertakings in the above-mentioned negotiations, the provisions set forth in paragraphs 5 to 14 below shall come into force immediately;

5. *Decides* that all States shall prevent the sale or supply, by their nationals or from their territories or using their flag vessels or aircraft, of petroleum or petroleum products or arms and related *matériel* of all types, including weapons and ammunition, military vehicles and equipment, police equipment and spare parts for the aforementioned, whether or not originating in their territories, to any person or body in Haiti or to any person or body for the purpose of any business carried on in or operated from Haiti, and any activities by their nationals or in their territories which promote or are calculated to promote such sale or supply;

6. *Decides* to prohibit any and all traffic from entering the territory or territorial sea of Haiti carrying petroleum or petroleum products, or arms and related *matériel* of all types, including weapons and ammunition, military vehicles and equipment, police equipment and spare parts for the aforementioned, in violation of paragraph 5 above;

7. *Decides* that the Committee established by paragraph 10 below may authorize on an exceptional case-by-case basis under a no-objection procedure the importation, in non-commercial quantities and only in barrels or bottles, of petroleum or petroleum products, including propane gas for cooking, for verified essential humanitarian needs, subject to acceptable arrangements for effective monitoring of delivery and use;

8. *Decides* that States in which there are funds, including any funds derived from property, *(a)* of the Government of Haiti or of the de facto authorities in Haiti, or *(b)* controlled directly or indirectly by such Government or authorities or by entities, wherever located or organized, owned or controlled by such Government or authorities, shall require all persons and entities within their own territories holding such funds to freeze them to ensure that they are not made available directly or indirectly to or for the benefit of the de facto authorities in Haiti;

9. *Calls upon* all States, and all international organizations, to act strictly in accordance with the provisions of the present resolution, notwithstanding the existence of any rights or obligations conferred or imposed by any international agreement or any contract entered into or any licence or permit granted prior to 23 June 1993;

10. *Decides* to establish, in accordance with rule 28 of its provisional rules of procedure, a Committee of the Security Council consisting of all the members of the Council to undertake the following tasks and to report on its work to the Council with its observations and recommendations:

(a) To examine the reports submitted pursuant to paragraph 13 below;

(b) To seek from all States further information regarding the action taken by them concerning the effective implementation of this resolution;

(c) To consider any information brought to its attention by States concerning violations of the measures imposed by this resolution and to recommend appropriate measures in response thereto;

(d) To consider and decide expeditiously requests for the approval of imports of petroleum and petroleum products for essential humanitarian needs in accordance with paragraph 7 above;

(e) To make periodic reports to the Security Council on information submitted to it regarding alleged violations of the present resolution, identifying where possible persons or entities, including vessels, reported to be engaged in such violations;

(f) To promulgate guidelines to facilitate implementation of this resolution;

11. *Calls upon* all States to cooperate fully with the Committee established by paragraph 10 in the fulfilment of its tasks, including supplying such information as may be sought by the Committee in pursuance of the present resolution;

12. *Calls upon* States to bring proceedings against persons and entities violating the measures imposed by this resolution and to impose appropriate penalties;

13. *Requests* all States to report to the Secretary-General by 16 July 1993 on the measures they have initiated for meeting the obligations set out in paragraphs 5 to 9 above;

14. *Requests* the Secretary-General to provide all necessary assistance to the Committee established by paragraph 10 and to make the necessary arrangements in the Secretariat for this purpose;

15. *Requests* the Secretary-General to report to the Security Council, not later than 15 July 1993, and earlier if he considers it appropriate, on progress achieved in the efforts jointly undertaken by him and the Secretary-General of the Organization of American States with a view to reaching a political solution to the crisis in Haiti;

16. *Expresses its readiness* to review all the measures in the present resolution with a view to lifting them if, after the provisions set forth in paragraphs 5 to 14 have come into force, the Secretary-General, having regard to the views of the Secretary-General of the Organization of American States, reports to the Council that the de facto authorities in Haiti have signed and have begun implementing in good faith an agreement to reinstate the legitimate Government of President Jean-Bertrand Aristide;

17. *Decides* to remain seized of the matter.

Security Council resolution 841(1993)

16 June 1993	Meeting 3238	Adopted unanimously

3-nation draft (S/25957).
Sponsors: France, United States, Venezuela.

Upon adoption of the resolution, the President announced that he had been asked by Council members to state that the resolution was warranted by the unique and exceptional situation in Haiti and should not be regarded as constituting a precedent.

Reports of the Secretary-General (July and August). As requested by the Security Council,

the Secretary-General reported to it in July[26] and August[28] that the efforts towards a political solution of the Haitian crisis had resulted in the signing of the Governors Island Agreement and of the New York Pact on 3 and 16 July, respectively (see below, under those topics).

The Secretary-General's recommendation, to which the Council agreed,[29] was to suspend the sanctions under resolution 841(1993) when implementation of the undertakings under the Agreement reached a particular stage, with the proviso that such suspension would be automatically terminated and the sanctions reimposed if the undertakings were not complied with by the parties to the Agreement or by any other authority in Haiti. The sanctions would be lifted definitively upon President Aristide's return to Haiti on 30 October.

In a follow-up report of 26 August,[28] the Secretary-General stated that Robert Malval, the Prime Minister–designate of Haiti, was ratified on 18 and 23 August by the Senate and by the Chamber of Deputies, from which he subsequently won a vote of confidence on his programme on 24 and 25 August. The Prime Minister having been confirmed and having assumed his functions in Haiti, the Secretary-General recommended the immediate suspension of the sanctions.

SECURITY COUNCIL ACTION (August, September and October)

In the light of the Secretary-General's report, the Security Council met on 27 August and invited Haiti, at its request, to participate in the discussions without the right to vote under rule 37.[a] Having considered also the Secretary-General's reports on the Governors Island Agreement and on the New York Pact, the Council unanimously adopted **resolution 861(1993)**.

The Security Council,

Recalling its resolution 841(1993) of 16 June 1993,

Commending the efforts undertaken by the Special Envoy for Haiti of the United Nations and Organization of American States Secretaries-General,

Having considered the relevant parts of the report of the Secretary-General of 12 July 1993,

Taking note with approval of the Governors Island Agreement between the President of the Republic of Haiti and the Commander-in-Chief of the Armed Forces of Haiti, including the provisions of point 4, under which the parties agreed that the sanctions should be suspended immediately after the Prime Minister is confirmed and assumes office in Haiti,

Having also considered the report of the Secretary-General of 13 August 1993 on the New York Pact of 16 July 1993,

Having received the report of the Secretary-General indicating that the Prime Minister of Haiti has been confirmed and has assumed office in Haiti,

Acting under Chapter VII of the Charter of the United Nations,

1. *Decides* that the measures set out in paragraphs 5 to 9 of resolution 841(1993) are suspended with immediate effect and requests all States to act consistently with this decision as soon as possible;

2. *Confirms its readiness,* as noted in the letter from the President of the Council of 15 July 1993, to terminate immediately the suspension of the measures referred to in paragraph 1 above if, at any time, the Secretary-General, having regard for the views of the Secretary-General of the Organization of American States, informs the Security Council that the parties to the Governors Island Agreement or any other authorities in Haiti have not complied in good faith with the Agreement;

3. *Expresses its readiness* to review all the measures in paragraphs 5 to 14 of resolution 841(1993) with a view to lifting them definitively once the Secretary-General, having regard for the views of the Secretary-General of the Organization of American States, informs the Security Council that the relevant provisions of the Governors Island Agreement have been fully implemented;

4. *Decides* to remain seized of the matter.

Security Council resolution 861(1993)

27 August 1993   Meeting 3271   Adopted unanimously

Draft prepared in consultations among Council members (S/26364).

The Security Council convened again on 17 September 1993 amidst reports of a recent upsurge of violence in Haiti, in particular the assassinations in September, and of the increasing incidence of threats to the joint United Nations/OAS International Civilian Mission (see above). Following consultations among Council members, the President made the following statement[30] on behalf of the Council:

Meeting number. SC 3278.

"The Security Council deplores the recent upsurge in violence in Haiti, particularly the events of 11 and 12 September, when at least a dozen people were assassinated, including a prominent supporter of President Aristide during a church service.

"The Council is deeply concerned at these developments as well as at the existence of organized armed civilian groups in the capital which are attempting to interfere with the new Constitutional Government's proper assumption of its functions.

"The Security Council considers it imperative that the Constitutional Government of Haiti assume control over the security forces of the country, and that those responsible for the activities of the organized armed civilian groups throughout the country, and particularly in Port-au-Prince, be held personally accountable for their actions and removed from their functions. The Council also urges the Haitian authorities to take immediate measures with a view to disarming these groups.

"The Council strongly calls on the Commander-in-Chief of the Armed Forces, also in his capacity as signatory to the Governors Island Agreement, to carry out his responsibilities to the fullest by ensuring immediate compliance with the letter and the spirit of the Governors Island Agreement.

"The Council will hold the Haitian military and security authorities personally responsible for the safety of all United Nations personnel in Haiti.

"Unless there is a clear and immediate effort by the security forces to put an end to the present levels of violence and intimidation and unless the above requirements are met, the Security Council will have no alternative but to consider that the authorities responsible for public order in Haiti are not complying in good faith with the Governors Island Agreement.

"Therefore, should the Secretary-General of the United Nations, in accordance with Security Council resolution 861(1993) and having received the views of the Secretary-General of the Organization of American States, inform the Security Council that, in his opinion, there is a serious and consistent non-compliance with the Governors Island Agreement, the Council will immediately reinstate those measures provided for in its resolution 841(1993) appropriate to the situation, with particular emphasis on those measures aimed at those deemed responsible for the non-compliance with the Agreement.

"The Council reaffirms that all the parties in Haiti are bound to comply with their obligations under the Governors Island Agreement, as well as with those embodied in the relevant international treaties to which Haiti is party and in all relevant Security Council resolutions.

"The Council will closely monitor the situation in Haiti in the coming days."

On 11 October, the Council convened urgently regarding that day's events which had prevented the seaborne military component of UNMIH from disembarking at Port-au-Prince (see below, under "UN Mission in Haiti"). Following consultations among Council members, the President made a statement on behalf of the Council deploring those events; reiterating his 17 September statement that serious and consistent non-compliance with the Governors Island Agreement would prompt the Council to reinstate immediately the sanctions under resolution 841(1993), with particular emphasis on measures aimed at those deemed responsible; and requesting an urgent report as to whether the 11 October incidents constituted such non-compliance.

Report of the Secretary-General (October). The Secretary-General submitted the requested report on 13 October.[31] It gave a factual account of the circumstances surrounding the 11 October incidents, including the 7 October general strike against UNMIH, and cited the series of violent incidents including assassinations that had occurred in Haiti during the previous few weeks. The facts led the Secretary-General to conclude that the incidents reflected a lack of will on the part of Haiti's military authorities to cooperate fully in a peaceful transition to a democratic society, as well as an explicit intent to prevent the democratic process agreed on in the Governors Island Agreement from taking its course.

In the light of the consistent non-compliance by the Haitian military and police with the Agreement, as borne out by the facts, the Secretary-

General, taking account also of the view of the OAS Secretary-General, considered it necessary, in accordance with resolution 861(1993), to terminate the suspension of measures set out in paragraphs 5 to 9 of resolution 841(1993).

SECURITY COUNCIL ACTION (13 October)

The Security Council met on 13 October 1993 to take action on the Secretary-General's report. At their request, Barbados, Belize, Dominica, Grenada, Haiti and Saint Vincent and the Grenadines were invited, under rule 37.[a] The Council unanimously adopted **resolution 873(1993)**.

The Security Council,

Recalling its resolutions 841(1993) of 16 June 1993, 861(1993) of 27 August 1993, 862(1993) of 31 August 1993 and 867(1993) of 23 September 1993,

Deeply disturbed by the continued obstruction of the arrival of the United Nations Mission in Haiti (UNMIH), dispatched pursuant to resolution 867(1993), and the failure of the Armed Forces of Haiti to carry out their responsibilities to allow the Mission to begin its work,

Having received the report of the Secretary-General informing the Council that the military authorities of Haiti, including the police, have not complied in good faith with the Governors Island Agreement,

Determining that their failure to fulfil obligations under the Agreement constitutes a threat to peace and security in the region,

Acting under Chapter VII of the Charter of the United Nations,

1. *Decides*, in accordance with paragraph 2 of resolution 861(1993), to terminate the suspension of the measures set out in paragraphs 5 to 9 of resolution 841(1993) as of 2359 hours Eastern Standard Time on 18 October 1993 unless the Secretary-General, having regard to the views of the Secretary-General of the Organization of American States, reports to the Council that the parties to the Governors Island Agreement and any other authorities in Haiti are implementing in full the agreement to reinstate the legitimate Government of President Jean-Bertrand Aristide and have established the necessary measures to enable UNMIH to carry out its mandate;

2. *Decides also* that funds that are required to be frozen pursuant to paragraph 8 of resolution 841(1993) may be released at the request of President Aristide or Prime Minister Malval of Haiti;

3. *Decides further* that the Committee established by paragraph 10 of resolution 841(1993) shall have the authority, in addition to that set forth in that paragraph, to grant exceptions to the prohibitions (other than those referred to in paragraph 2 above) referred to in paragraph 1 above on a case-by-case basis under the no-objection procedure in response to requests by President Aristide or Prime Minister Malval of Haiti;

4. *Confirms* its readiness to consider urgently the imposition of additional measures if the Secretary-General informs the Security Council that the parties to the Governors Island Agreement or any other authorities in Haiti continue to impede the activities of UNMIH or interfere with the freedom of movement and communication of UNMIH and its members as well as the other rights necessary for the performance of its mandate, or have not complied in full with relevant Security Council resolutions and the provisions of the Governors Island Agreement;

5. *Decides* to remain actively seized of the matter.

Security Council resolution 873(1993)
13 October 1993   Meeting 3291   Adopted unanimously
Draft prepared in consultations among Council members (S/26578).

Communication (15 October). On 15 October,[32] elected President Jean-Bertrand Aristide drew to the Secretary-General's attention the assassination on the previous day of the Minister of Justice, François-Guy Malary. In view of that and noting the violations of the Governors Island Agreement, he requested that the Security Council, under the authority vested in it by Chapter VII of the Charter, call on Member States to take the necessary measures to strengthen the provisions of resolution 873(1993).

SECURITY COUNCIL ACTION (16 and 25 October)

Responding to the Haitian President's request, the Security Council met on 16 October and invited Canada and Haiti, at their request, to participate without the right to vote under rule 37.[a] Following statements by several States, including Haiti, the Council unanimously adopted **resolution 875(1993)**.

The Security Council,

Reaffirming its resolutions 841(1993) of 16 June 1993, 861(1993) of 27 August 1993, 862(1993) of 31 August 1993, 867(1993) of 23 September 1993 and 873(1993) of 13 October 1993,

Noting resolutions MRE/RES.1/91, MRE/RES.2/91, MRE/RES.3/92 and MRE/RES.4/92 adopted by the Foreign Ministers of the Organization of American States, and resolution CP/RES.594(923/92) and declarations CP/DEC.8(927/93), CP/DEC.9(931/93), CP/DEC.10(934/93) and CP/DEC.15(967/93), adopted by the Permanent Council of the Organization of American States,

Deeply disturbed by the continued obstruction to the dispatch of the United Nations Mission in Haiti (UNMIH), pursuant to resolution 867(1993), and the failure of the Armed Forces of Haiti to carry out their responsibilities to allow the mission to begin its work,

Condemning the assassination of officials of the legitimate Government of President Jean-Bertrand Aristide,

Taking note of the letter of President Jean-Bertrand Aristide to the Secretary-General of 15 October 1993, in which he requested the Council to call on Member States to take the necessary measures to strengthen the provisions of Security Council resolution 873(1993),

Mindful of the report of the Secretary-General of 13 October 1993 informing the Council that the military authorities in Haiti, including the police, have not complied in full with the Governors Island Agreement,

Reaffirming its determination that, in these unique and exceptional circumstances, the failure of the military authorities in Haiti to fulfil their obligations under the

Agreement constitutes a threat to peace and security in the region,

Acting under Chapters VII and VIII of the Charter of the United Nations,

1. *Calls upon* Member States, acting nationally or through regional agencies or arrangements, cooperating with the legitimate Government of Haiti, to use such measures commensurate with the specific circumstances as may be necessary under the authority of the Security Council to ensure strict implementation of the provisions of resolutions 841(1993) and 873(1993) relating to the supply of petroleum or petroleum products or arms and related *matériel* of all types, and in particular to halt inward maritime shipping as necessary in order to inspect and verify their cargoes and destinations;

2. *Confirms* that it is prepared to consider further necessary measures to ensure full compliance with the provisions of relevant Security Council resolutions;

3. *Decides* to remain actively seized of the matter.

Security Council resolution 875(1993)

16 October 1993   Meeting 3293   Adopted unanimously

4-nation draft (S/26586).
Sponsors: Canada, France, United States, Venezuela.

The Council held another meeting on 25 October and, following consultations among its members, the President made the following statement[33] on behalf of the Council:

Meeting number. SC 3298.

"The Security Council reaffirms the necessity of full compliance with the Governors Island Agreement. It condemns the acts of the military authorities in Haiti, who continue to hamper the full implementation of the Agreement, in particular by permitting the development of acts of violence in violation of their obligations under the Agreement. It gives full support to the efforts of the Special Representative of the Secretary-General, Mr. Dante Caputo, to put an end to the crisis and to ensure the return, without delay, of democracy and the rule of law in Haiti.

"The Security Council, recalling points 7 and 8 of the Governors Island Agreement concerning the departure of the Commander-in-Chief of the Haitian Armed Forces and the appointment of a new Commander of the police force, insists that these provisions be implemented without further delay.

"The Security Council reiterates its support for the legitimate Government of Haiti and recalls that it holds the military authorities responsible for the security of that Government and of the parliamentarians. It also continues to hold the military authorities responsible for the safety and security of all United Nations personnel in Haiti.

"The Security Council warns that, should the Governors Island Agreement not be fully implemented, it will consider imposing measures additional to those imposed by resolutions 841(1993), 873(1993) and 875(1993).

"The Security Council underlines the importance of the full implementation of the measures contained in the above-mentioned resolutions by all States, including nearby countries.

"The Council will continue to monitor closely the situation in Haiti in the coming days."

Governors Island Agreement

In keeping with a Security Council request, the Secretary-General reported on 12 July 1993[26] that the Special Envoy had obtained the agreement of the President of Haiti, Jean-Bertrand Aristide, and the Commander-in-Chief of the Armed Forces of Haiti, General Raoul Cédras, to participate in a meeting with him at Governors Island, New York. The meeting took place from 27 June to 3 July and concluded with the signing, by the President and the General, of the Governors Island Agreement embodying arrangements, to be implemented in 10 stages, for the resolution of the Haitian crisis. The text of the Agreement was incorporated in the report. Both signatories pledged to cooperate fully in the peaceful transition to a stable and lasting democratic society in which all Haitians would be able to live in a climate of freedom, justice, security and respect for human rights.

The arrangements called for a dialogue among the political parties represented in the Haitian Parliament, in which the Presidential Commission would participate, to be organized under United Nations and OAS auspices, in order to agree on: a political truce and promotion of a social pact to create the conditions for a peaceful transition; a procedure for enabling Parliament to resume its normal functioning and for the speedy confirmation of a Prime Minister; and the adoption of laws necessary for the transition.

Also called for were: nomination by the President of a Prime Minister, his confirmation by the legally reconstituted Parliament and assumption to office in Haiti; followed by the suspension of the sanctions under Security Council resolution 841(1993) and of those adopted by OAS; technical and financial assistance for development, administrative and judicial reform and, with the presence of United Nations personnel, modernization of the Armed Forces of Haiti and creation of a new police force; an amnesty to be granted by the President; enactment of a law creating the new police force and providing for the appointment of its Commander-in-Chief by the President; appointment of a new Commander-in-Chief of the Armed Forces, in view of General Cédras's decision to take early retirement; and return to Haiti of President Jean-Bertrand Aristide on 30 October. Fulfilment of all the foregoing commitments would be subject to United Nations and OAS verification.

The Secretary-General stated his intention to entrust verification of the Agreement to the Special Envoy, who would report periodically to him and to the OAS Secretary-General. He would propose that MICIVIH remain in effect and recommend Council endorsement of the proposal to suspend the sanctions immediately after the duly nominated and confirmed Prime Minister assumed his functions in Haiti. However, the suspension should be automatically terminated if the parties, or any authorities in Haiti, failed to comply in good faith with the Agreement. He would report to the Council upon President Aristide's return to Haiti, with a view to having the sanctions lifted definitively.

On 15 July,[29] the Security Council declared its readiness to give the fullest possible support to the Agreement, to suspend the sanctions in force at the appropriate stage of the Agreement's implementation, with a provision for the automatic termination of the suspension as proposed, and to terminate the sanctions on receipt of the Secretary-General's confirmation that President Aristide had returned to Haiti.

SECURITY COUNCIL ACTION

The Security Council, in the statement of 25 October 1993[33] made by its President, reaffirmed the necessity of full compliance with the Agreement—as it did on 30 October[9]— and condemned the acts of the Haitian military who continued to hamper its full implementation, in particular by permitting the development of acts of violence in violation of their obligations under the Agreement. The Council insisted that the provisions of the Agreement concerning the departure of the Commander-in-Chief of the Armed Forces and the appointment of a new Commander of the police force be implemented without delay.

New York Pact

The Secretary-General reported on 13 August 1993[34] that, after the signing of the Governors Island Agreement, the inter-Haitian political dialogue it called for was convened by the Special Envoy. The dialogue took place at United Nations Headquarters, New York, from 14 to 16 July, at the conclusion of which the participants signed the New York Pact, providing for a six-month political truce, for a procedure to enable Parliament to resume its functioning and agreements for the early confirmation of a Prime Minister nominated by the President to head a Government of national concord, and for the adoption of the legal instruments necessary for ensuring the transition. The text of the Pact was annexed to the report.

Under the Pact, the political parties and parliamentary blocs undertook, among other things, to refrain from tabling in Parliament any motion of no-confidence against the new Government of national concord, to secure the immediate release of all persons detained for offences relating to their views and to have the status of prisoners reviewed, to promote the establishment of a compensation commission for the victims of the *coup d'état*,[35] and to ensure confirmation of the new Prime Minister without delay. They also

undertook to ensure passage by Parliament of a series of bills under an emergency procedure, including those relating to the setting up of a new police force, an amnesty, the abolition of all paramilitary forces, the creation of a Citizens' Protection Bureau, and reform of the judicial system. They reaffirmed the right of the Executive to review the various decrees and orders adopted from 30 September 1991 (the day after the *coup d'état*) to 3 July 1993 (the date of the Agreement) that were not in accord with the Constitution, particularly the order that created the Permanent Emergency Electoral Council.

With respect to the 13 Parliament members who derived their mandate from the partial elections held on 18 January, it was agreed that they should voluntarily refrain from occupying their seats until the Conciliation Commission—a constitutional organ whose functioning required the adoption by Parliament of a law under the emergency procedure—had definitively pronounced itself on the matter. Those elections were rejected as illegitimate by the OAS Permanent Council and by the General Assembly. During the dialogue, the Special Envoy stressed that the United Nations position on those elections remained unchanged.

Hence, it was the Secretary-General's understanding that, as agreed, those members of the Senate and the Chamber of Deputies who were in office by virtue of the contested 18 January elections were to abstain from participating in any Parliament business; failure to do so would constitute a serious breach of the Agreement, to be reported to the Security Council.

As with the undertakings under the Agreement, those under the Pact were subject to United Nations and OAS verification.

The Secretary-General further reported that President Aristide informed the Presidents of the two chambers of Parliament on 24 July of his intention to nominate Robert Malval as Prime Minister. A new Bureau was elected in the Chamber of Deputies on 22 and 28 July and in the Senate on 10 August. With the normalization of Parliament, the way had been cleared for the ratification of the Prime Minister.

UN Mission in Haiti

The Governors Island Agreement provided for, among other things, the presence of United Nations personnel to assist in modernizing the Armed Forces of Haiti and establishing a new police force. The President of Haiti, on 24 July 1993,[36] proposed terms of reference governing the assistance which Haiti hoped to receive in this regard.

Assistance to the police sector would be to enhance the functioning of the existing security forces until the new police force, which the United Nations would help to create, was capable of assuming its responsibilities. For this purpose, 500 to 600 United Nations police officers would be required. Assistance in respect of the Armed Forces would be to attain the degree of professionalism required to discharge their constitutional obligations, in particular to ensure the security and integrity of the Republic, assist in times of natural disasters and carry out development tasks pursuant to the relevant articles of the Constitution. United Nations personnel needed for those tasks would be 50 to 60 instructors and some 500 engineers and construction experts.

Report of the Secretary-General (August). On the basis of the President's proposal and taking account of the advice of the Special Envoy and the Friends of the Secretary-General for Haiti (Canada, France, United States, Venezuela), the Secretary-General, in a report of 25 August to the Security Council,[37] set out his recommendations for a United Nations Mission in Haiti, with civilian police and military components, to carry out the assistance called for.

Pending adoption of legislation necessary for the creation of the new police force and appointment of a Commander-in-Chief of the Police by the President, some 567 civilian police, to be known as United Nations police monitors, would assist the Government in monitoring the activities of those members of the Armed Forces charged with police functions, since the responsibilities of the Armed Forces currently included both military and police functions. The police monitors would provide guidance and training to all levels of the Haitian police and ensure that police actions were in keeping with legal requirements.

In order to perform their duties, the police monitors would require access to information on the deployment of all personnel charged with civilian police functions, including control of civil disturbances, and freedom of movement throughout Haiti. They should be entitled to hold discussions freely and confidentially with any individual or group, including those in the Armed Forces performing police functions, the Ministry of Justice and other components of the judicial system, as well as to submit recommendations regarding particular cases or situations and to make follow-up inquiries.

The task of modernizing the Armed Forces would be discharged by an average of five training teams of 12 trainers each, on duty in Haiti at any given time, and a military construction unit with a strength of approximately 500 all ranks. The teams would provide non-combat training in what would become their primary mission, as responsibility for internal security was transferred from the Armed Forces to the new police force. Training would aim to develop a range of capabilities in military engineering (such as road-

building and well-drilling), disaster relief, search and rescue operations, and border and coastal surveillance. The teams would work with the Haitian Government to develop a modern code of conduct, reform the military justice system and improve the effectiveness of the Inspector General of the Armed Forces.

The United Nations military construction unit would provide the Haitian military with on-the-job training in construction projects, to include the construction of new barracks; the conversion to civilian use of military facilities no longer required by the Armed Forces under their newly defined mission; the renovation of medical facilities; and road repair and well-drilling in rural areas. The projects would take six to eight months to complete.

UNMIH would be under the command of the United Nations, vested in the Secretary-General under the authority of the Security Council. It would be headed by a Special Representative of the Secretary-General, namely, the Special Envoy, who was already overseeing MICIVIH and who would coordinate the activities of the two missions. UNMIH would set up headquarters at Port-au-Prince, with sub-headquarters in other parts of the country as required.

The Secretary-General recommended that the Council authorize the establishment of UNMIH for an initial period of six months, to be dispatched as soon as the conditions set out in the Governors Island Agreement were met.

SECURITY COUNCIL ACTION (August)

The Security Council convened on 31 August 1993 regarding the Secretary-General's report and unanimously adopted **resolution 862(1993)**.

The Security Council,
Recalling its resolutions 841(1993) of 16 June 1993 and 861(1993) of 27 August 1993,
Recalling also the Governors Island Agreement between the President of the Republic of Haiti and the Commander-in-Chief of the Armed Forces of Haiti, of 3 July 1993, contained in the report of the Secretary-General of 12 July 1993, and the letter of the President of the Republic of Haiti to the Secretary-General of 24 July 1993,
Commending the efforts undertaken by the Special Envoy for Haiti of the United Nations and Organization of American States Secretaries-General,
Noting that point 5 of the Governors Island Agreement calls for international assistance in modernizing the armed forces of Haiti and establishing a new police force with the presence of United Nations personnel in these fields,
Reaffirming the international community's commitment to a resolution of the crisis in Haiti, including a restoration of democracy,
Recalling the situation in Haiti and the continuing responsibility of the Council under the Charter for the maintenance of international peace and security,

1. *Takes note* of the Secretary-General's report of 25 August 1993 to the Security Council, which contains recommendations concerning United Nations assistance in the modernization of the armed forces as well as in the establishment of a new police force in Haiti under a proposed United Nations Mission in Haiti;

2. *Approves* the dispatch as soon as possible of an advance team of not more than 30 personnel to assess requirements and prepare for the possible dispatch of both the civilian police and military assistance components of the proposed United Nations Mission in Haiti;

3. *Decides* that the mandate of the advance team will expire within one month, and contemplates that this advance team could be incorporated into the proposed United Nations Mission in Haiti if and when such a mission is formally established by the Council;

4. *Looks forward* to a further report of the Secretary-General on the proposed establishment of the United Nations Mission in Haiti, including in particular a detailed estimate of the cost and scope of this operation, a time-frame for its implementation, and the projected conclusion of this operation, and how to ensure coordination, *inter alia*, between it and the work of the Organization of American States, with a view to establishing the proposed mission on an expeditious basis, if the Council so decides;

5. *Urges* the Secretary-General to enter expeditiously into discussions with the Government of Haiti on a status-of-mission agreement to facilitate the early dispatch of the United Nations Mission in Haiti, if and when the Council so decides;

6. *Decides* to remain seized of the matter.

Security Council resolution 862(1993)

31 August 1993   Meeting 3272   Adopted unanimously

Draft prepared in consultations among Council members (S/26384).

Report of the Secretary-General (September). In keeping with paragraph 4 of resolution 862(1993), the Secretary-General submitted a further report on 21 September,[38] supplementing information provided in his August report.[37] It described the findings of an advance team of military, police and civilian specialists, led by the Special Envoy, dispatched to Haiti on 8 September. As instructed, the advance team undertook a detailed survey of requirements; a small group remained behind after the return of most of the team on 12 September to prepare for the eventual deployment of UNMIH if the Council so decided.

The advance team met with a number of Haitian officials representing the Constitutional Government, among them the new Prime Minister and the Armed Forces, including their Commander-in-Chief. Notwithstanding assurances by both sides of their desire to pursue implementation of the Governors Island Agreement, a gulf of mistrust and suspicion divided them. In the Special Envoy's opinion, that called for a tangible demonstration of the international community's commitment to solve the Haitian crisis.

For the organizational purpose of the police component, the territory of Haiti would be divided into four administrative divisions, with headquarters at Port-au-Prince. To the extent possible, United Nations police monitors would be deployed at the same locations as MICIVIH, but would maintain presence in all departmental capitals. They would adapt their deployment in such a manner as to encourage partnership between police and the communities they served.

Military assistance over the six-month mandate period would be a three-phased operation: the first phase would cover deployment of military units and installation of a base camp; the second would be devoted to training the Haitian military in various disciplines and initiating engineering and medical assistance projects; in the third and final phase, training would be expanded and projects completed. Parallel with those activities, the Armed Forces would be reorganized into five battalions and deployed throughout the country.

As to coordination between UNMIH and MICIVIH, both would operate under the overall authority of the Secretary-General's Special Representative (also the Special Envoy for Haiti). UNMIH police monitors would work with the Department of Investigation and Research within the MICIVIH Human Rights Division. MICIVIH would provide an orientation course for the police monitors, drawing on its experience and familiarity with the Haitian political and social environment. While separate budgets would be maintained for both missions, they would come under a single administrative unit under the Special Representative, with the unit's costs to be shared between the two budgets.

UNMIH and its personnel would be granted all relevant privileges and immunities provided for by the 1946 Convention on the Privileges and Immunities of the United Nations.[39] The status-of-mission agreement for UNMIH would be signed with the Government to facilitate the early dispatch of the mission. In view of the violence prevailing in the country, the Secretary-General would appoint a Security Adviser to coordinate the security requirements of the entire United Nations presence in Haiti.

In an addendum to his report,[40] the Secretary-General estimated the total operating cost for the six-month period at $49,856,000. The costs were to be considered an expense of the Organization to be borne by Member States; the assessments to be levied on them should be credited to a special account to be established for the purpose.

UNMIH personnel would consist of 99 international and 271 local civilian staff, 567 police monitors and 700 (rather than the original estimate of 500) military personnel, including 60 military trainers.

As later reported by the Secretary-General,[41] an advance team of 53 military and 51 police personnel was deployed at Port-au-Prince during September and October. The Status-of-Mission Agreement was signed by the new Prime Minister and the Secretary-General's Special Representative on 9 October.

Following consultations with Governments, the Secretary-General stated that the military component of UNMIH would be contributed by Argentina, Canada and the United States, and the police component by Algeria, Austria, Canada, France, Indonesia, Madagascar, the Russian Federation, Senegal, Spain, Switzerland, Tunisia and Venezuela.

SECURITY COUNCIL ACTION (September and October)

The Security Council, having before it the Secretary-General's September report, unanimously adopted **resolution 867(1993)** on 23 September.

The Security Council,

Recalling its resolutions 841(1993) of 16 June 1993, 861(1993) of 27 August 1993 and 862(1993) of 31 August 1993,

Recalling also relevant resolutions adopted by the General Assembly and the Organization of American States,

Noting the report of the Secretary-General of 21 September 1993, and the reports of the Secretary-General of 25 August 1993 and 26 August 1993, submitted pursuant to his reports to the Security Council dated 12 July 1993 and 13 August 1993,

Taking note of the letter dated 24 July 1993 from the Secretary-General to the President of the Security Council conveying a proposal from the Government of Haiti requesting the United Nations to provide assistance in creating a new police force and in modernizing the Haitian armed forces,

Stressing the importance of the Governors Island Agreement of 3 July 1993 between the President of the Republic of Haiti and the Commander-in-Chief of the Armed Forces of Haiti towards promoting the return of peace and stability in Haiti, including the provisions of paragraph 5, under which the parties call for assistance for modernizing the armed forces of Haiti and establishing a new police force with the presence of United Nations personnel in these fields,

Strongly supportive of the efforts to implement that Agreement, and to permit the resumption of the normal operations of government in Haiti, including police and military functions, under civilian control,

Recalling the situation in Haiti and the continuing responsibility of the Council under the Charter for the maintenance of international peace and security,

Concerned about the escalation of politically motivated violence in Haiti at this time of critical political transition, and recalling in this respect the statement of the President of the Security Council of 17 September 1993,

Considering that there is an urgent need to ensure conditions for the full implementation of the Governors Island Agreement and the political accords contained in the New York Pact as contained in the annex to the report of the Secretary-General of 13 August 1993,

1. *Approves* the recommendation of the Secretary-General contained in his report of 21 September 1993 and his report of 25 August 1993 to authorize the establishment and immediate dispatch of the United Nations Mission in Haiti (UNMIH) for a period of six months subject to the proviso that it will be extended beyond seventy-five days only upon a review by the Council to be based on a report from the Secretary-General on whether or not substantive progress has been made towards the implementation of the Governors Island Agreement and the political accords contained in the New York Pact;

2. *Decides* that, in accordance with the report of 21 September 1993, the United Nations Mission shall comprise up to 567 United Nations police monitors (UNPMs) and a military construction unit with a strength of approximately 700, including 60 military trainers;

3. *Determines* that the UNPMs shall provide guidance and training to all levels of the Haitian police and monitor the way in which the operations are implemented in accordance with paragraph 9 of the report of the Secretary-General of 21 September 1993;

4. *Also determines* that the military component of the Mission in charge of modernization of the armed forces shall have the following roles:

(a) The military training teams shall provide non-combat training, as outlined in paragraph 17 of the report of the Secretary-General of 21 September 1993, to meet requirements determined through coordination between the Chief of the United Nations Mission and the Government of Haiti;

(b) The military construction unit will work with the Haitian military to carry out projects, as specified in paragraph 15 of the report of the Secretary-General of 25 August 1993 and as described in paragraph 16 of his report of 21 September 1993;

5. *Welcomes* the intention of the Secretary-General to place the peace-keeping mission under the oversight of the Special Representative of the Secretaries-General of the United Nations and of the Organization of American States, who also oversees the activities of the International Civilian Mission (MICIVIH), so that the peace-keeping mission may benefit from the experience and information already obtained by MICIVIH;

6. *Calls upon* the Government of Haiti to take all appropriate steps to ensure the safety of United Nations personnel, as well as to ensure the freedom of movement and communication of the Mission and its members as well as the other rights necessary for the performance of its task, and in this regard urges the conclusion at the earliest possible stage of a Status-of-Mission Agreement;

7. *Notes* that such safety and freedoms are a prerequisite for the successful implementation of the Mission, and requests the Secretary-General to report to the Council in the event such conditions do not exist;

8. *Calls upon* all factions in Haiti explicitly and publicly to renounce, and to direct their supporters to renounce, violence as a means of political expression;

9. *Requests* the Secretary-General to dispatch the United Nations Mission in Haiti on an urgent basis;

10. *Encourages* the Secretary-General to establish a trust fund or make other arrangements to assist in the financing of the Mission, along the lines and conditions outlined in paragraph 26 of the report of the Secretary-

General of 21 September 1993, and to seek for this purpose pledges and contributions from Member States and others, and encourages Member States to make voluntary contributions to this fund;

11. *Requests* the Secretary-General to seek contributions of personnel from Member States for the civilian police and military components of the Mission, as specified in paragraph 18 of his report of 25 August 1993;

12. *Expresses the hope* that States will assist the legally constituted Government of Haiti in carrying out actions consistent with the restoration of democracy as called for by the Governors Island Agreement, the New York Pact and other relevant resolutions and agreements;

13. *Expresses its appreciation* for the constructive role of the Organization of American States in cooperation with the United Nations in promoting the solution of the political crisis and the restoration of democracy in Haiti and, in this context, stresses the importance of ensuring close coordination between the United Nations and the Organization of American States in their work in Haiti;

14. *Requests* the Secretary-General to submit progress reports to the Council on the implementation of the present resolution by 10 December 1993 and 25 January 1994, thus keeping the Council fully informed on actions taken to implement the Mission;

15. *Decides* to remain actively seized of the matter.

Security Council resolution 867(1993)
23 September 1993   Meeting 3282   Adopted unanimously

Draft by United States (S/26484), orally revised.

On 4 October, the Secretary-General informed the Council that, following the usual consultations, he intended to appoint Colonel Gregg Pulley (United States) as Commander of UNMIH's military unit[42] and Superintendent Jean-Jacques Lemay (Canada) as Commander of the police unit.[43] The Council agreed to those appointments on 6 October.[44]

The Council met again on 11 October regarding that day's events that prevented the military component of UNMIH aboard the USS *Harlan County* from landing at Port-au-Prince. Following consultations among Council members, the President was authorized to make the following statement[45] on behalf of the Council:

Meeting number. SC 3289.

"The Security Council is deeply concerned with the situation in Haiti and deeply deplores the events of 11 October 1993, when organized armed civilian groups ('attachés') threatened journalists and diplomats waiting to meet a contingent of the United Nations Mission in Haiti (UNMIH) dispatched pursuant to Security Council resolution 867(1993). Moreover, the disturbance created by these armed groups, and a lack of dock personnel, prevented the landing in Port-au-Prince of the ship carrying the contingent. The Security Council considers it imperative that the Armed Forces of Haiti carry out their responsibilities to ensure that obstructions such as these to the safe and successful dispatch of UNMIH end immediately.

"The Council reiterates, in accordance with its Presidential statement of 17 September 1993, that serious and consistent non-compliance with the Governors Island Agreement will prompt the Council to reinstate immediately those measures provided for in its resolution 841(1993) appropriate to the situation, with particular emphasis on those measures aimed at those deemed responsible for this non-compliance. In that context, the Security Council requests the Secretary-General to report urgently to the Council whether the incidents of 11 October constitute such non-compliance by the Armed Forces of Haiti with the Governors Island Agreement.

"The Council looks forward to the Secretary-General's report and will closely monitor the situation in Haiti in the coming days."

Reports of the Secretary-General (October and November). Replying to the Security Council's request to report whether the incident of 11 October constituted serious and consistent non-compliance by the Armed Forces of Haiti with the Governors Island Agreement, the Secretary-General submitted a report on 13 October,[46] describing the 11 October incidents as the nadir of a progressively deteriorating situation in Haiti.

The report pointed to the repeatedly observed lack of will on the part of the Armed Forces Command to facilitate deployment and operation of UNMIH, creating obstacles instead to delay its emplacement. Despite written commitments from the military and port authorities, the *Harlan County*, transporting the military component of UNMIH, was blocked from docking at Port-au-Prince. Port authorities denied having had contact with United Nations representatives and left the field clear for armed civilians who engaged in acts of intimidation, firing into the air and threatening Haitian and international journalists, as well as representatives of the international community. In spite of appeals to the Commander-in-Chief of the Armed Forces (General Cédras) and to the police chief (Lieutenant-Colonel Michel François), nothing was done to bring the situation under control.

A general strike had been declared against UNMIH earlier, on 7 October, instigated by a group known as Front pour l'avancement et le progrès d'Haïti, which on numerous occasions had threatened the Prime Minister and cabinet members, the Secretary-General's Special Representative and the French and Canadian personnel of UNMIH who were among the advance contingents of 53 military engineers and 51 civilian police deployed at Port-au-Prince during late September and early October.

The report also cited the attack on the Prime Minister's offices on 5 October by some 200 armed civilians, with police participating, as well as the complete disregard of government instructions by the military and police. All these examples, the report noted, reflected a clear and explicit intent to prevent the democratic process from taking its course.

The Secretary-General, taking account of the views of the OAS Secretary-General, was thus compelled to inform the Council that the Commander-in-Chief of the Armed Forces of Haiti, as one of the parties to the Agreement, and the police chief and commander of the Port-au-Prince metropolitan area, as one of the authorities in Haiti, had failed to fulfil the commitments entered into under the Agreement.

In a report of 26 November[47] on whether or not substantive progress had been made towards implementing the Governors Island Agreement and the New York Pact, the Secretary-General restated that various developments in Haiti had undermined the UNMIH mandate, in particular the 11 October incident. As a result of subsequent developments, the advance elements of UNMIH were withdrawn from Haiti, following the departure of the *Harlan County* on 13 October. The bulk of MICIVIH was likewise withdrawn on 15 October. The Special Representative and several assistants remained at Port-au-Prince.

The success of UNMIH, the Secretary-General stated, depended on the full and active cooperation of the two parties to the Governors Island Agreement; that cooperation had not been forthcoming from the Haitian military authorities. In the circumstances, he was obliged to conclude that the mandate entrusted to UNMIH by resolution 867(1993) could not be implemented until there was a clear and substantial change of attitude on the part of the Haitian military leaders.

The President of the Security Council stated on 10 December 1993[48] that, based on the Secretary-General's November report,[47] the Council had found no reason why the UNMIH mandate should not be continued for the full six-month period authorized by resolution 867(1993).

Financing

In a report of 9 December 1993[49] on the financing of 17 peace-keeping operations, including UNMIH, the Secretary-General stated that negotiations were continuing in Haiti among his Special Representative, the local authorities and the military regarding the emplacement of UNMIH. If and when the matter was resolved, the necessary resources would have to be provided.

For budgetary purposes, therefore, it was assumed that UNMIH would be continued at its current level, pending further developments. Requirements for its maintenance from its inception on 23 September 1993 to 30 April 1994 were estimated at $1,383,000, inclusive of the initial expenditures incurred by the survey and technical missions to Haiti ($59,500) and by the advance team ($137,500), estimated expenditures incurred until 31 October ($1,034,000) and maintenance costs from 1 November 1993 to 30 April 1994 ($152,000). A monthly maintenance cost of $25,300 as of 1 November 1993 was to cover the subsistence allowance for two liaison officers (military and police) and the salary and related costs for one P-5 officer (spokesman). A breakdown of the total requirement by major line-items of expenditure was also provided.

ACABQ, on 17 December,[50] recommended that, for the period indicated, the General Assembly authorize the Secretary-General to enter into commitments up to $1,383,000 gross ($1,364,000 net).

As requested by ACABQ,[51] the Secretary-General subsequently submitted a separate report on the financing of UNMIH, dated 22 December,[52] annexing a detailed table of cost estimates for 23 September 1993 to 22 March 1994, together with the usual supplementary information. It also contained a recommendation for the establishment of a special account for UNMIH.

The General Assembly, in December 1993, adopted **decision 48/477** without vote.

Financing of the United Nations Mission in Haiti

At its 87th plenary meeting, on 23 December 1993, the General Assembly, on the recommendation of the Fifth Committee, in accordance with the framework set out in its resolution 48/227 of 23 December 1993, having considered the report of the Secretary-General on the financing of seventeen peace-keeping operations and the related reports of the Advisory Committee on Administrative and Budgetary Questions, and concurring with the observations of the Advisory Committee:

(a) Authorized the Secretary-General, on an exceptional basis, to enter into commitments up to the amount of 1,383,000 United States dollars gross (1,364,000 dollars net) for the United Nations Mission in Haiti for the period from 23 September 1993 to 22 March 1994, and requested him to establish a special account for the Mission;

(b) Decided to apportion, as an ad hoc arrangement, the amount indicated in subparagraph *(a)* above among Member States in accordance with the composition of groups set out in paragraphs 3 and 4 of Assembly resolution 43/232 of 1 March 1989, as adjusted by the Assembly in its resolutions 44/192 B of 21 December 1989, 45/269 of 27 August 1991, 46/198 A of 20 December 1991 and 47/218 A of 23 December 1992 and its decision 48/472 of 23 December 1993, and taking into account the scale of assessments for the years 1992, 1993 and 1994 as set out in Assembly resolutions 46/221 A of 20 December 1991 and 48/223 A of 23 December 1993 and its decision 47/456 of 23 December 1992;

(c) Also decided that, in accordance with the provisions of its resolution 973(X) of 15 December 1955, there

should be set off against the apportionment among Member States, as provided for in subparagraph *(b)* above, their respective share in the Tax Equalization Fund of the estimated staff assessment income of 19,000 dollars for the period from 23 September 1993 to 22 March 1994.

General Assembly decision 48/477

Adopted without vote

Approved by Fifth Committee (A/48/826) without vote, 22 December (meeting 46); draft by Chairman (A/C.5/48/L.28); agenda item 165.
Meeting numbers. GA 48th session: 5th Committee 44, 46; plenary 87.

Also on 23 December, the Assembly, by **decision 48/484**, retained the item on the financing of UNMIH for consideration during its forty-eighth session.

REFERENCES

(1)S/25277. (2)YUN 1992, p. 234, GA res. 47/19, 24 Nov. 1992. (3)A/48/258. (4)A/48/463. (5)A/48/521. (6)A/48/529. (7)A/48/448 & Add.1. (8)A/INF/47/6 & Add.1. (9)S/26668. (10)S/26724 & Corr.1. (11)S/26725. (12)S/26747. (13)YUN 1992, p. 236, GA res. 47/20 A, 24 Nov. 1992. (14)A/47/908. (15)YUN 1992, p. 237. (16)A/47/960. (17)A/48/532. (18)A/48/532/Add.1. (19)A/C.5/47/93. (20)YUN 1991, p. 869, GA res. 46/187, 20 Dec. 1991. (21)A/47/7/Add.17. (22)A/C.5/48/27. (23)A/48/7/Add.3. (24)A/48/811. (25)S/25958. (26)A/47/975-S/26063. (27)S/25942. (28)S/26361. (29)S/26085. (30)S/26460. (31)S/26573. (32)S/26587. (33)S/26633. (34)A/47/1000-S/26297. (35)YUN 1991, p. 151. (36)S/26180. (37)S/26352. (38)S/26480. (39)YUN 1946-47, p. 100, GA res. 22 A (I), annex, 13 Feb. 1946. (40)S/26480/Add.1. (41)S/26802. (42)S/26537. (43)S/26539. (44)S/26538, S/26540. (45)S/26567. (46)S/26573. (47)S/26802. (48)S/26864. (49)A/C.5/48/40. (50)A/48/783. (51)A/48/778. (52)A/48/803.

Chapter III

Asia and the Pacific

The United Nations continued in 1993 to pursue its initiatives aimed at resolving conflicts and alleviating tensions in the Asia and Pacific region. Its operations were marked by encouraging success in one case and by significant progress in another.

The United Nations Transition Authority in Cambodia brought its mandate to a successful conclusion with the fulfilment of the final phase of its task, namely, the organization and supervision of elections in May. Certified free and fair by the Special Representative of the Secretary-General for Cambodia, those elections led to the formation in September of a new constitutional Government of Cambodia.

The United Nations Boundary Demarcation Commission completed its technical task in May of demarcating, for the first time, the precise coordinates of the international boundary between Iraq and Kuwait. More significantly, Iraq, towards the end of November, formally accepted its obligations under Security Council resolution 715(1991), thus enabling the United Nations Special Commission and the International Atomic Energy Agency (IAEA) to initiate the long-delayed full-scale ongoing monitoring and verification of Iraq's weapons-related activities on a routine basis.

In the Korean peninsula, the United Nations Command continued to monitor observance of the 1953 Armistice Agreement. The Democratic People's Republic of Korea (DPRK) called for the dissolution of the Command and for the replacement of the Agreement by one to be concluded between it and the Republic of Korea. In a disturbing development in March, the DPRK announced its decision to withdraw from the 1968 Treaty on the Non-Proliferation of Nuclear Weapons, following its refusal of repeated IAEA requests for access to and full inspection of its nuclear facilities. This non-compliance with its obligations under its agreement with IAEA for the application of safeguards in connection with the Treaty was, in April, brought before the Security Council, which urged the DPRK to reconsider its announcement and IAEA to continue to consult with that country in order to resolve the issue.

The Secretary-General, in pursuance of his mission of good offices on behalf of Cyprus, renewed and widened efforts to obtain the agreement of the Greek Cypriot and Turkish Cypriot communities to a package of confidence-building measures as a step towards reaching a mutually acceptable overall solution to the decades-long conflict between them. On his recommendation, the United Nations Peace-keeping Force in Cyprus, deemed vital to maintaining a climate conducive to negotiations, was extended by the Council twice during the year, the second time until June 1994.

The Assembly, in December, requested the Secretary-General to dispatch as soon as possible a United Nations special mission to Afghanistan to canvass a broad spectrum of that country's leaders to solicit their views on how the United Nations could best assist in facilitating national *rapprochement* and reconstruction. It also invited him to continue to monitor the overall situation in Afghanistan and make available his good offices as required.

East Asia

Korean question

On 15 June,[1] the United States, on behalf of the Unified Command, submitted to the Security Council the annual report of the United Nations Command (UNC) concerning the maintenance in 1992 of the 1953 Armistice Agreement.[2]

The report provided background information on UNC and its mission, as well as on the Armistice mechanism and procedures. This included the Neutral Nations Supervisory Commission (NNSC), originally composed of Czechoslovakia, Poland, Sweden and Switzerland and charged with conducting independent investigations of Armistice violations outside the demilitarized zone (DMZ); and the Military Armistice Commission (MAC), set up to supervise the implementation of the Agreement and to settle any violations reported to it by NNSC through negotiations with the Korean People's Army (KPA) and the Chinese People's Volunteers (CPV). MAC was composed of 10 military members—five senior officers from UNC and five from KPA/CPV. Its Joint Duty Office, located in the Joint Security Area, served as the basic channel of communications between the Democratic People's Republic of Korea (DPRK) and the Republic of Korea.

Appended to the report was an account of a 1992 Armistice violation[3] involving an armed infiltration by the DPRK through the DMZ into the Republic of Korea.

On 13 and 28 May 1992, the DPRK returned 30 sets of "United States war remains". Taking this as an indication that many more UNC war remains might be in the DPRK, UNC requested KPA to continue its search for and repatriation of such remains for humanitarian reasons.

By a letter of 11 October,[4] the DPRK asserted that the armistice mechanism had become worthless. NNSC had virtually ceased to function in 1956[5] when UNC unilaterally imposed limitations on it, and because of the withdrawal on 1 January 1993 of Czechoslovakia, whose replacement could be nominated solely by the DPRK. As to MAC, its major functions were paralysed in 1991[6] with the illegal appointment to it of a General of the Republic of Korea as a senior UNC member. The DPRK therefore called for the dissolution of UNC and the replacement of the Armistice Agreement with a peace agreement between the two Koreas, in accordance with a 1975 General Assembly resolution on the subject.[7]

By the same letter, the DPRK further cited several UNC violations of the Armistice between April and July 1993, including introducing heavy weapons into the DMZ, infiltrating combat vessels into the territorial waters of the DPRK and setting fire to its forests.

Following the announcement by the Republic of Korea and the United States on 26 January 1993 that they would resume their previously suspended joint "Team Spirit" military exercises, the DPRK, on 27 January, denounced the resumption as a provocative act intended to start a nuclear war in the Korean peninsula.[8] As a result, the country had been placed on semi-war alert on 8 March,[9] and, because of the coincidental demand by the International Atomic Energy Agency (IAEA) for a special inspection of its military installations not related to nuclear activities, it decided, on 12 March,[10] to withdraw from the 1968 Treaty on the Non-Proliferation of Nuclear Weapons (NPT)[11] until the United States nuclear threats and IAEA's unjust conduct had been recognized to have been removed. The DPRK also transmitted to the Security Council a 29 January memorandum[12] disclosing what it described as the true picture of the Republic of Korea's drive for nuclear-weapons development promoted with the tacit consent of the United States.

Compliance with non-proliferation and safeguards agreements

On 12 March 1993,[13] the DPRK informed the President of the Security Council that, owing to the abnormal situation currently prevailing, it was no longer able to fulfil its obligations under NPT and had decided to withdraw from it. The withdrawal was a defensive measure against the United States nuclear war manoeuvres, "Team Spirit", and the misapplication of NPT by some IAEA officials so as to jeopardize the country's sovereignty and security and stifle its socialist system.

The DPRK, on 15 March,[14] denied the inconsistencies first reported in 1992[15] between its declarations regarding quantities and composition of nuclear material and IAEA inspection findings, characterizing the latter as fabrication and the result of United States manipulation of IAEA.

Access to more information and to two additional locations in order to resolve the inconsistencies (referred to as a special inspection) were the subject of talks held between IAEA and the DPRK at Pyongyang from 20 to 28 January 1993; such access was subsequently requested by the Director General of IAEA, Hans Blix, on 9 February.

IAEA reports (March and April). The Secretary-General drew to the attention of the President of the Security Council an 18 March communication[16] from the Director General of IAEA, transmitting his report on the implementation of an IAEA Board of Governors resolution of 25 February and of the agreement between the Government of the Democratic People's Republic of Korea and the International Atomic Energy Agency for the application of safeguards in connection with the Treaty on the Non-Proliferation of Nuclear Weapons (safeguards agreement), which entered into force on 10 April 1992.[15]

The 25 February 1993 resolution called on the DPRK to extend full cooperation to IAEA to enable it to discharge its responsibilities under the safeguards agreement, and to respond positively and without delay to the Director General's request of 9 February for access to additional information and to two additional sites, which was essential and urgent in order to resolve the inconsistencies noted and to ensure verification of compliance with the agreement.

The resolution was forwarded to the DPRK the day after its adoption, with a request for cooperation in its implementation, in particular that the Government receive an IAEA inspection team scheduled to arrive at Pyongyang on 16 March. The DPRK, on 10 March, expressed reservations about receiving the inspection team, referring to the resumption of the joint Republic of Korea/United States military exercise, "Team Spirit", and to the semi-war state into which the country had been placed as a result of that upcoming exercise. Despite IAEA notification that that state could not impede implementation of the agreement, the DPRK issued a 12 March statement[13] declaring its decision to withdraw from NPT (see above). To IAEA's reiteration that the safeguards agreement remained in force until any withdrawal took effect—that is, after three months' advance notice to all other NPT parties and to the Security Council—and that a declaration of intention to withdraw should not impede the agreement's implementation, the DPRK none the less notified IAEA on 16 March that it could not receive the inspection team because, among other reasons, some IAEA officials had joined in a plot led by a party hostile to the DPRK and was trying to strangle its socialist system.

The Director General noted that: the safeguards agreement remained in force as long as the DPRK was a party to NPT; an NPT party had the right to withdraw from NPT if it decided that extraordinary events related to the subject-matter of the Treaty had jeopardized its supreme interests; and the withdrawal notice should state the nature of those extraordinary events.

In a second report, transmitted on 6 April,[17] the Director General stated that the IAEA Board of Governors, having been informed of the foregoing developments, adopted a further resolution on 18 March, by which it confirmed that, although the DPRK had announced its intention to withdraw from NPT, the safeguards agreement remained in force and compliance with it was essential; it requested the Director General to continue his dialogue with the DPRK.

In forwarding the 18 March resolution to the DPRK, the Director General reiterated his request that the IAEA inspection teams be granted access to the two locations specified, which, although described as military sites rather than nuclear facilities, in no way immunized them from inspection; if his request was not granted, he would have no choice but to report non-compliance to the Board at its 31 March meeting. A reply from the DPRK reaffirmed that the issue of special inspections could not be a matter for discussion.

Thus, the IAEA Board of Governors adopted a resolution on 1 April, by which it found the DPRK in non-compliance with its obligations under its safeguards agreement with IAEA and that IAEA had been unable to verify the non-diversion of nuclear material to nuclear weapons or other nuclear explosive devices; it decided to report the non-compliance to all IAEA members and to the Security Council and General Assembly.

Annexed to the report were the texts of the Board's February, March and April resolutions, the safeguards agreement and the communications exchanged between IAEA and the DPRK.

The DPRK, on 5 April,[18] rejected and condemned the Board's 1 April resolution as an encroachment on its sovereignty and dignity, asserting that it was preposterous for IAEA to charge it with non-compliance, that there was no basis for referring the matter to the United Nations and that to demand inspection based on spy-satellite intelligence information was to join the United States in its sinister purpose of exposing the military facilities of the DPRK so as to disarm it. The DPRK warned that, if the Security Council tried to pressure it by the application of collective sanctions, it would be compelled to take corresponding self-defensive measures.

SECURITY COUNCIL ACTION (April)

The Security Council, after consultations held on 8 April 1993, authorized its President to make the following statement[19] to the media on behalf of the Council members:

"The members of the Security Council take note of the oral statement on 6 April 1993 and the written report of the International Atomic Energy Agency (IAEA) Director General, Dr. Hans Blix. The members of the Council also take note of the letter of 12 March 1993 of the Permanent Representative of the Democratic People's Republic of Korea (DPRK) to the President of the Security Council, enclosing one from his Foreign Minister with reference to article X of the Treaty on the Non-Proliferation of Nuclear Weapons (NPT).

"The members of the Council are concerned at the situation which has arisen. In this connection they reaffirm the importance of NPT and of the parties to it adhering to it.

"The members of the Council also express their support for the North-South Joint Declaration on the Denuclearization of the Korean peninsula.

"The members of the Council welcome all efforts aimed at resolving this situation and in particular encourage IAEA to continue its consultations with the DPRK and its constructive endeavours for a proper settlement of the nuclear verification issue in the DPRK.

"The members of the Security Council will continue to follow the situation."

Communications. In a 10 April statement,[20] the DPRK asserted that its fictitious "nuclear problem" and its withdrawal from NPT—a matter pertaining to its sovereignty—were not issues for debate in the Security Council, an organ concerned with issues endangering world peace and security. If the Council wanted to deal with the nuclear problem from the standpoint of guaranteeing international peace and security, it must first call into question the actions of the United States, the first nation to develop nuclear weapons and the one with the largest nuclear arsenal. It asked how the Council could remain indifferent to the illegal acts of the United States, which had strained the situation in the Korean peninsula to the extreme by resuming the nuclear-war rehearsal "Team Spirit", and to those IAEA officials who violated the sovereignty and security of a non-nuclear State by abusing the IAEA statute, NPT and the safeguards agreement.

On 10 May,[21] the DPRK stated that some IAEA officials had demanded the inspection of military sites based on fabricated "satellite intelligence information" provided by the United States, in violation of the sovereign rights of States, had handed over confidential inspection information to the United States and had made it public. It asked the Council, when it convened on the matter of implementing the safeguards agreement, to consider the agreement's abuse by IAEA as it concerned the DPRK.

The IAEA Director General replied on 11 May[22] that IAEA had been guided by its statute and by the relevant provisions of the safeguards agreement, in conformity with which he had reported to the Board of Governors on the results of the agreement's implementation and had provided information concerning objections raised by the DPRK to IAEA's right of access to relevant sites. He pointed to the Board's 18 March resolution, in which it expressed its full confidence in the IAEA Director General and secretariat and its support for actions taken by them to implement the agreement in an impartial and objective manner.

SECURITY COUNCIL ACTION (May)

The Security Council met on 11 May to discuss the DPRK's notice of withdrawal from NPT. It invited that country and the Republic of Korea, at their request, to participate in the discussion without the right to vote, in accordance with the relevant provisions of the Charter and rule 37[a] of the Council's provisional rules of procedure.

The Council adopted **resolution 825(1993)**.

The Security Council,

Having considered with concern the letter from the Minister for Foreign Affairs of the Democratic People's Republic of Korea (DPRK) dated 12 March 1993 addressed to the President of the Council concerning the intention of the Government of the DPRK to withdraw from the Treaty on the Non-Proliferation of Nuclear Weapons (the Treaty) and the report of the Director General of the International Atomic Energy Agency (IAEA),

Recalling the Security Council Presidential statement of 8 April 1993 in which the members of the Council welcome all efforts aimed at resolving this situation and, in particular, encourage IAEA to continue its consultations with the DPRK for proper settlement of the nuclear verification issue in the DPRK,

Noting in that context the critical importance of the Treaty, emphasizing the integral role of IAEA safeguards in the implementation of the Treaty and in ensuring the peaceful uses of nuclear energy, and reaffirming the crucial contribution which progress in non-proliferation can make to the maintenance of international peace and security,

Recalling the Joint Declaration by the DPRK and the Republic of Korea (ROK) on the denuclearization of the Korean Peninsula, which includes establishment of a credible and effective bilateral inspection regime and

a pledge not to possess nuclear reprocessing and uranium enrichment facilities,

Noting that the DPRK is party to the Treaty and has concluded a full-scope safeguards agreement as required by that Treaty,

Having also considered with regret the IAEA Board of Governors' findings contained in its resolution of 1 April 1993 that the DPRK is in non-compliance with its obligations under the IAEA-DPRK safeguards agreement, and that IAEA is not able to verify that there has been no diversion of nuclear materials required to be safeguarded under the terms of the IAEA-DPRK safeguards agreement to nuclear weapons or other nuclear explosive devices,

Noting the 1 April 1993 statement by the Russian Federation, the United Kingdom and the United States, the depositories of the Treaty (S/25515), which questions whether the DPRK's stated reasons for withdrawing from the Treaty constitute extraordinary events relating to the subject-matter of the Treaty,

Noting the letter of reply by the DPRK to the Director General of IAEA dated 22 April 1993 which, *inter alia*, encourages and urges the Director General to hold consultations with the DPRK on the implementation of the safeguards agreement, and noting also that the DPRK has expressed its willingness to seek a negotiated solution to this issue,

Welcoming recent signs of improved cooperation between the DPRK and IAEA and the prospect of contacts between the DPRK and other Member States,

1. *Calls upon* the DPRK to reconsider the announcement contained in the letter of 12 March 1993 and thus to reaffirm its commitment to the Treaty;

2. *Further calls upon* the DPRK to honour its non-proliferation obligations under the Treaty and comply with its safeguards agreement with IAEA as specified by the IAEA Board of Governors' resolution of 25 February 1993;

3. *Requests* the Director General of IAEA to continue to consult with the DPRK with a view to resolving the issues which are the subject of the Board of Governors' findings and to report to the Security Council on his efforts in due time;

4. *Urges* all Member States to encourage the DPRK to respond positively to this resolution, and encourages them to facilitate a solution;

5. *Decides* to remain seized of the matter and to consider further Security Council action if necessary.

Security Council resolution 825(1993)

| 11 May 1993 | Meeting 3212 | 13-0-2 |

8-nation draft (S/25745).
Sponsors: France, Hungary, Japan, New Zealand, Russian Federation, Spain, United Kingdom, United States.

Vote in Council as follows:
In favour: Brazil, Cape Verde, Djibouti, France, Hungary, Japan, Morocco, New Zealand, Russian Federation, Spain, United Kingdom, United States, Venezuela.
Against: None.
Abstaining: China, Pakistan.

[a]Rule 37 of the Council's provisional rules of procedure states: "Any Member of the United Nations which is not a member of the Security Council may be invited, as the result of a decision of the Security Council, to participate, without vote, in the discussion of any question brought before the Security Council when the Security Council considers that the interests of that Member are specially affected, or when a Member brings a matter to the attention of the Security Council in accordance with Article 35(1) of the Charter."

In a statement to the Council, the DPRK asserted that neither legal nor technical grounds existed for a Council discussion of the so-called nuclear problem. It reiterated its reasons for withdrawing from NPT: the increasing nuclear threats from the United States and its manipulation of IAEA to demand opening military bases of the DPRK in order to disarm it. The "inconsistencies" and "suspicious locations" noted by IAEA were fabrications directed by the United States. The DPRK urged the Council not to deviate from justice and equity and to desist from applying a double standard by condoning the acts of the injurer while making an issue of the victim.

In China's view, the issue was mainly a matter between the DPRK and IAEA, the United States and the Republic of Korea, to be settled among them through dialogue and consultation. China was not in favour of having the Council deal with or adopt a resolution on the issue, for it could easily lead to complications and to an escalation of contradictions.

Pakistan said that, although many of its reservations on the original draft text had been resolved, those regarding paragraph 1 and the seventh preambular paragraph had not, hence its abstention.

On 12 May,[23] the DPRK characterized the resolution as unreasonable and resolutely rejected it as interference in its internal affairs and a grave infringement of its sovereignty. An ultimate imposition of sanctions based on the resolution could not but be construed as a declaration of war against the DPRK.

IAEA reports (September and October). As requested by the Security Council, the IAEA Director General continued to consult with the DPRK with a view to resolving the issues that were the subject of the Board of Governors' findings and reported to the Council on his efforts. His report covering developments from 1 April to 14 September was transmitted to the Council by the Secretary-General on 17 September.[24] During that period, the Director General and the DPRK had a continuous exchange of communications in an effort to fix dates for the IAEA special inspection requested in February; for routine and ad hoc inspections to ensure continuity of safeguards over declared nuclear activities; and for consultations on outstanding safeguards issues, for technical discussions to improve an understanding of the nuclear inventory presented to IAEA and on the issue of the impartial application of safeguards. Meetings were held between the parties at Vienna, on 8 April, 24 May, 7 June and 2 August; and at Pyongyang, from 1 to 3 September. Two inspection teams visited the DPRK: the seventh (10-14 May) and the eighth (3-10 August).

Several key points emerged from those activities: IAEA could not obtain access to additional information or to the two locations that could help resolve the inconsistencies found in 1992 and was thus unable to verify the correctness and assess the completeness of the initial declarations; the routine and ad hoc inspection activities required under the safeguards agreement were overdue and IAEA proposed that they be carried out between 25 September and 9 October for continuity of safeguards over the declared nuclear activities to be ensured; the seventh and eighth inspections were so restricted that, instead of the activities specified under the agreement, they were limited to containment, surveillance and maintenance activities at the 5 MW(e) reactor and the radiochemical laboratory; and refuelling of the 5 MW(e) reactor, an operation requiring IAEA presence, had been postponed.

In addition, the exchange of correspondence revealed that the DPRK decided on 11 June "unilaterally to suspend", as long as it considered it necessary, "the effectuation of its withdrawal" from NPT.

In an 11 October addendum to his report,[25] the Director General covered developments from 15 September to 1 October. In communications with the DPRK, he stressed that IAEA verification activities in respect of that country's declared nuclear material and facilities must continue to be performed fully. He observed that the DPRK seemed to be suggesting that its "unique and extraordinary situation with regard to a temporary suspension of the effectuation of its withdrawal from NPT" meant that all issues relating to the agreement's implementation were open and negotiable at consultations and he emphasized the imperative of viewing the specific safeguards activities and time-frame as an integral whole, not as a menu to select from. Furthermore, the Director General made clear that the only legal basis and guidance for the relations between IAEA and the DPRK was found in the safeguards agreement.

The Director General underscored the foregoing points to the Board of Governors at its meeting on 23 September, adding that the positive attitude of the DPRK towards continuing consultations in the near future had not yet been matched in its approach to the request for the required routine and ad hoc inspections. He reiterated his observation that the DPRK seemed to take the untenable position that all issues pertaining to safeguards implementation were open for negotiation. The Board, on 23 September, adopted a resolution, by which it decided that the situation was urgent and asked that the item be placed on the agenda of the thirty-seventh (1993) regular session of the IAEA General Conference. The DPRK rejected the resolution as unjust and a violation of its sovereign rights; the nuclear issue, it said, was political and military rather than technical and could be resolved only through talks between it and the United States.

At the General Conference on 1 October, the Director General stated that as long as the existing inconsistency was not resolved by credible explanations through additional information and visits to additional locations, IAEA would not be able to exclude the possibility that nuclear material in the DPRK had been diverted. That country's readiness to implement its safeguards agreement had diminished rather than increased; while it had previously not objected to routine and ad hoc inspections, it currently accepted only limited safeguards, mainly related to maintenance. Whereas earlier uncertainty had centred on the possible existence of non-declared nuclear material, in the current circumstances only the implementation of systematic, effective and timely safeguards could provide assurance about the exclusively peaceful use of the declared nuclear material and facilities.

On the same date, the General Conference adopted a resolution expressing grave concern that the DPRK had failed to discharge its safeguards obligations and urged it to cooperate fully with IAEA.

In a second addendum dated 3 December,[26] the Director General described developments from his 11 October report to 1 December, noting that the situation had deteriorated further. No consultations between the DPRK and IAEA and no inspections of any kind at that country's nuclear facilities had taken place. Surveillance equipment, such as cameras, had ceased to operate; seals had not been checked; and many items that, for reasonable assurance against misuse, required visits and verification at determined intervals had not been visited.

In his statement before the General Assembly on 1 November, the Director General reported that the central safeguards issue was that IAEA verification activities suggested that some nuclear material existed in the DPRK that had not been reported to IAEA. Hence, IAEA could not verify the correctness and assess the completeness of the declaration of material subject to safeguards. Until the inconsistency between that declaration and IAEA findings was satisfactorily resolved, the possibility that nuclear material had been diverted could not be excluded. The longer IAEA was precluded from conducting inspection, the more safeguards-related data deteriorated and the less assurance safeguards could provide that even the declared facilities were used exclusively for peaceful purposes.

In a 2 December statement, the Director General informed the Board of Governors that he was bound to conclude that the safeguards system in the DPRK could not be said to provide any meaningful assurance of the peaceful use of nuclear material and installations. That was not to say that the system could not, with renewed efforts, be fully or partially restored, if cooperation were forthcoming from that country.

He restated IAEA's readiness to receive at any time a team from the DPRK for consultations about the whole safeguards issue, including the need for additional information and visits to additional locations. It was also ready to send an inspection team to perform a full range of inspection activities, as communicated to the Government and of the kind previously performed without objection.

GENERAL ASSEMBLY ACTION

In **resolution 48/14** on the annual (1992) report of IAEA, adopted on 1 November, the General Assembly took note of the resolutions of the IAEA Board of Governors and expressed grave concern that the DPRK had failed to discharge its safeguards obligations and had recently widened the area of non-compliance. It commended the IAEA Director General and secretariat for their impartial efforts to implement the safeguards agreement still in force between IAEA and the DPRK and urged that country immediately to cooperate with IAEA.

REFERENCES

[1]S/25031. [2]YUN 1953, p. 136, GA res. 725(VIII), annex, 7 Dec. 1953. [3]YUN 1992, p. 241. [4]S/26568. [5]YUN 1956, p. 128. [6]YUN 1991, p. 154. [7]YUN 1975, p. 204, GA res. 3390 B (XXX), 18 Nov. 1975. [8]S/25191. [9]S/25386. [10]S/25405. [11]YUN 1968, p. 17, GA res. 2373(XXII), annex, 12 June 1968. [12]S/25370. [13]S/25407. [14]S/25422. [15]YUN 1992, p. 73. [16]S/25445. [17]A/48/133-S/25556. [18]S/25538 & Corr.1. [19]S/25562. [20]S/25595. [21]S/25747. [22]S/25774. [23]S/25768. [24]S/26456. [25]S/26456/Add.1. [26]S/26456/Add.2.

South-East Asia

Cambodia situation

The United Nations Transitional Authority in Cambodia (UNTAC), established by the Security Council in 1992,[1] brought its mandate to a successful conclusion in 1993. In cooperation with three of the four parties that had been involved in the Cambodian conflict and became signatories to the 1991 settlement agreements (Paris Agreements),[2] UNTAC saw to the implementation of those agreements as faithfully to their letter and spirit as was possible given the non-cooperation of one of the signatories. Thus, as envisioned by the agreements, the elections that created the Constituent Assembly took place as scheduled, leading to the formation of a new Government of Cambodia.

The three cooperating signatories were: the People's Revolutionary Party of Kampuchea, renamed the Cambodia People's Party (CPP) and also referred to as the party of the State of Cambodia (SOC); the National United Front for an Independent, Neutral, Peaceful and Cooperative Cambodia (FUNCINPEC, from its French name, Front uni national pour un Cambodge indépendant, neutre, pacifique et coopératif); and the Khmer People's National Liberation Front (KPNLF), also represented by the Buddhist Liberal Democratic Party (BLDP). The fourth signatory, the Party of Democratic Kampuchea (PDK), did not cooperate in the agreements' implementation.

The signatories' armed forces were, respectively, the Cambodian People's Armed Forces (CPAF), the National Army of Independent Kampuchea (ANKI), the Khmer People's National Liberation Armed Forces (KPNLAF) and the National Army of Democratic Kampuchea (NADK). Following the formation of the new Government, the first three armies merged to become the Cambodian Armed Forces (CAF).

By a number of resolutions, the Security Council endorsed the decision of the Supreme National Council (SNC)[2] to hold elections for a constituent assembly from 23 to 27 May and called on UNTAC to create a neutral political environment conducive to free and fair elections (resolution 810(1993)); reiterated that call (826(1993)); invited the Secretary-General promptly to report on the elections (835(1993)); endorsed the election results, certified free and fair by the United Nations and reported on by the Secretary-General on 10 June (840(1993)); confirmed that UNTAC should end upon the creation of a new government consistent with the 1991 Paris Agreements and that the UNTAC withdrawal should be completed on 15 November (860(1993)); welcomed the formation on 24 September of the new Government of all Cambodia; extended the withdrawal period of specific UNTAC elements, some until 30 November and the remainder until 31 December; and established, at the request of the new Government, a 20-member military liaison team at Phnom Penh for a six-month period (880(1993)).

The General Assembly provided the resources to maintain UNTAC to the end of its mandate and for the first phase of its liquidation (resolution 47/209 B), as well as for the final phase (decision 48/469) and the emplacement of the military liaison team (decision 48/480).

UN Transitional Authority in Cambodia

In the third[3] of four progress reports on UNTAC, requested by the Security Council in 1992[1] for submission at specific intervals, the Secretary-General described activities since the second (September 1992) progress report[4] up to 10 January 1993, as discharged by the seven UNTAC components: the human rights, electoral, military, civil administration, police, repatriation and rehabilitation components. The task of each was outlined when the Secretary-General proposed UNTAC's establishment in 1992.[5]

The human rights component expanded its education programme to include: the introduction of formal human rights courses in the educational system and the country-wide distribution of related curricular and other information materials; training sessions for judges and lawyers and for public administration officials in the provinces; dissemination of human rights concepts through radio programmes and video presentations; and collaboration with local human rights organizations, of which there were five. UNTAC investigated prisoners detained by the Phnom Penh authorities to determine whether or not their detention was politically motivated. In addition, an International Symposium on Human Rights in Cambodia was held (Phnom Penh, 30 November–2 December 1992), at which presentations on the future of human rights were given by FUNCINPEC, KPNLF and SOC.

Voter registration, begun in October 1992, went into high gear as its closure on 31 January 1993 drew near. Electoral teams were permitted to register applicants from PDK-controlled zones, mostly at registration points outside those zones. Of the more than 4 million registration cards issued, 2.6 million had been logged in by early January. Twenty political parties had provisionally registered. Each was entitled to post agents at registration points, in part to ensure that all voter registrants were qualified and to address the persistent claim that "Vietnamese" would try to register and vote. Only 0.3 per cent of all registrants, however, had been challenged by party agents.

Two revisions to the Electoral Law—one to enfranchise Khmer Krom residents in Cambodia (ethnic Cambodians born, or with a parent born, in southern Viet Nam) and the other to allow Cambodians overseas to register outside Cambodia (instead of in Cambodia as required)—were under proposal by FUNCINPEC and KPNLF. Having carefully considered the proposals, the Secretary-General instructed his Special Representative for Cambodia, Yasushi Akashi, that, unless the Security Council decided otherwise, he should not approve them: the first would not be consistent with the 1991 Paris Agreements; the second would entail administrative procedures that would make it impossible to hold the elections in May 1993 as scheduled.

The military situation had been marked by an increase in the daily count of cease-fire violations, mainly in central and northern Cambodia. The most serious occurred in the Bavel area of Battambang Province, where NADK had been attempting to consolidate territorial gains and disrupt CPAF communications. This led to continual shell-fire exchanges between the two armies throughout December 1992, in the course of which six bridges were blown up, 15,000 residents fled their homes and artillery shells landed in an area 50 kilometres north-east of Siem Reap where an UNTAC electoral team had recently been deployed.

PDK's refusal to participate in the cantonment, disarmament and demobilization of the four Cambodian armed forces made it necessary for the military component, originally deployed to meet the requirements of those three cease-fire provisions, to align its deployment with that of the electoral teams so as to protect them and enhance security in remote areas or areas of high conflict potential.

The civil administration component reported progress in developing procedures for expenditure control; establishing a border control mechanism to prevent the influx of Vietnamese into Cambodia and the export from it of round logs; planning specialized control operations for telecommunications and civil aviation; and advancing measures to foster a neutral political environment. With respect to foreign affairs, it supervised the abolition of entry and exit visas for holders of passports issued by Phnom Penh (SOC) and of the practice of retaining such passports after their holders had returned to Cambodia, as well as the streamlining of passport application and immigration procedures at Phnom Penh Airport.

As to national defence and public security, UNTAC proposed and obtained SOC approval of measures governing immovable assets and underlining the distinction between private and public assets, in view of widespread and complex land and property disputes. Incoming and outgoing correspondence of the SOC, FUNCINPEC and KPNLF administrations was monitored to prevent actions that might impair the neutrality of the political environment. A draft directive regarding political activity by CPAF, ANKI and KPNLAF was in preparation. An orientation programme on interim penal provisions was launched for about 200 magistrates, police officers, prosecutors and public defenders.

In the area of finance and information, UNTAC strengthened control over expenditure, revenue sources (taxes and customs duties), central bank functions and the sale of public assets. It monitored currency issuance by the national bank and began setting up a system to monitor its currency reserves and liabilities. It published media guidelines aimed at encouraging a free and responsible press.

The civilian police component organized training courses for the local police, awarding graduation certificates to 84 of those who had completed the course in basic police methods. To enable electoral activity to proceed under peaceful and orderly conditions, the police component, in cooperation with the human rights and civil administration components, developed measures to prevent and deal with threats to public order. Patrols and static guard duty were increased to bolster the security of political party offices regarded most vulnerable to attack. A special directive issued under the relevant articles of the Paris Agreements empowered UNTAC to arrest, detain and prosecute suspects in cases involving serious human rights violations.

Two thirds of an estimated 360,000 Cambodian refugees and displaced persons had been safely repatriated. Arrangements were made with the United States for resettling in North Carolina a group of 398 Vietnamese Montagnards, called the Front uni de libération des races opprimées, who had inhabited the forests of Mondolkiri Province during the last 15 years.

While the success of the voter registration exercise and repatriation process was remarkable and encouraging, some negative developments gave cause for concern. Chief among these were the continuing refusal of PDK to participate in phase II of the cease-fire implementation, making it impossible for UNTAC to carry out the agreed cantonment, disarmament and demobilization of the four parties' armed forces; the growing climate of violence as evidenced by politically motivated acts of intimidation and attacks against party workers and offices, apparently deliberate killings of ethnic Vietnamese and attacks on UNTAC; a growing reluctance of some administrative structures to accept the control and supervisory functions entrusted to UNTAC; and the infrequency of SNC meetings, not to mention the disappointing level of member participation.

On 13 February,[6] the Secretary-General submitted a report in response to the Council's 1992 call[7] for the implementation of measures to ensure the realization of the fundamental objectives of the Paris Agreements, in particular those required for the successful conduct of free and fair elections, including a presidential election.

In the context of Council instructions to proceed with the elections in all parts of Cambodia to which UNTAC had full access as at 31 January 1993, the Special Representative met with the President of PDK (Beijing, China, 27 January) in a renewed effort to secure his party's cooperation with UNTAC, stressing that it was in the long-term interests of PDK to take part in those elections. The PDK President insisted that before his party could join the peace process, its conditions must first be fulfilled, namely, the removal of foreign forces from Cambodia, the granting of greater powers to SNC and full UNTAC control over the five administrative areas of foreign affairs, national defence, public security, finance and information, as specified in the Paris Agreements.

At the first 1993 SNC meeting (Beijing, 28 January), it was agreed that the elections for a constituent assembly would be held from 23 to 25 May. Prince Norodom Sihanouk, who chaired the meeting, announced his decision not to advance his candidacy for the presidential elections until a new constitution was adopted, which would lay down the modalities for the election of the head of State and the related term of office and powers. Consequently, UNTAC preparations for holding a presidential election in conjunction with the constituent assembly elections were put on hold.

Despite additional protective measures for the electoral teams and political party offices and reinforced patrols in remote areas, incidents of violence and intimidation persisted mainly in the provinces of Battambang and Kompong Cham; in most cases the victims were FUNCINPEC members. Under investigation by UNTAC were two separate armed attacks (12 and 27 January) at Phum Angkrong and vicinity, Siem Reap Province, amidst indications that NADK might have been responsible; the two attacks killed 11 civilians, two of them UNTAC electoral workers, and injured 12 others. In early February, four FUNCINPEC members were detained at Battambang and an attack in the Bakan district, Pursat Province, killed five civilians and damaged UNTAC premises.

Attacks commonly levelled at UNTAC on PDK radio had become increasingly hostile. However, SOC had only recently begun a multi-media campaign to spread the message that UNTAC could not be trusted to protect Cambodians, and that only SOC could defend the country against PDK and so deserved electoral support.

To preserve Cambodia's natural resources, UNTAC deployed border control teams to monitor violations of the moratorium on the export of logs by land or sea, raised the number of its checkpoints along the Cambodia-Thailand border to 17 and appealed to the four Cambodian parties and neighbouring countries (the Lao People's Democratic Republic, Thailand and Viet Nam) to assist in implementing the moratorium. UNTAC observers recorded 46 violations between 1 January and 5 February, during which 46,507 cubic metres of logs were transported by three of the Cambodian parties (FUNCINPEC, PDK, SOC) to seven known destinations. At its 10 February meeting, SNC, on a proposal by UNTAC, asked the Technical Advisory Committee on Management and Sustainable Exploitation of Natural Resources to determine a ceiling on the export of sawn timber. Over PDK ob-

jections, it adopted a Declaration on Mining and Export of Minerals and Gems from Cambodia, placing a moratorium on the extraction and export of minerals and gems, effective 28 February.

Following UNTAC discussions with Thailand (which bordered on most of the PDK zones) regarding the Council's call for measures to prevent the supply of petroleum products to areas occupied by any Cambodian party not complying with the military provisions of the Paris Agreements, Thailand announced the suspension of its petroleum shipments to Cambodia pending establishment of a system, under UNTAC monitoring, to preclude petroleum shipments to those areas.

In the broader context of border control, the civil administration component was to monitor customs and immigration control. Each of the 23 checkpoints in operation was manned by an UNTAC team of military observers, armed soldiers and civilian police with communication support facilities, in which the three cooperating Cambodian parties were also represented.

At the 28 January SNC meeting, the Special Representative announced that some $540 million of the $880 million pledged at the 1992 Ministerial Conference on the Rehabilitation and Reconstruction of Cambodia[8] had been committed for specific rehabilitation activities; he conveyed UNTAC's concern, however, that the actual level of disbursements currently stood only at $95 million. Also of concern was the lack of funding for such specific activities as training and maintenance of essential social services that could compromise the overall rehabilitation effort. To address those concerns, it was agreed to hold a technical-level meeting, with the participation of donors, the Cambodian parties, all countries providing assistance to Cambodia and non-governmental organizations.

The Secretary-General stated that it was imperative for UNTAC to maintain the momentum towards the constituent assembly elections, due to start on 23 May. Meanwhile, he had instructed his Special Representative to assess post-election security requirements, as arrangements envisioned by the Paris Agreements would almost certainly be impossible to apply given PDK's decision not to enter into phase II of the cease-fire.

SECURITY COUNCIL ACTION

On 8 March, the Security Council unanimously adopted **resolution 810(1993)**.

The Security Council,
Reaffirming its resolutions 668(1990) of 20 September 1990 and 745(1992) of 28 February 1992 and other relevant resolutions,
Taking note of the report of the Secretary-General dated 13 February 1993,
Paying tribute to His Royal Highness Prince Norodom Sihanouk, President of the Supreme National Council

(SNC), for his continuing efforts to restore peace and national unity in Cambodia,

Recalling that under the Paris Agreements the Cambodian people have the right to determine their own political future through the free and fair election of a constituent assembly, which will draft and approve a new Cambodian constitution and transform itself into a legislative assembly, which will create the new Cambodian government,

Welcoming the achievements of the Secretary-General and UNTAC in the implementation of the Paris Agreements, in particular regarding voter registration and refugee repatriation, and reaffirming its continuing support for the activities of UNTAC,

Welcoming the decision taken by SNC at its meeting on 10 February 1993 to adopt a moratorium on the export of minerals and gems and to consider limits on the export of sawn timber from Cambodia in order to protect Cambodia's natural resources,

Deploring the violations of the cease-fire by PDK and SOC,

Concerned by the increasing number of acts of violence perpetrated on political grounds, in particular in areas under the control of SOC, and on ethnic grounds, and by the negative implications of such acts for the implementation of the Paris Agreements,

Underlining the importance of measures by UNTAC in order to ensure a neutral political environment in Cambodia,

Condemning attacks, threats and intimidation against UNTAC, in particular the recent detention of UNTAC personnel,

Deploring the failure of PDK to meet its obligations under the Paris Agreements, notably as regards unrestricted access by UNTAC to the areas under its control and as regards the application of phase II of the cease-fire, and urging the party concerned to join fully in the implementation of the Paris Agreements,

Expressing strong concern at recent reports by UNTAC of a small number of foreign military personnel serving with the armed forces of SOC in violation of the Paris Agreements; calling on all parties to cooperate fully with UNTAC investigations of reports of foreign forces within the territory under their control; and emphasizing the importance of the immediate removal of all foreign forces, advisers and military personnel from Cambodia,

1. *Approves* the report of the Secretary-General dated 13 February 1993;

2. *Endorses* the decision by the Supreme National Council that the election for the constituent assembly shall be held from 23 to 27 May 1993;

3. *Underlines* the crucial importance of national reconciliation for the attainment of lasting peace and stability in Cambodia;

4. *Urges* all Cambodian parties to cooperate fully with UNTAC in the preparation and holding of the election for the constituent assembly;

5. *Expresses its satisfaction* at the extent of voter registration;

6. *Calls on* UNTAC to continue to make every effort to create and maintain a neutral political environment conducive to the holding of free and fair elections, and requests the Secretary-General to inform the Security Council by 15 May 1993 of the conditions and preparations for the election;

7. *Urges* all Cambodian parties to help create in the minds of their followers tolerance for peaceful political competition and to ensure adherence to the code of conduct during the forthcoming political campaign;

8. *Urges in particular* all Cambodian parties to take all necessary measures to ensure freedom of speech, assembly and movement, as well as fair access to the media, including the press, television and radio, for all registered political parties during the electoral campaign starting on 7 April 1993, and to take all necessary steps to reassure the Cambodian people that the balloting for the election will be secret;

9. *Demands* that all Cambodian parties take the necessary measures to put an end to all acts of violence and to all threats and intimidation committed on political or ethnic grounds, and urges all those parties to cooperate with the UNTAC Special Prosecutor's Office in investigations of such acts;

10. *Expresses its full confidence* in the ability of UNTAC to conduct an election that is free and fair and its readiness to endorse the results of the election provided that the United Nations certifies it free and fair;

11. *Calls on* all Cambodian parties to abide by their commitment under the Paris Agreements to respect those results;

12. *Recognizes* that the Cambodians themselves bear primary responsibility for the implementation of the Paris Agreements and for the future stability and well-being of Cambodia;

13. *Recognizes in particular* that the Cambodians have the responsibility, after the election for the constituent assembly, to agree on a constitution and to create a government within three months and emphasizes the importance of completing that task on time;

14. *Expresses* its readiness to support fully the constituent assembly and the process of drawing up a constitution and establishing a new government for all Cambodia;

15. *Takes note* of the remarks of the Secretary-General in paragraph 44 of his report concerning the security situation in Cambodia during the period between the election for the constituent assembly and the end of the mandate of UNTAC upon the creation of a government, and welcomes his intention to submit recommendations in that connection;

16. *Commends* the decision of SNC at its meeting on 10 February 1993 to adopt measures for the protection of Cambodia's natural resources, and supports the measures taken by the Technical Advisory Committee on Management and Sustainable Exploitation of Natural Resources to implement these decisions;

17. *Reiterates its demand* that all parties honour in full their obligations under the Paris Agreements, in particular to desist from all offensive military activity;

18. *Demands* that all parties take all action necessary to safeguard the lives and the security of UNTAC personnel throughout Cambodia, and desist from all threats or intimidation against UNTAC personnel and from any interference with them in the performance of their mandate;

19. *Requests* the Secretary-General to report to the Council in the context of his fourth progress report in April 1993 on the implementation of this resolution, and on any further measures that may be necessary and appropriate to ensure the realization of the fundamental objectives of the Paris Agreements;

20. *Decides* to remain actively seized of the matter.

Security Council resolution 810(1993)
8 March 1993   Meeting 3181   Adopted unanimously
Draft prepared in consultations among Council members (S/25376).

Communications. On 11 March,[9] Viet Nam referred to the massacre of 33 Vietnamese and the wounding of 26 others during an attack on the fishing village of Chong Kneas, 10 kilometres south of Siem Reap. It denounced what it called the barbarous acts of terrorism against Vietnamese residents in Cambodia and demanded an immediate end to them. Viet Nam appealed to SNC and to UNTAC on 16 March[10] to take determined measures to stop the killing and, on 26 March,[11] issued a statement citing the relevant portions of the 1991 Paris Agreements obligating UNTAC morally and legally to protect ethnic Vietnamese residents in Cambodia.

Reports of the Secretary-General (3 and 15 May). In his fourth progress report, describing UNTAC activities up to 3 May,[12] the Secretary-General stated that the human rights education programme was accelerated, particularly in teacher training, dissemination of international human rights instruments, education of health professionals, training of public administration and political officials and support for local human rights organizations.

Revisions were made to the Electoral Law to ban public meetings before the official start of the election campaigns on 7 April, public opinion polls and the placing of party seals on ballot boxes at polling time; to amend provisions regarding the removal of names from the lists of candidates; and to permit polling stations to be set up in Paris, New York and Sydney, Australia, for overseas voters duly registered in Cambodia.

The computerized voter registration lists showed nearly 4.7 million registered voters, or about 96 per cent of the eligible voter population. Based on that number, 120 seats for the constituent assembly were allocated to the 21 provinces including the Phnom Penh special district. All 20 political parties—PDK not among them—had been officially registered and had submitted their lists of candidates. Preparations for the conduct of the elections were under way: 50,000 Cambodian electoral staff had been selected, the number and organization of polling stations were being finalized and plans had been made to recruit some 1,000 international polling station officers from more than 30 countries. Eleven countries were asked to provide a total of 50 fingerprint and five handwriting experts to check tendered ballots (ballots cast by voters whose cards had been lost or illegally confiscated or who had voted outside their province of registration).

One of the most serious violations of the ceasefire occurred on 3 May, when NADK elements attacked the town of Siem Reap with rockets, small arms and grenades. Targeted were a CPAF garrison, the airport and a number of buildings, including some occupied by UNTAC, which were also ransacked.

In cooperation with the civilian police component, the military component concluded security arrangements with FUNCINPEC, KPNLF and SOC applicable during the polling period. UNTAC alone would provide security at and around polling stations and for United Nations personnel and property; the armed forces of the three parties would assist UNTAC by reporting to it possible or actual threats to the election and by ensuring security in the zones they controlled.

On 1 March, UNTAC announced that, of the persons under investigation by the strategic investigation teams set up to examine allegations of the continued presence of foreign forces in Cambodia, three were Vietnamese who fell under the category of "foreign forces"; a fourth had since been similarly identified. However, UNTAC pointed out the complexities of the cases: the three Vietnamese were married to Cambodian women with whom they had children, and there was no suggestion that they were in any way under the control of Vietnamese authorities. UNTAC reported that Viet Nam had so far declined to receive the men back as Vietnamese nationals.

The five UNTAC engineering units, supplemented by the engineer platoons in 11 of the 12 infantry battalions, had repaired hundreds of bridges and improved scores of kilometres of roads, as well as airfields at Pochentong (Phnom Penh) and Stung Treng.

UNTAC efforts to stabilize the riel were hampered by the fact that support for it was perceived as partiality towards SOC. To avert social unrest from the unstable riel and spiralling food prices, UNTAC introduced additional rice supplies into the market to discourage hoarding and to bring down the price of that prime commodity. Besides making its television/video, radio and other information facilities available to the 20 participating parties, UNTAC exercised its right of direct control over existing administrative structures so as to secure for all parties access to the SOC public media facilities at Phnom Penh and to the FUNCINPEC and KPNLF radio stations.

On 30 March, a year after the repatriation component began operations, the Office of the United Nations High Commissioner for Refugees (UNHCR), the lead agency, closed the largest and last of the refugee camps. By the end of April, about 365,000 Cambodian refugees and displaced persons from camps along the Cambodia-Thailand border and elsewhere had been repatriated. Some 600 refugees on Thai territory had refused repatriation and would be deported by Thailand.

By March, only about $100 million of the $880 million pledged at the 1992 Ministerial Conference[8] had been disbursed for rehabilitation projects. Forty-five such projects, worth $366 million, had been approved by SNC. The rehabilitation component continued to monitor compliance with the moratorium on log export. On 9 March, SNC approved the UNTAC draft action plan for implementing the moratorium on the mining and export of minerals and gems.

The main emphasis of UNTAC efforts in information and education during the electoral campaign was on the secrecy of the ballot and on the production of broadcast campaign material.

Acts of violence and intimidation continued to undermine efforts to maintain a neutral political environment. About 100 persons were killed in March, including members of all four Cambodian parties and persons of Vietnamese descent. The UNTAC Special Prosecutor issued warrants for the arrest of 12 people including 7 CPAF officers in connection with the abduction and subsequent disappearance of 4 FUNCINPEC members in Battambang, 2 SOC officials for the murder of a BLDP member at Prey Veng, and an NADK officer in connection with a massacre at Chong Kneas, Siem Reap. The targets of violence were Vietnamese-speaking persons, including those born in Cambodia of Vietnamese descent; political party members and offices; and UNTAC military and civilian personnel.

The Secretary-General felt that, given the altered conditions for the UNTAC operations, the military component, which was to have been reduced after completion of the cantonment and demobilization process, should be maintained at its current level until the elections in May. Despite the imperfect conditions, he saw no reason to hold back the May elections, which were not the end but rather the beginning of the process of Cambodia's renewal.

Viet Nam, in a statement of 2 March[13] regarding the three men identified by UNTAC as "foreign forces", asserted that they did not fall under that category as defined by the 1991 Paris Agreements; thus, to label them as such and to demand their repatriation to Viet Nam was contrary to the letter and spirit of the agreements. The statement repeated what UNTAC itself recognized: that the three men returned to civilian life in 1983 and 1985, that they were married to Cambodian women and had children with them and that they were issued Cambodian identity cards. They had become Cambodian of Vietnamese origin, the statement continued, and Viet Nam had absolutely no jurisdiction over them.

In a further report of 15 May,[14] the Secretary-General described the final preparations for the elections. He referred to a meeting (Beijing,

6 May) at which FUNCINPEC, KPNLF and SOC reaffirmed their support for the elections. Technical preparations were virtually complete. Some 900 international polling officers recruited from 44 countries and the Geneva-based Inter-Parliamentary Union had arrived and were at a three-day training course (Bangkok, Thailand, 13-15 May); 130 staff members from the United Nations Secretariat and 370 UNTAC personnel were due to arrive at their duty stations by 18 May.

All political parties had campaigned vigorously. UNTAC itself organized multi-party meetings, granted access to its media facilities, provided air transport for campaign purposes to three parties, including FUNCINPEC, and stepped up publicity on the secrecy of the ballot through radio and television spots.

Incidents of banditry and lawlessness apart, violence to disrupt the electoral process continued: killings, including of ethnic Vietnamese, to pressure them into leaving Cambodia; SOC attacks and harassment to intimidate other political parties, primarily FUNCINPEC; and attacks on UNTAC personnel.

In the light of PDK's expressly repeated intention to oppose the elections even by violent means, UNTAC further refined the different levels of security measures applicable to what it designated as high-, medium- and low-risk zones. Measures for high-risk zones included reinforcement of physical fortifications, stationing armed UNTAC military personnel at and around polling stations, and provision of protective gear, as well as of quick reaction forces and medical support units. Equipment to enhance security had been obtained from five Governments; negotiations for more were in progress.

Owing to the heightened threat in Kompong Thom, UNTAC withdrew its civilian personnel from some locations and reduced the 102 polling stations in the area to 51. It made arrangements so that its civilian staff, including civilian police monitors, could directly seek the protection of the UNTAC Indonesian battalion on Kompong Thom, Stung and Baray; and so that all personnel at Siem Reap would be accommodated with military units at night. Movement in the provinces was subject to authorization and monitoring by UNTAC sector commanders.

The Secretary-General observed that, despite meticulous preparations by UNTAC, the conditions for the elections fell short of those envisioned by the Paris Agreements owing to PDK's progressive withdrawal from the peace process, starting with not complying with the Agreements' military provisions and moving to boycotting the elections and then to disrupting them through violence. Regrettably, SOC had also contributed to the climate of violence by resorting to intimidation of other political parties; it had, moreover, not responded satisfactorily to UNTAC's efforts to prevent it from using its administrative structures for political purposes. Nevertheless, the Secretary-General directed that the elections take place as scheduled, for that was clearly the will and intent of the Security Council and of the vast majority of the Cambodian people.

SECURITY COUNCIL ACTION

On 20 May, having considered the Secretary-General's reports of 3 and 15 May, the Security Council unanimously adopted **resolution 826(1993)**.

The Security Council,

Reaffirming its resolutions 668(1990) of 20 September 1990, 745(1992) of 28 February 1992, 810(1993) of 8 March 1993 and other relevant resolutions,

Taking note of the reports of the Secretary-General dated 3 May 1993 and 15 May 1993,

Expressing its strong support for the almost five million Cambodians who, in spite of violence and intimidation, have registered to vote in the election of a constituent assembly, and have broadly and actively participated in the electoral campaign,

Recognizing the great importance of His Royal Highness Prince Norodom Sihanouk, President of the Supreme National Council (SNC), continuing his invaluable efforts in Cambodia to achieve national reconciliation and restore peace,

1. *Approves* the reports of the Secretary-General dated 3 May 1993 and 15 May 1993;

2. *Expresses its satisfaction* with the arrangements made by the United Nations for the conduct of the election for the constituent assembly in Cambodia described in the report of the Secretary-General;

3. *Demands* that all the parties abide by the Paris Agreements and give UNTAC the full cooperation required under them;

4. *Commends* those participating in the election campaign in accordance with the Paris Agreements despite the violence and intimidation in order that the Cambodian people may have an opportunity to choose freely their own government;

5. *Deplores* all acts of non-cooperation with the Paris Agreements and condemns all acts of violence committed on political and ethnic grounds, intimidation and attacks on UNTAC personnel;

6. *Expresses its full support* for the measures taken by UNTAC to protect the safety of UNTAC personnel and underlines the need for UNTAC to continue its efforts in this regard;

7. *Demands* that all parties take all actions necessary to safeguard the lives and the security of UNTAC personnel throughout Cambodia, and desist from all threats or intimidation against UNTAC personnel and from any interference with them in the performance of their mandate;

8. *Expresses its appreciation* for the positive efforts and the achievements of UNTAC in preparation for the elections, in respect both of the registration of candidates and parties and of the holding of the electoral campaign, albeit under difficult conditions;

9. *Fully supports* the decision of the Secretary-General that the election be held as scheduled in accordance with the decision of SNC endorsed by the Security Council in its resolution 810(1993);

10. *Calls on* UNTAC to continue to work in accordance with resolution 810(1993) to ensure a neutral political environment conducive to the holding of free and fair elections;

11. *Reaffirms* its determination to endorse the results of the election for the constituent assembly provided that the United Nations certifies it free and fair;

12. *Reminds* all the Cambodian parties of their obligation under the Paris Agreements fully to comply with the results of the election;

13. *Warns* that the Council will respond appropriately should any of the parties fail to honour its obligations;

14. *Reaffirms* its readiness to support fully the constituent assembly and the process of drawing up a constitution and establishing a new government for all Cambodia and to support subsequent efforts to promote national reconciliation and peace building;

15. *Recognizes* that the Cambodians themselves bear primary responsibility for the implementation of the Paris Agreements and for the political future and well-being of their own country, and reaffirms that all Cambodian parties are expected to honour their obligations under the Paris Agreements and participate constructively and peacefully in the political process after the election;

16. *Requests* the Secretary-General to report promptly to the Council on the holding and results of the election, including on the conduct of the parties as regards their obligations under the Paris Agreements and, if necessary, to recommend any initiative and/or measures conducive to ensuring their full respect by all parties;

17. *Decides* to remain actively seized of the matter.

Security Council resolution 826(1993)

20 May 1993   Meeting 3213   Adopted unanimously

Draft prepared in consultations among Council members (S/25803), orally revised.

Safety of UNTAC personnel

The Secretary-General's third progress report on UNTAC[3] drew attention to the illegal detention of UNTAC personnel by NADK on two occasions: at O Sala, Kompong Thom, where four military observers and groups of soldiers from the Indonesian battalion were detained at different times during the three-day period from 15 to 18 December 1992; and in Kratie, where, on 18 December, 10 members of the Uruguayan battalion were detained overnight, together with four Russian personnel from a helicopter that inadvertently landed in an NADK defensive position. As a result of negotiations to secure agreement to procedures that would prevent the recurrence of such detentions, a joint PDK/NADK declaration was transmitted to the Special Representative on 20 December, enjoining UNTAC from entering PDK-controlled zones without prior authorization and holding UNTAC fully responsible for incidents that had resulted from its failure to obtain such authorization.

During the reporting period, 14 UNTAC personnel had been injured as a result of military activity by one Cambodian faction or another, nine of them from land-mine explosions in Banteay Meanchey, Kratie and Siem Reap provinces.

An armed attack at Phum Prek, Kompong Speu, on 2 April, that killed three members of the Bulgarian contingent and seriously wounded three others was the subject of a protest and condemnation by Bulgaria.[15]

SECURITY COUNCIL ACTION

After consultations among the members of the Security Council on 5 April, the President made the following statement[16] on behalf of the Council:

Meeting number. SC 3193.

"The Security Council strongly condemns all attacks on the United Nations Transitional Authority in Cambodia (UNTAC), particularly the recent attacks which have resulted in the death of two Bangladeshi members of UNTAC and the cowardly assassination of three members of the Bulgarian contingent of UNTAC on 2 April 1993.

"The Security Council expresses its strong support for UNTAC in carrying out its mandate within the framework of the Paris Agreements. It demands that all hostile acts against UNTAC cease immediately and that all parties take measures to safeguard the lives and the security of UNTAC personnel.

"It expresses its condolences to the Governments of Bangladesh and Bulgaria and to the families of the victims; it pays tribute to the latter for their courage and dedication. It requests the Secretary-General to report urgently to the Council on the circumstances of these murderous acts and the responsibility for them.

"The Security Council also expresses its determination that the election for the constituent assembly should be held on the dates decided by the Supreme National Council and endorsed by the Security Council in its resolution 810(1993). In this respect, the Council stresses the importance of ensuring a neutral political environment in Cambodia, as well as the cessation of acts of violence and of all threats and intimidation committed on political or ethnic grounds."

The Secretary-General's findings, communicated to the Council on 27 April,[17] revealed that an UNTAC post manned by a Bangladeshi unit at Angkor Chum, Siem Reap, was subjected to an hour-long mortar and small-arms fire on 27 March, during which a Bangladeshi soldier was wounded and later died from his wounds; four Cambodian civilians were also injured. An investigation strongly indicated that members of NADK had directed the attack.

On the night of 29 March, one of three Bangladeshi nationals (two of them UNTAC members) travelling by car was shot dead while passing a CPAF checkpoint. Two CPAF soldiers had since been arrested for that murder.

Shortly before midnight on 2 April, an 11-member Bulgarian battalion of UNTAC stationed at Phum Prek, Kompong Speu, was assaulted with automatic weapons and hand-grenades; three Bulgarians were killed and three others wounded. The attackers were 10 to 15 NADK soldiers, led by a commander who had earlier dined with the battalion. The UNTAC post was thereafter subjected to mortar and small-arms fire until dawn. The wounded were airlifted to the UNTAC field hospital at Phnom Penh and two were later evacuated to Bangkok for further treatment. On 5 April, the Bulgarian post at Amelean came under machine-gun fire; a sentry sustained a wound in the abdomen, which damaged his spinal cord and paralysed his legs.

The Secretary-General reported two further attacks, one on 8 April, in which a Japanese national serving with the UNTAC electoral component and his Cambodian interpreter were detained at Prasat Sambo District, Kompong Thom, and then shot; both died of their wounds. UNTAC had not been able to determine responsibility. The other attack, which occurred on 19 April, was on the UNTAC offices at Oaral District, Kompong Speu. An armoured personnel carrier, dispatched from a nearby Bulgarian contingent post to give assistance, was fired upon as it came within 1.5 kilometres of the UNTAC offices. An anti-tank grenade killed a Bulgarian soldier and wounded five others. In the ransacking of the UNTAC offices that ensued, an Indonesian civilian police monitor and a Cambodian interpreter were injured. Preliminary investigations indicated that NADK elements were responsible for the attack; however, since a CPAF camp was located near the UNTAC offices and seven non-UNTAC buildings were also destroyed, it could not be concluded that UNTAC was the prime target.

Reports of the Secretary-General. In his fourth periodic report on UNTAC, dated 3 May,[12] the Secretary-General indicated that the 27 March incident appeared to have been the first deliberate attack against UNTAC personnel. As to the 8 April incident, evidence ruled out involvement of any Cambodian faction.

In separate incidents on 30 April, an UNTAC vehicle carrying three civilian police monitors was fired upon in Kompong Cham, killing one and injuring another—a Colombian and a Malaysian, respectively; an attack on the Uruguayan detachment in Kratie wounded two soldiers. The assailants in both instances were unknown. On 1 May, a Dutch soldier was killed when three hand-grenades were hurled at the Dutch battalion camp in Banteay Meanchey; two days later, five soldiers from the Indian contingent were injured when their two-vehicle patrol was ambushed in Kompong Cham.

As a result of these attacks, UNTAC directed all of its military units to enhance security measures and procedures. Defensive positions, particularly in Siem Reap and Kompong Thom, were expanded to include bunkers, overhead protection and firing bays. Permanent guards and/or mobile patrols were used to improve the physical security of UNTAC premises and property at isolated locations. At UNTAC headquarters, the surrounding walls were heightened and illumination was improved. Military and civilian police monitors manned checkpoints and roadblocks, confiscating illegally held weapons.

In his 15 May report,[14] the Secretary-General noted that, between 4 and 11 May, UNTAC sustained five separate attacks: an ambush of one of its convoys in Banteay Meanchey; rocket and small-arms attacks on the Chinese engineering and Polish logistics companies in Kompong Thom and a similar assault on a Pakistani company at Choam Khsan, Preah Vihear; and, at Sisophon, Banteay Meanchey, a grenade attack on a vehicle driven by a civilian police monitor. The resultant UNTAC casualties were two dead and 17 wounded.

As at the reporting date, UNTAC personnel killed in the line of duty numbered 13 and the injured 52. Deaths through other causes totalled 39.

SECURITY COUNCIL ACTION

Following consultations among its members, the President of the Security Council, on 22 May, made the following statement[18] on behalf of the Council:

Meeting number. SC 3214.

"The Security Council strongly condemns the shelling on 21 May 1993 of the United Nations Transitional Authority in Cambodia (UNTAC), during which the Chinese engineering detachment suffered two deaths and seven wounded. It expresses its condolences to the Chinese Government and to the families of the victims; it pays tribute to the latter for their courage and dedication.

"The Security Council takes note of the preliminary report by the Secretariat indicating that the shelling was carried out by NADK. It requests the Secretary-General to investigate further and to report urgently to the Council.

"The Security Council expresses its strong support for UNTAC in carrying out its mandate within the framework of the Paris Agreements. It strongly condemns all attacks against UNTAC and demands that those responsible cease forthwith all hostile acts against UNTAC and take immediate measures to safeguard the lives and the security of UNTAC personnel.

"The Council recalls the warning contained in its resolution 826(1993) that it would respond appropriately should any of the parties fail to honour its obligations. It further warns that it will not countenance the use of violence to interfere with or overturn the

democratic process in Cambodia and will take further appropriate measures against any of the parties failing to honour its obligations.

"The Security Council also expresses its determination that the election for the constituent assembly should be held on the dates decided by the Supreme National Council and endorsed by the Security Council in its resolution 810(1993) and reaffirms its commitment to resolution 826(1993). The Council calls upon the Cambodian people fully to exercise their right to vote in the forthcoming elections. In this respect, the Council stresses the importance of ensuring the cessation of acts of violence and of all threats and intimidation, as well as of ensuring a neutral political environment in Cambodia."

As requested, the Secretary-General, on 28 May,[19] communicated the findings of the UNTAC investigations into the 21 May incident. They confirmed that the intended target of the NADK shelling was not the Chinese engineering company at Skon village, Kompong Cham, but rather an SOC police station located some 150 metres directly south of it. Being in the line of fire and owing to the inaccuracy of the firing, the UNTAC barracks was hit by a rocket that instantly killed a Chinese soldier and injured another who later died; seven others were injured.

SECURITY COUNCIL ACTION

On 8 June, following consultations among its members, the Security Council authorized its President to make the following statement[20] on behalf of the Council:

Meeting number. SC 3230.

"The Security Council strongly condemns the armed attack against a Pakistani platoon and another against a Malaysian platoon of the United Nations Transitional Authority in Cambodia (UNTAC), both on 7 June 1993. In the first incident, two Pakistani personnel were injured, one of them seriously; in the second, three Malaysian personnel were injured, one of them seriously.

"The Security Council takes note of the Secretariat's preliminary report that the first attack was launched against the Pakistani compound by the National Army of Democratic Kampuchea (NADK); the identity of the attackers in the second incident has not yet been determined. It requests the Secretary-General to investigate further and to report urgently to the Council.

"The Security Council demands that those responsible for the attacks cease immediately all attacks against UNTAC and reiterates its warning that it will take appropriate measures against those who are threatening the safety and security of UNTAC personnel and are trying to overturn the democratic process in Cambodia through violence."

The Secretary-General, on 22 June,[21] conveyed the results of the UNTAC investigation into the two attacks that occurred on 7 June. The attack on the Pakistani platoon encamped at Phum Tbeng, west of Preah Vihear, which injured two Pakistani soldiers, had been a deliberate action by some 170 NADK soldiers who attacked in waves. Evidence was provided by local villagers who identified two corpses on the scene as well-known NADK members. The Pakistani platoon had since been withdrawn from the area. The 45-minute assault, by rocket and small-arms fire, on the Malaysian platoon at Phum Tapoung, Battambang, which wounded three Malaysian soldiers, had in all probability been at the hands of CPAF elements. That conclusion was based on shell casings retrieved from the area and on the behaviour of the local CPAF and villagers.

Elections

The elections for the Constituent Assembly of Cambodia took place, as scheduled, from 23 to 28 May 1993. At the SNC meeting on 29 May, the Special Representative for Cambodia, in a statement made on behalf of the Secretary-General and the United Nations,[22] reported that the Cambodian electorate turned out in high numbers to exercise the right to vote without fear, in an atmosphere almost completely free of violence and intimidation, and concluded that the conduct of the elections had been free and fair. The counting and verification of ordinary and tendered ballots were under way, he said, adding that the outpouring of popular will demonstrated during the polling should reinforce the commitment already made by the parties to respect the election results.

Based on the certified results, the list of members of the Constituent Assembly would be drawn up, following which the date and venue of the first Assembly meeting would be fixed. The Special Representative announced that UNTAC stood ready to assist the Constituent Assembly and that a draft set of rules of procedure had been prepared for its consideration. He proposed that the modalities of the Assembly's functioning and its relationship with UNTAC, SNC and the existing administrative authorities should be discussed at the next SNC meeting on 5 June.

SECURITY COUNCIL ACTION

On 2 June, the Security Council unanimously adopted **resolution 835(1993)**.

The Security Council,

Reaffirming its resolutions 668(1990) of 20 September 1990, 745(1992) of 28 February 1992, 810(1993) of 8 March 1993, 826(1993) of 20 May 1993 and other relevant resolutions,

Expressing its appreciation to the United Nations Transitional Authority in Cambodia (UNTAC) and especially to the Special Representative of the Secretary-General, Yasushi Akashi, for their courage, dedication and per-

severance in providing the necessary support for the electoral process despite hardships and difficulties,

Paying tribute to the leadership and continuing role of His Royal Highness Prince Norodom Sihanouk, President of the Supreme National Council,

Noting with satisfaction the overwhelming number of Cambodians who demonstrated their patriotism and sense of responsibility in exercising their right to vote,

Endorsing the declaration of the Secretary-General's Special Representative to the Supreme National Council of 29 May 1993 that the conduct of the election had been free and fair,

1. *Salutes* the members of UNTAC, particularly those who gave their lives in order to make possible this extraordinary demonstration by the Cambodian people;

2. *Invites* the Secretary-General to make his report on the election available as soon as possible;

3. *Expresses its intention*, following certification of the election, to support fully the duly elected constituent assembly in its work of drawing up a constitution, according to the principles laid down in annex 5 to the Agreement on a Comprehensive Political Settlement of the Cambodia Conflict, and establishing a new government for all Cambodia;

4. *Calls upon* all parties to stand by their obligation to respect fully the results of the elections and urges them to do all in their power to bring about the peaceful establishment of a democratic government in accordance with the terms of the new constitution;

5. *Urges* the international community to contribute actively to the reconstruction and rehabilitation of Cambodia;

6. *Decides* to remain actively seized of the matter.

Security Council resolution 835(1993)
2 June 1993   Meeting 3227   Adopted unanimously
Draft prepared in consultations among Council members (S/25876).

Report of the Secretary-General. In a 10 June report,[23] the Secretary-General gave the official results of the elections. Of the 4,011,631 ballots (ordinary and tendered) verified as valid, FUNCINPEC won 1,824,188 votes (45.47 per cent of the votes); SOC (CPP) won 1,533,471 (38.23 per cent); and KNPLF (BLDP) won 152,764 (3.81 per cent). Based on those figures, the 120 seats in the Constituent Assembly were allocated as follows: 58 to FUNCINPEC, 51 to SOC (CPP), 10 to KNPLF (BLDP) and 1 to MOLINAKA (Molinaka and Naktaorsou Khmere for Freedom). A table giving the names of the 20 participating parties, with the number and percentage of votes won by each, was annexed to the report.

The Secretary-General authorized the Special Representative to issue a statement at the SNC meeting on 10 June, on behalf of the United Nations, that the elections had been free and fair. Voter turnout reached 4,267,192, representing 89.56 per cent of registered voters. Tendered ballots made up about 7 per cent of the votes cast. To ensure maximum accuracy and transparency, counting proceeded at a pace slower than anticipated and UNTAC released interim vote counts twice a day.

Certain irregularities were alleged by SOC (CPP): party agents were not able to inspect the ''safe havens'' where ballot boxes were stored overnight; the plastic seals of some boxes were ruptured; the indelible ink used was not efficacious; discrepancies were found in the ballot count of certain boxes; and some locally recruited Cambodian polling staff lacked impartiality. UNTAC investigations into some of these allegations were conducted to the complete satisfaction of party agents. As to the other allegations, details requested by UNTAC to enable investigations to proceed had not been forthcoming. UNTAC denied SOC's request for new elections in seven provinces and in Phnom Penh for lack of convincing evidence that irregularities and fraud had been such as to invalidate the poll.

SECURITY COUNCIL ACTION

The Security Council, having considered the Secretary-General's report on the conduct and results of the elections, unanimously adopted **resolution 840(1993)** on 15 June 1993.

The Security Council,

Reaffirming its resolutions 668(1990) of 20 September 1990, 745(1992) of 28 February 1992, 810(1993) of 8 March 1993, 826(1993) of 20 May 1993, 835(1993) of 2 June 1993 and other relevant resolutions,

Taking note of the report of the Secretary-General dated 10 June 1993, and in particular the statement contained therein concerning the election that took place in Cambodia from 23 to 28 May 1993,

Paying tribute to the leadership and continuing role of His Royal Highness Prince Norodom Sihanouk, President of the Supreme National Council, in bringing about national reconciliation and restoring peace in Cambodia,

Expressing its appreciation to the United Nations Transitional Authority in Cambodia (UNTAC) and especially to the Special Representative of the Secretary-General for the smoothness of the electoral process,

Reaffirming the national unity, territorial integrity and inviolability and independence of Cambodia,

Welcoming the fact that on 14 June 1993 the newly elected constituent assembly held its first meeting,

1. *Approves* the report of the Secretary-General;

2. *Endorses* the results of the election, which has been certified free and fair by the United Nations;

3. *Calls upon* all parties to stand by their obligation to respect fully the results of the election and to cooperate in securing a peaceful transition and welcomes, in this context, the efforts of His Royal Highness Prince Norodom Sihanouk to achieve national reconciliation and his leadership and continuing role in maintaining stability and in promoting cooperation among Cambodians by appropriate means;

4. *Fully supports* the newly elected constituent assembly which has begun its work of drawing up and approving a constitution according to the principles laid down in annex 5 to the Agreement on a Comprehensive Political Settlement of the Cambodia Conflict contained in the Paris Agreements, and will subsequently transform itself into a legislative assembly, which will establish a new government for all Cambodia;

5. *Emphasizes* the necessity to complete this work and to establish a new government for all Cambodia as soon as possible and within the time allotted by the Paris Agreements;

6. *Requests* UNTAC to continue to play its role in conjunction with SNC during the transitional period in accordance with the Paris Agreements;

7. *Requests also* the Secretary-General to report to the Security Council by the middle of July, including on his recommendations on the possible role the United Nations and its agencies might play after the end of the mandate of UNTAC according to the Paris Agreements;

8. *Urges* all States and relevant international organizations to contribute actively to the reconstruction and rehabilitation of Cambodia;

9. *Decides* to remain actively seized of the matter.

Security Council resolution 840(1993)

15 June 1993   Meeting 3237   Adopted unanimously

6-nation draft (S/25931), orally revised.

Sponsors: China, France, Japan, Russian Federation, United Kingdom, United States.

Post-election period and termination of UNTAC

Report of the Secretary-General (July). On 16 July,[24] the Secretary-General described post-election developments and the possible role of the United Nations after the end of the UNTAC mandate. As provided for by the Security Council in 1992,[1] that mandate was to extend for a period not to exceed 18 months until the end of the transitional period, that is, until the Constituent Assembly had drafted and approved a constitution, transformed itself into a legislative assembly and created a new Cambodian government—all to be performed within three months from the date of the election (23 to 28 May).

The duly elected Constituent Assembly held an inaugural meeting on 14 June. It elected its President and two Vice-Presidents and adopted its rules of procedure on 30 June. It established two permanent committees—the Committee for Drafting the Constitution and the Committee on Rules of Procedure. Elaboration of a draft constitution had begun, with UNTAC providing technical advice and logistical and operational assistance.

The post-election period had not been without difficulties. Some elements of SOC (CPP), which had made numerous allegations of electoral irregularities and had initially withheld recognition of the outcome of the elections, declared a short-lived ''secession'' in three eastern provinces that collapsed after a few days. SOC subsequently accepted the election results. None the less, the Electoral Advisory Committee, set up by the Special Representative, continued to review outstanding allegations.

Though not foreseen under the 1991 Paris Agreements,[2] an Interim Joint Administration

(Provisional National Government) was set up, with Prince Norodom Sihanouk as head of State, to serve as a cooperative framework, during the transitional period, between all parties holding seats in the Constituent Assembly. On 1 July, the Assembly gave its vote of confidence to the Administration and unanimously adopted the Programme of Action of the Provisional Government for the Coming Three Months. It agreed on the composition of the Council of Ministers, with Prince Norodom Ranariddh (head of FUNCINPEC) and Hun Sen (head of SOC (CPP)) as Co-Chairmen.

The Joint Administration was to be viewed as an attempt to fuse three of the existing administrative structures and as a manifestation of a common desire for peace, stability and national reconciliation. In accordance with the Paris Agreements, UNTAC continued to cooperate with SNC as the unique legitimate body and source of authority in Cambodia throughout the transition period.

Also declaring acceptance of the election results was PDK, which, although not a party to the Joint Administration, held tentative discussions with it aimed at achieving national reconciliation. In the meantime, low-level cease-fire violations and military activities, mainly involving NADK, continued to occur.

The Secretary-General outlined the plan for the orderly withdrawal of UNTAC to be completed by 15 November 1993. The military component would be withdrawn in three phases. Phase I (to end on 31 July) would entail the physical preparations for withdrawal. Under phase II (1-31 August), the infantry battalions and related field hospitals, engineering and other units would withdraw and infantry battalions in neighbouring sectors would redeploy to cover the vacated sectors. Under phase III (1 September-15 November), the remaining UNTAC elements would be completely withdrawn.

The 3,500 officers of the civilian police component were scheduled for withdrawal in three groups: 1,100 during 1 July–1 August; another 1,100 during 2-28 August; and 1,300 during 29 August–30 September.

Of the remaining 15 Professional staff of the human rights component at Phnom Penh and 18 others (with training assistants) in the provinces, eight were to leave by 31 July and the rest by 31 August.

More than 1,600 electoral staff (international polling station officers, fingerprint and handwriting experts and district electoral supervisors) were repatriated between 31 May and 15 June. Eight officers were to leave on 31 July and 16 others (including the Chief Electoral Officer and three staff assistants) were to remain at Phnom Penh until 31 August to assist the Electoral Advisory Committee.

Of the 172 international staff of the civil administration component (115 in provincial capitals, including the municipality of Phnom Penh, and at border checkpoints; and 57 at UNTAC headquarters), 32 were to depart before the end of July; the rest would remain until 31 August.

Twelve staff members of the rehabilitation component were scheduled to leave between 31 July and 22 August and the remaining 17 by 31 August. One third of the Information/Education Division's 45 staff had been released by 30 June; four were to leave by 31 July; and the rest would continue producing programmes on human rights education and on reconstruction and development until the end of August.

Various programmes and agencies of the United Nations system, as well as international financial institutions, would be prepared, in consultation with the Cambodian Government, to continue to play their traditional role in rehabilitation, reconstruction, development and humanitarian assistance during the immediate post-UNTAC period.

Communications. The Secretary-General supplemented his report with a letter to the Security Council President,[25] stating that, in the coming months, it was essential for the Interim Joint Administration to be able to function properly, and that neither social unrest nor macroeconomic disorder be allowed to take hold. It was also essential for those serving in the public domain—civil servants, police and the armed forces—to begin redirecting their allegiances from the factions of the past to the future constitutional Government.

Therefore, on the recommendation of the Special Representative and in consultation with concerned Governments, the Secretary-General concluded that urgent measures should be taken to enable UNTAC to provide, for the remainder of the transitional period, emergency financial assistance in support of the process of restructuring and adjustment of the administrative, police and military structures of the Joint Administration. The amount required would be $20 million—a relatively modest additional outlay to ensure non-interruption of the remarkable progress towards peace and the successful conclusion of United Nations endeavours on behalf of Cambodia.

The Security Council, on 16[26] and 26 July,[27] agreed with the Secretary-General's view regarding the proposed financial outlay and endorsed the overall concept and arrangements concerning the withdrawal of UNTAC from Cambodia.

Report of the Secretary-General (August). In a further report of 26 August,[28] the Secretary-General stated that agreement had been reached on some 120 articles of the draft constitution. With only two items outstanding—the status of the head of State and the post of prime minister—elaboration would be completed at the end of the month.

Relative calm lasting several weeks was broken in mid-August, when, as a result of NADK military activities in the north and west, CAF launched a military operation in Banteay Meanchey, surrounding a number of NADK strongholds and overrunning one at Phum Chat on the Thai border. Several hundred villagers were displaced or forcibly removed, including some 1,200 who reportedly crossed into Thailand.

NADK was further responsible for a mortar assault on a 21-man UNTAC checkpoint at Choam Khsan, Preah Vihear (1 August); and for attacks on two trains, one in Kampot and the other in Kompong Chhnang (2 and 15 August), that killed a total of 16 passengers and injured 40 others. Racist PDK radio broadcasts directed at ethnic Vietnamese were the subject of an UNTAC protest, which the PDK President rejected. UNTAC was investigating the murder of six such persons in Kompong Chhnang (10 August). In addition, a group of ethnic Vietnamese children had been abducted (13 August) and later released for ransom.

In another development, highly organized criminal gangs had been stealing UNTAC vehicles, sometimes at gunpoint. The Co-Presidents of the Interim Joint Administration, to whom representations were made, agreed to cooperate closely with UNTAC to prevent and punish such crimes.

The withdrawal of UNTAC was proceeding as planned, with some adjustments, including the retention until mid-September of 15 staff members in the Office of Economic Affairs and of 28 civilian police officers until 15 October.

The Secretary-General noted that urgent measures were required to assist the incoming Cambodian Government to meet a number of pressing needs: budgetary support, public administration reform, mine clearance, resettlement and reintegration of displaced persons, agriculture, social services including health care and education, maintenance of public utilities and repair of the infrastructure, especially the transportation system. These requirements were to be discussed at a meeting of the International Committee on Reconstruction of Cambodia (Paris, 8 and 9 September).

Noting that the future status of the Cambodia Mine Action Centre (CMAC) was to be taken up with the new Government, the Secretary-General stated that, since the inception of UNTAC, more than 4 million square metres had been cleared of mines and about 37,000 mines and other unexploded ordnance had been destroyed; some 2,330 Cambodians had been trained in mine-clearance techniques, of whom approximately 1,400 were currently employed. Pending alternative funding arrangements, he would maintain the United Nations Trust Fund for the Demining Programme in Cambodia. In the meantime, the CMAC Governing Council, on which Prince Sihanouk served as President and the Special Representative for Cambodia as Vice-President, was to meet at the end of August regarding the Council's mandate.

Article 17 of the Paris Agreements provided that, after the end of the transitional period, the United Nations Commission on Human Rights should continue to monitor the human rights situation in Cambodia and, if necessary, appoint a Special Rapporteur who would report his findings annually to the Commission and to the General Assembly. The Centre for Human Rights was scheduled to establish its operational presence in Phnom Penh upon the termination of the UNTAC mandate, with a total of 23 international and local staff, to be drawn in part from the UNTAC human rights component (see also PART THREE, Chapter X).

The Secretary-General indicated his intention to establish an integrated office at Phnom Penh, to be headed by a United Nations representative who would coordinate, in close consultation with the Cambodian Government, the full range of civilian activities to be undertaken by various programmes and agencies of the United Nations system to promote development, provide humanitarian assistance and foster respect for human rights in Cambodia. During the period immediately following the establishment of the new Government, the office would deal with a number of residual issues arising from the Paris Agreements and UNTAC's presence in the country.

SECURITY COUNCIL ACTION

On 27 August, the Security Council unanimously adopted **resolution 860(1993)**.

The Security Council,

Reaffirming its resolutions 668(1990) of 20 September 1990, 745(1992) of 28 February 1992, 840(1993) of 15 June 1993 and other relevant resolutions,

Taking note of the reports of the Secretary-General dated 16 July 1993 and 26 August 1993,

Paying tribute to the continuing role of His Royal Highness Prince Norodom Sihanouk in achieving peace, stability and genuine national reconciliation for all Cambodia,

Recalling that, according to the Paris Agreements, the transitional period shall terminate when the Constituent Assembly elected through free and fair elections, organized and certified by the United Nations, has approved the constitution and transformed itself into a legislative assembly, and thereafter a new government has been created,

Also taking note of the expressed wish of the Cambodian interim joint administration to maintain the mandate of the United Nations Transitional Authority in Cambodia (UNTAC) until the establishment of a new government in Cambodia as conveyed by the Secretariat,

1. *Welcomes* the reports of the Secretary-General dated 16 July 1993 and 26 August 1993, and approves the UNTAC withdrawal plan contained in document S/26090;

2. *Fully supports* the Constituent Assembly in its work of drawing up and approving a constitution, and stresses

the importance of completing this work in accordance with the Paris Agreements;

3. *Confirms* that UNTAC's functions under the Paris Agreements shall end upon the creation in September of a new government of Cambodia consistent with those Agreements;

4. *Decides* that, in order to ensure a safe and an orderly withdrawal of the military component of UNTAC, the period of such withdrawal shall end on 15 November 1993;

5. *Decides* to remain actively seized of the matter.

Security Council resolution 860(1993)

27 August 1993   Meeting 3270   Adopted unanimously

Draft prepared in consultations among Council members (S/26362).

On 28 October,[29] the Secretary-General informed the Council President of having received word from the UNTAC Officer-in-Charge of withdrawal that security in Cambodia had so deteriorated that theft of UNTAC equipment, often by armed elements, had increased; and that, at the next stage of withdrawal, equipment would need to be retrieved from outlying areas following the departure of military personnel, which could expose UNTAC civilian staff to heightened insecurity. In the circumstances, he requested that certain categories of UNTAC personnel remain deployed beyond 15 November, as follows: 71 military police officers from 16 to 30 November and 30 others from 1 to 31 December; 10 medical personnel from 16 November to 7 December and eight others from 8 to 31 December.

The Secretary-General advised that further United Nations involvement in the executive and managerial responsibilities of CMAC was inappropriate, but proposed extending to 30 November the deployment of 17 members of the UNTAC Mine Clearance and Training Unit.

Report of the Secretary-General (October). On 5 October,[30] the Secretary-General reported with great satisfaction that the new Government of Cambodia was formed on 24 September, based on the will of the people, expressed through free and fair elections organized and conducted by the United Nations.

The immediate steps leading to that historic event began on 19 September, when the 120-member Constituent Assembly concluded its deliberations on a new constitution; on 21 September, it formally adopted the Constitution by a vote of 113 to 5, with 2 abstentions, a greater margin than the two-thirds majority specified in the Paris Agreements.

On 24 September, Prince Sihanouk, as head of State of Cambodia, formally promulgated at Phnom Penh the Constitution according to which Cambodia became a constitutional monarchy, with the official name "The Kingdom of Cambodia", and an independent, sovereign, peaceful, neutral and non-aligned State. On the same date, Prince Sihanouk was elected King of Cambodia by the Royal Council of the Throne. The powers and duties of the monarch were set forth in the Constitution, article 7 of which stated that the King held the throne but should not hold power. In accordance with the Constitution and the Paris Agreements, the Constituent Assembly transformed itself into a legislative assembly.

The Constitution also stipulated that Cambodia should recognize and respect human rights in accordance with the Charter of the United Nations, the Universal Declaration of Human Rights[31] and all other international instruments related to human rights and the rights of women and children. Article 51 called for the adoption of a multi-party, free and democratic regime.

Following his election, King Sihanouk appointed Prince Norodom Ranariddh First Prime Minister, and Hun Sen, Second Prime Minister.

Thus UNTAC's mandate was successfully concluded on 24 September. Two days later, the Special Representative departed Cambodia. The departure by 15 November of most of UNTAC personnel was well under way.

The Secretary-General expressed his appreciation to the Security Council for its consistent support and guidance, as well as to all the countries that had contributed troops and/or police officers. He also expressed regret at the loss of UNTAC personnel and paid tribute to King Sihanouk, other leaders and the people of Cambodia for their historic achievement in overcoming two decades of strife and devastation and laying a sound foundation for a peaceful and democratic Cambodia.

SECURITY COUNCIL ACTION

The Security Council convened on 5 October. It had before it the Secretary-General's report (see above), as well as a statement of the Ministers for Foreign Affairs of the permanent Council members,[32] noting, among other things, the successful fulfilment of UNTAC's mandate and agreeing to consider how a continued United Nations presence would contribute further to peace and stability after UNTAC's departure.

At their request, Australia, Cambodia and Thailand were invited to participate in the deliberations without the right to vote under the relevant provision of the Charter and rule 37a of the Council's provisional rules of procedure.

After statements by 12 States, beginning with one by the First Prime Minister of Cambodia, the Council President made the following statement[33] on behalf of the Council:

Meeting number. SC 3287.

"On behalf of the members of the Security Council, I wish to thank His Royal Highness Prince Norodom Ranariddh, First Prime Minister, and His Excellency Mr. Hun Sen, Second Prime Minister, of the

Royal Government of Cambodia for their presence here and to express the satisfaction of the Security Council at the auspicious developments that have taken place in Cambodia since the holding of the elections of 23 to 28 May 1993, in particular the proclamation of the Cambodian Constitution on 24 September 1993 and the creation of the new Government of Cambodia.

"I also take this opportunity to congratulate His Majesty King Norodom Sihanouk, head of State of Cambodia, on his accession to the throne and to pay tribute to the continuing role played by His Majesty in the quest for national reconciliation and a better future for all Cambodia.

"In the light of the successful completion of the mandate of the United Nations Transitional Authority in Cambodia (UNTAC), the Security Council reiterates its recognition of the remarkable work carried out by UNTAC, under the leadership of the Secretary-General and his Special Representative, Mr. Yasushi Akashi.

"The Security Council stresses the importance of the continued support of the international community to the consolidation of peace and democracy and the promotion of development in Cambodia.

"Taking into account the letter dated 26 September 1993 addressed to the Secretary-General by His Royal Highness Prince Norodom Ranariddh, First Prime Minister, and His Excellency Mr. Hun Sen, Second Prime Minister, and the further report of the Secretary-General on the implementation of Security Council resolution 745(1992) which members of the Council have just received, the Council will continue to study the situation in Cambodia and will consider what action it should take."

(For the 26 September letter referred to in the statement, see below, under "UN Military Liaison Team in Cambodia".)

Financing

Report of the Secretary-General (July). In his 27 July report on the financing of UNTAC,[34] the Secretary-General indicated that, as at 30 June 1993, outstanding assessments of $290,533,100 were due from Member States: $4,645,300 for the United Nations Advance Mission in Cambodia (UNAMIC)[35] and $285,887,800 for UNTAC. Voluntary contributions consisted of cash contributions in the amounts of $1.1 million from Japan for costs incurred in reinforcing security measures undertaken by UNTAC and $25,807 from New Zealand for the air fare of international polling station officers. These items had been budgeted for.

The estimated amounts due to troop-contributing States for troop costs for the period 1 February to 31 May 1993 totalled $64,425,600. Troops were currently being provided by 25 Governments: Australia, Austria, Bangladesh, Bulgaria, Canada, Chile, China, France, Germany, Ghana, India, Indonesia, Japan, Malaysia, Namibia,[36] Netherlands, New Zealand, Pakistan, Philippines, Poland, Russian Federation, Singapore,[37] Thailand, Tunisia and Uruguay.

The appropriations for the combined UNAMIC and UNTAC operations from 1 November 1991 to 30 April 1993 totalled $1,161,191,600 gross ($1,143,038,800 net), of which $20,023,200 gross ($19,777,200 net) related specifically to UNAMIC.

Revised UNTAC requirements for the three-month period from 1 May to 31 July 1993 amounted to $301,181,600 gross ($292,829,700 net), representing an increase of $65,181,600 gross ($59,023,100 net) over the reduced commitment authorization of $236 million. The Advisory Committee on Administrative and Budgetary Questions (ACABQ) communicated to the Secretary-General on 13 April its concurrence in his request to enter into commitments up to that level. Requirements for the month of August amounted to $68,527,700 gross ($66,896,800 net).

The liquidation of UNTAC was projected to take 10 months; estimated costs for the first phase (1 September to 31 December 1993) amounted to $147,094,600 net. Proposals for the disposition of UNTAC property were annexed to the report, as was a list of UNTAC assets potentially available by 1 August.

To sum up, the financing of UNTAC required the appropriation of: $236 million gross ($233,806,600 net) to be authorized with prior ACABQ concurrence for operations from 1 May to 31 July 1993; $65,181,600 gross ($59,023,100 net) to meet additional requirements for the same period; and $68,527,700 gross ($66,896,800 net) for continued UNTAC operations for August. Also called for were: a decision to credit the unencumbered balance of $3,367,600 gross ($58,500 net) as of 30 April 1993 to Member States against their assessments for the additional requirements for 1 May to 31 July; approval, in principle, for the Secretary-General to proceed, upon the completion of UNTAC's mandate, to dispose of its property; and appropriation and/or commitment authorization in the amount of $150,515,700 gross ($147,094,600 net) to meet liquidation costs during the first phase.

In addition, the Secretary-General stated that assistance to the Interim Joint Administration in Cambodia was necessary to enable it to improve its capacity to generate revenue and meet minimal expenditure without provoking inflation. The assistance would allow the following to be undertaken with direct UNTAC involvement: unifying procedures for dealing with civil servants in zones administered by the three main parties of the Constituent Assembly; extending the use of the riel in the zones not hitherto using it; training public-sector employees in the responsibilities of a multi-party democracy; setting in motion the rationalization and streamlining of organizational structures and reduction of public-sector employment; and meeting the most pressing expenditures during July and August without resort to currency issuance.

The Secretary-General proposed that the assistance, calculated at $20 million for July and August, should be provided from the UNTAC budget. Since $3 million would be met from the Trust Fund for the Cambodian Peace Process, $17 million would be required from the UNTAC budget.

ACABQ,[38] noting that the Secretary-General's report was not available in time for detailed consideration and that performance report and cost estimates were incomplete, recommended, pending a detailed examination of an updated report, that the General Assembly appropriate and assess the amount of $85 million net to meet UNTAC's additional requirements from 1 May to 31 July 1993 and its continued operation during August. It recommended that the Secretary-General pursue his efforts to collect the outstanding assessments of $290.5 million from Member States for UNAMIC and UNTAC as at 30 June.

Annexed to the report of ACABQ was its letter of 15 July to the Secretary-General on financial assistance to the Interim Joint Administration, for which the Controller had requested commitment authority in the amount of $10 million under the terms of a 1991 Assembly resolution on unforeseen and extraordinary expenses.[39] ACABQ stated that, while such assistance could be within the overall scope of UNTAC, it could find no specific authority to support the financing of that activity from assessed contributions. It therefore decided not to act on that request.

As to the Secretary-General's request for $17 million from the UNTAC budget, ACABQ stated that, pending its consideration of that request, the Secretary-General could utilize $3 million from the Trust Fund for the Cambodian Peace Process. He could further utilize, on an exceptional and temporary basis, an amount from existing reserves equivalent to voluntary contributions pledged in response to his appeal of 9 July; repayment of reserves so utilized should be the first charge against contributions received until the amount utilized from the reserves was fully repaid.

GENERAL ASSEMBLY ACTION

On 14 September 1993, on the recommendation of the Fifth (Administrative and Budgetary) Committee, the General Assembly adopted **resolution 47/209 B** without vote.

Financing of the United Nations Transitional Authority in Cambodia

The General Assembly,

Having considered the report of the Secretary-General on the financing of the United Nations Transitional Authority in Cambodia and the related report of the Advisory Committee on Administrative and Budgetary Questions,

Bearing in mind Security Council resolutions 717(1991) of 16 October 1991, 718(1991) of 31 October 1991,

728(1992) of 8 January 1992, 745(1992) of 28 February 1992, 766(1992) of 21 July 1992, 783(1992) of 13 October 1992, 792(1992) of 30 November 1992, 810(1993) of 8 March 1993, 826(1993) of 20 May 1993, 835(1993) of 2 June 1993 and 840(1993) of 15 June 1993,

Reaffirming that the costs of the United Nations Advance Mission in Cambodia and the United Nations Transitional Authority in Cambodia are expenses of the Organization to be borne by Member States in accordance with Article 17, paragraph 2, of the Charter of the United Nations,

Recalling its previous decision regarding the fact that, in order to meet the expenditures caused by the Advance Mission and the Transitional Authority, a different procedure is required from the one applied to meet expenditures of the regular budget of the United Nations,

Taking into account the fact that the economically more developed countries are in a position to make relatively larger contributions and that the economically less developed countries have a relatively limited capacity to contribute towards such operations,

Bearing in mind the special responsibilities of the States permanent members of the Security Council, as indicated in General Assembly resolution 1874(S-IV) of 27 June 1963, in the financing of such operations,

Noting with appreciation that voluntary contributions have been made to the Advance Mission and the Transitional Authority by certain Governments,

Mindful of the fact that it is essential to provide the Transitional Authority with the necessary financial resources to enable it to fulfil its responsibilities under the relevant resolutions of the Security Council,

Expressing concern about the financial situation of the Transitional Authority, owing to overdue payments by Member States of their assessments, particularly Member States in arrears,

Expressing deep concern about the adverse effect that the deteriorating financial situation has on reimbursement to troop contributors, placing an additional burden on these countries,

Noting that the amount referred to in section IV of the report of the Secretary-General has been revised to 13 million United States dollars,

1. *Endorses* the observations and recommendations made by the Advisory Committee on Administrative and Budgetary Questions in its report;

2. *Urges* all Member States to ensure payment of their assessed contributions to the United Nations Advance Mission in Cambodia and the United Nations Transitional Authority in Cambodia promptly and in full;

3. *Requests* the Secretary-General to explore all possibilities in order to ensure prompt reimbursement to troop-contributing countries;

4. *Decides,* at this stage, to appropriate, in accordance with the recommendation contained in paragraph 14 of the report of the Advisory Committee, an amount of 85 million United States dollars net to meet the additional requirements of the Transitional Authority for the period from 1 May to 31 July 1993 and for the continued operation of the Transitional Authority from 1 August 1993 to the end of its mandate, in accordance with Security Council resolution 860(1993) of 27 August 1993, in addition to the total amount of 1,397,191,600 dollars gross (1,376,845,400 dollars net) already appropriated for the Advance Mission and the

Transitional Authority, inclusive of the amount of 236 million dollars authorized and apportioned with the prior concurrence of the Advisory Committee under the terms of paragraph 7 of General Assembly resolution 47/209 A of 22 December 1992 for the period from 1 May to 31 July 1993;

5. *Decides also*, as an ad hoc arrangement, to apportion the amount of 85 million dollars net, for the period from 1 May 1993 to the end of the mandate of the Transitional Authority, in accordance with Security Council resolution 860(1993), among Member States in accordance with the composition of groups set out in paragraphs 3 and 4 of General Assembly resolution 43/232 of 1 March 1989, as adjusted by the Assembly in its resolutions 44/192 B of 21 December 1989, 45/269 of 27 August 1991, 46/198 A of 20 December 1991 and 47/218 A of 23 December 1992, and taking into account the scale of assessments set out in Assembly resolution 46/221 A of 20 December 1991 and Assembly decision 47/456 of 23 December 1992;

6. *Decides further* to establish the contributions of Andorra, the Czech Republic, Eritrea, the former Yugoslav Republic of Macedonia, Monaco and Slovakia to the Transitional Authority in accordance with the rates of assessment to be adopted by the General Assembly for these Member States no later than at its forty-eighth session;

7. *Invites* the new Member States mentioned in paragraph 6 above to make advance payments against their assessed contributions, to be determined;

8. *Invites* voluntary contributions to the Transitional Authority in cash and in the form of services and supplies acceptable to the Secretary-General, to be administered, as appropriate, in accordance with the procedure established by the General Assembly in its resolutions 43/230 of 21 December 1988, 44/192 A of 21 December 1989 and 45/258 of 3 May 1991;

9. *Requests* the Secretary-General to submit to the General Assembly at its forty-eighth session a detailed and up-to-date performance report on the budget of the Advance Mission and the Transitional Authority for the period from 1 November 1991 to the end of the mandate of the Transitional Authority, in accordance with Security Council resolution 860(1993);

10. *Decides* that the disposition of the property of the Transitional Authority shall proceed on the basis of the principle that the equipment of the Transitional Authority should, wherever possible and cost-effective, be transferred to other missions, and, in this connection, endorses the recommendation of the Advisory Committee with regard to the disposition of the equipment, and requests the Secretary-General to proceed with the disposition on this basis;

11. *Requests* the Secretary-General to submit a report early at the forty-eighth session providing a detailed explanation for the donation of certain assets to the Government of Cambodia along with the proposals for the donation of any remaining assets which cannot be transferred to other missions;

12. *Decides*, with regard to section IV of the report of the Secretary-General, that the Secretary-General may use, on an extraordinary and temporary basis, an amount from the existing reserves equivalent to the pledges received and that repayment of any reserves so utilized shall be the first charge on receipts from voluntary contributions, and requests the Secretary-General to report to the General Assembly at its forty-eighth session, through the Advisory Committee, on the financial situation with regard to the joint interim administration referred to in section IV of his report, including proposals on this matter;

13. *Invites* Member States and other States in a position to do so to respond positively to the appeal of the Secretary-General for voluntary contributions for financial assistance to the joint interim administration of Cambodia;

14. *Requests* the Secretary-General to submit revised cost estimates related to the liquidation of the Transitional Authority, scheduled to start on 1 September 1993;

15. *Authorizes* the Secretary-General to enter into commitments of up to 100 million dollars to meet the costs associated with the initial liquidation of the Transitional Authority over the period from 1 September to 31 December 1993, subject to obtaining the prior concurrence of the Advisory Committee, the said amount to be apportioned among Member States in accordance with the scheme set out in the present resolution;

16. *Requests* the Advisory Committee to report to the General Assembly at its forty-eighth session on action taken with regard to paragraph 15 above;

17. *Requests* the Secretary-General to take all necessary action to ensure that the Transitional Authority is administered with a maximum of efficiency and economy.

General Assembly resolution 47/209 B

14 September 1993   Meeting 110   Adopted without vote

Approved by Fifth Committee (A/47/824/Add.1) without vote, 7 September (meeting 75); draft by Chairman (A/C.5/47/L.41); agenda item 123.
Meeting numbers. GA 47th session: 5th Committee 68, 69, 72, 75; plenary 110.

Report of the Secretary-General (December). On 8 December,[40] the Secretary-General submitted a further report on UNTAC's financing, giving updated information on assessed contributions, voluntary contributions, trust funds for Cambodia, reimbursements to troop-contributing States, financial performance from 1 November 1991 to 30 September 1993 and cost estimates for the initial stage of the liquidation phase of UNTAC, as revised, and for the final stage. The withdrawal plan for UNTAC was outlined, including the extension of deployment of certain categories of military personnel beyond 15 November 1993.

As at 31 October, a total of $230,689,200 in outstanding assessments was due from Member States for UNAMIC ($4,524,600) and UNTAC ($226,164,600).

Between 1 July and 31 October, voluntary contributions in the amount of $10.3 million were pledged to the Interim Joint Administration by six Member States (Australia, Japan, Netherlands, Philippines, United Kingdom and United States), of which $7.9 million had been paid and $2.4 million remained outstanding.

The four trust funds set up on behalf of Cambodia and the total contribution received by each as at 31 October were: the Trust Fund for the Cambodian Peace Process, set up by the Secretary-General in April 1990, received $8.7 million from

12 Member States ($6.8 million) and a private institution ($1.9 million); the Trust Fund for a Human Rights Education Programme in Cambodia, set up in June 1992, received $1.6 million from eight Member States and a private institution ($75,000); the Cambodia Trust Fund, set up in November 1992 to receive funds for rehabilitation activities, received $2.2 million from five Member States; and the Trust Fund for the Demining Programme in Cambodia, set up in July 1993 to support programmes in mine-awareness, mine-marking, mine-clearing and training in mine-clearing, received $713,400 from two Member States.

The estimated amounts due to troop-contributing States—currently 27 with the recent addition of Ireland and the United States—for troop costs for the period 1 March to 30 September 1993 totalled $105,738,100.

Between 1 November 1991 and 30 September 1993, apportionments were made to the combined operations of UNAMIC and UNTAC totalling $1,482,191,600 gross ($1,461,845,400 net), of which $20,023,200 gross ($19,777,200 net) related specifically to UNAMIC. Due to the extension of the UNTAC mandate through 24 September 1993, cost overruns of $65,660,300 gross ($61,850,600 net) had been incurred. Although the UNTAC mandate officially ended on 24 September, for financial reporting purposes, 30 September 1993 was used as the cut-off date for activities relating to the regular mandate. The liquidation phase would therefore begin on 1 October 1993.

The revised cost estimates for the liquidation of UNTAC from 1 October to 31 December amounted to $59,527,400 gross ($57,714,200 net). The costs associated with the final stage of liquidation, projected to be completed on 30 April 1994, amounted to $9,170,600 gross ($8,126,200 net).

In summary, the requirements called for appropriations of: $236 million gross ($233,806,600 net), authorized with prior ACABQ concurrence and apportioned under the terms of Assembly **resolution 47/209 B**, for the continued operation of UNTAC from 1 May to 31 July 1993; $65,660,300 gross ($61,850,600 net) to meet the additional requirements for 1 August to 30 September 1993; $59,527,400 gross ($57,714,200 net) and $9,170,600 gross ($8,126,200 net) to meet costs associated with, respectively, the liquidation of UNTAC from 1 October to 31 December 1993 and the final liquidation stage; and an additional amount of $34,358,300 gross ($27,691,000 net) to meet the additional requirements of UNTAC, including liquidation costs, taking account of the $100 million gross and net already apportioned in accordance with Assembly decision 48/469 below.

In a later addendum to the above report,[41] the Secretary-General outlined the plan for the disposition of UNTAC assets and gave the status of disposition of assets with a total residual value of $150.23 million as at 7 December 1993.

ACABQ,[42] referring to the Secretary-General's 9 December report[43] on the financing of 17 peace-keeping and other operations, including UNTAC, stated that it would review the full and separate report on UNTAC financing summarized above at the Assembly's resumed session in February 1994. Pending that review, it recommended that the existing commitment authority of $100 million be maintained through 31 March 1994 and assessed.

GENERAL ASSEMBLY ACTION

In December, the General Assembly adopted **decision 48/469** without vote.

Financing of the United Nations Transitional Authority in Cambodia

At its 87th plenary meeting, on 23 December 1993, the General Assembly, on the recommendation of the Fifth Committee, in accordance with the framework set out in its resolution 48/227 of 23 December 1993, having considered the report of the Secretary-General on the financing of seventeen peace-keeping operations and the related reports of the Advisory Committee on Administrative and Budgetary Questions, and concurring with the observations of the Advisory Committee:

(a) Authorized the Secretary-General, on an exceptional basis, to enter into commitments up to the amount of 100 million United States dollars gross and net for the United Nations Transitional Authority in Cambodia for the period from 1 September 1993 to 31 March 1994;

(b) Decided to apportion, as an ad hoc arrangement, the amount indicated in subparagraph *(a)* above among Member States in accordance with the composition of groups set out in paragraphs 3 and 4 of Assembly resolution 43/232 of 1 March 1989, as adjusted by the Assembly in its resolutions 44/192 B of 21 December 1989, 45/269 of 27 August 1991, 46/198 A of 20 December 1991 and 47/218 A of 23 December 1992 and its decision 48/472 of 23 December 1993, and taking into account the scale of assessments for the years 1992, 1993 and 1994 as set out in Assembly resolutions 46/221 A of 20 December 1991 and 48/223 A of 23 December 1993 and its decision 47/456 of 23 December 1992.

General Assembly decision 48/469

Adopted without vote

Approved by Fifth Committee (A/48/818) without vote, 22 December (meeting 46); draft by Chairman (A/C.5/48/L.21); agenda item 135.
Meeting numbers. GA 48th session: 5th Committee 44, 46; plenary 87.

UN Military Liaison Team in Cambodia

On 7 October 1993,[44] the Secretary-General reported having received a 26 September letter from the First and Second Prime Ministers of Cambodia requesting that he consider the possible dispatch of some 20 to 30 unarmed United Nations military observers to Cambodia for a period of six months following the end of the UNTAC mandate. The request was made in the context of security problems that would still remain in the country, especially in the provinces, after the withdrawal of UNTAC and of the need to build confidence among the Cambodian people. They reiterated their request on 4 October, convinced that a limited United Nations military presence at a crucial time would strengthen confidence among the people and thus enhance the stability of Cambodia and its new Government.

The Secretary-General restated his belief that United Nations efforts and resources in support of Cambodia should henceforth be concentrated on civilian activities in reconstruction and development, human rights protection, reintegration of refugees and displaced persons and mine clearance. He was not fully convinced that a small group of military officers based at Phnom Penh could play an effective part in controlling or resolving the country's remaining security problems; he also voiced doubt about deploying a merely symbolic military presence at a time of acute financial crisis.

However, should the Security Council respond positively to the request, the Secretary-General would recommend that a team of 20 military liaison officers be set up at Phnom Penh for a single six-month period, with a mandate limited to maintaining liaison with the Government on matters affecting security in Cambodia. The team would be separate from the proposed integrated office for United Nations civilian activities.[28]

The Council, on 12 October,[45] agreed in principle with the recommendation and asked the Secretary-General to submit the terms of reference of such a team, plans for its dispatch and the funding required. It further asked him to consider incorporating the team into the United Nations office that he intended to establish, also at Phnom Penh.

Accordingly, the Secretary-General, in a 27 October report,[46] informed the Council that the 20 military liaison officers would maintain liaison with the Government on matters affecting the country's security and assist it in tackling residual military matters related to the Paris Agreements. A Chief Military Liaison Officer (CMLO), reporting directly to the Secretary-General, would head the team. Activities outside the team's base at Phnom Penh would be undertaken at the CMLO's initiative or at the request of the Cambodian authorities.

The officers would be provided by Governments following consultations and with Council concurrence. To the extent possible, they would be drawn from UNTAC military personnel awaiting withdrawal from Cambodia. The team would be assisted by two international and 13 locally recruited civilian support staff. The bulk of the logistic equipment required would be drawn from UNTAC's existing resources.

The Secretary-General recommended that the military liaison team be separate from the proposed integrated office. However, the CMLO would

be in regular contact with the United Nations representative at that office regarding security of United Nations personnel. In the interests of economy, it was envisaged that administrative and logistic support services and resources would be shared where possible.

In a 7 November addendum to his report,[47] the Secretary-General estimated the cost of the team's operations at $1,060,000 gross, excluding requirements for air transportation within Cambodia, which he assumed the Government would provide free of charge. A breakdown of that figure by main categories of expenditure was annexed to the addendum. The costs should be considered an expense of the Organization to be borne by Member States, and the assessments to be levied on them should be credited to a special account to be set up for that purpose.

SECURITY COUNCIL ACTION

In the light of the Secretary-General's reports on the proposed military liaison team, as well as of the request to extend deployment of certain categories of UNTAC personnel beyond 15 November for security reasons,[29] the Security Council unanimously adopted **resolution 880(1993)** on 4 November.

The Security Council,
Recalling its resolution 745(1992) of 28 February 1992 concerning the implementation plan of the Paris Agreements on Cambodia and subsequent relevant resolutions,
Taking note of the reports of the Secretary-General dated 5 October 1993, 7 October 1993 and 27 October 1993, and of his letter to the President of the Security Council dated 28 October 1993,
Noting with satisfaction the success during the transitional period of the Cambodian people, under the leadership of His Majesty Samdech Preah Norodom Sihanouk, King of Cambodia, in promoting peace, stability and national reconciliation,
Welcoming the adoption of the constitution in accordance with the Paris Agreements on Cambodia,
Recognizing the termination of the United Nations Transitional Authority in Cambodia (UNTAC) mandate following the establishment of the constitutional government on 24 September 1993 in accordance with the Paris Agreements,
Noting with great satisfaction that, with the successful conclusion of the UNTAC mission following the election of 23-28 May 1993, the goal of the Paris Agreements of restoring to the Cambodian people and their democratically elected leaders their primary responsibility for peace, stability, national reconciliation and reconstruction in their country has been achieved,
Paying tribute to those Member States which contributed personnel to UNTAC and expressing sympathy and sorrow to those Governments whose nationals lost their lives or suffered casualties for the cause of peace in Cambodia as well as to their families,
Stressing the importance of consolidating the achievements of the Cambodian people by smooth and rapid

delivery of appropriate international assistance towards rehabilitation, reconstruction and development in Cambodia and towards peace-building in that country,

Noting the need to ensure the safe and orderly completion of the withdrawal of the military component of UNTAC from Cambodia, and the continuity of the vital mine clearance and training functions of the Cambodia Mine Action Centre (CMAC),

1. *Welcomes* the accession to the throne of His Majesty Samdech Preah Norodom Sihanouk, King of Cambodia, and stresses the importance of his continuing role in consolidating peace, stability and genuine national reconciliation in Cambodia;

2. *Welcomes also* the formation of the new Government of all Cambodia, established in accordance with the constitution and based upon the recent election;

3. *Pays tribute* to the work of UNTAC, whose success, under the authority of the Secretary-General and his Special Representative, constitutes a major achievement for the United Nations;

4. *Calls upon* all States to respect the sovereignty, independence, territorial integrity and inviolability, neutrality and national unity of Cambodia;

5. *Demands* the cessation of all illegal acts of violence, on whatever grounds, and the cessation of military activities directed against the democratically elected Government of Cambodia, as well as against the personnel of UNTAC and other United Nations and international agencies;

6. *Affirms* the importance, particularly in view of the recent tragic history of Cambodia, of ensuring respect for international humanitarian law in that country, welcomes in this regard the commitment of the First Prime Minister of the Royal Government of Cambodia to the implementation of the relevant provisions of the new Cambodian Constitution, and endorses the arrangements foreshadowed in paragraphs 27-29 of the Secretary-General's report of 26 August 1993 for appropriate United Nations activities in support of this commitment in accordance with the relevant provisions of the Paris Agreements;

7. *Urges* Member States to assist CMAC with technical experts and equipment, and to support de-mining work through voluntary contributions;

8. *Expresses the hope* that arrangements can be made as soon as possible so that relevant trust fund monies can be disbursed to CMAC and so that technical experts can be provided to CMAC through the United Nations Development Programme (UNDP);

9. *Notes* that, with the exceptions set out in paragraphs 10 and 11 below, the safe and orderly withdrawal of the military component of UNTAC provided for in resolution 860(1993) continues and will end on 15 November 1993;

10. *Decides* to extend the period of withdrawal of the mine clearance and training unit of UNTAC until 30 November 1993;

11. *Decides* to extend the period of withdrawal beyond 15 November 1993 for elements of the military police and medical components of UNTAC in accordance with the detailed recommendations set out in the Secretary-General's letter to the President of the Security Council of 28 October 1993, on the basis that all of these elements will be withdrawn by 31 December 1993;

12. *Decides* to establish a team of 20 military liaison officers for a single period of six months with a mandate to report on matters affecting security in Cambodia, to maintain liaison with the Government of Cambodia and to assist the Government in dealing with residual military matters relating to the Paris Agreements;

13. *Welcomes* the intention of the Secretary-General, in the light of the request by the Royal Government of Cambodia and the continuing commitment of the United Nations to Cambodia, to appoint, for a period to be agreed upon by the Secretary-General and the Government of Cambodia, a person to coordinate the United Nations presence in Cambodia, in accordance with the spirit and principles of the Paris Agreements;

14. *Urges* Member States to continue to help the Government of Cambodia in achieving its objectives of national reconciliation and rehabilitation of Cambodia, requests them to implement without delay the undertakings made during the meeting of the International Committee on Reconstruction of Cambodia and stresses the need for quick disbursing assistance to provide support for help to alleviate the fiscal crisis currently facing the new Government;

15. *Welcomes* the intention of the Secretary-General to report on the lessons learned during the course of UNTAC in the context of the Agenda for Peace.

Security Council resolution 880(1993)

4 November 1993   Meeting 3303   Adopted unanimously

Draft prepared in consultations among Council members (S/26687), orally revised.

On 16 November,[48] the Secretary-General, having completed the necessary consultations, proposed to the Council President that the military liaison team would be formed from contributions offered by the following 15 countries: Austria, Bangladesh, Belgium, China, France, India, Indonesia, Malaysia, New Zealand, Pakistan, Poland, Russian Federation, Singapore, Thailand and Uruguay. He also proposed to appoint Colonel A. N. M. Muniruzzaman (Bangladesh) as Chief Military Liaison Officer.

The Council agreed with those proposals on 19 November.[49]

Financing

The Secretary-General, on 12 November,[50] requested inclusion in the agenda of the forty-eighth session of the General Assembly of an additional item entitled: "Financing of the United Nations military liaison team in Cambodia". Owing to the nature of the item, he further requested that it be allocated to the Fifth Committee.

Report of the Secretary-General. In his 9 December report on the financing of 17 United Nations peace-keeping and other operations,[43] the Secretary-General included his estimates for the United Nations Military Liaison Team in Cambodia.

The requirements of the operation for the period from its inception to 30 April 1994 were estimated at $890,000 gross ($852,000 net). A breakdown by major line-items of expenditure was provided in an accompanying table. Calculations for subsistence allowance and travel costs took account of the fact that 13 officers were already on location and that 6 travelled to the mission area.

A detailed report covering the six-month period beginning 15 November 1993 was under preparation. ACABQ observed[51] that, pending its consideration of that report, it recommended that the Assembly authorize the Secretary-General to enter into commitments in an amount not exceeding $756,500 gross ($724,200 net) for the period from 4 November 1993 to 31 March 1994 and that that amount be assessed.

GENERAL ASSEMBLY ACTION

The General Assembly adopted **decision 48/480** without vote.

Financing of the United Nations Military Liaison Team in Cambodia

At its 87th plenary meeting, on 23 December 1993, the General Assembly, on the recommendation of the Fifth Committee, in accordance with the framework set out in its resolution 48/227 of 23 December 1993, having considered the report of the Secretary-General on the financing of seventeen peace-keeping operations and the related reports of the Advisory Committee on Administrative and Budgetary Questions, and concurring with the observations of the Advisory Committee:

(a) Authorized the Secretary-General, on an exceptional basis, to enter into total commitments up to the amount of 756,500 United States dollars gross (724,200 dollars net), inclusive of the amount authorized by the Advisory Committee in accordance with Assembly resolution 46/187 of 20 December 1991, for the United Nations Military Liaison Team in Cambodia for the period from 4 November 1993 to 31 March 1994, and requested him to establish a special account for the Liaison Team;

(b) Decided to apportion, as an ad hoc arrangement, the amount indicated in subparagraph (a) above among Member States in accordance with the composition of groups set out in paragraphs 3 and 4 of Assembly resolution 43/232 of 1 March 1989, as adjusted by the Assembly in its resolutions 44/192 B of 21 December 1989, 45/269 of 27 August 1991, 46/198 A of 20 December 1991 and 47/218 A of 23 December 1992 and its decision 48/472 of 23 December 1993, and taking into account the scale of assessments for the years 1992, 1993 and 1994 as set out in Assembly resolutions 46/221 A of 20 December 1991 and 48/223 A of 23 December 1993 and its decision 47/456 of 23 December 1992;

(c) Also decided that, in accordance with the provisions of its resolution 973(X) of 15 December 1955, there should be set off against the apportionment among Member States, as provided for in subparagraph (b) above, their respective share in the Tax Equalization Fund of the estimated staff assessment income of 32,300 dollars for the period from 4 November 1993 to 31 March 1994.

General Assembly decision 48/480

Adopted without vote

Approved by Fifth Committee (A/48/829) without vote, 22 December (meeting 46); draft by Chairman (A/C.5/48/L.31); agenda item 174
Meeting numbers. GA 48th session: 5th Committee 44, 46; plenary 87.

REFERENCES
[1]YUN 1992, p. 246, SC res. 745(1992), 28 Feb. 1992. [2]YUN 1991, p. 155. [3]S/25124. [4]YUN 1992, p. 253. [5]Ibid., p. 244. [6]S/25289. [7]YUN 1992, p. 258, SC res. 792(1992), 30 Nov. 1992. [8]Ibid., p. 252. [9]S/25409. [10]S/25455. [11]S/25497. [12]S/25719. [13]S/25366. [14]S/25784. [15]S/25565/Rev.1. [16]S/25530. [17]S/25669. [18]S/25822. [19]S/25871. [20]S/25896. [21]S/25988. [22]S/25879. [23]S/25913. [24]S/26090. [25]S/26095. [26]S/26096. [27]S/26150. [28]S/26360. [29]S/26675. [30]S/26529. [31]YUN 1948-49, p. 535, GA res. 217 A (III), 10 Dec. 1948. [32]S/26517. [33]S/26531. [34]A/47/733/Add.1. [35]YUN 1991, p. 157; YUN 1992, p. 248. [36]S/25770 & S/25771. [37]S/25816 & S/25817. [38]A/47/982. [39]YUN 1991, p. 869, GA res. 46/187, 20 Dec. 1991. [40]A/48/701 & Corr.1. [41]A/48/701/Add.1. [42]A/48/775. [43]A/C.5/48/40. [44]S/26546. [45]S/26570. [46]S/26649. [47]S/26649/Add.1. [48]S/26773. [49]S/26774. [50]A/48/244. [51]A/48/786.

Southern and Western Asia

Afghanistan situation

Following intensive consultations at Islamabad, Pakistan, eight Afghan leaders, including President Burhan-ud-Din Rabbani of Afghanistan, signed the Afghan Peace Accord on 7 March 1993. Held at the invitation of the Prime Minister of Pakistan, the consultations were also attended by the Deputy Foreign Minister of Iran and Prince Turki al-Faisal of Saudi Arabia. The document was transmitted to the Secretary-General by Pakistan on 10 March[1] and by Afghanistan on 17 March.[2]

By the Accord, the parties affirmed their commitment to preserving Afghanistan's unity, sovereignty and territorial integrity and recognized the urgency of rehabilitating and reconstructing the country and of facilitating the return of all Afghan refugees. They agreed: to form a Government for a period of 18 months, with President Rabbani to remain as President and Gulbadin Hikmatyar, or his nominee, as Prime Minister; to set in motion an electoral process of 18 months' duration, from 29 December 1992, including the formation of an election commission to hold elections for a constituent assembly within eight months of the signing of the Accord; to formulate a constitution setting forth the terms for the presidential and parliamentary elections; and to form a Defence Council comprising two members from each party, mainly to set up a national army under its authority.

The parties further agreed to: immediately and unconditionally release all Afghan detainees held by the Government and by the different parties during the armed hostilities; return to their original owners all public and private buildings, residential areas and properties occupied by the different armed groups, as well as displaced persons to their homes; constitute an all-party

committee to oversee the monetary system and
currency regulations; effect an immediate cease-
fire, to become permanent upon the formation of
the Cabinet; and create a Joint Commission, comprising representatives of the Organization of the
Islamic Conference and of all Afghan parties, to
monitor the cease-fire and cessation of hostilities.

The document established a division of powers
between the President and the Prime Minister, setting forth the specific powers and duties of each.

Report of the Secretary-General. In a September report[3] on emergency international assistance for peace, normalcy and reconstruction
of war-stricken Afghanistan (see PART THREE,
Chapter III), the Secretary-General stated that the
newly established Islamic State of Afghanistan[4]
had not yet succeeded in developing the political
and security conditions necessary for the urgent
task of rehabilitation. The country was undergoing a difficult transition, characterized by political discord over power sharing and a reluctance
to compromise. With the abundance of heavy
weaponry and ammunition, the situation often led
to intermittent fighting and a resort to blockades
and rocket attacks, particularly in Kabul.

A major effort launched early in the year by some
countries in the region and reinforced by intra-
Afghan negotiations had recently led to a *modus vivendi*
that offered encouraging prospects for peace. The
accords reached at Islamabad on 7 March and at
Jalalabad on 18 May, however, had neither resolved
difficulties within the Government nor removed the
potential threat of renewed fighting in Kabul. Acute
humanitarian problems were exacerbated by an outbreak of cholera and other diseases in Kabul and
elsewhere in the country. The armed conflict on
the Afghanistan-Tajikistan border (see below) further complicated the general situation. None the
less, authorities in many provinces had successfully
collected illegal arms, thus improving security, and
reopened major highways and roads, permitting
United Nations offices to operate.

Following consultations with Iran, Pakistan, the
Russian Federation, Saudi Arabia and the United
States, the Secretary-General issued a statement
on 22 June in which he encouraged the international community to support the peaceful political process in Afghanistan, in particular the efforts
to observe the cease-fire, and to ensure the safety
and well-being of the civilian population; he
reminded the donor Governments that his appeal
for humanitarian assistance remained seriously
underfunded so that essential United Nations programmes might have to be curtailed.

In the view of some Afghan leaders, political
normalization and peace in Afghanistan could be
reached ultimately through a national gathering,
while others favoured holding a general election,
as provided for in the Afghan Peace Accord. The

Ministry of Foreign Affairs, by a letter of 14 July,
formally informed the Office of the Secretary-
General in Afghanistan and Pakistan (OSGAP) of
a plan to hold such an election and invited the
United Nations to supervise it and provide financial assistance.

The Secretary-General drew attention to the situation of former President Mohammed Najibul-
lah, who, with members of his entourage, had been
in the OSGAP compound since April 1992.[4] He
was suffering from a serious kidney ailment and,
in conformity with international law and recognized standards of human rights, should be allowed to leave with his companions in order to receive medical treatment.

The Secretary-General stated that the two peace
accords reached in 1993 and the intention to seek
the will of the people through a national gathering or general election were encouraging developments; however, peace and stability in Afghanistan
were still far from being achieved. The process of
political normalization was not yet sufficiently
broad based. The paramount problem to be dealt
with, however, remained that of creating peace and
security in and around Kabul and the rest of the
country by collecting the heavy weapons that
abounded everywhere and by opening all roads to
civilian movement.

GENERAL ASSEMBLY ACTION (September and December)

By **decision 47/475** of 20 September, the
General Assembly deferred consideration of the
agenda item entitled "The situation in Afghanistan and its implications for international
peace and security", including it in the draft
agenda of its forty-eighth session.

On 21 December, in **resolution 48/208**, the Assembly encouraged the Government of Afghanistan to take immediate steps to consolidate
further the political process through national *rapprochement*, thus contributing to the creation of a
sound political situation and good security, which
would allow the holding of general, free and fair
elections in the country, to be observed by the
United Nations, as soon as circumstances permitted. It requested the Secretary-General to dispatch
as soon as possible a United Nations special mission to canvass a broad spectrum of Afghanistan's
leaders to solicit their views on how the United Nations could best assist Afghanistan in facilitating
national *rapprochement* and reconstruction, and to report their findings, conclusions and recommendations for appropriate action to the Secretary-General.
It also invited the Secretary-General to continue
to monitor the overall situation in Afghanistan and
make available his good offices as required.

(For information on the human rights situation
in Afghanistan, see PART THREE, Chapter X.)

Office of the Secretary-General in Afghanistan and Pakistan

The Office of the Secretary-General in Afghanistan and Pakistan (OSGAP), established in 1990, assisted the Secretary-General in monitoring the political situation in Afghanistan. The Office continued to be headed by the Personal Representative of the Secretary-General in Afghanistan and Pakistan, Sotirios Mousouris, who, since 1 January 1993, had been assisted by one Senior Military Adviser and one Senior Political Adviser. Owing to security concerns at Kabul, the international staff of the unit there had been operating from Islamabad, sharing temporary quarters with the United Nations Office for the Coordination of Humanitarian Assistance to Afghanistan.

In order to monitor developments and maintain contacts with Afghan government officials, political leaders and other personalities, the Personal Representative made four visits to Kabul, two to Herat and one to Mazar-i-Sharif. He also maintained contact with representatives of other countries in the region.

Financing

The Secretary-General, in December,[5] set out OSGAP's financial performance for the 1992-1993 biennium, which indicated an estimated total expenditure of $6,985,800 against revised appropriations of $7,764,300. The resultant net reduction of $778,500, attributable to savings under staff costs and military staff allowances ($528,500), general operating expenses ($169,600) and travel ($68,800), would be reflected in the second performance report of the 1992-1993 programme budget.

The estimated requirements for the period from 1 January to 31 December 1994 amounted to $1,279,800, which would be required to cover OSGAP costs, excluding provisions for staff assessment of $135,400, to be offset by the same amount under income.

ACABQ, noting that the estimates were based on expenditure in the operational area, recommended an amount of $1 million for OSGAP for 1994 under the proposed programme budget for 1994-1995, with no change in the number of posts requested. By **resolution 48/230, section V**, of 23 December, the Assembly took note of the Secretary-General's report and the ACABQ recommendations.

The foregoing figures were taken into account in the final programme budget appropriations adopted by the General Assembly for the 1992-1993 and 1994-1995 bienniums (**resolutions 48/219 A and 48/231 A**).

Afghanistan-Tajikistan

Tajikistan, on 13 July,[6] lodged a protest with the Consulate of Afghanistan at Dushanbe over an attack by some 200 armed persons and Afghan mujahidin on Sarigor village, Shurabad district. Tajikistan recalled that, in April and May, a group led by Kori Hamidullo, the same Afghan commander who launched the July attack, more than once violated the State frontier in the same district, looting and burning Sarigor and penetrating an area where Russian border troops were stationed. Those troops were currently engaged in combat operations to drive the armed bands from Tajik territory.

Tajikistan warned that it viewed the participation of Afghan citizens in those attacks—notably the commanding officer of Afghanistan's 55th Infantry Division, whom it named as being in overall command of the operation—as a hostile and dangerous provocation that could jeopardize its relations with Afghanistan.

The Russian Federation, on 14 July,[7] protested the same large-scale attack on Sarigor stating that it had been launched from Afghanistan and referring to the attackers as irregular forces and bandits. In appealing to Afghanistan to take immediate measures to prevent further attacks, the Russian Federation stressed that its troops would take the strongest action, using the entire military arsenal at their disposal to protect the Afghanistan-Tajikistan border in accordance with the Federation's obligations. It further spoke of the inevitability of retribution for any encroachments on the lives of Russian servicemen or of other Russians.

Afghanistan, on 22 July,[8] referred to a statement issued the day before by the spokesman for the Secretary-General regarding his concern over the border incidents, his appeal for restraint and his readiness to assist the parties to find a peaceful solution. Afghanistan stated that those incidents arose from a massive artillery attack on several Afghan villages on 15 and 16 July by the armed forces of the Russian Federation and Tajikistan. The casualties included 360 civilians killed, more than 400 others injured, over 6,000 families displaced, houses destroyed and wheat harvests burned. Afghanistan rejected as unfounded the accusations by the Russian Federation and Tajikistan, as well as the allegation that Tajik refugees had been trained and armed in Afghanistan and then sent to Tajikistan for destructive activities; it regretted the reference to retribution for the alleged attacks and to the irreparable blow to its good-neighbourly relations with Tajikistan. In response to the Secretary-General's appeal, Afghanistan said it was ready to engage in peaceful talks that would ensure the return of the Tajik refugees to their homeland in safety and honour.

Kazakhstan, Kyrgyzstan, the Russian Federation, Tajikistan and Uzbekistan, on 10 August,[9] transmitted a Declaration on the Inviolability of

Frontiers, signed by them in Moscow on 7 August, together with a document outlining measures for the normalization of the situation on the Afghanistan-Tajikistan border. By the declaration, the signatories pledged collective responsibility for the inviolability of their frontiers with third-party States but stated that none of them had the obligation unilaterally to ensure the security of another State's frontiers. In the second document, they stated that they were counting on the United Nations and the Conference on Security and Cooperation in Europe to support their efforts to normalize the situation on the Afghanistan-Tajikistan border and to send United Nations observers there to provide humanitarian and technical assistance.

In a 7 October letter,[10] Afghanistan assured the Secretary-General that it had not taken nor would it take armed action against Tajikistan. It also assured him of its full cooperation with his Special Envoy to Tajikistan, Ismat Kittani. It had undertaken negotiations with Tajikistan and planned to negotiate with UNHCR for the voluntary repatriation of Tajik refugees in Afghanistan. In a 25 October reply, the Secretary-General noted Afghanistan's efforts to reduce tensions with Tajikistan. In recognition of the strain placed on Afghanistan by Tajik refugees, he stated that the United Nations had recently dispatched an assessment mission to Kunduz and would soon re-establish its presence in the area to assist with problems, including those posed by the Tajik refugees. He stated that Afghanistan's continued assistance in addressing the security of United Nations staff would greatly facilitate United Nations work.

REFERENCES

[1]S/25398. [2]S/25435. [3]A/48/323 & Add.1. [4]YUN 1992, p. 263. [5]A/C.5/48/41. [6]S/26091. [7]S/26110. [8]S/26145. [9]A/48/304-S/26290. [10]S/26814.

Cyprus question

In continuance of his mission of good offices, the Secretary-General undertook new efforts in 1993 to enhance prospects for an overall settlement to the Cyprus problem. At his invitation, the leaders of the two Cypriot communities met in direct meetings for the purpose of agreeing to a number of confidence-building measures hammered out during a lengthy preparatory process at Nicosia, Cyprus. No agreement was reached, however. To forestall a set-back, the Secretary-General, through his Special Representative and two technical teams, immediately renewed contacts with the parties and Governments concerned, widening those contacts to include the leading citizens of both communities.

The United Nations Peace-keeping Force in Cyprus (UNFICYP), deemed vital for maintaining a climate conducive to continued negotiations, remained deployed, albeit at reduced strength. In December, the Security Council extended its mandate until 15 June 1994, the second extension authorized by the Council in 1993.

During the year, Cyprus and Turkey addressed a number of communications to the Secretary-General on several aspects of the Cyprus question. Those from Turkey transmitted letters from representatives of the Turkish Cypriot community, the majority from Osman Ertug, "Representative of the Turkish Republic of Northern Cyprus".

Among the aspects referred to were: the demographic structure of Cyprus,[1] confidence-building measures,[2] buffer zone violations,[3] the Greek Cypriot embargo imposed on the Turkish Cypriot community,[4] the application of Cyprus for membership in the European Community (subsequently renamed European Union),[5] the alleged destruction of Greek Cypriot cultural property[6] and the reported designation of an eminent European personality to act as an observer to the intercommunal talks.[7]

In the meantime, the General Assembly, by **decision 47/476** of 20 September 1993, included the item on the question of Cyprus in the draft agenda of its forty-eighth session.

Secretary-General's good offices

In pursuance of his good offices mission as mandated by the Security Council, the Secretary-General, on 18 March, informed the Council that, following the February elections in Cyprus, he had invited the leaders of the two Cypriot communities—Glafcos Clerides, President of Cyprus, and Rauf R. Denktas, "President of the Turkish Republic of Northern Cyprus"—to meet with him in New York on 30 March to discuss the timing, modalities and preparations for the resumption of substantive negotiations, based on the Set of Ideas that emerged from the 1991 talks[8] and endorsed by the Security Council in 1992.[9]

SECURITY COUNCIL ACTION

Following informal consultations by the Security Council on 26 March, its President was authorized to issue the following statement[10] on behalf of the Council in connection with its consideration of the item entitled "The situation in Cyprus":

> "The members of the Security Council have reviewed the situation related to the Secretary-General's mission of good offices in Cyprus.
> "The members of the Council welcomed the acceptance by the two leaders of the Secretary-General's invitation to attend a joint meeting on 30 March to discuss the timing, modalities, and preparation for the resumption of substantive direct negotiations as mandated by the Security Council.

"The members of the Council reaffirmed their position that the present status quo is not acceptable and that a mutually acceptable overall framework agreement should be achieved without delay on the basis of the Set of Ideas which have been endorsed by the Security Council.

"The members of the Council called on the leaders of the two communities in Cyprus to manifest their goodwill by cooperating fully with the Secretary-General so that the substantive direct negotiations which are due to resume shortly will result in significant progress.

"The members of the Council reaffirmed their determination to remain seized of the Cyprus question on an ongoing basis and to lend their active support to the Secretary-General's effort.

"The members of the Council requested the Secretary-General to report to the Council on the outcome of the 30 March meeting."

Accordingly, the Secretary-General, on 2 April,[11] informed the Council that the two leaders had met with him in New York as proposed, separately and then jointly on 30 March, followed by a working luncheon the next day. The outcome of the joint meeting was contained in a statement issued to the press by the Secretary-General's spokesperson on 31 March to the effect that the leaders had reaffirmed their commitment to cooperate with the Secretary-General in the context of his mission of good offices. They had declared their willingness to resume the joint negotiations in New York on 24 May, using the Set of Ideas for the purpose of freely reaching a mutually acceptable overall framework agreement.

Through a preparatory process, the Secretary-General's representatives would meet at Nicosia with the leaders for the purpose of clarifying their specific concerns relating to the draft overall framework agreement contained in the Set of Ideas, with a view to facilitating progress at the negotiations. They would also discuss implementation of the confidence-building measures set out in a 1992 Council resolution[12] to foster mutual confidence conducive to the success of the negotiating process.

Report of the Secretary-General (July). In a 1 July report[13] on his mission of good offices, the Secretary-General summarized the outcome of the preparatory work at Nicosia, from 15 April to 5 May and from 14 to 19 May. His Deputy Special Representative, Gustave Feissel, held a total of 34 meetings with the two leaders, amounting in duration to almost 50 hours. The extensive discussions made it possible to develop ample material to enable the two leaders, first, to reach agreement on a list of confidence-building measures, including on Varosha and Nicosia International Airport; and, second, to make progress towards reconciling differences on a number of substantive issues as part of the ongoing process to reach agreement

on the draft framework contained in the Set of Ideas.

Both leaders agreed on the need to identify issues in the Set that were significant and where an accommodation, to be reached *ad referendum*, would benefit both sides. In this connection, ways of reconciling differences in three areas were discussed: displaced persons and territorial adjustments; security and guarantee; and the workability of the federal Government.

By the leaders' preference, the focus was on confidence-building measures, discussions on which produced a significant number of measures that both sides would be prepared to implement. These included expert cooperation on the short- and long-term water problem, education, health and the environment; joint cultural and sports events; intra-party meetings; joint journalist meetings; joint commercial projects to be developed by the Chambers of Commerce and Industry of both sides; equitable distribution of international assistance; cooperative arrangements with respect to electric power supply; intercommunal cooperation in Pyla, including free movement of goods in the same manner as agreed in Varosha; identification of joint projects to benefit both communities in Nicosia; cooperation with UNFICYP in extending the unmanning agreement of 1989 to cover all areas of the United Nations–controlled buffer zone where the two sides were in close proximity to each other; a series of nine provisions concerning Varosha; a series of 10 provisions concerning Nicosia International Airport; and periodic meetings of representatives of the two communities to propose additional confidence-building measures.

A major portion of the discussions was devoted to securing agreement in respect of Varosha, specifically that part of it that had been a ghost town since 1974, when it was fenced off by Turkish forces. Bounded on three sides by land under Turkish Cypriot control and to the east by the sea, the fenced area extended approximately four kilometres north-south and about one and a half kilometres east-west. A 1979 high-level agreement[14] accorded high priority to its resettlement under United Nations auspices, and the Council, in 1984,[15] reserved it exclusively for settlement by its pre-August 1974 inhabitants (preponderantly Greek Cypriots).

Two proposals emerged during the discussions: one would place the fenced area under United Nations administration, pending a mutually agreed overall solution to the Cyprus problem, for bicommunal contact and commerce; the other would open the Nicosia International Airport for the equal benefit of both sides.

It had been stressed to the leaders that, given the purpose of confidence-building measures, it was essential that neither should seek political advantage or require the other to make political concessions; the benefits to accrue to either side would have to be significant in practical terms, but neither should be asked to adopt measures requiring it, directly or indirectly, to change its position on the political status of the other. It was also stressed that the United Nations would try its best to secure agreement on a package whose practical effect would be to lift most of the commercial obstacles encountered by the Turkish Cypriot side.

In the latter part of the discussions, the two leaders were prepared to consider a package deal including both Varosha and the reopening of Nicosia International Airport for unhindered international traffic of passengers and cargo to and from each side. Located in the United Nations Protected Area (UNPA) on the western outskirts of Nicosia, the airport had been out of use since 1974.

The intensive preparatory process produced three draft papers that brought the proposals to an advanced stage; they would serve as the basis for the joint meetings due to resume on 24 May. The first paper listed 14 confidence-building measures, 12 of which were taken to be acceptable to both sides. The second and third papers contained detailed provisions concerning Varosha and Nicosia International Airport.

The joint meetings resumed in New York on 24 May, under the chairmanship of the Secretary-General and with the newly appointed Special Representative for Cyprus, Joe Clark, in attendance.

The Greek Cypriot side voiced its agreement to the proposed arrangements for Varosha and Nicosia International Airport, provided that no provisions were added that would have the effect, directly or indirectly, of recognizing the "Turkish Republic of Northern Cyprus".

The Turkish Cypriot side reiterated that a proportionate compensation for relinquishing the fenced area of Varosha from its control, even when supplemented with the reopening of Nicosia International Airport, would be the removal of the embargo through the lifting of all restrictions on airports and seaports on the Turkish Cypriot side. The Turkish Cypriot airline should be able to fly from Erçan (Tymbou) airport directly to destinations in Western Europe and restrictions should be lifted from the port of Famagusta.

The International Civil Aviation Organization (ICAO) and its legal counsel, which were consulted on the matter, stated, however, that since international flights took place in the framework of air service agreements concluded exclusively between States, it did not seem possible, without recognizing a Turkish Cypriot State, to envisage the kind of arrangements requested by the Turkish Cypriot side. In an effort to accommodate the request for the operation of the Cyprus Turkish Airlines,

which was an airline registered in Turkey, it was agreed that Nicosia International Airport would be open to foreign airlines, including airlines registered in Turkey. The Greek Cypriot side moreover agreed that both sides would commit themselves to take no action that would in any way prevent or adversely affect the free movement of people or goods through Nicosia airport to and from both sides, that the United Nations would be empowered to look into any complaints by either side and that both would agree to abide by its recommendations.

As to Varosha, the Turkish Cypriot side stated that it would want to exclude from the fenced area to be placed under United Nations administration that part lying to the north of Dhimokratias Street, to serve as a security buffer between the United Nations–administered area and the port of Famagusta. Mr. Denktas added that he would wish to settle the retained section with Turkish Cypriots, in anticipation of the territorial arrangement that would constitute part of an ultimate overall settlement of the Cyprus problem—a position put forward by the Turkish Cypriot side in 1981.

On 28 May, when the leaders were asked to give their considered opinion on the papers, as further adjusted and supplemented during the joint meetings, Mr. Denktas stated that, before he could respond, he would need to consult with his "Government" and "Parliament", as well as with Turkey, giving 15 June as the date of his return to New York. He maintained that position despite the Secretary-General's suggestion that he return on 4 June and Mr. Clerides' stated readiness to wait until then.

A further joint meeting was held on 1 June in the presence of the President of the Security Council and the representatives of its permanent members. It was chaired by the Special Representative, who read out the Secretary-General's statement reviewing the events and concluding that the package of confidence-building measures was eminently fair, containing as it did significant and proportionate economic and other practical benefits for both sides and that the Varosha/Nicosia International Airport package required neither side to compromise on its substantive political positions and contained no surprises, all of its elements having been dealt with exhaustively during the preparatory process.

It was the Secretary-General's expectation, therefore, that both sides should have been able to reach agreement in New York; that the consultations Mr. Denktas intended to undertake would be to promote acceptance of the proposals; and that the two leaders would manifest their good will by taking the modest step proposed, which they owed to their people and to the international community. None the less, Mr. Denktas reiterated his desire to undertake consultations and return for a resumption of the joint meetings no later than 14 June.

During his visit to Ankara, between 8 and 11 June, Mr. Denktas addressed the Turkish Grand National Assembly and made numerous public statements expressing strong criticism of the package, which he would be obliged to reject if pressed for a positive or negative reply. In the circumstances, he saw no point in returning to New York. Consequently, the joint meeting scheduled for 14 June could not take place. The President and Acting Prime Minister of Turkey, however, indicated that Turkey supported the package and encouraged its acceptance.

Kenan Atakol, "Minister for Foreign Affairs and Defence of the Turkish Republic of Northern Cyprus", met with the Deputy Special Representative in New York on 14 and 15 June to convey Mr. Denktas's position: for the Varosha/Nicosia International Airport package to be acceptable, the northern part of Varosha, northwards from Dhimokratias Street, must remain with the Turkish Cypriot side. That, Mr. Atakol said, was the "bottom line". In addition, all air and seaport embargoes would have to be lifted from northern Cyprus. The return of Mr. Denktas to New York would depend on the Secretary-General's decision in the light of his evaluation of this message. Mr. Atakol asked no further questions relative to the package.

Despite this regrettable development, the Secretary-General was determined to persevere in his efforts to seek agreement on the package. To that end, he asked his Special Representative to visit Cyprus, Greece and Turkey in the next few weeks.

Security Council communication. The President of the Security Council wrote to the Secretary-General on 7 July[16] to convey the Council's full support for his efforts; its agreement with his assessment that implementation of the package of confidence-building measures relating in particular to Varosha and Nicosia International Airport would have a dramatic impact on overcoming the existing mistrust and in facilitating an overall settlement of the Cyprus problem; and its shared conviction that once the package was fully presented, its significant benefits would be recognized. The Council welcomed his decision to send his Special Representative to the three countries concerned and requested a report on the outcome and, if necessary, his recommendations for Council action.

Report of the Secretary-General (September). The Secretary-General further reported on 14 September,[17] that the Special Representative and his Deputy visited Cyprus from 13 to 18 July and held several meetings with the leaders of the two communities, leaders of the main political parties and key business organizations and with persons from the media, academia and other professions of both sides. They then visited Athens, Greece, on 19 and 20 July, where they met with the Prime Minister, and Ankara on 21 and 22 July, where they held meetings with Turkey's Prime Minister, Deputy Prime Minister and Foreign Minister. The Deputy Special Representative returned to Cyprus on 23 July, where he held further discussions with the leaders of the two communities.

The discussions with those two leaders did not reveal any change in their positions. Both affirmed their statements made in New York, with Mr. Denktas referring to the deep political division existing within the Turkish Cypriot community which, he maintained, prevented him from effectively fulfilling his functions as negotiator and was the reason why the questions about the package had not been submitted. That domestic problem would have to be resolved by elections, which he hoped would take place in November. Thus it was difficult for the negotiating process to move forward until then.

Several key conclusions emerged from the meeting with the Turkish Cypriot political party leaders and some 60 businessmen: inaccurate and incomplete information had been presented on the impact of the Varosha/Nicosia International Airport package, resulting in considerable confusion among Turkish Cypriots; they looked for guidance to Turkey, whose support for the package, expressed to the Special Representative, had not yet been conveyed either to them or to their leaders; and there was widespread interest in the package among Turkish Cypriots, who desired to consider it seriously and had many questions which they wished to have answered.

The Prime Minister of Greece expressed his full support for the package and for the position adopted by the Greek Cypriot side. The Prime Minister of Turkey and other Turkish leaders reaffirmed their own, as well as their country's, full support for the package, stating that the Turkish Cypriots were aware of that fact but that the ultimate decision was theirs to make. They agreed that all questions which the Turkish Cypriots had should be submitted as soon as possible, but noted that efforts to reach agreement on the package would inevitably be delayed until after the Turkish Cypriot elections.

Mr. Denktas, however, declined to provide any questions, but recognized that this should not prevent the United Nations from addressing Turkish Cypriot concerns, already presented informally at the meetings with political and business leaders.

The Secretary-General was obliged to report that the Turkish Cypriot side had not yet shown the good will and cooperation required to achieve an agreement on the package. However, as part of his determination to bring about such agreement, he proposed sending two teams to Cyprus in October. One, to be assembled with the help of UNDP, would consist of senior experts to address questions regarding the effects of the package, including those relating to the economic imbalance between the two communities. The other team, to be constituted jointly by ICAO and UNDP, would assess the technical requirements for reopening Nicosia airport.

Security Council communication. The Security Council President, by a 20 September letter to the Secretary-General,[18] stated that the Council, having considered his 14 September report, conveyed their continuing support for his efforts and full endorsement of his observations on the current Cyprus situation. In expressing disappointment that an agreement on the Varosha/Nicosia International Airport package had not been reached, they agreed that he could not continue his current effort indefinitely, called on the Turkish Cypriot side to give active support to that effort and recognized the important role that Turkey could play.

The Council looked forward to receiving a report on the outcome of his continued efforts, including that of the two technical missions. On the basis of that report, the Council would undertake a thorough review of the situation and, if necessary, consider alternative ways to promote implementation of the resolutions on Cyprus.

UNFICYP

The United Nations Peace-keeping Force in Cyprus, established by the Security Council in 1964,[19] continued in 1993 to discharge its main functions: to maintain the military status quo and prevent a recurrence of fighting; and humanitarian and economic activities to promote a return to normal conditions.

UNFICYP kept the United Nations buffer zone under constant surveillance through a system of observation posts and mobile and standing patrols, with the assistance of high-powered binoculars and night-vision devices.

In keeping with the requirements of the cease-fire called for by the Council in 1974,[20] the United Nations maintained that the opposing forces should remain behind their respective cease-fire lines and that neither could exercise authority or jurisdiction beyond its own line. There was no formal agreement between UNFICYP and the two sides on the complete delineation of the buffer zone as recorded by UNFICYP, nor on the zone's use and control. Thus, UNFICYP found itself supervising, by loose mutual consent, two constantly disputed cease-fire lines.

UNFICYP considered the main categories of cease-fire violations to be: any movement of military elements forward of their cease-fire line into the buffer zone; the discharge of any type of weapons or explosives along the lines or up to a distance of 1,000 metres behind them; building of new or strengthening of existing military positions within 400 metres of the opposing cease-fire line, or more than 400 metres from it, if UNFICYP considered this incompatible with the spirit of the cease-fire; overflights of the buffer zone by military or civilian aircraft, or by military aircraft of either side within 1,000 metres of the zone; troop deployment and training exercises in an area closer than 1,000 metres from their cease-fire line without prior notification; and provocative acts between the two sides, such as shouting abuse, indecent gestures or stone-throwing.

On the basis of proposals by the Secretary-General UNFICYP began to be restructured, as a first step, to a strength of three infantry battalions of approximately 350 personnel each, with the addition of a limited number of military observers for reconnaissance.

The operational plan would maintain the Force headquarters in UNPA at Nicosia. UNFICYP would continue to be divided into three sectors and six line companies: Sector West would be responsible for the area from Kokkina to the Ovgos River, Sector Centre for the area covering Nicosia, and Sector East for the area from Nicosia to the east coast. An armoured squadron and a helicopter flight unit would be based in UNPA.

The troop strength of the restructured Force was 1,323, to consist of infantry personnel (1,050), support personnel (223), including 37 military personnel forming the headquarters unit, civilian police (39) and military observers (12).

Civilian police, provided by Australia and Sweden and based in five stations across the island, were charged with: investigating criminal or other matters with inter-communal connotations or with the potential for escalating political tension; assisting in the prevention of civil disorder in the buffer zone; maintaining liaison with the civilian police of either side; and directly supporting the humanitarian activities of the Force. The military observers, provided by Austria, Ireland and Hungary, were assigned liaison and reconnaissance functions.

UNFICYP strength as at 15 November 1993 stood at 1,203 all ranks (down from 1,508 at 31 May). They were contributed by Argentina, Austria, Canada, Denmark, Finland, Hungary, Ireland and the United Kingdom.

On 21 May,[21] the Secretary-General informed the Council of his decision to appoint, with immediate effect, Joe Clark (former Prime Minister of Canada) as his Special Representative for Cyprus, a decision the Council welcomed on 24 May.[22]

Restructuring

As requested by the Security Council in 1992,[23] the Secretary-General submitted a report on the results of his consultations with troop-contributing States about restructuring UNFICYP.[24] He stated that, owing to successive reductions made by those States in the size of their contingents, the established strength of the Force (military personnel and civilian police) had been reduced from 2,141 in May 1992 to 1,513 in March 1993. Canada had announced that it would withdraw its contingent between mid-June and September. The United Kingdom would also reduce its support regiment by 145 personnel and would cease providing military police, mess staff, medical and dental care, the vehicle maintenance workshop or the transport squadron. These additional reductions would bring the Force strength down further to approximately 850. Unless the situation was redressed, UNFICYP would cease to be viable in June 1993.

All of the eight troop-contributing States consulted (Australia, Austria, Canada, Denmark, Finland, Ireland, Sweden and the United Kingdom) on possible options, within the context of the status of the political negotiations between the two communities, agreed on the urgency of taking remedial action.

Consultations focused on two alternative proposals for restructuring the Force. One would entrust its mandate to military observers, backed by a small infantry element. The other would restructure the Force and reduce it to the minimum number of infantry battalions required to maintain effective control of the buffer zone. Under the first proposal, for which most of the troop contributors expressed preference, a minimum of 200 United Nations military observers would patrol the buffer zone, provide random manning of observation posts, perform liaison functions between the parties and continuously monitor the buffer zone in central Nicosia. They would be supported by three or four infantry companies, which would occupy permanently a reduced number of observation posts and provide a reserve in the event of buffer-zone violations or other incidents. The restructured Force would be financed through the normal system of peace-keeping assessment.

The Secretary-General's representatives and advisers supported the second proposal. They pointed out that the conclusions of the 1990 review of the Force[25] remained operationally valid: the mandate and the resources required to carry it out had not been altered, nor had the political and military conditions prevailing in Cyprus, which did not justify converting the Force to an observer mission. Under the current mandate, the Force's strength could not be scaled down below six companies on the cease-fire line if it was to re-main able to fulfil its primary function of controlling the buffer zone. In a restructured Force retaining its international personality and flexibility, those six companies would be made up of three infantry battalions of at least 350 personnel each.

The battalions should be drawn from existing or new troop contributors under the same financing arrangement as other peace-keeping operations; that is, reimbursement of troop costs at the rates approved by the General Assembly from a special account funded through assessed contributions. The civilian police component, to be kept at its current strength, could assume some of the humanitarian tasks being discharged by the military. Headquarters staffing should be reduced from 56 to 37 military posts to reflect the reduced size of the Force.

It was the unanimous view of the Secretary-General's military and civilian advisers that, were UNFICYP to lose its capacity to maintain control of the buffer zone, there would be real danger that, without either party wishing it, small incidents could quickly escalate and threaten the cease-fire on which depended the security of the Cypriots and the maintenance of an atmosphere conducive to successful political negotiations.

The Secretary-General pointed out that the question was not whether the UNFICYP mandate could better be carried out by infantry or by a mix of infantry and military observers. The two options were comparable in cost (a 12-month estimated cost of $47,130,000 for the infantry-unit option and $47,400,000 for the military-observer option), but neither would be practicable unless the Council could accept funding by assessed contributions. The question before the Council was thus whether to decide on such funding or allow UNFICYP to dissolve into a token presence of a few military observers. He strongly recommended that the Council urgently decide to convert from voluntary to assessed funding, to allow him time to find States willing to contribute replacement contingents.

Cyprus, on 15 April,[26] confirmed in writing its offer to contribute, on a continuing basis, one third of the annual cost of UNFICYP, clarifying that the offer related to the Secretary-General's preferred option of infantry units estimated at $47,130,000, of which the Cyprus contribution would be $15,710,000.

SECURITY COUNCIL ACTION (11 and 27 May)

In the light of the Secretary-General's report, the Security Council convened on 11 May to consider a draft resolution sponsored by the United Kingdom[27] on the funding and restructuring of UNFICYP, which took account of the contribution offered by Cyprus. By a vote of 14 in favour to 1 against (Russian Federation), the draft was rejected owing to the negative vote of a permanent Council member.

The Russian Federation's vote reflected its objection to that provision of the draft which would have had the Council decide that, with effect from the next extension of UNFICYP's mandate on or before 15 June 1993, the costs of the Force should be treated as expenses of the Organization under Article 17(2) of the Charter of the United Nations.

Meeting number. SC 3211.

The Council met again on 27 May to consider a new draft text, which it adopted as **resolution 831(1993)**.

The Security Council,

Recalling its resolution 186(1964) and subsequent relevant resolutions,

Reaffirming that the extension of the mandate of the United Nations Peace-keeping Force in Cyprus (UNFICYP) should be considered every six months,

Noting the recent communication from the Government of Cyprus to the Secretary-General,

Noting that both voluntary and assessed methods of contribution are acceptable for United Nations peace-keeping operations and stressing the importance of maximizing voluntary contributions,

Stressing the importance it attaches to the achievement of early progress towards a political settlement in Cyprus, and also to the implementation of confidence-building measures,

Reiterating in particular its call to both sides to cooperate with UNFICYP in order to extend the unmanning agreement of 1989 to all areas of the United Nations-controlled Buffer Zone where the two sides are in close proximity to each other,

Reaffirming that the present status quo is not acceptable, and concerned that the United Nations should not be entering into open-ended peace-keeping commitments,

1. *Welcomes* the report of the Secretary-General on the United Nations operation in Cyprus;

2. *Expresses* its appreciation for past voluntary contributions to UNFICYP and for those that have recently been offered for the future, which are essential for the continuation of the Force;

3. *Stresses* the importance of the continuation of voluntary contributions to the Force and calls for maximum voluntary contributions in the future;

4. *Decides* that, with effect from the next extension of UNFICYP's mandate on or before 15 June 1993, those costs of the Force which are not covered by voluntary contributions should be treated as expenses of the Organization under Article 17(2) of the Charter of the United Nations;

5. *Decides also* that UNFICYP should be restructured as a first step on the basis of the proposal in paragraphs 16-19 of the Secretary-General's report, with the addition of a limited number of observers for reconnaissance and with a view to further restructuring in the light of the reassessment referred to in paragraph 7 below;

6. *Underlines* the responsibility of the parties for minimizing tension and facilitating the operation of UNFICYP, including through the implementation of confidence-building measures, including that the num-

ber of foreign troops in the Republic of Cyprus undergo a significant reduction and that a reduction of defence spending be effected in the Republic of Cyprus, as envisaged in its earlier relevant resolutions;

7. *Decides* to conduct a comprehensive reassessment of UNFICYP at the time of the consideration of the Force's mandate in December 1993, including of the implications of progress on confidence-building measures and towards a political settlement for the future of the Force;

8. *Requests* the Secretary-General to submit a report one month before that reassessment, to cover all aspects of the situation, including confidence-building measures, progress in political negotiations and possible progressive steps towards an observer force based on the proposal described in paragraph 12 of the Secretary-General's report;

9. *Invites* the Secretary-General to take the necessary steps to implement this resolution.

Security Council resolution 831(1993)

27 May 1993   Meeting 3222   14-0-1

Draft prepared in consultations among Council members (S/25831).

Vote in Council as follows:

In favour: Brazil, Cape Verde, China, Djibouti, France, Hungary, Japan, Morocco, New Zealand, Russian Federation, Spain, United Kingdom, United States, Venezuela.

Against: None.

Abstaining: Pakistan.

Pakistan said it would have been more appropriate if the text had retained its focus on the technical problem of financing UNFICYP, particularly since negotiations between the parties were at a critical juncture, requiring the Council to make every effort to induce the two sides to move towards a mutually acceptable political solution.

On 20 July,[28] the Secretary-General proposed, and the Council agreed,[29] that the group of 12 military observers, to be deployed in the first week of August, be composed of elements from Austria, Hungary and Ireland.

Operational activities

Report of the Secretary-General (June). In his report on UNFICYP operations for the period 1 December 1992 to 31 May 1993,[30] the Secretary-General described UNFICYP's relations with the parties, its maintenance of the cease-fire and the integrity of the buffer zone, its humanitarian work including the activities of the Committee on Missing Persons and the work of the various United Nations bodies and agencies to help promote a return to normal conditions throughout the island. He updated information on his mission of good offices (see above).

The report noted that the number of cease-fire violations had decreased slightly, but that air violations had increased: 30 overflights of the buffer zone by Turkish forces aircraft and 7 by National Guard aircraft; 53 overflights from the north and 5 from the south by civilian aircraft; and 9 by the Cyprus Police Airwing. The National Guard continued its programme of construction all along its cease-fire line, refusing to allow inspections of positions clearly emplaced within the buffer zone. The 1989 agreement on the unmanning of certain positions in Nicosia continued to hold and discussions were ongoing with both sides to extend the agreement to all areas of the zone where troops were in close proximity to each other. The report also noted threats to UNFICYP personnel.

In the mixed village of Pyla, located in the buffer zone, UNFICYP assisted the two mukhtars to exercise the full range of their responsibilities. It continued to urge removal of the Cyprus police control point on the Larnaca-Pyla road, south of the buffer zone, as it blocked the flow of tourists and other visitors to Pyla, severely disrupting its economy. The Turkish Cypriot side continued to restrict the freedom of movement of certain individuals to and from the northern part of the island, hampering UNFICYP's humanitarian work there.

Both sides were urged to take reciprocal measures to lower the tension, including mutual commitments, through UNFICYP, not to deploy along the cease-fire lines live ammunition or weapons other than hand-held ones and to prohibit weapons firing within sight or hearing of the buffer zone. They were also urged to work together so that their own agencies could assume the humanitarian functions carried out by UNFICYP over the years. Both sides had been made aware of the Secretary-General's anxiety over the situation in Pyla and of his view that the bicommunal nature of the village demanded special cooperation and understanding.

In view of the foregoing, the Secretary-General stated his belief that the continued presence of the Force remained indispensable and recommended that its mandate be extended for a further six months, until 15 December 1993.

In a 10 June addendum to his report,[31] the Secretary-General informed the Council that Cyprus, Greece and the United Kingdom had indicated their concurrence with the proposed extension. Turkey had also indicated its concurrence with and support of the position of the Turkish Cypriot side, as expressed at previous Council meetings on the extension of the UNFICYP mandate.

SECURITY COUNCIL ACTION

Having considered the Secretary-General's recommendation, the Security Council, on 11 June, unanimously adopted **resolution 839(1993)**.

The Security Council,

Noting the report of the Secretary-General on the United Nations operation in Cyprus of 9 June 1993,

Noting also the recommendation by the Secretary-General that the Security Council extend the station-

ing of the United Nations Peace-keeping Force in Cyprus for a further period of six months,

Noting further that the Government of Cyprus has agreed that, in view of the prevailing conditions in the island, it is necessary to keep the Force in Cyprus beyond 15 June 1993,

Recalling its resolution 831(1993) of 27 May 1993, and in particular its paragraphs 2, 3 and 4 on financing, as well as its paragraphs 5 and 7 on the restructuring of the Force and the comprehensive reassessment which is to be conducted in December 1993,

Reiterating in particular its call to both sides to cooperate with UNFICYP in order to extend the unmanning agreement of 1989 to all areas of the United Nations–controlled buffer zone where the two sides are in close proximity to each other,

Reaffirming the provisions of resolution 186(1964) of 4 March 1964 and other relevant resolutions,

1. *Extends once more* the stationing in Cyprus of the United Nations Peace-keeping Force established under resolution 186(1964) for a further period ending on 15 December 1993;

2. *Requests* the Secretary-General to continue his mission of good offices, to keep the Security Council informed of the progress made and to submit a report on the implementation of the present resolution by 15 November 1993 as part of the report called for in its resolution 831(1993);

3. *Supports* the recommendation of the Secretary-General expressed in paragraph 48 of his report that both sides take reciprocal measures to lower the tension, including mutual commitments, through UNFICYP, to prohibit along the cease-fire lines live ammunition or weapons other than those which are hand-held and to prohibit also firing of weapons within sight or hearing of the buffer zone and requests the Secretary-General to negotiate the necessary agreements between the parties to implement these measures;

4. *Calls upon* all the parties concerned to continue to cooperate with the Force on the basis of the present mandate;

5. *Calls on* both parties to carry forward expeditiously and in a constructive manner the intercommunal talks under the auspices of the Secretary-General, and requests the Secretary-General to report on progress in the current round.

Security Council resolution 839(1993)

11 June 1993   Meeting 3235   Adopted unanimously

Draft prepared in consultations among Council members (S/25927).

Report of the Secretary-General (November). On 22 November,[32] the Secretary-General submitted the report called for by resolution 831(1993) above. It provided: an overview of the United Nations Operation in Cyprus, including its costs; a description of the functions, strength and deployment of UNFICYP; a summary of its operations from 16 June to 15 December; and an update on developments in respect of the Secretary-General's good offices mission (see above).

The report noted a lack of progress in extending the 1989 unmanning agreement to all areas of the buffer zone, a decrease in the number of air violations by military aircraft, but an increase in violations by other aircraft. The National Guard programme of improving defensive positions along the cease-fire line continued, as did the violation by Greek Cypriot tourist and fishing boats of the seaward extensions of the cease-fire lines known as the maritime security lines. The Cyprus police control point on the Larnaca-Pyla road remained in place.

Two of several Greek Cypriot demonstrations and rallies were marked by serious violence. During one demonstration, a large number of Greek Cypriot motorcyclists entered the buffer zone more than once, confronting the Turkish forces; they also confronted UNFICYP at Ledra Crossing, tearing down UNFICYP barriers and injuring six Australian Civilian Police. Another demonstration of some 5,000 youths entered the buffer zone and injured five UNFICYP members who tried to restrain the demonstrators.

The report stated that the Force Commander had absorbed the effects of successive reductions in the strength of the Force, moving a greater proportion of battalion strengths into the buffer zone, reorganizing the system of observation posts and relying more heavily on mobile patrolling. He had also begun turning over certain UNFICYP humanitarian activities to the two sides. The 12 recently assigned military observers had been integrated into the three sectors to carry out reconnaissance, liaison and humanitarian tasks. On one-year assignments (against the six- to eight-month infantry tour), the observers provided useful continuity from one line unit to its replacement. The Force Commander believed 12 observers to be sufficient.

The report reviewed the options considered thus far for a restructured UNFICYP: an unarmed observer mission or an UNFICYP whose functions were divided between infantry and military observers—neither of which the Secretary-General recommended.

While UNFICYP had successfully kept the peace, the resulting opportunity had not been properly used by the two sides to reach an overall agreement. The question often asked was whether UNFICYP was not part of the problem rather than of the solution. The ancillary question was how long UNFICYP would remain on Cyprus. In weighing these questions, the Council might take account of the following considerations: each side had its own perception of the future of UNFICYP; with the Greek Cypriot side having a vital interest in seeing it maintained, while the Turkish Cypriot side neither objected to nor particularly desired its continued presence, as security was assured by the large-scale presence of Turkish forces; the withdrawal of UNFICYP would lead to incidents that could quickly escalate into a conflict, eliminating any hope of progress in a mission of good offices;

the status quo, deemed unacceptable by the Council, was established through the use of force and sustained by military strength—a situation not viable in the long term—so that a negotiated settlement was needed.

The Secretary-General was of the view that there was every justification for demanding that the two sides, as well as Turkey and Greece, work more effectively for a negotiated settlement in return for the great efforts of the international community. It was his intention to resume intensive contacts with both sides and with Turkey after the elections in the Turkish Cypriot community on 12 December. In the meantime, he urged once again that, as a first step towards the withdrawal of non-Cypriot troops envisaged in the Set of Ideas, the Turkish forces on the island be reduced to their level of 1982 and that this reduction be reciprocated by the Greek Cypriot side by a suspension of its weapons acquisition programmes.

Once again the Secretary-General recommended that the Council extend the UNFICYP mandate for a further six months, until 15 June 1994.

In a 13 December addendum to his report,[(33)] the Secretary-General informed the Council that Cyprus, Greece and the United Kingdom had indicated their concurrence with the proposed extension. Turkey had also indicated its concurrence with and support of the position of the Turkish Cypriot side, as expressed at previous Council meetings on the extension of the UNFICYP mandate.

Earlier, on 14 November,[(34)] Mr. Denktas referred to the Secretary-General's call to cooperate with UNFICYP in extending the 1989 unmanning agreement to all areas of the buffer zone, as well as his call for reciprocal measures to lower tension, including mutual commitments, through UNFICYP. He said discussions between the Turkish Cypriot side and UNFICYP on those issues could start without delay so as to reach a mutually acceptable arrangement. He called on the Council to ask the Greek Cypriot side to desist from all activities not conducive to a peaceful settlement, such as its demonstrations along the cease-fire lines.

SECURITY COUNCIL ACTION

On 15 December, the Security Council, having considered the Secretary-General's report, unanimously adopted **resolution 889(1993)**.

The Security Council,

Recalling its resolution 186(1964) and other relevant resolutions,

Having considered the report of the Secretary-General of 22 November 1993 submitted pursuant to resolutions 831(1993) of 27 May 1993 and 839(1993) of 11 June 1993 in connection with the Security Council's comprehensive reassessment of the United Nations operation in Cyprus,

Noting the recommendation by the Secretary-General that the Security Council extend the stationing of the United Nations Peace-keeping Force in Cyprus in its present strength and structure for a further period of six months,

Noting also that the Government of Cyprus has agreed that, in view of the prevailing conditions in the island, it is necessary to keep the Force in Cyprus beyond 15 December 1993,

1. *Extends* once more the stationing in Cyprus of the United Nations Peace-keeping Force established under resolution 186(1964) (UNFICYP) for a further period ending on 15 June 1994;

2. *Notes* the Secretary-General's conclusion that the present circumstances do not allow for any modification in the structure and strength of UNFICYP and requests him to keep those matters under constant review with a view to the further possible restructuring of UNFICYP;

3. *Calls upon* the military authorities on both sides to ensure that no incidents occur along the buffer zone and to extend their full cooperation to UNFICYP;

4. *Urges* all concerned once again to commit themselves to a significant reduction in the number of foreign troops in the Republic of Cyprus and a reduction of defence spending in the Republic of Cyprus to help restore confidence between the parties and as a first step towards the withdrawal of non-Cypriot forces as set out in the Set of Ideas;

5. *Calls upon* the military authorities on both sides, in line with paragraph 3 of resolution 839(1993) of 11 June 1993, to begin discussions with UNFICYP without further delay with a view to entering into mutual commitments to prohibit along the cease-fire lines live ammunition or weapons other than those which are handheld and to prohibit also the firing of weapons within sight or hearing of the buffer zone;

6. *Calls upon* the military authorities on both sides to cooperate with UNFICYP in extending the 1989 unmanning agreement to cover all areas of the buffer zone where the two sides are in close proximity to each other;

7. *Urges* the leaders of both communities to promote tolerance and reconciliation between the two communities as recommended in paragraph 102 of the Secretary-General's report of 22 November 1993;

8. *Reaffirms* that the status quo is unacceptable, and encourages the Secretary-General and his Special Representative to pursue the Secretary-General's mission of good offices on the basis of the Set of Ideas and the package of confidence-building measures relating to Varosha and Nicosia International Airport referred to in paragraph 45 of the Secretary-General's report of 22 November 1993;

9. *Notes with interest* the confirmation by the team of international economic experts that the package of confidence-building measures holds significant and proportionate benefits for both sides, and looks forward to receiving the full reports of the economic and civil aviation experts;

10. *Welcomes* in this context the decision of the Secretary-General to resume intensive contacts with both sides and with others concerned and to concentrate at this stage on achieving an agreement on the package of confidence-building measures, intended to

facilitate the political process towards an overall settlement;

11. *Further welcomes* the declared support of the Government of Turkey for the package of confidence-building measures, would also welcome a statement of support for that package by the Government of Greece and expresses the hope that rapid progress will now be made on achieving agreement on the package;

12. *Requests* the Secretary-General to submit a report by the end of February 1994 on the outcome of his efforts to achieve an agreement on the package of confidence-building measures;

13. *Decides* to undertake, on the basis of that report, a thorough review of the situation, including the future role of the United Nations, and, if necessary, to consider alternative ways to promote the implementation of its resolutions on Cyprus.

Security Council resolution 889(1993)

15 December 1993   Meeting 3322   Adopted unanimously

Draft prepared in consultations among Council members (S/26873), orally revised.

Financing

On 1 April[35] and again on 29 November,[36] the Secretary-General issued appeals to all Member States of the United Nations or members of the specialized agencies for voluntary contributions to finance UNFICYP. In his April appeal, he stated that as at mid-March, the accumulated shortfall in the UNFICYP Special Account for the mandate period ending 15 June 1993 was estimated at $204 million and that, for the current period, only $1.68 million had so far been pledged or received against projected expenditures of some $9.5 million. The United Nations had been able to meet the claims of troop-contributing countries only up to December 1981. It was unfair that those countries should have to absorb such a disproportionate share of the cost of UNFICYP.

In his November appeal, the Secretary-General stated that the accumulated shortfall had increased to $208.5 million by 15 June 1993, with only $6.8 million pledged for the mandate period 15 December 1992 to 15 June 1993. Since the Security Council had decided that the costs of UNFICYP not covered by voluntary contributions were to be treated as expenses of the Organization from the extension of its mandate on 15 June, the appeal was for special voluntary financial contribution towards the UNFICYP voluntary account for the period prior to 16 June 1993 to cover amounts remaining unreimbursed to troop contributors.

The Secretary-General, by a note of 15 June,[37] requested inclusion in the agenda of the forty-seventh session of the General Assembly an additional item, entitled "Financing of the United Nations Peace-keeping Force in Cyprus". Owing to the nature of the item, he further requested that it be allocated to the Fifth Committee. The Assembly inscribed and allocated the item, as requested, on 22 June.[38]

Report of the Secretary-General (August). In a 20 August report on the financing of UNFICYP,[39] the Secretary-General set out the operational plan of the Force and the cost estimates for its maintenance for the period 16 June to 15 December 1993. It also provided the historical background of the financing of the Force from its inception in 1964[19] to 15 June 1993, its financial administration, voluntary contributions received and the status of reimbursement to troop-contributing Governments.

Under agreements concluded prior to 15 June 1993, troop contributors volunteered to absorb the regular costs their contingents would incur (regular allowances and normal expenses for *matériel*) were they serving at home. However, the cost to the United Nations for maintaining UNFICYP included amounts to reimburse the troop contributors for certain of the expenses they incurred in providing troops, known as extra and extraordinary costs, for which reimbursement was being sought by the troop contributors. Owing to insufficient voluntary contributions, they were last reimbursed in June 1992 for claims pertaining to the six-month period ending December 1981. An amount of over $200 million remained outstanding, based on actual and estimated claims for the period from January 1982 through June 1993.

Beginning on 16 June 1993, cost estimates provided for standard reimbursement of troop costs, based on the rates established by the General Assembly in 1991[40] for peace-keeping operations. No reimbursement to the troop contributors had been made for this period.

The cost of maintaining UNFICYP for the current mandate period from 16 June to 15 December 1993 was estimated at $21,512,000 gross ($21,153,300 net). A summary by budget-line item and supplementary information were annexed to the report.

On 23 June, the Secretary-General sought the concurrence of ACABQ to enter into commitments in an amount not to exceed $6.9 million for the period from 16 June to 30 September 1993, pending submission of a detailed report on UNFICYP financing to the Assembly. Noting that voluntary contributions pledged and expected to be paid shortly exceeded the commitment authority sought and noting also that the Assembly had not yet considered the issue, ACABQ decided not to act on the request.

To enable UNFICYP to meet its operational requirements, and pending submission of the current report to the Assembly, spending authority in an amount not to exceed $2 million was authorized by the Controller under rule 110.6 of the Financial Regulations and Rules of the United Nations. On 4 August, payment of the pledged contribution by Cyprus in an amount of $18 million

was received, in addition to a payment of $500,000 previously received for the current mandate period.

The action thus required appeared to be an appropriation of $9,012,000 gross ($8,653,300 net) and the apportionment thereof, after taking into consideration voluntary contributions of $12,500,000 for the period 16 June to 15 December 1993.

Having examined the Secretary-General's report, ACABQ[41] believed that the cost for maintaining UNFICYP for the period specified should not exceed $21,271,000 gross ($20,943,000 net). Should the Assembly decide that the costs not covered by voluntary contributions should be assessed on Member States, the resulting appropriation should not exceed $8,771,000 gross ($8,443,000 net).

GENERAL ASSEMBLY ACTION

On 14 September, the General Assembly, on the recommendation of the Fifth Committee, adopted **resolution 47/236** without vote.

Financing of the United Nations Peace-keeping Force in Cyprus

The General Assembly,

Having considered the report of the Secretary-General on the financing of the United Nations Peace-keeping Force in Cyprus and the related report of the Advisory Committee on Administrative and Budgetary Questions,

Bearing in mind Security Council resolution 186(1964) of 4 March 1964, by which the Council established the United Nations Peace-keeping Force in Cyprus, and the subsequent resolutions by which the Council extended the mandate of the Force, the latest of which was resolution 839(1993) of 11 June 1993,

Recognizing that, in order to meet the expenditures caused by the Force with effect from 16 June 1993, a different procedure is required from the one applied to meet expenditures of the regular budget of the United Nations,

Taking into account the fact that the economically more developed countries are in a position to make relatively larger contributions and that the economically less developed countries have a relatively limited capacity to contribute towards such an operation,

Bearing in mind the special responsibilities of the States permanent members of the Security Council, as indicated in General Assembly resolution 1874(S-IV) of 27 June 1963, in the financing of such operations,

Noting with appreciation that voluntary contributions have been made to the Force by certain Governments,

Noting that voluntary contributions were insufficient to cover all of the costs of the operation, including those incurred by troop-contributing Governments prior to 16 June 1993, and regretting the absence of an adequate response to the various appeals for voluntary contributions, including the one contained in section IV of General Assembly resolution 47/218 A of 23 December 1992,

Appreciating the continued efforts of Governments providing troops to the Force,

Mindful of the fact that it is essential to provide the Force with the necessary financial resources to enable it to fulfil its mandate,

1. *Reaffirms*, in the context of paragraph 4 of Security Council resolution 831(1993) of 27 May 1993, in which the Council addressed the issue of the financing of the United Nations Peace-keeping Force in Cyprus, the role of the General Assembly, as set out in Article 17 of the Charter of the United Nations, as the organ to consider and approve the budget of the Organization, as well as the apportionment of its expenses among Member States;

2. *Expresses concern* that advice given to the Security Council by the Secretariat on the nature of the financing of the Force did not respect the role of the General Assembly as set out in Article 17 of the Charter;

3. *Requests* the President of the General Assembly to bring to the attention of the President of the Security Council the contents of the present resolution;

4. *Endorses* the observations and recommendations contained in the report of the Advisory Committee on Administrative and Budgetary Questions;

5. *Requests* the Secretary-General to take all necessary action, in accordance, *inter alia*, with the observations and recommendations of the Advisory Committee, to ensure that the Force is administered with a maximum of efficiency and economy, to improve management, and to include in his report on this item to the General Assembly information on the steps taken in this regard;

6. *Urges* all Member States to make every possible effort to ensure payment of their assessed contributions to the Force promptly and in full;

7. *Decides* that the costs of the Force for the period beginning 16 June 1993 that are not covered by voluntary contributions should be treated as expenses of the Organization to be borne by Member States in accordance with Article 17, paragraph 2, of the Charter;

8. *Decides also* to appropriate the amount of 8,771,000 United States dollars gross (8,443,000 dollars net) for the period from 16 June to 15 December 1993, and, accordingly, requests the Secretary-General to establish a special account for the United Nations Peace-keeping Force in Cyprus in accordance with paragraph 29 of his report;

9. *Decides further*, as an ad hoc arrangement, to apportion the amount of 8,771,000 dollars gross (8,443,000 dollars net) for the above-mentioned period among Member States, in accordance with the composition of groups set out in paragraphs 3 and 4 of General Assembly resolution 43/232 of 1 March 1989, as adjusted by the Assembly in its resolutions 44/192 B of 21 December 1989, 45/269 of 27 August 1991, 46/198 A of 20 December 1991 and 47/218 A of 23 December 1992, and taking into account the scale of assessments set out in Assembly resolution 46/221 A of 20 December 1991 and Assembly decision 47/456 of 23 December 1992;

10. *Decides* that, in accordance with the provisions of its resolution 973(X) of 15 December 1955, there shall be set off against the apportionment among Member States, as provided for in paragraph 9 above, their respective share in the Tax Equalization Fund of the estimated staff assessment income of 328,000 dollars for the period from 16 June to 15 December 1993 approved for the Force;

11. *Decides* to establish the contributions of Andorra, the Czech Republic, Eritrea, the former Yugoslav Republic of Macedonia, Monaco and Slovakia to the Force in accordance with the rates of assessment to be adopted by the General Assembly for these Member States at its forty-eighth session;

12. *Invites* the new Member States listed in paragraph 11 above to make advance payments against their assessed contributions, to be determined;

13. *Invites* voluntary contributions to the Force in cash and in the form of services and supplies acceptable to the Secretary-General, to be administered, as appropriate, in accordance with the procedure established by the General Assembly in its resolutions 43/230 of 21 December 1988, 44/192 A of 21 December 1989 and 45/258 of 3 May 1991;

14. *Decides* to maintain as separate the account established prior to 16 June 1993 for the Force, invites Member States to make voluntary contributions to that account, and, in this regard, requests the Secretary-General to intensify his efforts in appealing for voluntary contributions to this account;

15. *Requests* the Secretary-General, taking into account the voluntary nature of the financing of the Force prior to 16 June 1993, to report, no later than 31 January 1994, on the status of the account referred to in paragraph 14 above;

16. *Decides* to include in the draft agenda of its forty-eighth session the item entitled "Financing of the United Nations Peace-keeping Force in Cyprus".

General Assembly resolution 47/236

14 September 1993   Meeting 110   Adopted without vote

Approved by Fifth Committee (A/47/1015) without vote, 10 September (meeting 76); draft by Chairman (A/C.5/47/L.45); agenda item 157.
Meeting numbers. GA 47th session: 5th Committee 73, 76; plenary 110.

Report of the Secretary-General (December). In his 9 December report on the financing of 17 peace-keeping operations, including UNIFCYP,[42] the Secretary-General stated that, should the Security Council decide to extend the UNFICYP mandate beyond 15 December 1993, the estimated cost of UNFICYP for the period from 16 December 1993 to 30 April 1994 would amount to $17,559,000 gross ($17,232,000 net). The estimate took account of the ongoing restructuring of the Force. A breakdown of the requirements by major line-items of expenditure was provided in a table.

In accordance with the undertakings of Cyprus and Greece to make annual voluntary contributions to UNFICYP of $25 million, it was estimated that a portion of the cost indicated above would be offset by an amount of $9,375,000, representing the prorated share over four and one half months of the voluntary contributions. Therefore, the balance of resources required to maintain UNFICYP up to 30 April 1994 would amount to $8,184,000 gross ($7,857,000 net).

ACABQ[43] recommended that, for the period 16 December 1993 to 30 April 1994, the Secretary-General be authorized to commit an amount up to $8,184,000 gross ($7,857,000 net). This would also take into account the amount of $9,375,000 representing the prorated share of the pledged voluntary contributions. No assessment on Member States would be necessary for the time being since ACABQ had been informed that a cash balance of $28,500,000 was available to UNFICYP as at 13 December 1993.

GENERAL ASSEMBLY ACTION

In December, the General Assembly adopted **decision 48/474.**

Financing of the United Nations Peace-keeping Force in Cyprus

At its 87th plenary meeting, on 23 December 1993, the General Assembly, on the recommendation of the Fifth Committee, in accordance with the framework set out in its resolution 48/227 of 23 December 1993, having considered the report of the Secretary-General on the financing of seventeen peace-keeping operations and the related reports of the Advisory Committee on Administrative and Budgetary Questions, and concurring with the observations of the Advisory Committee:

(a) Authorized the Secretary-General, on an exceptional basis, to enter into commitments up to the amount of 6,365,300 United States dollars gross (6,111,000 dollars net), in addition to the pledged voluntary contributions of 9,375,000 dollars, for the United Nations Peace-keeping Force in Cyprus for the period from 16 December 1993 to 31 March 1994;

(b) Decided that no assessment on Member States would be necessary in the light of the current cash balance in the Special Account for the United Nations Peace-keeping Force in Cyprus.

General Assembly decision 48/474

Adopted without vote

Approved by Fifth Committee (A/48/822) without vote, 22 December (meeting 46); draft by Chairman (A/C.5/48/L.25); agenda item 160.
Meeting numbers. GA 48th session: 5th Committee 44, 46; plenary 87.

REFERENCES
[1]A/47/856-S/25063, A/47/999-S/26288, A/47/1007-S/26369, A/48/458-S/26506, A/48/546-S/26636. [2]A/47/878-S/25169, A/47/880-S/25196, A/48/706-S/26832. [3]A/47/924-S/25579, A/47/928-S/25628, A/47/934-S/25688, A/47/944-S/25740, A/47/993-S/26195. [4]A/47/972-S/26030. [5]A/47/989-S/26170 & Corr.1, A/47/998-S/26287. [6]A/48/583. [7]A/48/764-S/26880. [8]YUN 1991, p. 92. [9]YUN 1992, p. 268, SC res. 774(1992), 26 Aug. 1992. [10]S/25478. [11]S/25517. [12]YUN 1992, p. 269, SC res. 789(1992), 25 Nov. 1992. [13]S/26026. [14]YUN 1979, p. 422. [15]YUN 1984, p. 243, SC res. 550(1984), 11 May 1984. [16]S/26050. [17]S/26438. [18]S/26475. [19]YUN 1964, p. 165, SC res. 186(1964), 4 Mar. 1964. [20]YUN 1974, p. 291, SC res. 353(1974), 20 July 1974. [21]S/25832. [22]S/25833. [23]YUN 1992, p. 271, SC res. 796(1992), 14 Dec. 1992. [24]S/25492. [25]S/21982. [26]S/25647. [27]S/25693. [28]S/26178. [29]S/26179. [30]S/25912. [31]S/25912/Add.1. [32]S/26777. [33]S/26777/Add.1. [34]S/26833. [35]S/25502. [36]S/26813. [37]A/47/966. [38]A/47/252/Add.10. [39]A/47/1001. [40]YUN 1991, p. 862, GA res. 45/258, 3 May 1991. [41]A/47/1004. [42]A/C.5/48/40. [43]A/48/780.

Iran-Iraq

Iran and Iraq continued in 1993 to communicate to the Secretary-General allegations of violations of the cease-fire agreement concluded between the two countries in 1988.[1]

A majority of the allegations were of violations along the Iran-Iraq international boundary, consisting of intrusions by military elements of either side into the area of separation between the two countries, helicopter overflights of that area, small-arms firing within proximity of the boundary line, fortifying existing guard posts and observation towers within the area of separation or erecting new ones at points closer to it than agreed, digging slit trenches, erecting barbed-wire fences, installing or strengthening communication stations and provocative acts such as flag-raising.

Iran, however, alleged a number of Iraqi incursions into its territory, one of which, it said, took place on 8 February[2] by 70 well-trained, armed and equipped mercenaries from Iraq who entered Iran's border village of Beitoush, advanced to Nazarbad and then to Bizdeh, where they laid seige to two military bases, killing 14 Iranians and wounding two others; 33 persons were held captive but later released. The bases, as well as a local radio and television station that was emptied of its equipment, were set ablaze. Four other incursions from Iraq were alleged to have occurred between 7 and 10 April,[3] during which four Iranians were killed and civilian quarters and military and oil installations were damaged.

In retaliation for those attacks, Iran stated that, on 25 May,[4] it carried out what it described as a brief, necessary and proportionate operation against the military bases of the terrorist group where the attacks had originated. Iran added that its action was purely in exercise of its inherent right to self-defence, without prejudice to its policy of respecting the sovereignty and territorial integrity of Iraq and to its commitment to the cease-fire agreement between them.

In an 11 June letter,[5] Iran alleged that groups of anti-revolutionary elements infiltrated certain areas in the Shatit, Dehloran and Mehran regions on 12 May, attacking Iranian forces and a civilian vehicle; on 13 May, they exploded seven bombs around oil pipelines and an oil station at Abadan; and, on 15 May, a six-man group attacked Iranian forces in the Shalamcheh region and destroyed an ammunition depot. The attacks claimed the lives of 10 Iranians, including nine soldiers, and injured a number of others. Iran also alleged violations of its airspace on 23 June,[6] when six Iraqi war-planes overflew Mahabad, Sardasht, Bookan and Baneh; and, the following day, when two Iraqi war-planes flew over the southern section of western Azerbaijan province.

For its part, Iraq alleged a succession of bombardments, mainly by artillery, inflicted by Iran on areas in northern Iraq. On 13 March,[7] an aerial bombing of a civilian hospital in the

Raniyah district by six Iranian military aircraft claimed the lives of a number of Iraqi Kurdish citizens and caused extensive damage to the hospital. A further incident occurred on 20 April,[8] in the Qal'at Dizah valley, as Iranian forces massed on their side of the frontier to the east of the Iraqi town of Panjwin, causing the town's inhabitants to flee. On 19 April,[9] again in the Qal'at Dizah valley, as well as in Pishtashan and Qirnago, artillery bombarded civilian areas killing and injuring a number of civilians and forcing more than 3,000 persons to flee their homes. Similar attacks occurred on 26 April,[10] in the Tushman region and in the suburbs of Panjwin; on 7 May,[11] in Pusht and Parwin; and, on 14 May,[12] in Sar Qizil, Kalaw, Dustak and Shurladra slope.

Iraq reported that, on 25 May,[13] Iran carried out an aerial attack on Khalis and Jalula', causing damage to a medical depot, igniting fuel tanks and destroying two private houses. On 8 June,[14] Iraq condemned Iran's justification of this naked aggression on the basis of Article 51 of the Charter.[4]

On 16 June,[15] Iraq, in drawing attention to the continuing Iranian artillery bombardments of villages and townships in northern Iraq since May that had caused widespread death and injury, material damage and large-scale displacement of the populations who were fleeing farther inside Iraq, reiterated that such brutal bombardment constituted blatant and inadmissible aggression threatening security and stability in the region. On 10 June,[16] it reported that, from the night of 4 June and most of the following day, the northern section of Qal'at Dizah was subjected to sporadic shelling. Also subjected to intermittent and random bombardment were Shiyuzah and Bardi on 22 June; Ganaw and Qindil on 3/4 July; Shiyuzah, Sunah and Kometan on 15 July; and Qal'at Dizah and Panjwin during the following week.[17]

Iraq alleged that an Iranian Guard force entered two Iraqi villages in the Choarta sector on 20 July,[18] and, in the ensuing clash with local residents, an Iranian was killed and four were taken prisoner and handed over to United Nations representatives; three days later, Iranian forces fired Katyusha rockets during a three-hour bombardment of the Suleimaniyah area. On 30 and 31 July,[19] the border areas of Sunah, Shinah and Shiwarazah, as well as the Balinkan valley, were intermittently shelled. So were the following: on 31 July/1 August,[20] the Balinkan and Shahidan valleys, the villages of Wasan, Kuwaynah and Karalan, as well as villages on the western section of Qindil slope; and, on the night of 1/2 August, a number of villages in the Irbil Governorate.

On 23 August,[21] Iraq reported that the shelling of Dawlat Dizah on 9 August and of Duwayli the following day set fire to extensive sections of grain fields and displaced a number of families, as did the shelling, during the night of 14/15 August, of villages to the north of Hajj Umran. On 20 August,[22] the highway connecting Darbandikhan and Arabit and villages along the highway were shelled for most of the day, damaging a number of vehicles and injuring citizens; areas in Suleimaniyah Governorate were also bombarded, setting cultivated areas ablaze. The shelling of border areas continued into 21 August,[23] extending as far as 30 kilometres into Iraqi territory.

On the night of 27/28 August,[24] Iran bombarded a number of villages in Iraq as well as the Singasir area 20 kilometres inside Iraqi territory; and, on 1 September, two other villages north-east of Panjwin, burning farmlands in that area. Between 19 and 27 September,[25] Iran mounted a number of artillery attacks on villages around Qal'at Dizah.

In addition to those raids and bombardments, Iraq also alleged that, on 16 March,[26] a group of 50 to 60 armed Iranians mounted an assault on Iraqi positions from three directions, using medium machine-guns, 60-millimetre mortars and light rocket launchers; Iranian army identity papers were found on one of the eight bodies found after the encounter. On 6 October,[27] two Iranian military officers committed a provocative act by ordering individuals manning an Iraqi position in the demilitarized zone to pull back their position by afternoon the following day.

Iraq regarded the foregoing incidents as acts of renewed aggression and provocation and deplored the Security Council's failure to take appropriate measures despite repeated requests for United Nations intervention. It pointed out[13] that, since the United Nations Offices of the Secretary-General in Iran and in Iraq were closed on 31 December 1992, the absence of any machinery for monitoring the cease-fire undoubtedly encouraged Iran to engage in new armed aggressions against Iraq; there was therefore an urgent need to reconsider reopening those offices.

REFERENCES
[1]YUN 1988, p. 188. [2]S/25431. [3]S/25813. [4]S/25843. [5]S/25938. [6]S/26106. [7]S/25453 & S/25473. [8]S/25679. [9]S/25680. [10]S/25689. [11]S/25772. [12]S/25788. [13]S/25864. [14]S/25914. [15]S/25975. [16]S/25924. [17]S/26197. [18]S/26230. [19]S/26238. [20]S/26294. [21]S/26354. [22]S/26355. [23]26388. [24]S/26429. [25]S/26550. [26]S/25611. [27]S/26574.

Iraq-Kuwait situation

The United Nations continued in 1993 to oversee Iraq's fulfilment of its obligations under Security Council resolution 687(1991),[1] which set the terms of the cease-fire that formally brought to an end the 1991 military action taken to compel Iraq to withdraw from its occupation of Kuwait and provided for other conditions essential to restore peace and security in the Persian Gulf region. The Organization further sought Iraq's fulfilment of its obligations under resolutions 707(1991)[2] and 715(1991),[3] which were inextricably linked with and elaborated upon certain provisions of the cease-fire resolution.

The United Nations Special Commission, created as a subsidiary organ of the Council under the cease-fire resolution, and IAEA continued to discharge their mandate to ensure Iraq's compliance with its weapons-related obligations. Towards the end of 1993, both reported major positive developments in this regard, the most significant of which was the formal and unconditional acknowledgement by Iraq in November of its obligations under resolution 715(1991).

The United Nations Iraq-Kuwait Boundary Demarcation Commission, also created pursuant to the cease-fire resolution, completed its mandate of demarcating the international boundary between Iraq and Kuwait. It submitted its Final Report in May.

By **decision 47/477** of 20 September, the General Assembly included the item entitled "Consequences of the Iraqi occupation of and aggression against Kuwait" in the draft agenda of its forty-eighth session.

Cease-fire compliance

The status of Iraq's compliance with its weapons-related obligations was summarized by the Special Commission and by IAEA in semi-annual reports issued by each of them in June and December 1993 (see below, under "On-site inspections and ongoing monitoring and verification"). In the course of conducting on-site inspections in Iraq during the year, both bodies exerted efforts to obtain Iraq's full cooperation and compliance to enable both to complete the first and second phases of their work—inspection and survey, and disposal of weapons of mass destruction and the facilities for their production—and proceed to the third phase of ongoing monitoring and verification on a routine basis.

In its June report,[4] the Special Commission noted that Iraq's "full, final and complete" disclosures of its proscribed weapons programmes, due under resolution 707(1991), and its initial declarations under the two plans for ongoing monitoring and verification approved by resolution 715(1991) needed to be rectified if they were to form the basis for a definite material balance of Iraq's past weapons of mass destruction programmes and for effective monitoring and verification of compliance. One set of declarations, on Iraq's legal and administrative actions to give effect to its obligations in respect of ongoing monitoring and verification, had never been submitted. Iraq continued to refuse to divulge the names of foreign companies from which it had purchased equipment and materials. Accurate information was essential if the Commission was to establish a material balance for proscribed items and, in cooperation with IAEA and the Committee on sanctions, devise a workable and realistic mechanism for import control required by paragraph 7 of resolution 715(1991).

The IAEA June report[5] made similar observations in respect of Iraq's nuclear material declarations and procurement-related information.

Serious breaches of the Commission's rights, privileges and immunities included the denial by Iraq in January of the Commission's use of its own aircraft to transport personnel and equipment into and out of Iraq from Bahrain. In February, it threatened to shoot down a helicopter providing overhead surveillance for an inspection team if the aircraft did not leave the vicinity of the site and, in June, it blocked the installation of monitoring cameras at two rocket-test sites. It missed two deadlines for the removal and delivery to the Commission of equipment for the production of chemical-weapons precursors and delayed site inspection by a full day.

In their December reports, however, the Commission and IAEA reported major positive technical and political developments that had evolved during three rounds of talks held between the two bodies and Iraqi officials at the highest levels of Government. Iraq had acknowledged its obligations under resolution 715(1991) and the plans approved thereunder. It had confirmed that the significant new declarations it had made available during the talks and those it had previously presented had been made under and in conformity with that resolution. Its change in attitude had been reflected in the cooperation it had extended during the most recent on-site inspections. It had undertaken to cooperate with the Commission in implementing the plans in order to arrive, at the earliest feasible time, at the stage to permit both the Commission and IAEA to report to the Security Council that, in their view, Iraq was meeting all the requirements of section C of resolution 687(1991).

In the light of these positive developments, the Commission and IAEA were finally in a position to complete the first and second phases of their tasks and proceed to the third.

The status of Iraq's implementation of its other obligations under the cease-fire resolution and compliance with other related resolutions are reflected below, dealing with the Iraq-Kuwait international boundary, the repatriation of Kuwaiti nationals, the return of Kuwaiti property, and obligations with respect to all segments of the Iraqi civilian population.

For its part, Iraq issued a series of communications summarizing the measures it had taken each month between December 1992 and August 1993[6] to implement resolution 687(1991). They included cooperation extended to the inspection teams verifying Iraqi compliance with the military aspects of the resolution, as well as to the United Nations Iraq-Kuwait Observation Mission (UNIKOM); steps taken to locate missing Kuwaitis and to return Kuwaiti property; Iraq's participation in the work of the Governing Council of the United Nations Compensation Commission relating to claims for losses and damage resulting from the Iraqi invasion and occupation of Kuwait; and steps to implement the provisions of the 1992 Memorandum of Understanding[7] for the delivery of humanitarian relief to the civilian population of Iraq.

Financing of activities
arising from the cease-fire resolution

By **decision 47/471** of 14 September, the General Assembly decided to defer consideration of the item entitled "Financing of the activities arising from Security Council resolution 687(1991): other activities" and to include it in the agenda of its forty-eighth session.

Iraq-Kuwait boundary

In a number of communications to the Security Council President during 1993, Kuwait drew attention to continuing Iraqi assertions that Kuwait was part of Iraq. To illustrate, Kuwait, in an 8 March letter to the President of the Security Council,[8] cited: the evasive answer given by Iraq's Deputy Prime Minister when asked in a telephone interview (by British television, 31 January) whether, by his statement that the Kuwait chapter was closed, he meant Iraq's recognition of Kuwait as an independent sovereign State; and a press reference to Kuwait as part of Iraq's national territory (*Al-Jumhuriyah*, 28 February). On 23 March,[9] Kuwait reproduced two newspaper articles, one speaking of the "Governorate of Kuwait" (*Babil*, 6 March) and the other describing Iraq's acceptance of resolution 687(1991) as an imposed status quo paving the way to a time when it could be overcome and changed in a way to ensure the security and safety of Iraq's territory and people (*Al-Khuadissiyah*, 16 March).

Kuwait further transmitted samples of Iraqi school certificates of students born in Kuwait, recording their birthplace as the "Governorate of Kuwait";[10] it pointed to the standard Iraqi press practice of calling Kuwait an Iraqi Governorate (*Babil*, 8 November) and referring to the people of Kuwait as Iraqis (*Al-Thawra*, 8 November), and to general media references to the boundary between Kuwait and Iraq as the "administrative bound-

ary between the governorates of Basrah and Kuwait".[11] Also cited were Jordanian press reports of statements by the Iraqi Minister of Culture and Information to the effect that, while the major Powers might change geography, they could not change history: Kuwait remained a part of Iraq (*Al-Dustur*, 14 November) and the issue was not Kuwait but that Kuwait had been a part of Iraq until 1961 when the British made it a State, a situation which persisted until 1990 (*Sawt al-Sha'b*, 15 November).[12]

Demarcation Commission

The Chairman of the United Nations Iraq-Kuwait Boundary Demarcation Commission, on 20 May, submitted the Final Report on the Demarcation of the International Boundary between the Republic of Iraq and the State of Kuwait to the Secretary-General, who in turn transmitted it to the Security Council with a letter on 21 May.[13] The letter stated that, in addition to the Final Report, the Chairman submitted three certified copies of the list of geographic coordinates demarcating the international boundary between Iraq and Kuwait. In forwarding one copy to Iraq and the second to Kuwait for their archives, the Secretary-General drew attention to the Final Report and the large-scale maps of the boundary, along with technical documentation comprising certified records of survey stations and boundary pillars. The third copy was retained in the United Nations archives for safe keeping.

The Final Report described the Demarcation Commission's mandate and terms of reference, composition and rules of procedure, meetings and field sessions, participation, organization of work and its consideration of the historical background and definition of the boundary. It outlined the methods of mapping employed, decisions taken as to the demarcation of the western and northern sections and of the Khawr Abd Allah [Khor Abdullah], the physical representation of the boundary, recommendations for its maintenance, and demarcation documentation. The report presented the Commission's conclusion regarding the international boundary and listed coordinates demarcating it. An annex listed the Commission's documents and progress reports. The corresponding demarcation map was issued as an addendum to the Secretary-General's transmittal letter.[14]

The Final Report recorded that, to accomplish its mandate, as laid down in Council resolution 687(1991) and in the report of the Secretary-General[15] on the establishment of the Demarcation Commission pursuant to paragraph 3 of that resolution, the Commission drew upon appropriate material, including, in addition to the maps transmitted by Security Council document S/22412 (a set of 10 topographic maps by the

United Kingdom Director of General Military Survey), a 1932 Exchange of Letters referred to in the "Agreed Minutes between the State of Kuwait and the Republic of Iraq regarding the Restoration of Friendly Relations, Recognition and Related Matters", signed in 1963, containing the following description of "the existing frontier between the two countries", which constituted the delimitation formula for the demarcation.

"From the intersection of the Wadi-el-Audja with the Batin and thence northwards along the Batin to a point just south of the latitude of Safwan; thence eastwards passing south of Safwan Wells, Jebel Sanam and Um Qasr leaving them to Iraq and so on to the junction of the Khor Zobeir with the Khor Abdullah. The islands of Warbah, Bubiyan, Maskan (or Mashjan), Failakah, Auhah, Kubbar, Qaru and Umm-el-Maradim appertain to Koweit."

The Commission's task was thus technical, not political. As Council resolution 773(1992)[16] pointed out, the Commission was not reallocating territory between Kuwait and Iraq; it was simply carrying out the technical task necessary to demarcate for the first time the precise coordinates of the boundary set out in the Agreed Minutes, pursuant to resolution 687(1991). The Final Report stressed that the Commission had made every effort to confine itself strictly to that objective.

In its conclusion, the Final Report stated that the Demarcation Commission had fulfilled its mandate: it had demarcated in geographic coordinates of latitude and longitude the international boundary between Iraq and Kuwait set out in the Agreed Minutes, had made arrangements for the physical representation of the boundary through the emplacement of an appropriate number of boundary pillars or monuments and had provided for arrangements for continuing maintenance and location accuracy of the surficial boundary representation. The Commission stressed that it carried out this mandate and only this mandate.

Regarding boundary maintenance, the Commission recommended that the Secretary-General request the survey organizations that had been associated with the Commission to provide services, as follows: to inspect the pillars and markers of the boundary annually and report to him after each inspection; to take appropriate measures to reposition, repair or replace those pillars and markers, as necessary; and to monitor the adequacy of and emplace any additional boundary markers, such as buoys, pilings or other markers, as may be deemed useful. The Commission also recommended that an access road to the pillars be built to facilitate maintenance work, the costs to be shared by Iraq and Kuwait. These arrangements would remain in force until other technical arrangements were established between the parties.

In his transmittal letter, the Secretary-General stated that the coordinates established by the Commission constituted the final demarcation of the international boundary between Iraq and Kuwait set out in the Agreed Minutes. He also stated his intention to set in motion the mechanism for the recommended boundary maintenance, adding that the personnel to be involved, whether of the United Nations or of survey or similar organizations, were to enjoy unimpeded freedom of movement in the area of the demarcated boundary and all other privileges and immunities necessary for the fulfilment of their task.

SECURITY COUNCIL ACTION

On 27 May, the Security Council unanimously adopted **resolution 833(1993)**.

The Security Council,

Reaffirming its resolution 687(1991) of 3 April 1991, and in particular paragraphs 2, 3 and 4 thereof, its resolution 689(1991) of 9 April 1991, its resolution 773(1992) of 26 August 1992, and its resolution 806(1993) of 5 February 1993,

Recalling the report of the Secretary-General dated 2 May 1991 concerning the establishment of the United Nations Iraq-Kuwait Boundary Demarcation Commission (the Commission), the subsequent exchange of letters of 6 and 13 May 1991, and the acceptance of the report by Iraq and Kuwait,

Having considered the Secretary-General's letter of 21 May 1993 to the President of the Security Council transmitting the final report of the Commission dated 20 May 1993,

Recalling in this connection that through the demarcation process the Commission was not reallocating territory between Kuwait and Iraq, but it was simply carrying out the technical task necessary to demarcate for the first time the precise coordinates of the boundary set out in the "Agreed Minutes between the State of Kuwait and the Republic of Iraq regarding the Restoration of Friendly Relations, Recognition and Related Matters" signed by them on 4 October 1963, and that this task was carried out in the special circumstances following Iraq's invasion of Kuwait and pursuant to resolution 687(1991) and the Secretary-General's report for implementing paragraph 3 of that resolution,

Reminding Iraq of its obligations under resolution 687(1991), and in particular paragraph 2 thereof, and under other relevant resolutions of the Council, and of its acceptance of the resolutions of the Council adopted pursuant to Chapter VII of the Charter of the United Nations, which forms the basis for the cease-fire,

Noting with approval the Secretary-General's instruction to the United Nations Iraq-Kuwait Observation Mission (UNIKOM) to finalize the realignment of the demilitarized zone with the entire international boundary between Iraq and Kuwait demarcated by the Commission,

Welcoming the Secretary-General's decision to make the necessary arrangements for the maintenance of the physical representation of the boundary, as recommended by the Commission in section X *(c)* of its report, until other technical arrangements are established between Iraq and Kuwait for this purpose,

Acting under Chapter VII of the Charter of the United Nations,

1. *Welcomes* the Secretary-General's letter of 21 May 1993 to the President of the Council and the 20 May 1993 report of the Commission enclosed therewith;

2. *Welcomes also* the successful conclusion of the work of the Commission;

3. *Expresses its appreciation* to the Commission for its work on the land part of the boundary as well as the Khor Abdullah or offshore section of the boundary, and welcomes its demarcation decisions;

4. *Reaffirms* that the decisions of the Commission regarding the demarcation of the boundary are final;

5. *Demands* that Iraq and Kuwait in accordance with international law and relevant Security Council resolutions respect the inviolability of the international boundary, as demarcated by the Commission, and the right to navigational access;

6. *Underlines and reaffirms* its decision to guarantee the inviolability of the above-mentioned international boundary which has now been finally demarcated by the Commission and to take as appropriate all necessary measures to that end in accordance with the Charter, as provided for in paragraph 4 of resolution 687(1991) and paragraph 4 of resolution 773(1992);

7. *Decides* to remain seized of the matter.

Security Council resolution 833(1993)

27 May 1993   Meeting 3224   Adopted unanimously

Draft prepared in consultations among Council members (S/25852).

Venezuela stated its understanding that the resolution was not intended to establish any precedent affecting the general principle set forth in Article 33 of the Charter of the United Nations: that it was the parties directly involved in a dispute who must negotiate and reach an agreement to overcome their differences. In Brazil's view, questions related to definition and demarcation of international boundaries were to be settled directly by the States concerned. China observed that the demarcation of the boundary between Iraq and Kuwait was a special case arising from specific historical circumstance and as such was not generally applicable; for that reason the Council's invocation of Chapter VII of the Charter in that case must not be viewed as setting a precedent.

Communications. Kuwait, on 28 May,[17] expressed its appreciation to the Security Council members for adopting resolution 833(1992) and to the Demarcation Commission for their intensive efforts; on 16 June,[18] it transmitted a statement affirming that it would be bound by the decisions of the Commission and that it regarded resolution 833(1993) as an enlightened achievement to be added to the series of United Nations achievements in the promotion of international peace and justice.

Iraq, on 7 June,[19] reaffirmed its position on the question of demarcating the Iraq-Kuwait boundary on the basis of the Agreed Minutes as communicated to the Secretary-General in 1991,[20] when the Council adopted resolution 687(1991), and again in 1992.[21] Iraq also drew attention to what it said were blatant facts concerning the demarcation of the offshore boundary in the Khawr Abd Allah, which was endorsed by resolution 833(1993).

Iraq stated that when the Demarcation Commission first discussed the question at its third (1991) session,[22] the Chairman, Mochtar Kusuma-Atmadja (Indonesia), one of the three independent experts on the Commission, affirmed his understanding, shared by his fellow experts, that the mandate of the Commission did not authorize it to deal with the boundary line beyond the junction of the Khawr Zhobeir and the Khawr Abd Allah (i.e., in the sea) unless the two parties so agreed; and that, moreover, the Commission could not confer powers on itself.

The minutes of the Commission's sixth (1992) session recorded the differences that arose regarding the boundary section in question, particularly between the Kuwaiti representative and the Chairman, owing to Kuwaiti pressure on the experts to adopt Kuwait's position on the matter—a fact the Chairman did not hesitate to reveal, along with the interventions by the Deputy Legal Counsel of the United Nations Secretariat.

The letter transmitting the sixth session's report to the Council stated that, as far as the offshore boundary was concerned, the Council might wish to encourage the Commission to demarcate that part of the boundary as soon as possible and thus complete its work—this despite the Secretariat's full knowledge that the Commission had not yet agreed on its competence to do so under its terms of reference, and of the Chairman's position of implied resignation if that task was imposed on the Commission. Those facts, Iraq asserted, and the correspondence between the language of the transmittal letter and that of resolution 773(1992),[16] proved beyond doubt a coordinated effort by Kuwait and certain Council members and circles in the Secretariat to orient the Commission's work in a manner contrary to its mandate under resolution 687(1991), for to have amended the mandate would have meant a political and legal scandal that could not be covered up.

The 4 and 6 November letters of the Chairman explaining his resignation to the Secretary-General and to the Legal Counsel made clear that it was for two reasons. One was personal; the other was his reservation about the Commission's terms of reference: that is, the offshore boundary (Khawr Abd Allah) was not specifically mentioned in the 1932 Exchange of Letters referred to in the Agreed Minutes; hence, the Commission lacked an agreed delimitation on which to base a demarcation of that section. He described a situation that made it impossible for him to continue in office unless certain modifications were made to the Commission's mandate, which the Legal Counsel explained was out of the question.

Iraq asserted that the eighth session (Geneva, 14-16 December 1992), held under the newly appointed Chairman, Nicolas Valticos (Greece), hastily decided that the basic principle governing the demarcation of the offshore boundary must be the median line, it being understood that the purpose of the adjustment was to facilitate navigational access for both parties.

Iraq further asserted that the improper intervention and influence on the Commission's work gave rise to a number of legal questions: the description of the boundary endorsed by the Council for demarcation under resolution 687(1991) in no way touched on a description of the boundary in the Khawr Abd Allah and, since demarcation must be based on a delimitation (description) of the boundary agreed upon by the parties, the Commission had no basis for its demarcation of the Khawr Abd Allah; according to the boundary description in resolution 687(1991), the Khawr Abd Allah was not assigned the characteristic of territorial sea to justify its division between States with opposite or adjacent coasts according to sea law principles; the Khawr Abd Allah, even supposing it were a territorial sea, was correctly described as subject to "special circumstances" by two of the independent experts, which, under article 15 of the 1982 United Nations Convention on the Law of the Sea,[23] permitted delimitation of the boundary of the territorial sea to be made by a method other than the principle of the median line, failing agreement between the two parties on another principle and, since the delimitation of the boundary in this area was being effected for the first time, the "special circumstances" principle applied; since Iraq contended that it had historic rights in the Khawr Abd Allah area in which Kuwait carried no substantial navigation, according to the 1982 Convention on the Law of the Sea, the area was exempt from the median line rule; the Security Council had no right, pursuant to its functions and powers under the Charter, to impose a boundary delimitation on a Member State because, under international law, that sphere of competence was governed by the principle of agreement between the States concerned and, with the precision legally required, had no relation to questions of the maintenance of international peace and security that were the Council's sphere of competence; the Council had thus acted *ultra vires*.

Iraq stated that the imposition of the boundary in the Khawr Abd Allah area by the Demarcation Commission, on the basis of a purely political decision, presented a grave threat to Iraq's right to enjoy freedom of access to the sea by exercising its historic right to unrestricted and safe naviga- tion in the Khawr Abd Allah, to an extent that would place it in a position of a land-locked State.

Kuwait, in a detailed response of 21 July[24] to Iraq's arguments, drew attention to, among other things, paragraph 97 of the Demarcation Commission's Final Report guaranteeing the right to safe and unrestricted navigation in the offshore area for both Kuwait and Iraq. The paragraph stated in part that navigational access was possible for both States through the Khawr Zhobeir, the Khawr Shetana and the Khawr Abd Allah to and from all their own respective waters and territories bordering their boundary; that the right of navigation and access was provided for under the rules of international law as embodied in the 1982 Convention on the Law of the Sea; and that it was the Commission's view that the right of access implied a non-suspensible right of navigation for both States.

SECURITY COUNCIL ACTION

In the light of Iraq's comments on the Iraq-Kuwait international boundary as demarcated, the Security Council met on 28 June, and, after consultations among its members, authorized its President to make the following statement[25] on behalf of the Council:

Meeting number. SC 3246.

"The Security Council has noted with particular concern the letter of 6 June 1993 from the Minister for Foreign Affairs of the Republic of Iraq to the Secretary-General concerning resolution 833(1993).

"The Council recalls in this connection that the Iraq-Kuwait Boundary Demarcation Commission did not reallocate territory between Kuwait and Iraq, but simply carried out the technical task necessary to demarcate the precise coordinates for the first time, on the basis of 'The Agreed Minutes between the State of Kuwait and the Republic of Iraq regarding the Restoration of Friendly Relations, Recognition and Related Matters' signed by them on 4 October 1963, which were registered with the United Nations. The Council reminds Iraq that the Boundary Demarcation Commission acted on the basis of resolution 687(1991) and the Secretary-General's report on implementing paragraph 3 of that resolution, both of which were formally accepted by Iraq. In its resolution 833(1993), the Council reaffirmed that the decisions of the Commission were final, and demanded that Iraq and Kuwait respect the inviolability of the international boundary as demarcated by the Commission and the right to navigational access.

"The Council also reminds Iraq of its acceptance of resolution 687(1991) of the Council, which forms the basis for the cease-fire. The Council wishes to stress to Iraq the inviolability of the international boundary between Iraq and Kuwait, demarcated by the Commission and guaranteed by the Council pursuant to resolutions 687(1991), 773(1992) and 833(1993), and the serious consequences that would ensue from any breach thereof."

UN Iraq-Kuwait Observation Mission

The United Nations Iraq-Kuwait Observation Mission, established by the Security Council in 1991,[26] was mandated to monitor the Khawr Abd Allah waterway and the DMZ established by the Council along the boundary between Iraq and Kuwait, to deter DMZ violations through surveillance and to observe any hostile or potentially hostile action mounted from the territory of one State into the other. On 5 February 1993, the Council decided to extend the terms of reference of UNIKOM to include the capacity to take physical action to prevent or redress violations of the DMZ or of the Iraq-Kuwait boundary by civilians or police and to deal with problems that might arise from the presence of Iraqi installations, citizens and their assets in the DMZ on the Kuwaiti side of the newly demarcated Iraq-Kuwait international boundary.

The DMZ was described as measuring 200 kilometres long, to which the 40-kilometre-long Khawr Abd Allah waterway had to be added; it was mostly barren and uninhabited, except for the towns of Umm Qasr and Safwan, where there were airfields, as well as a port at Umm Qasr. The boundaries of the DMZ, which extended 10 kilometres into Iraq and five kilometres into Kuwait, had been realigned with the newly demarcated international boundary and marked at one-kilometre (1,000-metre) intervals and at major entry points; in addition, a road had been constructed along the entire length of the land portion of the boundary. As of 31 March, the DMZ was clearly identifiable on both sides.

UNIKOM maintained the DMZ in three operational sectors—northern, central and southern—with a headquarters in each. At the end of February, the emplacement of the 18 patrol/observation bases, six in each sector, was adjusted to strengthen the northern sector so that seven were placed there and six and five in the central and southern sectors respectively. UNIKOM's concept of operations was based on a combination of patrol/observation bases, observation points, ground and air patrols, investigation teams and liaison with Iraqi and Kuwaiti authorities at all levels. It employed surveillance aids, including maritime radar for the Khawr Abd Allah, night vision devices, high-powered binoculars and video cameras, as well as the Global Positioning System for the accurate determination of locations in the terrain.

In addition to its mandate, UNIKOM provided technical support to other United Nations missions in Iraq and Kuwait, in particular, air and ground transport, accommodation, communications and engineering support, on at-cost basis, to the Demarcation Commission; and escorts and accommodation to the United Nations Coordinator for the Return of Property from Iraq to Kuwait.

It continued to provide movement control in respect of all United Nations aircraft operating in the area.

UNIKOM maintained liaison offices at Baghdad and Kuwait City, and its Chief Military Observer and other senior staff remained in regular contact with the police of both sides. Iraq and Kuwait had each set up a liaison office in the DMZ; their Governments extended the cooperation necessary for UNIKOM to carry out its mandate.

On the Secretary-General's recommendation, the Council extended UNIKOM twice in 1993, each for a six-month period: the first time from 9 April until 8 October 1993 and the second from 9 October 1993 to 8 April 1994.

Special report of the Secretary-General (10 January). In a special report,[27] the Secretary-General drew to the Security Council's attention a number of serious developments casting doubt on Iraq's continued willingness to cooperate with UNIKOM and to abide by the commitments it had undertaken in this respect.

The developments concerned the former Iraqi naval base at Umm Qasr, comprising six ammunition bunkers and prefabricated buildings, including 19 such buildings in part of the base called Camp Khor, which Iraq had made available to UNIKOM and on which UNIKOM had put up additional prefabricated units. The Demarcation Commission had subsequently determined the naval base to be on Kuwaiti territory. UNIKOM informed the Iraqi authorities of this fact on 24 December 1992, stating that retrieval of Iraqi-owned items on the Kuwaiti side of the newly demarcated boundary would have to cease. Until then, that activity, which began in 1991 once Iraqi ownership had been established, had been allowed under close UNIKOM monitoring.

In accordance with procedures established by the Council and conveyed to the Chief Military Observer of UNIKOM, the contents of the bunkers were to be destroyed by UNIKOM or by a specialized firm under its supervision (letter of 3 November 1992) and removal of Iraqi property and assets was to be undertaken only with UNIKOM prior clearance, or by the Kuwaiti authorities through UNIKOM, and should be completed by 15 January 1993 (letter of 8 January).

On 2 January, however, unauthorized retrieval was conducted by some 250 Iraqis. This was repeated on 10 January, when some 200 Iraqis with trucks and heavy loading equipment forced entry into Umm Qasr, and, despite preventive steps taken by UNIKOM, succeeded in taking away most of the contents of the ammunition bunkers, including HY-2G anti-ship missiles. On the same date, up to 500 Iraqi personnel proceeded to dismantle the prefabricated buildings. Meanwhile, the Chief Military Observer was informed by the

Chairman of Iraq's Higher Committee for Coordination, responsible for liaison with UNIKOM, that on 11 January the dismantling operation would be extended to include the units housing UNIKOM and suggested evacuation of those premises. The Secretary-General recalled that, by an exchange of letters dated 15 April and 21 June 1992, the Government of Iraq had agreed that the land and premises made available to UNIKOM were inviolate and subject to the exclusive control and authority of the United Nations.

Annexed to the report were two Council letters establishing the procedures regarding the removal of Iraqi property, as well as a December 1992 letter from the Secretary-General to the Council President, drawing attention to some issues that had arisen as demarcation of the international boundary between Iraq and Kuwait neared completion. They concerned six Iraqi police posts, part of the Iraqi town of Umm Qasr, several Iraqi farms along the eastern part of the boundary and some well heads of the Ratqah oil field—all of which had been shown to be on Kuwaiti territory.

The Secretary-General's letter also referred to the three Iraqi and two Kuwaiti police posts that were closer to the boundary than the minimum of 1,000 metres from either side of it, which UNIKOM, with the concurrence of the two Governments, had established as a reasonable distance to prevent incidents. The Secretary-General stated that he had instructed UNIKOM to arrange with both parties for the removal of the police posts to the agreed distance, recalling in this connection Iraq's repeated assurance to abide by the Demarcation Commission's decision. He emphasized that the issue of the Iraqi citizens and their assets remaining on Kuwaiti territory was potentially volatile and apt to give rise to increased tension and that he was in touch with the parties in order to promote an early settlement.

In a 19 January addendum to his report,[28] the Secretary-General stated that, on 17 January, Iraq had withdrawn, under UNIKOM supervision, the six police posts located on Kuwaiti territory. As of midday on 13 January, the retrieval of Iraqi assets from Kuwaiti territory had ceased. As to the Iraqi and Kuwaiti posts that were nearer to the boundary than the agreed 1,000-metre distance from it, the Secretary-General stated that, through an oversight, two other Iraqi police posts set up in the central sector in early December 1992 were not included in the count; in Umm Qasr, where the boundary ran through a built-up area, three police checkpoints and a border post were also within the 1,000-metre range.

SECURITY COUNCIL ACTION

The Security Council met on 11 January and, after consultations among its members, authorized its President to make the following statement[29] on behalf of the Council:

Meeting number. SC 3162.

"The Security Council notes that there have been a number of recent actions by Iraq as part of its pattern of flouting relevant Security Council resolutions. One was the series of border incidents involving the United Nations Iraq-Kuwait Observation Mission (UNIKOM); another was the incident concerning the United Nations Special Commission (UNSCOM) and UNIKOM flights.

"The Security Council is deeply concerned at the incidents reported in the Secretary-General's special report of 10 January 1993 on UNIKOM. The Security Council recalls the provisions of resolution 687(1991) that established the Demilitarized Zone between Iraq and Kuwait and demanded that both countries respect the inviolability of the international boundary between them. It reaffirms that the boundary was at the very core of the conflict and that, in resolutions 687(1991) and 773(1991), it guaranteed the inviolability of the boundary and undertook to take, as appropriate, all necessary measures to that end in accordance with the Charter of the United Nations.

"The Council condemns the action taken by Iraq on 10 January 1993 to remove equipment by force from the Kuwaiti side of the demilitarized zone without prior consultation with UNIKOM, and through UNIKOM with the Kuwaiti authorities, as set out in the letter of 8 January 1993 from the President of the Security Council to the Secretary-General. In particular, the Council draws attention to the removal by Iraq of four HY-2G anti-ship missiles and other military equipment from the six bunkers in the former Iraqi naval base at Umm Qasr on Kuwaiti territory, in spite of the objections of UNIKOM and their efforts to prevent this. This action is a direct challenge to the authority of UNIKOM and amounts to clear-cut defiance by Iraq of the Council, which stipulated in the letter of 3 November 1992 from the President of the Council to the Secretary-General that the military equipment in the six bunkers should be destroyed by or under the supervision of UNIKOM. The Council demands that the anti-ship missiles and other military equipment removed by force from the six bunkers at Umm Qasr in Kuwaiti territory be returned immediately to the custody of UNIKOM for destruction, as previously decided.

"The Council also condemns further Iraqi intrusions into the Kuwaiti side of the demilitarized zone on 11 January 1993. It demands that any future retrieval mission be in accordance with the terms set out in the letter of 8 January 1993 from the President of the Council to the Secretary-General. On the UNIKOM facilities at Camp Khor, the Council stresses that the land and premises occupied by UNIKOM shall be inviolate and subject to the exclusive control and authority of the United Nations.

"The Council invites the Secretary-General, as a first step, to explore on an urgent basis the possibilities for restoring UNIKOM to its full strength and to consider in an emergency such as this the need for rapid reinforcement as set out in paragraph 18 of his report of 12 June 1991, as well as other suggestions that he might have to enhance the effectiveness of UNIKOM, and to report back to the Council.

"The Council is also alarmed by Iraq's refusal to allow the United Nations to transport its UNSCOM and UNIKOM personnel into Iraqi territory using its own aircraft. In this connection the Council reiterates the demand in its statement of 8 January 1993 that Iraq permit UNSCOM and UNIKOM to use their own aircraft to transport their personnel into Iraq. It rejects the arguments contained in the letter of 9 January 1993 from the Minister of Foreign Affairs of Iraq to the President of the Security Council.

"These latest developments concerning the activities of UNIKOM and UNSCOM constitute further material breaches of resolution 687(1991), which established the cease-fire and provided the conditions essential for the restoration of peace and security in the region, as well as other relevant resolutions and agreements. The Council demands that Iraq cooperate fully with UNIKOM, UNSCOM and other United Nations agencies in carrying out their mandates, and again warns Iraq of the serious consequences that will flow from such continued defiance. The Council will remain actively seized of the matter."

On 12 January,[30] Iraq reasoned that there could be no disputing the fact that the items retrieved from Umm Qasr belonged to it, that the retrieval was carried out in a peaceful and orderly manner and that the property did not include any item prohibited under resolution 687(1991). The clamour surrounding the matter had been contrived and the situation systematically escalated by the United States and its allies; and fragmentary and alarming information had been provided to the Council with the objective of depicting Iraq's position as one of flouting Council resolutions and defying the Council.

Special report of the Secretary-General (18 January). Responding to the Security Council's invitation to consider the need for rapid reinforcement of UNIKOM units in view of the January incidents, the Secretary-General, in a further special report,[31] observed that, in the circumstances, UNIKOM had performed the functions for which it was designed and for which its strength was sufficient. It had closely monitored the incidents, kept United Nations Headquarters informed and made immediate representations to the Iraqi personnel on the spot and to the Iraqi military authorities through the established liaison channel. For the most part, the representations with the Iraqis proved ineffective because UNIKOM's interlocutors stated that they were powerless to influence a course of events set in motion at the highest levels of the Iraqi Government. Similarly, representations to the United Nations remained without a positive response until the Security Council intervened and Member States threatened other measures, at which point the Council was informed that Iraq would suspend its unauthorized retrieval of property.

However, should the Council decide that UNIKOM's current mandate did not permit an adequate response to such violations as had occurred and that UNIKOM should be able to prevent and redress them, then it would require a capacity to take such physical action. Such action could be taken to prevent or, if that failed, redress small-scale violations of the DMZ, violations of the Iraq-Kuwait boundary by either civilians or police, and problems that might arise from the presence of Iraqi installations and Iraqi citizens and their assets in the DMZ on the Kuwaiti side of the newly demarcated boundary.

The Secretary-General estimated that three mechanized infantry battalions would be required to perform those functions. In addition, UNIKOM's airlift capability would need to be augmented to enable it to lift one company in one wave for rapid reaction. The total additional military support needed to enable UNIKOM to carry out its new mandate would comprise the following elements: 225 Headquarters and communications personnel; 2,250 infantry personnel; 750 logistics personnel; 200 engineers; 100 medical personnel and 120 personnel for the 20 helicopters that would also be required.

If the Council required UNIKOM also to prevent violations of the maritime boundary, it would additionally need naval assets, with the necessary docking facilities, to enable it to patrol the Khawr Abd Allah and intercept any violating vessels.

The current tasks of the unarmed military observers would be assigned to the infantry, which would be deployed at the existing patrol and observation bases and which would patrol the DMZ. The units would need to include a sufficient number of officers to carry out liaison, investigations and other special tasks. As in the past, the Governments of Iraq and Kuwait would be expected to consult with UNIKOM on the regulation of their activities within the DMZ. This would be of particular importance with regard to the maintenance of law and order, as UNIKOM would become an armed force with a mandate in some respects overlapping that of the local police.

UNIKOM would be provided with the weapons integral to its infantry battalions, to be used only in self-defence, which would include resistance to attempts by forceful means to prevent UNIKOM from discharging its mandated duties. UNIKOM would thus not be authorized to initiate enforcement action. It would need to retain the freedom of movement and the privileges and immunities it currently enjoyed; the arrangements governing its presence in Iraq and Kuwait should continue to apply *mutatis mutandis*.

The Secretary-General emphasized that the above arrangements were based on the assumption that the two Governments would cooperate with the restructured Mission. Without that cooperation, it would be impossible for UNIKOM to carry out its functions, in which case the Council would need to consider alternative measures. He further emphasized that, as restructured, UNIKOM would not have the capacity to prevent a significant military incursion. Should the Council consider that such risk existed, it would be necessary to make other arrangements for dealing with it, while at the same time ensuring the safety of UNIKOM.

In a 26 January addendum,[32] the Secretary-General estimated that the costs associated with strengthening UNIKOM would amount to some $112 million for the first six-month period, with an estimated additional monthly cost thereafter of approximately $12 million. A breakdown of the first figure by main categories of expenditure was annexed to the addendum. He recommended that the costs should be considered an expense of the Organization to be borne by Member States with the corresponding assessments to be levied on Member States to be credited to the UNIKOM special account.

SECURITY COUNCIL ACTION

On 5 February, the Security Council unanimously adopted **resolution 806(1993)**.

The Security Council,

Reaffirming its resolution 687(1991) of 3 April 1991, and in particular paragraphs 2, 3, 4 and 5 thereof, and its resolutions 689(1991) of 9 April 1991 and 773(1992) of 26 August 1992, and its other resolutions on this matter,

Having considered the report of the Secretary-General of 18 January 1993,

Noting with approval that work is being completed on the realignment of the demilitarized zone referred to in paragraph 5 of resolution 687(1991) to correspond to the international boundary demarcated by the United Nations Iraq-Kuwait Boundary Demarcation Commission,

Deeply concerned at recent actions by Iraq in violation of relevant Security Council resolutions, including the series of border incidents involving the United Nations Iraq-Kuwait Observation Mission (UNIKOM),

Recalling the statements made by the President on behalf of the Council on 8 January 1993 and on 11 January 1993,

Acting under Chapter VII of the Charter of the United Nations,

1. *Underlines once again* its guarantee of the inviolability of the international boundary between the State of Kuwait and the Republic of Iraq and its decision to take as appropriate all necessary measures to that end in accordance with the Charter, as provided for in paragraph 4 of resolution 687(1991);

2. *Approves* the report, and decides to extend the terms of reference of UNIKOM to include the functions contained in paragraph 5 of the report;

3. *Requests* the Secretary-General to plan and execute a phased deployment of the strengthening of UNIKOM taking into account the need for economy and other relevant factors and to report to the Council on

any step he intends to take following an initial deployment;

4. *Reaffirms* that the question of termination or continuation of UNIKOM and the modalities of UNIKOM will continue to be reviewed every six months pursuant to paragraphs 2 and 3 of resolution 689(1991), the next review to take place in April 1993;

5. *Decides* to remain seized of the matter.

Security Council resolution 806(1993)
5 February 1993   Meeting 3171   Adopted unanimously
Draft prepared in consultations among Council members (S/25244).

The Secretary-General, on 15 October,[33] notified the Council that, despite considerable effort, it had not been possible to identify a Member State able to provide a suitably equipped mechanized infantry battalion for the initial phasing in of three such battalions to reinforce UNIKOM. However, he proposed to accept the offer of Bangladesh to provide an infantry battalion, for which Kuwait had agreed to make available the necessary equipment and to build two camps to accommodate the battalion; he would expedite the battalion's deployment as soon as possible. The Council agreed to that proposal on 22 October.[34]

Reports of the Secretary-General (April and October). The Secretary-General submitted to the Security Council two reports, dated 2 April[35] and 1 October,[36] on the activities of UNIKOM in connection with the six-month review of its mandate. The first report covered the period 1 October 1992 to 31 March 1993 and the second, 1 April to 30 September 1993.

By 31 March, the engineering unit had disposed of 10,000 pieces of ordnance, constructed 3,000 metres of security fencing around UNIKOM headquarters and Camp Khor, built two new airstrips and maintained 1,500 kilometres of existing patrol routes. It assisted the Demarcation Commission by clearing or building access roads to 106 border-pillar sites along the DMZ and in transporting and emplacing the pillars. The unit also cleared and levelled three square kilometres of camp-site for the infantry battalions that were to reinforce UNIKOM and erected durable observation towers at all patrol/observation bases. The logistics unit continued to carry out vehicle maintenance, supply distribution and security-related tasks mainly for the headquarters facilities in the northern sector (Umm Qasr) and its extension, Camp Khor, and for the Doha logistic base. The medical unit, in addition to maintaining a sickbay facility at Umm Qasr in the northern sector and first-aid stations at the two other sectors, also provided emergency care to civilians injured in the DMZ, mostly by exploding ordnance.

Iran and Kuwait continued clearing their respective sides of the DMZ of unexploded ordnance and debris left over from the 1991 military action against Iraq, with which the Iraqi side particularly was littered.

In May, Kuwait informed the Secretary-General that it would set up a border security system, comprising a trench, an earthen embankment and a patrol road along the entire length of the land portion of the demarcated boundary between Kuwait and Iraq. The project began in June and was nearly completed in the southern and central sectors by the end of September. Four crossing points were constructed for UNIKOM use, one in each sector and a fourth on the main road at Safwan. This arrangement would be reviewed periodically in the light of UNIKOM's operational requirements.

Apart from the incidents described by the Secretary-General in his special report of 10 January,[27] UNIKOM observed three types of DMZ violations: minor incursions, often inadvertent, by military personnel on the ground; overflights by military aircraft, mostly unidentified; and violations involving the carrying and firing of weapons other than side-arms, committed mainly by policemen. There were 23 such violations by Iraq, 72 by Kuwait, 11 by Member States cooperating with Kuwait and 47 by unidentified parties.

By the end of September, UNIKOM had received 35 written complaints from Iraq and 46 from Kuwait, many of them alleging firings at police posts close to the boundary and airspace violations. Investigations into these complaints revealed the presence of rifles and machine-guns at the posts, in violation of the neutrality of the DMZ.

As at 31 March, there were 13 Iraqi facilities of various kinds (customs posts, police posts and control points) and two Kuwaiti police posts closer to the border than 1,000 metres. Seven of the Iraqi posts were in Safwan and Umm Qasr, which extended right up to the border and where a presence was required to maintain law and order and to control border crossings. The Chief Military Observer was in touch with the authorities concerned in order to reduce such presence in the 1,000-metre zone to the absolute minimum necessary to perform these functions.

As to issues that had arisen with respect to areas determined by the demarcation process to be on Kuwaiti territory and on which Iraqi citizens lived and Iraqi assets were located, including oil well heads at Ratqah and farms at Safwan, Kuwait had indicated that the Iraqis could not remain in those areas and had offered to compensate them for their private properties and assets. At the request of Kuwait, an assessment of those properties was being made by a neutral party designated by the Secretary-General on which to base appropriate compensation. Iraq stated that, while it rejected the principle of relocation and compensation, it would take no action that might provoke dispute or contention with the United Nations.

In his April report,[35] the Secretary-General observed that the events in January had demonstrated the importance of the United Nations presence at the Iraq-Kuwait border; he thus recommended that UNIKOM be maintained for a further six months until 30 September 1993, with which the Security Council concurred on 13 April.[36] In his October report,[37] he recommended extending UNIKOM until 8 April 1994, with which the Council likewise concurred, on 11 October.[38]

Communications. Subsequent to his October report on UNIKOM activities, the Secretary-General received several letters alleging violations in the DMZ.

Iraq wrote on 15 November[39] of intermittent firings from the Kuwaiti side in the direction of nearby Iraqi farms (26 September) and of 20 rounds fired at an Iraqi guard post (18 October).

Kuwait, on 16 November,[40] drew attention to orchestrated acts of provocation and incitement against its territorial integrity, including: a reported meeting on that date between Iraq's Minister of Agriculture and the Iraqi farmers on Kuwaiti territory, urging them to remain on their farms; a crowd of some 250 Iraqis in 60 vehicles converged at pillar 95 waving Iraqi flags, taunting and throwing stones at Kuwaiti workers engaged in building a trench; some Iraqis actually entered Kuwaiti territory in an attempt to level the trench and hoist Iraqi flags, bringing the construction to a halt.

On 22 November,[41] Kuwait reported a similar incident two days earlier: some 400 Iraqis in buses and jeeps converged on pillars 103 and 104, surrounding Kuwaiti workers; they retreated into Iraq only when a Kuwaiti policeman fired shots into the air. Also on 22 November,[42] Kuwait reported that two UNIKOM officers on patrol were intercepted 400 metres south of boundary pillar 95 by three Iraqis brandishing AK-47s. The officers were forced out of their vehicle and searched, after which the armed Iraqis hijacked the vehicle into Iraq. The officers were assisted at the Kuwaiti post at Al Mazari'.

SECURITY COUNCIL ACTION

In the light of the foregoing communications, the Security Council met on 23 November and, after consultations among its members, authorized its President to issue the following statement[43] on behalf of the Council:

Meeting number. SC 3319.

"The Security Council is seriously concerned about recent violations of the Iraq-Kuwait boundary as reported by the United Nations Iraq-Kuwait Observation Mission (UNIKOM), most notably those on 16 and 20 November 1993, when large numbers of Iraqi nationals crossed the boundary illegally. The Council holds the Government of Iraq responsible for these breaches of paragraph 2 of resolution 687(1991).

"The Security Council reminds Iraq of its obligations under resolution 687(1991), the acceptance of which forms the basis of the cease-fire, and under other relevant resolutions of the Council, including most recently resolution 833(1993).

"The Security Council demands that Iraq, in accordance with international law and relevant Security Council resolutions, respect the inviolability of the international boundary, and take all necessary measures to prevent any violations of that boundary."

Composition

UNIKOM continued under the command of Major-General T. K. Dibuama (Ghana), Chief Military Observer, until 20 August 1993; thereafter, Brigadier-General Vigar Aabrek (Norway) served as Acting Chief Military Observer. On 1 December, Major-General Krishna Narayan Singh Thapa (Nepal) assumed his functions as Chief Military Observer. His appointment had been proposed by the Secretary-General on 9 November[44] and agreed to by the Security Council on 12 November.[45]

As at September 1993, UNIKOM had a strength of 367 military personnel, all ranks,[36] of which 252 were military observers from 33 Member States and 115 were personnel in the engineering (50), logistics (45) and medical (20) units, provided by Argentina, Denmark and Norway, respectively. Of the 300 military observers authorized, 48 were on stand-by in their countries. UNIKOM strength had increased by 55 since March.

The civilian staff had been reduced from 188 in March to 185, of whom 79 were recruited internationally and 106 locally.

In addition to two small fixed-wing civilian aircraft contributed by Switzerland at no cost to the Organization and three chartered helicopters, UNIKOM had the use of a chartered aircraft for personnel and equipment transport between Baghdad and Kuwait City.

Pursuant to the expanded terms of reference of UNIKOM, calling for its reinforcement with three mechanized infantry battalions that were to be phased in, the military observers were to be retained during the first phase and reinforced with one mechanized battalion to be deployed in the northern sector, where Umm Qasr and Safwan were located. The Secretary-General's June report on UNIKOM financing (see below) reflected cost estimates for such a battalion, comprising 775 troops all ranks, plus 7 military observers and 15 medical and 5 logistics personnel. The battalion's deployment could not be envisaged before mid-September 1993.

Financing

Report of the Secretary-General (June). The Secretary-General's June report on the financing of UNIKOM[46] noted that, as at 24 May 1993, assessments totalling $159,592,821 had been apportioned among Member States in respect of UNIKOM from its inception on 9 April 1991 to 31 October 1993; contributions received for the same period amounted to $126,524,723, resulting in a shortfall of $33,068,098.

Voluntary contributions received between 21 November 1992 and 30 April 1993 for which no budgetary provision was made consisted of: the rental of four road graders, two bulldozers, two excavators and four tractors provided by Kuwait, which had yet to communicate their value to the Secretariat; and the service of two fixed-wing aircraft with crew, provided by Switzerland, valued at approximately $794,702 (SwF 1.2 million).

Resources made available to UNIKOM between 9 April 1991 and 31 October 1993 totalled $162,877,000 gross ($158,139,600 net), consisting of appropriations totalling $143,077,000 and a commitment authorization of $19,800,000. Estimated expenditures for the same period amounted to $151,572,633 gross ($147,827,860 net), resulting in an unencumbered balance of $11,304,367 gross ($10,311,740 net); interest and miscellaneous income totalled $631,929 and $1,685,902, respectively. The report noted that between 9 October 1991 and 31 December 1992, UNIKOM expenditures attributable to the Demarcation Commission amounted to $1,214,476 and were credited to the UNIKOM Special Account as miscellaneous income.

Due to the shortfall in payment of assessed contributions, $5 million had been borrowed from the Peace-keeping Reserve Fund to meet cash-flow requirements.

On 8 April, the Secretary-General requested authorization to enter into commitments for maintaining UNIKOM for the six-month period from 1 May to 31 October 1993 in the amount of $29,800,000 gross ($28,600,000 net)—composed of $19,800,000 gross ($18,600,000 net) as authorized by the General Assembly in 1992[47] for the same period and $10 million in accordance with the 1991 Assembly resolution on unforeseen and extraordinary expenses for the 1992-1993 biennium.[48] ACABQ's concurrence, conveyed on 14 April, was for $23,800,000 gross ($22,600,000 net), after having reduced the second component from $10 million to $4 million. The costs related to the strengthening of UNIKOM for the same six-month period were estimated at $24,616,100 gross ($24,505,700 net). Thus, the consolidated cost of maintaining UNIKOM for the period would be $44,416,100 gross ($43,105,700 net).

The Secretary-General estimated the cost of maintaining UNIKOM for the 12-month period from 1 November 1993 to 31 October 1994 at $6,250,825 gross ($6,064,700 net) per month. Should the Security Council decide to extend

UNIKOM beyond the expiration of its mandate on 31 October 1993, the Secretary-General requested the Assembly to make appropriate provision for UNIKOM expenses for the period beyond that date.

In sum, actions to be taken by the Assembly for UNIKOM financing were: for the period 1 May to 31 October 1993, the appropriation *(a)* of $19,800,000 gross ($18,600,000 net) for maintenance authorized with ACABQ concurrence and *(b)* of $24,616,100 gross ($24,505,700 net) and apportionment thereof for the enlargement of UNIKOM, inclusive of the $4 million authorized by ACABQ; *(c)* provision by means of appropriation and/or commitment authorization, based on the estimate of $6,250,825 gross ($6,064,700 net) a month, should the Council decide to continue UNIKOM beyond 31 October 1993; *(d)* a decision to retain the unencumbered balance of appropriations in the UNIKOM Special Account in the light of the outstanding assessed contributions; and *(e)* a decision to apply to UNIKOM the standing decision contained in the annex to a 1991 Assembly resolution,[(49)] whereby appropriations required in respect of obligations owed to Governments providing contingents and/or logistic support should be retained beyond the period stipulated under regulations 4.3 and 4.4 of the Financial Regulations and Rules of the United Nations.

ACABQ[(50)] recommended approval of the appropriation requested in *(a)*. In view of its observations and the uncertainty of the deployment date of the mechanized battalion, it recommended that the appropriation requested in *(b)* should not exceed $20 million gross. The total appropriation and apportionment for the period 1 May to 31 October 1993 should, therefore, not exceed $39.8 million gross. As to *(c)*, the Secretary-General was requested to submit a brief report to the Assembly outlining the projected requirements for the period beyond 31 October 1993 and requesting the necessary appropriation. ACABQ recommended acceptance of the requests in *(d)* and *(e)*.

GENERAL ASSEMBLY ACTION

On the recommendation of the Fifth Committee, the General Assembly, on 14 September, adopted **resolution 47/208 B** without vote.

Financing of the United Nations Iraq-Kuwait Observation Mission

The General Assembly,

Having considered the report of the Secretary-General on the financing of the United Nations Iraq-Kuwait Observation Mission and the related report of the Advisory Committee on Administrative and Budgetary Questions,

Bearing in mind Security Council resolutions 687(1991) of 3 April 1991 and 689(1991) of 9 April 1991, by which the Council decided to set up the United Nations Iraq-

Kuwait Observation Mission and to review the question of its termination or continuation every six months,

Recalling its resolution 45/260 of 3 May 1991 on the financing of the Observation Mission and its subsequent resolutions thereon, the latest of which was resolution 47/208 A of 22 December 1992,

Reaffirming that the costs of the Observation Mission are expenses of the Organization to be borne by Member States in accordance with Article 17, paragraph 2, of the Charter of the United Nations,

Recalling its previous decision regarding the fact that, in order to meet the expenditures caused by the Observation Mission, a different procedure is required from the one applied to meet expenditures of the regular budget of the United Nations,

Taking into account the fact that the economically more developed countries are in a position to make relatively larger contributions and that the economically less developed countries have a relatively limited capacity to contribute towards such an operation,

Bearing in mind the special responsibilities of the States permanent members of the Security Council, as indicated in General Assembly resolution 1874(S-IV) of 27 June 1963, in the financing of such operations,

Noting with appreciation that voluntary contributions have been made to the Observation Mission by certain Governments,

Mindful of the fact that it is essential to provide the Observation Mission with the necessary financial resources to enable it to fulfil its responsibilities under the relevant resolutions of the Security Council,

Expressing concern about the deteriorating financial situation with regard to peace-keeping activities owing to overdue payment by Member States of their assessments, particularly Member States in arrears,

Also expressing concern about the delays in submission of budget documents until well into the financial period of the Observation Mission, which have contributed to the deteriorating financial situation,

Expressing deep concern about the adverse effect that the deteriorating financial situation has on reimbursement to troop contributors, placing an additional burden on these countries and putting at risk the continuing supply of troops to the Observation Mission and, consequently, the success of the operation,

1. *Endorses* the observations and recommendations contained in the report of the Advisory Committee on Administrative and Budgetary Questions and approves on an exceptional basis the special arrangements for the United Nations Iraq-Kuwait Observation Mission with regard to the application of article IV of the Financial Regulations of the United Nations, whereby appropriations required in respect of obligations owed to Governments providing contingents and/or logistic support to the Observation Mission shall be retained beyond the period stipulated under financial regulations 4.3 and 4.4, as set out in the annex to the present resolution;

2. *Requests* the Secretary-General to take all necessary action to ensure that the Observation Mission is administered with a maximum of efficiency and economy, to improve management, and to include in his report on this item to the General Assembly information on the steps taken to improve management;

3. *Urges* all Member States to make every possible effort to ensure payment of their assessed contributions to the Observation Mission promptly and in full;

4. *Decides* to appropriate to the Special Account referred to in General Assembly resolution 45/260 the amount of 19.8 million United States dollars gross (18.6 million dollars net) authorized and apportioned with the prior concurrence of the Advisory Committee under the terms of paragraph 8 of Assembly resolution 47/208 A, for the operation of the Observation Mission for the period from 1 May to 31 October 1993;

5. *Decides also* to appropriate to the Special Account the amount of 20 million dollars gross (19,889,600 dollars net), inclusive of the amount of 4 million dollars authorized with the prior concurrence of the Advisory Committee under the terms of paragraph 1 of General Assembly resolution 46/187 of 20 December 1991, for the strengthening of the Observation Mission for the period from 1 May to 31 October 1993, inclusive;

6. *Decides further*, as an ad hoc arrangement, to apportion the amount of 20 million dollars gross (19,889,600 dollars net) for the above-mentioned period among Member States in accordance with the composition of groups set out in paragraphs 3 and 4 of General Assembly resolution 43/232 of 1 March 1989, as adjusted by the Assembly in its resolutions 44/192 B of 21 December 1989, 45/260 of 3 May 1991, 46/197 of 20 December 1991 and 47/218 A of 23 December 1992, and taking into account the scale of assessments set out in resolution 46/221 A of 20 December 1991 and Assembly decision 47/456 of 23 December 1992;

7. *Decides* that, in accordance with the provisions of its resolution 973(X) of 15 December 1955, there shall be set off against the apportionment among Member States, as provided for in paragraph 6 above, their respective share in the Tax Equalization Fund of the estimated staff assessment income of 110,400 dollars for the period from 1 May to 31 October 1993 approved for the Observation Mission;

8. *Decides also* that there shall be set off against the apportionment among Member States, as provided for in paragraph 6 above, their respective share in the unencumbered balance of 11,304,367 dollars gross (10,311,740 dollars net) for the period from 9 April 1991 to 31 October 1993;

9. *Authorizes* the Secretary-General to enter into commitments for the operation of the Observation Mission at a rate not to exceed 6,250,825 dollars gross (6,064,700 dollars net) per month for the period from 1 November 1993 to 28 February 1994, should the Security Council decide to continue the Mission beyond 31 October 1993, subject to obtaining the prior concurrence of the Advisory Committee for the actual level of commitments to be entered into for the period beyond 31 October 1993, the said amount to be apportioned among Member States in accordance with the scheme set out in the present resolution;

10. *Requests*, in this regard, the Secretary-General to submit to the General Assembly, no later than 8 February 1994, budget proposals, including revised estimates for the period the Security Council might have decided to continue the mandate of the Observation Mission beyond 31 October 1993, as well as budget proposals for the subsequent period of six months;

11. *Decides* to establish the contributions of Andorra, the Czech Republic, Eritrea, the former Yugoslav Republic of Macedonia, Monaco and Slovakia to the Observation Mission in accordance with the rates of assessment to be adopted by the General Assembly for these Member States at its forty-eighth session;

12. *Invites* the new Member States listed in paragraph 11 above to make advance payments against their assessed contributions, to be determined;

13. *Invites* voluntary contributions to the Observation Mission in cash and in the form of services and supplies acceptable to the Secretary-General, to be administered, as appropriate, in accordance with the procedure established by the General Assembly in its resolutions 43/230 of 21 December 1988, 44/192 A of 21 December 1989 and 45/258 of 3 May 1991.

ANNEX
Special arrangements with regard to the application of article IV of the Financial Regulations of the United Nations

1. At the end of the twelve-month period provided for in regulation 4.3, any unliquidated obligations of the financial period in question relating to goods supplied and services rendered by Governments for which claims have been received or which are covered by established reimbursement rates shall be transferred to accounts payable; such accounts payable shall remain recorded in the Special Account until payment is effected.

2. *(a)* Any other unliquidated obligations of the financial period in question owed to Governments for goods supplied and services rendered, as well as other obligations owed to Governments, for which required claims have not yet been received shall remain valid for an additional period of four years following the end of the twelve-month period provided for in regulation 4.3;

(b) Claims received during this four-year period shall be treated as provided under paragraph 1 of the present annex, if appropriate;

(c) At the end of the additional four-year period any unliquidated obligations shall be cancelled and the then remaining balance of any appropriations retained therefor shall be surrendered.

General Assembly resolution 47/208 B

14 September 1993   Meeting 110   Adopted without vote

Approved by Fifth Committee (A/47/823/Add.1) without vote, 3 September (meeting 74); draft by Chairman (A/C.5/47/L.39); agenda item 120 *(a)*.
Meeting numbers. GA 47th session: 5th Committee 68, 69, 72, 74; plenary 110.

Report of the Secretary-General (December). In a 9 December report on the financing of 17 peace-keeping operations including UNIKOM,[51] the Secretary-General estimated the cost of maintaining UNIKOM for the six-month period from 1 November 1993 to 30 April 1994 at $36,128,800 gross ($35,122,200 net), assuming full deployment of UNIKOM's enlarged military component by mid-December 1993. Of that amount, it was estimated that $23,414,800 would be received as a voluntary contribution from Kuwait, thereby leaving an unencumbered balance of $12,714,000 gross.

Since the strengthening of UNIKOM had not been implemented as planned, the amount of $20 million gross ($19,889,600 net) provided for by the Assembly in September remained available; consequently, the Secretary-General did not request additional resources for UNIKOM maintenance through 30 April 1994. He requested, however, authorization to enter into commitments up to the amount of $12,714,000 gross ($11,707,400 net) from the unencumbered balance of appropriations, for the period 1 November 1993 to 30 April 1994, should the Security Council continue UNIKOM beyond 8 April 1994. ACABQ, on 17 December,[52] recommended that the General Assembly grant that request.

GENERAL ASSEMBLY ACTION

In December, the General Assembly adopted **decision 48/466** without vote.

Financing of the United Nations Iraq-Kuwait Observation Mission

At its 87th plenary meeting, on 23 December 1993, the General Assembly, on the recommendation of the Fifth Committee, in accordance with the framework set out in its resolution 48/227 of 23 December 1993, having considered the report of the Secretary-General on the financing of seventeen peace-keeping operations and the related reports of the Advisory Committee on Administrative and Budgetary Questions, and concurring with the observations of the Advisory Committee:

(a) Authorized the Secretary-General, on an exceptional basis, to enter into commitments up to the amount of 8,687,800 United States dollars gross (8 million dollars net), in addition to the pledged voluntary contributions of 23,414,800 dollars for the United Nations Iraq-Kuwait Observation Mission for the period from 1 November 1993 to 28 February 1994;

(b) Decided that the amount of 8,687,800 dollars gross (8 million dollars net) referred to in paragraph *(a)* above shall be offset against the unencumbered balance of appropriations;

(c) Also decided that, in view of the expiration of the commitment authority on 28 February 1994, priority should be given to the cost estimates for the Observation Mission in the consideration by the General Assembly of peace-keeping budgets.

General Assembly decision 48/466

Adopted without vote

Approved by Fifth Committee (A/48/815) without vote, 22 December (meeting 46); draft by Chairman (A/C.5/48/L.18); agenda item 132 *(a)*.
Meeting numbers. GA 48th session: 5th Committee 44, 46; plenary 87.

On-site inspections and ongoing monitoring and verification

IAEA inspections

During 1993, IAEA, with the assistance and cooperation of the United Nations Special Commission (UNSCOM), conducted six on-site nuclear inspections in Iraq—the seventeenth to the twenty-second since it began such inspections in accordance with the relevant provisions of Security Council resolution 687(1991) of April 1991. The sites inspected were either previously or newly designated by the Special Commission and the inspection findings were summarized in reports transmitted to the Council by the Secretary-General.

The seventeenth inspection (25-31 January)[53] conducted: follow-up activities relating to the inventory of material, equipment and machine tools relevant to the revised (1992) annex 3[54] of the 1991 IAEA plan[55] for future ongoing monitoring and verification of Iraq's compliance with relevant paragraphs of resolutions 687(1991) and 707(1991), including a review of the inventory of machine tools under IAEA seal at the Al-Rabiya facility after a cruise missile attack on it; follow-up inspection of nuclear material stored at Tuwaitha, as well as of the Al-Jezira uranium waste pond and the Tarmiya uranium solution tanks; short-notice inspections at selected sites to check seals and verify utilization of key machine tools; and follow-up of the long-promised updated inventory required pursuant to annex 3.

After extensive questioning on the two *Arburg* jet moulding machines for the manufacture of centrifuge motors reported by a Member State to have been exported to Iraq, the Iraqi authorities acknowledged that the machine discovered in the Ash Shaykili warehouse in 1992 had been acquired for the manufacture of centrifuge motor stators, but firmly stood by their assertion that the only existing stator had been "potted" by hand; they denied knowledge of a second *Arburg* machine (which might have been procured for the Iraqi missile programme). The Inspectors reiterated that Iraq must locate and present the remaining mixer-settler units; whereas data supplied by a Member State indicated that 178 units had been exported to Iraq, only 70 had been inventoried.

The Al-Rabiya mechanical workshop facility, in the southern part of Baghdad, was targeted and largely destroyed by a cruise-missile attack on 17 January 1993. Documents removed from Iraq by the sixth (1991) inspection[56] had implicated the facility in the manufacture of EMIS (electromagnetic isotope separation) components. Three subsequent inspections of the site revealed it to be a modern facility with a sizeable machine tool inventory and supporting capabilities in material preparation, chemical cleaning and quality control, but yielded no evidence that the site had been involved in activities related to the nuclear programme code-named "Petrochemical Three" (PC-3), following the 1991 military action against Iraq.[57]

When the fifteenth (1992) inspection[58] revisited Al-Rabiya for the purpose of updating inventories of machine tools and other equipment, it was undergoing further development as an important part of Iraq's plan for reconstruction and industrialization. Its equipment inventory (primarily machine tools) had increased substantially, its workforce had doubled and a new administration and planning building was under construction. During the inspection on 27 January 1993, 10 days after its bombardment, intense round-the-clock rebuilding by thousands of people was in progress in a determined effort to restore the facility's operations. The inspection focused on accounting for the dual-use equipment of the facility's 86-item inventory as updated in 1992 (consisting of 80 items judged to be of general purpose and six of dual use and thus subject to control under annex 3 of the IAEA plan).

The irradiated fuel assemblies stored in the IRT-5000 reactor pool and adjacent storage pond at Al-Tuwaitha were verified by item counting. Seals were checked at Location B, where additional irradiated fuel assemblies were stored, as were seals at Location C, where the bulk of Iraqi uranium stock was stored, and in several Tuwaitha buildings where hot cells were located; all seals were found undisturbed. At the Al-Jezira plant, recovery from the waste retention basin of residual quantities of natural uranium, removal of uranium-bearing organic solutions and filters and entombment of drums of solid waste were awaiting warmer and drier weather for their completion. Iraq restated its intention to turn the site into a centre to develop processes for recovering minerals from indigenous ores and agreed to begin consolidating the storage of reactor components and spare parts in the Ash Shaykili warehouse.

The issue of procurement-related information was again taken up. Iraq's insistence on a consolidated list of outstanding IAEA and UNSCOM questions limited only to resolution 687(1991) was objected to by the Chief Inspector, as experience had shown that such an approach produced little information and generated further questions. At the end of the inspection, Iraq submitted a revised list of items required under annex 3 of the IAEA plan, described as including all existing items or items that were in existence in Iraq as at 1 January 1989 at facilities of the Iraqi Atomic Energy Commission (IAEC) and supporting universities and state establishments.

The eighteenth inspection (3-11 March)[59] covered 35 sites. Those relating to weaponization activities included the Al-Kindi establishment for military research and development, the Al-Qa'Qaa high-explosives plant and the Al-Hatteen State Establishment for the manufacture of military ordnance. The follow-up inspection of the RDX (high quality explosive with multiple applications) stored at Al-Hatteen was extended to include workshops; these were found to contain 242 machine tools, 94 of which (series-3 or -4 CNC turning machines manufactured by Matrix Churchill), in the inspectors' opinion, should have been among the dual-use items recently declared by Iraq under annex 3.

Clarification of inconsistencies between verification findings and Iraq's nuclear materials declaration under annex 3 was further sought, as was

detailed information about Iraq's foreign procurement and procurement network, including the manufacture and supplier of the 350-grade maraging steel. Negotiations for the removal from Iraq of irradiated fuel during the year were pursued.

Information suggesting possible underground nuclear facilities (not only reactors) led to the inspection of: a large dam under construction near Mosul; the nearby Jaber bin Haytham (SAAD-24) complex dedicated to the production of chemical warfare protective gear; and four sites declared by Iraq to have been considered as possible sites for an electrical power–producing reactor. The immediate in-field conclusions were negative. Based on information suggesting the dispersal of parts of the clandestine PC-3 nuclear programme, three facilities, including the College of Science at Saddam University at Baghdad, were inspected for the first time without prior notice. Iraq's first report under annex 2 of the IAEA plan, which remained outstanding at the end of the inspection, was delivered to IAEA on 22 April.

During the nineteenth inspection (30 April–7 May),[60] surface water, sediment and biota samples were collected from 15 locations along the Tigris-Euphrates watershed in fulfilment of the periodic radiometric survey of the main water bodies in Iraq required under the ongoing monitoring effort. A number of establishments were visited for the first time by a nuclear team for the specific purpose of continuing the verification of Iraq's equipment and materials declaration under annex 3; neither undeclared relevant equipment nor proscribed activities were discovered. Over Iraqi objections, 54 Matrix Churchill turning machines (in addition to the 94 discovered at the Al-Hatteen workshops by the previous inspection) were tag-sealed for identification. A technical evaluation of the 148 machines inventoried so far found 144 as not falling within annex 3 specifications; judgement was withheld on the remaining four that had a particular controller and encoder configuration, pending accuracy measurements planned for a future inspection.

The twentieth (25-30 June) and twenty-first (24-27 July) inspections[61] reviewed Iraqi preparations for the safe removal from Iraq of the remaining enriched uranium, in the form of 208 irradiated fuel assemblies from Iraqi research reactors. Civil engineering preparations were well under way and support equipment was being located and collected. The inspectors surveyed the route to the airport to ensure the shipment's smooth passage.

Independent information about machine tool deliveries to Iraq led to the inspection of a conventional munitions plant where 50 machines matching procurement data were found and marked for evaluation against the dual-use criteria.

The twenty-first inspection visited an industrial complex of facilities for the production of fibreglass, fibre composites, resin and new materials. None had a uniquely nuclear function, but future monitoring of the site was indicated. An assessment was made of the construction of non-nuclear facilities at the former nuclear sites of Al-Furat, Al-Jezira, Al-Sharqat and Al-Tarmiya, where the nuclear-related capabilities had been destroyed but not the infrastructure; the new activities at those sites bore no relationship to the former nuclear work. Preparations for installing surveillance cameras at machining facilities continued. Specific measurements and surveys were made to ensure the availability of utilities necessary to install surveillance test units at Um Al Ma'arik, where the major components of the EMIS modules had been fabricated.

Routine inventory and monitoring of dual-use equipment were carried out at a number of sites. Preparations began for consolidating the scattered quantities of HMX (high melting point explosive) in a single sealed location at the Muthana complex. The Al-Kindi small-missile development centre, which had capabilities for research with pyrotechnic materials, was also visited. Large-scale movement of equipment for safe keeping took place at Al-Nida (formerly Al-Rabiya) in June during the high political tension occasioned by Iraq's refusal to accept the installation of monitoring cameras at two missile test sites (see below, under "Special Commission activities").

During the twenty-second inspection (1-15 November),[62] surface water, sediment and biota samples were again collected at 15 locations along the Tigris-Euphrates watershed. Seventeen establishments were visited in an effort to reconcile Iraqi equipment declarations with information obtained outside of Iraq. Following further discussion and clarification of the reporting requirements, Iraq, by the conclusion of the inspection, submitted updated and revised declarations pursuant to annexes 2 and 3 of the IAEA plan for future ongoing monitoring and verification of Iraq's nuclear activities. (Previous annex 3 declarations had been submitted in January and August.)

Two meetings were held on the subject of technical advice obtained from foreign sources that enhanced Iraq's centrifuge enrichment efforts. The details provided with respect to individual components of the Iraqi prototype magnetic centrifuges and the process through which they evolved were consistent with available information. As to sources of technical expertise that aided Iraq's centrifuge development effort, Iraq would not disclose the names of individuals, the circumstances under which they got involved or details of the technical help provided pending the conclusion of legal action brought by Member States against those individuals. However, Iraq disclosed in general terms that technical help had been provided in respect of: machine tools, vacuum and clean-room technologies and heat treatment of maraging steel; simulation software for design and evaluation applications; procurement of specific components and equipment; two general assembly drawings and 10 to 12 drawings of specific components; and technical specifications for specific components. Iraq also identified an individual as its agent for the procurement of the 350-grade maraging steel, of which it received 100 tonnes in two consignments.

Detailed microscopic examination, bulk density assessment and sampling for chemical analysis were performed on the natural uranium oxide stocked in 201 drums and declared to have come from Brazil. The results of this work, not including the chemical analysis, suggested that in all likelihood the stock was of Brazilian origin, a finding requiring corroboration by Brazil.

Monitoring inspections were conducted at eight "core" sites of the former Iraqi nuclear programme and existing building modifications, new construction and future plans for converting four of them to non-nuclear applications were reviewed. In addition, the filling and sealing of a carbonate mine was completed during the inspection.

IAEA reports (June and December). During 1993, IAEA issued the fourth and fifth semi-annual reports on its implementation of the plan for the destruction, removal or rendering harmless of items listed in paragraph 12 of Security Council resolution 687(1991). The fourth report covered the period 17 December 1992 to 17 June 1993, and the fifth, the period 17 June to 17 December 1993. They were transmitted to the Council in June[5] and December,[63] respectively.

The reports updated the status of direct-use material, confirming that all of the known fresh (unirradiated) fuel for the IRT-5000 reactor had been removed from Iraq.[64] In June, IAEA concluded a contract with the Ministry for Atomic Energy of the Russian Federation, whose principal subcontractor was the Nuclear Assurance Corporation of the United States of America, for the removal from Iraq and subsequent disposal of the remaining enriched uranium in the form of 208 irradiated fuel assemblies from the Iraqi research reactors at Al-Tuwaitha and Location B. The airshipment out of Iraq of approximately 100 of those assemblies (all manufactured in the former USSR) to a facility in the Russian Federation was successfully completed on 4 December. Removal of the remaining assemblies was expected to take place during the first two months of 1994.

It had not been possible to establish the correctness and completeness of Iraqi nuclear material declarations through traditional material accountancy. Independent efforts to confirm quantities of such material not subject to safeguards inspection (much of it in the form of yellow cake delivered to Iraq by external sources) had not been successful. Despite considerable origin-based accountancy and highly precise isotopic and impurity measurements to match inspection-measured material with Iraqi declarations, the resulting picture did not provide assurance that all nuclear materials had been declared and presented. Thus, uncertainties remained to be clarified in respect of the inventory of natural uranium and the detailed utilization of part of this inventory in Iraq's past nuclear activities.

The Iraqi response to the remaining inconsistencies identified by IAEA in Iraq's "full, final and complete" declaration of 1992[65]—considerably revising the nuclear-material flow chart that Iraq first presented—was that they were attributable to losses during the 1991 bombing of Iraq, to the mixing of the material during evacuation, or to the inaccuracy of the sample analyses. Iraq considered the nuclear-material file closed and declined to provide further clarification, a position IAEA consistently rejected.

Significant progress had been made in verifying the origin of the large natural uranium oxide stock declared as being of Brazilian origin. By the end of the fifth semi-annual reporting period (17 December), most of the remaining natural uranium-containing slurries from Al-Jezira had been recovered and was being transferred in some 59 drums to Location C at Al-Tuwaitha.

As to installations, equipment and other materials relevant to enriched uranium production and to weaponization activities, Iraq had submitted an updated list of material, equipment and other items identified in annex 3 of the IAEA plan for future ongoing monitoring and verification of Iraq's compliance with paragraph 12 of Security Council resolution 687(1991).

Future actions included continuing efforts to resolve remaining uncertainties in the nuclear-material flow chart and verification of the completeness of the revised list of items submitted by Iraq pursuant to annex 3.

Special Commission activities

The United Nations Special Commission, headed by the Executive Chairman, Rolf Ekéus, continued to maintain three offices: the Office of the Executive Chairman in New York, a field office at Manama, Bahrain, and another at Baghdad.

Financing the Commission's operations remained a problem in the absence of Iraqi agreement to sell oil for the purposes set forth in resolution 706(1991)[66] and of Iraq's acknowledgement of its obligations under resolution 699 (1991)[67] to meet the full costs of the tasks authorized in section C of resolution 687(1991). Since the Commission's inception, its expenses had been met from voluntary contributions in cash or in kind (personnel, services, equipment) and advances from Member States, and from funds made available from frozen Iraqi assets as provided for in Council resolution 778(1992).[68]

According to the Secretary-General (see also below, under "Humanitarian assistance"),[69] the cumulative operational costs through the end of 1993 were estimated at over $72 million, of which only some $38 million would be covered from funds already designated in the escrow account and from other contributions. Further cash contributions had become urgent owing to the recently concluded contract for the removal from Iraq of irradiated uranium fuel currently stored at two sites,[63] involving the Commission in its largest expenditure to date: a fixed contract fee of $24,565,000 net, plus ancillary costs in the neighbourhood of $800,000.

The status, privileges and immunities of the Special Commission, IAEA and the United Nations specialized agencies involved in the implementation of resolution 687(1991) continued to be regulated by the relevant Council resolutions—687(1991),[1] 707(1991)[2] and 715(1991)[3]—and by a May 1991 exchange of letters between the Secretary-General and the Minister for Foreign Affairs of Iraq.

The agreement in the exchange of letters relating to the facilities, privileges and immunities of the Special Commission and IAEA in Bahrain was extended twice during the year, each for a six-month period, until 30 September 1993 and thereafter until 31 March 1994. Bahrain's formal agreement for the first extension was received by the Secretary-General on 29 April; the second was agreed upon in an exchange of letters dated 20 September and 23 October 1993.

As later reported by the Executive Chairman, Iraq had notified the Commission office at Baghdad in writing on 7 January that, effective immediately, the use of Habbaniyah airfield would be denied to the Commission, which should use either Iraqi aircraft to transport its personnel and equipment between Bahrain and Iraq or the land route from Amman, Jordan. This breach of Iraq's obligation to ensure the complete implementation of the privileges, immunities and facilities of Commission personnel, including their safety and freedom of movement, was orally reported to the Council on 8 January and confirmed in writing the same day.

SECURITY COUNCIL ACTION (8 and 11 January)

After consultations among its members, the Security Council, on 8 January, authorized its President to make the following statement[70] on behalf of the Council, in connection with its consideration of the item entitled "The situation between Iraq and Kuwait":

Meeting number. SC 3161.

"The Security Council is deeply disturbed by the Government of Iraq's recent Notes to the Office of the Special Commission in Baghdad and to the Headquarters of the United Nations Iraq-Kuwait Observation Mission (UNIKOM) that it will not allow the United Nations to transport its personnel into Iraqi territory using its own aircraft.

"The Security Council refers to resolution 687(1991) requiring Iraq to permit the Special Commission and IAEA to undertake immediate on-site inspection of any locations designated by the Commission. The agreement on facilities, privileges and immunities between the Government of Iraq and the United Nations, and resolutions 707(1991) and 715(1991) elaborated on Iraq's obligations by demanding, *inter alia,* that the Special Commission and IAEA be allowed, as they determined necessary, to use their own aircraft throughout Iraq and any airfield in Iraq without interference or hindrance of any kind. Concerning UNIKOM, Iraq is obligated by resolution 687(1991) and committed by an exchange of letters dated 15 April 1992 and 21 June 1992, respectively, to the unrestricted freedom of entry and exit without delay or hindrance of its personnel, property, supplies, equipment, spare parts and means of transport.

"The implementation of the measures set out in the recent communications of the Iraqi Government would seriously impede the activities of the Special Commission, IAEA and UNIKOM. Such restrictions constitute an unacceptable and material breach of the relevant provisions of resolution 687(1991), which established the cease-fire and provided the conditions essential to the restoration of peace and security in the region, as well as other relevant resolutions and agreements.

"The Council demands that the Government of Iraq abide by its obligations under all relevant Security Council resolutions and cooperate fully with the activities of the Special Commission, IAEA and UNIKOM. In particular, it demands that the Government of Iraq not interfere with the currently envisaged United Nations flights. The Security Council warns the Government of Iraq, as it has done in this connection in the past, of the serious consequences which would ensue from failure to comply with its obligations."

Iraq explained on 10 January[71] that its notification to the Special Commission to discontinue its use of foreign aircraft was a temporary decision dictated by United States threats to Iraq that endangered foreign flights in Iraqi airspace. Iraq described as incorrect the allegation that it had hampered the Commission's operations and again suggested that, rather than leasing foreign aircraft at Iraq's expense, the United Nations teams could lease Iraqi aircraft instead, or travel by land to Baghdad through Amman, as Iraqis did, including Government officials, who did not consider the United Nations teams higher in rank than themselves.

The Council, in a statement issued through its President on 11 January,[29] rejected Iraq's arguments. It reiterated its demand that the Special Commission be permitted to use its own aircraft to transport its personnel into Iraq, as well as its warning of serious consequences that would flow from continued Iraqi defiance.

Responding on 12 January,[30] Iraq denied having flouted the Council's resolutions or having any intention of defying the Council. It restated its position, namely, that in the event of military aggression against it by the United States and the United Kingdom, as was being persistently threatened, an Iraqi response in self-defence would put any foreign aircraft in danger; thus the suspension in question was not only temporary but logical and born of a sense of responsibility. Iraq failed to understand the legality or the logic of the Council's rejection of the request that Iraqi aircraft be used instead, or how that request could be interpreted as defiance of the Council. Iraq affirmed its wish for dialogue with the Council but asserted that it would neither relinquish its sovereignty and legitimate rights nor bargain in matters affecting their defence.

In a 2 March report to the Council,[72] the Executive Chairman summarized the exchanges of notes on the subject between the Commission and the Iraqi Ministry for Foreign Affairs and other Iraqi authorities between 7 and 19 January. On three occasions in the course of those exchanges, the Commission delivered to Iraq notifications of its flight plans in accordance with established procedures, expressing expectation of acknowledgement and acceptance. Iraq gave a number of reasons for refusing to permit Commission flights. It linked its refusal to the Sanctions Committee decision not to allow Iraqi Airways to resume international operations and restated the alternative transportation it had suggested. Subsequently, it stated that flights would be allowed on a case-by-case basis but that Iraq could bear no responsibility for the safety of Commission aircraft. Flights would be allowed to and from Habbaniyah provided they entered Iraqi airspace from Jordanian airspace and flight notifications were resubmitted accordingly. If the Commission flew the direct route, Iraq would be able to guarantee the safety of the Commission's aircraft, but only if the Commission guaranteed that "coalition" aircraft were not also flying in Iraqi airspace at the same time.

For its part, the Commission persisted in seeking resumption of its operations, immediately responding to each Iraqi note and offering a way for Iraq to meet its obligations by stating that, through the Commission's coordination with the States enforcing the "no-fly zone" (south of the 32nd parallel), the conditions for safe flight would be ensured, provided Iraq did not itself threaten the flights. The issue was resolved on 19 January, when Iraq informed the Commission that, on the basis of a statement by the Revolution Command Council, it would allow the resumption of Commission flights according to established procedures. By telephone, a guarantee was given that Iraq would ensure the safety of the Commission's aircraft.

Reports of the Special Commission (June). In 1993, the Executive Chairman of UNSCOM submitted his fifth and sixth semi-annual reports to the Secretary-General for transmittal to the Security Council. They described the Commission's activities and operational details, together with the main developments arising from those activities. Several appendices contained descriptions of: organizational and administrative issues; on-site inspections relating to chemical and biological weapons and ballistic missiles; the destruction of Iraq's chemical agents and munitions; activities of the Commission's Information Assessment Unit; ongoing monitoring and verification activities; and the monitoring of suppliers of materials and technical expertise to Iraq (fifth report only).

The fifth report, issued in June, covered the period from 14 December 1992 to 14 June 1993.[4] An account of UNSCOM's chemical-weapons inspections during that period included the results of the combined chemical and biological weapons inspection of December 1992,[73] according to which seven potential chemical weapons–related sites, including a pharmaceutical plant, and three biological sites, including the Al-Hakim Single Cell Production Facility, were visited. Three question-and-answer "seminars" were held with the Iraqi authorities on Iraq's "full, final and comprehensive report" on chemical weapons, while two were held on biological weapons issues. No useful information was obtained.

An additional chemical-weapons inspection (6-18 April 1993) visited a number of sites, notably the Fallujah sites, formerly part of the Muthanna State Establishment. The inspection required Iraq to remove by 31 May 11 specific items of equipment at Fallujah to Muthanna for destruction under Commission supervision. UNSCOM had taken account of Iraq's request to reuse the equipment for insecticide production, but decided that irreversible conversion was not an option on the grounds that, besides being readily reconvertible for proscribed use, they had been acquired specifically for the production of chemical-weapons precursors. Moreover, as Iraq still had not accepted the monitoring of dual-purpose equipment under the terms of the ongoing monitoring and verification plans approved by resolution 715(1991), UNSCOM could not guarantee their future use as proposed. Iraq accused the Commission of having gone to extremes in interpreting its mandate, criticizing it, the Sanctions Committee and the Council for their decisions relating to equipment destruction. Since the equipment had not been destroyed by 14 June, a formal report on the matter was made to the Council on 16 June (see below).

Biological weapons inspections (11-18 March) were made at seven sites, including one that had never previously been inspected; an examination of the research equipment, munitions and munition-filling equipment revealed them to be conventional items. However, some sites were found to have a dual-purpose capability; recommendations were made for future compliance-monitoring activities.

Two regular ballistic-missile inspections were undertaken. One (12-21 February) recorded serial numbers of specific machinery and details of raw materials (to assist in the determination of Iraq's supplier network) and assessed the capabilities of certain facilities, including the Taji-Nasr State Establishment, the Al-Yawm Al-Azim Facility and the TECO stand at Zaafaraniyah. The team also supervised the destruction at Taji of dies and moulds used, or intended for use, in proscribed missile activities. The other inspection (22 and 23 February), conducted on short notice, verified specific information that missiles with a range greater than 150 kilometres and their associated vehicles were present in an area west of Baghdad. Helicopter and high-altitude surveillance were integrated in the inspection. While no proscribed items or activities were observed, a serious breach of UNSCOM's surveillance rights occurred on 22 February: a helicopter was prevented from conducting aerial surveillance over a site by its Iraqi escort and openly threatened by anti-aircraft guns aimed at it. That incident was reported to the Council on 24 February.

In the absence of Iraq's acknowledgement of resolution 715(1991), which delayed long-term monitoring efforts across the whole spectrum of Iraqi missile-related activities, UNSCOM initiated interim monitoring, the first of which focused on work relating to liquid propulsion systems and associated technologies at the Ibn Al-Haytham Centre over eight weeks (25 January–23 March). A second team's investigations centred on the Al-Rasheed Factory and the Al-Qa'Qaa Establishment over a 52-day period (27 March–17 May), during which the team discussed with Iraq details of its missile designs, its knowledge of solid propellant technology, general capabilities in missile production, its ability to increase the range of existing systems, the current status of its production facilities and its plans for missile research, development, testing and production. The resultant information enhanced the Commission's understanding of Iraq's past weapons programmes and of its technology baseline.

The third interim monitoring team entered Iraq on 5 June. It was accompanied by a sub-team charged with installing remote-controlled cameras to monitor rocket test stands at two sites, of which Iraq was duly informed on 6 June. Iraq blocked the installation on the grounds that the cameras comprised sensors for monitoring under resolution 715(1991), a resolution Iraq would not accept despite its unanimous adoption under Chapter VII of the Charter of the United Nations.

In addition, the Commission participated in an IAEA survey of the sites (19-24 April) from which irradiated fuel was to be removed and air-shipped to the Russian Federation for reprocessing and permanent storage.

The report noted Iraq's continued refusal to cooperate. During the foregoing inspections, it had exhibited a most unwelcome trend of seeking to restrict the manner in which UNSCOM's rights were implemented. Iraq maintained its position, made known to the Council in 1991,[74] regarding the ongoing plans for monitoring and verification. It considered the new interim monitoring at Ibn Al-Haytham Centre to be conducted under the terms of resolution 687(1991) and installation of the surveillance cameras as falling within the framework of matters for discussion at a proposed dialogue between Iraq and the Commission, although later clarifying that its request was for a postponement of the installation in question until the dialogue took place.

The report drew attention to Iraqi declarations that required rectification and those that remained outstanding, as well as to Iraq's serious breaches of UNSCOM's rights, privileges and immunities. In consequence, the Commission had been unable to complete the inspection and survey and weapons-destruction phases of its work and proceed to ongoing monitoring and verification, for which preparations were under way.

In response to a wish expressed by Council members, the Executive Chairman prepared a detailed account of Iraq's attitude regarding the installation of monitoring cameras at Yawm Al-Azim and Al-Rafah and the destruction of chemical weapons production equipment, which was transmitted to the Council by the Secretary-General on 16 June.[75]

The Executive Chairman stated that, in his reply of 9 June to Iraq's position that the Commission limit itself to inspection activities specified by resolution 687(1991), under whose purview the installation of the cameras did not fall, he emphasized that the installation was in implementation of the mandate entrusted to the Commission by the same resolution and other relevant resolutions; he further stated his intention to inform the Council of Iraq's refusal to permit installation of essential equipment intended to allow continued determination of whether Iraq was meeting its unconditional undertaking not to use, develop, construct or acquire missiles prohibited under paragraph 8 of the same resolution. This breach of resolution 687(1991), he asserted, was compounded by a breach of the status arrangements of May 1991 between the United Nations and Iraq, pursuant to which the Commission had the "right to install equipment or construct facilities for observation, inspection, testing or monitoring activity".

Iraq, on 11 June, stated that it had requested a postponement of the decision to install the cameras pending a discussion of the matter, together with all other outstanding questions that were still the subject of dialogue. The Executive Chairman pointed out that Iraq's position ignored the fact that resolution 687(1991) called on the Secretary-General to draw up a plan for ongoing monitoring and verification of Iraq's obligations not to reacquire banned items or capabilities. That plan was unanimously approved by resolution 715(1991) and as such was mandatory and enforceable. Thus the issue was not even up for discussion, let alone "still the subject of dialogue". He characterized Iraq's insistence that the Commission limit itself to activities under resolution 687(1991) as a direct challenge to the authority of the Security Council and to the force of its resolutions adopted under Chapter VII of the Charter.

As to the required removal by 31 May of 11 pieces of equipment acquired for the production of chemical weapons precursors, along with a quantity of precursor chemicals, from Fallujah to Muthanna for destruction, Iraq remained insistent in its request for their reuse for insecticide production. UNSCOM explained that the equipment could not be rendered harmless, being intrinsically capable of use for prohibited purposes and quickly reconverted for such; it gave Iraq until 10 June to complete removal of the items, warning that failure to do so would have to be reported to the Council. Nevertheless, Iraq reiterated its proposal for a technical discussion in order to arrive at a formula that would assure practical guarantees for the peaceful use of the equipment. By 15 June, only five items had been removed. Such non-compliance was an outright violation of Iraq's obligations under resolution 687(1991) and put into question Iraq's overall readiness to implement that resolution and other relevant resolutions.

Among the most serious impediments to the Commission's task had been Iraq's attitude towards the use of helicopters for surveillance and operational support. Since its refusal of a helicopter surveillance flight in 1992,[76] Iraq had hindered the Commission's work by automatically objecting to any proposed helicopter flight that entailed a "box" in the vicinity of Baghdad. (A "box," usually in the order of 40 square kilometres, was given to Iraqi authorities the night before a flight to enable them to ensure that Iraqi air defences not treat the UNSCOM flight as a hostile intruder while not revealing the precise site to be surveyed.)

The Executive Chairman noted that Iraq, while not explicitly rejecting the monitoring provisions but rather expressing a willingness to renegotiate their terms, by its actions had prevented initiation of implementation of the plans for ongoing monitoring and verification approved by resolution 715(1991) and amounted to a de facto rejection of the Council's resolutions and decisions in this regard.

SECURITY COUNCIL ACTION

In the light of the Executive Chairman's 16 June report, the Security Council met on 18 June, and, after consultations among its members, authorized its President to make the following statement[77] on the Council's behalf:

Meeting number. SC 3242.

"The Security Council is deeply concerned by the Government of Iraq's de facto refusal to accept the United Nations Special Commission's (UNSCOM) installation of monitoring devices at rocket test sites and to transport chemical weapons–related equipment to a designated site for destruction, as set out in a report from the Executive Chairman of the Special Commission to the President of the Security Council.

"The Council refers to resolution 687(1991) requiring Iraq to permit the Special Commission and the International Atomic Energy Agency (IAEA) to undertake immediate on-site inspection of any locations designated by the Commission. The agreement on facilities, privileges and immunities between the Government of Iraq and the United Nations, and resolutions 707(1991) and 715(1991), clearly establish Iraq's obligation to accept the presence of monitoring equipment designated by the Special Commission, and that it is for the Special Commission alone to determine which items must be destroyed under paragraph 9 of resolution 687(1991).

"Iraq must accept installation by UNSCOM of monitoring devices at the rocket test sites in question and transport the chemical weapons–related equipment concerned to a designated site for destruction.

"The Council reminds Iraq that resolution 715(1991) approved plans for monitoring by the Special Commission and IAEA which clearly require Iraq to accept the presence of such monitoring equipment at Iraqi sites, designated by the Special Commission, to ensure continuing compliance with its obligations under Security Council resolution 687(1991).

"Iraq's refusal to comply with decisions of the Special Commission, as set out in the report of the Executive Chairman, constitutes a material and unacceptable breach of the relevant provisions of resolution 687(1991), which established the cease-fire and provided the conditions essential to the restoration of peace and security in the region, as well as violations of Security Council resolutions 707(1991) and 715(1991) and the plans for future ongoing monitoring and verification approved thereunder. In this context, it recalls the statements of 8 January 1993 and 11 January 1993, and warns the Government of Iraq of the serious consequences of material breaches of resolution 687(1991) and violations of its obligations under resolution 715(1991) and the above-mentioned plans.

"The Council reminds the Government of Iraq of its obligations under Security Council resolutions and its undertakings to provide for the safety of inspection personnel and equipment. The Council demands that the Government of Iraq immediately comply with its obligations under Security Council resolutions 687(1991), 707(1991) and 715(1991), and cease its attempts to restrict the Commission's inspection rights and operational capabilities."

Iraq, on 20 June,[78] clarified its position in writing since it had been denied the opportunity to do so when the Executive Chairman brought his views on the matters to the Council's attention. It stated that UNSCOM wanted to begin implementing resolution 715(1991) without informing the Council that Iraq had implemented all the fundamental parts of section C of resolution 687(1991) under UNSCOM supervision and that such compliance made it incumbent upon the Council to begin implementing in earnest that resolution's paragraph 22, that is, lifting the economic sanctions imposed on Iraq. That paragraph was as much mandatory as were all other parts of the resolution.

Iraq repeated its arguments regarding the installation of the cameras, stressing that it neither possessed nor produced any missiles with a range of over 150 kilometres and that the third interim monitoring team was currently discharging its tasks, with Iraq extending the required cooperation. Iraq likewise repeated its arguments for sparing the items of equipment ordered to be removed from Al-Fallujah for destruction at Muthanna, adding that they were brand new, never before used for either prohibited or non-prohibited purposes. Their proposed use in the production of pesticides would fill one of Iraq's agricultural needs, crucial under the deprivations of the current embargo. As to the helicopter flights over Baghdad, Iraq noted the existence of an agreement between its authorities and UNSCOM that no flights be conducted over populated areas anywhere in Iraq, including Baghdad.

Iraq expressed extreme surprise at what it called the Commission's attempt to distort the Iraqi position, to accuse it of non-compliance with resolution 687(1991) and to incite the Council against Iraq when it should be conveying to the Council that Iraq had gone a long way in implementing all the fundamental parts of section C of that resolution. It looked forward to the Council's initiating a professional, legal and technical review of what had been implemented with a view to lifting the three-year economic blockade on Iraq.

Special mission (July)

The UNSCOM Executive Chairman, accompanied by three members of his staff, undertook a special mission to Baghdad from 15 to 19 July 1993. The results, together with an account of the developments that had led to the mission, were described in a report of 20 July, transmitted to the Security Council through the Secretary-General the following day.[(79)]

The Executive Chairman stated that it had kept the Security Council informed of the status of Iraqi compliance with the Council President's statement, from its issuance on 18 June until 2 July. In that time, Iraq had removed all the chemical-weapons production equipment and precursor chemicals at Fallujah to Muthanna, where UNSCOM supervised and verified destruction of the equipment. The precursors would be destroyed in due course.

However, there had been no progress on the installation of the surveillance cameras at the two designated rocket-engine test sites, a measure that Iraq continued to block as falling within the monitoring plans approved by resolution 715(1991) and thus still a subject for discussion. The installation team, which had been in Iraq for over a month awaiting favourable developments to allow it to proceed with its task, was therefore instructed to withdraw on 5 July. As reported to the Council on 8 July, information had been received to the effect that Iraq had dismantled and removed equipment from the test sites, rendering them inoperative. The inspection team dispatched to Iraq to seal the equipment and facilities at both sites was thus informed by the Director of the Military Industrialization Corporation, General Amer Muhammad Rashid, that sealing was unnecessary and that the dismantled equipment could be inspected any time. The Chief Inspector nevertheless attempted to affix seals but was blocked from doing so. As instructed, the team left Iraq.

On 11 July, the Minister for Foreign Affairs of Iraq explained that the issue behind Iraq's refusal to permit sealing of the sites was that UNSCOM had begun implementing resolution 715(1991) without having committed itself to informing the Council that Iraq had complied with the provisions of section C of resolution 687(1991), making it incumbent on the Council to consider lifting the economic sanctions imposed on Iraq.

In reporting to the Council the outcome of the Commission's attempts to seal the two sites and equipment, the Executive Chairman referred to the failure of all efforts either to monitor the sites or to insure their non-use until effective monitoring could begin, as well as to the Iraqi Foreign Minister's 11 July letter. He concluded that Iraq had unequivocally raised the specific issue of monitoring two rocket-engine test sites to the level of the principle of Iraq's acceptance of ongoing monitoring and verification under resolution 715(1991).

The Executive Chairman noted that while an interim solution preventing the use of those sites might be possible, the permanent solution, through the installation of monitoring cameras, would not be found until Iraq could be convinced that it must accept and implement resolution 715(1991), adopted under Chapter VII of the Charter. The Commission had always understood resolutions 687(1991), 707(1991) and 715(1991) to constitute an indissoluble whole and had acted accordingly; it could not, therefore, consider reporting to the Council under paragraph 22 of resolution 687(1991) until it deemed Iraq to be in compliance, not only with that resolution, but also with the other two. In the circumstances, the Executive Chairman felt that it might be of some use to convey that message, with the Council's full support, to the highest levels of the Iraqi Government. At an informal session on 12 July, the Council decided that the Executive Chairman should visit Baghdad for that purpose.

The Executive Chairman, accompanied by three of his staff, travelled to Baghdad and held six meetings between 15 and 19 July with Iraqi officials including the Deputy Prime Minister, the Foreign Minister and an Under-Secretary in the Foreign Ministry, the IAEC Chairman, the Director of the Military Industrialization Corporation of Iraq and the Chief Iraqi counterpart in matters concerning the Special Commission inspections. The two sides exchanged position papers on specific points discussed at the first three meetings.

The nine-point Iraqi position paper contained proposed statements of undertakings: (1) by Iraq, on its readiness to comply with the plans approved by resolution 715(1991); (2) by the Security Council and UNSCOM, in implementing those plans, to respect Iraq's sovereignty, internal security and dignity, and (3) to guarantee its right to industrial, scientific and technological progress; (4) by UNSCOM to use Iraqi helicopters and reconnaissance aircraft for its aerial monitoring and verification tasks and (5) to conduct those tasks according to the rules of relevant international agreements; and (6 and 7) by the Council to implement paragraphs 22 and 24 of resolution 687(1991) and (8) to lift the embargo referred to in paragraph 14 of that resolution. The paper also contained (9) a demand that France, the United Kingdom and the United States end their air embargo to the south of parallel 32 and to the north of parallel 36 and cease violating Iraqi airspace and interfering in Iraq's internal affairs.

The Commission paper addressed two issues: acknowledgement by Iraq of its obligations under resolution 715(1991) and the plans approved thereunder; and monitoring of the rocket-engine test sites at Al-Yawm Al-Azim and Al-Rafah. On the first issue, the paper drew attention to part B of the monitoring plan to be executed by UNSCOM, particularly those paragraphs defining the Commission's general rights, which it would be obliged to insist upon if necessary. With Iraq's full cooperation and good will in carrying out the plan, a routine could be developed whereby the Commission could operate unobtrusively, without hampering or delaying normal activities at sites under inspection, with due regard to Iraq's sovereignty, independence, security and dignity.

Without prejudice to its rights to provide its own full logistical support, including transport, UNSCOM intended to avail itself of those provisions in the plan pursuant to which the Government was required to provide on request logistical and technical support, including flights for purposes specified in paragraph 17 of the plan—depending on the prevailing situation of confidence and availability of local logistical and technical support to meet Commission requirements. UNSCOM was further prepared to conduct with the Government a periodic review of the operations and execution of the plan and examine in good faith any Government concerns and determine what action, if any, it could take within the scope of its functions and responsibilities to the Council.

The Commission noted that the comprehensive nature of the Iraqi paper included issues (points 7 to 9) falling outside the Commission's competence; those relating to its responsibilities, however, contained positive elements, which would permit UNSCOM and Iraq to commence high-level technical talks in New York. UNSCOM suggested that point 2 be qualified by the phrase "in accordance with the Charter of the United Nations". Point 5 would be met if it would read ". . . carried out in the same spirit as relevant international agreements in the field of arms control and disarmament". As to point 6, the Commission would report to the Council when it was satisfied that Iraq was in compliance with its obligations under paragraphs 8 to 13 of that resolution; it was for the Council to decide on the action it would take in the light of such a report.

The Commission further noted Iraq's agreement, on an interim basis, to permit the cameras to be installed. A team would shortly be dispatched to perform the installation. It was agreed that the nature and implementation of the plans for ongoing monitoring and verification, as well as all other outstanding issues between Iraq and the Commission, would be discussed at the talks with a view to resolving them.

High-level talks (August/September)

High-level technical talks were held at United Nations Headquarters, New York, from 31 August

to 9 September, between an Iraqi delegation headed by the Director of the Military Industrialization Corporation, and the Special Commission and IAEA, led, respectively, by the Executive Chairman and by the IAEA Action Team Leader (Maurizio Zifferero) under Security Council resolution 687(1991).

A report on the talks, submitted by the Executive Chairman on 16 September,[80] gave the background, organization and objectives of the talks; outlined the outstanding issues for compliance as identified by five working groups (annex I); and described the discussions on the nature and manner of the implementation of ongoing monitoring and verification as set out in the plans of UNSCOM and IAEA (annex II), as well as outstanding matters to be resolved in a manner to permit the two bodies to make the reports required under paragraph 22 of resolution 687(1991) (annex III).

The outstanding issues, defined in great detail, were communicated to Iraq. In the category of chemical weapons, they concerned the production of chemical warfare agents, precursor chemicals, specific critical equipment suppliers, weaponization of produced agents, suppliers of unfilled munitions and chemical weapons facilities.

As to biological weapons, information was outstanding on: the location of inhalation chambers and aerosol generators known to have been imported into Iraq; the type, quantity, year since 1985, supplier and user of imports of toxins, specific micro-organisms and the complex media for their growth; and whether biological weapons-related activities were being conducted at facilities other than at the Section for Biological Research for Military Defence Purposes. UNSCOM assured Iraq of the expeditious processing of all allowable requests for exceptions to the general prohibition of activities relating to diseases other than those indigenous to Iraq or immediately expected to break out in its environment.

Unresolved missile issues included information on specific foreign suppliers, equipment delivered or ordered for project No. 1728 and the extent of possible foreign assistance in project No. B2000. Specific ways to address those issues were outlined.

Outstanding nuclear issues related primarily to procurement. IAEA restated its requests for the identities of: outside suppliers of the technical and design information for the Iraqi magnetic centrifuge; the manufacturers, suppliers, agents and shippers for the 350-grade maraging steel; the supplier of the carbon-fibre rotor tubes and the means whereby technical specifications were communicated to the manufacturer; and the manufacturer and procurement procedure for the HMX explosive declared by Iraq. Also outstanding was a description of the involvement of H&H Company in the Iraqi centrifuge enrichment programme.

Discussion of the plans for ongoing monitoring and verification focused on the three stages of implementation, the selection of sites for monitoring, the relationship of such monitoring to international disarmament agreements, the frequency and duration of inspections, and use of ground verification and its relation to Iraqi concerns regarding security, sovereignty and independence. It was UNSCOM's intention to implement the plans in the least intrusive manner and in the same spirit as relevant international agreements on arms control and disarmament were being carried out. It was recalled that paragraph 25 of the Secretary-General's plan[81] for on-site inspections foresaw that, at an appropriate time and after the entry into force of the Convention on the Prohibition of the Development, Production, Stockpiling and Use of Chemical Weapons and on Their Destruction,[82] the inspectorate envisaged in it might take over the function of monitoring and verification of compliance in the area of chemical weapons.

The Executive Chairman indicated that UNSCOM must continue to use its own aerial capability for logistical and technical support, as well as for surveillance, which would diminish in frequency as confidence-building measures bore fruit and baseline surveys were completed. The Commission would be prepared to enter into early discussions regarding the use, on a trial basis, of Iraqi helicopters for transportation from Baghdad to the Muthanna State Establishment. In the light of experience gained, discussions could be extended early in 1994 to the use of Iraqi aerial assets for other purposes.

It was pointed out that, for UNSCOM and IAEA to make the necessary reports under paragraph 22 of resolution 687(1991), they would need to be satisfied that Iraq had provided all information on outstanding issues in relation to its prohibited programmes to constitute the full, final and complete disclosure—as called for in resolutions 687(1991), 707(1991) and 715(1991)—of all programmes to develop prohibited weapons and of all holdings of such weapons, their components, production, research and development facilities and locations.

Given Iraq's fulfilment of its obligation to provide information on the outstanding issues as identified, the Commission and IAEA intended to complete the identification phase of their work under resolution 687(1991), probably before the end of December 1993, assuming Iraq accepted and facilitated forthcoming inspection activities; and to complete destruction of identified chemical weapons and precursors, as well as removal of the irradiated fuel from Iraq. In the same period, it would take decisions regarding the release of items connected with prohibited programmes. There would remain the initiation of the ongoing monitoring and verification required under paragraphs 10 and 13 of resolution 687(1991). With the necessary cooperation from Iraq, this should prove possible within a period of six months after receipt from it of comprehensive declarations on all facilities falling under the plans' provisions.

The Commission repeated its request to be allowed to use Rasheed airfield and to conduct aerial surveillance by both rotary- and fixed-wing aircraft. It reiterated the necessity of immediately activating the cameras at Al-Yawm Al-Azim and Al-Rafah.

High-level talks (October)

In advance of the resumed high-level talks (Baghdad, 2 to 8 October), UNSCOM technical experts went to Iraq in advance of the Executive Chairman to receive additional information from the Iraqi Government. The Executive Chairman's report on the October round of talks was transmitted to the Security Council through the Secretary-General on 12 October.[83]

The report stated that, with Iraq's provision of the necessary information on critical foreign suppliers, as defined in annex I of the 16 September report,[80] and upon its verification, the Commission could conclude as follows: (a) in the light of all the information made available to UNSCOM in respect of ballistic missiles and biological weapons, the Commission could state that Iraq had discharged its obligation to provide the information necessary to constitute full, final and complete disclosures of its past proscribed programmes in those areas, in compliance with paragraphs 8 and 9 (a) of resolution 687(1991); and (b) the substantial supplementary information relating to chemical weapons covered the full process of chemical weapons production, namely, the quantities of precursors imported, agent produced, equipment acquired for agent production indicating types and capacities, chemical munitions produced or imported and munitions filled by type of agent. The information would be used solely for the purposes of resolution 687(1991). The Commission hoped that verification, assessment and confirmation of the information, to be undertaken in New York, would enable it to make the same determination in the chemical weapons area as it had done in (a) above.

Iraq stated that the information, declarations and answers it had presented from 1991 until the current round of talks, as well as its actions during that period, represented full and complete implementation of its obligations under paragraphs 8, 9, 11, 12 and 13 of resolution 687(1991). It would be ready to declare formal acceptance of the plans for ongoing monitoring and verification when it became clear that the Council's obligations in relation to Iraq, especially under paragraph 22 of that resolution, would be implemented fully without obstructions, restrictions or additional conditions. Without prejudice to this position, it was immediately ready to present the declarations requested by UNSCOM and IAEA to complete the baseline information of the sites to be monitored.

The Commission explained that the most expeditious way for achieving that objective was for Iraq to provide forthwith formal acknowledgement of its obligations under resolution 715(1991) and the plans approved thereunder. UNSCOM could then set in motion full-scale ongoing monitoring and verification to the point where the plans were up and running within the briefest possible time.

The Commission also explained the framework within which it was required to operate: *(a)* resolutions 687(1991), 707(1991) and 715(1991), in respect of weapons of mass destruction, constituted an indissoluble whole, in that their implementation was not sequential and the various stages contained in 687(1991) and 715(1991) overlapped; *(b)* resolution 715(1991) was a mandatory resolution adopted unanimously under Chapter VII of the Charter and as such was automatically binding on Member States from the date of its adoption on 11 October 1991, and, while there was thus no issue of acceptance, Iraq's formal acknowledgement was a precondition for undertaking effective monitoring on Iraqi territory, with clearly defined rights and assurance of continuity; *(c)* the Council held[84] that Iraq's prior acknowledgement was an essential precondition to any reconsideration of the prohibitions (sanctions) referred to in paragraphs 21 and 22 of resolution 687(1991); and *(d)* as a subsidiary organ of the Council, the Commission was duty-bound to operate within the framework established by the Council and its officially expressed views. The Commission could thus not initiate full-scale ongoing monitoring and verification without the Council's first receiving Iraq's formal acknowledgement of its obligations under resolution 715(1991).

While welcoming Iraq's offer immediately to provide declarations prior to such acknowledgement, UNSCOM pointed out that, in order to achieve full legal value and credibility, declarations should be submitted formally under resolution 715(1991) and the plans approved thereunder. Furthermore, to be fully effective, baseline inspections and monitoring and verification had to be conducted under the acknowledged regime established by that resolution.

Iraq restated its concerns that, in the implementation of the plans, Iraqi aerial assets should replace those of the Commission; that its scientific, technical and economic development not be hindered; and that, in due course, the methods used should be revised to bring them in line with those used in international agreements and conventions.

In response, UNSCOM confirmed its position as recorded in its position paper,[79] discussed at Baghdad in July.

As to the periodic reviews agreed to in principle, agreement was reached that the first review could be held three months after the monitoring plans had been formally initiated and every three months thereafter. The plans themselves could only be revised by the Council, but UNSCOM considered that the annexes to the plans should be revised as and when necessary, in the light of experience and information obtained in the course of their implementation.

In the area of nuclear weapons, IAEA was confident that the essential elements of Iraq's nuclear weapons programme were understood and had been dismantled. Having provided the critical information on the suppliers of prohibited materials and sources of technical advice, Iraq had complied with all disclosure requirements concerning its previous nuclear weapons programme as contained in resolutions 687(1991) and 707(1991).

Over the preceding 15 months, IAEA had phased in certain elements of its plan for ongoing monitoring and verification. Those elements, of which Iraq had been aware, included: environmental sampling of air, water and surfaces; inspection of known sites relevant to the past nuclear programme and sites with potential to support a nuclear weapons programme; inspection of new sites that might be identified in the future; control of allowed nuclear materials and dual-use technical equipment; imagery; and surveillance equipment and use of sensors.

With a formal acceptance by Iraq of resolution 715(1991) and the two plans it approved for ongoing monitoring and verification, of which one was the IAEA plan, IAEA would be satisfied that Iraq had complied with the conditions laid down in paragraphs 11, 12 and 13 of section C of resolution 687(1991) and would accordingly report to the Council. Possible additional disclosures or discoveries would be dealt with during the ongoing monitoring and verification phase.

The two sides decided on a further high-level meeting in New York in mid-November.

High-level talks (November)

The high-level talks resumed in New York from 15 to 30 November.[85] The Iraqi technical team stated that its objectives were to follow up on the supplementary information provided by Iraq during the October talks at Baghdad so as to ensure that UNSCOM and IAEA were satisfied that Iraq's obligations under section C of resolution 687(1991) regarding past programmes had been discharged and to discuss ways of expediting the plans for ongoing monitoring and verification. IAEA and UNSCOM welcomed those objectives, and separate expert groups in the chemical, biological, ballistic missile and nuclear fields, as well as a group on operational issues, met to pursue them. In the course of the meetings, Iraq provided further details on past proscribed programmes and sites, equipment and materials to be monitored pursuant to the plans.

The Commission and IAEA informed the Iraqi side that the information available in all areas was deemed credible; they would deploy their best efforts to expedite the process of its further verification in order to arrive quickly at a definitive conclusion. In the firm conviction that that process could be completed substantially in advance of a determination that ongoing monitoring was under way and proceeding satisfactorily, UNSCOM emphasized the advisability of initiating full-scale ongoing monitoring while information verification was being completed. In the unlikely event that some verification elements were unduly held up, they would continue to be pursued during the monitoring phase so that the reporting under paragraph 22 of resolution 687(1991) was not needlessly delayed. The Commission and IAEA welcomed Iraq's express recognition of their right to undertake immediate on-site inspections should any new information on past programmes surface after paragraph 22 had been implemented.

In the light of its most recent inspections and the information currently available to it relating to Iraq's past programmes, UNSCOM was finally in a position to complete the identification phase of its work under resolution 687(1991).

Iraq reiterated its position on UNSCOM's use of Iraqi aerial assets, as well as its concerns relating to respect for its sovereignty, security and dignity of its people and to the realignment of the modalities for ongoing monitoring with those for implementing international instruments. On the first item, the Commission referred to its position as recorded in their joint report on the August/September talks,[80] adding that, at the beginning of 1994, it would be prepared to undertake a full survey of Iraqi air assets to determine their technical adequacy and stressing that the use of local logistical and technical aerial and other support would be dependent on the prevailing situation of confidence and availability of adequate assets. Both UNSCOM and IAEA stressed that it was their intention to implement the plans in the least intrusive manner and in the same spirit as relevant international agreements in the field of arms control and disarmament.

In reaffirming their agreement to undertake periodic reviews of the implementation of the plans, both sides agreed that the first such review should take place in February.

Political talks took place between the Deputy Prime Minister and the Executive Chairman on 22, 26 and 29 November, and with the IAEA Action Team Leader on 23 November. The Deputy Prime Minister indicated his intention to hold discussions separately with Council members and other interested Member States in order to assess their understandings of the conditions necessary for lifting the oil embargo in accordance with the terms of paragraph 22 of resolution 687(1991). Thereafter, he would meet again with the Executive Chairman to discuss future relations.

On 26 November,[86] the Minister for Foreign Affairs of Iraq formally informed the President of the Security Council that the Government of Iraq had decided to accept the obligations set forth in resolution 715(1991) and to comply with the two plans for monitoring and verification approved by that resolution. The Foreign Minister reiterated Iraq's requests as to the manner of implementing those plans. He conveyed Iraq's hope that, with this positive step, the Council would implement paragraph 22 of resolution 687(1991) speedily, in full and without obstacles, restrictions or additional conditions.

In the light of this acknowledgement, UNSCOM and IAEA requested Iraq to submit, as soon as possible, consolidated declarations under resolution 715(1991) and the plans. Responding on 30 November, the Government of Iraq issued a statement confirming that the declarations provided to UNSCOM in October 1993 and those provided to IAEA in November 1993, and previously in November 1991 and January and April 1993, were to be considered to have been made and submitted in conformity with the provisions of resolution 715(1991) and the plans.

The joint report on the foregoing talks, together with enclosures giving details of the technical talks (enclosure I) and reproducing the text of the Government's statement (enclosure II), was transmitted to the Council through the Secretary-General on 1 December.[85]

Report of the Special Commission (December). The sixth semi-annual report of the Special Commission, covering the period from 14 June to 14 December 1993, was transmitted to the Security Council on 21 December.[87]

The report noted that recent operational developments had been encouraging in that the inspection teams that had conducted activities in Iraq since the August/September high-level talks[80] had been well received and their tasks had been facilitated by Iraq.

Two chemical and biological weapons inspections were conducted during the period. One (10 and 11 July) was primarily to verify information that, contrary to initial declarations, Iraq had a larger stock of DB-0 bombs that might have had a biological warfare application. The inspection led to Iraq's declaration of larger stocks, stating that the bomb was a failed prototype munition for chemical weapons and that the larger numbers represented munitions scrapped during the production and testing phases.

A second inspection (19-22 November) was constituted on short notice to investigate persistent reports that chemical weapons had been used by Government troops against opposition elements in the southern marshes of Iraq. The team had come from a fact-finding mission to Iran to obtain clarification about the allegations from persons claiming to be eyewitnesses and about the exact location of the alleged attack. Using vehicles, boats and helicopters, the team conducted a thorough inspection of the alleged site. It collected large samples of soil, water, flora and fauna for analysis, which was under way, and obtained documents that were undergoing forensic examination.

In addition, a ballistic missile inspection (see below) also searched for possible hidden stocks of chemical and biological weapons facilities, but found no proscribed items or activities.

UNSCOM continued intensive and multifaceted inspection efforts in the area of ballistic missiles. A third interim monitoring team was dispatched (4-28 June) to assess existing Iraqi capabilities in the area of precision machining related to ballistic-missile production, in particular gyroscope devices and liquid-fuel engine manufacture. Two military sites and 16 industrial facilities were inspected.

Pursuant to interim arrangements agreed upon during the Executive Chairman's July mission to Baghdad,[79] the installation and testing of the surveillance camera systems at Al-Yawm Al-Azim and Al-Rafah rocket test sites, blocked by Iraq in June, were completed on 3 August. Missile experts were dispatched to Iraq (23 August–27 September) to observe any missile tests that might be declared to UNSCOM and to conduct detailed engineering surveys of test facilities at the two sites and five other test stands capable of performing missile and rocket engine tests. The camera systems were activated on 25 September following Iraq's agreement to the Commission's request for their immediate activation at the August/September high-level talks in New York.[80]

The cameras, arranged so as to enable UNSCOM to assess whether a test was of a prohibited missile, engine or motor, provided round-the-clock coverage of the missile-engine test stands. Missile test monitoring handbooks, including engineering baselines for the test sites, check-lists and reporting forms, were developed for Iraqi use. The camera systems were subsequently upgraded (2-10 December) to include radio links and improved lenses.

The objective of the largest ballistic missile inspection ever to be mounted (30 September–30 October) was twofold: to investigate reports of suspected prohibited activities in Iraq and of the continued concealment of proscribed items, notably missiles; and to verify Iraqi information on its past prohibited activities, especially on the operational use of missiles with a range greater than 150 kilometres. These tasks, identified as critical to UNSCOM's intention to complete the identification phase of its work under resolution 687(1991), required the largest inspection team to date, lengthy preparation and intensive training, in-depth analytical work, innovative use of advanced sensors and deployment of additional aerial assets in Iraq. Since much of the information to be checked referred to underground storage for prohibited items, the inspection employed, in addition to proven inspection procedures, new techniques, such as a custom-designed ground-penetrating radar (GPR) mounted on helicopters to maximize detection of prohibited items, especially missiles, missile launchers and possible hide sites. Two additional helicopters—manned and equipped specifically to meet the requirements of the inspection—were deployed to conduct GPR surveys and to perform aerial inspection of specific sites, including at night, using forward-looking infrared radar.

Ground inspections included a number of sites in and around Baghdad. Intensive GPR and ground searches were conducted around known launch positions of Al Hussein missiles in central and western Iraq, to verify critical information on the use of such missiles during the 1991 military action. Two additional sites were investigated on the ground and from the air to determine if they were or had been the locations of prohibited activities. Ground inspections and GPR surveys were made from 25 to 28 October.

In all, the inspection covered more than 30 sites and areas and flew more than 28 GPR missions, totalling more than 56 hours' flying time. Neither undeclared prohibited items nor activities were identified nor was evidence discovered to contradict the information provided by Iraq on issues related to the inspection. Iraq provided all the support requested for the inspection, granted access to all designated sites and areas and honoured all the inspection rights invoked; the inspection encountered no problems in executing its operational plan, including in the introduction and use of its aerial assets.

During the reporting period, UNSCOM introduced special aerial inspections focusing on the detection of gamma emissions, a technique to identify locations warranting more detailed ground inspections. The first such mission (10-25 September) began on 15 September, five days later than scheduled so that coverage was considerably reduced. The delay was due to a dispute regarding the installation of gamma detection sensors aboard an UNSCOM helicopter, which was quickly resolved, however. Partial surveys were conducted at Al-Tuwaitha, Al-Atheer and Al-Jezira, from multiple points of which gamma signals were detected. These sites were extensively covered during the second aerial inspection (2-15 December); the significance of the gamma signals detected from all sites would not be apparent until the results of the analysis became available.

The report summarized the technical and political developments, beginning with the issue that arose from the required removal of certain chemical weapons–production equipment and precursor chemicals from the Fallujah sites to Muthanna for destruction, and described how that became intertwined with the impasse occasioned by Iraq's blocking of UNSCOM's installation of remote-controlled monitoring cameras at two rocket-engine test stands and by the question of "dialogue" between Iraq, on the one hand, and UNSCOM and IAEA, or the Security Council, on the other. The report then traced the resolution of those issues through the Executive Chairman's July mission to Baghdad and the three high-level talks that culminated in Iraq's decision to accept its obligations under resolution 715(1991).

Long-term monitoring and verification

During 1993, the Security Council received from UNSCOM and IAEA their third and fourth reports on the status of the implementation of the plan of each for ongoing monitoring and verification of Iraq's compliance with relevant parts of section C of resolution 687(1991). UNSCOM's third report, covering the period 11 October 1992 to 10 April 1993,[88] was submitted by the Secretary-General on 19 April; the fourth report, submitted by UNSCOM's Executive Chairman and covering the period 11 April to 10 October 1993, was transmitted by the Secretary-General on 5 November.[89] The third and fourth IAEA reports were submitted by the IAEA Director General on 8 April[90] and 29 October;[91] they were subsequently transmitted to the Council by the Secretary-General.

Prepared in response to resolution 715(1991), which called for a status report at least every six months, the reports outlined the requirements that remained to be fulfilled by Iraq under the two plans approved by that resolution. The underlying obstacle in this connection was Iraq's desire to see an end to the first phase of implementation of its obligations under section C of resolution 687(1991), that is, the identification and elimination of proscribed weapons and weapons programmes, and for this to be followed by the Council's implementation of paragraph 22 of that resolution, namely, the lifting of the oil embargo,

before proceeding to ongoing monitoring and verification activities.

As a result of the July mission of the Executive Chairman and the three rounds of high-level talks between UNSCOM and IAEA, on the one hand and Iraq on the other (see above), Iraq, in November, formally accepted its obligations under resolution 715(1991) and committed itself to comply with the provisions of the plans for monitoring and verification, thus enabling the Special Commission and IAEA to initiate full-scale monitoring and verification of Iraq's weapons-related activities on a routine basis.

Kuwaiti property

In response to the Security Council's 1991 demand[92] that it immediately begin to return all seized Kuwaiti property, Iraq included, in its monthly communications to the Secretary-General on steps taken to implement its obligations under resolution 687(1991) (see above under "Cease-fire compliance"), a continuing account of the return of such property—an operation it conducted at the hand-over point south of Safwan.

On 6 January,[93] Iraq reported that, between 29 November and 31 December 1992, it had returned military equipment belonging to Kuwait's Air Force and Army Air Corps, including 2 damaged Skyhawk aircraft, 2 damaged Super Puma helicopters, 10 aircraft dollies, 10 items of equipment relating to aerial munitions, 21 pilot ejector seats for Skyhawk aircraft, 7 ground equipment items, the air defence computer and conditioning system, 10 radar systems and air-launched munitions (rockets and bombs). It stated on 8 March[94] that the return of all Air Force equipment and weapons had been completed on 16 February, except for a damaged C-130 aircraft for which repair bids were being awaited.

Iraq wrote on 5 April[95] of the return of the first batch of heavy military equipment. Begun on 28 February, it was completed in March with the hand-over of 18 French 155-mm guns, 18 French 120-mm mortars, 18 French ammunition carriers and 10 French command posts, 88 Ferret armoured cars, 20 American 155-mm guns and 40 Centurion tanks. The return in April of 74 Hawk missiles and related equipment was reported on 10 May,[96] and, on 10 June,[97] it was reported that, in May, the transfer had begun of the second batch of heavy equipment, comprising 27 Centurion and 20 Chieftain tanks, 124 Warrior and 37 Saladin armoured vehicles—all of British manufacture.

On 12 August,[98] Iraq stated that in July it had returned: 11 Chieftain tanks; armour replacement parts; a 20,000-line Swedish switchboard with computer, callback and other related equipment; 28 low-capacity exchanges; a telex exchange and power equipment; and navigation equipment. On 9 September,[99] it reported having returned the nose and stern of two destroyed A-4 aircraft.

Kuwait, by a letter of 17 May,[100] noted that, despite Iraq's apparent cooperation in returning Kuwaiti property, its implementation of that obligation was deficient for the following reasons. Most of the returned items had been intentionally sabotaged or destroyed, even just hours before being handed over, making them valueless or unfit for reuse. Whereas Iraq maintained that it was not responsible for the return of properties stolen from the private sector, valued at hundreds of millions of dollars, copies of officially signed and sealed Iraqi inventories, left behind in 1991 by the retreating Iraqis, proved that specialized Iraqi government agencies supervised the theft and removal of such properties from Kuwait. Moreover, Iraq had not abided by the lists agreed upon with the United Nations Coordinator for the return of property from Iraq to Kuwait and constantly delayed or hindered the hand-overs, resulting in additional administrative costs to Kuwait.

Kuwait repeated those same observations in letters to the Council President of 16 July[101] and 15 September.[102]

UN Compensation Commission and Compensation Fund

The United Nations Compensation Commission, established by the Security Council in 1991[103] for the resolution and payment of claims against Iraq for losses and damage resulting from its invasion and occupation of Kuwait, did not issue any reports in 1993.

At its March/April session, the Commission's Governing Council drew attention to the fact that, although $21 million had been deposited in the Compensation Fund in December 1992, the Commission's work continued to be jeopardized by a lack of financial resources. The Council thus requested its President to take steps to ensure that the Commission be given the necessary financial support. This was confirmed in May by the Secretary-General (see below, under "Escrow account"), who stated that the Commission had received funds to cover most of its projected operational and administrative costs for 1993, but that no funds were currently available to pay any significant amount of actual claims to injured parties.

Activities of the Governing Council. The Governing Council held three regular sessions in 1993, all at Geneva: the ninth (29 March–1 April),[104] tenth (26-28 July)[105] and eleventh (27-29 September)[106] sessions. It also held its first special session on 11 January.

At the ninth session, the Governing Council appointed nine Commissioners nominated by the Secretary-General, to constitute three panels of three members each, dealing with consolidated claims in categories A (departure from Iraq or Kuwait), B (death or serious personal injury) and C (individual claims for damages up to $100,000). The Council was informed that approximately 700,000 claims had been received. Owing to difficulties encountered by a number of Governments in meeting the 1 July 1993 deadline for submitting claims in the four categories, the Council authorized an extension to 1 October to any Government or entity requesting it by 1 July.

At its tenth session, the Governing Council decided that claims in categories B and C would be processed in chronological order. Those in category A would be processed in accordance with the criterion of proportionality, initially among the countries that had submitted claims prior to 1 July 1993; due consideration would be given to claims processed during the first stage of category A, if the criterion of chronological order had been applied. The Council decided to accept consolidated claims in categories A, B and C filed after the deadlines by the United Arab Emirates, Nigeria and Somalia, for processing after the claims submitted on time had been processed.

In view of the difficulties experienced by some Governments in making timely submissions of claims, the Governing Council decided, on an exceptional basis, to grant extensions until 1 January, 1 April and 1 May 1994 for claims in categories D, E and F, respectively, if the extensions were requested prior to the expiry of the current deadlines.

At the opening of its eleventh session on 27 September, the Governing Council was informed by its Executive Secretary that 2.2 million claims had been received. As at its previous two sessions, the Council authorized extensions, on request, this time until 1 January 1994 for the filing of claims in categories A, B and C. It decided to grant Egypt and Kuwait an extension until 1 April 1994 to file approximately 260,000 claims in category C, which were to be submitted in diskette form.

Communications. Iraq, on 12 February,[107] communicated its position on decision 16 concerning awards of interest on compensation, adopted by the Governing Council in 1992.[108]

Citing paragraphs 16 and 17 of resolution 687(1991) and the 1991 report of the Secretary-General[109] setting forth the institutional framework for the Compensation Commission and the Compensation Fund as approved by resolution 692(1991),[103] Iraq asserted that the texts neither stipulated nor mentioned interest. Had there been any intention to impose it on the compensation to be determined, there should have been some reference to it, however rudimentary. Thus, decision 16 was in conflict with resolution 687(1991), with the legal principles and the trend followed in peace treaties after the Second World War and with the principles of justice and fairness. Iraq therefore called on the Security Council to abrogate decision 16 and reaffirm compliance with its resolutions on this matter.

On 22 March,[110] Iraq drew attention to the fact that certain companies and individuals, instead of filing their claims with the Compensation Commission, had begun seeking compensation through their national courts, thereby aiming at Iraqi assets and reserves abroad.

By that procedure, the percentage deducted from Iraq's exports of petroleum and petroleum products would exceed the upper limit for compensation specified by the Council in resolution 705(1991),[111] i.e., 30 per cent of the annual value of those exports. The resultant harm to the Iraqi economy would be so severe as to curtail Iraq's ability to provide essentials for its people and make impossible the fulfilment of its obligations to the Compensation Fund itself. Iraq requested that the Council take appropriate measures to lay down guidelines to coordinate measures at the national and international levels in order to ensure that the percentage of compensation to be determined was not exceeded.

Arms and related sanctions

Reports of the Committee on sanctions. The Committee established by Security Council resolution 661(1990)[112] (Committee on sanctions) issued four reports—one every 90 days—during 1992, pursuant to the responsibilities entrusted to it under the guidelines approved by the Council in 1991[113] for monitoring the prohibitions against the sale or supply of arms to Iraq and related sanctions. The reports were transmitted to the Council on 19 March,[114] 7 June,[115] 7 September[116] and 13 December.[117]

Each report stated that, during the period under review, the Committee had received no information relating to possible violations of the arms and related sanctions against Iraq committed by other States or foreign nationals. It had not been consulted by States or international organizations on either the sale or supply of items to Iraq that might fall within the categories of proscribed items or of dual- or multiple-use items, nor had any allegations of violations in this regard been reported to it. No international organization had reported any relevant information that might have come to its attention.

Communications. Iraq addressed many communications to the Secretary-General during 1993 registering its protest against what it called the unfair practices of the Committee on sanctions. It cited objections raised by France, Japan, the United Kingdom and the United States to Iraqi

requests for the import of what it described as the most essential humanitarian and civilian needs, such as knitting-machine needles, textiles and thread for the manufacture of clothing and electrical materials.[118] Iraq illustrated, by counting the number of requests objected to by each of those countries, that the United States and the United Kingdom objected to the greatest number, on one occasion for nylon cloth, glue for textbooks, 120 tonnes of rock wool felt and blank audio cassettes;[119] on another, for Virginia tobacco, caustic soda for fertilizer, sodium phosphate for water treatment, cement, automotive supplies (tyres, oil filters, spare parts, paint) and detergent powder;[120] and authorization for Iraqi Airways to fly 2,000 pilgrims to Mecca.[121]

Other examples of requests rejected under one pretext or another were for 200 tonnes of polyester and acrylic yarn for textile production, 300 tonnes of polyvinyl chloride for hospital use, 103 rolls of galvanized steel plate, cable joints and about 26 tonnes of concrete additives,[122] 70 tonnes of wood glue,[123] brakes for agricultural tractors, pesticides, water taps, fans and paper products.[124]

Moreover, Iraq communicated periodic reports showing the impact of sanctions imposed on it: increased child morbidity and mortality,[125] increased malnutrition, diarrhoeal diseases and anaemia in both children and adults,[126] and an overall increase in the population's mortality rate.[127]

SECURITY COUNCIL ACTION

After each informal consultation held by the Security Council, on 25 January,[128] 24 May[129] and 20 September,[130] pursuant to paragraph 21 of resolution 687(1991), the Council President issued the following statement on behalf of the Council:

"After hearing all the opinions expressed in the course of the consultations, the President of the Council concluded that there was no agreement that the necessary conditions existed for a modification of the regimes established in paragraph 20 of resolution 687(1991), as referred to in paragraph 21 of that resolution."

The Council also held informal consultations on 23 and 29 March,[131] 21 July[132] and 18 November[133] pursuant to paragraphs 21 and 28 of resolution 687(1991) and paragraph 6 of resolution 700(1991). After each of those consultations, the President issued the following statement on behalf of the Council:

"After hearing all the opinions expressed in the course of the consultations, the President of the Security Council concluded that there was no agreement that the necessary conditions existed for a modification of the regimes established in paragraph 20 of Council resolution 687(1991), as referred to in paragraph 21 of that resolution; in paragraphs 22, 23, 24 and 25 of Council resolution 687(1991), as referred to in paragraph 28 of resolution 687(1991); and in paragraph 6 of Council resolution 700(1991).''

Repatriation of Kuwaitis

The question of the repatriation of Kuwaiti nationals in Iraq, including prisoners and detainees, and the status of missing persons were the subject of several communications from Kuwait to the Security Council President. On 2 March,[134] it stated that it had recently handed over to the International Committee of the Red Cross (ICRC) the individual files of 627 prisoners, detainees and missing persons. Each file contained full and detailed information on the individual concerned and the facts surrounding the place, date and circumstances of their detention as gathered from Iraqi documents left behind in Kuwait. In this connection, Kuwait reiterated its demands that Iraq provide information on all persons deported from Kuwait between 2 August 1990 and 26 February 1991 and release without delay those who might still be in detention; all persons arrested in Kuwait who died during or after the same period while in detention, including their grave sites; and all persons executed in Kuwait or Iraq during or after the same period, including the whereabouts of their remains. It also asked Iraq to search for persons listed as missing.

In May,[135] July,[136] September[137] and November,[138] Kuwait reported that no information had been received from Iraq about the 627 files, an indication that Iraq had reneged on its previous undertaking to reply within 10 days of receiving any file. Moreover, Iraq had prevented the efforts of the Secretary-General's Envoy to the League of Arab States, Rashid Idris, as well as of King Hassan II of Morocco, to secure the release of Kuwaiti prisoners and detainees. It had also refused to attend the last two meetings (Geneva, July and October) of the Tripartite Committee dealing with this issue.

For its part, Iraq, in its compliance reports for April[96] and May,[97] recalled its repeated affirmation that there were no so-called Kuwaiti detainees in Iraq. However, it reported having recently released to ICRC six Kuwaiti brothers who had illegally crossed over into Iraqi territory on 8 April.

Humanitarian assistance

In a May report,[69] the Secretary-General accounted for the funds transferred to an escrow account (see below, under that topic) to meet, among the specific purposes designated by the Security Council, the financing of a scheme for the purchase of foodstuffs, medicines, materials and supplies for essential civilian needs, in particular health-related materials, for distribution in all regions of Iraq and to all categories of the Iraqi civilian population.

The report stated that, as at 30 April, of the $101.5 million received into the escrow, $41.5 million had been designated for various humanitarian activities in Iraq. Of that amount, $38 million had been expended, primarily by transfer to other executing United Nations agencies; and $1.5 million, designated for activities after 1 April, had been transferred to the United Nations Children's Fund.

The report also gave cost estimates of the ongoing inter-agency humanitarian programme.

Inter-agency humanitarian programme

In its compliance report for the month of December 1992,[93] Iraq stated that, in accordance with the Memorandum of Understanding signed between Iraq and the United Nations for a six-month period ending 31 March 1993,[7] it had ensured all the necessary administrative requirements to facilitate the work of organizations and agencies operating within the framework of the relief programme, such as granting visas to additional personnel, issuing permits for the movement and passage of trucks, ensuring their safe arrival in all the country's governorates and making ready reserve depots for the storage of relief goods. Iraq had done so despite the fact that the United Nations had not seriously embarked on implementing the projects outlined in the action plan under the Memorandum.

According to the Secretary-General's May report,[69] (see below, under ''Escrow account'') the cost estimates of the ongoing United Nations Inter-agency Humanitarian Programme for Iraq had not been definitively established, but the projected total for specific project proposals submitted to date by various United Nations agencies and programmes for the period 1 April 1993 to 31 March 1994 amounted to $489 million. No further funds were currently available from the escrow account for those projects.

(For the extension of the Memorandum of Understanding and the new United Nations Inter-Agency Humanitarian Programme for Iraq, see PART THREE, Chapter III.)

Kurds and minority populations

On 2 April,[139] Iraq addressed identical letters to the Secretary-General and to the President of the Security Council, transmitting a copy of ''talking points'' delivered to four permanent Council members: France, the Russian Federation, the United Kingdom and the United States. Among the points made was that Iraq could not accept any formula that might be open to the interpretation that it agreed to the air exclusion zones imposed north of the 36th parallel and south of the 32nd. (The zones had been imposed on behalf of the Kurdish minority in the north and the Shi'a minority in the southern marshes.) Iraq called that action iniquitous and unlawful, with no basis in any United Nations resolution; its aim was political: to interfere in Iraq's internal affairs, undermine the situation in the country and dismember it on an ethnic and confessional basis.

Iraq stated that three countries (France, United Kingdom, United States) had imposed the aerial exclusion zones by unilateral decision and had used armed force to maintain them, as they had done in January 1992, had impeded Iraq's ability to defend its sovereignty against acts of aggression by the Iranian air force (April 1992 and March 1993), with those countries standing by watching the aggression take place. However, to avoid friction or misunderstanding, Iraq stressed that it was not opposed to an exchange of views with the States concerned.

On 10 June,[140] Iraq repeated the statement it had made in 1992[141] that the governorates of Dohuk, Erbil and Suleimaniyah had not been under the control of government authorities since the autumn of 1991. This anomalous situation resulted from the direct military intervention of France, the United Kingdom and the United States, which were preventing the Iraqi authorities from exercising their functions in those areas, even threatening to use force should they attempt to do so. As a result, the governorates had come under the control of armed bands and had become open to interference by Iran and other States and to widespread anarchy. Iraq could therefore not accept responsibility for incidents occurring there, including threats against United Nations personnel. Given the situation imposed on Iraq, it was surprising that the United Nations should ask it to take measures to improve the humanitarian situation in those governorates and ensure the security of their inhabitants.

Despite the anomalous situation, Iraq had provided facilities to relief convoys destined for the northern governorates and to United Nations personnel in all areas under Iraqi control to ensure implementation of the programmes approved under the action plan. It had cooperated with the humanitarian programme, which had been used for political purposes by certain States, as events had shown. Owing to pressure by these States, the programme had not attracted the necessary funding and had been beset by difficulties for which Iraq was in no way responsible.

War crimes

On 19 March,[142] the United States transmitted a "Report on Iraqi War Crimes" to the President of the Security Council. Prepared under the auspices of the Secretary of the Army of the United States, it was submitted in accordance with Council resolution 674(1990),[143] paragraph 2 of which invited States to collate substantiated information in

their possession or submitted to them on the grave breaches by Iraq of Council decisions,[144] the Charter of the United Nations, the 1949 Geneva Convention relative to the Protection of Civilian Persons in Time of War, the 1961 Vienna Convention on Diplomatic Relations,[145] the 1963 Vienna Convention on Consular Relations [146] and international law.

The six-part report comprised: a 19-page summary of Iraqi war crimes committed during Iraq's 1990 occupation of Kuwait and the 1991 military action taken against Iraq to compel it to withdraw from Kuwait; Iraqi treatment of United States prisoners of war (POWs); Iraqi treatment of protected persons and the occupation of Kuwait; specific examples of Iraqi war crimes in occupied Kuwait; pictorial documentation; and an index of files archived in the United States War Crimes Documentation Center.

According to the Army's investigations, Iraqi violations of the law of war were widespread and premeditated. Specific Iraqi war crimes, extensively documented by the War Crimes Documentation Center, included: the taking of Kuwaiti and third-country nationals in Kuwait as hostages and their individual or mass forcible deportation to Iraq; the taking of third-country nationals in Iraq as hostages and their forcible transfer within Iraq; compelling Kuwaiti and other foreign nationals to serve in Iraq's armed forces; the use of Kuwaiti and third-country nationals as human shields; inhumane treatment, including rape and wilful killing, of Kuwaiti and third-country civilians; the transfer of Iraq's civilian population into occupied Kuwait; and torture and other inhumane treatment of POWs of the United States and other countries cooperating with Kuwait.

Other specific war crimes were the unnecessary destruction of Kuwaiti private and public property; pillage, including that of Kuwaiti civilian hospitals; illegal confiscation or inadequate safeguarding of Kuwaiti public property; indiscriminate Scud-missile attacks against non-combatant civilians of Israel and Saudi Arabia; intentional release of oil into the Persian Gulf and sabotage of the Al-Burgan and Rumalia oil fields in Kuwait; and the employment of unanchored naval mines and mines without self-neutralizing devices.

The report stated that the War Crimes Documentation Center had accumulated several linear feet of files containing substantiating evidence of the crimes enumerated. The categories of documentation included United States documents, captured Iraqi documents, videotaped and written statements of eyewitnesses, POWs, "human shields" and Kuwaiti victims; graphic videotape and still photographic evidence; and general references dealing with the prosecution of war crimes cases.

In a preliminary response to the report, Iraq, on 17 June,[147] described it as full of arbitrary allegations formulated with public-relations assistance and given currency by the media for hostile purposes. It cited as an example the mendacious story of how infants were deprived of incubators at a Kuwait hospital, theatrically recounted by a Kuwaiti ambassador's daughter. As later revealed, an American public relations firm, engaged by the Embassy of Kuwait at Washington, D.C., coached the ambassador's daughter in the delivery of her so-called impartial testimony.

The purpose of the report, Iraq said, was twofold: to weaken Iraq in order to ensure Israel's ascendancy in the region and to control Iraq's natural resources, primarily oil. The information, gathered by intelligence sources of dubious objectivity and veracity, was compiled in a report by the United States, which was also a party to the conflict. That country alleged Iraqi violations while it ignored its own violations against Iraqi civilians: it had bombarded them savagely, leaving their homes, mosques and churches in ruins, destroying their drinking-water and sewage facilities, historic buildings, shelters where people had sought refuge and civilian plants such as the Baghdad infant formula factory.

Among its other comments on the report, Iraq pointed to the many contradictions it contained, particularly on the question of POWs. Its reference to Israel as being neutral to the conflict was patently untrue since it had carried out many hostile acts against Iraq, and Saudi Arabia was a principal party to the conflict; consequently, Iraqi response against those countries was in accord with the rules of armed conflict.

Escrow account

On 27 May,[69] the Secretary-General submitted a report pursuant to paragraph 5 of Security Council resolution 778(1992),[68] calling on him to ascertain the whereabouts and amounts of petroleum and petroleum products and the proceeds from their sale that were to be transferred to an escrow account to meet the purposes of resolutions 706 (1991)[66] and 712(1991).[148] Apart from financing purchases for the essential humanitarian needs of the Iraqi population (see above, under "Humanitarian assistance"), the proceeds in escrow were to be used to meet payments to the United Nations Compensation Fund, the full costs of carrying out the tasks authorized by section C of resolution 687(1991), the full costs incurred by the United Nations in facilitating the return of all Kuwaiti property seized by Iraq and half the costs of the Boundary Demarcation Commission.

As at 30 April 1993, 62 countries had replied to the Secretary-General's request for information on steps taken to implement resolution 778(1992). Of these, four indicated holding amounts, as follows: Greece, $276,000 in proceeds from the sale of Iraqi oil products; Japan, $48.88 million, subject to third-party rights so that none of it could be transferred to the escrow account; Tunisia, $15.8 million, already partially used to settle Iraq's debts to Tunisia; the United States, $637.4 million, $200 million of which it would transfer to the escrow account provided that amount at no time exceeded 50 per cent of total funds contributed or transferred to the account. The remaining 58 countries stated that they had no petroleum or petroleum products or frozen assets subject to the provisions of resolution 778(1992).

The Secretary-General provided a table showing the estimated expenditures for the various activities related to resolutions 687(1991) and 706(1991) from their inception to 31 December 1993, the resources made available from the escrow account or from direct contributions and the estimated amount of funding still needed in 1993.

As at 30 April 1993, a total of $101.5 million had been received into the escrow account, made up of voluntary contributions of $30 million from Saudi Arabia, $20 million from Kuwait and $1.5 million from the United Kingdom; and a transfer from the United States of $50 million in Iraqi frozen assets. As at the same date, the $101.5 million had been earmarked thus: $33 million for the United Nations Special Commission ($31.5 million had been expended); $21 million for the United Nations Compensation Commission ($6.6 million had been expended); $4 million for costs relating to the return of Kuwaiti property (with $2.7 million already expended); $2 million towards Iraq's share of the costs of the Boundary Demarcation Commission ($3.7 million had been expended by the Commission); and $41.5 million for various humanitarian activities in Iraq.

REFERENCES

[1]YUN 1991, p. 172, SC res. 687(1991), 3 Apr. 1991. [2]Ibid., p. 188, SC res. 707(1991), 15 Aug. 1991. [3]Ibid., p. 194, SC res. 715(1991), 11 Oct. 1991. [4]S/25977. [5]S/25983. [6]S/25064, S/25391, S/25535, S/25758, S/25928, S/26302, S/26427. [7]YUN 1992, p. 321. [8]S/25384. [9]S/25465. [10]S/26585 & Corr.1. [11]S/26740. [12]S/26887. [13]S/25811. [14]S/25811/Add.1. [15]YUN 1991, p. 177. [16]YUN 1992, p. 298, SC res. 773(1992), 26 Aug. 1992. [17]S/25865. [18]S/25963. [19]S/25905. [20]YUN 1991, p. 176. [21]YUN 1992, p. 297. [22]YUN 1991, p. 178. [23]YUN 1982, p. 181. [24]S/26132. [25]S/26006. [26]YUN 1991, p. 178, SC res. 689(1991), 9 Apr. 1991. [27]S/25085. [28]S/25085/Add.1. [29]S/25091. [30]S/25097. [31]S/25123. [32]S/25123/Add.1. [33]S/26621. [34]S/26622. [35]S/25514. [36]S/25588. [37]S/26520. [38]S/26566. [39]S/26755. [40]S/26758. [41]S/26784. [42]S/26786. [43]S/26787. [44]S/26735. [45]S/26736. [46]A/47/637/Add.1 & Corr.1. [47]YUN 1992, p. 300, GA res. 47/208 A, 22 Dec. 1992. [48]YUN 1991, p. 869, GA res. 46/187, 20 Dec. 1991. [49]Ibid., p. 135, GA res. 45/265, 17 May 1991. [50]A/47/987. [51]A/C.5/48/40. [52]A/48/772. [53]S/25411. [54]YUN 1992, p. 315. [55]YUN 1991, p. 193. [56]Ibid., p. 190. [57]Ibid., p. 167. [58]YUN 1992, p. 304. [59]S/25666. [60]S/25982. [61]S/26333. [62]S/1994/31. [63]S/26897. [64]YUN 1992, p. 305. [65]Ibid., pp. 303 & 316. [66]YUN 1991, p. 207, SC res. 706(1991), 15 Aug. 1991. [67]Ibid., p. 184, SC res. 699(1991), 17 June 1991. [68]YUN 1992, p. 320, SC res. 778(1992), 2 Oct. 1992. [69]S/25863. [70]S/25081. [71]S/25086. [72]S/25172. [73]YUN 1992, p. 312. [74]YUN 1991,

p. 194. [75]S/25960. [76]YUN 1992, p. 311. [77]S/25970. [78]S/25979. [79]S/26127. [80]S/26451. [81]YUN 1991, p. 183. [82]YUN 1992, p. 66, GA res. 47/39, 30 Nov. 1992. [83]S/26571. [84]YUN 1992, p. 306. [85]S/26825 & Corr.1. [86]S/26811. [87]S/26910. [88]S/25620. [89]S/26684. [90]S/25621. [91]S/26685. [92]YUN 1991, p. 171, SC res. 686(1991), 2 Mar. 1991. [93]S/25064. [94]S/25391. [95]S/25535. [96]S/25758. [97]S/25928. [98]S/26302. [99]S/26427. [100]S/25790. [101]S/26103. [102]S/26449. [103]YUN 1991, p. 196, SC res. 692(1991), 20 May 1991. [104]S/25717. [105]S/26251. [106]S/26544. [107]S/25305. [108]YUN 1992, p. 317. [109]YUN 1991, p. 195. [110]S/25462. [111]YUN 1991, p. 197, SC res. 705(1991), 15 Aug. 1991. [112]SC res. 661(1990), 6 Aug. 1990. [113]YUN 1991, p. 198, SC res. 700(1991), 17 June 1991. [114]S/25442. [115]S/25930. [116]S/26430. [117]S/26874. [118]S/25298. [119]S/25761 & Corr.1. [120]S/25961 & S/26027. [121]S/25836 & Corr.1. [122]S/26204. [123]S/26380. [124]S/26826. [125]S/25653. [126]S/25775. [127]S/26353, S/26504, S/26597. [128]S/25157. [129]S/25830. [130]S/26474. [131]S/25480. [132]S/26126. [133]S/26768. [134]S/25357. [135]S/25790. [136]S/26103. [137]S/26449. [138]S/26740. [139]S/25523. [140]S/25945. [141]YUN 1992, p. 322. [142]S/25441. [143]SC res. 674(1990), 29 Oct. 1990. [144]SC res. 664(1990), 666(1990), 667(1990) & 670(1990), 18 Aug., 13, 16 & 25 Sep. 1990, respectively. [145]YUN 1961, p. 512. [146]YUN 1963, p. 510. [147]S/25976. [148]YUN 1991, p. 209, SC res. 712(1991), 19 Sep. 1991.

Iraq–United States

Throughout 1993, Iraq addressed numerous communications to the Secretary-General alleging daily violations of its airspace by the United States and accusing it of frequently dropping heat flares on civilian areas and provocative leaflets over southern Iraq. It also transmitted a press account of the use by the United States and its allies of radioactive artillery shells in their 1991 aggression against Iraq and provided a count of hundreds of miscellaneous unexploded bombs, projectiles and missiles found in various parts of the country and disposed of by Iraq.

The United States, on 26 June,[1] informed the Security Council President that, in accordance with Article 51 of the Charter, it had exercised its right of self-defence by responding to Iraq's unlawful attempt to murder the former President of the United States, George Bush, for actions he had taken while he was President, as well as to its continuing threat to United States nationals. Based on the pattern of Iraqi behaviour, including the disregard for international law and Council resolutions, the United States concluded that there was no reasonable prospect that new diplomatic initiatives or economic measures could influence the Iraqi Government to cease planning attacks against the United States.

As a last resort, the United States had decided to respond by striking at an Iraqi military and intelligence target involved in such attacks. The target had been chosen carefully so as to minimize risks of collateral damage to civilians. It was hoped that such limited and proportionate action might discourage or pre-empt unlawful Iraqi activities.

Owing to the seriousness of Iraq's actions, the United States requested an urgent meeting of the Council.

SECURITY COUNCIL CONSIDERATION

The Security Council convened on 27 June to consider the matter. At its request, Iraq was invited to participate in the discussions without the right to vote, in accordance with the relevant provisions of the Charter and rule 37a of the Council's provisional rules of procedure.

Before the Council was Iraq's letter of 27 June[2] condemning what it called a cowardly act of military aggression against Iraq. United States warships stationed in the Red Sea and the "Arabian Gulf" had fired 23 Tomahawk cruise missiles at the information service headquarters and the nearby civilian districts of Al-Mansour and Al-Ma'moun in the centre of Baghdad, leaving a large number of dead and wounded civilians. The grounds for carrying out such a terrorist act had been concocted with the complicity of Kuwait. United Nations silence in the face of such crimes had encouraged the United States to persist in perpetrating State terrorism and blackmail.

During Council consideration of the matter, the United States declared that every State regarded an assassination attempt against its former head of State an attack against itself and would react. On April 14, at the start of President Bush's three-day visit to Kuwait City, authorities there thwarted a terrorist plot, seizing a powerful car bomb and other explosives and arresting 16 suspects. The ringleaders of the plot were two Iraqi nationals.

Based on investigations conducted by law enforcement, forensic and intelligence professionals of the United States, its Department of Justice and Central Intelligence Agency concluded that Iraq had planned, equipped and launched the terrorist operation that threatened the life of President Bush. Physical evidence supporting that conclusion included forensic data, interviews with the 16 suspects currently on trial in Kuwait and other intelligence.

Iraq denied any role in the alleged attempted assassination, challenging the parties concerned to come up with clear evidence acceptable to an impartial third party. It called the plot a complete fabrication by Kuwait and a pretext for United States aggression against Iraq.

No proposal was submitted on which the Council was required to take action.

Meeting number. SC 3245.

REFERENCES

[1]S/26003. [2]S/26004.

Chapter IV

Europe

United Nations concern in Europe in 1993 centred on the former Yugoslavia, on the Baltic States and on those fledgling countries of the Commonwealth of Independent States riven by civil unrest and ethnic strife.

Throughout the year, armed hostilities continued to rage in Bosnia and Herzegovina and in Croatia over the irreconcilable imperatives of State sovereignty, ethnic autonomy and territorial claims. Prospects for peace in Bosnia and Herzegovina receded in early May when the Bosnian Serbs rejected the peace package worked out in negotiations under the auspices of the International Conference on the Former Yugoslavia. The United Nations peace-keeping plan for Croatia remained unimplemented. Pending an overall solution to the conflict in those countries, the immediate objectives of the United Nations and the International Conference on the Former Yugoslavia continued to be to halt the fighting in order to facilitate negotiations and delivery of humanitarian assistance to the most affected populations, to stop the widespread violations of international humanitarian law and to reverse the effects of ethnic cleansing.

The Security Council adopted a number of resolutions strengthening the sanctions in force against Yugoslavia (Serbia and Montenegro), designating safe areas in Bosnia and Herzegovina and authorizing corresponding enforcement measures. It extended and enlarged the mandate of the United Nations Protection Force, and created the International Tribunal to Prosecute Persons Responsible for Serious Violations of International Humanitarian Law Committed in the Territory of the Former Yugoslavia since 1991. In December, the General Assembly urged the Council to lift the arms embargo applicable to the entire territory of the former Yugoslavia in respect of Bosnia and Herzegovina, to enable that country fully to exercise its right of self-defence against the unrelenting onslaught of the Bosnian Serbs—a proposal earlier rejected by the Council.

The United Nations Protection Force continued to maintain a presence in the former Yugoslav Republic of Macedonia as a preventive measure in that potential flashpoint of strife.

The Assembly welcomed the withdrawal of Russian military forces from Lithuania and called for the conclusion of agreements on the withdrawal of such forces from Estonia and Latvia. The Council, responding to the widening conflict in Azerbaijan, where Armenian and Azerbaijani inhabitants of the enclave of Nagorny Karabakh had been fighting for five years, demanded a cessation of hostilities and the withdrawal of forces that had recently occupied areas of Azerbaijan. The Council also authorized the deployment of a United Nations Observer Mission in Georgia, where Government and Abkhaz forces had been fighting for the control of Abkhazia. The Secretary-General dispatched a Special Envoy to Tajikistan to help obtain a cease-fire in the armed conflict between the Government and a coalition of so-called democratic and Islamist forces and to initiate negotiations.

Situation in the former Yugoslavia

General aspects

The complex crisis in the former Yugoslavia continued to elude resolution in 1993, notwithstanding international efforts to resolve it. Bosnia and Herzegovina, Croatia and the former Yugoslav Republic of Macedonia were the main focus of concern, but principally the first two where fighting persisted, adding to the already tens of thousands of people dead or wounded and to the more than 3 million refugees and displaced persons.

The Co-Chairmen of the International Conference on the Former Yugoslavia (ICFY) crafted a peace plan for Bosnia and Herzegovina that failed, however, to receive the approval of the Bosnian Serbs. In Croatia, the Co-Chairmen tried unsuccessfully to persuade the conflicting parties to implement fully the United Nations peace-keeping plan for that country. They also worked towards promoting a settlement of the dispute between Greece and the former Yugoslav Republic of Macedonia arising over the name of the latter. In addition, the United Nations Protection Force (UNPROFOR) continued to monitor the situation along that country's border with Albania and Yugoslavia (Serbia and Montenegro).

Several times during the year the Security Council extended and expanded UNPROFOR's mandate. The Council buttressed the sanctions regime in force against Yugoslavia (Serbia and Montenegro) and created, as its subsidiary organ, the International Tribunal to Prosecute Persons Responsible for Serious Violations of International Humanitarian Law Committed in the Territory of the Former Yugoslavia since 1991.

Following the decision by Yugoslavia (Serbia and Montenegro) to deny continuation in the country of missions by the Conference on Security and Cooperation in Europe (CSCE) that had been monitoring the situation in the towns of Kosovo, Sandjak and Vojvodina as a measure of preventive diplomacy, the Council called on the Government to reconsider that decision and to agree to the resumption of the missions' activities and to an increase in the number of monitors.

The international relief operation, led by the Office of the United Nations High Commissioner for Refugees (UNHCR), attempted to alleviate the suffering of the civilian population throughout the war-torn region by delivering convoys of basic humanitarian items and multi-sectoral assistance.

(For the human rights situation in the territory of the former Yugoslavia and General Assembly action on the subject, see PART THREE, Chapter X.)

International Conference on the Former Yugoslavia

The International Conference on the Former Yugoslavia, which in August 1992 replaced the Conference on Yugoslavia under the aegis of the European Community (EC),[1] continued in 1993 to serve as the forum for negotiations to resolve the crisis in the former Yugoslavia.

The Conference's Steering Committee was co-chaired by representatives of the Secretary-General and of the EC presidency, who were, respectively, Cyrus R. Vance (United States), succeeded by Thorvald Stoltenberg (Norway) with effect from 14 May,[2] and Lord David Owen (United Kingdom). The Steering Committee's membership included representatives of EC, CSCE, the Organization of the Islamic Conference (OIC), the five permanent members of the Security Council, representatives from neighbouring States, the International Committee of the Red Cross (ICRC) and UNHCR.

In addition to an Arbitration Commission and a secretariat, the Conference maintained six working groups whose work in 1993 was described in reports by the Secretary-General[3] and the Co-Chairmen.[4]

Between their first meeting in September 1992[1] and May 1993, the Co-Chairmen devoted their efforts towards hammering out a peace plan for Bosnia and Herzegovina that evolved into four constituent elements—a series of nine constitutional principles, a military agreement, a 10-province

map and an agreement on interim governmental arrangements—and to completing signature of the plan by the three Bosnian sides to the conflict (see below, under ''Bosnia and Herzegovina'').

In Croatia, the Co-Chairmen sponsored talks aimed at achieving a comprehensive cease-fire in and around the United Nations Protected Areas (UNPAs), to be followed by discussions on economic confidence-building steps. They also negotiated an agreement between the Government of Croatia and the local Serb authorities regarding implementation of Council resolution 802(1993), adopted in the wake of the January military incursion by Croatia into a pink zone and a UNPA around the Maslenica Bridge (see below, under ''Croatia'').

During April, the Co-Chairmen consulted with Greece and the former Yugoslav Republic of Macedonia in an attempt to settle their dispute over the latter's name in connection with its application for membership in the United Nations and to promote confidence-building measures between them (see PART ONE, Chapter V).

United Nations Protection Force

In 1993, the United Nations Protection Force, established in 1992[5] as an interim arrangement to create the conditions of peace and security required for the negotiation of an overall settlement of the Yugoslav crisis within the framework of the EC Conference on Yugoslavia (subsequently replaced by ICFY), was principally operational in Bosnia and Herzegovina, Croatia and the former Yugoslav Republic of Macedonia and had a liaison presence in Slovenia. It maintained its headquarters at Zagreb, Croatia.

In Croatia, the Force continued to be deployed in three UNPAs—areas where Serbs constituted a majority or a substantial minority of the population and where intercommunal tensions had led to armed conflict—divided into four sectors: Sector East (Eastern Slavonia, including Baranja and Western Srem), Sector North (northern Krajina), Sector South (southern Krajina) and Sector West (Western Slavonia). The cornerstone of its mandate remained the United Nations peace-keeping plan set out by the Secretary-General in a 1992 report, approved by the Council and based on which it created UNPROFOR (see below, under ''Croatia'').

The UNPROFOR mandate in Bosnia and Herzegovina was expanded and its strength correspondingly increased by the Council, which entrusted it with additional tasks: to modify the mechanism for approval and inspection of flights so as to provide for the authorization of humanitarian flights (resolution 816(1993)); and to take the necessary measures, including the use of force, in reply to bombardments of or armed incursions into the safe areas, or to any deliberate obstruction of UNPROFOR's freedom of movement or of protected humanitarian convoys (836(1993)). At the Council's request, the Secretary-General examined options (838(1993)) for deploying international observers on the borders of the country, with priority to its borders with Yugoslavia (Serbia and Montenegro), to monitor the arms embargo and other sanctions.

In the former Yugoslav Republic of Macedonia, UNPROFOR was to monitor and report any developments in the border areas that could undermine confidence and stability in that country and threaten its territory (see below, under "Former Yugoslav Republic of Macedonia"). It was also to coordinate closely with the CSCE mission there.[6]

The initial 12-month period for which UNPROFOR was established expired on 21 February 1993. It was, however, extended by Council resolutions during the year for successive additional interim periods ending on: 31 March (resolution 807(1993)), 30 June (815(1993)), 30 September (847(1993)), 1 and 5 October (for 24 hours and for four days (869(1993) and 870(1993)), and 31 March 1994 (871(1993)). The extensions were applicable to all UNPROFOR operations in the former Yugoslavia.

At the last mandate extension, the Council took note of the Secretary-General's intention to establish three subordinate commands within UNPROFOR—UNPROFOR (Croatia), UNPROFOR (Bosnia and Herzegovina) and UNPROFOR (the former Yugoslav Republic of Macedonia)—while retaining the existing dispositions in all other respects for the direction and conduct of the United Nations operation in the territory of the former Yugoslavia.

Composition

As at 31 December 1993, the strength of UNPROFOR in the former Yugoslavia stood at 26,947 troops, all ranks. Of that number, 675 were civilian police and 578 were military observers. The troops were provided by: Argentina, Belgium, Canada, Czech Republic, Denmark, Egypt, Finland, France, Jordan, Kenya, Malaysia, Nepal, Netherlands, Norway, Poland, Portugal, Russian Federation, Slovakia, Spain, Sweden, Ukraine, United Kingdom, United States.

Lieutenant-General Satish Nambiar (India) served as Force Commander from 4 March 1992 to 2 March 1993; he was replaced by Lieutenant-General Lars-Eric Wahlgren (Sweden), who served from 3 March to 30 June. General Jean Cot (France) was appointed Force Commander from 1 July.

On 1 December,[7] the Secretary-General proposed the appointment of Yasushi Akashi as his Special Representative for the former Yugoslavia and Chief of Mission of UNPROFOR, to which the Council agreed on 2 December.[8] The appointment was made to relieve Thorvald Stoltenberg of the duties of Special Representative, since, as Co-Chairman of the ICFY Steering Committee, he was heavily engaged in peace negotiations.

Financing

Report of the Secretary-General (June). According to a June report of the Secretary-General,[9] assessments apportioned among Member States in respect of UNPROFOR for the period from its inception on 12 January 1992 to 30 June 1993 totalled $716,754,979 as at 24 May 1993, while contributions received for that period amounted to $469,435,688, leaving a shortfall of $247,319,291. Voluntary contributions received from 15 October 1992 to 30 April 1993 in cash, services and supplies were valued at some $7.8 million. Contributions to the Trust Fund for the Common Costs of the Bosnia and Herzegovina Command, established in December 1992 to cover additional administrative expenses resulting from an enlargement of the Force in order to provide protection to humanitarian relief workers, totalled $4,024,261 as at 24 May 1993, while expenditures through 30 April 1993 amounted to $3,735,900.

Having been informed by the Secretary-General on 10 March that the cost of maintaining UNPROFOR for the mandate period from 21 February to 31 March 1993 was estimated at $61,184,000 gross ($60,440,000 net) and that an unencumbered balance of $33,424,100 gross ($33,170,700 net) remained from appropriations for the period 12 January 1992 to 20 February 1993, the Advisory Committee on Administrative and Budgetary Questions (ACABQ) concurred with his request for authorization to enter into commitments of $27,759,900 gross ($27,269,300 net) for the period from 21 February to 31 March 1993. These amounts represented the difference between estimated requirements for the extension period ending 31 March 1993, of $61,184,000 gross ($60,440,000 net) and unencumbered balance of appropriations for the period ending 20 February 1993 of $33,424,100 gross ($33,170,700 net). The Advisory Committee also concurred with the Secretary-General's requests to extend the first financial period of UNPROFOR by 39 days, up to and including 31 March 1993, and to consolidate and administer the resources provided to UNPROFOR from 12 January 1992 to 31 March 1993.

Expenditures from 12 January 1992 to 31 March 1993 totalled $579,309,400 gross ($575,583,200 net) and the cost of maintaining the Force for the period 1 April to 30 June 1993 was projected at $227,584,900 gross ($226,132,800 net). In April, the Secretary-General received ACABQ's concurrence to enter into reduced commitments of $151,193,575 gross ($149,477,002 net) for that period, inclusive of the $141,193,575 gross ($139,477,002 net) authorized by the General Assembly in 1992[10] and $10 million under the terms of a 1991 Assembly resolution on unforeseen and extraordinary expenses for the 1992-1993 biennium.[11] Not included in that amount were additional start-up requirements for expanded operations (in Bosnia and Herzegovina and in the former Yugoslav Republic of Macedonia) estimated at $79,137,400.

The estimated cost of maintaining UNPROFOR beyond 30 June 1993 to 30 June 1994, should its mandate be extended, was $77,065,450 gross ($76,484,725 net) per month, or $924,785,400 gross ($917,816,700 net) for the 12-month period. Reimbursements due to troop-contributing States through 30 April 1993 were estimated at $118,757,000.

The Secretary-General recommended that the Assembly extend the first UNPROFOR financial period to 31 March 1993; appropriate $255,344,800 gross ($253,402,100 net), including the amounts for which ACABQ concurrence had been received, for maintaining UNPROFOR from 21 February to 30 June; appropriate and apportion the amount for additional start-up requirements; and appropriate or grant commitment authorization of such additional amounts as necessary for maintaining UNPROFOR beyond 30 June. He also recommended that the Assembly establish for the Force a special financial period of 12 calendar months, from 1 July to 30 June, effective 1 July 1993, and apply special arrangements under article IV of the Financial Regulations of the United Nations dealing with retention beyond the financial period of unliquidated obligations owed to Governments.

ACABQ, in July,[12] reduced the cost of additional start-up requirements to $55 million gross and recommended appropriation and assessment of $200 million gross to maintain UNPROFOR from 1 July to 30 September 1993. It concurred with the Secretary-General's other requests for appropriations for the periods from 21 February to 30 June, including assessments of $86,391,325 gross ($86,655,798 net) for the maintenance of UNPROFOR from 1 April to 30 June. Also in July,[13] ACABQ considered that certain aspects of peace-keeping operations regarding international contractual personnel needed to be brought to the Assembly's attention, including whether remuneration of civilian staff should reflect primarily their country of recruitment or the quality of service delivered.

GENERAL ASSEMBLY ACTION (September)

On 14 September, the General Assembly, on the recommendation of the Fifth (Administrative and Budgetary) Committee, adopted **resolution 47/210 B** without vote.

Financing of the United Nations Protection Force

The General Assembly,

Having considered the report of the Secretary-General on the financing of the United Nations Protection Force and the related report of the Advisory Committee on Administrative and Budgetary Questions,

Bearing in mind Security Council resolutions 727(1992) of 8 January 1992 and 740(1992) of 7 February 1992, in which the Council endorsed the sending of a group of military liaison officers to Yugoslavia to promote maintenance of the cease-fire,

Bearing in mind also Security Council resolution 743(1992) of 21 February 1992, by which the Council established the United Nations Protection Force, and the subsequent resolutions by which the Council extended the mandate of the Force, the latest of which was resolution 847(1993) of 30 June 1993,

Recalling its resolutions 46/233 of 19 March 1992 and 47/210 A of 22 December 1992 on the financing of the Force,

Reaffirming that the costs of the Force are expenses of the Organization to be borne by Member States in accordance with Article 17, paragraph 2, of the Charter of the United Nations,

Recalling its previous decision regarding the fact that, in order to meet the expenditures caused by the Force, a different procedure is required from the one applied to meet expenditures of the regular budget of the United Nations,

Taking into account the fact that the economically more developed countries are in a position to make relatively larger contributions and that the economically less developed countries have a relatively limited capacity to contribute towards such an operation,

Bearing in mind the special responsibilities of the States permanent members of the Security Council, as indicated in General Assembly resolution 1874(S-IV) of 27 June 1963, in the financing of such operations,

Noting with appreciation that voluntary contributions have been made to the Force by certain Governments,

Mindful of the fact that it is essential to provide the Force with the necessary financial resources to enable it to fulfil its responsibilities under the relevant resolutions of the Security Council,

Expressing concern about the deteriorating financial situation with regard to the Force owing to overdue payments by Member States of their assessments, particularly Member States in arrears,

Also expressing concern about the delays in submission of budget documents until well into the financial period of the Force, which have contributed to the deteriorating financial situation,

Expressing deep concern about the adverse effect that the deteriorating financial situation has on reimbursement to troop contributors, placing an additional burden on these countries and putting at risk the continuing supply of troops to the Force and, consequently, the success of the operation,

1. *Endorses* the observations and recommendations contained in the report of the Advisory Committee on Administrative and Budgetary Questions, subject to the terms of the present resolution, and approves on an exceptional basis the special arrangements for the United

Nations Protection Force with regard to the application of article IV of the Financial Regulations of the United Nations, whereby appropriations required in respect of obligations owed to Governments providing contingents and/or logistic support to the Force shall be retained beyond the period stipulated under financial regulations 4.3 and 4.4, as set out in the annex to the present resolution;

2. *Requests* the Secretary-General to include in his report to the General Assembly at its forty-eighth session, referred to in paragraph 1 below, relevant information on the steps taken to comply with the recommendations of the Advisory Committee in its report and, in particular, the recommendation contained in paragraph 18 of the report of the Advisory Committee on the administrative and budgetary aspects of the financing of the United Nations peace-keeping operations;

3. *Also requests* the Secretary-General to take all necessary action to ensure that the Force is administered with a maximum of efficiency and economy, to improve management, and to include in his report to the General Assembly mentioned in paragraph 2 above the steps taken to improve management;

4. *Urges* all Member States to make every possible effort to ensure payment of their assessed contributions to the Force promptly and in full;

5. *Requests* the Secretary-General to explore all possibilities in order to ensure prompt reimbursement to troop-contributing countries;

6. *Decides* to extend the first financial period by thirty-nine days, up to and including 31 March 1993, and to consolidate and administer the resources provided to the Force for the period from its inception on 12 January 1992 to 31 March 1993, inclusive;

7. *Decides also* to appropriate to the Special Account referred to in General Assembly resolution 46/233 the amount of 27,759,900 United States dollars gross (27,269,300 dollars net), authorized and apportioned with the prior concurrence of the Advisory Committee under the terms of paragraph 7 of General Assembly resolution 47/210 A, for the operation of the Force for the period from 21 February to 31 March 1993;

8. *Decides further* to appropriate to the Special Account the amount of 227,584,900 dollars gross (226,132,800 dollars net), inclusive of the amount of 141,193,575 dollars gross (139,477,002 dollars net) authorized and apportioned with the prior concurrence of the Advisory Committee under the terms of paragraph 7 of General Assembly resolution 47/210 A, and the amount of 10 million dollars authorized by the Advisory Committee under the terms of paragraph 1 of Assembly resolution 46/187 of 20 December 1991, for the maintenance of the Force for the period from 1 April to 30 June 1993, inclusive;

9. *Decides* to appropriate to the Special Account an amount of 55 million dollars gross to meet the additional start-up requirements owing to the enlargement of the Force in the former Yugoslav Republic of Macedonia and in Bosnia and Herzegovina;

10. *Authorizes* the Secretary-General to enter into commitments for the operation of the Force in an amount not to exceed 200 million dollars gross (198,257,825 dollars net) for the period from 1 July to 30 September 1993, and, subject to the Security Council deciding to continue the Force beyond 30 September 1993 and to obtaining the prior concurrence of the Advisory Committee for the actual level of commitments to be entered into, to enter into commitments for the operation of the Force at a rate

not to exceed 65 million dollars gross (64,419,275 dollars net) per month for the period from 1 October to 31 December 1993, the said amounts to be apportioned among Member States in accordance with the scheme set out in the present resolution;

11. *Requests* the Secretary-General to submit to the General Assembly, prior to 1 November 1993, a full budget for the Force for the period from 1 July 1993 to 31 March 1994;

12. *Decides*, as an ad hoc arrangement, to apportion the amounts of 86,391,325 dollars gross (86,655,798 dollars net) for the period from 1 April to 30 June 1993, 55 million dollars gross for the additional start-up requirements owing to the enlargements of the Force in the former Yugoslav Republic of Macedonia and in Bosnia and Herzegovina and 200 million dollars gross (198,257,825 dollars net) for the period from 1 July to 30 September 1993 among Member States in accordance with the composition of groups set out in paragraphs 3 and 4 of General Assembly resolution 43/232 of 1 March 1989, as adjusted by the Assembly in its resolutions 44/192 B of 21 December 1989, 45/269 of 27 August 1991, 46/198 A of 20 December 1991 and 47/218 A, of 23 December 1992, and taking into account the scale of assessments for the years 1992, 1993 and 1994 set out in Assembly resolution 46/221 A of 20 December 1991 and Assembly decision 47/456 of 23 December 1992;

13. *Decides also* that, in accordance with the provisions of its resolution 973(X) of 15 December 1955, the apportionment among Member States, as provided for in paragraph 12 above, shall take into consideration the decrease in their respective share in the Tax Equalization Fund of the estimated staff assessment income of 264,473 dollars approved for the Force for the period from 1 April to 30 June 1993, inclusive;

14. *Decides further* that, in accordance with the provisions of its resolution 973(X), there shall be set off against the apportionment among Member States, as provided for in paragraph 12 above, their respective share in the Tax Equalization Fund of the estimated staff assessment income of 1,742,175 dollars for the period from 1 July to 30 September 1993 approved for the Force;

15. *Decides* to establish the contributions of Andorra, the Czech Republic, Eritrea, the former Yugoslav Republic of Macedonia, Monaco and Slovakia to the Force in accordance with the rates of assessment to be adopted by the General Assembly for these Member States at its forty-eighth session;

16. *Invites* the new Member States listed in paragraph 15 above to make advance payments against their assessed contributions, to be determined;

17. *Invites* voluntary contributions to the Force in cash and in the form of services and supplies acceptable to the Secretary-General, to be administered, as appropriate, in accordance with the procedure established by the General Assembly in its resolutions 43/230 of 21 December 1988, 44/192 A of 21 December 1989 and 45/258 of 3 May 1991.

ANNEX
Special arrangements with regard to the application of article IV of the Financial Regulations of the United Nations

1. At the end of the twelve-month period provided for in regulation 4.3, any unliquidated obligations of the financial period in question relating to goods supplied and services rendered by Governments for which claims

have been received or which are covered by established reimbursement rates shall be transferred to accounts payable; such accounts payable shall remain recorded in the Special Account until payment is effected;

2. *(a)* Any other unliquidated obligations of the financial period in question owed to Governments for goods supplied and services rendered, as well as other obligations owed to Governments, for which required claims have not yet been received shall remain valid for an additional period of four years following the end of the twelve-month period provided for in regulation 4.3;

(b) Claims received during this four-year period shall be treated as provided under paragraph 1 of the present annex, if appropriate;

(c) At the end of the additional four-year period, any unliquidated obligations shall be cancelled and the then remaining balance of any appropriations retained therefor shall be surrendered.

General Assembly resolution 47/210 B

14 September 1993   Meeting 110   Adopted without vote

Approved by Fifth Committee (A/47/825/Add.1) without vote, 3 September (meeting 74); draft by Chairman (A/C.5/47/L.42); agenda item 137.
Meeting numbers. GA 47th session: 5th Committee 68, 69, 72, 74; plenary 110.

Reports of the Secretary-General (December).

In a 3 December report,[14] the Secretary-General stated that assessments apportioned among Member States for the period 12 January 1992 to 31 December 1993 totalled $1,250,948,414 as at 12 November 1993, while contributions received for that period amounted to $873,685,791, leaving a shortfall of $377,262,623. The Trust Fund for the Common Costs of the Bosnia and Herzegovina Command received income of $5,426,621 as at 31 October, including contributions from Member States, public donations and interest, while Fund expenditures amounted to $3,131,600, resulting in an unencumbered balance of $2,295,021.

Resources made available to UNPROFOR from 12 January 1992 to 31 December 1993 totalled $1,256,894,300 gross ($1,248,231,650 net) and expenditures for that period were estimated at $1,237,223,600 gross ($1,228,633,650 net), leaving an unencumbered balance of $19,670,700 gross ($19,598,000 net). An additional $3,631,689 in interest and $75,372 in miscellaneous income were received for the same period. Estimated expenditures from 1 April to 30 June 1993 totalled $263,383,200 gross ($262,003,800 net), leaving an unencumbered balance of $19,201,700 gross ($19,129,000 net). Reimbursements due to troop-contributing States through 30 September 1993 were estimated at $75,201,700.

In a 9 December report on the financing of 17 peace-keeping operations,[15] including UNPROFOR, the Secretary-General indicated that the cost of maintaining UNPROFOR from 1 July 1993 to 31 March 1994 was estimated at $897,980,900 gross ($891,993,300 net), an increase of $502,980,900 gross ($500,477,700 net) above the amount already authorized. Cost estimates for the 12-month period

after 31 March 1994, should UNPROFOR's mandate be extended beyond that date, amounted to $1,244,806,200 gross ($1,232,835,900 net). The amount thus required for the 10-month period from 1 July 1993 to 30 April 1994 was estimated at $606,714,800 gross ($603,214,000 net), which represented the increased requirements, plus $103,733,900 gross ($102,736,300 net).

Pending consideration at its February 1994 session of the Secretary-General's full budget report, ACABQ, also in December,[16] recommended that the Secretary-General be authorized to enter into further commitments up to $450 million gross ($446 million net) until 31 March 1994, in addition to the existing commitment authority of $395 million through 31 December 1993.

In December, the General Assembly adopted **decision 48/470** without vote.

Financing of the United Nations Protection Force

At its 87th plenary meeting, on 23 December 1993, the General Assembly, on the recommendation of the Fifth Committee, in accordance with the framework set out in its resolution 48/227 of 23 December 1993, having considered the report of the Secretary-General on the financing of seventeen peace-keeping operations and the related reports of the Advisory Committee on Administrative and Budgetary Questions, and concurring with the observations of the Advisory Committee:

(a) Authorized the Secretary-General, on an exceptional basis, to enter into additional commitments up to the amount of $383,408,000 United States dollars gross (380 million dollars net) for the United Nations Protection Force for the period from 1 July 1993 to 28 February 1994;

(b) Decided at that time to apportion, as an ad hoc arrangement, the amount of 166,479,800 dollars gross (165 million dollars net) among Member States in accordance with the composition of groups set out in paragraphs 3 and 4 of Assembly resolution 43/232 of 1 March 1989, as adjusted by the Assembly in its resolutions 44/192 B of 21 December 1989, 45/269 of 27 August 1991, 46/198 A of 20 December 1991 and 47/218 A of 23 December 1992 and its decision 48/472 of 23 December 1993, and taking into account the scale of assessments for the years 1992, 1993 and 1994 as set out in Assembly resolutions 46/221 A of 20 December 1991 and 48/223 A of 23 December 1993 and its decision 47/456 of 23 December 1992;

(c) Also decided that, in accordance with the provisions of its resolution 973(X) of 15 December 1955, there should be set off against the apportionment among Member States, as provided for in subparagraph *(b)* above, their respective share in the Tax Equalization Fund of the estimated staff assessment income of 1,479,800 dollars for the period from 1 July 1993 to 28 February 1994;

(d) Further decided that, in view of the expiration of the commitment authority on 28 February 1994, priority should be given to the cost estimates for the Force

in the consideration by the General Assembly of peace-keeping budgets.

General Assembly decision 48/470

Adopted without vote

Approved by Fifth Committee (A/48/819) without vote, 22 December (meeting 46); draft by Chairman (A/C.5/48/L.22); agenda item 136.
Meeting numbers. GA 48th session: 5th Committee 44, 46; plenary 87.

International Tribunal

During the year, the Security Council created the International Tribunal for the Prosecution of Persons Responsible for Serious Violations of International Humanitarian Law Committed in the Territory of the Former Yugoslavia since 1991. The first in a series of steps leading to that action was the adoption by the Council in 1992 of two resolutions. One held that persons who committed or ordered the commission of grave breaches of the 1949 Geneva Conventions for the protection of war victims were individually responsible in respect of such breaches and called on States and international humanitarian organizations to collate substantiated information relating to such breaches (771(1992));[17] the other reiterated the call for substantiated information and requested the Secretary-General to establish an impartial Commission of Experts to examine information submitted and report to the Council on the Commission's conclusions (780(1992)).[18]

Communications. In accordance with the 1992 Security Council resolutions cited above, Austria,[19] Canada,[20] Switzerland,[21] and the United States[22] conveyed information to the Secretary-General on acts of wilful killing, torture of prisoners, abuse of civilians in detention centres, obstruction of the delivery of food and medical supplies to civilians, deliberate attacks on non-combatants, wanton devastation and destruction of property, and mass forcible expulsion and deportation of civilians in the territory of the former Yugoslavia.

Additional submissions and related information were provided by Bosnia and Herzegovina,[23] Croatia[24] and Yugoslavia (Serbia and Montenegro).[25]

Also drawn to the attention of the Council were the 1993 reports of the five-member Commission of Experts, a report on the preliminary exploration of a mass grave site near Vukovar, Croatia, and the periodic reports of the Special Rapporteur of the Commission on Human Rights on the human rights situation in the territory of the former Yugoslavia (see PART THREE, Chapter X) as well as the report of an EC investigative mission on the massive detention and rape of women, particularly Muslim women, in Bosnia and Herzegovina (see below, under "Bosnia and Herzegovina").

Preparatory to the Tribunal's creation, submissions were transmitted to the Council by France,[26] Italy,[27] and Sweden, on behalf of CSCE,[28] containing proposed modalities for the establishment

of such a tribunal, its attributes, features and institutional aspects.

In addition, the Commission of Experts, in its first interim report,[29] which concluded that grave breaches and other violations of international humanitarian law had been committed in the territory of the former Yugoslavia, noted that, should the Council or another competent organ of the United Nations decide to establish an ad hoc war crimes tribunal, such an initiative would be consistent with the direction of the Commission's work.

SECURITY COUNCIL ACTION (22 February)

The Security Council convened on 22 February to consider the question of establishing an international tribunal. It invited Bosnia and Herzegovina and Croatia, at their request, to participate without vote under rule 37[a] of the Council's provisional rules of procedure.

On the same date, the Council unanimously adopted **resolution 808(1993)**.

The Security Council,

Reaffirming its resolution 713(1991) of 25 September 1991 and all subsequent relevant resolutions,

Recalling paragraph 10 of its resolution 764(1992) of 13 July 1992, in which it reaffirmed that all parties are bound to comply with the obligations under international humanitarian law and in particular the Geneva Conventions of 12 August 1949, and that persons who commit or order the commission of grave breaches of the Conventions are individually responsible in respect of such breaches,

Recalling also its resolution 771(1992) of 13 August 1992, in which, *inter alia*, it demanded that all parties and others concerned in the former Yugoslavia, and all military forces in Bosnia and Herzegovina, immediately cease and desist from all breaches of international humanitarian law,

Recalling further its resolution 780(1992) of 6 October 1992, in which it requested the Secretary-General to establish, as a matter of urgency, an impartial Commission of Experts to examine and analyse the information submitted pursuant to resolutions 771(1992) and 780(1992), together with such further information as the Commission of Experts may obtain, with a view to providing the Secretary-General with its conclusions on the evidence of grave breaches of the Geneva Conventions and other violations of international humanitarian law committed in the territory of the former Yugoslavia,

Having considered the interim report of the Commission of Experts established by resolution 780(1992), in which the Commission observed that a decision to establish an ad hoc international tribunal in relation to events in the territory of the former Yugoslavia would be consistent with the direction of its work,

[a]Rule 37 of the Council's provisional rules of procedure states: "Any Member of the United Nations which is not a member of the Security Council may be invited, as the result of a decision of the Security Council, to participate, without vote, in the discussion of any question brought before the Security Council when the Security Council considers that the interests of that Member are specially affected, or when a Member brings a matter to the attention of the Security Council in accordance with Article 35(1) of the Charter."

Expressing once again its grave alarm at continuing reports of widespread violations of international humanitarian law occurring within the territory of the former Yugoslavia, including reports of mass killings and the continuance of the practice of "ethnic cleansing",

Determining that this situation constitutes a threat to international peace and security,

Determined to put an end to such crimes and to take effective measures to bring to justice the persons who are responsible for them,

Convinced that in the particular circumstances of the former Yugoslavia the establishment of an international tribunal would enable this aim to be achieved and would contribute to the restoration and maintenance of peace,

Noting in this regard the recommendation by the Co-Chairmen of the Steering Committee of the International Conference on the Former Yugoslavia for the establishment of such a tribunal,

Noting also with grave concern the "report of the European Community investigative mission into the treatment of Muslim women in the former Yugoslavia",

Noting further the report of the committee of jurists submitted by France, the report of the commission of jurists submitted by Italy, and the report transmitted by the Permanent Representative of Sweden on behalf of the Chairman-in-Office of the Conference on Security and Cooperation in Europe (CSCE),

1. *Decides* that an international tribunal shall be established for the prosecution of persons responsible for serious violations of international humanitarian law committed in the territory of the former Yugoslavia since 1991;

2. *Requests* the Secretary-General to submit for consideration by the Council at the earliest possible date, and if possible no later than 60 days after the adoption of the present resolution, a report on all aspects of this matter, including specific proposals and where appropriate options for the effective and expeditious implementation of the decision contained in paragraph 1 above, taking into account suggestions put forward in this regard by Member States;

3. *Decides* to remain actively seized of the matter.

Security Council resolution 808(1993)
22 February 1993   Meeting 3175   Adopted unanimously

Draft prepared in consultations among Council members (S/25314).

Communications. A number of States, responding to the Security Council's request for specific proposals for the establishment of an international tribunal, communicated their views to the Secretary-General. Egypt, Iran, Malaysia, Pakistan, Saudi Arabia, Senegal and Turkey (the OIC Contact Group on Bosnia and Herzegovina) submitted OIC's recommendations.[30] Also communicating their views were: Brazil,[31] Canada,[32] Mexico,[33] the Netherlands,[34] the Russian Federation,[35] Slovenia[36] and the United States.[37]

Yugoslavia (Serbia and Montenegro) said on 19 May[38] that all perpetrators of war crimes committed in the territory of the former Yugoslavia should be prosecuted and punished under national laws. Yugoslavia (Serbia and Montenegro), among those advocating the establishment of a permanent international tribunal, regarded as discriminatory the attempts to establish an ad hoc tribunal. War crimes, it said, were not committed in the territory of one State alone; hence, the selective approach to the former Yugoslavia was contrary to the principle of universality. The Council had no mandate to establish an international tribunal and Yugoslavia (Serbia and Montenegro) considered the drive to create one to be politically motivated.

Report of the Secretary-General. As requested by the Security Council, the Secretary-General submitted a 3 May report,[39] which took account of the suggestions put forward by the States mentioned above, in particular proposals submitted by France,[26] Italy[27] and Sweden on behalf of CSCE,[28] the views of the Commission of Experts and information gathered by that Commission. The report also took account of the suggestions or comments put forward by Australia, Austria, Belgium, Chile, China, Denmark, Germany, Ireland, Italy, New Zealand, Portugal, Spain, and the United Kingdom.

The report examined the legal basis for the establishment of the International Tribunal, set out in detail its competence in respect of the law it would apply, the persons to whom the law would be applied, including considerations as to the principle of individual criminal responsibility, its territorial and temporal reach and the relation of its work to that of national courts. It set out detailed views on the organization of the Tribunal (including the composition of the three Chambers, the qualification and election of judges, rules of procedure and evidence, the Prosecutor and the Registry responsible for servicing the Tribunal), on the investigation and pre-trial proceedings, on trial and post-trial proceedings, and on cooperation and judicial assistance. A concluding chapter dealt with a number of general and organizational issues.

The text of the Statute of the International Tribunal was annexed to the report.

With regard to the legal basis for establishing the Tribunal, the report stated that the Security Council would be establishing, as an enforcement measure under Chapter VII, a subsidiary organ within the terms of Article 29 of the Charter of the United Nations, but one of a judicial nature. That organ would perform its functions independently of political considerations and would not be subject to Council authority or control with regard to the performance of its judicial functions. However, the life span of the Tribunal would be linked to the restoration and maintenance of international peace and security in the territory of the former Yugoslavia, and Council decisions related thereto.

In a 19 May addendum to his report,[40] the Secretary-General estimated the costs of the Tribunal at approximately $31.2 million for its first year of operation.

SECURITY COUNCIL ACTION (25 May and 20 August)

The Security Council met on 25 May to consider the Secretary-General's 3 May report. At their request, Bosnia and Herzegovina and Croatia were invited to participate in the discussion without the right to vote under rule 37.[a] The Council unanimously adopted **resolution 827(1993)**.

The Security Council,

Reaffirming its resolution 713(1991) of 25 September 1991 and all subsequent relevant resolutions,

Having considered the report of the Secretary-General pursuant to paragraph 2 of resolution 808(1993),

Expressing once again its grave alarm at continuing reports of widespread and flagrant violations of international humanitarian law occurring within the territory of the former Yugoslavia, and especially in the Republic of Bosnia and Herzegovina, including reports of mass killings, massive, organized and systematic detention and rape of women, and the continuance of the practice of "ethnic cleansing", including for the acquisition and the holding of territory,

Determining that this situation continues to constitute a threat to international peace and security,

Determined to put an end to such crimes and to take effective measures to bring to justice the persons who are responsible for them,

Convinced that in the particular circumstances of the former Yugoslavia the establishment as an ad hoc measure by the Council of an international tribunal and the prosecution of persons responsible for serious violations of international humanitarian law would enable this aim to be achieved and would contribute to the restoration and maintenance of peace,

Believing that the establishment of an international tribunal and the prosecution of persons responsible for the above-mentioned violations of international humanitarian law will contribute to ensuring that such violations are halted and effectively redressed,

Noting in this regard the recommendation by the Co-Chairmen of the Steering Committee of the International Conference on the Former Yugoslavia for the establishment of such a tribunal,

Reaffirming in this regard its decision in resolution 808(1993) that an international tribunal shall be established for the prosecution of persons responsible for serious violations of international humanitarian law committed in the territory of the former Yugoslavia since 1991,

Considering that, pending the appointment of the Prosecutor of the International Tribunal, the Commission of Experts established pursuant to resolution 780(1992) should continue on an urgent basis the collection of information relating to evidence of grave breaches of the Geneva Conventions and other violations of international humanitarian law as proposed in its interim report,

Acting under Chapter VII of the Charter of the United Nations,

1. *Approves* the report of the Secretary-General;

2. *Decides* hereby to establish an international tribunal for the sole purpose of prosecuting persons responsible for serious violations of international humanitarian law committed in the territory of the former Yugoslavia between 1 January 1991 and a date to be determined by the Security Council upon the restoration of peace and to this end to adopt the Statute of the International Tribunal annexed to the above-mentioned report;

3. *Requests* the Secretary-General to submit to the judges of the International Tribunal, upon their election, any suggestions received from States for the rules of procedure and evidence called for in Article 15 of the Statute of the International Tribunal;

4. *Decides* that all States shall cooperate fully with the International Tribunal and its organs in accordance with the present resolution and the Statute of the International Tribunal and that consequently all States shall take any measures necessary under their domestic law to implement the provisions of the present resolution and the Statute, including the obligation of States to comply with requests for assistance or orders issued by a Trial Chamber under Article 29 of the Statute;

5. *Urges* States and intergovernmental and non-governmental organizations to contribute funds, equipment and services to the International Tribunal, including the offer of expert personnel;

6. *Decides* that the determination of the seat of the International Tribunal is subject to the conclusion of appropriate arrangements between the United Nations and the Netherlands acceptable to the Council, and that the International Tribunal may sit elsewhere when it considers it necessary for the efficient exercise of its functions;

7. *Decides* also that the work of the International Tribunal shall be carried out without prejudice to the right of the victims to seek, through appropriate means, compensation for damages incurred as a result of violations of international humanitarian law;

8. *Requests* the Secretary-General to implement urgently the present resolution and in particular to make practical arrangements for the effective functioning of the International Tribunal at the earliest time and to report periodically to the Council;

9. *Decides* to remain actively seized of the matter.

Security Council resolution 827(1993)

25 May 1993   Meeting 3217   Adopted unanimously

6-nation draft (S/25826).
Sponsors: France, New Zealand, Russian Federation, Spain, United Kingdom, United States.

Pursuant to article 13, subparagraph 2 *(a)*, of the Statute of the International Tribunal, the Legal Counsel, on behalf of the Secretary-General, invited, by a letter of 3 June, all Member States of the United Nations and non-member States maintaining a permanent observer mission to the United Nations to submit their nominations for judges of the Tribunal, up to two candidates, no two of whom were to be of the same nationality. The nominations were forwarded to the Council President in accordance with subparagraph 2 *(c)* of the same article of the Statute.

The Council convened on 20 August to draw up a list of candidates for judges from the nominations submitted. It unanimously adopted **resolution 857(1993)**.

The Security Council,

Recalling its resolutions 808(1993) of 22 February 1993 and 827(1993) of 25 May 1993,

Having decided to consider the nominations for Judges of the International Tribunal received by the Secretary-General before 16 August 1993,

Establishes the following list of candidates in accordance with Article 13 of the Statute of the International Tribunal:

Mr. Georges Michel Abi-Saab (Egypt)
Mr. Julio A. Barberis (Argentina)
Mr. Raphaël Barras (Switzerland)
Mr. Sikhe Camara (Guinea)
Mr. Antonio Cassese (Italy)
Mr. Hans Axel Valdemar Corell (Sweden)
Mr. Jules Deschenes (Canada)
Mr. Alfonso De los Heros (Peru)
Mr. Jerzy Jasinski (Poland)
Mr. Heike Jung (Germany)
Mr. Adolphus Godwin Karibi-Whyte (Nigeria)
Mr. Valentin G. Kisilev (Russian Federation)
Mr. Germain Le Foyer de Costil (France)
Mr. Li Haopei (China)
Ms. Gabrielle Kirk McDonald (United States of America)
Mr. Amadou N'Diaye (Mali)
Mr. Daniel David Ntanda Nsereko (Uganda)
Ms. Elizabeth Odio Benito (Costa Rica)
Mr. Hüseyin Pazarci (Turkey)
Mr. Moragodage Christopher Walter Pinto (Sri Lanka)
Mr. Rustam S. Sidhwa (Pakistan)
Sir Ninian Stephen (Australia)
Mr. Lal Chan Vohrah (Malaysia)

Security Council resolution 857(1993)

20 August 1993   Meeting 3265   Adopted unanimously

Draft prepared in consultations among Council members (S/26331).

Communications. Following adoption of Security Council resolution 827(1993), the Secretary-General, on 26 May,[41] requested the inclusion of an additional item in the agenda of the forty-seventh session of General Assembly entitled "Election of judges of the International Tribunal for the Prosecution of Persons Responsible for Serious Violations of International Humanitarian Law Committed in the Territory of the Former Yugoslavia since 1991". He also requested that the item be considered directly in plenary meeting. Based on the urgency of the request, the Assembly, on 28 May, decided to waive rule 40 of its rules of procedure requiring a meeting of the General Committee on the question and approved the request.

On 20 August,[42] the Security Council President transmitted resolution 857(1993) to the Assembly President. By a 26 August memorandum,[43] the Secretary-General transmitted the list of the 23 candidates nominated by the Council and the procedure for electing the 11 judges of the Tribunal. On 1 September,[44] he further transmitted the curricula vitae of the nominees.

GENERAL ASSEMBLY ACTION

On 17 September, following its consideration of the nominees, the General Assembly adopted **decision 47/328** without vote. By that decision it elected the following judges of the International Tribunal for a four-year term of office beginning on 17 November 1993: Georges Michel Abi-Saab (Egypt); Antonio Cassese (Italy); Jules Deschenes (Canada); Adolphus Godwin Karibi-Whyte (Nigeria); Germain Le Foyer De Costil (France); Li Haopei (China); Gabrielle Kirk McDonald (United States of America); Elizabeth Odio Benito (Costa Rica); Rustam S. Sidhwa (Pakistan); Ninian Stephen (Australia); Lal Chan Vohrah (Malaysia).

SECURITY COUNCIL ACTION

On 21 October, the Security Council convened to consider the appointment of the Prosecutor of the International Tribunal and adopted without vote **resolution 877(1993)**.

The Security Council,

Recalling its resolutions 808(1993) of 22 February 1993 and 827(1993) of 25 May 1993,

Having regard to Article 16 (4) of the Statute of the International Tribunal for the Prosecution of Persons Responsible for Serious Violations of International Humanitarian Law Committed in the Territory of the Former Yugoslavia since 1991,

Having considered the nomination by the Secretary-General of Mr. Ramon Escovar-Salom for the position of Prosecutor of the International Tribunal,

Appoints Mr. Ramon Escovar-Salom as Prosecutor of the International Tribunal.

Security Council resolution 877(1993)

21 October 1993   Meeting 3296   Adopted without vote

Draft prepared in consultations among Council members (S/26608).

Activities

Following their election on 17 September, the 11 judges of the International Tribunal began their four-year term on 17 November with an inaugural meeting at the Peace Palace (The Hague, Netherlands). They were scheduled to continue meeting until 30 November. At the inaugural meeting, the Tribunal elected Antonio Cassese (Italy) as President and Elizabeth Odio Benito (Costa Rica) as Vice-President, determined the membership of its Chambers, undertook a preliminary consideration of its rules of procedure and evidence, and discussed future working arrangements.

The Tribunal scheduled its second and third meetings to take place in 1994 at The Hague from 17 January to 4 February and from 11 to 22 April.

Financing

On 26 May,[41] the Secretary-General requested the inclusion in the agenda of the General Assembly of an item entitled "Financing of the International Tribunal for the Prosecution of Persons Responsible for Serious Violations of International Humanitarian Law Committed in the Territory of the Former Yugoslavia since 1991". The Assembly, on 28 May, approved that request.

ACABQ, on 22 July,[45] drew the Assembly's attention to a 2 July request from the Secretary-General, made under the terms of a 1991 resolution on unforeseen and extraordinary expenses for the 1992-1993 biennium,[11] to enter into commitments not exceeding $1,568,500 for the Tribunal's anticipated expenses in 1993. Pending an Assembly decision on the nature of the financing of the Tribunal, ACABQ granted the Secretary-General authority to enter into commitments in an amount not exceeding $500,000 for immediate requirements.

In a 20 August Secretariat note,[46] the Secretary-General proposed an article for inclusion in the Statute of the International Tribunal providing that its expenses would be borne by the regular budget of the Organization. The Security Council approved that approach and included the proposed article in the Statute adopted.

GENERAL ASSEMBLY ACTION

On 14 September, on the recommendation of the Fifth Committee, the General Assembly adopted **resolution 47/235** without vote.

Financing of the International Tribunal for the Prosecution of Persons Responsible for Serious Violations of International Humanitarian Law Committed in the Territory of the Former Yugoslavia since 1991

The General Assembly,

Having considered Security Council resolution 808(1993) of 22 February 1993, on the establishment of the International Tribunal for the Prosecution of Persons Responsible for Serious Violations of International Humanitarian Law Committed in the Territory of the Former Yugoslavia since 1991, and Council resolution 827(1993) of 25 May 1993, by which the Council adopted the statute of the International Tribunal,

Having also considered the note by the Secretariat on the financing of the International Tribunal and the report of the Advisory Committee on Administrative and Budgetary Questions,

Taking into account the views expressed by Member States in the Fifth Committee,

1. *Endorses* the observations and recommendations contained in the report of the Advisory Committee on Administrative and Budgetary Questions;

2. *Reaffirms*, in the context of Security Council resolution 827(1993) and with respect to the financing of the International Tribunal for the Prosecution of Persons Responsible for Serious Violations of International Humanitarian Law Committed in the Territory of the

Former Yugoslavia since 1991, the role of the General Assembly as set out in Article 17 of the Charter of the United Nations, as the organ to consider and approve the budget of the Organization, as well as the apportionment of its expenses among Member States;

3. *Expresses concern* that advice given to the Security Council by the Secretariat on the nature of the financing of the International Tribunal did not respect the role of the General Assembly as set out in Article 17 of the Charter;

4. *Requests* the President of the General Assembly to bring to the attention of the President of the Security Council the contents of the present resolution;

5. *Endorses* the recommendation of the Advisory Committee to authorize the Secretary-General to enter into commitments in an amount not to exceed 500,000 United States dollars to provide for the immediate and urgent requirements of the International Tribunal for its initial activities;

6. *Requests* the Secretary-General to submit, during the forty-eighth session of the General Assembly and before 31 December 1993, detailed cost estimates for the International Tribunal, separate from the proposed programme budget for the biennium 1994-1995, to be financed through assessed contributions and, pending a final decision on the manner of apportioning the expenses of the International Tribunal, to finance its activities through a separate account outside the regular budget;

7. *Invites* Member States and other interested parties to make voluntary contributions to the International Tribunal both in cash and in the form of services and supplies acceptable to the Secretary-General;

8. *Decides* to include in the draft agenda of its forty-eighth session the item entitled "Financing of the International Tribunal for the Prosecution of Persons Responsible for Serious Violations of International Humanitarian Law Committed in the Territory of the Former Yugoslavia since 1991".

General Assembly resolution 47/235

14 September 1993   Meeting 110   Adopted without vote

Approved by Fifth Committee (A/47/1014) without vote, 10 September (meeting 76); draft by Chairman (A/C.5/47/L.49); agenda item 155.
Meeting numbers. GA 47th session: 5th Committee 70, 72, 76; plenary 110.

Report of the Secretary-General. In an 8 December report,[47] the Secretary-General revised his initial estimate for financing the International Tribunal during 1993 from $1,568,500 to $450,800, based on the schedule established for the rest of the year.

The Secretary-General presented for approval estimated requirements of $33,200,000 for the Tribunal in the programme budget for the 1994-1995 biennium.

Requirements for staff assessment in respect of posts proposed for the Tribunal were estimated at $4,753,300 and would be offset in the same amount by income from staff assessment.

ACABQ noted on 15 December[48] that, pending a final decision on the manner of apportionment of the Tribunal's expenses, they were to be financed through a separate account outside the

United Nations regular budget and that the General Assembly had invited Member States and other interested parties to make voluntary contributions to the Tribunal. It further noted that pledges amounting to $3 million had been recorded in the trust fund established by the Secretary-General for that purpose.

ACABQ recommended that the Secretary-General be authorized to enter into commitments not exceeding $5.6 million for the first six months of 1994.

GENERAL ASSEMBLY ACTION

In December, on the recommendation of the Fifth Committee, the General Assembly adopted **decision 48/461** without a vote.

Financing of the International Tribunal for the Prosecution of Persons Responsible for Serious Violations of International Humanitarian Law Committed in the Territory of the Former Yugoslavia since 1991

At its 87th plenary meeting, on 23 December 1993, the General Assembly, on the recommendation of the Fifth Committee, having considered the report of the Secretary-General and the related report of the Advisory Committee on Administrative and Budgetary Questions:

(a) Endorsed the recommendations of the Advisory Committee contained in paragraphs 8 and 9 of its report;

(b) Authorized the Secretary-General to enter into commitments not to exceed $5.6 million United States dollars for the first six months of 1994, pending a final decision by the Assembly on the mode of financing the International Tribunal and without prejudice to recommendations that the Advisory Committee may make to the Assembly and the decisions that the Assembly may take thereon with regard to administrative matters, including the location of the Court, the levels and numbers of staff and the conditions of service of the judges and staff;

(c) Decided to consider at its resumed forty-eighth session the question of the mode of financing of the International Tribunal and the conditions of service and allowances of its members.

General Assembly decision 48/461

Adopted without vote

Approved by Fifth Committee (A/47/1014) without vote, 10 September (meeting 76); draft by Chairman (A/C.5/47/L.49); agenda item 155.
Meeting numbers. GA 48th session: 5th Committee 70, 72, 76; plenary 87.

Sanctions

In 1993, the Security Council took action to strengthen the sanctions regime against Yugoslavia (Serbia and Montenegro) that had been imposed by it in 1991 and 1992. The sanctions included a general and complete arms embargo applicable to the whole of the former Socialist Federal Republic of Yugoslavia (resolution 713(1991)),[49] comprehensive and mandatory sanctions to be implemented by all States (757(1992)),[50] and prohibition of transshipment through Yugoslavia (Serbia and Mon-

tenegro) of specific commodities and types of products (787(1992))[51] unless authorized by the Committee established pursuant to resolution 724(1991) (Committee on sanctions).[52]

In April, by resolution 819(1993), the Council demanded that Yugoslavia (Serbia and Montenegro) immediately cease the supply of arms, equipment and services to Bosnian Serb paramilitary units in Bosnia and Herzegovina and, by resolution 820(1993), it strengthened the sanctions regime against Yugoslavia (Serbia and Montenegro) effective nine days after the resolution's adoption, unless the Bosnian Serb party signed the Vance-Owen peace plan in full and ceased its military attacks in Bosnia and Herzegovina (see below). The strengthened sanctions would: prevent diversion to Yugoslavia (Serbia and Montenegro) of commodities and products, by land and sea, said to be destined for other places; require authorization by the Committee on sanctions for the transshipment of commodities and products through that country on the Danube River; forbid vessels registered in that country, owned or operated by it, or suspected of violating Council resolutions, to pass through installations within the territory of Member States; and authorize Member States to freeze any funds in their territories belonging to that country. Since the Bosnian Serb party maintained its rejection of the peace plan by the scheduled deadline, the new sanctions went into force on 26 April.

To facilitate the implementation of the sanctions regime, the Council further took action on the possible deployment of international observers on the borders of Bosnia and Herzegovina with Croatia and with Yugoslavia (Serbia and Montenegro), giving priority to its borders with the latter. An exemption from the arms embargo for Bosnia and Herzegovina was initiated by 22 Member States, as well as by that country itself, based on Article 51 of the Charter. (For details on these topics and on the related ban on military flights in the airspace of Bosnia and Herzegovina, see below, under ''Bosnia and Herzegovina''.)

During 1993, a number of States communicated to the Secretary-General the measures they had taken to implement the sanctions mandated by the Council.

Navigation on the Danube

Romania, in a 27 January declaration,[53] reported on measures it had taken to implement the sanctions in resolutions 757(1992) and 787(1992). The declaration also described how, on 18, 23 and 25 January, five separate convoys carrying petroleum products and towed by Yugoslav tugboats had succeeded in navigating the Danube from Ukraine to Yugoslavia (Serbia and Montenegro) despite Romania's efforts to intercept the convoy for inspection. On 28 January,[54] Bulgaria, referring to the 18 January convoy which had passed through the Bulgaria-Romania sector of the Danube, reported that its attempts to intercept it were likewise unsuccessful.

Both Bulgaria and Romania reported having brought these violations to the attention of all concerned, including Ukraine and the Committee on sanctions.

SECURITY COUNCIL ACTION

The Security Council, following consultations among its members on 28 January, authorized its President to make the following statement[55] to the media on behalf of the Council:

"In connection with letters of 27 January 1993 from the Chargés d'affaires of Bulgaria and Romania to the President of the Security Council, the members of the Council heard a report from the Chairman of the Committee established by resolution 724(1991) about Yugoslav vessels carrying oil from Ukraine to Serbia by way of the Danube, a flagrant violation of mandatory Security Council resolutions.

"The members of the Council are concerned that these shipments are reported to have left Ukrainian territory after the adoption of resolution 757(1992) and indeed may have left after the adoption of resolution 787(1992). They call on the Government of Ukraine to ensure that no further such shipments are permitted.

"The members of the Council are also extremely concerned that some of the vessels have already reached Serbia. In this regard, they demand that the authorities of the Federal Republic of Yugoslavia (Serbia and Montenegro) comply fully with the relevant resolutions. They have asked the President of the Council to convey their concern to the representatives of Romania and Bulgaria, to remind them of their clear obligations under the relevant resolutions and to seek an explanation of their failure to fulfil them. They have asked the President to draw particular attention to the relevant resolutions, which make clear the responsibility of all riparian States to take necessary measures to ensure that shipping on the Danube is in accordance with Security Council resolutions, including such enforcement measures commensurate with the specific circumstances as may be necessary to halt such shipping. The members of the Council reaffirm their support for vigorous enforcement of the relevant resolutions, and they are clear that the riparian States have the means to fulfil this obligation and that they must do so forthwith."

Communications. Ukraine responded on 29 January[56] that, according to its investigations, no oil or petroleum products had been shipped to Yugoslavia (Serbia and Montenegro) by Ukrainian flag vessels after the adoption of resolutions 757(1992) and 787(1992). Documents showed that the vessels referred to had been loaded in the Danube from tankers with petroleum products shipped by companies of Bulgaria, Cyprus, Greece, the Russian Federation, and Turkey among others, and that their destination was other than Yugoslavia (Serbia and Montenegro). Ukraine provided data relevant to the movement of vessels with petroleum products through Ukrainian waters in the Danube between 30 November 1992 and 23 January 1993.

Ukraine, in a 29 January statement,[57] said that it had been reliably established that the convoys were to deliver their cargo to Austria, Bosnia and Herzegovina, Croatia, the Czech Republic and Slovakia.

SECURITY COUNCIL ACTION

Following further consultations on 10 February regarding the situation on the Danube, the Security Council authorized its President to make the statement below to the media:[58]

"The members of the Security Council have heard a report from the Chairman of the Committee established by resolution 724(1991) about the detention of Romanian vessels on the Danube by the authorities of the Federal Republic of Yugoslavia (Serbia and Montenegro).

"They have learned that the Minister of Transport of the Federal Republic of Yugoslavia (Serbia and Montenegro) has threatened to detain more Romanian vessels if Romania does not allow the passage of Yugoslav vessels on the Danube. They have also learned that the Minister for Foreign Affairs of the Federal Republic of Yugoslavia (Serbia and Montenegro) has addressed a letter to the Chairman of the Committee established by resolution 724(1991) informing him that the Romanian vessels would be released without further delay, which according to information provided by the Chargé d'affaires of the Permanent Mission of Romania to the United Nations has not yet happened.

"The members of the Council recall their statement of 28 January 1993 about the responsibility of States to enforce mandatory Security Council resolutions, with particular reference to Yugoslav vessels attempting to violate those resolutions by way of the Danube. They commend the Romanian Government for the action it has since taken in this regard and reaffirm once again their full support for vigorous enforcement of the relevant resolutions.

"They also recall that under Article 103 of the Charter, the obligations of the Members of the United Nations under the Charter prevail over their obligations under any other international agreement.

"The members of the Council condemn any such retaliatory action and threats of such action by the authorities of the Federal Republic of Yugoslavia (Serbia and Montenegro). It is wholly unacceptable for those authorities to take retaliatory measures in response to action by a State in fulfilment of its obligations under the Charter of the United Nations. They demand that the authorities of the Federal Republic of Yugoslavia (Serbia and Montenegro) release forthwith the Romanian vessels they have unjustifiedly detained, and that they desist from further unlawful detentions."

Communications. On 26 February,[59] Hungary informed the Security Council President that because Romania had denied Yugoslav convoys access to the "Iron Gate" lock, some 45 Yugoslav barges were blocking the Danube, bringing navigation on that vital international waterway to a complete halt. The situation was inflicting further losses on the economies of the riparian States, already severely damaged by the sanctions regime. Austria, on 2 March,[60] referring to the blockade as illegal and retaliatory, asked the Council to remedy the situation.

On 10 March,[61] Yugoslavia (Serbia and Montenegro), replying to the Council President's call of 26 February demanding removal of the blockade, stated that all the barges and ships in question, owned by a Yugoslav private holding company, were removed on 2 March and that navigation in the Danube had been restored. The temporary blockade, neither caused nor encouraged by the Government of Yugoslavia (Serbia and Montenegro), had been instigated by independent trade unions of Yugoslav private shipping companies.

Hungary, on 18 May,[62] drew attention to the continued collection by Yugoslavia (Serbia and Montenegro) of transit charges from vessels passing through the Yugoslav sector of the Danube. Austria reported on 30 July[63] that the Danube situation was deteriorating owing to a recent blockade of the river at Belgrade; it expressed concern that States acting in accordance with the Council resolutions on sanctions were being confronted with acts of retortion. Hungary, referring to the same situation on 11 October,[64] stated that the blockade had been initiated in mid-July by two Serbian non-governmental organizations. Tolls had also begun to be imposed since 30 August by the so-called Republic of Serbian Krajina (also referred to as the Republic of Krajina).

SECURITY COUNCIL ACTION

The Security Council met on 13 October to consider the item "Navigation on the Danube river in the Federal Republic of Yugoslavia (Serbia and Montenegro)" and authorized its President to make the following statement[65] on the Council's behalf:

Meeting number. SC 3290.

"The Security Council has learned with deep concern that the blocking of the Danube by two Serbian non-governmental organizations is still continuing and deplores the acquiescence of the authorities of the Federal Republic of Yugoslavia (Serbia and Montenegro), which is reflected in the fact that they have failed to take any action to prevent these acts. It condemns these deliberate and unjustified acts of interference with the river traffic of several Member States of the United Nations. It emphasizes the importance it attaches to the free and unhindered navigation on the Danube which is essential for legitimate trade in the region. It reminds the authorities of the Federal Republic of Yugoslavia (Serbia and Montenegro) of their previous written commitment to secure free and safe navigation on this vital international waterway.

"The Security Council is also concerned that the authorities of the Federal Republic of Yugoslavia (Serbia and Montenegro) continue to impose tolls on foreign vessels transiting the section of the Danube which passes through the territory of the Federal Republic of Yugoslavia (Serbia and Montenegro). By extracting these payments, the Federal Republic of Yugoslavia (Serbia and Montenegro) violates its international obligations. The Security Council rejects any attempt to justify, on whatever ground, the imposition of tolls on the Danube. It demands that the authorities of the Federal Republic of Yugoslavia (Serbia and Montenegro) and any others imposing similar tolls cease such action immediately.

"The Security Council condemns these illegal actions and reaffirms that it is wholly unacceptable for the Federal Republic of Yugoslavia (Serbia and Montenegro) to take retaliatory measures in response to action by a State in fulfilment of its obligations under the Charter of the United Nations. It reminds the Federal Republic of Yugoslavia (Serbia and Montenegro) of its own international obligations and demands that its authorities ensure free movement of international traffic on the Danube.

"The Security Council remains seized of the matter."

On 20 December,[66] Ukraine drew attention to the customs law enacted by the Yugoslav authorities on 26 November, requiring vessels transiting through the Yugoslav sector of the Danube to pay a deposit equivalent to 50 per cent of the cargo's value. Ukraine asked that the Council take urgent measures to stop the illegal actions to which Yugoslavia (Serbia and Montenegro) was resorting.

Special economic assistance

Between January and June 1993, Bulgaria,[67] Hungary,[68] Romania,[69] Slovakia[70] and Ukraine[71] informed the Security Council President and the Secretary-General of economic difficulties they were undergoing as a result of their compliance with Council resolutions 757(1992), 787(1992) and 820(1993) and appealed for special economic assistance under the provisions of Article 50 of the Charter. The subject was further addressed in a letter to the Security Council President from Bulgaria, Romania and Ukraine[72] regarding sanctions implementation.

Yugoslavia (Serbia and Montenegro) reported the devastating impact of the sanctions on its economy and on the health and social well-being of its population, owing to the long procedure of the Committee on sanctions[52] for granting import approvals,[73] and complained about the Committee's failure to reply to its requests to import humanitarian items, to export certain commodities or to lift the freeze on its assets abroad.[74] It also provided data showing a serious decline in the country's health care services.[75] In November,[76] Yugoslavia (Serbia and Montenegro) transmitted an appeal by the Holy Synod of the Serbian Orthodox Church (Cetinje, 31 October–3 November) for the lifting of what the Synod called the inhuman sanctions.

SECURITY COUNCIL ACTION

The Security Council met on 18 June and unanimously adopted **resolution 843(1993)**.

The Security Council,

Recalling its resolution 724(1991) concerning Yugoslavia and all other relevant resolutions,

Recalling also Article 50 of the Charter of the United Nations,

Conscious of the fact that an increasing number of requests for assistance have been received under the provisions of Article 50 of the Charter of the United Nations,

Noting that the Security Council Committee established pursuant to resolution 724(1991), at its 65th meeting, set up a working group to examine the above-mentioned requests,

1. *Confirms* that the Committee established pursuant to resolution 724(1991) is entrusted with the task of examining requests for assistance under the provisions of Article 50 of the Charter of the United Nations;

2. *Welcomes* the establishment by the Committee of its working group and invites the Committee, as it completes the examination of each request, to make recommendations to the President of the Security Council for appropriate action.

Security Council resolution 843(1993)

18 June 1993   Meeting 3240   Adopted unanimously

Draft prepared in consultations among Council members (S/25956).

Recommendations of Committee on sanctions. On 2 July,[77] the Acting Chairman of the Committee on sanctions transmitted to the Security Council President recommendations for special economic assistance to five States—Bulgaria, Hungary, Romania, Uganda and Ukraine—together with their applications for such assistance and supporting explanatory material.

The Council President, on 6 July,[78] transmitted the Committee's recommendations to the Secretary-General with a request for their implementation (see PART THREE, Chapter III).

Humanitarian assistance programme

Under an international humanitarian assistance programme, various bodies of the United Nations system, EC, a number of non-governmental organizations and ICRC continued to deliver humanitarian assistance to the region. UNHCR remained the lead agency, with UNPROFOR providing escorts to humanitarian convoys, transport and engineering support, and determining the safest routes for the convoys.

The ICFY Working Group on Humanitarian Issues[4] reviewed the implementation of the programme at Geneva on 16 July. At a meeting on 8 October, it launched a new consolidated appeal revising needs for the period October to December 1993 and putting forward the requirements for the first half of 1994, totalling $697 million.

Contributions to the programme during the year consisted of $297,700,000 in cash and $206,700,000 in kind. Humanitarian assistance in metric tonnage provided to affected populations in the former Yugoslavia in 1993 was as follows: Bosnia and Herzegovina—267,763 metric tonnes; Croatia—92,193; the former Yugoslav Republic of Macedonia—2,967; Montenegro—3,953; and Serbia—38,614. Beneficiaries numbered 4,259,000 as at October 1993.

(See also below, under "Bosnia and Herzegovina"; and PART THREE, Chapters III and XV.)

Bosnia and Herzegovina

Despite numerous cease-fire agreements and reaffirmations of peace, the warring parties in Bosnia and Herzegovina, mainly the Muslim-dominated Government and the Bosnian Serbs, pursued throughout 1993 the armed hostilities that had raged between them since April 1992.

The year began with the assassination by Serbian extremists of Bosnia and Herzegovina's Deputy Prime Minister for Economic Affairs while under UNPROFOR protection. In March, the Bosnian Serbs intensified their offensive in eastern Bosnia and Herzegovina, leading the Security Council to declare the beseiged towns—Bihac, Gorazde, Sarajevo, Srebrenica, Tuzla and Zepa—and their surroundings as safe areas. The Council increased the presence of UNPROFOR in them, authorizing it to use force in self-defence and in reply to armed incursions and to obstructions of humanitarian convoys.

To further complicate an already complex situation, fighting erupted in April in the central part of the country between the formerly allied Bosnian Croats and Bosnian Muslims, blocking the supply routes for humanitarian assistance to the north. Hostilities between the two parties continued, despite Council calls for a halt to the fighting and a cease-fire arranged by the Co-Chairmen of the ICFY Steering Committee.

Against this background, the Co-Chairmen of the ICFY Steering Committee engaged the leaders of the conflicting parties in continual negotiations during the year to work out an acceptable peace plan. The negotiations resulted in the Vance-Owen peace package, rejected by the Bosnian Serbs in a referendum in May, however. As a result, the

Council strengthened the sanctions regime against Yugoslavia (Serbia and Montenegro) to induce acceptance of the plan, but to no avail. A confederal solution, distilled from the parties' own ideas, was alternatively under negotiation under the Co-Chairmen's auspices during the remainder of the year.

GENERAL ASSEMBLY ACTION

On 20 December, the General Assembly adopted **resolution 48/88** by recorded vote.

The situation in Bosnia and Herzegovina
The General Assembly,

Reaffirming its resolutions 46/242 of 25 August 1992 and 47/121 of 18 December 1992 and all relevant resolutions of the Security Council regarding the situation in the Republic of Bosnia and Herzegovina,

Reaffirming once again that, as the Republic of Bosnia and Herzegovina is a sovereign, independent State and a Member of the United Nations, it is entitled to all rights provided for in the Charter of the United Nations, including the right to self-defence under Article 51 thereof,

Gravely concerned that the unprovoked armed hostilities and aggression continue against Bosnia and Herzegovina and that the relevant resolutions of the Security Council remain unimplemented,

Recalling the report of the Committee on the Elimination of Racial Discrimination, in which the Committee "noted with great concern that links existed between the Federal Republic of Yugoslavia (Serbia and Montenegro) and Serbian militias and paramilitary groups responsible for massive, gross and systematic violations of human rights in Bosnia and Herzegovina and in Croatian territories controlled by Serbs",

Condemning the continuing hostilities by the Bosnian Serbs, particularly their abhorrent policy of "ethnic cleansing",

Alarmed at extremist Bosnian Croat military elements for their aggressive acts against Bosnia and Herzegovina,

Alarmed also at the collusion between Serbian forces and extremist Bosnian Croat elements and others to seek the dismemberment of the Republic of Bosnia and Herzegovina, in clear violation of the principles of the Charter of the United Nations and in total disregard of the relevant resolutions of the General Assembly and those of the Security Council,

Deploring the non-compliance with the relevant Security Council resolutions, especially by the Bosnian Serb Party,

Recalling the principles enunciated in its resolutions and the relevant resolutions of the Security Council, as well as those adopted by the International Conference on the Former Yugoslavia,

Reaffirming its determination to have the Republic of Bosnia and Herzegovina maintain its independence, unity and territorial integrity, and noting, in accordance with Article 24 of the Charter, the responsibility of the Security Council in that regard,

Also reaffirming its determination to prevent acts of genocide and crimes against humanity,

Reaffirming once again its total and complete rejection of the acquisition of territory through the use of force and the abhorrent practice of "ethnic cleansing",

Stressing that the continuation of aggression in Bosnia and Herzegovina is a serious impediment to the peace process,

Bearing in mind the obligation of all States to act in conformity with the principles and purposes of the Charter,

Stressing also that the full implementation of Security Council resolutions concerning the United Nations Protected Areas in the territory of the Republic of Croatia is of significant importance for the security, territorial integrity and stability of the Republic of Bosnia and Herzegovina,

Noting that the International Court of Justice, in its Order of 13 September 1993 in the case concerning application of the Convention on the Prevention and Punishment of the Crime of Genocide (Bosnia and Herzegovina v. Yugoslavia (Serbia and Montenegro)), indicated as a provisional measure that "the Government of the Federal Republic of Yugoslavia (Serbia and Montenegro) should immediately, in pursuance of its undertaking in the Convention on the Prevention and Punishment of the Crime of Genocide of 9 December 1948, take all measures within its power to prevent commission of the crime of genocide",

Taking note of the Order of the International Court of Justice of 13 September 1993, in which it stated that "the present perilous situation demands . . . [the] immediate and effective implementation of those [provisional] measures",

Commending the work of the Commission of Experts established pursuant to Security Council resolution 780(1992), of 6 October 1992, and noting with interest the first and second interim reports of the Commission,

Expressing its concern about the continuing siege of Sarajevo and other Bosnian cities and "safe areas", which endangers the well-being and safety of their inhabitants,

Aware, in the context of the character of Sarajevo as a multicultural, multi-ethnic and multireligious centre, of the need to preserve its plurality and avoid its further destruction,

Conscious that the grave situation in Bosnia and Herzegovina continues to be a threat to international peace and security,

1. *Reaffirms* the principles enunciated in its resolutions and the relevant resolutions of the Security Council and those adopted by the International Conference on the Former Yugoslavia pertaining to the Republic of Bosnia and Herzegovina;

2. *Demands* that all parties implement immediately, and scrupulously maintain in good faith, a cease-fire and agree to cease all hostilities throughout Bosnia and Herzegovina, in order to create an atmosphere conducive to the resumption of peace negotiations within the framework of the International Conference on the Former Yugoslavia;

3. *Reaffirms* that the consequences of "ethnic cleansing" will not be accepted by the international community and that those who have seized land by "ethnic cleansing" and by the use of force must relinquish those lands, in conformity with norms of international law;

4. *Condemns* the continued violation of the international border between the Republic of Bosnia and Herzegovina and the Republic of Croatia by Serbian forces, and thereby requests the Security Council to take all necessary measures in implementation of its resolution 769(1992) of 7 August 1992;

5. *Requests* the Security Council to follow and immediately implement its resolution 838(1993) of 10 June 1993 to ensure that the Federal Republic of Yugoslavia (Serbia and Montenegro) immediately ceases the supply of military arms, equipment and services to Bosnian Serb paramilitary units, as demanded in its resolution 819(1993) of 16 April 1993;

6. *Demands* that the Bosnian Serb party lift forthwith the siege of Sarajevo and other ''safe areas'', as well as other besieged Bosnian towns, and urges the Secretary-General to direct the United Nations Protection Force to take necessary measures, in accordance with relevant Security Council resolutions, for the protection of the ''safe areas'';

7. *Also demands* that, as a means of bringing about the cessation of hostilities and to facilitate delivery of humanitarian assistance, in accordance with paragraphs 5 and 9 of Security Council resolution 836(1993) of 4 June 1993, the Bosnian Serb party withdraw all its heavy weaponry and forces to areas outside the city of Sarajevo and other ''safe areas'' to a distance where they cease to constitute a menace to their security and that of their inhabitants and where they are to be monitored by United Nations military observers, and urges all parties to agree to implement further confidence-building measures;

8. *Reaffirms once again* the right of all refugees and displaced persons to return voluntarily to their homes in safety and dignity;

9. *Commends* the ongoing efforts of the Office of the United Nations High Commissioner for Refugees, the United Nations Protection Force and other international humanitarian agencies, and notes with the utmost appreciation those individuals who have shown exemplary bravery and courage and those who have made the ultimate sacrifice in carrying out their duties;

10. *Urges* the Office of the United Nations High Commissioner for Refugees, as part of its humanitarian assistance programme, to provide appropriate assistance to facilitate cultural exchanges between Sarajevo and the international community and to facilitate the delivery and installation of a reliable communication system in Sarajevo for the use of the civilian population;

11. *Urges* the Secretary-General to take immediate action to reopen Tuzla airport in order to facilitate the receipt and distribution of international humanitarian aid, consistent with the provisions of Security Council resolution 770(1992) of 13 August 1992;

12. *Demands* that all concerned facilitate the unhindered flow of humanitarian assistance, including the provision of water, electricity, fuel and communication, in particular to the ''safe areas'' in Bosnia and Herzegovina, and in this context urges the Security Council to implement fully its resolution 770(1992) to ensure the free flow of humanitarian assistance, particularly to the ''safe areas'';

13. *Commends* all States, and in particular the States bordering on the Federal Republic of Yugoslavia (Serbia and Montenegro) and the other Danube riparian States, for the measures they have taken to comply with the mandatory sanctions imposed by the Security Council against the Federal Republic of Yugoslavia (Serbia and Montenegro), and urges all States to continue their vigilant enforcement of those sanctions measures;

14. *Condemns vigorously* the violations of the human rights of the Bosnian people and of international humanitarian law committed by parties to the conflict, especially those violations committed as policy, flagrantly and on a massive scale, by the Federal Republic of Yugoslavia (Serbia and Montenegro) and the Bosnian Serbs;

15. *Urges* the Security Council, in fulfilling its responsibility under Article 24 of the Charter of the United Nations, to take all appropriate steps to uphold and restore fully the sovereignty, political independence, territorial integrity and unity of the Republic of Bosnia and Herzegovina, in cooperation with States Members of the United Nations and the Government of the Republic;

16. *Deeply alarmed* by the continuing systematic abuses committed against Albanians, Bosnians, Hungarians and Croatians, and others in Kosovo, Sandzak and Vojvodina, respectively, by the authorities of Serbia and Montenegro, and in that regard condemns the decision of those authorities not to renew the mandate of the monitoring missions of the Conference on Security and Cooperation in Europe in those regions;

17. *Also urges* the Security Council to give all due consideration, on an urgent basis, to exempt Bosnia and Herzegovina from the arms embargo as imposed on the former Yugoslavia under Security Council resolution 713(1991) of 25 September 1991;

18. *Urges* Member States, as well as other members of the international community, from all regions to extend their cooperation to the Republic of Bosnia and Herzegovina in exercise of its inherent right of individual and collective self-defence in accordance with Article 51 of Chapter VII of the Charter;

19. *Reaffirms* its resolution 47/1 of 22 September 1992, and urges Member States and the Secretariat in fulfilling the spirit of that resolution to end the de facto working status of the Federal Republic of Yugoslaia (Serbia and Montenegro);

20. *Requests* that the International Committee of the Red Cross be granted free access to all detention camps established by the Serbs in Serbia and Montenegro and in Bosnia and Herzegovina and to all persons imprisoned in those camps, and that all prisoners be notified of this action without delay;

21. *Requests* the Security Council to act immediately to close all detention camps in Bosnia and Herzegovina and further to close concentration camps established by the Serbs in Serbia and Montenegro and in Bosnia and Herzegovina and, until implementation, to assign international observers to those camps;

22. *Expresses its appreciation* to those States and international institutions which have provided humanitarian assistance to the people of Bosnia and Herzegovina, and appeals to all Member States to contribute generously towards alleviating their sufferings, including assistance to refugee centres for Bosnian refugees in other countries;

23. *Further affirms* individual responsibility for the perpetration of crimes against humanity committed in Bosnia and Herzegovina;

24. *Welcomes* the establishment of the International Tribunal for the Prosecution of Persons Responsible for Serious Violations of International Humanitarian Law Committed in the Territory of the Former Yugoslavia since 1991, constituted pursuant to Security Council resolution 827(1993) of 25 May 1993, and encourages the provision of all resources necessary, including voluntary con-

tributions from States and intergovernmental and non-governmental organizations, so that it can conduct its stipulated functions of trying and punishing those responsible for the perpetration of violations of international law;

25. *Encourages* the Commission of Experts established pursuant to Security Council resolution 780(1992), subject to the provisions of Council resolution 827(1993) and in cooperation with the Prosecutor of the International Tribunal, to facilitate the work of the International Tribunal, including the establishment of a record of violations such as "ethnic cleansing" and systematic rape;

26. *Requests* the Secretary-General to provide the necessary resources and support for the Commission to carry out its functions;

27. *Calls upon* the Security Council to ensure that the proposals contained in the "Geneva peace package" are in conformity with the Charter of the United Nations, the principles of international law, previous resolutions of the General Assembly and those adopted by the Security Council, and the principles adopted at the International Conference on the Former Yugoslavia;

28. *Calls* for the urgent reconvening of the International Conference on the Former Yugoslavia in order to arrive at just and equitable proposals for lasting peace in Bosnia and Herzegovina, and calls upon the parties to the conflict to show good faith as they continue to negotiate in order to reach a just, equitable and durable solution;

29. *Requests* the Secretary-General to submit a report on the implementation of the present resolution within 15 days of its adoption, as well as the report called for under the auspices of the London Conference, which, regrettably, has not yet been issued;

30. *Decides* to remain seized of the matter and to continue the consideration of this item.

General Assembly resolution 48/88

20 December 1993   Meeting 84   109-0-57 (recorded vote)

43-nation draft (A/48/L.50 & Add.1), orally revised; agenda item 42.
Sponsors: Afghanistan, Albania, Algeria, Azerbaijan, Bahrain, Bangladesh, Bosnia and Herzegovina, Brunei Darussalam, Burkina Faso, Colombia, Comoros, Costa Rica, Djibouti, Egypt, Gambia, Guinea, Guinea-Bissau, Indonesia, Iran, Jordan, Kuwait, Kyrgyzstan, Latvia, Lebanon, Libyan Arab Jamahiriya, Lithuania, Malaysia, Mali, Marshall Islands, Mauritania, Morocco, Niger, Oman, Pakistan, Qatar, Saudi Arabia, Senegal, Sierra Leone, Sudan, Tunisia, Turkey, United Arab Emirates, Yemen.
Meeting numbers. GA 48th session: plenary 82-84.

Recorded vote in Assembly as follows:

In favour: Afghanistan, Albania, Algeria, Antigua and Barbuda, Australia, Austria, Azerbaijan, Bahamas, Bahrain, Bangladesh, Barbados, Belize, Bhutan, Bolivia, Bosnia and Herzegovina, Botswana, Brunei Darussalam, Burkina Faso, Cameroon, Cape Verde, Central African Republic, Chad, Chile, Colombia, Comoros, Costa Rica, Croatia, Cyprus, Djibouti, Dominica, Dominican Republic, Ecuador, Egypt, El Salvador, Estonia, Fiji, Gambia, Grenada, Guatemala, Guinea, Guinea-Bissau, Guyana, Haiti, Honduras, Hungary, Indonesia, Iran, Iraq, Jamaica, Jordan, Kazakhstan, Kuwait, Kyrgyzstan, Latvia, Lebanon, Lesotho, Libyan Arab Jamahiriya, Lithuania, Madagascar, Malaysia, Maldives, Mali, Marshall Islands, Mauritania, Mauritius, Micronesia, Mongolia, Morocco, Mozambique, Namibia, Nepal, Nicaragua, Niger, Oman, Pakistan, Panama, Papua New Guinea, Paraguay, Peru, Philippines, Qatar, Republic of Moldova, Rwanda, Saint Lucia, Saint Vincent and the Grenadines, Samoa, Saudi Arabia, Senegal, Sierra Leone, Singapore, Slovenia, Solomon Islands, Sri Lanka, Sudan, Suriname, Syrian Arab Republic, Tajikistan, Thailand, the former Yugoslav Republic of Macedonia, Trinidad and Tobago, Tunisia, Turkey, Uganda, United Arab Emirates, United Republic of Tanzania, United States, Uruguay, Yemen, Zambia.
Against: None.
Abstaining: Andorra, Argentina, Armenia, Belarus, Belgium, Benin, Brazil, Bulgaria, Burundi, Canada, China, Côte d'Ivoire, Czech Republic, Denmark, Ethiopia, Finland, France, Gabon, Georgia, Germany, Ghana, Greece, Iceland, India, Ireland, Israel, Italy, Japan, Kenya, Liechtenstein, Luxem-

bourg, Malawi, Malta, Mexico, Monaco, Myanmar, Netherlands, New Zealand, Nigeria, Norway, Poland, Portugal, Republic of Korea, Romania, Russian Federation, San Marino, Slovakia, Spain, Swaziland, Sweden, Togo, Ukraine, United Kingdom, Venezuela, Viet Nam, Zaire, Zimbabwe.

The abstaining Member States believed that to lift the arms embargo on Bosnia and Herzegovina would only lead to further bloodshed; it would jeopardize the negotiating process and the mission of UNPROFOR and create a real possibility for the fighting to spill over into neighbouring countries in the region. The best means of resolving the conflict, they were convinced, was through a negotiated settlement.

Before adoption of the resolution, Kenya requested separate votes on paragraphs 17 and 19, to which Bosnia and Herzegovina, along with Costa Rica and the Comoros, objected. As a result, a vote was taken on Kenya's request, which was rejected by a recorded vote of 128 to 7, with 24 abstentions.

Armed incident

On 8 January, the Deputy Prime Minister for Economic Affairs of Bosnia and Herzegovina, Hakija Turajlic, was assassinated by Bosnian Serb forces as he was returning from Sarajevo's Butmir Airport in an UNPROFOR convoy on a United Nations controlled road. The convoy was blocked by two tanks belonging to Serbian extremists who entered the vehicle carrying Mr. Turajlic and shot him eight times. In bringing the incident to the Secretary-General's attention,[79] Bosnia and Herzegovina, which pointed to its understanding that UNPROFOR was not to stop or open their vehicles for inspection under any circumstances, demanded an explanation for UNPROFOR's conduct to the contrary at the time of the incident.

Bosnia and Herzegovina called for an emergency meeting of the Security Council, demanding immediate and resolute action, including the use of force under Chapter VII of the Charter.[80] A similar call was made by Turkey.[81]

SECURITY COUNCIL ACTION

The Security Council convened on 8 January and, following consultations among its members, authorized its President to make the following statement[82] on its behalf:
Meeting number. SC 3159.

"The Security Council is profoundly shocked to learn of the killing of Mr. Hakija Turajlic, Deputy Prime Minister for Economic Affairs of the Republic of Bosnia and Herzegovina, by Bosnian-Serb forces, while he was under the protection of the United Nations Protection Force (UNPROFOR).

"The Council strongly condemns this outrageous act of terrorism which is a grave violation of international humanitarian law and a flagrant challenge to the authority and the inviolability of UNPROFOR, as well as to the serious efforts undertaken with the aim of achieving an overall political settlement of the crisis.

"The Council urges all parties and others concerned to exercise the utmost restraint and to refrain from taking any action which might further exacerbate the situation.

"The Council requests the Secretary-General to undertake a full investigation of the incident and to report to it without delay. Upon receipt of that report the Council will consider the matter forthwith.

"The members of the Security Council extend their sincere condolences to the bereaved family of Mr. Turajlic and to the people and the Government of the Republic of Bosnia and Herzegovina."

On 10 January,[83] Bosnia and Herzegovina, while expressing deep gratitude to General Phillipe Morillon, Commander of UNPROFOR in that country, for his prompt release of information related to the assassination, stated that the circumstances leading to the Deputy Prime Minister's murder while under UNPROFOR protection demonstrated that UNPROFOR too often offered neither protection nor force. It laboured under a constricted mandate, passive rules of engagement and inadequate political support, all of which had proved counterproductive, permitting occupation forces to use it as an unwitting vehicle of aggression against Bosnia and Herzegovina.

Report of the Special Commission of Inquiry. Responding to the foregoing presidential statement, the Secretary-General, on 11 January, appointed a Special Commission of Inquiry to investigate the Deputy Prime Minister's assassination. Co-chaired by Sahabzada Yaqub-Khan (Pakistan), the Secretary-General's Special Representative for Western Sahara, and Lieutenant-General Lars-Eric Wahlgren (Sweden), Commander of the United Nations Interim Force in Lebanon, the Commission convened at Geneva on 12 January and visited the UNPROFOR mission area from 13 to 15 January. Its report established the facts and circumstances surrounding the incident, examined UNPROFOR's standing operating procedures and mandate in Bosnia and Herzegovina, and made recommendations relating to UNPROFOR's functioning.

In an 18 January letter[84] transmitting the report to the Security Council President, the Secretary-General drew attention to the following points made by the Commission of Inquiry: (1) Escorting members of the Presidency to and from the airport was not part of the UNPROFOR mandate, although it provided such service as a courtesy to the host Government. (2) The request for the transport of an official delegation to the airport was not in conformity with established procedures. (3) Consequently, UNPROFOR failed to adhere to the standing operating procedures normally applied to the escort of civilian officials. (4) Besides the considerable degree of mistrust surrounding the airport operation, false rumours that 60 mujahedin had flown

in on the aircraft Mr. Turajlic went to meet added to the tension at the Serb checkpoint. (5) Despite the 5 June 1992 agreement providing for the establishment of security corridors under UNPROFOR control between the airport and Sarajevo City, UNPROFOR vehicles were regularly subjected to inspection at checkpoints manned by all parties to the conflict. (6) The Commission of Inquiry concluded that the assassination was the work of a single assailant acting unilaterally.

Turkey, in a 28 January statement,[85] noted that the report played down what it called UNPROFOR's gross negligence. UNPROFOR had failed to exercise its authority and carry out its duty; the explanations provided to minimize those failures were inadmissible. Turkey said that the report, besides demonstrating the lack of coordination among United Nations entities, appeared to seek excuses for the Serb action. Turkey expected all who bore responsibility for Mr. Turajlic's death to be punished.

Based on its review of the report, Bosnia and Herzegovina requested the Council on 1 February[86] to authorize a supplementary investigation into the incident by an independent body, in cooperation with UNPROFOR and the Government of Bosnia and Herzegovina; to request the Secretary-General to report on steps to implement UNPROFOR control of the corridor linking Sarajevo with the airport; and to clarify UNPROFOR's mandate in relation to the provisions of Council resolution 770(1992)[87] on measures to facilitate the delivery of humanitarian assistance to Sarajevo and other parts of the country.

Safe areas

Communications. The United States, on 3 March,[88] requested an immediate meeting of the Security Council to discuss reports of continued fighting in Bosnia and Herzegovina. That country made a similar request, notifying the Council President on the same date[89] that Serbian and Montenegrin extremist forces had overrun the town of Cerska and its sourrounding villages pursuing a new round of expulsions and genocide. Srebrenica was under threat of imminent assault. The Serbian leaders had issued an order to wipe out or drive out the inhabitants of both towns and to blockade all humanitarian convoys. Within 72 hours, 2,000 innocent people had been murdered and thousands of others forcibly displaced. Some 40,000 people were in imminent danger of death from military attack, starvation, exposure to the elements and disease.

SECURITY COUNCIL ACTION

Responding to the foregoing requests, the Security Council met on 3 March and invited Bosnia and Herzegovina, at its request, to participate in the discussion without the right to vote under rule 37.[a]

After consultations among its members, the Council authorized its President to make the following statement[90] on the Council's behalf:

Meeting number. SC 3180.

"The Security Council, recalling all its relevant resolutions and statements, expresses its grave concern at and condemns the continuing unacceptable military attacks in eastern Bosnia and the resulting deterioration in the humanitarian situation in that region. It is appalled that, even as peace talks are continuing, attacks by Serb paramilitary units, including, reportedly, the killings of innocent civilians, continue in eastern Bosnia. In this connection, the Security Council is particularly concerned about the fall of the town of Cerska and the imminent fall of neighbouring villages. The Security Council demands that the killings and atrocities must stop and reaffirms that those guilty of crimes against international humanitarian law will be held individually responsible by the world community.

"The Security Council demands that the leaders of all the parties to the conflict in the Republic of Bosnia and Herzegovina remain fully engaged in New York in a sustained effort with the Co-Chairmen of the Steering Committee of the International Conference on the Former Yugoslavia to reach quickly a fair and workable settlement. In this connection, the Security Council also demands that all sides immediately cease all forms of military action throughout the Republic of Bosnia and Herzegovina, cease acts of violence against civilians, comply with their previous commitments including the cease-fire, and redouble their efforts to settle the conflict.

"The Security Council further demands that the Bosnian Serb side as well as all other parties refrain from taking any action which might endanger the lives and well-being of the inhabitants of eastern Bosnia, particularly in the areas near the town of Cerska, and that all concerned allow the unimpeded access of humanitarian relief supplies throughout the Republic of Bosnia and Herzegovina, especially humanitarian access to the besieged cities of eastern Bosnia, and permit the evacuation of the wounded.

"Having determined in the relevant resolutions that this situation constitutes a threat to international peace and security, the Security Council insists that these steps must be taken immediately.

"The Security Council also requests the Secretary-General to take immediate steps to increase UN-PROFOR's presence in eastern Bosnia.

"The Security Council remains seized of the matter and is ready to meet at any moment to consider further action."

Communications. In separate statements made on 3 March, EC[91] and OIC[92] expressed condemnation of and grave concern at the continuing aggression by Serbian paramilitary forces against the Muslim population in Bosnia and Herzegovina, in particular in the eastern part of the country.

Bosnia and Herzegovina, on 18 March,[93] requested an emergency meeting of the Security Council to consider further Serbian aggression against Srebrenica, Sarajevo and the Muslim town of Bjelina. A report followed four days later[94] to the effect that Serbian and Montenegrin forces had again attacked Srebrenica, as well as Gradacac and Tuzla.

The Secretary-General, on 19 March,[95] stated that the Prime Minister of France had expressed his concern over the situation unfolding in eastern Bosnia and Herzegovina. The UNPROFOR field commander had reported continuing obstruction by Serb forces of UNHCR relief efforts, despite negotiations with the political and military leaders of the Bosnian Serbs and with the Government of Yugoslavia (Serbia and Montenegro); the Force Commander had subsequently reported, however, that six United States aircraft had dropped 32 tonnes of food and one and a half tons of medical supplies in the area, with more air-drops planned, and that a land convoy had been able to enter Srebrenica. None the less, it was evident that a massive humanitarian tragedy might be in the making in eastern Bosnia and Herzegovina.

The United Nations High Commissioner for Refugees, Sadako Ogata, in a 2 April letter,[96] transmitted by the Secretary-General to the Council President, drew attention to the plight of Srebrenica, where thousands of Muslims fleeing from advancing Serb forces were converging. Despite the cease-fire and air-drops, the humanitarian situation was worsening. People, especially women and children, were dying in military attacks and from starvation, exposure to cold and lack of medical treatment.

UNHCR efforts, at best inadequate to address the increasing human suffering, were hampered by other difficulties. The stampede to flee Srebrenica resulted in people being crushed to death; the Bosnian authorities at Srebrenica and Tuzla (unable to absorb new arrivals of displaced persons) opposed continued evacuation, regarding it as facilitating the Serbian offensive; and the Bosnian Serb military permitted no further delivery of humanitarian aid into Srebrenica, allowing UNHCR only to evacuate civilians.

In the circumstances, the High Commissioner recommended that the enclave be turned into a United Nations protected area with an injection of massive life-sustaining assistance, or that there be a large-scale evacuation of the endangered population.

SECURITY COUNCIL ACTION

In the light of the UNHCR communication, the Security Council met on 3 April. At its request, Bosnia and Herzegovina was invited to participate in the discussions without the right to vote under rule 37.[a]

Following consultations among its members, the Council authorized its President to make the following statement:[(97)]

Meeting number. SC 3192.

"The Security Council is shocked by and extremely alarmed at the dire and worsening humanitarian situation which has developed in Srebrenica in the eastern part of the Republic of Bosnia and Herzegovina following the unacceptable decision of the Bosnian Serb party not to permit any further humanitarian aid to be delivered to that town, and to allow only evacuation of its civilian population. The relevant facts are contained in a letter dated 2 April 1993, addressed to the Secretary-General by the United Nations High Commissioner for Refugees.

"The Security Council recalls and reaffirms all its relevant resolutions and statements and condemns the continuing disregard and wilful flouting of the relevant Security Council resolutions and statements by the Bosnian Serb party, which once again, in pursuit of its unlawful, unacceptable and abhorrent policy of 'ethnic cleansing' aimed at territorial aggrandizement, has blocked the United Nations humanitarian relief efforts.

"Recognizing the imperative need to alleviate, with the utmost urgency, the sufferings of the population in and around Srebrenica who are in desperate need of food, medicine, clothes and shelter, the Security Council demands that the Bosnian Serb party cease and desist forthwith from all violations of international humanitarian law, including in particular the deliberate interference with humanitarian convoys, and allow all such convoys unhindered access to the town of Srebrenica and other parts in the Republic of Bosnia and Herzegovina. The Security Council demands that the Bosnian Serb party strictly comply with all relevant resolutions of the Security Council. It further demands that the Bosnian Serb party honour forthwith its most recent commitment 'to guarantee the free movement of humanitarian convoys and the protection of endangered civilians'. The Security Council also reaffirms that those guilty of crimes against international humanitarian law will be held individually responsible by the world community.

"The Security Council commends and strongly supports the efforts of the brave people who have undertaken to deliver urgently needed humanitarian assistance, under extremely trying conditions, to the civilian population in the Republic of Bosnia and Herzegovina, and in particular the efforts of the United Nations High Commissioner for Refugees (UNHCR) and the United Nations Protection Force (UNPROFOR).

"The Security Council recalls the request it made in its statement of 3 March 1993 to the Secretary-General to take immediate steps to increase UNPROFOR's presence in eastern Bosnia; welcomes the action taken already in that respect; and urges the Secretary-General and the United Nations High Commissioner for Refugees to use all the resources at their disposal within the scope of the relevant resolutions of the Council to reinforce the existing humanitarian operations in the Republic of Bosnia and Herzegovina.

"The Security Council will remain actively seized of the matter."

Communications. The foregoing statement notwithstanding, Bosnia and Herzegovina reported to the Security Council President on 5 April[(98)] that the Serbian and Montenegrin aggressors had continued their assault on the Srebrenica region, particularly on the town of Zeleni Jadar and on eastern Srebrenica. Bosnia and Herzegovina further reported on 8 April[(99)] that the level of humanitarian assistance, especially in Gorazde and Zepa, had proven largely ineffective because of the continuing blockade by Serbian and Montenegrin forces; it asked that the UNPROFOR mandate be expanded to include those two towns (and to the extent that it needed to be done in Srebrenica) to facilitate the delivery of humanitarian relief to them.

On 15 April,[(100)] Cape Verde, Djibouti, Morocco, Pakistan and Venezuela (Council members belonging to the Movement of Non-Aligned Countries) requested an urgent meeting of the Security Council to discuss the deteriorating situation in Bosnia and Herzegovina. That country, referring to the horrifying situation in Srebrenica, demanded on 16 April[(101)] that the Council take all necessary measures, as a matter of urgency, to guarantee the safety of the town's remaining inhabitants.

Also on 16 April,[(102)] Bosnia and Herzegovina wrote that forces directed, controlled and supported by Yugoslavia (Serbia and Montenegro) had intensified their assault on Srebrenica. It called the assault an act of genocide in violation of the 1948 Convention on the Prevention and Punishment of the Crime of Genocide[(103)] and a violation of the International Court of Justice (ICJ) Order of 8 April asking Yugoslavia (Serbia and Montenegro) immediately to take all measures within its power to prevent any military units under its direction or influence from committing genocide (see PART FIVE, Chapter I). Bosnia and Herzegovina requested that the Council take immediate measures, under Chapter VII of the Charter, to break the seige and enforce the ICJ Order.

SECURITY COUNCIL ACTION (16 April)

The Security Council convened on 16 April, inviting Bosnia and Herzegovina to participate in the discussion without the right to vote under rule 37.[a] On the same date, the Council unanimously adopted **resolution 819(1993)**.

The Security Council,

Reaffirming its resolution 713(1991) of 25 September 1991 and all its subsequent relevant resolutions,

Taking note that the International Court of Justice in its Order of 8 April 1993 in the case concerning application of the Convention on the Prevention and Punishment of the Crime of Genocide (Bosnia and Herzegovina v. Yugoslavia (Serbia and Montenegro)) unanimously indicated as a provisional measure that the Government of the Federal Republic of Yugoslavia (Serbia and Montenegro) should immediately, in pursuance of its undertaking in the Convention on the Prevention and Punishment of the Crime of Genocide of 9 December 1948, take all measures within its power to prevent the commission of the crime of genocide,

Reaffirming the sovereignty, territorial integrity and political independence of the Republic of Bosnia and Herzegovina,

Reaffirming its call on the parties and others concerned to observe immediately the cease-fire throughout the Republic of Bosnia and Herzegovina,

Reaffirming its condemnation of all violations of international humanitarian law, including, in particular, the practice of "ethnic cleansing",

Concerned by the pattern of hostilities by Bosnian Serb paramilitary units against towns and villages in eastern Bosnia and in this regard reaffirming that any taking or acquisition of territory by the threat or use of force, including through the practice of "ethnic cleansing", is unlawful and unacceptable,

Deeply alarmed at the information provided by the Secretary-General to the Security Council on 16 April 1993 on the rapid deterioration of the situation in Srebrenica and its surrounding areas, as a result of the continued deliberate armed attacks and shelling of the innocent civilian population by Bosnian Serb paramilitary units,

Strongly condemning the deliberate interdiction by Bosnian Serb paramilitary units of humanitarian assistance convoys,

Also strongly condemning the actions taken by Bosnian Serb paramilitary units against UNPROFOR, in particular their refusal to guarantee the safety and freedom of movement of UNPROFOR personnel,

Aware that a tragic humanitarian emergency has already developed in Srebrenica and its surrounding areas as a direct consequence of the brutal actions of Bosnian Serb paramilitary units, forcing the large-scale displacement of civilians, in particular women, children and the elderly,

Recalling the provisions of resolution 815(1993) on the mandate of UNPROFOR and in that context acting under Chapter VII of the Charter of the United Nations,

1. *Demands* that all parties and others concerned treat Srebrenica and its surroundings as a safe area which should be free from any armed attack or any other hostile act;

2. *Demands also* to that effect the immediate cessation of armed attacks by Bosnian Serb paramilitary units against Srebrenica and their immediate withdrawal from the areas surrounding Srebrenica;

3. *Demands* that the Federal Republic of Yugoslavia (Serbia and Montenegro) immediately cease the supply of military arms, equipment and services to the Bosnian Serb paramilitary units in the Republic of Bosnia and Herzegovina;

4. *Requests* the Secretary-General, with a view to monitoring the humanitarian situation in the safe area, to take immediate steps to increase the presence of UNPROFOR in Srebrenica and its surroundings; demands that all parties and others concerned cooperate

fully and promptly with UNPROFOR towards that end; and requests the Secretary-General to report urgently thereon to the Security Council;

5. *Reaffirms* that any taking or acquisition of territory by the threat or use of force, including through the practice of "ethnic cleansing", is unlawful and unacceptable;

6. *Condemns* and rejects the deliberate actions of the Bosnian Serb party to force the evacuation of the civilian population from Srebrenica and its surrounding areas as well as from other parts of the Republic of Bosnia and Herzegovina as part of its overall abhorrent campaign of "ethnic cleansing";

7. *Reaffirms its condemnation* of all violations of international humanitarian law, in particular the practice of "ethnic cleansing" and reaffirms that those who commit or order the commission of such acts shall be held individually responsible in respect of such acts;

8. *Demands* the unimpeded delivery of humanitarian assistance to all parts of the Republic of Bosnia and Herzegovina, in particular to the civilian population of Srebrenica and its surrounding areas, and recalls that such impediments to the delivery of humanitarian assistance constitute a serious violation of international humanitarian law;

9. *Urges* the Secretary-General and the United Nations High Commissioner for Refugees to use all the resources at their disposal within the scope of the relevant resolutions of the Council to reinforce the existing humanitarian operations in the Republic of Bosnia and Herzegovina, in particular Srebrenica and its surroundings;

10. *Further demands* that all parties guarantee the safety and full freedom of movement of UNPROFOR and of all other United Nations personnel as well as members of humanitarian organizations;

11. *Further requests* the Secretary-General, in consultation with UNHCR and UNPROFOR, to arrange for the safe transfer of the wounded and ill civilians from Srebrenica and its surrounding areas and to urgently report thereon to the Council;

12. *Decides* to send, as soon as possible, a mission of members of the Security Council to the Republic of Bosnia and Herzegovina to ascertain the situation and report thereon to the Security Council;

13. *Decides* to remain actively seized of the matter and to consider further steps to achieve a solution in conformity with relevant resolutions of the Council.

Security Council resolution 819(1993)

16 April 1993   Meeting 3199   Adopted unanimously

Draft prepared in consultations among Council members (S/25617).

The Council President, in a note of 21 April,[104] reported that, as a result of consultations among Council members, agreement had been reached that the mission referred to in paragraph 12 of the resolution would be composed of six members: France, Hungary, New Zealand, Pakistan, the Russian Federation and Venezuela.

SECURITY COUNCIL CONSIDERATION (19 and 20 April)

In response to a 15 April request from Turkey, on behalf of the OIC Contact Group on Bosnia and Herzegovina,[105] the Security Council held an open debate in three meetings on 19 and 20 April, following its adoption of resolutions 819(1993) and 820(1993) on 16 and 17 April, respectively. The debate focused on all aspects of the Bosnia and Herzegovina situation, especially the ongoing siege of the eastern part of the country.

At the 19 April meeting, the following States were invited, at their request, to participate in the discussions without the right to vote under rule 37:[a] Afghanistan, Albania, Algeria, Argentina, Austria, Bahrain, Bosnia and Herzegovina, Bulgaria, Canada, Comoros, Croatia, Denmark, Ecuador, Egypt, Germany, Indonesia, Iran, Ireland, Italy, Jordan, Lithuania, Malaysia, Malta, Qatar, Romania, Saudi Arabia, Senegal, Sierra Leone, Slovenia, Sweden, Turkey, Ukraine and the United Arab Emirates.

At Turkey's request,[106] the Permanent Observer of OIC was invited to address the Council under rule 39.[b] Ambassador Dragomir Djokic of Yugoslavia (Serbia and Montenegro), at his request, was also invited to address the Council.

Meeting numbers. SC 3201-3203.

During the debate, statements were made by 30 Member States, as well as by the OIC representative and the representative of Yugoslavia (Serbia and Montenegro).

Most of the speakers condemned the human rights violations perpetrated in the fighting, in particular the practice of ethnic cleansing, and the intransigence of the Bosnian Serbs. A number of States, besides calling for the creation of safe havens and for enforcement measures to stop Serbian bombardments and ensure the free flow of relief supplies, echoed Bosnia and Herzegovina's call for the placing of heavy weaponry under United Nations control, for the interdiction of supply lines from Yugoslavia (Serbia and Montenegro) to Bosnia and Herzegovina, and for excluding the Government of Bosnia and Herzegovina from the arms embargo in accordance with Article 51 of the Charter. Other States, said it was time to take more decisive steps, including further measures under Chapter VII of the Charter.

The representative of Yugoslavia (Serbia and Montenegro) pointed out that, despite its full cooperation with the Co-Chairmen of the ICFY Steering Committee to bring an end to the war in Bosnia and Herzegovina, its repeated statements that it had no territorial claims on any of its neighbours and the fact that, since 1992, not a single soldier of its army remained on Bosnia and Herzegovina's territory, the international community and the Council had persisted in treating Yugoslavia (Serbia and Montenegro) as party to the conflict and in calling for its punishment and isolation, thus holding it hostage to the Bos-

nian Croats, Muslims and Serbs. The conviction that Yugoslavia (Serbia and Montengro) could order the Bosnian Serbs to accept something that threatened their survival and that they were ready to obey orders from Belgrade was illusory and false. It was doing its utmost to advise the Bosnian Serbs but it could not order a people to capitulate who were dying and sacrificing all they had in order to survive on their land.

Report of the fact-finding mission. The six-member fact-finding mission[104] constituted pursuant to resolution 819(1993), visited Bosnia and Herzegovina, as well as Belgrade, Split and Zagreb to ascertain the situation on the ground. During its visit (22 to 27 April), the mission met with Bosnia and Herzegovina's President, Alija Izetbegović, and Vice-President, Ejup Ganic; Messrs. Radovan Karadzic and Mate Boban, leaders, respectively, of the Bosnian Serbs and Bosnian Croats; and Croatia's President, Franjo Tudjman. The mission also met with the UNPROFOR Commander and field commanders, representatives of UNHCR and ICRC, and local authorities of areas where hostilities were occurring: Gorazde, Sarajevo, Srebrenica, Tuzla and Zepa in eastern Bosnia and Herzegovina; and Vitez in central Bosnia. The mission's findings and recommendations were contained in a report transmitted to the Security Council President on 30 April.[107]

The mission found Srebrenica practically under seige, with access to it controlled by Bosnian Serb forces. The prevailing conditions were inhuman and reflected neither the spirit nor the intent of Council resolution 819(1993) declaring Srebrenica a safe area. The Serb forces did not appear ready to withdraw; on the contrary, their numbers increased, they maintained their own interpretation of the demilitarization agreement and had little respect for UNPROFOR's authority.

The mission recommended the withdrawal of Serb forces from Srebrenica to points from which they could not attack, harass or terrorize the town; expansion of the designated safe area; immediate restoration of the water supply; and a warning to the Serbs on the implications of international humanitarian law violations. Gorazde, Tuzla and Zepa should be declared safe areas, with UNPROFOR monitors to be deployed around the cease-fire lines in a way that would not prejudge the future implementation of the Vance-Owen peace plan. Sarajevo should immediately become a safe area.

The mission's meeting with President Tudjman and Mr. Boban focused on the hostilities between

---

[b]Rule 39 of the Council's provisional rules of procedure states: "The Security Council may invite members of the Secretariat or other persons, whom it considers competent for the purpose, to supply it with information or to give other assistance in examining matters within its competence."

Bosnian Croats and Bosnian Muslims at Vitez and on the massacres committed by one group against the other.

It was the mission's belief that the designation of certain towns or enclaves as safe areas deserved serious consideration as an act of preventive diplomacy, but should in no way undermine the Vance-Owen peace plan. The designations would require a larger UNPROFOR presence, a revised mandate to encompass cease-fire and safe area monitoring, and enforcement measures should the Serbs ignore the integrity of the safe areas.

Annexed to the report were: the mission's itinerary; an UNPROFOR-mediated agreement, signed at Sarajevo on 17 April by the military representatives of the Government and the Bosnian Serbs in the presence of UNPROFOR's Lieutenant-General Wahlgren, providing for a total cease-fire in the Srebrenica area effective 18 April and specific arrangements for the demilitarization of Srebrenica within 72 hours of the arrival of the UNPROFOR company to be deployed there; and a joint statement signed by President Izetbegović and Mr. Boban (for the Croatian Defence Council), witnessed by President Tudjman, by which they undertook to order their respective commanders and military units immediately to halt all hostilities and unconditionally to respect all agreements concluded thus far between the Bosnian Muslims and the Bosnian Croats.

Communications. Bosnia and Herzegovina brought the Security Council President up to date on the continuing armed attacks on several towns in eastern Bosnia and Herzegovina and the resultant humanitarian needs of their populations. It wrote on 17 April[108] that, notwithstanding Council resolution 819(1993), the attacks on Srebrenica had escalated. In view of evidence that the Serb commander, General Ratko Mladic, had ordered the massacre of defenceless civilians, Bosnia and Herzegovina asked that the President do all humanly possible to stop it.

A letter of 27 April[109] requested an expansion of UNPROFOR's mandate in Srebrenica. A new offensive was reported on 28 April[110] aimed at linking the Serb and Montenegrin territorial gains in the northern and eastern parts of the country to Serbia; Cazin, in the north-west, sustained the heaviest attack and Bihac the heaviest civilian casualties; the Posavina region, particularly the city of Gradacac, had come under renewed attack, as had Goradze, Srebrenica and Zepa.

Subsequent letters included: a formal request for an emergency meeting of the Council in the light of the four-hour attack on Zepa on 4 May;[111] appeals of 5 May for medical assistance and immediate deployment of UNPROFOR in the area[112] and for the Council to take all steps necessary to save Zepa;[113] and a letter of 6 May[114] giving an estimate of civilian casualties from the unremitting bombardment of Zepa and reporting the shelling of Tuzla and Sarajevo.

The report of the fact-finding mission[107] and the foregoing communications were before the Security Council when it met on 6 May. Bosnia and Herzegovina, at its request, was invited to participate without the right to vote under rule 37.ᵃ

The Council, acting under Chapter VII of the Charter, unanimously adopted **resolution 824(1993)**.

The Security Council,

Reaffirming all its earlier relevant resolutions,

Reaffirming also the sovereignty, territorial integrity and political independence of the Republic of Bosnia and Herzegovina,

Having considered the report of the Mission of the Security Council to the Republic of Bosnia and Herzegovina authorized by resolution 819(1993) and, in particular, its recommendations that the concept of safe areas be extended to other towns in need of safety,

Reaffirming again its condemnation of all violations of international humanitarian law, in particular "ethnic cleansing" and all practices conducive thereto, as well as the denial or the obstruction of access of civilians to humanitarian aid and services such as medical assistance and basic utilities,

Taking into consideration the urgent security and humanitarian needs faced by several towns in the Republic of Bosnia and Herzegovina as exacerbated by the constant influx of large numbers of displaced persons including, in particular, the sick and wounded,

Taking also into consideration the formal request submitted by the Republic of Bosnia and Herzegovina,

Deeply concerned at the continuing armed hostilities by Bosnian Serb paramilitary units against several towns in the Republic of Bosnia and Herzegovina and determined to ensure peace and stability throughout the country, most immediately in the towns of Sarajevo, Tuzla, Zepa, Gorazde, Bihac, as well as Srebrenica,

Convinced that the threatened towns and their surroundings should be treated as safe areas, free from armed attacks and from any other hostile acts which endanger the well-being and the safety of their inhabitants,

Aware in this context of the unique character of the city of Sarajevo, as a multicultural, multi-ethnic and pluri-religious centre which exemplifies the viability of coexistence and interrelations between all the communities of the Republic of Bosnia and Herzegovina, and of the need to preserve it and avoid its further destruction,

Affirming that nothing in the present resolution should be construed as contradicting or in any way departing from the spirit or the letter of the peace plan for the Republic of Bosnia and Herzegovina,

Convinced that treating the towns referred to above as safe areas will contribute to the early implementation of the peace plan,

Convinced also that further steps must be taken as necessary to achieve the security of all such safe areas,

Recalling the provisions of resolution 815(1993) on the mandate of UNPROFOR and in that context acting under Chapter VII of the Charter,

1. *Welcomes* the report of the Mission of the Security Council established pursuant to resolution 819(1993), and in particular its recommendations concerning safe areas;

2. *Demands* that any taking of territory by force cease immediately;

3. *Declares* that the capital city of the Republic of Bosnia and Herzegovina, Sarajevo, and other such threatened areas, in particular the towns of Tuzla, Zepa, Gorazde, Bihac, as well as Srebrenica, and their surroundings should be treated as safe areas by all the parties concerned and should be free from armed attacks and from any other hostile act;

4. *Further declares* that in these safe areas the following should be observed:

(a) The immediate cessation of armed attacks or any hostile act against these safe areas, and the withdrawal of all Bosnian Serb military or paramilitary units from these towns to a distance wherefrom they cease to constitute a menace to their security and that of their inhabitants to be monitored by United Nations military observers;

(b) Full respect by all parties of the rights of the United Nations Protection Force (UNPROFOR) and the international humanitarian agencies to free and unimpeded access to all safe areas in the Republic of Bosnia and Herzegovina and full respect for the safety of the personnel engaged in these operations;

5. *Demands* to that end that all parties and others concerned cooperate fully with UNPROFOR and take any necessary measures to respect these safe areas;

6. *Requests* the Secretary-General to take appropriate measures with a view to monitoring the humanitarian situation in the safe areas and, to that end, authorizes the strengthening of UNPROFOR by an additional 50 United Nations military observers, together with related equipment and logistical support; and in this connection, also demands that all parties and all others concerned cooperate fully and promptly with UNPROFOR;

7. *Declares* its readiness, in the event of the failure by any party to comply with the present resolution, to consider immediately the adoption of any additional measures necessary with a view to its full implementation, including to ensure respect for the safety of United Nations personnel;

8. *Declares also* that arrangements pursuant to the present resolution shall remain in force up until the provisions for the cessation of hostilities, separation of forces and supervision of heavy weaponry as envisaged in the peace plan for the Republic of Bosnia and Herzegovina, are implemented;

9. *Decides* to remain seized of the matter.

Security Council resolution 824(1993)

6 May 1993   Meeting 3208   Adopted unanimously

Draft prepared in consultations among Council members (S/25722).

Communications. Several countries conveyed their views to the Security Council President in May on various aspects relating to the safe areas and proposed ways for bringing about peace in Bosnia and Herzegovina.

By a 14 May memorandum,[115] Cape Verde, Djibouti, Morocco, Pakistan and Venezuela (Council members belonging to the Non-Aligned Movement) appealed to the Council to consider immediate adoption of measures, including: giving a new mandate for UNPROFOR to enable it to provide effective protection to the safe areas; recognizing Bosnia and Herzegovina's inherent right to self-defence; and extending economic sanctions to Croatia if its offensive actions continued, particularly in Mostar. A memorandum from France, transmitted on 19 May,[116] proposed options to ensure the protection of the safe areas, including new tasks for UNPROFOR and, to confer added credibility to the concept of safe areas, participation on the ground of the Russian Federation and the United States.

A communiqué issued by the Council of Ministers of the Western European Union (WEU) on 19 May[117] outlined the possible role that WEU might play in respect of the safe areas and UNPROFOR, as well as in the context of the Vance-Owen peace plan, in coordination with the North Atlantic Treaty Organization (NATO). A declaration of 24 May by OIC[118] urged forceful and decisive steps, including lifting the arms embargo against Bosnia and Herzegovina and a Council decision not to accept the unjust *fait accompli* in that country.

On 30 May,[119] Bosnia and Herzegovina wrote about a new offensive against Gorazde, the shelling of Sarajevo and the continuing attacks on the towns of Brcko and Maglaj and requested an emergency meeting of the Security Council. On 2 June,[120] it reported on the continued offensive against Gorazde.   Earlier, the Secretary-General, by a letter of 14 May to the Council President,[121] transmitted the text of an UNPROFOR-mediated cease-fire agreement concluded at Mostar on 12 May between the Generals of the Bosnian Muslim and Bosnian Croat parties. He stated that the situation in Mostar qualified the town as a "threatened area" under the terms of resolution 824(1993), which helped to set the terms of UNPROFOR's active involvement in the cease-fire and in deploying the Spanish battalion in an interposition role at Mostar. UNPROFOR's presence was an integral part of the cease-fire agreement and had helped to defuse the tension and stabilize the situation. None the less, concern had been expressed about the formal mandate of UNPROFOR in this regard, which also applied to the involvement of civilian police officers provided for in the cease-fire agreement, for which no authorization from the Council existed. The Secretary-General therefore requested confirmation as to whether the foregoing interpretation of the UNPROFOR mandate was acceptable. The Council's agreement with that interpretation was conveyed on 22 May.[122]

The Security Council convened on 4 June and invited Bosnia and Herzegovina and Turkey, at their request, to participate in the discussion without the right to vote under rule 37.ª Before it were the communications mentioned above.

By 13 votes to none, with 2 abstentions (Pakistan and Venezuela), the Council adopted **resolution 836(1993)**.

The Security Council,

Reaffirming its resolution 713(1991) of 25 September 1991 and all subsequent relevant resolutions,

Reaffirming in particular its resolutions 819(1993) of 16 April 1993 and 824(1993) of 6 May 1993, which demanded that certain towns and their surrounding areas in the Republic of Bosnia and Herzegovina should be treated as safe areas,

Reaffirming the sovereignty, territorial integrity and political independence of the Republic of Bosnia and Herzegovina and the responsibility of the Security Council in this regard,

Condemning military attacks, and actions that do not respect the sovereignty, territorial integrity and political independence of the Republic of Bosnia and Herzegovina, which, as a State Member of the United Nations, enjoys the rights provided for in the Charter of the United Nations,

Reiterating its alarm at the grave and intolerable situation in the Republic of Bosnia and Herzegovina arising from serious violations of international humanitarian law,

Reaffirming once again that any taking of territory by force or any practice of "ethnic cleansing" is unlawful and totally unacceptable,

Commending the Government of the Republic of Bosnia and Herzegovina and the Bosnian Croat party for having signed the Vance-Owen Plan,

Gravely concerned at the persistent refusal of the Bosnian Serb party to accept the Vance-Owen Plan and calling upon that party to accept the Peace Plan for the Republic of Bosnia and Herzegovina in full,

Deeply concerned by the continuing armed hostilities in the territory of the Republic of Bosnia and Herzegovina which run totally counter to the Peace Plan,

Alarmed by the resulting plight of the civilian population in the territory of the Republic of Bosnia and Herzegovina, in particular in Sarajevo, Bihac, Srebrenica, Gorazde, Tuzla and Zepa,

Condemning the obstruction, primarily by the Bosnian Serb party, of the delivery of humanitarian assistance,

Determined to ensure the protection of the civilian population in safe areas and to promote a lasting political solution,

Confirming the ban on military flights in the airspace of the Republic of Bosnia and Herzegovina, established by resolutions 781(1992) of 9 October 1992, 786(1992) of 10 November 1992 and 816(1993) of 31 March 1993,

Affirming that the concept of safe areas in the Republic of Bosnia and Herzegovina as contained in resolutions 819(1993) and 824(1993) was adopted to respond to an emergency situation, and noting that the concept proposed by France in document S/25800 and by others could make a valuable contribution and should not in any way be taken as an end in itself, but as a part of the Vance-Owen process and as a first step towards a just and lasting political solution,

Convinced that treating the towns and surrounding areas referred to above as safe areas will contribute to the early implementation of that objective,

Stressing that the lasting solution to the conflict in the Republic of Bosnia and Herzegovina must be based on the following principles: immediate and complete cessation of hostilities; withdrawal from territories seized by the use of force and "ethnic cleansing"; reversal of the consequences of "ethnic cleansing" and recognition of the right of all refugees to return to their homes; and respect for the sovereignty, territorial integrity and political independence of the Republic of Bosnia and Herzegovina,

Noting also the crucial work being done throughout the Republic of Bosnia and Herzegovina by the United Nations Protection Force (UNPROFOR), and the importance of such work continuing,

Determining that the situation in the Republic of Bosnia and Herzegovina continues to be a threat to international peace and security,

Acting under Chapter VII of the Charter of the United Nations,

1. *Calls* for the full and immediate implementation of all its relevant resolutions;

2. *Commends* the Peace Plan for the Republic of Bosnia and Herzegovina as contained in document S/25479;

3. *Reaffirms* the unacceptability of the acquisition of territory by the use of force and the need to restore the full sovereignty, territorial integrity and political independence of the Republic of Bosnia and Herzegovina;

4. *Decides* to ensure full respect for the safe areas referred to in resolution 824(1993);

5. *Decides* to extend to that end the mandate of UNPROFOR in order to enable it, in the safe areas referred to in resolution 824(1993), to deter attacks against the safe areas, to monitor the cease-fire, to promote the withdrawal of military or paramilitary units other than those of the Government of the Republic of Bosnia and Herzegovina and to occupy some key points on the ground, in addition to participating in the delivery of humanitarian relief to the population as provided for in resolution 776(1992) of 14 September 1992;

6. *Affirms* that these safe areas are a temporary measure and that the primary objective remains to reverse the consequences of the use of force and to allow all persons displaced from their homes in the Republic of Bosnia and Herzegovina to return to their homes in peace, beginning, *inter alia*, with the prompt implementation of the provisions of the Vance-Owen Plan in areas where those have been agreed by the parties directly concerned;

7. *Requests* the Secretary-General, in consultation, *inter alia*, with the Governments of the Member States contributing forces to UNPROFOR:

(a) To make the adjustments or reinforcement of UNPROFOR which might be required by the implementation of the present resolution, and to consider assigning UNPROFOR elements in support of the elements entrusted with protection of safe areas, with the agreement of the Governments contributing forces;

(b) To direct the UNPROFOR Force Commander to redeploy to the extent possible the forces under his command in the Republic of Bosnia and Herzegovina;

8. *Calls upon* Member States to contribute forces, including logistic support, to facilitate the implementa-

tion of the provisions regarding the safe areas, expresses its gratitude to Member States already providing forces for that purpose and invites the Secretary-General to seek additional contingents from other Member States;

9. *Authorizes* UNPROFOR, in addition to the mandate defined in resolutions 770(1992) of 13 August 1992 and 776(1992), in carrying out the mandate defined in paragraph 5 above, acting in self-defence, to take the necessary measures, including the use of force, in reply to bombardments against the safe areas by any of the parties or to armed incursion into them or in the event of any deliberate obstruction in or around those areas to the freedom of movement of UNPROFOR or of protected humanitarian convoys;

10. *Decides* that, notwithstanding paragraph 1 of resolution 816(1993), Member States, acting nationally or through regional organizations or arrangements, may take, under the authority of the Security Council and subject to close coordination with the Secretary-General and UNPROFOR, all necessary measures, through the use of air power, in and around the safe areas in the Republic of Bosnia and Herzegovina, to support UNPROFOR in the performance of its mandate set out in paragraphs 5 and 9 above;

11. *Requests* the Member States concerned, the Secretary-General and UNPROFOR to coordinate closely on the measures they are taking to implement paragraph 10 above and to report to the Council through the Secretary-General;

12. *Invites* the Secretary-General to report to the Council, for decision, if possible within seven days of the adoption of the present resolution, on the modalities of its implementation, including its financial implications;

13. *Further invites* the Secretary-General to submit to the Council, not later than two months after the adoption of the present resolution, a report on the implementation of and compliance with the present resolution;

14. *Emphasizes* that it will keep open other options for new and tougher measures, none of which is prejudged or excluded from consideration;

15. *Decides* to remain actively seized of the matter, and undertakes to take prompt action, as required.

Security Council resolution 836(1993)

4 June 1993	Meeting 3228	13-0-2

5-nation draft (S/25870).

Sponsors: France, Russian Federation, Spain, United Kingdom, United States.

Vote in Council as follows:

In favour: Brazil, Cape Verde, China, Djibouti, France, Hungary, Japan, Morocco, New Zealand, Russian Federation, Spain, United Kingdom, United States.

Against: None.

Abstaining: Pakistan, Venezuela.

Before adoption of the resolution, Pakistan stated that the text did not address certain core issues of the Bosnia and Herzegovina conflict. Unless the measures it specified were supplemented by further enforcement actions by the Council within a given time-frame and as part of an overall plan, the situation on the ground might be frozen to the advantage of the Bosnian Serbs. It believed that the modality of safe areas as contained in the text could be acceptable only if and when the international community committed itself to the full implementation of the Vance-Owen peace plan, in particular to its provisions on territorial arrangements for Bosnian Muslim communities. All Bosnian Muslim regions, as specified in that plan, should be declared protected areas and those already so declared should be given maximum protection.

Venezuela said that it had serious difficulties with the text. It proposed an initiative incomplete in scope and contrary to its own objectives. Venezuela disagreed with the way in which extending protective measures for a number of urban centres with a predominantly Muslim population was to be achieved. It added that the Council, although traditionally attentive to the opinions of parties to a conflict, did not even consider Bosnia and Herzegovina's position, namely, its rejection of the particular modality of "safe areas" as contained in the text.

Report of the Secretary-General. As requested by the Security Council, the Secretary-General, on 14 June, provided an analysis[123] of the modalities for implementing resolution 836(1993), for which the tasks under the existing UNPROFOR mandate for Bosnia and Herzegovina would be combined with tasks specifically related to the safe areas, as follows: deterrence of attacks; monitoring of the cease-fire; promotion of the withdrawal of military or paramilitary units other than those of the Government of Bosnia and Herzegovina; occupation of key points; protection of humanitarian relief delivery and distribution.

To perform these tasks, UNPROFOR would need to deploy within the safe areas, around their perimeters and at other important points and to respond to attacks against such areas, humanitarian convoys and UNPROFOR personnel. It would have to monitor cease-fire breaches and the surrounding areas for current military actions and future intentions, as well as areas from which units might be withdrawn to ensure that they remained demilitarized.

Any forces deployed must possess appropriate levels of protection, mobility and fire-power, including the availability of a credible air-strike capability provided by Member States.

The analysis included details of the categories of additional Force requirements, currently estimated at some 7,600 personnel, as well as additional equipment, winterized troop accommodations, and civilian personnel.

In a 17 June addendum,[124] the Secretary-General estimated the cost associated with the additional responsibilities to be undertaken by UNPROFOR at $249.9 million for an initial six-month period and the monthly cost thereafter at approximately $26 million.

He recommended that the additional cost should be considered an expense of the Organization to be borne by Member States and that the assessments to be levied on them should be credited to the UNPROFOR special account.

SECURITY COUNCIL ACTION

The Security Council met on 18 June. It had before it, besides the Secretary-General's report, several communications from Bosnia and Herzegovina stating that the attacks on the safe area of Gorazde continued unabated and that its 70,000 inhabitants were vulnerable to genocidal slaughter.[125] At its request, Bosnia and Herzegovina was invited to participate without the right to vote under rule 37.[a]

The Council unanimously adopted **resolution 844(1993)**.

The Security Council,

Reaffirming its resolution 713(1991) of 25 September 1991 and all subsequent relevant resolutions,

Having considered the report of the Secretary-General pursuant to paragraph 12 of resolution 836(1993) concerning the safe areas in the Republic of Bosnia and Herzegovina,

Reiterating once again its alarm at the grave and intolerable situation in the Republic of Bosnia and Herzegovina arising from serious violations of international humanitarian law,

Recalling the overwhelming importance of seeking a comprehensive political solution to the conflict in the Republic of Bosnia and Herzegovina,

Determined to implement fully the provisions of resolution 836(1993),

Acting under Chapter VII of the Charter of the United Nations,

1. *Approves* the report of the Secretary-General;

2. *Decides* to authorize the reinforcement of the United Nations Protection Force (UNPROFOR) to meet the additional force requirements mentioned in paragraph 6 of the report of the Secretary-General as an initial approach;

3. *Requests* the Secretary-General to continue the consultations, *inter alia*, with the Governments of the Member States contributing forces to UNPROFOR, called for in resolution 836(1993);

4. *Reaffirms* its decision in paragraph 10 of resolution 836(1993) on the use of air power, in and around the safe areas, to support UNPROFOR in the performance of its mandate, and encourages Member States, acting nationally or through regional organizations or arrangements, to coordinate closely with the Secretary-General in this regard;

5. *Calls upon* Member States to contribute forces, including logistic support and equipment to facilitate the implementation of the provisions regarding the safe areas;

6. *Invites* the Secretary-General to report to the Council on a regular basis on the implementation of resolution 836(1993) and this resolution;

7. *Decides* to remain actively seized of the matter.

Security Council resolution 844(1993)

18 June 1993   Meeting 3241   Adopted unanimously

5-nation draft (S/25966).

Sponsors: France, Russian Federation, Spain, United Kingdom, United States.

The Secretary-General informed the Council on 29 July of his proposal to pursue offers of troops and equipment made by France, Jordan, Malaysia, the Netherlands and Pakistan in respect of the implementation of resolutions 836(1993) and 844(1993)—to which the Council agreed on 2 August.[126] He also notified the Council on 18 August that the United Nations had acquired the initial operational capability for the use of air power in support of UNPROFOR in Bosnia and Herzegovina; the President acknowledged the information on 22 August.[127]

Communications. On 2 July,[128] Bosnia and Herzegovina requested the Security Council for an air evacuation of Gorazde, which was under a new artillery offensive; a UNHCR humanitarian convoy destined for it had been blocked. On 19 July,[129] it reported that Sarajevo was under a two-pronged offensive and that Mount Igman, southwest of Sarajevo, was being targeted.

SECURITY COUNCIL ACTION

At a meeting on 22 July in connection with the reported offensive on Mount Igman and Sarajevo, the Security Council invited Bosnia and Herzegovina to participate in the discussion without the right to vote under rule 37.[a]

Following consultations among its members, the Council authorized its President to make the following statement[130] on behalf of the Council:

Meeting number. SC 3257.

"The Security Council has noted with grave concern the letter of 19 July 1993 from the President of the Presidency of the Republic of Bosnia and Herzegovina addressed to the President of the Security Council about the Bosnian Serb military offensive in the area of Mount Igman, close to Sarajevo, a city which has stood for centuries as an outstanding example of a multicultural, multi-ethnic and pluri-religious society, which needs to be protected and preserved.

"The Security Council renews its demand that all hostilities in the Republic of Bosnia and Herzegovina cease and that the parties and others concerned refrain from any hostile acts. It supports the call from the Co-Chairmen of the International Conference on the Former Yugoslavia in this regard, designed to facilitate the peace talks.

"The Security Council reaffirms its resolutions 824(1993) and 836(1993), in the first of which the Council declared Sarajevo a safe area that should be free from armed attacks and any hostile acts, and from which Bosnian Serb military or paramilitary units should be withdrawn to a distance wherefrom they cease to constitute a menace to its security and that of its inhabitants. It condemns the offensive by the Bosnian Serbs on Mount Igman aimed at further isolating Sarajevo and escalating the recent unprecedented and unacceptable pressures on the Government and people of the Republic of Bosnia and Herzegovina before the forthcoming talks in Geneva. It demands an immediate end to this offensive and to all attacks on Sarajevo. It also demands an immediate end to all violations of international humanitarian law. It demands an end to the disruption of public utilities (including water, electricity, fuel and communications) by the Bosnian Serb party and to the blocking of, and interference with, the delivery of humanitarian relief by both the Bosnian Serb and the Bosnian Croat parties.

"The Security Council calls on the parties to meet in Geneva under the auspices of the co-Chairmen of the International Conference on the Former Yugoslavia. It calls on the parties to negotiate in earnest with the aim of achieving a just and equitable settlement on the basis of the sovereignty, territorial integrity and political independence of the Republic of Bosnia nad Herzegovina and the principles agreed at the International Conference on the Former Yugoslavia in London on 26 August 1992 and supported by the Council in its statement of 2 September 1992. In particular it reaffirms the unacceptability of ethnic cleansing, or the acquisition of territory by the use of force, or any dissolution of the Republic of Bosnia and Herzegovina.

"The Security Council emphasizes that it will keep open all options, none of which is prejudged or excluded from consideration."

Communications. Between 23 July and 3 December, Bosnia and Herzegovina addressed further communications to the Security Council President relating to safe areas.

Three of the letters[131] reported the continuing armed attack on the Muslim city of Mostar and its surroundings by the Bosnian Croats and reiterated its request that the Council convene in emergency meeting to designate Mostar as a safe area.

Seven letters spoke of the continuing siege of Sarajevo. They drew attention to: the intensification of an already heavy Serb offensive on Mount Igman;[132] the resultant subhuman level to which humanitarian conditions in Sarajevo had deteriorated;[133] President Izetbegović's conditioning his continued attendance at the Geneva peace talks on the United States commitment, in conjunction with NATO, to halt the brutal siege of Sarajevo and induce Serb withdrawal from newly occupied positions;[134] the Serbs' use of helicopters in the assault around Sarajevo, in violation of the ban on military flights (see below);[135] the death of 536 civilians and the wounding of 3,306 others since the declaration of Sarajevo as a safe area in May due to the slow, inconsistent and indecisive implementation of resolution 836(1993);[136] the targeting of Sarajevans by new and more vicious weapons;[137] and the daily shelling of Sarajevo, to which NATO and the United States had not responded, despite their commitments to do so.[138]

Further letters concerned the repeated artillery bombardment of Gorazde;[139] and the intense attacks on Tuzla with ground-to-ground and air-to-ground rockets.[140]

Bosnian Croats–Bosnian Muslims

Complicating the Serbian aggression against the territory of Bosnia and Herzegovina was the outbreak in April of renewed military hostilities between Government forces and Bosnian Croat paramilitary units in central Bosnia and Herzegovina. The fighting intensified in May and widened to other parts of the country, with reports of violations of human rights and international humanitarian law perpetrated by both sides.

SECURITY COUNCIL ACTION (21 April and 10 May)

After consultations among its members on 21 April, the Security Council authorized its President to make the following statement[141] to the media on the Council's behalf:

"The members of the Security Council are deeply concerned by the reports on the outbreak of military hostilities between Bosnian governmental forces and Bosnian Croat paramilitary units north and west of Sarajevo. They are appalled by the reports corroborated by UNPROFOR of atrocities and killings, in particular the setting on fire of Muslim houses and the shooting of entire families in two villages by Bosnian Croat paramilitary units.

"The members of the Security Council strongly condemn this new outbreak of violence undermining the overall efforts to establish a cease-fire and achieve a political solution of the conflict in the Republic of Bosnia and Herzegovina and demand that Bosnian governmental forces and Bosnian Croat paramilitary units cease immediately those hostilities and that all parties refrain from taking any action which endangers the lives and well-being of the inhabitants of the region, strictly comply with their previous commitments including the cease-fire and redouble their efforts to settle the conflict. They call upon all the parties to cooperate with the current efforts in this regard by UNPROFOR and Lord Owen, Co-Chairman of the Steering Committee of the International Conference on the Former Yugoslavia.

"The members of the Security Council also demand that the Bosnian Serbs fully implement resolution 819(1993), including the immediate withdrawal from the areas surrounding Srebrenica, and allow UNPROFOR personnel unimpeded access to the town."

Through the efforts of the ICFY Co-Chairmen, a cease-fire agreement between the two forces, including joint military arrangements to eliminate conflict between them in central Bosnia and Herzegovina, was reached on 25 April. The agreement was embodied in a joint statement signed at Zagreb on that date by President Izetbegović and Mr. Boban (as "President of the Croatian Union of Herceg-Bosna") and witnessed by President Tudjman.[142]

Despite that agreement, fighting continued, as evidenced by Croatia's appeal of 10 May[143] to President Izetbegović and Mr. Boban immediately to do their utmost to put an end to a renewed widening of conflict between Bosnian Croats and Bosnian Muslims and restore cooperation between them in their joint struggle against the Serb aggressor. Also on 10 May,[144] Croatia, while welcoming the recently concluded cease-fire between Croat and Muslim forces, denounced the Bosnian Croat offensive around the Muslim town of Mostar, as it did the Bosnian Muslim offensive on the Croat towns of Jablanica and Konjic.

The Council, after consultations among its members on 10 May, authorized its President to make the followng statement[145] on the Council's behalf:

Meeting number. SC 3210.

"The Security Council, recalling its statement of 21 April 1993 concerning the atrocities and killings in areas north and west of Sarajevo, expresses its grave concern at the major new military offensive launched by Bosnian Croat paramilitary units in the areas of Mostar, Jablanica and Dreznica.

"The Security Council strongly condemns this major military offensive launched by Bosnian Croat paramilitary units which is totally inconsistent with the signature of the Peace Plan for the Republic of Bosnia and Herzegovina by the Bosnian Croat party. The Council demands that the attacks against the areas of Mostar, Jablanica and Dreznica cease forthwith; that Bosnian Croat paramilitary units withdraw immediately from the area and that all the parties strictly comply with their previous commitments as well as the cease-fire agreed to today between the Government of the Republic of Bosnia and Herzegovina and the Bosnian Croat party.

"The Security Council also expresses its deep concern that the UNPROFOR battalion in the area has been forced under fire to redeploy as a result of this latest offensive and condemns the refusal of Bosnian Croat paramilitary units to allow the presence of United Nations military observers, in particular in the city of Mostar.

"The Security Council once again reiterates its demand that UNPROFOR personnel be allowed unimpeded access throughout the Republic of Bosnia and Herzegovina and, in this particular case, demands that the Bosnian Croat paramilitary units ensure the safety and security of UNPROFOR as well as all United Nations personnel in the areas of Mostar, Jablanica and Dreznica. In this connection, the Council expresses its deep concern at the increasing hostile attitude of Bosnian Croat paramilitary units towards UNPROFOR personnel.

"The Security Council calls upon the Republic of Croatia, in accordance with the commitments under the Zagreb agreement of 25 April 1993, to exert all its influence on the Bosnian Croat leadership and paramilitary units with a view to ceasing immediately their attacks, particularly in the areas of Mostar, Jablanica and Dreznica. It further calls on the Republic of Croatia to adhere strictly to its obligations under Security Council resolution 752(1992), including putting an end to all forms of interference and respecting the territorial integrity of the Republic of Bosnia and Herzegovina.

"The Security Council once again reaffirms the sovereignty, territorial integrity and independence of the Republic of Bosnia and Herzegovina and the inacceptability of the acquisition of territory by force and the practice of 'ethnic cleansing'.

"The Security Council remains seized of the matter and is ready to consider further measures to ensure that all parties and others concerned abide by their commitments and fully respect relevant Council decisions."

Communication. Bosnia and Herzegovina, on 26 October,[146] informed the Security Council President of the destruction by Croat extremist forces of the Muslim village of Stupni Do in central Bosnia. More than 80 Muslim civilians, including women, children and the elderly, were reported massacred. Bosnia and Herzegovina urged the Council to take all necessary measures to deter further acts of aggression and slaughter of civilians.

SECURITY COUNCIL ACTION

The Security Council, following consultations among its members on 28 October, authorized its President to make the following statement[147] on the Council's behalf:

"The members of the Council have heard an initial oral report by the Secretariat concerning the massacre of the civilian population in the village of Stupni Do on 23 October 1993 by troops of the Croatian Defence Council (HVO). They also heard accounts of attacks against UNPROFOR by armed persons bearing uniforms of the Bosnian Government forces, and of an attack to which a humanitarian convoy under the protection of UNPROFOR was subjected on 25 October 1993 in central Bosnia.

"The members of the Council unreservedly condemn these acts of violence. They express their profound concern about the preliminary information to the effect that regular and organized armed forces were probably involved. They have requested the Secretary-General to submit as soon as possible a complete report on the responsibility for these acts. The members of the Council are prepared to draw all the relevant conclusions from this report, which will also be transmitted to the Commission of Experts established by resolution 780(1992).

"The members of the Council reiterate their demand that all the parties in the former Yugoslavia comply with their obligations under international humanitarian law, and that those responsible for such violations of international humanitarian law should be held accountable in accordance with the relevant resolutions of the Council. The members of the Council call upon all the parties in the former Yugoslavia to guarantee the unimpeded access to humanitarian assistance and the security of the personnel responsible for it."

UNPROFOR report. On 12 November,[148] the Secretary-General transmitted to the Security Council President a report by UNPROFOR regard-

ing the 25 October incident in which two humanitarian aid convoys were attacked near Novi Travnik in central Bosnia and Herzegovina resulting
in one fatality and ten casualties.

The Secretary-General suspended humanitarian convoys in central Bosnia and Herzegovina
until an investigation of the incident had been carried out and credible guarantees for safe passage
obtained from the warring parties.

Communications. Croatia, on 3 November,[149] requested an urgent meeting of the Security Council to address the situation in and around
the Bosnian Croat town of Vares, in central Bosnia and Herzegovina, under seige by the Bosnian
Muslim army. Six days later,[150] it reported that
the town of Vitez was threatened by the same
army, which had already overrun the bordering
villages of Zabrdje and Jelike. It warned that ethnic cleansing of the over 40,000 refugees of mostly
Bosnian Croats would create a catastrophe; an ammunition factory there, if destroyed, could threaten
the town's security. Croatia urged the Council to
address this imminent humanitarian tragedy.

Bosnia and Herzegovina also called for an emergency Council session to respond to hostage-taking
by Serb forces on 8 November.[151] It informed the
Council President that a delegation headed by
Archbishop Vinko Puljic of Sarajevo, while travelling under UNPROFOR protection to Vares on a
peace mission, had been intercepted at Rajlovac
near Sarajevo by Bosnian Serb forces who then
took his two Bosnian Croat escorts hostage.

SECURITY COUNCIL ACTION

In accordance with Croatia's request, the Security Council met on 9 November. It invited Bosnia and Herzegovina, at its request, to participate
in the discussion without the right to vote, under
rule 37.[a]

Following consultations among its members, the
Council authorized its President to make the following statement[152] on the Council's behalf:

Meeting number. SC 3308.

"The Security Council expresses its deep concern
at the reports on the deterioration of the situation in
Central Bosnia where increased military activities are
seriously threatening security of the civilian population.

"The Security Council demands that all parties and
others concerned refrain from taking any action that
threatens the safety and well-being of the civilian
population.

"The Security Council is equally concerned at the
overall humanitarian situation prevailing in the
Republic of Bosnia and Herzegovina. It reiterates its
demand to all parties and others concerned to guarantee unimpeded access for humanitarian assistance.

"The Security Council, aware of the heavy burden that these developments add to the existing precarious humanitarian situation of the refugees and dis-

placed persons in the Republic of Bosnia and
Herzegovina and in the surrounding countries, calls
on all parties to assist the competent United Nations
agencies and other humanitarian organizations in
their efforts to provide relief to the affected civilian
population in those countries.

"The Security Council urges all parties and others
concerned to exert the utmost restraint and refrain
from taking any action which might exacerbate the
situation."

The President was further authorized to make
a second statement[153] as follows:

"The Security Council is profoundly shocked to
learn of the incident which took place on 8 November 1993 in which two persons were taken hostage by
the Bosnian Serb forces, while members of a delegation headed by Monsignor Vinko Puljic, the Archbishop of Sarajevo, travelling to the city of Vares on
a mission of peace, under the protection of the United
Nations Protection Force (UNPROFOR).

"The Security Council strongly condemns this outrageous act, which is a flagrant challenge to the
authority and inviolability of UNPROFOR.

"The Security Council takes note that, despite the
prompt and commendable intervention of the Special
Representative of the Secretary-General, neither of the
hostages has been released and demands that the Bosnian
Serb forces proceed immediately to release them. The
Council reminds the perpetrators of this act that they
are obligated to ensure that no harm comes to the individuals being held and that those responsible for violations of international humanitarian law will be held
personally accountable for their actions.

"The Security Council requests the Secretary-
General to undertake a thorough investigation of the
incident and to report to the Council without delay.
It urges all parties and others concerned to refrain
from taking any action which might further exacerbate the situation.

"The Security Council condemns all attacks and
hostile acts against UNPROFOR by all parties in the
Republic of Bosnia and Herzegovina, as well as in the
Republic of Croatia, which have become more frequent over the last weeks, and demands that they cease
forthwith."

Report of the Secretary-General. Pursuant to
the second presidential statement of 9 November,
the Secretary-General transmitted to the Security
Council President an extensive UNPROFOR report
regarding the two hostages. The report provided
details of the circumstances surrounding the incident. It noted the meticulous observance by
UNPROFOR of the normal operating procedures
for the escort mission; the refusal of the Serb
checkpoint to allow the convoy to proceed to Vares
or to return to its unit until the two Bosnian
Croats, reported by the Serbs to be war criminals,
were surrendered; the negotiations conducted by
the escort commander; and the forcible opening
of the armoured personnel carrier by the Serbs,
who took away the two men.

The Secretary-General's letter of 11 November transmitting the report[154] informed the President that, following intensive negotiations under the direct supervision of his Special Representative for the Former Yugoslavia, the two persons concerned had been released to UNPROFOR on the same date. According to the report, they were to be handed over to the Government of Bosnia and Herzegovina for trial.

Ban on military flights

The Secretary-General, by letters, dated 12[155] and 16 March,[156] informed the President of the Security Council of the first violations of the 1992 ban on military flights in the airspace of Bosnia and Herzegovina, one of them involving combat activity on 13 March 1993. The ban was established by Council resolution 781(1992)[157] and reaffirmed by resolution 786(1992),[158] for the safe delivery of humanitarian assistance and as a decisive step for the cessation of hostilities in Bosnia and Herzegovina.

SECURITY COUNCIL ACTION

Following consultations on 17 March, the Security Council authorized its President to make the following statement[159] on behalf of the Council:

Meeting number. SC 3184.

"The Security Council has been informed by the Secretary-General in a letter of 12 March 1993 of the violation on 11 March 1993 by military jets, proceeding from the airport of Banja Luka, of Security Council resolution 781(1992), relating to the prohibition of military flights in the airspace of the Republic of Bosnia and Herzegovina, notwithstanding the fact that the Bosnian Serbs at the airport had received appropriate notification by United Nations observers that such flights would constitute a violation of the said resolution.

"The Security Council equally takes note of the report by the Secretary-General in his letter of 16 March 1993 indicating that on 13 March 1993 new violations of the no-fly zone took place by planes that proceeded to bomb the villages of Gladovici and Osatica in the Republic of Bosnia and Herzegovina before leaving in the direction of the Federal Republic of Yugoslavia (Serbia and Montenegro). The above flights are the first violations of Security Council resolution 781(1992) observed by UNPROFOR which involved combat activity.

"The Security Council strongly condemns all violations of its relevant resolutions and underlines the fact that since the beginning of the monitoring operations in early November 1992, the United Nations has reported 465 violations of the no-fly zone over the Republic of Bosnia and Herzegovina.

"The Security Council demands that these violations cease forthwith and reiterates its strong determination to ensure full respect of its resolutions. It particularly underlines its condemnation of all violations, especially those reported by the Secretary-General in his letters referred to above, at a time when

the peace process has reached a critical juncture and when humanitarian relief efforts require full cooperation by all parties.

"The Security Council demands from the Bosnian Serbs an immediate explanation of the aforementioned violations and particularly of the aerial bombardment of the villages of Gladovici and Osatica.

"It requests the Secretary-General to ensure that an investigation is made of the reported possible use of the territory of the Federal Republic of Yugoslavia (Serbia and Montenegro) to launch air attacks against the territory of the Republic of Bosnia and Herzegovina.

"The Security Council has mandated its President to convey to the Minister for Foreign Affairs of the Federal Republic of Yugoslavia (Serbia and Montenegro) and to the leader of the Bosnian Serbs its deepest concern about the above-mentioned developments, and its demand that they take immediate action to prevent any repetitions of these attacks.

"The Security Council will continue to consider what additional steps may be required to secure implementation of the provisions of relevant Security Council resolutions."

Communications by the Secretary-General. In accordance with the foregoing presidential statement, the Secretary-General reported on 27 April[160] that only Yugoslavia (Serbia and Montenegro) had responded to his request for information on the violations. In a statement[161] denying the alleged violations of the airspace of Bosnia and Herzegovina, it described the alleged combat use of aircraft on 13 March as a premeditated fraud intended to pressure the Council at a moment when important agreements to end the war were to be reached.

On 22 March,[162] the Secretary-General informed the Council of the UNPROFOR Commander's concern about the proposed enforcement by Member States of the interdiction on military flights. The Commander was apprehensive that the proposed enforcement action would have negative consequences for the viability of UNPROFOR. In particular, its work of protecting the delivery of humanitarian aid would be seriously jeopardized. He was, moreover, worried about the safety and security of UNPROFOR's military observers and civilian personnel, especially those stationed at airfields.

SECURITY COUNCIL ACTION

The Security Council convened on 31 March to consider a draft resolution relating to the Force Commander's concerns. Bosnia and Herzegovina was invited, at its request, to participate without the right to vote under rule 37.ᵃ

The Council adopted **resolution 816(1993)** by 14 votes to none, with 1 abstention (China).

The Security Council,

Recalling its resolutions 781(1992) of 9 October 1992 and 786(1992) of 10 November 1992,

Recalling paragraph 6 of resolution 781(1992) and paragraph 6 of resolution 786(1992) in which the Council undertook to consider urgently, in the case of violations of the ban on military flights in the airspace of the Republic of Bosnia and Herzegovina, the further measures necessary to enforce the ban,

Deploring the failure of some parties concerned to cooperate fully with United Nations Protection Force (UNPROFOR) airfield monitors in the implementation of resolutions 781(1992) and 786(1992),

Deeply concerned by the various reports of the Secretary-General concerning violations of the ban on military flights in the airspace of the Republic of Bosnia and Herzegovina,

Deeply concerned in particular by the Secretary-General's letters to the President of the Security Council of 12 and 16 March 1993 concerning new blatant violations of the ban on military flights in the airspace of the Republic of Bosnia and Herzegovina, and recalling in this regard the statement by the President of the Security Council of 17 March 1993, and in particular the reference to the bombing of villages in the Republic of Bosnia and Herzegovina,

Recalling the provisions of Chapter VIII of the Charter of the United Nations,

Determining that the grave situation in the Republic of Bosnia and Herzegovina continues to be a threat to international peace and security,

Acting under Chapter VII of the Charter of the United Nations,

1. *Decides* to extend the ban established by resolution 781(1992) to cover flights by all fixed-wing and rotary-wing aircraft in the airspace of the Republic of Bosnia and Herzegovina, this ban not to apply to flights authorized by UNPROFOR in accordance with paragraph 2 below;

2. *Requests* UNPROFOR to modify the mechanism referred to in paragraph 3 of resolution 781(1992) so as to provide for the authorization, in the airspace of the Republic of Bosnia and Herzegovina, of humanitarian flights and other flights consistent with relevant resolutions of the Council;

3. *Requests* UNPROFOR to continue to monitor compliance with the ban on flights in the airspace of the Republic of Bosnia and Herzegovina, and calls on all parties urgently to cooperate with UNPROFOR in making practical arrangements for the close monitoring of authorized flights and improving the notification procedures;

4. *Authorizes* Member States, seven days after the adoption of this resolution, acting nationally or through regional organizations or arrangements, to take, under the authority of the Security Council and subject to close coordination with the Secretary-General and UNPROFOR, all necessary measures in the airspace of the Republic of Bosnia and Herzegovina, in the event of further violations, to ensure compliance with the ban on flights referred to in paragraph 1 above, and proportionate to the specific circumstances and the nature of the flights;

5. *Requests* the Member States concerned, the Secretary-General and UNPROFOR to coordinate closely on the measures they are taking to implement paragraph 4 above, including the rules of engagement, and on the starting date of its implementation, which should be no later than seven days from the date when the authority conferred by paragraph 4 above takes effect, and to report the starting date to the Council through the Secretary-General;

6. *Decides* that, in the event of the Co-Chairmen of the Steering Committee of the International Conference on the Former Yugoslavia notifying the Council that all the Bosnian parties have accepted their proposals on a settlement before the starting date referred to in paragraph 5 above, the measures set forth in the present resolution will be subsumed into the measures for implementing that settlement;

7. *Also requests* the Member States concerned to inform the Secretary-General immediately of any actions they take in exercise of the authority conferred by paragraph 4 above;

8. *Requests further* the Secretary-General to report regularly to the Council on the matter and to inform it immediately of any actions taken by the Member States concerned in exercise of the authority conferred by paragraph 4 above;

9. *Decides* to remain actively seized of the matter.

Security Council resolution 816(1993)

31 March 1993   Meeting 3191   14-0-1

6-nation draft (S/25440).
Sponsors: France, Morocco, Pakistan, Spain, United Kingdom, United States.
Vote in Council as follows:

In favour: Brazil, Cape Verde, Djibouti, France, Hungary, Japan, Morocco, New Zealand, Pakistan, Russian Federation, Spain, United Kingdom, United States, Venezuela.
Against: None.
Abstaining: China.

After the vote, China placed on record its reservations on the invocation of Chapter VII of the Charter to authorize the use of force to ensure compliance with the ban on military flights.

On 9 April,[163] the Secretary-General informed the Council President that Member States concerned had been coordinating with him and UNPROFOR regarding measures to ensure compliance with the ban. The North Atlantic Council of NATO had adopted necessary arrangements for the operation. The rules of engagement established by the Member States concerned were in conformity with paragraph 4 of resolution 816(1993). Liaison cells had been set up at UNPROFOR headquarters at Zagreb and at Kiseljak in Bosnia and Herzegovina, with an UNPROFOR liaison team to be dispatched to the command headquarters designated by Member States. As requested, UNPROFOR had modified the mechanism referred to in paragraph 3 of resolution 781(1992).

The Secretary-General further informed the Council on 16 April[164] that France, the Netherlands, Turkey, the United Kingdom and the United States had offered to make aircraft available; those from France, the Netherlands and the United States had been deployed. He transmitted the further revised guidelines for the authorization of non-UNPROFOR and non-UNHCR flights in the airspace of Bosnia and Herzegovina. The Council took note of the information on 21 April.[165]

Violations

The Secretary-General, in a 10 February report,[166] stated that the interdiction of military flights in the airspace of Bosnia and Herzegovina had been violated, by the parties to the conflict on nearly 400 occasions since its imposition. However, the frequency of violations had dropped and, in the four weeks to 8 February, averaged about two violations a day.

In addition, by numerous notes verbales addressed to the Security Council President throughout 1993,[167] the Secretary-General reported all instances of unauthorized flights, as received by UNPROFOR, in apparent violation of the ban.

Arms embargo: request for exemption

During the general debate held by the Security Council on 19 and 20 April on the situation in Bosnia and Herzegovina, a number of States, invoking Article 51 of the United Nations Charter, called for exempting that country from the 1991 arms embargo on the former Yugoslavia[49] to enable it to exercise its right of self-defence.

A draft resolution to that effect[168] was submitted for Council consideration in June by 22 nations: Afghanistan, Albania, Algeria, Cape Verde, Comoros, Djibouti, Egypt, Estonia, Indonesia, Iran, Jordan, Latvia, Libya Arab Jamahiriya, Malaysia, Morocco, Pakistan, Senegal, Syrian Arab Republic, Turkey, Tunisia, United Arab Emirates, Venezuela.

By that draft, the Council would have reaffirmed the sovereignty, territorial integrity and political independence of Bosnia and Herzegovina, demanded that all hostilities within the country be halted forthwith, and would have decided to exempt the Government of Bosnia and Herzegovina from the arms embargo imposed on the former Yugoslavia by resolution 713(1991) with the sole purpose of enabling it to exercise its inherent right of self-defence.

SECURITY COUNCIL CONSIDERATION

The Security Council convened on 29 June to consider the draft resolution.

At their request, Afghanistan, Albania, Bangladesh, Bosnia and Herzegovina, the Comoros, Costa Rica, Croatia, Egypt, Estonia, Indonesia, Iran, Jordan, Latvia, the Libyan Arab Jamahiriya, Malaysia, Senegal, Slovenia, the Syrian Arab Republic, Tunisia, Turkey and the United Arab Emirates were invited to participate in the discussion without the right to vote under rule 37.[a] At his request, Dragomir Djokic, Ambassador of Yugoslavia (Serbia and Montenegro), was also invited to address the Council.

Following statements by some 29 States, the Council voted on the draft resolution, which received 6 votes to none, with 9 abstentions.

In favour: Cape Verde, Djibouti, Morocco, Pakistan, United States, Venezuela.

Against: None.

Abstaining: Brazil, China, France, Hungary, Japan, New Zealand, Russian Federation, Spain, United Kingdom.

The draft was not adopted, having failed to obtain the required number of votes.

The United Kingdom stated that it was simply not credible that lifting the arms embargo would result in arms reaching only the Bosnian Government forces; already a substantial proportion of the arms clandestinely destined for the Bosnian Government had fallen into other hands. Lifting the embargo would provide an irresistible temptation to the Bosnian Serbs and Bosnian Croats to intensify their military efforts and to ensure that, by the time any substantial delivery of weapons was made, the military threat posed to them by the Bosnian Government forces had been neutralized.

For France, deciding selectively to lift the arms embargo would only interfere with the ongoing negotiating process—a view shared by Japan and the Russian Federation.

The Russian Federation stated that adopting the draft would intensify the fighting, endanger the security of United Nations troops and cause the conflict to spread beyond the country's boundaries. Japan added that ongoing humanitarian assistance could be jeopardized and the possibility of resolving the conflict by peaceful political means would be eliminated.

Hungary wanted to give a last chance to the tireless efforts aimed at achieving a solution to the crisis.

Meeting number. SC 3247.

Subsequently, Bosnia and Herzegovina informed the Secretary-General that it had issued a statement of intention, dated 15 November,[169] to institute legal proceedings against the United Kingdom before ICJ for violating the terms of the 1948 Convention on the Prevention and Punishment of the Crime of Genocide,[103] of the 1965 International Convention on the Elimination of All Forms of Racial Discrimination[170] and of the other sources of general international law set forth in Article 38 of the ICJ Statute. The application, besides charging the United Kingdom with failure in its affirmative obligation to prevent genocide against the people of Bosnia and Herzegovina, would further charge it, as a permanent Council member, with having illegally maintained an arms embargo on the Republic in violation of Article 51 of the Charter.

The United Kingdom, on 6 December,[171] rejected the statement as totally without foundation. On 17 December,[172] Bosnia and Herzegovina notified the Council President of its decision not to proceed with its application.

Earlier, on 27 October,[173] Yugoslavia (Serbia and Montenegro) drew attention to a 20 October

UNPROFOR report, according to which a commander of the Army of Bosnia and Herzegovina admitted that chemical grenades had been used against the Bosnian Serb forces. In addition to that Army's repeated threats to use chemical weapons, President Izetbegović was quoted by the Turkish News Agency in June as saying he would not rule out the use of such weapons if the United Nations did not exempt Bosnia and Herzegovina from the arms embargo.

World Conference on Human Rights. The 1993 World Conference on Human Rights (see PART THREE, Chapter X) adopted a special declaration on Bosnia and Herzegovina, in which it urged lifting the embargo against it to enable it to exercise its right to self-defence.

GENERAL ASSEMBLY ACTION

In **resolution 48/88** of 20 December on the situation in Bosnia and Herzegovina, the General Assembly urged the Security Council to consider exempting Bosnia and Herzegovina from the arms embargo as imposed on the former Yugoslavia under Council resolution 713(1991). It likewise urged Member States and the international community to cooperate with Bosnia and Herzegovina in exercise of its inherent right of self-defence in accordance with Article 51 of Chapter VII of the Charter.

Border control

SECURITY COUNCIL ACTION

On 10 June, the Security Council considered a draft resolution relating to the deployment of international observers on the borders of Bosnia and Herzegovina to facilitate implementation of the sanctions regime mandated by Council resolutions 713(1991),[49] 757(1992),[50] 787(1992),[51] 819(1993) and 820(1993), as well as of resolution 752(1992)[174] demanding immediate cessation of all outside interference.

Before the Council were: the 1992 report of the Secretary-General[175] presenting three options for such deployment; a 24 May letter[176] from France, the Russian Federation, Spain, the United Kingdom and the United States offering to provide jointly, among other assistance, border monitors or technical expertise or aerial surveillance; a 1 June letter from Croatia[177] accepting international control of its entire border with Bosnia and Herzegovina; and an 8 June letter from Bosnia and Herzegovina[178] supporting the deployment of monitors along its border with Yugoslavia (Serbia and Montenegro) to enable effective control of all border traffic between the two countries.

The Council unanimously adopted **resolution 838(1993)**.

The Security Council,

Reaffirming its resolution 713(1991) of 25 September 1991 and all subsequent relevant resolutions,

Reaffirming the sovereignty, territorial integrity and political independence of the Republic of Bosnia and Herzegovina and the responsibility of the Security Council in this regard,

Reiterating the demands in its resolution 752(1992) and subsequent relevant resolutions that all forms of interference from outside the Republic of Bosnia and Herzegovina cease immediately and that its neighbours take swift action to end all interference and respect its territorial integrity,

Recalling the demand in its resolution 819(1993) that the Federal Republic of Yugoslavia (Serbia and Montenegro) immediately cease the supply of military arms, equipment and services to Bosnian Serb paramilitary units,

Taking into account the report of the Secretary-General dated 21 December 1992 on the possible deployment of observers on the borders of the Republic of Bosnia and Herzegovina,

Expressing its condemnation of all activities carried out in violation of resolutions 757(1992), 787(1992) and 820(1993) between the territory of the Federal Republic of Yugoslavia (Serbia and Montenegro) and the United Nations Protected Areas in the Republic of Croatia and those areas of the Republic of Bosnia and Herzegovina under the control of Bosnian Serb forces,

Considering that, in order to facilitate the implementation of the relevant Security Council resolutions, observers should be deployed on the borders of the Republic of Bosnia and Herzegovina, as indicated in its resolution 787(1992),

Taking note of the earlier preparedness of the authorities in the Federal Republic of Yugoslavia (Serbia and Montenegro) to stop all but humanitarian supplies to the Bosnian Serb party, and urging full implementation of that commitment,

Considering that all appropriate measures should be undertaken to achieve a peaceful settlement of the conflict in the Republic of Bosnia and Herzegovina provided for in the Vance-Owen Peace Plan,

Bearing in mind paragraph 4 *(a)* of its resolution 757(1992) concerning the prevention by all States of imports into their territories of all commodities and products originating in or exported from the Federal Republic of Yugoslavia (Serbia and Montenegro) and paragraph 12 of its resolution 820(1993) concerning import to, export from and transshipment through those areas of the Republic of Bosnia and Herzegovina under the control of Bosnian Serb forces,

1. *Requests* the Secretary-General to submit to the Council as soon as possible a further report on options for the deployment of international observers to monitor effectively the implementation of the relevant Security Council resolutions, to be drawn from the United Nations and, if appropriate, from Member States acting nationally or through regional organizations and arrangements, on the borders of the Republic of Bosnia and Herzegovina, giving priority to the border between the Republic of Bosnia and Herzegovina and the Federal Republic of Yugoslavia (Serbia and Montenegro) and taking into account developments since his report of 21 December 1992 as well as the differing circum-

stances affecting the various sectors of the borders and the need for appropriate coordination mechanisms;

2. *Invites* the Secretary-General to contact immediately Member States, nationally or through regional organizations or arrangements, to ensure the availability to him on a continuing basis of any relevant material derived from aerial surveillance and to report thereon to the Security Council;

3. *Decides* to remain seized of the matter.

Security Council resolution 838(1993)
10 June 1993   Meeting 3234   Adopted unanimously
5-nation draft (S/25798).
Sponsors: France, Russian Federation, Spain, United Kingdom, United States.

Report of the Secretary-General. In response to the Security Council's request, the Secretary-General submitted a further report, dated 1 July,[179] on options for the deployment of international observers on the borders of Bosnia and Herzegovina, giving priority to its border with Yugoslavia (Serbia and Montenegro) and taking account of the 1993 Council resolutions strengthening the sanctions regime against Yugoslavia (Serbia and Montenegro).

Two options for monitoring were developed by UNPROFOR. One option called for the deployment of international monitors at 48 major crossing points on the borders between Bosnia and Herzegovina and Yugoslavia (Serbia and Montenegro) and at 75 crossing points between Bosnia and Herzegovina and Croatia, in addition to those where the international borders of Croatia coincided with those of the UNPAs, making a total of 123 crossing points along 1,100 kilometres of borderline. The monitoring activity would involve observing and reporting traffic at the crossing points but not checking outgoing and incoming goods. Eight observers and/or troops and four interpreters would be required at each point. For its effectiveness, this option would depend largely on the cooperation of Croatian and Yugoslav customs officers.

The Force Commander suggested dividing the work between UNPROFOR and European Community Monitoring Mission teams, with UNPROFOR in command of arrangements and acting as the sole reporting body to the Council. To reduce military staff requirements and the training time required, the Secretary-General suggested using civilian police monitors and former customs and retired border police officials, to be identified by Member States.

The other option was for full border control, requiring a capability, not only to observe and report, but also to search, to deny passage and to interdict in cases where the borders had been already crossed. UNPROFOR would in effect supersede national authorities in respect of certain national border control functions.

UNPROFOR estimated that such a mission would need an infantry platoon at each crossing point, with a total troop requirement of over 10,000, augmented by a logistics battalion of 1,000 to 1,200 all ranks and a number of civilian police monitors, interpreters, and civilian affairs and administrative personnel. Thus, the total additional essential requirements would range from 10,300 to 10,500 troops and civilian personnel.

The Secretary-General advised that it would be unrealistic for the Council to authorize the second option. As for the first, for which substantial additional observers and equipment would be required, the Council might wish to establish whether Member States would be ready to make available the qualified staff required and to take account of the Organization's precarious financial situation. It might also wish to note that the effectiveness of the first option would depend entirely on the cooperation of the neighbouring countries and the parties concerned in Bosnia and Herzegovina.

In an addendum to his report, dated 13 July,[180] the Secretary-General estimated that the total cost of the first option would amount to some $94.8 million for an initial six-month period and approximately $8.1 million a month thereafter.

The additional costs should be considered an expense of the Organization to be borne by Member States and the assessments to be levied on them should be credited to the UNPROFOR Special Account.

The Council President, on 7 July,[181] informed the Secretary-General that the Council continued to believe that international observers should be deployed on the borders of Bosnia and Herzegovina, with priority given to the border between it and Yugoslavia (Serbia and Montenegro). The Council invited him to establish whether Member States were ready to make qualified personnel available, to explore all possibilities for implementing of the border monitors concept, and to seek the full cooperation of the neighbouring countries.

Activities of the Co-Chairmen of the ICFY Steering Committee

Efforts to bring peace to Bosnia and Herzegovina proceeded on the basis of the principles of the Charter of the United Nations, the relevant decisions of the Security Council and the principles adopted by ICFY at its London session in August 1992.[182] Since that session, the Co-Chairmen of the ICFY Steering Committee had held intensive negotiations with the three sides to the conflict, namely, the Bosnian Government, the Bosnian Serbs and the Bosnian Croats, as well as with Croatia and Yugoslavia (Serbia and Montenegro).

In seven rounds of talks during 1993 that took place between 2 January and 2 May—three at Geneva, followed by three in New York and one at Athens, Greece—the Co-Chairmen devoted their efforts to hammering out a peace plan for Bosnia and Herzegovina and to getting the three sides to sign the plan. Known as the Vance-Owen peace plan, it included a set of nine constitutional principles, an agreement on military and related issues, a map reflecting the country's organization into 10 provinces, and an agreement on interim governmental arrangements. It was endorsed by EC and by the Secretary-General. Although signed by the three sides by 2 May, the plan was rejected three days later by the "assembly" of the Bosnian Serbs and in a mid-May referendum.

Despite this set-back, the Co-Chairmen continued to search for a peaceful settlement.

Vance-Owen peace plan

Report of the Secretary-General (6 January). In a 6 January report,[183] the Secretary-General gave an account of the first of the three rounds of talks at Geneva held from 2 and 4 January. The report stated that it was the first time since September 1992[1] that the three sides to the conflict in Bosnia and Herzegovina were represented at the highest political and military levels: Bosnia and Herzegovina was led by President Alija Izetbegović; the Bosnian Croats by Mate Boban; and the Bosnian Serbs by Radovan Karadzic. Also attending were the delegations of Yugoslavia (Serbia and Montenegro) and of Croatia, led, respectively, by President Dobrica Cosic and by President Franjo Tudjman.

Before the talks adjourned, the Co-Chairmen placed before the delegations a comprehensive package that they believed represented a fair, just and lasting peace in Bosnia and Herzegovina. Referred to as the Vance-Owen peace plan, the package consisted of a draft agreement relating to Bosnia and Herzegovina dealing with the delimitation of provinces in accordance with a map suggesting a future 10-province structure of the republic, with a constitutional framework of 10 principles and with humanitarian issues; and a draft agreement for peace in Bosnia and Herzegovina dealing with the observance and monitoring of the cessation of hostilities, restoration of infrastructure, opening of routes, separation of forces, demilitarization of Sarajevo, monitoring of borders and return of forces to designated provinces. It was explained to the three sides that the two agreements were inextricably linked and that any mutually agreed changes they might propose would be incorporated.

SECURITY COUNCIL ACTION

Following the first round of talks at Geneva, the Security Council held consultations on 8 January,

after which it authorized its President to make the following statement:[184]

Meeting number. SC 3160.

"The Security Council fully supports the efforts of the Co-Chairmen of the Steering Committee of the International Conference on the Former Yugoslavia aimed at achieving an overall political settlement of the crisis through a complete cessation of hostilities and the establishment of a constitutional framework for the Republic of Bosnia and Herzegovina. In this connection, the Council reaffirms the need to respect fully the sovereignty, territorial integrity and political independence of the Republic of Bosnia and Herzegovina.

"The Council fully endorses the view of the Secretary-General described in his report that it is the duty of all the parties involved in the conflict in the Republic of Bosnia and Herzegovina, despite the recent provocation, to cooperate with the Co-Chairmen in bringing this conflict to an end swiftly.

"The Council appeals to all the parties involved to cooperate to the fullest with the peace efforts and warns any party which would oppose an overall political settlement against the consequences of such an attitude; lack of cooperation and non-compliance with its relevant resolutions will compel the Security Council to review the situation in an urgent and most serious manner, and to consider further necessary measures."

Reports of the Secretary-General (13 January, 2 and 8 February). In a 13 January report,[185] the Secretary-General covered the resumed talks from 10 to 12 January, during which the Co-Chairmen considered eight constitutional principles suggested by Mr. Karadzic and arrived at a new version of nine consolidated principles, on the basis of which a new constitution would be drafted. They reviewed the international monitoring and control arrangements envisaged with regard to: interprovincial throughways, a constitutional court, progressive demilitarization of the country, non-discriminatory composition of the police, an international commission of human rights, ombudsmen, and a human rights court.

At the conclusion of the talks, Mr. Boban signed the agreement setting out the constitutional principles together with the provincial map and the agreement on military and related issues. President Izetbegović accepted the constitutional principles and the agreement on military and related issues, but not the provincial map. Mr. Karadzic stated his agreement with the proposed constitutional principles provided his "assembly" confirmed that agreement within seven days; he did not accept the provincial map and had some questions about the agreement on military and related issues.

In a 2 February report,[186] the Secretary-General covered the third round of Geneva talks (23 to 30 January). At the end of that round, devoted to the question of the provincial boundaries, the Co-Chairmen informed the parties of their conclusion that the proposed provincial map proposed should be maintained and invited them to sign it. Mr. Boban reconfirmed his acceptance of the map and signed it. President Izetbegović maintained his non-acceptance because, in his view, the map had the effect of rewarding the ethnic cleansing that had taken place. Mr. Karadzic stated that he could formally accept the map on the understanding that the populations in certain areas would be democratically consulted—a condition which the Co-Chairmen ruled as tantamount to non-acceptance of the map.

The Co-Chairmen also invited the three sides to sign the agreement on military and related issues. Messrs. Boban and Karadzic signed the agreement. His earlier acceptance notwithstanding, President Izetbegović declined to sign because he felt that the arrangements on the control of heavy weapons were not strong enough. He was therefore invited to clarify his concerns with the UNPROFOR Commander so as to enable him to sign the agreement.

In addition, the Co-Chairmen submitted for comment to the three sides a working paper on interim arrangements for governing Bosnia and Herzegovina as a whole and each of the provinces during a transitional period until a constitution was drafted and elections held.

The next three rounds of talks took place in New York to take advantage of the Security Council's good offices to help the three sides to overcome their outstanding difficulties. The Secretary-General's report of 8 February,[187] on the round held from 3 to 8 February, noted the extensive discussions on 2 February with the Council's President and permanent members, in which the Co-Chairmen explained the process leading up to the peace package and the factors that had influenced its contents.

The Co-Chairmen explained their priorities in terms of the principles laid down by the Council and at the 1992 ICFY London session.[182] They also expressed concerns about the danger of the conflict spreading and their view that even a selective lifting of the arms embargo would not be in the interests of peace or human rights, and could lead instead to a devastating conflagration engulfing the Balkan region.

The Co-Chairmen conveyed their assessment that the peace package was enforceable and would require a United Nations force of 15,000 to 25,000 to implement it. They urged the establishment of an international criminal court to try persons accused of grave breaches of international humanitarian law in the former Yugoslavia.

The Co-Chairmen also consulted with the OIC Contact Group and, on 6 and 7 February, briefed the Minister for Foreign Affairs of Yugoslavia (Serbia and Montenegro).

The possibility of reaching agreed solutions among the three sides was reduced by the refusal of the Bosnian Government side to meet with the other sides or to discuss provincial boundaries. That Government suggested that work should rather concentrate on the drafting of a new constitution and that the interim governmental arrangements should be built around the existing Government of Bosnia and Herzegovina. It proposed that the Serb side immediately place its heavy weapons under international control, offering to do the same.

The Bosnian Serb side continued to express its readiness to accept and sign the map only if the populations of contested areas were consulted and submitted a map suggesting changes in the proposed provincial boundaries. It could not accept interim arrangements based on the premise that the existing Constitution of Bosnia and Herzegovina continued to be valid or that the interim Government—which it preferred to call the "central coordinating body"—would be a continuation of the current Presidency.

The Bosnian Croat side was prepared to entertain some changes to make the proposed provincial boundaries more acceptable to the other two sides. It advanced a number of suggestions, particularly in respect of the eastern border of Travnik and the western border of Posavina provinces. Since the revised map was rejected by the Bosnian Serb side, which also reconfirmed its position on the proposed original map, the Co-Chairmen remained committed to their original proposal.

SECURITY COUNCIL ACTION

At its 24 February meeting, the Security Council invited Bosnia and Herzegovina, at its request, to participate in the discussion without the right to vote under rule 37.[a] Following consultations among its members, the President was authorized to make the following statement[188] on behalf of the Council:

Meeting number. SC 3176.

"The Security Council, having heard a report from the Co-Chairmen of the Steering Committee of the International Conference on the Former Yugoslavia, is concerned that the present opportunity to reach a negotiated settlement in Bosnia and Herzegovina should not be allowed to slip by. It endorses fully the statement by the President of the United States of America and the Secretary-General of the United Nations on 23 February, calling on the leaders of the parties involved in the peace talks on Bosnia and Herzegovina to come to New York immediately to resume discussions with a view to the early conclusion of an agreement to end the conflict. The Council urges these leaders to respond quickly and positively to that call, and stands ready to give its full support to the efforts of the Co-Chairmen to bring the talks to a successful conclusion.''

Report of the Secretary-General (12 March).
According to the Secretary-General's report of 12 March,[189] significant progress was achieved during the resumed New York talks from 1 to 6 March. The Bosnian Government signed the agreement on military and related issues. It took this action in the light of the following important developments: a Canadian battalion had been deployed to Sarajevo near the airport; certain countries had indicated their preparedness to help the United Nations implement an agreed peace settlement; discussions had taken place on the matter of implementing a viable agreement containing enforcement provisions, which involved the Secretariat's Department of Peace-keeping Operations, UNPROFOR, NATO and the Supreme Headquarters of the Allied Powers in Europe. Moreover, the UNPROFOR Commander had informed the Co-Chairmen that, once substantial numbers of additional troops arrived in Bosnia and Herzegovina, it would be possible to undertake control of heavy weapons and ensure the physical separation of opposing forces.

As a result of meetings on the legitimacy of the State of Bosnia and Herzegovina, the Bosnian Government side and the Bosnian Croat side on 3 March signed a provisional agreement on interim governmental arrangements, in particular with respect to the interim presidency.

Discussions proceeded on the basis that, until the entry into force of a new constitution and the holding of elections, the current Constitution of Bosnia and Herzegovina should continue in force, except to the extent required to implement the proposed provisions in respect of human rights and the reversal of ethnic cleansing, and of the agreed interim governmental arrangements mentioned above. The current powers of the *opstinas* (municipalities) would continue, as would their boundaries, except as required to conform to the agreed provisional boundaries, or when changed by consensus.

With the Bosnian Government's signature of the military agreement, seven out of nine signatures required for the conclusion of the peace settlement plan had been obtained. Outstanding was the agreement of the Bosnian Government and Bosnian Serbs to the provincial map.

SECURITY COUNCIL ACTION

The Security Council met on 25 March and invited Bosnia and Herzegovina, at its request, to participate in the discussion without the right to vote, in accordance with rule 37.[a] After consultations among its members, the Council author-

ized its President to make the following statement[190] on behalf of the Council:

Meeting number. SC 3186.

''The Security Council warmly welcomes the signature by President Alija Izetbegović and Mr. Mate Boban of all four documents of the Peace Plan for Bosnia and Herzegovina worked out by the Co-Chairmen of the Steering Committee of the International Conference on the Former Yugoslavia.

''On this important occasion the Security Council pays tribute to the untiring efforts of the Co-Chairmen, Secretary Vance and Lord Owen.

''The Council commends the action of the two parties who have signed all the documents and calls on the remaining party to sign without delay the two documents of the Peace Plan that it has not already signed and to cease its violence, offensive military actions, 'ethnic cleansing' and obstruction of humanitarian assistance.

''The Council calls for an immediate cessation of hostilities by all parties.

''The Council looks forward to receiving a report from the Secretary-General on the developments in the International Conference and stands ready to take action to follow up on the report and to take the steps required to bring about the peace settlement.''

Report of the Secretary-General (26 March).
The Secretary-General's report of 26 March[191] covered the round of talks held from 16 to 25 March, at which the interim governmental arrangements were discussed further. The Bosnian Government and the Bosnian Croats felt that Sarajevo province should be increased in size, making it less dominated by Sarajevo City; the province should be governed according to the proportional formula applicable to the other nine provinces and the city itself should be governed by an interim Executive Mayor and Executive Board, under the nominal supervision of the Presidency.

The Bosnian Serb side, whose initial position had been for Sarajevo's governance by Muslims and Serbs on a 50-50 basis, would accept a capital *opstina* governed equally among the Bosnian Croats, Muslims and Serbs. It continued to argue for the division of Bosnia and Herzegovina into what would effectively be three separate states, taking the view that the nine constitutional principles it had signed were relevant only to the drafting of a new constitution and not applicable for the interim period.

The Bosnian Serb side insisted on the continuation of legislation adopted by its ''Republika Srpska''. It could not accept the case for any form of interim central government, arguing instead for a central coordinating body with as few functions as possible relating to the coordination of the three peoples' interim constituent structures.

However, the Bosnian Serb side expressed support for the proposed international human rights monitoring mission, with open access to all provinces. It was not convinced of the case for ombudsmen at the national level but considered that each side should appoint four ombudsmen for its constituent structure. Similarly, any human rights court should operate within each constituent structure.

It was thus clear to the Co-Chairmen that the Bosnian Serb position had hardened appreciably on many of the political aspects of an overall settlement since the January round of negotiations.

The Co-Chairmen considered that the interim arrangements should form part of the peace package. Thus, at the last plenary meeting of this round of talks, they presented for signature the final peace package, consisting of the constitutional principles, the map of the provincial boundaries, the military agreement, and the interim governmental arrangements. All had been signed, with the exception of the provincial map and the agreement on interim arrangements, which lacked the signature of the Bosnian Serb side.

In the circumstances, the Co-Chairmen recommended that any enforcement action of the ban on military flights or toughening of sanctions, or the placing of United Nations military observers around the border of Bosnia and Herzegovina, in Croatia and Yugoslavia (Serbia and Montenegro), should be accompanied by the Security Council's endorsement of the peace package.

The Secretary-General observed that the peace package provided the only mechanism for re-establishing peace, with justice and respect for human rights, in Bosnia and Herzegovina. He strongly urged the Council to approve the whole peace package and to call on the Bosnian Serbs to sign the remaining two parts so that attention might be concentrated on its implementation.

The Secretary-General also recommended the early establishment of an international human rights monitoring mission, which all three sides had accepted.

SECURITY COUNCIL ACTION

The Council convened on 17 April in response to two 17 April requests, from France[192] and from Cape Verde, Djibouti, Morocco, Pakistan and Venezuela (Council members that were members of the Non-Aligned Movement).[193] Before it were the reports of the Secretary-General on the activities of the Co-Chairmen of the ICFY Steering Committee describing developments regarding the peace package for Bosnia and Herzegovina.

Also before the Council were a number of communications, to the effect that there was no alternative to the peace plan worked out by the Co-Chairmen; that, if accepted in full by the Bosnian Serb side, there would be a gradual lifting of the sanctions in force against Yugoslavia (Serbia and Montenegro), leading to its full readmittance into the international community; otherwise, the strengthened economic sanctions proposed should be adopted as a measure necessary for the immediate acceptance of the peace package and thereafter for its full implementation in good faith. They included an EC declaration;[194] a statement by France, Spain, the United Kingdom and the United States;[195] a statement by Cape Verde, Djibouti, Morocco, Pakistan and Venezuela;[196] and a letter from Turkey on behalf of the OIC Contact Group.[197]

At its request, Bosnia and Herzegovina was invited to participate in the discussion without the right to vote, in accordance with rule 37.[a] With the Council's consent, Cyrus Vance (United States), Co-Chairman of the ICFY Steering Committee, was invited under rule 39.[b] Ambassador Dragomir Djokic of Yugoslavia (Serbia and Montenegro), at his request, was also invited to address the Council.

In his address, Mr. Vance stated that he and his Co-Chairman, Lord Owen, hoped that the Council would adopt the draft resolution at hand in order to send the very clear message to the Bosnian Serb side and its supporters that time was running out and the international community would no longer wait. If the measures envisaged in the resolution should fail to achieve the desired effect, they should be followed by additional measures of sterner persuasion. Mr. Vance added that everything possible must be done to bring humanitarian relief and assistance to the suffering communities in Bosnia and Herzegovina.

Following an oral revision to the text, the Council adopted **resolution 820(1993)** by a vote of 13 to none, with 2 abstentions (China, Russian Federation).

The Security Council,

Reaffirming all its earlier relevant resolutions,

Having considered the reports of the Secretary-General on the peace talks held by the Co-Chairmen of the Steering Committee of the International Conference on the Former Yugoslavia,

Reaffirming the need for a lasting peace settlement to be signed by all of the Bosnian parties,

Reaffirming the sovereignty, territorial integrity and political independence of the Republic of Bosnia and Herzegovina,

Reaffirming once again that any taking of territory by force or any practice of "ethnic cleansing" is unlawful and totally unacceptable, and insisting that all displaced persons be enabled to return in peace to their former homes,

Reaffirming in this regard its resolution 808(1993) in which it decided that an international tribunal shall be established for the prosecution of persons responsible for serious violations of international humanitarian law committed in the territory of the former Yugoslavia since

1991 and requested the Secretary-General to submit a report at the earliest possible date,

Deeply alarmed and concerned about the magnitude of the plight of innocent victims of the conflict in the Republic of Bosnia and Herzegovina,

Expressing its condemnation of all the activities carried out in violation of resolutions 757(1992) and 787(1992) between the territory of the Federal Republic of Yugoslavia (Serbia and Montenegro) and Serb-controlled areas in the Republic of Croatia and the Republic of Bosnia and Herzegovina,

Deeply concerned by the position of the Bosnian Serb party as reported in paragraphs 17, 18 and 19 of the report of the Secretary-General of 26 March 1993,

Recalling the provisions of Chapter VIII of the Charter of the United Nations,

A

1. *Commends* the peace plan for Bosnia and Herzegovina in the form agreed to by two of the Bosnian parties and set out in the report of the Secretary-General of 26 March 1993, namely the Agreement on Interim Arrangements (annex I), the nine Constitutional Principles (annex II), the provisional provincial map (annex III) and the Agreement for Peace in Bosnia and Herzegovina (annex IV);

2. *Welcomes* the fact that this plan has now been accepted in full by two of the Bosnian parties;

3. *Expresses* its grave concern at the refusal so far of the Bosnian Serb party to accept the Agreement on Interim Arrangements and the provisional provincial map, and calls on that party to accept the peace plan in full;

4. *Demands* that all parties and others concerned continue to observe the cease-fire and refrain from any further hostilities;

5. *Demands* full respect for the right of the United Nations Protection Force (UNPROFOR) and the international humanitarian agencies to free and unimpeded access to all areas in the Republic of Bosnia and Herzegovina, and that all parties, in particular the Bosnian Serb party and others concerned, cooperate fully with them and take all necessary steps to ensure the safety of their personnel;

6. *Condemns once again* all violations of international humanitarian law, including in particular the practice of "ethnic cleansing" and the massive, organized and systematic detention and rape of women, and reaffirms that those who commit or have committed or order or have ordered the commission of such acts will be held individually responsible in respect of such acts;

7. *Reaffirms* its endorsement of the principles that all statements or commitments made under duress, particularly those relating to land and property, are wholly null and void and that all displaced persons have the right to return in peace to their former homes and should be assisted to do so;

8. *Declares* its readiness to take all the necessary measures to assist the parties in the effective implementation of the peace plan once it has been agreed in full by all the parties, and requests the Secretary-General to submit to the Council at the earliest possible date, and if possible not later than nine days after the adoption of the present resolution, a report containing an account of the preparatory work for the implementation of the proposals referred to in paragraph 28 of the Secretary-General's report of 26 March 1993 and detailed proposals for the implementation of the peace plan, including arrangements for the effective international control of heavy weapons, based *inter alia* on consultations with Member States, acting nationally or through regional organizations or arrangements;

9. *Encourages* Member States, acting nationally or through regional organizations or arrangements, to cooperate effectively with the Secretary-General in his efforts to assist the parties in implementing the peace plan in accordance with paragraph 8 above;

B

Determined to strengthen the implementation of the measures imposed by its earlier relevant resolutions,

Acting under Chapter VII of the Charter of the United Nations,

10. *Decides* that the provisions set forth in paragraphs 12 to 30 below shall, to the extent that they establish obligations beyond those established by its earlier relevant resolutions, come into force nine days after the date of the adoption of the present resolution unless the Secretary-General has reported to the Council that the Bosnian Serb party has joined the other parties in signing the peace plan and in implementing it and that the Bosnian Serbs have ceased their military attacks;

11. *Decides further* that if, at any time after the submission of the above-mentioned report of the Secretary-General, the Secretary-General reports to the Council that the Bosnian Serbs have renewed their military attacks or failed to comply with the peace plan, the provisions set forth in paragraphs 12 to 30 below shall come into force immediately;

12. *Decides* that import to, export from and transshipment through the United Nations Protected Areas in the Republic of Croatia and those areas of the Republic of Bosnia and Herzegovina under the control of Bosnian Serb forces, with the exception of essential humanitarian supplies including medical supplies and foodstuffs distributed by international humanitarian agencies, shall be permitted only with proper authorization from the Government of the Republic of Croatia or the Government of the Republic of Bosnia and Herzegovina respectively;

13. *Decides* that all States, in implementing the measures imposed by resolutions 757(1992), 760(1992), 787(1992) and the present resolution, shall take steps to prevent diversion to the territory of the Federal Republic of Yugoslavia (Serbia and Montenegro) of commodities and products said to be destined for other places, in particular the United Nations Protected Areas in the Republic of Croatia and those areas of the Republic of Bosnia and Herzegovina under the control of Bosnian Serb forces;

14. *Demands* that all parties and others concerned cooperate fully with UNPROFOR in the fulfilment of its immigration and customs control functions deriving from resolution 769(1992);

15. *Decides* that transshipments of commodities and products through the Federal Republic of Yugoslavia (Serbia and Montenegro) on the Danube shall be permitted only if specifically authorized by the Committee established by resolution 724(1991) and that each vessel so authorized must be subject to effective monitoring while passing along the Danube between Vidin/Calafat and Mohacs;

16. *Confirms* that no vessels *(a)* registered in the Federal Republic of Yugoslavia (Serbia and Montenegro) or *(b)* in which a majority or controlling interest is held by a person or undertaking in or operating from the Federal Republic of Yugoslavia (Serbia and Montenegro) or *(c)* suspected of having violated or being in violation of resolutions 713(1991), 757(1992), 787(1992) or the present resolution shall be permitted to pass through installations, including river locks or canals within the territory of Member States, and calls upon the riparian States to ensure that adequate monitoring is provided to all cabotage traffic involving points that are situated between Vidin/Calafat and Mohacs;

17. *Reaffirms* the responsibility of riparian States to take necessary measures to ensure that shipping on the Danube is in accordance with resolutions 713(1991), 757(1992), 787(1992) and the present resolution, including any measures under the authority of the Security Council to halt or otherwise control all shipping in order to inspect and verify their cargoes and destinations, to ensure effective monitoring and to ensure strict implementation of the relevant resolutions, and reiterates its request in resolution 787(1992) to all States, including non-riparian States, to provide, acting nationally or through regional organizations or arrangements, such assistance as may be required by the riparian States, notwithstanding the restrictions on navigation set out in the international agreements which apply to the Danube;

18. *Requests* the Committee established by resolution 724(1991) to make periodic reports to the Security Council on information submitted to the Committee regarding alleged violations of the relevant resolutions, identifying where possible persons or entities, including vessels, reported to be engaged in such violations;

19. *Reminds* States of the importance of strict enforcement of measures imposed under Chapter VII of the Charter, and calls upon them to bring proceedings against persons and entities violating the measures imposed by resolutions 713(1991), 757(1992), 787(1992) and the present resolution and to impose appropriate penalties;

20. *Welcomes* the role of the international Sanctions Assistance Missions in support of the implementation of the measures imposed under resolutions 713(1991), 757(1992), 787(1992) and the present resolution and the appointment of the Sanctions Coordinator by the Conference on Security and Cooperation in Europe and invites the Sanctions Coordinator and the Sanctions Assistance Missions to work in close cooperation with the Committee established by resolution 724(1991);

21. *Decides* that States in which there are funds, including any funds derived from property, *(a)* of the authorities in the Federal Republic of Yugoslavia (Serbia and Montenegro), or *(b)* of commercial, industrial or public utility undertakings in the Federal Republic of Yugoslavia (Serbia and Montenegro), or *(c)* controlled directly or indirectly by such authorities or undertakings or by entities, wherever located or organized, owned or controlled by such authorities or undertakings, shall require all persons and entities within their own territories holding such funds to freeze them to ensure that they are not made available directly or indirectly to or for the benefit of the authorities in the Federal Republic of Yugoslavia (Serbia and Montenegro) or to any commercial, industrial or public utility undertaking in

the Federal Republic of Yugoslavia (Serbia and Montenegro), and calls on all States to report to the Committee established by resolution 724(1991) on actions taken pursuant to this paragraph;

22. *Decides* to prohibit the transport of all commodities and products across the land borders or to or from the ports of the Federal Republic of Yugoslavia (Serbia and Montenegro), the only exceptions being:

(a) The importation of medical supplies and foodstuffs into the Federal Republic of Yugoslavia (Serbia and Montenegro) as provided for in resolution 757(1992), in which connection the Committee established by resolution 724(1991) will draw up rules for monitoring to ensure full compliance with this and other relevant resolutions;

(b) The importation of other essential humanitarian supplies into the Federal Republic of Yugoslavia (Serbia and Montenegro) approved on a case-by-case basis under the no-objection procedure by the Committee established by resolution 724(1991);

(c) Strictly limited transshipments through the territory of the Federal Republic of Yugoslavia (Serbia and Montenegro), when authorized on an exceptional basis by the Committee established by resolution 724(1991), provided that nothing in this paragraph shall affect transshipment on the Danube in accordance with paragraph 15 above;

23. *Decides* that each State neighbouring the Federal Republic of Yugoslavia (Serbia and Montenegro) shall prevent the passage of all freight vehicles and rolling stock into or out of the Federal Republic of Yugoslavia (Serbia and Montenegro), except at a strictly limited number of road and rail border crossing points, the location of which shall be notified by each neighbouring State to the Committee established by resolution 724(1991) and approved by the Committee;

24. *Decides* that all States shall impound all vessels, freight vehicles, rolling stock and aircraft in their territories in which a majority or controlling interest is held by a person or undertaking in or operating from the Federal Republic of Yugoslavia (Serbia and Montenegro) and that these vessels, freight vehicles, rolling stock and aircraft may be forfeit to the seizing State upon a determination that they have been in violation of resolutions 713(1991), 757(1992), 787(1992) or the present resolution;

25. *Decides* that all States shall detain pending investigation all vessels, freight vehicles, rolling stock, aircraft and cargoes found in their territories and suspected of having violated or being in violation of resolutions 713(1991), 757(1992), 787(1992) or the present resolution, and that, upon a determination that they have been in violation, such vessels, freight vehicles, rolling stock and aircraft shall be impounded and, where appropriate, they and their cargoes may be forfeit to the detaining State;

26. *Confirms* that States may charge the expense of impounding vessels, freight vehicles, rolling stock and aircraft to their owners;

27. *Decides* to prohibit the provision of services, both financial and non-financial, to any person or body for purposes of any business carried on in the Federal Republic of Yugoslavia (Serbia and Montenegro) the only exceptions being telecommunications, postal services, legal services consistent with resolution 757(1992) and, as approved, on a case-by-case basis by the Com-

mittee established by resolution 724(1991), services whose supply may be necessary for humanitarian or other exceptional purposes;

28. *Decides* to prohibit all commercial maritime traffic from entering the territorial sea of the Federal Republic of Yugoslavia (Serbia and Montenegro) except when authorized on a case-by-case basis by the Committee established by resolution 724(1991) or in case of *force majeure*;

29. *Reaffirms* the authority of States acting under paragraph 12 of resolution 787(1992) to use such measures commensurate with the specific circumstances as may be necessary under the authority of the Security Council to enforce the present resolution and its other relevant resolutions, including in the territorial sea of the Federal Republic of Yugoslavia (Serbia and Montenegro);

30. *Confirms* that the provisions set forth in paragraphs 12 to 29 above, strengthening the implementation of the measures imposed by its earlier relevant resolutions, do not apply to activities related to UNPROFOR, the International Conference on the Former Yugoslavia or the European Community Monitor Mission;

C

Desirous of achieving the full readmittance of the Federal Republic of Yugoslavia (Serbia and Montenegro) to the international community once it has fully implemented the relevant resolutions of the Council,

31. *Expresses its readiness*, after all three Bosnian parties have accepted the peace plan and on the basis of verified evidence, provided by the Secretary-General, that the Bosnian Serb party is cooperating in good faith in effective implementation of the plan, to review all the measures in the present resolution and its other relevant resolutions with a view to gradually lifting them;

32. *Invites* all States to consider what contribution they can make to the reconstruction of the Republic of Bosnia and Herzegovina;

33. *Decides* to remain actively seized of the matter.

Security Council resolution 820(1993)

17 April 1993   Meeting 3200   13-0-2

9-nation draft (S/25558), orally revised.
Sponsors: Cape Verde, Djibouti, France, Morocco, Pakistan, Spain, United Kingdom, United States, Venezuela.

Vote in Council as follows:

In favour: Brazil, Cape Verde, Djibouti, France, Hungary, Japan, Morocco, New Zealand, Pakistan, Spain, United Kingdom, United States, Venezuela.
Against: None.
Abstaining: China, Russian Federation.

Explaining its intention to abstain, the Russian Federation stated that, although it supported the Part A provisions of the text, strengthening sanctions against Yugoslavia (Serbia and Montenegro) was quite untimely. The most reasonable approach would be to delay voting on the draft until 26 April, as previously agreed. It would not, however, hinder adoption of the draft since it would enter into force only nine days after its adoption, thus allowing the Bosnian Serb side to sign the peace plan.

China, while welcoming those elements of the resolution that commended the unremitting efforts of the Co-Chairmen, found it difficult to support the adoption of enforcement measures and

strengthening and expanding existing sanctions against Yugoslavia (Serbia and Montenegro). In China's view, the international community should continue to promote negotiations and avoid taking action that might further complicate the issue.

Reports of the Secretary-General (30 April and 3 May). In a 30 April report[198] covering the activities of the Co-Chairmen since 26 March, the Secretary-General described their continued efforts to help alleviate the humanitarian situation in Bosnia and Herzegovina, to persuade the Bosnian Serb side to sign the two remaining documents of the peace plan, and to prepare, with the UNPROFOR Commander, for the implementation of the plan upon completion of its signature.

Between 21 and 25 April, Lord Owen, accompanied by Mr. Vance's Special Adviser, led a delegation on behalf of the Co-Chairmen to the area of the former Yugoslavia and held a series of meetings with all the parties at the highest levels at Zagreb and at Belgrade. Despite the urgings of the three Presidents for acceptance of the plan, the Bosnian Serb "assembly", on 26 April, voted against it and decided to put it to a referendum. On 29 April, while continuing efforts to persuade the Bosnian Serb side to sign the outstanding two documents of the peace plan, the Co-Chairmen were informed that the referendum had been superseded by a decision of the "assembly" to hold a fresh meeting on 5 May to reconsider its previous decision against signing the peace plan.

In his report of 3 May,[199] the Secretary-General reported that, in the light of these developments, the Co-Chairmen, together with Mr. Stoltenberg, Co-Chairman-designate to succeed Mr. Vance, held a further round of talks at Athens on 1 and 2 May with the Presidents of Bosnia and Herzegovina, Croatia, Yugoslavia (Serbia and Montenegro), Serbia and Montenegro, and the leaders of the Bosnian Croats and Bosnian Serbs. Also in attendance were observers from the host Government, EC, the Russian Federation and the United States.

During that meeting Mr. Vance provided additional amplifications on the concept of the northern corridor, consisting of the internationally controlled throughway linking the provinces of Banja Luka and Bijeljina and a demilitarized zone extending five kilometres into either side of the throughway in the territory of Bosnia and Herzegovina. The status of the explanations and amplifications was confirmed in a letter from the Co-Chairmen to President Izetbegović and Messrs. Boban and Karadzic.

On 2 May, Mr. Karadzic signed the agreement on interim arrangements and the provisional provincial map, thus completing all signatures required on the peace plan. He also issued a statement, to be made part of the ICFY official documents, that the signature of the Bosnian Serb side would become invalid, null and void if not supported by the "assembly" of the "Republic of Sprska", scheduled to meet at Pale on 5 May.

Mr. Karadzic's signature was annulled almost immediately by the Bosnian Serb "assembly" at that meeting and by the subsequent referendum on 15 and 16 May, notwithstanding intervention in the plan's favour by Serbia's President and Prime Minister. Immediately after the 5 May meeting, Yugoslavia (Serbia and Montenegro) announced that it was cutting off all but humanitarian supplies to the Bosnian Serbs.

Statements by the Secretary-General and Security Council. On 6 May, the spokesman for the Secretary-General issued a statement to the effect that the Secretary-General believed that the last word had not been spoken by the Bosnian Serbs, that there would be more negotiations and efforts would continue to overcome the current difficulties to obtaining agreement on the Vance-Owen peace plan.

Following informal consultations by the Security Council on 7 May, its President made a statement to the press reaffirming that the Vance-Owen peace plan remained the basis for a peaceful solution to the conflict in Bosnia and Herzegovina and that the Bosnian Serbs must return to it. The statement also expressed the conviction that preparatory work for the plan's implementation should continue in the interim.

Confederation proposals

Reports of ICFY Steering Committee Co-Chairmen (July-August). Following the rejection of the Vance-Owen peace plan by the Bosnian Serb "assembly" on 5 May, the Co-Chairmen of the ICFY Steering Committee maintained contact with the different sides to the conflict.

In their 8 July report,[(200)] the Co-Chairmen noted that implementation of the Vance-Owen peace plan, in the absence of agreement by the Bosnian Serbs, was premised on, among other things, continued cooperation between the Muslim-led Bosnian Government and the Bosnian Croats. By the second week of May, however, major fighting broke out again between these two sides in central Bosnia.

On 18 May, the Co-Chairmen met with Bosnia and Herzegovina's President Izetbegović, the Bosnian Croat leader, Mr. Boban, and Croatia's President Tudjman. President Izetbegović and Mr. Boban reached understandings on: a cessation of hostilities between the Bosnian Croats and the Bosnian Muslims; cooperation in implementing the peace plan in the six predominantly Muslim or Croat provinces; further meetings of the Coordination Body (under the interim arrangements of the Vance-Owen peace plan, the nine-member body for implementing the peace in Bosnia and Herzegovina); organization of regular meetings of the Presidency; and formation of a Government with agreed allocations of ministries and diplomatic posts.

On 20 and 21 May, the Foreign Ministers of France, Spain, the Russian Federation, the United Kingdom and the United States met to discuss the situation.

In the meantime, the fighting in central Bosnia and Herzegovina increased between the Muslims and Croats as each side tried to contest as much territory as possible, thereby bringing to an end the cooperation that existed between them since the March 1992 referendum.

The Co-Chairmen met with Presidents Milosevic and Tudjman (Belgrade and Zagreb, 9-11 June), who revived the concept of a confederation for Bosnia and Herzegovina. First proposed in March 1992 by Ambassador José Cutileiro at Lisbon, Portugal, the concept of a confederal solution had initially been accepted by all three sides; however, from the time President Izetbegović withdrew his support for the proposal, it had been vigorously opposed by the Bosnian Government side in the context of ICFY.

On 23 June at Geneva, Presidents Milosevic and Tudjman informed the Co-Chairmen that consultations had taken place between the Bosnian Croat and Bosnian Serb leaders, Messrs. Boban and Karadzic, and that a draft providing for the organization of Bosnia and Herzegovina into a confederation of three constituent republics had been prepared, based on the agreed constitutional principles of the Vance-Owen peace plan.

The Co-Chairmen suggested additional elements to the draft, including: establishment of a Confederated Council of Ministers whose Chairman would be Prime Minister, rotating at agreed intervals among the three republics, with a similar rotation for the Foreign Minister; referral of disputes that could not be settled in the Constitutional Court by consensus for binding arbitration by a Chamber of five drawn from ICJ judges; and international monitoring of throughways so as to ensure freedom of movement.

Messrs. Boban and Karadzic reconfirmed their acceptance of the Vance-Owen peace plan's military agreement, subject to updating and consequential amendment; they also agreed on texts that maintained key parts of the Vance-Owen agreement on interim arrangements, including those for the protection of human rights. No specific map had been put forward, but the Bosnian Croats and Bosnian Serbs offered to negotiate directly along the lines they had already explained to President Izetbegović and the collective Presidency.

On 1 July, the Co-Chairmen convened a meeting of the Steering Committee at which they stressed the deteriorating security situation facing UNPROFOR, UNHCR and humanitarian workers; the lack of resources for humanitarian operations; the lack of troops in UNPROFOR to fulfil its various mandates; the importance of continuing the search for negotiated solutions; and the dangers of escalation of the conflict if the parties turned their backs on that search.

The Co-Chairmen circulated the Bosnian Croat-Bosnian Serb revised constitutional principles, military agreements and interim arrangements and gave a detailed presentation on how, as a result of their clarification meetings, a confederation of three republics in Bosnia and Herzegovina might look in terms of territorial boundaries.

In their 3 August report,[201] which covered negotiations during July, the Co-Chairmen said that, owing to the deteriorating humanitarian situation and the persistence of conflict, they had arranged for a resumption of peace talks, which began on 27 July. Discussions concentrated on securing a cease-fire; humanitarian issues; future constitutional arrangements; and allocation of territory to the constituent entities.

On 30 July, acting on the directives of their respective authorities, the military commanders of the three sides signed an agreement providing for a full cease-fire, a freeze on all military activities and free passage for UNPROFOR and humanitarian aid convoys.

Also on 30 July, all sides agreed to a Constitutional Agreement for a Union of Republics of Bosnia and Herzegovina, to form part of an overall peace settlement. Under consideration were the establishment of an Access Authority (foreseen under the Vance-Owen peace plan) to ensure movement throughout the country; and a map, regarding which the Co-Chairmen were determined to ensure that a Muslim-majority republic should have at least 30 per cent of the territory of Bosnia and Herzegovina and have access to the Sava River and to the sea at Ploce.

The Co-Chairmen's report, transmitted on 6 August,[202] noted that, in reply to President Izetbegović's request for clarification of chapter I, article 1, of the Constitutional Agreement, the Co-Chairmen wrote that Bosnia and Herzegovina was already a recognized State Member of the United Nations and, in the spirit of the Charter, the principles of the 1992 London Conference, and those laid down by the Security Council, confirmed their understanding that the meaning of article 1 was that the Union of Republics of Bosnia and Herzegovina would continue as a State Member of the United Nations. They suggested to the Presidency that it could ask the Council to put the matter beyond doubt, adding that the provisions of the Constitutional Agreement made it legally impossible to dissolve the Union without the free consent of all three Constituent Republics.

In subsequent discussions, the following annexes to the Constitutional Agreement were prepared and were accepted by all three sides: composition and competence of the Human Rights Court, list of human rights instruments incorporated in the Constitutional Agreement, and initial appointment and functions of the Ombudsmen.

All three sides agreed that the name of each Constituent Republic would be determined by the competent authorities of that Republic. They also agreed that the map of the three Constituent Republics would be referred to the Boundary Commission established in accordance with article 1 *(b)* of the Agreement, which should ensure that the territory of the Republic marked as No. 1 on the map should not be less than 30 per cent of the entire territory of the Union of Republics of Bosnia and Herzegovina.

The three sides reaffirmed their acceptance of the Agreement for peace in Bosnia and Herzegovina, which dealt with the military aspects of implementing a peaceful settlement for the republic, and agreed that the document would be updated by the Mixed Military Working Group under the chairmanship of UNPROFOR. They also agreed on the core areas to be allocated to each of the three Constituent Republics. However, unresolved questions relating to Brcko, eastern Bosnia, the Bihac pocket, Posavina and eastern Herzegovina and Sarajevo remained. The last was the most contentious issue, with positions deeply entrenched.

The report provided details of the responsibilities envisaged for a proposed Implementation Force, to be established by the United Nations.

On 9 August,[203] Croatia registered its exception to certain passages in the report which it felt could lead to misunderstandings and confusion as to Croatia's position on the peace talks and the conflict in Bosnia and Herzegovina. Bosnia and Herzegovina's objections to the same report were communicated to the Council on 11 August.[204]

In their report transmitted on 20 August,[205] the Co-Chairmen stated that, as of that date, the parties had worked out arrangements to place Sarajevo under United Nations administration for a period of up to two years and Mostar under EC administration for a similar period. Detailed arrangements were worked out in respect of demarcations in the town of Brcko and discussions held regarding the towns of Gornji Vakuf, Donji Vakuf, Bugojno and Travnik. The Bosnian Serb side agreed to a special road linking Gorazde and Zepa, which would be part of the territory of, and administered and policed by, the Muslim-majority republic.

In the light of these developments, the parties issued a 20 August statement acknowledging receipt of constitutional papers and a map, based on the constitutional and related documents already worked out and reflecting the discussions that had taken place, and undertaking to go home to explain the map and return to Geneva for a final meeting on Monday, 30 August.

Those constitutional and related papers were reproduced in an addendum to the report,[206] as was the map indicating the boundaries of the constituent republics, to be incorporated in annex A of the Constitutional Agreement.[207]

SECURITY COUNCIL ACTION

Following receipt of the August reports of the Co-Chairmen, the Security Council convened on 24 August. At its request, Bosnia and Herzegovina was invited to participate in the discussion without the right to vote under rule 37.[a]

The Council unanimously adopted **resolution 859(1993)**.

The Security Council,

Recalling all its previous resolutions on the conflict in the Republic of Bosnia and Herzegovina,

Reaffirming the sovereignty, territorial integrity and political independence of the Republic of Bosnia and Herzegovina and the responsibility of the Security Council in this regard,

Reaffirming further that the Republic of Bosnia and Herzegovina, as a State Member of the United Nations, enjoys the rights provided for in the Charter of the United Nations,

Noting that the Republic of Bosnia and Herzegovina has continued to be subject to armed hostilities in contravention of Security Council resolution 713(1991) and other relevant Security Council resolutions and that, despite all efforts by the United Nations as well as regional organizations and arrangements, there is still no compliance with all relevant Security Council resolutions, in particular by the Bosnian Serb party,

Condemning once again all war crimes and other violations of international humanitarian law, by whomsoever committed, Bosnian Serbs or other individuals,

Deeply concerned at the deterioration of humanitarian conditions in the Republic of Bosnia and Herzegovina, including in and around Mostar, and determined to support in every possible way the efforts by the United Nations Protection Force (UNPROFOR) and the United Nations High Commissioner for Refugees (UNHCR) to continue providing humanitarian assistance to civilian populations in need,

Concerned about the continuing siege of Sarajevo, Mostar and other threatened cities,

Strongly condemning the disruption of public utilities (including water, electricity, fuel and communications), in particular by the Bosnian Serb party, and calling upon all parties concerned to cooperate in restoring them,

Recalling the principles for a political solution adopted by the London International Conference on the Former Yugoslavia,

Reaffirming once again the unacceptability of the acquisition of territory through the use of force and the practice of "ethnic cleansing",

Stressing that an end to the hostilities in the Republic of Bosnia and Herzegovina is necessary to achieve meaningful progress in the peace process,

Mindful of its primary responsibility under the Charter of the United Nations for the maintenance of international peace and security,

Taking into account the reports of the Co-Chairmen of the Steering Committee of the International Conference on the Former Yugoslavia contained in documents S/26233, S/26260 and S/26337,

Determining that the grave situation in the Republic of Bosnia and Herzegovina continues to be a threat to international peace and security,

Acting under Chapter VII of the Charter of the United Nations,

1. *Notes with appreciation* the report by the Secretary-General's Special Representative on the latest developments at the Geneva peace talks and urges the parties, in cooperation with the Co-Chairmen, to conclude as soon as possible a just and comprehensive political settlement freely agreed by all of them;

2. *Calls* for an immediate cease-fire and cessation of hostilities throughout the Republic of Bosnia and Herzegovina as essential for achieving a just and equitable political solution to the conflict in Bosnia and Herzegovina through peaceful negotiations;

3. *Demands* that all concerned facilitate the unhindered flow of humanitarian assistance, including the provision of food, water, electricity, fuel and communications, in particular to the "safe areas" in Bosnia and Herzegovina;

4. *Demands also* that the safety and operational effectiveness of UNPROFOR and UNHCR personnel in Bosnia and Herzegovina be fully respected by all parties at all times;

5. *Notes with appreciation* the Secretary-General's letter of 18 August 1993, stating that the United Nations has now the initial operational capability for the use of air power in support of UNPROFOR in Bosnia and Herzegovina;

6. *Affirms* that a solution to the conflict in the Republic of Bosnia and Herzegovina must be in conformity with the Charter of the United Nations and the principles of international law; and further affirms the continuing relevance in this context of:

(a) The sovereignty, territorial integrity and political independence of the Republic of Bosnia and Herzegovina;

(b) The fact that neither a change in the name of the State nor changes regarding the internal organization of the State such as those contained in the constitutional agreement annexed to the Co-Chairmen's report in document S/26337 would affect the continued membership of Bosnia and Herzegovina in the United Nations;

(c) The principles adopted by the London International Conference on the Former Yugoslavia, including the need for a cessation of hostilities, the principle of a negotiated solution freely arrived at, the unacceptability of the acquisition of territory by force or by "ethnic cleansing" and the right of refugees and others who have suffered losses to compensation in accordance with the statement on Bosnia adopted by the London Conference;

(d) Recognition and respect for the right of all displaced persons to return to their homes in safety and honour;

(e) The maintenance of Sarajevo, capital of Bosnia and Herzegovina, as a united city and a multicultural, multi-ethnic and pluri-religious centre;

7. *Recalls* the principle of individual responsibility for the perpetration of war crimes and other violations of international humanitarian law and its decision in resolution 827(1993) to establish an International Tribunal;

8. *Declares its readiness* to consider taking the necessary measures to assist the parties in the effective implementation of a fair and equitable settlement once it has been freely agreed by the parties, which would require a decision by the Council;

9. *Decides* to remain actively seized of the matter.

Security Council resolution 859(1993)

24 August 1993   Meeting 3269   Adopted unanimously

Draft prepared in consultations among Council members (S/26182).

Further reports of the Co-Chairmen. The Co-Chairmen's report covering the resumed talks on 31 August and 1 September[208] noted that at the end of the talks the Co-Chairmen had put to the parties the peace package distilled from the parties' own ideas. The Bosnian Croat and Bosnian Serb sides were ready to sign the package and collateral agreements, but the Bosnian Government side wanted further consideration of the question of access to the Adriatic Sea and some of the territorial issues.

A report transmitted to the Council on 23 September[209] provided an account of deliberations on the *HMS Invincible* in the Adriatic Sea on 20 September. On that occasion, President Izetbegović and Messrs. Boban and Karadzic met in the presence of the Co-Chairmen; Presidents Bulatovic, Milosevic and Tudjman; and Deputy Foreign Minister Vitaly Churkin (Russian Federation) and Ambassador Charles Redman (United States), who attended as observers. At that meeting, provisions for the promotion and protection of human rights were reconfirmed, as were arrangements for implementing and monitoring a cessation of hostilities. Agreements were also worked out providing the Muslim-majority republic with access to the Adriatic Sea via the Neretva River, giving that republic a 99-year lease on an area for the construction of a port at Ploce (in addition to the use of the port of Rijeka) and assuring freedom of transit between the Union of Republics of Bosnia and Herzegovina and Croatia.

The three sides informed the Co-Chairmen that they would submit the package arrived at on the *Invincible* to their respective assemblies for ratification. The Bosnian Croat and the Bosnian Serb sides subsequently informed the Co-Chairmen that their assemblies had ratified the package; the Bosnian Presidency reported that its expanded assembly did not.

Both the Bosnian Croat and Bosnian Serb sides then informed the Co-Chairmen that they had made concessions on the *HMS Invincible* conditional on the acceptance of the package by all sides. They therefore intended to withdraw their concessions. The Co-Chairmen appealed to them not to do so and to continue the search for peace.

In their final report of the year, transmitted on 29 December,[210] the Co-Chairmen described the extensive discussions held with the three sides, as well as with neighbouring countries, between 29 November and 23 December, in a determined push for a peace agreement.

The situation after the meetings held at Geneva and Brussels (Belgium) between 21 and 23 December was summarized by the Co-Chairmen as follows. There was agreement among all three sides (1) that Bosnia and Herzegovina should be organized as a union of three republics and (2) that the Muslim-majority republic should have 33.3 per cent of the territory and the Croat-majority republic, 17.5 per cent. (3) All three leaders accepted the Co-Chairmen's appeal to observe a holiday truce from 23 December 1993 to 15 January 1994 and undertook to instruct their military commanders down to the local level to observe the cease-fire faithfully and (4) agreed to return to Geneva on 15 January 1994 to continue the search for peace. (5) Working groups were set up to help reach agreement, by 15 January, on: the definition of the Mostar City area to be placed under the temporary administration of the European Union (formerly EC); technical arrangements for providing the Muslim-majority republic with road and rail access to Brcko and the Sava River, without prejudice to that republic's continued support for the arrangements agreed on the *HMS Invincible*; access of the Muslim-majority republic to the sea; and continued discussions on territorial delimitation. (6) All three sides were asked to consult their respective "assemblies" beforehand so that any agreement concluded at Geneva would enter into force immediately upon signature.

Violations of international humanitarian law

Mass rape

Report of EC mission. In response to a 1992 Security Council request,[211] Denmark, as representative of the EC Presidency, transmitted to the Council on 2 February 1993 the report[212] of the mission dispatched to the former Yugoslavia at the initiative of the EC European Council to investigate reports of massive, organized and systematic detention and rape of Muslim women in the former Yugoslavia.

The mission, headed by Dame Ann Warburton, visited Croatia and Bosnia and Herzegovina from 18 to 24 December 1992 and from 19 to 26 January 1993, meeting with a wide range of interlocutors including leaders of Catholic and Muslim communities, field staff of international agencies, representatives of the Government of Croatia, governmental and non-governmental organizations, women's groups, gynaecology specialists and mental health experts. It visited refugee centres, shelters for displaced persons, hospitals and food distribution centres. It interviewed victims and eyewitnesses of human rights violations, and examined documentation detailing the process of clearing villages. The mission sought to determine the scale of the problem and whether or not it could be described as systematic.

Reasoned estimates placed the number of victims at around 20,000. Indications were that the rapes had been particularly sadistic in some cases and that, in many, the intention was to make women pregnant and to detain them long enough to make termination of the pregnancy impossible. This raised the problem of adoption of children conceived under those circumstances.

While the majority of victims were Muslim women, the mission also received reports of the rape of Croat and Serb women and children, as well as the sexual abuse of men in detention camps.

The mission concluded that the wide-scale rape of Muslim women and its clearly recognizable pattern suggested that it was an important element of war strategy.

The mission made recommendations calling for coordination of assistance; physical facilities to house the victims of rape; access to psychiatric and counselling services, to gynaecological treatment and to facilities for the termination of pregnancy. Immediate measures included: screening procedures and counselling by cross-disciplinary teams of gynaecological, psychiatric, psychological and other medical expertise; an emergency ambulance service; installation of sanitation and washing facilities at refugee centres; adequate nutrition and health care by mobile medical teams; removal from the refugee camps of the most vulnerable individuals, particularly women victims of trauma and abuse, to better living arrangements. Other recommendations included development of rehabilitation programmes for victims, rapid visa procedures by EC Governments for refugees from Bosnia and Herzegovina, particularly victims of rape, and temporary accommodation of Muslim women needing medical treatment.

Annexed to the report was a Declaration on the follow-up to the mission, adopted at Brussels on 1 February, by which EC Governments stated their intention to implement the mission's recommendations and to urge the parties to the conflict to bring an end to their abhorrent practices. (See also PART THREE, Chapter X.)

Detainees

SECURITY COUNCIL ACTION (April)

Following consultations held on 8 April, the President of the Security Council, on behalf of the Council

members, made the following statement to the media:[213]

"The members of the Security Council express their concern at the report of the International Committee of the Red Cross, according to which 17 detainees lost their lives on 26 March 1993 in the Republic of Bosnia and Herzegovina, when the vehicle transporting them from the Batkovic Camp (under the control of Serb forces) for work at the front was ambushed.

"The members of the Council, recalling all the relevant resolutions and statements of the Council, remind all the parties that they are responsible at all times for the detainees' safety and that they must not compel detainees to do work of a military nature or destined to serve a military purpose. The ICRC had already repeatedly called on all parties to the conflict in the Republic of Bosnia and Herzegovina strictly to observe the provisions of international humanitarian law.

"The members of the Council condemn all violations of the Third and Fourth Geneva Conventions, which the parties have undertaken to respect, and reaffirm once again that those who commit or order the commission of such acts will be held personally responsible.

"The members of the Council request the Commission of Experts established pursuant to Security Council resolution 780(1992) to carry out an investigation of these abominable practices and to make a report."

Communication. On 7 September,[214] Croatia communicated to the Secretary-General an appeal of its President calling on the Bosnian Croats to ensure forthwith humane treatment of all detainees and to allow ICRC free access to detention camps. The appeal also called for the prevention and removal of obstacles to the delivery of humanitarian aid and for every assistance to the United Nations and international humanitarian organizations. It invited the other warring parties in Bosnia and Herzegovina to do the same.

SECURITY COUNCIL ACTION (September)

The Security Council met on 14 September, inviting Bosnia and Herzegovina, at its request, to participate without the right to vote under rule 37.[a] Following consultations, the Council authorized its President to make the following statement[215] on behalf of the Council:

Meeting number. SC 3276.

"The Security Council expresses its profound concern over recent reports that Bosnian Croats have been holding Bosnian Muslims in detention camps under deplorable conditions. The Council recalls the international revulsion and condemnation that accompanied revelations last year of the conditions under which Bosnian Muslims and Bosnian Croats were being held in Bosnian Serb detention camps.

"The Council reiterates the principle that the International Committee of the Red Cross (ICRC) must be given access to all detainees in Bosnia wherever they may be held. It notes that ICRC has recently been given access to some detainees, but recalls with condemnation the obstacles which the Bosnian Croats have previously placed in the way of ICRC's attempts to gain access to the camps in order to ascertain the conditions of the detained. It also notes the recent appeal addressed by the President of Croatia to the Bosnian Croats.

"The Council emphasizes the fact that inhumane treatment and abuses in detention centres violates international humanitarian law. Moreover, as the Council has previously recalled, persons who commit or order the commission of grave breaches of the Geneva Conventions are individually responsible in respect of such breaches.

"The Council calls upon the Bosnian Croats to supply immediately to ICRC complete information on all camps where Bosnian Muslim and other prisoners are being held, and to assure ICRC and all other legitimately concerned international bodies free and unhindered access to the detained, wherever they may be held.

"The Council believes that the Government of Croatia has a responsibility to use its influence with the Bosnian Croats to secure compliance with this statement and calls on the Government of Croatia to take immediate steps to that end.

"The Council further reaffirms that all parties to the conflict are bound to comply with their obligations under international humanitarian law and in particular the Geneva Conventions of 12 August 1949, and reminds them of its willingness to consider appropriate actions if any of them should fail to abide scrupulously by their obligations.

"The Council decides to remain seized of the matter."

Genocide

In April,[216] the Secretary-General transmitted to the Security Council an ICJ Order of 8 April indicating provisional measures in the case concerning *Application of the Convention on the Prevention and Punishment of the Crime of Genocide (Bosnia and Herzegovina v. Yugoslavia (Serbia and Montenegro))*. Also in April,[217] Bosnia and Herzegovina requested the Council to take immediate measures under Chapter VII of the Charter to stop the continuing assault on the country and enforce that Order. On 15 September,[218] it requested the Council to enforce a further ICJ Order concerning the case, made on 13 September, in view of the continuing aggression and genocide against the country and its people (see PART FIVE, Chapter I).

Humanitarian assistance

Bosnia and Herzegovina informed the President of the Security Council on 12 January[219] that the unsatisfactory conditions surrounding the delivery of humanitarian supplies to destinations within the country—to remedy which the Council had adopted resolution 770(1992)[220]—remained unchanged. It drew attention to reports confirmed by the UNHCR Director of Relief Operations in Bosnia and Herzegovina of deaths from cold and starvation, especially in the eastern part of the country. It also attached a report of 11 January from *New York Newsday* raising concerns warranting an urgent response from

the Council about UNPROFOR's ability to deliver humanitarian aid effectively.

On 18 January,[221] Bosnia and Herzegovina drew attention to the UNHCR report of the denial by Serbian and Montenegrin military forces of access for food deliveries to Gorazde and Srebrenica in Bosnia and Herzegovina. It asked the Council to issue a statement emphasizing the severity and urgency of the situation, requesting UNPROFOR-participating States fully to invoke resolution 770(1992) in the delivery of humanitarian assistance, and requesting also that air drops of food commence immediately.

SECURITY COUNCIL ACTION (25 January and 17 February)

The Security Council met on 25 January and, following consultations among its members, authorized its President to make the following statement below[222] on the Council's behalf:

Meeting number. SC 3164.

"The Security Council notes with appreciation the efforts of the international community to alleviate the plight of the civilian population in the Republic of Bosnia and Herzegovina, whose lives have been severely affected by the fighting there. The Council has the highest regard for the efforts of the brave people who have undertaken to deliver urgently needed humanitarian assistance under extremely trying conditions to the civilian population in the Republic of Bosnia and Herzegovina, in particular the efforts of the United Nations Protection Force (UNPROFOR) and the United Nations High Commissioner for Refugees (UNHCR). However, the Council deeply regrets that the situation there has imposed great limits on the international community in the fulfilment of its humanitarian mandate.

"The Council reaffirms its demand that all parties and others concerned, in particular Serb paramilitary units, cease and desist forthwith from all violations of international humanitarian law being committed in the territory of the Republic of Bosnia and Herzegovina, including in particular the deliberate interference with humanitarian convoys. The Council warns the parties concerned of serious consequences, in accordance with relevant resolutions of the Security Council, if they continue to impede the delivery of humanitarian relief assistance.

"The Council invites the Secretary-General to keep under continuous review the possibility of air-dropping humanitarian assistance to areas isolated by the conflict in the Republic of Bosnia and Herzegovina.

"The Council will remain actively seized of the matter."

The Council met again on 17 February and, after consultations among its members on the same subject, authorized its President to make the following statement[223] on the Council's behalf:

Meeting number. SC 3173.

"The Security Council recalls all relevant resolutions of the Council and its statement of 25 January concerning the provision of humanitarian relief in the Republic of Bosnia and Herzegovina. It notes with deep concern that, notwithstanding the Council's demand in that statement, relief efforts continue to be impeded. It condemns the blocking of humanitarian convoys and the impeding of relief supplies, which place at risk the civilian population of the Republic of Bosnia and Herzegovina and endanger the lives of personnel delivering such supplies. It remains deeply concerned at reports of pressing humanitarian need in the Republic of Bosnia and Herzegovina, particularly in the eastern part of the country.

"The Council reiterates its demand that the parties and all others concerned allow immediate and unimpeded access to humanitarian relief supplies. It further demands that the parties and others concerned give the United Nations High Commissioner for Refugees the guarantees she has sought that they will abide by the promises they have made to comply with the Council's decisions in this regard, and thus facilitate the resumption of the full humanitarian relief programme, to which the Council attaches the greatest importance."

Communication. Yugoslavia (Serbia and Montenegro) drew to the attention of the Security Council President on 23 February[224] information it had received from the United States that it intended to air-drop humanitarian assistance into areas of eastern Bosnia and Herzegovina, citing Council resolution 770(1992)[220] as a legal basis for the operation. The United States had stated that the operation was a temporary emergency effort and had warned the Yugoslav Army not to disrupt it in any way. Yugoslavia (Serbia and Montenegro), in reaffirming its support for the delivery of relief supplies to all warring sides, stressed that the decision could have some negative and grave, though possibly unintended, implications for the ICFY negotiations in progress. It pointed out that it could not be held responsible for incidents that might take place over Bosnia and Herzegovina in the wake of that decision.

Yugoslavia (Serbia and Montenegro) assured the Council President that it would not interfere with the air-drops on the understanding that neither its territory nor its airspace would be intruded upon.

SECURITY COUNCIL ACTION

At its meeting on 25 February, the Security Council invited Bosnia and Herzegovina to participate without the right to vote under rule 37.[a] Following consultations among its members, the Council authorized its President to make the following statement[225] on the Council's behalf:

Meeting number. SC 3177.

"The Security Council, having received a report from the Secretary-General, recalls all its relevant resolutions and its statements of 25 January 1993 and 17 February 1993 concerning the provision of humanitarian relief in the Republic of Bosnia and Herzegovina. It is deeply concerned that, in spite of its repeated demands, relief efforts continue to be impeded by Serb paramilitary units, especially in the

eastern part of the country, namely in the enclaves of Srebrenica, Cerska, Gorazde and Zepa.

"The Security Council deplores the deterioration of the humanitarian situation in the Republic of Bosnia and Herzegovina at a time when discussions are to resume with a view to reaching a just and durable agreement to end the conflict. It regards the blockade of relief efforts as a serious impediment to a negotiated settlement in the Republic of Bosnia and Herzegovina and to the efforts of the Co-Chairmen of the Steering Committee of the International Conference on the Former Yugoslavia. It notes with concern that the measures taken by Serb paramilitary units to interdict humanitarian convoys, in flagrant violation of relevant Security Council resolutions, expose the personnel of UNPROFOR and UNHCR as well as other humanitarian organizations to physical harm.

"The deliberate impeding of the delivery of food and humanitarian relief essential for the survival of the civilian population in the Republic of Bosnia and Herzegovina constitutes a violation of the Geneva Conventions of 1949, and the Security Council is committed to ensuring that individuals responsible for such acts are brought to justice.

"The Security Council strongly condemns once again the blocking of humanitarian convoys that has impeded the delivery of humanitarian supplies. It reiterates its demand that the Bosnian parties grant immediate and unimpeded access for humanitarian convoys and fully comply with the Security Council's decisions in this regard. The Security Council expresses its strong support for the use, in full coordination with the United Nations and in accordance with the relevant Security Council resolutions, of humanitarian air drops in isolated areas of the Republic of Bosnia and Herzegovina that are in critical need of humanitarian supplies and cannot be reached by ground convoys. It reaffirms its firm commitment to the full implementation of the humanitarian relief programme in the Republic of Bosnia and Herzegovina.

"The Security Council remains actively seized of the matter and continues its consideration of further steps, in accordance with its relevant resolutions."

ICFY Working Group on Humanitarian Issues

The Working Group on Humanitarian Issues met on 16 July at Geneva.[201] The meeting was attended by the Co-Chairmen and representatives of the region's Governments, ICRC, the United Nations Children's Fund, the World Health Organization and the World Food Programme. Sadako Ogata, United Nations High Commissioner for Refugees and Chairperson of the Group, informed the meeting of the serious obstacles affecting international relief efforts, including the ongoing denial and obstruction of humanitarian access in many areas of Bosnia and Herzegovina and attacks on and harassment of relief staff. She highlighted the dire conditions of the population of Sarajevo and of those populations trapped in many other areas, such as Srebrenica and Mostar in central Bosnia and Herzegovina. She also cited the shortfall in funding for all United Nations relief agencies as a further serious obstacle, resulting in cut-backs in various support programmes.

The meeting recognized the need to provide temporary protection for refugees and to ease the burden of refugee-receiving States in the region.

On 18 November, Mrs. Ogata, together with the ICRC President, met with the Foreign Minister of Bosnia and Herzegovina and the leaders of the Bosnian Croats and Bosnian Serbs, Messrs. Boban and Karadzic, in order to seek their commitment to create conditions that would allow the international community to provide the necessary humanitarian assistance to the country's population.

On the same date, Mrs. Ogata and the parties signed a joint declaration ensuring the delivery of humanitarian assistance by suspending hostilities and allowing free and unconditional access by the most effective land routes; ensuring complete and secure freedom of movement for all United Nations personnel and international humanitarian organizations; allowing UNHCR and ICRC to determine the content of humanitarian assistance; ensuring that the humanitarian deliveries reached their intended civilian beneficiaries and were not diverted for military or other uses; releasing all civilians unlawfully detained; and ensuring that the military and civilian administrations at all levels honoured the foregoing and previous commitments regarding respect for the freedom of movement and other human rights, the 1949 Geneva Conventions and other applicable international humanitarian law and principles.

During the year, some 267,763 metric tonnes of humanitarian assistance was provided to Bosnia and Herzegovina.

Croatia

In 1993, the armed forces of the Government of Croatia launched two incursions into the Serb-controlled UNPAs, one in January and another in September. This undermined efforts by ICFY and the United Nations to nurture a climate of cooperation and confidence between the Government of Croatia and the local Serb authorities in order to get the two parties to implement the United Nations peace-keeping plan for Croatia. The incursions, together with related Government actions regarded by the local Serb authorities as provocations, led to an escalation of the fighting, in particular in September, and, for most of the year at least, to the hardening of what appeared to be irreconcilable positions, putting in doubt the usefulness of UNPROFOR's presence in the country.

By December, however, the Secretary-General was able to report of continuing talks between the parties within the ICFY framework aimed at a comprehensive cease-fire and at implementing the peacekeeping plan.

UNPAs and pink zones

Although the only major success achieved by UNPROFOR in relation to its basic mandate in Croatia had been the 1992 withdrawal of the Yugoslav People's Army (JNA) forces from Croatian territory,[226] law and order had been enhanced through the gradual reorganization and redeployment of the local police so that, by the beginning of 1993, the position of minority groups had been stabilized somewhat, both inside and outside the UNPAs.

On 22 January, the Croatian Army launched an offensive on Maslenica and other locations in the southern part of Sector South and the adjacent pink zones, claiming the lives of two UNPROFOR soldiers (France) and injuring four others. The attack was immediately brought to the attention of the President of the Security Council by Yugoslavia (Serbia and Montenegro), claiming that it had taken place in the territory of the so-called Republic of Serb Krajina (also ''Republic of Krajina'').[227]

Croatia explained[228] that its action had been aimed at securing the site for the rebuilding of the Maslenica Bridge; it added that, although it had adopted the general amnesty required as a condition for a reinstatement of Croatian authority in the pink zones, neither the process of reintegrating those zones into Croatia's legal, economic and social systems had begun, nor had Croatian authority in those zones been restored and local police forces re-established in proportion to the zones' demographic structure prior to the conflict, in accordance with the peace-keeping plan. Croatia attributed the deteriorating situation in the UNPAs to the decision by the Knin authorities to create new paramilitary forces there and in the pink zones—an action inconsistent with the demilitarization called for by the plan.

SECURITY COUNCIL ACTION (25 and 27 January)

The Security Council met on 25 January in response to a letter of the same date from France[229] requesting an immediate meeting to consider the grave situation in the UNPAs, especially the attacks to which UNPROFOR had been subjected. Yugoslavia (Serbia and Montenegro) had made a similar request the day before.[230]

The Council unanimously adopted **resolution 802(1993)**.

The Security Council,
Reaffirming its resolution 713(1991) of 25 September 1991 and all subsequent relevant resolutions,
Reaffirming in particular its commitment to the United Nations peace-keeping plan,
Deeply concerned by the information provided by the Secretary-General to the Security Council on 25 January 1993 on the rapid and violent deterioration of the situation in Croatia as a result of military attacks by Croatian armed forces on the areas under the protection of the United Nations Protection Force (UNPROFOR),

Strongly condemning those attacks which have led to casualties and loss of life in UNPROFOR, as well as among the civilian population,

Deeply concerned also by the lack of cooperation in recent months by the Serb local authorities in the areas under the protection of UNPROFOR, by the recent seizure by them of heavy weapons under UNPROFOR control, and by threats to widen the conflict,

1. *Demands* the immediate cessation of hostile activities by Croatian armed forces within or adjacent to the United Nations Protected Areas and the withdrawal of the Croatian armed forces from these areas;

2. *Strongly condemns* the attacks by these forces against UNPROFOR in the conduct of its duty of protecting civilians in the United Nations Protected Areas and demands their immediate cessation;

3. *Demands also* that the heavy weapons seized from the UNPROFOR-controlled storage areas be returned immediately to UNPROFOR;

4. *Demands* that all parties and others concerned comply strictly with the cease-fire arrangements already agreed and cooperate fully and unconditionally in the implementation of the United Nations peace-keeping plan, including the disbanding and demobilization of Serb Territorial Defence units or other units of similar functions;

5. *Expresses* its condolences to the families of the UNPROFOR personnel who have lost their lives;

6. *Demands* that all parties and others concerned respect fully the safety of United Nations personnel;

7. *Invites* the Secretary-General to take all necessary steps to ensure the safety of the UNPROFOR personnel concerned;

8. *Calls upon* all parties and others concerned to cooperate with UNPROFOR in resolving all remaining issues connected with the implementation of the peace-keeping plan, including allowing civilian traffic freely to use the Maslenica crossing;

9. *Calls again upon* all parties and others concerned to cooperate fully with the International Conference on the Former Yugoslavia and to refrain from any actions or threats which might undermine the current efforts aimed at reaching a political settlement;

10. *Decides* to remain actively seized of the matter.

Security Council resolution 802(1993)

25 January 1993   Meeting 3163   Adopted unanimously

Draft prepared in consultations among Council members (S/25160), orally revised.

On 27 January, the Council, after consultations among its members, authorized its President to make the following statement[231] on behalf of the Council, in connection with its consideration of the item entitled "The situation prevailing in and adjacent to the United Nations Protected areas in Croatia":

Meeting number. SC 3165.

"The Security Council is deeply concerned to learn from the Secretary-General that the offensive by the Croatian armed forces continues unabated in flagrant violation of resolution 802(1993) of 25 January 1993, at a crucial time in the peace process.

"The Council demands that military action by all parties and others concerned cease immediately. It further demands that all parties and others concerned comply fully and immediately with all the provisions of resolution 802(1993) and with other relevant Security Council resolutions.

"The Council once again demands that all parties and others concerned respect fully the safety of United Nations personnel and guarantee their freedom of movement. The Council reiterates that it will hold the political and military leaders involved in the conflict responsible and accountable for the safety of the United Nations peace-keeping personnel in the area.

"The Security Council will remain actively seized of the matter, in particular with a view to considering what further steps might be necessary to ensure that resolution 802(1993) and other relevant Security Council resolutions are fully implemented."

Report of the Secretary-General (February).

As reported by the Secretary-General on 10 February,[232] UNPROFOR made repeated representations with the Croatian Government, the Serb leaders in Zadar and Knin (UNPAs) and with the Government of Yugoslavia (Serbia and Montenegro) aimed at halting hostile activities and encouraging compliance with the cease-fire arrangements, as called for by resolution 802(1993). Croatia informed the Force Commander on 26 January that it would remove its military, but not its police, from the areas it had taken upon Serb compliance with the resolution. The Serb leaders, however, demanded a return of the Croatian forces to their pre-offensive positions before it could consider compliance.

Following the offensive, President Tudjman of Croatia indicated that his Government was prepared to invade the UNPAs if UNPROFOR was unable to fulfil its mandate in Croatia. The Serb leaders had re-armed, reinforced and remobilized their forces. They had also refused to negotiate with the Croats or to return the heavy weapons wrested from storage unless the Croatian armed forces withdrew to their pre-offensive positions, as called for by resolution 802(1993). Croatia categorically rejected such a withdrawal, claiming that the only issue to negotiate was the return of the UNPAs and the pink zones to Croatian control, with the Serb minority enjoying the rights granted to it by the Croatian Constitution, the Constitutional Law on Human Rights and Rights of National and Ethnic Communities of Minorities in the Republic of Croatia (8 May 1992) and other relevant national legislation. The Serb leadership in the UNPAs, however, refused to regard these territories as part of Croatia and rejected talks on this basis, recalling that the peace-keeping plan was explicitly not intended to prejudge a political solution to the Yugoslav crisis. It argued that two parties to the original plan, the President of Serbia and the Federal Yugoslav military authorities at Belgrade, no longer had any *locus standi* in the areas where UNPROFOR was deployed. The UNPROFOR mandate and deployment, they insisted, must be discussed anew with them as the sovereign "Republic of Serb Krajina".

These positions appeared to be irreconcilable and the Secretary-General warned that, unless they were addressed, a sound basis would not exist for renewing the UNPROFOR mandate in Croatia. As he had informed the Council on 27 January, Croatia's unilateral military offensive had seriously undermined confidence, disrupted the negotiation process, affected cooperation between it and the local Serb authorities and had put in doubt a return to the original peace-keeping plan.

In the circumstances, the Secretary-General presented three possible options regarding the UNPROFOR mandate in Croatia: to renew the mandate entrusted to UNPROFOR by resolution 743(1992), to modify it, or to give UNPROFOR no mandate in Croatia. Analysis of those options indicated no clear way forward in a difficult situation not foreseen when the Council established UNPROFOR and attributable to the failure to implement the United Nations peace-keeping plan and to negotiate an agreed settlement to the conflict between Croatia and the Serb populations living in the UNPAs and the pink zones.

The Secretary-General accordingly asked the Co-Chairmen of the ICFY Steering Committee to address these questions so that he could make a substantive recommendation for an extension of the UNPROFOR mandate. As it was unlikely that results could be achieved by the expiration date of the current mandate on 21 February 1993, the Secretary-General recommended that the Council extend the existing mandate for an interim period up to 31 March 1993, in order to give the Co-Chairmen the necessary time.

SECURITY COUNCIL ACTION

The Security Council met on 19 February and, acting under Chapter VII of the United Nations Charter, unanimously adopted **resolution 807(1993)**.

The Security Council,

Reaffirming its resolution 743(1992) and all subsequent resolutions relating to the United Nations Protection Force (UNPROFOR),

Having considered the report of the Secretary-General dated 10 February 1993,

Deeply concerned by the lack of cooperation of the parties and others concerned in implementing the United Nations peace-keeping plan in Croatia,

Deeply concerned also by the recent and repeated violations by the parties and others concerned of their cease-fire obligations,

Determining that the situation thus created constitutes a threat to peace and security in the region,

Taking note in that context of the Secretary-General's request to the Co-Chairmen of the Steering Committee of the International Conference on the Former Yugoslavia, mentioned in his report, to establish as soon as possible, through discussions with the parties, a basis on which UNPROFOR's mandate could be renewed,

Determined to ensure the security of UNPROFOR and to this end, acting under Chapter VII of the Charter of the United Nations,

1. *Demands* that the parties and others concerned comply fully with the United Nations peace-keeping plan in Croatia and with the other commitments they have undertaken and in particular with their cease-fire obligations;

2. *Demands further* that the parties and others concerned refrain from positioning their forces in the proximity of UNPROFOR's units in the United Nations Protected Areas (UNPAs) and in the pink zones;

3. *Demands also* the full and strict observance of all relevant Security Council resolutions relating to the mandate and operations of UNPROFOR in the Republic of Bosnia and Herzegovina;

4. *Demands also* that the parties and others concerned respect fully UNPROFOR's unimpeded freedom of movement enabling it *inter alia* to carry out all necessary concentrations and deployments, all movements of equipment and weapons and all humanitarian and logistical activities;

5. *Decides*, in the context of these demands, to extend UNPROFOR's mandate for an interim period terminating on 31 March 1993;

6. *Urges* the parties and others concerned fully to cooperate with the Co-Chairmen of the Steering Committee of the International Conference on the Former Yugoslavia in the discussions under their auspices in order to ensure full implementation of the United Nations peace-keeping mandate in Croatia, including *inter alia* through the collection and supervision of heavy weapons by UNPROFOR and the appropriate withdrawal of forces;

7. *Invites* the Secretary-General to work to achieve the rapid implementation of the United Nations peace-keeping mandate and of relevant Security Council resolutions, including resolution 802(1993), thus to ensure security and stability throughout the UNPAs and the pink zones;

8. *Invites further* the Secretary-General, during the interim period and in consultation with the force-contributing States, to take, in accordance with paragraph 17 of his report, all appropriate measures to strengthen the security of UNPROFOR, in particular by providing it with the necessary defensive means, and to study the possibility of carrying out such local redeployment of military units as is required to ensure their protection;

9. *Requests* the Secretary-General to submit a report on the further extension of UNPROFOR's mandate, including financial estimates for all UNPROFOR's activities as proposed in his report of 10 February 1993;

10. *Decides* to remain actively seized of the matter.

Security Council resolution 807(1993)
19 February 1993   Meeting 3174   Adopted unanimously

Draft prepared in consultations among Council members (S/25306).

Report of the Secretary-General (March). In a 25 March report with a later addendum,[233] the Secretary-General stated that, pursuant to Security Council resolution 807(1993), the Co-Chairmen of the ICFY Steering Committee had held talks in New York and Geneva with representatives of the Government of Croatia and the Serb populations living in the UNPAs and pink zones. While progress had been made, fundamental differences remained between the two sides. More time was thus needed to bring the negotiations to a meaningful conclusion.

Since a termination of the UNPROFOR mandate in Croatia would very likely result in an outbreak of renewed hostilities, the Secretary-General recommended that it be extended for a further interim period of three months, from 1 April to 30 June 1993. He urged the parties to cooperate with UNPROFOR to resolve any remaining differences. He also asked the ICFY Co-Chairmen to continue their efforts to obtain from the parties a renewed commitment to the elements of the United Nations peace-keeping plan and to the implementation of Security Council resolution 802(1993) and other relevant resolutions.

In the addendum to his report, the Secretary-General estimated the total cost of maintaining UNPROFOR for the period of the extension at $336.2 million. He recommended that the additional cost should be considered an expense of the Organization to be borne by Member States; the assessments to be levied on them should be credited to the UNPROFOR Special Account.

SECURITY COUNCIL ACTION

In the light of the Secretary-General's report, the Security Council convened on 30 March. At its request, Croatia was invited to participate in the discussion without the right to vote under rule 37.[a]

The Council unanimously adopted **resolution 815(1993)**.

The Security Council,

Reaffirming its resolution 743(1992) and all subsequent resolutions relating to the United Nations Protection Force (UNPROFOR),

Reaffirming in particular its commitment to ensure respect for the sovereignty and territorial integrity of Croatia and of the other Republics where UNPROFOR is deployed,

Having considered the report of the Secretary-General dated 25 March 1993,

Deeply concerned by the continuing violations by the parties and others concerned of their cease-fire obligations,

Determining that the situation thus created continues to constitute a threat to peace and security in the region,

Determined to ensure the security of UNPROFOR and its freedom of movement for all its missions, and to these ends acting under Chapter VII of the Charter of the United Nations,

1. *Approves* the report of the Secretary-General, in particular its paragraph 5;

2. *Reaffirms* all the provisions of its resolutions 802(1993) and 807(1993);

3. *Decides* to reconsider one month after the date of this resolution, or at any time at the request of the Secretary-General, UNPROFOR's mandate in light of developments of the International Conference on the Former Yugoslavia and the situation on the ground;

4. *Decides*, in this context, further to extend UN-PROFOR's mandate for an additional interim period terminating on 30 June 1993;

5. *Supports* the Co-Chairmen of the Steering Committee of the International Conference on the Former Yugoslavia in their efforts to help to define the future status of those territories comprising the United Nations Protected Areas (UNPAs), which are integral parts of the territory of the Republic of Croatia, and demands full respect for international humanitarian law, and in particular the Geneva Conventions, in these Areas;

6. *Requests* the Secretary-General to report urgently to the Council on how the United Nations Peace Plan for Croatia can be effectively implemented;

7. *Decides* to remain actively seized of the matter.

Security Council resolution 815(1993)

30 March 1993   Meeting 3189   Adopted unanimously

Draft prepared in consultations among Council members (S/25481).

Reports of the Secretary-General (April and May). On 8 April,[234] the Secretary-General reported that the Croatian Government and the Serb local authorities had signed an agreement at Geneva on 6 April for the full implementation of Security Council resolution 802(1993). The result of negotiations conducted under the auspices of the Co-Chairmen of the ICFY Steering Committee from mid-February was that the agreement would enter into force when the Co-Chairmen received both parties' assurances that neither would station any police in the areas from which the Croatian armed forces were to withdraw and that UNPROFOR would fulfil all police functions in those areas during an interim period. Croatian assurance was given orally at the time of signature, while assurance from the Serb side required approval of its "assembly".

The agreement provided for: a cessation of hostilities by the Croatian armed forces on the fourth day after the agreement's entry into force and, simultaneously, strict compliance by the Croatian Government and the Serb local authorities with the already agreed 1991 cease-fire arrangements,[235] together with the 1992 implementing accords;[236] withdrawal of the Croatian armed forces to the lines of confrontation existing before the outbreak of hostilities on 22 January, to be completed within a further five days, and the vacated areas not to be occupied by Serb armed forces; in parallel to that withdrawal, placing all heavy weapons under UNPROFOR supervision; placing the Maslenica Bridge, Zemunik Airport and Peruca Dam, and their facilities, and the roads from Zadar to the bridge and to the airport, from the bridge to Seline via Rovanjska, and from Sinj to the dam under exclusive UNPROFOR control.

The agreement further provided for the immediate implementation by the parties of the remaining provisions of the peace-keeping plan and of all relevant Council resolutions, including 762(1992);[237] to that end, talks between them, under the Co-Chairmen's auspices, would be undertaken no later than 15 days after the agreement's entry into force. UNPROFOR would re-establish and strengthen its military and police presence in each area from which the Croatian armed forces would withdraw before the area was vacated. The parties would request the United Nations to strengthen UNPROFOR to carry out these functions under the peace-keeping plan.

It was the Force Commander's assessment that, to implement the agreement, UNPROFOR would additionally require two mechanized infantry battalions each of 900 troops all ranks, one engineer company of up to 150 troops all ranks, and 50 military observers. Civilian police requirements would be met by temporary redeployment from existing UNPROFOR resources. The Secretary-General recommended Council approval of the proposed changes.

The Secretary-General's report of 30 April[238] on the Co-Chairmen's activities (which also summarized the 6 April agreement) stated that approval of the agreement from the Serb "assembly" had not been received when the parties resumed talks at Geneva on 30 April.

In his May report,[239] submitted pursuant to Security Council resolution 815(1993), the Secretary-General pointed out that the Council, by that resolution, had explicitly referred to the UNPAs as integral parts of the territory of the Republic of Croatia, thus formally making clear that the international community would not entertain the local Serb authorities' claim to recognition as a sovereign entity (the so-called Republic of Krajina).

That aspiration to sovereignty, the Secretary-General noted, had largely been the reason for the local Serbs' refusal either to demilitarize or to cooperate in the implementation of resolution 769(1992)[240] authorizing UNPROFOR to establish border controls at the international borders of the UNPAs. In the absence of such controls, resolution 820(1993), imposing additional sanctions against Yugoslavia (Serbia and Montenegro), established a regime providing that import to, export from, and transshipment through the UNPAs in Croatia, with the exception of humanitarian supplies, was to be permitted only with proper authorization from Croatia. A meeting held on 27 April by UNPROFOR with the local Serb authorities to secure their agreement to resolution 769(1992) resulted in their declaration that, in view of resolution 820(1993), such agreement could not be considered; they regarded the idea of Croatia regulating UNPA commerce and trade as being in direct breach of the peace-keeping plan.

Regarding resolution 802(1993), the ICFY Co-Chairmen had negotiated with both parties to secure endorsement of the 6 April provisional agreement.[234] However, an endorsement from the Serb side had still not materialized by 10 May.

Prospects for the amicable coexistence of the two sides had receded and the situation was likely to deteriorate further. The remaining Croats in the UNPAs had been subjected to relentless persecution,

murder, assault, threats, armed robbery and arson. UNPROFOR had had to establish protected villages and relocate several hundred civilians to security in Croatia. UNHCR had put the number of Croatian Serbs who had fled to Serbia as of 19 March at approximately 251,000. Hostilities continued, including repeated shelling of civilian targets by both sides, and reports of further imminent incursions had raised tensions in the UNPAs.

The fighting had also inflicted casualties on UNPROFOR. In addition, the local Serb authorities had imposed greater restrictions on its freedom of movement on the ground and in the air and manifested their hostility towards UNPROFOR. UNPROFOR was thus severely handicapped in the performance of its functions.

The Serb authorities in UNPAs remained unwilling to accept the premises of UNPROFOR's mandate as defined in the Council resolutions. On 30 April, the Secretary-General received a letter from those authorities asking him to clarify whether the original peace-keeping plan still existed, to "relocate" UNPROFOR "along the line of confrontation as it existed in January 1993" and warning of the possible escalation of military conflicts if their demands were not met.

The Secretary-General noted that, although UNPROFOR had succeeded in ensuring the complete withdrawal of JNA, in maintaining peace and reducing the intimidation of civilians in UNPAs, it had not been able to fulfil other aspects of the original peace-keeping plan. The Serbs had failed to demilitarize UNPAs (resolution 743(1992))[5] so that little progress had been made towards the return of refugees and displaced persons; they had refused to cooperate with UNPROFOR in returning the pink zones to Croatian authority (resolution 762(1992))[237] and to permit establishment of controls at the international borders of UNPAs. Restrictions imposed by them on the freedom of movement of UNPROFOR crippled its monitoring functions. The Croatian side, in turn, had manifested its impatience with the United Nations (June 1992, and January and April 1993), launching military offensives across the lines of confrontation on three occasions. Croatia's view—reiterated in March,[241] April[242] and May[243]—was that UNPROFOR should be given enforcement powers to oblige the Serbs to comply with Council resolutions within a fixed timetable. Failing that, Croatia made clear that it would not agree to further extensions of the UNPROFOR mandate.

Given these virtually irreconcilable positions, the Secretary-General presented three options for the future of UNPROFOR in Croatia, together with their advantages and disadvantages. One would be to declare the UNPROFOR mandate unworkable due to Serb non-cooperation and withdraw the Force, or decide that, unless the two sides made progress in political negotiations before the end of the current mandate, the Force would be withdrawn. A withdrawal would almost certainly lead to a resumption of hostilities that the United Nations would again be called upon to end. A second option would be to accept the Croatian view and approve enforcement action to exact compliance from the Serbs, which would put UNPROFOR at war with the Serbs in the UNPAs and pink zones. A third option would be to keep the Force in place, with no change in mandate but with limited enhancements of its military capacity.

The Secretary-General decided not to recommend any of those options, but to await a report from the newly appointed United Nations Co-Chairman of the ICFY Steering Committee and Special Representative in the former Yugoslavia, Thorvald Stoltenberg, before making any recommendation on UNPROFOR.

The Secretary-General reiterated the requirements for UNPROFOR's reinforcement in the hope that the Serb authorities would endorse the provisional agreement for the implementation of 802(1991). He called for continued negotiations under ICFY auspices and noted that, even if implementation of the cease-fire agreement became feasible, the Secretariat knew of no Member State willing to contribute the infantry battalion required.

In a 25 May addendum[244] to his report, the Secretary-General stated that enhancements of UNPROFOR in accordance with the third option mentioned above would require an additional 2,650 troops and 100 military observers costing some $91.2 million for an initial six-month period. Should the Security Council enlarge the mandate and strength of UNPROFOR as proposed, the related costs should be considered an expense of the Organization to be borne by Member States and the assessments to be levied on them should be credited to the UNPROFOR special account.

On 18 October, the Secretary-General proposed, and on 22 October received the Council's concurrence, to accept Indonesia's offer of 25 military observers in the context of resolution 847(1993).[245]

Communications. On 27 May,[246] Croatia informed the Security Council President that local Serb leaders had failed to attend the talks under UNPROFOR's auspices at Zagreb on 26 May, indicating their unwillingness to continue the ongoing dialogue aimed at normalizing the situation in the UNPAs. That meeting had been agreed upon between representatives of Croatia and the local Serbs at a previous meeting (Topusko, 18 May). They had also refused to sign the 6 April agreement on the implementation of resolution 802(1993), scheduled to take effect on 20 May.

Croatia emphasized that it remained open to dialogue with the local Serb leaders and had created a governmental committee to normalize relations with the Serbian population in Croatia. It would continue to follow strictly the relevant Council resolutions, 815(1993) in particular, emphasizing that the UNPAs were an integral part of the territory of Croatia. Croatia stressed that dialogue between the Government and the Serbian population on Croatian territory was an essential part of restoring peace and stability in the entire Balkan region, but must in no way jeopardize Croatia's sovereignty and territorial integrity.

SECURITY COUNCIL ACTION

The Security Council met on 8 June and invited Croatia, at its request, to participate in the discussion under rule 37.[a] Following consultations among its members, the Council authorized its President to make the following statement below[247] on the Council's behalf:

Meeting number. SC 3231.

"Having examined the situation in the United Nations Protected Areas (UNPAs) in the Republic of Croatia, the Security Council is deeply concerned by the failure of the Krajina Serbs to participate in talks on the implementation of its resolution 802(1993) which were to be held in Zagreb on 26 May 1993. It deplores the interruption of the dialogue between the parties, which had recently produced encouraging signs of progress.

"The Council stresses its support for the peace process under the auspices of the Co-Chairmen of the International Conference on the Former Yugoslavia and urges the parties to solve all problems which might arise by peaceful means and resume the talks immediately with a view to the rapid implementation of resolution 802(1993) and all other relevant resolutions. The Council expresses its willingness to help ensure the implementation of an agreement on this basis reached by the parties, including respect for the rights of the local Serb population.

"The Council reminds the parties that the UNPAs are integral parts of the territory of the Republic of Croatia, and that no action inconsistent with this would be acceptable.

"The Council reiterates its demand that international humanitarian law be fully respected in the UNPAs.

"The Council urges the Government of the Republic of Croatia, in cooperation with other interested parties, to take all necessary measures to ensure the full protection of the rights of all residents of the UNPAs when the Republic of Croatia exercises fully its authority in these Areas."

Report of the Secretary-General. Following receipt of advice from his Special Representative, the Secretary-General stated in a 24 June report[248] to the Security Council that the renewal of the UNPROFOR mandate would apply to all the republics of the former Yugoslavia in which UNPROFOR was deployed. He reiterated that a sound basis would not exist for renewing the UNPROFOR mandate in Croatia unless two factors were addressed—the failure of the parties, particularly the Serb side, to permit implementation of the United Nations peace-keeping plan, and their failure to cooperate in establishing a political process that would offer the prospect of an early agreed settlement. He noted, nevertheless, that the presence of UNPROFOR was indispensable to control the conflict. UNPROFOR not only fulfilled a role in respect of the UNPAs, but also played, in both Sector East and Dalmatia, a deterrent and mediating role between Croatia and Yugoslavia (Serbia and Montenegro); it provided an operational link between other areas of Croatia to contiguous areas of Bosnia and Herzegovina; and its logistics bases at Zagreb and Split were essential to the support of its operations within Bosnia and Herzegovina. Consequently, the best option for the moment was to keep UNPROFOR with its current mandate in place, in the hope that a changing international environment would facilitate intensified peacemaking efforts by the ICFY Co-Chairmen, with UNPROFOR support.

Although such an option fell short of Croatia's wish that the mandate have enforcement powers, he would seek Croatia's consent to a limited further extension of three months.

The Secretary-General also said that, should the already unacceptable level of threats to the safety and security of United Nations personnel increase, he would have to conclude that a viable basis for their functioning no longer existed.

In recommending that the Council extend the UNPROFOR mandate by a further three months, to 30 September 1993, the Secretary-General stated that significant progress would be required in the peacemaking efforts of the Co-Chairmen if any further renewal was to be contemplated beyond that date.

SECURITY COUNCIL ACTION

The Security Council convened on 30 June and invited Croatia, at its request, to participate in the discussion without the right to vote under rule 37.ᵃ Before the Council were the Secretary-General's reports of 15 May and 24 June.

Also before the Council was a 25 June letter from Croatia[249] indicating acceptance of only a one-month extension of UNPROFOR's mandate. If progress were made during that time, Croatia would be willing to accept the prolongation of UNPROFOR's role in the country under a new mandate to be concluded only between Croatia and the United Nations and separated from the UNPROFOR mandates in Bosnia and Herzegovina and in the former Yugoslav Republic of Macedonia. The new mandate must give UNPROFOR the authority and instructions to enforce and implement all of the relevant Council resolutions within a specific timetable.

The Council unanimously adopted **resolution 847(1993)**.

The Security Council,

Reaffirming its resolution 743(1992) and all subsequent resolutions relating to the United Nations Protection Force (UNPROFOR),

Having considered the reports of the Secretary-General of 15 May 1993 and of 25 June 1993,

Having considered also the letter by the President of the Republic of Croatia of 26 June 1993 addressed to the Secretary-General,

Recalling the overwhelming importance of seeking, on the basis of the relevant resolutions of the Security Council, comprehensive political solutions to the conflicts in the territory of the former Yugoslavia, and of sustaining confidence and stability in the former Yugoslav Republic of Macedonia,

Strongly condemning continuing military attacks within the territory of the Republics of Croatia and of Bosnia and Herzegovina, and reaffirming its commitment to ensure respect for the sovereignty and territorial integrity of the Republic of Croatia and of the other Member States where UNPROFOR is deployed,

Calling on the parties and others concerned to reach an agreement on confidence-building measures in the territory of the Republic of Croatia, including the opening of the railroad between Zagreb and Split, the highway between Zagreb and Zupanja, and the Adriatic oil pipeline, securing the uninterrupted traffic across the Maslenica straits, and restoring the supply of electricity and water to all regions of the Republic of Croatia including the United Nations Protected Areas,

Determined to ensure the security of UNPROFOR and its freedom of movement for all its missions, and to these ends, as regards UNPROFOR in the Republic of Croatia and the Republic of Bosnia and Herzegovina, acting under Chapter VII of the Charter of the United Nations,

1. *Approves* the report of the Secretary-General of 25 June 1993 and the request for additional resources contained in paragraphs 22, 24 and 25 of his report of 15 May 1993;

2. *Requests* the Secretary-General to report one month after the adoption of the present resolution on progress towards implementation of the United Nations peacekeeping plan for Croatia and all relevant Security Council resolutions, taking into account the position of the Croatian Government, and decides to reconsider, in the light of that report, UNPROFOR's mandate in the territory of the Republic of Croatia;

3. *Decides*, in this context, to extend UNPROFOR's mandate for an additional interim period terminating on 30 September 1993;

4. *Requests* the Secretary-General to keep the Council regularly informed on developments in regard to the implementation of UNPROFOR's mandate;

5. *Decides* to remain actively seized of the matter.

Security Council resolution 847(1993)

30 June 1993   Meeting 3248   Adopted unanimously

Draft prepared in consultations among Council members (S/26014).

The Adriatic oil pipeline mentioned in the resolution was the subject of letters of 30 June from the States participating in the Central European Initiative—Austria, Bosnia and Herzegovina, Croatia, the Czech Republic, Hungary, Italy, Poland,

Slovakia and Slovenia[250]—and of 19 July from Ukraine.[251] In the view of those States, UNPROFOR could play a crucial role in the early reactivation of the pipeline, which had been blocked since September 1991.

Communications. Croatia, on 12 July,[252] informed the Security Council President of its intention to reopen the Maslenica Bridge to traffic on 18 July. Croatia also advised of its determination to reopen nearby Zemunik Airport to civilian traffic. These steps, it said, were essential to normalize living conditions in the country and to facilitate post-war recovery. It would welcome the help of the Council and UNPROFOR to ensure that the reopening of the bridge would not be interrupted.

Those developments and the danger they posed were drawn to the attention of the Council President by the Secretary-General on 14 July[253] for appropriate action. The authorities of both the local Serbs and Yugoslavia (Serbia and Montenegro) perceived the planned events as a provocation, said the Secretary-General. On his instructions, the Force Commander had advised Croatia of the need for all concerned to act in a manner conducive to the maintenance of peace, pointing out that the event planned for 18 July was not in keeping with Council resolutions 802(1993) and 847(1993). The Force Commander moreover reminded Croatia that having excluded UNPROFOR from entering the Maslenica area, it could hardly ensure the reopening of the bridge without incident.

SECURITY COUNCIL ACTION (15 and 30 July)

The Security Council convened on 15 July 1993 and, after consultations among its members, authorized its President to make the following statement[254] on its behalf:

Meeting number. SC 3255.

"The Security Council is deeply concerned at the information contained in the letter of the Secretary-General of 14 July 1993 on the situation in and around the United Nations Protected Areas (UNPAs) in the Republic of Croatia. It recalls its resolutions 802(1993) and 847(1993) and in particular the demand in the former that all parties and others concerned comply strictly with the cease-fire arrangements already agreed and the call on them in the latter to reach an agreement on confidence-building measures.

"The Security Council expresses its deep concern at the latest report on hostilities in the UNPAs, including in particular by the Krajina Serbs, and demands that these hostilities cease immediately.

"The Security Council continues to attach the highest importance to securing the reopening of the Maslenica crossing to civilian traffic. In this context it reaffirms its support for the sovereignty and territorial integrity of the Republic of Croatia. It recognizes the real and legitimate concern of the Government of the Republic of Croatia in such reopening, as set out in the letter of 12 July 1993 from the Permanent Representative of the Republic of Croatia. It also recalls the demand

in its resolution 802(1993) that the Croatian armed forces withdraw from the areas in question.

"The Security Council considers that the planned unilateral reopening of the Maslenica Bridge and of Zemunik Airport on 18 July 1993, in the absence of agreement between the parties and others concerned in cooperation with the United Nations Protection Force (UNPROFOR), would jeopardize the objectives of the Council's resolutions and in particular the call in its resolution 847(1993) for agreement on confidence-building measures and the efforts of the Co-Chairmen of the International Conference on the Former Yugoslavia and UNPROFOR to achieve a negotiated settlement to the problem. It urges the Government of the Republic of Croatia to refrain from this action.

"The Security Council expresses its support for the efforts of the Co-Chairmen and UNPROFOR and calls on the parties and others concerned to cooperate fully with them in this regard and to conclude rapidly the agreement on confidence-building measures called for in its resolution 847(1993). It joins the Secretary-General in his call to the parties and others concerned to act in a manner conducive to the maintenance of peace and to refrain from any action which would undermine these efforts, and calls upon the parties to assure UNPROFOR's freedom of access in particular to the area surrounding the Maslenica crossing."

In the light of information subsequently received from the Special Representative regarding an agreement reached by the parties at Erdut and Zagreb on 15 and 16 July (described below by the Co-Chairmen of the ICFY Steering Committee), the Council convened on 30 July, following which it authorized its President to make the following statement:[255]

Meeting number. SC 3260.

"The Security Council has heard with deep concern the report from the Special Representative of the Secretary-General for the Former Yugoslavia on the situation in and around the United Nations Protected Areas (UNPAs) in the Republic of Croatia and in particular in respect of the Maslenica crossing.

"The Security Council reaffirms the presidential statement of 15 July 1993. Following this statement the parties reached an agreement on 15 and 16 July 1993 at Erdut which requires the withdrawal of Croatian armed forces and police from the area of the Maslenica Bridge by 31 July 1993 and the placing of the bridge under the exclusive control of the United Nations Protection Force (UNPROFOR).

"The Security Council demands that the Croatian forces withdraw forthwith in conformity with the above-mentioned agreement, and that they permit the immediate deployment of UNPROFOR. The Council also demands that the Krajina Serb forces refrain from entering the area. The Council calls for maximum restraint from all the parties, including the observance of a cease-fire.

"The Security Council warns of the serious consequences of any failure to implement the above-mentioned agreement.

"The Council will remain actively seized of the matter."

Report of the Co-Chairmen of ICFY Steering Committee. According to the Co-Chairmen's report, transmitted to the President of the Security Council on 3 August,[(201)] an agreement for implementing resolution 802(1993) was signed by the Government of Croatia and the local Serb authorities on 15 and 16 July, following the Co-Chairmen's contacts with Presidents Milosevic and Tudjman and subsequent discussions at Erdut and Zagreb.

The agreement provided that there would be no Croatian armed forces or police in the areas specified in the agreement after 31 July; UNPROFOR would move into those areas. In the villages of Islam Crcki, Smokovic and Kasic, Serb police, together with United Nations civilian police (UNCIVPOL), would be present. With the withdrawal of the Croatian armed forces and police, Maslenica Bridge, Zemunik Airport and Peruca Dam would be under the exclusive control of UNPROFOR. The building of a pontoon bridge could proceed after the agreement had been signed by both parties. They would intensify efforts to reach a negotiated solution to all problems existing between them, starting with a cease-fire to be negotiated by UNPROFOR.

A cease-fire text, prepared by UNPROFOR, was examined by the parties at Vienna. However, the Croatian Government considered the cease-fire as not linked to the Erdut/Zagreb agreement, while the Serbs insisted that they would not sign any cease-fire before the withdrawal of Croatian forces in accordance with that agreement.

On 23 July, the Croatian authorities signed a unilateral undertaking to the agreement to permit UNPROFOR to start deploying in the Zemunik/Maslenica area and to assume full control by 31 July. The undertaking further provided that, from 1 August, UNCIVPOL, together with five Serb police, armed only with side-arms, would establish their presence in each of the three villages named in the agreement.

On 25 July, UNPROFOR obtained an undertaking from the Serb leadership to refrain from all armed hostilities until 31 July and to allow the withdrawal of the Croatian armed forces and police, as stipulated by the agreement. The Croatian authorities failed to comply with the agreement and the Serbs indicated that they would feel free to resume armed hostilities after 31 July.

Reports of the Secretary-General (August and September). The Secretary-General, reporting on 16 August 1993 on the implementation of the United Nations peace-keeping plan for Croatia,[(256)] stated that, despite determined efforts by the Co-Chairmen of the ICFY Steering Committee for implementing resolutions 802(1993) and 847(1993), the situation had not changed. Subsequent to the 30 July presidential statement, 2,000

UNPROFOR troops moved towards the areas from which the Croatian forces were to withdraw but were unable to deploy because the Croatian military authorities restricted access to the areas concerned and did not cooperate in the planning or reconnaissance of the operation.

Following Serb shelling of the area on 2 August, which sank one of the Maslenica Bridge pontoons, the Co-Chairmen arranged for talks between the parties (Geneva, 12 August) on a cease-fire to include the elements of the Erdut/Zagreb agreement.

Pending the outcome of current efforts to persuade both sides to cooperate with UNPROFOR in implementing the two resolutions above, the Secretary-General withheld recommendation on the future of the UNPROFOR mandate in Croatia. In this connection, he referred to Croatia's 18 June proposal,[(257)] elaborated upon on 30 July,[(258)] for the separation of the UNPROFOR mandate into three independent mandates, for Croatia, Bosnia and Herzegovina and the Former Yugoslav Republic of Macedonia, which he intended to keep under review.

The Secretary-General subsequently reported in September[(259)] that the intensive discussions between the Co-Chairmen and the parties at Geneva, Zagreb and Knin, most recently on 9 and 10 September, produced an agreement to hold a further meeting, aboard a ship on the Adriatic on 12 September, between the parties' military experts.

Meanwhile, in the UNPAs and pink zones, shelling intensified on both sides of the confrontation line, and, on 9 September, the Croatian Army launched a military incursion into the Medak pocket, destroying three Serb villages. Hostilities worsened on 10 and 11 September. The intervention of the Special Representative and the Force Commander, as well as a call from the Security Council (see immediately below), brought about a cease-fire on 15 September. Some 500 to 600 UNPROFOR troops moved into the areas vacated by the withdrawal of Croatian forces. Efforts continued to reschedule the postponed meeting aboard ship on the Adriatic.

SECURITY COUNCIL ACTION

Meeting on 14 September, the Security Council invited Croatia, at its request, to participate in the discussion without the right to vote in accordance with rule 37.[a] The President was authorized to make the following statement[(260)] on behalf of the Council, in connection with its consideration on the item entitled ''The situation in Croatia'':
Meeting number. SC 3275.

''The Security Council expresses its profound concern at the reports from the Secretariat of recent military hostilities in Croatia, in particular the escalation of the means employed, and the grave threat they pose to the peace process in Geneva and overall stability in the former Yugoslavia.

"The Council reaffirms its respect for the sovereignty and territorial integrity of the Republic of Croatia, and calls on both sides to accept UNPROFOR's proposal of an immediate cease-fire. It calls on the Croatian Government to withdraw its armed forces to positions occupied before 9 September 1993, on the basis of that proposal, and calls on the Serbian forces to halt all provocative military actions."

Report of the Secretary-General. In his 20 September report,[259] the Secretary-General referred to Croatia's proposal that UNPROFOR be divided into three parts—UNPROFOR (Croatia), UNPROFOR (Bosnia and Herzegovina) and UNPROFOR (the former Yugoslav Republic of Macedonia)—while retaining its integrated military, logistical and administrative structure under the command of one Special Representative of the Secretary-General and one Force Commander. The Secretary-General instructed his Special Representative to put such a division into effect, provided there were no additional financial implications and overall command and coordination were not weakened.

He recommended that the Council renew UNPROFOR's mandate for a further six months, to 31 March 1994; demand that the parties in Croatia conclude an immediate cease-fire and cooperate with UNPROFOR, which must be enabled to fulfil the peace-keeping aspects of its mandate; and direct the parties to cooperate with UNPROFOR in restoring water, power, communications and other economic necessities. By 30 November, he would report to the Council on progress made by the Co-Chairmen and UNPROFOR and make further recommendations on the basis of developments during those two months.

In an addendum to his report,[261] the Secretary-General stated that the monthly cost of maintaining the Force would be limited initially to the commitment authority contained in General Assembly **resolution 47/210 B** and that he would report on additional requirements.

Communication. Croatia, on 24 September,[262] informed the Security Council President that its Parliament supported the Government decision to terminate the UNPROFOR mandate in Croatia in its current form, for it was undermining Croatia's sovereignty and territorial integrity. The major changes it wanted to the UNPROFOR mandate were based on existing Security Council resolutions and reports of the Secretary-General, including guarantees for the full protection of human rights and minority rights. If these were not incorporated in the resolution extending the UNPROFOR mandate, then, upon the expiration of the current interim extension, Croatia would con-

sider the mandate terminated and would request UNPROFOR's withdrawal by 30 November 1993.

SECURITY COUNCIL ACTION (30 September, 1 and 4 October)

In the light of the Secretary-General's 30 September report and of the foregoing letter from Croatia, the Security Council, at its meeting on 30 September, unanimously adopted **resolution 869(1993)**.

The Security Council,

Reaffirming its resolution 743(1992) and all subsequent resolutions relating to the United Nations Protection Force (UNPROFOR),

Reiterating its determination to ensure the security of UNPROFOR and its freedom of movement for all its missions, and to these ends, as regards UNPROFOR in the Republic of Croatia and in the Republic of Bosnia and Herzegovina, acting under Chapter VII of the Charter of the United Nations,

1. *Decides* to extend UNPROFOR's mandate for an additional period terminating on 1 October 1993;

2. *Decides* to remain actively seized of the matter.

Security Council resolution 869(1993)
30 September 1993   Meeting 3284   Adopted unanimously
Draft prepared in consultations among Council members (S/26513).

Before the expiry of the 24-hour extension, the Council met again on 1 October and unanimously adopted **resolution 870(1993)**.

The Security Council,

Reaffirming its resolution 743(1992) and all subsequent resolutions relating to the United Nations Protection Force (UNPROFOR),

Reiterating its determination to ensure the security of UNPROFOR and its freedom of movement for all its missions, and to these ends, as regards UNPROFOR in the Republic of Croatia and in the Republic of Bosnia and Herzegovina, acting under Chapter VII of the Charter of the United Nations,

1. *Decides* to extend UNPROFOR's mandate for an additional period terminating on 5 October 1993;

2. *Decides* to remain actively seized of the matter.

Security Council resolution 870(1993)
1 October 1993   Meeting 3285   Adopted unanimously
Draft prepared in consultations among Council members (S/26525), orally revised.

The Council met again on 4 October, the day before the expiry of the above extension. Acting under Chapter VII of the Charter, the Council unanimously adopted **resolution 871(1993)**.

The Security Council,

Reaffirming its resolution 743(1992) and all subsequent resolutions relating to the United Nations Protection Force (UNPROFOR),

Reaffirming also its resolution 713(1991) and all subsequent relevant resolutions,

Having considered the report of the Secretary-General of 20 September 1993,

Having also considered the letter of the Minister for Foreign Affairs of the Republic of Croatia dated 24 September 1993,

Deeply concerned that the United Nations peace-keeping plan for the Republic of Croatia, and all relevant Security Council resolutions, in particular resolution 769(1992), have not yet been fully implemented,

Reiterating its determination to ensure the security of UNPROFOR and its freedom of movement for all its missions, and to these ends, as regards UNPROFOR in the Republic of Croatia and in the Republic of Bosnia and Herzegovina, acting under Chapter VII of the Charter of the United Nations,

1. *Welcomes* the report of the Secretary-General of 20 September 1993, in particular its paragraph 16;

2. *Takes note* of the intention of the Secretary-General to establish, as described in his report, three subordinate commands within UNPROFOR—UNPROFOR (Croatia), UNPROFOR (Bosnia and Herzegovina) and UNPROFOR (the former Yugoslav Republic of Macedonia)—while retaining the existing dispositions in all other respects for the direction and conduct of the United Nations operation in the territory of the former Yugoslavia;

3. *Condemns once again* continuing military attacks within the territory of the Republic of Croatia and the Republic of Bosnia and Herzegovina, and reaffirms its commitment to ensure respect for the sovereignty and territorial integrity of the Republic of Croatia, the Republic of Bosnia and Herzegovina and the former Yugoslav Republic of Macedonia, where UNPROFOR is deployed;

4. *Reaffirms* the crucial importance of the full and prompt implementation of the United Nations peace-keeping plan for the Republic of Croatia including the provisions of the plan concerning the demilitarization of the United Nations Protected Areas (UNPAs) and calls upon the signatories of that plan and all others concerned, in particular the Federal Republic of Yugoslavia (Serbia and Montenegro), to cooperate in its full implementation;

5. *Declares* that continued non-cooperation in the implementation of the relevant resolutions of the Security Council or external interference, in respect of the full implementation of the United Nations peace-keeping plan for the Republic of Croatia would have serious consequences and in this connection affirms that full normalization of the international community's position towards those concerned will take into account their actions in implementing all relevant resolutions of the Security Council including those relating to the United Nations peace-keeping plan for the Republic of Croatia;

6. *Calls* for an immediate cease-fire agreement between the Croatian Government and the local Serb authorities in the UNPAs, mediated under the auspices of the International Conference on the Former Yugoslavia, and urges them to cooperate fully and unconditionally in its implementation, as well as in the implementation of all the relevant resolutions of the Council;

7. *Stresses* the importance it attaches, as a first step towards the implementation of the United Nations peace-keeping plan for the Republic of Croatia, to the process of restoration of the authority of the Republic of Croatia in the "pink zones", and in this context calls for the revival of the Joint Commission established under the chairmanship of UNPROFOR;

8. *Urges* all the parties and others concerned to cooperate with UNPROFOR in reaching and implementing an agreement on confidence-building measures including the restoration of electricity, water and communications in all regions of the Republic of Croatia, and stresses in this context the importance it attaches to the opening of the railroad between Zagreb and Split, the highway between Zagreb and Zupanja, and the Adriatic oil pipeline, securing the uninterrupted traffic across the Maslenica strait, and restoring the supply of electricity and water to all regions of the Republic of Croatia including the United Nations Protected Areas;

9. *Authorizes* UNPROFOR, in carrying out its mandate in the Republic of Croatia, acting in self-defence, to take the necessary measures, including the use of force, to ensure its security and its freedom of movement;

10. *Decides* to continue to review urgently the extension of close air support to UNPROFOR in the territory of the Republic of Croatia as recommended by the Secretary-General in his report of 20 September 1993;

11. *Decides* in this context to extend UNPROFOR's mandate for an additional period terminating on 31 March 1994;

12. *Requests* the Secretary-General to report two months after the adoption of the present resolution on progress towards implementation of the United Nations peace-keeping plan for the Republic of Croatia and all relevant Security Council resolutions, taking into account the position of the Croatian Government, as well as on the outcome of the negotiations within the International Conference on the Former Yugoslavia, and decides to reconsider UNPROFOR's mandate in the light of that report;

13. *Requests further* the Secretary-General to keep the Council regularly informed on developments in regard to the implementation of UNPROFOR's mandate;

14. *Decides* to remain actively seized of the matter.

Security Council resolution 871(1993)

4 October 1993   Meeting 3286   Adopted unanimously

Draft prepared in consultations among Council members (S/26518).

Report of the Secretary-General. On 1 December,[263] the Secretary-General reported on the continuing (November) talks within the ICFY framework aimed at achieving a comprehensive cease-fire in and around the UNPAs and on UNPROFOR efforts towards implementing the United Nations peace-keeping plan for Croatia.

The talks took account of the Croatian President's "peace initiative" of 2 November,[264] advancing proposals on the question, and measures to be undertaken by the three parties to the conflict in Bosnia and Herzegovina and by all States in the area of the former Yugoslavia for the permanent consolidation of peace.

Further talks chaired by ICFY were held from 1 to 3 November, at which the parties accepted a three-step strategy: discussion of a cease-fire, consideration of economic reconstruction, and discussion of political questions.

The key elements of a cease-fire agreement were the separation of forces along the confrontation lines, with UNPROFOR interposed between the two sides and monitoring heavy weapons on either side. In areas of withdrawal, UNPROFOR would be interposed between the forces at the Maslenica Bridge, Zemunik Airport, Peruca Dam and Miljevci Plateau, all of which would remain under Croatian control. Three villages near Maslenica and a key feature overlooking Obrovac would revert to Serb control.

The main areas of economic interest related to infrastructure and communications, energy and water supply. The parties concurred on the establishment of joint commissions to examine and finalize practical arrangements.

The road from Zagreb to Slavonski Brod, via Kucani was a priority for the Croatian side, which indicated that, following a cease-fire, Zemunik Airport and Maslenica Bridge would be opened for use by both sides. The Serb side asked that a route be opened between Western Slavonia and Hungary, as well as road and railway traffic between Western Slavonia and Baranja, via Osijek; it also asked for access to the open sea from Rovanjska harbour and use of a part of Zadar harbour.

After further talks in November, the Croatian side stated that, with one modification, it could sign the cease-fire proposal. Remaining on the table were modifications proposed by the Serb side, without which it stated it could not sign the document. The parties agreed, however, to set up a military joint commission to continue practical work on outstanding areas of dispute on the lines of separation to be used once a cease-fire was in place.

UNPROFOR had reinforced its support to the ICFY-sponsored talks and to promoting measures in the UNPAs to reduce tensions and thereby establish conditions favourable to a comprehensive cease-fire. The Secretary-General did not recommend reconsideration of UNPROFOR's mandate by the Security Council. However, he pointed out that it was essential for the two sides to intensify their efforts for achieving a cease-fire agreement, for the institution of practical measures of economic cooperation and for the negotiation of a lasting political settlement—an observation which the Council shared.[265]

Violations of international humanitarian law

Subsequent to a report brought to the attention of the Security Council in February on the preliminary excavation of a mass grave near Vukovar in northern Croatia (see PART THREE, Chapter X), the Secretary-General, by a letter of 20 August,[266] informed the Council President that the Netherlands had offered to provide, free of cost to the United Nations, an armed military engineer unit of up to 50 personnel to assist in the excavation of mass grave sites in the UNPAs. The

Secretary-General proposed including the unit in UNPROFOR on a temporary basis, to be deployed in the area for a period of 10 weeks starting on 1 September, subject to the extension of the current UNPROFOR mandate beyond 30 September.

On 27 August,[267] the Council President conveyed the Council's agreement to the proposal, adding that it was the Council's understanding that UNPROFOR's connection with the engineering unit would be to provide administrative and logistic support and protection.

Earlier, on 2 February, the report of an EC mission that visited Bosnia and Herzegovina and Croatia to investigate massive and systematic detention and rape of women was also brought to the attention of the Council. (See "Mass rape" above, under "Bosnia and Herzegovina".)

Humanitarian assistance

The overall United Nations humanitarian effort in Croatia was the subject of a report by the Secretary-General in 1993. Based on that report, the General Assembly adopted **resolution 48/204** on 21 December, calling on all States to provide special and other assistance to Croatia and asking the Secretary-General to carry out an assessment of the country's needs for rehabilitation, reconstruction and development (see PART THREE, Chapter III).

Former Yugoslav Republic of Macedonia

During 1993, the former Yugoslav Republic of Macedonia was admitted to membership in the United Nations, amid differences with Greece over the name of that republic. The Co-Chairmen of the ICFY Steering Committee conducted negotiations with the two countries in order to settle their differences and to promote confidence-building measures between them (see PART ONE, Chapter V).

On 27 August, ICFY[4] mediated "Agreed Minutes" between the former Yugoslav Republic of Macedonia and the local Serbs that embodied undertakings and understandings reflecting the requests and complaints put to ICFY by the latter. The Minutes recorded the Government's undertaking to treat the Serbs equally with other nationalities living in the republic, to provide them with instruction in the Serbian language, to guarantee them constitutional religious freedom, to provide equal support to the Serbian-language media, to protect historical monuments and other cultural inheritance of the Serbs in the republic, and to conduct a national census in 1994.

Communication from the Secretary-General. The Secretary-General, on 15 June,[268] drew to the attention of the President of the Security Council an 11 June letter from the United States offering a reinforced company team of approximately 300 troops to operate with UNPROFOR in the former Yugoslav Republic of Macedonia. The United States stated that its offer was intended to augment the UNPROFOR units already deployed in there, not to replace them.

The Secretary-General estimated that the cost associated with the deployment of the additional troops to reinforce UNPROFOR would amount to some $10.5 million for an initial six-month period and approximately $1.5 million per month thereafter. A breakdown of the estimate, by main categories of expenditure, was also provided. The Secretary-General recommended that, should the Council decide to approve the proposed deployment, the related cost should be considered an expense of the Organization to be borne by Member States and the assessment to be levied on them should be credited to the UNPROFOR special account.

SECURITY COUNCIL ACTION

On 18 June, the Security Council, having considered the Secretary-General's letter, unanimously adopted **resolution 842(1993)**.

The Security Council,

Reaffirming its resolution 743(1992) and all subsequent resolutions relating to the United Nations Protection Force (UNPROFOR),

Recalling in particular resolution 795(1992) of 11 December 1992 which authorized the UNPROFOR presence in the former Yugoslav Republic of Macedonia,

Welcoming the important contribution of the existing UNPROFOR presence in the former Yugoslav Republic of Macedonia to stability in the region,

Seeking to support efforts for a peaceful resolution to the situation in the former Yugoslavia as it relates to the former Yugoslav Republic of Macedonia as provided for in the Secretary-General's report of 10 December 1992 and approved by resolution 795(1992) of 11 December 1992,

Noting with appreciation the offer made by a Member State to contribute additional personnel to the UNPROFOR presence in the former Yugoslav Republic of Macedonia, and the latter Government's favourable response thereto,

1. *Welcomes* the offer made by a Member State to contribute additional personnel to the UNPROFOR presence in the former Yugoslav Republic of Macedonia and decides to expand the size of UNPROFOR accordingly and to authorize the deployment of these additional personnel;

2. *Decides* to remain seized of the matter.

Security Council resolution 842(1993)

18 June 1993   Meeting 3239   Adopted unanimously

Draft prepared in consultations among Council members (S/25955).

Report of the Secretary-General. In keeping with a 1992 Security Council request,[(6)] the Secretary-General reported on 13 July 1993[(269)] on the deployment and activities of UNPROFOR in

the former Yugoslav Republic of Macedonia prior to its reinforcement with United States troops.

The Secretary-General stated that the first UNCIVPOL monitors arrived on 27 December 1992. A Canadian company arrived on 7 January 1993 and remained until 18 February, when its operation was taken over by a 434-man joint battalion from Finland, Norway and Sweden. As at May 1993, there were 18 permanently manned observation posts, 4 along the border with Albania and 14 along the border with Yugoslavia (Serbia and Montenegro). United States troops numbering about 300 arrived during the first two weeks in July.

Since early January, the northern border and the western border north of Debar had been constantly monitored from observation posts and by regular patrols, first by the Canadian company and then by the Nordic battalion, with a view to reporting activities that might increase tension or threaten peace and stability. UNPROFOR military personnel had a number of encounters with Yugoslav soldiers claiming that UNPROFOR had intruded into the territory of Yugoslavia (Serbia and Montenegro). That the border, previously an internal one, had not been definitively delineated was a source of potential conflict. The two Governments had yet to set up a joint border commission to resolve the matter conclusively.

The 19 United Nations Military Observers (UNMOs) covering the western border area south of Debar were based at Ohrid. Eleven were responsible for patrolling the area south of Debar; the remaining eight patrolled the northern border area or served at headquarters near Skopje. In connection with their programme of visits to border villages aimed at gaining the confidence of their inhabitants and assisting in defusing possible inter-ethnic tensions, the UNMOs referred complaints about alleged discriminatory practices against the ethnic Albanian population to the relevant national authorities, to ICFY or to the Commission on Human Rights, as appropriate.

UNCIVPOL regularly patrolled specific crossings and the border areas in general to monitor the work of local border police. They reported two shooting incidents on the border with Albania that occurred on 22 February and 19 April resulting from illegal border crossings. An Albanian national, who was shot in the February incident, was believed to have been involved in smuggling arms into the country.

The Secretary-General observed that UNPROFOR had so far been successful in its preventive mandate in the country. He intended to keep the situation there under close review and would report to the Council, as appropriate, in the months to come.

On 22 July,[270] the Council President informed the Secretary-General that the Council had taken note of his report; it welcomed the completion of UNPROFOR's reinforcement and the establishment of close coordination with the CSCE mission.

Yugoslavia (Serbia and Montenegro)

CSCE missions

By a 20 July letter,[271] transmitted by Sweden, the Chairman of the CSCE Council informed the President of the Security Council that, at the end of June, Yugoslavia (Serbia and Montenegro) withdrew its acceptance of the CSCE missions in Kosovo, Sandjac and Vojvodina. As recognized by the Government, the missions—established in September 1992 to promote dialogue between the authorities and communities in the three regions, collect information on human rights violations and promote solutions to such problems—had proved invaluable in promoting stability and counteracting the risk of ethnically motivated violence. Hence, their discontinuance would aggravate existing threats to peace and security in the region.

The CSCE Council Chairman, on 23 July,[272] underscoring the basic condition as defined by the CSCE Council for the gradual readmittance of Yugoslavia (Serbia and Montenegro) to the international community, called on the Government to revoke its decision and live up to the norms and principles it had accepted as a CSCE participating State.

That Government, responding on 28 July 1993,[273] said that a normalization of cooperation between it, as an equal partner, and CSCE would facilitate the future acceptance of the CSCE missions in the country. Despite its unjust suspension from CSCE meetings in July 1992, Yugoslavia (Serbia and Montenegro) had continued its CSCE commitments. The Government stressed that its isolation from CSCE activities was not conducive to continued cooperation and was in nobody's interest. It further stressed, on 3 August,[274] that it was not Yugoslavia (Serbia and Montenegro) that had refused to allow the continued functioning of the CSCE missions, but rather CSCE which had rejected the cooperation offered on a number of occasions. It assured CSCE that the situation in Kosovo, Metohija, Raska and Vojvodina, was under control and posed no danger to international peace and security. It reiterated those views on 9 August.[275]

SECURITY COUNCIL ACTION

The Security Council convened on 9 August, inviting without objection Dragomir Djokic, Ambassador of Yugoslavia (Serbia and Montenegro), to be present at the discussion.

By a recorded vote of 14 to none, with 1 abstention (China), the Council adopted **resolution 855(1993)**.

The Security Council,

Taking note of the letters of 20 July 1993 and 23 July 1993 from the Chairman-in-Office of the Council of Ministers of the Conference on Security and Cooperation in Europe (CSCE),

Further taking note of the letters of 28 July 1993 and 3 August 1993 circulated by the authorities of the Federal Republic of Yugoslavia (Serbia and Montenegro),

Deeply concerned at the refusal of the authorities in the Federal Republic of Yugoslavia (Serbia and Montenegro) to allow the CSCE missions of long duration to continue their activities,

Bearing in mind that the CSCE missions of long duration are an example of preventive diplomacy undertaken within the framework of the CSCE, and have greatly contributed to promoting stability and counteracting the risk of violence in Kosovo, Sandjak and Vojvodina, the Federal Republic of Yugoslavia (Serbia and Montenegro),

Reaffirming its relevant resolutions aimed at putting an end to conflict in the former Yugoslavia,

Determined to avoid any extension of the conflict in the former Yugoslavia and, in this context, attaching great importance to the work of the CSCE missions and to the continued ability of the international community to monitor the situation in Kosovo, Sandjak and Vojvodina, the Federal Republic of Yugoslavia (Serbia and Montenegro),

Stressing its commitment to the territorial integrity and political independence of all States in the region,

1. *Endorses* the efforts of the CSCE as described in the letters noted above from the Chairman-in-Office of the Council of Ministers of the Conference on Security and Cooperation in Europe (CSCE);

2. *Calls upon* the authorities in the Federal Republic of Yugoslavia (Serbia and Montenegro) to reconsider their refusal to allow the continuation of the activities of the CSCE missions in Kosovo, Sandjak and Vojvodina, the Federal Republic of Yugoslavia (Serbia and Montenegro), to cooperate with the CSCE by taking the practical steps needed for the resumption of the activities of these missions and to agree to an increase in the number of monitors as decided by the CSCE;

3. *Further calls upon* the authorities in the Federal Republic of Yugoslavia (Serbia and Montenegro) to assure the monitors' safety and security, and to allow them free and unimpeded access necessary to accomplish their mission in full;

4. *Decides* to remain seized of the matter.

Security Council resolution 855(1993)

9 August 1993   Meeting 3262   14-0-1

5-nation draft (S/26263).
Sponsors: France, Hungary, Spain, United Kingdom, United States.

Vote in Council as follows:

In favour: Brazil, Cape Verde, Djibouti, France, Hungary, Japan, Morocco, New Zealand, Pakistan, Russian Federation, Spain, United Kingdom, United States, Venezuela.
Against: None.
Abstaining: China.

China was of the view that the issue of Kosovo was an internal affair of Yugoslavia (Serbia and

Montenegro), whose sovereignty, political independence and territorial integrity should be respected in line with the basic principles of the United Nations Charter and international law. China cautioned the Council to exercise extreme prudence and act in strict conformity with the Charter's purposes and principles, especially non-interference in internal affairs of States. The CSCE missions to Kosovo and other areas of Yugoslavia (Serbia and Montenegro) were sent with the consent of that country, and the question of their continuation should be solved through continued dialogue and consultation.

Yugoslavia (Serbia and Montenegro)–Albania

During 1993, Albania and Yugoslavia (Serbia and Montenegro) addressed a number of communications to the President of the Security Council and the Secretary-General alleging hostile incidents by one against the other along their common border and in the Yugoslav region of Kosovo, whose population included more than 2 million ethnic Albanians.

Albania's concern focused on Kosovo, where it reported, on 24 April,[276] daily evidence of Serbia's plans for the ethnic cleansing of the Albanians there and asked the Council urgently to take preventive measures, such as deploying United Nations troops, to prevent such an occurrence and armed conflict. On 27 April,[277] Albania drew attention to two border incidents in the previous two days in which six Albanians were killed when Serb forces opened fire on Albanian villages along the border. On 26 May,[278] Albania reported a shooting incident at the town of Gllogovc in Kosovo on 22 May, during which two Serbian policemen were killed by unidentified gunmen; as a result, 100 Albanians were arrested and beaten. A series of incidents were also reported on 18 June:[279] explosions and shootings in the town of Gjakova on 14 June; destructive raids on 12 ethnic Albanian households in the village of Gllanaselle on 17 June under the pretext of an arms search; and, on the same day, an explosion in Pristina (Prishtina) that severely wounded an Albanian woman. In view of what it described as the grave situation in Kosovo, Albania, on 8 July,[280] expressed concern at the discontinuance of the CSCE mission there.

Albania alleged on 6 August[281] that Serbian military forces perpetrated two successive acts of provocation by opening automatic rifle fire in the direction of Albanian territory; in view of the escalating tension on its border with Yugoslavia (Serbia and Montenegro), Albania requested an urgent Council meeting to consider the situation. Another border incident was reported to have taken place on 6 August,[282] when Yugoslav military forces fired into Albania's territory across the

border near Tropoja in northern Albania, killing an Albanian and wounding another. Albania said that, in the first four months of 1993, 14 Albanian nationals had been shot dead by Serbian border guards at different points along its border with Yugoslavia (Serbia and Montenegro).

Albania also transmitted to the Secretary-General a statement and reports of the "Council for the Protection of Human Rights and Freedoms of the Republic of Kosovo" on 14 September, alleging increased repression by Serbian police in Kosovo.[283]

For its part, Yugoslavia (Serbia and Montenegro), on 30 April,[284] accused Albania of flagrant interference in its internal affairs. In categorically rejecting Albania's allegations with respect to Kosovo, it said that it found it absurd that a sovereign State could be charged with attacking its own territory; Albania's main goal, it said, was to further encourage secessionist and terrorist forces in Kosovo and Metohija by provoking incidents at the common border. A letter of 11 June[285] listed 18 incidents of border violations committed by Albanian nationals between 12 January and 30 May. By a 20 August letter,[286] Yugoslavia (Serbia and Montenegro) condemned the armed ambush and killing of a Yugoslav guard on Yugoslav territory near the border with Albania. On 15 November,[287] it refuted each and every allegation made by Albania during the 1993 General Assembly debate as part of that country's anti-Yugoslav campaign. It asserted on 19 November[288] that Albania's accusations were but a screen to conceal its responsibility for providing support to the Albanian secessionist movement in the former Yugoslav Republic of Macedonia. On 15 December,[289] Yugoslavia (Serbia and Montenegro) accused the Albanian President of openly expressing territorial claims towards it by calling for a "Greater Albania".

The Co-Chairmen of the ICFY Steering Committee[4] raised the situation of ethnic Albanians in Kosovo several times in meetings with President Slobodan Milosevic of Yugoslavia (Serbia and Montenegro) during the year and, in particular, urged a reconsideration of the decision not to renew the mandate of the CSCE mission there. The Government did not attend a meeting scheduled by ICFY at Geneva on 8 September for the resumption of talks on educational problems in Kosovo, claiming that minority issues were internal matters. It had not been possible since then to find a mutually agreeable venue for the parties to meet.

A representative of the ICFY Working Group on Ethnic and National Communities and Minorities travelled to Pristina on 26 August to meet with the local Serb authorities and local Albanian representatives.

Related questions

Development of good-neighbourly relations among Balkan States

Within the context of its consideration of disarmament and international security issues, the General Assembly adopted a resolution on the development of good-neighbourly relations among Balkan States, calling for confidence-building measures, particularly within the framework of CSCE; emphasizing the importance of promoting cooperation in various fields, including advancement of democratic processes and promotion of human rights; and stressing their closer engagement in cooperation arrangements as a favourable influence on the political and economic situation in the region.

GENERAL ASSEMBLY ACTION

On 16 December, on the recommendation of the First Committee, the General Assembly adopted **resolution 48/84 B** without vote.

Developments of good-neighbourly relations among Balkan States

The General Assembly,

Recalling its resolutions 2625(XXV) of 24 October 1970 and 46/62 of 9 December 1991,

Affirming its determination that all nations should live together in peace with one another as good neighbours,

Emphasizing the urgency of the consolidation of the Balkans as a region of peace, security, stability and good-neighbourliness, thus contributing to the maintenance of international peace and security and so enhancing the prospects for sustained development and prosperity for its peoples,

Noting the desire of the Balkan States to develop good-neighbourly relations among themselves and friendly relations with all nations in accordance with the Charter of the United Nations,

1. *Calls upon* all Balkan States to endeavour to promote good-neighbourly relations and continually to undertake unilateral and joint activities, particularly confidence-building measures as appropriate, in particular within the framework of the Conference on Security and Cooperation in Europe;

2. *Emphasizes* the importance for all Balkan States to promote mutual cooperation in all fields and, *inter alia*, in trade and other forms of economic cooperation, transport and telecommunications, protection of the environment, advancement of democratic processes, promotion of human rights and development of cultural and sport relations;

3. *Stresses* that closer engagement of Balkan States in cooperation arrangements on the European continent will favourably influence the political and economic situation in the region, as well as the good-neighbourly relations among Balkan States;

4. *Requests* the Secretary-General to seek the views of Member States, particularly those from the Balkan region, of international organizations, as well as of competent organs of the United Nations, on the development of good-neighbourly relations in the region and on measures and preventive activities aimed at creation of a stable zone of peace and cooperation in the Balkans by the year 2000;

5. *Decides* to consider the report of the Secretary-General on the subject at its fiftieth regular session.

General Assembly resolution 48/84 B

16 December 1993   Meeting 81   Adopted without vote

Approved by First Committee (A/48/685) without vote, 18 November (meeting 29); draft by the former Yugoslav Republic of Macedonia (A/C.1/48/L.26/Rev.3); agenda item 80.
Meeting numbers. GA 48th session: 1st Committee 3-14, 24-26, 29; plenary 81.

Introducing the first revision to the draft text, the former Yugoslav Republic of Macedonia explained that paragraph 3 had been reworded to make it fully acceptable to all EC members, while paragraph 4 had been rearranged to make it clear that the resolution entailed no financial implications. The former Yugoslavia Republic of Macedonia considered it very important from the standpoint of the maintenance of international security that no efforts be spared to keep at least a minimal light of hope alive in the Balkans.

REFERENCES

[1]YUN 1992, p. 327. [2]S/25806 & S/25807. [3]S/25490. [4]S/1994/83. [5]YUN 1992, p. 333, SC res. 743(1992), 21 Feb. 1992. [6]Ibid., p. 386, SC res. 795(1992), 11 Dec. 1992. [7]S/26838. [8]S/26839. [9]A/47/741/Add.1 & Corr.1. [10]YUN 1992, p. 385, GA res. 47/210 A, 22 Dec. 1992. [11]YUN 1991, p. 869, GA res. 46/187, 20 Dec. 1991. [12]A/47/986. [13]A/47/990. [14]A/48/690. [15]A/C.5/48/40. [16]A/48/776. [17]YUN 1992, p. 366, SC res. 771(1992), 13 Aug. 1992. [18]Ibid., p. 370, SC res. 780(1992), 6 Oct. 1992. [19]S/25377 & S/25613. [20]S/25392 & S/26016. [21]S/26737. [22]S/25171, S/25393, S/25586 & S/25969. [23]S/25205 & S/26737. [24]S/25082, S/25094, S/25129, S/25702, S/26454, S/26455 & S/26617. [25]A/48/77-S/25231, S/25345, S/25346, S/25421 & Add.1 & S/26894. [26]S/25266. [27]S/25300. [28]S/25307. [29]S/25274. [30]A/47/920-S/25512. [31]A/47/922-S/25540. [32]S/25504 & S/25594. [33]S/25417. [34]S/25716. [35]S/25537. [36]S/25652. [37]S/25575. [38]A/48/170-S/25801. [39]S/25704. [40]S/25704/Add.1. [41]A/47/955. [42]A/47/1003. [43]A/47/1005. [44]A/47/1006. [45]A/47/980. [46]A/47/1002. [47]A/C.5/48/44. [48]A/48/765. [49]YUN 1991, p. 215, SC res. 713(1991), 25 Sep. 1991. [50]YUN 1992, p. 352, SC res. 757(1991), 30 May 1992. [51]Ibid., p. 375, SC res. 787(1992), 16 Nov. 1992. [52]YUN 1991, p. 219, SC res 724(1991), 15 Dec. 1991. [53]S/25189. [54]S/25182. [55]S/25190. [56]S/25195. [57]S/25201. [58]S/25270. [59]S/25347. [60]S/25351. [61]S/25396. [62]S/25808. [63]S/26206. [64]S/26562. [65]S/26572. [66]S/26903. [67]S/25743, S/25804 & S/26041. [68]S/25683. [69]S/25207. [70]S/25894. [71]S/25630, S/25636 & S/25682. [72]S/25322. [73]S/25869. [74]S/26167 & S/26673. [75]A/48/408-S/26461. [76]A/48/602-S/26749. [77]S/26040. [78]S/26056. [79]A/47/859-S/25087. [80]S/25074. [81]S/25077. [82]S/25079. [83]A/47/862-S/25089. [84]S/25130. [85]A/47/879-S/25194. [86]S/25204. [87]YUN 1992, p. 365, SC res. 770(1992), 13 Aug. 1992. [88]S/25353. [89]S/25358. [90]S/25361. [91]S/25367. [92]A/47/903-S/25372. [93]S/25434. [94]S/25459. [95]S/25456. [96]S/25519. [97]S/25520. [98]S/25529. [99]S/25566. [100]S/25604. [101]S/25609. [102]S/25616. [103]YUN 1948-49, p. 959, GA res. 260 A (III), annex, 9 Dec. 1948. [104]S/25645. [105]S/25607. [106]S/25615. [107]S/25700. [108]S/25624 & S/25629. [109]S/25670. [110]S/25681. [111]S/25718. [112]S/25728. [113]S/25730. [114]S/25731. [115]S/25782. [116]S/25800. [117]S/25823. [118]A/47/958-S/25860. [119]S/25872.

(120)S/25877. (121)S/25824. (122)S/25825. (123)S/25939 & Corr.1.
(124)S/25939/Add.1. (125)S/25908, S/25909, S/25933, S/25943 &
S/25959. (126)S/26223 & S/26224. (127)S/26335 & S/26336.
(128)S/26042. (129)S/26107. (130)S/26134. (131)S/26144, S/26754
& S/26782. (132)S/26227. (133)S/26232. (134)S/26244. (135)S/26245.
(136)S/26367. (137)S/26601. (138)S/26815. (139)S/26607 & S/26704.
(140)S/26870. (141)S/25646. (142)S/25659. (143)S/25749.
(144)S/25748. (145)S/25746. (146)S/26641. (147)S/26661.
(148)S/26742. (149)S/26690. (150)S/26715. (151)S/26692.
(152)S/26716. (153)S/26717. (154)S/26726. (155)S/25443.
(156)S/25444. (157)YUN 1992, p. 371, SC res. 781(1992),
9 Oct. 1992. (158)Ibid., p. 373, SC res. 786(1992), 10 Nov. 1992.
(159)S/25426. (160)S/25691. (161)S/25450. (162)S/25457.
(163)S/25567. (164)S/25608. (165)S/25649. (166)S/25264 & Corr.1.
(167)S/24900/Add.8-65, Add.66 & Corr.1, Add.67-70, Add.71 &
Corr.1, Add.72 & Corr.1 & Add.73-103. (168)S/25997.
(169)A/48/659-S/26806. (170)YUN 1965, p. 440, GA res.
2106 A (XX), annex, 21 Dec. 1965. (171)A/48/736-S/26847.
(172)S/26908. (173)S/26672. (174)YUN 1992, p. 350, SC res.
752(1992), 5 May 1992. (175)Ibid., p. 378. (176)S/25829.
(177)S/25874. (178)S/25907. (179)S/26018 & Corr.1. (180)S/26018/
Add.1. (181)S/26049. (182)YUN 1992, p. 344. (183)S/25050.
(184)S/25080. (185)S/25100. (186)S/25221. (187)S/25248.
(188)S/25328. (189)S/25403. (190)S/25471. (191)S/25479.
(192)S/25622. (193)S/25623. (194)S/25546. (195)S/25580.
(196)S/25605. (197)S/25607. (198)S/25708. (199)S/25709.
(200)S/26066. (201)S/26233. (202)S/26260. (203)S/26281.
(204)S/26309. (205)S/26337. (206)S/26337/Add.1. (207)S/26337/
Add.2. (208)S/26395. (209)S/26486. (210)S/26922. (211)YUN 1992,
p. 378, SC res. 798(1992), 18 Dec. 1992. (212)S/25240.
(213)S/25557. (214)S/26419. (215)S/26437. (216)S/25686.
(217)S/25616. (218)S/26442. (219)S/25099. (220)YUN 1992, p. 365,
SC res. 770(1992), 13 Aug. 1992. (221)A/47/871-S/25120.
(222)S/25162. (223)S/25302. (224)S/25330. (225)S/25334. (226)YUN
1992, p. 328. (227)S/25139. (228)S/25145. (229)S/25156.
(230)S/25154. (231)S/25178. (232)S/25264 & Corr.1. (233)S/25470
& Add.1. (234)S/25555. (235)YUN 1991, p. 217. (236)YUN 1992,
p. 329. (237)YUN 1992, p. 339, SC res. 762(1992), 30 June
1992. (238)S/25708. (239)S/25777. (240)YUN 1992, p. 341, SC
res. 769(1992), 7 Aug. 1992. (241)S/25447. (242)S/25601.
(243)S/25766. (244)S/25777/Add.1. (245)S/26619 & S/26620.
(246)S/25854. (247)S/25897. (248)S/25993. (249)S/26002.
(250)S/26017. (251)S/26128. (252)S/26074. (253)S/26082. (254)S/26084.
(255)S/26199. (256)S/26310. (257)A/47/967-S/25973. (258)S/26220.
(259)S/26470. (260)S/26436. (261)S/26470/Add.1. (262)S/26491.
(263)S/26828. (264) S/26681. (265)S/26890. (266)S/26373. (267)S/26374.
(268)S/25954 & Add.1. (269)S/26099. (270)S/26130. (271)S/26121.
(272)S/26148. (273)S/26210. (274)A/48/290-S/26234. (275)S/26279.
(276)S/25662. (277)S/25672. (278)S/25866. (279)S/25997.
(280)A/48/257-S/26070. (281)S/26277. (282)S/26278. (283)A/48/395-
S/26439. (284)S/25711. (285)S/25934. (286)S/26346. (287)A/48/603.
(288)A/48/638-S/26788. (289)S/26879.

Baltic States

The Secretary-General kept himself closely informed of the negotiations between the three Baltic States—Estonia, Latvia and Lithuania—and the Russian Federation on the withdrawal of the armed forces of the former Soviet Union from the Baltic States and related issues. The Baltic States had been pressing for the removal from their territories of Soviet, and then Russian, forces since the restoration of their independence in 1991.

In August 1993, the Secretary-General appointed Professor Tommy Koh of Singapore as his Special Envoy to lead a good offices mission to the Russian Federation and the Baltic States. The results of his mission, which visited all four States from 29 August to 9 September, and other related developments were outlined in an October report of the Secretary-General.[1]

The situation with respect to Lithuania had almost been resolved, as the last Russian combat unit was withdrawn from that country on 31 August, and a few hundred remaining unarmed Russian troops were to be withdrawn shortly. Russian officials confirmed to the Special Envoy their readiness to withdraw their remaining troops from Estonia and Latvia, but stated that there were outstanding problems regarding the terms and conditions of their withdrawal, as well as the satisfactory resolution of some related issues. These included the status and social benefits of retired Russian military personnel in Estonia and Latvia, an agreement on a former Soviet submarine training centre in Estonia, and three strategic facilities in Latvia. Both Estonia and Latvia wished all Russian troops to be withdrawn before the end of the year, but the Russian Federation offered to withdraw them by the end of 1994.

Following the departure of the Special Envoy from the area, further rounds of negotiations were held between Estonia and the Russian Federation on 14 and 15 September, and between Latvia and the Russian Federation on 27 and 28 September. However, no major progress was achieved on the issue of troop withdrawal.

The Secretary-General urged Member States and regional organizations, such as CSCE and the Council of Europe, to continue to take all possible actions to help resolve remaining questions. He commended countries that had joined in a multinational effort to help the Russian Federation build the necessary housing for troops and their families returning from the Baltic States.

During the year, Latvia, Lithuania and the Russian Federation sent communications to the Secretary-General relating to the troop withdrawal.[2]

GENERAL ASSEMBLY ACTION

On 15 November, the General Assembly adopted without vote **resolution 48/18**.

Complete withdrawal of foreign military forces from the territories of the Baltic States

The General Assembly,

Reaffirming its resolution 47/21 of 25 November 1992,

Having considered the report of the Secretary-General on the complete withdrawal of foreign military forces from the territories of the Baltic States,

Conscious of the statement in the report of the Secretary-General that "delay in completing the withdrawal of foreign military forces from the territories"

of Estonia and Latvia "is rightly a matter of concern to the international community",

Considering that the United Nations, pursuant to the provisions of its Charter, has a major role to play in, and responsibility for, the maintenance of international peace and security,

Mindful that the timely application of preventive diplomacy is the most desirable and efficient means of easing tensions before they result in conflict,

Recalling with particular satisfaction that independence was restored in Estonia, Latvia and Lithuania through peaceful and democratic means,

Recognizing that the stationing of foreign military forces in the territories of Estonia and Latvia without the required consent of those countries is a problem remaining from the past that must be resolved in a peaceful manner,

Welcoming the withdrawal of the military forces of the Russian Federation from the territory of Lithuania, which was completed on 31 August 1993 in accordance with a previously agreed timetable,

Welcoming also the progress achieved in reducing the foreign military presence in Estonia and Latvia,

Concerned that the bilateral talks on the complete withdrawal of foreign military forces from the territories of Estonia and Latvia, initiated in February 1992, have not yet yielded agreements, as called for in resolution 47/21,

Recognizing that the completion of the withdrawal of foreign military forces from the territories of Estonia and Latvia will facilitate the consolidation of their restored independence and the rebuilding of their economies,

Welcoming further the good offices mission that the Secretary-General recently sent to the Baltic States and the Russian Federation in pursuit of the implementation of resolution 47/21,

Recalling the "Helsinki Document 1992 - the Challenges of Change", in particular paragraph 15 of the Helsinki Summit Declaration, agreed upon at the meeting of the Conference on Security and Cooperation in Europe held at Helsinki on 9 and 10 July 1992,

Recognizing also that the Conference on Security and Cooperation in Europe is a regional arrangement, and as such provides an important link between European and global security,

Recognizing further that regional organizations participating in complementary efforts with the United Nations may encourage States outside the region to act supportively,

1. *Calls again upon* the States concerned, in line with the basic principles of international law and in order to prevent any possible conflict, to conclude without delay appropriate agreements, including timetables, for the early, orderly and complete withdrawal of foreign military forces from the territories of Estonia and Latvia;

2. *Reaffirms its support* for the efforts made by the States participating in the Conference on Security and Cooperation in Europe to remove the foreign military forces stationed in the territories of Estonia and Latvia without the required consent of those countries, in a peaceful manner and through negotiations;

3. *Welcomes* the multilateral efforts to help the Russian Federation build housing for troops and their families returning from Estonia and Latvia;

4. *Invites* the States concerned to avoid any statements or actions that may be provocative or unfriendly;

5. *Expresses its appreciation* for the efforts of the Secretary-General aimed at the implementation of resolution 47/21,

including the sending of a good offices mission to the Baltic States and the Russian Federation;

6. *Urges* the Secretary-General to continue to use his good offices to facilitate the complete withdrawal of foreign military forces from the territories of Estonia and Latvia;

7. *Requests* the Secretary-General to keep Member States informed of progress towards the implementation of the present resolution and to report thereon to the General Assembly at its forty-ninth session;

8. *Decides* to include in the provisional agenda of its forty-ninth session the item entitled "Complete withdrawal of foreign military forces from the territories of the Baltic States".

General Assembly resolution 48/18

15 November 1993   Meeting 55   Adopted without vote

3-nation draft (A/48/L.17/Rev.2); agenda item 32.
Sponsors: Estonia, Latvia, Lithuania.

Introducing the draft, Latvia said there had not been significant progress on the part of the Russian Federation in adhering to a 1992 Assembly request[3] for the early, orderly and complete withdrawal of its troops. In fact, the Russian Federation had put forward several conditions and acted in contradiction to such requirements. Rhetoric regarding the Russian-speaking population in Latvia and the desire to retain some military facilities left room for doubt as to whether the Russian Federation had the political will to remove its troops from Latvia, and gave the impression that it still wanted to keep its military presence in the region. Latvia urged the Russian Federation, other Member States and the international community to continue working towards the withdrawal of foreign military forces from Latvia and Estonia.

The Russian Federation stated that it was making active efforts to build full-fledged good-neighbourly relations with Latvia and Estonia and to ensure the earliest possible settlement of problems in those relations, including the presence of military forces of the former Soviet Union in the two States. The full withdrawal of troops from Lithuania within the agreed time-frame showed Russia's good will. Considerable progress had been achieved in reducing the numbers of Russian troops in Latvia and Estonia, where their numbers had been reduced from 57,000 to 17,000, and from 25,000 to 4,000, respectively. The problem of troop withdrawal from those two countries was not political and the Russian Federation was attempting to complete it as early as technically possible. One serious obstacle to speedy withdrawal was the lack of housing in Russia for returning troops and family members. Another problem was that of approximately 90,000 retired Russian military personnel and family members permanently residing in Latvia and Estonia, whose situation could only be described as tragic. The Russian Federation expected that that acute humanitarian aspect of the problem would soon find a civilized solution.

REFERENCES
(1)A/48/501. (2)A/48/161, S/26104, A/48/328-S/26334, A/48/343-S/26343, A/48/348, A/48/352-S/26370, A/48/361, A/48/386. (3)YUN 1992, p. 387, GA res. 47/21, 25 Nov. 1992.

Other States

Armenia-Azerbaijan

The year 1993 marked over five years of fighting between Armenian and Azerbaijani inhabitants in and around Nagorny Karabakh, an enclave in Azerbaijan. Armenia and Azerbaijan— two newly independent States, admitted to the United Nations in 1992—were involved in the situation, and submitted numerous communications regarding it throughout the year to the Security Council.

Armenia, on 22 January 1993,[1] circulated a statement by the Chairman of the Legislature of Nagorny Karabakh, stating that the recognition of the Nagorny Karabakh Republic as a full party to negotiations would help the peace process. Azerbaijan, on 27 January,[2] protested that that statement, from a citizen of Azerbaijan claiming to be the leader of a non-existent administrative-territorial entity in Azerbaijan, was circulated as a Council document. On the same date,[3] Armenia warned that its blockade by Azerbaijan turned a critical situation into a catastrophe.

SECURITY COUNCIL ACTION (29 January)

After Security Council consultations held on 29 January, the President of the Council made a statement to the media on behalf of Council members:[4]

"The members of the Security Council express their deep concern at the devastating effect of interruptions in the supply of goods and materials, in particular energy supplies, to Armenia and to the Nakhichevan region of Azerbaijan. They note with serious concern that these interruptions, combined with an unusually harsh winter, have brought the economy and infrastructure of the region to near collapse and created a real threat of starvation.

"The members of the Council urge all countries in a position to help to facilitate the provision of fuel and humanitarian assistance and call on Governments in the region, with a view to preventing a further deterioration of the humanitarian situation, to allow humanitarian supplies to flow freely, in particular fuel to Armenia and to the Nakhichevan region of Azerbaijan.

"The members of the Council reaffirm their full support for the CSCE efforts, designed to bring the parties together and achieve peace in the region. They call upon the parties to agree to an immediate cease-fire, and an early resumption of talks within the CSCE framework.

"The members of the Security Council will keep the matter under consideration."

Communications (February-5 April). Between February and April, Azerbaijan repeatedly accused Armenia of new attacks against its territory, including seizing seven villages in the northern part of Upper Karabakh on 6 and 7 February,[5] and launching an attack on the Kelbadjar district on 27 March.[6]

Armenia, on 1 April,[7] denied the accusations, saying that Azerbaijani forces had launched a massive military offensive on 23 March against the Mardakert area in Nagorny Karabakh and the humanitarian corridor in Lachin. Karabakh Self-Defence Forces had been compelled to take decisive countermeasures, while no military forces from Armenia had taken part in any of those actions.

On 5 April,[8] Azerbaijan charged that Armenian armed forces had virtually completed their occupation of the highland part of Karabakh and the Kelbadjar and Lachin districts of Azerbaijan, and were extending their aggression to the northwest and south of Nagorny Karabakh.

By a joint statement of 16 March,[9] the Presidents of France and the Russian Federation reaffirmed their strong support for settling the conflict in Nagorny Karabakh, within the framework of the Minsk Conference under the auspices of CSCE, and called on all parties to the conflict to bring about an immediate de-escalation in the fighting and an effective cease-fire.

SECURITY COUNCIL ACTION (6 April)

On 3 April,[10] Turkey requested the Security Council urgently to consider the situation between Armenia and Azerbaijan, citing reports of a large-scale offensive by Armenian armed forces in the Azerbaijani district of Kelbadjar. Accordingly, the Council convened on 6 April. Following consultations with the members of the Council, the President made a statement[11] on behalf of the Council, in connection with the item entitled "The situation relating to Nagorny Karabakh":

Meeting number. SC 3194.

"The Security Council expresses its serious concern at the deterioration of relations between the Republic of Armenia and the Republic of Azerbaijan, and at the escalation of hostile acts in the Nagorny Karabakh conflict, especially the invasion of the Kelbadjar district of the Republic of Azerbaijan by local Armenian forces. The Council demands the immediate cessation of all such hostilities, which endanger peace and security of the region, and the withdrawal of these forces.

"In this context, the Security Council, reaffirming the sovereignty and territorial integrity of all States of the region and the inviolability of their borders, expresses its support for the CSCE peace process. It expresses the hope that the recent preliminary agreement reached by the Minsk Group will be expeditiously followed by agreements on a cease-fire, a timetable for the deployment of the monitors, a draft political declaration and the convening, as soon as possible, of the Minsk Conference.

"The Security Council urges the parties involved to take all necessary steps to advance the CSCE peace process and refrain from any action that will obstruct a peaceful solution to the problem.

"The Council also calls for unimpeded access to international humanitarian relief efforts in the region and in particular in all areas affected by the conflict in order to alleviate the suffering of the civilian population.

"The Security Council requests the Secretary-General, in consultation with CSCE, to ascertain facts, as appropriate, and to submit urgently a report to the Council containing an assessment of the situation on the ground.

"The Council will remain seized of the matter."

Communications (7-27 April). Azerbaijan, in numerous communications, accused Armenia of ignoring the Council's requests and of continuing and escalating its aggression against Azerbaijani territory. On 12 April,[12] Azerbaijan said troops from Armenia had launched an attack in the Zangelan and Kubadly districts, and continued attacking and bombarding in some other districts. On 20 April,[13] Azerbaijan said that the armed forces of Armenia had occupied areas in nine Azerbaijani districts and subjected their inhabitants to "ethnic cleansing", and that areas in 11 districts were being systematically subjected to aggression and aerial, artillery and tank bombardment. Also, some 54,000 Azerbaijanis had been the victims of ethnic cleansing in the Nagorny Karabakh area of Azerbaijan. On 29 April,[14] Azerbaijan said that a three-day emergency meeting of the Committee of Senior Officials of CSCE had been counter-productive because of Armenia's unyielding position.

On 17 April,[15] Armenia reported that Azerbaijan had spread its scope of military activity by directing several attacks towards frontier villages on the Armenian side, which were clearly attempts to draw Armenia into the armed confrontation. Several districts in Armenia had been shelled and, on 10 April, Azerbaijani forces had captured the villages of Srashen and Nerkin Hand in the Kapan region of Armenia, but were driven away the next day. Attacks had also taken place against Nagorny Karabakh. Armenia said that Turkey had followed unfriendly statements with some practical actions, including delivering weapons to Azerbaijan and cutting completely the flow of humanitarian shipments destined for Armenia.

Turkey, on 16 April,[16] said allegations of weapons shipment to Azerbaijan, as well as of transportation from Turkey of servicemen disguised as civilians to Nakhichevan, were totally unfounded and deliberately fabricated by the Armenian authorities.

EC, in a 7 April statement,[17] urged Armenia to use its influence on the Nagorny Karabakh forces for an immediate withdrawal from the Azeri territory in the Kelbadjar and Fizuli areas, and requested all parties not to withdraw from the negotiations of the Minsk Group.

Report of the Secretary-General (14 April). In accordance with the Security Council's request of 6 April, the Secretary-General, on 14 April, submitted a report[18] in connection with the situation relating to Nagorny Karabakh. He reported that he had instructed the heads of the United Nations Interim Offices in Armenia and Azerbaijan to undertake field missions to the areas of conflict, which took place between 6 and 12 April.

The United Nations representative in Azerbaijan stated that authorities in the district of Ganja indicated that Azeri forces had lost control over the entire Kelbadjar district, and the fighting in Kelbadjar had led to the displacement of 40,000-50,000 residents. The town of Fizuli appeared to be under military attack. At Koubatly, the mission was told that shelling had occurred from the territory of the Republic of Armenia, as well as from the Lachin corridor and Nagorny Karabakh itself.

In Armenia, the acting United Nations representative reported that there was evidence of substantial destruction, resulting from mortar shelling, in several villages near the Azeri border. Also, a shell exploded near a United Nations vehicle in the town of Khndzorask, and the mission had to leave the village of Korndzor when tank fire began, apparently from the territory of Azerbaijan. A helicopter reconnaissance of the border between Armenia and the Kelbadjar district of Azerbaijan saw no sign of hostilities, military movements or presence of the armed forces of Armenia.

In his observations, the Secretary-General said that the intensification of fighting in and around Nagorny Karabakh, especially the recent attacks against the Kelbadjar and Fizuli districts of Azerbaijan, posed a serious threat to peace and security in the entire Transcaucasus region. He strongly urged all parties to cease fighting and return to the negotiating table within CSCE's Minsk process.

SECURITY COUNCIL ACTION (30 April)

On 30 April, the Security Council convened to consider the Secretary-General's report. The Council invited Armenia and Azerbaijan to participate in the discussion without the right to vote under rule 37ᵃ of its provisional rules of procedure. The Council unanimously adopted **resolution 822(1993)**.

The Security Council,

Recalling the statements of the President of the Security Council of 29 January 1993 and of 6 April 1993 concerning the Nagorny Karabakh conflict,

Taking note of the report of the Secretary-General dated 14 April 1993,

Expressing its serious concern at the deterioration of the relations between the Republic of Armenia and the Republic of Azerbaijan,

Noting with alarm the escalation in armed hostilities and, in particular, the latest invasion of the Kelbadjar district of the Republic of Azerbaijan by local Armenian forces,

Concerned that this situation endangers peace and security in the region,

Expressing grave concern at the displacement of a large number of civilians and the humanitarian emergency in the region, in particular in the Kelbadjar district,

Reaffirming the respect for sovereignty and territorial integrity of all States in the region,

Reaffirming also the inviolability of international borders and the inadmissibility of the use of force for the acquisition of territory,

Expressing its support for the peace process being pursued within the framework of the Conference on Security and Cooperation in Europe and deeply concerned at the disruptive effect that the escalation in armed hostilities can have on that process,

1. *Demands* the immediate cessation of all hostilities and hostile acts with a view to establishing a durable cease-fire, as well as immediate withdrawal of all occupying forces from the Kelbadjar district and other recently occupied areas of Azerbaijan;

2. *Urges* the parties concerned immediately to resume negotiations for the resolution of the conflict within the framework of the peace process of the Minsk Group of the Conference on Security and Cooperation in Europe and refrain from any action that will obstruct a peaceful solution of the problem;

3. *Calls* for unimpeded access for international humanitarian relief efforts in the region, in particular in all areas affected by the conflict in order to alleviate the suffering of the civilian population and reaffirms that all parties are bound to comply with the principles and rules of international humanitarian law;

4. *Requests* the Secretary-General, in consultation with the Chairman-in-Office of the Conference on Security and Cooperation in Europe as well as the Chairman of the Minsk Group of the Conference, to assess the situation in the region, in particular in the Kelbadjar district of Azerbaijan, and to submit a further report to the Council;

5. *Decides* to remain actively seized of the matter.

Security Council resolution 822(1993)

30 April 1993   Meeting 3205   Adopted unanimously

Draft prepared in consultations among Council members (S/25695).

Communications (1 May–27 July). Armenia accused Azerbaijan several times of aggression against it, including shelling of border areas and penetrating into Armenian territory in May,[19] and an air attack on the city of Vardenis in July.[20] On 22 July,[21] Armenia countered what it said was disinformation about the capture of the city of Agdam, stating that Azerbaijani forces had attacked the Karabakh Self-Defence Forces from near Agdam, and that the Karabakh forces had then gone on a counter-offensive to repel the adversary.

Azerbaijan also repeatedly charged Armenia with continued acts of aggression, including: seizing villages in the Kazakh district in May;[22] beginning an offensive, including air attacks, in the direction of the Agdam and Agjabedi districts in Azerbaijan in June;[23] and occupying the city of Agdam on 23 July, and bombarding villages where refugees from Agdam were settled in tent encampments.[24]

An outline of the diplomatic efforts of CSCE was contained in a 27 July report[25] by the Chairman of the Minsk Conference of CSCE on Nagorny Karabakh. He said that both the President of Armenia and the acting President of Azerbaijan had reconfirmed their support for the Minsk Group's timetable of steps to implement Security Council resolution 822(1993), but that the attitude of local Armenian community leaders in Nagorny Karabakh appeared to be rigid and governed by military rather than diplomatic considerations. The Chairman convened a meeting of the nine countries of the Minsk Group in Rome on 22 and 23 July. While the meeting was in process, news was received of the seizure of the Azerbaijani city of Agdam, which prompted a statement unanimously endorsed by the nine States. They strongly condemned the seizure, calling it an unacceptable act, and stated that it was in the interest of the Armenian community of Nagorny Karabakh to withdraw immediately from territories recently seized by force.

SECURITY COUNCIL ACTION (29 July)

In response to requests of Azerbaijan[26] and Turkey,[27] the Security Council convened on 29 July to consider the situation relating to Nagorny Karabakh. The Council invited Armenia, Azerbaijan and Turkey to participate in the discussion without the right to vote under rule 37ᵃ of its provisional rules of procedure. It unanimously adopted **resolution 853(1993)**.

The Security Council,

Reaffirming its resolution 822(1993) of 30 April 1993,

Having considered the report issued on 27 July 1993 by the Chairman of the Minsk Group of the Conference on Security and Cooperation in Europe (CSCE),

Expressing its serious concern at the deterioration of relations between the Republic of Armenia and the Azerbaijani Republic and at the tensions between them,

Welcoming acceptance by the parties concerned of the timetable of urgent steps to implement its resolution 822(1993),

Noting with alarm the escalation in armed hostilities and, in particular, the seizure of the district of Agdam in the Azerbaijani Republic,

Concerned that this situation continues to endanger peace and security in the region,

Expressing once again its grave concern at the displacement of large numbers of civilians in the Azerbaijani Republic and at the serious humanitarian emergency in the region,

Reaffirming the sovereignty and territorial integrity of the Azerbaijani Republic and of all other States in the region,

Reaffirming also the inviolability of international borders and the inadmissibility of the use of force for the acquisition of territory,

1. *Condemns* the seizure of the district of Agdam and of all other recently occupied areas of the Azerbaijani Republic;

2. *Further condemns* all hostile actions in the region, in particular attacks on civilians and bombardments of inhabited areas;

3. *Demands* the immediate cessation of all hostilities and the immediate, complete and unconditional withdrawal of the occupying forces involved from the district of Agdam and all other recently occupied areas of the Azerbaijani Republic;

4. *Calls on* the parties concerned to reach and maintain durable cease-fire arrangements;

5. *Reiterates* in the context of paragraphs 3 and 4 above its earlier calls for the restoration of economic, transport and energy links in the region;

6. *Endorses* the continuing efforts by the Minsk Group of CSCE to achieve a peaceful solution to the conflict, including efforts to implement resolution 822(1993), and expresses its grave concern at the disruptive effect that the escalation of armed hostilities has had on these efforts;

7. *Welcomes* the preparations for a CSCE monitor mission with a timetable for its deployment, as well as consideration within CSCE of the proposal for a CSCE presence in the region;

8. *Urges* the parties concerned to refrain from any action that will obstruct a peaceful solution to the conflict, and to pursue negotiations within the Minsk Group of CSCE, as well as through direct contacts between them, towards a final settlement;

9. *Urges* the Government of the Republic of Armenia to continue to exert its influence to achieve compliance by the Armenians of the Nagorny Karabakh region of the Azerbaijani Republic with its resolution 822(1993) and the present resolution, and the acceptance by this party of the proposals of the Minsk Group of CSCE;

10. *Urges* States to refrain from the supply of any weapons and munitions which might lead to an intensification of the conflict or the continued occupation of territory;

11. *Calls once again* for unimpeded access for international humanitarian relief efforts in the region, in particular in all areas affected by the conflict, in order to alleviate the increased suffering of the civilian population and reaffirms that all parties are bound to comply with the principles and rules of international humanitarian law;

12. *Requests* the Secretary-General and relevant international agencies to provide urgent humanitarian assistance to the affected civilian population and to assist displaced persons to return to their homes;

13. *Requests* the Secretary-General, in consultation with the Chairman-in-Office of CSCE as well as the Chairman of the Minsk Group, to continue to report to the Council on the situation;

14. *Decides* to remain actively seized of the matter.

Security Council resolution 853(1993)

29 July 1993   Meeting 3259   Adopted unanimously

Draft prepared in consultations among Council members (S/26190), orally corrected.

Communications (14 August). Azerbaijan, on 14 August,[28] said that despite Armenia's stated commitment to implement resolution 853(1993), Armenian armed forces had considerably stepped up their military operations in the territory of Azerbaijan, including seizing six populated areas in the Agdam district. Armenia, also on 14 August,[29] said Azerbaijani armed forces had bombarded towns in the Tavush and Ijevan regions in the north-eastern part of Armenia with unprecedented intensity.

SECURITY COUNCIL ACTION (18 August)

On 17 August,[30] Azerbaijan requested a convening of the Security Council, accusing Armenia of continuing aggression and of ignoring previous Council resolutions. Turkey, on the same date,[31] also charged Armenia with continuing its aggression and occupying more Azerbaijani territory, namely in the Fizuli, Djabrail and Agdam districts. Armenia, on 18 August,[32] requested an urgent meeting of the Council to assess the most recent evidence of Azerbaijani aggression and to condemn Azerbaijan's continuing policy of expanding its war against Nagorny Karabakh to the borders of Armenia.

The Council convened accordingly on 18 August. Following consultations with the members of the Council, the President made the following statement[33] on behalf of the Council:

Meeting number. SC 3264.

"The Security Council expresses its serious concern at the deterioration of relations between the Republic of Armenia and the Azerbaijani Republic and at the tensions between them. The Council calls upon the Government of the Republic of Armenia to use its influence to achieve compliance by the Armenians of the Nagorny Karabakh region of the Azerbaijani Republic with its resolutions 822(1993) and 853(1993).

"The Council also expresses its deep concern at the recent intensification of fighting in the area of Fizuli. The Council condemns the attack on the Fizuli region from the Nagorny Karabakh region of the Azerbaijani Republic, just as it has previously condemned the invasion and seizure of the districts of Kelbadjar and Agdam of the Azerbaijani Republic. The Council demands a stop to all attacks and an immediate cessation of the hostilities and bombardments, which endanger peace and security in the region, and an immediate, complete and unconditional withdrawal of occupying forces from the area of Fizuli, and from the districts of Kelbadjar and Agdam and other recently occupied areas of the Azerbaijani Republic. The Council calls upon the Government of the Republic of Armenia to use its unique influence to this end.

"The Council reaffirms the sovereignty and territorial integrity of the Azerbaijani Republic and of all other States in the region and the inviolability of their borders, and expresses its grave concern at the effect these hostilities have had on the efforts of the Minsk Group of the Conference on Security and Cooperation in Europe (CSCE) to achieve a peaceful solution to the conflict. The Council stresses its full support of the CSCE peace process, and notes particularly the opportunity that the current round of Minsk Group talks have afforded the parties to the conflict to present their views directly. In this context, the Council calls upon all of the parties to respond positively and within the agreed time-frame to the 13 August adjusted version of the Minsk Group's 'Timetable of urgent steps to implement United Nations Security Council resolutions 822(1993) and 853(1993)' and to refrain from any actions that would obstruct a peaceful solution. The Council welcomes the intention of CSCE to send a mission to the region to report on all aspects of the situation.

"In the light of this most recent escalation of the conflict, the Council strongly reaffirms its call in resolution 853(1993) for States to refrain from supplying any weapons and munitions which might lead to an intensification of the conflict or the continued occupation of territory of the Azerbaijani Republic. The Council calls upon the Government of the Republic of Armenia to ensure that the forces involved are not provided with the means to extend their military campaign still further.

"The Council also renews its calls in resolutions 822(1993) and 853(1993) for unimpeded access for international humanitarian relief efforts in the region, in all areas affected by the conflict, in order to alleviate the continually increasing suffering of the civilian population. The Council reminds the parties that they are bound by and must adhere to the principles and rules of international humanitarian law.

"The Security Council will remain actively seized of the matter and will be ready to consider appropriate steps to ensure that all parties fully respect and comply with its resolutions."

Communications (1 September–8 October).

On 1 September,[34] Armenia notified the Security Council that Azerbaijan and the Republic of Nagorny Karabakh had signed a cease-fire on 31 August and that their leaders had agreed to meet by 10 September. By a statement of 6 September,[35] EC condemned the recent offensives by local Armenian forces in Nagorny Karabakh, which were making deeper and deeper incursions into Azerbaijani territory.

On 1 October,[36] the Chairman of the Minsk Conference reported on efforts for a peaceful settlement of the Nagorny Karabakh conflict. He said contacts between the parties to the conflict in Moscow on 12 and 13 September and again

around 24 September resulted in the cease-fire of 31 August being extended to 5 October. The consultations had led to the creation of an adjusted timetable of urgent steps to implement Council resolutions 822(1993) and 853(1993) between 18 October and 18 November. Those steps included: the announcement by the Nagorny Karabakh leadership of readiness to withdraw from all recently occupied areas of Azerbaijan, and subsequent gradual withdrawal of forces; the reopening of the main gas pipeline from Azerbaijan into Armenia and Nakhichevan; the reopening of communications and transportation; and the exchange of hostages and prisoners of war. Those and other steps were to be verified by a CSCE mission.

Armenia, on 6 October,[37] said the adjusted timetable was acceptable, while Azerbaijan, on 8 October,[38] said it could not agree to the timetable as it stood, citing, among other things, the following reasons: it introduced prior conditions for a withdrawal of forces from the occupied areas of Azerbaijan, in violation of the Council's demand for unconditional withdrawal; it did not mention the Lachin district or occupied areas in the Zangelan and Kazakh districts, or measures for the liberation of localities in the Nagorny Karabakh region in Azerbaijan; and it did not provide for measures to solve the problem of refugees and displaced persons in Azerbaijan.

SECURITY COUNCIL ACTION (October/November)

In accordance with an understanding reached in prior consultations, the Security Council convened on 14 October to consider the situation relating to Nagorny Karabakh and unanimously adopted **resolution 874(1993)**.

The Security Council,

Reaffirming its resolutions 822(1993) of 30 April 1993 and 853(1993) of 29 July 1993, and recalling the statement read by the President of the Council, on behalf of the Council, on 18 August 1993,

Having considered the letter dated 1 October 1993 from the Chairman of the Conference on Security and Cooperation in Europe (CSCE) Minsk Conference on Nagorny Karabakh addressed to the President of the Security Council,

Expressing its serious concern that a continuation of the conflict in and around the Nagorny Karabakh region of the Azerbaijani Republic, and of the tensions between the Republic of Armenia and the Azerbaijani Republic, would endanger peace and security in the region,

Taking note of the high-level meetings which took place in Moscow on 8 October 1993 and expressing the hope that they will contribute to the improvement of the situation and the peaceful settlement of the conflict,

Reaffirming the sovereignty and territorial integrity of the Azerbaijani Republic and of all other States in the region,

Reaffirming also the inviolability of international borders and the inadmissibility of the use of force for the acquisition of territory,

Expressing once again its grave concern at the human suffering the conflict has caused and at the serious humanitarian emergency in the region and expressing in particular its grave concern at the displacement of large numbers of civilians in the Azerbaijani Republic,

1. *Calls upon* the parties concerned to make effective and permanent the cease-fire established as a result of the direct contacts undertaken with the assistance of the Government of the Russian Federation in support of the CSCE Minsk Group;

2. *Reiterates again* its full support for the peace process being pursued within the framework of CSCE, and for the tireless efforts of the CSCE Minsk Group;

3. *Welcomes and commends* to the parties the "Adjusted timetable of urgent steps to implement Security Council resolutions 822(1993) and 853(1993)" set out on 28 September 1993 at the meeting of the CSCE Minsk Group and submitted to the parties concerned by the Chairman of the Group with the full support of nine other members of the Group, and calls on the parties to accept it;

4. *Expresses the conviction* that all other pending questions arising from the conflict and not directly addressed in the "Adjusted timetable" should be settled expeditiously through peaceful negotiations in the context of the CSCE Minsk process;

5. *Calls* for the immediate implementation of the reciprocal and urgent steps provided for in the CSCE Minsk Group's "Adjusted timetable", including the withdrawal of forces from recently occupied territories and the removal of all obstacles to communications and transportation;

6. *Calls also* for an early convening of the CSCE Minsk Conference for the purpose of arriving at a negotiated settlement to the conflict as provided for in the timetable, in conformity with the 24 March 1992 mandate of the CSCE Council of Ministers;

7. *Requests* the Secretary-General to respond favourably to an invitation to send a representative to attend the CSCE Minsk Conference and to provide all possible assistance for the substantive negotiations that will follow the opening of the Conference;

8. *Supports* the monitoring mission developed by CSCE;

9. *Calls on* all parties to refrain from all violations of international humanitarian law and renews its call in resolutions 822(1993) and 853(1993) for unimpeded access for international humanitarian relief efforts in all areas affected by the conflict;

10. *Urges* all States in the region to refrain from any hostile acts and from any interference or intervention which would lead to the widening of the conflict and undermine peace and security in the region;

11. *Requests* the Secretary-General and relevant international agencies to provide urgent humanitarian assistance to the affected civilian population and to assist refugees and displaced persons to return to their homes in security and dignity;

12. *Requests also* the Secretary-General, the Chairman-in-Office of CSCE and the Chairman of the CSCE Minsk Conference to continue to report to the Council on the progress of the Minsk process and on all aspects of the situation on the ground, and on present and future cooperation between CSCE and the United Nations in this regard;

13. *Decides* to remain actively seized of the matter.

Security Council resolution 874(1993)
14 October 1993   Meeting 3292   Adopted unanimously
Draft prepared in consultations among Council members (S/26582).

On 8 November,[39] in connection with the consideration of the situation in Georgia, the President of the Council, in a statement on behalf of the Council, noted the effects of the continuing disorder in the Republic of Georgia on the humanitarian situation in neighbouring Armenia and Azerbaijan (see below).

Azerbaijan, on 26 October,[40] charged that the armed forces of Armenia had violated the cease-fire agreement and launched a massive attack in the Djebrail, Fizuli, Zangelan and Kubatly districts of Azerbaijan, and had reached the frontier between Azerbaijan and Iran. Turkey, on 27 October,[41] requested the Council to convene urgently in order to take effective enforcement measures to stop the Armenian aggression. Iran, on 28 October,[42] also requested an urgent Council meeting, as fresh Armenian military offensives close to Iran's northern border endangered peace and security in the entire area and threatened the national security of Iran.

On 9 November,[43] the Chairman-in-Office of the Minsk Conference transmitted a declaration by the nine countries of the Minsk Group, condemning the most recent cease-fire violation and seizure of additional territory by force. He also presented a package proposal resulting from a meeting of the Group from 2 to 8 November. The proposal contained a new version of the adjusted timetable of urgent steps to implement Council resolutions 822(1993) and 853(1993) (see above), to which the parties were required to reply by 22 November.

In accordance with the above requests, the Council convened on 12 November. It invited Armenia, Azerbaijan, Iran and Turkey to participate in the discussion without the right to vote under rule 37 of its provisional rules of procedure.[a] The Council unanimously adopted **resolution 884(1993)**.

The Security Council,

Reaffirming its resolutions 822(1993) of 30 April 1993, 853(1993) of 29 July 1993 and 874(1993) of 14 October 1993,

Reaffirming its full support for the peace process being pursued within the framework of the Conference on Security and Cooperation in Europe (CSCE), and for the tireless efforts of the CSCE Minsk Group,

Taking note of the letter dated 9 November 1993 from the Chairman-in-Office of the Minsk Conference on Nagorny Karabakh addressed to the President of the Security Council and its enclosures,

Expressing its serious concern that a continuation of the conflict in and around the Nagorny Karabakh region of the Azerbaijani Republic, and of the tensions between the Republic of Armenia and the Azerbaijani Republic, would endanger peace and security in the region,

Noting with alarm the escalation in armed hostilities as consequence of the violations of the cease-fire and excesses in the use of force in response to those violations, in particular the occupation of the Zangelan district and the city of Goradiz in the Azerbaijani Republic,

Reaffirming the sovereignty and territorial integrity of the Azerbaijani Republic and of all other States in the region,

Reaffirming also the inviolability of international borders and the inadmissibility of the use of force for the acquisition of territory,

Expressing grave concern at the latest displacement of a large number of civilians and the humanitarian emergency in the Zangelan district and the city of Goradiz and on Azerbaijan's southern frontier,

1. *Condemns* the recent violations of the cease-fire established between the parties, which resulted in a resumption of hostilities, and particularly condemns the occupation of the Zangelan district and the city of Goradiz, attacks on civilians and bombardments of the territory of the Azerbaijani Republic;

2. *Calls upon* the Government of Armenia to use its influence to achieve compliance by the Armenians of the Nagorny Karabakh region of the Azerbaijani Republic with resolutions 822(1993), 853(1993) and 874(1993), and to ensure that the forces involved are not provided with the means to extend their military campaign further;

3. *Welcomes* the Declaration of 4 November 1993 of the nine members of the CSCE Minsk Group and commends the proposals contained therein for unilateral cease-fire declarations;

4. *Demands* from the parties concerned the immediate cessation of armed hostilities and hostile acts, the unilateral withdrawal of occupying forces from the Zangelan district and the city of Goradiz, and the withdrawal of occupying forces from other recently occupied areas of the Azerbaijani Republic in accordance with the "Adjusted timetable of urgent steps to implement Security Council resolutions 822(1993) and 853(1993)" as amended by the CSCE Minsk Group meeting in Vienna of 2 to 8 November 1993;

5. *Strongly urges* the parties concerned to resume promptly and to make effective and permanent the cease-fire established as a result of the direct contacts undertaken with the assistance of the Government of the Russian Federation in support of the CSCE Minsk Group, and to continue to seek a negotiated settlement of the conflict within the context of the CSCE Minsk process and the "Adjusted timetable" as amended by the CSCE Minsk Group meeting in Vienna of 2 to 8 November 1993;

6. *Urges again* all States in the region to refrain from any hostile acts and from any interference or intervention, which would lead to the widening of the conflict and undermine peace and security in the region;

7. *Requests* the Secretary-General and relevant international agencies to provide urgent humanitarian assistance to the affected civilian population, including that in the Zangelan district and the city of Goradiz and on Azerbaijan's southern frontier, and to assist refugees and displaced persons to return to their homes in security and dignity;

8. *Reiterates* its request that the Secretary-General, the Chairman-in-Office of CSCE and the Chairman of the CSCE Minsk Conference continue to report to the Council on the progress of the Minsk process and on all aspects of the situation on the ground, in particular on the implementation of its relevant resolutions, and on present and future cooperation between CSCE and the United Nations in this regard;

9. *Decides* to remain actively seized of the matter.

Security Council resolution 884(1993)

12 November 1993   Meeting 3313   Adopted unanimously

Draft prepared in consultations among Council members (S/26719).

Georgia
Report of the Secretary-General (January).

On 28 January,[44] the Secretary-General reported on developments in Abkhazia, in the northwestern part of Georgia, where armed conflict had broken out in 1992.[45] He said the situation in Abkhazia had further deteriorated since he reported to the Security Council in November 1992.[46] An agreement resulting from a meeting between the President of the Russian Federation and the Chairman of the State Council of the Republic of Georgia on 3 September 1992[47] still offered the best basis for a resumption of the peace process.

The main military confrontation lines between the Georgian and Abkhaz forces had remained virtually unchanged since early October 1992, despite intensified fighting in some areas. The unabated fighting in Abkhazia had led to the displacement of tens of thousands of civilians and created a serious humanitarian situation which had been aggravated by the winter season. The Georgian authorities had expressed concern that some of the Russian military units stationed in Abkhazia were supporting the Abkhaz forces. In order to assess the situation, the Secretary-General considered dispatching a new mission.

SECURITY COUNCIL ACTION (January)

In accordance with an understanding reached in prior consultations and in response to a request by Georgia contained in a letter of December 1992,[46] the Security Council convened on 29 January to consider the situation in Georgia, including the Secretary-General's 28 January report. At its request, the President of the Council invited Georgia under rule 37 of the Council's provisional rules of procedure.[a] The President made a statement on behalf of the Council:[48]

Meeting number. SC 3169.

"The Security Council notes with appreciation the report of the Secretary-General on the situation in Abkhazia, Republic of Georgia.

"The Council expresses its grave preoccupation regarding the further deterioration of the situation in Abkhazia and calls on all the parties immediately to cease the fighting and to observe and implement faith-fully the terms of the agreement of 3 September 1992, which affirms that the territorial integrity of Georgia shall be ensured, which provides for a cease-fire and the commitment by the parties not to resort to the use of force, and which constitutes the basis for an over-all political solution.

"The Council shares the observation of the Secretary-General that the restoration of a viable peace process in Abkhazia, based on the agreement of 3 September 1992, may require more active sup-port by the international community to assist the par-ties to agree to a cease-fire, to the return of refugees and to work out a political settlement; and in that con-text, the Council reiterates its support for the current efforts undertaken by the Conference on Security and Cooperation in Europe (CSCE).

"The Council endorses, to this end, the proposal of the Secretary-General to send a new mission to Georgia to review the situation in Abkhazia and it stresses the need to ensure effective coordination be-tween the activities of the United Nations and those of CSCE aiming at restoring peace. The Council be-lieves that it is necessary to assess the overall political situation and to discuss and provide advice on prac-tical matters such as the establishment and monitor-ing of an immediate cease-fire, the monitoring of the border in Abkhazia between Georgia and the Rus-sian Federation, and the protection of the railway and communication links in Abkhazia.

"The Council also endorses the proposal of the Secretary-General to send a fact-finding mission to Abkhazia to look into the allegation of violations of international humanitarian law by both sides.

"The Council requests the Secretary-General to re-port on the outcome of the mission and to propose measures to consolidate the cease-fire and for an over-all political settlement."

Communications and report of the Secretary-General (May and July). On 5 May,[49] the Secretary-General notified the President of the Security Council that in view of the further de-terioration of the situation in Abkhazia, he found the dispatch of another visiting mission an inade-quate approach to revive the peace process and had decided to appoint Edouard Brunner of Swit-zerland as his Special Envoy for Georgia. His tasks would be to: obtain a cease-fire agreement; assist the parties in reviving the process of negotiations to find a political solution to the conflict; and en-list the support of neighbouring countries and others concerned for those objectives. The Coun-cil members welcomed the Secretary-General's de-cision, according to a letter of 11 May from its President.[50]

In a 1 July report,[51] the Secretary-General described the first mission of his Special Envoy to Georgia from 20 to 25 May, as well as intensified efforts of the United Nations to seek a settlement of the conflict in Abkhazia. He characterized the situation in Georgia as deteriorating and as hav-ing a devastating effect on the country's economy.

A cease-fire agreement, which came into effect on 20 May, held for two weeks or so, but later was violated daily, especially by Abkhaz shelling of Sukhumi, the capital of Abkhazia, which was still held by forces loyal to the Government. Civilian casualties were on the rise, and Eduard Shevard-nadze, Georgia's head of State, feared an immi-nent assault on Sukhumi across the river Gumista, which constituted a no-man's land between the op-posing forces to the north of the city itself.

The Special Envoy met with Georgian officials at Tblisi, the capital of Georgia, and Sukhumi, and with Abkhaz leaders at Gudauta, the seat of the Abkhaz party. In Moscow, he met with Rus-sian leaders, and at Stockholm, with the Minister for Foreign Affairs of Sweden, who was Chairman-in-Office of CSCE. Those consultations revealed that the Georgian Government and its supporters at Sukhumi supported the Secretary-General's ap-proach of a solution along three tracks: consoli-dation of the cease-fire, the launching of a politi-cal negotiating process, and support for those processes by neighbouring countries, pre-eminently the Russian Federation. The Abkhaz side favoured a United Nations–sponsored peace conference, but not the deployment of military ob-servers, while the Russian side favoured such deployment, but had reservations about a con-ference.

In view of the urgent need to get the conflict under control, the Secretary-General recom-mended that a group of 50 United Nations mili-tary observers be deployed to Georgia, initially in the Sukhumi and Ochamchira districts of Abkha-zia, with a mandate to: discourage further escala-tion of the conflict; use its good offices to reinstate the cease-fire agreement; report cease-fire viola-tions and endeavour to restore the status quo; and attempt to establish communications between the two sides to forestall violations.

On 7 July,[52] the Secretary-General, describing a serious deterioration in the military situation in and around Sukhumi, said that it would not be wise to proceed with the actual deployment of 50 military observers until the cease-fire was re-established and was being respected.

SECURITY COUNCIL ACTION (July and August)

On 2 July,[53] Georgia requested an emergency meeting of the Security Council, citing intense ar-tillery bombardment of the residential areas of Sukhumi, causing civilian casualties at a catas-trophic rate. Abkhazian separatists had com-menced a wide-scale offensive along the entire front, Georgia said, and, in the coastal area con-trolled by frontier troops of the Russian Federa-tion, assault forces were landing, consisting primarily of citizens of the Russian Federation.

Following consultations with the members of the Council, the President made the following statement on 2 July[54] on behalf of the Council:

Meeting number. SC 3249.

"The Security Council has considered the letter dated 2 July 1993 from the Head of State of the Republic of Georgia concerning the situation in Abkhazia, Republic of Georgia. The Council expresses its deep concern at the reports of increased fighting around Sukhumi. The Council calls on all the parties to cease military action immediately, and to respect the cease-fire agreement of 14 May 1993. The Council will consider without delay the report of the Secretary-General of 1 July 1993, and the recommendations therein."

On 9 July, the Council convened again to consider the situation in Georgia, including the Secretary-General's July report. The Council invited Georgia to participate in the discussion without the right to vote under rule 37 of its provisional rules of procedure.[a] The Council adopted unanimously **resolution 849(1993)**.

The Security Council,

Having considered the report of the Secretary-General of 1 July 1993,

Recalling the statements made by the President of the Security Council on 10 September 1992, 8 October 1992 and 29 January 1993 concerning the situation in Abkhazia, Republic of Georgia,

Recalling the Moscow Agreement of 3 September 1992,

Endorsing the approach set out in the Secretary-General's letter of 5 May 1993 to the President of the Security Council,

Noting with concern the recent intensification of fighting around Sukhumi,

Reaffirming the statement made by the President of the Security Council on 2 July 1993, which called in particular on all parties to respect the cease-fire agreement of 14 May 1993,

Stressing the importance it attaches, in the context of the deployment of military observers, to the existence and implementation of a cease-fire and a peace process with the effective involvement of the United Nations,

1. *Notes with appreciation* the observations contained in the Secretary-General's report;

2. *Requests* the Secretary-General to send his Special Envoy to the region to assist in reaching agreement on the implementation of the cease-fire; and to begin immediately the necessary preparations, including contacting Member States which may be able to make observers available and sending a planning team to the area, for the dispatch of 50 military observers to Georgia once the cease-fire is implemented;

3. *Further requests* the Secretary-General to notify the Council, for its decision, when the cease-fire has been implemented and in his view conditions permit the deployment of the observers, and to make recommendations at that stage for their mandate, and declares its readiness to act expeditiously upon such notification;

4. *Welcomes* in this context the Secretary-General's continuing efforts to launch a peace process involving the parties to the conflict and with the participation of the Government of the Russian Federation as a facilitator;

5. *Supports* the Secretary-General's continuing cooperation with the Chairman-in-Office of the Conference on Security and Cooperation in Europe in their efforts to bring peace to the region;

6. *Calls on* the Government of the Republic of Georgia to enter expeditiously into discussion with the United Nations on a status of forces agreement to facilitate early deployment of observers when the Council so decides;

7. *Decides* to remain seized of the matter.

Security Council resolution 849(1993)

9 July 1993   Meeting 3252   Adopted unanimously

Draft prepared in consultations among Council members (S/26053), orally revised.

On 2 August,[55] Georgia stated that an agreement on a cease-fire in Abkhazia had been signed. On 4 August,[56] the Secretary-General informed the Council that he had dispatched a planning team to Abkhazia on 19 July, which returned to New York on 27 July. In view of the fact that the cease-fire agreement of 27 July took effect on 28 July and conditions now permitted the immediate deployment of observers, he proposed to dispatch an advance team of 5-10 observers to the conflict area as soon as possible.

The Council convened on 6 August, in accordance with an understanding reached in prior consultations, to consider the Secretary-General's 4 August letter. It unanimously adopted **resolution 854(1993)**.

The Security Council,

Recalling its resolution 849(1993) of 9 July 1993, which reserved to the Council a decision on the deployment of military observers, following implementation of a cease-fire,

Welcoming the signing on 27 July 1993 of the agreement establishing the cease-fire in Abkhazia, Republic of Georgia,

1. *Approves* the Secretary-General's proposal as contained in his letter of 4 August 1993 to the President of the Security Council that an advance team of up to ten United Nations military observers be deployed to the region as soon as possible to begin to help to verify compliance with the cease-fire as envisaged in the cease-fire agreement, the mandate of the team to expire within three months, and contemplates that this advance team will be incorporated into a United Nations observer mission if such a mission is formally established by the Council;

2. *Looks forward* to the report of the Secretary-General on the proposed establishment of a United Nations observer mission, including in particular a detailed estimate of the cost and the scope of this operation, a timeframe for its implementation, and the projected conclusion of this operation;

3. *Decides* to remain seized of the matter.

Security Council resolution 854(1993)

6 August 1993   Meeting 3261   Adopted unanimously

Draft prepared in consultations among Council members (S/26258), orally revised.

Report of the Secretary-General (August). On 6 August,[57] the Secretary-General reported on the efforts of his Special Envoy and an international planning team to prepare for the deployment of military observers in the light of the 27 July cease-fire agreement, which was annexed to the report. He described his concept of operation for a military observer mission to be known as the "United Nations Observer Mission in Georgia" (UNOMIG) which, he said, would provide a major stabilizing effect for the observance of the cease-fire. After considering the findings of the planning team, the Secretary-General reached the conclusion that the dispatch of 50 military observers would not be sufficient to cope with the situation that had developed since the 27 July agreement, so he suggested that its mandate be expanded to include 88 military observers and supporting staff.

SECURITY COUNCIL ACTION (August and September)

The Security Council convened on 24 August to consider the Secretary-General's report and unanimously adopted **resolution 858(1993)**.

The Security Council,

Recalling its resolution 849(1993) of 9 July 1993, which reserved to the Council a decision on the deployment of observers, following implementation of a cease-fire,

Welcoming the signing of the cease-fire agreement of 27 July 1993 between the Republic of Georgia and forces in Abkhazia,

Recalling its resolution 854(1993) of 6 August 1993, in which the Council approved the deployment of an advance team of observers for a period of three months,

Having considered the Secretary-General's report,

Reaffirming previous statements which underscored the vital importance of the maintenance of cease-fire agreements, in particular the statement of the President of the Security Council on 2 July 1993,

Determining that continuation of the conflict in Georgia threatens peace and stability in the region,

Noting that the parties to the conflict have committed themselves to withdrawal of forces from Abkhazia and that this withdrawal is at present under way,

1. *Welcomes* the Secretary-General's report of 6 August 1993;

2. *Decides* to establish a United Nations Observer Mission in Georgia (UNOMIG) in accordance with the above-mentioned report, comprising up to eighty-eight military observers, plus minimal staff necessary to support UNOMIG, with the following mandate:

  (a) To verify compliance with the cease-fire agreement of 27 July 1993 with special attention to the situation in the city of Sukhumi;

  (b) To investigate reports of cease-fire violations and to attempt to resolve such incidents with the parties involved;

  (c) To report to the Secretary-General on the implementation of its mandate including, in particular, violations of the cease-fire agreement;

3. *Decides* that UNOMIG is established for a period of six months subject to the proviso that it will be extended beyond the initial ninety days only upon a re-view by the Council based on a report from the Secretary-General whether or not substantive progress had been made towards implementing measures aimed at establishing a lasting peace;

4. *Requests* the Secretary-General to report as appropriate, but in any event within three months, on the activities of UNOMIG;

5. *Decides* to keep under constant review the operational arrangements to implement the mandate contained in this resolution, in the light of any further recommendations that the Secretary-General may make in this regard;

6. *Welcomes* the proposed deployment of mixed interim monitoring groups of Georgian/Abkhaz/Russian units designed to consolidate the cease-fire, and requests the Secretary-General to facilitate cooperation between the United Nations observers and these units within their respective mandates;

7. *Calls on* all parties to respect and implement the Cease-fire Agreement of 27 July 1993 and to cooperate fully with UNOMIG and ensure the safety of all United Nations personnel and all other peace-keeping and humanitarian personnel within Georgia;

8. *Calls on* the Government of the Republic of Georgia to conclude expeditiously with the United Nations a status of forces agreement to facilitate deployment of UNOMIG;

9. *Requests* the Secretary-General to pursue energetically, through his Special Envoy, efforts to facilitate the peace process and negotiations, starting as soon as possible, towards the achievement of a comprehensive political settlement;

10. *Expresses its continuing support* for the Secretary-General's ongoing cooperation with the Chairman-in-Office of the Conference on Security and Cooperation in Europe in efforts to bring peace to Georgia and elsewhere in the region;

11. *Decides* to remain seized of the matter.

Security Council resolution 858(1993)
24 August 1993   Meeting 3268   Adopted unanimously

Draft prepared in consultations among Council members (S/26348).

On 16 September,[58] Georgia requested an urgent Council meeting to discuss what it called a full-scale offensive by the Gudauta grouping of Abkhazia against the cities of Sukhumi and Ochamchira.

The Council convened accordingly on 17 September. Following consultations among its members, the President of the Council made the following statement[59] on behalf of the Council:

Meeting number. SC 3279.

"The Security Council expresses its extreme concern at the outbreak of fighting in Abkhazia, Republic of Georgia, arising from the attacks by the Abkhaz forces on the towns of Sukhumi and Ochamchira.

"The Council strongly condemns this grave violation by the Abkhaz side of the Sochi cease-fire agreement of 27 July 1993, which was mediated by the Russian Federation and welcomed by the Security Council in resolutions 854(1993) of 6 August 1993 and 858(1993) of 24 August 1993.

"The Council strongly demands that the Abkhaz leadership end immediately the hostilities and promptly withdraw all its forces to the cease-fire lines agreed upon in Sochi on 27 July 1993. Failure to take such action can entail the risk of serious consequences.

"The Council urges all countries to encourage the re-establishment of the cease-fire and the resumption of the peace process.

"The Council expresses its strong desire to see the Abkhaz side enter fully into the peace process without further delay.

"The Council notes the oral report of the Secretary-General on 17 September 1993 regarding the situation in Abkhazia, Republic of Georgia, and welcomes his intention to send his Special Envoy for Georgia to Moscow and to the area to assess the situation and to establish a way forward to a peaceful settlement to the dispute.

"The Council looks forward to receiving the Secretary-General's report at an early date."

Report and communications (September and October). On 7 October,[60] the Secretary-General reported on the initial efforts to implement the mandate of UNOMIG and the efforts to start a political process in view of the collapse of the cease-fire and the military advances by the Abkhaz party.

UNOMIG had been in its early stages of deployment when the cease-fire broke down on 16 September and Abkhaz forces launched attacks on Sukhumi and Ochamchira. Patrols and further deployment of both civilian and military staff were suspended, with the strength of the mission standing at 12 military observers. On 27 September, Sukhumi was occupied by Abkhaz forces, and all efforts by Georgian forces to defend their remaining positions in Abkhazia ceased on 1 October.

It was evident that UNOMIG's mandate had been invalidated as a result of the general breakdown of the cease-fire and the collapse of the tripartite machinery responsible for its implementation. The Secretary-General proposed to maintain the current strength of UNOMIG at Sukhumi, where the Chief Military Observer had established contact with officials that arrived with the Abkhaz forces.

Expressing sadness at the suffering inflicted by the fighting on civilians, the Secretary-General said he was particularly shocked by the deliberate attacks on Georgian aircraft on three consecutive days, which had resulted in a heavy toll on human life, and by the large number of displaced persons. There were also alarming reports of atrocities and allegations of ethnic cleansing. He called on the Abkhaz leadership to exercise maximum restraint regarding the civilian population remaining at Sukhumi and elsewhere in Abkhazia.

Georgia sent several communications to the Council after the breakdown of the cease-fire, including a statement of 23 September,[61] accusing Abkhaz forces of carrying out a massacre in the village of Akhaldaba and of shooting down two ci-vilian aircraft with the loss of 67 lives. On 2 October,[62] Georgia said that the Gudauta separatists continued hostilities in the direction of Ochamchira and Gali, even as the defenders of Sukhumi had left the city, and over 100,000 refugees were seeking shelter in the mountainous region of Svaneti.

SECURITY COUNCIL ACTION (19 October)

In response to a request by Georgia,[63] the Security Council convened on 19 October to consider the situation there. The Council again invited Georgia to participate in the discussion without the right to vote under rule 37 of its provisional rules of procedure.[a] The Council unanimously adopted **resolution 876(1993)**.

The Security Council,

Reaffirming its resolutions 849(1993) of 9 July 1993, 854(1993) of 6 August 1993 and 858(1993) of 24 August 1993,

Recalling the statement made by the President of the Council on 17 September 1993, in which the Security Council expressed its extreme concern for the situation in Abkhazia, Republic of Georgia, and urged all countries to encourage the resumption of the peace process,

Having considered the letter from the Chairman of the Parliament, head of State of the Republic of Georgia, dated 12 October 1993,

Having also considered the Secretary-General's report of 7 October 1993,

Deeply concerned at the human suffering caused by conflict in the region, and at reports of "ethnic cleansing" and other serious violations of international humanitarian law,

Determining that continuation of the conflict in Abkhazia, Republic of Georgia, threatens peace and stability in the region,

1. *Affirms* the sovereignty and territorial integrity of the Republic of Georgia;

2. *Reaffirms* its strong condemnation of the grave violation by the Abkhaz side of the cease-fire agreement of 27 July 1993 between the Republic of Georgia and forces in Abkhazia, and subsequent actions in violation of international humanitarian law;

3. *Condemns also* the killing of the Chairman of the Defence Council and Council of Ministers of the Autonomous Republic of Abkhazia;

4. *Demands* that all parties refrain from the use of force and from any violations of international humanitarian law, and welcomes the decision of the Secretary-General to send a fact-finding mission to the Republic of Georgia in this regard, in particular to investigate reports of "ethnic cleansing";

5. *Affirms* the right of refugees and displaced persons to return to their homes, and calls on the parties to facilitate this;

6. *Welcomes* the humanitarian assistance already provided, including by international aid agencies, and urges Member States to contribute towards the relief efforts;

7. *Calls* for unimpeded access for international humanitarian relief assistance in the region;

8. *Calls on* all States to prevent the provision from their territories or by persons under their jurisdiction of all assistance, other than humanitarian assistance, to the Abkhaz side and in particular to prevent the supply of any weapons and munitions;

9. *Reiterates* its support for the efforts of the Secretary-General and his Special Envoy, in cooperation with the Chairman-in-Office of the Conference on Security and Cooperation in Europe and with the assistance of the Government of the Russian Federation as a facilitator, to carry forward the peace process with the aim of achieving an overall political settlement;

10. *Notes* the provisional steps the Secretary-General has taken with regard to the United Nations Observer Mission in Georgia (UNOMIG), and welcomes his intention to provide a further report both on the future of UNOMIG and on the political aspects of the United Nations role in trying to end the conflict in Abkhazia;

11. *Decides* to remain seized of the matter.

Security Council resolution 876(1993)

19 October 1993   Meeting 3295   Adopted unanimously

Draft prepared in consultations among Council members (S/26592).

Report of the Secretary-General (27 October). A report of the Secretary-General dated 27 October[64] updated his political efforts and those of his Special Envoy, as well as the status of UNOMIG. The Special Envoy had discussions at Geneva with the Abkhaz side on 6 and 7 October and with Georgian representatives on 17 and 18 October. In view of the expressed willingness of both sides to meet, the Secretary-General planned for the Special Envoy to hold a first round of discussions with both parties in late November, under United Nations auspices and with the Russian Federation as facilitator. The mandate of UNOMIG having been invalidated by the military developments of 16 to 27 September, he recommended that the Mission be continued at its current military strength of five observers with minimal support staff for a further three months.

SECURITY COUNCIL ACTION (November)

The Council convened on 4 November to consider the Secretary-General's report. It invited Georgia to participate in the discussion without the right to vote under rule 37 of its provisional rules of procedure.[a]

It unanimously adopted **resolution 881(1993)**.

The Security Council,

Reaffirming its resolutions 849(1993) of 9 July 1993, 854(1993) of 6 August 1993, 858(1993) of 24 August 1993 and 876(1993) of 19 October 1993,

Recalling in particular resolution 858(1993) of 24 August 1993, in which the Council decided to establish a United Nations Observer Mission in Georgia (UNOMIG),

Having considered the Secretary-General's report of 27 October 1993 concerning the situation in Abkhazia, Republic of Georgia,

Noting with concern that the original mandate of UNOMIG has been overtaken by the military developments of 16 to 27 September 1993,

Expressing its serious concern that continuation of the conflict in Abkhazia, Republic of Georgia, threatens peace and stability in the region,

1. *Welcomes* the Secretary-General's report of 27 October 1993;

2. *Welcomes also* the continued efforts of the Secretary-General and his Special Envoy, in cooperation with the Chairman-in-Office of the Conference on Security and Cooperation in Europe and with the assistance of the Government of the Russian Federation as facilitator, to carry forward the peace process with the aim of achieving an overall political settlement, and in particular to bring both parties together in late November 1993 in Geneva;

3. *Reiterates* the demand in its resolution 876(1993) that all the parties to the conflict in Abkhazia, Republic of Georgia, refrain from the use of force and from any violation of international humanitarian law, and looks forward to the report of the fact-finding mission sent by the Secretary-General to the Republic of Georgia in this regard;

4. *Approves* the continued presence of UNOMIG in Georgia until 31 January 1994 comprising up to five military observers plus minimal support staff, with the following interim mandate:

(a) To maintain contacts with both sides to the conflict and military contingents of the Russian Federation;

(b) To monitor the situation and report to headquarters, with particular reference to any developments relevant to the efforts of the United Nations to promote a comprehensive political settlement;

5. *Decides* that UNOMIG will not be extended beyond 31 January 1994 unless the Secretary-General reports to the Council that substantive progress has been made towards implementing measures aimed at establishing a lasting peace or that the peace process will be served by the prolongation of its mandate, and requests the Secretary-General to report as appropriate, but in any event by late January 1994, on the activities of UNOMIG;

6. *Requests* the Secretary-General to take planning steps which would enable, upon a further decision by the Council, prompt deployment of additional personnel within the originally authorized strength of UNOMIG if the Secretary-General reports that the situation on the ground and in the peace process warrants it;

7. *Decides* to remain seized of the matter.

Security Council resolution 881(1993)

4 November 1993   Meeting 3304   Adopted unanimously

Draft prepared in consultations among Council members (S/26688).

At an 8 November meeting, the President made the following statement on behalf of the Council:[39]

Meeting number. SC 3307.

"The Security Council is following with deep concern developments in the Republic of Georgia, where the continuing disorder has led to mass suffering of the civilian population and threatens to worsen seriously the humanitarian situation in neighbouring Azerbaijan and Armenia.

"In this connection, the Security Council notes the appeal by the Government of the Republic of Georgia to the Russian Federation, the Azerbaijani Republic and the Republic of Armenia for assistance to protect and ensure the uninterrupted operation of railroads in the Republic of Georgia. These are crucial communication links for the three Transcaucasian countries. The Council welcomes the improvement in security for the lines of communication that has followed the Russian Federation's response, which was made in accordance with the wishes of the Government of the Republic of Georgia.

"The Security Council appeals to the international community to continue its efforts to provide emergency humanitarian assistance to the population of the Republic of Georgia.

"The Security Council will remain seized of the matter, and asks to be kept informed of developments by the parties concerned on a regular basis."

Report of the fact-finding mission. On 17 November,[65] the Secretary-General submitted a report of a fact-finding mission he dispatched to investigate the situation of human rights violations in Abkhazia, Georgia, including allegations of "ethnic cleansing". The mission visited the area from 22 to 30 October, interviewing authorities, as well as victims and witnesses to human rights violations, in Abkhazia and Tbilisi.

The mission concluded that numerous and serious human rights violations had been committed and continued to be committed in Abkhazia since the outbreak of the armed conflict between Georgian government forces and Abkhazian forces in August 1992. Violations of the right to life had taken place on a large scale; the victims were mainly civilians, but also many combatants had been wounded or captured. Other human rights violations included torture and ill-treatment, property rights violations and forced displacements. Both Georgian government forces and Abkhazian forces, as well as irregulars and civilians, had been responsible for such human rights violations, and the victims included members of all ethnic groups inhabiting Abkhazia. The conflict had led to almost complete devastation of huge areas of the country and a massive displacement of population.

In its recommendations, the mission said that investigations should be carried out by both parties to the conflict into all allegations of human rights violations, with a view to clarifying the circumstances and identifying those responsible. Compensation should be granted to the victims or, in the case of extrajudicial executions, to their families, and all illegally occupied houses should be restored to their owners. The right of displaced persons to return to Abkhazia should be ensured. Measures should be taken to ensure that, in carrying out their tasks, the security forces fully respected human rights and observed, in particular, the restrictions on the use of force and firearms as set out in international human rights instruments.

SECURITY COUNCIL ACTION (December)

By a letter to the Security Council President dated 16 December,[66] the Secretary-General stated that a Memorandum of Understanding between the parties, signed at Geneva on 1 December, manifested encouraging progress towards lasting peace in the area. Therefore, he was seeking from the Council a contingent authority to deploy up to 50 additional military observers. The Memorandum of Understanding, signed in the presence of representatives of the United Nations, the Russian Federation and CSCE, was appended to a 9 December letter from Georgia.[67]

The Council convened on 22 December to consider the Secretary-General's letter. It invited Georgia to participate in the discussion without the right to vote, under rule 37 of its provisional rules of procedure,[a] and adopted unanimously **resolution 892(1993)**.

The Security Council,

Reaffirming its resolutions 849(1993) of 9 July 1993, 854(1993) of 6 August 1993, 858(1993) of 24 August 1993, 876(1993) of 19 October 1993 and 881(1993) of 4 November 1993,

Also reaffirming its resolution 868(1993) of 29 September 1993 concerning the security of United Nations operations,

Having considered the Secretary-General's letter of 16 December 1993 concerning the situation in Abkhazia, Republic of Georgia,

Noting the letter of 9 December 1993 from the Permanent Representative of Georgia to the United Nations addressed to the Secretary-General, transmitting the Memorandum of Understanding between the Georgian and Abkhazian sides signed in Geneva on 1 December 1993,

Welcoming the signature of the Memorandum of Understanding,

Taking note that the parties to the Memorandum of Understanding consider that the maintenance of peace would be promoted by an increased international presence in the zone of conflict,

Taking note also of the first expert-level talks held between the parties in Moscow on 15 and 16 December 1993 and of the intention to convene a new round of negotiations in Geneva on 11 January 1994 with a view to achieving a comprehensive political settlement of the conflict,

Noting that encouraging progress has been achieved in the negotiations between the parties, which justifies the deployment of additional United Nations military observers,

Noting also the decisions of the ministerial meeting of the Conference on Security and Cooperation in Europe (CSCE) held in Rome on 30 November and 1 December 1993, and welcoming further the continuing cooperation between the United Nations and CSCE in this matter,

Deeply concerned at the humanitarian situation in Georgia, in particular at the number of displaced persons and refugees,

1. *Welcomes* the Secretary-General's letter of 16 December 1993;

2. *Authorizes* the phased deployment of up to 50 additional United Nations military observers to UNOMIG as recommended by the Secretary-General in his letter to perform the functions described in paragraph 4 of Security Council resolution 881(1993) and in this manner to contribute to the implementation by the parties of the provisions of the Memorandum of Understanding of 1 December 1993; and requests the Secretary-General to inform the Council on the duties of new observers as additional deployments beyond the initial 10 referred to in the Secretary-General's letter are undertaken;

3. *Notes* the intention of the Secretary-General to plan and prepare for a possible further expansion of UNOMIG to ensure prompt deployment should the situation on the ground and the course of negotiations warrant it;

4. *Expresses its willingness* to review the existing mandate of UNOMIG taking into account any progress achieved towards the promotion of a comprehensive political settlement and in the light of the report of the Secretary-General due late January 1994; this report should cover, *inter alia*, the specific activities UNOMIG will undertake, prospects for the mission, and anticipated costs, in the light of the situation on the ground and in the negotiations;

5. *Urges* the parties to comply fully with all the commitments they have undertaken in the Memorandum of Understanding, and in particular with the commitments undertaken in accordance with the main provisions of the cease-fire agreement of 27 July 1993, set out in paragraph 1 of the Memorandum of Understanding;

6. *Urges also* the parties to take all steps necessary to ensure the security of UNOMIG personnel and welcomes the readiness of the Government of the Russian Federation to assist the Secretary-General in this regard;

7. *Urges also* the parties fully to comply with their undertakings in the Memorandum of Understanding to create conditions for the voluntary, safe and speedy return of refugees to the places of their permanent residence and to facilitate the provision of humanitarian assistance to all victims of the conflict;

8. *Urges also* the parties not to take any political or any other steps that could aggravate the existing situation or hinder the process towards a comprehensive political settlement;

9. *Encourages* donor States to make contributions in response to the United Nations humanitarian appeal;

10. *Decides* to remain actively seized of the matter.

Security Council resolution 892(1993)

22 December 1993   Meeting 3325   Adopted unanimously

Draft prepared in consultations among Council members (S/26909).

UN Observer Mission in Georgia

The United Nations Observer Mission in Georgia was established in August 1993 by Security Council **resolution 858(1993)**, with a threefold mandate: to verify compliance with the cease-fire

agreement of 27 July 1993, with special attention to the situation in the city of Sukhumi; to investigate and attempt to resolve cease-fire violations; and to report to the Secretary-General on the implementation of its mandate (see above).

UNOMIG was to establish its headquarters at Sukhumi and maintain three sector headquarters (at Sukhumi and Ochamchira, and at the Psou River) and a liaison office at Tbilisi.

When the cease-fire in Abkhazia broke down on 16 September, UNOMIG consisted of the Chief Military Observer, 10 military observers and 11 civilian staff. The Secretary-General noted that, as a result of the breakdown, UNOMIG's mandate was invalidated, and further deployment of both military and civilian staff was suspended.

On 27 October, the Secretary-General, noting ongoing efforts towards a political settlement of the conflict in Abkhazia, recommended the continuation of UNOMIG for a further three months. The Council, by **resolution 881(1993)** of 4 November, approved the continued presence of UNOMIG in Georgia until 31 January 1994, comprising up to five military observers, with the following interim mandate: to maintain contacts with both sides to the conflict and military contingents of the Russian Federation; and to monitor the situation and report to United Nations Headquarters, with particular reference to any developments relevant to United Nations efforts to promote a comprehensive political settlement. The Council also decided that the mandate of UNOMIG would not be extended beyond 31 January 1994 unless the Secretary-General reported that substantial progress had been made towards a lasting peace or that the peace process would be served by the prolongation of its mandate.

In response to a 27 August letter by the Secretary-General,[68] the Security Council, on 31 August,[69] agreed with his proposal to appoint Brigadier-General John Hvidegaard of Denmark as Chief Military Observer of UNOMIG. On 3 September,[70] the Council agreed to the Secretary-General's 1 September proposal[71] that the military observers of UNOMIG come from the following States: Austria, Bangladesh, the Czech Republic, Denmark, Germany, Greece, Poland, Sierra Leone, Sweden and Switzerland.

Financing of UNOMIG

On 7 July,[72] the Secretary-General estimated the total cost of UNOMIG at $9,005,000 gross for an initial six months. He said that he would recommend to the General Assembly that the costs relating to UNOMIG be considered an expense of the Organization to be borne by Member States in accordance with Article 17, paragraph 2, of the Charter of the United Nations and that the assessments to be levied on Member States be credited to a special account to be established for that purpose.

On 7 August,[73] the Secretary-General estimated that an operation consisting of 88 instead of 50 military observers would cost $16,195,000 gross for a six-month period, and $1,950,000 gross per month after that. On 3 November,[74] he stated that the cost of the continuation of UNOMIG at its then current strength—consisting of the Chief Military Observer, four military observers and six international staff—would amount to $612,000 gross for a further three months, with monthly costs thereafter of $204,000 gross.

In a 6 December report to the Assembly[75] on the financing of UNOMIG, as well as in a 9 December report to the Fifth Committee on the financing of 17 peace-keeping operations,[76] the Secretary-General stated that the cost of UNOMIG from its inception in August 1993 to 31 January 1994 would amount to $2,278,800 gross ($2,198,400 net). Should the Council decide that UNOMIG be maintained beyond 31 January 1994, its monthly maintenance cost was estimated at $252,800 gross ($240,900 net); consequently the cost of the Mission from inception to 30 April 1994 would amount to $3,037,200 gross ($2,921,100 net). ACABQ, also in December,[77] recommended that the Assembly authorize the commitment and assessment of that amount.

GENERAL ASSEMBLY ACTION

In December, the General Assembly adopted without vote **decision 48/475**.

Financing of the United Nations Observer Mission in Georgia

At its 87th plenary meeting, on 23 December 1993, the General Assembly, on the recommendation of the Fifth Committee, in accordance with the framework set out in its resolution 48/227 of 23 December 1993, having considered the report of the Secretary-General on the financing of seventeen peace-keeping operations and the related report of the Advisory Committee on Administrative and Budgetary Questions, and concurring with the observations of the Advisory Committee:

(a) Authorized the Secretary-General, on an exceptional basis, to enter into commitments up to the amount of 2,786,600 United States dollars gross (2,680,100 dollars net) for the United Nations Observer Mission in Georgia for the period from 24 August 1993 to 31 March 1994, should the Security Council extend the mandate beyond 31 January 1994, and requested the Secretary-General to establish a special account for the Observation Mission;

(b) Decided at that time to apportion, as an ad hoc arrangement, the amount of 2,536,200 dollars gross (2,439,300 dollars net) for the period ending 31 January 1994 among Member States in accordance with the composition of groups set out in paragraphs 3 and 4 of Assembly resolution 43/232 of 1 March 1989, as adjusted by the Assembly in its resolutions 44/192 B of 21 December 1989, 45/269 of 27 August 1991, 46/198 A of 20 December 1991, 47/218 A of 23 December 1992 and its decision 48/472 of 23 December 1993, and taking into account the scale of assessments for the years 1992, 1993 and 1994 as set out in Assembly resolutions 46/221 A of 20 December 1991 and 48/223 A of 23 December 1993 and its decision 47/456 of 23 December 1992;

(c) Also decided that, in accordance with the provisions of its resolution 973(X) of 15 December 1955, there should be set off against the apportionment among Member States, as provided for in subparagraph (b) above, their respective share in the Tax Equalization Fund of the estimated staff assessment income of 96,900 dollars for the period from 24 August 1993 to 31 January 1994.

General Assembly decision 48/475

Adopted without vote

Approved by Fifth Committee (A/48/823) without vote, 22 December (meeting 46); draft by Chairman (A/C.5/48/L.26); agenda item 162.
Meeting numbers. GA 48th session: 5th Committee 44, 46; plenary 87.

Republic of Moldova

In 1993, the Republic of Moldova addressed letters to the Secretary-General concerning the presence of Russian troops in the country. On 19 February,[78] it said that the fourteenth Army of the Russian Federation had started large-scale military manoeuvres, ignoring Moldova's opposition to such action. On 16 June,[79] Moldova declared unacceptable a proposal of the President of the Russian Federation regarding the possible creation of military bases on the territories of some former Soviet republics, but considered his second proposal to withdraw Russian military forces from all former Soviet republics a realistic and just solution. On 16 September,[80] Moldova reported that the Commander of the Fourteenth Russian Army had been elected a member of the so-called parliament of the self-proclaimed Dniester Moldovan Republic, an act which Moldova considered a new attempt by certain forces in Russia for a de facto recognition of the Dniester Republic, as well as a clear signal of the unwillingness of the Russian side to withdraw its military units.

Tajikistan

The United Nations Mission of Observers in Tajikistan (UNMOT) became operational on 21 January 1993. It provided the Secretary-General with up-to-date information on the conflict in Tajikistan, and was instrumental in coordinating the international community's response to the humanitarian situation in the country, the Secretary-General said in a 26 April letter[81] to the President of the Security Council.

In that letter, he also announced his decision to appoint Ismat Kittani as his Special Envoy for Tajikistan, with the mandate to: obtain agreement on a cease-fire and make recommendations on an international monitoring mechanism; ascertain the positions of all the concerned parties and make good offices available to help establish negotiations for a political solution; and enlist the help of neighbouring countries and others concerned in achieving the above objectives.

The Secretary-General stated that recent reports from UNMOT had led him to conclude that there could be an escalation of the confrontation, especially in the border areas between Tajikistan and Afghanistan, unless urgent action was taken to establish a cease-fire and start a political dialogue. He suggested an extension of the mandate of UNMOT for another three months.

The Secretary-General's proposals were welcomed by the members of the Security Council, as stated in a letter of 29 April of its President.[82]

On 30 April,[83] the Russian Federation informed the Secretary-General that it had agreed to make available up to 500 men to participate in the military contingent of joint forces for the maintenance of peace in Tajikistan, together with Kazakhstan, Kyrgyzstan and Uzbekistan.

In statements of 13[84] and 15 July,[85] Tajikistan said that, on 13 July, anti-government troops, supported by Afghan mujahidin and subunits under the Ministry of Defence of Afghanistan, had attacked the frontier village of Sarigor in the Shurabad district, resulting in loss of life and injury. Terrorist groups had entrenched themselves in Afghanistan, threatening the situation in Tajikistan as it was healing from its civil war and welcoming returning refugees. On 14 July,[86] the Russian Federation protested to Afghanistan about the 13 July attack on Sarigor and the twelfth frontier post of the Moscow border detachment of the Russian border troops in Tajikistan. The Russian Federation regarded that attack launched from Afghan territory as an act of aggression against its troops and against Tajikistan. (See also PART TWO, Chapter III, on Afghanistan-Tajikistan situation.)

On 4 August,[87] Tajikistan said it had just concluded an operation to rout anti-government guerrillas and Afghan mujahidin from one border area, but the build-up of Tajik armed opposition forces and Afghan mujahidin was continuing in Afghanistan along the frontier with Tajikistan.

The heads of State of Kazakhstan, Kyrgyzstan, the Russian Federation, Tajikistan and Uzbekistan, at a 7 August meeting, adopted a declaration on the inviolability of frontiers; an announcement of measures for the normalization of the situation on the Tajik-Afghan border; and a message of the five countries to the Secretary-General,[88] in which the Foreign Ministers stated that, recently, specific military operations had been undertaken aimed at breaching the frontier and stirring up armed conflict in Tajikistan. The five countries—in accordance with the Treaty on Col-

lective Security that they had signed within the framework of the Commonwealth of Independent States (CIS), and in implementation of the right of individual and collective self-defence under Article 51 of the United Nations Charter—had decided to provide Tajikistan with emergency supplementary assistance, including military assistance.

Report of the Secretary-General (August). On 16 August,[89] the Secretary-General reported on the efforts of his Special Envoy for Tajikistan and on developments in that country. The Special Envoy arrived at Dushanbe, the capital of Tajikistan, on 14 May, where he held talks with the President and other officials. At Khorog, the regional capital of Gorno-Badakhshan, he had discussions with various groups, including the field commanders of the major groups opposing the central Government. He also visited neighbouring and other concerned States for talks with their leaders.

In outlining the background to the situation, the Secretary-General said the conflict in Tajikistan had resulted in thousands of deaths and more than 400,000 refugees and displaced persons. The political and economic structures of the country were disrupted by the disintegration of the Soviet Union, resulting in a struggle between different clans for a redistribution of power. Some members of the Islamic clergy were active in the opposition to the current Government, much of which was based in northern Afghanistan, where there were approximately 60,000 Tajik refugees. As for the latest developments, the Secretary-General said the most serious one was a large-scale attack on 13 July by fighters who crossed in from Afghanistan and occupied a Russian military border post, resulting in 27 deaths.

A solution to the problems of Tajikistan, as emphasized by the Special Envoy, could come about only through peaceful reconciliation with the widest possible participation of all political groups and regions of the country. Given the escalating crisis on the Tajik-Afghan border, the Secretary-General asked the Special Envoy to visit Kabul for discussions with government leaders there. The situation in Tajikistan contained the seeds of a major threat to peace and security for Central Asia and beyond, and required a concerted effort to persuade the Government and the opposition to accept the need for a political solution and to participate in a negotiating process.

SECURITY COUNCIL ACTION

The Security Council convened on 23 August to consider the situation in Tajikistan and along the Tajik-Afghan border. It invited Tajikistan, at its request, to participate in the discussion without the right to vote, in accordance with rule 37 of the Council's provisional rules of procedure.[a] Following consultations with the Council members, the President made a statement on their behalf:[90]

Meeting number. SC 3266.

"The Security Council expresses its deep concern at the continuing violence and armed conflict in Tajikistan, at the escalating crisis along the Tajik-Afghan border, and at the risk of the conflict threatening the peace and stability of Central Asia and beyond.

"The Council stresses the urgent need for the cessation of all hostile actions on the Tajik-Afghan border. It urges the Government of Tajikistan and all opposition groups to accept as soon as possible the need for an overall political solution and to participate in a negotiating process for the early establishment of a cease-fire and eventual national reconciliation with the widest possible participation of all political groups and all the regions of the country. The Council looks to the Government of Tajikistan and all opposition groups to observe basic political rights of all groups in Tajikistan, in order to promote a lasting reconciliation and to achieve full compliance with the principles to which Tajikistan is committed as a participating State in the Conference on Security and Cooperation in Europe (CSCE).

"The Council reaffirms the necessity to respect the sovereignty and territorial integrity of Tajikistan and all other countries of the region and the inviolability of their borders.

"The Council welcomes efforts by regional parties aimed at stabilizing the situation. In particular, the Council welcomes the 7 August 1993 Moscow summit of heads of State and Government from the Republic of Kazakhstan, the Kyrgyz Republic, the Russian Federation, the Republic of Tajikistan and the Republic of Uzbekistan, at the initiative of the Russian Federation, and the 6-7 July 1993 Istanbul summit of the Economic Cooperation Organization, and their decisions aimed at peaceful solutions to the problems on the border between Tajikistan and Afghanistan. Furthermore, it welcomes the efforts of CSCE. The Council recognizes the actions of the Governments of Afghanistan and Tajikistan which created new negotiating bodies aimed at reducing tension along their common border.

"The Council draws attention to the critical humanitarian situation in Tajikistan and the Tajik refugee camps in northern Afghanistan and the need for additional humanitarian assistance. Stabilizing the situation along the Tajik-Afghan border should assist UNHCR in performing its mission. The Council calls upon the Government of Tajikistan to continue to assist in the return and reintegration of all Tajiks who fled this civil war and who wish to return to their homes.

"The Council expresses appreciation for the Secretary-General's report of 16 August 1993 and welcomes the Secretary-General's proposals to extend the mandate of his Special Envoy until 31 October 1993 and to extend the tenure of United Nations officials currently in Tajikistan for a period of three months. In the light of the unstable situation on the Tajik-Afghan border, the Council welcomes the Secretary-General's decision to dispatch his Special Envoy to Afghanistan and other countries in the region. The Council also welcomes the receptivity of the Secretary-General to possible requests from the parties for United Nations assistance in their efforts already under way and requests that he and his Special Envoy maintain close contact with the parties.

"The Council looks forward to receiving periodic reports from the Secretary-General on his Special Envoy's mission and the Secretary-General's recommendations for ways the United Nations may assist in resolving the situation and for defining more clearly the possible ambit of United Nations involvement.

"The Security Council will remain seized of the matter."

Communications (August-October). On 24 August,[91] Kazakhstan, Kyrgyzstan, the Russian Federation, Tajikistan and Uzbekistan announced an agreement of that date concerning the situation on the Tajik-Afghan border, concluded at a joint meeting of the Ministers for Foreign Affairs and the Ministers of Defence of the States members of CIS in Moscow. The agreement provided for the establishment of coalition defence forces in Tajikistan, which was viewed as a regional arrangement concluded in accordance with the purposes and principles of Chapter VIII of the Charter. The text of the agreement and other documents relating to the coalition forces were contained in a 20 October letter[92] from the Russian Federation.

On 7 October,[93] Afghanistan said it had not taken nor would it take armed action against Tajikistan. It assured the Secretary-General of its full cooperation with his Special Envoy. On 25 October, the Secretary-General expressed his appreciation for such assurances.

The establishment in Tajik territory of coalition forces from five States members of CIS was an important step in the de-escalation of the conflict, Tajikistan said on 27 October.[94] There was continued tension along the Tajik-Afghan border, but Tajikistan appreciated the efforts of the Afghan authorities to improve the situation.

In a 10 September letter to the Security Council President,[95] the Secretary-General discussed the outcome of discussions that his Special Envoy had with leaders in Afghanistan, Iran, Pakistan and Tajikistan from 17 to 26 August. All the Afghan leaders stated that the conflict in Tajikistan was a purely internal matter that should be resolved through discussions between the Tajik Government and opposition. The Tajik opposition leaders said they too favoured a peaceful solution through negotiations, but wanted to hold discussions with the Russian Federation before they would consider discussions with the Tajik Government. The Government of Tajikistan indicated that it wanted a peaceful settlement and supported the idea of negotiations with opposition leaders who accepted the existence and structures of the State of Tajikistan, and did not wish to impose an Islamic State on it.

The Secretary-General stated that the Minister for Foreign Affairs of the Russian Federation had expressed the belief that the United Nations and the Russian Federation could cooperate closely together to bring about a political settlement in Tajikistan. The Secretary-General welcomed the Russian initiative and stated that it was clear that a consensus was emerging on the need for a political settlement.

Report of the Secretary-General (November). In a 14 November report,[96] the Secretary-General stated that recent developments in Tajikistan and the neighbouring region gave grounds both for hope for a political solution of the conflict and for serious concern about the risk of further deterioration of the situation.

Fighting, however, continued to escalate. Cross-border infiltration by armed opposition groups from Afghanistan and fighting between them and government and CIS forces occurred almost on a daily basis, and the armed confrontation inside Tajikistan was intensifying, particularly in Khatlon and Gorno-Badakhshan regions.

The Secretary-General said he hoped that the implementation of the decision to establish CIS coalition peace-keeping forces in Tajikistan could contribute to the achievement of early agreement on political dialogue, cessation of hostilities and national reconciliation.

Concerted efforts were needed to overcome the remaining difficulties and persuade the Government as well as the major opposition groups to start a serious negotiation process without further delay. The Secretary-General stood ready to respond to any reasonable request by the parties and to recommend to the Security Council an international monitoring mechanism to help implement any agreement concluded by them. In those circumstances, he added, he had decided to extend the mandate of his Special Envoy for a further five months, until 31 March 1994.

On 22 December,[97] the Security Council welcomed the Secretary-General's decision, transmitted in a 16 December letter,[98] to appoint Ramiro Piriz-Ballon as Mr. Kittani's successor as Special Envoy for Tajikistan.

Ukraine

Responding to a request by Ukraine,[99] the Security Council convened on 20 July to discuss a complaint by Ukraine regarding the Decree of the Supreme Soviet of the Russian Federation concerning Sevastopol.

In forwarding its request, Ukraine said the Ukrainian city of Sevastopol alleged so-called

"Russian federal status" for the city and entrusted the Government of the Russian Federation with the task of working out a State programme to ensure the city's status. That, Ukraine said, was a flagrant disregard of international law and overt encroachment on its territorial inviolability. Implementation by Russian authorities of the Decree would have led to adequate actions by Ukraine in defence of its sovereignty and territorial integrity.

The Russian Federation,[100] on 19 July, transmitted a statement by its Ministry of Foreign Affairs stating that the Decree departed from the policy followed by the President and the Government in upholding Russian interests with regard to matters relating to the Black Sea fleet and in maintaining bases for the Russian Navy on the territory of Ukraine, in the Crimea and Sevastopol. It impeded the already difficult task of reaching a settlement; any problem could be settled only through political dialogue.

After consultations among the Security Council members, the President made a statement on their behalf:[101]

Meeting number. SC 3256.

"The Security Council has considered the letter dated 13 and 16 July 1993 from the Permanent Representative of Ukraine to the President of the Council, transmitting a statement by the President of Ukraine on the Decree adopted by the Supreme Soviet of the Russian Federation on 9 July 1993 concerning Sevastopol and a letter from the Minister for Foreign Affairs of Ukraine on the same matter.

"The Security Council has also considered the letter dated 19 July 1993 from the Permanent Representative of the Russian Federation, circulating a statement by the Ministry of Foreign Affairs of the Russian Federation concerning the aforementioned Decree.

"The Security Council shares the deep concern, and welcomes the position, expressed by the President and the Minister for Foreign Affairs of Ukraine concerning the Decree of the Supreme Soviet of the Russian Federation. In this context, it also welcomes the position taken by the Ministry of Foreign Affairs on behalf of the Government of the Russian Federation.

"The Security Council reaffirms in this connection its commitment to the territorial integrity of Ukraine, in accordance with the Charter of the United Nations. The Security Council recalls that in the Treaty between the Russian Federation and Ukraine, signed at Kiev on 19 November 1990, the High Contracting Parties committed themselves to respect each other's territorial integrity within their currently existing frontiers. The Decree of the Supreme Soviet of the Russian Federation is incompatible with this commitment as well as with the purposes and principles of the Charter of the United Nations, and without effect.

"The Security Council welcomes the efforts of the Presidents and the Governments of the Russian Federation and Ukraine to settle any differences between them by peaceful means and urges that they take all steps to ensure the avoidance of tension.

"The Security Council will remain seized of the matter."

United Nations interim offices

During the year, United Nations interim offices were established in Armenia, Azerbaijan, Belarus, Georgia, Kazakhstan, Ukraine and Uzbekistan for the purpose of coordinating operational development activities of the Organization in those countries (see PART THREE, Chapter II; see also PART ONE, Chapter V, for the funding of those offices).

As reported by the Secretary-General in November,[96] Tajikistan had requested him to establish a United Nations integrated office at Dushanbe to provide advice and assistance in developing the country's economic and social infrastructure, as well as to coordinate the humanitarian efforts of the international community. The Government had also sought United Nations advisory services in the field of human rights and democratic institutions. Pending a decision by the General Assembly, a small team of United Nations officials would continue to perform their functions until the establishment of an integrated office.

REFERENCES

[1]S/25142.   [2]S/25186.   [3]S/25181.   [4]S/25199.   [5]S/25254.
[6]S/25491.   [7]S/25510.   [8]S/25527.   [9]S/25499.   [10]S/25524.
[11]S/25539.   [12]S/25582.   [13]S/25650.   [14]S/25687.   [15]S/25626.
[16]S/25671.   [17]S/25564.   [18]S/25600.   [19]S/25712.   [20]S/26157.
[21]S/26135.   [22]S/25736.   [23]S/25952.   [24]S/26163.   [25]S/26184.
[26]S/26164.   [27]S/26168.   [28]S/26305.   [29]S/26312.   [30]S/26318.
[31]S/26319.   [32]S/26322.   [33]S/26326.   [34]S/26393.   [35]S/26417.
[36]S/26522.   [37]S/26543.   [38]S/26556.   [39]S/26706.   [40]S/26647.
[41]S/26650.   [42]S/26662.   [43]S/26718.   [44]S/25188.   [45]YUN
1992, p. 391.   [46]Ibid., p. 393.   [47]Ibid., p. 392.   [48]S/25198.
[49]S/25756.   [50]S/25757.   [51]S/26023.   [52]S/26023/Add.2.
[53]S/26031.   [54]S/26032.   [55]S/26222.   [56]S/26254.   [57]S/26250
& Add.1.   [58]S/26462.   [59]S/26463.   [60]S/26551.   [61]S/26487.
[62]S/26528.   [63]S/26576.   [64]S/26646 & Add.1.   [65]S/26795.
[66]S/26901.   [67]S/26875.   [68]S/26391.   [69]S/26392.   [70]S/26405.
[71]S/26404.   [72]S/26023/Add.1.   [73]S/26250/Add.1.
[74]S/26646/Add.1.   [75]A/48/699.   [76]A/C.5/48/40.   [77]A/48/781.
[78]S/25321.   [79]A/48/213-S/25962.   [80]A/48/404-S/26452.
[81]S/25697.   [82]S/25698.   [83]S/25720.   [84]S/26091.   [85]S/26092.
[86]S/26110.   [87]S/26241.   [88]A/48/304-S/26290.   [89]S/26311.
[90]S/26341.   [91]A/48/347-S/26357.   [92]S/26610.   [93]S/26814.
[94]S/26659.   [95]S/26744.   [96]S/26743.   [97]S/26913.   [98]S/26912.
[99]S/26100.   [100]S/26109.   [101]S/26118.

Other questions relating to Europe

Cooperation with CSCE

Pursuant to a 1992 General Assembly request,[1] the Secretary-General submitted in November 1993 a report[2] on cooperation between the United Nations and the Conference on Security and Cooperation in Europe, including a practical division of labour. Thus, CSCE had taken the lead in peacemaking efforts in Nagorny Karabakh, Moldova and South Ossetia, Georgia, while the United Nations had the lead in Tajikistan and Abkhazia, Georgia. In the former Yugosla-

via, cooperation had taken place between the two organizations in the former Yugoslav Republic of Macedonia, and CSCE long-term missions in Kosovo, Sandjak and Vojvodina provided the only international presence at the governmental level.

The text of a framework for cooperation and coordination between the United Nations Secretariat and CSCE, signed on 26 May, was annexed to a letter to the Secretary-General from Sweden.[3]

GENERAL ASSEMBLY ACTION

On 16 November, the General Assembly adopted without vote **resolution 48/19.**

Cooperation between the United Nations and the Conference on Security and Cooperation in Europe

The General Assembly,

Recalling its resolution 47/10 of 28 October 1992 on cooperation between the United Nations and the Conference on Security and Cooperation in Europe,

Welcoming its resolution 48/5 of 13 October 1993 on observer status for the Conference on Security and Cooperation in Europe in the General Assembly,

Welcoming also the declaration at the 1992 Helsinki Summit by the heads of State or Government of the participating States of the Conference on Security and Cooperation in Europe of their understanding that the Conference is a regional arrangement in the sense of Chapter VIII of the Charter of the United Nations, and as such provides an important link between European and global security,

Recalling also the documents of the Conference, in particular the Final Act signed at Helsinki on 1 August 1975, the Charter of Paris for a New Europe, the Prague Document on Further Development of the Institutions and Structures of the Conference on Security and Cooperation in Europe, the Vienna Document 1992 on Confidence- and Security-building Measures, the Helsinki Document 1992 and the Summary of Conclusions of the Third Meeting of the Council of the Conference on Security and Cooperation in Europe, held at Stockholm on 14 and 15 December 1992,

Noting the crucial role of the Conference in the efforts to forestall aggression and violence in the Conference area by addressing the root causes of problems and to prevent, manage and settle conflicts peacefully by appropriate means,

Noting also the comprehensive character of the commitments of the Conference and its concept of indivisible security; its role in promoting human rights, the rule of law and democratic values; its increased capabilities in early warning, conflict prevention, crisis management and security cooperation, including the appointment of the High Commissioner on National Minorities of the Conference; planning for peace-keeping operations and initiatives for further enhancing mechanisms for the peaceful settlement of disputes,

Noting further that the new tasks before the Conference are of an evolving character and require enhanced coordination and cooperation with international organizations, in particular with the United Nations,

Noting with satisfaction the concrete results in the field already yielded as a result of the framework for cooperation and coordination between the United Nations Secretariat and the Conference, signed on 26 May 1993,

Taking note of the report of the Secretary-General on the cooperation between the United Nations and the Conference on Security and Cooperation in Europe,

1. *Reiterates* the need for enhanced cooperation and coordination between the United Nations and the Conference on Security and Cooperation in Europe;

2. *Endorses* the Framework for cooperation and coordination between the United Nations Secretariat and the Conference;

3. *Requests* the Secretary-General to submit to the General Assembly at its forty-ninth session a report on cooperation and coordination between the United Nations and the Conference;

4. *Decides* to include in the provisional agenda of its forty-ninth session the item entitled ''Cooperation be- tween the United Nations and the Conference on Secu- rity and Cooperation in Europe''.

General Assembly resolution 48/19

16 November 1993   Meeting 56   Adopted without vote

43-nation draft (A/48/L.18 & Add.1); agenda item 26.
Sponsors: Albania, Armenia, Austria, Azerbaijan, Belarus, Belgium, Bulgaria, Canada, Croatia, Cyprus, Czech Republic, Denmark, Finland, France, Geor- gia, Germany, Greece, Hungary, Iceland, Ireland, Italy, Kazakhstan, Kyr- gyzstan, Liechtenstein, Luxembourg, Malta, Netherlands, Norway, Poland, Portugal, Republic of Moldova, Romania, Russian Federation, San Mar- ino, Slovenia, Spain, Sweden, Tajikistan, the former Yugoslav Republic of Macedonia, Turkey, Ukraine, United Kingdom, United States.

REFERENCES
[1]YUN 1992, p. 146, GA res. 47/10, 28 Oct. 1992. [2]A/48/549. [3]A/48/185.

Chapter V

Middle East

United Nations efforts in 1993 focused on helping to bring about a comprehensive settlement of the complex Middle East conflict, while the parties to the conflict themselves were engaged in an ongoing peace process sponsored by the Russian Federation and the United States and aided by Norway. In its multilateral negotiations, the United Nations acted as a full participant. Those negotiations resulted in the signing, on 13 September in Washington, D.C., of the Declaration of Principles on Interim Self-Government Arrangements between Israel and the Palestine Liberation Organization (PLO), a historic breakthrough that was welcomed by many States and international organizations. The handshake at that ceremony between Israeli Prime Minister Yitzhak Rabin and PLO Chairman Yasser Arafat provided a compelling symbol of the possibility of peace between former enemies. Prior to that, on 9 September, Israel and PLO had exchanged letters of mutual recognition, thereby paving the way to further political negotiations. The General Assembly expressed full support for the Declaration of Principles as well as the Agreement between Israel and Jordan on the Common Agenda, signed on 14 September, as an important initial step in achieving a comprehensive, just and lasting peace in the Middle East, and urged all parties to implement the agreements (resolution 48/58).

In addressing the question of Palestine, reaffirmed to be the epicentre of the Arab-Israeli conflict, the Assembly stressed the need for the United Nations to play a more active and expanded role in the current peace process and in the implementation of the Declaration of Principles. It urged Member States to provide economic and technical assistance to Palestinians and underlined that the realization of their legitimate national rights, primarily to self-determination, withdrawal of Israel from Palestinian territory; guaranteeing arrangements for peace and security of all States in the region and resolution of the refugee and settlements problems were elements of a comprehensive peace (48/158 D). The United Nations system also addressed the Palestine question and the policies and practices of Israel in the occupied territory including Jerusalem, and other Arab territories occupied since 1967, while a variety of United Nations organizations and specialized agencies maintained their programmes of economic and social assistance to Palestinians throughout the year. The Assembly welcomed the results of the Conference to Support Middle East Peace, convened in Washington, D.C., in October, and the Secretary-General's establishment in September of a high-level United Nations task force to support the economic and social development of the Palestinian people. It also urged Member States to provide economic, financial and technical assistance to the Palestinians during the interim period (48/58).

The Committee on the Exercise of the Inalienable Rights of the Palestinian People (Committee on Palestinian rights) continued to press for the implementation of its original (1976) recommendations—on Israeli withdrawal from the occupied Palestinian territory and on the rights of the Palestinians to return to their homes and property and to achieve self-determination, national independence and sovereignty in Palestine.

To help keep the region's latent volatility in check, the Security Council twice extended the mandate of the United Nations Interim Force in Lebanon and that of the United Nations Disengagement Observer Force in the Golan Heights, so that both peacekeeping forces remained operative during the year.

Israel's policies and practices in the Arab territories it occupied were monitored constantly by the Special Committee to Investigate Israeli Practices Affecting the Human Rights of the Palestinian People and Other Arabs of the Occupied Territories (Committee on Israeli practices), whose findings in 1993 reflected a critically tense situation and a high level of violence engendered by the uprising and Israel's suppression of it by military force and collective punishment, including the closure of the territories in March and mass deportations of Palestinians despite political breakthroughs at the negotiation table between Israel and PLO. The refusal by Israel to ensure the safe and immediate return, as demanded by the Security Council in resolution 799(1992), of the 415 Palestinians whom Israel had deported in December 1992 to Marj al Zahour in southern Lebanon, challenged, in the Secretary-General's view, the Council's authority. It was not until 15 December 1993 that Israel heeded the Council's demand and allowed the return of all deportees.

The Commission on Human Rights reiterated the Palestinians' right to self-determination and called on Israel to desist from human rights violations in the territories.

The United Nations Relief Works and Agency for Palestine Refugees in the Near East continued to provide a wide-ranging programme of education, health, relief and social services for the Palestine refugees. It appealed for increased contributions from Governments to meet the anticipated needs of a refugee population of 2.8 million (48/40 A). By a series of resolutions, the Assembly addressed specific aspects of the refugee problem.

The Economic and Social Council deplored Israel's confiscation of land, appropriation of water resources and depletion of other economic resources, (1993/52), while the Assembly reaffirmed the inalienable right of Palestinians to their natural and all other economic resources and regarded any infringement thereof as illegal (48/212).

Middle East peace process

Multilateral negotiations among Israel, Arab countries and other States, in which the United Nations acted as a full participant and which were sponsored by the Russian Federation and the United States and assisted by Norway, as well as bilateral talks between Israel and the Palestine Liberation Organization (PLO), resulted in the signing, on 13 September in Washington, D.C., of the Declaration of Principles on Interim Self-Government between Israel and PLO (see below). In December, the General Assembly, by adopting resolution 48/58, sponsored by 110 nations, welcomed the peace process started in 1991 at Madrid,[1] Spain, and supported the subsequent bilateral negotiations. It expressed full support for the achievements of that process thus far, in particular the Declaration of Principles and the Agreement between Israel and Jordan on the Common Agenda, which constituted an important initial step in achieving a comprehensive, just and lasting peace in the Middle East. The Assembly urged all parties to implement the agreements reached and stressed the need to achieve rapid progress on the other tracks of the Arab-Israeli negotiations. Welcoming the results of the Conference to Support Middle East Peace (Washington, D.C., 1 October) and the establishment of a high-level United Nations task force to support the economic and social development of the Palestinian people, it urged Member States to provide economic and other assistance to Palestinians during the interim period. It finally considered that an active United Nations role in the Middle East peace process and in assisting in the implementation of the Declaration of Principles could make a positive contribution.

Despite the large number of sponsors of the text, reflecting almost universal support for the Middle East peace process, it proved impossible to reach consensus on it, owing to the lack of a reference to Security Council resolution 425(1978) relating to Lebanon.

Effective January 1993, Chinmaya Rajaninath Gharekhan (India), as the Secretary-General's Special Representative, coordinated the role of the United Nations in the working groups on arms control and regional security, economic and regional development, environment, refugees and water, having been appointed in November 1992[2] after the United Nations was invited to be a full participant in the multilateral negotiations following the Madrid Peace Conference.

Declaration of Principles on Interim Self-Government Arrangements between Israel and PLO

Israel and PLO signed, on 13 September in Washington, D.C., the Declaration of Principles on Interim Self-Government Arrangements, which emanated from previous bilateral and multilateral negotiations. Prior to that, on 9 September, the two parties had exchanged letters of mutual recognition, whereby PLO recognized the right of Israel to exist in peace and security, accepted Security Council resolutions 242(1967) and 338(1973) and renounced terrorism and violence, while Israel recognized PLO as the representative of the Palestinian people. The signed Declaration, consisting of 17 articles, 4 annexes and agreed minutes, was transmitted to the Secretary-General on 8 October[3] by the Russian Federation and the United States, co-sponsors of the peace process. The Declaration, which was to enter into force one month after its signing, pertained to the aim of the negotiations (Article I), the framework for the interim period (II), elections (III), jurisdiction (IV), the transitional period and permanent status negotiations (V), the preparatory transfer of powers and responsibilities (VI), an interim agreement (VII), public order and security (VIII), laws and military orders (IX), a joint Israeli-Palestinian Liaison Committee (X), Israeli-Palestinian cooperation in economic fields (XI), liaison and cooperation with Jordan and Egypt (XII), the redeployment of Israeli forces (XIII), Israeli withdrawal from the Gaza Strip and Jericho area (XIV), the resolution of disputes (XV), Israeli-Palestinian cooperation concerning regional programmes (XVI) and miscellaneous provisions (XVII). Attached to the Declaration were protocols on the mode and conditions of elections (Annex I), on withdrawal of Israeli forces from the Gaza Strip and Jericho area (II), on Israeli-Palestinian cooperation in economic and development programmes (III), and on Israeli-Palestinian cooperation concerning regional development programmes (IV).

By the Declaration, Israel and PLO agreed that it was time to recognize their mutual legitimate and political rights, to strive to live in peaceful coexistence and mutual dignity and security and to achieve a just, lasting and comprehensive peace settlement and reconciliation through the agreed political process. According to the text, the aim of the Israeli-Palestinian negotiations within the current Middle East peace process was to establish a Palestinian Interim Self-Government Authority, as proposed by PLO in 1992,[4] as the elected Council for Palestinians in the West Bank and Gaza, for a transitional period of not more than five years, leading to a permanent settlement based on Security Council resolutions 242(1967)[5] and 338(1973).[6] It was understood that the interim arrangements were an integral part of the peace process and that the permanent status negotiations would lead to the implementation of those resolutions.

In order that the Palestinian people in the West Bank and Gaza might govern themselves according to democratic principles, direct, free and general political elections would be held for the Palestinian Council not later than nine months after the Declaration's entry into force under agreed supervision and international observation, with the Palestinian police ensuring public order. The Council's jurisdiction would cover West Bank and Gaza territory, except for issues to be negotiated in the permanent status negotiations. The two sides viewed the West Bank and Gaza as a single territorial unit, whose integrity was to be preserved during the interim period. The five-year transitional period would begin upon Israeli withdrawal from the Gaza and Jericho areas. Permanent status negotiations between Israel and Palestinian representatives were to commence as soon as possible, but not later than the third year of the interim period, and were to cover remaining issues, including Jerusalem, refugees, settlements, security arrangements, borders, and relations and cooperation with other neighbours.

The agreement provided that upon the entry into force of the Declaration and Israeli withdrawal, authority would be transferred from the Israeli military government and its Civil Administration to the Palestinians authorized for that task until the inauguration of the Palestinian Council. With a view to promoting economic development, authority would also be transferred to the Palestinians in the spheres of education and culture, health, social welfare, direct taxation and tourism. The Palestinian side was further to begin to build a Palestinian police force. Not later than the eve of elections for the Council, Israeli forces in the West Bank and Gaza were to be redeployed outside populated areas, in addition to the military withdrawal (see below).

An interim agreement was to be negotiated specifying the structure of the Council, the number of its members, the transfer of powers to it from Israel, its executive and legislative authorities and independent Palestinian judicial organs. In order to promote economic growth, the Council would establish a Palestinian Electricity Authority, a Gaza Sea Port Authority, a Palestinian Development Bank, a Palestinian Export Promotion Board, a Palestinian Environmental Authority, a Palestinian Land Authority, a Palestinian Water Administration Authority, and any other authorities agreed upon. After the Council's inauguration, the Israeli Civil Administration would be dissolved and its military government withdrawn. The Council was charged with establishing a strong police force to guarantee public order and internal security for Palestinians in the West Bank and Gaza, while Israel was to continue to bear the responsibility of defending against external threats, as well as for the overall security of Israelis.

In order to ensure the smooth implementation of the Declaration and subsequent agreements pertaining to the interim period, a Joint Israeli-Palestinian Liaison Committee was to be established to deal with issues requiring coordination, other issues of common interest and disputes. The Joint Liaison Committee was also to resolve disputes arising out of the Declaration's application or interpretation. Any disputes not settled through conciliation would be addressed by an Arbitration Committee to be established by the parties. The parties agreed to invite Egypt and Jordan to participate in establishing further liaison and cooperation arrangements between Israeli and Palestinian representatives on the one hand, and Egypt and Jordan on the other, including the constitution of a Continuing Committee which would decide by agreement on the modalities of admitting persons displaced from the West Bank and Gaza in 1967, together with measures necessary to prevent disruption and disorder. In addition, an Israeli-Palestinian Economic Cooperation Committee was envisaged to develop and implement economic and regional development programmes as provided for in Annexes III and IV to the Declaration.

The Protocol on the Mode and Conditions of Elections provided Palestinians living in Jerusalem with the right to participate in the election process, while not prejudicing the future status of those registered as displaced on 4 June 1967 as a result of their being unable to participate in elections owing to practical considerations. In accordance with the Protocol on Withdrawal of Israeli Forces from the Gaza Strip and Jericho Area, the two sides would conclude and sign an agreement on such withdrawal within two months of the Declaration's entry into force. Israel would implement an accelerated and scheduled withdrawal immediately after signing the agreement and complete it within four months. The agreement would include arrangements for a smooth and peaceful transfer of authority from the Israeli military government and its Civilian Administration to Palestinian representatives; the structure, powers and responsibilities of the Palestinian authorities in the two areas except for matters relating to external security, settlements, Israeli citizens and foreign relations; and arrangements for the assumption of internal security and public order by a Palestinian police force consisting of locally recruited officers and officers recruited from abroad holding Jordanian passports or Palestinian documents issued by Egypt. The withdrawal agreement would also provide for a temporary international or foreign presence; establishment of a joint Palestinian-Israeli Coordination and Cooperation Committee for mutual security purposes; an economic development and stabilization programme, including an emergency fund, to encourage foreign investment and financial and economic support; and safe passage for persons and transportation between Gaza and Jericho.

The Protocol on Israeli-Palestinian Cooperation in Economic and Development Programmes set out terms of reference for establishment of an Israeli-Palestinian Continuing Committee for Economic Cooperation, focusing on water, electricity, energy, finance, transport and communications, trade, industry, labour relations and social welfare issues, human resource development and cooperation, environmental protection, and communications and media. The Protocol on Israeli-Palestinian Cooperation concerning Regional Development Programmes outlined a two-part development programme for the region, including an economic development programme for the West Bank and Gaza and a regional economic development programme, to be initiated by the seven most powerful industrialized nations (Group of Seven). The West Bank and Gaza programme would deal with social rehabilitation, including housing and construction; small and medium business development; infrastructure development; and human resources. The regional programme might address the establishment of a Middle East Development Fund, to be followed by a Middle East Development Bank; a joint Israeli-Palestinian-Jordanian plan for coordinated exploitation of the Dead Sea area; the Mediterranean Sea-Dead Sea Canal; desalinization and water development; a regional plan for agricultural development and the prevention of desertification; interconnection of electricity grids; transfer, distribution and industrial exploitation of gas, oil and other energy resources; and a regional tour-

ism, transportation and telecommunications development plan.

Subsequent to the signing of the Declaration, Israel and Jordan agreed on 14 September in Washington, D.C., to a Common Agenda which searched for steps to arrive at a state of peace based on resolutions 242(1967) and 338(1973) in all their aspects, and regulated matters in the fields of security, water, refugees and displaced persons and borders, and explored potentials of future bilateral cooperation in natural and human resources, infrastructure and economic areas, including tourism.

By a decision taken on 4 November at Tunis, Tunisia, the PLO Executive Committee established the Palestinian Economic Council for Development and Construction, which was to define the priorities of development projects, as well as their implementation, control and management.

GENERAL ASSEMBLY ACTION

During the General Assembly's consideration of the Middle East situation in December, Israel stated that the political breakthroughs represented by the signing of the Camp David Accords in 1978,[7] the Declaration of Principles and the Common Agenda must be accompanied by economic growth and development in order to build stable peace. Economic and human progress were twin pillars supporting the political achievements.

Israel noted that 46 countries and organizations had come together at the Conference to Support Middle East Peace (Washington, D.C., 1 October), pledging $2 billion over five years to finance social and economic development in the West Bank and Gaza Strip, and that the United Nations had established a high-level task force to achieve the same goal. Israel further noted that it was making progress with the Palestinians and 13 other Arab delegations in the multilateral negotiations, thus creating opportunities for regional cooperation. Forty-seven countries and international organizations, including the United Nations, were participating in those multilateral talks, and five working groups were discussing refugees, arms control, regional economic cooperation, water and environment. For the first time, Israel went on to say, all States participating in the talks on regional economic development had agreed on a plan of action, which included 35 projects, workshops and studies in diverse areas. Also for the first time in the multilateral negotiations, talks about the Middle East were being held in the Middle East.

Israel said it sought a quiet and secure border with Lebanon, on which it had no territorial claims. It looked forward to a peace treaty and hoped that the Lebanese Government would assert its sovereignty and disarm those who used its land as a base for attacks on Israel. It called upon King Hussein of Jordan to sign a peace treaty with it and expressed desire for a comprehensive peace, based on individual treaties with the Gulf States, the North African States and all other Arab and Muslim countries. It further called on its negotiating partners to lay down economic weapons and end the Arab boycott, which was an obstacle to peace, impeding prosperity and hurting all societies in the Middle East. Science, education, health and technology would advance as countries of the region diverted human energies and resources away from conflict and shifted funds from the military to the civilian sector.

Jordan termed the Israeli-Palestinian Declaration of Principles the first tangible step towards peace. Progress on the Israeli-Jordanian, Israeli-Lebanese and Israeli-Syrian talks would ensure movement towards the comprehensive peace which the countries of the region and the international community had longed for as a prelude to lasting regional peace and security. The multilateral track was no less important than the bilateral track, as it involved 13 Arab States and Israel, together with the two co-sponsors of the peace process—the Russian Federation and the United States—in addition to other participants from outside the region, as well as the United Nations and the World Bank. So far, that track had yielded results which went beyond the exchange of abstract ideas to cover tangible matters, such as feasibility studies, training programmes and the establishment of a joint American-Israeli-Jordanian committee. Jordan maintained that the United Nations had a still more vital and larger role to play along two lines: it should continue acting as the baseline of international legality and conscience in its reaffirmation of Security Council resolutions 242(1967)[5] and 338(1973)[6] and all other relevant resolutions, and should explore ways to reinforce the two peace camps on the Arab and Israeli sides by providing support and assistance. The United Nations must continue to play an active role until the protagonists reach the stage of implementing resolution 242(1967)[5] and the Palestinians were able to exercise their inalienable right to self-determination on their national territory and establish an independent State of their own with Arab Al-Quds as its capital.

In the continuing debate, Lebanon said it understood that the Declaration of Principles would lead to the transfer from Israel to the Palestinians of authority over East Jerusalem and all of the cities, towns and villages of the West Bank and Gaza. Equally, it emphasized that the signing of the agreement in Washington would not achieve genuine peace unless there was substantive progress on the Lebanese and Syrian tracks of the Arab-Israeli negotiations, leading to full Israeli withdrawal from southern Lebanon and the Golan Heights. It stressed the need for the United Na-

tions to play a more active role in the peace process, the success of which, it said, was dependent on implementing resolutions 242(1967), 338(1973) and 425(1978).[8] Lebanon expressed alarm at what it called Israel's opposition to internationally recognized principles central to the achievement of a comprehensive peace settlement, over which discussion had been postponed, and which included Israeli withdrawal from all occupied territory, including Jerusalem, the dismantling of all settlements in those lands and the repatriation of Palestinian refugees.

On 14 December, Norway, introducing the draft resolution on the Middle East peace process,[9] noted that paragraph 4 stressed the need for achieving rapid progress on the other tracks of the Arab-Israeli negotiations, those between Israel and the Syrian Arab Republic, and between Israel and Lebanon. With regard to the latter, it said that, though not mentioned in the text, resolution 425(1978) would be an important point of reference. Norway introduced the draft together with the Russian Federation and the United States on behalf of 87 additional sponsors,[10] who were joined later by 20 others.

The Russian Federation underlined that, besides the mutual recognition by Israel and PLO and their signing of the Declaration of Principles, no less vital for a comprehensive and lasting settlement was the task of spurring talks between Israel and the Syrian Arab Republic and Lebanon. Success required stalwart diplomatic efforts through the framework defined by the Madrid process. The goals for settling the key problems, especially in southern Lebanon, were set out in resolution 425(1978). The Russian Federation was convinced that adoption of what it called the constructive, balanced and non-confrontational draft would open a new page in the history of United Nations consideration of the situation in the Middle East and enable the Organization to be more fully included in the agreements.

According to the United States, the draft allowed the Assembly to record for the first time its support for the Middle East peace process inaugurated at Madrid and to speak, after decades of division and discord, with one voice about the imperative of a Middle East peace.

Before voting on the draft, Lebanon pointed out that it had not been a party to the wars of 1967 and 1973 and, as a result, neither resolutions 242(1967) or 338(1973) nor the "land for peace" formula was applicable to it. Therefore, resolution 425(1978) must be mentioned in the text if the Assembly was seriously to consider it as a show of support for the Madrid Conference and subsequent negotiations. Lebanon said that it and the entire Arab Group had worked hard to impress on the sponsors the imperative of including a reference to resolution 425(1978), without which the text could be misconstrued to mean that Lebanon had participated in the Madrid Conference and subsequent negotiations on the basis of Council resolutions 242(1967) and 338(1973). Although it was committed to continuing the bilateral negotiations based on all three resolutions, Lebanon would refrain from entering into the multilateral talks until there was real progress in the bilateral negotiations.

Similarly, the Syrian Arab Republic said it could not agree to a text on the Middle East peace process that failed to make reference to resolution 425(1978) concerning Lebanon, which had participated in the Madrid Conference and subsequent bilateral talks on the basis of that resolution.

On 14 December 1993, the Assembly adopted **resolution 48/58** by recorded vote.

Middle East peace process

The General Assembly,

Stressing that the achievement of a comprehensive, just and lasting settlement of the Middle East conflict will constitute a significant contribution to strengthening international peace and security,

Recalling the convening of the Peace Conference on the Middle East at Madrid on 30 October 1991, on the basis of Security Council resolutions 242(1967) of 22 November 1967 and 338(1973) of 22 October 1973, and the subsequent bilateral negotiations, as well as the meetings of the multilateral working groups, and noting with satisfaction the broad international support for the peace process,

Noting the continuing positive participation of the United Nations as a full extraregional participant in the work of the multilateral working groups,

Bearing in mind the Declaration of Principles on Interim Self-Government Arrangements, signed by the Government of the State of Israel and the Palestine Liberation Organization in Washington, D.C., on 13 September 1993,

Also bearing in mind the Agreement between Israel and Jordan on the Common Agenda, signed in Washington, D.C., on 14 September 1993,

1. *Welcomes* the peace process started at Madrid and supports the subsequent bilateral negotiations;

2. *Stresses* the importance of, and need for, achieving a comprehensive, just and lasting peace in the Middle East;

3. *Expresses its full support* for the achievements of the peace process thus far, in particular the Declaration of Principles on Interim Self-Government Arrangements signed by the State of Israel and the Palestine Liberation Organization, and the Agreement between Israel and Jordan on the Common Agenda, which constitute an important initial step in achieving a comprehensive, just and lasting peace in the Middle East, and urges all parties to implement agreements reached;

4. *Stresses* the need for achieving rapid progress on the other tracks of the Arab-Israeli negotiations within the peace process;

5. *Welcomes* the results of the Conference to Support Middle East Peace, convened in Washington, D.C., on 1 October 1993, and the establishment of the high-level United Nations task force to support the economic and social development of the Palestinian people, and urges Member States to provide economic, financial and technical assistance to the Palestinian people during the interim period;

6. *Calls upon* all Member States also to extend economic, financial and technical assistance to States in the region and to render support for the peace process;

7. *Considers* that an active United Nations role in the Middle East peace process and in assisting in the implementation of the Declaration of Principles can make a positive contribution;

8. *Encourages* regional development and cooperation in the areas where work has already begun within the framework of the Madrid Conference.

General Assembly resolution 48/58

14 December 1993   Meeting 79   155-3-1 (recorded vote)

110-nation draft (A/48/L.32 & Add.1); agenda item 34.

Sponsors: Albania, Angola, Argentina, Armenia, Australia, Austria, Azerbaijan, Barbados, Belarus, Belgium, Benin, Bhutan, Bolivia, Bosnia and Herzegovina, Botswana, Brazil, Bulgaria, Burundi, Cambodia, Canada, Cape Verde, Central African Republic, Chile, Comoros, Congo, Costa Rica, Côte d'Ivoire, Croatia, Czech Republic, Denmark, Ecuador, Egypt, El Salvador, Estonia, Ethiopia, Fiji, Finland, Georgia, Germany, Ghana, Greece, Guatemala, Guinea, Guinea-Bissau, Haiti, Honduras, Hungary, Iceland, Ireland, Israel, Italy, Jamaica, Japan, Jordan, Kazakhstan, Kenya, Kyrgyzstan, Latvia, Lesotho, Liechtenstein, Lithuania, Luxembourg, Madagascar, Malawi, Malta, Marshall Islands, Mauritius, Micronesia, Mongolia, Morocco, Myanmar, Nepal, Netherlands, New Zealand, Nicaragua, Norway, Papua New Guinea, Paraguay, Peru, Philippines, Poland, Portugal, Republic of Korea, Republic of Moldova, Romania, Russian Federation, Rwanda, Saint Vincent and the Grenadines, Samoa, San Marino, Singapore, Slovakia, Slovenia, Solomon Islands, Spain, Suriname, Sweden, Tajikistan, Thailand, the former Yugoslav Republic of Macedonia, Togo, Tunisia, Turkey, Turkmenistan, Ukraine, United Kingdom, United States, Uruguay, Venezuela, Zambia.

Meeting numbers. GA 48th session: plenary 67, 68, 79.

Recorded vote in Assembly as follows:

In favour: Albania, Algeria, Angola, Antigua and Barbuda, Argentina, Armenia, Australia, Austria, Azerbaijan, Bahamas, Bahrain, Bangladesh, Barbados, Belarus, Belgium, Benin, Bhutan, Bolivia, Botswana, Brazil, Brunei Darussalam, Bulgaria, Burkina Faso, Cambodia, Cameroon, Canada, Central African Republic, Chad, Chile, China, Colombia, Comoros, Congo, Costa Rica, Côte d'Ivoire, Croatia, Cuba, Cyprus, Czech Republic, Democratic People's Republic of Korea, Denmark, Djibouti, Dominica, Dominican Republic, Ecuador, Egypt, El Salvador, Estonia, Ethiopia, Fiji, Finland, France, Gabon, Gambia, Germany, Ghana, Greece, Guatemala, Guinea, Guinea-Bissau, Guyana, Haiti, Hungary, Iceland, India, Indonesia, Ireland, Israel, Italy, Jamaica, Japan, Jordan, Kazakhstan, Kenya, Kuwait, Lao People's Democratic Republic, Latvia, Lesotho, Liechtenstein, Lithuania, Luxembourg, Madagascar, Malawi, Malaysia, Maldives, Mali, Malta, Marshall Islands, Mauritania, Mauritius, Mexico, Micronesia, Monaco, Mongolia, Morocco, Mozambique, Myanmar, Namibia, Nepal, Netherlands, New Zealand, Nicaragua, Niger, Nigeria, Norway, Oman, Pakistan, Panama, Papua New Guinea, Paraguay, Peru, Philippines, Poland, Portugal, Qatar, Republic of Korea, Republic of Moldova, Romania, Russian Federation, Rwanda, Saint Lucia, Saint Vincent and the Grenadines, Samoa, San Marino, Saudi Arabia, Senegal, Sierra Leone, Singapore, Slovakia, Slovenia, Solomon Islands, Spain, Sri Lanka, Sudan, Suriname, Swaziland, Sweden, Thailand, the former Yugoslav Republic of Macedonia, Togo, Trinidad and Tobago, Tunisia, Turkey, Uganda, Ukraine, United Arab Emirates, United Kingdom, United Republic of Tanzania, United States, Uruguay, Venezuela, Viet Nam, Yemen, Zambia, Zimbabwe.

Against: Iran, Lebanon, Syrian Arab Republic.

Abstaining: Libyan Arab Jamahiriya.

Proposed peace conference under UN auspices

As requested by the General Assembly in 1992,[11] the Secretary-General submitted a progress report on 19 November 1993[12] on his continuing efforts and developments in regard to convening an international peace conference on the Middle East under United Nations auspices, which was first endorsed by the Assembly in 1983.[13] The report stated that no reply had been received from the Security Council to his request for its views. However, Israel and PLO had communicated their positions in response to a note verbale of 14 September seeking information on steps taken to implement the 1992 resolution.

In its note of 12 October, Israel said it had long advocated direct negotiations as the only framework to advance peace in the Middle East, an approach vindicated by the negotiations currently taking place in the framework of the Madrid peace process and recent achievements in the Israeli-Palestinian and Israeli-Jordanian talks. The 1992 resolution on the conference ran counter to the principle of direct negotiations, Israel continued, stating that while the resolution referred to Security Council resolutions 242(1967)[5] and 338(1973),[6] it also offered a series of principles that prejudged and even predetermined the outcome of those negotiations. Israel said that the resolution was outdated and out of touch with reality, and that it continued to oppose it and believed such a text should not be adopted again by the Assembly in 1993.

The Permanent Observer of Palestine stated in his note of 21 October that the most significant development emanating from the peace process, the recent signing of the Declaration of Principles between Israel and PLO containing agreement on mutual recognition, was an important and positive step towards a comprehensive, just and lasting peace. The most crucial elements yet to be negotiated included the final status of Jerusalem, the illegal settlements, the rights of Palestinian refugees and border questions. Similar progress on other tracks of the peace process between the concerned Arab States and Israel was necessary for the process to proceed smoothly. PLO strongly stressed the need for the United Nations to play a more active and expanded role in the peace process and called for the Organization's full engagement in it, as well as in the provision of assistance to Palestinians in their efforts to build their new life and own authority and effectively to implement the Declaration. It believed that the Assembly should reaffirm once more the principles for achieving a comprehensive peace and emphasized the permanent responsibility of the United Nations regarding the question of Palestine until its resolution in all aspects. PLO stood ready to cooperate fully with the Secretary-General to carry out his efforts to promote peace, as called for in the 1992 Assembly resolution, in an effective and successful manner.

The Secretary-General observed that the United Nations had always supported a comprehensive, just and lasting peace based on resolutions 242(1967) and 338(1973), taking into account the legitimate political rights of the Palestinians, including self-determination. In that connection, he welcomed the Declaration, hoping that it would lead to a peace acceptable to all parties concerned. The United Nations stood ready to support the peace process and had, over the past year, participated actively in the multilateral working groups established in the framework of the Madrid Conference in 1991.[1] To help sustain the momentum of the Israeli-Palestinian negotiations and in an effort to support the implementation of the Declaration of Principles, the United Nations had begun to enhance its economic and social assistance to the West Bank and Gaza, which would intensify in the months ahead.

United Nations Truce Supervision Organization

Three peace-keeping operations remained in place in the region: two peace-keeping forces—the United Nations Disengagement Observer Force (UNDOF) (see below, under "Israel and the Syrian Arab Republic") and the United Nations Interim Force in Lebanon (UNIFIL) (see below, under "Lebanon")—and an observer mission, the United Nations Truce Supervision Organization (UNTSO). Headquartered at Jerusalem, with liaison offices at Amman, Jordan, and Beirut, Lebanon, UNTSO's 57 unarmed military observers continued to assist UNDOF and UNIFIL in performing their tasks. They manned five observation posts along the Lebanese side of the Israel-Lebanon armistice demarcation line and operated four mobile teams in the Israeli-controlled section of the UNIFIL area. Two observers were assigned to UNIFIL headquarters.

REFERENCES

[1]YUN 1991, p. 221. [2]YUN 1992, p. 396. [3]A/48/486-S/26560. [4]YUN 1992, p. 399. [5]YUN 1967, p. 257, SC res. 242(1967), 22 Nov. 1967. [6]YUN 1973, p. 213, SC res. 338(1973), 22 Oct. 1973. [7]YUN 1978, p. 327. [8]Ibid., p. 312, SC res. 425(1978), 19 Mar. 1978. [9]A/48/L.32. [10]A/48/755. [11]YUN 1992, p. 397, GA res. 47/64 D, 11 Dec. 1992. [12]A/48/607-S/26769. [13]YUN 1983, p. 278, GA res. 38/58 C, 13 Dec. 1983.

Palestine question

During 1993, the question of Palestine continued to be of undiminishing concern to the General Assembly, which, aware of the mutual recognition between Israel and PLO and the signing between the two parties of the Declaration of Principles, reaffirmed the need to achieve a peaceful settlement. Following its consideration of the 1993 report of the Committee on Palestinian rights, the Assembly in December adopted four resolutions addressing the question.

By resolution 48/158 D, the Assembly stressed the need for the United Nations to play a more active and expanded role in the current peace process and in the implementation of the Declaration of Principles; urged Member States to provide economic and technical assistance to the Palestinian people; and reaffirmed the following principles for the achievement of a final settlement and comprehensive peace: realization of the legitimate national rights of Palestinians, primarily to self-determination; withdrawal of Israel from Palestinian territory occupied since 1967, including Jerusalem, and from other occupied Arab territories; guaranteeing arrangements for peace and security of all States in the region within secure and internationally recognized boundaries; and resolution of the problem of the Palestine refugees and the illegal Israeli settlements. By adopting resolution 48/158 A, it endorsed the Committee's recommendations on the Palestine question and, requesting it to keep the situation under review, to make suggestions to it and the Security Council, as appropriate. It once again requested resources for the Division for Palestinian Rights, as well as continued cooperation with it (48/158 B); and further requested the Department of Public Information (DPI) to continue its special information programme on the question during the 1994-1995 biennium (48/158 C). It again determined that Israel's 1980 decision[1] to impose its laws, jurisdiction and administration on Jerusalem was illegal and therefore null and void; and deplored the transfer by some States of their diplomatic missions to Jerusalem in violation of Security Council resolution 478(1980)[2] (48/59 A).

Having reviewed the assistance provided by the United Nations system to Palestinians throughout the year, the Assembly (48/213) and the Economic and Social Council (1993/78) appealed for increased international assistance to the Palestinian people, in cooperation with PLO. The Assembly urged States to open their markets to exports from the West Bank and Gaza on the most favourable terms.

In related actions, the Assembly demanded that Israel acknowledge the *de jure* applicability of the 1949 Geneva Convention relative to the Protection of Civilian Persons in Time of War (fourth Geneva Convention) to the occupied Palestinian territory, including Jerusalem and other Arab territories occupied since 1967, and to comply scrupulously with that Convention. It determined that all measures and actions taken by Israel with respect to those territories in violation of the Convention were illegal and without validity, demanding that it desist forthwith from any such actions; called on Israel to respect all fundamental freedoms of Palestinians, including education; and reaffirmed that the Israeli settlements in the above territories were illegal and an obstacle to peace (see below,

under "Territories occupied by Israel"). The Assembly again proposed the establishment of a university "Al-Quds" for Palestine refugees and called on Israel to remove the hindrances it had put in the way of its establishment (see below, under "Palestine refugees").

On 29 November, the Committee on Palestinian rights organized at the United Nations Headquarters and Offices at Geneva and Vienna observances of the International Day of Solidarity with the Palestinian people.

Activities of the Committee on Palestinian rights. As mandated by the General Assembly in 1992,[3] the Committee on Palestinian rights, established in 1975,[4] continued to observe developments in the Israeli-occupied territories and actions by Israel which the Committee regarded as violations of international law or of United Nations resolutions. It brought such actions—including Israeli settlement activities, Israeli exploitation of Arab-owned land and human rights violations such as deportations and other matters affecting Palestinian rights—to the attention of the Assembly and the Security Council.[5] It continued to press for the implementation of its original (1976) recommendations[6]—on Israeli withdrawal from the occupied Palestinian territory and on the rights of Palestinians to return to their homes and property and to achieve self-determination, national independence and sovereignty in Palestine. The Committee considered that the principled position adopted by the international community on the Palestine question had begun to bear fruit due to the shift from confrontation to cooperation and a renewed determination to resolve long-standing regional conflicts.

The Committee submitted a report on its activities to the Assembly in November 1993,[7] reiterating its invitation to all Member States and Permanent Observers, as well as PLO, to participate as observers in its work. It also re-established its Working Group to assist in the preparation and expedition of its work.

The Committee and, under its guidance, the Division for Palestinian Rights, continued to expand cooperation with non-governmental organizations (NGOs) in order to promote awareness of the Palestine question and create conditions favourable for the implementation of its recommendations. To that end, the Committee carried out its approved programme of regional NGO symposia and seminars for 1993. It affirmed the importance of the contribution of the NGO community to international efforts on behalf of the Palestinian people and considered that its support would become even more necessary during the future transition period.

The Committee decided to devote its seminar for the European region to assistance to the Palestinian people (see below under "Assistance to Palestinians"). The North American regional seminar (New York, 28 and 29 June), the theme of which was priorities for United Nations action, discussed the United Nations and the implementation of international human rights instruments and relevant Security Council resolutions; the role of the Organization in promoting economic development in the occupied Palestinian territories; and the United Nations and the peace process. It was followed immediately by an NGO symposium, which included several workshops and four panels: building for peace and Palestine: priorities for the second decade of the NGO movement; rights, resources, refugees: the need for protection; ending the occupation: a prelude to peace and security; and NGO priorities for the second decade. The African regional seminar (Dakar, Senegal, 30 August–3 September) was held jointly with an NGO Symposium and addressed Africa, the Middle East, and the question of Palestine. Discussions topics were: towards a just solution of the Palestine question; building peace in Jerusalem—the holy city of three religions; towards self-determination and statehood; and the need to revive the economy in the occupied territories, including Jerusalem. Two additional workshops for NGOs dealt with action by African NGOs to promote efforts to end Israel's violation of human rights of Palestinians; and mobilization and networking by NGOs to promote a just, comprehensive and lasting solution to the Palestine question. The European regional NGO symposium (Vienna, 23 and 24 August) was on the Middle East peace process: Palestinian rights and development—a challenge to Europe. It was immediately followed by an international NGO meeting (25-27 August), the theme of which was renewing the NGO commitment to Palestinian national and human rights.

In order to strengthen its programme of research, monitoring and publications, the Division for Palestinian Rights during 1993 continued work on the establishment of a computer-based United Nations information system on the question of Palestine (UNISPAL), as requested by the Committee and endorsed by the Assembly in 1992.[8] The Committee requested that provision for further development of the system be made in the 1994-1995 budget, stressing the importance and usefulness of UNISPAL for the work of the Committee, the United Nations and the international community.

In its 1993 recommendations, the Committee welcomed the peace process started at Madrid in 1991,[9] the exchange of letters of mutual recognition between Israel and PLO and the subsequent signing by the two sides of the Declaration of Principles as important steps towards a comprehensive, just and lasting peace in accordance with Security Council resolutions 242(1967)[10] and 338-

(1973).[11] It called for intensified international support and assistance to Palestinians, with PLO as its recognized leadership, to ensure the successful implementation of the agreements reached. It further stressed the need for full United Nations engagement in the peace process and in building the forthcoming Palestinian National Authority, as well as providing assistance to Palestinians in all fields.

The Committee considered that the following priority tasks required immediate and sustained attention in its future programme of work: promoting support for the ongoing peace process and for the Declaration of Principles, and monitoring closely the situation to promote effective implementation of the agreements reached and full realization of Palestinian rights; promoting intensified assistance to the Palestinian people by the whole United Nations system and other donors, for immediate relief and nation-building; and encouraging constructive debate of the major issues to be negotiated at a later stage with a view to promoting a final settlement based on international legitimacy. Finally, it attached greatest importance to the intensified mobilization of NGOs throughout the transitional period to monitor developments, promote the full exercise of Palestinian rights in accordance with United Nations resolutions and provide the assistance needed for institution-building.

GENERAL ASSEMBLY ACTION

Addressing the question of Palestine before the General Assembly in November, the Chairman of the Committee on Palestinian rights stated that the Declaration of Principles had opened a new chapter in the long history of that question, symbolized by the handshake between Israeli Prime Minister Rabin and PLO Chairman Arafat. The Committee supported those developments and strongly urged the parties to continue their efforts so as to ensure that the process led to a definitive peace, especially since many sensitive aspects relating to implementing the Declaration, such as Israeli withdrawal, permanent status arrangements regarding Jerusalem, refugees, settlements, security arrangements, borders and other issues remained to be negotiated. He stressed once again the need for full United Nations engagement in the peace process and in building the national Palestinian institutions as well as in providing broad assistance, in which regard he welcomed the Secretary-General's efforts to develop a concerted United Nations response to support implementation of the Declaration.

The Observer of Palestine noted that the Declaration left for negotiations at a later stage issues of paramount importance, such as Al-Quds, settlements, refugees and boundaries. He emphasized that their solution and form of final settlement must be based fully on international legality, in particular on relevant Security Council and Assembly resolutions that conformed to international law in addition to providing a pragmatic and practicable solution. The Security Council in particular had a clear position on Israeli settlements, having in 1980[12] declared them to be a violation of the fourth Geneva Convention and a serious obstruction to peace, and calling for their dismantlement. He stressed that the settlements continued to be illegal regardless of any political developments.

Israel told the Assembly that, far from the limelight, Israeli-Palestinian committees were working hard to negotiate security arrangements and modalities of transferring authority in Gaza and Jericho. The Economic Cooperation Committee had begun its work in Paris, guided by the principles of reciprocity, equity and fair relationships, and exploring joint action in water, energy, industry and infrastructure, on which issues specific working groups were established. Commending activities of the United Nations Development Programme (UNDP) and the United Nations Relief and Works Agency for Palestine Refugees in the Near East (UNRWA), Israel appealed to the Secretary-General to double their budgets and the efforts of the United Nations.

Following consideration of the report of the Committee on Palestinian rights, the General Assembly, on 20 December, adopted four resolutions on the question of Palestine, all by recorded vote. **Resolution 48/158 D** reaffirmed the need for a peaceful settlement of that question.

Peaceful settlement of the question of Palestine

The General Assembly,

Recalling its relevant resolutions, the most recent of which was resolution 47/64 D of 11 December 1992,

Having considered the report of the Secretary-General of 19 November 1993,

Stressing that achieving a comprehensive settlement of the Middle East conflict, the core of which is the question of Palestine, will constitute a significant contribution to international peace and security,

Noting the convening at Madrid, on 30 October 1991, of the Peace Conference on the Middle East and the subsequent bilateral negotiations, as well as meetings of the multilateral working groups,

Noting also that the United Nations has participated as a full, extraregional participant in the work of the multilateral working groups,

Aware of the mutual recognition between the Government of the State of Israel and the Palestine Liberation Organization, as the representative of the Palestinian people, and the signing between the two parties of the Declaration of Principles on Interim Self-Government Arrangements in Washington, D.C., on 13 September 1993, as well as their subsequent negotiations,

Welcoming the convening of the Conference to Support Middle East Peace in Washington, D.C., on 1 October 1993,

1. *Reaffirms* the need to achieve a peaceful settlement of the question of Palestine, the core of the Arab-Israeli conflict, in all its aspects;

2. *Expresses* its support for the ongoing peace process, which began in Madrid, and the Declaration of Principles on Interim Self-Government Arrangements, and expresses the hope that the process will lead to the establishment of a comprehensive, just and lasting peace in the Middle East;

3. *Stresses* the need for the United Nations to play a more active and expanded role in the current peace process and in the implementation of the Declaration of Principles;

4. *Urges* Member States to provide economic and technical assistance to the Palestinian people;

5. *Also stresses* the upcoming negotiations on the final settlement, and reaffirms the following principles for the achievement of a final settlement and comprehensive peace:

(a) The realization of the legitimate national rights of the Palestinian people, primarily the right to self-determination;

(b) The withdrawal of Israel from the Palestinian territory occupied since 1967, including Jerusalem, and from the other occupied Arab territories;

(c) Guaranteeing arrangements for peace and security of all States in the region, including those named in resolution 181(II) of 29 November 1947, within secure and internationally recognized boundaries;

(d) Resolving the problem of the Palestine refugees in conformity with General Assembly resolution 194(III) of 11 December 1948, and subsequent relevant resolutions;

(e) Resolving the problem of the Israeli settlements, which are illegal and an obstacle to peace, in conformity with relevant United Nations resolutions;

(f) Guaranteeing freedom of access to Holy Places and religious buildings and sites;

6. *Requests* the Secretary-General to continue his efforts with the parties concerned, and in consultation with the Security Council, for the promotion of peace in the region and to submit progress reports on developments in this matter.

General Assembly resolution 48/158 D

20 December 1993   Meeting 85   92-5-51 (recorded vote)

12-nation draft (A/48/L.44 & Add.1); agenda item 35.
Sponsors: Afghanistan, Comoros, Cuba, India, Indonesia, Jordan, Malaysia, Malta, Pakistan, Senegal, Tunisia, Yemen.
Meeting numbers. GA 48th session: plenary 65, 66, 85.

Recorded vote in Assembly as follows:

In favour: Algeria, Antigua and Barbuda, Azerbaijan, Bahamas, Bahrain, Bangladesh, Barbados, Benin, Bhutan, Bolivia, Bosnia and Herzegovina, Botswana, Brazil, Brunei Darussalam, Burkina Faso, Burundi, Cambodia, Cape Verde, Chad, Chile, China, Colombia, Comoros, Costa Rica, Cuba, Cyprus, Democratic People's Republic of Korea, Djibouti, Ecuador, Egypt, El Salvador, Gambia, Guatemala, Guinea-Bissau, Guyana, Haiti, Honduras, India, Indonesia, Jamaica, Jordan, Kuwait, Lao People's Democratic Republic, Lebanon, Lesotho, Libyan Arab Jamahiriya, Madagascar, Malawi, Malaysia, Maldives, Mali, Malta, Mauritania, Mauritius, Mexico, Mongolia, Morocco, Mozambique, Namibia, Nepal, Nicaragua, Niger, Nigeria, Oman, Pakistan, Peru, Philippines, Qatar, Rwanda, Saint Lucia, Saint Vincent and the Grenadines, Saudi Arabia, Senegal, Sierra Leone, Singapore, Sri Lanka, Sudan, Suriname, Swaziland, Syrian Arab Republic, Thailand, Togo, Trinidad and Tobago, Tunisia, Turkey, United Arab Emirates, United Republic of Tanzania, Venezuela, Viet Nam, Yemen, Zambia, Zimbabwe.

Against: Dominican Republic, Israel, Marshall Islands, Micronesia, United States.

Abstaining: Argentina, Armenia, Australia, Austria, Belarus, Belgium, Belize, Bulgaria, Canada, Côte d'Ivoire, Croatia, Czech Republic, Denmark, Dominica, Estonia, Ethiopia, Finland, France, Georgia, Germany, Ghana, Greece, Hungary, Iceland, Ireland, Italy, Japan, Kazakhstan, Kenya, Latvia, Liechtenstein, Lithuania, Luxembourg, Netherlands, New Zealand, Norway, Panama, Poland, Portugal, Republic of Korea, Republic of Moldova, Romania, Russian Federation, Slovakia, Slovenia, Spain, Sweden, the former Yugoslav Republic of Macedonia, Ukraine, United Kingdom, Uruguay.

In explanation of its vote, Israel asserted that the principles contained in the resolution prejudged and even predetermined the outcome of the ongoing negotiations, thus contradicting itself. On the one hand, the text claimed to support the peace process begun in Madrid, while on the other, it ignored the basic principle of direct negotiations without preconditions on which that very process was based. Israel had long advocated direct negotiations as the only framework for advancing Middle East peace, and recent achievements vindicated that approach. Any attempt to internationalize the issues or to perpetuate the existence of bodies which did so would lead nowhere.

The United States said that the resolution was greatly improved over its predecessor texts that called for convening an international peace conference on the Middle East; however, it spoke conclusively to issues under direct negotiation between the parties. Instead, the Assembly should support those negotiations without prejudice in order for all the parties to resolve their differences directly and avoid focusing on divisive and polarizing statements.

The Russian Federation regretted that the text had retained the traditional array of principles for a Middle East settlement, which, it said, were an attempt to predetermine the bilateral Arab-Israeli negotiations and could complicate their course.

A draft resolution[13] on the uprising (*intifadah*) of the Palestinian people, which was tabled under the agenda item on the Palestine question, was withdrawn by its sponsors (Afghanistan, Cuba, Indonesia, Jordan, Malaysia, Malta, Senegal, Tunisia and Yemen). The text condemned those Israeli policies and practices which violated the human rights of Palestinians in the occupied territories, and requested the Security Council to examine with urgency the situation in the territories with a view to considering measures needed to provide international protection to Palestinian civilians.

By adopting **resolution 48/158 A**, the Assembly requested the Committee on Palestinian rights to keep under review the situation relating to the Palestine question.

Committee on the Exercise of the Inalienable Rights of the Palestinian People

The General Assembly,

Recalling its resolutions 181(II) of 29 November 1947, 194(III) of 11 December 1948, 3236(XXIX) of 22 November 1974, 3375(XXX) and 3376(XXX) of 10 November 1975, 31/20 of 24 November 1976, 32/40 A

of 2 December 1977, 33/28 A and B of 7 December 1978, 34/65 A of 29 November 1979 and 34/65 C of 12 December 1979, ES-7/2 of 29 July 1980, 35/169 A and C of 15 December 1980, 36/120 A and C of 10 December 1981, ES-7/4 of 28 April 1982, 37/86 A of 10 December 1982, 38/58 A of 13 December 1983, 39/49 A of 11 December 1984, 40/96 A of 12 December 1985, 41/43 A of 2 December 1986, 42/66 A of 2 December 1987, 43/175 A of 15 December 1988, 44/41 A of 6 December 1989, 45/67 A of 6 December 1990, 46/74 A of 11 December 1991 and 47/64 A of 11 December 1992,

Having considered the report of the Committee on the Exercise of the Inalienable Rights of the Palestinian People,

Welcoming the signing of the Declaration of Principles on Interim Self-Government Arrangements, including its Annexes and Agreed Minutes, by the Government of the State of Israel and the Palestine Liberation Organization on 13 September 1993 in Washington, D.C.,

Reaffirming that the United Nations has a permanent responsibility with respect to the question of Palestine until the question is resolved in all its aspects in a satisfactory manner in accordance with international legitimacy,

1. *Expresses its appreciation* to the Committee on the Exercise of the Inalienable Rights of the Palestinian People for its efforts in performing the tasks assigned to it by the General Assembly;

2. *Considers* that the Committee can make a valuable and positive contribution to international efforts to promote the effective implementation of the Declaration of Principles on Interim Self-Government Arrangements and to mobilize international support for and assistance to the Palestinian people during the transitional period;

3. *Endorses* the recommendations of the Committee contained in paragraphs 85 to 96 of its report;

4. *Requests* the Committee to continue to keep under review the situation relating to the question of Palestine and to report and make suggestions to the General Assembly or the Security Council, as appropriate;

5. *Authorizes* the Committee to continue to exert all efforts to promote the exercise of the inalienable rights of the Palestinian people, to make such adjustments in its approved programme of work as it may consider appropriate and necessary in light of developments, to give special emphasis to the need to mobilize support for and assistance to the Palestinian people and to report thereon to the General Assembly at its forty-ninth session and thereafter;

6. *Also requests* the Committee to continue to extend its cooperation to non-governmental organizations in their contribution towards heightening international awareness of the facts relating to the question of Palestine and promoting support and assistance to meet the needs of the Palestinian people, and to take the necessary steps to involve additional non-governmental organizations in its work;

7. *Requests* the United Nations Conciliation Commission for Palestine, established under General Assembly resolution 194(III), as well as other United Nations bodies associated with the question of Palestine, to continue to cooperate fully with the Committee and to make available to it, at its request, the relevant information and documentation which they have at their disposal;

8. *Requests* the Secretary-General to circulate the report of the Committee to all the competent bodies of

the United Nations, and urges them to take the necessary action, as appropriate;

9. *Also requests* the Secretary-General to continue to provide the Committee with all the necessary facilities for the performance of its tasks.

General Assembly resolution 48/158 A

20 December 1993   Meeting 85   106-3-40 (recorded vote)

14-nation draft (A/48/L.41 & Add.1); agenda item 35.
Sponsors: Afghanistan, Comoros, Cuba, India, Indonesia, Jordan, Madagascar, Malaysia, Malta, Pakistan, Senegal, Tunisia, Ukraine, Yemen.
Financial implications. 5th Committee, A/48/787; S-G, A/C.5/48/43.
Meeting numbers. GA 48th session: 5th Committee 43; plenary 65, 66, 85.

Recorded vote in Assembly as follows:

In favour: Algeria, Antigua and Barbuda, Armenia, Azerbaijan, Bahamas, Bahrain, Bangladesh, Barbados, Belarus, Belize, Benin, Bhutan, Bolivia, Bosnia and Herzegovina, Botswana, Brazil, Brunei Darussalam, Burkina Faso, Burundi, Cambodia, Cape Verde, Chad, Chile, China, Colombia, Comoros, Costa Rica, Côte d'Ivoire, Cuba, Cyprus, Democratic People's Republic of Korea, Djibouti, Ecuador, Egypt, El Salvador, Ethiopia, Gambia, Ghana, Greece, Guatemala, Guinea-Bissau, Guyana, Haiti, Honduras, India, Indonesia, Iran, Iraq, Jamaica, Jordan, Kazakhstan, Kuwait, Lao People's Democratic Republic, Lebanon, Lesotho, Libyan Arab Jamahiriya, Madagascar, Malaysia, Maldives, Mali, Malta, Mauritania, Mauritius, Mexico, Mongolia, Morocco, Mozambique, Namibia, Nepal, Nicaragua, Niger, Nigeria, Oman, Pakistan, Panama, Peru, Philippines, Qatar, Republic of Korea, Rwanda, Saint Lucia, Saint Vincent and the Grenadines, Saudi Arabia, Senegal, Sierra Leone, Singapore, Spain, Sri Lanka, Sudan, Suriname, Swaziland, Syrian Arab Republic, Thailand, Togo, Trinidad and Tobago, Tunisia, Turkey, Ukraine, United Arab Emirates, United Republic of Tanzania, Uruguay, Venezuela, Viet Nam, Yemen, Zambia, Zimbabwe.

Against: Dominican Republic, Israel, United States.

Abstaining: Argentina, Australia, Austria, Belgium, Bulgaria, Canada, Croatia, Czech Republic, Denmark, Dominica, Estonia, Finland, France, Georgia, Germany, Hungary, Iceland, Ireland, Italy, Japan, Kenya, Latvia, Liechtenstein, Lithuania, Luxembourg, Marshall Islands, Micronesia, Netherlands, New Zealand, Norway, Poland, Portugal, Republic of Moldova, Romania, Russian Federation, Slovakia, Slovenia, Sweden, the former Yugoslav Republic of Macedonia, United Kingdom.

Resolution 48/158 B dealt with the Secretariat's Division for Palestinian Rights.

Division for Palestinian Rights of the Secretariat

The General Assembly,

Having considered the report of the Committee on the Exercise of the Inalienable Rights of the Palestinian People,

Taking note, in particular, of the relevant information contained in paragraphs 46 to 68 of that report,

Recalling its resolutions 32/40 B of 2 December 1977, 33/28 C of 7 December 1978, 34/65 D of 12 December 1979, 35/169 D of 15 December 1980, 36/120 B of 10 December 1981, 37/86 B of 10 December 1982, 38/58 B of 13 December 1983, 39/49 B of 11 December 1984, 40/96 B of 12 December 1985, 41/43 B of 2 December 1986, 42/66 B of 2 December 1987, 43/175 B of 15 December 1988, 44/41 B of 6 December 1989, 45/67 B of 6 December 1990, 46/74 B of 11 December 1991, and 47/64 B of 11 December 1992,

1. *Notes with appreciation* the action taken by the Secretary-General in compliance with its resolution 47/64 B;

2. *Requests* the Secretary-General to provide the Division for Palestinian Rights of the Secretariat with the resources it requires, including the continuing development of the computer-based information system on the question of Palestine, and to ensure that it continues to discharge the tasks detailed in paragraph 1 of resolution 32/40 B, paragraph 2 *(b)* of resolution 34/65 D, paragraph 3 of resolution 40/96 B, paragraph 2 of resolution 42/66 B, paragraph 2 of resolution 44/41 B and

paragraph 2 of resolution 46/74 B, in consultation with the Committee on the Exercise of the Inalienable Rights of the Palestinian People and under its guidance;

3. *Also requests* the Secretary-General to ensure the continued cooperation of the Department of Public Information and other units of the Secretariat in enabling the Division to perform its tasks and in covering adequately the various aspects of the question of Palestine;

4. *Invites* all Governments and organizations to lend their cooperation to the Committee and the Division in the performance of their tasks;

5. *Notes with appreciation* the action taken by Member States to observe annually on 29 November the International Day of Solidarity with the Palestinian People and requests them to continue to give the widest possible publicity to the observance, and requests the Committee to continue to organize, as part of the observance of the Day of Solidarity, an annual exhibit on Palestinian rights in cooperation with the Office of the Permanent Observer for Palestine to the United Nations.

General Assembly resolution 48/158 B

20 December 1993   Meeting 85   107-2-41 (recorded vote)

14-nation draft (A/48/L.42 & Add.1); agenda item 35.
Sponsors: Afghanistan, Comoros, Cuba, India, Indonesia, Jordan, Madagascar, Malaysia, Malta, Pakistan, Senegal, Tunisia, Ukraine, Yemen.
Financial implications. 5th Committee, A/48/787; S-G, A/C.5/48/43.
Meeting numbers. GA 48th session: 5th Committee 43; plenary 65, 66, 85.

Recorded vote in Assembly as follows:

In favour: Algeria, Angola, Antigua and Barbuda, Armenia, Azerbaijan, Bahamas, Bahrain, Bangladesh, Barbados, Belarus, Belize, Benin, Bhutan, Bolivia, Bosnia and Herzegovina, Botswana, Brazil, Brunei Darussalam, Burkina Faso, Burundi, Cambodia, Cape Verde, Chad, Chile, China, Colombia, Comoros, Costa Rica, Côte d'Ivoire, Cuba, Cyprus, Democratic People's Republic of Korea, Djibouti, Ecuador, Egypt, El Salvador, Ethiopia, Gambia, Ghana, Greece, Guatemala, Guinea-Bissau, Guyana, Haiti, Honduras, India, Indonesia, Iran, Iraq, Jamaica, Jordan, Kazakhstan, Kuwait, Lao People's Democratic Republic, Lebanon, Lesotho, Libyan Arab Jamahiriya, Madagascar, Malaysia, Maldives, Mali, Malta, Mauritania, Mauritius, Mexico, Mongolia, Morocco, Mozambique, Namibia, Nepal, Nicaragua, Niger, Nigeria, Oman, Pakistan, Panama, Peru, Philippines, Qatar, Republic of Korea, Rwanda, Saint Lucia, Saint Vincent and the Grenadines, Saudi Arabia, Senegal, Sierra Leone, Singapore, Spain, Sri Lanka, Sudan, Suriname, Swaziland, Syrian Arab Republic, Thailand, Togo, Trinidad and Tobago, Tunisia, Turkey, Ukraine, United Arab Emirates, United Republic of Tanzania, Uruguay, Venezuela, Viet Nam, Yemen, Zambia, Zimbabwe.

Against: Israel, United States.

Abstaining: Argentina, Australia, Austria, Belgium, Bulgaria, Canada, Croatia, Czech Republic, Denmark, Dominica, Dominican Republic, Estonia, Finland, France, Georgia, Germany, Hungary, Iceland, Ireland, Italy, Japan, Kenya, Latvia, Liechtenstein, Lithuania, Luxembourg, Marshall Islands, Micronesia, Netherlands, New Zealand, Norway, Poland, Portugal, Republic of Moldova, Romania, Russian Federation, Slovakia, Slovenia, Sweden, the former Yugoslav Republic of Macedonia, United Kingdom.

A fourth resolution, **48/158 C**, concerned United Nations information activities on the Palestine question.

Public information activities

The Committee on Palestinian rights[7] followed up on the implementation of a 1992 General Assembly request[14] that DPI continue its 1992-1993 special information programme on the Palestine question, with emphasis on public opinion in Europe and North America.

DPI in 1993 accordingly continued to provide press coverage of all United Nations meetings relevant to the question, including those of the Security Council and the Committee, and issued 47 press releases in English and 43 in French containing statements by the Secretary-General relating to it and the situation in the occupied Arab territories. Ongoing coverage of United Nations activities on the question was provided by the United Nations Information Centres, which produced and distributed newsletters, press releases and television news programmes and regularly briefed media representatives. The _UN Chronicle_ continued to publish stories relating to Palestinian issues, while the Department's Public Inquiries Unit responded to 324 information requests on the topic. The issue was also included in the presentation made during the guided tour of Headquarters, and the Group Programme and Community Liaison Unit of DPI arranged briefings on Palestine.

The Department continued to distribute its publications, including the booklet _Building for Peace in the Middle East: An Israeli-Palestinian Dialogue_ and a revised edition of _For the Rights of Palestinians: The Work of the Committee on the Exercise of the Inalienable Rights of the Palestinian People_. Cooperation with the French production company Point du Jour resulted in the production of a two-hour video documentary on the history of Palestine. DPI was currently editing a 30-minute version of that documentary to highlight United Nations involvement, as well as the struggle of Palestinians to achieve their national rights. It further provided feature coverage of various aspects of the question in its weekly radio news magazines, highlighting in particular the deportation of Palestinians. It produced feature programmes on assistance to the Palestinian people and on international protection of Palestinian refugees in Arabic, Bangla, English, French, Hindi, Indonesian, Kiswahili, Portuguese, Russian, Spanish and Urdu.

In cooperation with Greece, DPI sponsored an encounter for Greek journalists (Athens, 27 and 28 April) on the theme of Jerusalem: visions of reconciliation, that brought together 11 international expert panellists. The Department sponsored an international encounter for European journalists (London, 9-11 June) in cooperation with the United Kingdom and supported by _The Guardian_ on promoting a culture for peace in the Middle East. Based on those encounters, DPI initiated the production of three publications.

Among its recommendations, the Committee considered that the bulletins published by the Division for Palestinian rights should be expanded and restructured, and that the Division's studies, information notes, reports and other material should focus specifically on the main issues addressed by the Committee to enhance their usefulness. It believed that the information work of

the United Nations related to the Palestine question would become even more important. Thus, the information programme should follow and reflect the realities and experiences of Palestinians, provide assistance to Palestinian media development and continue disseminating information about the just cause of the Palestinian people, in addition to supporting dialogue in the effort to build peace.

GENERAL ASSEMBLY ACTION

On 20 December 1993, the General Assembly adopted **resolution 48/158 C** by recorded vote.

Department of Public Information of the Secretariat
The General Assembly,

Having considered the report of the Committee on the Exercise of the Inalienable Rights of the Palestinian People,

Taking note, in particular, of the information contained in paragraphs 71 to 84 of that report,

Recalling its resolution 47/64 C of 11 December 1992,

Convinced that the world-wide dissemination of accurate and comprehensive information and the role of non-governmental organizations and institutions remain of vital importance in heightening awareness of and support for the inalienable rights of the Palestinian people,

Aware of the Declaration of Principles on Interim Self-Government Arrangements, signed in Washington, D.C., on 13 September 1993 by the Government of the State of Israel and the Palestine Liberation Organization, and of its positive implications,

1. _Notes with appreciation_ the action taken by the Department of Public Information of the Secretariat in compliance with General Assembly resolution 47/64 C;

2. _Requests_ the Department of Public Information, in full cooperation and coordination with the Committee on the Exercise of the Inalienable Rights of the Palestinian People, to continue, with the necessary flexibility as may be required by developments affecting the question of Palestine, its special information programme on the question of Palestine for the biennium 1994-1995, with particular emphasis on public opinion in Europe and North America, and in particular:

_(a)_ To disseminate information on all the activities of the United Nations system relating to the question of Palestine, including reports of the work carried out by the relevant United Nations organizations;

_(b)_ To continue to issue and update publications on the various aspects of the question of Palestine in all fields, including all information relating to the recent events concerning this question;

_(c)_ To expand its audiovisual material on the question of Palestine, including the production of such material;

_(d)_ To organize and promote fact-finding news missions for journalists to the area, including the occupied territories;

_(e)_ To organize international, regional and national encounters for journalists;

_(f)_ To provide, in cooperation with specialized agencies of the United Nations system, particularly the United Nations Educational, Scientific and Cultural Organization, assistance to the Palestinian people in the field of media development.

General Assembly resolution 48/158 C

20 December 1993   Meeting 85   147-2-2 (recorded vote)

13-nation draft (A/48/L.43 & Add.1); agenda item 35.
Sponsors: Afghanistan, Comoros, Cuba, India, Indonesia, Jordan, Madagascar, Malaysia, Malta, Pakistan, Senegal, Tunisia, Yemen.
Financial implications. 5th Committee, A/48/787; S-G, A/C.5/48/43.
Meeting numbers. GA 48th session: 5th Committee 43; plenary 65, 66, 85.

Recorded vote in Assembly as follows:

In favour: Algeria, Angola, Antigua and Barbuda, Argentina, Armenia, Australia, Austria, Azerbaijan, Bahamas, Bahrain, Bangladesh, Barbados, Belarus, Belgium, Belize, Benin, Bhutan, Bolivia, Bosnia and Herzegovina, Botswana, Brazil, Brunei Darussalam, Bulgaria, Burkina Faso, Burundi, Cambodia, Canada, Cape Verde, Chad, Chile, China, Colombia, Comoros, Costa Rica, Côte d'Ivoire, Croatia, Cuba, Cyprus, Czech Republic, Democratic People's Republic of Korea, Denmark, Djibouti, Dominica, Dominican Republic, Ecuador, Egypt, El Salvador, Estonia, Ethiopia, Finland, France, Gambia, Germany, Ghana, Greece, Guatemala, Guinea-Bissau, Guyana, Haiti, Honduras, Hungary, Iceland, India, Indonesia, Iran, Iraq, Ireland, Italy, Jamaica, Japan, Jordan, Kazakhstan, Kenya, Kuwait, Lao People's Democratic Republic, Latvia, Lebanon, Lesotho, Libyan Arab Jamahiriya, Liechtenstein, Lithuania, Luxembourg, Madagascar, Malawi, Malaysia, Maldives, Mali, Malta, Marshall Islands, Mauritania, Mauritius, Mexico, Micronesia, Mongolia, Morocco, Mozambique, Namibia, Nepal, Netherlands, New Zealand, Nicaragua, Niger, Nigeria, Norway, Oman, Pakistan, Panama, Peru, Philippines, Poland, Portugal, Qatar, Republic of Korea, Republic of Moldova, Romania, Rwanda, Saint Lucia, Saint Vincent and the Grenadines, Saudi Arabia, Senegal, Sierra Leone, Singapore, Slovakia, Slovenia, Spain, Sri Lanka, Sudan, Suriname, Swaziland, Sweden, Syrian Arab Republic, the former Yugoslav Republic of Macedonia, Thailand, Togo, Trinidad and Tobago, Tunisia, Turkey, Ukraine, United Arab Emirates, United Kingdom, United Republic of Tanzania, Uruguay, Venezuela, Viet Nam, Yemen, Zambia, Zimbabwe.
Against: Israel, United States.
Abstaining: Georgia, Russian Federation.

Jerusalem

In October 1993,[15] the Secretary-General submitted a report containing the replies of two Member States to his request for information on steps taken or envisaged to implement a 1992 resolution of the General Assembly deploring the transfer by some States of their diplomatic missions to Jerusalem and calling on them to abide by the relevant United Nations resolutions.[16] Of those States, Ecuador pointed out that it maintained its embassy at Tel Aviv. Ghana stated that, since it had severed all relations with Israel in 1975, the resolution did not apply to it.

GENERAL ASSEMBLY ACTION

On 14 December 1993, the General Assembly adopted **resolution 48/59 A** by recorded vote.

Jerusalem

The General Assembly,

Recalling its resolutions 36/120 E of 10 December 1981, 37/123 C of 16 December 1982, 38/180 C of 19 December 1983, 39/146 C of 14 December 1984, 40/168 C of 16 December 1985, 41/162 C of 4 December 1986, 42/209 D of 11 December 1987, 43/54 C of 6 December 1988, 44/40 C of 4 December 1989, 45/83 C of 13 December 1990, 46/82 B of 16 December 1991 and 47/63 B of 11 December 1992, in which it determined that all legislative and administrative measures and actions taken by Israel, the occupying Power, which had altered or purported to alter the character and status of the Holy City of Jerusalem, in particular the so-called

"Basic Law" on Jerusalem and the proclamation of Jerusalem as the capital of Israel, were null and void and must be rescinded forthwith,

Recalling also Security Council resolution 478(1980) of 20 August 1980, in which the Council, *inter alia*, decided not to recognize the "Basic Law" and called upon those States that had established diplomatic missions at Jerusalem to withdraw such missions from the Holy City,

Having considered the report of the Secretary-General of 25 October 1993,

1. *Determines* that the decision of Israel to impose its laws, jurisdiction and administration on the Holy City of Jerusalem is illegal and therefore null and void and has no validity whatsoever;

2. *Deplores* the transfer by some States of their diplomatic missions to Jerusalem in violation of Security Council resolution 478(1980), and their refusal to comply with the provisions of that resolution;

3. *Calls once more upon* those States to abide by the provisions of the relevant United Nations resolutions, in conformity with the Charter of the United Nations;

4. *Requests* the Secretary-General to report to the General Assembly at its forty-ninth session on the implementation of the present resolution.

General Assembly resolution 48/59 A

14 December 1993   Meeting 79   141-1-11 (recorded vote)

16-nation draft (A/48/L.34 & Add.1); agenda item 34.
Sponsors: Afghanistan, Algeria, Egypt, Indonesia, Jordan, Malaysia, Mauritania, Morocco, Pakistan, Qatar, Saudi Arabia, Senegal, Sudan, Tunisia, United Arab Emirates, Yemen.
Meeting numbers. GA 48th session: plenary 67, 68, 79.

Recorded vote in Assembly as follows:

In favour: Albania, Algeria, Antigua and Barbuda, Argentina, Armenia, Australia, Austria, Azerbaijan, Bahamas, Bahrain, Bangladesh, Barbados, Belarus, Belgium, Benin, Bhutan, Bolivia, Bosnia and Herzegovina, Brazil, Brunei Darussalam, Bulgaria, Burkina Faso, Cameroon, Canada, Central African Republic, Chad, Chile, China, Colombia, Comoros, Congo, Croatia, Cuba, Cyprus, Czech Republic, Democratic People's Republic of Korea, Denmark, Djibouti, Ecuador, Egypt, Estonia, Ethiopia, Finland, France, Gambia, Germany, Greece, Guatemala, Guinea, Guinea-Bissau, Guyana, Haiti, Hungary, India, Indonesia, Iran, Iraq, Ireland, Italy, Jamaica, Japan, Jordan, Kazakhstan, Kenya, Kuwait, Lao People's Democratic Republic, Latvia, Lebanon, Lesotho, Libyan Arab Jamahiriya, Liechtenstein, Lithuania, Luxembourg, Madagascar, Malawi, Malaysia, Maldives, Mali, Malta, Mauritania, Mauritius, Mexico, Monaco, Mongolia, Morocco, Mozambique, Myanmar, Namibia, Nepal, Netherlands, New Zealand, Nicaragua, Niger, Norway, Oman, Pakistan, Panama, Paraguay, Peru, Philippines, Poland, Portugal, Qatar, Republic of Korea, Republic of Moldova, Romania, Russian Federation, Rwanda, Saint Lucia, Saint Vincent and the Grenadines, San Marino, Saudi Arabia, Senegal, Sierra Leone, Singapore, Slovak Republic, Slovenia, Spain, Sri Lanka, Sudan, Suriname, Swaziland, Sweden, Syrian Arab Republic, Thailand, the former Yugoslav Republic of Macedonia, Togo, Trinidad and Tobago, Tunisia, Turkey, Uganda, Ukraine, United Arab Emirates, United Kingdom, United Republic of Tanzania, Uruguay, Venezuela, Viet Nam, Yemen, Zambia, Zimbabwe.
Against: Israel.
Abstaining: Botswana, Fiji, Ghana, Iceland, Marshall Islands, Micronesia, Nigeria, Papua New Guinea, Samoa, Solomon Islands, United States.

Following the vote, the United States emphasized that, after the breakthroughs that changed traditional approaches to the Arab-Israeli conflict, it was important to avoid focusing on divisive or polarizing statements. It was convinced that Jerusalem must remain undivided, but that its final status should be decided through negotiations. Instead of addressing the issue in the manner of this resolution, the United States said that the parties had agreed that Jerusalem would be considered in the final status negotiations.

Assistance to Palestinians

In an effort to support the momentum of the Israeli-Palestinian peace talks, and in response to requests received from Israel and PLO, the Secretary-General on 8 September established a high-level United Nations task force on economic and social development of the Gaza Strip and Jericho. Members of the task force included UNDP Administrator James G. Speth, United Nations Children's Fund (UNICEF) Executive Director James Grant, UNRWA Commissioner-General Ilter Türkmen, Under-Secretary-General for Humanitarian Affairs Jan Eliasson, Under-Secretary-General for Political Affairs James Jonah and Special Political Adviser to the Secretary-General Chinmaya Rajaninath Gharekhan. The priorities of the task force, whose work commenced immediately, were to establish an integrated United Nations approach towards development in Gaza and Jericho, with a particular focus on Gaza, where needs were greatest; to coordinate with other institutions, agencies and NGOs involved in ongoing development projects; and to mobilize international financial support.

Overall, the United Nations system in 1993 expanded its programmes of assistance to the Palestinian people, as requested by the General Assembly in 1992.[17] Summaries of the assistance activities undertaken by 10 bodies and 6 specialized agencies of the system were contained in a report submitted by the Secretary-General to the Assembly, through the Economic and Social Council, in September 1993,[18] and later updated.[19]

In early September 1993, when news of the breakthrough in Israeli-Palestinian negotiations became public, the Secretary-General established a high-level task force to identify new activities and projects that could be rapidly implemented by UNRWA, UNDP and UNICEF, and the United Nations agencies with an established presence in the occupied territories. Those activities would be carried out in addition to the agencies' regular programmes and would be launched as soon as funding was secured. The report of the task force, which identified immediate additional needs for the Palestinian people at $138 million, was circulated to the Conference to Support Middle East Peace on 1 October. Conference participants acknowledged that, in view of its extensive operations in the area, the United Nations would be an effective channel for such assistance, especially in the short term.

In addition to implementing projects with an immediate impact on the economy of the West Bank and Gaza, thereby generating new employment, with a resulting multiplier effect, the Secretary-General was committed to strengthening Palestinian institutions, in particular those which would support the Palestinian Authority. On 14 September, the day after the signing of the Declaration of Principles, PLO Chairman Arafat, in a meeting with the Secretary-General, requested United Nations technical assistance in a variety of sectors, in particular for building the Palestinian administration to be entrusted with the tasks of self-government. He subsequently requested, in a letter of 10 December to the Secretary-General, United Nations assistance in training the Palestinian police force envisaged in the Declaration.

In response to those requests, the Secretary-General in October dispatched a technical mission to Tunis and the occupied territories, for consultation with the Palestinian leadership. The mission also met with officials in Egypt, Israel and Jordan. The parties welcomed the Secretary-General's intention to ensure a unified and coherent approach in the provision of economic, social and other assistance in the territories. The mission also met with representatives of the United Nations agencies and programmes in the West Bank and Gaza, as well as the World Bank team visiting the area at the time. In the light of the mission's findings, the Secretary-General was persuaded of the need to appoint a high-level personality who would serve as a focal point for all United Nations assistance to the Palestinians in the territories.

Conference to Support Middle East Peace. The Conference to Support Middle East Peace, co-sponsored by the Russian Federation and the United States, was held at the United States Department of State (Washington, D.C., 1 October). Forty-six attending States and international organizations, including the United Nations, pledged $2 billion over five years to finance social and economic development in the West Bank and Gaza Strip. At the occasion of the Conference, the UNDP Administrator stated that the United Nations system was in 1993 providing services and implementing special projects in the West Bank and Gaza that amounted to $250 million, a figure accounting for one third of all public expenditure in the West Bank and about one half in Gaza. The system employed more than 8,000 Palestinians and some 70 international staff. He estimated the cost of additional activities in economic and social infrastructure, education, health, public management and training, social services, agriculture, industry and emergency activities, that were to be carried out by UNDP, UNICEF and UNRWA, at $138,250,000.

In November, the Observer of Palestine welcomed before the Assembly the results of the Conference; meanwhile the Palestinian side had established the Palestinian Economic Council for Development and Reconstruction and had maintained constant contact with donor countries and international institutions. PLO expected more United Nations organizations to establish a presence in the Palestinian territory and further expected their close coordination under the direct supervision of the Secretrary-General or his representative.

Report of the Secretary-General. According to the Secretary-General's June 1993 report,[18] the United Nations Centre for Human Settlements (Habitat) prepared and submitted to the April/May session of the Commission on Human Settlements a report on housing requirements of the Palestinian people[20] as part of a plan for the implementation of a shelter strategy for Palestinians to the year 2000. After consideration of the report, the Commission on Human Settlements on 5 May adopted a resolution by recorded vote, requesting the Secretary-General, in consultation with Habitat's Executive Director and in cooperation with PLO, to take all appropriate measures for implementing a national Palestinian housing strategy in accordance with the Global Strategy for Shelter to the Year 2000. It also requested the Executive Director to take all appropriate measures and conduct consultations with a view to facilitating the training and formation of the Palestinian technical cadres necessary to the secure national housing requirements for the Palestinians.[21]

In implementing its 1992-1994 programme of cooperation for the West Bank and Gaza Strip, UNICEF was committed to providing $2,175,000 from its general resources and was to seek an additional $2,175,000 from specific-purpose contributions, of which almost $1 million had been received during the programme's first year, with additional pledges under negotiation. Major objectives included the reduction of child and maternal mortality, the expansion and upgrading of early childhood development activities, educational improvements, and the extension of rehabilitation services for disabled children, while UNICEF's overall strategy was to strengthen the implementation capacity of local organizations and promote cooperation among service providers through joint policy planning, information sharing and implementation. UNICEF was committed to providing support to 42 local clinics run by UNRWA to sustain and expand immunization coverage for 200,000 Palestinian children, aimed at controlling diarrhoeal diseases; reaching 500,000 mothers and children under the anaemia control project; strengthening the capacity of 200 local clinics to control acute respiratory infections; supporting 500 primary schools; providing training for 5,000 teachers as well as local physiotherapists and social and health workers; providing physiotherapy to 3,000 children and supporting the rehabilitation of children with psychological and social problems arising from exposure to conflict situations. UNICEF undertook those activities in close cooperation and coordination with international and national agencies, notably UNRWA and the Palestinian Red Crescent Society.

UNICEF implemented specific programmes of assistance to Palestinian children in Jordan, Lebanon and the Syrian Arab Republic. The programme in Jordan, with annual funding of $200,000 from general resources and the same amount from specific-purpose contributions, was directed at the needs of Palestinians who resided not in camps but in squatter and poor areas of the Amman-Zarqa region and other major urban areas. To better reach this target group, the Fund cooperated with more than 40 international and local NGOs in carrying out the programme which included three components: child and maternal health, education and the urban family. The programme in Lebanon had an approved annual financing level of $350,000 from general resources and the same amount from specific-purpose contributions. Its objectives included the reduction of child and maternal mortality; promotion of early childhood stimulation opportunities and facilities; empowering women with education and vocational skills; and expanding and improving water supply and sanitation, primarily for displaced Palestinians. The programme in the Syrian Arab Republic was based on the same funding scheme as that for Jordan, and comprised three elements: child and maternal health, women's development and early childhood development, while special emphasis was placed on fostering community action and mobilizing the extensive network of NGOs in the Palestinian community.

The Economic and Social Commission for Western Asia (ESCWA), in collaboration with the Food and Agriculture Organization of the United Nations (FAO), fielded a joint project identification/formulation mission to the occupied territories (10 February–2 March) in order to prepare a plan of action for the rehabilitation of the agricultural sector and to make recommendations for developing the institutional structure as well as to prepare priority project documents. Based on the mission's findings, ESCWA in November completed a study on the rehabilitation of the agricultural sector in the occupied Palestinian territories.[22] The study concluded that, since the beginning of occupation, the policy pursued by the Israeli military authority was to expedite the integration of the territories' economy with that of Israel, to discourage indigenous economic development and to ensure the suppression of any competition that could prove detrimental to Israeli interests. Now the territories were almost totally dependent on trade with Israel, and many Palestinians earned their income either by working as labourers in Israel or through subcontracting work with Israeli firms. The sharp reduction in remittances by Palestinians who worked in the Gulf States exacerbated that dependency. The outstanding issues facing the agricultural sector were defined as confiscations and restrictions, reduced services, lack of infrastructure, market constraints, particularly with respect to access to export markets, institutional handicaps and the absence of planning and coordination. Project documents on land reclamation and development, rehabilitation of deep wells for irrigation purposes, rehabilitation of springs and irrigation canals, establishment of a central laboratory for veterinary services and establishing a dairy production training centre in the West Bank were finalized and annexed to the study.

At the conclusion of a mission fielded by the United Nations Environment Programme (UNEP) to Egypt, Jordan, the Syrian Arab Republic and PLO headquarters at Tunis, it was noted that the establishment of environmental information systems for the occupied Palestinian territories was a necessary first step for assessing the environmental situation. The mission, which was unable to visit the occupied territories, recommended that such an information system be established with technical, financial and training support and a back-up system at an institution in the West Bank with a sub-centre in Gaza. The findings and recommendations of the mission were discussed by UNEP's Governing Council, which, by a decision of 21 May,[23] expressed concern over the deterioration of the environmental conditions in the territories, stressed the need for protecting their environment and natural resources and requested UNEP's Executive Director to implement the recommendations. The Council also requested him to complete and update the report on the state of the environment in the territories for submission to the Council's 1994 session, and to provide the necessary technical assistance in Palestinian institutional and self-capacity building, including training (see PART THREE, Chapter VIII). UNEP further participated in a working group on environment (Tokyo, 24 and 25 May), which conducted discussions in the framework of the Middle East peace process.

In accordance with a General Assembly resolution of 1992,[17] the Committee on Palestinian rights devoted its 1993 seminar for the European region[24] to assistance to the Palestinian people. Held at the headquarters of the United Nations Educational, Scientific and Cultural Organization (UNESCO) (Paris, 26-29 April), the seminar considered assistance to the Palestinian people: priorities and needs and the role and experience of the United Nations system, regional organizations, countries involved in assistance projects in the occupied territories and of Palestinian and interna-

tional NGOs. The seminar underlined the need for coordination between various donors and United Nations organizations and agencies on the one hand, and the Palestinian central authority on the other. In this connection, it welcomed the introduction of the Palestine Development Programme prepared by the Department of Economic Affairs and Planning of PLO. The seminar asked the Committee to recommend that the Secretary-General convene a meeting of representatives of the United Nations system and PLO officials to consider mechanisms for coordinating and channelling assistance, as well as for deciding on priorities. It finally called for urgent action by the international community to meet the emergency needs of Palestinians living under occupation. ESCWA contributed actively to the discussions at the seminar and gave a presentation that centred on its recent experience and priority areas and projects related to Palestinian development assistance. UNESCO itself granted Palestine, under its Participation Programme for 1992-1993, financial aid amounting, in February 1993, to $93,000.

UNRWA maintained an extensive programme of education, health and relief services and other humanitarian assistance to Palestine refugees (see below, under "Palestine refugees").

As to assistance by specialized agencies, the current projects of the International Labour Organisation (ILO) in the territories covered trade union training and vocational rehabilitation for handicapped persons. A continuation of activities was foreseen in other areas, with ILO attaching considerable importance to the extension of its technical cooperation programmes to assist Palestinians. A multidisciplinary ILO mission to the territories in October, which explored modalities of future ILO involvement, received logistical support from UNDP.

The World Health Organization (WHO) cooperated with the Union of Palestinian Medical Relief Committees in completing a study of rural health centres and services in the occupied territories to locate the infrastructure, analyze the services it offered and establish how that infrastructure could form the backbone of a cohesive primary health care system. Work financed by WHO to remodel a maternity wing in the Red Crescent Society hospital in Jerusalem was completed in late 1992. During the period under review, two donations totalling $230,000 were received from Belgium and Italy in response to an appeal for $3.5 million.

UNDP activities. UNDP's Programme of Assistance to the Palestinian People in 1993 achieved a substantially increased level of expenditures over previous years. Its overall objectives evolved in response to the rapidly changing political situation and especially the signing in September of the

Declaration of Principles between Israel and PLO (see above). To help meet the challenge, UNDP formulated 34 capacity-building projects involving governance, agriculture, industry, urban development, trade promotion, statistics, water, sanitation and environment and gender in development. By the end of 1993, Governments had pledged more than one third of the $75 million required to complete those projects. During the year, UNDP investment in the occupied Palestinian territories totalled $15 million, bringing its total investment there to more than $50 million.

The programme strategy for 1993, formulated in full collaboration with Palestinian counterparts, focused on four primary development areas. The first of those represented a concerted effort to support the public sector, especially in the emerging central governance institutions, such as the Palestinian Bureau of Statistics, local public institutions, municipalities and water departments. UNDP extended assistance to the newly established Palestinian institutional structures to enable them to rise to their substantive challenges. The second area of focus stimulated and encouraged economic development, particularly in industry, commerce and trade, agriculture and tourism. Human development, the third area, sought to alleviate poverty and narrow the social, economic and gender gaps in the West Bank and Gaza. The fourth strategic development objective addressed environmental protection and development.

The programme launched a number of projects in 1993 aimed at economic expansion and employment generation. Six industrial companies benefited from the Business Development Centre revolving loan fund, which also provided technical cooperation to the Palestinian Chambers of Commerce and to vocational training institutions through advisory services. A modern irrigation project provided some 600 farmers in Gaza with irrigation equipment and training, enabling them to save water and increase productivity in a cost-effective manner. Under an integrated rural development project, two villages in the northern West Bank were selected on a pilot basis, with the aim of alleviating poverty, upgrading health and education services, and improving water and sanitation systems. The completion of the Princess Alia Hospital at Hebron and the start of construction on the Beit Jala Hospital brought expanded and improved health care facilities to the West Bank, while ambulances, medical equipment and assistance to the handicapped were provided to various health institutions. The construction of nine schools, mainly in rural areas, allowed better access to education facilities, particularly for girls, improved the physical classroom environment and reduced the teacher-student ratio. As the integration of women into the economy and their em-

powerment in governance structures continued to be a main thrust of the programme, UNDP launched a project that particularly targeted women and their promotion in the Palestinian society and economy. UNDP designed and began construction of water distribution networks to improve the quality and quantity of the water supply to 20,000 residents of the old city of Nablus and for nearly 100,000 residents of Rafah in the Gaza Strip. The completion of a project to deepen and upgrade the well at Ein Samia provided 200,000 residents with a better and more reliable water supply. Under the water resources action programme, launched by UNDP in 1993, the efforts of a task force of Palestinian professionals was coordinated to plan for and manage the region's water resources.

The World Food Programme launched, in close cooperation with UNDP, a $3.4 million project for emergency food assistance to Gaza's non-refugee population. A joint UNDP/UNICEF/UNRWA project was initiated in the context of the Middle East peace process's multilateral working group on refugees to expand community services serving children and youth. The programme provided considerable logistical and advisory support to World Bank missions fielded to the West Bank and Gaza throughout 1993. In July, UNDP published and widely circulated the second *Compendium of Ongoing Technical Assistance Projects in the Occupied Palestinian Territories.*

By a decision of 18 June,[(25)] the UNDP Governing Council took note of the Administrator's 1993 report on the programme of assistance,[(26)] recommending that it continue to address the serious economic and social situation of the Palestinians, and appealing to the international community, Governments and intergovernmental organizations to expand financial and other support for activities of the programme to cover the projected shortfall in resources available to UNDP's fifth (1992-1996) programming cycle.

The *Report of the Mission to Review UNDP's Programme in the Occupied Palestinian Territories* (10-31 October 1992), which was published in March 1993, stated that Gaza's aquifers were severely overexploited and salinated to the extent that wells were going out of operation and water was becoming unpalatable or even unusable for irrigation. That was the core of Gaza's environmental problems, which were compounded by abundant waste water and solid waste throughout the urban landscape. Only 20 per cent of the refugee camp population and 40 per cent of those outside were served by sewers, which posed health risks. UNDP reported a life expectancy at birth of 65 years in the occupied territories as opposed to 76 years in Israel. While the estimated infant mortality rate ranged from 40 to 70 per 1,000 live birth in the occupied territories, it was 10 per 1,000 for Israel. The mission concluded that the constraints imposed by the Civil Administration, insecurity, civil strife and strikes created an extremely unfavourable climate for economic activities, while Israeli practices and the Arab economic boycott hampered exports. The suspension of concessional flows, especially from the Gulf countries, seriously threatened the functioning of public services, while the economic situation in Israel, combined with the inflow of new immigrants, reduced opportunities for Palestinian workers on Israel's labour market. Among its recommendations, the mission deemed it important that UNDP not wait for agreement in the peace process before it launched a more coherent programme, requiring increased financial resources. It should assist Palestinian efforts to draw up an initial development plan, as well as sector plans based on it. An economic adviser of international reputation should be sent to Jerusalem, to be attached to the Special Representative's Office for a period of three to six months. Those initiatives were to involve from the beginning major bilateral donors as well as interested neighbours such as Egypt and Jordan, and be undertaken in close cooperation with the World Bank. The mission identified as the main objective of any development effort the strengthening of the self-reliance of the Palestinian economy and people and the gradual movement of Palestinians out of dependency into a phase of rehabilitation and revitalization. UNDP should thus, in accordance with Palestinian priorities, focus on three themes: human resources development, including institution-building at central and local levels; employment and income-generating projects; and infrastructural improvements. Within this context, environment, water and sanitation were to receive priority attention. The mission finally recommended the strengthening of the Office of the Programme of Assistance to the Palestinian People in New York so as to facilitate a policy dialogue between Headquarters and the Office at Jerusalem on major issues and to ensure the provision of highly qualified technical advice.

UNCTAD activities. Assistance to Palestinians by the secretariat of the United Nations Conference on Trade and Development (UNCTAD) from March 1992 to March 1993 was intensified in four main areas: monitoring and analysis of Israeli policies and practices hampering Palestinian economic development; investigation of the impact of those policies and practices on the main economic sectors; development of a database on the economy in the territories and information dissemination; and coordination of activities with other United Nations organs. This assistance, including recent developments in the Palestinian economy, the status of the environment and measures to improve it, were reviewed in a July report of the UNCTAD secretariat.[27] On 1 October, the Trade and Development Board[28] took note of the report.

Within the context of the intersectoral UNCTAD project investigating prospects of sustained economic and social development in the West Bank and Gaza, work was intensified on the preparation of 25 in-depth field studies covering the main economic and social sectors. As part of the project's requirements, work on the secretariat's database on the economy of the occupied Palestinian territory was intensified. A statistical series covering national income, population, labour and employment, balance of payments and external trade for the period 1968-1987 was standardized and classified along the lines of the economic time series in use in the secretariat and stored in its computer facilities for future reference. The series was also published[29] and widely disseminated to research and educational institutions so as to provide a uniform set of economic statistics on the West Bank and Gaza. In September, UNCTAD reported on the prospects for sustained development of the Palestinian economy in the West Bank and Gaza Strip,[30] whereby it assessed the main economic and social problems, identified needs and specific measures for immediate action and outlined prospects for sustained development.

In accordance with principle 23 of the 1992 Rio Declaration on Environment and Development,[31] stating that the environment and natural resources of people under oppression, domination and occupation shall be protected, the UNCTAD secretariat initiated an in-depth study of the environmental dimension of Israeli policies in the West Bank and Gaza and their impact on the economic and social situation of Palestinians. Another UNCTAD study on the agricultural sector of the West Bank and Gaza Strip, issued in October,[32] identified as strategic objectives of agricultural development generating the maximum number of employment opportunities; targeting the production process to cater for domestic consumption needs; maximizing the area of land under cultivation; expanding the irrigated farming area; and striving to improve the competitiveness of farmers as regards produce quality, production costs and level of auxiliary marketing services. The study recommended policies and projects in the planning of agricultural development, credit, education and research, land, water, agricultural trade, infrastructure and auxiliary services, diversification of cropping patterns, livestock, subsidiary components, and cooperatives.

ECONOMIC AND SOCIAL COUNCIL ACTION

On 30 July 1993, the Economic and Social Council adopted **resolution 1993/78** by roll-call vote.

Assistance to the Palestinian people

The Economic and Social Council

Recommends to the General Assembly the adoption of the following draft resolution:

"Assistance to the Palestinian people

"*The General Assembly,*

"*Recalling* its resolution 47/170 of 22 December 1992,

"*Taking into account* the *intifadah* of the Palestinian people in the occupied Palestinian territory against the Israeli occupation, including Israeli economic and social policies and practices,

"*Rejecting* Israeli restrictions on external economic and social assistance to the Palestinian people in the occupied Palestinian territory,

"*Concerned* about the economic losses sustained by the Palestinian people as a result of Israeli closures and isolation of the Palestinian territory, including Jerusalem, occupied since 1967,

"*Affirming* that the Palestinian people cannot develop their national economy as long as the Israeli occupation persists,

"*Taking into account* developments in the peace talks and their implications for the Palestinian people,

"*Welcoming* the United Nations Seminar on Assistance to the Palestinian People, held in Paris from 26 to 29 April 1993 in response to General Assembly resolution 47/170,

"*Aware* of the increasing need to provide economic and social assistance to the Palestinian people,

"1.   *Takes note* of the report of the Secretary-General;

"2.   *Expresses its appreciation* to the States, United Nations bodies and intergovernmental and non-governmental organizations that have provided assistance to the Palestinian people;

"3.   *Requests* the international community, the United Nations system and intergovernmental and non-governmental organizations to sustain and increase their assistance to the Palestinian people, in close cooperation with the Palestine Liberation Organization;

"4.   *Urges* the Government of Israel to accept *de jure* applicability of the Geneva Convention relative to the Protection of Civilian Persons in Time of War, of 12 August 1949, to all territories occupied by Israel since 1967 and to abide scrupulously by the provisions of that Convention;

"5.   *Calls for* treatment on a transit basis of Palestinian exports and imports passing through neighbouring ports and points of exit and entry;

"6.   *Also calls for* the granting of trade concessions and concrete preferential measures for Palestinian exports on the basis of Palestinian certificates of origin;

"7.   *Further calls for* the immediate lifting of Israeli restrictions and obstacles hindering the implementation of assistance projects by the United Nations bodies and others providing economic and social assistance to the Palestinian people in the occupied Palestinian territory;

"8.   *Reiterates its call* for the implementation of development projects in the occupied Palestinian territory, including the projects mentioned in its resolution 39/223 of 18 December 1984;

"9.   *Calls for* facilitation of the establishment of Palestinian economic and social institutions in the occupied Palestinian territory;

"10.   *Suggests* that the Committee on the Exercise of the Inalienable Rights of the Palestinian People consider, in its future programmes, convening seminars on economic and social assistance to the Palestinian people, taking into account their assistance needs in the light of developments in the region;

"11.   *Requests* the Secretary-General to seek ways and means of mobilizing and coordinating assistance to the Palestinian people, taking into account the outcome of the United Nations Seminar on Assistance to the Palestinian People, held in Paris from 26 to 29 April 1993;

"12.   *Requests* the Secretary-General to report to the General Assembly at its forty-ninth session, through the Economic and Social Council, on the progress made in the implementation of the present resolution."

Economic and Social Council resolution 1993/78

30 July 1993   Meeting 46   45-1 (roll-call vote)

11-nation draft (E/1993/L.43 & Corr.1), orally revised; agenda item 4 *(b)*.
Sponsors: Algeria, Cuba, Iraq, Lebanon, Malaysia, Morocco, Senegal, Somalia, Syrian Arab Republic, Tunisia, Yemen.
Meeting numbers. ESC 41, 43, 45, 46.

Roll-call vote in Council as follows:

In favour: Angola, Argentina, Australia, Austria, Bahamas, Bangladesh, Belarus, Belgium, Benin, Bhutan, Botswana, Brazil, Canada, Chile, China, Colombia, Cuba, Denmark, France, Germany, Guinea, India, Italy, Japan, Kuwait, Madagascar, Malaysia, Mexico, Morocco, Nigeria, Norway, Peru, Philippines, Poland, Republic of Korea, Romania, Russian Federation, Sri Lanka, Suriname, Swaziland, Syrian Arab Republic, Trinidad and Tobago, Turkey, Ukraine, United Kingdom.
Against: United States.

The United States rejected the text on the grounds that it was political in nature as well as controversial and would not help to resolve the fundamental issues currently the subject of direct negotiations between Israel and the Palestinians.

GENERAL ASSEMBLY ACTION

On 21 December, acting on the recommendation of the Second (Economic and Financial) Committee, the General Assembly adopted **resolution 48/213** without vote.

Assistance to the Palestinian people

The General Assembly,

Recalling its resolution 47/170 of 22 December 1992,

Welcoming the signing of the Declaration of Principles on Interim Self-Government Arrangements, including its Annexes and its Agreed Minutes, by the Government of the State of Israel and the Palestine Liberation Organization, in Washington, D.C., on 13 September 1993,

Gravely concerned about the difficult economic and employment conditions facing the Palestinian people throughout the occupied territory,

Conscious of the need for improvement in the economic and social infrastructure of the occupied territory and in the living conditions of the Palestinian people,

Aware that development is difficult under occupation and is best promoted in circumstances of peace and stability,

Noting, in the light of the recent developments, the great economic and social challenges facing the Palestinian people and their leadership,

Conscious also of the urgent necessity for international assistance to the Palestinian people, taking into account the Palestinian priorities,

Noting also the convening of the United Nations Seminar on Assistance to the Palestinian People, held at the headquarters of the United Nations Educational, Scientific and Cultural Organization from 26 to 29 April 1993,

Stressing the need for the full engagement of the United Nations in the process of building Palestinian institutions and in providing broad assistance to the Palestinian people,

Welcoming the convening of the Conference to Support Middle East Peace, held in Washington, D.C., on 1 October 1993, and the establishment of the high-level United Nations task force to support the economic and social development of the Palestinian people,

Having considered the report of the Secretary-General,

1. *Takes note* of the report of the Secretary-General;

2. *Expresses its appreciation* to the Secretary-General for his rapid response and efforts regarding assistance to the Palestinian people;

3. *Expresses its appreciation also* to the Member States, United Nations bodies and intergovernmental and non-governmental organizations that have provided and continue to provide assistance to the Palestinian people;

4. *Welcomes* the results of the Conference to Support Middle East Peace, convened in Washington, D.C., on 1 October 1993;

5. *Urges* Member States, international financial institutions of the United Nations system, international intergovernmental and non-governmental organizations and regional and interregional organizations to extend, as rapidly and as generously as possible, economic and social assistance to the Palestinian people in order to assist in the development of the West Bank and Gaza, and to do so in close cooperation with the Palestine Liberation Organization and through official Palestinian institutions;

6. *Considers* that an active United Nations role in assisting in the implementation of the Declaration of Principles on Interim Self-Government Arrangements, including its Annexes and its Agreed Minutes, can make a positive contribution;

7. *Calls upon* relevant organizations and agencies of the United Nations system to intensify their assistance in response to the urgent needs of the Palestinian people and to improve coordination through an appropriate mechanism under the auspices of the Secretary-General;

8. *Urges* Member States to open their markets to exports from the West Bank and Gaza on the most favourable terms, consistent with appropriate trading rules;

9. *Suggests* the convening in 1993/94, under the appropriate United Nations auspices, of a seminar on Palestinian trade and investment needs in light of the new developments;

10. *Requests* the Secretary-General to ensure the coordinated work of the United Nations system for an adequate response to the needs of the Palestinian people and to mobilize financial, technical, economic and other assistance;

11. *Also requests* the Secretary-General to submit a report to the General Assembly at its forty-ninth session, through the Economic and Social Council, on the implementation of the present resolution, containing:

(a) An assessment of the assistance actually received by the Palestinian people;

(b) An assessment of the needs still unmet and specific proposals for responding effectively to them;

12. *Decides* to include in the provisional agenda of its forty-ninth session an item entitled "Assistance to the Palestinian people".

General Assembly resolution 48/213

21 December 1993   Meeting 86   Adopted without vote

Approved by Second Committee (A/48/715) without vote, 13 December (meeting 48); draft by Vice-Chairman (A/C.2/48/L.90), based on informal consultations on 12-nation draft (A/C.2/48/L.18); agenda item 12. *Meeting numbers.* GA 48th session: 2nd Committee 12-14, 45, 48; plenary 86.

Assistance to Palestinian women

In response to the Economic and Social Council's 1992 request[33] that he review the situation of Palestinian women and children in the occupied territory and in the refugee camps, the Secretary-General submitted a report to the Commission on the Status of Women at its 1993 session.[34] In a later report[35] covering developments during 1993, the Secretary-General noted that during that year no missions of experts to the territory, requested by the Council in resolution 1993/15 of July 1993 (see below), could take place in view of the changing political situation. He stated that despite positive developments and increased hope for peace after the signing of the Declaration of Principles[36] in September between Israel and PLO, no substantive or immediate improvement of living conditions of Palestinian women and children, whose status was profoundly affected by the political consequences of occupation, could be reported.

The number of fatalities and injuries, particularly among children, was significantly higher in 1993 than during the preceding year. UNRWA reported that Israeli security forces were responsible for the deaths of 80 Palestinians from the West Bank, including 8 children, and 120 persons from Gaza, among them 28 children. Approximately one fourth of all fatalities continued to be children under 16 years of age. Palestinian women similarly experienced violence and maltreatment caused by the unrest and armed conflict. In Gaza, 722 women reported serious injuries requiring medical treatment, as did 108 women in the West Bank. Eight of 48 female prisoners suffering from injuries and maltreatment were reportedly denied adequate medical treatment, and 9 Palestinian females were said to have been killed through actions of the Israeli security forces and settlers, among them three schoolgirls under 13 years of age and one 4-year-old girl. Women and children were especially affected by measures of collective punishment.

The Israeli-ordered closure of Gaza and the West Bank on 30 and 31 March, respectively, resulted in a substantial rise in socio-economic hardship since some 130,000 Palestinians were suddenly cut off from their income sources, which in turn changed consumption patterns and nutritional habits. Concern was expressed that the percentage of growth-retarded children under three years of age and the number of child deaths could rise, since protein-energy malnutrition was closely associated with infant and child mortality. The rapidly worsening dimension of environmental contamination and degradation in the territories, especially in Gaza, which stemmed mostly from the over-exploitation by Israeli authorities and settlers of the available water resources, the lack of adequate waste management systems and destruction of thousands of olive and fruit trees, presented a direct health threat to the population, in particular to children.

The life of Palestinian families was characterized by frequent separations, and the absence of male family members due to detention, expulsion, imprisonment or death increased the number of female-headed households. That number was likewise high among the Palestinian refugee population since men tended to leave the camps in search of work. Thus, the camps' population consisted mainly of women, children and the elderly, women being the backbone of refugee camp life. According to UNRWA, some 30 per cent of households in the West Bank's refugee population and 20 per cent in Gaza were female-headed. A reported 22 per cent of families qualifying for UNRWA's special hardship programme were headed by women. In addition, family reunification laws led to the deportation of family members, including children, denying them the right to permanent return, while children were even denied registration.

Female-headed households were particularly vulnerable to poverty, as women had traditionally depended on men as providers. Impeded by lack of education, vocational training, skills and employment, and subject to socio-cultural restrictions in their freedom of movement, the majority of Palestinian women could not ensure a living for their families. The condition of widows was exceedingly difficult, not having received sufficient attention regarding *de jure* headship, property rights and guardianship of the children. Social and legal pressures often forced single women and their children to join the household of their kin and give up independent living in the absence of a male head of family. Thirty-seven per cent of the female population married under the minimum legal age of 17, with the increase in such early marriages reportedly linked to long-term school closures and the deteriorating economic situation, which discouraged parents from continuing their daughters' education.

The Secretary-General anticipated, however, that the implementation of the Declaration of Principles would have an impact on the situation of Palestinian women as it transformed the region's political perspective. With political developments entering a new phase, the concerns of women could be considered part of the development agenda. All areas addressed in the Agreement,

starting from direct, free and general elections for the Palestinian Council to human resources development, environmental protection and communications and media, could benefit from the scrutiny of women. Development projects in agriculture and the setting up of infrastructure, housing, education and health facilities could best be elaborated with the participation of female experts. At the outset, it was of paramount importance to strive for *de jure* equality for women.

The Secretary-General stated that the Palestinian Federation of Women's Action recognized the urgent need for women's equality to be enshrined in the constitutional declaration of the national authority and for women's participation in the drafting of laws and regulations and in the new legislature and community life to be guaranteed. The Federation asked for the participation of leading female professionals in the formation of the transitional national government and for a larger proportion of women in principal and subsidiary organizations and institutions dealing with social, economic, educational, administrative and other matters. Its request covered civil rights, education, health provision, the planning and implementation of growth and development and the media.

Adequate funds and resources should be given to women-in-development programmes, and female personnel of sufficient authority should be included in all policy, planning and programming activities, the Secretary-General continued. Appropriate quantitative and qualitative national targets needed to be identified, and while a national machinery for the advancement of Palestinian women was already in place, it was in need of recognition, authority and influence at the highest political level. Women needed to participate in future governance structures and existing development institutions and, most importantly, be involved in the formulation of development strategies. Skills training and gender awareness were important tools for achieving those goals. The most important programme, besides providing adequate health services and improving education, the Secretary-General concluded, was the development of sustainable income-generation activities for women, which required the identification of realistic, feasible possibilities and basic support facilities, as well as support from the international community, NGOs and donor agencies.

ECONOMIC AND SOCIAL COUNCIL ACTION

On 27 July, the Economic and Social Council, on the recommendation of its Social Committee, adopted **resolution 1993/15** by roll-call vote.

Situation of and assistance to Palestinian women
The Economic and Social Council,
Having considered with appreciation the report submitted by the Secretary-General on the situation of Palestinian

women in the occupied territory and previous reports concerning the situation of Palestinian women inside and outside the occupied Palestinian territory,

Recalling the Nairobi Forward-looking Strategies for the Advancement of Women, in particular paragraph 260 thereof,

Recalling also its resolution 1992/16 of 30 July 1992 and its other relevant resolutions,

Deeply concerned about the additional suffering of women and children living under occupation,

Expressing special concern about the tragic situation of the Palestinian women in the occupied Palestinian territory, which has been dangerously deteriorating at all levels,

Deeply alarmed by the deteriorating situation of Palestinian women and children in the occupied Palestinian territory, including Jerusalem, as a result of the continued Israeli violation of Palestinian human rights and oppressive measures, including collective punishments, curfews, demolition of houses, closure of schools and universities, mass deportation, confiscation of land and settlement activities and denial of family unification, which are illegal and contrary to the relevant provisions of the Geneva Convention relative to the Protection of Civilian Persons in Time of War, of 12 August 1949,

1. *Reaffirms* that for Palestinian women, equality, self-reliance and integration in the national development plan can be achieved only through the termination of the Israeli occupation and the attainment of the inalienable rights of the Palestinian people;

2. *Demands* that Israel, the occupying Power, accept the *de jure* applicability of the Geneva Convention relative to the Protection of Civilian Persons in Time of War, of 12 August 1949, to the occupied Palestinian territory, including Jerusalem, and to respect the provisions of the Convention;

3. *Appeals* to Governments, financial organizations of the United Nations system, non-governmental organizations and other relevant institutions to provide financial assistance to Palestinian women towards the creation of specific projects for them, in support of their attempts to achieve full integration in the development process of their society;

4. *Requests* the Commission on the Status of Women to continue monitoring the implementation of the Nairobi Forward-looking Strategies for the Advancement of Women, in particular paragraph 260 concerning assistance to Palestinian women;

5. *Requests* the Secretary-General to assist in the review of the situation of Palestinian women using all available resources, including missions of experts to the occupied Palestinian territory, and to submit to the Commission, at its thirty-eighth session, a report on the implementation of the present resolution, containing recommendations and a programme of action aimed at improving the situation of Palestinian women under Israeli occupation.

Economic and Social Council resolution 1993/15

27 July 1993   Meeting 43   32-1-11 (roll-call vote)

Approved by Social Committee (E/1993/105) by recorded vote (31-1-11), 14 July (meeting 9); draft by Commission on women (E/1993/27); agenda item 19.

Roll-call vote in Council as follows:

In favour: Argentina, Australia, Austria, Bahamas, Bangladesh, Belarus, Benin, Bhutan, Botswana, Brazil, Chile, China, Colombia, Cuba, Guinea, India, Kuwait, Madagascar, Malaysia, Mexico, Morocco, Nigeria, Peru,

Philippines, Republic of Korea, Russian Federation, Suriname, Swaziland, Syrian Arab Republic, Togo, Trinidad and Tobago, Ukraine.
   Against: United States.
   Abstaining: Belgium, Canada, Denmark, France, Germany, Italy, Japan, Norway, Poland, Romania, United Kingdom.

REFERENCES

[1]YUN 1980, p. 399. [2]Ibid., p. 426, SC res. 478(1980), 20 Aug. 1980. [3]YUN 1992, p. 401, GA res. 47/64 A, 11 Dec. 1992. [4]YUN 1975, p. 248, GA res. 3376(XXX), 10 Nov. 1975. [5]A/47/874-S/25136, A/47/893-S/25311, A/47/911-S/25464, A/47/959-S/25862. [6]YUN 1976, p. 235. [7]A/48/35. [8]YUN 1992, p. 402, GA res. 47/64 B, 11 Dec. 1992. [9]YUN 1991, p. 221. [10]YUN 1967, p. 257, SC res. 242(1967), 22 Nov. 1967. [11]YUN 1973, p. 213, SC res. 338(1973), 22 Oct. 1973. [12]YUN 1980, p. 427, SC res. 465(1980), 1 Mar. 1980. [13]A/48/L.45. [14]YUN 1992, p. 403, GA res. 47/64 C, 11 Dec. 1992. [15]A/48/522. [16]YUN 1992, p. 403, GA res. 47/63 B, 11 Dec. 1992. [17]Ibid., p. 406, GA res. 47/170, 22 Dec. 1992. [18]A/48/183-E/1993/74 & Add.1. [19]A/49/263-E/1994/112. [20]HS/C/14/2/Add.1. [21]A/48/8 (res. 14/9). [22]E/ESCWA/AGR/1993/9. [23]A/48/25 (dec. 17/31). [24]A/48/168-E/1993/62 & Corr.1. [25]E/1993/35 (dec. 93/19). [26]DP/1993/19. [27]TD/B/40(1)/8. [28]A/48/15. [29]UNCTAD/RDP/SEU/6, UNCTAD/DSD/SEU/1. [30]UNCTAD/DSD/SEU/2. [31]YUN 1992, p. 672. [32]UNCTAD/DSD/SEU/Misc.5. [33]YUN 1992, p. 876, ESC res. 1992/16, 30 July 1992. [34]E/CN.6/1993/10. [35]E/CN.6/1994/6. [36]A/48/486-S/26560, annex.

Incidents and disputes involving Arab countries and Israel

Iraq and Israel

By **decision 48/436** of 20 December 1993, the General Assembly deferred consideration of the item on armed Israeli aggression against Iraqi nuclear installations and included it in the draft agenda of its forty-ninth (1994) session. The item had been inscribed yearly on the Assembly's agenda since 1981,[1] following the bombing by Israel of a nuclear research centre near Baghdad.

Israel and Lebanon

The overall situation in Lebanon improved at a steady pace during 1993 following the election of a new Government, which put national reconciliation and reconstruction at the top of its agenda. The extension of governmental authority throughout the country progressed further, and the security situation improved as political stability returned after nearly 16 years of conflict. However, continued military and civil violence characterized a tense security situation in the southern part of the country, which remained under Israeli occupation. The area north of the border with Israel and the western Bekaa were theatres for frequent armed confrontations between Israeli and South Lebanon Army (SLA) troops on the one hand and Islamic guerrilla resistance groups, most notably Hezbollah, on the other. Sporadic fighting also occurred involving Israeli troops and SLA personnel. In July, Israel launched an unprecedented week-long military campaign into southern Lebanon, which erased entirely dozens of villages, left some 130 people dead and many hundreds wounded and caused an exodus of an estimated half a million people fleeing towards Beirut and northern areas of the country.

Following the establishment of a cease-fire on 31 July and after consultations with the United Nations, the Lebanese Government, on 9 August, sent an army unit to the area of operation of the United Nations Interim Force in Lebanon (UNIFIL) for the purpose of maintaining law and order. The unit, which comprised some 300 personnel of all ranks, remained deployed in garrisons at Qana, Jwayya, Arzun and Bir as Sanasil.

Lebanon continued in 1993 to press for the withdrawal of Israel from that part of southern Lebanon proclaimed a "security zone" by Israel and manned by the Israel Defence Force (IDF), with the assistance of the so-called South Lebanon Army, referred to as the de facto forces (DFF). The boundaries of the Israeli-controlled Lebanese territory—an area along the armistice demarcation line—were determined by the forward positions of DFF and IDF. As of July 1993, the two forces maintained 72 military positions. Within the Israeli-controlled area, Israel maintained, in addition to DFF, a civil administration and a security service with broad powers to pursue suspected opponents of the occupation. Movement between that area and the rest of Lebanon was strictly controlled, and the area remained largely dependent on Israel for economic assistance. An estimated 3,000 jobs in Israel were held by Lebanese from that area, and access to them was controlled by DFF and the security services. In justification of its refusal to withdraw, Israel maintained that its presence was in self-defence against attacks on northern Israel by what it claimed were several terrorist factions, particularly the Shiite Muslim group Hezbollah, which used Lebanese territory as their staging area.

The situation in Lebanon, as well as Israel's and Lebanon's positions on issues related to it, were reflected in the Secretary-General's reports on UNIFIL (see below), as well as in a number of communications addressed to the Secretary-General and the President of the Security Council during the year.[2]

In connection with its requests to the Security Council to further extend UNIFIL's mandate, which was due to expire on 31 January and 31 July (see below), Lebanon reported on positive developments in the country. They included, according to a letter of January,[3] the formation of a new Government headed by Prime Minister Rafic Hariri, which commenced its agenda to broaden and strengthen national reconciliation, accelerate reconstruction and development, and promote national stability and security through social, economic and administrative reform and the liberation of occupied Lebanese territory. In spite of those developments and contrary to the participation of both countries in the peace talks, Israel intensified its efforts to destabilize Lebanon by perpetuating its occupation of the south. Recently, it had uprooted 415 Palestinians from their homes and deported them to Lebanon in violation of Lebanese sovereignty and territorial integrity and the principles of the Charter (see below, under "Expulsion and deportation of Palestinians").

Throughout 14 months of negotiations, Lebanon worked to secure implementation of resolution 425(1978),[4] which Israel, however, refused to implement. The time had come for the Security Council to demonstrate its clout as the ultimate guarantor of Member States' compliance with international law and invoke Chapter VII of the Charter. In this context, the presence of UNIFIL remained of utmost necessity to provide assistance and international support to the civilian population facing occupation. However, this assistance could not be substituted for the fulfilment of UNIFIL's original mandate as stipulated in resolution 425(1978) to ensure Israeli withdrawal and assist the Lebanese Government in re-establishing its authority.

In July,[5] Lebanon reported that major positive developments had accelerated the establishment of national peace, stability and security on its territory. The Lebanese army and internal security forces deployed throughout the country, with the exception of the Israeli-occupied area, were constantly being upgraded. Law and order were rigorously enforced and travel throughout the country was safe and unrestricted. Those achievements allowed the Government to focus on its reconstruction and development plans, for which the World Bank had approved a $175 million loan. Concurrently, Lebanon was exerting great efforts to resettle thousands of civilians displaced by civil strife, two Israeli invasions and the sustained occupation of the south. Despite the ongoing bilateral peace negotiations which had commenced in Madrid, Israel continued to perpetuate its occupation irrespective of Lebanon's significant achievements in consolidating national unity and central authority. As long as Israel continued its occupation, hostilities and bloodshed on Lebanese soil would persist, while its people would exercise their legal right, as sanctioned by the Charter, of individual and collective resistance until Israel withdrew all its forces in accordance with resolution 425(1978). Lebanon reaffirmed UNIFIL's valuable international commitment to its sovereignty and population which, however, could not substitute for its original mandate as stipulated in resolution 425(1978).

The Committee on Palestinian rights[6] expressed alarm at those persistent Israeli air, naval and ground assaults against vast areas of Lebanon in July, which caused the displacement of and high numbers of casualties and suffering among Palestinians living in refugee camps of Beddawi and Nahr el-Bared in northern Lebanon, and Ein el-Hilweh, Mieh Mieh and Rashidieh in the country's southern part.

During the General Assembly's debate on the Middle East situation in December, Lebanon called it unfortunate that in the face of optimistic developments, it remained crippled by a painful thorn in its side, the Israeli occupation of parts of southern Lebanon and the western Bekaa valley. The international community had permitted that ordeal to continue for 15 years in spite of Security Council resolutions 425(1978)[4] and 426(1978).[7] As Israel and Lebanon were sitting at the conference table at Madrid in 1991, shells came raining down on Lebanon. In Washington, Lebanon was presented with vague promises for future withdrawal, while being subjected on the ground to bombardment for the slightest "provocation", which was, in fact, Lebanese resistance against occupation as sanctioned under Article 51 of the Charter. Such was the case in July and August, when Israeli military, in retaliation for the killing of seven of its soldiers on Lebanese soil, killed 140 civilians, levelled scores of villages and caused the exodus of half a million people in response to Prime Minister Rabin's announcement that a major objective of his so-called "operation accountability" was the displacement of the civilian population and the flooding of Beirut with refugees.

UNIFIL

The Security Council twice extended the mandate of UNIFIL during 1993, in January and July, each time for a six-month period.

Established by the Council in 1978,[4] following Israel's invasion of Lebanon in March of that year,[8] UNIFIL was entrusted with confirming the withdrawal of Israeli forces, restoring international peace and security, and assisting the Government of Lebanon in ensuring the return of its effective authority in the area. A second Israeli invasion, launched in June 1982,[9] radically altered the situation in which UNIFIL had to function. Shortly thereafter, the Council authorized the Force to carry out, in addition to its original mandate, the interim tasks of providing protection and humanitarian assistance to the local population, while maintaining its positions in its area of deployment,[10] which tasks it continued to carry out during 1993. The Force was assisted by the Ob-

server Group Lebanon, composed of 57 unarmed military observers organized from the United Nations Truce Supervision Organization and under the operational control of the UNIFIL Commander.

Composition and deployment

As at January 1993,[11] UNIFIL had a strength of 5,250 military personnel provided by 10 countries: Fiji, Finland, France, Ghana, Ireland, Italy, Nepal, Norway, Poland and Sweden, reflecting a 10 per cent reduction in its military strength, as requested by the Security Council in 1992.[12] In addition, UNIFIL had reduced the number of internationally recruited civilian staff by 17 per cent. Civilian support was provided by a staff of 524, of whom 155 were recruited internationally and 369 locally. By July,[13] at the beginning of the second mandate period, the numbers had changed to 526, 161 and 365, respectively, while troop strength had decreased slightly, to 5,247.

UNIFIL remained deployed in southern Lebanon in six sectors: the Fijian, Finnish, Ghanaian, Irish, Nepalese and Norwegian battalion sectors. The entire Norwegian battalion sector was within the Israeli-controlled area, as were parts of the other five sectors. In accordance with operational requirements, the Force adjusted the boundaries of the battalion sectors and relocated a number of positions. In mid-February, the headquarters of the Ghanaian battalion was moved from Marakah to Al Qaranis near Bir as Sanasil. On 16 February, UNIFIL handed over to the Lebanese army an area comprising the villages of Marakah, Jinnata and Yanuh, including the former Ghanaian headquarters complex. Work continued on the new Irish battalion headquarters near Tibnin. Military logistic support was provided by the Swedish logistic battalion, elements of the French composite battalion, the Norwegian maintenance company, the Ghanaian engineer company, the Italian helicopter unit and some civilian staff, especially in communications and vehicle maintenance.

The Force Mobile Reserve, a composite mechanized company, consisting of elements from seven contingents (Fiji, Finland, Ghana, Ireland, Nepal, Norway and Sweden), frequently reinforced UNIFIL battalions when serious incidents occurred and during rotations. One platoon of the Reserve was deployed in the Nepalese battalion sector.

As proposed by the Secretary-General and agreed to by the Security Council in 1992,[14] Major-General Trond Furuhovde (Norway) took over as Force Commander on 22 February to succeed Lieutenant-General Lars-Eric Wahlgren (Sweden), who had been appointed in 1988.[15]

Activities

Report of the Secretary-General (January). The Secretary-General gave an account of developments in the UNIFIL area between 22 July 1992 and 22 January 1993.[11] During that period, UNIFIL suffered two casualties due to firing (Ireland, Nepal), while 12 others were injured as a result of firing or explosions. This brought the number of soldiers who had died since UNIFIL's inception to 190 and the wounded to 292.

UNIFIL continued to oppose attempts by armed elements to enter or operate within its area of deployment, which at times led to friction or violent incidents at its checkpoints. During the review period, 19 operations by resistance groups against IDF/DFF were recorded by the Force, and other attacks against IDF/DFF were reported north of the Litani River, in which armed elements employed rockets, mortars, rocket-propelled grenades and AT-3 anti-tank missiles. The use of roadside bombs continued, especially in the Israeli-controlled area. In responding to such attacks or initiating action themselves, IDF/DFF employed artillery, mortars, tanks and aircraft, often firing into villages. Over 6,000 rounds of artillery mortar and tank fire were recorded as being fired by IDF/DFF during the reporting period, and 242 instances of their firing at or close to UNIFIL positions, which marked a 67 per cent increase over the previous six months. UNIFIL carried out 180 controlled explosions in connection with a programme to clear its deployment area of various types of unexploded ordnance. It continued to extend humanitarian assistance to the civilian population in the form of food, fuel, water, electricity, clothes, medical supplies, engineering work and repairs to buildings damaged as a result of fighting, as well as providing escorts to farmers. From resources made available by troop-contributing countries, it provided water projects, school materials and equipment, and supplies for social services. UNIFIL medical centres and mobile teams rendered care to an average of 2,000 patients a month, and a field dental programme was established. Its personnel contributed some $11,000 for humanitarian work.

The Secretary-General observed that during a period of high tension, volatility and unpredictability, UNIFIL continued to prevent its area from being used for hostile activities and to protect its inhabitants. In carrying out its tasks, the Force was again severely hampered by the amount of fire directed against it, in which respect he appealed to all parties concerned to respect UNIFIL's international and impartial status. In view of UNIFIL's contribution to stability in such a volatile area, the Secretary-General recommended that the Council accept Lebanon's request[3] for an extension of the UNIFIL mandate for another six months, until 31 July 1993.

SECURITY COUNCIL ACTION (January)

The Security Council met on 28 January 1993 to consider the Secretary-General's report and the request by Lebanon, following which the Council unanimously adopted **resolution 803(1993)**.

The Security Council,

Recalling its resolutions 425(1978) and 426(1978) of 19 March 1978, 501(1982) of 25 February 1982, 508(1982) of 5 June 1982, 509(1982) of 6 June 1982 and 520(1982) of 17 September 1982, as well as all its resolutions on the situation in Lebanon,

Having studied the report of the Secretary-General on the United Nations Interim Force in Lebanon of 22 January 1993 and taking note of the observations expressed therein,

Taking note of the letter dated 18 January 1993 from the Permanent Representative of Lebanon to the United Nations addressed to the Secretary-General,

Responding to the request of the Government of Lebanon,

1. *Decides* to extend the present mandate of UNIFIL for a further interim period of six months, that is, until 31 July 1993;

2. *Reiterates* its strong support for the territorial integrity, sovereignty and independence of Lebanon within its internationally recognized boundaries;

3. *Re-emphasizes* the terms of reference and general guidelines of the Force as stated in the report of the Secretary-General of 19 March 1978, approved by resolution 426(1978), and calls upon all parties concerned to cooperate fully with the Force for the full implementation of its mandate;

4. *Reiterates* that the Force should fully implement its mandate as defined in resolutions 425(1978), 426(1978) and all other relevant resolutions;

5. *Requests* the Secretary-General to continue consultations with the Government of Lebanon and other parties directly concerned with the implementation of the present resolution and to report to the Security Council thereon.

Security Council resolution 803(1993)

28 January 1993   Meeting 3167   Adopted unanimously

Draft prepared in consultations among Council members (S/25180).

Following adoption of the resolution and consultations among Council members, the President made a statement[16] on behalf of the Council:

"The members of the Security Council have noted with appreciation the report of the Secretary-General on the United Nations Interim Force in Lebanon (UNIFIL) submitted in conformity with resolution 768(1992).

"They reaffirm their commitment to the full sovereignty, independence, territorial integrity and national unity of Lebanon within its internationally recognized boundaries. In this context, they assert that any State shall refrain from the threat or use of force against the territorial integrity or political independence of any State, or in any other manner inconsistent with the purposes of the United Nations.

"As the Security Council extends the mandate of UNIFIL for a further interim period on the basis of resolution 425(1978), the members of the Council again stress the urgent need for the implementation of that resolution in all its aspects. They reiterate their full support for the Taif Agreement and for the continued efforts of the Lebanese Government to consolidate peace, national unity and security in the country, while successfully carrying out the reconstruction process. The members of the Council commend the Lebanese Government for its successful efforts to extend its authority in the south of the country in full coordination with UNIFIL.

"The members of the Security Council express their concern over the continuing violence in southern Lebanon, regret the loss of civilian life and urge all parties to exercise restraint.

"The members of the Security Council take this opportunity to express their appreciation for the continuing efforts of the Secretary-General and his staff in this regard and commend UNIFIL's troops and troop-contributing countries for their sacrifices and commitment to the cause of international peace and security under difficult circumstances."

Report of the Secretary-General (July). In his report to the Security Council on developments during the six-month period from 23 January to 20 July 1993,[13] the Secretary-General noted that one Nepalese soldier had lost his life as a result of firing and two others had suffered injuries. This brought the number of UNIFIL's accumulated casualties to 192 and of those wounded to 294.

In continuing to oppose attempts by armed elements to operate in its area of deployment, UNIFIL noted an increase in dangerous confrontations between them and the Force. It recorded 63 operations by resistance groups against IDF/DFF—44 more than in the previous six-month period. Altogether, there were 168 instances of firing at or close to UNIFIL positions, for which the Irish and Finnish battalion sectors accounted for more than 70 per cent. The Force carried out 44 controlled explosions to clear undetonated remnants of war.

The Secretary-General observed that during the reporting period, attacks by armed elements against Israel and associated military targets on Lebanese territory were generally more effective than in the past, and the severity of Israeli retaliation rose concomitantly. Despite repeated appeals, the highly escalatory practice of firing into populated areas continued, causing casualties among men, women and children. Meanwhile, UNIFIL ensured to the best of its abilities the peaceful character of its operation area, limited the conflict to the extent possible and protected the inhabitants from the effects of violence. He stressed again that respect by all concerned for the Force's international and impartial status was essential for its effective functioning. He noted with satisfaction the improvement of the situation in other parts of Lebanon, which made it possible to use Beirut's international airport for the rotation of UNIFIL's contingents. The hand-over of a part of UNIFIL's area of operation to the Lebanese army was another step forward. Referring to UNIFIL's contribution to stability and protection

in the area, he recommended that the Council accept Lebanon's request of 14 July[5] for an extension of the Force for a further six months, until 31 January 1994.

SECURITY COUNCIL ACTION (July)

On 28 July 1993, the Security Council, having considered the Secretary-General's report and by Lebanon's request, unanimously adopted **resolution 852(1993)**.

The Security Council,

Recalling its resolutions 425(1978) and 426(1978) of 19 March 1978, 501(1982) of 25 February 1982, 508(1982) of 5 June 1982, 509(1982) of 6 June 1982 and 520(1982) of 17 September 1982, as well as all its resolutions on the situation in Lebanon,

Having studied the report of the Secretary-General on the United Nations Interim Force in Lebanon of 20 July 1993, and taking note of the observations expressed therein,

Taking note of the letter dated 14 July 1993 from the Permanent Representative of Lebanon to the United Nations addressed to the Secretary-General,

Responding to the request of the Government of Lebanon,

1. *Decides* to extend the present mandate of the United Nations Interim Force in Lebanon for a further interim period of six months, that is, until 31 January 1994;

2. *Reiterates* its strong support for the territorial integrity, sovereignty and independence of Lebanon within its internationally recognized boundaries;

3. *Re-emphasizes* the terms of reference and general guidelines of the Force as stated in the report of the Secretary-General of 19 March 1978, approved by resolution 426(1978), and calls upon all parties concerned to cooperate fully with the Force for the full implementation of its mandate;

4. *Reiterates* that the Force should fully implement its mandate as defined in resolutions 425(1978), 426(1978) and all other relevant resolutions;

5. *Requests* the Secretary-General to continue consultations with the Government of Lebanon and other parties directly concerned with the implementation of the present resolution and to report to the Security Council thereon.

Security Council resolution 852(1993)

28 July 1993   Meeting 3258   Adopted unanimously

Draft prepared in consultations among Council members (S/26177).

Following the vote and consultations among Council members, the President made the following statement[17] on behalf of the Council:

"The members of the Security Council have noted with appreciation the report of the Secretary-General on the United Nations Interim Force in Lebanon (UNIFIL) submitted in conformity with resolution 803(1993) of 28 January 1993.

"They reaffirm their commitment to the full sovereignty, independence, territorial integrity and national unity of Lebanon within its internationally recognized boundaries. In this context, they assert that any State shall refrain from the threat or use of force against the territorial integrity or political independence of any State, or in any other manner inconsistent with the purposes of the United Nations.

"As the Security Council extends the mandate of UNIFIL for a further interim period on the basis of resolution 425(1978) of 19 March 1978, the members of the Council again stress the urgent need for the implementation of that resolution in all its aspects. They reiterate their full support for the Taif Agreement and for the continued efforts of the Lebanese Government to consolidate peace, national unity and security in the country, while successfully carrying out the reconstruction process. The members of the Council commend the Lebanese Government for its successful efforts to extend its authority in the south of the country in full coordination with UNIFIL.

"The members of the Security Council express their concern over the continuing violence in southern Lebanon, regret the loss of civilian life and urge all parties to exercise restraint.

"The members of the Security Council take this opportunity to express their appreciation for the continuing efforts of the Secretary-General and his staff in this regard and commend UNIFIL's troops and troop-contributing countries for their sacrifices and commitment to the cause of international peace and security under difficult circumstances."

Financing

A report of the Secretary-General on the financing of UNIFIL[18] indicated that as at 31 October 1993, assessments totalling $2,152.3 million had been apportioned among Member States from UNIFIL's inception on 19 March 1978 to 31 January 1994, against which contributions of $2,044.9 million had been received. Additional commitments were authorized in the amount of $146.3 million less applied credits of $22.2 million. The resulting outstanding balance due of $231.5 million included an amount of $19.6 million due from China, transferred to a special account in accordance with a 1981 General Assembly resolution,[19] leaving $211.9 million due as at 31 October 1993. The budget performance for the period from 1 February 1993 to 31 January 1994 reflected estimated savings of $1,194,000.

Voluntary contributions in services and supplies continued to be received from Switzerland. Cash contributions to the Suspense Account, created in 1979,[20] amounted to $9.8 million as at 31 October 1993, of which $1.4 million was received from Switzerland.

As at 31 October 1993, amounts due to former and current troop-contributing States for troop costs stood at $65.6 million, and an additional $6.2 million was owed to Governments for contingent-owned equipment. Unpaid assessed contributions to the UNIFIL Special Account for the period since its inception amounted to $228.1 million as at 31 January[11] and to $228.7 million as at 31 July.[13] Reimbursements due were met only up to 31 January 1991.

In a December report on the financing of peace-keeping operations,[21] the Secretary-General proposed that the General Assembly authorize monthly commitments for UNIFIL for the period beginning 1 February 1994 at the current level of $12,190,000 gross ($11,931,500 net), should the Security Council decide to continue the Force beyond 31 January 1994. Based on those estimates, the amount required for the period from 1 February to 30 April 1994 would be $36,570,000 gross ($35,403,000 net).

The Advisory Committee on Administrative and Budgetary Questions (ACABQ) recommended[22] that the Secretary-General be authorized to enter into commitments for the Force in an amount up to $24 million gross ($23.5 million net) for the period 1 February to 31 March 1994, and that that amount be assessed to Member States.

In a second report,[23] ACABQ noted that its recommendations were for commitment authority rather than appropriation in view of the fact that the relevant budgets had not been considered and approved; however, consistent with past practice, amounts authorized by the Assembly for commitment could be assessed and apportioned. The Committee further pointed out that in a number of instances its recommendations related only to periods up to 31 March 1994 rather than 30 April. The amounts it would recommend in the future would take into account the performance during the initial months, thereby effecting a de facto adjustment as necessary to the amounts now being recommended.

GENERAL ASSEMBLY ACTION

In December 1993, acting on the recommendation of the Fifth (Administrative and Budgetary) Committee, the General Assembly adopted **decision 48/464** without vote.

Financing of the United Nations Interim Force in Lebanon

At its 87th plenary meeting, on 23 December 1993, the General Assembly, on the recommendation of the Fifth Committee, in accordance with the framework set out in its resolution 48/227 of 23 December 1993, having considered the report of the Secretary-General on the financing of seventeen peace-keeping operations and the related reports of the Advisory Committee on Administrative and Budgetary Questions, and concurring with the observations of the Advisory Committee:

(a) Authorized the Secretary-General, on an exceptional basis, to enter into commitments up to the amount of 24 million United States dollars gross (23.5 million dollars net) for the United Nations Interim Force in Lebanon for the period from 1 February to 31 March 1994, should the Security Council decide to extend the Force beyond 31 January 1994;

(b) Decided at that time to apportion, as an ad hoc arrangement, the amount of 22,876,000 dollars gross

(22.4 million dollars net) among Member States in accordance with the composition of groups set out in paragraphs 3 and 4 of Assembly resolution 43/232 of 1 March 1989, as adjusted by the Assembly in its resolutions 44/192 B of 21 December 1989, 45/269 of 27 August 1991, 46/198 A of 20 December 1991 and 47/218 A of 23 December 1992 and its decision 48/472 of 23 December 1993, and taking into account the scale of assessments for the years 1992, 1993 and 1994 as set out in Assembly resolutions 46/221 A of 20 December 1991 and 48/223 A of 23 December 1993 and its decision 47/456 of 23 December 1992;

(c) Also decided that, in accordance with the provisions of its resolution 973(X) of 15 December 1955, there should be set off against the apportionment among Member States, as provided for in subparagraph *(b)* above, their respective share in the Tax Equalization Fund of the estimated staff assessment income of 476,600 dollars for the period from 1 February to 31 March 1994.

General Assembly decision 48/464

Adopted without vote

Approved by Fifth Committee (A/48/813) without vote, 22 December (meeting 46); draft by Chairman (A/C.5/48/L.16), orally revised; agenda item 130 *(b)*. *Meeting numbers*. GA 48th session: 5th Committee 44, 46; plenary 87.

Israel and the Syrian Arab Republic

The General Assembly in 1993 continued to call for Israel's withdrawal from the Golan Heights, a part of the Syrian Arab Republic near its borders with Israel and Lebanon, which came under Israeli occupation in 1967. Israel effectively annexed the area when it decided to extend its laws, jurisdiction and administration to the territory towards the end of 1981,[24] and the annexation was confirmed by a decision of the Israeli Knesset in November 1991.[25]

The issue of Israeli practices affecting the human rights of the population in the Syrian Arab Golan was continuously monitored by the Committee on Israeli practices and was the subject of resolutions by the Commission on Human Rights and the General Assembly (see below, under "Territories occupied by Israel").

Report of the Secretary-General. Pursuant to a 1992 General Assembly resolution[26] calling on the international community to urge Israel to withdraw from the Syrian Golan Heights, the Secretary-General in October 1993 submitted a report[27] on steps taken or envisaged by Member States in implementing that resolution. As at 1 October, replies from Ecuador and Ghana had been received in reply to his notes verbales of 16 August requesting information in that regard.

GENERAL ASSEMBLY ACTION

On 14 December, the General Assembly adopted **resolution 48/59 B** by recorded vote.

Syrian Golan
The General Assembly,

Having considered the item entitled "The situation in the Middle East",

Taking note of the report of the Secretary-General of 25 October 1993,

Recalling Security Council resolution 497(1981) of 17 December 1981,

Recalling also its resolution 3314(XXIX) of 14 December 1974, in the annex to which it defined an act of aggression, *inter alia*, as "the invasion or attack by the armed forces of a State of the territory of another State, or any military occupation, however temporary, resulting from such invasion or attack, or any annexation by the use of force of the territory of another State or part thereof" and provided that "no consideration of whatever nature, whether political, economic, military or otherwise, may serve as a justification for aggression",

Reaffirming the fundamental principle of the inadmissibility of the acquisition of territory by force,

Reaffirming once more the applicability of the Geneva Convention relative to the Protection of Civilian Persons in Time of War, of 12 August 1949, to the occupied Syrian Golan,

Noting that Israel has refused, in violation of Article 25 of the Charter of the United Nations, to accept and carry out Security Council resolution 497(1981),

Deeply concerned that Israel has not withdrawn from the Syrian Golan, which has been under occupation since 1967, contrary to the relevant Security Council and General Assembly resolutions,

Noting with satisfaction the convening at Madrid of the Peace Conference on the Middle East on the basis of Security Council resolutions 242(1967) of 22 November 1967 and 338(1973) of 22 October 1973, but regretting that a just and comprehensive peace has not yet been achieved after two years of negotiation in Washington, D.C.,

1. *Declares* that Israel has failed so far to comply with Security Council resolution 497(1981);

2. *Declares once more* that Israel's decision to impose its laws, jurisdiction and administration on the occupied Syrian Golan is illegal and therefore null and void and has no validity whatsoever;

3. *Declares also* that the Knesset decision of 11 November 1991 annexing the occupied Syrian Golan constitutes a grave violation of Security Council resolution 497(1981) and therefore is null and void and has no validity whatsoever;

4. *Declares further* all Israeli policies and practices of, or aimed at, annexation of the occupied Arab territories since 1967, including the occupied Syrian Golan, to be illegal and in violation of international law and of the relevant United Nations resolutions;

5. *Determines once more* that all actions taken by Israel to give effect to its decisions relating to the occupied Syrian Golan are illegal and invalid and shall not be recognized;

6. *Reaffirms its determination* that all relevant provisions of the Regulations annexed to the Hague Convention IV of 1907, and the Geneva Convention relative to the Protection of Civilian Persons in Time of War, of 12 August 1949, continue to apply to the Syrian territory occupied by Israel since 1967, and calls upon the parties thereto to respect and ensure respect for their obligations under those instruments in all circumstances;

7. *Determines once more* that the continued occupation of the Syrian Golan since 1967 and its de facto annexation by Israel on 14 December 1981, following Israel's decision to impose its laws, jurisdiction and administration on that territory, constitute a continuing threat to peace and security in the region;

8. *Firmly emphasizes once more* its demand that Israel, the occupying Power, rescind forthwith its illegal decision of 14 December 1981 to impose its laws, jurisdiction and administration on the Syrian Golan, and its decision of 11 November 1991, which resulted in the effective annexation of that territory;

9. *Demands once more* that Israel withdraw from the occupied Syrian Golan in implementation of the relevant Security Council resolutions;

10. *Calls upon* the international community to urge Israel to withdraw from the occupied Syrian Golan and other occupied Arab territories for the establishment of a just, comprehensive and lasting peace in the region;

11. *Requests* the Secretary-General to report to the General Assembly at its forty-ninth session on the implementation of the present resolution.

General Assembly resolution 48/59 B

14 December 1993   Meeting 79   65-2-83 (recorded vote)

11-nation draft (A/48/L.46 & Add.1); agenda item 34.
Sponsors: Bahrain, Cuba, Indonesia, Kuwait, Lebanon, Malaysia, Qatar, Sudan, Syrian Arab Republic, United Arab Emirates, Yemen.
Meeting numbers. GA 48th session: plenary 67, 68, 79.

Recorded vote in Assembly as follows:

In favour: Algeria, Armenia, Azerbaijan, Bahrain, Bangladesh, Bhutan, Bolivia, Brunei Darussalam, Burkina Faso, Chad, China, Comoros, Costa Rica, Cuba, Cyprus, Democratic People's Republic of Korea, Djibouti, Egypt, El Salvador, Guatemala, Guinea, Guinea-Bissau, India, Indonesia, Iran, Iraq, Jordan, Kuwait, Lao People's Democratic Republic, Lebanon, Lesotho, Libyan Arab Jamahiriya, Madagascar, Malawi, Malaysia, Maldives, Mauritania, Mauritius, Morocco, Myanmar, Namibia, Niger, Nigeria, Oman, Pakistan, Philippines, Qatar, Saint Lucia, Saudi Arabia, Senegal, Sierra Leone, Sri Lanka, Sudan, Suriname, Swaziland, Syrian Arab Republic, Trinidad and Tobago, Tunisia, Turkey, Uganda, United Arab Emirates, United Republic of Tanzania, Viet Nam, Yemen, Zimbabwe.

Against: Israel, United States.

Abstaining: Albania, Antigua and Barbuda, Argentina, Australia, Austria, Bahamas, Barbados, Belarus, Belgium, Bosnia and Herzegovina, Botswana, Brazil, Bulgaria, Cameroon, Canada, Chile, Colombia, Czech Republic, Denmark, Dominica, Dominican Republic, Ecuador, Estonia, Ethiopia, Fiji, Finland, France, Gambia, Germany, Ghana, Greece, Guyana, Haiti, Hungary, Iceland, Ireland, Italy, Jamaica, Japan, Kazakhstan, Kenya, Latvia, Liechtenstein, Lithuania, Luxembourg, Malta, Marshall Islands, Mexico, Micronesia, Monaco, Nepal, Netherlands, New Zealand, Nicaragua, Norway, Panama, Papua New Guinea, Paraguay, Peru, Poland, Portugal, Republic of Korea, Republic of Moldova, Romania, Russian Federation, Rwanda, Saint Vincent and the Grenadines, Samoa, San Marino, Singapore, Slovakia, Slovenia, Solomon Islands, Spain, Sweden, Thailand, the former Yugoslav Republic of Macedonia, Togo, Ukraine, United Kingdom, Uruguay, Venezuela, Zambia.

After adoption of the resolution, the United States expressed disappointment and indicated that it had already outlined its position on the status of the Golan Heights by voting in favour of Security Council resolution 497(1981).[28] Israel and the Syrian Arab Republic would again soon engage in bilateral negotiations, and it was important not to prejudge or prejudice the outcome of those talks.

UNDOF

The United Nations Disengagement Observer Force (UNDOF), established by the Security Council in 1974,[29] as called for by the Agreement on Disengagement of Forces between Israel and the Syrian Arab Republic concluded that year,[30] was charged with supervising the observance of the cease-fire between the two countries in the Golan Heights area and ensuring the separation of their forces. Assisting the Force as required were observers from UNTSO.

The UNDOF mandate was renewed twice in 1993, in May and November, each time for a six-month period.

Composition

In November 1993, UNDOF had a strength of 1,110 military troops (reduced from 1,124 in May) from Austria, Canada, Finland and Poland, plus five observers from UNTSO. In addition, it was assisted by 85 UNTSO observers assigned to the Israel-Syria Mixed Armistice Commission.

UNDOF, under the command of Major-General Roman Misztal (Poland), remained deployed within and close to the area of separation, with most of the military component of its headquarters located at Camp Faouar and some elements deployed in Camp Ziouani. Its civilian administrative staff operated at Damascus, while the Force Commander maintained offices at both Camp Faouar and Damascus. The Austrian battalion, based at Camp Faouar, maintained 16 positions (reduced from 18 in May) and 9 outposts (up from 7 in May) in the northern operational area, conducting 26 patrols daily at irregular intervals on predetermined routes. In the southern area, the Finnish battalion, which was based at Camp Ziouani, manned 14 positions and 8 outposts (16 and 6, respectively, in May), patrolling 19 times daily. The military police had detachments at Camps Faouar and Ziouani, in addition to Checkpoint C.

Damascus international airport served as UNDOF's airhead; the Tel Aviv airport was also used. The seaports of Latakia, Ashdod and Haifa were used for sea shipments, while in-theatre air support was provided by UNTSO on request.

On 2 August,[31] the Secretary-General informed the Security Council that the Finnish infantry battalion would be replaced by a Polish unit and that logistic support for the Force would be consolidated in the Canadian logistic unit. The Council took note of the foregoing on the same date.[32] The Canadian logistic unit was reinforced on 1 October by 26 men. In addition to its previous functions, it commenced to perform second-line general transport tasks, ration transport, and control and management of goods received by UNDOF, as well as maintenance of heavy equipment, for which reason part of the unit was deployed to Camp Faouar. The Polish logistic unit ceased to function on that date, leaving behind a team of 25 for hand-over and preparations for the arrival of the Polish infantry battalion, whose advance party arrived on 1 November, the full unit being scheduled to replace the Finnish battalion by mid-December.

A restructuring of the Force was put into effect following Finland's withdrawal of its battalion on 9 December, at which time its operational responsibilities were handed over to the Polish battalion. As a consequence of the restructuring, UNDOF's authorized military strength was reduced by 88.

Activities

Reports of the Secretary-General (May and November). Before the expiration of the mandate of UNDOF on 31 May and 30 November 1993, the Secretary-General reported to the Security Council on UNDOF activities for the mandate periods, covering 20 November 1992 to 21 May 1993[33] and 22 May to 22 November 1993.[34] UNDOF suffered one fatality due to natural causes, bringing the number of deaths to 32 since its inception, 19 as a result of hostile action or accidents and 13 from other causes.

The reports noted that the Force continued to perform its functions effectively with the cooperation of Israel and the Syrian Arab Republic. The cease-fire was maintained and the operational situation in UNDOF's area of supervision remained calm. To ensure that no military forces were deployed in the area of separation, UNDOF supervised it from permanently manned positions and observation posts and by foot and mobile patrols operating day and night at irregular intervals on predetermined routes. Temporary outposts were set up and additional patrols were conducted as necessary. In the Wadi Ar Raqqad, new patrol paths were created enabling UNDOF to operate more easily on the difficult terrain. Through frequent patrolling and the establishment of standing patrols, it continued its efforts to prevent incidents involving Syrian shepherds who grazed their flocks close to and west of the A-line. UNDOF conducted fortnightly inspections of armaments and force levels in the area of limitation, accompanied by liaison officers from the two parties. As in the past, both sides restricted the movement of inspection teams, denying access to some positions.

The Syrian authorities continued to lay mines and replace old ones along the eastern edge of the separation area. As reported in May, the Polish mine-clearing teams cleared a total area of 21,965 square metres and destroyed a number of other explosive devices. UNDOF assisted the International Committee of the Red Cross (ICRC) with mail facilities and safe passage of persons—a total of 533 between May and November. It also provided medical treatment to the local population within available means.

In his observations, the Secretary-General cautioned that despite the relative quiet in the Israel–Syrian Arab Republic sector, the situation as a whole remained potentially dangerous, unless and until a comprehensive Middle East settlement was reached. Stating in each report that he considered UNDOF's continued presence in the area to be essential, the Secretary-General, with the Syrian Arab Republic's assent and Israel's agreement, recommended that its mandate be extended for a further six months, until 30 November 1993 in the first instance and until 31 May 1994 in the second.

SECURITY COUNCIL ACTION (May and November)

Meeting on 26 May 1993, the Security Council, without debate, unanimously adopted **resolution 830(1993)**.

The Security Council,
Having considered the report of the Secretary-General on the United Nations Disengagement Observer Force,
Decides:
(*a*) To call upon the parties concerned to implement immediately its resolution 338(1973) of 22 October 1973;
(*b*) To renew the mandate of the United Nations Disengagement Observer Force for another period of six months, that is, until 30 November 1993;
(*c*) To request the Secretary-General to submit, at the end of this period, a report on the development in the situation and the measures taken to implement Security Council resolution 338(1973).

Security Council resolution 830(1993)
26 May 1993   Meeting 3220   Adopted unanimously
Draft prepared in consultations among Council members (S/25838).

On 29 November, the Council, also without debate, unanimously adopted **resolution 887(1993)**.

The Security Council,
Having considered the report of the Secretary-General on the United Nations Disengagement Observer Force,
Decides:
(*a*) To call upon the parties concerned to implement immediately its resolution 338(1973) of 22 October 1973;
(*b*) To renew the mandate of the United Nations Disengagement Observer Force for another period of six months, that is, until 31 May 1994;
(*c*) To request the Secretary-General to submit, at the end of this period, a report on the development in the situation and the measures taken to implement Security Council resolution 338(1973).

Security Council resolution 887(1993)
29 November 1993   Meeting 3320   Adopted unanimously
Draft prepared in consultations among Council members (S/26808).

Following the adoption of each resolution, the President stated that he had been authorized to make the following complementary statement on behalf of the Council:[35]

"As is known, the report of the Secretary-General on the United Nations Disengagement Observer Force states, in paragraph 19 [21 in the May report]: 'Despite the present quiet in the Israel-Syria sector, the situation ["in the Middle East as a whole" added in the May report] continues to be potentially dangerous and is likely to remain so, unless and until a comprehensive setlement covering all aspects of the

Middle East problem can be reached.' That statement of the Secretary-General reflects the view of the Security Council.''

Financing

In a December report on the financing of UNDOF,[36] the Secretary-General indicated that assessed contributions apportioned to Member States in respect of the Force—from its inception in 1974[37] to 30 November 1993—and of the United Nations Emergency Force II (UNEF II) (from its inception at the end of 1973 to its liquidation in 1980)—totalled $1,034.1 million, against which $968.3 million had been received as at 31 October 1993. The resultant outstanding balance of $58.6 million included $36 million due from China, which was transferred to a special account pursuant to a 1981 General Assembly resolution,[19] leaving $22.6 million in unpaid contributions.

UNDOF's performance record for 1 December 1992 to 30 November 1993 showed estimated savings of $706,000 gross ($640,000 net), which the Secretary-General recommended to the Assembly for credit to Member States against their assessments for future mandate periods.

The unaudited UNDOF/UNEF II financial statement, as at 30 June 1993, covering the 12 months from 1 December 1991 to 30 November 1992, showed a ''surplus'' balance of $5,109,799, representing excess of income (including assessed contributions, irrespective of collectibility) over expenditure and consisting of interest income ($1,309,685) and other accrued miscellaneous credits including savings from liquidation of prior obligations. The Secretary-General proposed that, until the level of $22.6 million unpaid contributions was reduced, that surplus, which otherwise would be surrendered as credits to Member States under certain provisions of the Financial Regulations, be entered into the Suspense Account set up by the Assembly in 1978.[38]

For the 12-month period beginning 1 December 1993, the average Force strength would be reduced, due to the Finnish withdrawal, by 88, from 1,124 to 1,036 troops, for an overall reduction of 7.8 per cent in military personnel. Likewise, the civilian staff was to be reduced by 6 to 120, including 84 recruited locally, in line with a proposed 6.7 per cent reduction in local-level posts. On this basis, and assuming continuation of its existing responsibilities, the Secretary-General estimated the cost of maintaining UNDOF at $32,160,000 gross ($31,188,000 net) for the 12-month period from 1 December 1993 to 30 November 1994, which equalled $2,680,000 gross ($2,599,000 net) monthly. Accordingly, subject to the renewal of UNDOF's mandate, he requested the Assembly to make appropriate provision for UNDOF's expenses for the period from 1 December 1993 to 30 November 1994.

ACABQ, in December,[39] concurred with the Secretary-General in his December report on the financing of peace-keeping operations,[21] and recommended that he be authorized to enter into commitments for UNDOF up to $13,400,000 gross ($12,995,000 net) for the period from 1 December 1993 to 30 April 1994 inclusive. However, no assessment on Member States would be necessary in this connection since the cash balance available to UNDOF as at 13 December stood at $30,700,000.

In a second report,[23] ACABQ pointed out that its recommendations were for commitment authority rather than appropriation in view of the fact that the relevant budgets had not been considered and approved; however, consistent with past practice, amounts authorized by the Assembly for commitment could be assessed and apportioned.

GENERAL ASSEMBLY ACTION

On 23 December 1993, acting on the recommendation of the Fifth Committee, the General Assembly adopted **decision 48/463** without vote.

Financing of the United Nations Disengagement Observer Force

At its 87th plenary meeting, on 23 December 1993, the General Assembly, on the recommendation of the Fifth Committee, in accordance with the framework set out in its resolution 48/227 of 23 December 1993, having considered the report of the Secretary-General on the financing of seventeen peace-keeping operations and the related reports of the Advisory Committee on Administrative and Budgetary Questions, and concurring with the observations of the Advisory Committee:

(a) Authorized the Secretary-General, on an exceptional basis, to enter into commitments up to the amount of 10,720,000 United States dollars gross (10,396,000 dollars net) for the United Nations Disengagement Observer Force for the period from 1 December 1993 to 31 March 1994;

(b) Decided that no assessment on Member States would be necessary in the light of the current cash balance in the Special Account for the United Nations Disengagement Observer Force.

General Assembly decision 48/463

Adopted without vote

Approved by Fifth Committee (A/48/812) without vote, 22 December (meeting 46); draft by Chairman (A/C.5/48/L.15); agenda item 130 *(a)*.
Meeting numbers. GA 48th session: 5th Committee 44, 46; plenary 87.

REFERENCES

[1]YUN 1981, p. 275. [2]A/47/891-S/25308, S/25352, S/26151, S/26152, A/47/988-S/26165, A/47/992-S/16192, A/47/994-S/26196, A/47/995-S/26202, A/47/996-S/26221, A/48/284-S/16191, A/48/287-S/26201. [3]S/25125. [4]YUN 1978, p. 312, SC res. 425(1978), 19 Mar. 1978. [5]S/26083. [6]A/48/35. [7]YUN 1978, p. 312, SC res. 426(1978), 19 Mar. 1978. [8]Ibid., p. 296. [9]YUN 1982, p. 428. [10]Ibid., p. 450, SC res. 511(1982), 18 June 1982. [11]S/25150 & Add.1. [12]YUN 1992, p. 411, SC res. 734(1992), 29 Jan. 1992. [13]S/26111. [14]YUN 1992, p. 410. [15]YUN 1988, p. 220. [16]S/25185. [17]S/26183. [18]A/48/841. [19]YUN 1981, p. 1299, GA res. 36/116 A, 10 Dec. 1981. [20]YUN 1979, p. 352, GA res. 34/9 D, 17 Dec. 1979. [21]A/C.5/48/40. [22]A/48/770. [23]A/48/778. [24]YUN 1981, p. 309. [25]YUN 1992, p. 415. [26]Ibid., GA res. 47/63 A, 11 Dec. 1992. [27]A/48/522. [28]YUN 1981, p. 313, SC

res. 497(1981), 17 Dec. 1981.[29]YUN 1974, p. 205, SC res. 350(1974), 31 May 1974. [30]Ibid., p. 198. [31]S/26225. [32]S/26226. [33]S/25809. [34]S/26781. [35]S/25849, S/26809. [36]A/48/700. [37]YUN 1974, p. 205, SC res. 350(1974), 31 May 1974. [38]YUN 1978, p. 323, GA res. 33/13 E, 14 Dec. 1978. [39]A/48/769.

Territories occupied by Israel

The Palestine territory and other Arab territories occupied by Israel as a result of previous armed conflicts in the Middle East comprised the West Bank of the Jordan River, including East Jerusalem, the Gaza Strip and the Golan Heights in the Syrian Arab Republic. The inhabitants of those territories, which in 1993 had been under Israeli occupation for more than a quarter of a century, continued to reject the occupation as a permanent fact, which was manifested by the widespread uprising (*intifadah*) that persisted during the year. Israel's policies and actions in the territories remained under constant monitoring by the Committee on Israeli practices, whose reports in 1993 reflected a critically tense situation and a high level of violence engendered by the uprising and Israel's suppression of it by military force and collective punishment, including mass deportations of Palestinians despite political breakthroughs at the negotiation table between Israel and PLO.

Transmitting the report of the Committee, the Chairman stated that the civilian population of the occupied territories continued to suffer a heavy toll of casualties due to the disproportionately harsh and violent methods employed by the Israeli authorities to repress the popular Palestinian uprising. Those measures resulted in an increased loss of life and severe injuries among civilians, including small children who clearly represented no security threat.[1] According to the report of the Committee on Palestinian rights,[2] the total number of Palestinians killed as a result of shooting, beating and tear-gas from the beginning of the *intifadah* in December 1987[3] up to August 1993 had risen to 1,240, approximately 25 per cent of whom were children under 16 years of age.

The continued deployment of Israeli undercover units, a further relaxation of the rules for opening fire and the use of live ammunition as well as rubber and plastic-coated bullets led to a greater than 180 per cent increase in fatalities among children alone. At the end of 1992, IDF started to carry out a new form of collective punishment, which consisted of destroying entire neighbourhoods with heavy artillery fire during searches for wanted persons. A number of such operations aimed at capturing a single fugitive left scores of innocent people homeless.

The increase in violence in both the territories and Israel, specifically the killing of an Israeli in the Nissanit settlement in Gaza on 28 March and the killing of two Israeli policemen inside Israel on 30 March, led Israeli authorities to impose a complete closure of the territories on 31 March, which virtually divided them into five distinct areas, namely: Gaza, the northern West Bank, the southern West Bank, Jerusalem and the Syrian Golan Heights. The closure created unprecedented hardship to the population of the territories, the majority of whom already lived below the poverty line. It also deprived approximately 120,000 persons of their means of livelihood, as they were suddenly cut off from $2.75 million per day in wages previously earned in Israel. As special permits were required for entry into Jerusalem and Israel as well as for travel between the West Bank and Gaza and within the West Bank itself, the measure had a seriously negative impact on commerce, medical care, education and access to services, including those provided by UNRWA, according to the Secretary-General's report on assistance to the Palestinian people.[4] In some areas, roadblocks created enclaves, depriving Palestinians living in them of access to their families, work, schools, medical facilities, utility services and places to worship in Jerusalem.

Commerce was rendered virtually impossible, and agriculture was similarly affected by the drop in consumer income, the closure of external markets and the division of the territories itself. Unemployment rose to nearly 60 per cent in Gaza and to almost that level in the West Bank during April and May, as noted in the annual report of the Commissioner-General of UNRWA.[5] Palestinians began liquidating savings and selling personal belongings to purchase food, pay debts and cover rents.

Freedom of movement was further restricted by the continued practice of imposing prolonged curfews on refugee camps and entire localities. Many families requested urgent food aid. In addition, difficulty and delay in obtaining permits to circulate from one area to the other prevented numerous farmers from reaching the markets for their products. The closure had a negative bearing on the health situation in the territories, since the most important medical facilities serving Palestinians were located in Jerusalem. It was felt in the education sector as students were prevented from attending classes in areas in which they did not reside, with more than 25 per cent of them unable to register in schools and universities despite the prolongation of registration periods. Those limitations furthermore negatively affected access to both Christian and Muslim holy sites.

Restrictions regarding freedom of expression continued as the Israeli authorities, on 31 March

1993, closed the Hebron-based Al Zahra Press Service for six months on charges that seditious material had been found on its premises. Journalists were often harassed, beaten or arrested when covering confrontations between Palestinians and Israeli soldiers. On the positive side, however, military authorities in June issued licences for a new Palestinian weekly and a new daily to be distributed in Jerusalem and the West Bank.

The administration of justice continued to be a source of concern, as it was characterized by a lack of due process of laws and the frequent absence of basic legal safeguards for the Arab population. In addition, the practice of torture and ill-treatment during interrogation and even after sentencing continued. It was revealed that physicians were required to examine prisoners for the purpose of determining whether they were physically fit for certain types of interrogation practices.

The General Assembly, in four resolutions adopted in December, demanded that Israel desist from taking any measures or actions in the occupied Palestinian territory, including Jerusalem, that were in violation of the fourth Geneva Convention, determining them to be illegal and without validity; demanded that Israel facilitate the return of all deported Palestinians and accelerate the release of all Palestinians arbitrarily detained or imprisoned; and reaffirmed that the Israeli settlements were illegal and an obstacle to peace (48/41 C). It demanded that Israel accept the *de jure* applicability of the fourth Geneva Convention in those territories, including Jerusalem, and other Arab territories occupied by Israel since 1967 (48/41 B), and expressed the hope that, in the light of the recent positive political developments, those policies and practices of Israel which violated the human rights of Palestinians and other Arabs there would be brought to an immediate end (48/41 A). The Assembly also condemned Israel's persistence in changing the physical character, demographic composition, institutional structure and legal status of the occupied Syrian Golan, in particular the establishment of settlements, and determined that all measures and actions by Israel purporting to alter the character and legal status of the Syrian Golan were null and void (48/41 D). In addition, both the Economic and Social Council (1993/52) and the Assembly (48/212) recognized the economic and social repercussions of the Israeli settlements on Palestinians and deplored Israel's confiscation of land, appropriation of water resources, depletion of other economic resources and displacement and deportation of the population of the territories, reaffirming the inalienable right of the Palestinian people and the population of the occupied Syrian Golan to their natural and all other economic resources, any infringement thereof being without legal validity.

Earlier, in February, the Commission on Human Rights adopted five resolutions relating to the occupied territories, specifically on: the situation in occupied Palestine,[6] Israeli settlements,[7] human rights violations[8] and human rights in the Syrian Golan[9] (see PART THREE, Chapter X).

Numerous communications addressed to the Secretary-General throughout 1993 drew attention to an escalation of Israeli acts of repression that caused many casualties and resulted in a dangerously deteriorating security situation in the occupied territories. The reported incidents involved the killing and wounding of Palestinians, including women, youth and children, by Israeli armed forces and settlers. In those communications, the Permanent Observer of Palestine[10] as well as the Chairman of the Committee on Palestinian rights[11] appealed urgently and repeatedly to the Security Council to ensure the protection of Palestinians in accordance with resolution 681(1990).[12]

In view of the serious situation, Egypt, chairing the Group of Arab States, on 22 March[13] requested a formal meeting of the Security Council.

Israel, on the other hand, on 29 March[14] stated that militant Islamic fundamentalist groups, such as Hamas and the Islamic Jihad, as well as PLO, had blazed a trail of bloodshed and violence as a diversion away from the road towards reconciliation and peace. Meanwhile, Palestinians, resorting to stabbings, shootings and stonings, had stepped up their campaign of iniquity. It noted that Palestinians were also targeted, 864 of them having been killed since the start of the *intifadah* and 2,242 injured by fellow Palestinians. On 2 July,[15] Israel, giving an account of an attack against a bus at the northern entrance to Jerusalem, expressed its commitment to doing its utmost to promote the peace process, despite provocations and terrorist attacks.

Reports of the Committee on Israeli practices. As requested by the General Assembly in 1992,[16] the Committee on Israeli practices in 1993 presented three periodic reports—in April,[17] August[18] and November[1]—covering developments in the occupied territories between 27 August 1992 and 27 August 1993. The reports incorporated excerpts or details of written information from various sources, including individuals, organizations and the Israeli and Arab press; oral testimonies of 42 persons with first-hand experience of the human rights situation in the territories, obtained through hearings conducted between 28 April and 7 May at Damascus (Syrian Arab Republic), Amman (Jordan) and Cairo (Egypt); and official Israeli statements reflecting Israel's policies in the territories, as well as reports on measures taken to implement them.

On the basis of the information placed before it, the Committee concluded[1] that the situation of basic human rights and fundamental freedoms for Palestinians and other Arabs in the occupied territories continued to be critical. In violation of its obligations as a State party to the fourth Geneva Convention, Israel continued to implement its policy based on the consideration that the territories it had occupied since 1967 constituted a part of the State of Israel, and persistently imposed its laws, jurisdiction and administration on them. It pursued a policy of annexation which resulted in the expropriation of land, the diversion of water resources, the uprooting of trees and the building of an infrastructure of roads linking settlements. Although Israeli authorities suggested a shift in budget allocations away from settlements, the expansion of existing ones continued.

Detailing its observations, the Committee noted that Israel had been implementing unproportionally harsh measures to quell the uprising and resistance to occupation. It was concerned by the increasing fatalities of innocent civilians, particularly small children, as the result of indiscriminate and random shooting by Israeli troops. Numerous persons who were killed had not been involved in violent actions but were simply bystanders. According to B'tselem, the Israeli Information Centre for Human Rights in the Occupied Territories, 125 Palestinians were killed during the first nine months of the new Israeli administration of Yitzhak Rabin, as opposed to 79 during the last nine months of the Shamir Government. The number of children killed during the first six months of the current Government represented a 180 per cent increase in comparison with the corresponding period of the previous administration. In a report published in the *Jerusalem Post* on 18 May, B'tselem maintained that more youths under 16 (a total of 34) had been killed between 9 December 1992 and 16 May 1993 than in any corresponding period during the past five years. The pronounced increase in the number of deaths among the civilian population was attributed to an additional modification of instructions issued to soldiers regarding rules for opening fire. On 31 March, *Ha'aretz* and the *Jerusalem Post* reported the implementation of new measures by the army, which included the opening of fire without warning at armed Palestinians. According to instructions issued by the IDF Judge Advocate-General's office, soldiers and other security personnel were now authorized to shoot Palestinians carrying guns even if they did not actually threaten to open fire at them, and in all cases of riots.

During the reporting period, Israel implemented on a large scale new and particularly harsh measures of collective punishment. Entire blocks of houses and apartments in which wanted persons were suspected to be hiding were destroyed in the search for such persons. Those measures were completely disproportionate to the alleged offence, as they affected several unrelated houses or neighbourhoods at a time. At incidents in both Gaza and the West Bank, the army shelled entire neighbourhoods with heavy artillery fire, including anti-tank missiles and attacks from helicopters. The reason invoked was to avoid Israeli soldiers' finding themselves in a life-threatening situation while searching for fugitives. Many houses were looted during those operations or destroyed by mistake.

Proclaiming the closure of the territories on 31 March, Israel denied all Palestinian-owned vehicles the right of entry into them. Palestinians were forbidden to stay overnight and were subject to a $358 fine if caught. Those restrictions had particularly severe repercussions on health services, since the principal hospitals serving the territories were located in East Jerusalem. In April, Palestinians were reportedly denied access to the only hospital for registered refugees (August Victoria), to the largest and most advanced hospital in the territories (Makassed) and to the area's only ophthalmological hospital (St. John's), all of which were located in East Jerusalem. The closure left approximately 120,000 Palestinians and Arabs without work, and numerous Palestinians who used to work inside Israel were not remunerated for their work during March, compounding an already serious economic situation resulting from the replacement of Arab workers in Israel by new immigrants and the significant decrease in transfers of funds from Palestinians abroad in the aftermath of the Gulf war. The loss of earnings for the population of the territories was estimated at $100 million for April alone. In June, 50,000 residents of Gaza reportedly received food and financial aid from the Israeli Civil Administration. The dire circumstances caused the European Union on 9 July to announce that it would send $2.82 million worth of urgent food aid to Palestinian families in Gaza.

Deliberate economic pressure, which included the uprooting of trees, tax raids and administrative harassment, continued to be applied. The uneven application of laws and preferential treatment of Israeli companies reduced the competitiveness and number of Palestinian enterprises and factories. Unlike settlers, the population of the territories was systematically denied access to water resources and permission to repair old artesian wells and drill new ones. The systematic diversion of water led, especially in Gaza, to its scarcity. The problem of insufficient water was often tied to its excessive use by settlers who were not subjected to any quantitative restrictions, which resulted in an ecological imbalance and increased water salinity, making it unfit for domestic consumption and unsuitable for the cultivation of certain crops.

In view of these policies, the Committee on Israeli practices once again stressed the need for urgent measures to ensure effective protection of the basic rights and freedoms of the inhabitants of the territories. Pending a comprehensive, just and lasting settlement of the Arab-Israeli conflict, it recommended: full application by Israel of the fourth Geneva Convention, the main international instrument of humanitarian law applicable to the territories; full compliance with all resolutions relevant to the Palestine question adopted by the United Nations and by ILO, UNESCO and WHO; full Israeli cooperation with ICRC in its efforts to gain access to and protect detained persons; full support by member States of ICRC activities on behalf of the unprecedentedly increasing number of detained persons, as well as of UNRWA activities on behalf of the refugee population; and full respect by the Israeli authorities of UNRWA's privileges and immunities. The Committee further recommended renewed efforts by Member States to convince Israel of the need for increased human rights protection through international monitoring, *inter alia* by granting it access to the territories; and full recognition of the need to give priority consideration in the peace negotiations to protection of the population's basic rights.

Consideration by the Committee on Palestinian rights. The Committee on Palestinian rights,[2] while welcoming the positive developments between Israel and PLO, remained greatly concerned at the continued grave situation in the occupied Palestinian territories and called on Israel to recognize the applicability of the fourth Geneva Convention, implement its provisions immediately, and restore respect for human rights. In particular, it called on Israel to end the shooting of unarmed demonstrators by IDF and its undercover activities, which had resulted in many summary executions; to release all political prisoners and detainees; and to end the imposition of collective punishments such as curfews, closures of the territories, the destruction or sealing of houses and the deportation of Palestinians, calling for the return of all those deported since 1967. It further called on Israel, pending its complete withdrawal from the territories, including Jerusalem, immediately to end its confiscation of Palestinian land and its settlement activities, including the building of roads and control over water resources, and to repeal military orders restricting political, economic and social activities by Palestinians.

Reports reaching the Committee left no doubt that the continuation of occupation, buttressed by armed force, increasingly endangered the very fabric of Palestinian society and its livelihood, and resulted in grave human rights violations. In this context, the Committee welcomed the appointment by the Commission on Human Rights of a Special Rapporteur mandated to investigate Israel's violations of the principles and bases of international law, international humanitarian law and the fourth Geneva Convention (see PART THREE, Chapter X). Also reported was the continuation of repressive measures by the occupation forces and armed settlers despite the ongoing peace process and the election of a new Israeli Government in 1992. The Committee expressed great concern that the number of Palestinians killed by the armed forces or their agents following the killings of Israelis had risen sharply in the year under review. Since the beginning of the *intifadah*[3] until August 1993, the total number of Palestinian casualties by shooting, beating or tear-gas had risen to 1,240, while 130,000 were estimated to have been injured.

The Committee noted an intensification of the campaign by the previous Israeli Government to pursue persons declared as "wanted" by the authorities, primarily through increased harassment of their families, increased use of large-scale military operations using excessive force and the application of Israel's military order No. 1076 of April 1992, which permitted a seven-year prison term without trial for failure to respond to a summons, as well as the widespread use of undercover units engaged in extrajudicial killings. Military assaults against the homes of fugitives, using large-calibre machine-gun ammunition, anti-tank missiles and dynamite, took place in February and April in Gaza, thereby rendering hundreds of Palestinians homeless. The Committee furthermore deplored that in October, after the signing of the Declaration of Principles, a similar attack took place, in which the homes of another 18 families in Gaza were blasted. Human rights organizations reported that from the *intifadah's* beginning to August 1993, more than 2,400 homes had been demolished or sealed, over 166,000 trees had been uprooted, and curfews had been imposed in more than 12,000 instances.

According to the Committee, the closure in March of the West Bank, including Jerusalem, and Gaza had a particularly negative effect on the Palestinian residents of East Jerusalem, who became almost totally isolated and deprived of any freedom of movement.

The Committee also observed with the greatest concern the rapid worsening of the environmental situation in the territories, due mostly to over-exploitation by Israeli authorities and settlers of the water resources, the lack of an adequate waste management system and the destruction of thousands of olive and fruit trees. Contamination and degradation of the environment reached especially severe proportions in the overpopulated Gaza Strip, where the problem acquired crisis dimensions representing a direct health threat to the population, especially children.

Report of the Secretary-General. The Secretary-General reported to the General Assembly in October 1993[19] that Israel had not replied to his July request for information on steps taken or envisaged to implement a 1992 Assembly resolution[16] demanding *inter alia* that Israel allow the Committee on Israeli practices access to the occupied territories and condemning certain Israeli policies and practices there. He also drew the attention of States and international organizations, including the specialized agencies, to the Assembly's call not to recognize any changes carried out by Israel in the territories and to avoid actions, including those in the field of aid, that might be used by Israel in its annexation or other policies.

The Secretary-General noted that, in response to the resolution's request that he ensure the widest circulation of the reports of the Committee and of information on its activities and findings, DPI continued to provide press coverage of all meetings of the Special Committee on Israeli practices and of the Commission on Human Rights, published stories relating to Palestinian issues in the *UN Chronicle*, covered various aspects of the Palestine question in weekly radio news and feature programmes, continued distributing its booklet *Life of Palestinians under Israeli Occupation*[20] and publicized the Committee's 1993 mission to the Middle East. (For further details on DPI activities, see above, under ''Public information activities''.)

GENERAL ASSEMBLY ACTION

Following consideration of the report of the Committee on Israeli practices and acting on the recommendation of the Fourth (Special Political and Decolonization) Committee, the General Assembly, on 10 December 1993, adopted **resolution 48/41 A** by recorded vote.

The General Assembly,

Guided by the purposes and principles of the Charter of the United Nations,

Guided also by the principles of international humanitarian law, in particular the Geneva Convention relative to the Protection of Civilian Persons in Time of War, of 12 August 1949, as well as international standards of human rights, in particular the Universal Declaration of Human Rights and the International Covenants on Human Rights,

Recalling its relevant resolutions, including resolution 2443(XXIII) of 19 December 1968, and relevant resolutions of the Commission on Human Rights,

Recalling also relevant resolutions of the Security Council,

Aware of the uprising (*intifadah*) of the Palestinian people,

Convinced that occupation itself represents a primary violation of human rights,

Having considered the reports of the Special Committee to Investigate Israeli Practices Affecting the Human Rights of the Palestinian People and Other Arabs of the Occupied Territories and the relevant reports of the Secretary-General,

Noting the signing of the Declaration of Principles on Interim Self-Government Arrangements, including its Annexes, and its Agreed Minutes, by the Government of the State of Israel and the Palestine Liberation Organization at Washington, D.C., on 13 September 1993,

1. *Commends* the Special Committee to Investigate Israeli Practices Affecting the Human Rights of the Palestinian People and Other Arabs of the Occupied Territories for its efforts in performing the tasks assigned to it by the General Assembly and for its impartiality;

2. *Demands* that Israel cooperate with the Special Committee in implementing its mandate;

3. *Deplores* the policies and practices of Israel violating the human rights of the Palestinian people and other Arabs of the occupied territories, as reflected in the reports of the Special Committee covering the reporting period;

4. *Expresses the hope* that, in the light of the recent positive political developments, those policies and practices will be brought to an end immediately;

5. *Requests* the Special Committee, pending complete termination of the Israeli occupation, to continue to investigate Israeli policies and practices in the occupied Palestinian territory, including Jerusalem, and other Arab territories occupied by Israel since 1967, to consult, as appropriate, with the International Committee of the Red Cross according to its regulations in order to ensure that the welfare and human rights of the peoples of the occupied territories are safeguarded and to report to the Secretary-General as soon as possible and whenever the need arises thereafter;

6. *Also requests* the Special Committee to submit regularly to the Secretary-General periodic reports on the current situation in the occupied Palestinian territory;

7. *Further requests* the Special Committee to continue to investigate the treatment of prisoners in the occupied Palestinian territory, including Jerusalem, and other Arab territories occupied by Israel since 1967;

8. *Requests* the Secretary-General:

(*a*) To provide all necessary facilities to the Special Committee, including those required for its visits to the occupied territories, so that it may investigate the Israeli policies and practices referred to in the present resolution;

(*b*) To continue to make available such additional staff as may be necessary to assist the Special Committee in the performance of its tasks;

(*c*) To circulate regularly to Member States the periodic reports mentioned in paragraph 6 above;

(*d*) To ensure the widest circulation of the reports of the Special Committee and of information regarding its activities and findings, by all means available, through the Department of Public Information of the Secretariat and, where necessary, to reprint those reports of the Special Committee that are no longer available;

(*e*) To report to the General Assembly at its forty-ninth session on the tasks entrusted to him in the present resolution;

9. *Decides* to include in the provisional agenda of its forty-ninth session the item entitled ''Report of the Spe-

cial Committee to Investigate Israeli Practices Affecting the Human Rights of the Palestinian People and Other Arabs of the Occupied Territories''.

General Assembly resolution 48/41 A

10 December 1993   Meeting 75   93-2-65 (recorded vote)

Approved by Fourth Committee (A/48/647) by recorded vote (81-2-52), 8 December (meeting 27); 16-nation draft (A/C.4/48/L.32); agenda item 86.
Sponsors: Bahrain, Bangladesh, Brunei Darussalam, Comoros, Cuba, Egypt, Indonesia, Jordan, Malaysia, Mauritania, Qatar, Saudi Arabia, Sudan, Tunisia, United Arab Emirates, Yemen.
Meeting numbers. GA 48th session: 4th Committee 20, 21, 27; plenary 75.

Recorded vote in Assembly as follows:

   In favour: Afghanistan, Algeria, Angola, Azerbaijan, Bahrain, Bangladesh, Benin, Bhutan, Bosnia and Herzegovina, Botswana, Brazil, Brunei Darussalam, Burkina Faso, Cameroon, Cape Verde,* Chad, Chile, China, Colombia, Comoros, Costa Rica, Côte d'Ivoire, Cuba, Cyprus, Democratic People's Republic of Korea, Djibouti, Ecuador, Egypt, El Salvador, Gambia, Ghana, Guatemala, Guinea, Guinea-Bissau, Haiti, Honduras, India, Indonesia, Iran, Jordan, Kuwait, Lao People's Democratic Republic, Lebanon, Lesotho, Libyan Arab Jamahiriya, Madagascar, Malawi, Malaysia, Maldives, Mali, Mauritania, Mauritius, Mexico, Mongolia, Morocco, Mozambique, Myanmar, Namibia, Nepal, Nicaragua, Niger, Nigeria, Oman, Pakistan, Peru, Philippines, Qatar, Republic of Korea, Rwanda, Saint Lucia, Saint Vincent and the Grenadines, Saudi Arabia, Senegal, Sierra Leone, Singapore, Sri Lanka, Sudan, Suriname, Syrian Arab Republic, Thailand, Togo, Trinidad and Tobago, Tunisia, Turkey, Uganda, Ukraine, United Arab Emirates, United Republic of Tanzania, Venezuela, Viet Nam, Yemen, Zaire, Zimbabwe.

   Against: Israel, United States.

   Abstaining: Antigua and Barbuda, Argentina, Armenia, Australia, Austria, Bahamas, Barbados, Belarus, Belgium, Belize, Bolivia, Bulgaria, Canada, Central African Republic, Congo, Czech Republic, Denmark, Dominica, Dominican Republic, Estonia, Fiji, Finland, France, Gabon, Georgia, Germany, Greece, Grenada, Guyana, Hungary, Iceland, Ireland, Italy, Jamaica, Japan, Kazakhstan, Kenya, Latvia, Liechtenstein, Lithuania, Luxembourg, Malta, Marshall Islands, Micronesia, Netherlands, New Zealand, Norway, Panama, Papua New Guinea, Paraguay, Poland, Portugal, Republic of Moldova, Romania, Russian Federation, Samoa, San Marino, Slovakia, Slovenia, Spain, Swaziland, Sweden, the former Yugoslav Republic of Macedonia, United Kingdom, Uruguay.

   *Later advised the Secretariat it had intended to abstain.

On the same date, the Assembly adopted **resolution 48/41 C**, as recommended by the Fourth Committee, also by recorded vote.

The General Assembly,

Bearing in mind the relevant resolutions of the Security Council,

Recalling its relevant resolutions and the resolutions of the Commission on Human Rights,

Aware of the responsibility of the international community to promote human rights and ensure respect for international law,

Reaffirming the principle of the inadmissibility of the acquisition of territory by force,

Gravely concerned about the violations of the human rights of the Palestinian people, as described in the reports of the Special Committee to Investigate Israeli Practices Affecting the Human Rights of the Palestinian People and Other Arabs of the Occupied Territories, especially in the fields of collective punishment, closure of areas, annexation, establishment of settlements and mass deportation,

Gravely concerned also about the situation in the occupied Palestinian territory, including Jerusalem, and the other Arab territories occupied by Israel since 1967, resulting from the measures and actions taken by Israel, the occupying Power, designed to change the legal status, geographical nature and demographic composition of those territories,

Concerned about the dangerous situation resulting from actions taken by the illegal, armed settlers in the occupied territory,

Convinced of the positive impact of an international presence in the occupied Palestinian territory to ensure compliance with the provisions of the Geneva Convention relative to the Protection of Civilian Persons in Time of War, of 12 August 1949,

Reaffirming the applicability of the Convention to the occupied Palestinian territory, including Jerusalem, and the other Arab territories occupied by Israel since 1967,

Welcoming the signing of the Declaration of Principles on Interim Self-Government Arrangements, including its Annexes, and its Agreed Minutes, by the Government of the State of Israel and the Palestine Liberation Organization, at Washington, D.C., on 13 September 1993,

1. *Determines* that all measures and actions taken by Israel, the occupying Power, in the occupied Palestinian territory, including Jerusalem, in violation of the relevant provisions of the Geneva Convention relative to the Protection of Civilian Persons in Time of War, of 12 August 1949, and contrary to the relevant resolutions of the Security Council, are illegal and have no validity, and demands that Israel desist forthwith from taking any such measures or actions;

2. *Demands* that Israel, the occupying Power, facilitate the return of all Palestinians deported from the occupied Palestinian territory since 1967;

3. *Calls upon* Israel, the occupying Power, to accelerate the release of all Palestinians arbitrarily detained or imprisoned;

4. *Calls* for complete respect by the occupying Power of all fundamental freedoms of the Palestinian people, such as the freedom of education, including the free operation of schools, universities and other educational institutions;

5. *Reaffirms* that the Israeli settlements in the occupied Palestinian territory, including Jerusalem, and the other Arab territories occupied by Israel since 1967 are illegal and an obstacle to peace;

6. *Requests* the Secretary-General to report to the General Assembly at its forty-ninth session on the implementation of the present resolution.

General Assembly resolution 48/41 C

10 December 1993   Meeting 75   106-2-48 (recorded vote)

Approved by Fourth Committee (A/48/647) by recorded vote (96-2-36), 8 December (meeting 27); 16-nation draft (A/C.4/48/L.34); agenda item 86.
Sponsors: Bahrain, Bangladesh, Brunei Darussalam, Comoros, Cuba, Egypt, Indonesia, Jordan, Malaysia, Mauritania, Qatar, Saudi Arabia, Sudan, Tunisia, United Arab Emirates, Yemen.
Meeting numbers. GA 48th session: 4th Committee 20, 21, 27; plenary 75.

Recorded vote in Assembly as follows:

   In favour: Afghanistan, Algeria, Australia, Austria, Azerbaijan, Bahamas, Bahrain, Bangladesh, Belarus, Belize, Benin, Bhutan, Bolivia, Bosnia and Herzegovina, Botswana, Brazil, Brunei Darussalam, Burkina Faso, Cameroon, Cape Verde, Chad, Chile, China, Colombia, Comoros, Congo, Côte d'Ivoire, Cuba, Cyprus, Democratic People's Republic of Korea, Djibouti, Ecuador, Egypt, El Salvador, France, Gambia, Ghana, Greece, Grenada, Guatemala, Guinea, Guinea-Bissau, Guyana, Haiti, Honduras, India, Indonesia, Iran, Ireland, Jordan, Kazakhstan, Kuwait, Lao People's Democratic Republic, Lebanon, Lesotho, Libyan Arab Jamahiriya, Madagascar, Malawi, Malaysia, Maldives, Mali, Malta, Mauritania, Mauritius, Mexico, Mongolia, Morocco, Mozambique, Myanmar, Namibia, Nepal, New Zealand, Nicaragua, Niger, Nigeria, Oman, Pakistan, Peru, Philippines, Qatar, Republic of Korea, Rwanda, Saudi Arabia, Senegal, Sierra Leone, Singapore, Spain, Sri Lanka, Sudan, Suriname, Sweden, Syrian Arab Republic, Thailand, Togo, Trinidad and Tobago, Tunisia, Turkey, Uganda,

Ukraine, United Arab Emirates, United Republic of Tanzania, Uruguay, Viet Nam, Yemen, Zaire, Zimbabwe.
Against: Israel, United States.
Abstaining: Antigua and Barbuda, Argentina, Armenia, Barbados, Belgium, Bulgaria, Canada, Central African Republic, Costa Rica, Czech Republic, Denmark, Dominica, Dominican Republic, Estonia, Fiji, Finland, Georgia, Germany, Hungary, Iceland, Italy, Jamaica, Japan, Kenya, Latvia, Liechtenstein, Lithuania, Luxembourg, Marshall Islands, Micronesia, Netherlands, Norway, Panama, Papua New Guinea, Paraguay, Poland, Portugal, Republic of Moldova, Romania, Russian Federation, Saint Lucia, Saint Vincent and the Grenadines, Samoa, San Marino, Slovakia, Slovenia, the former Yugoslav Republic of Macedonia, United Kingdom.

In the Fourth Committee, Israel said the draft resolutions based on the report of the Committee on Israeli practices, though somewhat modified, ignored the recently signed Declaration of Principles and disregarded the understandings reached. Moreover, they touched on the subjects of boundaries, settlements and Jerusalem, which should properly be discussed only in the negotiations stipulated in the Declaration. The resolutions under consideration prejudged the outcome of the negotiations. Since the Committee on Israeli practices was established in 1968 in an atmosphere of open hostility, it should be disbanded and the resolutions based on its reports discontinued.

Fourth Geneva Convention

Report of the Committee on Israeli practices. In its November 1993 report,[1] the Committee on Israeli practices underlined that the fourth Geneva Convention stipulated that military occupation was to be considered a temporary, de facto situation giving no right whatsoever to the occupying Power over the territorial integrity of the territories it occupied. The Israeli authorities, however, continued to pursue their policy of annexation, which resulted in the expropriation of land, diversion of water resources, uprooting of trees and building of an infrastructure of roads linking its settlements, in violation of the Convention. Thus, the Committee recommended full application by Israel of the Convention as the main international instrument of humanitarian law applicable to the territories, which had been repeatedly reaffirmed by the Security Council, the General Assembly and other relevant United Nations organs.

Report of the Secretary-General. In October 1993,[21] the Secretary-General informed the Assembly that Israel had not replied to his April request for information on steps taken or envisaged to implement a 1992 Assembly resolution[22] demanding that it accept the *de jure* applicability of the fourth Geneva Convention and comply with its provisions in the occupied Palestinian territory, including Jerusalem, and other Arab territories it had occupied since 1967.

GENERAL ASSEMBLY ACTION

On 10 December 1993, on the recommendation of the Fourth Committee, the General Assembly adopted **resolution 48/41 B** by recorded vote.

The General Assembly,
Bearing in mind the relevant resolutions of the Security Council,
Recalling its relevant resolutions,
Having considered the reports of the Special Committee to Investigate Israeli Practices Affecting the Human Rights of the Palestinian People and Other Arabs of the Occupied Territories and the relevant reports of the Secretary-General,
Considering that the promotion of respect for the obligations arising from the Charter of the United Nations and other instruments and rules of international law is among the basic purposes and principles of the United Nations,
Stressing that Israel, the occupying Power, should strictly comply with its obligations under international law,
    1. *Reaffirms* that the Geneva Convention relative to the Protection of Civilian Persons in Time of War, of 12 August 1949, is applicable to the occupied Palestinian territory, including Jerusalem, and other Arab territories occupied by Israel since 1967;
    2. *Demands* that Israel accept the *de jure* applicability of the Convention in the occupied Palestinian territory, including Jerusalem, and other Arab territories occupied by Israel since 1967, and that it comply scrupulously with the provisions of the Convention;
    3. *Calls upon* all States parties to the Convention, in accordance with article 1 common to the four Geneva Conventions, to exert all efforts in order to ensure respect for its provisions by Israel, the occupying Power, in the occupied Palestinian territory, including Jerusalem, and other Arab territories occupied by Israel since 1967;
    4. *Requests* the Secretary-General to report to the General Assembly at its forty-ninth session on the implementation of the present resolution.

General Assembly resolution 48/41 B
10 December 1993   Meeting 75   152-1-6 (recorded vote)

Approved by Fourth Committee (A/48/647) by recorded vote (130-1-7), 8 December (meeting 27); 17-nation draft (A/C.4/48/L.33); agenda item 86.
Sponsors: Bahrain, Bangladesh, Brunei Darussalam, Comoros, Cuba, Egypt, India, Indonesia, Jordan, Malaysia, Mauritania, Qatar, Saudi Arabia, Sudan, Tunisia, United Arab Emirates, Yemen.
Meeting numbers. GA 48th session: 4th Committee 20, 21, 27; plenary 75.

Recorded vote in Assembly as follows:
In favour: Afghanistan, Algeria, Antigua and Barbuda, Argentina, Armenia, Australia, Austria, Azerbaijan, Bahamas, Bahrain, Bangladesh, Barbados, Belarus, Belgium, Belize, Benin, Bhutan, Bolivia, Bosnia and Herzegovina, Botswana, Brazil, Brunei Darussalam, Bulgaria, Burkina Faso, Cameroon, Canada, Cape Verde, Chad, Chile, China, Colombia, Comoros, Congo, Costa Rica, Côte d'Ivoire, Cuba, Cyprus, Czech Republic, Democratic People's Republic of Korea, Denmark, Djibouti, Dominican Republic, Ecuador, Egypt, El Salvador, Estonia, Fiji, Finland, France, Gabon, Georgia, Germany, Ghana, Greece, Grenada, Guatemala, Guinea, Guinea-Bissau, Guyana, Haiti, Honduras, Hungary, Iceland, India, Indonesia, Iran, Iraq, Ireland, Italy, Jamaica, Japan, Jordan, Kazakhstan, Kenya, Kuwait, Lao People's Democratic Republic, Latvia, Lebanon, Lesotho, Libyan Arab Jamahiriya, Liechtenstein, Lithuania, Luxembourg, Madagascar, Malawi, Malaysia, Maldives, Mali, Malta, Mauritania, Mauritius, Mexico, Mongolia, Morocco, Mozambique, Myanmar, Namibia, Nepal, Netherlands, New Zealand, Nicaragua, Niger, Nigeria, Norway, Oman, Pakistan, Panama, Papua New Guinea, Paraguay, Peru, Philippines, Poland, Portugal, Qatar, Republic of Korea, Republic of Moldova, Romania, Rwanda, Saint Lucia, Saint Vincent and the Grenadines, San Marino, Saudi Arabia, Senegal, Sierra Leone, Singapore, Slovakia, Slovenia, Spain, Sri Lanka, Sudan, Suriname, Swaziland, Sweden, Syrian Arab Republic, the former Yugoslav Republic of Macedonia, Thailand, Togo, Trinidad and Tobago, Tunisia, Turkey, Turkmenistan, Uganda, Ukraine, United Arab Emirates, United Kingdom, United Republic of Tanzania, Uruguay, Venezuela, Viet Nam, Yemen, Zaire, Zimbabwe.
Against: Israel.
Abstaining: Central African Republic, Marshall Islands, Micronesia, Russian Federation, Samoa, United States.

Expulsion and deportation of Palestinians

As the latest incident in a series of expulsions and deportations, Israel had, on 17 December 1992,[23] expelled on alleged security grounds 415 Palestinians, in violation of article 49 of the fourth Geneva Convention, from the occupied territories to Marj al Zahour in its so-called security zone in southern Lebanon, apparently in punishment for the recent killing of an Israeli soldier. The deportation was to be for a period of two years. On the following day, the Security Council adopted resolution 799(1992),[24] by which it demanded the immediate return to the territories of all those deported. It was not before December 1993 that Israel heeded the Council's demand and allowed the return of the last remaining deportees.

Report of the Secretary-General. Pursuant to resolution 799(1992), the Secretary-General on 25 January submitted a report[25] on developments in the deportation case. He had informed Israeli Foreign Minister Shimon Peres of his decision to send the Under-Secretary-General for Political Affairs, James Jonah, to the region, and expressed hope that a solution would be achieved in conformity with the position unanimously adopted by the Security Council.

The Under-Secretary-General visited the area from 27 to 30 December 1992. While in Israel, he held extensive discussions with Prime Minister Yitzhak Rabin and the Foreign Minister. In Jerusalem, he met with a group of Palestinians, led by Faisal Husseini, the head of the Palestinian delegation to the peace talks with Israel. In Lebanon, he convened with President Elias Hrawi and Prime Minister Rafik Hariri, as well as with the Minister of Health and Acting Minister for Foreign Affairs, Marwan Hamadieh. Although he was prevented from meeting with the deportees themselves, the Under-Secretary-General met with representatives of their families, at their request, as well as with Israeli families who had suffered from acts of terrorism. In addition, he was briefed by representatives of UNIFIL and UNRWA, it being noted that 16 of the deportees were UNRWA staff members.

On 2 January 1993, Mr. Jonah briefed the Secretary-General in Addis Ababa on his discussions in the region, which had been inconclusive because it had not proved possible to persuade Israel to fulfil its obligations under resolution 799(1992). The Secretary-General subsequently informed Prime Minister Rabin of his intention to deploy a second mission, led by his Special Political Adviser and representative to the multilateral Middle East talks, Under-Secretary-General Chinmaya Gharekhan, in order to achieve a solution in accordance with the will of the Security Council. On 4 January, the Secretary-General conveyed to the Council President that an impor-tant principle was at stake, as Israel's deportation of 415 Palestinian civilians was illegal under international law, in contravention of the fourth Geneva Convention and in fundamental disregard of the 1948 Universal Declaration of Human Rights,[26] as well as of repeated Council resolutions, most recently resolution 799(1992). The Secretary-General regretted that Mr. Jonah's mission had been unsuccessful, which was attributable to Israel's non-compliance with that resolution. Recalling the unanimous and unequivocal position taken by the Council in that resolution, he said there was no alternative to the safe and immediate return to the territories of all those deported. If Israel did not recognize the need to comply with resolution 799(1992), he might have to recommend that the Council consider taking further steps to ensure respect for its decision.

The Secretary-General briefed Mr. Gharekhan at Cairo on 6 January about his renewed mission, stressing that, in his discussions with Israel, he should focus solely on implementation of resolution 799(1992). While the United Nations was concerned over the humanitarian plight of the deportees, this aspect was not addressed by the Council. Rather, it was appropriate for ICRC, which under the fourth Geneva Convention had special responsibility for civilians under occupation, to address the humanitarian needs of the deportees.

Visiting Israel from 7 to 12 January, Under-Secretary-General Gharekhan conferred extensively with Israeli authorities, including the Prime Minister and the Foreign Minister. The Prime Minister emphasized that the "temporary expulsion" could not be rescinded. The decision had been taken in the light of acts of violence by supporters of the Hamas and Islamic Jihad movements against Israeli citizens, which had culminated in the kidnapping and murder of an Israeli border policeman. He mentioned that a number of petitions had been filed with the Israeli High Court of Justice, including one that challenged the legality of the deportation decision which, unlike previous ones, did not stem from the British Mandatory Emergency Regulations of 1945. Should the High Court rule that the decision was illegal, the deportees would be returned. Otherwise, each expelled individual had the right to appeal. In Israel's opinion, the expulsion orders were not inconsistent with the position taken by the Security Council. All those deported would be permitted to return, as requested by the Council; the only difference was regarding the timing. Each deportee had been informed, at the time of his expulsion, of the period he would have to remain away. If the Council were to adopt measures against Israel, it might lead to a collapse of the peace process, for which the Council would be held responsible.

For his part, Mr. Gharekhan underlined that the objective of his mission was to find a solution in accordance with resolution 799(1992). If Israel failed to fulfil its obligations under that resolution, the Secretary-General would have no choice but to submit an unambiguous report to the Security Council as a follow-up to his 4 January communication to its President. He firmly rejected the view that the Council could be held responsible for a collapse in the Middle East peace process. Should such an eventuality arise, Israel alone would be responsible. Israel could place the deportees in prison or under administrative detention, which, at least, would not violate the fourth Geneva Convention. During his visit to Jerusalem, Mr. Gharekhan met, at their request, with a representative group of Palestinians led by Faisal Husseini, who said that unless the deportees were permitted to return, the Palestinian delegation would not resume peace talks with Israel.

While his mission did not concern humanitarian matters, the Under-Secretary-General conferred twice with the head of the ICRC delegation at Tel Aviv, who briefed him on the visit of ICRC to the deportees on 9 January, which had been agreed to on a one-time basis by Lebanon, Israel and UNIFIL. The ICRC delegate and the medical doctor conducting the visit had decided, and were given permission by Israel, to evacuate two deportees on humanitarian grounds. One, a 16-year-old boy, had been expelled "by mistake", while the other was evacuated for medical reasons.

On 13 January, the Secretary-General met in Paris with the Israeli Foreign Minister, reiterating to him the need for Israel to comply immediately with the Security Council decision. On the following day, agreement was reached with the Prime Minister to send Mr. Gharekhan again to Jerusalem in a further effort to secure implementation of resolution 799(1992).

During the Under-Secretary-General's return trip to Israel, from 19 to 22 January, he again met with the Prime Minister and the Foreign Minister. In the meantime, the Israeli High Court, on 17 January, had begun consideration of the appeal challenging the deportation order's legality. As at the date of the present report, the Court hearings were continuing. Mr. Gharekhan again received a group of Palestinians who expressed support for the efforts of the Secretary-General and demanded implementation of resolution 799(1992) without delay. The Palestinians reiterated their position that they could not take part in the peace talks unless the deportation issue was resolved.

Summing up his observations, the Secretary-General underlined that in order to understand fully the gravity of the situation addressed in resolution 799(1992), it was important to recall that the deportations of 17 December 1992 were only the most recent in a series of Israeli violations of the fourth Geneva Convention. To ensure the safety and protection of Palestinian civilians under Israeli occupation, he intended to initiate discussions with Israel regarding the establishment of a United Nations monitoring mechanism in the occupied territories, as suggested by the Council in resolution 681(1990).[12] The Palestinians' need for safety and protection had to be met regardless of progress in the peace talks.

Israel's refusal to ensure the safe and immediate return of the deportees challenged, in the Secretary-General's view, the authority of the Security Council. Additionally, there was a growing perception throughout the international community that the Council, by not pressing for Israeli compliance, did not attach equal importance to the implementation of all of its decisions. In these circumstances, he would be failing in his duty by not recommending that the Council take whatever measures were required to ensure that its unanimous decision, as set out in resolution 799(1992), was respected. The developments outlined above underscored the need to achieve a comprehensive, just and lasting Middle East peace, and the international community should spare no effort in its pursuit of a settlement. For his own part, the Secretary-General remained committed to doing everything possible to help in that endeavour.

Report of the Committee on Israeli practices. The Committee on Israeli practices[1] reported that, as at August 1993, 396 deportees still remained at the Marj al Zahour tent camp.

On 28 January, Israel's High Court of Justice had ruled the expulsion order to be invalid but indicated that Israel was not obliged to return the deportees and allowed the order to remain in force because of an emergency mandatory regulation providing for individual deportations. The judges concluded that the deportations amounted to 415 individual expulsions, with each man deported on the basis of evidence brought against him. The Committee emphasized, however, that under article 49 of the fourth Geneva Convention, individual or mass forcible transfers, as well as deportations of protected persons from occupied territory to the territory of the Occupying Power or to that of any other country, occupied or not, were prohibited, regardless of their motive. On 1 February, the Israeli Government voted unanimously to allow some 100 selected deportees to return and reduced the duration of expulsion of those remaining by half. The deportees refused this "package deal", and 396 remained at the Marj al Zahour camp; but in August, they accepted Israel's offer to allow them to return from exile in two stages.

In another case, Israel announced on 28 April that it would allow 30 long-term Palestinian deportees to return to the territories, of whom the first 15 returned on 30 April, with the rest returning on 3 May.

Consideration by the Committee on Palestinian rights. The Committee on Palestinian rights, extremely concerned by the deportation of the 415 Palestinians, on 21 January adopted a statement[27] by which it strongly condemned that action as contrary to the fourth Geneva Convention and numerous Security Council resolutions. The Committee noted that the deportees were enduring extremely harsh conditions, being exposed to winter weather and lacking adequate food, water and medical care. They also faced the threat of possible violent actions, including artillery shelling, from Israeli or Israeli-controlled forces. The Committee called on the Security Council to take all necessary measures, including the application of Chapter VII of the Charter, to bring about the implementation of resolution 799(1992). It again urgently appealed to the Council to provide protection to Palestinians in the territories, including Jerusalem, in accordance with the fourth Geneva Convention, and in particular with resolution 681(1990).[12]

In its November report,[2] the Committee expressed the view that in spite of having permitted some of the deportees to return to their homes, Israel had yet to implement resolution 799(1992).[24]

Communications. In a memorandum[28] of 8 January to the Secretary-General on the December 1992 deportations by Israel and Israeli deportations as a whole, the Permanent Observer of Palestine stated that, as the deportees, who had been blindfolded and bound and driven in buses to Israel's northern border, tried to return on foot, they were prevented from doing so by shooting and shelling directed at them by the Israeli army. Such shelling was repeated several times at later dates. He noted that the situation of the deportees was deteriorating due to the harshness of weather and a lack of all essentials, including water, medicine and foodstuffs. A number of them had become sick and several were injured. Meanwhile, Israel rejected a formal request by ICRC to provide the deportees with the essential materials through Israel's borders. According to the memorandum, Israel had deported some 2,500 Palestinian civilians since 1967. The Permanent Observer concluded that the deportation was illegal under international law and the fourth Geneva Convention, in violation of the Universal Declaration of Human Rights[26] and all other human rights instruments and standards, as well as applicable domestic law. The deportation of December 1992 also constituted a form of collective punishment, which had a detrimental effect on the peace process and which could not succeed as long as that situation

was not brought to an end. He emphasized that the Security Council was duty-bound to compel Israel to abide by its obligations under Article 25 of the Charter and to guarantee respect for international law. PLO called on the Council to adopt a new resolution under Chapter VII of the Charter to ensure Israel's acceptance and implementation of resolution 799(1992).

On 4 February,[29] the Permanent Observer brought to the Secretary-General's attention statements reportedly made by Prime Minister Rabin to the Israeli Parliament to the effect that an "agreement" had been negotiated between Israel and the United States on the deportation issue. *The New York Times* had quoted the Prime Minister as saying that "his agreement with the United States to bring back a quarter of the 400 Palestinians banished to Lebanon had preserved his right to deport hundreds of more people in the future". Such an "agreemeent", PLO said, was not in accordance with resolution 799(1992), and its acceptance would be tantamount to legitimizing deportation. It called on the Council to consider immediately the Secretary-General's January report[25] on the matter and keep it actively under review, a demand which was reiterated on 16 February.[30]

Israel informed the Secretary-General on 9 February[31] of a government decision of 1 February which allowed the return of 101 Palestinians to the locations from which they had been temporarily deported. Those returning would be persons whose circumstances surrounding their temporary deportation were relatively less severe in comparison to others. Also, the military commanders would be instructed to reduce by one half the term of deportation of those still remaining under the deportation order. With regard to them, the decisions of the Supreme Court were to be carried out, including their right to appeal before an advisory committee and contact with an attorney, in addition to a review of the security information concerning those who did not appeal. The delivery of necessary humanitarian provisions to the deportees would be allowed by helicopter. Israel noted that this decision provided for the return of all excluded persons before the end of 1993.

Accordingly, Israel reported, on 20 December,[32] the phased return of the deportees during the year. In January and February, 19 deportees who were either ill or mistakenly expelled were returned. On 1 February, Israel decided to allow the return of 101 Palestinians to their original locations, and to reduce by one half the term of exclusion for those against whom the deportation orders remained in force. However, the deportees whose exclusion was lifted chose not to return at that time. On 9 September, 181 persons were allowed to return, and on 15 December, the remaining 215 deportees were allowed to do so, of whom 197 returned while 18 chose not to.

Report of the Secretary-General. The Secretary-General informed the General Assembly in October 1993[33] that no reply had been received from Israel to his note verbale of April requesting information on steps it had taken or envisaged to implement the 1992 Assembly demand[34] that Israel rescind the illegal deportation of Palestinians and facilitate their immediate return.

Palestinian detainees

Report of the Committee on Israeli practices. The Committee on Israeli practices in November[1] reported that the status and treatment of Arab prisoners in Israeli custody continued to be critical. Detainees were still subjected in a systematic manner to various forms of both physical and psychological torture and ill-treatment, such as long periods in isolation cells, uninterrupted interrogation sessions, food and sleep deprivation, denial of use of sanitary facilities, having to remain in uncomfortable positions for long periods, confinement in refrigerated rooms with cold water poured over them and having their heads covered with sacks. According to statistics on 500 local residents, over 96 per cent reported having been subjected to various forms of torture while in prison or detention, for periods ranging from 6 months to 10 years (*Ha'aretz* and *Jerusalem Post*, 9 June). It was revealed that doctors examining security detainees had to sign a form declaring that prisoners were medically fit to be chained and blindfolded (*Jerusalem Post*, 14 June).

Deaths in custody and suicides of prisoners continued to occur. Ayman Nasser, a 23-year-old member of the Fatah Hawks, died on 3 April in Barzilai Hospital as a result of lung damage and septic shock reportedly caused by smoke inhalation and injuries sustained during his arrest on 20 March and the ensuing extensive interrogation. He was said to have been beaten, handcuffed, hooded and subjected to food and sleep deprivation and did not receive adequate medical care in time. On 15 February, a 34-year-old security prisoner was found hanging in his cell in Beersheba prison after having served almost eight years of his 18-year sentence.

Consideration by the Committee on Palestinian rights. The Committee on Palestinian rights in November[2] noted with concern that approximately 14,000 Palestinian political prisoners were still being held in Israeli prisons and detention camps, many of whom were in administrative detention without having been brought to trial. Reports of inhuman conditions in jails and mistreatment of prisoners included beatings and tor-

ture. The Committee observed with alarm that 14 Palestinians had died in custody since the beginning of the *intifadah* in 1987.[3]

Report of the Secretary-General. The Secretary-General reported to the General Assembly in October 1993[35] that Israel had not replied to his April request for information on steps taken or envisaged to implement an Assembly resolution of 1992[36] calling on it to release all Palestinians and other Arabs arbitrarily detained or imprisoned.

Israeli measures against educational institutions

Report of the Committee on Israeli practices. In November,[1] the Committee on Israeli practices reported that the closure on 31 March of the occupied territories by Israel had had adverse consequences on education since more than 25 per cent of the students there were unable to register at universities or attend classes. Students living in a location different from that of their educational facility were denied permits to commute, while many were unable even to register despite the extension of registration periods. Children whose parents were residents of different localities were at times denied education altogether. The Committee was also informed of the persistent lack of appropriate educational infrastructure, manifested in a severe shortage of classrooms, buildings that failed to meet the requisite standards and extremely short teaching hours due to overcrowding and inadequate teaching conditions.

The Committee was informed of the closure on 21 November 1992 by IDF of the UNRWA Technical Training Centre in Gaza for one month because its students were celebrating the declaration of independence of the Palestinian State. The Gaza Secondary School was ordered closed for the same reason. On 5 April 1993, the Hashimiya Secondary School for Boys was closed for two weeks following student protests. As a positive development, the Committee noted the opening on 4 October 1992 of the first four-year college in Gaza.

Report of the Secretary-General. The Secretary-General informed the General Assembly in October 1993[37] that no reply had been received from Israel in response to his note verbale of April requesting information on steps it had taken or envisaged to implement the 1992 Assembly demand[38] that it rescind all actions and measures against educational institutions, ensure their freedom and refrain from hindering their effective operation.

Golan Heights

Report of the Committee on Israeli practices. The Syrian Arab Republic provided the Committee on Israeli practices[1] with information on the situation in the occupied Syrian Arab Golan Heights. It referred to the lack of most health and educational services and the neglect of public utilities, which had led to a constant deterioration of the situation in the villages. Israeli settlements were given names derived from the Torah, and Arabic signboards were replaced with Hebrew and English ones, which revealed attempts to endow that territory with a Hebrew identity and the intention to perpetuate the Israeli occupation. Many archaeological sites were reportedly destroyed as a result of military manoeuvres by IDF, which used various types of explosives and armour-piercing shells. Israeli agricultural exploitation continued to be characterized by the expropriation of land and the seizure and exploitation of water resources. While the Arab population was prohibited from drilling new wells or even using old ones, Israeli authorities drilled numerous wells for the benefit of the settlements. As to educational affairs, Arab students were forced to learn Hebrew as a basic subject and therefore had to study three languages, to the detriment of scientific and social subjects. In health services, there was a shortage of all types of first-aid facilities and of medical specialists. Israel furthermore did not abandon its attempts to impose compulsory conscription on young Arabs and enlist them in the ranks of the very army which occupied their land.

The Committee also observed the pursuance by Israel of its policy of annexation and settlements in the Golan Heights. In addition to the expropriation of land, its inhabitants were coerced into selling land at prices considerably lower than its real value.

Report of the Secretary-General. In October 1993,[39] the Secretary-General informed the General Assembly that no reply had been received from Israel to his April request for information on steps it had taken or envisaged to implement a 1992 Assembly resolution[40] condemning the persistence of Israel in changing the physical character, demographic composition, institutional structure and legal status of the occupied Golan and calling on it to desist from repressive measures against the population there.

GENERAL ASSEMBLY ACTION

On 10 December 1993, the General Assembly, on the recommendation of the Fourth Committee, adopted **resolution 48/41 D** by recorded vote.

The General Assembly,

Deeply concerned that the Arab territories occupied since 1967 have been under continued Israeli military occupation,

Recalling Security Council resolution 497(1981) of 17 December 1981,

Recalling also its resolutions 36/226 B of 17 December 1981, ES-9/1 of 5 February 1982, 37/88 E of 10 December 1982, 38/79 F of 15 December 1983, 39/95 F of 14 December 1984, 40/161 F of 16 December 1985, 41/63 F of 3 December 1986, 42/160 F of 8 December 1987, 43/21 of 3 November 1988, 43/58 F of 6 December 1988, 44/2 of 6 October 1989, 44/48 F of 8 December 1989, 45/74 F of 11 December 1990, 46/47 F of 9 December 1991 and 47/70 F of 14 December 1992,

Having considered the report of the Secretary-General of 29 October 1993,

Recalling further its previous resolutions, in particular resolutions 3414(XXX) of 5 December 1975, 31/61 of 9 December 1976, 32/20 of 25 November 1977, 33/28 and 33/29 of 7 December 1978, 34/70 of 6 December 1979 and 35/122 E of 11 December 1980, in which, *inter alia*, it called upon Israel to put an end to its occupation of the Arab territories,

Reaffirming once more the illegality of the decision of 14 December 1981 taken by Israel to impose its laws, jurisdiction and administration on the occupied Syrian Golan, which has resulted in the effective annexation of that territory,

Reaffirming that the acquisition of territory by force is inadmissible under the Charter of the United Nations,

Recalling the Geneva Convention relative to the Protection of Civilian Persons in Time of War, of 12 August 1949,

Reaffirming the applicability of the Convention to the occupied Syrian Golan,

Bearing in mind Security Council resolution 237(1967) of 14 June 1967,

1. *Condemns* Israel, the occupying Power, for its refusal to comply with the relevant resolutions on the occupied Syrian Golan, and in particular Security Council resolution 497(1981), in which the Council, *inter alia*, decided that the Israeli decision to impose its laws, jurisdiction and administration on the occupied Syrian Arab Golan was null and void and without international legal effect and demanded that Israel, the occupying Power, should rescind forthwith its decision;

2. *Also condemns* the persistence of Israel in changing the physical character, demographic composition, institutional structure and legal status of the occupied Syrian Golan and in particular the establishment of settlements;

3. *Determines* that all legislative and administrative measures and actions taken or to be taken by Israel, the occupying Power, that purport to alter the character and legal status of the occupied Syrian Golan are null and void, constitute a flagrant violation of international law and of the Geneva Convention relative to the Protection of Civilian Persons in Time of War, of 12 August 1949, and have no legal effect;

4. *Denounces* attempts by Israel forcibly to impose Israeli citizenship and Israeli identity cards on the Syrian citizens in the occupied Syrian Golan, and calls upon it to desist from its repressive measures against the population of the occupied Syrian Golan;

5. *Deplores* the violations by Israel of the Convention;

6. *Calls once again upon* Member States not to recognize any of the legislative or administrative measures and actions referred to above;

7. *Requests* the Secretary-General to report to the General Assembly at its forty-ninth session on the implementation of the present resolution.

General Assembly resolution 48/41 D

10 December 1993   Meeting 75   85-1-68 (recorded vote)

Approved by Fourth Committee (A/48/647) by recorded vote (74-1-55), 8 December (meeting 27); 8-nation draft (A/C.4/48/L.35); agenda item 86.

Sponsors: Bangladesh, Brunei Darussalam, Comoros, Cuba, Indonesia, Lebanon, Malaysia, Syrian Arab Republic.
Meeting numbers. GA 48th session: 4th Committee 20, 21, 27; plenary 75.
Recorded vote in Assembly as follows:

In favour: Afghanistan, Algeria, Armenia, Azerbaijan, Bahrain, Bangladesh, Belarus, Benin, Bhutan, Bolivia, Bosnia and Herzegovina, Botswana, Brazil, Brunei Darussalam, Burkina Faso, Cameroon, Chad, Chile, China, Colombia, Comoros, Cuba, Cyprus, Democratic People's Republic of Korea, Djibouti, Ecuador, Egypt, Ghana, Guinea, India, Indonesia, Iran, Iraq, Jordan, Kazakhstan, Kuwait, Lao People's Democratic Republic, Lebanon, Lesotho, Libyan Arab Jamahiriya, Madagascar, Malaysia, Maldives, Mali, Malta, Mauritania, Mauritius, Mexico, Micronesia, Mongolia, Morocco, Mozambique, Myanmar, Namibia, Nepal, Niger, Oman, Pakistan, Peru, Philippines, Qatar, Republic of Korea, Rwanda, Saint Lucia, Saudi Arabia, Senegal, Sierra Leone, Singapore, Sri Lanka, Sudan, Suriname, Syrian Arab Republic, Thailand, Togo, Trinidad and Tobago, Tunisia, Turkey, Uganda, Ukraine, United Arab Emirates, United Republic of Tanzania, Venezuela, Viet Nam, Yemen, Zaire, Zimbabwe.

Against: Israel.

Abstaining: Antigua and Barbuda, Argentina, Australia, Austria, Bahamas, Barbados, Belgium, Belize, Bulgaria, Canada, Central African Republic, Congo, Costa Rica, Côte d'Ivoire, Czech Republic, Denmark, Dominica, Dominican Republic, Estonia, Fiji, Finland, France, Gabon, Gambia, Georgia, Germany, Greece, Guinea-Bissau, Guyana, Haiti, Hungary, Iceland, Ireland, Italy, Jamaica, Japan, Kenya, Latvia, Liechtenstein, Lithuania, Luxembourg, Malawi, Marshall Islands, Micronesia, Netherlands, New Zealand, Nigeria, Norway, Panama, Papua New Guinea, Paraguay, Poland, Portugal, Republic of Moldova, Romania, Russian Federation, Saint Vincent and the Grenadines, Samoa, San Marino, Slovakia, Slovenia, Spain, Swaziland, Sweden, the former Yugoslav Republic of Macedonia, United Kingdom, United States, Uruguay.

Israeli settlements

Report of the Committee on Israeli practices. In its November 1993 report,[1] the Committee on Israeli practices noted that, although Israel had pledged not to build any new settlements, the expansion of existing ones was pursued. At the settlements of Asfad, Enab, Kfar Sifar, Kiryat, Kiryat Sefer, Ma'aleh Adumim, Ma'ali Amos, Moshav Ganai Tal, Ofra, Sweish and Takoa, the construction of 1,800 new housing units reportedly began on 6 July. According to *Al-Tali'ah* of 11 March, 43 settlements were being expanded, with those activities being especially intensive in the district of Bethlehem, followed by Nablus and Tulkarm. Although the Committee received no evidence that new settlements had been established since the new Rabin Government took office, *Al-Tali'ah* reported on 1 July that work was under way for the construction of a new settlement to be named Talmoun 4.

The Council of Jewish Communities in the West Bank and Gaza indicated that 127,000 Jews were already living in settlements. *Ha'aretz* and the *Jerusalem Post* reported on 1 December 1992 that according to a demographic study by the Peace Now movement, 144 settlements existed in the territories. Another survey indicated new settlement activities under the Rabin Government, in addition to the pledged completion of 11,000 housing units. Some 277,000 dunums of land were confiscated during the first five years of the *intifadah*, and the total of confiscated land amounted to 3,700,944 dunums. Those figures represented, at the end of 1992, 63 per cent of the total land surface in the West Bank and 44 per cent in Gaza.

The period under consideration was marked by frequent acts of violence and aggression by settlers

against Palestinians and other Arabs in the territories. Jewish settlers engaged in and on occasion stepped up indiscriminate attacks against individuals and raided villages and refugee camps, wantonly destroying Arab-owned property, as well as places of worship, and uprooting trees. According to witness testimony before the Committee, Israeli settlers stormed the Al Akkad Mosque in Khan Younis on 29 March and burnt it down. On 11 April, the mosque of Al Bureij was desecrated, and four days later the mosque of Al Isslah in the Shejaya district was profaned.

Consideration by the Committee on Palestinian rights. The Committee on Palestinian rights noted in November[2] that construction in the critical area of greater Jerusalem proceeded apace, with the Government considering ambitious plans to link the city centre with the southern block of settlements. Among those plans was completing the Jerusalem-Efrat highway, an estimated $42 million project intended to link the Jerusalem suburb of Gilo with the Etzion block of settlements and to benefit the economic development of Jerusalem's so-called "bedroom suburbs". The Committee reaffirmed that those settlement policies and practices were in violation of the fourth Geneva Convention.

Report of the Secretary-General. The Secretary-General informed the General Assembly in October 1993[41] that no reply had been received from Israel to his April request for information on steps it had taken or envisaged to implement the 1992 Assembly demand[42] that it desist from taking any action that would result in changing the legal status, geographical nature or demographic composition of the territories.

Economic and social repercussions of Israeli settlements

In a report of July 1993,[43] the Secretary-General highlighted the economic and social consequences of the establishment of settlements by Israel in the Palestinian territory, including Jerusalem, as well as in the Syrian Golan. Prepared in response to a General Assembly request of 1992,[44] the report was submitted to the Assembly through the Economic and Social Council.

According to the report, settlers were encouraged to settle in the territories through financial and tax incentives offered by the Government. Loans were more concessionary, infrastructure was provided free of charge and taxes were substantially discounted. *The New York Times* had reported in 1990 that settlers who built their own houses received the land virtually for free, while more than 50 per cent of the mortgage was interest-free. In addition, the Jewish Agency reported that the Government provided contractor subsidies that included interim financing for construction, a grant of 50 per cent of the cost of development (some $20,000 per housing unit), and a government guarantee of partial purchase of apartments not sold. The Government also provided buyer subsidies, under which the average mortgage for a family of three in development areas amounted to $32,000.

A report by UNCTAD[45] was cited as stating that the new "Stars Plan" settlement programme envisaged the establishment of a dozen new settlements, including many in the northern West Bank along its pre-1967 border with Israel. Another important plan under implementation was the continued expansion of Maaleh Adumin, which recently became the first Israeli "city" in the occupied territories. Its extension was intended to link up with settlements encircling East Jerusalem and with other settlements planned for construction west of the Palestinian city of Jericho. Israeli officials reportedly said that their settlement activity until mid-1992 was aimed at boxing in Palestinian areas, establishing Palestinian "islands of autonomy" and preventing Palestinian territorial congruity. It was estimated that by 1993 an additional 50,000 Israelis might reside in those settlements under construction. By the end of 1992, around 247,000 to 290,000 Jewish settlers lived in the following areas: East Jerusalem (120,000-140,000 settlers and 8 settlements); West Bank (110,000-130,000 settlers and 156 settlements); Gaza (4,000-5,000 settlers and 18 settlements); and Golan Heights (13,000-15,000 settlers and 33 settlements).

Since mid-1992, two main political issues affected the pace of Israeli settlement: the formation of a Labour coalition Government in July 1992 and American loan guarantees which were approved in October 1992. Those loan guarantees, as requested by Israel and approved by the President of the United States, stipulated that Israel would receive up to $2 billion annually in United States guarantees for fiscal years 1993-1997, but could not use them for activities outside its pre-1967 borders, and that the United States President retained the right to suspend or terminate the loans if their terms or conditions were violated. He was also entitled to reduce the loans by the amount Israel had spent in previous years on settlement construction and other activities deemed inconsistent with the agreements. However, it was nearly impossible to determine the source of funding of settlements, since the Israeli Government and the Jewish Agency could free funds for use in the territories by using money obtained under the United States loan guarantees for projects inside Israel.

As to the policies of the new Labour coalition Government, it had announced a change of national priorities by giving more attention to the absorption of immigrants, and had declared its intention to curtail its housing programme in the occupied territories. A careful review of that new policy revealed, however, that settlement construction was not frozen since the Government remained committed to continuing the construction of 11,000 housing units in the territories, while it simultaneously intended to halt construction of 6,681 units approved by the Shamir Government in the 1992 budget. According to the Minister of Construction and Housing, it was decided to complete 9,850 units in settlements throughout the West Bank, and 1,200 each in Gaza and the Golan Heights. Of those units approved for the West Bank, 1,700 were in Greater Jerusalem; 2,150 were located throughout the area and were in the framing stage; 5,000 were near completion; while 1,000 were being constructed by individual settlers. As at September 1992, Israeli settlements in the Greater Jerusalem region had a population of 184,878, and 16,235 housing units were under construction.

Land, the mainstay of the territories' economy, continued to be subject to expropriation and confiscation for the purpose of establishing new settlements and expanding old ones. A total of 19,145 dunums were confiscated during 1992, and 3,381 dunums were confiscated for settlements during the first four months of 1993.

Along with land confiscation, water continued to be one of the most sensitive issues affecting economic and social development. A series of military orders established rules and regulations on water extraction, consumption, sale and distribution; control of water use; sharing and rationing; construction of water installations; drilling of wells; and granting of permits, making it easier for Israeli authorities and settlers to seize and utilize the resource. They regulated all matters regarding water resources, whether groundwater or surface water, including springs, ponds, streams and rivers, as well as price-setting and quantities allowed for use by Arab inhabitants and farmers. As a result, Israeli authorities continued to gain control over water resources. Settlements were often established on sites with good quality and quantity of groundwater as well as fertile land. Many existing Arab wells were blocked or sealed by the occupation authorities to protect the wells drilled for Israeli settlements. Other wells had dried up owing to overexploitation of the groundwater reservoirs in upstream areas by new wells drilled for settlements. Out of the total annual water supply of 700 million cubic metres in the West Bank and 60 million cubic metres in Gaza, between 515 million and 530 million cubic metres were transferred for use by Israel and its settlements. About 30 per cent of the total water used in Israel was taken from resources of the West Bank, representing 80 per cent of its groundwater potential. This water distribution policy, combined with over-pumping in some areas, severely strained the availability of Palestinian water resources and their ability to meet growing needs. Palestinians' access to water resources remained far less than that afforded to settlers, whose allowance per capita for agricultural use was 13 times greater than that for Palestinians in the West Bank and 7 times the entitlement of those living in Gaza. Private water consumption among Palestinians in the West Bank amounted to approximately 35 cubic metres per year per person, compared to 100 cubic metres for settlers. Deep wells drilled by Israeli authorities affected the level and quantity of water in Arab wells, resulting in a reduction in their productive capacity and the drying up of some wells and, consequently, of agricultural land that depended on them for irrigation water. Additionally, overexploitation of groundwater in Gaza and the great increase in water use by settlers augmented salinity due to sea-water intrusion. As in the West Bank and Gaza, continued arbitrary Israeli practices of land confiscation and water control reduced the cultivation area, curtailed local development and lowered the local level of income from agriculture in the Syrian Golan.

Agriculture was also heavily affected by such Israeli policies as curfews, military orders, uprooting of trees, land confiscation and the establishment of new settlements, under which circumstances it operated on the basis of a decreasing cultivated area and limited water supply, coupled with low productivity, cyclical fluctuations, insufficient diversification and often unequal competition with Israeli exports to the territories, which received generous government subsidies. With the justification of "security requirements", Israeli authorities engaged in an unprecedented practice of uprooting olive and fruit trees, thereby depriving farmers of their main source of income and forcing them to leave their land. During the first four months of 1993, approximately 3,180 trees were uprooted in the territories. The occupation authorities followed the same policy in the Syrian Golan by uprooting tree seedlings planted by Arab farmers for their failure to obtain permits for planting from the so-called Israel Land Administration.

Curfews imposed by Israel brought hardship to all spheres of daily life in the territories and halted all economic activities, sometimes being the first step which enabled settlers to establish new settlements or expand existing ones. After curfews were lifted, those settlements became "de facto" and gained the protection of the military authorities. Fishing in Gaza was also affected by curfews and Israeli seaside settlements, reducing the area allowed for fishing.

Consideration by the Committee on Palestinian rights. It was noted by the Committee on Pal-

estinian rights in November[2] that the Palestinian economy, which witnessed significant structural changes over 26 years of Israeli occupation, was made dependent on and inferior to the highly capitalized and technologically advanced Israeli economy. Continued human rights violations by Israeli authorities, control of water resources, the demolition of houses and other property and the destruction of olive trees and crops further exacerbated the living conditions of the Palestinian population.

ECONOMIC AND SOCIAL COUNCIL ACTION

On 29 July, the Economic and Social Council, on the recommendation of its Economic Committee, adopted **resolution 1993/52** by recorded vote.

Economic and social repercussions of the Israeli settlements on the Palestinian people in the Palestinian territory, including Jerusalem, occupied since 1967, and on the Arab population of the occupied Syrian Golan

The Economic and Social Council,

Taking note of General Assembly resolution 47/172 of 22 December 1992,

Recalling its resolution 1992/57 of 31 July 1992,

Guided by the principles of the Charter of the United Nations, affirming the inadmissibility of the acquisition of territory by force and recalling Security Council resolutions 242(1967) of 22 November 1967 and 497(1981) of 17 December 1981,

Recalling also Security Council resolution 465(1980) of 1 March 1980 and other resolutions affirming the applicability of the Geneva Convention relative to the Protection of Civilian Persons in Time of War, of 12 August 1949, to the occupied Palestinian territory, including Jerusalem, and other Arab territories occupied by Israel since 1967,

Expressing its concern at the establishment by Israel, the occupying Power, of settlements in the occupied Palestinian territory and other Arab territories occupied since 1967, including the settlements of new immigrants therein,

Welcoming the Middle East peace process started at Madrid on 30 October 1991 and recognizing that a complete freeze of settlement activity would significantly enhance the prospects for progress in that process,

1. *Takes note* of the report of the Secretary-General on the economic and social consequences of the establishment of settlements by Israel in the Palestinian territory, including Jerusalem, occupied since 1967, and the Syrian Golan;

2. *Deplores* the establishment of settlements by Israel in the Palestinian territory, including Jerusalem, and the other Arab territories occupied since 1967, and regards the settlements as illegal and an obstacle to peace;

3. *Recognizes* the economic and social repercussions of the Israeli settlements on the Palestinian people in the Palestinian territory, including Jerusalem, occupied by Israel since 1967, and on the Arab population of the occupied Syrian Golan;

4. *Strongly deplores* Israel's practices in the occupied Palestinian territory and other Arab territories occupied since 1967, in particular its confiscation of land, its ap-

propriation of water resources, its depletion of other economic resources and its displacement and deportation of the population of those territories;

5. *Reaffirms* the inalienable right of the Palestinian people and the population of the occupied Syrian Golan to their natural and all other economic resources, and regards any infringement thereof as being without any legal validity;

6. *Requests* the Secretary-General to submit to the General Assembly at its forty-ninth session, through the Economic and Social Council, a report on the progress made in the implementation of the present resolution.

Economic and Social Council resolution 1993/52

29 July 1993   Meeting 45   41-1-3 (roll-call vote)

Approved by Economic Committee (E/1993/114) by roll-call vote (40-1-3), 26 July (meeting 15); 18-nation draft (E/1993/C.1/L.4), orally revised following informal consultations; agenda item 16.

Sponsors: Algeria, Angola, Cuba, Democratic People's Republic of Korea, Egypt, Iraq, Madagascar, Malaysia, Morocco, Nigeria, Pakistan, Qatar, Saudi Arabia, Senegal, Sudan, Syrian Arab Republic, Tunisia, Yemen.

Roll-call vote in Council as follows:

In favour: Angola, Argentina, Australia, Bahamas, Bangladesh, Belarus, Belgium, Benin, Bhutan, Botswana, Brazil, Canada, Chile, China, Colombia, Cuba, Denmark, France, Germany, Guinea, India, Italy, Kuwait, Madagascar, Malaysia, Mexico, Morocco, Nigeria, Norway, Peru, Philippines, Republic of Korea, Romania, Sri Lanka, Suriname, Swaziland, Syrian Arab Republic, Trinidad and Tobago, Turkey, Ukraine, United Kingdom.

Against: United States.

Abstaining: Japan, Poland, Russian Federation.

In the view of the United States, the text was politically inflammatory and could compromise the peace process. The Economic and Social Council, which was not the appropriate body to settle political questions, should not compete with the negotiations that had been initiated.

GENERAL ASSEMBLY ACTION

On 21 December, the General Assembly, acting on the recommendation of the Second Committee, adopted **resolution 48/212** by recorded vote.

Economic and social repercussions of the Israeli settlements on the Palestinian people in the Palestinian territory, including Jerusalem, occupied since 1967, and on the Arab population of the Syrian Golan

The General Assembly,

Recalling its resolution 47/172 of 22 December 1992,

Taking note of Economic and Social Council resolution 1993/52 of 29 July 1993,

Reaffirming the principle of the permanent sovereignty of people under foreign occupation over their national resources,

Guided by the principles of the Charter of the United Nations, affirming the inadmissibility of the acquisition of territory by force, and recalling Security Council resolutions 242(1967) of 22 November 1967 and 497(1981) of 17 December 1981,

Recalling Security Council resolution 465(1980) of 1 March 1980 and other resolutions affirming the applicability of the Geneva Convention relative to the Protection of Civilian Persons in Time of War, of 12 August 1949, to the occupied Palestinian territory, including Jerusalem, and other Arab territories occupied by Israel since 1967,

Aware of the negative and grave economic and social repercussions of the Israeli settlements on the Palestinian people in the Palestinian territory occupied since 1967, including Jerusalem, and on the Arab population of the Syrian Golan,

Welcoming the ongoing Middle East peace process started at Madrid, and in particular the signing of the Declaration of Principles on Interim Self-Government Arrangements, including its Annexes and its Agreed Minutes, by the Government of the State of Israel and the Palestine Liberation Organization, in Washington, D.C., on 13 September 1993,

1. *Takes note* of the report of the Secretary-General on the economic and social consequences of the establishment of settlements by Israel in the Palestinian territory, including Jerusalem, occupied since 1967, and the Syrian Golan;

2. *Reaffirms* that Israeli settlements in the Palestinian territory, including Jerusalem, and other Arab territories occupied since 1967 are illegal and an obstacle to economic and social development;

3. *Recognizes* the economic and social repercussions of the Israeli settlements on the Palestinian people in the Palestinian territory occupied by Israel since 1967, including Jerusalem, and on the Arab population of the Syrian Golan;

4. *Reaffirms also* the inalienable right of the Palestinian people and the population of the Syrian Golan to their natural and all other economic resources, and regards any infringement thereof as being illegal;

5. *Requests* the Secretary-General to submit to the General Assembly at its forty-ninth session, through the Economic and Social Council, a report on the progress made in the implementation of the present resolution.

General Assembly resolution 48/212

21 December 1993   Meeting 86   143-3-13 (recorded vote)

Approved by Second Committee (A/48/715) by recorded vote (113-2-13), 10 December (meeting 47); 13-nation draft (A/C.2/48/L.17), orally revised following informal consultations; agenda item 12.

Sponsors: Algeria, Cuba, Democratic People's Republic of Korea, Djibouti, Egypt, Indonesia, Jordan, Malaysia, Mauritania, Morocco, Sudan, Tunisia, Yemen.

Meeting numbers. GA 48th session: 2nd Committee 12-14, 45, 47; plenary 86.

Recorded vote in Assembly as follows:

In favour: Afghanistan, Albania, Algeria, Angola, Antigua and Barbuda, Argentina, Armenia, Australia, Austria, Azerbaijan, Bahamas, Bahrain, Bangladesh, Barbados, Belgium, Belize, Bhutan, Bolivia, Brazil, Brunei Darussalam, Bulgaria, Burkina Faso, Burundi, Cameroon, Canada, Cape Verde, Chad, Chile, China, Colombia, Comoros, Congo, Costa Rica, Cuba, Cyprus, Czech Republic, Democratic People's Republic of Korea, Denmark, Djibouti, Ecuador, Egypt, El Salvador, Estonia, Ethiopia, Fiji, Finland, France, Gambia, Germany, Greece, Grenada, Guatemala, Guinea-Bissau, Guyana, Haiti, Honduras, Hungary, Iceland, India, Indonesia, Iran, Iraq, Ireland, Italy, Jamaica, Japan, Jordan, Kazakhstan, Kuwait, Kyrgyzstan, Lao People's Democratic Republic, Latvia, Lebanon, Lesotho, Libyan Arab Jamahiriya, Liechtenstein, Lithuania, Luxembourg, Madagascar, Malawi, Malaysia, Maldives, Mali, Malta, Mauritania, Mauritius, Mexico, Monaco, Mongolia, Morocco, Myanmar, Namibia, Nepal, Netherlands, New Zealand, Nicaragua, Niger, Norway, Oman, Pakistan, Panama, Paraguay, Peru, Philippines, Poland, Portugal, Qatar, Republic of Korea, Republic of Moldova, Romania, Rwanda, Saint Lucia, Saint Vincent and the Grenadines, Saudi Arabia, Senegal, Sierra Leone, Singapore, Slovakia, Slovenia, Spain, Sri Lanka, Sudan, Suriname, Swaziland, Sweden, Syrian Arab Republic, Tajikistan, the former Yugoslav Republic of Macedonia, Thailand, Togo, Trinidad and Tobago, Tunisia, Turkey, Uganda, Ukraine, United Arab Emirates, United Kingdom, United Republic of Tanzania, Venezuela, Viet Nam, Yemen, Zambia, Zimbabwe.

Against: Israel, Marshall Islands, United States.

Abstaining: Belarus, Botswana, Central African Republic, Croatia, Dominican Republic, Kenya, Micronesia, Nigeria, Papua New Guinea, Russian Federation, Samoa, Turkmenistan, Uruguay.

Speaking before the vote, Israel said the resolution ran counter to the modalities envisaged in the Declaration of Principles signed on 13 September between Israel and PLO and prejudged the outcome of the negotiations, which were the proper forum in which to resolve such issues as the settlements.

Living conditions of Palestinians

The Secretary-General informed the Economic and Social Council by a note of May 1993[46] that a progress report on the implementation of a 1991 General Assembly resolution[47] concerning the living conditions of Palestinians was being finalized for submission directly to the General Assembly. On 29 July, by **decision 1993/309**, the Economic and Social Council deferred the issue to its resumed substantive 1993 session, since the report was not yet available.

By a letter of 11 March,[48] Israel brought to the Secretary-General's attention steps it had taken to improve the welfare and standard of living of Palestinians in the territories. According to that communication, emphasis was recently placed on expanding employment opportunities and developing the local economy. This policy was pursued through legislation to encourage private initiative and local industry in order to promote investment and provide jobs, and through improvement of the general climate in the territories in order to create an attractive environment for investment. As a means of encouraging investment and employment, Israel had recently introduced income tax reform, encouraged capital and foreign investments and legislated labour rights for Palestinians working in Israel. Under those provisions, every Israeli employer was required to record officially employees from the territories to ensure that they received appropriate wages and social benefits. As a result, 70 per cent of those employed in Israel were legally registered, compared to 30 per cent in the past. All restrictions on the transfer of funds to the territories were rescinded. Israel also encouraged: the establishment of new banks and financial establishments; exports; new factories; conversion of agricultural land to increase profitability; and industrial parks. It rescinded or reformed legislation dealing with arrest, detention and legal procedures in security-related cases. Additionally, the automobile surtax was abolished, all universities were reopened, and the opening of new polytechnic colleges at Khan Younis and Gaza was approved. Elections were conducted for chambers of commerce in all municipalities except Bethlehem; the age below which persons required a permit to enter Israel was lowered from 60 to 50 years; houses sealed for security reasons over five years ago were reopened on a case-by-case basis; and the distribu-

tion of Arabic newspapers was expanded to include el-Ittihad, Sabah al-Hir, el Khateb and Kol el-Arab.

REFERENCES

[1]A/48/557. [2]A/48/35. [3]YUN 1987, p. 296. [4]A/48/183-E/1994/74/Add.1. [5]A/48/13. [6]E/1993/23-E/CN.4/1993/122 (res. 1993/4). [7]Ibid. (res. 1993/3). [8]Ibid. (res. 1993/2 A & B). [9]Ibid. (res. 1993/1). [10]A/47/888-S/25282, A/47/892-S/25309, A/47/909-S/25458, A/48/253-S/26045, A/48/263-S/26078. [11]A/47/893-S/25311, A/47/911-S/15464, A/47/959-S/25862. [12]SC res. 681(1990), 20 Dec. 1990. [13]S/25460. [14]S/25485. [15]S/26029. [16]YUN 1992, p. 425, GA res. 47/70 A, 14 Dec. 1990. [17]A/48/96. [18]A/48/278. [19]A/48/537. [20]DPI/1192. [21]A/48/538. [22]YUN 1992, p. 427, GA res. 47/70 B, 14 Dec. 1992. [23]Ibid., p. 429. [24]Ibid., p., 429, SC res. 799(1992), 18 Dec. 1992. [25]S/25149. [26]YUN 1948-49, p. 535, GA res. 217 A(III), 10 Dec. 1948. [27]A/47/874-S/25136. [28]A/47/858-S/25075. [29]A/47/882-S/25242. [30]A/47/890-S/25294. [31]S/25258. [32]S/26907. [33]A/48/541. [34]YUN 1992, p. 431, GA res. 47/70 E, 14 Dec. 1992. [35]A/48/540. [36]YUN 1992, p. 432, GA res. 47/70 D, 14 Dec. 1992. [37]A/48/543. [38]YUN 1992, p. 433, GA res. 47/70 G, 14 Dec. 1992. [39]A/48/542. [40]YUN 1992, p. 434, GA res. 47/70 F, 14 Dec. 1992. [41]A/48/539. [42]YUN 1992, p. 436, GA res. 47/70 C, 14 Dec. 1992. [43]A/48/188-E/1993/78. [44]YUN 1992, p. 439, GA res. 47/172, 22 Dec. 1992. [45]Ibid., p. 407. [46]E/1993/64. [47]YUN 1991, p. 265, GA res. 46/162, 19 Dec. 1992. [48]A/48/112.

Palestine refugees

The number of Palestine refugees registered with UNRWA as at 30 June 1993, was 2,797,179.[1] They lived in and outside camps in the Israeli-occupied West Bank (479,023) and Gaza Strip (603,380), Jordan (1,072,561), Lebanon (328,176) and the Syrian Arab Republic (314,039). By the end of 1993, UNRWA put the total number of refugees at over 2.9 million.

The various aspects of the Palestine refugee problem, as well as the activities of UNRWA, were addressed by the General Assembly through 10 resolutions, adopted in December, concerning: assistance to Palestine refugees (48/40 A) and to displaced persons (48/40 C); the Working Group on the Financing of UNRWA (48/40 B); scholarships for higher education and vocational training (44/40 D); refugees in Israeli-occupied territory (48/40 E); return of displaced population and refugees (48/40 F); revenues from refugees' properties (48/40 G); refugee protection (48/40 H); proposed University of Jerusalem "Al-Quds" for Palestine refugees (48/40 I); and protection of Palestinian students and educational institutions and safeguarding of UNRWA facilities (44/40 J). In addition, the Assembly adopted a decision on the participation of Palestine in the Advisory Commission of UNRWA (48/417).

UN Agency for Palestine refugees

The UNRWA Commissioner-General observed in the Agency's report covering the period 1 July 1992 to 30 June 1993[1] that the exchange of letters on recognition and the signing of the Declaration of Principles between PLO and Israel marked a turning point in the region. It was clear that the political developments would have an impact on UNRWA's operations and programmes. Because of the scale of its presence in the area, its largely Palestinian staff and its historical experience, UNRWA was predestined to be a major contributor to a combined effort to assist in the economic and social development of the West Bank and Gaza. At the same time, the need for continued assistance to Palestine refugees in Jordan, Lebanon and the Syrian Arab Republic should not be overlooked. He noted that, unfortunately, the negotiations had not been accompanied by an improvement in the political, security and economic environment affecting Palestinians. On the contrary, there had been a serious deterioration in the situation, culminating in the highest fatality figures recorded in Gaza since the beginning of the *intifadah* and an unprecedented worsening of economic and social conditions. A new dimension was introduced by the closure of the occupied territories on 31 March, with UNRWA responding to the resulting hardship by distributing food to nearly 80,000 persons. The closure, accompanied by stern security measures, including an intensified military presence in refugee camps, severely disrupted the Agency's efforts to render medical and educational services, particularly in Jerusalem.

Against this background of setbacks, UNRWA in 1993 provided a wide-ranging programme of education, health, relief and social services for Palestine refugees in its five areas of operation. The Agency also continued to undertake extraordinary measures of assistance for Lebanon and the occupied territories. Following the signing of the Declaration of Principles, UNRWA on 6 October launched a new initiative, the Peace Implementation Plan (PIP), to enhance services and infrastructure for Palestine refugees, as well as to create new job opportunities through expanded project investment. Under the plan, which was developed in close consultation with UNRWA's Advisory Commission, major donors and the Palestinian leadership, the Agency began to undertake special construction and development projects that addressed the needs of Palestine refugees in education, environmental health, primary health care, income generation and social services. Its projects responded to objectives identified by the Secretary-General's Task Force on Economic and Social Development of the Gaza Strip and Jericho and formed part of the United Nations' integrated approach in support of the transition period. As at 31 December, total pledges for PIP amounted to over $30 million.

The 2.8 million registered refugees had access to UNRWA schools and training centres and specialist clinics, as well as to basic food and clothing if they had no resources of their own. Agency-wide, more than 392,000 pupils were enrolled in 641 elementary and preparatory schools, and more than 5,000 in eight training centres. Refugees had guaranteed access to primary health care through the Agency's health centres and clinics. Social services, increasingly provided with the active participation of Palestine refugee communities, were available through 71 women's programme centres, reaching 12,800 women. Eighteen locally run community rehabilitation centres provided services for disabled persons and their families, including 1,500 disabled refugee children and adolescents, with technical assistance from UNRWA. Agency-wide, 6.5 per cent of the refugee population were registered as special hardship cases, qualifying them for basic food rations, childrens' clothing, shelter rehabilitation and preferential access to vocational training centres.

The education programme, UNRWA's largest activity, grew substantially during the reporting period as a result of adding a tenth year to the basic education cycle in Jordan in conformity with that Government's reform programme. A total of 392,757 elementary and preparatory pupils attended 641 schools, 18,350 more than in the previous year. Vocational training, comprising two-year post-preparatory trade courses and post-secondary technical courses, expanded as well, with the number of training places increasing to 4,496 from 4,296. The number of education staff benefiting from the in-service training programme increased to 1,075 from 857, while university scholarships for outstanding students rose to 746 from 661. The education programme followed the host Government's curricula, in close cooperation with UNESCO, which seconded 12 of its staff to UNRWA. To meet the changing educational needs of the Palestine refugee community and to provide more technical support to the five fields, the Agency reorganized its department of education by integrating all divisions into the UNRWA Institute of Education at Amman and by moving the office of the Director of Education from Vienna to the UNRWA Headquarters Branch at Amman effective 1 July. Another aspect of education reform in Jordan was the raising of minimum qualifications for certification of basic-education-cycle teachers to include possession of a four-year university degree. In line with UNRWA's decision to phase out its two-year teacher training programme in June, the number of teacher training places Agency-wide was reduced to 645 from 850. Following consultations with Jordan and Palestinians, UNRWA decided to replace the phased-out teacher training courses in Jordan and in the West Bank with educational science faculties offering a first-level university degree.

The 201 UNRWA schools in Jordan provided basic education to 152,350 pupils, an increase of 12,350 over the previous year. The schools operated normally, as did the Amman and Wadi Seer training centres. To accommodate the increased school population, UNRWA employed more than 450 additional teachers and constructed over 60 new classrooms. In addition, it built three new schools in the Baqa'a, Marka and Suf camps to replace dilapidated prefabricated buildings. Five other schools were under construction. More than 180 Palestine refugee students received UNRWA scholarships to Jordanian universities. The 76 schools in Lebanon, attended by 33,172 pupils, enjoyed an almost normal school year owing to the improved security situation in the country. The Siblin Training Centre provided training places for 644 students during the 1992/93 academic year. UNRWA awarded 42 university scholarships to refugee students in Lebanon. Enrolment in UNRWA's 111 schools in the Syrian Arab Republic increased by 1,427 students to 60,216, while 857 trainees were enrolled in 20 courses at the Damascus Training Centre, exceeding its 776 budgeted places. Agency premises in the country remained inadequate, insufficient and severely overcrowded, with 97.3 per cent of elementary classes operating on a double shift. Furthermore, 24.3 per cent of schools were accommodated in unsatisfactory rented premises lacking proper facilities, such as adequate light and space, laboratories, libraries and playgrounds. Some progress was nevertheless achieved, including the building of two new schools, two specialized rooms and 26 classrooms to avoid the need for triple shifts.

As a result of school closures due to military orders, curfews and general strikes, the Agency's 100 schools in the West Bank, which served a population of 42,310 pupils, lost 14.8 per cent of school days and were particularly hard hit by the closure of the territories in March. The three Agency training centres at Kalandia and Ramallah provided a total of 1,156 additional training places, 84 more than in the previous academic year. New courses in ceramic production, social work and marketing and financial management were introduced at the two Ramallah centres, while the institution at Kalandia received a special contribution of $2 million to upgrade its facilities and services. The Agency's 153 schools in

Gaza served a student population of 104,709, an increase of more than 4,650 pupils over the preceding school year, including some 800 new returnees from the Gulf States. However, 16.4 per cent of school days had been lost by the end of June due to military-ordered closures, curfews and general strikes. The Gaza Training Centre, which offered 728 training places in 13 two-year courses in mechanical, electrical and building trades and three two-year semi-professional courses in physiotherapy, industrial electronics and business and office practice was closed twice during the academic year by military order for periods exceeding one month in each case. In response to lost teaching time, UNRWA applied exceptional measures, such as extending the school day by one or two periods, extending the training year, distributing self-learning materials and offering special classes to pupils with learning problems.

UNRWA's primary health care included both preventive and curative medical care, environmental health services and supplementary nutritional assistance to pregnant and nursing women and children under the age of three. Medical care at the primary level was complemented by secondary services such as hospitalization and other referral and support services. More than 3,000 professional and support staff, the majority of whom were locally recruited Palestinians, provided those services through a network of 119 health centres or points and mother and child health clinics; 62 dental clinics; 65 laboratories; 39 specialist clinics for paediatrics, obstetrics and gynaecology, cardiology, ophthalmology, chest diseases and ear, nose and throat illnesses; and 204 special care clinics for the treatment of diabetes mellitus and hypertension. UNRWA's health clinics received nearly 6.1 million patient visits during the reporting period. The Agency introduced or expanded a number of services during the year. Of particular significance was the integration of family planning services, comprising health education, counselling and provision of contraceptive techniques, within the maternal and child health care programme. New efforts were made to control non-communicable diseases such as diabetes mellitus, hypertension, hereditary anaemia and management of iron-deficiency anaemia. UNRWA further developed its mental health programmes in the West Bank and Gaza, with special emphasis on post-traumatic stress disorders among children. In Jordan, the increase in demand for health services created by the influx of more than 300,000 Palestinians from the Gulf States continued to be felt, thus medical, dental and other consultations increased by 10 per cent over 1991 to exceed 1.5 million. To prepare for the introduction of family planning services in all health centres in 1993, UNRWA, in coordination with UNICEF, conducted nine workshops to train

130 medical and nursing staff in planned parenthood education and family planning. In cooperation with the Jordan University of Science and Technology, the Agency held a workshop for its staff from all fields (Irbid, Jordan, January). UNRWA continued with its project to construct, equip and commission a 232-bed hospital in Gaza at a cost of $35 million, $20 million of which represented capital cost and $15 million operating cost for the first three years.

The demand for relief and social services grew beyond the Agency's financial capacity. The drastic curtailment in Palestinian economic activity in the occupied territory and continued restrictions on obtaining work permits in Lebanon further reduced self-reliance. Deteriorating socio-economic conditions, especially in the Gaza Strip, led to increased insistence by refugees that UNRWA provide sustained direct relief for larger numbers. By 30 June, the number of refugees qualifying for special hardship assistance rose to 180,647 from 178,323 one year earlier. The difficulties were exacerbated through the increase of registered refugees to 2.8 million from 2.65 million one year earlier, partly as a result of refugees' requesting the updating of their files. Palestinians remaining in Kuwait were particularly concerned with ensuring that their records were correct. During the year, 1,102 of those families requested and received certification of their status as registered refugees. A major effort was directed at building up the community's capacity to provide social services of its own, with technical support and additional funding from UNRWA. By the end of the reporting period, 5 of the 71 women's programme centres were managed by committees of Palestine refugee women themselves. Locally run community rehabilitation projects for disabled refugees increased to 18 from 14, with growing attention to home-based intervention and vocational rehabilitation. The number of active self-support projects for the poorest refugees, assisted by grants or, increasingly, loans, rose to 672, of which 593 were ongoing.

For the sixth successive year, UNRWA ran a programme of extraordinary measures for refugees in Lebanon and the occupied territory (EMLOT) to alleviate the difficulties experienced as a result of the *intifadah* and the Israeli response to it. The programme provided assistance to refugees in Lebanon, where the socio-economic conditions remained precarious despite the improved security situation. The measures included a refugee affairs officer programme, a legal assistance scheme, emergency food distribution, cash grants to families in distress and a variety of emergency health services, including increased hospitalization subsidies. During the five-year period ending December 1992, expenditures on EMLOT totalled more

than $139 million. For 1993, $2.6 million in cash and in kind was budgeted for Lebanon, $8.8 million for the West Bank and $14 million for Gaza. To meet the demands for emergency food distribution during the review period, food commodities amounting to 14,270 tonnes in Gaza and 7,237 tonnes in the West Bank were budgeted at a cost of $7.7 million. However, curfews and closures and the resulting lack of income meant that the demand for emergency food aid greatly exceeded those amounts. In May, the Agency began distributing available stocks and issued an urgent appeal for special donations of flour, rice and sugar for 120,000 families in Gaza and 39,000 families in the West Bank. UNRWA provided $1,044,000 in cash plus tents and blankets worth $46,000 for emergency assistance to needy refugee families whose breadwinners were detained, deported, killed or injured, or whose shelters had been damaged or demolished by military orders. In response to the severe damage to 58 homes, 26 of which were rendered uninhabitable, caused by military operations between February and April, the Agency expended $10,000 for immediate in-kind emergency assistance. An additional $60,250 in emergency cash assistance was disbursed to the affected families. Among other extraordinary measures, UNRWA maintained, in cooperation with UNICEF, six physiotherapy clinics in the West Bank and six in Gaza. It also provided $895,000 from emergency funds to infants considered to be nutritionally at risk as well as to school-age children and pregnant and nursing mothers.

In Lebanon, flour, rice, sugar, oil, skim milk and other commodities were distributed to 15,700 families, totalling 81,000 persons, and financial assistance amounting to $461,000 was provided to assist refugees with repair or reconstruction of their shelters. The Agency subsidized hospital expenses for registered as well as needy non-registered refugees in the amount of $104,000. In the initial period following the deportation of 415 Palestinians from the occupied territory to southern Lebanon, a group that included 16 UNRWA staff members, the Agency provided medical care and relief assistance, including water, food, tents, blankets, heating oil, medical supplies and other essential items.

Under the expanded programme of assistance (EPA), set up in 1988 with a target of $65 million, some $54 million had been received or pledged by mid-1993. The objectives of the programme were to improve living conditions in camps and upgrade the infrastructure through which Agency services were delivered. EPA also included specific objectives such as promoting sustainable employment, upgrading Agency installations, rehabilitating infrastructure and improving sanitation in the camps. In October, with the introduction of the

Peace Implementation Plan, it was decided to phase out EPA. Projects under implementation would be completed, but no additional funding would be sought.

Under a revolving loan fund set up in 1991 to assist the local Palestinian economy in the aftermath of the Persian Gulf war, 105 loans amounting to over $2 million had been disbursed in Gaza by the end of June. In the West Bank, 37 projects had received loans amounting to $1.3 million, including some $250,000 which had been repaid by borrowers and disbursed as new loans. The Agency disbursed 28 loans totalling $180,000 in Jordan and 13 loans totalling $82,000 in Lebanon. By the end of the reporting period, donors had contributed or pledged $4.2 million specifically for revolving loan funds.

Approximately $10.7 million was allocated to address environmental conditions in refugee camps through sewerage schemes, water supply projects and improved refuse disposal systems. Some $3.6 million was budgeted for housing improvement in camps in the occupied territory and Jordan. As at 30 June, 45 projects with a value of $27.7 million were under negotiation with potential donors, and 142 projects amounting to $46.1 million were being implemented. The Agency employed approximately 20,800 staff, the majority of whom were themselves Palestine refugees, and was thus one of the largest employers in the Middle East.

Introducing the report to the Fourth Committee, the UNRWA Commissioner-General pointed out that the establishment of a Palestinian authority would put the Agency in a radically different position, for it would continue its activities to the extent requested by that authority, in close coordination and consultation with it. PLO had indicated its desire to see UNRWA continue its programmes of assistance to Palestinian refugees and had asked the Agency to expand them to promote social and economic development. Notwithstanding the above, UNRWA was coming to the end of a task entrusted to it 40 years earlier, and its main concern was to complete that task as successfully as possible.

GENERAL ASSEMBLY ACTION

On 10 December 1993, on the recommendation of the Fourth Committee, the General Assembly adopted **resolution 48/40 A** by recorded vote. Passed in the wake of the signing by Israel and PLO of the Declaration of Principles, its text was amended from that of recent years. In broadening UNRWA's role, it called on the Agency to make a decisive contribution towards giving a fresh impetus to the economic and social stability of the occupied territories.

Assistance to Palestine refugees

The General Assembly,

Recalling its resolution 47/69 A of 14 December 1992 and all its previous resolutions on the question, including resolution 194(III) of 11 December 1948,

Taking note of the report of the Commissioner-General of the United Nations Relief and Works Agency for Palestine Refugees in the Near East covering the period from 1 July 1992 to 30 June 1993, and, in particular, of the hope expressed by the Commissioner-General "that this report covers an era which is gone forever",

Welcoming the signature by the Government of the State of Israel and the Palestine Liberation Organization of the Declaration of Principles on Interim Self-Government Arrangements, including its Annexes and its Agreed Minutes, at Washington, D.C., on 13 September 1993,

1. *Notes with regret* that repatriation or compensation of the refugees, as provided for in paragraph 11 of General Assembly resolution 194(III), has not yet been effected and that, therefore, the situation of the refugees continues to be a matter of concern;

2. *Expresses its thanks* to the Commissioner-General and to all the staff of the United Nations Relief and Works Agency for Palestine Refugees in the Near East, recognizing that the Agency is doing all it can within the limits of available resources, and also expresses its thanks to the specialized agencies and to private organizations for their valuable work in assisting the refugees;

3. *Requests* that the headquarters of the Agency be transferred as soon as practicable to its area of operations;

4. *Notes with regret* that the United Nations Conciliation Commission for Palestine has been unable to find a means of achieving progress in the implementation of paragraph 11 of General Assembly resolution 194(III), and requests the Commission to exert continued efforts towards the implementation of that paragraph and to report to the Assembly as appropriate, but no later than 1 September 1994;

5. *Notes* that the new context created by the Declaration of Principles on Interim Self-Government, including its Annexes and its Agreed Minutes, signed by the Government of the State of Israel and the Palestine Liberation Organization, will have major consequences for the activities of the Agency, which is henceforth called upon, within the framework of strengthened cooperation with the specialized agencies and the World Bank, to make a decisive contribution towards giving a fresh impetus to the economic and social stability of the occupied territories, and notes also that the functioning of the Agency remains essential throughout its area of operations;

6. *Welcomes* the results of the Conference to Support Middle East Peace, held in Washington, D.C., on 1 October 1993, concerning urgent financial and economic assistance in support of the Israeli-Palestinian accord, and urges all Member States to extend aid and assistance with a view to the economic development of the occupied territories;

7. *Directs attention* to the continuing seriousness of the financial position of the Agency, as outlined in the report of the Commissioner-General;

8. *Notes with profound concern* that, despite the commendable and successful efforts of the Commissioner-

General to collect additional contributions, the increased level of income to the Agency is still insufficient to cover essential budget requirements in the current year and that, at the currently foreseen levels of contributions, deficits will recur each year;

9. *Calls upon* all Governments, as a matter of urgency, to make the most generous efforts possible to meet the anticipated needs of the Agency, and therefore urges non-contributing Governments to contribute regularly and contributing Governments to consider increasing their regular contributions.

General Assembly resolution 48/40 A

10 December 1993   Meeting 75   159-0-2 (recorded vote)

Approved by Fourth Committee (A/48/646) by recorded vote (137-0-2), 8 December (meeting 27); 12-nation draft (A/C.4/48/L.20); agenda item 85.
Sponsors: Belgium, Denmark, France, Germany, Greece, Ireland, Italy, Luxembourg, Netherlands, Portugal, Spain, United Kingdom.
Meeting numbers. GA 48th session: 4th Committee 18, 19, 23-27; plenary 75.

Recorded vote in Assembly as follows:

In favour: Afghanistan, Algeria, Angola, Antigua and Barbuda, Argentina, Armenia, Australia, Austria, Azerbaijan, Bahamas, Bahrain, Bangladesh, Barbados, Belarus, Belgium, Belize, Benin, Bhutan, Bolivia, Bosnia and Herzegovina, Botswana, Brazil, Brunei Darussalam, Bulgaria, Burkina Faso, Cambodia, Cameroon, Canada, Cape Verde, Central African Republic, Chad, Chile, China, Colombia, Comoros, Congo, Costa Rica, Côte d'Ivoire, Cuba, Cyprus, Czech Republic, Democratic People's Republic of Korea, Denmark, Djibouti, Dominica, Dominican Republic, Ecuador, Egypt, El Salvador, Estonia, Ethiopia, Fiji, Finland, France, Gabon, Gambia, Georgia, Germany, Greece, Grenada, Guatemala, Guinea, Guinea-Bissau, Guyana, Haiti, Honduras, Hungary, Iceland, India, Indonesia, Iran, Ireland, Italy, Jamaica, Japan, Jordan, Kazakhstan, Kenya, Kuwait, Lao People's Democratic Republic, Latvia, Lebanon, Lesotho, Libyan Arab Jamahiriya, Liechtenstein, Lithuania, Luxembourg, Madagascar, Malawi, Malaysia, Maldives, Mali, Malta, Marshall Islands, Mauritania, Mauritius, Mexico, Micronesia, Mongolia, Morocco, Mozambique, Myanmar, Namibia, Nepal, Netherlands, New Zealand, Nicaragua, Niger, Nigeria, Norway, Oman, Pakistan, Panama, Papua New Guinea, Paraguay, Peru, Philippines, Poland, Portugal, Qatar, Republic of Korea, Republic of Moldova, Romania, Russian Federation, Rwanda, Saint Lucia, Saint Vincent and the Grenadines, San Marino, Saudi Arabia, Senegal, Sierra Leone, Singapore, Slovakia, Slovenia, Spain, Sri Lanka, Sudan, Suriname, Swaziland, Sweden, Syrian Arab Republic, the former Yugoslav Republic of Macedonia, Thailand, Togo, Trinidad and Tobago, Tunisia, Turkey, Turkmenistan, Uganda, Ukraine, United Arab Emirates, United Kingdom, United Republic of Tanzania, Uruguay, Venezuela, Viet Nam, Yemen, Zaire, Zimbabwe.
Against: None.
Abstaining: Israel, United States.

On the proposal of the Chairman of the Fourth Committee, the Assembly, also on 10 December, agreed to the understanding that the Advisory Commission of UNRWA would establish a working relationship with PLO (**decision 48/417**).

UNRWA financing

The UNRWA Commissioner-General, in his report to the General Assembly,[1] stated that the financial outlook for 1993 was critical, with a deficit of $28.5 million projected at the beginning of the year: $17 million in the regular budget and $11.5 million in the EMLOT budget. Despite concerted efforts to expand the donor base, particularly among countries in the region, and secure additional contributions from the Agency's traditional major donors, only $6.5 million was provided to UNRWA by the end of June. Merely to maintain a constant level of services, the Agency's budget had to increase by 5 per cent per annum to accommodate population growth and

rising costs. However, more than at any other time in recent years, UNRWA's financial needs competed with shrinking donor aid budgets and the large increase in emergencies worldwide. Exchange rate losses incurred as a result of the fluctuating currency markets further exacerbated the Agency's financial situation. In anticipation of the shortfall, the Agency was forced to implement austerity measures, which had an immediate impact on the quality of its services.

The General Fund budget approved for 1992-1993 amounted to $572 million, of which $297.2 million represented the 1993 portion. With the additional sums earmarked for EMLOT, EPA and the Gaza Hospital project, the grand total for the biennium amounted to $644.7 million.

In 1992-1993, a total of $473.4 million (including $34.4 million in late arrivals) was received under the UNRWA General Fund ($443.5 million in cash and $30 million in kind). An additional $52.5 million (including $3.9 million in late arrivals) was received for funded ongoing activities ($18.7 million in cash and $33.8 million in kind). Expenditures for the biennium totalled $476.5 million under the General Fund and $50.7 million for funded ongoing activities. For the 1994-1995 biennium, expenditures under the General Fund were estimated at $632.3 million (including $79.4 million in food donations), representing an increase of $60.3 million, or about 10 per cent, over the approved General Fund budget for 1992-1993.

The regular budget was not completely funded for 1993, and substantial amounts were still required for EMLOT, EPA and the Gaza Hospital project. Only limited success was achieved in broadening the Agency's donor base. None the less, donor and host government support remained strong, as Agency services alone were not sufficient to maintain even basic life-sustaining needs.

Working Group on UNRWA financing

The Chairman of the Working Group on the Financing of UNRWA, by a letter dated 7 April 1993,[2] expressed concern at the Agency's critical financial situation, as the budget constraints faced by it could not have come at a worse time. With efforts under way to invigorate the Middle East peace process, a reduction in services by the Agency charged with providing for the basic human needs of Palestine refugees would send the wrong signal. The peace process should at all stages be accompanied by socio-economic measures to increase confidence in the negotiations. The UNRWA Commissioner-General had issued three appeals to major donors, most recently in February, and followed up with visits to the capitals of Bahrain, Qatar, Saudi Arabia and the United Arab Emirates to increase their hitherto limited contributions. A special meeting of the

UNRWA Advisory Commission was held at Vienna in March, followed by a briefing to major donors. The Chairman added the voice of the Working Group to those appealing for increased financial support to the Agency's vital humanitarian programme.

The Working Group held two meetings in 1993, on 9 September and 22 October.[3] In its report to the General Assembly, the Working Group noted that UNRWA ended the first year of the 1992-1993 biennium with a deficit of $10.2 million. This included a shortfall of $2.6 million in its General Fund, which reduced its working capital by the same amount, from $33.7 million to $31.1 million. The working capital was sufficient only to cover expenditures for the Agency's regular operations for about five or six weeks. In addition to that working capital, $6.5 million remained set aside for emergencies and other contingencies. The total 1992 deficit also reflected an accumulated deficit of $6.4 million, which was related to major funded ongoing activities that were a core part of the Agency's regular programmes.

The EMLOT fund also showed a negative balance—$1.2 million—at the end of 1992, which remained a matter of serious concern. In addition to the shortfalls in the Agency's regular and emergency programmes, the Agency's Fund for capital and special projects, which was budgeted at $12.8 million for 1992, was only partially funded by special contributions. Consequently, the implementation of a number of construction projects had to be deferred to 1993 or even later.

UNRWA's financial prospects for 1993 were unfavourable due to the fact that growth in the level of contributions was not keeping pace with the combined factors of growth in the number of beneficiaries of its programmes and their rising costs. At the beginning of the year, the Commissioner-General informed donor Governments of the projected cash shortfall for 1993 of $28.5 million. To avoid further serious deterioration of the financial situation, he decided to introduce a number of austerity measures amounting to some $13.5 million, aimed at reducing planned expenditures, particularly in travel and recruitment. Those measures, while reducing expenditures in the immediate term, would be difficult to sustain beyond 1993. The Working Group felt that the negative cumulative impact such measures had on the level and quality of the services could adversely affect the region's overall situation at a critical time. In view of the above, the Commissioner-General appealed in February to Governments and intergovernmental organizations for increased funding to compensate for the anticipated cash budget deficit. Another appeal for additional food donations for emergency distribution was issued after Israel's closure in March of

the occupied territories, but responses fell far short of the Agency's requirements.

The report also noted that in response to recent political developments and in order to support the peace process, UNRWA had introduced PIP to cover an improvement in, and expansion of, ongoing programmes and services, as well as short-term projects related to the infrastructure of basic and social services. Although the initial focus of the latest development towards peace was on the West Bank and Gaza, it was important that the needs of the 1.7 million refugees in Jordan, Lebanon and the Syrian Arab Republic not be overlooked. Therefore, UNRWA had to maintain and improve the services that it provided in all five fields of operation.

Sharing the Commissioner-General's concern about the funding prospects for 1994, the Working Group strongly urged Governments to continue making generous contributions and consider making additional contributions in support of both emergency-related programmes and special projects, as well as to expanded programmes planned by the Agency in response to the peace process and special contributions for construction projects.

GENERAL ASSEMBLY ACTION

On 10 December 1993, on the recommendation of the Fourth Committee, the General Assembly adopted **resolution 48/40 B** without vote.

Working Group on the Financing of the United Nations Relief and Works Agency for Palestine Refugees in the Near East

The General Assembly,

Recalling its resolutions 2656(XXV) of 7 December 1970, 2728(XXV) of 15 December 1970, 2791(XXVI) of 6 December 1971, 47/69 B of 14 December 1992 and the previous resolutions on this question,

Recalling also its decision 36/462 of 16 March 1982, by which it took note of the special report of the Working Group on the Financing of the United Nations Relief and Works Agency for Palestine Refugees in the Near East,

Having considered the report of the Working Group,

Taking into account the report of the Commissioner-General of the United Nations Relief and Works Agency for Palestine Refugees in the Near East, covering the period from 1 July 1992 to 30 June 1993,

Deeply concerned about the critical financial situation of the Agency, which has affected and affects the continuation of the provision of the necessary Agency services to the Palestine refugees, including the emergency-related programmes,

Emphasizing the continuing need for extraordinary efforts in order to maintain, at least at the present minimum level, the activities of the Agency, as well as to enable the Agency to carry out essential construction,

1. *Commends* the Working Group on the Financing of the United Nations Relief and Works Agency for

Palestine Refugees in the Near East for its efforts to assist in ensuring the financial security of the Agency;

2. *Takes note with approval* of the report of the Working Group;

3. *Requests* the Working Group to continue its efforts, in cooperation with the Secretary-General and the Commissioner-General, for the financing of the Agency for a further period of one year;

4. *Requests* the Secretary-General to provide the necessary services and assistance to the Working Group for the conduct of its work.

General Assembly resolution 48/40 B

10 December 1993   Meeting 75   Adopted without vote

Approved by Fourth Committee (A/48/646) without vote, 8 December (meeting 27); 25-nation draft (A/C.4/48/L.21); agenda item 85.

Sponsors: Australia, Austria, Bangladesh, Belgium, Canada, Denmark, France, Germany, Greece, Indonesia, Ireland, Italy, Japan, Luxembourg, Malaysia, Netherlands, New Zealand, Pakistan, Philippines, Portugal, Spain, Sweden, Turkey, United Kingdom, United States.

Meeting numbers. GA 48th session: 4th Committee 18, 19, 23-27; plenary 75.

Legal matters

UNRWA staff

The Commissioner-General reported that for the period from 1 July 1992 to 30 June 1993,[1] there was a substantial increase over the preceding year in the number of staff members arrested in the occupied territory and held in detention without trial. The number of staff arrested and detained in Jordan and Lebanon decreased, while three new cases were reported in the Syrian Arab Republic. The total number of staff detained during the reporting period was 71, of whom 40 were arrested and released without charge or trial, 3 were charged, tried and sentenced, and 28 remained in detention. Of the 415 Palestinians who were deported into southern Lebanon in December 1992,[5] 16 were UNRWA staff members. None of them were among those who returned with Israeli permission in the subsequent months; the Agency's protests against those deportations were to no avail.

Two UNRWA staff members were killed by Israeli security forces in Gaza. In February, a 28-year-old nurse was shot in the back of the head while rendering assistance to a wounded youth in Rafah. In March, a 47-year-old teacher was shot and killed outside a wake house, also in Rafah. One locally recruited staff member was killed by Palestinians in Gaza for alleged collaboration with the Israeli authorities.

In spite of the Agency's frequent approaches to the relevant authorities, it was not provided with adequate and timely information on the reasons for the arrest and detention of its staff members. It could thus not determine whether their arrest and detention arose out of their official duties. However, it had access to 18 staff members from Gaza and 11 from the West Bank who were in prisons and detention centres in the occupied terri-

tory and in Israel. The treatment of staff members in detention remained of major concern, with staff members upon their release complaining of ill treatment, including beatings and psychological abuse. Despite efforts on the part of the Agency, it was unable to visit staff in detention elsewhere. In the performance of their duties, both international and locally recruited staff continued to be subjected to various forms of mistreatment by Israeli security forces, including beatings, threats, insults, intimidation and temporary detention. Thirty-nine such cases of mistreatment were recorded in Gaza and 64 in the West Bank.

Difficulties related to the movement of locally recruited staff in and out of the West Bank increased substantially. There were lengthy delays in clearance by the Israeli authorities of staff members for travel on official duty. These included difficulties in obtaining entry for locally recruited drivers to Ben Gurion international airport in Israel, despite assurances from the authorities that such entry would be facilitated. The freedom of movement of staff members was further impeded by frequent curfews and the continued insistence of Israeli authorities that locally recruited staff members be in possession of curfew permits. The Agency's efforts to obtain curfew permits for such staff in Gaza were subjected to lengthy bureaucratic delays, and the number made available consistently fell short of that requested by the Agency. The arbitrary designation of closed military areas also impeded the legitimate movement of staff members, including international staff.

UNRWA services and premises

The Commissioner-General reported[1] that between 1 July 1992 and 30 June 1993 Israeli security forces made 77 incursions into UNRWA installations in the West Bank and 186 in Gaza, at times resulting in injury to staff and damage to property. There were 78 recorded intrusions into health clinic premises, and Israeli security forces on occasion also used Agency premises during military operations. Particularly in Gaza, UNRWA schools were at times used as temporary interrogation centres. The Agency protested such actions as a violation of its privileges and immunities.

Interference by the security forces with UNRWA ambulance and medical services became more frequent. In Gaza, 61 incidents were recorded in which ambulances were stopped, searched and on occasion shot at, and ambulance drivers and accompanying medical personnel were at times beaten and had their identity documents confiscated. There were 11 such incidents in the West Bank. Israeli authorities continued to object to the Agency's reconstruction of demolished camp shelters, despite assurances by Israel's Ministry of Foreign Affairs that there would be no objection to it. Construction projects were also subjected to detailed and time-consuming procedures. At least 105 homes in the West Bank and 38 in Gaza were demolished by Israeli authorities on the grounds that proper building permits had not been obtained by the owners. Restrictions were imposed on the quantity of items imported for the Agency's essential operations, and incoming goods were often subjected to delays at the port of entry.

As from 1 January 1992, Israel resumed payment of current charges for clearance, warehousing and transport of UNRWA supplies, for which it was responsible under the 1967 Comay-Michelmore Agreement and which it had suspended from 1988 to 1991. Israel also agreed to reimburse the Agency 4.2 million, which it had advanced to cover payments during the suspension, in three equal instalments, the first of which was paid in April 1993.

In **resolution 48/40 J** (see below), the General Assembly condemned the repeated Israeli raids on UNRWA premises and installations and called on Israel to refrain from such acts.

Compensation claims

In 1993, UNRWA reported[1] that no progress had been made with regard to its claims against the Governments of: Israel (for loss and damage to UNRWA property during the 1967 Middle East hostilities, Israel's invasion of Lebanon in 1982 and its military action before then); Jordan (arising from the 1967 hostilities and the disturbances of 1970 and 1971); and the Syrian Arab Republic (relating mainly to the levy of certain taxes from which UNRWA believed it was exempt under existing agreements). Those claims had been reported in 1986.[6] The Secretary-General, in September 1993,[7] also stated that there had been no progress with regard to UNRWA claims against Israel resulting from its 1982 invasion of Lebanon.

In **resolution 48/40 H** (see below), the General Assembly called on Israel to compensate UNRWA for damages to its property and facilities resulting from its invasion of Lebanon, without prejudice to Israel's responsibility for all damages resulting from that invasion.

Other aspects

Displaced persons

During the reporting period, the future of displaced Palestinians and the need to provide housing for them became an even larger concern to UNRWA. Among the displaced in Lebanon were some 6,000 Palestinian families, or about 30,000 persons, who were identified by UNRWA as requiring assistance. The return of property to the lawful owners involved evicting displaced Palestinians squatting on those sites. By June, more than 1,000 Palestinian families had been served with official

eviction notices. The situation of 315 displaced families living along the coastal road between Beirut and Saida was the focus of discussions between representatives of Lebanon, UNRWA and the Palestinians. Many displaced families continued to live in intolerable conditions, having taken refuge years earlier in shacks which lacked decent sanitary facilities and access to safe water supply. The Agency reprogrammed funds for the reconstruction of damaged shelters, but those amounts fell far short of what was required for rehousing.

Humanitarian assistance

In 1993, in addition to providing relief in the form of basic food commodities, blankets, clothing, shelter repair and cash grants, UNRWA continued to provide a small measure of humanitarian assistance to persons who had been displaced as a result of the June 1967 war and subsequent hostilities in the Middle East but who were not registered with UNRWA as refugees.

GENERAL ASSEMBLY ACTION

On 10 December 1993, the General Assembly, on the recommendation of the Fourth Committee, adopted **resolution 48/40 C** without vote.

Assistance to persons displaced as a result of the June 1967 and subsequent hostilities
The General Assembly,
Recalling its resolution 47/69 C of 14 December 1992 and all its previous resolutions on the question,
Taking note of the report of the Commissioner-General of the United Nations Relief and Works Agency for Palestine Refugees in the Near East, covering the period from 1 July 1992 to 30 June 1993,
Concerned about the continued human suffering resulting from the hostilities in the Middle East,
1. *Reaffirms* its resolution 47/69 C and all its previous resolutions on the question;
2. *Endorses,* bearing in mind the objectives of those resolutions, the efforts of the Commissioner-General of the United Nations Relief and Works Agency for Palestine Refugees in the Near East to continue to provide humanitarian assistance as far as practicable, on an emergency basis and as a temporary measure, to other persons in the area who are currently displaced and in serious need of continued assistance as a result of the June 1967 and subsequent hostilities;
3. *Strongly appeals* to all Governments and to organizations and individuals to contribute generously for the above purposes to the United Nations Relief and Works Agency for Palestine Refugees in the Near East and to the other intergovernmental and non-governmental organizations concerned.

General Assembly resolution 48/40 C

10 December 1993   Meeting 75   Adopted without vote

Approved by Fourth Committee (A/48/646) without vote, 8 December (meeting 27); 25-nation draft (A/C.4/48/L.22); agenda item 85.
Sponsors: Austria, Bangladesh, Belgium, Canada, Comoros, Cyprus, Denmark, Finland, France, Germany, Greece, India, Indonesia, Ireland, Italy,

Japan, Luxembourg, Malaysia, Netherlands, Norway, Pakistan, Philippines, Sri Lanka, Sweden, United Kingdom.
Meeting numbers. GA 48th session: 4th Committee 18, 19, 23-27; plenary 75.

Repatriation of refugees

The Secretary-General reported in September 1993[8] on compliance with the General Assembly's 1992 call on Israel to take immediate steps for the return of all displaced inhabitants and to desist from measures obstructing their return.[9] By a note of 15 June, Israel had stated that its position on the matter had been detailed fully in successive annual replies, the latest of which was included in a 1992 report by the Secretary-General.[10] Because of Israel's continued effort to review individual cases of resettlement based on the merits of each case, 94,439 persons had returned to the administered territories.

The Secretary-General also included information from UNRWA on the return of refugees registered with it. Since the Agency was not involved in arrangements for either refugees or displaced persons not registered as refugees, its information was based on requests by returning registered refugees for the transfer of their service entitlements to their areas of return; UNRWA was not necessarily aware of the return of registered refugees who had not made such requests. Its records indicated that, between 1 July 1992 and 30 June 1993, 275 registered refugees had returned to the West Bank and 65 to the Gaza Strip. Some of them might not have been displaced in 1967 but might be family members of a displaced registered refugee whom they had accompanied on return or later joined. Displaced refugees known by UNRWA to have returned to the occupied territories since June 1967 numbered about 12,740. The Agency was unable to estimate the total number of displaced inhabitants who had returned, as it kept records only of registered refugees, and even those records, particularly with respect to the location of registered refugees, might be incomplete.

GENERAL ASSEMBLY ACTION

On 10 December 1993, on the recommendation of the Fourth Committee, the General Assembly adopted **resolution 48/40 F** by recorded vote.

Return of population and refugees displaced since 1967

The General Assembly,

Recalling Security Council resolution 237(1967) of 14 June 1967,

Recalling also its resolutions 2252(ES-V) of 4 July 1967, 2452 A (XXIII) of 19 December 1968, 2535 B (XXIV) of 10 December 1969, 2672 D (XXV) of 8 December 1970, 2792 E (XXVI) of 6 December 1971, 2963 C and D (XXVII) of 13 December 1972, 3089 C (XXVIII) of 7 December 1973, 3331 D (XXIX) of 17 December 1974, 3419 C (XXX) of 8 December 1975, 31/15 D of 23 November 1976, 32/90 E of 13 December 1977, 33/112 F of 18 December 1978, 34/52 E of 23 November 1979, ES-7/2 of 29 July 1980, 35/13 E of 3 November 1980, 36/146 B

of 16 December 1981, 37/120 G of 16 December 1982, 38/83 G of 15 December 1983, 39/99 G of 14 December 1984, 40/165 G of 16 December 1985, 41/69 G of 3 December 1986, 42/69 G of 2 December 1987, 43/57 G of 6 December 1988, 44/47 G of 8 December 1989, 45/73 G of 11 December 1990, 46/46 G of 9 December 1991 and 47/69 G of 14 December 1992,

Having considered the report of the Secretary-General,

Having also considered the report of the Commissioner-General of the United Nations Relief and Works Agency for Palestine Refugees in the Near East, covering the period from 1 July 1992 to 30 June 1993,

Taking note of the relevant provisions of the Declaration of Principles on Interim Self-Government Arrangements, including its Annexes and its Agreed Minutes, signed in Washington, D.C., on 13 September 1993 by the Government of the State of Israel and the Palestine Liberation Organization,

1. *Reaffirms* the inalienable right of all displaced inhabitants to return to their homes or former places of residence in the territories occupied by Israel since 1967;

2. *Calls upon* Israel to accelerate the necessary steps for the unimpeded return of all displaced inhabitants;

3. *Requests* the Secretary-General, after consulting with the Commissioner-General of the United Nations Relief and Works Agency for Palestine Refugees in the Near East, to report to the General Assembly, before the opening of its forty-ninth session, on the compliance of Israel with paragraph 2 above.

General Assembly resolution 48/40 F

10 December 1993   Meeting 75   152-2-5 (recorded vote)

Approved by Fourth Committee (A/48/646) by recorded vote (127-2-6), 8 December (meeting 27); 10-nation draft (A/C.4/48/L.26/Rev.1); agenda item 85.
Sponsors: Afghanistan, Bangladesh, Brunei Darussalam, Comoros, Cuba, Indonesia, Madagascar, Malaysia, Mali, Pakistan.
Meeting numbers. GA 48th session: 4th Committee 18, 19, 23-27; plenary 75.

Recorded vote in Assembly as follows:

In favour: Afghanistan, Algeria, Angola, Antigua and Barbuda, Argentina, Armenia, Australia, Austria, Azerbaijan, Bahamas, Bahrain, Bangladesh, Barbados, Belarus, Belgium, Belize, Benin, Bhutan, Bolivia, Bosnia and Herzegovina, Botswana, Brazil, Brunei Darussalam, Bulgaria, Burkina Faso, Cameroon, Canada, Cape Verde, Chad, Chile, China, Colombia, Comoros, Congo, Costa Rica, Côte d'Ivoire, Cuba, Cyprus, Czech Republic, Democratic People's Republic of Korea, Denmark, Djibouti, Dominican Republic, Ecuador, Egypt, El Salvador, Estonia, Ethiopia, Fiji, Finland, France, Gambia, Georgia, Germany, Ghana, Greece, Grenada, Guatemala, Guinea, Guinea-Bissau, Guyana, Haiti, Honduras, Hungary, Iceland, India, Indonesia, Iran, Ireland, Italy, Jamaica, Japan, Jordan, Kazakhstan, Kenya, Kuwait, Lao People's Democratic Republic, Latvia, Lebanon, Lesotho, Libyan Arab Jamahiriya, Liechtenstein, Lithuania, Luxembourg, Madagascar, Malawi, Malaysia, Maldives, Mali, Malta, Mauritania, Mauritius, Mexico, Mongolia, Morocco, Mozambique, Myanmar, Namibia, Nepal, Netherlands, New Zealand, Nicaragua, Niger, Norway, Oman, Pakistan, Panama, Papua New Guinea, Paraguay, Peru, Philippines, Poland, Portugal, Qatar, Republic of Korea, Republic of Moldova, Romania, Rwanda, Saint Lucia, Saint Vincent and the Grenadines, San Marino, Saudi Arabia, Senegal, Sierra Leone, Singapore, Slovakia, Slovenia, Spain, Sri Lanka, Sudan, Suriname, Swaziland, Sweden, Syrian Arab Republic, the former Yugoslav Republic of Macedonia, Thailand, Togo, Trinidad and Tobago, Tunisia, Turkey, Turkmenistan, Uganda, Ukraine, United Arab Emirates, United Kingdom, United Republic of Tanzania, Uruguay, Venezuela, Viet Nam, Yemen, Zaire, Zimbabwe.

Against: Israel, United States.

Abstaining: Central African Republic, Marshall Islands, Micronesia, Nigeria, Russian Federation.

Food aid

The Secretary-General reported in September 1993[11] that UNRWA continued to provide food assistance to the neediest of the refugee population, known as special hardship cases, who had numbered 179,397 persons in December 1992. It also continued emergency distributions of basic commodities, such as flour, rice, sugar, animal protein and skim milk to the needy, including non-registered Palestinians, in the occupied territory and Lebanon. In 1992, 15,036 tons of those commodities were distributed in Gaza, 7,970 tons in the West Bank and 3,202 tons in Lebanon. Given the lack of additional resources, it had not been possible for the Commissioner-General to consider resuming the interrupted general distribution of basic food rations to all refugees, as requested by the Assembly in several resolutions, most recently in 1992.[12]

On 8 December, the Fourth Committee decided not to take action[13] on a draft resolution on the resumption of the ration distribution to Palestine refugees,[14] which was therefore not considered by the General Assembly at its 1993 session. Introducing the draft on behalf of the sponsors (Afghanistan, Bangladesh, Brunei Darussalam, Comoros, Cuba, India, Indonesia, Madagascar, Malaysia, Mali, Pakistan), Indonesia stated that they would not insist on a vote on the understanding that UNRWA and the Commissioner-General would respond positively within the available resources should the need for ration distribution arise.

Education and training services

Protection of Palestinian
students and educational institutions

In September 1993,[15] the Secretary-General reproduced Israel's reply of 15 June to his 18 February note verbale referring to a 1992 General Assembly resolution[16] calling on Israel to open immediately all closed educational and vocational institutions, a large number of which were operated by UNRWA, and to refrain from closing them thereafter.

Describing the resolution as unbalanced, Israel reiterated its position that it distorted the Government's role and policy, which had always been to encourage development of the educational system in Judea, Samaria and the Gaza District. During its administration, the level of education and literacy in those territories had markedly improved and many new institutions of learning had been established. Since December 1987, however, the schools had frequently been exploited as centres for organizing and launching violent activities. Measures taken by the authorities were in reaction to activities having nothing to do with education. Those measures had enabled Israel to permit the reopening of all educational institutions, including all seven institutions of higher education, as recently recognized by UNESCO.

The Secretary-General also quoted reports of the UNRWA Commissioner-General to the effect

that of 77 cases of unauthorized entry into UNRWA premises in the West Bank during the period 1 July 1992 to 30 June 1993, 34 related to schools; of the 186 such cases in Gaza, 86 related to schools. During the same period, two deaths and 39 cases of injury among students and trainees occurred at UNRWA educational institutions in the West Bank, and 20 deaths and 1,077 injuries occurred at institutions in the Gaza Strip, all of which were attributable to beatings, tear-gas inhalation, rubber bullets and live ammunition. In addition, 76 students and trainees in the West Bank and 159 in Gaza were detained, of whom 53 and 94, respectively, had been released by 30 June 1993.

During the 1992/93 academic year, an average of 21 per cent of training time was lost at the Kalandia and Ramallah men's and women's training centres in the West Bank due to general strikes, curfews and severe weather conditions. The Gaza training centre lost 29 per cent of days as a result of military closure orders and 10 per cent owing to general strikes and curfews. Of the 361 students from Gaza attending the three training centres in the West Bank, 33 did not receive permits to study there after the March closure. Between September 1992 and June 1993, 8 per cent of school days were lost in the West Bank and 16.8 per cent in the Gaza Strip, owing primarily to military closures, general strikes and curfews. Alternative places were used for teaching classes from schools closed by military order. The Agency provided students in the territories with distance education and self-learning materials, but such measures could only partially compensate for lost classroom time, which had a detrimental effect on educational performance.

GENERAL ASSEMBLY ACTION

On 10 December, on the recommendation of the Fourth Committee, the General Assembly adopted **resolution 48/40 J** by recorded vote.

Protection of Palestinian students and educational institutions and safeguarding of the security of the facilities of the United Nations Relief and Works Agency for Palestine Refugees in the Near East in the occupied Palestinian territories

The General Assembly,

Recalling Security Council resolution 605(1987) of 22 December 1987,

Recalling also its resolutions 43/21 of 3 November 1988, 43/57 I of 6 December 1988, 44/2 of 6 October 1989, 44/47 K of 8 December 1989, 45/73 K of 11 December 1990, 46/46 K of 9 December 1991 and 47/69 K of 14 December 1992,

Taking note of the report of the Secretary-General dated 21 January 1988, submitted in accordance with Security Council resolution 605(1987), the report dated 31 October 1990, submitted in accordance with Council resolution 672(1990) of 12 October 1990, and the report dated 9 April 1991, submitted in accordance with Council resolution 681(1990) of 20 December 1990,

Having considered the report of the Secretary-General,

Having also considered the report of the Commissioner-General of the United Nations Relief and Works Agency for Palestine Refugees in the Near East, covering the period from 1 July 1992 to 30 June 1993,

Taking note, in particular, of section IV of that report, especially paragraphs 88 and 89,

Concerned about the situation in the Palestinian territory occupied by Israel since 1967, including Jerusalem,

1. *Condemns* the repeated Israeli raids on the premises and installations of the United Nations Relief and Works Agency for Palestine Refugees in the Near East, and calls upon Israel, the occupying Power, to refrain from such raids;

2. *Deplores* the policy and practices of Israel, the occupying Power, which have led to the prolonged closure of educational and vocational institutions, a large number of which are operated by the Agency, and the repeated disruption of medical services;

3. *Requests* the Secretary-General to report to the General Assembly at its forty-ninth session on the implementation of the present resolution.

General Assembly resolution 48/40 J

10 December 1993   Meeting 75   159-2 (recorded vote)

Approved by Fourth Committee (A/48/646) by recorded vote (136-2), 8 December (meeting 27); 9-nation draft (A/C.4/48/L.30); agenda item 85.

Sponsors: Afghanistan, Bangladesh, Brunei Darussalam, Comoros, Cuba, Indonesia, Madagascar, Malaysia, Pakistan.

Meeting numbers. GA 48th session: 4th Committee 18, 19, 23-27; plenary 75.

Recorded vote in Assembly as follows:

In favour: Afghanistan, Algeria, Angola, Antigua and Barbuda, Argentina, Armenia, Australia, Austria, Azerbaijan, Bahamas, Bahrain, Bangladesh, Barbados, Belarus, Belgium, Belize, Benin, Bhutan, Bolivia, Bosnia and Herzegovina, Botswana, Brazil, Brunei Darussalam, Bulgaria, Burkina Faso, Cameroon, Canada, Cape Verde, Central African Republic, Chad, Chile, China, Colombia, Comoros, Congo, Costa Rica, Côte d'Ivoire, Cuba, Cyprus, Czech Republic, Democratic People's Republic of Korea, Denmark, Djibouti, Dominican Republic, Ecuador, Egypt, El Salvador, Estonia, Ethiopia, Fiji, Finland, France, Gabon, Gambia, Georgia, Germany, Ghana, Greece, Grenada, Guatemala, Guinea, Guinea-Bissau, Guyana, Haiti, Honduras, Hungary, Iceland, India, Indonesia, Iran, Iraq, Ireland, Italy, Jamaica, Japan, Jordan, Kazakhstan, Kenya, Kuwait, Lao People's Democratic Republic, Latvia, Lebanon, Lesotho, Libyan Arab Jamahiriya, Liechtenstein, Lithuania, Luxembourg, Madagascar, Malawi, Malaysia, Maldives, Mali, Malta, Marshall Islands, Mauritania, Mauritius, Mexico, Micronesia, Mongolia, Morocco, Mozambique, Myanmar, Namibia, Nepal, Netherlands, New Zealand, Nicaragua, Niger, Nigeria, Norway, Oman, Pakistan, Panama, Papua New Guinea, Paraguay, Peru, Philippines, Poland, Portugal, Qatar, Republic of Korea, Republic of Moldova, Romania, Russian Federation, Rwanda, Saint Lucia, Saint Vincent and the Grenadines, San Marino, Saudi Arabia, Senegal, Sierra Leone, Singapore, Slovakia, Slovenia, Spain, Sri Lanka, Sudan, Suriname, Swaziland, Sweden, Syrian Arab Republic, the former Yugoslav Republic of Macedonia, Thailand, Togo, Trinidad and Tobago, Tunisia, Turkey, Turkmenistan, Uganda, Ukraine, United Arab Emirates, United Kingdom, United Republic of Tanzania, Uruguay, Venezuela, Viet Nam, Yemen, Zaire, Zimbabwe.

Against: Israel, United States.

Proposed University of Jerusalem "Al Quds"

In keeping with a General Assembly request of 1992[17] the Secretary-General reported in October 1993[18] on the establishment of a university for Palestine refugees at Jerusalem. The proposed university, first considered by the Assembly in 1980,[19] had since been the subject of annual reports by the Secretary-General with regard to

measures taken towards its establishment, including a functional feasibility study.

To assist in the preparation of the study and at the Secretary-General's request, the Rector of the United Nations University made available the services of a highly qualified expert, Dr. Mihaly Simai, who would visit the area and meet with competent Israeli officials. By a note verbale of 16 August, the Secretary-General had requested Israel to facilitate the expert's visit at a mutually convenient time. Recalling the position of Israel on the proposed university and the questions it had raised, as well as the clarifications already given by the Secretariat, the Secretary-General expressed the opinion that those questions could best be discussed during the proposed visit.

Israel had replied on 23 August that its position remained unchanged, and recalled its note of 15 June underscoring its consistent vote against the Assembly resolutions calling for the establishment of the proposed university, whose sponsors sought to exploit higher education in order to politicize issues extraneous to genuine academic pursuits. In Israel's opinion, a visit by the expert would serve no useful purpose, and so it was unable to assist in taking this matter further.

The Secretary-General thus concluded that the feasibility study could not be completed as planned.

GENERAL ASSEMBLY ACTION

On 10 December 1993, on the basis of the Fourth Committee's recommendation, the General Assembly adopted **resolution 48/40 I** by recorded vote.

University of Jerusalem "Al-Quds" for Palestine refugees

The General Assembly,

Recalling its resolutions 36/146 G of 16 December 1981, 37/120 C of 16 December 1982, 38/83 K of 15 December 1983, 39/99 K of 14 December 1984, 40/165 D and K of 16 December 1985, 41/69 K of 3 December 1986, 42/69 K of 2 December 1987, 43/57 J of 6 December 1988, 44/47 J of 8 December 1989, 45/73 J of 11 December 1990, 46/46 J of 9 December 1991 and 47/69 J of 14 December 1992,

Having considered the report of the Secretary-General,

Having also considered the report of the Commissioner-General of the United Nations Relief and Works Agency for Palestine Refugees in the Near East, covering the period from 1 July 1992 to 30 June 1993,

1. *Emphasizes* the need for strengthening the educational system in the Palestinian territory occupied by Israel since 5 June 1967, including Jerusalem, and specifically the need for the establishment of the proposed university;

2. *Requests* the Secretary-General to continue to take all necessary measures for establishing the University of Jerusalem "Al-Quds", in accordance with General Assembly resolution 35/13 B of 3 November 1980, giving due consideration to the recommendations consistent with the provisions of that resolution;

3. *Calls once more upon* Israel, the occupying Power, to cooperate in the implementation of the present resolution and to remove the hindrances that it has put in the way of establishing the University of Jerusalem "Al-Quds";

4. *Also requests* the Secretary-General to report to the General Assembly at its forty-ninth session on the progress made in the implementation of the present resolution.

General Assembly resolution 48/40 I

10 December 1993   Meeting 75   156-2-2 (recorded vote)

Approved by Fourth Committee (A/48/646) by recorded vote (133-2-2), 8 December (meeting 27); 11-nation draft (A/C.4/48/L.29); agenda item 85.
Sponsors: Afghanistan, Bangladesh, Brunei Darussalam, Comoros, Cuba, India, Indonesia, Jordan, Madagascar, Malaysia, Pakistan.
Meeting numbers. GA 48th session: 4th Committee 18, 19, 23-27; plenary 75.

Recorded vote in Assembly as follows:

In favour: Afghanistan, Algeria, Angola, Antigua and Barbuda, Argentina, Armenia, Australia, Austria, Azerbaijan, Bahamas, Bahrain, Bangladesh, Barbados, Belarus, Belgium, Belize, Benin, Bhutan, Bolivia, Bosnia and Herzegovina, Botswana, Brazil, Brunei Darussalam, Bulgaria, Burkina Faso, Cameroon, Canada, Cape Verde, Chad, Chile, China, Colombia, Comoros, Congo, Costa Rica, Côte d'Ivoire, Cuba, Cyprus, Czech Republic, Democratic People's Republic of Korea, Denmark, Djibouti, Dominican Republic, Ecuador, Egypt, El Salvador, Estonia, Ethiopia, Fiji, Finland, France, Gabon, Gambia, Georgia, Germany, Ghana, Greece, Grenada, Guatemala, Guinea, Guinea-Bissau, Guyana, Haiti, Honduras, Hungary, Iceland, India, Indonesia, Iran, Iraq, Ireland, Italy, Jamaica, Japan, Jordan, Kazakhstan, Kenya, Kuwait, Lao People's Democratic Republic, Latvia, Lebanon, Lesotho, Libyan Arab Jamahiriya, Liechtenstein, Lithuania, Luxembourg, Madagascar, Malawi, Malaysia, Maldives, Mali, Malta, Marshall Islands, Mauritania, Mauritius, Mexico, Micronesia, Mongolia, Morocco, Mozambique, Myanmar, Namibia, Nepal, Netherlands, New Zealand, Nicaragua, Niger, Nigeria, Norway, Oman, Pakistan, Panama, Papua New Guinea, Paraguay, Peru, Philippines, Poland, Portugal, Qatar, Republic of Korea, Republic of Moldova, Romania, Rwanda, Saint Lucia, Saint Vincent and the Grenadines, San Marino, Saudi Arabia, Senegal, Sierra Leone, Singapore, Slovakia, Slovenia, Spain, Sri Lanka, Sudan, Suriname, Sweden, Syrian Arab Republic, the former Yugoslav Republic of Macedonia, Thailand, Togo, Trinidad and Tobago, Tunisia, Turkey, Turkmenistan, Uganda, Ukraine, United Arab Emirates, United Kingdom, United Republic of Tanzania, Uruguay, Venezuela, Viet Nam, Yemen, Zaire, Zimbabwe.
Against: Israel, United States.
Abstaining: Central African Republic, Russian Federation.

Scholarships

The Secretary-General reported in September 1993[20] on responses to the General Assembly's 1992 appeal[21] to augment special allocations for scholarships and grants to Palestine refugees, for which UNRWA acted as recipient and trustee.

In the 1992/93 academic year, Japan offered 23 vocational fellowships for study in that country to Palestine refugees in UNRWA's employ. Under the UNRWA university scholarship programme for secondary school graduates, 135 Palestine refugee students received scholarships funded by Japan's contribution of $1 million in 1989, to be spread over five years. An additional 68 Palestinian students participated in the programme in 1992/93 under another five-year grant of $400,000 made by Japan in 1992, and 169 Palestinians were awarded scholarships made possible by a contribution from Switzerland of $197,300 in 1992. Twenty-nine applications from Palestine refugee students were referred to Iranian authorities, whose Government had offered 30 university scholarships in 1992. Those awards, while not spe-

cifically in response to Assembly resolutions, were in keeping with their spirit. In addition, 119 Palestinian students at Egyptian universities benefited from a 1992 contribution from the Netherlands, which granted $426,533 to cover their tuition.

During the 1992/93 academic year, UNESCO awarded 13 scholarships to Palestinians from its regular programme and budget, and four under its Participation Programme. Four Palestinians were awarded international fellowships under the WHO postgraduate fellowship programme aimed at developing technical and managerial skills of UNRWA's Department of Health staff and at meeting future replacement needs under various health disciplines.

GENERAL ASSEMBLY ACTION

On 10 December, on the recommendation of the Fourth Committee, the General Assembly adopted **resolution 48/40 D** by recorded vote.

Offers by Member States of grants and scholarships for higher education, including vocational training, for Palestine refugees

The General Assembly,

Recalling its resolution 212(III) of 19 November 1948 on assistance to Palestine refugees,

Recalling also its resolutions 35/13 B of 3 November 1980, 36/146 H of 16 December 1981, 37/120 D of 16 December 1982, 38/83 D of 15 December 1983, 39/99 D of 14 December 1984, 40/165 D of 16 December 1985, 41/69 D of 3 December 1986, 42/69 D of 2 December 1987, 43/57 D of 6 December 1988, 44/47 D of 8 December 1989, 45/73 D of 11 December 1990, 46/46 D of 9 December 1991 and 47/69 D of 14 December 1992,

Cognizant of the fact that the Palestine refugees have, for the last four decades, lost their homes, lands and means of livelihood,

Having considered the report of the Secretary-General,

Having also considered the report of the Commissioner-General of the United Nations Relief and Works Agency for Palestine Refugees in the Near East, covering the period from 1 July 1992 to 30 June 1993,

1. *Urges* all States to respond to the appeal in its resolution 32/90 F of 13 December 1977 and reiterated in subsequent relevant resolutions in a manner commensurate with the needs of Palestine refugees for higher education, including vocational training;

2. *Strongly appeals* to all States, specialized agencies and non-governmental organizations to augment the special allocations for grants and scholarships to Palestine refugees, in addition to their contributions to the regular budget of the United Nations Relief and Works Agency for Palestine Refugees in the Near East;

3. *Expresses its appreciation* to all Governments, specialized agencies and non-governmental organizations that responded favourably to its resolutions 41/69 D, 42/69 D, 43/57 D, 44/47 D, 45/73 D, 46/46 D and 47/69 D;

4. *Invites* the relevant specialized agencies and other organizations of the United Nations system to continue, within their respective spheres of competence, to extend assistance for higher education to Palestine refugee students;

5. *Appeals* to all States, specialized agencies and the United Nations University to contribute generously to the Palestinian universities in the Palestinian territory occupied by Israel since 1967, including, in due course, the proposed University of Jerusalem "Al-Quds" for Palestine refugees;

6. *Appeals* to all States, specialized agencies and other international bodies to contribute towards the establishment of vocational training centres for Palestine refugees;

7. *Requests* the Agency to act as the recipient and trustee for the special allocations for grants and scholarships and to award them to qualified Palestine refugee candidates;

8. *Requests* the Secretary-General to report to the General Assembly at its forty-ninth session on the implementation of the present resolution.

General Assembly resolution 48/40 D

10 December 1993   Meeting 75   161-0-1 (recorded vote)

Approved by Fourth Committee (A/48/646) by recorded vote (139-0-1), 8 December (meeting 27); 12-nation draft (A/C.4/48/L.23); agenda item 85.
Sponsors: Afghanistan, Bangladesh, Brunei Darussalam, Comoros, Cuba, India, Indonesia, Jordan, Madagascar, Malaysia, Mali, Pakistan.
Meeting numbers. GA 48th session: 4th Committee 18, 19, 23-27; plenary 75.

Recorded vote in Assembly as follows:

In favour: Afghanistan, Algeria, Angola, Antigua and Barbuda, Argentina, Armenia, Australia, Austria, Azerbaijan, Bahamas, Bahrain, Bangladesh, Barbados, Belarus, Belgium, Belize, Benin, Bhutan, Bolivia, Bosnia and Herzegovina, Botswana, Brazil, Brunei Darussalam, Bulgaria, Burkina Faso, Cambodia, Cameroon, Canada, Cape Verde, Central African Republic, Chad, Chile, China, Colombia, Comoros, Congo, Costa Rica, Côte d'Ivoire, Cuba, Cyprus, Czech Republic, Democratic People's Republic of Korea, Denmark, Djibouti, Dominica, Dominican Republic, Ecuador, Egypt, El Salvador, Estonia, Ethiopia, Fiji, Finland, France, Gabon, Gambia, Georgia, Germany, Greece, Grenada, Guatemala, Guinea, Guinea-Bissau, Guyana, Haiti, Honduras, Hungary, Iceland, India, Indonesia, Iran, Iraq, Ireland, Italy, Jamaica, Japan, Jordan, Kazakhstan, Kenya, Kuwait, Lao People's Democratic Republic, Latvia, Lebanon, Lesotho, Libyan Arab Jamahiriya, Liechtenstein, Lithuania, Luxembourg, Madagascar, Malawi, Malaysia, Maldives, Mali, Malta, Marshall Islands, Mauritania, Mauritius, Mexico, Micronesia, Mongolia, Morocco, Mozambique, Myanmar, Namibia, Nepal, Netherlands, New Zealand, Nicaragua, Niger, Nigeria, Norway, Oman, Pakistan, Panama, Papua New Guinea, Paraguay, Peru, Philippines, Poland, Portugal, Qatar, Republic of Korea, Republic of Moldova, Romania, Russian Federation, Rwanda, Saint Lucia, Saint Vincent and the Grenadines, San Marino, Saudi Arabia, Senegal, Sierra Leone, Singapore, Slovakia, Slovenia, Spain, Sri Lanka, Sudan, Suriname, Swaziland, Sweden, Syrian Arab Republic, the former Yugoslav Republic of Macedonia, Thailand, Togo, Trinidad and Tobago, Tunisia, Turkey, Turkmenistan, Uganda, Ukraine, United Arab Emirates, United Kingdom, United Republic of Tanzania, United States, Uruguay, Venezuela, Viet Nam, Yemen, Zaire, Zimbabwe.
Against: None.
Abstaining: Israel.

Property rights

Report of the Secretary-General. In response to a 1992 General Assembly resolution,[22] the Secretary-General, in August 1993,[23] submitted a report on the status of steps taken to protect and administer Arab property, assets and property rights in Israel and to establish a fund for income derived therefrom, on behalf of the rightful owners. The Secretary-General indicated that he had transmitted the resolution to Israel and to all other Member States for their comments, as well as to the Chairman of the United Nations Conciliation Commission for Palestine.

According to Israel's reply of 15 June, reproduced in the report, the 1992 resolution demonstrated misuse of the Assembly for an on-going propaganda campaign against Israel. Its position had been set out in statements to the then Special Political Committee on three occasions and in a 1992 report of the Secretary-General.[24] Israel again asserted that there was no legal basis for taking the steps proposed, as property rights within the borders of a sovereign State were subject exclusively to that State's domestic laws; the rights of States to regulate and dispose of property within their territory (and income derived from that property) was a generally accepted principle. Significantly, the resolution's sponsors had not proposed that similar steps be taken regarding the confiscated Jewish property in Arab countries—suggesting that Israel's sovereignty was limited or restricted by some provision that did not apply to other States Members of the United Nations. The property left behind by approximately 800,000 Jewish refugees who resettled in Israel as a result of the 1948 war, estimated to be in the billions of dollars, was expropriated by the Arab countries in which they had lived. Israel stressed that there could be no difference in law, justice or equity between the claims of the Arab and Jewish property owners.

The Secretary-General added that no reply had been received from any other Member State regarding implementation of the resolution.

Report of the Conciliation Commission. The United Nations Conciliation Commission for Palestine, in its report covering the period from 1 September 1992 to 31 August 1993,[25] stated that it had nothing new to report since the submission of its September 1992 report,[24] in which it had noted that the circumstances which unfortunately limited its possibilities of action regarding compensation for Palestine refugee properties remained unchanged.

GENERAL ASSEMBLY ACTION

On 10 December, on the recommendation of the Fourth Committee, the General Assembly adopted **resolution 48/40 G** by recorded vote.

Revenues derived from Palestine refugees' properties

The General Assembly,

Recalling its resolutions 35/13 A to F of 3 November 1980, 36/146 C of 16 December 1981, 37/120 H of 16 December 1982, 38/83 H of 15 December 1983, 39/99 H of 14 December 1984, 40/165 H of 16 December 1985, 41/69 H of 3 December 1986, 42/69 H of 2 December 1987, 43/57 H of 6 December 1988, 44/47 H of 8 December 1989, 45/73 H of 11 December 1990, 46/46 H of 9 December 1991, 47/69 H of 14 December 1992 and all its previous resolutions on the question, including resolution 194(III) of 11 December 1948,

Taking note of the report of the Secretary-General,

Taking note also of the report of the United Nations Conciliation Commission for Palestine, covering the period from 1 September 1992 to 31 August 1993,

Recalling that the Universal Declaration of Human Rights and the principles of international law uphold the principle that no one shall be arbitrarily deprived of his or her private property,

Considering that the Palestine Arab refugees are entitled to their property and to the income derived therefrom, in conformity with the principles of justice and equity,

Recalling in particular its resolution 394(V) of 14 December 1950, in which it directed the United Nations Conciliation Commission for Palestine, in consultation with the parties concerned, to prescribe measures for the protection of the rights, property and interests of the Palestine Arab refugees,

Taking note of the completion of the programme of identification and evaluation of Arab property, as announced by the United Nations Conciliation Commission for Palestine in its twenty-second progress report, and of the fact that the Land Office had a schedule of Arab owners and file of documents defining the location, area and other particulars of Arab property,

1. *Requests* the Secretary-General to take all appropriate steps, in consultation with the United Nations Conciliation Commission for Palestine, for the protection of Arab property, assets and property rights in Israel and to establish a fund for the receipt of income derived therefrom, on behalf of the rightful owners;

2. *Calls once more upon* Israel to render all facilities and assistance to the Secretary-General in the implementation of the present resolution;

3. *Calls upon* the Governments of all the other Member States concerned to provide the Secretary-General with any pertinent information in their possession concerning Arab property, assets and property rights in Israel which would assist the Secretary-General in the implementation of the present resolution;

4. *Requests* the Secretary-General to report to the General Assembly at its forty-ninth session on the implementation of the present resolution.

General Assembly resolution 48/40 G

10 December 1993   Meeting 75   114-2-44 (recorded vote)

Approved by Fourth Committee (A/48/646) by recorded vote (91-2-43), 8 December (meeting 27); 9-nation draft (A/C.4/48/L.27), orally revised; agenda item 85.

Sponsors: Afghanistan, Bangladesh, Brunei Darussalam, Comoros, Cuba, Indonesia, Madagascar, Malaysia, Pakistan.

Meeting numbers. GA 48th session: 4th Committee 18, 19, 23-27; plenary 75.

Recorded vote in Assembly as follows:

In favour: Afghanistan, Algeria, Angola, Antigua and Barbuda, Australia,* Azerbaijan, Bahamas, Bahrain, Bangladesh, Barbados, Belarus, Belize, Benin, Bhutan, Botswana, Brazil, Brunei Darussalam, Burkina Faso, Cameroon, Canada,* Cape Verde, Chad, Chile, China, Colombia, Comoros, Congo, Costa Rica, Côte d'Ivoire, Cuba, Cyprus, Democratic People's Republic of Korea, Djibouti, Dominican Republic, Ecuador, Egypt, El Salvador, France, Gabon, Gambia, Ghana, Greece, Grenada, Guatemala, Guinea, Guinea-Bissau, Guyana, Haiti, Honduras, India, Indonesia, Iran, Iraq, Jamaica, Jordan, Kazakhstan, Kenya, Kuwait, Lao People's Democratic Republic, Latvia, Lebanon, Lesotho, Libyan Arab Jamahiriya, Madagascar, Malawi, Malaysia, Maldives, Mali, Malta, Mauritania, Mauritius, Mexico, Mongolia, Morocco, Mozambique, Myanmar, Namibia, Nepal, New Zealand,* Nicaragua, Niger, Oman, Pakistan, Panama, Peru, Philippines, Qatar, Republic of Korea, Rwanda, Saint Lucia, Saint Vincent and the Grenadines, Saudi Arabia, Senegal, Sierra Leone, Singapore, Spain, Sri Lanka, Sudan, Suriname, Syrian Arab Republic, Thailand, Togo, Trinidad and Tobago, Tunisia, Uganda, Ukraine, United Arab Emirates, United Republic of Tanzania, Uruguay, Venezuela, Viet Nam, Yemen, Zaire, Zimbabwe.

Against: Israel, United States.

Abstaining: Argentina, Armenia, Austria, Belgium, Bolivia, Bulgaria, Central African Republic, Czech Republic, Denmark, Dominica, Estonia, Ethiopia, Fiji, Finland, Georgia, Germany, Hungary, Iceland, Ireland, Italy, Japan,

Liechtenstein, Lithuania, Luxembourg, Marshall Islands, Micronesia, Netherlands, Nigeria, Norway, Papua New Guinea, Paraguay, Poland, Portugal, Republic of Moldova, Romania, Russian Federation, San Marino, Slovakia, Slovenia, Swaziland, Sweden, the former Yugoslav Republic of Macedonia, Turkey, United Kingdom.

*Later advised the Secretariat they had intended to abstain.

Refugee protection

The Secretary-General reported in September 1993[26] on implementation of a 1992 General Assembly resolution[27] holding Israel responsible for the security of the Palestine refugees in the occupied territory, including Jerusalem, and calling on it to compensate UNRWA for the damage to its property and facilities resulting from Israel's 1982 invasion of Lebanon and its policies and practices in the occupied territory.

The report reproduced Israel's note verbale of 15 June 1993 to the Secretary-General's request for information on steps taken or envisaged to comply with the resolution. Israel said that it had fully set forth its position on the subject in statements to the then Special Political Committee and in a 1992 report of the Secretary-General.[28] The note stated that adopting the resolution was hypocritical, anachronistic and out of place. Despite its withdrawal from Lebanon in 1985, Israel was still being blamed for the "suffering" of Palestinians there and, not surprisingly, for Arab persecution of Palestinian refugees. In recent years, thousands of Palestinians had been killed and wounded in Lebanese refugee camps in vicious fighting totally unconnected with Israel; likewise, Palestinian refugee camps in Jordan and the Syrian Arab Republic were the scenes of considerable human misery. The selective and distorted presentation of the Palestinian refugees' situation in Arab countries clearly illustrated the resolution's double standards and its blatant disregard for the refugees' general welfare. Israel emphasized that, in keeping with international law, it alone was competent to ensure full protection to all inhabitants of Judaea, Samaria and the Gaza District.

The Secretary-General went on to cite the UNRWA Commissioner-General's report for the period 1 July 1992 to 30 June 1993,[1] to the effect that the Commissioner-General had continued his efforts in support of the Palestine refugees' safety and legal and human rights, as called for in the 1992 Assembly resolution. UNRWA international staff, in particular the refugee affairs and legal officers, continued to help reduce tension and prevent maltreatment of refugees, especially vulnerable groups such as women and children. The Commissioner-General also protested to Israel against the excessive use of force and collective punishments, such as the punitive demolition and sealing of shelters, as a failure on Israel's part to uphold standards required under international humanitarian law. As part of the Commissioner-General's efforts in that regard, legal advice and financial assistance were provided for refugees seeking to assert their legal rights.

GENERAL ASSEMBLY ACTION

On 10 December, on the recommendation of the Fourth Committee, the General Assembly adopted **resolution 48/40 H** by recorded vote.

Protection of Palestine refugees

The General Assembly,

Recalling in particular Security Council resolutions 605(1987) of 22 December 1987, 607(1988) of 5 January 1988, 608(1988) of 14 January 1988, 636(1989) of 6 July 1989, 641(1989) of 30 August 1989, 672(1990) of 12 October 1990, 673(1990) of 24 October 1990, 681(1990) of 20 December 1990, 694(1991) of 24 May 1991 and 726(1992) of 6 January 1992,

Recalling its resolutions ES-7/5 of 26 June 1982, ES-7/6 and ES-7/8 of 19 August 1982, ES-7/9 of 24 September 1982, 37/120 J of 16 December 1982, 38/83 I of 15 December 1983, 39/99 I of 14 December 1984, 40/165 I of 16 December 1985, 41/69 I of 3 December 1986, 42/69 I of 2 December 1987, 43/21 of 3 November 1988, 43/57 I of 6 December 1988, 44/47 I of 8 December 1989, 45/73 I of 11 December 1990, 46/46 I of 9 December 1991 and 47/69 I of 14 December 1992,

Taking note of the report of the Secretary-General dated 21 January 1988, submitted in accordance with Security Council resolution 605(1987), the report dated 31 October 1990, submitted in accordance with Council resolution 672(1990), and the report dated 9 April 1991, submitted in accordance with Council resolution 681(1990),

Having considered the report of the Secretary-General,

Having also considered the report of the Commissioner-General of the United Nations Relief and Works Agency for Palestine Refugees in the Near East, covering the period from 1 July 1992 to 30 June 1993,

Concerned about the situation in the Palestinian territory occupied by Israel since 1967, including Jerusalem,

Taking into account the need to consider measures for the impartial protection of the Palestinian civilian population under Israeli occupation,

Referring to the humanitarian principles of the Geneva Convention relative to the Protection of Civilian Persons in Time of War, of 12 August 1949, and to the obligations arising from the regulations annexed to the Hague Convention IV of 1907,

Deeply distressed that, notwithstanding the improved security situation owing to the deployment of the Lebanese army, the Lebanese and Palestinian populations are still suffering from continuing Israeli acts of aggression against Lebanon and from other hostile acts,

1. *Holds* Israel responsible for the security of the Palestine refugees in the occupied Palestinian territory, including Jerusalem, and calls upon it to fulfil its obligations as the occupying Power in this regard, in accordance with the pertinent provisions of the Geneva Convention relative to the Protection of Civilian Persons in Time of War, of 12 August 1949;

2. *Calls upon* all the High Contracting Parties to the Convention to take appropriate measures to ensure respect by Israel, the occupying Power, for the Convention in all circumstances, in conformity with their obligation under article 1 thereof;

3. *Urges* the Security Council to remain seized of the situation in the occupied Palestinian territory;

4. *Urges* the Secretary-General and the Commissioner-General of the United Nations Relief and Works Agency for Palestine Refugees in the Near East to continue their efforts in support of the upholding of the safety and security and the legal and human rights of the Palestine refugees in all the territories under Israeli occupation since 1967;

5. *Calls once again upon* Israel to desist forthwith from acts of aggression against the Lebanese and Palestinian populations in Lebanon in violation of the Charter of the United Nations and the norms of international law;

6. *Demands* that Israel, the occupying Power, release forthwith all arbitrarily detained Palestine refugees, including the employees of the Agency;

7. *Calls once again upon* Israel to compensate the Agency for damages to its property and facilities resulting from the invasion of Lebanon by Israel in 1982, without prejudice to the responsibility of the latter for all damages resulting from that invasion, as well as for other damages resulting from the policies and practices of Israel, the occupying Power, in the occupied Palestinian territory;

8. *Requests* the Secretary-General, in consultation with the Commissioner-General, to report to the General Assembly, before the opening of its forty-ninth session, on the implementation of the present resolution.

General Assembly resolution 48/40 H

10 December 1993   Meeting 75   153-2-6 (recorded vote)

Approved by Fourth Committee (A/48/646) by recorded vote (134-2-2), 8 December (meeting 27); 9-nation draft (A/C.4/48/L.28); agenda item 85.
Sponsors: Afghanistan, Bangladesh, Brunei Darussalam, Comoros, Cuba, Indonesia, Madagascar, Malaysia, Pakistan.
Meeting numbers. GA 48th session: 4th Committee 18, 19, 23-27; plenary 75.

Recorded vote in Assembly as follows:

In favour: Afghanistan, Algeria, Angola, Antigua and Barbuda, Argentina, Armenia, Australia, Austria, Azerbaijan, Bahamas, Bahrain, Bangladesh, Barbados, Belarus, Belgium, Belize, Benin, Bhutan, Bolivia, Bosnia and Herzegovina, Botswana, Brazil, Brunei Darussalam, Bulgaria, Burkina Faso, Cameroon, Cape Verde, Chad, Chile, China, Colombia, Comoros, Congo, Costa Rica, Côte d'Ivoire, Cuba, Cyprus, Czech Republic, Democratic People's Republic of Korea, Denmark, Djibouti, Dominican Republic, Ecuador, Egypt, El Salvador, Estonia, Ethiopia, Fiji, Finland, France, Gabon, Gambia, Germany, Ghana, Greece, Grenada, Guatemala, Guinea, Guinea-Bissau, Guyana, Haiti, Honduras, Hungary, Iceland, India, Indonesia, Iran, Iraq, Ireland, Italy, Jamaica, Japan, Jordan, Kazakhstan, Kuwait, Lao People's Democratic Republic, Latvia, Lebanon, Lesotho, Libyan Arab Jamahiriya, Liechtenstein, Lithuania, Luxembourg, Madagascar, Malawi, Malaysia, Maldives, Mali, Malta, Marshall Islands, Mauritania, Mauritius, Mexico, Micronesia, Mongolia, Morocco, Mozambique, Myanmar, Namibia, Nepal, Netherlands, Nicaragua, Niger, Nigeria, Norway, Oman, Pakistan, Panama, Papua New Guinea, Paraguay, Peru, Philippines, Poland, Portugal, Qatar, Republic of Korea, Republic of Moldova, Romania, Rwanda, Saint Lucia, Saint Vincent and the Grenadines, San Marino, Saudi Arabia, Senegal, Sierra Leone, Singapore, Slovakia, Slovenia, Spain, Sri Lanka, Sudan, Suriname, Swaziland, Sweden, Syrian Arab Republic, the former Yugoslav Republic of Macedonia, Thailand, Togo, Trinidad and Tobago, Tunisia, Turkey, Turkmenistan, Uganda, Ukraine, United Arab Emirates, United Kingdom, United Republic of Tanzania, Uruguay, Venezuela, Viet Nam, Yemen, Zaire, Zimbabwe.
Against: Israel, United States.
Abstaining: Canada,* Central African Republic, Georgia, Kenya, New Zealand,* Russian Federation.

*Later advised the Secretariat they had intended to vote in favour.

Removal and resettlement of refugees

In a September 1993 report,[29] the Secretary-General reproduced Israel's reply of 15 June to his note verbale of 18 February referring to a 1992

General Assembly resolution[30] demanding that Israel desist from removing and resettling Palestine refugees in the Palestinian territory occupied by it since 1967 and from destroying their shelters. The reply stated that Israel's position had been made known in successive annual replies to the Secretary-General in recent years, the latest of which was contained in his 1992 report on the subject.[31]

Israel considered the resolution unbalanced and distorted in that it intentionally ignored the improved living conditions in Gaza since 1967. Nothing could be more indicative of that approach than the resolution's condemnation of refugee rehabilitation projects. By initiating community development projects in Gaza, Israel had enabled some 20,000 families (approximately 150,000 persons) to leave the refugee camps on a voluntary basis and relocate to nearby residential areas. Its vital role in planning and implementing those housing projects had been recognized in 1985 by both the Secretary-General[32] and the Commissioner-General. Israel continued to do as much as it could to improve living conditions of Palestinians in the territories; it had outlined recent steps to the Secretary-General in March[33] (see above, under "Living conditions of Palestinians").

The resolution's request that the Secretary-General resume issuing identity cards irrespective of the refugees' need for them was yet another indication of its patent political bias. Notwithstanding subversive efforts to the contrary, Israel was determined to pursue the task of improving the refugees' living conditions through projects such as the refugee housing programmes, welcoming all assistance from the international community in that regard.

The Secretary-General stated that, according to information from UNRWA, Israeli authorities continued to inflict collective punishment through punitive demolition and sealing of refugee shelters in the West Bank and Gaza. As at 30 June 1993, of the 87 refugee families affected by the 1971 demolition of shelters in Gaza,[34] 12 continued to live in conditions of hardship and 19 remained in unsatisfactory housing. Despite assurances by Israel that those families would be rehoused, no progress had been made.

The situation of the families living on the northern perimeter of Jabalia camp,[35] who had been told to remove some of their shelter extensions, remained the same: no demolitions had taken place, but the shelters remained isolated by the bulldozing of sand around them. Of the 35 families whose shelters on the perimeter of Beach camp were demolished in 1983,[36] 18 had been allocated plots of land at the Sheikh Radwan and Beit Lahiya housing projects, one was housed in a vacant shelter at Beach camp, and the other 16 remained

in the same situation as previously reported—in temporary shelters near the camp site. Of the 12 families at Rafah camp who had agreed, at the request of the Israeli authorities, to relocate to the Israeli-sponsored Tel-es-Sultan housing project,[37] two had moved there, leaving the remaining 10 shelters isolated by sand ramparts. Thirty families (150 persons) from Canada camp in Egypt had returned to Gaza to accommodations at Tel-es-Sultan.

The Israeli authorities had to date allocated approximately 3,914 plots of land in the Gaza Strip for housing projects. A total of 2,605 plots had been built on by 3,714 refugee families comprising 22,946 persons; buildings on 236 plots were under construction, while 936 plots were still vacant and 137 had been built on by non-refugee families. In addition, 3,034 refugee families, consisting of 18,823 persons, had moved into 2,666 completed housing units consisting of 5,893 rooms.

As to the Assembly's request that he address the acute situation of the refugees, the Commissioner-General advised that UNRWA, in addition to extending to refugees its regular services plus emergency food, medical and other assistance, also pursued its long-term programme to upgrade infrastructure, especially in the camps, and, in general, to improve the economic and social welfare of the refugees.

The Secretary-General regretted his inability to comply with the Assembly's request that he resume issuing identification cards to all Palestine refugees and their descendants in the occupied territory, whether or not they were recipients of UNRWA rations and services. Under an arrangement in effect for 40 years, all families registered with UNRWA were in possession of Agency-issued registration cards indicating the number of family members and their eligibility for services. However, the Commissioner-General did not have the means to issue identity cards as such. He would keep the matter under review to see whether appropriate documentation regarding the registration status of individual members of refugee families could be issued.

GENERAL ASSEMBLY ACTION

On 10 December 1993, on the recommendation of the Fourth Committee, the General Assembly adopted **resolution 48/40 E** by recorded vote.

Palestine refugees in the Palestinian territory occupied by Israel since 1967

The General Assembly,

Recalling Security Council resolution 237(1967) of 14 June 1967,

Recalling also its resolutions 2792 C (XXVI) of 6 December 1971, 2963 C (XXVII) of 13 December 1972, 3089 C (XXVIII) of 7 December 1973, 3331 D (XXIX) of 17 December 1974, 3419 C (XXX) of 8 December

1975, 31/15 E of 23 November 1976, 32/90 C of 13 December 1977, 33/112 E of 18 December 1978, 34/52 F of 23 November 1979, 35/13 F of 3 November 1980, 36/146 A of 16 December 1981, 37/120 E and I of 16 December 1982, 38/83 E and J of 15 December 1983, 39/99 E and J of 14 December 1984, 40/165 E and J of 16 December 1985, 41/69 E and J of 3 December 1986, 42/69 E and J of 2 December 1987, 43/57 E of 6 December 1988, 44/47 E of 8 December 1989, 45/73 E of 11 December 1990, 46/46 E of 9 December 1991 and 47/69 E of 14 December 1992,

Having considered the report of the Secretary-General,

Having also considered the report of the Commissioner-General of the United Nations Relief and Works Agency for Palestine Refugees in the Near East, covering the period from 1 July 1992 to 30 June 1993,

Recalling the provisions of paragraph 11 of its resolution 194(III) of 11 December 1948, and considering that measures to resettle Palestine refugees in the Palestinian territory occupied by Israel since 1967 away from their homes and property from which they were displaced constitute a violation of their inalienable right of return,

Alarmed by the reports received from the Commissioner-General that the Israeli occupying authorities, in contravention of the obligation of Israel under international law, persist in their policy of demolishing shelters occupied by refugee families,

1. *Demands once again* that Israel desist from the removal and resettlement of Palestine refugees in the Palestinian territory occupied by Israel since 1967 and from the destruction of their shelters;

2. *Requests* the Commissioner-General of the United Nations Relief and Works Agency for Palestine Refugees in the Near East to address the acute situation of the Palestine refugees in the Palestinian territory occupied by Israel since 1967 and accordingly to extend all the services of the Agency to those refugees;

3. *Requests* the Secretary-General, in cooperation with the Commissioner-General, to resume issuing identification cards to all Palestine refugees and their descendants in the occupied Palestinian territory, irrespective of whether or not they are recipients of rations and services of the Agency;

4. *Also requests* the Secretary-General, after consulting with the Commissioner-General, to report to the General Assembly, before the opening of its forty-ninth session, on the implementation of the present resolution and, in particular, on the compliance of Israel with paragraph 1 above.

General Assembly resolution 48/40 E

10 December 1993   Meeting 75   157-2 (recorded vote)

Approved by Fourth Committee (A/48/646) by recorded vote (135-2), 8 December (meeting 27); 9-nation draft (A/C.4/48/L.24/Rev.1); agenda item 85.

Sponsors: Afghanistan, Bangladesh, Brunei Darussalam, Comoros, Cuba, Indonesia, Madagascar, Malaysia, Pakistan.

Meeting numbers. GA 48th session: 4th Committee 18, 19, 23-27; plenary 75.

Recorded vote in Assembly as follows:

In favour: Afghanistan, Algeria, Angola, Antigua and Barbuda, Argentina, Armenia, Australia, Austria, Azerbaijan, Bahamas, Bahrain, Bangladesh, Barbados, Belarus, Belgium, Belize, Benin, Bhutan, Bolivia, Bosnia and Herzegovina, Botswana, Brazil, Brunei Darussalam, Bulgaria, Burkina Faso, Cameroon, Canada, Cape Verde, Chad, Chile, China, Colombia, Comoros, Congo, Costa Rica, Côte d'Ivoire, Cuba, Cyprus, Czech Republic, Democratic People's Republic of Korea, Denmark, Djibouti, Dominican Republic, Ecuador, Egypt, El Salvador, Estonia, Ethiopia, Fiji, Finland, France, Gabon, Gambia, Georgia, Germany, Ghana, Greece, Grenada, Guatemala, Guinea, Guinea-Bissau, Guyana, Haiti, Honduras, Hungary, Iceland, India, Indonesia, Iran, Iraq, Ireland, Italy, Jamaica, Japan, Jordan, Kazakhstan, Kenya, Kuwait, Latvia, Lebanon, Lesotho, Libyan Arab Jamahiriya, Liechtenstein, Lithuania, Luxembourg, Madagascar, Malawi, Malaysia, Maldives, Mali, Malta, Marshall Islands, Mauritania, Mauritius, Mexico, Micronesia, Mongolia, Morocco, Mozambique, Myanmar, Namibia, Nepal, Netherlands, New Zealand, Nicaragua, Niger, Nigeria, Norway, Oman, Pakistan, Panama, Papua New Guinea, Paraguay, Peru, Philippines, Poland, Portugal, Qatar, Republic of Korea, Republic of Moldova, Romania, Russian Federation, Rwanda, Saint Lucia, Saint Vincent and the Grenadines, San Marino, Saudi Arabia, Senegal, Sierra Leone, Singapore, Slovakia, Slovenia, Spain, Sri Lanka, Sudan, Suriname, Swaziland, Sweden, Syrian Arab Republic, Thailand, the former Yugoslav Republic of Macedonia, Togo, Trinidad and Tobago, Tunisia, Turkey, Turkmenistan, Uganda, Ukraine, United Arab Emirates, United Kingdom, United Republic of Tanzania, Uruguay, Venezuela, Viet Nam, Yemen, Zaire, Zimbabwe.

Against: Israel, United States.

REFERENCES

[1]A/48/13 & Add.1 & Add.1/Corr.1. [2]A/48/132. [3]A/48/554. [4]YUN 1992, p. 1042, GA res. 47/211, 23 Dec. 1992. [5]Ibid., p. 429. [6]YUN 1986, p. 342. [7]A/48/376. [8]A/48/375. [9]YUN 1992, p. 446, GA res. 47/69 G, 14 Dec. 1992. [10]Ibid., p. 446. [11]A/48/374. [12]YUN 1992, p. 447, GA res. 47/69 F, 14 Dec. 1992. [13]A/48/646. [14]A/C.4/48/L.25. [15]A/48/377. [16]YUN 1992, p. 448, GA res. 47/69 K, 14 Dec. 1992. [17]Ibid., p. 449, GA res. 47/69 J, 14 Dec. 1992. [18]A/48/431. [19]YUN 1980, p. 443, GA res. 35/13 B, 3 Nov. 1980. [20]A/48/372. [21]YUN 1992, p. 450, GA res. 47/69 D, 14 Dec. 1992. [22]Ibid., p. 452, GA res. 47/69 H, 14 Dec. 1992. [23]A/48/275. [24]YUN 1992, p. 451. [25]A/48/474. [26]A/48/376. [27]YUN 1992, p. 453, GA res. 47/69 I, 14 Dec. 1992. [28]Ibid., p. 452. [29]A/48/373. [30]YUN 1992, p. 455, GA res. 47/69 E, 14 Dec. 1992. [31]Ibid., p. 454. [32]YUN 1985, p. 367. [33]A/48/112. [34]YUN 1971, p. 198. [35]YUN 1985, p. 366. [36]YUN 1983, p. 358. [37]YUN 1986, p. 351.

Chapter VI

Regional economic and social activities

During 1993, the five United Nations regional commissions continued to promote economic and social development in their respective regions. Three of the five commissions held their regular sessions during the year. The Economic Commission for Africa (ECA) held its twenty-eighth session/nineteenth meeting of the Conference of Ministers and the fourteenth meeting of the Technical Preparatory Committee of the Whole at Addis Ababa, Ethiopia; the Economic and Social Commission for Asia and the Pacific (ESCAP) held its forty-ninth session at Bangkok, Thailand; and the Economic Commission for Europe (ECE) held its forty-eighth session at Geneva. However, the Economic Commission for Latin America and the Caribbean (ECLAC) and the Economic and Social Commission for Western Asia (ESCWA) did not meet in 1993. In July, the Economic and Social Council called for the role of the regional commissions to be strengthened (resolution 1993/61).

The Council amended the terms of reference of ECE, to allow Member States located in the Central Asian part of the former USSR to be admitted to the Commission (decision 1993/317). It also upheld ECE's decision to bar the participation of Yugoslavia (Serbia and Montenegro) in the Commission's work as long as it did not participate in the work of the General Assembly (1993/316).

The Council endorsed ESCAP's resolution on population and sustainable development, dealing with goals and strategies into the twenty-first century (1993/319) and ECA's resolution on preparations for the 1995 World Summit for Social Development (1993/64), and called for a constructive dialogue between industrialized and developing countries (1993/62). It recommended to the General Assembly a resolution on resource mobilization to implement the regional action programme for phase II (1992-1996) of the Transport and Communications Decade for Asia and the Pacific (1993/63), subsequently adopted by the Assembly in December (resolution 48/177). The Council also called for resource mobilization and financial support to implement the programmes of the Second Industrial Decade for Africa, 1993-2002 (1993/65) and the Second Transport and Communications Decade in Africa, 1991-2000 (1993/66). It further addressed ECA activities in its resolutions on strengthening development information systems for regional cooperation and integration in Africa (1993/67) and the African Institute for Economic Development and Planning (1993/68).

In November, the Assembly urged United Nations agencies and organizations to continue and intensify their cooperation with the Latin American Economic System (48/22) and in December, it invited the United Nations Conference on Trade and Development to elaborate a programme for improving transit facilities in the land-locked States of Central Asia (48/170). It renewed its appeal for increased financial and technical support to the Southern African Development Community (48/173).

Regional cooperation

During 1993, the General Assembly continued to consider the restructuring and revitalization of the United Nations in the economic, social and related fields, including the regional commissions. By **resolution 47/212 B** of 6 May, the Assembly noted that the Secretary-General had indicated, in 1992,[1] that further restructuring of the Secretariat would entail decentralization of activities to the field and to the regional commissions. It requested him to review the role of the commissions, with a view to improving the distribution of responsibilities among them on the basis of their relative advantages.

The Secretary-General established the interdepartmental Task Force on Decentralization at the Secretariat level, with the participation of the regional commissions, to examine Headquarters activities that could be carried out more effectively at the regional level. Following working-level consultations and deliberations within the framework of the Task Force, from 3 to 7 May, the executive secretaries of the regional commissions met in New York on 10 and 11 May. They agreed on a number of principles for the distribution of responsibilities and tasks between global components of the United Nations and the commissions. They identified several types of activities for decentralization including empirical research and analysis of data and information within the regional or subregional context; regional, subregional and national follow-up to global events; planning and management of human resources development; preparation of inventories of specific capabilities and capacities; promotion of economic and technical cooperation among developing countries; identification of priority subprogrammes providing comparative advantages to their respective commissions and possibilities for a cost-effective decentralization; and advisory services.

The executive secretaries proposed: a new ratio for the distribution of advisory services; a high degree of decentralization in natural resources and energy and adjustments in a variety of other programmes; ways to make the commissions' contribution to major humanitarian assistance programmes more continuous and systematic and to establish or strengthen joint units and develop joint programmes; and the establishment of a task force comprising the United Nations Department for Economic and Social Information and Policy Analysis and the commissions' statistical divisions to enhance interaction in the information area.

The executive secretaries highlighted important issues that had emerged from the recent sessions of ESCAP, ECE and ECA and examined preparations for and follow-up to global programmes and conferences and interregional cooperation in energy, trade facilitation and transport. They expressed concern about the sharp decline in funds available to the commissions under the fifth (1992-1996) programming cycle of the United Nations Development Programme (UNDP) and a reduction of funding support from the United Nations Population Fund (UNFPA).

Report of the Secretary-General. In a June report to the Economic and Social Council on regional cooperation,[2] the Secretary-General outlined the work of the five regional commissions, including matters and decisions requiring action by or brought to the attention of the Council. In response to a 1992 Council request for information on action taken to strengthen the role of the regional commissions,[3] the Secretary-General provided a detailed account of the May meeting of the executive secretaries and the extensive consultations which took place on that matter and on the question of decentralization within the framework of the interdepartmental Task Force. The Secretary-General pointed to the commissions' joint recommendation that the Council consider the question of their contributions to the implementation of Agenda 21,[4] adopted by the 1992 United Nations Conference on Environment and Development (UNCED).

ECONOMIC AND SOCIAL COUNCIL ACTION

On 2 February, by **decision 1993/202**, the Economic and Social Council took note of the Secretary-General's 1992 report on regional cooperation.[5] By **decision 1993/213** of 12

February, the Council requested the regional commissions to report on their plans to implement Agenda 21 and to make those reports available to the Commission on Sustainable Development in 1994 at the latest.

On 30 July, the Council on the recommendation of its Economic Committee, adopted **resolution 1993/61** without vote.

Strengthening the role of the regional commissions
The Economic and Social Council,

Recalling its resolution 1992/43 of 31 July 1992 and General Assembly resolutions 32/197 of 20 December 1977, 45/264 of 13 May 1991, 46/145 of 17 December 1991 and 46/235 of 13 April 1992,

Noting with interest the recommendations made by the regional commissions, in response to General Assembly resolution 46/235, to strengthen their effectiveness, as contained in the report of the Secretary-General on restructuring and revitalization of the United Nations in the economic, social and related fields,[a]

Welcoming the report of the Secretary-General on regional cooperation, including the account of steps being taken to decentralize functions and responsibilities to the regional commissions in order to strengthen the regional presence of the Organization and to enhance its effectiveness,

1. *Reaffirms* its support for decentralization in order to achieve a more effective distribution of responsibilities and tasks between global, regional and national entities in the economic, social and related fields;

2. *Takes note* of the measures taken by the Secretary-General to strengthen the work of the Organization at the regional level, and urges him to continue his efforts in that direction, as appropriate;

3. *Recommends* to the General Assembly that, in connection with the restructuring and revitalization of the United Nations in the economic, social and related fields, it consider the recommendations made by the regional commissions.

---

[a]A/47/534.

Economic and Social Council resolution 1993/61
30 July 1993   Meeting 46   Adopted without vote

Approved by Economic Committee (E/1993/109) without vote, 26 July (meeting 15); 11-nation draft (E/1993/C.1/L.2), orally revised following informal consultations; agenda item 14.
Sponsors: Algeria, Benin, Brazil, Chile, Ethiopia, Guinea, Mexico, Nigeria, Senegal, Suriname, Togo.

REFERENCES
[1]YUN 1992, p. 456. [2]E/1993/85. [3]YUN 1992, p. 458, ESC res. 1992/43, 31 July 1992. [4]YUN 1992, p. 672. [5]Ibid., p. 457.

Africa

On 12 February, the Economic and Social Council decided that the 1993 session of ECA/nineteenth meeting of the Conference of Ministers of the Commission would be held at Libreville, Gabon, from 19 to 22 April (**decision 1993/203**).

However, no action was taken on that decision and ECA held its twenty-eighth session/nineteenth meeting of the Conference of Ministers at Addis Ababa, Ethiopia, from 3 to 6 May.[1] The Conference had as its theme: perspectives of Africa's socio-economic development into the twenty-first century; implementation of the 1991 Abuja Treaty, adopted by the Organization of African Unity (OAU) in 1991, establishing the African Economic Community; and Agenda 21, adopted by UNCED in 1992.[2] The Ministers reviewed issues related to development management and the human development agenda, trade, industrial and infrastructural development, preparations for forthcoming international conferences, and programme, administrative and organizational questions.

In his message to the Conference, the Secretary-General stated that implementation of the United Nations New Agenda for the Development of Africa in the 1990s, adopted by the General Assembly in 1991,[3] was a key United Nations priority. He urged African countries to seize the opportunity of the International Conference on African Development, to be held in October in Tokyo (see PART THREE, Chapter III), to work towards a new partnership based on a clear rationalization of the region's development needs and priorities. However, he stressed the vital importance of achieving peace, stability and security as integral components of development through prevention and peaceful resolution of conflicts, respect for human rights and fundamental freedoms and greater government responsiveness and accountability. The continent also had to develop political institutions capable of building and sustaining a competitive economy and expand its production and market opportunities through regional economic integration and cooperation to facilitate Africa's integration into the global economy.

In his statement to the Conference, the Executive Secretary of ECA noted the need for a pragmatic approach to socio-economic restructuring, so as to preserve an equitable social structure in spite of rapid transformation and for galvanizing national consensus behind economic reforms. He observed that the structural adjustment programmes applied since the mid-1980s were taking too long to achieve self-sustained growth, because they did not go far enough in correcting the structural causes of Africa's underdevelopment and because of continued administrative and political instabilities.

He called for bold initiatives to reduce external debt and increase official development assistance (ODA) to Africa, along with private credit and foreign direct investment (FDI).

The Conference of Ministers was preceded by the fourteenth meeting of the Technical Prepara-

tory Committee of the Whole (Addis Ababa, 26 April–2 May),[4] which considered strategic objectives for Africa's socio-economic development in the 1990s,[5] noting that Africa's efforts and those of its partners should focus on issues of a negotiated continental framework for regional security, stability and peace; implementation of the Abuja Treaty establishing the African Economic Community; effective participation in all ongoing global negotiation processes; a comprehensive programme for building human capacities, including entrepreneurial skills, coupled with the indigenization of science and technology; redefining the role of the state in Africa and improving the quality of governance; sustainable development of the continent's agricultural potential; sustainable industrialization; upgrading of continental transport, communications and energy infrastructures for the creation of a single African market; a new pragmatic approach to Africa's external cooperation; and mobilization of the required financial resources, with primary emphasis on domestic resources.

The Committee also reviewed the continent's economic performance in 1992 and the outlook for 1993 and examined strategies for financial resource mobilization for Africa's development in the 1990s.[6] It studied proposals for the implementation of the Abuja Treaty establishing the African Economic Community[7] and for the African Strategies for the implementation of Agenda 21,[8] and issues relating to regional cooperation for development. The Committee noted that, in response to the Commission's 1992 resolution on strengthening ECA,[9] subsequently endorsed by the Economic and Social Council,[10] steps had been taken to reinforce ECA's internal capacity, strengthen its programmes of assistance to member States and enhance its advocacy role with regard to the region's economic and social policy.

The Committee endorsed the proposed new structure of the Commission's intergovernmental machinery[11] and made recommendations concerning rationalization and harmonization of ECA-sponsored institutions and strengthening of the ECA Multidisciplinary Regional Advisory Group and its Multinational Programming and Operational Centres (MULPOCs). It also endorsed the proposed programme of work and priorities for the biennium 1994-1995[12] and took note of the first revisions to the medium-term plan for 1992-1997.[13] (For more details, see below, under specific headings.)

The Conference of Ministers reviewed, amended and adopted the Committee's report,[4] including its resolutions and declaration on the implications of the Uruguay Round on Africa's trade. It called on member States to be guided by the strategic objectives for Africa's economic development in the 1990s in their programmes of structural adjustment, transformation and development.[14] The Ministers also called on the Secretary-General to strengthen ECA's role as team leader and coordinator of United Nations activities with a regional perspective in Africa in order to ensure rational implementation of the strategic objectives for Africa's economic development within the context of the New Agenda, called on the Economic and Social Council and the General Assembly to provide an updated legislative framework for the regional commissions and urged United Nations bodies active in Africa to work in close partnership with ECA.[15]

The Conference of Ministers adopted a new structure of the Commission's intergovernmental machinery,[16] which would consist of the following: the Conference of Ministers responsible for economic and social development and planning (the Commission) and its Technical Preparatory Committee of the Whole; intergovernmental committees of experts of MULPOCs; seven thematic conferences of ministers (on human development; sustainable development and the environment; finance; trade and regional cooperation and integration; transport and communications; industry; and on development and utilization of mineral resources and energy) and their committees of experts; and four technical subsidiary bodies: the United Nations Regional Cartographic Conference for Africa; the African Regional Conference for Science and Technology; the Joint Conference of African Planners, Statisticians, Demographers and Information Scientists; and the Africa Regional Coordinating Committee for the Integration of Women in Development. The terms of reference of those bodies were annexed to the Conference's resolution.

The Conference agreed to revive its Ad Hoc Committee of 10 member States to examine proposals on the harmonization and rationalization of ECA-sponsored institutions, requested the Executive Secretary to undertake a cost-benefit analysis on institutions to be merged and urged United Nations organizations to make greater use of their services.[17] It further requested the Executive Secretary to prepare a programme for the strengthening and rationalization of MULPOCs, and urged MULPOCs to assist intergovernmental organizations to coordinate, harmonize and rationalize activities with a view to establishing a single community in their subregions.[18] The Conference called on member States to make increasing use of the resources and expertise of the Multidisciplinary Regional Advisory Group in seeking solutions to their socio-economic development problems.[19]

In a Declaration on the implications of the Uruguay Round of international trade negotiations on Africa's trade, adopted on 6 May, the Conference called on African countries to establish strong common positions in multilateral trade negotiations. It urged the major negotiating partners to set aside, in an annex to the Final Act of the Uruguay Round negotiations, African preferences and derogations for a transitional period of economic restructuring and called on ECA, the United Nations Conference on Trade and Development (UNCTAD) and the General Agreement on Tariffs and Trade (GATT) to undertake studies on the potential impacts of the post–Uruguay Round trading regime on specific economic sectors of African countries and develop measures to mitigate the negative effects (see also PART THREE, Chapter IV).

Economic and social trends

Economic trends

Africa's economic situation remained precarious and disturbing in 1993, according to a summary of the survey of economic conditions in its various subregions.[20] Overall regional output grew by only 1 per cent, after virtually stagnating in 1992, perpetuating the decline in per capita income. The combined gross domestic product (GDP) of the continent's non-oil-exporting countries increased by 1.4 per cent, having declined by 0.7 per cent in 1992, while the growth rate of the oil-exporting States declined from 1.1 per cent in 1992 to 0.8 per cent in 1993, as a result of lower oil prices, persistent structural problems and reduced external demand. Output in the mineral-exporting countries was estimated to have declined by 3.2 per cent, following a 3.6 per cent fall in 1992, whereas beverage-exporting States were expected to have registered a 3.2 per cent growth, compared with a 0.3 per cent fall in 1992.

Manufacturing value-added increased by a mere 1.3 per cent in 1993, from a decline of 0.8 per cent in 1992. The manufacturing sector was adversely affected by a host of structural problems, including the non-availability and high cost of imported inputs, difficulties with domestic supply of raw materials and rising costs of labour, credit and other supporting facilities. Civil wars and widespread political conflicts paralysed industrial production in many countries resulting in the virtual stagnation of industrial output. Drastic reduction of public investment under structural adjustment programmes, coupled with a lack of private and foreign investment also weakened the industrial sectors.

In the mining sector, total oil production fell by an estimated 1.1 per cent to 338.2 million tons, as a result of lower outputs in member States of the Organization of Petroleum Exporting Countries (OPEC) (Algeria and the Libyan Arab Jamahiriya) and in Angola, Cameroon and Tunisia. Oil production increased only in the Congo, Egypt and Nigeria. Overall mineral production was hard hit by the collapse of the mining industry in Zaire, a drop in international prices of ores and metals and sluggish growth of the world economy and the destabilization of markets by unusually large volumes of mineral exports from countries of the former USSR.

The annual inflation rate decreased slightly in 1993 but remained high at 35.5 per cent, compared with 40 per cent in 1992, largely as a result of the impact of devaluation of national currencies, removal of subsidies, higher tariffs on utilities and the rise in import prices which coincided with generally poor output growth. The greatest inflationary tendencies were in Nigeria, Sudan, Zaire, Zambia and Zimbabwe. However, the franc zone economies (Benin, Cameroon, Central African Republic, Chad, Comoros, Congo, Côte d'Ivoire, Equatorial Guinea, Gabon, Mali, Niger, Senegal, Togo) had an average inflation of only 1.4 per cent.

The average budget deficit as a proportion of GDP was 6.5 per cent in the 1992/93 fiscal year, an increase from 5.4 per cent the previous year. However, many countries pursued rigorous fiscal measures aimed at rationalizing expenditure through reducing wage bills and retrenching staff in the wider public sector. On the revenue side, an increasing number of countries were placing more emphasis on revenue generation through broadening the tax base, changing the tax rate and improving the collection of revenue arrears. Some rationalization measures, however, caused substantial economic dislocations in the development of infrastructure, health and education services and aggravated overall unemployment and poverty.

External debt

Africa's external debt reached $285.4 billion in 1993, a 2.4 per cent increase over 1992. The debt-to-GDP ratio increased to 95.9 per cent of regional GDP, from 89.6 per cent in 1992. The debt/export ratio also rose from 287.4 per cent in 1992 to 288.9 per cent in 1993. Actual debt services, however, fell slightly from 26.3 per cent of exports to 24.4 per cent, due to debt rescheduling for major indebted countries, but remained unmanageable for the greater number of States. In addition, some 21 per cent of the African debt was owed to multilateral institutions, which could not engage in debt rescheduling in accordance with their statutes. The debt burden compromised the creditworthiness of most Governments and imposed additional constraints on their ability to obtain new credits and loans. During the year, there was no change in the strategy adopted by the donor community to address the African debt problem, nor any measurable progress in implementing recent initiatives on debt.

Agriculture

Total agricultural output for the region as a whole grew by 3.1 per cent in 1993, compared to a decline of 3.7 per cent in 1992, owing to favourable rainfall in southern Africa after the severe drought the previous year. Food production rose by 3.3 per cent, having decreased by 3.7 per cent in 1992. Total cereal output reached 80.3 million tons from 70.1 million tons in 1992, representing a 15 per cent increase. The cereal crop increased from 9.8 million tons to 19.6 million tons in East and southern Africa, but declined by 1.1 million tons, to 8.7 million tons, in such countries as Algeria, the Libyan Arab Jamahiriya, Morocco and Tunisia. The production of roots and tubers increased by 12 per cent, from 81.9 million tons to some 91.7 million tons in 1993, owing largely to a 48 per cent expansion in Nigeria, which compensated for production shortages in strife-torn Angola, Burundi, Liberia, Rwanda and elsewhere. The production of coffee and tea was also on the rise, while cocoa output declined by 4 per cent, from 1,287 tons in 1992 to 1,236 tons in 1993. Production gains in coffee and tea were offset, however, by declining world prices for those commodities. In an effort to boost agricultural exports, many African countries continued to pursue liberalization policies. However, despite the increase in agricultural output, the aggregate food aid needs of the region for 1993-1994 remained high, with 14 countries financing exceptional food emergencies and drought relief and recovery continuing to be a major focus of agricultural development policy.

Trade

Africa's external sector continued to be affected by falling export prices, deteriorating terms of trade, compressed imports, rising debt and reduced resource flows. Despite an impressive 8 per cent growth in the volume of African exports, their value decreased by 0.2 per cent to $74.3 billion in 1993, following a 1.7 per cent contraction in 1992. The oil-exporting countries accounted for $47.6 billion, or 64.1 per cent, of the region's total exports, compared with $50.2 billion, or 67.5 per cent, in 1992. The drop of 12 per cent resulted from the decline in oil prices. At the same time, import values rose by 1.3 per cent to $75.9 billion, with volumes increasing by 3.5 per cent. Thus, Africa's terms of trade deteriorated by 5.5 per cent in 1993, compared with a 4.1 per cent drop the previous year.

As a result of those trends in exports and imports, coupled with the persistent deficit on the services account, Africa's overall balance of payments amounted to a deficit of some $500 million, compared to a surplus of $700 million in 1992. The trade balance and services account registered higher deficits in 1993 and unrequited transfers grew by $400 million. Total ODA receipts by developing Africa fell from $24.7 billion in 1991 to $23.3 billion in 1992, which included a decline from $17.2 billion to $16.7 billion in sub-Saharan Africa alone.

Subregional economic performance

Central Africa was the continent's only subregion to register a negative growth rate in 1993, with output falling by 4.6 per cent, following a 4.8 per cent contraction in 1992. GDP fell by 13 per cent in Zaire, after a 12 per cent decline the previous year, as the continuing political and economic crisis paralysed that country's institutions and brought its major economic infrastructure into a state of disrepair. The subregion's three oil-producing countries (Cameroon, Congo and Gabon) also experienced serious economic difficulties. Economic growth in North Africa fell to 0.8 per cent in 1993 from 0.9 per cent in 1992, due largely to the drought in the Maghreb countries and difficulties in the oil sector, with the exception being Tunisia which recorded a 4.1 per cent increase in GDP. In West Africa, 1992/93 was a good agricultural season and, as a result, GDP increased by 2.7 per cent, although slightly down from the 3 per cent growth level experienced the previous year. Nigeria, the largest economy in the subregion, grew by 4.5 per cent, somewhat slower than in 1992. Southern Africa's aggregate output rose by 1.2 per cent, after a 1.3 per cent decline in 1992, while that of East Africa grew by 2.6 per cent, compared with a fall of 1.4 per cent the previous year. A huge 9.3 per cent increase was registered in Ethiopia, as the country was recovering from years of low output growth because of civil war and drought, while the Sudan's economy expanded by an estimated 5.9 per cent, down from 12.9 per cent in 1992.

The economies of Africa's least developed countries (LDCs) grew by 1.9 per cent in 1993, having contracted by 0.7 per cent in 1992. The positive growth rate was mainly due to the improved performance of the Sahel group, whose GDP increased by 2.4 per cent. The economic performance of many LDCs, however, was adversely affected by the decline in their terms of trade, insufficient ODA flows and the growing burden of debt service obligations, as well as by political conflicts and civil wars, which were destroying physical and social infrastructure and precipitating an escalation of refugees and displaced persons.

Social trends

Unemployment, poor health facilities, high levels of illiteracy and general instability characterized the social scene in Africa in 1993.[20] The situation was aggravated by internal strife, political crisis and civil war in several countries and by the high social cost of adjustment programmes, as previous economic strategies paid scant attention to social development issues. Unemployment continued to be a major problem, with few countries having any effective plan to combat it, and the development of the rural sector was marginal in contrast to the limited progress made in respect of urban development. The legacy of the region's economic crisis in the 1980s continued to manifest itself in deteriorating social and human conditions and escalating absolute and relative poverty. An estimated 220 million Africans—almost half of the population in sub-Saharan Africa—lived in absolute poverty, unable to meet their most basic needs. Efforts to overcome problems of education and health were still wanting in the face of high population growth and inadequate resources.

As national development strategies were characterized by massive underinvestment in human and social development, due priority had to be given to social planning and social programmes, focusing on employment generation, poverty alleviation, environmental protection, family planning, health, education, and the nutrition of Africa's children. Efforts for social integration also focused on the protection of children's rights and welfare, promotion of the status of women and enhancement of the capacity of African families to meet their socio-economic needs.

Activities in 1993

The biennial report of the Executive Secretary for 1992-1993[21] focused on ECA's activities to promote reform measures and bring about structural change in the region, as advocated in major regional development policy and strategy frameworks such as the 1980 Lagos Plan of Action,[22] the United Nations New Agenda for the Development of Africa in the 1990s,[3] the African Alternative Framework to Structural Adjustment Programmes for Socio-Economic Recovery and Transformation (AAF-SAP)[23] and the Abuja Treaty establishing the African Economic Community. Those activities covered a wide range of issues and concerns, including development policies, human resources development and utilization, information systems development, economic cooperation and integration, agriculture and rural development, marine affairs, special problems of the least developed, land-locked and island developing countries, public administration and fiscal affairs, social development, women in development, the environment and development, human settlements, industrial development, trade development and cooperation, the external debt crisis, monetary and financial policies and strategies, natural resources and energy, science and technology, population, transport and communications, tourism, and statistical development. The report grouped the activities under four main categories, namely conferences and meetings; research and analysis; information packaging and dissemination; and technical assistance through advisory services, workshops, seminars and training, fellowships and operational field projects.

Development policy and regional economic cooperation activities

At its 1993 meeting, the ECA Technical Preparatory Committee of the Whole reviewed a preliminary study of proposed strategies for financial resource mobilization[6] to implement the New Agenda during the period 1993-2005. Africa's external financial requirements for that period were estimated at $950 billion, comprising $490 billion for debt-service obligations and $460 billion for capital investment. However, the dominant share of gross domestic investment had to be financed from domestic savings—between 52 and 78 per cent in the lower-income group of countries and between 87 and 93 per cent in the upper-income group. To meet the growth target set in the New Agenda, gross domestic investment in the former group had to increase to 26 per cent of GDP in 1993, 40.7 per cent in 1998 and 37.3 per cent in 2005, and in the latter group to 24.4 per cent, 32.8 per cent and 33.5 per cent. In turn, that strategy required the gross domestic savings rate to reach 20.5 per cent of GDP in 1993, 26.1 per cent in 1998 and 19.5 per cent in 2005 in the former group and 22.9 per cent, 28.6 per cent and 31.4 per cent for the same years in the latter group.

The Committee emphasized the importance of the region's public and private sectors in boosting aggregate savings rates and urged African Governments to draw a lesson from Asian countries in that regard. It called on them to improve conditions conducive to the mobilization of domestic resources, particularly through the establishment of a peaceful political, social and economic environment as a prerequisite for attracting foreign investment.

Having considered proposals for implementing the Abuja Treaty,[7] the Committee noted that regional cooperation and economic integration were key to Africa's accelerated economic development and stressed the need to establish national institutional mechanisms to deal with those issues.

In May,[24] the Conference of Ministers called on member States to speed up the ratification of the Treaty and its protocols and establish sound structures to further the objectives of the African Economic Community. It urged ECA, OAU and the African Development Bank (AfDB) to assist in furthering subregional economic integration

programmes and in setting up self-financed mechanisms to fund Community activities, and appealed for measures to facilitate the integration of subregional economic institutions.

In a 4 May resolution on strategic objectives for Africa's economic development in the 1990s,[14] the Conference called on African Governments to boost their economies' absorptive capacities for external resources, improve their investment climate and implement financial sector reforms to raise the gross domestic saving rate to 25 to 30 per cent of GDP and the gross domestic investment rate to the range of 30 to 35 per cent. The Ministers appealed for increased ODA to the continent, the opening of external markets to Africa's non-traditional agricultural and industrial exports and for external measures to encourage investment and reduce the region's external debt.

The ECA secretariat and MULPOCs coordinated their efforts to assist subregional economic groupings to rationalize their respective programmes. In March, the five MULPOCs organized meetings of their intergovernmental committees of experts for each subregion, to review progress made in economic cooperation and integration at the subregional level. A joint meeting of chief executives of African intergovernmental organizations and United Nations specialized agencies (Addis Ababa, April) considered system-wide proposals for the implementation of the Abuja Treaty, while a conference of chief executives of ECA-sponsored institutions, also held in April, examined proposals for merging and streamlining their activities. A regional seminar on the African Economic Community was conducted in July.

ECA's annual report, covering 7 May 1993 to 5 May 1994,[25] noted that the Multidisciplinary Regional Advisory Group provided technical support for training, seminars and workshops for improving public sector performance, privatization and public enterprise, public financial management, and strengthening the capabilities of national and subregional training and research institutions.

Major reports prepared by ECA in the socio-economic area included a survey of economic and social conditions in Africa for 1992/1993 and an annual economic report on the region which reviewed the economic situation in African countries, including the structure of GDP, developments in major economic sectors, development policy analysis, assessment of trade and balance of payments, debt issues, general forecasts for the region as a whole and its main subregions, as well as the implications for growth and development. Other studies dealt with issues of production bases, strategic planning of the food sector, trade structures and liberalization in the context of structural adjustment programmes, the debt crisis, policy constraints in implementing health programmes, the continent's growth performance, determinants for private investment and macroeconomic policy responses to external shocks in Africa. ECA also organized an ad hoc expert group meeting on the revitalization of investment for Africa's development (Addis Ababa, 29 November–1 December).

The United Nations Trust Fund for African Development continued to finance various projects in the economic and social fields. At a biennial pledging conference, held in conjunction with ECA's 1993 session, the Fund received total contributions in excess of $1 million, compared with $285,000 in 1991. Also at the 1993 session, the Commission recommended for adoption by the Economic and Social Council a resolution on the African Institute for Economic Development and Planning.[(26)]

ECONOMIC AND SOCIAL COUNCIL ACTION

On 30 July, the Economic and Social Council, on the recommendation of its Economic Committee, adopted **resolution 1993/68** without vote.

African Institute for Economic Development and Planning

The Economic and Social Council,

Recalling resolutions 285(XII) of 28 February 1975, 433(XVII) of 30 April 1982, 537(XX) of 29 April 1985, 574(XXI) of 19 April 1986, 612(XXII) of 24 April 1987 and 622(XXIII) of 15 April 1988 of the Conference of Ministers of the Economic Commission for Africa on the financing and future development of the African Institute for Economic Development and Planning,

Recalling also resolutions 669(XXIV) of 7 April 1989 and 680(XXV) of 19 May 1990 of the Conference of Ministers of the Economic Commission for Africa, in which the Conference of Ministers appealed to the General Assembly, as a matter of urgency, to approve the incorporation of four core posts of the Institute into the regular budget,

Bearing in mind resolution 726(XXVII) of 22 April 1992 of the Conference of Ministers of the Economic Commission for Africa on strengthening the Economic Commission for Africa to face Africa's development challenges in the 1990s, in which the Conference of Ministers expressed gratitude to the General Assembly for providing the Institute with a grant to cover the costs of four Professional posts for the biennium 1992-1993, thus enabling the Institute to contribute to the process of strengthening the operational capacity of the Commission in meeting the challenges facing Africa in the 1990s,

Recalling its resolutions 1985/62 of 26 July 1985 and 1990/72 of 27 July 1990, in which the Council, *inter alia*, recommended the incorporation of four core Professional posts into the United Nations regular budget as a contribution to the long-term financing of the Institute and to enable it to carry out its approved work programme and functions on a continued and sustained basis,

Noting that the Joint Inspection Unit, after a thorough examination of the Institute's situation, had recommended in its 1990 report that eight permanent posts be created in the regular budget to erase annual uncertainty about the Institute's budget and to offset dependency on United Nations Development Programme funding,

Bearing in mind that United Nations Development Programme policy requires that funding of core posts in institutions such as the African Institute for Economic Development and Planning should be discouraged, and that the Programme is currently supporting a preparatory-phase project designed to improve operational capacities for research, short-term training and networking, advisory/consultancy services and management audit,

Commending the increasing efforts of member States to meet their obligations to the Institute on a regular basis by paying their annual assessed contributions,

Noting with appreciation that the resources put at the disposal of the Institute, in the form of a grant for the four Professional posts for the years 1991 to 1993, have been productively used and that recent achievements in revitalizing the Institute and in improving its delivery capacities would not have been realized without those resources,

Noting with interest the increasingly successful attempts to generate independent income by various means and to develop operational projects for possible funding from diversified bilateral and other donor agencies,

Convinced that, with the expansion in the fields of its activities to include subject areas related to development management in general, the Institute will, in future years, play an even more important role in the promotion of the sustained development of Africa,

Considering that the Institute is the only bilingual regional institution of its kind in Africa and that it has an outstanding record of providing training and research services to African countries in the area of economic development and planning,

Considering also that there are increasing demands being made by member States and their intergovernmental organizations for the services of the Institute, particularly for tailor-made training programmes,

Considering further that counterpart United Nations institutions in other regions have benefited from regular budget posts,

Conscious of the urgency of stabilizing the financing of the core posts in the Institute,

1. *Calls upon* the General Assembly, in considering the proposed programme budget for the Economic Commission for Africa for the biennium 1994-1995, to take adequate steps to ensure sufficient staffing at the Professional level for the Commission to implement its mandates;

2. *Appeals* to all States to provide extrabudgetary resources for programme implementation, as requested in the Institute's component of the proposed programme budget for the Commission for the biennium 1994-1995;

3. *Requests* all States to sustain their support to the Institute through payment of their contributions and increased use of the various types of services it provides;

4. *Urges* the Executive Secretary of the Economic Commission for Africa and the management of the Institute to continue their efforts to mobilize extrabudgetary and other supplementary resources in order to enable the Institute to implement its expanded programmes.

Economic and Social Council resolution 1993/68

30 July 1993   Meeting 46   Adopted without vote

Approved by Economic Committee (E/1993/109) without vote, 23 July (meeting 14); draft by ECA (E/1993/85), orally amended following informal consultations; agenda item 14.

Financial implications. S-G, E/1993/85/Add.1.

GENERAL ASSEMBLY ACTION

By **decision 48/454** of 21 December, the General Assembly endorsed the Council's resolution and agreed to take steps to meet ECA's staffing requirements under the 1994-1995 programme budget.

Statistical development

During the year, the ECA secretariat continued to provide assistance in implementing the Addis Ababa Plan of Action for Statistical Development in Africa in the 1990s[27] and to support national programmes in the collection, analysis and dissemination of socio-economic statistics. The Coordinating Committee on African Statistical Development held its annual meeting at Addis Ababa in July. The secretariat produced draft guidelines for the development of quantitative indicators for monitoring statistical development and guidelines for statistical needs assessment and strategy development. It assisted 14 countries in conducting needs assessment and strategy development exercises and undertook some 45 technical advisory missions to provide on-the-job training in the area of statistics. The secretariat issued a publication on African socio-economic indicators for 1992, a bibliography of African statistical publications for 1992-1993 and the *African Statistical Yearbook, 1990-1991, Volume I, Part 2: West Africa* and *Volume I, Part 3: East and Southern Africa.* Other publications related to the contribution of women to statistics in the informal sector, the role of the International Comparison Programme in strengthening price statistics, development of statistical databases and the impact of new technology on statistical computing and concepts, definition and classification used in Africa's demographic surveys.

Information for development

The Regional Technical Committee for the Pan-African Development Information System (PADIS), at its sixth meeting (Addis Ababa, 21 and 22 April), reviewed activities of subregional centres—the West African Development Information System (WADIS) and the East and Southern African Development Information System (ESADIS), the latter having become operational in February 1993. In May, ECA, on the recommendation of the meeting, requested the General Assembly, through the Economic and Social Council, to ensure staffing and resources to strengthen information systems development for regional cooperation and integration in Africa.[28] The Council and the Assembly both took action on that request (see below). The

Subregional Technical Committee for PADIS in North Africa also held a meeting in 1993 (Tangier, Morocco, 30 March-3 April).

PADIS continued to assist member States to improve their information infrastructure in support of development planning and management through feasibility and needs assessment missions, training in software and database management and information management methodologies, and in the use of electronic mail and computer-mediated communications. Workshops were organized on networking among libraries and documentation centres in southern Africa (Harare, Zimbabwe, February), communication in Ethiopian government offices (Addis Ababa, 6-8 December) and electronic communications for West African universities (Accra, Ghana, 15-17 December).

PADIS continued to publish its quarterly newsletter on information management and technology in the region and produced databases on socio-economic, scientific and technical aspects of development in Africa and on African experts in those aspects.

ECONOMIC AND SOCIAL COUNCIL ACTION

On 30 July, the Economic and Social Council, on the recommendation of its Economic Committee, adopted **resolution 1993/67** without vote.

Strengthening development information systems for regional cooperation and integration in Africa

The Economic and Social Council,

Concerned about the wide North-South gap in the flow of vital information and in the acquisition and utilization of information technology,

Conscious of the importance of information in fostering African regional cooperation and integration, in particular through the strengthening of existing regional groupings and the establishment of the African Economic Community,

Bearing in mind the need to establish data networks and databases as specified in the Treaty Establishing the African Economic Community, as well as the emphasis on information technology delineated in the Fourth Lomé Convention, signed at Lomé on 15 December 1989,

Recalling resolutions 716(XXVI) of 12 May 1991 and 726(XXVII) and 732(XXVII) of 22 April 1992 of the Conference of Ministers of the Economic Commission for Africa,

Appreciating the continuing support given by the International Development Research Centre to the Pan-African Development Information System in order to carry out activities to strengthen the information capabilities of member States,

Appreciating also the support given by eleven member States for the submission of the project on information technology for Africa for further consideration by the Commission of the European Communities in the framework of the Fourth Lomé Convention,

Noting with satisfaction the performance of the Pan-African Development Information System of the Economic

Commission for Africa in the delivery of technical assistance to member States,

Also noting with satisfaction the proposal of the Executive Secretary of the Economic Commission for Africa
to incorporate the activities of the System into the programme budget of the Commission,

Bearing in mind the need to strengthen the subregional
development information centres of the Commission as
information support for subregional economic cooperation and integration,

Noting with concern the decreasing availability of extrabudgetary resources for implementation and utilization
of development information systems and technology,

Also noting with concern the precarious financial situation of the Pan-African Development Information System and the need to end its reliance on extrabudgetary
sources of funding,

Welcoming the intention of the Secretary-General of the
United Nations to provide adequate resources for mandated programmes in Africa, with special attention to
those programmes in science and technology for development, in the preparation of the proposed programme
budget for the biennium 1994-1995,

1. *Requests* the Pan-African Development Information System to build elements of cost recovery into its
delivery of information services and products;

2. *Urges* member States, in order to receive further
needed technical assistance in information systems
development:

(a) To give priority to information systems development in the use of their United Nations Development
Programme country indicative planning figures;

(b) To consider development information activities
in their 1993 pledges to the United Nations Trust Fund
for African Development;

(c) To use, where appropriate, the financial provision
under the Fourth Lomé Convention for this purpose;

3. *Urgently appeals* to the donor community to support the activities of the Economic Commission for
Africa to strengthen development information capabilities in the African region;

4. *Requests* the Commission to continue its leadership role in the coordination of development information and technology to respond to pressing development
problems of Africa;

5. *Requests* the Executive Secretary of the Economic
Commission for Africa to seek additional resources,
through voluntary contributions, for the subregional development information centres of the Commission in
the framework of the subprogramme on statistical and
information systems development;

6. *Requests* the General Assembly to ensure the provision of adequate staffing and resources to permit the implementation of activities under the subprogramme of the
Commission on information systems development, beginning
with the programme budget for the biennium 1994-1995.

Economic and Social Council resolution 1993/67

30 July 1993   Meeting 46   Adopted without vote

Approved by Economic Committee (E/1993/109) without vote, 23 July (meeting 14); draft by ECA (E/1993/85/Add.1), orally amended following informal consultations; agenda item 14.
Financial implications. S-G, E/1993/85/Add.1.

GENERAL ASSEMBLY ACTION

By **decision 48/453** of 21 December, the General
Assembly endorsed the Council's resolution and

agreed to ensure the provision of staff and resources
to permit the delivery of activities on information
systems development under the 1994-1995 programme budget.

Public administration and finance

An international conference on development
management in Africa (Addis Ababa, 8-12 March)
reviewed the region's past experience, emerging
challenges and future priorities in that field and
emphasized the need for a new approach of shared
responsibility among national, regional and external actors to enhance development management
capacity in Africa. The conference adopted the
Strategic Agenda for Development Management
in Africa in the 1990s,[29] which identified priorities for enhancing development management, including improving the public policy-making process; enhancing efficiency and quality of African
civil services; promoting ethics and strengthening
accountability mechanisms as well as the resource
mobilization and financial management capacity
of African Governments; undertaking public enterprise sector reforms to improve public enterprise performance and privatization; promoting
economic and institutional decentralization for
sustained development; enhancing entrepreneurial capacity and promoting private sector development; ensuring effective popular participation
in development and governance; enhancing the
participation and skills of women in development
management; and optimizing the use of information technology in African public administration.

In May,[30] the Conference of Ministers endorsed the Strategic Agenda, recommended its use
as a guide for action by African Governments as
well as by regional and international organizations,
and requested the Executive Secretary to coordinate and monitor its implementation. It also
called on member States and international organizations to mobilize support to continue the Special Action Programme for Public Administration
and Management in Africa and to ensure the realization of the Agenda's objectives.

The secretariat's work in public administration
and fiscal affairs focused on research to identify
policy options and measures to improve the operations of public institutions and enhance their role
in the development process. It conducted studies
on improving government financial management,
tax reforms and administration. It organized a
national training workshop on senior financial
management in the public sector (Lusaka,
Zambia, March) and prepared a directory of African institutions offering management education
and training. Other areas of research dealt with
the legal and regulatory constraints to private sector development, strengthening of credit and capital markets and the development of human

resources, fiscal policies to promote indigenous private investment, assessment of the performance of reformed public and recently privatized enterprises, various approaches to privatization in Africa and measures for stimulating, developing and promoting indigenous entrepreneurial capability.

International trade and development finance

ECA activities in international trade and development finance continued to focus on mobilizing financial resources for development and Africa's international trade.

The Technical Preparatory Committee of the Whole considered issues related to the Uruguay Round of multilateral trade negotiations and their implications for Africa's trade. It expressed concern that issues of importance to African and other developing countries had been sidetracked in those negotiations and that could result in an inequitable international trading system after their conclusion. The Committee noted that, given its vulnerable position, Africa needed to be granted preferential treatment and longer transitional periods of adjustment for implementing structural reforms. The Committee also observed that the region's access to markets of industrialized countries was becoming more restricted and called on African States to exercise pragmatism in their trade liberalization policies. It underlined the need for members of the African, Caribbean and Pacific (ACP) Group to prepare for the mid-term review of the Lomé IV Convention on trade between the Group and the European Community. On the Committee's recommendation, the Conference of Ministers called on African countries to establish strong common positions on key issues in the forthcoming mid-term review of the Lomé Convention, with the objective of expanding their exports to the European Community.[31]

In 1993, the secretariat assisted African countries to formulate and implement policies and measures to expand domestic and intra-African trade and the continent's international trade, alleviate the debt burden and improve their debt management capabilities and to facilitate monetary and financial integration in Africa. It undertook studies on Africa's competitiveness in traditional markets, on its export prospects after the Uruguay Round, on mechanisms for facilitating the development of rural trade and stabilizing export earnings and on factors contributing to the underdevelopment of African domestic trade. It also continued to publish the *African Trade Bulletin* and its *Flash* newsletter on trade opportunities and issued an African trade directory dealing with the external debt crisis and the fourth edition of a directory of chambers of commerce, agriculture and mines.

The secretariat initiated the creation of a database on the region's external debt profile and organized a seminar on the impact of declining commodity prices on Africa's capacity to grow and service its external debt (Addis Ababa, 15 and 16 November), followed by a workshop on ways of alleviating Africa's debt burden (Addis Ababa, 17 and 18 November).

The Conference of African Ministers of Trade (twelfth session, Tunis, Tunisia, 22-24 October)[32] considered issues related to the region's effective participation in international trade, the impact of the Uruguay Round and preparations for the mid-term review of the Lomé IV Convention, focusing on policies, strategies and measures to foster an enabling environment for Africa's trade. The Conference also discussed the continuing decline in prices of commodities of export interest to Africa, the role of the private sector in promoting intra-African trade, and policy measures to enhance the role of women in domestic trade and to facilitate the development of rural trade through the provision of services and rural credit. The Conference adopted the Tunis Declaration on the Uruguay Round of Multilateral Trade Negotiations and agreed that an international conference on technical assistance to African countries to assist them to adapt their economies to the new trade environment should be organized jointly by ECA, OAU, UNCTAD and GATT. It also adopted recommendations concerning the promotion and expansion of intra-African trade and strategies for the revitalization, recovery and growth of Africa's trade in the 1990s and beyond.

Transnational corporations

Activities of the Joint ECA/UNCTAD Unit on Transnational Corporations (TNCs) focused on research to encourage private sector activities and enhance the role of foreign direct investment (FDI) in the financing of African development. The Unit carried out case studies on FDI from developing countries, the role of trading TNCs on industrialization in developing countries, investment flows from Central and Eastern Europe, Japanese FDI and prospects for future increased activity, and technology transfer through Japanese foreign investment.

Industrial development

The secretariat continued to assist member States in formulating and implementing industrial policies and programmes aimed at the revitalization and restructuring of the region's industrial sector. It published the annual bulletin entitled *Focus on African Industry* and a study of investment and financial policies and their impact on the development of indigenous industries. It organized an ad hoc expert group meeting on the possibility of producing basic chemicals from natural gas and a seminar on policy options for Africa in the 1990s in the light of the report of the South Commission on South-South economic cooperation (Addis Ababa, 15 and 16 September) (see PART THREE, Chapter I).

In the context of the second Industrial Development Decade for Africa (IDDA II), 1993-2002, publications were issued on lessons and experiences from selected newly industrialized countries for the Decade's implementation, application of compact mini-plant technology to manufacture steel products in African countries and production and utilization of nitrogen, phosphate and potash fertilizers in Africa and perspectives for their integrated development, as well as a technical handbook on composite and non-wheat flours. The secretariat provided technical assistance to promote 11 selected subregional projects in the priority areas of metal, chemicals, engineering and agro-industries and organized an ad hoc expert group meeting on the promotion of investment in industrial projects (Addis Ababa, 22-25 November).

Second Industrial Development Decade for Africa

The ECA Technical Preparatory Committee of the Whole emphasized the need for harmonization and coordination of the programme of IDDA II, which was endorsed by the Economic and Social Council in 1992[33] and later adopted by the General Assembly,[34] and the programme of the Second United Nations Transport and Communications Decade in Africa (see below). The Committee considered a proposed programme for the coordination of activities.[35] In May, on the Committee's recommendation, the Conference of Ministers adopted a resolution on IDDA II,[36] elements of which were included in action taken by the Economic and Social Council later in the year.

The Conference of African Ministers of Industry (Port Louis, Mauritius, 31 May–3 June) adopted the Plan of Action for the harmonization of the implementation of IDDA II and requested the Executive Secretary of ECA and the Director-General of the United Nations Industrial Development Organization (UNIDO) to take concrete action to coordinate related activities. The Conference called on African Governments, ECA and UNIDO to support the development of the private sector for the accelerated implementation of IDDA II and the development of basic industries for the structural transformation of African economies. It adopted the Mauritius Declaration on Africa's accelerated industrial recovery and development in the context of IDDA II and beyond, underscoring the importance of the private sector and natural resource-based core industries in the continent's self-reliant and self-sustained development. It also

adopted the African common position for the fifth session of the General Conference of UNIDO, to be held at Yaoundé, Cameroon, in December (see PART SIX, Chapter XVII). That common position emphasized the importance of UNIDO's contribution to the implementation of IDDA II, human resources development through industrial and technical training, the development and transfer of technology and rehabilitation of existing industries, industrialization of African LDCs, external debt and the industrial sector and new concepts and approaches for industrial development cooperation.

Follow-up meetings on the implementation of subregional programmes for IDDA II were held for West Africa (Abidjan, Côte d'Ivoire, 14-18 June), North Africa (Tunis, 22-26 November) and eastern and southern Africa (Addis Ababa, 16-19 December).

ECONOMIC AND SOCIAL COUNCIL ACTION

On 30 July, the Economic and Social Council, on the recommendation of its Economic Committee, adopted **resolution 1993/62** without vote.

Second Industrial Development Decade for Africa (1993-2002), and fifth session of the General Conference of the United Nations Industrial Development Organization

The Economic and Social Council,

Recalling decision IDB.9/Dec.16 of 22 May 1992 of the Industrial Development Board of the United Nations Industrial Development Organization, in which the Board accepted the offer of the Government of Cameroon to act as host to the fifth session of the General Conference of the United Nations Industrial Development Organization at Yaoundé from 6 to 10 December 1993,

Considering the importance of the Conference, one of whose objectives will be to reassess the role and mission of the United Nations Industrial Development Organization with a view to increasing its effectiveness and enabling it to respond more fully to the needs and interests of all member States, in particular developing countries,

Bearing in mind the joint African position on the revitalization of the United Nations Industrial Development Organization adopted by the Conference of African Ministers of Industry at its eleventh meeting, held at Port Louis from 31 May to 3 June 1993,

Aware of the need to give high priority to the implementation of the programme for the Second Industrial Development Decade for Africa,

1. *Invites* Member States and intergovernmental organizations to participate in the fifth session of the General Conference of the United Nations Industrial Development Organization;

2. *Calls for* a constructive dialogue between industrialized and developing countries, with a view to taking satisfactorily into account the legitimate interests and aspirations of Africa in the field of industrialization;

3. *Notes with satisfaction* the offer of the Government of Cameroon to act as host to the fifth session of the

General Conference of the United Nations Industrial Development Organization;

4. *Welcomes* the measures adopted and those still to be taken by the Government of Cameroon with a view to ensuring the success of the Conference, and invites States Members and the organizations of the United Nations system to contribute to its full success.

Economic and Social Council resolution 1993/62

30 July 1993   Meeting 46   Adopted without vote

Approved by Economic Committee (E/1993/109) without vote, 22 July (meeting 13); 14-nation draft (E/1993/C.1/L.3), orally revised following informal consultations; agenda item 14.
Sponsors: Algeria, Benin, Botswana, Cameroon, Cuba, Ethiopia, Guinea, Kenya, Morocco, Nigeria, Senegal, Swaziland, United Republic of Tanzania, Yemen.

On the same date, the Council, also on the recommendation of its Economic Committee, adopted **resolution 1993/65** without vote.

Second Industrial Development Decade for Africa
The Economic and Social Council,

Recalling General Assembly resolution 44/237 of 22 December 1989, by which the Assembly proclaimed the period 1991-2000 the Second Industrial Development Decade for Africa,

Taking note of General Assembly resolution 47/177 of 22 December 1992, in which the Assembly adopted the programme for the Second Decade and decided to adjust the period for the programme for the Decade to cover the years 1993-2002,

Bearing in mind resolution 739(XXVII) and decision 1 (XXVII) of 22 April 1992, of the Conference of Ministers of the Economic Commission for Africa,

Aware of the need to harmonize the Second Industrial Development Decade for Africa and the Second Transport and Communications Decade in Africa,

Considering the relevant provisions of Agenda 21, adopted by the United Nations Conference on Environment and Development,

1. *Notes* that the Conference of African Ministers of Industry, at its eleventh meeting, held at Port Louis from 31 May to 3 June 1993, examined the plan of action to harmonize the Second Industrial Development Decade for Africa and the Second Transport and Communications Decade in Africa and made recommendations thereon;

2. *Reiterates* its appeal to the United Nations Development Programme to consider allocating under the regional component of its fifth programming cycle for Africa (1992-1996) adequate resources for supporting the activities of the programme for the Second Industrial Development Decade for Africa;

3. *Appeals* to financial institutions, in particular the World Bank and the African Development Bank, to consider providing full support to the programme for the Second Industrial Development Decade for Africa and to contribute effectively to the financing of identified projects in the implementation of the programme at the national, subregional and regional levels;

4. *Urges* African countries to give priority to the mobilization of their own financial resources, through increased domestic savings and better management of national resources, for the financing and implementation of the programme for the Second Decade;

5. *Invites* African countries and African development institutions to take the measures necessary to create an enabling environment conducive to domestic, foreign, private and public industrial investment;

6. *Urges* African countries to promote the private sector and to involve it fully in decision-making and in the implementation of the programme for the Second Decade;

7. *Invites* African countries to provide adequate support to African entrepreneurs in order to promote the development of small- and medium-scale industries;

8. *Requests* the General Assembly to provide adequate resources to the Economic Commission for Africa for the Second Decade, especially to strengthen industrial cooperation in the implementation of the programme for the Decade;

9. *Requests* the Executive Secretary of the Economic Commission for Africa and the Director-General of the United Nations Industrial Development Organization to harmonize further their activities to support member States in their efforts to ensure the effective implementation of the Second Decade.

Economic and Social Council resolution 1993/65

30 July 1993   Meeting 46   Adopted without vote

Approved by Economic Committee (E/1993/109) without vote, 23 July (meeting 14); draft by ECA (E/1993/85/Add.1), orally amended following informal consultations; agenda item 14.
Financial implications. S-G, E/1993/85/Add.1.

GENERAL ASSEMBLY ACTION

By **decision 48/456** of 21 December, the General Assembly endorsed the Council resolution on IDDA II and agreed to provide adequate resources for the Decade's implementation.

Transport and communications

Activities in the field of transport and communications focused on projects dealing with human resources and institutional development, transport data gathering and processing for the eventual establishment of a transport database, and the feasibility of manufacturing transport equipment in Africa. The secretariat organized an ad hoc expert group meeting to review guidelines on development of subregional cooperation in shipping and issued guidelines for improving clearing and forwarding operations in the region, management of shipping, coordination among port authorities and port users, inland water port efficiency and intra-African mail routing plans, developing human resources in freight forwarding and efficient transport chains along transit corridors. The secretariat prepared a report on the status of cooperation among African ports and its promotion for an intergovernmental meeting of African port experts and senior officials and published newsletters on activities of the Second United Nations Transport and Communications Decade in Africa.

Transport and Communications Decade

The Conference of African Ministers of Transport, Communications and Planning (ninth meeting, Addis Ababa, 12 and 13 March) reviewed the implementation of the Second United Nations Transport and Communications Decade in Africa

(UNTACDA II), which was adopted by the Economic and Social Council in 1991[37] and endorsed by the General Assembly later that year.[38] Acting on the recommendation of the Conference, the ECA Conference of Ministers adopted a resolution on UNTACDA II,[39] which the Economic and Social Council drew on later in the year in taking action on the subject. Also on the Conference's recommendation, the Ministers appealed to African Governments to give priority to the employment of skilled Africans, particularly in the transport and communications sector, and the establishment of an incentive package to retain such skilled manpower, and called on agencies financing projects in Africa to use skilled Africans in implementing those projects.[40]

In other action,[41] the Conference of Ministers decided to reactivate the Trans-African Highway Bureau and called for every effort to enable the Bureau to start functioning in 1994. In response to that resolution, a meeting of plenipotentiaries (Rabat, Morocco, 14 September) adopted the statutes of the Bureau, which were to become effective after their ratification by 26 member States.

ECONOMIC AND SOCIAL COUNCIL ACTION

On 30 July, the Economic and Social Council, on the recommendation of its Economic Committee, adopted **resolution 1993/66** without vote.

Second Transport and Communications Decade in Africa

The Economic and Social Council,

Recalling resolution 710(XXVI) of 12 May 1991 of the Conference of Ministers of the Economic Commission for Africa, in which the Conference of Ministers adopted the programme for the Second Transport and Communications Decade in Africa,

Recalling also its resolution 1991/83 of 26 July 1991, in which it requested the General Assembly formally to launch the Second Transport and Communications Decade in Africa,

Referring to General Assembly decision 46/456 of 20 December 1991, in which the Assembly approved the programme for the Second Decade, including the provision of resources for its implementation,

Referring also to resolutions 91/84 of 8 February 1991 and 93/89 of 12 March 1993 of the Conference of African Ministers of Transport, Communications and Planning,

Having considered the report of the Conference of African Ministers of Transport, Communications and Planning on its ninth meeting, held in Addis Ababa on 12 and 13 March 1993,

Bearing in mind that the first mid-term evaluation and review of the programme for the Second Decade is scheduled to take place in 1994,

Noting that new projects are to be prepared for inclusion in the programme in 1995,

Recognizing the importance of resource mobilization and other promotional activities for the successful implementation of the programme for the Second Decade and the new projects at the national, subregional and regional levels,

Noting with appreciation the immense support that the United Nations Development Programme has provided for the preparation and launching of the programme for the Second Decade,

1. *Requests* the Governing Council of the United Nations Development Programme to consider favourably and to continue to finance activities in support of the implementation of the programme for the Second Transport and Communications Decade in Africa during the fifth programming cycle of the United Nations Development Programme;

2. *Appeals* to individual African and international financial institutions to increase their support for and facilitate the financing of projects and activities of the programme for the Second Decade;

3. *Appeals* to African member States to ensure and actively pursue the implementation of the new projects to be included in the programme for the Decade;

4. *Calls upon* the member institutions of the Resource Mobilization Committee for the Second Transport and Communications Decade in Africa, especially the African Development Bank as Chairman of the Committee, to carry out resource mobilization and promotional activities to enhance the successful implementation of the programme;

5. *Requests* the Economic Commission for Africa, in its capacity as lead agency, together with all the relevant mechanisms of the Second Transport and Communications Decade:

(a) To carry out in 1994 the first mid-term evaluation of the programme for the Second Decade, as stipulated in the implementation strategy;

(b) To revise the objectives and strategy of the programme for the Second Decade in the light of changed circumstances, if need be, in consultation with member States;

(c) To assist member States and African intergovernmental organizations to prepare and screen new projects for inclusion in the programme in 1995 as stipulated in the programme implementation plan, in consultation with member States;

(d) To organize two regional workshops on the Second Decade to disseminate the strategy and promote the objectives of the Second Decade in Africa;

6. *Requests* the General Assembly to provide the Economic Commission for Africa, in its capacity as lead agency for the Second Decade, with adequate resources, allocated within the regular budget, to enable it to carry out effectively and efficiently the activities listed in paragraphs 5 *(a)* to *(d)* above;

7. *Requests* the Executive Secretary of the Economic Commission for Africa to report to the Conference of Ministers at its twentieth meeting on the progress made in the implementation of the present resolution.

Economic and Social Council resolution 1993/66

30 July 1993   Meeting 46   Adopted without vote

Approved by Economic Committee (E/1993/109) without vote, 23 July (meeting 14); draft by ECA (E/1993/85/Add.1), orally amended following informal consultations; agenda item 14.
Financial implications. S-G, E/1993/85/Add.1.

By **decision 48/455** of 21 December, the General Assembly endorsed the Council's resolution and agreed to provide adequate resources for the Decade's implementation.

Europe-Africa permanent link through the Strait of Gibraltar

In response to a 1991 Economic and Social Council request,[42] the Secretary-General submitted a June evaluation report, prepared by the Executive Secretaries of ECA and ECE, on the Europe-Africa permanent link through the Strait of Gibraltar.[43] The report analysed studies carried out on the project between 1982 and 1992, under 1980 and 1989 cooperation agreements between Morocco and Spain, dealing with its geological, economic and legal aspects, as well as with traffic estimates and the feasibility of a tunnel or a bridge. The report concluded that the project was technically feasible and economically acceptable, and that it could be justified as a multilateral project because some 40 per cent of the gain from constructing a permanent link would be for users in countries other than Morocco and Spain. The report recommended that additional studies be carried out on the project's impact on local development and that structures built in similar terrain elsewhere in the region be examined, a parallel analysis of one tunnel option and two bridge options be undertaken and the impact of the construction of bridge piers on the undersea environment and the technical, economic and financial feasibility of the partial start-up of the project be evaluated.

On 30 July, the Economic and Social Council, on the recommendation of its Economic Committee, adopted **resolution 1993/60** without vote.

Europe-Africa permanent link through the Strait of Gibraltar

The Economic and Social Council,

Recalling its resolutions 1982/57 of 30 July 1982, 1983/62 of 29 July 1983, 1984/75 of 27 July 1984, 1985/70 of 26 July 1985, 1987/69 of 8 July 1987, 1989/119 of 28 July 1989, 1991/74 of 26 July 1991 and 1992/45 of 31 July 1992,

Referring to General Assembly resolution 43/179 of 20 December 1988, by which the Assembly declared the period 1991-2000 the Second Transport and Communications Decade in Africa,

Also referring to resolution 912(1989), adopted on 1 February 1989 by the Parliamentary Assembly of the Council of Europe regarding measures to encourage the construction of a major traffic artery in south-western Europe and to study thoroughly the possibility of a permanent link through the Strait of Gibraltar,

Conscious that the project for the permanent link will help offer better prospects for the improvement of the transport networks connected to it and for the development of broader cooperation between Europe and Africa,

Also conscious of the economic impact and regional and interregional integration effects of the project,

Taking account, firstly, of the considerable work done on the project in terms of the surveying of the Strait of Gibraltar site and the engineering and socio-economic studies carried out and, secondly, of the ongoing programme of work, which, by the end of the year, should lead to the choice of the most advantageous solution,

Taking note of the recommendations and conclusions of the evaluation report on the studies relating to the project undertaken during the period 1982-1993, prepared by the Economic Commission for Africa and the Economic Commission for Europe in accordance with Council resolution 1991/74,

1. *Welcomes* the cooperation on the project among the Governments of Morocco and Spain, the Economic Commission for Africa and the Economic Commission for Europe;

2. *Also welcomes* the favourable response of the International Tunnelling Association and the Transport Study Centre for the Western Mediterranean to the appeal made by the Economic and Social Council in resolution 1991/74;

3. *Commends* the Economic Commission for Africa and the Economic Commission for Europe on the work done in preparing the project evaluation report requested by the Council in resolution 1991/74;

4. *Invites* the scientific and technical institutions concerned to take part in the special session on the permanent link through the Strait of Gibraltar, to be held at Cairo in April 1994 under the auspices of the Economic Commission for Africa, the Economic Commission for Europe and the International Tunnelling Association;

5. *Invites* the States concerned and the competent bodies to cooperate with the Governments of Morocco and Spain in carrying out studies for the implementation of the project and to take part in the International Colloquium on the Permanent Link, to be held at Seville, Spain, in 1994;

6. *Requests* the Executive Secretaries of the Economic Commission for Africa and the Economic Commission for Europe to take an active part in the follow-up to the project and to report thereon to the Economic and Social Council at its substantive session of 1995;

7. *Calls upon* the Secretary-General to give his full support to the Economic Commission for Africa and the Economic Commission for Europe to enable them to carry out the activities mentioned above and, within existing priorities, to provide them with the necessary resources.

Economic and Social Council resolution 1993/60

30 July 1993   Meeting 46   Adopted without vote

Approved by Economic Committee (E/1993/109) without vote, 22 July (meeting 13); 4-nation draft (E/1993/C.1/L.1); agenda item 14.
Sponsors: France, Italy, Morocco, Spain.

Tourism

In the area of tourism development, the ECA Conference of Ministers recommended[44] that member States should take steps to recognize the positive role of tourism in socio-economic development, allocate necessary resources to it and develop human resources for tourism development; improve and develop the quality and diversity of tourism products; protect the natural and human environment for sustainable tourism; constitute an African association of tourism and hotel training establishments; facilitate tourist flows through a concerted policy; and establish inter-State tourism circuits based on complementarity, on joint promotion of tourism products and on African integration policies.

ECA organized an experts workshop on tourism development (Addis Ababa, 16 and 17 June), conducted a study on traditional crafts-producers in Kenya and prepared project proposals for the integration of traditional arts and crafts into African tourism products and for the development of human resources for tourism. It participated in a meeting of European tourism operators in Africa, convened by the European Community in November, and provided assistance in developing terms of reference for a pan-African tourism organization, organizing a festival of arts and culture in Madagascar and elaborating a tourism programme and a strategy for tourism development in the Preferential Trade Area for Eastern and Southern African States.

Science and technology

ECA's activities in science and technology focused on strengthening the infrastructure for policy-making and planning in the development and application of science and technology, human resources development and utilization and promotion of subregional and regional cooperation. The secretariat undertook a study on the subregional and regional professional scientific and technical associations and institutions in the area of science and technology and organized a training workshop on integration of science and technology and economic development policies (Kampala, Uganda 17-21 May). It also carried out a feasibility study on the proposed establishment of an African Foundation for Research and Development (AFRAND), and set up a Task Force on AFRAND. The proposal was supported by the Presidential Forum on Management of Science and Technology for Development in Africa (Gaborone, Botswana, 31 October–1 November). Science and technology issues were also considered by the North Africa Subregional Working Group (Tunis, 13-16 December), which examined the basis for a subregional policy in that field.

The eighth meeting of the Intergovernmental Committee of Experts on Science and Technology Development (Addis Ababa, 22-26 November) welcomed the Committee's upgrading to the African Regional Conference on Science and Technology, in accordance with the new structure of ECA,[16] and requested ECA, UNESCO, OAU and

UNIDO to develop and recommend mechanisms for evaluating developments in and management of science and technology in member States. It also made recommendations on methodologies for planning and managing science and technology policy, the role of subregional and regional technology associations and professional institutions, acquisition and transfer of nuclear science and technology for agricultural production and food preservation, institutional capacity-building, integrating science and technology and economic development policies, and technology assessment for better technological priorities and choices.

Marine affairs

In the marine affairs area, the ECA secretariat provided advisory services in the application of legal mechanisms established by the 1982 United Nations Convention on the Law of the Sea[45] for the exploitation of non-living marine resources. It undertook missions to various States and conducted a technical study on the status of awareness, ratification and progress in implementing the Convention's provisions.

Natural resources

Natural resources activities covered the exploration and development of mineral resources, the development and management of water resources and the development and provision of cartographic and remote-sensing services.

On the recommendation of the Eighth United Nations Cartographic Conference for Africa (Addis Ababa, 22-26 February), the Conference of Ministers requested the Executive Secretary to assist member States in coordinating their activities in cartography, remote sensing and geographic information systems (GIS) and called for action to establish hydrographic services in eastern and southern Africa and extend them to the rest of the continent. It urged industrialized countries and the international community to strengthen efforts for the education of African scientists and users of earth observation data, GIS and cartography, and requested countries advanced in space technology to facilitate access to satellite data and extend their data acquisition network to improve coverage of African countries.[46] The Ministers also called for efforts to set up suitable facilities for data acquisition, processing and dissemination at the Regional Centre for Services in Surveying, Mapping and Remote Sensing in Nairobi and the Regional Remote Sensing Centre in Ouagadougou, Burkina Faso, and appealed to ECA and UNDP to set up, strengthen and support national, subregional and regional environment information systems programmes.[47] The Ministers also invited ECA and the African Organization for Cartography and Remote Sensing to work to establish a cartographic data bank for Africa.[48]

ECA assisted member States and relevant institutions to obtain information on surveying, mapping, remote sensing and GIS and prepared technical papers for a meeting on international mapping from space (Hanover, Germany, September) and the United Nations Regional Conference on Space Technology for Sustainable Development in Africa (Dakar, Senegal, 25-29 October). It published the sixth issue of the *MAJI* annual information bulletin on water resources activities and undertook studies on problems and prospects for integrated development of the Nile basin, existing transboundary river/lake basin organizations and conservation and rational use of water resources in selected North African countries.

The secretariat carried out a comparative study of policies for mineral resources development in the region and provided technical assistance for a round-table meeting on small-scale gold mining (Niamey, Niger, October) and a conference on financial and technical support for mining ventures (Johannesburg, South Africa, November). It also provided assistance in the restructuring of Equatorial Guinea's Mining Department, in preparing studies on copper and aluminium fabricating facilities in Africa and in small-scale gold mining activities in Côte d'Ivoire, Ghana and Guinea. ECA organized and serviced the fifth Regional Conference on Mineral Resources Development and Utilization in Africa (Addis Ababa, 10-17 November), which made a wide range of recommendations concerning mineral development policies, national legislation on environmental impact assessment, resource mobilization and strengthening of geological and mining institutions, small-scale mining and the environment, the establishment of data banks, and cooperation and integration in mineral resources and energy development and utilization.

Energy

ECA continued to assist member States in developing indigenous energy sources, formulating adequate energy policy and strengthening institutional capacity through training African experts in the energy sector. An ad hoc expert group meeting was held for senior advisers (Addis Ababa, 17-19 May) on energy policy and strategies in Africa, and publications were prepared on energy supply and use and related policy options in African countries, as well as on the potential contribution of new and renewable sources of energy to the African energy supply.

Food and agriculture

Activities in the field of food and agricultural development included a workshop on the improvement of public sector capacities in project management and administration. Technical publications were prepared on measures for the increased operational effectiveness of planning and policy-making institutions, on the promotion, rehabilitation and conservation of green belts and soils in North Africa, and on approaches to improve agricultural data collection, processing and interpretation in eastern and southern Africa. The secretariat developed curricula for training in agricultural marketing extension services and in basic marketing principles and prepared a comparative analysis of the structural advantages of agricultural export-oriented products of Africa and South-East Asia. Other studies dealt with measures for alleviating infrastructural constraints to intraregional food trade, intervention policies and measures for enhancing small farmers' access to credit facilities, and small-farmer credit programmes.

ECA convened meetings on critical food security issues for Central and West African countries and produced a manual on measures to expand food availability through the exploitation of non-conventional food resources. It provided assistance in programming and promoting comprehensive food security programmes, improving national capacities in food security policy analysis and developing an information base for maize and non-conventional food resources. It also carried out the testing of livestock models in Central and West Africa, prepared an in-depth study on land privatization in Africa and launched a project on massive rehabilitation and development of agriculture in Ethiopia's Tigray region. It published one issue of the *Rural Progress* newsletter and produced a report on strengthening financial institutions for rural Africa and providing credit for agricultural and other income-generating activities in selected countries.

Fisheries

Activities in the areas of fisheries and living marine resources included seminars on the continent's aquaculture sector and on fisheries policies and strategy in Ethiopia. ECA also provided advisory services on fisheries-related issues for the post-conflict reconstruction and rehabilitation of affected African countries, such as Mozambique, and a follow-up fact-finding mission to Eritrea to formulate a master plan for reconstruction, rehabilitation and development. It assisted in developing a subregional maritime data bank for members of the Indian Ocean Commission and in elaborating aquaculture development strategies in various subregions. Several publications were prepared, dealing with cooperation in the exploitation and management of shared inland fisheries resources, updating and treatment of data in agriculture and fisheries, cooperation in the implementation of exclusive economic zones in fisheries, the status of agriculture and fisheries in Africa and analysis of fisheries activities, a proposed strategy for developing the fisheries sector and harmonizing and coordinating its activities, and aquaculture development in selected African countries.

Environment

The ECA Technical Preparatory Committee of the Whole considered the African Strategies for the implementation of Agenda 21[8] in seven priority areas: managing demographic change and population pressures; achieving food self-sufficiency and security; ensuring efficient and equitable use of water resources; securing greater energy self-sufficiency; optimizing environmentally clean industrial production; managing species and ecosystems; and preventing and reversing desertification. The Committee noted the general inadequacy of human resources and institutional capacity in the priority sectoral programmes and made recommendations to mitigate the situation. It welcomed measures to prepare an African common position in negotiations on an international convention to combat desertification and urged that the position should include modalities for eradicating poverty through sustainable development, promoting alternative development of livelihoods for people, assessing and monitoring drought and desertification and their interaction with climate change, and reaching consensus on the role of multilateral institutions, NGOs and the private sector.

On the Committee's recommendation, the Conference of Ministers adopted the African Strategies for the implementation of Agenda 21 and urged member States to incorporate them into national strategies and to mobilize resources for their implementation.[49] The Ministers also urged ECA, OAU and AfDB to explore the possibility of establishing an African environment fund in support of the Strategies' implementation and requested the Executive Secretary to organize a ministerial conference to evaluate negotiations on the Convention to combat desertification.

In other action,[50] the Ministers urged member States to advocate greater support for the African Centre of Meteorological Applications for Development in Niamey, called on them to ratify the Centre's constitution and appealed for financial support.

The fifth session of the African Ministerial Conference on the Environment (Addis Ababa, 22-27 November) took note of the Strategies and encouraged African countries and organizations to use them as a framework for formulating their national action programmes in the implementation of Agenda 21. The Conference adopted a new policy orientation and its indicative programme for 1994-1995, which focused on combating poverty and environmental degradation. It also considered issues related to desertification, natural disasters and a proposed African regional meeting on biological diversity.

ECA's activities in environment and development focused on developing common interpretations, strategies and action programmes as a follow-up to UNCED, ensuring coordination of regional and subregional activities and contributing to Africa's regional position at the World Conference on Natural Disaster Reduction, to be held in 1994, and an African perspective on the international convention to combat desertification. The secretariat assisted in servicing an expert group meeting on the convention (Addis Ababa, 5-8 August) and a high-level meeting of the Intergovernmental Authority on Drought and Development (Addis Ababa, September).

Social development and humanitarian affairs

The ECA Technical Preparatory Committee of the Whole noted the widespread deterioration in living conditions in Africa as a result of continuing disease, illiteracy, undernourishment and malnutrition, unemployment and poverty. A comprehensive and integrated strategy for development and structural transformation, centred on human development, was required to bring about improvements in those conditions. The Committee adopted the Human Development Agenda for Africa in the 1990s,[51] which outlined a human-centred programme of action in the priority areas of education for development, improved health care, food security and nutrition, safe water and sanitation, generation of productive employment opportunities and promotion of popular participation, good governance and civic society, and set out financial requirements for the programme's implementation.

The ECA Conference of Ministers endorsed the Agenda and urged African Governments to give priority to improving human development conditions and to redirect their policies to ensure the implementation of human-centred development strategies.[52] The Ministers requested the Executive Secretary to initiate actions for the establishment of a regional human development fund in Africa, as outlined in the Agenda. In separate action, the Ministers recommended for adoption by the Economic and Social Council a resolution on the preparations for the 1995 World Summit for Social Development[53] (see below).

The Ministers further called on African Governments to intensify preparations for the observance of and follow-up to the International Year of the Family (1994) and urged that observance activities be concentrated at the local and national levels.[54] It invited African Governments to develop policies to support, strengthen and protect the family and to provide mechanisms for mitigating negative socio-economic consequences of national development policies. It urged them to develop measures to address and resolve the problems of armed and civil conflicts, hunger and famine and their impact on the family. The Ministers noted the recommendations of the United Nations Africa and Western Asia Preparatory Meeting for the International Year of the Family (Tunis, 29 March–2 April), which examined the situation of families in the ECA and ESCWA regions.

The secretariat carried out several activities to promote human resources development, including measures to establish a human development fund, which would subsume the previously proposed African fund for youth. Technical publications were produced dealing with status, policies and programmes on human resources development and utilization in Africa; the impact of structural adjustment programmes on the effective utilization of human resources; refinement of human development indicators; an exchange programme of high-level manpower in the region; problems and constraints on productivity in agriculture; planning, development and utilization of human resources for industrial development; and measures for employment generation and stimulation of growth in the urban informal sector and among women workers in rural areas. It also organized workshops, seminars and symposia to assist member States in various fields. National workshops were held on enhancing cooperation and interface between the Government and popular development organizations in Namibia (Windhoek, 11-13 August) and on creating an enabling environment for the informal sector in Ethiopia (Addis Ababa, 12-14 October). In collaboration with the United States Institute for Peace, a symposium was organized on cooperation in the Horn of Africa (Addis Ababa, 8-12 July) to consider the socio-economic and cultural content of the conflict in the Horn of Africa and the human dimensions of the post-conflict reconstruction and development.

In the area of education, ECA carried out research on the role of Africa's higher-education institutions in economic integration, implications of regional development strategies for education, the status of and requirements for training programmes and organizational development policies for university staff, non-formal education and

training, guidelines for the preparation of manpower profiles and identification of training needs, and problems, constraints and methods of identifying alternative sources of financing higher education in Africa. Curriculum development was another area of research and included publications on past attempts towards curriculum reform, further steps in curriculum development for socio-economic transformation in the region, curriculum development for promoting self-confidence, assessment of confidence-building factors in school curricula and attitude formation. The secretariat, in cooperation with UNESCO, organized an ad hoc expert group meeting on curriculum reform for development and self-confidence-building in Africa (Addis Ababa, 18-21 October).

Activities in the social development area focused on issues concerning youth, the family, disabled and ageing persons and crime. The secretariat conducted research on the role and contribution of youth to conserving the African environment and on the administration of juvenile justice in eastern and southern Africa, and cooperated with OAU in organizing a meeting on youth and development (Cotonou, Benin, 19 and 20 August). It undertook a study on the social and economic situation of the ageing in Africa, and organized an ad hoc expert group meeting on the impact of economic and social changes on the African family (Addis Ababa, 13-17 December), which reviewed long-term strategies and programmes. The secretariat continued to provide technical and substantive support to the United Nations African Institute for the Prevention of Crime and the Treatment of Offenders, and participated in the fourth meeting of its Governing Board (Kampala, 22 and 23 November).

ECONOMIC AND SOCIAL COUNCIL ACTION

On 30 July, the Economic and Social Council, on the recommendation of its Economic Committee, adopted **resolution 1993/64** without vote.

Preparations for the World Summit for Social Development
The Economic and Social Council,

Taking note of General Assembly resolution 47/92 of 16 December 1992 on the convening in 1995 of a world summit for social development,

Convinced that the World Summit for Social Development would provide a unique opportunity to focus the attention of all countries on the main social and human concerns and to promote policies and strengthen international cooperation in order to effectively address those concerns,

Further convinced that Africa has a special stake in the Summit and its outcome,

Cognizant of the continuing severe deterioration of social and human conditions in Africa and the need to reverse this unacceptable situation as a matter of urgency,

Determined to ensure the effective participation of Africa in the preparatory process for the Summit and at the Summit itself,

1. *Urges* States members of the Economic Commission for Africa to participate actively in the preparatory activities for the World Summit for Social Development, particularly the meetings of the Preparatory Committee established by the General Assembly;

2. *Stresses* the need for members of the Commission to adopt an African common position on the issues to be discussed at the Summit;

3. *Decides* that an African common position on the issues before the Summit should be formulated by the meeting of the Conference of African Ministers Responsible for Human Development, to be held in January 1994, which should serve as the regional preparatory meeting for the Summit;

4. *Requests* the Executive Secretary of the Economic Commission for Africa to prepare, in cooperation with the Organization of African Unity and other African regional and subregional organizations, the necessary documentation for the meeting, including a draft African common position on the issues before the Summit;

5. *Further requests* the Executive Secretary of the Commission to transmit the African common position to the Preparatory Committee for the Summit, at its first session, which is scheduled to be held in New York from 31 January to 11 February 1994.

Economic and Social Council resolution 1993/64

30 July 1993   Meeting 46   Adopted without vote

Approved by Economic Committee (E/1993/109) without vote, 23 July (meeting 14); draft by ECA (E/1993/85); agenda item 14.

Population

The ECA Conference of Ministers, in May,[55] approved the Dakar/Ngor Declaration on Population, Family and Sustainable Development, adopted by the third African Population Conference in 1992,[56] and requested African Governments to use the Declaration in preparing for the 1994 International Conference on Population and Development. The Executive Secretary was invited to have the Declaration's principles, objectives and recommendations incorporated in ECA's work programme and to establish a follow-up committee of member States on the Declaration's implementation.

Activities in population issues emphasized the integration of population factors in development planning and research in population dynamics, family planning and HIV/AIDS and their interrelationships with sustainable development. The secretariat prepared an assessment of national population programmes in member States during the 1990s and a manual for the integration of population factors in human resources development. Other publications dealt with the correlation of changing infant and child mortality and fertility to development programmes in selected countries; mortality levels, patterns, trends, differentials and their socio-economic interrelationships in Africa; the relationship between population and the environment; alternatives to traditional approaches in family planning programmes in Africa; and consistency of United Nations projections with those produced in selected ECA member States. In addition, ECA continued to provide advisory services to the region in the field of population.

Human settlements

On the recommendation of the seventh meeting of the Joint Intergovernmental Regional Committee on Human Settlements and Environment (Addis Ababa, 29 March–2 April), the ECA Conference of Ministers supported the development of the ECA project on the building materials industry in Africa and invited African Governments to support its implementation and ensure the use of environmentally acceptable materials and practices under the project. The Ministers requested the Executive Secretary to mobilize resources and ensure the continuation of the project and its extension to other African countries under the programme of IDDA II dealing with industrial development.[57] They further called for cooperation in implementing projects to promote local building materials, provide manpower training in the production of those materials and construction techniques, and formulate unified standards for building materials to ensure product quality.

The secretariat's work in human settlements focused on redressing the rural/urban imbalance in the region. It developed and promoted guidelines for the formulation and implementation of national policies on settlements, aimed at balanced spatial distribution of population and economic activities in the context of a sound environment, land reforms, promotion of rural townships and strengthening the indigenous construction sector through the development of indigenous skills, low-cost building materials and small-scale production units and transfer of appropriate technology. Pilot plants were introduced or under construction in selected countries for the commercial manufacture of stabilized soil blocks, fibre concrete roofing tiles and lime kilns. The secretariat published a bulletin on human settlements in Africa, prepared guidelines on shelter indicators in the region and issued publications on the formulation of efficient land-use planning within the framework of the urban economy and physical planning, applicable to arid and semi-arid areas as well as coastal and tropical forest zones.

Integration of women in development

At its fourteenth meeting, the Africa Regional Coordinating Committee for the Integration of Women in Development (Addis Ababa, 19-21 April) reviewed ECA's activities and programme on women in development; discussed implementation of the Abuja Declaration on Participatory Development: the role of women in Africa in the 1990s, adopted by the 1989 Conference on the Integration of Women in Development and endorsed by the ECA Conference of Ministers in 1990;[58] considered a progress report on establishing a federation of African women entrepreneurs and an African bank for women; and reviewed preparations for the fifth African Regional Conference on Women, scheduled for Dakar in November 1994 in preparation for the 1995 World Conference on Women. The Committee's draft provisional agenda for the Regional Conference focused on women in the peace process; equality, education and social issues; women empowerment; and women, environment and sustainable development. Other matters considered by the Committee included violence against women and strategies for improving the flow of information on gender issues in Africa.

On the Committee's recommendation, the ECA Conference of Ministers adopted the agenda and thematic outline of the fifth African Regional Conference on Women, urged African Governments to initiate preparation of national reports for submission to the Conference and to institute information and communication campaigns and called on them to establish national preparatory coordinating committees.[59] The Ministers also called on ECA, OAU and the Africa Regional Coordinating Committee to help define Africa's plan of action for consideration by the World Conference as part of the global platform for action, appealed for support to subregional and regional women's programmes and efforts to create a federation of African women entrepreneurs and an African bank for women, and urged ECA and OAU to assist Uganda in organizing the Regional Conference on Women, Peace and Development to be held in Kampala in 1993.

Activities for the integration of women in development focused on preparations for the fifth African Regional Conference and on enhancement of women's role in mainstream development by reinforcing their business and managerial capabilities and strengthening the database and information network on women. Following a regional inter-agency meeting at Addis Ababa in March, an Inter-Agency Task Force was established to coordinate preparations for the Regional Conference. At meetings at Addis Ababa in April and September, the Task Force adopted information and communication strategies for the Conference and agreed on regional and agency inputs. ECA also developed guidelines for preparing national reports and participated in a preparatory meeting for the Conference of French- and Portuguese-speaking African Ministers of Women's Affairs and Rural Development in November and the Regional Conference on Women and Peace (Kampala, 22-25 November), which adopted the Kampala Action Plan on Women and Peace.

The African Training and Research Centre for Women (ATRCW) organized a training-of-trainers workshop for promotion of women entrepreneurs and their access to credit and an ad hoc expert group meeting on strategies for the enhancement of women's skills in mainstreaming and decision-making (Addis Ababa, 6-10 December). The African Federation of Women Entrepreneurs was established in 1993 and held its inaugural meeting (Accra, Ghana, 1-3 June) and a pre-feasibility study was carried out on the establishment of an African bank for women. Other studies dealt with the external debt crisis and its impact on African women and the participation of women in food processing, preservation, storage and agro-industries. The secretariat continued to issue the *ATRCW Update* newsletter and launched the *FEMME-LINE* newsletter covering preparations for the Regional Conference.

Programme, administrative and organizational questions

The ECA Technical Preparatory Committee of the Whole considered a report on the medium-term plan for 1992-1997,[13] the first revision of which was undertaken by the Committee for Programme and Coordination (CPC) in 1992[60] following that year's session of the Commission. Under the revised plan, ECA's activities were clustered around nine subprogramme areas: development issues and policies; trade, regional economic cooperation and integration; poverty alleviation through sustainable development; development administration and management; human resources development and social transformation; statistical and information systems development; natural resources and energy development; infrastructural and structural transformation; and women in development. The Committee took note of the first revision, called on the secretariat to continue efforts for greater programme focus and urged ECA to be more proactive in its advocacy role on African development issues.

The Committee also considered the proposed programme of work and priorities for the biennium 1994-1995,[12] prepared within the framework of the medium-term plan. The programme focused on factors required to sustain rehabilitation, long-term development and transformation in Africa, with an emphasis on strengthening institutional capacities for development management in the public and private sectors, and specifically addressed the debt problem and issues related to human development, poverty alleviation, women in development and popular participation. The Committee further reviewed the Commission's programme evaluation[61] and underscored the need for reforms to bring ECA's activities in line with priorities identified in the medium-term plan.

In May,[62] the Conference of Ministers endorsed the 1994-1995 work programme and called for allocation of adequate resources under the United Nations programme budget to implement programmes for African development under the 1992-1997 medium-term plan.

Cooperation between SADC and the United Nations

In response to a 1991 General Assembly request,[63] the Secretary-General submitted an October report on cooperation between the United Nations and the Southern African Development Community (SADC).[64] SADC was established in 1992 at Windhoek as successor to the 10-member Southern African Development Coordination Conference. The report described assistance provided to southern African countries by the United Nations system and by various Member States.

The United Nations Secretariat continued to implement the United Nations Educational and Training Programme for Southern Africa, which was expanded to include educational and training assistance to disadvantaged South Africans. ECA cooperated with SADC in promoting the southern African community, organizing seminars and workshops, conducting various studies, drafting protocols, managing negotiations and promoting trade and industrial cooperation. UNDP-assisted projects on trade development and promotion generated more than $120 million in additional trade among eastern and southern African countries and was expected to bring $300 million more in new trade. UNDP also supported an expanded fever vaccine production programme for the east coast within the framework of a $15 million tick-borne diseases programme.

Other United Nations programmes and agencies provided support to SADC members in such areas as environmental issues, food and agriculture, human settlements, employment and training, industrialization and health.

Financial assistance totalling more than $1 billion for the 1993 fiscal year was provided by the International Monetary Fund and the World Bank through their lending operations. The International Fund for Agricultural Development extended 24 loans in excess of $234 million for 22 projects in SADC countries, with a total commitment of $486.7 million, focusing on drought relief and agricultural rehabilitation.

GENERAL ASSEMBLY ACTION

On 21 December, the General Assembly, on the recommendation of its Second Committee, adopted **resolution 48/173** without vote.

Cooperation between the United Nations and the Southern African Development Community

The General Assembly,

Reaffirming its resolutions 37/248 of 21 December 1982, 38/160 of 19 December 1983, 39/215 of 18 December 1984, 40/195 of 17 December 1985, 42/181 of 11 December 1987, 44/221 of 22 December 1989 and 46/160 of 19 December 1991, in which, *inter alia*, it requested the Secretary-General to promote cooperation between the organs, organizations and bodies of the United Nations system and the Southern African Development Coordination Conference and urged intensification of contacts in order to accelerate the achievement of the objectives of the Lusaka Declaration of 1 April 1980, by which the Conference was established,

Having considered the report of the Secretary-General,

Welcoming the transformation of the Southern African Development Coordination Conference into the Southern African Development Community, which is aimed at deepening and expanding the process of economic integration and cooperation in the region, involving the full participation of all citizens of the member States of the Community,

Commending States members of the Community for demonstrating their support and commitment to deeper and more formal arrangements for cooperation within the new Community,

Noting the efforts made by the Community to implement its programme of action,

Reaffirming that the successful implementation of the development programmes of the Community can be achieved only if the Community has adequate resources at its disposal,

Welcoming the endorsement by the Multi-party Negotiating Forum of South Africa of the reintegration of Walvis Bay and the offshore islands into Namibia and the agreement reached between the Governments of Namibia and South Africa to complete the reintegration process by 28 February 1994,

Noting also that the effects of war, drought, loss of life and destruction of economic and social infrastructure in southern Africa demand the continuation and strengthening of rehabilitation programmes to regenerate the economies of the countries of the region,

Recognizing the positive developments that have taken place in South Africa, including the decisions to establish a Transitional Executive Council and to hold democratic elections on 27 April 1994,

Expressing grave concern at the unsettled and deteriorating political and military situation in Angola, noting with continued concern the grave humanitarian situation and emphasizing the importance of a continued and effective United Nations presence in promoting a negotiated settlement in Angola with a view to fostering the peace process,

Noting with satisfaction the progress made so far in the implementation of the General Peace Agreement for Mozambique between the Government of Mozambique and the Resistência Nacional Moçambicana, observing that, as a result, life is gradually returning to normal in Mozambique, and emphasizing the continuing need for positive action by all parties concerned,

Noting the progress made by some organs, organizations and bodies of the United Nations system in formulating mechanisms for cooperation with the Community,

1. *Takes note* of the report of the Secretary-General, in which he describes progress made in the implementation of the resolutions of the General Assembly dealing with cooperation between the United Nations and the Southern African Development Community;

2. *Commends* the Member States and organs, organizations and bodies of the United Nations system that have maintained, enhanced and initiated development cooperation with the Community;

3. *Calls upon* the Member States and organs, organizations and bodies of the United Nations system that have not yet established contact and relationships with the Community to explore the possibility of doing so;

4. *Commends* the members of the Community for the progress achieved so far in implementing its programme of action and encouraging further such efforts;

5. *Renews its appeal* to the international community to increase its financial, technical and material support for the Community in order to enable it to implement fully its programme of action and to meet the reconstruction and rehabilitation needs;

6. *Appeals* to the international community and relevant organizations of the United Nations system to extend appropriate assistance to the Community in order to enable it to advance the process of regional economic integration, including the participation in the process of a democratic, non-racial South Africa as soon as possible;

7. *Welcomes* the economic and political reforms under way within the Community, which are intended better to address the challenges of regional cooperation and integration in the 1990s;

8. *Calls upon* the South African authorities and all parties concerned to redouble efforts to end the violence and build a stronger foundation for the emergence of democracy in South Africa;

9. *Regrets* the unbecoming actions of the National Union for the Total Independence of Angola, which are increasing the suffering of the civilian population of Angola, which is increasingly in need of help, causing an intolerable refugee problem and damaging the Angolan economy, and demands that the Union permanently cease such actions;

10. *Welcomes also* the steps taken by the Secretary-General to implement the emergency humanitarian assistance plan for Angola, and appeals to Member States to make generous contributions;

11. *Notes with appreciation* the assistance and pledges made by Member States in support of the peace process in Mozambique, and encourages the donor community to provide appropriate and prompt assistance for the implementation of all aspects of the General Peace Agreement for Mozambique;

12. *Reaffirms its appeal* to the international community to continue extending assistance to Namibia at this stage of its independence, to enable it to implement its national development programme;

13. *Invites* the donor community and other cooperating partners to participate at a high level in the Annual Consultative Conference of the Southern African Development Community, to be held at Gaborone from 26 to 28 January 1994;

14. *Commends* the Secretary-General and members of the international community for their timely response

to the drought situation in southern Africa, which has averted famine in the region and has initiated a process that will ensure a rapid response to situations of a similar nature in the future, and in this regard encourages the international community to assist countries of the region in overcoming the effects of drought on a sustained basis;

15. *Requests* the Secretary-General, in consultation with the Executive Secretary of the Southern African Development Community, to continue to intensify contacts aimed at promoting and harmonizing cooperation between the United Nations and the Community;

16. *Also requests* the Secretary-General to report to the General Assembly at its fiftieth session on the implementation of the present resolution.

General Assembly resolution 48/173

21 December 1993   Meeting 86   Adopted without vote

Approved by Second Committee (A/48/717/Add.5) without vote, 9 December (meeting 46); draft by Vice-Chairman (A/C.2/48/L.73), based on informal consultations on 10-nation draft (A/C.2/48/L.25); agenda item 91 *(d)*.

Meeting numbers. GA 48th session: 2nd Committee 15-17, 40, 46; plenary 86.

REFERENCES

(1)E/1993/38. (2)YUN 1992, p. 672. (3)YUN 1991, p. 402, GA res. 46/151, annex II, 18 Dec. 1991. (4)E/ECA/CM.19/26/Rev.1. (5)E/ECA/CM.19/4. (6)E/ECA/CM.19/5. (7)E/ECA/CM.19/7. (8)E/ECA/CM.19/8 & Add.1. (9)YUN 1992, p. 461. (10)Ibid., ESC res. 1992/51, 31 July 1992. (11)E/ECA/CM.19/19. (12)E/ECA/CM.19/22 & Corr.1,2 & Add.1. (13)E/ECA/CM.19/21. (14)E/1993/38 (res. 742(XXVIII)). (15)Ibid. (res. 769(XXVIII)). (16)Ibid. (res. 757(XXVIII)). (17)Ibid. (res. 754(XXVIII)). (18)Ibid. (res. 745(XXVIII)). (19)Ibid. (res. 756(XXVIII)). (20)E/1994/54. (21)E/ECA/CM.20/4. (22)YUN 1980, p. 548. (23)GA res. 44/24, 17 Nov. 1989. (24)E/1993/38 (res. 743(XXVIII)). (25)E/1994/40. (26)E/1993/38 (res. 768(XXVIII)). (27)YUN 1991, p. 304. (28)E/1993/38 (res. 766(XXVIII)). (29)E/ECA/CM.19/11. (30)E/1993/38 (res. 747(XXVIII)). (31)Ibid. (res. 751(XXVIII)). (32)E/ECA/TRADE/93/23. (33)YUN 1992, p. 468, ESC res. 1992/44, 31 July 1992. (34)Ibid., p. 469, GA res. 47/177, 22 Dec. 1992. (35)E/ECA/CM.19/14 & Add.1. (36)E/1993/38 (res. 752(XXVIII)). (37)YUN 1991, p. 301, ESC res. 1991/83, 26 July 1991. (38)Ibid., p. 302, GA dec. 46/456, 20 Dec. 1991. (39)E/1993/38 (res. 761(XXVIII)). (40)Ibid. (res. 763(XXVIII)). (41)Ibid. (res. 762(XXVIII)). (42)YUN 1991, p. 303, ESC res. 1991/74, 26 July 1991. (43)E/1993/80. (44)E/1993/38 (res. 765(XXVIII)). (45)YUN 1982, p. 178. (46)E/1993/38 (res. 758(XXVIII)). (47)Ibid. (res. 759(XXVIII)). (48)Ibid. (res. 760(XXVIII)). (49)Ibid. (res. 744(XXVIII)). (50)Ibid. (res. 755(XXVIII)). (51)E/ECA/CM.19/9. (52)E/1993/38 (res. 746(XXVIII)). (53)Ibid. (res. 749(XXVIII)). (54)Ibid. (res. 750(XXVIII)). (55)Ibid. (res. 748(XXVIII)). (56)YUN 1992, p. 476. (57)E/1993/38 (res. 764(XXVII)). (58)E/1990/42 (res. 686(XV)). (59)E/1993/38 (res. 753(XXVIII)). (60)YUN 1992, p. 477. (61)E/ECA/CM.19/23. (62)E/1993/38 (res. 767(XXVIII)). (63)YUN 1991, p. 305, GA res. 46/160, 19 Dec. 1991. (64)A/48/495 & Add.1.

Asia and the Pacific

The Economic and Social Commission for Asia and the Pacific, at its forty-ninth session (Bangkok, Thailand, 21-29 April 1993),[1] had as its theme topic ''Expansion of investment and intraregional trade as a vehicle for enhancing regional economic cooperation and development in Asia and the Pacific''. On 29 April,[2] it called on its Executive Secretary to give priority to the implementation of the action programme for regional economic cooperation in trade and investment, especially the review and analysis of regional trade patterns; the strengthening of the Regional Trade Information Network; the establishment of a regional investment information and promotion service; networking of trade-related research institutions; the enhancement of national capabilities in quality control; sectoral foreign direct investment (FDI) inflows and analysis of FDI policies; the development of export-oriented small and medium enterprises; environmental issues related to trade and investment; assistance to disadvantaged economies in transition; the integration of the Central Asian economies into the region; and inter-subregional cooperation in trade and investment. The Commission called for the active participation of its members and the collaboration of international donors in the programme's implementation, and requested the Executive Secretary to report annually, beginning in 1994, on the progress made.

ESCAP reviewed the implementation of its 1992 resolution on its role and functions in the context of United Nations restructuring.[3] It reaffirmed its recommendations,[4] which were included in the Secretary-General's report[5] submitted in response to a 1992 General Assembly resolution,[6] calling for the strengthening of the regional commissions. In a resolution on the strengthening of its role in the coordination of regional operational activities,[7] ESCAP called for measures to enhance the efficiency and effectiveness of the United Nations system at the regional level. It urged that ESCAP's role be strengthened in the coordination of operational activities among United Nations organizations, programmes, funds and specialized agencies, taking into account its comparative advantages in collecting information, monitoring economic developments and promoting cooperation with and among its member Governments. The Executive Secretary was requested to continue following the reform process and to report in 1994 on developments in that regard.

The Commission also adopted resolutions on the second phase (1992-1996) of the Transport and Communications Decade for Asia and the Pacific; the Tehran Declaration on Strengthening Regional Cooperation for Technology-led Industrialization in Asia and the Pacific; goals and strategies for population and sustainable development into the twenty-first century; the regional programme on space applications for development; the Proclamation and Agenda for Action for the Asian and Pacific Decade of Disabled Persons, 1993-2002; implementation of General Assembly decisions on UNCED in the ESCAP region; the strengthening of

assistance to LDCs; and the eradication of preventable diseases in the region. (For information on those resolutions, see below, under relevant subject headings.)

In a message to the session, the Secretary-General observed that political progress following the relaxation of tensions in the post-cold-war era would be difficult to sustain without improvements in economic and social conditions. He emphasized that the United Nations political mission was inseparable from its economic and social mission and that the regional commissions should continue to play an important role in the strengthening of regional cooperation. Despite the recent slow-down in the global economy, many Asian and Pacific countries continued to show a capacity for sustained economic growth and were a source of encouragement to developing countries in other parts of the world. The continued expansion of intra-regional trade, investment and technology contributed to a dynamism that was characteristic of much of the region. At the same time, however, poverty, malnutrition, disease and illiteracy were widespread in Asia and the Pacific. The least developed and Pacific island countries, as well as ESCAP's new members from Central Asia, had generally failed to make significant economic progress and needed special assistance to accelerate their development. The Secretary-General called for support for ESCAP as the main regional arm of the United Nations in Asia and the Pacific.

Economic and social trends

Economic trends

The *Economic and Social Survey of Asia and the Pacific 1993*[8] reviewed world economic developments and their implications for the ESCAP region. It discussed the region's macroeconomic performance and policies, regional performance and policies in international trade and balance of payments, fiscal reforms, economic transformation and social development, and population dynamics and their implications for development.

A summary of the survey[9] noted that the region's robust economic performance in 1993 was remarkable given the recession in the world economy. The average rate of growth for its developing economies was estimated at 6.7 per cent, unchanged from 1992. China achieved a spectacular growth rate of 13 per cent and India's economy was expected to grow by 4.6 per cent. Although the economic performance of various groups of countries continued to diverge, their approaches to development policy, and to some extent their performance, converged, giving greater scope for private participation and market forces. Economic growth rates exceeded 5 per cent in most South Asian countries and ranged between 6 and 8 per cent in South-East Asia, with the exception of the Philippines. Although the small island economies of the Pacific remained vulnerable to external factors, some achieved success in their stabilization and restructuring efforts, and their overall economic performance was expected to improve. Growth rates also strengthened in most of the region's LDCs, ranging from 5 to 7 per cent.

In 1993, the region's three developed economies (Australia, Japan, New Zealand) suffered from the recessionary symptoms that had affected all industrialized countries since 1990. Japan's economy stagnated, having seen its growth rate fall from 4 per cent in 1991 to 1.3 per cent in 1992. Despite the lowest interest rates in decades, Japan's recovery was expected to be slow given the need for economic adjustment after years of high growth, large trade and balance-of-payments surpluses and unrealistically high asset values. Australia and New Zealand, however, showed definite signs of recovery. Their output grew by 2.4 per cent and 3.6 per cent, respectively, and annual inflation rates fell below 2 per cent.

In East Asia, the high rate of growth in China's GDP, buttressed by a 20 per cent increase in industrial production and an estimated 4 per cent growth in agricultural output, raised concern that the economy was overheating and that inflation was out of control. The annual inflation rate rose from 5.4 per cent in 1992 to 12.3 per cent in 1993. Following government policy action, however, the economy appeared well positioned towards the end of the year to restrain inflation without a drastic reduction in growth. Hong Kong reduced its annual rate of inflation from 9.3 per cent in 1992 to about 8.5 per cent in 1993, while in the Republic of Korea the inflation rate rose from 4.5 to 5 per cent over the same period.

The economy of the Democratic People's Republic of Korea made no progress towards growth or stability in 1993, having contracted by 5.2 per cent in 1991 and 5 per cent in 1992. The Government attempted to redress the situation with cautious reform measures, relaxing its central planning regime and encouraging foreign investment and trade, especially with neighbouring countries. In Mongolia, which initiated major reforms for transition from a centrally planned economy to a market system, price adjustments resulted in high inflation and real national income decreased by 33 per cent in 1992. Mongolia's economic situation was aggravated by a severe winter and internal dislocations that affected domestic production.

The six Central Asian economies that became members of ESCAP in 1992 also faced the daunting task of transition to a market system. The challenges included the reorientation of their foreign trade, the settling of national currency and

exchange rate questions, the establishment of a viable banking and credit network, and the restructuring, revitalization and reorientation of production and trade. Their situation in 1992-1993 was characterized by high inflation and falling production, resulting from the disruption of supplies and the loss of markets after the dissolution of the USSR. In 1992, the net material product had dropped by 31 per cent in Tajikistan, 28.2 per cent in Azerbaijan, 26 per cent in Kyrgyzstan, 14.2 per cent in Kazakhstan and 12.9 per cent in Uzbekistan, while inflation rates varied from 640 per cent in Uzbekistan and 980 per cent in Turkmenistan to 1,450 per cent in Tajikistan, more than 1,700 per cent in Kazakhstan and Kyrgyzstan and 2,280 per cent in Azerbaijan. At the same time, the terms of trade improved significantly in Turkmenistan and Kazakhstan and marginally in Kyrgyzstan, owing to a shift to world prices, but worsened in the three other countries, especially in Azerbaijan and Tajikistan where armed conflicts added to the economic disruption. During 1993, all six countries except Tajikistan introduced national currencies and were becoming more diverse in their macroeconomic policies, as evidenced by the encouragement of foreign investment in Kazakhstan, economic conservatism in Turkmenistan and Uzbekistan and the dominance of security concerns over reform issues in Azerbaijan and Tajikistan.

The South Asian countries achieved considerable success in reducing their budgetary and balance-of-payments deficits and inflation rates. Iran's economy was expected to grow by 6.2 per cent in 1993, compared with 6.6 per cent in 1992, while its inflation declined from 21.6 per cent in 1992 to 10 per cent. Sri Lanka's GDP increased from 4.3 per cent in 1992 to about 5.8 per cent in 1993, while its inflation rate was expected to remain at 11.5 per cent. India registered growth in its industrial, agricultural and services sectors and a drop in inflation. Pakistan's growth rate fell from 7.7 per cent in 1992 to 3 per cent, following extensive flood damage to agriculture, physical infrastructure and related manufacturing activities. It also suffered the effects of global recession on its terms of trade and political uncertainties prior to the October 1993 general elections.

In South-East Asia, Singapore's growth rate accelerated from 5.8 per cent in 1992 to 8.1 per cent in 1993 and Indonesia's economy was estimated to grow from 5.8 to 6.3 per cent over the same period. The Philippine GDP increased by 1.8 per cent compared with 0.3 per cent in 1992, and Thailand sustained a 7.5 per cent growth rate for the second consecutive year. Growth rates were expected to decline in Malaysia from 8 per cent in 1992 to 7.6 per cent in 1993 and in Viet Nam from 8.3 per cent to 7.5 per cent over the same period.

The annual inflation rate rose to 9.5 per cent in Indonesia and remained at about 2.5 per cent in Singapore. It fell in all other countries.

Among the subregion's LDCs, Cambodia's GDP growth rate slowed from 7.6 per cent in 1991 to 7 per cent in 1992, due largely to a downturn in agricultural production caused by late and insufficient rainfall. Its growth was expected to increase steadily in 1993, however, with the expansion of its industrial and services sectors. The economy of the Lao People's Democratic Republic was also expected to grow steadily, having achieved a 4 per cent rate of increase in 1991 and a 7 per cent growth rate in 1992. Myanmar anticipated a 5.8 per cent growth rate after 10.9 per cent growth in 1992. Although inflation rates remained high, they had decreased between 1991 and 1992 from 197 to 75 per cent in Cambodia, from 32.3 to 21.9 per cent in Myanmar and from 13.4 to 9.8 per cent in the Lao People's Democratic Republic.

The fortunes of South Asia's five LDCs were mixed. Afghanistan's war-ravaged infrastructure and lack of civil order contributed to crop yields that were up to 70 per cent lower than pre-war levels and manufacturing output that was well below capacity. Bangladesh expected growth to expand from 4 per cent in 1992 to 5 per cent in 1993, while inflation fell from 5.1 per cent in 1992 to an all-time low of 1.4 per cent in 1993. Real GDP growth in the Maldives was projected to be around 6 per cent in 1993 compared with 7.6 per cent in 1991 and 6.3 per cent in 1992. The economy of Nepal grew by 2.9 per cent in 1993 following sharp increases in industrial output and tourism, and inflation stabilized at an annual average of 11 per cent, down from 21 per cent in 1992. Bhutan's growth had stabilized at 5 per cent a year in 1991-1992.

With Australia and New Zealand recovering from recession, the economies of most Pacific island countries were expected to grow in 1993 despite cyclones in Samoa and Vanuatu and a drought in Tonga. GDP growth rates were estimated to rise from 8.6 per cent in 1992 to 10.6 per cent in 1993 in Papua New Guinea, from 2.8 to 4.5 per cent in Fiji and from 1.9 to 2.5 per cent in Tonga. Vanuatu's economy expanded by 1.9 per cent, having stagnated in 1992. Samoa rebounded with 1.9 per cent growth after a 5 per cent contraction the previous year. The growth rate was expected to decline in the Solomon Islands, however, from 8.2 per cent in 1992 to 4.8 per cent in 1993. Inflation increased from 4.1 to 7.5 per cent in Vanuatu, but declined to 7 per cent in Samoa and was stable at 4.5 per cent in Papua New Guinea, about 5 per cent in Fiji, 8 per cent in Tonga and 10 per cent in the Solomon Islands.

International trade continued to underpin the economic resilience of the ESCAP region. In 1993, growth rates appeared to have slowed somewhat, but ranged between 12 and 16 per cent in a number of countries. Regional imports accelerated in several countries, spurred by the rapid pace of domestic economic activities, infrastructural investment and growing consumer demand in response to rising income.

Among the factors contributing to high growth rates were a shift in export composition from primary commodities to manufactured goods; sustained demand for manufactured products in the developed economies despite the recession; the successful diversification of markets; capital inflows, encouraged by policy reforms; and increasing foreign participation in the region's emerging capital markets.

The region received more than half of all FDI and over 70 per cent of the medium- and long-term international bank lending directed to developing countries in 1991-1992. The total volume of capital inflows to Asian countries was estimated at $144 billion for the period 1989-1992, compared with $82 billion during 1985-1989; FDI accounted for 44 per cent of the increase.

Exports from the region in 1992 totalled $893.8 billion, an 11.2 per cent increase over the previous year, with the developing economies accounting for more than half of that amount, having increased their exports by 13.9 per cent in 1992. Total regional imports for 1992 grew by 8.2 per cent over 1991 to reach some $812.6 billion. The developing countries' share was about 65 per cent, as they expanded their imports by 13.3 per cent for the year. Exports increased by 28.7 per cent in the Pacific island economies, 15.7 per cent in East Asia, 12 per cent in South-East Asia, 7.9 per cent in the developed countries and 7.4 per cent in South Asia.

Policy liberalization and initiatives for regional economic cooperation in Asia and the Pacific included efforts to form subregional free trade areas, notably the ASEAN (Association of South-East Asian Nations) Free Trade Area and the South Asia Preferential Trading Arrangement, as well as the establishment and expansion of regional and subregional organizations, such as the Asia-Pacific Economic Cooperation, the East Asia Economic Caucus, the South Asian Association for Regional Cooperation (SAARC), the Economic Cooperation Organization (ECO) and the South Pacific Forum. Localized economic cooperation zones, dubbed growth triangles, also emerged among countries at different stages of development to exploit complementarities arising from differences in their labour, capital and natural resources. The most successful growth triangles were those linking southern China, Hong Kong and Taiwan, and Singapore, the Johore State of Malaysia and the island of Batam in Indonesia. There were also proposals to establish five new triangles.

Social trends

The quality of life in many ESCAP countries improved in terms of health, nutrition, literacy and education, life expectancy and mortality, and a sizeable proportion of the population achieved truly affluent living standards. At the same time, however, structural transformations resulted in wide income and welfare disparities, and persistent poverty remained the most crucial of the region's problems. The rapid pace of urbanization led to growing urban slums and squalor, and concern was also growing about the lack of safety, security and health protection in industrial workplaces. Atmospheric pollution was also a serious health hazard, among wide-ranging environmental problems. Many epidemic diseases re-emerged, and the AIDS pandemic posed a serious threat to public health.

Among other emerging issues were the declining influence of the family and the high incidence of divorce, single parenthood and parentless childhood, homelessness and street-begging by children, young adults and elderly people. Child and sex abuse, drug abuse and homicidal and suicidal violence were also increasing.

Although annual population growth rates in many parts of the region slowed considerably from the 2 to 3 per cent of earlier decades, a current average growth rate of 1.7 per cent meant that more than 50 million people were being added annually to the total population of Asia and the Pacific in the 1990s and that about 48 million people were likely to be added annually from 2000 to 2010. Population growth rates in South Asia were well above the regional average and were expected to account for 60 per cent of the region's population increase between 2000 and 2010. While expanded education programmes in many countries enabled high levels of basic literacy, opportunities for higher education remained much more limited. In most countries, there were also considerable deficiencies in health services, particularly for the rural majority. To cope with the enormous projected cost of future health needs, Governments adopted the goal of "Health for All by the Year 2000", based on the use of less costly primary health-care methods and emphasis on the need to control epidemic and vector-borne diseases and to provide adequate prenatal and postnatal care and health education.

Population dynamics demanded that some countries expand employment opportunities beyond the traditional agricultural sector. Population growth also contributed to greater exploitation of natural resources and the serious depletion of forests, flora and fauna, water and soil resources. Industrialization, more intense land use and technological changes also had adverse environmental consequences. However, awareness of the interaction between population, environment and development was growing, and population policies were increasingly being integrated with other economic and social development policies.

Activities in 1993

Development policy and regional economic cooperation

At its 1993 session,[1] the Commission had before it a study on the expansion of investment and intraregional trade as a vehicle for enhancing regional economic cooperation and development in Asia and the Pacific.[10] The report examined regional links in trade and investment and analysed the trade-investment nexus, including the integration of FDI and trade flows and the role of foreign investment in industrial restructuring. It also reviewed constraints on the expansion of intraregional trade and investment, specific problems of the Pacific island countries, LDCs and economies in transition, and policy options for enhancing cooperation and development. During its discussion of the study, the Commission emphasized that, despite the rapid rise of intraregional investment in recent years, the distribution of such flows and the impact of the trade- and investment-led growth strategy remained skewed, and it recommended measures to balance that situation. It endorsed the study's contention that long-term regional and global prosperity lay in multilateralism and the openness of economies.

The Committee for Regional Economic Cooperation, at its second session (Bangkok, 19 and 20 April 1993),[11] adopted the action programme for regional economic cooperation in trade and investment, approved by the Committee's Steering Group at its first meeting in 1992[12] and revised at the Group's second meeting (Bangkok, 15, 16 and 19 April 1993). The programme called for activities and studies dealing with the growth of intraregional trade, the role of foreign investment and the private sector, the development of small and medium-sized enterprises, emerging trade and investment-related concerns, economies in transition and inter-subregional cooperation. At its 1993 session, the Commission endorsed the action programme and adopted a resolution on its implementation (see above). It agreed that priority should be given to studies on trade and investment flows in the region and to the requirements of the Pacific island and land-locked countries, LDCs and economies in transition.

The ESCAP secretariat organized a meeting of consultants during 1993 to discuss recent tax system reforms and their impact on income distribution and poverty (Bangkok, 27-29 September) and an expert group meeting on development issues and policies (Bangkok, 7-9 December). ESCAP also signed memoranda of understanding with the Asian Development Bank and with ECO, and prepared a draft framework agreement for cooperation with SAARC and a memorandum of understanding with ASEAN. In December, the SAARC Standing Committee endorsed the framework agreement.

Least developed and
land-locked developing countries

The Special Body on Least Developed and Land-locked Developing Countries (first session, Bangkok, 22-24 February 1993)[13] reviewed development trends, issues and policies of those countries, international cooperation for their development and implementation of the Programme of Action for LDCs for the 1990s, adopted in 1990 by a United Nations conference (known as the Paris Conference)[14] and endorsed by the General Assembly later that year.[15] The Special Body also endorsed the proposed programme of work for 1994-1995, which concentrated on macroeconomic policies, trade, transport and private foreign investment.

Discussions focused on political, economic and social reforms launched by LDCs, as well as on issues related to official development assistance (ODA), external debt, international trade and regional cooperation. It was noted that, despite gains by some LDCs including Bhutan and Maldives, progress since the Paris Conference had been discouraging. LDCs continued to face an uncertain global economic environment, mounting obstacles to their exports, a heavy debt burden and major dislocations stemming from natural disasters, wars, civil unrest and ethnic strife. The Special Body urged donor countries to increase substantially their assistance to LDCs that remained critically dependent on ODA, and emphasized the importance of promoting economic and technical cooperation among developing countries (ECDC/TCDC) as well as intra- and inter-subregional economic cooperation. It noted the growing assistance to LDCs by China, India, Indonesia, the Republic of Korea and Thailand, and it welcomed an offer by UNCTAD to assist with a feasibility study on a proposed centre for research on LDCs at Dhaka, Bangladesh.

On 29 April,[16] ESCAP reaffirmed that LDCs had the primary responsibility for their own development and called on its members and international organizations to support their efforts to implement the Programme of Action for the 1990s. It invited member Governments to assist with preparations for the 1995 mid-term regional review of the Programme's implementation. It urged the secretariat to strengthen programmes that focused on the priority needs of LDCs in the region.

The Executive Secretary was requested to report in 1994 on the progress made.

ESCAP activities to assist LDCs during 1993 included nine country courses, four fellowship programmes, seven training courses and 61 advisory and other missions to 12 countries. The secretariat sponsored a comparative study programme on management of technical cooperation for Nepal and an exhibition of gift items from Asian LDCs (Tokyo, 16-18 November), and organized study visits on urban development for Samoa and on TCDC national focal points and on innovative slum improvement for Bangladesh. It also convened a training workshop on information technologies and population science (Beijing, 12-21 October) and workshops on the transport, financial and economic planning model for inland container depots (Phnom Penh, Cambodia, 26 April–4 May), information needs assessment (Kuala Lumpur, Malaysia, 8-11 November) and expansion of trade and the promotion of business opportunities (Dhaka, 29 November).

A consultative expert group meeting on technological upgrading of agro-based industries (Bangkok, 22-26 November) focused on the development and popularization of food-processing technology in LDCs and land-locked developing countries. Seminar topics included Japan's generalized system of preferences (Vientiane, Lao People's Democratic Republic, 1-3 March), comprehensive flood-loss prevention and management (Yangon, Myanmar, 30 and 31 March), access to the Japanese market (Tokyo, 15 and 19 November) and manpower development in trade facilitation (Male, Maldives, 12-16 December). LDCs also participated in activities organized for developing countries in general.[17]

Land-locked States in Central Asia

The newly independent States in Central Asia had the additional disadvantage of being landlocked and, in 1993, the Meeting of Governmental Experts from Land-locked and Transit Developing Countries and Representatives of Donor Countries and Financial and Development Institutions (New York, 17-19 May),[18] convened by UNCTAD, concluded, *inter alia*, that to enter world markets those countries required a complex multi-country transit system, including links between the Central Asian States and neighbouring and southern Asian transit countries. The Meeting proposed an evaluation of Central Asian transit systems and a programme to improve the transit environment (see also PART THREE, Chapter I).

GENERAL ASSEMBLY ACTION

On 21 December, the General Assembly, on the recommendation of the Second Committee, adopted **resolution 48/170** without vote.

Assistance to land-locked States in Central Asia

The General Assembly,

Bearing in mind its resolution 48/169 of 21 December 1993, entitled "Specific actions related to the particular needs and problems of land-locked developing countries", and expecting that the newly independent land-locked States in Central Asia will participate in the activities and meetings referred to in that resolution,

Recalling the agreed conclusions and recommendations on priority areas and modalities for further action to improve transit systems in land-locked and transit developing countries of the Meeting of Governmental Experts from Land-locked and Transit Developing Countries and Representatives of Donor Countries and Financial and Development Institutions, convened by the Trade and Development Board in New York from 17 to 19 May 1993, as set forth in the report of the Meeting of Governmental Experts,

Recalling in particular those paragraphs of the agreed conclusions and recommendations of the Meeting of Governmental Experts pertaining to the newly independent and developing land-locked States in Central Asia and their transit developing country neighbours,

Noting that those countries are seeking to enter world markets and that such an objective requires the establishment of a multi-country transit system,

Emphasizing the importance of elaborating a programme for improving the efficiency of the current transit environment, including better coordination between railway and highway transport, in the newly independent and developing land-locked States in Central Asia and their transit developing country neighbours,

Recognizing the important role played by bilateral cooperative arrangements, multilateral agreements and regional and subregional cooperation and integration in comprehensively solving the transit problems of the land-locked developing countries and improving the transit transport systems in the newly independent and developing land-locked States in Central Asia and their transit developing country neighbours,

1. _Recognizes_ that various forms of international technical and financial assistance will be required to improve the efficiency of the current transit environment in the newly independent and developing land-locked States in Central Asia and their transit developing country neighbours, including a general survey of transit infrastructure and rehabilitation needs in support of national and regional efforts and programmes;

2. _Also recognizes_ that the work being done in this context by the Economic and Social Commission for Asia and the Pacific and by the Economic Cooperation Organization can provide a basis for further elaboration;

3. _Invites_ the Secretary-General of the United Nations Conference on Trade and Development, in cooperation with the United Nations Development Programme, to evaluate the transit system of the newly independent and developing land-locked States in Central Asia and their transit developing country neighbours and to elaborate a programme for improving their transit facilities, and to report to the General Assembly at its forty-ninth session on the implementation of the present resolution.

General Assembly resolution 48/170

21 December 1993   Meeting 86   Adopted without vote

Approved by Second Committee (A/48/717/Add.2) without vote, 10 December (meeting 47); draft by Vice-Chairman (A/C.2/48/L.79), based on informal consultations on 3-nation draft (A/C.2/48/L.23); agenda item 91 (a). _Meeting numbers._ GA 48th session: 2nd Committee 30-32, 39, 47; plenary 86.

Special problems of Pacific island countries

The Special Body on Pacific Island Developing Countries (first session, Bangkok, 25-27 February 1993)[19] reviewed recent development trends and their policy implications for economic growth and structural transformation, considered ESCAP activities in the Pacific and adopted the proposed work programme for 1994-1995. The Special Body noted that a lack of marketing expertise and market opportunities, as well as volatile export demand conditions, constrained economic activity in several island countries. It emphasized the need to develop human resources and to improve trade and investment relationships between the subregion and East and South-East Asia. It expressed concern at the marked decline in ESCAP activities in the Pacific and requested the secretariat to make every effort to reverse that trend. The Special Body noted the environmental problems faced by many Pacific island countries and reviewed contributions from the ESCAP region to the Global Conference on the Sustainable Development of Small Island Developing States, scheduled for 1994, including the South Pacific Regional Environment Programme.

In April, the Commission emphasized the need to put the technical assistance activities of the Pacific Operations Centre on a more permanent basis. It welcomed the secretariat's decision to resume the ESCAP training and orientation programme in 1994, and to increase the Centre's advisory staff to 10. The Pacific Trust Fund, which was established to ensure the participation of Pacific island countries in ESCAP's annual sessions, had received contributions from 20 members and two associate members of ESCAP by 1993; its balance was projected to reach $299,400 by the end of the year.

ESCAP transition economies

The 10 Asian and Pacific disadvantaged economies in transition to a market system (Azerbaijan, Cambodia, Kazakhstan, Kyrgyzstan, Lao People's Democratic Republic, Mongolia, Tajikistan, Turkmenistan, Uzbekistan, Viet Nam) needed various forms of assistance to develop their financial, industrial, infrastructural, trading and other institutional frameworks in 1993. They also needed assistance in the areas of human resources and social development. In April, the Commission noted their need for price and enterprise reforms and identified a number of economic and social problems requiring immediate attention. They included a lack of competitive structure, the need for military conversion and the valuation of assets for privatization, and a social safety net to protect those who suffered as a consequence of reforms. The Commission also noted the closed nature of existing trading systems and the absence of transport and communications links with market-oriented neighbours.

Activities to address those concerns were incorporated into ESCAP's work programme for 1994-1995 and into the action programme for regional cooperation in trade and investment (see above). Advisory missions during the year included extended visits to Azerbaijan, Kyrgyzstan and Mongolia.[20] The secretariat provided advice to the Lao People's Democratic Republic on the utilization of GSP schemes and the introduction of multimodal transport; to Viet Nam on the social integration of disabled persons, census data preparation and the processing and compilation of price data; and to Cambodia and Viet Nam on population censuses and surveys.

The secretariat established a trust fund and orientation programme for the Asian republics of the Commonwealth of Independent States, and conducted a number of training projects, seminars and workshops for them. These included national workshops on economic reform in Kazakhstan (Almaty, July) and Mongolia (Ulan Bator, September); a training workshop on environmental issues associated with the use of fertilizers in the Lao People's Democratic Republic (October); training courses on statistics and various aspects of trade and investment for Cambodia, the Lao People's Democratic Republic, Mongolia and Viet Nam; and national seminars on Japan's GSP scheme in the Lao People's Democratic Republic (March) and Viet Nam (September). An international symposium on the development of transitional economies through intraregional trade expansion and economic cooperation with neighbouring countries (Chanchun, China, June/July) was based on a case-study of the North-East Asian subregion.

Other activities included advisory services on the rehabilitation of the Port of Sihanoukville in Cambodia, the preparation of a seminar on population, environment and development in the Lao People's Democractic Republic, and a needs assessment mission on population policy and development planning in Cambodia.

Economic and technical cooperation

During 1993, ESCAP received $16.02 million in contributions for technical cooperation activities, 18 per cent less than in 1992.[21] The decrease was mainly due to reduced funding by UNDP. Donor States and developing member countries provided 230.25 work-months of expert services, compared with 300.25 in 1992. The Project Review Committee considered 109 new project proposals for bilateral funding in 1994 (compared with 135 in 1992), and recommended 91 of them, totalling $8.47 million, for approval and submission to potential donors. Bilateral donors approved 78 projects, totalling $6.27 million, for execution under ESCAP's work programme, excluding special projects and regional institutions. A corps of 10 regional advisers undertook 40 missions to 34 developing countries of the region.

The Commission urged the secretariat to enhance its catalytic role as a regional focal point for TCDC for the benefit of the least developed, landlocked and island developing countries, using the ESCAP TCDC supplementary fund.

During the year, the secretariat carried out more than 80 promotional TCDC activities financed from extrabudgetary resources.[22] With the support of China, the Netherlands, Norway and the Republic of Korea, 33 operational TCDC activities were implemented through the supplementary fund, 25 of them for least developed, land-locked and island developing countries and economies in transition. Overall, 22 ESCAP members benefited from the fund in 1993. Areas of TCDC activity included agriculture, the environment, human settlements, natural resources, population, rural development, social development and issues related to disabled and elderly persons, statistics, telecommunications, trade promotion and women in development. Training courses within the framework of TCDC were offered by China, India, Indonesia, Malaysia, Pakistan, the Philippines, the Republic of Korea, Singapore and Thailand. A workshop for TCDC national focal points was organized and funded by UNDP (Colombo, Sri Lanka, 5-7 April). Technical cooperation activities, however, continued to suffer from a lack of commitment by the region's developing countries, the inadequacy of financial and human resources for national follow-up activities, and ineffective TCDC national focal points.

International trade and finance

The year's activities in international trade and finance focused on implementation of the action programme for regional economic cooperation in trade and investment, which was endorsed by the Commission in April (see above, under "Development policy and regional economic cooperation"). The secretariat prepared studies on intraregional trade flows in Asia and the Pacific; patterns and policies that determine intraregional commodity trade flows; FDI flows and policies; the feasibility of developing a regional investment-information and promotion service; and the development of electronic goods for export.[23] The secretariat began to develop a regional database on goods and services under the ESCAP/UNDP Regional Trade Programme, and made an arrangement to link the Regional Trade Information Network with the electronic trading opportunities system, developed under UNCTAD's Special Programme for Trade Efficiency.

A seminar was held on the expansion of manufactured exports by small and medium enterprises (Bangkok, 30 November–2 December), and projects were formulated to enhance indigenous quality control, to promote investment in the least developed and island developing countries and economies in transition, and to analyse interrelationships between trade and the environment. The secretariat also designed programmes to promote intraregional trade in agricultural commodities and to stimulate intraregional trade research through a network of research institutions. The latter programme was finalized at a regional workshop (Kathmandu, Nepal, 8-10 December). Other activities included consultations among jute-producing countries (Bangkok, 12-14 May), an expert group meeting on an international silk information system (Bangkok, 14-17 September), a second symposium on economic and trade cooperation between China and the Asian and Pacific region (Beijing, 20-26 October), and a seminar on the enhancement of national trade information capabilities through modern technology (Manila, Philippines, 9-11 November). The Asia-Pacific Consultative Forum on Coffee held its first session in 1993 (Bangkok, 17 and 18 March).

Implementation of the action programme was reviewed by the Steering Group of the Committee for Regional Economic Cooperation at its third session (Tokyo, 12-15 October).

Transnational corporations

In 1993, the ESCAP/TCMD (United Nations Transnational Corporations and Management Division) Joint Unit on Transnational Corporations continued to facilitate a better understanding of TNCs and their impact on host countries in Asia and the Pacific, and to help the region's developing countries attract FDI. The Unit prepared policy recommendations for publication and distribution among ESCAP members and collected data on FDI in the region. It also initiated a project on the impact of service regulations on FDI and organized an expert group meeting on TNCs and backward linkages in the electronics industries (Bangkok, 30 November–4 December).

Transport and communications

The Committee on Transport and Communications held its first session under the new ESCAP conference structure in Bangkok from 13 to 17 December.[24] The Committee reviewed regional developments in transport and communications, including activities under phase II (1992-1996) of the Transport and Communications Decade for Asia and the Pacific (see below).

The Committee recognized that further expansion in transport and communications was indispensable for economic and social development in the region, and requested that in future research the secretariat highlight the impact of infrastructure and transport development on poverty alleviation. It emphasized the need to promote land transportation links between Eastern Asia and Western Europe through the Asian land transport infrastructure development (ALTID) project, and proposed the creation of a special body to act as a focal point for infrastructure development in the region. It supported the development of a Maritime Policy Planning Model within its regional maritime strategy study project, and endorsed further studies and databases on trade, shipping and ports. The Committee also proposed an expert group meeting on the development of transport management information systems.

A study on the development of the Asian Highway network under the ALTID project was endorsed at an expert group meeting (Bangkok, 29 November–3 December). Other activities included a review seminar on multimodal transport (Karachi, Pakistan, 18 February), country-level workshops on a container terminal module (Kota Kinabalu, Malaysia, 22-26 February) and the facilitation of maritime traffic (Manila, November), and a fellowship scheme in port middle management, offered by Australia in May/June. A seminar-cum-study tour on compressed natural gas for road transport was held in Germany (30 August–11 September) and an Asian road-safety conference was held at Kuala Lumpur (25-28 October). A meeting of Transport Ministers of ECO members (Almaty, Kazakhstan, 25-27 October) adopted an outline plan for the development of the transport sector in the ECO region.

Transport and Communications Decade for Asia and the Pacific

In April 1993, the Commission endorsed decisions of the 1992 Meeting of Ministers Responsible for Transport and Communications[25] relating to phase II (1992-1996) of the Transport and Communications Decade for Asia and the Pacific, 1985-1994.[26] The Commission adopted a resolution on resource mobilization for phase II.[27]

The Committee for Transport and Communications, in December,[24] endorsed the regional action programme and its activities and took note of developments related to resource mobilization.

ECONOMIC AND SOCIAL COUNCIL ACTION

On 30 July, the Economic and Social Council, on the recommendation of its Economic Committee, adopted **resolution 1993/63** without vote.

Resource mobilization for the implementation of the regional action programme for phase II (1992-1996) of the Transport and Communications Decade for Asia and the Pacific

The Economic and Social Council

Recommends to the General Assembly the adoption of the following draft resolution:

[For text, see General Assembly resolution 48/177 below.]

Economic and Social Council resolution 1993/63

30 July 1993   Meeting 46   Adopted without vote

Approved by Economic Committee (E/1993/109) without vote, 23 July (meeting 14); draft by ESCAP (E/1993/85), orally amended following informal consultations; agenda item 14.

GENERAL ASSEMBLY ACTION

On 21 December, the General Assembly, on the recommendation of the Second Committee, adopted **resolution 48/177** without vote.

Resource mobilization for the implementation of the regional action programme for phase II (1992-1996) of the Transport and Communications Decade for Asia and the Pacific

The General Assembly,

Taking note of resolution 49/2 of 29 April 1993 of the Economic and Social Commission for Asia and the Pacific on resource mobilization for the implementation of the regional action programme for phase II (1992-1996) of the Transport and Communications Decade for Asia and the Pacific,

Recalling its resolution 39/227 of 18 December 1984, by which it proclaimed the period 1985-1994 the Transport and Communications Decade for Asia and the Pacific, and Economic and Social Council resolution 1984/78 of 27 July 1984 on the Transport and Communications Decade for Asia and the Pacific, 1985-1994,

Recalling also Economic and Social Council resolution 1991/75 of 26 July 1991, in which the Council urged all appropriate international organizations, particularly the United Nations Development Programme, to contribute effectively to the formulation and implementation of a regional action programme for the second half of the Decade, and General Assembly decision 46/453 of 20 December 1991, in which the Assembly endorsed Council resolution 1991/75,

Reaffirming the importance of phase II (1992-1996) of the Transport and Communications Decade for Asia and the Pacific,

Noting that it may not be possible to implement the regional action programme effectively and efficiently without adequate funds, and noting the decision of the Governing Council of the United Nations Development Programme in this regard,

1. *Requests* the Governing Council of the United Nations Development Programme to keep under review the level of funding to be provided for the implementation of the regional action programme, so that phase II (1992-1996) of the Transport and Communications Decade for Asia and the Pacific will have a greater impact;

2. *Requests* bilateral donors to take note of General Assembly decision 46/453, so as to ensure that the programme approved by the Meeting of Ministers Responsible for Transport and Communications held at Bang-

kok from 3 to 5 June 1992 will be implemented effectively;

3. *Invites* all Governments in a position to do so to contribute to the implementation of the programme approved by the Meeting of Ministers Responsible for Transport and Communications;

4. *Requests* the Secretary-General to report to the General Assembly at its forty-ninth session on the implementation of the present resolution.

General Assembly resolution 48/177

21 December 1993   Meeting 86   Adopted without vote

Approved by Second Committee (A/48/717/Add.8) without vote, 13 December (meeting 48); draft in ESC resolution 1993/63; agenda item 91 *(g)*.
Meeting numbers. GA 48th session: 2nd Committee 36-40, 48; plenary 86.

Tourism

In April, the Commission recognized the linkage between the development of transport and communications and the increasingly important role of tourism in Asian and Pacific countries. The Committee for Transport and Communications observed that the rapid growth of tourism had created a pressing need for planned tourism development to maximize its socio-economic benefits and minimize its adverse impact.

Activities during the year included expert group meetings on the environmental management of coastal tourism development (Bali, Indonesia, 8-12 March) and tourism training (Bangkok, 30 November–3 December), and a seminar on investment and economic cooperation in the tourism sector in Pacific island countries (Tokyo, 18-23 October). The secretariat continued to disseminate technical information and data on tourism development through the *ESCAP Tourism Review* and the *ESCAP Tourism Newsletter.*

Industrial and technological development

At its 1993 session, the Commission endorsed the Regional Strategy and Action Plan for Industrial and Technological Development, and the Tehran Declaration on Strengthening Regional Cooperation for Technology-led Industrialization in Asia and the Pacific, adopted at the 1992 Meeting of Ministers of Industry and Technology.[25] The Commission invited the international community to provide technical and financial support for the early implementation of both and called on the Executive Secretary to report on progress in 1995.[28] The Executive Secretary was also requested to convene a regional conference in 1996 to review and assess progress, and to report in 1994 on an offer by Iran to upgrade the Institute for Research in Planning and Development at Tehran to provide regional and subregional facilities.

The Commission urged the secretariat to strengthen activities to promote enterprise-to-enterprise cooperation; to explore innovative means of industrial financing; and to mobilize resources to assist Central Asian States, especially in the areas of market-oriented reforms, industrial restructuring and rehabilitation. The secretariat was requested to develop special programmes for newly independent States in the areas of industrial restructuring and technological development and the development of human resources in technology and vocational training. The Commission also suggested that the secretariat study the impact of liberalization, deregulation and restructuring measures on small and medium industries, and their regional export experience in the areas of textiles, leather and electronics. It was asked to organize a regional seminar on the subject. The Commission urged its members to strengthen their economic, industrial and technological reform efforts and to participate in the Taejon International Exposition in the Republic of Korea (August-November).

The main focus of the secretariat's efforts during the year was related to the promotion of industrial restructuring, investment, skills development, enhancement of the role of the private sector and privatization, small and medium industries, and the participation of women in industrial development. Activities included a national seminar on private sector growth, technology choice and investment in the industrial development of Bangladesh (Dhaka, 23-25 January), a regional seminar on investment promotion and enhancement of the role of the private sector (Dhaka, 26-30 January), an expert group consultation on strategies for technology-led industrial development and restructuring in the region (Bangkok, 26-28 October), an expert group meeting on the financing of small and medium enterprises (New Delhi, India, 12 and 13 November), and a regional forum for sustainable industrial restructuring (Kuala Lumpur, 6-12 December). The secretariat also co-sponsored the World Convention of Small and Medium Enterprises in Beijing in March, and studied options for regional and subregional cooperation with the Tehran Institute for Research in Planning and Development.

Asian and Pacific Development Centre

The Asian and Pacific Development Centre (APDC) issued seven publications and carried out 19 projects in 1993 in the programme areas of energy, economic management, information technology, poverty alleviation, public management, regional cooperation and women in development. Eight projects were funded by UNDP and 11 by other agencies and countries, including Canada, Germany, the Netherlands and Sweden. Total funds available to APDC for 1993 amounted to $3,047,377, an increase of 2.4 per cent over 1992. The 1993 operating budget, however, showed a deficit of $81,497 compared with a surplus in 1992. On 4 October, Macau signed the Charter of APDC, bringing to 22 the total number of the Centre's members and associate members.

Natural resources and marine affairs

Mineral resources

Mineral resources activities in 1993 concentrated on geological and mineral resource assessments in selected LDCs, and on mineral commodities such as gold, base metals, bauxite, non-metallic and fertilizer minerals and construction materials. The secretariat continued to promote foreign investment in the mining industry and assisted with mineral development strategies, mining codes and related investments in Bhutan, Cambodia, China, Kazakhstan, Kyrgyzstan, Sri Lanka and Viet Nam. Those countries also received assistance with the formulation of project proposals and national policies, and with the evaluation of their minerals potential. Two projects were under way on a review of policies for mining development and investment promotion in selected Asian and Pacific countries and on training and other support for mineral-based industries in Central Asian States. Efforts were made to integrate geoscientific knowledge into land-use planning, and the secretariat organized round-table conferences on legal and fiscal regimes for foreign investment in the mining industry (Beijing, May), and on mining law (Hanoi, October). The final meeting of the working group on quaternary correlation in the region was held at Khon Kaen, Thailand (October), and a second workshop-cum-study tour on industrial minerals development was held at Hangzhou, China (26 October–1 November).

The 1993 activities of the Committee for Coordination of Joint Prospecting for Mineral Resources in Asian Offshore Areas focused on fundamental geological research and offshore oil and gas exploration.

Water resources

The secretariat continued to provide advisory services on water resources development and management. During the year, it organized a regional workshop on computer applications for groundwater assessment and management (Bangkok, 19-28 January), regional and national seminars on water management in urban areas (see below, under "Human settlements") and roving seminars on comprehensive flood-loss prevention and management in Iran, Myanmar, Pakistan and Solomon Islands. The secretariat also participated in the international conference on environmentally sound water resources utilization (Bangkok, November). The Inter-Agency Task Force on Water for Asia met at Bangkok in May and December.

Marine affairs

Work in marine affairs centred on the evaluation of offshore construction aggregates in East Asia and the development of an integrated marine policy within the framework of the 1982 United Nations

Convention on the Law of the Sea[29] (see PART FOUR, Chapter III). A study was undertaken on protection of the marine environment in Sri Lanka, and a workshop was held on management strategies for the protection of the coastal and marine environment in the South Asian Seas region (Colombo, December).

Mekong River basin development

The Interim Committee for Coordination of Investigations of the Lower Mekong Basin[30] had resumed its operations in 1992, following agreements among the four riparian States (Cambodia, the Lao People's Democratic Republic, Thailand and Viet Nam) on basic principles for future cooperation. These were officially signed at their 1993 meeting (Hanoi, February) and the future modality for cooperation was being discussed by a Mekong Working Group, established in December 1992.

The Committee's activities, implemented through its annual work programme, comprised feasibility studies on the delta master plan, run-of-the-river hydropower possibilities, the Srepok action plan, a development plan for Tonle Sap and the identification of priority hydropower projects in Cambodia, and the Ya-Soup multi-purpose project in Viet Nam. Other projects dealt with the development of the Mekong geographic information system, aerial photography for resources mapping in Cambodia, assessment and monitoring of the forest cover and the sustainable protection of natural resources, updating of the hydrographic atlas, and participation in the UNEP/WHO Global Environmental Monitoring System. Investment in data and information systems provided capabilities for annual flooding and salinity-intrusion forecasting and water-quality assessment, while rural projects addressed the development of fishermen's communities in the Lao People's Democratic Republic and the improvement of land and water use in northern Thailand. Programmes were formulated to support fisheries and navigation along the Mekong River from China to the South China Sea. An expert group meeting on Mekong water-quality monitoring and assessment was held at Bangkok in November.

New donor commitments for the Committee totalled more than $16 million in 1993, while financing of its project portfolio rose to about 40 per cent, from 7 per cent in 1985. The portfolio for 1994 included 117 projects with a funding requirement of $197 million. During 1993, the Republic of Korea joined the Committee's donor community, and Denmark and UNDP made considerable new contributions.

Energy

In 1993, the secretariat prepared six country reports on sectoral energy demand, issued eight publications on energy issues and completed five others. Advisory services were provided to Cambodia on hydrocarbon exploration and hydrocarbon contract agreements, and to the Philippines on industrial energy conservation. Activities under the UNDP-funded Programme for Asian Cooperation in Energy and the Environment included an executive seminar on coal technology and the environment (Sydney, Australia, July), a training course on coal production, utilization and environmental protection (Sydney, August-October), and two workshops on coal technology (Bangkok, October; Kuala Lumpur, November). Among other activities were a regional workshop on environmentally sound coal technologies (Bangkok, 7-10 April), TCDC consultations on wind energy in Fiji, a mission to Indonesia and New Zealand in November/December to prepare for activities related to natural gas, a training workshop on the promotion of energy consultancy services, and a training course on business opportunities in marketing energy efficiency (Bangkok, December).

Agricultural and rural development

ESCAP activities in agriculture and rural development during 1993 continued to focus on the alleviation of rural poverty, integrated rural development, and interdivisional, inter-agency and multisectoral activities. The secretariat implemented a project to promote rural non-farm employment and initiated, in cooperation with FAO, a project to assist LDCs in formulating macroeconomic strategies for sustainable agricultural development. Drought early-warning teams to analyse rainfall data and satellite images were established under phase II of the satellite crop-monitoring project. The secretariat organized a workshop on employment strategies for the rural poor (Bangkok, 14-16 July) and an expert group meeting on the sensitizing of agricultural research to community development needs (Bangkok, 17-20 August).

The ESCAP/FAO/UNIDO/Fertilizer Advisory, Development and Information Network for Asia and the Pacific continued to provide training activities, information dissemination and advisory services for its members. It carried out a marketing management training programme (Kathmandu, 13-22 September), and convened a regional workshop on cooperation in soil-testing (Bangkok, 16-18 August), a regional consultation on the sustainability of national cooperation centres (Bangkok, 8-12 November) and a regional fertilizer conference (Manila, 30 November–3 December). Activities under the Inter-Agency Coordinated Plan of Action for Integrated Rural Development in the ESCAP Region included publication of the *Poverty Alleviation Initiatives* newsletter and preparation of a compendium of United Nations programmes on rural poverty alleviation.

In April, the Commission urged the donor community to fund activities of the Regional Network for Agricultural Machinery (RNAM) during its fifth phase (1992-1996), and approved Viet Nam's application for membership in RNAM. In 1993,[31] RNAM carried out expert missions to eight countries under a UNIDO special project on the promotion and development of agro-related metalworking industries in LDCs, organized the third Agricultural Machinery Exhibition and Symposium (Jakarta, Indonesia, 6-12 December), and conducted a tour for manufacturers from Indonesia, Pakistan, the Philippines and Thailand to study the production of agricultural equipment in China. It also prepared a paper on international cooperation among small- and medium-scale industries in agricultural machinery manufacturing in RNAM countries, presented at a colloquium on small farm equipment and a workshop on micro-enterprise development (Los Baños, Philippines, June); produced a document on existing policies and strategies for agricultural mechanization in RNAM countries; and published three issues of the *RNAM Newsletter*. The Network's activities were reviewed by its Technical Advisory Committee (Jakarta, 6-8 December) and by its Governing Body (Jakarta, 9-11 December).

The Regional Coordination Centre for Research and Development of Coarse Grains, Pulses, Roots and Tuber Crops in the Humid Tropics of Asia and the Pacific completed a regional cooperative programme for the improvement of food legumes and coarse grains, which included eight country studies on the employment and income-generation effects of their processing and marketing, and a related workshop on the expansion of rural employment in Asia (Serdang, Malaysia, May). The Centre began to implement projects on women's role in upland farming development and farmers' strategies for agricultural diversification, organized a seminar on upland agriculture in Asia (Bogor, Indonesia, April), and provided training courses on the application of regional crop databases. Data collection and compilation activities were carried out in Pakistan, Sri Lanka and Viet Nam, and related training was provided to Indonesia, Myanmar and Pakistan. Indonesia and Myanmar also received assistance with agricultural planning, research and development. In addition to its quarterly newsletter, *Palawija News*, the Centre issued several publications dealing with soybeans, vegetables and other crops in Asia. It also provided five databases on crop production and costs in Viet Nam.

The Centre's activities were reviewed by its Governing Board at its eleventh and twelfth sessions, held at Bogor in January[32] and December.[33]

Science and technology

At its 1993 session, the Commission noted the secretariat's efforts to create a climate conducive to technology transfer, the development of human resources in science and technology, and the development, transfer and application of new and emerging technologies. It stated that the secretariat should strengthen its efforts to help countries adopt appropriate industrial technologies, including advanced materials technologies, biotechnology, automated manufacturing systems and process planning controls, and to facilitate the technology flow from the most advanced developing countries to the less developed economies.

On 29 April,[34] the Commission decided to convene a ministerial-level meeting in Beijing in September 1994 to launch a regional space applications programme for development. It urged ESCAP members to participate actively in the meeting and urged the secretariat to continue to promote the integration of Earth space-information technology with the management of natural resources and with development planning. The Executive Secretary was requested to report on progress in 1994.

A meeting of directors of national remote-sensing centres and programmes in the region was held in preparation for the ministerial meeting in conjunction with the ninth session of the Intergovernmental Consultative Committee on the Regional Remote-Sensing Programme (Islamabad, Pakistan, 8-12 May).[35] The meeting adopted a conceptual framework for the space applications programme, which was intended to increase the awareness, knowledge and understanding of space applications for natural resource accounting, environmental monitoring, disaster mitigation and development planning. The framework was subsequently revised and endorsed by the Committee on Environment and Sustainable Development (see below, under "Environment").

A meeting of experts on space applications in the Asia-Pacific region (Bangkok, 27-30 October) also proposed general guidelines for the meeting's preparations. Other activities during the year included a workshop-cum-study tour on science and technology for plant-growth regulators (Beijing, 25-27 August), a regional remote-sensing seminar on tropical ecosystem management (Kuching, Malaysia, 8-14 September), and an international seminar on remote sensing for coastal zone and coral reef applications (Bangkok, 25 October– 1 November). In May, UNDP approved a new geographic information systems/remote-sensing programme for 1993-1996.

Asian and Pacific Centre for Technology Transfer

In April, the Commission reviewed activities of the Asian and Pacific Centre for Transfer of Technology, suggested further action and elected members of its Governing Board for 1993-1996. In July, the Centre was relocated from Bangalore to New Delhi.

During 1993, the Centre completed the first phase of a UNDP-funded project on technology transfer and management, and began to implement a project on the transfer of small-scale productive technologies to encourage entrepreneurship among rural women. A regional expert group meeting was held (New Delhi, 29 and 30 July) to evaluate printed resource materials for the women's project, and the first in a series of national workshops for participating countries was organized (Kathmandu, December). The Centre also organized a demonstration workshop on solar cookers (New Delhi, April) and an international exhibition-cum-seminar on selected technologies from India and China (New Delhi, April). It assisted with technology exchanges among small and medium-sized enterprises and issued a number of publications dealing with waste management and recycling, technology transfer contracts, the preparation of the solar cooking device, hydrogen energy for developing countries and the dimensions of technology exchange. Six issues of the *Asia-Pacific Tech Monitor* were published in 1993, as well as a compendium of 101 environmentally friendly technologies. A Value-Added Technology Information Service was initiated to disseminate information on new ideas, technologies, products, processes and machinery, and trade and technology policies.

The Centre's activities were reviewed by its Technical Advisory Committee (New Delhi, 16 and 17 November) and by its Governing Board (eighth session, New Delhi, 18 and 19 November).[36]

Social development

At its 1993 session, the Commission reviewed implementation of the Social Development Strategy for the ESCAP Region Towards the Year 2000 and Beyond, adopted in 1991.[37] It observed that the Strategy's principal objective was poverty alleviation and that priority attention should continue to focus on health, education, disability and ageing. Other priorities included cooperation between Governments and NGOs, and policies to strengthen the role of the family in society, to enhance the participation of youth in development, to prevent juvenile delinquency, to increase collaboration with the Commission on Human Rights, and to promote functional literacy, especially among girls and young women.

In a resolution on the eradication of preventable diseases in Asia and the Pacific,[38] the Commission urged ESCAP members to achieve the WHO goal of eradicating poliomyelitis in the region by the year 2000, and to coordinate action against the spread of AIDS and other sexually transmitted diseases by, *inter alia*, providing health information and education to promote responsible behaviour. It encouraged its members to give priority to preventive health care. WHO was urged to strengthen its collaboration with ESCAP members and was invited to report in 1994 to the regional ministerial preparatory conference for the

1995 World Summit for Social Development. The Executive Secretary was requested to work closely with WHO in preparing that report.

The Committee on Poverty Alleviation through Economic Growth and Social Development (first session, Bangkok, 20-24 September)[39] reviewed regional poverty, national policy approaches and international initiatives, and examined strategies to promote people's participation in poverty alleviation. It considered the recommendations of an expert group meeting on national poverty concepts and measurement in Asia and the Pacific (Bangkok, 15-17 September) and adopted its own recommendations for action by Governments and by ESCAP.

Among other activities in 1993 were a senior officials meeting on the strengthening of the Regional Network of National Focal Points on Drug Abuse Demand Reduction (Bangkok, 1-4 February), three subregional workshops on the subject (Bangkok, 9-13 August and 16-20 August; Port Moresby, Papua New Guinea, 18-21 October), a training course on demand reduction for narcotics in border areas of China and Myanmar (Bangkok, 20 September–15 October) and a regional preparatory meeting (Beijing, 24-28 May) for the International Year of the Family (1994). The implementation of the Social Development Strategy was considered at the second session of the Inter-Agency Task Force on the subject (Bangkok, 26 November). The secretariat initiated a project to strengthen the integration of youth into the development process, and two case-studies were prepared on policies and programmes for the integration of elderly persons in development.

Disabled persons

On 29 April,[40] the Commission adopted the Agenda for Action for the Asian and Pacific Decade of Disabled Persons, 1993-2002, having proclaimed the Decade in 1992.[41] It urged ESCAP members to sign the Proclamation on the Full Participation and Equality of People with Disabilities in the Asian and Pacific Region, adopted at the launching of the Decade,[41] and to implement the Agenda for Action. It also called for contributions to the trust fund for the Decade. The Executive Secretary was requested to develop regional activities supporting the Agenda for Action and to report on the progress achieved at the 1994 ministerial preparatory conference for the 1995 World Summit for Social Development.

The Agenda for Action covered 12 areas of concern: national coordination, legislation, information, public awareness, accessibility and communication, education, training and employment, prevention of causes of disability, rehabilitation services, assistive devices, self-help organizations and regional cooperation.[42] The secretariat launched two regional projects related to self-help organizations and the promotion of non-handicapping environments, and held a South Asia workshop on the management of self-help organizations for disabled persons (Dhaka, 5-14 December). The workshop led to the establishment of a South Asian network of self-help organizations.

The secretariat joined a number of NGOs in organizing a Conference of Deaf People in Asia (Bangkok, 9-12 March) and the First Regional Conference of NGOs on the Asian and Pacific Decade of Disabled Persons (Okinawa, Japan, October). The Okinawa Conference led to the establishment of a regional NGO network to promote the Decade, several commemorative publications and a directory of self-help organizations of disabled people in the region. Other regional activities included a leadership training seminar for the disabled (Dhaka, November/December), a consultative expert meeting on national disability legislation for Asia and the Pacific (Kuala Lumpur, December) and a conference on independent living and changing attitudes (Singapore, April). The revitalized Asia-Pacific Inter-organizational Task Force on Disability-related Concerns held its seventh meeting in 1993 (Bangkok, 29 March).

Women in development

At its 1993 session, the Commission considered preparations for the Second Asian and Pacific Ministerial Conference on Women in Development, to be held in 1994, and endorsed the Seoul Statement on Empowering Women in Politics, adopted in 1992.[43] The Commission urged its members to establish national preparatory committees for the Conference, and made suggestions for a regional plan of action for the advancement of women.

ESCAP convened a second inter-agency meeting on preparations for the Conference (Bangkok, 18 May) and an Asian and Pacific symposium of NGOs on women in development (Manila, 16-20 November).[44] The symposium comprised workshops dealing with health, labour rights, agriculture, culture and education, political empowerment, economic empowerment, violence against women, human rights, science and technology, indigenous women, family and the environment, and it initiated a regional NGO plan of action. In addition, ESCAP organized a workshop on a women's information network in Mongolia (9-11 November), and published a 1993 directory of national focal points for the advancement of women in Asia and the Pacific, and a directory of women experts in the region.

Population

In April, the Commission endorsed the Bali Declaration on Population and Sustainable Development, adopted by the Fourth Asian and Pacific Popula-

tion Conference in 1992.[41] The Declaration was the main regional input to the 1994 International Conference on Population and Development; ESCAP urged the secretariat to play a greater role in creating awareness of its implications and monitoring its implementation. The Commission urged countries with high infant, child and maternal mortality rates to strengthen efforts to improve health conditions, and to ensure that women's concerns were addressed in all population and development activities and programmes. The Commission adopted a resolution on population and sustainable development,[45] which was brought to the attention of the General Assembly by the Economic and Social Council (see below).

As a follow-up to the Fourth Asian and Pacific Conference, ESCAP convened a number of subregional meetings and conferences on population issues.[46] The Ministerial Meeting on Population and Sustainable Development in the Pacific (Port Vila, Vanuatu, 9 and 10 September) adopted the Port Vila Declaration, which highlighted the interrelationship between population and sustainable economic growth and development, the need for gender equality and empowerment of women, the role and importance of the family, and issues of reproductive rights, reproductive health and family planning. The SAARC Ministerial Conference on Women and Family Health (Kathmandu, 21-23 November) was held in compliance with the Dhaka Declaration of the Seventh Summit Conference of SAARC (Dhaka, April). It adopted the Kathmandu Resolution, which identified major factors underlying high maternal and child mortality rates in the subregion, and pledged to take steps to reduce those rates. The Fourth Conference of the Asian Forum of Parliamentarians on Population and Development (Kuala Lumpur, 26-28 October) reviewed the population and development situation in Asian countries and discussed the status of family planning and maternal and child health; the status of women and health; population growth, ageing and youth; and population, the environment and food.

A round table on population and development strategies (Bangkok, 17-19 November), organized jointly by ESCAP and UNFPA, adopted 13 recommendations dealing with institutional arrangements for integrated population and development planning. Other activities included a country case-study on the integration of the elderly into the mainstream of economic and social development in Bangladesh; a training workshop on field research on ageing issues (Beijing, August/September); study directors' meetings on local-level policy development to deal with ageing (Chiang Mai, Thailand, 2-5 November) and on rural-urban migration (Bangkok, 8-10 December); an ASEAN and East-Asia workshop on the Population Information Network (Kuala Lumpur,

12 and 13 November); and an international seminar on the consequences of replacement and below-replacement level fertility in East and South-East Asia (Seoul, 29 November–3 December). A regional conference on family planning (Tehran, September) identified the urgent maternal and child-health and family-planning needs of Central Asian States.

The secretariat assisted Governments in analysing trends associated with urbanization.

ECONOMIC AND SOCIAL COUNCIL ACTION

On the recommendation of its Economic Committee, the Economic and Social Council adopted **decision 1993/319** without vote.

Population and sustainable development: goals and strategies into the twenty-first century

At its 46th plenary meeting, on 30 July 1993, the Economic and Social Council decided to bring to the attention of the General Assembly at its forty-eighth session resolution 49/4 of 29 April 1993, adopted by the Economic and Social Commission for Asia and the Pacific at its forty-ninth session, the text of which is annexed to the present decision.

ANNEX
Resolution 49/4 of 29 April 1993, adopted by the Economic and Social Commission for Asia and the Pacific at its forty-ninth session

Population and sustainable development: goals and strategies into the twenty-first century

The Economic and Social Commission for Asia and the Pacific,

Recalling its resolution 48/4 of 23 April 1992 on the Fourth Asian and Pacific Population Conference, held at Denpasar, Indonesia, from 19 to 27 August 1992, in which it recalled its decision to organize the Conference as a ministerial meeting jointly with the United Nations Population Fund in order to review the changes in the population situation that had occurred during the 1980s and highlight the perspectives of population policies and programmes during the 1990s in countries and areas of Asia and the Pacific,

Recognizing that integration of population factors in the socio-economic development process is crucial and that the alleviation of poverty is fundamental to the achievement of sustainable development,

Mindful of the substantial progress achieved by members and associate members in responding to the Asia-Pacific Call for Action on Population and Development adopted by the Third Asian and Pacific Population Conference, held at Colombo from 20 to 29 September 1982, and the role played by the secretariat and donors, particularly the United Nations Population Fund, in its implementation,

Taking note of the importance of the International Conference on Population and Development, to be held at Cairo from 5 to 13 September 1994,

1. *Welcomes* the adoption by the Fourth Asian and Pacific Population Conference, held at Denpasar, Indonesia, from 19 to 27 August 1992, of the Bali Declaration on Population and Sustainable Development, and endorses the recommendations of that Declaration;

2. *Urges* all members and associate members to take early and effective action to implement the Bali Decla-

ration through the provision of adequate financial and human resources;

3. *Also urges* all members, associate members and the Executive Secretary to make every effort to incorporate population, environment and development concerns in their inputs to the forthcoming International Conference on Population and Development;

4. *Calls upon* donor countries and funding agencies, in particular the United Nations Population Fund, United Nations bodies and specialized agencies, intergovernmental organizations and non-governmental organizations, to provide substantive and financial support for the implementation of the Bali Declaration;

5. *Requests* the Executive Secretary, as head of the main centre within the United Nations system for the general economic and social development of the Asian and Pacific region:

(*a*) To assist the members and associate members in the implementation of the Bali Declaration by initiating appropriate activities, and to review and appraise their progress;

(*b*) To cooperate with members and associate members in implementing the Bali Declaration and, in the light of the declining financial and human resources devoted to the Asian and Pacific regional population programme, to seek to mobilize resources for this purpose;

(*c*) To continue to play an advocacy role in the planning and implementation of population programmes in the Economic and Social Commission for Asia and the Pacific region, and even more vigorously in the light of the Bali Declaration;

(*d*) To disseminate information through regular publications and other appropriate means concerning the implementation of the Bali Declaration and the challenges faced by countries in the region in its implementation;

(*e*) To report to the Commission at periodic intervals on the progress made;

(*f*) To organize a meeting of senior planners and policy makers to incorporate concretely the recommendations of the Bali Declaration within the regional document for the International Conference on Population and Development;

6. *Invites* the Executive Secretary, in transmitting the present resolution to the Economic and Social Council, to request that it be brought to the attention of the General Assembly.

Economic and Social Council decision 1993/319

Adopted without vote

Approved by Economic Committee (E/1993/109) without vote, 23 July (meeting 14); oral proposal by Chairman; agenda item 14.

Human settlements

The highlight of 1993 activities associated with human settlements was the Ministerial Conference on Urbanization in Asia and the Pacific (Bangkok, 27 October–2 November).[47] The Conference adopted the Bangkok Declaration on Sustainable Urban Development and Management in Asia and the Pacific and endorsed a Regional Action Plan on Urbanization. It incorporated a preparatory meeting of senior officials, and symposia of local authorities, NGOs and the media, and it established an Asia-Pacific Urban Forum, which held its first meeting in conjunction with the Conference.

The Bangkok Declaration urged ESCAP members to prepare national strategies and action plans on urban development; strengthen interagency coordination to ensure an integrated approach to decision-making in urban development; recognize housing construction as a productive sector of the economy; ensure cooperation between all urban actors; strengthen the planning and management capacity of local authorities to deal effectively with urban poverty and environmental issues; and improve the availability of information, research, monitoring and evaluation mechanisms in the urban sector. ESCAP members were urged to appoint focal points for the implementation of the Regional Action Plan, and the Executive Director was requested to convene a ministerial conference on urbanization and the Asia-Pacific Urban Forum in 1998. The Conference also called on ESCAP members to promote broad-based participation in preparations for the United Nations Conference on Human Settlements (Habitat II), to be held in 1996 (see PART THREE, Chapter IX).

The Regional Action Plan on Urbanization[48] contained 40 proposals for action and seven recommendations related to urbanization strategies and policies, resource allocations, intragovernmental coordination and cooperation, human resources development, information and research, and monitoring and evaluation.

The Network of Training, Research and Information Institutes in Human Settlements in Asia and the Pacific was formally established at a meeting convened for that purpose (New Delhi, 27-29 September), and its Steering Committee held two meetings in 1993 (New Delhi, September/October; Bangkok, October). The ESCAP secretariat organized an intergovernmental expert group meeting on urbanization (Colombo, 30 March–1 April), a workshop on subnational area planning (Ho Chi Minh City, July), a high-level seminar on shelter for the urban poor (Bombay, India, 24 November) and an international training course on dwelling construction technology (Nanjing, China, 1-19 December). It launched a project on urban water management, which included a regional seminar on water management in urban areas (Bangkok, 22-26 March) and a workshop on urban water management in Viet Nam (Hanoi, November). It also published a directory of research and training institutes in human settlements and the _State of Urbanization in Asia and the Pacific, 1993_ report.

The secretariat assisted the Regional Network of Local Authorities for the Management of Human Settlements (CITYNET) to convene the fourth session of its Executive Committee (Colombo, 2-3 April) and the third CITYNET Congress (Bombay, 20-24 November).

Environment

The focus of ESCAP's environment subprogramme in 1993 was on the integration of environmental considerations into planning and decision-making.

The ESCAP/UNDP High-level Meeting on Environmentally Sound and Sustainable Development in Asia and the Pacific (Kuala Lumpur, 15-19 February)[49] reviewed the regional dimensions of Agenda 21, adopted by UNCED in 1992,[50] and implementation of the Regional Strategy on Environmentally Sound and Sustainable Development, endorsed by ESCAP in 1991.[51] It also developed a regional framework of action for sustainable development.

On 29 April,[52] the Commission requested the General Assembly to reinforce ESCAP's technical capacity for coordinating the implementation of Agenda 21 at the regional and subregional levels. The Executive Secretary was requested to explore the needs of Governments for its implementation, identify cooperation among Governments on environment and development issues, seek the cooperation and involvement of subregional organizations and NGOs, seek funding support from donors and the Global Environmental Facility, report in 1994 on the implementation of Agenda 21, and convene a ministerial-level conference on environment and development in 1995.

The ESCAP Committee on Environment and Sustainable Development held its first session at Bangkok from 4 to 8 October,[53] preceded by a preparatory expert group meeting (Bangkok, 30 September–2 October). The Committee considered Agenda 21 priorities and their implications for the Regional Strategy, examined environment and sustainable development issues and policies, and adopted 51 recommendations concerning, _inter alia_, energy and sustainable development, natural resources development and management, the integration of environmental considerations into economic decision-making, the impact of population growth and distribution on the environment, natural disaster reduction, and programme planning and implementation.

Following up on the Committee's recommendations, the secretariat initiated work on a state-of-the-environment database, studied models of national strategies for sustainable development in Mongolia, Nepal and the Philippines, held a workshop on environmental awareness (Kathmandu, November) and launched a UNDP/ESCAP programme for Asian cooperation in energy and the environment in Beijing in October. It also conducted case-studies on environmentally sound and sustainable development issues, including the development of environmentally sound coastal tourism and national plans of action to combat desertification. The Regional Network of Research and Training Centres on Desertification Control in Asia and the Pacific cooperated with UNEP to promote a methodology for mapping desertification and to establish an intergovernmental mechanism for capacity-building in desertification control. The Inter-Agency Committee on Environment and Development in Asia and the Pacific held its fourth meeting in 1993 (Manila, 15 and 16 March), and its Working Group met at Bangkok in February and September.

Among other activities were a meeting of senior officials on environmental cooperation in North-East Asia (Seoul, 8-11 February), a second Asia-Pacific seminar on climate change (Bangkok, 29-31 March), a regional meeting on the financing of environmentally sound development (Bangkok, June), a workshop on hazardous waste management (Bangkok, August), and consultative meetings on the development of a regional strategy on climate change (Bangkok, October) and on resource valuation in subnational planning (Bangkok, December).

Natural disaster reduction

The Typhoon Committee (twenty-sixth session, Quezon City, Philippines, 2-8 November)[54] reviewed, *inter alia*, ESCAP activities related to natural disaster reduction, including advisory services on flood-loss prevention and management; the preparation of guidelines for storm-surge mapping; the assessment of preparedness programmes, forecasting systems and operational methods for water-related natural disaster reduction; a publication on natural disaster reduction in Asia and the Pacific; and an exhibition on the International Day for Natural Disaster Reduction (13 October).

The ESCAP secretariat also organized a South and East Asia symposium on tropical storm and related flooding (Guangzhou, China, 22-25 November). The WMO/ESCAP Panel on Tropical Cyclones held its twentieth session in 1993 (Karachi, Pakistan, 16-22 February).

Statistics

Statistics development activities in 1993 continued to focus on the strengthening of national capabilities. The secretariat initiated projects on the development of gender statistics and on environmental and resource accounting, and sent 36 advisory missions to address various aspects of national accounts, the compilation of price and expenditure statistics, the use of statistical software packages and planning, and the processing and analysis of population censuses and surveys. It also

continued to gather demographic, social, economic and other statistics on the Asian and Pacific countries and to issue regular statistical publications.

In April, the Commission endorsed the 1992 recommendations of the Committee on Statistics[55] and urged the secretariat to undertake activities to improve statistics on trade in services and indicators on poverty. The secretariat was also urged to support implementation of the 1993 System of National Accounts.

During the year, ESCAP organized an expert group meeting on environment statistics (Bangkok, 9-12 March) and a workshop on the development and improvement of environment statistics (Kathmandu, 31 May-4 June). A workshop on the management of national statistical services in the 1990s (Bangkok, November) focused on data dissemination in monitoring human development. The Working Group of Statistical Experts held its eighth session (Bangkok, November).

Statistical Institute for Asia and the Pacific

The Statistical Institute for Asia and the Pacific[56] (Tokyo) continued to train statisticians in government services. In April, the Commission urged it to expand its programme on analysis and statistical interpretation and to increase its number of in-country courses. It was requested to provide training in techniques of data dissemination, expand the training of trainers, and produce printed and audiovisual training materials to support national training capability.

During the year, 610 people participated in the Institute's training courses on practical statistics, automatic data processing, analysis and interpretation of statistics and training of trainers in microcomputers, as well as its 21 in-country courses and a subregional course on food security statistics. Two research projects and a meeting of national focal points for human development indicators were held in conjunction with the workshop on the management of national statistical services in the 1990s (see above). The modalities of the sixth phase of the Institute's work, which commenced in 1992, were considered by its Advisory Council (Tokyo, 20 and 21 October).

Programme and organizational questions
Work programmes
for 1992-1993 and 1994-1995

In April,[1] the Commission reviewed the implementation of its 1992-1993 programme of work and endorsed the proposed programme changes for 1993.[57] The changes related to the special needs of children, the elderly and disabled persons; ESCAP urged the secretariat to involve NGOs and the private sector in services to enhance governmental support for those groups.

The Commission also adopted the draft programme of work and priorities for 1994-1995,[58] with modifications. The programme focused on regional economic cooperation, environment and sustainable development, poverty alleviation through economic growth and social development, transport and communications, statistics, and the least developed, land-locked and island developing countries. The Commission stressed that higher priority should also be given to macroeconomic policies and mineral resources development.

Fiftieth session of ESCAP

At its forty-ninth session, the Commission decided to hold its fiftieth session at New Delhi, India, between February and April 1994. It chose "Infrastructure development as key to economic growth and regional economic cooperation" as its theme topic for that session.

By **decision 1993/318** of 30 July, the Economic and Social Council endorsed the Commission's decision regarding the time and venue of its fiftieth session.

REFERENCES

[1]E/1993/36. [2]Ibid. (res. 49/1). [3]YUN 1992, p. 478. [4]E/ESCAP/891 & Corr.1. [5]YUN 1992, p. 934. [6]Ibid., p. 932, GA res. 46/235, 13 Apr. 1992. [7]E/1993/36 (res. 49/10). [8]*Economic and Social Survey of Asia and the Pacific 1993* (ST/ESCAP/1363), Sales No. E.94.II.F.8. [9]E/1994/52. [10]E/ESCAP/925 & Corr.1. [11]E/ESCAP/898 & Corr.1. [12]YUN 1992, p. 482. [13]E/ESCAP/899. [14]A/CONF.147/18. [15]GA res. 45/206, 21 Dec. 1990. [16]E/1993/36 (res. 49/8). [17]E/ESCAP/951 & Corr.1. [18]TD/B/40(1)/2. [19]E/ESCAP/900 & Corr.1. [20]E/ESCAP/934 & Corr.1. [21]E/ESCAP/969 & Corr.1. [22]E/ESCAP/933. [23]E/ESCAP/932 & Corr.1. [24]E/ESCAP/948 & Corr.1. [25]YUN 1992, p. 486. [26]YUN 1984, p. 624, GA res. 39/227, 18 Dec. 1984. [27]E/1993/36 (res. 49/2). [28]Ibid. (res. 49/3). [29]YUN 1982, p. 181. [30]E/ESCAP/960/Rev.1. [31]E/ESCAP/955. [32]E/ESCAP/908 & Corr.1. [33]E/ESCAP/954 & Corr.1. [34]E/1993/36 (res. 49/5). [35]E/ESCAP/938. [36]E/ESCAP/952. [37]YUN 1991, p. 316. [38]E/1993/36 (res. 49/9). [39]E/ESCAP/939. [40]E/1993/36 (res. 49/6). [41]YUN 1992, p. 490. [42]E/ESCAP/945 & Corr.1. [43]YUN 1992, p. 491. [44]E/ESCAP/944. [45]E/1993/36 (res. 49/4). [46]E/ESCAP/947. [47]E/ESCAP/940. [48]E/ESCAP/941 & Corr.1. [49]E/ESCAP/915. [50]YUN 1992, p. 670. [51]YUN 1991, p. 318. [52]E/1993/36 (res. 49/7). [53]E/ESCAP/936. [54]E/ESCAP/961. [55]YUN 1992, p. 492. [56]E/ESCAP/953 & Add.1. [57]E/ESCAP/917 & Corr.1. [58]E/ESCAP/914.

Europe

The forty-eighth session of the Economic Commission for Europe was held at Geneva from 19 to 27 April 1993,[1] at a time when unprecedented changes in ECE countries continued to pose new challenges to regional cooperation.

The dominant concerns in the period following the 1992 session included the continuing, and in some cases deepening, recession, high levels of unemployment, slow economic recovery in Europe and North America, currency fluctuations in Europe, increased protectionist pressures, slow and difficult adjustment to market economies in Eastern Europe and the former USSR, and migration policies. The economic outlook in Western Europe in 1993 was judged to be rather bleak, with high and rising unemployment.

The process of transition to a market economy in Central and Eastern European countries continued to require international financial and technical assistance and counselling, although reforms were beginning to bear fruit and economic indicators were improving. The establishment of a single internal market for capital, labour, goods and services was completed in Western Europe, and integration continued at the regional and subregional levels with the completion of cooperation and free-trade agreements.

At its 1993 session, the Commission reviewed its implementation of the relevant provisions of the Final Act, the 1990 Charter of Paris for a New Europe and the 1992 Helsinki Declaration of the Conference on Security and Cooperation in Europe (CSCE). Particular attention was given to the strengthening of security and economic cooperation in the Mediterranean region. On 26 April,[2] the Commission stressed the need for continued efforts to protect the Mediterranean ecosystem. The ECE Executive Secretary was requested to continue efforts to increase interregional cooperation on matters within the competence of ECE and of common interest to Mediterranean countries, and to facilitate consultations on the Mediterranean Technical Assistance Programme and the Mediterranean Special Programme of Action to strengthen environmental management and development in the subregion. He was to report in 1994 on the progress made.

During the year, ECE participated in the first CSCE Economic Forum (Prague, Czech Republic, 16-18 March), the CSCE Mediterranean seminar on environmental issues of importance to the subregion (Valletta, Malta, 17-21 May) and the CSCE Council meeting (Rome, Italy, 30 November and 1 December). In April, the Commission invited its subsidiary bodies to contribute to the follow-up of the Economic Forum and requested them to take provisions of the CSCE documents into account in their work.[3] It requested the subsidiary bodies to implement its 1990 decisions on restructuring within ECE and asked the Executive Secretary to report on the subject in 1994. The Commission considered its activities and future work in the priority areas of environment, transport, statistics, trade facilitation and economic analysis. It discussed its efforts to assist countries in transition to a market economy and international cooperation to address the consequences of the 1986 nuclear accident at Chernobyl (see PART THREE, Chapter III).

The Commission adopted organizational decisions related to resources for its priority and other sectors;[4] reporting from its subsidiary bodies;[5] the preparation and organization of its annual session;[6] and the amendment of its rules of procedure.[7] The Commission approved its work programme for 1993-1994 and endorsed the programme for 1993-1997,[3] subject to review at its 1994 session. The programme of work included its five priority areas, as well as energy, international trade, industry and technology, agriculture and timber, and human settlements.

On 26 April,[8] the Commission recommended to the Economic and Social Council amendments to its terms of reference to the effect, *inter alia*, that new Member States of the United Nations located in the Asian part of the former USSR were entitled to be members of ECE insofar as the former USSR was a European Member of the United Nations. By **decision 1993/317** of 30 July, the Council approved the amendments and modified ECE's terms of reference accordingly.

As a result of that decision, seven countries that were admitted to the United Nations in 1992 (Armenia, Azerbaijan, Georgia, Kazakhstan, Kyrgyzstan, Turkmenistan and Uzbekistan) became members of ECE in 1993, and five other countries (Andorra, the Czech Republic, Monaco, Slovakia and the former Yugoslav Republic of Macedonia) automatically gained membership by virtue of their admission to the United Nations in 1993, bringing ECE membership at the end of 1993 to 54.

In response to a 1991 Commission request,[9] its Chairman continued to convene ad hoc informal meetings of ECE to consult on policy matters, assist with preparations for the annual sessions, monitor progress in the work programmes and offer guidance to the Executive Secretary. In accordance with a 1992 Commission decision on the provision of adequate resources,[10] the Chairman also arranged consultations between the Executive Secretary and ECE's subsidiary bodies.

As agreed at an ad hoc informal meeting on 24 September, the Commission, at a special session on 26 November,[11] designated its Vice-Chairman as the new Chairman and elected a new Vice-Chairman.

The Commission continued to provide a bridge between the United Nations and other regional economic institutions, including the European Community (EC), the Organisation for Economic Cooperation and Development (OECD), the Council of Europe and the European Bank for Reconstruction and Development.

On 20 April,[12] the Commission, by 34 votes to 2, with 2 abstentions, recommended to the Economic and Social Council that the Federal Republic of Yugoslavia (Serbia and Montenegro) should not participate in the work of ECE as long as it did not participate in the work of the General Assembly pursuant to a 1992 Assembly resolution.[13] By **decision 1993/316** of 30 July, the Council endorsed that decision.

Economic trends

The economic situation in the ECE region in 1993 was characterized by continuing recession in Western Europe and recovery in North America. The United States and Canada registered growth rates of about 3 per cent and 3.6 per cent, respectively, while the economy of EC as a whole was estimated to have contracted by 0.3 per cent. The United Kingdom was the only country in the region to have shown signs of recovery. Output grew by an estimated 1.5 per cent in the United Kingdom and a mere 0.5 per cent in Italy, but stagnated in France and declined by almost 1 per cent in Germany, although eastern Germany recorded growth of about 8 per cent because of government consumption and investment. Regional unemployment rose to exceed 10 per cent in 1993, but, by the end of the year, the recession appeared to have bottomed out in Western Europe and a modest recovery was forecast for 1994.

In Eastern Europe, total output fell by 3 per cent in 1993, less than half the 1992 rate of decline, according to the summary of the survey of economic conditions in the ECE region, 1993-1994.[14] However, the collapse in output continued virtually unchecked in the Russian Federation and other members of the Commonwealth of Independent States (CIS), with an average drop of 13 per cent following a 20 per cent drop in 1992. The depression in CIS was greatly intensified by the collapse of trade among its members. Following the breakup of the rouble zone in 1993, most CIS countries faced a large deterioration in their terms of trade with the Russian Federation and with other suppliers of energy, which raised their oil and gas prices to world market levels. They also suffered interruptions in deliveries because of nonpayment of debts and inadequacies in their distribution systems. Similar problems in the Baltic States were aggravated by the loss of markets in the former USSR and the introduction of tough stabilization policies. At the same time, GDP rose by 4 per cent in Poland and increased modestly in Romania and Slovenia. Output was on the rise in Hungary and Albania, due to a sharp increase in agricultural production, and the recession was levelling out in the Czech Republic. With the exception of Slovenia and Albania, however, production continued to fall in other southern European economies in transition, especially in Yugoslavia (Serbia and Montenegro) and the former Yugoslav Republic of Macedonia.

The economic transition in Central and Eastern European countries was accompanied by a pronounced deterioration in social indicators for poverty, mortality, marriages and births, preschool and youth education, and crime. The unemployment level rose threefold in Eastern Europe between 1991 and the end of 1993 to almost 7.6 million people, or some 14 per cent of the labour force, although national figures ranged from 3.5 per cent in the Czech Republic to about 30 per cent in Albania and the former Yugoslav Republic of Macedonia. Official unemployment rates ranged between 0.2 per cent and 1.3 per cent in CIS countries, except Armenia (6.2 per cent), and began to increase sharply in the Baltic States. Although the official rate in the Russian Federation was 1.1 per cent, the unofficial rate was more than 10 per cent.

Annual inflation rates ranged from between 20 and 37 per cent in the Czech Republic, Hungary, Poland, Slovakia and Slovenia to more than 70 per cent in Bulgaria and 350 per cent in the former Yugoslav Republic of Macedonia. The rate was between 20 and 26 per cent per month in the Russian Federation and averaged more than 1,000 per cent for 1993 in virtually all other CIS States. Hyperinflation continued unchecked in Yugoslavia (Serbia and Montenegro), while a number of other countries, including Georgia and Ukraine, had passed, or were dangerously close to, that threshold. The year also brought a sharp deterioration in the current account balances of all economies in transition except that of the Czech Republic, as export growth declined and imports expanded, in many cases substantially. Export values fell by 13 per cent in Bulgaria and 16 per cent in Hungary but increased by 7 per cent and 17 per cent in Poland and the Czech Republic, respectively. The growth of imports ranged from less than 1 per cent in Bulgaria to about 25 per cent in Poland. Hungary had the largest current account deficit ($3.5 billion), followed by Poland ($2.3 billion) and Romania ($1.5 billion). A large reduction in subsidized imports, coupled with weak domestic demand and the depreciation of the rouble, brought a 27 per cent drop in imports into the Russian Federation, while exports continued to rise, creating a $15 billion surplus in the current account balance.

Although the transition to a market economy in Central and Eastern European countries led to a drastic reduction in both agricultural and industrial output, restructuring and privatization yielded an expansion of the services sector, improvements in the availability, range and quality of goods and services and the re-emergence of an entrepreneurial middle class. The private sector's share of total output increased from 29 per cent of GDP in Poland to 47 per cent in 1992 and from virtually zero in the Czech Republic to around 50 per cent in 1993. Agricultural land was returned to private ownership in Albania and Romania, and the mass privatization of medium- and large-sized enterprises began in the Russian Federation. By the end of 1993, about 85 per cent of small enterprises employing fewer than 200 people had been privatized. Nevertheless, industrial sectors continued to be dominated by large State-owned enterprises whose share in output and employment remained considerable, and some countries made little progress in the transition process in general.

The economic situation in 1993 was also characterized by the collapse of fixed investment, which had declined since 1989 by an average of 40 per cent in Eastern Europe, 56 per cent in the Russian Federation and Ukraine and 80 per cent in the Baltic States. In 1993, some recovery of fixed investment appeared to be taking place in Poland and Hungary and in some sectors in the Czech Republic. Investment rose by about 11 per cent in Slovenia. At the same time, deficiencies in traditional fiscal and monetary policy instruments caused the emphasis of macroeconomic stabilization policies to be placed on reductions in government expenditure, threatening further unemployment and cuts in social security benefits. Attempts to cut large budget deficits by increasing tax revenue were inhibited by underdeveloped tax collection systems and widespread tax evasion.

**Western economic
assistance to Eastern Europe**

Gross financial flows to the economies in transition from western market economies and international financial institutions increased from $31.3 billion in 1990 to an estimated $45 billion in 1993, with special financing (debt write-offs, rescheduling, deferrals and arrears) accounting for more than half of the total. About two thirds of the total went to the Russian Federation and other CIS States. Inflows to Eastern Europe concentrated on four "advanced" transition economies (the Czech Republic, Hungary, Poland and Slovenia), which had received more than 70 per cent of development bank commitments to the subregion and more than 90 per cent of FDI flows since 1990. During that period, development bank loans to Eastern Europe totalled about $5 billion, to which $5.4 billion in official grants from western Governments could be added.

ODA, excluding bilateral credits, for the period 1990-1993 was roughly equal to FDI flows and totalled less than $10 billion, including $3.5 billion for 1993. The level of FDI was considerably less than hoped for, because of the perceived high risks and uncertainty of investment in transition economies and operational problems encountered by foreign investors. According to the survey summary,[14] economies in transition needed to concentrate on the creation of essential infrastructure for a market economy, including a non-discriminatory legal framework for foreign investment. Given the relatively small size of domestic markets, they also needed to facilitate intraregional trade and access to the much larger markets of the successor States of the former USSR as a means of attracting FDI.

Activities in 1993

The main emphasis of ECE activities in 1993 remained on the transition process in Central and Eastern European countries and their integration into the European and global economies.[15] Since the inception of its programme to assist economies in transition in 1990, ECE had organized a total of 113 workshops, including 30 in 1993, on issues relating to energy, human settlements, industrial development, statistics, environment, transport, trade, timber, agriculture, and development issues and policies. Its subsidiary bodies continued their special assistance programmes in these and other areas, including trade, population activities, industry and technology. The United Nations/ECE Trust Fund for Assistance to Countries in Transition became operational in 1993, received $130,657 in contributions during the year and had a balance of $70,000 by year's end. ECE was introducing a programme of regional advisory services and considered proposals to diversify and strengthen its assistance. Particular attention was paid to market access for countries in transition, which assumed special importance late in the year with the successful conclusion of the Uruguay Round of multilateral trade negotiations (see PART THREE, Chapter IV).

In April,[16] the Commission requested its Executive Secretary to present proposals for the diversification of ECE assistance to the General Assembly at its forty-eighth (1993) session and to report on the subject in 1994.

Other areas of concern were ECE's continuing assistance to developing countries of other regions and its contribution to United Nations global programmes,[17] as well as its participation in CSCE.[18] In April,[19] the Commission decided to convene a high-level regional preparatory meeting in 1994 for the fourth World Conference on Women (1995) and invited member States and relevant international organizations to contribute to its preparation.

International trade

In accordance with the 1992-1995 programme of work of the Committee on the Development of Trade, endorsed by ECE in April 1993, activities focused on trade facilitation, promotion and analysis. The ECE secretariat continued to publish its quarterly *East-West Investment News* and prepared studies on the implications of privatization for economies in transition, their place in the world market, and conditions conducive to expanded trade among those economies. A business forum was organized in Belarus (Minsk, November) and a workshop was held on the promotion of FDI in a small country in transition (Ljubljana, Slovenia, 29 and 30 November). A guide on financing East-West trade and privatization in Central and Eastern Europe was revised at a seminar on the subject (Geneva, 13 September) and approved for publication by the Working Party on International Contract Practices in Industry (forty-second session, Geneva, 13-15 September). The Working Party also began to prepare a new guide on property law in Central and Eastern Europe, which dealt with questions of ownership, valuation, security and restitution.

The Working Party on Facilitation of International Trade Procedures held two sessions at Geneva in 1993 (thirty-seventh, 16-19 March; thirty-eighth, 21-24 September). It approved a number of new messages for the United Nations Electronic Data Interchange for Administration, Commerce and Transport (UN/EDIFACT) as a standard for world trade. In total, there were 168 messages at various stages of development by the Working Party. It also approved the establishment of an African EDIFACT Board, in addition to existing regional boards for Pan America, Western Europe, Eastern Europe, Australia/New Zealand and Asia.

An intersecretariat task force of ECE, UNCTAD and the International Trade Centre was also established in 1993 to coordinate activities among the three bodies, and the Inter-Agency Working Group for Coordinated Open Electronic Data Interchange Standards Development approved its final report.

Industry

In April 1993, ECE stressed the importance of follow-up to the 1992 high-level meeting on cooperation and sustainable development in the chemical industry[20] and encouraged the Working Party on the Chemical Industry to continue its efforts to achieve sustainable development in that sector.[21]

As a follow-up to the high-level meeting, a meeting of experts was held (Warsaw, Poland, 15 and 16 April) to assist with a detailed project proposal and feasibility study for the establishment of a Regional Environmental Management Centre for the Chemical Industry. The Working Party (third session, Geneva, 6-8 October)[22] welcomed the proposal in principle and invited interested parties to help fund the Centre. It endorsed the reports of the meeting of experts on the periodic survey of the chemical industry and of the annual meeting of rapporteurs on aromatic hydrocarbons and olefins. It also organized a round-table discussion on conditions for economic recovery and sustainable development in the chemical industry. Discussion focused on the competitiveness of the European chemical industry.

The Working Party took note of the study on the management of plastic wastes in the region and of progress in preparing the *ECE Directory of Chemical Producers and Products*. It was agreed that the secretariat should publish an annual review of the chemical industry in 1993. The Working Party considered proposals for a pilot project to demonstrate the clean-up of selected chemical waste sites and for a comparative study of chemical legislation in ECE member countries. It noted proposals to hold workshops in 1994 on waste treatment in industrial parks and on the rational use of raw materials and energy in the chemical industry. It decided to convene a preparatory meeting in 1994 for the seminar on the complex utilization of raw materials using advanced low- and non-waste process technologies. The seminar was scheduled to be held in Moscow in 1995. The Working Party adopted its programme of work for 1994-1998 and agreed to include a study on trends in structural and ownership changes in the chemical industries of the economies in transition.

The Working Party on Engineering Industries and Automation (twelfth session, Geneva, 24-26 February)[23] considered the report of the first ad hoc meeting on the study of medium- and long-term trends and prospects in the sector, endorsed annual reviews of the sector for 1990 and 1991 and decided to add short-term forecasts of research, production and trade in engineering industries for selected countries to the annual review. It examined studies of low-waste technologies in engineering industries and of food-processing machinery and packaging techniques, as well as the results of workshops on rehabilitation engineering for disabled and elderly persons. It took note of preparations for a workshop on industrial robots, automatic handling and assembly equipment in present and future manufacturing systems, scheduled for 1994, and for a seminar on foundry production and ecology, held at Minsk (24-28 May).

The Working Party also considered reports of the thirteenth and fourteenth meetings on statistical questions concerning engineering industries and automation and agreed to organize a workshop on PRODCOM—EC's system of product statistics. It reviewed seminars and workshops held in 1992, discussed proposals for future workshops and adopted its work programme for 1993-1997.

The Working Party on Steel (third session, Geneva, 20-22 October)[24] considered reports of a meeting of experts on the steel market and of an intersecretariat meeting on steel statistics. It examined developments in 1993 and prospects for 1994. It reviewed the preparation of bulletins on steel statistics and a study on iron and steel scrap, and considered a study on the impact of scrap reclamation and preparation on the world steel industry. It also considered the report of the first ad hoc meeting for a study on recent developments in steel consumption and trade in ECE member countries. The Working Party was informed of a study tour of steel plants in the Czech Republic and Slovakia (6-11 June) and accepted Japan's invitation for a study tour of its steel installations in 1994.

Acting on a recommendation of a seminar on metallurgy and ecology (Nancy, France, 10-14 May), the Working Party decided to convene an expert group meeting in 1994 on ecological issues in the iron and steel industry. Discussion was to focus on environmental management, the recycling of iron and steel products and by-products, environmental safety standards and the harmonization of regulations in ECE member countries. The programme of work for 1994-1998 included seminars on recycling, privatization and structural changes in the steel industry of countries in transition, a workshop on restructuring the iron and steel industry in Ukraine, and a study on restructuring and changing ownership in the steel industry.

In April, ECE endorsed the 1993-1997 work programmes of the three Working Parties.

Transport

The Inland Transport Committee (fifty-fifth session, Geneva, 1-5 February 1993)[25] analysed the transport situation in member countries and considered activities to assist economies in transition. It discussed, among other things, transport policy and economics; road, rail and inland water transport; customs questions; the transport of dangerous goods and perishable foodstuffs; follow-up to the 1991 Pan-European Transport Conference (the Prague Conference); traffic flows; transport in the Mediterranean; road traffic safety; international harmonization of technical requirements for the construction of road vehicles; and preparation of the 1995 census of road traffic.

The Committee decided to study further the feasibility of organizing a regional conference on transport and the environment. It also decided to convene an ad hoc expert group meeting on the development of a European railway network and to launch a study on the establishment of a main inland waterways network. It endorsed the draft Convention on Customs Treatment of Pool Containers used in International Transport (Container Pool Convention), prepared by its Working Party on Customs Questions affecting Transport. By three separate resolutions, the Committee decided to designate a second Road Safety Week in the spring of 1995; approved provisions relating to inland water transport and requested its Working Party on Combined Transport to study possibilities for establishing a legally binding international instrument on combined inland water transport, to deal with, *inter alia*, coastal shipping and the handling of dangerous goods; and endorsed recommendations for the introduction of larger containers in combined transport, adopted by a 1992 global seminar on the subject. In April, ECE acted on those resolutions by adopting a decision on cooperation in the field of transport.[26]

In another resolution, the Committee recommended that Governments harmonize customs controls at border crossings to improve traffic flow. It also adopted its revised terms of reference and its programme of work for 1993-1997, endorsed by ECE in April.

Also in April, the Commission stressed the need to complete provisions for the carriage of dangerous goods by inland waterways, and underlined the need to harmonize further international regulations for their transportation. It welcomed the revision of the 1968 Convention on Road Signs and Signals and the 1971 European Agreement supplementing it. It called for the early completion of joint road and rail infrastructure projects and invited the Inland Transport Committee to consider ECE's role in implementing a coherent European system of transport infrastructure networks.

During the year, the ECE secretariat continued to participate in preparations for the second Pan-European Transport Conference, scheduled for 1994, including its draft Declaration and a European Transport Charter. It supported the Trans-European North-South Motorway (TEM) and Trans-European Railways (TER) projects and undertook studies on traffic forecasting and the upgrading of non-motorway sections of the TEM network. A trust fund agreement for the TER project became operational in 1993. The secretariat studied bottlenecks and gaps in international infrastructure networks and completed its revision of provisions concerning the carriage of dangerous goods by inland waterways.

During 1993, 23 States, including one non-ECE member, became contracting parties to a total of 31 ECE legal instruments. An ECE infrastructure agreement for combined transport entered into force on 20 October, and an inventory of its infrastructure parameters was published. The Conference of the Contracting Parties to the 1957 European Agreement concerning the International Carriage of Dangerous Goods by Road (first session, Geneva, 28 October) adopted a Protocol amending the definition of vehicles and the procedure for amendments to the annexes. Other activities included workshops on privatization of the road haulage industry (Berlin, 1 and 2 April) and on transport infrastructure planning for economies in transition (Aachen, Germany, 8 and 9 April), and ad hoc meetings at Geneva on the development of a European railway network (15 September), the facilitation of border crossings for international rail transport (16 September) and the road traffic census (22 and 23 November).

Energy

At its third session (Geneva, 9-11 November),[27] the Committee on Energy reviewed the energy situation and policies in the region, particularly the economies in transition. It adopted its programme of work for 1993-1997, covering energy reform in Central and Eastern Europe and the broad objectives of more rational energy use and sustainable development. The Committee also reviewed activities to enhance energy efficiency, promote cooperation in the field of renewable sources of energy and assist in the transition of the coal, gas and electric power industries in Central and Eastern Europe. It agreed, in principle, to create a working party on renewable sources of energy, and requested the secretariat to reconvene the Steering Committee of the project entitled "Global Energy Efficiency 21: An Interregional Approach", in consultation with other regional commissions and relevant United Nations bodies.

The Working Parties on Coal, Gas and Electric Power held their third sessions at Geneva. The Working Party on Coal (11-13 October) focused on the transition of coal industries in Central and Eastern Europe to market economy conditions. Its emphasis was on the social and environmental consequences of restructuring, as well as the use of clean technologies and environmental impact assessments in underground and opencast coal mining, international coal trade and transport. It also examined the prospects for coal in the ECE region. Activities during the year included a symposium on new coal utilization technologies (Helsinki, Finland, 10-13 May), which focused on gasification, liquefaction, combustion and environmental issues; and a preparatory meeting for the symposium on the sustainable development of opencast coal mining regions (Most, Czech Republic, 11 November). Workshops were held on the restructuring of coal industries in Central and Eastern Europe (Katowice, Poland, 1-3 June) and on opportunities to develop new economic activities in the coal mining regions of Central and Eastern Europe (Brussels, Belgium, 18-21 October).

The Working Party on Gas (25-27 January) considered a programme to assist the adaptation of gas industries in Central and Eastern Europe to market conditions and approved a technical cooperation programme to promote and develop a market-based gas industry. The programme was to be operated through a trust fund, which was further considered at an ad hoc meeting (Geneva, 10 May). Workshops were held on gas pricing and gas market structure (Groningen, Netherlands, April), the rehabilitation of gas transportation systems (Minsk, Belarus, 8 and 9 June) and coal-bed methane recovery (Donetsk, Ukraine, 15-17 June). A symposium (Istanbul, Turkey, 4-8 October) addressed prospects for gas markets and the region's gas industry in the years 2000-2010. In November, the Committee on Energy invited European Governments and gas enterprises to follow up on the symposium's recommendations.

The Working Party on Electric Power (11-13 May) concentrated on the implications of economic reforms in Central and Eastern Europe for electric power demand and supply, the environment, sustainable development, and energy policies and strategies. A study was carried out on prospects for the natural gas and electric power industries, and a workshop was organized on the possibilities of refurbishing fossil-fired power stations, taking environmental requirements into account (Ankara, Turkey, April).

The Steering Committee of the "Energy Efficiency 2000" project to reduce the gap between energy-intensive industries in Eastern Europe and the energy-saving technologies of the West held its third and fourth meetings in 1993 at Geneva (2-4 March and 12-14 October). The Committee considered developing a new UNDP/ECE project on demonstration zones for the implementation of energy-efficiency strategies in Central and Eastern Europe, supported by the Global Environment Facility. Activities during the year included a seminar on energy efficiency and economic transition in Central and Eastern Europe (Paris, 25-28 May), an ad hoc meeting on methods of financing energy-efficiency demonstration zones (Newcastle, United Kingdom, 15 and 16 June), and a symposium on the environmental benefits of energy conservation (Moscow, 20-24 September). In November, the Committee on Energy invited its members to meet their pledges to the project trust fund, and requested the Executive Secretary to determine requirements for the second phase of the project, including work on energy-efficiency standards.

The secretariat issued a publication on solar power systems and made a presentation at a UNESCO high-level meeting for a world solar summit (Paris, July).

Agriculture

The Committee on Agriculture (forty-fourth session, Geneva, 8-10 March)[28] reviewed recent developments and prospects for agriculture in the region, and agricultural policy reforms in the economies in transition in particular. It adopted its work programme for 1993-1997, focusing on economic analysis of the agri-food sector and farm management, agriculture and the environment, the standardization and quality of perishable produce, and food and agricultural statistics. The Committee also reviewed European trade in agricultural products and the market situation for selected commodities, including grains, livestock and meat, and dairy products. The Committee welcomed the 1992 decision by the FAO Council to establish Working Parties on the Economics of the Agri-food Sector and Farm Management, and on Relations between Agriculture and the Environment, as joint FAO/ECE bodies. The Working Parties held their second sessions at Geneva in 1993 (15-18 February and 24-28 May, respectively).

The Committee requested its Working Party on Standardization of Perishable Produce and Quality Development to study the legal aspects of commercial standards for perishable produce in economies in transition. The Senior Advisers to ECE Governments on Environmental and Water Problems (see below, under "Environment") were requested to consider establishing a task force on the prevention and control of water pollution from fertilizers and pesticides.

ECE endorsed the Committee's programme of work in April, and the coordination of related activities between ECE and FAO was examined at a joint meeting of the Committee's Bureau and the Executive Committee of the FAO European Commission for Agriculture (Budapest, Hungary, 5-7 July).

The Timber Committee held its fifty-first session in 1993 (Rome, 11-15 October),[29] jointly with the twenty-sixth session of the FAO European Forestry Commission. The joint session reviewed market developments for forest products in 1993 and prospects for 1994, and considered the policy implications of and follow-up to the 1990 ECE/FAO forest resource assessment (temperate zones) and preparations for the assessment 2000. It also examined the implications of UNCED for forestry in Europe. It was informed of the outcome of the second Ministerial Conference on the Protection of Forests in Europe (Helsinki, June) and of a seminar on the sustainable development of boreal and temperate forests (Montreal, Canada, September), sponsored by CSCE. The joint session endorsed the programme of assistance to countries in transition and agreed that a team of specialists should monitor its implementation at regular intervals. It also endorsed the terms of reference for a team of public relations specialists to prepare a "public relations tool kit" for those countries that wished to use it in the forestry and forest industries sector.

Acting on the recommendations of an ad hoc meeting (Geneva, 15-17 February) and the Joint FAO/ECE Working Party on Forest Economics and Statistics (nineteenth session, Geneva, 7-9 June), the joint session approved proposals to improve the collection and dissemination of statistics. On the recommendation of another ad hoc meeting (Geneva, 22-24 February), it agreed to launch a study on the outlook for non-wood forest goods and services. The joint session also reviewed developments in the tropical forests action programme, progress with the European timber trends and prospects study, and a pilot study of long-term historical changes in temperate-zone forest resources. The Timber Committee approved its programme of work for 1994-1998, focusing on developments affecting forestry and forests products; the collection, dissemination and improvement of statistics on forests and forest products; forest technology, management and training; the sustainable development of forests and forest products; and assistance to economies in transition.

Activities during the year included an ad hoc FAO/ECE meeting on global forest resource assessment (Kotka, Finland, 3-7 May), a seminar on the use of multifunctional machinery and equipment in logging operations (Olenino, Russian Federation, 22-28 August), and workshops on new forestry law for countries in transition (Debe, Poland, 27 September–1 October) and on sustainable development in the management of a forest enterprise (Switzerland, 21-26 November). The Steering Committee of the Joint FAO/ECE/ILO Committee on Forest Technology, Management and Training held its eleventh session (Geneva, 21 and 22 September). A team of specialists established to discuss problems in the forestry and forest industries arising from radiation contamination, and from the Chernobyl disaster in particular, met for the first time in November. The secretariat issued forest and forest-products country profiles for Albania, Estonia, Hungary, Poland and Romania.

Economic analysis

The Senior Economic Advisers to ECE Governments (twenty-ninth session, Geneva, 7-11 June)[30] held a round-table conference on structural change, employment and unemployment in market and transition economies. The conference discussed the factors necessary for economic recovery in the transition countries, long-term projections and perspectives for the world economy, and issues related to interregional and intraregional trade, sustainable economic development, and structural changes in employment, labour productivity and working patterns and their impact on economic growth.

During 1993, the secretariat's activities in the field of economic analysis and projections focused

on population research dealing with international migration, the elderly, fertility and family surveys, and population-related policies. ECE cooperated in organizing the European Population Conference, held at Geneva in March in preparation for the 1994 International Conference on Population and Development (see PART THREE, Chapter IX).

Environment

The Senior Advisers to ECE Governments on Environmental and Water Problems (sixth session, Geneva, 16-19 March)[31] reviewed preparations for the "Environment for Europe" conference, to be held later in the year (see below), and adopted their contribution to it. They also reviewed the implementation of ECE Conventions, on Environmental Impact Assessment in a Transboundary Context, on the Transboundary Effects of Industrial Accidents and on the Protection and Use of Transboundary Watercourses and International Lakes. They also examined the implications of UNCED for the ECE region and progress towards cooperation in water management, environmentally sound technology and products, the management of hazardous chemicals, integrated pollution prevention and control, environment and economics, and bilateral and multilateral financial cooperation.

The Senior Advisers adopted recommendations on water-quality criteria, including the control of water pollution from fertilizers and pesticides, and requested the secretariat to publish them in the *Water Series*. They endorsed the work programme of the Joint Working Group on Environment and Economics (third session, Geneva, 19-21 January), as well as their own, which focused on policy issues, environmental impact assessment, environmentally sound technology and products, water management and industrial accidents.

In April, ECE endorsed the Senior Advisers' work programme and adopted a decision on cooperation in the field of environment and sustainable development.[32] It called on member States to ratify or accede to the ECE environmental Conventions, underlined the need to extend the OECD system of environmental performance reviews to other ECE countries, and requested the Executive Secretary to carry out a feasibility study on the organization of a regional conference on transport and the environment (see also above, under "Transport"). In separate action,[33] ECE called on its subsidiary bodies to participate in international activities to mitigate the consequences of the Chernobyl accident, and requested the Executive Secretary to study the possibility of contributing to the United Nations review of those activities.

The Declaration of the Ministerial Conference "Environment for Europe" (Lucerne, Switzerland,

28-30 April) provided for ECE to have a central role in coordinating the "Environment for Europe" process, including follow-up to the Conference, preparations for the next conference in 1995, and development of the environmental programme for Europe. Pursuant to the Declaration, the Senior Advisers, at a special session (Geneva, 21 October),[34] established the Working Group of Senior Governmental Officials "Environment for Europe" and invited it to give particular consideration to the short-term needs of economies in transition. The Senior Advisers also recommended that they become the Committee on Environmental Policy.

At its eleventh session (Geneva, 1-3 December), the Executive Body for the 1979 Convention on Long-range Transboundary Air Pollution adopted the introduction and part I of the revised technical annex to the protocol for the control of nitrogen oxide emissions, and adopted a framework for a second protocol for the further reduction of sulphur emissions, expected to be finalized early in 1994. It reviewed activities of the Working Group on Effects (twelfth session, Geneva, 6-8 July) and requested it to prepare information on the critical-loads approach and its application for the new sulphur protocol. The Executive Body also considered activities of the Steering Body to the Cooperative Programme for Monitoring and Evaluation of the Long-range Transmission of Air Pollutants in Europe (EMEP) (seventeenth session, Geneva, 6-8 September).

By the end of 1993, there were 37 parties to the 1979 Convention. There were 35 parties to its protocol on long-term financing for EMEP, 21 to the protocol on the reduction of sulphur emissions, 23 to the protocol on the control of nitrogen oxide emissions, and four to the protocol on the control of emissions of volatile organic compounds. The 1991 Convention on Environmental Impact Assessment in a Transboundary Context had been ratified by four Governments. The 1992 Convention on the Protection and Use of Transboundary Watercourses and International Lakes had been ratified or acceded to by three countries, and the 1992 Convention on the Transboundary Effects of Industrial Accidents had been approved by one Government. In 1993, the status and implementation of the last Convention was reviewed at the second meeting of its signatories (Geneva, 14-17 June).

The Working Group on Strategies met three times at Geneva during the year, for its ninth (1-5 March), tenth (24-28 May) and eleventh sessions (30 August–3 September), and the Working Group on Technology held its second session (Geneva, 28 and 29 June). Other activities included workshops on costing techniques for environmental policies (Geneva, 18 and 19 January) and on the impact of economic restructuring on the environment (Budapest, 9 and 10 March), and a seminar on low-waste technology and environmentally sound products (Warsaw, 24-28 May).

Human settlements

The Committee on Human Settlements (fifty-fourth session, Geneva, 21-23 September)[35] discussed the human settlements situation in the region and related trends and policies. It reviewed work accomplished or in progress on the promotion of sustainable human settlements policies; practical transition problems; modernization policies for built-up areas; the management of land, housing and building; major trends influencing human settlements development; housing forecasting; building pathology and prevention of disorders; cooperation with the Energy Efficiency 2000 project (see above, under "Energy"); development of human settlements statistics; human settlements problems in southern Europe; and the ECE compendium of model provisions for building regulations. The Committee also discussed its contribution to the second United Nations Conference on Human Settlements (Habitat II), to be held in 1996 (see PART THREE, Chapter IX). It recommended that ECE convene a high-level regional preparatory meeting for Habitat II.

The Committee adopted terms of reference for its new Working Parties on Sustainable Human Settlements Planning and on Housing Development, Modernization and Management (formerly Housing, Modernization and Management), and agreed on a draft programme of work, focusing on the sustainable development of human settlements and the process of socio-economic transition. It established a task force to elaborate draft guidelines on sustainable human settlements planning and management and approved a new set of regional recommendations on current housing and building statistics.

In 1993, the Working Parties on Housing, Modernization and Management and on Sustainable Human Settlements Planning held their first sessions at Geneva (2-4 June and 28-30 June, respectively). The secretariat convened a consultation with NGOs to intensify their involvement in the Committee's programme of work. It issued housing policy guidelines with special reference to economies in transition, as well as an information leaflet on human settlements in the 1990s. During the period from September 1992 to September 1993, 12 workshops and three seminars were organized on issues related to human settlements. They included a seminar on reform of real property, land registration and cadastre for promoting economic development and improving urban management and planning (Copenhagen, Denmark, 25-29 October).

Standardization

The Working Party on Standardization Policies (third meeting, Geneva, 12-14 May)[36] reviewed developments in the field of standardization, including coordination, harmonization, conformity assessment and metrology in testing. The Working Party and the Committee on Energy organized a seminar on energy-efficiency standards and labelling systems (Geneva, 11 May), and the Working Party adopted its programme of work for 1993-1997.

In October, the Working Party decided to publish a third revised version of the ECE recommendations on standardization policies and a list of contact points in ECE member countries, which provided information on national standards, conformity assessment procedures and metrology.

Statistics

The Conference of European Statisticians (forty-first session, Geneva, 14-18 June)[37] considered the consequences of increased ECE membership, recent developments in countries in transition and a framework for priority-setting. It examined ways to improve the efficiency of the statistical process and discussed the proposed new economic classification for the United States. The Conference reviewed activities in its programme areas, including the organization and operation of statistical services, statistical information technology, and support for ECE publications, studies and projects. It noted the report of a seminar for statistical offices of Mediterranean countries (Palermo, Italy, September 1992) and adopted recommendations concerning electronic data processing and statistical metadata, statistical data editing and survey processing, the European Comparison Programme (a comparative analysis of national accounts), labour statistics, cultural statistics, fertility and family surveys and migration statistics, housing and building statistics, quality measures and specific methodological issues in environment statistics, and physical environmental accounting.

The Conference welcomed the publication by the ECE secretariat of a guide to statistics on the hidden and informal economy, and commended activities to assist economies in transition to establish agricultural statistics. It expressed satisfaction with the activities of the Intersecretariat Working Group on Service Statistics to coordinate work between ECE, the Statistical Office of EC (EUROSTAT) and OECD. It approved proposals to improve the *Annual Bulletin of Housing and Building Statistics for Europe* and the ECE specialized energy bulletins, and agreed to discontinue the *Annual Bulletin of General Energy Statistics* and to incorporate it in the ad hoc publication on energy balances for Europe and North

America for 1970-2000. It considered its programme of work for 1993-1994, requested its Bureau to develop a minimum programme of recommended statistics for countries at the initial stages of transition, and agreed to establish a new Intersecretariat Working Group on Censuses with the participation of ECE and EUROSTAT.

The Bureau of the Conference, at a meeting with directors of EUROSTAT and OECD (Geneva, 15 and 16 February), reviewed cooperation and coordination through intersecretariat working groups and joint programme review meetings, and agreed to integrate the draft work programmes of the three bodies in all fields of statistics into a single document.

The Joint ECE/OECD Meeting on National Accounts (Paris, 21-25 June) reviewed implementation of the revised System of National Accounts (SNA) (see PART THREE, Chapter XVII) and considered statistics on the hidden and informal economy. The implications of the revised SNA for consumer price indices were among matters considered at a joint ECE/ILO meeting (Geneva, 25-28 October). The effectiveness of technical assistance programmes in statistics was discussed by major donors and recipient countries at a workshop in Romania. Participants noted that a lack of electronic data-processing equipment in recipient countries was a particular problem. Activities of the ECE secretariat during the year focused on the development of classifications and other norms in the areas of agriculture, the hidden economy, international price statistics, environment, transport, energy, housing, population censuses and electronic data processing.

REFERENCES

[1]E/1993/37. [2]Ibid. (dec. C(48)). [3]Ibid. (dec. D(48)). [4]Ibid. (dec. E(48)). [5]Ibid. (dec. I(48)). [6]Ibid. (dec. L(48)). [7]Ibid. (dec. M(48)). [8]Ibid. (dec. N(48)). [9]YUN 1991, p. 320. [10]YUN 1992, p. 493. [11]E/1993/37/Add.1. [12]E/1993/37 (dec. A(48)). [13]YUN 1992, p. 139, GA res. 47/1, 22 Sep. 1992. [14]E/1994/51. [15]E/ECE/1287. [16]E/1993/37 (dec. B(48)). [17]E/ECE/1293. [18]E/ECE/1288. [19]E/1993/37 (dec. K(48)). [20]YUN 1992, p. 497. [21]E/1993/37 (dec. H(48)). [22]ECE/CHEM/92. [23]ECE/ENG.AUT/51. [24]ECE/STEEL/83. [25]ECE/TRANS/97. [26]E/1993/37 (dec. G(48)). [27]ECE/ENERGY/24. [28]ECE/AGRI/122. [29]ECE/TIM/71. [30]ECE/EC.AD/42. [31]ECE/ENVWA/29. [32]E/1993/37 (dec. F(48)). [33]Ibid. (dec. J(48)). [34]ECE/ENVWA/34. [35]ECE/HBP/89. [36]ECE/STAND/38. [37]ECE/CES/43.

Latin America and the Caribbean

The Economic Commission for Latin America and the Caribbean did not meet in 1993. In accordance with a 1992 Economic and Social Council decision,[1] the Commission's twenty-fifth session was to be held at Cartagena de Indias, Colombia, in 1994.

Economic trends

A summary of the 1993 economic survey of Latin America and the Caribbean[2] stated that economic activity in the region as a whole increased by 3.2 per cent during the year, while regional per capita output rose by 1.3 per cent. Unlike previous years, Brazil was a major positive factor in the region's continued recovery. After three years of poor performance, Brazil registered a 4.5 per cent increase in its GDP. If Brazil's growth were excluded, the region's growth rate would have declined from 4.3 per cent in 1992 to 2.6 per cent in 1993. Other positive influences on regional performance in 1993 were the cumulative effect of adjustment policies and reforms adopted in previous years and a drop in international interest rates. At the same time, however, limited growth in global demand and the deterioration of international commodity prices had adverse consequences for the region's economic performance.

Growth rates varied considerably among countries, reaching 6 per cent in Argentina, Chile and Costa Rica and 5.5 per cent in Panama, but only 1 per cent in Mexico. Peru registered a 6.5 per cent expansion after five years of recession, while GDP in Belize, Bolivia, Honduras and Paraguay grew by between 3 and 3.5 per cent. Brazil, Colombia, El Salvador, Guatemala and Guyana showed a 4 to 5 per cent increase. Growth rates in the Bahamas, Dominica, the Dominican Republic, Ecuador, Jamaica and Uruguay varied between 1.5 and 2.5 per cent. Output fell by 1 per cent in Nicaragua, Trinidad and Tobago and Venezuela and by 11 per cent in Haiti, while Cuba's level of activity worsened for the fourth consecutive year.

Economic expansion generally exceeded population growth, with increases in per capita output of more than 3 per cent in Argentina, Chile, Costa Rica, Panama and Peru and between 1 and 3 per cent in eight other countries. In another 10 States, however, per capita output grew only slightly or shrank. The unemployment rate was largely unchanged. It declined significantly only in Colombia and Panama, while Argentina, Ecuador, Honduras and Mexico registered higher rates. Slight decreases occurred in Bolivia, Brazil, Guatemala, Uruguay and Venezuela.

The annual regional inflation rate, excluding Brazil, declined from 22 per cent in 1992 to 19 per cent in 1993 and was below 15 per cent in most countries. Brazil was the exception, with its three-digit inflation rate soaring even higher.

The unit value of exports from Latin America and the Caribbean was adversely affected by foreign markets; it fell by 4 per cent in 1993 and slowed growth in the unit value of imports to only 1 per cent. The result was an almost 5 per cent decline in the terms of trade in most countries. Argentina, El Salvador, Nicaragua, Paraguay and Uruguay were exceptions. Due to an increase of some 9 per cent in export volume, however, the total value of regional exports grew by 4.5 per cent to reach $133 billion. The value of exports increased considerably in Costa Rica (11.7 per cent), El Salvador (22.7 per cent), Nicaragua (19.3 per cent) and Paraguay (32.6 per cent), by between 6 and 8 per cent in Argentina, Brazil, Colombia and Mexico, and by 3 to 5 per cent in Bolivia, Guatemala, Honduras and Panama. It fell by 3 to 8 per cent in the Dominican Republic, Chile, Ecuador, Peru and Uruguay and by almost 32 per cent in Haiti.

Total merchandise imports to Latin America and the Caribbean increased for the third consecutive year, growing by 6.5 per cent in volume and by 8 per cent in value, to reach $147.7 billion. The expansion of imports, facilitated by large capital inflows, was widespread in the region. The oil-exporting countries registered a 3 per cent rise in their imports, largely due to increased unit values, while the non-oil-exporting States saw their imports grow by 13 per cent through expanded volume. Brazil and Colombia accounted for 25 per cent of the region's import growth, expanding by $5 billion and $2.7 billion, respectively. They were followed by Argentina and Chile, with increases of almost $1 billion each. Imports declined in Bolivia, Ecuador, Haiti, Nicaragua, Peru and especially Venezuela, where they fell by $1 billion after two years of vigorous expansion.

A more rapid growth of imports over exports, and the resultant deterioration of trade balances in Brazil, Chile and Colombia, was only partially offset by better results in Mexico and Venezuela, causing an increase in the region's trade deficit from $10 billion in 1992 to $15 billion in 1993 and a $43 billion deficit on the current account of the balance of payments. Net capital inflows declined slightly but continued to be very positive, amounting to $55 billion. The largest reductions were registered in Argentina, Brazil and Chile. Uruguay and Paraguay recorded strong increases.

Most capital entering the region came from private non-banking sources and consisted of foreign direct investment (FDI), trade credits, time deposits in local banks and public debt instruments denominated in local currency. Most countries also attracted new kinds of foreign capital from non-banking sources, including bond issues and stock portfolio investments. With capital inflows exceeding the deficit on the current account, the global balance of payments fell from $25 billion in 1992 to $12 billion in 1993, resulting in considerably increased reserves in all but five countries.

Real exchange rates also declined in all but five countries of the region. Real parity remained unchanged in Chile and Venezuela, while exchange rates increased in Honduras, Paraguay and Peru.

The net transfer of financial resources was positive for the third consecutive year and stood at $25.7 billion. Many countries improved their fiscal management as a result of ongoing stabilization programmes. Nine had their fiscal accounts under control, three had imbalances of less than 2 per cent of GDP, and seven had major financial deficits.

External debt

The region's external debt grew by 4 per cent in 1993 to $487 billion on the strength of bond placements totalling $19 billion, loans from bilateral and multilateral sources, and debt in the form of trade credits. At the same time, financing, in such forms as direct investment, time deposits and fund-raising through equity markets, limited debt growth. Some debt reduction operations also took place during the year, especially in Argentina. Although debt increased in most countries, it contracted by 14 per cent in El Salvador, 12 per cent in Trinidad and Tobago, 4 per cent in Guatemala and 1 per cent in Panama. The debt increase rate varied from almost 10 per cent in Mexico and 6 per cent in Paraguay to between 4 and 5 per cent in Argentina, Chile, Costa Rica and Ecuador and 1 to 3 per cent in the rest of the region.

The region's external debt burden continued to fall during 1993, prolonging the trend of the past decade. The share of debt interest in total exports from Latin America and the Caribbean declined from 19.2 per cent in 1992 to 17.6 per cent in 1993, but still ranged from 116 per cent in Nicaragua to between 20 and 25 per cent in Argentina, Bolivia, Brazil, Honduras and Peru, and 10 to 20 per cent in most other countries. Only five States (Chile, Costa Rica, Guatemala, Haiti and Paraguay) were below 10 per cent.

Activities in 1993

Development policy and regional economic cooperation

The economic development work of the ECLAC secretariat included studies by the Economic Development Division and information and documentation activities carried out by the Latin American Centre for Economic and Social Documentation (CLADES). The Economic Development Division monitored the economic evolution of countries in the region, including their economic and social policies and development strategies to harmonize macroeconomic stability with social equity and structural change.

The report on the Commission's activities between its 1992 and 1994 sessions[3] stated that ECLAC continued to publish the annual *Economic*

Panorama of Latin America, Preliminary Overview of the Economy of Latin America and the Caribbean and *Economic Survey of Latin America and the Caribbean.* These publications presented, respectively, a timely overview of economic trends in the nine major economies of the region for the first eight months of the year, the performance of the entire region during 1993, and complete and comparable breakdowns on the region's economic trends. ECLAC also examined alternative policies for managing the external debt, for bringing about expansive adjustments and lowering inflation without causing recession, and for analysing the impact of real exchange rates on exports from Chile and Brazil.

In 1993, a regional project on fiscal decentralization included case-studies in Argentina, Brazil, Chile and Colombia and technical seminars in Porto Alegre, Brazil (7 July), Bogotá, Colombia (26 July) and Medellín, Colombia (28 July). A fifth regional seminar on fiscal policy, stabilization and adjustment (Santiago, Chile, 25-28 January) examined the relationships between fiscal policy and other macroeconomic factors. A workshop on public policy reforms and social spending (Santiago, 14-15 June) discussed policies for providing services and government regulation in the social sectors of Latin America. A seminar on fiscal decentralization in the region was held in Argentina (Buenos Aires, 20 October) and a technical cooperation programme on fiscal issues was initiated between ECLAC and Cuba.

CLADES focused its activities on strengthening the management of information and documentation for economic and social development in the region. It held two regional meetings on information management (Santiago, 17-21 May; San José, Costa Rica, 8-12 November), continued to issue the periodicals *PLANINDEX* and *Informativo terminológico* and published an edition dedicated to the Southern Common Market (MERCOSUR) as part of its *INFOPLAN* series.

The Latin American and Caribbean Institute for Economic and Social Planning (ILPES) organized a high-level international training programme in regional development (Santa Cruz, Bolivia, 9 August–10 September). It also organized a number of courses, including one on the Integrated Laboratory on the Design of Regional Strategies (Popayán, Colombia, 31 May–2 July). Others were held on policy formulation and project evaluation (Santiago, 4 October–6 November) and economic reforms and strategic public management (Santiago, 5 November–10 December). Special attention was given during the year to budget policies in public sector programming, resource allocation and social spending, and the strengthening and development of municipal management. ILPES organized workshops on integrated systems of financial administration (Santiago, 28-30 April), methodological problems in the measurement of public social spending and its redistributive impact (Santiago, 3 and 4 June), a seminar on municipal management and training (Santiago, 27 and 28 September) and an inter-American seminar on local statistical information systems to help overcome poverty (Santiago, 28 and 29 October). Advisory assistance missions were undertaken to more than 15 countries at the request of their Governments, and progress was made in the conceptualization of regional development management and its interaction with decentralization processes and international competitiveness.

The Presiding Officers of the Regional Council for Planning, at their sixteenth meeting (Brasilia, Brazil, 24 and 25 November) emphasized the need for ILPES to continue to promote technical cooperation in public sector restructuring, regulation and privatization; citizen participation in quality control of public services; and financial relations between different levels of government. They endorsed the Institute's new training policy, noting in particular an international course on economic reforms and strategic State management.

Industrial, scientific and technological development

The Joint ECLAC/UNIDO Industrial and Technological Development Unit assigned special importance in 1993 to industrial restructuring to achieve competitiveness. Its efforts were channelled through the ECLAC/UNDP project on "Design of policies to strengthen the capacity for technological innovation and enhance the international competitiveness in the Latin American entrepreneurial environment". Technical advisory services in export policies, technological innovation and human resources development were provided to Chile, Mexico and Venezuela and studies were prepared on regional technological policies, innovations and the impact of regional integration on long-term growth. A two-year project on production restructuring, industrial organization and international competitiveness in Argentina, Brazil, Chile, Colombia and Mexico was initiated with the International Development Research Centre, and a joint study on health system reforms in the region was launched by ECLAC and the Pan-American Health Organization.

Competitiveness was the subject of two informal forums on the quality of education in Chile (Santiago, 15 April and 24 May), a meeting of authors on the integration of competitiveness, sustainability and social development (Paris, 17-19 June), and of seminars on industrial organization, innovation systems and international competitiveness in Latin America and the Caribbean (Termas de Cauquenes, Chile, 15 and 16 July), and policies for technological innovation, human resources development and international competitiveness (Santiago, 2 and 3 December).

ECLAC continued its cooperation with the Latin American Association of Capital Goods Industries and published a regional directory of capital goods manufacturers for 1993.

Other publications included a book on competitiveness, technological policies and industrial innovation in Uruguay; essays on industrial policy and on FDI by leading Latin American companies; articles on the region's experience with technological policies and innovation systems; a document on policies, institutional mechanisms and measures to support small and medium-sized industries and extraregional industrial cooperation; and two issues (Nos. 14 and 15) of the journal *Industrialización y Desarrollo Tecnológico*.

International trade and development finance

The activities of the ECLAC International Trade and Development Division focused mainly on the design of policies and mechanisms to permit the continued expansion and improvement of the commercial linkages of the region in the changing world economy. A number of documents were prepared on aspects of trade and economic relations. The role of foreign ministries in the cooperation process was discussed at a seminar on the management of international cooperation between Latin America and the European Community (Rome, 15 and 16 April).

In the context of its activities in regional integration and cooperation, ECLAC published a document on Latin American economic integration and cooperation among developing countries (South-South cooperation), conducted studies on various aspects of integration, gave a course on international trade and integration (Quito, Ecuador, 19-25 May), co-sponsored a conference with the Inter-American Development Bank (IDB) on trade liberalization in the Western Hemisphere (Santiago, 24 and 25 May), and organized a meeting of representatives of Latin American and Spanish diplomatic academies (Santiago, 29 and 30 November).

Activities in development finance included studies on financing for small and medium-sized enterprises, a technical seminar on the development of regional capital markets (Santiago, 18 and 19 October) and a regional seminar on pension system reform and the development of capital markets in Latin America (Asunción, Paraguay, 22 and 23 November). The development of capital markets was also considered at a seminar in Chile (Santiago, 11 and 12 January) and pension system reform was the subject of a seminar-workshop in El Salvador (San Salvador, 31 March and 1 April).

Seminars dealing with bank regulation and supervision were held in Honduras (Tegucigalpa, 28-30 March) and in Brazil (Brasilia, 26 November). A seminar-workshop on social security was held in Paraguay (Asunción, 26-28 May).

Natural resources and energy

ECLAC's support for natural resources and energy management included workshops on water resources management (Lima, Peru, 6 and 7 August) and on the development of small-scale mining in Latin America and the Caribbean (Santiago, 15-17 November). A meeting of the expert group on the possible effects of climate change on regional water resources was held in Chile (Santiago, 23-25 November) and courses on integrated water resources management and on water resources legislation were held at Guatemala City, from 15 to 25 March and from 24 to 28 May, respectively. ECLAC also offered training in the management of hydrographic basins (Temuco and Concepción, Chile, 7-12 May and 28 May), the sound management of hazardous wastes (Santiago, 2-13 August), and natural resources management (Mendoza, Argentina, 22 November–15 December).

In the area of marine resources, the secretariat supported UNCED follow-up related to coastal management, fishing on the high seas, the transboundary shipment of wastes by sea, the establishment of protected coastal and marine areas, and the influence of coastal human settlements on marine ecosystems.

Studies were prepared on the technological research and financial development needs of the mining and metallurgy sector and ECLAC assisted in a study of the mineral trade in the Latin American Integration Association. Presentations were made on trends in metal consumption within regional blocs at an international seminar on regionalism and mining resources (Santiago, 4-6 October); on economic reforms and energy policy at the Energy Conference of Latin America and the Caribbean (Bogotá, 15-18 June); and on the role of the state in the energy sector at the first Latin American energy seminar (Rio de Janeiro, Brazil, 18-22 October). ECLAC launched a technical cooperation project with the Latin American Energy Organization to recommend policies for regional economic development and undertook various other tasks related to the economic appraisal of the region's natural resources, the maintenance of mining statistics, and natural resources management.

Transport

The focus of ECLAC's transport programme was on technical cooperation among Latin American countries in railways, urban public transport, port management and road maintenance. It published eight issues (Nos. 101-108) of its *Boletín FAL* on the facilitation of trade and transport in the region and supported national seminars on road network conservation and management in Argentina, Brazil, the Dominican Republic, Ecuador, El Salvador, Guatemala, Honduras, Nicaragua, Panama, Paraguay, Peru, Puerto Rico and Venezuela. Activities included a seminar on multimodal transport in Latin America (Montevideo, Uruguay, 21-23 June), organized jointly with the Latin American Integration Association, and the first maritime trade meeting (Santiago, 10 and 11 November), co-sponsored by the Chilean Maritime League.

Social development

During 1993, the ECLAC Social Development Division continued to study characteristics and trends of poverty and policies to overcome it. It also served as the regional focal point for youth and social policy activities in the United Nations system.

The Division played a key role in the Latin American and Caribbean Regional Preparatory Meeting for the International Year of the Family (Cartagena, 9-13 August), which reviewed the situation and prospects of the family in the region and adopted the Cartagena Declaration. As a follow-up to the Meeting, a book was published on changes that had affected families in the region over the past three decades and a meeting of experts was held on indicators in family policy issues (Mar del Plata, Argentina, 16 and 17 December).

The Division participated in the international Conference on Social Development and Poverty (Oaxaca, Mexico, 8-11 September), organized by Mexico with the support of UNDP and the World Bank, and published the 1993 edition of *Panorama social de América Latina*, which reviewed recent employment indicators, poverty and its impact on youth, and the effect of family organization on children's educational performance.

Seminars were held on postgraduate training in social policies (Santiago, 13 and 14 December), social policy and project management and evaluation (Santiago, 14-16 December), rural youth, modernity and democracy in Latin America (Santiago, 26-28 October), and global youth policies (Santa Cruz, 22-25 November). Training courses during the year dealt with social planning and project evaluation (Santiago, March-July and October-November; Buenos Aires, November), youth policies (Caracas, Venezuela, 26 April–8 May), development cooperation (Madrid, Spain, 7-27 May), social policy rationalization (Tegucigalpa, July) and social policy and governability in Latin America (Madrid, 22-29 September).

Integration of women

The Presiding Officers of the Regional Conference on the Integration of Women into the Economic and Social Development of Latin America and the Caribbean met twice in 1993. At their sixteenth meeting (Caracas, 27 and 28 May), they analysed ongoing activities, considered the first draft of the new regional programme of action and made recommendations on national and regional preparations for the 1995 World Conference on Women.

Studies were under way on the situation of women in the region, new theoretical approaches to understanding women's status in society, the gender perspective and its links with development issues, women's participation in decision-making, women in the informal sector, domestic violence against women, women and culture, and teenage pregnancy. Comparative studies of active legislation on women were also conducted under a technical cooperation project in Colombia, Ecuador, Honduras and Paraguay, along with analyses of relevant government agencies and NGOs and technical meetings aimed at improving the legal and institutional framework for including women in development activities.

Other activities included meetings on teenage pregnancy and women heads of household (Santiago, 2 March) and on women leaders (Santiago, 4 and 5 June), a seminar on culture, modernity and gender (Santiago, 1-3 December) and courses on gender policies (Santiago, 15 March–15 December) and social policies in relation to gender (Santiago, 4 October–6 November).

Environment

A primary task of ECLAC's Environment and Human Settlements Division was the implementation of Agenda 21, adopted by UNCED in 1992,[4] in which ECLAC was assigned the role of regional coordination body.

A regional meeting was convened on the application of the 1989 Basel Convention on the Control of Transboundary Movements of Hazardous Wastes and their Disposal[5] (Santiago, 15-19 November). The meeting discussed the environmentally sound management of hazardous wastes in Latin America and the Caribbean. The legal aspects of waste management were considered at a national seminar on environmental law in Chile (Santiago, 7 October). Activities under an ongoing technical cooperation project for environmental planning and management dealt with environmentally sustainable agricultural development in Chile, Mexico and Peru, and ways of incorporating the environmental dimension into development management. ECLAC also continued work on the management of urban and industrial waste (see below) and organized a meeting of the regional expert group on deep sea fishing (Santiago, 25 and 26 November).

Human settlements

The Joint ECLAC/UNEP Development and Environment Unit had under execution a project on controlled environmentally sound waste management. The project provided guidelines and advisory services for municipalities in Argentina, Brazil, Chile, Colombia, Costa Rica and Ecuador. Legal, institutional and technological policy aspects of waste management were addressed and a seminar was held on municipal policies (Córdoba, Argentina, 9-12 June).

A project on urban management in selected medium-sized Latin American cities, focused on the refinement of urban management tools, environmental questions and citizen participation in the cities of San Pedro Sula (Honduras), Córdoba, Ibagué (Colombia) and Temuco (Chile). Studies were conducted on industrial development and municipal plans for waste management in Buenos Aires and Cartagena and two international courses were offered on policies for the environmentally sound management of urban and industrial wastes (Cartagena, 19-30 July; Santiago, 2-13 August). ECLAC continued a study of the environmental information needed for development management in the region's human settlements and participated in the Second Regional Meeting of Ministers and Senior Authorities of the Housing and Urban Development Sector in Latin America and the Caribbean (Santiago, 29 November–2 December).

Population

The Latin American Demographic Centre (CELADE), the institution responsible for ECLAC's regional population programme, focused its activities during 1993 on applied research, technical cooperation, training and dissemination of demographic data. The Centre fielded some 40 missions and provided advisory services in such areas as census processing, demographic analysis, the elderly, maternal and infant mortality, computerized birth and other data, population and the environment, population projections, spatial distribution, the demographic dynamics of poverty, and population policies.

CELADE's training and teaching activities included a third postgraduate course on population and development under the UNFPA Global Programme of Training in Population and Development (Santiago, 15 March–15 December), the sixteenth intensive regional course on demographic analyses for development (Santiago, 17 August–17 December), intensive national courses on population and development in Colombia (Santa Fe de Bogotá, 1 March–28 May) and El Salvador (1 October 1993–June 1994), and three workshops on the application of a population database programme (Concepción, Chile, 4-8 January; El Salvador, 8-19 March; Caracas, 22-26 November).

In preparation for the 1994 International Conference on Population and Development, the Centre joined ECLAC and UNFPA in organizing the Latin American and Caribbean Regional Conference on Population and Development (Mexico City, 29 April–4 May),[6] attended by representatives of 52 Governments, United Nations agencies and NGOs. The Conference adopted the Latin American and Caribbean Consensus on Population and Development and recommended guidelines for preparing a regional programme of action.

Among other activities in 1993 were a meeting on indigenous reservations (Temuco, 15 and 16 January), a seminar-workshop on contemporary socio-demographic research on indigenous peoples (Santa Cruz, 18-22 October) and seminars on new international migration patterns and trends in the context of integration (Montevideo, 27-29 October) and on the regional population information network (Santiago, 17-19 November). The Centre continued to publish research studies on population and produced several issues of *DOCPAL: Latin American Population Abstracts*, *Notas de Población* and the *Demographic Bulletin*.

Food and agriculture

Most Latin American and Caribbean countries in 1993 were seeking to increase their exportable supply of non-traditional agricultural goods, and a number of ECLAC documents reviewed aspects of recent experience in agro-exports. An analysis was begun of the experiences of such traditional extraregional exporters of horticultural products as Australia, New Zealand and South Africa to determine the implications for the ECLAC region of its efforts to diversify exports. Although there were some instances of successful trade expansion within the region, serious constraints were encountered in exporting those goods to other regions. An ongoing project on policy formulation for the transformation of agricultural production included a seminar on policies for agricultural restructuring in Paraguay (Asunción, 2-4 November) and missions to several Central American countries to discuss this subject with government authorities and the private sector.

Statistics and economic projections

The ECLAC Statistics and Economic Projections Division continued to analyse the region's position in the global economy, to carry out activities to expand the regional network of statistical information and to undertake medium- and long-term studies on Latin American and Caribbean development. The Division was developing a database of short-term indicators, a regional data bank on external trade, a household survey data bank, and databases on external debt and on social statistics. It participated in a technical meeting of the United Nations working group on the implementation of the System of National Accounts (Santiago, 26-30 July) and organized a regional seminar on the subject (Santiago, 22-26 November). The Division supported national efforts to develop statistical databases to measure poverty and to implement the Harmonized Commodity Description and Coding System. It helped convene an international workshop on poverty and a colloquium on measuring and analysing poverty (Aguascalientes, Mexico, 20 March–3 April and 21 and 22 October) and provided technical assistance and training for government officials in Brazil and Mexico for the management of social indicators. Information on the situation of women was prepared from household survey data.

Transnational corporations

The joint ECLAC/UNCTAD unit on TNCs continued to research the contribution by and impact of TNCs on the region's development. The unit concentrated on: legal and statistical information on FDI and TNCs in the region; TNCs and changes in the world economy; the role of TNCs in industrial restructuring of the region's economies; and technical cooperation related to TNCs and international competitiveness.

Documents published in 1993 dealt with legal and statistical information on foreign investment in the region and with TNCs in relation to economic transition in Argentina, industrial modernization in Brazil and Colombia, and the restructuring of Brazil's manufacturing sector. Surveys of the main foreign-owned manufacturing companies were carried out in Costa Rica. The unit also issued a study on structural aspects of the "new international industrial order". It examined the impact of global economic changes on developing countries and the role of foreign investment and technology in the region's development and on restructuring of the automotive industry in particular.

Technical cooperation assistance

During 1993, the ECLAC Programme Planning and Operations Division completed 20 regional, 8 subregional and 17 country projects funded from multilateral and bilateral extrabudgetary funds. It launched 12 new projects and a further 22 projects were at various stages of implementation. The new projects focused on the areas of poverty, the reformulation of Argentina's foreign trade system, welfare and social assistance in Brazil, demographic analysis and policy formulation in the British Virgin Islands, rural economic organization in Mexico, and energy and petroleum supply questions in Central America. A technical cooperation agreement was signed between ECLAC and Saint Lucia.

Technical cooperation among developing countries

During 1993, the Programme Planning and Operations Division continued its work within the framework of the 1978 Buenos Aires Plan of Action for Promoting and Implementing Technical Cooperation among Developing Countries.[7] Its efforts focused on the incorporation of TCDC elements in projects to strengthen national institutions, support for cooperation networks and information systems to expedite the flow of technical cooperation, and the consolidation of national TCDC focal points. The Division also supported seminars and technical meetings to exchange experiences. Those activities were coordinated through a regional mechanism, established by ECLAC and the Latin American Economic System (SELA) with UNDP support, and were reviewed at the eighth meeting of the Coordination Mechanism for International Bodies and Regional Forums Engaged in TCDC Activities (Montevideo, 29-31 March). TCDC issues were also considered at a regional meeting of national directors for international technical cooperation (Caracas, 24-26 August).

ECLAC also collaborated with SELA and UNCTAD in preparing a regional TCDC programming exercise in international trade, and with UNCTAD and ESCAP in a joint project to promote cooperation among countries of the Pacific Rim. It continued to publish the quarterly bulletin *Cooperation and Development*, which described the Commission's TCDC initiatives.

Subregional activities

Caribbean

The ECLAC subregional headquarters for the Caribbean, at Port of Spain, Trinidad and Tobago, continued to analyse socio-economic development in the subregion and to support the activities of subregional bodies, including the Caribbean Development and Cooperation Committee (CDCC), the Caribbean Council for Science and Technology (CCST) and the Caribbean Documentation Centre (CDC). It also provided technical assistance to the Organization of Eastern Caribbean States (OECS) in an effort to achieve a closer political union of countries in the subregion. The subregional headquarters continued to review the economic performance of Caribbean countries and relevant international economic developments, to publish technical studies and reports on research activities and projects and to disseminate information on economic development and trade and related activities through its quarterly bulletin, *External Sector Briefing Notes* and the quarterly newsletter, *Focus*. It prepared the second edition of the *Women in Development Bibliography* and documents on the implications of the North American Free Trade Agreement (NAFTA) from the Caribbean perspective and on the use of basic indicators to construct databases on women engaged in selected activities.

An ad hoc expert group meeting of national economic managers and planners of CDCC countries (Port of Spain, 23 and 24 November) reviewed the state of national economic management and planning in the Caribbean and examined issues relating to development with social equity from the subregional perspective. Social development questions in the context of the structural adjustment process in the subregion were considered at another expert group meeting (Port of Spain, 25 and 26 November). The subregional headquarters continued to issue the CCST quarterly newsletter and the *PATNEWS* update, which provided patent information in support of industrial development and technology transfer.

Activities for the integration of women in development included an ad hoc meeting of experts to consider a framework for discussing relations between men and women in changing Caribbean social structures (Port of Spain, 22 and 23 March). Preparations for the 1994 International Conference on Population and Development concentrated on national policy formulation and the analysis of census data and population projections. The framework of a Caribbean plan of action on population and development was adopted at the first meeting of a working group set up for that purpose (Port of Spain, 29 and 30 July). Training courses were offered in the use of demographic variables for a national work plan on population (Port of Spain, 6 and 7 April), the analysis of census data using a computerized database (Saint Lucia, 19-21 April), and the preparation of population projections and the creation of a data bank (Saint Lucia, 14-18 June). A training workshop was held on adolescent fertility and population policy (Castries, Saint Lucia, 15 June).

The subregional headquarters studied the consequences of climate change and the rise in sea level, in collaboration with UNEP and the University of Miami, and analysed the vulnerability of coastal areas in the Caribbean basin. It established an electronic system for the exchange of environmental information (AMBIONET) and offered a training workshop on AMBIONET's implementation (Mexico City, 25-28 April). A technical meeting was held for the Atlantic, Caribbean and Mediterranean island countries (Port of Spain, 12-16 July) in preparation for the 1994 Global Conference on the Sustainable Development of Small Island Developing Countries.

Mexico and Central America

The ECLAC subregional headquarters for Mexico and Central America (Mexico City) continued its activities in Central America, Cuba, the Dominican Republic, Haiti and Mexico, with the aim of reviving and modernizing the subregion's economies and consolidating Central American integration. A significant share of the work, focusing on economic, social and industrial development, international trade, food and agriculture and energy, was devoted to analysing stabilization and structural adjustment policies implemented in the 1980s and Central America's development options for the 1990s. Studies were made of the subregion's strategic options in trade negotiations, the financing of micro-enterprises through NGOs, investment initiatives for reviving the industrial sector and methodologies for evaluating the international economic situation and its impact on the subregion. An investment and technical cooperation project bank was established under a project sponsored by Italy.

The financial implications of the El Salvador peace agreement and their impact on the economic stabilization programme were analysed by the subregional headquarters, which also examined the possibility of growing medicinal plants and industrializing their cultivation in the subregion. Two seminars were organized on the subregion's economy (Guatemala City, 22 and 23 February; Tegucigalpa, 22 and 23 July). Through the subregional headquarters, ECLAC provided advisory services to Cuba on free trade agreements, analysed the implications of NAFTA for the subregion and conducted studies on economic relations between Mexico and Central America, various aspects of Mexican agriculture, recent trends in traditional exports, the incorporation of women into changing production patterns in Mexico, and the health situation and health policies in Central America.

In the field of energy, a frame of reference was formulated for an electrical interconnection project between Guatemala and Mexico and work was completed on a load shedding plan for the interconnected systems of El Salvador and Guatemala. The subregional headquarters assisted Mexico in organizing discussion panels on electrical integration and on the exchange of experiences in efficient energy use. It cooperated with the Latin American Energy Organization in formulating alternatives for the supply of hydrocarbons for electricity generation and cooperated with IDB in a study of problems in Central America's electricity subsector. Project profiles and studies on electrical interconnection were prepared under a joint project with the World Bank, co-sponsored by UNDP.

Cooperation between the United Nations and the Latin American Economic System

In response to a 1992 General Assembly request,[8] the Secretary-General submitted an October 1993 report on cooperation between the United Nations and the Latin American Economic System.[9]

Cooperation between SELA and the United Nations system had intensified since SELA's establishment in 1975, particularly through ECLAC, which provided support to various SELA projects and participated in its meetings. The two organizations collaborated on matters related to social policy, population, information and trade development. Within the framework of the inter-agency group on integrated social policies, they studied the feasibility of establishing a social project bank and an information and communications network. They updated their database on regional cooperation and cooperated on projects to form a network of regional development financing institutions and to train managers of regional information networks.

Under the SELA/UNESCO/IDB Simón Bolívar Programme, launched in 1992, 120 projects were identified to establish links between the productive sector and the main research centres and universities of the region.

SELA, UNDP, UNCTAD and the Governments of Honduras and Italy held a regional seminar on external debt conversion for economic, social and environmental projects (Tegucigalpa, 19-21 May), and SELA, UNDP and WHO collaborated on "Project Convergence" which was designed to promote technological development in the region's health sector. An agreement establishing an Inter-Agency Committee to support Project Convergence was signed by SELA, UNDP, WHO, ECLAC and UNESCO.

Joint activities of SELA and UNCTAD focused on a new regional programme of technical cooperation in international trade and trade relations (LATINTRADE) and included collaboration on the sixth consultative meeting on the Uruguay Round of multilateral trade negotiations and on the needs of countries in the region for technical assistance in trade negotiations (Geneva, 12 and 13 July).

The Latin American Council of SELA held its nineteenth ordinary ministerial meeting in Caracas, Venezuela, from 25 to 29 October.[10]

GENERAL ASSEMBLY ACTION

On 22 November, the General Assembly adopted **resolution 48/22** without vote.

Cooperation between the United Nations and the Latin American Economic System

The General Assembly,

Recalling its resolution 47/13 of 29 October 1992 on cooperation between the United Nations and the Latin American Economic System,

Having considered the report of the Secretary-General on cooperation between the United Nations and the Latin American Economic System,

Bearing in mind the Agreement between the United Nations and the Latin American Economic System, in which the parties agree to strengthen and expand their cooperation in matters which are of common concern in the field of their respective competence pursuant to their constitutional instruments,

Considering that the Economic Commission for Latin America and the Caribbean has developed ties of cooperation with the Latin American Economic System which have grown stronger in recent years,

Bearing in mind also that the Permanent Secretariat of the Latin American Economic System has carried out several programmes with the support of the United Nations Development Programme in areas that are considered of priority for the economic development of the region,

Considering also that the Latin American Economic System is developing joint activities with the specialized agencies and other organizations and programmes of the United Nations system, such as the United Nations Conference on Trade and Development, the United Nations Educational, Scientific and Cultural Organization, the United Nations Industrial Development Organization, the World Meteorological Organization, the World Health Organization, the World Intellectual Property Organization, the United Nations Environment Programme, the Department for Development Support and Management Services, the Department for Economic and Social Information and Policy Analysis, the Department for Policy Coordination and Sustainable Development, the Office of the United Nations Disaster Relief Coordinator, the United Nations Institute for Training and Research and the International Telecommunication Union,

Welcoming the recent decision of the Latin American Council which expresses appreciation to the international organizations and other institutions providing support to the Permanent Secretariat of the Latin American Economic System,

1. *Takes note with satisfaction* of the report of the Secretary-General;

2. *Urges* the Economic Commission for Latin America and the Caribbean to continue broadening and deepening its coordination and mutual support activities with the Latin American Economic System;

3. *Urges* the United Nations Development Programme to strengthen and expand its support to the programmes that the Permanent Secretariat of the Latin American Economic System is carrying out, aimed at complementing the technical assistance activities conducted by the Latin American Economic System;

4. *Urges* the specialized agencies and other organizations and programmes of the United Nations system to continue and intensify their support for, and cooperation in the activities of, the Latin American Economic System;

5. *Requests* both the Secretary-General of the United Nations and the Permanent Secretary of the Latin American Economic System to assess, at the appropriate time, the implementation of the Agreement between the United Nations and the Latin American Economic System and to report thereon to the General Assembly at its forty-ninth session;

6. *Requests* the Secretary-General to submit to the General Assembly at its forty-ninth session a report on the implementation of the present resolution.

General Assembly resolution 48/22

22 November 1993   Meeting 60   Adopted without vote

27-nation draft (A/48/L.20); agenda item 28.

Sponsors: Argentina, Barbados, Belize, Bolivia, Brazil, Chile, Colombia, Costa Rica, Cuba, Dominican Republic, Ecuador, El Salvador, Grenada, Guatemala, Guyana, Haiti, Honduras, Jamaica, Mexico, Nicaragua, Panama, Paraguay, Peru, Suriname, Trinidad and Tobago, Uruguay, Venezuela.

REFERENCES

[1]YUN 1992, p. 515, ESC dec. 1992/291, 31 July 1992. [2]E/1994/53. [3]LC/G.1803(SES.25/6). [4]YUN 1992, p. 672. [5]UNEP/WG.190/4. [6]LC/G.1762(Conf.83/4). [7]YUN 1978, p. 467. [8]YUN 1992, p. 514, GA res. 47/13, 29 Oct. 1992. [9]A/48/409. [10]A/48/597.

Western Asia

The Economic and Social Commission for Western Asia did not meet in 1993, having held its sixteenth session at Amman, Jordan, in 1992. On 2 February 1993, the Economic and Social Council endorsed the Commission's 1992 decision[1] to convene sessions of the ESCWA Technical Committee in alternate years when no Commission session was held, starting with a three-day meeting in 1993 (**resolution 1993/1**).

The Technical Committee held its eighth session at Amman (11-13 October).[2] It reviewed activities of the ESCWA secretariat, examined economic and social developments in the region, and considered a proposed work programme for the 1994-1995 biennium. The main discussion themes included obstacles facing the Commission, the strengthening of interaction between ESCWA and its members, coordination questions, and the impact of the Persian Gulf crisis on labour in the region. The Committee recommended to the Commission a resolution by which meetings of the Technical Committee would be linked with the Commission's sessions, in accordance with previous practice, and that ESCWA sessions would be held in odd years, beginning in 1995.

Economic trends

Overall economic performance in the region slowed considerably in 1993, according to a summary of the survey of economic and social developments in the ESCWA region, 1993.[3] All countries except Qatar and Yemen recorded positive growth rates, but the aggregate GDP growth rate was estimated at 3.5 per cent, compared with 6.8 per cent in 1992. Factors contributing to the slow-down in economic activity included lower oil prices and revenues, depressed export performance, continued economic sanctions against Iraq and their adverse impact on countries with traditional economic ties with Iraq, limited progress in mobilizing resources for reconstruction, attacks on tourists in Egypt and their negative effect on the confidence of foreign investors, a persistent political crisis in Yemen, and the depressed state of regional cooperation in general. The slow-down was partially offset, however, by the momentum of economic reforms in Egypt, Jordan, Lebanon, Saudi Arabia and the Syrian Arab Republic, which were aimed at stabilization, deregulation and a greater role for the private sector. Other positive developments included good harvests, a rise in domestic demand in the oil-producing countries, and buoyant private sector activity, including significant private sector capital repatriation.

Economic activity in the Gulf Cooperation Council (GCC) group of countries grew by an estimated 3.3 per cent, compared with 7.5 per cent in 1992. The highest growth, 25 per cent, was recorded in Kuwait, which sharply increased its oil production and revenues for the second consecutive year and continued its reconstruction and rehabilitation activities. The oil sector in the other GCC countries declined by more than 10 per cent, and growth in the non-oil sector failed to compensate. GDP growth rates between 1992 and 1993 fell from 6.8 per cent to 4 per cent in Oman and from 4.3 per cent to about 1 per cent in Saudi Arabia. Growth held at 2 per cent in Bahrain over the same period, and the United Arab Emirates' economy grew by 1 per cent. With the decline in oil revenues, GCC countries had to borrow from international markets and draw on their financial assets to meet the high costs of defence, reconstruction and rehabilitation. The downturn also provoked more intense efforts to privatize the non-oil sector and to rationalize public expenditure.

With the exception of Lebanon and the Syrian Arab Republic, economic growth in the more diversified economies also slowed to an estimated 4.1 per cent in 1993, against 5.6 per cent the previous year. Although well below the 11 per cent expansion of 1992, Jordan's growth rate was estimated at a still impressive 6 per cent, due to the success of structural adjustment policies which reduced external and internal imbalances and created a favourable investment climate. Egypt's economy grew by 1.8 per cent, compared with 3 per cent in 1992, as tourism revenues fell by some 30 per cent and difficulties persisted with privatization, trade liberalization and regulation of the labour market. Economic and social conditions in Iraq continued to deteriorate as a consequence of the Persian Gulf hostilities and United Nations sanctions. This was reflected in the depreciation of its currency, high inflation and shortages of foodstuffs, medicines and intermediate products.

Lebanon's GDP growth accelerated from 5 per cent in 1992 to 7 per cent in 1993, reflecting an improved investment environment and increasing donor confidence. The economy of the Syrian Arab Republic grew at an estimated 6 per cent compared with 5 per cent in 1992, following the promotion of private sector investment, a good harvest, a budget deficit reduction, and the gradual elimination of price distortions. In Yemen, however, GDP declined by 1 per cent, owing to a political crisis that aggravated economic conditions and reduced the availability of external financial resources such as workers' remittances and aid.

With the exception of Iraq and Yemen, inflation in the region ranged between 1 and 4 per cent in the GCC countries and between about 5 and 12 per cent in the rest of Western Asia. The inflation rate hit a three-year low of 7.4 per cent in Egypt and fell from 131 per cent to 8.9 per cent in Lebanon, its lowest level in 10 years. Inflation fell below 5 per cent in Jordan, but rose in the Syrian Arab Republic from 9 per cent in 1992 to 12 per cent in 1993, following the gradual elimination of subsidies. Shortages of foreign currency and a widening budget deficit boosted inflation in Yemen to 55 per cent. Iraq also continued to suffer from excessively high inflation. Although significant progress was achieved in reducing macroeconomic imbalances in some of the more diversified economies, unemployment remained a major problem. The official unemployment rate in Egypt was some 12 per cent of the labour force but unofficial estimates ran as high as 20 per cent. In Jordan, unemployment declined but remained high at 11 per cent. The unofficial rate in Yemen was estimated at 25 per cent in 1993.

Fiscal developments in the GCC countries in 1993 were still affected by the ramifications of the Gulf crisis as well as by the drop in oil revenues, which increased projected budget deficits significantly, especially in Kuwait, Oman and Saudi Arabia. Budget deficits decreased in most other countries except Yemen, where it was more than double the projection. At the same time, banks in Western Asia continued to suffer under a mounting burden of non-performing loans. These were estimated at $25 billion at the end of 1993 and constituted about 35 per cent of total bank lending, 9 per cent of total bank assets and five times the banks' combined profits. Regional stock markets surged however, with the value of traded shares reaching some $7.6 billion, 31 per cent more than in 1992 and 65 per cent above the 1991 figure. In 1993, the International Finance Corporation included the Jordanian stock market among the 20 emerging markets of the developing countries. The Saudi Arabian stock market became the largest in the ESCWA region in terms of capitalization, although it remained closed to foreign investors. Plans were being made to open the Bahrain stock market to foreign investors, and to modernize the trading system at the Cairo stock exchange in Egypt and introduce new legislation to regulate its activities.

The external debt of the ESCWA region increased from $180 billion in 1992 to $186 billion in 1993. This represented 62 per cent of the region's aggregate GDP of about $298.8 billion and 11.5 per cent of the total debt of the developing countries. The GCC countries accounted for some 60 per cent of the region's total debt and for its overall increase. Debt-reduction agreements were reached between Egypt and IMF and between Jordan and commercial lenders.

Sectoral developments

Oil and natural gas

In 1993, oil prices averaged $16.3 per barrel, the lowest level in four years and 11.3 per cent less than in the previous year. Underlying factors included a 0.2 per cent drop in world demand, the inability of the OPEC countries to agree on lower production ceilings, higher output by non-OPEC members and speculation about the lifting of sanctions against Iraq's oil exports. As a result, oil revenues in the region declined by 8.2 per cent from $78.1 billion in 1992 to $72.5 billion in 1993. The drop in revenues came despite a 4.5 per cent increase in production and ranged from 18.6 per cent in Qatar and 15.9 per cent in Saudi Arabia to 8.3 per cent in Egypt and 2 per cent in the United Arab Emirates. Output declined by 2.1 and 2.3 per cent in the United Arab Emirates and Saudi Arabia respectively. Revenues grew, however, by 46.8 per cent in Kuwait and by 12.6 per cent in the Syrian Arab Republic where daily production increased by 75.5 per cent and 7.5 per cent, respectively. Iraq's oil exports were limited under United Nations sanctions to 50,000 barrels a day to Jordan as debt payment.

Proven oil reserves in Western Asia declined by 0.4 per cent to 572.3 billion barrels, but they accounted for 57.3 per cent of the world's total. Proven reserves in Saudi Arabia, which accounted for 45.2 per cent of the regional total and some 26 per cent of global oil reserves, decreased by 0.6 per cent and totalled 258.7 billion barrels. Iraq followed with 100 billion barrels, the United Arab Emirates with 98.1 billion and Kuwait with 94 billion. The region's production in 1993 rose from 22.9 per cent to 24 per cent of the world's total.

Proven gas reserves in the ESCWA region reached 24,619 billion cubic metres in 1993, an 18.9 per cent increase over three years, accounting for about 17 per cent of the world total. Since 1990, marketed production of natural gas had grown by more than 78 per cent in Qatar, which had some 20 per cent of the region's total reserves, and by almost 50 per cent in the United Arab Emirates.

Most of that production was intended for local consumption, but Western Asian countries with large reserves also pursued export strategies. Oman was analysing export opportunities in southern Europe and planned to export gas to India. Qatar's marketed output had increased by 78 per cent since 1990 and the United Arab Emirates planned to increase its liquefied natural gas production in 1993 following a Japanese undertaking to double imports over a 25-year period.

Agriculture

The region's agricultural production index grew by 2.6 per cent in 1993. Growth rates varied from 7.5 per cent in Iraq to 4.8 per cent in the Syrian Arab Republic, 3.8 per cent in Lebanon, 2.6 per cent in Egypt and 1.2 per cent in Yemen. Jordan and Saudi Arabia registered decreases of 5.9 per cent and 0.5 per cent, respectively. The region's food production index increased by almost 3 per cent and its cereal production by 7.5 per cent, due mainly to a 30 per cent expansion in the Syrian Arab Republic and 9.1 per cent growth in Iraq. Regional wheat production was 4.7 per cent higher than in 1992. The Syrian Arab Republic achieved the largest growth rate (21.5 per cent), followed by Iraq (18 per cent), and Egypt (3.6 per cent). Growth declined by 29.3 per cent in Jordan, 8.5 per cent in Saudi Arabia, 7.9 per cent in Yemen, and 3.8 per cent in Lebanon.

The value of Western Asian agricultural exports totalled $2.6 billion in 1992, the most recent date for which statistics were available, compared with $2.4 billion in 1991, but agricultural imports also grew from $13.8 billion to $15.4 billion over the same period.

Industrial development

The rate of industrialization in Western Asia continued to advance, albeit at a slower pace. Most countries gave greater emphasis to export-oriented small- and medium-scale private industries, while the GCC countries paid increased attention to downstream operations to accelerate the diversification of their economies. The expansion of industrial capacity, in that subregion in particular, through heavy industries such as petrochemicals and basic metal industries, created opportunities for the further development of downstream industries and for greater integration of the subregional industrial sector. Apart from cost and revenue incentives to improve the investment environment in the GCC subregion, most Western Asian countries granted additional benefits to foreign investors to help upgrade industries with better technologies, management and marketing techniques.

The relative contribution of the industrial sector, however, declined from 11 per cent of GDP in 1989 to 9.7 per cent in 1991, due largely to the devastating effects of the Persian Gulf hostilities on Iraq and Kuwait. The region's manufacturing sector continued to be constrained by the size of the domestic market and a contraction in aggregate demand, while global recession, competition from industrialized countries and protectionist measures against manufacturing products, particularly petrochemicals, caused the loss of traditional markets and increased difficulties in accessing new ones.

Trade

The total value of exports from the region reached $99.2 billion in 1992, 10.3 per cent more than in 1991. The increase was attributed entirely to the GCC subregion. Exports from other ESCWA countries declined slightly. The value of Kuwait's exports rose from $0.5 billion in 1991 to $6.5 billion in 1992, followed by Saudi Arabia with an increase of some $2 billion. Although the developed market economies remained the region's main trading partners, their share of its total exports fell from an average of 54 per cent in previous years, to an estimated 51.3 per cent in 1993. Intraregional exports accounted for about 10 per cent, while exports to other developing countries reached 26.3 per cent of the total, the highest level since 1985. The share of the former centrally planned economies dropped by more than 40 per cent against the 1992 level, to 1.3 per cent.

Imports to the region totalled $87.1 billion in 1992, a 16 per cent increase over 1991. They grew by $4.5 billion in Saudi Arabia, $3.6 billion in the United Arab Emirates and $2.7 billion in other ESCWA countries. The share of the developed economies in the regional total remained more than 60 per cent in 1993, with the United States accounting for 17 per cent. Intraregional imports rose from 6 per cent in 1992 to 6.3 per cent in 1993, considerably less than the 1989-1990 level of 10.4 per cent. As imports increased faster than exports, the region's export/import ratio declined in 1992 from 1.44 in 1990 and 1.21 in 1991 to 1.14.

The combined current account balance of the region, excluding Iraq, Lebanon, Qatar, the United Arab Emirates and Yemen, showed a deficit of $19.6 billion in 1992, compared with a 1991 deficit of $39.3 billion. The GCC countries reduced their deficit from $42.4 billion to $21.7 billion, owing to a significant drop in the deficit in services and unrequited transfers, while the surplus of the more diversified economies fell from $3.1 billion to $2.1 billion. At the same time, the international reserves of Western Asia, excluding Iraq, the Syrian Arab Republic and Yemen, reached about $38 billion in 1992, up from $36.4 billion in 1991, following a $5.5 billion increase in Egypt's reserves. Reserves of the GCC countries, however, decreased by $3.8 billion in 1992 and continued to decline in the first nine months of 1993, from $19.4 billion to $18.4 billion, excluding Oman, while the reserves of other ESCWA countries grew by $0.7 billion over the same period. The reserves/import ratio for the region dropped from 5.86 months in 1991 to 5.23 months in 1992.

Social trends

While the quality of life in the ESCWA region continued to improve in general, rapid political, economic and social developments and the inequitable distribution of the benefits of development increased the gap between the rich and poor in some countries. The poor and rural populations in most countries continued to be deprived and marginalized. In Jordan, the number of families living below the poverty line rose by 6.6 per cent in 1992 and accounted for 21.3 per cent of the total number of households in the country, up from 18.7 per cent in 1989. The impoverishment of Iraq's population also increased as a consequence of the Persian Gulf crisis and the Government's impaired ability, because of economic sanctions, to act as a welfare State.

Despite improvements in basic health conditions, children in Western Asia continued to suffer from malnutrition in poor and war-torn communities. Unemployment was running high among young people in 1993 as education geared towards "prestigious" professions, rather than technical and vocational training, caused surplus labour in certain occupations. Although progress was made in channelling human and physical resources towards the prevention of disability and care for the disabled, most disabled persons, particularly in rural areas, were marginalized from the mainstream of development in ESCWA countries. Disability-related problems increased in size and scope as a result of armed conflicts, civil unrest and the suppression of Palestinians in the occupied territories (see PART TWO, Chapter V). Minimal progress was made towards improving the status of women by giving them a voice at decision-making levels or creating legal awareness. Failure to make progress was attributed largely to political instability, increasing economic vulnerability and external dependence, coupled with inappropriate legislation that limited women's contribution to economic activity and withheld their full integration into the development process in Western Asia.

On the positive side, mortality rates for children under five decreased significantly in all countries of the region. Many ESCWA members pursued policies and measures to ensure higher standards of health and to provide free health care services to their citizens. Public expenditure on preventive and curative health services increased, as did the number of hospitals. Improvements in the overall health situation and access to health facilities had a positive impact on infant and maternal mortality, fertility and life expectancy. Better health and rising literacy rates also correlated favourably with family planning, resulting in lower birth rates in the region.

Encouraging results were achieved in education, health and employment for women and the literacy gap between men and women narrowed considerably through the promotion of higher enrolment rates for women in schools under the new "Education for All" policy. Women's literacy rates ranged from 83 per cent in the case of the former Democratic Yemen and about 70 per cent in Jordan, Kuwait and Lebanon to a low of 34 per cent in Egypt and 28 per cent in Yemen. The share of education in total expenditures grew significantly, although the situation remained critical in rural areas.

Activities in 1993

Development planning, development finance and international trade

Activities under ESCWA's subprogramme on development issues and policies during 1993[4] included the annual survey of economic and social developments in the ESCWA region. The survey considered, among other things, the implications of economic reform and structural adjustment policies in Egypt, Jordan and Lebanon. Other studies outlined a conceptual and methodological framework for poverty alleviation in Western Asia and discussed major economic issues and challenges facing unified Yemen. Four quarterly notes were issued on major economic developments in the region.

In the area of international trade and development finance, the secretariat issued an analytical review of developments in the external trade and payments situation of Western Asian countries, which focused on the commodity structure and geographical distribution of trade, intraregional trade, balance-of-payments flows and international reserves. Another review dealt with the region's monetary and financial sectors and covered privatization issues in particular. The secretariat also prepared regional studies on export finance mechanisms, the link between production policies and export activity, finance and development in the region, management and the organization of Government, and external debt problem.

Consultations were held with member Governments and relevant agencies on financing the Reconstruction and Rehabilitation Decade for Western Asia, 1994-2003, which was declared by the Commission in 1992.[5] ESCWA also cooperated with the League of Arab States (LAS) and OAU in organizing the First Arab-African Trade Fair (Tunis, Tunisia, October) and prepared a paper on trade relations between Western Asia and African countries.

Food and agriculture

Activities under ESCWA's food and agriculture subprogramme focused on resource conservation, rural development, rehabilitation of the agricultural sector, project planning and policy analysis, food consumption and distribution, and dissemination of information on agriculture. ESCWA continued to issue its annual publication *Agriculture and Development in Western Asia* and prepared national farm data handbooks for Jordan and Lebanon. The secretariat assisted Oman and the United Arab Emirates in formulating national plans of action to combat desertification and completed desertification control projects in Bahrain and Yemen. It recommended a plan of action to restrict the use of qat and to ensure its eventual eradication in Yemen and undertook studies on the rehabilitation of agriculture in Lebanon and in the occupied Palestinian territories. Two project documents were prepared on the rehabilitation of deep wells and springs and related irrigation canals.

Policies and programmes for rural development were assessed at an ad hoc expert group meeting (Amman, 10-14 October) and in a regional study and country studies of Lebanon and Oman. Another study examined intraregional trade in agricultural commodities and related trade policies and identified constraints and prospective improvements in that field. Activities in project planning and analysis included the third Arab symposium on the planning and development of fisheries and crustacea in the Arab world (Damascus, Syrian Arab Republic, 9-12 May) and the fifth regional training workshop on food and agricultural policy analysis (Cairo, 21 November–8 December). The secretariat also organized a national training workshop on farm management, project planning and analysis (Beirut, Lebanon, 13-25 September) and a two-stage training workshop on the planning and appraisal of agricultural and rural development projects (Amman, 22-26 August and 21-25 November).

In 1993, ESCWA signed a memorandum of understanding for collaboration and coordination with the International Centre for Agricultural Research in Dry Areas and concluded agreements with FAO and the Near East and North Africa Regional Agricultural Credit Association, for the preparation of a textbook on agricultural credit for Arab universities, and with the Arab Centre for the Study of Arid Zones and Dry Lands on cooperation in the fields of desertification and natural resources.

Industrial development

Under its industrial development subprogramme, ESCWA published a biennial review of recent developments in manufacturing and industrial prospects in the region. It prepared an assessment of the industrial sector in Yemen and sectoral studies on the manufacture of machinery for agro-food industries and the development of the pulp and paper industry in a number of Arab countries. A regional survey of the production and consumption of substances harmful to the ozone layer was completed and case studies of Egypt, Jordan and the Syrian Arab Republic formed the basis for a publication dealing with the productive employment of women in the Western Asian pharmaceuticals and electronics industries. Missions were fielded to the Syrian Arab Republic (6-8 April), the United Arab Emirates (10-23 May) and Lebanon (28 June–13 July) to provide advice on existing industries in those countries.

The ESCWA Industry Division gave special attention to the promotion of entrepreneurship in the region. An expert group meeting on the creation of indigenous entrepreneurship and opportunities for small- and medium-scale industrial investment (Damascus, 11-14 April) identified obstacles to and perspectives for the development of entrepreneurship in Western Asia. Another expert group meeting, on the operation of enterprises under severe and fast-changing conditions (Beirut, 24-26 November), made recommendations on enhancing disaster management at the level of industrial enterprises, firms and institutions. A regional training-of-trainers workshop (Cairo, 23 October–11 November) addressed ways to start a small business. Efforts to promote the diffusion of advanced industrial technologies included a joint UNIDO/ESCWA expert group meeting on automation and microprocessor controls (Amman, 15-17 November) and a training course on tissue culture techniques and applications in industry and agriculture (Cairo, 9-21 October). The Second Arab Conference on Perspectives of Modern Biotechnology (Amman, 24-28 April), co-sponsored by FAO and UNEP, dealt with applications for biotechnology and genetic engineering in industry, agriculture, pharmaceuticals and medicine, as well as investment in biotechnology-based projects and their commercialization.

Natural resources and energy

ESCWA's activities under the natural resources subprogramme addressed water resources management and conservation, the promotion of regional cooperation in water resources development and the establishment of an ESCWA water resources database (EWDB). A regional survey of water resources activities was prepared, together with studies on the operation and maintenance of dams in selected countries and on water resources planning, management, use and conservation. Another publication dealt with the planning and design of EWDB. A symposium on water use and conservation (Amman, 28 November–2 December) examined ways to meet the growing demand for water as well as problems aggravated by the region's limited water resources. It also discussed mechanisms for regional and interregional cooperation in the water sector. The secretariat completed the preparatory stage of a three-year regional project to assess water resources using remote-sensing techniques and reviewed cooperation among ESCWA members in the area of shared water resources. It also produced reports on the proposed establishment of a regional committee on natural resources and on the implementation of the Mar del Plata Action Plan adopted by the 1977 United Nations Water Conference.[6] In the area of mineral resources, a regional study was completed on down-stream phosphate industries and their prospects.

During the year, ESCWA cooperated with LAS in studying the possible establishment of a regional training network on water issues and a regional water resources council and of conducting a conference on water resources in the occupied Arab territories. It coordinated its activities with the Inter-Islamic Network on Water Resources Development and Management and participated in the first meeting of the Inter-Agency Task Force on Land and Water Resources (Alexandria, Egypt, 22 February), which discussed cooperation and coordination among United Nations organizations and the Arab regional agencies. A Steering Committee was set up by ESCWA, UNESCO and the Arab Centre for the Study of Arid Zones and Dry Lands to coordinate water-related activities, including projects on remote sensing, sea water intrusion, and the preparation of a water atlas for the Arab world.

The secretariat continued to promote regional energy strategies and policies, the use of renewable and non-conventional energy technologies and energy conservation through good management. It published the annual survey and assessment of energy-related activities in the ESCWA region and undertook a study on optimal energy use in oil-refining, based on case studies of oil refineries in Jordan and Yemen. It also reviewed the promotion of selected renewable energy projects and implementation of the 1981 Nairobi Programme of Action for the Development and Utilization of New and Renewable Sources of Energy.[7]

Science and technology

Activities under the Commission's science and technology subprogramme included a study on the integration of science and technology in the region's development planning and management process, a workshop on the same subject (Amman, 27-30 September) and an expert group meeting on the substitution of ozone-depleting substances (ODS) in Western Asia (Amman, 1-2 December). The expert group reviewed national and regional ODS use, considered ways of controlling ODS consumption and of implementing ODS-substitution strategies. The secretariat also continued preparations for the establishment of a regional centre for space science and technology education.

Transport and communications

Activities under the transport and communications subprogramme in 1993 included studies on the assessment of manpower development in the transport sector of selected ESCWA countries and on maritime hydrographic surveying and the maintenance of hydrographic surveying equipment in Western Asia. They also included the publication of documents on maritime transport statistics, information classification, the coordination of investments in the transport sector, pricing policies for port services and facilities and the use of computers in transport management. The secretariat continued to publish its annual _Transport Bulletin_ and co-sponsored, with UNCTAD, a workshop for senior officials on multimodal transport (Amman, 25-27 January). Advisory services were provided on the creation of free zones and port tariffs in Jordan and for evaluating a study on a new seaport in Oman. Expert group meetings were held on training needs in the transport sector (Amman, 23 and 24 January) and transport information systems (Beirut, 15-18 November).

Environment

Work under the environment subprogramme was directed towards the implementation of Agenda 21, adopted by the 1992 United Nations Conference on Environment and Development,[8] and the 1991 Arab Declaration on Environment and Development and Future Prospects,[9] which was endorsed by the Commission in 1992.[10] It also focused on the incorporation of the environmental dimension in the development process and the establishment of an environment database.

In accordance with the Arab Declaration and a 1992 Commission resolution on the subject,[10] a Joint Committee on Environment and Development in the Arab Region was established at a preparatory meeting (Amman, 7 and 8 April), organized by ESCWA, LAS, FAO and UNEP. The Joint Committee's objectives were to coordinate environment and development activities among members of the United Nations system, the LAS system and other Arab and international organizations, to develop proposals for an Arab environmental work programme, and to attract financial

and other support. At its first session (Cairo, 15 and 16 September),[11] the Joint Committee adopted the revised Integrated Environmental Information Network, approved in 1992 by the Council of Arab Ministers Responsible for Environment as part of the Arab Programme of Action for Sustainable Development. The Joint Committee appealed to its members for greater efforts to implement Arab environmental action programmes and activities. It also invited the ECA to join the Committee and decided to convene an Arab Ministerial Conference on Sustainable Agricultural and Rural Development in November 1994. A Preparatory Committee for the Conference held its first meeting on 13 September to consider technical, financial and organizational requirements.

ESCWA operational activities in the area of environment and sustainable development were directed towards capacity-building programmes to enable member States to identify and solve their environmental problems, formulate policies to encourage sustainable development, prepare management plans for environmentally sensitive States and areas, assess national and regional conditions and trends in environment and development, develop regional and subregional environmental legislation, rationalize the use of natural resources, and encourage follow-up to Agenda 21. The Commission also identified priority areas for action under Agenda 21, including the consideration of environment and development issues in decision-making; sustainable agriculture and rural development; water resources management; changing consumption and production patterns; poverty, sustainable development and human well-being; and technologies for sustainable development. An Environment Coordination Unit was set up within ESCWA in July.

During the year, the ESCWA secretariat reviewed the follow-up to Agenda 21 and the implementation of the Arab Declaration and compiled and computerized an environment database. It convened a national workshop on environmental planning and management capabilities in Jordan (Amman, 12 and 13 December).

Social development and the role of women

In 1993, the secretariat issued the biennial _Survey of Social Trends and Indicators in Countries of the ESCWA Region_ and parts of the Commission's contribution to the 1995 World Summit for Social Development. It prepared a study on the impact of drug abuse among youth in Western Asia, and substantially completed a study of the social impact of the Persian Gulf crisis on the region. A project on rural community development in Egypt and the Syrian Arab Republic was in the formulation stage. The secretariat organized a workshop on prosthetics and orthotics for key medical and technical personnel in Western Asia and the Eastern Mediterranean (Amman, 8-15 October). An expert group meeting on policies and programmes for the elderly in the ESCWA region was held in Cairo (19-21 October).

The women and development subprogramme included preparations for the International Year of the Family (1994) and the Fourth World Conference on Women (1995) and activities to integrate women into the development process. A study on the reintegration of women returnees and their families into their societies of origin compared the socio-economic problems facing women returnees and their families affected by crises in Egypt, Jordan and Yemen and proposed ways of alleviating them. The secretariat updated the directory of professional Arab women for technical cooperation projects and substantially completed a regional guide on employment laws and legislation for Arab women, a survey of the situation and needs of women in southern Yemen and a study on the socialization of children in the Persian Gulf region. It also reviewed technical assistance projects for the development and empowerment of women and the eradication of legal illiteracy among women. ESCWA cooperated with the United Nations Development Fund for Women in a project to strengthen statistics on women in development.

A technical assistance project to set up national preparatory committees for the Fourth World Conference on Women included missions in November/December to Bahrain, Egypt, Kuwait, Lebanon, Qatar, the Syrian Arab Republic, the United Arab Emirates and Yemen. Expert consultations on a policy framework and regional programme of action for Arab women in agriculture in the Near East (Cairo, 29 November–2 December) were held in cooperation with FAO and a UNICEF/UNDP/ESCWA workshop and briefing on regional preparations for the World Conference was convened for Egyptian NGOs (Cairo, 14 and 15 December). Other activities included a proposal for an expert group meeting on the Arab family in a changing society, to be held in 1994 in the context of the International Year of the Family, and a regional and national seminar for business and professional women (Amman, 26-28 April), which discussed the participation of Arab women in business and professional fields and their access to higher education and vocational training.

Population and human settlements

During the year, the secretariat published three issues of the *Population Bulletin of ESCWA*, produced the biennial demographic and related socio-economic data sheets for countries of Western Asia, issued a bibliography of population literature in the Arab world and prepared a computer-ized database on population and labour. Studies dealt with return migration, instructors and trainers in the Arab world and the spatial distribution of population. Expert group meetings were held on unemployment in ESCWA countries (Amman, 26-29 July) and human development in the Arab world (Cairo, 6-9 December). Regional population trends, policies and activities were reviewed at the Arab Population Conference (Amman, 4-8 April). The Conference adopted the Second Amman Declaration on Population and Development in the Arab World as a regional input to the 1994 International Conference on Population and Development.

Work in the field of human settlements focused on urban development, affordable housing and planning and design standards and techniques. Studies were prepared on housing trends during the last two decades, shelter and public amenities in urban areas, planning and design standards and community cohesiveness in urban life. Advisory missions were fielded to Yemen to help upgrade secondary settlements in the city of Thula (October) and to provide advice on a proposed national housing strategy (December). An expert group meeting was held on the social and cultural context of physical planning of the Arab city (Amman, 6-9 June). A cooperation agreement was reached between ESCWA and LAS concerning preparations for the 1996 United Nations Conference on Human Settlements (Habitat II).

Statistics

In February 1993 (see below), the Economic and Social Council established a Statistical Committee within ESCWA, as recommended by the Commission in 1992.[1] The Fourth Meeting of Heads of Central Statistical Organizations in the ESCWA Region (Amman, 26-28 October)[12] decided on the Committee's composition and activities. The Meeting also considered the implementation of its previous recommendations, technical cooperation in statistics, issues related to the United Nations System of National Accounts, the improvement of civil registration and vital statistics systems, the development of indicators and improved statistics on the status of Arab women and the National Household Survey Capability Programme.

Three biennial publications were issued in 1993: the *Bulletin of Industrial Statistics for the Arab Countries*, *Prices and Financial Statistics in the ESCWA Region* and *Compendium of Social Statistics and Indicators*. The status of civil registration and vital statistics systems in Western Asia and strategies for their improvement were the subject of a regional workshop (Damascus, 20-24 June). The first in a series of studies on social statistics in the region was issued, which also dealt with civil registration and vital statistics. A computerized database on labour statistics was produced and a database software program for registering live births and generating statistical reports was being developed. ESCWA continued to provide its members with advisory and training services under the Regional Household Survey Project.

ECONOMIC AND SOCIAL COUNCIL ACTION

On 2 February, the Economic and Social Council adopted **resolution 1993/2** without vote.

Establishment of a statistical committee within the Economic and Social Commission for Western Asia

The Economic and Social Council,

Realizing the importance of coordinating statistical work at the regional level and of standardizing statistical methods and concepts in accordance with the circumstances and potential of the countries of the region covered by the Economic and Social Commission for Western Asia and their economic and social development requirements, which induced other United Nations regional commissions to establish standing statistical committees to undertake the coordination of statistical work in their regions,

Aware of the necessity of supporting the participation of the statistical organizations of States members of the Commission in planning and developing statistical activities and in identifying the priority of statistical plans and programmes in the regions,

Aware also of the need to strengthen coordination and integration with regard to statistical policies, programmes and activities between regional Arab organizations and the Commission, with a view to meeting the needs and requirements of statistical organizations in member States and to developing those organizations in order to achieve the economic and social development goals of the countries of the region,

Noting that the meetings of heads of central statistical organizations of the States members of the Commission, held in 1985, 1987 and 1989, have proved effective in directing, coordinating and evaluating the statistical programmes of the Commission and in associating them with the statistical programmes and activities of regional Arab organizations and of member States,

Stressing the need for the meetings of heads of central statistical organizations of the States members of the Commission to assume a permanent institutional form,

1. *Decides* to establish a Statistical Committee of the Economic and Social Commission for Western Asia comprising representatives of the central statistical organizations of the States members of the Commission to undertake the following activities:

(a) To familiarize itself with the statistical activities of the States members of the Commission and to follow up the progress made in those countries in the development of their statistical programmes, drawing up recommendations regarding the status, implementation and evaluation of programmes of statistical work and organizing symposia, workshops and seminars related to statistics;

(b) To study international statistical systems, classifications and projects, adapting them to suit the conditions and priorities of the countries of the region;

(c) To provide advice on the statistical training requirements of the States members of the Commission,

proposing training programmes in coordination with appropriate regional institutions as needed;

(d) To standardize national statistics to make them more comparable at regional and international levels, taking into consideration relevant recommendations of the Statistical Commission and other appropriate bodies;

(e) To coordinate the exchange of statistical data and information between the Commission and its member States for the benefit of all concerned;

(f) To coordinate the statistical programmes of the States members of the Commission, in particular in matters relating to statistical surveys and censuses and dates of implementation;

2. *Recommends* that the Statistical Committee meet biennially;

3. *Calls upon* the Executive Secretary of the Commission to follow up the present resolution and to submit to the Commission at its seventeenth session a report on the achievements of the Statistical Committee.

Economic and Social Council resolution 1993/2

2 February 1993   Meeting 2   Adopted without vote

Draft by ESCWA (E/1992/65/Add.1); agenda item 2.

Technical cooperation

ESCWA continued its technical cooperation activities through short-term regional advisory services and the monitoring and substantive support of technical assistance projects.[13] During 1993, the secretariat continued to implement projects to encourage industrial ventures in ESCWA countries; establish engineering-infrastructure projects; conduct household surveys; and provide advice on data processing, energy, environment, human resource development, development planning and policy, promotion and industrial management, national accounts and economic statistics, science and technology, transport and communications, water resources development and social statistics.

Organizational questions

During the Persian Gulf hostilities, ESCWA's headquarters were temporarily relocated from Baghdad to Amman and, at its 1992 session,[1] the Commission considered offers to host its permanent headquarters and recommended a resolution for adoption by the Economic and Social Council.

On 2 February, the Council adopted **resolution 1993/3** without vote.

Permanent headquarters of the Economic and Social Commission for Western Asia

The Economic and Social Council,

Referring to the request submitted by the Government of Lebanon regarding the transfer and hosting of the permanent headquarters of the Economic and Social Commission for Western Asia in Beirut,

Referring also to the memorandum of the Government of Iraq, containing a request that the staff of the Commission return to Baghdad by 31 December 1992, failing which the Government would take back the present buildings, but would be prepared to provide other buildings for the same purpose,

Referring further to the request submitted by the Government of Jordan regarding the transfer and hosting of the permanent headquarters of the Commission in Amman,

Referring to the note by the Executive Secretary concerning the permanent headquarters of the Commission,

Taking into consideration the need to provide stability for the secretariat of the Commission, which is vital for the performance of the tasks entrusted to it,

1. *Requests* the Executive Secretary of the Economic and Social Commission for Western Asia to take the necessary measures to study the requests submitted by the Government of Lebanon and the Government of Jordan, as well as any other request that may be received from any State member of the Commission regarding the transfer and hosting of the permanent headquarters of the Commission, and also requests the Executive Secretary to submit to the Commission at its next special session a detailed report on the contacts he makes with regard to the Commission's permanent headquarters, which should contain an appraisal of the offers made in that respect;

2. *Decides* that a special session of the Commission shall be held at Beirut within one year of the date of the adoption of the present resolution to discuss the question of the permanent headquarters of the Commission;

3. *Expresses its appreciation* to the Government of Lebanon for its offer to act as host to the special session of the Commission and for being prepared to meet the expenses involved;

4. *Expresses its thanks* to the Government of Iraq, as the present host of the Commission, for the facilities it has provided and is providing to the Commission, and appeals to that Government to consult with the Executive Secretary of the Commission before taking any measures related to buildings allocated for the permanent headquarters of the Commission at Baghdad in the light of the agreement concluded between the United Nations and the Government of the Republic of Iraq relating to the headquarters of the Economic and Social Commission for Western Asia, signed at Baghdad on 13 June 1979;

5. *Expresses its thanks also* to the Government of Jordan for hosting the Commission on a temporary basis since August 1991 and for providing it with all the necessary facilities.

Economic and Social Council resolution 1993/3

2 February 1993   Meeting 2   Adopted without vote

Draft by ESCWA (E/1992/65/Add.1); agenda item 2.

By September 1993, no written offers to host ESCWA's permanent headquarters had been received, despite several indications of interest from member States. The special session of the Commission on that subject was cancelled as the issue was included as an agenda item of ESCWA's seventeenth (1994) session.

REFERENCES

(1)YUN 1992, p. 522. (2)E/ESCWA/17/16. (3)E/1994/55. (4)E/ESCWA/17/4 (Part I). (5)YUN 1992, p. 515. (6)YUN 1977, p. 555. (7)YUN 1981, p. 689. (8)YUN 1992, p. 672. (9)YUN 1991, p. 338. (10)YUN 1992, p. 521. (11)E/ESCWA/17/5/Add.2. (12)E/ESCWA/17/5/Add.1. (13)E/ESCWA/17/4 (Part II).

PART THREE

Economic and social questions

Chapter I

Development policy and international economic cooperation

The world economy continued to be sluggish in 1993, after three years of virtual stagnation. This was largely a reflection of the persistent weakness of the developed economies, which accounted for over 70 per cent of world output, and, to a lesser extent, of the decline in output in countries in transition from centrally planned to market economies. As to the developing countries, there was improvement in all major regions except Western Asia.

The issue of sustainable development received considerable attention throughout the United Nations system during 1993. The Economic and Social Council established a Commission on Sustainable Development, which held its first session in June, and a High-level Advisory Board on Sustainable Development met in organizational session in September. The Administrative Committee on Coordination established an Inter-agency Committee on Sustainable Development.

Eradication of poverty was also widely discussed during the year. The newly established Standing Committee on Poverty Alleviation of the United Nations Conference on Trade and Development met in January and the General Assembly considered the matter in December. The Assembly stressed the importance of domestic policies to mobilize resources to eradicate poverty and requested the Secretary-General to urge United Nations organizations to strengthen implementation of their poverty eradication programmes (resolution 48/184). The Assembly also proclaimed 1996 International Year for the Eradication of Poverty (48/183).

Preparations began for the Global Conference on the Sustainable Development of Small Island Developing States; the first session of the Conference's Preparatory Committee was held in August/September. In December, the Assembly decided to convene the Conference from 25 April to 6 May 1994 in Barbados and requested the Secretary-General to ensure that its goals and purposes received the widest possible dissemination (48/193).

The Assembly also considered the particular needs and problems of land-locked developing countries. It called on donor countries and multilateral financial and development institutions to assist them in the construction, maintenance and improvement of their transport and related facilities (48/169).

International economic relations

Development and international economic cooperation

Many aspects of development and international economic cooperation were discussed in 1993 by the General Assembly, the Economic and Social Council and other United Nations bodies. However, the Committee for Development Planning did not meet in 1993.

GENERAL ASSEMBLY ACTION

The Second (Economic and Financial) Committee considered various issues of development and international economic cooperation during the forty-eighth (1993) session of the General Assembly and made a number of recommendations. By **decision 48/441** of 21 December, the Assembly took note of part one of the Committee's report.[1]

Also on 21 December, on the recommendation of the Second Committee, the Assembly adopted **resolution 48/165** without vote.

Renewal of the dialogue on strengthening international economic cooperation for development through partnership

The General Assembly,

Reaffirming the validity of the objectives and commitments with regard to development adopted by the General Assembly and other United Nations bodies, especially the Declaration on International Economic Cooperation, in particular the Revitalization of Economic Growth and Development of the Developing Countries, the International Development Strategy for the Fourth United Nations Development Decade, the Declaration on the Right to Development, the United Nations New Agenda for the Development of Africa in the 1990s, the Programme of Action for the Least Developed Countries for the 1990s, the Cartagena Commitment, the Rio Declaraton on Environment and Development and Agenda 21, which provide an overall framework for furthering international economic cooperation for development,

Noting the ongoing work of the Secretary-General in the preparation of a report on an agenda for development, as requested by the General Assembly in its resolution 47/181 of 22 December 1992,

Recognizing the trends towards regional cooperation and integration, interdependence of nations and the globalization of economic issues and problems,

Convinced that universal peace, security and prosperity cannot be fully achieved in the absence of economic and social development and improvements in international economic relations,

Bearing in mind the interlinkages between economic problems and between the economic and social aspects of development, and aware that among the most compelling challenges facing the world community are the acceleration of development, the eradication of poverty, and the need to address disparities among countries and to forge genuine international economic cooperation and partnership for development,

Reaffirming that the United Nations has a central role to play in promoting international cooperation for development and in bringing development issues to the attention of the international community,

Noting the role of the Secretary-General in encouraging all countries to engage in a constructive dialogue for advancing development and in facilitating their efforts in that regard,

Convinced that the commitment to cooperation and partnership for development, which has been evolving in various forums in recent years, constitutes a good foundation from which to advance and promote international economic cooperation for development, the commitment to which has been clearly manifested in several documents, especially the Declaration on International Economic Cooperation, in particular the Revitalization of Economic Growth and Development of the Developing Countries, the International Development Strategy for the Fourth United Nations Development Decade, the Declaration on the Right to Development, the United Nations New Agenda for the Development of Africa in the 1990s, the Programme of Action for the Least Developed Countries for the 1990s, the Cartagena Commitment, the Rio Declaration on Environment and Development and Agenda 21,

Also convinced of the importance of continuing to build upon the spirit of cooperation and partnership for development through constructive dialogue among all countries, in particular between the developed and developing countries, for the purpose of promoting an international economic environment conducive to sustainable development,

1. *Reaffirms* the need to strengthen constructive dialogue and partnership in order to promote further international economic cooperation for development;

2. *Also reaffirms* that such a dialogue should be conducted in response to the imperatives of mutual interests and benefits, genuine interdependence, shared responsibilities and the partnership for sustainable development as established at the United Nations Conference on Environment and Development, and that the United Nations system should play a central role in facilitating such a dialogue;

3. *Further reaffirms* that the United Nations has a central role to play in promoting international cooperation for development and in bringing development issues to the attention of the international community;

4. *Requests* the Secretary-General to submit to the General Assembly at its forty-ninth session an analysis and recommendations on ways and means to promote such a dialogue, reflecting the ongoing work on an agenda for development and taking into account the progress achieved in fulfilment of the commitment referred to in the eighth preambular paragraph above.

General Assembly resolution 48/165

21 December 1993   Meeting 86   Adopted without vote

Approved by Second Committee (A/48/717/Add.12) without vote, 10 December (meeting 47); draft by Australia, Canada, China, Colombia (for Group of 77), Czech Republic, Estonia, Hungary, Indonesia (for Non-Aligned Movement), Japan, Latvia, Lithuania, New Zealand, the former Yugoslav Republic of Macedonia and United States (A/C.2/48/L.28/Rev.1); agenda item 91.

Meeting numbers. GA 48th session: 2nd Committee 8, 9, 15-17, 20, 30-32, 36-40, 42-45, 47; plenary 86.

In other action, the Assembly, by **decision 48/437** of 20 December, deferred consideration of the launching of global negotiations on international economic cooperation for development and decided to include it in the provisional agenda of its forty-ninth (1994) session.

Agenda for development

In a note of 29 November,[2] the Secretary-General reported on progress in implementing a 1992 General Assembly resolution[3] on the preparation of an agenda for development. The note provided information on 17 replies received from Member States to a communication from the Secretary-General eliciting their views on the agenda. Based on those replies and on consultations within the United Nations Secretariat and with organizations of the United Nations system, including at the Administrative Committee on Coordination (ACC) session of 28 and 29 October 1993,[4] the note also presented initial indications of approaches and broad themes that the Secretary-General proposed to pursue in an agenda for development. He also referred to the subject in his report on the work of the Organization (see p. 3).

In view of the complexity of the issues to be addressed in an agenda for development, the Secretary-General proposed that the subject be considered by the Economic and Social Council and the Assembly in 1994.

GENERAL ASSEMBLY ACTION

On 21 December, on the recommendation of the Second Committee, the General Assembly adopted **resolution 48/166** without vote.

An agenda for development

The General Assembly,

Recalling its resolution 47/181 of 22 December 1992,

Convinced of the need to elaborate a framework to promote international consensus in the field of development,

Committed to strengthening the effectiveness of the United Nations in the economic and social sectors, and recognizing, in this respect, the need to revive the role of the United Nations in fostering and promoting international cooperation for economic and social development,

Taking note of the views expressed by States on an agenda for development,

Welcoming the intention of the Secretary-General to issue in the early months of 1994 the report requested in its resolution 47/181,

1. *Takes note with appreciation* of the note by the Secretary-General on progress in the implementation of General Assembly resolution 47/181;

2. *Decides* that the intergovernmental discussions to consider an agenda for development and the reports of the Secretary-General thereon should be held at the substantive session of 1994 of the Economic and Social Council and at the forty-ninth session of the General Assembly;

3. *Invites* the President of the General Assembly to promote, as early as possible in 1994, in an open-ended format, broad-based discussions and an exchange of views on an agenda for development, on the basis of the report of the Secretary-General requested in its resolution 47/181;

4. *Also invites* the President of the General Assembly, in order to ensure the broad-based nature of those discussions, to invite relevant programmes, funds and agencies of the United Nations system, relevant multilateral institutions and other relevant organizations, including scientific and academic institutions, to participate fully in or present their views during those discussions;

5. *Requests* the Secretary-General to submit to the General Assembly at its forty-ninth session further recommendations, as appropriate, to follow up his report on an agenda for development, taking into account the views expressed during the substantive session of 1994 of the Economic and Social Council, as well as the views expressed during the discussions promoted by the President of the General Assembly and summarized under his own responsibility;

6. *Recommends* that the Economic and Social Council, at its organizational session for 1994, consider "An agenda for development" as a possible topic for the high-level segment of its substantive session of 1994;

7. *Decides* to hold special plenary meetings at a high level, at its forty-ninth session, to consider ways of promoting and giving political impetus to an agenda for development;

8. *Also decides* to include in the provisional agenda of its forty-ninth session an item entitled "An agenda for development".

General Assembly resolution 48/166

21 December 1993   Meeting 86   Adopted without vote

Approved by Second Committee (A/48/717/Add.12) without vote, 13 December (meeting 48); draft by Vice-Chairman (A/C.2/48/L.87), based on informal consultations on draft by China, and Colombia (for Group of 77) (A/C.2/48/L.74); agenda item 91.
Meeting numbers. GA 48th session: 2nd Committee 8, 9, 15-17, 20, 30-32, 36-40, 43-46, 48; plenary 86.

UN initiative on opportunity and participation

On 28 April 1993,[5] Papua New Guinea requested that an item entitled "United Nations initiative on opportunity and participation" be included in the agenda of the General Assembly's 1993 session. It expressed appreciation for the work being carried out by the United Nations, particularly in the context of the Fourth United Nations Development Decade (1991-2000) and preparation of a proposed agenda for development, to identify, publicize and deal with the international aspects of the difficulties limiting economic opportunity and participation in developing countries. However, it believed that it would be appropriate in 1993 to establish a panel to study and report on opportunity and participation in the economies of developing countries, since it was the International Year of the World's Indigenous People, the year immediately following the United Nations Conference on Environment and Development (UNCED), and the year preceding the International Conference on Population and Development and the Global Conference on the Sustainable Development of Small Island Developing States.

On 22 October,[6] Papua New Guinea submitted supplementary documentation on its proposal.

GENERAL ASSEMBLY ACTION

On 14 December, the General Assembly adopted **resolution 48/60** by consensus.

United Nations initiative on opportunity and participation

The General Assembly,

Reaffirming the Declaration on International Economic Cooperation, in particular the Revitalization of Economic Growth and Development of the Developing Countries, contained in the annex to its resolution S-18/3 of 1 May 1990, and the International Development Strategy for the Fourth United Nations Development Decade, contained in the annex to its resolution 45/199 of 21 December 1990, which provide the overall framework for economic growth and development,

Recalling its resolutions 46/144 of 17 December 1991 on the implementation of the commitments and policies agreed upon in the Declaration on International Economic Cooperation, in particular the Revitalization of Economic Growth and Development of the Developing Countries, and 47/181 of 22 December 1992 on an agenda for development,

Taking into account the Cartagena Commitment, the United Nations New Agenda for the Development of Africa in the 1990s, the Programme of Action for the Least Developed Countries for the 1990s and Agenda 21 and all other relevant decisions of the United Nations Conference on Environment and Development,

Bearing in mind that the reactivation of economic growth and sustainable development in all countries requires, *inter alia*, a dynamic and a supportive international economic environment,

Noting the views of the Secretary-General on an agenda for development, as contained in his report on the work of the Organization, and his note of 29 November 1993 on the progress in the implementation of General Assembly resolution 47/181,

Determined to uphold the Charter of the United Nations, in particular the commitment to employ international machinery for the promotion of the economic and social advancement of all peoples,

Recognizing that one of the fundamental prerequisites for the achievement of sustainable development is broad public participation in decision-making,

Acknowledging the relevance of the issue of opportunity and participation in the economic and social development agenda of the United Nations system,

Pledged to support efforts, particularly of the developing countries, to increase their opportunity and participation in the world economy and those of the individuals and communities in those countries for accelerated and sustainable development,

Taking special note of the request dated 28 April 1993 for the inclusion of the present item in the provisional agenda of the forty-eighth session, and of all related documents on the United Nations initiative on opportunity and participation, including the document of 26 October 1993,

1. *Takes note* of the report of the Secretary-General on the work of the Organization, in particular as it concerns the preparation of the report on an agenda for development, and his note on the progress in the implementation of General Assembly resolution 47/181;

2. *Decides* that an ad hoc panel of distinguished, expert and experienced persons, broadly representative of the international community, to be known as the "United Nations Panel on Opportunity and Participation", funded from within existing resources and supported by voluntary contributions, shall be appointed to conduct a comprehensive study on opportunity and participation for the economic and social advancement of all peoples, with particular reference to the economies of developing countries;

3. *Requests* the Secretary-General, in consultation with Member States, to appoint the members of the Panel from lists of experts within the United Nations system, in particular members of the Committee for Development Planning, taking into account the outcome of discussions on Economic and Social Council resolution 1993/81 of 30 July 1993 and the relevant provisions of General Assembly resolution 47/191 of 22 December 1992, so that they will commence their study as early as possible in 1994 in order to prepare a comprehensive, systematic and thorough report, including appropriate conclusions and practical recommendations, guided by the consensus and principles on international cooperation for development as enshrined in various agreements and declarations referred to in the preamble of the present resolution, and based on their own independent judgement, in time for consideration by the General Assembly at its fiftieth session in 1995;

4. *Invites* Member States and international organizations to contribute on a voluntary basis towards implementation of the present resolution;

5. *Invites* the United Nations Panel on Opportunity and Participation, in the preparation of the above-mentioned study, to draw, *inter alia*, on the ongoing discussions in the context of the preparation of an agenda for development;

6. *Requests* the Secretary-General to submit to the General Assembly at its forty-ninth session a progress report on the work of the Panel;

7. *Decides* to include in the provisional agenda of its forty-ninth session a sub-item entitled "United Nations initiative on opportunity and participation" under the item entitled "Development and international economic cooperation".

General Assembly resolution 48/60

14 December 1993   Meeting 79   Adopted by consensus

51-nation draft (A/48/L.19/Rev.1 & Add.1), orally revised; agenda item 151.
Sponsors: Algeria, Antigua and Barbuda, Argentina, Australia, Bahamas, Barbados, Belize, Benin, Brunei Darussalam, Cape Verde, Chile, Costa Rica, El Salvador, Fiji, Grenada, Guatemala, Guinea, Guinea-Bissau, Guyana,

India, Indonesia, Israel, Jamaica, Madagascar, Malawi, Maldives, Mali, Marshall Islands, Micronesia, Mongolia, Morocco, Namibia, Nepal, New Zealand, Nicaragua, Nigeria, Pakistan, Panama, Papua New Guinea, Paraguay, Republic of Korea, Rwanda, Saint Lucia, Saint Vincent and the Grenadines, Samoa, Sierra Leone, Solomon Islands, Togo, United Republic of Tanzania, Vanuatu, Zambia.
Meeting numbers. GA 48th session: plenary 55-57, 79.

International cooperation for economic growth and development

In response to a 1991 General Assembly request,[7] the Secretary-General submitted a report on regional economic integration among developing countries,[8] which was discussed by the Second Committee in the context of the implementation of the Declaration on International Economic Cooperation, in particular the Revitalization of Economic Growth and Development of the Developing Countries,[9] and the International Development Strategy for the Fourth United Nations Development Decade,[10] both adopted by the Assembly in 1990.

The report described measures to promote regional economic integration envisaged by the United Nations Conference on Trade and Development (UNCTAD), the Economic Commission for Latin America and the Caribbean, the Economic and Social Commission for Asia and the Pacific, the Economic Commission for Africa and the Economic and Social Commission for Western Asia. It noted that the efforts of UNCTAD and the regional commissions in preparing, formulating and implementing joint projects to promote regional economic integration could help to avoid duplication and mobilize the required extra-budgetary resources.

GENERAL ASSEMBLY ACTION

On 21 December, on the recommendation of the Second Committee, the General Assembly adopted **resolution 48/185** without vote.

Implementation of the commitments and policies agreed upon in the Declaration on International Economic Cooperation, in particular the Revitalization of Economic Growth and Development of the Developing Countries, and implementation of the International Development Strategy for the Fourth United Nations Development Decade

The General Assembly,

Reaffirming the Declaration on International Economic Cooperation, in particular the Revitalization of Economic Growth and Development of the Developing Countries, contained in the annex to its resolution S-18/3 of 1 May 1990, and the International Development Strategy for the Fourth United Nations Development Decade, contained in the annex to its resolution 45/199 of 21 December 1990, which provide the overall framework for economic growth and development,

Recalling its resolutions 46/144 of 17 December 1991 and 47/152 of 18 December 1992 on the implementation of the Declaration and the International Development Strategy,

1. *Takes note* of the report submitted by the Secretary-General, as requested in its resolution 46/145 of 17 December 1991, on regional economic integration among developing countries;

2. *Stresses* the need for the full and timely implementation of the commitments and policies agreed upon in the Declaration on International Cooperation, in particular the Revitalization of Economic Growth and Development of the Developing Countries, and in the International Development Strategy for the Fourth United Nations Development Decade;

3. *Encourages* Member States that have not yet submitted their reports on the implementation of the commitments and policies agreed upon in the Declaration and in the International Development Strategy to do so;

4. *Decides*, in order to monitor the progress made in the implementation of the Declaration and the International Development Strategy and to facilitate the deliberations on the analytical and comprehensive report of the Secretary-General on the subject, as requested in its resolution 47/152, to include in the provisional agenda of its forty-ninth session the item entitled "International cooperation for economic growth and development: *(a)* Implementation of the commitments and policies agreed upon in the Declaration on International Economic Cooperation, in particular the Revitalization of Economic Growth and Development of the Developing Countries; *(b)* Implementation of the International Development Strategy for the Fourth United Nations Development Decade";

5. *Requests* the Secretary-General to include in his analytical and comprehensive report on the implementation of the commitments and policies agreed upon in the Declaration and in the International Development Strategy information on the difficulties encountered in implementing the commitments and the measures that have to be taken by Member States for the expeditious and full implementation of the agreements contained therein.

General Assembly resolution 48/185

21 December 1993   Meeting 86   Adopted without vote

Approved by Second Committee (A/48/721) without vote, 6 December (meeting 45); draft by China, and Colombia (for Group of 77) (A/C.2/48/L.10), orally amended following informal consultations; agenda item 95.
Meeting numbers. GA 48th session: 2nd Committee 21, 22, 26, 45; plenary 86.

Integration of economies in transition into the world economy

In response to a 1992 General Assembly request,[11] the Secretary-General submitted, in October 1993, a report on the role of the United Nations in the integration of the economies in transition into the world economy.[12]

The report described the overall setting of the transition economies—that is, countries in Eastern Europe formerly characterized by one-party rule and by an economic system anchored to some form of administrative planning—and discussed the process of their integration into the world economy. It further addressed the need to promote the flow of information for a market-based economy, and particularly to transform statistical capabilities. With regard to the role of the United Nations,

the report noted that most agencies were already involved in the issues of the transition economies, with many of them rendering assistance indirectly. More direct assistance was being provided by the Bretton Woods institutions (the International Monetary Fund and the World Bank). The report also provided information received from a number of United Nations bodies, programmes and agencies on assistance provided to those economies.

The report concluded that a more buoyant international economy, particularly in Western Europe, and increased access to markets could do much to quicken the process of integrating the transition economies into the world economy. However, international cooperation policies also had a major role to play in enhancing that process. Most United Nations bodies had been involved in this regard, either by transferring financial resources or by delivering technical assistance, including information about the broader environment into which the transition economies wished to integrate. Far more technical assistance, including information aid, could be rendered by United Nations agencies to enhance the integration process, but financial constraints had restricted many agencies from doing so. Nevertheless, policy makers in the transition economies and technical assistance institutions recognized that the aid provided by the international community in general and United Nations agencies in particular could be improved through better coordination and more effective targeting, and by concentrating on: needs assessments carried out by transition economies themselves; ascertaining the commitment of donors to transferring resources, the form of aid and the timetable for its availability; and sequencing of aid delivery from donors to potential recipients.

In response to a 1992 General Assembly request,[13] the Secretary-General, in a September report,[14] reviewed the impact of the recent evolution of the economies in transition on the world economy. The report, in part an update of reports on the subject submitted to the Economic and Social Council in 1991[15] and to the Assembly in 1992,[16] discussed the process of transition of the economies of Eastern Europe and the former USSR from central planning and autarky to price mechanisms and openness, as well as the evolution of trade relationships of those economies. It also described the impact of the changes in Eastern Europe on some developing countries and the need for external resources for the transition process, including the implications that the large additional demand for financial resources would have for finance for the development of developing countries.

The report concluded by noting that the economies in transition needed greater opportunities to trade with the rest of the world, as well as among themselves. Their trade expansion could take place with less friction in export markets when world output and trade were growing reasonably fast. In addition, the need for increased external resources for the transition process could be met without impinging on the needs of other countries only if the industrial economies were growing and generating sufficient resources. Although an assessment of those implications was bound to be speculative, there was little doubt that, in the long term, the impact of the changes in the transition economies would be positive for the growth of the world economy.

UNDP action. In his annual report covering 1992,[17] the Administrator of the United Nations Development Programme (UNDP) described programmes under way or planned for Europe and the Commonwealth of Independent States.[18]

On 18 June 1993,[19] the UNDP Governing Council requested the Administrator to develop further UNDP's strategy in assisting the countries in transition to a market economy and encouraged him to share the experience gained with interested countries. It invited the international community to increase resources to assist those countries through UNDP's technical cooperation activities, taking fully into account that it should not be to the detriment of existing programmes.

GENERAL ASSEMBLY ACTION

On 21 December, the General Assembly, on the recommendation of the Second Committee, adopted **resolution 48/181** without vote.

Integration of the economies in transition into the world economy

The General Assembly,

Reaffirming its resolutions 47/175 and 47/187 of 22 December 1992 and all its other relevant resolutions,

Taking note of the relevant decisions of the Governing Council of the United Nations Development Programme, decision B(48), adopted by the Economic Commission for Europe on 26 April 1993, and resolution 49/1, adopted by the Economic and Social Commission for Asia and the Pacific on 29 April 1993,

Taking note also of the report of the Secretary-General on the role of the United Nations system in addressing problems facing countries with economies in transition, including the difficulties that those countries are encountering as they integrate their economies into the world economy,

1. *Reaffirms* the need for the full integration of the countries with economies in transition as well as of all other countries into the world economy, in particular through improved market access for their exports of goods and services, which integration will simultaneously support the systemic transformation of countries with economies in transition towards market-oriented policies and have a positive impact on world trade and global economic growth and development;

2. *Requests* the Secretary-General to strengthen, within existing resources and through appropriate ar-

rangements within the United Nations Secretariat, the ability of the United Nations system to conduct analytical activities and provide policy advice and technical assistance to the countries with economies in transition, as well as to promote and enhance mutual cooperation with the International Monetary Fund and the World Bank, within their respective mandates;

3. *Also requests* the Secretary-General to study, within the scope of the implementation of the present resolution and while continuing the existing cooperation with relevant international institutions and entities, possible areas of economic and technical cooperation among countries with economies in transition, as well as with the developing countries, identifying the role that the United Nations system could play in this field, with a view to encouraging greater participation by those countries in the world economy;

4. *Further requests* the Secretary-General to submit to the General Assembly at its forty-ninth session, and biennially thereafter, a report on the implementation of the present resolution.

General Assembly resolution 48/181

21 December 1993   Meeting 86   Adopted without vote

Approved by Second Committee (A/48/717/Add.11) without vote, 6 December (meeting 45); 44-nation draft (A/C.2/48/L.6/Rev.1), orally revised; agenda item 91 (j).

Sponsors: Albania, Armenia, Azerbaijan, Belarus, Belgium, Bulgaria, Croatia, Czech Republic, Denmark, Estonia, Finland, France, Georgia, Germany, Greece, Hungary, Iceland, Ireland, Italy, Japan, Kazakhstan, Kyrgyzstan, Latvia, Lithuania, Luxembourg, Netherlands, Norway, Poland, Portugal, Republic of Moldova, Romania, Russian Federation, Slovakia, Slovenia, Spain, Sweden, Tajikistan, the former Yugoslav Republic of Macedonia, Turkey, Turkmenistan, Ukraine, United Kingdom, United States.

Meeting numbers. GA 48th session: 2nd Committee 8, 9, 18, 45; plenary 86.

The private sector in development

Entrepreneurship and national development

In response to General Assembly requests of 1991[20] and 1992,[21] the Secretary-General submitted a report in October 1993 on entrepreneurship and national development.[22] The report discussed possible government policies to create an enabling environment that would allow entrepreneurship to flourish, suggested possible sources of entrepreneurial ability and measures for the development of entrepreneurship, and described the role of the international community in encouraging the growth of entrepreneurship.

The report concluded by noting that an increasing number of Governments had privatized activities by either selling them, contracting out activities or withdrawing from particular sectors, thus opening up wider vistas for private entrepreneurs. Although insufficient attention had been paid to primary, technical and commercial education, that imbalance was slowly being corrected and the process was likely to accelerate in the 1990s. Governments and non-governmental organizations (NGOs) had made efforts to broaden entrepreneurial sources and mobilize the talents of women and other groups who were formerly limited to microenterprises. They had also moved to reduce discrimination against entrepreneurs in the informal sector, which had formerly been considered as a negative social phenomenon, and had sought to draw informal entrepreneurs into the general economy. All those trends would require support from the international community, including maintaining open markets and increasing flows of investment and economic assistance to permit the newly entrepreneurial economies to flourish.

Measures undertaken by Governments included providing credit facilities, training and extension services and special programmes for women entrepreneurs and others from previously disadvantaged groups, promoting technology parks, incubators and industrial estates, subcontracting, franchising and licensing, as well as funding institutions for promoting new enterprises. In the 1980s and 1990s those measures were being subjected further to market forces and entrepreneurship promotion was also being pursued.

Privatization

The Ad Hoc Working Group on Comparative Experiences with Privatization, established by the UNCTAD Trade and Development Board (TDB) in 1992,[23] held its second and third sessions in 1993. At the second (Geneva, 7-11 June),[24] it reviewed 31 country presentations that had been submitted to the secretariat. It also had before it an UNCTAD secretariat report on the design, implementation and results of privatization programmes, including a cross-country analysis of national experiences,[25] and a preliminary version of a directory of national focal points dealing with privatization.[26] The Working Group also considered techniques for privatization and financing of privatization, including the role of foreign investment, international agencies and bilateral donors.

It annexed to its report a summary of the main points made in its discussion of policy issues and approaches relating to the techniques and financing of privatization.

At its third session (Geneva, 29 November–3 December),[27] the Working Group continued its consideration of the design, implementation and results of privatization programmes as presented in updated versions of the report on those issues[28] and of the directory of national focal points dealing with privatization.[29] It also had before it an issues paper by the UNCTAD secretariat, dealing with competition and the regulation of privatized monopolies and social impact and socially related support measures,[30] as well as five country presentations.

A summary of the Working Group's discussion on competition and the regulation of privatized monopolies and social impact and socially related support measures was annexed to its report.

Documents prepared by the UNCTAD secretariat for the Working Group were also submitted to the UNCTAD Intergovernmental Group of Experts on Restrictive Business Practices (Geneva, 18-22 October).[31]

On 21 December, on the recommendation of the Second Committee, the General Assembly adopted **resolution 48/180** without vote.

Entrepreneurship and privatization for economic growth and sustainable development

The General Assembly,

Recalling its resolutions 45/98 of 14 December 1990, 45/188 of 21 December 1990, 46/166 of 19 December 1991 and 47/171, 47/181 and 47/199 of 22 December 1992,

Taking note of Agenda 21, the Cartagena Commitment, the International Development Strategy for the Fourth United Nations Development Decade and the Declaration on International Economic Cooperation, in particular the Revitalization of Economic Growth and Development of the Developing Countries,

Taking note with appreciation of the report of the Secretary-General on entrepreneurship and national development,

Taking note also of chapter VII of the *World Economic Survey, 1993,*

Taking into account the activities of the Ad Hoc Working Group on Comparative Experiences with Privatization and the Intergovernmental Working Group of Experts on Restrictive Business Practices, of the United Nations Conference on Trade and Development,

Recognizing the importance of the market and the private sector for the efficient functioning of economies in various stages of development,

Recognizing also the sovereign right of each State to decide on the development of its private and public sectors, taking into account the comparative advantages of each sector, bearing in mind the economic, social and cultural diversity in the world,

Acknowledging that broad participation by individuals and major groups in decision-making is a fundamental prerequisite for the achievement of economic growth and sustainable development, with entrepreneurship as an important element of that goal,

Noting that many countries continue to attach major importance to the privatization of enterprises, demonopolization and administrative deregulation in the context of their economic restructuring policies, as a means to increase efficiency, economic growth and sustainable development,

Recognizing further the important role of Governments in creating, through transparent and participatory processes, the enabling environment supportive of entrepreneurship and facilitative of privatization, in particular the establishment of the judicial, executive and legislative frameworks necessary for a market-based exchange of goods and services and for good management, as described in paragraphs 27 and 28 of the Cartagena Commitment,

Emphasizing the importance of a supportive international economic environment, including investment and trade, for the promotion of entrepreneurship and privatization in all countries,

Noting also the difficulties that countries encounter in promoting entrepreneurship and in implementing privatization programmes owing to a lack of appropriate experience and technical capacities in those areas,

Welcoming the activities that have been and will be undertaken by the organizations, bodies, programmes and specialized agencies of the United Nations system for the benefit of recipient countries and in conformity with their own policies and priorities for development, in supporting national efforts aimed at creating enabling environments for entrepreneurship and for the implementation of privatization programmes,

Recalling with satisfaction the active collaboration between the United Nations system and private-sector associations, such as the ongoing efforts of the United Nations Development Programme with the International Chamber of Commerce, the Business Council for Sustainable Development and the Chamber of Commerce and Industry of the Group of 77,

Mindful of the resource constraints of the Secretariat and, therefore, of the need to rationalize related agenda items and requests for reports,

1. *Invites* interested Member States to enhance the exchange of information among themselves and all relevant organs, organizations and bodies of the United Nations system on activities, programmes and experiences of Member States and the United Nations system concerning entrepreneurship, privatization, demonopolization and administrative deregulation, in order to increase the efficiency and effectiveness of technical cooperation in this field;

2. *Requests* the Secretary-General to strengthen, within existing resources and with due priority, the activities of the United Nations system related to the promotion of entrepreneurship and to the implementation of privatization programmes, demonopolization and administrative deregulation, through, *inter alia*, better coordination;

3. *Calls upon* the relevant organs, organizations and programmes of the United Nations system, according to their mandates, to develop and, upon request, increase technical assistance and to incorporate in their respective programming and activities specific objectives that will:

(*a*) Facilitate, as appropriate, the creation of enabling environments for the establishment and growth of small and medium-size enterprises and for the support of local entrepreneurs;

(*b*) Facilitate, as appropriate, the design and implementation of privatization, demonopolization and administrative deregulation policies and assist relevant national institutions in developing the capacities to institute appropriate policy, legal, regulatory and fiscal frameworks and incentives to promote entrepreneurship;

4. *Encourages* the relevant organs, organizations and bodies of the United Nations system, in pursuing those activities, to foster active partnerships between public and private entities, taking into account the capacities for self-organization of entrepreneurs, through, for example:

(*a*) Mechanisms for discussion and consultation by relevant parties as to the appropriate ways to enhance the environment for entrepreneurship, privatization, demonopolization and administrative deregulation;

(*b*) Promoting initiatives, such as national and, where appropriate, regional workshops, to review and disseminate experience and lessons learned locally and internationally on the promotion of entrepreneurship and on the implementation of privatization, demonopolization and administrative deregulation;

5. *Also requests* the Secretary-General to prepare a biennial report, in consultation with the heads of relevant organs, organizations and programmes of the United Nations system, on policies and activities related to entrepreneurship, privatization, demonopolization and administrative deregulation, clarifying the focus of their respective activities;

6. *Decides* to review and appraise at its fiftieth session the activities related to the present resolution under an item entitled "Development and international economic cooperation: Entrepreneurship and privatization for economic growth and sustainable development".

General Assembly resolution 48/180

21 December 1993   Meeting 86   Adopted without vote

Approved by Second Committee (A/48/717/Add.10) without vote, 13 December (meeting 48); 50-nation draft (A/C.2/48/L.34/Rev.1); agenda item 91 *(i)*.
Sponsors: Argentina, Armenia, Australia, Austria, Belarus, Belgium, Benin, Bulgaria, Canada, Czech Republic, Denmark, El Salvador, Estonia, Finland, France, Germany, Greece, Iceland, Ireland, Israel, Italy, Japan, Kazakhstan, Latvia, Liechtenstein, Lithuania, Luxembourg, Marshall Islands, Mongolia, Morocco, Netherlands, New Zealand, Norway, Poland, Portugal, Republic of Korea, Republic of Moldova, Romania, Russian Federation, Singapore, Slovakia, Slovenia, Spain, Sweden, Tajikistan, Thailand, the former Yugoslav Republic of Macedonia, Ukraine, United Kingdom, United States.
Meeting numbers. GA 48th session: 2nd Committee 30-32, 42, 48; plenary 86.

Coercive economic measures

In response to a 1991 General Assembly request,[32] the Secretary-General submitted a note in October 1993 on economic measures as a means of political and economic coercion against developing countries.[33] He described his recent restructuring of the economic and social sectors of the Secretariat and drew attention to the fact that UNCTAD VIII, held in 1992,[34] had redefined UNCTAD's programme of work. In view of those new arrangements and newly established priorities, and due to the fact that no further conceptual work had been carried out on the subject, the assignment of responsibilities for further work in the area had yet to be determined.

The Secretary-General stated that the conclusions of a 1989 expert group on coercive economic measures[35] should be considered. They included the precise definition and classification of coercive economic measures; the further elaboration of specific legal norms; the refinement of methodologies to measure the impact of such measures; the establishment of adequate monitoring procedures; the definition of specific criteria to assess coercive measures; the consideration of options for possible compensation mechanisms in qualified cases; the examination of an appropriate institutional capacity to deal with information gathering and assessment of concrete cases; and the examination of common conceptual features and differences between economic sanctions imposed by the United Nations and coercive economic measures.

GENERAL ASSEMBLY ACTION

On 21 December, on the recommendation of the Second Committee, the General Assembly adopted **resolution 48/168** by recorded vote.

Economic measures as a means of political and economic coercion against developing countries

The General Assembly,

Recalling the relevant principles set forth in the Charter of the United Nations,

Reaffirming that no State may use or encourage the use of economic, political or any other type of measures to coerce another State in order to obtain from it the subordination of the exercise of its sovereign rights,

Bearing in mind the general principles governing international trade and trade policies for development contained in the relevant resolutions and rules of the United Nations Conference on Trade and Development and the General Agreement on Tariffs and Trade,

Reaffirming also its resolutions 44/215 of 22 December 1989 and 46/210 of 20 December 1991,

Gravely concerned that the use of coercive economic measures adversely affects the economy and development efforts of developing countries and has a general negative impact on international economic cooperation and on the world-wide effort to move towards a non-discriminatory, open trading system,

Having considered the note by the Secretary-General prepared pursuant to General Assembly resolution 46/210 and the ideas contained therein,

Concerned that the mandate referred to in paragraph 4 of its resolution 46/210 has not been fully implemented,

Taking into account the restructuring of the United Nations Secretariat and the consequent reallocation of functions,

1. *Calls upon* the international community to adopt urgent and effective measures to eliminate the use by some developed countries of unilateral economic coercive measures against developing countries that are not authorized by relevant organs of the United Nations or are inconsistent with the principles contained in the Charter of the United Nations, as a means of forcibly imposing the will of one State on another;

2. *Urges* the implementation of its resolutions 44/215 and 46/210;

3. *Requests* the Secretary-General to assign to the Department of Economic and Social Information and Policy Analysis of the Secretariat, in cooperation with the United Nations Conference on Trade and Development, the function of continuing to monitor the imposition of measures of this nature, as well as to continue the preparation of studies in this field as mandated by the General Assembly in its resolutions 44/215 and 46/210;

4. *Also requests* the Secretary-General to report to the General Assembly at its fiftieth session on the implementation of the present resolution.

General Assembly resolution 48/168

21 December 1993   Meeting 86   116-32-16 (recorded vote)

Approved by Second Committee (A/48/717/Add.2) by recorded vote (85-33-14), 10 December (meeting 47); draft by China, Colombia (for Group of 77) and Ukraine (A/C.2/48/L.21); agenda item 91 *(a)*.

Meeting numbers. GA 48th session: 2nd Committee 30-32, 39, 47; plenary 86.

Recorded vote in Assembly as follows:

In favour: Algeria, Angola, Antigua and Barbuda, Argentina, Bahamas, Bahrain, Bangladesh, Barbados, Belize, Benin, Bhutan, Bolivia, Brazil, Brunei Darussalam, Burkina Faso, Burundi, Cambodia, Cameroon, Cape Verde, Central African Republic, Chad, Chile, China, Colombia, Comoros, Congo, Costa Rica, Côte d'Ivoire, Cuba, Democratic People's Republic of Korea, Denmark, Djibouti, Dominica, Dominican Republic, Ecuador, Egypt, El Salvador, Eritrea, Ethiopia, Fiji, Gabon, Gambia, Grenada, Guatemala, Guinea-Bissau, Guyana, Haiti, Honduras, India, Indonesia, Iran, Iraq, Jamaica, Jordan, Kenya, Kuwait, Lao People's Democratic Republic, Lebanon, Lesotho, Libyan Arab Jamahiriya, Madagascar, Malawi, Malaysia, Maldives, Mali, Marshall Islands, Mauritania, Mauritius, Mexico, Micronesia, Mongolia, Morocco, Mozambique, Myanmar, Namibia, Nepal, Nicaragua, Niger, Nigeria, Oman, Pakistan, Papua New Guinea, Paraguay, Peru, Philippines, Qatar, Rwanda, Saint Lucia, Saint Vincent and the Grenadines, Samoa, Saudi Arabia, Senegal, Sierra Leone, Singapore, Solomon Islands, Sri Lanka, Sudan, Suriname, Swaziland, Syrian Arab Republic, Thailand, the former Yugoslav Republic of Macedonia, Togo, Trinidad and Tobago, Tunisia, Uganda, Ukraine, United Arab Emirates, United Republic of Tanzania, Uruguay, Venezuela, Viet Nam, Yemen, Zaire, Zambia, Zimbabwe.

Against: Australia, Austria, Belgium, Bulgaria, Canada, Czech Republic, Estonia, Finland, France, Germany, Hungary, Iceland, Ireland, Israel, Italy, Japan, Liechtenstein, Lithuania, Luxembourg, Netherlands, New Zealand, Norway, Poland, Portugal, Republic of Moldova, Slovakia, Slovenia, Sweden, Turkey, United Kingdom, United States.

Abstaining: Albania, Armenia, Belarus, Botswana, Croatia, Cyprus, Greece, Kazakhstan, Kyrgyzstan, Malta, Panama, Republic of Korea, Russian Federation, Spain, Tajikistan, Turkmenistan.

Economic stabilization programmes

Pursuant to a 1991 General Assembly request,[36] the Secretary-General submitted a report in September 1993 on economic stabilization programmes in developing countries.[37] He discussed the broadening of the debate on adjustment, noting that views on stabilization and adjustment had changed between the start of the debt crisis in 1982 and the end of the 1980s, when structural adjustment programmes came to encompass a far broader range of policy areas than balance-of-payments and price stability. He also considered changes in the international environment in the 1990s and the effect of those changes on the developing countries.

The Secretary-General concluded that successful adjustment creating the conditions for resumption of economic growth depended on three main elements: there had to be government commitment to a consistent set of macroeconomic and sectoral policies for a period of time sufficient to create confidence in the rules concerning investment and production; the international economic environment to which each country was adjusting needed to be more stable; and there was a need for international economic cooperation, which could increase the chances of success of adjustment policies.

By **decision 48/440** of 21 December, the General Assembly took note of the Secretary-General's report.

Economic cooperation among developing countries

The UNCTAD Standing Committee on Economic Cooperation among Developing Countries (ECDC), established in 1992,[38] held its first session at Geneva from 11 to 15 January 1993.[39] It had before it a note by the UNCTAD secretariat on issues for consideration in the establishment of the Committee's work programme[40] and a report reviewing major developments in the area of ECDC.[41]

The Committee adopted its programme of work which consisted of: promotion and expansion of trade; cooperation at the enterprise level; policy dialogue to mobilize support and explore potentials for cooperation among developing countries and with other interested countries and groupings; strengthening integration and fostering inter-regional cooperation; enlarging and deepening monetary, financial and investment cooperation; and technical support and skill development. It also adopted the provisional agenda for its second session, to be held in 1994.

South Commission report

In accordance with a 1991 General Assembly request,[42] the Secretary-General submitted in September 1993 a report[43] on developments pertaining to the implementation of the recommendations of *The Challenge to the South: The Report of the South Commission*.[44] The report considered South consciousness, including the reflection of South-South cooperation priorities in national development plans and the establishment of national follow-up mechanisms; examined progress in financial cooperation in the areas of clearing, payments and credit arrangements, the proposed debtors forum and the South Bank; and reviewed progress within the global system of trade preferences (GSTP) among developing countries, including the launching of the second round of GSTP negotiations and a summary of South-South trade flows. It also discussed cooperation among developing-country producers of agricultural commodities, within the context of the renewal of global commodity agreements, and cooperation among enterprises to foster contacts and encourage businesses; considered cooperation in promoting food security and in education, science and technology; appraised the recently resumed dynamism of regional and subregional cooperation and integration processes in the South; and considered the call for improved cooperation and organization of the South at the global level, including regular consultations of heads of State.

The report noted that, at the sectoral level, South-South initiatives had been vigorously promoted, for example, in the food security sector. A more significant development was the resumed dynamism of regional and subregional cooperation and integration processes in Africa, Asia and Latin America and the Caribbean. Those changes also presented a case for the United Nations, multilateral financial institutions and developed countries to provide significant assistance to the South-South cooperation process. Support by the United Nations at the sectoral, regional and thematic levels needed to be monitored and analysed by the General Assembly on a comprehensive and regular basis; the Secretary-General's report represented a start in that direction.

GENERAL ASSEMBLY ACTION

On 21 December, the General Assembly, on the recommendation of the Second Committee, adopted **resolution 48/164** without vote.

Follow-up to the report of the South Commission
The General Assembly,

Recalling its resolution 46/155 of 19 December 1991, in which it recognized the relevance of the report entitled *The Challenge to the South: The Report of the South Commission* in addressing the issues of interest to the South in the 1990s, especially the North-South dialogue, trade, finance, technology, regional cooperation and integration among developing countries,

Taking note of the report of the Secretary-General on developments pertaining to the implementation of the recommendations of the report of the South Commission, in which he proposed a comprehensive approach to the questions of South-South cooperation,

Welcoming the support given by the United Nations Development Programme in distributing copies of the report of the South Commission in developing countries,

1. *Requests* the Secretary-General to draw upon the discussions and conclusions in the report in elaborating an agenda for development;

2. *Considers* that a comprehensive and systematic overview and analysis of South-South cooperation worldwide is required to stimulate intergovernmental debate, decisions and actions, as appropriate, within the United Nations system and to promote such cooperation within and between regions of the South, and globally;

3. *Also requests* the Secretary-General to prepare a comprehensive report entitled ''State of South-South cooperation'', containing quantitative data and indicators on all aspects of South-South cooperation and prepared with the help of all relevant organizations of the United Nations, in particular the United Nations Conference on Trade and Development;

4. *Calls upon* all organs, organizations and agencies of the United Nations system, in particular the regional commissions and subregional organizations, to provide analytical and empirical materials for the preparation of the report;

5. *Further requests* the Secretary-General to submit his report on the state of South-South cooperation to the General Assembly at its fiftieth session, at which time the Assembly will decide on the need for further reports on the matter.

General Assembly resolution 48/164
21 December 1993   Meeting 86   Adopted without vote

Approved by Second Committee (A/48/717/Add.12) without vote, 9 December (meeting 46); draft by Vice-Chairman (A/C.2/48/L.67), based on informal consultations on draft by China, Colombia (for Group of 77) and the former Yugoslav Republic of Macedonia (A/C.2/48/L.3); agenda item 91.
Meeting numbers. GA 48th session: 2nd Committee 8, 9, 15-17, 20, 30-32, 36-40, 43-46; plenary 86.

Sustainable development

Commission on Sustainable Development

In response to a 1992 General Assembly request,[45] the Secretary-General submitted a note to the Economic and Social Council on the establishment of the Commission on Sustainable Development,[46] which was to be part of an institutional structure for ensuring the implementation of Agenda 21, adopted by UNCED in 1992.[47] The Secretary-General drew the Council's attention to the Assembly's recommendations with regard to the Commission's establishment and noted that action to be taken by the Council included: establishment of the Commission; the regional allocation of seats; the date of elections; rules of procedure; agenda for the organizational session; and dates for the organizational and first substantive sessions. Also before the Council was a report of the Secretary-General on the Commission's rules of procedure.[48]

ECONOMIC AND SOCIAL COUNCIL ACTION

In February, the Council adopted **decision 1993/207** without vote.

Establishment of the Commission on Sustainable Development

At its 3rd plenary meeting, on 12 February 1993, the Economic and Social Council, having considered the note by the Secretary-General, and in accordance with General Assembly resolution 47/191 of 22 December 1992:

(a) Decided to establish the Commission on Sustainable Development as a functional commission of the Council with the functions as enumerated in paragraphs 3 to 5 of General Assembly resolution 47/191;

(b) Also decided that the Commission should be composed of fifty-three members elected from among the States Members of the United Nations and members of the specialized agencies for a term of office of three years according to the following allocation of seats:

(i) Thirteen seats for African States;
(ii) Eleven seats for Asian States;
(iii) Six seats for Eastern European States;
(iv) Ten seats for Latin American and Caribbean States;
(v) Thirteen seats for Western European and other States;

(c) Further decided that elections for membership in the Commission should be held on 16 February 1993;

(d) Recommended that the General Assembly, taking into account its resolution 1798(XVII) of 11 December 1962, should make the necessary provisions so that travel expenses for one of the representatives of each Member State elected to the Commission on Sustainable Development participating in a session of the Commission or its subsidiary organs would be paid from the regular budget of the United Nations;

(e) Decided that the Commission should meet annually for a period of two to three weeks and that, as a transitional measure, an organizational session of the Commission should be held at Headquarters from 24 to 26 February 1993 and that the first substantive session of the Commission should be held at Headquarters from 14 to 25 June 1993;

(f) Approved the following provisional agenda for the organizational session of the Commission:
1. Election of the Chairman and other members of the Bureau
2. Provisional agenda and organization of work of the Commission at its first substantive session

3. Outline of a multi-year thematic programme of work for the Commission
4. Other organizational issues.

Economic and Social Council decision 1993/207
                                    Adopted without vote

Draft by President and Bureau (E/1993/L.9 & Add.1), based on informal consultations; agenda items 2 & 3.
Meeting numbers. ESC 2, 3.

Also in February, the Council adopted **decision 1993/215** without vote.

Procedural arrangements for the Commission on Sustainable Development

At its 3rd plenary meeting, on 12 February 1993, the Economic and Social Council:

(a) Decided that, with the following supplementary arrangements, the rules of procedure of the functional commissions of the Economic and Social Council should apply to the Commission on Sustainable Development:

Participation of and consultation with specialized agencies and participation of other intergovernmental organizations

1. While the participation of and consultation with specialized agencies and the participation of other intergovernmental organizations are governed by rules 71 to 74 of the rules of procedure of the functional commissions of the Economic and Social Council, the Commission on Sustainable Development or a subsidiary organ thereof shall invite relevant intergovernmental organizations within and outside the United Nations system, including multilateral financial institutions, to appoint special representatives to the Commission to serve as focal points for the Commission's members and the Secretariat.

Representation of and consultation with non-governmental organizations

2. Representation of and consultation with non-governmental organizations would be governed by the following arrangements, which would supplement, solely for the purposes of the Commission, rules 75 and 76 of the rules of procedure of the functional commissions of the Economic and Social Council:

(i) Non-governmental organizations in consultative status with the Council, category I or II, or relevant and competent non-governmental organizations on the Roster may designate authorized representatives to be present at and observe the meetings of the Commission and its subsidiary organs;

(ii) These non-governmental organizations may, at their own expense, make written presentations to the Commission and its subsidiary organs, through the Secretariat, in the official languages of the United Nations, as they deem appropriate. Such written presentations will not be issued as official documents;

(iii) These non-governmental organizations may be given an opportunity to briefly address the meetings of the Commission and its subsidiary organs. Taking into account the number of non-governmental organizations expressing a desire to be accorded that opportunity, the Chairman of the Commission or its subsidiary organ may request the non-governmental organizations concerned to address the meetings through one or more spokespersons. Any oral intervention by a representative of a non-governmental organization shall be made at the discretion of the Chairman of the Commission or its subsidiary organ and with the consent of the members of the Commission or its subsidiary organ, as the case may be;

(iv) Non-governmental organizations shall not have any negotiating role in the work of the Commission and its subsidiary organs;

(v) The Commission may consult with and/or hear, as appropriate, non-governmental organizations in consultative status with the Council, category I or II, or relevant and competent non-governmental organizations on the Roster either directly or through a committee or committees established for that purpose;

(vi) The relevance and competence of non-governmental organizations to be included in the Roster shall be determined by the Council on the recommendation of the Secretary-General;

(b) Requested the Commission to encourage equitable representation of non-governmental organizations from the developed and developing countries and from all regions, and also to strive to ensure a fair balance between non-governmental organizations with an environment focus and those with a development focus;

(c) Decided that any non-governmental organization which was accredited to participate in the work of the Preparatory Committee for the United Nations Conference on Environment and Development by the conclusion of its fourth session could apply for and should be granted Roster status, subject to approval by the Council and bearing in mind the provisions of Article 71 of the Charter of the United Nations;

(d) Invited non-governmental organizations, with a view to enhancing their effective and coordinated contribution to the work of the Commission and to the follow-up to the United Nations Conference on Environment and Development in general, to consider or continue organizing themselves in various constituencies and interest groups and to set up non-governmental networks, including electronic networks, for the exchange of relevant information and documentation;

(e) Decided further, in the light of paragraph 2 of the supplementary arrangements outlined above and Council decision 1993/207 of 12 February 1993, to make the following changes to the rules of procedure of the functional commissions of the Council:

(i) In footnote 1, add ''Commission on Sustainable Development'';

(ii) Footnote 4 should read:

''4Not applicable to the Commission on Narcotic Drugs or the Commission on Sustainable Development, which are composed of States whose representatives are appointed by Governments without consultation with the Secretary-General and without confirmation by the Council.'';

(iii) Add a footnote to rules 75 and 76, inserting indicator after ''*Representation*'' and ''*Consultation*'', to read:

''9The terms of representation of and consultations with the non-governmental organizations in the Commission on Sustainable Development have been further determined by the Economic and Social Council in its decision 1993/215 of 12 February 1993.''

Economic and Social Council decision 1993/215

Adopted without vote

Draft by President and Bureau (E/1993/L.11), based on informal consultations; agenda item 5.
Meeting numbers. ESC 2, 3.

In other action, the Council, by **decision 1993/219** of 29 April, decided that the Commission's Bureau would consist of a Chairman and four Vice-Chairmen, one of whom would also serve as Rapporteur. By **decision 1993/220** of 26 May, the Council decided to accredit to the Commission NGOs listed in a Secretariat note.[49]

Activities of the Commission. The Commission on Sustainable Development held an organizational session in New York from 24 to 26 February.[50] It considered a report by the Secretary-General containing an outline of the Commission's multi-year (1993-1997) thematic programme of work[51] and reviewed the provisional agenda for its first session as well as issues relating to its future work.

By **decision 1993/217** of 29 April, the Council took note of the Commission's report on its organizational session and approved the provisional agenda for its first session.

The Commission held its first session in New York from 14 to 25 June.[50] Among other documents, the Commission had before it a revised programme of work;[52] a report by the Secretary-General on progress in incorporating UNCED (1992) recommendations[53] in the programmes of the United Nations system;[54] his recommendations and proposals for improving coordination of programmes related to development data in existence within the United Nations system;[55] his report on the transfer of environmentally sound technology, cooperation and capacity-building (see PART THREE, Chapter VII); his report on financial arrangements to give effect to UNCED decisions;[56] and his notes on information provided by the UNCTAD Trade and Development Board[57] and the United Nations Environment Programme[58] on the implementation of Agenda 21.

The Commission brought a number of matters to the attention of the Economic and Social Council, including its multi-year thematic programme of work; issues relating to its future work; information regarding the implementation of Agenda 21 at the national level; the incorporation of UNCED recommendations in the activities of international organizations and action taken by ACC to ensure incorporation of sustainable development principles in United Nations programmes and processes; progress in the transfer of environmentally sound technology, cooperation and capacity-building; financial arrangements to give effect to UNCED decisions; and the provisional agenda for its second (1994) session.

By **decision 1993/314** of 29 July, the Council took note of the report of the Commission on its first session,[50] endorsed its decisions and recommendations and approved the provisional agenda for its second session. By **resolution 1993/72**, the Council called on the Commission on Sustainable Development to work closely with the Commission on Science and Technology for Development (see PART THREE, Chapter VII) and to take advantage of its work while reviewing the implementation of Agenda 21.

High-level Advisory Board

Following the General Assembly's 1992 endorsement[45] of his view concerning the establishment of a High-level Advisory Board on Sustainable Development, the Secretary-General submitted to the Economic and Social Council in February 1993 a report[59] describing the proposed functions of and arrangements for the Board.

By **decision 1993/216** of 12 February, the Council took note of the Secretary-General's proposals on the Board and decided to revert to the matter at its resumed organizational session in April. However, at that session, the Council had before it a revised version of the Secretary-General's report[60] but took no action on it.

The High-level Advisory Board, appointed by the Secretary-General in July, held its first (organizational) session on 13 and 14 September in New York. The Board focused on the themes: linkages between economic, social and political development; new approaches to finance and technology; and establishment of new partnerships between the United Nations system and other bodies active in the field of sustainable development. It established panels to carry forward work on those themes between its first and second sessions.[61]

Inter-agency Committee

The Inter-agency Committee on Sustainable Development, established by ACC in 1992,[62] held its first meeting in New York from 23 to 25 March 1993.[63] With regard to the review of ACC's subsidiary bodies, the Inter-agency Committee recommended that: the Intersecretariat Group for Water Resources should be continued and its terms of reference updated to include the implementation of Agenda 21; the Task Force on Rural Development should be retained and consideration given to reassessing its terms of reference; and there should be a coordination mechanism for the oceans under the Inter-agency Committee. It also recommended that a draft statement on the follow-up to UNCED, annexed to its report, should be considered and adopted by ACC (see PART THREE, Chapter VIII).

The Inter-agency Committee held its second meeting in New York from 8 to 10 September.[64] It brought to ACC's attention its recommendation regarding the establishment of an ACC subcommittee on oceans and coastal areas and its conclusions relating to Agenda 21 financing and reporting requirements of the United Nations system.

At its second regular session of 1993 (New York, 28 and 29 October),[65] ACC established a Subcommittee on Oceans and Coastal Areas.

Other action

On 26 March,[66] the UNCTAD Trade and Development Board decided on areas of future activities for UNCTAD in sustainable development and agreed that the theme of trade and environment should feature on the agenda of its future sessions (see PART THREE, Chapter IV). It annexed to its decision a report on its specific plans to implement Agenda 21 and transmitted it to the General Assembly, through the Commission on Sustainable Development and the Economic and Social Council.

The Governing Council of UNDP, on 18 June,[67] noted the establishment of a sustainable development network by UNDP and requested the Administrator to ensure that the network took into consideration other similar networks to avoid duplication and to provide linkage between them. The Council also made recommendations regarding UNDP's Capacity 21 initiative (see PART THREE, Chapter VIII).

The Joint Meeting (twenty-seventh series) of the Committee for Programme and Coordination and the Administrative Committee on Coordination (New York, 27 October) considered the results of UNCED and their implications for the United Nations system.[68] The meeting had before it a paper[69] that highlighted matters related to coordination, financing and programme questions. The meeting concluded that policy coordination should start at the national level through establishing national coordinating structures, while the United Nations system, through its resident coordinator network, could play a key role in coordinating international support for national follow-up activities. In addition, adequate support should be given to elaborating national sustainable development strategies. The meeting considered it essential to ensure effective interaction and collaborative arrangements in the area of transfer of environmentally sound technologies, cooperation and capacity-building (see PART THREE, Chapter VII) and recommended that the Economic and Social Council consider science and technology at the coordination segment of its 1994 session. It underscored the need for broader agency participation in the Global Environment Facility and UNDP's Capacity 21 Programme and for further development of partnership between the United Nations system and NGOs, as well as the private sector.

Eradication of poverty
Report of the Secretary-General. In a November 1993 report,[70] prepared in response to a 1992

General Assembly request,[71] the Secretary-General reviewed progress achieved since 1992 in coordinating action in the fight against poverty. With regard to general trends, he noted that a preliminary review had indicated that poverty alleviation programmes were becoming central to technical cooperation provided by the United Nations in most developing countries and that there was broad recognition that a multisectoral, coordinated response by the system was essential. Because of the complex, cross-sectoral nature of poverty, agencies had found it effective to work together and, as a result, United Nations technical cooperation efforts were increasingly characterized by broad inter-agency collaboration.

At the conceptual level, there was recognition that poverty eradication required a two-pronged approach: employment creation and the increase of household income; and provision of basic human services. Even when both approaches were being promoted, it might be necessary to create social safety nets to protect the most vulnerable. It was apparent that the United Nations development system had taken many steps to meet the challenge of poverty, and initiatives were being taken to further ensure a coordinated response.

The report further described the scope of coordination at the country level and the strengthening of the preparatory stages of poverty-oriented programmes, including data collection and analysis. It also discussed efforts to establish new partnerships to promote an integrated and participatory approach, resource mobilization and the inter-agency focus on improved technical cooperation for poverty alleviation.

UNCTAD action. The Standing Committee on Poverty Alleviation, established by the UNCTAD Trade and Development Board in 1992,[72] held its first session at Geneva from 18 to 22 January 1993.[73] On 22 January, it adopted and annexed to its report its work programme, which consisted of the following: review of existing information and analyses on causes of poverty; programmes and policies; development assistance and poverty; international trade and poverty alleviation; alleviation of poverty and sustainable development; and population, migration and poverty alleviation. In addition, the Committee would identify, for further consideration, areas in which technical cooperation should be strengthened. For consideration of the work programme, the Committee had before it two notes by the UNCTAD secretariat, one on the issues[74] and the other giving background information.[75]

The Committee recommended that its second session take place in early 1994 and that an intergovernmental group of experts meet to exchange experiences on poverty reduction impacts of social funds and safety nets, including mobilization of

domestic and external resources for poverty alleviation.

With the support of UNDP and the Netherlands, the UNCTAD Secretary-General convened a workshop on social mobilization and organization of the poor (Tunis, Tunisia, 15-18 November 1993).[76]

GENERAL ASSEMBLY ACTION

On 21 December, the General Assembly, on the recommendation of the Second Committee, adopted **resolution 48/184** without vote.

International cooperation for the eradication of poverty in developing countries

The General Assembly,

Reaffirming its resolutions 43/195 of 20 December 1988, 44/212 of 22 December 1989, 45/213 of 21 December 1990, 46/141 of 17 December 1991 and 47/197 of 22 December 1992 related to international cooperation for the eradication of poverty in developing countries,

Reaffirming also its resolutions S-18/3 of 1 May 1990 and 45/199 of 21 December 1990, as well as all the declarations, commitments, plans and programmes of action containing provisions related to the eradication of poverty in the framework of activities of the United Nations system,

Reaffirming further the Rio Declaration on Environment and Development, in particular principle 5 thereof, Agenda 21, in particular chapter 3 thereof entitled "Combating poverty", the Non-legally Binding Authoritative Statement of Principles for a Global Consensus on the Management, Conservation and Sustainable Development of All Types of Forests, in particular principle 7 (a) thereof, and all other decisions and recommendations adopted by the United Nations Conference on Environment and Development relating to the eradication of poverty,

Underlining that the eradication of poverty, especially in developing countries, is one of the priority development objectives for the 1990s,

Recognizing that poverty is a complex and multidimensional problem with origins in both the national and international domains, and that its eradication constitutes an important factor in ensuring sustainable development,

Recognizing also the central role that women play in the eradication of poverty and the necessity of addressing the needs of women in poverty eradication programmes,

Considering that the efforts made at the national and international levels need to be enhanced to ensure the eradication of poverty, in particular in the least developed countries, the countries in sub-Saharan Africa and other countries that have areas of concentrated poverty,

Reaffirming the need for the organs, organizations and bodies of the United Nations system to coordinate better and harmonize their activities in the field of the eradication of poverty, bearing in mind the relevant paragraphs of General Assembly resolution 47/199 of 22 December 1992, in particular the paragraphs dealing with mechanisms and instruments of coordination at the field level,

Taking note of the report of the Secretary-General,

1. *Stresses* the importance of domestic policies, including effective budgetary policies, to mobilize and allocate domestic resources for the eradication of poverty through, *inter alia*, the creation of employment and

income-generating programmes, the implementation of food security, health, education, housing and population programmes and the strengthening of national capacity-building execution programmes;

2. *Reaffirms* that a supportive international economic environment which takes into account resource flows and structural adjustment programmes, in which social and environmental dimensions are integrated, is vital to the success of efforts of developing countries, in particular, to deal with the eradication of poverty;

3. *Invites* all countries to undertake national strategies and programmes for the eradication of poverty that are, *inter alia*, sensitive to gender considerations, taking into account cultural, religious and social particularities, and that involve more active participation by the targeted communities, as well as by the most vulnerable groups, in initiating, implementing, following up and evaluating specific projects;

4. *Reiterates its request* to the international community to adopt specific and effective measures designed to increase financial flows to developing countries, and urges the developed countries, which have reaffirmed their commitment to reach the accepted United Nations target of 0.7 per cent of gross national product for official development assistance, to the extent that they have not yet achieved that target, to agree to augment their aid programmes in order to reach that target as soon as possible, some developed countries having agreed to reach the target by the year 2000, while other developed countries, in line with their support for reform efforts in developing countries, agree to make their best efforts to increase their level of official development assistance;

5. *Invites* the international community and the organs, organizations and bodies of the United Nations system to continue to support development programmes in developing countries, including the implementation of the decisions and recommendations of the United Nations Conference on Environment and Development related to the eradication of poverty, particularly chapter 3 of Agenda 21 entitled "Combating poverty";

6. *Requests* the Secretary-General to urge the organs, organizations and bodies of the United Nations system, in the framework of the help they give to developing countries, to strengthen their institutional capacities for implementing their poverty eradication programmes and to adopt a coordinated and integrated approach that takes into account, *inter alia*, the role and needs of women, with attention to social services, income generation and the increased participation of local communities;

7. *Invites* preparatory bodies and all relevant forthcoming major meetings and conferences of the United Nations system, particularly the International Conference on Population and Development, the World Summit for Social Development, the Fourth World Conference on Women: Action for Equality, Development and Peace and the United Nations Conference on Human Settlements (Habitat II), to take specific measures and decisions to meet, by the early part of the twenty-first century, the challenge of the eradication of poverty;

8. *Requests* the Secretary-General to submit to the General Assembly at its forty-ninth session an updated report focusing, *inter alia*, on the development of appropriate inputs to country programmes by relevant agencies and organizations of the United Nations system, based on exchange of information on and analysis of the operations of actual programmes and on the iden-

tification of constraints and weaknesses of operational and coordinating capacities owing to a lack of resources, as well as focusing on elements for the elaboration of multisectoral strategies;

9. *Decides* to include in the provisional agenda of its forty-ninth session the item entitled "International cooperation for the eradication of poverty in developing countries".

General Assembly resolution 48/184

21 December 1993   Meeting 86   Adopted without vote

Approved by Second Committee (A/48/719) without vote, 13 December (meeting 48); draft by Vice-Chairman (A/C.2/48/L.89), based on informal consultations on draft by China, and Colombia (for Group of 77) (A/C.2/48/L.61); agenda item 93.
Meeting numbers. GA 48th session: 2nd Committee 41, 45, 48; plenary 86.

International Year for the Eradication of Poverty (1996)

On 21 December 1993, on the recommendation of the Second Committee, the General Assembly adopted **resolution 48/183** without vote.

International Year for the Eradication of Poverty

The General Assembly,

Recalling its resolution 47/196 of 22 December 1992 entitled "Observance of an international day for the eradication of poverty",

Reaffirming its resolutions 43/195 of 20 December 1988, 44/212 of 22 December 1989, 45/213 of 21 December 1990, 46/141 of 17 December 1991 and 47/197 of 22 December 1992 related to international cooperation for the eradication of poverty in developing countries,

Recognizing that poverty is a complex and multidimensional problem with origins in both the national and international domains, and that its eradication in all countries, in particular in developing countries, has become one of the priority development objectives for the 1990s in order to promote sustainable development,

Noting that the efforts made at the national and international levels need to be enhanced to ensure the eradication of poverty, in particular in the least developed countries, the countries in sub-Saharan Africa and other countries which have areas of concentrated poverty,

Welcoming the success achieved in organizing and observing the International Day for the Eradication of Poverty,

Taking into account its decision 35/424 of 5 December 1980 and Economic and Social Council resolution 1980/67 of 25 July 1980 on guidelines for international years and anniversaries,

Taking note of the report of the Secretary-General on international cooperation for the eradication of poverty in developing countries,

Stressing the positive impact of a favourable international economic environment, in particular in the area of trade, on combating poverty in all countries, especially in developing countries,

Stressing also the importance of international cooperation in combating poverty through, *inter alia*, exchange among Governments that have had successful experiences in the field,

1. *Proclaims* 1996 International Year for the Eradication of Poverty;

2. *Decides* that the major activities for the observance of the Year should be undertaken at the local, national and international levels, and that assistance should be

provided by the United Nations system with a view to creating among States, policy makers and international public opinion a greater awareness that the eradication of poverty is fundamental to reinforcing peace and achieving sustainable development;

3. *Requests* the Secretary-General, in consultation with States, the specialized agencies and intergovernmental and non-governmental organizations concerned, to prepare a draft programme on the preparations for and observance of the Year, setting out the objectives, principles and main recommendations for the Year, and to submit a progress report thereon to the General Assembly at its forty-ninth session;

4. *Also requests* the Secretary-General to give widespread publicity to the activities of the United Nations system, including those described in chapter 3 of Agenda 21, related to the eradication of poverty;

5. *Invites* all States, organizations of the United Nations system, intergovernmental organizations concerned and interested national organizations, including non-governmental organizations, to exert every possible effort in the preparations for and observance of the Year and to cooperate with the Secretary-General in achieving the objectives of the Year;

6. *Designates* the Department for Policy Coordination and Sustainable Development of the Secretariat as the preparatory body, and the Economic and Social Council as the coordinating body, for the International Year for the Eradication of Poverty;

7. *Recommends* that the preparatory body and the coordinating body work in close collaboration with all relevant organizations inside and outside the United Nations system in the preparations for and observance of the Year;

8. *Decides* to include in the provisional agenda of its forty-ninth session, under the item entitled "International cooperation for the eradication of poverty in developing countries", a sub-item on the International Year for the Eradication of Poverty.

General Assembly resolution 48/183

21 December 1993   Meeting 86   Adopted without vote

Approved by Second Committee (A/48/719) without vote, 13 December (meeting 48); draft by Vice-Chairman (A/C.2/48/L.86), based on informal consultations on draft by China, and Colombia (for Group of 77) (A/C.2/48/L.60); agenda item 93.

Meeting numbers. GA 48th session: 2nd Committee 41, 45, 48; plenary 86.

Rural development

In April 1993, the ACC Task Force on Rural Development was renamed the Subcommittee on Rural Development.[77] The Subcommittee, which met in Washington, D.C., from 5 to 7 May,[78] considered work accomplished by agencies during 1992 in rural development and related areas. It also discussed the report of a joint session of the Panels on Monitoring and Evaluation and on People's Participation (Washington, D.C., 3 May) and the report of the Working Group on Industrial Contribution to Rural Development (Washington, D.C., 4 May). Other issues addressed by the Subcommittee included coordination and collaboration on rural development and agrarian reform activities and programmes (1993-1994 biennium); the impact of national macroeconomic policies on the rural poor;

implementation of the 1985 Nairobi Forward-looking Strategies for the Advancement of Women[79] as they related to rural women; an enabling approach to shelter improvement in rural areas as a contribution to sustainable rural development and poverty alleviation; women and the environment; refugee/returnee aid and development; and the programme of work and time-frame for 1993-1994.

The Subcommittee agreed that its main focus in future should be on sustainable rural development and that the thematic topic for its next (1994) meeting would be policy approaches to rural poverty alleviation.

REFERENCES

[1]A/48/717. [2]A/48/689. [3]YUN 1992, p. 528, GA res. 47/181, 22 Dec. 1992. [4]ACC/1993/28. [5]A/48/142. [6]A/48/544. [7]YUN 1991, p. 287, GA res. 46/145, 17 Dec. 1991. [8]A/48/505. [9]GA res. S-18/3, annex, 1 May 1990. [10]GA res. 45/199, annex, 21 Dec. 1990. [11]YUN 1992, p. 529, GA res. 47/187, 22 Dec. 1992. [12]A/48/317. [13]YUN 1992, p. 530, GA res. 47/175, 22 Dec. 1992. [14]A/48/331. [15]YUN 1991, p. 345. [16]YUN 1992, p. 529. [17]DP/1993/10/Add.1. [18]YUN 1992, p. 561. [19]E/1993/35 (dec. 93/15). [20]YUN 1991, p. 349, GA res. 46/166, 19 Dec. 1991. [21]YUN 1992, p. 533, GA res. 47/171, 22 Dec. 1992. [22]A/48/472. [23]YUN 1992, p. 533. [24]TD/B/40(1)/11. [25]TD/B/WG.3/7. [26]UNCTAD/DSD/Misc.8 & Add.1. [27]TD/B/40(2)/5. [28]TD/B/WG.3/7/Rev.1. [29]UNCTAD/DSD/Misc.8/Rev.1 & Add.1. [30]TD/B/WG.3/11. [31]TD/B/40(2)/2. [32]YUN 1991, p. 348, GA res. 46/210, 20 Dec. 1991. [33]A/48/535. [34]YUN 1992, p. 611. [35]A/44/510. [36]YUN 1991, p. 347, GA res. 46/154, 19 Dec. 1991. [37]A/48/380. [38]YUN 1992, p. 613. [39]TD/B/39(2)/16. [40]TD/B/CN.3/2. [41]TD/B/CN.3/3. [42]YUN 1991, p. 352, GA res. 46/155, 19 Dec. 1991. [43]A/48/350. [44]A/45/810 & Corr.1. [45]YUN 1992, p. 676, GA res. 47/191, 22 Dec. 1992. [46]E/1993/14. [47]YUN 1992, p. 672. [48]E/1993/12. [49]E/1993/65. [50]E/1993/25/Rev.1. [51]E/CN.17/1993/2. [52]E/CN.17/1993/5. [53]YUN 1992, p. 670. [54]E/CN.17/1993/8. [55]E/CN.17/1993/9. [56]E/CN.17/1993/11 & Add.1. [57]E/CN.17/1993/13. [58]E/CN.17/1993/14. [59]E/1993/15 & Corr.1. [60]E/1993/15/Rev.1. [61]E/CN.17/1994/13. [62]YUN 1992, p. 681. [63]ACC/1993/11. [64]ACC/1993/24. [65]ACC/1993/28. [66]A/48/15 (dec. 402(XXXIX)). [67]E/1993/35 (dec. 93/12). [68]E/1994/4. [69]E/1993/121. [70]A/48/545. [71]YUN 1992, p. 537, GA res. 47/197, 22 Dec. 1992. [72]Ibid., p. 536. [73]TD/B/39(2)/13. [74]TD/B/CN.2/2. [75]TD/B/CN.2/3. [76]TD/B/CN.2/7. [77]ACC/1993/2/Add.2. [78]ACC/1993/15. [79]YUN 1985, p. 937.

Economic and social trends and policy

Economic surveys and trends

The *World Economic Survey 1993*[1] noted that in 1993, for the third year in succession, the rate of growth of world output would be below that of world population. While stagnation characterized the developed market economies and decline continued to be a feature of the economies in transition from centrally planned to market economy, the developing countries were growing at a pace not seen since the 1970s. Those in Asia, including the most populous, and in the Southern Cone of Latin America were expanding rapidly. The growth was widely dispersed, helping to raise the living standards of a large majority of the population of the developing countries and about 60 per cent of the world population. However, in a large number of countries, particularly in Africa, which accounted for as much as a fifth of the population of the developing countries, per capita output continued to decline. While world output barely increased, world trade grew surprisingly fast. The volume of world exports increased by about 4.5 per cent in 1992, after a 3.6 per cent growth in 1991.

The Economic and Social Council took note of the *Survey* by **decision 1993/303** of 29 July.

In a note giving an update of the world economy at the end of 1993,[2] the Secretary-General stated that total world output was estimated to have increased by only 1 per cent in 1993, after three years of virtual stagnation.

The United States economy was estimated to have grown by around 3 per cent, close to its projected rate, but Japan's economy did not grow at all in 1993 and the economies of the European Union (formerly the European Community) contracted by around 0.3 per cent. In the transition economies, output declined by some 10 per cent in 1993, following a 30 per cent drop over the previous three years. However, the rate of decline differed widely among countries, and in Poland output actually increased.

In the developing countries, overall output increased by slightly over 5 per cent in 1993, with much of the growth contributed by China and South and East Asia. In Africa, the production growth rate remained considerably below the population growth rate.

As to the outlook for 1994, the world economy was expected to grow at a modest pace of 2.5 per cent, with recovery largely based on an expected acceleration of growth in the developed economies from 1 per cent in 1993 to slightly over 2 per cent in 1994. The transition economies were expected to stop contracting, while the growth of developing countries was likely to remain unchanged at around 5 per cent.

In the context of the stagnating world economy, the *Trade and Development Report, 1993*[3] noted that, as a result of the North's failure to recover, commodity prices were falling yet again, intensifying poverty in the South, and the unemployed were multiplying, intensifying poverty in the North. Prospects for recovery in the developed world continued to be affected by persistent high interest rates in Europe, adjustment to debt deflation in some major industrial countries, tensions in currency markets, weak business and consumer confidence and efforts to reduce budget deficits. Prospects for developing countries that had been

expanding continuously were positive, but overshadowed by the threat of increasing protectionism through the formation of trading blocs, and by managed trade. The increasing need to adopt or strengthen environmental measures could also have significant macroeconomic implications. Crucial to the prospects of the Asian economies was the sustainability of China's economic performance, which was already showing signs of overheating and was confronted by serious bottlenecks in transportation, energy and raw material production. Growth in Africa continued to depend on the evolution of terms of trade, external aid and the weather, as well as on progress in resolving armed conflicts and civil strife. Latin America's prospects depended to a large extent on the continuity of capital inflows and the ability to translate them into investment-led growth.

UNCTAD action. On 1 October,[4] the Trade and Development Board, in its conclusion on the international implications of macroeconomic policies and issues concerning global interdependence, noted the effects of the continuing recession in the developed market economies. It recognized that, while stimulative macroeconomic policies might overcome the recession, many Governments faced the dilemma that demand and employment-generating fiscal policies would further raise government deficits and debt, whereas fiscal retrenchment would exacerbate unemployment. Some support was expressed for the solution put forward in the *Trade and Development Report, 1993*, advocating relaxation of monetary and fiscal stances to boost activity, combined with privatization and a one-time capital levy to reduce public indebtedness. It was recognized that the global financial and trading environment was important for growth of the world economy. The Board agreed that the growth that had occurred in certain developing regions had been a source of strength for the world economy, and that more rapid growth in developing countries would be of benefit all round. Attention was also drawn to the need for adequate and stable levels of financing, both public and private, to underpin growth-oriented domestic policies. Calls were made for multilateral modalities to improve the perception of commercial banks of the creditworthiness of developing countries, for universally accepted guidelines for supervisory and regulatory procedures of financial markets and for the replenishment of international financial institutions. Reference was also made to the trade measures needed to stimulate growth (see PART THREE, Chapter IV).

REFERENCES

[1] *World Economic Survey 1993: Current Trends and Policies in the World Economy* (E/1993/60), Sales No. E.93.II.C.1. [2] E/1994/INF/1. [3] *Trade and Development Report, 1993* (UNCTAD/TDR/13), Sales No. E.93.II.D.10. [4] A/48/15 (conclusion 405(XL)).

Development planning and public administration

Development planning

In his April report to the Economic and Social Council on the establishment of the High-level Advisory Board on Sustainable Development,[1] the Secretary-General recalled that the General Assembly, in 1992,[2] had noted his view that areas covered by the Committee for Development Planning (CDP) were potentially similar to those of the Advisory Board and his proposal that a single body should be established to provide high-level advice on all questions relating to environment and development. He noted that CDP's mandate, which was to be subsumed under that of the Advisory Board, had evolved from providing assistance to the Council in evaluating United Nations activities relating to economic planning and programming towards consideration of world development trends and prospects and formulation of recommendations in the areas of development and international economic and financial cooperation. Within CDP itself, it had been suggested that there was a need to strengthen the capacity of its membership to deal with sustainable development issues.

Since the Secretary-General's proposal that CDP's functions should be subsumed under those of the High-level Advisory Board was under consideration by the Council, expert members were not appointed in time for CDP's scheduled April 1993 session, thus resulting in the session not taking place.

ECONOMIC AND SOCIAL COUNCIL ACTION

On 30 July, the Economic and Social Council adopted **resolution 1993/81** without vote.

Committee for Development Planning
The Economic and Social Council,

Recalling its resolution 1079(XXXIX) of 28 July 1965 on economic planning and projections,

Recalling also its resolution 1625(LI) of 30 July 1971 on the Committee for Development Planning,

Taking note of General Assembly resolution 47/191 of 22 December 1992 on institutional arrangements to follow up the United Nations Conference on Environment and Development,

1. *Reaffirms* the existing mandate of the Committee for Development Planning, as set out in relevant resolutions of the Economic and Social Council, without prejudice to the outcome of the ongoing process of reform of the United Nations in the economic, social and related fields;

2. *Expresses its deep concern* that the experts members of the Committee for Development Planning were not appointed in time for the session of the Committee scheduled for 1993;

3. *Requests* the Secretary-General to take the necessary measures to convene the 1993 session of the Committee for Development Planning no later than December.

Economic and Social Council resolution 1993/81

30 July 1993   Meeting 46   Adopted without vote

Draft by China, and Colombia (for Group of 77) (E/1993/L.45), orally revised; agenda item 15.

By **decision 1993/334** of 30 July, the Council decided to consider an item entitled "Committee for Development Planning" at its resumed substantive session of 1993. At that session, on 8 December, the Council had before it a draft resolution[3] by which it would have established a Group of Experts on Development to replace CDP. Consideration of that draft text was deferred to a later date. On 8 December, by **decision 1993/338**, the Council decided that the twenty-ninth session of CDP should be held in New York from 12 to 14 January 1994.

Public administration

In accordance with Economic and Social Council **decision 1993/228** of 16 July, the Eleventh Meeting of Experts on the United Nations Programme in Public Administration and Finance was held at Geneva from 6 to 14 October 1993.[4] The Experts reviewed current issues in public administration and finance in developing countries, development management in Africa in the 1990s and the public management problems of transition economies. They also discussed the United Nations work programme in public administration and finance and public administration and finance issues for the turn of the century. The Experts recommended action on those issues at both national and international levels.

Commenting on the Experts' recommendations, the Secretary-General noted that actions at the national level were the responsibility of Member States and suggested that the Economic and Social Council might wish to call their attention to those recommendations. Actions recommended at the international level would be implemented within resources available for the United Nations programme in public administration and development management. The Secretary-General believed that every attempt should be made to incorporate those recommendations within the broad framework of the medium-term plan for 1992-1997.

The Experts recommended that their next meeting be convened in 1995 to review current issues and problems in public administration and development management in developing and transition-economy countries; examine progress made in implementing recommendations made at the Eleventh Meeting; and review the United Nations regular programme of work. The Secretary-General suggested that future Meetings focus mainly on prevailing public management issues, especially in the context of global concerns such as governance, accountability, productivity and responsiveness with a view to providing timely policy and technical guidance to developing countries.

REFERENCES

[1]E/1993/15/Rev.1. [2]YUN 1992, p. 676, GA res. 47/191, 22 Dec. 1992. [3]E/1993/L.46. [4]E/1994/56.

Developing countries

Least developed countries

During 1993, the General Assembly, the UNCTAD Trade and Development Board, the UNDP Governing Council and other United Nations bodies reviewed the problems of the officially designated least developed countries (LDCs).

The number of countries on the United Nations list of LDCs remained at 47, namely: Afghanistan, Bangladesh, Benin, Bhutan, Botswana, Burkina Faso, Burundi, Cambodia, Cape Verde, Central African Republic, Chad, Comoros, Djibouti, Equatorial Guinea, Ethiopia, Gambia, Guinea, Guinea-Bissau, Haiti, Kiribati, Lao People's Democratic Republic, Lesotho, Liberia, Madagascar, Malawi, Maldives, Mali, Mauritania, Mozambique, Myanmar, Nepal, Niger, Rwanda, Samoa, Sao Tome and Principe, Sierra Leone, Solomon Islands, Somalia, Sudan, Togo, Tuvalu, Uganda, United Republic of Tanzania, Vanuatu, Yemen, Zaire, Zambia.

In June, the UNDP Administrator submitted to the Governing Council a communication from Albania,[1] in which it requested classification as an "as if" LDC and provided information on its socio-economic situation. In a May note,[2] the Administrator outlined Albania's economic reform efforts during its transition from a rigid form of communism to democracy and a market-oriented economy. He observed that it was expected that Albania's per capita gross national product (GNP) in 1992 or 1993 would fall below the threshold for LDC eligibility but that there was difficulty in obtaining accurate data, particularly for 1990 and earlier. Noting that the granting of "as if" LDC status would give Albania access to increased UNDP and United Nations resources, which would greatly facilitate its efforts to overcome the extraordinary difficulties it was facing, the Administrator recommended that the Governing Council grant such status.

On 18 June,[3] the Governing Council requested the Administrator to provide additional information on the subject for further consideration at its 1994 special session.

Programme of Action for the 1990s

Several United Nations bodies reviewed progress in the implementation of the Programme of Action for the Least Developed Countries for the 1990s, adopted by the Second (1990) United Nations Conference on the Least Developed Countries (Paris Conference)[4] and endorsed by the General Assembly the same year.[5]

Report of the Secretary-General. In response to requests by the General Assembly in 1991[6] and 1992,[7] the Secretary-General submitted a report in September 1993 on the implementation of the Programme of Action.[8] The report, which covered the period up to the end of June 1993, gave special attention to the outcome of the third annual review of the Programme undertaken by the UNCTAD Trade and Development Board (TDB) (see below). Several sections of the report drew on the report entitled *The Least Developed Countries— 1992 Report.*[9]

The Secretary-General noted that most LDCs had made substantial efforts to reorient their macroeconomic and sectoral policies with a view to creating a favourable environment and sound basis for sustained growth and development. They had also taken steps to expand and modernize their economic base, promote popular participation in the development process, and enhance human and institutional capacities, as recommended in the Programme of Action. Although the LDCs' drive towards policy reform was one of the most striking aspects of the Programme's implementation and that drive continued to gather momentum in a growing number of countries, it was faltering in certain others.

With regard to recent economic performance, for the LDCs as a whole there had been economic stagnation and a fall in per capita income since 1990, with negative to zero real growth in overall gross domestic product (GDP) in 1991 and 1992. Population growth continued to outpace the rise in output. However, a slight recovery in growth was forecast for 1993, with overall GDP being projected to increase at a rate of 1.4 per cent.

The report concluded that the fledgling reform process in many LDCs needed to be nurtured, while in others even more fundamental conditions for reactivating growth and development had to be promoted. A significant improvement in the external environment would be a critical factor in the LDCs' attaining the Programme's objectives.

In accordance with the Assembly's 1990 decision[5] that the UNCTAD Intergovernmental Group on LDCs should carry out a mid-term review of the situation in those countries in 1995, TDB planned to convene the Group in September/

October of that year and stressed the need for adequate and timely preparations for it.

UNCTAD action. At its March 1993 session,[10] TDB carried out its annual review of progress in implementing the Programme of Action for LDCs. As decided in 1992,[11] the Board reviewed two issues in depth: domestic and external resource mobilization, including the debt situation and management; and improving trading opportunities.

TDB had before it *The Least Developed Countries—1992 Report*,[9] which reviewed the recent economic performance of LDCs against the background of the slow-down of the world economy, analysed demographic trends and policies in those countries, examined food-security issues and reviewed progress in implementing support measures for LDCs' efforts, particularly with regard to resource flows to them and their debt and debt-service burden. It also discussed issues of domestic resource mobilization in LDCs, the impact of the Uruguay Round of trade negotiations on trading opportunities for them and the role of NGOs in LDCs.

On 26 March,[12] TDB noted that LDCs had reaffirmed their commitment to implementing reforms, including structural adjustment programmes. It emphasized the need to formulate medium- to long-term strategies for socio-economic development, for which a stable political environment was necessary, and stressed that Governments should prioritize their short-, medium- and long-term objectives, and the mechanisms for achieving them. It was agreed that progress could not be achieved without sustainable good governance and economic and social development efforts. Among priorities emphasized were the need for human resource development; strengthened policies to combat population growth; revitalization of the agricultural sector and improvement in food security; mobilization and effective use of domestic savings; and fiscal reforms and rationalization of public expenditure in coordination with other macroeconomic and sectoral reforms, including trade-policy reforms.

Both LDCs and donor countries noted with concern that in 1991 official development assistance to LDCs fell from 0.09 per cent to 0.08 per cent of Development Assistance Committee (DAC) (of the Organisation for Economic Cooperation and Development) donors' combined GNP in the preceding two years. DAC donors were urged to fulfil aid targets and commitments to LDCs. In addition, urgent consideration should be given to the implications of the enlarged list of LDCs on their resource requirements. The heavy debt burden of LDCs continued to be a major strain on export earnings and a hindrance to their efforts to adjust and expand their economies. LDCs and some donors called for improvements in the scope and coverage of debt-relief schemes and mechanisms, including those relating to debt-service obligations to multilateral institutions.

It was stressed that properly conceived foreign direct investment could be an important vehicle for stimulating the manufacturing and processing sectors, for mobilizing savings in LDCs and for the transfer of technology and managerial skills. Fair access to all markets was also stressed as a key instrument for promoting trade and development. LDCs proposed that the Final Act of the Uruguay Round should include a chapter embodying provisions for LDCs covering the elimination of tariff and non-tariff barriers for both primary and processed products. LDCs, and a number of other delegations, requested that a high-level group be organized to examine the provisions of the draft Final Act of the Uruguay Round as they related to LDCs and to propose measures for inclusion in the Final Act.

The need for adequate preparations for the 1995 mid-term review of the Programme of Action was stressed. It was felt that UNCTAD's participation in country-level monitoring should be strengthened, notably through enhanced participation in the country review process.

UNDP action. In response to a 1991 UNDP Governing Council request,[13] the Administrator submitted in May 1993 a report on matters relating to LDCs.[14] The report discussed UNDP's financial contributions to the development of LDCs, aid coordination and economic management, and human development.

The report concluded that, while UNDP support to LDCs included the whole range of sectors and activities in the Programme of Action, the areas of aid coordination and economic management and human development had been recognized as priorities for UNDP. UNDP had developed various instruments in the area of aid coordination, such as the round-table process, which assisted LDCs to obtain financial resources from donor countries, the national technical cooperation assessments and programmes, and the programme approach. The challenge would be to integrate those mechanisms into a comprehensive strategy for strengthening the national institutions in charge of defining and implementing development policies. With regard to human development, UNDP had traditionally been active in various sectors that were included under the human development concept. However, following the recommendations contained in the Programme of Action and in line with the *Human Development Report* (see PART THREE, Chapter XII), it appeared necessary to define comprehensive approaches to human development in LDCs. UNDP was following that strategy in a growing number of LDCs and it was being reflected in their country programmes.

On 18 June,[15] the Governing Council endorsed the priorities identified by the Administrator to assist in implementing the Programme of Action, namely, aid coordination and economic management and human development. It stressed the need to strengthen the national capacities of LDCs and requested the Administrator to strengthen UNDP's efforts to address their special needs and priorities, particularly in the areas of environment and poverty alleviation. The Council invited UNDP to contribute towards forging stronger links between national and global follow-up of the Programme of Action by enhancing its collaboration with UNCTAD, and requested it to assist in the preparations for the 1995 mid-term review of the Programme and in mobilizing funding for the participation of LDCs. The Council reiterated its appeal to all countries to support LDCs through UNDP facilities that focused on their needs, such as the United Nations Capital Development Fund, trust funds and cost-sharing arrangements. It requested the Administrator to strengthen UNDP's overall capacity to deal with the needs of LDCs in line with the Programme of Action's recommendations and to report to the Council in 1995 on specific measures taken by UNDP to address the special needs and priorities of LDCs.

GENERAL ASSEMBLY ACTION

On 21 December, on the recommendation of the Second Committee, the General Assembly adopted **resolution 48/171** without vote.

Implementation of the Programme of Action for the Least Developed Countries for the 1990s

The General Assembly,

Recalling its resolutions 45/206 of 21 December 1990, in which it endorsed the Paris Declaration and the Programme of Action for the Least Developed Countries for the 1990s, 46/156 of 19 December 1991 on the implementation of the Programme of Action and 47/173 of 22 December 1992 on the implications of the application of the new criteria for identifying the least developed countries in the implementation of the Programme of Action,

Recalling also its resolutions S-18/3 of 1 May 1990, the annex to which contains the Declaration on International Economic Cooperation, in particular the Revitalization of the Economic Growth and Development of the Developing Countries, and 45/199 of 21 December 1990, the annex to which contains the International Development Strategy for the Fourth United Nations Development Decade, as well as the document entitled ''A New Partnership for Development: The Cartagena Commitment'', adopted by the United Nations Conference on Trade and Development at its eighth session, and the texts adopted by the United Nations Conference on Environment and Development, particularly Agenda 21,

Taking note of the declaration adopted at the Ministerial Meeting of the Least Developed Countries, held in New York on 30 September 1993, in pursuance of the deci-

sion taken at the Ministerial Meeting held at Dhaka in February 1990,

Recalling further that the prime objective of the Programme of Action is to arrest the further deterioration in the socio-economic situation of the least developed countries, to reactivate and accelerate their growth and development and to set them on the path of sustained growth and development,

Noting that while many least developed countries, for their part, have been implementing courageous and far-reaching policy reforms and adjustment measures in line with the Programme of Action, implementation of international support measures and commitments by a number of donor countries has fallen short of the provisions of the Programme of Action,

Expressing serious concern about the continued deterioration in the socio-economic situation of the least developed countries as a whole,

Also expressing concern about the heavy debt stock and debt-service burden of the least developed countries, the limited market for their products and the reduced flow of development resources,

Stressing that the mid-term review of the implementation of the Programme of Action provides a unique opportunity for the least developed countries and their development partners to take new measures as necessary, with a view to enhancing the implementation of the Programme of Action during the rest of the 1990s,

Also stressing that the implementation of the Programme of Action provides for a mid-term review conducted by the United Nations Conference on Trade and Development in accordance with paragraph 140 of the Programme of Action, the results of which will be submitted to the General Assembly,

Taking note with appreciation of the report of the Secretary-General,

1. *Reaffirms* the Paris Declaration and the Programme of Action for the Least Developed Countries for the 1990s;

2. *Calls upon* all Governments, international organizations, multilateral financial institutions and development funds, the organs, organizations and programmes of the United Nations system and all other organizations concerned to take concrete measures to implement fully the Programme of Action as a matter of urgency;

3. *Welcomes* the fundamental and far-reaching domestic reforms that have been or are being implemented by the least developed countries, and notes that such efforts should be continued;

4. *Notes* the efforts of the international community, in particular the donor countries, to try to fulfil their commitments in all areas, as set out in the Programme of Action, and urges the provision of adequate external support to the efforts of the least developed countries, keeping under review the possibility of implementing further new steps in specific areas of importance to the least developed countries;

5. *Calls upon* the donor countries to fulfil their aid commitments as contained in the Programme of Action on a priority basis and to adjust them upwardly so as to reflect fully the additional resource requirements of the least developed countries, including those added to the list of least developed countries following the Second United Nations Conference on the Least Developed Countries;

6. *Stresses* that progress in the implementation of the Programme of Action will require effective implementation of national policies and priorities by the least developed countries for their economic growth and development, as well as a strong and committed partnership between those countries and their development partners;

7. *Requests* the Secretary-General, in conformity with paragraph 142 of the Programme of Action, to continue to ensure the full mobilization and coordination of all organs, organizations and bodies of the United Nations system in the implementation of and follow-up to the Programme of Action, in close collaboration with the Secretary-General of the United Nations Conference on Trade and Development, the secretariats of the regional commissions and the lead agencies of aid programmes;

8. *Calls upon* the United Nations Conference on Trade and Development to initiate further innovative measures to provide and mobilize financial and technical support for the effective implementation of the Programme of Action;

9. *Also stresses* the importance of effective follow-up and monitoring mechanisms for the Programme of Action, and notes that the annual follow-up of progress in the implementation of the Programme of Action undertaken by the Trade and Development Board on the basis of the annual report on the least developed countries helps to contribute to the development dialogue between those countries and their development partners, and urges that that exercise be strengthened;

10. *Notes with concern* the constrained resource position of the United Nations Development Programme during its fifth programming cycle and its impact on the least developed countries, and urges all concerned to take steps to carry out their agreed development programmes;

11. *Welcomes* the initiatives of some donor countries to write off and/or reduce, as appropriate, the official debt of the least developed countries, and invites others to take similar measures;

12. *Reiterates* that increased opportunities for trade can help reactivate economic growth in the least developed countries, and calls for significantly improved market access for their products, particularly through the elimination, wherever possible, or substantial reduction of tariff and non-tariff barriers, as well as giving special attention to the problems of the least developed countries within the context of the Final Act of the Uruguay Round of multilateral trade negotiations, with a view to integrating them in the global trading system;

13. *Also notes with concern* the environmental and development challenges facing the least developed countries and their vulnerability in this regard, and urges development partners to provide those countries with additional resources to enhance their capacity to achieve sustainable development;

14. *Invites* the preparatory bodies and all relevant forthcoming major meetings and conferences of the United Nations system, particularly the International Conference on Population and Development, the World Summit for Social Development, the Fourth World Conference on Women: Action for Equality, Development and Peace and the United Nations Conference on Human Settlements (Habitat II), to take into account the particular needs and requirements of the least developed countries in formulating their final documents;

15. *Welcomes* the positive contribution of the non-governmental organizations in the least developed countries in the field of socio-economic development;

16. *Decides* to convene a high-level intergovernmental meeting to conduct a mid-term global review, in accordance with paragraph 140 of the Programme of Action and General Assembly resolution 45/206, on the implementation of the Programme of Action, to be held in the early part of September 1995 or at any other suitable date during the second half of 1995;

17. *Stresses* the importance of timely, adequate and thorough preparations for the mid-term global review;

18. *Requests* the Trade and Development Board to consider, at its spring session in 1994, the elaboration of the preparatory activities for the mid-term global review meeting, including intergovernmental, expert, sectoral and inter-agency preparatory meetings and the substantive documentation;

19. *Urges* all Governments and international organizations, including multilateral and bilateral financial and technical assistance institutions, in particular the United Nations Development Programme, to take adequate steps to ensure appropriate preparations for an in-depth mid-term global review of the Programme of Action;

20. *Requests* all relevant organs, organizations and bodies of the United Nations system to submit reports containing a review of the implementation of the Programme of Action within their respective fields of competence, with special emphasis on areas where commitments have remained unfulfilled, and proposals for new measures, as necessary, as further inputs to the preparation for the mid-term global review;

21. *Stresses* the importance of maintaining the institutional identity and visibility of the Division for the Least Developed Countries in the secretariat of the United Nations Conference on Trade and Development, which is entrusted with the task of global-level monitoring of and follow-up to the Programme of Action, and welcomes the action taken by the Secretary-General to fill the vacant post of Director of the Division;

22. *Reiterates* its request to the Secretary-General, in resolution 46/156, to mobilize extrabudgetary resources to ensure the participation of at least one representative from each least developed country at the spring sessions of the Trade and Development Board, as well as at the intergovernmental, expert, sectoral and inter-agency preparatory meetings for the mid-term review process;

23. *Decides* to consider at its forty-ninth session the recommendations of the Trade and Development Board on preparations for the mid-term global review, as well as the question of meeting the cost of full and effective participation of representatives of the least developed countries at that meeting;

24. *Requests* the Secretary-General to submit to the General Assembly at its fiftieth session a report on the progress made in the implementation of the present resolution.

General Assembly resolution 48/171

21 December 1993   Meeting 86   Adopted without vote

Approved by Second Committee (A/48/717/Add.3) without vote, 10 December (meeting 47); draft by Vice-Chairman (A/C.2/48/L.76), based on informal consultations on draft by Colombia (for Group of 77) (A/C.2/48/L.8); agenda item 91 *(b)*.
Meeting numbers. GA 48th session: 2nd Committee 15-17, 19, 47; plenary 86.

Island developing countries

1994 Global Conference on the Sustainable Development of Small Island Developing States

As decided by the General Assembly in 1992,[16] the Preparatory Committee for the Global Conference on the Sustainable Development of Small Island Developing States, to be held in 1994, held its organizational and first sessions in 1993.[17]

At the organizational session (New York, 15 and 16 April), the Committee had before it reports of the Secretary-General on the preparations for the Conference[18] and on its draft provisional rules of procedure.[19] On 16 April, the Committee adopted a decision, which it drew to the attention of the Assembly, recommending the participation of associate members of regional commissions in the Conference and its preparatory process. It also adopted guidelines for its work, recommended to the Conference for adoption a set of provisional rules of procedure, decided to invite NGOs to contribute to the Conference and its preparatory process and adopted the provisional agenda for its first session.

At the first session (New York, 30 August–10 September), the Secretary-General submitted a report on sustainable development of small island developing States (SIDS).[20] The report described trends in the socio-economic development of SIDS and the major constraints to their sustainable development, their special vulnerabilities and options for their sustainable development. Basic constraints on the sustainable development of SIDS were the lack of land-based and proved marine resources; susceptibility to natural disasters; fragility of ecosystems; depletion of non-renewable resources and, in some, problems of obtaining freshwater supplies; limited resource assessment capabilities; high costs of infrastructure and public service provision associated with a lack of economies of scale; high internal transport costs and deteriorating inter-island transport services in archipelago States; poor accessibility to markets and sources of supply; a demographic structure with a large proportion of young and old people because of emigration; shortage of skilled personnel, both entrepreneurial and administrative; high dependence on foreign capital but little attractiveness for foreign investment; and small internal markets.

Sustainable development options open to SIDS included export of services, such as tourism, offshore financial activities, electronic data entry and flexible specialization as a method of organizing export production of light manufactures that offered the potential to increase international competitiveness and responsiveness to external economic changes.

The report identified the major priority areas for the sustainable development of SIDS as being environmental problems, management of re-

sources and external transport constraints. It then discussed policies and measures for addressing those issues at the national, regional and international levels.

Also before the Preparatory Committee were reports of the Secretary-General on a review of activities being carried out within the United Nations system in the area of the sustainable development of SIDS[21] and on the activities of the Conference secretariat.[22] In addition, the Committee considered the provisional agenda for the Conference[23] and a paper outlining the position of the Group of 77 developing countries and China on basic elements for an action programme for the sustainable development of SIDS.[24]

The Preparatory Committee also considered the reports of two regional technical meetings held during the year—one for the Indian and Pacific Oceans (Port Vila, Vanuatu, 31 May–4 June)[25] and the other for the Atlantic/Caribbean/Mediterranean (Port-of-Spain, Trinidad, 12-16 July).[26]

The Preparatory Committee adopted three decisions requiring action by the General Assembly, on the dates of the Conference, the date for pre-session consultations and options for the continuation of the Committee's preparatory work. Other decisions, which were brought to the Assembly's attention, dealt with the accreditation of NGOs to the Conference and its preparatory process; the position of the Group of 77 and China on basic elements for an action programme; information needs on donor activities in support of sustainable development in SIDS; a statement by Vanuatu on behalf of the member States and observers of the Alliance of Small Island States, which was annexed to the Committee's report; and the provisional agenda for the Conference. Also annexed to the Committee's report was the text of a draft programme of action for the sustainable development of SIDS.

GENERAL ASSEMBLY ACTION

On 21 December, on the recommendation of the Second Committee, the General Assembly adopted **resolution 48/193** without vote.

Global Conference on the Sustainable Development of Small Island Developing States

The General Assembly,

Recalling the report of the United Nations Conference on Environment and Development, and in particular Agenda 21, chapter 17, section G, relating to the sustainable development of small island developing States,

Recalling also its resolution 47/186 of 22 December 1992 on specific measures in favour of island developing countries,

Reaffirming its resolution 47/189 of 22 December 1992, in which it decided to convene the first Global Conference on the Sustainable Development of Small Island Developing States,

Reaffirming, in particular, the goals and objectives of the Global Conference identified in paragraphs 4 and 5 of resolution 47/189, and mindful of the important contribution that their successful accomplishment could make to the promotion of sustainable and environmentally sound development with respect to small island developing States,

Stressing that, because the development options of small island developing States are limited, there are special challenges to planning for and implementing sustainable development, and that small island developing States will be constrained in meeting those challenges without the cooperation and assistance of the international community,

Also stressing the need for the intergovernmental preparatory process for the Global Conference on the Sustainable Development of Small Island Developing States to be completed before the Conference itself,

1. *Takes note* of the report of the Preparatory Committee for the Global Conference on the Sustainable Development of Small Island Developing States on its organizational and first sessions;

2. *Decides* to convene the first Global Conference on the Sustainable Development of Small Island Developing States in Barbados from 25 April to 6 May 1994, including a high-level segment on 5 and 6 May;

3. *Urges once again* that representation at the Conference be at the highest possible level;

4. *Also decides* to convene one day of pre-Conference consultations at the venue of the Conference on 24 April 1994;

5. *Further decides* that the first session of the Preparatory Committee shall be resumed in New York for a period of five working days, from 7 to 11 March 1994, to complete the preparatory work assigned to it in paragraph 11 of resolution 47/189, including the draft programme of action for the sustainable development of small island developing States contained in annex III to the report of the Preparatory Committee, and that adequate facilities shall be made available for this purpose within the approved budget limit set for the biennium 1994-1995;

6. *Endorses* Preparatory Committee decisions 1 and 4 concerning the participation of associate members of regional commissions and of non-governmental organizations, including major groups, in the Conference and its preparatory process;

7. *Also endorses* Preparatory Committee decisions 3 and 13 and decides to transmit the provisional rules of procedure and the provisional agenda to the Conference for adoption;

8. *Requests* the Secretary-General, in consultation with the relevant United Nations agencies and organizations, and taking into account the submissions he may receive from bilateral, regional and multilateral donor agencies as well as from non-governmental organizations, to ensure the timely submission to the Preparatory Committee, at its resumed session, of the report requested in decision 11 of the Preparatory Committee;

9. *Also requests* the Secretary-General, through the Department of Public Information of the Secretariat, to ensure that the goals and purposes of the Conference receive the widest possible dissemination within Member States, non-governmental organizations and na-

tional, regional and international media, with a view to encouraging their active contribution to and support for the Conference and its preparatory process;

10. *Expresses its appreciation* for the contributions made to the voluntary fund established for the purpose of assisting small island developing States and the least developed countries to participate fully and effectively in the Conference and its preparatory process, and invites all Member States and organizations in a position to do so to contribute generously to the fund;

11. *Decides* to include in the agenda of its forty-ninth session, under the item entitled "Implementation of decisions and recommendations of the United Nations Conference on Environment and Development", the sub-item entitled "Global Conference on the Sustainable Development of Small Island Developing States", and requests the Secretary-General to submit to the General Assembly at its forty-ninth session the report of the Global Conference.

General Assembly resolution 48/193

21 December 1993   Meeting 86   Adopted without vote

Approved by Second Committee (A/48/725) without vote, 10 December (meeting 47); draft by Vice-Chairman (A/C.2/48/L.78), based on informal consultations on draft by China, and Colombia (for Group of 77) (A/C.2/48/L.12); agenda item 99 *(b)*.

Meeting numbers. GA 48th session: 2nd Committee 36-43, 47; plenary 86.

Land-locked developing countries

In response to a 1991 General Assembly request,[27] the UNCTAD Secretary-General convened in 1993 a Meeting of Governmental Experts from Land-locked and Transit Developing Countries and Representatives of Donor Countries and Financial and Development Institutions (New York, 17-19 May).[28] The Meeting reviewed the problems of land-locked and transit developing countries and considered action to address them. It adopted and annexed to its report a set of conclusions and recommendations which identified priority areas for transit cooperation and suggested modalities for action to improve transit systems at the national, subregional and international levels. As follow-up action, the Meeting recommended the holding of similar meetings of governmental experts every two years and of regular regional symposiums to monitor progress of implementation of the conclusions.

At its September/October 1993 session, TDB had before it, in addition to the report of the Meeting, reports by the UNCTAD secretariat on the results of studies related to transit and its alternatives,[29] and on information received from Governments, international and intergovernmental organizations and NGOs regarding action taken by them in favour of land-locked developing countries.[30]

On 1 October,[10] TDB endorsed the conclusions and recommendations of the Meeting of Governmental Experts,[28] and took note of the reports by the UNCTAD secretariat. It decided to forward those documents, together with its comments, to the General Assembly for action.

On 19 October,[31] the Secretary-General transmitted to the General Assembly the UNCTAD Secretary-General's report on progress in implementing specific action related to the particular needs and problems of land-locked developing countries. The report comprised the conclusions and recommendations of the Meeting of Governmental Experts, the results of studies related to transit and its alternatives, and information received from the international community on action taken in favour of land-locked developing countries.

GENERAL ASSEMBLY ACTION

On 21 December, the Assembly, on the recommendation of the Second Committee, adopted **resolution 48/169** without vote.

Specific actions related to the particular needs and problems of land-locked developing countries

The General Assembly,

Recalling the provisions of its resolutions 44/214 of 22 December 1989 and 46/212 of 20 December 1991,

Recognizing that the lack of territorial access to the sea, aggravated by remoteness and isolation from world markets, and prohibitive transit costs and risks impose serious constraints on the overall socio-economic development efforts of the land-locked developing countries,

Recognizing also that fifteen of the land-locked developing countries are also classified by the United Nations as least developed countries and that their geographical situation is an added constraint on their overall ability to cope with the challenges of development,

Recognizing further that most transit countries are themselves developing countries facing serious economic problems, including the lack of adequate infrastructure in the transport sector,

Recalling that measures to deal with the transit problems of land-locked developing countries require closer and even more effective cooperation and collaboration between those countries and their transit neighbours,

Recalling also the United Nations Convention on the Law of the Sea, adopted on 10 December 1982,

Recognizing the important role played by bilateral cooperative arrangements and regional and subregional cooperation and integration in comprehensively solving the transit problems of the land-locked developing countries and improving the transit transport systems in land-locked and transit developing countries,

Noting the importance of strengthening the existing international support measures with a view to addressing further the problems of land-locked developing countries,

1. *Reaffirms* the right of access of land-locked countries to and from the sea and freedom of transit through the territory of transit States by all means of transport, in accordance with international law;

2. *Also reaffirms* that transit developing countries, in the exercise of their full sovereignty over their territory, have the right to take all measures necessary to ensure that the rights and facilities provided for land-locked developing countries in no way infringe upon their legitimate interests;

3. *Calls upon* both the land-locked developing countries and their transit neighbours, in the spirit of South-

South cooperation, including bilateral cooperation, to implement measures to strengthen further their cooperative and collaborative efforts in dealing with their transit problems;

4. *Appeals once again* to all States, international organizations and financial institutions to implement, as a matter of urgency and priority, the specific actions related to the particular needs and problems of land-locked developing countries envisaged in the previous resolutions adopted by the General Assembly and the United Nations Conference on Trade and Development, and in the International Development Strategy for the Fourth United Nations Development Decade and the Declaration on International Economic Cooperation, in particular the Revitalization of Economic Growth and Development of the Developing Countries, adopted at the eighteenth special session of the General Assembly and contained in the annex to its resolution S-18/3 of 1 May 1990, as well as the relevant provisions of the Programme of Action for the Least Developed Countries for the 1990s;

5. *Invites* the land-locked developing countries and their transit neighbours to intensify further their cooperative arrangements for the development of transit infrastructures, institutions and services to facilitate the faster movement of goods in transit with financial and technical assistance from donors and financial agencies;

6. *Emphasizes* that assistance for the improvement of transport-transit facilities and services should be integrated into the overall economic development strategies of the land-locked and transit developing countries and that donor assistance should consequently take into account the requirements for long-term restructuring of the economies of the land-locked developing countries;

7. *Calls upon* donor countries and multilateral financial and development institutions to provide land-locked and transit developing countries with appropriate financial and technical assistance in the form of grants or concessional loans for the construction, maintenance and improvement of their transport, storage and other transit-related facilities, including alternative routes and improved communications;

8. *Invites* the United Nations Development Programme further to promote, as appropriate, subregional, regional and interregional projects and programmes and to expand its support in the transport and communications sectors to the land-locked and transit developing countries and its technical cooperation for development geared towards promoting national and collective self-reliance among them;

9. *Takes note* of the report of the Meeting of Governmental Experts from Land-locked and Transit Developing Countries and Representatives of Donor Countries and Financial and Development Institutions held in New York from 17 to 19 May 1993, and endorses the conclusions and recommendations contained therein;

10. *Requests* the Secretary-General to convene in 1995, within the overall level of resources for the biennium 1994-1995, another meeting of governmental experts from land-locked and transit developing countries, representatives of donor countries and financial and development institutions to review progress in the development of the transit systems in the land-locked and transit developing countries on the basis of an evaluation of the transit systems of those countries to be made by the Secretary-General of the United Nations Con-

ference on Trade and Development in cooperation with the Administrator of the United Nations Development Programme and to recommend further appropriate action, including elaboration of programmes for further improvement of those transit systems, to the Trade and Development Board and to the General Assembly at its fiftieth session;

11.   *Takes note* of the results of the specific studies on transit issues prepared by the secretariat of the United Nations Conference on Trade and Development, and encourages the international community to make use of them, as appropriate, when devising strategies to address the particular needs and problems of land-locked developing countries;

12.   *Invites* the Secretary-General of the United Nations Conference on Trade and Development to organize, within the overall level of resources for the biennium 1994-1995 and in collaboration with the Administrator of the United Nations Development Programme and the executive heads of the regional commissions, a symposium in 1994 for land-locked and transit developing countries to address specific regional problems in implementing the recommendations of the Meeting of Governmental Experts held in May 1993 and to submit the results of the studies referred to in paragraph 11 above to that symposium;

13.   *Requests* the Secretary-General of the United Nations Conference on Trade and Development to seek voluntary contributions to ensure participation of representatives of land-locked and transit developing countries in the meeting and symposium referred to, respectively, in paragraphs 10 and 12 above;

14.   *Takes note with appreciation* of the contribution of the United Nations Conference on Trade and Development in formulating international measures to deal with the special problems of the land-locked developing countries, and urges the Conference, *inter alia*, to keep under constant review the evolution of transport-transit infrastructure facilities, institutions and services, monitor the implementation of agreed measures, collaborate in all relevant initiatives, including those of private-sector and non-governmental organizations, and serve as a focal point on cross-regional issues of interest to land-locked developing countries;

15.   *Invites* the Secretary-General of the United Nations, in consultation with the Secretary-General of the United Nations Conference on Trade and Development, to take appropriate measures to enhance the capacity of the Conference, within existing resources for the biennium 1994-1995, in the area dealing with land-locked developing countries so as to ensure the effective im-

plementation of the activities called for in the present resolution and of existing measures in support of land-locked developing countries;

16.   *Invites* the international community and the preparatory bodies for all relevant forthcoming major meetings and conferences of the United Nations system to take into account, in the preparation of documentation, the specific needs and requirements of land-locked and transit developing countries and the participation of those countries in those meetings and conferences;

17.   *Welcomes* the reports of the Secretary-General of the United Nations and of the Secretary-General of the United Nations Conference on Trade and Development on specific action related to the specific needs and problems of land-locked developing countries, and requests the Secretary-General of the United Nations Conference on Trade and Development to prepare another report, taking into account the provisions of the present resolution, for submission to the General Assembly at its fiftieth session.

General Assembly resolution 48/169

21 December 1993   Meeting 86   Adopted without vote

Approved by Second Committee (A/48/717/Add.2) without vote, 10 December (meeting 47); draft by Vice-Chairman (A/C.2/48/L.81), based on informal consultations on 20-nation draft (A/C.2/48/L.22); agenda item 91 (a).

Meeting numbers. GA 48th session: 2nd Committee 30-32, 39, 47; plenary 86.

In other action, the Assembly, by **resolution 48/170**, invited the UNCTAD Secretary-General, in cooperation with UNDP, to evaluate the transit system of the newly independent and developing land-locked States in Central Asia (see PART TWO, Chapter VI).

REFERENCES

[1]DP/1993/67/Add.1. [2]DP/1993/67. [3]E/1993/35 (dec. 93/23). [4]A/CONF.147/18. [5]GA res. 45/206, 21 Dec. 1990. [6]YUN 1991, p. 358, GA res. 46/156, 19 Dec. 1991. [7]YUN 1992, p. 544, GA res. 47/173, 22 Dec. 1992. [8]A/48/333. [9]*The Least Developed Countries—1992 Report* (TD/B/39(2)/10), Sales No. E.93.II.D.3. [10]A/48/15. [11]YUN 1992, p. 544. [12]A/48/15 (conclusion 404(XXXIX)). [13]YUN 1991, p. 357. [14]DP/1993/18. [15]E/1993/35 (dec. 93/18). [16]YUN 1992, p. 547, GA res. 47/189, 22 Dec. 1992. [17]A/48/36. [18]A/CONF.167/PC/2. [19]A/CONF.167/PC/3. [20]A/CONF.167/PC/10 & Corr.1. [21]A/CONF.167/PC/6. [22]A/CONF.167/PC/9. [23]A/CONF.167/PC/11. [24]A/CONF.167/PC/L.5/Rev.1. [25]A/CONF.167/PC/7. [26]A/CONF.167/PC/8. [27]YUN 1991, p. 359, GA res. 46/212, 20 Dec. 1991. [28]TD/B/40(1)/2. [29]TD/B/40(1)/4. [30]TD/B/40(1)/5 & Add.1. [31]A/48/487.

Chapter II

Operational activities for development

In 1993, the United Nations system experienced a significant downturn in contributions for operational activities for development, which obliged organizations to restrict assistance commitments.

The Economic and Social Council, in following up the 1992 biennial policy review of operational activities, requested the Secretary-General to set result-oriented targets (resolution 1993/7). The General Assembly authorized the establishment of nine field offices of the United Nations development system in successor States of the USSR and reaffirmed that they should be funded through voluntary contributions (resolution 48/209).

During 1992, the most recent year for which detailed figures were available, expenditure by the United Nations system on operational activities for development totalled $8.9 billion. Of that amount, $4.6 billion was in the form of development grants and $4.3 billion in concessional loans.

The United Nations Development Programme—the central funding body in the United Nations system for providing technical assistance to developing countries—spent $1.031 billion on programme activities in 1993, compared with $1.027 billion in 1992. The organizational entities of the United Nations—mainly through the newly established Department for Development Support and Management Services—delivered a technical cooperation programme of $209 million in 1993, compared with $243 million in 1992.

Expenditure in 1993 by the United Nations Capital Development Fund, a multilateral agency providing small-scale capital assistance to the least developed countries, amounted to $59 million.

With regard to technical cooperation among developing countries, the Assembly endorsed the decisions of the May/June meeting of the High-level Committee on the Review of Technical Cooperation Among Developing Countries and urged that high priority be given to cooperation in science and technology, transfer of technology, capacity-building, education and technical training and know-how (48/172).

General aspects

Strengthening operational activities

In 1993, the General Assembly (**resolution 48/162**), within the context of restructuring and revitalizing the United Nations in the economic, social and related fields, stated that the aim of the segment of the Economic and Social Council dealing with the operational activities of the United Nations for international development cooperation would be to improve the quality and impact of the United Nations operational activities through an integrated approach and to ensure that policies formulated by the Assembly, particularly during the triennial policy review of operational activities, were implemented on a system-wide basis. The segment would also include a high-level meeting on international development cooperation.

With regard to the need for increased resources for operational development, the Assembly requested the Secretary-General to analyse possible improvements in the present funding system, including multi-year negotiated pledges, and to submit recommendations to the United Nations Development Programme (UNDP) Governing Council in April 1994. He could also assess the likely impact of various options on overall levels of funding and contributions.

The Assembly decided to review efforts to improve United Nations functioning in operational activities, as well as decisions on financing, possibly at a high-level meeting of the Council and at the Assembly in 1995. (See also PART THREE, Chapter XVIII.)

Follow-up to the 1992 triennial policy review

ACC consideration. Implementation of 1992 General Assembly resolution 47/199[1] on the triennial policy review of operational activities for development within the United Nations system was discussed in committees of the Administrative Committee on Coordination (ACC) during 1993. The Consultative Committee on Substantive Questions (Geneva, 16-19 March)[2] discussed and adopted guidelines with regard to the country strategy note called for in the resolution. It also agreed on a common interpretation of national execution.

At the first session of the newly established ACC Consultative Committee on Programme and Operational Questions (CCPOQ) (New York, 20-24 September),[3] a work programme for implementing resolution 47/199 was discussed in response to a request contained in Economic and Social Council **resolution 1993/7** (see below). CCPOQ also reviewed the resident coordinator system, decentralization, operational activities training, monitoring of ACC guidelines, evaluation and programme coordination issues.

UNDP action. In May,[4] the UNDP Administrator reported on measures taken to implement resolution 47/199. He stated that UNDP was reviewing the concept of a country strategy note for the United Nations system, which would serve as a framework and a reference for organizations and their governing bodies when considering country programmes. In terms of a common programme approach, UNDP had issued its own guiding principles for use by its field offices and had introduced a programme support document for building capacity for implementing and sustaining national programmes. As regards a common interpretation of national execution, it had revised its operational guidelines and was ensuring that those activities were appropriately supported. Considerable progress had been made in harmonizing the programme exercises and cycles of organizations in about 33 per cent of countries, and a work plan had been developed to increase synchronization. UNDP was collaborating with its partners in the United Nations system in formulating common processes, formats and procedures and in producing a common manual. It was also co-financing a study on rationalizing aid accountability requirements among multilateral and bilateral donors, and had proposed the development of system-wide approaches to harmonize monitoring and evaluation. The pool of candidates for the selection of resident representatives/resident coordinators was being widened, and, in collaboration with the United Nations Children's Fund (UNICEF), UNDP was studying the possible expansion of the number of their common premises.

On 18 June,[5] the UNDP Governing Council requested the UNDP Administrator to strengthen implementation of resolution 47/199 and to ensure feedback to the Council, especially at the field level. He was asked to report to the Council in 1994.

Report of the Secretary-General. In a June report to the Economic and Social Council,[6] the Secretary-General described progress in implementing resolution 47/199. He outlined the current context of operational activities for development and progress made in relation to programme development, implementation and support. He also discussed efforts to strengthen the resident coordinator system and addressed a number of thematic issues. Annexed to the report were the work programme for implementing resolution 47/199 and texts developed by ACC on the country strategy note, the programme approach and national execution.

In addition to summarizing ACC's efforts to implement resolution 47/199, the report stated that the Joint Consultative Group on Policy (JCGP),

comprising UNDP, UNICEF, the United Nations Population Fund (UNFPA), the International Fund for Agricultural Development (IFAD) and the World Food Programme (WFP), had also initiated action on various aspects of the resolution and assigned specific tasks to its subgroups.

Both CCPOQ and JCGP were devoting attention to evaluation, monitoring and auditing, the expansion of common premises and training. CCPOQ had established a working group to consider the functioning of the resident coordinator system. Communication with resident coordinators was being reinforced to ensure that guidance was available to them when needed, and the provision of additional support to resident coordinators was being reviewed by a CCPOQ working group.

In a later report,[7] the Secretary-General stated that a country strategy workshop had been held at Turin, Italy, from 11 to 14 October. The workshop, attended by 11 senior national officials, resident coordinators and other United Nations officials, had helped to clarify some practical questions in connection with the country strategy note and the ACC guidelines.

As to the adaptation and harmonization of programme cycles, JCGP had established several targets: to achieve, by 1996, 80 per cent harmonization of countries with the programming cycles of UNDP, UNFPA and UNICEF and to relate them to WFP projects; in countries with a national plan, to adapt UNDP, UNFPA and UNICEF programming cycles to the plan; and, in countries without formal plans, to harmonize the programming cycles among themselves.

Based on those targets, JCGP, in late 1993, issued a joint UNDP/UNFPA/UNICEF letter to resident coordinators, country directors and field representatives containing guiding principles on how to proceed with country programme cycle harmonization.

ECONOMIC AND SOCIAL COUNCIL ACTION

On 22 July, the Economic and Social Council adopted **resolution 1993/7** without vote.

Operational activities for development

The Economic and Social Council,

Recalling General Assembly resolution 44/211 of 22 December 1989 and taking note of Assembly resolution 47/199 of 22 December 1992,

Noting with concern that the results of the 1992 United Nations Pledging Conference for Development Activities were well below expected levels and that the current trend of contributions in real terms to funds and programmes, particularly core contributions, is downward,

Reiterating that the fundamental characteristics of the operational activities of the United Nations system should be, *inter alia*, their universal, voluntary and grant nature, neutrality and multilateralism, and that recipient Governments have the primary responsibility for coordinating all types of external assistance,

1. *Takes note* of the progress report of the Secretary-General on the implementation of General Assembly resolution 47/199, including the annexes thereto on the country strategy note, national execution and the programme approach;

2. *Urges* the heads of the funds, programmes and specialized agencies of the United Nations system to make every effort further to improve the efficiency and effectiveness of their organizations, and to inform their governing bodies of measures taken in this regard in their annual reports;

3. *Urges* developed countries, in particular those countries whose overall performance is not commensurate with their capacity, taking into account established official development assistance targets, including targets established at the Second United Nations Conference on the Least Developed Countries and current levels of contribution, to increase their official development assistance substantially, including contributions to the operational activities of the United Nations system;

4. *Requests* the Secretary-General to seek to ensure that an effective methodology for evaluation of the programme approach, as called for in paragraph 13 of Assembly resolution 47/199, has been developed by June 1994, and to review the progress made by the United Nations system in promoting greater integration of its activities with national development programmes and in providing more coherent United Nations system support, including an assessment of the experience gained in the implementation at the field level of the common United Nations system framework for the programme approach;

5. *Also requests* the Secretary-General to undertake a review of the progress made by the United Nations system in applying national execution at the country level, including an assessment of the experience gained in the implementation at the field level of the common United Nations system guiding principles for national execution, contained in the progress report on the implementation of Assembly resolution 47/199;

6. *Invites* the Secretary-General to provide information on a regular basis to all participating countries regarding the steps being taken in accordance with the provisions of paragraph 9 of Assembly resolution 47/199 dealing with the country strategy note, including information on the forthcoming seminar on this topic, to be held at the International Training Centre of the International Labour Organisation at Turin, Italy;

7. *Emphasizes* the need to take full account of the factors outlined in paragraph 38 of Assembly resolution 47/199 in order to ensure an effectively functioning resident coordinator system, and invites the organs of the United Nations system, at the country level, to contribute, where appropriate, to the provision of the resources necessary to assist the resident coordinator in fulfilling his responsibilities;

8. *Stresses* the importance it attaches to the early and complete implementation of paragraphs 39 to 41 of Assembly resolution 47/199, on the strengthening and support of the resident coordinator system, including paragraphs 39 (*d*) and (*g*) on widening the pool of qualified development professionals eligible for appointment as United Nations Development Programme resident representatives or resident coordinators and on enhancing the responsibility and authority of the resident coordinator for the planning and coordination of programmes;

9. *Underlines* the importance of making early progress on decentralization and delegation of authority to field offices, including approval authority within approved programmes, in the context of enhanced accountability;

10. *Requests* the Secretary-General to develop further the work programme for the implementation of Assembly resolution 47/199, contained in annex I to his report, with a view to setting result-oriented targets;

11. *Stresses* the need for future reports on the implementation of Assembly resolution 47/199 to focus on the outcome and output of the activities of the United Nations system, in particular at the field level, rather than on the input;

12. *Requests* the United Nations system, including the Department for Policy Coordination and Sustainable Development of the Secretariat, to devote sufficient resources to the coordinated and effective implementation of Assembly resolution 47/199, including through temporary secondment of staff from the funds, programmes and specialized agencies of the United Nations system;

13. *Decides* to review the implementation of the present resolution at its substantive session of 1994, as part of the review of the implementation of Assembly resolution 47/199 called for in paragraph 54 of that resolution.

Economic and Social Council resolution 1993/7

22 July 1993   Meeting 40   Adopted without vote

Draft by Vice-President (E/1993/L.28), based on informal consultations; agenda item 3.
Meeting numbers. ESC 24-29, 35, 38, 40.

Financing of operational activities

A significant downturn in contributions to operational activities within the United Nations system was registered in 1993.[7] Voluntary pledges to UNDP totalled $910 million, a reduction of 15 per cent from 1992, forcing it to restrict commitments to only 70 per cent of indicative planning figures (IPFs). Contributions to UNICEF totalled $539 million, a drop of 22 per cent from 1992, while UNFPA's overall income fell by almost 8 per cent, to $219.6 million. A target of $1.5 billion was established for WFP for the 1993-1994 biennium (the same level as for 1991-1992); the pace of pledges being made towards that target was far below that of the previous biennium and was also cause for concern.

Expenditures

During 1992,[8] expenditures by the United Nations system on operational activities totalled $8.9 billion. Of that amount, $4.6 billion was distributed in development grants through UNDP, UNFPA, UNICEF, WFP and specialized agencies and other organizations, and $4.3 billion was disbursed in concessional loans by the International Development Association (IDA) ($4.1 billion) and IFAD ($131 million). Non-concessional loans, disbursed through the World Bank and the International Finance Corporation (IFC), had a negative balance of $6.9 billion in 1992. Grants to finance refugee, humanitarian, special economic and disaster relief activities totalled $1.2 billion.

Of total expenditures on grant-financed development activities in 1992, WFP accounted for 34.4 per cent; UNDP and UNDP-administered funds, 25.4 per cent; UNICEF, 16.2 per cent; specialized agencies, 15.9 per cent; regular budgets, 5.3 per cent; and UNFPA, 2.8 per cent.

By region, approximately 45.5 per cent of expenditures went to Africa; 35.8 per cent to Asia and the Pacific; 7.5 to the Americas; and 0.6 per cent to Europe. Interregional and global activities received 7.9 per cent.

Expenditures by sector on grant-financed development activities were as follows: humanitarian aid and relief, 28 per cent; health, 19 per cent; agriculture, forestry and fisheries, 11 per cent; general development issues, policy and planning, 9 per cent; education and natural resources, 6 per cent each; industry, 4 per cent; population, social conditions and equity, and transport and communications, 3 per cent each; employment and science and technology, 2 per cent each; and human settlements and international trade and development finance, 1 per cent each.

Contributions

Contributions from Governments and other sources for operational activities of the United Nations system, including IFAD and the World Bank group (World Bank, IDA and IFC), totalled $11.2 billion in 1992.[8]

In addition, contributions for refugees, humanitarian, special economic and disaster relief activities totalled $1.1 billion, and for the United Nations Environment Programme Environment Fund $77 million.

UN Pledging Conference for Development Activities

The 1993 United Nations Pledging Conference for Development Activities was held in New York on 2 and 3 November to receive government pledges for 1994 to United Nations funds and programmes concerned with development and related assistance.

In an October note[9] to the General Assembly, the Secretary-General listed contributions pledged or paid at the 1992 pledging conference to 24 United Nations funds and programmes, as at 30 June 1993, totalling approximately $1.4 billion, with $760 million designated for UNDP.

United Nations field offices

In a July report,[10] the Secretary-General assessed the experience gained in the establishment and functioning of the seven United Nations interim offices, in Armenia, Azerbaijan, Belarus, Georgia, Kazakhstan, Ukraine and Uzbekistan, which he decided to set up in 1992.[11]

On 9 November,[12] the Under-Secretary-General for Policy Coordination and Sustainable Development, in a statement before the General Assembly's Second (Economic and Financial) Committee, said that the establishment of the interim offices represented an advance towards a unified, cost-effective United Nations presence in the field. It responded to demands for a better coordinated and multi-disciplinary response to the needs of recipient countries, and was intended to reduce administrative costs and maximize resources for programme delivery. The offices would be headed by the United Nations Representative, who would function as team leader and also serve as UNDP resident coordinator. He wished to dispel concerns that the offices might, without mandate, perform political functions, become a politicized new model of United Nations offices in the field or be used for human rights monitoring. The main function of the offices was, and would continue to be, to respond to the development needs of the countries concerned, including the provision of coordinated humanitarian assistance. United Nations public information activities were also an integral component of the interim offices (see PART ONE, Chapter V).

GENERAL ASSEMBLY ACTION

On 21 December, the General Assembly, on the recommendation of the Second Committee, adopted **resolution 48/209** without vote.

Operational activities for development: field offices of the United Nations development system
The General Assembly,
Reaffirming its resolutions 34/213 of 19 December 1979, 44/211 of 22 December 1989, 46/182 of 19 December 1991 and 47/199 of 22 December 1992,
Having considered the statement made on behalf of the Secretary-General by the Under-Secretary-General for Policy Coordination and Sustainable Development before the Second Committee on 9 November 1993,
Reaffirming that the fundamental characteristics of the operational activities of the United Nations system should be, *inter alia*, their universal, voluntary and grant nature, and their neutrality and multilateralism,
Reaffirming also the importance of a more effective and coherent coordinated approach by the United Nations system to the needs of recipient countries, particularly at the field level,
Reaffirming further that the mandates of the separate United Nations sectoral and specialized entities, funds, programmes and specialized agencies should be respected and enhanced, taking into account their complementarities,
Reaffirming that assistance should be based on an agreed division of responsibility among the funding organizations, under the coordination of the Government concerned, in order to integrate their response into the development needs of recipient countries,
1. *Reaffirms* the principle that the assistance provided by the United Nations system should be in conformity

with the national objectives and priorities of the recipient countries, that the coordination of various assistance inputs at the national level is the prerogative of the Government concerned and that the overall responsibility for, and coordination of, operational activities for development of the United Nations system carried out at the country level is entrusted to the resident coordinator;

2. *Authorizes* the establishment of field offices in Armenia, Azerbaijan, Belarus, Eritrea, Georgia, Kazakhstan, the Russian Federation, Ukraine and Uzbekistan, and decides that those offices shall be field offices of the United Nations development system;

3. *Reaffirms* that the field offices of the United Nations development system at the country level shall be coordinated by resident coordinators and shall comply fully with the provisions laid down by the General Assembly relating to the organizational structure, mandates and functions of the offices of the United Nations development system and to the role of the resident coordinator, in particular those provisions contained in its resolutions 34/213, 46/182 and 47/199;

4. *Stresses* that all field offices should comply fully with the provisions of its resolution 47/199 relating to the role and functions of the resident coordinator, in particular paragraphs 38 and 39 thereof, and reaffirms that the resident representative of the United Nations Development Programme shall normally be designated as the resident coordinator and that, in accordance with its resolution 46/182, the resident coordinator shall normally coordinate the humanitarian assistance of the United Nations system at the country level;

5. *Reaffirms* that field office activities related to public information, where in place, should follow the relevant provisions of resolutions of the General Assembly, in particular its resolution 48/44 B of 10 December 1993;

6. *Also reaffirms* the need to increase the number of common premises, in cooperation with host Governments, in a way that increases efficiency through, *inter alia*, consolidation of administrative infrastructures of the organizations concerned, but does not increase the costs for the United Nations system or for developing countries;

7. *Further reaffirms* that all field offices should operate on a sound financial basis;

8. *Reaffirms* that all field offices are to be funded through voluntary contributions, including those from the host country, and that the United Nations regular budget is a financial source for currently mandated activities related to public information;

9. *Decides* to review the situation of all field offices as part of the next triennial policy review of operational activities for development within the United Nations system, through the procedures established for that purpose in its resolution 47/199;

10. *Stresses* that field offices in any new recipient country shall be based on the relevant provisions of General Assembly resolutions, including those contained in the present resolution.

General Assembly resolution 48/209

21 December 1993   Meeting 86   Adopted without vote

Approved by Second Committee (A/48/733) without vote, 13 December (meeting 48); draft by Vice-Chairman (A/C.2/48/L.70), based on informal consultations; agenda item 154.
Financial implications. 5th Committee, A/48/792; S-G, A/C.2/48/L.85, A/C.5/48/55.
Meeting numbers. GA 48th session: 2nd Committee 26-29, 46, 48; 5th Committee 43; plenary 86.

By **decision 48/451** of 21 December, the Assembly took note of the Secretary-General's report.[10]

In related action, the Assembly, in **resolution 48/44 B** of 10 December, requested the Secretary-General to ensure that his proposals relating to the structure, functions and activities of the United Nations interim offices in Armenia, Azerbaijan, Belarus, Georgia, Kazakhstan, Ukraine and Uzbekistan fully complied with the mandates of relevant Assembly resolutions pertaining to operational activities and dissemination of information.

REFERENCES

[1]YUN 1992, p. 552, GA res. 47/199, 22 Dec. 1992. [2]ACC/1993/10. [3]ACC/1993/25. [4]DP/1993/10. [5]E/1993/35 (dec. 93/16). [6]E/1993/73. [7]E/1994/64. [8]E/1994/64/Add.2. [9]A/CONF.160/2. [10]A/48/146/Add.1. [11]YUN 1992, p. 126. [12]A/48/585.

Technical cooperation through UNDP

In his annual report for 1993,[1] the UNDP Administrator discussed changes in the international community's thinking and approaches with regard to development. He stated that the mixed record of development and of development cooperation resulted largely from the failure to acknowledge that the political and cultural framework as well as governance of countries were part of the development process, and that development must be owned by the potential beneficiaries. UNDP's contribution to the conceptual debate on development was based on the concept of sustainable human development involving poverty alleviation, employment generation, empowerment of disadvantaged groups in society, equity and the regeneration of the environment. It was promoting the concept and reorienting its cooperation at all levels to support national efforts to achieve and sustain human development in economic, socio-cultural, environmental, political and other terms. The challenge for UNDP was to remain relevant and accountable and to seek more effective ways of supporting countries.

In 1993, estimated UNDP income was some $1,371 million, a decrease from $1,620 million in 1992. Of the 1993 total, approximately $891 million came from voluntary pledges, compared to $1,778 million in 1992. Other major sources included cost-sharing contributions by recipient Governments ($376 million), trust funds established by the Administrator, excluding the Global Environment Facility (GEF) ($71 million), contributions to local office costs ($17 million), government cash counterpart contributions ($12 million), extrabudgetary activities ($4 million) and contributions to the Special Measures Fund for the Least Developed Countries

(LDCs) ($0.26 million). An additional $149 million was received through management service agreements.

In addition, eight funds administered by UNDP provided approximately $76.8 million during 1993, bringing total income to $1,588.6 million. Those funds were the United Nations Capital Development Fund (UNCDF), the United Nations Revolving Fund for Natural Resources Exploration (UNRFNRE), the United Nations Sudano-Sahelian Office (UNSO), the United Nations Volunteers (UNV), the United Nations Fund for Science and Technology for Development (UNFSTD), the United Nations Development Fund for Women (UNIFEM), the UNDP Energy Account and the UNDP Study Programme.

Of the donor country members of the Development Assistance Committee of the Organisation for Economic Cooperation and Development, Austria, Germany, Luxembourg, the Netherlands, Norway and Portugal maintained their 1994 contributions at the previous year's levels, while Denmark, Finland, Ireland and Sweden increased their contributions. Of the programme countries, Bangladesh, Honduras, India, Mongolia, Mali, Morocco, Namibia, Niue, the Republic of Korea, Romania, Samoa, Uganda, the United Republic of Tanzania and Viet Nam increased their contributions. India continued to be the largest donor in that group, while the Republic of Korea pledged an increase of over 50 per cent.

Field programme expenditures, including IPF resources, Special Programme Resources (SPR), the Special Measures Fund for LDCs, cost-sharing and government cash counterpart contributions amounted to $1.031 billion in 1993. Of field programme expenditures, 49.2 per cent went to project personnel, which included internationally and nationally recruited experts and UNV specialists, 19.3 per cent to subcontracts, 15.4 per cent to project equipment, 9.3 per cent to training and the remainder to miscellaneous expenses such as maintenance and operational costs.

By region, both sub-Saharan Africa and Asia and the Pacific absorbed about 37 per cent of IPF resources in 1993; Latin America and the Caribbean 10 per cent; the Arab States 8 per cent; and Europe and the Commonwealth of Independent States 1 per cent. Global and interregional projects absorbed 6 per cent.

Project approvals during 1993 totalled 954, a decline from 972 in 1992. The value of new project approvals was $782 million, compared to $642 million the previous year.

UNDP Governing Council

In 1993, the UNDP Governing Council held both its organizational meeting and a special session to discuss pending issues from 16 to 19 February, and its fortieth session from 1 to 18 June in New York.[2] A special session to discuss the 1994-1995 programme budget and the question of integrating the UNDP Office of Project Services into the United Nations Department for Development Support and Management Services (DDSMS) was held in New York on 16 December.[3]

At the organizational meeting, the Council adopted a decision on its schedule of meetings and other organizational matters.[4] At the February special session, it adopted eight decisions, which are dealt with below.

During its fortieth session, the Council adopted 37 decisions. Those not dealt with in this chapter related to the United Nations humanitarian programme, follow-up to the United Nations Conference on Environment and Development (UNCED), regional cooperation for the protection of vulnerable ecosystems, human immunodeficiency virus/acquired immunodeficiency syndrome (HIV/AIDS), technical cooperation in support of the transition to a market economy and democracy in countries of Eastern and Central Europe and the Commonwealth of Independent States, UNDP's role in implementing the United Nations New Agenda for the Development of Africa in the 1990s, LDCs, the programme of assistance to the Palestinian people, UNFPA and its financial budgetary and administrative matters, UNIFEM and UNSO.

On 16 December, the Council's special session adopted a decision on the Office for Project Services (see below).

On 1 June,[5] the Council approved the agenda and organization of work for its fortieth session, and on 9 June,[6] deferred consideration of the venue of Council sessions pending the outcome of the restructuring of the economic and social sectors of the United Nations. On 16 June,[7] the Council paid tribute to William H. Draper, the UNDP Administrator from 1986 to 1993. On 17 June, it took note of a number of reports and documents;[8] decided to review the provisional agenda of its forty-first session at its organizational session;[9] and agreed on the schedule of its future sessions and that of its subsidiary bodies.[10]

The General Assembly, by **decision 48/447** of 21 December, took note of the report of the UNDP Governing Council on its organizational meeting for 1993, its special session and its fortieth session.[2]

In **resolution 48/162** of 20 December, the Assembly decided to transform the current governing body of UNDP/UNFPA into an Executive Board.

Standing Committee for Programme Matters. The Standing Committee for Programme Matters held an in-sessional meeting during the special session of the Governing Council

(16-19 February).[11] It considered reports on field visits, country programmes and projects and its future programme of work, including the tentative timetable for mid-term reviews by country and intercountry programmes to be carried out between 1993 and 1995. The Committee recommended that the Council adopt a draft decision approving a number of country programmes.

The Standing Committee also held an in-sessional meeting during the fortieth session of the Council (1-18 June),[12] covering country, intercountry and global programmes, UNFPA, field visits, evaluation, programme management issues, including decentralization and the country programme approach, and its future programme of work. The Committee recommended that the Council adopt draft decisions approving a number of UNDP and UNFPA country programmes, on assistance to Myanmar and on evaluation. It approved revised terms of reference for field visits.

UNDP operational activities
Country and intercountry programmes

On 19 February,[13] the UNDP Governing Council approved country programmes for 18 countries: 6 in Africa, 4 in Arab States, 3 in Europe, 1 in Asia and the Pacific, and 4 in Latin America and the Caribbean. It approved a fifth country programme for Rwanda with the provision that the Administrator present an interim report on its implementation and on the impact which the evolution of the general context of the country might have on the programme's implementation. It also approved the extension of the third country programme for Cyprus. The Council noted the Administrator's intention to continue to approve projects on a case-by-case basis for Somalia, pending normalization of the situation there, and requested the Administrator to report to its fortieth session and its special session in February 1994 on the results and progress of UNDP efforts in that country. The Council noted the tentative timetable for the mid-term reviews to be carried out between 1993 and 1995.[14]

On 18 June,[15] the Council approved country programmes for 25 countries: 10 in Africa, 9 in Asia and the Pacific, 4 in the Arab States, and 2 in Latin America and the Caribbean. It approved the fifth country programme for the United Republic of Tanzania, subject to the Administrator's reporting to it in 1994 on the advancement of the programme in the light of comments made by the Standing Committee for Programme Matters. The fourth programme for Sudan was approved on the understanding that the proposed activities would have a primary focus on food security and sustainable rural agriculture devel-

opment and would be subject to a policy review after one year. The Council endorsed the Administrator's recommendation[16] to continue the country programme for Malawi, maintaining the focus on human development through poverty alleviation while encouraging and facilitating the process of political change and its contribution to the achievement of the programme goals. It approved amendments to the country programme for Rwanda[17] and took note of an oral report on assistance to Cambodia. The Council approved a one-year extension of the country programmes for 15 countries: 6 in Africa, 1 in Europe and the Commonwealth of Independent States, and 8 in Latin America and the Caribbean. It also noted the Administrator's intention[18] to continue to approve projects in Iraq on a case-by-case basis.

In response to a 1992 Council request,[19] the Administrator, in April, submitted a note[20] summarizing the outcome of a resource allocation review of ongoing fourth cycle (1987-1991) projects, carried out with Myanmar and executing agencies in 1992. As a result of the review, $8.4 million was released by curtailing several projects and was being applied to high-priority projects with greater grass-roots-level impact. The report also presented the major findings of an evaluation of Myanmar's fifth country programme, which highlighted the need to restore curtailed projects. The report recommended that the sixth country programme be submitted to the Council in 1995 and outlined areas where continuing UNDP technical cooperation would be needed during the transitional period from July 1993 to December 1995. An amount of $40 million from the fifth cycle (1992-1996) IPF for Myanmar was proposed to meet those needs.

On 18 June,[21] the Council decided that, until a country programme for Myanmar was considered, all future assistance from UNDP and related funds should be targeted towards programmes having a grass-roots-level impact, particularly in the areas of primary health care, the environment, HIV/AIDS, training and education, and food security. It approved, in addition to the amounts released from the reallocation of carried-over fourth cycle resources, an expenditure of up to $18 million from fifth cycle IPF allocations for the 18-month period to December 1994. The Administrator was requested to continue to approve assistance on a project-by-project basis and to submit to the Council in 1994 a report on the status of approval and implementation of new projects and recommendations for future programming.

Mid-term reviews. In response to a 1992 request,[19] the Administrator presented to the Council's February special session a tentative timetable and reporting proposals for 1993-1995 mid-term reviews.[22] On 19 February,[13] the

Council took note of the tentative timetable and decided to examine it further in the light of views expressed at the special session.

In a November report,[23] the Administrator gave an overview of mid-term reviews carried out in 1993 of the country programmes for India, Indonesia and Zambia. He also submitted a revised timetable for 1993-1995 reviews. The reviews indicated that UNDP's programmes remained valid and that existing projects had only required re-organization around sectoral or thematic clusters to sharpen focus, impact and continued relevance. The reviews also examined experience gained in national execution; UNDP assistance in national capacity-building for policy and programme formulation, management and evaluation; experience with new support cost arrangements, including implementation problems; and experience with the programme approach and the extent to which alternative programme mechanisms changed the focus of country programmes. With regard to the resource situation, the Administrator stated that IPF resources were nearly fully committed, with a significant proportion having been carried over from preceding programmes. The decline in available resources limited the capacity of UNDP country programmes to adjust to changing circumstances and/or initiate new activities.

Country programmes by region

Africa

UNDP, through its Regional Bureau for Africa, continued to support the United Nations New Agenda for the Development of Africa in the 1990s[24] (see next chapter), mainly through its project executed by the Economic Commission for Africa. It provided assistance at central and local government levels for strengthening economic management capacity in several countries. It also collaborated with other bodies and agencies in identifying priority areas for government/donor cooperation and funded studies in preparation for a 1994 donors' conference on human resource development for post-apartheid South Africa. Under its African Capacity-Building Initiative, eight more projects were approved, bringing the total to 18, with a total commitment of $46.3 million. The National Long-Term Perspective Studies Programme, designed to help countries define national priorities to guide their development over a 25-year period, became fully operational in 1993 in six countries. A number of seminars, conferences and workshops were held to sensitize African countries to the initiative.

Seventy-five nationally executed projects were approved for some $60 million, representing 45 per cent of new projects approved and about 60 per cent of the total value in 1993. To help strengthen indigenous capacity for national execution, UNDP conducted a number of seminars and workshops on the subject. It collaborated with other agencies and bilateral partners in alleviating poverty through a comprehensive approach encompassing macroeconomic policy reforms and sectoral interventions. Efforts were made to operationalize the human development concept, with particular attention being paid to the promotion of women's participation in the development process. In the area of private sector development, UNDP assisted in improving management capabilities and promoting trade and investment. By the end of 1993, the Africa Project Development Facility, a joint effort with the African Development Bank, IFC and bilateral donors, had completed more than 130 projects in 25 countries, helping entrepreneurs to identify financial resources and obtain technical and managerial expertise.

UNDP programmes also addressed environmental management, including conservation, pollution control and desertification. Some 14 projects were approved for funding under GEF, including $16 million for regional water pollution control and biodiversity preservation for Lake Tanganyika and the Gulf of Guinea. Support was also provided to a number of countries to prepare national environment programmes.

Two round-table meetings were held: the one for Burkina Faso focused on economic management and a policy framework paper, while that for Equatorial Guinea concentrated on aid coordination, support to the structural adjustment programme and the development of long-term perspective policies. Sectoral consultations were held in Benin, Burkina Faso, Cape Verde, the Central African Republic and the Niger. UNDP supported the democratization process in a number of countries, including Burundi, Eritrea, Malawi, Mali, Namibia, the Niger and Sierra Leone, while humanitarian assistance was provided to several countries in conflict.

Concerning HIV/AIDS, UNDP approved a $15.5 million programme for capacity-building to support national programmes in Uganda. It also developed training materials for use in Kenya, Senegal, Uganda and Zimbabwe.

Asia and the Pacific

By the end of 1993, the fifth (1992-1996) cycle IPF resources for Asia and the Pacific were estimated to amount to $1.3 billion. Cost-sharing contributions from recipient countries and third parties were expected to provide another $100 million. During the year, some 210 projects were approved with a value of about $187 million from IPF and

SPR, and the total expenditure for the region was estimated at $250 million.

The regional programme utilized the programme approach to facilitate the integration of cross-cutting issues into a rational programme with strategic aims. Region-wide projects were focused on only 16 key programmes under the three themes of economic reform, environmental management, and poverty alleviation and human development.

Two large programmes on jute and leather in India gathered momentum, while in Bangladesh, UNDP assisted in developing two major programmes in the urban and education sectors. Thailand was assisted in developing strategies to enhance incomes of the rural population.

Some 125 nationally executed projects were approved for $113 million, representing 59 per cent of the total number of new projects approved and 56 per cent of the total value. China and India were the leading countries implementing projects through national execution, accounting for 35 per cent of total projects under the fifth cycle. A regional centre was opened at Kuala Lumpur, Malaysia, to help Governments discharge their accounting and reporting responsibilities.

In the area of aid coordination, UNDP assisted Viet Nam in preparing and conducting its first donor conference, held in Paris in November, resulting in pledges of $1.86 billion. Agreement was reached with the Asian Development Bank, key Pacific island intercountry organizations, the World Bank and the Pacific island countries that UNDP would continue to be the lead agency supporting the round-table process for interested Governments. Six Pacific island countries were preparing for round-table and sectoral meetings. UNDP helped Mongolia to prepare for its donor meeting and provided support to Cambodia in preparing its national strategy.

A major emphasis was being placed on improving inter-agency coordination, especially among the JCGP partners. In that context, UNDP established a United Nations Inter-Agency Support Unit in Pakistan to assist with planning and implementing the local United Nations common agenda—a methodology for joint programming in population, education, and income generation and employment.

In the human development area, UNDP supported a project in India to collect and analyse human development indicators and the establishment of the Parliamentarians Forum for Human Development. Under the regional programme, NGO assistance was sought to collate seven case studies of successful people's participation in six countries. UNDP's sustainable human development initiative resulted in the publication of the *Pacific Sustainable Human Development Report*, addressing new development options, policies and strategies for the Pacific

islands. Implementation of community-based sustainable human development schemes started on a pilot basis to ensure improved and sustainable quality of life under small island conditions.

With regard to poverty alleviation, UNDP supported the development of a national strategy and action plan for Nepal, implemented a programme in Sri Lanka, and, with other agencies and the World Bank, supported a successful rural water supply and sanitation programme in Pakistan. It also assessed the poverty situation in rural Mongolia, as a result of which the Government and donors requested UNDP to develop a multisectoral comprehensive framework for coordinated donor effort in poverty alleviation.

In environment and natural resources management, UNDP assisted China to formulate a national Agenda 21 programme to form the basis of a high-level donors' conference in 1994. At the regional level, consultative and planning meetings were convened for programmes in agricultural resource management and marine pollution. Under GEF, $36 million, covering activities in over 20 countries and territories in the region, was approved. GEF pre-investment activities in six countries resulted in follow-up capital and technical cooperation investments of about $92 million.

In other action, UNDP developed a comprehensive framework for addressing governance issues in Mongolia and assisted in modernizing election machinery in the Philippines. Also in the Philippines, a significant step was taken towards establishing a regional framework to address the legal, ethical and human rights dimensions of HIV/AIDS with the holding of the Inter-country Consultation on Law, Ethics and HIV (Cebu, 3-6 May).

The regional programme was instrumental in facilitating information and data-sharing among countries in the region, and a database of telecommunication and socio-economic data for telecommunication planning activities was established at the Asian-Pacific Telecommunity, an intergovernmental body.

UNDP, through its resident representatives, coordinated relief assistance in Nepal and Sri Lanka and assumed responsibility in Cambodia for providing and channelling international assistance for demining operations.

Arab States

Programming for the Arab States region for the fifth (1992-1996) cycle was practically finalized during 1993. The Governing Council had approved programmes for all countries except Iraq and Somalia (where the situation did not allow the development of country programmes and where the Administrator would approve programmes on a case-by-case basis) and Oman, where it was decided not to develop a country programme.

A substantial part of technical cooperation in the region was directed at supporting macroeconomic reforms, economic policy development, economic and social development and administrative reform. Social policy, concern with human development and environment and natural resources management were featured in several programmes.

The regional programme for the Arab States was developed in 1993 and approved by an intergovernmental meeting at Sana'a, Yemen, in December. It envisaged launching programmes in sustainable human development, economic integration and trade, and energy. Many projects would be implemented by Arab regional organizations and institutions, and the programme would also cooperate with the Palestinians in the occupied territories.

In Somalia, UNDP supported community-based small-scale programmes in the more peaceful northern region, cooperated with the humanitarian programme of the United Nations Operation in Somalia and, with the World Bank, developed a medium-term rehabilitation plan for the country. It restored drinking water production in Mogadishu and financed the rehabilitation of its airport and seaport. It developed a programme to demobilize and reintegrate the militia in the northwest (see next chapter). The area development schemes programme continued to be successfully implemented in the Sudan, and its philosophy was applied to developing the rehabilitation programme in northern Somalia.

UNDP continued to support economic reform in Egypt and administrative reforms in Kuwait. In Algeria, UNDP supported policy development and mobilized resources and expertise to draw up a new investment code to promote private domestic and foreign investments. It financed the preparation of the programme of administrative rehabilitation in Lebanon and co-sponsored a round table on human development with Tunisia. It supported Djibouti and Morocco in combating the HIV epidemic and Morocco and Lebanon in eliminating illegal drug production.

Europe and the Commonwealth of Independent States

UNDP opened seven new country offices in the region during 1993, bringing the total number of offices in the region to 19 by the end of the year (see also under "Organizational issues" below). The wide area network (WAN), a donor-funded, satellite-based communications network, was operational in seven countries of the region, and a proposal had been prepared to extend the system to additional countries. Once established in all country offices, the WAN would be made available to other users, such as government aid coordination agencies, parliamentarians, NGOs and the media.

In collaboration with the International Atomic Energy Agency (IAEA), UNDP launched an initiative to strengthen nuclear safety and radiation protection infrastructures in the Commonwealth of Independent States (CIS). Following a ministerial-level forum on the subject (Vienna, May), IAEA and UNDP began to prepare a large-scale programme involving all concerned United Nations agencies and interested donors to cover all sectors affected by nuclear safety problems.

The economic and societal transition of the countries of Eastern Europe and the former USSR, including transition to a market economy, privatization, democracy and governance and the social impact of transition, was the focus of a workshop (Berlin, 27 September–7 October), held in cooperation with the East-West Economic Academy. All resident representatives from the region as well as several resident representatives from other regions facing similar transitional problems attended. (For further information on transition economies, see the previous chapter and under "New recipient countries" below.)

Support for building national capacity for external resource management was a top priority for UNDP activities in the region. In collaboration with the World Bank, UNDP established external resource management agencies in Kazakhstan and Kyrgyzstan and trained government officials in several countries. It also supported Belarus in designing its aid management mechanism.

A number of integrated regional programmes were designed or launched in 1993, covering local economic development, inter-modal transport information systems, economic and social statistics and human development data, inter-republic trade, water and civil society, and strengthening of foreign affairs ministries. UNDP also supported projects in democratization, improved governance and strengthened local participation in the countries in transition.

In the area of energy and the environment, the project document for the GEF Black Sea programme was signed, and the Programme Coordination Unit was opened at Istanbul, Turkey. The work plan of the GEF Danube River Basin programme was completed and work on a strategic action plan started. Programmes were also launched in the human and social sector development sectors.

UNDP participated in United Nations consolidated appeals for Armenia, Azerbaijan and the former Yugoslavia for projects related to rehabilitation and reconstruction. It carried out a number of humanitarian assistance and reconstruction activities in the former Yugoslavia, including Croatia.

Latin America and the Caribbean

In 1993, as an important part of its agenda in Latin America and the Caribbean, UNDP addressed the problem of social reform.

That subject and its main issue, poverty, were addressed by the Forum on Social Reform and Poverty, jointly organized with the Inter-American Development Bank (IDB) in February. Joint IDB/UNDP meetings were also held in several countries to define social reform policies and specific problems to be financed by IDB with UNDP execution of technical cooperation elements. Other major items on the UNDP agenda for the region were: governance and UNDP's capacity to exercise leadership in defining relations between various segments of society; the need for State reform and guarantees to citizens affected by the privatization process; and environment and development. Those items constituted the basis for UNDP advocacy in sustainable human development, which had been well received in many countries.

UNDP-supported activities at the national level on social reform and poverty alleviation were most evident in Argentina. Colombia also channelled a large share of its IPF resources and cost-sharing funds to improve health and education. Activities in this area were continued in Chile, Mexico, Peru and Central America.

In the area of governance, UNDP facilitated equal opportunities in health and education and continued to strengthen municipal and provincial governments. Ecuador addressed this issue and the consolidation of democracy through an education programme on human rights for the armed forces, and Panama requested UNDP assistance in organizing a national meeting on unity and human development. The Dominican Republic requested assistance in launching the National Consultation on Strategic Development Challenges, in preparation for the 1994 Presidential elections.

UNDP helped Peru to re-establish its rating on the international credit market and supported its privatization programme, and assisted Brazil in its efforts to become a global trader in computer software. In Colombia, a UNDP project covering 47 per cent of the indigenous population in the rural areas addressed the need to empower communities affected by armed conflict, poverty and lack of social services.

In the area of the environment, the portfolio of approved projects financed by GEF grew to 18, for a total of some $60 million.

Global and interregional programmes

UNDP's global and interregional programmes helped developing countries to benefit from international scientific knowledge, research and experience while enhancing their own national capacities.

UNDP investments in high-risk/high-reward activities achieved breakthroughs in a number of fields vital to developing countries and attracted complementary funding. The global programme supported non-governmental research institutes, which had developed improved strains of rice, potatoes, fish and other foods, and helped establish networks to study and monitor global environmental concerns. It promoted the sharing of knowledge and applied research and information exchanges and databanks.

In terms of environmental activities, the UNDP global programme undertook six GEF projects valued at $20.4 million, including a $4.8 million programme to establish monitoring stations in Algeria, Argentina, Brazil, China, Indonesia and Kenya to measure concentrations of harmful gases in the atmosphere and a $2.6 million project to establish centres for training in integrated ocean and coastal management in Africa, Asia, Latin America and Oceania.

In 1993, UNDP increased by $1 million its support to sustainable development networks, seven of which were in operation at the end of the year. It supported high-priority agricultural research to create and disseminate high-yielding, disease- and pest-resistant food products and funded a $4.6 million project to reduce the use of costly and dangerous pesticides in potato farming.

UNDP helped other United Nations specialized agencies and organizations to respond to the HIV epidemic. Several joint activities were initiated with specialized agencies, financial institutions and NGOs. It sought to strengthen national capacity to undertake research and study the extent and nature of the psychological, social and economic causes and consequences of the epidemic and to link research to policy and programme development. UNDP also facilitated the establishment of networks on law, ethics, and human rights and HIV in Africa, Asia and the Pacific, and Latin America and the Caribbean to strengthen their capacity to respond to the epidemic.

Regional integration

In a January report to the Governing Council,[(25)] the UNDP Administrator described UNDP's support for regional economic integration during the fourth (1987-1991) cycle and the approach for the fifth (1992-1996) cycle. He stated that the most visible motor of regional economic integration was the development of trade and the creation of institutions to promote the expansion of intraregional trade. The emphasis for the future might shift towards regional economic cooperation rather than economic integration. In this regard, the emerging priorities of UNDP were consistent with changes taking place at the global level, with emphasis on cooperation in those areas linking regional efforts with changes in global trading arrangements. The Trade and Development Board of the United Nations Conference on Trade and Development (UNCTAD) also considered regional integration issues (see PART THREE, Chapter IV).

On 17 June,[8] the Council took note of the Administrator's report.

Programme planning and management

In response to a 1991 Governing Council request,[26] the Administrator, in March, submitted a report on the efficiency of programming and the comparative advantages of UNDP.[27] He stated that UNDP's comparative advantage in providing technical cooperation was created by international agreements and mandates; the resources available for administration and technical cooperation programmes and its managerial capacity to implement them effectively; and the resulting development of products, expertise and relationships. UNDP's technical cooperation was based on ideological and commercial neutrality and impartiality in sensitive areas; multilateralism and universality; its multisectoral nature; and its network of field offices. The combination of those characteristics was unique to UNDP.

UNDP was extremely effective in the areas for which it had functional comparative advantages, particularly in relation to multisectoral and cross-sectoral activities, donor coordination, promotion of regional integration and South-South cooperation, global initiatives on issues of major significance, and the development of innovative approaches to the design and delivery of technical cooperation. There was a major opportunity for UNDP to develop further its comparative advantages in the four substantive areas that were emerging as key priorities: economic management and public sector reform; social development, poverty alleviation and community participation in development; environmental protection and sustainable natural resource management; and productive capacity, involving technology transfer and private sector development support. Full realization of UNDP's comparative advantages would involve better utilization of the field office network, more effective mobilization of the expertise of the United Nations system, more effective networking with research institutions, NGOs and other sources of expertise, and recruitment of more specialized and technically qualified staff.

It would also be necessary to identify more precisely UNDP's role in the four substantive areas mentioned, refine its relationship with other agencies in similar fields, maximize linkages and complementarity in specific fields, and assist national authorities to identify more exactly their needs and priorities. There was also a need for greater dynamism in realigning resources to address new and emerging problems, to reformulate objectives and to reshape the institution.

In response to a 1992 Council request,[19] the Administrator submitted a report on progress in harmonizing programme cycles and programme procedures among members of JCGP,[28] particularly the harmonization of terminology, the simplification of financial and reporting procedures and payments to government staff. He stated that harmonization had occurred in about one third of the countries served.

National execution

In response to a 1992 Governing Council request,[29] the Administrator, in May, presented a report on national execution and agency support costs.[30] He stated that new projects approved for national execution amounted to 30 per cent of all new approvals in 1991 and to 37 per cent in 1992. This trend was expected to accelerate in 1993 and future years. Preliminary data also indicated that agency implementation of nationally executed projects had increased significantly over the fourth (1987-1991) cycle. Under the fifth (1992-1996) cycle, it was estimated that 40 per cent of all new approvals of IPF-financed activities would be assigned for national execution. The Administrator also discussed new support cost arrangements (see below).

On 18 June,[31] the Council welcomed the increased use of national execution in UNDP-assisted programmes and projects and called on recipient countries, with the assistance of UNDP, to assess national capacities for carrying out execution responsibilities before project approval. It encouraged greater use of United Nations specialized agencies in the design, technical appraisal and backstopping of nationally executed projects.

Capacity-building

In response to a 1992 Governing Council request that he report to it annually on national capacity-building, the Administrator, in January, submitted a report on the subject.[32] The report examined the background and conceptual framework of capacity-building, discussed ways of assessing its achievements and outlined a framework for national capacity-building. Although some valuable capacities were built as a result of efforts by UNDP and other donors, especially in the areas of infrastructure, vocational training, health statistics, civil aviation and meteorology, there was concern within the development community regarding the identification of more coherent strategies and instruments.

The report listed issues to be addressed in formulating capacity-building activities, including its relevance to core national development objectives;

the national policy context for the programme activities; the extent to which the capacity of non-governmental as well as governmental institutions was being built; coordination mechanisms and sustainability; and incorporation of past lessons in the delivery of technical cooperation in support of capacity-building. UNDP support included the programme approach, national execution and aid coordination. In addition, the successor arrangement for agency support costs facilitated the development of programme frameworks. UNDP support to Governments included the capacity to define and manage a long-term vision of social and economic development, to formulate policies and substantive orientations for the short and medium term; to manage and implement national programmes; and to monitor and evaluate the impact of national programmes. The UNDP country strategy document also addressed capacity-building issues and set out the specific instruments through which the national strategy for capacity-building would be supported by UNDP.

On 17 June,[8] the Council took note of the Administrator's report.

Capacity 21

In a January report on environment and development,[33] the Administrator stated that Capacity 21, launched by him and noted by the General Assembly in 1992,[34] was designed to aid developing countries in formulating and implementing sustainable development strategies and national capacity-building programmes. It had been established following the adoption by the United Nations Conference on Environment and Development of Agenda 21,[35] which UNDP had been given a significant role in implementing.

The programme, which became fully operational in June 1993, would be managed within the provisions for SPR. A management committee had been established to screen programme proposals, approve funding, monitor and evaluate implementation and ensure coordination with regional and country programmes. An initial target of $100 million was proposed for its pilot phase. By the end of 1993, 11 Governments had pledged a total of $33 million.

On 19 February,[36] the Governing Council approved the Administrator's decision to launch Capacity 21 and decided that UNDP should present specific and detailed proposals for its implementation to the Council in June, including recommendations on the distribution of resources.

In response to that request, the Administrator issued in May a report[37] in which he stated that Capacity 21 was to complement capacity-building initiatives of such facilities as GEF, the 1987 Montreal Protocol for the Protection of the Ozone Layer,[38] UNSO, UNCDF and country IPFs. Con-

sultations on the programme's scope and focus had taken place with donor and recipient countries, United Nations system agencies and other partners, which had provided a basis for identifying programmes for funding. The programme was to begin in 10 countries in 1993 and in a further 15 to 20 in 1994. Preparatory activities in some 30 to 40 countries would form the basis for full programmes in the 1995-1996 period.

On 18 June,[39] the Council requested the Administrator to proceed with implementing Capacity 21. It decided to distribute resources according to the criteria applied to SPR and supported the Administrator's intention to devote 40 per cent of the overall budget of Capacity 21 to LDCs. The Council endorsed the proposal to evaluate Capacity 21 at the end of the fifth (1992-1996) programming cycle with a view to incorporating its activities into UNDP's regular programming.

NGO collaboration and grass-roots activities

In response to a 1990 Governing Council decision,[40] the Administrator submitted a report on UNDP cooperation with NGOs and grass-roots organizations.[41] The report indicated an expansion in the scope and level of this cooperation through programmes that supported participatory, community-based development; promoted dialogue and collaboration between NGOs and grass-roots organizations, Governments and multilateral agencies; encouraged and supported their involvement in sustainable development activities; and strengthened the impact of the development efforts of NGOs and grass-roots groups. In particular, cooperation expanded in the areas of grass-roots participation in poverty eradication and environment and natural resource management. Such cooperation was increasingly reflected in country and regional programmes and initiatives. Activities were funded from IPF, global and inter-regional programmes, SPR and extrabudgetary funds.

The report proposed measures for strengthening cooperation, including adjusting UNDP's policies and procedures within the framework of country programmes; consulting with NGOs and grass-roots organizations during the elaboration of advisory notes and country programmes; participation of programme beneficiaries in the elaboration and evaluation of UNDP-funded programmes and projects; and including NGOs and grass-roots organizations in the consultative process at the country, regional and global levels regarding the development of strategies, programmes and projects addressing areas of focus for the fifth cycle.

On 17 June,[8] the Governing Council took note of the Administrator's report.

Management Development Programme

In a February report,[42] the Administrator described the implementation of the Management Development Programme (MDP), established by the Governing Council in 1988.[43] By December 1992, project activities for management improvement, fully or partially financed by UNDP, had been approved in 51 countries for a total expenditure of $50 million of MDP funds, $26 million of IPF resources, and $10 million from non-UNDP sources. UNDP also attracted cost-sharing and parallel financing from other bilateral and multilateral agencies. The programme was to be evaluated during 1993, and guidelines and working manuals were to be issued to promote needs assessment and provide guidance for programme design and formulation. Special attention was given to the role of and opportunities for women in management positions. National execution was used as the preferred mode of project implementation.

The shift to market economies, the rise in democratic systems and the collapse of the USSR provided new impetus for MDP-assisted reforms. In this context, MDP would help Governments to build the institutional and organizational capacity to manage economic, financial and administrative reform, including civil service and organizational development.

On 17 June,[8] the Council took note of the Administrator's report.

Programme evaluation

The Administrator's tenth annual report on programme evaluation[44] presented a synopsis of the evaluation strategy being pursued during the fifth (1992-1996) programming cycle and summarized the findings and recommendations of major evaluations undertaken in 1992. It examined the status of other work undertaken by the Central Evaluation Office (CEO), including a study of the extent to which feedback and lessons from evaluation reports were internalized within the UNDP system; highlighted cross-cutting issues emerging from CEO's work in 1992; and gave an account of other evaluation work. It also presented the CEO work plan for evaluation activities in 1993-1994.

On 18 June,[45] the Governing Council noted the impending issuance of revised and strengthened guidelines for country programme evaluations and requested the Administrator to include, as a biennial element in his annual report on evaluation, a statistical and quantitative analysis of evaluation reports. He was also requested to report in 1994 on the ongoing study on and proposal for a strategic approach to feedback throughout UNDP, including at the field level, and to undertake more joint evaluations with other United Nations organizations and Member States to promote common evaluation principles and practices. The Council urged the Administrator to continue supporting action towards a common system for reporting the degree and rate of success or failure in the achievement of programme and project objectives.

Programme management

In April,[46] in response to a 1992 Governing Council request,[47] the Administrator presented a report on programme management issues, including decentralization and the programme approach. He stated that the emphasis of country programmes in the fifth programming cycle was on supporting major national priorities with the aim of achieving identifiable and sustainable results in institutional and ecological terms. At the same time, monitoring and evaluation procedures were being revised to strengthen the capacity of in-country systems to keep track of programme implementation. They would also provide early warning for issues requiring corrective action. UNDP's guiding principles for its programme approach were issued in April, and the outline of a programme support document had been elaborated as the standard format for UNDP support to national programmes. The latter, which was being used on a trial basis, was designed to be responsive to different country situations and requirements as well as to provide information on progress in capacity-building and other outputs and to ensure financial accountability.

In relation to decentralization, emphasis was placed on expanding the scope of resident representatives for managing country programmes and their own administrative affairs. It aimed at improving UNDP's efficiency and effectiveness in the context of increased budgetary constraints. Accordingly, financial authority for project approvals was increased to $1 million for resident representatives and to $3 million for directors of the regional bureaux. Authority was delegated to resident representatives to formulate and approve the individual components of national programmes cleared by the Action Committee. Procedures were also introduced to balance this increased financial authority with more accountability and to review programme progress through the field office work-planning process. UNDP was also working with inter-agency groups to coordinate and harmonize programme management issues.

On 18 June,[15] the Council took note of the Administrator's report.

Fifth and sixth programming cycles

In May, the Administrator submitted a report on matters relating to the fifth (1992-1996) and sixth (1997-2001) programming cycles.[48] He provided information on the status of fifth cycle resources and programmes, the planning framework for the remaining years of the cycle, and a list of and explanations for IPFs for the cycle. It also discussed the methodology for allocating programme resources in the sixth cycle. The Administrator reported that in 1993 there was a further erosion of resources due to reductions in contributions and the strengthening of the dollar. Based on estimates of contributions for the remaining years of the fifth cycle, he had established a revised planning framework in 1992, assuming a growth rate of resources of only 4 per cent rather than the target of 8 per cent set in 1990.[49] After further monitoring of the resource outlook, it had become necessary to revise again the planning parameters for the fifth cycle and to advise UNDP field offices that programme planning should be carried out under the assumption that only 75 per cent of established IPFs would be available. Accordingly, IPF expenditure targets for 1993 and 1994 were revised further to $640 million and $590 million, respectively. Those resource constraints and reductions in expenditure targets had obviously affected programme approvals during 1992 and 1993. The projected reductions in IPF expenditures would require reformulation of expenditure patterns of certain approved country programmes and even deferral or elimination of priority programmes and projects.

In response to a 1991 Governing Council request,[50] the Administrator also presented his preliminary views on issues relating to the mobilization and allocation of resources for the sixth programming cycle, based on experience with earlier cycles. He stated that UNDP would contribute to the discussion currently going on in the General Assembly on funding mechanisms for operational activities, including the possibility of multi-year negotiated pledges, and would report to the Council in 1994.

On 17 June,[51] the Council requested the Administrator to continue consultations on the preparations for the sixth programming cycle and to submit a conceptual paper on the issue to its 1994 session.

New recipient countries

In response to a 1992 Governing Council request,[52] the Administrator, in January, submitted a report on provisional activities of programmes undertaken between June and December 1992 in the Baltic States and CIS.[53] He had proposed an integrated strategy for United Nations assistance in those countries, with the highest priority being support for the transition process for which UNDP had established short-term strategies. Inter-agency coordination was being pursued with JCGP and ACC, while specific agreements were being reached with several international organizations. Nine field offices were being opened, and arrangements were under way to attend to requests for field offices for the remaining countries. The total cost of activities for the 1992-1993 biennium amounted to $5.5 million. High priority was being given to capacity-building, particularly aid management and resource mobilization. Programme resources came from core funds, trust funds and product-specific fund-raising, mainly through multilateral regional packages. A target of $100 million per year had been set. UNDP's role was evolving towards human development and the establishment of new equitable forms of regional cooperation.

On 19 February,[54] the Council took note of the Administrator's report.

Also on 19 February,[55] the Council, welcoming Bosnia and Herzegovina, Croatia, the Czech Republic, Georgia, the Slovak Republic, Slovenia and Tajikistan as recipient countries in UNDP, approved the allocation of IPFs and requested the Administrator to inform it at its fortieth session of any revised basic data and the effect on IPF computation. The Administrator was authorized to proceed with programme development in those countries, taking into account other development activities being carried out there.

On 18 June,[56] the Council also welcomed Eritrea and the former Yugoslav Republic of Macedonia as recipient countries in UNDP. It approved the allocation of IPFs and requested the Administrator to inform it in 1994 of any revised basic data and its effect on IPF computation. It authorized the Administrator to proceed with programme development in the two countries, taking into account other development activities being undertaken.

Financing

In his annual review of the financial situation,[57] the Administrator reported that total income in 1993 was $1.35 billion, compared with $1.53 billion in 1992, while expenditures remained at the same level of $1.4 billion. Consequently, UNDP's general resources declined to $149 million as at 31 December 1993 from $221 million as at 31 December 1992. Income from voluntary contributions totalled $897 million, a reduction of $180 million, or 15 per cent, from 1992 final figures. Miscellaneous income increased to $23.9 million as a result of reduced foreign exchange losses, while interest income remained stable. Cost-sharing contributions grew from $294 million in 1992 to $376 million in 1993.

IPF expenditures decreased by some 16 per cent to $609 million in 1993, in line with the need to reduce IPF targets, while cost-sharing expenditure increased from $225 million to $341 million. SPR expenditures fell from $50.6 million in 1992 to $46 million in 1993. Expenditure under national execution rose to $173 million, representing a 72 per cent increase over 1992 levels. Overall, 1993 expenditure exceeded income by $67 million.

The Administrator reported that the situation with respect to the growth levels of voluntary contributions had stabilized but the decline in UNDP general resources was expected to continue, despite expected reductions in total expenditure and modest growth in income. He urged Governments to increase voluntary contributions to the core resources of the organization, which were expected to remain flat in 1994.

On 18 June,[58] the Governing Council took note of the annual review of the financial situation for 1992.[59] It noted with concern the level of resources expected to be available in 1993 and 1994 and urged Governments to increase their contributions to UNDP in line with the planning assumptions of the fifth (1992-1996) programming cycle.

The Council noted the Administrator's efforts to develop strategies to reduce expenditure due to the reduced resource flows and requested him to protect UNDP's continued financial viability and integrity. It approved the retroactive request of the United Nations Educational, Scientific and Cultural Organization for additional support costs arising from the significant appreciation of the French franc over the period 1989 and 1990. In addition, it noted the intention of the Administrator to provide a final report upon the closure of the Special Measures Fund for LDCs.

Budgets

Revised 1992-1993 budget

The Administrator presented to the Governing Council revised budget estimates for 1992-1993,[60] along with observations of the Advisory Committee on Administrative and Budgetary Questions (ACABQ).[61] Estimates for UNDP core activities amounted to $479.6 million gross and $447.6 million net, representing a decrease of $1.5 million. There was a volume decrease for UNV of $438,000 due to the application of the staffing formula, and a volume increase for the Office of Project Services (OPS) of $526,000 relating to the core budget and $3.2 million relating to the extrabudgetary account.

On 18 June,[62] the Council approved the revised budget estimates for OPS and the UNV programme, as well as revised appropriations of $609,564,700 gross to finance the 1992-1993 biennial budget. It resolved that income estimates of $32 million should be used to offset the gross appropriations, resulting in net appropriations of $577,564,700. The Council requested the Ad-

ministrator, in line with the recommendation of ACABQ, to include a concise statement of the Programme's current and projected income in the executive summary of future submissions of the biennial budget estimates, and invited him to consider further changes to achieve consistency among budget documents and financial review and expenditure reports.

1994-1995 budget

UNDP budget estimates for 1994-1995, submitted by the Administrator in March,[60] totalled $628.4 million. That amount comprised appropriations of $486.1 million gross, or $449.4 million net, for UNDP core activities, $111.5 million for programme support and development activities, and $30.8 million for trust funds (UNCDF, UNFSTD/UNRFNRE, UNSO and UNIFEM).

The net core budget of $449.4 million, which included support for United Nations operational activities, compared with the appropriation level for 1992-1993 of $449.1 million. The overall volume reduction totalled $41.8 million. Of the total core budget, $336.7 million related to the field, while $149.4 related to headquarters, representing a reduction of $31.3 million and $10.5 million respectively. However, there were core field budget increases of $880,000 for implementation of the regional service centre concept and $1 million for use in CIS.

The total increase for the programme support and development activities budget for 1994-1995 was $10.2 million, mainly due to cost adjustments. Concerning trust funds, with budgets estimated at $30.8 million, there were volume reductions of $1.4 million and an increase of $0.3 million.

In its observations on the 1994-1995 budget estimates,[61] ACABQ recommended that a concise statement of UNDP's current and projected income be included in the executive summary of the Administrator's future report on the budget.

On 18 June,[62] the Governing Council approved appropriations in the amount of $628,421,000 gross to finance the 1994-1995 biennial budget and resolved that the income estimates of $36,700,000 be used to offset the gross appropriations, resulting in net appropriations of $591,721,100. It endorsed the Administrator's proposal, in relation to alternative sources of financing for the non-UNDP-related workload, to charge the full costs of such support to the UNDP budget and to reflect them separately by introducing a new appropriation line entitled "Support to the operational activities of the United Nations".

The Council welcomed the Administrator's proposal to implement volume reductions in the core budget of both headquarters and field offices without negatively affecting programme delivery and approved his proposals relating to cost adjustments, in particular the application of savings earned in 1993 up to a ceiling of 1.5 per cent of the 1992-1993 core appropriation. The Council urged the Administrator to be innovative and cost-effective in utilizing core resources allocated to the field presence in the Baltic States, CIS and Georgia; to give priority, when allocating core resources, to those countries with the lowest levels of per capita gross national product and the highest level of IPF and aggregate programme resources; and to ensure an integrated United Nations approach and presence. It requested him to conclude an agreement with the United Nations on the joint funding of the United Nations interim field offices in CIS and Georgia and to report to the Council on the question in 1994 in his revised budget estimates for 1994-1995.

It supported the Administrator's initiatives with regard to a regional service centre concept, in particular the involvement of commercial audit and accounting firms in providing audit and accounts examination services to field offices, and requested him to keep it informed of further developments in the context of the revised budget estimates for 1994-1995. It approved the continuation of posts for the Humanitarian Programme and called on the Administrator to include separate presentations on the programme in future budget documents, delineating all costs to be charged to it.

Under programme support and development activities, the Council approved the establishment of 41 sustainable development national officer posts and the request to establish a limited network of up to 22 national officer posts to support the resident coordinator/resident representative in the national response to the HIV/AIDS pandemic, subject to review.

The Council also approved the proposed 1994-1995 budget estimates for the Office for Project Services and the budget and staffing proposals relating UNCDF, UNIFEM, UNRFNRE/UNFSTD and UNSO.

It requested the Administrator to report in 1994 on experience gained in the piloting of short-term, non-permanent contracts, including consultations with the International Civil Service Commission. It decided to extend the pilot phase relating to reclassification and to review the implementation of the pilot arrangement, including its continuation, and reclassifications made on the basis of a report which the Administrator was requested to submit in the context of his budget proposals for 1996-1997.

Audit reports

The Governing Council considered the financial report and audited financial statements of the Board of Auditors on UNDP for the biennium ending 31 December 1991,[63] the views of ACABQ

thereon,[64] and the comments of the Administrator on the Board of Auditors' report.[65] It also examined the audited accounts of the participating and executing agencies as at December 1991[66] and a note by the Administrator summarizing observations of the external auditors of the executing agencies on their 1991 accounts relating to funds allocated to them by UNDP.[67]

On 18 June,[68] the Council noted with approval the Administrator's proposal to institutionalize a mechanism to follow up the external and internal audit recommendations as part of the proposed Office of Budget and Management. It supported his expansion of audit coverage through the regional service centre concept and urged him to take up the issue of timely audited statements from executing agencies in the appropriate inter-agency forums and to ensure strict adherence to established rules and procedures regarding the hiring of consultants. He was also urged to monitor the implementation of the revised instructions to be issued in 1993.

The Council requested the Administrator to streamline UNDP's project appraisal and approval procedures and to finalize measures to address the recommendations of the Board of Auditors regarding adequate property control, including accountability.

Financial regulations

In May,[69] the Administrator submitted a report on proposed financial regulation 4.6, which defined the term "readily usable" with respect to the currency of voluntary contributions, and on other matters on which consensus had not been achieved in 1992. The report reproduced the texts of those items for consideration by the Council.

On 18 June,[70] the Council approved the following text as Financial Regulation 4.6:

"In view of the multilateral nature of the Programme, non-recipient donor countries which make their voluntary contributions wholly or partly in non-convertible currencies are requested to pay a gradually increasing share of their contributions in convertible currencies."

The Council also approved the following text as Financial Regulation 4.7:

"Meanwhile, entities headquartered in a net donor country which has contributed in a non-convertible currency shall be reimbursed for services and equipment purchased under the Programme only in the currency of that country where such a currency is accumulated and until such accumulation is used; conversely, if, when utilizing a non-convertible contribution, costs are incurred in other currencies, these shall be reimbursed to UNDP in a convertible currency."

The Financial Regulations were renumbered appropriately.

Procurement

In response to a 1991 Governing Council request,[26] the Administrator, in May, submitted a report on the procurement of goods and services from developing countries.[71] The report provided an overview of procurement from developing countries by the United Nations system between 1988 and 1992, discussed improvements made to increase such procurement and identified the main constraints and limitations preventing further procurement from developing countries. The Administrator confirmed that procurement from developing countries under UNDP funding had increased significantly since 1988 (from $78 million to $103 million in 1992), due to an increase in national execution and additional delegation of authority by OPS to the field. However, there were still many constraints on the part of developing countries themselves. The Administrator believed that the Inter-Agency Procurement Services Office (IAPSO) should continue to enhance its service and coordinating role for research and development and information-sharing activities. He recommended that the Inter-Agency Procurement Working Group (IAPWG) develop guidelines based on those measures, including the strengthening of focal points and the establishment of databases at the field and country level as well as training programmes for procurement staff. He cautioned the Council as to its expectations of significant results in the near future, especially in percentage terms, but stressed that progress would continue to be made in terms of the greater delegation of authority and decentralization of functions and processes and with the increased use of national execution as the modality of preference.

On 18 June,[72] the Council commended the progress made in increasing procurement from developing countries, as well as the research and development activities of IAPSO. It encouraged Governments to address the constraints and limitations, including attitudinal barriers, to promoting procurement from developing countries. It urged UNDP, through IAPWG, to encourage the United Nations, its funds, programmes and specialized agencies to increase procurement from developing and underutilized major donor countries and supported IAPWG in further defining and improving the accuracy of the data provided to IAPSO for its annual reporting to the Governing Council and to the Economic and Social Council. The Council requested UNDP, through IAPWG, to improve existing procurement or supplier databases to include greater product and skill specification, and stressed the need for the United Nations system to improve its rostering and shortlisting systems and procedures to ensure greater geographical representation from suppliers from developing countries and underutilized major donor countries.

UNDP-administered funds

During 1993, 10 new trust funds were established by the Administrator on behalf of UNDP.[73] They were the Trust Fund for the UNDP History Project, Trust Fund in Support of Peace-Building Activities in El Salvador, Trust Fund for Democratization Support and the Electoral Process in Guinea-Bissau, UNDP/Denmark Trust Fund for Electoral Assistance Project in Burundi, UNDP Trust Fund for Human Resources Development in South Africa, UNDP Trust Fund for Capacity-Building in De-mining Operations for Cambodia, UNDP Trust Fund for Council on Health Research for Development, UNDP Trust Fund for the Reintegration of Demobilized Military Personnel in Mozambique, UNDP/Norway Trust Fund for Assistance to the Electoral Process in Mozambique and the UNDP/Switzerland Trust Fund for Aid Management and Aid Coordination in Kyrgyzstan. Contributions received for those funds totalled $16.3 million. In addition, one trust fund was established on behalf of UNCDF and eight on behalf of UNV. Contributions for those arrangements totalled $1.6 million.

During 1993, contributions to the 75 trust funds and sub-trust funds in operation totalled $73.8 million, while expenditures amounted to $76.5 milllion.[74]

Special Programme Resources

In 1993,[57] total SPR expenditures, representing resources set aside by the Governing Council to finance specified types of programme activities during each programming cycle, amounted to $74 million, of which $27.6 million was charged against cost-sharing contributions, resulting in a net expenditure of $46.4 million. Expenditures on SPR activities approved by the Council in 1992 were grouped under the categories of disaster mitigation, thematic activities, other special/and or new activities, aid coordination and programme development.

Support cost arrangements

In response to a 1992 Governing Council request,[75] the Administrator submitted a report on national execution and agency support costs,[30] which examined the status of implementation of the new support cost arrangements established in 1992,[75] training programmes on their application and the status of financial provisions for them. It also reported on implementation of the technical support services at the programme level (TSS-1) work programme for 1992-1993; preparation of the TSS-1 work programme for 1994-1995; status of the technical support services at the project level (TSS-2) facility; issues relating to the smaller technical agencies; and monitoring and evaluation of the cost arrangements.

The report stated that, following field testing of the guidelines for implementation of the new agency support cost arrangements, several improvements and refinements had been incorporated and a revised version had been issued. The guidelines would continue to be field tested in 1993 and incorporated into UNDP's Programme and Projects Manual. Some 12 subregional and 9 national workshops were held between October 1992 and February 1993 to train field representatives from Governments, agencies and UNDP in the new arrangements.

With regard to financial provisions, the Administrator noted that the considerable erosion in the resource outlook for 1993 and future years had obliged him to establish a revised planning framework for the fifth (1992-1996) programming cycle. Since the financial provisions for SPR, approved by the Council in 1991,[76] were based on higher projections for programmable resources, adjustments to individual components of the provisions had become necessary.

In 1991,[76] the Council had provided that, in respect of the first $140 million of nationally implemented projects approved for the fifth cycle, 10 per cent of their value should be added to the relevant IPF sub-lines and $17 million had been earmarked for that purpose. However, nationally executed projects approved under the old arrangements amounted to $304 million, far exceeding the original estimate, and the identification of the first $140 million of nationally implemented projects had proven to be operationally difficult. In addition, in a 1990 decision,[77] the Council had specified that IPF add-on would continue to be paid for nationally executed projects approved before the end of the fourth (1987-1991) cycle, leading several Governments and UNDP field offices to continue planning utilization of such add-on resources for an interim period in the fifth cycle.

The Administrator proposed, therefore, that instead of adding the specific resources to the IPF sub-line, the provisions for the IPF add-on legislation continue for one more year. Thus, he intended to provide 13 per cent of 1992 project expenditures relating to nationally executed projects approved before 1 January 1992 as an add-on to IPFs of the countries concerned. From 1993 onwards, the 1991 provisions relating to the IPF sub-line would be applicable.

On 18 June,[31] the Council encouraged further training in the new arrangements for agency support costs and endorsed the Administrator's proposals on the provisions of IPF add-on in respect of nationally implemented projects approved before 1 January 1992. It welcomed progress in implementing the TSS-1 work programme for 1992-1993 and agreed that the formulation of the 1994-1995 work programme should be governed by national priorities and needs. The Administrator was requested to submit the 1994-1995 work programme in 1994. The Council urged that approvals of TSS-2 funding of UNDP-financed projects be accelerated and that specialized agencies be more involved in the design and formulation of such projects. It invited the Administrator to continue consultations with the smaller technical agencies on their full incorporation in the new support cost arrangements. The Council requested the Administrator to consult with Member States on the implementation of an external evaluation of the new arrangements to be carried out during 1994 and to report back to it.

Sectoral support

In a report to the Governing Council's special session,[78] the Administrator stated that the Industrial Development Board of the United Nations Industrial Development Organization (UNIDO) had requested the Council to consider increasing the annual allocation as of 1993 for the UNIDO Country Director Programme. The current allocation of $3.8 million had been established in 1991.[79] The Administrator therefore proposed an annual allocation of $5.4 million for 1992 and $4.8 million for 1993.

On 18 February,[80] the Council authorized an amount of up to $10.2 million for the UNIDO Country Director Programme for 1992 and 1993, from the total of $19 million earmarked for funding the programme in the fifth (1992-1996) programming cycle under the Sectoral Support Programme. The authorized reallocation would result in a corresponding reduction of yearly allocations for the last three years of the cycle. The Council invited UNIDO to manage the programme within the overall resources allocated and to sustain it through its own resources, subject to review by the Council in 1994.

Preparatory assistance

In a report to the Governing Council's special session,[81] the Administrator stated that, following the Council's 1992 approval of global and interregional programmes for the fifth programming cycle,[82] a number of new initiatives had been launched, necessitating approval of preparatory assistance projects. In view of the increase of the global IPF from $63 million to $112 million for the fifth cycle, due to escalating costs of short-term consultancy services and increased time required for preparatory work on research-oriented projects, the Administrator recommended that the authority granted to him for all global preparatory assistance projects be increased from its current level of $125,000 to $250,000.

On 18 February,[83] the Council approved the Administrator's recommendation.

Organizational issues

Staff-related matters

In response to a 1992 Governing Council request,[47] the Administrator included in his revised budget estimates for 1994-1995[60] a report on his review of the senior management structure of UNDP against the background of the restructuring of the United Nations Secretariat. In line with the Secretary-General's policy of reducing overall the number of high-level posts in the United Nations, the Administrator proposed the elimination or downgrading of two posts at the Assistant Secretary-General (ASG) level (the post of Assistant Administrator for the Bureau for External Relations and one of the posts of Director, Regional Bureau) and 10 posts at the D-2 level.

On 18 June,[62] the Council endorsed the Administrator's proposals with regard to the senior management structure of UNDP, especially those maintaining the level of posts of Directors of Regional Bureaux, Director of the Bureau for Programme Policy and Evaluation and Director of the Bureau for Finance and Administration at the ASG level, with the exception of the proposal to downgrade the post of Director, Regional Bureau of Arab States from ASG to the D-2 level. He was asked to review the senior management structure and report to the Council in 1994.

Office of Project Services

As part of the second phase of the restructuring of the United Nations Secretariat, the Secretary-General created DDSMS, into which he proposed incorporating the functions of OPS.

On 19 February,[84] the Governing Council requested its President to bring to the attention of the General Assembly and the Fifth (Administrative and Budgetary) Committee its concerns regarding the need to consider the Council's continuing role in relation to OPS; the need for OPS to maintain its autonomy and improve its effectiveness and efficiency; the financial, administrative and personnel implications for the UNDP budget; and the need to ensure the maximum delegation of authority to the resident coordinator for implementing OPS activities.

General Assembly consideration. Following Fifth Committee consideration of a March report of the Secretary-General,[85] in which he outlined OPS functions and indicated that he had established a task force to review procedures for incorporating OPS into DDSMS on 1 January 1994, the Assembly, on 6 May, adopted **resolution 47/212 B**, in which it noted that the modalities for integrating OPS into DDSMS would first be considered by the UNDP Governing Council and then by the Assembly, in the light of the work of the Secretary-General's task force.

Governing Council consideration. By a June note,[86] the Secretary-General submitted the report of his task force on OPS to the Governing Council. The task force defined the mandate, functions and governance of and the basic authorities for OPS, which would be a semi-autonomous and self-financing body within DDSMS. It proposed the establishment of an OPS management board reporting to the Governing Council and the General Assembly.

The UNDP Administrator, in a June report,[87] discussed the task force's recommendations and addressed the Council's concerns, raised in February. It recommended that the Council endorse the modalities for the transfer of OPS as set out by the task force and approved by the Secretary-General.

On 18 June,[88] the Council noted that its present supervisory responsibilities for OPS and those of the Economic and Social Council and the General Assembly, including the Council's responsibility for approving the OPS administrative budget, would remain unchanged. It underlined the continuing need for transparent reporting on OPS activities, including through annual financial statements and audit reports. The Council requested the Secretary-General to report in 1994 on steps taken to integrate DDSMS and OPS functions and to eliminate duplication between them. It accepted the modalities for the transfer, as outlined by the task force, subject to a number of requirements and on the understanding that the modalities would be further clarified prior to the transfer, and that 1 January 1994 should be regarded as a target date pending review by the General Assembly. The Council drew attention to the fact that ACABQ had requested the Secretary-General to report on the modalities before 1 January 1994, including information on how conditions of operation were to be met. ACABQ believed that the primary focus should be on resolving issues prior to implementation rather than on a predetermined target date.[61] The requirements cited by the Council were that: OPS had to have the maximum possible degree of autonomy; it should continue to work closely with UNDP, in particular maintaining close links with resident representatives; it should further develop collaboration with other parts of the United Nations system, particularly the specialized agencies; and it should maintain its high level of expertise and staff commitment, remain self-financing, have the freedom to utilize the most cost-effective central services, retain and improve its rules of procurement and have the power to negotiate and conclude agreements for its implementation services.

The Council supported the continuing role to be played by UNDP in developing management service agreements and stressed that OPS should not develop fund-raising capacities. The Administrator, together with DDSMS and other relevant bodies, was requested to prepare a timetable for the OPS transfer, and the Secretary-General, in collaboration with the Administrator, was asked to address the Council's concerns, expressed in its requirements for accepting the modalities, in the context of the proposed programme budget for 1994-1995. He was also asked, in cooperation with the Administrator, to present by 1 September 1993 detailed information regarding staffing arrangements.

The Administrator, in collaboration with the Secretary-General, was asked to convene informal consultations on the modalities prior to their consideration by the Assembly. The Council decided to reconvene for a one-day special session to make recommendations on the modalities detailed in the programme budget for 1994-1995, also prior to Assembly consideration. It decided to review the impact of the OPS transfer on UNDP activities and functions in 1994, on the basis of a report by the Administrator, and to review the implementation of OPS staffing arrangements in 1995, on the basis of a report by the Secretary General.

Secretary-General's report. In an October/November report,[89] the Secretary-General provided information on the institutional and administrative arrangements governing the integration of UNDP/OPS into DDSMS. The Secretary-General addressed the Governing Council's concerns, as cited in its 18 June decision, as requirements for accepting the modalities for the transfer, including its request for detailed information on staffing arrangements. He noted that a detailed report on integration of implementation functions would be submitted to the Council in 1994.

Commenting in November on the Secretary-General's report,[90] ACABQ questioned the viability of the 1 January 1994 integration date and recommended to the Assembly that it take place on 1 January 1995. The Secretary-General was requested to submit a report to ACABQ's spring 1994 session on all modalities and working arrangements, in particular those which remained to be resolved, and include an operational budget, based on the merger of the portfolios of UNDP/OPS and DDSMS, with a clear indication of the personnel to be drawn from the existing UNDP/OPS and DDSMS. The report should also include information on the projected magnitude of the OPS portfolio and its internal organization.

In **decision 48/459** of 23 December, the Assembly decided to defer consideration of the Secretary-General's report[89] to its resumed session.

Governing Council consideration (special session). In accordance with its 18 June decision on OPS,[88] the Governing Council reconvened for a special session on 16 December to consider the question of the integration of OPS into DDSMS. It had before it the Secretary-General's report on institutional and administrative arrangements governing the transfer[89] and ACABQ's report on the issue.[90]

On 16 December,[91] the Council recommended that OPS remain within UNDP until 1 January 1995 and decided to review the modalities for its transfer to DDSMS. It requested the OPS Management Board to clarify further the arrangements for the transfer and asked the Council President to inform the President of the General Assembly of its decision. The Secretary-General was requested to report to the Council a soon as possible on steps taken to clarify the modalities for the transfer.

Proposal on the location of UNDP

In response to a 1992 Governing Council request,[92] the Administrator submitted a report on a proposal to relocate UNDP and UNFPA headquarters from New York to Bonn, Germany,[93] including its potential impact on the United Nations system and Member States, and its programme-related, budgetary, legal and administrative implications. The report stated that UNDP had held discussions with Germany, the United States and the United Nations Secretariat on Germany's proposal to host at Bonn the headquarters of UNDP, its affiliated funds and UNFPA. The Secretary-General had also requested the views of UNDP Member States on the impact of the proposed move for the United Nations system. As at 20 May 1993, the Secretary-General had received replies from or on behalf of 46 States. Of those, 41 indicated negative implications of relocation, 3 indicated positive implications, while 2 considered it too early to give a definitive response.

As for the impact of the relocation on Member States, by 23 March 1993, replies had been received from 72 States, including a common position taken by the 35 members of the Alliance of Small Island States and by 9 South Pacific Forum United Nations Members. Four Member States that replied in favour cited advantages ranging from better communications and proximity to German Federal Ministries and the North-South Centre at Bonn, to shorter travel distance to European capitals and Africa. A total of 58 States saw only disadvantages to relocating, stating that it would hamper developing countries in their efforts to interact with UNDP and UNIFEM. They also cited the lack of representation in Germany and Europe; functional difficulties for their representatives covering the General Assembly's Second Committee, the Economic and Social Council, UNDP and UNFPA; and financial burdens ranging from opening new missions or maintaining some form of diplomatic presence in Bonn to increased travel expenditures. Four States saw both advantages and disadvantages, and seven States were neutral on the issue.

With regard to programme-related, budgetary, legal and administrative implications, the Administrator reported that consultations were held within the United Nations system and with the German Government, and an inter-secretariat working group had been established to identify indicative costs and issues to be addressed. The working group concluded that there would be major human resource implications, some programme-related implications not yet fully identified or elaborated on, and a range of other issues and implications requiring further study. There were also constraints relating to services currently provided to UNDP and UNFPA by the United Nations Secretariat in New York and the related impact on the United Nations budget. Additionally, the German offer would require further elaboration regarding specific buildings or alternative options; the transition costs, which at 1992 prices could range from $88 million to $125 million; the possible savings in current expenditure, which could range from $10.1 million to $14.4 million per annum; and implications that might arise from the restructuring process within the United Nations.

On 16 June,[94] the Council recalled with appreciation Germany's proposal to host the headquarters of UNDP, of its affiliated funds and of UNFPA at Bonn from 1996 onwards. In the context of the restructuring and revitalization of the United Nations system in the economic, social and related fields, it invited those Member States that had not yet transmitted their views on the proposal to do so prior to its next session. The Council also invited Member States to continue to review the Administrator's report on the issue and decided to consult further on the matter at its 1994 session.

Coordination with other organizations

In response to a 1992 Governing Council request,[92] the Administrator, in March, submitted a report on multilateral coordination and complementarity.[95] He stated that the role of UNDP and of multilateral financial institutions had changed significantly, and that the division of labour provided in their mandates regarding activities at the country level was no longer clear. At the global level, there was a trade-off for UNDP between greater decentralization of its programmes and participation in global initiatives.

The report suggested two possible approaches for dealing with the issue: one would be based on a new division of labour, involving a redefinition of the functions and responsibilities of each agency, by sector and region, and the other, based on competition, while stressing the need for coordination and complementarity, would involve the acceptance of the idea of a market in technical cooperation services. To contribute to a rational and effective use of technical cooperation by recipient countries, it was imperative that UNDP develop cost-effective and flexible modalities for programming and designing technical cooperation. Its relationship with multilateral financial institutions should therefore not be adversarial nor overtly accommodating, but should be based on the best use of its comparative advantages, in particular those derived from its field presence in virtually all countries. It should develop its in-house analytical and policy advisory capacity, strengthen the information network and build a roster of consultants of high calibre. It should review existing collaborative arrangements and improve the effectiveness of its operations. UNDP should collaborate with other United Nations agencies in identifying its comparative advantages as a basis for redefining relationships with multilateral financial institutions. Within the United Nations system itself, the agencies and UNDP should forge a new alliance to support national development strategies.

By a 17 June decision,[8] the Council took note of the Administrator's report.

REFERENCES

[1]DP/1994/10 & Add.1-5. [2]E/1993/35. [3]E/1993/35/Add.1. [4]E/1993/35 (dec. 93/1). [5]Ibid. (dec. 93/10). [6]Ibid. (dec. 93/40). [7]Ibid. (dec. 93/9). [8]Ibid. (dec. 93/43). [9]Ibid. (dec. 93/44). [10]Ibid. (dec. 93/45). [11]DP/1993/68 (Parts I & II). [12]DP/1993/73. [13]E/1993/35 (dec. 93/4). [14]DP/1993/6. [15]E/1993/35 (dec. 93/20). [16]DP/1993/62. [17]DP/1993/64. [18]DP/1993/71. [19]YUN 1992, p. 559. [20]DP/1993/60. [21]E/1993/35 (dec. 93/21). [22]DP/1993/6. [23]DP/1994/6. [24]YUN 1991, p. 397, GA res. 46/151, annex, 18 Dec. 1991. [25]DP/1993/14. [26]YUN 1991, p. 378. [27]DP/1993/28. [28]DP/1993/27. [29]YUN 1992, p. 563. [30]DP/1993/22. [31]DP/1993/35 (dec. 93/25). [32]DP/1993/23. [33]DP/1993/3. [34]YUN 1992, p. 680, GA res. 47/194, 22 Dec. 1992. [35]Ibid., p. 672. [36]E/1993/35 (dec. 93/2). [37]DP/1993/11. [38]YUN 1987, p. 686. [39]E/1993/35 (dec. 93/12). [40]E/1990/29 (dec. 90/18). [41]DP/1993/15. [42]DP/1993/16. [43]YUN 1988, p. 349. [44]DP/1993/26. [45]E/1993/35 (dec. 93/26). [46]DP/1993/24. [47]YUN 1992, p. 569. [48]DP/1993/21. [49]E/1990/29 (dec. 90/34). [50]YUN 1991, p. 378. [51]E/1993/35 (dec. 93/24). [52]YUN 1992, p. 565. [53]DP/1993/5. [54]E/1993/35 (dec. 93/8). [55]Ibid. (dec. 93/3). [56]Ibid. (dec. 93/22). [57]DP/1994/34. [58]E/1993/35 (dec. 93/34). [59]DP/1993/44 & Add.1-3 & Corr.1. [60]DP/1993/45. [61]DP/1993/46. [62]E/1993/35 (dec. 93/35). [63]A/47/5/Add.1. [64]A/47/500. [65]DP/1993/47. [66]DP/1993/48/Add.1. [67]DP/1993/48. [68]E/1993/35 (dec. 93/36). [69]DP/1993/49. [70]E/1993/35 (dec. 93/37). [71]DP/1993/50. [72]E/1993/35 (dec. 93/38). [73]DP/1994/34/Add.3. [74]DP/1994/34/Add.2. [75]YUN 1992, p. 568. [76]YUN 1991, p. 382. [77]E/1990/29 (dec. 90/21). [78]DP/1993/61. [79]YUN 1991, p. 383. [80]E/1993/35 (dec. 93/6). [81]DP/1993/51. [82]YUN 1992, p. 558. [83]DP/1993/35 (dec. 93/5). [84]Ibid. (dec. 93/7). [85]A/C.5/47/88. [86]DP/1993/70. [87]DP/1993/20. [88]E/1993/35 (dec. 93/42). [89]A/48/502 & Add.1,2. [90]A/48/7/Add.1. [91]E/1993/35/Add.1 (dec. 93/46). [92]YUN 1992, p. 570. [93]DP/1993/55 & Add.1-3. [94]DP/1993/35 (dec. 93/41). [95]DP/1993/25.

Other technical cooperation

UN programmes

The newly created DDSMS, established as part of the restructuring of the United Nations in the economic, social and related fields, incorporated the technical cooperation functions of the former Department of Economic and Social Development, created in 1992.[1] The reorganization was designed to sharpen the focus and enhance the impact of United Nations technical cooperation. Other organizational entities engaged in providing technical cooperation assistance during 1993 included the regional commissions, the United Nations Centre for Human Settlements (Habitat) and UNCTAD.

In 1993, the organizational entities of the United Nations delivered a technical cooperation programme of $209 million, compared with $243 million in 1992.

DDSMS activities

In his annual report to the UNDP Governing Council on technical cooperation activities,[2] the Secretary-General stated that in 1993 DDSMS had more than 700 technical cooperation projects under execution in a dozen substantive sectors, with a total project expenditure of some $126 million. Projects financed by UNDP represented $63.5 million; those by trust funds, $42.5 million; by UNFPA, $12.1 million and by the United Nations regular programme of technical cooperation, $8.2 million.

On a geographical basis, the DDSMS-executed programme included expenditures of $55.2 million in Africa; $28.6 million in Asia and the Pacific; $23.2 million for interregional and global programmes; $12.1 million in Arab States; $6.1 million in the Americas; and $1.1 million in Europe. Project delivery in Africa remained the largest, with a 44 per cent share of total delivery.

Distribution of expenditures by substantive sectors was as follows: natural resources and energy planning, $29.9 million; development policies and planning, $24.8 million; sustainable development and environmental management, $17.4 million; statistics, $14.9 million; governance and public administration, $12.9 million; public finance and enterprise management, $6.4 million; population, $6 million; United Nations Educational and Training Programme for Southern Africa, $5.3 million; human resources and social development, $4.4 million; national execution and capacity-building, $2.1 million; advisory services and training, $1.6 million; and social development, $0.5 million. Of the total of $126.3 million, natural resources and

energy planning comprised 24 per cent; development policies and planning, 20 per cent; and sustainable development, 14 per cent.

On 18 June,[3] the UNDP Governing Council took note of the Secretary-General's report on the 1992 technical cooperation activities of the United Nations.[1] It stressed the need to improve the technical focus of DDSMS, especially through the United Nations regular programme of technical cooperation, and encouraged the Department to help strengthen national capacities for programme management, execution and implementation. The Council requested DDSMS to improve its preparation and appraisal of projects and its capacity-building techniques and to ensure that its activities were undertaken with full attention to the 1992 General Assembly resolution on the triennial policy review of operational activities for development in the United Nations system,[4] particularly to the functions and responsibilities of recipient Governments and resident coordinators. It stressed the importance of clarifying the division of labour between DDSMS and other United Nations organs dealing with technical cooperation, especially UNDP, and requested the Administrator to report to the Council in 1994 on progress made in coordination. The Secretary-General was requested to provide a more analytical review of DDSMS technical cooperation.

United Nations Volunteers

In a report on UNV for the biennium 1992-1993,[5] the Administrator stated that an average of 3,500 assignments had been undertaken each year, with over 2,000 ongoing at any given moment. On 31 December 1993, 2,085 UNV specialists were serving the Organization. The major focus of UNV activities remained unchanged (classic technical cooperation activities, community-based initiatives, peace-related activities, humanitarian relief and rehabilitation), but were now interrelated due to the interlocking nature of relief, peace-building and development activities. The UNV approach was to support the efforts of low-income and vulnerable community groups. Its closeness to the local level of resources, knowledge and experience was its chief distinguishing characteristic.

In his annual report covering 1993,[6] the Administrator stated that UNV participation in humanitarian relief activities was very significant during 1993; by the end of the year, 300 UNV specialists had served in humanitarian programmes in 34 countries. In the areas of peace-building and the electoral process, 465 volunteers from 45 countries, serving as district electoral supervisors under the auspices of the United Nations Transitional Authority in Cambodia (see PART

TWO, Chapter III), prepared for and administered the elections in Cambodia. In Mozambique, 105 UNVs working under the United Nations Operation in Mozambique (see PART TWO, Chapter I) assisted in the demobilization process, the registration of demobilized soldiers and the coordination of humanitarian assistance at the provincial level.

At the policy level, with the evolution of United Nations responsibilities, volunteer roles had proved to be particularly appropriate in the areas of peace-building and humanitarian relief. UNV had elaborated a strategic approach for the period 1993 to 1996 and was giving focus and relevance to its programme through identification with the special volunteer perspective and style of operation, derived from its solid base at the community level. UNV priorities were to mobilize resources from all sources, widen the range of UNV partners to involve local community groups, local governments and municipalities, development banks, and national and international NGOs, and make use of a full spectrum of assignment periods ranging from three months to a cumulative total of six years.

With regard to funding sources, the Administrator stated that the decline in UNDP's share of total resources (primarily IPFs), which had fallen from 70.1 per cent in 1991 to an estimated 49.9 per cent in 1993, pointed to the need for greater awareness of UNV's relevance to the more focused country programmes funded by UNDP. He considered UNV to be an essential instrument in furthering the overall UNDP objective of promoting sustainable human development and, in that context, UNV would also be able to draw on many non-IPF resources. UNDP would continue to work with UNV in seeking additional financial support for its Domestic Development Services programme. Contributions to the Special Voluntary Fund (SVF) had increased but remained modest. The level of SVF-supported activity was constrained by its inability to commit funds beyond actual cash in hand. The Administrator proposed that UNV be authorized to commit funds, on a fully funded basis, on receipt of written pledges rather than on receipt of the funds, so as to facilitate higher programme delivery and provide more accurate information on the utilization of funds for existing and potential donors.

UNISTAR

The Administrator, in a report on the United Nations International Short-Term Advisory Resources (UNISTAR) programme for 1991-1993,[7] stated that, with effect from 1 June 1993, he had merged UNISTAR with UNV. UNISTAR, which provided short-term, highly specialized volunteer services to the private and public sectors of de-veloping countries, would now serve as the UNV focal point for entrepreneurship promotion and development. The merger enabled UNISTAR to expand its activities beyond its present programme countries and focus in support of the broader spectrum of sustainable human development.

During the reporting period, UNISTAR completed 518 volunteer assignments to private and State-owned enterprises and government institutions in 41 countries. The services contributed were equivalent to more than $7 million in technical cooperation. Asia, Europe and CIS were the fastest-growing regions for UNISTAR cooperation. Activities during the reporting period included helping India to investigate new product uses and outlets for jute and assisting Mongolia in drafting its first company law and in introducing the concept of mutual funds through its stock exchange. At the enterprise level, it assisted printers, furniture makers, food processors and garment manufacturers, and organized workshops for enterprises too small to afford its services. It was also advising Governments and business associations on developing indigenous UNISTAR programmes.

Technical cooperation among developing countries

In his annual report for 1993,[6] the UNDP Administrator stated that technical cooperation among developing countries (TCDC) had increased and high priority was being given to the TCDC modality. Promotional and operational activities supported by the system were increasing, as were financial contributions for TCDC from national budgets of developing countries.

The sensitization to TCDC was being expanded through a training-of-trainers approach at the national, regional and subregional levels, targeting private and public sector development professionals and United Nations development system staff. Orientation on the TCDC modality was also provided as part of other promotional activities, and information activities were strengthened through a number of publications, such as the magazine *Cooperation South* and the TCDC newsletter *Focus*. Two regional workshops (Asia/Pacific and Africa) were held to develop further the role of focal points in promoting and advising on the application of TCDC. Updating of the TCDC-INRES database on available capacities and expertise gathered momentum, and software was redesigned to offer greater compatibility with other database systems. Capacities and needs-matching consultations, aimed at enhancing the exchange of technical capacities between developing countries, were held in Bangladesh, Nigeria, Uganda and Zimbabwe. In the area of intercountry networking, a study of resource mobilization through aid cooperation covering nine countries in Latin America and the Caribbean was coordinated by Chile, and a network arrangement in inter-university cooperation on policy research, coordinated by the Addis Ababa University (Ethiopia), was launched.

Action by Committee on TCDC

The eighth session of the High-level Committee on the Review of Technical Cooperation among Developing Countries was held in New York from 25 to 28 May and on 4 June 1993.[8]

The Committee had before it the following: a review of progress in implementing the 1978 Buenos Aires Plan of Action for Promoting and Implementing TCDC[9] and decisions taken by the High-level Committee on the Plan of Action;[10] a report covering several TCDC issues (the Expert Group Meeting on TCDC held at Rabat, Morocco, on 10 and 11 February 1993; the extent to which the recommendations of the 1990 report, *The Challenge to the South: The Report of the South Commission*, pertaining to TCDC, could be implemented; the preparation of guidelines to review policies and procedures of the United Nations development system concerning TCDC; and intergovernmental programming exercises for TCDC);[11] a report on developing a TCDC strategy in the United Nations development system;[12] and a report on staffing the UNDP Special Unit for TCDC.[13]

On 4 June, the Committee adopted three decisions. Regarding progress in implementing the Buenos Aires Plan of Action,[14] the Committee encouraged Governments and United Nations organizations to improve the methodology for reporting on progress and requested its Bureau to adjust the dates for submission of information by Governments, organizations of the United Nations system and intergovernmental organizations. Developing countries and United Nations organizations were invited to examine, for possible inclusion in their activities, the recommendations of the South Commission. The Committee called on United Nations organizations to apply, on an experimental basis, ACC guidelines for reviewing policies and procedures in the United Nations, in particular those relating to refinement and improvement, and called on ACC to monitor their implementation.

In a decision on an overall framework for promoting and applying TCDC in the 1990s,[15] the Committee welcomed the development of such a strategy[12] and called on all parties to implement it as a priority. It expressed reservations about the proposed establishment of an interregional fund to finance the foreign exchange components of TCDC and requested the UNDP Administrator to consult Governments on the matter and report on the outcome. It also encouraged consideration of regional and subregional mecha-

nisms to support countries in implementing the strategy. The Committee requested developing countries and United Nations organizations to strengthen their focal points for TCDC by according them appropriate status and providing adequate staff and resources. It recognized the importance and potential for TCDC in countries with economies in transition and invited interested developed countries and donors to support the TCDC modality through their respective bilateral and trilateral arrangements. It expressed concern over the financial constraints affecting UNDP, including the decrease in the SPR allocation for TCDC, and invited the UNDP Governing Council to ensure that the increasing work of the Special Unit for TCDC was not adversely affected. It also invited UNDP to maintain the approved SPR allocation for TCDC for the 1992-1996 cycle so as to ensure implementation of the Special Unit's activities. The Committee urged United Nations organizations, in particular UNDP, to increase their support of TCDC activities and improve financing mechanisms, including regional, interregional and global resources, and called on developed and developing countries to increase their support of TCDC.

By its third decision,[16] the High-level Committee approved the agenda for its ninth (1995) session.

On 18 June,[17] the UNDP Governing Council noted the report of the High-level Committee and requested the Administrator to facilitate implementation of its decisions.

On 29 July, the Economic and Social Council, by **decision 1993/307**, took note of the Committee report.

Report of the Secretary-General. In response to a 1991 General Assembly request,[18] the Secretary-General, in October, submitted a report on economic and technical cooperation among developing countries.[19] He stated that United Nations organizations had reported an increased emphasis on TCDC as reflected in the large number of promotional and operational TCDC activities supported by them, including activities facilitating the participation of women. They had also adopted, or were in the process of adopting, policies to accelerate the use of the TCDC modality. Through its Special Unit for TCDC, UNDP had adopted a multi-pronged approach to promoting TCDC and had increased its collaboration with United Nations agencies. The new subprogrammes prepared in the context of the overall strategy for the 1990s would cover compilation and dissemination of information on successful TCDC; identification of institutions in developing countries that had successfully applied the TCDC modality; expansion of the database on technical expertise and capacities of developing country institutions; funding training activities and networking or twinning arrangements; strengthening institutions to serve as centres of excellence; and assistance in developing strategies, policies and procedures for promoting TCDC.

GENERAL ASSEMBLY ACTION

On 21 December, the General Assembly, on the recommendation of the Second Committee, adopted **resolution 48/172** without vote.

Economic and technical cooperation among developing countries

The General Assembly,

Reaffirming its resolutions 33/134 of 19 December 1978, in which it endorsed the Buenos Aires Plan of Action for Promoting and Implementing Technical Cooperation among Developing Countries, and 46/159 of 19 December 1991, as well as other relevant resolutions of the General Assembly and Economic and Social Council resolution 1992/41 of 30 July 1992,

Stressing that technical cooperation among developing countries remains a key element in international cooperation, that it has a complementary role with respect to other forms of international technical cooperation and that its final purpose is to promote economic growth and development, in particular human resource development, utilizing the capacities of developing countries,

Reaffirming also that, while developing countries have the primary responsibility for promoting and implementing technical cooperation among themselves, the United Nations system and developed countries should assist and support such activities, and that the United Nations system should continue to play a prominent role as promoter and catalyst of technical cooperation among developing countries, in accordance with the Buenos Aires Plan of Action,

Taking note with satisfaction of the statement in the report of the Secretary-General on the implementation of General Assembly resolution 45/159 that the organizations of the United Nations system had reported an increased emphasis on activities in technical cooperation among developing countries and that nearly all of the responding organizations had reported having adopted or being in the process of adopting policies to accelerate the use of the modality of such cooperation, and stressing the role of the operational activities segment of the Economic and Social Council in monitoring the use of this modality,

1. *Endorses* the report of the High-level Committee on the Review of Technical Cooperation among Developing Countries on its eighth session and the decisions adopted by the High-level Committee in annex I of its report;

2. *Urges* all Member States, in particular the developed countries among them, the United Nations Development Programme and other programmes and bodies whose work is related to that of the Economic and Social Council, as well as the specialized agencies, to give high priority and full support in their specific fields of operational activities to technical cooperation among developing countries, in the fields of, *inter alia*, science and technology, transfer of technology, capacity-building, education and technical training and know-how;

3. *Requests* all parties involved in the implementation of the strategy for the promotion and application of technical cooperation among developing countries in the 1990s, as referred to in the report of the High-level Committee, to ensure the widespread use of such cooperation;

4. *Requests* the Secretary-General to report to the General Assembly at its fiftieth session on the implementation of technical cooperation among developing countries in the United Nations development system and on the follow-up to the present resolution.

General Assembly resolution 48/172

21 December 1993   Meeting 86   Adopted without vote

Approved by Second Committee (A/48/717/Add.5) without vote, 6 December (meeting 45); draft by Vice-Chairman (A/C.2/48/L.54), based on informal consultations on draft by Colombia (for Group of 77 and China) (A/C.2/48/L.7); agenda item 91 *(d)*.
Meeting numbers. GA 48th session: 2nd Committee 19, 40, 45; plenary 86.

REFERENCES
[1]YUN 1992, p. 570. [2]DP/1994/26 & Add.1,2. [3]E/1993/35 (dec. 93/30). [4]YUN 1992, p. 552, GA res. 47/199, 22 Dec. 1992. [5]DP/1994/28. [6]DP/1994/10/Add.1. [7]DP/1994/31. [8]A/48/39. [9]YUN 1978, p. 467. [10]TCDC/8/2 & Add.1. [11]TCDC/8/3. [12]TCDC/8/4. [13]TCDC/8/5. [14]A/48/39 (dec. 8/1). [15]Ibid. (dec. 8/2). [16]Ibid. (dec. 8/3). [17]E/1993/35 (dec. 93/39). [18]YUN 1991, p. 391, GA res. 46/159, 19 Dec. 1991. [19]A/48/491.

UN Capital Development Fund

During 1993, an estimated $45.6 million in resources was made available to UNCDF, a multilateral agency providing small-scale assistance to officially designated LDCs and other countries regarded as LDCs. The total comprised $31.5 million in voluntary contributions, a $7.2 million reduction in operational reserve, $5.8 million in other income, and $800,000 in loan repayments. A further $90.5 million was available from previous years.

Resources used during the year totalled $59 million, including $53.6 million in project expenditures, $4.4 million in administrative expenditures and $1 million in technical support costs.

Nineteen new projects were approved for Bhutan (2), Burundi, Cambodia, Guinea, Madagascar, Malawi, Mali (2), Mauritania (4), Mozambique, the Niger and Yemen, and 3 inter-regional projects. The total value of projects approved by UNCDF in 1993 was $36.9 million.

In his annual report for 1993,[1] the Administrator stated that UNCDF had launched its new programme approach, emphasizing partnership with local governments and institutions and geographical concentration in the provision of infrastructure, micro-credit and local development funds. It had also channelled resources directly to local governing bodies and had empowered local communities with decision-making authority. To adjust to the UNDP-wide resource constraints, completed projects were closed, with savings reverting to general resources. A comprehensive review of the pipeline for new projects led to its reduction by approximately 32 per cent over the next two to four years. At the same time, the Fund had been exploiting new avenues for resource mobilization, including the establishment of regional trust funds and increased contact with foundations and associations of local authorities. However, these initiatives could not substitute for core contributions in enabling UNCDF to fulfil its mandate.

In response to a 1981 General Assembly request,[2] the Administrator submitted his biennial policy review of the operations of UNCDF for the period 1991-1992.[3]

On 18 June,[4] the UNDP Governing Council noted that the implementation of a partial funding formula had allowed for the highest level ever of programming in 1991 and a record level of programme expenditure in 1992. It was, however, concerned that the commitment capacity of UNCDF would be impaired by current funding trends, including the continuing decline in voluntary contributions. The Council invited the Administrator to mobilize additional resources, to cooperate more closely with other multilateral financing institutions and to submit recommendations to the Council in 1994. It endorsed the Administrator's proposal to continue the loan facility within UNCDF and invited him to submit an outline of his plans for the Fund's future in 1995, including identification of any potential reorientation of the Fund's original mandate and preservation of its autonomy and identity. It renewed its appeal for voluntary financial support to UNCDF so that it could continue to respond to the growing needs of its recipient countries.

REFERENCES
[1]DP/1994/10/Add.1. [2]YUN 1981, p. 435, GA res. 36/200, 17 Dec. 1981. [3]DP/1993/42 & Corr.1. [4]E/1993/35 (dec. 93/32).

Chapter III

Special economic and humanitarian assistance

In 1993, the United Nations continued to respond to the escalation of complex emergencies and humanitarian situations worldwide. The Economic and Social Council considered the coordination of humanitarian assistance and adopted recommendations to strengthen delivery. The General Assembly endorsed those conclusions and emphasized the leadership role of the Secretary-General, through the Emergency Relief Coordinator, in coordinating coherent and timely responses to humanitarian emergencies. It requested the Inter-Agency Standing Committee to ensure the availability of adequate resources for rapid and coordinated responses (resolution 48/57).

The Governing Council of the United Nations Development Programme reviewed the implementation of the United Nations New Agenda for the Development of Africa in the 1990s. The Assembly called on the international community to pursue vigorously its responsibilities under the New Agenda and to support fully the African effort (48/214). The agencies of the United Nations system provided emergency disaster relief and other humanitarian assistance to various countries in Africa, Asia, Europe and Latin America.

The Assembly decided to convene the World Conference on Natural Disaster Reduction at Yokohama, Japan, from 23 to 27 May 1994 (48/188).

Special economic assistance

In 1993, the United Nations continued to mobilize and provide special economic assistance to a number of developing countries facing severe economic problems, often caused by armed conflict, civil strife or natural disasters.

Critical situation in Africa

New Agenda for the Development of Africa

United Nations organizations continued to implement the United Nations New Agenda for the Development of Africa in the 1990s, adopted by the General Assembly in 1991.[1] The Panel of High-Level Personalities on African Development, appointed by the Secretary-General in 1992[2] to assist and advise him on the implementation of

the New Agenda, held its second meeting at Rome, Italy, on 17 and 18 April 1993. The Panel reviewed implementation of the New Agenda and coordination of the activities of non-governmental organizations (NGOs), Governments and the United Nations system. A third meeting (New York, 2 and 3 December) focused on long-term development in Africa, security and development, and regional integration and cooperation. It also discussed the diversification of African economies and the feasibility of a diversification fund. Japan hosted the Tokyo International Conference on African Development (5 and 6 October). The Conference adopted the Tokyo Declaration on African Development, pledging to give further impetus to economic and political reforms adopted by African countries.

UNCTAD action. In March,[3] the Trade and Development Board (TDB) of the United Nations Conference on Trade and Development (UNCTAD), in response to the commitment made at UNCTAD VIII in 1992,[4] discussed issues relating to the New Agenda as well as regional integration and technical cooperation issues. It considered reports of the UNCTAD Secretary-General on regional integration issues in Africa[5] and UNCTAD's technical cooperation activities in that region.[6]

TDB observed that Africa risked further marginalization if it did not pursue cooperation and regional integration. It stressed the importance of strengthening regional infrastructures and harmonizing policies, and urged the international community to increase its financial support for regional integration projects. It also urged the UNCTAD secretariat to be closely associated with the Tokyo International Conference on African Development.

The Board called for an evaluation of UNCTAD's technical cooperation activities to improve their effectiveness and to reflect the priorities of African countries. It suggested that African countries should intensify their collaboration with UNCTAD and use the round-table forum to broaden the dialogue on regional cooperation projects. It recommended that greater efforts be made to mobilize resources for UNCTAD's technical cooperation activities, as well as for projects supporting technical cooperation among developing countries. It stressed the need to continue the African multilateral trade negotiations project beyond the conclusion of the Uruguay Round of multilateral trade negotiations (see PART THREE, Chapter IV). The Board suggested that there should be closer dialogue between Africa and its development partners, similar to that organized by the Southern African Development Community, and greater collaboration with the Global Coalition for Africa.

The Board requested the Working Party on the Medium-term Plan and the Programme Budget to strengthen UNCTAD's Africa Unit.

UNDP action. In response to a 1992 decision of the Governing Council of the United Nations Development Programme (UNDP),[7] the UNDP Administrator submitted in April 1993 a report[8] on UNDP's role in the implementation of the New Agenda. The report explained UNDP's integrated approach to African development and outlined the thrust of its interventions and plans for strengthening future support.

On 18 June,[9] the Governing Council asked the Administrator to contribute fully to the implementation of the New Agenda and to strengthen coordination with the United Nations system and with the Office of the Special Coordinator of Assistance to Africa and the Least Developed Countries (LDCs) in particular. It called on African countries to follow up on the New Agenda to achieve sustainable growth and development, to promote cooperation and regional and subregional integration, to intensify the process of democratization, to encourage investment, and to integrate population issues into the development process. The Council called on the international community to help African countries by solving the African debt crisis, providing adequate resource flows, diversifying African economies, enhancing market access and supporting regional integration. It appealed for increased contributions to cover the projected shortfall in resources for the fifth programming cycle (1992-1996), and encouraged UNDP to focus its National Long-Term Perspective Studies and African Capacity-Building Initiative on a holistic and coordinated approach to development. The Council welcomed the Capacity 21 initiative to support UNDP's follow-up to the 1992 United Nations Conference on Environment and Development (UNCED), and called on the Administrator to continue implementing UNCED's Agenda 21,[10] *inter alia*, in the context of the elaboration of the International Convention on Drought and Desertification. The Council asked the Administrator to work closely with the Department of Humanitarian Affairs to ensure effective and coordinated responses to emergency situations in Africa and to encourage a rapid transition from emergencies to rehabilitation and sustainable development. It also requested UNDP to support regional and subregional cooperation and integration in Africa to enhance the efficiency of the related institutions.

In a later report on implementation of the New Agenda,[11] the Administrator stated that during 1993 UNDP supported the Secretary-General's Panel of High-Level Personalities, provided follow-up and monitoring of networks, strengthened mechanisms for policy dialogue on Africa, reinforced the capacity of the Special Coordinator of Assistance to Africa and LDCs in New York, and supported the *Africa Recovery* magazine. In collaboration with Japan and Indonesia, it co-sponsored follow-up workshops to the Tokyo International Conference on African Development (see above). It also supported the establishment of the African Economic Community and the strengthening of selected subregional bodies and programmes.

UNDP's National Long-Term Perspective Studies Programme became operational, with programmes in a number of African countries. By the end of 1993, the African Capacity-Building Foundation, which managed donor funds, was aiding training institutions in Benin, Guinea, Nigeria and Zimbabwe, and operational work was under way in other countries. UNDP was supporting 24 countries in political transition and was developing a programme for sustainable political systems and better governance as the basis for continued UNDP backing. It also provided humanitarian assistance and support for economic reforms, private sector development, aid coordination, human resources development and the environment.

The number of UNDP projects for Africa was reduced significantly during 1993, but the volume of resources executed by national authorities continued to grow. At the end of 1993, over $50 million in project funds were approved for national execution, compared with $32 million in 1992.

Report of the Secretary-General. The Secretary-General, in a September report,[12] submitted the first preliminary assessment of the New Agenda since its adoption in 1991. The report focused on global factors relevant to the Agenda's successful implementation; reviewed major support of African socio-economic recovery and development; analysed specific concerns within the African region; and outlined action to reinforce implementation.

Major action in support of the New Agenda in 1993 included the second meeting of the Panel of High-Level Personalities on African Development, the Tokyo Conference on African Development and adoption of the Tokyo Declaration, and revitalization of the Inter-Agency Task Force on African Recovery and Development. Several bilateral creditors provided debt relief to support economic growth, environmental management and poverty alleviation programmes. Multilateral financial assistance was provided by the World Bank Group, the International Monetary Fund

(IMF), the African Development Bank (AfDB), the International Fund for Agricultural Development (IFAD) and the European Community. The Food and Agriculture Organization of the United Nations (FAO) contributed towards food security through early-warning and disaster-preparedness projects, and, on behalf of the Secretary-General, undertook a feasibility study on the establishment of a $50 million-$75 million Diversification Facility for African Commodities.[13] It was proposed that the Facility be set up in AfDB for an initial period of three to four years. Assistance was also provided in the areas of education and training, the African Capacity-Building Initiative, national shelter strategies, the environment and population. United Nations agencies, particularly UNCTAD, took action to promote regional economic cooperation and integration.

The Secretary-General, in October,[14] submitted a study on overall resource flows to Africa and proposed ways of mobilizing additional resources in the 1990s.

In a January report to the Commission for Social Development on the critical social situation in Africa,[15] the Secretary-General identified obstacles to implementation of the United Nations Programme of Action for African Economic Recovery and Development 1986-1990,[16] and the major social development issues facing Africa, including their impact on women, youth and refugees.

GENERAL ASSEMBLY ACTION

On 23 December, the General Assembly adopted **resolution 48/214** without vote.

United Nations New Agenda for the Development of Africa in the 1990s

The General Assembly,

Reaffirming its resolution 46/151 of 18 December 1991, the annex to which contains the United Nations New Agenda for the Development of Africa in the 1990s,

Also reaffirming its resolution 45/253 of 21 December 1990 on programme planning, in which the economic recovery and development of Africa are spelt out as one of the five overall priorities reflected in the medium-term plan for the period 1992-1997,

Recalling its resolutions 45/178 A to C of 19 December 1990 and 45/200 of 21 December 1990 on the critical economic situation in Africa and on African commodity problems, respectively,

Taking note of decisions 92/19 of 26 May 1992 and 93/17 of 18 June 1993 adopted by the Governing Council of the United Nations Development Programme on the New Agenda,

Taking note also of resolution CM/Res.1415(LVI) of 28 June 1992 of the Council of Ministers of the Organization of African Unity on the New Agenda,

Noting the continuing efforts of the Secretary-General to ensure the successful implementation of the New Agenda,

Convinced that growth and development on a sustained and sustainable basis can come about only as a result, *inter alia*, of the full participation of the people, particularly women, in the development process,

Recognizing the persistent efforts undertaken by many African countries to implement political and economic reform policies, and reaffirming the crucial importance of adequate social services and facilities to meet the basic needs of the populations and economic human-centred development, further recognizing the importance of good governance to meet overall development objectives,

Mindful of the need for African countries to diversify their economies, particularly their primary commodities, with a view to modernizing African production, distribution and marketing systems, enhancing productivity and stabilizing and increasing African export earnings in the face of the persistent decline of the prices of many primary commodities and the continuous deterioration in the terms of trade of African economies,

Reaffirming the importance of addressing the challenges facing African agricultural sectors, *inter alia*, drought, desertification, land degradation, locust infestation, land management and incentive structures, so as to achieve African food security as outlined in the New Agenda,

Deeply concerned by the constrained financial resource flows to Africa aggravated by rising debt and debt-service obligations and low private investment flows, and noting that Africa is the only continent experiencing a negative net transfer of resources in the 1990s,

Acknowledging the positive impact of substantive official development assistance transfers to Africa,

Reaffirming also the commitments on resource flows, including private direct investment, as contained in paragraphs 29 and 30 of the New Agenda,

Mindful of the need for African countries to increase and mobilize internal resources for sustainable development through, *inter alia*, policies for the promotion of domestic savings, improved and accessible banking facilities and further improvements in traditional practices of capital formation at local levels,

Taking note of the Tokyo International Conference on African Development, held on 5 and 6 October 1993, and of the Declaration adopted at that Conference,

Having considered the report of the Secretary-General on the preliminary consideration of the implementation of the New Agenda, the report transmitted by the Secretary-General on the need for and feasibility of the establishment of a diversification fund for Africa's commodities, and the report of the Secretary-General on financial resource flows to Africa,

1. *Reaffirms* the high priority attached, in the medium-term plan for the period 1992-1997, to Africa's economic recovery and development, including the effective implementation of the United Nations New Agenda for the Development of Africa in the 1990s as integrated in programme 45;

2. *Notes with appreciation* the establishment of a panel of high-level personalities to advise and assist the Secretary-General on African development, in particular on the implementation of the New Agenda, and requests that this panel continue to meet regularly under the chairmanship of the Secretary-General and that its recommendations be made available to the Member States;

3. *Commends* African countries for the actions undertaken to promote an economic environment conducive

to growth and development, in conformity with their commitments under the New Agenda, and calls upon them to pursue vigorously those responsibilities and commitments in order to achieve growth and development on a sustained and sustainable basis;

4. *Urges* all United Nations organs, organizations and programmes to integrate the priorities of the New Agenda in their mandates, to allocate sufficient resources for their operation and to improve further the use of available resources;

5. *Recommends* that, as part of capacity-building assistance, interested African countries be assisted in the monitoring of the impact of the work being undertaken in the context of the implementation of the New Agenda and in ensuring the participation of community-based groups, particularly women;

6. *Renews its call upon* the international community to pursue vigorously its responsibilities and commitments under the New Agenda in order to provide full and tangible support to the African efforts;

7. *Recognizes* the importance and high priority to be given to African regional and subregional cooperation and integration, and urges the United Nations system and its organizations to allocate sufficient technical and financial support to African regional economic groupings, including the African Economic Community, in order to contribute to their effectiveness in the process of African economic development;

8. *Urges* the multilateral financial institutions, recipient countries and donor countries, within the conceptual framework and design and implementation of structural adjustment policies in Africa, to pay special attention to eradicating poverty and addressing the social impact of these policies, while focusing on public investment, fiscal reform, reform of public enterprises, export expansion and efficient public administration;

9. *Invites* the preparatory bodies of all forthcoming conferences of the United Nations system to take into account the specific needs, requirements and priorities of the African countries, as outlined in the New Agenda;

10. *Invites* the Secretary-General to strengthen the capacity and capability of the Secretariat to raise international awareness of the urgent international and African actions needed to overcome the economic crisis in Africa, and to reinforce the capabilities of the Office of the Special Coordinator for Africa and the least developed countries to follow up, monitor and evaluate implementation of the New Agenda and, in the process, provide an effective framework for the Economic and Social Council to consider the implementation of the New Agenda in 1995 as part of its high-level segment, as well as for the General Assembly to conduct a midterm review of the implementation of the New Agenda in 1996, in accordance with paragraph 43 *(b)* and *(c)* thereof;

11. *Calls upon* the Secretary-General of the United Nations to work in close coordination and cooperation with the Secretary-General of the Organization of African Unity, in particular, on the follow-up to and review and evaluation of the implementation of the New Agenda;

12. *Welcomes* the report prepared by the Food and Agriculture Organization of the United Nations and transmitted by the Secretary-General entitled "Need for and feasibility of the establishment of a diversification fund for Africa's commodities";

13. *Affirms* the need for further efforts to promote the diversification of African economies;

14. *Stresses* the importance that the Secretary-General, Africa and an increasing number of countries attach to the necessity of the proposed establishment and operationalization of a diversification fund for Africa's commodities;

15. *Stresses also* the need, in developing diversification projects and programmes, to make full and effective use of existing funding mechanisms;

16. *Stresses further* the need to fill gaps that may exist in funding available for diversification of related activities in Africa;

17. *Decides* to address rigorously the full range of issues related to the diversification of African economies, with particular attention to the issues outlined in paragraphs 14, 15 and 16 of the present resolution, and for this purpose to convene in the first quarter of 1994, on the basis of background documents to be prepared by the Secretary-General, intensive consultations involving concerned and interested States, together with relevant financial institutions and United Nations organizations, including, *inter alia*, the African Development Bank, the World Bank, the United Nations Conference on Trade and Development, the Economic Commission for Africa, the United Nations Development Programme, the Food and Agriculture Organization of the United Nations and the United Nations Industrial Development Organization;

18. *Decides also* to take full account of the conclusions of those consultations in determining, during its resumed forty-eighth session, the appropriate actions to be taken to strengthen support for the diversification of African economies, including the proposed establishment of new funding arrangements, together with the organization of follow-up activities, such as seminars or expert workshops;

19. *Encourages* African countries to establish national diversification councils, as recommended in the report transmitted by the Secretary-General, including representatives from the Government and the private sector;

20. *Urges* the international community to increase financial resource flows to Africa, as these are crucial to regenerate growth and sustainable development of the African economies, to provide effective support to the political and economic reforms in which many African countries are now engaged and to help cushion adverse social impact;

21. *Reaffirms* the recommendations stipulated in paragraphs 23 to 28 of the New Agenda concerning Africa's debt problem, and in that context invites the international community to address Africa's external debt crisis and debt problems of African countries, including continuing to give serious consideration to the proposal for the convening of an international conference on Africa's external indebtedness;

22. *Urges* States to implement the undertakings they have made to attain the agreed international targets of devoting 0.7 per cent of gross national product to official development assistance and 0.15 per cent to least developed countries as soon as possible and to provide a better environment for the realization of the suggested estimate of the need to achieve an average of a 4 per cent real growth in annual financial resource flows to Africa, as outlined in paragraph 29 of the New Agenda;

23.　*Requests* the Secretary-General to undertake a study, in consultation with relevant financial institutions, recommending appropriate measures further to improve financial intermediation systems and practices in African countries to be submitted to the General Assembly at its fiftieth session, which should take into account an in-depth analysis of the current traditional systems and practices of capital formation at the local level and the kind of support measures the international community could provide;

24.　*Urges* African countries to continue their efforts for the improvement of the investment climate, and urges donor countries to support those efforts by, *inter alia*, providing increasing assistance to human resources development and to the rehabilitation and development of the social and economic infrastructure;

25.　*Requests* Governments and organs, organizations and bodies of the United Nations system and intergovernmental and non-governmental organizations, within their respective spheres of competence, to take appropriate measures in order to implement the commitments contained in the Tokyo Declaration of 6 October 1993 and to take other initiatives, as may be necessary, with the participation of interested parties from Africa and the international community, to ensure an effective follow-up of the Tokyo International Conference on African Development;

26.　*Decides* to include an item entitled "Implementation of the United Nations New Agenda for the Development of Africa in the 1990s" in the agenda of its fiftieth session.

General Assembly resolution 48/214

23 December 1993　　　Meeting 87　　　Adopted without vote

Draft by Norway (A/48/L.24/Rev.2), orally corrected by Egypt; agenda item 24.
Financial implications. 5th Committee, A/48/810; S-G, A/C.5/48/64.
Meeting numbers. GA 48th session: 5th Committee 45; plenary 49, 50, 87.

Special assistance to Djibouti

The Secretary-General, responding to a 1992 General Assembly request,[17] submitted in August 1993 a report[18] on assistance for the reconstruction and development of Djibouti. He reported that Djibouti's only resources were geothermal energy, which had not been tapped, and fisheries, and that the country's ecosystem was threatened by increasing desertification, soil erosion and groundwater depletion. He noted that Djibouti's transit trade with neighbouring Ethiopia and Somalia made its economy very sensitive to political developments in those countries. The crisis in Ethiopia and the prolonged closure of the border with Somalia had caused trade to shrink between 1989 and 1991, and the situation had been exacerbated by the Persian Gulf crisis, which had caused the collapse of the national airline, Air Djibouti. Other adversities, including increased fuel prices, delays in investment projects and internal conflict, demonstrated an urgent need to diversify the economy. Accordingly, the priorities of the 1991-1995 development plan were to promote the development of infrastructure and human resources.

The report noted also that an influx of refugees had imposed additional burdens on social services, including the education and health systems. Unemployment was high, and there was a shortage of skilled labour. The Government planned to expand primary and secondary education, improve technical vocational training and strengthen planning and management.

The UNDP country programme for Djibouti focused on the development of human resources and infrastructure. Its implementation was, however, delayed by disturbances in the north of the country. United Nations agencies were also planning assistance for the refugees in Djibouti.

GENERAL ASSEMBLY ACTION

On 21 December, the General Assembly, on the recommendation of the Second (Economic and Financial) Committee, adopted **resolution 48/198** without vote.

Assistance for the reconstruction and development of Djibouti

The General Assembly,

Recalling its resolution 47/157 of 18 December 1992 and its previous resolutions on economic assistance to Djibouti,

Recalling also the Paris Declaration and the Programme of Action for the Least Developed Countries for the 1990s, adopted by the Second United Nations Conference on the Least Developed Countries on 14 September 1990, as well as the mutual commitments undertaken on that occasion and the importance attached to the follow-up to that Conference,

Aware that the economic and social development efforts of Djibouti, which is included in the list of least developed countries, are constrained by the extremes of the local climate, in particular cyclical droughts and torrential rains and floods such as those which occurred in 1989, and that the implementation of reconstruction and development programmes requires the deployment of resources that exceed the real capacity of the country,

Noting with concern that the situation in Djibouti has been adversely affected by the evolving critical situation in the Horn of Africa, and noting the presence of over 100,000 refugees and persons displaced from their countries, which has, on the one hand, placed serious strains on the fragile economic, social and administrative infrastructure of the country and, on the other, raised serious security concerns,

Noting the critical economic situation of Djibouti resulting from the number of priority development projects that have been suspended in the light of the new critical regional and international situation,

Taking note of the report of the Secretary-General,

Recalling with gratitude the support provided to emergency relief operations during the floods in 1989 by various countries and intergovernmental and non-governmental organizations,

1.　*Declares its solidarity* with the Government and people of Djibouti in the face of the devastating consequences of the torrential rains and floods and the new adverse economic realities of Djibouti resulting, in particular, from the new critical situation in the Horn of Africa;

2. *Expresses its appreciation* to the Secretary-General for his efforts to make the international community aware of the difficulties faced by Djibouti in particular and the Horn of Africa in general;

3. *Invites* the United Nations system, in particular the United Nations Development Programme, to assist the Government of Djibouti, in the context of the scheduled round-table meeting, in preparing an urgent programme of rehabilitation and reconstruction, as well as a sustainable and adequate long-term development programme;

4. *Calls upon* all States, all regional and interregional organizations, non-governmental organizations and other intergovernmental agencies, in particular the United Nations Development Programme, the United Nations Children's Fund, the World Food Programme, the United Nations Industrial Development Organization, the Food and Agriculture Organization of the United Nations, the International Fund for Agricultural Development and the World Bank, to provide Djibouti with appropriate assistance, on a bilateral as well as a multilateral basis, to enable it to cope with its special economic difficulties;

5. *Requests* the Secretary-General to continue his efforts to mobilize the resources necessary for an effective programme of financial, technical and material assistance to Djibouti;

6. *Also requests* the Secretary-General to prepare a study of the progress made with economic assistance to that country, in time for the question to be considered by the General Assembly at its forty-ninth session.

General Assembly resolution 48/198

21 December 1993   Meeting 86   Adopted without vote

Approved by Second Committee (A/48/726) without vote, 6 December (meeting 45); draft by Algeria (for African States), Bahrain, Bangladesh, China, Djibouti, Jordan, Kuwait, Lebanon, Saudi Arabia, Suriname and Yemen (A/C.2/48/L.33), orally revised following informal consultations; agenda item 100.
Meeting numbers. GA 48th session: 2nd Committee 33-35, 42, 45; plenary 86.

Namibia

The Secretary-General, in an October report to the General Assembly,[19] recalled that the Assembly had in 1991[20] endorsed an Economic and Social Council resolution inviting the United Nations system and donor agencies to grant Namibia assistance comparable to that given to LDCs for a number of years immediately after its independence. He noted that the Governing Council of UNDP had granted Namibia "as if" LDC status in 1991, making it eligible for additional assistance from specialized funds and the Special Programme Reserve for LDCs. Under that arrangement, Namibia was eligible for loans on concessional terms and full LDC privileges in United Nations conferences and donor negotiations. The UNDP Trust Fund for Namibia, established in 1989, had successfully completed priority projects in agriculture and rural development, education and training,

health and housing. At the end of 1992, the Fund had received contributions of $4.4 million and would continue to co-finance ongoing projects under the first country programme for Namibia (1993-1997). Total indicative planning figure (IPF) resources under that programme amounted to $14.4 million, with Government cost-sharing projected at $1.2 million. The Namibian Government had agreed to a round-table conference and a National Technical Cooperation and Assessment Programme. The United Nations Capital Development Fund and the United Nations Sudano-Sahelian Office conducted missions to Namibia and identified specific areas for intervention. IFAD was hoping to conclude a $12.5 million loan for livestock development, and AfDB concluded a concessional loan agreement of 36 million rand for education.

However, Namibia was unable to obtain International Development Association (IDA) loans from the World Bank, because the Bank did not recognize its assumed LDC status. The Secretary-General concluded that the United Nations should continue to accord Namibia "as if" LDC status to facilitate its efforts at mobilizing development resources.

The General Assembly, by **decision 48/452** of 21 December, took note of the Secretary-General's report.

Other economic assistance

Yemen

In July,[21] Yemen informed the Economic and Social Council that the first parliamentary elections since unification in 1990 had been held in April 1993, and the new Government was formulating a general development strategy to deal with its economic problems. The country continued to face heavy burdens on its administrative and financial resources, including those associated with the Persian Gulf war, unification, the return of migrants and refugees from neighbouring countries, the loss of remittances from returnees, and natural disasters. The deficit on its current account balance averaged about 22 per cent of gross domestic product (GDP). Yemen needed large-scale foreign assistance, particularly grants and soft loans, to rectify a deplorable socio-economic situation, and the Government believed that the methodology applied to determine the magnitude and management of aid to the country should be reviewed.

The Secretary-General, responding to a 1992 request of the General Assembly,[22] submitted in August 1993[23] a report on assistance to Yemen. He stated that the World Bank and Yemen, in collaboration with UNDP, had developed a $245 million multisectoral emergency recovery programme. The World Bank had so far mobilized $60 million in credits and grants, including $33 million from the World Bank/IDA, $15 million from the United States Agency for International Development and $4.5 million from Germany. UNDP provided $400,000 from Special Programme Resources. Total funds available for the programme amounted to $86 million, leaving a funding gap of $159 million. To date, 55 per cent of the World Bank/IDA funds and 90 per cent of the German funds had been disbursed. Other agencies contributing to the programme were UNICEF, FAO, WFP and UNFPA.

In November, a UNDP representative informed the Assembly's Second Committee that the round-table process had been reactivated and a second meeting was planned to discuss Yemen's financial needs. UNDP and IMF were preparing a programme to strengthen Yemen's economic and financial management and to lay the foundation for sustainable and equitable growth. UNDP was also supporting the rehabilitation and privatization of public enterprises in the southern part of the country, and was working with the United Nations Industrial Development Organization and the Government to develop a free-trade zone.

ECONOMIC AMD SOCIAL COUNCIL ACTION

On 29 July, the Economic and Social Council adopted **resolution 1993/58** without vote.

Assistance to Yemen

The Economic and Social Council,

Convinced of the need for further cooperation with Yemen in its efforts, which began with the unification of Yemen and culminated in the holding of the first parliamentary elections in April 1993,

Recognizing that Yemen is one of the least developed countries and that it still faces major economic and social challenges as a result of unification, the return of Yemeni expatriates, the flow of refugees from the Horn of Africa, in particular from Somalia, and recent natural disasters,

Taking into consideration previous resolutions of the General Assembly, the Economic and Social Council and other international organizations in this regard, in particular Assembly resolutions 45/193 and 45/222 of 21 December 1990, 46/174 of 19 December 1991 and 47/179 of 22 December 1992, and Council resolutions 1990/65 of 26 July 1990, 1991/62 of 26 July 1991 and 1992/61 of 31 July 1992,

Bearing in mind the letter dated 2 July 1993 from the representative of Yemen to the United Nations Office at Geneva addressed to the Secretary-General,

Having heard the oral report on assistance to Yemen made on behalf of the Secretary-General at the 38th plenary meeting, on 21 July 1993, by the representative of the United Nations Development Programme,

1. *Encourages* the international community to respond actively to the needs of Yemen, and requests donor States to continue to provide assistance on a bilateral and multilateral basis, with a view to enabling Yemen to address the emergency situation;

2. *Calls upon* Member States and all organizations of the United Nations system, including the specialized agencies, as well as financial institutions, to provide assistance to the Government of Yemen in its reconstruction and development efforts;

3. *Expresses its appreciation* to the Secretary-General for his efforts and requests him to continue to coordinate the activities of the organizations of the United Nations system with a view to intensifying their cooperation with and their assistance to Yemen, in order to assist Yemen in the mobilization of its own resources;

4. *Requests* the Secretary-General to submit to the Economic and Social Council at its substantive session of 1994 a written report on the progress made in the implementation of the present resolution.

Economic and Social Council resolution 1993/58

29 July 1993   Meeting 45   Adopted without vote

16-nation draft (E/1993/L.38), orally revised following informal consultations; agenda item 6 *(a)*.
Sponsors: Algeria, Benin, Bhutan, Egypt, France, Guinea, India, Indonesia, Japan, Lebanon, Malaysia, Morocco, Pakistan, Syrian Arab Republic, Tunisia, Yemen.
Meeting numbers. ESC 38, 44, 45.

GENERAL ASSEMBLY ACTION

On 21 December, the General Assembly, on the recommendation of the Second Committee, adopted **resolution 48/195** without vote.

Assistance to Yemen

The General Assembly,

Taking note of the report of the Secretary-General,

Recalling its resolutions 45/193 and 45/222 of 21 December 1990, 46/174 of 19 December 1991 and 47/179 of 22 December 1992 and Economic and Social Council resolution 1991/62 of 26 July 1991, taking note of Council resolution 1993/58 of 29 July 1993, and recalling decisions 91/19 and 91/20 of 25 June 1991 of the Governing Council of the United Nations Development Programme,

Stressing the importance of implementing all relevant General Assembly and Economic and Social Council resolutions, and relevant decisions of the Governing Council of the United Nations Development Programme,

Requests the Secretary-General to keep under review the implementation of all relevant resolutions and to submit to the General Assembly at its fiftieth session a comprehensive report on that implementation.

General Assembly resolution 48/195

21 December 1993   Meeting 86   Adopted without vote

Approved by Second Committee (A/48/726) without vote, 6 December (meeting 45); 3-nation draft (A/C.2/48/L.29); agenda item 100.
Sponsors: Oman, United States, Yemen.
Meeting numbers. GA 48th session: 2nd Committee 33-35, 41, 45; plenary 86.

States affected by sanctions against Yugoslavia (Serbia and Montenegro)

In 1992,[24] and in 1993 by **resolution 820(1993)**, the Security Council imposed an arms embargo against the territory of the former Socialist Federal Republic of Yugoslavia and a comprehensive set of mandatory trade and economic sanctions against the Federal Republic of Yugoslavia (Serbia and Montenegro). In 1992, the Council had agreed that appropriate consideration should be given to the special economic problems of States resulting from sanctions imposed under Chapter VII of the Charter of the United Nations, and invited the Secretary-General to consult with the heads of international financial institutions, other components of the United Nations system and Member States and to report to the Council.[25] On 18 June 1993, the Council, by **resolution 843(1993)**, confirmed that its Committee on the former Yugoslavia[26] was entrusted with examining requests for assistance and invited it to make recommendations to the President of the Council for appropriate action. By July 1993, Albania, Bulgaria, Hungary, Romania, Slovakia, the former Yugoslav Republic of Macedonia, Uganda and Ukraine had requested consultations with the Council and had provided information regarding their special economic problems as a result of the sanctions.

Albania reported that, in addition to direct economic losses, the country's capacity to respond to new market-oriented incentives in its economic programme had been hampered by the sanctions. Total estimated losses to its economy were between $300 million and $400 million. Bulgaria said that by the end of 1992, its economy had suffered losses amounting to $1.2 billion in the areas of industry, trade, transport, energy, tourism and construction, and for the period May to December 1993 it estimated losses of $1.9 billion. Hungary reported that, in addition to economic difficulties stemming from the sanctions, restrictions on navigation on the Danube River were particularly serious. It estimated that since May 1992 it had incurred losses of $800 million. Romania stated that by the end of 1992, direct and indirect losses to its economy since the beginning of the sanctions totalled about $7 billion. The sanctions had seriously affected all branches of the economy, including industry, transport, agriculture and tourism. The social costs included increasing unemployment, a lack of consumer goods and migration of the labour force. Uganda stated that following the imposition of sanctions, work on the construction of the Mityana–Fort Portal road in western Uganda by a Yugoslav construction company had come to a standstill. Uganda requested Council authorization for payments to be made to allow completion of the project.

Ukraine reported discussions with the United Nations concerning reimbursement for heavy losses arising from strict implementation of the sanctions. It drew particular attention to international trade on the Danube and requested a simpler procedure for obtaining transshipment authorization and coordination with the Danube States regarding expansion of the list of articles requiring authorization.

The Committee on Sanctions recommended that the Council appeal to all States to provide immediate technical, financial and material assistance to the affected countries to mitigate the adverse impact on their economies. It also invited competent organs and specialized agencies of the United Nations system, including international financial institutions and regional development banks, to consider how their assistance programmes could alleviate special economic problems arising from the sanctions. It requested the Secretary-General to seek information from States and concerned United Nations organs and agencies on action taken to alleviate those problems.

By a letter of 6 July,[27] the President of the Security Council informed the Secretary-General of the Committee's recommendations and requested him to implement the actions contained therein.

On 20 September, the General Assembly, by **resolution 47/120 B**, invited the Council to consider appropriate measures by the United Nations system and international financial institutions to solve the special problems of States arising from the measures imposed by the Council.

Report of the Secretary-General. As requested by the Council in December 1992,[25] the Secretary-General reported in November 1993[28] on the special economic problems of States resulting from the imposition of the sanctions. The report outlined the Council's application of Article 50 of the Charter and deliberations on the issue by other United Nations intergovernmental bodies. It examined the experience gained and summarized replies received by the Secretary-General on the application of Article 50. The Secretary-General concluded that the Council's response to special economic problems resulting from sanctions had been flexible and that that flexibility should be preserved. He proposed measures to improve international responses, including the establishment of a permanent fund or individual trust funds to assist the affected States. He said that the General Assembly and the Economic and Social Council should support the Security Council's appeal for assistance in order to emphasize and enhance the commitment of the international community.

GENERAL ASSEMBLY ACTION

On 21 December, the General Assembly, on the recommendation of the Second Committee, adopted **resolution 48/210** without vote.

Economic assistance to States affected by the implementation of the Security Council resolutions imposing sanctions against the Federal Republic of Yugoslavia (Serbia and Montenegro)
The General Assembly,
Recalling the provisions of Articles 25, 48, 49 and 50 of the Charter of the United Nations,
Recalling also its resolution 47/120 B of 20 September 1993 entitled ''An Agenda for Peace'', and in particular section IV thereof,

Recalling further Security Council resolutions 713(1991) of 25 September 1991, 724(1991) of 15 December 1991, 757(1992) of 30 May 1992, 787(1992) of 16 November 1992 and 820(1993) of 17 April 1993, in which the Council decided to impose an arms embargo against the territory of the former Socialist Federal Republic of Yugoslavia and a comprehensive set of trade and economic sanctions against the Federal Republic of Yugoslavia (Serbia and Montenegro),

Taking note of Security Council resolution 843(1993) of 18 June 1993, in which the Council entrusted the Committee established pursuant to its resolution 724(1991) concerning Yugoslavia with the task of examining requests for assistance under the provisions of Article 50 of the Charter, as well as other relevant resolutions,

Commending the efforts of the Security Council Committee established pursuant to resolution 724(1991) aimed at improving the efficiency of its work,

Expressing concern at the special economic problems confronting States and in particular the States that border the Federal Republic of Yugoslavia (Serbia and Montenegro), the other Danube riparian States and other States in the region adversely affected by the severance of their economic relations with the Federal Republic of Yugoslavia (Serbia and Montenegro) and the disruption of traditional transport and communications links in that part of Europe,

Noting the information provided by States regarding the measures taken to give full effect to the sanctions as laid down in the relevant Security Council resolutions, as well as the information concerning the special economic problems they have been confronted with as a result of the implementation of those measures,

Recalling the recommendations adopted by the Security Council Committee established pursuant to resolution 724(1991) with regard to the States confronted with special economic problems arising from the application of sanctions against the Federal Republic of Yugoslavia (Serbia and Montenegro) pursuant to Security Council resolutions 757(1992), 787(1992) and 820(1993),

Recognizing that the continued full implementation of Security Council resolutions 713(1991), 724(1991), 757(1992), 760(1992) of 18 June 1992, 787(1992) and 820(1993) by all States will support measures to ensure compliance with these and other relevant resolutions,

Taking note of the report of the Secretary-General prepared pursuant to the note by the President of the Security Council regarding the question of special economic problems of States as a result of sanctions imposed under Chapter VII of the Charter,

1. *Commends* the States bordering on the Federal Republic of Yugoslavia (Serbia and Montenegro), the other Danube riparian States and all other States for the measures they have taken to comply with Security Council resolutions 713(1991), 724(1991), 757(1992), 760(1992), 787(1992) and 820(1993), and urges all States to continue to observe those resolutions strictly;

2. *Recognizes* the urgent need to assist States in coping with their special economic problems arising from the implementation of sanctions against the Federal Republic of Yugoslavia (Serbia and Montenegro), *inter alia*, through consideration of assistance for the promotion of the exports of the affected countries and for the promotion of investments in those countries;

3. *Supports* the recommendations of the Security Council Committee established pursuant to resolution 724(1991) concerning Yugoslavia, in response to requests for assistance received by the Security Council from certain States confronting special economic problems under the provisions of Article 50 of the Charter of the United Nations, in which the Committee, *inter alia:*

(a) Appealed to all States on an urgent basis to provide immediate technical, financial and material assistance to the affected States to mitigate the adverse impact on their economies of the application by those States of sanctions against the Federal Republic of Yugoslavia (Serbia and Montenegro) pursuant to Security Council resolutions 757(1992), 787(1992) and 820(1993);

(b) Invited the competent organs and specialized agencies of the United Nations system, including the international financial institutions and the regional development banks, to consider how their assistance programmes and facilities might be helpful to the affected States, with a view to alleviating their special economic problems arising from the application of sanctions against the Federal Republic of Yugoslavia (Serbia and Montenegro) pursuant to Security Council resolutions 757(1992), 787(1992) and 820(1993);

4. *Appeals* to all States and invites the competent organs and specialized agencies of the United Nations system to fulfil these recommendations of the Security Council Committee established pursuant to resolution 724(1991);

5. *Requests* the Secretary-General to seek on a regular basis information from States and the concerned organs and agencies of the United Nations system on action taken to alleviate the special economic problems of the affected States and to report thereon to the Security Council, as well as to submit a report on the implementation of the present resolution to the General Assembly at its forty-ninth session.

General Assembly resolution 48/210

21 December 1993   Meeting 86   Adopted without vote

Approved by Second Committee (A/48/734) without vote, 6 December (meeting 45); 18-nation draft (A/C.2/48/L.27), orally revised following informal consultations; agenda item 169.

Sponsors: Albania, Bulgaria, Cyprus, Czech Republic, Germany, Greece, Hungary, Netherlands, Poland, Republic of Moldova, Romania, Russian Federation, Slovakia, the former Yugoslav Republic of Macedonia, Uganda, Ukraine, United Kingdom, United States.

Meeting numbers. GA 48th session: 2nd Committee 33-35, 40, 45; plenary 86.

On 17 December,[29] the Federal Republic of Yugoslavia (Serbia and Montenegro) complained to the Chairman of the Committee on Yugoslavia about the Committee's rejection of the Russian Federation's request to export natural gas for humanitarian purposes to the Federal Republic of Yugoslavia, and the position of France, the United Kingdom and the United States that they would allow only strictly limited quantities of fuel for certain institutions whose needs were verified by humanitarian agencies.

REFERENCES
(1)YUN 1991, p. 402, GA res. 46/151, annex II, 18 Dec. 1991. (2)YUN 1992, p. 575. (3)A/48/15 (conclusions 403(XXXIX)). (4)YUN 1992, p. 611. (5)TD/B/39(2)/11. (6)TD/B/39(2)/12 & Corr.1 & Add.1. (7)YUN 1992, p. 576. (8)DP/1993/17.

(9)E/1993/35 (dec. 93/17). (10)YUN 1992, p. 672. (11)DP/1994/12. (12)A/48/334. (13)A/48/335 & Add.1,2. (14)A/48/336 & Corr.1. (15)E/CN.5/1993/11. (16)YUN 1986, p. 446, GA res. S-13/2, annex, 1 June 1986. (17)YUN 1992, p. 580, GA res. 47/157, 18 Dec. 1992. (18)A/48/319. (19)A/48/498. (20)YUN 1991, p. 409, GA res. 46/204, 20 Dec. 1991. (21)E/1993/101. (22)YUN 1992, p. 583, GA res. 47/179, 22 Dec. 1992. (23)A/48/320. (24)YUN 1992, pp. 352 & 375, SC res. 757(1992) & 787(1992), 30 May & 16 Nov. 1992. (25)Ibid., p. 88. (26)YUN 1991, p. 219, SC res. 724(1991), 15 Dec. 1991. (27)S/26056. (28)A/48/573-S/26705. (29)A/48/799-S/26900.

Humanitarian assistance

Coordination

On 12 February, the Economic and Social Council, by **decision 1993/205**, decided that its coordination segment should consider the theme "Coordination of humanitarian assistance: emergency relief and the continuum to rehabilitation and development" and make recommendations for implementation by the United Nations system.

In response to that decision, the Secretary-General submitted in June a report[1] outlining United Nations efforts to achieve coordinated humanitarian responses that treated relief, rehabilitation and development as an integrated whole. The Council also had before it a statement by the International Federation of Red Cross and Red Crescent Societies.[2] The Council's conclusions[3] emphasized the important leadership role of the Secretary-General, through the Emergency Relief Coordinator, in coordinating coherent and timely responses to major and complex emergencies and natural disasters. It also emphasized the need for Governments, the United Nations system and NGOs to support fully the coordinating role of the Secretariat's Department of Humanitarian Affairs (DHA). It stressed the need for the Emergency Relief Coordinator to ensure that the humanitarian dimensions of relief assistance were taken fully into account, and called on the operational agencies of the United Nations system to implement, through the Inter-Agency Standing Committee (IASC), the agreed division of responsibilities.

The Council also stressed that coordination should be field-oriented, and emphasized the important role of the Emergency Relief Coordinator in facilitating access to emergency areas, coordinating inter-agency needs assessment missions, preparing consolidated appeals and supporting field coordination. It further stressed the importance of adequate financial resources both for relief and for the continuum to development. The Council requested the governing bodies of relevant United Nations organizations to support the implementation of its conclusions.

The Council also made specific recommendations in various operational areas. It recommended, among other things, that: DHA intensify its promotion of disaster preparedness and consider the deployment of an inter-agency emergency response team in situations where there was no United Nations field presence; IASC serve as the primary policy coordinator in complex emergencies and be more action-oriented; DHA consider entrusting primary responsibility in specific complex emergencies to operational agencies, under the overall leadership of the Emergency Relief Coordinator; the Secretary-General review the financial regulations governing the Central Emergency Revolving Fund (CERF) to ensure quick disbursement; the General Assembly increase the size and scope of CERF; consolidated appeals be used selectively for a system-wide response and their projected requirements be realistic; and Governments, United Nations development organizations, the Bretton Woods institutions and regional commissions be involved early in an emergency to ensure that needs assessments took account of rehabilitation and long-term requirements, promoted national capacity-building and helped to prevent and mitigate future emergencies.

The issue was also considered in April by the Administrative Committee on Coordination,[4] whose recommendations were incorporated into the Secretary-General's report.[1]

Report of the Secretary-General. In accordance with a 1992 General Assembly resolution,[5] the Secretary-General, in November,[6] reported on strengthening the coordination of United Nations humanitarian emergency assistance. The report covered the activities of DHA and IASC, the system's response to disasters and emergencies, information management, and relief, rehabilitation and development efforts.

DHA coordinated responses to an increasing number of emergencies and disasters and established or strengthened mechanisms and procedures to implement Assembly resolutions. It also set up and managed CERF. It continued to adjust its organizational structure and management and coordination mechanisms, including IASC. DHA clarified and rationalized the division of work between its Geneva and New York offices, including the merging of the International Decade for Natural Disaster Reduction secretariat and the Disaster Mitigation Branch. It also proposed integrating the Relief Coordination and Complex Emergencies Branches. DHA also strengthened its cooperation with the operational agencies of the United Nations system, particularly UNDP.

DHA assisted in formulating technical programmes and in channelling external assistance to 18 of the most disaster-prone countries. It helped to launch collective programmes for groups of neighbouring countries with similar needs in Africa, the Andes, Asia, the Mediterranean and the South Pacific. New country-specific programmes were launched in Argentina in 1993. In Asia, the priorities for a new programme of technical cooperation were identified, while in Africa, field missions went to seven of the more disaster-prone countries and a region-wide survey was conducted on the status of national disaster mitigation and future assistance needs.

In the 20 months ending October 1993, DHA addressed 107 disasters worldwide and launched 41 appeals for international assistance. Inter-agency field missions supported national authorities, working closely with the resident coordinator and the disaster management team. DHA provided $1.12 million in emergency grants, established the United Nations Disaster Assessment and Coordination Stand-by Team, which began operating in September 1993, and was preparing operational guidelines for the use of military and civil defence assets to deliver relief assistance following large-scale natural disasters or similar emergencies. DHA was also developing standard operating procedures for a coordinated response to technological disasters, establishing a Central Register of Disaster Management Capacities and incorporating basic specifications for the most frequently used disaster relief items into the stockpile registry.

A dramatic increase in the number and scale of complex emergencies during the year presented new challenges to the United Nations system, particularly DHA. A variety of structures and processes were put in place in different countries to ensure field-level coordination; however, in many cases, intense conflict hampered humanitarian access to those in need. The Secretary-General noted that the financial and human resources available to the United Nations system were insufficient to respond to the increasing number of disasters and emergencies.

DHA was involved in policy coordination and resource mobilization for the clearing of land-mines and was collaborating in the establishment of a database on various aspects of the problem. It was also working with the United Nations Security Coordinator to safeguard humanitarian personnel.

In February, DHA established an informal IASC task force on internally displaced persons and took steps to assist displaced persons in the Sudan and Zaire. It was also involved in the establishment of a new emergency operations centre at Geneva.

Central Emergency Revolving Fund. Concerns were expressed during the year about some of the constraints in utilizing CERF and the desirability of strengthening and expanding it. CERF had disbursed a total of $52.6 million since becom-

ing operational in 1992. Of that amount, $22.5 million had been reimbursed and the balance stood at $19.5 million. In response to recommendations of the Economic and Social Council,[3] DHA advocated the Fund's use for early relief efforts and planned to review its financial regulations to ensure quick disbursements.

Inter-agency coordination. During 1993, IASC provided clear guidelines and made specific policy decisions on a number of substantive issues relating to United Nations responses to complex emergencies in Angola, Somalia, the Sudan and the newly independent States of the former USSR. It also focused on the formulation of system-wide policies and strategies for addressing the problems of internally displaced persons and the relief-rehabilitation continuum. In response to the recommendations of the Economic and Social Council[3] on its role and activities in coordinating assistance during complex emergencies, IASC agreed that terms of reference should be drafted to enhance its decision-making and follow-up. The first meeting of the IASC Task Force on the Relief-to-Development Continuum (New York, 6 October) established two working groups, the first to discuss a unified definition of the concept and development of a system-wide operational framework, and the second to elaborate a financial strategy.

The Commission on Human Settlements, in May,[7] recommended that the United Nations Centre for Human Settlements (Habitat) play an active role in the work of IASC.

UNDP action. On 18 June,[8] the Governing Council requested UNDP to work closely with the secretariat of the International Decade for Natural Disaster Reduction in disaster prevention and mitigation, and to participate in the 1994 World Conference on Natural Disaster Reduction. It urged that a more structured working relationship between UNDP and DHA be put into effect as soon as possible. The Council requested the UNDP Administrator to support DHA initiatives to develop an operational framework identifying the roles and responsibilities of all the system's operational entities at the various stages of the relief-to-development continuum.

In his annual report for 1993,[9] the Administrator reported that UNDP took several important steps during the year in the area of the relief-to-development continuum, in collaboration with DHA. It made 54 approvals under the disaster mitigation category of the Special Programme Resources and initiated support for the reintegration of uprooted populations in Cambodia, Djibouti, Kenya, Liberia, Mozambique, Rwanda, Sierra Leone and Somalia.

In the area of disaster mitigation, assistance was directed towards coordination, with special emphasis on those activities not covered by other

United Nations agencies. Allocations focused on vulnerability reduction, multisectoral needs assessments for the internally displaced, refugees and returnees, and short-term support to resident coordinators to enhance the field-level coordination of emergency assistance provided by the United Nations system. The main objective was to build the capacity of national disaster-management institutions. It also conducted 15 workshops under its Disaster Management Training Programme, jointly managed with DHA.

UNICEF action. The Executive Board of the United Nations Children's Fund (UNICEF) (26 April–7 May)[10] urged that UNICEF country programmes, especially in emergency-prone countries, give increased attention to disaster prevention, preparedness and vulnerability analysis. It recommended that country programmes link rehabilitation to sustainable development programmes; suggested that UNICEF increase the evaluation of its emergency programmes, as well as its participation in system-wide evaluations of those activities; confirmed that its emergency support should be financed primarily from supplementary funds and that, in view of the complementarity of the Emergency Programme Fund (EPF) and CERF, funding from EPF should be used only for rapid responses to emergencies not covered by DHA and CERF. The Board requested the Executive Director to collaborate with DHA and other United Nations agencies providing humanitarian assistance in order to make CERF more accessible to the United Nations development system, and recommended a level of $14 million for EPF for 1994-1995, subject to review.

In a follow-up report,[11] UNICEF reviewed progress in responding to emergencies in 1993. It provided an overview of UNICEF assistance and discussed its support to the United Nations coordination system, the continuum from relief to development, policy and programme development and humanitarian mandates. It also discussed UNICEF action to streamline its operational procedures and guidelines for responding rapidly and effectively to emergencies. Annexed to the report were a report on UNICEF assistance in support of complex emergencies and details on the utilization of EPF.

Consolidated appeals

Consolidated inter-agency appeals issued or remaining in effect as at 24 September 1993 related to Afghanistan, Angola, Armenia, Azerbaijan, Eritrea, Ethiopia, Georgia, Haiti, Iraq, Kenya, Lebanon, Liberia, Mozambique, Rwanda, Somalia, the Sudan, Tajikistan, the former Yugoslavia, southern Africa and Zaire. However, only 56 per cent of their requirements had been met and other funding mechanisms and resource mobilization strategies were being studied. IASC was formulating guidelines to ensure the consistency, effectiveness, field orientation and priority focus of the appeals.

GENERAL ASSEMBLY ACTION

On 14 December, the General Assembly adopted **resolution 48/57** without vote.

Strengthening of the coordination of humanitarian emergency assistance of the United Nations

The General Assembly,

Reaffirming its resolutions 46/182 of 19 December 1991 and 47/168 of 22 December 1992,

Reaffirming also the guiding principles contained in section I of the annex to its resolution 46/182,

Noting that States have submitted replies to the Secretary-General pursuant to paragraphs 7 and 8 of its resolution 47/168,

Taking note of the relevant decisions of operational agencies, organizations, programmes and funds of the United Nations system concerning their participation in a coordinated response to humanitarian emergencies,

Deeply concerned about the increasing number and growing magnitude and complexity of natural disasters and other emergencies,

Concerned about the impediments created by natural disasters and other emergencies to the efforts of the affected countries to achieve development,

Emphasizing the importance of a timely, prompt and effective humanitarian response,

Stressing the importance of a coordinated response to natural disasters and of technical and financial assistance to the natural-disaster-prone countries in the fields of disaster preparedness and mitigation, including exchange of information and post-disaster development activities,

Noting the encouraging results of the operation of the Central Emergency Revolving Fund and its increasing utilization by the operational agencies,

Recognizing the increasing need for humanitarian assistance and adequate financial resources to ensure a prompt response by the United Nations to humanitarian emergency situations, both for relief and for the continuum to development,

Recognizing also the need to strengthen coordination further, in particular field coordination, on humanitarian assistance, bearing in mind that coordination should be field-oriented,

Noting also the humanitarian and rehabilitation aspects of the problem of mine clearance, in the context of its resolution 48/7 of 19 October 1993,

Welcoming the efforts being undertaken in the Inter-Agency Standing Committee to develop a coherent and complementary approach on the part of the relevant operational and development actors to the continuum-related activities,

Stressing the need for adequate protection of personnel involved in humanitarian operations in accordance with relevant norms and principles of international law and within the context of General Assembly resolutions 47/120 A of 18 December 1992 and 47/120 B of 20 September 1993, taking into account recent initiatives in this regard,

1. *Takes note* of the report of the Secretary-General;

2. *Agrees fully* with the agreed conclusions of the Economic and Social Council, the implementation of which

will be reviewed by the Council at its substantive session of 1994;

3. *Emphasizes* the leadership role of the Secretary-General, through the Emergency Relief Coordinator and working closely with him, in coordinating a coherent and timely response to humanitarian emergencies;

4. *Stresses* the essential need for improved coordination within the United Nations system, and, while reaffirming the mandate and functions of the Department of Humanitarian Affairs to that end, requests the Emergency Relief Coordinator to improve coordination and management further, both at Headquarters and at the field level, including the coordination of the work of the relevant operational agencies;

5. *Invites* the intergovernmental bodies of the relevant operational organizations and agencies to provide full support for system-wide coordination, under the leadership of the Emergency Relief Coordinator, in order to facilitate an effective response at Headquarters and at the field level to natural disasters and other emergencies;

6. *Also stresses*, in this regard, that the Inter-Agency Standing Committee, under the leadership of the Emergency Relief Coordinator, should serve as the primary mechanism for inter-agency coordination, meet more frequently and act therefore in an action-oriented manner on policy issues related to humanitarian assistance and on formulating a coherent and timely United Nations response to humanitarian emergencies;

7. *Further stresses* the necessity of accelerating the development of an emergency information system, within the Department of Humanitarian Affairs, to collect and disseminate timely information on natural disasters and other humanitarian emergencies, including information provided by the national Government, United Nations agencies, donors and relief organizations, to provide early warning of a crisis, to assess needs on a continuing basis and to track financial and other contributions;

8. *Recognizes* the need to increase the resources available in the Central Emergency Revolving Fund, including through timely repayment of funds, invites potential donors to make additional contributions to the Fund, and requests the Secretary-General to conduct consultations to that effect, taking fully into account the need to secure contributions to the Fund on an assured, broad-based and additional basis;

9. *Decides* to expand the scope of the Central Emergency Revolving Fund to include the International Organization for Migration;

10. *Invites* operational agencies to contribute to field-level coordination in the early stages of an emergency;

11. *Requests* the Inter-Agency Standing Committee to agree, as a matter of urgency, on the best means and guidelines to ensure adequate human and financial resources for rapid response coordination, including the provision of resources that could be drawn on by the Emergency Relief Coordinator for establishing special coordination arrangements in the initial stage of an emergency, taking into account the relevant provisions of General Assembly resolutions 46/182 and 47/199 of 22 December 1992 and of the agreed conclusions of the Economic and Social Council related to field-level coordination;

12. *Decides also*, pending a final decision to be taken by the Economic and Social Council at its substantive session of 1994, on the basis of the recommendations of the Inter-Agency Standing Committee, as well as on

the experience gained, to authorize, in exceptional circumstances, on a time-bound basis and while preserving the revolving nature of the Central Emergency Revolving Fund, the Emergency Relief Coordinator and relevant operational agencies, under the leadership of the Coordinator, to draw from the interest earned by the Revolving Fund to enhance rapid response coordination where insufficient capacity exists at the field level;

13. *Also requests* the Inter-Agency Standing Committee to provide recommendations on other issues related to field coordination, including measures taken for clear allocations of responsibilities at an early stage of an emergency, in particular by entrusting the primary responsibility to the operational agencies, as appropriate, and on standardized procedures for joint emergency needs assessment missions, under the overall leadership and coordination of the Emergency Relief Coordinator;

14. *Requests* the Secretary-General to include in his annual report on the coordination of humanitarian emergency assistance recommendations on practical measures to enhance the coordinated system-wide support for efforts to facilitate the transition from emergency relief to rehabilitation and development and, particularly in the context of activities of the International Decade for Natural Disaster Reduction, the promotion of national capacity-building to help prevent and mitigate future emergencies;

15. *Also requests* the Secretary-General to continue to strengthen the consolidated appeals process, making it more field-oriented, and to ensure that such appeals are based on specific priorities resulting from comprehensive and realistic projections of relief requirements for natural disasters and other emergencies requiring a coordinated response, and in this context invites all concerned operational and humanitarian organizations and agencies to cooperate and fully participate in the preparation of these appeals;

16. *Calls upon* States to respond quickly and generously to consolidated appeals for humanitarian assistance, taking into account rehabilitation and long-term development requirements;

17. *Invites* the Secretary-General to examine further all possible ways and means to provide, within existing resources, adequate qualified personnel and administrative resources commensurate with the responsibilities of the Department of Humanitarian Affairs in dealing with the increasing number of natural disasters and other emergencies;

18. *Stresses* the importance of the Emergency Relief Coordinator participating fully in the overall United Nations planning of responses to emergencies in order to serve as the humanitarian advocate in ensuring that the humanitarian dimension, particularly the principles of humanity, neutrality and impartiality of relief assistance, is taken fully into account;

19. *Emphasizes* the importance of the role of the Emergency Relief Coordinator in facilitating access by the operational organizations to emergency areas for the rapid provision of emergency assistance by obtaining the consent of all parties concerned, through modalities such as the establishment of temporary relief corridors where needed, days and zones of tranquillity and other forms, including facilitating for those organizations the return of refugees and displaced persons;

20. *Requests* the Secretary-General to include in his annual report to the General Assembly at its forty-ninth

session recommendations on ways and means to improve the operational capacity of the emergency stockpiles, as well as an analysis of the advantages or disadvantages, including promptness of the response and cost-effectiveness, of the establishment of regional warehouses, taking into account the existing facilities and the possibility of strengthening them;

21. *Also requests* the Secretary-General to include in his report to the Economic and Social Council at its substantive session of 1994 the recommendations of the Inter-Agency Standing Committee requested in paragraphs 11 and 13 of the present resolution;

22. *Further requests* the Secretary-General to include in his annual report on the coordination of humanitarian emergency assistance to the General Assembly at its forty-ninth session information on the progress made in the implementation of the present resolution and on ways of further strengthening coordination of humanitarian emergency assistance within the United Nations system.

General Assembly resolution 48/57

14 December 1993   Meeting 78   Adopted without vote

31-nation draft (A/48/L.47 & Add.1); agenda item 44.

Sponsors: Armenia, Australia, Austria, Azerbaijan, Belarus, Belgium, Canada, China, Colombia, Denmark, Finland, France, Germany, Greece, Ireland, Italy, Japan, Kazakhstan, Luxembourg, Netherlands, New Zealand, Norway, Poland, Portugal, Russian Federation, Spain, Sweden, Turkey, Ukraine, United Kingdom, United States.

Meeting numbers. GA 48th session: plenary 58, 59, 63, 78.

The Assembly, in **resolution 48/162**, outlined its organizational approach to discussions on the strengthening of the coordination of humanitarian and disaster relief assistance of the United Nations, including special economic assistance.

Activities

Africa

Special Emergency Programme for the Horn of Africa

In May, DHA reported that United Nations consolidated inter-agency appeals were launched in 1993 for Eritrea, Ethiopia, Kenya, Somalia and the Sudan under the Special Emergency Programme for the Horn of Africa (SEPHA). However, the response to the appeals was weak. Of the $921.8 million requested for the five countries, only $172,174,350, or 18.7 per cent, was received or firmly committed as at 10 May. As a result, most agencies either scaled down or failed to implement many humanitarian aid efforts.

In Eritrea, which became independent on 24 May, a plan was being finalized for the return and rehabilitation of refugees. The total 1993 appeal for Eritrea was $80.5 million, and a pledging conference for refugee reintegration and rehabilitation of resettlement areas was held on 6 July. In Ethiopia, improvements in the general situation significantly reduced the number of people requiring assistance, and total funding requests for Ethiopia in 1993 amounted to $299,871,748 for relief, rehabilitation and refugee assistance activi-

ties. In Kenya, the need for aid for drought victims, refugees and displaced people continued, although the numbers requiring assistance declined. The 1993 appeal for Kenya totalled $192.2 million. There were no major unmet humanitarian needs in Djibouti, but further assistance was given for the expansion of refugee camps and for the repatriation of refugees to Somalia. In Somalia, there were significant improvements in the provision of relief aid during the first months of 1993 and mortality and morbidity dropped sharply.

Angola

In response to a 1992 General Assembly request,[12] the Secretary-General reported in October 1993 on international assistance for the economic rehabilitation of Angola.[13] The report described the humanitarian assistance programme, including sectoral interventions and organizational arrangements, and outlined the assistance provided by Member States and the United Nations system. The Secretary-General said that the prospect of favourable conditions for the economic and social rehabilitation of Angola was extinguished with the advent of an undeclared state of war following the 1992 elections. Major hostilities through September 1993 had devastated Angola's population and caused the virtual collapse of its social and economic system, posing special challenges to all relief agencies. Efforts to establish a cease-fire to permit the provision of humanitarian assistance had proved unsuccessful, and reconstruction and development plans had been transformed into emergency humanitarian assistance programmes. The United Nations focused on immediate humanitarian needs and preventive approaches in fields such as health and nutrition. In February, UNICEF applied its adaptive programming approach for a country in difficult circumstances, and subsequently launched a 90-day Plan of Action. The Office of the United Nations High Commissioner for Refugees (UNHCR) modified its programme to concentrate on repatriates and to extend support to non-returnee populations bordering Zaire and Zambia. Various NGOs also reoriented their strategies and programmes to cope with the wide-scale civil conflict.

In May, DHA issued a consolidated inter-agency appeal for $226 million in humanitarian assistance. Contributions of $60 million were reported, including $48 million in food aid. Following discussions in July and August, the Special Representative of the Secretary-General, the Government of Angola and the National Union for the Total Independence of Angola (UNITA) agreed to a revised emergency relief plan targeting areas considered insecure. In October, the first relief flights in nine months reached the town of Cuito, and all besieged cities received humanitarian assistance.

A United Nations Humanitarian Assistance Coordination Unit, under the supervision of the Special Representative, was established to coordinate the activities and contributions of the international community, NGOs and United Nations agencies. The Unit developed an emergency relief plan to deliver humanitarian relief items to sites that remained accessible and to negotiate with the Government and UNITA for access to locations under siege. The Secretary-General concluded that comprehensive and lasting peace was essential for the adequate provision of humanitarian assistance to Angola.

GENERAL ASSEMBLY ACTION

On 21 December, the General Assembly, on the recommendation of the Second Committee, adopted **resolution 48/202** without vote.

International assistance for the economic rehabilitation of Angola

The General Assembly,

Recalling its resolutions 47/164 of 18 December 1992, 46/142 of 17 December 1991, 45/233 of 21 December 1990 and 44/168 of 15 December 1989 on international assistance for the economic rehabilitation of Angola,

Recalling also that the Security Council in its resolutions 387(1976) of 31 March 1976, 475(1980) of 27 June 1980, 628(1989) of 16 January 1989 and other resolutions on international assistance for the economic rehabilitation of Angola had, *inter alia*, requested the international community to render assistance to Angola,

Deeply concerned about the critical economic and political situation prevailing in Angola, aggravated by the renewal in October 1992 of hostilities which continue to destroy the economic and social infrastructure,

Concerned about the serious deterioration of the humanitarian situation, as a result of which an estimated 3 million people are in need of emergency aid,

Gravely concerned about the drought, which has devastated the centre and south of the country, causing suffering for millions of people,

Taking into consideration the fact that the implementation of the Peace Accords for Angola would create favourable conditions for the economic and social rehabilitation of the country,

Aware of the need for a greater effort and commitment on the part of the international community to assist Angola in rehabilitating its economy,

Conscious of the fact that during 1993, owing to the prevailing situation in the country, the Government of Angola was unable to organize a round-table conference of donors as planned,

1. *Takes note* of the report of the Secretary-General;

2. *Calls upon* all parties to do their utmost to achieve the full and effective implementation of the Peace Accords for Angola in order to bring peace and stability to Angola, thus creating conditions conducive to its economic rehabilitation;

3. *Expresses its appreciation* to all States, United Nations organizations and other donors for the emergency humanitarian assistance rendered to Angola through the Special Relief Programme for Angola, and appeals for continued and generous contributions for emergency humanitarian assistance;

4. *Reiterates its appeal* to the international community to continue to render the material, technical and financial assistance necessary for the economic rehabilitation of Angola;

5. *Requests* the Secretary-General, in cooperation with the international community, to continue to mobilize organizations and organs of the United Nations system in order to ensure an appropriate level of economic assistance for Angola;

6. *Welcomes* the decision of the Government of Angola to organize in 1994 a round-table conference of donors for the rehabilitation and reconstruction of Angola, in collaboration with the United Nations Development Programme, the African Development Bank, the Government of Portugal and other interested countries;

7. *Also requests* the Secretary-General to report to the General Assembly at its fiftieth session on the implementation of the present resolution;

8. *Decides* to include in the provisional agenda of its fiftieth session the item entitled "International assistance for the economic rehabilitation of Angola".

General Assembly resolution 48/202

21 December 1993   Meeting 86   Adopted without vote

Approved by Second Committee (A/48/727) without vote, 6 December (meeting 45); draft by Algeria (for African States), Antigua and Barbuda, Bosnia and Herzegovina, Brazil, Cambodia, China, Colombia, Cuba, El Salvador, Guatemala, Guyana, Honduras, Italy, Portugal, Spain, Suriname and the former Yugoslav Republic of Macedonia (A/C.2/48/L.36), orally revised following informal consultations; agenda item 101.

Meeting numbers. GA 48th session: 2nd Committee 33-35, 41, 45; plenary 86.

Burundi

On 27 October,[14] Burundi informed the Secretary-General of violence and the risk of civil war in the country following a military coup on 21 October. The number of refugees and displaced persons at that time was estimated at more than 300,000. Burundi requested the international community to intervene urgently to restore democratic institutions and provide emergency humanitarian assistance.

On 3 November, the General Assembly, by **resolution 48/17**, requested Member States and international, intergovernmental and non-governmental organizations to provide emergency humanitarian assistance and/or other assistance to the people of Burundi.

On 16 November,[15] the President of the Security Council stated that the Council was alarmed at the movement of over 700,000 refugees into neighbouring countries and an increasing number of displaced persons throughout the country. The Council appealed to all States, international agencies and other humanitarian organizations to provide prompt humanitarian assistance to the af-

fected civilian population in Burundi and neighbouring countries.

In response to that situation, the United Nations, on 23 November, launched an appeal for
$9.5 million to meet the basic survival needs of
the displaced. UNHCR also appealed for $17 mil-
lion for assistance to Burundi refugees in Rwanda,
the United Republic of Tanzania and Zaire.

Liberia

The Secretary-General submitted in September
a report on assistance for the rehabilitation and
reconstruction of Liberia,[16] as requested by the
Assembly in 1992.[17] The report provided sectoral
reviews of assistance and requirements and outlined contributions from Member States and the
United Nations system.

The report noted that the security and socio-
economic situation in Liberia continued to deteriorate and that the October 1992 attack on Monrovia and subsequent hostilities had led to massive
population displacements and damage to infrastructure. As a result of the new emergency situation, a special emergency appeal for $7.5 million
was issued in November 1992. Donations received
since the outbreak of the Liberia crisis totalled $147.4
million. The signing, on 25 July 1993, of the Cotonou
Peace Agreement[18] created the prospect of more
effective relief operations and the implementation
of rehabilitation and reconstruction programmes.
By mid-August, the United Nations had resumed
humanitarian relief to parts of Liberia controlled
by the National Patriotic Front and had sent a mission to assess needs.

The Secretary-General said that it was necessary
to maintain a range of humanitarian assistance activities to deal with the return of refugees, the resettlement of displaced persons, and the demobilization and reintegration of troops. The programme
should also shift its emphasis from relief to reconstruction and rehabilitation.

On 26 March, by **resolution 813(1993)**, the Security Council reaffirmed its support for increased
humanitarian assistance to Liberia and demanded
that parties to the conflict refrain from impeding
its delivery. It also called on the parties to ensure
the safety of all humanitarian assistance personnel. On 22 September, by **resolution 866(1993)**,
the Council established the United Nations Observer Mission in Liberia, which would assist in
the coordination of humanitarian activities in the
field. It also welcomed the Secretary-General's establishment of a Trust Fund to assist in mine-clearing,
humanitarian and development activities.

GENERAL ASSEMBLY ACTION

On 21 December, the General Assembly, on the
recommendation of the Second Committee,
adopted **resolution 48/197** without vote.

Assistance for the rehabilitation and reconstruction of Liberia

The General Assembly,

Recalling its resolutions 45/232 of 21 December 1990,
46/147 of 17 December 1991 and 47/154 of 18 December 1992,

Taking note of Security Council resolutions 813(1993)
of 26 March 1993, 856(1993) of 10 August 1993 and
866(1993) of 22 September 1993, in which the Council,
inter alia, decided to establish the United Nations Observer Mission in Liberia, under its authority and under
the direction of the Secretary-General through his Special Representative, for a period of seven months,

Taking note also of Security Council resolution 868(1993)
of 29 September 1993, in which the Council, *inter alia*,
urged States and parties to a conflict to cooperate closely
with the United Nations to ensure the security and safety
of United Nations forces and personnel,

Having considered the report of the Secretary-General,

Noting that, even though a viable country-wide emergency assistance programme has been instituted, security and logistic problems continue to hamper relief assistance, particularly in the interior, and have prevented
the transition from emergency relief to reconstruction
and development,

Gravely concerned about the devastating effects of the protracted conflict on the socio-economic conditions in Liberia, and noting the urgent need to rehabilitate, in an
atmosphere of peace and stability, basic sectors of the
country in order to restore normalcy,

Welcoming the signing on 25 July 1993 at Cotonou,
Benin, under the auspices of the Economic Community
of West African States, by the Interim Government of
National Unity of Liberia, the National Patriotic Front
of Liberia and the United Liberation Movement of Liberia for Democracy, of a peace agreement providing
for a cease-fire, disarmament and demobilization of the
warring parties, formation of a transitional government
and the holding of general and presidential elections,

1. *Expresses its gratitude* to the States and international
and non-governmental organizations that have
responded and continue to respond to appeals by the
Interim Government of Liberia, as well as to appeals
by the Secretary-General for emergency relief and other
assistance;

2. *Expresses its gratitude* to the Secretary-General for
his continued efforts in mobilizing the international
community, the United Nations and other organizations
to provide emergency assistance to Liberia, and urges
that such assistance be continued;

3. *Calls upon* the international community and intergovernmental organizations to continue to provide
Liberia, as appropriate, with technical, financial and
other assistance for the repatriation and resettlement of
Liberian refugees, returnees and displaced persons and
for the rehabilitation of combatants, which constitute
important elements for facilitating the holding of
democratic elections in Liberia;

4. *Appeals* to the international community and intergovernmental organizations to provide adequate assistance
to programmes identified in the report of the Secretary-
General, including through contributions to the Trust
Fund established by the Secretary-General, in order, *inter
alia*, to help defray the cost of the deployment of additional peace-keeping forces of the Military Observer Group
of the Economic Community of West African States;

5. *Calls upon* all parties and factions in Liberia to ensure fully the security and safety of personnel of the United Nations and its specialized agencies, as well as of non-governmental organizations, and to guarantee their complete freedom of movement throughout Liberia, and to take all steps necessary to create an atmosphere conducive to the successful implementation of the Cotonou Agreement;

6. *Requests* the Secretary-General:

(a) To continue his efforts to coordinate the work of the United Nations system and to mobilize financial, technical and other assistance for the rehabilitation and reconstruction of Liberia;

(b) To undertake, when conditions permit, in close collaboration with the authorities of Liberia, an overall assessment of needs, with the objective of holding, when appropriate, a round-table conference of donors for the rehabilitation and reconstruction of Liberia;

7. *Also requests* the Secretary-General to report to the General Assembly at its forty-ninth session on the implementation of the present resolution;

8. *Decides* to include in the provisional agenda of its forty-ninth session an item entitled ''International assistance for the reconstruction and rehabilitation of Liberia''.

General Assembly resolution 48/197

21 December 1993   Meeting 86   Adopted without vote

Approved by Second Committee (A/48/726) without vote, 6 December (meeting 45); draft by Vice-Chairman (A/C.2/48/L.63), based on informal consultations on draft by Algeria (for African States), Guyana and United States (A/C.2/48/L.32); agenda item 100.
Meeting numbers. GA 48th session: 2nd Committee 33-35, 41, 45; plenary 86.

Rwanda

The Secretary-General reported[19] to the Security Council in August that the number of displaced persons in Rwanda resulting from the conflict there was estimated at 900,000. The situation was exacerbated by Rwanda's already precarious economic condition, high population density and rapidly declining agricultural production. Following an inter-agency mission to Rwanda in March, DHA on 15 April launched a consolidated appeal for $78 million to meet the needs of those displaced from April to December.

In March, the Security Council (**resolution 812(1993)**) expressed alarm at the humanitarian consequences of the latest resumption of fighting in Rwanda and called on the parties to allow the delivery of humanitarian supplies and the return of displaced persons. In September,[20] the Secretary-General stated that the international community had contributed up to $100 million since January 1993. Since the signing of the Arusha peace agreement in August (see PART TWO, Chapter I), 600,000 individuals had returned home, and assistance would continue to be provided to those remaining in camps. The United Nations was encouraging the donor community to pool resources for a comprehensive programme of assistance to demobilized soldiers, UNHCR was coordinating refugee activities, and

a mine-clearing programme was to be initiated. UNDP and DHA were planning a round-table meeting on humanitarian assistance in 1994.

The Security Council in October (**resolution 872(1993)**) established the United Nations Assistance Mission for Rwanda, to assist in the coordination of humanitarian assistance activities. It urged Member States, the specialized agencies and NGOs to intensify their economic, financial and humanitarian assistance.

Also in October,[21] Rwanda informed the General Assembly that, although the April appeal had improved the humanitarian situation, the war had destroyed a substantial amount of socio-economic and administrative infrastructure and had prevented Rwanda from achieving the macroeconomic and sectoral objectives of its 1990 structural adjustment programme. Further international assistance was requested to revive the economy and rebuild and rehabilitate national infrastructure.

In December,[22] the Secretary-General stated that emergency and rehabilitation efforts for displaced persons had been complicated by an influx of some 375,000 refugees from Burundi, due to ethnic violence and drought in that country.

GENERAL ASSEMBLY ACTION

On 21 December, on the recommendation of the Second Committee, the General Assembly adopted **resolution 48/211** without vote.

Emergency assistance for the socio-economic rehabilitation of Rwanda

The General Assembly,

Recalling Security Council resolutions 812(1993) of 12 March 1993 and 846(1993) of 22 June 1993 on the situation in Rwanda,

Recalling also Security Council resolution 872(1993) of 5 October 1993, in which the Council urged Member States, United Nations agencies and non-governmental organizations to provide and intensify their economic, financial and humanitarian assistance in favour of the Rwandese population and of the democratization process in Rwanda,

Noting with satisfaction the signing, on 4 August 1993 at Arusha, United Republic of Tanzania, of the Peace Agreement between the Government of Rwanda and the Rwandese Patriotic Front, which put an end to the armed conflict,

Taking into account the serious consequences of the breakdown of the national economy and the destruction of important social, economic and administrative infrastructures in the areas affected by the war, as well as the imperious necessity to satisfy the needs of the displaced persons and the refugees,

Taking into consideration the fact that the implementation of the Arusha Peace Agreement would create favourable conditions for the socio-economic rehabilitation of Rwanda,

Also taking into consideration the fact that the insufficiency of economic and financial resources of Rwanda requires the assistance of the international community in order to enable the implementation of the Arusha Peace Agreement,

Noting the recent large-scale inflow of refugees from Burundi into Rwanda,

1. *Calls upon* all parties to do their utmost to achieve the full and effective implementation of the Arusha Peace Agreement and national reconciliation goals, thus creating conditions conducive to the socio-economic rehabilitation of Rwanda;

2. *Expresses its appreciation* to all States, United Nations organizations and intergovernmental and non-governmental organizations for the emergency humanitarian assistance rendered to Rwanda since the beginning of hostilities;

3. *Welcomes* the United Nations Consolidated Inter-Agency Appeal for Rwanda, launched in April 1993 by the Department of Humanitarian Affairs of the Secretariat in favour of displaced persons in Rwanda;

4. *Urges* all States, United Nations organizations and intergovernmental and non-governmental organizations to intensify, in favour of Rwanda, economic, financial, material and technical assistance in order to encourage the process of rehabilitation and sustained development, especially by raising its economy, rebuilding and rehabilitating various infrastructures destroyed by the war;

5. *Invites* all States, United Nations organizations and intergovernmental and non-governmental organizations to provide to Rwanda adequate assistance for the settlement of displaced persons and the repatriation of refugees, the demobilization of soldiers and reintegration of demobilized soldiers into civil life, the clearance of mines and the completion of the democratic process;

6. *Requests* the Secretary-General to support with all possible assistance the consolidation of peace in Rwanda and to submit a report to the General Assembly at its forty-ninth session on the implementation of the present resolution;

7. *Decides* to include in the provisional agenda of its forty-ninth session the item entitled "Emergency assistance for the socio-economic rehabilitation of Rwanda".

General Assembly resolution 48/211

21 December 1993   Meeting 86   Adopted without vote

Approved by Second Committee (A/48/735) without vote, 6 December (meeting 45); draft by Algeria (for African States), Belgium, Democratic People's Republic of Korea, El Salvador, Honduras and Republic of Korea (A/C.2/48/L.35), orally revised, and further orally revised following informal consultations; agenda item 171.

Meeting numbers. GA 48th session: 2nd Committee 33-35, 42, 45; plenary 86.

Sierra Leone

The Cotonou Peace Agreement,[18] signed in July, provided for the sealing of borders with Côte d'Ivoire, Guinea and Sierra Leone to prevent cross-border attacks, infiltration or the importation of arms. In September, the Security Council (**resolution 866(1993)**) established a United Nations Observer Mission (see above), *inter alia*, to monitor compliance with that Agreement.

GENERAL ASSEMBLY ACTION

On 21 December, the General Assembly, on the recommendation of the Second Committee, adopted **resolution 48/196** without vote.

International assistance to Sierra Leone
The General Assembly,

Recalling its resolutions 37/158 of 17 December 1982, 38/205 of 20 December 1983 and 39/192 of 17 December 1984, in which it appealed to all States, the specialized agencies and international development and financial institutions to provide all possible assistance for the development of Sierra Leone,

Recalling also its resolution 37/133 of 17 December 1982, in which it decided to include Sierra Leone in the list of the least developed countries,

Taking note of Security Council resolution 866(1993) of 22 September 1993, in which the Council decided to establish, under its authority, the United Nations Observer Mission in Liberia to, *inter alia*, monitor compliance with the peace agreement, including at points on Liberia's borders with Sierra Leone and other neighbouring countries,

Aware that the Government of Sierra Leone, in cooperation with the Governments of the other States members of the Economic Community of West African States, embarked, at the height of the Liberian crisis, upon a peace-keeping/peace-monitoring exercise at Monrovia, capital of neighbouring Liberia,

Aware also of the serious destruction and devastation of the productive areas of the territory of Sierra Leone, and of its economy as a whole, brought about by the spill-over effect of the conflict in Liberia,

Concerned at the consequent devastating effects on the lives and properties of Sierra Leoneans in the eastern and southern provinces, which have resulted in massive outflows of refugees and displaced persons,

Alarmed at the astronomical cost to the Government of Sierra Leone of protecting its territory and people from the spill-over effect of the conflict in Liberia,

Conscious of the need for the international community to assist Sierra Leone in the rehabilitation of its economy and the effective implementation of reconstruction and rehabilitation programmes, which require the mobilization of substantial resources that are beyond the current means of the country,

Aware that the financial crisis that Sierra Leone is undergoing has led to a slowing down of its economic and social development,

1. *Expresses its gratitude* to the Secretary-General for his efforts in mobilizing the international community, the United Nations system and other organizations to provide assistance to Sierra Leone;

2. *Calls upon* the international community and intergovernmental and non-governmental organizations to provide Sierra Leone with technical, financial and other forms of assistance for the repatriation and resettlement of Sierra Leonean refugees, returnees and displaced persons;

3. *Appeals* to the international community and intergovernmental and non-governmental organizations to provide adequate assistance for the rehabilitation of the economy of Sierra Leone and the reconstruction of its devastated areas;

4. *Urges* all States and relevant United Nations bodies to provide all possible assistance to help the Government of Sierra Leone meet the critical humanitarian needs of the population and to provide, as appropriate, food, medicine and essential equipment for hospitals and schools;

5. *Urgently reiterates its appeal* to the international community, including the specialized agencies and other or-

ganizations and bodies of the United Nations system, to contribute generously, through bilateral and multilateral channels, to the economic and social development of Sierra Leone;

6. *Requests* the Secretary-General to continue his efforts to mobilize the resources necessary for an effective programme of financial, technical and material assistance to Sierra Leone;

7. *Also requests* the Secretary-General to report to the General Assembly at its forty-ninth session on the implementation of the present resolution;

8. *Decides* to include in the provisional agenda of its forty-ninth session an item entitled "International assistance to Sierra Leone".

General Assembly resolution 48/196

21 December 1993   Meeting 86   Adopted without vote

Approved by Second Committee (A/48/726) without vote, 6 December (meeting 45); draft by Vice-Chairman (A/C.2/48/L.64), based on informal consultations on draft by Algeria (for African States), Cuba, Grenada, Guyana, Papua New Guinea, Saint Kitts and Nevis, Saint Vincent and the Grenadines, Singapore and Solomon Islands (A/C.2/48/L.31); agenda item 100.

Meeting numbers. GA 48th session: 2nd Committee 33-35, 41, 45; plenary 86.

Somalia

Responding to a 1992 General Assembly request,[23] the Secretary-General, in an October report on emergency assistance for humanitarian relief and the economic and social rehabilitation of Somalia,[24] provided information on the 100-Day Action Programme for Accelerated Humanitarian Assistance, the 1993 relief and rehabilitation programme, challenges facing the humanitarian mission, and assistance provided by the United Nations system and by Member States.

The 100-Day Action Programme, initiated in October 1992,[25] was extended to the end of March 1993 and received $74 million of the $83 million required. The Unified Task Force (UNITAF) helped to open access to remote areas and enabled the delivery of relief supplies. It opened the port of Mogadishu and repaired major supply routes. The combined efforts of humanitarian organizations and security forces dramatically reduced levels of malnutrition and mortality; however, theft, looting and extortion plagued relief efforts, and the resettlement of internally displaced persons and refugees was affected by ongoing security problems.

At the beginning of 1993, the worst of the emergency appeared to be over and the focus of the operation started to shift from relief to rehabilitation. The 1993 relief and rehabilitation programme, with requirements of $166.5 million, was launched at the Third Coordination Meeting for Humanitarian Assistance for Somalia (Addis Ababa, Ethiopia, 11-13 March). The Conference on National Reconciliation (15 March) endorsed the outcome of the Meeting and condemned attacks on relief personnel and supplies.

The mandate of the United Nations Operation in Somalia (UNOSOM) was expanded by the Security Council in March (**resolution 814(1993)**), following reports by the Secretary-General.[26] The Council requested him to provide assistance covering: economic relief and rehabilitation; the repatriation of refugees and resettlement of displaced persons; the re-establishment of national and regional institutions, civil administration and the Somali police force; and mine clearance. UNOSOM II took over from UNITAF the task of facilitating the delivery of humanitarian assistance and expanding efforts to establish security throughout Somalia.

In July, the Secretary-General reported to the Council[27] on attacks on UNOSOM II forces on 5 June. The attack and insecurity in Mogadishu South resulted in the temporary curtailment of many humanitarian programmes, but relief operations in the country were not disrupted. Pockets of acute malnutrition and medical problems persisted and about 1 million Somalis required shelter and life-sustaining assistance. Of the 1.7 million Somalis forced to leave their homes, over 1 million had crossed into Kenya and Ethiopia, while others moved to Mogadishu, Kismayo and Baidoa.

The rehabilitation of social services also continued, with NGOs reporting that some 23,000 primary grade students had enrolled in 22 schools in the Bay, Bakool, Mogadishu and Lower Shabelle regions. In the Juba Valley, schools were rehabilitated and provided with textbooks and other equipment. An education development centre was established at Mogadishu, together with a scholarship programme to allow Somali university students to complete their studies abroad. Some 32 hospitals and 81 child health centres were operating throughout the country, and mobile vaccination teams were providing immunization. The water supply systems at Mogadishu, Afgoi, Hargeisa and Berbera were rehabilitated and sanitation projects were maintained. Some success was reported with the reactivation of food-crop and livestock production. Commercial and trading activities showed encouraging signs of recovery, limited telecommunication services were available and local companies provided fuel throughout the country. UNOSOM II, the World Bank and UNDP developed a draft planning framework for the reconstruction and recovery of Somalia, which was reviewed by the third informal meeting of donors, United Nations agencies and NGOs, sponsored by the World Bank (Paris, 22 October).

On 16 November, the Under-Secretary-General for Humanitarian Affairs told the Assembly's Second Committee that Somalia required short-term assistance and rehabilitation measures and long-term development and reconstruction work. The Fourth Coordination Meeting for Humanitarian

Assistance for Somalia (Addis Ababa, 29 November–1 December) considered implementation of those measures.

The Secretary-General, in a later report to the Council,[28] stated that UNOSOM II had highlighted, at the Fourth Coordination Meeting, its efforts to place humanitarian assistance at the forefront of its work in Somalia. Somali delegates and international donors had reaffirmed their commitment to accelerate Somali control of the recovery and development process, and the Meeting had agreed on a strategy for the mobilization and allocation of resources and the development of programmes and projects. Agreements were also reached on the establishment of development committees in the various regions and the formation of a Development Council to mobilize resources. An aid coordination body was to be set up to coordinate donor assistance. The strategy was to be implemented in regions where a large measure of stability and security prevailed.

The Secretary-General also reported that the donor community's willingness to commit further resources to Somalia's rehabilitation and reconstruction was conditional on national reconciliation and at least minimum levels of security.

In November,[29] the UNDP Administrator informed the Governing Council that he would continue to approve projects in Somalia on a case-by-case basis, pending normalization of the situation in the country. UNDP would concentrate on rehabilitation and reconstruction activities, particularly in the water, health, sanitation, education and infrastructure sectors.

GENERAL ASSEMBLY ACTION

On 21 December, on the recommendation of the Second Committee, the General Assembly adopted **resolution 48/201** without vote.

Assistance for humanitarian relief and the economic and social rehabilitation of Somalia

The General Assembly,

Recalling its resolutions 43/206 of 20 December 1988, 44/178 of 19 December 1989, 45/229 of 21 December 1990, 46/176 of 19 December 1991 and 47/160 of 18 December 1992 and the resolutions and decisions of the Economic and Social Council on emergency assistance to Somalia,

Recalling also Security Council resolution 733(1992) of 23 January 1992 and all subsequent relevant resolutions, in which the Council, *inter alia*, urged all parties, movements and factions in Somalia to facilitate the efforts of the United Nations, its specialized agencies and humanitarian organizations to provide urgent humanitarian assistance to the affected population in Somalia and reiterated the call for the full respect of the security and safety of the personnel of those organizations and the guarantee of their complete freedom of movement in and around Mogadishu and other parts of Somalia,

Noting the cooperation between the United Nations, the Organization of African Unity, the League of Arab States, the Organization of the Islamic Conference, the countries of the Horn of Africa and the countries of the Non-Aligned Movement in their efforts to resolve the humanitarian, security and political crisis in Somalia,

Noting with appreciation the continued efforts made by the Secretary-General to assist the Somali people in their efforts to promote peace, stability and national reconciliation,

Welcoming the results of the Fourth Coordination Meeting for Humanitarian Assistance for Somalia, held at Addis Ababa from 29 November to 1 December 1993,

Noting also the significant improvement in the situation in most parts of the country achieved by the United Nations Operation in Somalia,

Taking note of the report of the Secretary-General on emergency assistance for humanitarian relief and the economic and social rehabilitation of Somalia, and the statement made before the Second Committee of the General Assembly on 16 November 1993 by the Under-Secretary-General for Humanitarian Affairs,

Deeply appreciative of the humanitarian assistance rendered by a number of States to alleviate the hardship and suffering of the affected Somali population,

Emphasizing the importance of the further implementation of its resolution 47/160 to rehabilitate basic social and economic services at the local and regional levels throughout the country,

Recognizing that the emergency phase of the present crisis is almost over and that the focus is shifting to rehabilitation and recovery,

1. *Expresses its gratitude* to all States and the intergovernmental and non-governmental organizations that have responded to the appeals of the Secretary-General and others by extending assistance to Somalia;

2. *Expresses its appreciation* to the Secretary-General for his continued and tireless efforts to mobilize assistance to the Somali people;

3. *Welcomes* the ongoing efforts of the United Nations, the Organization of African Unity, the League of Arab States, the Organization of the Islamic Conference, the countries of the Horn of Africa and the countries of the Non-Aligned Movement to resolve the situation in Somalia;

4. *Urges* all States and relevant intergovernmental and non-governmental organizations to continue the further implementation of resolution 47/160 in order to assist the Somali people to embark on the rehabilitation of basic social and economic services as well as institution-building aimed at the restoration of civil administration at the local level in all those parts of the country where peace, security and stability prevail;

5. *Appeals* to all the Somali parties concerned to terminate hostilities on the basis of the Addis Ababa Agreement of 27 March 1993, and to engage in a national reconciliation process leading to the re-establishment of peace, order and stability, which are essential if relief and rehabilitation efforts are to be successful;

6. *Calls upon* all parties, movements and factions in Somalia to respect fully the security and safety of personnel of the United Nations and its specialized agencies and of non-governmental organizations and to guarantee their complete freedom of movement throughout Somalia;

7. *Calls upon* the Secretary-General to continue to mobilize international humanitarian and rehabilitation assistance for Somalia;

8. *Requests* the Secretary-General, in view of the critical situation in Somalia, to take all measures necessary for the implementation of the present resolution, to apprise the Economic and Social Council at its substantive session of 1994 of the progress made and to report thereon to the General Assembly at its forty-ninth session.

General Assembly resolution 48/201

21 December 1993   Meeting 86   Adopted without vote

Approved by Second Committee (A/48/726) without vote, 9 December (meeting 46); draft by Vice-Chairman (A/C.2/48/L.69), based on informal consultations on 11-nation draft (A/C.2/48/L.40); agenda item 100.
Meeting numbers. GA 48th session: 2nd Committee 33-35, 41, 46; plenary 86.

Sudan

In response to a 1992 General Assembly request,[30] the Secretary-General submitted in October 1993 a report on emergency assistance to the Sudan.[31] The report provided an update on the situation and emergency responses, including Operation Lifeline Sudan. It also provided information on action by Member States and organizations of the United Nations system.

The report stated that the ongoing conflict in the Sudan had displaced hundreds of thousands of people. Malnutrition rates in some areas were high and the delivery of emergency relief had been hindered by a lack of security and heavy rains. Cattle herds had been decimated by raids and disease, and crop planting had been constrained by the lack of security. Some 700,000 people in the south were at risk of starvation, while another 1.5 million were in urgent need of food. In January,[32] the Sudan briefed the Secretary-General on the activities of the rebel movement, which was obstructing the distribution of relief supplies to the southern part of the country.

The growth forecast under the Sudan's economic reform programme had not materialized. Inflation and a devalued pound had caused a surge in prices of basic commodities and shortages of other necessities. Pay increases had not kept pace with inflation and the World Bank had suspended its operations pending repayment of outstanding loans.

Emergency requirements for the Sudan for 1993, as reflected in the January 1993 United Nations consolidated appeal, amounted to $130 million for food aid and $74 million for the non-food sector. By July, contributions totalled $65 million for food aid and $17 million for non-food aid. The Government had requested that donors concentrate humanitarian aid in the areas of development, basic needs, transport and logistics. In January, the Government and international NGOs agreed on a wide range of issues, including cooperation on national capacity-building, administrative procedures to facilitate relief work and the need to shift from relief to rehabilitation. A Commission of Voluntary Agencies, the Government's

focal point for the concerns and activities of NGOs, became operational in July. In August, the United Nations Special Envoy for the Sudan met with the Government and faction leaders. Agreement was reached on measures to expedite the delivery of assistance and on access by United Nations monitors to all United Nations relief locations. Similar agreements were made with NGOs.

In September, an informal consultation on the Sudan's priority needs was convened at Geneva.

On 16 November, the Sudan informed the Second Committee that it had signed various agreements consolidating cooperation between the Government, the United Nations, the International Committee of the Red Cross (ICRC) and NGOs. Those agreements resulted in increased food delivery, the streamlining of administrative procedures, greater participation by NGOs and the entry of ICRC into southern Sudan. Agreements were also signed with WFP to take advantage of cheap river transport, and with Sudan Railways to increase the frequency and capacity of rail trips to the south.

GENERAL ASSEMBLY ACTION

On 21 December, on the recommendation of the Second Committee, the General Assembly adopted **resolution 48/200** without vote.

Emergency assistance to the Sudan
The General Assembly,

Recalling its resolutions 43/8 of 18 October 1988, 43/52 of 6 December 1988, 44/12 of 24 October 1989, 45/226 of 21 December 1990, 46/178 of 19 December 1991 and 47/162 of 18 December 1992 on assistance to the Sudan,

Noting that, despite the progress made in the Sudan Emergency Operation and Operation Lifeline Sudan, considerable relief needs still remain to be addressed, particularly in the areas of non-food assistance, logistics and emergency recovery and rehabilitation,

Recognizing the need in emergency situations to address the continuum of relief, rehabilitation and development,

Taking note of the report of the Secretary-General, and of the statement made by the representative of the Sudan before the Second Committee of the General Assembly on 16 November 1993,

1. *Notes with appreciation* the cooperation between the Government of the Sudan and the United Nations, which has resulted in a number of agreements and arrangements to facilitate relief operations and enhance their efficiency and effectiveness, and encourages the Government of the Sudan to continue to improve their implementation;

2. *Calls upon* the international community to continue to contribute generously to the emergency needs of the country, including its recovery and rehabilitation needs, as well as to national capacity-building in the areas of emergency management, preparedness and prevention;

3. *Appeals* to all parties concerned to continue to pursue dialogue and negotiations and to terminate hostilities in order to allow for the re-establishment of peace, order and stability and also to facilitate relief efforts;

4. *Stresses* the importance of assuring safe access for personnel providing relief assistance to all in need;

5. *Urges* all parties involved to continue to offer all feasible assistance, including facilitating the movement of relief supplies and personnel, so as to guarantee maximum success of the Sudan Emergency Operation in all parts of the country;

6. *Requests* the Secretary-General to continue to mobilize and coordinate resources and support for the Sudan Emergency Operation and Operation Lifeline Sudan, to assess the emergency situation in the country and to report thereon, as well as on the recovery and rehabilitation of the country, to the General Assembly at its forty-ninth session.

General Assembly resolution 48/200

21 December 1993   Meeting 86   Adopted without vote

Approved by Second Committee (A/48/726) without vote, 9 December (meeting 46); draft by Vice-Chairman (A/C.2/48/L.68), based on informal consultations on 11-nation draft (A/C.2/48/L.39) and orally revised; agenda item 100.

Meeting numbers. GA 48th session: 2nd Committee 33-35, 41, 46; plenary 86.

Zaire

In August, the Secretary-General dispatched an inter-agency mission to Zaire to assess the humanitarian needs of the people affected by economic and social turmoil and to identify ways to meet their needs. The general economic and social situation had deteriorated and a combination of political and economic problems had brought about civil and ethnic strife. That situation had resulted in the collapse of administrative, social and economic structures, hyperinflation, high unemployment, a shortage of basic goods and large numbers of internally displaced persons. Some United Nations agencies, ICRC, international and local NGOs and church organizations had managed to bring some relief to the displaced, but their resources were overstretched and additional assistance was urgently needed to prevent a human tragedy of massive proportions. In December, the United Nations and the International Organization for Migration launched an appeal for $84,248,520 to provide urgent assistance in the fields of transport, health, sanitation, agriculture and shelter.

Asia

Afghanistan

In response to a 1992 General Assembly request,[33] the Secretary-General submitted in September 1993 a report, with a later addendum,[34] on emergency international assistance for peace, normalcy and reconstruction of war-stricken Afghanistan. He outlined emergency humanitarian and relief assistance and described the current political situation. Following his revision of United Nations coordination arrangements in Afghanistan, the United Nations Office for the Coordination of Humanitarian Assistance to Afghanistan, under the auspices of DHA, was responsible for coordinating humanitarian programmes as of 1 January. Also in January, the Secretary-General launched an updated consolidated appeal for Afghanistan for $138.2 million to support mine clearance, voluntary repatriation, food aid, health, water supply and sanitation, emergency agricultural inputs and relief management. He said that, because of continued insecurity, the projected number of returning refugees had been reduced from 2 million to 1.3 million; as a result, the overall programme requirements were reduced to $112.6 million. In June, the Secretary-General reminded donor Governments that his appeal for humanitarian assistance remained seriously underfunded and programmes might have to be curtailed. As at 15 August, $45.8 million had been either pledged or contributed.

During May/June, a group of experts prepared a comprehensive draft Action Plan for Immediate Rehabilitation, which was expected to be transformed into a full-scale rehabilitation strategy for presentation to donors in 1994.

The security of United Nations staff in Afghanistan remained a major concern and a short-term strategy was developed to maintain and strengthen the United Nations international presence in safe areas of the country, while continuing delivery of assistance to other areas with the help of national staff and NGOs. In mid-July, a lull in the fighting enabled the deployment of a small number of international staff at Kabul on a rotating basis.

The mine-clearing programme continued uninterrupted. Some 2,000 trained Afghan mine clearers were employed to clear unexploded ordnance from access roads, villages, irrigation canals and agricultural land, and a nationwide survey started to identify more accurately the areas affected by mines. Of the $15 million requested in the January appeal for mine clearance, $12.4 million had been made available.

The first meeting of the Tripartite Commission, comprising the Governments of Afghanistan and Iran and UNHCR, met in May to discuss the return and rights of refugees and operational matters. Also in May, Pakistan agreed to allow refugees from Iran to transit through Baluchistan; by July, over 15,197 persons from Pakistan and 28,732 returnees from Iran had been assisted.

In June, a cholera epidemic spread rapidly to 21 of the country's 29 provinces and a United Nations task force was established to address the problem. WHO and UNICEF chlorinated wells and conducted a public awareness campaign through local media. By August, however, there had been no donor response to the January appeal for $2 million to carry out emergency repairs to water supply systems in several Afghan cities. In the meantime, UNDP provided IPF funds to restore the water supply to 300,000 persons.

GENERAL ASSEMBLY ACTION

On 21 December, on the recommendation of the Second Committee, the General Assembly adopted **resolution 48/208** without vote.

Emergency international assistance for peace, normalcy and reconstruction of war-stricken Afghanistan

The General Assembly,

Recalling its resolution 47/119 of 18 December 1992 on emergency international assistance for the reconstruction of war-stricken Afghanistan,

Taking note of the report of the Secretary-General,

Noting that the establishment of the Islamic State in Afghanistan provides a new opportunity for the reconstruction of the country,

Wishing the people of Afghanistan peace and prosperity,

Deeply concerned about the massive destruction of property and the serious damage to the economic and social infrastructure of Afghanistan caused by fourteen years of war,

Stressing the importance of the rehabilitation and reconstruction of Afghanistan for the prosperity of its people, who have suffered many hardships during fourteen years of war and devastation and who have lost the chance for development throughout the conflict,

Aware that Afghanistan continues to suffer from an extremely critical economic situation as a land-locked, least developed and war-stricken country,

Affirming the urgent need to initiate international action to assist Afghanistan in restoring basic services and in rebuilding the country,

Expressing its hope that the international community will respond adequately to the consolidated appeal for emergency humanitarian assistance for Afghanistan, launched by the Secretary-General for the period October 1993 to March 1994,

Thanking all Governments that have rendered assistance to Afghan refugees, in particular the Governments of Pakistan and the Islamic Republic of Iran, and recognizing the need for international assistance for the repatriation and resettlement of refugees and internally displaced persons,

Bearing in mind the close interrelationship between the revitalization of the economy and the strengthening of the ability of Afghanistan to take effective steps towards those objectives and the ensuring of peace and normalcy in the country,

Stressing the important role that the United Nations can play in the further consolidation of peace and stability by assisting the process of national *rapprochement*, reconstruction and rehabilitation in Afghanistan,

Expressing its appreciation to the States and the intergovernmental and non-governmental organizations that have responded positively and continue to respond to the humanitarian needs of Afghanistan, as well as to the Secretary-General and his Personal Representative for mobilizing and coordinating the delivery of appropriate humanitarian assistance,

Welcoming the Action Plan for immediate rehabilitation, dated October 1993, prepared by the United Nations Development Programme, as lead agency, in cooperation with the Government of Afghanistan, as a first step towards reconstruction and as a framework for the mobilization of international assistance for the reconstruction and rehabilitation of the country,

Appreciating the assistance of the Office of the United Nations High Commissioner for Refugees in its continued support for the repatriation of Afghan refugees from neighbouring countries,

1. *Encourages* the Government of Afghanistan to take immediate steps to consolidate further the political process through national *rapprochement*, thus contributing to the creation of a sound political situation and good security, which would allow the holding of general, free and fair elections in the country, observed by the United Nations, as soon as circumstances permit;

2. *Welcomes with appreciation* the efforts of the Secretary-General to draw the attention of the international community to the acute problems of Afghanistan;

3. *Urgently appeals* to all States, organizations and programmes of the United Nations system, specialized agencies and other intergovernmental and non-governmental organizations, as well as to the international financial and development institutions, to provide, on a priority basis, all possible financial, technical and material assistance for the restoration of basic services and for the reconstruction of Afghanistan and for the resettlement of refugees and internally displaced persons, having in mind the availability of the Afghanistan Emergency Trust Fund referred to in paragraph 6 below;

4. *Requests* the Secretary-General:

(a) To dispatch to Afghanistan, as soon as possible, a United Nations special mission to canvass a broad spectrum of the leaders of Afghanistan soliciting their views on how the United Nations can best assist Afghanistan in facilitating national *rapprochement* and reconstruction, and to submit its findings, conclusions and recommendations to the Secretary-General for appropriate action;

(b) To develop the Action Plan for immediate rehabilitation, prepared by the United Nations Development Programme, into a full-scale strategy for rehabilitation and reconstruction, based on an in-country assessment by a team of experts of the war damage and destruction;

(c) To initiate, taking into account the conclusions and recommendations of the United Nations special mission to Afghanistan, a plan for mobilizing financial, technical and material assistance, including the possibility of convening a conference of donor States and international financial institutions;

5. *Invites* the Secretary-General to continue to monitor the overall situation in Afghanistan and make available his good offices as required, and to report thereon to the General Assembly at its forty-ninth session;

6. *Appeals* to all Member States, in particular donor countries, to provide emergency financial assistance through the Afghanistan Emergency Trust Fund established in August 1988 and the consolidated appeals by the Secretary-General for emergency humanitarian assistance for Afghanistan;

7. *Invites* the international financial institutions, specialized agencies, organizations and programmes of the United Nations system, where appropriate, to bring the special needs of Afghanistan to the attention of their respective governing bodies for their consideration and

to report on the decisions of those bodies to the Secretary-General;

8. *Requests* the Secretary-General to report to the General Assembly at its forty-ninth session on the progress made in the implementation of the present resolution;

9. *Decides* to include in the provisional agenda of its forty-ninth session the item entitled "Emergency international assistance for peace, normalcy and reconstruction of war-stricken Afghanistan".

General Assembly resolution 48/208

21 December 1993   Meeting 86   Adopted without vote

Approved by Second Committee (A/48/716) without vote, 6 December (meeting 45); 34-nation draft (A/C.2/48/L.19), orally revised following informal consultations; agenda item 105.
Sponsors: Armenia, Barbados, Benin, Belarus, Brazil, Brunei Darussalam, Bulgaria, Colombia, Cuba, Cyprus, Czech Republic, Georgia, Guinea-Bissau, Hungary, Israel, Japan, Kazakhstan, Kyrgyzstan, Latvia, Malaysia, Marshall Islands, Mexico, Namibia, Poland, Republic of Korea, Republic of Moldova, Romania, Russian Federation, Slovakia, Slovenia, Thailand, Tunisia, Turkey, Ukraine.
Meeting numbers. GA 48th session: 2nd Committee 33-35, 39, 45; plenary 86.

Iraq

The Plan of Action of the United Nations Inter-Agency Humanitarian Cooperation Programme for Iraq, established in 1991,[35] was completed in March 1993. The Plan, under which relief supplies were transported by the United Nations from southern Turkey to northern Iraq, was supported by $165 million in voluntary contributions and funds from the United Nations escrow account. A United Nations inter-agency assessment mission visited Iraq from 5 to 16 March. It confirmed the need to expand the ongoing humanitarian programme to cover the period 1 April 1993 to 31 March 1994 and to include relief and rehabilitation activities to promote self-reliance. It concluded that conditions in all sectors had deteriorated and the numbers registering for destitute status had increased as living standards declined. A new United Nations Inter-Agency Humanitarian Cooperation Programme requiring $489.2 million was finalized to succeed the Plan of Action. The new Programme included relief and humanitarian assistance projects in the areas of food and nutrition; agricultural assistance and rehabilitation; health; community rehabilitation and infrastructure; and programme support and coordination. Agreement was reached in principle between the United Nations and Iraq on the extension of the existing Memorandum of Understanding providing a framework for the humanitarian programme.

The United Nations Guards contingent was increased in October to cope with an increase in security incidents affecting the programme.

In a progress report on the implementation of the 1993/94 cooperation programme, DHA stated that, as at 10 December, resources available or pledged for humanitarian activities totalled $200 million against revised estimated requirements of $467 million. Activities by United Nations agencies involved a total of $93 million.

In June,[36] the UNDP Administrator informed the Governing Council that he intended to continue approving projects in Iraq on a case-by-case basis within the framework of the new United Nations Inter-Agency Humanitarian Programme for Iraq. The projects would be implemented in cooperation with the Coordinator of the Programme.

Lebanon

In response to requests in 1992 by the General Assembly[37] and the Economic and Social Council,[38] the Secretary-General reported in October 1993 on assistance for the reconstruction and development of Lebanon.[39]

The report stated that 1993 was expected to be a year of vigorous recovery characterized by better control over inflation and the exchange rate, better balance in public finance, real growth of GDP and a return to normal interest rates. The Government launched the National Emergency Rehabilitation Programme (NERP), a multisectoral operation focusing on emergency repairs and the rehabilitation of physical and social infrastructure. It comprised $1.7 billion of public infrastructure investment, $250 million for private sector credit and $300 million for technical assistance. The Government also formulated a programme of institutional renewal and development to accompany NERP. In April, a draft 10-year (1993-2002) national reconstruction plan, costed at $10 billion, was disclosed. By 31 May, external funds secured for the reconstruction of Lebanon totalled $1,020 million, of which $630 million was identified for NERP. United Nations assistance for reconstruction amounted to $30 million. The World Bank approved a $175 million loan to finance high-priority reconstruction in the areas of electricity, water, waste water and solid waste, education, housing and technical assistance. The International Finance Corporation granted a $45 million loan to commercial banks for onlending to industrial and tourism enterprises.

Under the programme of United Nations Assistance for Reconstruction and Development of Lebanon (UNARDOL), the resident coordinator continued to promote cooperation and coordination of system-wide activities. The United Nations presence in Lebanon was strengthened, as an increasing number of projects became operational and field operations for development activities were extended outside Beirut for the first time. In July, the United Nations responded to an emergency created by armed conflict in southern Lebanon and the West Bekaa region and, in August, an inter-agency humanitarian needs assessment mission to the region identified short-term humanitarian needs totalling about $30 million for housing, the repair and reconstruction of schools and agricultural inputs. An appeal for humanitarian assistance, amounting to $28,745,200, was launched on 20 August, following a visit to Lebanon by the Under-Secretary-General for Humanitarian Affairs. On the advice of UNARDOL, the Government was preparing, with lead support from UNDP, a two-phase needs assessment programme for the reactivation of public administration. UNARDOL was finalizing a priority humanitarian assistance programme.

The UNDP Governing Council approved the third country programme for Lebanon,[40] which focused on building national capacity for human development. UNDP's technical cooperation for 1992-1996 was to concentrate on social reconstruction, economic revitalization and reactivation of the public sector. UNDP developed a comprehensive programme for fiscal reform and administration for co-financing with IMF, and also helped to finance and establish a technical cooperation unit.

The General Assembly, by **decision 48/450** of 21 December, took note of the Secretary-General's report.

ECONOMIC AND SOCIAL COUNCIL ACTION

On 29 July, the Economic and Social Council adopted **resolution 1993/59** without vote.

Assistance for the reconstruction and development of Lebanon

The Economic and Social Council,

Taking note of General Assembly resolution 47/155 of 18 December 1992 on assistance for the reconstruction and development of Lebanon, and recalling previous resolutions adopted by the Economic and Social Council, in which the specialized agencies and other organizations and bodies of the United Nations system were called upon to expand and intensify their programmes of assistance in response to the urgent needs of Lebanon,

Aware of the deteriorating economic and social conditions of Lebanon and the magnitude of the country's needs, subsequent to the serious destruction of the infrastructure which adversely affected the social conditions, and the efforts to rebuild and develop the country,

Noting with great concern the high rate of inflation in Lebanon during the past few years, and its still pervasive negative consequences, and the serious erosion of the value of the country's currency,

Reaffirming the great need for a regional and international initiative to assist the Government of Lebanon in the reconstruction of the country and the recovery of its human and economic potential,

Expressing its appreciation for the efforts of the Secretary-General in mobilizing assistance for Lebanon,

1. *Appeals* to all Member States and all organizations of the United Nations system to intensify their efforts to mobilize all possible assistance for the Government of Lebanon in its reconstruction and development efforts, in accordance with the relevant resolutions and decisions of the General Assembly and the Economic and Social Council;

2. *Requests* all organizations and programmes of the United Nations system to intensify their assistance in response to the urgent needs of Lebanon, and invites them to take the necessary measures to assign an adequate number of employees to their offices in Beirut as soon as possible;

3. *Invites* the Secretary-General to inform the Council at its substantive session of 1994 of the progress made in the implementation of the present resolution.

Economic and Social Council resolution 1993/59

29 July 1993   Meeting 45   Adopted without vote

36-nation draft (E/1993/L.40), orally revised following informal consultations; agenda item 6 (a).

Sponsors: Algeria, Argentina, Bahrain, Benin, Chile, China, Czech Republic, Egypt, France, Greece, Guinea, Iraq, Italy, Japan, Jordan, Kuwait, Lebanon, Madagascar, Malaysia, Mexico, Morocco, Oman, Poland, Qatar, Romania, Russian Federation, Saudi Arabia, Spain, Sudan, Swaziland, Syrian Arab Republic, Togo, Tunisia, Turkey, United Arab Emirates, Yemen.

Meeting numbers. ESC 38, 44, 45.

Europe

Croatia

By a letter of 18 June,[41] Croatia drew the Secretary-General's attention to the large-scale destruction caused by war, the significant human losses and suffering of the expelled and displaced population, as well as the inability of its economy to cope with the cost of displaced persons and refugees and the reconstruction of destroyed and damaged property. The destruction and blockade of certain sections of the infrastructure had led to economic fragmentation and had paralysed economic activity in some areas. About a third of the country's industrial facilities had been destroyed or damaged, together with other infrastructure, housing and cultural treasures. Major damage had also been inflicted on social welfare infrastructure. In addition, Croatia was caring for about 270,000 refugees from Bosnia and Herzegovina. The Government had prepared a survey of programmes for humanitarian aid, reconstruction and development, for which it was requesting assistance in the form of donations, favourable credit and joint ventures. It asked the Secretary-General to set up a United Nations mission of experts, as recommended by the General Assembly in 1992,[42] to assess the nation's war damage and reconstruction and development needs.

The Secretary-General, in response to a 1992 Assembly request,[42] reported in October on international cooperation to alleviate the consequences of war in Croatia and to facilitate its recovery.[43] The report covered the United Nations consolidated inter-agency appeals and the role of the international community in the reconstruction of Croatia.

The report stated that, following the consolidated appeal for humanitarian programmes launched in 1992 for the countries of the former

Yugoslavia, a new appeal was launched in March to cover the 1993 humanitarian needs of over 3.8 million people, of whom 800,000 were in Croatia. Besides focusing on short-term humanitarian needs, the appeal reflected a commitment to post-emergency economic recovery and rehabilitation and included projects in the areas of agriculture, income generation and post-emergency shelters, sponsored by UNDP, FAO and UNIDO. The appeal included reconstruction and rehabilitation projects for Croatia totalling $158,237,587.

In May, on the initiative of the Croatian Government, UNDP and the private sector sponsored an international conference on the role of international institutions in the reconstruction and development of the Croatian economy. The conference estimated war damage to the Croatian economy at $20 billion. The World Bank initiated lending activities in Croatia for an emergency operation, adjustment lending, a credit line to local banks and infrastructure projects. The European Bank for Reconstruction and Development targeted its lending on the Government's stabilization programme and selected industries. The conference also resulted in a series of conferences on the role of the public and private sectors in the reconstruction and transition process, and the United Nations presented a project to strengthen the management of external support to Croatia. Following the conference, the Prime Minister of Croatia indicated that his country was seeking loans from the international community totalling $20.7 billion for reconstruction and rehabilitation. UNDP was assisting in the assessment of war damage needs and was discussing a country programme with the Government.

GENERAL ASSEMBLY ACTION

On 21 December, on the recommendation of the Second Committee, the General Assembly adopted **resolution 48/204** without vote.

International cooperation and assistance to alleviate the consequences of war in Croatia and to facilitate its recovery

The General Assembly,

Reaffirming its resolution 47/166 of 18 December 1992,

Having considered the report of the Secretary-General, in which he summarized the international community's humanitarian effort in Croatia within United Nations consolidated inter-agency appeals and reviewed the role of the international community in the reconstruction of Croatia,

Taking note of the letter dated 18 June 1993 from the Prime Minister of Croatia to the Secretary-General,

Noting the continuous efforts of the Government of Croatia to solve the problems of postwar reconstruction of the national infrastructure and, at the same time, to solve the existing problem of refugees, displaced persons and victims of war within Croatia,

Recognizing the importance of the United Nations overall humanitarian effort in Croatia, in particular its involvement in specific actions aimed at transforming humanitarian relief into longer-term development projects,

1. *Reaffirms its appeal* to all States, regional, inter-governmental and non-governmental organizations and other relevant bodies to provide cooperation in various forms and special and other assistance, in particular in the most severely affected areas and with a view to facilitating the return of refugees and internally displaced persons to those areas;

2. *Requests* the Secretary-General, taking into account the circumstances in the region, to carry out, in cooperation with the Government of Croatia, an assessment of needs for the rehabilitation, reconstruction and development of Croatia and to launch, if appropriate, an international appeal for the funding of a programme for rehabilitation, reconstruction and development;

3. *Also requests* the Secretary-General to submit to the General Assembly at its forty-ninth session a comprehensive report on the implementation of the present resolution.

General Assembly resolution 48/204

21 December 1993   Meeting 86   Adopted without vote

Approved by Second Committee (A/48/729) without vote, 6 December (meeting 45); 21-nation draft (A/C.2/48/L.26); agenda item 103.
Sponsors: Albania, Argentina, Austria, Bosnia and Herzegovina, Costa Rica, Croatia, Czech Republic, Dominican Republic, El Salvador, Guatemala, Hungary, Israel, Latvia, Mexico, Poland, Romania, Slovakia, Slovenia, the former Yugoslav Republic of Macedonia, Turkey, Ukraine.
Meeting numbers. GA 48th session: 2nd Committee 33-35, 40, 45; plenary 86.

Other territories of former Yugoslavia

In 1993, the situation in the territories of the former Yugoslavia, other than Croatia, grew increasingly difficult in the face of continuing armed hostilities. The United Nations humanitarian assistance programme operated under unpredictable conditions due to a lack of security and to obstruction by the warring parties of the delivery of such assistance. The situation was especially difficult in Bosnia and Herzegovina, where humanitarian aid had to be delivered to a number of areas under siege in the eastern part of the country. Yugoslavia (Serbia and Montenegro) was experiencing serious economic difficulties owing to the sanctions regime imposed against it by the Security Council and to the large number of refugees to whom it was giving asylum. Likewise the former Yugoslav Republic of Macedonia's economy was deteriorating due to the interruption of trade in the region.

The United Nations estimated that by March the number of people requiring assistance in the entire region had reached some 3.8 million. It launched a consolidated inter-agency appeal for $1,335.3 million for the period 1 April to 31 December. As the situation worsened, an inter-agency mission visited the region and a new United Nations inter-agency appeal for $522 million was launched on 8 October to provide assistance from January to June 1994 for some 4.3 million people.

Newly independent States

On the recommendation of the Inter-Agency Task Force on the Newly Independent States, a special emergency programme for those countries was launched within DHA-Geneva. The Task Force was concerned with follow-up to the consolidated inter-agency appeals for the four newly independent countries and the lack of donor response.

In June, an appeal was issued for Armenia totalling $22.5 million for the period 10 July 1993 to 31 March 1994, to meet the needs of refugees and displaced persons following two earthquakes and continued armed conflict.

The United Nations also issued an appeal for Azerbaijan in June for $12.5 million to assist over 500,000 refugees and displaced persons as a result of the five-year old conflict over Nagorno-Karabakh.

In Georgia, conflicts in Abkhazia and South Ossetia resulted in the displacement of an estimated 250,000 persons. The United Nations issued an appeal in March, updated in December, for $20 million to cover them through May 1994.

An urgent preliminary appeal for $20.4 million for humanitarian assistance to Tajikistan was launched on 11 January to cover the needs of some 400,000 internally displaced persons and Tajik refugees in Afghanistan through May 1993. Civil strife and fighting throughout the southern provinces, particularly along the border with Afghanistan, had created a volatile situation with potentially grave consequences for Central Asia.

Latin America and the Caribbean

Central America

In response to a 1991 General Assembly resolution,[44] the Secretary-General submitted in October 1993 a report[45] on implementation of the Special Plan of Economic Cooperation for Central America, which commenced in 1988[46] and was extended to 1993.[47] An updated strategy framework for the Plan was approved by Governments in February, defining sectoral/thematic priorities. Under the revised strategy, the Plan retained its primary objective, but incorporated two new priority areas: productive modernization and human resources development. Since 1988, 71 technical assistance projects had been approved (of which 15 had been completed) at a cost of $138 million. In addition to those projects, investment portfolios and technical cooperation projects had been formulated, requiring $2.3 billion in external resources. Sectoral/thematic meetings with Governments, institutions and donors had resulted

in commitments totalling $643 million, while another $442 million was being negotiated. Under the Plan, assistance was provided in the areas of refugees, returnees and displaced persons, food aid, external debt and financial support to the Central American Common Market, industrial rehabilitation and reconversion, agricultural development, external trade, physical infrastructure, the energy sector, programmes against poverty, micro-, small- and medium-sized business, food security, tourism, the environment, and support for the Central American Bank for Economic Integration.

The Secretary-General stated that the Plan had contributed to peace through development and had facilitated dialogue within the subregion and the international community. Those achievements needed to be consolidated, as advocated by the Presidents of Costa Rica, El Salvador, Guatemala, Honduras, Nicaragua and Panama in a Joint Declaration,[48] signed at Guatemala City on 17 June 1993. The Secretary-General suggested that the international community continue its support, particularly in easing the transition from humanitarian assistance to development cooperation. He pledged United Nations assistance in the renewed effort to consolidate peace and democracy with human development.

GENERAL ASSEMBLY ACTION

On 21 December, the General Assembly, on the recommendation of the Second Committee, adopted **resolution 48/199** without vote.

Special Plan of Economic Cooperation for Central America

The General Assembly,

Recalling its resolutions 42/1 of 7 October 1987, 43/24 of 15 November 1988, 44/10 of 23 October 1989 and 45/15 of 20 November 1990,

Recalling in particular its resolutions 42/204 of 11 December 1987, 42/231 of 12 May 1988, 43/210 of 20 December 1988, 44/182 of 19 December 1989, 45/231 of 21 December 1990 and 46/170 of 19 December 1991,

Recalling also the importance of the efforts made by the Secretary-General with respect to the situation in Central America and the continuing involvement of the United Nations in economic cooperation in the region,

Particularly interested in ensuring that the critical situation in Central America continues to be addressed, especially in view of the severe economic and social crises that still affect the region,

Recognizing the work being done by the United Nations Development Programme in discharging the responsibilities entrusted to it for the coordination of the Special Plan of Economic Cooperation for Central America, in accordance with the decisions that the Central American Governments have taken on the subject,

Recognizing also the importance of the Special Plan, especially in promoting intraregional and international consensus on securing and coordinating cooperation, the assistance provided to Central American countries in setting priorities for their development, the involvement of the international community in attaining priority goals, the strengthening of regional organizations, including the General Secretariat of the Central American Integration System, the Central American Bank for Economic Integration, the Permanent Secretariat of the General Treaty on Central American Economic Integration and the Central American Parliament, the mobilization of international resources for the region and the gearing of programmes to the social sector, and the role of the International Conference on Central American Refugees as a vital tool of the emergency programme of the Special Plan,

Bearing in mind that establishing a region of peace, freedom, democracy and development is a fundamental goal in Central America,

Recognizing further the commitments assumed at the presidential summits, especially the commitments on establishing a framework of priorities with a view to preventing any reversal of the achievements in Central America and to building a firm and lasting peace, with human development, in the region, which calls for the identification of fundamentally new courses of action and the preparation of a new integrated and sustained development strategy,

Noting that, in the Guatemala Declaration, adopted on 29 October 1993 at the conclusion of the fourteenth summit of Central American Presidents, the Presidents underlined that Central America offered the conditions necessary for establishing interdependence between peace and development and that the building of peace would be strengthened if such interdependence was made effective through an integrated approach, and appealed to the international community to support the efforts of the Governments of the subregion to alleviate poverty by carrying out programmes and projects oriented to human development,

1. *Takes note* of the report of the Secretary-General on the Special Plan of Economic Cooperation for Central America, which describes the status of implementation of the Special Plan, together with requirements in terms of the resources and financial assistance indispensable to the completion of priority programmes and projects for peace-building;

2. *Supports* the efforts of the Central American Governments in their commitments to poverty alleviation and sustainable human development, and urges them to implement further appropriate policies and programmes in executing those commitments;

3. *Requests*, given the need to anticipate the depletion of resources under the Special Plan and the conclusion in May 1994 of the process established by the International Conference on Central American Refugees, that the necessary resources be provided for the establishment of updated and new regional programmes, through arrangements that the Central American countries are to determine jointly with the cooperating community and the agencies of the United Nations system, especially the United Nations Development Programme, in support of the efforts of the Central American Governments with a view to preventing any reversal of the achievements in Central America and to building peace in the region through integrated and sustained development;

4. *Urges* all States, intergovernmental organizations, international financial institutions, the organs and specialized agencies of the United Nations system and

regional and subregional organizations to step up support for the implementation of the goals and objectives of the Special Plan, taking into account the severe economic and social crises facing the region;

5. *Again stresses* the urgent need for the international community to maintain its cooperation with the Central American countries and to provide them, in a sustained manner, with adequate financial and technical resources on appropriate terms, with a view to promoting effectively the development and economic growth of the region;

6. *Commends* the efforts of the Central American peoples and Governments to consolidate peace by implementing the agreements adopted at the summit meetings held since 1987, urges them to continue with their efforts to consolidate a firm and lasting peace in Central America, and requests the Secretary-General to continue to afford the fullest possible support for the initiatives and efforts of the Central American Governments;

7. *Supports* the decision taken by the Presidents of the Central American countries at their fourteenth summit meeting with respect to the adoption of decentralization policies oriented to human development at the local level and linked where necessary to macroeconomic policies, given the need to ensure a continuum from humanitarian assistance to development cooperation;

8. *Notes with appreciation* the effective support extended by international and regional financial institutions to the priority programmes and projects that the Central American countries have identified as regards energy, communications, roads and agriculture within the framework of the Special Plan;

9. *Requests* the Secretary-General to submit to the General Assembly at its forty-ninth session a report on the implementation of the Special Plan;

10. *Decides* to examine and evaluate the implementation of the Special Plan at its forty-ninth session.

General Assembly resolution 48/199

21 December 1993   Meeting 86   Adopted without vote

Approved by Second Committee (A/48/726) without vote, 6 December (meeting 45); draft by Vice-Chairman (A/C.2/48/L.65), based on informal consultations on 15-nation draft (A/C.2/48/L.42); agenda item 100.
Meeting numbers. GA 48th session: 2nd Committee 33-35, 42, 45; plenary 86.

El Salvador

In response to a 1992 General Assembly request,[49] the Secretary-General submitted in September a report on assistance for the reconstruction and development of El Salvador.[50] The report outlined the economic situation in 1992 and the Government's plan for 1993, examined the advances, limitations and prospects for national reconstruction and the strengthening of democratic institutions, and discussed challenges and expectations.

The end of 1992 was marked by increased production despite an incomplete stabilization and adjustment effort and an accumulation of social problems. In 1993, the main macroeconomic objectives were to maintain the rate of economic growth (4.5-5 per cent), to reduce inflation and the fiscal deficit, and to strengthen the current balance-of-payments account.

The short-term contingency phase of El Salvador's National Reconstruction Plan was successfully executed. However, implementation was affected by a number of factors, including delays in the provision of external resources and the Government's limited financial capacity to respond to the priorities of the 1992 Peace Accords and agreements reached with different beneficiaries. The second phase of the Plan, a five-year medium-term phase, was being implemented in 115 of El Salvador's 265 municipalities.

The Government submitted priority programmes totalling $1,533 million over four years to the Consultative Group of donors (Paris, 1 April). That included $1,161 million for the Reconstruction Plan. The Government undertook to provide $403 million in addition to $362 million in external assistance already promised, leaving a funding deficit of $768 million.

The Government's land-transfer programme was not advancing as quickly as desired. Only 59 per cent of the land included in the first phase of the programme had been handed over and only 25 of the negotiations for private properties had been finalized. Nevertheless, the second phase of the programme had begun and had benefited some 623 ex-combatants. The emergency demobilization programme for the reintegration of ex-combatants was formulated and executed, with UNDP as the lead agency. The second phase of the programme for the war-disabled was also being implemented and the Law on the Protection of the War-Disabled entered into force on 22 January. However, a lack of resources for the fund established under the Law raised concern about its viability. The European Economic Community was financing a project for the productive reintegration of the war-disabled and the United Nations Observer Mission in El Salvador (ONUSAL) was coordinating negotiations on a housing programme under the Reconstruction Plan for ex-combatants and the disabled of the Armed Forces and of the Frente Farabundo Martí para la Liberación Nacional. The Government submitted the financial and technical assistance requirements for that programme to the Consultative Group meeting. The Secretary-General noted that the shortfall in resources to finance an important part of the reconstruction and development programmes and to strengthen democratic institutions threatened the consolidation of the peace process.

In a November report[51] to the Security Council on ONUSAL, the Secretary-General stated that donors had shown a preference for financing infrastructure and environment projects, with the result that commitments for the reintegration of ex-combatants and the promotion of democratic institutions had fallen short of expectations. The Government had, however, been reallocating funds

intended for other purposes to peace-related projects, and continued to mobilize external financing for that purpose. The Secretary-General noted that implementation of the peace process had progressed well and elections in March 1994 should be the culminating point in the process (see PART TWO, Chapter II).

GENERAL ASSEMBLY ACTION

On 21 December, on the recommendation of the Second Committee, the General Assembly adopted **resolution 48/203** without vote.

Assistance for the reconstruction and development of El Salvador

The General Assembly,

Recalling Security Council resolution 784(1992) of 30 October 1992 and reaffirming its resolution 47/158 of 18 December 1992,

Having considered the report of the Secretary-General on assistance for the reconstruction and development of El Salvador, and the further report of the Secretary-General on the United Nations Observer Mission in El Salvador,

Noting the progress made in implementing the commitments assumed as a result of the signing, on 16 January 1992 at Mexico City, of the Chapultepec Agreement between the Government of El Salvador and the Frente Farabundo Martí para la Liberación Nacional, which put an end to the armed conflict in El Salvador through a process developed under the auspices of the Secretary-General,

Recognizing that El Salvador is at a critical stage of transition and that international cooperation will help to overcome the difficulties that have arisen and to implement fully the commitments assumed under the Chapultepec Agreement,

Noting also that, in spite of national efforts and the support given by the international community to the implementation of priority programmes in the National Reconstruction Plan and the strengthening of democratic institutions, some of these programmes have been affected by, *inter alia*, the limited availability of financial resources,

1. *Expresses its appreciation* to the Secretary-General and the Governments of Colombia, Mexico, Spain and Venezuela, which make up the Group of Friends of the Secretary-General, and to the Government of the United States of America and other Governments that are helping to build peace in El Salvador;

2. *Expresses its gratitude* to the international community, especially the cooperating community, to the specialized agencies of the United Nations and to other governmental and non-governmental organizations for the technical and financial assistance they have provided to El Salvador to supplement the effort to build peace;

3. *Recognizes* that the implementation of the National Reconstruction Plan and the strengthening of democratic institutions are efforts complementary to the peace process: they reflect the collective aspirations and needs of the country, being means of overcoming the root causes of the crisis and of consolidating peace, democracy and human development;

4. *Calls upon* the signatories to the Chapultepec Agreement to expedite the implementation of any remaining commitments under that Agreement, in order to guarantee fully the building of peace in El Salvador and hence to encourage the international community to increase the level of financial resources accorded to priority projects for reconstruction, development and the strengthening of democratic institutions in El Salvador;

5. *Calls upon* the Government of El Salvador to consider the possibility, in the implementation of projects under the National Reconstruction Plan in areas affected by the conflict, of greater involvement of non-governmental organizations that have addressed the needs of the populations of those areas, with a view to making the projects more sustainable and facilitating increased participation by civilian society in decisions affecting its future;

6. *Emphasizes* the importance of external technical and financial assistance to the implementation of the complementary efforts for building peace;

7. *Again requests* the Secretary-General to take the necessary measures and make every possible effort to mobilize material and financial resources, in keeping with the requirements for the progress of priority programmes in El Salvador;

8. *Decides* to include in the provisional agenda of its forty-ninth session the item entitled "Assistance for the reconstruction and development of El Salvador", and requests the Secretary-General to submit a report on the implementation of the present resolution.

General Assembly resolution 48/203

21 December 1993   Meeting 86   Adopted without vote

Approved by Second Committee (A/48/728) without vote, 6 December (meeting 45); 23-nation draft (A/C.2/48/L.43), orally revised following informal consultations; agenda item 102.
Sponsors: Angola, Belize, Bolivia, Chile, Colombia, Costa Rica, Croatia, Cyprus, Ecuador, El Salvador, Guatemala, Guyana, Honduras, Jamaica, Mexico, Nicaragua, Panama, Paraguay, Russian Federation, Rwanda, Spain, Suriname, Venezuela.
Meeting numbers. GA 48th session: 2nd Committee 33-35, 42, 45; plenary 86.

Nicaragua

In response to a 1992 General Assembly request,[52] the Secretary-General reported in August on international assistance for the rehabilitation and reconstruction of Nicaragua in the aftermath of the war and natural disasters.[53] The report described the activities of the United Nations system in Nicaragua during the transition to peace. It stated that since the end of the war in 1990, a Programme of National Reconciliation and Rehabilitation had been implemented and a stabilization programme had reduced the annual rate of inflation from a five-digit figure to 4 per cent in 1992 and less than 20 per cent in early 1993. It had also reduced the overall cash deficit from 31.2 per cent to 10.8 per cent of GDP in 1993. Structural adjustments included the abolition of a State monopoly in banking and traditional exports, a unified foreign exchange rate and the privatization of public enterprises. However, those programmes had not been sufficient to reactivate

the Nicaraguan economy and a further deterioration in social conditions had undermined the credibility of democratic political institutions. The report also noted that Nicaragua had been affected by a series of natural disasters.

Various United Nations agencies, particularly UNDP, provided support to Nicaragua. UNDP assisted in emergency agricultural projects, as well as projects to strengthen the rule of law, institutional development and the private sector. It also assisted those affected by natural disasters. UNDP helped the Government design a development strategy, announced by the President in January, to improve the quality of and access to social services, and to activate the productive resources of the poor. It was also supporting a national dialogue on economic, political and social themes and was instrumental in creating a Ministry of Social Action. In addition, the World Bank and IMF provided technical and financial support to the Government's Economic Stabilization and Structural Adjustment Programme and for a reform of the State banking system. The report suggested that the United Nations help Nicaragua to renegotiate its external debt, which stood at over $10 billion, and to define future assistance needs.

GENERAL ASSEMBLY ACTION

On 22 October, the General Assembly adopted **resolution 48/8** without vote.

International assistance for the rehabilitation and reconstruction of Nicaragua: aftermath of the war and natural disasters

The General Assembly,

Recalling its resolutions 45/15 of 20 November 1990, 46/109 A and B of 17 December 1991 and 47/118 of 18 December 1992 concerning the situation in Central America, in which it welcomed the implementation of phases I and II of the National Conciliation Agreement on Economic and Social Matters concluded in Nicaragua on 26 October 1990 and 15 August 1991, and endorsed, in particular, the provision concerning exceptional circumstances of Nicaragua and the invitation to the international community and the international funding agencies to provide effective and efficient support for the implementation of the Agreement,

Recalling its resolution 47/169 of 22 December 1992 concerning the item entitled "International assistance for the rehabilitation and reconstruction of Nicaragua: aftermath of the war and natural disasters", in which it commended the international community for its work in the rehabilitation and reconstruction of Nicaragua and requested the continuation of the support to overcome the aftermath of the war and natural disasters and to stimulate the process of reconstruction and development,

Deeply concerned at the fact that the recent natural disasters and the burden of foreign debt are impeding Nicaragua's efforts to overcome the consequences of the war within the framework of a democracy and in the macroeconomic conditions already achieved,

Recognizing the efforts of the international community and the Government of Nicaragua to provide relief and emergency assistance to persons affected by the aftermath of the war, the floods, the volcanic eruption, the tidal wave and the recent hurricane,

Recognizing also that the intensive efforts of the Government of Nicaragua to promote economic reactivation within the framework of a process of adjustment with economic growth and development with equity have been hindered by situations of violence resulting from the aftermath of the war and by the needs of thousands of displaced persons, refugees and unemployed persons who must be integrated into the economic life of the country, as well as by the effects of natural disasters,

Recognizing further that the Government of Nicaragua is making considerable progress in securing a broad social consensus by means of a process of national dialogue for the adoption of measures to lay the foundations for reconstruction and economic and social development,

1. *Commends* the efforts made by the international community, including the organs and organizations of the United Nations system, to supplement the action undertaken by the Government of Nicaragua in the task of rehabilitation and national reconstruction, as well as in providing emergency assistance;

2. *Encourages* the Government of Nicaragua to continue its efforts for reconstruction and national reconciliation;

3. *Requests* all Member States, the international funding agencies and regional, intraregional and non-governmental organizations to continue providing, in a flexible form, support to Nicaragua at the required levels, giving particular attention to the exceptional circumstances in Nicaragua, both to overcome the aftermath of the war and natural disasters and to stimulate the process of reconstruction, social investment, stabilization and development;

4. *Requests* the Secretary-General, in cooperation with the relevant organs and organizations of the United Nations system and in close cooperation with the Nicaraguan authorities, to provide all necessary assistance to activities for the rehabilitation, reconstruction, stabilization and development of that country and to continue to ensure the timely, comprehensive, flexible and effective formulation and coordination of programmes of the United Nations system in Nicaragua, given the importance of those activities for the consolidation of peace;

5. *Also requests* the Secretary-General to provide Nicaragua, at the request of its Government, with all possible assistance to support the consolidation of peace, in areas such as the settlement of displaced and demobilized persons and refugees, land ownership and land tenure in rural areas, direct care for war victims, mine clearance and the overcoming of difficulties in the restoration of the productive areas of the country, and, in general, a process of sustained economic and social recovery and development that will render the peace and democracy achieved irreversible;

6. *Further requests* the Secretary-General to submit a report to the General Assembly at its forty-ninth session on the action taken to implement the present resolution;

7. *Decides* to include in the provisional agenda of its forty-ninth session the item entitled "International assistance for the rehabilitation and reconstruction of Nicaragua: aftermath of the war and natural disasters".

General Assembly resolution 48/8

22 October 1993   Meeting 35   Adopted without vote

38-nation draft (A/48/L.10 & Add.1), orally revised; agenda item 45.
Sponsors: Antigua and Barbuda, Argentina, Bahamas, Bangladesh, Barbados, Bolivia, Chile, Colombia, Costa Rica, Cuba, Dominican Republic, Ecuador, El Salvador, Guatemala, Guyana, Haiti, Honduras, Indonesia, Italy, Jamaica, Japan, Mexico, Mongolia, Nepal, Nicaragua, Norway, Panama, Paraguay, Peru, Philippines, Saint Vincent and the Grenadines, Spain, Suriname, Sweden, Trinidad and Tobago, United States, Uruguay, Venezuela.

Haiti

The United Nations and the Organization of American States (OAS) responded to the worsening situation in Haiti by formulating, through a coordinating committee for humanitarian assistance to Haiti, a joint Consolidated Humanitarian Plan of Action. The Plan, covering needs totalling $62.7 million, was launched in March and included emergency programmes in the fields of health, nutrition and food aid, water supply and sanitation, and agriculture, as well as support services and some education and other social needs. A United Nations/OAS Steering Committee was established to coordinate its implementation.

The Assistant Secretary-General of OAS and the Under-Secretary-General for Humanitarian Affairs of the United Nations renewed the March appeal in June, and again in August, urging the international community to respond to Haiti's deteriorating economic and social circumstances. They said they were encouraged by the signing of the Governors Island Agreement in July (see PART TWO, Chapter II) and the promise it held for restoring normal political, social and economic activity. They noted that the renewed appeal focused on immediate emergency needs and that a comprehensive emergency economic recovery programme, under the auspices of the World Bank, IMF, UNDP and the United States Agency for International Development, was being formulated.

On 16 June, the Security Council, by **resolution 841(1993)** and consistent with the trade embargo recommended by OAS, imposed an oil embargo on Haiti. The Committee established to monitor the embargo was able, however, to authorize the importation, in non-commercial quantities, of petroleum and petroleum products for verified essential humanitarian needs.

The General Assembly, in December, by **resolution 48/151**, called on Member States to intensify their humanitarian assistance to the people of Haiti, and welcomed the decision of the Secretary-General to dispatch a team of additional humanitarian personnel there. In April, by **resolution 47/20 B** and again in December, by **resolution 48/27**, the Assembly confirmed that the international community intended to increase technical, economic and financial cooperation when constitutional order was established in Haiti.

REFERENCES
[1]E/1993/90. [2]E/1993/NGO/4. [3]A/48/3/Rev.1. [4]ACC/1993/14. [5]YUN 1992, p. 585, GA res. 47/168, 22 Dec. 1992. [6]A/48/536. [7]A/48/8 (res. 14/5). [8]E/1993/35 (dec. 93/11). [9]DP/1994/10/Add.1. [10]E/1993/34 (dec. 1993/7). [11]E/ICEF/1994/11. [12]YUN 1992, p. 589, GA res. 47/164, 18 Dec. 1992. [13]A/48/473. [14]A/48/240. [15]S/26757. [16]A/48/392 & Corr.1. [17]YUN 1992, p. 591, GA res. 47/154, 18 Dec. 1992. [18]S/26272. [19]S/26350. [20]S/26488. [21]A/48/241. [22]S/26927. [23]YUN 1992, p. 594, GA res. 47/160, 18 Dec. 1992. [24]A/48/504. [25]YUN 1992, p. 593. [26]S/25168, S/25354 & Add.1,2. [27]S/26022. [28]S/1994/12. [29]DP/1993/59. [30]YUN 1992, p. 596, GA res. 47/162, 18 Dec. 1992. [31]A/48/434. [32]A/48/60. [33]YUN 1992, p. 598, GA res. 47/119, 18 Dec. 1992. [34]A/48/323 & Add.1. [35]YUN 1991, p. 205. [36]DP/1993/71. [37]YUN 1992, p. 600, GA res. 47/155, 18 Dec. 1992. [38]Ibid., ESC res. 1992/42, 30 July 1992. [39]A/48/453. [40]E/1993/35 (dec. 93/4). [41]A/48/215. [42]YUN 1992, p. 601, GA res. 47/166, 18 Dec. 1992. [43]A/48/534. [44]YUN 1991, p. 431, GA res. 46/170, 19 Dec. 1991. [45]A/48/405. [46]YUN 1988, p. 306. [47]GA res. 45/231, 21 Dec. 1990. [48]A/47/971. [49]YUN 1992, p. 602, GA res. 47/158, 18 Dec. 1992. [50]A/48/310. [51]S/26790. [52]YUN 1992, p. 607, GA res. 47/169, 22 Dec. 1992. [53]A/48/318.

Disaster relief

International Decade for Natural Disaster Reduction

In response to a 1991 General Assembly request,[1] the Secretary-General submitted in June 1993 a report with later addendum,[2] on the implementation of the International Framework of Action for the International Decade for Natural Disaster Reduction (IDNDR), proclaimed by the Assembly in 1989[3] and reiterated in 1990.[4] The report described activities in support of national disaster reduction strategies, demonstration projects for the Decade and plans for the World Conference on Natural Disaster Reduction (see below). The two international organs of the Decade—the Special High-Level Council and the Scientific and Technical Committee—met during 1993. The Council adopted a 12-point Plan of Action for the Conference and the Committee recommended action to strengthen the Decade.

In July, the Under-Secretary-General for Humanitarian Affairs told the Economic and Social Council that it was important to harmonize the work of disaster mitigation with IDNDR and that arrangements were being made to integrate the IDNDR secretariat into DHA. The IDNDR Director reported that a steering committee had been established to coordinate United Nations contributions to the Decade; however, national commitment to the Decade was uneven and the resources available were insufficient. He suggested that technical and financial support should be consolidated, either through the Decade Trust Fund or bilaterally.

Major meetings organized in connection with the Decade included the IDNDR Chiba International Conference (Japan, 27-30 November 1992) and the IDNDR Aichi Nagoya International Conference (Japan, 1-4 November 1993).[5]

1994 World Conference on Natural Disaster Reduction

The General Assembly in 1991[1] had endorsed the recommendation of the Scientific and Technical Committee of IDNDR to convene a World Conference on Natural Disaster Reduction in 1994 as a contribution to the mid-term review of the Decade.

In January 1993, the Special High-Level Council of IDNDR, at its second session, adopted a 12-point Plan of Action for the Conference, recommending measures to be taken by the Secretary-General. It undertook to mobilize support and resources for the Conference and promote the adoption of national disaster mitigation policies.

In April, the Scientific and Technical Committee, as the Preparatory Committee for the Conference, finalized a conference programme, which included national risk assessments and national and regional meetings to review progress towards Decade goals. The aims of the Conference were to review the national, regional and international accomplishments of the Decade, chart an action programme for the future, exchange information on the implementation of programmes, and increase awareness of the importance of disaster reduction policies. Major themes for the Conference included the cost benefits of hazard mitigation, construction of safer buildings, drought management, disaster warning and preparedness systems, interaction between natural and technological disasters, and the vulnerability of communities and special groups.

On 30 July, the Economic and Social Council, by **decision 1993/328**, took note of the Secretary-General's report[2] and expressed its support for the preparatory work on the Conference. It welcomed the offer of the Government of Japan to host the Conference at Yokohama (23-27 May 1994) and recommended that the General Assembly further consider the plans and preparations for the Conference.

GENERAL ASSEMBLY ACTION

On 21 December, the General Assembly, on the recommendation of the Second Committee, adopted **resolution 48/188** without vote.

International Decade for Natural Disaster Reduction

The General Assembly,

Expressing its support to all countries that have suffered a heavy loss of human life, as well as serious damage, both material and economic, as a result of natural disasters,

Recalling its resolutions 44/236 of 22 December 1989, in which it proclaimed the International Decade for Natural Disaster Reduction, and 46/182 of 19 December 1991, in the annex to which it called for substantive improvements in international humanitarian emergency assistance and which led to the establishment of the Department of Humanitarian Affairs of the Secretariat,

Recalling also its resolution 46/149 of 18 December 1991, in which it endorsed the convening in 1994 of a world conference of representatives of national committees for the Decade,

Taking note of Economic and Social Council decision 1993/328 of 30 July 1993 on the World Conference on Natural Disaster Reduction,

Recognizing the important contribution the Decade can make to the improvement of emergency management in general and to capacity-building for disaster preparedness and mitigation at the national level,

Emphasizing the important role of professional and other non-governmental organizations, particularly scientific and technological societies, humanitarian groups and investment institutions, in the implementation of programmes and activities of the Decade,

Having considered the 12-point Plan of Action for the Conference, adopted by the Special High-Level Council for the Decade at its second session,

Having also considered the recommendations made by the Secretary-General with the purpose of providing guidance for the continuing implementation of the Decade and the effective preparation and convening of the Conference,

Recognizing the close interrelationship between disaster prevention and sustainable development, which was already recognized at the United Nations Conference on Environment and Development and taken account of in chapter 7, section F, of Agenda 21,

Convinced that each country bears the primary responsibility for protecting its people, infrastructure and other national assets from the impact of natural disasters,

Taking note of the report of the Secretary-General on the Decade, which contains, *inter alia*, the second annual report of the Scientific and Technical Committee on the Decade,

1. *Commends* those countries exposed to disasters that have already taken initiatives to reduce their vulnerability, encourages them to continue in the context of their socio-economic process, with the implementation of natural disaster mitigation policies during the International Decade for Natural Disaster Reduction, taking into account the targets for progress in disaster reduction defined by the Scientific and Technical Committee on the Decade, and also encourages them to pursue the possibilities of regional cooperation within the framework of the Decade;

2. *Encourages* the members of the Special High-Level Council for the Decade, on the basis of the advice they have provided to the Secretary-General, to embark actively, individually and as a group, on measures to increase public awareness of the potential for disaster reduction and raise support for the activities of the Decade from Governments, international financing institutions and other funding organizations, and the business community;

3. *Commends* the Scientific and Technical Committee for the work accomplished in 1992, and endorses its

proposals for the preparations for the World Conference on Natural Disaster Reduction;

4. *Calls upon* Member States and all other participants in the Decade to participate actively in the financial and technical support of Decade activities, including those of the secretariat of the Decade;

5. *Calls upon* the Department of Humanitarian Affairs of the Secretariat, of which the secretariat of the Decade has become an integral part, to continue to bring closer together the operational and promotional efforts in disaster preparedness and mitigation, thus paving the way for the successful attainment of the goals and objectives of the Decade;

6. *Decides* to convene in 1994 the World Conference on Natural Disaster Reduction with the following objectives:

(a) To review the accomplishments of the Decade at the national, regional and international levels;

(b) To chart a programme of action for the future;

(c) To exchange information on the implementation of Decade programmes and policies;

(d) To increase awareness of the importance of disaster reduction policies;

7. *Accepts with deep appreciation* the generous offer of the Government of Japan to host the World Conference, and decides that the Conference will be held at Yokohama from 23 to 27 May 1994;

8. *Decides* to establish a Preparatory Committee for the World Conference on Natural Disaster Reduction, which will meet for five days at Geneva, no later than March 1994, to review organizational and substantive preparations for the Conference, approve the programme of work of the Conference and propose rules of procedure for adoption by the Conference, on the basis of recommendations submitted by the secretariat of the Decade, after consultation with the host country;

9. *Requests* the secretariat of the Decade to serve as the secretariat of the Conference and to coordinate preparatory activities, in close cooperation with the host Government and the Preparatory Committee for the Conference, with the full support of relevant departments and offices of the United Nations Secretariat;

10. *Recognizes* the importance of broad and multidisciplinary participation in the Conference, and to this end requests the Secretary-General to invite to the Conference all States, national committees for the Decade, and organs, organizations and programmes of the United Nations system, as well as the intergovernmental organizations and scientific associations concerned, relevant non-governmental organizations and the private sector;

11. *Calls upon* all Governments to take an active part in the Conference and its preparatory process, in particular by:

(a) Undertaking systematic assessments of national and local hazards and risks, with the assistance of the intersectoral national committees for the Decade;

(b) Organizing multidisciplinary national and regional conferences and technical meetings, so as to ensure that the entire potential of each country, both at the national level and within the context of regional cooperation, including its scientific and technical capability, is fully utilized in disaster reduction;

(c) Preparing comprehensive reports on progress achieved and plans for further action to be presented at the Conference;

12. *Calls upon* all United Nations bodies and specialized agencies to participate actively in the Conference, as well as its preparatory process, and commends those organizations which, in line with the open and participatory nature of the Decade, have assumed responsibility for the organization of technical committees at the Conference;

13. *Decides* that the preparatory process and the Conference itself should be funded through existing budgetary resources, without negatively affecting programmed activities, and through voluntary contributions to the Trust Fund established for the Decade;

14. *Requests* the Secretary-General to appeal to all Member States to contribute generously to the Trust Fund with a view to financing the additional activities required in preparing for and holding the Conference;

15. *Expresses its deep appreciation* to those countries that have provided generous support for the activities of the Decade by making voluntary contributions to its Trust Fund, making available scientific and technical knowledge, developing and implementing innovative disaster reduction projects and hosting activities or meetings of importance to the Decade;

16. *Also expresses its deep appreciation* to those national committees and focal points for the Decade that have participated actively in the process of attaining the goals and objectives of the Decade;

17. *Requests* the Secretary-General to submit to the General Assembly at its forty-ninth session a report on progress made in the implementation of the present resolution, including the findings of the mid-term review of the implementation of the International Framework of Action for the International Decade for Natural Disaster Reduction, to be carried out by the Economic and Social Council at its substantive session of 1994.

General Assembly resolution 48/188

21 December 1993   Meeting 86   Adopted without vote

Approved by Second Committee (A/48/724) without vote, 10 December (meeting 47); draft by Belgium (for European Union), Canada, China, Colombia (for Group of 77), Finland, Israel, Japan, Kazakhstan, Norway, Poland, Russian Federation, the former Yugoslav Republic of Macedonia and United States (A/C.2/48/L.24), orally revised following informal consultations; agenda item 98.
Financial implications. 5th Committee, A/48/793; S-G, A/C.2/48/L.62, A/C.5/48/58.
Meeting numbers. GA 48th session: 2nd Committee 33-35, 38, 47; 5th Committee 43; plenary 86.

Drought-stricken areas

Southern Africa

DHA stated in a June situation report that the 1992/93 regional drought emergency, which affected more than 20 million people in southern Africa (Angola, Botswana, Lesotho, Malawi, Mozambique, Namibia, Swaziland, United Republic of Tanzania, Zambia and Zimbabwe), was over. Improved crop and food supply estimates and the mobilization of local and regional resources had averted a major famine. DHA stated that $708 million of the $951 million requested had been received following the joint Southern African Development Community (SADC)/United Nations appeal launched in 1992. Contributions to the appeal totalled 1.5 million metric tons of target food,

2 million tons of programme food, and $76 million for non-food requirements. In addition, Governments in the region had diverted large amounts of their own resources for food imports and the distribution of relief assistance. DHA noted that the SADC region usually exported food, but had been forced to import 11.6 million tons of food valued at $4 billion, including transportation costs. Efforts were under way at the national and regional levels to review the response to the 1991/92 drought to see how the region's capacity to respond to future droughts might be improved. A number of SADC initiatives were also focusing on regional food security. A key factor in the effective coordination of the flow of food was the SADC/WFP Logistics Advisory Centre. NGOs assisted with the feeding of vulnerable groups, emergency water and sanitation activities and the implementation of nutrition and health programmes.

With widespread rains in Mozambique, the United Republic of Tanzania and Zambia during the 1992/93 growing season, the forecast for total 1993 cereal production in the SADC region was around 11.5 million metric tons—almost double that of the 1992 harvest. Although much of the food deficit for the 1993/94 marketing year would be covered by commercial imports, several countries would require substantial food aid. The impact of the drought on the water supply and health sectors continued to be felt and additional assistance was required to prevent further deterioration in health conditions. The continued effects of the drought were also being felt in the areas of livestock, industry, infrastructure and social institutions. Close collaboration at the national level by United Nations agencies, NGOs, the World Bank, IMF and the African Development Bank would be necessary during the transition to the post-emergency phase.

DHA continued to cooperate with SADC in identifying ways to enhance the emergency response and drought management capacities of its member countries. An SADC regional drought management workshop was held (Harare, Zimbabwe, 13-16 September) to determine the most effective strategies for dealing with future drought; it was followed by workshops in each of the SADC countries. The SADC initiative was intended to complement activities undertaken or planned for countries of the region by the DHA-UNDP Disaster Management Training Programme.

Sudano-Sahelian region

In a report on the activities of the United Nations Sudano-Sahelian Office (UNSO),[6] the UNDP Administrator noted that UNSO programme activities, totalling about $60 million, supported the broad areas of environmental planning, the development of local natural-resource management capacities, environmental information systems, coordination and information, and the negotiation of an international convention to combat desertification. During 1993, UNSO-supported drought and desertification strategies were adopted by Benin, Burkina Faso, the Gambia, Mali and Mauritania, and were in different stages of preparation in other countries. UNSO also supported local-level natural resources management, traditional land-use systems, and the decentralization of resources management to land users. It helped to formulate Environmental Information Systems programmes in Chad, the Gambia, Mali, the Niger, Uganda and the United Republic of Tanzania, and to prepare desertification case-studies for Uganda and Mali.

On 21 May,[7] the Governing Council of the United Nations Environment Programme (UNEP) requested the Executive Director, in consultation with UNDP, to amend the UNEP/UNDP joint undertaking to allow UNSO to intensify its involvement in desertification control.

On 18 June,[8] the UNDP Governing Council recognized the important role of UNSO in implementing follow-up activities to the 1992 United Nations Conference on Environment and Development (UNCED)[9] and encouraged the Administrator to strengthen the role of UNSO as the UNDP focal point for all matters related to drought and desertification control. It requested the Administrator to report in 1994 on alternative ways of financing the work of UNSO and reconfirmed its support for the UNSO/UNEP joint venture to implement the drought and desertification programmes of UNCED's Agenda 21, particularly in Africa.

UNSO prepared UNDP's system-wide desertification strategy, which was adopted in November.

The Secretary-General, in a June report on the implementation of the 1977 Plan of Action to Combat Desertification[10] and the medium-term recovery and rehabilitation programme in the Sudano-Sahelian region,[11] stated that UNSO, in collaboration with the Permanent Inter-State Committee for Drought Control in the Sahel and the Intergovernmental Authority on Drought and Development, was creating closer ties with SADC and the Maghreb Arab Union and was strengthening its collaboration with the Organization of African Unity, the Economic Commission for Africa and the African Development Bank in subregional consultations and joint strategic programmes related to provisions of Agenda 21.

The Economic and Social Council, on 29 July, by **decision 1993/312**, took note of the Secretary-General's report.

Storms and cyclones

Cuba

On 31 March,[12] Barbados, on behalf of the Group of Latin American and Caribbean Member States, reported that on 12 March Cuba was battered by winds of up to 200 kilometres per hour and waves up to 25 feet. Eight of Cuba's 14 provinces were seriously affected by winds and sea-water flooding in coastal areas. Five people died and tens of thousands were displaced when homes were destroyed or damaged. Preliminary estimates of losses to personal property, industrial installations, public service facilities and crops exceeded $1 billion.

Although national efforts had been fully deployed to counter the effects of the storm, and some international aid had been received, the Group considered it necessary for the United Nations to encourage massive international assistance to counter the widespread damage to the Cuban economy.

GENERAL ASSEMBLY ACTION

On 15 April, the General Assembly adopted **resolution 47/228** without vote.

Emergency assistance to Cuba

The General Assembly,

Deeply concerned about the extensive damage and devastation in Cuba caused by the very severe storm that affected that country on 12 and 13 March 1993,

Noting with concern the loss of life, the destruction of thousands of dwellings and the severe damage to major sectors of the national infrastructure,

Acknowledging the efforts of the Government and the people of Cuba to provide relief and emergency assistance to the people affected by the storm,

Noting that the continuing efforts of the Government of Cuba to promote economic growth and development will be hampered by this calamity,

1. *Declares its solidarity* with the Government and the people of Cuba in this hour of trial;

2. *Notes with appreciation* the efforts of the Government of Cuba to provide speedy relief to the storm victims from national resources;

3. *Commends* the efforts of the international community to supplement the relief operations and emergency assistance provided by the Government of Cuba;

4. *Calls upon* the Secretary-General, in cooperation with the relevant organs and organizations of the United Nations system and in close collaboration with the Government authorities, to assist in the rehabilitation efforts of the Government and the people of Cuba;

5. *Requests* all States and international organizations and other intergovernmental agencies to extend emergency support to Cuba for the duration of the emergency and the ensuing rehabilitation process to alleviate the plight of the afflicted people of Cuba, including their economic and financial burden.

General Assembly resolution 47/228
15 April 1993   Meeting 99   Adopted without vote

3-nation draft (A/47/L.55 & Add.1), orally revised; agenda item 154.
Sponsors: Belize, Democratic People's Republic of Korea, Togo.

Iran

Floods caused by heavy rains in Iran between February and April resulted in severe loss of life and livestock and damage to farmlands, housing and infrastructure. Total damage was estimated at $350 million to $400 million. International responses included contributions in cash, through the Iranian Red Crescent Society, and in kind. DHA made an emergency grant for the purchase of rice and vegetable oil, and conducted a mission in May, in collaboration with UNDP Tehran, the Government and non-governmental institutions.

The National Disaster Task Force had overall responsibility for relief programmes.

Other disasters

Earthquake in India

On 30 September, the south-eastern area of India's Maharashtra State was struck by an earthquake measuring 6.4 on the Richter scale. DHA dispatched its United Nations Disaster Assessment and Coordination Stand-by Team, and the international response to cover United Nations relief activities was reported at over $6 million as at 4 October. The Indian Government launched a major relief operation, using army teams who worked with thousands of volunteers. The earthquake was the strongest in India in 50 years, killing more than 11,000 people and causing extensive property damage.

Locust infestation in Africa

Countries in the Maghreb/Sahel region reported a resurgence of the desert locust in September. Infestations were reported in the Sudan and Somalia. In West Africa, a first wave had passed through Chad, eastern Niger and Mauritania. Reproduction of locust populations had also been observed in Mali and Mauritania. Available data suggested that ecological conditions were generally favourable to the locusts in West Africa and that swarms from the current reproduction cycle would move towards central and northern Mauritania, and possibly to Morocco or south-west Algeria. India and Pakistan also faced serious infestations and it was feared that those populations, if not destroyed, could aggravate the situation in central and western regions in 1994.

An ad hoc meeting of experts from the countries of the Arab Maghreb Union and the Sahel discussed the locust infestations (Tunis, Tunisia, 1 and 2 September)[13] and described action taken by FAO to organize prevention and control oper-

ations and raise the necessary financial resources. The meeting elaborated an emergency plan to contain the locust invasion in the short and medium term. Its recommendations were adopted by a meeting of FAO and Ministers of Agriculture responsible for locust control in the countries of the Maghreb and the Sahel (Algiers, Algeria, 27 September).[14] The latter meeting invited FAO, as an immediate measure, to implement the emergency plan quickly, and to undertake complementary activities to manage the situation in the front-line countries and in Mauritania in particular. FAO was asked to formulate a medium-term preventive control programme for the entire desert locust invasion area and to develop training and research in scientific and technical areas of locust control. The establishment of a regional training and research centre for West Africa was recommended.

GENERAL ASSEMBLY ACTION

On 19 November, the General Assembly adopted **resolution 48/20 without vote.**

Emergency action to combat locust infestation in Africa
The General Assembly,
Recalling the international strategy for the fight against locust infestation, particularly in Africa, adopted by the Economic and Social Council in its resolution 1989/98 of 26 July 1989 and endorsed by the General Assembly in its decision 44/438 of 19 December 1989,
Also recalling its resolution 42/169 of 11 December 1987 on the International Decade for Natural Disaster Reduction, which included locust infestations among the types of natural disasters to be covered by the Decade,
Deeply concerned at the exceptional seriousness and real dangers of the current locust infestation in Africa and concerned at its resulting economic, social and environmental consequences, including the reduction of agricultural output and the displacement of affected populations,
Aware that current campaigns for locust control have so far been unable to put an end to the infestation, in particular because of the limited financial resources of the affected countries, and convinced that the fight against this plague, because of its recurrent nature, requires increased and coordinated mobilization of appropriate human, scientific, technical, material and financial resources,
Bearing in mind the recommendations of the meeting of the Ministers of Agriculture responsible for locust control of the countries of the Maghreb and of the Sahel, held at Algiers on 27 September 1993,
1. *Expresses its deep concern* at the worsening locust infestation in Africa, especially in the Sahel and Maghreb regions, which threatens other regions of Africa, and reaffirms the need to accord high priority to locust control and eradication;
2. *Notes with appreciation* the efforts of the affected countries, and expresses its gratitude to donor countries, the Food and Agriculture Organization of the United Nations and other competent institutions of the United

Nations system for their efforts to contain the locust infestation in Africa;

3. *Calls upon* the international community, particularly the developed countries and the United Nations system, to support fully the locust control programmes undertaken at the national, subregional and regional levels by the affected countries;

4. *Invites* the Food and Agriculture Organization speedily to implement the emergency plan adopted by the experts from the region at their meeting held at Tunis on 1 and 2 September 1993 and to undertake the relevant complementary activities with a view to controlling the situation in the front-line countries;

5. *Requests* the Director-General of the Food and Agriculture Organization, in collaboration with the Secretary-General, to keep the situation under constant review and to organize a pledging conference as early as possible in the first quarter of 1994 with a view to mobilizing the necessary financial and other resources such as aircraft, appropriate chemicals and technical personnel to provide effective assistance to affected countries in their efforts to combat the locust infestation in Africa;

6. *Requests* the Secretary-General, in collaboration with the Director-General of the Food and Agriculture Organization, to submit to the General Assembly at its forty-ninth session a report on the implementation of the present resolution.

General Assembly resolution 48/20

19 November 1993   Meeting 58   Adopted without vote

22-nation draft (A/48/L.22); agenda item 175.

Sponsors: Algeria, Belgium, Canada, China, Denmark, Finland, France, Germany, Greece, Iceland, Ireland, Italy, Japan, Luxembourg, Netherlands, Norway, Portugal, Russian Federation, Spain, Sweden, United Kingdom, United States.

Chernobyl aftermath

On 22 June,[15] the Russian Federation communicated to the Secretary-General an appeal to parliaments, Governments and the international community issued by participants in the International Conference on the Scientific and Practical Aspects of Medical and Social Problems and the Role of the Sanatorium and Spa System in Improving the Health of the Population Exposed to the Effects of Radiation as a Consequence of the Accident at the Chernobyl Nuclear Power Plant, and of Other Radiological Disasters (Golitsyno, Russian Federation, 10 and 11 February). The Conference appealed for greater efforts to save the lives and protect the health of people affected by the accident, and to revitalize the regions exposed to radioactive contamination.

In July, the Under-Secretary-General for Humanitarian Affairs reported orally to the Economic and Social Council on strengthening international cooperation and coordination of efforts to study and mitigate the consequences of Chernobyl. On 22 July, the Council, by **decision 1993/232**, took note of the oral report and decided to keep the matter under review.

In September,[16] the Secretary-General, as requested by the General Assembly in 1992,[17] presented the conclusions of an analytical review of all United Nations activities related to the accident, summarized action by the international community and made recommendations for further action to stimulate and coordinate assistance. The report noted that in March 1993 the post of United Nations Coordinator of International Cooperation on Chernobyl was conferred upon the Under-Secretary-General for Humanitarian Affairs, who convened a meeting of the Inter-Agency Task Force for Chernobyl (Geneva, 16 April). That meeting launched a new approach to the Chernobyl problem and submitted priority projects with clearly defined time-frames to the Coordinator.

In May, the Coordinator went to Belarus, the Russian Federation and Ukraine. He took part in a coordination meeting with their Ministers responsible for Chernobyl relief (Minsk, Belarus, 26 May), which emphasized the importance of openness and transparency in issues of nuclear safety and waste management. It recommended that the United Nations promote closer cooperation and a more effective division of labour among the States affected, the United Nations system and international organizations, and agreed on the need for a flexible funding strategy. In the communiqué issued following the meeting, the three Ministers and the Coordinator agreed to increase efforts to implement priority projects; to identify possible sources of funding on a bilateral, regional and multilateral basis; to encourage the incorporation of the Chernobyl problem into the regular activities of the specialized agencies; to request the Director-General of the World Health Organization (WHO) to conduct a study on the treatment of the health of the persons who took part in the immediate post-Chernobyl relief efforts; and to create a quadripartite coordination committee. That new high-level coordinating mechanism would meet regularly to exchange information on the efforts of the United Nations system, to provide for more precise coordination of international efforts, and to promote and strengthen efforts to study, mitigate and minimize the consequences of the disaster. The first meeting of the committee was held on 17 November.

The Management Committee of the WHO International Programme on the Health Effects of the Chernobyl Accident met in May and reported that, due to financial constraints, so far only five health projects had been implemented. The Coordinator held meetings with the European Community in June and with the Commission of the European Communities in July as part of the initiative to strengthen cooperation, and a further meeting of the Inter-Agency Task Force was convened in July to determine ways of approaching potential donors to finance specific projects. The meeting urged that preference be given to projects that promised tangible results for the affected population, rather than purely research projects.

The results of the analytical review of United Nations activities indicated that an appropriate balance had to be achieved between the United Nations approach, which addressed the issue within the more complex economic and social context of the affected States, and the interests of the international community, which lay principally in research. The two approaches were considered complementary, and it was noted that areas of overlap provided opportunities for collaboration, for combining resources and for pooling expertise and knowledge. It was felt that the United Nations should cultivate an interdisciplinary focus and mobilize support for organizations that could effectively respond to priority needs.

GENERAL ASSEMBLY ACTION

On 21 December, the General Assembly, on the recommendation of the Second Committee, adopted **resolution 48/206** without vote.

Strengthening of international cooperation and coordination of efforts to study, mitigate and minimize the consequences of the Chernobyl disaster

The General Assembly,

Reaffirming its resolutions 45/190 of 21 December 1990 and 46/150 of 18 December 1991,

Recalling Economic and Social Council resolutions 1990/50 of 13 July 1990, 1991/51 of 26 July 1991 and 1992/38 of 30 July 1992 and taking note of Council decision 1993/232 of 22 July 1993,

Taking note of the decisions adopted by the organs, organizations and programmes of the United Nations system in the implementation of General Assembly resolutions 45/190 and 46/150,

Noting with appreciation the contribution made by Member States and by organizations of the United Nations system in the development of cooperation to mitigate and minimize the consequences of the Chernobyl disaster, the activities of regional and other organizations, in particular the Commission of the European Communities, as well as bilateral activities and those of the non-governmental sector,

Bearing in mind the communiqué on the meeting of the Governments of Belarus, the Russian Federation and Ukraine and the United Nations Coordinator of International Cooperation on Chernobyl, held at Minsk on 26 May 1993,

Recognizing the importance of providing international support to the ongoing national efforts to mitigate and minimize the radiological, health, socio-economic, psychological and environmental consequences of the Chernobyl disaster, taking into consideration the subsequent social, economic and other changes that have occurred in the countries most affected by the Chernobyl disaster,

Taking note of the report of the Secretary-General on the implementation of General Assembly resolution 47/165 of 18 December 1992 and the conclusions of the analytical review of all United Nations activities to study, mitigate and minimize the consequences of the Chernobyl disaster,

1. *Requests* the Secretary-General to continue his efforts in the implementation of General Assembly resolutions 45/190, 46/150 and 47/165 and, in particular, to continue to maintain close contacts with the Commission of the European Communities and regional and other relevant organizations, with a view to encouraging the regular exchange of information, cooperation, coordination and complementarity in the multilateral and bilateral efforts in those areas, while implementing programmes and specific projects;

2. *Invites* the Secretary-General to consider the possibility of a further exchange of information between the United Nations, as a catalyst, existing coordination mechanisms and Member States on the activities related to Chernobyl;

3. *Also requests* the Secretary-General to submit to the General Assembly for consideration at its fiftieth session, under a separate agenda item, a report on the implementation of the present resolution.

General Assembly resolution 48/206

21 December 1993   Meeting 86   Adopted without vote

Approved by Second Committee (A/48/731) without vote, 6 December (meeting 45); 34-nation draft (A/C.2/48/L.19), orally revised following informal consultations; agenda item 105.

Sponsors: Armenia, Barbados, Benin, Belarus, Brazil, Brunei Darussalam, Bulgaria, Colombia, Cuba, Cyprus, Czech Republic, Georgia, Guinea-Bissau, Hungary, Israel, Japan, Kazakhstan, Kyrgyzstan, Latvia, Malaysia, Marshall Islands, Mexico, Namibia, Poland, Republic of Korea, Republic of Moldova, Romania, Russian Federation, Slovakia, Slovenia, Thailand, Tunisia, Turkey, Ukraine.

Meeting numbers. GA 48th session: 2nd Committee 33-35, 39, 45; plenary 86.

REFERENCES
[1]YUN 1991, p. 412, GA res. 46/149, 18 Dec. 1991. [2]A/48/219-E/1993/97 & Add.1. [3]GA res. 44/236, 22 Dec. 1989. [4]GA res. 45/185, 21 Dec. 1990. [5]A/C.2/48/9. [6]DP/1994/10/Add.1. [7]A/48/25 (dec. 17/19 C). [8]E/1993/35 (dec. 93/33). [9]YUN 1992, p. 670. [10]YUN 1977, p. 509. [11]A/48/216-E/1993/92. [12]A/47/917. [13]A/C.2/48/6. [14]A/48/552. [15]A/48/218-E/1993/96. [16]A/48/406. [17]YUN 1992, p. 610, GA res. 47/165, 18 Dec. 1992.

Chapter IV

International trade, finance and transport

The growth of both world output and world trade accelerated in 1992 for the first time since 1988. While the recovery in output was modest, the volume growth of world trade was much greater, due to the recovery in the United States, the import boom in Latin America and the continued expansion of intra-Asian trade. However, international trade continued to be affected by structural and policy-driven changes as well as by macroeconomic developments in the world economy, including the recession and large currency misalignments.

An important landmark in the liberalization of global trade was the successful conclusion on 15 December, seven years after it was launched, of the Uruguay Round of multilateral trade negotiations. The General Assembly had earlier urged participants to complete the Round by that date, taking into account the particular interests of the developing countries (resolution 48/55).

The Assembly examined various aspects of international trade, finance and development and decided to convene, in 1995, under the auspices of the United Nations Conference on Trade and Development (UNCTAD), the Third United Nations Conference to Review All Aspects of the Set of Multilaterally Agreed Equitable Principles and Rules for the Control of Restrictive Business Practices (decision 48/442). It emphasized the importance of monitoring the implementation of the Cartagena Commitment, adopted by UNCTAD VIII in 1992, and requested UNCTAD to continue its special role in trade and environment (resolution 48/55). With regard to the debt problems of developing countries, the Assembly called on the international community to implement additional relief measures, including further cancellation or reduction of debt and debt service related to official debt, and to take urgent action with regard to the remaining commercial debt owed by the developing countries (48/182).

In the area of transport, the International Convention on Maritime Liens and Mortgages was adopted at a Conference convened by UNCTAD and the International Maritime Organization.

UNCTAD VIII follow-up

In a September 1993 report on strengthening international organizations in the area of multilateral trade,[1] prepared in response to a 1992 General Assembly request,[2] the Secretary-General reported on developments within UNCTAD and its subsidiary bodies since the eighth session (1992) of the United Nations Conference on Trade and Development (UNCTAD VIII).[3] UNCTAD's work had concentrated on the implementation of the Cartagena Commitment, focusing on reforms to its intergovernmental machinery and working methods and on reorienting and enhancing its activities in the areas of trade and development through the adoption and implementation of work programmes for all its new intergovernmental organs. Although those reforms were largely implemented, further work was needed to address outstanding institutional issues, such as optimal forms of the outcome of the intergovernmental deliberations. Recent activities in UNCTAD had demonstrated the willingness of member States to assign it a wider scope for policy analysis and UNCTAD was well placed to contribute to the processes of consensus-building and policy-making regarding the post–Uruguay Round trade agenda.

The report also described developments in the Uruguay Round of trade negotiations and addressed the question of strengthening international organizations in the area of multilateral trade (see below).

At the second part of its thirty-ninth session (Geneva, 15-26 March),[4] the UNCTAD Trade and Development Board (TDB) discussed follow-up action to the recommendations adopted at UNCTAD VIII. It had before it a report by the UNCTAD Secretary-General[5] on the development of human resources for trade. The report discussed human resources development as a strategic factor in international trade and competitiveness and the formulation and implementation of human resources development in international trade, and outlined UNCTAD's future role in supporting developing countries and economies in transition in their human resources development efforts. The report recommended that UNCTAD familiarize policy makers with the subject, promote exchanges of views and disseminate information and databases; pursue on-the-job training in the context of advisory services; expand its TRAINMAR and TRAINFORTRADE programmes in cooperation with the International Trade Centre (ITC) and other United Nations organizations; cooperate with research and training institutions; and develop a research programme in human resources development for trade.

TDB adopted a report of one of its Vice-Presidents, which noted that the Board's discussion supported the continuation and implementation of UNCTAD's human resources development activities in trade and trade-related areas. Such activities should be carried out in collaboration with ITC and other organizations, paying special attention to the needs of the least developed countries (LDCs) and geographically disadvantaged countries. The Board approved of the approach of TRAINMAR and TRAINFORTRADE, particularly their long-term approach to capacity-building and network development. The discussion highlighted the need for UNCTAD to develop human resources development networks among research, training and technological institutions in trade and trade-related areas and noted that the work of UNCTAD's intergovernmental experts contributed to the development of appropriate human resources development policies. TDB invited donor countries to increase their contributions to UNCTAD and drew attention to the desirability of developing countries using bilateral and multilateral funds to enable them to benefit from UNCTAD's technical cooperation activities in human resources development.

At the first part of its fortieth session (Geneva, 20 September–1 October),[4] TDB reviewed the evolution and consequences of emerging free trade and economic integration agreements. It had before it an UNCTAD secretariat report,[6] which analysed the recent evolution and consequences of economic spaces and regional integration processes, and examined European integration, economic integration in the western hemisphere, in Asia and the Pacific and among developing countries, and the dynamic effects of regional integration on the international trading system. The UNCTAD Secretary-General submitted to the Board's March session a report on regional integration issues in Africa.[7]

On 1 October,[8] TDB stated that, to maintain the positive aspects of integration arrangements and their dynamic growth effects, member States and groupings should be supportive of the multilateral trading system; integration groupings should observe multilateral disciplines and rules in devising their policies and ensure transparency of their rules, regulations and standards, taking into account the effects on third countries; intensification or extension of integration schemes should lead to further multilateral trade liberalization and global integration; integration groupings should bear special responsibility for their weaker trading partners, particularly developing countries, identify new opportunities for economic interaction with developing countries, and en-

courage investment cooperation, joint ventures and other measures to help third countries to expand trade and economic cooperation with groupings; and, in accepting new members, they should avoid adverse effects on liberal market access for developing countries. The UNCTAD secretariat should provide technical advice, analysis and training to facilitate information, dialogue and evaluation for a better understanding of integration schemes, and UNCTAD bodies, including its Standing Committee on Economic Cooperation among Developing Countries (see PART THREE, Chapter I), should intensify their work on strengthening economic integration of developing countries.

TDB recommended that the secretariat should provide it with information on significant new developments in regional integration groupings and on their implications for other countries.

REFERENCES

[1]A/48/363. [2]YUN 1992, p. 617, GA res. 47/184, 22 Dec. 1992. [3]Ibid., p. 611. [4]A/48/15. [5]TD/B/39(2)/14 & Corr.1. [6]TD/B/40(1)/7. [7]TD/B/39(2)/11. [8]A/48/15 (conclusions 408(XL)).

International trade

The *Trade and Development Report, 1993*[1] noted that international trade in 1992 was affected by structural and policy changes as well as by macroeconomic developments in the world economy. These included the recession in the developed economies and large currency misalignments and realignments; the collapse of the economic and political systems of the former socialist countries of Eastern Europe; the unification of Germany; initiatives regarding regional trading blocs; new environmental policies; trade conflicts and protectionism in member countries of the Organisation for Economic Cooperation and Development (OECD); the trade-liberalization and export-expansion policies of developing countries; increased productivity of primary commodities; the conflict in the Persian Gulf; the emergence of China as a major participant in world trade; and uncertainties due to the failure to complete the Uruguay Round of multilateral trade negotiations until the end of 1993 (see below). While some developments enlarged developing countries' trading opportunities, others intensified competition in OECD markets, in some cases accompanied by reduced predictability and greater risks, threatening the momentum of export expansion in developing countries and those of Central and Eastern Europe and of the former USSR.

The *World Economic Survey 1993*[2] reported that the pattern of trade flows did not suggest a large change from recent trends. The volume of world exports grew by 4.5 per cent in 1992, compared with around 3.5 per cent in 1991. Growth in trade reflected the regional pattern of the growth of output, differing widely among countries and regions. The developed market economies gave only weak impetus to world trade in 1992, except for North America, which increased imports by 11 per cent, reflecting the economic recovery in the United States and Canada that began to take hold during the year. United States exports grew by 7 per cent, almost twice the global growth rate, despite the sluggish nature of its markets in Europe and Japan. Japan's imports contracted and exports fell steeply as growth of its economy slowed. There was a sharp reduction in German import growth after two years of double-digit growth. The weak import demand in Germany and in other European economies had important repercussions on their European trading partners.

In the transition economies, the attempt to redirect trade resulted in a sharp decline in both exports and imports. The States of the former USSR entered deeply into that process in 1992, while in Eastern Europe the overall contraction in trade appeared to have ended. Although the rate of growth of trade of developing countries as a whole slowed somewhat, exports grew by 7 per cent and imports by 10 per cent. In Latin America and the Caribbean, trade expanded rapidly, especially imports. The volume of exports increased by over 6 per cent, with Brazil and Chile registering rapid expansion. Africa's exports, dominated by primary products, grew by only 4 per cent compared to 7 per cent in 1991. Imports recovered modestly from 1991 levels, mostly food imports to supplement production shortfalls. Trade in South and East Asia continued its strong growth, although at a much slower rate than in 1991. Exports grew by 11 per cent and imports by 10 per cent compared with 15 per cent in 1991. China's trade continued to expand vigorously; the value of its exports grew by some 14 per cent and imports by 22 per cent. Depressed oil prices resulted in only a modest increase in the value of exports of the countries of Western Asia, while imports expanded by 7 per cent.

UNCTAD action. At its September/October session, TDB considered, on the basis of the *Trade and Development Report, 1993*, the international implications of macroeconomic policies and issues concerning global interdependence. On 1 October,[3] it expressed concern over the continuing recession in the developed market economies. It noted that the slow growth, in addition to adding to unemployment in the developed countries, was exacerbating protectionist pressures and limiting the demand for, and hence putting downward pressure on, the prices of their imports from develop-

ing countries. The terms of trade for developing countries' commodity and manufactured exports were deteriorating continuously, with adverse consequences for their development performance and prospects. TDB emphasized that the failure of developed countries to improve access to their markets posed a danger for the efforts of other countries to accelerate development by opening up their own economies and integrating into the world economy. The need for an early-warning mechanism to address key emerging issues was stressed, as was the need to adhere to the principles and rules of the multilateral trading system. There was consensus on the importance of an early and balanced conclusion of the Uruguay Round of trade negotiations, taking into account the interests of developing countries. TDB also identified global economic measures to stimulate growth (see PART THREE, Chapter I).

GENERAL ASSEMBLY ACTION

On 10 December, on the recommendation of the Second (Economic and Financial) Committee, the General Assembly adopted **resolution 48/55** without vote.

International trade and development

The General Assembly,

Reaffirming the importance and continuing validity of the Declaration on International Economic Cooperation, in particular the Revitalization of Economic Growth and Development of the Developing Countries, the International Development Strategy for the Fourth United Nations Development Decade, the United Nations New Agenda for the Development of Africa in the 1990s, the Programme of Action for the Least Developed Countries for the 1990s, the Cartagena Commitment, and the various agreements, in particular Agenda 21, that provide an overall framework for developing cooperative action to address the development challenges of the 1990s,

Recalling its resolutions 1995(XIX) of 30 December 1964, as amended, on the establishment of the United Nations Conference on Trade and Development as an organ of the General Assembly and 47/183 of 22 December 1992 on the eighth session of the Conference,

Noting the progress made by the United Nations Conference on Trade and Development in the implementation of the outcome of its eighth session, in particular its contribution, within its mandate, to trade and environmental issues,

Noting with concern that, although a number of developing countries have experienced higher rates of growth and an expansion of their trade, the current international economic situation, characterized by slow growth and a fragile economic recovery, has adversely affected the growth and development of all countries, in particular the developing countries,

Emphasizing the importance of an open, equitable, secure, non-discriminatory and predictable multilateral trading system that is consistent with the goals of sustainable development and that leads to the optimal distribution of global production in accordance with comparative advantage, and of a stable international financial environment for economic recovery and growth in all parts of the world economy, in particular in the developing countries,

Noting with serious concern the intensification of pressures for protectionism and unilateralism, in particular in many developed countries, and stressing in this regard the need for all countries to halt and reverse protectionism and respect multilaterally agreed trade rules,

Emphasizing also that the high economic cost of protectionist policies has a negative impact on the economic growth and sustainable development of all countries, in particular the developing countries, and emphasizing further that within this context such policies in no case constitute an appropriate means of addressing the serious problems of unemployment,

Recognizing that improved access to external markets and further multilateral trade liberalization are very important prerequisites for the reactivation of growth in all parts of the world economy, in particular in the developing countries,

Recognizing with satisfaction that major structural economic reforms, as well as trade policy liberalization and regional economic integration efforts, are being undertaken by many developing countries, as well as by a number of other countries, and that such policies have contributed to the expansion of world trade and enhanced export possibilities and economic growth prospects for all countries,

Recognizing also that regional economic integration processes, including those among developing countries, which have intensified in recent years, impart substantial dynamism to global trade and enhance trade and development possibilities for all countries, and stressing that in order to maintain the positive aspects of such integration arrangements and assure the prevalence of their dynamic growth effects, Member States and groupings should strive to be outward-oriented and supportive of the multilateral trading system,

Emphasizing the need for increased international support for the reforms being undertaken by many developing countries and by countries with economies in transition, including the provision of increased global market access for their exports, which is of critical importance for the success and further encouragement of those reforms,

Reaffirming the need to give priority to problems facing the least developed countries, owing to the fragility of their economies and their particular vulnerability to external shocks and natural calamities,

Reaffirming also the message from the Trade and Development Board to the Governments participating in the Uruguay Round of multilateral trade negotiations, adopted by the Board at the second part of its thirty-ninth session, in which the Board stressed that an early and successful conclusion of the Uruguay Round should be viewed as a prerequisite to a return to the path of growth, trade expansion and an improved world economic climate,

Stressing that, for the Uruguay Round to be concluded in a balanced manner, issues of particular interest to developing countries and their development must be taken fully into account,

Emphasizing that a failure of the Uruguay Round would seriously risk eroding business confidence, intensify trade differences and disputes, retard global economic growth and recovery, encourage and protect uncompetitive sectors of the economy and undermine the outward-oriented reforms being undertaken by many developing countries,

Reaffirming the need for a balanced and integrated approach to environment, trade and development issues within the context of a new global partnership for sustainable development,

Recognizing that the complex linkages between trade and environment pose significant challenges to the pursuit of sustainable development and to the maintenance of a free and open trading system,

Welcoming Trade and Development Board decision 402(XXXIX) of 26 March 1993 on sustainable development and its conclusions 407(XL) of 1 October 1993 regarding the contribution of the United Nations Conference on Trade and Development, within its mandate and in the context of sustainable development, to the study of the interlinkages between trade and environment,

1. *Takes note* of the reports of the Trade and Development Board on the second part of its thirty-ninth session and the first part of its fortieth session, and calls upon all States to take appropriate action to implement the outcome of those sessions;

2. *Emphasizes* the importance of follow-up and monitoring of the implementation of the policies and measures contained in the Cartagena Commitment;

3. *Takes note* of the conclusions derived from the debate of the Trade and Development Board, which was underpinned, *inter alia*, by the *Trade and Development Report, 1993*, on the international implications of macroeconomic policies and issues concerning interdependence, as constituting a concrete contribution to the changing of perceptions on issues concerning growth dynamics in various regions, particularly with respect to the conceptual framework, design and implementation of structural adjustment policies;

4. *Recognizes* that trade liberalization by all countries, in particular the developed countries, is an important tool for increasing economic efficiency and improving resource allocation, economic growth, sustainable development and employment in all countries;

5. *Stresses* in this context the urgent need for trade liberalization and improved access to the markets of all countries, in particular those of the developed countries, in order to generate global economic growth and sustainable development for the benefit of all countries, in particular the developing countries, as well as countries with economies in transition;

6. *Emphasizes* that, in order to promote sustainable development through trade, the removal of existing distortions in international trade is essential; emphasizes, in particular, the need for a substantial and progressive reduction in the support and protection of agriculture, covering internal regimes, market access and export subsidies, as well as of industry and other sectors, so as to avoid inflicting large losses on the more efficient producers, especially in developing countries; and in this context further emphasizes that trade liberalization should be pursued on a global basis across economic sectors so as to contribute to sustainable development;

7. *Deplores* the repeated delays in concluding the Uruguay Round of multilateral trade negotiations;

8. *Urges* all countries, in particular the major developed countries, to resolve all outstanding differences in

all areas of the negotiations in order to ensure a successful conclusion of the Uruguay Round;

9. *Strongly urges* all participants in the Uruguay Round to complete the Round by 15 December 1993, taking into account issues of particular interest to the developing countries and providing a comprehensive market access package on goods and services, including items of export interest to those countries, and stresses in this regard the need for a full contribution by all parties;

10. *Urges* all participants to give special attention to the least developed countries with a view to enhancing their full participation in the multilateral trading system;

11. *Stresses* that the ability of many developing countries to mobilize, through international trade, the resources needed to finance investments required for sustainable development may be impaired by tariff and non-tariff impediments, including tariff escalation, limiting their access to export markets, and also that a comprehensive and balanced conclusion to the Uruguay Round would help all countries mobilize financing for sustainable development;

12. *Emphasizes* that an open, equitable, secure, non-discriminatory and predictable multilateral trading system that is consistent with the goals of sustainable development and that leads to the optimal distribution of global production in accordance with comparative advantage is of benefit to all trading partners, and in this context also emphasizes that improved market access for the exports of developing countries in conjunction with sound macroeconomic and environmental policies would have a positive environmental impact and would therefore make an important contribution towards sustainable development;

13. *Also emphasizes* that environment and trade policies should be made mutually supportive, with a view to achieving sustainable development;

14. *Further emphasizes* that environmental measures addressing transborder or global environmental problems should, as far as possible, be based on an international consensus, and in this context emphasizes still further that the international community should strive for the broadest possible international coordination of environmental and trade policies through intergovernmental cooperation, taking into account the complex linkages between environment, trade and sustainable development;

15. *Emphasizes* that trade policy measures for environmental purposes should not constitute a means of arbitrary or unjustifiable discrimination or a disguised restriction on international trade and that, in this respect, unilateral actions to deal with environmental challenges outside the jurisdiction of the importing country should be avoided;

16. *Requests* the United Nations Conference on Trade and Development to continue its special role in the field of trade and environment, including policy analysis, conceptual work and consensus-building, with a view to ensuring transparency and coherence in making environmental and trade policies mutually supportive, and taking into account the work being done by the General Agreement on Tariffs and Trade and other competent international and regional economic institutions;

17. *Invites* the General Agreement on Tariffs and Trade and requests the United Nations Conference on Trade and Development, in accordance with their respective mandates and competencies and in close cooperation with other competent United Nations bodies and the regional commissions, to address trade and environmental matters comprehensively, and to submit, through the Com-

mission on Sustainable Development, a report thereon to the Economic and Social Council at its substantive session of 1994.

General Assembly resolution 48/55

10 December 1993   Meeting 75   Adopted without vote

Approved by Second Committee (A/48/717/Add.1) without vote, 6 December (meeting 45); draft by Vice-Chairman (A/C.2/48/L.57), based on informal consultations on draft by China and Colombia, for Group of 77 (A/C.2/48/L.15); agenda item 91 *(a)*.

Meeting numbers. GA 48th session: 2nd Committee 30-32, 34, 45; plenary 75.

Trade policy

The *Trade and Development Report, 1993*[1] noted that the process of trade liberalization in developing countries continued, with many countries taking steps to open their economies, foster their integration into world markets, and reduce tariff rates or simplify or bind most of their tariffs. Import-liberalization measures in the non-tariff area were also implemented and anti-dumping and anti-subsidy legislation was adopted. Countries in Central and Eastern Europe also embarked on fundamental economic reforms embracing liberal trade policies and the newly independent States of the former USSR declared their intention to adopt outward-oriented policies, despite the disruption of trade that accompanied the difficult transition process. By contrast, trade liberalization in the developed countries was modest. Some of them made liberalization contingent upon attaining their objectives in international trade negotiations, while others implemented tariff reductions provisionally pending a satisfactory outcome of the Uruguay Round. Only a few developed countries reduced trade restrictions on a most-favoured-nation (MFN) basis. The move towards regional and subregional integration accelerated with the completion of a number of integration schemes and trading arrangements.

The *World Economic Survey 1993*[2] reported that the resort to bilateral, regional or mini-multilateral trading arrangements was a concomitant of the growing disenchantment with multilateralism. However, concern over the wisdom of such trading blocs had arisen with their proliferation.

Some proponents of trade blocs viewed them as building blocks of an open international trading system. However, the many protectionist and discriminatory practices associated with the formation and functioning of trading blocs cast doubt on that view. Indeed, blocs could provide greater incentives for applying trade-management devices such as anti-dumping measures and voluntary export restraints.

A multilateral trading system in which all countries traded freely with one another remained the best way to increase world welfare. To ensure that trade blocs did not ultimately fragment the multilateral trading system, it was necessary to strengthen the rules of the General Agreement on Tariffs and Trade (GATT) (see PART SIX, Chapter XVIII), especially those relating to transparency and non-discrimination, and the commitment to abide by those rules.

Trade policy reforms in developing countries

In a January report on trade policy reforms in developing countries and the international support required,[4] the UNCTAD secretariat noted that an increasing number of developing countries had embarked on far-reaching economic reforms with the active collaboration of international financial institutions. Trade policy reforms, which were usually important components of the broader reform efforts, were increasingly directed towards trade liberalization. While some progress had been made, many reforms had yet to achieve their objective. Only a few of the more advanced developing countries had managed to increase exports and investments significantly. The report recommended an expansion of external support through unhindered access to export markets and the development of an equitable, secure and predictable international trading system; the promotion of competitive market structures; incentives and assistance conducive to technology transfer and direct foreign investment in developing countries; and the provision of technical cooperation. Since there was no standard trade-policy approach applicable to all developing countries, international support should allow for policy pluralism and flexible approaches to policy reforms.

UNCTAD action. In conclusions adopted on 26 March,[5] TDB considered that developing countries' trade policy reforms and structural adjustment should be pursued, consistent with their trade, financial and development needs, and should incorporate a social component, especially with regard to vulnerable social groups. It agreed that the international community should support developing countries, particularly LDCs, through improved market access, increased flows of financial resources and debt relief. It also agreed that UNCTAD should identify and propose treatment of key emerging trade and development issues, including an early-warning perspective. The Intergovernmental Group of Experts on Restrictive Business Practices should pursue its work with regard to policies and rules to control such practices, in order to encourage competition, promote proper functioning of markets and efficient resource allocation, and bring about further liberalization of international trade. TDB invited the Ad Hoc Working Group on Expansion of Trading Opportunities for Developing Countries to support those countries' reforms. It agreed that the secretariat should refine a proposal on the study of market-based price mechanisms to assist technology transfer to developing countries, and

suggested that further study of national policies in developing countries and of appropriate external support measures to ensure long-term success of trade policy reforms should be carried out.

Uruguay Round

In response to a 1992 General Assembly request,[6] the Secretary-General submitted a September 1993 report on strengthening international organizations in the area of multilateral trade,[7] in which he reviewed developments in the Uruguay Round—the eighth round of multilateral trade negotiations, launched in 1986[8] under the aegis of GATT.

The Secretary-General noted that the prospects for a successful conclusion of the Round had brightened with the Tokyo Summit (7-9 July 1993),[9] where leaders of the seven major industrialized countries and the European Community (EC) renewed their determination to achieve a global and balanced agreement before the end of the year. In addition, an agreement on market access issues was reached by Canada, Japan, the United States and EC on 7 July, which led to the resumption of negotiations in the middle of that month. The Secretary-General said it was expected that the negotiations would accelerate with the aim of concluding them by 15 December.

In **resolution 48/55**, the Assembly deplored the repeated delays in concluding the negotiations and urged all participants to complete the Round by 15 December.

The negotiations, which were concluded on that date, proved to be a landmark in the international trade endeavour to strengthen the multilateral trading system. However, some countries expressed concern over the balance between the likely benefits and shortcomings of the outcome.

UNCTAD action. In March,[10] TDB adopted a message to Governments participating in the Uruguay Round. It stated that the draft Final Act should take into account issues of interest to developing countries and their development, financial and trade needs, and be supplemented by a comprehensive market-access package on goods and services. Special attention should be given to the problems of LDCs in order to integrate them into the global trading system. TDB also transmitted to its third executive session (Geneva, 27 April) the report of the Chairman of its Sessional Committee I. The Group of 77 developing countries issued a declaration entitled "Developments in the Uruguay Round", which TDB annexed to its report on that session.[11]

On 1 October,[10] the Board, in a statement by its President, said that special efforts should be made in the market-access negotiations for improvements for products of export interest to developing countries, and stressed that evaluation of the Round's results in terms of differential and more favourable treatment for developing countries should be undertaken well in advance to provide sufficient time for possible corrective measures. It recognized UNCTAD's important role in considering developments in the Round, as well as in analysing and assessing the outcome, particularly through technical assistance to developing countries.

Trade and environment

In response to a 1992 General Assembly request,[12] TDB examined the issue of trade and environment at its 1993 sessions. On 26 March,[13] it decided to consider the theme "trade and environment" at the first part of each of its annual sessions and, at the first part of its fortieth session in September/October 1993, the specific issue of trends in the field of trade and environment within the framework of international cooperation. For subsequent sessions, the theme to be discussed would be determined through consultation. TDB transmitted to the General Assembly, through the Commission on Sustainable Development (see PART THREE, Chapter I) and the Economic and Social Council, its report on UNCTAD's plans to implement Agenda 21,[14] adopted by the 1992 United Nations Conference on Environment and Development, which it annexed to its decision.

At its September/October session, TDB considered an UNCTAD secretariat report on trends in the field of trade and environment in the framework of international cooperation.[15] The report described the linkages between trade and environment, trends in environmental policy and trade, the use of trade measures for environmental purposes, international cooperation on environmental standards, and proposals for strengthening international cooperation. The following were identified as important objectives of strengthened cooperation in trade and environment: expansion of trading opportunities for developing countries; prevention of trade conflicts and maintenance of an open trading system; greater coherence between policies and measures implemented by individual countries; prevention of the detrimental effects of environmental policies and measures on the economic growth of developing countries; and greater integration of trade and environmental policies.

In 1 October conclusions,[16] TDB agreed that UNCTAD's role in trade and environment should lie in policy analysis and debate, conceptual work, the building of consensus among member States on the interaction between environmental and trade policies, the dissemination of information to policy makers and assistance in capacity-building, paying attention to the problems and special circumstances of developing countries, including

LDCs, as well as to countries in transition. The Ad Hoc Working Group on Expansion of Trading Opportunities for Developing Countries should study the economic costs of reducing the negative environmental effects of production processes and consumption, and the market opportunities for exporters flowing from the demand for such "friendly products". Increased attention should be paid to environmentally motivated policy instruments with a trade impact, such as those on packaging, labelling and recycling, particularly their impact on exporters in developing countries and countries in transition, and eco-labelling programmes should take into account the trade and sustainable development interests of producing countries. TDB also stated that the effects of OECD procedural guidelines on integrating trade and environment policies and its future work programme needed to be studied, and interaction between UNCTAD and OECD and other intergovernmental and regional organizations in the field of trade and environment should continue to be developed. Technical assistance in trade and environment should be pursued by UNCTAD, and donor countries, other countries in a position to do so and multilateral agencies should increase significantly their funds for technical assistance, particularly for LDCs. Countries should reply to the UNCTAD secretariat questionnaire on environmental measures which could have an impact on trade.

The Board recommended that it consider the themes "the effect of the internalization of external costs on sustainable development" and "the impact of environment-related policies on export competitiveness and market access" at its 1994 sessions.

In **resolution 48/55**, the General Assembly requested UNCTAD to continue its special role in trade and environment and invited it, and GATT, to submit to the 1994 substantive session of the Economic and Social Council, through the Commission on Sustainable Development, a report on trade and environmental matters.

Strengthening institutional trade arrangements

In response to a 1992 General Assembly request,[6] the Secretary-General submitted in September 1993 a report on strengthening international organizations in the area of multilateral trade,[7] in which he stated that no further replies had been received from Governments or international organizations to the UNCTAD Secretary-General's request for their views on the subject, made in response to a 1991 Assembly request.[17]

The report also discussed developments since UNCTAD VIII and the status of the Uruguay Round (see above).

Taking into account the views of Governments, which had stressed that, given the unfinished state of the Uruguay Round, the time might not be ripe to define a clear line of action or to draw conclusions as to the institutional needs of a global trading system, the Secretary-General stated that it might be advisable for the Assembly to review the matter again in 1994.

GENERAL ASSEMBLY ACTION

On 10 December, on the recommendation of the Second Committee, the General Assembly adopted **resolution 48/54** without vote.

Strengthening international organizations in the area of multilateral trade

The General Assembly,

Reaffirming the importance and continuing validity of the Declaration on International Economic Cooperation, in particular the Revitalization of Economic Growth and Development of the Developing Countries, the International Development Strategy for the Fourth United Nations Development Decade, the United Nations New Agenda for the Development of Africa in the 1990s, the Programme of Action for the Least Developed Countries for the 1990s, the document entitled "A New Partnership for Development: the Cartagena Commitment", and the various agreements, in particular Agenda 21, that provide an overall framework for developing cooperative action to address the development challenges of the 1990s,

Recalling its resolutions 45/201 of 21 December 1990, 46/207 of 20 December 1991 and 47/184 of 22 December 1992,

Welcoming the progress made by the United Nations Conference on Trade and Development in the implementation of the outcome of its eighth session, in particular the institutional reforms within the organization,

Taking note of the report of the Secretary-General concerning institutional developments related to the strengthening of international organizations in the area of multilateral trade,

Deeply concerned by the repeated delays in concluding the Uruguay Round of multilateral trade negotiations,

Stressing the urgent need for the Uruguay Round to be concluded in a balanced manner, taking into account issues of particular interest to developing countries and their development,

Emphasizing the importance of a strengthened multilateral trading system and of the respect by all countries for multilaterally agreed rules,

1. *Once again urges* all Governments, competent regional economic integration organizations, and the executive heads of the competent specialized agencies and of other organizations and programmes of the United Nations system to continue to present their views to the Secretary-General on this matter;

2. *Requests* the Secretary-General to prepare, for submission to the General Assembly at its forty-ninth session, an updated report taking into account the positive institutional outcome and implementation of the results of the eighth session of the United Nations Conference on Trade and Development and the developments in the Uruguay Round of multilateral trade negotiations.

General Assembly resolution 48/54

10 December 1993   Meeting 75   Adopted without vote

Approved by Second Committee (A/48/717/Add.1) without vote, 6 December (meeting 45); draft by Vice-Chairman (A/C.2/48/L.55), based on informal consultations on draft by China and Colombia, for Group of 77 (A/C.2/48/L.13); agenda item 91 *(a)*.

Meeting numbers. GA 48th session: 2nd Committee 30-32, 34, 45; plenary 75.

Structural adjustment

Structural adjustment for transition to disarmament

As follow-up to the establishment by TDB in 1992[18] of an ad hoc working group to explore the issue of structural adjustment for the transition to disarmament, the UNCTAD secretariat submitted a February 1993 report on the activities of the United Nations in that area.[19] The report surveyed the activities of United Nations organizations and identified the major issues that UNCTAD could consider through its Ad Hoc Working Group. They included the global impacts on trade and development of the adjustment to disarmament and the conversion of military capacities to civilian uses; economic and social policy issues and options; connections and interactions between debt, trade, growth, military expenditures and sustainable development; and consensus-building on policies and measures at the local, national, regional and global levels.

On 26 March,[10] TDB requested its President to hold informal consultations on the draft terms of reference of the Ad Hoc Working Group, and asked the UNCTAD Secretary-General to prepare draft terms of reference and a compendium of comments submitted by member States. It agreed to establish, at its September/October session, the Working Group's terms of reference and timetable.

In September,[20] the United Nations Secretary-General stated that he had requested the UNCTAD secretariat to coordinate the establishment of a United Nations interdepartmental task force to provide Member States with political, technical and economic advice on the transition from military to civilian production (see PART ONE, Chapter II, under "Economic aspects of disarmament").

TDB members held informal consultations on the Ad Hoc Working Group's terms of reference on 8 September. The Board's fourth executive session (Geneva, 13 September)[21] had before it an UNCTAD secretariat note containing suggested terms of reference[22] and a compendium of comments on the terms of reference[23] by four member States (Brazil, China and Japan, and Denmark on behalf of EC). TDB agreed that further consultations should be held on the issue on 17 September and that the results would be communicated to the Board in September/October.

TDB was informed that, at the 17 September consultations, an open-ended drafting group was established to work on the draft terms of reference. That group met on 30 September and a number of amendments were made. On 1 October,[10] TDB noted that further consultations were required and asked the President of its thirty-ninth session, who was chairing the consultations, to continue his mandate and report to the Board at its next (1994) executive session. Further consultations were held on 11 and 12 November, which resulted in revised draft terms of reference.[24]

Trade preferences

Generalized system of preferences

TDB's Special Committee on Preferences held its twentieth session at Geneva from 10 to 14 May 1993.[25] It considered the sixteenth general report[26] by the UNCTAD secretariat on the implementation of the generalized system of preferences (GSP), which described changes and improvements in the system and updated information on its trade effects. It noted that, with the exception of a few technical changes, the EC scheme would be applied *mutatis mutandis* from 1 January to 31 December 1993. The countries of the Commonwealth of Independent States and Georgia were added to the list of beneficiaries under the EC scheme. However, benefits were not extended to cover textiles, iron and steel and finishing products. Namibia and the former Czechoslovakia became beneficiaries under Japan's scheme. Croatia, the Marshall Islands, Micronesia, Saint Kitts and Nevis and Slovenia were added to the beneficiary list of Finland. Bosnia and Herzegovina was added to Norway's beneficiaries, while Israel and Turkey were withdrawn, following the entry into force of trade agreements between them and Norway. Sweden also removed Turkey from its beneficiaries as a result of a free trade agreement, while it provided GSP-LDC treatment to Namibia. Turkey was withdrawn from Switzerland's list of beneficiaries as well. The United States designated the successor States of the former Yugoslavia, other than Serbia and Montenegro, as beneficiaries under its scheme. The Russian Federation implemented a temporary preferential scheme whereby imports from developing countries were subject to a 50 per cent MFN rate of its import customs tariffs. The scheme also provided for duty-free treatment for goods originating in LDCs and established a list of beneficiary developing countries, including LDCs.

In a summary of discussions annexed to the Special Committee's report,[25] the Chairman said that developing countries felt that there was a need to expand product coverage of the schemes to include all products of export interest to developing countries, and to grant those products

deeper tariff cuts, including duty-free treatment. In that connection, concern was expressed over the possible erosion of preferential margins resulting from MFN tariff reductions after the conclusion of the Uruguay Round. There was also a need for multilaterally agreed criteria for applying the built-in limitation measures of the schemes, as well as graduation. With regard to the rules of origin, it was felt that harmonization would simplify the rules and lead to better equivalence of access to preference-giving country markets. As to technical cooperation, developing countries expressed concern over the decline in resources available and appealed to potential donors and the United Nations Development Programme (UNDP) to provide further assistance. It was agreed that technical assistance activities should be practical and pragmatic, provide for informal consultations to solve immediate problems and pay attention to the requests of LDCs. A number of countries felt that GSP should be revitalized and that the Committee should conduct a policy review at its next session. Countries were encouraged to submit information to the secretariat on utilization of the schemes, particularly with regard to the rules of origin, in preparation for the review.

In a text, which it attached to its report,[25] the Committee decided to begin preparations for the 1995 policy review of GSP and to consider its 1994 session as a preparatory meeting for that review. It requested the UNCTAD secretariat to study ways to improve and enhance the impact of GSP in the new international economic and political environment, in consultation with experts and eminent personalities.

On 13 September, at its fourth executive session,[21] TDB endorsed the Committee's decision on preparations for the 1995 policy review.

Technical cooperation

The delivery of technical cooperation with regard to GSP and other trade laws remained high in 1993[27] owing to increased interest shown by beneficiaries and made possible by UNDP and trust fund contributions to the GSP programme by UNCTAD member States. Extrabudgetary funding for global GSP activities in 1993 totalled $877,780, of which UNDP accounted for approximately $256,000 or 29 per cent, with the remainder coming from trust fund contributions. Trust fund contributions for specific purposes amounted to $487,250, in-kind contributions to $55,395 and central trust fund contributions to $79,135, or 13 per cent of total funding. During the year, some 45 activities were undertaken in all regions of the world, including 30 training seminars/workshops and 7 advisory missions aimed primarily at assisting preference-receiving countries to make better use of the system and to establish or upgrade GSP focal points. In all, 1,204 participants from 31 preference-receiving countries benefited from those training activities.

Countries in Africa and Central and Eastern Europe showed increasing interest in GSP, leading to more requests for training activities. Furthermore, as the Uruguay Round had been successfully concluded, more requests for seminars and advisory missions on GSP and other trade laws were anticipated.

Trade promotion and facilitation

During 1993, United Nations bodies continued to assist developing countries to promote their exports and to facilitate the movement of their goods in international commerce. The main originator of technical cooperation projects in that area was ITC.

International Trade Centre

During 1993, ITC, under the joint sponsorship of UNCTAD and GATT, continued its technical cooperation activities, serving as a focal point for United Nations assistance to developing countries in formulating and implementing trade promotion programmes. ITC held a technical meeting (Geneva, 16 and 17 February)[28] to consider the 1992 evaluation of its activities in commodity trade, development and promotion,[29] to examine the evaluator's findings and recommendations and to make recommendations to the Joint Advisory Group (JAG) (see below). The meeting concentrated on key issues raised in the evaluation, such as ITC's role within the international producer-consumer cooperation system, particularly relationships with the Common Fund for Commodities, the optimal use of available resources, and the extension of interregional work to activities at the national level. It recommended that ITC should continue to support commodity diversification and processing by promoting the export development of derivatives from natural resources. Commodity-specific work should be complemented by more attention to cross-commodity issues. With regard to ITC's coverage of its commodity work, the meeting recommended that the issue be kept under review. As to funding, ITC should seek non-traditional sources of financing.

In comments on the evaluation's specific recommendations, the meeting emphasized the importance of expanding programme activities at the country and regional levels, and suggested that ITC seminars could be used to identify its potential role in implementing national project activities. Concerning the extension of ITC's work to metals and minerals, it suggested that ITC should assess its impact in this area with its current staff and resources. In sustaining an ongoing ITC commitment in relation to a given commodity, the meeting recommended that priorities should be kept under review in the light of available resources. ITC should try to align its practices to those of other United Nations organizations in carrying out the evaluation's recommendations.

The meeting had reservations on the recommendation relating to ITC's commodity work and stressed that ITC should continue to provide technical assistance to international commodity bodies for the elaboration of projects for submission to the Common Fund.

JAG action. The Joint Advisory Group on ITC held its twenty-sixth session at Geneva from 8 to 11 November 1993.[30] It had before it a report on ITC's 1992 activities,[31] the report of the 1992 ITC technical meeting,[32] an evaluation of the ITC subprogramme on institutional infrastructure for trade promotion at the national level,[33] ITC's comments on the recommendations contained in the evaluation of that subprogramme,[34] the report of the 1993 technical meeting (see above), and the report on the 1992 evaluation of ITC's activities in commodity trade, development and promotion.[29]

JAG regretted the postponement of a decision on the appointment of an Executive Director of ITC and the filling of other key management posts, and called on UNCTAD and GATT urgently to arrive at an appropriate solution. Donor countries expressed support in principle for ITC's activities, but some indicated that uncertainties surrounding management posts would affect consideration of their trust fund contributions. JAG noted the innovative steps that ITC was taking in the environmental aspects of trade.

China, Denmark, Finland, France, Germany, India and Japan announced their trust fund contributions for 1994. However, the Netherlands, Norway, Sweden and Switzerland indicated their intention either not to contribute to the fund or to reduce contributions substantially until an Executive Director was appointed.

JAG agreed that its Bureau should initiate informal consultations on the terms of reference and timing of a review of ITC's mandate, financial and personnel situation, general structure and relations with UNCTAD and GATT.

In **resolution 47/212 B** of 6 May, the General Assembly requested the Secretary-General to pursue as a matter of urgency his efforts to agree with the GATT Director-General on a prompt appointment to the post of Executive Director of ITC at its current level. The Assembly reiterated the request in **resolution 48/228** of 23 December.

Trade efficiency

The Ad Hoc Working Group on Trade Efficiency—established by TDB in 1992[35]—held its second session at Geneva from 15 to 19 November 1993.[36] It considered an UNCTAD secretariat note containing a compendium of trade facilitation recommendations[37] and a consultant's report on draft guidelines on better trade practices.[38] The Group agreed that the compendium should be part of the background documentation for the 1994 International Symposium on Trade Efficiency (see below). It also agreed that delegations' views concerning the recommendations relating to preshipment inspection should be brought to the attention of the Working Party on Facilitation of International Trade Procedures of the Economic Commission for Europe (ECE), and that its Bureau and that of the ECE Working Party should cooperate further in implementing international standards to enhance trade efficiency.

The Ad Hoc Working Group also had before it the UNCTAD secretariat's interim report[39] on the first evaluation of the trade point programme to establish, operate and interconnect trade points (trade facilitation centres), a key component of the Trade Efficiency Initiative, launched by UNCTAD VIII. In his summary of the discussions on this item, the Chairman indicated that several countries had reported on the status of their trade points and that trade point directors had made a number of recommendations and identified issues requiring further consideration.

The Ad Hoc Working Group also considered an UNCTAD secretariat progress report[40] on measures taken by the UNCTAD Secretary-General, in response to a 1992 General Assembly request,[41] to prepare for the convening in 1994 of the United Nations International Symposium on Trade Efficiency. The Group was informed of the schedule for the preparations for the Symposium, to be held at Columbus, Ohio, United States.

**Trading opportunities
for developing countries**

The Ad Hoc Working Group on Expansion of Trading Opportunities for Developing Countries, established in 1992,[42] held its second session at Geneva from 22 to 26 November 1993.[43] It had before it reports by the UNCTAD secretariat on market opportunities, covering environmental measures, structural adjustment policies and restrictive business practices,[44] and trade measures and implications of regional integration arrangements.[45] A number of countries made presentations to the Working Group on their national experiences, export capabilities, market opportunities and export promotion and marketing. In his summary of the Group's discussion, which covered the building of export capabilities, expanding export market opportunities, and export promotion and marketing, the Chairman stated that

a number of prerequisites for building internationally competitive export capabilities had been identified. The Group recommended that the subsidy element of export incentives should be kept moderate and be subject to review; high priority should be given to investments in the area of human resource development; and consideration should be given to the impact of environmentally motivated policy instruments on trading partners, particularly exporters in developing countries and countries in transition. It also recommended that countries adopt and enforce competition policy and strengthen cooperation to prevent restrictive business practices from impeding or negating market opportunities of developing countries, and that the Intergovernmental Group of Experts on Restrictive Business Practices study the interface between competition and international trade and prepare guidelines on competition policy. The need for more countries to assist LDCs in export promotion and marketing was highlighted.

Restrictive business practices

The Intergovernmental Group of Experts on Restrictive Business Practices held its twelfth session at Geneva from 18 to 22 October 1993.[46] It had before it an UNCTAD secretariat note[47] containing replies from nine countries on steps taken to meet their commitment to the 1980 Set of Multilaterally Agreed Equitable Principles and Rules for the Control of Restrictive Business Practices (known as the Set).[48] Other secretariat notes dealt with activities relating to specific provisions of the Set, including technical assistance, advisory and training programmes,[49] and information and consultation on restrictive business practices.[50] The Group also had before it draft commentaries to possible elements for articles of a model law or laws on restrictive business practices,[51] a note on the compilation of a handbook on restrictive business practices legislation,[52] an UNCTAD study on the role of competition policy in economic reforms in developing and other countries,[53] and a revised report on concentration of market power, through mergers, take-overs, joint ventures and other acquisitions of control, and its effects on international markets, in particular the markets of developing countries.[54]

On 22 October,[46] the Group of Experts adopted a series of conclusions, in which it agreed that the UNCTAD secretariat should publish the study on concentration of market power[54] and revise the study on the role of competition policy in economic reforms;[53] finalize a check-list for requests for information and consultations; circulate an updated directory on competition authorities; and continue elaboration of the commentary to the model law or laws and compilation of the handbook on restrictive business practices legislation. It requested the UNCTAD secretariat to provide technical assistance, advisory and training services in the area of competition policy to developing countries and countries in transition; called on intergovernmental organizations, financing programmes and member States to provide the necessary resources and to inform the secretariat of programmes eligible for technical assistance; and called on intergovernmental organizations to cooperate in this area.

On 21 December, by **decision 48/442**, the General Assembly, taking note of the recommendation of the Second (1990) United Nations Conference to Review All Aspects of the Set of Multilaterally Agreed Equitable Principles and Rules for the Control of Restrictive Business Practices,[55] decided to convene a Third Conference, under the auspices of UNCTAD, at Geneva in 1995.

Commodities

The *World Economic Survey 1993*[2] stated that the prices of non-oil commodities, as measured by UNCTAD's combined index of nominal dollar prices, declined in 1992 for the third successive year, by 3.4 per cent. The decline was attributed to weak demand for raw materials in most industrialized economies; contraction of demand in the former USSR and Eastern Europe, combined with high levels of exports of minerals and metals from those areas; and a chronic excess supply of a wide range of agricultural commodities on world markets. However, despite the overall decline, there were indications of recovery in some prices due to the resumption of growth in the United States, increased imports by some developing countries, the continued strong demand of Asian exporters of manufactures and the emergence of China as a growing market for industrial raw materials.

Among the major commodity groups, prices of tropical beverages fell by 14 per cent and coffee prices plummeted to their lowest level in 22 years, 21 per cent lower than in 1991. Cocoa prices declined by around 8 per cent, while tea prices improved to their highest level in three years. Wheat prices showed some strength, but later weakened when the United States and other countries suspended exports to the Russian Federation when it defaulted on repayments of 1991 loans for grain imports. Prices of vegetable oils and oil-seeds increased by 7.5 per cent. Prices of agricultural raw materials as a whole declined by 3.1 per cent, and the UNCTAD index of minerals and base metals prices declined by 3 per cent.

The *Trade and Development Report, 1993*[1] stated that, in addition to the recession in the main consuming countries and changes in the formerly centrally planned economies, economic reforms introduced in developing countries had had mixed effects on commodity supply and export earnings. While many inefficiencies were corrected by those reforms, established export structures were destroyed and new difficulties emerged in commodity exports. Devaluations contributed to reducing real wages in many developing countries, resulting in lower prices for commodity exports. Several longer-term factors also contributed to the emergence of depressed commodity markets, including the increased importance in developed countries of relatively less commodity-intensive sectors, the substitution of traditional materials by synthetics and composites, and the saturation point reached in per capita consumption of many foods in developed countries.

Common Fund for Commodities

The Agreement Establishing the Common Fund for Commodities, a mechanism intended to stabilize the commodities market by helping to finance buffer stocks of specific commodities as well as commodity development activities such as research and marketing, entered into force in 1989, and the Fund became operational that year.

Signatures and ratifications

As at 31 December 1993,[56] the 1980 Agreement Establishing the Common Fund for Commodities had been signed by 118 States and the European Economic Community (EEC)/European Union, and, with the accession of Mozambique on 30 September 1993, 106 States and EEC had become parties to it.

Individual commodities

Agricultural commodities

Bananas. In order to complete a single market in respect of bananas, EEC proposed a common import regime to allow duty-free access for African, Caribbean and Pacific (ACP) suppliers and to impose a tariff quota and import duties on other suppliers. The new regime came into effect on 1 July 1993.

On 13 April,[57] Panama transmitted to the Secretary-General the 2 April Declaration on Bananas issued by the Ministers for Foreign Affairs of Colombia, Costa Rica, Ecuador, El Salvador, Guatemala, Honduras, Nicaragua and Panama, rejecting the new EEC regime as a violation of GATT principles. It also rejected an EEC proposal to establish a compensation fund in respect of certain Latin American banana-producing countries.

On 10 May,[58] Saint Lucia rejected the assertions made in both the Declaration on Bananas and the 11 February Declaration of Santiago de Guayaquil, which was presented to the Permanent

Council of the Organization of American States by the Presidents of the Central American banana-producing countries. It submitted the text of a statement on the subject that it had made to the Permanent Council, in which it stated that the small banana-producing countries of the Caribbean would suffer severe economic and social difficulties if the international commitments in favour of ACP countries under the Lomé Convention were not honoured.

Cocoa. The United Nations Cocoa Conference, 1992, held two sessions at Geneva in 1993 (22 February–5 March, 5-16 July) to negotiate a successor arrangement to the International Cocoa Agreement, 1986,[59] which had been extended in part for two years, effective 1 October 1990.

On 16 July,[60] the Conference established the text of the International Cocoa Agreement, 1993,[61] which was open for signature at United Nations Headquarters from 16 August to 30 September. The Agreement would come into force on 1 October 1993 if at least five exporting countries, accounting for at least 80 per cent of total exports, and Governments representing importing countries having at least 60 per cent of total imports deposited their instruments of ratification. If they could not complete their constitutional procedures before then, in accordance with article 55, the Agreement could be applied provisionally.

As at 31 December 1993,[56] 15 States had signed the Agreement, 4 States had formally ratified or accepted it, and 8 States had provided notification of provisional application.

Coffee. The International Coffee Agreement, 1983, the economic provisions of which were suspended in 1989, was extended in 1991 to 30 September 1993.[62] At a 29 April meeting, the Executive Board of the International Coffee Organization recommended a one-year extension until 30 September 1994. On 4 June 1993, the International Coffee Council agreed to the extension to allow for negotiation of a new Agreement.

Olive oil. The United Nations Conference on Olive Oil and Table Olives, 1993, was held at Geneva from 8 to 10 March. It established the text of the 1993 Protocol[63] extending the International Agreement on Olive Oil and Table Olives, 1986,[64] with amendments. The Protocol, which was open for signature at United Nations Headquarters from 1 May to 31 December 1993, was to enter into force on 1 January 1994 if instruments of ratification were deposited by Governments holding at least 85 per cent of the participation shares.

As at 31 December 1993,[56] eight States and EEC had signed the Protocol and two States and EEC had formally ratified or approved it.

Sugar. On 20 January 1993,[65] those States which had deposited instruments of ratification to the International Sugar Agreement, 1992,[66] or had notified that they would apply it provisionally, met to decide whether to put the Agreement into force provisionally or definitively among themselves. Since the target of 60 per cent of the votes required for the Agreement's entry into force had been exceeded, the 20 States represented and EEC decided to put the Agreement into force provisionally as of that date.

As at 31 December,[56] the International Sugar Agreement, 1992, had been signed by 26 States and EEC, 21 States and EEC had formally become parties to it, and 14 States had provided notification of provisional application.

Tropical timber. The International Tropical Timber Agreement, 1983,[67] was due to expire on 31 March 1994. In accordance with a 1991 request of the International Tropical Timber Council, the UNCTAD Secretary-General convened the United Nations Conference for the Negotiation of a Successor Agreement to the International Tropical Timber Agreement, 1983 (Geneva, 13-16 April, 21-25 June and 4-15 October 1993). The Conference considered the composite text of a draft successor agreement,[68] prepared by the UNCTAD secretariat in cooperation with the Executive Director of the International Tropical Timber Organization, based on proposals submitted by producer and consumer groups.[69] It also had before it an UNCTAD secretariat note on the background, status and operation of the Agreement, 1983, and recent developments of relevance to the negotiation of a successor agreement.[70] By a 15 October resolution,[71] the Conference, noting the status of the negotiations, requested the International Tropical Timber Council to facilitate consultations on the main issues before the Conference. It invited its President to recommend that the UNCTAD Secretary-General reconvene the Conference in January 1994.

Minerals and metals

Bauxite. The Second Ad Hoc Review Meeting on Bauxite of the Standing Committee on Commodities (Geneva, 29 and 30 April 1993)[72] reviewed the current market situation and outlook for bauxite, alumina and aluminium. The Chairman, in his summary of the discussions, stated that there were significant gaps in available information on several important items, including data on trade, aluminium stocks and secondary aluminium, and that improvements in statistics on production, consumption and trade of bauxite, alumina and aluminium in the republics of the former USSR would contribute significantly to a better understanding of the dynamics of the markets for those commodities. The meeting was informed of the publication by the International Primary Aluminium Institute of the *Bauxite Mine*

Rehabilitation Survey, detailing information on the environmental impact and rehabilitation of bauxite mines.

Iron ore. The second session of the Intergovernmental Group of Experts on Iron Ore of the Standing Committee on Commodities was held at Geneva from 25 to 27 October 1993.[73] The Group reviewed iron ore statistics, the current situation and outlook for iron ore and a bibliography of relevant studies on iron ore. It also considered its possible application to the Common Fund for Commodities and decided to reconsider the question in 1994.

Tungsten. The Intergovernmental Group of Experts on Tungsten held its second session at Geneva from 8 to 10 November 1993.[74] It had before it an UNCTAD secretariat review of the current tungsten market situation and medium- and long-term outlook.[75] The Group examined statistics and reviewed the current market situation and outlook; and considered industry views on particular aspects of the industry and ways to improve the functioning and stability of the tungsten market through strengthened international cooperation between Governments and industries of producing and consuming countries. In addition, it discussed project proposals by Governments and industry for possible financing under the Second Account of the Common Fund for Commodities. The Group agreed that projects should meet Common Fund criteria and should be sent to the UNCTAD secretariat for examination by other members.

Services

The Standing Committee on Developing Services Sectors: Fostering Competitive Services Sectors in Developing Countries, established by TDB in 1992,[76] held its first session on insurance at Geneva from 1 to 5 February 1993.[77] The Committee had before it reports on issues for consideration in the establishment of the work programme on insurance[78] and on agricultural insurance in developing countries;[79] a review of developments in insurance markets;[80] and a report on privatization of insurance enterprises and liberalization of insurance markets in developing countries.[81] Also before it was the report of the Group of Experts on Agricultural Insurance in Developing Countries (Geneva, 28 and 29 January).[82]

The Standing Committee adopted its work programme in the field of insurance, under which it intended to promote transparency, foster competitive insurance services and strengthen technical cooperation and human resources development.

In carrying out its work, the Committee would give due regard to the work of the former Committee on Invisibles and Financing related to Trade and of the UNCTAD secretariat.

REFERENCES

[1]*Trade and Development Report, 1993* (UNCTAD/TDR/13), Sales No. E.93.II.D.10. [2]*World Economic Survey 1993: Current Trends and Policies in the World Economy* (E/1993/60), Sales No. E.93.II.C.1. [3]A/48/15 (conclusions 405(XL)). [4]TD/B/39(2)/3. [5]A/48/15 (conclusions 401(XXXIX)). [6]YUN 1992, p. 617, GA res. 47/184, 22 Dec. 1992. [7]A/48/363. [8]YUN 1986, p. 1210. [9]A/48/353-S/26372. [10]A/48/15. [11]TD/B/EX(3)/3. [12]YUN 1992, p. 676, GA res. 47/191, 22 Dec. 1992. [13]A/48/15 (dec. 402(XXXIX)). [14]YUN 1992, p. 672. [15]TD/B/40(1)/6 & Corr.1. [16]A/48/15 (conclusions 407(XL)). [17]YUN 1991, p. 440, GA res. 46/207, 20 Dec. 1991. [18]YUN 1992, p. 613. [19]TD/B/39(2)/20. [20]TD/B/48/400. [21]TD/B/EX(4)/3. [22]TD/B/40(1)/Misc.1. [23]TD/B/EX(4)/2. [24]TD/B/40(1)/Misc.1/Rev.1. [25]TD/B/40(1)/10. [26]TD/B/SCP/3 & Add.1 & Add.1/Corr.1. [27]TD/B/SCP/7. [28]ITC/AG(XXVI)/136. [29]YUN 1992, p. 619. [30]ITC/AG(XXVI)/139. [31]ITC/AG(XXVI)/137 & Add.1. [32]YUN 1992, p. 620. [33]ITC/AG(XXV)/129. [34]ITC/INF/66. [35]YUN 1992, p. 621. [36]TD/B/40(2)/3. [37]TD/B/WG.2/6. [38]TD/B/WG.2/6/Add.1, Parts I & II. [39]TD/B/WG.2/7 & Add.1. [40]TD/B/WG.2/8. [41]YUN 1992, p. 613, GA res. 47/183, 22 Dec. 1992. [42]Ibid., p. 622. [43]TD/B/40(2)/4. [44]TD/B/WG.4/6. [45]TD/B/WG.4/7. [46]TD/B/40(2)/2. [47]TD/B/RBP/95 & Add.1. [48]YUN 1980, p. 626. [49]TD/B/RBP/97 & Add.1. [50]TD/B/RBP/78/Rev.2 & Corr.1. [51]TD/B/RBP/81/Rev.2. [52]TD/B/RBP/94. [53]TD/B/RBP/96. [54]TD/B/RBP/80/Rev.2. [55]TD/RBP/CONF.3/9. [56]*Multilateral Treaties Deposited with the Secretary-General: Status as at 31 December 1993* (ST/LEG/SER.E/12), Sales No. E.94.V.11. [57]A/48/139. [58]A/48/164. [59]YUN 1986, p. 502. [60]TD/COCOA.8/16. [61]TD/COCOA.8/17. [62]YUN 1991, p. 446. [63]TD/OLIVE OIL.9/6. [64]YUN 1986, p. 503. [65]TD/SUGAR.12/8. [66]YUN 1992, p. 625. [67]YUN 1983, p. 556. [68]TD/TIMBER.2/R.3. [69]TD/TIMBER.2/R.1. [70]TD/TIMBER.2/3. [71]TD/TIMBER.2/12. [72]TD/B/CN.1/RM/BAUXITE/4. [73]TD/B/CN.1/17. [74]TD/B/CN.1/18. [75]TD/B/CN.1/TUNGSTEN/7. [76]YUN 1992, p. 630. [77]TD/B/39(2)/19. [78]TD/B/CN.4/15. [79]UNCTAD/SDD/INS/1 & Summary. [80]UNCTAD/SDD/INS/2. [81]UNCTAD/SDD/INS/3. [82]UNCTAD/SDD/INS/4.

Finance

Financial policy

The *World Economic Survey 1993*[1] stated that, in 1992, the major industrialized countries began to look at fiscal and monetary means to stimulate their economies. Inflation fell to relatively low rates in several countries and monetary restraints were eased. There was also room for a non-inflationary fiscal stimulus in some countries. Fiscal actions were taken or announced in 1992 in Japan, the United Kingdom and the United States and at the European Community Summit, but each stimulus was a modest one. However, following the meeting of finance ministers of the seven major economies in February 1993, discussions began on arranging credible steps in a new spirit of cooperation to strengthen economic growth.

In giving a preliminary assessment of the world economic situation at the end of 1993,[2] the Secretary-General noted that the steady fall in inflation in most developed economies offered an important opportunity for putting into effect some macroeconomic policies to stimulate demand. While the scope for fiscal stimulus appeared limited, there was significant room for monetary easing, especially in Europe where real interest rates were still high in most countries.

Although the short-term growth outlook of the developing countries was encouraging, two sources of concern remained: Latin America's recovery of growth could prove fragile, as inflation and large budget deficits remained a major concern in some countries; and Africa's need for aid was increasing in order to facilitate the reform process and support investment in human and physical infrastructure, even as aid fatigue seemed to be setting in.

The task of reform in the transition economies, particularly the faster-changing ones, had had a much more inflationary aspect than had been foreseen. External assistance could ease some economic constraints to reform and make the political tasks of reform less onerous.

Net transfer of resources

The turn-around in the transfer of resources between developed and developing countries which began in 1991 continued into 1992. The *World Economic Survey 1993*[1] reported on the subject, as requested by the General Assembly in 1992,[3] noting that developed market economies transferred over $50 billion to other countries in 1992, $17 billion more than in 1991, while the developing countries received a similar amount in transfers, marking the second year of very large aggregate net inflows. It was estimated that the transition economies transferred about $1 billion in hard currency to other countries.

In 1992, for the first time in a decade, the deficit energy-exporter countries again became net recipients of external resource transfers. African oil exporters, however, were still making net transfers abroad and Egypt had begun to do so to reduce its trade deficit as part of its adjustment programme. Africa was the only region of the developing world that had a negative transfer in 1992, although the smaller countries of the sub-Saharan region continued to register a modest overall positive transfer of about $10 billion. Latin America and the Caribbean registered a net inflow of $7 billion, compared with negative transfers of between $20 billion and $30 billion in the late 1980s. Although the region of China, South and East Asia and the Pacific made substantial net transfers abroad during the late 1980s, most transfers were to build up official reserves, repay external debts and invest in other countries. However, as a whole, the region was a net recipient of financial resources in 1992.

Developing countries as a whole were expected to continue to absorb net resource transfers in the next few years, as some countries had regained access to private credit markets, interest rates were not expected to rise strongly and there was no shortage of private finance at the global level, or of official credit on commercial terms. That did not mean, however, that the overall resource constraint on the economic growth of the developing countries had been removed.

Development financing

The *World Economic Survey 1993*[1] stated that the trend in the flow of official development finance, which had been rising steadily in dollar terms in recent years, was expected to continue in 1992, after reaching almost $56 billion in 1991. However, in real terms it had fluctuated, rising by 2.5 per cent in 1991 after falling to the 1988 level in 1990. The pattern of flows from donor countries seemed to be changing, with growth hinging almost completely on aid from industrialized countries, as flows from Arab donor countries and the former centrally planned economies declined. Although developed countries had reaffirmed their commitment to reach the United Nations target of 0.7 per cent of gross national product (GNP) for official development assistance (ODA), there was little change in the ODA/GNP ratio. In many developed countries, there had been a major rethinking of aid, while in others budget exigencies had caused aid cut-backs. However, Japan had made a major commitment to expand its aid programme and was likely to be the premier donor of the 1990s. Nevertheless, the *Survey* stated, the political and economic role of ODA needed to be rethought and the image and effectiveness of aid policies reexamined if a voter constituency for international assistance was to be rebuilt in donor countries.

Report of the Secretary-General. In the context of the General Assembly's 1991 decision[4] to consider convening an international conference on the financing of development and its 1992 decision[5] to continue exploring the issue, the Secretary-General, in response to a request in the latter decision, submitted a September 1993 report on sources of financing for development.[6] The report described the situation in development finance, covering both domestic and international resources. It also put forward a number of current domestic and international policy issues.

GENERAL ASSEMBLY ACTION

On 21 December, the General Assembly, on the recommendation of the Second Committee, adopted **resolution 48/187** without vote.

International conference on the financing of development

The General Assembly,

Reaffirming the importance and continued validity of the Declaration on International Economic Cooperation, in particular the Revitalization of Economic

Growth and Development of the Developing Countries, the International Development Strategy for the Fourth United Nations Development Decade, the Cartagena Commitment, the United Nations New Agenda for the Development of Africa in the 1990s, the Programme of Action for the Least Developed Countries for the 1990s, and the various consensus agreements and conventions, especially Agenda 21, adopted during the United Nations Conference on Environment and Development,

Recalling its resolution 46/205 of 20 December 1991 on the convening of an international conference on the financing of development, and its decision 47/436 of 18 December 1992,

Noting with interest the analysis of the current international financial situation outlined in the report of the Secretary-General, and recalling the link between peace, security, growth and development,

Recalling also its resolution 47/181 of 22 December 1992 on an agenda for development,

1. *Decides* to continue to explore the issue of the financing of development and its potential funding sources, in close consultation and cooperation with the World Bank, the International Monetary Fund and the United Nations Conference on Trade and Development;

2. *Requests* the Secretary-General to submit to the General Assembly at its fiftieth session a report on the situation of all potential sources of financing for development, including sources of new and additional financing for development, in order to consider the issue of the convening of an international conference on the financing of development;

3. *Also decides* to include in the provisional agenda of its fiftieth session, under the item "International cooperation for economic growth and development", the issue of the financing of development.

General Assembly resolution 48/187

21 December 1993   Meeting 86   Adopted without vote

Approved by Second Committee (A/48/723) without vote, 9 December (meeting 46); draft by China, Colombia (for Group of 77) and the former Yugoslav Republic of Macedonia (A/C.2/48/L.4), orally revised following informal consultations; agenda item 97.

Meeting numbers. GA 48th session: 2nd Committee 8, 9, 15, 46; plenary 86.

Debt problems of developing countries

The *World Economic Survey 1993*[1] stated that, at the aggregate level, the debt crisis appeared past. However, for the crisis to be over, developing countries needed to be perceived as creditworthy and to maintain a sustainable relationship between debt levels and other variables. The relationship between debt servicing and export earnings, in particular, had to appear to be stable over the long run, meaning that the ratio of debt to exports and debt to GNP did not grow on average over long periods of time. If trends in debt ratios were useful indicators of the long-run sustainability of debt, the debt-servicing ratio indicated the current burden of the debt. Overall, the ratio of debt service to exports of goods and services in 1992 was virtually unchanged from 1991. There was a rise in principal repayments, which was offset by a decline in the interest-servicing ratio associated with the decline in average interest rates. Evidence of

the debt crisis being over could also be gathered from the secondary market for commercial bank debt. However, the picture was mixed, with demand having strengthened in the secondary market for some countries' debt, while cautious with others and quite pessimistic with yet others. The conclusion was that, while for some countries the debt crisis had at last been overcome, for others it remained a pressing concern.

The *Trade and Development Report, 1993*[7] stated that the character of the debt crisis in the early 1990s was substantially different from that of the early 1980s. For a number of major middle-income debtors it had become much less acute, though at a high price in terms of development progress and falling per capita income. At the global level, the major problem was debt owed to official creditors and, to an increasing extent, to international financial institutions. The growing share of multilateral debt had also made the debt structure less flexible. Although the current crisis mainly affected low-income countries, mostly in Africa, several lower-middle-income countries had yet to graduate from the debt rescheduling process. In addition, while the major Latin American debtors were leaving the rescheduling scene, the Russian Federation had entered it. Despite recent improvements, the terms of reschedulings of the Paris Club (a group of creditors) were not yet well adapted to debtors' capacity to pay and were likely to lead to further pressures on external payments. Improvements were required in the scale of debt reduction, eligibility criteria and the time-frame for implementation. There had been calls for closer coordination between the Paris Club and donor groups (such as the consultative groups and consortia chaired by the World Bank and round tables chaired by UNDP) or for shifting the official bilateral debt rescheduling for low-income countries to such forums. A single meeting on debt and finance would reduce the high transaction cost for separate uncoordinated meetings of the Paris Club and make it possible to detect and act on a country's debt-servicing difficulties early, before arrears started to accumulate.

Report of the Secretary-General. In response to a 1992 General Assembly request,[8] the Secretary-General submitted in September 1993 a report on the international debt strategy as at mid-1993.[9] It discussed the current debt situation of developing countries and current issues in international debt policy, including the overall policy environment, the Paris Club and difficulties in servicing multilateral debt.

The report concluded that solving the debt problem of the developing countries would not *ipso facto* solve external financial constraints, much less their development problems. Restructuring debt so as to remove the debt overhang needed to be part of a package of measures leading to a sustainable external payments situation with adequate economic growth. Even the countries that were furthest along in working their way out of their debt crisis had not yet fully reached that goal. In many cases, their recovery remained fragile and would have to be watched closely. Many other countries remained even further behind and were not yet out of the debt crisis. Continued intensified international cooperation was thus warranted to assist countries still mired in the debt crisis and to help others restore adequate economic growth.

Tokyo Summit. The seven major industrial nations, at their Economic Summit (Tokyo, 7-9 July),[10] confirmed the validity of the international debt strategy and invited the Paris Club to continue reviewing the question of debt relief for the poorest highly indebted countries, especially with regard to earlier reductions in the stock of debt, on a case-by-case basis. They welcomed the United States decision to join them in debt reduction for those countries.

UNCTAD action. On 1 October,[11] TDB welcomed the recent improvements in the international debt strategy and noted that there was a need for continuing efforts by debtors and the international community to resolve the remaining problems, paying special attention to LDCs. It also noted the role that increased external financial flows, particularly non-debt-creating flows, could play in helping to prevent and overcome debt difficulties. TDB observed that Paris Club practices had improved, particularly with the adoption of enhanced concessional terms for the poorest, most indebted countries. It emphasized the crucial role of the international financial institutions in supporting developing countries and endorsed the principle that the preferred creditor status of those institutions should not be impaired.

Calls were made by a number of TDB members for a review of the eligibility criteria for debt reduction so as to include all heavily indebted low-income countries. Attention was also drawn to the urgent needs of the lower-middle-income countries for debt reduction. As to multilateral debt, it was stressed that a substantial increase in net transfers from international financial institutions was particularly important for heavily indebted countries and would help them to avoid the emergence of arrears. Some members called for an adequate replenishment of the soft windows of those institutions, and others pointed to the need for an agreement on a new IMF enhanced structural adjustment facility to be reached before the end of 1993, with the concessional element being no less than in the previous scheme. As regards commercial bank debt, Governments of creditor countries were urged to ensure that the Brady deals being negotiated, that is, arrangements for restructur-

ing such debt, brought about a significant reduction in the total external debt of the countries concerned.

GENERAL ASSEMBLY ACTION

On 21 December, the General Assembly, on the recommendation of the Second Committee, adopted **resolution 48/182** by recorded vote.

Enhanced international cooperation towards a durable solution to the external debt problems of developing countries

The General Assembly,

Reaffirming its resolutions 41/202 of 8 December 1986, 42/198 of 11 December 1987, 43/198 of 20 December 1988, 44/205 of 22 December 1989, S-18/3 of 1 May 1990, 45/199 of 21 December 1990, 45/214 of 21 December 1990, 46/148 and 46/151 of 18 December 1991 and 47/198 of 22 December 1992,

Noting that, owing to uneven developments in the context of the evolving international debt strategy, further progress and further concrete measures are essential for the solution of the external debt problems of a large number of developing countries,

Welcoming the fact that some developing countries have made substantial progress towards resolving their debt difficulties,

Noting with concern the continuing debt and debt-service problems of indebted developing countries, which adversely affect their development efforts and economic growth, and reiterating the need to address and solve those problems through effective debt-relief measures, bearing in mind, in this context, the special and critical situation of the most indebted developing countries of Africa,

Noting also that a number of countries with economies in transition are experiencing debt-servicing difficulties, while recognizing that the Paris Club has adopted a flexible and innovative approach to deal with these problems, and calling upon private creditors to adopt similar measures,

Stressing the importance of alleviating the onerous debt and debt-service burdens connected with all types of debt of developing countries, taking into account the urgent need for an equitable and durable approach,

Emphasizing the importance for debtor developing countries of continuing to pursue and intensify their efforts in their economic reform, stabilization and structural adjustment programmes, in order to raise savings and investment, reduce inflation and improve economic efficiency, taking into account their individual characteristics and the vulnerability of the poorer strata of their populations,

Stressing also the necessity of a supportive international economic environment as regards, *inter alia*, terms of trade, commodity prices, improved market access, trade practices, exchange rates and international interest rates, and noting the continued need for resources for the implementation of international consensus agreements for the promotion of sustainable development,

Expressing its concern that, in many developing countries, the burden of debt and debt service constitutes one of the major obstacles to the revitalization of growth and development, despite the often strenuous economic reforms of those countries,

Noting that those developing countries which have continued, at great cost, to meet their international debt and debt-service obligations in a timely fashion have done so despite severe external and domestic financial constraints,

1. *Takes note* of the report of the Secretary-General on the external debt crisis and development;

2. *Notes* the fact that some debtor developing countries with commercial external debt have been able to conclude agreements on commercial bank debt-service reduction, and calls for the conclusion of similar agreements with other interested developing countries;

3. *Calls upon* the international community to explore ways to implement additional measures, including further cancellation or reduction of debt and debt service related to official debt, and to take more urgent action with regard to, *inter alia*, the remaining commercial debt owed by the developing countries;

4. *Welcomes* the write-off by certain donors of a significant part of the bilateral official debt of the least developed countries, and urges those countries which have not done so to cancel or provide equivalent relief for the official development assistance debt of the least developed countries;

5. *Calls* for the rapid and effective implementation of the measures taken to address the debt problem of certain middle-income African countries, and invites all creditors to consider taking appropriate measures for middle-income debtor developing countries, taking into account the special and critical situation of those in Africa;

6. *Calls upon* the donor countries and multilateral financial institutions, within their prerogatives, to consider appropriate new measures for substantial relief of the debt of low-income countries;

7. *Stresses* the need for the broadest and most expeditious implementation of the recent initiatives and the need to continue to build upon them, and calls upon the developed countries to adopt and implement further debt-alleviating terms, including consideration of the Trinidad terms, as appropriate;

8. *Recognizes* the urgent need to continue to provide a social safety net to vulnerable groups most adversely affected by the implementation of economic reform programmes in the debtor countries, particularly low-income groups, in order to ensure social and political stability;

9. *Emphasizes* the importance for developing countries of continuing their efforts to promote a favourable environment for attracting foreign investment, thereby promoting growth and sustainable development;

10. *Stresses also* that concerted action by the international community, in particular by developed countries, to alleviate the debt burden of developing countries is vital to growth in the developing countries, which, in turn, would promote the growth of the world economy;

11. *Recognizes also* the need of debtor developing countries for a supportive international economic environment as regards, *inter alia*, terms of trade, commodity prices, improved market access and trade practices, and stresses the urgent need for a balanced and successful outcome of the Uruguay Round of multilateral trade negotiations, which would result in the liberalization and expansion of world trade to the benefit of all countries, in particular the developing countries;

12. *Stresses further* the need, in addition to debt-relief measures that include debt and debt-service reduction, for new financial flows to debtor developing countries, and urges the creditor countries and the multilateral financial institutions to continue to extend concessional financial assistance, as appropriate, in order to support the implementation by the developing countries of their economic reforms, stabilization and structural adjustment programmes, so as to enable them to extricate themselves from the debt overhang and to assist them in achieving economic growth and development;

13. *Urges* the international community to consider wider application of innovative measures, such as debt-for-equity, debt-for-nature and debt-for-development swaps, without prejudice to more durable solutions such as debt reduction and/or cancellation;

14. *Calls upon* private creditors and, in particular, commercial banks to renew and expand initiatives and efforts to tackle the commercial debt problems of the least developed countries and of low- and middle-income developing countries;

15. *Urges* the multilateral financial institutions to continue to provide support for debt and debt-service reduction packages with the necessary flexibility under their established guidelines, and also urges that earnest attention be given to continuing to work towards a growth-oriented solution to the problems of developing countries that are having serious debt-servicing difficulties, including those countries whose debt is mainly to official creditors or to multilateral financial institutions;

16. *Urges* creditor countries, private banks and, within their prerogatives, multilateral financial institutions to consider the extension of appropriate new financial support to developing countries, in particular the low-income countries with substantial debt burdens that continue, at great cost, to service the debt and meet their international obligations;

17. *Requests* the Secretary-General to report to the General Assembly at its forty-ninth session on the implementation of the present resolution.

General Assembly resolution 48/182

21 December 1993   Meeting 86   164-1 (recorded vote)

Approved by Second Committee (A/48/718) by recorded vote (152-1), 13 December (meeting 48); draft by China and Colombia (for Group of 77) (A/C.2/48/L.5/Rev.1), orally revised; agenda item 92.

Meeting numbers. GA 48th session: 2nd Committee 10, 11, 18, 48; plenary 86.

Recorded vote in Assembly as follows:

In favour: Afghanistan, Albania, Algeria, Angola, Antigua and Barbuda, Argentina, Armenia, Australia, Austria, Azerbaijan, Bahamas, Bahrain, Bangladesh, Barbados, Belarus, Belgium, Belize, Benin, Bhutan, Bolivia, Botswana, Brazil, Brunei Darussalam, Bulgaria, Burkina Faso, Burundi, Cambodia, Cameroon, Canada, Cape Verde, Central African Republic, Chad, Chile, China, Colombia, Comoros, Congo, Costa Rica, Côte d'Ivoire, Croatia, Cuba, Cyprus, Czech Republic, Democratic People's Republic of Korea, Denmark, Djibouti, Dominica, Dominican Republic, Ecuador, Egypt, El Salvador, Eritrea, Estonia, Ethiopia, Fiji, Finland, France, Gabon, Gambia, Germany, Greece, Grenada, Guatemala, Guinea-Bissau, Guyana, Haiti, Honduras, Hungary, Iceland, India, Indonesia, Iran, Iraq, Israel, Italy, Jamaica, Japan, Jordan, Kazakhstan, Kenya, Kuwait, Kyrgyzstan, Lao People's Democratic Republic, Latvia, Lebanon, Lesotho, Libyan Arab Jamahiriya, Liechtenstein, Lithuania, Luxembourg, Madagascar, Malawi, Malaysia, Maldives, Mali, Malta, Marshall Islands, Mauritania, Mauritius, Mexico, Micronesia, Monaco, Mongolia, Morocco, Mozambique, Myanmar, Namibia, Nepal, Netherlands, New Zealand, Nicaragua, Niger, Nigeria, Norway, Oman, Pakistan, Panama, Papua New Guinea, Paraguay, Peru, Philippines, Poland, Portugal, Qatar, Republic of Korea, Republic of Moldova, Romania, Russian Federation, Rwanda, Saint Lucia, Saint Vincent and the Grenadines, Samoa, Saudi Arabia, Senegal, Sierra Leone, Singapore, Slovakia, Slovenia, Spain, Sri Lanka, Sudan, Suriname, Swaziland, Sweden,

Syrian Arab Republic, Tajikistan, Thailand, the former Yugoslav Republic of Macedonia, Togo, Trinidad and Tobago, Tunisia, Turkey, Turkmenistan, Uganda, Ukraine, United Arab Emirates, United Kingdom, United Republic of Tanzania, Uruguay, Venezuela, Viet Nam, Yemen, Zambia, Zimbabwe.
Against: United States.

Investment and financial flows

The Ad Hoc Working Group on Investment and Financial Flows; Non-debt-creating Finance for Development; New Mechanisms for increasing Investment and Financial Flows, established by TDB in 1992,[12] held its second session at Geneva from 28 June to 2 July 1993.[13] The Working Group considered global trends and issues, including foreign investors' motivations, and host and home country policies and measures to promote foreign direct investment (FDI), including export processing zones (EPZs) and special economic zones. It had before it UNCTAD secretariat reports on recent trends and policy issues in FDI in developing countries,[14] the role of FDI in EPZs and the developmental impact of EPZs,[15] and a study on selected country experiences of EPZs.[16] A number of countries presented case-studies on the subject of EPZs.

The Working Group concluded that the upward trend of FDI flows to developing countries and economies in transition was expected to continue in the 1990s. However, constraints could emerge if economic uncertainty and high unemployment in developed countries continued. The Group noted that economic liberalization policies had helped to increase FDI flows for some countries, while for others, especially LDCs, flows had fallen short of expectations. It considered that regional trading groupings would have an important impact on the FDI pattern. Concern was expressed by some countries about the low level of large-scale FDI and FDI in high-technology sectors flowing to them.

On the question of EPZs, the Working Group considered that, although they had largely met their objectives by attracting FDI, backward and forward linkages with the domestic economy had not in general developed to a significant degree. Despite the growing trend towards trade liberalization, there was still a role for EPZs as windows for attracting FDI and for introducing market reforms. They also had an important demonstration effect and could be used to promote new activities.

REFERENCES

[1]*World Economic Survey 1993: Current Trends and Policies in the World Economy* (E/1993/60), Sales No. E.93.II.C.1. [2]E/1994/INF/1. [3]YUN 1992, p. 632, GA res. 47/178, 22 Dec. 1992. [4]YUN 1991, p. 450, GA res. 46/205, 20 Dec. 1991. [5]YUN 1992, p. 635, GA dec. 47/436, 18 Dec. 1992. [6]A/48/367. [7]*Trade and Development Report, 1993* (UNCTAD/TDR/13), Sales No. E.93.II.D.10. [8]YUN 1992, p. 637, GA res. 47/198, 22 Dec. 1992. [9]A/48/345. [10]A/48/353-S/26372. [11]A/48/15 (conclusions 406(XL)). [12]YUN 1992, p. 638. [13]TD/B/40(1)/12. [14]TD/B/WG.1/7. [15]TD/B/WG.1/6. [16]UNCTAD/GID/DF/2.

Transport

Maritime transport

Shipping

In response to a 1992 request of the Standing Committee on Developing Services Sectors (Shipping),[1] the UNCTAD secretariat submitted a note on the specific outputs and activities of its work programme on shipping[2] to TDB's March 1993 executive session. The note provided lists of meetings on shipping projected for the period 1993-1995, of reports, studies and background documents to be prepared for those meetings, and of recurrent publications and technical material. Operational activities, including advisory services, group training and field projects, would be provided at the request of Governments. The activities listed were also reflected in UNCTAD's proposals for the 1994-1995 United Nations programme budget.

The main developments of 1992 in international shipping and related fields were analysed in UNCTAD's *Review of Maritime Transport 1992*.[3]

Multimodal transport

A global meeting, under the aegis of TRAIN-MAR (Valencia, Spain, November), was held to improve consensus building and to share experiences from various regions of the world in the field of multimodal transport. It brought together regional multimodal-transport lecturing teams in the commercial transport industry in an effort to reach consensus on a future action programme for human resources development in multimodal transport. An association (the Club of Valencia) was established to act as a catalyst for the exchange of ideas on modern trade and transport technologies and serve as a pool of experts on multimodal transport issues. The secretariat continued to collect and disseminate information on technologies and structural changes in multimodal transport and on measures affecting access to markets for such transport.

Ports

Following approval of its terms of reference by TDB on 26 March,[4] the Intergovernmental Group of Experts on Ports held its first meeting at Geneva from 25 to 29 October.[5] It had before it UNCTAD secretariat reports on port organization and management,[6] port marketing and the challenge of the third generation port,[7] strategic planning for port authorities,[8] the management and development of human resources in ports,[9] legal aspects of port management,[10] the principles of modern port management and organization,[11] and sustainable development for ports.[12]

The Group of Experts recommended that Governments reflect on the importance of ports and their potential for fostering trade and development; that they adopt long-term and business planning methodologies in adopting their port policies; that port matters be included more often as specific items on the agendas of national, regional, intergovernmental and international meetings concerning trade, development and environmental issues; and that further study and analysis be conducted on the strengths/weaknesses of the concepts of privatization/commercialization of port organization and management structures. It also recommended that UNCTAD identify and document cooperative efforts among ports. The Group supported the conclusions and recommendations of a 1991 informal meeting of legal experts on port matters,[9] and made a number of recommendations on ports in relation to the environment and development.

With regard to specific aspects of port organization and management, the Group recommended that port policy should reflect the importance of ports as a link in the transport chain (railways, roads, waterways), with other integrated functionaries (customs, police, local authorities) comprising the others. Port policy should be implemented by optimum labour use, more efficient cargo handling, intensive use of electronic data interchange, streamlined procedures and efficient use of equipment. The current port system should be modernized and supported by an appropriate legal framework that would take account of the division of responsibilities between central, regional and local levels, and the roles of private entities and port labour. Port management should be market-oriented and port policy defined, with clear objectives and development strategies. The Group recommended further studies on: survey of national port systems; analysis of the relationship between the city and the port; and human resource development in ports. It also recommended that the necessary resources be assured for training, that UNCTAD training programmes be maintained and reinforced, and that the TRAINMAR network be extended and strengthened.

The Group further recommended that donor countries and ports in a position to do so contribute to the full rehabilitation of the Somalia port system, and that UNCTAD act as an information exchange point for ports seeking information on technical cooperation cases like those of Liberia and Somalia. It also recommended that a list of ports, private companies and individuals offering port management expertise be drawn up for the reference of Governments and ports.

Technical assistance and training

UNCTAD's technical and training activities in shipping, ports, multimodal transport and maritime legislation recovered in 1993 from a decline the previous year. A total of 34 projects were carried out, with expenditures of $3 million, compared to 32 projects totalling $2 million in 1992. Activities included the management of the ports of Kismayu and Mogadishu, in Somalia, and the surveying and drawing up of a rehabilitation programme for those ports and the ports of Berbera and Bosasso. UNCTAD continued to develop and implement the Advance Cargo Information System (ACIS)—a collection of computer applications designed to produce management information. By the end of 1993, the ACIS tracking module for railway cargo was operational in 13 African countries and the port module was operational in Dar es Salaam, United Republic of Tanzania, and Mombasa, Kenya.

The TRAINMAR programme, which supported institutions providing training for officials and managers in the maritime sector, continued to expand. By the end of 1993, 51 bodies in 46 countries were involved, and projects totalling over $1 million were executed. New projects related to strengthening training institutions in the southern cone of South America and developing a new course on short sea multimodal transport. Assistance was provided in modernizing maritime legislation at national and regional levels.

UNCTAD delivered 30 policy seminars in shipping, ports and multimodal transport during 1993, including new ones on the commercial role of ports and strategic port pricing.

Maritime liens and mortgages

In accordance with a 1991 General Assembly resolution,[13] the Secretaries-General of UNCTAD and the International Maritime Organization (IMO) convened the Conference of Plenipotentiaries on a Convention on Maritime Liens and Mortgages at Geneva from 19 April to 6 May 1993.[14] The Conference had before it draft articles for the convention;[15] the report of the Joint UNCTAD/IMO Intergovernmental Group of Experts on Maritime Liens and Mortgages and Related Subjects on its sixth session, held in 1989;[16] that Group's final report, adopted in 1989;[17] and a compilation of comments and proposals by Governments and intergovernmental and non-governmental organizations on the draft convention.[18]

On 6 May, the Conference adopted its Final Act and the text of the International Convention on Maritime Liens and Mortgages, 1993.[19] The Convention was to be open for signature at United Nations Headquarters from 1 September 1993 until 31 August 1994. Also on 6 May, the Conference adopted a resolution recommending that UNCTAD and IMO, in the light of the Conference's outcome, reconvene the Joint Intergovernmental Group of Experts to review the International Convention for the Unification of Certain Rules relating to the Arrest of Sea-going Ships, 1952.

As at 31 December 1993,[20] the Convention had been signed by Guinea and Tunisia.

Transport of dangerous goods

The Secretary-General submitted to the Economic and Social Council in May 1993 a report on the work of the Committee of Experts on the Transport of Dangerous Goods during 1991-1992.[21] The Committee paid special attention to coordinating its activities with those of other international organizations connected with the transport of dangerous goods and established liaison with the secretariats of the International Labour Organisation, the World Health Organization and the United Nations Environment Programme to avoid duplicating work connected with existing agreements and instruments on the safe transport of dangerous goods. The Committee expressed concern over the possible duplication of work in harmonizing systems of classification and labelling of chemicals due to the possible creation of new United Nations bodies in the context of the implementation of chapter 19 (environmentally sound management of toxic chemicals, including prevention of illegal international traffic in toxic and dangerous products) of Agenda 21, adopted by the United Nations Conference on Environment and Development in 1992.[22] It requested the Economic and Social Council to call on Governments and international organizations involved in implementing that chapter to avoid such duplication and to ensure that the new system drew on, or was compatible with, that developed by the Committee.

The Committee requested the Secretariat to publish the new and amended recommendations on the transport of dangerous goods (eighth revised edition) before the end of 1993. It stressed the role of the Secretariat in implementing the recommendations and requested that adequate funding be provided to support its work. The Committee agreed on the work programme of its Subcommittee of Experts on the Transport of Dangerous Goods.

The Subcommittee held its seventh (Geneva, 12-21 July)[23] and eighth (Geneva, 22-30 November)[24] sessions in 1993, while the Committee itself was scheduled to meet again in 1994.

ECONOMIC AND SOCIAL COUNCIL ACTION

On 29 July, the Economic and Social Council, on the recommendation of its Economic Committee, adopted **resolution 1993/50** without vote.

Work of the Committee of Experts on the Transport of Dangerous Goods

The Economic and Social Council,

Recalling its resolutions 468(XV) of 15 April 1953, 1983/7 of 26 May 1983, 1985/9 of 28 May 1985, 1986/66 of 23 July 1986, 1987/54 of 28 May 1987, 1989/104 of 27 July 1989 and 1991/57 of 26 July 1991,

Noting the ever-increasing volume of dangerous goods in world-wide commerce and the rapid expansion of technology and innovation,

Noting also that the United Nations Conference on Environment and Development recommended, in chapter 19 of Agenda 21, that international bodies, including the International Programme on Chemical Safety of the World Health Organization, the International Labour Organisation and the United Nations Environment Programme, as well as the Food and Agriculture Organization of the United Nations, the International Maritime Organization, the Committee of Experts on the Transport of Dangerous Goods and the Organisation for Economic Cooperation and Development, in cooperation with regional and national authorities having existing classification and labelling systems and other systems for the dissemination of information, should establish a coordinating group with a view to establishing and elaborating a harmonized classification and labelling system for chemicals,

Noting further that, in response to its requests made in its resolutions 1983/7, 1985/9, 1986/66, 1987/54, 1989/104 and 1991/57 for adequate staff resources for servicing the Committee, an additional Professional post was granted but has not yet been filled officially, in spite of temporary redeployment arrangements,

Bearing in mind the continuing need to meet the growing concern for the protection of life, property and the environment through the safe transport of dangerous goods while facilitating trade,

Aware that, in order to achieve internationally harmonized legislation, the specialized agencies and other international organizations involved in activities related to the transport of dangerous goods, as well as interested Member States, have responded positively to the relevant resolutions adopted since Council resolution 468 G (XV) and are committed to taking the recommendations of the Committee of Experts on the Transport of Dangerous Goods as a basis for the formulation of their requirements and regulations, including those concerning classification and labelling, and, therefore, rely on the work of the Committee,

Aware of the concern expressed by the Assembly of the International Maritime Organization, in its resolution A.717(17) of 6 November 1991, with regard to the development of new conventions, legislation and recommendations relating to dangerous goods or to the management of chemicals outside the coordinated forum of the Committee of Experts on the Transport of Dangerous Goods, and aware also that the Assembly had urged all United Nations and other intergovernmental bodies concerned working on various aspects of the management of chemicals to coordinate their efforts in order to ensure the compatibility of any legislation on chemicals with established transport rules and regulations,

Recognizing the increasing need for cooperation between international bodies involved in activities related to the transport of dangerous goods and those involved in other aspects of chemical safety,

Confirming the need for the Committee of Experts on the Transport of Dangerous Goods to participate actively in relevant activities associated with the implementation of Agenda 21,

Reaffirming the desirability of widening the decision-making base of the Committee by encouraging the participation of developing countries and other non-member countries in its future work,

1. *Takes note* of the report of the Secretary-General on the work of the Committee of Experts on the Transport of Dangerous Goods during the biennium 1991-1992 and of the new and amended recommendations approved by the Committee for inclusion in its existing recommendations;

2. *Requests* the Secretary-General:

(a) To incorporate in the existing recommendations of the Committee of Experts on the Transport of Dangerous Goods all the new and amended recommendations approved by the Committee at its seventeenth session, held at Geneva from 7 to 16 December 1992;

(b) To publish the new and amended recommendations in all the official languages of the United Nations, in the most cost-effective manner, not later than the end of 1993;

(c) To circulate the new and amended recommendations immediately after their publication to the Governments of Member States, the specialized agencies, the International Atomic Energy Agency and the other international organizations concerned;

3. *Invites* all Governments, the specialized agencies, the International Atomic Energy Agency and the other international organizations concerned to transmit to the Secretary-General their views on the work of the Committee, together with any comments they may wish to make on the amended recommendations;

4. *Invites* all interested Governments and the international organizations concerned, when developing appropriate codes and regulations, to take full account of the recommendations of the Committee;

5. *Invites* all Governments and the international organizations concerned with the implementation of chapter 19 of Agenda 21, and participating in the development of a globally harmonized system of classification and labelling of chemicals, to avoid duplication of work and to ensure that, to the greatest extent possible, the new system draws on, or is compatible with, the internationally well-recognized and implemented system developed by the Committee of Experts on the Transport of Dangerous Goods;

6. *Requests* the Secretary-General to take all steps necessary to ensure representation of the secretariat of the Committee of Experts on the Transport of Dangerous Goods at appropriate meetings of international organizations committed to implementing the recommendations of the Committee or involved in the process of global harmonization of classification and labelling systems for chemicals;

7. *Recommends once again* that adequate funding be provided to support the work of the Committee;

8. *Recommends* that the staff necessary for the adequate servicing of the Committee continue to be made available, and that the vacant Professional post be filled as a matter of priority;

9. *Requests* the Secretary-General to submit to the Council in 1995 a report on the implementation of the present resolution.

Economic and Social Council resolution 1993/50

29 July 1993   Meeting 45   Adopted without vote

Approved by Economic Committee (E/1993/111) without vote, 23 July (meeting 14); draft by Committee of Experts on Transport of Dangerous Goods (E/1993/57); agenda item 15 (j).

REFERENCES
[1]YUN 1992, p. 639. [2]TD/B/EX(2)/3. [3]*Review of Maritime Transport 1992* (TD/B/CN.4/27), Sales No. E.94.II.D.2. [4]A/48/15. [5]TD/B/CN.4/28. [6]TD/B/CN.4/GE.1/2. [7]TD/B/C.4/AC.7/14. [8]UNCTAD/SHIP/646. [9]UNCTAD/SHIP/644. [10]UNCTAD/SHIP/639. [11]TD/B/C.4/AC.7/13. [12]UNCTAD/SDD/PORT/1. [13]YUN 1991, p. 455, GA res. 46/213, 20 Dec. 1991. [14]A/CONF.162/8. [15]A/CONF.162/4. [16]TD/B/C.4/326. [17]TD/B/C.4/327. [18]A/CONF.162/3 & Add.1-3. [19]A/CONF. 162/7. [20]*Multilateral Treaties Deposited with the Secretary-General: Status as at 31 December 1993* (ST/LEG/SER.E/12), Sales No. E.94.V.11. [21]E/1993/57. [22]YUN 1992, p. 672. [23]ST/SG/AC.10/C.3/14. [24]ST/SG/AC.10/C.3/16.

UNCTAD structure, programme and finances

UNCTAD programme

The Trade and Development Board—the executive body of UNCTAD—held two regular sessions and three executive sessions in 1993, at Geneva. It held the second part of its thirty-ninth session from 15 to 26 March and the first part of its fortieth session from 20 September to 1 October.[1] In March, it adopted a decision on sustainable development (see PART THREE, Chapter I) and agreed conclusions on trade policies, structural adjustment and economic reform, UNCTAD's contribution to implementation of the United Nations New Agenda for the Development of Africa in the 1990s (see preceding chapter), and a review of progress in implementing the Programme of Action for LDCs for the 1990s (see PART THREE, Chapter I). It also sent a message to Governments participating in the Uruguay Round of multilateral trade negotiations. In September/October, it adopted agreed conclusions on global interdependence, debt issues, trade and environment and economic spaces and regional integration processes.

In accordance with its new working methods, TDB also held its second (5 March),[2] third (27 April)[3] and fourth (13 September)[4] executive sessions. At the second session, it took note of the reports of its subsidiary bodies and endorsed their work programmes and activities. It also discussed the restructuring process. At the third session, it reviewed developments in the Uruguay Round and discussed the report on the twenty-second session of the Working Party on the Medium-term Plan and the Programme Budget (see below). At the fourth session, it also considered reports of its subsidiary bodies and discussed procedural and administrative matters.

On 12 February, the Economic and Social Council, by **decision 1993/208 A**, decided to consider at its 1993 substantive session TDB's report on the second part of its thirty-ninth session. It authorized the Secretary-General to transmit directly to the General Assembly's forty-eighth (1993) session the report on the first part of its fortieth session.

On 29 July, by **decision 1993/301**, the Council took note of TDB's report on the second part of its thirty-ninth session.

Restructuring

As part of the ongoing process of restructuring the economic and social sectors of the United Nations Secretariat, the Secretary-General transferred to UNCTAD responsibility for activities under the programme on transnational corporations and three subprogrammes of the programme on science and technology for development, formerly carried out by the Department of Economic and Social Development in New York.

Programme budget

At its twenty-second session (Geneva, 5-8 April, 17 September and 13 October),[5] the UNCTAD Working Party on the Medium-term Plan and the Programme Budget reviewed proposed revisions and adopted amendments to the UNCTAD sections of the United Nations programme budget for the biennium 1994-1995. In April, it stressed the need for increased transparency in the United Nations budget process as it applied to UNCTAD and identified a number of factors which inhibited efficient and effective review of the programme budget. To address those concerns, it recommended that: future sessions of the Working Party should be provided with financial tables; in preparing documents for the Working Party or other groups involved in the programme and budget planning/review, the mandate from which a specified activity was drawn should be indicated; the narrative should clearly identify activities financed from the regular budget, those to be funded from extrabudgetary resources and those dependent on extrabudgetary resources being made available; there should be consistency in the application of definitions and presentation of the materials between and within subprogrammes; and the nomenclature should clearly distinguish between those ad hoc expert groups established by the UNCTAD Secretary-General and intergovernmental groups of experts mandated by intergovernmental bodies.

In terms of priorities, the Working Party recommended that those areas designated as "high priority" should be given a larger share of overall UNCTAD resources, and the division of resources among the "high priority" areas should be equitable according to the work programmes approved in the relevant intergovernmental bodies.

In September/October, the Working Party requested that the UNCTAD Secretary-General review all aspects relating to conference facilities and services and make proposals for improving the current situation, taking into account the financial situation of the United Nations.

The Committee for Programme and Coordination, in October,[6] recommended approval by the General Assembly of the programme narrative of the proposed programme budget for 1994-1995 relating to UNCTAD. The Assembly endorsed the recommendation in **resolution 48/228**.

On 23 December, by **resolution 48/231 A**, the Assembly approved an appropriation of $108,296,400 for UNCTAD for the 1994-1995 biennium.

Technical cooperation

In 1993, some $20 million was allocated to UNCTAD technical cooperation activities. UNDP remained the largest single source of funds, while bilateral donors and other sources, including the European Union (formerly EC), provided increasing amounts. Activities in the area of trade included continued assistance to developing countries participating in the Uruguay Round of multilateral trade negotiations; development of the service sector; utilization of GSP; competition policies; transfer of technology; and UNCTAD's programmes for the development of human resources for trade and for helping developing countries to manage better their external trade liabilities. Activities were also pursued with regard to insurance, selected international monetary issues, commodities, and diversification and marketing. Work was undertaken on the transit problems of land-locked developing countries in Africa, the development of shipping services, including assistance for the better management of ports, multimodal transport and the human resources development programme for the maritime sector. UNCTAD also assisted in making operational the port of Mogadishu, Somalia. UNCTAD's largest technical cooperation programme assisted over 50 countries to improve their management of customs. Operational activities were also initiated under a new UNCTAD programme on trade efficiency.

Thirtieth anniversary of UNCTAD in 1994

In a note to TDB's second executive session,[7] the UNCTAD secretariat presented preliminary thoughts on possible events to be organized in 1994 to mark UNCTAD's thirtieth anniversary. Suggested events included a Raúl Prebisch lecture; a one-day symposium of eminent panellists on selected themes on the development agenda; a special event hosted by a member State and to include non-governmental organizations, the enterprise sector, trade unions and academics; the issue of several publications and a special exhibition; the preparation of a film on UNCTAD; the production of special issues of UNCTAD publications; and various activities in collaboration with the media. The United Nations Postal Administration had already agreed to issue a commemorative stamp. Those activities, including a special meeting of TDB at which it could adopt a declaration to mark the anniversary and activities at the national level, would require support by member States.

On 5 March,[2] TDB agreed that its President, regional coordinators and China should hold consultative meetings with the secretariat on the preparations for the anniversary.

In an oral report to TDB's fortieth (September/October) session, the President of the thirty-ninth session stated that, during the consultations, it had been agreed that a two-day high-level meeting should be held during the autumn 1994 session and that the output of the celebrations should serve as an input for the preparation of the fifti-eth anniversary of the United Nations in 1995. Switzerland's offer to host and finance the proposed seminar/symposium was welcomed; the theme would be discussed further. The UNCTAD secretariat was requested to contact regional commissions and development banks with regard to organizing and financing regional seminars. It had been agreed that the secretariat proposal for a film could be envisaged only on the basis of voluntary contributions. The secretariat was requested to examine the feasibility and financial implications of organizing an international competition among universities throughout the world on a theme in relation to UNCTAD.

On 1 October,[1] TDB mandated the President of the thirty-ninth session to continue to coordinate arrangements for the celebration of the anniversary and to pursue further consultations.

REFERENCES
[1]A/48/15. [2]TD/B/EX(2)/2. [3]TD/B/EX(3)/3. [4]TD/B/EX(4)/3. [5]TD/B/39(2)/25 & Add.1. [6]A/48/16. [7]TD/B/EX(2)/INF.2.

Chapter V

Transnational corporations

The role of transnational corporations (TNCs) in
economic development continued to grow in 1993
as foreign direct investment flows into developing
countries reached record levels. The newly opened
economies of Central and Eastern Europe provided further scope for TNCs to make a positive
contribution to the world economy.

The role of TNCs in the transitional economies
of Central and Eastern Europe was a new item on
the agenda of the Commission on TNCs, which
met in New York in April. The Commission also
discussed trends in foreign direct investment in developing countries and the role of TNCs in services, including banking. The Intergovernmental
Working Group of Experts on International Standards of Accounting and Reporting met in March.

In July, the Economic and Social Council requested the Secretary-General to prepare reports
on how to improve flows of foreign direct investment to African and other developing countries
(resolution 1993/49). It invited TNCs to continue
to contribute to the demise of apartheid in South
Africa and to take appropriate measures regarding the vulnerable and critical process there.

The United Nations programme on TNCs underwent a second phase of restructuring during the
year, when programmes relating to TNCs were integrated within the United Nations Conference on
Trade and Development (UNCTAD) on 1 September. UNCTAD established a new Division on TNCs
and Investment to implement the programme on
TNCs and related activities.

Bilateral, regional and international arrangements

In a March report on an international framework for TNCs,[1] the Secretary-General reviewed
trends and developments in law- and policy-
making concerning the emerging international
framework for foreign direct investment and the
operation of TNCs.

At the multilateral level, the most significant developments were the adoption of guidelines on the
treatment of foreign direct investment and the continuing negotiation of agreements on international
trade in services, trade-related investment measures and trade-related aspects of intellectual prop-

erty. At the regional and interregional levels, the
main treaty-making activity occurred in the context of regional integration schemes and the
expansion of free trade zones. Also of importance
for foreign investment operations was the 1991
review of the Declaration on International Investment and Multinational Enterprises of the
Organisation for Economic Cooperation and Development. At the bilateral level, the network of
bilateral treaties for the promotion and protection
of foreign direct investment continued to expand;
cooperation agreements were concluded between
the United States and a number of developing
countries. Various instruments were also successfully concluded on specific aspects relative to the
operations of TNCs, notably on environmental
protection, antitrust and banking supervision.

Those developments confirmed a trend already
established in the 1980s; Governments from both
developed and developing countries continued to
be preoccupied with the provision of policy conditions under a legal framework that would attract
foreign direct investment flows into their countries.
A preliminary assessment of the contribution of
the new instruments to the international framework suggested a further strengthening of principles on the treatment of foreign investors, while
the elaboration of standards on TNC activities had
proceeded mainly through the conclusion of instruments dealing with specific issues, such as environmental protection, banking and financial
markets supervision and illicit payments in international business transactions.

At its April session,[2] the Commission on TNCs
took note of the Secretary-General's report.

Draft code of conduct

In his report, mentioned above, on the international framework for TNCs,[1] the Secretary-
General referred to the draft code of conduct on
TNCs, first considered in 1975,[3] as well as to
other international arrangements and agreements
relating to TNCs.

He noted that informal consultations, held in
July 1992,[4] had concluded that no consensus was
currently possible on the draft code of conduct.
It was generally recognized that the code negotiations, which spanned a period of more than 15
years and involved all countries and regions, con-

tributed significantly to the elaboration of principles and standards on foreign direct investment. The negotiations, in addition to elaborating general principles to guide the treatment of foreign investors by host Governments, had suggested a set of rules of good conduct to guide foreign investors' behaviour.

REFERENCES

(1)E/C.10/1993/8. (2)E/1993/30. (3)YUN 1975, p. 484. (4)YUN 1992, p. 644.

Standards of accounting and reporting

At its eleventh session (New York, 4-12 March 1993),[1] the Intergovernmental Working Group of Experts on International Standards of Accounting and Reporting had before it reports of the Secretary-General on a global review of the state of accounting and auditing education and training,[2] as well as on regional reviews in Africa,[3] Asia and Latin America[4] and Europe and North America.[5] Other reports before the Working Group were on: responsibilities of the accounting profession and direction of accounting and auditing education;[6] requirements for professional accounting education for the year 2000 and beyond;[7] recent developments affecting the European accountancy profession;[8] and education of European accountants and challenges of the international economy.[9]

Following a discussion of accounting education and strengthening of the profession, the Group expressed concern that accountants and auditors were not being properly prepared to meet their global responsibilities. There was consensus on the need to develop standards for a global qualification that would make the accounting profession equal around the world. The Group suggested that two new designations be established—that of United Nations registered accountant and (on a higher level) that of United Nations registered auditor.

The Group called upon the International Federation of Accountants to focus on education problems globally and to consider developing global qualification standards for accountants and auditors to be endorsed by the United Nations. The Group also requested the Secretary-General to explore with interested parties—international, public and private—ways of launching a consultation process with a view to promoting global interaction for the advancement of accounting and professional education.

In other action, the Group recommended for adoption by the Commission on TNCs three draft resolutions, by which the Economic and Social

Council would be requested to increase the Group's membership from 34 to 50; the General Assembly would be requested to grant financial assistance to developing countries that were members of the Group; and the Secretary-General would be called on to ensure an appropriate structure and resources within the Secretariat so that the Group could carry out its mandate effectively.

On the recommendation of the Commission,[10] the Economic and Social Council, in **resolution 1993/49**, decided that consideration of the Group's proposals should be deferred until the Commission's 1994 session. It took note of the report of the Group and reaffirmed the importance of its work in contributing to greater transparency in the activities of TNCs.

REFERENCES

(1)E/C.10/1993/12. (2)E/C.10/AC.3/1993/2. (3)E/C.10/AC.3/1993/4. (4)E/C.10/AC.3/1993/5. (5)E/C.10/AC.3/1993/6. (6)E/C.10/AC.3/1993/3. (7)E/C.10/AC.3/1993/7. (8)E/C.10/AC.3/1993/8. (9)E/C.10/AC.3/1993/9. (10)E/1993/30.

Commission on TNCs

The Commission on Transnational Corporations held its nineteenth session in New York from 5 to 15 April 1993.[1] It discussed the role of TNCs in the world economy and trends in foreign direct investment in developing countries; the role of TNCs in the newly opened economies of Central and Eastern Europe; TNCs in services, including banking; international, regional and bilateral arrangements and agreements relating to TNCs; and the activities of the United Nations TNCs and Management Division and its joint units. It also considered the provisional agenda for its twentieth (1994) session.

On 29 July, the Economic and Social Council took note of the Commission's report on its nineteenth session[1] (**decision 1993/306**) and approved the provisional agenda and documentation for the twentieth session (**decision 1993/304**).

ECONOMIC AND SOCIAL COUNCIL ACTION

On 29 July, the Economic and Social Council, on the recommendation of its Economic Committee, adopted **resolution 1993/49** without vote.

Strengthening the role of the Commission on Transnational Corporations

The Economic and Social Council

1. *Takes note* of the reports prepared for the Commission on Transnational Corporations at its nineteenth session;

2. *Reaffirms* the validity of the Commission on Transnational Corporations and the need further to strengthen its role as the focal point within the United Nations system for comprehensive intergovernmental consideration

of issues concerning foreign direct investment as related to transnational corporations;

3. *Emphasizes* the need for the Secretary-General to reinforce the role of the United Nations system, including the joint units established with the regional commissions, in strengthening the capacity of developing countries, in particular, at their request, in the field of foreign direct investment by providing technical cooperation, consultative and advisory services, training, research and information to those countries;

4. *Requests* the Secretary-General, in coordination with multilateral organizations and financial institutions, to give priority to strengthening technical cooperation in order to enhance the capacities of developing countries and other recipient countries to create a favourable investment climate, including in the services sector, in the context of their economic programmes;

5. *Invites* the Governments of developed countries to increase their activities aimed at assisting, in particular, developing countries, in the development of an environment favourable to foreign investment;

6. *Requests* the Secretary-General to give priority to analytical studies, including those on global trends and determinants of foreign direct investment flows, as related, *inter alia*, to transnational corporations, and on the impact of those trends, flows and stocks on all countries, in particular developing countries;

7. *Also requests* the Secretary-General to submit to the Commission at its twentieth session an analytical and comparative report on the role of foreign direct investment in Africa, with recommendations on ways and means of improving foreign direct investment inflows throughout the African continent;

8. *Further requests* the Secretary-General to submit to the Commission at its twentieth session an analytical report on the flows of foreign direct investment, paying special attention to the situation of the least developed countries, and other developing countries outside Africa, with recommendations on how to improve flows to developing countries;

9. *Requests* the Secretary-General to take steps to ensure that the work of the United Nations system in the field of transnational corporations and related issues is undertaken in a coordinated manner that avoids duplication of work, and to submit a report to the Commission at its twentieth session on the steps taken;

10. *Takes note* of the regional conference held in 1992 on foreign investment flows in Latin America and welcomes the initiative taken by the Secretariat in organizing a similar meeting in 1993 in Africa, at the ministerial level;

11. *Requests* the Secretary-General, with regard to technical cooperation activities, to continue to promote and to provide advice on the interrelationship between foreign direct investment and interregional, regional and subregional economic integration and technical and economic cooperation among developing countries;

12. *Requests* the Secretary-General to continue activities in matters relating to the role of transnational corporations in the development of small and medium-sized enterprises;

13. *Stresses* the importance of the role of foreign direct investment, in particular that of transnational corporations, in privatization processes, and reiterates the invitation to the Secretary-General to enhance studies and technical cooperation programmes in this area, in

accordance with Economic and Social Council resolution 1992/36 of 30 July 1992;

14. *Takes note* of the results of the consultations on the draft code of conduct on transnational corporations held by the President of the General Assembly from 21 to 23 July 1992;

15. *Invites* Member States, in particular developed countries, to increase financial support flows for research and advisory and information work as it relates to foreign investment;

16. *Takes note* of the report of the Intergovernmental Working Group of Experts on International Standards of Accounting and Reporting and decides that consideration of the draft resolutions contained therein should be deferred to the twentieth session of the Commission, and reaffirms the importance of the work of the Group in contributing to greater transparency in the activities of transnational corporations;

17. *Recognizes* the need for the integration of the economies in transition into the world economy through, *inter alia*, an increase in inflows of foreign direct investment, and recognizes also the contribution that the United Nations system can make in this regard, taking into account General Assembly resolutions 47/175 and 47/187 of 22 December 1992;

18. *Calls upon* Member States to exchange information among themselves, their relevant private sectors and all competent organs, organizations and bodies of the United Nations system on their activities, programmes and experiences related to the promotion of foreign direct investment, in particular in developing countries;

19. *Reiterates* the urgent need for the removal of the remaining obstacles to the creation of an atmosphere conducive to constitutional negotiations in South Africa in order to build upon the significant developments already achieved;

20. *Recognizes* that some financial institutions are unable to resume their lending activities to South Africa as a result of the inhibiting economic and political difficulties in that country, such as the ongoing violence;

21. *Reiterates further* its obligations towards the complete eradication of apartheid, reaffirmed in General Assembly resolutions 45/176 A of 19 December 1990, 46/79 A of 13 December 1991 and 47/116 A of 18 December 1992 and in the Declaration on Apartheid and its Destructive Consequences in Southern Africa, contained in the annex to General Assembly resolution S-16/1 of 14 December 1989;

22. *Reaffirms* that Governments, entrepreneurs and enterprises, including transnational corporations, have contributed to the demise of the apartheid system, and invites them to give their full and concerted support to that end and to take appropriate measures regarding the vulnerable and critical process currently under way in South Africa, with the aim of achieving the total eradication of the apartheid system and the establishment of a united non-racial and democratic South Africa;

23. *Requests* the Secretary-General:

(a) To continue, in close cooperation with the relevant organs of the United Nations, the work of collecting and disseminating information on the activities of transnational corporations conducting operations in South Africa;

(b) To continue preparing studies on the scale, form and responsibilities of the operations of transnational corporations in South Africa, including their non-equity business arrangements and their involvement in particular sectors of the South African economy;

(c) To continue examining possible contributions of transnational corporations to the construction of a united and non-racial democratic South Africa in the economic and social fields, taking into account the special need for the development of human resources, particularly the training of black South African entrepreneurs, and for employment, housing and health;

24. *Decides* that the Commission should review its future activities at its twentieth session and, if appropriate, make recommendations to the General Assembly, through the Economic and Social Council, in the context of the ongoing restructuring of the United Nations in the economic and social fields;

25. *Requests* the Secretary-General to report to the Commission at its twentieth session on the implementation of the present resolution.

Economic and Social Council resolution 1993/49

29 July 1993   Meeting 45   Adopted without vote

Approved by Economic Committee (E/1993/111) without vote, 23 July (meeting 14); draft by Commission on TNCs (E/1993/30); agenda item 15 *(d)*.

TNCs in South Africa

A March report of the Secretary-General on the role of TNCs in South Africa[2] dealt with the involvement and possible contributions of TNCs to the South African economy as it was going through a period of adjustment.

The Secretary-General discussed South Africa's economy in the context of world recessionary conditions, addressing in particular external and internal constraints, favourable balance-of-payments, currency, monetary and fiscal developments, the more optimistic long-term outlook for gold, and the recent involvement of TNCs in South Africa. In addition, he considered possible economic policy measures that would encourage long-term inward foreign investments by TNCs, including abolishing the dual exchange rate system, privatizing industry, restructuring the economy by focusing on projects aimed at beneficiating South Africa's mineral wealth other than gold, and fostering a favourable tax regime.

The Secretary-General concluded that South Africa was faced not only with an urgent need for cyclical recovery, but also with the need for some structural readjustments to bring its economy back on to a path of sustainable higher-level growth and provide employment for the masses of unemployed. He noted that all the policy measures discussed in the report would encourage the inflow of foreign investments by TNCs.

In an addendum to the report,[3] the Secretary-General provided lists of TNCs from 18 countries that had disposed of their equity interests in South Africa and of those from 20 countries with equity interests of more than 10 per cent. Annexed to the addendum was a Code of Conduct for Multinational Companies Investing in South Africa, submitted by the Congress of South African Trade Unions (COSATU), and a Platform of Guiding Principles for Foreign Investors, formulated by COSATU and the African National Congress.

On the recommendation of the Commission on TNCs,[1] the Economic and Social Council, in resolution 1993/49, reaffirmed that Governments, entrepreneurs and enterprises, including TNCs, had contributed to the demise of the apartheid system, and invited them to take appropriate measures regarding the vulnerable and critical process under way in South Africa, with the aim of achieving the total eradication of the apartheid system. The Secretary-General was requested to continue preparing studies on TNC operations in South Africa and to examine their possible contribution to the construction of a united and non-racial democratic society.

Follow-up to UNCED

In a March report[4] on follow-up to the 1992 United Nations Conference on Environment and Development (UNCED)[5] as related to TNCs, the Secretary-General summarized the discussions on business and industry that took place during the UNCED preparatory process. He also provided an overview of emerging positive trends in the role of TNCs in environment and development; discussed the implications of UNCED agreements for TNCs, and business in general; and suggested how the Commission on TNCs could organize future work on TNCs and the environment in order to maintain and broaden the momentum gained at UNCED regarding the corporate role in sustainable development.

Numerous chapters of Agenda 21[6]—the action plan for sustainable development adopted by UNCED—contained references to TNCs, including issues such as business and hazardous waste; business and biodiversity; and international banking and the debt crisis. The Secretary-General noted that Agenda 21 suggested that the best environmental practices of TNCs could be promoted with wider adoption of and reporting on implementation of environmental codes of conduct; adoption of voluntary information-sharing programmes, based on the spirit of international guidelines; and development of sectoral trade association guidelines on cleaner production.

The TNCs and Management Division informed more than 2,000 TNCs of the results of UNCED, and asked for their appraisal of it. A preliminary reading of the responses indicated that the business community was overwhelmingly positive in its assessment of the Conference; the responding corporations looked forward to working with the United Nations in implementing Agenda 21, and it was clear that they had seriously considered the implications of sustainable development for their activities.

In discussing the near-term role of the United Nations in the business-related recommendations of Agenda 21, the Secretary-General said that future environmental work relevant to TNC activities could focus on six areas: integrating environment and development into corporate decision-making in all countries; building the institutional capacity of developing and transitional economies to manage large-scale projects, investments and technologies in an environmentally sound manner; examining the linkages between trade, foreign investment and the environment; evaluating market and regulatory instruments that sought to increase the use of "green" products, processes and services; supporting full internationalization of environmental costs and transparency in accounting and reporting; and contributing to the further expansion of corporate international environmental laws, agreements and guidelines.

On 29 July, the Economic and Social Council, on the recommendation of the Commission on TNCs,[1] took note of the Secretary-General's report and requested the Chairman of that Commission to transmit it to the Commission on Sustainable Development for substantive consideration (**decision 1993/305**).

TNCs in transition economies

In a March report on foreign direct investment in the newly opened economies of Central and Eastern Europe,[7] the Secretary-General addressed the main issues associated with such investment in those economies, including the countries of the former USSR, during their transition from centrally planned to market-oriented structures. He discussed the structure of and trends in foreign direct investment, and policy, legal and institutional frameworks covering investment in Central and Eastern European countries. He also addressed some policy implications of foreign direct investment in those countries.

The Secretary-General concluded that foreign direct investment could play an important role as a catalyst in opening up the economies of Central and Eastern Europe, enhancing labour productivity and transferring management techniques and skills. Foreign direct investment in those economies remained in the early stages, but substantial opportunities were available for investment development. There was an urgent need, however, for strategic international technical support to assist the transition economies in their efforts to strengthen foreign direct investment policy formulation and management capacity. Technical assistance should focus in particular on the analysis, design and implementation of national trans-

formation and privatization policies, the training of entrepreneurs, financiers and corporate managers, and specific investment promotion activities at the regional or country levels. Assistance could also be provided in drafting investment legislation, tax and other fiscal regulations affecting TNCs, and natural resource legislation for programmes affecting the environment. Considering the challenge of establishing and maintaining an internationally competitive private sector, entailing the establishment and management of advanced infrastructure and communication networks, investment frameworks and economy-wide technologies, there was an urgent need for assistance in institution-building and human resource development.

United Nations cooperation in promoting foreign direct investment in transition economies included the design by the TNCs and Management Division of a programme of integrated technical assistance and human resource development aimed at strengthening national capacity for the effective assimilation of foreign investment, and the establishment of a Section on Economies in Transition and Free Economic Zones. The Division, in collaboration with Bulgaria, organized an Ad Hoc Expert Group Meeting on the Role of Foreign Direct Investment in the Newly Opened Economies of Central and Eastern Europe (Sofia, 5-7 January).

In April,[1] the Commission on TNCs reaffirmed the importance it attached to the research and technical assistance activities of the TNCs and Management Division in countries with transitional economies and requested the Secretary-General to report in 1994 on the Division's analytical and technical assistance activities in all transitional economies, as well as on the progress and activities of foreign direct investment and TNCs operating in such economies.

TNCs and international economic relations

In April, the Commission on TNCs had before it three reports dealing with TNCs in the world economy and trends in foreign direct investment in developing countries, as well as a related report on the universe of TNCs.

In a March report,[8] the Secretary-General reviewed global trends in foreign direct investment, as well as regional trends in developed and developing countries and in the transitional economies of Central and Eastern Europe. He noted that inflows of foreign direct investment to all regions of the developing world had increased in absolute and relative terms, despite the decline in such flows worldwide in 1991 and in inflows to the developed countries. The reason for that trend in 1991 was, on the one hand, the continued economic uncertainty in the developed countries and, on the other, the maintenance or resurgence of economic growth and sustained profitability in developing countries in Asia and Latin America, together with the continuing trend towards liberalization and privatization.

The decline in world-wide flows of foreign direct investment in 1991 represented the first downturn since 1982 and occurred largely because of recessionary conditions in major industrialized countries and structural weaknesses in the financial systems in a number of countries, which made finance capital for investment more difficult to obtain. Despite those declines, the importance of the activities of TNCs in the world economy continued to increase as net additions to the world-wide stock of foreign direct investment and their pace of growth were faster relative to exports, domestic output and domestic investment. Several structural changes in the world economy, combined with a number of anticipated policy-related changes, were likely to contribute to an upward trend in foreign direct investment flows during the 1990s.

Another March report[9] examined the growth of foreign direct investment in the 1980s and attempted to determine whether the surge in investment flows in the latter half of that decade signified a new trend or if it was just a temporary bulge.

The Secretary-General stated that cyclical factors alone did not explain the size of the investment flow between 1985 and 1990, which grew at an annual rate of 28 per cent, the highest ever recorded. A contributing factor in the increase was the response of TNCs to policy changes and to structural changes in the world economy. Policy-related factors included trade liberalization, changes in exchange rates, the liberalization of foreign direct investment regimes, privatization, non-tariff barriers and regional integration schemes. Structural factors included the existence of a stock of foreign direct investment already in place and the emergence of an integrated international production system. The influence of those factors suggested that investment flows would probably continue to increase, despite the fact that cyclical factors were currently having the opposite effect.

The emergence of an integrated international production system and its implications for developing countries were discussed by the Secretary-General in another March report.[10] He noted that the rapid growth of foreign direct investment in the 1980s was evidence of the growing importance of TNCs in the world economy. Foreign direct investment had grown three times faster than world exports and almost four times faster than world output between 1983 and 1990. TNCs also influenced international production through non-equity linkages, such as franchising and joint ven-

tures. In addition to providing capital through inflows of foreign direct investment, TNCs also had an impact on host economies through the transfer of technology and skills to host country nationals, expansion of the host country's role in international trade and stimulating host country business enterprise through the local purchasing of raw inputs, services and manufactured components.

As TNCs were adopting new strategies and organizational structures, the functional and geographic scope of international production was undergoing significant change. While TNCs applied different strategies under different circumstances, there appeared to be a definite evolution towards those involving a more complex type of cross-border, intra-firm integration of the value chain over a wider geographical area. As those new strategies and structures evolved, host economies—especially those of developing countries—needed to evaluate and update their policy frameworks for attracting foreign direct investment and the activities of TNCs.

In a report[11] on the universe of TNCs, the Secretary-General outlined its dimensions and the characteristics, utilizing the results of efforts to establish an information system on TNCs by the Centre on TNCs and its successor, the TNCs and Management Division and its joint units.

At the beginning of the 1990s, there were about 35,000 parent TNCs with some 175,000 affiliates covering all sectors of the economy and regions of the world. A relatively small number of large companies accounted for a significant share of TNC activity as measured by foreign assets. A relatively small group of TNCs also played a major role in determining flows of foreign direct investment and associated technology and the integration of a country within the international production system. While the majority of TNCs originated in developed countries, during the 1980s a growing number of firms headquartered in developing countries had also become part of the universe of TNCs.

In April,[1] the Commission on TNCs requested the Secretary-General to continue the research programme on TNCs in the world economy and flows of foreign direct investment to developing countries, and to disseminate the results through publications such as the *World Investment Report* and the *World Investment Directory*.

Foreign direct investment in services

In a report[12] on issues related to the liberalization of foreign direct investment in services, including banking, the Secretary-General noted that services had maintained their role as the largest and fastest growing sector in both the flows and stocks of foreign direct investment, mainly as a result of investment among developed countries. A number of countries were doing what, a decade earlier, would have been unthinkable: permitting TNCs into their financial, air-transportation, telecommunication and utilities industries. Foreign direct investment in services was likely to continue to grow rapidly and extend into such capital-intensive service industries as telecommunications and air transport in both developed and developing countries.

Foreign direct investment policies in services were being increasingly liberalized as a means to increase the efficiency and competitiveness of local service industries. As the experience of many countries showed, the opening of key services could lead to productivity gains that could improve overall economic performance.

In April,[1] the Commission requested the Secretary-General to strengthen in-depth research and technical cooperation in the area of services and to report in 1994.

REFERENCES

[1]E/1993/30. [2]E/C.10/1993/13. [3]E/C.10/1993/13/Add.1. [4]E/C.10/1993/7. [5]YUN 1992, p. 670. [6]Ibid., p. 672. [7]E/C.10/1993/5. [8]E/C.10/1993/2. [9]E/C.10/1993/3. [10]E/C.10/1993/4. [11]E/C.10/1993/11. [12]E/C.10/1993/6.

UN programme on TNCs

Administrative questions

In September 1993, the Secretary-General, in a report on the restructuring and efficiency of the Secretariat,[1] informed the General Assembly that the programme relating to TNCs had been integrated within UNCTAD. That action was taken in accordance with Assembly **resolution 47/212 B** of 6 May on the review of the efficiency of the administrative and financial functioning of the United Nations and programme budget for the biennium 1992-1993, in which the Secretary-General was requested to ensure that all activities related to TNCs were integrated. The UNCTAD programme on TNCs became operational at Geneva on 1 September.

UNCTAD established a new Division on TNCs and Investment to implement the programme, as well as related UNCTAD activities in the areas of foreign direct investment, privatization and enterprise development.

In March,[2] the Secretary-General informed the Commission on TNCs that, in the first phase of restructuring in 1992, the mandate of the former United Nations Centre on TNCs and its joint units was subsumed under the Department of Economic and Social Development, as the TNCs and Management Division.[3]

The main thrust of the Division became to respond to the challenge of strengthening national capabilities and supporting the move to market structures.

Some of the new priorities of the TNC programme were in the fields of sustainable development, information management, privatization and private sector development, and assistance to economies in transition. In order to develop and implement activities to support the process of economic reform and restructuring, a special Section on Economies in Transition and Free Economic Zones was set up within the TNCs and Management Division.

Implementation of the TNC programme

In a March report,[2] the Secretary-General discussed implementation of the United Nations programme on TNCs by the TNCs and Management Division and its joint units. In addition to reviewing the evolution of the programme since its establishment by the Economic and Social Council in 1974,[4] he described its major accomplishments in 1992.

Information activities

The information system on TNCs continued to provide products and services in the areas of corporate information; aggregate economic and financial information; laws, regulations and policies; contracts and agreements; industries and sectors; and business reference.[2] It also expanded the range of topics on which information services were provided. The restructuring of the Secretariat resulted in increased demands being placed on the information-on-demand component of the system, as that was recognized as a comprehensive repository capable of serving expanded needs. Work was begun on coordinating the provision of information services, with the goal of expanding services while realizing economies.

Particular effort was devoted to strengthening the legal component of the information system, as access to a store of legal and contractual information could facilitate the move of many countries towards liberalization of investment and market activities. The TNC programme had built a database and issued an inventory of investment contracts; it had also begun an inventory of current full-text investment legislation available in-house, or from electronic information services or research institutions.

The store of corporate information continued to expand. The pilot phase of an information network on foreign investors and investment services (FIND) was launched, its objective being to enhance the flow of information on investment opportunities and to match investors and projects.

In 1993, the programme completed the development and testing of TRANSCIS, a microcomputer-based system for the storage, processing and retrieval of bibliographic and textual information for users at the country level. Three bibliographic databases with a total of 12,000 records were incorporated into the system.

Joint units with the regional commissions

The joint units of the TNC programme with the five regional commissions were responsible for preparing case-studies on economic, social and institutional aspects of TNC activities in their regions.

The joint unit with the Economic Commission for Africa (ECA) focused its efforts on research on the operations of TNCs in the region, with emphasis on alternative forms of investment and cooperation. It also examined the role of Japanese foreign direct investment in Africa, with particular emphasis on technology transfer and home country policy development. Missions were undertaken to Burkina Faso and the Niger on the role of joint ventures in Africa, to Ghana and Nigeria on transnational trading companies, and to Tokyo on Japanese investment in Africa.

The joint unit with the Economic Commission for Europe focused on providing direct support to the economies in transition of Central and Eastern Europe in the area of industrial enterprise restructuring through foreign direct investment and external financing. In cooperation with Governments, support was directed towards helping individual Eastern European enterprises to define their specific problems and their possibilities for obtaining outside assistance through investment by specific Western enterprises.

The joint unit with the Economic and Social Commission for Asia and the Pacific undertook a number of research projects, including an evaluation of the contribution of TNCs to the development of backward linkages in the electrical and electronic industry (funded by Japan); an update of service industries in Asia; and a study on management contracts for international chain hotels in Thailand. The unit continued to collect, analyse and disseminate information and data on the activities of TNCs and on changes in foreign direct investment legislation in the region. The unit provided technical support to an International Conference on TNCs and China (Beijing, 9-11 September).

The joint unit established with the Economic Commission for Latin America and the Caribbean (ECLAC) focused its research primarily on TNCs and the industrial restructuring process in selected countries of the region, and on TNCs and the process of change in the international economy. It prepared the final version of the *Directory on Foreign Investment in Latin America and the Caribbean 1993: Legal Framework and Statistical Information*. In the area of technical cooperation, the unit cooperated with the Andean Development Corporation in preparing for a second regional high-level symposium on the contribution of TNCs to the growth and development of Latin America and the Caribbean, to be held in 1994.

The joint unit established with the Economic and Social Commission for Western Asia (ESCWA) contributed to the preparation of the *World Investment Directory*, volume V: *Africa and West Asia*, which was being finalized. The unit's activities were reduced in 1993 because of the temporary deployment of responsible ESCWA staff to New York in the wake of the war in the Persian Gulf.

Research

The research activities of the TNCs and Management Division bore directly on policy debates concerning the role of TNCs.

In July 1992, the Division published the *World Investment Report 1992: Transnational Corporations as Engines of Growth*,[5] the second in an annual series begun in 1991. A study entitled *Transnational Corporations from Developing Countries: Impact on Their Home Countries*[6] was finalized, examining how TNCs from developing countries could make positive contributions to their home economies. The Division also published a study entitled *The Impact of Trade-related Investment Measures on Trade and Development*, to promote a better understanding of issues related to the role of TNCs in several areas affected by the Uruguay Round of multilateral trade negotiations. Other research publications included: a study entitled *From the Common Market to EC92: Regional Economic Integration in the European Community and Transnational Corporations*;[7] three volumes of the *World Investment Directory 1992*, covering Asia and the Pacific,[8] Central and Eastern Europe,[9] and the developed countries;[10] and studies on small and medium-sized TNCs.

As a complement to the statistical information contained in those volumes, the Division embarked on the publication of 20 volumes of analytical studies entitled *United Nations Library on Transnational Corporations*.

A series of case-studies on the activities of TNCs in Africa was prepared by the joint unit established with ECA, and the joint unit with ECLAC continued its work on a global overview of the industrial restructuring process in Latin America, based on case-studies of Brazil, Chile, Colombia and Mexico.

Technical cooperation

Despite some institutional difficulties, the programme on TNCs was able to execute a large number of technical cooperation activities in 1992. Particular emphasis was placed on economic reform and marketization; human resources development; environment and natural resources management; private sector development and privatization; and assisting tax reform.

In Latin America and the Caribbean, Cuba was assisted in promoting foreign investment in and export of health-care products, and Antigua and Barbuda, Honduras and Peru were advised on privatization projects. In Africa, assistance was provided to Mozambique in developing a legal and institutional framework to negotiate effectively with TNCs, and to Algeria and Tunisia in drafting foreign investment laws and codes. In Asia and the Pacific, members of the Indian Ocean Commission were aided in harmonizing foreign investment and development policies, and advice on foreign investment and technology transfer was provided to Fiji, Malaysia, Samoa, Tonga and Vanuatu. In Central and Eastern Europe, the TNC programme helped with projects dealing with developing legal infrastructure in Albania, privatization and restructuring in Romania, and the development of export markets for the scientific resources of Estonia, Latvia and Lithuania.

Training projects intended to enhance human resources development included workshops in several African countries—Ghana, Nigeria, Sierra Leone, Uganda and the United Republic of Tanzania—on topics such as international commercial arbitration, negotiating joint ventures, and fraud in international banking and financial transactions. In Asia and the Pacific, round tables were held for officials in Pakistan and the Philippines, and on-the-job training on the legal aspects of natural resources and other projects was provided at the Attorney-General's Office in Papua New Guinea. In Latin America and the Caribbean, workshops were held in Colombia, Cuba and Jamaica on environmental protection policy, intellectual property rights and negotiating joint ventures. In Central and Eastern Europe, workshops were held on privatization in Hungary and on international industrial contracts in Romania.

In the area of environment and natural resources management, the programme helped Colombia, Ecuador and Nicaragua to draft policies, laws and regulations on environmental protection, and reviewed a proposal for an ethanol plant in Grenada. The programme drafted the Solomon Islands Environmental Law and assisted Bangladesh and Papua New Guinea in negotiations with companies in the petrochemical and mining industries. Assistance was provided to Angola in the natural resources sector, a gold-mining contract was reviewed for the United Republic of Tanzania, and Sierra Leone was helped in drafting a Mines and Minerals Act. Legislation per-

taining to the tourism industry in Mozambique was reviewed.

Privatization and foreign investment

In a March report,[11] the Secretary-General provided the Commission on TNCs with information on experience gained in technical assistance and advice on foreign investment projects, with particular reference to privatization. He noted that the core belief behind the transfer to private ownership or operation of commercial interests of the State was that goods and services would be more efficiently provided by the private sector under competitive conditions. At least 80 countries had active privatization programmes and some 8,500 State enterprises worldwide had been privatized over the preceding 12 years. The former German Democratic Republic accounted for two thirds of completed privatizations, while a small number of countries in Latin America accounted for nearly 60 per cent of all privatizations in the developing world.

The Secretary-General discussed foreign investment policy issues in privatization, organizing privatization and the role of foreign participation, regulation and privatization, and modalities in privatization transactions. He concluded that the privatization process was still at an early stage in most countries, with foreign investor participation playing a significant though not dominant part in the process so far. Foreign participation could contribute to the goals of privatization by bringing skills, capital, markets and technology that were not available domestically.

There was considerable need and scope for training and advisory support to the developing and transitional economies covering policy and regulatory review and subsequent implementation, enterprise reform, and development of supporting business disciplines and institutions, as well as in the design and negotiation of divestments involving foreign investors.

With many countries in Africa about to undertake large-scale privatization and divestiture programmes, the TNC programme had provided advice to Kenya, Uganda and the United Republic of Tanzania. Assistance had also been provided to the Gambia, Sierra Leone and Zimbabwe.

Financing

Resources for implementing the programme on TNCs were made available from the United Nations regular budget and from extrabudgetary funds.

During 1992,[2] nine States contributed or pledged some $1.3 million to the Trust Fund of the United Nations TNCs and Management Division. Total extrabudgetary disbursements amounted to about $5.7 million, of which $2.9 million came from UNDP and $2.8 million from trust funds.

Expenditures on workshops and other training activities in 1992 amounted to about $1.6 million, while extrabudgetary expenditures on advisory projects totalled some $2.4 million.

REFERENCES

(1)A/48/428. (2)E/C.10/1993/9. (3)YUN 1992, p. 644. (4)YUN 1974, p. 484, ESC res. 1908(LVII), 2 Aug. 1974. (5)*World Investment Report 1992: Transnational Corporations as Engines of Growth*, Sales No. E.92.II.A.19. (6)*Transnational Corporations from Developing Countries: Impact on Their Home Countries*, Sales No. E.93.II.A.8. (7)*From the Common Market to EC92: Regional Economic Integration in the European Community and Transnational Corporations*, Sales No. E.93.II.A.2. (8)*World Investment Directory 1992*, vol. I: *Asia and the Pacific*, Sales No. 92.II.A.11. (9)Ibid., vol. II: *Central and Eastern Europe*, Sales No. 93.II.A.1. (10)Ibid., vol. III: *Developed Countries*, Sales No. E.93.II.A.9. (11)E/C.10/1993/10.

Chapter VI

Natural resources, energy and cartography

The use and conservation of natural resources and energy continued to be considered by a number of United Nations bodies in 1993. The Committee on Natural Resources held its first session as an expert committee in March/April following the 1992 restructuring of the United Nations in the economic and social fields. The Committee discussed, among other things, permanent sovereignty over mineral and water resources, new techniques for identifying those resources, small-scale mining activities in developing countries, and relevant matters arising from the 1992 United Nations Conference on Environment and Development (UNCED). The importance of the water and mineral resources programme in the context of sustainable development was brought to the attention of the Economic and Social Council.

In his report to the General Assembly, the Director General of the International Atomic Energy Agency (IAEA) also referred to UNCED, noting that IAEA could play an important role in achieving the objective of sustainable development by facilitating the transfer of nuclear techniques to promote health, ensure greater availability of fresh water and secure data on the atmosphere and seas. The Assembly, in November, urged States to strive for effective international cooperation in carrying out IAEA's work in promoting the use of nuclear energy (resolution 48/14).

The Fifth United Nations Regional Cartographic Conference for the Americas was held in New York in January.

Natural resources

Exploration

UN Revolving Fund for Natural Resources Exploration

During 1993, the United Nations Revolving Fund for Natural Resources Exploration (UNRFNRE), established by the General Assembly in 1973,[1] continued to assist developing countries in the exploration of minerals, water and energy resources, and to help attract investment to exploit them. During its 20 years of operation, the Fund—administered by the United Nations Development Programme (UNDP)—expended a total of $78 million and dis-

covered mineral resources having an estimated potential value of $1.5 billion.[2]

In the Philippines, metallurgical tests on a pilot-plant scale were carried out in 1993, following exploration for secondary chromite deposits on Dinagat Island. Gold exploration at Mapawa was initiated and fieldwork completed by the end of the year. With UNRFNRE support, a gold deposit was discovered in the United Republic of Tanzania and an initial drilling programme was designed. In Guatemala, a call for bids to develop the gold deposit at El Pato was prepared. UNRFNRE received requests for assistance in mineral exploration programmes from Guinea, Sri Lanka and Viet Nam. Potential recipients also included Cuba, the Democratic People's Republic of Korea, Estonia, Mongolia, Myanmar and Namibia.

In the area of geothermal energy, the Fund had in the pipeline projects in Argentina, China, Costa Rica, Mexico, Nicaragua and the Russian Federation, but project execution awaited sufficient funding.

New techniques for natural resources exploration and assessment

In response to a 1991 request of the Economic and Social Council,[3] the Secretary-General submitted to the March/April 1993 session of the Committee on Natural Resources a report on new techniques, including remote sensing, for identifying, exploring for and assessing mineral and water resources.[4] The report provided information on features of remote-sensing systems available through commercial outlets, including price schedules, and summarized the activities of the Department of Economic and Social Development (DESD) in remote sensing, particularly with regard to strengthening the capabilities of developing countries.

DESD, with the Office of Outer Space Affairs, prepared a training programme on the use of microwave sensors in the Sahel region of Africa, and similar arrangements were made for such a training course for countries in Latin America (see PART ONE, Chapter IV).

On 8 April,[5] the Committee on Natural Resources emphasized that new techniques, such as remote sensing, played a complementary role in identifying, exploring for, developing and managing mineral and water resources. It was of the view that they would be of paramount importance for monitoring and understanding the global hydrologic cycle. It recommended that the Economic and Social Council request the Secretary-General to prepare, for the second (1994) or third (1996) Committee session, a note giving information on existing internationally agreed principles, rules and regulations governing the relationship between the owner of data collected through remote-sensing techniques and the country to which such data were related, as well as information on United Nations activities related to the issue.

Disaster prevention and mitigation

In the mineral resources and mining area, United Nations activities in disaster mitigation and prevention were carried out in worker safety in the mining and mineral industries and in areas where mineral resource and geological expertise and technology were applicable, such as the monitoring and prediction of earthquakes, landslides and volcanic eruptions. Such activities were mainly implemented by the International Labour Organisation (ILO).

In Malaysia, the Department for Development Support and Management Services (DDSMS), formerly DESD, began a project in 1993 to enhance the Government's regulatory and administrative systems for managing worker safety in the minerals industry.

The geological expertise of DDSMS was being used to provide input to the Technical Committee of the United Nations Working Group on Mine Clearance, which had the objective of creating a centralized and systematic means of assisting countries in the clearance of land-mines and munitions. DDSMS would prepare maps, identify geophysical companies having technology and equipment for mine clearance, and establish a computerized database.

On 8 April,[5] the Committee on Natural Resources stressed the importance of effective and coordinated implementation of the International Decade for Natural Disaster Reduction (see PART THREE, Chapter III) and the need for countries to adopt proactive strategies for water- and mining-related disasters. It recommended that United Nations organizations devote priority attention to developing strategies and programmes that integrated water and land issues and that the Secretariat be asked to prepare a study on non-structural measures taken by Governments to prevent disasters related to water and mineral resources.

Permanent sovereignty over natural resources

In response to a 1991 Economic and Social Council request,[6] the Secretary-General submitted to the Committee on Natural Resources a report on permanent sovereignty over natural resources.[7] It reviewed trends with respect to the exercise of permanent sovereignty in the context of sustainable development, discussed salient issues affecting water resources and described the focus of DESD's technical cooperation activities.

Special mention was made of the facility for technical support services at the programme level (TSS-1), which was established to contribute to, among other things, achieving a sharper technical focus by agencies and enhancing agency technical support to developing countries in the upstream stages of programme and project cycles.

The United Nations could contribute to a common thematic approach to developing resources for the benefit of all, while the sovereignty of a country was maintained in order to determine the mode and timing of development of its resources. The use of TSS-1 studies and evaluations to formulate such an approach could be beneficial to developing countries in ensuring that the economic, scientific and technological objectives of developing a resource were achieved, while acknowledging and protecting the concerns of other countries.

On 8 April,[5] the Committee on Natural Resources recommended that the issue of permanent sovereignty over mineral and water resources no longer be included in its agenda as a standing item, but that specific aspects be brought to its attention under other relevant items. It also recommended that the Economic and Social Council request the Secretary-General to update the section of his report dealing with water and the exercise of permanent sovereignty, devoting special attention to issues related to shared water resources, taking into account comments by Committee members, Member States and non-governmental organizations, and including an analysis of trends in recent negotiations and agreements related to shared water resources. The Committee further recommended that the Council request the Secretary-General to prepare a study reviewing the mining legislation of selected countries.

Committee on Natural Resources

The new expert Committee on Natural Resources, established by the Economic and Social Council in 1992[8] to replace the former standing committee of the same name, held its first session in New York from 29 March to 8 April 1993.[5] It discussed permanent sovereignty over mineral and water resources; new techniques, including remote sensing, for identifying and assessing those resources; disaster prevention and mitigation in developing and utilizing mineral and water resources; activities of the United Nations system in the fields of water and mineral resources; matters arising from

UNCED[9] in the field of water resources; issues concerning the 1991 International Round-table on Mining and the Environment;[10] small-scale mining activities in developing countries; and priority programmes for coordinated action by the United Nations system in both water and mineral resources.

The Committee issued statements on some of those issues and recommended that its second session be held in 1994 instead of 1995. It also made recommendations regarding its terms of reference and future work.

ECONOMIC AND SOCIAL COUNCIL ACTION

On 29 July, by **decision 1993/302**, the Economic and Social Council decided that the second session of the Committee on Natural Resources should be held in 1994, that the normal two-year cycle of meetings would resume at that time and that the third session would be held in 1996. It approved the provisional agenda and documentation for the second session, with the inclusion of an additional item entitled ''Review and recasting of the recommendations made by the Committee at its first session'', and requested the Secretariat to prepare reports related to that agenda item. The Council requested the Committee to review in 1994 its recommendations relating to water, with a view to making a contribution to the work of the Commission on Sustainable Development at its 1994 session, and to review and recast the recommendations it made at its 1993 session by following a standard pattern of reporting when submitting its recommendations to the Council.

Mineral resources

The Committee on Natural Resources, at its March/April 1993 session, had before it four reports of the Secretary-General concerning mineral resources, three of which were submitted in response to a 1991 Economic and Social Council request.[11]

In a report on ways and means of facilitating the flow of financial resources and transfer of technology to develop the mineral resources of developing countries,[12] the Secretary-General discussed recent trends in prices, supply and demand of metals and minerals, ways to facilitate the flows of financial resources, existing programmes to support the efforts of developing countries in securing investments for the development of mineral resources, the transfer of technology to developing countries, and the recommendations of two 1991 United Nations seminars on mining taxation and applied finance for natural resources.[10] The report stated that, since modern mining and processing methods were very capital-intensive, developing countries would have to rely increasingly on foreign investment. In attracting foreign capital, those countries should pay particular attention to their policies and procedures as they applied to foreign enterprises and attempt to make them competitive.

On 8 April,[5] the Committee recommended that the Economic and Social Council request the Secretary-General to update his report for its 1994 session, taking into account the special needs of economies in transition and requirements for environmental protection.

The Secretary-General submitted a report[13] in which he reviewed the outcome of the 1991 International Round-table on Mining and the Environment[10] and the mining-related recommendations of UNCED. The report discussed the environmental challenges facing the mining sector and the impact of environmental policies on its growth, and outlined the environmental aspects of mineral development activities in 1991-1992 and those planned for 1993.

On 8 April,[5] the Committee recommended that the Council request the Secretary-General to prepare for its 1994 session a report on the effects of changing environmental legislation and regulations applicable to the mining industry on a global basis. It also recommended that studies be prepared by entities of the United Nations system on the impact on the environment of exploration and mining in developing countries and economies in transition, starting with precious and base metals, and that a review be carried out of state-of-the-art technologies dealing with processing of mining waste and tailings for the recovery of useful mineral components in order to alleviate disposal problems.

A third report[14] considered recent achievements in small-scale mining activities in developing countries. It addressed the issue of transformation to full commercialization of artisanal or informal mining and discussed recent national legislation, progress in technology transfer, promotion of small-scale mining, the contribution of women in such mining, and environmental considerations. The report concluded that artisanal mining should be rationalized and, in the developing countries, strengthened, given its contribution to rural economic and social development.

On 8 April,[5] the Committee recommended that the Council ask the Secretary-General to prepare a report for its 1994 session on the impact of small-scale mining on environmental and social aspects of selected regions (giving priority to precious metals, industrial minerals and construction materials); the drawing up and/or adaptation of related legislation and regulations; and typical, mechanized small-scale mining operations, conditions and possibilities for implementing them, and improvement of miners' working conditions. Particular attention should be given to the position and role of women in small-scale mining.

In a February report,[15] the Secretary-General submitted to the Committee a proposal for a mechanism to monitor and gather information on a regular basis on issues concerning the flow of investment in the mineral sector of developing countries and capacity-building in investment promotion. The creation of such a mechanism might be considered as developing countries were actively seeking new investment inflows and there was a critical need for accurate data because of a lack of comparability between countries.

On 8 April,[5] the Committee, taking into account the problems identified in obtaining data on foreign direct investment and the existing economic analyses of activity in the mining sector undertaken by the United Nations Conference on Trade and Development and the World Bank, considered that a study of proposed procedures, costs and benefits should be undertaken before any comprehensive analysis of foreign direct investment flows began. Existing analyses could be further enhanced by reflecting major geological regions controlling mineral deposit types as well as purely geographical or socio-economic groups. Also, increased attention should be given to building systematic knowledge bases concerning the nature, quantity and location of mineral resources and of mineral resource potential. The Committee recommended that the United Nations system encourage strategic programmes of regional resource assessment and land classification at the national and international levels and that the Council request the Secretary-General to prepare a summary review of regional mineral resource assessment programmes.

Technical cooperation activities

DDSMS was the principal United Nations office responsible for executing and coordinating technical cooperation activities in mineral resource development. Areas addressed included exploration, evaluation and feasibility studies, mining and ore processing, investment promotion and marketing.[16]

In response to increased requests from developing countries for assistance in formulating and designing foreign investment policy and regulatory and tax legislation and in negotiating terms and conditions of foreign investment with potential investors, DDSMS completed projects involving foreign investment policy development in 1992 and 1993 in Ethiopia, Guinea-Bissau, Malaysia, the Philippines and Yemen. It was also involved in assisting such policy development in Burkina Faso, Chad, Kenya, the Niger and Viet Nam. Three projects involving negotiation preparation or assistance were completed in Bolivia, Burundi and Jamaica, and projects with negotiation components were under way in Burkina Faso, the Niger

and the United Republic of Tanzania. Advice was provided regarding a privatization project in Bolivia.

On 8 April,[5] the Committee on Natural Resources recommended that the Economic and Social Council request the Secretary-General to prepare for its 1994 session a report on technical cooperation activities of the United Nations system in the mining sector, paying special attention to projects aimed at enhancing the capacity of the developing countries and economies in transition to develop effective foreign investment policies, negotiate mining investment agreements and develop and implement adequate social policies to respond to the ongoing trend towards privatizing the mining sector. It also recommended that the Council invite the UNDP Administrator to report to it in 1994 on UNRFNRE activities, including current administrative mechanisms and financing arrangements, as well as an extensive assessment of achievements and future programmes of activities.

Water resources

The Committee on Natural Resources, at its March/April session, had before it five reports of the Secretary-General regarding water resources.

In February,[17] the Secretary-General reported on the activities of the United Nations system in the field of water resources. The Mar del Plata Action Plan, adopted in 1977 by the United Nations Water Conference,[18] provided the basis for coordination and cooperation efforts among the 21 organizations within the system that were active in the field of water resources. The report outlined coordination efforts at the global and regional levels, and presented the results of various meetings held during 1990-1992, including the 1992 International Conference on Water and the Environment.[19]

On 8 April,[5] the Committee recommended that the Economic and Social Council encourage United Nations organs and organizations to adopt and implement more coherent perceptions of water-related issues and to address the cognitive problems involved through intersectoral, interprofessional and interdisciplinary cooperation and joint programming in water resources. It drew to the Council's attention the following: that the Committee was the appropriate forum to provide expertise and advice on the parts of Agenda 21, adopted by UNCED in 1992,[20] related to water and mineral resources; that interrelated water and land issues were inseparable components of sustainable development; and that it acknowledged and supported the important role of the Intersecretariat Group for Water Resources of the Administrative Committee on Coordination (ACC) in the exchange of information and coordination of programmes aimed at the sustainable development of water resources.

The Committee also recommended that the Council invite United Nations organs and organizations to enhance their cooperation with organizations outside the system and that the theme for World Water Day, 1994, should be public participation in the sustainable development and management of water resources.

The Secretary-General submitted two reports on cross-sectoral priority programmes for coordinated action by the United Nations system in water resources, one on information management[21] and the other on capacity-building for water resources management.[22]

The former report described the objectives and scope of an integrated information system and discussed information management issues at the national, regional and global levels. It stated that the integrated management of information on water resources—together with other physical, environmental, demographic and socio-economic data—was an essential component in the rational use and protection of finite and vulnerable water resources. It suggested that the objective of a monitoring system should be to act as an indicator of areas of opportunity and as a warning system of areas at risk.

On 8 April,[5] the Committee recommended that United Nations organizations assist Governments to establish or strengthen their databases as tools for integrated action in developing and managing water resources; priority attention needed to be given to drought-prone countries where haphazard development of water resources, particularly groundwater, was common. It also recommended that they give urgent consideration to establishing a system-wide integrated monitoring and assessment network, with a view to evaluating periodically the state of freshwater resources on a global basis.

The latter report[22] noted that, as far as water resource development and management were concerned, capacity-building could be defined in terms of four elements: information development and management; human resources development; institutional and legal arrangements; and public awareness. It discussed the evolution of the concept of capacity-building and reviewed what might constitute the elements of a capacity-building strategy.

On 8 April,[5] the Committee recommended that United Nations organizations promote capacity-building as a component of all technical cooperation programmes and that United Nations assistance with regard to capacity-building for water resources development and management be increased. Besides training and the transfer of technology, assistance should include provision of equipment and machinery, and on-the-job training programmes should take into consideration the wider requirements of capacity-building for water resources planning and management. Noting that the diversity of conditions faced by water-short regions called for case-studies to identify their underlying causes and characteristics, the Committee recommended that the studies consider both bio-geo-chemical and socio-technological cycles of water, with a view to supporting human resources development in developing countries, and that priority be assigned to drought-stricken regions of developing countries.

In a February report,[23] the Secretary-General summarized the provisions of Agenda 21 relevant to the area of freshwater resources. He stated that, although the challenge of securing a reliable supply of fresh water, adequate in quantity and quality, for all people, was perhaps the most fundamental issue related to both environment and development, UNCED had not fully addressed the issue.

On 8 April,[5] the Committee recognized the importance of formalizing the rights of humanity and duties of Governments in relation to the water cycle, decided to study the issue in depth in 1994 and invited the Economic and Social Council to bring the question to the attention of the Commission on Sustainable Development. The Secretary-General was requested to report in 1994 on existing instruments in other areas, which would be pertinent to global action on the water cycle. The Committee also invited the Council to take freshwater issues into account when deciding on the agenda of forthcoming conferences and to recommend to the Intergovernmental Negotiating Committee for the Elaboration of an International Convention to Combat Desertification in Those Countries Experiencing Serious Drought and/or Desertification, Particularly in Africa (see PART THREE, Chapter VIII) that it pay particular attention to the most salient water interlinkages involved in desertification. The Committee recommended that greater external financial support be given to developing countries to improve their capacity to manage their soil and water resources, that countries consider adopting water-pricing policies and that the Council invite the World Bank to strengthen the activities of the International Programme for Technology Research for Irrigation and Drainage. The Council and the Commission on Sustainable Development were invited to consider modalities to enable the Committee to assist them in reviewing the relevant chapters of Agenda 21.

With regard to other issues arising from UNCED, the Committee recommended that the Secretary-General submit in 1994 reports on action taken by Governments concerning integrated water resources development and management, and on institutional and legal issues related to such management. It further recommended that the Council recommend to the United Nations Educational, Scientific and Cultural Organization (UNESCO) and the World Meteorological Organization (WMO) that they take steps to promote a dialogue between the scientific community and decision makers in the area of water management and invite the Food and Agriculture Organization of the United Nations to take steps to develop integrated water, soil and land-use management strategies for sustainable development and conservation of the natural resource base.

In a report on human development issues and water resources development in the 1990s,[24] the Secretary-General put forward a set of proposals for implementing a sustainable water resources development strategy. Particular attention was given to the institutional and financial factors required to implement such a strategy, and the importance of public participation and involvement by local communities was stressed. Areas in which reforms had to be undertaken to achieve compatible human and water resources development included poverty, human development, research into water- and land-use practices, public participation, environment, subsidies and cost recovery for water projects, water rights, national water plans, organizational arrangements, macroeconomic and structural adjustment programmes and development assistance. The reduction of poverty was seen as one of the basic conditions for reducing destructive environmental activities and achieving sustainable development.

Technical cooperation activities

A number of United Nations organizations were involved in activities in the field of water resources in 1993 in the context of the programme areas outlined in Agenda 21,[20] namely: integrated water resources development and management; water resources assessment and impacts of climate change on water resources; protection of water resources, water quality and aquatic ecosystems; drinking-water supply and sanitation; water and sustainable urban development; and water for sustainable food production and rural development.

In the area of integrated water resources development and management, DDSMS, together with UNDP, carried out a number of pilot sector assessments or diagnostic studies in countries such as Bolivia, India, Morocco, Nepal, Peru and Yemen.[25] Further work was envisaged in China, Madagascar, Papua New Guinea and the countries of the Southern Africa Development Community. The first Freshwater Consultative Forum took place from 13 to 16 December at Geneva, and the Working Group on Water Resources of the

Multilateral Middle East Peace Process held meetings in April. A macroeconomic-based, multi-objective planning model in the field of integrated water resources development and management was successfully developed and applied in a north China project, which concluded in November.

Water resources assessment activities continued to occupy a major place in UNESCO and WMO programmes. The fourth UNESCO/WMO/International Council of Scientific Unions Conference on Hydrology, held in Paris from 22 to 27 March, highlighted those programmes and agreed to the Paris Statement, which recommended an even closer partnership between the two agency programmes.

Regarding the impacts of climatic change on water resources, WMO convened a workshop in Trinidad and Tobago from 5 to 9 July that dealt with water-quality issues in small islands. The Economic Commission for Latin America and the Caribbean convened a regional expert meeting in November on the possible effects of climate change on water resources in the region.

Inter-agency coordination

The ACC Subcommittee on Water Resources met at Santo Domingo, Dominican Republic, from 6 to 8 October[26] and was preceded by a meeting of the Inter-agency Steering Committee for Water Supply and Sanitation (4 and 5 October). Issues discussed by the Subcommittee included arrangements for the system-wide monitoring of the water-related provisions of Agenda 21, its own terms of reference and those of the Steering Committee.

REFERENCES

[1]YUN 1973, p. 408, GA res. 3167(XXVIII), 17 Dec. 1973. [2]E/C.7/1994/12. [3]YUN 1991, p. 470, ESC res. 1991/89, 26 July 1991. [4]E/C.7/1993/3. [5]E/1993/28. [6]YUN 1991, p. 471, ESC res. 1991/88, 26 July 1991. [7]E/C.7/1993/2. [8]YUN 1992, p. 655, ESC dec. 1992/218, 30 Apr. 1992. [9]Ibid., p. 670. [10]YUN 1991, p. 473. [11]Ibid., p. 474, ESC res. 1991/87, 26 July 1991. [12]E/C.7/1993/9. [13]E/C.7/1993/10. [14]E/C.7/1993/11. [15]E/C.7/1993/12. [16]E/C.7/1994/3. [17]E/C.7/1993/4. [18]YUN 1977, p. 555. [19]YUN 1992, p. 656. [20]Ibid., p. 672. [21]E/C.7/1993/7. [22]E/C.7/1993/8. [23]E/C.7/1993/5. [24]E/C.7/1993/6. [25]E/C.7/1994/2. [26]ACC/1993/3.

Energy

Many entities within the United Nations system were active in 1993 in all aspects of energy. Activities focused on environmental aspects of energy development and use, including energy conservation and efficiency, inter-fuel substitution and promotion of the development and increased use of new and renewable sources of energy.

The Committee on New and Renewable Sources of Energy and on Energy for Development, established in 1992,[1] was to hold its first session in 1994.

Energy resources development

During 1993, a large number of programmes of technical cooperation with developing countries were carried out by various United Nations organizations. They included advisory services, training workshops and seminars, publications and database management.[2] Practically all of them involved energy conservation and efficiency of use and issues relating to energy and the environment. Activities promoting the development and more widespread use of new and renewable sources of energy were on the increase.

DDSMS fielded technical advisory services to 60 countries in 1993. At the end of the year, 115 energy projects were being executed in 40 developing countries, with a total budget of $110 million. The DDSMS energy programme focused on operational activities, including advisory services, project formulation and implementation, organization of meetings, symposia and workshops and publications. It maintained an ongoing programme of research in support of technical cooperation. Its publications in 1993 included *Power Generation Options*,[3] *Energy Efficiency in Transportation*[4] and *Trends in Environmental Impact Assessment of Energy Projects*.[5]

Meetings organized during 1993 by DDSMS included: Workshop on Economic Restructuring and Environmental Management in the Coal Sector, Prague, Czech Republic, 15 and 16 March; Symposium on Safety and Mechanization in Underground Coal Mining, Omuta City, Japan, 13-16 October; Symposium on Coal Preparation and Beneficiation, China, 26-31 October; Seminar on System Planning in the Power Sector, New York, 8-12 November; Regional Workshop on Energy Efficiency and Control of Environmental Emissions, Lima, Peru, 22 November–4 December; and Conference on the Clean and Efficient Use of Coal and Lignite, Hong Kong, 30 November–3 December.

The Department for Policy Coordination and Sustainable Development was engaged in three energy subprogrammes: monitoring and analysis of global energy trends and prospects and their impact on development and environment; promotion of sustainable energy exploration and development in developing countries; and furthering the development and use of new and renewable sources of energy.

The Department for Economic and Social Information and Policy Analysis also carried out activities in energy. Its Statistical Division compiled energy information, and its Macroeconomic and Social Policy Analysis Division was involved in analysing current and long-term energy developments and prospects and their impact on the world economy and development efforts.

UNDP was in the process of formulating an overall strategy on energy and the environment as part of its continuing activities. There were 122 ongoing projects under UNDP indicative planning figure funding, representing some $104 million in UNDP funding and $46 million in cost-sharing from other sources. UNDP Global Environment Facility energy projects totalled some $86 million and ranged from the installation of renewable energy systems to monitoring greenhouse gases.

Energy account

The United Nations Fund for Science and Technology for Development (UNFSTD) funded energy projects through the Energy Account of UNDP.[6] The projects focused mainly on energy efficiency and on the use of renewable sources of energy to meet the basic needs of rural communities.

Financing Energy Services for Small-Scale Energy Users (FINESSE) was initiated in 1989 by the World Bank, in collaboration with the Netherlands Ministry of Development Cooperation, the United States Department of Energy and UNFSTD, and resulted from the recognition that traditional energy-sector lending by multilateral and bilateral institutions was biased towards large-scale, supply-oriented fossil fuels and hydro-based projects. Its objective was to identify and promote ways to provide technically feasible and economically viable renewable energy as well as energy efficiency services to end-users. The Netherlands provided a trust fund of almost $900,000 for FINESSE.

Another large-scale proposal, the Programme for Asian Cooperation on Energy and the Environment, was funded by a trust fund of over $2 million from Australia. Its objective was to assist developing countries in the environmentally responsible production and efficient use of energy from coal. Through a related project, funded by Germany, international conferences were organized in China and India to enhance their efforts in the clean and efficient use of coal.

Other activities funded under the Energy Account included the installation of solar water-heating systems at three hospitals in Grenada and assistance to the Solar Energy Company in Kiribati in the design, installation, maintenance and management of solar photovoltaic home systems.

UNFSTD participated in the funding and organization of an international workshop on renewable energy project implementation and management (New Delhi, India, March). Also, in cooperation with the Latin American Energy Organization and the Treaty for Amazonian Cooperation, a training workshop on photovoltaic systems for rural electrification was organized in November in Ecuador.

Nuclear energy

IAEA report

On 23 August 1993,[7] the Secretary-General transmitted the 1992 report of the International Atomic Energy Agency to the General Assembly. Presenting and updating the report in the Assembly on 1 November, the IAEA Director General said that mankind seemed to stand on the threshold of an era in which many nuclear techniques might be disseminated for peaceful purposes, especially for the benefit of the developing world; in which nuclear power could help reduce environmental threats; and in which one might even begin to think seriously about how to organize a nuclear-weapon-free world (see PART SIX, Chapter I, for further information on IAEA activities).

The Director General addressed the issues of environmental protection and radioactive waste, as well as nuclear non-proliferation (see PART ONE, Chapter II) and IAEA's nuclear safeguards system, including inspection missions in Iraq and verification activities in the Democratic People's Republic of Korea (see PART TWO, Chapter III).

Nuclear techniques had much to contribute to the objective of sustainable development as outlined in Agenda 21, adopted by UNCED in 1992.[8] IAEA, as the central intergovernmental mechanism in the nuclear sphere, could play an important role in that regard, and not only in the areas of safe generation of energy and safe disposal of radioactive waste. It could facilitate the transfer of nuclear techniques to promote health, to ensure greater availability of fresh water and to secure data on the atmosphere and the seas. The IAEA laboratories helped institutes in Africa to use nuclear techniques for conducting element analysis in air, water, soil and biological samples, and helped marine laboratories in developing countries by providing expertise and training.

Agenda 21 had called for the design and implementation of environmentally sound energy strategies, which was not an easy task as all forms of energy generation entailed some risks. A mix of energy sources was needed to minimize those risks. IAEA was engaged, along with other organizations, in obtaining data about the implications of different energy policy scenarios, including the assessment of the potential of nuclear power for mitigating greenhouse emissions.

IAEA's efforts to develop not only recommendations but legally binding safety standards for nuclear powerplants continued, and there was a consensus about the structure and main content of a

nuclear safety convention, the scope of which would be limited to civil nuclear-power reactors.

On 1 November, the General Assembly, by recorded vote, adopted **resolution 48/14**.

Report of the International Atomic Energy Agency
The General Assembly,
Having received the report of the International Atomic Energy Agency to the General Assembly for the year 1992,
Noting the statement of the Director General of the International Atomic Energy Agency of 1 November 1993, in which he provided additional information on the main developments in the activities of the Agency during 1993,
Recognizing the importance of the work of the Agency in promoting the further application of nuclear energy for peaceful purposes, as envisaged in its statute,
Also recognizing the special needs of the developing countries for technical assistance from the Agency in order to benefit effectively from the application of nuclear technology for peaceful purposes as well as from the contribution of nuclear energy to their economic development,
Conscious of the importance of the work of the Agency in the implementation of the safeguards provisions of the Treaty on the Non-Proliferation of Nuclear Weapons and other international treaties, conventions and agreements designed to achieve similar objectives, as well as in ensuring, as far as it is able, that the assistance provided by the Agency or at its request or under its supervision or control is not used in such a way as to further any military purpose, as stated in article II of its statute,
Further recognizing the importance of the work of the Agency on nuclear power, applications of nuclear methods and techniques, nuclear safety, radiological protection and radioactive waste management, including its work directed towards assisting developing countries in all these fields,
Again stressing the need for the highest standards of safety in the design and operation of nuclear plants so as to minimize risks to life, health and the environment,
Noting the statements and actions of the Agency concerning non-compliance by Iraq with its non-proliferation obligations,
Taking note of resolutions GOV/2636 of 25 February 1993, GOV/2639 of 18 March 1993, GOV/2645 of 1 April 1993 and GOV/2692 of 23 September 1993 of the Board of Governors of the International Atomic Energy Agency in connection with the implementation of the agreement between the Agency and the Democratic People's Republic of Korea for the application of safeguards in connection with the Treaty on the Non-Proliferation of Nuclear Weapons, as well as Security Council resolution 825(1993) of 11 May 1993, and expressing its grave concern that the Democratic People's Republic of Korea has failed to discharge its safeguards obligations and has recently widened the area of non-compliance,
Bearing in mind resolutions GC(XXXVII)/RES/614 on measures to resolve international radioactive waste management issues, GC(XXXVII)/RES/615 on strengthening nuclear safety through the early conclusion of

a nuclear safety convention, GC(XXXVII)/RES/616 on practical utilization of food irradiation in developing countries, GC(XXXVII)/RES/617 on a plan for producing potable water economically, GC(XXXVII)/RES/618 on the strengthening of the Agency's main activities, GC(XXXVII)/RES/619 on strengthening the effectiveness and improving the efficiency of the safeguards system, GC(XXXVII)/RES/624 on the implementation of the agreement between the Agency and the Democratic People's Republic of Korea for the application of safeguards in connection with the Treaty on the Non-Proliferation of Nuclear Weapons, GC(XXXVII)/RES/625 on a nuclear-weapon-free zone in Africa, GC(XXXVII)/RES/626 on the implementation of Security Council resolutions 687(1991), 707(1991) and 715(1991) relating to Iraq and GC(XXXVII)/RES/627 on application of Agency safeguards in the Middle East, adopted on 1 October 1993 by the General Conference of the Agency at its thirty-seventh regular session,

1. *Takes note* of the report of the International Atomic Energy Agency;

2. *Affirms its confidence* in the role of the Agency in the application of nuclear energy for peaceful purposes;

3. *Welcomes* the reappointment of Mr. Hans Blix as Director General of the Agency;

4. *Urges* all States to strive for effective and harmonious international cooperation in carrying out the work of the Agency, pursuant to its statute; in promoting the use of nuclear energy and the application of the necessary measures to strengthen further the safety of nuclear installations and to minimize risks to life, health and the environment; in strengthening technical assistance and cooperation for developing countries; and in ensuring the effectiveness and efficiency of the safeguards system of the Agency;

5. *Welcomes* the decisions taken by the Agency to strengthen its safeguards system;

6. *Welcomes also* the decisions taken by the Agency to strengthen its technical assistance and cooperation activities;

7. *Commends* the Director General and the secretariat of the Agency for their impartial efforts to implement the safeguards agreement still in force between the Agency and the Democratic People's Republic of Korea, and urges the Democratic People's Republic of Korea to cooperate immediately with the Agency in the full implementation of the safeguards agreement;

8. *Also commends* the Director General of the Agency and his staff for their strenuous efforts in the implementation of Security Council resolutions 687(1991) of 3 April 1991, 707(1991) of 15 August 1991 and 715(1991) of 11 October 1991, and endorses his efforts to put in place the necessary measures for the implementation of the plan for future ongoing monitoring, in accordance with Security Council resolution 715(1991);

9. *Requests* the Secretary-General to transmit to the Director General of the Agency the records of the forty-eighth session of the General Assembly relating to the activities of the Agency.

General Assembly resolution 48/14

1 November 1993   Meeting 46   140-1-9 (recorded vote)

59-nation draft (A/48/L.13 & Corr.1 & Add.1); agenda item 14.
Sponsors: Afghanistan, Albania, Argentina, Armenia, Australia, Belgium, Bhutan, Bulgaria, Canada, Colombia, Costa Rica, Croatia, Czech Republic, Denmark, Dominica, Ecuador, Egypt, Ethiopia, Fiji, Finland, France, Gambia, Germany, Greece, Hungary, Ireland, Israel, Italy, Japan, Latvia, Lesotho,

Liberia, Lithuania, Luxembourg, Marshall Islands, Micronesia, Netherlands, New Zealand, Nicaragua, Nigeria, Norway, Papua New Guinea, Poland, Portugal, Republic of Korea, Romania, Russian Federation, Singapore, Slovakia, Slovenia, Solomon Islands, Spain, Sweden, the former Yugoslav Republic of Macedonia, Turkey, Ukraine, United Kingdom, United States, Venezuela.
Meeting numbers. GA 48th session: plenary 45, 46.

Recorded vote in Assembly as follows:

In favour: Afghanistan, Albania, Algeria, Andorra, Argentina, Armenia, Australia, Austria, Bahamas, Bahrain, Bangladesh, Barbados, Belarus, Belgium, Belize, Benin, Bhutan, Bolivia, Botswana, Brazil, Brunei Darussalam, Bulgaria, Burkina Faso, Cambodia, Cameroon, Canada, Cape Verde, Chad, Chile, Colombia, Congo, Costa Rica, Côte d'Ivoire, Croatia, Cyprus, Czech Republic, Denmark, Djibouti, Dominica, Ecuador, Egypt, Estonia, Ethiopia, Fiji, Finland, France, Germany, Greece, Guatemala, Guinea-Bissau, Guyana, Hungary, Iceland, India, Indonesia, Iran, Ireland, Israel, Italy, Jamaica, Japan, Jordan, Kazakhstan, Kenya, Kuwait, Kyrgyzstan, Lao People's Democratic Republic, Latvia, Lesotho, Libyan Arab Jamahiriya, Liechtenstein, Lithuania, Luxembourg, Madagascar, Malaysia, Maldives, Malta, Marshall Islands, Mauritania, Mauritius, Mexico, Micronesia, Mongolia, Morocco, Myanmar, Namibia, Nepal, Netherlands, New Zealand, Nicaragua, Niger, Nigeria, Norway, Oman, Pakistan, Panama, Papua New Guinea, Paraguay, Peru, Philippines, Poland, Portugal, Qatar, Republic of Korea, Republic of Moldova, Romania, Russian Federation, Rwanda, Samoa, San Marino, Saudi Arabia, Sierra Leone, Singapore, Slovakia, Slovenia, Spain, Sri Lanka, Sudan, Suriname, Swaziland, Sweden, Syrian Arab Republic, Thailand, the former Republic of Macedonia, Togo, Tunisia, Turkey, Uganda, Ukraine, United Arab Emirates, United Kingdom, United Republic of Tanzania, United States, Uruguay, Vanuatu, Venezuela, Yemen, Zaire, Zambia, Zimbabwe.

Against: Democratic People's Republic of Korea.

Abstaining: Angola, China, Cuba, Ghana, Guinea, Iraq, Mali, Senegal, Viet Nam.

REFERENCES

[1]YUN 1992, p. 659, ESC dec. 1992/218, 30 Apr. 1992. [2]E/C.13/1994/4. [3]*Power Generation Options*, Sales No. E.94.II.A.1. [4]*Energy Efficiency in Transportation*, Sales No. E.93.II.A.4. [5]*Trends in Environmental Impact Assessment of Energy Projects*, Sales No. E.94.II.A.6. [6]DP/1994/29. [7]A/48/341. [8]YUN 1992, p. 672.

Cartography

UN Regional Cartographic Conference for the Americas

The Fifth United Nations Regional Cartographic Conference for the Americas was held in New York from 11 to 15 January 1993.[1]

The Conference, noting the importance of technology transfer in the mapping sciences, recommended that the United Nations, together with the international scientific community, convene a small meeting to examine the feasibility of establishing an international advisory group available to developing nations wishing to acquire modern technologies in the mapping sciences. It recognized the need to establish environmental information systems and to bring up to date global, regional and national geographic information for sustainable development, using geographic information system (GIS) technology, and recommended that ways be devised to overcome problems of introducing GIS systems into developing countries.

The Conference recognized the need for the region's smaller nations to develop geographic information systems and recommended that available information on such systems be collected and disseminated through regional seminars. It noted that constraining or impeding the conservation or development communities from acquiring land or geographical data and information was in conflict with the aims and spirit of UNCED. It therefore recommended that Member States make available all publicly funded land and geographical data sets and that self-teaching packages be produced for training in cartography and geo-information.

The Conference also recommended: that developing countries use new technologies, such as aerial triangulation by global positioning systems, image motion compensation aerial survey cameras and digital technology in orthophotography, and that aerial survey specifications be adapted to reflect new technologies; that training and cooperative assistance activities be supported by awarding fellowships to developing-country personnel and by workshops on surveying and mapping; that the United Nations continue to cooperate with scientific and professional organizations in surveying, mapping, GIS and cartography and to select authors for background papers in collaboration with them; and that the United Nations collaborate with all oganizations dealing with issues relating to women in cartography to increase their participation in all fields of cartography.

ECONOMIC AND SOCIAL COUNCIL ACTION

On 12 July, by **decision 1993/225**, the Economic and Social Council took note of the Secretary-General's report on the Fifth Conference,[1] and requested him to implement the Con-

ference's recommendations. It endorsed the Conference's recommendation to convene the Sixth United Nations Regional Cartographic Conference for the Americas during the first half of 1997.

**UN Regional Cartographic
Conference for Asia and the Pacific**

In a note verbale to the Secretary-General,[2] China offered to host the Thirteenth United Nations Regional Cartographic Conference for Asia and the Pacific in Beijing in May 1994.

On 30 July, by **decision 1993/327**, the Economic and Social Council accepted the invitation with gratitude.

Standardization of geographical names

On 12 July, by **decision 1993/226**, the Economic and Social Council took note of the Secretary-General's report on the Sixth (1992) United Nations Conference on the Standardization of Geographical Names.[3] It endorsed the Conference's recommendation to convene the Seventh Conference during the second half of 1997 and accepted the offer of Iran to host it. The Secretary-General was requested to take measures to implement the Conference's other recommendations. The Council approved the statute of the United Nations Group of Experts on Geographical Names, which was annexed to the Secretary-General's report on the Conference.[4]

REFERENCES

[1]E/1993/39. [2]E/1993/11. [3]YUN 1992, p. 662. [4]E/1993/21 & Corr.1.

Chapter VII

Science and technology

In 1993, the United Nations continued its efforts to strengthen the scientific and technological areas of development. As a result of the restructuring of the United Nations in the economic and social fields, programmes in science and technology were integrated within the Department for Policy Coordination and Sustainable Development of the Secretariat and the United Nations Conference on Trade and Development, whose Ad Hoc Working Group on the Interrelationship between Investment and Technology Transfer met twice during the year.

The Commission on Science and Technology for Development, at its first session, considered issues related to scientific and technological capacity-building in developing countries, technology transfer, conversion of military technology for civilian use, application of science and technology for sustainable development and mobilization of financial resources for science and technology. In July, the Economic and Social Council acted on the Commission's recommendations in seven resolutions and two decisions, endorsed by the General Assembly in December (resolution 48/179). In the same resolution, the Assembly reaffirmed the validity of the Vienna Programme of Action on Science and Technology for Development and stressed the need to strengthen the role of the United Nations in those fields.

Science and technology for development

Implementation of the Vienna Programme of Action

General aspects

The 1979 Vienna Programme of Action on Science and Technology for Development[1] continued to be implemented by several United Nations bodies and organizations in 1993. Its main goal, reaffirmed by the General Assembly in 1989 following an end-of-decade review,[2] was to strengthen the scientific and technological capabilities of developing countries as a basis for their social and economic development.

The Secretary-General, in a March report to the Commission on Science and Technology for Development,[3] stated that, although many of the hopes raised in the Vienna Programme of Action remained unfulfilled, the 1992 United Nations Conference on Environment and Development (UNCED)[4] had revitalized the idea of technology cooperation between developed and developing countries and had added the new paradigm of "sustainability" to the agenda of science and technology as a cross-cutting issue to be reflected in the further implementation of the Programme of Action.

Endogenous capacity-building

In a March report[5] to the Commission on Science and Technology for Development, the Secretary-General assessed the effect of United Nations activities related to endogenous capacity-building in science and technology, one of the three major issues of the Vienna Programme of Action. It focused on a pilot programme executed in 10 developing countries since 1986 to assist in establishing appropriate national policies and programmes. The programme included pilot projects in Jordan, Nepal, Thailand and the United Republic of Tanzania and an interregional project in six other countries (see below), as well as inter-agency missions to coordinate and review various science and technology programmes undertaken by the United Nations system. The report recommended that endogenous capacity-building be one of the major guidelines in the development process and a major objective of all long-term projects, and that donors coordinate their efforts at the country level to improve the use of resources and complementarity of programmes. It also recommended that cross-sectoral technological projects be executed through national organizations; that capacity-building projects be incorporated into national plans and programmes; and that greater attention be given to the quality of experts, the supply, maintenance and modernization of equipment, and training.

The Commission also had before it a 1992 review of United Nations operational activities related to the enhancement of national capacity-building in science and technology[6] and reports on the 1992 Meeting of High-level Experts on Science and Technology for Development,[7] on the activities of the Department of Economic and Social Development in science and technology[8] and on improving coordination and cooperation in that field (see below, under "Organizational matters"). It emphasized that endogenous capacity-building should become a key area in its work and that the pilot programme for developing countries should be integrated with sustainable development and made available to other States, including economies in transition.

Report of the Secretary-General. In response to a 1991 General Assembly resolution,[9] the Secretary-General reported in October 1993 on the strengthening of endogenous capacity-building in science and technology in developing countries.[10] The report reviewed the development of world scientific and technological capacities in 1970-1990 and noted that the gap between the developed and developing countries had widened during that period, with the former accounting for 96 per cent of global research and development expenditure and 85.5 per cent of all the research scientists and engineers. Developing countries, under the pressure of economic and social problems, were being forced to abandon their long-term capacity-building plans in science and technology. Massive flows of external cooperation and the role of the international donor community would be critical in building their capabilities in science and technology. That conclusion was also reached at the Conference on the Development and Strengthening of Research Capacity in Developing Countries (The Hague, Netherlands, 2 and 3 September). The Conference agreed that there should be no division in scientific research between the North and the South and called for a global research system.

The report identified components essential for strengthening the process of endogenous capacity-building and described activities under an interregional technical cooperation project on endogenous capacity, which included pilot projects in Cape Verde, Jamaica, Pakistan, Togo, Uganda and Viet Nam. The project, totalling $2.2 million, was financed by Germany through the United Nations Fund for Science and Technology for Development. Its goal was to enhance human and institutional capacity in developing countries to make autonomous decisions on the development, acquisition, deployment and diffusion of technologies; to integrate science and technology into the national development process; and to introduce a cohesive approach to achieve that objective. In 1993, policy dialogues under the project were carried out in Viet Nam (31 March–2 April), Cape Verde (11-14 October) and Uganda (15 and 16 November).

The report outlined possible actions for strengthening capacity-building, including coordination of sources of financing, technology assessment and forecasting, and operational activities of the United Nations. It also provided background information on the International Association of Technology Assessment and Forecasting Institutions—a non-governmental organization established in Bergen, Norway, in July 1993.

GENERAL ASSEMBLY ACTION

On 21 December, the General Assembly, on the recommendation of the Second (Economic and Financial) Committee, adopted **resolution 48/179** without vote.

Science and technology for development

The General Assembly,

Reaffirming the continuing validity of the Vienna Programme of Action on Science and Technology for Development, adopted by the United Nations Conference on Science and Technology for Development, which the General Asssembly endorsed in its resolution 34/218 of 19 December 1979 and subsequently reaffirmed in its resolution 44/14 A of 26 October 1989,

Recalling the Declaration on International Economic Cooperation, in particular the Revitalization of Economic Growth and Development of the Developing Countries, the International Development Strategy for the Fourth United Nations Development Decade, the Cartagena Commitment, adopted by the United Nations Conference on Trade and Development at its eighth session, the recommendations and decisions adopted by the United Nations Conference on Environment and Development, particularly those contained in Agenda 21, General Assembly resolution 46/165 of 19 December 1991, and other resolutions and decisions adopted by the organizations and bodies of the United Nations system concerning science and technology for development,

Recognizing, in the context of relevant measures to restructure the Secretariat and of General Assembly resolution 47/212 of 23 December 1992, the role of the United Nations Conference on Trade and Development in this respect,

Bearing in mind the vital contribution of science and technology, including new and emerging technologies, to the reactivation of economic growth and development of the developing countries and their efforts to achieve the objectives set forth by the United Nations Conference on Environment and Development,

Reaffirming that capacity-building in science and technology for development in the developing countries should remain one of the priority issues on the agenda of the United Nations,

Recognizing also that the United Nations should play a central role in the enhancement of support and assistance to the developing countries in their efforts to build their endogenous capacity in science and technology,

Recalling the need to promote, facilitate and finance, as appropriate, access to and the transfer of environmentally sound technologies and corresponding know-how, in particular to the developing countries, on favourable terms, including on concessional and preferential terms, as mutually agreed, taking into account the need to protect intellectual property rights as well as the special needs of the developing countries for the implementation of Agenda 21,

Stressing the need for developed countries and international organizations to continue to support the efforts of developing countries to create and develop endogenous scientific and technological capabilities,

Taking note of the report of the Secretary-General on ways and means of strengthening endogenous capacity-building in science and technology in the developing countries,

1. *Endorses* the relevant resolutions and decisions adopted by the Economic and Social Council at its substantive session of 1993 on the basis of the report of the Commission on Science and Technology for Development on its first session, including the recommendation that the Council, at its organizational session for 1994, include science and technology for development as a priority subject to be considered for the coordination segment of the Council in 1994;

2. *Stresses* that endogenous capacity-building in science and technology in the developing countries is indispensable to their efforts to mobilize indigenous resources for science and technology for development;

3. *Emphasizes* the vital role of the United Nations in supporting the developing countries in endogenous capacity-building in the field of science and technology;

4. *Urges* that national efforts and international development cooperation, in particular through supportive financial and technical assistance from donor Governments, multilateral lending institutions and international agencies, be intensified and strengthened towards endogenous capacity-building in science and technology in the developing countries;

5. *Welcomes* the initiative for a consultative meeting to consider ways and means for organizing a more effective coalition of resources to meet the scientific and technological needs of the developing countries, and requests the Secretary-General to make provisions for convening such a meeting, within existing resources, as soon as possible;

6. *Requests* the Secretary-General to take all necessary measures to ensure the full implementation of programme 17, science and technology for development, of the medium-term plan for the period 1992-1997 and the activities planned for the biennium 1994-1995 in the field of science and technology for development, in accordance with the specific mandates provided for in relevant General Assembly resolutions;

7. *Stresses* the urgent need to strengthen the vital role of the United Nations in the field of science and technology, particularly through better coordination, including in the fields of technology assessment, monitoring and forecasting;

8. *Calls upon* the Commission on Science and Technology for Development and the Commission on Sustainable Development to interact effectively, through the Economic and Social Council, in carrying out their respective mandates;

9. *Recognizes* the importance of cooperation among the developing countries in the field of science and technology, building on their comparative advantages and complementarities, and urges the organizations and bodies of the United Nations system and other relevant international, regional or subregional organizations and programmes to provide continued and enhanced support, through technical assistance and financing, as appropriate, for such efforts;

10. *Recognizes also* the potentially important role of the United Nations Fund for Science and Technology for Development in enhancing endogenous capacity-building in science and technology in the developing countries, and calls upon all countries in a position to do so to contribute generously to the Fund;

11. *Requests* the Secretary-General to submit a report to the General Assembly at its fiftieth session on progress in the implementation of the present resolution, as well as on ways and means of reinvigorating the Fund and ensuring its effective operation.

General Assembly resolution 48/179

21 December 1993   Meeting 86   Adopted without vote

Approved by Second Committee (A/48/717/Add.9) without vote, 10 December (meeting 47); draft by Vice-Chairman (A/C.2/48/L.77), based on informal consultations on draft by China and Colombia (for Group of 77) (A/C.2/48/L.16) and orally amended by China; agenda item 91 *(h)*.
Meeting numbers. GA 48th session: 2nd Committee 8, 9, 15-17, 20, 30-32, 34, 36-40, 43-45, 47; plenary 86.

Strengthening technological capacity in developing countries

Activities of the United Nations system

The Commission on Science and Technology for Development, at its first session (New York, 12-23 April),[11] considered as its substantive theme the contribution of technologies, including new and emerging ones, to the industrialization of developing countries and to the strengthening of regional and global integration processes, including proposals for transferring such technologies and incorporating them in the productive sector of those countries.

The Commission had before it a report of the Secretary-General on the contribution of technology to industrialization and regional and global integration.[12] The report reviewed the impact of global technological and managerial transformations on the developing countries' economies and the extent to which regional and global economic integration could contribute to their technological modernization and economic performance. It emphasized the need to integrate science and technology policies in developing countries so as to upgrade their scientific and technological base and strengthen the linkages between national research and development and private firms. It also underscored the new conditions for regional economic integration, resulting from the globalization of research and development and inter-firm collaborative agreements.

The Commission also took note of a 1991 report[13] of the Director-General for Development and International Economic Cooperation on new developments and trends in the activities of the United Nations in science and technology for development.

The Commission concluded that it should serve as a global framework for the assessment of scientific and technological advancement and of its impact on developing countries and economies in transition. It should review and reassess the new and emerging technologies which would affect development in those countries, particularly in the areas of international competitiveness, sustainable development and employment trends. It should also disseminate the knowledge and experience of the technologically developed countries and encourage regional and global integration through science and technology. Institutional mechanisms should be established to implement technological cooperation projects.

In other activities, DESD convened, in cooperation with the United Nations Educational, Scientific and Cultural Organization, an expert group meeting on technology assessment, monitoring and forecasting (Paris, 25-28 January), which examined the methodological issues of introducing technology assessment in developing countries. It discussed economic, social and environmental impact assessment methodologies and practices and the major factors likely to foster technology assessment in the government and private sectors. It specified the role a technology assessment focal point could play within the United Nations system.

ECONOMIC AND SOCIAL COUNCIL ACTION

On 30 July, the Economic and Social Council, on the recommendation of its Economic Committee, adopted **resolution 1993/69** without vote.

Contribution of technologies, including new and emerging technologies, to the industrialization of developing countries and the strengthening of regional and global integration processes, and proposed ways and means of transferring such technologies and incorporating them into the productive sector of those countries

The Economic and Social Council,

Taking note with appreciation of the report of the Secretary-General on the contribution of technology to industrialization and regional and global integration,

Recognizing that appropriate action at the subregional, regional, interregional and international levels can considerably broaden the scope for equitable, sustainable and efficient industrial development at the national level,

Considering that ongoing globalization trends define new modalities of international specialization, to which developing countries and economies in transition must respond,

Bearing in mind the fruitful experience gained from innovative approaches to technological cooperation at the regional and subregional levels,

Emphasizing that priority attention must be given to support activities at the national level, as the basis both for national development and for cooperation at the subregional, regional and interregional levels,

Considering the contribution of technologies, including new and emerging ones, to the industrialization of developing countries and the strengthening of regional and global integration processes,

Pursuing its mandate of promoting and catalysing international cooperation in the field of science and technology for development, in particular in developing countries, and in helping to solve global scientific and technological problems,

Bearing in mind the theme and contents of Agenda 21, in particular paragraphs 31.2, 34.13 and 35.3 thereof,

Taking into account General Assembly resolutions 46/165 of 19 December 1991 and 47/153 of 18 December 1992,

Recognizing the strong interest expressed by the Commission on Science and Technology for Development in enhancing the linkages between research and development activities and the productive sector, and the related policy measures,

Taking note with appreciation of the report of the Director-General for Development and International Economic Cooperation on new developments and trends in the programmes and activities of the United Nations system in science and technology for development,

1. *Decides* to form an ad hoc panel of experts from the members of the Commission on Science and Technology for Development, aided by the relevant organs, organizations and bodies of the United Nations system, to study in depth the various issues related to the substantive theme and the report of the Secretary-General so as to formulate recommendations for consideration by the Commission at its second session, under an agenda item entitled "Action arising from the first session", concentrating on the following issues:

(a) Policies and mechanisms for promoting linkages among national, subregional, regional and global science and technology systems and between those science and technology systems and the industrial sector of developing countries;

(b) The development of internal linkages within the United Nations system for effective coordination of the work dealing with the promotion of sustainable industrial development;

(c) Past, present and future trends in science and technology, including the transfer of technology, and their implications for the sustainable industrial development of developing countries;

(d) Strategies for using science and technology in promoting exports in selected sectors;

2. *Requests* the Secretary-General of the United Nations Conference on Trade and Development to submit to the Commission on Science and Technology for Development at its second session a report on the results obtained from the work of the Ad Hoc Working Group on the Interrelationship between Investment and Technology Transfer;

3. *Requests* the relevant organs, organizations and bodies of the United Nations system, in particular the United Nations Industrial Development Organization, the International Labour Organisation and the Food and Agriculture Organization of the United Nations, to update the section of the report of the Secretary-General concerning the problems and policy measures related to promoting effective linkages between research and development and the productive sector, with particular attention to the new developments and approach being effected in support of Agenda 21, and with an indication of any major new opportunities open for international cooperation in this matter; the updated section

will be included in the report of the Secretary-General on the coordination of United Nations activities in science and technology, to be submitted to the Economic and Social Council at its substantive session of 1994.

Economic and Social Council resolution 1993/69

30 July 1993   Meeting 46   Adopted without vote

Approved by Economic Committee (E/1993/110) without vote, 26 July (meeting 15); draft by Commission on Science and Technology for Development (E/1993/31); agenda item 15 (c).

UNCTAD activities. The United Nations Conference on Trade and Development (UNCTAD) conducted various activities to strengthen the technological capacity of developing countries. Under its project on endogenous capacity-building, policy dialogues were carried out in Cape Verde, Uganda and Viet Nam. It organized a seminar on the strengthening of national technological capabilities (Bujumbura, Burundi, 24-26 February), which identified problems and suggested measures for establishing closer links between research institutions and enterprises in the productive sector. It also discussed institutional arrangements, incentives, research and development projects design and financing, human resources development and international cooperation. A workshop was held prior to the seminar on the legal aspects of the transfer of technology, in particular contractual arrangements for the acquisition of technology. Other activities included a workshop on recent trends in promoting innovativeness and technology transfer (Bangkok, Thailand, 21-24 September), which focused on policies and instruments for the creation, transfer, adaptation and absorption of technology, with particular reference to the role of intellectual property protection. Several publications were also issued on industry and case-studies on technology transfer and development.

UNCTAD had three ongoing new information technology programmes, designed to improve transit systems. They were: the Advance Cargo Information System, providing information on movements of cargo and transport equipment, which was being implemented in several African countries; the Automated System for Customs Data and Management for modernizing and streamlining customs administrations and their operational procedures, which was being implemented in 51 countries; and the Trade Point Programme, designed to set up trade facilitation centres for foreign trade transactions.

UNCTAD also completed a study on research and development collaboration agreements among enterprises.

ECONOMIC AND SOCIAL COUNCIL ACTION

On 30 July, the Council, on the recommendation of its Economic Committee, adopted **resolution 1993/71** without vote.

Activities of the United Nations system in science and technology for development

The Economic and Social Council,

Having considered the reports of the Secretary-General on ways and means of improving the quality of coordination and cooperation in science and technology for development, the assessment of the effect of activities of the United Nations system related to the process of creating and strengthening endogenous capacity-building in science and technology in developing countries, and the activities of the Department of Economic and Social Development of the Secretariat in science and technology for development, the report of the Meeting of High-level Experts on Science and Technology for Development and the note by the Secretariat on the Expert Group Meeting on Technology Assessment, Monitoring and Forecasting,

Taking note of General Assembly resolution 47/199 of 22 December 1992, in particular paragraph 20 thereof,

Having examined the note by the Secretary-General on the comprehensive policy review of operational activities of the United Nations system as a means of examining the contribution of the operational activities of the United Nations system to the enhancement of the national capacities of developing countries in the field of science and technology,

1. *Recommends* that the Economic and Social Council, at its organizational session for 1994, include science and technology for development as a priority subject to be considered at the coordination segment of the Economic and Social Council in 1994;

2. *Requests* the Secretary-General to prepare, for that purpose, a report containing an analysis of and action-oriented proposals to improve the coordination mechanisms of organs, programmes and specialized agencies, including the World Bank, which are involved in the science and technology activities of the United Nations system; the report should take into account the implications of the recent reforms of the Secretariat, as well as ways and means of improving the coordination of the United Nations system with other relevant intergovernmental institutions and private organizations involved in science and technology activities;

3. *Considers* the note by the Secretary-General on the comprehensive policy review of operational activities of the United Nations system a valuable input to the consideration of science and technology activities at the coordination segment of its substantive session of 1994;

4. *Requests* the Commission on Science and Technology for Development to consider, at its second session, the outcome of the coordination segment of the substantive session of the Council of 1994;

5. *Stresses* that endogenous capacity-building in science and technology is an indispensable component of any country's effort to mobilize science and technology for development and that it should hence remain a priority issue on the United Nations agenda;

6. *Requests* the Secretary-General to inform the Commission on Science and Technology for Development at its biennial sessions of the progress being achieved and any major problems encountered in the application of science and technology for sustainable development at the national, subregional and regional levels, with a view to identifying new options for international action;

7. *Expresses its approval* of the activities undertaken so far by the United Nations system to assist the develop-

ing countries in enhancing their national capacities in the field of science and technology;

8. *Expresses its approval* of the innovative features of the series of ten pilot projects being undertaken by the United Nations system to develop endogenous capacity, such as the participatory approach, demand-driven and developmental orientation and country-level coordination, and requests that those projects be completed and evaluated, with a view to disseminating information on their successful features;

9. *Invites* the United Nations Development Programme, the World Bank, the regional development banks and other multilateral and bilateral cooperation agencies to give priority to endogenous capacity-building in their respective projects on science and technology for development and to integrate appropriate participatory approaches into the planning and evaluation cycles of their projects;

10. *Stresses* the need for national policies in support of science and technology communities in order to enhance information-management capacity and to facilitate affordable and widespread access to international on-line science and technology information networks and their connectivity to global and regional networks in all countries, and the need to make them available to all countries through on-line access, floppy disks, and other electronic and traditional means;

11. *Urges* organizations of the United Nations system and their collaborating institutions to coordinate their activities aimed at information management, including the upgrading and updating of their databases in the field of science and technology;

12. *Calls upon* all Governments to promote further harmonized and coherent approaches to and policies on science and technology for development at the national level and to reflect such harmonized approaches in their multilateral activities throughout the United Nations system;

13. *Invites* the Commission on Science and Technology for Development to develop an appropriate, dynamic mechanism for its interaction with intergovernmental organizations that are not part of the United Nations system, as well as with non-governmental organizations, institutions, foundations and the private sector concerned with science and technology for development and wishing to make common cause with the Commission;

14. *Also invites* the organs, organizations and bodies of the United Nations system, in their activities related to science and technology, to take full advantage of the potential contribution of relevant intergovernmental organizations outside the United Nations system and of non-governmental organizations;

15. *Welcomes*, in this connection, such initiatives as that of the Third World Academy of Sciences in establishing regional centres for the application of science and technology for sustainable development in the developing countries, and urges donor agencies and Member States to support such initiatives.

Economic and Social Council resolution 1993/71

30 July 1993   Meeting 46   Adopted without vote

Approved by Economic Committee (E/1993/110) without vote, 26 July (meeting 15); draft by Commission on Science and Technology for Development (E/1993/31), orally amended following informal consultations; agenda item 15 *(c)*.

Science for sustainable development

In March 1993,[14] the Secretary-General submitted to the Commission a report on implications arising from Agenda 21, adopted by UNCED,[4] for the Commission's work.

The Secretary-General identified the four areas of activities in science and technology which fell under Agenda 21 as technology transfer and cooperation, endogenous capacity-building, technology assessment in support of the effective management of technologies, and science for sustainable development. He suggested that assistance to Member States in those areas should focus on formulating policies and programmes to facilitate access to and transfer of environmentally sound technologies; building national consensus on the use of science and technology options most suitable to countries' needs and developing appropriate decision-making mechanisms; strengthening the international network of regional and national technology assessment institutions and building technology assessment capabilities, including environmental risk assessment; and improving Member States' capacities to generate scientific knowledge and technical know-how in the areas of environment and development.

The Commission also considered a report on the transfer of environmentally sound technologies (see below, under "Technology transfer") and proposals by Austria for university cooperation for sustainable development.[15] It requested the Secretariat to examine further the relationship between science and technology and sustainable development, as well as modalities for effective interaction with the Commission on Sustainable Development (see PART THREE, Chapter I).

Commission action. The Commission[16] emphasized the role of the educational sector for science and technology transfer and encouraged Member States to adopt measures promoting: educational cooperation with industrial enterprises; establishment of regional training and research centres in developing countries and economies in transition; South-South university scholarship programmes and North-South university partnerships and networks; and equitable access of all people to science and technology education and information. It requested the Secretary-General to study and report on strengthening United Nations activities in science and technology through educational measures; to review the United Nations science and technology information networks; and to explore the feasibility of providing developing countries and economies in transition with access to international scientific data networks, with a view to creating a global means of scientific communication and information transmission. The Commission also recommended that the Economic and Social Council invite relevant United Nations bodies to consider ways of harnessing resources to enhance science, technology and research capacity-building in developing countries and economies in transition.

ECONOMIC AND SOCIAL COUNCIL ACTION

On 30 July, the Council, on the recommendation of its Economic Committee, adopted **resolution 1993/72** without vote.

Science and technology for sustainable development
The Economic and Social Council,

Taking note of General Assembly resolution 47/191 of 22 December 1992 on institutional arrangements to follow up the United Nations Conference on Environment and Development,

Emphasizing the importance of effective interaction between the Commission on Science and Technology for Development and the Commission on Sustainable Development,

1. *Takes note* of the following documentation considered by the Commission on Science and Technology for Development at its first session under the agenda item entitled "Science and technology for sustainable development":

(*a*) Note by the Secretary-General on the implications of the outcome of the United Nations Conference on Environment and Development, including Agenda 21, for the work of the Commission on Science and Technology for Development;

(*b*) Report of the Secretary-General on the utilization and marketing of energy technologies, focusing on policy issues and options for the effective transfer and application of environmentally sound energy technologies;

2. *Stresses* the critical importance of supporting countries, in particular the developing countries, in harnessing the potential of science and technology, with a view to achieving the objectives set forth by the United Nations Conference on Environment and Development;

3. *Emphasizes*, in this respect, the relevance of the activities of the United Nations system in the areas of science and technology, particularly in endogenous capacity-building, including the improvement of traditional technologies, as well as aspects related to technology transfer, technology assessment and forecasting, science and technology information dissemination and management, and science for sustainable development;

4. *Decides* that the Commission on Science and Technology for Development should place particular emphasis in its work on policy issues and options related to the development, transfer and utilization of technologies that promote sustainable development objectives, in accordance with the mandate of the Commission and taking into account the provisions of Agenda 21 concerning science and technology;

5. *Supports* the activities of the United Nations system and the international cooperation aimed, taking into account the elements of chapter V.B of the report of the Commission on Science and Technology for Development on its first session, at promoting the use of the following:

(*a*) New and renewable sources of energy technologies;

(*b*) Clean coal, fossil fuels and other energy technologies;

(*c*) Alternative fuel technologies;

6. *Encourages* bilateral and multilateral donors to provide further support for the development, transfer and application of environmentally sound technologies;

7. *Calls upon* the Commission on Sustainable Development to interact closely with the Commission on Science and Technology for Development and to take advantage of its work while reviewing the implementation of Agenda 21;

8. *Requests* the Secretary-General to ensure that information on those aspects of the work of the Commission on Sustainable Development that have a bearing on the work of the Commission on Science and Technology for Development is distributed to members of the latter Commission and that the work of the two Commissions is coordinated effectively.

Economic and Social Council resolution 1993/72

30 July 1993   Meeting 46   Adopted without vote

Approved by Economic Committee (E/1993/110) without vote, 26 July (meeting 15); draft by Commission on Science and Technology for Development (E/1993/31), orally amended following informal consultations; agenda item 15 (c).

Conversion of military technologies

On 30 July, the Economic and Social Council, on the recommendation of its Economic Committee, adopted **resolution 1993/70** without vote.

Scientific and technological aspects of the conversion of military capacity for civilian use and sustainable development
The Economic and Social Council,

Recalling principle 25 of the Rio Declaration on Environment and Development, adopted by the United Nations Conference on Environment and Development, which states that peace, development and environmental protection are interdependent and indivisible,

Recalling also General Assembly resolution 46/36 C of 6 December 1991, in which the Assembly stressed the growing importance of the relationship between disarmament and development in current international relations, and Assembly resolution 46/36 B of 6 December 1991, in which the Assembly recalled the report of the Secretary-General transmitting the study on charting potential uses of resources allocated to military activities for civilian endeavours to protect the environment,

Stressing that science and technology could contribute greatly to the elaboration of a strategy for the conversion of military technologies for civilian use, sustainable development and environmental protection, affecting the most fundamental interests of all Member States,

Recalling General Assembly resolution 44/14 E of 26 October 1989, in which the Assembly decided, *inter alia*, to entrust the Centre for Science and Technology for Development of the Secretariat to serve as the focal point for technological assessment within the United Nations system and, where possible, for relations with Governments and non-governmental organizations concerning technological assessment activities in Member States, and Assembly resolution 46/165 of 19 December 1991, in which the Assembly reaffirmed the role of the Centre,

Noting the deliberations at the recent United Nations conferences held at Beijing from 22 to 26 October 1991, at Dortmund, Germany, from 24 to 27 February 1992 and in Moscow from 12 to 17 October 1992 on the scientific and technological aspects of the conversion of military capacity, as well as the activities of the United Nations system in this field, in particular those of the United Nations Industrial Development Organization and the United Nations Conference on Trade and Development,

1. *Reaffirms* that, in the era of global concern for the environment and in the new political climate, the conversion of military technologies for civilian use and sustainable development should receive increased international attention, with the appropriate support and involvement of the United Nations;

2. *Requests* the Secretary-General to submit to the Commission on Science and Technology for Development at its second session a report on the scientific and technological aspects of the conversion of military capacity for civilian use and sustainable development, with a focus on technology assessment issues, particularly the economic effects, employment implications and environmental consequences of alternative technological choices;

3. *Requests* the Secretary-General to elaborate that report by drawing from the United Nations conferences and other United Nations activities referred to in the fifth preambular paragraph above, particularly those of the United Nations Conference on Trade and Development in the Ad Hoc Working Group on the Interrelationship between Investment and Technology Transfer, and to explore the issue of strengthening agreement on the transition to disarmament.

Economic and Social Council resolution 1993/70

30 July 1993   Meeting 46   Adopted without vote

Approved by Economic Committee (E/1993/110) without vote, 26 July (meeting 15); draft by Commission on Science and Technology for Development (E/1993/31); agenda item 15 (c).

Financial resources for science and technology

In March, the Secretary-General reported to the Commission on the organization of a coalition of resources to finance science and technology for development.[17] The report reviewed the existing experience of mobilizing financial resources and outlined a concept for organizing a coalition and proposals for action. According to the report, such a coalition should be based on programmes oriented to attract potential donors and should focus on coordination and policy coherence and not on the establishment of a new funding body. It should emphasize qualitative additionality, with clearly defined programme coverage centring on endogenous capacity-building. It should give priority to programmes resulting from dialogues among participants in the development process and provide for maximum flexibility and diversity in their approaches.

The Secretary-General examined alternative models for resource mobilization, including an inter-institutional mechanism for information exchange and policy coherence, to facilitate coordination and assist in developing guidelines, or

the creation of an international association or council for science and technology, to mobilize resources and allocate funds to specific capacity-building projects. The report outlined the structure, functions and mode of operation of the second alternative.

On 30 July, the Economic and Social Council, on the recommendation of its Economic Committee, adopted **resolution 1993/73** without vote.

Financing science and technology for development
The Economic and Social Council,

Acknowledging the significant role of the United Nations in the field of science and technology for development,

Recognizing that there is a need to harmonize the efforts of different sources of funding for science and technology for development,

Recognizing also that the increasing need for cooperation in programmes of endogenous capacity-building requires adequate financial support,

Taking note of General Assembly resolution 47/190 of 22 December 1992, in which the Assembly called upon all concerned to implement all commitments, agreements and recommendations reached at the United Nations Conference on Environment and Development, especially by ensuring provision of the means of implementation,

Taking note also of the report of the Secretary-General on the organization of a coalition of resources to finance science and technology for development, submitted to the Commission on Science and Technology for Development at its first session,

1. *Decides* to maintain as a priority its efforts to enable developing countries to address their needs for funds and cooperation to enhance the input of science and technology into their development programmes and to build up an endogenous capacity on the basis of the priorities and plans of developing countries; due attention should be paid in this regard to the needs of the countries with economies in transition, in accordance with the relevant mandates of the General Assembly;

2. *Requests* the Secretary-General, in pursuance of General Assembly resolution 46/165 of 19 December 1991, in which the Assembly requested concrete proposals for organizing a more effective coalition of resources to meet the scientific and technological needs of developing countries, to convene a consultative meeting in 1993;

3. *Decides* that the consultative meeting shall:

(a) Compare and exchange views on portfolios of programmes and projects in science and technology in support of endogenous capacity-building at the national, regional and global levels;

(b) Consider ways and means of securing continual interaction and complementarity of the institutions involved in the financing of science and technology and suggest specific ways in which such cooperation could continue for the harmonization of their policies and the enhancement of specific opportunities for a coalition of resources among the interested financing and funding institutions;

4. *Also decides* that the participants in the consultative meeting should include representatives from multilateral development financial institutions, including the United Nations Development Programme, the World Bank and the regional development banks, together with private and international foundations and bilateral donors interested in science and technology for development;

5. *Requests* the Administrator of the United Nations Development Programme to consider providing the consultative meeting with a review of the United Nations Fund for Science and Technology for Development aimed at redefining its role in this context;

6. *Requests* the Secretary-General to submit to the Economic and Social Council at its substantive session of 1994 a report on the implementation of the present resolution.

Economic and Social Council resolution 1993/73

30 July 1993　　　　Meeting 46　　　　Adopted without vote

Approved by Economic Committee (E/1993/110) without vote, 26 July (meeting 15); draft by Commission on Science and Technology for Development (E/1993/31), orally amended following informal consultations; agenda item 15 *(c)*.

Financial implications. S-G, E/1993/31/Add.1.

The consultative meeting requested by the Council was subsequently postponed until 1994.

UN Fund for Science and Technology for Development

During 1993, the United Nations Fund for Science and Technology for Development, including the Energy Account of the United Nations Development Programme (UNDP), received an estimated $1.04 million in resources from voluntary and cost-sharing contributions and from interest and other income. A total of $7.83 million was carried over from 1992. During the year, the Fund's expenditure amounted to $2.94 million, leaving a balance of $6.93 million, less $5.44 million in unspent project allocations.

The endogenous capacity-building programme in science and technology accelerated with the organization of a second group of policy dialogues in Cape Verde, Jamaica, Pakistan, Uganda and Viet Nam. The Fund complemented that programme with new projects on management of technology and technology assessment, both addressing the needs of the middle-income and least developed countries (LDCs) in Asia. Its programme of assistance in establishing technology business incubators, implemented in some 14 countries, produced 50 operational incubators, mostly in China. The Science and Technology Referral Services for Journalists, designed to improve the quality of media reporting in science and technology, was extended, and included Malaysia, the Philippines and Sri Lanka. The Fund completed the establishment of a computerized data bank for mineral resources in Mongolia and a quality control project for heavy industry in Latin America, as well as a project to set national standards for quality control in China. More than 800 scientific instruments were repaired under a repair and maintenance project in southern Africa, which evolved into a broader programme covering West Africa and South Asia. Activities dealing with transfer of knowledge through expatriate nationals were also expanded to include 39 countries.

Poverty alleviation was also addressed by the programme on financing energy services for small-scale energy-users, which targeted the rural poor and placed emphasis on new and renewable sources of energy and energy conservation.

REFERENCES
[1]YUN 1979, p. 636. [2]GA res. 44/14 A, 26 Oct. 1989. [3]E/CN.16/1993/5. [4]YUN 1992, p. 670. [5]E/CN.16/1993/4. [6]YUN 1992, p. 666. [7]Ibid., p. 664. [8]Ibid., p. 668. [9]YUN 1991, p. 482, GA res. 46/165, 19 Dec. 1991. [10]A/48/465. [11]E/1993/31. [12]E/CN.16/1993/2. [13]A/CN.11/1991/5. [14]E/CN.16/1993/8. [15]E/CN.16/1993/11. [16]E/1993/31 (res. 1/1). [17]E/CN.16/1993/10.

Technology transfer

During the year, activities in the field of technology transfer were geared towards the implementation of relevant provisions of the Cartagena Commitment, adopted in 1992 by the eighth session of UNCTAD (UNCTAD VIII).[1]

The Ad Hoc Working Group on the Interrelationship between Investment and Technology Transfer, established by the UNCTAD Trade and Development Board (TDB) in 1992,[2] held two sessions in 1993. At its first session (Geneva, 25-29 January),[3] the Group adopted its programme of work in the areas of investment flows, transfer of technology and competitiveness; technological capacity-building in developing countries, particularly LDCs, and in economies in transition; and transfer and development of environmentally sound technologies (ESTs).

At its second session (Geneva, 13-17 December),[4] the Group reviewed the work of the United Nations system and a number of intergovernmental, national and non-governmental organizations (NGOs) dealing with investment-related technology issues,[5] and discussed evolving approaches to technology capacity-building and competitiveness.[6] It also considered 14 country case-studies and the report of a workshop on the transfer and development of ESTs (see below).[7]

In March,[8] TDB agreed that the proposal on the study on market-based price mechanisms as a means of assisting technology transfer to developing countries should be further refined. In September,[8] it referred the issue to the Working Group.

By **decision 1993/322** of 30 July, the Economic and Social Council requested the Secretary-General to provide a brief report to the General Assembly in early 1994 on technology transfer activities and coordination mechanisms within the United Nations system.

Transfer of environmentally sound technology

The Secretary-General submitted to the Commission on Science and Technology for Development in March 1993[9] a report on utilization and marketing of energy technologies, focusing on policy issues and options for the effective transfer and application of ESTs. The report recommended that developed countries finance demonstration and development of energy technologies in developing countries and provide them with information on product and service vendors; the developing countries should create better policy environments for investment in energy-efficient goods and services. The report also recommended that developed and developing countries establish joint research and development strategies for the generation, transfer and use of ESTs.

In April, the Commission underscored the need for funding for technology transfer and placed special emphasis on modalities for fostering the development and transfer of clean energy technologies, as well as increasing energy efficiency.

The workshop on the transfer and development of ESTs (Oslo, Norway, 13-15 October),[7] organized by UNCTAD and the Government of Norway, reviewed environment-related technology issues and examined the role of private firms in generating and transferring ESTs and the demand side of the transfer process. It also considered priority elements for an action programme covering technological capacity-building, access to technology, activities relating to the private sector, actions for recipient Governments, finance for the transfer of ESTs, related standards and regulations and their enforcement, and international institutional aspects.

The workshop recommended studies on technology information and assessment; extension of the effectiveness of benchmarking and incorporation of environmental benchmarks into measures to attract foreign direct investment; upgrading of environmental standards and incentives for technological initiatives in the private sector; a multi-donor approach to the provision of environmental services and institutional capacity-building; the selection and transfer of effective measures already introduced in developing countries; and establishment of a financial instrument for addressing local problems with environmental, technological and developmental dimensions.

Action by the Commission on Sustainable Development. In June, the Secretary-General reported to the Commission on Sustainable Development

on the progress achieved in facilitating and promoting the transfer of environmentally sound technology.[10] The report considered trends and issues related to such transfers, initiatives being undertaken by the United Nations, the private sector, Governments and NGOs, and issues concerning the future work of the Commission.

The Commission (New York, 14-25 June)[11] stressed the need to facilitate and finance access to and the transfer of ESTs and know-how, in particular to developing countries, on favourable terms; to promote long-term technological cooperation and partnership between holders and potential users of such technologies; and to improve the endogenous capacities of developing countries to develop, assess, manage and use ESTs through, *inter alia*, research and development, education and training. The Commission urged donors and Governments to increase financial support for the transfer and management of ESTs. It recognized the need to develop methodologies and establish institutions for technology assessment and stressed the importance of strengthening national capacities in the field of new technologies. Governments were urged to promote access to and the transfer of ESTs by developing or modifying appropriate policies and mechanisms, providing incentives for the private sector and supporting the required investment and infrastructure. The Commission recommended strengthening measures promoting information exchange on hazardous technologies and discouraging their transfer, and called on the international community to support technological cooperation and capacity-building among developing countries, as well as their initiatives in the field of environmentally sound technology. It requested the Secretary-General to implement the relevant sections of Agenda 21, including the designation of a focal point for United Nations activities in technology assessment, the collection and dissemination of information on environmental emergencies, and the establishment of a network of national, subregional and regional information systems.

The Commission decided to establish an intersessional ad hoc open-ended working group to review progress in technology transfer and capacity-building, and invited Governments and intergovernmental bodies to provide information on their activities in those areas. Emphasizing the need for effective interaction with intergovernmental bodies, it invited the Economic and Social Council to consider the intergovernmental machinery related to science and technology at the coordination segment of its 1994 substantive session so as to clarify the distribution of labour and cooperation mechanisms.

Draft code of conduct

In response to a 1992 General Assembly request,[12] the UNCTAD Secretary-General submitted in November 1993 a report[13] on consultations carried out in 1993 on an international code of conduct on the transfer of technology. He recalled that UNCTAD VIII had recognized that conditions did not exist to reach full agreement on outstanding issues in the draft code of conduct.

The report stated that the future of the negotiations on the draft code could be influenced by the work of the Ad Hoc Working Group on the Interrelationship between Investment and Technology Transfer. A clearer understanding of the issues being discussed by the Group could contribute to a better perception of the initiatives Governments might wish to take. The UNCTAD Secretary-General therefore proposed to undertake consultations with Governments after completion of the Working Group's activities and to report to the General Assembly on further action to be taken.

GENERAL ASSEMBLY ACTION

On 21 December, the General Assembly, on the recommendation of the Second Committee, adopted **resolution 48/167** without vote.

International code of conduct on the transfer of technology

The General Assembly

1. *Recognizes* that the conditions do not currently exist to reach full agreement on all outstanding issues in the draft international code of conduct on the transfer of technology and also that, should Governments indicate, either directly or through the Secretary-General of the United Nations Conference on Trade and Development reporting in accordance with General Assembly resolution 46/214 of 20 December 1991, that there is the convergence of views necessary to reach agreement on all outstanding issues, then the Trade and Development Board should re-engage and continue its work aimed at facilitating agreement on the code;

2. *Invites* the Secretary-General of the United Nations Conference on Trade and Development, based on the relevant provisions of the Cartagena Commitment and taking into account the findings of the Ad Hoc Working Group on the Interrelationship between Investment and Technology Transfer, to report to the General Assembly at its fiftieth session on the state of the discussion.

General Assembly resolution 48/167

21 December 1993   Meeting 86   Adopted without vote

Approved by Second Committee (A/48/717/Add.2) without vote, 10 December (meeting 47); draft by Chairman (A/C.2/48/L.14/Rev.1); agenda item 91 *(a)*.

Meeting numbers. GA 48th session: 2nd Committee 8, 9, 15-17, 20, 30-32, 36-40, 43-45, 47; plenary 86.

REFERENCES

[1]YUN 1992, p. 612. [2]Ibid., p. 666. [3]TD/B/39(2)/18. [4]TD/B/40(2)/10. [5]TD/B/WG.5/6. [6]TD/B/WG.5/7. [7]*Report of the Workshop on the Transfer and Development of Environmentally Sound Technologies (ESTs)*, Sales No. E.94.II.D.1. [8]A/48/15. [9]E/CN.16/1993/9. [10]E/CN.17/1993/10. [11]E/1993/25/Add.1. [12]YUN 1992, p. 667, GA res. 47/182, 22 Dec. 1992. [13]A/48/533.

Organizational matters

Commission on Science and Technology for Development

The Commission on Science and Technology for Development, established in 1992,[1] held its first session in 1993 (New York, 12-23 April).[2]

The Commission considered as its substantive theme the contribution of technologies to the industrialization of developing countries and the strengthening of regional and global integration processes, including proposals for transferring such technologies and incorporating them in the productive sector of those countries. It also examined United Nations activities in science and technology and matters relating to science and technology for sustainable development, the financing of science and technology for development, the organization of ad hoc panels and workshops on specific science and technology issues, and programme questions. The Commission recommended seven draft resolutions and two decisions for action by the Economic and Social Council and brought to its attention one resolution and one decision.

The Economic and Social Council, by **decision 1993/321** of 30 July, took note of the Commission's report, endorsed the resolution and decision brought to its attention and approved the provisional agenda and documentation for the Commission's second session.

Future work of the Commission

The Commission on Science and Technology for Development suggested criteria for the selection of substantive themes for its future sessions and topics for consideration, including science and technology and women; the conversion of military technology to civilian use; information science and technologies; application of biotechnology to agriculture, health and other areas; ecology; educational technologies for children; linkage between research and development and the production sector; and the role of science and technology in the informal sector. It stressed that the topics chosen should aim at achieving holistic and multidisciplinary approaches and that it should focus on two or three themes at each session. Topics considered by the former Advisory Committee on Science and Technology for Development could be updated and taken into account in the selection of future themes. The Commission felt that its work should be directed towards a clearly defined, specific and pragmatic programme that could be effectively implemented.

Expert panels

In a March report,[3] the Secretary-General recommended that the Commission on Science and

Technology for Development continue the practice established by the former Advisory Committee on Science and Technology for Development of convening ad hoc panels/workshops of experts on specific issues of science and technology. He suggested organizing up to four ad hoc panels each biennium to advise the relevant operational agencies of the United Nations system.

The Commission pointed out that the themes chosen for the ad hoc panels should deal with policy analysis, research and coordination. Among topics proposed for future panels were science and technology for ensuring food security, environmentally sound technology for waste management, science and technology in meeting the basic needs of the population and application of science and technology in improving the productivity of the informal sector. The Commission stressed the importance of obtaining adequate resources and expert advice for its work and of maintaining relationships with other entities within and outside the United Nations system.

On 23 April,[(4)] the Commission took note of the Secretary-General's report.

ECONOMIC AND SOCIAL COUNCIL ACTION

On 30 July, the Economic and Social Council, on the recommendation of its Economic Committee, adopted **resolution 1993/74** without vote.

Future work plan of the Commission on Science and Technology for Development

The Economic and Social Council,

Noting with appreciation the report of the Secretary-General on the organization of ad hoc panels/workshops on specific issues of science and technology for development,

Taking into account the need to focus the work of the Commission on Science and Technology for Development during its two-year inter-sessional periods through the preparation of analytical reports on a limited number of substantive themes,

Recognizing that the opportunity of organizing ad hoc panels or workshops during the inter-sessional period can at least in part be used for deepening the analytical work on the substantive themes chosen for each period, while in the same period ad hoc panels or workshops can still be organized on specific issues of science and technology for development,

Noting the offer of some member States to host such panels or workshops and the offer of one member State to finance a panel on a substantive theme, preferably to be held in a developing country, in order to encourage the new style of work on the substantive themes, thus enabling one extrabudgetary panel to be convened in addition to the four panels or workshops provided for in the regular programme budget,

Considering the desirability of connecting the work of the Commission on Science and Technology for Development with the concrete experiences of member States in the area of science and technology for development and with policies in that area,

Emphasizing, inter alia, the following criteria for choosing substantive themes for the inter-sessional work:

(a) The themes and the work thereon should, whenever possible, be timely and directed at the broad interests of organizations of the United Nations system;

(b) They should serve the mandate of the Commission by making it possible to:

(i) Synthesize relevant issues and insights without conducting extensive new research;

(ii) Provide advice on science and technology policies in the developing countries and facilitate discussion thereon at the national and regional levels;

(iii) Formulate recommendations within the United Nations system;

(c) They should fall within the mandate of the Commission and reflect the comparative advantage of the Commission *vis-à-vis* other United Nations bodies;

(d) They should be of wide interest to end-users, in particular in developing countries, and be relevant to the least developed countries;

1. *Decides* that the following three substantive themes shall be the focus of the work of the Commission on Science and Technology for Development during the inter-sessional period 1993-1995:

(a) Technology for small-scale economic activities to address the basic needs of low-income populations; the theme should be examined by one of the panels of experts, which would build upon relevant studies from inside and outside the United Nations system, including the regional commissions, the United Nations Conference on Trade and Development, the United Nations Industrial Development Organization, the International Labour Organisation, the Food and Agriculture Organization of the United Nations, the World Bank and regional development banks. A diagnosis and action-oriented proposals would be made with regard to the following issues:

(i) Access to and adaptation of technology, and North-South and South-South transfer of technology;

(ii) Effects of productivity;

(iii) Generation of jobs and income to combat poverty by addressing the basic needs (education, health, housing and food) of low-income populations, including issues related to gender and age;

(iv) Dissemination mechanisms, including training, regional and international cooperation and networking, data banks and project banks;

(v) Interrelation with other endogenous capacity-building and research and development activities;

(vi) Finance and monitoring;

(b) The gender implications of science and technology for developing countries; the following topics would be analysed, taking into account cultural and social aspects and the knowledge of indigenous people:

(i) The implications of technological change for employment and skills;

(ii) The health implications of advances in medical knowledge;

(iii) Energy technologies;

(iv) Agricultural technologies;

(v) Science and technology education and entry into the professions.

The work would include an analysis of activities, both within and outside the United Nations system, on these topics and would lead to science and technology recommendations for national Governments and the relevant United Nations bodies;

(c) The science and technology aspects of the sectoral issue to be discussed by the Commission on Sustainable Development in 1995; the purpose is to relate the expertise of the Commission on Science and Technology for Development directly to the work of the Commission on Sustainable Development;

2. *Also decides* to assign responsibility for the intersessional work on each of the substantive themes to a member of the Commission on Science and Technology for Development who would call together a panel of experts with the help of the Secretariat; other members of the Commission would be invited to join the assigned member in that task;

3. *Further decides* to have, in addition to the three panels of members of the Commission on Science and Technology for Development and outside experts, panels of experts or workshops on the following specific issues:

(a) The contribution of technologies, including new and emerging ones, to industrialization in developing countries;

(b) Information technologies and their role in the field of science and technology, in particular in relation to the needs of developing countries; once the relevant issues have been made clear by the panel, this issue might be selected as a substantive theme of the Commission for the inter-sessional period 1995-1997;

4. *Requests* the organs, organizations and bodies of the United Nations system that provide technical cooperation assistance in the field of science and technology to take full advantage of the expertise of the Commission on Science and Technology for Development and its willingness to participate actively in the provision of such technical cooperation.

Economic and Social Council resolution 1993/74

30 July 1993   Meeting 46   Adopted without vote

Approved by Economic Committee (E/1993/110) without vote, 26 July (meeting 15); draft by Commission on Science and Technology for Development (E/1993/31); agenda item 15 *(c)*.

Also on the recommendation of the Economic Committee, the Council adopted **decision 1993/320** without vote.

Preparation of analytical reports by the Commission on Science and Technology for Development

At its 46th plenary meeting, on 30 July 1993, the Economic and Social Council decided that the Commission on Science and Technology for Development should adopt, within existing resources, the procedures for preparing analytical reports contained in the annex to the present decision.

ANNEX
Tasks of the Commission on Science and Technology for Development and preparation of analytical reports by the Commission

1. The tasks of the Commission on Science and Technology for Development include:

(a) Assisting the Economic and Social Council in providing science and technology policy guidelines and recommendations to Member States, in particular developing countries;

(b) Providing innovative approaches to improving the quality of coordination and cooperation within the United Nations system in the area of science and technology, with a view to ensuring optimum mobilization of resources;

(c) Providing expert advice to other parts of the United Nations system.

2. In order to fulfil its tasks, the work of the Commission should include the preparation of reports on a limited number of substantive topics. In preparing those reports the Commission should adopt the following procedures:

(a) The substantive themes for each session of the Commission should be determined by the Commission at its previous session, taking into account the agenda of the General Assembly and other agreed criteria. The Secretary-General will be invited to suggest possible themes after consultation with relevant agencies of the United Nations system;

(b) For each theme chosen, the Commission will establish a panel of its own members having responsibility for preparing a draft report for consideration by the Commission as a whole at its next session. Other experts may also be involved in the preparatory process. The panels will appoint their own chairman and rapporteur and determine their method of work. They will be assisted by the secretariat of the Commission. A lead agency of the United Nations system may be invited to work with the panel in identifying the activities relevant to the theme within the United Nations system;

(c) Once adopted by the Commission, the reports on substantive themes will be submitted to the Economic and Social Council as representing a major output from a particular session of the Commission and will also be given wider distribution throughout the development community;

(d) In order for the Commission to evaluate the reports effectively at its plenary meetings, its consideration of those reports will occur in two stages. The first stage will be devoted primarily to technical discussion of the draft chapters and selection of substantive themes for the next session of the Commission. The second stage will be devoted, as necessary, to intergovernmental negotiations concerning draft recommendations and resolutions. The total duration of a given session of the Commission will be kept as short as possible.

3. The use and application of the content and recommendations of the analytical reports of the Commission will be monitored to ensure that they are having the desired effects.

4. The Secretariat should seek to establish a computer network for communication between the Secretariat and the members of the Commission and among the members of the Commission, so that the products of the deliberations of each panel can be made available to the members of the Commission in a timely manner. The network should allow for computer conferencing on the substantive themes.

5. These methods of work will be implemented within the existing resources for science and technology. To supplement those resources, Member States and relevant organizations are encouraged to provide voluntary contributions.

Economic and Social Council decision 1993/320

Adopted without vote

Approved by Economic Committee (E/1993/110) without vote, 26 July (meeting 15); draft by Commission on Science and Technology for Development (E/1993/31); agenda item 15 *(c)*.

Programme of work for 1994-1995

The Commission's programme proposals for the biennium 1994-1995 covered four sub-programmes: proposed activities in endogenous capacity-building and resource mobilization; the Advanced Technology Assessment System (ATAS), with a special focus on the conversion of military technology to civilian applications; coordination and harmonization of United Nations activities; and information services.

The Commission generally supported the programme of work and emphasized the role of the regional commissions in coordinating the programme at the regional level.

ECONOMIC AND SOCIAL COUNCIL ACTION

On 30 July, the Economic and Social Council adopted without vote **resolution 1993/75**.

Programme of work for 1994-1995 in the field of science and technology for development

The Economic and Social Council,

Transmits to the General Assembly, for further consideration, the following draft resolution, as approved by the Commission on Science and Technology for Development at its first session:

"*The General Assembly,*

"*Recalling* its resolutions 46/235 of 13 April 1992 and 47/212 and 47/214 of 23 December 1992,

"*Having considered* the note by the Secretariat on programme proposals for the biennium 1994-1995 in the field of science and technology for development, in particular paragraphs 2 and 5 thereof,

"1. *Reaffirms* the mandates and functions of the Commission on Science and Technology for Development as the main substantive organ of the Economic and Social Council dealing with the global issue of science and technology for development;

"2. *Also reaffirms* the need to count on the substantive support of an efficient Secretariat unit provided with a level of resources commensurate with its functions;

"3. *Requests* the Secretary-General to take all necessary measures to ensure the full implementation of programme 17 of the medium-term plan for the period 1992-1997 and, in particular, to provide resources for the implementation of the activities proposed for the biennium 1994-1995 in the field of science and technology for development, taking into account the priority attached to these activities within the medium-term plan;

"4. *Also requests* the Secretary-General to ensure that the Secretariat unit having primary responsibility for the implementation of programme activities in the field of science and technology for development, including the substantive servicing of the Commission, will be managed in an integrated manner, and further requests the Secretary-General to provide for its strengthening in terms of the efficient organization of the Secretariat;

"5. *Further requests* the Secretary-General to make sufficient provisions within the programme budget for the biennium 1994-1995 for the implementation of technical cooperation activities in the field of science and technology;

"6. *Requests* the Secretary-General to clarify the division of labour and coordination arrangements for the efficient functioning of Secretariat units in the field of science and technology for development, particularly the Department for Policy Coordination and Sustainable Development, the Department for Development Support and Management Services, the United Nations Conference on Trade and Development and the regional commissions;

"7. *Expresses concern* regarding the proposed abolition of the Task Force on Science and Technology for Development of the Administrative Committee on Coordination and the negative impact this may have on the quality of the coordination of system-wide activities in these fields;

"8. *Requests* the Secretary-General to provide the resources necessary for convening at least four intersessional ad hoc panels/workshops on specific issues in the field of science and technology, which will provide crucial input into the work of the Commission in terms of independent, specialized and expert advice;

"9. *Urges* the Secretary-General to make every possible effort to adhere strictly to existing rules and to avoid the repetition of the regrettable experience of the late issuance of documentation for the first session of the Commission."

Economic and Social Council resolution 1993/75

30 July 1993   Meeting 46   Adopted without vote

Referred by Economic Committee (E/1993/110), 26 July (meeting 15); draft by Commission on Science and Technology for Development (E/1993/31), orally amended in Council following informal consultations; agenda item 15 *(c)*.

Financial implications. S-G, E/1993/31/Add.1.

Following the adoption of the resolution, Belgium, on behalf of the European Community (EC), indicated that it could not support the draft resolution for three reasons: the text was not discussed by the Commission on Science and Technology for Development and was not therefore accepted by all its members; the draft resolution had unspecified financial implications for the 1994-1995 programme budget; and it prejudged the results of the restructuring of the Secretariat of the United Nations. However, conscious of the importance of international cooperation, the EC members agreed that the text should be forwarded to the General Assembly at its forty-eighth session for an in-depth examination.

Restructuring in the UN system

In 1993, as part of the restructuring in the United Nations system, programmes relating to science and technology for development were integrated within UNCTAD and the Department for Policy Coordination and Sustainable Development of the United Nations Secretariat, established on 1 February. Within the Administrative Committee on Coordination (ACC), functions of the Task Force on Science and Technology for Development were absorbed by the Consultative Committee on Programme and Operational Questions and the Inter-Agency Committee on Sustainable Development.

On 6 May, by section III of **resolution 47/212 B**, the General Assembly requested the Secretary-General, in implementing the restructuring of the Secretariat and in preparing the proposed programme budget for 1994-1995, to provide adequate resources and to identify clearly units for the implementation of all programmes and activities, including science and technology for development, and to strengthen coordination of the activities on science and technology within UNDP for better management of the United Nations Fund for Science and Technology for Development.

Coordination in the UN system

In a March report[5] to the Commission on Science and Technology for Development, the Secretary-General provided proposals for improving coordination and cooperation in the United Nations system. He recommended placing greater emphasis on coordination at country and regional levels, adopting a coherent approach to national capacity-building, ensuring harmonization of activities at the headquarters level, facilitating coordination through a framework of policy studies, organizing early consultations on programmes requiring joint action and financing, and establishing a United Nations scientific and technological information network. Other recommendations dealt with ATAS as the United Nations focal point for technology assessment and coordination on identified specific activities.

In April, the Commission considered that special priority should be assigned to enhancing the complementarity of all components of the system in science and technology and underscored the importance of coherence and harmonized national policies in that field. It recommended that an effective coordination mechanism for science and technology be maintained within the restructured ACC.

The ACC Inter-Agency Committee on Sustainable Development, at its second meeting (New York, 8-10 September),[6] designated task managers for follow-up to and reporting on, *inter alia*, education and science, the transfer of ESTs, cooperation and capacity-building and biotechnology. The ACC Consultative Committee on Programme and Operational Questions, at its first session (New York, 20-24 September),[7] decided to focus on linkages between science and technology and development, and included an item on science and technology for development in its programme of work for 1994.

The Joint Meetings (twenty-seventh series) of the Committee for Programme and Coordination and ACC (New York, 27 October), in considering the results of UNCED and their implications for the United Nations system,[8] identified the transfer of ESTs, cooperation and capacity-building as an important area of coordination. They considered it essential to ensure effective interaction and collaborative arrangements in this area within the framework of the Economic and Social Council based on clear division of labour and responsibilities. They recommended that the Council consider science and technology at the coordination segment of its 1994 substantive session.

REFERENCES

(1)YUN 1992, p. 935, ESC dec. 1992/218, 30 Apr. 1992. (2)E/1993/31. (3)E/CN.16/1993/7. (4)E/1993/31 (dec. 1/101). (5)E/CN.16/1993/3. (6)ACC/1993/24. (7)ACC/1993/25. (8)E/1994/4.

Chapter VIII

Environment

Follow-up on the 1992 United Nations Conference on Environment and Development (UNCED) and efforts to implement its Agenda 21 dominated the major environment-related activities of the United Nations system in 1993. Intergovernmental meetings were held on such issues as desertification and fisheries, and environmental concerns were integrated into many economic and social development programmes.

The General Assembly noted progress made by the Intergovernmental Negotiating Committee towards elaboration of an international convention to combat desertification (resolution 48/191) and by the Conference on Straddling Fish Stocks and Highly Migratory Fish Stocks (48/194). The Convention on Biological Diversity entered into force in December 1993.

The Governing Council of the United Nations Environment Programme (UNEP) held its seventeenth session in 1993 (Nairobi, 10-21 May), adopting 45 decisions on environmental and administrative matters. The Assembly (48/174) called for the strengthening of UNEP and welcomed its action-oriented approach to UNCED follow-up.

UNCED follow-up

In 1993, institutional structures were established and other activities pursued to follow up on UNCED and implement the main texts adopted at the Conference: the Rio Declaration on Environment and Development; the comprehensive plan of action for sustainable development into the twenty-first century, also known as Agenda 21; and the Non-legally Binding Authoritative Statement of Principles for a Global Consensus on the Management, Conservation and Sustainable Development of All Types of Forests.[1]

Progress was made with ratification of two conventions opened for signature at UNCED: the International Framework Convention on Climate Change and the International Framework Convention on the Conservation of Biological Diversity.

Other developments on UNCED issues included meetings of a United Nations Conference on Straddling Fish Stocks and Highly Migratory Fish Stocks and preparations for an international convention to combat desertification.

By its **resolution 48/193** of 21 December, the General Assembly decided to convene, in Barbados from 25 April to 6 May 1994, the first Global Conference on the Sustainable Development of Small Island Developing States, as called for in Agenda 21 (see PART THREE, Chapter I).

UNDP activities. In May,[2] the Administrator of the United Nations Development Programme (UNDP) submitted a report on UNCED follow-up and on UNDP's strategy for sustainable development. He stated that UNDP had intensified its efforts to integrate environmental concerns into the mainstream of its development activities and had launched a major programme in support of Agenda 21 that included Capacity 21, a programme designed to help developing nations to implement Agenda 21 (see PART THREE, Chapter II). The report discussed the implications of Agenda 21 for UNDP and described Capacity 21.

On 18 June,[3] the Council welcomed the Administrator's report[2] and requested that he proceed with implementing Capacity 21.

The Governing Council supported UNDP's goal of devoting 40 per cent of the Capacity 21 budget to the least developed countries and requested the Administrator to report annually on follow-up to UNCED and on UNDP activities in the field of sustainable development.

UNEP activities. In February,[4] the Executive Director of the United Nations Environment Programme (UNEP) submitted a note describing how UNEP proposed to follow up on three subjects emanating from UNCED: the global conference on the sustainable development of small island States; the elaboration of an international convention to combat desertification; and the convening of an intergovernmental meeting on the protection of the marine environment from land-based activities. The UNEP Governing Council, on 21 May,[5] endorsed the actions proposed by the Executive Director regarding those issues.

Institutional arrangements

In an October report,[6] the Secretary-General discussed the establishment of and secretariat support arrangements for the Commission on Sustainable Development;[7] the Inter-Agency Committee on Sustainable Development; and the

High-Level Advisory Board on Sustainable Development (see PART THREE, Chapter I).

On 21 May,[8] UNEP's Governing Council requested the Executive Director to coordinate UNEP's programme activities with the outcome of the first session of the Commission on Sustainable Development and to ensure that adequate staff resources were available for collaboration with the newly restructured Global Environment Facility (GEF). The Executive Director was encouraged to refocus UNEP's offices so that they could also collaborate with the Department for Policy Coordination and Sustainable Development.

Dissemination of Rio Declaration

At its June session,[9] the Commission on Sustainable Development reported on its first session and proposed programme of work. It noted initial efforts to incorporate into the programmes and processes of the United Nations system the Rio Declaration on Environment and Development, consisting of 27 principles as a basis for negotiation of an Earth Charter that could be approved on the fiftieth anniversary of the United Nations in 1995.[10] It also requested that the Secretary-General keep it informed of measures taken for the effective functioning of the Inter-Agency Committee on Sustainable Development.

GENERAL ASSEMBLY ACTION

On 21 December, on the recommendation of the Second (Economic and Financial) Committee, the General Assembly adopted without vote **resolution 48/190**.

Dissemination of the principles of the Rio Declaration on Environment and Development

The General Assembly,

Convinced that the Rio Declaration on Environment and Development contains fundamental principles for the achievement of sustainable development, based on a new and equitable global partnership,

Conscious of the fact that the dissemination of the principles contained in the Declaration will contribute to increasing public awareness of the need to take a balanced and integrated approach to development and environment questions,

Bearing in mind its resolution 47/191 of 22 December 1992, in particular paragraph 4 *(a)* thereof, in which it recommended that the Commission on Sustainable Development promote the incorporation of the principles of the Declaration in the implementation of Agenda 21, and taking note of paragraphs 32 and 42 of chapter I of the report of the Commission on Sustainable Development on its first session,

Recalling that the ministers and other participants at the high-level meeting of the first session of the Commission emphasized the need to promote broad dissemination of the principles of the Declaration at all levels with a view to promoting public awareness regarding sustainable development,

Recalling also chapter 36 of Agenda 21, entitled "Promoting education, public awareness and training",

1. *Urges* all Governments to promote widespread dissemination of the Rio Declaration on Environment and Development in the public and private sectors;

2. *Requests* the Secretary-General to ensure that the Declaration is widely disseminated by the competent organs and bodies of the United Nations system and that its principles are incorporated in their programmes and processes, in accordance with paragraphs 32 and 42 of chapter I of the report of the Commission on Sustainable Development on its first session.

General Assembly resolution 48/190

21 December 1993   Meeting 86   Adopted without vote

Approved by Second Committee (A/48/725) without vote, 9 December (meeting 46); draft by China and Colombia (for Group of 77) (A/C.2/48/L.46); agenda item 99.

Meeting numbers. GA 48th session: 2nd Committee 36-43, 46, 47; plenary 86.

Coordination within the UN system

The Inter-Agency Committee on Sustainable Development (IACSD), established by the Administrative Committee on Coordination (ACC) in 1992,[11] held two meetings in 1993 (New York, 23-25 March and 8-10 September).

At its September session,[12] IACSD discussed the sharing of responsibilities for implementation of Agenda 21 among the organizations of the United Nations system. It designated task managers and cooperating organizations for the various chapters and programme areas of Agenda 21, agreed on the responsibilities and functions of the task managers and established a process for inter-agency consultations and coordination.

An ad hoc inter-agency meeting was convened in Paris on 23 and 24 August to work out arrangements for an inter-agency mechanism that would deal with broad development issues related to the oceans and report to IACSD. As a result, IACSD recommended the establishment of an ACC Subcommittee on Oceans and Coastal Areas to meet the coordination needs broadly defined in chapter 17 of Agenda 21.

The results of UNCED and their implications for the United Nations system was the topic of the twenty-seventh series of Joint Meetings of the Committee for Programme and Coordination (CPC) and ACC (New York, 27 October).[13]

The Joint Meetings concluded that harmonized policy guidance on sustainable development issues by various governing bodies throughout the United Nations system was crucial, and recommended that the Commission on Sustainable Development assist the Economic and Social Council with coordination.

The Joint Meetings had before them a background paper,[14] which drew attention to a number of issues addressed by ACC, IACSD and the Commission on Sustainable Development and discussed financial constraints on the implementation of Agenda 21, as well as coordination questions.

In a March report,[15] the UNEP Executive Director proposed that ACC remain the central body responsible for coordination in the field of environment. She also stated that in April she would inform ACC of the establishment of an Inter-Agency Environment Coordination Group as a possible successor arrangement to the system of Designated Officials for Environmental Matters. On 21 May,[16] UNEP's Governing Council took note of those proposals, and welcomed the new machinery developed by ACC for the system-wide follow-up to UNCED, particularly the creation of IACSD.

The Governing Council requested that ACC, in future, report only in those years when the Council met in regular session,[17] and focus its reports on policy matters related to UNCED, particularly those regarding system-wide coordination and emerging and important environmental issues of system-wide interest.

System-wide medium-term environment programme

In April, the UNEP Executive Director reported on implementation of the second system-wide medium-term environment programme, 1990-1995 (SWMTEP II), and on the results of the mid-term review of SWMTEP for the period 1990-1995.[18] The Executive Director recommended that, in view of the proposal for a new system-wide coordinating arrangement, UNEP's coordinating mandate be assessed at a later stage. She also recommended that proposals for a future planning and strategy document be made to the UNEP Governing Council at its 1995 session.

On 21 May,[19] the Governing Council endorsed that recommendation.

Cooperation between UNEP and Habitat

On 21 May,[20] the UNEP Governing Council requested the Executive Director to continue her efforts to increase cooperation between UNEP and the United Nations Centre for Human Settlements (Habitat) in the implementation of Agenda 21, and to report to the Governing Council's eighteenth regular session on the outcome.

REFERENCES
[1]YUN 1992, p. 670. [2]DP/1993/11. [3]E/1993/35 (dec. 93/12). [4]UNEP/GC.17/20. [5]A/48/25 (dec. 17/2). [6]A/48/442. [7]YUN 1992, p. 676, GA res. 47/191, 22 Dec. 1992. [8]A/48/25 (dec. 17/1). [9]E/1993/25/Add.1. [10]YUN 1992, p. 670. [11]YUN 1992, p. 681. [12]ACC/1993/24. [13]E/1994/4. [14]E/1993/121. [15]UNEP/GC.17/12/Add.1. [16]A/48/25 (dec. 17/9). [17]Ibid. (dec. 17/11). [18]UNEP/GC.17/6. [19]A/48/25 (dec. 17/16). [20]Ibid. (dec. 17/10).

General aspects

Environmental perspective

On 21 December, by **decision 48/449**, the General Assembly decided to discontinue the reporting it requested in 1987[1] related to the Environmental Perspective to the Year 2000 and Beyond, and the report of the World Commission on Environment and Development.[2]

Women and environment

On 21 May,[3] the UNEP Governing Council requested the Executive Director, as UNEP's contribution to the Fourth World Conference on Women to be held in Beijing in 1995, to ensure that gender considerations were well integrated into all policies, programmes and activities of UNEP and to prepare concrete proposals for the integration of concerns related to women and environment into the process of sustainable development.

In its **resolution 1993/12**, adopted on 27 July, the Economic and Social Council requested, among other things, that, in their reports for the 1995 Beijing Conference, Governments include information on the extent to which objectives proposed in Agenda 21, chapter 24, relating to women, had been met, and how the recommended activities had been implemented (see PART THREE, Chapter XIII).

International conventions

Climate change convention

By the end of 1993, 166 States had signed the United Nations Framework Convention on Climate Change,[4] which had been opened for signature at UNCED in 1992.[5] The goal of the Convention was to limit the emission into the atmosphere of carbon dioxide and other "greenhouse gases" that might cause a change in the Earth's climate.

By the end of the year, the Convention had been ratified by 51 States and the European Economic Community. The date for the Convention's entry into force was set at 21 March 1994, 90 days after the deposit of the fiftieth instrument of ratification, acceptance, approval or accession.

The Intergovernmental Negotiating Committee for a Framework Convention on Climate Change held its seventh session in New York from 15 to 20 March.[6] It discussed, among other things, matters relating to the financial mechanism and technical and financial support to developing country parties, and the activities of the Convention's interim secretariat.

The Committee's eighth session was held at Geneva from 16 to 27 August.[7] It discussed national communications and other statements relating to the Convention, and Convention-related activities of the United Nations system. In an October note by the Secretary-General,[8] the General Assembly was asked to accept Germany's invitation to host the first session of the Conference of Parties to the Framework Convention at Berlin, 28 March–7 April 1995.

GENERAL ASSEMBLY ACTION

On 21 December, on the recommendation of the Second Committee, the General Assembly adopted without vote **resolution 48/189**.

United Nations Framework Convention on Climate Change

The General Assembly,

Recalling the United Nations Framework Convention on Climate Change, negotiated under its auspices and opened for signature at Rio de Janeiro on 4 June 1992, during the United Nations Conference on Environment and Development,

Noting with satisfaction the progress being made towards fulfilling the requirements for entry into force stipulated in article 23 of the Convention and the preparatory work undertaken by the Intergovernmental Negotiating Committee for a Framework Convention on Climate Change in pursuance of General Assembly resolution 47/195 of 22 December 1992,

Noting that, in accordance with article 7, paragraph 4, of the Convention, the first session of the Conference of the Parties to the Convention shall be convened by the interim secretariat of the Convention and shall take place not later than one year after the date of entry into force of the Convention,

Having considered the recommendation made by the Intergovernmental Negotiating Committee at its eighth session regarding the Conference of the Parties and the related note by the Secretary-General,

Taking into account the basic provisions of General Assembly resolution 40/243 of 18 December 1985,

1. *Decides* that the first session of the Conference of the Parties to the United Nations Framework Convention on Climate Change shall be held from 28 March to 7 April 1995, subject to the applicable provisions of the United Nations Framework Convention on Climate Change;

2. *Accepts with deep appreciation* the generous offer of the Government of Germany to host at Berlin the first session of the Conference of the Parties;

3. *Also decides* to include the first session of the Conference of the Parties in the calendar of conferences and meetings for 1994-1995.

General Assembly resolution 48/189

21 December 1993   Meeting 86   Adopted without vote

Approved by Second Committee (A/48/725) without vote, 10 December (meeting 47); draft by China and Colombia (for Group of 77) (A/C.2/48/L.38), orally revised following informal consultations; agenda item 99.

Meeting numbers. GA 48th session: 2nd Committee 36-43, 46, 47; plenary 86.

Convention on Biological Diversity

The Convention on Biological Diversity, which was opened for signature at UNCED in 1992,[9] became international law on 29 December 1993, 90 days after its thirtieth ratification. At the time of its entry into force, 37 States had ratified the Convention and 167 States had signed it. The first Conference of Parties to the Convention was tentatively scheduled for the period 28 November to 9 December 1994.

The UNEP Governing Council, in May,[10] established the Intergovernmental Committee on the Convention on Biological Diversity to prepare for the first meeting of the Conference of Parties to the Convention. On 21 September, UNEP announced the appointment of seven specialists to the Interim Secretariat of the Convention on Biological Diversity at Geneva.

Montreal Protocol and Ozone Convention

Parties to the 1987 Montreal Protocol on Substances that Deplete the Ozone Layer[11] held their fifth meeting at Bangkok, Thailand, from 17 to 19 November. The meeting agreed to phase out the production of halons in developed countries at the end of 1993. A $510 million replenishment of the Multilateral Fund was approved for the next three years to help developing countries phase out the use of ozone-depleting substances. The meeting concluded that, when selecting alternatives and substitutes for hydrochlorofluorocarbons, factors such as environmental health and safety, technical feasibility, commercial availability and performance must be considered.

The Montreal Protocol meeting was followed by the Third Meeting (Bangkok, 23-24 November) of the Conference of the Parties of the 1985 Vienna Convention for the Protection of the Ozone Layer,[12] which pledged to protect human health and the environment from the effects of ozone depletion by coordinating international research. It was recommended, among other things, that States parties to the Convention contribute to the World Meteorological Organization's special fund for environmental monitoring of the Global Ozone Observing System, in order to expand the station network in developing countries.

At the end of 1993 there were 133 States parties to the Vienna Convention and 131 States parties to the Montreal Protocol.[4]

Global Environment Facility

The pilot phase of the Global Environment Facility (GEF)—a joint effort of the World Bank, UNDP and UNEP established in 1991[13]—entered its third and final year in 1993. The purpose of GEF was to help developing countries respond to environmental problems in four programme areas:

climate change, ozone depletion, pollution of international waters and biodiversity.

GEF member Governments met in Rome, Beijing, Washington, D.C., Paris and Cartagena, Colombia, in 1993.

The Cartagena meeting in December was billed as the final round of negotiations on the new facility. Although it failed to reach agreement on key operational arrangements, it did make progress on the institutional framework, and donors reconfirmed their intention to contribute to the $2 billion target for GEF II.

Forty-five projects totalling $288.7 million had been approved by the implementing agencies at the end of 1993: 22 by UNDP, 20 by the World Bank and 3 by UNEP. There were 113 projects in the GEF work programme for a total commitment of $727 million.

On 21 May,[14] the UNEP Governing Council requested the Executive Director to continue to cooperate closely with the World Bank and UNDP in the successful completion of GEF's pilot phase.

REFERENCES

[1]YUN 1987, p. 661, GA res. 42/186, 11 Dec. 1992. [2]YUN 1987, p. 679, GA res. 42/187, 11 Dec. 1992. [3]A/48/25 (dec. 17/4). [4]*Multilateral Treaties Deposited with the Secretary-General: Status as at 31 December 1993* (ST/LEG/SER.E/12), Sales No. E.94.V.11. [5]YUN 1992, p. 681. [6]A/AC.237/31. [7]A/AC.237/41. [8]A/48/563. [9]YUN 1992, p. 683. [10]A/48/25 (dec. 17/30). [11]YUN 1987, p. 686. [12]YUN 1985, p. 804. [13]YUN 1991, p. 505. [14]A/48/25 (dec. 17/40).

Environmental activities

Environmental monitoring and assessment

The Executive Director of UNEP reported to the Governing Council in February[1] that uncertainties over the outcome of the United Nations Conference on Environment and Development (UNCED) and restructuring within the United Nations system had prevented UNEP from completing detailed proposals for adequate financial and institutional support as requested by the Governing Council at its previous (sixteenth) session.

Earthwatch, the environmental assessment arm of UNEP in cooperation with the United Nations specialized agencies, shares its activities among the Global Environment Monitoring System (GEMS), the International Environmental Information System (INFOTERRA) and the International Register of Potentially Toxic Chemicals (IRPTC), aiming to make the provision of reliable information for decision-making on the global environment a more coherent and effective process.

Following inter-agency discussions for strengthening Earthwatch, it was decided that its institu-

tional framework could only be determined once the rationalization of inter-agency bodies and the establishment of new structures for sustainable development were more advanced.

The Executive Director suggested that, in view of the prevailing circumstances, the Governing Council request that she continue efforts to strengthen Earthwatch and report to the next (eighteenth) session in 1994.

State of the environment

On 21 May,[2] the UNEP Governing Council took note of three reports dealing with the state of the environment.

The first report, the Executive Summary of the Comprehensive State-of-the-Environment Report: 1972-1992,[3] examined the major environmental issues of the day and how they had evolved over the last two decades, and the manner in which developments in different sectors of the economy had impacted on the environment and affected the human condition. It also analysed the range of responses to developments at the scientific, public, national and international levels and sociopolitical, economic and technological developments and the challenges and opportunities implied by them.

The second report, the Executive Summary of the State-of-the-Environment Report 1992: Poverty and the Environment,[4] addressed poverty and its variations within and between countries and between rich and poor; the economic and physical environment and its impact on the poor; migration; and the persistence of poverty.

The third report,[5] on emerging environmental issues, was divided into two main parts. Part I covered such issues as the re-use of waste water, volatile organic compounds in air, and tropospheric ozone. Part II briefly updated issues examined in a report to the sixteenth session on new technologies, plastics, municipal wastes and the ecological situation in the Arctic.

Environmental indicators

In February,[1] the UNEP Executive Director discussed the development and use of environmental indicators in connection with Earthwatch to monitor the state of the environment and detect changing conditions over time.

On 21 May,[6] UNEP's Governing Council requested UNEP to continue to develop environmental indicators in cooperation with the United Nations Statistical Office and relevant specialized agencies. The Executive Director was requested to submit to the Council in 1994 a progress report and plan of action on the development and use of environmental indicators.

Protection against harmful products and wastes

UNEP policy and activities in the area of hazardous waste were among topics covered in a February report by the Executive Director.[7]

Effective 1 January, the Executive Director established a permanent Secretariat at Geneva for the Basel Convention on the Control of Transboundary Movements of Hazardous Wastes and Their Disposal. UNEP had been performing the functions of the Convention Secretariat on an interim basis since its adoption in 1989. Its main tasks were to implement the Convention and the decisions adopted by the Conference of its parties; to implement technical assistance projects; and to respond to requests for assistance related to the environmentally sound management of hazardous wastes, the development of national legislation in that field and capacity-building. (See also action by the Commission on Human Rights, PART THREE, Chapter X.)

On 21 May,[8] the UNEP Governing Council urged Governments that had not already done so to ratify or accede to the Basel Convention, and requested the Executive Director to examine its implementation to date and any issues that might have resulted in its slow ratification. As at 13 October, the Basel Convention had been ratified or acceded to by 49 countries.

The Council urged developed countries to assist in technology transfer to developing countries and countries in transition to a market economy in order to minimize the generation of hazardous wastes, and requested the Executive Director to continue to promote an international strategy for the environmentally sound management of hazardous wastes through the Secretariat of the Basel Convention.[9]

In a related decision,[10] the Council requested the Executive Director to replace a list of environmentally harmful chemical substances, processes and phenomena of global significance[11] with an assessment, every four years, of chemical issues that were critical globally.

Irradiated nuclear fuel

UNEP participated in a Joint Working Group on the Carriage of Irradiated Nuclear Fuel by Sea, together with the International Atomic Energy Agency (IAEA) and the International Maritime Organization (IMO). The Working Group met in London (8-11 December 1992) and at Vienna (26-30 April 1993) following letters of concern from a number of Governments and non-governmental organizations about the planned shipment by sea of plutonium from France to Japan and the possible implications for human life and the environment if an accident occurred. The Joint Working Group completed a draft Code for the Safe Carriage of Irradiated Nuclear Fuel, Plutonium, and High-Level Radioactive Wastes in Flasks on Board Ships at the Vienna meeting in April, and on 21 May UNEP's Governing Council requested that the Executive Director report on future developments resulting from the Group's work.[12]

Forum on Chemical Risk Assessment

On 21 May,[13] the UNEP Governing Council requested the Executive Director to convene, together with the executive heads of the World Health Organization and the International Labour Organisation, a meeting of experts from Governments and relevant intergovernmental organizations that could constitute the first Intergovernmental Forum on Chemical Risk Assessment and Management. The Council noted an offer by the Swedish Government to host a meeting on chemical risk assessment and management at Stockholm in April 1994.

Environmental emergencies

In April,[14] the Executive Director submitted a report on the United Nations Centre for Urgent Environmental Assistance (UNCUEA), summarizing and evaluating its activities and experiences. Established experimentally in 1991,[15] the Centre aimed to assess and respond to man-made environmental emergencies in cooperation with other United Nations agencies.

The Executive Director recommended, among other things, that UNCUEA remain in UNEP, that its experimental phase be extended and that its role be defined more precisely.

On 21 May,[16] UNEP's Governing Council decided to extend the experimental stage for a further twelve months, during which time the Centre should identify the specific needs of countries faced with different types of environmental emergencies; analyse the ability of the United Nations and other organizations to respond; review the major disasters of the last 10 years and identify gaps in responses to them; and develop concrete proposals for an enhanced international response capacity, focusing on the United Nations system in particular.

GENERAL ASSEMBLY ACTION

On 21 December, on the recommendation of the Second Committee, the General Assembly adopted without vote **resolution 48/192**.

Strengthening international cooperation in the monitoring of global environmental problems

The General Assembly,

Reaffirming its resolutions 44/224 of 22 December 1989 and 46/217 of 20 December 1991 on international cooperation in the monitoring, assessment and anticipation of environmental threats and in assistance in cases of environmental emergency,

Reaffirming also the relevant provisions of Agenda 21 and the Rio Declaration on Environment and Development, adopted by the United Nations Conference on Environment and Development, including principle 2 of the Declaration, which states that States have, in accordance with the Charter of the United Nations and the principles of international law, the sovereign right to exploit their own resources pursuant to their own environmental and developmental policies, and the responsibility to ensure that activities within their jurisdiction or control do not cause damage to the environment of other States or of areas beyond their national jurisdiction,

Recalling decision 16/37 of 31 May 1991 of the Governing Council of the United Nations Environment Programme on early warning and forecasting of environmental emergencies, and taking note of Governing Council decision 17/26 of 21 May 1993 on the United Nations Centre for Urgent Environmental Assistance,

Taking note of the relevant parts of the reports of the Committee on the Peaceful Uses of Outer Space on its thirty-fifth and thirty-sixth sessions in particular, in which the Committee noted the importance of remote sensing by satellites for monitoring the Earth's environment and, in particular, for studying and monitoring global change,

Taking into account the ongoing activities of the Committee on Earth Observation Satellites in support of global environment monitoring and related applications,

Bearing in mind the importance of the participation of relevant organs, specialized agencies and other organizations of the United Nations system, within their respective mandates, in Earthwatch, in particular in its environmental monitoring programmes, and the need for early warning capabilities in those programmes,

Recognizing the need to make Earthwatch a more efficient instrument for environmental sensing and assessment of all elements influencing the global environment in order to ensure a balanced approach in serving, in particular, the needs of developing countries,

Recognizing also the potential and importance of current available methods, technologies and techniques for monitoring, assessment and anticipation of global environmental problems, including remote sensing and monitoring from outer space,

1. *Invites* Governments, relevant organizations of the United Nations system, within their respective mandates, and other relevant entities to review, as appropriate, their contribution to international cooperation in environmental monitoring, including environmentally related remote sensing and data assessment, and to provide appropriate support for such activities within existing resources;

2. *Requests* the Executive Director of the United Nations Environment Programme to prepare and to submit to the Governing Council of the United Nations Environment Programme at its eighteenth session a report on the activities of the Programme in environmental monitoring, containing proposals and recommendations within the context of Agenda 21 and a review of Earthwatch, taking into account the decisions adopted by the Governing Council at its seventeenth session, in cooperation with relevant entities within the United Nations system and, where appropriate, outside the United Nations system;

3. *Invites* the Governing Council of the United Nations Environment Programme to consider the above-mentioned report at its eighteenth session and to submit its conclusions and recommendations to the General Assembly at its fiftieth session, through the Economic and Social Council.

General Assembly resolution 48/192

21 December 1993   Meeting 86   Adopted without vote

Approved by Second Committee (A/48/725) without vote, 10 December (meeting 47); draft by Vice-Chairman (A/C.2/48/L.80), based on informal consultations on 14-nation draft (A/C.2/48/L.47); agenda item 99 *(a)*.

Sponsors: Armenia, Belarus, Canada, Czech Republic, Georgia, Hungary, Kazakhstan, Kyrgyzstan, Republic of Moldova, Romania, Russian Federation, Tajikistan, Turkmenistan, Ukraine.

Meeting numbers. GA 48th session: 2nd Committee 36-43, 46, 47; plenary 86.

Ecosystems

Global climate

In a February report,[17] the Executive Director of UNEP transmitted two documents to the Governing Council: the report on the progress and future activities of the World Climate Impact Assessment and Response Strategies Programme (WCIRP); and the report of the Chairman of the Intergovernmental Panel on Climate Change (IPCC), discussing the IPCC budget and work programme in 1991 and 1992. On 21 May,[18] the UNEP Governing Council took note of both reports and adopted a three-part decision on climate change.

The Governing Council urged Governments to increase their support for IPCC and endorse its revised structure and future work plans. It requested the Executive Director to further develop WCIRP and ensure the preparation of an integrated proposal concerning the Programme's coordination and resource needs. It also urged Governments to ensure early implementation of the recommendations of the Intergovernmental Meeting on the World Climate Programme.

Desertification and drought control

The Intergovernmental Negotiating Committee for the Elaboration of an International Convention to Combat Desertification in those Countries Experiencing Serious Drought and/or Desertification, particularly in Africa, held its organizational session in New York from 26 to 29 January,[19] its first session at Nairobi from 24 May to 3 June,[20] and its second session at Geneva from 13 to 24 September.[21]

The General Assembly established the Committee in 1992[22] and, with a view to finalizing a convention by June 1994, invited UNEP, UNDP, the United Nations Sudano-Sahelian Office (UNSO) and other international organizations dealing with desertification to contribute to its work.

At its first substantive session, the Committee established two working groups. Working Group I was responsible for the elaboration of the preamble, principles, objectives and commitments, including financial arrangements and capacity-building. Working Group II was responsible for the elaboration of institutional, administrative, technological and scientific aspects, research, data collection and exchange of information, procedural arrangements and legal provisions. The Committee decided that an instrument on Africa should be negotiated once the main structure of the convention had been defined, and should be adopted as an integral part of the convention. It encouraged Governments to make written submissions on the contents of the convention.

At its second session, the Committee requested the Secretariat to continue to support the preparation of a regional instrument on Africa and similar instruments for Asia and Latin America and the Caribbean, and to take into account other affected regions.

The Committee also requested the Secretariat to draft a single negotiating text to the convention, which would serve as the basis for discussions in the Committee's two working groups at its third substantive session in 1994. That text, contained in a November note by the Secretariat,[23] drew heavily on views submitted by Governments, as well as on statements by the two working groups at the Committee's second session. The negotiating text contained 42 articles.

GENERAL ASSEMBLY ACTION

On 21 December, on the recommendation of the Second Committee, the General Assembly adopted without vote **resolution 48/191**.

Elaboration of an international convention to combat desertification in countries experiencing serious drought and/or desertification, particularly in Africa

The General Assembly,

Recalling its resolutions 44/172 of 19 December 1989, 44/228 of 22 December 1989 and other relevant General Assembly resolutions, as well as decisions of the United Nations Conference on Environment and Development, in particular the recommendation by which the Conference invited the General Assembly to establish, under its auspices, an intergovernmental negotiating committee for the elaboration of an international convention to combat desertification in those countries experiencing serious drought and/or desertification, particularly in Africa,

Recalling also its resolution 47/188 of 22 December 1992, by which it established the Intergovernmental Negotiating Committee for the Elaboration of an International Convention to Combat Desertification in those Countries Experiencing Serious Drought and/or Desertification, particularly in Africa, with a view to finalizing such a convention by June 1994,

Recalling further that in Agenda 21, chapter 12, in particular paragraphs 12.1 to 12.4 thereof, desertification and/or drought is recognized as a problem of global dimension, in that it affects one sixth of the world population and one quarter of the total land area of the world and requires a broad response, as set out in paragraph 12.4 of Agenda 21, and that concrete measures have to

be taken in all regions, particularly in Africa, within the framework of the convention,

Reiterating the objective of finalizing the convention by June 1994 and of implementing it as soon as possible,

Noting with appreciation the work of the Intergovernmental Negotiating Committee at its first and second substantive sessions,

Having considered the note by the Secretary-General concerning the progress of the negotiations on the convention,

1. *Urges* the Intergovernmental Negotiating Committee for the Elaboration of an International Convention to Combat Desertification in those Countries Experiencing Serious Drought and/or Desertification, particularly in Africa, to complete the negotiations successfully by June 1994, in accordance with resolution 47/188;

2. *Decides* that the Intergovernmental Negotiating Committee shall hold one session after the adoption of the convention in order to review the situation in the interim period pending its entry into force, in particular with regard to the implementation of provisions adapted to the specific needs of each region;

3. *Also decides* that the session of the Intergovernmental Negotiating Committee after the adoption of the convention shall be held not later than 31 January 1995, and requests the Secretary-General to make appropriate arrangements for the functioning of the ad hoc secretariat and the multidisciplinary panel of experts to service that session;

4. *Further decides* that the negotiating process shall continue to be funded through existing United Nations budgetary resources, without negatively affecting its programmed activities, and through voluntary contributions to the trust fund established pursuant to its resolution 47/188 specifically for that purpose for the duration of the negotiations and administered by the head of the ad hoc secretariat under the authority of the Secretary-General, with the possibility of carrying over contributed resources from one fiscal year to the next;

5. *Notes* the contributions to the work of the Intergovernmental Negotiating Committee in the conduct of its mandate made by the United Nations Development Programme, the United Nations Sudano-Sahelian Office, the United Nations Environment Programme, the Food and Agriculture Organization of the United Nations, the United Nations Conference on Trade and Development, the United Nations Educational, Scientific and Cultural Organization, the World Meteorological Organization, the International Fund for Agricultural Development and other relevant international organizations dealing with desertification, drought and development, and invites them to continue to provide such support;

6. *Notes with appreciation* the initial contributions made to the trust fund, and invites Governments, regional economic integration organizations and other interested organizations, including non-governmental organizations, to continue their support for the fund;

7. *Invites* the international community, in particular the developed countries and other countries in a position to do so, to make voluntary contributions to the secretariat of the Intergovernmental Negotiating Committee and/or the United Nations Sudano-Sahelian Office of the United Nations Development Programme and any other relevant international and regional organizations to allow them to assist countries affected by drought

and/or desertification in all regions, particularly in Africa, in their preparation for the negotiating process;

8. *Also notes with appreciation* the contributions made to the special voluntary fund established pursuant to resolution 47/188 to assist developing countries affected by desertification and drought, in particular the least developed countries, to participate fully and effectively in the negotiating process, and invites Governments, regional economic integration organizations and other interested organizations, including non-governmental organizations, to continue to contribute generously to the fund;

9. *Notes* the arrangements made by the Secretary-General and the welcome support of relevant or interested organizations, organs, programmes and concerned agencies of the United Nations system and intergovernmental, subregional and regional organizations in the work of the Intergovernmental Negotiating Committee, and invites them to continue to participate actively in the work of the Committee in the future;

10. *Urges* Governments to continue, in close collaboration with the regional commissions and national, subregional and regional organizations, to organize activities to support the process of the Intergovernmental Negotiating Committee, involving, as appropriate, the scientific and industrial communities, trade unions, the relevant non-governmental organizations and other interested groups;

11. *Notes also* the assistance provided by the United Nations Sudano-Sahelian Office to the countries covered under its mandate in their preparations for and participation in the negotiating process, and invites the Office to continue to support the Governments concerned and to continue to mobilize resources for that purpose;

12. *Notes further* the constructive contribution of relevant non-governmental organizations to the success of the negotiating process, in accordance with the rules of procedure of the Intergovernmental Negotiating Committee and taking into account procedures used in the process of the United Nations Conference on Environment and Development, and encourages them, particularly non-governmental organizations from developing countries, to continue to contribute to the success of the negotiating process;

13. *Reiterates its request* to the Chairman of the Intergovernmental Negotiating Committee to continue to submit progress reports on the negotiations to the Commission on Sustainable Development and other appropriate bodies;

14. *Requests* the Secretary-General to bring the present resolution to the attention of all Governments, relevant intergovernmental and non-governmental organizations and scientific and other institutions concerned;

15. *Also requests* the Secretary-General to submit to the General Assembly at its forty-ninth session a report on the implementation of the present resolution;

16. *Decides* to include in the provisional agenda of its forty-ninth session, under the item entitled ''Implementation of decisions and recommendations of the United Nations Conference on Environment and Development,'' the sub-item entitled ''Elaboration of an international convention to combat desertification in those countries experiencing serious drought and/or desertification, particularly in Africa''.

General Assembly resolution 48/191

21 December 1993   Meeting 86   Adopted without vote

Approved by Second Committee (A/48/725) without vote, 9 December (meeting 46); draft by Intergovernmental Negotiating Committee (A/48/226/Add.1), orally revised; agenda item 99 *(a)*.
Meeting numbers. GA 48th session: 2nd Committee 36-43, 46, 47; plenary 86.

UNEP activities. On 21 May,[24] the UNEP Governing Council adopted a three-part decision on desertification issues. In the first, on the implementation in 1991-1992 of the 1977 United Nations Plan of Action to Combat Desertification (PACD),[25] the Governing Council requested UNEP to provide to the Governments of affected countries information gathered by monitoring. It requested the Executive Director to continue to promote international cooperation, to expand UNEP's regional/subregional joint ventures for implementation of a coordinated plan of action to combat desertification, as recommended in chapter 12 of Agenda 21, and to continue to cooperate fully in the preparations of the desertification convention by the Intergovernmental Negotiating Committee.

In the second part, the Executive Director was requested to intensify UNEP's interaction with UNDP and the World Bank on funding activities to combat land degradation through the Global Environment Facility (GEF) following discontinuation of the global financing mechanisms of PACD.

In the third part, the Executive Director was authorized to continue supporting UNSO as a joint venture with UNDP, at least until the conclusions of the Intergovernmental Negotiating Committee for the desertification convention became clear.

A report by the Executive Director[26] on the implementation of PACD in 1991 and 1992 was included in a June report of the Secretary-General[27] to the Economic and Social Council and the General Assembly.

In another June report,[28] the Secretary-General presented the results of a study on land degradation in South Asia, undertaken in response to a 1991 Economic and Social Council request.[29] The report covered the status, causes and consequences of land degradation; institutions and programmes to combat it; and proposals for action.

UNDP activities. In an April report,[30] the UNDP Administrator summarized UNSO's activities during 1991-1992 and discussed the implications of a 1992 review of UNSO in the light of UNCED. That review had resulted in a redefinition of goals and the reorientation of major UNSO activities to emphasize its role as the United Nations focal point on issues concerning drought and desertification.

On 18 June,[31] the UNDP Governing Council recognized the important role of UNSO in follow-up activities to UNCED, and reconfirmed its support to the UNDP-UNSO/UNEP joint venture to implement chapter 12 of Agenda 21. The UNDP Administrator was requested to report to the Governing Council at its 1994 session on the implementation of the Governing Council's decision.

ECONOMIC AND SOCIAL COUNCIL ACTION

On 29 July, by **decision 1993/312**, the Council took note of the Secretary-General's report on the implementation of PACD and of the medium-term recovery and rehabilitation programme in the Sudano-Sahelian region,[27] and of the Secretary-General's report on combating aridity, soil erosion, salinity, waterlogging, desertification and the effects of drought in South Asia.[28]

GENERAL ASSEMBLY ACTION

On 21 December, on the recommendation of the Second Committee, the General Assembly adopted without vote **resolution 48/175**.

Drought and desertification

The General Assembly,

Recalling its resolution 32/172 of 19 December 1977, in which it approved the report of the United Nations Conference on Desertification, containing the Plan of Action to Combat Desertification, and its subsequent resolutions on the subject,

Recalling also the decisions of the United Nations Conference on Environment and Development set forth in chapter 12, entitled "Managing fragile ecosystems: combating desertification and drought", of Agenda 21, which develop and complete the decisions contained in the Plan of Action,

Concerned about the continued world-wide degradation of soil resources, particularly in Africa,

Bearing in mind that in the long term the problems of drought, desertification and degradation of the productive capacity of the soil have serious world-wide economic and social consequences that threaten the security and well-being of all affected countries,

Stressing the importance of the ongoing negotiations to elaborate an international convention to combat desertification in those countries experiencing serious drought and/or desertification, particularly in Africa,

Noting the active role played by the United Nations Sudano-Sahelian Office in combating drought and the important contribution of that Office to African countries in the ongoing process of negotiating an international convention to combat desertification,

Taking note of the recommendation contained in paragraph 38.27 of Agenda 21 and of decision 93/33 of 18 June 1993 of the Governing Council of the United Nations Development Programme, in which the Governing Council encouraged the Administrator to strengthen the substantive role and maintain the identity of the United Nations Sudano-Sahelian Office as the focal point within the Programme for all matters related to drought and desertification control, in particular those in Africa, in accordance with the ongoing process of integrating the Office into the core programme of the Programme,

Recalling the appeals to the United Nations Development Programme and the United Nations Environment Programme to continue and strengthen their cooperation in combating desertification, notably through support for the United Nations Sudano-Sahelian Office by the joint venture programme,

Having examined the report of the Secretary-General on the implementation of the Plan of Action to Combat Desertification and of the medium-term recovery and rehabilitation programme in the Sudano-Sahelian region,

1. *Welcomes* the support of the international community and urges it to continue its financial, technical and material support to the countries most affected by drought and desertification in order to support their effort to translate the decisions of the United Nations Conference on Environment and Development into concrete activities to implement the programmes outlined in chapter 12 of Agenda 21, duly taking into account the provisions of the future international convention to combat desertification in those countries experiencing serious drought and/or desertification, particularly in Africa;

2. *Takes note with satisfaction* of decision 93/33 of the Governing Council of the United Nations Development Programme, in which the Governing Council decided that the experience and technical expertise of the United Nations Sudano-Sahelian Office in drought and desertification control should be made available to all affected countries, in particular those in Africa;

3. *Recommends* that the cooperation between the United Nations Development Programme and the United Nations Environment Programme, ensured by the joint agreement to support the United Nations Sudano-Sahelian Office in the implementation in the Sudano-Sahelian region of the Plan of Action to Combat Desertification in a manner consistent with the provisions of the future convention, be strengthened and enlarged in the context of implementing Agenda 21, but without prejudice to the particular attention that must be paid to the countries of the Sudano-Sahelian region;

4. *Appeals* to donor countries to contribute to the United Nations fund for the Sudano-Sahelian region to allow it to continue to bring effective assistance to African countries within the framework of the negotiation process for an international convention to combat desertification and to assist the affected countries in implementing chapter 12 of Agenda 21;

5. *Appeals urgently* to the members of the international community, particularly donor countries, to support the effort being exerted to combat drought and desertification on affected subregional levels, *inter alia*, within subregional intergovernmental organizations such as the Intergovernmental Authority on Drought and Development, the Permanent Inter-State Committee for Drought Control in the Sahel, the Southern African Development Community and the Arab Maghreb Union, as well as within the programmes, funds and relevant agencies of the United Nations system, including the Food and Agriculture Organization of the United Nations, the United Nations Environment Programme and the United Nations Development Programme;

6. *Requests* the Secretary-General to report to the General Assembly at its fiftieth session on the implementation of the present resolution.

General Assembly resolution 48/175
21 December 1993   Meeting 86   Adopted without vote

Approved by Second Committee (A/48/717/Add.7) without vote, 6 December (meeting 45); draft by Vice-Chairman (A/C.2/48/L.66), based on informal consultations on draft by China and Colombia (for Group of 77) (A/C.2/48/L.45); agenda item 91 *(f)*.
Meeting numbers. GA 48th session: 2nd Committee 36-40, 42, 45; plenary 86.

Marine ecosystems

Straddling and highly migratory fish stocks

Pursuant to chapter 17 of Agenda 21 and a 1992 General Assembly resolution,[32] the United Nations Conference on Straddling Fish Stocks and Highly Migratory Fish Stocks met in New York in 1993 for an organizational session from 19 to 23 April and for a second session from 12 to 30 July. A summary of the discussions and recommendations was contained in an October report by the Secretary-General.[33] The Conference recommended that two further sessions be convened in 1994 and that the Food and Agriculture Organization of the United Nations (FAO) prepare information papers on the precautionary approach in fisheries management and on the concept of maximum sustainable yield.

A negotiating text prepared by the Conference Chairman was contained in an annex to the Secretary-General's report.

GENERAL ASSEMBLY ACTION

On 21 December, on the recommendation of the Second Committee, the General Assembly adopted without vote **resolution 48/194**.

United Nations Conference on Straddling Fish Stocks and Highly Migratory Fish Stocks

The General Assembly,

Reaffirming its resolution 47/192 of 22 December 1992, concerning the United Nations Conference on Straddling Fish Stocks and Highly Migratory Fish Stocks (the Conference),

Noting that the Conference held its organizational session in New York from 19 to 23 April 1993 and its second session, also in New York, from 12 to 30 July 1993,

Noting with appreciation that the Food and Agriculture Organization of the United Nations has agreed to prepare two information papers, one on the precautionary approach and the other on the concept of maximum sustainable yield,

Welcoming the report of the Secretary-General on the progress made by the Conference during 1993,

Taking note of the recommendation of the Conference to the General Assembly, as set forth in the report of the Conference on its second session, regarding the convening of two further sessions in 1994, required by the Conference in order to complete its work,

Convinced that the widest possible participation in the Conference is important to ensure its success,

1. *Notes* the progress made by the United Nations Conference on Straddling Fish Stocks and Highly Migratory Fish Stocks;

2. *Reaffirms* that the Conference should complete its work before the forty-ninth session of the General Assembly;

3. *Approves* the convening in New York of two further sessions of the Conference, to be held from 14 to 31 March 1994 and from 15 to 26 August 1994, in accordance with the recommendation of the Conference;

4. *Requests* the Secretary-General to provide services for these two sessions of the Conference, with facilities enabling the Conference to hold two simultaneous meetings during the sessions;

5. *Renews its request* to Governments and regional economic integration organizations to contribute to the voluntary fund established in accordance with paragraph 9 of General Assembly resolution 47/192 for the purpose of assisting developing countries, especially those most concerned by the subject-matter of the Conference, in particular the least developed among them, to participate fully and effectively in the Conference, and expresses its appreciation for the contributions to the fund made so far;

6. *Also requests* the Secretary-General to circulate to delegations as early as possible the information papers being prepared by the Food and Agriculture Organization of the United Nations;

7. *Further requests* the Secretary-General to submit to the General Assembly at its forty-ninth session the final report on the work of the Conference;

8. *Decides* to include in the provisional agenda of its forty-ninth session, under the item entitled "Implementation of decisions and recommendations of the United Nations Conference on Environment and Development," the sub-item entitled "Sustainable use and conservation of marine living resources of the high seas: United Nations Conference on Straddling Fish Stocks and Highly Migratory Fish Stocks".

General Assembly resolution 48/194
21 December 1993   Meeting 86   Adopted without vote

Approved by Second Committee (A/47/725) without vote, 10 December (meeting 47); draft by Fiji (A/C.2/48/L.44), orally revised following informal consultations; agenda item 99 *(c)*.
Meeting numbers. GA 48th session: 2nd Committee 36-43, 47; plenary 86.

Drift-net fishing

In response to a 1992 General Assembly request,[34] the Secretary-General submitted in October a report on large-scale pelagic drift-net fishing and its impact on living marine resources.[35] The report discussed the activities of intergovernmental organizations regarding pelagic drift-net fishing and reviewed the situation in the Pacific, Atlantic and Indian Oceans, the Baltic Sea and the Mediterranean.

GENERAL ASSEMBLY ACTION

On 21 December, the General Assembly adopted **decision 48/445**, by which it took note with appreciation of the report of the Secretary-General.[35] It called on all members of the international community, intergovernmental organizations, regional economic integration organizations and appropriate non-governmental organizations to provide the Secretary-General with information relevant to the implementation of a 1991 Assembly resolution.[36] It requested the Secretary-General to report to it in 1994, and to submit subsequently annual updates on further developments relevant to the implementation of that resolution.

Marine pollution from terrestrial sources

UNEP was invited, in chapter 17 of Agenda 21, to convene an intergovernmental meeting on protection of the marine environment from land-based activities. In a March report,[37] UNEP's Executive Director discussed that request and suggested a work plan, timetable and budget for the meeting.

On 21 May,[38] UNEP's Governing Council asked the Executive Director to coordinate preparations for the intergovernmental meeting to be held in 1995. It decided that the preparatory process should include, among other things, a preliminary meeting of experts in late 1993 to assess the effectiveness of selected regional agreements and a one-week meeting of Government-designated experts to focus on the 1985 Montreal Guidelines for the Protection of the Marine Environment against Pollution from Land-based Sources,[39] to be held in June 1994.

Conservation of wildlife

In a March report,[40] the UNEP Executive Director reviewed the Programme's efforts since 1990 to protect the African elephant and the African and Asian rhinoceros. She stated that in the last 20 years the world's rhinoceros population had declined by 85 per cent and that over the last decade African elephant populations had also declined rapidly, mainly as a result of intensive ivory poaching and the encroachment of human populations on their habitats.

The UNEP Governing Council, on 21 May,[41] requested the Executive Director to assist collaborative approaches to elephant conservation in Africa and to establish an African elephant conservation facility within UNEP. It also requested the Executive Director to establish an African and Asian rhinoceros conservation facility if requested by a forthcoming conference of range States and donors.

Regional cooperation

UNDP action. On 18 June,[42] the UNDP Governing Council asked the Administrator to recognize the need to protect vulnerable ecosystems such as large bodies of water bounded by more than one country, and urged him to use programming mechanisms available to him to respond to those problems if necessary. In adopting the decision, the Council took note of the need to protect

such large bodies of water as the Caspian Sea and Lake Victoria.

REFERENCES

[1]UNEP/GC.17/5/Add.2. [2]A/48/25 (dec. 17/6). [3]UNEP/GC.17/9. [4]UNEP/GC.17/15. [5]UNEP/GC.17/18. [6]A/48/25 (dec. 17/22). [7]UNEP/GC.17/5. [8]A/48/25 (dec. 17/14). [9]Ibid. (dec. 17/18). [10]Ibid. (dec. 17/15). [11]UNEP/GC.17/24. [12]A/48/25 (dec. 17/13). [13]Ibid. (dec. 17/29). [14]UNEP/GC.17/29. [15]YUN 1991, p. 495. [16]A/48/25 (dec. 17/26). [17]UNEP/GC.17/5/Add.1. [18]A/48/25 (dec. 17/24). [19]A/AC.241/4. [20]A/48/226. [21]A/48/226/Add.1. [22]YUN 1992, p. 686, GA res. 47/188, 22 Dec. 1992. [23]A/AC.241/15. [24]A/48/25 (dec. 17/19). [25]YUN 1977, p. 509. [26]UNEP/GC.17/14. [27]A/48/216-E/1993/92. [28]E/1993/55 & Corr.1. [29]YUN 1991, p. 501, ESC res. 1991/97, 26 July 1991. [30]DP/1993/43. [31]E/1993/35 (dec. 93/33). [32]YUN 1992, p. 688, GA res. 47/192, 22 Dec. 1992. [33]A/48/479. [34]YUN 1992, p. 689, GA dec. 47/443, 22 Dec. 1992. [35]A/48/451 & Corr.1,2. [36]YUN 1991, p. 503, GA res. 46/215, 20 Dec. 1991. [37]UNEP/GC.17/5/Add.3. [38]A/48/25 (dec. 17/20). [39]YUN 1985, p. 815. [40]UNEP/GC.17/5/Add.4. [41]A/48/25 (dec. 17/23). [42]E/1993/35 (dec. 93/13).

Programme and finances of UNEP

Finances

On 21 May,[1] the UNEP Governing Council requested the Executive Director to maintain a clear distinction between programme deliveries and administrative overheads in the Programme's budget format and presentation. The Council requested that the revised 1994-1995 and proposed 1996-1997 budgets be presented to its 1995 session in a more transparent format.

Environment Fund

On 21 May,[2] the UNEP Governing Council approved revised appropriations of $37,818,600 for the programme and programme support costs budget for 1992-1993, including $3,490,000 on a loan basis towards the construction of new office accommodation. It also approved an initial appropriation of $41,829,500 for the programme and programme support costs budget for the biennium 1994-1995.

Also on 21 May,[3] the Council approved an appropriation of $120/130 million for a core Environment Fund programme activity for the biennium 1994-1995. The budget subprogrammes receiving the largest share were: capacity-building for environmentally sound and sustainable development; environmental management of terrestrial ecosystems and their resources; and Earthwatch data, information, assessment and early warning. The Council approved an additional appropriation of up to $10 million for use as and when additional resources became available for a supplementary programme, particularly for further implementation of Agenda 21.

Trust funds

On 21 May,[4] the UNEP Governing Council took note of a report of the Executive Director,[5] which discussed the management and finances of 45 general and technical cooperation trust funds administered by UNEP. The Council approved the establishment of three general trust funds and four technical cooperation funds by the Executive Director since the Council's 1991 session.

UNEP regional offices

On 21 May,[6] the UNEP Governing Council requested the Executive Director to review UNEP's representation with a view to strengthening its regional and liaison offices.

UNEP Council

1993 session

At its seventeenth session, held at Nairobi from 10 to 21 May 1993, the UNEP Governing Council adopted 45 decisions on environmental and administrative matters,[7] including follow-up actions to UNCED; the role of women in environment and development; the environmental effects of the Iraq-Kuwait conflict; movements of hazardous wastes and irradiated nuclear fuel; transfer of environmentally sound technology; desertification; protection of the marine environment; measures for the conservation of elephant and rhinoceros populations; and climate.

On 12 February, in **decision 1993/208 C**, the Economic and Social Council decided that, when reviewing at its substantive session of 1993 the report of the Governing Council of UNEP on its seventeenth session, it would not consider new draft proposals except for specific recommendations requiring action by the Council and proposals relating to coordination aspects of the work of those bodies.

On 29 July, by **decision 1993/311**, the Economic and Social Council took note of the report of the Governing Council of UNEP on its seventeenth session.[7]

GENERAL ASSEMBLY ACTION

On 21 December, on the recommendation of the Second Committee, the General Assembly adopted without vote **resolution 48/174**.

Strengthening of the United Nations Environment Programme

The General Assembly,

Recalling its resolution 2997(XXVII) of 15 December 1972, in which it decided to establish a Governing Council of the United Nations Environment Programme,

Recalling also decision 15/1 of 25 May 1989 of the Governing Council of the United Nations Environment Programme, in which the Governing Council, *inter alia*, reaffirmed the central role of the United Nations Environment Programme as the central catalysing, coordinating and stimulating body in the field of environment within the United Nations system,

Recalling further decisions 16/1 and 16/6, both of 31 May 1991, of the Governing Council of the United Nations Environment Programme, in the first of which the Council expressed its support for retaining at the headquarters of the United Nations Environment Programme at Nairobi the programme activity centres already located there, decided that future major extensions to the physical or other infrastructure of the Programme, particularly those with global functions, would be centred principally at Nairobi, and requested the Executive Director to examine the feasibility of providing on-site interpretation facilities and to continue negotiations with the host Government with a view to improving the facilities available at the headquarters office at Nairobi, including external communication services,

Reaffirming paragraphs 38.21 and 38.23 of Agenda 21, in which it was stated that there would be a need for an enhanced and strengthened role for the United Nations Environment Programme and its Governing Council, that, *inter alia*, the regional offices of the Programme should be strengthened without weakening its headquarters at Nairobi and that its liaison and interaction with the United Nations Development Programme and the World Bank should be reinforced and intensified,

Reaffirming also paragraphs 25, 26 and 32 (c) of its resolution 47/191 of 22 December 1992,

Commending the United Nations Environment Programme for its leading role in the negotiation of many international conventions on the environment, its mobilization of global environmental awareness and its contribution in the area of capacity-building in regard to the preservation of the environment and its integration into sustainable development,

Mindful of the need to rationalize meetings related to the United Nations Environment Programme so as to ensure effective capacity utilization at the headquarters of the Programme,

1. *Endorses* the report of the Governing Council of the United Nations Environment Programme on the work of its seventeenth session and the decisions contained therein;

2. *Stresses* the need for close cooperation between the United Nations Environment Programme and the Commission on Sustainable Development in implementing the recommendations of the United Nations Conference on Environment and Development, in accordance with the relevant provisions of chapter 38 of Agenda 21;

3. *Welcomes* the action-oriented approach of the Governing Council towards the implementation of the follow-up activities to the Conference, as outlined in its report;

4. *Expresses its gratitude* to the Government of Kenya for the grant of an additional forty acres of land for the expansion of office facilities and the improvement of the communications network, and encourages it to continue to ensure that the United Nations Environment Programme and other United Nations organs, agencies and programmes based at Nairobi work in a conducive and hospitable environment;

5. *Invites* the Secretary-General to strengthen further the liaison function at Nairobi for the secretariat of the Commission on Sustainable Development, on the basis of arrangements made at the United Nations Conference on Environment and Development, duly taking into account all relevant provisions of paragraph 32 *(c)* of General Assembly resolution 47/191;

6. *Urges* Member States to make their contributions to the Environment Fund in accordance with Governing Council decision 17/32 of 21 May 1993;

7. *Notes with appreciation* the efforts of the Executive Director of the United Nations Environment Programme to ensure that as many meetings related to the Programme as possible are held at the headquarters of the Programme so as to maximize utilization of conference facilities and services;

8. *Requests* the Secretary-General to ensure that the programming of meetings related to the Programme is rationalized to facilitate economy and more effective capacity utilization at the headquarters of the Programme;

9. *Also requests* the Secretary-General to report to the General Assembly at its fiftieth session on the implementation of the present resolution.

General Assembly resolution 48/174

21 December 1993   Meeting 86   Adopted without vote

Approved by Second Committee (A/48/717/Add.6) without vote, 10 December (meeting 47); draft by Vice-Chairman (A/C.2/48/L.83), based on informal consultations on draft by China and Colombia (for Group of 77) (A/C.2/48/L.58) and orally revised and further orally amended by Australia and Belgium (for EU); agenda item 91 *(e)*.

Meeting numbers. GA 48th session: 2nd Committee 36-40, 43, 47; plenary 86.

REFERENCES

[1]A/48/25 (dec. 17/41). [2]Ibid. (dec. 17/33). [3]Ibid. (dec. 17/32). [4]Ibid. (dec. 17/39). [5]UNEP/GC.17/19. [6]A/48/25 (dec. 17/28). [7]A/48/25.

Environmental aspects of political, economic and other issues

Military conflicts and the environment

On 21 May,[1] the UNEP Governing Council encouraged Governments to establish a national environmental policy for the military sector and requested the Executive Director to report on the application of environmental norms for the treatment and disposal of hazardous wastes by military establishments.

Also on that date,[2] the Council requested the Executive Director to maintain UNEP's leading role in coordinating the efforts of the United Nations and other international organizations to assess the environmental effects of the conflict between Iraq and Kuwait, and to mobilize funds for assessment and rehabilitation programmes.

Environmental assistance to Israeli-occupied territories

On 21 May,[3] the UNEP Governing Council expressed concern over deteriorating environmental conditions in the occupied Palestinian and other Arab territories. It requested the Executive Director to provide technical assistance for Palestinian institutional and capacity-building in the environment field and to submit an updated report on the state of the environment in the occupied territories to the Council's eighteenth regular session.

Environmental problems of economies in transition

On 21 May,[4] the UNEP Governing Council requested the Executive Director to consider how UNEP could best assist those countries with economies in transition with their environmental problems. She was requested to participate fully in the follow-up to the 1993 Lucerne Conference on Environment for Europe.

Transfer of environmentally sound technology

On 21 May,[5] the UNEP Governing Council requested the Executive Director to examine the feasibility of developing international guidelines for information on potential environmental impacts that technology exporters should provide to importers, and to report to the Council on the results of that study at its 1995 session.

In February,[6] the Executive Director suggested that the establishment of three international environmental technology centres, in addition to the UNEP International Environment Centre in Japan, might be warranted. She suggested a centre for industrial pollution control technologies in Eastern Europe or nearby; a centre for forestry, agroforestry, afforestation and soil management technologies in Latin America and the Caribbean; and a centre for rangeland management and desertification control technologies in Africa. On 21 May,[7] the Council requested the Executive Director to strengthen existing links between UNEP and relevant centres of excellence, and to keep the establishment of technology centres under review.

Environmental Law

On 21 May,[8] the Governing Council adopted the Programme for the Development and Periodic Review of Environmental Law for the 1990s.[6] The Programme, which earlier had been adopted by a Meeting of Senior Government Officials Expert in Environmental Law that met in November 1991 and in September 1992, identified 18 programme areas and their respective objectives, strategies and activities for action by UNEP in the light of experience and new developments, including Agenda 21, since the 1982 adoption by the UNEP Governing Council of the 1981

Montevideo Programme for the Development and Periodic Review of Environmental Law,[9] which had provided the basis for UNEP activities in the field of environmental law for the following decade.

The 1993 Programme defined a broad strategy for UNEP activities in the field of environmental law for the 1990s. The Governing Council requested the Executive Director to prepare and disseminate analytical reports, organize intergovernmental meetings and contribute to capacity-building in the field of environmental law. The Council was to review the Programme's implementation not later than its regular session in 1997.

Environment and criminal law

In its **resolution 1993/28** on the role of criminal law in the protection of the environment, the Economic and Social Council, among other things, requested the Secretary-General to consider the possibility of undertaking activities in the field of environmental crime in the United Nations crime prevention and criminal justice programme (see PART THREE, Chapter XII).

REFERENCES

[1]A/48/25 (dec. 17/5). [2]Ibid. (dec. 17/7). [3]Ibid. (dec. 17/31). [4]Ibid. (dec. 17/27). [5]Ibid. (dec. 17/17). [6]UNEP/GC.17/5. [7]A/48/25 (dec. 17/21). [8]A/48/25 (dec. 17/25). [9]YUN 1981, p. 839.

Chapter IX

Population and human settlements

The United Nations Population Fund, while addressing the problems of population growth, distribution and movement, focused in 1993 on improving the quality of family-planning services, integrating them with reproductive health care, empowering women to make free and informed reproductive choices, and strengthening information, education and communication activities. It continued to assist Governments with the formulation, implementation and evaluation of population policies and programmes and with the collection of population data.

As part of preparations for the 1994 International Conference on Population and Development, the Economic and Social Council adopted a conceptual framework for the Conference's draft recommendations, including the outline of a new plan of action on population, sustained economic growth and sustainable development (decision 1993/323). Both the Council and the General Assembly emphasized the importance of a thorough intergovernmental preparatory process for the success of the Conference and action to publicize its objectives and the issues on its agenda (resolutions 1993/76 and 48/186).

The United Nations Centre for Human Settlements continued to assist developing countries in all aspects of human settlements activities, through research and development, technical cooperation and information dissemination. As the United Nations lead agency coordinating activities related to the Global Strategy for Shelter to the Year 2000, the Centre's objective remained adequate shelter for all.

The Commission on Human Settlements, at its fourteenth session, considered as its major themes a strategy for improving municipal management, intermediate and cost-effective building materials, and technologies and transfer mechanisms for housing delivery. In December, the General Assembly adopted a Plan of Action for 1994-1995 to implement the Global Strategy, as recommended by the Commission (48/178).

The Preparatory Committee for the United Nations Conference on Human Settlements (Habitat II), scheduled for 1996, held its organizational session in 1993. The preparatory process for the Conference was officially launched on 4 October.

Population

1994 International Conference on Population and Development

In 1992,[1] the General Assembly had endorsed a decision by the Economic and Social Council earlier that year[2] to hold the International Conference on Population and Development at Cairo, Egypt, from 5 to 13 September 1994.

In a note[3] to the Council in January 1993, the Secretary-General proposed that the second session of the Preparatory Committee for the Conference be advanced from August to mid-May 1993 and extended from four to eight days. It was also proposed that the Population Commission's twenty-seventh session be deferred until April 1994 when it could be held in conjunction with the third session of the Preparatory Committee. The Secretary-General recommended similar arrangements for the participation of non-governmental organizations (NGOs) to those adopted by the 1992 United Nations Conference on Environment and Development, but with improvements in the accreditation procedures.

ECONOMIC AND SOCIAL COUNCIL ACTION

On 12 February, the Economic and Social Council adopted **resolution 1993/4** without vote.

International Conference on Population and Development and its preparatory process
The Economic and Social Council,
Recalling its resolutions 1989/91 of 26 July 1989, 1991/93 of 26 July 1991 and 1992/37 of 30 July 1992, in which it decided on the convening, mandate and preparatory process of the International Conference on Population and Development,
Taking note of General Assembly resolution 47/176 of 22 December 1992, in which, *inter alia*, the Assembly recognized the importance of ensuring an adequate intergovernmental preparatory process for the Conference, as well as the importance of the participation in the Conference and its preparatory process of all relevant non-governmental organizations from developed and developing countries,
1. *Decides* that the second session of the Preparatory Committee for the International Conference on Population and Development shall be rescheduled to take place from 10 to 21 May 1993 in New York;

2. *Also decides* to convene the third session of the Preparatory Committee from 11 to 22 April 1994, within the overall resources of the proposed programme budget for the biennium 1994-1995 to be approved by the General Assembly at its forty-eighth session in accordance with its resolution 47/213 of 23 December 1992 and without prejudice to the utilization of resources available through contributions to the voluntary trust funds for the Conference, taking fully into account the need to ensure the success of the Conference in fulfilling its mandate and the need to ensure an adequate intergovernmental preparatory process for it;

3. *Further decides* to postpone the twenty-seventh session of the Population Commission to 1994 and to consider at the Council's substantive session of 1993 the possibility of scheduling it in conjunction with the third session of the Preparatory Committee, within the overall resources of the proposed programme budget for the biennium 1994-1995 to be approved by the General Assembly at its forty-eighth session in accordance with its resolution 47/213;

4. *Adopts* the modalities for the participation in and contribution to the Conference and its preparatory process of non-governmental organizations, as set out in the annex to the present resolution;

5. *Decides* that, in order to support the full and effective participation of developing countries, in particular the least developed among them, in the Conference and its preparatory process, each least developed country, to the extent that extrabudgetary funds are available, may be provided, from the voluntary trust funds for the Conference, with travel expenses and, on an exceptional basis, daily subsistence allowance for one representative attending the sessions of the Preparatory Committee and the Conference itself;

6. *Recognizes* the importance of non-governmental participation in the preparatory process and the Conference itself and encourages all support to enable representatives of non-governmental organizations from developing countries to participate fully.

ANNEX
Participation of non-governmental organizations in the International Conference on Population and Development and its preparatory process

1. Non-governmental organizations in consultative status with the Economic and Social Council which express their wish to attend the International Conference on Population and Development and the meetings of the Preparatory Committee for the Conference shall be accredited for participation. Others wishing to be accredited may apply to the secretariat of the Conference for this purpose in accordance with the requirements of the present resolution.

2. The secretariat of the Conference shall be responsible for the receipt and preliminary evaluation, in accordance with the provisions of the present resolution, of requests from non-governmental organizations for accreditation to the Conference and its preparatory process.

3. All such applications must be accompanied by information on the competence of the organization and the relevance of its activities to the work of the Preparatory Committee, with an indication of the particular areas of the Conference preparations to which such competence and relevance pertain, and should include the following:

(a) The purposes of the organization;

(b) Information on its programmes and activities in areas relevant to the Conference and its preparatory process and in which country or countries they are carried out;

(c) Confirmation of its activities at the national and/or international level;

(d) Copies of its annual reports with financial statements, and a list of members of the governing body and their countries of nationality;

(e) A description of its membership, indicating the total number of members and their geographical distribution.

4. In the evaluation of the relevance of applications of non-governmental organizations for accreditation to the Conference and its preparatory process, it is agreed that a determination will be made based on their background and involvement in population issues or population and development issues, including those mentioned in paragraph 4 of Economic and Social Council resolution 1991/93 of 26 July 1991.

5. Non-governmental organizations seeking accreditation shall be asked to confirm their interest in the goals and objectives of the Conference.

6. In cases where the secretariat of the Conference believes, on the basis of the information provided in accordance with the present resolution, that the organization has established its competence and the relevance of its activities to the work of the Preparatory Committee, it will recommend to the Preparatory Committee that the organization be accredited. In cases where the secretariat does not recommend the granting of accreditation, it will make available to the Preparatory Committee its reasons for not doing so. The secretariat should ensure that its recommendations are available to members of the Preparatory Committee at least one week prior to the start of each session.

7. The Preparatory Committee will decide on all proposals for accreditation within twenty-four hours after the recommendations of the secretariat of the Conference have been taken up by the Preparatory Committee in plenary meeting. In the event of a decision not being taken within this period, interim accreditation shall be accorded until such time as a decision is taken.

8. A non-governmental organization that has been granted accreditation to attend a session of the Preparatory Committee may attend all its future sessions.

9. In recognition of the intergovernmental nature of the Conference, non-governmental organizations shall have no negotiating role in the work of the Conference and its preparatory process.

10. Relevant non-governmental organizations in consultative status with the Economic and Social Council may be given an opportunity to briefly address the Preparatory Committee in plenary meeting and its subsidiary bodies. Other relevant non-governmental organizations may also ask to speak briefly at such meetings. If the number of requests is too large, the Preparatory Committee shall request the non-governmental organizations to form themselves into constituencies, each constituency to speak through one spokesperson. Any oral intervention by a non-governmental organization should, in accordance with normal United Nations practice, be made at the discretion of the chairman and with the consent of the Preparatory Committee.

11. Relevant non-governmental organizations may, at their own expense, make written presentations dur-

ing the preparatory process in the official languages of the United Nations, as they deem appropriate. Those written presentations will not be issued as official documents except in accordance with United Nations rules of procedure.

Economic and Social Council resolution 1993/4

12 February 1993   Meeting 3   Adopted without vote

Draft by President and members of Bureau based on informal consultations (E/1993/L.10/Rev.1); agenda item 4.
Meeting numbers. ESC 2, 3.

Preparatory activities

During 1993, preparatory activities for the 1994 International Conference on Population and Development were undertaken by the United Nations Population Fund (UNFPA), the Population Division of the Secretariat's Department of Economic and Social Development—which was incorporated into the Department for Economic and Social Information and Policy Analysis later in the year—and Conference focal points designated by 19 units, programmes and organizations of the United Nations system. They focused on priority issues, including population growth and demographic structure; population policies and programmes; population, environment and development; population distribution and migration; status of women and population; and family-planning programmes, health and family well-being.

The Population Commission, acting as the Preparatory Committee, reviewed preparatory activities at its second session (New York, 10-21 May 1993)[4] and agreed on provisional rules of procedure for the Conference. It also considered the conceptual framework of draft recommendations of the Conference, proposed by the Conference Secretary-General.[5] The framework provided the outline of a new plan of action on population, sustained economic growth and sustainable development, to be adopted by the Conference; it was based on a number of international instruments, including the 1974 World Population Plan of Action[6] and the recommendations of the 1984 International Conference on Population.[7]

The Preparatory Committee decided to approve a list of NGOs to be accredited to the Conference. On 30 July, the Economic and Social Council endorsed that decision, took note of the Committee's report[4] and approved the provisional agenda and documentation for the Committee's third session (**decision 1993/325**). By **decision 1993/324** of the same date, the Council endorsed the Committee's recommendation that representatives designated by associate members of the regional commissions could participate as observers, without the right to vote, in the deliberations of the Conference, the preparatory process and any other appropriate committee or working group.

In October,[8] the United Nations Secretary-General drew the attention of the General Assembly

to the report of the Preparatory Committee on its second session. By **decision 48/448** of 21 December, the Assembly took note of the information.

ECONOMIC AND SOCIAL COUNCIL ACTION

The Economic and Social Council, in July, adopted **decision 1993/323** without vote.

Proposed conceptual framework of the draft recommendations of the International Conference on Population and Development

At its 46th plenary meeting, on 30 July 1993, the Economic and Social Council decided to request the Secretary-General of the International Conference on Population and Development, in preparing documentation for the Conference, to be guided by the views expressed by delegations and other participants at the second session of the Preparatory Committee for the International Conference on Population and Development, and to take into account the Chairman's summary annexed to the present decision.

ANNEX
Chairman's summary concerning the conceptual framework

1.   The purpose of the present summary is to provide guidance to the secretariat of the International Conference on Population and Development for further work on the draft of the Cairo document, to be submitted to the Preparatory Committee at its third session, based on the discussions that took place at the second session of the Preparatory Committee on the proposed conceptual framework of the draft recommendations of the Conference.

2.   Discussions on the structure of the document took place in a subgroup of the informal consultations of the whole and led to the following draft structure:

Preamble
Principles/fundamental considerations
Choices and responsibilities

Chapter I.   The interrelationships between population, sustained economic growth and sustainable development
Chapter II.   Gender equality and empowerment of women
Chapter III.   Population growth and structure
Chapter IV.   The family, its role and composition
Chapter V.   Reproductive rights, reproductive health and family planning
Chapter VI.   Health and mortality
Chapter VII.   Population distribution, urbanization and internal migration
Chapter VIII.   International migration
Means of implementation
Chapter IX.   Promotion of population information, education and communication
Chapter X.   Capacity-building
Chapter XI.   Technology, research and development
Partnership in population—actors and resources
Chapter XII.   National action
Chapter XIII.   International cooperation
Chapter XIV.   Partnerships with non-governmental sectors
From commitment to action
Chapter XV.   Follow-up to the Conference

3. The discussions on the content of the document in both plenary meetings and the informal consultations of the whole covered the entire range of topics proposed in the conceptual framework, as well as the issue of goals for the year 2015 proposed by the Secretary-General of the International Conference on Population and Development. Those discussions are summarized as follows.

4. Several delegations spoke on the importance of ensuring that the preamble defined the context of the Conference document and conveyed to a broader public the vision and purpose of the Conference. It was suggested that, in addition to the items contained in paragraph 13 of the conceptual framework, the preamble should include reference to past experiences with population policies and programmes; contain strengthened demographic data that was focused on the twenty-year framework; and indicate action necessary to attain population objectives in the context of sustained economic growth and sustainable development, with emphasis on human rights and giving special attention to the developing countries, particularly the least developed countries. The preamble should also draw attention to the magnitude of resources required for implementing commitments made by the Conference. The list of instruments mentioned in paragraph 14 of the conceptual framework should be expanded for balance and coverage and should include key regional documents.

5. All delegations agreed that the principles would be an essential part of any document emanating from the Conference and would form the basis for the new plan of action. That section of the document should ensure that the plan of action was action-oriented and would form the basis for international consensus. While circumstances would change and priorities vary, the principles agreed on at the Conference would provide the guiding philosophy in the area of population and development well into the twenty-first century.

6. Most delegations stressed that the principles should be built as much as possible on agreed international instruments, including the World Population Plan of Action, the recommendations of the International Conference on Population, the Amsterdam Declaration on a Better Life for Future Generations, the Rio Declaration on Environment and Development and Agenda 21. Many delegations considered that the right to development was an essential principle, as was the sovereignty of nations.

7. Numerous delegations favoured a group of principles in which the importance of human rights was fundamental and provided the main point of departure. It was hoped that the principles would be concise and easily readable so as to have maximum public appeal.

8. It was generally agreed that the International Conference on Population and Development should concentrate on its overall theme of population, sustained economic growth and sustainable development. Issues and recommendations relating to this theme should be forward-looking, operational and pragmatic.

9. Many delegations mentioned the new climate of agreement and the spirit of cooperation regarding population issues. They also noted the lack of major differences between the approaches of the developing and the developed regions on substantive issues and the broad consensus on the need to examine population matters in the context of development. They further stressed the central importance of the human being in all questions of population and development and the need for population policies and programmes to be based on the fundamental rights and freedoms of individuals and couples.

10. While building on the important achievements of the 1974 and 1984 population conferences, many delegations endorsed the suggestion of the Secretary-General of the Conference for a new plan of action that would be free-standing and operational in nature. They also stressed the importance of ensuring that the recommendations were formulated in a manner that clearly identified their innovative aspects and priorities. In addition, the recommendations of the regional conferences and expert group meetings should be fully taken into account in preparing the Cairo document.

11. Many delegations emphasized the need for recommendations to reflect the considerable demographic, social and economic diversity that existed among and within countries. Traditional classifications of development were considered inadequate, given the social and economic changes of recent years. The economies in transition of Europe, for example, had very complex demographic and socio-economic problems that differed markedly from those of the more developed European countries. Recommendations for action should take into account regional diversity and country-specific conditions.

12. All delegations agreed that population, environment and development were inextricably interrelated. Many delegations stressed, however, that the Conference should not run the risk of being too diffuse in its deliberations, but rather should focus most particularly on population-related issues, while taking note of complementary issues. In this regard, it was recognized that the Conference should build on existing international agreements, especially those adopted at the United Nations Conference on Environment and Development, including Agenda 21. Merely renegotiating those agreements would serve no purpose.

13. Many delegations strongly emphasized that sustained economic growth and socio-economic development had a fundamental impact on population. Highest priority must therefore be accorded to improving the quality of life for all people, notably through the alleviation of poverty; the creation of employment; the guarantee of human rights; and the improvement of health, education and housing, and economic opportunities, particularly for women.

14. In order to promote sustained economic growth and sustainable development, many delegations stressed the importance of a supportive international economic environment. The debt burden of poorer countries remained a major constraint to their socio-economic development. Restrictive trade policies inhibited economic growth and led to inefficient patterns of production and resource use. Structural adjustment programmes could have the effect of weakening social services, placing added stress on vulnerable groups, including women and children, and encouraging over-exploitation of natural resources and environmental degradation. Emphasis was also placed on science and technology and the development of relevant new technologies and their accessibility by countries in need. Building domestic capacities and strengthening institutions to meet the challenges of demographic change were further priorities.

15. Many delegations pointed out that achieving the objectives of sustained economic growth, sustainable de-

velopment and effective population policies would require mobilization of substantial additional financial resources from the international community as well as within countries. It would not be useful to adopt objectives without considering the means of implementation and the resources required. In this regard, the model provided by Agenda 21 could be considered.

16.   There was general agreement that population factors had significant impact on and were in turn influenced by continued widespread poverty and inequality of wealth between and within nations, as well as by wasteful patterns of production and consumption, unsustainable use of natural resources and environmental degradation and serious social and gender inequalities.

17.   An important priority, it was pointed out, was the development of adaptive strategies to address the implications for sustainable development and the environment resulting from the inevitable increase in population numbers and changes in concentration and distribution, particularly in ecologically vulnerable areas and urban agglomerations. Related to this were strategies to minimize dislocations of populations due to environmental factors and natural disasters. Such policies would need to address the underlying causes, promote emergency preparedness and establish mechanisms to aid the victims, both within and outside their own country.

18.   Several delegations noted the importance of maintaining a balance between human needs and aspirations on the one hand and the natural resource base and environmental conditions on the other. It was recognized that inefficient and unsustainable use of natural resources and environmental degradation, whether caused by rapid population growth, poverty or unsustainable consumption patterns, could constrain prospects for socio-economic development. In this connection, some delegations underscored the importance of changing values, behaviour patterns and the distribution of power within society.

19.   Social and economic factors could influence the impact of population on both local and global environmental problems. Many delegations referred to increasing demographic-related pressures on the environment and natural resources, whether associated with numbers, urban concentrations, migration or consumption patterns. Concern was expressed about effects on natural life-support capacities in different ecological zones.

20.   It was considered important to promote more effective partnerships between Governments and the private sector in addressing population and development issues. Greater involvement and participation in the process of both policy-making and implementation by local communities, industry, non-governmental organizations and indigenous groups should be stimulated.

21.   There was unanimous agreement that the empowerment of women was an essential factor in achieving population objectives, sustained economic growth and sustainable development. Existing gender inequalities and barriers to women should be eliminated and their participation in all levels of policy-making and implementation should be increased. Opportunities should be enhanced for leadership roles and for greater access to education, jobs and improved health services, including sexual and reproductive health services and family planning. The role and responsibility of men in bringing about gender equity, policy and value changes was repeatedly emphasized.

22.   Delegations expected that in the Cairo document issues of gender equality, equity and rights that were specific to particular chapters would be addressed in those chapters. Gender issues (such as achieving gender equality in education and training; enactment and/or enforcement of laws pertaining to minimum age at marriage; proposals concerning women's opportunities for productive and remunerative employment; and women's rights, health and advancement at the workplace), which cut across many of the chapters and could not be adequately dealt with under any single heading, such as health or reproduction, should be addressed under chapter II of the document, to be entitled "Gender equality and empowerment of women". Many delegations emphasized the need to present the recommendations in a systematic manner, and a suggestion was made to structure them according to four categories: legal, economic, educational and cultural. Some delegations called attention to issues such as power-sharing in decision-making in the family, violence against women, prostitution and the special needs of women for protection in times of war. Genital mutilation, which some delegations saw as both a health issue and a rights issue, also needed to be addressed in the Conference document. In general, it was felt that the document should give greater emphasis to the comprehensive relationship between women's empowerment, development and population.

23.   Some delegations emphasized that the document should not merely reiterate general principles that had already been accepted but should go further than earlier agreements and make concrete proposals for action that would lead to those accepted goals, or else should elaborate or extend earlier language regarding rights and responsibilities pertaining to gender issues, as they were linked to population and development. It was also felt that there was a need to develop indicators to monitor progress in this area. Specific suggestions were made in some areas, such as goals for achieving gender equality in education and universal primary education for both girls and boys. Delegations also emphasized the need to include concrete steps to improve women's access to productive and remunerative employment, as well as measures to eliminate negative stereotypes against women.

24.   While many delegations emphasized the importance of rapid population growth as one of the main challenges faced by the world community, it was also recognized that there existed considerable variation in population growth rates among regions and countries. Consequently, any recommendations concerning population growth should take this diversity into account and be formulated accordingly. Some delegations noted that there was a growing international consensus on the importance of achieving stabilization of population. A few delegations suggested that specific demographic targets should be set, including targets for population growth.

25.   Trends in population growth and structure, many delegations agreed, should be clearly highlighted in the final document, since they provided the necessary background against which population and development relationships interacted. In this regard, a number of delegations stressed the special situation of the least developed countries, which needed special atten-

tion. Also, mention was made of the importance of future levels of population in relation to consumption and production.

26. Many delegations noted that population growth and poverty were closely related but that simplistic cause and effect notions should be avoided. Many socio-economic variables affected population growth, in particular gender equality and human resources development, in the areas, *inter alia*, of education, health, family planning and employment. These linkages should be brought out in the final document.

27. While the discussion on population structure covered all age groups, many delegations focused particularly on population ageing and agreed that the consequences of ageing required close scrutiny. The issue of ageing was of immediate concern in a number of the developed countries, but it was pointed out that problems of ageing could become overwhelmingly large in the developing countries, where the bulk of the elderly would be living.

28. Rapidly ageing populations represented a new phenomenon in human history that required urgent attention, particularly when viewed over a longer time perspective. It was pointed out that women would make up a disproportionate share of the elderly, making it all the more crucial to integrate women in the development process.

29. Several delegations expressed the need for the document to take into account the perspective of particular population groups, such as indigenous peoples and the disabled, whose needs concerning, *inter alia*, sexual and reproductive health, including family-planning services, should be recognized. It was also suggested that the Conference document should address the specific forms of discrimination that disabled people may face with regard to international migration.

30. Many delegations requested that there should be a separate chapter on the family, emphasizing its central role in society. Delegations emphasized the importance of addressing within this issue the diversity of families and their varied experiences.

31. Many delegations suggested that the Cairo document should recognize that women, regardless of age, marital status, sexual orientation and other social conditions, have the right to have access to information, education and services to exercise their reproductive and sexual rights.

32. The reproductive rights of couples and individuals to decide freely and responsibly the number and spacing of their children, as stated in the World Population Plan of Action, was reaffirmed by a large majority of delegations. A few speakers suggested some modification of the rights to make them apply to couples only, to individuals only or to women only.

33. In relation to sexual and reproductive health, many delegations reiterated that reproductive health programmes should protect women of all ages. Such programmes should have a client-centred approach. Some delegations recommended the inclusion of proper prevention, treatment and referral of sexually transmitted diseases and infertility.

34. Family-planning services were widely recognized as a means of fulfilling reproductive rights as well as of promoting maternal and child health. Such services, it was strongly recommended, should be voluntary, accessible, acceptable and affordable. Improving the qual-

ity of services and choice of available methods was also recognized as an important priority. Many delegations reiterated the need to promote research and development on both male and female family-planning methods. The role that men can play in the practice of family planning was also suggested as an important topic of attention. Many participants recommended a special mention of the need to remove legal barriers to the wider social dissemination and marketing of family-planning methods.

35. Human sexuality and sexual behaviour were recognized as a neglected area that required special attention. In this respect, it was recommended that sexuality and gender relationships be treated as closely interrelated and as factors that affect sexual health and reproductive behaviour. Many delegations suggested specific action covering a wide range of activities, such as behavioural research, sex education for boys and girls, counselling, and the consideration of parents as a major channel for ensuring responsible parenthood.

36. Adolescents also received particular attention. Many delegations recommended the inclusion in the Cairo document of specific actions aimed at facilitating informed decisions regarding their sexual behaviour, sexual health and the prevention of sexually transmitted diseases, as well as the removal of barriers to the access by adolescents to reproductive health-care services.

37. It was pointed out that among the issues that the Conference needed to address was the unacceptably high levels of maternal mortality and morbidity in many developing countries. Unsafe and illegal abortion, which in many countries was an important cause of maternal morbidity and mortality, constituted one of the most neglected problems affecting women's lives. It was seen by most delegations as a major public health issue which the Conference needed to recognize and address as such. While many delegations suggested that all women should have access to safe abortion, others suggested that the best way to eliminate abortions was the provision of effective, modern contraception information and services; a few delegations reiterated that abortion should not be promoted as a method of family planning.

38. Several delegations emphasized the importance of primary health care in combating infant, child and maternal mortality and expressed concern about the reduction of social investment in health as a result of structural adjustment programmes. It was recommended that, with respect to child survival, the Conference take into account the strategies and goals agreed upon at the World Summit for Children. The situation prevailing in the countries in economic transition regarding mortality levels and trends, especially adult male mortality, preoccupied several delegations and should also be addressed in the final document.

39. Many delegations stressed the need for the Conference document to pay particular attention to those issues that had come to light since the International Conference on Population in 1984, such as the acquired immunodeficiency syndrome (AIDS) pandemic. The Cairo document was seen as a unique opportunity to articulate a consensus on strategies for the prevention of human immunodeficiency virus (HIV) infection. In this respect, it was noted that information, education and communication campaigns were vital for preventing the

spread of AIDS and that information about the prevention of HIV/AIDS infection should be included as an element in family-planning programmes. The issue of international cooperation in research on drugs to treat and prevent AIDS should receive adequate attention.

40.   With respect to themes related to population distribution and internal migration, delegations supported the need for decentralization and the strengthening of local government. Support was also expressed for the elimination of generalized subsidies in urban areas, the adoption of appropriate pricing policies for services and agricultural goods and the introduction of cost-recovery schemes. Subsidies must be directed only to the urban poor, whose productivity had to be enhanced as part of any strategy of poverty alleviation. Inclusion of environmental issues related to population distribution was welcomed. There was support for the need to promote balanced urban and rural development and to create jobs in rural areas. Redirecting migration from large to small or medium-sized urban centres as a means of achieving a balanced population distribution was endorsed. Some delegations suggested that recommendations to enhance data sources on internal migration were needed, as well as studies on the causes of internal migration.

41.   With respect to international migration, several delegations stressed the need to consider different types of migrants. It was important to use the appropriate terminology, especially in the area of rights. With respect to migrant workers, mention of the relevant International Labour Organisation conventions and recommendations was suggested, although caution had to be exercised in citing international instruments that had not yet been ratified. Delegations from the developed countries underscored the relevance of the recommendations on international migration made by the European Population Conference, held at Geneva from 23 to 26 March 1993, whose language already represented the broad consensus of countries that were members of the Economic Commission for Europe.

42.   The generally positive tone adopted in discussing international migration was welcomed. It was pointed out that in many circumstances migration was beneficial both to countries of origin and to receiving countries. The challenge was to reduce pressures leading to uncontrolled migration. Several delegations pointed out the difficulty of the task, particularly because the development process was likely to increase migration pressures in the short term. A few delegations noted that strong migratory pressures could be generated in the economies in transition if their serious demographic problems were not solved, in conjunction with job-creation. It was suggested that a special subsection on international migration and development be included. That subsection should contain recommendations regarding the causes of migration, particularly relative to those areas where economic growth and sustainable development could be fostered by international cooperation. Some delegations stressed the need for bilateral or multilateral negotiations and agreements regarding particular aspects of international migration, such as the treatment of migrant workers and their families or the migration of skilled personnel. The need to protect female migrant workers from exploitation was underscored.

43.   Several delegations noted that it was important to prevent racism and xenophobia not only with respect to long-term migrants but rather with respect to all migrants. The integration of long-term migrants was to be pursued while at the same time respecting their cultural background.

44.   The need to improve statistics on both migrants and their remittances was stressed by a number of delegations. The interchange of information between the sending and the receiving countries had to be fostered. Further studies on the causes of international migration and the effects of remittances were suggested.

45.   With respect to refugees, delegations indicated that the relevant international instruments should be mentioned and that it was important to reiterate the international consensus on protection. Mention should be made of the right to seek asylum and not to the right to asylum. It was stressed that refugee assistance was needed both in the developing countries and in the countries that were in economic transition. The provision of adequate health and sexual and reproductive health services for female refugees was suggested.

46.   Many speakers emphasized the major role of population information, education and communication and motivational activities in bringing a diverse cross-section of policy makers, planners, programme managers, administrators, field workers and the general public to new levels of awareness about the implications of emerging population issues. In order to achieve responsible choices in all aspects of population, including fertility and migration, better communication was needed to reach all segments of the population. Individuals, families and communities should know what choices were available to them and how best to make them. At the same time, Governments should recognize their responsibility at every level to avoid coercion and to promote informed choice. It was pointed out that, with the wide variety of forms of information and communication channels available for awareness creation and the delivery of motivational messages, Governments should carefully examine their information, education and communication programmes to ensure that they employ appropriate information-processing and repackaging techniques in order to achieve maximum results with their specific target audiences.

47.   Mere awareness was no longer sufficient. It would be appropriate to move from awareness to action. It was therefore appropriate to spell out for the 1990s, in the fields of information, education and communication, specific options and opportunities that would enhance individual, family, community and national choices.

48.   The importance of timely dissemination of reliable and up-to-date information in appropriate formats for the formulation of effective population policies and the implementation of efficient programmes should be stressed in the Conference document. It should emphasize that the development of national population information systems was an effective means of organizing the data and information that constituted the knowledge-base on population. The document should recommend that the use of modern information-handling technologies be promoted to develop databases, facilitate the processing and analysis of population data and improve the exchange of information.

49.   Many delegations considered the collection and analysis of population and related statistics to be essential for a complete and accurate understanding of popu-

lation trends in the formulation, implementation and monitoring of population plans and programmes. Research, both scientific and policy related, was emphasized as an essential ingredient of population and development efforts. In addition, research should pay proper attention to gender issues and considerations of special population groups, such as indigenous peoples and the disabled.

50. Several delegations pointed out the need to give greater emphasis to data-generation, training (including research training) and research in the area of population. In many developing countries, the paucity of population data and the insufficiency of research capabilities had adversely affected the possibility of meaningfully integrating population perspectives into development plans and strategies.

51. A number of speakers stressed the importance of research and technology in responding to population and development issues, particularly with regard to contraception, infant and child survival, disability and environmental degradation. The Cairo document should reflect the vital contributions that technology and research could make in improving human lives and living conditions.

52. There was a broad consensus among delegations that strong emphasis needed to be placed in the Cairo document on the need for broadened national action aimed at social development. More resources, both national and international, should be assigned to social programmes. Several delegations endorsed the view of the Secretary-General of the Conference that the share of total national expenditure going to the social sectors should rise to at least 20 per cent. It was underscored that, within social-sector expenditure, the population sector should be given high priority, commensurate with the crucial linkages between that sector and socio-economic development.

53. National action in population-related matters concerned developing and developed countries alike. The theme of the Conference—population, sustained economic growth and sustainable development—made it clear that a reciprocity of actions was needed, with the North re-examining its lifestyles and unsustainable consumption patterns while the South acted to bring population growth down to a level compatible with sustainable development. Many delegations highlighted the necessity of including in the Cairo document this broad perspective of population and development.

54. Delegations suggested a broadening of the scope of resource mobilization beyond family planning to encompass sexual and reproductive health care. Further, many delegations were of the opinion that an even broader message must come out of the Conference, namely that reproductive health and family planning were linked to other factors, such as education and women's status, which were equally important for the achievement of socio-economic development.

55. On the matter of increased allocation of national resources for population, delegations were in broad agreement. None the less, increased allocations should be made within the constraints of overall resource availability and perceived national development priorities. International bilateral and multilateral assistance, which had been declining in recent years, had played an important part in facilitating national action in the area of population. In the view of many delegations, assistance for population should be increased in line with an overall increase in overseas development assistance to 0.7 per cent of gross national product.

56. Delegations broadly supported the need for a partnership for national action on population between Governments, non-governmental organizations and other organizations outside government, as well as the private sector. Non-governmental organizations were seen not as substitutes for government action but as partners acting as catalysts for change, setting quality standards for population programmes and developing innovative approaches.

57. Delegations also considered it important for the Cairo document to address the issue of adequate and reliable funding for the activities of non-governmental organizations. Both Governments and donor agencies should develop mechanisms for assuring a regular flow of resources to non-governmental organizations. In the view of some delegations, this policy should include increasingly direct reliance on national non-governmental organizations, in order to profit from their knowledge of local socio-cultural conditions.

58. Similarly, the complementary role of the private sector in the area of population should be clearly spelt out in the Cairo document. Legal and regulatory barriers impeding full access to reproductive health and family-planning services should be reviewed. The contribution of services supplied by the private sector to promoting cost-effectiveness in reproductive health care and other social sectors should be given full recognition.

59. Many delegations noted the need for updated estimates for resource requirements in order to achieve global population goals of the sort proposed by the Secretary-General of the Conference. The Amsterdam Declaration on a Better Life for Future Generations, the only international forum to have addressed the issue of resource mobilization for population activities, should be refined in this respect, so as to provide the Cairo Conference with more precise estimates of the resources required over the next decade. In this connection, various delegations suggested that relevant recommendations made by the European Population Conference regarding resource mobilization be consulted.

60. The appeal to increase resources for population activities could be strengthened by emphasizing the developmental successes achieved by investments in population programmes and the high rates of return observed on such investments. Other delegations noted that post-cold-war circumstances presented the opportunity to increase investments in social sectors substantially, including the population sector.

61. The need for international cooperation for technical assistance to help resolve various population issues was underscored. The special needs of the economies in transition for such cooperation was noted and it was suggested that the corresponding recommendations made by the European Population Conference be consulted.

62. There was general support for the proposal of the Secretary-General of the Conference to include a set of quantitative goals in the Cairo document. Such goals must take into account regional and national variations. Some delegations suggested that the proposed time-frame of twenty years be segmented into five- and ten-year frames. Progress towards achieving the goals should be monitored.

63. The point was made by many delegations that the goals must be consistent with each other and with those set at other international forums. There must be no coercion of any kind involved in the programmes formulated to achieve those goals. Some delegations suggested the possibility of including other social and economic goals.

64. Some delegations suggested that the Cairo document also include qualitative goals and objectives.

65. Additional resources would be required to achieve those goals. Estimates in this regard should be prepared by the Secretariat, taking into account current and proposed levels of national expenditure in the social sector.

66. Several delegations emphasized the need for the Cairo document to make adequate provision for the follow-up to commitments made at the Conference, including mechanisms for the review and appraisal of progress made towards implementation of Conference objectives. Some delegations also suggested that the document include recommendations on institutional arrangements for the implementation of the new plan of action.

Economic and Social Council decision 1993/323

Adopted without vote

Referred by Economic Committee (E/1993/112), 26 July (meeting 15); draft by Preparatory Committee (E/1993/69); agenda item 15 *(f)*.

Reports of the Secretary-General of the Conference. In response to a 1991 Economic and Social Council resolution,[9] the Secretary-General of the Conference, Dr. Nafis Sadik, Executive Director of UNFPA, submitted a progress report in April 1993[10] reviewing preparations and related financial and organizational questions.

She noted that, in response to her request, more than 80 national committees related to the Conference preparatory process had been set up as of early 1993, and that the Conference secretariat had developed an outline for use by Governments in preparing their national reports on population. As part of its information activities, the secretariat continued to publish a newsletter covering Conference preparations. The newsletter, *Population 94,* was renamed *ICPD 94* in early 1993 and was to be issued every two months in English, French and Spanish. Issues related to the participation of NGOs were discussed further by the NGO Planning Committee for the Conference and its Steering Committee at meetings in New York on 8 January and 11 and 12 March, respectively. The report noted the ongoing seventh population inquiry and exercises to monitor population trends and policies and multilateral population programmes. The financial requirements for the Conference were estimated at $5,651,000 and included $2,650,300 for conference servicing and some $3 million in non-conference-servicing costs.

In response to a 1992 General Assembly request,[1] the Secretary-General of the Conference submitted a further progress report on Conference preparations in October.[11] The report noted that national preparatory committees had been established in more than 100 countries and that the Conference secretariat continued to disseminate information on the objectives and activities of the Conference through its newsletter and other information materials. In accordance with Economic and Social Council **resolution 1993/4,** 332 NGOs received accreditation for the Conference, while 69 others also participated in the preparatory process.

Coordination within the United Nations system was ensured through the Administrative Committee on Coordination and its Ad Hoc Inter-Agency Meeting for the Conference, which met for the second time in 1993 (Geneva, 13 July).[12] The Meeting reviewed Conference preparations and discussed the contributions of United Nations bodies to the review and appraisal of the World Population Plan of Action, as well as the proposed action programme to be adopted at the Conference.

An addendum to the Secretary-General's report[13] provided an annotated outline of the final Conference document, dealing with the interrelationships between population, sustained economic growth and sustainable development; gender equality and empowerment of women; roles, composition and structure of the family; population growth and structure; reproductive rights, reproductive health and family planning; health and mortality; population distribution, urbanization and internal migration; international migration; population information, education and communication; capacity-building; technology, research and development; national action; international cooperation; partnerships with NGOs, the private sector and local community groups; and follow-up to the Conference.

Expert group meetings

In 1991,[9] the Economic and Social Council had authorized the Secretary-General of the Conference to convene six expert group meetings on population and development issues, five of which had been held in 1992.[14] The sixth meeting, on population distribution and migration (Santa Cruz, Bolivia, 18-22 January 1993), was attended by 16 internationally renowned experts and adopted 37 recommendations to the Preparatory Committee, dealing with internal and international migration, refugees, and data and research needs regarding population distribution and migration. The expert group's findings were summarized in a progress report on Conference preparations by the Secretary-General of the Conference.[10] In April 1993, she also submitted to the Preparatory Committee a synthesis of the six meetings.[15]

As a follow-up to those meetings, several round-table meetings were held on topics relevant to the

Conference:[16] women's perspectives on family planning and reproductive health and rights (Ottawa, Canada, 26 and 27 August); population policies, programmes and HIV/AIDS (Berlin, 28 September–1 October); population and development strategies (Bangkok, Thailand, 17-19 November); population, environment and sustainable development (Geneva, 24-26 November); and population and communication (Vienna, 2 and 3 December). In addition, the Twenty-second General Population Conference of the International Union for the Scientific Study of Population (Montreal, Canada, 24 August–1 September) devoted a one-day session to issues on the agenda of the International Conference.

Regional activities

In 1991,[9] the Economic and Social Council had invited the regional commissions to convene conferences on the status of population policies and programmes in their regions. Two of them were held in 1992[14] and regional activities in 1993 were described in progress reports of the Conference Secretary-General, submitted to the Economic and Social Council[10] and the General Assembly.[11]

The European Population Conference (Geneva, 23-26 March), jointly sponsored by the Economic Commission for Europe, the Council of Europe and UNFPA, involved countries in Europe and North America. It adopted a set of recommendations on: fertility, the status of women and the family; health and mortality; selected consequences of population growth and age structure; international migration; international cooperation in the field of population; and the generation and use of policy-relevant knowledge.

The Arab Population Conference (Amman, Jordan, 4-8 April), organized by the Economic and Social Commission for Western Asia, the League of Arab States and UNFPA, adopted the Second Amman Declaration on Population and Development in the Arab World,[17] further to the Amman Declaration adopted at the Third Regional Population Conference in the Arab World in 1984.[18] The Second Amman Declaration established general principles and objectives for population policies to: achieve appropriate population growth rates; reduce maternal child and infant mortality in particular; and achieve a geographical population distribution consistent with sound development and a healthy environment, by rationalizing urban growth and improving the quality of life in rural areas. The Declaration also contained recommendations on human development; population, environment and development; population distribution and urbanization; international migration; women, population and development; maternal and child health and fam-

ily planning; information, education and communication; the role of national NGOs in development; special categories of population; structural adjustment and population policies; data, research, information exchange and training; and regional and international cooperation.

The Latin American and Caribbean Regional Conference on Population and Development (Mexico City, 29 April–4 May), convened by the Economic Commission for Latin America and the Caribbean and UNFPA, adopted a consensus statement,[19] which reviewed the population situation in the region and made recommendations on population growth and structure; population distribution, development and the environment; women and population dynamics; population policies and programmes; development, health, family planning and well-being; international migration and development; training, data production and research; and international cooperation in the population field.

Several subregional meetings were also held during the year as a follow-up to the regional conferences.[16] The conference of the Maghreb countries (Algeria, Libyan Arab Jamahiriya, Mauritania, Morocco, Tunisia) (Tunis, Tunisia, 7-10 July) adopted the Tunis Plan of Action on Population and Development in the Arab Maghreb.[20] The South Pacific Ministerial Meeting on Population and Sustainable Development (Port Vila, Vanuatu, 6-10 September) adopted the Port Vila Declaration on Population and Sustainable Development.[21] The Ministerial Meeting on Population of the Non-Aligned Movement (Bali, Indonesia, 9-13 November) adopted the Denpasar Declaration on Population, a statement of issues and recommendations for the International Conference and a statement of support for South-South collaboration in population and family planning.[22]

Other subregional activities included the South Asian Ministerial Conference on Women and Family Health (Kathmandu, Nepal, 21-23 November), organized by the South Asian Association for Regional Cooperation and UNFPA; a meeting of the Andean countries (Bolivia, Colombia, Ecuador, Peru, Venezuela) (Lima, Peru, 1-3 December), which adopted the Andean Declaration on Population and Development; and the Caribbean Meeting of Experts for a Regional Plan of Action on Population and Development (Port-of-Spain, Trinidad, 2 and 3 December).

Trust funds

Two trust funds were established by the United Nations Secretary-General to support the Conference.[11] The first, the Trust Fund for the 1994 International Conference on Population and Development (General Trust Fund), was to be used for preparatory activities. By October, contributions to the Fund totalled $939,769. The second fund, the Voluntary Fund for Supporting Developing Countries' Participation in the Conference, had received $663,080 in contributions or pledges. A Trust Fund of UNFPA was also established to support national preparatory activities, including meetings and studies at the country level, activities to disseminate information and increase awareness of the Conference, and other conference-related costs. A total of $3,124,579 had been contributed or pledged to the Fund.

ECONOMIC AND SOCIAL COUNCIL ACTION

On 30 July, the Economic and Social Council adopted **resolution 1993/76** without vote.

Preparations for the International Conference on Population and Development

The Economic and Social Council,

Reaffirming General Assembly resolutions 45/216 of 21 December 1990 and 47/176 of 22 December 1992, and reaffirming Economic and Social Council resolutions 1989/91 of 26 July 1989, 1991/93 of 26 July 1991 and 1993/4 of 12 February 1993,

Reaffirming also Council resolution 1992/37 of 30 July 1992, in which it accepted the offer of the Government of Egypt to host the International Conference on Population and Development and decided to convene the Conference at Cairo from 5 to 13 September 1994,

Reaffirming further General Assembly resolutions S-18/3 of 1 May 1990, the annex to which contains the Declaration on International Economic Cooperation, in particular the Revitalization of Economic Growth and Development of the Developing Countries, 45/199 of 21 December 1990, the annex to which contains the International Development Strategy for the Fourth United Nations Development Decade, 45/206 of 21 December 1990 on the implementation of the Programme of Action for the Least Developed Countries for the 1990s, 45/217 of 21 December 1990 on the World Summit for Children and 46/151 of 18 December 1991, the annex to which contains the United Nations New Agenda for the Development of Africa in the 1990s, as well as the Rio Declaration on Environment and Development and Agenda 21, adopted by the United Nations Conference on Environment and Development,

Recognizing the particular importance of population issues in the context of sustained economic growth and sustainable development processes, and conscious of the need to give priority to the issues related to population and development,

Aware of the political impetus given to the issue of population on the international agenda since the decision of the United Nations to hold a conference on population,

Noting the appointment of the Executive Director of the United Nations Population Fund as Secretary-General of the International Conference on Population and Development and of the Director of the Population Division of the Department for Economic and Social Information and Policy Analysis of the Secretariat as Deputy Secretary-General of the Conference,

Stressing the need for the intergovernmental preparatory process for the International Conference on Popu-

lation and Development to be completed before the holding of the Conference itself,

1. *Recommends* that the Preparatory Committee for the International Conference on Population and Development be made a subsidiary body of the General Assembly, without prejudice to current arrangements for participation in the International Conference on Population and Development and its preparatory process and, in that context, decides that the report of the Preparatory Committee on its second session shall be submitted, through the Economic and Social Council, to the General Assembly at its forty-eighth session, to be considered under the item entitled "International Conference on Population and Development", as stipulated in General Assembly resolution 47/176;

2. *Requests* the Secretary-General of the International Conference on Population and Development to prepare for the information of delegations, by February 1994, the first draft of the final substantive document of the Conference, taking into account the views expressed by participants during the second session of the Preparatory Committee and the forty-eighth session of the General Assembly;

3. *Decides* to extend the third session of the Preparatory Committee for the Conference by one week, starting on 4 April 1994, and to ensure that adequate facilities are available for it, all within the approved budget limit set by the General Assembly for the biennium 1994-1995;

4. *Also decides* to convene two-day pre-Conference consultations at the venue of the Conference;

5. *Expresses its appreciation* for the extrabudgetary contributions to the trust funds established to assist developing countries, in particular the least developed among them, in preparing for and participating fully and effectively in the Conference and its preparatory process, and invites all Member States and organizations in a position to do so to support these trust funds further;

6. *Reaffirms* the significance of the media, and requests the Secretary-General of the United Nations to promote the objectives and activities of the Conference;

7. *Requests* the Secretary-General of the United Nations, in collaboration with the Secretary-General of the International Conference on Population and Development, to include in the report referred to in paragraph 20 of General Assembly resolution 47/176 an annotated outline of the final document of the Conference, as well as information on the implementation of the present resolution.

Economic and Social Council resolution 1993/76

30 July 1993   Meeting 46   Adopted without vote

Referred by Economic Committee (E/1993/112), 26 July (meeting 15); draft by Preparatory Committee (E/1993/69), orally amended; agenda item 15 *(f)*. *Financial implications.* S-G, E/1993/116.

GENERAL ASSEMBLY ACTION

On 21 December, the General Assembly, on the recommendation of the Second (Economic and Financial) Committee, adopted **resolution 48/186** without vote.

International Conference on Population and Development

The General Assembly,

Recalling its resolution 47/176 of 22 December 1992 on the International Conference on Population and Development, to be held at Cairo from 5 to 13 September 1994,

Recalling also Economic and Social Council resolutions 1989/91 of 26 July 1989, 1991/93 of 26 July 1991 and 1992/37 of 30 July 1992, and taking note of Council resolution 1993/4 of 12 February 1993,

Recognizing the importance of population issues in the context of sustained economic growth and sustainable development, and the need to treat population issues in their proper developmental perspective,

Taking note of the report of the Preparatory Committee for the International Conference on Population and Development on its second session,

Emphasizing the importance of a thorough intergovernmental preparatory process for the success of the Conference,

1. *Takes note with appreciation* of the progress report of the Secretary-General on the preparations for the International Conference on Population and Development and the accompanying annotated outline of the draft final document of the Conference;

2. *Endorses fully* Economic and Social Council resolution 1993/76 of 30 July 1993 on the preparations for the Conference;

3. *Decides* that the Preparatory Committee for the International Conference on Population and Development shall become a subsidiary body of the General Assembly, without prejudice to current arrangements for participation in the Conference and its preparatory process;

4. *Expresses its appreciation* to States and organizations for the extrabudgetary contributions made so far to the three trust funds that have been established to support preparatory activities, including national activities, as well as to support the participation in the Conference and its preparatory process of developing countries, particularly the least developed among them, and calls upon all States and organizations in a position to do so to support those trust funds further;

5. *Requests* the Secretary-General of the Conference, in preparing the draft final document of the Conference, to be guided by the views expressed by delegations and groups of delegations on the annotated outline, including those expressed at the forty-eighth session of the General Assembly;

6. *Also requests* the Secretary-General of the Conference, in recognition of the importance to the preparations for the Conference of the regional and subregional population conferences, to submit to the Preparatory Committee at its third session a report synthesizing the results of those conferences;

7. *Further requests* the Secretary-General of the Conference to convene, within existing resources, informal consultations at United Nations Headquarters in the period prior to the third session of the Preparatory Committee, to exchange views in preparation for negotiations on the draft final document of the Conference;

8. *Reaffirms* the importance of the participation in and contribution to the preparatory process and the Conference itself of non-governmental organizations, in accordance with the relevant provisions of Economic and Social Council resolution 1993/4;

9. *Emphasizes* the particular importance of immediate action in widely publicizing the objectives of the Conference and the issues to be discussed at it;

10. *Requests* the Secretary-General of the United Nations, in close consultation with the Secretary-General of the Conference, to ensure implementation of the present resolution;

11. *Decides* to include in the provisional agenda of its forty-ninth session an item entitled "Report of the International Conference on Population and Development".

General Assembly resolution 48/186

21 December 1993   Meeting 86   Adopted without vote

Approved by Second Committee (A/48/722) without vote, 6 December (meeting 45); draft by Australia, Austria, Belgium, Canada, China, Colombia (for Group of 77), Denmark, Finland, France, Germany, Greece, Ireland, Italy, Japan, Luxembourg, Netherlands, Norway, Portugal, Russian Federation, Spain, Sweden, United Kingdom and United States (A/C.2/48/L.11/Rev.1); agenda item 96.

Meeting numbers. GA 48th session: 2nd Committee 23-26, 45; plenary 86.

UN Population Fund

UNFPA activities

According to a report of the UNFPA Executive Director on 1993 activities,[23] the bulk of UNFPA assistance again went to family-planning services, followed by communication and education programmes, population-policy formulation and evaluation, population dynamics, basic data collection, special programmes and multisectoral activities.

At the end of 1993, the Fund was assisting 1,560 projects—493 country projects in Africa, 384 in Asia and the Pacific, 208 in Latin America and the Caribbean and 177 in the Arab States and Europe, as well as 127 regional and 171 interregional projects.

Family-planning programmes received $104.1 million of the total allocation of $206.1 million. UNFPA programmes focused on improving the quality of family-planning services, adopting a more comprehensive approach to reproductive health care, and empowering women in terms of reproductive rights and freedom. The Fund also formulated a policy paper to guide its humanitarian assistance during emergencies and other difficult situations. Thematic evaluations of family-planning services carried out in Botswana, Ecuador, Indonesia, Mexico, the Niger, Pakistan, Turkey and Viet Nam highlighted limitations in the choice of contraceptive methods available to clients, varied technical competence of service providers, a lack of infrastructure and equipment, and inadequate follow-up mechanisms and record-keeping. They also found that projects and activities in maternal and child health/family planning (MCH/FP) did not focus adequately on the quality of services. The evaluations resulted in recommendations that the mix of contraceptive methods should be sufficiently diverse to meet the needs of all users, that the choice of method should rest with users and not with service providers, and that users should be provided with complete and accurate information on available methods. Other recommendations dealt with promoting male contraception, training service providers and their supervisors, and developing adequate follow-up mechanisms and record-keeping systems.

As the cost of providing family-planning services continued to escalate, UNFPA supported case-studies on cost-recovery schemes in Brazil, Colombia, Egypt, Kenya, Indonesia and Thailand, and an in-depth review and appraisal of global experiences in shifting a significant share of funding from Governments and donors to the private sector. The Fund also prepared a policy proposal to support national efforts to integrate family planning into reproductive health care through primary health care systems. According to the proposal, integrated care would provide information and services aimed at all couples and individuals, including adolescents; treatment of gynaecological problems related to contraception; information, education and services dealing with prenatal and postnatal care and with childbirth; information and services regarding the prevention of sexually transmitted diseases; diagnosis and treatment of infertility and sub-fecundity and referral services for follow-up care; and routine reproductive health check-ups for women. It was also proposed that integrated services be extended to poor women, minorities, unmarried women and adolescents, to promote healthy and responsible reproductive behaviour as well as the use of condoms and other barrier methods of contraception, and to pay special attention to young adults and men.

The prevention and treatment of sexually transmitted diseases, including HIV/AIDS, was an integral component of reproductive health care and an important concern of the UNFPA programme. The Fund helped to organize a round table on the impact of HIV/AIDS on population policies and programmes (Berlin, September/October), which emphasized that commitment to combat the disease should be an essential part of sound population and related family-planning policies. UNFPA also participated in inter-agency discussions on the feasibility of establishing a joint and co-sponsored United Nations programme on AIDS, called for by the World Health Assembly (see PART THREE, Chapter XI). On 18 June,[24] the Governing Council of the United Nations Development Programme (UNDP) supported the initiative and noted the UNFPA Executive Director's intent to cooperate fully in consultations on its implementation. In 1993, the Fund prepared and distributed the *1992 AIDS Update*, providing information on UNFPA assistance in supplying condoms, training MCH/FP service providers and promoting HIV/AIDS information and education activities. Under its Global Initiative on Contraceptive Requirements and Logistics Management Needs in Developing Countries in the 1990s, UNFPA collaborated with the World Health Organization in preparing estimates for condom requirements for HIV/AIDS prevention as part of in-depth studies in the Philippines, Turkey and Viet Nam. The esti-

mates were included in an update of global contraceptive requirements for 1994-2005, prepared by UNFPA in cooperation with the Population Council.

The Fund's assistance for information, education and communication (IEC) activities totalled $37.7 million, or 18.3 per cent of all programme allocations. Activities aimed at creating demand for reproductive health care and family-planning services and changing people's behaviour by helping to: generate political commitment to and community support for such services; improve the quality of services; train service providers in interpersonal communications and motivational skills; change people's perceptions of family planning; inform potential clients about the availability of services; and enable them to choose a contraceptive method. UNFPA organized a thematic evaluation of seven IEC projects in support of MCH/FP activities in the Comoros, India, the Philippines, Rwanda and Zambia. It found that projects needed to be less ambitious, have a realistic time-frame and emphasize quality as well as quantity. The shortcomings identified in the evaluation were addressed in a technical paper on developing IEC strategies for population programmes. A technical note was also prepared on the relationship between IEC and family-planning service delivery. It focused on the need for: close cooperation between service providers and IEC personnel in identifying desired changes in behaviour and targeting different population groups; strong intra- and inter-sectoral coordination; the use of mass media and interpersonal communications to disseminate and personalize IEC messages; a sound service-delivery system to meet demand created by IEC activities; integration and coordination of IEC and family-planning activities; and the incorporation of monitoring and evaluation mechanisms in project design.

The Fund allocated some $17.9 million, or 8.7 per cent of its assistance, for the formulation, evaluation and implementation of population policies and programmes, and some $14 million (6.8 per cent) to population dynamics programmes. Assistance to national project execution was provided through country support teams, all eight of which—three in Africa, three in Asia, one in the Arab States and one in Latin America and the Caribbean—became fully operational in 1993. The teams fielded missions to some 100 countries, providing technical support for the formulation of projects to strengthen family-planning services and delivery to remote areas in Egypt, to expand and upgrade MCH/FP services in Yemen and MCH/birth spacing in Cambodia, and to strengthen training for expanded family health services in the Syrian Arab Republic. Focus-group discussions on women's reproductive health care and family-planning concerns were organized in Nepal. Assistance was also extended to Viet Nam to formulate a comprehensive population education project and to China to train 22 high-level educators to plan population education programmes. Technical back-stopping was provided to the Sudan for a project on family-welfare planning, education, motivation and services in industrial areas of Khartoum. Training and orientation were provided to three senior Mongolian officials in population and development planning, and to 110 Latin American professionals in programme management.

Basic data collection received some $13.2 million in assistance, or 6.4 per cent of the total allocation. The Fund continued to help developing countries generate population data and improve their capacity to collect, analyse and disseminate information on a timely basis. It assisted in developing a management information system for contraceptive supplies in Viet Nam and in designing a questionnaire for a migration and labour force survey in the Sudan, and it emphasized efforts to improve the capacity of Latin American countries in obtaining and using demographic data to support decentralized social policies.

Other allocations included some $10.6 million, or 5.1 per cent of total assistance, for special programmes, and $8.6 million (4.2 per cent) for multisectoral activities. Another $6 million was delivered through population projects under the United Nations regular programme of technical cooperation.

UNFPA continued to seek ways of linking family-planning activities with efforts to improve the social and economic status of women in society. It published a comprehensive assessment of its experimental projects to help women secure credit and set up micro-enterprises, to provide technical assistance and training in small-business management and to promote family planning. The assessment was based on the findings of four project evaluation missions to Egypt, Ghana, India, Kenya, Paraguay and the Philippines, which recommended the introduction of MCH/FP, IEC and other population components into existing micro-enterprise programmes and the linking of micro-enterprise projects for women with UNFPA country-level population programmes, and especially those activities to enhance women's reproductive rights.

The Fund continued to coordinate with agencies and organizations within and outside the United Nations system. In March, an inter-agency task force discussed questions concerning the division of labour between the various actors in country-level activities and the operations of country support teams, and emphasized the need to improve the quality of technical back-stopping plans.

The task force also considered technical support in December. In accordance with a 1992 General Assembly resolution on the streamlining of United Nations operational activities for development,[25] the Fund participated in the development of a system-wide interpretation of the programme approach; collaboration in the area of evaluation; and the drafting of system-wide guidelines for United Nations contributions and programmatic responses. UNFPA, UNDP and the United Nations Children's Fund (UNICEF) agreed to fund an umbrella project on a system-wide integrated approach to country-level technical assistance activities, and reached agreement on an integrated development package for the Governate of Assiut in Egypt. The Fund convened working groups to harmonize programming cycles for Latin America and the Caribbean and for the Middle East and North Africa within the three bodies. A UNFPA/UNICEF integrated planning model was being developed for Bangladesh, to include modules on literacy, nutrition, health and women's status.

In March,[26] the Executive Director submitted a report on the Fund's collaboration with the World Bank and regional development banks. The report examined the rationale for close collaboration between those organizations, analysed their collaborative programming activities at the global, regional, national and headquarters level, and identified further actions.

On 18 June,[24] the UNDP Governing Council took note of the report and endorsed actions to strengthen collaboration.

UNFPA's *The State of World Population 1993*, entitled "The Individual and the World: Population, Migration and Development in the 1990s", called for urgent action to establish common international classifications of migrants and migration. It also sought increased attention to relevant international legislation, the effects of development policies on migration flows and the needs of migrant women in particular.

UNDP Governing Council action. On 18 June,[24] the Governing Council took note of the Executive Director's report on the 1992 activities of the Fund[27] and encouraged UNFPA to heighten the strategic focus of its programmes to maximize their effectiveness. It welcomed an increase in resources allocated to MCH/FP and called for stronger IEC activities, focused on the needs of adolescents. It noted the status report[28] on the implementation of the strategy for UNFPA assistance to sub-Saharan Africa,[29] and requested the Executive Director to strengthen the Fund's activities in Africa and to report in 1995 on the strategy's implementation. The Fund was encouraged to monitor the impact of its activities in the area of women, population and development and to pursue links with women's organizations at the country and intercountry levels. The Council commended progress on the Fund's Global Initiative on Contraceptive Requirements and Logistics Management Needs, and requested that the Executive Director report on the subject in 1994 and continue the Initiative beyond that year. It welcomed the Fund's efforts to harmonize its programme cycles with those of other bodies and to adapt them to national development plans, and encouraged it to involve NGOs in population programme activities in the field. The Executive Director was requested to report in 1994 on the implementation of the 1992 Assembly resolution,[25] to submit in 1994 an updated review and assessment of UNFPA, synthesizing its experience over the last 25 years, and to present proposals on programme priorities and the future direction of UNFPA in 1995.

Country and intercountry programmes

In an April 1993 report,[30] the Executive Director provided the status of financial implementation of Governing Council–approved UNFPA country programmes and projects for the period 1985-1992, plus estimates of $118.5 million, including $77.7 million from regular funds, for 15 new programmes. The balance of UNFPA commitments for ongoing and new programmes amounted to $525.1 million.

The Governing Council, on 18 June,[31] approved the 15 country programmes—11 in sub-Saharan Africa and 2 each in Asia and the Pacific and in Latin America and the Caribbean—and made a provision that the Executive Director should present interim reports in 1994 on implementation of the programmes for Equatorial Guinea and Rwanda.

The combined allocation for country and intercountry programmes was $206.1 million in 1993, up from $163.6 million in 1992.[23] UNFPA concentrated on programmes in 58 priority countries (32 in Africa, 17 in Asia and the Pacific, 5 in Latin America and the Caribbean and 4 in the Arab States), which received $119 million, or 72.6 per cent, of the $164.1 million allocated to country programmes overall. The resources allocated to priority programmes increased in absolute terms from $77.9 million spent in 1992, but dropped by 3.2 per cent from that year's share in the total. Allocations for intercountry activities (regional and interregional) amounted to some $42 million, or 20.4 per cent of the total in 1993, compared with $25.5 million (19.8 per cent) of expenditures in 1992.

In a March report,[32] the Executive Director reviewed implementation of the Fund's priority-country system and criteria for determining priority status. The report noted that allocations to

priority countries increased from $277 million during 1983-1987 to $411 million for 1988-1992, or from 70 per cent of the total country programme expenditure in 1983 to 75 per cent in 1992. It recommended that the existing criteria for determining priority status and their threshold levels be retained and that the list of priority countries be updated more frequently. On 18 June,[24] the Governing Council took note of the report and the January 1992 update of the list, and reaffirmed the continued use of the criteria. It requested the Executive Director to study the feasibility of including the maternal mortality rate as a criterion and to report on the subject in 1995.

Allocations to programmes for sub-Saharan Africa totalled $59.3 million in 1993, up from $37 million in 1992. Most resources (62.4 per cent) were allocated to family-planning and communication and education programmes. The Fund's strategy for assistance to Africa was modified to reflect growing governmental awareness of population problems, the establishment of at least rudimentary family-planning services in all but 2 of the 44 countries covered, and the emergence of new population issues. During the year, however, UNFPA-supported activities were disrupted by political and social unrest in Angola, Burundi, Cameroon, the Congo, Liberia, Mali, Nigeria, Togo and Zaire; improved conditions facilitated programmes in Ethiopia and Mozambique. The Fund fielded its first mission to the new nation of Eritrea and developed four projects to bridge the 1993-1994 period while the first country programme was being formulated (for details on Eritrea's independence, see PART TWO, Chapter I). A fact-finding mission went to South Africa to identify priorities and modalities for future assistance.

The Arab States and Europe received $23.2 million in 1993, compared with $10.7 million spent in 1992. Of that total, more than $19 million was allocated to the Arab States and some $4 million to Europe and the newly independent States of the former USSR. Family-planning programmes accounted for 54.9 per cent of the total allocation and were being increasingly introduced to the Arab States, along with action programmes in reproductive health and communication and education. Family-planning and related activities were also the focus of UNFPA assistance to Europe, which had high rates of induced abortion. More than 85 technical assistance missions were undertaken to 20 countries during the year.

Some $76.8 million was allocated to Asia and the Pacific in 1993, an increase from $49.5 million spent in 1992. Family-planning programmes received 64 per cent of allocations. The Fund initiated assistance programmes for five countries of Central Asia and provided emergency relief in the areas of children's health and women's reproductive health. It provided more than $2 million for procurement of contraceptives and training in their use. Two project-formulation missions were fielded to Cambodia to assess priority needs related to a national census and MCH/birth-spacing services. In total, some 150 technical advisory missions were carried out in more than 30 countries in the region.

UNFPA resources allocated to Latin America and the Caribbean increased in 1993 to $21.3 million from the 1992 expenditures of $15.4 million. Of that, 51.7 per cent was allocated to family planning, which, along with reproductive health, was among the region's priorities. Country support teams based in the region fielded 125 missions in response to 170 requests.

Allocations for interregional programmes in 1993 totalled some $24.4 million, of which $8.3 million, or 22.1 per cent, went to family planning. Policy formulation and population and development received $5 million, or 20.5 per cent. Major activities focused on training and research and the dissemination of population information.

Work programmes

In an April report on the UNFPA work plan and proposed programme expenditure for 1994-1997,[33] the Executive Director provided information on resource utilization and the distribution of programmable resources among country and intercountry activities for 1989-1992, 1993-1996 and 1994-1997.

On 18 June,[34] the UNDP Governing Council approved the work plan for 1994-1997 and the request for new programme expenditure authority of $217.3 million for 1994, and endorsed the following estimates for new programmable resources for 1995-1997, subject to actual contributions: $234.1 million for 1995, $246.8 million for 1996 and $260.4 million for 1997. It also endorsed an estimated $15 million per year in multi-bilateral funding for 1994-1997.

Programme planning and evaluation

During the year, UNFPA continued its efforts to enhance the impact of its programmes by reviewing programme strategies and evaluating performance through its programme review and strategy development (PRSD) exercise.[23] Five PRSD missions were organized in 1993—two in Africa (Chad, Zambia) and three in Asia and the Pacific (Iran, Maldives, Philippines)—bringing the total number of missions conducted since 1977 to 189. UNFPA analysed the quality and impact of 29 PRSD reports, covering the period 1989-1992, and examined the PRSD process as a whole. The reviews reaffirmed the exercise as a powerful approach to population programming and noted that the objectives and strategies of the corresponding

UNFPA country programmes were clearly based on PRSD recommendations. It was recommended that more attention be given to PRSD follow-up.

On 18 June,[24] the Governing Council underlined the need to strengthen further the capacity of recipient countries to formulate well-coordinated, monitored and evaluated programmes, and noted that experience gained through the PRSD exercise enabled the Fund to contribute to the formulation of the country strategy note and the development of a common programme approach. It encouraged the Executive Director to continue efforts to improve evaluation activities and requested her to report in 1994 on progress made in decentralizing to the field the decision-making process, including project approval.

During 1992-1993, UNFPA carried out 220 project evaluations and a series of thematic evaluations in three programme areas. In 1993, it launched another thematic evaluation, on local production of contraceptives, and conducted desk reviews for future evaluations on community participation in family-planning programmes and on information and service programmes for adolescents. To ensure proper feedback and use of evaluation results, the Fund began to redesign its evaluation database and to publish the *Evaluation Findings* bulletin. It also revised its guidelines on decentralization and extended total programme approval authority, on a trial basis, to field offices in 12 countries.

Financial and administrative questions

The Fund's estimated income in 1993 fell by 7.8 per cent from $238.2 million in 1992,[23] to $219.6 million, while provisional expenditures totalled $215.4 million, up from $193.6 million the previous year. During the year, 101 Governments pledged $216.6 million, $17.2 million (7.4 per cent) less than in 1992. An additional $14.8 million for multi-bilateral projects and $10.9 million for programmes were generated through other financial arrangements.

On 18 June,[35] the UNDP Governing Council took note of the annual review of activities financed by UNFPA in 1992[36] and requested the Executive Director to include in future annual reviews, in line with revised financial regulations, an overview of cost-sharing contributions and their distribution among programme areas. It expressed concern at a higher ratio of administrative costs to programme delivery in 1992-1993 and requested the Executive Director to include a progress report on budget implementation in the annual financial review and to report in 1994 on administrative cost savings achieved. She was urged to institute guidelines to delineate programme, programme-support and administrative expenditures. The Council reconfirmed its 1991 decision[37] to keep the annual level of the Fund's operational reserve at 20 per cent of general resources income.

Noting progress in implementing recommendations of the Board of Auditors on management issues, the Governing Council called for audited financial statements by executing agencies and Governments on their activities on behalf of UNFPA, requested a summary of observations thereon by external auditors and of corrective action taken by the agencies, and urged the Executive Director to avoid duplication of procurement capacities in the United Nations system.

The Council also had before it a progress report[38] on UNFPA successor support-cost arrangements,[37] which provided proposals to improve the implementation of technical support services arrangements. The Council welcomed the proposals, noted the establishment of UNFPA country support teams, authorized the Executive Director to take steps to improve technical support services further, and requested her to report on the subject in 1995.[24]

In response to a 1992 decision of the Governing Council,[39] the Executive Director submitted in April 1993 proposed amendments[40] to the UNFPA financial regulations relating to procurement and cost-sharing. On 18 June,[41] the Council approved the revised financial regulations dealing with trust funds, internal control, the definition of cost-sharing and UNFPA funds.

1994-1995 budget

In April 1993, the Executive Director submitted to the UNDP Governing Council budget estimates for UNFPA administrative and programme support services for the 1994-1995 biennium.[42] The total biennial budget amounted to $120.1 million gross, or an 8.6 per cent increase over revised 1992-1993 estimates of $110.6 million.

On 18 June,[35] the Council, having considered the budget estimates, audit reports for the year ended 31 December 1991[43] and a report of the Advisory Committee on Administrative and Budgetary Questions (ACABQ),[44] approved gross appropriations of $120,092,200 to finance 1994-1995 administrative and programme support services. The Council agreed that overhead credits estimated at $6.5 million and miscellaneous income of $500,000 from trust funds for support services should be used to offset the gross amount, resulting in net appropriations of $113,092,200. The Executive Director was authorized to transfer credits between programmes within reasonable limits, with the concurrence of ACABQ. The Council also approved changes in the level of posts and additional posts requested in the budget estimates, and invited the Executive Director to make further

proposals for the level of Country Director posts in the 1996-1997 budget.

UN Population Award

In September, the Secretary-General presented the 1993 United Nations Population Award to Dr. Fred T. Sai (Ghana) for his leadership in family planning and population and contributions to research on nutrition and community welfare; and to the Mainichi Shimbun Population Problems Research Council (Japan) for creating awareness of population issues and for its population studies and publications. Each received a diploma, a gold medal and a monetary prize. The Award was established by the General Assembly in 1981[45] to be presented annually to individuals or institutions for outstanding contributions to increased awareness of population problems and to their solutions. The Award's Trust Fund totalled $627,471 as at 31 December 1992.

In August,[46] the Secretary-General transmitted to the Assembly the UNFPA Executive Director's report on the status of the Award. The Assembly took note of it by **decision 48/452** of 21 December.

REFERENCES

[1]YUN 1992, p. 695, GA res. 47/176, 22 Dec. 1992. [2]Ibid., ESC res. 1992/37, 30 July 1992. [3]E/1993/13. [4]E/1993/69. [5]E/CONF.84/PC/11. [6]YUN 1974, p. 552. [7]YUN 1984, p. 714. [8]A/48/492. [9]YUN 1991, p. 510, ESC res. 1991/93, 26 July 1991. [10]E/1993/49. [11]A/48/430. [12]ACC/1993/17. [13]A/48/430/Add.1. [14]YUN 1992, p. 694. [15]E/CONF.84/PC/12. [16]A/CONF.171/PC/2. [17]E/CONF.84/PC/16. [18]YUN 1984, p. 642. [19]E/CONF.84/PC/17. [20]A/C.2/48/7. [21]A/C.2/48/3. [22]A/48/746. [23]DP/1994/44. [24]E/1993/35 (dec. 93/27 A). [25]YUN 1992, p. 552, GA res. 47/199, 22 Dec. 1992. [26]DP/1993/34 & Corr.1. [27]YUN 1992, p. 696. [28]Ibid., p. 699. [29]YUN 1987, p. 634. [30]DP/1993/31. [31]E/1993/35 (dec. 93/27 C). [32]DP/1993/33. [33]DP/1993/30. [34]E/1993/35 (dec. 93/27 B). [35]Ibid. (dec. 93/28). [36]YUN 1992, p. 700. [37]YUN 1991, p. 515. [38]DP/1993/32 & Corr.1. [39]YUN 1992, p. 701. [40]DP/1993/63. [41]E/1993/35 (dec. 93/29). [42]DP/1993/35. [43]DP/1993/37. [44]DP/1993/38. [45]YUN 1981, p. 792, GA res. 36/201, 17 Dec. 1981. [46]A/48/276.

Human settlements

Commission on Human Settlements

The Commission on Human Settlements held its fourteenth session at Nairobi, Kenya, from 26 April to 5 May 1993, adopting 20 resolutions and five decisions. It considered activities of the United Nations Centre for Human Settlements (UNCHS) in 1992-1993[1] and requested[2] the UNCHS Executive Director to assess in future reports the relevance of United Nations system-wide activities to the Centre's work. He was also requested[3] to strengthen the Centre's regional activities, restructure its network of regional offices, and report on progress in 1995.

The Commission decided[4] that the Committee of Permanent Representatives to UNCHS would meet at least four times a year to assess human settlements problems and the implementation of the Commission's decisions. The Commission considered the Executive Director's draft of its third report to the General Assembly on the implementation of the Global Strategy for Shelter to the Year 2000,[5] adopted by the Assembly in 1988,[6] and the proposed plan of action and timetable for 1994-1995.[7] It decided[8] to incorporate into the draft additions and amendments submitted by national delegations, and to submit the revised report,[9] including the 1994-1995 plan of action, to the Assembly.

On 29 July, the Economic and Social Council, by **decision 1993/310**, took note of the Commission's report on its fourteenth session[10] and of its third report on the Strategy's implementation.[9]

1995 session

On 5 May,[11] the Commission, recalling its 1987 resolution[12] regarding the selection of two themes for each session and having considered the Executive Director's report[13] on themes for the fifteenth (1995) session, requested the Executive Director to prepare papers for the 1995 session, reviewing national action on housing since the 1976 Habitat: United Nations Conference on Human Settlements[14] and on sustainable human settlements in an urbanizing world. It also decided to take up in 1997 the contribution of the private and non-governmental sectors to shelter for low-income groups, and the management of natural resources in the context of sustainable human settlements.

GENERAL ASSEMBLY ACTION

On 21 December, the General Assembly, on the recommendation of the Second Committee, adopted **resolution 48/176** without vote.

Human settlements

The General Assembly,

Recalling its resolution 32/162 of 19 December 1977, by which it established the Commission on Human Settlements and its secretariat, the United Nations Centre for Human Settlements (Habitat), to serve as the institutional focus for human settlements activities within the United Nations system,

Recalling also its resolution 43/181 of 20 December 1988, in which it designated the Commission on Human Settlements as the intergovernmental body responsible for coordinating, evaluating and monitoring the Global Strategy for Shelter to the Year 2000,

Cognizant of the importance of maintaining the momentum already generated at the national and international level for the implementation of the Strategy,

Recognizing the role of the United Nations Centre for Human Settlements (Habitat) in the implementation of the Strategy and of the human settlement aspects of Agenda 21 and in the preparatory work for the United Nations Conference on Human Settlements (Habitat II),

Noting with appreciation that the Commission on Human Settlements and the Centre, in line with the objectives and responsibilities set out in General Assembly resolution 32/162, have succeeded in placing human settlements high on the agenda for national action and international cooperation and in promoting increased understanding of the links among people, settlements, environment and development,

Noting with concern that, in many developing countries, the achievements in terms of policies, programmes and projects at the national level in the field of human settlements have not been sufficient to arrest or reverse the deterioration in the living conditions of their populations, in both urban and rural areas,

Convinced that proper planning, development and management of human settlements will lead to economic and social progress and thereby alleviate poverty and promote development that is environmentally sound and sustainable in the long run, and aware that widespread civil conflicts and wars have left many cities and villages totally destroyed,

Reaffirming the importance of its resolution 47/180 of 22 December 1992 on the United Nations Conference on Human Settlements (Habitat II),

Recalling its resolution 47/212 B of 6 May 1993, in which, *inter alia*, it requested the Secretary-General to reconsider his proposal to abolish the post of Under-Secretary-General of the United Nations Centre for Human Settlements (Habitat), taking into account the views and recommendations of the Commission on Human Settlements and the Governing Council of the United Nations Environment Programme and the views expressed by Member States regarding the question of separate senior management arrangements for the Centre,

1. *Endorses* the report of the Commission on Human Settlements on the work of its fourteenth session;

2. *Also endorses* Commission resolutions 14/7 of 5 May 1993 on the strengthening of regional activities, 14/19 of 5 May 1993 on the role and place of the United Nations Centre for Human Settlements (Habitat) in the United Nations system and 14/20 of 5 May 1993 on the preparations for the United Nations Conference on Human Settlements (Habitat II);

3. *Requests* the Secretary-General to ensure that the United Nations Environment Programme and the United Nations Centre for Human Settlements (Habitat) are kept under distinct and separate management and direction, in accordance with their specific mandates and activities;

4. *Also requests* the Secretary-General—in the context of ensuring high-level leadership of the United Nations Centre for Human Settlements (Habitat) through distinct and separate management and direction as contemplated in General Assembly resolution 32/162, taking into account relevant recommendations on the ongoing restructuring of the economic and social sectors of the United Nations system as it prepares for the challenges of human settlement development and management in the twenty-first century, as well as prepa-

rations for Habitat II—to give full consideration to the views expressed by Member States regarding the leadership of the Centre;

5. *Further requests* the Secretary-General to ensure that, in the restructuring of the United Nations system, the Centre is maintained as the global focal point for human settlements and that its institutional capabilities are strengthened at its headquarters, maximizing the effectiveness of national and regional operations;

6. *Urges* all Member States, intergovernmental and non-governmental organizations and organs, organizations and bodies of the United Nations system to contribute to and participate actively in adequate preparations for Habitat II;

7. *Invites* the Secretary-General to submit to the General Assembly at its forty-ninth session a report on the implementation of the present resolution and on the progress made in preparations for the United Nations Conference on Human Settlements (Habitat II).

General Assembly resolution 48/176

21 December 1993   Meeting 86   Adopted without vote

Approved by Second Committee (A/48/717/Add.8) without vote, 13 December (meeting 48); draft by China and Colombia (for Group of 77) (A/C.2/48/L.37), orally revised following informal consultations; agenda item 91 *(g)*.

Meeting numbers. GA 48th session: 2nd Committee 36-41, 48; plenary 86.

Global Strategy for Shelter to the Year 2000

The UNCHS Executive Director presented a report[15] to the Commission on the implementation of the Global Strategy for Shelter to the Year 2000.[6] It covered the period 1991-1992 and described action taken by UNCHS, Member States, the United Nations system and bilateral and multilateral agencies and intergovernmental and non-governmental organizations. It noted that the Centre's activities promoted wider understanding of the links between shelter, the living environment and sustainable development, provided substantive support to Member States and disseminated information on the Strategy, as well as on areas such as research and development, women in shelter and services development, and cooperation with NGOs and other organizations. The Executive Director concluded that, although many Governments had taken positive steps towards national shelter strategies, their impact on the living environment of the poor remained rather limited, and that action should be intensified in the areas of access to land, infrastructure and finance.

On 5 May,[16] the Commission adopted its third report on the Strategy's implementation, including the plan of action for 1994-1995.[9] It urged Governments to continue preparing annual progress reports for submission to the Executive Director and to publicize them within their countries. Governments were also invited to intensify efforts to formulate and implement national shelter strategies, using the guidelines for national ac-

tion contained in the Strategy[17] and the plan of action for 1994-1995, and to pay particular attention to specific recommendations of Agenda 21, adopted by the 1992 United Nations Conference on Environment and Development (UNCED).[18] The Commission recommended that Governments adopt a cost-effective monitoring system for national shelter strategies by applying shelter sector performance indicators (see below). It requested the Executive Director to continue disseminating information to Member States on successful country experiences, and providing technical assistance and training in policy formulation and implementation. He was also requested to collaborate with relevant capacity-building and other programmes within the United Nations system, to have country experiences reflected in the Strategy's mid-term review for the second United Nations Conference on Human Settlements (Habitat II) (see below), and to report on the Strategy's implementation in 1995.

GENERAL ASSEMBLY ACTION

On 21 December, the General Assembly, on the recommendation of the Second Committee, adopted **resolution 48/178** without vote.

Global Strategy for Shelter to the Year 2000
The General Assembly,

Recalling its resolution 43/181 of 20 December 1988, in which it adopted the Global Strategy for Shelter to the Year 2000 and designated the Commission on Human Settlements as the United Nations intergovernmental body responsible for coordinating, evaluating and monitoring the Strategy,

Recalling also its resolution 47/180 of 22 December 1992 on the United Nations Conference on Human Settlements (Habitat II), in which it affirmed that a mid-term review of the implementation of the Global Strategy should be conducted at the Conference,

Noting with satisfaction the recognition of the renewed commitment to the Global Strategy expressed in Agenda 21, adopted by the United Nations Conference on Environment and Development,

Bearing in mind the high potential of enabling shelter strategies, which rely on labour-intensive and locally based technologies, to generate employment, demand for local products and savings, and thereby promote economic development and poverty reduction,

Bearing in mind also that enabling strategies typically include activities, such as institutional reform, revision of building codes and regulations and steps aimed at facilitating the access of the poor to critical resources, especially land and finance, which can best be implemented through partnership arrangements among the public, private and community sectors and the empowerment of the poor and of women,

Convinced that the concept of enabling strategies synthesizes the lessons learned in the development of living conditions since Habitat: United Nations Conference on Human Settlements, held at Vancouver from 31 May to 11 June 1976, and that broad commitment to the implementation of such strategies represents the only viable way of reversing the trend towards deterioration of those conditions,

Recognizing that, since the adoption of the Global Strategy, additional weight has been given to and further insights have been reached into several essential aspects of enabling shelter strategies, such as the requirement for sensitivity to gender considerations, and their potential for contributing to environmentally sustainable development,

Aware that adequate information plays a pivotal role in the proper analysis of the outcome, opportunities and constraints of current housing processes, and in assessing the impact of policies, strategies and programmes thereon,

Having considered the third report of the Commission on Human Settlements on the implementation of the Global Strategy for Shelter to the Year 2000,

Noting with satisfaction that a number of Governments have initiated or reformulated their national shelter strategies based on the principle of enabling all actors in the shelter sector, that many other Governments have initiated action on particular components of a national shelter strategy and, furthermore, that a number of Governments have commenced a process for applying selected indicators for monitoring the progress and efficiency of their national shelter strategies,

Noting also with satisfaction the support given to the implementation of the Global Strategy by donor Governments, international bodies and intergovernmental and non-governmental organizations,

Cognizant of the importance of maintaining the momentum already generated at the national and international levels for the implementation of the Global Strategy,

1. *Commends* Governments that are already revising, consolidating, formulating or implementing their national shelter strategies based on the enabling principles of the Global Strategy for Shelter to the Year 2000;

2. *Urges* all Governments to adopt and/or strengthen integrated national shelter strategies based on the enabling approach and principles of social, economic and environmental sustainability, and to review them regularly with a view to ensuring the improvement of living conditions, particularly of the rural and urban poor, women and the homeless;

3. *Recommends* that all Governments adopt a cost-effective system for monitoring the progress of their national shelter strategy and, when assessing the performance of the shelter sector, also adopt, as far as is feasible, taking into account local conditions and sensitivity to gender considerations, guidelines for monitoring national shelter strategies and the application of shelter sector performance indicators, and publicize the guidelines within their countries, particularly on World Habitat Day, and also submit them to the Executive Director of the United Nations Centre for Human Settlements (Habitat), in order to enable him to prepare the reports on the implementation of the Global Strategy for consideration by the Commission on Human Settlements;

4. *Urges* Governments to integrate fully the environmental dimension in the formulation and implementation of national shelter strategies, taking into account the relevant components of Agenda 21;

5. *Invites* Governments to make voluntary contributions to the United Nations Habitat and Human Settlements Foundation in order to facilitate the implementation and monitoring of the Global Strategy;

6. *Urges* the international community to strengthen its support for national efforts to formulate and implement enabling shelter strategies in developing countries, as recommended in Agenda 21;

7. *Urges* the organizations of the United Nations system, particularly the United Nations Development Programme, and other multilateral and bilateral agencies to provide, on the basis of an approach consistent with the Global Strategy, increased financial and other support to Governments for the implementation of the Global Strategy Plan of Action for 1994-1995;

8. *Adopts* the Global Strategy Plan of Action for 1994-1995, and urges all Governments, relevant United Nations and private sector organizations and intergovernmental and non-governmental organizations to prepare and implement their specific plans of action.

General Assembly resolution 48/178

21 December 1993   Meeting 86   Adopted without vote

Approved by Second Committee (A/48/717/Add.8) without vote, 13 December (meeting 48); draft by Commission on Human Settlements (A/48/8); agenda item 91 *(g)*.

Meeting numbers. GA 48th session: 2nd Committee 36-40, 48; plenary 86.

Shelter sector performance indicators

In response to a 1991 Commission request,[19] the Executive Director submitted a report on shelter sector performance indicators[20] designed to help Governments monitor progress towards the objectives of the Global Strategy. The report provided a conceptual framework for the UNCHS/World Bank Housing Indicators Programme, a plan for its globalization, and an overview of progress based on a survey of 52 countries. It proposed 12 key indicators—grouped under the headings of price, quantity, quality, supply and demand—to capture the essential elements of shelter sector performance worldwide, and described their uses and the criteria for their selection.

On 5 May,[21] the Commission urged Governments to intensify their monitoring of housing sector performance through use of the key indicators, the findings of which should be the basis for national reports on the status of human settlements to Habitat II. The Commission recommended technical and financial assistance for monitoring, and the Executive Director was requested to coordinate the activities of the Housing Indicators Programme with programmes related to women's participation, the urban environment and the city database. He was also asked to initiate action to introduce housing indicators into the *Global Report on Human Settlements*, the *World Development Report* and other reports published on a regular basis, and to report on the subject in 1995.

Building materials for housing

Pursuant to a 1991 Commission request,[22] the Executive Director presented a report on appropriate, intermediate, cost-effective building materials, technologies and transfer mechanisms for housing delivery.[23] The report reviewed recent production, import and price trends underlying the housing crisis in developing countries, and outlined an operational strategy for the sector's development. It suggested that the Commission might consider national and international action to enhance the supply of durable and affordable building materials using renewable resources and energy-efficient technologies and to minimize the adverse environmental impact caused by the extraction of raw materials and the production of building materials.

On 5 May,[24] the Commission recommended that Governments consider implementing national strategies for the sustainable supply of affordable building materials. Governments were urged to facilitate the role of non-governmental and community-based organizations, households and women's groups in the design, promotion, production and use of environmentally sound buildings and household energy technologies. The Commission called on Governments to create an environment conducive to greater decentralization, innovation and competition, increased investment and improved technological capacity and organization in the sector; to support the transfer of appropriate and environmentally sound technologies and related equipment; to support domestic capacity for research and development, standardization training and awareness creation; and to organize training in support of ecologically friendly and low-cost informal-sector building schemes and household energy programmes.

The Commission further recommended that Governments: support the development, transfer and diffusion of technologies that made efficient use of natural resources and agricultural and industrial wastes, improved energy efficiency and reduced environmental pollution; provide industrial extension services to small-scale producers of building materials and encourage their cooperation; improve the availability of venture capital, equity and term-loan support for technological upgrading of the building-materials sector; support the adoption of appropriate building codes, regulations and standards; disseminate information on available cost-effective and environmentally sound building materials; set up appropriate technology transfer mechanisms to enhance the application of technology options; and incorporate building technologies in the educational curricula of professional institutes. It also recommended greater efforts to enhance the recycling of building materials. The Executive Director was asked to present in 1995 a list of building materials that were potentially harmful to human health and the environment, and to continue UNCHS publications and training programmes to facilitate the environmentally sound production of cost-effective and durable building materials.

1996 Conference on human settlements

In 1992,[25] the General Assembly had decided to convene the second United Nations Conference on Human Settlements (Habitat II) in 1996 and to establish a Preparatory Committee for the Conference.

The Preparatory Committee held an organizational session in 1993 (New York, 3-5 March).[26] It had before it a report of the Secretary-General on Conference preparations,[27] containing recommendations on substantive issues. Topics suggested for consideration by the Conference included a general declaration of principles; a review of global conditions, trends and issues, and of the role and institutional arrangements for human settlements in the United Nations system; resource mobilization for a global action plan; and programmes and subprogrammes dealing with development, settlement policies and strategies, new and emerging technologies, capacity-building and institutional strengthening, and finance. The report also noted decisions to set up an ad hoc Conference secretariat as part of UNCHS and to establish two voluntary trust funds—one to meet general Conference costs and the other to support the participation of developing countries. It further proposed a procedure for determining NGOs' relevance to the Preparatory Committee's work and outlined an information programme for the Conference.

On 5 March, the Preparatory Committee invited the Commission on Human Settlements to provide recommendations on substantive issues for the Conference and to draft guidelines for a harmonized approach to national preparations and reporting. The Secretary-General of the Conference (to be appointed) was asked to assist developing countries, at their request, to prepare national reports to the Conference. The Committee also requested the United Nations Secretary-General to consider the results of the review of Agenda 21[18] on human settlements issues by the Commission on Sustainable Development (see PART THREE, Chapter I) and the outcome of regional and subregional preparatory meetings when making recommendations on a global action plan. It urged United Nations bodies to provide inputs to the preparatory process and asked Governments to contribute to the Conference's voluntary funds. The Committee further decided on the organization and agenda of its first session, to be held in April 1994, and adopted rules of procedure for the participation of NGOs in the Conference and its preparatory process.

In response to the Committee's request, the UNCHS Executive Director reported to the Commission on Human Settlements in April on substantive issues and draft guidelines for preparations and reporting at the country level.[28] The report grouped the issues under three central themes—policies and strategies for an urbanizing world, democratization and capacity-building, and investment in sustainable settlements development. It also suggested criteria for the organization and support of country-based preparatory activities and modalities for action.

In May,[29] the Commission revised the Executive Director's report and asked him to forward it to the Preparatory Committee. It recommended that the Conference programme focus on: the main future challenges and problems in the field of human settlements; the implementation of programmes resulting from Agenda 21; international coordination of strategies and development projects; and strengthening the basis for international cooperation in human settlements. The Commission also recommended that Governments initiate their preparatory activities in line with the proposed guidelines, that national and international preparations integrate NGOs, local governments, communities and the private sector, and that national focal points for the Conference be established as soon as possible. The Executive Director was asked to draft guidelines for the focal points, to test the feasibility of the guidelines for national and thematic global reports through the establishment of ad hoc working groups, and to support the preparatory process at the country and regional levels. The Commission requested the United Nations Secretary-General to appoint urgently a Secretary-General of the Conference, and decided to include an item on preparations for the Conference in the provisional agenda of its 1995 session and to discuss the mid-term review of the Global Strategy for Shelter to the Year 2000 at that session.

Preparations for Habitat II were officially launched in New York on 4 October, World Habitat Day. UNCHS made presentations on the Conference at the Second Annual Meeting of Ministers for Housing and Urban Development in Latin America (Cartagena de Indias, Colombia, 29 November–1 December) and at a meeting of cities from Europe, North America and Latin America (Barcelona, Spain, 1-3 December). The Centre also initiated information activities for the Conference and published the first issue of the *Habitat II Bulletin*.

The Ministerial Conference on Urbanization in Asia and the Pacific (Bangkok, Thailand, 27 October–2 November) adopted a Regional Plan of Action on Urbanization and called for broad-based participation in the preparatory process for Habitat II as part of the Plan's implementation.

Human settlements and political, economic and social issues

Assistance to victims of apartheid

On 5 May,[30] the Commission on Human Settlements, noting discussions between the South African Government and representatives of the black majority and other interested groups, expressed the hope that they would have a positive effect on the deplorable housing situation of the South African majority. It commended the Organization of African Unity and others for supporting the struggle against apartheid and called on the international community to continue its assistance to displaced and homeless victims of apartheid. The Executive Director was asked to intensify efforts to provide technical training and other forms of assistance.

Housing strategy for Palestinians

In response to a 1991 Commission request,[31] the Executive Director submitted a report on the housing requirements of the Palestinian people,[32] which reviewed the land use and demographic situation in the occupied territories, provided a profile of the Palestinian housing sector, examined housing demand and supply trends and proposed a Palestinian housing strategy. The Executive Director also considered future housing delivery mechanisms in the territories and recommended an action plan, comprising background studies, the development of a national housing strategy and institutional capacity, and the establishment of a housing-finance system. He listed housing institutions that needed to be created and suggested an investment plan totalling $2.37 billion.

By 16 votes to 1, with 24 abstentions, the Commission[33] requested the Secretary-General, in consultation with the Executive Director and in cooperation with the Palestine Liberation Organization, to implement a national Palestinian housing strategy in accordance with the Global Strategy for Shelter to the Year 2000, and called on international donors to increase their assistance in that area. It called on Israel to end the confiscation of Palestinian lands, the establishment of settlements for new immigrants and the application of laws preventing Palestinians from establishing national housing-finance institutions. It also called on Israel to refrain from policies preventing building permits for Palestinians and prohibiting production of local building materials, and to lift sanctions on financial aid for housing from international, Arab and regional organizations. The Commission asked the Preparatory Committee for Habitat II to consider the housing requirements of Palestinians in the Conference agenda. The Executive Director was requested to facilitate training for Palestinian technical personnel and to report in 1995 on progress made.

Women and human settlements

On 5 May,[34] the Commission urged Governments to develop a shelter strategy that strengthened the participation of women in settlement development and management locally, nationally and regionally, and to review and repeal gender-discriminatory legislation in human settlements development. It called for active collaboration between Governments and UNCHS to improve the condition of women in the design, development, governing and management of human settlements, and asked the Executive Director to increase support to Governments for the development of gender-sensitive shelter strategies. The Executive Director was also requested to review key shelter sector performance indicators for gender sensitivity and to supplement them with indicators identifying the possibly disadvantaged position of women in the housing sector. He was also requested to formulate guidelines on women's legal rights to house and land tenure and access to credit; to incorporate those measures into the work programme of the Centre for 1994-1995; to prepare a substantive contribution to the Fourth (1995) World Conference on Women; to include the outcome of that Conference in documentation for Habitat II; and to report on the subject in 1995.

Shelter, employment and poverty

Pursuant to a 1991 Commission request,[35] the Executive Director submitted a report on the relationship between underemployment and unemployment and shelter provision.[36] The report provided the rationale for linking shelter and employment in the context of the Global Strategy for Shelter to the Year 2000, examined linkages between housing, human settlements development and employment generation, and appraised the scope and modalities for increasing employment opportunities in poor communities by supporting labour-intensive technologies. It also reviewed recent United Nations efforts to integrate employment-generation and shelter provision, and made suggestions for future research and action. Calling for a common strategy to promote shelter and employment for the poor, the Executive Director recommended that international and national efforts concentrate on projects to test employment-intensive approaches to housing and service supply, the mixed use of residential areas, and technical and organizational skills training.

On 5 May,[37] the Commission called on UNCHS and the International Labour Organisation to intensify their coordination and cooperation in the areas of employment-generation and labour-intensive programmes. It urged Governments to support labour-intensive technologies in the delivery of shelter, infrastructure and services and to encourage the training and use of the unemployed in those activities. It also called on Governments to introduce legislation bridging the gap between formal-sector and informal-sector activities and to promote building codes, standards

and regulations for the use of locally available materials and labour-intensive technologies. Governments were urged to support the establishment and expansion of community-based credit mechanisms for the urban poor, and credit and loan systems for small-scale enterprises. The Executive Director was asked to convene an intergovernmental meeting on strategies for poverty reduction through employment-intensive modes of delivering shelter, infrastructure and services in low-income urban communities, and to increase support to countries interested in new building legislation. He was also urged to increase assistance for employment-intensive approaches to housing, infrastructure and services supply. The Commission recommended that Governments involve small-scale, labour-intensive enterprises in public works activities, and asked the Executive Director to report on the potential of employment-intensive shelter programmes to the World Summit for Social Development in 1995.

The right to adequate housing

On 5 May,[38] the Commission encouraged all States that had not done so to ratify all international treaties containing the human right to adequate housing, in particular the 1966 International Covenant on Economic, Social and Cultural Rights.[39] It invited all States to repeal, reform or amend legislation, policies or programmes negatively affecting that right and to provide the Special Rapporteur of the Commission on Human Rights with any relevant information. Governments were urged to cease practices such as forced evictions and any other form of discrimination in the housing sphere, and to establish mechanisms for monitoring homelessness, inadequate housing conditions, persons without security of tenure and other related issues impeding the efficiency of the shelter sector. The Commission encouraged States to take legislative action for the realization of the right to adequate housing, and recommended that the issue be considered by the Preparatory Committee for Habitat II. The Executive Director was asked to solicit States' views on the most effective ways of implementing and monitoring the right to adequate housing and to report in 1995 on possible contributions by UNCHS towards that end, including the development of an integrated monitoring system by the Centre and United Nations human rights bodies.

Environmental aspects of human settlements

In response to a 1991 Commission request,[40] the Executive Director reported in February 1993 on the outcome of UNCED, with special reference to human settlements issues, and the follow-up activities of UNCHS.[41] The report outlined ongoing and planned activities to promote: the development of sustainable human settlements and adequate shelter for all; improved settlements management; sustainable land-use planning and management; the integrated provision of environmental infrastructure, including water, sanitation and solid-waste disposal; sustainable energy and transportation systems in human settlements; settlement planning and management in disaster-prone areas; sustainable construction industry activities; and human resource development and capacity-building. Other related areas addressed by UNCED included protection of the atmosphere, oceans and coastal areas and human settlements activities involving NGOs and women.

Urban areas, environment and energy

An expert group meeting (Lund, Sweden, 8-12 March), convened by UNCHS in cooperation with the Governments of the Netherlands and Sweden, discussed strategies for implementing Agenda 21 as it related to human settlements, with special emphasis on urban areas, the environment and energy. The meeting stressed the need to provide access to environmentally sound basic services for all, and to maximize public participation and the use of local resources in urban development programmes. It emphasized the central role of women in energy and environmental management, suggested the development of a framework to evaluate the sustainability of urban development, and recommended the establishment of a network for interregional and intercountry exchanges of information, and monitoring of the implementation of Agenda 21 in the context of urban energy and shelter.

On 5 May,[42] the Commission requested the UNCHS Executive Director to integrate the meeting's conclusions into the Centre's work programme and to disseminate its recommendations within and outside the United Nations system. The Preparatory Committee for Habitat II was invited to use the report and its recommendations in its work.

Disaster and post-war reconstruction

On 5 May, the Commission recommended[43] that UNCHS play an active role in the work of the recently established Inter-Agency Standing Committee (see PART THREE, Chapter III). It also requested[44] the Executive Director to make arrangements for assistance to Cuba, which had recently suffered considerable loss of life and damage to its economy, housing and other infrastructure during a severe storm. It was requested that assistance focus on the reconstruction and development of Cuba's housing sector and the preservation of urban areas in disaster-prone zones. (For further details, see PART THREE, Chapter III.)

UN Centre for Human Settlements (Habitat)

Activities

In 1993, UNCHS supported 257 technical cooperation programmes and projects in 95 countries, with an overall budget in excess of $42 million. A total of 42 new projects were approved and became operational during the year, while 48 others were completed. The Centre provided special advisory services in human settlements finance, building materials and construction technology, and the application of microcomputer technology to data management. It fielded a total of 10 technical assistance missions to Brazil, Costa Rica, Egypt, Italy, Japan, Myanmar, the Philippines and the United States. Another mission went to Ghana as part of the Sustainable Cities Programme (see below).

The 1992-1993 UNCHS work programme was structured under eight subprogrammes: global issues and strategies; national policies and instruments; integrated settlements management; financial resources; land management; infrastructure development and operation; housing production; and the construction sector. In 1993, the Commission on Human Settlements had before it a report of the Executive Director on the implementation of the work programme.[1]

The first subprogramme helped developing countries to formulate and implement national shelter strategies in accordance with the Global Strategy for Shelter. Its *GSS in Action* provided an overview of the Strategy's main recommendations and highlighted them in 22 success stories from 17 countries. The Strategy was reviewed at a regional seminar for South Pacific countries (Brisbane, Australia, 13-17 April).

The objective of the second subprogramme was to analyse national human settlements policies and instruments, prepare policy options and guidelines for sustainable human settlements programmes, and assist with investment planning and translation of the Global Strategy at the national level. Activities in that area included a workshop on gender-aware approaches to human settlements development (Colombo, Sri Lanka, 11-13 June) and the training of trainers in local government management for east and southern African countries (Livingstone, Zambia, 9-29 May).

The third subprogramme focused on metropolitan, secondary-centre and subnational systems management and human resources development. The Centre continued its research project on metropolitan planning and management in the developing world, initiated in 1990, and issued a related publication on spatial decentralization policies implemented in Bombay, India, and Cairo, Egypt. Among other publications were the *Gestión urbana en ciudades intermedias de América Latina* and *The*

Management of Human Settlements: The Municipal Level.
The Centre also participated in the World Conference on Metropolitan Governance, held in Tokyo, which focused on decentralization and modernization of metropolitan management as well as on city-to-city and private/public co-operation.

The financial resources subprogramme analysed the ability of housing-finance institutions to address the increasing demand for housing and services. The Centre was preparing technical publications on selected national proposals for housing-finance programmes, and case-studies of innovative housing-finance institutions and housing as a source of economic activity. Another publication dealt with the role of cooperatives and credit unions in mobilizing finance for the improvement of low-income human settlements. UNCHS also co-sponsored a course on housing in development, attended by housing officials from east and southern Africa (Nairobi, 27 March–24 April).

The fifth subprogramme focused on land management and ways of ensuring a steady, adequate and affordable supply of land for all settlement needs. Work continued on reviewing and updating technical and administrative requirements to improve the operation of land registration and information systems. In 1993, the Centre published a study of Australia's experience in the development of land-title registration systems and organized an international seminar on new approaches to land regularization policies in developing countries (Mexico City, 23-26 February).

Activities under the infrastructure development and operation subprogramme were carried out under the Settlement Infrastructure and Environment Programme, which was initiated in 1992 to develop an integrated approach to the planning, delivery, maintenance and management of environmental infrastructure and services in human settlements. In 1993, as part of the Programme's waste-management component, the Centre started a project on small-scale composting and digestion of organic municipal refuse and held a regional workshop on solid-waste recycling and reuse in developing countries (Manila, Philippines, 20-22 January). It was also formulating projects for the development of waste-management tools at the municipal level and on environmental and health risk assessment of solid-waste management. The Centre began field research activities on the integrated management of water resources and environmental infrastructure in Ecuador, the Lao People's Democratic Republic, Nicaragua and Zambia, and continued studies of urban water-resource management in eight Asian megacities. The environmental health component included a project on crowding and health in low-income

settlements and related workshops in Indonesia (Jakarta, 16 February) and Guinea-Bissau (Bissau, 13 May).

The seventh subprogramme, on housing production, paid special attention to the needs and potentials of the poorest groups. A regional workshop on community participation and training for settlement development was held (Ndola, Zambia, 7-11 June), and an international seminar on enabling community management was organized in October for high-level government officials, community leaders and project personnel from Bolivia, Costa Rica, Ecuador, Ghana, Sri Lanka, Uganda and Zambia.

The eighth subprogramme focused on the construction sector, the transfer of small-scale technologies to local building materials industries, and skills development and upgrading. In collaboration with the United Nations Industrial Development Organization, the Centre convened the first global consultation on the construction industry (Tunis, Tunisia, 3-7 May) to discuss natural resource consumption by the industry, physical disruption caused by construction activities and increased environmental pollution. It also continued to publish its *Journal of the Network of African Countries on Local Building Materials and Technologies.*

UNCHS participated in the annual Conference of Ministers responsible for human settlements in Central and Eastern Europe (Romania, 24-26 March), a conference on habitat: proposals for a "liveable" environment (Bormio, Italy, May), and a design workshop on regional development for east and southern Africa (Harare, Zimbabwe, 1-5 June). The Centre continued to issue *Habitat News* and the *UNCHS (Habitat) Shelter Bulletin*, and prepared a number of technical publications, audio-visual aids and information kits.

The 1993 Habitat Scroll of Honour Awards for outstanding contributions by individuals, organizations and projects to the shelter delivery process were presented to the Cités Unies Développement (France), the Build-Together Programme (Namibia) and, posthumously, to Anthony William Bullard (United Kingdom) and Zia ul Haq (Afghanistan)—UNCHS staff members killed in an ambush in Afghanistan.

Improvement of municipal management

The UNCHS/UNDP/World Bank 10-year Urban Management Programme (UMP) was designed to strengthen the contribution of municipalities in developing countries towards human development, economic growth, poverty alleviation and environmental enhancement. Its first phase (1986-1991) focused on land management, municipal finance and administration, infrastructure, urban environment and, as of 1991, urban poverty alleviation. The second phase (1992-1996) was aimed at building the capacity of developing countries to address those five programme areas. It included city and country consultations; technical cooperation through regional panels of experts in Africa, Asia and the Pacific, Latin America and the Caribbean and the Arab States; and global support from UMP nucleus teams to continue research on efficient urban management, to synthesize past experiences and to disseminate UMP-related materials. Aggregate resources for the second phase were in excess of $25 million. The first African regional workshop on urban management was held at Nairobi (11-15 January) and the sixth annual review meeting of UMP also took place (The Hague, Netherlands, 30 June and 1 July).

An operational arm of UMP's urban environmental component, the Sustainable Cities Programme, was launched by UNCHS in 1990 to help municipal authorities improve their environmental planning and management capacity. The Programme's demonstration projects resulted in broad-based environmental strategies, priority capital investment projects and strengthened urban management capacities. City-level demonstration activities were under way in 12 countries and UNCHS began projects in four cities—Dar es Salaam (United Republic of Tanzania), Ismailia (Egypt), Concepción (Chile) and Madras (India). The project in Ismailia was reviewed at a consultation on the city's sustainable growth and development (Abu Sultan, Egypt, 5-8 July). Six more city-level demonstrations were to be launched in 1993-1994 in Accra (Ghana), Ibadan (Nigeria), Tunis (Tunisia), Jakarta (Indonesia), Guayaquil (Ecuador) and Katowice (Poland). In addition, Berlin, Moscow, Tianjin (China) and Plovdiv (Bulgaria) expressed interest in participating in the Programme.

Another joint UNCHS/UNDP/World Bank initiative, the City Data Programme, was launched in 1991 to identify key urban indicators for planning and management decisions and promote data collection and dissemination. Programme activities included the UNCHS-CitiBase project to develop a global urban-data collection and dissemination system, pilot projects in Kenya and Romania, and the development of a visual settlement planning approach to improve low-income and informal settlements. Activities in 1993 included a regional seminar on strategic options for public transport improvements in large cities of developing countries (Pune, India, 27 and 28 January) and a capacity-building workshop on information dissemination strategies for urban management (Dakar, Senegal, 6-8 July).

In January 1993, the Executive Director submitted to the Commission a report on the improvement of municipal management.[45] It discussed the need for a radically new look at the role of cit-

ies in national and global development, and for municipal management that involved the whole population in city development. It identified the key areas for improved municipal management as land management, infrastructure and services, transport, financial management and organizational performance. The report suggested options for partnerships between municipalities, for central-government support and for international cooperation. The Executive Director recommended that the Commission consider: ways for municipal management to address urban poverty issues; ways of promoting institutional and sectoral partnerships; steps to strengthen institutional capacity-building; the issue of metropolitan management; and possible new initiatives under the Centre's technical support programmes.

On 5 May,[46] the Commission adopted a broader concept of municipal management and recommended that the authority of municipal governments to develop and manage local revenues according to principles of efficiency, equity and fairness be recognized. It urged municipal governments to cooperate with NGOs, community organizations and the private sector in identifying priority problems and facilitating public-private partnerships. The Executive Director was requested to develop guidelines to improve the management and living conditions in different settlements and to report on the subject in 1995.

Work programme

In February, the Executive Director submitted to the Commission a draft 1994-1995 work programme for UNCHS,[47] based on the eight subprogramme areas of the 1992-1997 medium-term plan.

On 5 May,[48] the Commission adopted the work programme having amended specific programme outputs and added activities in such areas as comparative shelter strategy development, municipal management, settlements financing, infrastructure development and technology transfer. It also designated 16 programme priorities.

Coordination

In May, the Commission had before it a joint progress report of the Executive Directors of UNCHS and the United Nations Environment Programme[49] describing cooperation in such areas as the assessment of environmental conditions in human settlements; environmental aspects of policies, planning and management in rural and urban settlements; environmentally sound human settlements technology; and research, training and the dissemination of information.

The Commission, having considered the joint report as well as the UNCHS Executive Director's reports on coordination and cooperation,[50] requested[51] him to intensify the coordination of United Nations system-wide activities, particularly those relating to implementation of the Global Strategy for Shelter and the human settlements aspects of Agenda 21, and to report in 1995 on further areas of collaboration emerging from Agenda 21. He was also asked to continue close cooperation between the Centre, universities, research and scientific institutes, NGOs and voluntary groups, and to report on the results in 1995.

The Commission confirmed[52] the importance of UNCHS as a focal point for human settlements action within the United Nations system and recommended that it increase its assistance to countries in formulating solutions to human settlements problems. The Executive Director was asked to report in 1995 on the Centre's new objectives and its role within the United Nations system.

The Commission endorsed[53] the conclusions and recommendations of the 1992 Meeting on Governmental-Non-Governmental Cooperation in the Field of Human Settlements[54] and encouraged Member States to cooperate with non-governmental and community-based organizations. Member States were urged to involve NGOs in the promotion of public awareness and implementation and monitoring of the Global Strategy for Shelter and relevant parts of Agenda 21. The Executive Director was requested to consult regularly with representatives of those organizations and to strengthen their research, training and dissemination capacity. The Commission asked the Secretary-General of Habitat II to facilitate their involvement in the Conference and its preparations.

As a follow-up to the 1992 Meeting, the Centre organized an international seminar in 1993 in Tokyo on housing settlement policy. It examined prospects for partnerships between Governments and NGOs, prepared several reports for the 1993 meeting of the Subcommittee on Rural Development (formerly the Task Force on Rural Development) of the Administrative Committee on Coordination, and issued a related publication on rural regional settlement systems in Africa.

Triennial policy review of human settlements activities

In 1992,[55] the General Assembly had requested executive heads of United Nations agencies to submit progress reports to their governing bodies concerning the triennial policy review of operational activities of the United Nations development system in their respective fields. In a March 1993 report,[56] the Executive Director analysed issues to be addressed in the policy review and suggested that the Commission consider measures to strengthen the UNCHS capacity to

provide policy advice and technical support at the country level, and to strengthen and expand the Centre's training programmes.

In May,[57] the Commission supported the Centre's initiatives to expand its programme for in-country human settlements analysis and needs assessment, and its shelter sector indicators programme. It also endorsed efforts to expand in-country capacity-building.

CPC consideration. In March, the Secretary-General presented to the Committee for Programme and Coordination (CPC) a triennial review of the implementation of its recommendations concerning the evaluation of the human settlements programme.[58] He assessed the implementation of CPC's recommendations on coordination, programme planning, information dissemination and the intergovernmental review of the in-depth evaluation, and provided suggestions for national focal points and NGOs to improve United Nations activities in human settlements. The Secretary-General recommended that UNCHS and the regional units adopt the suggestions, agree on their respective roles and appropriate coordination mechanisms, and reflect the views of governmental experts and NGOs in proposed work programmes. He also recommended that the Preparatory Committee for Habitat II be informed of CPC's decisions on coordination.

In May,[59] CPC endorsed the Secretary-General's recommendations.

Global Parliamentarians on Habitat

At their seventh meeting (Nairobi, 3 May 1993), the Global Parliamentarians on Habitat agreed to raise major human settlements problems in their national parliaments. They decided to become an incorporated body and to participate in the preparations for Habitat II, and asked the UNCHS Executive Director to extend support to their 1994 meeting, to be held in Mexico.

On 5 May,[60] the Commission took note of and annexed to its resolution the conclusion reached by the meeting.

Financing

The Centre's work programme was financed from the United Nations regular budget and from extrabudgetary resources. UNCHS project delivery in 1993 amounted to $44.4 million, including projects financed by UNDP ($22.3 million), the United Nations Habitat and Human Settlements Foundation ($12.7 million) and other sources ($9.4 million).

UN Habitat and Human Settlements Foundation

As at 1 March 1993,[61] voluntary contributions to the United Nations Habitat and Human Settlements Foundation consisted of unpaid pledges of $937,612 and pledges for 1993 of $6.68 million. Income for the biennium ended 31 December 1993 was estimated at $22,680,746, against estimated expenditures of $23,628,142. Combined pledges by Governments for the same period amounted to $20,562,254.

At a pledging meeting held during the Commission's 1993 session, 18 countries made pledges to the Centre and the Foundation. In addition, some 40 States pledged $758,025 at the November United Nations Pledging Conference for Development Activities.

1994-1995 budget

In February 1993, the Executive Director reported on the Foundation's proposed budget for the biennium 1994-1995.[62] The report estimated income for that period at $21,741,700, including $18.2 million in expected contributions and pledges. Estimated expenditures totalled $19,842,300 plus an allocation of $600,000 to the reserve fund, leaving an expected balance of $1,299,400. The concurring report of ACABQ and the projected use of the Centre's extrabudgetary resources in 1994-

1995 were submitted as addenda to the proposed budget.

The Commission adopted the budget on 5 May.[63]

REFERENCES

[1]YUN 1992, p. 705. [2]A/48/8 (res. 14/2). [3]Ibid. (res. 14/7). [4]Ibid. (res. 14/10). [5]HS/C/14/4 & Corr.1. [6]YUN 1988, p. 478, GA res. 43/181, 20 Dec. 1988. [7]HS/C/14/4/Add.1 & Corr.2. [8]A/48/8 (dec. 14/21). [9]A/48/8/Add.1. [10]A/48/8. [11]A/48/8 (dec. 14/25). [12]YUN 1987, p. 715. [13]HS/C/14/15. [14]YUN 1976, p. 441. [15]HS/C/14/3. [16]A/48/8 (res. 14/1). [17]YUN 1988, p. 478. [18]YUN 1992, p. 672. [19]YUN 1991, p. 520. [20]HS/C/14/3/Add.1. [21]A/48/8 (res. 14/13). [22]YUN 1991, p. 519. [23]HS/C/14/7. [24]A/48/8 (res. 14/16). [25]YUN 1992, p. 702, GA res. 47/180, 22 Dec. 1992. [26]A/48/37. [27]A/CONF.165/PC/2. [28]HS/C/14/14/Add.1. [29]A/48/8 (res. 14/20). [30]Ibid. (res. 14/11). [31]YUN 1991, p. 522. [32]HS/C/14/2/Add.1. [33]A/48/8 (res. 14/9). [34]Ibid. (res. 14/4). [35]YUN 1991, p. 523. [36]HS/C/14/2/Add.2. [37]A/48/8 (res. 14/3). [38]Ibid. (res. 14/6). [39]YUN 1966, p. 419, GA res. 2200 A (XXI), annex, 16 Dec. 1966. [40]YUN 1991, p. 524. [41]HS/C/14/5. [42]A/48/8 (res. 14/14). [43]Ibid. (res. 14/5). [44]Ibid. (res. 14/8). [45]HS/C/14/6. [46]A/48/8 (res. 14/15). [47]HS/C/14/8. [48]A/48/8 (dec. 14/22). [49]HS/C/14/11. [50]YUN 1992, p. 706. [51]A/48/8 (res. 14/18). [52]Ibid. (res. 14/19). [53]Ibid. (res. 14/17). [54]YUN 1992, p. 707. [55]Ibid., p. 552, GA res. 47/199, 22 Dec. 1992. [56]HS/C/14/14/Add.2. [57]A/48/8 (dec. 14/24). [58]E/AC.51/1993/4. [59]A/48/16. [60]A/48/8 (res. 14/12). [61]HS/C/14/INF.6. [62]HS/C/14/9 & Corr.1,2 & Add.1,2. [63]A/48/8 (dec. 14/23).

Chapter X

Human rights

In 1993—the forty-fifth anniversary of the adoption of the Universal Declaration of Human Rights—the United Nations continued its efforts to promote and protect human rights and fundamental freedoms.

The World Conference on Human Rights, which was held at Vienna in June, adopted the Vienna Declaration and Programme of Action, by which participating Governments reaffirmed their solemn commitment to a broad range of human rights and fundamental freedoms and called for measures to strengthen international human rights instruments and their monitoring mechanisms. As recommended in the Declaration, the General Assembly, in December, created the post of High Commissioner for Human Rights (resolution 48/141).

The year marked the International Year of the World's Indigenous People. In December, the Assembly proclaimed the International Decade of the World's Indigenous People, to begin on 10 December 1994 (Human Rights Day), with the goal of strengthening international cooperation to solve problems faced by indigenous people in areas such as human rights, the environment, development, education and health (48/163). It also proclaimed the third Decade to Combat Racism and Racial Discrimination, beginning in 1993, and adopted the Programme of Action for the Decade (48/91).

The Human Rights Commission established a Working Group on the Right to Development to ensure the promotion, encouragement and reinforcement of the principles contained in the 1986 Declaration on the Right to Development. Progress was made by the Working Group to Elaborate a Draft Optional Protocol to the 1984 Convention against Torture and Other Cruel, Inhuman or Degrading Treatment or Punishment. Work continued on a draft declaration on the right and responsibility of individuals, groups and organs of society to promote and protect universally recognized human rights and fundamental freedoms and on a draft declaration defining gross and large-scale violations of human rights as an international crime.

Alleged violations of human rights on a large scale in several countries were again examined.

The Commission on Human Rights held its forty-ninth session at Geneva from 1 February to 12 March, during which it adopted 98 resolutions and 16 decisions.

The Subcommission on Prevention of Discrimination and Protection of Minorities held its forty-fifth session at Geneva from 2 to 27 August. At that session, it adopted 46 resolutions and 11 decisions.

Discrimination

Racial discrimination

Second Decade to Combat Racism and Racial Discrimination (1983-1993)

Implementation of the Programme for the Decade

In 1993, United Nations efforts to implement the Programme of Action for the Second Decade to Combat Racism and Racial Discrimination continued to be carried out in accordance with the plan of activities for 1985-1989 put forward in 1984[1] and the plan approved by the General Assembly in 1987,[2] covering the remainder of the Decade, 1990-1993.

Reports of the Secretary-General. In response to a 1992 Commission on Human Rights request,[3] the Secretary-General reported on progress made in carrying out the plan of activities to implement the Programme of Action.[4] He described United Nations seminars, publications and studies, action taken by United Nations bodies, and the status of the Trust Fund for the Programme for the Decade. He presented perspectives on proclaiming a third decade to combat racism and racial discrimination, which might serve as a basis for the Commission's debate on the subject.

Pursuant to an Economic and Social Council 1985 request,[5] the Secretary-General, in a May report,[6] described recent activities by United Nations bodies to implement the Programme for the Second Decade and stated that the International Day for the Elimination of Racial Discrimination (22 March 1993) had focused on the theme "Racism, racial discrimination, xenophobia and violence: what can the United Nations do?". As authorized by the Council in 1990,[7] a meeting of representatives of national institutions and organizations promoting tolerance and harmony and combating racism and racial discrimination took place (Sydney, Australia, 19-23 April). The

Secretary-General reported on the status of the Trust Fund for the Programme for the Decade.

As requested by the General Assembly in 1992,[8] the final draft of the model legislation to guide Governments in enacting legislation against racial discrimination, as revised by the Secretariat in accordance with comments made by members of the Committee on the Elimination of Racial Discrimination, was submitted in October.[9]

On 20 December, the Assembly, by **decision 48/426**, took note of the draft model legislation.

Third Decade to Combat Racism and Racial Discrimination (1993-2003)

Draft programme of action

Reports of the Secretary-General. In response to a 1992 Economic and Social Council request,[10] the Secretary-General, in May 1993,[6] presented a revised draft programme of action for the third decade in light of observations made in the General Assembly and the Commission on Human Rights. The revisions were based on the elements for the programme of action put forward by the Secretary-General in 1992.[11]

As requested by the Assembly in 1992,[8] the Secretary-General submitted in October a new draft programme of action for the third decade, taking into account comments made by the Assembly in 1992 and by the Economic and Social Council, the Commission on Human Rights and its Subcommission on Prevention of Discrimination and Protection of Minorities in 1993.[12] The draft also included proposals put forward in 1993 by the World Conference on Human Rights (see below, under "Advancement of human rights"), suggestions made at a non-governmental organization (NGO) forum (Vienna, 10-12 June 1993) and recommendations adopted by an international consultation of NGOs on racism, xenophobia, racial and ethnic intolerance and conflicts (Geneva, 15-17 September 1993) organized by the NGO Subcommittee on Racism, Racial Discrimination, Apartheid and Decolonization in cooperation with the United Nations Centre for Human Rights. Those recommendations were annexed to the Secretary-General's report.

The new draft elements emphasized measures to be taken by the Assembly and Security Council for the complete elimination of apartheid and support for the establishment of a united, non-racial and democratic South Africa and to counteract the legacy of cultural, economic and social inequality left by apartheid. Actions proposed at the international, national and regional levels included ratification and implementation of international instruments to combat racism and racial discrimination; activities by the United Nations Department of Public Information (DPI), the

United Nations Educational, Scientific and Cultural Organization (UNESCO) and the International Labour Organisation (ILO); basic research and studies; resolution of ethnic conflicts; cooperation with United Nations efforts; measures in the areas of teaching, education and culture; activities involving the mass media; and measures to protect vulnerable groups and populations disadvantaged as a result of racism or racial discrimination. The importance of coordination and reporting between United Nations bodies was also discussed.

The Secretary-General suggested that the goals and objectives of the third decade be the same as those adopted by the Assembly in 1973 for the first Decade.[13]

Human Rights Commission action. On 26 February 1993,[14] the Commission appealed to all States that had not ratified or acceded to the relevant international instruments to combat racism and racial discrimination to do so. It urged Governments to combat new forms of racism and asked them, and international organizations and NGOs, to increase their activities to combat racism, racial discrimination and apartheid. It asked the Secretary-General to continue to study the effects of racial discrimination on children of minorities and those of migrant workers in the areas of education, training and employment, and to submit recommendations on measures to combat those effects. The Commission asked UNESCO to expedite the preparation of teaching materials and aids to promote educational and training activities on human rights and against racism and racial discrimination. Member States were called on to consider signing and ratifying the 1992 International Convention on the Protection of the Rights of All Migrant Workers and Members of Their Families[15] as a matter of priority.

Regretting that most activities scheduled for 1992-1993 had not been implemented due to lack of resources, the Commission called on the international community to provide financial resources for efficient action against racism and racial discrimination and appealed for generous contributions to the Trust Fund. It asked Governments, United Nations bodies and specialized agencies, other intergovernmental organizations and NGOs to participate in activities scheduled for 1990-1993 that had not yet been carried out.

The Commission recommended that activities related to a draft programme of action for a third decade, as contained in a 1992 report of the Secretary-General,[11] be undertaken and reviewed at mid-term. It asked the Secretary-General, in preparing the draft programme of action, to accord the highest priority to activities for monitoring the transition to a non-racist society in South Africa. Governments were called on to encourage further positive change in South Africa, based on guidelines contained in the 1989 Declaration on Apartheid and its Destructive Consequences in Southern Africa.[16] It recommended that 1992-1993 activities that had not been implemented because of lack of resources be included in the draft programme of action for the third decade along with other proposed activities annexed to its resolution. It decided to consider the draft programme of action in 1994.

On 2 March,[17] the Commission took note of a 1992 report by the Secretary-General[3] describing trends in racism, racial discrimination, intolerance and xenophobia and recommended that the General Assembly take steps to launch a third decade, beginning in 1993. The Commission confirmed the importance of a complementarity of economic, social, educational and information measures at the national level, including legislative, administrative and penal measures, and of international measures, and urged Governments to take measures and develop policies to combat racism and eliminate discrimination. It decided to appoint, for three years, a special rapporteur to address contemporary forms of racism, racial discrimination and xenophobia who would report to the Commission annually, beginning in 1994. The Secretary-General was asked to assist the special rapporteur in performing his or her functions.

The Economic and Social Council, by **decision 1993/258** of 28 July, approved the Commission's decision to appoint a special rapporteur and its request to the Secretary-General for assistance.

The Chairman of the Commission appointed Robert Dossou (Benin) as Special Rapporteur.

Subcommission action. On 16 August,[18] the Subcommission recommended that the Special Rapporteur examine situations in various regions, beginning with incidents that were increasing in the developed countries, and the theories and attitudes of racial superiority that incited them. It recommended that he report to the Subcommission in 1994 and that arrangements be made to convene, at that time, a joint meeting between the Subcommission and the Committee on the Elimination of Racial Discrimination, with a view to elaborating recommendations concerning the importance of the complementarity of economic, social, educational and information measures at the national level, including legislative, administrative and penal measures, and of international measures. The Subcommission asked the Secretary-General to prepare, for that meeting, a survey of efforts by United Nations bodies to prevent and combat racism, racial discrimination, xenophobia and related intolerance, together with proposals on how those efforts could be strengthened and better coordinated.

Other action. In March,[19] the Committee on the Elimination of Racial Discrimination discussed

a possible third decade and expressed interest in holding seminars on themes, including the effectiveness of national legislation and recourse procedures available to victims of racism; the eradication of incitement to racial hatred and discrimination; and the problem of refugee flows resulting from ethnic conflicts or political restructuring.

The Committee Chairman informed the Commission on Human Rights of the Committee's readiness to cooperate with the Special Rapporteur on contemporary forms of racism, racial discrimination and xenophobia and related forms of intolerance.

ECONOMIC AND SOCIAL COUNCIL ACTION

On 27 July, the Economic and Social Council, on the recommendation of its Social Committee, adopted **resolution 1993/8** without vote.

Third decade to combat racism and racial discrimination

The Economic and Social Council,

Recalling its resolution 1992/13 of 20 July 1992,

Reaffirming the purpose set forth in the Charter of the United Nations of achieving international cooperation in solving international problems of an economic, social, cultural or humanitarian character and in promoting and encouraging respect for human rights and fundamental freedoms for all, without distinction as to race, sex, language or religion,

Recalling that in resolution 1992/13, it requested the Secretary-General to prepare a draft programme of action for the third decade to combat racism and racial discrimination and to submit it to the General Assembly at its forty-seventh session, taking into account, *inter alia,* the elements of the Programme of Action for the Second Decade to Combat Racism and Racial Discrimination that had not yet been fully implemented,

Recalling also that the General Assembly, in its resolution 47/77 of 16 December 1992, took note of the report of the Secretary-General on the implementation of the Programme of Action for the Second Decade, and requested him to submit to the Assembly, at its forty-eighth session, a new draft programme of action for the third decade,

Having examined the report of the Secretary-General on the implementation of the Programme of Action for the Second Decade,

Convinced that it is necessary that the General Assembly proclaim in 1993 a third decade to combat racism and racial discrimination as a means of intensifying national and international efforts in this field,

Taking into account the progress made towards building a democratic and united South Africa not based on racial prejudice,

Emphasizing that it is the responsibility of the Government of South Africa to take all necessary measures to stop immediately the violence in that country and to protect the life and property of all South Africans,

Emphasizing also the need for all parties to cooperate in combating violence and to exercise restraint,

Bearing in mind the Declaration on Apartheid and its Destructive Consequences in Southern Africa, adopted by the General Assembly in its resolution S-16/1 of 14 December 1989 and contained in the annex thereto,

Deeply concerned about the prevalence of racism and racial tensions, as well as of the rising tide of xenophobia,

Stressing the need to continue the coordination of activities undertaken by various United Nations bodies and specialized agencies for the purpose of implementing the Programme of Action for the Second Decade,

1. *Declares* that all forms of racism and racial discrimination, particularly in their institutionalized forms, such as apartheid, or resulting from official doctrines of racial superiority or exclusivity, are among the most serious violations of human rights in the contemporary world and must be combated by all available means;

2. *Recommends* that the General Assembly at its forty-eighth session proclaim a third decade to combat racism and racial discrimination;

3. *Requests* the Secretary-General, in preparing the draft programme of action for the third decade, to accord the highest priority to activities aimed at monitoring the transition from apartheid to a non-racist society in South Africa;

4. *Also requests* the Secretary-General to take into account the results of the World Conference on Human Rights and the discussion held during the substantive session of 1993 of the Council in the preparation of the programme of action for the third decade;

5. *Considers* that voluntary contributions to the Trust Fund for the Programme for the Decade for Action to Combat Racism and Racial Discrimination are indispensable for the implementation of the above-mentioned programmes;

6. *Calls upon* the international community to provide the Secretary-General with appropriate financial resources for efficient action against racism and racial discrimination;

7. *Decides* to accord the highest priority to the question of the implementation of the programme of action for the third decade to combat racism and racial discrimination.

Economic and Social Council resolution 1993/8

27 July 1993   Meeting 43   Adopted without vote

Approved by Social Committee (E/1993/104) without vote, 14 July (meeting 9); draft by France and Senegal (for African States) (E/1993/C.2/L.1), orally revised; agenda item 17.

GENERAL ASSEMBLY ACTION

On 20 December, the General Assembly, on the recommendation of the Third (Social, Humanitarian and Cultural) Committee, adopted **resolution 48/91** without vote.

Third Decade to Combat Racism and Racial Discrimination

The General Assembly,

Reaffirming its objectives set forth in the Charter of the United Nations to achieve international cooperation in solving problems of an economic, social, cultural or humanitarian character and in promoting and encouraging respect for human rights and fundamental freedoms for all without distinction as to race, sex, language or religion,

Reaffirming also its firm determination and its commitment to eradicate totally and unconditionally racism in all its forms, racial discrimination and apartheid,

Recalling the Universal Declaration of Human Rights, the International Convention on the Elimination of All Forms of Racial Discrimination, the International Convention on the Suppression and Punishment of the Crime of Apartheid, and the Convention against Discrimination in Education adopted by the United Nations Educational, Scientific and Cultural Organization on 14 December 1960,

Recalling also the outcome of the two World Conferences to Combat Racism and Racial Discrimination, held at Geneva in 1978 and 1983,

Welcoming the outcome of the World Conference on Human Rights, and, in particular, the attention given in the Vienna Declaration and Programme of Action to the elimination of racism, racial discrimination, xenophobia and other forms of intolerance,

Welcoming also decision 1993/258 taken by the Economic and Social Council on 28 July 1993 concerning the appointment of a special rapporteur on contemporary forms of racism, racial discrimination, xenophobia and related intolerance,

Recalling its resolution 38/14 of 22 November 1983, the annex to which contains the Programme of Action for the Second Decade to Combat Racism and Racial Discrimination,

Noting with grave concern that despite the efforts of the international community, the principal objectives of the two Decades for Action to Combat Racism and Racial Discrimination have not been attained and that millions of human beings continue to this day to be the victims of varied forms of racism, racial discrimination and apartheid,

Deeply concerned about the current trend of the evolution of racism into discriminatory practices based on culture, nationality, religion or language,

Recalling in particular its resolution 47/77 of 16 December 1992,

Having considered the report submitted by the Secretary-General within the framework of the implementation of the Programme of Action for the Second Decade,

Firmly convinced of the need to take more effective and sustained measures at the national and international levels for the elimination of all forms of racism and racial discrimination,

Welcoming the proposal to launch a third decade to combat racism and racial discrimination,

Convinced of the need to ensure and support the peaceful transition towards a democratic and non-racial South Africa,

Recognizing the importance of strengthening national legislation and institutions for the promotion of racial harmony,

Aware of the importance and the magnitude of the phenomenon of migrant workers, as well as the efforts undertaken by the international community to improve the protection of the human rights of migrant workers and members of their families,

Recalling the adoption at its forty-fifth session of the International Convention on the Protection of the Rights of All Migrant Workers and Members of Their Families,

Acknowledging that indigenous people are at times victims of particular forms of racism and racial discrimination,

Reaffirming the Declaration on Apartheid and its Destructive Consequences in Southern Africa, unanimously adopted by the General Assembly at its sixteenth special session, on 14 December 1989, which offers guidelines on how to end apartheid,

1. *Declares once again* that all forms of racism and racial discrimination, whether in their institutionalized form, such as apartheid, or resulting from official doctrines of racial superiority and/or exclusivity, such as "ethnic cleansing", are among the most serious violations of human rights in the contemporary world and must be combated by all available means;

2. *Decides* to proclaim the ten-year period beginning in 1993 as the Third Decade to Combat Racism and Racial Discrimination, and to adopt the Programme of Action proposed for the Third Decade contained in the annex to the present resolution;

3. *Calls upon* Governments to cooperate with the Special Rapporteur on contemporary forms of racism, racial discrimination, xenophobia and related intolerance to enable him to fulfil his mandate;

4. *Urges* all Governments to take all necessary measures to combat new forms of racism, in particular by adapting constantly the methods provided to combat them, especially in the legislative, administrative, educational and information fields;

5. *Decides* that the international community in general and the United Nations in particular should continue to give the highest priority to programmes for combating racism, racial discrimination and apartheid and intensify their efforts, during the Third Decade, to provide assistance and relief to the victims of racism and all forms of racial discrimination and apartheid;

6. *Requests* the Secretary-General to continue to accord special attention to the situation of migrant workers and members of their families and to include regularly in his reports all information on such workers;

7. *Calls upon* all Member States to consider signing and ratifying or acceding to the International Convention on the Protection of the Rights of All Migrant Workers and Members of Their Families as a matter of priority, to enable its entry into force;

8. *Also requests* the Secretary-General to continue the study on the effects of racial discrimination on the children of minorities, in particular those of migrant workers, in the fields of education, training and employment, and to submit, *inter alia*, specific recommendations for the implementation of measures to combat the effects of that discrimination;

9. *Urges* the Secretary-General, United Nations bodies, the specialized agencies, all Governments, intergovernmental organizations and relevant non-governmental organizations, in implementing the Programme of Action for the Third Decade, to pay particular attention to the situation of indigenous people;

10. *Further requests* the Secretary-General to revise and finalize the draft model legislation for the guidance of Governments in the enactment of further legislation against racial discrimination, in the light of comments made by members of the Committee on the Elimination of Racial Discrimination at its fortieth and forty-first sessions and to publish and distribute the text as soon as possible;

11. *Renews its invitation* to the United Nations Educational, Scientific and Cultural Organization to expedite the preparation of teaching materials and teaching aids to promote teaching, training and educational activities on human rights and against racism and racial dis-

crimination, with particular emphasis on activities at the primary and secondary levels of education;

12. *Considers* that all the parts of the Programme of Action for the Third Decade should be given equal attention in order to attain the objectives of the Third Decade;

13. *Regrets* that some of the activities scheduled for the Second Decade to Combat Racism and Racial Discrimination have not been implemented because of lack of adequate resources;

14. *Requests* the Secretary-General to ensure that the necessary financial resources are provided for the implementation of the activities of the Third Decade during the biennium 1994-1995;

15. *Also requests* the Secretary-General to accord the highest priority to the activities of the Programme of Action for the Third Decade that aim at monitoring the transition from apartheid to a non-racist society in South Africa;

16. *Further requests* the Secretary-General to submit each year to the Economic and Social Council a detailed report on all activities of United Nations bodies and the specialized agencies containing an analysis of information received on such activities to combat racism and racial discrimination;

17. *Invites* the Secretary-General to submit proposals to the General Assembly with a view to supplementing, if necessary, the Programme of Action for the Third Decade;

18. *Invites* all Governments, United Nations bodies, the specialized agencies and other intergovernmental organizations, as well as interested non-governmental organizations in consultative status with the Economic and Social Council, to participate fully in the Third Decade;

19. *Invites* all Governments, intergovernmental and non-governmental organizations and individuals in a position to do so to contribute generously to the Trust Fund for the Programme for the Decade for Action to Combat Racism and Racial Discrimination, and to this end requests the Secretary-General to continue to undertake appropriate contacts and initiatives;

20. *Decides* to keep the item entitled "Elimination of racism and racial discrimination" on its agenda and to consider it as a matter of the highest priority at its forty-ninth session.

ANNEX
Programme of Action for the Third Decade to Combat Racism and Racial Discrimination (1993-2003)

Introduction

1. The goals and objectives of the Third Decade to Combat Racism and Racial Discrimination are those adopted by the General Assembly for the first Decade and contained in paragraph 8 of the annex to its resolution 3057(XXVIII) of 2 November 1973:

"The ultimate goals of the Decade are to promote human rights and fundamental freedoms for all, without distinction of any kind on grounds of race, colour, descent or national or ethnic origin, especially by eradicating racial prejudice, racism and racial discrimination; to arrest any expansion of racist policies, to eliminate the persistence of racist policies and to counteract the emergence of alliances based on mutual espousal of racism and racial discrimination; to resist any policy and practices which lead to the strengthening of the racist regimes and contribute to the sus-

tainment of racism and racial discrimination; to identify, isolate and dispel the fallacious and mythical beliefs, policies and practices that contribute to racism
and racial discrimination; and to put an end to racist
regimes.''

2. In drawing up suggested elements for the
Programme of Action for the Third Decade, account
has been taken of the fact that current global economic
conditions have caused many Member States to call for
budgetary restraint, which in turn requires a conservative approach to the number and type of programmes
of action that may be considered at this time. The
Secretary-General also took into account the relevant
suggestions made by the Committee on the Elimination
of Racial Discrimination at its forty-first session. The
elements presented below have been suggested as those
which are essential, should resources be made available to implement them.

Measures to ensure a peaceful transition
from apartheid to a democratic,
non-racial regime in South Africa

3. Recently, there have been signs of change in South
Africa, notably the abolition of such legal pillars of apartheid as the Group Areas Act, the Land Areas Act and
the Population Registration Act. Although there is reason to be hopeful that South Africa is moving into the
mainstream of the international community, the transition period may prove to be difficult and dangerous.
Fierce political competition between political parties and
ethnic groups has in fact already led to bloodshed.

4. The General Assembly and the Security Council should therefore continue to exercise constant
vigilance with regard to South Africa until a democratic
regime is installed in that country. These two bodies
might, moreover, consider initiating a mechanism to advise and assist the parties concerned in order to bring
apartheid to an end, not only in law but also in fact.
Reference should be made to Security Council resolution 765(1992) of 16 July 1992 urging the South African authorities to bring an effective end to the violence
and bring those responsible to justice.

5. The General Assembly will continue to examine
the relevant work undertaken by the established United
Nations bodies in the fight against apartheid, that is,
the Special Committee against Apartheid, the Group
of Three and the Ad Hoc Working Group of Experts
on Southern Africa.

Measures to remedy the legacy of cultural,
economic and social disparities left by apartheid

6. Action will be needed to rectify the consequences
of apartheid in South Africa, since the policy of apartheid has entailed the use of State power to increase inequalities between racial groups. The knowledge and experience of human rights bodies dealing with racial
discrimination could be most useful in promoting equality. Assistance to the victims of the political antagonisms
resulting from the process of dismantling apartheid must
also be given the greatest attention, and international
solidarity on their behalf should be intensified.

7. The Centre for Human Rights should offer technical assistance in the field of human rights to South
Africa during and after the transition period. A cycle
of seminars intended to encourage the advent of an
egalitarian society should be envisaged, in cooperation
with the concerned specialized agencies and units of the

United Nations Secretariat, which could include the following:

(a) Seminar on measures to be taken on behalf of
the disadvantaged groups in South African society in
the cultural, economic and social fields (''positive discrimination'');

(b) Seminar on the effects of racial discrimination
on the health of members of disadvantaged groups;

(c) Training courses in human rights for the South
African police force, military and judiciary.

8. In addition, in cooperation with the democratically elected Government of South Africa, the United
Nations Educational, Scientific and Cultural Organization might undertake a project for the total revision
of the South African educational system in order to
eliminate all methods and references of a racist character.

Action at the international level

9. During the discussion at the substantive session
of 1992 of the Economic and Social Council concerning the Second Decade to Combat Racism and Racial
Discrimination, many delegations expressed their concern with regard to new expressions of racism, racial
discrimination, intolerance and xenophobia in various
parts of the world. In particular, these affect minorities,
ethnic groups, migrant workers, indigenous populations,
nomads, immigrants and refugees.

10. The biggest contribution to the elimination of
racial discrimination will be that which results from the
actions of States within their own territories. International action undertaken as part of any programme for
the Third Decade should therefore be directed so as to
assist States to act effectively. The International Convention on the Elimination of All Forms of Racial Discrimination has established standards for States, and
every opportunity should be seized to ensure that these
are universally accepted and applied.

11. The General Assembly should consider more effective action to ensure that all States parties to the International Convention on the Elimination of All Forms
of Racial Discrimination fulfil their reporting and financial obligations. National action against racism and racial discrimination should be monitored and improved
by requesting an expert member of the Committee on
the Elimination of Racial Discrimination to prepare a
report on obstacles encountered with respect to the effective implementation of the Convention by States parties and suggestions for remedial measures.

12. The General Assembly requests the Secretary-
General to organize regional workshops and seminars.
A team from the Committee should be invited to monitor these meetings. The following themes are suggested
for the seminars:

(a) Seminar to assess the experience gained in the implementation of the International Convention on the Elimination of All Forms of Racial Discrimination. The seminar
would also assess the efficiency of national legislation and
recourse procedures available to victims of racism;

(b) Seminar on the eradication of incitement to racial hatred and discrimination, including the prohibition of propaganda activities and of organizations involved in them;

(c) Seminar on the right to equal treatment before
tribunals and other judicial institutions, including the
provision of reparation for damages suffered as a result
of discrimination;

(d) Seminar on the transmission of racial inequality from one generation to another, with special reference to the children of migrant workers and the appearance of new forms of segregation;

(e) Seminar on immigration and racism;

(f) Seminar on international cooperation in the elimination of racial discrimination, including cooperation between States, the contribution of non-governmental organizations, national and regional institutions, United Nations bodies and petitions to treaty-monitoring bodies;

(g) Seminar on the enactment of national legislation to combat racism and racial discrimination affecting ethnic groups, migrant workers and refugees (in Europe and North America);

(h) Seminar on flows of refugees resulting from ethnic conflicts or political restructuring of multi-ethnic societies in socio-economic transition (Eastern Europe, Africa and Asia) and their link with racism in the host country;

(i) Training course on national legislation prohibiting racial discrimination for nationals from countries with and without such legislation;

(j) Regional seminars on nationalism, ethnonationalism and human rights could also provide an opportunity for broadening knowledge of the causes of today's ethnic conflicts and particularly of the so-called policy of "ethnic cleansing", in order to provide solutions.

13. The General Assembly requests the Department of Public Information of the Secretariat to undertake specific activities that could be carried out by Governments and relevant national non-governmental organizations to commemorate the International Day for the Elimination of Racial Discrimination on 21 March each year. Support should be sought from artists, as well as religious leaders, trade unions, enterprises and political parties, to sensitize the population on the evils of racism and racial discrimination.

14. The Department of Public Information should also publish its posters for the Third Decade and informative brochures on the activities planned for the Decade. Documentary films and reports, as well as radio broadcasts on the damaging effects of racism and racial discrimination, should, moreover, be considered.

15. In cooperation with the United Nations Educational, Scientific and Cultural Organization and the Department of Public Information, the General Assembly supports the organization of a seminar on the role of mass media in combating or disseminating racist ideas.

16. In cooperation with the International Labour Organisation, the possibility of organizing a seminar on the role of trade unions in combating racism and racial discrimination in employment should be explored.

17. The General Assembly invites the United Nations Educational, Scientific and Cultural Organization to expedite the preparation of teaching materials and teaching aids to promote teaching, training and educational activities against racism and racial discrimination, with particular emphasis on activities at the primary and secondary levels of education.

18. The General Assembly calls upon Member States to make special efforts:

(a) To promote the aim of non-discrimination in all educational programmes and policies;

(b) To give special attention to the civic education of teachers. It is essential that teachers be aware of the principles and essential content of the legal texts relevant to racism and racial discrimination and of how to deal with the problem of relations between children belonging to different communities;

(c) To teach contemporary history at an early age, presenting children with an accurate picture of the crimes committed by fascist and other totalitarian regimes, and more particularly of the crimes of apartheid and genocide;

(d) To ensure that curricula and textbooks reflect anti-racist principles and promote intercultural education.

Action at the national and regional levels

19. The following questions are addressed in the context of action to be taken at the national and regional levels: have there been any successful national models to eliminate racism and racial prejudices that could be recommended to States, for example, for educating children, or principles of equality to tackle racism against migrant workers, ethnic minorities or indigenous people? What kind of affirmative action programmes are there at the national or regional level to redress discrimination against specific groups?

20. The General Assembly recommends that States that have not yet done so adopt, ratify and implement legislation prohibiting racism and racial discrimination, such as the International Convention on the Elimination of All Forms of Racial Discrimination, the International Convention on the Suppression and Punishment of the Crime of Apartheid and the International Convention on the Protection of the Rights of All Migrant Workers and Members of Their Families.

21. The General Assembly recommends that Member States review their national programmes to combat racial discrimination and its effects in order to identify and to seize opportunities to close gaps between different groups, and especially to undertake housing, educational and employment programmes that have proved to be successful in combating racial discrimination and xenophobia.

22. The General Assembly recommends that Member States encourage the participation of journalists and human rights advocates from minority groups and communities in the mass media. Radio and television programmes should increase the number of broadcasts produced by and in cooperation with racial and cultural minority groups. Multicultural activities of the media should also be encouraged where they can contribute to the suppression of racism and xenophobia.

23. The General Assembly recommends that regional organizations cooperate closely with United Nations efforts to combat racism and racial discrimination. Regional organizations dealing with human rights issues could mobilize public opinion in their regions against the evils of racism and racial prejudices directed towards disadvantaged racial and ethnic groups. These institutions could serve an important function in assisting Governments to enact national legislation against racial discrimination and promote adoption and application of international conventions. Regional human rights commissions should be called upon to publicize widely basic texts on existing human rights instruments.

Basic research and studies

24. The long-term viability of the United Nations programme against racism and racial discrimination will depend in part on continuing research into the causes of racism and into the new manifestations of racism and racial discrimination. The General Assembly may wish to examine the importance of preparing studies on racism. The following are some aspects to be studied:

(a) Application of article 2 of the International Convention on the Elimination of All Forms of Racial Discrimination. Such a study might assist States to learn from one another the national measures taken to implement the Convention;

(b) Economic factors contributing to perpetuation of racism and racial discrimination;

(c) Integration or preservation of cultural identity in a multiracial or multi-ethnic society;

(d) Political rights, including the participation of various racial groups in political processes and their representation in government service;

(e) Civil rights, including migration, nationality and freedom of opinion and association;

(f) Educational measures to combat racial prejudice and discrimination and to propagate the principles of the United Nations;

(g) Socio-economic costs of racism and racial discrimination;

(h) Global integration and the question of racism and the nation State;

(i) National mechanisms against racism and racial discrimination in the fields of immigration, employment, salary, housing, education and ownership of property.

Coordination and reporting

25. It may be relevant to recall that in its resolution 38/14 of 22 November 1983, in which it proclaimed the Second Decade to Combat Racism and Racial Discrimination, the General Assembly charged the Economic and Social Council with coordinating the implementation of the Programme of Action for the Second Decade and evaluating the activities. The Assembly decides that the following steps should be taken to strengthen the United Nations input into the Third Decade to Combat Racism and Racial Discrimination:

(a) The General Assembly entrusts the Economic and Social Council and the Commission on Human Rights, in cooperation with the Secretary-General, with the responsibility for coordinating the programmes and evaluating the activities undertaken in connection with the Third Decade;

(b) The Secretary-General is invited to provide specific information on activities against racism, to be contained in one annual report, which should be comprehensive in nature and allow a general overview of all mandated activities. This will facilitate coordination and evaluation;

(c) An open-ended working group of the Commission on Human Rights, or other appropriate arrangements under the Commission, may be established to review Decade-related information on the basis of the annual reports referred to above, as well as relevant studies and reports of seminars, to assist the Commission in formulating appropriate recommendations to the Economic and Social Council on particular activities, allocation of priorities and so on.

26. Furthermore, an inter-agency meeting should be organized immediately after the proclamation of the Third Decade, in 1994, with a view to planning working meetings and other activities.

Regular system-wide consultations

27. On an annual basis, consultations between the United Nations, specialized agencies and non-governmental organizations should take place to review and plan Decade-related activities. In this framework, the Centre for Human Rights should organize inter-agency meetings to consider and discuss further measures to strengthen the coordination and cooperation of programmes related to the issues of combating racism and racial discrimination.

28. The Centre should also strengthen the relationship with non-governmental organizations fighting against racism and racial discrimination by holding consultations and briefings with the non-governmental organizations. Such meetings could help them to initiate, develop and present proposals regarding the struggle against racism and racial discrimination.

29. The Secretary-General should include the activities to be carried out during the Decade, as well as the related resource requirements, in the proposed programme budgets, which will be submitted biennially, during the Decade, starting with the proposed programme budget for the biennium 1994-1995.

General Assembly resolution 48/91

20 December 1993   Meeting 84   Adopted without vote

Approved by Third Committee (A/48/625/Add.1) without vote, 8 December (meeting 54); draft by Algeria for African Group (A/C.3/48/L.13/Rev.1); agenda item 107.
Financial implications. S-G, A/C.3/48/L.80.
Meeting numbers. GA 48th session: 3rd Committee 3-10, 25, 32, 33, 48, 54; plenary 84.

Convention on the Elimination of All Forms of Racial Discrimination

Accessions and ratifications

As at 31 December 1993,[20] there were 137 parties to the International Convention on the Elimination of All Forms of Racial Discrimination, adopted by the General Assembly in 1965[21] and in force since 1969.[22] Armenia, Bosnia and Herzegovina, the Czech Republic, the Republic of Moldova and Slovakia became parties during 1993.

Implementation of the Convention

The Committee on the Elimination of Racial Discrimination (CERD), set up under article 8 of the Convention, held two sessions in 1993, both at Geneva: the forty-second session from 1 to 19 March and the forty-third from 2 to 20 August.[19]

Most of CERD's work was devoted to examining reports submitted by States parties on measures taken to implement the Convention's provisions. The Committee considered the reports of 23 States. In its report, it summarized its members' views on each country report and the statements made by the States parties concerned. CERD adopted an amendment to its general guidelines regarding the form and content of reports to be submitted under article 9, which consisted of inserting a new paragraph concerning information on the ethnic characteristics of the country. Regarding reporting obligations under article 9, it requested the Secretary-General to continue to send reminders to States parties from which two or more reports were due but had not been received before 20 August—the closing date of its session—asking them to submit their reports by 31 December 1993. Also in accordance with article 9, CERD, on 19 March, requested further information by 31 July 1993 from Croatia and Serbia and Montenegro,[23] where continuing ethnic conflict was cause for concern. It also encouraged Bosnia and Herzegovina to confirm its adherence to the Convention and, if it proceeded accordingly, to submit information by 31 July 1993 on the implementation of the Convention (for details on the situation in the former Yugoslavia, see below, under "Human rights violations"). All three of the States concerned submitted the requested information, which was considered by CERD in August.

The Committee adopted general recommendations concerning non-citizens; training of law enforcement officials in human rights protection; adherence to the Convention by successor States; article 1.1 of the Convention concerning the definition of racial discrimination; article 4 of the Convention dealing with the penalization of certain categories of misconduct; the application of article 9 of the Convention; and the establishment of national institutions to facilitate the Convention's implementation.

CERD also considered, in conformity with article 14, communications from individuals or groups of individuals claiming violation of their rights under the Convention by a State party recognizing CERD competence to receive and consider such communications. Eighteen States parties—Algeria, Australia, Bulgaria, Costa Rica, Denmark, Ecuador, France, Hungary, Iceland, Italy, the Netherlands, Norway, Peru, the Russian Federation, Senegal, Sweden, Ukraine and Uruguay—had declared such recognition. The text of the Committee's opinion on one communication was annexed to its report.

Under article 15 of the Convention, the Secretary-General transmitted to CERD documents related to Trust and Non-Self-Governing Territories. The Committee observed that it found it impossible to fulfil its function under article 15 as the documents did not include copies of petitions and did not contain valid information concerning legislative, judicial, administrative or other measures directly related to the Convention's principles and objectives. The Committee asked that appropriate information be furnished.

CERD considered activities to implement the Programme of Action for the Second Decade to Combat Racism and Racial Discrimination and the launching of a third decade (see above). In August, it discussed the outcome of the 1993 World Conference on Human Rights (see below, under "Advancement of human rights") and its possible implications for the Committee's work.

In October,[24] the Secretary-General informed the General Assembly that, on 1 March 1993, he had communicated to all States parties an amendment to the Convention, adopted in 1992,[25] regarding the financing of CERD. As at 15 September 1993, the amendment, which was to enter into force when accepted by a two-thirds majority of States parties, had been accepted by five of them. The Secretary-General reported that, as at 31 August, outstanding assessments and arrears totalled $311,540 from 90 States.

On 26 February,[26] the Commission on Human Rights urged States parties to notify the Secretary-General, as depositary of the International Convention on the Elimination of All Forms of Racial Discrimination, of their acceptance of the amendment and welcomed a 1992 General Assembly decision on the financing of CERD.[27]

GENERAL ASSEMBLY ACTION

On 20 December, the General Assembly, on the recommendation of the Third Committee, adopted **resolution 48/90** without vote.

Report of the Committee on the Elimination of Racial Discrimination

The General Assembly,

Recalling its previous resolutions concerning the reports of the Committee on the Elimination of Racial Discrimination and its resolutions on the status of the International Convention on the Elimination of All Forms of Racial Discrimination,

Reiterating the importance of the Convention, which is one of the most widely accepted human rights instruments adopted under the auspices of the United Nations,

Aware of the importance of the contributions of the Committee to the efforts of the United Nations to combat racism and all other forms of discrimination based on race, colour, descent or national or ethnic origin,

Reiterating once again the need to intensify the struggle for the elimination of racism and racial discrimination throughout the world, especially its most brutal forms,

Emphasizing the obligation of all States parties to the Convention to take legislative, judicial and other measures in order to secure full implementation of the provisions of the Convention,

Bearing in mind the Vienna Declaration and Programme of Action, adopted by the World Conference on Human Rights on 25 June 1993, in particular section II.B, relating to equality, dignity and tolerance,

Calling upon States parties expeditiously to notify the Secretary-General in writing of their agreement to the amendment to the Convention regarding the financing of the Committee, as decided upon at the Fourteenth Meeting of States Parties to the International Convention on the Elimination of All Forms of Racial Discrimination on 15 January 1992 and endorsed in General Assembly resolution 47/111 of 16 December 1992,

Welcoming efforts of the Secretary-General to ensure interim financial arrangements for the financing of the expenses incurred by the Committee,

Stressing the importance of enabling the Committee to function smoothly and to have all necessary facilities for the effective performance of its functions under the Convention,

Having considered the report of the Secretary-General on the financial situation of the Committee,

1. *Commends* the Committee on the Elimination of Racial Discrimination for its work with regard to the implementation of the International Convention on the Elimination of All Forms of Racial Discrimination and the Programme of Action for the Second Decade to Combat Racism and Racial Discrimination and for its contribution to the preparation of the Third Decade to Combat Racism and Racial Discrimination;

2. *Welcomes* the innovatory procedures adopted by the Committee for reviewing the implementation of the Convention in States whose reports are overdue and for formulating concluding observations on State party reports;

3. *Takes note* of the general recommendations adopted by the Committee, which concretize the obligations of States parties with regard to the provisions of the Convention, especially General Recommendation XII (42), on successor States, and General Recommendation XV (42), on article 4 of the Convention;

4. *Encourages* the Committee to continue to exert its efforts to enhance its contributions in the area of prevention of racial discrimination, including early warning and urgent procedures;

5. *Expresses its profound concern* at the fact that a number of States parties to the Convention still have not fulfilled their financial obligations, as shown in the report of the Secretary-General;

6. *Remains fully aware* of the fact that such a situation may lead to a further delay in the discharge by the Committee of its substantive obligations under the Convention;

7. *Takes note with appreciation* of the report of the Committee on the work of its forty-second and forty-third sessions;

8. *Urges* States parties to accelerate their domestic ratification procedures with regard to the amendment concerning the financing of the Committee;

9. *Requests* the Secretary-General to continue to ensure adequate financial arrangements and appropriate means to enable the functioning of the Committee;

10. *Calls upon* States parties to fulfil their obligations under article 9, paragraph 1, of the Convention, to submit in due time their periodic reports on measures taken to implement the Convention and to pay their outstanding contributions and, if possible, their contributions for 1994 before 1 February 1994, so as to enable the Committee to meet regularly;

11. *Strongly appeals* to all States parties, especially those in arrears, to fulfil their financial obligations under article 8, paragraph 6, of the Convention;

12. *Also requests* the Secretary-General to invite those States parties which are in arrears to pay the amounts in arrears, and to report thereon to the General Assembly at its forty-ninth session;

13. *Decides* to consider at its forty-ninth session, under the item entitled "Elimination of racism and racial discrimination", the report of the Secretary-General on the financial situation of the Committee and the report of the Committee.

General Assembly resolution 48/90

20 December 1993   Meeting 84   Adopted without vote

Approved by Third Committee (A/48/625) without vote, 12 November (meeting 32); 28-nation draft (A/C.3/48/L.16), orally revised; agenda item 107.

Sponsors: Australia, Austria, Bangladesh, Bosnia and Herzegovina, Bulgaria, Canada, Costa Rica, Cyprus, Czech Republic, Denmark, Ecuador, Egypt, Finland, Germany, Hungary, Iceland, Morocco, Netherlands, New Zealand, Nigeria, Norway, Pakistan, Poland, Romania, Slovakia, Slovenia, Sweden, the former Yugoslav Republic of Macedonia.

Meeting numbers. GA 48th session: 3rd Committee 3-10, 25, 32; plenary 84.

Other aspects of discrimination

Religious freedom

Report of the Secretary-General. As requested by the Commission on Human Rights in 1992,[28] the Secretary-General, in a January 1993 report,[29] described activities to encourage understanding, tolerance and respect in matters relating to freedom of religion or belief being carried out by the United Nations University (UNU), DPI and under the World Public Information Campaign for Human Rights. He reported on progress made in preparing a general comment to be adopted by the Human Rights Committee concerning article 18 of the International Covenant on Civil and Political Rights, adopted by the General Assembly in 1966[30] and in force since 1976,[31] dealing with freedom of thought, conscience and religion (see below, under "Civil and political rights"). He stated that the Special Rapporteur on religious intolerance had received substantive assistance in fulfilling his mandate and his report had been issued.

Report of the Special Rapporteur. In a January report[32] to the Commission on Human Rights, Special Rapporteur Angelo Vidal d'Almeida Ribeiro (Portugal) stated that he had transmitted to 24 Governments allegations regarding situations which seemed to be inconsistent with the provisions of the 1981 Declaration on the Elimination of All Forms of Intolerance and of Discrimination Based on Religion or Belief.[33] The allegations were reproduced in the report as were comments received from Governments in response. The majority of allegations pointed to the violation of the right to have the religion or belief of one's choice, the right to change one's religion or belief, the right to manifest and practise one's religion in public and in private, the right to celebrate holidays and ceremonies in accordance with the precepts of one's religion or belief and the right not to be subjected to discrimination on those grounds by any State, institution or group of persons.

The Special Rapporteur stated that many acts of religious intolerance and discrimination continued to be characterized by violence or the threat of its use, including extrajudicial killings, arbitrary imprisonment, enforced disappearance and abduction. He noted, however, continued progress in the area of religious freedom by countries in Eastern Europe, the establishment of diplomatic relations between the Holy See and Israel and efforts to set up a dialogue and create greater understanding between the Catholic and Jewish communities in Spain.

The Special Rapporteur invited Governments facing religious tensions to avail themselves of the advisory services and technical assistance offered by the Centre for Human Rights. He urged States to ratify the relevant international human rights instruments and recommended that they continue to consider preparing a separate binding international instrument on the elimination of intolerance and discrimination based on religion or belief. He believed that States should adapt legislation to existing international standards, particularly the 1981 Declaration, and make available effective administrative and judicial remedies. The Special Rapporteur advocated creating national institutions to promote tolerance in matters of religion and belief and underlined the importance of promoting religious tolerance and understanding by introducing national and international human rights standards in school and university curricula and through teacher training. He emphasized the significant role of media briefings and information seminars aimed at the broadest possible dissemination of the Declaration's principles.

Human Rights Commission action. As requested by the General Assembly in 1992,[34] the Commission on Human Rights continued in 1993 to consider measures to implement the Declaration. On 5 March,[35] it urged States to provide adequate constitutional and legal guarantees of freedom of thought, conscience, religion and belief and called on them to encourage understanding, tolerance and respect for freedom of religion or belief and to ensure that members of law enforcement bodies, civil servants, educators and other public officials respected different religions and beliefs. It further called on States to recognize, as provided in the Declaration, the right of all persons to worship or assemble for religious purposes, establish and maintain places to do so and ensure that such places were fully respected and protected. The Commission considered it desirable to enhance United Nations promotional and public information activities relating to freedom of religion or belief and to ensure that measures were taken to that end in the World Public Information Campaign for Human Rights (see below, under "Advancement of human rights").

The Commission asked the Secretary-General to accord high priority to disseminating the Declaration in all United Nations official languages and to make the text available for use by United Nations information centres (UNICs) and other interested bodies. States were called on to consider facilitating the text's dissemination in national and local languages and interested NGOs were asked to consider what further role they play in implementing the Declaration and disseminating it in national and local languages. The Commission asked the Secretary-General to assist the Special Rapporteur to enable him to report to the Commission in 1994 and also to report himself in 1994.

Following the resignation of the Special Rapporteur on religious intolerance during the Commission's 1993 session, the Chairman of the Commission appointed Abdelfattah Amor (Tunisia) as his replacement.

Subcommission action. On 13 August,[36] the Subcommission recommended to the Commission that it consider organizing, in cooperation with UNESCO, UNU, interested governmental organizations and NGOs and academic and research organizations, a global consultation on the positions and approaches of different religions and beliefs to human rights and fundamental freedoms.

GENERAL ASSEMBLY ACTION

On 20 December, the General Assembly, on the recommendation of the Third Committee, adopted **resolution 48/128** without vote.

Elimination of all forms of religious intolerance
The General Assembly,
Recalling that all States have pledged themselves, under the Charter of the United Nations, to promote and encourage universal respect for and observance of human rights and fundamental freedoms for all without distinction as to race, sex, language or religion,
Recognizing that those rights derive from the inherent dignity of the human person,
Reaffirming that discrimination against human beings on the grounds of religion or belief constitutes an affront to human dignity and a disavowal of the principles of the Charter,
Reaffirming also its resolution 36/55 of 25 November 1981, by which it proclaimed the Declaration on the Elimination of All Forms of Intolerance and of Discrimination Based on Religion or Belief,
Recalling its resolution 47/129 of 18 December 1992, in which it requested the Commission on Human Rights to continue its consideration of measures to implement the Declaration,
Taking note of Commission on Human Rights resolution 1993/25 of 5 March 1993,
Reaffirming the call of the World Conference on Human Rights for all Governments to take all appropriate measures in compliance with their international obligations and with due regard to their respective legal systems to counter intolerance and related violence based on religion or belief, including practices of discrimination

against women and the desecration of religious sites, recognizing that every individual has the right to freedom of thought, conscience, expression and religion,

Recalling Commission on Human Rights resolution 1992/17 of 21 February 1992, in which the Commission decided to extend for three years the mandate of the Special Rapporteur appointed to examine incidents and governmental actions in all parts of the world that are incompatible with the provisions of the Declaration and to recommend remedial measures, as appropriate, and recalling also Economic and Social Council decision 1992/226 of 20 July 1992,

Welcoming the appointment of Abdelfattah Amor as Special Rapporteur of the Commission on Human Rights, and calling upon all Governments to cooperate with the Special Rapporteur to enable him to carry out his mandate fully,

Recognizing that it is desirable to enhance the promotional and public information activities of the United Nations in matters relating to freedom of religion or belief and that both Governments and non-governmental organizations have an important role to play in this domain,

Emphasizing that non-governmental organizations and religious bodies and groups at every level have an important role to play in the promotion of tolerance and the protection of freedom of religion or belief,

Conscious of the importance of education in ensuring tolerance of religion and belief,

Alarmed that serious instances, including acts of violence, of intolerance and discrimination on the grounds of religion or belief occur in many parts of the world, as evidenced in the report of the former Special Rapporteur of the Commission on Human Rights, Angelo Vidal d'Almeida Ribeiro,

Reaffirming the dismay and condemnation expressed by the World Conference on Human Rights at the continued occurrence of gross and systematic violations and situations that constitute serious obstacles to the full enjoyment of all human rights, including religious intolerance,

Believing that further efforts are therefore required to promote and protect the right to freedom of thought, conscience, religion and belief and to eliminate all forms of hatred, intolerance and discrimination based on religion or belief,

1. *Reaffirms* that freedom of thought, conscience, religion and belief is a human right derived from the inherent dignity of the human person and guaranteed to all without discrimination;

2. *Urges* States to ensure that their constitutional and legal systems provide full guarantees of freedom of thought, conscience, religion and belief, including the provision of effective remedies where there is intolerance or discrimination based on religion or belief;

3. *Recognizes* that legislation alone is not enough to prevent violations of human rights, including the right to freedom of religion or belief;

4. *Urges* all States therefore to take all appropriate measures to combat hatred, intolerance and acts of violence, including those motivated by religious extremism, and to encourage understanding, tolerance and respect in matters relating to freedom of religion or belief;

5. *Urges* States to ensure that, in the course of their official duties, members of law enforcement bodies, civil servants, educators and other public officials respect different religions and beliefs and do not discriminate against persons professing other religions or beliefs;

6. *Calls upon* all States to recognize, as provided in the Declaration on the Elimination of All Forms of Intolerance and of Discrimination Based on Religion or Belief, the right of all persons to worship or assemble in connection with a religion or belief, and to establish and maintain places for those purposes;

7. *Also calls upon* all States in accordance with their national legislation to exert utmost efforts to ensure that religious places and shrines are fully respected and protected;

8. *Considers it desirable* to enhance the promotional and public information activities of the United Nations in matters relating to freedom of religion or belief and to ensure that appropriate measures are taken to this end in the World Public Information Campaign for Human Rights;

9. *Invites* the Secretary-General to continue to give high priority to the dissemination of the text of the Declaration, in all the official languages of the United Nations, and to take all appropriate measures to make the text available for use by the United Nations information centres, as well as by other interested bodies;

10. *Encourages* the continuing efforts on the part of the Special Rapporteur appointed to examine incidents and governmental actions in all parts of the world that are incompatible with the provisions of the Declaration and to recommend remedial measures as appropriate;

11. *Encourages* Governments to give serious consideration to inviting the Special Rapporteur to visit their countries so as to enable him to fulfil his mandate even more effectively;

12. *Recommends* that the promotion and protection of the right to freedom of thought, conscience and religion be given appropriate priority in the work of the United Nations programme of advisory services in the field of human rights, including work on the drafting of basic legal texts in conformity with international instruments on human rights and taking into account the provisions of the Declaration;

13. *Notes with interest* the adoption by the Human Rights Committee of a general comment on article 18 of the International Covenant on Civil and Political Rights, dealing with freedom of thought, conscience and religion;

14. *Welcomes* the efforts of non-governmental organizations to promote the implementation of the Declaration;

15. *Requests* the Secretary-General to invite interested non-governmental organizations to consider what further role they could envisage playing in the implementation of the Declaration and in its dissemination in national and local languages;

16. *Urges* all States to consider disseminating the text of the Declaration in their respective national languages and to facilitate its dissemination in national and local languages;

17. *Requests* the Commission on Human Rights to continue its consideration of measures to implement the Declaration;

18. *Decides* to consider the question of the elimination of all forms of religious intolerance at its forty-ninth session under the item entitled "Human rights questions".

General Assembly resolution 48/128
20 December 1993   Meeting 85   Adopted without vote

Approved by Third Committee (A/48/632/Add.2) without vote, 6 December
(meeting 52); 53-nation draft (A/C.3/48/L.48); agenda item 114 *(b)*.
Sponsors: Albania, Argentina, Australia, Austria, Bahamas, Belarus, Belgium,
Bulgaria, Canada, Chile, Costa Rica, Côte d'Ivoire, Croatia, Cyprus, Czech
Republic, Denmark, Finland, France, Georgia, Germany, Greece, Guatemala,
Honduras, Hungary, Iceland, Ireland, Israel, Italy, Latvia, Liechtenstein,
Lithuania, Luxembourg, Malta, Marshall Islands, Morocco, Netherlands,
New Zealand, Norway, Peru, Poland, Portugal, Romania, Russian Federa-
tion, San Marino, Sierra Leone, Slovenia, Spain, Sweden, Ukraine, United
Kingdom, United States, Uruguay, Venezuela.
Meeting numbers. GA 48th session: 3rd Committee 36-52; plenary 85.

Indigenous populations

Draft declaration on indigenous rights

Human Rights Commission action. On 5
March,[37] the Commission recommended to the
Economic and Social Council that the Working
Group on Indigenous Populations (see below) be
authorized to meet for 10 days prior to the 1993
session of the Subcommission on Prevention of
Discrimination and Protection of Minorities to intensify efforts to complete a draft declaration on
indigenous rights and to issue, following the final
adoption of the draft, a United Nations sales publication. It asked the Secretary-General to assist
the Group and its Chairman-Rapporteur, to transmit the Group's 1992 report[38] to Governments,
indigenous peoples' and intergovernmental organizations and NGOs for comments and suggestions, and to ensure that the Group's sessions were
provided with interpretation and documentation
in English and Spanish. The Commission appealed to Governments, organizations and individuals to consider favourably requests for contributions to the United Nations Voluntary Fund
for Indigenous Populations.

Also on 5 March,[39] the Commission asked the
Working Group and the Subcommission to make
their best effort to complete their consideration of
the draft declaration and to report to the Commission in 1994.

On 28 July, the Economic and Social Council,
by **decision 1993/262**, authorized the Group to
meet for 10 working days prior to the Subcommission's 1993 session and approved the Commission's request to the Secretary-General to assist
the Group.

Working Group activities. At its eleventh
session (Geneva, 19-30 July), the Working Group
on Indigenous Populations[40] agreed on a final
text of the draft declaration on the rights of indigenous peoples, which was based on a revised
working paper prepared by the Chairperson-
Rapporteur[41] and a relevant explanatory
note.[42] The Group decided to submit the final
draft text, which was annexed to its report, to the
Subcommission in August. It recommended that
the Subcommission request the Secretary-General
to send the text to United Nations editorial and
translation services as soon as possible and circu-

late it to indigenous peoples, Governments, intergovernmental organizations and NGOs, indicating
that there would be no further discussion of the
text in the Working Group. It further recommended that the Commission and the Economic
and Social Council enable indigenous peoples to
participate in the consideration of the draft declaration by the Subcommission and other United
Nations bodies and that the draft be submitted to
the Commission in 1995.

(For the Group's action on the International
Year of the World's Indigenous People and the international decade of the world's indigenous people, see below.)

Subcommission action. On 26 August,[43] the
Subcommission decided to entitle the draft declaration on indigenous rights, "United Nations
Declaration on the Rights of Indigenous Peoples",
to postpone until 1994 consideration of the draft
and to submit it to the Commission in 1995 for
consideration and adoption, on the understanding that the Working Group's 1994 session would
contain a summary of general views expressed by
the participants on the draft declaration. It asked
the Secretary-General to submit the draft for technical revision as soon as possible and to transmit
it to indigenous peoples and organizations, Governments and intergovernmental organizations and
NGOs upon completion of the revision and not
later than 31 March 1994 and to include in the
note of transmittal a reference that no further
amendments to the revised text would be accepted
during future standard-setting proceedings of the
Working Group. It recommended that the Commission on Human Rights and the Economic and
Social Council enable indigenous peoples to participate in the consideration of the draft.

On the same date,[44] the Subcommission requested the Commission to recommend to the
Economic and Social Council that the Working
Group's annual report be issued as a United Nations sales publication and that a seminar on indigenous land rights and claims be held. It requested the Secretary-General to consider
establishing a permanent forum for indigenous
peoples in the United Nations system and to prepare an annotated agenda for the Working
Group's 1994 session.

Protection of indigenous heritage

In July,[45] the Subcommission's Special Rapporteur, Erica-Irene A. Daes (Greece), submitted
a study on the protection of the cultural and intellectual property of indigenous peoples. She
described contemporary issues involving indigenous heritage and discussed existing legal instruments and mechanisms applicable to indigenous peoples' collective rights to their heritage.
The Special Rapporteur recommended measures

to: recognize indigenous peoples as the true collective owners of their works, art and ideas; recover loss of dispersed heritage; prevent further losses of heritage; and continue her study with a mandate to draft basic principles and guidelines related to the protection of indigenous heritage.

Subcommission action. On 26 August,[46] the Subcommission decided that the Special Rapporteur's study should be entitled ''Protection of the heritage of the indigenous peoples'' and asked her to expand her study with a view to elaborating draft principles and guidelines for the protection of the heritage of indigenous peoples and to submit a preliminary report thereon in 1994.

Study on treaties, agreements and other constructive arrangements

Human Rights Commission action. On 5 March,[47] the Commission endorsed the Subcommission's 1992 request[48] to Special Rapporteur Miguel Alfonso Martínez (Cuba) to prepare a second progress report on treaties, agreements and other constructive arrangements between States and indigenous populations for submission to the Working Group on Indigenous Populations and the Subcommission in 1994.

On 28 July 1993, the Economic and Social Council, by **decision 1993/289**, approved the Commission's endorsement.

Subcommission action. On 26 August,[49] the Subcommission reiterated its request to the Special Rapporteur to submit a second progress report to the Group and the Subcommission in 1994.

International Year of the World's Indigenous People (1993)

Human Rights Commission action. On 5 March,[39] the Commission called on the United Nations system and Governments to develop policies to support the objectives and the theme of the International Year of the World's Indigenous People and to strengthen the institutional framework to implement them. It recommended that all thematic rapporteurs, special representatives, independent experts and working groups pay particular attention to the situation of indigenous people and asked the Coordinator of the Year, in the report to the 1994 General Assembly on the activities and results of the Year, to include an account of the response of the United Nations system to the needs of indigenous people. The Commission urged the Coordinator to continue to solicit the cooperation of the specialized agencies, regional commissions, financial and development institutions and other relevant organizations of the United Nations system to promote the Year's programme of activities, adopted by the General Assembly in 1991,[50] and appealed to those bodies to take into account the needs of in-

digenous people in their budgeting and programming.

The Commission encouraged the Preparatory Committee for the World Conference on Human Rights (1993) to consider how issues pertinent to the Year could be addressed within the framework of the Conference and authorized the Working Group's Chairman-Rapporteur to represent the Group at the Conference. It appealed to Governments, intergovernmental organizations and NGOs to contribute to the Voluntary Fund for the International Year.

Subcommission action. On 26 August,[44] the Subcommission decided to request the Commission to recommend to the Economic and Social Council that it approve the participation of the Working Group's Chairperson-Rapporteur in the closing ceremony of the International Year.

Other action. In accordance with a 1992 General Assembly request,[51] the Coordinator of the International Year of the World's Indigenous People reconvened the technical meeting on the International Year of the World's Indigenous People (Geneva, 14-16 July)[52] to examine progress during the first six months of the Year and consider suggestions for the final six months. The meeting adopted a series of recommendations concerning coordination within the United Nations system; indigenous people's health issues; dissemination of information; the proclamation of an international decade of the world's indigenous people; and financial assistance for projects and activities of indigenous people. The technical meeting of agencies, regional commissions and other organizations of the United Nations system with representatives of States, organizations of indigenous peoples and other NGOs having a special interest in indigenous matters was held at Geneva from 9 to 11 March 1992[48] and from 3 to 5 August.[53] In July 1993,[40] the Working Group on Indigenous Populations endorsed the recommendations made at the final technical meeting (see below).

On 18 June,[54] the World Conference on Human Rights commemorated the International Year.

GENERAL ASSEMBLY ACTION

On 20 December, the General Assembly, on the recommendation of the Third Committee, adopted **resolution 48/133** without vote.

International Year of the World's Indigenous People, 1993

The General Assembly,

Bearing in mind that one of the purposes of the United Nations set forth in the Charter is the achievement of international cooperation in solving international problems of an economic, social, cultural or humanitarian character, and in promoting and encouraging respect for human rights and for fundamental freedoms for all without discrimination as to race, sex, language or religion,

Recognizing and respecting the value and the diversity of cultures, as well as the cultural heritage and the forms of social organization of the world's indigenous people,

Recalling its resolution 45/164 of 18 December 1990, in which it proclaimed 1993 the International Year of the World's Indigenous People, with a view to strengthening international cooperation for the solution of problems faced by indigenous communities in areas such as human rights, the environment, development, education and health,

Conscious of the need to improve the economic, social and cultural situation of the indigenous people with full respect for their distinctiveness and their own initiatives,

Appreciative of the contributions made to the voluntary fund for the Year opened by the Secretary-General,

Noting the establishment of the fund for the development of indigenous peoples of Latin America and the Caribbean as one kind of support for the objectives of the Year,

Taking note of the recommendation of the World Conference on Human Rights, held at Vienna from 14 to 25 June 1993, that an international decade of the world's indigenous people should be proclaimed,

Noting the need to continue strengthening the initiatives taken as a result of the Year,

Recalling the request to the Subcommission on Prevention of Discrimination and Protection of Minorities that it should complete its consideration of the draft universal declaration on the rights of indigenous peoples,

1. *Calls upon* the United Nations system and Governments that have not yet done so to develop policies in support of the objectives and the theme of the International Year of the World's Indigenous People and to strengthen the institutional framework for their implementation;

2. *Recommends* to all thematic rapporteurs, special representatives, independent experts and working groups that they pay particular attention, within the framework of their mandates, to the situation of indigenous people;

3. *Urges* the Assistant Secretary-General for Human Rights to continue to solicit actively the cooperation of specialized agencies, regional commissions, financial and development institutions and other relevant organizations of the United Nations system for the promotion of a programme of activities in support of the objectives and the theme of the Year;

4. *Appeals* to the specialized agencies, regional commissions and financial and development institutions of the United Nations system to continue to increase their efforts to take into special account the needs of indigenous people in their budgeting and in their programming;

5. *Requests*:

(a) That reports of the three technical meetings, first provided for in paragraph 8 of General Assembly resolution 46/128 of 17 December 1991, be included in the final assessment proceedings provided for in paragraph 12 of the same resolution and that their conclusions be included in the report of the Coordinator for the Year to be submitted to the General Assembly at its forty-ninth session;

(b) That the Commission on Human Rights convene, from within existing resources, a meeting of participants in the programmes and projects of the Year, in the three days preceding the twelfth session of the Working Group on Indigenous Populations of the Subcommission on Prevention of Discrimination and Protection of Minorities, to report to the Working Group on the conclusions that can be drawn from the activities of the Year with a view to the elaboration of a detailed plan of action and the establishment of a funding plan for the International Decade of the World's Indigenous People;

6. *Stresses* the relevance for the solution of problems faced by indigenous communities of the recommendations contained in chapter 26 of Agenda 21, including their implementation;

7. *Notes with satisfaction* the holding at Manila of a Global Youth Earth-saving Summit which, by its reaffirmation of the role of traditional cultures in the preservation of the environment, underscored the right to cultural survival;

8. *Welcomes* the proposal for a gathering of indigenous youth in 1995, an "Indigenous Youth Cultural Olympics", as a follow-up to the Year, to be held in conjunction with the International Decade of the World's Indigenous People and the fiftieth anniversary of the United Nations, to reaffirm the value of traditional cultures, folk arts and rituals as effective expressions of respective national identities and as a foundation for a shared vision for peace, freedom and equality;

9. *Also stresses* that the governmental and intergovernmental activities undertaken within the context of the Year and beyond should take fully into account the development needs of indigenous people and that the Year should contribute to enhancing and facilitating the coordination capabilities of Member States for collecting and analysing information;

10. *Notes* that there is a continuing need within the United Nations system to aggregate data specific to indigenous people by means of enhancing and facilitating the coordination capabilities of Member States for collecting and analysing such data;

11. *Requests* the Subcommission on Prevention of Discrimination and Protection of Minorities, at its forty-sixth session, to complete its consideration of the draft universal declaration on the rights of indigenous peoples and to submit its report to the Commission on Human Rights at its fifty-first session;

12. *Requests* the Coordinator for the Year, in the report to be submitted to the General Assembly at its forty-ninth session on the activities developed and the results achieved within the context of the Year, to include an account of the response of the United Nations system to the needs of indigenous people;

13. *Expresses its appreciation* for the work undertaken for the Year by Governments, the Coordinator for the Year, the International Labour Organisation, the Goodwill Ambassador, Rigoberta Menchu, indigenous and non-governmental organizations, the Commission on Human Rights and the Working Group on Indigenous Populations.

General Assembly resolution 48/133

20 December 1993   Meeting 85   Adopted without vote

Approved by Third Committee (A/48/632/Add.2) without vote, 6 December (meeting 53); 31-nation draft (A/C.3/48/L.60); agenda item 114 (b).

Sponsors: Antigua and Barbuda, Australia, Bahamas, Bolivia, Canada, Chile, Colombia, Costa Rica, Cuba, Cyprus, Denmark, Dominican Republic, Ecuador, Finland, Greece, Guatemala, Guyana, Hungary, Mexico, New

Zealand, Nicaragua, Nigeria, Norway, Panama, Peru, Philippines, Russian Federation, Senegal, Slovenia, Sweden, Trinidad and Tobago.
Meeting numbers. GA 48th session: 3rd Committee 36-53; plenary 85.

International Decade of the World's Indigenous People

The Vienna Declaration and Programme of Action, adopted by the World Conference on Human Rights (Vienna, 14-25 June),[55] recommended that the General Assembly proclaim an international decade of the world's indigenous people, to begin in January 1994. In July,[40] the Working Group on Indigenous Populations welcomed that recommendation and, in August,[44] the Subcommission endorsed it.

GENERAL ASSEMBLY ACTION

On 21 December, the General Assembly, on the recommendation of the Third Committee, adopted **resolution 48/163** without vote.

International Decade of the World's Indigenous People

The General Assembly,

Bearing in mind that one of the purposes of the United Nations, as set forth in its Charter, is the achievement of international cooperation in solving international problems of an economic, social, cultural or humanitarian character and in promoting and encouraging respect for human rights and for fundamental freedoms for all without distinction as to race, sex, language or religion,

Recalling its resolution 45/164 of 18 December 1990, in which it proclaimed 1993 as the International Year of the World's Indigenous People, with a view to strengthening international cooperation for the solution of problems faced by indigenous people in areas such as human rights, the environment, development, education and health,

Acknowledging the significance of the Year in raising international awareness of the contribution of, and problems faced by, indigenous people throughout the world, and aware of the need to build on the results and lessons of the Year,

Recognizing the importance of consulting with indigenous people, the need for financial support from the international community, with support from within the United Nations system, including the specialized agencies, the need for a strategic planning framework and the need for adequate coordination and communication channels,

Expressing its appreciation for the work undertaken by the Coordinator for the Year, the Centre for Human Rights of the Secretariat, the Goodwill Ambassador, Rigoberta Menchu, and the Working Group on Indigenous Populations of the Subcommission on Prevention of Discrimination and Protection of Minorities,

Recognizing the value and the diversity of the cultures and the forms of social organization of the world's indigenous people,

Welcoming the report of the United Nations Conference on Environment and Development, in which the vital role of indigenous people and their communities in the interrelationship between the natural environment and its sustainable development is recognized, including their holistic traditional scientific knowledge of their lands, natural resources and environment,

Recognizing the importance of considering the establishment of a permanent forum for indigenous people in the framework of an international decade,

Taking note of the recommendation in the Vienna Declaration and Programme of Action, adopted by the World Conference on Human Rights, held at Vienna from 14 to 25 June 1993, that the General Assembly should proclaim an international decade of the world's indigenous people, which should begin from 1994 and should include action-oriented programmes to be decided upon in partnership with indigenous people,

1. *Proclaims* the International Decade of the World's Indigenous People, commencing on 10 December 1994, the period from 1 January to 9 December 1994 to be set aside for planning for the Decade in partnership with indigenous people;

2. *Decides* that the goal of the Decade should be the strengthening of international cooperation for the solution of problems faced by indigenous people in such areas as human rights, the environment, development, education and health;

3. *Also decides* that, beginning in the first year of the Decade, one day of every year shall be observed as the International Day of Indigenous People;

4. *Requests* the Commission on Human Rights, at its fiftieth session, to invite the Working Group on Indigenous Populations of the Subcommission on Prevention of Discrimination and Protection of Minorities to identify at its next session an appropriate date for this purpose;

5. *Requests* the Secretary-General to appoint the Assistant Secretary-General for Human Rights as the Coordinator for the Decade;

6. *Requests* the Coordinator to coordinate the programme of activities for the Decade in full collaboration and consultation with Governments, competent bodies, the International Labour Organisation and other specialized agencies of the United Nations system, and indigenous and non-governmental organizations;

7. *Requests* competent United Nations bodies and specialized agencies to designate focal points for coordination with the Centre for Human Rights of the Secretariat of activities related to the Decade;

8. *Invites* Governments to ensure that activities and objectives for the Decade are planned and implemented on the basis of full consultation and collaboration with indigenous people;

9. *Requests* specialized agencies, regional commissions and other organizations of the United Nations system to consider with Governments and in partnership with indigenous people how they can contribute to the success of the Decade, and to transmit their recommendations to the Economic and Social Council;

10. *Appeals* to its specialized agencies, regional commissions, financial and development institutions and other relevant organizations of the United Nations system to increase their efforts to take into special account the needs of indigenous people in their budgeting and in their programming;

11. *Invites* indigenous organizations and other interested non-governmental organizations to consider the contributions they can make to the success of the Decade, with a view to presenting them to the Working Group on Indigenous Populations;

12. *Requests* the Commission on Human Rights to ask the Working Group on Indigenous Populations to identify possible programmes and projects in connection with the Decade and to submit them through the Subcommission on Prevention of Discrimination and Protection of Minorities to the Commission for its consideration;

13. *Recommends* that adequate human and financial resources be made available to the Centre for Human Rights in support of its activities related to indigenous people, within the overall framework of strengthening its activities envisaged in the Vienna Declaration and Programme of Action;

14. *Requests* the Secretary-General to establish a voluntary fund for the Decade, and authorizes him to accept and administer voluntary contributions from Governments, intergovernmental and non-governmental organizations and other private institutions and individuals for the purpose of funding projects and programmes during the Decade;

15. *Urges* Governments and intergovernmental and non-governmental organizations to contribute to the voluntary fund for the Decade to be established by the Secretary-General, and invites indigenous organizations to do likewise;

16. *Invites* Governments, competent United Nations bodies and specialized agenices and other intergovernmental institutions, including financial institutions, to consider providing additional resources to finance the attachment of suitable staff, including indigenous staff, to the Centre for Human Rights on a regionally balanced basis;

17. *Encourages* Governments to establish national committees or other more permanent structures involving indigenous representatives to plan activities for the Decade;

18. *Requests* that the meeting to be convened in accordance with its resolution 46/128 of 17 December 1991 to review the Year also consider preparations for the Decade, giving full participation to indigenous people, particularly with regard to the elaboration of a detailed plan of action, including an evaluation mechanism, and the establishment of a funding plan for the Decade, and that the meeting report to the Working Group on Indigenous Populations;

19. *Urges* the competent United Nations organs, programmes and specialized agencies, in planning activities for the Decade, to examine how existing programmes and resources might be utilized to benefit indigenous people more effectively, including through the exploration of ways in which indigenous perspectives and activities can be included or enhanced;

20. *Requests* the Commission on Human Rights at its fiftieth session to give priority consideration to the establishment of a permanent forum for indigenous people in the United Nations system;

21. *Requests* the Secretary-General to give all the assistance necessary to ensure the success of the Decade;

22. *Also requests* the Secretary-General to submit to it a preliminary report at its forty-ninth session and a final report at its fiftieth session on a comprehensive programme of action for the Decade;

23. *Decides* to include in the provisional agenda of its forty-ninth session an item entitled ''Programme of activities of the International Decade of the World's Indigenous People''.

General Assembly resolution 48/163

21 December 1993   Meeting 86   Adopted without vote

Approved by Third Committee (A/48/632/Add.2) without vote, 8 December (meeting 54); 34-nation draft (A/C.3/48/L.54), orally revised; further orally revised in Assembly; agenda item 114 *(b)*.
Sponsors: Antigua and Barbuda, Australia, Bahamas, Barbados, Bolivia, Brazil, Canada, Chile, Colombia, Costa Rica, Cuba, Denmark, Dominica, Dominican Republic, Ecuador, El Salvador, Fiji, Gambia, Greece, Grenada, Guatemala, Guyana, Jamaica, Marshall Islands, Mexico, New Zealand, Nicaragua, Norway, Papua New Guinea, Peru, Philippines, Sierra Leone, Suriname, Trinidad and Tobago.
Meeting numbers. GA 48th session: 3rd Committee 36-54; plenary 86.

Migrant workers

International Convention

As at 31 December 1993,[20] Morocco had ratified, Egypt had acceded to and Chile, Mexico and the Philippines had signed the International Convention on the Protection of the Rights of All Migrant Workers and Members of Their Families, adopted by the General Assembly in 1990.[56]

The Secretary-General reported that, as at 1 August 1993, Morocco had ratified, Egypt had acceded to and Mexico had signed the Convention.[57] In a later report, he stated that, as at 1 December 1993, Chile and the Philippines had also signed the Convention.[58]

Human Rights Commission action. On 10 March,[59] the Commission urged all States to consider signing and ratifying or acceding to the Convention and invited United Nations agencies and organizations, intergovernmental organizations and NGOs to disseminate information on it. It asked the Secretary-General to provide all the assistance necessary to promote the Convention through the World Public Information Campaign on Human Rights and the programme of advisory services in the field of human rights (see below, under ''Advancement of human rights'') and to report on the Convention's status in 1994.

GENERAL ASSEMBLY ACTION

On 20 December, the General Assembly, on the recommendation of the Third Committee, adopted **resolution 48/148** without vote.

International Convention on the Protection of the Rights of All Migrant Workers and Members of Their Families

The General Assembly,

Reaffirming once more the permanent validity of the principles and standards set forth in the basic instruments regarding the international protection of human rights, in particular in the Universal Declaration of Human Rights, the International Covenants on Human Rights, the International Convention on the Elimination of All Forms of Racial Discrimination, the Convention on the Elimination of All Forms of Discrimination against Women and the Convention on the Rights of the Child,

Bearing in mind the principles and standards established within the framework of the International Labour Organisation and the importance of the work done in connection with migrant workers and members of their families in other specialized agencies and in various organs of the United Nations,

Reiterating that, in spite of the existence of an already established body of principles and standards, there is a need to make further efforts to improve the situation and to ensure the human rights and dignity of all migrant workers and members of their families,

Aware of the situation of migrant workers and members of their families and the marked increase in migratory movements that has occurred, especially in certain parts of the world,

Considering that in the Vienna Declaration and Programme of Action, adopted by the World Conference on Human Rights, held at Vienna from 14 to 25 June 1993, all States are urged to guarantee the protection of the human rights of all migrant workers and members of their families,

Underlining the importance of the creation of conditions to foster greater harmony and tolerance between migrant workers and the rest of the society of the State in which they reside,

Recalling its resolution 45/158 of 18 December 1990, in which it adopted and opened for signature, ratification and accession the International Convention on the Protection of the Rights of All Migrant Workers and Members of Their Families,

Bearing in mind that in the Vienna Declaration and Programme of Action States are invited to consider the possibility of signing and ratifying the Convention at the earliest possible time,

Recalling that, in its resolution 47/110 of 16 December 1992, it requested the Secretary-General to submit to it at its forty-eighth session a report on the status of the Convention,

1. *Takes note* of the report of the Secretary-General on the status of the International Convention on the Protection of the Rights of All Migrant Workers and Members of Their Families;

2. *Welcomes* the signature or ratification of, or accession to, the Convention by some Member States;

3. *Calls upon* all Member States to consider signing and ratifying or acceding to the Convention as a matter of priority, and expresses the hope that it will enter into force at an early date;

4. *Requests* the Secretary-General to provide all facilities and assistance necessary for the promotion of the Convention, through the World Public Information Campaign on Human Rights and the programme of advisory services in the field of human rights;

5. *Invites* the organizations and agencies of the United Nations system and intergovernmental and non-governmental organizations to intensify their efforts with a view to disseminating information on and promoting understanding of the Convention;

6. *Also requests* the Secretary-General to submit to the General Assembly at its forty-ninth session a report on the status of the Convention;

7. *Decides* to consider the report of the Secretary-General at its forty-ninth session under the sub-item entitled "Implementation of human rights instruments".

General Assembly resolution 48/148

20 December 1993   Meeting 85   Adopted without vote

Approved by Third Committee (A/48/632/Add.3) without vote, 6 December (meeting 53); 27-nation draft (A/C.3/48/L.67); agenda item 114 *(c)*.
Sponsors: Algeria, Argentina, Chile, Colombia, Costa Rica, Croatia, Cuba, Ecuador, Egypt, Ghana, Guatemala, Guinea, Guinea-Bissau, India, Mex-

ico, Morocco, Nicaragua, Peru, Philippines, Russian Federation, Rwanda, Senegal, Sierra Leone, Sudan, Tunisia, Turkey, Uruguay.
Meeting numbers. GA 48th session: 3rd Committee 36-53; plenary 85.

Freedom of movement

Subcommission action. On 20 August,[60] the Subcommission requested host countries to continue efforts to improve the situation and ensure the human rights and dignity of all migrant workers and their families and to protect them against violence, bodily injury, threats and intimidation.

Protection of minorities

Declaration

Human Rights Commission action. On 5 March,[61] the Commission called on States to promote and give effect to the principles contained in the 1992 Declaration on the Rights of Persons Belonging to National or Ethnic, Religious and Linguistic Minorities,[62] and urged all treaty bodies and special representatives, special rapporteurs and working groups of the Commission and Subcommission to give due regard to the Declaration. It invited intergovernmental organizations and NGOs to promote and protect the rights of persons belonging to national or ethnic, religious and linguistic minorities. It called on the Secretary-General to make available, as part of the programme of advisory services and technical assistance of the Centre for Human Rights, qualified experts familiar with minority issues and encouraged Governments to consider availing themselves of such services and assistance. The Secretary-General was asked to provide additional resources for such services and assistance and to report on the implementation of the Commission's resolution in 1994.

Subcommission action. On 26 August,[63] the Subcommission appealed to States to take municipal, legislative, administrative and other measures to promote and give effect to the principles in the Declaration and to conclude bilateral or, where possible, multilateral agreements to ensure the rights of national or ethnic minorities in their countries and to observe them in accordance with the standards of international humanitarian law in cases of armed conflict. It asked the Secretary-General to make available the resources to provide monitoring, advisory assistance and financing to States for activities related to the protection of minorities.

Report of the Secretary-General. As requested by the General Assembly in 1992,[62] the Secretary-General presented, in November 1993, an overview of activities for the effective promotion of the Declaration taken by United Nations bodies, specialized agencies, treaty bodies, special rapporteurs and independent experts and NGOs and human rights institutes.[64] The Secretary-General advocated dialogue by means of negotiations and consultations to improve the situation of persons belonging to minorities. He stated that the promotion of dialogue between States, and between States and persons belonging to minorities, with a view to implementing the Declaration should be encouraged.

GENERAL ASSEMBLY ACTION

On 20 December, the General Assembly, on the recommendation of the Third Committee, adopted **resolution 48/138** without vote.

Declaration on the Rights of Persons Belonging to National or Ethnic, Religious and Linguistic Minorities

The General Assembly,

Recalling its resolution 47/135 of 18 December 1992, in which it adopted the Declaration on the Rights of Persons Belonging to National or Ethnic, Religious and Linguistic Minorities,

Conscious of the need effectively to promote and protect the rights of persons belonging to minorities, as set out in the Declaration,

Noting the importance of an even more effective implementation of international human rights instruments with regard to the rights of all persons, including those belonging to national or ethnic, religious and linguistic minorities,

Welcoming Commission on Human Rights resolution 1993/24 of 5 March 1993 on the rights of persons belonging to national or ethnic, religious and linguistic minorities,

Noting that resolutions 1993/42 and 1993/43 adopted by the Subcommission on Prevention of Discrimination and Protection of Minorities on 26 August 1993 are to be considered by the Commission on Human Rights at its fiftieth session,

Aware of the provisions of article 27 of the International Covenant on Civil and Political Rights concerning the rights of persons belonging to ethnic, religious or linguistic minorities,

Acknowledging that the United Nations has an increasingly important role to play regarding the protection of minorities by, *inter alia*, taking due account of the Declaration,

Concerned by the growing frequency and severity of disputes and conflicts concerning minorities in many countries, and their often tragic consequences,

Affirming that effective measures and the creation of favourable conditions for the promotion and protection of the rights of persons belonging to national or ethnic, religious and linguistic minorities, ensuring effective non-discrimination and equality for all, contribute to the prevention and peaceful solution of human rights problems and situations involving minorities,

Considering that the promotion and protection of the rights of persons belonging to national or ethnic, religious and linguistic minorities contribute to political and social stability and peace, and enrich the cultural heritage of society as a whole of the States in which such persons live,

Reaffirming the obligation of States to ensure that persons belonging to minorities may exercise fully and effectively all human rights and fundamental freedoms without any discrimination and in full equality before the law in accordance with the Declaration,

Welcoming initiatives aiming at disseminating information on the Declaration and at promoting understanding thereof,

Having considered the report of the Secretary-General on the effective promotion of the Declaration,

Mindful of the recommendations contained in section II, paragraphs 25 to 27, of the Vienna Declaration and Programme of Action, adopted unanimously by the World Conference on Human Rights, held at Vienna from 14 to 25 June 1993,

1. *Takes note* of the report of the Secretary-General on the effective promotion of the Declaration on the Rights of Persons belonging to National or Ethnic, Religious and Linguistic Minorities;

2. *Urges* States and the international community to promote and protect the rights of persons belonging to national or ethnic, religious and linguistic minorities, as set out in the Declaration, including through the facilitation of their full participation in all aspects of the political, economic, social, religious and cultural life of society and in the economic progress and development of their country;

3. *Calls upon* the Commission on Human Rights to examine ways and means to promote and protect effectively the rights of persons belonging to minorities, as set out in the Declaration;

4. *Calls upon* the Secretary-General to provide through the Centre for Human Rights of the Secretariat, at the request of Governments concerned and as part of the programme of advisory services and technical assistance of the Centre, qualified expertise on minority issues and human rights, as well as on the prevention and resolution of disputes, to assist in existing or potential situations involving minorities;

5. *Appeals* to States to take all the necessary legislative and other measures to promote and give effect, as appropriate, to the principles of the Declaration;

6. *Also appeals* to States to make bilateral and multilateral efforts, as appropriate, to protect the rights of persons belonging to national or ethnic, religious and linguistic minorities in their countries, in accordance with the Declaration;

7. *Urges* all treaty bodies and special representatives, special rapporteurs and working groups of the Commission on Human Rights and the Subcommission on Prevention of Discrimination and Protection of Minorities to give due regard to the promotion and protection of the rights of persons belonging to minorities, as set forth in the Declaration, as appropriate, within their mandates;

8. *Encourages* intergovernmental and non-governmental organizations to continue to contribute to the promotion and protection of the rights of persons belonging to national or ethnic, religious and linguistic minorities;

9. *Invites* the Secretary-General to continue the dissemination of information on the Declaration and the promotion of understanding thereof, including, as appropriate, in the context of the training of United Nations personnel;

10. *Requests* the Secretary-General to report to the General Assembly at its forty-ninth session on the implementation of the present resolution under the item entitled "Human rights questions".

General Assembly resolution 48/138
20 December 1993 Meeting 85 Adopted without vote

Approved by Third Committee (A/48/632/Add.2) without vote, 6 December (meeting 53); 46-nation draft (A/C.3/48/L.71); agenda item 114 *(b)*.
Sponsors: Albania, Argentina, Armenia, Australia, Austria, Belarus, Benin, Bosnia and Herzegovina, Canada, Costa Rica, Croatia, Czech Republic, Denmark, Estonia, Ethiopia, Finland, Gambia, Georgia, Greece, Guatemala, Guinea-Bissau, Hungary, Iceland, India, Italy, Kyrgyzstan, Latvia, Liechtenstein, Lithuania, Malawi, Morocco, Nepal, Netherlands, Norway, Poland, Republic of Korea, Russian Federation, Rwanda, Senegal, Slovakia, Slovenia, Sweden, the former Yugoslav Republic of Macedonia, Ukraine, United States, Uruguay.
Meeting numbers. GA 48th session: 3rd Committee 36-53; plenary 85.

Minority problems

Report of the Special Rapporteur. In August, Special Rapporteur Asbjorn Eide (Norway) submitted his final report on ways to facilitate the peaceful and constructive solution of problems involving minorities.[65] In addenda,[66] he reported on replies to a questionnaire on minorities received from 25 Governments and 4 NGOs. A reply from Yugoslavia (Serbia and Montenegro) was submitted separately,[67] as were recommendations for measures to be taken at the national and international level.[68]

Other action. In accordance with a 1992 Economic and Social Council decision,[69] a technical meeting of experts on minorities from different regions of the world was held (Geneva, 2-4 February 1993)[70] to exchange views on the Special Rapporteur's progress reports and to provide guidance for his final report.

In July, UNESCO submitted to the Subcommission a report describing its 1993 activities to promote and protect the rights of persons belonging to national or ethnic, religious and linguistic minorities and those planned for 1994 and 1995.[71]

Subcommission action. On 26 August,[72] the Subcommission recommended that the Special Rapporteur's study be published in all official United Nations languages and given the widest circulation possible. It endorsed his recommendations and urged relevant treaty bodies to take note of recommendations 48 to 55 and recommendation 65; the specialized agencies and other United Nations bodies to take account of recommendations 56 to 63; States to note and act on recommendations 4 to 22 and to take into account recommendations 25 to 34; and NGOs to study and act on recommendations 66 to 68. The Subcommission recommended that the Commission study a proposal in recommendation 44 to establish a working group on minority issues and to study and give advice to the Centre for Human Rights concerning recommendations 46 and 47, in particular on ways in which the programme of technical assistance and advisory services could help in preventing group conflicts. It decided to consider in 1994 the follow-up to the report, including the feasibility and usefulness of preparing a more comprehensive programme for the preven-

tion of discrimination and protection of minorities, and entrusted the Special Rapporteur with preparing a working paper containing suggestions for such a programme.

HIV- and AIDS-related discrimination

Human Rights Commission action. On 9 March,[73] the Commission called on States to take steps to ensure the full enjoyment of civil, political, economic, social and cultural rights by people infected with the human immunodeficiency virus (HIV) or with acquired immunodeficiency syndrome (AIDS), their families, those associated with them and people presumed to be at risk of infection, paying particular attention to women, children and other vulnerable groups, in order to prevent discrimination against them. It urged them to include in their AIDS programmes measures to combat discrimination and to take steps to develop a supportive social environment for effective AIDS prevention and care. The Commission asked the Human Rights Committee, the Committee on Economic, Social and Cultural Rights and similar bodies to monitor States parties' compliance with their commitments under the relevant human rights instruments regarding the rights of people infected with HIV or AIDS, their families and people with whom they lived, or people presumed to be at risk. It welcomed a 1990 preliminary report[74] and the 1991[75] and 1992[76] progress reports of the Subcommission's Special Rapporteur (Luis Varela Quirós, Costa Rica), and endorsed requests made by the Subcommission in 1992 that he submit his final report in 1993 and that the Secretary-General give him any assistance he required. The Commission decided to consider the final report in 1994.

On 28 July, the Economic and Social Council, by **decision 1993/269**, approved the Commission's endorsement of the Subcommission's requests.

Report of the Special Rapporteur. In August, the Subcommission's Special Rapporteur, Luis Varela Quirós, submitted a final report on discrimination against HIV-infected people or people with AIDS.[77] In his conclusions and recommendations, the Special Rapporteur stated that discriminatory practices could be eradicated only by national and international education programmes. As women and children stood out as being the ones most unfairly affected by the disease, the Special Rapporteur called for special emphasis to be placed on the provisions of the 1979 Convention on the Elimination of All Forms of Discrimination against Women[78] and for the Subcommission to condemn the exploitation of children and child prostitution. He called for the provision of appropriate hospital treatment and psychological care for those suffering from the disease.

Subcommission action. On 25 August,[79] the Subcommission called on States to take steps, including protective legislation and appropriate education, to ensure the full enjoyment of civil, political, economic, social and cultural rights by people with HIV and AIDS, their families, those associated with them and people presumed to be at risk of infection, paying particular attention to women, children and other vulnerable groups, in order to prevent discrimination against them. It also called on them to advance the legal, economic and social status of women and indigenous peoples, as well as of minorities and other groups suffering discrimination, to render them less vulnerable to HIV infection and to the adverse socio-economic consequences of the pandemic. The Subcommission urged relevant United Nations working groups and special rapporteurs to consider the impact of AIDS and AIDS-related discrimination in their reports, and asked the Secretary-General to bring its resolution to their attention, as well as to treaty-monitoring bodies and those bodies concerned with the status and rights of women. It further asked the Secretary-General to report in 1994 on developments concerning the possibility of establishing a joint United Nations programme on HIV and AIDS between the United Nations system and the World Health Organization. The Subcommission expressed grave concern at the continued exploitation of children and child prostitution and called on the Working Group on Contemporary Forms of Slavery to pay urgent attention to the matter.

REFERENCES

[1]YUN 1984, p. 785. [2]YUN 1987, p. 732, GA res. 42/47, annex, 30 Nov. 1987. [3]YUN 1992, p. 710. [4]E/CN.4/1993/55. [5]YUN 1985, p. 836, ESC res. 1985/19, 29 May 1985. [6]E/1993/71. [7]ESC dec. 1990/224, 25 May 1990. [8]YUN 1992, p. 711, GA res. 47/77, 16 Dec. 1992. [9]A/48/558. [10]YUN 1992, p. 710, ESC res. 1992/13, 30 July 1992. [11]Ibid., p. 709. [12]A/48/423. [13]YUN 1973, p. 523, GA res. 3057(XXVIII), 2 Nov. 1973. [14]E/1993/23 (res. 1993/11). [15]YUN 1992, p. 721, GA res. 47/110, 16 Dec. 1992. [16]GA res. S-16/1, 14 Dec. 1989. [17]E/1993/23 (res. 1993/20). [18]E/CN.4/1994/2 (res. 1993/3). [19]A/48/18. [20]*Multilateral Treaties Deposited with the Secretary-General: Status as at 31 December 1993* (ST/LEG/SER.E/12), Sales No. E.94.V.11. [21]YUN 1965, p. 440, GA res. 2106 A (XX), annex, 21 Dec. 1965. [22]YUN 1969, p. 488. [23]A/48/18 (dec. 1 (42)). [24]A/48/439. [25]YUN 1985, p. 714. [26]E/1993/23 (res. 1993/16). [27]YUN 1992, p. 769, GA res. 47/111, 16 Dec. 1992. [28]Ibid., p. 716. [29]E/CN.4/1993/63. [30]YUN 1966, p. 423, GA res. 2200 A (XXI), annex, 16 Dec. 1966. [31]YUN 1976, p. 609. [32]E/CN.4/1993/62 & Corr.1 & Add.1. [33]YUN 1981, p. 881, GA res. 36/55, 25 Nov. 1981. [34]YUN 1992, p. 716, GA res. 47/129, 18 Dec. 1992. [35]E/1993/23 (res. 1993/25). [36]E/CN.4/1994/2 (res. 1993/2). [37]E/1993/23 (res. 1993/31). [38]YUN 1992, p. 718. [39]E/1993/23 (res. 1993/30). [40]E/CN.4/Sub.2/1993/29 & Add.1,2. [41]E/CN.4/Sub.2/1993/26. [42]E/CN.4/Sub.2/1993/26/Add.1. [43]E/CN.4/1994/2 (res. 1993/46). [44]Ibid. (res. 1993/45). [45]E/CN.4/Sub.2/1993/28. [46]E/CN.4/1994/2 (res. 1993/44). [47]E/1993/23 (dec. 1993/105). [48]YUN 1992, p. 719. [49]E/CN.4/1994/2 (dec. 1993/110). [50]YUN 1991, p. 539, GA res. 46/128, annex, 17 Dec. 1991. [51]YUN 1992, p. 720, GA res. 47/75, 14 Dec. 1992. [52]E/CN.4/1994/86. [53]E/CN.4/ 1992/AC.4/TM2/3. [54]A/CONF.157/24. [55]A/CONF.157/23. [56]GA res. 45/158, annex, 18 Dec. 1990. [57]A/48/471. [58]E/CN.4/1994/62. [59]E/1993/23 (res. 1993/89). [60]E/CN.4/1994/2 (res. 1993/21). [61]E/1993/23 (res. 1993/24). [62]YUN 1992, p. 722, GA res. 47/135, 18 Dec. 1992. [63]E/CN.4/1994/2 (res. 1993/42). [64]A/48/509 & Corr.1 & Add.1. [65]E/CN.4/Sub.2/1993/34. [66]E/CN.4/Sub.2/1993/34/Add.1,2. [67]E/CN.4/Sub.2/1993/34/Add.3. [68]E/CN.4/Sub.2/1993/34/Add.4. [69]YUN 1992, p. 725, ESC dec. 1992/254, 20 July 1992. [70]E/CN.4/1993/85. [71]E/CN.4/Sub.2/1993/4. [72]E/CN.4/1994/2 (res. 1993/43). [73]E/1993/23 (res. 1993/53). [74]E/CN.4/Sub.2/1990/9. [75]YUN 1991, p. 543. [76]YUN 1992, p. 725. [77]E/CN.4/Sub.2/1993/9. [78]YUN 1979, p. 895, GA res. 34/180, annex, 18 Dec. 1979. [79]E/CN.4/1994/2 (res. 1993/31).

Civil and political rights

Covenant on Civil and Political Rights and Optional Protocols

Accessions and ratifications

As at 31 December, parties to the International Covenant on Civil and Political Rights and the Optional Protocol thereto, adopted by the General Assembly in 1966[1] and in force since 1976,[2] totalled 125 and 74 States respectively.[3] Armenia, Bosnia and Herzegovina, Cape Verde, Czech Republic, Dominica, Ethiopia, Malawi, Mozambique, Nigeria, Republic of Moldova and Slovakia became parties to the Covenant in 1993; Armenia, Czech Republic, Germany, Guinea, Guyana, Romania, Slovakia and Slovenia acceded or succeeded to or ratified the Optional Protocol.

Parties to the Second Optional Protocol, aiming at the abolition of the death penalty—adopted by the Assembly in 1989[4] and in force since July 1991[5]—totalled 19 States as at 31 December 1993.[3] Austria, Ecuador, Ireland, Mozambique, Panama, Uruguay and Venezuela ratified or acceded to it in 1993.

In a report to the Commission,[6] the Secretary-General provided information on the status of the Covenant and the Optional Protocols as at 1 December (see below, under "Advancement of human rights").

Human Rights Commission action. On 26 February,[7] the Commission appealed to States that had not done so to become parties to the Covenant and Optional Protocols and to consider making the declaration provided for in article 41 of the Covenant. A similar appeal was made in December by the General Assembly in **resolution 48/119**. The Commission requested the Secretary-General to report in 1994 on the status of the Covenant and its Optional Protocols.

Implementation

Human Rights Committee activities. The Human Rights Committee, established under article 28 of the Covenant, held three sessions in 1993: its forty-seventh from 22 March to 8 April in New York, and forty-eighth from 12 to 30 July and forty-ninth from 18 October to 5 November, both at Geneva.

At those sessions, the Committee considered reports from 15 States—Bulgaria, Dominican Republic, Egypt, Guinea, Hungary, Iceland, Iran, Ireland, Japan, Libyan Arab Jamahiriya, Malta, Niger, Norway, Romania and Uruguay—under article 40 of the Covenant. It adopted views on 22 communications from individuals claiming that their rights under the Covenant had been violated. The Committee decided that 19 other such communications were inadmissible.

The Committee adopted and annexed to its report[8] a general comment on article 18 of the Covenant concerning the right to freedom of thought, conscience and religion. The comments were intended to assist States parties to fulfil their reporting obligations and promote the Covenant's implementation.

In October,[9] the Committee requested Angola and Burundi, following recent events in those countries (see PART TWO, Chapter I for details), to submit reports on their application of rights protected under the Covenant relating to the imposition of a state of emergency, the right to life, torture, personal security, freedom of movement and the right to participate in public life.

State of siege or emergency

Human Rights Commission action. On 5 March,[10] the Commission recommended the inclusion in the agenda of the 1993 World Conference on Human Rights (see below, under "Advancement of human rights") an item on strengthening protection of human rights during states of emergency. It also recommended to the Economic and Social Council a draft decision concerning the work of the Special Rapporteur on human rights and states of emergency (Leandro Despouy, Argentina).

On 26 February,[7] the Commission underlined, as did the General Assembly later in the year in **resolution 48/119**, the necessity for strict observance of the agreed conditions and procedures for derogation under article 4 of the Covenant and the need for States parties to provide full and timely information during states of emergency, so that the justification and appropriateness of measures taken in those circumstances could be assessed.

ECONOMIC AND SOCIAL COUNCIL ACTION

On 28 July, the Economic and Social Council, by **decision 1993/265**, endorsed a 1992 Subcommission request[11] to the Special Rapporteur to continue updating the list of states of emergency and to include in his annual report to the Subcommission and the Commission recommendations on inalienable or non-derogable rights. It also endorsed the Subcommission's request that the Secretary-General provide the Special Rapporteur with all the assistance he might require.

Report of the Special Rapporteur. In June, Special Rapporteur Leandro Despouy submitted his sixth annual report containing information on 83 States or territories which, since 1 January 1985, had proclaimed, extended or terminated a state of emergency.[12] Previous reports were issued in 1987,[13] 1988,[14] 1989,[15] 1991[16] and 1992.[11]

As requested by the Subcommission on 25 August 1992,[17] the Special Rapporteur revised and updated his sixth report,[18] which the Secretary-General transmitted to the Commission in November.[19]

Self-determination of peoples

By three resolutions adopted in 1993, the Commission on Human Rights reaffirmed the right to self-determination of the people of Cambodia,[20] Palestine[21] and Western Sahara.[22] A fourth resolution[23] adopted under the item pertained to the use of mercenaries as a means to impede the exercise of the right of peoples to self-determination.

Report of the Secretary-General. In September,[24] the Secretary-General summarized action taken in 1993 by the Commission and the Economic and Social Council on the right of peoples to self-determination. He also summarized replies received from five Governments in response to his request for information from States for inclusion in his report, prepared in response to two 1992 Assembly resolutions.[25]

GENERAL ASSEMBLY ACTION

In 1993, the General Assembly adopted two resolutions and one decision on the right to self-determination, a right it repeatedly reaffirmed for individual Non-Self-Governing Territories (see PART ONE, Chapter III).

On 20 December, the Assembly, on the recommendation of the Third Committee, adopted **resolution 48/93** without vote.

Universal realization of the right of peoples to self-determination

The General Assembly,

Reaffirming the importance, for the effective guarantee and observance of human rights, of the universal realization of the right of peoples to self-determination enshrined in the Charter of the United Nations and embodied in the International Covenants on Human Rights, as well as in the Declaration on the Granting of Independence to Colonial Countries and Peoples contained in General Assembly resolution 1514(XV) of 14 December 1960,

Welcoming the progressive exercise of the right to self-determination by peoples under colonial, foreign or alien occupation and their emergence into sovereign statehood and independence,

Deeply concerned at the continuation of acts or threats of foreign military intervention and occupation that are threatening to suppress, or have already suppressed, the right to self-determination of an increasing number of sovereign peoples and nations,

Expressing grave concern that, as a consequence of the persistence of such actions, millions of people have been and are being uprooted from their homes as refugees and displaced persons, and emphasizing the urgent need for concerted international action to alleviate their condition,

Recalling the relevant resolutions regarding the violation of the right of peoples to self-determination and other human rights as a result of foreign military intervention, aggression and occupation, adopted by the Commission on Human Rights at its thirty-sixth, thirty-seventh, thirty-eighth, thirty-ninth, fortieth, forty-first, forty-second, forty-third, forty-fourth, forty-fifth, forty-sixth, forty-seventh, forty-eighth and forty-ninth sessions,

Reaffirming its resolutions 35/35 B of 14 November 1980, 36/10 of 28 October 1981, 37/42 of 3 December 1982, 38/16 of 22 November 1983, 39/18 of 23 November 1984, 40/24 of 29 November 1985, 41/100 of 4 December 1986, 42/94 of 7 December 1987, 43/105 of 8 December 1988, 44/80 of 8 December 1989, 45/131 of 14 December 1990, 46/88 of 16 December 1991 and 47/83 of 16 December 1992,

Taking note of the report of the Secretary-General on the right of peoples to self-determination,

1. *Reaffirms* that the universal realization of the right of all peoples, including those under colonial, foreign and alien domination, to self-determination is a fundamental condition for the effective guarantee and observance of human rights and for the preservation and promotion of such rights;

2. *Declares its firm opposition* to acts of foreign military intervention, aggression and occupation, since these have resulted in the suppression of the right of peoples to self-determination and other human rights in certain parts of the world;

3. *Calls upon* those States responsible to cease immediately their military intervention in and occupation of foreign countries and territories and all acts of repression, discrimination, exploitation and maltreatment, particularly the brutal and inhuman methods reportedly employed for the execution of those acts against the peoples concerned;

4. *Deplores* the plight of the millions of refugees and displaced persons who have been uprooted as a result of the aforementioned acts, and reaffirms their right to return to their homes voluntarily in safety and honour;

5. *Requests* the Commission on Human Rights to continue to give special attention to the violation of human rights, especially the right to self-determination, resulting from foreign military intervention, aggression or occupation;

6. *Requests* the Secretary-General to report on this question to the General Assembly at its forty-ninth session under the item entitled "Right of peoples to self-determination".

General Assembly resolution 48/93

20 December 1993   Meeting 85   Adopted without vote

Approved by Third Committee (A/48/626) without vote, 12 November (meeting 32); 35-nation draft (A/C.3/48/L.15); agenda item 108 (a).

Sponsors: Afghanistan, Albania, Azerbaijan, Bahrain, Bosnia and Herzegovina, Brunei Darussalam, Cape Verde, Chile, Colombia, Comoros, Costa Rica, Djibouti, Dominican Republic, Ecuador, Egypt, El Salvador, Gabon, Guatemala, Honduras, Iran, Jordan, Kuwait, Malaysia, Mauritania, Morocco, Nicaragua, Oman, Pakistan, Papua New Guinea, Qatar, Saudi Arabia, Sierra Leone, Singapore, Thailand, United Arab Emirates.

Meeting numbers. GA 48th session: 3rd Committee 3-10, 25, 32; plenary 85.

Also on 20 December, on the Third Committee's recommendation, the Assembly adopted **resolution 48/94** by recorded vote.

Importance of the universal realization of the right of peoples to self-determination and of the speedy granting of independence to colonial countries and peoples for the effective guarantee and observance of human rights

The General Assembly,

Reaffirming its faith in the importance of the implementation of the Declaration on the Granting of Independence to Colonial Countries and Peoples contained in its resolution 1514(XV) of 14 December 1960,

Reaffirming the importance of the universal realization of the right of peoples to self-determination, national sovereignty and territorial integrity and of the speedy granting of independence to colonial countries and peoples as imperatives for the full enjoyment of all human rights,

Reaffirming also the obligation of all Member States to comply with the principles of the Charter of the United Nations and the resolutions of the United Nations regarding the exercise of the right to self-determination by peoples under colonial and foreign domination,

Recalling the Vienna Declaration and Programme of Action adopted at the World Conference on Human Rights,

Considering the urgent need of Namibia for assistance in its efforts to reconstruct and strengthen its fledgling economic and social structures,

Recalling the Abuja Declaration on South Africa, adopted by the Assembly of Heads of State and Government of the Organization of African Unity at its twenty-seventh ordinary session, held at Abuja in June 1991, and the statement on developments in South Africa adopted by the Ad Hoc Committee on Southern Africa of the Organization of African Unity at its extraordinary session of the Ministers for Foreign Affairs, held in New York on 29 September 1993,

Affirming the need to exercise vigilance with respect to developments in South Africa to ensure that the common objective of the international community and the peoples of South Africa is achieved by the establishment of a united, democratic and non-racial South Africa without deviation or obstruction,

Recalling the signing of the General Peace Agreement for Mozambique at Rome on 4 October 1992, which provides for the termination of the armed conflict in that country,

Reaffirming the national unity and territorial integrity of the Comoros,

Deeply concerned by Israel's continuing occupation of parts of southern Lebanon and its frequent attacks against Lebanese territory and people, as well as its refusal to implement Security Council resolution 425(1978) of 19 March 1978,

Bearing in mind United Nations resolutions related to the question of Palestine,

Taking note of the recent positive evolution in the Middle East peace process, in particular the signing on 13 September 1993 of the Declaration of Principles on Interim Self-Government Arrangements by the Government of the State of Israel and the Palestine Liberation Organization,

1. *Calls upon* all States to implement fully and faithfully all the relevant resolutions of the United Nations regarding the exercise of the right to self-determination and independence by peoples under colonial and foreign domination;

2. *Reaffirms* the legitimacy of the struggle of peoples for independence, territorial integrity, national unity and liberation from colonial domination, apartheid and foreign occupation, in all its forms and by all available means;

3. *Reaffirms also* the inalienable right of the Palestinian people and all peoples under foreign occupation and colonial domination to self-determination, independence and sovereignty;

4. *Calls upon* those Governments which do not recognize the right to self-determination and independence of all peoples still under colonial domination, alien subjugation and foreign occupation to do so;

5. *Calls upon* Israel to refrain from violation of the fundamental rights of the Palestinian people and from denial of its right to self-determination;

6. *Urges* all States, the specialized agencies and organizations of the United Nations system, as well as other international organizations, to extend their support to the Palestinian people through its sole and legitimate representative, the Palestine Liberation Organization, in its struggle to regain its right to self-determination and independence in accordance with the Charter of the United Nations;

7. *Urgently appeals* to all States, the organizations of the United Nations system and other international organizations to render assistance to Namibia in order to enhance its efforts to promote democracy and economic development;

8. *Strongly urges* the Government of South Africa to take additional steps to implement fully the provisions of the statement on developments in South Africa adopted on 29 September 1993 by the Ad Hoc Committee of the Organization of African Unity on Southern Africa, in order to achieve the objectives of the Declaration on Apartheid and its Destructive Consequences in Southern Africa;

9. *Calls upon* all parties to refrain immediately from acts of violence, and calls upon the Government of South Africa to exercise its responsibility to end the ongoing violence through, *inter alia*, strict adherence to the National Peace Accord signed on 14 September 1991;

10. *Calls upon* all signatories to the National Peace Accord to manifest their commitment to peace by fully implementing its provisions, and calls upon other parties to contribute to the attainment of its objectives;

11. *Strongly condemns* the establishment and use of armed groups with a view to pitting them against the national liberation movements;

12. *Demands* that the Government of South Africa repeal the security legislation that remains in force, which inhibits free and peaceful political activity;

13. *Requests* the Secretary-General to act speedily to implement Security Council resolution 772(1992) of 17 August 1992 in its entirety, including those parts pertaining to the investigation of criminal conduct and the monitoring of all armed formations in the country;

14. *Demands* the full application of the mandatory arms embargo against South Africa, imposed under Security Council resolution 418(1977) of 4 November 1977, by all countries and more particularly by those countries which maintain military and nuclear cooperation with the Government of South Africa and continue to supply it with related *matériel*;

15. *Appeals* to the international community, pursuant to General Assembly resolution 47/82 of 16 December 1992, to continue to extend assistance to Lesotho to enable it to fulfil its international humanitarian obligations towards refugees;

16. *Pays tribute* to the Government and people of Angola for their noble contribution to the evolving climate of peace in southern Angola, and addresses its strongest appeal to the National Union for the Total Independence of Angola to undertake to commit itself to the peace process that will lead to a comprehensive settlement in Angola on the basis of the Peace Accords;

17. *Demands* that the Government of South Africa pay compensation to Angola for damages caused, in accordance with the relevant resolutions and decisions of the Security Council;

18. *Demands also* that the Government of South Africa pay full and adequate compensation to Botswana for the loss of life and damage to property resulting from the unprovoked and unwarranted military attacks of 14 June 1985, 19 May 1986 and 20 June 1988 on the capital of Botswana;

19. *Calls upon* the international community to continue to extend its generous support to the ongoing efforts aimed at ensuring respect for and the successful implementation of the General Peace Agreement for Mozambique and at assisting the Government of Mozambique in the establishment of lasting peace and democracy and in the promotion of an effective programme of national reconstruction in that country;

20. *Fully supports* the Secretary-General in his efforts to implement the plan for the settlement of the question of Western Sahara by organizing, in cooperation with the Organization of African Unity, a referendum for the self-determination of the people of Western Sahara;

21. *Notes* the contacts between the Government of the Comoros and the Government of France in the search for a just solution to the problem of the integration of the Comorian island of Mayotte into the Comoros, in accordance with the resolutions of the Organization of African Unity and the United Nations on the question;

22. *Strongly condemns* the continued violation of the human rights of the peoples still under colonial domination and alien subjugation;

23. *Calls* for a substantial increase in all forms of assistance given by all States, United Nations organs, the specialized agencies and non-governmental organizations to the victims of racism, racial discrimination and apartheid through anti-apartheid organizations and national liberation movements recognized by the Organization of African Unity;

24. *Reaffirms* that the practice of using mercenaries against sovereign States and national liberation movements constitutes a criminal act, and calls upon the Governments of all countries to enact legislation declaring the recruitment, financing and training of mercenaries in their territories and the transit of mercenaries through their territories to be punishable offences and prohibiting their nationals from serving as mercenaries, and to report on such legislation to the Secretary-General;

25. *Demands* the immediate and unconditional release of all persons detained or imprisoned as a result of their struggle for self-determination and independence, full respect for their fundamental individual rights and compliance with article 5 of the Universal Declaration of Human Rights, under which no one shall be subjected to torture or to cruel, inhuman or degrading treatment;

26. *Expresses its appreciation* for the material and other forms of assistance that peoples under colonial rule continue to receive from Governments, organizations of the United Nations system and other intergovernmental organizations, and calls for a substantial increase in that assistance;

27. *Urges* all States, the specialized agencies and other competent organizations of the United Nations system to do their utmost to ensure the full implementation of the Declaration on the Granting of Independence to Colonial Countries and Peoples and to intensify their efforts to support peoples under colonial, foreign and racist domination in their just struggle for self-determination and independence;

28. *Decides* to consider this question at its forty-ninth session under the item entitled "Right of peoples to self-determination".

General Assembly resolution 48/94

20 December 1993   Meeting 85   101-26-36 (recorded vote)

Approved by Third Committee (A/48/626) by recorded vote (87-25-34), 12 November (meeting 32); draft by Algeria, for African Group (A/C.3/48/L.19); agenda item 108 *(a)*.

Meeting numbers. GA 48th session: 3rd Committee 3-10, 25, 32; plenary 85.

Recorded vote in Assembly as follows:

In favour: Afghanistan, Algeria, Angola, Antigua and Barbuda, Bahamas, Bahrain, Bangladesh, Barbados, Belize, Benin, Bhutan, Bolivia, Botswana, Brazil, Brunei Darussalam, Burkina Faso, Burundi, Cameroon, Cape Verde, Central African Republic, Chad, Chile, China, Colombia, Comoros, Congo, Côte d'Ivoire, Cuba, Cyprus, Democratic People's Republic of Korea, Djibouti, Dominica, Ecuador, Egypt, Ethiopia, Gabon, Gambia, Ghana, Guatemala, Guinea, Guinea-Bissau, Guyana, Haiti, India, Indonesia, Iran, Iraq, Jordan, Kenya, Kuwait, Lao People's Democratic Republic, Lebanon, Lesotho, Libyan Arab Jamahiriya, Malawi, Malaysia, Maldives, Mali, Mauritania, Mauritius, Mexico, Mongolia, Morocco, Mozambique, Myanmar, Namibia, Nepal, Niger, Nigeria, Oman, Pakistan, Papua New Guinea, Peru, Philippines, Qatar, Rwanda, Saint Lucia, Saint Vincent and the Grenadines, Saudi Arabia, Senegal, Sierra Leone, Singapore, Solomon Islands, Sri Lanka, Sudan, Suriname, Swaziland, Syrian Arab Republic, Thailand, Togo, Trinidad and Tobago, Tunisia, Uganda, United Arab Emirates, United Republic of Tanzania, Venezuela, Viet Nam, Yemen, Zaire, Zambia, Zimbabwe.

Against: Argentina, Belgium, Bulgaria, Canada, Czech Republic, Denmark, Finland, France, Georgia, Germany, Hungary, Iceland, Israel, Italy, Japan, Luxembourg, Monaco, Netherlands, Norway, Poland, Romania, Russian Federation, Slovakia, Sweden, United Kingdom, United States.

Abstaining: Albania, Armenia, Australia, Austria, Azerbaijan, Belarus, Costa Rica, Croatia, Dominican Republic, Estonia, Fiji, Greece, Honduras, Ireland, Jamaica, Kazakhstan, Kyrgyzstan, Latvia, Liechtenstein, Lithuania, Malta, Marshall Islands, Micronesia, New Zealand, Nicaragua, Panama, Paraguay, Portugal, Republic of Korea, Republic of Moldova, San Marino, Slovenia, Spain, the former Yugoslav Republic of Macedonia, Turkey, Ukraine, Uruguay.

By **decision 48/427** of 20 December, the Assembly deferred to a future session consideration of the question of the effective realization of the right of self-determination through autonomy.

Cambodia

Human Rights Commission action. On 19 February,[20] the Commission requested the Secretary-General to ensure a continued United Nations human rights presence in Cambodia after the expiry of the mandate of the United Nations Transitional Authority in Cambodia (UNTAC) (see PART TWO, Chapter III). He was asked to appoint a special representative to maintain contact with the people and Government of Cambodia; guide and coordinate the United Nations human rights presence; assist the Government to promote and protect human rights; and report to the Commission in 1994. Those requests were approved by the Economic and Social Council in its **decision 1993/254** of 28 July. The Commission further asked him to communicate the contents of its resolution to, and seek the consent and cooperation of, the newly elected Government of Cambodia to facilitate the tasks of the special representative and the Centre for Human Rights in fulfilling their respective mandates.

On 23 November, the Secretary-General appointed Michael Kirby (Australia) as his Special Representative.

(For General Assembly action on the human rights situation in Cambodia, see below, under "Human rights violations".)

Palestinians

Human Rights Commission action. By a 19 February resolution,[21] adopted by a roll-call vote of 27 to 1, with 19 abstentions, the Commission reaffirmed the right of the Palestinians to self-determination and called on Israel to withdraw from the Palestinian and other Arab territories, including Jerusalem, in accordance with United Nations resolutions. It asked the Secretary-General to transmit its resolution to Israel and all other Governments, to distribute it as widely as possible and to make available to the Commission, prior to its 1994 session, all information pertaining to its implementation by Israel.

Subcommission action. On 20 August,[26] the Subcommission, by a secret ballot of 17 votes to 2, with 5 abstentions, condemned Israel for its gross violations of the rules of international law; its policy of deporting Palestinian citizens and expelling them from their homeland; establishing Israeli settlements in the Palestinian and other occupied Arab territories; its continued occupation of the Syrian Golan and defiance of United Nations resolutions; and the inhuman treatment and terrorist practices exercised against Syrian Arab citizens in the occupied Golan. It called on Israel to withdraw from the Palestinian and other occupied Arab territories; to refrain from deporting and expelling Palestinian citizens from their homeland; and to dismantle Israeli settlements in the occupied territories. It asked all States and international organizations not to recognize any Israeli laws, jurisdiction or administration in respect of the occupied Syrian Golan. The Secretary-General was requested to provide in 1994 an updated list of reports, studies, statistics and other documents relating to the question of Palestine and other occupied Arab territories, with texts of relevant United Nations decisions and resolutions, the report of the Special Committee to Investigate Israeli Practices Affecting the Human Rights of the Palestinian People and Other Arabs of the Occupied Territories, and other relevant information.

Report of the Secretary-General. In accordance with a 1992 Commission request,[27] the Secretary-General reported in January 1993[28] that he had asked Israel for information on the Commission's 1992 resolution on the situation in occupied Palestine and had received no reply.

Western Sahara

Human Rights Commission action. On 26 February 1993,[22] the Commission endorsed the content of a 1992 letter from the President of the Security Council to the Secretary-General[29] in which Council members expressed the view that Morocco and the Frente Popular para la Liberación de Saguia el-Hamra y de Río de Oro must abide by the 1991 cease-fire agreement and abstain from any provocative behaviour endangering the Secretary-General's 1991 settlement plan.[30] It decided to follow the situation in Western Sahara and to consider the matter in 1994.

Mercenaries

Human Rights Commission action. On 19 February,[23] the Commission, reaffirming that the recruitment, use, financing and training of mercenaries should be considered as offences of grave concern, called on all States to consider acceding to or ratifying the 1989 International Convention against the Recruitment, Use, Financing and Training of Mercenaries[31] and urged them to prevent mercenaries from using any part of their territory to destabilize any sovereign State. It asked the Special Rapporteur to report in 1994.

On 9 March,[32] the Commission asked all special rapporteurs and working groups to continue to pay particular attention to the adverse effect on the enjoyment of human rights of acts of violence committed by armed groups that spread terror among the population, and by drug traffickers, in their forthcoming reports on the situation of human rights in countries where such acts of violence occurred. It also asked the Secretary-General to continue to collect information on the question

and to make it available to the special rapporteurs and working groups concerned.

Reports of the Special Rapporteur. In response to a 1992 Assembly request,[33] the Secretary-General, in September 1993,[34] transmitted a report containing information on mercenary activities covering February to July 1992, prepared by Special Rapporteur Enrique Bernales Ballesteros (Peru). He noted that there had been a growing trend towards recourse to the use of mercenaries, chiefly due to the outbreak of new armed conflicts and to the establishment of new States. He also noted that standard legal procedures were resorted to in order to conceal a mercenary. The Special Rapporteur recommended that the Assembly, among other things, advise States to be more alert to the dangers in tolerating, permitting or acquiescing in the recruitment, hiring and training of mercenaries; ask Member States to adopt domestic legislation prohibiting organizations that traffic in mercenaries; consider establishing a group of experts to determine the criteria for defining the real mercenary status of an individual having dual or multiple nationality or who had benefited from the purported granting of nationality; and call on States that had not yet ratified or acceded to the 1989 Convention to speed up the process of doing so.

In a later report,[35] the Special Rapporteur discussed the use of mercenaries as a means of violating human rights and impeding the exercise of the right of peoples to self-determination. He described his activities during 1993 and correspondence received from Member States concerning mercenary activities. He reported on mercenary activities in Africa, the former Yugoslavia and a number of republics of the former USSR (Armenia, Azerbaijan, Georgia, the Republic of Moldova, Tajikistan) and the consequences for human rights of violent acts committed by armed groups and drug traffickers.

As to the status of the 1989 International Convention,[31] the Special Rapporteur stated that only seven States had become parties to the Convention—Barbados, Cyprus, Maldives, Seychelles, Suriname, Togo and Ukraine; an additional 13 States had signed it—Angola, Belarus, Cameroon, Congo, Germany, Italy, Morocco, Nigeria, Poland, Romania, Uruguay, Yugoslavia and Zaire. The Convention was to enter into force on the thirtieth day following the date of deposit with the Secretary-General of the twenty-second instrument of ratification or accession.

Among recommendations for action by the Commission on Human Rights made by the Special Rapporteur were that it should condemn mercenary activities and consider appointing a working group to evaluate reports and communications on acts of violence committed by armed groups and drug traffickers.

On 20 December, the General Assembly, on the recommendation of the Third Committee, adopted **resolution 48/92** by recorded vote.

Use of mercenaries as a means to violate human rights and to impede the exercise of the right of peoples to self-determination

The General Assembly,

Recalling its resolution 47/84 of 16 December 1992 on the use of mercenaries as a means to violate human rights and to impede the exercise of the right of peoples to self-determination,

Reaffirming the purposes and principles enshrined in the Charter of the United Nations concerning the strict observance of the principles of sovereign equality, political independence, territorial integrity of States and self-determination of peoples,

Urging strict respect for the principle of the non-use or threat of the use of force in international relations, as developed in the Declaration on Principles of International Law concerning Friendly Relations and Cooperation among States in accordance with the Charter of the United Nations,

Reaffirming also the legitimacy of the struggle of peoples and their liberation movements for their independence, territorial integrity, national unity and liberation from colonial domination, apartheid and foreign intervention and occupation, and that their legitimate struggle can in no way be considered as or equated to mercenary activity,

Convinced that the use of mercenaries is a threat to international peace and security,

Deeply concerned about the menace that the activities of mercenaries represent for all States, particularly African and other developing States,

Profoundly alarmed at the continued international criminal activities of mercenaries in collusion with drug traffickers,

Alarmed by the growing linkage observed between mercenary activities and terrorist practices,

Recognizing that the activities of mercenaries are contrary to the fundamental principles of international law, such as non-interference in the internal affairs of States, territorial integrity and independence, and impede the process of the self-determination of peoples struggling against colonialism, racism and apartheid and all forms of foreign domination,

Deeply concerned about the continuing participation of South Africa in mercenary-related activities, as highlighted in the report of the Special Rapporteur of the Commission on Human Rights,

Recalling all of its relevant resolutions, in which, *inter alia,* it condemned any State that permitted or tolerated the recruitment, financing, training, assembly, transit and use of mercenaries with the objective of overthrowing the Governments of States Members of the United Nations, especially those of developing countries, or of fighting against national liberation movements, and recalling also the relevant resolutions of the Security Council, the Economic and Social Council and the Organization of African Unity,

Deeply concerned also about the loss of life, the substantial damage to property and the short-term and long-term negative effects on the economy of southern African countries resulting from mercenary aggression,

Convinced that it is necessary to develop international cooperation among States for the prevention, prosecution and punishment of such offences,

Recalling with satisfaction the adoption of the International Convention against the Recruitment, Use, Financing, and Training of Mercenaries,

1. *Takes note with appreciation* of the report of the Special Rapporteur of the Commission on Human Rights;

2. *Condemns* the continued recruitment, financing, training, assembly, transit and use of mercenaries, as well as all other forms of support to mercenaries, for the purpose of destabilizing and overthrowing the Governments of African States and other developing States and fighting against the national liberation movements of peoples struggling for the exercise of their right to self-determination;

3. *Reaffirms* that the use of mercenaries and their recruitment, financing and training are offences of grave concern to all States and violate the purposes and principles enshrined in the Charter of the United Nations;

4. *Denounces* any State that persists in, permits or tolerates the recruitment of mercenaries and provides facilities to them for launching armed aggression against other States;

5. *Urges* all States to take the necessary steps and to exercise the utmost vigilance against the menace posed by the activities of mercenaries and to ensure, by both administrative and legislative measures, that their territory and other territories under their control, as well as their nationals, are not used for the recruitment, assembly, financing, training and transit of mercenaries or for the planning of activities designed to destabilize or overthrow the Government of any State and to fight the national liberation movements struggling against racism, apartheid, colonial domination and foreign intervention or occupation;

6. *Calls upon* all States to extend humanitarian assistance to victims of situations resulting from the use of mercenaries, as well as from colonial or alien domination or foreign occupation;

7. *Reaffirms* that to use channels of humanitarian and other assistance to finance, train and arm mercenaries is inadmissible;

8. *Calls upon* all States that have not yet done so to consider taking early action to sign or to ratify the International Convention against the Recruitment, Use, Financing and Training of Mercenaries;

9. *Requests* the Centre for Human Rights of the Secretariat to organize, within the framework of its existing resources, working meetings to analyse the philosophical, political and legal aspects of this question, in the light of the recommendations contained in the report of the Special Rapporteur;

10. *Requests* the Special Rapporteur of the Commission on Human Rights to report to the General Assembly at its forty-ninth session on the use of mercenaries, especially in view of the additional elements highlighted in his report.

General Assembly resolution 48/92

20 December 1993   Meeting 85   108-14-39 (recorded vote)

Approved by Third Committee (A/48/626) by recorded vote (100-14-35), 12 November (meeting 32); 12-nation draft (A/C.3/48/L.12), orally revised; agenda item 108 *(a)*.

Sponsors: Angola, Cuba, Ghana, Lesotho, Malawi, Namibia, Nigeria, Uganda, United Republic of Tanzania, Viet Nam, Zambia, Zimbabwe.

Meeting numbers. GA 48th session: 3rd Committee 3-10, 25, 32; plenary 85.

Recorded vote in Assembly as follows:

In favour: Algeria, Angola, Antigua and Barbuda, Bahamas, Bahrain, Bangladesh, Barbados, Belize, Benin, Bhutan, Bolivia, Botswana, Brazil, Brunei Darussalam, Burkina Faso, Burundi, Cambodia, Cameroon, Cape Verde, Central African Republic, Chad, Chile, China, Colombia, Congo, Costa Rica, Côte d'Ivoire, Cuba, Cyprus, Democratic People's Republic of Korea, Djibouti, Dominica, Dominican Republic, Ecuador, Egypt, Ethiopia, Fiji, Gabon, Gambia, Ghana, Guinea, Guinea-Bissau, Guyana, Honduras, India, Indonesia, Iran, Iraq, Jamaica, Jordan, Kenya, Kuwait, Lao People's Democratic Republic, Lebanon, Lesotho, Libyan Arab Jamahiriya, Malawi, Malaysia, Maldives, Mali, Mauritania, Mauritius, Mexico, Mongolia, Morocco, Mozambique, Myanmar, Namibia, Nepal, Nicaragua, Niger, Nigeria, Oman, Pakistan, Panama, Papua New Guinea, Paraguay, Peru, Philippines, Qatar, Republic of Moldova, Rwanda, Saint Lucia, Saint Vincent and the Grenadines, Saudi Arabia, Senegal, Sierra Leone, Singapore, Sri Lanka, Sudan, Suriname, Swaziland, Syrian Arab Republic, Thailand, Togo, Trinidad and Tobago, Tunisia, Uganda, Ukraine, United Arab Emirates, United Republic of Tanzania, Uruguay, Venezuela, Viet Nam, Yemen, Zaire, Zambia, Zimbabwe.

Against: Belgium, Bulgaria, Canada, Czech Republic, France, Germany, Italy, Luxembourg, Monaco, Netherlands, Portugal, Romania, United Kingdom, United States.

Abstaining: Albania, Argentina, Armenia, Australia, Austria, Azerbaijan, Belarus, Croatia, Denmark, Estonia, Finland, Georgia, Greece, Hungary, Iceland, Ireland, Israel, Japan, Kazakhstan, Kyrgyzstan, Latvia, Liechtenstein, Lithuania, Malta, Marshall Islands, Micronesia, New Zealand, Norway, Poland, Republic of Korea, Russian Federation, San Marino, Slovakia, Slovenia, Solomon Islands, Spain, Sweden, the former Yugoslav Republic of Macedonia, Turkey.

Rights of detained persons

Administration of justice

Human Rights Commission action. On 5 March,[36] the Commission called on its subsidiary bodies, including its special rapporteurs and working groups, to give special attention to questions relating to the effective protection of human rights in the administration of justice and to provide specific recommendations, including proposals for possible concrete measures under advisory services programmes. It requested its Subcommission to continue to create a sessional working group on detention to draw up proposals regarding human rights in the administration of justice, and to formulate proposals to the Secretary-General on the utility and format of his reports prepared in pursuance of a 1974 Subcommission resolution.[37] It invited the Commission on Crime Prevention and Criminal Justice (see PART THREE, Chapter XII) to explore ways of cooperating with the human rights programme in the administration of justice.

Also on 5 March,[38] the Commission urged Governments to pay more attention to the needs of institutions concerned with the administration of justice by allocating more resources to them and to strengthen existing national and regional human rights institutions. It appealed to them to include in their national development plans the administration of justice as an integral part of the development process and to allocate adequate resources for the provision of legal aid services to promote and protect human rights. The Commission appealed to the international community to provide assistance for the provision of legal aid services to ensure the promotion, protection and full enjoyment of human rights in African and other developing countries and asked the international community to respond favourably to requests for financial and technical assistance made by institutions concerned with such matters. It urged the Secretary-General to consider favourably applications for assistance by African Member States and other developing countries regarding the creation and strengthening of national institutions concerned with the administration of justice within the framework of the United Nations programme of advisory services and technical cooperation in the field of human rights.

Report of the Secretary-General. As requested by the General Assembly in 1991,[39] the Secretary-General, in November,[40] presented an overview of advisory services and technical assistance, activities of United Nations bodies, dissemination of relevant international instruments and coordination of activities in the area of human rights in the administration of justice. He concluded that United Nations standards should remain the focus of sustained and effective dissemination and technical assistance efforts, particularly through the programme of advisory services and technical assistance of the Centre for Human Rights.

GENERAL ASSEMBLY ACTION

On 20 December, the General Assembly, on the recommendation of the Third Committee, adopted **resolution 48/137** without vote.

Human rights in the administration of justice

The General Assembly,

Recalling its resolution 46/120 of 17 December 1991,

Bearing in mind the principles embodied in articles 3, 5, 9, 10 and 11 of the Universal Declaration of Human Rights and the relevant provisions of the International Covenant on Civil and Political Rights and the Optional Protocols thereto, in particular article 6 of the Covenant, in which it is stated explicitly that no one shall be arbitrarily deprived of his life and prohibits the imposition of the death penalty for crimes committed by persons below eighteen years of age,

Bearing in mind also the relevant principles embodied in the Convention against Torture and Other Cruel, Inhuman or Degrading Treatment or Punishment and in the International Convention on the Elimination of All Forms of Racial Discrimination,

Mindful of the Convention on the Elimination of All Forms of Discrimination against Women, in particular of the obligation of States parties to treat men and women equally in all stages of procedures in courts and tribunals,

Calling attention to the numerous international standards in the field of the administration of justice, such as the Body of Principles for the Protection of All Persons under Any Form of Detention or Imprisonment, the Declaration of Basic Principles of Justice for Victims of Crime and Abuse of Power, the safeguards guaranteeing protection of the rights of those facing the death penalty, the Basic Principles on the Independence of the Judiciary, the Basic Principles on the Role of Lawyers, the Model Agreement on the Transfer of Foreign Prisoners and recommendations on the treatment of foreign prisoners, the Code of Conduct for Law Enforcement Officials, the Basic Principles on the Use of Force and Firearms by Law Enforcement Officials, the Standard Minimum Rules for the Treatment of Prisoners, the Basic Principles for the Treatment of Prisoners, the United Nations Rules for the Protection of Juveniles Deprived of their Liberty, the Guidelines on the Role of Prosecutors, the United Nations Standard Minimum Rules for Non-Custodial Measures (the Tokyo Rules), the United Nations Standard Minimum Rules for the Administration of Juvenile Justice (the Beijing Rules), the Model Treaty on the Transfer of Proceedings in Criminal Matters and the Model Treaty on the Transfer of Supervision of Offenders Conditionally Sentenced or Conditionally Released,

Recalling its resolution 47/133 of 18 December 1992, by which it adopted the Declaration on the Protection of All Persons from Enforced Disappearance,

Welcoming the important work of the Commission on Human Rights and of the Subcommission on Prevention of Discrimination and Protection of Minorities in the field of human rights in the administration of justice, in particular regarding the independence of the judiciary, the independence of judges and lawyers, the right to a fair trial, habeas corpus, human rights and states of emergency, the question of arbitrary detention, the human rights of juveniles in detention, the privatization of prisons and the question of the impunity of perpetrators of violations of human rights,

Taking note of resolution 1993/39 of 26 August 1993 of the Subcommission on Prevention of Discrimination and Protection of Minorities, entitled "Independence of the judiciary",

Welcoming Commission on Human Rights resolutions 1993/32 of 5 March 1993, entitled "The administration of justice and human rights", and 1993/41 of 5 March 1993, entitled "Human rights in the administration of justice",

Welcoming also the important work of the Commission on Crime Prevention and Criminal Justice in the field of human rights in the administration of justice, as reflected in section III of Economic and Social Council resolution 1993/34 of 27 July 1993,

Recognizing that the rule of law and the proper administration of justice are prerequisites for sustainable economic and social development,

Recognizing also the central role of the administration of justice in the promotion and protection of human rights,

Aware of the importance of national and regional intergovernmental human rights bodies and institutions in the promotion and protection of human rights,

Having considered the report of the Secretary-General,

Mindful of the recommendations relating to human rights in the administration of justice contained in the Vienna Declaration and Programme of Action adopted by the World Conference on Human Rights, held at Vienna from 14 to 25 June 1993,

1. *Takes note with appreciation* of the report of the Secretary-General;

2. *Reaffirms* the importance of the full and effective implementation of all United Nations standards on human rights in the administration of justice;

3. *Acknowledges* that it is the primary responsibility of all Governments to promote and protect human rights;

4. *Acknowledges also* that the administration of justice, including law enforcement and prosecutorial agencies and, especially, an independent judiciary and legal profession in full conformity with applicable standards contained in international human rights instruments, are essential to the full and non-discriminatory realization of human rights and indispensable to the processes of democracy and sustainable development;

5. *Once again calls upon* all States to pay due attention to United Nations norms and standards on human rights in the administration of justice in developing national and regional strategies for their practical implementation and to spare no effort in providing for effective legislative and other mechanisms and procedures, as well as for adequate financial resources to ensure more effective implementation of those norms and standards;

6. *Appeals* to Governments to include in their national development plans the administration of justice as an integral part of the development process and to allocate adequate resources for the provision of legal-aid services with a view to the promotion and protection of human rights;

7. *Urges* the Secretary-General to consider favourably requests for assistance by States in the field of the administration of justice within the framework of the United Nations programme of advisory services and technical cooperation in the field of human rights, and to strengthen coordination of activities in this field;

8. *Strongly recommends*, in this context, that the establishment of a comprehensive programme within the system of advisory services and technical assistance be considered in order to help States in the task of building and strengthening adequate national structures that have a direct impact on the overall observance of human rights and the maintenance of the rule of law; such a programme should provide, upon the request of the interested Governments, technical and financial assistance to national projects for the reform of penal and correctional establishments and for the education and training of lawyers, judges and security forces in human rights and in any other sphere of activity relevant to the good functioning of the rule of law;

9. *Acknowledges* that institutions concerned with the administration of justice should be properly funded and that an increased level of both technical and financial assistance should be provided by the international community;

10. *Appeals* to the international community to provide assistance, at the request of the Governments concerned, for the provision of legal-aid services with a view to ensuring the promotion, protection and full enjoyment of human rights;

11. *Invites* the international community to respond favourably to requests for financial and technical assistance made by institutions concerned with the promotion and protection of human rights, with a view to enhancing and strengthening their national capacities to promote and protect human rights consistent with the standards set forth in international and other human rights instruments;

12. *Acknowledges* the important role of the regional commissions, specialized agencies and United Nations institutes in the area of human rights and crime preven-

tion and criminal justice, and of other organizations of the United Nations system, as well as intergovernmental and non-governmental organizations, including national professional associations concerned with promoting United Nations standards in this field;

13. *Invites* the Commission on Crime Prevention and Criminal Justice to pay particular attention to questions relating to the administration of justice, with special emphasis on the effective implementation of norms and standards;

14. *Decides* to consider the question of human rights in the administration of justice at its fiftieth session under the item entitled "Human rights questions".

General Assembly resolution 48/137

20 December 1993   Meeting 85   Adopted without vote

Approved by Third Committee (A/48/632/Add.2) without vote, 6 December (meeting 53); 34-nation draft (A/C.3/48/L.69); agenda item 114 *(b)*.

Sponsors: Albania, Andorra, Argentina, Australia, Austria, Belgium, Canada, Costa Rica, Côte d'Ivoire, Cyprus, Denmark, Ethiopia, Finland, France, Gambia, Germany, Hungary, Iceland, Italy, Lesotho, Liechtenstein, New Zealand, Nicaragua, Nigeria, Norway, Poland, Rwanda, San Marino, Senegal, Slovenia, Spain, Sweden, Uganda, United Republic of Tanzania.

Meeting numbers. GA 48th session: 3rd Committee 36-53; plenary 85.

Treatment of prisoners and detainees

A five-member sessional Working Group on Detention, established by the Subcommission on 3 August,[41] met at Geneva on 5, 9 and 16 August.[42] The Group decided to recommend to the Subcommission that the report of the Secretary-General and the annual synopsis of materials provided by Governments, special agencies and NGOs on the human rights of detained or imprisoned persons, prepared pursuant to a 1974 Subcommission resolution,[37] be discontinued.

On 25 August,[43] the Subcommission decided to stop considering information received pursuant to its 1974 resolution[37] and recommended to the Secretary-General that he no longer issue reports and synopses of material on the subject.

The Working Group on Detention decided to postpone until 1994 examination of *habeas corpus* as a non-derogable right and as one of the requirements for the right to a fair trial, pending consideration by the Subcommission of a 1992 report on the right to a fair trial.[44]

As to the death penalty, the Group recommended that its agenda item should be formulated as: issues related to the deprivation of the right to life, with special reference to imposition of the death penalty on persons under 18 years of age and on the mentally and physically disabled; and questions relating to summary, arbitrary and extrajudicial executions.

In its discussion of juvenile justice, the Group recommended that the Subcommission urge States to make greater efforts to separate adults and juveniles in prisons.

In response to a 1992 Subcommission request,[45] Claire Palley (United Kingdom) was preparing an outline of a study of the privatiza-

tion of prisons. The Group, having heard Ms. Palley's description of her outline, recommended that the Subcommission recommend to the Commission that she be requested to carry out a further special study on the subject. On 5 March,[46] the Commission endorsed the Subcommission's request to Ms. Palley to prepare an outline of the possible utility, scope and structure of a special study on the issue of privatization of prisons and to the Secretary-General to provide her with all the assistance she needed. In June,[47] she submitted the outline to the Subcommission. The Subcommission, on 25 August,[48] requested the Commission to authorize it in 1994 to appoint one of its members to conduct a special study on issues raised in the outline.

In other matters, the Group requested the secretariat to draft a report on coordination between the Centre for Human Rights and the United Nations Crime Prevention and Criminal Justice Branch and decided to consider in 1994 follow-up measures to the 1992 Declaration on the Protection of All Persons from Enforced Disappearance.[49]

Torture and cruel treatment

Report of the Special Rapporteur. Special Rapporteur Peter H. Kooijmans (Netherlands), in his eighth report to the Commission on questions relevant to torture,[50] said that he continued to receive requests for urgent action or information concerning persons who were allegedly being tortured or about whom fears were expressed that they might be. He brought 79 of those cases to the immediate attention of 31 Governments, appealing to them to ensure humane treatment of the persons concerned while in detention. Details on the contents of those appeals and of government replies were given in the report.

The Special Rapporteur reported on his participation in the second mission of the Special Rapporteur on the situation of human rights in the former Yugoslavia in 1992.[51]

The Special Rapporteur made a number of recommendations, some of which were taken up by the Commission in a March resolution.

Human Rights Commission action. On 5 March,[52] the Commission, commending the Special Rapporteur for his report, stressed his conclusions and recommendations concerning: instituting a system of periodic visits by independent experts to places of detention; guaranteeing to detainees by the judiciary their rights in accordance with international and national standards; forbidding illegal incommunicado detention; adopting legal provisions giving a detainee access to legal counsel and the right to initiate promptly after arrest proceedings before a court on the lawfulness of the detention; taking strict measures against members of the medical profession who practised torture; interrogating detainees at official interrogation centres, recording such interrogations and forbidding blindfolding or hooding; and establishing at the national level an independent authority to receive complaints about torture or other maltreatment. It endorsed the recommendation that those responsible for acts of torture should be brought to trial and, if found guilty, severely punished. The Commission called on all States to sign and accede to or ratify the 1984 Convention against Torture and Other Cruel, Inhuman or Degrading Treatment or Punishment.[53] It urged the Secretary-General to make available, as part of the programme of human rights advisory services, qualified experts in law enforcement, detention and medicine to assist Governments in preventing torture. The Commission noted with regret the resignation of the Special Rapporteur and asked the Chairman of the Commission to appoint a replacement. The Secretary-General was asked to provide all the assistance the special rapporteur might require.

In April, the Commission appointed Nigel S. Rodley (United Kingdom) as Special Rapporteur.

Convention against torture

As at 31 December 1993, 79 States had become parties to the 1984 Convention against Torture and Other Cruel, Inhuman and Degrading Treatment or Punishment,[53] nine of them (Antigua and Barbuda, Armenia, Bosnia and Herzegovina, Burundi, Costa Rica, Czech Republic, Morocco, Slovakia and Slovenia) in 1993.[3] The Convention had entered into force in 1987.[54] The optional provisions of articles 21 and 22 (under which a party recognized the competence of the Committee against Torture, set up under the Convention, to receive and consider communications to the effect that a party claimed that another was not fulfilling its obligations under the Convention, and to receive communications from or on behalf of individuals claiming to be victims of a violation of the Convention by a State party) also entered into force in 1987; 34 parties had made the required declarations. The Secretary-General reported on the status of the Convention as at 1 December 1993.[55]

Human Rights Commission action. On 5 March,[56] the Commission urged all States to become parties to the Convention as a matter of priority; it asked all ratifying or acceding States and those States parties that had not done so to consider making the declaration provided for in articles 21 and 22 and to consider withdrawing their reservations to article 20. States parties were encouraged to notify the Secretary-General of their acceptance of the amendments to articles 17 and

18 of the Convention adopted in 1992.[57] The Commission requested the Secretary-General to continue submitting annual reports on the Convention's status and to ensure appropriate staff and facilities for the effective functioning of the Committee against Torture.

Draft optional protocol

Human Rights Commission action. On 5 March,[58] the Commission welcomed progress made by the Working Group to Elaborate a Draft Optional Protocol to the Convention against Torture and Other Cruel, Inhuman or Degrading Treatment or Punishment at its first (1992) session.[57] It asked the Working Group to meet between sessions for a period of two weeks prior to the Commission's 1994 session to continue its work and to report to the Commission. It asked the Secretary-General to transmit the Working Group's report to Governments, specialized agencies, chairmen of the human rights treaty bodies, the Special Rapporteur on the question of torture and intergovernmental organizations and NGOs concerned so that they could submit their observations to the Group. It also asked him to invite Governments, specialized agencies, NGOs, the Chairman of the Committee against Torture and the Special Rapporteur to participate in the Working Group's activities and to extend all the necessary facilities to the Group for its meeting.

Working group activities. The Working Group on the Draft Optional Protocol to the Convention against Torture and Other Cruel, Inhuman or Degrading Treatment or Punishment (Geneva, 25 October–5 November 1993)[59] examined and revised the text of articles 1 to 7 of the draft as submitted by Costa Rica in 1991,[60] completing its first reading of those articles, which it annexed to its report. The Group also considered articles 8 to 19 of the draft.

ECONOMIC AND SOCIAL COUNCIL ACTION

On 28 July, the Economic and Social Council, on the recommendation of its Social Committee, adopted **resolution 1993/46** without vote.

Question of a draft optional protocol to the Convention against Torture and Other Cruel, Inhuman or Degrading Treatment or Punishment

The Economic and Social Council,

Taking note of Commission on Human Rights resolution 1993/34 of 5 March 1993,

1. *Authorizes* the open-ended working group of the Commission on Human Rights to meet for a period of two weeks prior to the fiftieth session of the Commission with a view to continuing the elaboration of the draft optional protocol to the Convention against Torture and Other Cruel, Inhuman or Degrading Treatment or Punishment;

2. *Requests* the Secretary-General to extend to the working group all necessary facilities for its meetings

and to transmit the report of the working group to Governments, the specialized agencies, the chairmen of the human rights treaty bodies, the Special Rapporteur on the question of torture and the intergovernmental and non-governmental organizations concerned.

Economic and Social Council resolution 1993/46

28 July 1993   Meeting 44   Adopted without vote

Approved by Social Committee (E/1993/108) without vote, 22 July (meeting 17); draft by Commission on Human Rights (E/1993/23); agenda item 18.

Committee against Torture

The Committee against Torture, established as a monitoring body under the Convention, held its tenth session at Geneva from 19 to 30 April.[61] It examined reports submitted by Canada, China, Hungary, Panama, Spain and Sweden under article 19 of the Convention.

In eight closed meetings devoted to its activities under article 20, the Committee studied confidential information which appeared to contain well-founded indications that torture was systematically practised in a State party to the Convention. Under article 22, the Committee continued to consider a communication, which was declared admissible in 1992,[62] from an individual claiming to be a victim of violations by a State party. Annexed to the Committee's report was a list of States that had signed, ratified or acceded to the Convention as at 30 April 1993.

An addendum to the Committee's report[63] summarized the results of an inquiry on Turkey, carried out under article 20 of the Convention. The inquiry, which began in 1990 following the receipt of information alleging the systematic practice of torture in Turkey, concluded in 1993. The Committee's conclusions covered legislation enacted in Turkey covering criminal procedures and the treatment of detained persons, allegations received during the inquiry and places of detention.

The Committee noted with satisfaction the cooperation of the Turkish authorities and congratulated them on having acted on many of its recommendations and improved the human rights situation. It remained concerned at the number and substance of allegations of torture, which confirmed the existence and systematic character of the practice of torture in Turkey and expressed the hope that the new Government, formed in June 1993, would take measures to end the practice.

The Committee held its eleventh session, also at Geneva, from 8 to 19 November, examining reports submitted by Cyprus, Ecuador, Egypt, Paraguay, Poland and Portugal. It studied seven communications and adopted its final views on one of them.

By **decision 48/430** of 20 December, the General Assembly, on the recommendation of the Third Committee, took note of the Committee's report on its ninth (1992) and tenth sessions.

On 24 November 1993, the fourth meeting of the States parties to the Convention elected five members of the Committee to replace those whose terms of office would expire on 31 December and to consider the question of the responsibilities of States parties for the expenses referred to in article 17, paragraph 7, and in article 18, paragraph 5, of the Convention. The meeting had before it a November report of the Secretary-General[64] on the status of contributions received from States parties, actual expenditures for the financial periods covering 1987-1992, estimated expenditure for 1993 and anticipated commitments for 1994 and 1995.

Fund for victims of torture

On 5 March,[65] the Commission on Human Rights appealed to Governments, organizations and individuals to contribute to the United Nations Voluntary Fund for Victims of Torture, established in 1981.[66] It called on the Secretary-General to consider arranging a special pledging session for the Fund in the context of the 1993 World Conference on Human Rights (see under "Advancement of human rights") and asked him to transmit to Governments its appeals for contributions, ensure the provision of adequate staff and computer equipment to operate the Fund and inform the Commission annually of the Fund's operations.

In response to a 1992 Commission request,[67] the Secretary-General, by a January note with later addenda[68] submitted a consolidated report on the Fund's activities during the preceding ten years (1982-1992). The note gave amounts of donor contributions and programmes and reflected donor trends. The Secretary-General concluded that, despite limited means and little fund-raising time, the Fund had proven to be a useful tool in assisting torture victims and their families.

By the same note, the Secretary-General transmitted the text of the Istanbul Declaration adopted by the International Rehabilitation Council for Torture Victims, issued following a 1992 symposium organized by the Rehabilitation and Research Centre for Torture Victims (Denmark) and the Human Rights Foundation of Turkey and the Turkish Medical Association, which appealed for an increase in national governments' contributions to the Fund from $1.6 million in 1992 to $25 million in 1995 and at least $100 million in 1999.

In his annual report to the Assembly on the status of the Fund,[69] the Secretary-General stated that, at its twelfth session (Geneva, 19-28 April), the Fund's Board of Trustees recommended approval of grants for 67 projects in 50 countries in the amount of $2,111,880. The projects recommended by the Board focused on supporting programmes providing direct medical, psychological, social and other assistance to torture victims and their families. The Board also recommended four new guidelines dealing with applications for grants, the reporting procedure, pledges, refunding grants, termination of projects and established channels of assistance, which were annexed to the Secretary-General's report.

During 1993, the Fund received $1,892,630 from 25 States. Contributions were also received from a number of individuals.

By **decision 48/430** of 20 December, the Assembly took note of the Secretary-General's annual report.

Detention of juveniles

Human Rights Commission action. On 10 March,[70] the Commission welcomed a 1992 proposal by the Secretary-General[71] to organize in 1994 a meeting of experts on the application of international standards concerning the human rights of detained juveniles. It endorsed the Subcommission's 1992 request to the Secretary-General to provide all necessary assistance for the meeting[72] and asked him to report on the meeting's results.

On 28 July, the Economic and Social Council, by **decision 1993/280**, approved both the Secretary-General's proposal to organize a meeting of experts and the representation of the Committee on the Rights of the Child, the Working Group on Contemporary Forms of Slavery and the Working Group on Detention at the meeting. It also approved the Commission's endorsement of the Subcommission's request to the Secretary-General to provide all necessary assistance for the meeting.

Note by the Secretary-General. By a June note,[73] the Secretary-General reported on progress in arranging the meeting.

Subcommission action. On 25 August,[74] the Subcommission requested the Secretary-General to provide all necessary assistance for the meeting and asked him to report on its results.

Detention without charge or trial

Human Rights Commission action. On 5 March,[75] the Commission asked the Working Group on Arbitrary Detention, created in 1991[76] for a three-year period, to investigate cases of detention imposed arbitrarily or otherwise inconsistently with the international standards set forth in the 1948 Universal Declaration of Human Rights[77] or in relevant international legal instruments. The Commission considered that the Group, within its mandate, could take up cases on its own initiative. It asked the Group to report in 1994 on its activities and to make suggestions and recommendations to enable it better to carry out its task. The Commission asked the Group to continue to seek information from Governments, in-

tergovernmental organizations, NGOs and individuals concerned or their representatives. The Secretary-General was requested to assist the Group, particularly with regard to staffing and appropriate resources to discharge its mandate, including the organization, carrying out and follow-up of missions in countries wishing to invite the Group. The request to the Secretary-General was approved by the Economic and Social Council on 28 July by **decision 1993/264**.

Working Group activities. The Working Group on Arbitrary Detention held three sessions at Geneva in 1993 (26-30 April, 27 September–1 October, 1-10 December).[78] The activities of the five-member group of independent experts consisted of transmitting letters to the Governments of countries where cases of alleged arbitrary detention were reported to have occurred, asking them to make inquiries and inform the Group of the results within 90 days. The Group sent communications to 32 countries concerning 183 cases of arbitrary detention, to which 15 countries replied. In addition, the Group received five replies to letters transmitted prior to 1993. The Group also addressed 17 urgent-action appeals to 14 countries. Most of these concerned cases of alleged arbitrary detention which had endangered the health or life of the detainees.

The Group stated that timely and comprehensive information from Governments was the main factor in the success of the Group's work and appealed to Governments that maintained states of emergency for long periods to limit their use. It recommended strengthening *habeas corpus* and recommended that the Commission on Human Rights support its Subcommission's efforts to elaborate a declaration on *habeas corpus* with a view to arriving at an additional protocol to the 1966 International Covenant on Civil and Political Rights (see below).[1] Annexed to the report were the Group's methods of work, as revised in December, and decisions adopted by the Group concerning communications transmitted in 1992 and 1993.

Detained UN staff members

Report of the Secretary-General. The Secretary-General submitted to the Commission a report updating developments pertaining to the detention of international civil servants and their families.[79] Annexed to the report was a consolidated list of staff members under arrest and detention or missing.

Human Rights Commission action. On 5 March,[80] the Commission appealed to Member States to respect and ensure respect for the rights of staff members and others acting under United Nations authority and their families, and urged them, in accordance with the 1988 Body of Principles for the Protection of All Persons under Any Form of Detention or Imprisonment,[81] to provide adequate and prompt information concerning their arrest or detention. It further urged Member States to allow medical teams to investigate the health of detained staff members, experts and their families in order to provide them with medical treatment, and called on them to allow representatives of international organizations to attend hearings. It asked the Secretary-General to continue to ensure that the human rights, privileges and immunities of United Nations staff members, experts and their families were fully respected and to seek compensation for damage suffered, as well as their full reintegration. It also asked him to take steps to ensure the application of the recommendations contained in the final report of the Special Rapporteur on the protection of the human rights of United Nations staff members, experts and their families[72] and to submit in 1994 an updated report on the situation of United Nations staff members, experts and their families detained, imprisoned, missing or held in a country against their will, including those cases that had been successfully settled since his last report.[82]

Extra-legal executions

The Commission on Human Rights had before it the first report submitted by its new Special Rapporteur on summary or arbitrary executions, Bacre Waly Ndiaye (Senegal).[83] He addressed a series of issues related to his mandate and described urgent appeals and other communications transmitted to Governments, together with any replies or observations received from them. There were grounds, the Special Rapporteur stated, for believing that armed conflicts and political violence had resulted in an increase in violations of the right to life. He expressed concern at the high number of allegations concerning violations of the right to life in the context of violence against participants in demonstrations and other public manifestations, journalists and members of trade unions or political movements.

The Special Rapporteur made recommendations concerning: violations of the right to life in connection with the death penalty; deaths in custody; deaths due to use of force by law enforcement officials; violations of the right to life during armed conflicts; expulsion of persons to a country where their life was in danger; genocide; and victims' rights.

In August,[84] the Special Rapporteur submitted a report on his visit to Rwanda (8-17 April) where he investigated allegations of grave and massive violations of the right to life in the context of an armed conflict between Rwandese Government forces and the armed opposition movement, the Rwandese Patriotic Front.

From 24 May to 2 June, he had visited Peru to look into allegations of violations of the right to life there.[85]

Human Rights Commission action. On 10 March,[86] the Commission, strongly condemning the large number of extrajudicial, summary or arbitrary executions taking place, appealed to Governments, United Nations bodies, specialized agencies, intergovernmental organizations and NGOs to take action to combat and eliminate them. It welcomed the appointment of the new Special Rapporteur for extrajudicial, summary or arbitrary executions and requested him to continue examining such executions, to pay special attention to executions of children and allegations concerning violations of the right to life in the context of violence against participants in demonstrations, and to respond to information he received, particularly when a summary or arbitrary execution was imminent or threatened or when such an execution had occurred. The Commission asked the Secretary-General to provide assistance to the Special Rapporteur and to consider ways to publicize his work and recommendations. It urged Governments to cooperate with and assist the Special Rapporteur and to take measures to lower the level of violence and needless loss of life during situations of internal violence, disturbances, tensions and public emergency.

Disappearance of persons

Human Rights Commission action. On 5 March,[87] the Commission requested the Working Group on Enforced or Involuntary Disappearances to submit all information it deemed necessary and any specific recommendations it might have regarding the fulfilment of its task; pay attention to cases of children subjected to enforced disappearance and children of disappeared persons; take account of the provisions of the Declaration on the Protection of All Persons from Enforced Disappearances;[49] and modify its working methods if necessary. The Commission encouraged Governments concerned to consider inviting the Group to visit their countries and asked the Secretary-General to ensure that the Group received all necessary assistance, in particular staff and resources, especially in carrying out missions and holding sessions in countries prepared to receive it. It further asked him to inform the Group of steps he had taken to secure the widespread dissemination and promotion of the Declaration.

Also on 5 March,[88] the Commission, noting the proposed model autopsy protocol prepared under United Nations auspices,[89] asked the Secretary-General to consult with Governments, United Nations bodies, professional organizations of forensic experts, and other interested institutions to identify experts who could join forensic teams or provide advice or assistance to thematic or country mechanisms, advisory services and technical assistance programmes. It also requested him to establish a list of forensic experts and experts in related fields and to make that list available to special rapporteurs and human rights experts so that they might request the forensic experts to assist them in evaluating documents and other evidence and to accompany them on country visits. The Commission further asked the Secretary-General to inform it in 1994 of progress made.

On 9 March,[90] the Commission, commending Governments that had invited any of the thematic special rapporteurs or the Working Group on Enforced or Involuntary Disappearances to visit their countries, encouraged them to respond expeditiously to requests for information. It invited Governments to study carefully the recommendations addressed to them under the thematic procedures and to keep the relevant mechanisms informed on progress made in implementing them. The Commission requested special rapporteurs and working groups to include in their reports gender-disaggregated data, as well as comments on problems of responding and the results of analyses. It asked the Secretary-General to consider convening a meeting of all thematic special rapporteurs and working group Chairmen to enable an exchange of views and closer cooperation; to issue annually the conclusions and recommendations of special rapporteurs and working groups; and to ensure the availability of resources for effective implementation of all thematic mandates.

Report of the Secretary-General. In a February report,[91] the Secretary-General described the activities of forensic scientists that helped to combat human rights violations and reported on consultations conducted by the Working Group on Enforced or Involuntary Disappearances with organizations concerned with forensic science and human rights. He stated that the Working Group had elaborated a preliminary scheme consisting of: maintaining a list of experienced organizations in human rights and forensic science; the designation of experts by the organizations; establishing three types of programmes for forensic activities, including programmes requested by Governments, programmes initiated at the request of special rapporteurs, working groups or other United Nations organs, and programmes requested by NGOs; and granting experts the legal status of experts on mission in accordance with the 1946 Convention on the Privileges and Immunities of the United Nations.[92] Recommendations for further activities included consultations with NGOs experienced in human rights and forensic science

and studying various legal and practical issues in detail. Annexed to the report was the text of a cooperation service agreement between the United Nations and Physicians for Human Rights, a United States-based NGO.

Working Group activities. The five-member Working Group on Enforced or Involuntary Disappearances, established in 1980,[93] held three sessions in 1993: its thirty-ninth in New York (17-21 May) and its fortieth and forty-first at Geneva (24 September–1 October and 24 November–3 December).[94] The Group examined information on enforced or involuntary disappearances received from Governments and NGOs.

A member of the Group carried out a mission to parts of the territory of the former Yugoslavia (4-13 August) to determine how the problem of disappearances there could best be approached,[95] and recommended that the special process should be entrusted to the Special Rapporteur on the situation of human rights in the former Yugoslavia in a joint mandate with a member of the Group, resulting in joint annual reports to the Commission on Human Rights and, possibly, the General Assembly. The total number of reports of enforced or involuntary disappearances received from the former Yugoslavia numbered 11,103. (For further details, see below, under "Human rights violations".)

In 1993, the total number of cases worldwide being kept under active consideration stood at 33,843. The Group continued to process a backlog of some 2,639 reports submitted in 1991 and received some 5,523 new reports of disappearances in 30 countries. It transmitted 3,162 newly reported cases to the Governments concerned, of which some 523 were received in 1993, while the rest were part of the backlog. It also transmitted to Governments 151 cases under its urgent-action procedure, of which 18 were clarified during the year.

The Group concluded that the phenomenon of disappearances was still rampant and that the policy and practice of many States ran counter to the provisions of the Declaration on the Protection of All Persons from Enforced Disappearances.[49] It noted, however, that cooperation with most Governments was improving. The Group appealed for increased human resources to carry out its mandate effectively.

Annexed to the Group's report was a list of new NGOs that had contacted the Group and graphs showing the development of disappearances during the period 1973-1992 in countries with more than 50 transmitted cases.

By **decision 1993/263** of 28 July, the Economic and Social Council approved the Commission's request to the Secretary-General to establish a list of forensic experts and experts in related fields who could provide advice in regard to the monitoring of human rights violations and training of local teams and/or assistance in the reunification of families of the disappeared. It also approved the Commission's request that the Secretary-General provide resources to fund Centre for Human Rights activities to implement the Commission's resolution on human rights and forensic science.[88]

Other aspects of civil and political rights

Slavery

Working Group activities. The Subcommission's five-member Working Group on Contemporary Forms of Slavery, at its eighteenth session (Geneva, 17-27 May),[96] focused on the training of law enforcement officials and police, economic development programmes, information campaigns, education programmes for children in danger, new forms of legislation, rehabilitation measures and the protection of working children. It also considered the Programme of Action for the Prevention of the Sale of Children, Child Prostitution and Child Pornography[97] and the mandate of the Special Rapporteur on the sale of children, child prostitution and child pornography (see below, under "Other human rights questions") and reviewed developments in other contemporary forms of slavery, including slavery and the slave trade, debt bondage, forced labour and exploitation and traffic affecting children, including child soldiers and illegal traffic for the purposes of adoption and organ transplants, and incest.

Human Rights Commission action. On 5 March,[98] the Commission asked the Secretary-General to invite States parties to the 1926 Slavery Convention, the 1956 Supplementary Convention on the Abolition of Slavery, the Slave Trade, and Institutions and Practices Similar to Slavery,[99] and the 1949 Convention for the Suppression of the Traffic in Persons and of the Exploitation of the Prostitution of Others[100] to submit regular reports to the Subcommission on the situation in their countries. It invited States that had not ratified the relevant Conventions to do so, or to explain in writing why they felt unable to. Intergovernmental organizations, relevant United Nations organizations and NGOs were asked to supply information to the Working Group on Contemporary Forms of Slavery. The Commission encouraged its Subcommission to elaborate recommendations on ways to establish an effective mechanism to implement the slavery Conventions on the basis of a 1989 study by the Secretary-General.[101] It asked the Secretary-General to designate the Centre for Human Rights as the focal point for coordinating United Nations activities to suppress contemporary forms of slavery and

to report in 1994 on measures taken to that end. It asked the Special Rapporteur on the sale of children to examine ways of cooperating with the Working Group and asked Governments to pursue a policy of information, prevention and rehabilitation of women victims of prostitution and to take appropriate economic and social measures to that effect. The Secretary-General was to report to the Economic and Social Council on steps taken to implement a 1983 Council resolution on suppression of the traffic in persons and of the exploitation of the prostitution of others.[102]

On 10 March,[103] the Commission approved a number of requests made by its Subcommission in 1992 pertaining to organizational matters of the Working Group.

Subcommission action. On 20 August, the Subcommission adopted a resolution concerning matters considered by the Working Group,[104] another on additional assistance in studying ways of resolving problems arising from slavery[105] and a third on the Group's mandate.[106]

Report of the Secretary-General. In response to a 1992 Economic and Social Council request,[107] the Secretary-General submitted a May 1993 report summarizing information from 12 Governments, two specialized agencies, one regional commission and two other United Nations bodies on the suppression of traffic in persons and of the exploitation of the prostitution of others.[108]

ECONOMIC AND SOCIAL COUNCIL ACTION

On 28 July, on the recommendation of its Social Committee, the Economic and Social Council adopted **resolution 1993/48** without vote.

Suppression of the traffic in persons
The Economic and Social Council,
Recalling Commission on Human Rights resolution 1982/20 of 10 March 1982 on the question of slavery and the slave trade in all their practices and manifestations, including the slavery-like practices of apartheid and colonialism, 1988/42 of 8 March 1988, 1989/35 of 6 March 1989, 1990/63 of 7 March 1990, 1991/58 of 6 March 1991 and 1992/47 of 3 March 1992 on the report of the Working Group on Contemporary Forms of Slavery of the Subcommission on Prevention of Discrimination and Protection of Minorities, taking note of Commission resolution 1993/27 of 5 March 1993 and decision 1993/112 of 10 March 1993, also on the report of the Working Group, and recalling Commission resolution 1992/74 of 5 March 1992 on programmes of action for the prevention of the sale of children, child prostitution and child pornography and for the elimination of the exploitation of child labour,
Recalling also Council resolutions 1982/20 of 4 May 1982 and 1983/30 of 26 May 1983 on the suppression of the traffic in persons and of the exploitation of the prostitution of others, 1988/34 of 27 May 1988 and 1989/74 of 24 May 1989 on the Working Group, and 1990/46 of 25 May 1990, 1991/35 of 31 May 1991 and 1992/10 of 20 July 1992 on the suppression of the traffic in persons,

Recalling further Commission on Human Rights resolution 1992/36 of 28 February 1992 on a draft programme of action for the prevention of traffic in persons and the exploitation of the prostitution of others,

Considering that the report of the Special Rapporteur of the Economic and Social Council on the suppression of the traffic in persons and the exploitation of the prostitution of others still constitutes a useful basis for further action,

Having examined the report of the Secretary-General on the implementation of Council resolution 1983/30 on the suppression of the traffic in persons and of the exploitation of the prostitution of others,

Noting that only a few Member States, United Nations organizations and other intergovernmental organizations have submitted information on the steps taken to implement the recommendations contained in Council resolution 1983/30,

Gravely concerned that slavery, the slave trade and slavery-like practices still exist, that there are modern manifestations of those phenomena and that such practices represent some of the gravest violations of human rights,

Convinced that the United Nations Trust Fund on Contemporary Forms of Slavery will play an important role in the protection of the human rights of victims of contemporary forms of slavery,

Aware of the complexity of the issue of the suppression of the traffic in persons and the exploitation of the prostitution of others, and the need for further coordination and cooperation to implement the recommendations made by the Special Rapporteur and by various United Nations bodies,

Sharing the grave concern, expressed by the Commission on Human Rights in paragraph 2 of its resolution 1993/27, at manifestations of contemporary forms of slavery as reported to the Working Group,

Mindful of the resolutions on violence against women, adopted by the Commission on Human Rights, the Commission on the Status of Women and the Commission on Crime Prevention and Criminal Justice,

Welcoming the determined stance taken in the Vienna Declaration and Programme of Action adopted by the World Conference on Human Rights held at Vienna from 14 to 25 June 1993 against gender-based violence and all forms of sexual harassment and exploitation, including those resulting from cultural prejudice and international trafficking and the pertinent reference made in that Declaration to legal measures, national action and international cooperation in such fields as economic and social development, education, safe maternity and health care, and social support,

1. *Reminds* States parties to the Slavery Convention of 1926, the Supplementary Convention on the Abolition of Slavery, the Slave Trade and Institutions and Practices Similar to Slavery of 1956, and the Convention for the Suppression of the Traffic in Persons and of the Exploitation of the Prostitution of Others of 1949 that they should submit to the Working Group on Contemporary Forms of Slavery of the Subcommission on Prevention of Discrimination and Protection of Minorities regular reports on the situation in their countries, as provided for under the relevant conventions and under Council decision 16(LVI) of 17 May 1974;

2. *Takes note with appreciation* of the report of the Secretary-General on the implementation of Council resolution 1983/30 on the suppression of the traffic in

persons and of the exploitation of the prostitution of others;

3. *Requests* the Secretary-General to submit a further report to the Council, at its substantive session of 1994, on the steps taken to implement the recommendations contained in Council resolution 1983/30 by those Member States, United Nations organizations and other intergovernmental organizations which have not yet submitted such information and to make that report available to the Working Group;

4. *Also requests* the Secretary-General to continue to include in the abovementioned report, or to make available to the Council in some way, information on activities of the supervisory bodies of the International Labour Organisation regarding the implementation of provisions and standards designed to ensure the protection of children and other persons exposed to contemporary forms of slavery;

5. *Takes note* in this connection of the information on activities of the supervisory bodies of the International Labour Organisation regarding the implementation of provisions and standards designed to ensure the protection of children and other persons exposed to contemporary forms of slavery;

6. *Requests* the Secretary-General to include in the abovementioned report information on any operational activities of the United Nations system that can foster the implementation of standards designed to ensure the protection of children and other persons exposed to contemporary forms of slavery and activities that might be geared to the prevention of violations and alleviation of the plight, or rehabilitation, of victims;

7. *Also requests* the Secretary-General to include in the abovementioned report information on the matter of the close collaboration of the Commission on the Status of Women and the Commission on Crime Prevention and Criminal Justice with the Centre for Human Rights of the Secretariat on the issue of the suppression of contemporary forms of slavery;

8. *Urges* the Secretary-General to ensure effective servicing of the Working Group and of other activities related to the suppression of contemporary forms of slavery and slavery-like practices, and requests him to report to the Council at its substantive session of 1994 on the steps taken in that regard;

9. *Reiterates its request* to the Secretary-General to designate the Centre for Human Rights as the focal point for the coordination of activities in the United Nations for the suppression of contemporary forms of slavery, and requests the Secretary-General to report on the follow-up to this request;

10. *Urges* the Commission on the Status of Women and the Commission on Crime Prevention and Criminal Justice to collaborate closely with the Centre for Human Rights on the issue of the suppression of contemporary forms of slavery;

11. *Welcomes* the establishment of the United Nations Trust Fund on Contemporary Forms of Slavery;

12. *Approves* the endorsement by the Commission on Human Rights in its resolution 1993/27 of the recommendation made by the Subcommission on Prevention of Discrimination and Protection of Minorities, in its resolution 1992/2 of 14 August 1992, that the arrangements regarding the organization of the sessions of the Working Group, as contained in Commission decision

1992/115 of 3 March 1992, should be repeated in subsequent years;

13. *Welcomes* Commission on Human Rights decision 1993/112 to authorize the Subcommission to consider the possibility of appointing a special rapporteur to update the report of the Special Rapporteur on the exploitation of child labour, Mr. Abdelwahab Bouhdiba;

14. *Concurs* with the Centre for Social Development and Humanitarian Affairs of the Secretariat in its assessment of the relevance of the United Nations Guidelines for the Prevention of Juvenile Delinquency (The Riyadh Guidelines) contained in the annex to General Assembly resolution 45/112 of 14 December 1990;

15. *Decides* to consider the question of the suppression of the traffic in persons at its substantive session of 1994 under the item entitled "Human rights questions".

Economic and Social Council resolution 1993/48

28 July 1993   Meeting 44   Adopted without vote

Approved by Social Committee (E/1993/108) without vote, 22 July (meeting 17); 18-nation draft (E/1993/C.2/L.4); agenda item 18.
Sponsors: Belgium, Czech Republic, Ecuador, Finland, Ireland, Morocco, Netherlands, Nigeria, Norway, Peru, Philippines, Poland, Romania, Russian Federation, Senegal, Slovakia, Uruguay, Venezuela.

Sexual exploitation of women during wartime

Subcommission action. On 25 August,[109] the Subcommission decided to entrust Linda Chavez (United States), as Special Rapporteur, with undertaking an in-depth study on the situation of systematic rape, sexual slavery and slavery-like practices during wartime, including internal armed conflict. It asked her to submit a preliminary report.

Report of the Special Rapporteur. In September,[110] the Special Rapporteur submitted a preparatory document on systematic rape, sexual slavery and slavery-like practices during wartime, presenting background information for the in-depth study, the object of the study and its outline. (For information on rape and abuse of women in the territory of the former Yugoslavia, see below under "Human rights violations".)

UN Voluntary Trust Fund on Contemporary Forms of Slavery

On 5 March,[111] the Commission on Human Rights welcomed the Secretary-General's appointment of a Board of Trustees of the United Nations Voluntary Trust Fund on Contemporary Forms of Slavery, established by the General Assembly in 1991,[112] and asked him to assist the Board in its efforts to make the Fund and its humanitarian work better known. It appealed to Governments, organizations and individuals to respond favourably to requests for contributions to the Fund and asked the Secretary-General to transmit its appeal to all Governments.

Freedom of movement

Population transfer

Human Rights Commission action. On 4 March,[113] the Commission, by a vote of 48 to 1, endorsed the Subcommission's 1992 decision[114] to entrust Special Rapporteurs Awn Shawkat Al-Khasawneh (Jordan) and Ribot Hatano (Japan) with preparing a preliminary study, for submission in 1993, on the human rights dimensions of population transfer and its request to the Secretary-General to give them all the assistance they required. The Commission's endorsements were approved by the Economic and Social Council by **decision 1993/288** of 28 July.

Report of the Special Rapporteurs. In July,[115] the Special Rapporteurs on the human rights dimensions of population transfer, including the implantation of settlers, described the circumstances under which population transfers occurred as well as their cumulative effects and listed applicable international standards and regional human rights instruments and bilateral population exchange agreements and treaties. The Special Rapporteurs recommended that a specific legal instrument should clarify that population transfer was, *prima facie*, unlawful and elaborate the circumstances under which, in exceptional cases, population transfer would be permitted. They made a number of recommendations, several of which were incorporated into a Subcommission resolution.

Subcommission action. On 25 August,[116] the Subcommission endorsed the preliminary report's conclusions and recommendations. Regretting the inability of Special Rapporteur Hatano to continue his duties, it asked Special Rapporteur Awn Shawkat Al-Khasawneh to continue the study on population transfer and to submit a progress report in 1994. The Subcommission asked the Commission to request the Secretary-General to organize an expert seminar in 1995 and to ask the Special Rapporteur to undertake on-site visits to diverse, ongoing cases of population transfer. It requested the Secretary-General to invite Governments, United Nations bodies and intergovernmental organizations and NGOs to provide the Special Rapporteur with relevant information and to provide him with all the assistance he might require.

Freedom of speech

Human Rights Commission action. On 5 March,[117] expressing concern at the extensive occurrence of detention of persons exercising their right to freedom of opinion and expression, the Commission appealed to States to ensure respect and support for that right. It also appealed to them to ensure that persons seeking to exercise those rights and freedoms were not discriminated against or harassed, in areas such as employment, housing and social services. It asked its Chairman to appoint for three years a special rapporteur on the right to freedom of opinion and expression and asked the Secretary-General to provide all the assistance he or she might require. It asked the Special Rapporteur to note the relevant work being carried out in the specialized agencies and other United Nations organizations and to submit a report in 1994.

On 28 July, the Economic and Social Council, by **decision 1993/268**, approved the appointment of a special rapporteur, the request to the Secretary-General to assist him or her and the request to the Special Rapporteur to submit a report in 1994.

The Commission's Chairman appointed Mr. A. Hussain (India) as Special Rapporteur on the rights to freedom of opinion and expression.

Cooperation with UN human rights bodies

Report of the Secretary-General. In February 1993,[118] the Secretary-General, in response to a 1992 Commission request,[119] provided information on specific cases in which persons alleged that they had suffered reprisals for availing or attempting to avail themselves of United Nations human rights procedures or had been subjected to intimidation to prevent them from doing so. He also described decisions and measures taken by United Nations policy-making organs in that regard. Annexed to the report were allegations of intimidation and reprisal received and processed by United Nations human rights bodies.

Human Rights Commission action. On 10 March,[120] the Commission urged Governments to refrain from acts of intimidation or reprisal against individuals or groups seeking access to United Nations human rights bodies. It requested representatives of those bodies and treaty bodies monitoring the observance of human rights to help prevent the hampering of access to United Nations human rights procedures and to continue to take urgent steps to prevent the occurrence of intimidation or reprisal. It also requested them to include in their reports a reference to allegations of intimidation or reprisal, as well as an account of action taken by them. It asked the Secretary-General to report in 1994.

Conscientious objectors

Report of the Secretary-General. In January,[121] the Secretary-General summarized replies from 24 Governments and one NGO received in accordance with a 1991 Commission request[122] for comments or information on conscientious objection to military service.

Human Rights Commission action. On 10 March,[123] the Commission requested the Secretary-General to report in 1995 on conscientious objection to military service, taking into account comments by Governments and further information received by him.

Amnesty

Human Rights Commission action. On 5 March,[124] the Commission endorsed a 1992 Subcommission decision[119] to entrust Special Rapporteurs El Hadji Guissé (Senegal) and Louis Joinet (France) with drafting a study on the question of impunity of perpetrators of human rights violations and asked the Secretary-General to provide the Special Rapporteurs with any assistance they might require.

The Economic and Social Council, by **decision 1993/266** of 28 July, approved the Commission's endorsement and its request to the Secretary-General.

Report of the Special Rapporteurs. As requested by the Subcommission in 1992,[119] the Special Rapporteurs submitted a progress report on the question of impunity of perpetrators of serious human rights violations.[125] They recommended that ways to eradicate the practice of death squads be studied; guidelines for implementing national reconciliation policies drawn up; NGOs given a greater role in a strategy for combating impunity; comparative study of various experiences of truth-finding commissions undertaken; guidelines for conserving and regulating access to the files and records of the security and intelligence services drawn up; a study on the scope of the right of every person to a hearing prepared; and a comparative analysis of various purging policies carried out.

Subcommission action. On 26 August,[126] the Subcommission requested the Special Rapporteurs to submit a report in 1994 on the question of impunity for perpetrators of violations of civil and political rights and to continue their study on perpetrators of violations of economic and social rights. It asked the Secretary-General to provide the Special Rapporteurs with any assistance they might need.

Independence of the judicial system

Human Rights Commission action. On 5 March,[127] the Commission endorsed the Subcommission's 1992 decision[119] to entrust Louis Joinet with preparing a report on practices and measures which had served to strengthen or weaken the independence of the judiciary and on the protection of members of the legal profession. It requested the Secretary-General to provide Mr. Joinet with all the assistance necessary to prepare the report.

By **decision 1993/267** of 28 July, the Economic and Social Council approved the Commission's endorsement and request.

Report of the Special Rapporteur. In July, Special Rapporteur Joinet presented information collected from 25 States on measures they had taken to strengthen the safeguards of independence and protection of judges and lawyers and analysed advisory services and technical assistance programmes in that area.[128] He also examined cases of measures and practices that had weakened those safeguards, based on information received from 17 States. The Special Rapporteur discussed cooperation between the United Nations Crime Prevention and Criminal Justice Programme and the United Nations human rights programme and the establishment of a monitoring mechanism for reviewing the independence and impartiality of the judiciary.

Subcommission action. On 28 August,[129] the Subcommission recommended that the Commission create a monitoring mechanism in the form of a special rapporteur to follow up the question of the independence and impartiality of the judiciary. It asked the Secretary-General to provide the special rapporteur with the assistance he or she might need.

Right to a fair trial

Human Rights Commission action. On 5 March,[130] the Commission decided to endorse a 1992 request of the Subcommission[131] to two Special Rapporteurs to continue their study on the right to a fair trial.

On 28 July, the Economic and Social Council, by **decision 1993/290**, approved the Commission's endorsement of the Subcommission's request.

Report of the Special Rapporteurs. In June,[132] Special Rapporteurs Stanislav Chernichenko (Russian Federation) and William Treat (United States) submitted their fourth report on the right to a fair trial, in which they recommended the development of a third optional protocol to the 1966 International Covenant on Civil and Political Rights,[1] aiming at guaranteeing under all circumstances the right to a fair trial and a remedy. A preliminary draft of the optional protocol was annexed to their report, as was a supplemental bibliography of relevant material. In separate addenda, the Special Rapporteurs submitted a resolution and draft declaration on the right to a fair trial and a remedy for future discussion by the Subcommission[133] and a summary of information received from NGOs and bar associations concerning national laws and practices relating to the right to a fair trial.[134].

Subcommission action. On 25 August,[135] the Subcommission asked the Special Rapporteurs to submit in 1994 a final report, including recommendations for strengthening the implementation of the right to a fair trial, together with a draft optional protocol to the International Covenant on Civil and Political Rights[1] and to consider elaborating a draft

declaration or body of principles on the right to a fair trial and a remedy. It asked the Secretary-General to transmit the draft third optional protocol to Governments, NGOs and the Human Rights Committee for comments and suggestions. The Subcommission decided to consider in 1994 the advisability of elaborating a third optional protocol to the Covenant and other recommendations of the Special Rapporteurs.

REFERENCES

[1]YUN 1966, p. 423, GA res. 2200 A (XXI), annex, 16 Dec. 1966. [2]YUN 1976, p. 609. [3]*Multilateral Treaties Deposited with the Secretary-General: Status as at 31 December 1993* (ST/LEG/SER.E/12), Sales No. E.94.V.11. [4]GA res. 44/128, annex, 15 Dec. 1989. [5]YUN 1991, p. 544. [6]E/CN.4/1994/67. [7]E/1993/23 (res. 1993/15). [8]A/48/40. [9]A/49/40. [10]E/1993/23 (res. 1993/42). [11]YUN 1992, p. 727. [12]E/CN.4/Sub.2/1993/23. [13]YUN 1987, p. 741. [14]YUN 1988, p. 499. [15]E/CN.4/Sub.2/1989/30/Rev.2. [16]YUN 1991, p. 545. [17]E/CN.4/1994/2 (res. 1993/28). [18]E/CN.4/Sub.2/1993/23/Rev.1. [19]E/CN.4/1994/32. [20]E/1993/23 (res. 1993/6). [21]Ibid. (res. 1993/4). [22]Ibid. (res. 1993/17). [23]Ibid. (res. 1993/5). [24]A/48/384. [25]YUN 1992, pp. 727 & 728, GA res. 47/83 & 47/82, 16 Dec. 1992. [26]E/CN.4/1994/2 (res. 1993/15). [27]YUN 1992, p. 731. [28]E/CN.4/1993/17. [29]YUN 1992, p. 963. [30]YUN 1991, p. 793. [31]GA res. 44/34, annex, 4 Dec. 1989. [32]E/1993/23 (res. 1993/48). [33]YUN 1992, p. 733, GA res. 47/84, 16 Dec. 1992. [34]A/48/385. [35]E/CN.4/1994/23. [36]E/1993/23 (res. 1993/41). [37]YUN 1974, p. 676. [38]E/1993/23 (res. 1993/32). [39]YUN 1991, p. 553, GA res. 46/120, 17 Dec. 1991. [40]A/48/575. [41]E/CN.4/1994/2 (dec. 1993/103). [42]E/CN.4/Sub.2/1993/22 & Corr.1-3. [43]E/CN.4/1994/2 (res. 1993/25). [44]YUN 1992, p. 751. [45]YUN 1992, p. 734. [46]E/1993/23 (dec. 1993/108). [47]E/CN.4/Sub.2/1993/21. [48]E/CN.4/1994/2 (dec. 1993/109). [49]YUN 1992, p. 744, GA res. 47/133, 18 Dec. 1992. [50]E/CN.4/1993/26. [51]YUN 1992, p. 797. [52]E/1993/23 (res. 1993/40). [53]YUN 1984, p. 813, GA res. 39/46, annex, 10 Dec. 1984. [54]YUN 1987, p. 775. [55]E/CN.4/1994/28. [56]E/1993/23 (res. 1993/37). [57]YUN 1992, p. 735. [58]E/1993/23 (res. 1994/34). [59]E/CN.4/1994/25 & Add.1. [60]YUN 1991, p. 555. [61]A/48/44. [62]YUN 1992, p. 736. [63]A/48/44/Add.1. [64]CAT/SP/16 & Add.1. [65]E/1993/23 (res. 1993/38). [66]YUN 1981, p. 906, GA res. 36/151, 16 Dec. 1981. [67]YUN 1992, p. 737. [68]E/CN.4/1993/23 & Add.1,2. [69]A/48/520. [70]E/1993/23 (res. 1993/80). [71]YUN 1992, p. 738. [72]YUN 1992, p. 739. [73]E/CN.4/Sub.2/1993/20. [74]E/CN.4/1994/2 (res. 1993/27). [75]E/1993/23 (res. 1993/36). [76]YUN 1991, p. 557. [77]YUN 1948-49, p. 535, GA res. 217 A (III), 10 Dec. 1948. [78]E/CN.4/1994/27. [79]E/CN.4/1993/22. [80]E/1993/23 (res. 1993/39). [81]YUN 1988, p. 510, GA res. 43/173, annex, 9 Dec. 1988. [82]YUN 1991, p. 558. [83]E/CN.4/1993/46. [84]E/CN.4/1994/7/Add.1. [85]E/CN.4/1994/7/Add.2. [86]E/1993/23 (res. 1993/71). [87]Ibid. (res. 1993/35). [88]Ibid. (res. 1993/33). [89]*Manual on the Effective Prevention and Investigation of Extra-legal, Arbitrary and Summary Executions* (ST/CSDHA/12), Sales No. E.91.IV.1. [90]E/1993/22 (res. 1993/47). [91]E/CN.4/1993/20. [92]YUN 1946-47, p. 100, GA res. 22 A(I), annex, 13 Feb. 1946. [93]YUN 1980, p. 843. [94]E/CN.4/1994/26 & Corr.1. [95]E/CN.4/1994/26/Add.1. [96]E/CN.4/Sub.2/1993/30. [97]YUN 1992, p. 814. [98]E/1993/23 (res. 1993/27). [99]YUN 1956, p. 228. [100]YUN 1948-49, p. 613, GA res. 317(IV), annex, 2 Dec. 1949. [101]E/CN.4/Sub.2/1989/37. [102]YUN 1983, p. 918, ESC res. 1983/30, 26 May 1983. [103]E/1993/23 (dec. 1993/112). [104]E/CN.4/1994/2 (res. 1993/5). [105]Ibid. (res. 1993/6). [106]Ibid. (res. 1993/7). [107]YUN 1992, p. 748, ESC res. 1992/10, 20 July 1992. [108]E/1993/61 & Add.1. [109]E/CN.4/1994/2 (res. 1993/24). [110]E/CN.4/Sub.2/1993/44. [111]E/1993/23 (res. 1993/26). [112]YUN 1991, p. 563, GA res. 46/122, 17 Dec. 1991. [113]E/1993/23 (dec. 1993/104). [114]YUN 1992, p. 749. [115]E/CN.4/Sub.2/1993/17 & Corr.1.

[116]E/CN.4/1994/2 (res. 1993/34). [117]E/1993/23 (res. 1993/45).[118]E/CN.4/1993/38. [119]YUN 1992, p. 750. [120]E/1993/23 (res. 1993/64). [121]E/CN.4/1993/68 & Add.1-3. [122]YUN 1991, p. 565. [123]E/1993/23 (res. 1993/84). [124]Ibid. (res. 1993/43). [125]E/CN.4/Sub.2/1993/6. [126]E/CN.4/1994/2 (res. 1993/37). [127]E/1993/23 (res. 1993/44). [128]E/CN.4/ Sub.2/1993/25. [129]E/CN.4/1994/2 (res. 1993/39). [130]E/1993/23 (dec. 1993/106). [131]YUN 1992, p. 751. [132]E/CN.4/Sub.2/ 1993/24. [133]E/CN.4/Sub.2/1993/24 & Add.1. [134]E/CN.4/ Sub.2/1993/24 & Add.2. [135]E/CN.4/1994/2 (res. 1993/26).

Economic, social and cultural rights

Expert seminar. As requested by the Commission on Human Rights in 1991,[1] the Secretary-General organized an expert seminar to discuss indicators to measure achievements in the progressive realization of economic, social and cultural rights (Geneva, 25-29 January 1993).[2] Given the nature of the seminar's objectives, it was considered a satellite meeting to the World Conference on Human Rights (see below under "Advancement on human rights"). The seminar concluded that the first priority was to identify and clarify the content of specific rights and States parties' obligations in order to identify the most appropriate way to assess progressive achievement, which might or might not involve the use of statistical indicators. It also concluded that monitoring the performance of States in the progressive realization of economic, social and cultural rights required new approaches in data collection analysis and interpretation that focused on poor and disadvantaged groups. The seminar outlined the objectives necessary to promote the progressive realization of economic, social and cultural rights and made a number of general recommendations for action by United Nations bodies, including the specialized agencies, and States.

Human Rights Commission action. On 26 February,[3] the Commission on Human Rights requested the Secretary-General to bring the conclusions and recommendations of the expert seminar to the attention of Member States, the Commission, other United Nations bodies, the specialized agencies, financial institutions and NGOs.

The Commission encouraged States parties to the International Covenant on Economic, Social and Cultural Rights[4] to support and cooperate with the Committee on Economic, Social and Cultural Rights and asked the Economic and Social Council to identify ways in which international cooperation and technical assistance could contribute to the effective implementation of the rights recognized in the Covenant. Taking note of the final report of the Special Rapporteur on the realization of economic, social and cultural rights, submitted in 1992,[5] the Commission requested the

Secretary-General to ensure wide distribution of that report and the Special Rapporteur's 1990[6] and 1991[7] progress reports throughout the United Nations, in particular by publishing them in a single document. It also requested the Secretary-General to invite international financial institutions to consider organizing an expert seminar on their role in realizing economic, social and cultural rights; prepare basic policy guidelines on structural adjustment and economic, social and cultural rights; and promote coordination of United Nations human rights activities and those of development agencies, with a view to drawing on their expertise and support.

On the same date,[8] by a roll-call vote of 36 to 2, with 12 abstentions, the Commission asked the Secretary-General to submit in 1994, in consultation with Governments, specialized agencies, intergovernmental organizations and NGOs concerned, a report on the repercussions and prospects of the debt crisis and structural adjustment programmes on the effective enjoyment of economic, social and cultural rights of developing countries.

Report of the Secretary-General. In response to a 1992 Subcommission request,[5] the Secretary-General in July highlighted activities undertaken by the Centre for Human Rights in the field of economic, social and cultural rights.[9] Annexed to the report was a list of United Nations bodies and agencies having mandates bearing directly on those rights. A separate addendum[10] provided a list of documents relating to economic, social and cultural rights issued in preparation for the World Conference on Human Rights.

Covenant on Economic, Social and Cultural Rights

As at 31 December 1993, the International Covenant on Economic, Social and Cultural Rights, adopted by the General Assembly in 1966[4] and in force since 1976,[11] had been ratified or acceded to by 127 States. Armenia, Benin, Bosnia and Herzegovina, Cape Verde, the Czech Republic, Dominica, Ethiopia, Malawi, Nigeria, Republic of Moldova and Slovakia became parties in 1993.[12]

The Secretary-General provided information on the status of ratifications of or accessions to and signatures of the Covenant as at 1 December 1993[13] (see also below, under "Advancement of human rights").

Implementation of the Covenant

Human Rights Commission action. On 26 February,[14] the Commission appealed to all States that had not done so to become parties to the Covenant. It welcomed the efforts of the Committee on Economic, Social and Cultural Rights in preparing general comments on the provisions of the Covenant and encouraged Governments to publish the Covenant in as many languages as possible and to disseminate it widely. It asked the Secretary-General to report in 1994 on the status of the Covenant.

Committee on Economic, Social and Cultural Rights. The Committee on Economic, Social and Cultural Rights, established in 1985,[15] held its eighth (extraordinary) session at Geneva from 10 to 28 May.[16] The session was authorized by the Economic and Social Council in 1992[17] owing to the long-standing backlog of States parties' reports awaiting the Committee's consideration. Its pre-sessional five-member working group, established in 1988[18] to meet for one week prior to each session, convened at Geneva from 28 June to 2 July. The Committee held its ninth (regular) session, also at Geneva, from 22 November to 10 December.[16]

Concerning the rights covered by articles 6 to 9 of the Covenant (the right to work and to favourable conditions of work, trade union rights and the right to social security) the Committee examined a report from Senegal.[19] Rights covered under articles 10 to 12 (the protection of the family, mothers and children, and the right to an adequate living standard and to physical and mental health) were examined in reports submitted by Nicaragua.[20] As to the rights covered by articles 13 to 15 (education, including compulsory education, and cultural participation), the Committee considered reports from Australia[21] and Germany.[22] Under articles 10 to 15, the Committee examined a report from Canada.[23]

Under articles 1 to 15, the Committee examined reports from Iceland,[24] Iran,[25] Lebanon,[26] Mexico,[27] New Zealand,[28] Niue,[29] Tokelau[30] and Viet Nam.[31]

The Committee reviewed the state of implementation of the economic, social and cultural rights contained in the Covenant by Kenya which, although a party to the Covenant since 1976, had not fulfilled its reporting obligations.

The Committee's day of general discussion in May focused on the rights of the ageing and the elderly and, in December, on the right to health.

ECONOMIC AND SOCIAL COUNCIL ACTION

The Economic and Social Council, by **decision 1993/296** of 28 July, noting the longstanding backlog of States parties' reports awaiting consideration, authorized the holding of an extraordinary additional three-week session of the Committee on Economic, Social and Cultural Rights in the first half of 1994. It also authorized a special three-day meeting of the Committee's pre-sessional working group, to be held immediately following the

conclusion of the Committee's ninth session. Also on 28 July, the Council, by **decision 1993/297,** endorsed the Committee's request to the General Assembly to authorize payment to each Committee member of an honorarium equivalent to that payable to members of other treaty bodies. By **decision 1993/298** of the same date, the Council decided to consider in 1994 the allocation of resources to enable the Committee to involve experts in its general discussion. In addition, by **decision 1993/295** of 28 July, it renewed its endorsement of the Committee's 1992 decision[32] to send one or two of its members to advise the Dominican Republic regarding efforts to promote full compliance with the Covenant in the case of large-scale evictions, subject to acceptance by the Government. On the same date, the Council, by **decision 1993/294,** approved the Committee's offer of technical assistance to Panama.

On 28 July, the Council, by **decision 1993/299,** took note of the Committee's report on its 1992 session[32] and of an extract from the Committee's report on its 1993 extraordinary session.[33]

Right to development

Report of the Secretary-General. In response to a 1992 General Assembly request,[34] the Secretary-General submitted proposals in January 1993[35] for the implementation and promotion of the 1986 Declaration on the Right to Development.[36] He addressed obstacles to the implementation of the right to development and examined the criteria to measure progress in the realization of that right. Among his proposals was the setting up of a supervisory mechanism such as a group of independent experts, or an interagency advisory group or the appointment of a special rapporteur.

Human Rights Commission action. On 4 March,[37] the Commission, by a roll-call vote of 36 to 1, with 13 abstentions, established, initially for a three-year period, a working group on the right to development to identify obstacles to the implementation and realization of the 1986 Declaration[36] and to recommend ways towards the realization of that right by all States. It asked the working group to submit to it a report on the obstacles affecting the implementation of the Declaration and to report annually on its work. The Commission requested the Secretary-General to ensure that the group received all necessary assistance and asked him to invite Governments and intergovernmental organizations to communicate to the Advisory Services, Technical Assistance and Information Branch of the Centre for Human Rights sample projects on the effective implementation of the Declaration. It requested the Economic and Social Council and the General Assembly to give attention in 1993 to the implementation of the principles in the Declaration. Noting with concern the lack of coordination in the United Nations system of the implementation of the principles contained in the 1986 Declaration, the Commission urged all relevant bodies, particularly the specialized agencies, to take due account of the Declaration and to make efforts to contribute to its application.

Subcommission action. On 26 August,[38] the Subcommission decided to entrust Asbjorn Eide (Norway) with producing a preparatory document on the relationship between the enjoyment of human rights, in particular economic, social and cultural rights, and income distribution, taking into account matters related to the realization of the right to development, with a view to determining how to strengthen activities in that area. It asked him to consult the widest possible variety of sources in preparing the document, which it would examine in 1994.

Working Group activities. The Working Group on the Right to Development, at its first session (Geneva, 8-19 November 1993),[39] elected its officers, adopted its agenda and defined its methods of work. The 15-member Group reviewed major developments since the adoption of the Declaration, discussed its mandate and considered obstacles to the realization of the Declaration. The Group recommended that additional information be sought from Governments, international institutions, regional economic commissions, the Commission on Social Development and the Commission on the Status of Women, as well as other international bodies. Annexed to the Group's report were preliminary guidelines and a checklist which would facilitate the collection of information from those sources. The Group proposed holding two sessions in 1994 and a meeting between its Chairman and the chairpersons of other human rights bodies prior to its second session. It further recommended that: the Secretary-General be asked to provide the Centre for Human Rights with a unit to follow up on the Declaration and its implementation and to give logistical support to the Group; the Executive Secretaries of the regional commissions be invited to a future session; Governments and the international community be encouraged to incorporate the right to development into their activities; the right to development be put on the agenda of forthcoming United Nations meetings; and NGOs and other grass-roots organizations be enabled to play a major role in activities relating to the right to development.

Note by the Secretary-General. In November,[40] the Secretary-General submitted to the General Assembly his 1992 report to the Commission[32] on the implementation of the 1986 Declaration, as requested by the Assembly in 1992.[34]

On 20 December, the General Assembly, by **decision 48/430**, took note of the Secretary-General's note on the right to development.

ECONOMIC AND SOCIAL COUNCIL ACTION

On 28 July, the Economic and Social Council, on the recommendation of its Social Committee, adopted **decision 1993/260** by a roll-call vote.

Right to development
At its 44th plenary meeting, on 28 July 1993, the Economic and Social Council, taking note of Commission on Human Rights resolution 1993/22 of 4 March 1993, approved:

(a) The Commission's decision to establish, initially for a three-year period, a working group on the right to development, to identify obstacles to the implementation and realization of the Declaration on the Right to Development and to recommend ways and means towards the realization of the right to development by all States;

(b) The Commission's request to the working group to submit to the Commission at its fiftieth session an initial, comprehensive report and to continue reporting to the Commission, on a yearly basis, on its work;

(c) The Commission's request to the Secretary-General to ensure that the working group received all necessary assistance, in particular the staff and resources required to fulfil its mandate, and to invite Governments and intergovernmental organizations to communicate to the Advisory Services, Technical Assistance and Information Branch of the Centre for Human Rights of the Secretariat sample projects on the effective implementation of the Declaration on the Right to Development.

Economic and Social Council decision 1993/260

44-1-4 (roll-call vote)

Approved by Social Committee (E/1993/108) by roll-call vote (38-1-6), 22 July (meeting 17); draft by Commission on Human Rights (E/1993/23); agenda item 18.

Roll-call vote in Council as follows:

In favour: Angola, Argentina, Australia, Austria, Bahamas, Bangladesh, Belarus, Belgium, Benin, Bhutan, Botswana, Brazil, Chile, China, Colombia, Cuba, Denmark, France, Guinea, India, Italy, Kuwait, Madagascar, Malaysia, Mexico, Morocco, Nigeria, Norway, Peru, Philippines, Poland, Republic of Korea, Romania, Russian Federation, Spain, Sri Lanka, Suriname, Swaziland, Syrian Arab Republic, Togo, Trinidad and Tobago, Turkey, Ukraine, Zaire.

Against: United States.

Abstaining: Canada, Germany, Japan, United Kingdom.

GENERAL ASSEMBLY ACTION

On 20 December, the General Assembly, on the recommendation of the Third Committee, adopted **resolution 48/130** without vote.

Right to development
The General Assembly,

Reaffirming the Declaration on the Right to Development, which it proclaimed at its forty-first session,

Recalling its resolutions 45/97 of 14 December 1990, 46/123 of 17 December 1991 and 47/123 of 18 December 1992, and those of the Commission on Human Rights relating to the right to development, and taking note of Commission resolution 1993/22 of 4 March 1993,

Recalling also the report on the Global Consultation on the Realization of the Right to Development as a Human Right,[a]

Recalling further the principles proclaimed in the Rio Declaration on Environment and Development of 14 June 1992,

Reiterating the importance of the right to development for all countries, in particular the developing countries,

Mindful that the Commission on Human Rights entered a new phase at its forty-ninth session in its consideration of this matter, which is directed towards the implementation and further enhancement of the right to development,

Reaffirming the need for an evaluation mechanism so as to ensure the promotion, encouragement and reinforcement of the principles contained in the Declaration on the Right to Development, and welcoming in this regard, the decision of the Commission at its forty-ninth session, in its resolution 1993/22, to establish a working group on the right to development,

Noting that the World Conference on Human Rights, held at Vienna from 14 to 25 June 1993, examined the relationship between development and the enjoyment by everyone of economic, social and cultural rights as well as civil and political rights, recognizing the importance of creating the conditions whereby everyone may enjoy those rights as set out in the International Covenants on Human Rights,

Recalling that, in order to promote development, equal attention and urgent consideration should be given to the implementation, promotion and protection of civil, political, economic, social and cultural rights,

Welcoming the Vienna Declaration and Programme of Action, adopted by the World Conference on Human Rights, which reaffirms the right to development as a universal and inalienable right and an integral part of fundamental human rights and reaffirms that the human person is the central subject of development,

Having considered the comprehensive report of the Secretary-General prepared pursuant to resolution 47/123,

1. *Reaffirms* the importance of the right to development for all countries, in particular the developing countries;

2. *Takes note with interest* of the comprehensive report of the Secretary-General prepared in accordance with General Assembly resolution 47/123;

3. *Requests* the Secretary-General to submit to the Commission on Human Rights at its fiftieth session concrete proposals on the effective implementation and promotion of the Declaration on the Right to Development, taking into account the views expressed on the issue at the forty-ninth session of the Commission as well as any further comments and recommendations that may be submitted pursuant to paragraph 10 of Commission resolution 1993/22;

4. *Notes with appreciation* the convening of the first meeting of the Working Group on the Right to Development from 8 to 19 November 1993 at Geneva;

5. *Also requests* the Secretary-General to continue coordination of the various activities with regard to the implementation of the Declaration;

6. *Urges* all relevant bodies of the United Nations system, particularly the specialized agencies, when planning their programmes of activities, to take due account of the Declaration and to make efforts to enhance their cooperation in its application;

7. *Urges* the regional commissions and regional intergovernmental organizations to convene meetings of governmental experts and representatives of non-governmental and grass-roots organizations for the purpose of seeking agreements for the implementation of the Declaration through international cooperation;

8. *Further requests* the Secretary-General to inform the Commission on Human Rights at its fiftieth session and the General Assembly at its forty-ninth session of the activities of the organizations, programmes and agencies of the United Nations system for the implementation of the Declaration;

9. *Calls upon* the Commission on Human Rights to continue to make proposals to the General Assembly, through the Economic and Social Council, on the future course of action on the question, in particular on practical measures for the implementation and enhancement of the Declaration, taking into account the conclusions and recommendations of the Global Consultation on the Realization of the Right to Development as a Human Right and the report of the Working Group on the Right to Development;

10. *Takes note with satisfaction* of the results of the World Conference on Human Rights, including its reaffirmation that all human rights are universal, indivisible, interdependent and interrelated and that democracy, development and respect for human rights and fundamental freedoms are interdependent and mutually reinforcing;

11. *Decides* to consider this question at its forty-ninth session under the sub-item entitled "Human rights questions, including alternative approaches for improving the effective enjoyment of human rights and fundamental freedoms".

---

[a]E/CN.4/1990/9/Rev.1.

General Assembly resolution 48/130

20 December 1993   Meeting 85   Adopted without vote

Approved by Third Committee (A/48/632/Add.2) without vote, 6 December (meeting 52); draft by Argentina, Armenia, Australia, Austria, Belgium, Brazil, China, Costa Rica, Denmark, Dominican Republic, France, Indonesia (for Non-Aligned Movement), Mexico, Norway, Spain and Uruguay (A/C.3/48/L.50); agenda item 114 (b).

Meeting numbers. GA 48th session: 3rd Committee 36-52; plenary 85.

Extreme poverty

Human Rights Commission action. On 26 February,[41] the Commission endorsed the Subcommission's appointment in 1992 of Leandro Despouy (Argentina) as Special Rapporteur on human rights and extreme poverty.[42] It asked him to pay special attention to several aspects of the subject and to consider the possibility of organizing a seminar on extreme poverty and denial of human rights. It called on States, specialized agencies, United Nations bodies and other international organizations to continue to make their views on human rights and extreme poverty known to the Secretary-General, and to give due attention each International Day for the Elimination of Poverty (17 October) to the situation of the poorest and to inform the Secretary-General of activities undertaken in that regard. It asked the

Secretary-General to take into account, in preparing the programme for the International Day, of the relationship between extreme poverty and the full realization of human rights and to report to the Commission in 1994 on the subject.

Report of the Special Rapporteur. In July,[43] Special Rapporteur Despouy, in his preliminary report on human rights and extreme poverty, proposed holding a seminar on extreme poverty and denial of human rights. He outlined the plan of work for his progress report which would offer a definition of extreme poverty, discuss problems of poverty and work of the agencies and organizations, consider a human rights approach to extreme poverty and present conclusions and recommendations. It would also discuss the history of the subject, review his mandate and outline his sources of information.

Subcommission action. On 25 August,[44] the Subcommission approved the Special Rapporteur's proposals for the seminar on extreme poverty and the denial of human rights and asked him to submit an interim report in 1994. It requested the Secretary-General to assist the Special Rapporteur and to inform him of the conclusions of any consultations held on human rights and extreme poverty with Governments, specialized agencies, intergovernmental organizations and NGOs.

ECONOMIC AND SOCIAL COUNCIL ACTION

On 28 July, the Economic and Social Council, on the recommendation of its Social Committee, adopted **resolution 1993/44** without vote.

Human rights and extreme poverty

The Economic and Social Council,

Taking note of Commission on Human Rights resolution 1993/13 of 26 February 1993 and recalling resolution 1992/27 of 27 August 1992 of the Subcommission on Prevention of Discrimination and Protection of Minorities,

1. *Approves* the appointment of Mr. Leandro Despouy as Special Rapporteur on the question of human rights and extreme poverty with responsibility for preparing a study on this subject on the basis of the aspects set out by the Commission on Human Rights in its resolutions 1989/10 of 2 March 1989, 1990/15 of 23 February 1990 and 1991/14 of 22 February 1991, bearing particularly in mind the approach defined in Commission resolution 1992/11 of 21 February 1992;

2. *Requests* the Secretary-General to continue his consultations on the topic of human rights and extreme poverty with Governments, specialized agencies and intergovernmental and non-governmental organizations and to inform the Special Rapporteur of the conclusions of those consultations;

3. *Also requests* the Secretary-General to provide the Special Rapporteur with all necessary assistance for the fulfilment of his mandate, including, as appropriate, assistance from consultants with specialized knowledge of the subject.

Economic and Social Council resolution 1993/44

28 July 1993   Meeting 44   Adopted without vote

Approved by Social Committee (E/1993/108) without vote, 22 July (meeting 17); draft by Commission on Human Rights (E/1993/23); agenda item 18.

Right to own property

Report of the independent expert. In 1993,[45] the Commission had before it the final report of independent expert Luis Valencia Rodríguez (Ecuador) on the right of everyone to own property alone as well as in association with others. He discussed the significance of the right to own property as a contribution to securing peace and the goals of economic and social development enshrined in the Charter. The expert discussed the legal protection of the right to own property as a human right and its implementation; presented national and international policies, national legislation and practical measures in the field; and described the restrictions and limitations in exercising the right. He recommended retaining the subject on the agendas of the General Assembly and the Commission; maintaining a link between the right to own property, the right to adequate housing and other relevant human rights; supporting property rights reforms in ex-socialist States and some developing countries; convening a seminar in an Eastern European country on ensuring the right to own property; and the routine provision of remedies by local courts, administrative tribunals and other authorities. He outlined action that should be taken by CERD and the Committee on the Elimination of Discrimination against Women.

Human Rights Commission action. On 4 March,[46] the Commission renewed the independent expert's mandate for one year in order for him to complete his report using observations and comments submitted by Governments, intergovernmental organizations and NGOs that were not included due to the time when they were received. It requested the Secretary-General to assist the independent expert and decided to consider the report in 1994.

On 28 July, the Economic and Social Council, by **decision 1993/259**, approved the Commission's decision and its request to the Secretary-General.

Right to adequate housing

Human Rights Commission action. On 4 March,[47] the Commission endorsed the Subcommission's 1992 decision[48] to appoint Rajinder Sachar (India) as Special Rapporteur on promoting the realization of the right to adequate housing.

By **decision 1993/287** of 28 July, the Economic and Social Council approved the Commission's endorsement of the Subcommission's requests to the Special Rapporteur to submit to the Subcommission in 1993 a progress report on the promotion of the realization of the right to adequate housing and to the Secretary-General to provide assistance to him.

Report of the Special Rapporteur. In June,[49] Special Rapporteur Sachar elaborated and clarified States' obligations concerning the right to adequate housing, as well as other legal dimensions of that right. He proposed that the United Nations Advisory Services Programme develop expertise in the area of housing rights and recommended developing legal and political procedures to enhance Government accountability regarding housing rights. The Special Rapporteur considered visits to countries as an indispensable component of his future work and asked for the support of the Subcommission in that regard.

Subcommission action. On 25 August,[50] the Subcommission endorsed the Special Rapporteur's preliminary conclusions and recommendations and decided to renew his mandate for one year to enable him to explore fully the issues arising from the right to adequate housing. It asked the Special Rapporteur to submit in 1994 a second progress report and to examine the need to adopt an international declaration or convention on the right to adequate housing. The Subcommission requested the Secretary-General to assist the Special Rapporteur in preparing the study.

Forced evictions

Human Rights Commission action. On 23 March,[51] the Commission urged Governments to take measures to eliminate the practice of forced evictions, to confer legal security of tenure on all persons so threatened and to adopt measures giving full protection against forced eviction. It recommended that Governments provide restitution, compensation and/or appropriate and sufficient alternative accommodation or land to persons and communities forcibly evicted, following mutually satisfactory negotiations. The Commission requested the Secretary-General to transmit its resolution to Governments, United Nations bodies, specialized agencies, regional and intergovernmental organizations, NGOs and community-based organizations to solicit their views and comments. It also requested him to compile an analytical report on the practice, based on an analysis of international law and jurisprudence and information provided in response to his request and to submit the report in 1994.

Subcommission action. On 26 August,[52] the Subcommission recommended that Governments provide immediate restitution, compensation and/or sufficient alternative accommodation or land to persons and communities that had been forcibly evicted.

Human rights education

On 9 March,[53] the Commission on Human Rights recommended that the General Assembly take measures to declare a decade for human rights education in the light of recommendations of the UNESCO International Congress on Education for Human Rights and Democracy (Montreal, Canada, 8-11 March). It asked the Secretary-General to submit in 1994 a report on action taken in relation to the declaration of a decade for human rights education. The Commission called on States to increase their efforts to eradicate illiteracy and provide the necessary facilities to ensure that the entire population had access to all-round education.

GENERAL ASSEMBLY ACTION

On 20 December, the General Assembly, on the recommendation of the Third Committee, adopted **resolution 48/127** without vote.

Decade for human rights education
The General Assembly,

Guided by the fundamental and universal principles enshrined in the Charter of the United Nations and the Universal Declaration of Human Rights,

Reaffirming article 26 of the Universal Declaration of Human Rights, according to which "education shall be directed to the full development of the human personality and to the strengthening of respect for human rights and fundamental freedoms",

Recalling the provisions of other international human rights instruments, such as those of article 13 of the International Covenant on Economic, Social and Cultural Rights and article 20 of the Convention on the Rights of the Child, that reflect the aims of the aforementioned article,

Convinced that human rights education is a universal priority in that it contributes to a concept of development consistent with the dignity of the human person, which must include consideration of the diversity of groups such as children, women, youths, persons with disabilities, the ageing, indigenous people, minorities and other groups,

Aware that human rights education involves more than providing information but rather is a comprehensive life-long process by which people at all levels of development and in all strata of society learn respect for the dignity of others and the means and methods of ensuring that respect within a democratic society,

Taking into account the efforts made by educators and non-governmental organizations in all parts of the world, as well as by intergovernmental organizations, including the United Nations Educational, Scientific and Cultural Organization, the International Labour Organisation and the United Nations Children's Fund, to promote education in accordance with the aforementioned principles,

Considering the World Plan of Action on Education for Human Rights and Democracy, adopted by the International Congress on Education for Human Rights and Democracy convened by the United Nations Educational, Scientific and Cultural Organization at Montreal from 8 to 11 March 1993, according to which education for human rights and democracy is itself a human right and a prerequisite for the realization of human rights, democracy and social justice,

Aware of the experience in human rights education of United Nations peace-building operations, including the United Nations Observer Mission in El Salvador and the United Nations Transitional Authority in Cambodia,

Taking into account Commission on Human Rights resolution 1993/56 of 9 March 1993, in which the Commission recommended that knowledge of human rights, both in its theoretical dimension and in its practical application, should be established as a priority in educational policies,

Bearing in mind the Vienna Declaration and Programme of Action, adopted by the World Conference on Human Rights at Vienna on 25 June 1993, in particular section II, paragraphs 78 to 82,

1. *Appeals* to all Governments to step up their efforts to eradicate illiteracy and to direct education towards the full development of the human personality and to the strengthening of respect for human rights and fundamental freedoms;

2. *Urges* governmental and non-governmental educational agencies to intensify their efforts to establish and implement programmes of human rights education, as recommended in the Vienna Declaration and Programme of Action;

3. *Takes note* of the World Plan of Action on Education for Human Rights and Democracy and recommends that Governments and non-governmental organizations consider it in preparing national plans for human rights education;

4. *Requests* the Commission on Human Rights, in cooperation with Member States, human rights treaty-monitoring bodies, other appropriate bodies and competent non-governmental organizations, to consider proposals for a United Nations decade for human rights education, which should be incorporated by the Secretary-General into a plan of action for such a decade and submitted, through the Economic and Social Council, to the General Assembly at its forty-ninth session, with a view to the proclamation of a decade for human rights education;

5. *Requests* the Secretary-General to consider the establishment of a voluntary fund for human rights education, with special provision for the support of the human rights education activities of non-governmental organizations, to be administered by the Centre for Human Rights of the Secretariat;

6. *Invites* the specialized agencies and United Nations programmes to develop suitable activities in their respective fields of competence to further the objectives of human rights education;

7. *Also requests* the Secretary-General to bring the present resolution to the attention of all members of the international community and to intergovernmental and non-governmental organizations concerned with human rights and education;

8. *Calls upon* international, regional and national non-governmental organizations, in particular those concerned with women, labour, development and the environment, as well as all other social justice groups, human rights advocates, educators, religious organizations and the media, to increase their involvement in formal and non-formal education in human rights and to cooperate with the Centre for Human Rights in preparing for a United Nations decade for human rights education;

9. *Urges* the existing human rights monitoring bodies to place particular emphasis on the implementation by Member States of their international obligation to promote human rights education;

10. *Decides* to consider this matter at its forty-ninth session under the item entitled "Human rights questions".

General Assembly resolution 48/127

20 December 1993   Meeting 85   Adopted without vote

Approved by Third Committee (A/48/632/Add.2) without vote, 6 December (meeting 52); 24-nation draft (A/C.3/48/L.47), orally revised; agenda item 114 (b).

Sponsors: Angola, Cameroon, Chile, Costa Rica, Côte d'Ivoire, Cyprus, Dominican Republic, Ethiopia, Gambia, Guatemala, Malawi, Monaco, Mongolia, Morocco, Mozambique, Namibia, Nicaragua, Nigeria, Philippines, Poland, Senegal, Sierra Leone, Slovenia, Uganda.

Meeting numbers. GA 48th session: 3rd Committee 36-52; plenary 85.

REFERENCES

(1)YUN 1991, p. 567. (2)A/CONF.157/PC/73. (3)E/1993/23 (res. 1993/14). (4)YUN 1966, p. 419, GA res 2200 A (XXI), annex, 16 Dec. 1966. (5)YUN 1992, p. 752. (6)E/CN.4/Sub.2/1990/19. (7)YUN 1991, p. 568. (8)E/1993/23 (res. 1993/12). (9)E/CN.4/Sub.2/1993/18. (10)E/CN.4/Sub.2/1993/18/Add.1. (11)YUN 1976, p. 609. (12)*Multilateral Treaties Deposited with the Secretary-General: Status as at 31 December 1993* (ST/LEG/SER.E/12), Sales No. E.94.V.11. (13)E/CN.4/1994/67. (14)E/1993/23 (res. 1993/15). (15)YUN 1985, p. 878, ESC res. 1985/17, 28 May 1985. (16)E/1994/23. (17)YUN 1992, p. 753, ESC dec. 1992/259, 20 July 1992. (18)YUN 1988, p. 527, ESC res. 1988/4, 24 May 1988. (19)E/1984/6/Add.22. (20)E/1986/3/Add.15 & 16. (21)E/1990/7/Add.13. (22)E/1990/7/Add.12. (23)E/1990/6/Add.3. (24)E/1990/5/Add.6 & 14. (25)E/1990/5/Add.9. (26)E/1990/5/Add.16. (27)E/1990/6/Add.4. (28)E/1990/5/Add.5. (29)E/1990/5/Add.12. (30)E/1990/5/Add.11. (31)E/1990/5/Add.10. (32)YUN 1992, p. 753. (33)E/1993/L.23. (34)YUN 1992, p. 753, GA res. 47/123, 18 Dec. 1992. (35)E/CN.4/1993/16. (36)YUN 1986, p. 717, GA res. 41/128, annex, 4 Dec. 1986. (37)E/1993/23 (res. 1993/22). (38)E/CN.4/1994/2 (res. 1993/40). (39)E/CN.4/1994/21. (40)A/48/576. (41)E/1993/23 (res. 1993/13). (42)YUN 1992, p. 755. (43)E/CN.4/Sub.2/1993/16. (44)E/CN.4/1994/2 (res. 1993/35). (45)E/CN.4/1993/15. (46)E/1993/23 (res. 1993/21). (47)Ibid. (dec. 1993/103). (48)YUN 1992, p. 756. (49)E/CN.4/Sub.2/1993/15. (50)E/CN.4/1994/2 (res. 1993/36). (51)E/1993/23 (res. 1993/77). (52)E/CN.4/1994/2 (res. 1993/41). (53)E/1993/23 (res. 1993/56).

Advancement of human rights

On 20 December, the General Assembly, on the recommendation of the Third Committee, adopted **resolution 48/123** by recorded vote.

Alternative approaches and ways and means within the United Nations system for improving the effective enjoyment of human rights and fundamental freedoms

The General Assembly,

Recalling that in the Charter of the United Nations the peoples of the United Nations declared their determination to reaffirm faith in fundamental human rights, in the dignity and worth of the human person and in the equal rights of men and women and of nations large and small and to employ international machinery for the promotion of the economic and social advancement of all peoples,

Recalling also that one of the purposes of the United Nations, as set forth in the Charter, is to achieve international cooperation in solving international problems of an economic, social, cultural or humanitarian character and in promoting and encouraging respect for human rights and for fundamental freedoms for all without distinction as to race, sex, language or religion,

Emphasizing the significance and validity of the Universal Declaration of Human Rights and of the International Covenants on Human Rights in promoting respect for and observance of human rights and fundamental freedoms,

Recalling further its resolution 32/130 of 16 December 1977, in which it decided that the approach to future work within the United Nations system with respect to human rights questions should take into account the concepts set forth in that resolution,

Noting with concern that many of the principles enunciated in resolution 32/130 have not yet been taken into consideration by the international community with all the necessary dynamism and objectivity,

Emphasizing the special importance of the purposes and principles proclaimed in the Declaration on the Right to Development, contained in the annex to its resolution 41/128 of 4 December 1986,

Reaffirming that the implementation of the right to development is an indispensable element in the process of creating the appropriate conditions for the full enjoyment and preservation of all human rights and fundamental liberties,

Taking into account the final documents of the Tenth Conference of Heads of State or Government of Non-Aligned Countries, held at Jakarta in September 1992,

Reiterating that the right to development is an inalienable human right and that equality of development opportunities is a prerogative both of nations and of individuals within nations,

Expressing its particular concern about the progressive worsening of living conditions in the developing world and the negative impact thereof on the full enjoyment of human rights, and especially about the very serious economic situation of the African continent and the disastrous effects of the heavy burden of the external debt for the peoples of Africa, Asia and Latin America,

Reiterating its profound conviction that all human rights and fundamental freedoms are indivisible and interdependent and that equal attention and urgent consideration should be given to the implementation, promotion and protection of civil and political rights and of economic, social and cultural rights,

Deeply convinced that, today more than ever, economic and social development and human rights are complementary elements leading to the same goal, that is, the maintenance of peace and justice among nations as the foundation for the ideals of freedom and well-being to which mankind aspires,

Reiterating that cooperation among all nations on the basis of respect for the independence, sovereignty and territorial integrity of each State, including the right of every people to choose freely its own socio-economic and political system, is essential for the promotion of peace and development,

Reiterating also that, in order to ensure the full implementation of the right to development, international cooperation should be conducive to an improvement of relations among States as well as to the commitment of States to refrain from conditioning their economic assistance to developing countries,

Considering that the efforts of the developing countries to promote their own development should be supported by an increased flow of resources and by the adoption of appropriate and substantive measures for creating an external environment conducive to such development,

1. *Reiterates its request* that the Commission on Human Rights continue its current work on overall analysis with a view to further promoting and strengthening human rights and fundamental freedoms, including the question of the programme and working methods of the Commission, and on the overall analysis of the alternative approaches and ways and means for improving the effective enjoyment of human rights and fundamental freedoms in accordance with the provisions and ideas set forth in General Assembly resolution 32/130;

2. *Affirms* that a primary aim of international cooperation in the field of human rights is a life of freedom, dignity and peace for all peoples and for every human being, that all human rights and fundamental freedoms are indivisible and interrelated and that the promotion and protection of one category of rights should never exempt or excuse States from promoting and protecting the others;

3. *Reaffirms* that equal attention and urgent consideration should be given to the implementation, promotion and protection of civil and political rights and of economic, social and cultural rights;

4. *Reiterates once again* that the international community should accord, or continue to accord, priority to the search for solutions to mass and flagrant violations of human rights of peoples and individuals affected by situations such as those mentioned in paragraph 1 *(e)* of General Assembly resolution 32/130, paying due attention also to other situations of violations of human rights;

5. *Notes* that the questions mentioned in paragraph 4 above were discussed during the World Conference on Human Rights held at Vienna from 14 to 25 June 1993 and are referred to in the Vienna Declaration and Programme of Action as obstacles still prevailing to the achievement of further progress in the field of human rights;

6. *Reaffirms* that the right to development is an inalienable human right;

7. *Reaffirms also* that international peace and security are essential elements for achieving the full realization of the right to development;

8. *Recognizes* that all human rights and fundamental freedoms are indivisible and interdependent;

9. *Considers it necessary* for all Member States to promote international cooperation on the basis of respect for the independence, sovereignty and territorial integrity of each State, including the right of every people to choose freely its own socio-economic and political system, with a view to solving international economic, social and humanitarian problems;

10. *Urges* all States to cooperate with the Commission on Human Rights in the promotion and protection of human rights and fundamental freedoms;

11. *Also urges* all States to promote international cooperation which contributes to the enhancement of the promotion and preservation of human rights, unbiased by any political motivation or condition whatsoever;

12. *Decides* that the approaches to future work within the United Nations system on human rights matters should take into account the content of the Declaration on the Right to Development and the need for the implementation thereof;

13. *Decides* to consider this question at its forty-ninth session.

General Assembly resolution 48/123

20 December 1993   Meeting 85   115-34-21 (recorded vote)

Approved by Third Committee (A/48/632/Add.2) by recorded vote (99-36-20), 6 December (meeting 52); 21-nation draft (A/C.3/48/L.43); agenda item 114 *(b)*.

Sponsors: Algeria, Angola, Central African Republic, Cuba, Democratic People's Republic of Korea, Gambia, India, Iran, Iraq, Lao People's Democratic Republic, Mexico, Namibia, Nigeria, Peru, Sierra Leone, Sudan, Uganda, Viet Nam, Yemen, Zambia, Zimbabwe.

Meeting numbers. GA 48th session: 3rd Committee 36-52; plenary 85.

Recorded vote in Assembly as follows:

In favour: Afghanistan, Algeria, Angola, Antigua and Barbuda, Armenia, Bahamas, Bahrain, Bangladesh, Barbados, Belize, Benin, Bhutan, Bolivia, Botswana, Brazil, Brunei Darussalam, Burkina Faso, Burundi, Cambodia, Cameroon, Cape Verde, Central African Republic, Chad, Chile, China, Colombia, Comoros, Congo, Costa Rica, Côte d'Ivoire, Cuba, Cyprus, Democratic People's Republic of Korea, Djibouti, Dominica, Dominican Republic, Ecuador, Egypt, El Salvador, Ethiopia, Gabon, Gambia, Ghana, Grenada, Guatemala, Guinea, Guinea-Bissau, Guyana, Haiti, Honduras, India, Indonesia, Iran, Iraq, Jamaica, Jordan, Kenya, Kuwait, Kyrgyzstan, Lao People's Democratic Republic, Lebanon, Lesotho, Libyan Arab Jamahiriya, Madagascar, Malawi, Malaysia, Maldives, Mali, Mauritania, Mauritius, Mexico, Mongolia, Morocco, Mozambique, Myanmar, Namibia, Nepal, Nicaragua, Niger, Nigeria, Oman, Pakistan, Papua New Guinea, Paraguay, Peru, Philippines, Qatar, Rwanda, Saint Lucia, Saint Vincent and the Grenadines, Saudi Arabia, Senegal, Sierra Leone, Singapore, Sri Lanka, Sudan, Suriname, Swaziland, Syrian Arab Republic, Thailand, the former Yugoslav Republic of Macedonia, Togo, Trinidad and Tobago, Tunisia, Turkmenistan, Uganda, United Arab Emirates, United Republic of Tanzania, Uruguay, Venezuela, Viet Nam, Yemen, Zaire, Zambia, Zimbabwe.

Against: Albania, Australia, Austria, Belgium, Bulgaria, Canada, Croatia, Czech Republic, Denmark, Finland, France, Germany, Greece, Hungary, Iceland, Ireland, Israel, Italy, Japan, Liechtenstein, Luxembourg, Malta, Monaco, Netherlands, Norway, Poland, Portugal, Republic of Moldova, Romania, San Marino, Spain, Sweden, United Kingdom, United States.

Abstaining: Argentina, Azerbaijan, Belarus, Bosnia and Herzegovina, Estonia, Fiji, Georgia, Kazakhstan, Latvia, Lithuania, Marshall Islands, Micronesia, New Zealand, Panama, Republic of Korea, Russian Federation, Slovakia, Slovenia, Solomon Islands, Turkey, Ukraine.

National institutions for human rights protection

Reports of the Secretary-General. As requested by the Commission on Human Rights in 1992,[1] the Secretary-General reported in January[2] on steps taken to plan a follow-up workshop, following the World Conference on Human Rights, to the 1991 International Workshop on National Institutions for the Promotion and Protection of Human Rights.[3] The Secretary-General suggested holding consultations during the Commission's 1993 session so that a Member State could offer to host the workshop.

In response to a 1991 General Assembly request,[4] the Secretary-General, in November,[5] reported on activities undertaken to enhance the dissemination of principles relating to the status of national institutions[1] and thus trigger the promotion of such institutions in countries that had none. It stressed the role of national institutions and their activities during the World Conference on Human Rights and described technical assistance programmes and advisory services being carried out by the Centre for Human Rights. Annexed to the report was the text of principles relating to the status of national institutions.

Human Rights Commission action. On 9 March,[6] the Commission requested the Secretary-General to give high priority to requests from Member States for assistance in establishing and strengthening national institutions for the promotion and protection of human rights as part of the programme of advisory services and technical assistance in the field of human rights. It asked the Centre for Human Rights to enhance cooperation between the United Nations and regional and national institutions. The Commission welcomed the holding of a meeting of national institutions within the framework of the World Conference on Human Rights (see above) and the invitation to representatives of national institutions to participate as observers in the Conference. It requested the Secretary-General to finance developing countries' attendance at the World Conference from the voluntary fund for the Conference and asked Governments and intergovernmental organizations and NGOs to contribute to the fund. The Secretary-General was asked to: bring the Commission's resolution to the attention of the Preparatory Committee of the Conference; prepare a report for the Conference on possible means to assist in establishing and strengthening national institutions through international cooperation; organize, following the Conference, an international workshop as a follow-up to the 1991 International Workshop on National Institutions for the Promotion and Protection of Human Rights;[3] and consider the results of the 1991 workshop and other international meetings when preparing a manual on national institutions. It asked the Conference's Preparatory Committee to promote the principles[1] and to bear in mind the report of the 1991 Workshop.

On 28 July, by **decision 1993/270**, the Economic and Social Council approved the Commission's requests to the Secretary-General to finance developing countries' attendance at the World Conference on Human Rights and to continue organizing an international workshop.

International workshop. The second International Workshop on National Institutions for the Promotion and Protection of Human Rights (Tunis, 13-17 December 1993)[7] made recommendations on strengthening national institutions; protecting the rights of disabled persons, women, children and migrant workers; the release of hostages and victims of arbitrary detention; and on torture.

GENERAL ASSEMBLY ACTION

On 20 December, the General Assembly, on the recommendation of the Third Committee, adopted **resolution 48/134** without vote.

National institutions for the promotion and protection of human rights

The General Assembly,

Recalling the relevant resolutions concerning national institutions for the protection and promotion of human rights, notably its resolutions 41/129 of 4 December 1986 and 46/124 of 17 December 1991 and Commission on Human Rights resolutions 1987/40 of 10 March 1987, 1988/72 of 10 March 1988, 1989/52 of 7 March 1989, 1990/73 of 7 March 1990, 1991/27 of 5 March 1991, 1992/54 of 3 March 1992, and taking note of Commission resolution 1993/55 of 9 March 1993,

Emphasizing the importance of the Universal Declaration of Human Rights, the International Covenants on Human Rights and other international instruments for promoting respect for and observance of human rights and fundamental freedoms,

Affirming that priority should be accorded to the development of appropriate arrangements at the national level to ensure the effective implementation of international human rights standards,

Convinced of the significant role that institutions at the national level can play in promoting and protecting human rights and fundamental freedoms and in developing and enhancing public awareness of those rights and freedoms,

Recognizing that the United Nations can play a catalytic role in assisting the development of national institutions by acting as a clearing-house for the exchange of information and experience,

Mindful in this regard of the guidelines on the structure and functioning of national and local institutions for the promotion and protection of human rights endorsed by the General Assembly in its resolution 33/46 of 14 December 1978,

Welcoming the growing interest shown worldwide in the creation and strengthening of national institutions, expressed during the Regional Meeting for Africa of the World Conference on Human Rights, held at Tunis from 2 to 6 November 1992, the Regional Meeting for Latin America and the Caribbean, held at San José from 18 to 22 January 1993, the Regional Meeting for Asia, held at Bangkok from 29 March to 2 April 1993, the Commonwealth Workshop on National Human Rights Institutions, held at Ottawa from 30 September to 2 October 1992 and the Workshop for the Asia and Pacific Region on Human Rights Issues, held at Jakarta from 26 to 28 January 1993, and manifested in the decisions announced recently by several Member States to establish national institutions for the promotion and protection of human rights,

Bearing in mind the Vienna Declaration and Programme of Action, in which the World Conference on Human Rights reaffirmed the important and constructive role played by national institutions for the promotion and protection of human rights, in particular in their advisory capacity to the competent authorities, their role in remedying human rights violations, in the dissemination of human rights information and education in human rights,

Noting the diverse approaches adopted throughout the world for the promotion and protection of human rights at the national level, emphasizing the universality, indivisibility and interdependence of all human rights, and emphasizing and recognizing the value of such approaches to promoting universal respect for, and observance of, human rights and fundamental freedoms,

1. *Takes note with satisfaction* of the updated report of the Secretary-General, prepared in accordance with its resolution 46/124 of 17 December 1991;

2. *Reaffirms* the importance of developing, in accordance with national legislation, effective national institutions for the promotion and protection of human rights and of ensuring the pluralism of their membership and their independence;

3. *Encourages* Member States to establish or, where they already exist, to strengthen national institutions for the promotion and protection of human rights and to incorporate those elements in national development plans;

4. *Encourages* national institutions for the promotion and protection of human rights established by Member States to prevent and combat all violations of human rights as enumerated in the Vienna Declaration and Programme of Action and relevant international instruments;

5. *Requests* the Centre for Human Rights of the Secretariat to continue its efforts to enhance cooperation between the United Nations and national institutions, particularly in the field of advisory services and technical assistance and of information and education, including within the framework of the World Public Information Campaign for Human Rights;

6. *Also requests* the Centre for Human Rights to establish, upon the request of States concerned, United Nations centres for human rights documentation and training and to do so on the basis of established procedures for the use of available resources within the United Nations Voluntary Fund for Advisory Services and Technical Assistance in the Field of Human Rights;

7. *Requests* the Secretary-General to respond favourably to requests from Member States for assistance in the establishment and strengthening of national institutions for the promotion and protection of human rights as part of the programme of advisory services and technical cooperation in the field of human rights, as well as national centres for human rights documentation and training;

8. *Encourages* all Member States to take appropriate steps to promote the exchange of information and experience concerning the establishment and effective operation of such national institutions;

9. *Affirms* the role of national institutions as agencies for the dissemination of human rights materials and for other public information activities, prepared or organized under the auspices of the United Nations;

10. *Welcomes* the organization, under the auspices of the Centre for Human Rights, of a follow-up meeting at Tunis in December 1993 with a view, in particular, to examining ways and means of promoting technical assistance for the cooperation and strengthening of national institutions, and to continue to examine all issues relating to the question of national institutions;

11. *Welcomes also* the Principles relating to the status of national institutions, annexed to the present resolution;

12. *Encourages* the establishment and strengthening of national institutions having regard to those principles and recognizing that it is the right of each State to choose the framework that is best suited to its particular needs at the national level;

13. *Requests* the Secretary-General to report to the General Assembly at its fiftieth session on the implementation of the present resolution.

ANNEX
Principles relating to the status of national institutions for the promotion and protection of human rights

Competence and responsibilities

1. A national institution shall be vested with competence to promote and protect human rights.

2. A national institution shall be given as broad a mandate as possible, which shall be clearly set forth in a constitutional or legislative text, specifying its composition and its sphere of competence.

3. A national institution shall, *inter alia*, have the following responsibilities:

(*a*) To submit to the Government, Parliament and any other competent body, on an advisory basis either at the request of the authorities concerned or through the exercise of its power to hear a matter without higher referral, opinions, recommendations, proposals and reports on any matters concerning the promotion and protection of human rights; the national institution may decide to publicize them; these opinions, recommendations, proposals and reports, as well as any prerogative of the national institution, shall relate to the following areas:

(i) Any legislative or administrative provisions, as well as provisions relating to judicial organizations, intended to preserve and extend the protection of human rights; in that connection, the national institution shall examine the legislation and administrative provisions in force, as well as bills and proposals, and shall make such recommendations as it deems appropriate in order to ensure that these provisions conform to the fundamental principles of human rights; it shall, if necessary, recommend the adoption of new legislation, the amendment of legislation in force and the adoption or amendment of administrative measures;

(ii) Any situation of violation of human rights which it decides to take up;

(iii) The preparation of reports on the national situation with regard to human rights in general, and on more specific matters;

(iv) Drawing the attention of the Government to situations in any part of the country where human rights are violated and making proposals to it for initiatives to put an end to such situations and, where necessary, expressing an opinion on the positions and reactions of the Government;

(*b*) To promote and ensure the harmonization of national legislation regulations and practices with the international human rights instruments to which the State is a party, and their effective implementation;

(*c*) To encourage ratification of the above-mentioned instruments or accession to those instruments, and to ensure their implementation;

(*d*) To contribute to the reports which States are required to submit to United Nations bodies and committees, and to regional institutions, pursuant to their treaty obligations and, where necessary, to express an opinion on the subject, with due respect for their independence;

(*e*) To cooperate with the United Nations and any other organization in the United Nations system, the regional institutions and the national institutions of other countries that are competent in the areas of the promotion and protection of human rights;

(*f*) To assist in the formulation of programmes for the teaching of, and research into, human rights and to take part in their execution in schools, universities and professional circles;

(*g*) To publicize human rights and efforts to combat all forms of discrimination, in particular racial discrimination, by increasing public awareness, especially through information and education and by making use of all press organs.

Composition and guarantees of independence and pluralism

1. The composition of the national institution and the appointment of its members, whether by means of an election or otherwise, shall be established in accordance with a procedure which affords all necessary guarantees to ensure the pluralist representation of the social forces (of civilian society) involved in the promotion and protection of human rights, particularly by powers which will enable effective cooperation to be established with, or through the presence of, representatives of:

(*a*) Non-governmental organizations responsible for human rights and efforts to combat racial discrimination, trade unions, concerned social and professional organizations, for example, associations of lawyers, doctors, journalists and eminent scientists;

(*b*) Trends in philosophical or religious thought;

(*c*) Universities and qualified experts;

(*d*) Parliament;

(*e*) Government departments (if these are included, the representatives should participate in the deliberations only in an advisory capacity).

2. The national institution shall have an infrastructure which is suited to the smooth conduct of its activities, in particular adequate funding. The purpose of this funding should be to enable it to have its own staff and premises, in order to be independent of the Government and not be subject to financial control which might affect its independence.

3. In order to ensure a stable mandate for the members of the institution, without which there can be no real independence, their appointment shall be effected by an official act which shall establish the specific duration of the mandate. This mandate may be renewable, provided that the pluralism of the institution's membership is ensured.

Methods of operation

Within the framework of its operation, the national institution shall:

(*a*) Freely consider any questions falling within its competence, whether they are submitted by the Government or taken up by it without referral to a higher authority, on the proposal of its members or of any petitioner;

(*b*) Hear any person and obtain any information and any documents necessary for assessing situations falling within its competence;

(*c*) Address public opinion directly or through any press organ, particularly in order to publicize its opinions and recommendations;

(*d*) Meet on a regular basis and whenever necessary in the presence of all its members after they have been duly convened;

(*e*) Establish working groups from among its members as necessary, and set up local or regional sections to assist it in discharging its functions;

(f) Maintain consultation with the other bodies, whether jurisdictional or otherwise, responsible for the promotion and protection of human rights (in particular ombudsmen, mediators and similar institutions);

(g) In view of the fundamental role played by the non-governmental organizations in expanding the work of the national institutions, develop relations with the non-governmental organizations devoted to promoting and protecting human rights, to economic and social development, to combating racism, to protecting particularly vulnerable groups (especially children, migrant workers, refugees, physically and mentally disabled persons) or to specialized areas.

Additional principles concerning the status of commissions with quasi-jurisdictional competence

A national institution may be authorized to hear and consider complaints and petitions concerning individual situations. Cases may be brought before it by individuals, their representatives, third parties, non-governmental organizations, associations of trade unions or any other representative organizations. In such circumstances, and without prejudice to the principles stated above concerning the other powers of the commissions, the functions entrusted to them may be based on the following principles:

(a) Seeking an amicable settlement through conciliation or, within the limits prescribed by the law, through binding decisions or, where necessary, on the basis of confidentiality;

(b) Informing the party who filed the petition of his rights, in particular the remedies available to him, and promoting his access to them;

(c) Hearing any complaints or petitions or transmitting them to any other competent authority within the limits prescribed by the law;

(d) Making recommendations to the competent authorities, especially by proposing amendments or reforms of the laws, regulations and administrative practices, especially if they have created the difficulties encountered by the persons filing the petitions in order to assert their rights.

General Assembly resolution 48/134

20 December 1993   Meeting 85   Adopted without vote

Approved by Third Committee (A/48/632/Add.2) without vote, 6 December (meeting 53); 21-nation draft (A/C.3/48/L.63), orally revised; agenda item 114 *(b)*.

Sponsors: Australia, Belarus, Cameroon, Colombia, Costa Rica, Cyprus, France, Gambia, Guatemala, Guyana, India, Mongolia, Morocco, New Zealand, Nigeria, Peru, Philippines, Russian Federation, Senegal, Ukraine, United Kingdom.

Meeting numbers. GA 48th session: 3rd Committee 36-53; plenary 85.

UN machinery

Commission on Human Rights

The Commission on Human Rights held its forty-ninth session at Geneva from 1 February to 12 March 1993, during which it adopted 98 resolutions and 16 decisions. In addition, the Commission recommended for adoption by the Economic and Social Council four draft resolutions and 44 draft decisions.

The Economic and Social Council, by **decision 1993/300** of 28 July, took note of the Commission's report on its forty-ninth session.[8]

On 11 March,[9] the Commission decided that reports submitted to it should, as much as possible, not exceed 32 pages and should be distributed in all official languages no less than six weeks before Commission consideration. It authorized special representatives, special rapporteurs, independent experts and thematic working groups to begin their work immediately following approval by the Commission, on the understanding that if the Economic and Social Council did not approve the initiation or extension of a mandate, work on that mandate would cease. On the same date,[10] the Commission requested its Chairman to ensure, when appointing special representatives, special rapporteurs and independent experts, that the appointments were made on as wide a geographical basis as possible to correct a current geographical imbalance.

With regard to the organization of its work, the Commission decided, on 2 February,[11] to invite a number of experts, special rapporteurs, special representatives and chairman-rapporteurs of working groups to participate in the meetings at which their reports were to be considered.

On 26 February,[12] the Commission expressed its gratitude to the outgoing Under-Secretary-General for Human Rights, Antoine Blanca, for his services and dedication.

Emergency mechanism of the Commission

On 13 March,[13] the Commission postponed consideration of a 1992 proposal[1] to establish an emergency mechanism of the Commission to enable the United Nations to react appropriately and immediately to acute situations arising from gross human rights violations.

Organization of the work of the 1994 session

On 12 March,[14] the Commission recommended that the Economic and Social Council authorize 40 fully serviced additional meetings for the Commission's fiftieth (1994) session and requested that the Chairman organize the session's work within the time normally allotted, the additional meetings to be utilized only if absolutely necessary.

On 28 July, by **decision 1993/293**, the Council approved the request.

Rationalization of work

On 12 March,[15] the Commission established an open-ended inter-sessional working group, to be convened after the World Conference on Human Rights and chaired by the Chairman of the Commission, to consider the rationalization of the work of the Commission and submit specific proposals for consideration at its 1994 session.

Procedure for special sessions

On 11 March,[16] the Commission recommended to the Economic and Social Council for adoption a draft decision concerning the procedure for holding special sessions of the Commission, which the Council adopted on 28 July.

ECONOMIC AND SOCIAL COUNCIL ACTION

In July, the Economic and Social Council, on the recommendation of its Social Committee, adopted **decision 1993/286** without vote.

Procedure for special sessions of the Commission on Human Rights

At its 44th plenary meeting, on 28 July 1993, the Economic and Social Council, taking note of Commission on Human Rights resolution 1993/96 of 11 March 1993, recalling Council resolution 1990/48 of 25 May 1990, in which it authorized the Commission to meet exceptionally between its regular sessions, provided that a majority of States members of the Commission so agreed, mindful of the need for the Commission to deal with urgent and acute human rights situations in the most expeditious way, and recognizing the need to specify the procedure to be followed in the case of a request for a special session of the Commission, decided that the procedure for convening special sessions of the Commission in accordance with its resolution 1990/48 should be that contained in the annex to the present decision.

ANNEX
Procedure for Special Sessions of the Commission on Human Rights

1. Any State Member of the United Nations may request the Secretary-General to convene a special session of the Commission on Human Rights. Such a request shall be submitted, together with the reasons for the request, to the Assistant Secretary-General for Human Rights at Geneva.

2. The following rules shall apply for the consideration of such requests:

(*a*) The Assistant Secretary-General shall immediately transmit the request, together with the reasons given, to the States members of the Commission by the most expeditious means of communication available and inquire whether or not they support the request;

(*b*) States members of the Commission shall, within four United Nations working days from the date of the communication from the Assistant Secretary-General, express in writing their views concerning the request;

(*c*) The replies from States members of the Commission must reach the office of the Assistant Secretary-General for Human Rights not later than 6 p.m. (Geneva time) on the fourth day;

(*d*) The Assistant Secretary-General shall duly inform the States members of the Commission of the results of the inquiry and, if the majority of States members have expressed support for the convening of a special session of the Commission within the deadline referred to in paragraph 2 (*c*) above, in conformity with Economic and Social Council resolution 1990/48 of 25 May 1990, the Assistant Secretary-General shall communicate the opening date of the special session;

(*e*) The special session shall open between the fourth and the sixth United Nations working day after the deadline referred to in paragraph 2 (*c*) above.

3. In considering the appropriateness of holding a special session, States members of the Commission may take into consideration whether the Economic and Social Council or the General Assembly is in regular session and is, or is likely to be, seized of the matter concerned.

4. The duration of the special session shall, in principle, not exceed three days.

5. The rules of procedure of such a special session shall be the rules of procedure of the functional commissions of the Economic and Social Council.

6. The Commission meeting in special session may take the same decisions as at its regular sessions.

7. If the Commission meeting in special session requests the submission of a report on the matter under consideration, the report, together with any information provided by the State concerned, shall be distributed promptly by the Assistant Secretary-General to all States members of the Commission.

8. If the report and the information referred to in paragraph 7 above are not considered by the Commission meeting in special session on the issue, they shall be considered at the next regular session of the Commission or the General Assembly or at the next substantive session of the Economic and Social Council, whichever occurs earlier.

Economic and Social Council decision 1993/286

Adopted without vote

Approved by Social Committee (E/1993/108) without vote, 22 July (meeting 17); draft by Commission on Human Rights (E/1993/23); agenda item 18.

Subcommission on Prevention of Discrimination and Protection of Minorities

Subcommission session

The Subcommission on Prevention of Discrimination and Protection of Minorities held its forty-fifth session at Geneva from 2 to 27 August 1993.[17] At that session, it adopted 46 resolutions and 11 decisions. In addition, it recommended to the Commission on Human Rights, its parent body, six draft resolutions and 14 decisions for adoption.

The Subcommission adopted decisions relating to the composition of its pre-sessional working groups,[18] methods of voting on proposals pertaining to allegations of human rights violations in countries,[19] and its 1993 agenda.[20] It also adopted a decision[21] on the communications procedure established by the Economic and Social Council in 1970[22] and decided to invite a number of experts and special rapporteurs to participate in the meetings at which their reports were to be considered.[23]

Report of the Subcommission Chairman. In February,[24] the Subcommission's 1992 Chairman, Miguel Alfonso Martínez (Cuba), submitted a report on the work of the 1992 intersessional Working Group on the methods of work of the Subcommission.[25]

Human Rights Commission action. On 5 March,[26] the Commission called on the Subcommission, in fulfilling its functions and duties, to be guided by the relevant resolutions of the Economic and Social Council. Taking note of the steps taken by the Subcommission to rationalize and streamline its work, the Commission invited the Subcommission to consider ways to improve its work further. It asked the Subcommission to restrict its requests to the Secretary-General to ask Governments, intergovernmental organizations, the specialized agencies and other bodies for their views and comments to requests relating to studies that had received prior approval from the Commission. It invited the 1992 Subcommission Chairman to consult with members of the Bureau of the Commission and asked the 1993 Subcommission Chairman to report on progress made with regard to the work of the Subcommission.

On 28 July, the Economic and Social Council, by **decision 1993/261**, approved the Commission's decision.

Subcommission action. On 20 August,[27] the Subcommission decided to convene in 1994 a sessional working group to continue to study its methods of work, emphasizing the methods to be used and procedures to be followed under item 6 of its agenda (human rights violations and fundamental freedoms).

Strengthening the Centre for Human Rights

Human Rights Commission action. On 9 March,[28] the Commission on Human Rights requested the Secretary-General to enhance the coordinating role and importance of the Centre for Human Rights within the United Nations system and to ensure that it was provided with sufficient resources. It asked the Secretary-General and United Nations bodies to implement the relevant recommendations of the World Conference on Human Rights with regard to securing the financial and other resources to strengthen the Centre (see below).

Reports of the Secretary-General. In accordance with a 1992 General Assembly request,[29] the Secretary-General submitted to the Commission, in February, an interim report on developments relating to the activities of the Centre for Human Rights,[30] and, in November, a report to the General Assembly on the proposed programme budget for 1994-1995 to strengthen the Centre.[31]

By **decision 48/430** of 20 December, the General Assembly took note of the Secretary-General's November report.

GENERAL ASSEMBLY ACTION

On 20 December, the General Assembly, on the recommendation of the Third Committee, adopted **resolution 48/129** without vote.

Strengthening of the Centre for Human Rights of the Secretariat

The General Assembly,

Recalling its resolutions 44/135 of 15 December 1989, 45/180 of 21 December 1990, 46/118 and 46/111 of 17 December 1991, and 47/127 of 18 December 1992, and bearing in mind all relevant resolutions of the Economic and Social Council and the Commission on Human Rights,

Considering that the promotion of universal respect for and observance of human rights and fundamental freedoms is one of the basic purposes of the United Nations enshrined in the Charter of the United Nations and of high importance to the Organization,

Noting that in the Vienna Declaration and Programme of Action, adopted by the World Conference on Human Rights, held at Vienna from 14 to 25 June 1993, the importance of strengthening the Centre for Human Rights of the Secretariat is stressed,

Bearing in mind that the Secretary-General, in his reports on the work of the Organization for 1992 and 1993, stated that "the Charter of the United Nations places the promotion of human rights as one of our priority objectives, along with promoting development and preserving international peace and security", and that "in the course of 1993, the activities of the Centre for Human Rights at Geneva underwent a significant expansion in the five main areas of its work",

Noting also that the difficult financial situation of the Centre has created considerable obstacles to the implementation of the various procedures and mechanisms, has negatively influenced the servicing by the Secretariat of the bodies concerned and has impaired the quality and precision of the reporting,

1. *Supports* the efforts of the Secretary-General to enhance the role and importance of the Centre for Human Rights of the Secretariat as the coordinating unit, within the United Nations system, of bodies dealing with the promotion and the protection of human rights;

2. *Requests* the Secretary-General to make additional proposals to increase further the resources of the human rights programme in 1994-1995, so as to enable the Centre fully to discharge its duties implementing all the mandates assigned to it by the General Assembly and other legislative bodies;

3. *Welcomes* the recommendations of the World Conference on Human Rights concerning the strengthening of the Centre, as contained in the Vienna Declaration and Programme of Action;

4. *Takes note* of the recommendation of the Committee for Programme and Coordination that the General Assembly approve the programme narratives of section 21 of the proposed programme budget for the biennium 1994-1995;

5. *Takes note also* of the statement by the Secretary-General in his report concerning the implications of organizational changes in the Secretariat[a] that he would propose to use the remaining vacant posts now available in the Secretariat in the light of new initiatives and emerging mandates and priorities;

6. *Requests* the Secretary-General and Member States to ensure that appropriate additional resources from within the existing and future regular budgets of the United Nations are accorded to the Centre to enable

---

[a]A/C.5/47/2 & Corr.1.

it to carry out, in full and on time, the mandates contained in the Vienna Declaration and Programme of Action without diverting resources from development programmes and activities of the United Nations;

7. *Also requests* the Secretary-General to submit an interim report to the Commission on Human Rights at its fiftieth session and a final report to the General Assembly at its forty-ninth session on the strengthening of the Centre and on the measures taken to implement the present resolution.

General Assembly resolution 48/129

20 December 1993   Meeting 85   Adopted without vote

Approved by Third Committee (A/48/632/Add.2) without vote, 8 December (meeting 54); 90-nation draft (A/C.3/48/L.49); agenda item 114 *(b)*.

Sponsors: Afghanistan, Albania, Andorra, Argentina, Armenia, Australia, Austria, Bahamas, Belarus, Belgium, Benin, Bolivia, Bulgaria, Cambodia, Canada, Central African Republic, Chad, Chile, Costa Rica, Croatia, Cyprus, Czech Republic, Denmark, Egypt, Estonia, Ethiopia, Finland, France, Gambia, Georgia, Germany, Ghana, Greece, Grenada, Guatemala, Guinea, Guinea-Bissau, Guyana, Hungary, Iceland, Indonesia, Ireland, Italy, Latvia, Lesotho, Liechtenstein, Luxembourg, Madagascar, Malta, Marshall Islands, Mauritania, Mauritius, Monaco, Morocco, Namibia, Nepal, Netherlands, New Zealand, Nicaragua, Niger, Nigeria, Norway, Pakistan, Panama, Peru, Philippines, Poland, Portugal, Republic of Korea, Republic of Moldova, Romania, Russian Federation, Rwanda, Senegal, Sierra Leone, Slovakia, Slovenia, Spain, Suriname, Sweden, Tajikistan, the former Yugoslav Republic of Macedonia, Togo, Tunisia, Turkey, Ukraine, United Kingdom, United Republic of Tanzania, Uruguay, Venezuela.

Meeting numbers. GA 48th session: 3rd Committee 36-54; plenary 85.

Strengthening United Nations action

Human Rights Commission action. On 9 March,[32] the Commission reiterated that all peoples had the right to determine freely their political status and pursue their economic, social and cultural development, and that every State had the duty to respect that right within the provisions of the United Nations Charter, including respect for territorial integrity. It called on Member States to base their activities for the promotion, protection and full realization of human rights and fundamental freedoms, including the development of further international cooperation in that area, on the Charter, the 1966 International Covenants on Human Rights[33] and other relevant international instruments, and to refrain from activities inconsistent with that international legal framework. It underlined the need for accurate, impartial and objective information on political, economic and social situations and events in all countries and asked United Nations human rights bodies and special rapporteurs, special representatives, independent experts and working groups to take into account its resolution in carrying out their respective responsibilities. The Commission requested the Secretary-General to continue gathering information and comments from Member States on the basis of its resolution for consideration by the World Conference on Human Rights. It also asked him to submit in 1994, based on comments by Governments, proposals for promoting international cooperation and strengthening United Nations action in the area of human rights.

Also on 9 March,[34] by a roll-call vote of 33 to 16, with 3 abstentions, the Commission expressed its conviction that strengthening the United Nations role in the promotion, protection and full realization of all human rights required increasingly efficient functioning of all mechanisms, as well as suitable methods of work of the Commission. It requested the Secretary-General to submit a report in 1994 on various aspects of treaty and non-treaty mechanisms established to supervise, investigate and monitor the implementation of the provisions of international legal instruments and on the criteria used by the Centre for Human Rights to channel communications received either to existing public machinery or to bodies provided for in a confidential procedure established under a 1970 Economic and Social Council resolution.[22] It also asked him to make the report available to the World Conference on Human Rights.

Report of the Secretary-General. As requested by the Commission in 1992,[35] the Secretary-General submitted comments received from States (Cuba, Mexico, Nicaragua) on possible means to ensure that accurate, impartial and objective information on the political, economic and social situations and events in all countries was made regularly available to human rights bodies and international public opinion.[36]

GENERAL ASSEMBLY ACTION

On 20 December, the General Assembly, on the recommendation of the Third Committee, adopted **resolution 48/125** without vote.

Strengthening of United Nations action in the human rights field through the promotion of international cooperation and the importance of non-selectivity, impartiality and objectivity

The General Assembly,

Reaffirming its faith in fundamental human rights, in the dignity and worth of the human person and the equal rights of men and women and of nations large and small, and its determination to promote social progress and better standards of living in greater freedom,

Bearing in mind that one of the purposes of the United Nations is to develop friendly relations among nations based on respect for the principle of equal rights and self-determination of peoples and to take other appropriate measures to strengthen universal peace,

Bearing in mind also that one of the purposes of the United Nations is to achieve international cooperation in solving international problems of an economic, social, cultural or humanitarian character and in promoting and encouraging respect for human rights and fundamental freedoms for all without distinction as to race, sex, language or religion,

Recalling that, in accordance with Article 55 of the Charter of the United Nations, the Organization shall promote universal respect for and observance of human rights and fundamental freedoms for all, with a view to the creation of conditions of stability and well-being that are necessary for peaceful and friendly relations among nations, based on respect for the principle of equal rights and self-determination of peoples and that, in accordance with Article 56, all Members pledge themselves to take joint and separate action in cooperation with the Organization for the achievement of the purposes set forth in Article 55,

Reiterating that Member States should continue to act in the human rights field in conformity with the provisions of the Charter,

Desirous of achieving further progress in international cooperation in promoting and encouraging respect for human rights and fundamental freedoms,

Considering that such international cooperation should be based on the principles embodied in international law, especially the Charter, as well as the Universal Declaration of Human Rights, the International Covenants on Human Rights and other relevant instruments,

Deeply convinced that United Nations action in this field should be based not only on a profound understanding of the broad range of problems existing in all societies but also on full respect for the political, economic and social realities of each of them, in strict compliance with the purposes and principles of the Charter and for the basic purpose of promoting and encouraging respect for human rights and fundamental freedoms through international cooperation,

Reaffirming its resolutions 45/163 of 18 December 1990, 46/129 of 17 December 1991 and 47/131 of 18 December 1992,

Bearing in mind its resolutions 2131(XX) of 21 December 1965, 2625(XXV) of 24 October 1970 and 36/103 of 9 December 1981,

Taking into account Commission on Human Rights resolution 1993/59 of 9 March 1993,

Reaffirming the importance of ensuring the universality, objectivity and non-selectivity of the consideration of human rights issues, as affirmed in the Vienna Declaration and Programme of Action, adopted by the World Conference on Human Rights, held at Vienna from 14 to 25 June 1993,

Aware of the fact that the promotion, protection and full exercise of all human rights and fundamental freedoms as legitimate concerns of the world community should be guided by the principles of non-selectivity, impartiality and objectivity and should not be used for political ends,

Affirming the importance of the objectivity, independence and discretion of the special rapporteurs and representatives on thematic issues and countries, as well as of the members of the working groups, in carrying out their mandates,

Underlining the obligation that Governments have to promote and protect human rights and to carry out the responsibilities that they have undertaken under international law, especially the Charter, as well as various international instruments in the field of human rights,

1. *Reiterates* that, by virtue of the principle of equal rights and self-determination of peoples enshrined in the Charter of the United Nations, all peoples have the right freely to determine, without external interference, their political status and to pursue their economic, social and cultural development, and that every State has the duty to respect that right within the provisions of the Charter, including respect for territorial integrity;

2. *Reaffirms* that it is a purpose of the United Nations and the task of all Member States, in cooperation with the Organization, to promote and encourage respect for human rights and fundamental freedoms and to remain vigilant with regard to violations of human rights wherever they occur;

3. *Calls upon* all Member States to base their activities for the protection and promotion of human rights, including the development of further international cooperation in this field, on the Charter, the Universal Declaration of Human Rights, the International Covenant on Economic, Social and Cultural Rights, the International Covenant on Civil and Political Rights and other relevant international instruments, and to refrain from activities that are inconsistent with that international framework;

4. *Considers* that international cooperation in this field should make an effective and practical contribution to the urgent task of preventing mass and flagrant violations of human rights and fundamental freedoms for all and to the strengthening of international peace and security;

5. *Affirms* that the promotion, protection and full realization of all human rights and fundamental freedoms, as legitimate concerns of the world community, should be guided by the principles of non-selectivity, impartiality and objectivity, and should not be used for political ends;

6. *Requests* all human rights bodies within the United Nations system, as well as the special rapporteurs and representatives, independent experts and working groups, to take duly into account the contents of the present resolution in carrying out their mandates;

7. *Expresses its conviction* that an unbiased and fair approach to human rights issues contributes to the promotion of international cooperation as well as to the effective promotion, protection and realization of human rights and fundamental freedoms;

8. *Stresses*, in this context, the continuing need for impartial and objective information on the political, economic and social situations and events of all countries;

9. *Invites* Member States to consider adopting, as appropriate, within the framework of their respective legal systems and in accordance with their obligations under international law, especially the Charter, and international human rights instruments, the measures that they may deem appropriate to achieve further progress in international cooperation in promoting and encouraging respect for human rights and fundamental freedoms;

10. *Requests* the Commission on Human Rights, at its fiftieth session, to continue to examine ways and means to strengthen United Nations action in this regard on the basis of the present resolution and of Commission resolution 1993/59;

11. *Decides* to consider this matter at its forty-ninth session under the item entitled "Human rights questions".

General Assembly resolution 48/125

20 December 1993   Meeting 85   Adopted without vote

Approved by Third Committee (A/48/632/Add.2) without vote, 6 December (meeting 52); 24-nation draft (A/C.3/48/L.45), orally amended by Australia; agenda item 114 *(b)*.

Sponsors: Afghanistan, Bangladesh, China, Cuba, Democratic People's Republic of Korea, Gabon, Gambia, Ghana, Indonesia, Iran, Iraq, Lao People's Democratic Republic, Malaysia, Mexico, Mozambique, Namibia, Nigeria, Pakistan, Peru, Sudan, United Republic of Tanzania, Viet Nam, Zambia, Zimbabwe.

Meeting numbers. GA 48th session: 3rd Committee 36-52; plenary 85.

Rule of law

On 9 March,[37] the Commission on Human Rights reiterated the need to consider ways by which the United Nations could better contribute to the development and strengthening by Member States of the rule of law. It requested the Secretary-General of the World Conference on Human Rights to bring its resolution to the attention of the Conference's Preparatory Committee.

On 20 December, the General Assembly, on the recommendation of the Third Committee, adopted **resolution 48/132** without vote.

Strengthening of the rule of law

The General Assembly,

Recalling that the achievement of international cooperation in promoting and encouraging respect for human rights and fundamental freedoms for all without distinction as to race, sex, language and religion is one of the purposes of the United Nations,

Recalling also that, by adopting the Universal Declaration of Human Rights, Member States have pledged themselves to achieve, in cooperation with the United Nations, the promotion of universal respect for and observance of human rights and fundamental freedoms,

Firmly convinced that, as stressed in the Universal Declaration of Human Rights, the rule of law is an essential factor in the protection of human rights,

Convinced that through their own national legal and judicial systems States must provide appropriate civil, criminal and administrative remedies for violations of human rights,

Aware of the need for the implementation of strengthened advisory services and technical assistance activities in the field of human rights,

Mindful of the significant role played by national institutions in the promotion and protection of universally recognized human rights and fundamental freedoms in their respective countries,

Convinced that the Centre for Human Rights of the Secretariat should play an important role in coordinating system-wide attention for human rights,

Recalling Commission on Human Rights resolution 1992/51 of 3 March 1992 and taking note of Commission resolution 1993/50 of 9 March 1993, both entitled "Strengthening of the rule of law",

Noting with appreciation that in the Vienna Declaration and Programme of Action, adopted by the World Conference on Human Rights on 25 June 1993, the Conference recommended that priority be given to national and international action to promote democracy, development and human rights,

1. *Endorses* the recommendation of the World Conference on Human Rights that a comprehensive programme be established within the United Nations and under the coordination of the Centre for Human Rights of the Secretariat, with a view to helping States in the task of building and strengthening adequate national structures which have a direct impact on the overall observance of human rights and the maintenance of the rule of law;

2. *Expresses its conviction* that such a programme should be able to provide, upon the request of the interested Government, technical and financial assistance for the implementation of national plans of action as well as specific projects for the reform of penal and correctional establishments, and the education and training of lawyers, judges and security forces in human rights, and in any other sphere of activity relevant to the good functioning of the rule of law;

3. *Requests* the Secretary-General, in accordance with the request contained in section II, paragraph 70, of the Vienna Declaration and Programme of Action, to submit concrete proposals to the General Assembly at its forty-ninth session containing alternatives for the establishment, structure, operational modalities and funding of the proposed programme, taking into account existing programmes and activities already undertaken by the Centre for Human Rights;

4. *Requests* the Commission on Human Rights to remain actively seized of this question, with a view to further elaborating the outline of the proposed programme;

5. *Decides* to continue its consideration of this question at its forty-ninth session in the light of the proposals of the Secretary-General.

General Assembly resolution 48/132

20 December 1993   Meeting 85   Adopted without vote

Approved by Third Committee (A/48/632/Add.2) without vote, 6 December (meeting 52); 47-nation draft (A/C.3/48/L.56); agenda item 114 *(b)*.
Sponsors: Andorra, Argentina, Australia, Belarus, Bolivia, Brazil, Bulgaria, Cambodia, Canada, Chad, Chile, Colombia, Costa Rica, Côte d'Ivoire, Denmark, Dominican Republic, France, Gambia, Georgia, Guatemala, Guinea, Guinea-Bissau, Honduras, India, Japan, Kyrgyzstan, Malawi, Morocco, Nepal, Nicaragua, Norway, Pakistan, Peru, Philippines, Portugal, Republic of Korea, Republic of Moldova, Romania, Russian Federation, Samoa, Senegal, Sudan, Togo, Uganda, Ukraine, Uruguay, Venezuela.
Meeting numbers. GA 48th session: 3rd Committee 36-52; plenary 85.

High Commissioner for Human Rights

The Vienna Declaration and Programme of Action,[38] adopted by the World Conference on Human Rights on 25 June (see below), in addressing the need to strengthen United Nations machinery for human rights, called for the General Assembly to consider, as a matter of priority, the establishment of the post of High Commissioner for Human Rights.

Pursuant to that recommendation, the Assembly's Third Committee established an open-ended working group to consider that question and other aspects of applying the Vienna Declaration's recommendations.

On 20 December, the General Assembly, on the recommendation of the Third Committee, adopted **resolution 48/141** without vote.

High Commissioner for the promotion and protection of all human rights

The General Assembly,

Reaffirming its commitment to the purposes and principles of the Charter of the United Nations,

Emphasizing the responsibilities of all States, in conformity with the Charter, to promote and encourage respect for all human rights and fundamental freedoms for all, without distinction as to race, sex, language or religion,

Emphasizing also the need to observe the Universal Declaration of Human Rights and for the full implementation of the human rights instruments, including the International Covenant on Civil and Political Rights, the International Covenant on Economic, Social and Cultural Rights, as well as the Declaration on the Right to Development,

Reaffirming that the right to development is a universal and inalienable right which is a fundamental part of the rights of the human person,

Considering that the promotion and the protection of all human rights is one of the priorities of the international community,

Recalling that one of the purposes of the United Nations enshrined in the Charter is to achieve international cooperation in promoting and encouraging respect for human rights,

Reaffirming the commitment contained under Article 56 of the Charter of the United Nations to take joint and separate action in cooperation with the United Nations for the achievement of the purposes set forth in Article 55,

Emphasizing the need for the promotion and protection of all human rights to be guided by the principles of impartiality, objectivity and non-selectivity, in the spirit of constructive international dialogue and cooperation,

Aware that all human rights are universal, indivisible, interdependent and interrelated and that as such they should be given the same emphasis,

Affirming its commitment to the Vienna Declaration and Programme of Action, adopted by the World Conference on Human Rights, held at Vienna from 14 to 25 June 1993,

Convinced that the World Conference on Human Rights made an important contribution to the cause of human rights and that its recommendations should be implemented through effective action by all States, the competent organs of the United Nations and the specialized agencies, in cooperation with non-governmental organizations,

Acknowledging the importance of strengthening the provision of advisory services and technical assistance by the Centre for Human Rights of the Secretariat and other relevant programmes and bodies of the United Nations system for the purpose of the promotion and protection of all human rights,

Determined to adapt, strengthen, and streamline the existing mechanisms to promote and protect all human rights and fundamental freedoms while avoiding unnecessary duplication,

Recognizing that the activities of the United Nations in the field of human rights should be rationalized and enhanced in order to strengthen the United Nations machinery in this field and to further the objectives of universal respect for observance of international human rights standards,

Reaffirming that the General Assembly, the Economic and Social Council and the Commission on Human Rights are the responsible organs for decision- and policy-making for the promotion and protection of all human rights,

Reaffirming also the necessity for a continued adaptation of the United Nations human rights machinery to the current and future needs in the promotion and protection of human rights and the need to improve its coordination, efficiency and effectiveness, as reflected in the Vienna Declaration and Programme of Action and within the framework of a balanced and sustainable development for all people,

Having considered the recommendation contained in paragraph 18 of section II of the Vienna Declaration and Programme of Action,

1. *Decides* to create the post of the United Nations High Commissioner for Human Rights;

2. *Decides* that the High Commissioner shall:

(*a*) Be a person of high moral standing and personal integrity and shall possess expertise, including in the field of human rights, and the general knowledge and understanding of diverse cultures necessary for impartial, objective, non-selective and effective performance of the duties of the High Commissioner;

(*b*) Be appointed by the Secretary-General of the United Nations and approved by the General Assembly, with due regard to geographical rotation, and have a fixed term of four years with a possibility of one renewal for another fixed term of four years;

(*c*) Be of the rank of Under-Secretary-General;

3. *Also decides* that the High Commissioner shall:

(*a*) Function within the framework of the Charter of the United Nations, the Universal Declaration of Human Rights, other international instruments of human rights and international law, including the obligations, within this framework, to respect the sovereignty, territorial integrity and domestic jurisdiction of States and to promote the universal respect for and observance of all human rights, in the recognition that, in the framework of the purposes and principles of the Charter, the promotion and protection of all human rights is a legitimate concern of the international community;

(*b*) Be guided by the recognition that all human rights—civil, cultural, economic, political and social—are universal, indivisible, interdependent and interrelated and that, while the significance of national and regional particularities and various historical, cultural and religious backgrounds must be borne in mind, it is the duty of States, regardless of their political, economic and cultural systems, to promote and protect all human rights and fundamental freedoms;

(*c*) Recognize the importance of promoting a balanced and sustainable development for all people and of ensuring realization of the right to development, as established in the Declaration on the Right to Development;

4. *Further decides* that the High Commissioner shall be the United Nations official with principal responsibility for United Nations human rights activities under the direction and authority of the Secretary-General and that within the framework of the overall competence, authority and decisions of the General Assembly, the Economic and Social Council and the Commission on Human Rights, the High Commissioner's responsibilities shall be:

(*a*) To promote and protect the effective enjoyment by all of all civil, cultural, economic, political and social rights;

(*b*) To carry out the tasks assigned to him/her by the competent bodies of the United Nations system in the field of human rights and to make recommendations to them with a view to improving the promotion and protection of all human rights;

(c) To promote and protect the realization of the right to development and to enhance support from relevant bodies of the United Nations system for this purpose;

(d) To provide, through the Centre for Human Rights and other appropriate institutions, advisory services and technical and financial assistance, at the request of the State concerned and, where appropriate, the regional human rights organizations, with a view to supporting actions and programmes in the field of human rights;

(e) To coordinate relevant United Nations education and public information programmes in the field of human rights;

(f) To play an active role in removing the current obstacles and in meeting the challenges to the full realization of all human rights and in preventing the continuation of human rights violations throughout the world, as reflected in the Vienna Declaration and Programme of Action;

(g) To engage in a dialogue with all Governments in the implementation of his/her mandate with a view to securing respect for all human rights;

(h) To enhance international cooperation for the promotion and protection of all human rights;

(i) To coordinate the human rights promotion and protection activities throughout the United Nations system;

(j) To rationalize, adapt, strengthen and streamline the United Nations machinery in the field of human rights with a view to improving its efficiency and effectiveness;

(k) To carry out overall supervision of the Centre for Human Rights;

5. *Requests* the High Commissioner to report annually on his/her activities, in accordance with his/her mandate, to the Commission on Human Rights and, through the Economic and Social Council, to the General Assembly;

6. *Decides* that the Office of the United Nations High Commissioner for Human Rights shall be located at Geneva and shall have a liaison office in New York;

7. *Requests* the Secretary-General to provide appropriate staff and resources, within the existing and future regular budgets of the United Nations, to enable the High Commissioner to fulfil his/her mandate, without diverting resources from the development programmes and activities of the United Nations;

8. *Also requests* the Secretary-General to report to the General Assembly at its forty-ninth session on the implementation of the present resolution.

General Assembly resolution 48/141

20 December 1993   Meeting 85   Adopted without vote

Approved by Third Committee (A/48/632/Add.4) by consensus, 16 December (meeting 57); draft by Working Group on establishment of a High Commissioner (A/C.3/48/L.85), orally revised; agenda item 114 *(b)*.
Meeting numbers. GA 48th session: 3rd Committee 36-58; plenary 85.

1993 World Conference on Human Rights

The World Conference on Human Rights took place at Vienna from 14 to 25 June 1993.[39] On 25 June, it adopted the Vienna Declaration and Programme of Action,[38] in which participating Governments reaffirmed their solemn commitment to a broad range of human rights and fundamental freedoms, called for specific measures to strengthen international human rights instruments and their monitoring mechanisms.

The Declaration's recommendations addressed racism, racial discrimination, xenophobia and other forms of intolerance; national or ethnic, religious and linguistic minorities; the status and human rights of women; children's rights; freedom from torture; rights of disabled persons; national and international action to promote democracy, development and human rights; and human rights education.

It also called for increased coordination on human rights within the United Nations system, a substantial increase in resources for the human rights programme and strengthening the Centre for Human Rights and United Nations human rights machinery, including establishing the post of High Commissioner for Human Rights.

The Conference adopted two declarations calling on the international community, particularly the Security Council, to take forceful and decisive steps to bring peace to Angola and to Bosnia and Herzegovina. It commemorated the 1993 International Year of the World's Indigenous People (see above) and designated commemorative days during the Conference dedicated to various themes, such as peace, development, women, children and democracy.

The Conference was attended by representatives of 171 States, 2 national liberation movements, 15 United Nations bodies, 10 specialized agencies, 18 intergovernmental organizations, 24 national institutions and 6 ombudsmen, 11 United Nations human rights and related bodies, 9 other organizations, 248 NGOs in consultative status with the Economic and Social Council and 593 other NGOs. A number of eminent persons attended and addressed the Conference at the invitation of the Secretary-General.

Prior to the Conference, consultations took place among senior officials of participating States Members (Vienna, 9-12 June).

Preparatory Committee

The Preparatory Committee for the World Conference on Human Rights, at its fourth session (Geneva, 19 April–7 May 1993),[40] adopted and transmitted to the Conference paragraphs of the draft final document of the Conference, based on declarations adopted at regional preparatory meetings: Africa (Tunis, 2-6 November 1992),[41] Asia (Bangkok, 29 March–2 April 1993)[42] and Latin America and the Caribbean (San José, Costa Rica,

18-22 January 1993)[43] and on other documents, including an April note by the Secretary-General containing elements for possible inclusion in the draft.[44]

GENERAL ASSEMBLY ACTION

On 20 December, on the recommendation of the Third Committee, the General Assembly adopted **resolution 48/121** without vote.

World Conference on Human Rights

The General Assembly,

Recalling its resolutions 45/155 of 18 December 1990, in which it decided, *inter alia*, to convene at a high level a World Conference on Human Rights in 1993, and its resolutions 46/116 of 17 December 1991 and 47/122 of 18 December 1992,

Taking note with appreciation of the Vienna Declaration and Programme of Action, adopted by the World Conference on Human Rights, held at Vienna from 14 to 25 June 1993,

Bearing in mind the view of the Conference that the promotion and protection of human rights is a matter of priority for the international community,

Convinced that the Conference has made an important contribution to the cause of human rights and that its results have to be translated into effective action by States, the competent organs of the United Nations and its family of organizations and other organizations concerned, as well as non-governmental organizations,

Bearing in mind the recommendation of the Conference that the General Assembly, the Commission on Human Rights and other organs and bodies of the United Nations system related to human rights consider ways and means for the full implementation, without delay, of the recommendations contained in the Vienna Declaration and Programme of Action,

Expressing its gratitude to the Government and people of Austria for acting as hosts to the Conference, for the excellent arrangements and for the hospitality extended to all participants,

Expressing its appreciation to the Secretary-General of the United Nations, the Secretary-General of the Conference and the members of the Secretariat for effectively preparing for and servicing the Conference,

1. *Takes note* of the report of the World Conference on Human Rights;

2. *Endorses* the Vienna Declaration and Programme of Action, adopted by the Conference on 25 June 1993;

3. *Expresses its satisfaction* with the work of the Conference, which constitutes a solid foundation for further action and initiatives by the United Nations and other interested international bodies, as well as by the States and national organizations concerned;

4. *Confirms* the views of the Conference on the urgency of eliminating denials and violations of human rights;

5. *Requests* the Secretary-General to ensure the distribution of the Vienna Declaration and Programme of Action as widely as possible and to include the text of the Declaration in the next edition of *Human Rights: A Compilation of International Instruments*;

6. *Also requests* the Secretary-General to transmit to the competent organs of the United Nations and the spe-

cialized agencies the Vienna Declaration and Programme of Action;

7. *Urges* all States to give widespread publicity to the Vienna Declaration and Programme of Action and the work of the Conference in order to promote increased awareness of human rights and fundamental freedoms;

8. *Calls upon* all States to take further action with a view to the full realization of human rights in the light of the recommendations of the Conference;

9. *Endorses* the recommendations of the Conference that the Secretary-General, the General Assembly, the Commission on Human Rights and other organs and bodies of the United Nations system related to human rights should take further action with a view to the full implementation of all recommendations of the Conference;

10. *Requests* the Secretary-General to report annually to the General Assembly on the measures taken and the progress achieved in the implementation of the recommendations of the Conference;

11. *Decides* to include in the agenda of its forthcoming sessions, under the item entitled "Human rights questions", a standing sub-item entitled "Comprehensive implementation of and follow-up to the Vienna Declaration and Programme of Action".

General Assembly resolution 48/121

20 December 1993   Meeting 85   Adopted without vote

Approved by Third Committee (A/48/632/Add.2) without vote, 8 December (meeting 54); 115-nation draft (A/C.3/48/L.38); agenda item 114 *(b)*.

Sponsors: Afghanistan, Albania, Angola, Argentina, Armenia, Australia, Austria, Azerbaijan, Bahamas, Bangladesh, Barbados, Belarus, Belgium, Bolivia, Bosnia and Herzegovina, Bulgaria, Cambodia, Canada, Chile, Colombia, Costa Rica, Côte d'Ivoire, Croatia, Cuba, Cyprus, Czech Republic, Denmark, Dominican Republic, Ecuador, Egypt, El Salvador, Estonia, Ethiopia, Finland, France, Gambia, Georgia, Germany, Greece, Guatemala, Guinea, Haiti, Honduras, Hungary, Iceland, India, Indonesia, Ireland, Italy, Jamaica, Japan, Kazakhstan, Kenya, Kuwait, Kyrgyzstan, Latvia, Lesotho, Libyan Arab Jamahiriya, Liechtenstein, Lithuania, Luxembourg, Madagascar, Malawi, Malta, Marshall Islands, Mauritania, Mexico, Micronesia, Monaco, Mongolia, Morocco, Myanmar, Namibia, Nepal, Netherlands, New Zealand, Nicaragua, Nigeria, Norway, Pakistan, Panama, Papua New Guinea, Peru, Philippines, Poland, Portugal, Republic of Korea, Republic of Moldova, Romania, Russian Federation, Rwanda, Senegal, Singapore, Slovakia, Slovenia, Solomon Islands, Spain, Sri Lanka, Sudan, Suriname, Sweden, Tajikistan, Thailand, the former Yugoslav Republic of Macedonia, Tunisia, Turkey, Uganda, Ukraine, United Kingdom, United States, Uruguay, Venezuela, Viet Nam, Yemen, Zambia.

Financial implications. 5th Committee, A/48/795; S-G, A/C.3/48/L.80, A/C.5/48/46.

Meeting numbers. GA 48th session: 3rd Committee 36-54; 5th Committee 43; plenary 85.

Public information activities

In response to a 1992 request of the Human Rights Commission,[45] the Secretary-General submitted a report on public information activities in the human rights field, including the World Public Information Campaign on Human Rights launched by the General Assembly in 1988,[46] carried out by the Centre for Human Rights and the United Nations Department of Public Information (DPI).[47] He also discussed coordination and cooperation within and outside the United Nations system, human rights observances and national focal points and assessed the Campaign's impact.

Human Rights Commission action. On 9 March,[48] the Commission encouraged Member

States to provide, facilitate and promote publicity for United Nations human rights activities and to accord priority to disseminating in their national and local languages the 1948 Universal Declaration of Human Rights,[49] the 1966 International Covenants on Human Rights[33] and other international instruments. Urging Member States to include in their educational curricula materials relevant to a comprehensive understanding of human rights issues, it encouraged the Centre for Human Rights to produce materials for that purpose. It welcomed the Centre's decision to convene a series of expert meetings in 1993 to elaborate training manuals. The Commission asked DPI to use fully its available resources in human rights to produce materials on such issues. It stressed the need for close cooperation between the Centre and DPI in implementing the World Campaign and asked the Secretary-General to take advantage of the collaboration of NGOs in that process. It also emphasized the need for the Secretariat to harmonize its public information activities with those of other international bodies with regard to the dissemination of information on international humanitarian law. The Commission asked the Secretary-General to ensure that recent periodic reports of States parties to treaty-monitoring bodies and summary records of discussions on them in the treaty bodies be made available in UNICs in the submitting countries; to increase resources for the Public Information Campaign; to review the human rights information programmes and any views expressed on them during the World Conference; to consider a recommendation of the fourth (1992) meeting of persons chairing the human rights treaty bodies;[50] that an expert group from outside the Secretariat be appointed to review the Centre's information programme; and to submit in 1994 a report on public information activities.

Advisory services

In 1993,[51] under the United Nations programme of advisory services in human rights established in 1955,[52] activities funded by the United Nations regular budget included the establishment of a human rights field office at Phnom Penh, Cambodia, on 1 October, the appointment of a human rights officer in Guatemala to monitor the return of refugees from Mexico and provide advisory services and technical assistance and the appointment of an independent expert to assist the Special Representative of the Secretary-General for Somalia to re-establish human rights and the rule of law, as well as the eventual holding of elections. The Centre for Human Rights provided electoral assistance to South Africa and advisory services to assist in constitutional drafting pro-

cesses attending democratic transition in Malawi, South Africa and Tajikistan. Among seminars and training courses held were: a seminar on free and fair elections and human rights in a democratic society (Maseru, Lesotho, January); a workshop on human rights and the resolution of conflicts between citizens and state organs (Bucharest, Romania, 10-14 May); and a colloquium on human rights and the media (Bucharest, 16-20 August). Two meetings of national institutions were held (Sydney, Australia, 19-23 April; Tunis, 13-17 December). Fellowships were awarded to 47 candidates and 120 internships were offered to graduate students. Needs assessment missions were fielded to Burundi, Malawi, Romania, and South Africa.

Under the Voluntary Fund for Technical Cooperation in the Field of Human Rights, established in 1987,[53] support was given to regional institutions in Africa and an Asian and Pacific workshop on human rights issues was held (Jakarta, Indonesia, 26-28 January). Ongoing projects were under way in Africa (Benin, Burundi, Cameroon, Côte d'Ivoire, Egypt, Ethiopia, Guinea, Lesotho, Malawi, Mozambique, Namibia, Sao Tome and Principe, Somalia, South Africa, United Republic of Tanzania); Asia and the Pacific (Cambodia, Mongolia, Papua New Guinea, Tajikistan); Europe (Albania, Armenia, Azerbaijan, Belarus, Georgia, Hungary, Lithuania, Poland, Romania, the Russian Federation, Slovakia, the former Yugoslav Republic of Macedonia); and Latin America (Argentina, Bolivia, Colombia, Ecuador, Guatemala, Mexico, Paraguay).

The Secretary-General reported that, as at 31 December 1993, the Fund had a negative balance of $1,172,076. Annexed to the report was an account of the Fund's income and expenditures, utilization and project commitments in 1993.

Human Rights Commission action. On 10 March,[54] the Commission, taking note of the Secretary-General's report on advisory services in human rights during 1992, including the Voluntary Fund for Technical Cooperation in the Field of Human Rights,[55] asked him to implement all activities under the programme of advisory services on the basis of clearly defined objectives and themes; provide urgently more human and financial resources to enlarge advisory services; pursue efforts towards a comprehensive plan for advisory services and technical cooperation; and give special attention to proposals for the implementation of advisory services made by United Nations human rights treaty bodies, special representatives, special rapporteurs and working groups and to report on follow-up activities undertaken as a result. It requested its special rapporteurs and representatives, as well as the Working Group on

Enforced or Involuntary Disappearances and the Working Group on Arbitrary Detention, to recommend specific projects under the programmes of advisory services and encourage Governments to avail themselves of the services provided for under the programmes.

Concerning the Voluntary Fund, the Commission asked the Secretary-General to appoint a board of trustees; to include the Board's report in his annual report on advisory services and technical cooperation; and to guarantee transparency of the criteria and rules of procedure to be followed in carrying out human rights technical cooperation. It asked the Board to assist the Secretary-General to streamline and rationalize the Fund's working methods and procedures and to promote and solicit contributions and pledges. Regarding system-wide cooperation, the Commission asked the Secretary-General to explore further the possibilities offered by cooperation between the Centre for Human Rights and specialized bodies of the system; bring the need for further technical assistance in the legal field to the attention of the relevant United Nations bodies and specialized agencies; and report to the Commission annually on progress made in implementing the programme of advisory services.

By **decision 1993/283** of 28 July, the Economic and Social Council approved the Commission's requests to the Secretary-General to provide urgently more human and financial resources to enlarge human rights advisory services and to appoint a board of trustees for the Fund.

Georgia

On 10 March,[56] the Commission requested the Secretary-General to evaluate the needs for human rights support and technical assistance to Georgia by providing advisory services aimed at furthering legislation in constitutional and institutional matters and at providing institutions with the expertise to implement international human rights standards. The Commission's request to the Secretary-General was approved by the Economic and Social Council by **decision 1993/281** of 28 July.

Guatemala

Human Rights Commission action. Taking note of the report by independent expert Christian Tomuschat (Germany) on the situation of human rights in Guatemala,[57] the Commission, on 10 March,[58] asked the Secretary-General to continue to provide that country and NGOs with advisory services and to extend the independent expert's mandate. Urging Guatemala to intensify investigations to identify and bring to justice those responsible for human rights violations, the Commission appealed for intensified efforts to ensure that its authorities and security forces fully

respected the human rights of the Guatemalan people. It also asked that the expert report in 1994 on measures taken by Guatemala.

By **decision 1993/335** of 30 July, the Economic and Social Council postponed consideration of a draft decision on assistance to Guatemala which would have approved the extension of the expert's mandate.[59] On 21 October, by **decision 1993/336**, the Council approved the extension.

Subcommission action. On 20 August,[60] the Subcommission adopted a resolution on the situation of human rights in Guatemala.

Somalia

Human Rights Commission action. On 10 March,[61] the Commission asked the Secretary-General to appoint for one year an independent expert to assist the Special Representative of the Secretary-General for Somalia to develop a long-term programme of advisory services; to give priority to implementing the programme recommended by the independent expert; and to provide additional resources to fund the activities of the independent expert and the Centre for Human Rights in implementing its resolution. Those requests were approved by the Economic and Social Council by **decision 1993/282** of 28 July. The Commission asked the independent expert to report in 1994 on conditions in Somalia to the General Assembly, the Commission and, if needed, to the Economic and Social Council. The Secretary-General was urged to recommend the establishment of a unit within the United Nations operation in Somalia to assist in promoting and protecting human rights, in encouraging respect for humanitarian law and in implementing the independent expert's recommendations.

Report of the independent expert. In October,[62] independent expert Fanuel Jarirentundu Kozonguizi (Namibia) concluded that it was premature to propose any concrete activity under the advisory services programme. If the situation did not improve, he would consider recommending that the Commission change his mandate or revert the situation to other United Nations bodies. He recommended establishing an independent group of human rights monitors to receive complaints and collect and investigate reports of human rights violations and humanitarian law.

GENERAL ASSEMBLY ACTION

On 20 December, the General Assembly, on the recommendation of the Third Committee, adopted **resolution 48/146** without vote.

Situation of human rights in Somalia

The General Assembly,

Guided by the principles embodied in the Charter of the United Nations, the International Bill of Human Rights and other applicable human rights instruments,

Gravely concerned by the situation in Somalia, including the extensive damage and destruction of villages, towns and cities, the heavy damage inflicted by the civil conflict on the country's infrastructure and the still widespread disruption of many public facilities and services and the lack of a governmental authority to ensure even basic human rights,

Deploring the loss of human life in Somalia and attacks against personnel of the United Nations and other humanitarian organizations in Somalia, which sometimes result in serious injuries or deaths,

Recalling Security Council resolution 733(1992) of 21 January 1992, all subsequent relevant Security Council resolutions and General Assembly resolution 47/167 of 18 December 1992, and taking note of Commission on Human Rights resolution 1993/86 of 10 March 1993,

Commending the ongoing efforts in Somalia of the United Nations, the specialized agencies, humanitarian organizations, non-governmental organizations, countries in the region and regional organizations,

Taking note with appreciation of the report of the independent expert on the conditions in Somalia, dated 26 October 1993,

1. *Commends* the independent expert for his report on the conditions in Somalia, in which he cited an increase in human rights violations fuelled by the absence of an accountable government and the lack of infrastructure;

2. *Urges* all Somali parties to the conflict to confirm their commitment to the Addis Ababa agreement of 27 March 1993;

3. *Urges* all Somalis to work together towards peace and security in Somalia and to guarantee the protection of all human rights and fundamental freedoms for all Somalis;

4. *Calls upon* all parties to protect civilians, United Nations personnel and humanitarian relief workers from being killed, tortured or arbitrarily detained;

5. *Requests* that, following the restoration of political stability and security in Somalia, the Commission on Human Rights, in accordance with the Charter of the United Nations, consider establishing a group of independent human rights monitors, funded from within existing United Nations resources, to receive complaints and collect and investigate reports of violations of human rights and to transmit them, where appropriate, to the Centre for Human Rights of the Secretariat, in an effort to prevent human rights violations;

6. *Decides* to continue its consideration of this question at its forty-ninth session.

General Assembly resolution 48/146

20 December 1993   Meeting 85   Adopted without vote

Approved by Third Committee (A/48/632/Add.3) without vote, 6 December (meeting 53); 44-nation draft (A/C.3/48/L.62/Rev.1); agenda item 114 *(c)*.
Sponsors: Andorra, Armenia, Australia, Austria, Belgium, Canada, Costa Rica, Czech Republic, Denmark, Djibouti, Ethiopia, Finland, France, Georgia, Germany, Greece, Guinea, Hungary, Iceland, Ireland, Italy, Japan, Luxembourg, Monaco, Morocco, Netherlands, New Zealand, Nicaragua, Norway, Pakistan, Poland, Portugal, Republic of Korea, Republic of Moldova, Romania, San Marino, Sierra Leone, Slovakia, Solomon Islands, Spain, Sweden, Turkey, United Kingdom, United States.
Meeting numbers. GA 48th session: 3rd Committee 36-53; plenary 85.

International human rights instruments

Human rights treaty bodies

In 1993, there were seven human rights treaty instruments in force providing for monitoring treaty implementation by expert bodies. Those instruments and their respective treaty bodies were the: 1965 International Convention on the Elimination of All Forms of Racial Discrimination[63] (CERD); 1966 International Covenant on Economic, Social and Cultural Rights[33] (Committee on Economic, Social and Cultural Rights); 1966 International Covenant on Civil and Political Rights[33] (Human Rights Committee); 1979 Convention on the Elimination of All Forms of Discrimination against Women[64] (Committee on the Elimination of Discrimination against Women); 1984 Convention against Torture and Other Cruel, Inhuman or Degrading Treatment or Punishment[65] (Committee against Torture); 1989 Convention on the Rights of the Child[66] (Committee on the Rights of the Child); and the 1973 International Convention on the Suppression and Punishment of the Crime of Apartheid[67] (Group of Three).

Human Rights Commission action. On 26 February,[68] the Commission endorsed continuing efforts to streamline, rationalize and improve reporting procedures by treaty bodies and by the Secretary-General, as well as the recommendations made at the meeting of persons chairing the human rights treaty bodies, on ensuring financing and adequate staffing for operating those bodies. It requested that a 1989 study by the independent expert on possible long-term approaches to enhance the effective operation of existing and prospective bodies established under United Nations human rights instruments[69] be updated for submission in 1994 and that an interim report be presented to the General Assembly in 1993 and made available to the World Conference on Human Rights. The Commission asked the Secretary-General to give high priority to establishing a computerized database to improve the efficiency and effectiveness of the functioning of treaty bodies; to expedite implementation of the 1990 recommendations of the Task Force on Computerization[70] by asking Member States to contribute voluntarily to cover the cost of the proposed system; to prepare an inventory of all international human rights standard-setting activities to facilitate better-informed decision-making; to ensure that recent periodic reports of States parties to treaty-monitoring bodies and summary records of committee discussions pertaining to them were made available in the UNICs in countries submitting the reports; and to ensure that the *Manual on Human Rights Reporting*[71] was available in all official languages at the earliest opportunity.

Report of the Independent Expert. Independent Expert Philip Alston (Australia) presented in April 1993[72] an interim report updating his 1989 study on possible long-term approaches to enhance the effective operation of existing and prospective bodies established under United Nations human rights instruments.[69] He concluded that existing levels of secretariat servicing provided to the treaty bodies was inadequate and made recommendations regarding reporting procedures, steps to remedy the problem of overdue reports by States parties and financing arrangements.

By a November note,[73] the Secretary-General stated that the interim report was presented to the World Conference on Human Rights and was being made available to the General Assembly.

By **decision 48/430** of 20 December, the General Assembly took note of the Secretary-General's note.

Reports of the Secretary-General. In response to a 1992 General Assembly request,[74] the Secretary-General submitted an October report[75] examining the conclusions and recommendations of the fourth (1992) meeting of persons chairing the human rights treaty bodies.[50]

Also in response to a 1992 Assembly request,[74] the Secretary-General, in November, discussed the need to ensure financing and adequate staffing resources for the operations of the treaty bodies.[76]

GENERAL ASSEMBLY ACTION

On 20 December, on the recommendation of the Third Committee, the General Assembly adopted **resolution 48/120** without vote.

Effective implementation of international instruments on human rights, including reporting obligations under international instruments on human rights
The General Assembly,

Recalling its resolution 47/111 of 16 December 1992, as well as other relevant resolutions,

Reaffirming that the effective implementation of United Nations human rights instruments is of major importance to the efforts of the Organization, pursuant to the Charter of the United Nations and the Universal Declaration of Human Rights, to promote universal respect for and observance of human rights and fundamental freedoms,

Reaffirming its responsibility to ensure the proper functioning of treaty bodies established pursuant to instruments adopted by the General Assembly and, in this connection, further reaffirming the importance of:

(a) Ensuring the effective functioning of systems of periodic reporting by States parties to these instruments,

(b) Securing sufficient financial resources to overcome existing difficulties with their effective functioning,

(c) Addressing questions of both reporting obligations and financial implications whenever elaborating any further instruments on human rights,

Recalling the conclusions and recommendations of the second meeting of persons chairing the human rights treaty bodies, held at Geneva in October 1988, and the endorsement of the recommendations aimed at streamlining, rationalizing and otherwise improving reporting procedures by the General Assembly in its resolution 47/111 and the Commission on Human Rights in its resolution 1993/16 of 26 February 1993,

Noting the meeting, within the framework of the World Conference on Human Rights, of persons chairing treaty bodies together with those persons chairing each of the principal regional and other human rights bodies,

Recalling in particular the conclusions and recommendations of the third and fourth meetings of persons chairing the human rights treaty bodies, held at Geneva in October 1990,[a] and in October 1992, respectively,

Expressing concern about the increasing backlog of reports on implementation by States parties of United Nations instruments on human rights and about delays in consideration of reports by the treaty bodies,

Taking note of the reports of the Secretary-General on progress achieved in enhancing the effective functioning of the treaty bodies,

Taking note also of the relevant paragraphs of the Vienna Declaration and Programme of Action adopted by the World Conference on Human Rights, held from 14 to 25 June 1993,

Welcoming the interim report of the updated study by the independent expert on possible long-term approaches to enhancing the effective operation of the human rights treaty system,

1. *Endorses* the conclusions and recommendations of the meetings of persons chairing the human rights treaty bodies aimed at streamlining, rationalizing and otherwise improving reporting procedures, as well as the continuing efforts in this connection by the treaty bodies and the Secretary-General within their respective spheres of competence;

2. *Takes note with satisfaction* of the interim report of the updated study by the independent expert on possible long-term approaches to enhancing the effective operation of the human rights treaty system, and requests that the Commission on Human Rights review the proposals to be submitted in the final report of the independent expert with a view to recommending further action;

3. *Requests* the Secretary-General to give high priority to establishing a computerized database to improve the efficiency and effectiveness of the functioning of the treaty bodies;

4. *Again urges* States parties to make every effort to meet their reporting obligations and to contribute, individually and through meetings of States parties, to identifying and implementing ways of further streamlining and improving reporting procedures as well as enhancing coordination and information flow between the treaty bodies and with relevant United Nations bodies, including specialized agencies;

5. *Welcomes* the emphasis placed by the meeting of persons chairing the human rights treaty bodies and by the Commission on Human Rights on the importance of technical assistance and advisory services, and further to this end:

(a) Endorses the request of the Commission that the Secretary-General report regularly to the Commission on possible technical assistance projects identified by the treaty bodies;

(b) Invites the treaty bodies to give priority attention to identifying such possibilities in the regular course of their work of reviewing the periodic reports of States parties;

6. *Endorses* the recommendations of the meetings of persons chairing the human rights treaty bodies on the need to ensure financing and adequate staffing resources for the operations of the treaty bodies, and with this in mind:

(a) Reiterates its request that the Secretary-General provide adequate resources in regard to the various treaty bodies;

(b) Requests that the Secretary-General report on this question to the Commission on Human Rights at its fiftieth session and to the General Assembly at its forty-ninth session;

7. *Urges* States parties to notify the Secretary-General, as depository of the International Convention on the Elimination of All Forms of Racial Discrimination and the Convention against Torture and Other Cruel, Inhuman or Degrading Treatment or Punishment, of their acceptance of the amendments approved by the States parties and by the General Assembly in its resolution 47/111, for the purpose of funding the respective committees from the regular budget;

8. *Calls upon* all States parties to fulfil without delay and in full their financial obligations, including their arrears, under the International Convention on the Elimination of All Forms of Racial Discrimination and the Convention against Torture and Other Cruel, Inhuman or Degrading Treatment or Punishment until the amendments enter into force;

9. *Requests* the Secretary-General to continue to take the necessary measures to ensure that the two committees established under the International Convention on the Elimination of All Forms of Racial Discrimination and the Convention against Torture and Other Cruel, Inhuman or Degrading Treatment or Punishment meet as scheduled until the amendments enter into force;

10. *Welcomes* the report of the Secretary-General on the effective implementation of the conclusions and recommendations of the fourth meeting of persons chairing human rights treaty bodies, held in October 1992, particularly the holding of the meeting of chairpersons and those persons chairing each of the principal regional and other human rights bodies at Vienna on 15 and 16 June 1993, within the framework of the World Conference on Human Rights, at which the "Vienna statement of the international human rights treaty bodies" was adopted;[b]

11. *Also requests* the Secretary-General to take the appropriate steps in order to continue financing the biennial meetings of persons chairing the human rights treaty bodies from the available resources of the regular budget of the United Nations;

12. *Decides* to continue giving priority consideration, at its forty-ninth session, to the conclusions and recommendations of the meetings of persons chairing human rights treaty bodies, in the light of the deliberations of the Commission on Human Rights, under the item entitled "Human rights questions".

---

[a]A/45/636.

[b]A/CONF.157/TBB/4 & Add.1.

General Assembly resolution 48/120

20 December 1993   Meeting 85   Adopted without vote

Approved by Third Committee (A/48/632/Add.1) without vote, 3 December (meeting 50); 29-nation draft (A/C.3/48/L.61); agenda item 114 *(a)*.
Sponsors: Argentina, Australia, Austria, Belgium, Cameroon, Canada, Chile, Costa Rica, Cyprus, Czech Republic, Denmark, Finland, France, Germany, Hungary, Iceland, Ireland, Italy, Luxembourg, Netherlands, New Zealand, Norway, Philippines, Poland, Portugal, Slovakia, Spain, Sweden, United Kingdom.
Meeting numbers. GA 48th session: 3rd Committee 36-50; plenary 85.

In other action, the General Assembly, by **decision 48/430** of 20 December, took note of the Secretary-General's report on the need to ensure adequate resources for the operations of human rights treaty bodies.[76]

On the same date, the Assembly, by **decision 48/429**, took note of a report of the Third Committee, which contained its recommendations on a number of human rights–related topics (see APPENDIX IV, agenda item 114).[77]

Reporting obligations of States parties

On 26 February,[68] the Commission urged States parties to fulfil their reporting obligations and to contribute to identifying and implementing ways to further streamline and improve reporting procedures.

Successor States and human rights treaties

On 5 March,[78] the Commission urged successor States that had not done so to accede to or ratify those international human rights treaties to which the predecessor States were not parties. It requested the Secretary-General to render advisory services with respect to succession or accession to successor States that were United Nations Members and to report in 1994 on action taken.

International Covenants on Human Rights

Human Rights Commission action. On 26 February,[79] the Commission adopted a resolution on the 1966 International Covenants on Human Rights,[33] which corresponded largely to a resolution adopted by the General Assembly later in the year. The Commission asked the Secretary-General to report in 1994 on the status of the Covenants and on the work of the Committee on Economic, Social and Cultural Rights.

Report of the Secretary-General. In October, the Secretary-General reported on the status of the Covenants as at 1 August 1993.[80]

GENERAL ASSEMBLY ACTION

On 20 December, the General Assembly, on the recommendation of the Third Committee, adopted **resolution 48/119** without vote.

International covenants on human rights

The General Assembly,

Recalling its resolution 46/113 of 17 December 1991, and taking note of Commission on Human Rights resolution 1993/15 of 26 February 1993,

Mindful that the International Covenants on Human Rights constitute the first all-embracing and legally binding international treaties in the field of human rights and, together with the Universal Declaration of Human Rights, form the core of the International Bill of Human Rights,

Taking note of the report of the Secretary-General on the status of the International Covenant on Economic, Social and Cultural Rights, the International Covenant on Civil and Political Rights and the Optional Protocols to the International Covenant on Civil and Political Rights,

Welcoming the fact that the total number of States parties to each of the Covenants has increased significantly through recent ratifications or accessions, while noting at the same time that many States Members of the United Nations have yet to become parties to them or to the Optional Protocols to the International Covenant on Civil and Political Rights,

Recalling the International Covenant on Economic, Social and Cultural Rights and the International Covenant on Civil and Political Rights and reaffirming that all human rights and fundamental freedoms are indivisible and interrelated and that the promotion and protection of one category of rights should never exempt or excuse States from the promotion and protection of the other rights,

Recognizing the important role of the Human Rights Committee in the implementation of the International Covenant on Civil and Political Rights and the Optional Protocols thereto,

Also recognizing the important role of the Committee on Economic, Social and Cultural Rights in the implementation of the International Covenant on Economic, Social and Cultural Rights,

Welcoming the submission to the General Assembly of the annual report of the Human Rights Committee and the report of the Committee on Economic, Social and Cultural Rights on its seventh session,

Considering that the effective functioning of treaty bodies established in accordance with the relevant provisions of international instruments on human rights plays a fundamental role and hence represents an important continuing concern of the United Nations,

Noting with satisfaction the ongoing efforts of the Human Rights Committee and the Committee on Economic, Social and Cultural Rights to improve their methods of work,

Noting with concern the critical situation with regard to overdue reports from States parties to the International Covenants on Human Rights,

Bearing in mind the successful conclusion of the World Conference on Human Rights, held at Vienna from 14 to 25 June 1993, and the adoption of the Vienna Declaration and Programme of Action, and taking into account in particular the call for strengthening and further implementation of the human rights instruments,

1. *Reaffirms* the importance of the International Covenants on Human Rights as major parts of international efforts to promote universal respect for and observance of human rights and fundamental freedoms;

2. *Once again urges* all States that have not yet done so to become parties to the International Covenant on Economic, Social and Cultural Rights and the International Covenant on Civil and Political Rights and to consider acceding to the Optional Protocols to the International Covenant on Civil and Political Rights;

3. *Welcomes* the intention of the Secretary-General to intensify systematic efforts to encourage States to become parties to the Covenants and, through the programme of advisory services in the field of human rights, to assist such States, at their request, in ratifying or acceding to the Covenants;

4. *Invites* the States parties to the International Covenant on Civil and Political Rights to consider making the declaration provided for in article 41 of the Covenant;

5. *Emphasizes* the importance of the strictest compliance by States parties with their obligations under the International Covenant on Economic, Social and Cultural Rights and the International Covenant on Civil and Political Rights and, where applicable, the Optional Protocols to the International Covenant on Civil and Political Rights;

6. *Stresses* the importance of avoiding the erosion of human rights by derogation, and underlines the necessity of strict observance of the agreed conditions and procedures for derogation under article 4 of the International Covenant on Civil and Political Rights, bearing in mind the need for States parties to provide the fullest possible information during states of emergency, so that the justification for and appropriateness of measures taken in these circumstances can be assessed;

7. *Also stresses* the importance of taking fully into account the specific needs and situation of women in the implementation of the Covenants at the national level, particularly in the national reports, and in the work of the Human Rights Committee and the Committee on Economic, Social and Cultural Rights;

8. *Encourages* States to consider limiting the extent of any reservations they lodge to the International Covenants on Human Rights, to formulate any reservations as precisely and narrowly as possible and to ensure that no reservation is incompatible with the object and purpose of the relevant treaty or is otherwise contrary to international law;

9. *Encourages* the States parties to review regularly any reservations made in respect of the provisions of the International Covenants on Human Rights with a view to withdrawing them;

10. *Takes note with appreciation* of the annual reports of the Human Rights Committee submitted to the General Assembly at its forty-seventh and forty-eighth sessions;

11. *Also takes note with appreciation* of the reports of the Committee on Economic, Social and Cultural Rights on its sixth and seventh sessions;

12. *Expresses its satisfaction* with the serious and constructive manner in which both Committees are carrying out their function;

13. *Welcomes* the efforts of the Committees to further improve their working methods, in particular by adopting concluding observations containing specific suggestions and recommendations concerning steps States parties could take to implement the Covenants more effectively;

14. *Invites* the Committees to identify specific needs of States parties that might be addressed through the advisory services and technical assistance programme of the Centre for Human Rights of the Secretariat, with the possible participation of members of the Committees where appropriate;

15. *Encourages* the Human Rights Committee and the Committee on Economic, Social and Cultural Rights to consider further innovations in their working methods, in particular aiming at the prevention of serious human rights violations in their respective fields of competence and the promotion of peaceful solutions;

16. *Welcomes* the continuing efforts of the Human Rights Committee to strive for uniform standards in the implementation of the provisions of the International Covenant on Civil and Political Rights, and appeals to other bodies dealing with similar human rights questions to respect these uniform standards, as expressed in the general comments of the Human Rights Committee;

17. *Also welcomes* the efforts of the Committee on Economic, Social and Cultural Rights in the preparation of general comments on the provisions of the International Covenant on Economic, Social and Cultural Rights;

18. *Urges* States parties to fulfil in good time such reporting obligations under the International Covenants on Human Rights as may be requested;

19. *Urges* States parties to the International Covenant on Economic, Social and Cultural Rights, the specialized agencies and other relevant United Nations bodies to extend their full support and cooperation to the Committee on Economic, Social and Cultural Rights;

20. *Also urges* States parties to take duly into account, in implementing the provisions of the Covenants, the observations made at the conclusion of the consideration of their reports by the Human Rights Committee and by the Committee on Economic, Social and Cultural Rights;

21. *Invites* States parties to give particular attention to the dissemination at the national level of the reports they have submitted to the Human Rights Committee and the Committee on Economic, Social and Cultural Rights, as well as the summary records relating to the examination of those reports by the Committees;

22. *Encourages* all Governments to publish the texts of the International Covenant on Economic, Social and Cultural Rights, the International Covenant on Civil and Political Rights and the Optional Protocols to the International Covenant on Civil and Political Rights in as many local languages as possible and to distribute them and make them known as widely as possible in their territories;

23. *Requests* the Secretary-General to consider ways and means of assisting States parties to the Covenants in the preparation of their reports, including seminars or workshops at the national level for the purpose of training government officials engaged in the preparation of such reports, and the exploration of other possibilities available under the regular programme of advisory services in the field of human rights;

24. *Also requests* the Secretary-General, in accordance with the Vienna Declaration and Programme of Action, to make appropriate arrangements for additional resources from within the regular budget to be provided to the Human Rights Committee for dealing in an effective and timely manner with the increasing workload under the first Optional Protocol to the International Covenant on Civil and Political Rights;

25. *Further requests* the Secretary-General to ensure that the Centre for Human Rights of the Secretariat effectively assists the Human Rights Committee and the Committee on Economic, Social and Cultural Rights in the implementation of their respective mandates;

26. *Once again urges* the Secretary-General, taking into account the suggestions of the Human Rights Committee, to take determined steps to give more publicity to the work of that Committee and, similarly, to the work of the Committee on Economic, Social and Cultural Rights;

27. *Requests* the Secretary-General to submit to the General Assembly at its fiftieth session, under the item entitled "Human rights questions", a report on the status of the International Covenant on Economic, Social and Cultural Rights, the International Covenant on Civil and Political Rights and the Optional Protocols

to the International Covenant on Civil and Political Rights, including all reservations and declarations.

General Assembly resolution 48/119

20 December 1993   Meeting 85   Adopted without vote

Approved by Third Committee (A/48/632/Add.1) without vote, 3 December (meeting 50); 31-nation draft (A/C.3/48/L.53); agenda item 114 *(a)*.
Sponsors: Australia, Austria, Belarus, Canada, Costa Rica, Cyprus, Czech Republic, Denmark, El Salvador, Finland, Gambia, Guatemala, Hungary, Iceland, Italy, Lithuania, Netherlands, New Zealand, Norway, Peru, Philippines, Poland, Portugal, Romania, Russian Federation, Senegal, Slovakia, Slovenia, Spain, Sweden, Venezuela.
Meeting numbers. GA 48th session: 3rd Committee 36-56; plenary 85.

Universal Declaration of Human Rights

Report of the Secretary-General. In accordance with a General Assembly resolution on the fortieth (1988) anniversary of the Universal Declaration of Human Rights,[81] the Secretary-General submitted in December 1993 a report[82] on activities undertaken since 1988 towards the universal ratification of or accession to United Nations human rights instruments. New mechanisms included the establishment of additional treaty bodies, special procedures—such as thematic and country-oriented rapporteurs—advisory services and the Working Group on the Right to Development. The Secretary-General reviewed measures taken by the Commission and the Subcommission to improve the effectiveness of existing mechanisms for the promotion and protection of human rights and those under consideration by the Commission. He discussed instruments being drafted and new topics presented in studies, reports and working papers. He also described developments under advisory services, public information activities and activities to strengthen national and existing regional institutions for the promotion of human rights.

GENERAL ASSEMBLY ACTION

By **decision 48/410 A** of 7 December, the General Assembly increased from five to nine the number of award winners of human rights prizes to be presented to mark the forty-fifth anniversary of the 1948 Universal Declaration.[49]

By **decision 48/410 B** of 10 December, the Assembly, in accordance with its 1966 resolution,[83] its 1992 decision[84] and decision 48/410 A, awarded nine prizes to individuals and organizations that had made outstanding contributions to promote and protect human rights (see APPENDIX III).

The Assembly, by **decision 48/416** of 10 December, reaffirmed, on the occasion of the forty-fifth anniversary of the Universal Declaration, the Declaration's significance as a source of inspiration for national and international efforts for the promotion and protection of human rights, and decided to include in the provisional agenda of its fifty-third (1998) session an item on the fiftieth anniversary of the Declaration.

Electoral processes

Periodic and genuine elections

As requested by the General Assembly in 1992,[85] the Secretary-General submitted in November 1993 a report on enhancing the effectiveness of the principle of periodic and genuine elections.[86] Between 16 October 1992 and 15 October 1993, 27 requests were received from 24 Member States for electoral assistance. Of those requests, 21 related to technical assistance or advisory activities, compared to 14 the previous year. Annexed to the report were details of the status of 35 Member States' requests, including the nature of the requests and action taken in response. The Secretary-General discussed major United Nations missions, including UNTAC (see PART TWO, Chapter III), the United Nations Angola Verification Mission II (see PART TWO, Chapter I) and the United Nations Mission for the Referendum in Western Sahara (see PART ONE, Chapter III).

The United Nations Trust Fund for Electoral Observation, established in 1991,[87] for cases in which requesting Member States were unable to finance in whole or in part the electoral verification, had received contributions of $569,069.

By **decision 48/430** of 20 December, the Assembly took note of the Secretary-General's report.

GENERAL ASSEMBLY ACTION

On 20 December, the General Assembly, on the recommendation of the Third Committee, adopted **resolution 48/131** by recorded vote.

Enhancing the effectiveness of the principle of periodic and genuine elections

The General Assembly,

Recalling its resolutions 44/146 of 15 December 1989, 45/150 of 18 December 1990, and especially 46/137 of 17 December 1991 and 47/138 of 18 December 1992, as well as the annex to Commission on Human Rights resolution 1989/51 of 7 March 1989,

Bearing in mind the Vienna Declaration and Programme of Action, adopted by the World Conference of Human Rights, held at Vienna from 14 to 25 June 1993, especially the recognition therein that assistance provided upon the request of Governments for the conduct of free and fair elections, including assistance in the human rights aspects of elections and public information about elections, is of particular importance in the strengthening and building of institutions relating to human rights and the strengthening of a pluralistic civil society, and that special emphasis should be given to measures that assist in achieving those goals;

Reaffirming that electoral assistance is provided only at the specific request of the Member State concerned,

Having considered the report of the Secretary-General,

Noting the high level of requests for electoral assistance by Member States,

1. *Takes note with appreciation* of the report of the Secretary-General on United Nations activities aimed at enhancing the effectiveness of the principle of periodic and genuine elections;

2. *Commends* the electoral assistance provided to Member States at their request by the United Nations, requests that such assistance continue on a case-by-case basis in accordance with the proposed guidelines on electoral assistance, recognizing that the fundamental responsibility for ensuring free and fair elections lies with Governments, and also requests the Electoral Assistance Unit of the Secretariat to inform Member States on a regular basis about the requests received, the responses given to those requests and the nature of the assistance provided;

3. *Requests* that the United Nations attempt to ensure, before undertaking to provide electoral assistance to a requesting State, that there is adequate time to organize and carry out an effective mission for providing such assistance, that conditions exist to allow a free and fair election and that provisions can be made for adequate and comprehensive reporting of the results of the mission;

4. *Recommends* that the United Nations, in order to ensure the continuation and consolidation of the democratization process in Member States requesting assistance, provide assistance before and after elections have taken place, including needs-assessment missions aimed at recommending programmes which might contribute to the consolidation of the democratization process;

5. *Recalls* the establishment by the Secretary-General of the United Nations Trust Fund for Electoral Observation and the establishment by the Administrator of the United Nations Development Programme of a separate fund, the Trust Fund for Technical Assistance to Electoral Processes, and calls upon Member States to consider contributing to the funds;

6. *Stresses* the importance of coordination by the focal point within the United Nations system, commends the Centre for Human Rights of the Secretariat for the advisory services and technical assistance it provides and the Department for Development Support and Management Services of the Secretariat and the United Nations Development Programme for the technical assistance they provide to requesting Member States, and requests the focal point to strengthen its collaboration with the Centre for Human Rights, including through an exchange of personnel when appropriate, and with the Department for Development Support and Management Services and the United Nations Development Programme and inform them of requests submitted in the area of electoral assistance;

7. *Recommends* that the United Nations continue and strengthen its coordination of election preparation and observation with intergovernmental and non-governmental organizations which have an interest in such activities;

8. *Requests* the Secretary-General to provide the Electoral Assistance Unit with adequate human and financial resources, under the regular budget of the United Nations and within existing resources, to allow it to carry out its mandate;

9. *Also requests* the Secretary-General to reinforce the Centre for Human Rights through the redeployment of resources and personnel, so as to enable it to answer, in close coordination with the Electoral Assistance Unit, the increasing number of requests from Member States for advisory services in the area of electoral assistance;

10. *Recommends* that the Secretary-General, on the basis of the guidelines proposed in his report and on the basis of experience acquired over the last two years, provide a revised set of guidelines for consideration at its forty-ninth session;

11. *Further requests* the Secretary-General to report to the General Assembly at its forty-ninth session on the implementation of resolution 47/138 and the present resolution, in particular on the status of requests from Member States for electoral assistance and verification, and on the validity of the guidelines in the light of experience.

General Assembly resolution 48/131

20 December 1993   Meeting 85   153-0-13 (recorded vote)

Approved by Third Committee (A/48/632/Add.2) by recorded vote (138-1-15), 6 December (meeting 52); 43-nation draft (A/C.3/48/L.55); agenda item 114 *(b)*.

Sponsors: Albania, Argentina, Armenia, Australia, Belgium, Bulgaria, Canada, Central African Republic, Chad, Costa Rica, Cyprus, Czech Republic, Denmark, Ethiopia, Finland, Gambia, Greece, Hungary, Iceland, Ireland, Israel, Italy, Latvia, Lithuania, Luxembourg, Malawi, Netherlands, Nicaragua, Norway, Panama, Poland, Republic of Korea, Romania, Russian Federation, Rwanda, San Marino, Slovakia, Turkey, Ukraine, United Kingdom, United States, Yemen.

Meeting numbers. GA 48th session: 3rd Committee 36-52; plenary 85.

Recorded vote in Assembly as follows:

In favour: Afghanistan, Albania, Algeria, Angola, Antigua and Barbuda, Argentina, Armenia, Australia, Austria, Azerbaijan, Bahamas, Bahrain, Bangladesh, Barbados, Belarus, Belgium, Belize, Benin, Bhutan, Bolivia, Bosnia and Herzegovina, Botswana, Brazil, Bulgaria, Burkina Faso, Burundi, Cambodia, Cameroon, Canada, Cape Verde, Central African Republic, Chad, Chile, Colombia, Comoros, Congo, Costa Rica, Côte d'Ivoire, Croatia, Cyprus, Czech Republic, Denmark, Djibouti, Dominica, Dominican Republic, Ecuador, Egypt, El Salvador, Estonia, Ethiopia, Fiji, Finland, France, Gabon, Gambia, Georgia, Germany, Ghana, Greece, Grenada, Guatemala, Guinea, Guinea-Bissau, Guyana, Haiti, Honduras, Hungary, Iceland, India, Indonesia, Ireland, Israel, Italy, Jamaica, Japan, Jordan, Kazakhstan, Kenya, Kuwait, Kyrgyzstan, Latvia, Lebanon, Lesotho, Liechtenstein, Lithuania, Luxembourg, Madagascar, Malawi, Malaysia, Maldives, Mali, Malta, Marshall Islands, Mauritania, Mauritius, Mexico, Micronesia, Monaco, Mongolia, Morocco, Mozambique, Namibia, Nepal, Netherlands, New Zealand, Nicaragua, Niger, Nigeria, Norway, Oman, Pakistan, Panama, Papua New Guinea, Paraguay, Peru, Poland, Portugal, Qatar, Republic of Korea, Republic of Moldova, Romania, Russian Federation, Rwanda, Saint Lucia, Saint Vincent and the Grenadines, San Marino, Senegal, Sierra Leone, Singapore, Slovakia, Slovenia, Solomon Islands, Spain, Sri Lanka, Suriname, Swaziland, Sweden, Thailand, the former Yugoslav Republic of Macedonia, Togo, Trinidad and Tobago, Tunisia, Turkey, Turkmenistan, Ukraine, United Arab Emirates, United Kingdom, United States, Uruguay, Venezuela, Yemen, Zaire, Zambia.

Against: None.

Abstaining: China, Cuba, Democratic People's Republic of Korea, Iraq, Libyan Arab Jamahiriya, Myanmar, Philippines, Sudan, Syrian Arab Republic, Uganda, United Republic of Tanzania, Viet Nam, Zimbabwe.

In the Committee, before approval of the draft as a whole, paragraphs 3 and 4 were adopted by recorded votes of 129 to 5, with 13 abstentions, and by 129 to 5, with 14 abstentions, respectively.

In the Assembly, paragraph 3 was retained by a recorded vote of 149 to 5, with 9 abstentions, and paragraph 4 by 150 to 5, with 8 abstentions.

Respect for the principles of national sovereignty and non-interference

In response to a 1992 General Assembly request,[88] the Secretary-General submitted in October a report[89] summarizing action taken by the Commission on Human Rights concerning respect for the principles of national sovereignty and non-interference in the internal affairs of States in their electoral processes. He stated that, while no specific action had been taken by the Commission to review the fundamental factors negatively affecting the observance of those principles, a number of its resolutions referred to the issue of elections in the context of guaranteeing the free expression of the will of people. They addressed the questions of Afghanistan,[90] Georgia,[56] Myanmar,[91] Somalia,[61] consequences for the enjoyment of human rights of acts of violence committed by armed groups that spread terror among the population and by drug traffickers,[92] and strengthening United Nations action in the field of human rights through the promotion of international cooperation and the importance of non-selectivity, impartiality and objectivity.[34]

By **decision 48/430** of 20 December, the Assembly took note of the Secretary-General's report.

GENERAL ASSEMBLY ACTION

On 20 December, the General Assembly, on the recommendation of the Third Committee, adopted **resolution 48/124** by recorded vote.

Respect for the principles of national sovereignty and non-interference in the internal affairs of States in their electoral processes

The General Assembly,

Reaffirming the purpose of the United Nations to develop friendly relations among nations based on respect for the principle of equal rights and self-determination of peoples and to take other appropriate measures to strengthen universal peace,

Recalling its resolution 1514(XV) of 14 December 1960, containing the Declaration on the Granting of Independence to Colonial Countries and Peoples,

Recalling also its resolution 2625(XXV) of 24 October 1970, by which it approved the Declaration on Principles of International Law concerning Friendly Relations and Cooperation among States in accordance with the Charter of the United Nations,

Recalling further the principle enshrined in Article 2, paragraph 7, of the Charter of the United Nations, which establishes that nothing contained in the Charter shall authorize the United Nations to intervene in matters which are essentially within the domestic jurisdiction of any State or shall require the Members to submit such matters to settlement under the Charter,

Reaffirming the legitimacy of the struggle of peoples for independence, territorial integrity, national unity and for liberation from colonial domination and apartheid, and for the establishment of a society in which the people, irrespective of race, colour or creed, will fully enjoy political and other rights on a basis of equality and participate freely in the determination of their destiny,

Reaffirming also the legitimacy of the struggle of all peoples under colonial and foreign domination, particularly the Palestinian people, for the exercise of their inalienable right to self-determination and national independence, which will enable them to decide freely on their own future,

Recognizing that the principles of national sovereignty and non-interference in the internal affairs of any State should be respected in the holding of elections,

Recognizing also that there is no single political system or single model for electoral processes equally suited to all nations and their peoples, and that political systems and electoral processes are subject to historical, political, cultural and religious factors,

Convinced that the establishment of the necessary mechanisms and means to guarantee full popular participation in electoral processes corresponds to States,

Recalling its resolutions in this regard, in particular resolution 47/130 of 18 December 1992,

Welcoming the Vienna Declaration and Programme of Action, adopted by the World Conference on Human Rights, held at Vienna from 14 to 25 June 1993, in which the Conference reaffirmed that the processes of promoting and protecting human rights should be conducted in conformity with the purposes and principles of the Charter,

1. *Reiterates* that, by virtue of the principle of equal rights and self-determination of peoples enshrined in the Charter of the United Nations, all peoples have the right, freely and without external interference, to determine their political status and to pursue their economic, social and cultural development, and that every State has the duty to respect that right in accordance with the provisions of the Charter;

2. *Reaffirms* that it is the concern solely of peoples to determine methods and to establish institutions regarding the electoral process, as well as to determine the ways for its implementation according to their constitution and national legislation, and that, consequently, States should establish the necessary mechanisms and means to guarantee full popular participation in those processes;

3. *Reaffirms also* that any activities that attempt, directly or indirectly, to interfere in the free development of national electoral processes, in particular in the developing countries, or that are intended to sway the results of such processes, violate the spirit and letter of the principles established in the Charter and in the Declaration on Principles of International Law concerning Friendly Relations and Cooperation among States in accordance with the Charter of the United Nations;

4. *Reaffirms further* that there is no universal need for the United Nations to provide electoral assistance to Member States, except in special circumstances such as cases of decolonization, in the context of regional or international peace processes or at the request of specific sovereign States, by virtue of resolutions adopted by the Security Council or the General Assembly in each case, in strict conformity with the principles of sovereignty and non-interference in the internal affairs of States;

5. *Urges* all States to respect the principle of non-interference in the internal affairs of States and the sovereign right of peoples to determine their political, economic and social systems;

6. *Strongly appeals* to all States to refrain from financing or providing, directly or indirectly, any other form of overt or covert support for political parties or groups and from taking actions to undermine the electoral processes in any country;

7. *Condemns* any act of armed aggression or threat or use of force against peoples, their elected Governments or their legitimate leaders;

8. *Reiterates* that only the total eradication of apartheid and the establishment of a non-racial, democratic society based on majority rule, through the full and free exercise of universal suffrage, can lead to a just and lasting solution to the situation in South Africa;

9. *Reaffirms* the legitimacy of the struggle of all peoples under colonial and foreign domination, particularly of the Palestinian people, for the exercise of their inalienable right to self-determination and national independence, which will enable them to determine their political, economic and social system, without interference;

10. *Calls upon* the Commission on Human Rights at its fiftieth session to continue giving priority to the review of the fundamental factors that negatively affect the observance of the principles of national sovereignty and non-interference in the internal affairs of States in their electoral processes and to report to the General Assembly at its forty-ninth session, through the Economic and Social Council;

11. *Requests* the Secretary-General to report to the General Assembly at its forty-ninth session on the implementation of the present resolution, under the item entitled ''Human rights questions''.

General Assembly resolution 48/124

20 December 1993   Meeting 85   101-51-17 (recorded vote)

Approved by Third Committee (A/48/632/Add.2) by recorded vote (86-52-18), 6 December (meeting 52); 10-nation draft (A/C.3/48/L.44), orally corrected; agenda item 114 *(b)*.
Sponsors: China, Cuba, Democratic People's Republic of Korea, Gambia, Lao People's Democratic Republic, Namibia, Sudan, United Republic of Tanzania, Viet Nam, Zimbabwe.
Meeting numbers. GA 48th session: 3rd Committee 36-52; plenary 85.

Recorded vote in Assembly as follows:

In favour: Afghanistan, Algeria, Angola, Antigua and Barbuda, Bahamas, Bahrain, Bangladesh, Barbados, Benin, Bhutan, Botswana, Brazil, Brunei Darussalam, Burkina Faso, Burundi, Cambodia, Cameroon, Cape Verde, Central African Republic, Chad, China, Colombia, Comoros, Congo, Côte d'Ivoire, Cuba, Cyprus, Democratic People's Republic of Korea, Djibouti, Dominica, Dominican Republic, Ecuador, Egypt, Ethiopia, Gabon, Gambia, Ghana, Grenada, Guatemala, Guinea, Guinea-Bissau, Guyana, Haiti, Honduras, India, Indonesia, Iran, Iraq, Jordan, Kenya, Kuwait, Kyrgyzstan, Lao People's Democratic Republic, Lebanon, Lesotho, Libyan Arab Jamahiriya, Madagascar, Malawi, Malaysia, Maldives, Mali, Mauritania, Mexico, Mongolia, Morocco, Mozambique, Myanmar, Namibia, Nepal, Niger, Nigeria, Oman, Pakistan, Papua New Guinea, Peru, Qatar, Rwanda, Saint Lucia, Saint Vincent and the Grenadines, Saudi Arabia, Senegal, Sierra Leone, Singapore, Sri Lanka, Sudan, Suriname, Swaziland, Syrian Arab Republic, Thailand, the former Yugoslav Republic of Macedonia, Togo, Trinidad and Tobago, Tunisia, Uganda, United Arab Emirates, United Republic of Tanzania, Venezuela, Viet Nam, Yemen, Zaire, Zimbabwe.

Against: Albania, Argentina, Armenia, Australia, Austria, Azerbaijan, Belarus, Belgium, Bulgaria, Canada, Croatia, Czech Republic, Denmark, Estonia, Finland, France, Germany, Greece, Hungary, Iceland, Ireland, Israel, Italy, Japan, Kazakhstan, Latvia, Liechtenstein, Lithuania, Luxembourg, Malta, Marshall Islands, Monaco, Netherlands, New Zealand, Norway, Panama, Poland, Portugal, Republic of Korea, Republic of Moldova, Romania, Russian Federation, San Marino, Slovakia, Slovenia, Spain, Sweden, Turkey, Ukraine, United Kingdom, United States.

Abstaining: Belize, Bolivia, Chile, Costa Rica, El Salvador, Fiji, Georgia, Jamaica, Mauritius, Micronesia, Nicaragua, Paraguay, Philippines, Solomon Islands, Turkmenistan, Uruguay, Zambia.

Regional arrangements

Report of the Secretary-General. As requested by the Commission on Human Rights in 1992,[93] the Secretary-General submitted in January 1993 a report[94] describing action taken by the Centre for Human Rights to cooperate with regional bodies and commissions in Africa, the Americas, Asia and the Pacific and Europe with regard to promoting and protecting human rights.

The Secretary-General stated that he would continue to strengthen exchanges between the United Nations and regional intergovernmental organizations dealing with human rights. Such organizations were in a valuable position to strengthen human rights norms, and cooperation could only be mutually beneficial.

Human Rights Commission action. On 9 March,[95] the Commission asked States in areas where regional arrangements in the field of human rights did not exist to consider establishing regional machinery to promote and protect human rights. It welcomed the continued cooperation of the Centre for Human Rights with the Executive Secretary of the Economic and Social Commission for Asia and the Pacific (ESCAP) in establishing a depository centre for United Nations human rights materials at ESCAP headquarters (Bangkok). The Commission asked the Secretary-General, as foreseen in the medium-term plan for 1992-1997, to continue to strengthen exchanges between the United Nations and regional intergovernmental organizations dealing with human rights, and welcomed the continued organization, by the Centre, of national, regional and subregional workshops and training courses for government officials engaged in the administration of justice and in implementing international human rights instruments. It asked him to submit a further report on the state of regional arrangements in 1995.

Asia and the Pacific

The General Assembly, in 1990,[96] had welcomed the designation of the ESCAP library at Bangkok as a depository centre for United Nations human rights materials within ESCAP. The library's functions included the collection, processing and dissemination of such materials in the Asia and Pacific region.

Report of the Secretary-General. In a January progress report to the Commission on regional arrangements for the promotion and protection of human rights in Asia and the Pacific,[97] the Secretary-General described cooperation between the Centre for Human Rights and ESCAP and summarized replies from two specialized agencies and two United Nations bodies containing their suggestions for activities. He also discussed consultations taking place between the United Nations and countries in the region.

Human Rights Commission action. On 9 March,[98] the Commission encouraged ESCAP member States and associate members and other parties to use ESCAP's depository centre and asked the Secretary-General to ensure a continuing flow of human rights materials to the library. It encouraged States in Asia and the Pacific to consider establishing regional arrangements to promote and protect human rights and appealed to Governments

in the region to consider using the United Nations programme of advisory services and technical assistance in human rights to organize information and training courses for government personnel on the application of international human rights standards and the experience of relevant international organs. The Commission welcomed the interest of some Governments in hosting a regional meeting for Asia and the Pacific in 1993 or 1994 to follow up the discussion on the region's consultative mechanism and requested the Secretary-General to facilitate the realization of that activity. The Commission's request to the Secretary-General was approved by the Economic and Social Council in **decision 1993/271** of 28 July. The Commission also requested the Secretary-General to consult the States in the region in the implementation of its resolution and to submit a report in 1994 on the progress achieved.

Responsibility to promote and protect human rights

Working Group activities. The Working Group to draft a declaration on the right and responsibility of individuals, groups and organs of society to promote and protect universally recognized human rights and fundamental freedoms held its eighth session at Geneva from 18 to 29 January and on 1 March 1993.[99] The Group completed the first reading of the text of articles 3 and 4 of chapter III and of article 5 of chapter V, and began the second reading of the preamble of the draft declaration. Annexed to the Group's report were a first reading text of the draft declaration and compilations of first and second reading proposals.

Human Rights Commission action. On 10 March,[100] the Commission urged the Working Group to complete its task and submit the draft declaration in 1994, and requested the Secretary-General to circulate the Group's report to Member States, specialized agencies, intergovernmental organizations and NGOs for their comments on the first reading text. The Commission decided to continue elaborating the draft declaration at its 1994 session and to make meeting time available to the Working Group prior to and during that session.

ECONOMIC AND SOCIAL COUNCIL ACTION

On 28 July, on the recommendation of its Social Committee, the Economic and Social Council adopted **resolution 1993/47** without vote.

Question of a draft declaration on the right and responsibility of individuals, groups and organs of society to promote and protect universally recognized human rights and fundamental freedoms

The Economic and Social Council,

Taking note of Commission on Human Rights resolution 1993/92 of 10 March 1993,

1. *Authorizes* the open-ended working group of the Commission on Human Rights to meet for a period of two weeks prior to the fiftieth session of the Commission in order to continue its work on the elaboration of a draft declaration on the right and responsibility of individuals, groups and organs of society to promote and protect universally recognized human rights and fundamental freedoms;

2. *Requests* the Secretary-General to extend all necessary facilities to the working group for its meetings;

3. *Also requests* the Secretary-General to circulate the report of the working group, including the text of the draft declaration adopted at first reading, to the Governments of all States Members of the United Nations and members of competent specialized agencies and to interested intergovernmental and non-governmental organizations, with an invitation to submit written comments on the text adopted on first reading for consideration by the working group at its forthcoming session.

Economic and Social Council resolution 1993/47

28 July 1993   Meeting 44   Adopted without vote

Approved by Social Committee (E/1993/108) without vote, 22 July (meeting 17); draft by Commission on Human Rights (E/1993/23); agenda item 18.

Internally displaced persons and humanitarian assistance

On 11 March,[101] the Commission on Human Rights, taking note of the comprehensive study prepared by the representative of the Secretary-General on internally displaced persons,[102] prepared in response to a 1992 Commission request,[103] asked him to renew the mandate of the representative for two years with a view to identifying ways to improve protection for and assistance to such persons. It asked the representative to submit annual reports on his activities to the Commission and the General Assembly and to make suggestions and recommendations to enable him to carry out his activities better. The Economic and Social Council approved the Commission's requests on 28 July by **decision 1993/285**.

Note by the Secretary-General. In November,[104] the Secretary-General transmitted to the Assembly a report prepared by his representative on internally displaced persons, as requested by the Commission. The report described the activities of the representative and those that he planned to undertake.

GENERAL ASSEMBLY ACTION

On 20 December, the General Assembly, on the recommendation of the Third Committee, adopted **resolution 48/135** without vote.

Internally displaced persons

The General Assembly,

Deeply disturbed by the large number of internally displaced persons throughout the world, and conscious of the serious problem this is creating for the international community,

Recalling the relevant norms of international human rights instruments as well as of international humanitarian law,

Conscious of the human rights as well as the humanitarian dimensions of the problem of internally displaced persons,

Conscious also of the need for the United Nations system to gather information comprehensively on the issues of the protection of the human rights of and assistance to internally displaced persons,

Welcoming the initiative of the Commission on Human Rights on this question and, in particular, its resolution 1992/73 of 5 March 1992, by which it requested the Secretary-General to appoint a representative to study the human rights issues related to internally displaced persons, and Commission resolution 1993/95 of 11 March 1993, by which it requested the Secretary-General to mandate his representative for two years to continue his work aimed at a better understanding of the problems faced by internally displaced persons and their possible long-term solutions,

Bearing in mind the Vienna Declaration and Programme of Action, which calls for a comprehensive approach by the international community with regard to refugees and displaced persons,

Welcoming the support provided to the representative of the Secretary-General by the Office of the United Nations High Commissioner for Refugees, the Department for Humanitarian Affairs of the Secretariat and other intergovernmental and non-governmental organizations,

Welcoming also the decision by the Executive Committee of the Programme of the United Nations High Commissioner for Refugees to extend, on a case-by-case basis and under specific circumstances, protection and assistance to the internally displaced,

Taking note of the comprehensive study of the representative of the Secretary-General, submitted to the Commission on Human Rights at its forty-ninth session, and the useful suggestions and recommendations contained therein,

1. *Takes note with appreciation* of the report of the representative of the Secretary-General;

2. *Encourages* the representative, through dialogue with Governments, to continue his review of the needs for international protection of and assistance to internally displaced persons, including his compilation and analysis of existing rules and norms;

3. *Invites* the representative to present suggestions and recommendations with regard to ways and means, including the institutional aspects, of providing effective protection of and assistance to internally displaced persons;

4. *Calls upon* all Governments to continue to facilitate the activities of the representative, encourages them to give serious consideration to inviting the representative to visit their countries so as to enable him to study and analyse more fully the issues involved, and thanks those Governments which have already done so;

5. *Urges* all concerned United Nations agencies and organizations to provide all possible assistance and support to the representative in the implementation of his programme of activities;

6. *Decides* to continue its consideration of this question at its fiftieth session.

General Assembly resolution 48/135
20 December 1993   Meeting 85   Adopted without vote

Approved by Third Committee (A/48/632/Add.2) without vote, 6 December
(meeting 53); 40-nation draft (A/C.3/48/L.64); agenda item 114 *(b)*.

Sponsors: Afghanistan, Angola, Argentina, Australia, Austria, Belarus, Canada, Chile, Costa Rica, Cyprus, Czech Republic, Denmark, Ethiopia, Finland, France, Gambia, Georgia, Germany, Greece, Guatemala, Honduras, Hungary, Iceland, Italy, Lesotho, Mozambique, Namibia, Norway, Peru, Poland, Russian Federation, Rwanda, Slovakia, Sudan, Sweden, the former Yugoslav Republic of Macedonia, United Kingdom, United States, Zambia.

Meeting numbers. GA 48th session: 3rd Committee 36-53; plenary 85.

Humanitarian assistance

By a vote of 14 to none, with 7 abstentions, the Subcommission, on 26 August,[105] expressed its appreciation to Claire Palley (United Kingdom) for her preparatory document on the role of the United Nations in international humanitarian activities and assistance and human rights enforcement.[106] It recommended that the Commission authorize the Subcommission to appoint her as special rapporteur on humanitarian assistance, taking into account the need to develop international cooperation in the humanitarian field and to promote and protect human rights. It asked the Special Rapporteur to submit a preliminary report in 1994, a progress report in 1995 and, if possible, a final report in 1996, and requested the Secretary-General to provide her with the necessary assistance. The Subcommission invited its members to submit their views on the question and recommended a draft decision for adoption by the Commission in 1994.

REFERENCES

[1]YUN 1992, p. 758. [2]E/CN.4/1993/33. [3]YUN 1991, p. 573. [4]Ibid., GA res. 46/124, 17 Dec. 1991. [5]A/48/340. [6]E/1993/23 (res. 1993/55). [7]E/CN.4/1994/45. [8]E/1993/23 & Add.1. [9]Ibid. (res. 1993/94 A). [10]Ibid. (res. 1993/94 B). [11]Ibid. (dec. 1993/101). [12]Ibid. (dec. 1993/102). [13]Ibid. (dec. 1993/115). [14]Ibid. (dec. 1993/116.) [15]Ibid. (res. 1993/98). [16]Ibid. (res. 1993/96). [17]E/CN.4/1994/2. [18]Ibid. (dec. 1993/111). [19]Ibid. (dec. 1993/106). [20]Ibid. (dec. 1993/102). [21]Ibid. (dec. 1993/104). [22]YUN 1970, p. 530, ESC res. 1503(XLVIII), 27 May 1970. [23]E/CN.4/1994/2 (dec. 1993/101). [24]E/CN.4/1993/60. [25]YUN 1992, p. 759. [26]E/1993/23 (res. 1993/28). [27]E/CN.4/1994/2 (res. 1993/4). [28]E/1993/23 (res. 1993/52). [29]YUN 1992, p. 760, GA res. 47/127, 18 Dec. 1992. [30]E/CN.4/1993/87. [31]A/48/589. [32]E/1993/23 (res. 1993/59). [33]YUN 1966, pp. 419 & 423, GA res. 2200 A (XXI), annex, 16 Dec. 1966. [34]E/1993/23 (res. 1993/58). [35]YUN 1992, p. 761. [36]E/CN.4/1993/30. [37]E/1993/23 (res. 1993/50). [38]A/CONF.157/23. [39]A/CONF.157/24. [40]A/CONF.157/PC/98. [41]A/CONF.157/PC/57. [42]A/CONF.157/PC/59. [43]A/CONF.157/PC/58. [44]A/CONF.157/PC/82. [45]YUN 1992, p. 765. [46]YUN 1988, p. 539, GA res. 43/128, 8 Dec. 1988. [47]E/CN.4/1993/29 & Add.1. [48]E/1993/23 (res. 1993/49). [49]YUN 1948-49, p. 535, GA res. 217 A (III), 10 Dec. 1948. [50]YUN 1992, p. 769. [51]E/CN.4/1994/78. [52]YUN 1955, p. 164, GA res. 926(X), 14 Dec. 1955. [53]YUN 1987, p. 790, ESC dec. 1987/147, 29 May 1987. [54]E/1993/23 (res. 1993/87). [55]YUN 1992, p. 766. [56]E/1993/23 (res. 1993/85). [57]E/CN.4/1993/10 & Corr.1. [58]E/1993/23 (res. 1993/88). [59]E/1993/122. [60]E/CN.4/1994/2 (res. 1993/16). [61]E/1993/23 (res. 1993/86). [62]A/48/510. [63]YUN 1965, p. 440, GA res. 2106 A (XX), annex, 21 Dec. 1965. [64]YUN 1979, p. 895, GA res. 34/180, annex, 18 Dec. 1979. [65]YUN 1984, p. 813, GA res. 39/46, 16 Dec. 1984. [66]GA res. 44/22, 20 Nov. 1989. [67]YUN 1973, p. 103, GA res. 3068(XXVIII), annex, 30 Nov. 1973. [68]E/1993/23 (res. 1993/16). [69]A/44/668. [70]E/CN.4/1990/39. [71]*Manual on Human Rights Reporting*, Sales No. E.91.XIV.1. [72]A/CONF.157/PC/62/Add.11/Rev.1. [73]A/48/556. [74]YUN 1992, p. 769, GA res. 47/111, 16 Dec. 1992. [75]A/48/508 & Corr.1. [76]A/48/560. [77]A/48/632. [78]E/1993/23 (res. 1993/23). [79]Ibid. (res. 1993/15). [80]A/48/507 & Corr.1. [81]YUN 1988, p. 548, GA res. 43/90, 8 Dec. 1988. [82]A/48/506. [83]YUN 1966, p. 457, GA res. 2217(XXI), 19 Dec. 1966. [84]YUN 1992, p. 772, GA dec. 47/429, 18 Dec. 1992. [85]Ibid., GA res. 47/138, 18 Dec. 1992. [86]A/48/590. [87]YUN 1991, p. 588, GA res. 46/137, 19 Dec. 1991. [88]YUN 1992, p. 773, GA res. 47/130, 18 Dec. 1992. [89]A/48/425. [90]E/1993/23 (res. 1993/66). [91]Ibid. (res. 1993/73). [92]Ibid. (res. 1993/48). [93]YUN 1992, p. 775. [94]E/CN.4/1993/32. [95]E/1993/23 (res. 1993/51). [96]GA res. 45/168, 18 Dec. 1990. [97]E/CN.4/1993/31. [98]E/1993/23 (res. 1993/57). [99]E/CN.4/1993/64. [100]E/1993/23 (res. 1993/92). [101]Ibid. (res. 1993/95). [102]E/CN.4/1993/35. [103]YUN 1992, p. 777. [104]A/48/579. [105]E/CN.4/1994/2 (res. 1993/38). [106]E/CN.4/Sub.2/1993/39.

Human rights violations

Alleged violations of human rights on a large scale in several countries were again examined during 1993 by the General Assembly, the Economic and Social Council and the Commission on Human Rights, as well as by special bodies and officials appointed to examine some of those allegations.

Also discussed were alleged human rights violations involving the self-determination of peoples (see above, under "Civil and political rights") with regard to Cambodia, Western Sahara and the Palestinian people.

Under a procedure established by the Council in 1970 to deal with communications alleging denial or violation of human rights,[1] the Commission held closed meetings in 1993 to study confidential documents and a confidential report by a working group set up in 1990.[2] Those documents dealt ·with human rights situations in Bahrain, Chad, Kenya, Rwanda, Somalia, the Sudan and Zaire. The Commission decided to discontinue its consideration of the human rights situation in Bahrain and Kenya. It also decided that it would no longer examine the human rights situation in the Sudan and Zaire under the Council's confidential procedure, given the public procedure adopted by the Commission with regard to both in 1993.[3,4]

Africa

Chad

On 20 August,[5] the Subcommission strongly condemned the gross and continuing human rights violations in Chad and appealed to the international community to take measures to enhance the promotion and protection of human rights and fundamental freedoms in that country.

Equatorial Guinea

On 10 March,[6] the Commission on Human Rights, taking note of a report by Expert Fernando Volio Jiménez (Costa Rica),[7] expressed concern at the persistence of politically motivated human rights violations in Equatorial Guinea, a lack of cooperation with the Expert, and the fact that the Government had neither implemented the 1980 Plan of Action prepared by the Expert[8] nor approved his 1992 emergency plan of action.[9] It called on Equatorial Guinea to permit the establishment of an independent judiciary, to promote harmonious coexistence of the peoples of the country and to free all political prisoners. The Commission requested its Chairman to appoint a special rapporteur to study human rights violations by Equatorial Guinea and report in 1994, and asked the Secretary-General to assist him or her.

On 28 July, the Economic and Social Council, by **decision 1993/277**, approved the appointment of a special rapporteur on the situation of human rights in Equatorial Guinea and the Commission's request to the Secretary-General for assistance. Alejandro Artucio Rodríguez (Uruguay) was appointed Special Rapporteur.

South Africa

Working Group activities. In 1993, the six-member Ad Hoc Working Group of Experts on southern Africa, established by the Commission on Human Rights in 1967,[10] submitted to the Commission a final report[11] and prepared an interim report to be submitted in 1994.[12]

The Group, in its interim report, re-examined its mandate and discussed the organization of its work concerning fact-finding missions to gather testimony from witnesses (Gaborone, Botswana, 16-19 August; Harare, Zimbabwe, 20-27 August). Subjects of inquiry concerned the right to life, detention without trial, detention and deaths in police custody, political trials, political prisoners, executions, the system of "homelands", freedom of the press, the right to education, trade union rights (see below), constitutional negotiations and proposed electoral law (see PART TWO, Chapter I, for details on the political situation in South Africa).

The Working Group invited the new Government of South Africa to adopt and ratify some of the more important international covenants and asked the Commission on Human Rights to invite the Government to create an independent and impartial judiciary, and a police force to serve the entire population without discrimination. It further recommended retraining for security forces in accordance with international standards; encouraging black people to serve as members of the

judiciary; abolishing repressive regulations, including those applicable to "homelands"; unconditional amnesty for all sentences arising from anti-apartheid activities regarded as politically motivated; abolition of the death penalty and replacement with other forms of punishment for prisoners on death row; abolition of the "homelands" system; provision of human and material resources for education; inviting ILO to advise on labour laws; and human rights monitoring during the post-election transitional period. The Group noted that the international community had a vital role to play in assisting the new South Africa.

Human Rights Commission action. On 26 February,[13] the Commission demanded that the South African authorities fully respect section 29 of the Prisons Act, prevent the inhuman treatment of children in South Africa and ensure their basic and legitimate freedoms of movement, association and education. It called on the authorities to release all political prisoners; allow the safe return of political exiles and refugees; maintain law and order; abolish the system of "homelands"; repeal remaining discriminatory laws; accede to the 1966 International Covenants on Human Rights[14] and the 1965 International Convention on the Elimination of All Forms of Racial Discrimination;[15] implement the recommendations of and cooperate with the Commission of Inquiry regarding the Prevention of Public Violence and Intimidation (see PART TWO, Chapter I); and allow the Ad Hoc Working Group of Experts on southern Africa to visit South Africa.

The Commission called on the international community to support the process of transition in South Africa; assist and enhance the role of humanitarian and human rights groups in extending assistance to apartheid victims and monitoring the human rights situation; assist the Office of the United Nations High Commissioner for Refugees (UNHCR) and other humanitarian organizations in repatriating and reintegrating South African refugees; observe fully the mandatory arms embargo and the Security Council's 1977 request to monitor effectively the implementation of the arms embargo against South Africa;[16] support the peace process in Angola and Mozambique; and assist non-racial sports bodies in redressing structural inequalities in sports. The Commission called on the Centre for Human Rights to respond to South Africa's needs during its period of transition, in accordance with a 1992 General Assembly resolution.[17] It decided to renew the Group's mandate for an additional two years—a decision approved by the Economic and Social Council by **decision 1993/257** of 28 July—and asked the Group to submit its interim report in 1994 and its final report in 1995 and a preliminary report to the General Assembly in 1993 (see below) and 1994.

Subcommission action. On 20 August,[18] the Subcommission called on South African authorities to maintain law and order, stop the violence that continued to devastate South Africa, prosecute its perpetrators and protect all citizens, irrespective of their political affiliation. It called on South Africa not to execute persons convicted and sentenced to death for "security", "security-related" or "unrest-related" offences and to bring before the courts any members of the security forces or other government organs or other persons against whom *prima facie* evidence of participation in killing residents in black areas or in murdering political opponents of apartheid existed. It condemned all military collaboration with South Africa, particularly in the nuclear field.

Note by the Secretary-General. In November,[19] the Secretary-General transmitted to the General Assembly a preliminary report on the situation of human rights in South Africa, prepared by the Ad Hoc Working Group of Experts on southern Africa. The report evaluated the principal developments of the human rights situation in South Africa between February and September 1993; its recommendations were similar to those made in the interim report (see above).

Transition to democracy

On 26 February,[20] the Commission recommended a draft text to the Economic and Social Council.

ECONOMIC AND SOCIAL COUNCIL ACTION

On 28 July, the Economic and Social Council, on the recommendation of its Social Committee, adopted **resolution 1993/45** without vote.

Monitoring the transition to democracy in South Africa

The Economic and Social Council,

Recalling its resolution 1992/3 of 20 July 1992,

Noting the statement of the Special Rapporteur of the Subcommission on Prevention of Discrimination and Protection of Minorities, Mr. Ahmed Khalifa, in presenting his last report, that in the light of recent events the list of institutions giving support to the South African regime should be discontinued,

Noting also that it is of paramount importance to monitor the process towards democracy and social justice in South Africa,

1. *Expresses its appreciation* to the Special Rapporteur, Mr. Ahmed Khalifa, for his considerable contribution to the cause of eliminating the policy of apartheid;

2. *Expresses its thanks* to all Governments and organizations that supplied the Special Rapporteur with information;

3. *Authorizes* the Subcommission on Prevention of Discrimination and Protection of Minorities to entrust Ms. Judith Sefi Attah with the task of submitting annually a report on the transition to democracy in South Africa, including therein:

(a) Steps taken in accordance with international human rights instruments to prevent violence between different groups in South Africa;

(b) Steps taken to investigate the alleged involvement of the South African security forces in fomenting violence and how this problem is being addressed;

(c) Steps taken to ensure equal political participation for all South Africans, including those removed under the apartheid system to the so-called homelands;

(d) Steps taken to ensure the enjoyment by all South Africans, without discrimination, of economic and social rights;

(e) An analysis of the obstacles preventing the democratization of South Africa and ways and means of eliminating them;

4. *Requests* the Secretary-General to extend to Ms. Attah, the Special Rapporteur, all the assistance that she may require in the exercise of her mandate.

Economic and Social Council resolution 1993/45

28 July 1993   Meeting 44   Adopted without vote

Approved by Social Committee (E/1993/108) without vote, 22 July (meeting 17); draft by Commission on Human Rights (E/1993/23); agenda item 18.

Reports of the Special Rapporteur. In July, Special Rapporteur Judith Sefi Attah (Nigeria) presented a preliminary report on monitoring the transition to democracy in South Africa, in which she considered the political process in the country, political violence, inequality of economic and social rights and impediments to the transition.[21] She observed that the process of change through peaceful negotiations remained fragile and made recommendations to facilitate the full democratization of the country.

In a later addendum,[22] the Special Rapporteur described a mission to South Africa (24 November–2 December) that coincided with a period in the transition process during which important negotiated transitional legislation had either been concluded or was nearing completion. The mission recommended that the United Nations initiate and coordinate detailed planning of socio-economic assistance programmes; the international community support NGOs involved in voter education and other aspects of the transition; NGOs assist in consolidating democratic change through development-related activities; all groups and parties participate in elections; use of violence and intimidation by political leaders discontinue; the private sector support youth programmes; the new Multi-Party Peace-keeping Force receive support; the international community cooperate and coordinate activities under United Nations auspices; and sound preparations be made to ensure the success of United Nations monitoring of the elections.

Subcommission action. On 13 August,[23] the Subcommission requested the Secretary-General to bring the Special Rapporteur's report to the attention of the Government of South Africa and to contact the Government to enable the Special Rapporteur to undertake a special mission to South Africa while preparing her next report. It asked the Special Rapporteur to submit her second report in 1994 and requested the Secretary-General to provide her with all the assistance she needed.

1973 Convention against apartheid

As at 31 December 1993, there were 98 parties to the International Convention on the Suppression and Punishment of the Crime of Apartheid,[24] which was adopted by the General Assembly in 1973[25] and entered into force in 1976.[26] In 1993, Armenia, Bosnia and Herzegovina, the Czech Republic and Slovakia became parties to the Convention. In his annual report to the General Assembly on the status of the Convention,[27] the Secretary-General provided a list of States that had signed, ratified, acceded or succeeded to it as at 31 August.

Activities of the Group of Three. The Group of Three—established under article IX of the Convention to consider reports of States parties on measures taken to implement the Convention—held its fifteenth session at Geneva from 25 to 29 January.[28] The Group examined the reports of Algeria, Colombia, Mexico, Senegal, Tunisia and Venezuela.[29] It continued to examine whether the actions of transnational corporations (TNCs) operating in South Africa came under the definition of the crime of apartheid and whether legal action could be taken against them under the Convention. The Group called on States parties to incorporate in their legislation provisions relating to the crime of apartheid and invited Governments, entrepreneurs and enterprises to support the transition in South Africa. The Group recommended to the Commission that it request the Secretary-General to invite the States parties to the Convention which had not done so to express their views on the extent and nature of the responsibility of TNCs for the continued existence of apartheid in South Africa.

Human Rights Commission action. On 26 February,[30] by a roll-call vote of 30 to none, with 21 abstentions, the Commission urged States that had not done so to accede to the Convention against apartheid and recommended once again that all States parties take account of the guidelines laid down by the Group of Three in 1978 for submission of reports.[31] It requested the Secretary-General to intensify his efforts to disseminate information on the Convention and its implementation. The Commission requested the international community to urge South Africa to repeal the remaining apartheid laws and introduce legal and administrative measures to correct socioeconomic inequalities. It asked the Group of Three to continue to meet every two years and the Secretary-General to provide assistance to it.

On 20 December, the General Assembly, on the recommendation of the Third Committee, adopted **resolution 48/89** by recorded vote.

Status of the International Convention on the Suppression and Punishment of the Crime of Apartheid

The General Assembly,

Recalling its resolutions 41/103 of 4 December 1986, 42/56 of 30 November 1987, 43/97 of 8 December 1988, 44/69 of 8 December 1989, 45/90 of 14 December 1990, 46/84 of 16 December 1991 and 47/81 of 16 December 1992,

Mindful that the International Convention on the Suppression and Punishment of the Crime of Apartheid constitutes an important international treaty in the field of human rights and serves to implement the ideals of the Universal Declaration of Human Rights,

Reaffirming its conviction that apartheid is a crime against humanity and constitutes a total negation of the purposes and principles of the Charter of the United Nations and a gross violation of human rights, seriously threatening international peace and security,

Condemning the abhorrent system of apartheid wherever it exists, as well as the repression it engenders,

Convinced that universal ratification of or accession to the Convention and the immediate implementation of its provisions will contribute to the eradication of the crime of apartheid,

1. *Takes note* of the report of the Secretary-General;

2. *Commends* those States parties to the International Convention on the Suppression and Punishment of the Crime of Apartheid which have submitted their reports under article VII thereof;

3. *Appeals* to all States, United Nations organs, the specialized agencies and international and national non-governmental organizations to step up their activities to enhance public awareness by denouncing the crimes of apartheid;

4. *Underlines* the importance of the universal ratification of the Convention, which would be an effective contribution to the fulfilment of the ideals of the Universal Declaration of Human Rights and other human rights instruments;

5. *Appeals once again* to those States which have not yet done so to ratify or to accede to the Convention without further delay;

6. *Requests* the Secretary-General to intensify his efforts, through appropriate channels, to disseminate information on the Convention and its implementation with a view to promoting further ratification of or accession to the Convention;

7. *Also requests* the Secretary-General to include in his next annual report under General Assembly resolution 3380(XXX) of 10 November 1975 a special section concerning the implementation of the Convention.

General Assembly resolution 48/89

20 December 1993   Meeting 84   119-1-48 (recorded vote)

Approved by Third Committee (A/48/625) by recorded vote (103-1-46), 12 November (meeting 32); 7-nation draft (A/C.3/48/L.14); agenda item 107.
Sponsors: Angola, Mozambique, Namibia, Nigeria, United Republic of Tanzania, Zambia, Zimbabwe.
Meeting numbers. GA 48th session: 3rd Committee 3-10, 25, 32; plenary 84.

Recorded vote in Assembly as follows:

In favour: Afghanistan, Albania, Algeria, Angola, Antigua and Barbuda, Armenia, Bahamas, Bahrain, Bangladesh, Barbados, Belarus, Belize, Benin,

Bhutan, Bolivia, Bosnia and Herzegovina, Botswana, Brunei Darussalam, Burkina Faso, Burundi, Cambodia, Cameroon, Cape Verde, Central African Republic, Chad, Chile, China, Colombia, Comoros, Congo, Costa Rica, Côte d'Ivoire, Cuba, Cyprus, Democratic People's Republic of Korea, Djibouti, Dominica, Dominican Republic, Ecuador, Egypt, El Salvador, Ethiopia, Fiji, Gabon, Gambia, Ghana, Grenada, Guatemala, Guinea, Guinea-Bissau, Guyana, Haiti, Honduras, India, Indonesia, Iran, Iraq, Jamaica, Jordan, Kenya, Kuwait, Lao People's Democratic Republic, Lebanon, Lesotho, Libyan Arab Jamahiriya, Madagascar, Malawi, Malaysia, Maldives, Mali, Mauritania, Mauritius, Mexico, Mongolia, Morocco, Mozambique, Myanmar, Namibia, Nepal, Nicaragua, Niger, Nigeria, Oman, Pakistan, Panama, Papua New Guinea, Paraguay, Peru, Philippines, Qatar, Rwanda, Saint Lucia, Saint Vincent and the Grenadines, Saudi Arabia, Senegal, Sierra Leone, Singapore, Slovenia, Solomon Islands, Sri Lanka, Sudan, Suriname, Swaziland, Syrian Arab Republic, Thailand, Togo, Trinidad and Tobago, Tunisia, Uganda, Ukraine, United Arab Emirates, United Republic of Tanzania, Uruguay, Venezuela, Viet Nam, Yemen, Zaire, Zambia, Zimbabwe.

Against: United States.

Abstaining: Andorra, Argentina, Australia, Austria, Azerbaijan, Belgium, Brazil, Bulgaria, Canada, Croatia, Czech Republic, Denmark, Estonia, Finland, Georgia, Germany, Greece, Hungary, Iceland, Ireland, Israel, Italy, Japan, Kazakhstan, Kyrgyzstan, Latvia, Liechtenstein, Lithuania, Luxembourg, Malta, Marshall Islands, Micronesia, Netherlands, New Zealand, Norway, Poland, Portugal, Republic of Moldova, Romania, Russian Federation, San Marino, Slovakia, Spain, Sweden, the former Yugoslav Republic of Macedonia, Turkey, Turkmenistan, United Kingdom.

Foreign support of South Africa

Human Rights Commission action. On 28 February,[32] by a roll-call vote of 30 to 12, with 9 abstentions, the Commission condemned assistance to South Africa, particularly in the military and nuclear fields. It called on Governments that had not done so to take measures to end military cooperation with South Africa and assistance in the manufacture of arms and military supplies there and to cease nuclear collaboration. The Commission further called on them to maintain pressure against South Africa until agreement was reached on drawing up and adopting a new constitution and holding elections. Noting with appreciation measures taken by some States, parliamentarians, institutions, trade unions and NGOs to exert pressure on South Africa, the Commission called on them to maintain their efforts to urge South Africa to comply with United Nations resolutions and decisions.

The Commission appealed to the international community to assist the front-line and neighbouring States and to increase its contributions to the victims and opponents of apartheid. It also appealed to the international community, specialized agencies and intergovernmental organizations and NGOs to increase humanitarian and legal assistance to apartheid victims, returning refugees and exiles and released political prisoners.

The Commission asked the Secretary-General to continue to ensure the coordination of activities of the United Nations system in accordance with the 1989 Declaration on Apartheid and its Destructive Consequences in Southern Africa,[33] to continue to monitor its implementation and to pursue initiatives leading to the eradication of apartheid. Expressing appreciation to the Subcommission's Special Rapporteur, Ahmed Mohamed Khalifa (Egypt), for his updated 1992 report on

the adverse consequences for the enjoyment of human rights of political, military, economic and other forms of assistance given to South Africa,[34] the Commission asked the Secretary-General to give the report the widest dissemination and to issue it as a United Nations publication. It further requested him to report on the implementation of its resolution in 1994.

Note by the Secretary-General. In June,[35] the Secretary-General informed the Economic and Social Council that the Government of South Africa had submitted directly to ILO its report on measures taken in response to the 1992 report of the ILO Fact-finding and Conciliation Commission on Freedom of Association[36] concerning allegations of infringements of trade union rights in South Africa. In accordance with a 1992 Council request,[37] the Government of South Africa was to submit its report to the Secretary-General who in turn would transmit the document to ILO.

By **decision 1993/299** of 28 July, the Economic and Social Council took note of the Secretary-General's note.

Sudan

Human Rights Commission action. By a roll-call vote of 35 to 9, with 8 abstentions, the Commission, on 10 March,[3] expressing its deep concern at the serious human rights violations in the Sudan, urged the Government to respect human rights and called on all parties to the hostilities to cooperate to ensure such respect. The Commission also called on all parties to respect the provisions of international humanitarian law, including the Geneva Conventions of 12 August 1949 for the protection of war victims, to halt the use of weapons against the civilian population and to protect civilians from violations. It further called on them to permit international agencies, humanitarian organizations and donor Governments to deliver humanitarian assistance and to cooperate with the United Nations Department of Humanitarian Affairs. The Commission called on the Sudan to comply with applicable international human rights instruments and to ensure a full investigation of the killings of Sudanese employees of foreign relief organizations, to bring to justice those responsible and to provide just compensation to the victims' families.

The Commission requested its Chairman to appoint a special rapporteur on the situation of human rights in the Sudan and asked him or her to seek and receive credible and reliable information from Governments, NGOs and any other parties and to report to the General Assembly in 1993 and the Commission in 1994. It called on the Sudan to cooperate fully and to ensure that the Special Rapporteur had free and unlimited access to any person with whom he or she wished to meet, and asked the Secretary-General to provide assistance to the Special Rapporteur.

On 30 March, the Chairman appointed Dr. Gáspár Bíró (Hungary) as Special Rapporteur.

The Economic and Social Council, by **decision 1993/272** of 28 July, approved the Commission's decision to appoint a special rapporteur on the situation of human rights in the Sudan, and its requests to the Special Rapporteur to report to the Commission in 1994 and to the Secretary-General to assist him.

Report of the Special Rapporteur. On 18 November, the Secretary-General transmitted to the General Assembly an interim report of the Special Rapporteur.[(38)] He visited the Sudan from 11 to 23 September where he met with government authorities, representatives of humanitarian organizations and individual citizens and detainees, and visited displaced-persons camps and prisons. The Special Rapporteur received reports of extrajudicial killings and summary executions; enforced or involuntary disappearances; torture and other cruel, inhuman or degrading treatment; arbitrary arrest and detention; and reprisals by police and security forces. He drew attention to specific cases of human rights violations by the Sudanese army and paramilitary forces under its control having occurred in the Nuba Mountains area in central Sudan, an area he visited between 17 and 21 September.

The Special Rapporteur concluded that the seriousness of the human rights situation in the Sudan demanded continuing and intensified monitoring. He recommended that the Government abide by its human rights obligations under international law; ensure training for its security and police forces, army, paramilitary or civil defence groups; grant free access to regional and international humanitarian and human rights organizations; complete investigations into the arrest, disappearance and killing of hundreds of civilians and army officers following an attack by the Sudan People's Liberation Army in Juba in 1992; carry out investigations into human rights violations in the Nuba Mountains; cease attacks on civilians; ensure access to food and health care; agree on a cease-fire; and address the problem of displaced persons.

GENERAL ASSEMBLY ACTION

On 20 December, the General Assembly, on the recommendation of the Third Committee, adopted **resolution 48/147** by recorded vote.

Situation of human rights in the Sudan

The General Assembly,

Guided by the principles embodied in the Charter of the United Nations, the Universal Declaration of Human Rights, the International Covenants on Human Rights, and the International Convention on the Elimination of All Forms of Racial Discrimination,

Reaffirming that all Member States have an obligation to promote and protect human rights and fundamental freedoms and to comply with the obligations laid down in the various instruments in this field,

Recalling resolution AHG/Res.213(XXVIII) on the strengthening of cooperation and coordination among African States, adopted by the Assembly of Heads of State and Government of the Organization of African Unity at its twenty-eighth ordinary session, held at Dakar in June and July 1992, as well as the declaration AHG/Decl.1(XXVI), adopted at the twenty-sixth ordinary session, held at Addis Ababa in July 1990,[a]

Noting with deep concern reports of grave human rights violations in the Sudan, particularly summary executions, detentions without trial, forced displacement of persons and torture, described in part in the reports submitted to the Commission on Human Rights at its forty-ninth session by the Special Rapporteurs on the question of torture and extrajudicial summary or arbitrary executions,

Disturbed by the failure of the Government of the Sudan to provide for a full impartial investigation of the killings of Sudanese nationals employed by foreign government relief organizations, despite the announcement by the Government of its intention to convene an independent judicial inquiry commission,

Concerned over the reported attack on 12 November 1993 by aeroplanes of the Government of the Sudan on an airstrip in Thiet that resulted in injuries to three relief workers, and further concerned by the reported bombing of civilian areas in Loa and Pageri on 23 November 1993 that may have resulted in deaths or injuries,

Deeply concerned that access by the civilian population to humanitarian assistance is being impeded, which represents a threat to human life and an offence to human dignity, but welcoming the continuing dialogue between the Government of the Sudan and other parties, donor Governments and international private voluntary agencies regarding the delivery of humanitarian aid, and expressing the hope that such dialogue will result in improved cooperation for the delivery of humanitarian assistance,

Alarmed by the large number of internally displaced persons and victims of discrimination in the Sudan, including members of minorities who have been forcibly displaced in violation of their human rights and who are in need of relief assistance and of protection,

Alarmed also by the mass exodus of refugees to neighbouring countries and conscious of the burden that this places on those countries, but expressing its appreciation for the continuing efforts to assist them, thereby easing the burden on host countries,

Emphasizing that it is essential to put an end to the serious deterioration of the human rights situation in the Sudan, including that in the Nuba Mountains,

Recognizing the fact that the Sudan has been hosting large numbers of refugees from several neighbouring countries over the last three decades,

Welcoming the efforts of the United Nations and other humanitarian organizations to provide humanitarian relief to those Sudanese in need,

---

[a]A/45/482.

Noting with appreciation the efforts of the Special Rapporteur of the Commission on Human Rights, and commending him for his interim report on the situation of human rights in the Sudan,

1. *Expresses its deep concern* at the continuing and serious human rights violations in the Sudan, including summary executions, detentions without due process, forced displacement of persons and torture;

2. *Takes note* of paragraph 24 of the interim report of the Special Rapporteur of the Commission on Human Rights on the situation of human rights in the Sudan, in which he stated that the Government of the Sudan had cooperated with him by arranging the meetings he had requested and further facilitated visits to the locations he had wished to see;

3. *Notes with concern* the reprisals taken by the Government of the Sudan against those who contacted or attempted to contact the Special Rapporteur;

4. *Urges* the Government of the Sudan fully to respect human rights, and calls upon all parties to cooperate in order to ensure such respect;

5. *Calls upon* the Government of the Sudan to comply with applicable international human rights instruments, in particular the International Covenants on Human Rights and the International Convention on the Elimination of All Forms of Racial Discrimination, to which the Sudan is a party, and to ensure that all individuals in its territory and subject to its jurisdiction, including members of all religious and ethnic groups, enjoy the rights recognized in those instruments;

6. *Calls upon* all parties to the hostilities to respect fully the applicable provisions of international humanitarian law, including article 3 common to the Geneva Conventions of 12 August 1949, and the Additional Protocols thereto, of 1977, to halt the use of weapons against the civilian population and to protect all civilians from violations, including arbitrary detention, ill-treatment, torture and summary execution;

7. *Expresses its appreciation* to the humanitarian organizations for their work in helping displaced persons and drought and conflict victims in the Sudan, and calls upon all parties to protect humanitarian relief workers;

8. *Calls upon* the Special Rapporteur of the Commission on Human Rights on extrajudicial, summary or arbitrary executions again to address the killing of Sudanese nationals employed by foreign government relief organizations;

9. *Calls upon* the Government of the Sudan to explain fully the actions to obstruct the efforts of the Special Rapporteur, especially the ill-treatment afforded those who contacted or attempted to contact him;

10. *Also calls upon* the Government of the Sudan to ensure a full, thorough and prompt investigation by the independent judicial inquiry commission of the killings of Sudanese nationals employed by foreign government relief organizations, to bring to justice those responsible for the killings and to provide just compensation to the families of the victims;

11. *Further calls upon* the Government of the Sudan to investigate and explain without delay the circumstances behind the air attacks on 12 and 23 November 1993;

12. *Strongly urges* all parties to the hostilities to redouble their efforts to negotiate an equitable solution to the civil conflict to ensure respect for the human rights and fundamental freedoms of the Sudanese people and thereby create the necessary conditions to end the exodus of Sudanese refugees to neighbouring countries and facilitate their early return to the Sudan, and welcomes efforts to facilitate dialogue among the parties to that end;

13. *Notes with appreciation*, in this connection, the current regional efforts of heads of State of States members of the Intergovernmental Authority on Drought and Development (Eritrea, Ethiopia, Kenya and Uganda) to assist parties to the conflict in the Sudan to reach a peaceful settlement;

14. *Calls upon* the Government of the Sudan and other parties to permit international agencies, humanitarian organizations and donor Governments to deliver humanitarian assistance to the civilian population and to cooperate with the recent initiatives of the Department of Humanitarian Affairs of the Secretariat to deliver humanitarian assistance to all persons in need;

15. *Recommends* that the serious human rights situation in the Sudan be monitored, and invites the Commission on Human Rights to give urgent attention to this question at its fiftieth session;

16. *Decides* to continue its consideration of this question at its forty-ninth session.

General Assembly resolution 48/147

20 December 1993   Meeting 85   111-13-30 (recorded vote)

Approved by Third Committee (A/48/632/Add.3) by recorded vote (102-11-31), 6 December (meeting 53); 25-nation draft (A/C.3/48/L.65/Rev.1), orally revised; agenda item 114 *(c)*.
Sponsors: Argentina, Australia, Austria, Belgium, Canada, Denmark, Finland, Georgia, Germany, Ghana, Greece, Honduras, Hungary, Iceland, Ireland, Israel, Italy, Luxembourg, Netherlands, Norway, Portugal, Spain, Sweden, United Kingdom, United States.
Meeting numbers. GA 48th session: 3rd Committee 36-53; plenary 85.

Recorded vote in Assembly as follows:

In favour: Albania, Algeria, Antigua and Barbuda, Argentina, Armenia, Australia, Austria, Azerbaijan, Bahamas, Barbados, Belarus, Belgium, Belize, Benin, Bolivia, Botswana, Brazil, Bulgaria, Canada, Cape Verde, Chile, Colombia, Congo, Costa Rica, Croatia, Cyprus, Czech Republic, Denmark, Dominica, Dominican Republic, Ecuador, El Salvador, Estonia, Fiji, Finland, France, Gabon, Gambia, Georgia, Germany, Ghana, Greece, Grenada, Guatemala, Guinea-Bissau, Guyana, Haiti, Honduras, Hungary, Iceland, Ireland, Israel, Italy, Japan, Kazakhstan, Kuwait, Kyrgyzstan, Latvia, Lesotho, Liechtenstein, Lithuania, Luxembourg, Madagascar, Malawi, Malta, Marshall Islands, Mauritius, Mexico, Micronesia, Monaco, Mongolia, Namibia, Nepal, Netherlands, New Zealand, Nicaragua, Norway, Panama, Papua New Guinea, Paraguay, Peru, Poland, Portugal, Republic of Korea, Republic of Moldova, Romania, Russian Federation, Rwanda, Saint Lucia, Saint Vincent and the Grenadines, San Marino, Saudi Arabia, Singapore, Slovakia, Slovenia, Solomon Islands, Spain, Suriname, Sweden, the former Yugoslav Republic of Macedonia, Trinidad and Tobago, Turkey, Ukraine, United Kingdom, United Republic of Tanzania, United States, Uruguay, Venezuela, Zaire, Zambia, Zimbabwe.
Against: Afghanistan, China, Cuba, India, Indonesia, Iran, Iraq, Libyan Arab Jamahiriya, Myanmar, Pakistan, Sudan, Syrian Arab Republic, Viet Nam.
Abstaining: Angola, Bangladesh, Bhutan, Brunei Darussalam, Burkina Faso, Burundi, Cameroon, Central African Republic, Comoros, Côte d'Ivoire, Eritrea, Guinea, Jamaica, Kenya, Lao People's Democratic Republic, Malaysia, Maldives, Mali, Mauritania, Mozambique, Niger, Nigeria, Philippines, Sierra Leone, Sri Lanka, Swaziland, Thailand, Togo, Tunisia, Uganda.

In the Third Committee, paragraphs 12 and 2 were adopted by recorded votes of 147 to none, with 1 abstention, and 148 to none, respectively. The eleventh preambular paragraph was adopted by 148 votes to none.

Togo

On 10 March,[39] the Commission, deploring the obstacles standing in the way of a democratic transition in Togo and the use of violence by the armed forces against peaceful demonstrators, called on the authorities to take measures to create conditions conducive to the return of Togolese refugees in security and dignity and to guarantee the security of all Togolese, including political opponents. It requested the Secretary-General to bring its resolution to the attention of the Togolese authorities, asking them to indicate action taken thereon, and to report to the Commission in 1994 on the basis of any information obtained on the human rights situation in Togo, including information furnished by NGOs.

Zaire

On 10 March 1993,[4] the Commission on Human Rights deplored the continuing serious violations of human rights and fundamental freedoms in Zaire and expressed concern about discriminatory measures affecting persons belonging to minority groups. It recommended that thematic rapporteurs and working groups of the Commission should continue to keep a close watch on the human rights situation in Zaire, and requested the Secretary-General to bring its resolution to the attention of Zairian authorities and to report in 1994.

Asia and the Pacific

Afghanistan

Report of the Special Rapporteur. Special Rapporteur Felix Ermacora (Austria) presented to the Commission on Human Rights in February a report on the human rights situation in Afghanistan.[40] He visited Pakistan from 29 January to 3 February and Afghanistan on 31 January 1993 to gather up-to-date material following the submission of his 1992 interim report.[41] At the request of the Russian Federation, the Special Rapporteur visited Moscow on 28 January to discuss the situation of former Soviet prisoners of war held in Afghanistan, and that of Afghan children who had been brought from Afghanistan to study in the former USSR.

The Special Rapporteur stated that, although the 1992 change in power had taken place peacefully,[42] it was followed by increasingly violent clashes between armed groups of various political factions. It appeared that the decision concerning the political status of the country was still dependent on the outcome of an armed struggle for political power, which the Secretary-General's 1991 five-point peace plan had sought to prevent.[43]

He had received reliable information regarding the existence of some 1,500 prisoners who were detained by different mujahidin groups. In addition, the fate of former Soviet prisoners had not been clarified. The enjoyment of economic, social and cultural rights was not guaranteed and genuine elections had not taken place.

In addition to his 1992 recommendations,[41] the Special Rapporteur recommended that Afghanistan respect humanitarian law; issue a declaration on article 4 of the International Covenant on Civil and Political Rights (relating to human rights in emergency situations);[44] allow the International Committee on the Red Cross (ICRC) to visit places of detention; limit the period of detention on remand or preventive detention to a reasonable term; not discriminate against refugees who had been associated with the former Government and to whom amnesty applied; and apply the country's general amnesty without discrimination. He stated that the United Nations should invite the Afghan Government to accept United Nations monitoring or advisory services; collaborate with it in studying the human rights situation; initiate the process of periodic and genuine elections; and cooperate with the Special Rapporteur. He advocated a systematic search into the whereabouts of disappeared persons and support by the international community to the repatriation of some 4 million Afghan refugees.

Human Rights Commission action. On 10 March,[45] the Commission urged the Afghan parties to undertake all efforts to achieve a comprehensive political solution, respect the humanitarian rules set out in the 1949 Geneva Conventions and their Additional Protocols of 1977,[46] halt the use of weapons against civilians and protect them from reprisals and violence, including ill-treatment, torture and summary execution, and expedite the exchange of prisoners. It called on States and parties concerned to implement a 1992 General Assembly decision concerning prisoners of war and persons missing as a result of war in Afghanistan[47] and to make efforts to release all prisoners of war, particularly former Soviet prisoners of war, since the hostilities in which the former USSR was involved had legally ended. The Commission urged the unconditional release of all prisoners detained without trial in Afghanistan by rival groups and called on all conflicting parties to investigate the fate of disappeared persons, apply amnesty decrees equally to all detainees, reduce the period during which prisoners awaited trial, treat all prisoners in accordance with the Standard Minimum Rules for the Treatment of Prisoners[48] and apply to all convicted persons the relevant articles of the International Covenant on Civil and Political Rights.

Expressing concern at reports that the living conditions of refugees, especially those of women and children, were becoming increasingly difficult, the Commission urgently appealed to Member States and humanitarian organizations to promote the implementation of projects envisaged by the

Coordinator for United Nations Humanitarian and Economic Assistance to Afghanistan (see PART THREE, Chapter III) and UNHCR programmes (see PART THREE, Chapter XV). It also appealed to Member States, humanitarian organizations and all parties concerned to cooperate fully, especially on the subject of mine detection, in facilitating the return of refugees and displaced persons to their homes in safety and dignity. The Commission urged all parties to ensure the safety of personnel involved in implementing United Nations humanitarian and economic assistance programmes and to extend their cooperation to the Commission and its Special Rapporteur. The Commission extended the Special Rapporteur's mandate for one year and asked him to report to the Assembly in 1993 and the Commission in 1994. The Secretary-General was asked to give him all necessary assistance.

By **decision 1993/275** of 28 July, the Economic and Social Council approved the extension of the Special Rapporteur's mandate and the Commission's request that he report in 1993 and 1994.

Interim report of the Special Rapporteur. In November, the Secretary-General transmitted to the General Assembly an interim report of the Special Rapporteur on the situation of human rights in Afghanistan from March to October 1993.[49] The Special Rapporteur had visited Pakistan and Afghanistan in September.

Despite the formation of an Islamic Government, the rivalry between the groups whose leaders or members were ministers in the coalition Government had continued and their difference had not been resolved through negotiation. The Special Rapporteur concluded that the human rights situation was far from satisfactory. Fighting continued in Kabul, where some 36,000 houses were partly or fully destroyed and more than 30,000 damaged. Some 110,000 families were displaced and thousands of persons were killed or wounded. Numerous cases of rape and ill-treatment by armed persons had been reported. In 1993, a relatively small number of refugees chose to return from Pakistan. An estimated 2 million remained in Pakistan and some 2.15 million were in Iran. More than 90,000 new refugees had arrived in Pakistan since April 1992. Numerous members from the Afghan Sikh and Hindu communities had fled Kabul owing to the insecurity caused by shelling and looting. Death sentences continued to be pronounced and were reportedly carried out.

The Special Rapporteur recommended abolishing prisons run by political parties and releasing their prisoners; broadening and accelerating mine clearance; enabling displaced persons to return safely to their homes and to rebuild them; ensuring respect for women; and solving political con-

flicts peacefully and democratically. He further recommended that the United Nations try to bring the conflicting groups to the negotiating table and urged it to continue to monitor the human rights situation. He appealed to the international community to continue its efforts in favour of mine clearance.

GENERAL ASSEMBLY ACTION

On 20 December, the General Assembly, on the recommendation of the Third Committee, adopted **resolution 48/152** without vote.

Situation of human rights in Afghanistan
The General Assembly,

Guided by the principles embodied in the Charter of the United Nations, the Universal Declaration of Human Rights and the International Covenants on Human Rights and accepted humanitarian rules, as set out in the Geneva Conventions of 12 August 1949 and the Additional Protocols thereto, of 1977,

Aware of its responsibility to promote and encourage respect for human rights and fundamental freedoms for all and resolved to remain vigilant with regard to violations of human rights wherever they occur,

Reaffirming that all Member States have an obligation to promote and protect human rights and fundamental freedoms and to fulfil the obligations they have freely undertaken under the various international instruments,

Recalling Economic and Social Council resolution 1984/37 of 24 May 1984, in which the Council requested the Chairman of the Commission on Human Rights to appoint a special rapporteur to examine the situation of human rights in Afghanistan, with a view to formulating proposals that could contribute to ensuring full protection of the human rights of the inhabitants of the country before, during and after the withdrawal of all foreign forces,

Recalling also its resolution 47/141 of 18 December 1992 and all its other relevant resolutions, as well as the resolutions of the Commission on Human Rights and the decisions of the Economic and Social Council,

Taking note, in particular, of Commission on Human Rights resolution 1993/66 of 10 March 1993, in which the Commission decided to extend the mandate of its Special Rapporteur on the situation of human rights in Afghanistan for one year and to request him to report to the General Assembly at its forty-eighth session, and of Economic and Social Council decision 1993/275 of 28 July 1993, in which the Council approved the Commission's decision,

Noting that, following the demise of the former Afghan Government, a transitional Islamic State of Afghanistan was established,

Noting with deep concern that in spite of the efforts and initiatives taken by the Government of Afghanistan towards ensuring complete peace and stability, a situation of armed confrontation, affecting mainly the civilian population, which is still the target of indiscriminate military attacks by rival groups, continues to exist in parts of the territory of Afghanistan, and in particular in Kabul, and has also caused a dramatic rise in the number of persons displaced inside the country,

Concerned that the prevailing situation in the country as regards the political and legal order is affecting the security of members of all ethnic and religious groups, including minorities,

Noting with concern reports of violations of rights enshrined in the International Covenant on Civil and Political Rights, such as the right to life, liberty and security of person and to freedom of opinion, expression and association,

Deeply concerned about the violation of the human rights of women by warring factions in Afghanistan, and about the lack of respect towards them and their honour, physical integrity and dignity, as reported by the Special Rapporteur,

Concerned at reports of detainees who are being held for political reasons by rival groups, in particular in prisons run by political parties, among whom are several members of the former Government,

Noting that much remains to be done for the treatment of prisoners to be in conformity with the provisions of the Geneva Conventions of 12 August 1949 and the Additional Protocols thereto, of 1977,

Deeply concerned that the repatriation of Afghan refugees has dramatically declined in 1993, owing to the prevailing situation in Afghanistan, and expressing the hope that conditions in the country will allow those still in exile to return as soon as possible,

Aware that peace and security in Afghanistan are prerequisites for the successful repatriation of about four million refugees, in particular the achievement of a comprehensive political solution and the establishment of a freely and democratically elected government, the end of armed confrontation in Kabul and in some provinces, the clearance of the minefields that have been laid in many parts of the country, the restoration of an effective authority in the whole country and the reconstruction of the economy,

Affirming that the declaration of general amnesty issued by the Islamic State of Afghanistan should be applied in a strictly non-discriminatory manner and that prisoners detained by rival groups without trial on Afghan territory should be released unconditionally,

Commending the activity carried out by the Office of the United Nations High Commissioner for Refugees and the International Committee of the Red Cross in cooperation with the Afghan authorities, as well as non-governmental organizations, in favour of the people of Afghanistan,

Taking note with appreciation of the report of the Special Rapporteur and of the conclusions and recommendations contained therein,

Welcoming the fact that the Special Rapporteur was able to visit the capital of Afghanistan, Kabul,

1. *Welcomes* the cooperation that authorities in Afghanistan have extended to the Special Rapporteur of the Commission on Human Rights on the situation of human rights in Afghanistan, in view of the circumstances prevailing in the country;

2. *Also welcomes* the cooperation that the authorities in Afghanistan have extended, in particular to the Coordinator for Humanitarian and Economic Assistance Programmes Relating to Afghanistan and to international organizations, such as the specialized agencies, the Office of the United Nations High Commissioner for Refugees and the International Committee of the Red Cross;

3. *Urges* all the Afghan parties to undertake, where appropriate under the auspices of the United Nations, all possible efforts in order to achieve a comprehensive political solution, which is the only way to bring about peace and the full restoration of human rights in Afghanistan, based on the free exercise of the right to self-determination by the people, including free and genuine elections, the cessation of armed confrontation and the creation of conditions that will permit the free return, as soon as possible, of about four million refugees to their homeland in safety and dignity, whenever they wish, and the full enjoyment of human rights and fundamental freedoms by all Afghans;

4. *Welcomes* all the efforts towards reaching a comprehensive, peaceful political solution to the conflict in Afghanistan;

5. *Urges* all the parties to carry out as soon as possible a disarmament process, which constitutes a prerequisite of a solution to the conflict, as decided also in the Afghan peace accord signed by the Afghan parties at Islamabad on 7 March 1993;

6. *Invites* the United Nations to offer, upon request of the Government of Afghanistan and with due regard to the Afghan tradition, advisory services and technical assistance concerning the drafting of a Constitution, which should embody internationally accepted human rights principles, and the holding of direct elections;

7. *Recognizes* that the promotion and protection of human rights should be an essential element in the achievement of a comprehensive solution to the crisis in Afghanistan, and calls upon all the Afghan parties to respect human rights;

8. *Urges* all the Afghan parties to respect accepted humanitarian rules, as set out in the Geneva Conventions of 12 August 1949 and the Additional Protocols thereto, of 1977, to halt the use of weapons against the civilian population, to protect all civilians from acts of reprisal and violence, including ill-treatment, torture and summary executions, and to expedite the simultaneous release of prisoners wherever they may be held;

9. *Strongly urges* all Afghan parties to ensure respect for the human rights and fundamental freedoms of women, so that their honour and dignity would be ensured in accordance with the provisions of international human rights instruments and the humanitarian law;

10. *Calls upon* all States and parties concerned to make all efforts for the realization of its decision 47/428 of 16 December 1992 entitled "Prisoners of war and persons missing as a result of war in Afghanistan", and calls upon them to make all efforts for the immediate release of all prisoners of war, and in particular of former Soviet prisoners of war, as provided for under article 118 of the Geneva Convention relative to the Treatment of Prisoners of War, of 12 August 1949, considering that the hostilities in which the former Soviet Union was involved have legally and effectively ended, and also in particular for the tracing of the many Afghans still missing as a result of the war;

11. *Urges* the unconditional release of all prisoners detained without trial on the Afghan territory by rival groups, and calls for the abolition of prisons run by political parties;

12. *Calls upon* the authorities in Afghanistan to investigate thoroughly the fate of those persons who have disappeared during the conflict, to apply amnesty decrees equally to all detainees, to reduce the period dur-

ing which prisoners await trial, to treat all prisoners, especially those awaiting trial or those in custody in juvenile rehabilitation centres, in accordance with the Standard Minimum Rules for the Treatment of Prisoners, adopted by the First United Nations Congress on the Prevention of Crime and the Treatment of Offenders, and to apply to all suspected or convicted persons article 14, paragraphs 3 *(d)* and 5 to 7, of the International Covenant on Civil and Political Rights;

13. *Appeals* to all Member States to provide adequate humanitarian assistance to Afghanistan in order to contribute to the alleviation of the suffering of refugees and especially to the improvement of the living conditions of women and children;

14. *Urgently appeals* to all Member States and humanitarian organizations to continue to promote the implementation of the projects envisaged by the Coordinator for Humanitarian and Economic Assistance Programmes Relating to Afghanistan and the programmes of the United Nations High Commissioner for Refugees, especially the pilot projects for the repatriation of refugees;

15. *Reiterates its appeal* to all Member States, humanitarian organizations and all parties concerned to cooperate fully on the question of mine detection and clearance, in order to facilitate the return of refugees and displaced persons to their homes in safety and dignity;

16. *Strongly urges* all the parties to the conflict to undertake all necessary measures to ensure the safety of the personnel of humanitarian organizations involved in the implementation of the United Nations humanitarian and economic assistance programmes relating to Afghanistan and the programmes of the United Nations High Commissioner for Refugees, in order to avoid further deplorable incidents such as those which have caused loss of life among that personnel;

17. *Invites* the United Nations Educational, Scientific and Cultural Organization, once the situation is back to normal and upon the invitation of the Afghan Government, to study the situation of the Kabul Museum and of the national archives and to take proper action to preserve the Afghan cultural heritage;

18. *Recommends* the translation of the report of the Special Rapporteur into the Dari and Pashtu languages;

19. *Urges* the authorities in Afghanistan to continue to extend their full cooperation to the Commission on Human Rights and its Special Rapporteur;

20. *Requests* the Secretary-General to give all necessary assistance to the Special Rapporteur;

21. *Decides* to keep under consideration during its forty-ninth session the situation of human rights in Afghanistan, in the light of additional elements provided by the Commission on Human Rights and the Economic and Social Council.

General Assembly resolution 48/152

20 December 1993   Meeting 85   Adopted without vote

Approved by Third Committee (A/48/632/Add.3) without vote, 6 December (meeting 53); draft by Chairman (A/C.3/48/L.73), orally revised; agenda item 114 *(c)*.
Meeting numbers. GA 48th session: 3rd Committee 36-53; plenary 85.

Cambodia

The Commission on Human Rights and the Economic and Social Council expressed concern about the protection of human rights in Cambodia (see above, under "Civil and political rights").

GENERAL ASSEMBLY ACTION

On 20 December, the General Assembly, on the recommendation of the Third Committee, adopted **resolution 48/154** without vote.

Situation of human rights in Cambodia

The General Assembly,

Guided by the principles embodied in the Charter of the United Nations, the Universal Declaration of Human Rights and the International Covenants on Human Rights,

Taking note of the Agreement on a Comprehensive Political Settlement of the Cambodia Conflict, signed on 23 October 1991, including part III thereof, relating to human rights,

Taking note also of Commission on Human Rights resolution 1993/6 of 19 February 1993,

Bearing in mind the role and responsibilities of the United Nations and the international community in the process of the rehabilitation and reconstruction of Cambodia,

Recognizing that the tragic recent history of Cambodia requires special measures to assure the protection of the human rights of all people in the country and the non-return to the policies and practices of the past, as stipulated in the agreements signed in Paris on 23 October 1991,

Welcoming the elections of May 1993 and the inauguration of the Government of the Kingdom of Cambodia,

1. *Welcomes* the establishment in Cambodia of an operational presence of the Centre for Human Rights of the Secretariat:

(*a*) To manage the implementation of educational and technical assistance and advisory services programmes, and to ensure their continuation;

(*b*) To assist the Government of Cambodia established after the election, at its request, in meeting its obligations under the human rights instruments recently adhered to, including the preparation of reports to the relevant monitoring committees;

(*c*) To provide support to bona fide human rights groups in Cambodia;

(*d*) To contribute to the creation and/or strengthening of national institutions for the promotion and protection of human rights;

(*e*) To continue to assist with the drafting and implementation of legislation to promote and protect human rights;

(*f*) To continue to assist with the training of persons responsible for the administration of justice;

2. *Requests* the Secretary-General, in line with all effective measures, to assure the protection of the human rights of all people in Cambodia and to ensure adequate resources, from within existing overall United Nations resources, for the functioning of the operational presence of the Centre for Human Rights in Cambodia;

3. *Welcomes also* the appointment by the Secretary-General of a Special Representative to undertake the tasks set out in paragraph 6 of Commission on Human Rights resolution 1993/6;

4. *Requests* the Secretary-General to provide all necessary resources, from within existing resources, to enable

the Special Representative to fulfil those tasks expeditiously;

5. *Also requests* the Secretary-General to report to the General Assembly at its forty-ninth session on the role of the Centre for Human Rights in assisting the Cambodian Government and people in the promotion and protection of human rights and on any recommendations made by the Special Representative on matters within his mandate;

6. *Decides* to continue its consideration of the situation of human rights in Cambodia at its forty-ninth session.

General Assembly resolution 48/154

20 December 1993   Meeting 85   Adopted without vote

Approved by Third Committee (A/48/632/Add.3) without vote, 6 December (meeting 53); 15-nation draft (A/C.3/48/L.75), orally revised; agenda item 114 *(c)*.

Sponsors: Australia, Austria, Cambodia, Cameroon, Canada, France, Indonesia, Japan, Netherlands, New Zealand, Russian Federation, Sweden, United Kingdom, United States, Uruguay.

Meeting numbers. GA 48th session: 3rd Committee 36-53; plenary 85.

China

On 11 March,[50] the Commission, by a roll-call vote of 22 to 17, with 12 abstentions, decided to take no action on a draft resolution concerning the situation in China.

By that draft, the Commission would have expressed concern over continuing reports of human rights violations in China and called on the Government to ensure the observance of human rights and improve the administration of justice.

East Timor

Report of the Secretary-General. In a February report to the Commission on Human Rights on the situation in East Timor,[51] the Secretary-General discussed his good-offices activities aimed at achieving a just, comprehensive and internationally acceptable settlement of the question of East Timor. He also described action taken by the Working Group on Enforced or Involuntary Disappearances in 1992,[52] the Special Rapporteur on extrajudicial, summary or arbitrary executions[53] and the Special Rapporteur on the question of torture.[54] Annexed to the report was information received from the Governments of Indonesia and Portugal and NGOs regarding the trials surrounding November 1991 incidents of violence at Dili, which resulted in loss of life, injuries and disappearances among civilians.[55] (See also PART ONE, Chapter III.)

Human Rights Commission action. On 11 March,[56] by a roll-call vote of 22 to 12, with 15 abstentions, the Commission expressed deep concern at the reports of continuing human rights violations in East Timor and, referring to the trials surrounding the 1991 incident at Dili, regretted the disparity in sentences imposed on those civilians not indicted for violent activities—who should have been released—and on the military involved. It called on Indonesia to ensure that all East Timorese in custody were treated humanely, all trials were fair, just and public, and those not involved in violent activities were released, and urged it to invite the Special Rapporteurs on torture and on extrajudicial, summary or arbitrary executions and the Working Group on Enforced or Involuntary Disappearances to visit East Timor. It decided to consider the situation in East Timor in 1994 on the basis of the reports of the Special Rapporteurs and Working Groups and that of the Secretary-General, which would include an analytical compilation of information received from Governments, intergovernmental organizations and NGOs.

Subcommission action. The Subcommission had before it a July note by the Secretariat,[57] updating the good-offices activities of the Secretary-General, including a visit to Indonesia and East Timor from 3 to 8 April by his Personal Envoy, S. Amos Wako (Kenya).

By a secret ballot of 13 votes to 10, with 2 abstentions, the Subcommission, on 20 August,[58] urged the Indonesian authorities to implement the Commission's 1993 decisions concerning East Timor and to honour the provisions of the 1949 Geneva Convention relative to the Protection of Civilian Persons in Time of War regarding the prohibition on removing prisoners from their original place of residence.

Indonesia

On 25 August,[59] the Subcommission, by a secret ballot of 17 votes to 7, with 1 abstention, decided to take no action on a draft resolution concerning human rights violations in Indonesia. By that draft, the Subcommission would have encouraged the Indonesian authorities to invite the Special Rapporteurs on the question of torture and on extrajudicial, summary and arbitrary executions to visit Aceh and other parts of Indonesia. The Special Rapporteur on torture, Peter H. Kooijmans (Netherlands), had been prevented from visiting Aceh province during a November 1991 visit to Indonesia.[60]

Iran

Report of the Special Representative. Special Representative Reynaldo Galindo Pohl (El Salvador) submitted to the Commission on Human Rights a January report on the human rights situation in Iran.[61] He had received information on alleged incidents and cases concerning the right to life; enforced or involuntary disappearances; the right to freedom from torture or cruel, inhuman or degrading treatment or punishment; the administration of justice; freedom of expression, opinion and association and the right to peaceful assembly; political rights; the situation of women and children; the right to education; the right to own property; the right to leave one's country and to return; freedom of religion; and the Baha'i community. The detailed allegations had been transmitted to Iran to enable it to verify their accuracy; Iran's replies were reflected in the Special Representative's report. He also discussed repressive aspects in Iran's fight against drug trafficking, the refugee population and military and civilian victims of chemical-weapons attacks during the hostilities between Iran and Iraq.

The Special Representative noted that there was continued uncertainty about the official reaction to dissidence; self-censorship was widespread in the media; several guarantees of due process were still the letter of the law or the subject of proposed legislation; the right of free association had been denied; ICRC continued to be prevented from performing its function in prisons; the restrictions on non-Islamic religious groups were manifold; and the situation of women left much to be desired. The number of judicial executions continued to exceed the very restrictive terms of the 1966 International Covenant on Civil and Political Rights and there had been cases of torture and cruel, inhuman or degrading treatment or punishment.

The Special Representative recommended making urgent appeals to Iran to implement fully the international human rights standards in force and the 1991 agreement concluded with ICRC concerning visits to prisons and prisoners.[62] He stated that the urgent need to reduce drastically the number of executions should be emphasized and that Iran should be asked to resume a policy of full cooperation with the Commission.

In a later addendum,[63] the Special Representative presented Iran's replies to questions raised in his 1992 interim report.[62]

Human Rights Commission action. On 10 March,[64] by a roll-call vote of 23 to 11, with 14 abstentions, the Commission, expressing concern at continuing reports of human rights violations in Iran, called on that country to intensify its efforts to investigate and rectify the human rights issues raised by the Special Representative, comply with international human rights instruments and ensure that all individuals enjoyed the rights recognized in those instruments. It encouraged Iran to continue to cooperate with ICRC and the Special Representative. The Commission endorsed the Special Representative's view that international monitoring of human rights in Iran should continue. Deciding to extend the Special Representative's mandate for another year, the Commission asked him to submit an interim report to the General Assembly in 1993 (see below) and a final report to the Commission in 1994. The Secretary-General was asked to assist him. Those requests were approved by the Economic and Social Council by **decision 1993/273** of 28 July.

Note by the Secretary-General. On 3 August,[65] the Secretary-General drew the Subcommission's attention to reports by special rapporteurs or human rights bodies, as well as to steps which had been or were being taken by the Economic and Social Council, the General Assembly and the Commission on Human Rights to prevent human rights violations in Iran since August 1992.

Subcommission action. On 20 August 1993,[66] the Subcommission, by a secret ballot of 20 votes to 3, with 2 abstentions, asked the Special Representative to consider and recommend the strongest measures that could be adopted within the United Nations to eliminate human rights violations in Iran, and asked the Secretary-General to inform it in 1994 of the reports and measures towards that end, implemented or under way by United Nations bodies.

Interim report of the Special Representative. In November, the Secretary-General transmitted to the General Assembly the Special Representative's interim report on the human rights situation in Iran,[67] which summarized allegations of human rights violations received by him between January and September 1993 and which he had communicated to Iran. They concerned the right to life; enforced or involuntary disappearances; the right to freedom from torture or cruel, inhuman or degrading treatment or punishment; the administration of justice; freedom of expression, opinion and the press; freedom of religion and the situation of the Baha'is; the situation of women and children; and the rights to work, education and to own property. Information was also received on the 25 May 1993 air attacks by the Iranian Air Force on military bases in Iraq, which belonged to the Iran National Liberation Army of the People's Mujahidin, and on tensions between the Government and the Kurdish and Naraoui people.

The Special Representative recommended that Iran be urged to: stop its intelligence agents from threatening or attempting to kill members of the Iranian opposition abroad and to investigate the incidents that had been reported; give effect to the guarantees of due process of law in its courts and tribunals; recognize that men and women were equal before the law; examine the problem of intimidating the media and adopt legal measures to protect the press; implement a 1991 agreement between ICRC and the Government;[68] and resume full cooperation with the Special Representative by allowing him to revisit the country. He stated that the human rights situation in Iran should remain under international scrutiny.

In a later addendum,[69] the Special Representative presented Iran's replies to allegations of human rights violations presented in his interim report.

GENERAL ASSEMBLY ACTION

On 20 December, on the recommendation of the Third Committee, the General Assembly adopted **resolution 48/145** by recorded vote.

Situation of human rights in the Islamic Republic of Iran

The General Assembly,

Guided by the principles embodied in the Charter of the United Nations, the Universal Declaration of Human Rights and the International Covenants on Human Rights,

Reaffirming that all Member States have an obligation to promote and protect human rights and fundamental freedoms and to fulfil the obligations they have undertaken under the various international instruments in this field,

Bearing in mind its relevant resolutions, including the most recent, resolution 47/146 of 18 December 1992, as well as those of the Commission on Human Rights, including the most recent, resolution 1993/62 of 10 March 1993, and those of the Subcommission on Prevention of Discrimination and Protection of Minorities, including the most recent, resolution 1993/14 of 20 August 1993,

Noting that the Government of the Islamic Republic of Iran has responded to the request of the Special Representative of the Commission on Human Rights for information concerning allegations of human rights violations in that country, but that it did not allow him to pay a fourth visit to the country so that he might obtain direct and first-hand information on the current human rights situation there,

Reaffirming that Governments are accountable for assassinations and attacks by their agents against persons on the territory of another State, as well as for the incitement, approval or wilful condoning of such acts,

Noting the observation of the Special Representative that there is enough evidence to show that it is entirely proper for the human rights situation in the Islamic Republic of Iran to remain under international scrutiny,

Noting also that the Subcommission on Prevention of Discrimination and Protection of Minorities, in its resolution 1993/14, has condemned the continuing flagrant violations of human rights in the Islamic Republic of Iran,

Noting further the concluding observations of the Committee on the Elimination of Racial Discrimination, the Human Rights Committee and the Committee on Economic, Social and Cultural Rights on the human rights situation in the Islamic Republic of Iran,

1. *Takes note with appreciation* of the interim report of the Special Representative of the Commission on Human Rights and the considerations and observations contained therein;

2. *Expresses its deep concern* at continuing reports of violations of human rights in the Islamic Republic of Iran;

3. *Expresses its concern* more specifically at the main criticisms of the Special Representative with regard to the human rights situation in the Islamic Republic of Iran, namely, the high number of executions, cases of torture and cruel, inhuman or degrading treatment or punishment, the standard of the administration of justice, the absence of guarantees of due process of law, discriminatory treatment of certain groups of citizens by reason of their religious beliefs, notably the Baha'is, whose existence as a viable religious community is threatened, and restrictions on the freedom of expression, thought, opinion and the press, and that, as noted by the Special Representative, there is continued discrimination against women;

4. *Expresses its grave concern* at the continued use of the death penalty, which the Special Representative has described as excessive;

5. *Also expresses its grave concern* that there are continuing threats to the life of a citizen of another State, whose case is mentioned in the interim report of the Special Representative, as well as to individuals associated with his work, which appear to have the support of the Government of the Islamic Republic of Iran;

6. *Urges* the Government of the Islamic Republic of Iran to refrain from activities such as those mentioned in the interim report of the Special Representative against members of the Iranian opposition living abroad;

7. *Regrets* that the Government of the Islamic Republic of Iran has still not permitted the Special Representative to visit the country and has thus not enabled him fully to discharge his mandate by according him full cooperation;

8. *Also urges* the Government of the Islamic Republic of Iran to implement existing agreements with international humanitarian organizations;

9. *Calls upon* the Government of the Islamic Republic of Iran to intensify its efforts to investigate and rectify the human rights issues raised by the Special Representative in sections IV and V of his interim report, in particular as regards the administration of justice and due process of law;

10. *Also calls upon* the Government of the Islamic Republic of Iran to comply with international instruments on human rights, in particular the International Covenant on Civil and Political Rights, to which the Islamic Republic of Iran is a party, and to ensure that all individuals within its territory and subject to its jurisdiction, including religious groups, enjoy the rights recognized in those instruments;

11. *Endorses* the view of the Special Representative that the international monitoring of the human rights situation in the Islamic Republic of Iran should be continued;

12. *Further calls upon* the Government of the Islamic Republic of Iran to cooperate fully with the Special Representative;

13. *Requests* the Secretary-General to give all necessary assistance to the Special Representative;

14. *Decides* to continue the examination of the situation of human rights in the Islamic Republic of Iran, including the situation of minority groups, such as the Baha'is, during its forty-ninth session, under the item entitled "Human rights questions" in the light of additional elements provided by the Commission on Human Rights and the Economic and Social Council.

General Assembly resolution 48/145

20 December 1993   Meeting 85   74-23-51 (recorded vote)

Approved by Third Committee (A/48/632/Add.3) by recorded vote (68-22-45), 6 December (meeting 53); 23-nation draft (A/C.3/48/L.58); agenda item 114 *(c)*.

Sponsors: Australia, Belgium, Canada, Costa Rica, Denmark, Finland, France, Germany, Greece, Iceland, Ireland, Italy, Japan, Liechtenstein, Luxembourg, Netherlands, Norway, Portugal, San Marino, Spain, Sweden, United Kingdom, United States.

Meeting numbers. GA 48th session: 3rd Committee 36-53; plenary 85.

Recorded vote in Assembly as follows:

In favour: Algeria, Antigua and Barbuda, Argentina, Australia, Austria, Bahamas, Barbados, Belgium, Belize, Bolivia, Botswana, Brazil, Canada, Chile, Costa Rica, Czech Republic, Denmark, Dominica, Dominican Republic, Ecuador, Egypt, El Salvador, Finland, France, Germany, Greece, Grenada, Guatemala, Guyana, Haiti, Honduras, Iceland, Iran, Ireland, Israel, Italy, Jamaica, Japan, Latvia, Liechtenstein, Luxembourg, Malawi, Malta, Marshall Islands, Mauritius, Mexico, Micronesia, Monaco, Netherlands, New Zealand, Nicaragua, Norway, Panama, Papua New Guinea, Paraguay, Peru, Portugal, Russian Federation, Rwanda, Saint Lucia, Saint Vincent and the Grenadines, San Marino, Slovenia, Solomon Islands, Spain, Suriname, Swaziland, Sweden, Trinidad and Tobago, United Kingdom, United States, Venezuela, Zaire, Zambia.

Against: Afghanistan, Armenia, Azerbaijan, Bangladesh, Brunei Darussalam, China, Cuba, Democratic People's Republic of Korea, Guinea-Bissau, India, Indonesia, Iran, Libyan Arab Jamahiriya, Malaysia, Myanmar, Oman, Pakistan, Qatar, Sri Lanka, Sudan, Syrian Arab Republic, Turkmenistan, Viet Nam.

Abstaining: Albania, Angola, Belarus, Benin, Bhutan, Bulgaria, Burkina Faso, Burundi, Cameroon, Central African Republic, Chad,* Colombia, Comoros, Congo, Côte d'Ivoire, Cyprus, Eritrea, Ethiopia, Fiji, Gabon, Georgia, Ghana, Guinea, Kazakhstan, Kenya, Lao People's Democratic Republic, Lesotho, Maldives, Mali, Mauritania, Mozambique, Namibia, Nepal, Niger, Nigeria, Philippines, Poland, Republic of Korea, Saudi Arabia, Sierra Leone, Singapore, Slovakia, Thailand, the former Yugoslav Republic of Macedonia, Togo, Tunisia, Uganda, Ukraine, United Republic of Tanzania, Uruguay, Zimbabwe.

*Later informed the Secretariat it had intended to vote in favour.

Iraq

Report of the Special Rapporteur. In February,[70] Special Rapporteur Max van der Stoel (Netherlands) reported on the human rights situation in Iraq, including allegations of violations he had received regarding summary or arbitrary execution; enforced or involuntary disappearances; torture and other cruel, inhuman or degrading treatment; arbitrary arrest and detention and due process of law; freedom of association and expression; and access to food and health care. He also received information on human rights violations in Iraq affecting the Kurdish population, the Assyrian and Turkoman communities, the indigenous Ma'dan and others in the southern marsh area and the Shiah of southern Iraq. The report contained Iraq's replies to the Special Rapporteur's inquiries and to the allegations of human rights violations reported by him in 1992.[71]

The Special Rapporteur concluded that there had been massive human rights violations of the gravest nature by Iraq. He recommended that Iraq: bring the activities of its security services into conformity with the standards of international law; set up a commission on disappearances and cooperate with the Working Group on Enforced or Involuntary Disappearances; end its interference in the religious activities of the Shiahs and compensate them for damages; end its internal economic embargoes; take advantage of the food-for-oil formula to enable Iraq to finance humanitarian assistance; and approve his previous recommendation to send human rights monitors to the country.[71]

Human Rights Commission action. By a roll-call vote of 36 to 1, with 15 abstentions, the Commission, on 10 March,[72] expressed strong con-

demnation of massive human rights violations by Iraq, in particular: summary and arbitrary executions; systematic torture; enforced or involuntary disappearances; suppression of freedom of thought, expression and association; and violations of property and economic rights. It called on Iraq to release persons arbitrarily arrested and detained, including Kuwaitis and nationals of other States, and, as a State party to the International Covenants on Human Rights,[14] to abide by its obligations under them. The Commission urged Iraq to set up an independent commission of inquiry to look into the fate of tens of thousands of disappeared persons and to bring its security services into line with the standards of international law.

Regretting Iraq's failure to provide satisfactory replies concerning human rights violations brought to the Special Rapporteur's attention, it called on Iraq to reply without delay to enable him to formulate recommendations to improve the human rights situation there. It asked the Secretary-General, in consultation with the Special Rapporteur, to send monitors to Iraq to help verify reports on the human rights situation and to provide additional resources for that purpose. The Commission decided to extend for one year the Special Rapporteur's mandate as defined in a 1992 Commission resolution,[71] and urged Iraq to cooperate with him, notably during his next visit. It asked the Special Rapporteur to submit an interim report to the General Assembly in 1993 and to report to the Commission in 1994. The Commission asked the Secretary-General to give him all the assistance he needed. The decision to extend the mandate and the Commission's requests to the Special Rapporteur and the Secretary-General, including the provision of additional resources to send human rights monitors to Iraq, were approved by the Economic and Social Council by **decision 1993/279** of 28 July.

Subcommission action. By a secret ballot of 14 votes to 9, with 2 abstentions, the Subcommission, on 20 August,[73] condemned the human rights violations by the Government of Iraq.

Interim report of the Special Rapporteur. In August, the Secretary-General transmitted to the Assembly an interim report by the Special Rapporteur,[74] in which he described grave human rights violations in the marshes of southern Iraq and the situation of economic rights throughout the country. He concluded that the Government had discriminated in its distribution of food and health care to the detriment of the human rights of the general populations living in the northern and southern parts of the country. He recommended that Iraq end its military activities against civilians in the southern marsh area; allow the stationing of human rights monitors; cooperate with the United Nations Special Commission (see PART TWO, Chapter III); end activities that might cause environmental damage to the southern marsh area; take action towards securing the economic, social and cultural rights of peoples of the southern marsh; allow unhindered access of United Nations humanitarian agencies throughout the country; remove interferences with the fair and equitable access to food, medical supplies and essential resources; cease its artillery shelling of farms and communities in the northern Kurdish territory; contribute to the United Nations humanitarian programme in Iraq; and take advantage of the food-for-oil formula. In December,[75] Hungary requested that the Special Rapporteur's interim report be circulated to the Security Council.

In a later addendum to his report,[76] the Special Rapporteur presented a reply by the Government of Iraq to the allegations of human rights violations contained therein.

GENERAL ASSEMBLY ACTION

On 20 December, on the recommendation of the Third Committee, the General Assembly adopted **resolution 48/144** by recorded vote.

Situation of human rights in Iraq

The General Assembly,

Guided by the principles embodied in the Charter of the United Nations, the Universal Declaration of Human Rights and the International Covenants on Human Rights,

Reaffirming that all Member States have an obligation to promote and protect human rights and fundamental freedoms and to fulfil the obligations they have undertaken under the various international instruments in this field,

Mindful that Iraq is a party to the International Covenants on Human Rights,

Recalling its resolution 47/145 of 18 December 1992, in which it expressed its deep concern at flagrant violations of human rights by the Government of Iraq,

Recalling also Security Council resolution 688(1991) of 5 April 1991, in which the Council demanded an end to the repression of the Iraqi civilian population and insisted that Iraq should cooperate with humanitarian organizations and ensure that the human and political rights of all Iraqi citizens were respected,

Recalling in particular Commission on Human Rights resolution 1991/74 of 6 March 1991, by which the Commission requested its Chairman to appoint a Special Rapporteur to make a thorough study of the violations of human rights by the Government of Iraq, based on all information the Special Rapporteur might deem relevant, including information provided by intergovernmental and non-governmental organizations and any comments and material provided by the Government of Iraq,

Bearing in mind the pertinent resolutions of the Commission on Human Rights condemning the flagrant violations of human rights by the Government of Iraq, including its most recent resolution, 1993/74 of 10 March

1993, by which the Commission extended the mandate of the Special Rapporteur for a further year and requested him to submit an interim report to the General Assembly at its forty-eighth session and a final report to the Commission at its fiftieth session,

Recalling Security Council resolutions 687(1991) of 3 April 1991, 706(1991) of 15 August 1991, 712(1991) of 19 September 1991 and 778(1992) of 2 October 1992,

Deeply concerned by the massive and grave violations of human rights by the Government of Iraq, such as summary and arbitrary executions, torture and other cruel, inhuman or degrading treatment, enforced or involuntary disappearances, arbitrary arrests and detention and lack of due process and the rule of law and of freedom of thought, of expression, of association and of access to food and health care,

Deeply concerned also by the fact that chemical weapons have been used on the Iraqi civilian population, by the forced displacement of hundreds of thousands of Iraqi civilians and by the destruction of Iraqi towns and villages, as well as by the fact that tens of thousands of displaced Kurds have had to take refuge in camps and shelters in the north of Iraq,

Deeply concerned further by the increasingly severe and grave violations of human rights by the Government of Iraq against the civilian population in southern Iraq, in particular in the southern marshes, a large part of which has sought refuge on the border between Iraq and the Islamic Republic of Iran,

Expressing concern in particular at the fact that there are no signs of improvement in the general situation of human rights in Iraq, and, therefore, welcoming the decision to deploy a team of human rights monitors to such locations as would facilitate improved information flows and assessment and would help in the independent verification of reports on the situation of human rights in Iraq,

Regretting that the Government of Iraq has not seen fit to respond to requests for a visit of the Special Rapporteur on the situation of human rights in Iraq, and noting that, despite the formal cooperation extended to the Special Rapporteur by the Government, such cooperation needs to be substantially improved, in particular by giving full replies to the inquiries of the Special Rapporteur about acts being committed by the Government that are incompatible with the international human rights instruments that are binding on that country,

1. *Takes note with appreciation* of the interim report submitted by the Special Rapporteur of the Commission on Human Rights and the observations, conclusions and recommendations contained therein;

2. *Expresses its strong condemnation* of the massive violations of human rights of the gravest nature, for which the Government of Iraq is responsible and to which the Special Rapporteur has referred in his recent reports, in particular:

(a) Summary and arbitrary executions, orchestrated mass executions and burials, extrajudicial killings, including political killings, in particular in the northern region of Iraq, in southern Shiah centres and in the southern marshes;

(b) The widespread routine practice of systematic torture in its most cruel forms;

(c) Enforced or involuntary disappearances, routinely practised arbitrary arrest and detention, including arrest and detention of women, the elderly and children, and consistent and routine failure to respect due process and the rule of law;

(d) Suppression of freedom of thought, expression and association and violations of property rights;

(e) The unwillingness of the Government of Iraq to honour its responsibilities in respect of the economic rights of the population;

3. *Deplores* the refusal of Iraq to cooperate in the implementation of Security Council resolutions 706(1991) and 712(1991) and its failure to provide the Iraqi population with access to adequate food and health care;

4. *Calls upon* the Government of Iraq to release immediately all persons arbitrarily arrested and detained, including Kuwaitis and nationals of other States;

5. *Calls once again upon* Iraq, as a State party to the International Covenant on Economic, Social and Cultural Rights and to the International Covenant on Civil and Political Rights, to abide by its obligations freely undertaken under the Covenants and under other international instruments on human rights and, particularly, to respect and ensure the rights of all individuals, irrespective of their origin within its territory and subject to its jurisdiction;

6. *Recognizes* the importance of the work of the United Nations in providing humanitarian relief to the people of Iraq, and calls upon Iraq to allow unhindered access of the United Nations humanitarian agencies throughout the country, including ensuring the safety of United Nations personnel and humanitarian workers, *inter alia*, through the continued implementation of the Memorandum of Understanding signed by the United Nations and the Government of Iraq;

7. *Expresses special alarm* at the repressive practices directed against the Kurds, which continue to have an impact on the lives of the Iraqi people as a whole;

8. *Also expresses special alarm* at the resurgence of grave violations of human rights in southern Iraq, which is the result of a policy directed against the marsh Arabs in particular, many of whom have sought refuge outside the country;

9. *Welcomes* the sending of human rights monitors to the border between Iraq and the Islamic Republic of Iran, and calls upon the Government of Iraq to allow immediate and unconditional stationing of human rights monitors throughout the country, especially the southern marsh area;

10. *Expresses its special alarm* at all internal embargoes, which permit essentially no exceptions for humanitarian needs and which prevent the equitable enjoyment of basic foodstuffs and medical supplies, and calls upon the Government of Iraq, which has sole responsibility in this regard, to remove them and to take steps to cooperate with international humanitarian agencies in the provision of relief to those in need throughout Iraq;

11. *Urges once more* the Government of Iraq to set up an independent commission of inquiry to look into the fate of tens of thousands of persons who have disappeared;

12. *Regrets* the failure of the Government of Iraq to provide satisfactory replies concerning the violations of human rights brought to the attention of the Special Rapporteur, and calls upon the Government fully to cooperate and to reply without delay in a comprehensive and detailed manner so as to enable the Special Rapporteur to formulate the appropriate recommendations to improve the situation of human rights in Iraq;

13. *Requests* the Secretary-General to provide the Special Rapporteur with all assistance necessary to carry out his mandate;

14. *Decides* to continue its consideration of the situation of human rights in Iraq during its forty-ninth session under the item entitled "Human rights questions" in the light of additional elements provided by the Commission on Human Rights and the Economic and Social Council.

General Assembly resolution 48/144

20 December 1993   Meeting 85   116-2-43 (recorded vote)

Approved by Third Committee (A/48/632/Add.3) by recorded vote (105-2-41), 6 December (meeting 52); 32-nation draft (A/C.3/48/L.57); agenda item 114 (c).

Sponsors: Andorra, Argentina, Australia, Austria, Belgium, Bulgaria, Canada, Costa Rica, Czech Republic, Denmark, Finland, France, Germany, Greece, Hungary, Iceland, Ireland, Italy, Japan, Kuwait, Liechtenstein, Luxembourg, Netherlands, Norway, Panama, Portugal, Romania, San Marino, Spain, Sweden, United Kingdom, United States.

Meeting numbers. GA 48th session: 3rd Committee 36-52; plenary 85.

Recorded vote in Assembly as follows:

In favour: Afghanistan, Albania, Antigua and Barbuda, Argentina, Armenia, Australia, Austria, Azerbaijan, Bahamas, Barbados, Belarus, Belgium, Belize, Benin, Bhutan, Bolivia, Bosnia and Herzegovina, Botswana, Brazil, Bulgaria, Canada, Cape Verde, Chile, Colombia, Comoros, Costa Rica, Croatia, Cyprus, Czech Republic, Denmark, Djibouti, Dominica, Dominican Republic, Ecuador, Egypt, El Salvador, Estonia, Finland, France, Gambia, Georgia, Germany, Ghana, Greece, Grenada, Guinea, Guyana, Haiti, Honduras, Hungary, Iceland, Iran, Ireland, Israel, Italy, Jamaica, Japan, Kazakhstan, Kuwait, Kyrgyzstan, Latvia, Liechtenstein, Lithuania, Luxembourg, Malawi, Maldives, Malta, Marshall Islands, Mauritius, Mexico, Micronesia, Monaco, Mongolia, Nepal, Netherlands, New Zealand, Nicaragua, Niger, Norway, Panama, Papua New Guinea, Paraguay, Peru, Poland, Portugal, Republic of Korea, Republic of Moldova, Romania, Russian Federation, Rwanda, Saint Lucia, Saint Vincent and the Grenadines, Samoa, San Marino, Saudi Arabia, Senegal, Singapore, Slovakia, Slovenia, Solomon Islands, Spain, Suriname, Swaziland, Sweden, Syrian Arab Republic, the former Yugoslav Republic of Macedonia, Trinidad and Tobago, Turkey, Ukraine, United Arab Emirates, United Kingdom, United States, Uruguay, Venezuela, Zaire, Zambia.

Against: Iraq, Sudan.

Abstaining: Algeria, Angola, Bangladesh, Brunei Darussalam, Burundi, Cambodia, Cameroon, Central African Republic, Chad, China, Congo, Côte d'Ivoire, Cuba, Democratic People's Republic of Korea, Eritrea, Ethiopia, Fiji, Gabon, Guinea-Bissau, India, Indonesia, Kenya, Lao People's Democratic Republic, Lesotho, Libyan Arab Jamahiriya, Malaysia, Mali, Mauritania, Morocco, Mozambique, Namibia, Nigeria, Pakistan, Philippines, Sierra Leone, Sri Lanka, Thailand, Togo, Tunisia, Uganda, United Republic of Tanzania, Viet Nam, Zimbabwe.

Myanmar

Report of the Special Rapporteur. In February,[77] Special Rapporteur Yozo Yokota (Japan) reported on the human rights situation in Myanmar. He had visited the country from 7 to 14 December 1992, when he met with government officials, visited a prison and spoke with Muslim village leaders whom he asked about religious and ethnic tolerance.

The Special Rapporteur received information of alleged human rights violations relating to the right to life; torture, cruel, inhuman or degrading punishment; disappearances; arbitrary and prolonged detention; and freedom of expression. He discussed the systematic repression of the Muslims of Rakhine State which was based on ethnic and racial intolerance. He was informed that the provisions of Myanmar's Citizenship Law, under which persons must prove that they had Burmese nationality back to eight great-grandparents, were directed at the Rakhine Muslim population to forbid them from gaining nationality or associate nationality, a category of second-class citizenship.

He recommended that the Government of Myanmar transfer power to the elected civilian government; fulfil its obligations under articles 55 and 56 of the United Nations Charter; consider acceding to the International Covenants on Human Rights,[14] the Convention against Torture and Other Cruel, Inhuman or Degrading Treatment or Punishment[78] and the 1977 Protocols to the Geneva Conventions of 1949,[46] and withdraw its reservations to articles 15 (freedom of association) and 37 (prohibition of the torture of minors) of the Convention on the Rights of the Child;[79] comply with its obligations under ILO Conventions relating to forced labour and the existence and practice of free trade unions; revise its Citizenship Law; respect the human rights of Muslims and other minorities; and try, by a properly constituted and independent civilian court, Daw Aung San Suu Kyi and all other political leaders arrested or detained under martial law following demonstrations in 1988 and 1990. He advocated lifting the state of emergency in the country, abolishing martial law and bringing Myanmar law concerning the protection of physical integrity rights into line with accepted international standards.

In a February note verbale to the Secretary-General,[80] the Government of Myanmar made rebuttals concerning certain allegations presented by the Special Rapporteur.

Human Rights Commission action. On 10 March,[81] the Commission, deploring the continued seriousness of the human rights situation in Myanmar and the fact that political leaders, including Daw Aung San Suu Kyi and other leaders of the National League for Democracy, remained deprived of their liberty, urged the Government to release her and other detained political leaders and all political prisoners. The Commission further urged the Government to take steps towards establishing a democratic State; adopt measures recommended by the General Assembly in 1992;[82] and take measures to allow all citizens to participate freely in the process of transition to democracy by convening the Parliament elected in May 1990, lifting restraining orders on political leaders, releasing detainees, ensuring the normal function of political parties and lifting restrictions on the rights of association and assembly and of freedom of opinion and expression. It called on Myanmar to lift emergency measures; end the flow of Myanmar refugees to neighbouring countries and facilitate their early repatriation and full reintegration; and pay particular attention to the conditions of its prisons. The Commission asked the Government to ensure that all persons were afforded the minimum guarantees for a fair trial,

that laws were given due publicity and that the principle of non-retroactivity was respected. It urged Myanmar to cooperate with the Special Rapporteur. It decided to extend the Special Rapporteur's mandate for one year and asked him to report to the General Assembly in 1993 and to the Commission in 1994. The Economic and Social Council approved that decision and request by **decision 1993/278** of 28 July.

Subcommission action. On 20 August,[83] the Subcommission, by a secret ballot of 17 votes to 2, with 5 abstentions, called on the Government of Myanmar to ensure respect for human rights and fundamental freedoms and to allow full implementation of the May 1990 election, in accordance with a 1992 General Assembly resolution.[82]

Interim report of the Special Rapporteur. In November,[84] the Special Rapporteur stated that in September and early October he had transmitted to the Government of Myanmar a memorandum of allegations of human rights violations concerning arbitrary detention; torture, cruel, inhuman or degrading treatment; disappearances; summary or arbitrary execution; repatriated Muslims from northern Arakan State; labour rights; rights of the child; compliance with the May 1990 elections and principles and guidelines of the National Convention; rights devolved from citizenship status; improving the human rights situation; social, cultural and economic rights; arrests and detentions; the administration of justice; restrictions as to movement, residence and possession of articles under the 1975 Law Safeguarding the State against the Dangers of Subversive Elements; and the repatriation of Muslims. The Government's October response to some of the allegations was reproduced in the Special Rapporteur's report.

The Special Rapporteur observed that there were arrests of persons attempting to voice political dissent and arrests under emergency decrees. The arrest of some labour activists was reported, as was the continued practice of forced labour. He described forms of torture and cruel, inhuman or degrading treatment that took place during interrogation, forced portering and forced labour and forced relocations in the context of military operations. Although all death sentences had been commuted to life imprisonment, reports continued to be received of extrajudicial executions carried out by the army in the context of forced portering and labour, most frequently against ethnic minorities. Over 35,000 Myanmar Muslims from northern Rakhine State had returned from Bangladesh; their residency and citizenship status remained unclear and they were not entitled to freedom of movement, to enrol in institutions of higher learning or to enter certain professions. He stated that the Government had replied that disappearances could not occur because the law required keeping a register of all detainees; regarding extrajudicial executions, inquests were made into unknown causes of death; allegations of summary or arbitrary executions were false and unfounded; returnees were resettled into their original villages; people in the border areas contributed voluntary labour; and the army had prevented Myanmar from disintegrating and had safeguarded national sovereignty.

In a later report,[85] the Special Rapporteur described his visit to Myanmar from 9 to 16 November.

GENERAL ASSEMBLY ACTION

On 20 December, the General Assembly, on the recommendation of the Third Committee, adopted **resolution 48/150** without vote.

Situation of human rights in Myanmar

The General Assembly,

Reaffirming that all Member States have an obligation to promote and protect human rights and fundamental freedoms as stated in the Charter of the United Nations and elaborated in the Universal Declaration of Human Rights, the International Covenants on Human Rights and other applicable human rights instruments,

Aware that, in accordance with the Charter, the Organization promotes and encourages respect for human rights and fundamental freedoms for all and that the Universal Declaration of Human Rights states that "the will of the people shall be the basis of the authority of government",

Recalling its resolution 47/144 of 18 December 1992,

Recalling also Commission on Human Rights resolution 1992/58 of 3 March 1992, in which the Commission, *inter alia*, decided to nominate a special rapporteur to establish direct contacts with the Government and with the people of Myanmar, including political leaders deprived of their liberty, their families and their lawyers, with a view to examining the situation of human rights in Myanmar and following any progress made towards the transfer of power to a civilian Government and the drafting of a new Constitution, the lifting of restrictions on personal freedoms and the restoration of human rights in Myanmar,

Taking note of Commission on Human Rights resolution 1993/73 of 10 March 1993, in which the Commission decided to extend for one year the mandate of the Special Rapporteur,

Gravely concerned that the Government of Myanmar still has not implemented its commitments to take all necessary steps towards democracy in the light of the results of the elections held in 1990,

Gravely concerned also at the continued violations of human rights in Myanmar, as reported by the Special Rapporteur, in particular summary and arbitrary executions, torture, forced labour, abuse of women, restrictions on fundamental freedoms, including the freedom of expression and assembly, and the imposition of oppressive measures directed in particular at ethnic and religious minorities,

Noting that the human rights situation in Myanmar has consequently resulted in flows of refugees to neighbouring countries, thus creating problems for the countries concerned,

Noting also the measures taken by the Government of Myanmar, including its accession to the Geneva Conventions of 12 August 1949 for the protection of victims of war, and the release of a number of political prisoners in response to the concerns expressed by the international community, including the General Assembly and the Commission on Human Rights,

Welcoming the signing of the Memorandum of Understanding between the Government of Myanmar and the Office of the United Nations High Commissioner for Refugees on 5 November 1993 on the voluntary repatriation of refugees from Bangladesh to Myanmar,

Noting further the cease-fire that has been reached between the Government of Myanmar and several groups of ethnic and religious minorities in Myanmar,

1. *Expresses its appreciation* to the Special Rapporteur of the Commission on Human Rights for his interim report and the conclusions and recommendations contained therein;

2. *Deplores* the continued violations of human rights in Myanmar;

3. *Again urges* the Government of Myanmar, in conformity with its assurances given at various times, to take all necessary steps towards the restoration of democracy in accordance with the will of the people as expressed in the democratic elections held in 1990, and to ensure that political parties can function freely;

4. *Notes with concern* the observation of the Special Rapporteur, with regard to the National Convention, that no evident progress has been made towards turning over power to a freely elected civilian Government;

5. *Also notes with concern* in this respect that most of the representatives duly elected in 1990 have been excluded from participating in the meetings of the National Convention, created to prepare basic elements for the drafting of a new Constitution, and that one of the objectives of the National Convention is to maintain the participation of the armed forces in a leading role in the future political life of the State;

6. *Strongly urges* the Government of Myanmar to take all appropriate measures to allow all citizens to participate freely in the political process in accordance with the principles of the Universal Declaration of Human Rights and to accelerate the process of transition to democracy, in particular through the transfer of power to the democratically elected representatives;

7. *Urges* the Government of Myanmar to ensure full respect for human rights and fundamental freedoms, including freedom of expression and assembly, and the protection of the rights of persons belonging to ethnic and religious minorities and to put an end to violations of the right to life and integrity of the human being, to the practices of torture, abuse of women and forced labour and to enforced disappearances and summary executions;

8. *Appeals* to the Government of Myanmar to consider becoming a party to the International Covenant on Civil and Political Rights and the International Covenant on Economic, Social and Cultural Rights and to the Convention against Torture and Other Cruel, Inhuman or Degrading Treatment or Punishment;

9. *Stresses* the importance of free and confidential access to prisoners by international humanitarian agencies;

10. *Regrets* the recent harsh sentences meted out to a number of dissidents, including persons voicing dissent in regard to the procedures of the National Convention;

11. *Regrets also* that, while a certain number of political prisoners have been released, many political leaders are still deprived of their freedom and their fundamental rights;

12. *Strongly urges* the Government of Myanmar to release unconditionally and immediately the Nobel Peace Prize Laureate Aung San Suu Kyi, who is now in her fifth year of detention without trial, and other political leaders and remaining political prisoners;

13. *Calls upon* the Government of Myanmar to respect fully the obligations of the Geneva Conventions of 12 August 1949, in particular the obligations in article 3 common to the Conventions, and to make use of such services as may be offered by impartial humanitarian bodies;

14. *Encourages* the Government of Myanmar fully to implement the Memorandum of Understanding between the Government of Myanmar and the Office of the United Nations High Commissioner for Refugees of 5 November 1993 and to create the necessary conditions to ensure an end to the flows of refugees to neighbouring countries and to facilitate their speedy repatriation and their full reintegration, in conditions of safety and dignity;

15. *Requests* the Secretary-General to assist in the implementation of the present resolution and to report to the General Assembly at its forty-ninth session;

16. *Decides* to continue its consideration of this question at its forty-ninth session.

General Assembly resolution 48/150
20 December 1993   Meeting 85   Adopted without vote

Approved by Third Committee (A/48/632/Add.3) without vote, 6 December (meeting 53); 31-nation draft (A/C.3/48/L.70); agenda item 114 (c).
Sponsors: Argentina, Armenia, Australia, Austria, Belgium, Bulgaria, Canada, Chile, Costa Rica, Denmark, Estonia, Finland, France, Germany, Greece, Hungary, Iceland, Ireland, Italy, Liechtenstein, Lithuania, Luxembourg, Netherlands, Norway, Panama, Poland, Portugal, Romania, Spain, Sweden, United Kingdom.
Meeting numbers. GA 48th session: 3rd Committee 36-53; plenary 85.

Papua New Guinea

On 10 March,[86] the Commission urged the Government of Papua New Guinea to permit international fact-finding missions access to that country, particularly Bougainville, to assist in resolving the conflict there, and to recommence negotiations with all factions of the Bougainville peoples to achieve peace and a mutually satisfactory solution to the armed conflict. It asked the Secretary-General to transmit to the Commission in 1994 information on the situation in Bougainville from the Government of Papua New Guinea.

On the same date,[87] the Commission endorsed a 1992 Subcommission request[88] to the Special Rapporteur on the study of treaties, agreements and other constructive arrangements between States and indigenous populations to include in his report the case of the agreements entered into between the indigenous people of Bougainville and the Government of Papua New Guinea.

Tibet

On 20 August,[89] the Subcommission, by a secret ballot of 17 votes to 6, with 2 abstentions, decided to take no action on a draft resolution concerning the situation in Tibet. By that text, the Subcommission would have urged China to facilitate access to all parts of Tibet by the Special Rapporteur of the Commission and asked the Secretary-General to report to the Commission in 1994 on the situation in Tibet.

Europe and the Mediterranean

Albania

In February,[90] the Secretary-General provided information on steps that Albania had taken to implement a 1992 Commission resolution concerning its human rights situation.[88] Included in the report was a communication from Albania describing measures taken in 1992 to guarantee and promote human rights.

The Commission, on 10 March,[91] called on Albania to continue to adopt legislative and administrative measures to meet the requirements of relevant international human rights instruments and to respect the rights of minorities living there. It asked the Secretary-General to bring its resolution to Albania's attention, request information regarding its implementation and report to the Commission in 1994.

Cyprus

In February,[92] the Secretary-General, pursuant to a 1992 Commission decision,[88] reported on human rights in Cyprus. He described action taken in 1992 by the Security Council and the Committee on Missing Persons in Cyprus (see PART TWO, Chapter III).

On 8 March,[93] the Commission postponed debate on the question of human rights in Cyprus until 1994, on the understanding that action required by previous resolutions would continue to remain operative, including the Commission's request to the Secretary-General to provide a report on their implementation.

Estonia and Latvia

As requested by the General Assembly in 1992,[94] the Secretary-General reported in October on progress made in the area of human rights in Estonia and Latvia.[95] A fact-finding mission visited Estonia from 7 to 11 February 1993 to investigate alleged human rights abuses against minorities. The mission focused on the issue of Estonian citizenship and on the language requirements established for obtaining it. It also inquired into the cultural rights of minorities and their religious freedom but found no evidence of discrimination on ethnic or religious grounds. The mission observed that the country's transition from a centralized to a market-oriented economy limited the possibilities to promote faster integration of Estonian residents of non-ethnic Estonian origin. It recommended measures to improve the teaching of the Estonian language and stated that the United Nations Centre for Human Rights was prepared to offer advisory services and technical assistance to Estonia.

A fact-finding mission to Latvia took place in 1992.[96]

GENERAL ASSEMBLY ACTION

On 20 December, the General Assembly, on the recommendation of the Third Committee, adopted **resolution 48/155** without vote.

Situation of human rights in Estonia and Latvia
The General Assembly,

Recalling its resolution 47/115 of 16 December 1992,

Taking into account the provisions of the Declaration on the Human Rights of Individuals Who Are not Nationals of the Country in which They Live,

Having considered the report of the Secretary-General,

1. *Takes note* of the report of the Secretary-General and of the conclusions and recommendations therein of the United Nations fact-finding missions to Estonia and Latvia;

2. *Welcomes* the cooperation that the Governments of Estonia and Latvia have extended to various international fact-finding missions;

3. *Notes* the existence of unresolved issues that involve large groups of population of different ethnic origin;

4. *Requests* the Secretary-General to keep Member States informed of the situation of human rights in Estonia and Latvia, and decides to consider this item at one of its future sessions.

General Assembly resolution 48/155

20 December 1993   Meeting 85   Adopted without vote

Approved by Third Committee (A/48/633) without vote, 8 December (meeting 54); draft by Russian Federation (A/C.3/48/L.37/Rev.2), orally amended by Chairman; agenda item 115.
Meeting numbers. GA 48th session: 3rd Committee 36-54; plenary 85.

Romania

In February,[97] the Secretary-General reported on action taken pursuant to a 1992 Commission resolution on human rights in Romania,[96] noting that he had requested information from Romania on the implementation of the resolution's provisions. Included in the report was a communication from Romania describing steps it had taken in 1992 to guarantee and promote human rights. The report also described advisory services and technical assistance during 1992 and provided information on relevant activities of the Commission's special rapporteurs.

On 10 March,[98] the Commission urged the Government of Romania and its authorities to continue their efforts to ensure respect for human rights and encouraged their cooperation in the area of advisory services. It requested the Secretary-General to bring the resolution to Romania's attention, ask it to provide information on its implementation and report in 1994.

The former Yugoslavia

Human rights situation

Commission of Experts. In February,[99] the Secretary-General transmitted to the Security Council the first interim report of the Commission of Experts to examine evidence of human rights violations in the former Yugoslavia, established by the Secretary-General in accordance with a 1992 Security Council request.[100] The Commission discussed and adopted the report at its third session (Geneva, 25 and 26 January 1993). The report, covering the period November 1992 to January 1993, provided a broad view of the Commission's work and presented its preliminary conclusions on evidence examined and its views on a number of legal issues. It described the Commission's projected plan of work, which included in-depth investigations into mass killings and destruction of property; treatment of prisoners and detainees; systematic sexual assualts; and ethnic cleansing. In the light of the need for additional financial and personnel resources to carry out the in-depth investigations, the Commission requested the Secretary-General to establish a trust fund.

In its concluding remarks, the Commission noted that the establishment of an ad hoc war crimes tribunal, by the Security Council or another international body, would be consistent with the direction of its work.

Annexed to the Commission's report was the report of a December 1992 preliminary site exploration of a mass grave near Vukovar, Croatia.[101] The report also contained photographs, maps of the area, preliminary forensic reports and a list of missing persons from the Vukovar Hospital and the Vukovar area, prepared by the Joint Commission to Trace Missing Persons and Mortal Remains, based at the University of Zagreb Medical School.

In October,[102] the Secretary-General transmitted the second interim report, describing the work of the Commission from February to August 1993, during which time the Commission had held, at Geneva, its fourth (1-3 March), fifth (24 and 25 May), sixth (13 and 14 July) and seventh (30 and 31 August) sessions. The report outlined the steps the Commission had taken to implement the programme of work established in January and progress achieved.

Investigative missions were sent to Belgrade, Ljubljana, Sarajevo and Zagreb (18-29 April), Knin (17-19 May), and to Sarajevo again (20 June–9 July). In addition, interviews with five prisoners of war were held at Zagreb (11-14 August). Reconnaissance missions were set to Vukovar (5-16 March) to prepare for the excavation of a mass grave at Ovcara and to Dubrovnik (20-22 May) to explore the possibility of an on-site investigation into targeting, indiscriminate attacks, destruction of cultural property and ethnic cleansing. As to allegations of systematic rape, the Commission was forming female investigative teams. It had to postpone or limit the scale and scope of its investigative missions and major projects owing to the volatile military and political situation in the former Yugoslavia and to the fact that voluntary contributions of financial and human resources did not start to come in on a sufficient scale until July/August.

The Commission had set up a database to record all alleged grave breaches of the Geneva Conventions and other human rights violations. As at 31 August, the database contained over 3,000 cases, representing thousands of alleged violations and incidents of victimization.

Pursuant to the Commission's request, the Secretary-General set up a Trust Fund, to which a number of Governments made contributions or pledges. As at 31 August, the balance of the Fund amounted to some $730,000 in cash and over $380,000 in pledges.

The Commission's future projects included further investigative missions to Sarajevo and other regions of the former Yugoslavia, investigations of mass graves, systematic rape, and detention centres and prison camps, and continued work on the database.

The Security Council, in **resolution 827(1993)** of 25 May, established the International Tribunal for the Prosecution of Persons Responsible for Serious Violations of International Humanitarian Law Committed in the Former Yugoslavia (see PART TWO, Chapter IV, for information on the situation in the former Yugoslavia).

Reports of the Special Rapporteur. In February,[103] Special Rapporteur Tadeusz Mazoweicki (Poland) described the human rights situation in Bosnia and Herzegovina, the Federal Republic of Yugoslavia (Serbia and Montenegro), Croatia, Slovenia and the former Yugoslav Republic of Macedonia. He visited the last three countries from 10 to 17 January. He also discussed a visit that took place from 12 to 23 January by medical and psychiatric experts, the Director of the United Nations Division for the Advancement of Women and staff from the Centre for Human Rights to investigate allegations of rape in Croatia, Bosnia and Herzegovina and the Federal Republic of Yugoslavia (Serbia and Montenegro).

The Special Rapporteur concluded that ethnic cleansing violated fundamental human rights principles and that Bosnian Serb political and military leaders bore responsibility for that policy. Evidence of war crimes in Croatia and Bosnia and Herzegovina was mounting, and the rape of women had been widespread in both conflicts. In Bosnia and Herzegovina, thousands of persons, mainly civilians, were still imprisoned. Convoys attempting to deliver humanitarian aid were repeatedly attacked. Indoctrination and misinformation continued to encourage national and religious hatred.

The Special Rapporteur recommended releasing all detainees; creating security zones in Bosnia and Herzegovina; ending blockades of cities and regions and opening humanitarian relief corridors; providing victims of rape access to medical and psychological care; expanding the mandate of the United Nations Protection Force (UNPROFOR); allowing Croatian refugees to cross the border for temporary protection or in transit to third States; guaranteeing the right to seek asylum; providing support to democratically oriented groups; guaranteeing the right of return to all victims of ethnic cleansing; further investigating the creation of an international war crimes tribunal; improving coordination of human rights activities; and providing sufficient resources to the Centre for Human Rights so that the Special Rapporteur could carry out his mandate effectively. Annexed to the report was a summary of the report of the Special Rapporteur on extrajudicial, summary or arbitrary executions on his December 1992 mission to investigate allegations of mass graves,[101] the report of the team of medical and psychiatric experts on their January 1993 mission to investigate allegations of rape in the former Yugoslavia, and the programme of action on humanitarian issues agreed between the Co-Chairmen of the 1992 International Conference on the Former Yugoslavia[104] and the parties to the conflict.

By a 26 February note,[105] the Secretary-General transmitted the Special Rapporteur's report to the Security Council and the General Assembly.

On 20 December, the Assembly, by **decision 48/430**, took note of the Secretary-General's note.

Human Rights Commission action. On 23 February,[106] the Commission condemned in the strongest terms all human rights violations in the former Yugoslavia and called on Serbian authorities to refrain from the use of force and the practice of ethnic cleansing and to respect fully the rights of persons belonging to minority groups. It demanded that all parties notify ICRC of the location of all places of detention and that ICRC, the Special Rapporteur, UNHCR, the missions of the European Community and the Conference on Security and Cooperation in Europe (CSCE) and other international and regional organizations be granted immediate, unimpeded and continued access to such places. It also demanded the immediate internationally supervised release of all persons arbitrarily or illegally detained in the former Yugoslavia and the immediate closure of all detention facilities not authorized by and in compliance with the 1949 Geneva Conventions.

It welcomed the work of the Commission of Experts (see above), asked the Secretary-General to provide additional resources to enable it to fulfil its mandate effectively and urged States to do the same. The Commission on Human Rights also welcomed Security Council **resolution 808(1993)** of 22 February by which it decided that an international tribunal should be established to prosecute persons responsible for serious violations of international humanitarian law in the former Yugoslavia. It asked the Secretary-General in his report to the Council to propose that the tribunal should also determine whether the crimes committed fell within the scope of the 1948 Convention on the Prevention and Punishment of the Crime of Genocide.[107] The Commission asked the Council to consider establishing a United Nations observer mission to investigate and report on alleged human rights violations in Kosovo, Sandjak and Vojvodina (see also PART TWO, Chapter IV).

The Commission extended its Special Rapporteur's mandate for one year and asked him to submit periodic reports. The Secretary-General was requested to continue to make those reports available to the Security Council. The Special Rapporteur was asked, in consultation with the Working Group on Enforced or Involuntary Disappearances and ICRC, to propose a mechanism to address the subject of disappearances. The Commission asked all United Nations bodies, Governments and informed intergovernmental organizations and NGOs to cooperate fully with the Special Rapporteur and to provide him with accurate information on the human rights situation in the former Yugoslavia. It asked the Secretary-General to ensure the cooperation of all United Nations bodies in implementing its resolution and, in accordance with a 1992 General Assembly request,[108] to provide the Special Rapporteur with the necessary assistance to enable him to fulfil his mandate and, in particular, to appoint field staff in the former Yugoslavia to provide first-hand, timely reports on observance or violations of human rights.

ECONOMIC AND SOCIAL COUNCIL ACTION

In July, the Economic and Social Council, on the recommendation of its Social Committee, adopted **decision 1993/255** without vote.

Situation of human rights in the territory of the former Yugoslavia

At its 44th plenary meeting, on 28 July 1993, the Economic and Social Council, taking note of Commission on Human Rights resolution 1993/7 of 23 February 1993, approved:

(*a*) The Commission's request to the Secretary-General immediately to provide additional resources and personnel to the Commission of Experts that are sufficient to enable it to fulfil its mandate effectively;

(*b*) The Commission's decision to extend the mandate of the Special Rapporteur for one year;

(*c*) The Commission's request to the Secretary-General to take steps to ensure the full and effective cooperation of all United Nations bodies to implement Commission resolution 1993/7 and, pursuant to paragraph 21 of General Assembly resolution 47/147 of 18 December 1992, to provide the Special Rapporteur on the situation of human rights in the former Yugoslavia, within the overall budgetary framework of the United Nations, with additional resources and all other necessary assistance to enable him to fulfil his mandate and, in particular, to provide for the appointment of field staff in the territory of the former Yugoslavia to provide first-hand, timely reports on observance or violations of human rights in their area of assignment.

Economic and Social Council decision 1993/255

Adopted without vote

Approved by Social Committee (E/1993/108) without vote, 22 July (meeting 17); draft by Commission on Human Rights (E/1993/23); agenda item 18.

Subcommission action. On 20 August,[109] the Subcommission, by a secret ballot of 17 votes to 4, with 3 abstentions, vigorously condemned the violation of the human rights of the ethnic Albanians of Kosovo committed by the authorities of the Federal Republic of Yugoslavia (Serbia and Montenegro). It urged the authorities to bring the human rights violations to a halt, revoke all discriminatory legislation and re-establish Kosovo's democratic institutions. The Commission requested the Federal Republic to facilitate the appointment of field staff and allow CSCE missions of long duration to continue their activities, pursuant to the terms of Security Council **resolution 855(1993)**.

Also on 20 August,[110] the Subcommission, by a secret ballot of 22 votes to 1, with 1 abstention, urged the establishment of an international tribunal to prosecute those responsible for violations of international law in the former Yugoslavia, and called on the relevant United Nations bodies to ensure the urgent allocation of sufficient funds to the Commission of Experts.

On the same date,[111] the Subcommission urged United Nations Member States to bring to justice, in accordance with internationally recognized principles of due process, all those involved in the crimes committed in Bosnia and Herzegovina and elsewhere in the territory of the former Yugoslavia.

Periodic reports of the Special Rapporteur. As requested by the Commission in February, the Special Rapporteur submitted a series of periodic reports on the human rights situation in the former Yugoslavia.

In May,[112] he stated that a team of his field staff had visited Bosnia and Herzegovina (1-16 April) to gather information regarding alleged human rights violations in the eastern part of the country. He described the human rights situation and events in the enclaves of Cerska, Konjevic Polje, Srebrenica, Gorazde and Zepa; the humanitarian situation of those forcibly displaced in the east; forced recruitment into military service by all parties; and the situation of Serbians in Tuzla. The Special Rapporteur concluded that massive and repeated violations of the 1949 Geneva Conventions were perpetrated by Serb forces in Cerska, Konjevic Polje and Srebrenica and by government forces who refused the evacuation of civilians from Srebrenica. He recommended that the parties to the conflict release all detainees; end blockades and open humanitarian relief corridors; expand the safe area concept, especially to Gorazde and Zepa; and guarantee the right to flight and the right to seek asylum. He also recommended expanding UNPROFOR's mandate and an immediate response by the international community to UNHCR and World Food Programme appeals for financing humanitarian aid.

In his second periodic report, also submitted in May,[113] the Special Rapporteur reviewed a visit by his field staff (30 April–7 May) to the Lasva valley area of central Bosnia and Herzegovina, the scene of fighting between government and Croat forces. He described ethnic cleansing by Croat forces in the town of Vitez, the village of Ahmici and the city of Mostar, as well as arbitrary executions by government forces in the Vitez area. He concluded that hostilities between the two parties involved massive and systematic violations of human rights and international law; ethnic cleansing by Croat forces included forced displacement and detentions of civilians, arbitrary executions, attacks on towns, and destruction of villages and religious sites; government forces had carried out arbitrary executions and torture; there had been systematic violations of commitments by all parties to respect human rights and international agreements; and the peace plan designed to divide Bosnia and Herzegovina along ethnic lines had been used to create ethnically homogenous areas.

In August,[114] the Special Rapporteur discussed his visit to Sarajevo on 11 and 12 August, noting that conditions there had deteriorated dramatically since his October 1992 visit.[115] He concluded that hostilities were being conducted in ways that violated the most basic human rights and were in fundamental breach of the laws of war. Those breaches included the starvation of a besieged population as a method of warfare; using civilians as military targets and deliberately killing and wounding them; denying and destroying electric, water and gas supplies and food and medical supplies; repeated hospital shellings; and detaining civilians as hostages. He recommended opening an overland relief route to Sarajevo; setting up energy and water installations under in-

ternational protection; placing the central Kosovo hospital under international protection; administering relief as a priority to those in need of special protection; creating trust necessary for the release of prisoners of war and the closure of detention camps; protecting civilians from hostage-taking; and trying and sentencing snipers who killed or wounded civilians.

The Special Rapporteur's fourth periodic report, submitted in September,[116] was based on information gathered by two field officers during nine days of on-site investigations and interviews in the city of Mostar and surrounding towns of Capljina, Citluk, Medjugorje and Pocitelj. He described the situation in Mostar, giving details of ethnic cleansing, arbitrary arrests and detentions resulting from forced evictions and the use of civilians as targets of military attacks. He concluded that those practices deserved the strongest possible condemnation and called for the restoration of respect for international humanitarian law. Stating that impeding humanitarian aid by any party to the conflict violated international law on the conduct of war, he demanded that immediate, unimpeded access to Mostar be guaranteed and that medical services be restored. He called for the release of all detainees with guarantees for their safe return.

In November,[117] the Special Rapporteur provided a wide-ranging assessment of the human rights situation in Croatia, Bosnia and Herzegovina and the Federal Republic of Yugoslavia (Serbia and Montenegro), based on a fact-finding mission by two staff members from the Centre for Human Rights (13-26 October).

Describing the situation in Bosnia and Herzegovina, he stated that 2.1 million people had been displaced from their homes since the war began—nearly 50 per cent of the population recorded in the 1991 census. At least 100 women were reportedly raped by Bosnian Croat soldiers between April and October 1993, a figure believed to be incomplete because of limited access to Mostar and the dispersal of refugees from western Herzegovina. Soldiers acting for the Government allegedly committed human rights abuses, including summary executions, arbitrary arrests and detention and violations of the rights of detainees. Human rights violations allegedly committed by Bosnian Croat forces were summary executions; mass deportations; arbitrary arrests and detention and violations of the rights of detainees; military attacks on civilians; and the imposition of exorbitant taxes on foreign aid convoys. As to violations by Bosnian Serb forces, the Special Rapporteur noted that the expulsion of non-Serbs from Serb-held territories was in some areas nearly complete. Summary executions and disappearances had occurred, as had arbitrary arrests and detention and the ill-treatment of detainees. He observed that through administrative measures alone, Bosnian Serb authorities had stripped non-Serbs of many basic human rights since 1992. There were military attacks on civilians, the imposition of taxes on foreign aid convoys and the destruction of mosques. The Special Rapporteur urged the international community to respond generously and speedily to the needs of Bosnia and Herzegovina by providing the necessary humanitarian aid. He stated that the Muslim community there was threatened with extermination, condemned the crime of rape and all other forms of sexual abuse, and reiterated his conviction that perpetrators of violations of humanitarian law should be held accountable and punished.

In Croatia, there were reports of arbitrary executions and ethnic cleansing committed by Croatian armed forces in the villages of Divoselo, Citluk and Pocitelj, situated in the Medak "pocket", and of the killing of Serbs, where it was alleged that Croatian authorities had failed to conduct proper investigations. There were cases of arbitrary detention, violations of the right to a fair trial, denials of citizenship, illegal evictions, damage to and destruction of buildings belonging to Croatians of Serbian ethnic origin and government influence over the media. He described the situation of the Muslim minority and refugees and the situation in United Nations Protected Areas (UNPAs). The Special Rapporteur requested Croatian authorities to ensure punishment for those responsible for the contravention of human rights and international humanitarian standards in the Medak pocket and also requested that the parties to the conflict in the UNPAs refrain from shelling civilian targets.

With regard to the Federal Republic of Yugoslavia (Serbia and Montenegro), he stated that the use of brutal and excessive force by the police had been reported to him throughout Serbia. Violations had been reported of the rights to freedom of assembly and association and expression. Residents of the area who could not prove their Serbian citizenship faced discrimination in employment, housing and education. There were some 530,000 refugees in Serbia from other territories of the former Yugoslavia. In Kosovo, the polarization of the Albanian and Serb populations continued, with reports of Albanians, who represented 90 per cent of the Kosovo population, being illtreated and tortured, evicted from their homes and discriminated against through language and education. He also described the situation in Sandzak, Vojvodina and Montenegro. The Special Rapporteur advocated giving special attention to developing an independent, democratically oriented communications media; amending the law to allow persons immediate access to a lawyer

after arrest; and rescinding a May 1993 instruction not to register as refugees men of military age from areas of Bosnia and Croatia regarded as safe municipalities. He drew attention to deaths of Albanians while in police detention in Kosovo and called for Serbian authorities to identify and punish those responsible.

In his sixth periodic report,[118] the Special Rapporteur discussed events that occurred in November and December in Bosnia and Herzegovina, Croatia, the Federal Republic of Yugoslavia (Serbia and Montenegro), the former Yugoslav Republic of Macedonia and Slovenia.

Regarding Bosnia and Herzegovina, he observed that ethnic cleansing continued. Citing the continuing war and the use of access to aid as an instrument of war as main causes of the severe suffering, he called for the immediate cessation of interference with aid deliveries. He drew attention to the fact that military attacks on civilians committed by Bosnian Serb and Croat forces exceeded that of the other warring parties. He reiterated his conviction that perpetrators of human rights violations must be held accountable and punished.

As to Croatia, the Special Rapporteur condemned the continuing practice of illegal and forced evictions by members of the Croatian armed forces and called on the Government to restore the rights of affected tenants and prevent the recurrence of such acts. He recommended establishing a court of human rights and reminded the international community of the urgent need for humanitarian assistance for refugees and displaced persons.

The Special Rapporteur noted with concern the continuing serious human rights violations in the Federal Republic of Yugoslavia (Serbia and Montenegro). He recommended the adoption of legislation to remove the legal uncertainty surrounding citizenship and possible discrimination on grounds of ethnic, religious or other origin, and international support to develop a democratic opposition in Serbia. As to conscientious objection to military service, he recommended adoption of a law on amnesty and the introduction of alternative forms of service that were non-combatant or civilian.

The Special Rapporteur observed progress in the former Yugoslav Republic of Macedonia in eliminating discriminatory practices and in freedom of the media. He urged donor countries to consider providing that country with bilateral technical and financial assistance to foster its overall development.

He observed that the human rights situation was satisfactory in Slovenia and recommended that the country be excluded from his mandate.

The Special Rapporteur discussed the problem of disappearances and the situation of children in the former Yugoslavia, including refugee and displaced children and children living in the territories of the former Yugoslavia that had not been directly involved in the war, and reiterated his previous recommendations and his call for follow-up action to them.

Activities of the Working Group on disappearances. In accordance with the Commission's request to the Special Rapporteur to develop, in consultation with the Working Group on Enforced or Involuntary Disappearances and ICRC, proposals for a mechanism to address the subject of disappearances in the former Yugoslavia, a mission was undertaken by a member of the Working Group and a Zagreb-based field officer of the Centre for Human Rights (4-13 August).[119] The members of the mission visited Belgrade and Zagreb and two UNPAs.

The Working Group member proposed that United Nations action on missing persons in the former Yugoslavia should meet minimum standards of effectiveness, take a pragmatic approach, use the predicament of the relatives of missing persons as its point of departure and formulate a sensible response to it. In addition, it should take a strictly humanitarian, non-accusatory approach to clarifying cases of missing persons and incorporate requirements that interlocutors act on behalf of the relatives and that the identity of sources be kept confidential. He recommended entrusting such action to the Special Rapporteur in a joint mandate with one member of the Working Group, resulting in joint annual reports to the Commission and possibly the General Assembly.

GENERAL ASSEMBLY ACTION

On 20 December, on the recommendation of the Third Committee, the General Assembly adopted **resolution 48/153** without vote.

Situation of human rights in the territory of the former Yugoslavia: violations of human rights in the Republic of Bosnia and Herzegovina, the Republic of Croatia and the Federal Republic of Yugoslavia (Serbia and Montenegro)

The General Assembly,

Guided by the purposes and principles of the Charter of the United Nations, the Universal Declaration of Human Rights, the International Covenants on Human Rights, the International Convention on the Elimination of All Forms of Racial Discrimination, the Convention on the Rights of the Child, the Convention on the Prevention and Punishment of the Crime of Genocide, the Convention against Torture and Other Cruel, Inhuman or Degrading Treatment or Punishment and other instruments of international humanitarian law, including the Geneva Conventions of 12 August 1949 for the protection of victims of war and the Additional Protocols thereto, of 1977, as well as the principles and commitments undertaken by States members of the Conference on Security and Cooperation in Europe,

Gravely concerned at the human tragedy in the territories of the Republic of Bosnia and Herzegovina, the Republic of Croatia and the Federal Republic of Yugoslavia (Serbia and Montenegro) and at the continuing massive and systematic violations of human rights occurring in most of those areas, particularly in the areas of Bosnia and Herzegovina under Bosnian Serb control,

Bearing in mind its resolution 47/147 of 18 December 1992, Commission on Human Rights resolutions 1992/S-1/1 of 14 August 1992, 1992/S-2/1 of 1 December 1992 and 1993/7 of 23 February 1993 and relevant resolutions of the Security Council,

Recalling specifically Security Council resolutions 771(1992) of 13 August 1992, 780(1992) of 6 October 1992, 787(1992) of 16 November 1992, 808(1993) of 22 February 1993 and 827(1993) of 25 May 1993 in which the Council demanded, *inter alia*, that all parties and others concerned in the former Yugoslavia immediately cease and desist from all breaches of international humanitarian law, requested the Secretary-General to establish a commission of experts to examine and analyse information relating to serious violations of such law being committed in the territory of the former Yugoslavia, and decided to establish an international tribunal for the prosecution of persons responsible for such violations,

Welcoming the convening of the International Tribunal for the Prosecution of Persons Responsible for Serious Violations of International Humanitarian Law Committed in the Territory of the Former Yugoslavia since 1991 and the naming of its Chief Prosecutor,

Welcoming also Security Council resolutions 824(1993) of 6 May 1993 and 836(1993) of 4 June 1993, in which the Council declared that Sarajevo, Tuzla, Zepa, Gorazde, Bihac, Srebrenica and their surroundings should be treated as safe areas and that international humanitarian agencies should be given free and unimpeded access to those areas,

Welcoming further the interim reports and recommendations of the Special Rapporteur of the Commission on Human Rights,

Expressing its appreciation to all States that have cooperated with the United Nations High Commissioner for Refugees,

Recalling its resolutions 47/80 of 16 December 1992, in which it condemned unreservedly "ethnic cleansing" and acts of violence arising from racial hatred, and reiterated its conviction that those who committed or ordered the commission of acts of "ethnic cleansing" were individually responsible and should be brought to justice, and its resolution 47/121 of 18 December 1992, in which it, *inter alia*, stated that the abhorrent policy of "ethnic cleansing" was a form of genocide,

Noting with appreciation the efforts of the Special Rapporteur, as well as those of the Chairman of the Working Group on Arbitrary Detention, the Special Rapporteur on extrajudicial, summary or arbitrary executions, the Special Rapporteur on the question of torture and the representative of the Secretary-General on internally displaced persons, who accompanied him on his missions,

Encouraging the continuing efforts made in the framework of the International Conference on the Former Yugoslavia to find a peaceful solution,

Welcoming the ongoing efforts of the Conference on Security and Cooperation in Europe to re-establish its presence in the Federal Republic of Yugoslavia (Serbia and Montenegro) in order to prevent further human rights violations, and deeply concerned about the decision of the authorities in the Federal Republic of Yugoslavia (Serbia and Montenegro) to expel the monitoring missions of long duration of the Conference on Security and Cooperation in Europe and the European Union to Kosovo, Sandjak and Vojvodina, where the human rights situation remains a cause of great concern,

Welcoming also the efforts of the European Union, *inter alia*, through its monitoring missions, to promote respect for human rights and fundamental freedoms in the territory of the former Yugoslavia,

Gravely concerned at the human rights situation in Bosnia and Herzegovina, Croatia and the Federal Republic of Yugoslavia (Serbia and Montenegro), and in particular at the continuing, odious practice of "ethnic cleansing", which is the direct cause of the vast majority of human rights violations there and whose principal victims are the Muslim population threatened with virtual extermination,

Noting the discriminatory policies, measures and violent actions committed against ethnic Albanians in Kosovo, and aware of the possible escalation of the situation into a violent conflict there,

Strongly rejecting policies and ideologies aimed at "ethnic cleansing" and at promoting racial and religious hatred in any form,

Alarmed that, although the conflict in Bosnia and Herzegovina is not a religious conflict, it has been characterized by the systematic destruction and profanation of mosques, churches and other places of worship, as well as other sites of cultural heritage, in particular in areas currently or previously under Bosnian Serb and Bosnian Croat control,

1.   *Commends* the Special Rapporteur on the situation of human rights in the territories of the successor States of the former Yugoslavia for his reports;

2.   *Expresses its grave concern* at the Special Rapporteur's detailed reports of massive and systematic violations of human rights and humanitarian law in the Republic of Bosnia and Herzegovina, the Republic of Croatia and the Federal Republic of Yugoslavia (Serbia and Montenegro);

3.   *Notes with grave concern* the Special Rapporteur's conclusions about the impending humanitarian disaster in Bosnia and Herzegovina this winter;

4.   *Condemns in the strongest terms* all violations of human rights and international humanitarian law in Bosnia and Herzegovina, Croatia and the Federal Republic of Yugoslavia (Serbia and Montenegro) by all sides to the conflict, recognizing that the leadership in territory under the control of Serbs in Bosnia and Herzegovina and Croatia, the commanders of Serb paramilitary forces and political and military leaders in the Federal Republic of Yugoslavia (Serbia and Montenegro) bear primary responsibility for most of those violations;

5.   *Condemns* the specific violations identified by the Special Rapporteur, most of which are committed in connection with "ethnic cleansing" and which include killings, torture, beatings, arbitrary searches, rape, disappearances, destruction of houses and other acts or threats of violence aimed at forcing individuals to leave their homes, as well as reports of violations of human rights in connection with detention;

6.   *Condemns* the indiscriminate shelling of cities and civilian areas, the systematic terrorization and murder of non-combatants, the destruction of vital services, and besieging of cities and the use of military force against civilian populations and relief operations by all sides, recognizing that the main responsibility lies with the Bosnian Serbs, who have used such tactics as a matter of policy, and the Bosnian Croats;

7.   *Supports* the determination of the Security Council that all persons who perpetrate or authorize violations of international humanitarian law are individually responsible for those breaches and that the international community shall exert every effort to bring them to justice;

8.   *Urges* all States, United Nations bodies, including the specialized agencies, and the Special Rapporteur and, as appropriate, international humanitarian organizations to make available substantiated information in their possession or submitted to them relating to violations and the perpetrators of such violations of international humanitarian law, including grave breaches of the Geneva Conventions of 12 August 1949, in Bosnia and Herzegovina, Croatia and the Federal Republic of Yugoslavia (Serbia and Montenegro) to the International Tribunal for the Prosecution of Persons Responsible for Serious Violations of International Humanitarian Law Committed in the Territory of the Former Yugoslavia since 1991, established by the Security Council in its resolution 827(1993) for prosecution, as appropriate, by the Chief Prosecutor;

9.   *Expresses deep concern* at the number of disappearances and missing persons in Bosnia and Herzegovina, Croatia and the Federal Republic of Yugoslavia (Serbia and Montenegro), and reiterates calls on all parties to make all possible efforts to account for those missing;

10.   *Urges* that an immediate end be brought to the continuing practice of "ethnic cleansing", and in particular that the authorities of the Federal Republic of Yugoslavia (Serbia and Montenegro) use their influence with the self-proclaimed Serbian authorities in Bosnia and Herzegovina and Croatia to bring the practice of "ethnic cleansing" to an immediate end and to reverse the effects of that practice;

11.   *Urges* the Government of Croatia to use its influence with the self-proclaimed Croatian authorities in Bosnia and Herzegovina to bring the practice of "ethnic cleansing" to an immediate end and to reverse the effects of that practice;

12.   *Reaffirms* that States are to be held accountable for violations of human rights which their agents commit on their own territory or on the territory of another State;

13.   *Expresses its complete support* for the victims of those violations, reaffirms the right of all persons to return to their homes in safety and dignity, considers invalid all acts made under duress affecting ownership of property and other related questions, recognizes the right of victims of "ethnic cleansing" to receive just reparation for their losses, and urges all parties to fulfil their agreements to this end;

14.   *Condemns in particular* the violations of human rights and humanitarian law in connection with detention, including killings, torture and the systematic practice of rape, and urges the immediate, internationally supervised release of all persons arbitrarily or illegally detained in Bosnia and Herzegovina, Croatia and the

Federal Republic of Yugoslavia (Serbia and Montenegro);

15. *Calls* for the immediate closure of all detention facilities not in compliance with the Geneva Conventions of 12 August 1949;

16. *Urges* all parties to notify immediately the International Committee of the Red Cross of the locations of all camps, prisons and other places of detention within Bosnia and Herzegovina, Croatia, and Serbia and Montenegro, and urges that the International Committee, the Special Rapporteur and his staff, the United Nations High Commissioner for Refugees, the monitoring and other missions of the European Union and the Conference on Security and Cooperation in Europe and other relevant international and regional organizations be granted immediate, unimpeded and continued access to such places of detention;

17. *Expresses its grave concern* at the deteriorating human rights situation in the Federal Republic of Yugoslavia (Serbia and Montenegro), particularly in Kosovo, as described in the reports of the Special Rapporteur, and strongly condemns the violations of human rights occurring there;

18. *Strongly condemns* in particular the measures and practices of discrimination and the violations of the human rights of the ethnic Albanians of Kosovo, as well as the large-scale repression committed by the Serbian authorities, including:

(a) Police brutality against ethnic Albanians, arbitrary searches, seizures and arrests, torture and ill-treatment during detention and discrimination in the administration of justice, which leads to a climate of lawlessness in which criminal acts, particularly against ethnic Albanians, take place with impunity;

(b) The discriminatory removal of ethnic Albanian officials, especially from the police and judiciary, the mass dismissal of ethnic Albanians from professional, administrative and other skilled positions in State-owned enterprises and public institutions, including teachers from the Serb-run school system, and the closure of Albanian high schools and universities;

(c) Arbitrary imprisonment of ethnic Albanian journalists, the closure of Albanian-language mass media and the discriminatory removal of ethnic Albanian staff from local radio and television stations;

(d) Repression by the Serbian police and military;

19. *Urges* the authorities in the Federal Republic of Yugoslavia (Serbia and Montenegro):

(a) To take all necessary measures to bring to an immediate end the human rights violations inflicted on the ethnic Albanians in Kosovo, including, in particular, discriminatory measures and practices, arbitrary detention and the use of torture and other cruel, inhuman or degrading treatment and the occurrence of summary executions;

(b) To revoke all discriminatory legislation, in particular that which has entered into force since 1989;

(c) To re-establish the democratic institutions of Kosovo, including the parliament and the judiciary;

(d) To resume dialogue with the ethnic Albanians in Kosovo, including under the auspices of the International Conference on the Former Yugoslavia;

20. *Also urges* the authorities of the Federal Republic of Yugoslavia (Serbia and Montenegro) to respect the human rights and fundamental freedoms of ethnic Albanians in Kosovo, and expresses the view that the best means to safeguard human rights in Kosovo is to restore its autonomy;

21. *Expresses its grave concern* at the report by the Special Rapporteur of violations of human rights occurring in Sandjak and Vojvodina, particularly acts of physical harassment, abductions, the burning of homes, warrantless searches, confiscation of property, arbitrary arrests, the closure of political parties, and other discriminatory practices in favour of the Serbian population, which are intended to change the ethnic structure of those areas;

22. *Calls upon* the authorities of the Federal Republic of Yugoslavia (Serbia and Montenegro) to allow the immediate entry of an international human rights monitoring presence into the country, particularly into Kosovo, and strongly urges them to reconsider their refusal to allow the continuation of the activities of the missions of the Conference on Security and Cooperation in Europe in Kosovo, Sandjak and Vojvodina and to cooperate with the Conference by taking the practical steps needed for the resumption of the activities of those missions, called for by the Security Council in its resolution 855(1993) of 22 February 1993 in order to prevent the extension of the conflict to those areas;

23. *Reaffirms* that all parties to the conflict in the territories of Bosnia and Herzegovina, Croatia and the Federal Republic of Yugoslavia (Serbia and Montenegro) share the responsibility for finding a peaceful solution through negotiations under the auspices of the International Conference on the Former Yugoslavia, urges that human rights concerns be given proper priority in the peace process, and calls upon the parties to implement immediately all commitments made in the framework of the Conference and to reach a just and durable solution as soon as possible;

24. *Urges* all United Nations bodies, including the United Nations Protection Force, the United Nations human rights treaty bodies and the specialized agencies, and Governments and informed intergovernmental and non-governmental organizations to cooperate fully with the Special Rapporteur, and in particular to provide him on a continuing basis with all relevant and accurate information in their possession on the situation of human rights in Bosnia and Herzegovina, Croatia and the Federal Republic of Yugoslavia (Serbia and Montenegro);

25. *Urges* all States and competent organizations to consider implementation of the recommendations of the Special Rapporteur in his recent reports, and in particular:

(a) Welcomes the call of the Special Rapporteur for the opening of humanitarian relief corridors to prevent the imminent death of tens of thousands of persons, especially in view of the lack of access to many areas in the face of the coming winter;

(b) Supports the call of the Special Rapporteur for the immediate release of detainees into conditions of safety;

(c) Draws the attention of the international community to the need for an effective response to counter the policy of "ethnic cleansing" perpetrated by any side, particularly the Bosnian Serb forces, who have used such tactics as a matter of policy, and Bosnian Croat forces;

(d) Supports the request of the Special Rapporteur to the Croatian authorities to take action against those who have committed human rights violations and contravened international humanitarian standards in the Medak Pocket and to take steps to punish those responsible to prevent such incidents in the future;

(e) Welcomes the signing of the Joint Declaration with respect to Freedom of Movement of 18 November 1993, in which the signatories have solemnly agreed to ensure complete and secure freedom of movement for all personnel of the United Nations and international humanitarian organizations and which was solemnly renewed at a meeting held at Geneva on 29 November 1993 within the framework of the International Conference on the Former Yugoslavia;

26.　*Urges* the Secretary-General to take all necessary steps to ensure the full and effective coordination of the activities of all United Nations bodies in implementing the present resolution, and urges those bodies concerned with the situation in the territories of Bosnia and Herzegovina, Croatia and the Federal Republic of Yugoslavia (Serbia and Montenegro) to coordinate closely with the Special Rapporteur and the International Tribunal;

27.　*Also urges* the Secretary-General, within existing resources, to make all necessary resources available for the Special Rapporteur to carry out his mandate and in particular to provide him with adequate staff based in the territories of Bosnia and Herzegovina, Croatia and the Federal Republic of Yugoslavia (Serbia and Montenegro) to ensure effective continuous monitoring of the human rights situation there and coordination with other United Nations bodies involved, including the United Nations Protection Force;

28.　*Requests* the Secretary-General to give all other necessary assistance to the Special Rapporteur to enable him to fulfil his mandate;

29.　*Calls upon* the States concerned to cooperate fully with the Special Rapporteur so as to enable him to fulfil his mandate;

30.　*Invites* the Chief Prosecutor of the International Tribunal to consider the appointment to his office of experts in the prosecution of crimes of sexual violence;

31.　*Calls upon* States to put experts, including experts in the prosecution of crimes of sexual violence, at the disposal of the Chief Prosecutor and the International Tribunal;

32.　*Invites* the Commission on Human Rights at its fiftieth session to request the Special Rapporteur to report to the General Assembly at its forty-ninth session;

33.　*Decides* to continue its examination of this question at its forty-ninth session under the item entitled "Human rights questions".

General Assembly resolution 48/153

20 December 1993　　　Meeting 85　　　Adopted without vote

Approved by Third Committee (A/48/632/Add.3) without vote, 8 December (meeting 55); 52-nation draft (A/C.3/48/L.74/Rev.1), orally corrected; agenda item 114 *(c)*.

Sponsors: Afghanistan, Albania, Andorra, Australia, Austria, Azerbaijan, Bangladesh, Belgium, Bosnia and Herzegovina, Bulgaria, Canada, Costa Rica, Czech Republic, Denmark, Djibouti, Egypt, Finland, France, Georgia, Germany, Hungary, Iceland, Indonesia, Ireland, Iran, Italy, Japan, Kuwait, Liechtenstein, Luxembourg, Malaysia, Marshall Islands, Morocco, Netherlands, New Zealand, Norway, Pakistan, Papua New Guinea, Poland, Portugal, Samoa, Saudi Arabia, Senegal, Sierra Leone, Spain, Sudan, Sweden, Tunisia, Turkey, United Kingdom, United States, Yemen.

Financial implications. 5th Committee, A/48/797; S-G, A/C.3/48/L.81, A/C.5/48/47.

Meeting numbers. GA 48th session: 3rd Committee 36-55; 5th Committee 43; plenary 85.

Rape and abuse of women

Human Rights Commission action. On 23 February,[120] the Commission strongly condemned the rape and abuse of women and children in the

former Yugoslavia and demanded that those involved cease those acts and take action to ensure the enjoyment of human rights and fundamental freedoms. Welcoming the initiative of the European Council on the rapid dispatch of a mission to investigate the treatment of Muslim women (see PART TWO, Chapter IV),[121] the Commission requested the Special Rapporteur on the situation of human rights in the former Yugoslavia to pursue a specific investigation into the rape and abuse of women and children, including the dispatch of a qualified team of experts, to coordinate with the relevant thematic special rapporteurs, with the mission dispatched by the European Council and with any other missions and to report further to the Commission. It asked the Secretary-General to provide the Special Rapporteur with the means to enable any future missions to have free and secure access to places of detention and to submit a report on the implementation of the Commission's resolution not later than 30 June 1993.

ECONOMIC AND SOCIAL COUNCIL ACTION

In July, the Economic and Social Council, on the recommendation of its Social Committee, adopted **decision 1993/256** without vote.

Rape and abuse of women in the territory of the former Yugoslavia

At its 44th plenary meeting, on 28 July 1993, the Economic and Social Council, taking note of Commission on Human Rights resolution 1993/8 of 23 February 1993, approved the Commission's requests:

(a) To the Special Rapporteur on the situation of human rights in the former Yugoslavia to pursue a specific investigation into the rape and abuse of women and children in the former Yugoslavia, including the dispatch of a qualified team of experts, to coordinate with the relevant thematic special rapporteurs of the Commission, with the mission dispatched by the European Council and with any other missions and to present a further report to the Commission;

(b) To the Secretary-General to provide such necessary means as are available to him in the area to enable any future missions to have free and secure access to places of detention.

Economic and Social Council decision 1993/256

　　　　　　　　　　　　　　　　　Adopted without vote

Approved by Social Committee (E/1993/108) without vote, 22 July (meeting 17); draft by Commission on Human Rights (E/1993/23); agenda item 18.

Report of the Secretary-General. As requested by the Commission in February, the Secretary-General submitted in June a report on rape and abuse of women in the former Yugoslavia.[122] He discussed action taken by the United Nations to prevent the rape and abuse and summarized information received concerning the activities of ICRC and the International Federation of Red Cross and Red Crescent Societies.

He concluded that female human rights monitors would be essential to obtain first-hand evidence. Public education through dissemination of pamphlets, radio programmes and other mass media was an important element in collective healing.

GENERAL ASSEMBLY ACTION

On 20 December, the General Assembly, on the recommendation of the Third Committee, adopted **resolution 48/143** without vote.

Rape and abuse of women in the areas of armed conflict in the former Yugoslavia

The General Assembly,

Guided by the purposes and principles of the Charter of the United Nations, the Universal Declaration of Human Rights, the International Covenants on Human Rights, the International Convention on the Elimination of All Forms of Racial Discrimination, the Convention on the Prevention and Punishment of the Crime of Genocide, the Convention against Torture and Other Cruel, Inhuman or Degrading Treatment or Punishment, the Convention on the Elimination of All Forms of Discrimination against Women, the Convention on the Rights of the Child and other instruments of international humanitarian law, including the Geneva Conventions of 12 August 1949 and the Additional Protocols thereto, of 1977,

Recalling its resolution 3074(XXVIII) of 3 December 1973, entitled "Principles of international cooperation in the detection, arrest, extradition and punishment of persons guilty of war crimes and crimes against humanity",

Taking note of Commission on Human Rights resolution 1993/8 of 23 February 1993, entitled "Rape and abuse of women in the territory of the former Yugoslavia",

Appalled at the recurring and substantiated reports of widespread rape and abuse of women and children in the areas of armed conflict in the former Yugoslavia, in particular its systematic use against the Muslim women and children in Bosnia and Herzegovina by Serbian forces,

Reaffirming the relevant Security Council resolutions, in particular resolution 798(1992) of 18 December 1992, in which, *inter alia*, the Council strongly condemned those acts of unspeakable brutality,

Convinced that this heinous practice constitutes a deliberate weapon of war in fulfilling the policy of "ethnic cleansing" carried out by Serbian forces in Bosnia and Herzegovina, and recalling its resolution 47/121 of 18 December 1992, in which it stated, *inter alia*, that the abhorrent policy of "ethnic cleansing" was a form of genocide,

Welcoming the initiatives taken by the Special Rapporteur of the Commission on Human Rights on the situation of human rights in the former Yugoslavia, particularly his prompt dispatch of a team of experts to the former Yugoslavia to investigate the allegations of rape and abuse of women,

Welcoming also the initiative of the European Council in the rapid dispatch of a mission to investigate the treatment of Muslim women in the former Yugoslavia, and the report of the mission,

Taking note with deep concern of the findings of the team of experts dispatched by the Special Rapporteur, and those of the mission dispatched by the European Council,

Welcoming the establishment of the International Tribunal for the Prosecution of Persons Responsible for Serious Violations of International Humanitarian Law Committed in the Territory of the Former Yugoslavia since 1991, in pursuance of Security Council resolutions 808(1993) of 22 February 1993 and 827(1993) of 25 May 1993,

Also taking note with deep concern of the reports on the findings of the Special Rapporteur and the Secretary-General, assisted by the staff of the Special Rapporteur, regarding rape and abuse of women in the territory of the former Yugoslavia, particularly Bosnia and Herzegovina,

Deeply alarmed at the situation facing victims of rape in the conflicts in different parts of the world, in particular in Bosnia and Herzegovina, and the continuing use of rape as a weapon of war,

Desirous of ensuring that persons accused of upholding and perpetrating rape and sexual violence as a weapon of war in the areas of armed conflict in the former Yugoslavia will be brought to justice by the International Tribunal where appropriate,

Recognizing the extraordinary suffering of the victims of rape and sexual violence and the necessity for an appropriate response to provide assistance to those victims,

Taking into account resolution 37/3 of 24 March 1993 of the Commission on the Status of Women,

Noting with appreciation the work of humanitarian organizations aimed at supporting the victims of rape and abuse and alleviating their suffering,

1. *Strongly condemns* the abhorrent practice of rape and abuse of women and children in the areas of armed conflict in the former Yugoslavia, which constitutes a war crime;

2. *Expresses its outrage* that the systematic practice of rape is being used as a weapon of war and an instrument of "ethnic cleansing" against the women and children in the areas of armed conflict in the former Yugoslavia, in particular against Muslim women and children in Bosnia and Herzegovina;

3. *Demands* that those involved immediately cease those outrageous acts, which are in gross violation of international humanitarian law, including the Geneva Conventions of 12 August 1949 and the Additional Protocols thereto, of 1977, and take immediate action to ensure the enjoyment of human rights and fundamental freedoms in accordance with their obligations under those instruments and other applicable international human rights instruments;

4. *Urges* all Member States to take joint and separate action, in cooperation with the United Nations, to bring about an end to that despicable practice;

5. *Reaffirms* that all persons who perpetrate or authorize crimes against humanity and other violations of international humanitarian law are individually responsible for those violations, and that those in positions of authority who have failed adequately to ensure that persons under their control comply with the relevant international instruments are accountable together with the perpetrators;

6. *Urges* Member States to exert every effort to bring to justice, in accordance with internationally recognized principles of due process, all those individuals directly or indirectly involved in those outrageous international crimes;

7. *Commends* the Special Rapporteur for his report on the situation of human rights in the territory of the former Yugoslavia;

8. *Urges* all States and all relevant intergovernmental and non-governmental organizations, including the United Nations Children's Fund, the Office of the United Nations High Commissioner for Refugees and the World Health Organization, to provide to the victims of such rape and abuse appropriate assistance for their physical and mental rehabilitation;

9. *Invites* the Commission on Human Rights to request the Special Rapporteur to continue investigation into the rape and abuse of women and children in the areas of armed conflict in the former Yugoslavia, in particular in Bosnia and Herzegovina;

10. *Declares* that rape is a heinous crime, and encourages the International Tribunal for the Prosecution of Persons Responsible for Serious Violations of International Humanitarian Law Committed in the Territory of the Former Yugoslavia since 1991 to give due priority to the cases of the victims of rape in the areas of armed conflict in the former Yugoslavia, in particular in Bosnia and Herzegovina;

11. *Requests* the Secretary-General to provide such necessary means as are available to him in the area to enable any future missions to have free and secure access to places of detention;

12. *Also requests* the Secretary-General to submit a report on the implementation of the present resolution to the General Assembly not later than 31 January 1994;

13. *Decides* to continue the consideration of this question at its forty-ninth session.

General Assembly resolution 48/143

20 December 1993   Meeting 85   Adopted without vote

Approved by Third Committee (A/48/632/Add.3) without vote, 6 December (meeting 52); 66-nation draft (A/C.3/48/L.51/Rev.1), orally revised; agenda item 114 *(c)*.

Sponsors: Afghanistan, Albania, Andorra, Australia, Austria, Azerbaijan, Bangladesh, Belgium, Bolivia, Bosnia and Herzegovina, Cambodia, Cameroon, Canada, Costa Rica, Denmark, Djibouti, Dominican Republic, Egypt, Finland, France, Gambia, Georgia, Germany, Greece, Guatemala, Guinea, Honduras, Iceland, Iran, Iraq, Ireland, Israel, Italy, Japan, Kyrgyzstan, Liechtenstein, Luxembourg, Madagascar, Malaysia, Morocco, Nepal, Netherlands, New Zealand, Nicaragua, Norway, Oman, Pakistan, Peru, Philippines, Portugal, Republic of Korea, Samoa, San Marino, Saudi Arabia, Senegal, Slovenia, Solomon Islands, Spain, Sudan, Sweden, Tunisia, Turkey, United Kingdom, United States, Uruguay, Yemen.

Meeting numbers. GA 48th session: 3rd Committee 36-52; plenary 85.

The Americas and the Caribbean

Cuba

Report of the Special Rapporteur. In February,[123] Special Rapporteur Carl-Johan Groth (Sweden) reported on the human rights situation in Cuba. He stated that the Government of Cuba had refused to cooperate because it questioned the legality of the Special Rapporteur's appointment and maintained that there were no human rights violations. He based his report on information received from Cubans living outside the country and information that Cuban citizens living in the country had sent abroad. Allegations of human rights abuses dealt with the rights to freedom of opinion, assembly and association, trade union freedom, religious freedom, the right to enter and leave the country and prison conditions.

The Special Rapporteur, through the Commission on Human Rights, recommended that Cuba

ratify the principal human rights instruments to which it was not a party; end persecution for reasons related to the freedom of peaceful expression and association; permit legalization of independent groups; respect the guarantees of due process; ensure greater transparency and guarantees in the prison system; review sentences imposed for political offences and for trying to leave the country illegally; and expedite and make more transparent the procedure of applying for permission to leave and enter the country. Annexed to the report was a note verbale of 27 April 1992 from Cuba to the Secretary-General, giving its legal interpretation of a 1992 Commission resolution,[124] and a legal opinion thereon by the United Nations Office of Legal Affairs.

Human Rights Commission action. By a roll-call vote of 27 to 10, with 15 abstentions, the Commission, on 10 March,[125] called on Cuba to permit the Special Rapporteur to carry out his mandate in full, particularly by allowing him to visit the country. It expressed concern that Cuba, a member of the Commission, had failed to cooperate with it and regretted the numerous unanswered reports of human rights violations described in the report, particularly intolerance for freedom of speech and assembly. It called on Cuba to carry out the measures recommended by the Special Rapporteur. The Commission affirmed and extended the Special Rapporteur's mandate for one year and asked him to maintain direct contact with the Government and citizens of Cuba, to submit an interim report to the Assembly in 1993 and to report to the Commission in 1994. The Commission requested the Secretary-General to assist him.

On 28 July, the Economic and Social Council, by **decision 1993/274**, approved the extension of the Special Rapporteur's mandate and the Commission's requests to him and the Secretary-General.

Interim report of the Special Rapporteur. In November,[126] the Secretary-General transmitted the Special Rapporteur's interim report on the situation of human rights in Cuba. The Special Rapporteur stated that he had not been able to secure Cuba's permission to visit the country. Thus, his report was based on meetings with individuals and representatives of organizations and groups concerned with human rights in Cuba operating in New York and Washington, D.C. He had travelled to New York and Washington (15-22 September) and to Madrid, Spain (24 September), where he met with Cuban citizens in exile and representatives of human rights organizations.

The Special Rapporteur received information on alleged violations of freedom of opinion and expression, the right to leave the country, the right to an effective recourse and alleged conditions in prisons and labour camps.

The Special Rapporteur proposed that Cuba ratify the human rights instruments to which it was not a party; end persecution for reasons related to the freedom of peaceful expression and association; permit legalization of independent groups; respect the guarantees of due process; ensure guarantees in prison; review sentences imposed for political offences and for trying to leave the country unlawfully; and expedite and make more explicit the procedure of applying for a permit to leave the country. Appended to the report were a note verbale of 24 August from the Special Rapporteur to Cuba requesting its cooperation in carrying out his mandate and a note verbale of 8 October 1992 from Cuba to the Special Rapporteur rejecting a 1992 Commission resolution.[124]

GENERAL ASSEMBLY ACTION

On 20 December, on the recommendation of the Third Committee, the General Assembly adopted **resolution 48/142** by recorded vote.

Situation of human rights in Cuba

The General Assembly,

Reaffirming that all Member States have an obligation to promote and protect human rights and fundamental freedoms as stated in the Charter of the United Nations and elaborated in the Universal Declaration of Human Rights, the International Covenants on Human Rights and other applicable human rights instruments,

Reaffirming also that all Member States have an obligation to fulfil the commitments they have freely undertaken under the various international instruments,

Taking particular note of Commission on Human Rights resolution 1993/63 of 10 March 1993, in which the Commission recognized with deep appreciation the efforts of the Secretary-General and of the Special Rapporteur of the Commission on Human Rights to carry out the mandate concerning the situation of human rights in Cuba,

Noting concern about ongoing reports of serious violations of human rights in Cuba, as outlined in the interim report submitted to the General Assembly by the Special Rapporteur,

Recalling the failure of the Government of Cuba to cooperate with the Commission on Human Rights with regard to its resolution 1992/61 of 3 March 1992 by refusing to permit the Special Rapporteur to visit Cuba, and noting its response, as cited in appendix II to the interim report of the Special Rapporteur, in which it states: "we emphatically reject resolution 1992/61 and, accordingly, we cannot cooperate in its implementation in any way",

1. *Commends* the Special Rapporteur of the Commission on Human Rights for his interim report;

2. *Expresses its full support* for the work of the Special Rapporteur;

3. *Calls upon* the Government of Cuba to cooperate fully with the Special Rapporteur by permitting him full and free access to establish contact with the Government and the citizens of Cuba so that he may fulfil the mandate entrusted to him;

4. *Regrets profoundly* the numerous uncontested reports of violations of basic human rights and fundamental freedoms that are described in the report of the Special Rapporteur to the Commission on Human Rights and in his interim report;

5. *Calls upon* the Government of Cuba to adopt measures proposed by the Special Rapporteur and ratify international human rights instruments, cease the persecution and punishment of citizens for reasons related to freedom of expression and peaceful association, permit legalization of independent groups, respect guarantees of due process, permit access to the prisons by national independent groups and international humanitarian agencies, review sentences for crimes of a political nature and cease retaliatory measures towards those seeking permission to leave the country;

6. *Decides* to continue its consideration of this question at its forty-ninth session.

General Assembly resolution 48/142

20 December 1993   Meeting 85   74-20-61 (recorded vote)

Approved by Third Committee (A/48/632/Add.3) by recorded vote (62-18-52), 6 December (meeting 52); 24-nation draft (A/C.3/48/L.36/Rev.1); agenda item 114 *(c)*.

Sponsors: Australia, Belgium, Bulgaria, Canada, Czech Republic, Denmark, Finland, France, Gambia, Germany, Hungary, Iceland, Ireland, Japan, Luxembourg, Netherlands, Norway, Poland, Portugal, Republic of Moldova, Romania, Sweden, United Kingdom, United States.

Meeting numbers. GA 48th session: 3rd Committee 36-52; plenary 85.

Recorded vote in Assembly as follows:

In favour: Albania, Argentina, Armenia, Australia, Austria, Bangladesh, Belgium, Bulgaria, Canada, Chile, Costa Rica, Croatia, Cyprus, Czech Republic, Denmark, Dominica, Dominican Republic, Ecuador, El Salvador, Estonia, Fiji, Finland, France, Gambia, Georgia, Germany, Greece, Honduras, Hungary, Iceland, Ireland, Israel, Italy, Japan, Kuwait, Latvia, Liechtenstein, Lithuania, Luxembourg, Malawi, Malta, Marshall Islands, Mauritius, Micronesia, Monaco, Nepal, Netherlands, New Zealand, Nicaragua, Norway, Panama, Papua New Guinea, Paraguay, Poland, Portugal, Republic of Korea, Republic of Moldova, Romania, Russian Federation, Samoa, San Marino, Saudi Arabia, Singapore, Slovakia, Slovenia, Solomon Islands, Spain, Sweden, the former Yugoslav Republic of Macedonia, Turkey, United Kingdom, United States, Uruguay, Zaire.

Against: China, Cuba, Democratic People's Republic of Korea, Ghana, India, Indonesia, Iran, Iraq, Lao People's Democratic Republic, Libyan Arab Jamahiriya, Malaysia, Myanmar, Namibia, Sudan, Syrian Arab Republic, Uganda, United Republic of Tanzania, Viet Nam, Zambia, Zimbabwe.

Abstaining: Afghanistan, Algeria, Antigua and Barbuda, Azerbaijan, Bahamas, Barbados, Belarus, Belize, Benin, Bhutan, Bolivia, Botswana, Brazil, Brunei Darussalam, Burkina Faso, Burundi, Cambodia, Cameroon, Cape Verde, Central African Republic, Chad, Colombia, Comoros, Congo, Côte d'Ivoire, Egypt, Eritrea, Ethiopia, Gabon, Grenada, Guinea, Guinea-Bissau, Guyana, Jamaica, Kazakhstan, Kenya, Kyrgyzstan, Lesotho, Maldives, Mali, Mauritania, Mexico, Mozambique, Niger, Nigeria, Pakistan, Peru, Philippines, Rwanda, Saint Lucia, Saint Vincent and the Grenadines, Sierra Leone, Sri Lanka, Suriname, Swaziland, Thailand, Togo, Trinidad and Tobago, Tunisia, Ukraine, Venezuela.

El Salvador

Report of the Independent Expert. Independent Expert Pedro Nikken (Venezuela) submitted to the Commission in February a report on human rights in El Salvador, based on his visits to the country from 27 September to 4 October 1992 and from 7 to 14 January 1993.[127] He stated that the restoration of peace did not automatically mean the establishment of a climate in which human rights were fully observed and safeguarded. However, there were positive signs. There had been a decrease in extrajudicial, summary or arbitrary executions and there had been no sign of enforced or involuntary disappearance. Arbitrary arrests continued and there had been a significant increase in the number of homicides attributed to persons unknown or common criminals. Structural deficiencies in the judicial system violated the right to due process and were seen as an obstacle to the safeguarding of human rights.

The Independent Expert recommended that the Government of El Salvador take advantage of the presence of the Human Rights Division of the United Nations Observer Mission in El Salvador (ONUSAL) and implement the recommendations of the Ad Hoc Commission on the Purification of the Armed Forces. He called on the Frente Farabundo Martí para la Liberación Nacional (FMLN) to destroy all its weapons. He advocated strengthening the Office of the National Counsel for the Defence of Human Rights; setting up the National Civil Police; guaranteeing the independence of judges and lawyers; revising the approved text of the National Council of the Judiciary; satisfying the economic, social and cultural rights of Salvadorians; and providing support from the international community through the National Reconstruction Plan.

Human Rights Commission action. On 10 March,[128] the Commission, welcoming the February signing of the agreements and principles of the Forum for Economic and Social Consultation proposed in the 1992 Peace Agreement between El Salvador and FMLN,[129] urged both parties to abide by them.

The Commission expressed its gratitude to El Salvador for ending the armed conflict and its positive impact on the observance of human rights, and welcomed the integration of FMLN into the civil life of the country. It expressed concern at continued reports of human rights violations and urged both parties to carry out fully the remaining agreements, together with the recommendations by ONUSAL and by the Ad Hoc Commission on the Purification of the Armed Forces and those to be produced by the Commission on the Truth. Endorsing the Independent Expert's recommendations, it requested the Secretary-General to extend his mandate for one year and asked the Expert to report in 1994. Those requests were approved by the Economic and Social Council by **decision 1993/284** of 28 July.

(For details of the political situation in El Salvador, see PART TWO, Chapter II.)

ONUSAL

In accordance with a 1991 Security Council resolution,[130] the Secretary-General, in February, transmitted an ONUSAL report which discussed ONUSAL as a mechanism for active verification of human rights.[131] Active verification involved a continuous presence, for an adequate length of time, in the territory of the country which was the subject of verification; acceptance by the warring parties of the mission's powers to observe,

investigate and make recommendations; protection of human rights on the basis of undertakings sovereignly adopted within the State; and the capacity to promote meaningful change on the basis of the parties' acceptance of international verification of compliance with political or legal obligations. The report stated that ONUSAL's approach represented a valid option for improving the human rights situation in El Salvador.

GENERAL ASSEMBLY ACTION

On 20 December, on the recommendation of the Third Committee, the General Assembly adopted **resolution 48/149** without vote.

Situation of human rights in El Salvador

The General Assembly,

Guided by the international human rights instruments,

Recalling its resolution 47/140 of 18 December 1992, and taking note of Commission on Human Rights resolution 1993/93 of 10 March 1993 and the statement of 20 August 1993 by the Chairman of the Subcommission on Prevention of Discrimination and Protection of Minorities on support for the peace process in El Salvador, as well as Security Council resolution 888(1993) of 30 November 1993,

Taking into account the reports of the Secretary-General and the Director of the Human Rights Division of the United Nations Observer Mission in El Salvador,

Convinced that full and speedy implementation of the outstanding commitments of the peace agreements is necessary in order to guarantee full respect for human rights and the consolidation of the reconciliation and democratization process under way in El Salvador,

Welcoming the fact that most of the agreements have already been put into effect by the Government of El Salvador and the Frente Farabundo Martí para la Liberación Nacional,

Concerned none the less that problems persist and that there are continuing delays in the implementation of several important elements of the peace agreements, referred to in Security Council resolution 832(1993) of 27 May 1993, and that there have also been some irregularities in the implementation of those relating to public security,

Noting with concern the recent acts of violence in El Salvador, which may indicate renewed activity by illegal armed groups, and could, if left unchecked, negatively affect the peace process in El Salvador, including the elections scheduled for March 1994,

Also noting with concern the seemingly politically motivated murders of, and threats against, members of the different political parties, including the Frente Farabundo Martí para la Liberación Nacional and the Alianza Republicana Nacionalista,

Welcoming in this regard the efforts of the Secretary-General in cooperation with the Government of El Salvador towards the establishment of a mechanism to investigate illegal armed groups and their possible connection with renewed political violence,

Noting that El Salvador has entered a decisive phase in the peace process and that political parties have just begun a campaign for the elections to be held in March 1994, which should take place in a peaceful environment,

Noting also the importance of the fact that reforms of the judicial system have been adopted, as well as the need for the adoption of both the reforms in the process of being approved and those recommended by the Commission on the Truth, which are designed to contribute to the elimination of the existing impunity and consequently to the full attainment of the rule of law,

Recalling the role that the Office of the National Counsel for the Defence of Human Rights is called upon to play in the promotion and protection of human rights,

Considering that the international community must follow closely and continue to support all efforts to consolidate peace, ensure full respect for human rights and undertake the reconstruction of El Salvador,

1. *Commends* the Government of El Salvador and the Frente Farabundo Martí para la Liberación Nacional for having fulfilled most of their commitments and for having overcome a number of obstacles to the implementation of their agreements;

2. *Expresses its concern* that there are important elements of the peace agreements that have been only partially implemented and therefore calls upon the Government of El Salvador and the Frente Farabundo Martí to step up their efforts to complete as agreed, by the proposed dates, the programme for the transfer of land, the reintegration programme for ex-combatants, the deployment of the National Civil Police and the phasing out of the National Police, as well as the collection of weapons issued for the exclusive use of personnel of the armed forces and the adoption of the Act on Private Security Services;

3. *Condemns* the recent acts of violence that may be politically motivated, which have been repudiated by the various sectors of Salvadorian society, and considers it inadmissible that such acts, perpetrated by a small minority, should jeopardize the progress made in implementing the agreements and hamper the holding of free elections in March 1994;

4. *Supports*, in this context, the efforts of the Secretary-General, in cooperation with the Government of El Salvador, to initiate immediately an impartial, independent and credible investigation of illegal armed groups, as recommended by the Commission on the Truth, and urges all sectors of society in El Salvador to cooperate with such an investigation;

5. *Notes with satisfaction* the statement of 5 November 1993, entitled "Commitment of the presidential candidates to peace and stability in El Salvador", in which the candidates, *inter alia*, solemnly committed themselves to maintaining the constructive evolution of the peace process and to implementing all the commitments contained in the peace agreements and rejected any politically motivated violence or intimidation;

6. *Calls upon* all Governments to contribute to the consolidation of peace and the attainment of full respect for human rights in El Salvador by supporting full compliance with the peace agreements;

7. *Reiterates its gratitude* for the important work being carried out by the Secretary-General and his representative and by the United Nations Observer Mission in El Salvador, and extends to them its support so that they can continue to take all necessary steps to contribute to the successful implementation of the peace agreements;

8. *Acknowledges with satisfaction* the continuing efforts of the Governments of Colombia, Mexico, Spain and Venezuela, which make up the Group of Friends of the Secretary-General, as well as the Government of the United States of America, in support of the steps being taken by the Secretary-General to consolidate the peace process in El Salvador;

9. *Notes* that, as has been pointed out by the Secretary-General, the human rights situation in El Salvador continues to evolve in a somewhat ambivalent fashion, since, on the one hand, there continue to be signs of improvement and, on the other, violations persist, particularly as regards the right to life, and the capacity of the judicial system to clarify and punish such violations continues to be unsatisfactory;

10. *Urges* all States, as well as the international financial and development institutions, promptly and generously to provide financial contributions to support the fulfilment of all aspects of the peace agreements, including the National Reconstruction Plan;

11. *Urges* the Government of El Salvador and all other institutions involved in the electoral process to adopt the necessary measures to create an atmosphere conducive to ensuring that the elections scheduled for March 1994 are free, representative and authentic, since they are a key element in the consolidation of the peace process.

General Assembly resolution 48/149

20 December 1993   Meeting 85   Adopted without vote

Approved by Third Committee (A/48/632/Add.3) without vote, 8 December (meeting 54); 15-nation draft (A/C.3/48/L.68/Rev.1), orally revised; agenda item 114 *(c)*.
Sponsors: Canada, Colombia, Costa Rica, El Salvador, France, Guatemala, Honduras, Hungary, Mexico, Nicaragua, Panama, Spain, Sweden, United States, Venezuela.
Meeting numbers. GA 48th session: 3rd Committee 36-54; plenary 85.

Haiti

Report of the Special Rapporteur. In February, Special Rapporteur Marco Tulio Bruni Celli (Venezuela) submitted to the Commission a report covering the human rights situation in Haiti during 1992.[132] He visited Haiti from 18 to 21 August 1992 and requested two additional visits, in December 1992 and January 1993, but was refused permission by the Haitian Government.

The Special Rapporteur noted that the human rights situation in Haiti had deteriorated in 1992, which had seen deaths, disappearances and murders, preventive repression, persecution, arbitrary detention, torture, extortion of protection money from citizens by security forces, the dropping of legislative programmes, the re-emergence of section chiefs, the banning of demonstrations, and police repression of all anti-government protests. There was virtually no rule of law.

The Special Rapporteur recommended that the Commission express its deep concern at the widespread violence and condemn systematic human rights violations; continue to monitor the human rights situation; inform the de facto Government that the fact that it had not been recognized by the international community did not exempt the State from its obligations to the Haitian people;

inform the de facto Government that the systematic violation of human rights represented a breach of the principles enshrined in the United Nations Charter; express its concern at the fate of Haitians who were being sent back to the country after attempting to flee abroad; express satisfaction at the cooperation between United Nations organizations and those of the inter-American system; recognize the efforts taken by the inter-American system to resolve the political crisis and ask the Secretary-General to continue cooperating with the other bodies, especially with the Organization of American States (OAS); and continue to appoint a Special Rapporteur. He recommended that the Secretary-General send to Haiti human rights specialists to be permanently based at the United Nations Development Programme office at Port-au-Prince.

Human Rights Commission action. On 10 March,[133] the Commission strongly condemned the overthrow of Haiti's constitutionally elected President, the use of violence and military coercion and the subsequent deterioration of the human rights situation. It expressed deep concern over the substantial deterioration of the human rights situation since the September 1991 *coup d'état*.[134] Drawing the attention of the international community to the fate of Haitians who were fleeing the country, the Commission asked for support in assisting them. It decided to extend the Special Rapporteur's mandate for one year and asked him to submit a provisional report to the General Assembly in 1993 and a final report to the Commission in 1994. It requested the Secretary-General to provide the Special Rapporteur with all the assistance he needed. The extension of the Special Rapporteur's mandate and the Commission's requests were approved by the Economic and Social Council by **decision 1993/276** of 28 July.

Subcommission action. On 20 August,[135] the Subcommission, noting with satisfaction the agreements signed between the constitutional President of Haiti and the Commander-in-Chief of the armed forces, called on all sectors of Haitian society to ensure that a peaceful transition could take place and that democracy could be firmly established (see PART TWO, Chapter II).

Provisional report of the Special Rapporteur. As requested by the Commission, the Secretary-General, in November,[136] transmitted the provisional report of the Special Rapporteur to the Assembly. In the course of his work, the Special Rapporteur had travelled to Washington, D.C. (13 August), New York (19 August) and Haiti (22-26 August).

The Special Rapporteur stated that, since his last report, repression and politically motivated violence had persisted. Human rights violations

had remained systematic and widespread; harassment, intimidation, attacks, arbitrary arrests, summary executions and torture continued to be carried out with impunity by members of the military and civilians working with them. Those violations continued throughout the year, even after the signing in July of the Governors Island Agreement and the New York Pact (see PART TWO, Chapter II).

The Special Rapporteur recommended that the Assembly express its satisfaction with the agreements reached for restoring the constitutional Government, while regretting the obstacles to their full implementation, and express its gratitude to the International Civilian Mission, deployed jointly by the United Nations and OAS. He further recommended that the United Nations continue to observe and remain apprised of the human rights situation in Haiti; Haiti be required to honour the obligations assumed when it ratified international human rights instruments; the Government of Haiti be required to honour its pledge to conduct programmes relating to the administration of justice, prison administration, the updating of civil and criminal legislation, the separation of the police from the armed forces, the training of the police and modernization of the army and the investigation of crimes committed by the military, the authorities, security agents and those under their orders in violation of human rights; the joint United Nations/OAS Civilian Mission remain in Haiti for as long as was deemed necessary; and a programme be established for the promotion of human rights.

GENERAL ASSEMBLY ACTION

On 20 December, on the recommendation of the Third Committee, the General Assembly adopted **resolution 48/151** without vote.

Human rights in Haiti

The General Assembly,

Recalling its resolutions 46/7 of 11 October 1991, 46/138 of 17 December 1991, 47/20 of 24 November 1992 and 47/143 of 18 December 1992,

Guided by the principles embodied in the Charter of the United Nations, the Universal Declaration of Human Rights and the International Covenants on Human Rights,

Aware of its responsibility for the promotion and encouragement of respect for human rights and fundamental freedoms for all, and resolved to keep a close watch on human rights violations wherever they may occur,

Reaffirming that all Member States are required to promote and protect human rights and to comply with the obligations laid down in the various instruments in this field,

Taking note of Commission on Human Rights resolution 1993/68 of 10 March 1993, in which the Commission decided to extend the mandate of its Special Rapporteur for one year, with a view to having him submit an interim report to the General Assembly at its forty-eighth session and a final report to the Commission at its fiftieth session,

Taking note also of the report submitted in accordance with General Assembly resolution 47/20 B of 20 April 1993 by the International Civilian Mission to Haiti, established by the United Nations and the Organization of American States,

Deeply concerned about the grave events occurring in Haiti since 29 September 1991, when the democratic process in that country was abruptly and violently interrupted, which have resulted in the loss of human lives and violations of human rights,

Concerned at the exodus of Haitian nationals from the country because of the deteriorating political and economic situation since 29 September 1991,

Deeply alarmed by the persistence and worsening of serious violations of human rights, in particular summary and arbitrary executions, forced disappearances, of torture and rape, arbitrary arrests and detentions and denial of freedom of expression, assembly and association,

Deeply concerned by the increase in acts of violence and intimidation against the Government of Haiti, especially the assassination of the Minister of Justice, François Guy Malary, which have contributed to the temporary withdrawal of the International Civilian Mission,

Recognizing the important role played by the International Civilian Mission, whose presence in Haiti has prevented greater violations of human rights, and encouraging its earliest possible return to Haiti,

1. *Commends* the Special Rapporteur of the Commission on Human Rights, Mr. Marco Tulio Bruni Celli, for his report on the situation of human rights in Haiti, and supports the recommendations contained therein;

2. *Once again condemns* the overthrow of the constitutionally elected President, Mr. Jean-Bertrand Aristide, and the use of violence and military coercion, and the subsequent deterioration of the situation of human rights in Haiti;

3. *Expresses its conviction* that the full implementation of the Governors Island Agreement, which was signed by all parties, is essential for the improvement of the situation of human rights in Haiti and that the refusal by one of the parties to implement this Agreement has led to a further deterioration of the human rights situation;

4. *Expresses its deep concern* about the continuing worsening of the human rights situation in Haiti during 1993 and the resulting increase in violations of the human rights embodied in the International Covenant on Civil and Political Rights, the International Covenant on Economic, Social and Cultural Rights, the American Convention on Human Rights: "Pact of San José, Costa Rica" and other international human rights instruments;

5. *Condemns* the recurrence of the flagrant human rights violations committed under the illegal government that took power following the coup of 29 September 1991, in particular, summary executions, political assassinations, arbitrary arrests and detentions, torture, searches without warrant, rape, restrictions on freedom of movement, expression, assembly and association and of the press and the repression of popular demonstrations calling for the return of President Jean-Bertrand Aristide;

6. *Calls* for the early return of the International Civilian Mission to Haiti as a means of preventing further violations of human rights;

7. *Calls the attention* of the international community to the fate of the Haitian nationals who are fleeing the country and requests its support for the efforts being made to assist them;

8. *Expresses its appreciation* to the Office of the United Nations High Commissioner for Refugees for the work it is doing in favour of the Haitian nationals fleeing the country, and invites Member States to continue to give financial and material support to its efforts;

9. *Calls upon* Member States to continue and to intensify their humanitarian assistance to the people of Haiti, and welcomes in this regard the decision of the Secretary-General to dispatch a team of additional humanitarian personnel to Haiti;

10. *Decides* to keep the situation of human rights and fundamental freedoms in Haiti under review during its forty-ninth session and to consider it further in the light of the information supplied by the Commission on Human Rights and the Economic and Social Council.

General Assembly resolution 48/151

20 December 1993   Meeting 85   Adopted without vote

Approved by Third Committee (A/48/632/Add.3) without vote, 6 December (meeting 53); 54-nation draft (A/C.3/48/L.72), orally revised; agenda item 114 *(c)*.

Sponsors: Andorra, Antigua and Barbuda, Argentina, Australia, Austria, Bahamas, Barbados, Belgium, Belize, Benin, Bolivia, Brazil, Cambodia, Canada, Chile, Colombia, Costa Rica, Cuba, Denmark, Ecuador, El Salvador, Finland, France, Germany, Greece, Grenada, Guatemala, Guyana, Haiti, Honduras, Hungary, Iceland, Ireland, Italy, Jamaica, Japan, Luxembourg, Mexico, Netherlands, Nicaragua, Norway, Panama, Peru, Portugal, San Marino, Spain, Suriname, Sweden, Trinidad and Tobago, United Kingdom, United States, Uruguay, Vanuatu, Venezuela.

Meeting numbers. GA 48th session: 3rd Committee 36-53; plenary 85.

In **resolution 48/27** of 6 December, the Assembly strongly condemned the attempted illegal replacement of the constitutional President of Haiti, the use of violence and military coercion and the violation of human rights in the country.

Peru

On 23 August,[137] the Subcommission noted with interest the electoral processes, monitored by OAS, to elect a new Congress and renew the municipal authorities in Peru. It strongly condemned the human rights violations committed by the terrorist groups Sendero Luminoso and Movimiento Revolucionario Tupac Amaru. The Subcommission urged the Peruvian authorities to adopt the necessary measures to guarantee full compliance with the State's obligations to investigate and penalize those responsible for human rights violations, as well as to compensate the victims.

United States

On 16 August,[138] the Subcommission, by 6 votes to 4, with 7 abstentions, asked its Chairman to request the United States to provide information on an incident that took place on 29 July 1993 at Laredo, Texas, in connection with a donation intended for religious institutions in Cuba, which resulted in a hunger strike maintained for 17 days by 13 persons who considered that they were prevented from exercising their civil rights and whose health was deteriorating.

Middle East

Lebanon

Human Rights Commission action. On 10 March,[139] the Commission, by a roll-call vote of 50 to 1, condemned ongoing Israeli human rights violations in southern Lebanon, manifested by arbitrary detention of civilians, destruction of their homes, confiscation of their property, their expulsion from the occupied area and bombardment of villages. It demanded that Israel end such practices immediately and implement relevant Security Council resolutions requiring its immediate, total and unconditional withdrawal from all Lebanese territory and respect for Lebanon's sovereignty, independence and territorial integrity. It also demanded that Israel end immediately its policy of forced deportation and implement a 1992 Security Council resolution,[140] comply with the 1949 Geneva Convention relative to the Protection of Civilian Persons in Time of War (fourth Geneva Convention) and facilitate the humanitarian mission of ICRC and similar organizations. It asked the Secretary-General to bring the resolution to Israel's attention and to invite Israel to provide information on its implementation. He was asked to report to the General Assembly in 1993 and to the Commission in 1994 on the results of his efforts.

Reports of the Secretary-General. In accordance with the Commission's request, the Secretary-General reported to the Assembly in November[141] that he had asked Israel for information on the implementation of the Commission's resolution and had received no reply.

On 20 December, by **decision 48/430**, the Assembly took note of the Secretary-General's report.

As requested by the Commission in 1992,[142] the Secretary-General submitted in January 1993 a report[143] in which he stated that he had asked Israel for information on the implementation of the Commission's 1992 resolution and had received no reply.

Territories occupied by Israel

In 1993, the question of human rights violations in the territories occupied by Israel as a result of the 1967 hostilities in the Middle East was again considered by the Commission. Political and other aspects were considered by the General Assembly, its Special Committee to Investigate Israeli Practices Affecting the Human Rights of the Palestinian People and Other Arabs of the Occupied Territories (Committee on Israeli practices) and other bodies (see PART TWO, Chapter V).

Reports of the Secretary-General. In a January report to the Commission,[144] the Secretary-General stated that he had brought the Commission's two 1992 resolutions on human rights violations in the Israeli-occupied territories[142] to the attention of Governments, the Committee on Israeli practices and the Committee on the Exercise of the Inalienable Rights of the Palestinian People. They had also been transmitted to the specialized agencies, the United Nations Relief and Works Agency for Palestine Refugees in the Near East, international humanitarian organizations and NGOs. Information was also disseminated through United Nations press releases, publications, audiovisual programmes and journalists' encounters on the question of Palestine.

Also in January,[145] the Secretary-General submitted a list of all United Nations reports issued since 6 March 1992 on the situation of the population of the occupied Arab territories.

In accordance with a 1992 Subcommission request,[146] the Secretary-General provided in July[147] an updated list of reports, studies, statistics and other documents relating to the question of Palestine and other occupied Arab territories.

Human Rights Commission action. By a 19 February resolution,[148] adopted by a roll-call vote of 26 to 16, with 5 abstentions, the Commission condemned Israel's policies and practices that violated the human rights of Palestinians in the Israeli-occupied territories. Affirming the right of the Palestinians to resist the Israeli occupation by all means, the Commission called on Israel to desist from all human rights violations in the Palestinian and other occupied Arab territories, to respect the principles of international law and its commitments to the United Nations Charter, and to withdraw from the Palestinian territory, including Jerusalem, and other occupied Arab territories, in accordance with United Nations and Commission resolutions. It decided to appoint a special rapporteur and called on Israel to cooperate with him or her. The Commission requested the Secretary-General to bring its resolution to the attention of the Government of Israel and to all other Governments, concerned United Nations organs, the specialized agencies, regional intergovernmental organizations and international humanitarian organizations, to disseminate it as widely as possible and to report to the Commission in 1994 on its implementation by Israel. It also asked him to provide the Commission with all United Nations reports issued between sessions of the Commission that dealt with the conditions in which the Palestinians were living under Israeli occupation.

René Felber (Switzerland) was appointed as Special Rapporteur.

By another resolution, adopted on the same day by a roll-call vote of 27 to 1, with 19 abstentions,[149] the Commission, reaffirming the applicability of the fourth Geneva Convention to the territories, including Jerusalem, strongly condemned Israel for refusing to apply that Convention and for the ill-treatment and torture of Palestinian detainees and prisoners. It also condemned Israel for deporting Palestinians, calling on it to comply with Security Council, General Assembly and Commission resolutions providing for their return to their homeland and to desist from that policy. The Commission asked the Secretary-General to report in 1994 on progress in implementing the resolution, after bringing it to the attention of Governments, United Nations organs and agencies, intergovernmental and international humanitarian organizations and NGOs.

Also on 19 February,[150] by a roll-call vote of 29 to 1, with 17 abstentions, the Commission strongly condemned Israel for refusing to comply with United Nations resolutions on the Syrian Golan. Condemning Israel's persistence in changing the physical character, demographic composition, institutional structure and legal status of the Syrian Golan, the Commission emphasized that displaced persons must be allowed to return and recover their property. It determined that all Israeli measures that altered the character and legal status of the Syrian Golan were null and void, violated international law and the fourth Geneva Convention and had no legal effect. Strongly condemning Israel for attempting to impose Israeli citizenship and identity cards on Syrians and for its practices of annexation, establishing settlements, confiscating lands, diverting water resources and imposing a boycott on agricultural products, the Commission called on Israel to desist from its settlement designs and policies aimed against academic institutions and from its repressive measures. It again called on Member States not to recognize any of those measures or actions. The Secretary-General was asked to give the resolution wide publicity and to report to the Commission in 1994.

By a further 19 February resolution,[151] adopted by a roll-call vote of 46 to 1, the Commission reaffirmed that the installation of Israeli civilians in the occupied territories was illegal and constituted a violation of the fourth Geneva Convention. Regretting that Israel had not complied with its resolutions adopted in 1990,[152] 1991[153] and 1992,[154] it urged Israel to abstain from installing settlers, including immigrants, in the occupied territories.

ECONOMIC AND SOCIAL COUNCIL ACTION

In July, the Economic and Social Council, on the recommendation of its Social Committee, adopted **decision 1993/253** by roll-call vote.

Question of the violation of human rights in the occupied Arab territories, including Palestine

At its 44th plenary meeting, on 28 July 1993, the Economic and Social Council, taking note of Commission on Human Rights resolution 1993/2 A of 19 February 1993, approved the Commission's decision to appoint a special rapporteur with the following mandate:

(*a*) To investigate Israel's violations of the principles and bases of international law, international humanitarian law and the Geneva Convention relative to the Protection of Civilian Persons in Time of War, of 12 August 1949, in the Palestinian territories occupied by Israel since 1967;

(*b*) To receive communications, to hear witnesses, and to use such modalities of procedure as he may deem necessary for his mandate;

(*c*) To report, with his conclusions and recommendations, to the Commission on Human Rights at its future sessions, until the end of the Israeli occupation of those territories.

Economic and Social Council decision 1993/253

26-12-8 (roll-call vote)

Approved by Social Committee (E/1993/108) by roll-call vote (22-11-10), 22 July (meeting 17); draft by Commission on Human Rights (E/1993/23); agenda item 18.

Roll-call vote in Council as follows:

In favour: Bahamas, Bangladesh, Benin, Bhutan, Botswana, Brazil, Chile, China, Colombia, Cuba, Guinea, India, Kuwait, Madagascar, Malaysia, Mexico, Morocco, Nigeria, Peru, Philippines, Sri Lanka, Suriname, Swaziland, Syrian Arab Republic, Trinidad and Tobago, Turkey.

Against: Australia, Belarus, Canada, Denmark, Germany, Japan, Norway, Poland, Romania, Russian Federation, United Kingdom, United States.

Abstaining: Argentina, Austria, Belgium, France, Italy, Republic of Korea, Spain, Ukraine.

Mass exoduses

Human Rights Commission action. On 10 March,[155] the Commission again invited Governments and intergovernmental and humanitarian organizations to intensify their cooperation in addressing problems resulting from mass exoduses of refugees and displaced persons (see PART THREE, Chapter XV) and the causes of such exoduses. It asked all United Nations bodies, the specialized agencies, governmental and intergovernmental organizations and NGOs to cooperate with it and to provide information on the human rights situations creating or affecting refugees and displaced persons within their mandates. The Commission urged the Secretary-General to allocate resources to consolidate the system for early-warning activities by designating the United Nations Department of Humanitarian Affairs as the focal point for early warning and strengthening coordination among Secretariat offices concerned, in order to ensure that effective action was taken to identify human rights abuses contributing to mass exoduses. The Commission requested the Secretary-General to ask Governments, intergovernmental organizations, specialized agencies and NGOs for information and to submit in 1994 a report outlining the principal developments in the United Nations system regarding early warning and preventive diplomacy since the issuance in 1992 of "An Agenda for Peace".[156]

On 20 December, on the recommendation of the Third Committee, the General Assembly adopted **resolution 48/139** without vote.

Human rights and mass exoduses

The General Assembly,

Mindful of its general humanitarian mandate under the Charter of the United Nations to promote and encourage respect for human rights and fundamental freedoms,

Noting that the report of the Secretary-General entitled "An Agenda for Peace" identifies the protection of human rights as an important element of peace, security and economic well-being and highlights the importance of preventive diplomacy,

Deeply disturbed by the increasing scale and magnitude of exoduses of refugees and displacements of population in many regions of the world and by the suffering of millions of refugees and displaced persons,

Conscious of the fact that human rights violations are one of the multiple and complex factors causing mass exoduses of refugees and displaced persons,

Deeply preoccupied by the increasingly heavy burden being imposed, particularly upon developing countries with limited resources of their own and upon the international community as a whole, by these sudden mass exoduses and displacements of population,

Stressing the need for strengthening international cooperation aimed at averting new massive flows of refugees while providing durable solutions to actual refugee situations,

Reaffirming its resolution 41/70 of 3 December 1986, in which it endorsed the conclusions and recommendations contained in the report of the Group of Governmental Experts on International Cooperation to Avert New Flows of Refugees,

Bearing in mind its resolution 46/127 of 17 December 1991 and Commission on Human Rights resolution 1993/70 of 10 March 1993, as well as all previous relevant resolutions of the General Assembly and the Commission,

Noting that the Secretary-General, in his report on the strengthening of the coordination of humanitarian emergency assistance of the United Nations, states that in complex emergencies, humanitarian assistance is essential but must be complemented by measures to address the root causes of such emergencies, and that the establishment of the inter-agency consultation on early warning serves the purposes of both prevention and preparedness,

Noting also that the Executive Committee of the Programme of the United Nations High Commissioner for Refugees has specifically acknowledged the direct relationship between the observance of human rights standards, refugee movements and problems of protection,

1. *Recalls its endorsement,* in its resolution 41/70, of the recommendations and conclusions contained in the report of the Group of Governmental Experts on International Cooperation to Avert New Flows of Refugees, including, *inter alia,* the call upon all States to promote human rights and fundamental freedoms and to refrain from denying these to individuals in their population because of nationality, ethnicity, race, religion or language;

2. *Once again invites* all Governments and intergovernmental and humanitarian organizations concerned to intensify their cooperation with and assistance to worldwide efforts to address the serious problems resulting from mass exoduses of refugees and displaced persons, and also the causes of such exoduses;

3. *Requests* all Governments to ensure the effective implementation of the relevant international instruments, in particular in the field of human rights and humanitarian law, as this would contribute to averting new massive flows of refugees and displaced persons;

4. *Requests* all United Nations bodies, including the United Nations human rights treaty bodies, the specialized agencies and governmental, intergovernmental and non-governmental organizations, to cooperate fully with all mechanisms of the Commission on Human Rights and, in particular, to provide them with all relevant and accurate information in their possession on the human rights situations creating or affecting refugees and displaced persons within their mandates;

5. *Welcomes* the recommendation in Commission on Human Rights resolution 1993/70 that special rapporteurs, special representatives and working groups studying situations of violation of human rights pay attention to problems resulting in mass exoduses of populations and, where appropriate, report and make relevant recommendations to the Commission;

6. *Notes* that the Executive Committee of the Programme of the United Nations High Commissioner for Refugees has specifically acknowledged the direct relationship between the observance of human rights standards, refugee movements, problems of protection and solutions;

7. *Welcomes* the contributions of the United Nations High Commissioner for Refugees to the deliberations of international human rights bodies, and encourages her to seek ways to make these contributions even more effective;

8. *Also welcomes* the statement made by the High Commissioner at the forty-ninth session of the Commission on Human Rights, on 3 March 1993, in which she emphasized the need for early response by the international community to human rights situations that threaten to generate refugees and displaced persons or that impede their voluntary return;

9. *Encourages* States that have not already done so to accede to the 1951 Convention relating to the Status of Refugees and the Protocol thereto of 1967;

10. *Takes note with appreciation* of the emphasis placed by the Secretary-General in his report to the General Assembly at its forty-seventh session on the need to develop the capacity of the United Nations for early warning and preventive diplomacy to help deter humanitarian crises;

11. *Reaffirms,* in this regard, its previous resolutions on the question of human rights and mass exoduses, and requests the Secretary-General, in the further development of the capacity of the Secretariat for early warning and preventive diplomacy, to pay particular attention to international cooperation to avert new flows of refugees;

12. *Notes,* in this connection, that mass movements of populations are caused by multiple and complex factors, which indicates that early warning requires an intersectoral and multidisciplinary approach;

13. *Encourages* the Secretary-General especially to continue to discharge the task described in the report of the Group of Governmental Experts on International

Cooperation to Avert New Flows of Refugees, including the continuous monitoring of all potential outflows, and to implement the recommendations of the Joint Inspection Unit contained in its report on the coordination of activities related to early warning of possible refugee flows;

14. *Urges* the Secretary-General to attach high priority and to allocate the necessary resources from the regular budget of the United Nations to the consolidation and strengthening of the system for undertaking early-warning activities in the humanitarian area by, *inter alia*, the designation of the Department of Humanitarian Affairs of the Secretariat as the focal point for early warning in this area and strengthened coordination between relevant offices of the Secretariat concerned with early warning and organizations of the United Nations system, for the purpose of ensuring, *inter alia*, that effective action is taken to identify human rights abuses that contribute to mass outflows of persons;

15. *Welcomes* the decision by the Administrative Committee on Coordination to establish a regular United Nations inter-agency early-warning consultation related to possible flows of refugees and displaced persons, based on the sharing and analysis of relevant information between United Nations bodies and the development of collective recommendations for action to alleviate, *inter alia*, the possible causes of new flows of refugees and displaced persons;

16. *Also welcomes* the decision by the Administrative Committee on Coordination to designate the Department of Humanitarian Affairs as the focal point of the United Nations inter-agency early-warning consultation;

17. *Urges* the Department of Humanitarian Affairs to take the necessary steps to function effectively as the focal point of the inter-agency early-warning consultation;

18. *Urges* all the bodies involved in the inter-agency consultation to cooperate fully in, and devote the necessary resources to, the successful operation of the consultation;

19. *Invites* the Commission on Human Rights to keep the question of human rights and mass exoduses under review with a view to supporting the early-warning arrangement instituted by the Secretary-General to avert new massive flows of refugees and displaced persons;

20. *Requests* the Secretary-General to report to the General Assembly at its fiftieth session on the strengthened role that he is playing in undertaking early-warning activities, especially in the areas of human rights and humanitarian assistance, as well as on any further developments relating to the recommendations contained in the report of the Group of Governmental Experts on International Cooperation to Avert New Flows of Refugees and the recommendations of the Joint Inspection Unit;

21. *Invites* the Secretary-General to include in his report to the General Assembly at its fiftieth session detailed information on the programmatic, institutional, administrative, financial and managerial efforts instituted to enhance the capacity of the United Nations to avert new flows of refugees and to tackle the root causes of such outflows;

22. *Decides* to continue its consideration of the question of human rights and mass exoduses at its fiftieth session.

General Assembly resolution 48/139
20 December 1993   Meeting 85   Adopted without vote

Approved by Third Committee (A/48/632/Add.2) without vote, 6 December (meeting 53); 23-nation draft (A/C.3/48/L.76); agenda item 114 *(b)*.
Sponsors: Albania, Australia, Cameroon, Canada, Costa Rica, Côte d'Ivoire, Finland, France, Gambia, Germany, Hungary, Ireland, Italy, Japan, Jordan, Luxembourg, Netherlands, New Zealand, Nigeria, Philippines, Poland, United Kingdom, United States.
Meeting numbers. GA 48th session: 3rd Committee 36-53; plenary 85.

Genocide

Status of the 1948 Convention

As at 31 December 1993,[24] 112 States had become parties to the 1948 Convention on the Prevention and Punishment of the Crime of Genocide.[107] In 1993, Armenia, the Czech Republic, Georgia, the Republic of Moldova and Slovakia became parties to the Convention.

Subcommission action. On 20 August,[111] the Subcommission affirmed that all persons who perpetrated or authorized the commission of genocide were individually responsible for such actions and urged United Nations Member States to bring to justice those involved in the crimes committed in Bosnia and Herzegovina, elsewhere in the territory of the former Yugoslavia or in any other part of the world.

Terrorism

On 20 August,[157] the Subcommission called on Governments, in accordance with international human rights standards and internationally recognized principles of due process, to take measures to prevent and combat terrorism and called on the international community to enhance cooperation in the fight against the spread of terrorism.

GENERAL ASSEMBLY ACTION

On 20 December, the General Assembly, on the recommendation of the Third Committee, adopted **resolution 48/122** without vote.

Human rights and terrorism

The General Assembly,

Guided by the principles embodied in the Charter of the United Nations, the Universal Declaration of Human Rights and the International Covenants on Human Rights,

Bearing in mind that the most essential and basic human right is the right to life,

Bearing in mind also the Vienna Declaration and Programme of Action, adopted by the World Conference on Human Rights, held at Vienna from 14 to 25 June 1993,

Reiterating that all Member States have an obligation to promote and protect human rights and fundamental freedoms, and also that every individual should strive to secure their universal and effective recognition and observance,

Seriously concerned at the gross violations of human rights perpetrated by terrorist groups,

Profoundly deploring the increasing number of innocent persons, including women, children and the elderly, killed, massacred and maimed by terrorists in indiscriminate and random acts of violence and terror, which cannot be justified under any circumstances,

Noting with great concern the growing connection between the terrorist groups and the illegal traffic in arms and drugs,

Mindful of the need to protect human rights of and guarantees for the individual in accordance with the relevant international human rights principles and instruments, particularly the right to life,

1. *Unequivocally condemns* all acts, methods and practices of terrorism in all its forms and manifestations, wherever and by whomever committed, as activities aimed at the destruction of human rights, fundamental freedoms and democracy, threatening the territorial integrity and security of States, destabilizing legitimately constituted Governments, undermining pluralistic civil society and having adverse consequences on the economic and social development of States;

2. *Calls upon* States, in accordance with international standards of human rights, to take all necessary and effective measures to prevent, combat and eliminate terrorism;

3. *Urges* the international community to enhance cooperation in the fight against the threat of terrorism at national, regional and international levels;

4. *Requests* the Secretary-General to transmit the text of the present resolution to all Member States and to competent specialized agencies and intergovernmental organizations;

5. *Decides* to consider this question at its forty-ninth session under the item entitled "Human rights questions".

General Assembly resolution 48/122

20 December 1993   Meeting 85   Adopted without vote

Approved by Third Committee (A/48/632/Add.2) without vote, 6 December (meeting 53); 25-nation draft (A/C.3/48/L.42); agenda item 114 (b).

Sponsors: Afghanistan, Albania, Algeria, Azerbaijan, Bosnia and Herzegovina, Colombia, Croatia, Cuba, Egypt, Guatemala, India, Kazakhstan, Kyrgyzstan, Morocco, Nigeria, Peru, Republic of Korea, Sierra Leone, Sri Lanka, Sudan, Tajikistan, the former Yugoslav Republic of Macedonia, Tunisia, Turkey, Turkmenistan.

Meeting numbers. GA 48th session: 3rd Committee 36-53; plenary 85.

Other aspects of human rights violations

Declaration on gross and large-scale human rights violations

In accordance with a 1992 Subcommission decision,[158] Stanislav Chernichenko (Russian Federation) submitted the proposed core text of a draft declaration defining gross and large-scale violations of human rights as an international crime.[159]

On 25 August,[160] the Subcommission recommended that the Commission appoint Mr. Chernichenko as Special Rapporteur to prepare a report on the recognition of gross and large-scale violations of human rights perpetrated on the orders of Governments or sanctioned by them as an international crime. It recommended that the Special Rapporteur include in his report a draft

declaration on the subject; it would consider the report in 1994.

Restitution for human rights violations

Human Rights Commission action. On 5 March,[161] the Commission endorsed a request made by its Subcommission in 1992[162] concerning the preparation by the Special Rapporteur on the right to restitution, compensation and rehabilitation for victims of gross violations of human rights and fundamental freedoms of a final report and its request that the Secretary-General provide the Special Rapporteur with all necessary assistance.

The Economic and Social Council, by **decision 1993/291** of 28 July, approved the Commission's endorsement of the Subcommission's requests.

Report of the Special Rapporteur. In July, the Subcommission's Special Rapporteur, Theo van Boven (Netherlands), submitted his final report,[163] in which he proposed basic principles and guidelines for a set of standards to strengthen the right to restitution, compensation and rehabilitation for victims of gross violations of human rights and fundamental freedoms. He discussed crime prevention and criminal justice and international humanitarian law, reviewed decisions and views of United Nations human rights bodies, and discussed compensation to victims of gross human rights violations resulting from the invasion and occupation of Kuwait by Iraq. He recommended that the United Nations adopt a set of principles and guidelines and include provisions on reparations in new human rights instruments. Further recommendations were made to States, specialized agencies, international treaty bodies, working groups, rapporteurs and NGOs.

Subcommission action. On 27 August,[164] the Subcommission decided to transmit the Special Rapporteur's study to the Commission with a view to its publication and dissemination, and to examine further in 1994 the proposed basic principles and guidelines and to establish, if necessary, a sessional working group with a view to adopting a body of such principles and guidelines. It asked the Secretary-General to invite Governments, intergovernmental organizations and NGOs to submit their comments on the proposed principles and guidelines.

Civil defence forces

Report of the Secretary-General. In January,[165] the Secretary-General summarized comments received from 18 Member States, two intergovernmental organizations and three NGOs concerning domestic law and practice relating to civil defence forces and the relationship between such forces and human rights.

Human Rights Commission action. On 9 March,[166] the Commission requested the Secretary-General to submit in 1994 a report containing a summary of additional information and comments received concerning civil defence forces and their relation to human rights protection and fundamental freedoms. It invited special rapporteurs and working groups concerned to continue to pay attention to the issue.

REFERENCES

[1]YUN 1970, p. 530, ESC res. 1503(XLVIII), 27 May 1970. [2]ESC res. 1990/41, 25 May 1990. [3]E/1993/23 (res. 1993/60). [4]Ibid. (res. 1993/61). [5]E/CN.4/1994/2 (res. 1993/10). [6]E/1993/23 (res. 1993/69). [7]E/CN.4/1993/48. [8]YUN 1981, p. 938. [9]YUN 1992, p. 767. [10]YUN 1967, p. 509. [11]YUN 1992, p. 778. [12]E/CN.4/1994/15. [13]E/1993/23 (res. 1993/9). [14]YUN 1966, pp. 419 & 423, GA res. 2200 A (XXI), annex, 16 Dec. 1966. [15]YUN 1965, p. 440, GA res. 2106 A (XX), annex, 21 Dec. 1965. [16]YUN 1977, p. 161, SC res. 418(1977), 4 Nov. 1977. [17]YUN 1992, p. 162, GA res. 47/116 A, 18 Dec. 1992. [18]E/CN.4/1994/2 (res. 1993/11). [19]A/48/525. [20]E/1993/23 (res. 1993/19). [21]E/CN.4/Sub.2/1993/11. [22]E/CN.4/Sub.2/1993/11/Add.1. [23]E/CN.4/1994/2 (res. 1993/1). [24]*Multilateral Treaties Deposited with the Secretary-General: Status as at 31 December 1993* (ST/LEG/SER.E/12), Sales No. E.94.V.11. [25]YUN 1973, p. 103, GA res. 3068(XXVIII), annex, 30 Nov. 1973. [26]YUN 1976, p. 575. [27]A/48/438. [28]E/CN.4/1993/54 & Corr.1. [29]E/CN.4/1993/52/Add.1-6. [30]E/1993/23 (res. 1993/10). [31]YUN 1978, p. 677. [32]E/1993/23 (res. 1993/18). [33]GA res. S-16/1, annex, 14 Dec. 1989. [34]YUN 1992, p. 781. [35]E/1993/95. [36]YUN 1992, p. 782. [37]Ibid., ESC res. 1992/12, 20 July 1992. [38]A/48/601. [39]E/1993/23 (res. 1993/75). [40]E/CN.4/1993/42. [41]YUN 1992, p. 785. [42]Ibid., p. 263. [43]YUN 1991, p. 161. [44]YUN 1966, p. 423, GA res. 2200 A (XXI), annex, 16 Dec. 1966. [45]E/1993/23 (res. 1993/66). [46]YUN 1977, p. 706. [47]YUN 1992, p. 787, GA dec. 47/428, 16 Dec. 1992. [48]YUN 1955, p. 209. [49]A/48/584. [50]E/1993/23 (dec. 1993/110). [51]E/CN.4/1993/49. [52]YUN 1992, p. 739. [53]E/CN.4/1993/46. [54]E/CN.4/1993/26. [55]YUN 1991, p. 798. [56]E/1993/23 (res. 1993/97). [57]E/CN.4/Sub.2/1993/14. [58]E/CN.4/1994/2 (res. 1993/12). [59]Ibid. (dec. 1993/108). [60]YUN 1992, p. 787. [61]E/CN.4/1993/41. [62]YUN 1992, p. 788. [63]E/CN.4/1993/41/Add.1. [64]E/1993/23 (res. 1993/62). [65]E/CN.4/Sub.2/1993/12. [66]E/CN.4/1994/2 (res. 1993/14). [67]A/48/526. [68]YUN 1991, p. 601. [69]A/48/526/Add.1. [70]E/CN.4/1993/45. [71]YUN 1992, p. 790. [72]E/1993/23 (res. 1993/74). [73]E/CN.4/1994/2 (res. 1993/20). [74]A/48/600. [75]S/26869. [76]A/48/600/Add.1. [77]E/CN.4/1993/37. [78]YUN 1984, p. 813, GA res. 39/46, annex, 10 Dec. 1984. [79]GA res. 44/25, annex, 20 Nov. 1989. [80]E/CN.4/1993/105. [81]E/1993/23 (res. 1993/73). [82]YUN 1992, p. 793, GA res. 47/144, 18 Dec. 1992. [83]E/CN.4/1994/2 (res. 1993/19). [84]A/48/578. [85]E/CN.4/1994/57. [86]E/1993/23 (res. 1993/76). [87]Ibid. (dec. 1993/111). [88]YUN 1992, p. 794. [89]E/CN.4/1994/2 (dec. 1993/107). [90]E/CN.4/1993/43. [91]E/1993/23 (res. 1993/65). [92]E/CN.4/1993/36. [93]E/1993/23 (dec. 1993/109). [94]YUN 1992, p. 795, GA res. 47/115, 16 Dec. 1992. [95]A/48/511. [96]YUN 1992, p. 795. [97]E/CN.4/1993/40. [98]E/1993/23 (res. 1993/72). [99]S/25274. [100]YUN 1992, p. 370, SC res. 780(1992), 6 Oct. 1992. [101]Ibid., p. 797. [102]S/26545. [103]E/CN.4/1993/50. [104]YUN 1992, p. 327. [105]A/48/92-S/25341. [106]E/1993/23 (res. 1993/7). [107]YUN 1948-49, p. 959, GA res. 260 A (III), annex, 9 Dec. 1948. [108]YUN 1992, p. 799, GA res. 47/147, 18 Dec. 1992. [109]E/CN.4/1994/2 (res. 1993/9). [110]Ibid. (res. 1993/17). [111]Ibid. (res. 1993/8). [112]E/CN.4/1994/3. [113]E/CN.4/1994/4. [114]E/CN.4/1994/6. [115]YUN 1992, p. 796. [116]E/CN.4/1994/8. [117]E/CN.4/1994/47. [118]E/CN.4/1994/110. [119]E/CN.4/1994/26/Add.1. [120]E/1993/23 (res. 1993/8). [121]E/CN.4/1993/92. [122]E/CN.4/1994/5. [123]E/CN.4/1993/39. [124]YUN 1992, p. 801. [125]E/1993/23 (res. 1993/63). [126]A/48/562. [127]E/CN.4/1993/11. [128]E/1993/23 (res. 1993/93). [129]YUN 1992, p. 222. [130]YUN 1991, p. 149, SC res. 693(1991), 20 May 1991. [131]E/CN.4/1993/96. [132]E/CN.4/1993/47. [133]E/1993/23 (res. 1993/68). [134]YUN 1991, p. 151. [135]E/CN.4/1994/2 (res. 1993/18). [136]A/48/561. [137]E/CN.4/1994/2 (res. 1993/23). [138]Ibid. (dec. 1993/105). [139]E/1993/23 (res. 1993/67). [140]YUN 1992, p. 429, SC res. 799(1992), 18 Dec. 1992. [141]A/48/577. [142]YUN 1992, p. 808. [143]E/CN.4/1993/44. [144]E/CN.4/1993/12. [145]E/CN.4/1993/13. [146]YUN 1992, p. 731. [147]E/CN.4/Sub.2/1993/12. [148]E/1993/23 (res. 1993/2 A). [149]Ibid. (res. 1993/2 B). [150]Ibid. (res. 1993/1). [151]Ibid. (res. 1993/3). [152]E/1990/22 (res. 1990/1). [153]YUN 1991, p. 612. [154]YUN 1992, p. 809. [155]E/1993/23 (res. 1993/70). [156]YUN 1992, p. 35. [157]E/CN.4/1994/2 (res. 1993/13). [158]YUN 1992, p. 810. [159]E/CN.4/Sub.2/1993/10 & Corr.1. [160]E/CN.4/1994/2 (res. 1993/30). [161]E/1993/23 (dec. 1993/107). [162]YUN 1992, p. 811. [163]E/CN.4/Sub.2/1993/8. [164]E/CN.4/1994/2 (res. 1993/29). [165]E/CN.4/1993/34. [166]E/1993/23 (res. 1993/54).

Other human rights questions

Additional Protocols I and II to the 1949 Geneva Conventions

In August 1993,[1] the Secretary-General provided information on the status of the two 1977 Protocols Additional to the Geneva Conventions of 12 August 1949 for the protection of war victims.[2] As at 16 July, 126 States had ratified or acceded to Protocol I (on protection of victims of international armed conflicts); 13 States—Albania, Armenia, Bosnia and Herzegovina, Burundi, Czech Republic, Egypt, Estonia, Greece, Kyrgystan, Republic of Moldova, Slovakia, Tajikistan, Zimbabwe—had done so since the Secretary-General's report in 1992.[3] All but 11 of the 126 also adhered to Protocol II (on protection of victims of non-international conflicts). Two States—France and the Philippines—adhered only to Protocol II.

Rights of the child

Convention on the Rights of the Child

Accessions and ratifications

As at 31 December 1993,[4] there were 154 parties to the Convention on the Rights of the Child, adopted by the General Assembly in 1989[5] and in force since 2 September 1990. In 1993, 28 States became parties to the Convention.

The Secretary-General reported on the status of the Convention in November 1993.[6]

CRC activities. In 1993, the Committee on the Rights of the Child held its third (11-29 January) and fourth (20 September–8 October) sessions, both at Geneva.[7]

The Committee considered initial reports from 11 States parties—Bolivia, Costa Rica, Egypt, El Salvador, Indonesia, Peru, Russian Federation, Rwanda, Sudan, Sweden, Viet Nam—under article 44 of the Convention. It recommended that the General Assembly request the Secretary-General to study ways to improve the protection of children from the adverse effects of armed conflicts and asked him to bring its recommendation to the Assembly's attention, which he did by a note of 3 August.[8] The working group established in 1992[3] to submit final proposals on the subject presented an oral report to the Committee on its activities (see below for action concerning children in armed conflicts). The Committee asked the Secretary-General to transmit to the Commission on Human Rights in 1994 a preliminary draft optional protocol on involvement of children in armed conflicts, which it prepared at its January session.[9] It made recommendations on the dissemination of information, cooperation with United Nations bodies and the establishment of a documentation unit on the rights of the child, and continued to discuss its participation in the preparatory activities for the 1993 World Conference on Human Rights.

In accordance with article 43 of the Convention, the Third Meeting of the States Parties to the Convention met (New York, 23 February) to elect five members of the Committee to replace those whose terms were due to expire on 28 February 1993.[10]

Human Rights Commission action. On 10 March,[11] the Commission called on States that had not done so to sign, ratify or accede to the Convention as a matter of priority and appealed to States parties that had made reservations to review the compatibility of their reservations with article 51 of the Convention and other relevant rules of international law. It asked the Secretary-General to continue to assist in disseminating information on the Convention and in its implementation with a view to promoting further ratification of or accession to it; to ensure the provision of staff and facilities for the effective performance of the Committee; and to report on the status of the Convention in 1994.

Sale of children, child prostitution and pornography

Report of the Special Rapporteur. In January,[12] Special Rapporteur Vitit Muntarbhorn (Thailand) submitted a report to the Commission on Human Rights on the sale of children for, among other things, adoption, labour, prostitution and pornography and organ transplants. He summarized communications which he had sent to five States, prompted by reports concerning situations affecting children's rights and calling for clarification and response. The Special Rapporteur discussed his 1992 visit to Australia to study the situation

there and recommended a number of preventive measures, among them: effective monitoring and law enforcement against criminal elements seeking to exploit children; a more active role by the private sector; improved information-gathering on child exploitation; making more visible the issues of child abuse and exploitation; enacting new laws on the sale of children; and improved law enforcement against the customers of child prostitution. Annexed to the report was a list of 46 States that had replied to a questionnaire on child prostitution and pornography,[13] together with a questionnaire on the sale of children's organs and a list of 24 States that had replied to it.

Human Rights Commission action. On 10 March,[14] the Commission appealed to Governments to cooperate with and assist the Special Rapporteur and asked him to continue to pay attention to insufficiently documented areas and to set short- and medium-term priorities in his recommendations. It also asked him to seek credible and reliable information from Governments, specialized agencies, intergovernmental organizations and NGOs. The Commission invited the Special Rapporteur to cooperate with the Committee, the Subcommission and its Working Group on Contemporary Forms of Slavery, as well as with other United Nations bodies dealing with questions covered by his mandate. It asked the Secretary-General to assist the Special Rapporteur to carry out his mandate and enable him to report in 1994.

GENERAL ASSEMBLY ACTION

On 20 December, the General Assembly, on the recommendation of the Third Committee, adopted **resolution 48/156** without vote.

Need to adopt efficient international measures for the prevention of the sale of children, child prostitution and child pornography

The General Assembly,

Recalling the Convention on the Rights of the Child, adopted in its resolution 44/25 of 20 November 1989,

Recalling also the World Declaration on the Survival, Protection and Development of Children and the Plan of Action for Implementing the World Declaration on the Survival, Protection and Development of Children in the 1990s, adopted by the World Summit for Children, held in New York in September 1990, and recalling that in the Declaration States made a solemn commitment to give priority to the rights of the child and to his or her survival, protection and development, thus contributing to the welfare of every society,

Mindful of the Vienna Declaration and Programme of Action, adopted by the World Conference on Human Rights, held at Vienna from 14 to 25 June 1993, which requires effective measures against female infanticide, harmful child labour, sale of children and organs, child prostitution, child pornography, as well as other forms of sexual abuse,

Bearing in mind Commission on Human Rights resolution 1992/74 of 5 March 1992, in which the Commission adopted the Programme of Action for the Prevention of the Sale of Children, Child Prostitution and Child Pornography,

Recognizing the enormous efforts made in this field by the United Nations, particularly the United Nations Children's Fund, the Committee on the Rights of the Child and the Special Rapporteur of the Commission on Human Rights on the sale of children, child prostitution and child pornography,

Deeply concerned by the persistence of the practice of the use of children for prostitution, sexual abuse and other activities, which may also often constitute exploitation of child labour,

Deeply disturbed by the persistence of the practice of the sale of children and other practices, which may be linked to related disappearances, illegal adoptions, abandonment, kidnapping and abductions for commercial purposes,

Regretting that one of the main difficulties found by the Special Rapporteur has been the lack of information on this issue,

Bearing in mind the different causes that influence the emergence and continuation of these special circumstances, including in particular poverty, natural disasters and armed conflicts, and their harmful effects on the rights of children,

Considering that it is necessary to redouble greater efforts at the national and international level to promote and protect the rights of children all over the world,

Expressing its interest in benefiting from the studies, conclusions and recommendations of the Special Rapporteur,

1. *Expresses great concern* at the growing number of incidents worldwide related to the sale of children, child prostitution and child pornography;

2. *Urges* Governments to continue searching for solutions as well as ways and means of enhancing international cooperation to eradicate such aberrant practices;

3. *Expresses its support* for the work of the Special Rapporteur appointed by the Commission on Human Rights to examine all over the world the question of the sale of children, child prostitution and child pornography, and urges him to continue his efforts in the discharge of his mandate;

4. *Urges* all Governments to collaborate with the Special Rapporteur and to assist him by providing him with all the requested information;

5. *Calls upon* those States which have not done so to become parties to the Convention on the Rights of the Child, and calls upon the States parties to the Convention to implement national measures aimed at fulfilling the provisions of the Convention;

6. *Requests* the Commission on Human Rights to consider, during its fiftieth session, the creation of a working group to study, as a matter of priority and in close contact with the Special Rapporteur, the elaboration of guidelines for a possible draft convention on the issues related to the sale of children, child prostitution and child pornography, as well as the basic measures required for preventing and eradicating these serious problems;

7. *Requests* the Centre for Human Rights of the Secretariat to transmit paragraph 6 above to the Committee on the Rights of the Child so that it can express its comments;

8. *Invites* the Special Rapporteur, within the framework of his mandate, to continue giving attention to the

economic, social, legal and cultural factors affecting these phenomena;

9. *Requests* the Special Rapporteur to submit a provisional report to the General Assembly at its forty-ninth session;

10. *Requests* the Secretary-General, from within existing resources, to provide the Special Rapporteur and the working group of the Commission on Human Rights with every necessary assistance;

11. *Decides* to consider this question at its forty-ninth session under the item entitled "Necessity of adopting effective measures for the promotion and protection of the rights of children throughout the world who are victims of especially difficult circumstances, including armed conflicts".

General Assembly resolution 48/156

20 December 1993   Meeting 85   Adopted without vote

Approved by Third Committee (A/48/634) without vote, 6 December (meeting 52); 42-nation draft (A/C.3/48/L.39/Rev.1); agenda item 172.

Sponsors: Antigua and Barbuda, Argentina, Australia, Bahamas, Barbados, Belize, Bolivia, Brazil, Burkina Faso, Cambodia, Chile, Colombia, Costa Rica, Côte d'Ivoire, Cuba, Dominica, Dominican Republic, Ecuador, El Salvador, Grenada, Guatemala, Guinea-Bissau, Guyana, Haiti, Honduras, India, Jamaica, Mexico, Mongolia, Morocco, Nicaragua, Panama, Paraguay, Peru, Philippines, Saint Kitts and Nevis, Saint Lucia, Saint Vincent and the Grenadines, Suriname, Trinidad and Tobago, Uruguay, Venezuela.

Meeting numbers. GA 48th session: 3rd Committee 36-52; plenary 85.

Programme of action

Pursuant to a 1992 Subcommission request,[15] the Working Group on Contemporary Forms of Slavery in July[16] presented replies received from 20 States, one specialized agency, one regional commission, two intergovernmental organizations and one NGO on measures adopted to implement the 1992 Programme of Action for the Prevention of the Sale of Children, Child Prostitution and Child Pornography.[13]

On 20 August,[17] the Subcommission decided to transmit the Group's report to the Commission in 1994. It requested the Secretary-General to invite Governments, United Nations bodies and intergovernmental organizations and NGOs to investigate allegations of the removal of organs from children and indicate measures taken to counteract that practice.

Child labour

On 10 March,[18] the Commission adopted the Programme of Action for the Elimination of the Exploitation of Child Labour and recommended that all States adopt legislative and administrative measures to carry it out. It urged United Nations bodies and intergovernmental organizations to bear in mind the Programme when drawing up policies and developing programmes related to children and the family. It also urged NGOs to adopt the Programme. It asked all States to report to the Subcommission on measures adopted to implement the Programme and on their efficacy. The Commission asked the Subcommission to submit a report every two years on the implementation of the Programme by States, and asked the

Under-Secretary-General for Human Rights to support the Subcommission in fulfilling that mandate. The Programme of Action was annexed to the Commission's resolution.

Children in armed conflicts

On 10 March,[(19)] the Commission, expressing its deep concern at the serious consequences of armed conflicts for children, who were often the main victims of the indiscriminate use of anti-personnel mines, asked all States to prevent such indiscriminate use and to protect and assist the victims. It asked relevant United Nations organizations and other intergovernmental organizations to intensify their efforts to assist child victims of anti-personnel mines and to support the activities of NGOs in that regard.

GENERAL ASSEMBLY ACTION

On 20 December, the General Assembly, on the recommendation of the Third Committee, adopted **resolution 48/157** without vote.

Protection of children affected by armed conflicts

The General Assembly,

Reaffirming its resolution 44/25 of 20 November 1989, in which it adopted the Convention on the Rights of the Child, and its resolution 3318(XXIX) of 14 December 1974, in which it proclaimed the Declaration on the Protection of Women and Children in Emergency and Armed Conflict,

Recalling that the Geneva Conventions of 12 August 1949 and the Additional Protocols thereto, of 1977, as well as article 38 of the Convention on the Rights of the Child, accord children special protection and treatment,

Recalling the World Declaration on the Survival, Protection and Development of Children and the Plan of Action for Implementing the World Declaration on the Survival, Protection and Development of Children in the 1990s, adopted by the World Summit for Children, held in New York in September 1990, and stressing the necessity of implementing their provisions,

Taking note of the report of the Committee on the Rights of the Child on its third session, held at Geneva from 11 to 29 January 1993, in particular its recommendation to the General Assembly that the Secretary-General should undertake a study of the ways and means of improving the protection of children from the adverse effects of armed conflicts,

Taking note also of Commission on Human Rights resolution 1993/83 of 10 March 1993,

Mindful of the strong support of the World Conference on Human Rights, held at Vienna from 14 to 25 June 1993, for the proposed study by the Secretary-General, as reflected in paragraph 50 of section II of the Vienna Declaration and Programme of Action,

Profoundly concerned about the grievous deterioration in the situation of children in many parts of the world as a result of armed conflicts, and convinced that immediate and concerted action is called for,

Convinced that children affected by armed conflicts require the special protection of the international community and that there is a need for all States to work towards the alleviation of their plight,

Recognizing the valuable work done in this field by United Nations bodies and organizations, as well as by other relevant intergovernmental and non-governmental organizations,

1. *Expresses grave concern* about the tragic situation of children in many parts of the world as a result of armed conflicts;

2. *Calls upon* States fully to respect the provisions of the Geneva Conventions of 12 August 1949 and the Additional Protocols thereto, of 1977, as well as those of the Convention on the Rights of the Child, which accord children affected by armed conflicts special protection and treatment;

3. *Urges* all Member States to continue seeking comprehensive improvement of the situation of children affected by armed conflicts with appropriate and concrete measures;

4. *Requests* bodies and organizations of the United Nations, as well as intergovernmental and non-governmental organizations, within the scope of their respective mandates, to cooperate in order to ensure more effective action in addressing the problem of children affected by armed conflicts;

5. *Requests* the Secretary-General to submit to the General Assembly at its forty-ninth session a report on those concrete measures which have been taken, pursuant to paragraphs 3 and 4 above, to alleviate the situation of children in armed conflict;

6. *Takes note with appreciation* of the report of the Committee on the Rights of the Child on its third session and the recommendations contained therein concerning the situation of children affected by armed conflict;

7. *Requests* the Secretary-General to appoint an expert, working in collaboration with the Centre for Human Rights of the Secretariat and the United Nations Children's Fund, to undertake a comprehensive study of this question, including the participation of children in armed conflict, as well as the relevance and adequacy of existing standards, and to make specific recommendations on ways and means of preventing children from being affected by armed conflicts and of improving the protection of children in armed conflicts and on measures to ensure effective protection of these children, including from indiscriminate use of all weapons of war, especially anti-personnel mines, and to promote their physical and psychological recovery and social reintegration, in particular, measures to ensure proper medical care and adequate nutrition, taking into account the recommendations by the World Conference on Human Rights and the Committee on the Rights of the Child;

8. *Requests* Member States and United Nations bodies and organizations, as well as other relevant intergovernmental and non-governmental organizations, including the Committee on the Rights of the Child, the United Nations Children's Fund, the Office of the United Nations High Commissioner for Refugees, the World Health Organization and the International Committee of the Red Cross, to contribute to the study requested in paragraph 7 above;

9. *Also requests* the Secretary-General to submit a progress report on the study to the General Assembly at its forty-ninth session;

10. *Invites* the Commission on Human Rights to consider the study at its fifty-first session;

11. *Decides* to consider this question at its forty-ninth session under the item entitled ''Necessity of adopting effective measures for the promotion and protection of the rights of children throughout the world who are victims of especially difficult circumstances, including armed conflicts''.

General Assembly resolution 48/157

20 December 1993   Meeting 85   Adopted without vote

Approved by Third Committee (A/48/634) without vote, 8 December (meeting 54); 74-nation draft (A/C.3/48/L.40), orally revised; agenda item 172.
Sponsors: Afghanistan, Andorra, Angola, Antigua and Barbuda, Argentina, Australia, Austria, Azerbaijan, Bahamas, Barbados, Belgium, Belize, Bolivia, Bosnia and Herzegovina, Botswana, Brazil, Burkina Faso, Cambodia, Cameroon, Canada, Chile, Colombia, Costa Rica, Côte d'Ivoire, Cuba, Cyprus, Denmark, Dominica, Dominican Republic, Ecuador, Egypt, El Salvador, Ethiopia, Finland, France, Grenada, Guatemala, Guinea-Bissau, Guyana, Haiti, Honduras, Iceland, Ireland, Jamaica, Kyrgyzstan, Liechtenstein, Mexico, Monaco, Mongolia, Morocco, Namibia, New Zealand, Nicaragua, Nigeria, Norway, Pakistan, Panama, Paraguay, Peru, Philippines, Portugal, Rwanda, Saint Kitts and Nevis, Saint Lucia, Saint Vincent and the Grenadines, Solomon Islands, Spain, Suriname, Sweden, Tajikistan, Togo, Trinidad and Tobago, Uruguay, Venezuela.
Financial implications. 5th Committee, A/48/798; S-G, A/C.3/48/L.82, A/C.5/48/49.
Meeting numbers. GA 48th session: 3rd Committee 36-54; 5th Committee, 43; plenary 85.

Street children

On 10 March,[20] the Commission called on all States that had not done so to become parties to the Convention on the Rights of the Child and called on the international community to support the efforts of States to improve the situation of street children by supporting development projects that had a positive effect on them. It recommended that the Committee on the Rights of the Child and other treaty bodies bear the plight of street children in mind when examining States parties' reports and called on special rapporteurs, special representatives and working groups to pay particular attention to the problem.

GENERAL ASSEMBLY ACTION

On 20 December, the General Assembly, on the recommendation of the Third Committee, adopted **resolution 48/136** without vote.

Plight of street children

The General Assembly,

Recalling its resolution 47/126 of 18 December 1992,

Taking note of Commission on Human Rights resolution 1993/81 of 10 March 1993,

Welcoming the special attention given to the rights of children by the World Conference on Human Rights, held at Vienna from 14 to 25 June 1993, and welcoming in particular section I, paragraph 21, of the Vienna Declaration and Programme of Action,

Recalling the Convention on the Rights of the Child as a major contribution to the protection of the rights of all children, including street children,

Reaffirming that children are a particularly vulnerable section of society whose rights require special protection and that children living under especially difficult circumstances, such as street children, deserve special attention, protection and assistance from their families and communities and as part of national efforts and international cooperation,

Recognizing that all children have the right to health, shelter and education, to an adequate standard of living and to freedom from violence and harassment,

Deeply concerned about the growing number of street children worldwide and the squalid conditions in which these children are often forced to live,

Profoundly concerned that the killing of and violence against street children threatens the most fundamental right of all, the right to life,

Alarmed at continuing serious offences of this nature against street children,

Recognizing the responsibility of Governments to investigate all cases of offences against children and to punish offenders,

Recognizing also that legislation *per se* is not enough to prevent violations of human rights, including those of street children, and that Governments should implement their laws and complement legislative measures with effective action, *inter alia*, in the fields of law enforcement and in the administration of justice,

Welcoming the efforts made by some Governments to take effective action to address the question of street children,

Welcoming also the publicity given to, and the increased awareness of, the plight of street children and the achievements of non-governmental organizations in promoting the rights of these children and in providing practical assistance to improve their situation, and expressing its appreciation for their continued efforts,

Welcoming further the valuable work of the United Nations Children's Fund and its National Committees in reducing the suffering of street children,

Noting with appreciation the important work carried out in this field by the United Nations, in particular the Committee on the Rights of the Child, the Special Rapporteur of the Commission on Human Rights on the sale of children, child prostitution and child pornography and the United Nations International Drug Control Programme,

Bearing in mind the diverse causes of the emergence and marginalization of street children, including poverty, rural-to-urban migration, unemployment, broken families, intolerance and exploitation, and that such causes are often aggravated and their solution made more difficult by serious socio-economic difficulties,

Bearing in mind also that in the Vienna Declaration and Programme of Action, the World Conference on Human Rights urged all States, with the support of international cooperation, to address the acute problem of children in especially difficult circumstances and urged that national and international mechanisms and programmes should be strengthened for the defence and protection of children, including street children,

Recognizing that the prevention and solution of certain aspects of this phenomenon could also be facilitated in the context of economic and social development,

1. *Expresses grave concern* at the continued growth in the number of incidents worldwide and at reports of street children being involved in or affected by serious crime, drug abuse, violence and prostitution;

2. *Urges* Governments to continue actively to seek comprehensive solutions to tackle the problems of street children and to take measures to restore their full participation in society and to provide, *inter alia*, adequate nutrition, shelter, health care and education;

3. *Strongly urges* Governments to respect fundamental human rights, particularly the right to life, and to take urgent measures to prevent the killing of street children and to combat torture and violence against them;

4. *Emphasizes* that strict compliance with the provisions of the Convention on the Rights of the Child constitutes a significant step towards solving the problems of street children, and calls upon all States that have not done so to become parties to the Convention as a matter of priority;

5. *Calls upon* the international community to support, through effective international cooperation, the efforts of States to improve the situation of street children, and encourages States parties to the Convention, in preparing their reports to the Committee on the Rights of the Child, to bear this problem in mind and to consider requesting, or indicating their need for, technical advice and assistance for initiatives aimed at improving the situation of street children, in accordance with article 45 of the Convention;

6. *Reiterates its invitation* to the Committee on the Rights of the Child to consider the possibility of a general comment on street children;

7. *Recommends* that the Committee on the Rights of the Child and other relevant treaty-monitoring bodies bear this growing problem in mind when examining reports from States parties;

8. *Invites* Governments, United Nations bodies and organizations and intergovernmental and non-governmental organizations to cooperate and to ensure greater awareness and more effective action to solve the problem of street children by, among other measures, supporting development projects that can have a positive impact on the situation of street children;

9. *Calls upon* special rapporteurs, special representatives and working groups of the Commission on Human Rights and the Subcommission on the Prevention of Discrimination and Protection of Minorities, within their mandates, to pay particular attention to the plight of street children;

10. *Decides* to consider the question further at its forty-ninth session under the item entitled "Human rights questions".

General Assembly resolution 48/136

20 December 1993   Meeting 85   Adopted without vote

Approved by Third Committee (A/48/632/Add.2) without vote, 6 December (meeting 53); 79-nation draft (A/C.3/48/L.66); agenda item 114 *(b)*.
Sponsors: Afghanistan, Andorra, Angola, Armenia, Australia, Austria, Belarus, Belgium, Benin, Botswana, Bolivia, Burkina Faso, Cambodia, Cameroon, Canada, Central African Republic, Chad, Colombia, Costa Rica, Côte d'Ivoire, Cyprus, Denmark, Dominican Republic, Ethiopia, Finland, France, Gabon, Gambia, Germany, Ghana, Greece, Guinea, Guinea-Bissau, Guyana, Haiti, Honduras, Iceland, India, Iraq, Ireland, Italy, Jamaica, Lesotho, Liechtenstein, Luxembourg, Madagascar, Malawi, Mali, Marshall Islands, Mexico, Monaco, Mongolia, Morocco, Namibia, Nepal, Netherlands, New Zealand, Nicaragua, Niger, Norway, Pakistan, Peru, Philippines, Portugal, Republic of Moldova, Russian Federation, Rwanda, Senegal, Sierra Leone, Slovenia, Spain, Swaziland, Sweden, Thailand, Togo, Turkey, Ukraine, United Kingdom, Uruguay.
Meeting numbers. GA 48th session: 3rd Committee 36-53; plenary 85.

Youth and human rights

Conscientious objection to military service

In 1993, the Commission on Human Rights had before it a report of the Secretary-General in which he presented information on conscientious objec-

tion to military service received from 24 Governments and one NGO.[21]

Women

Discrimination

In July 1993,[22] the Secretary-General reported on the implementation of a 1992 Subcommission resolution requesting information on the equality and empowerment of women.[23] He stated that, as at 1 June, information had been received from Senegal.

Violence against women

On 8 March,[24] the Commission, condemning human rights violations against women, requested special rapporteurs and working groups, in carrying out their mandates, to include in their reports information on human rights violations affecting women. It asked the secretariat to ensure that special rapporteurs, experts and working groups were fully apprised of the particular ways in which the rights of women were violated. The Commission decided to consider appointing in 1994 a special rapporteur on violence against women and asked the Secretary-General to consult with all United Nations human rights bodies on the implementation of its resolution. It asked him to report to the General Assembly in 1993 and to the Commission in 1994.

By **resolution 48/104** of 20 December, the Assembly proclaimed the Declaration on the Elimination of Violence against Women (see PART THREE, Chapter XIII).

Traditional practices affecting the health of women and children

On 25 August,[25] the Subcommission, welcoming Sri Lanka's offer to host a regional seminar on the elimination of harmful traditional practices affecting the health of women and children, recommended a draft text on the subject to be considered by the Commission in 1994.

Science and technology

Bioethics

On 10 March,[26] the Commission asked Governments, specialized agencies and other United Nations organizations, intergovernmental organizations and NGOs to inform the Secretary-General of activities being carried out to ensure that the life sciences were developing in a manner respectful of human rights. It also asked States to inform the Secretary-General of legislative or other measures taken on the subject. The Commission asked the Subcommission to consider ways to ensure that the life sciences developed in a manner respectful of human rights and to make recommendations to that effect. It asked the Secretary-General to report in 1995.

Computerized personal files

On 10 March,[27] the Commission, referring to the guidelines for the regulation of computerized personal data files,[28] adopted by the General Assembly in 1990,[29] requested the Secretary-General to report in 1995 on the application of the guidelines within the United Nations and on information collected from States, intergovernmental and regional organizations and NGOs concerning the follow-up to the guidelines.

On 20 December, the General Assembly, on the recommendation of the Third Committee, adopted **resolution 48/140** without vote.

Human rights and scientific and technological progress

The General Assembly,

Noting that scientific and technological progress is one of the decisive factors in the development of human society,

Bearing in mind the relevant provisions of the Universal Declaration of Human Rights, the International Covenant on Economic, Social and Cultural Rights, the International Covenant on Civil and Political Rights, and the Declaration on Social Progress and Development,

Reaffirming the importance of its resolution 45/95 of 14 December 1990, in which it adopted guidelines for the regulation of computerized personal data files, and its resolution 46/119 of 17 December 1991, in which it adopted the Principles for the Protection of Persons with Mental Illness and for the Improvement of Mental Health Care,

Welcoming with satisfaction Commission on Human Rights resolution 1993/91 entitled "Human rights and bioethics" and Commission decision 1993/113 entitled "Question of the follow-up to the guidelines for the regulation of computerized personal files", adopted on 10 March 1993,

Welcoming the relevant paragraphs of the Vienna Declaration and Programme of Action, adopted by the World Conference on Human Rights, held at Vienna from 14 to 25 June 1993,

Aware that everyone has the right to enjoy the benefits of scientific progress and its applications,

Reaffirming the need to respect human rights and fundamental freedoms and the dignity of the human person in the conditions of scientific and technological progress,

Noting that certain advances, notably in the biomedical and life sciences as well as in information technology, may have potentially adverse consequences for the integrity, dignity and human rights of the individual, and that illicit dumping of toxic and dangerous substances and waste potentially constitutes a serious threat to the human rights, the life and health of everyone,

Considering that the human being is in the centre of social and economic development,

Conscious that modern science and technology give the possibility to create material conditions for the prosperity of society and for the thorough development of the human person,

Recognizing the need for international cooperation so that all mankind can benefit from the achievements of scientific and technological progress and so that their use in favour of economic and social progress can be to the benefit of all,

Convinced of the need to develop life science ethics both nationally and internationally,

1. *Calls upon* all Member States to ensure that the achievements of scientific and technological progress and the intellectual potential of mankind are used for promoting and encouraging universal respect for human rights and fundamental freedoms;

2. *Once again calls upon* Member States to take the necessary measures to ensure that the results of science and technology are used only for the benefit of the human being and do not lead to the disturbance of the ecological environment, that is, *inter alia*, measures against the illicit dumping of toxic and dangerous products and waste;

3. *Emphasizes* the fact that many advances in scientific knowledge and technology in health, education, housing and other social spheres should be readily available to the populations as the heritage of humanity, with a view to sustainable development, taking into account the need to protect intellectual property rights;

4. *Requests* the specialized agencies and other United Nations bodies to inform the Secretary-General of the activities and programmes carried out to ensure development of life and technical sciences respectful of human rights, in order to contribute to the reports of the Secretary-General requested in resolution 1993/91 and decision 1993/113 of the Commission on Human Rights;

5. *Decides* to consider the question of human rights and scientific and technological progress at its fiftieth session under the item entitled "Human rights questions".

General Assembly resolution 48/140

20 December 1993   Meeting 85   Adopted without vote

Approved by Third Committee (A/48/632/Add.2) without vote, 13 December (meeting 56); 13-nation draft (A/C.3/48/L.77), orally revised and further amended by Ireland; agenda item 114 *(b)*.
Sponsors: Andorra, Argentina, Austria, Belarus, Belgium, Chile, Costa Rica, France, Guatemala, Madagascar, Monaco, Poland, Senegal.
Meeting numbers. GA 48th session: 3rd Committee 36-56; plenary 85.

Human rights and the environment

Human Rights Commission action. On 10 March,[30] the Commission endorsed a 1992 Subcommission request[23] that Special Rapporteur Fatma Zohra Ksentini (Algeria) be entrusted with preparing in 1993 a second progress report on human rights and the environment and that the Secretary-General be asked to give her all the assistance she might require.

The Economic and Social Council approved those requests by **decision 1993/292** of 28 July.

Report of the Special Rapporteur. In July, the Subcommission's Special Rapporteur submitted a second progress report,[31] reviewing developments regarding the recognition and implementation of environmental rights as human rights. She noted that environmental damage had direct effects on the enjoyment of human rights, such as the right to life, health, a satisfactory standard of living, sufficient food, housing, education, work, culture, non-discrimination, dignity and the harmonious development of one's personality, security of person and family, development and peace. She suggested that guidelines be drawn up to address the environmental aspects of universally recognized human rights and that a meeting of experts be organized to work out recommendations on incorporating the right to a satisfactory environment into the activities of human rights bodies. She also suggested that the right to a satisfactory environment be included in the agenda of the meeting of chairmen of human rights bodies. The Special Rapporteur further recommended that various themes be examined, among them, the rights of women and the environment, children and the environment, racial discrimination and the environment, interaction of the environment with economic, social and cultural rights, the right to life and the environment, and environment and development. She also proposed establishing a mechanism for monitoring situations, possibly in the form of a special rapporteur. The Special Rapporteur's first progress report was submitted in 1992.[23]

Subcommission action. On 25 August,[32] the Subcommission requested the Special Rapporteur to submit in 1994 a final report, including recommendations aimed at developing basic principles and guidelines concerning human rights and the environment. It asked the Secretary-General to organize an expert meeting prior to the final report's preparation to draw up recommendations on incorporating the right to environment in the activities of human rights bodies. The Subcommission asked him to invite Governments, United Nations bodies, specialized agencies, intergovernmental organizations and NGOs, indigenous peoples' organizations and international human rights organizations to provide the Special Rapporteur with information relating to her report. It also asked him to provide the Special Rapporteur with all the assistance she needed. The Subcommission recommended a draft decision for adoption by the Commission in 1994.

Movement and dumping of toxic and dangerous products and wastes

By a roll-call vote of 34 to 1, with 17 abstentions, the Commission, on 10 March,[33] welcomed the final declaration adopted by the 1992 regional meeting for Africa of the World Conference on Human Rights,[34] especially where it related to the environmental consequences of dumping toxic and dangerous products and wastes and its effect on human life. It invited Governments, through legislative and other measures, to prevent illegal international traffic in such products. It also in-

vited the United Nations Environment Programme, ILO, the World Health Organization, the International Atomic Energy Agency and the Organization of African Unity and other regional organizations to intensify their cooperation and assistance on environmentally sound management of toxic chemicals, including their transboundary movement. The Commission decided to continue consideration of the subject in 1995.

Human rights of disabled persons

Human Rights Commission action. On 5 March,[35] the Commission expressed its appreciation to the United Nations Centre for Social Development and Humanitarian Affairs for its efforts to coordinate and supervise the implementation of the 1982 World Programme of Action concerning Disabled Persons.[36] It appealed to Member States to highlight the observance of the International Day of Disabled Persons on 3 December every year and encouraged them to implement the standard rules on equal opportunities for disabled persons. The Commission invited human rights treaty bodies to monitor the compliance of States with their commitments under the relevant human rights instruments to ensure the full enjoyment of those rights by disabled persons.

Subcommission action. On 27 August,[37] the Subcommission requested the Commission to take into consideration the recommendations of its Special Rapporteur, Leandro Despouy (Argentina),[38] and to appoint an international ombudsman for the human rights of disabled persons. It asked the Secretary-General to report to the Commission and the Subcommission on the coordination efforts of United Nations organs and bodies concerned with the protection of disabled persons, and to establish a mechanism to facilitate such coordination and cooperation.

REFERENCES

[1]A/INF/48/3. [2]YUN 1977, p. 706. [3]YUN 1992, p. 812. [4]*Multilateral Treaties Deposited with the Secretary-General: Status as at 31 December 1993* (ST/LEG/SER.E/12), Sales No. E.94.V.11. [5]GA res. 44/25, annex, 20 Nov. 1989. [6]E/CN.4/1994/83. [7]A/49/41. [8]A/48/280. [9]CRC/C/16. [10]CRC/SP/9 & Add.1. [11]E/1993/23 (res. 1993/78). [12]E/CN.4/1993/67 & Add.1. [13]YUN 1992, p. 814. [14]E/1993/23 (res. 1993/82). [15]YUN 1992, p. 747. [16]E/CN.4/Sub.2/1993/31 & Add.1. [17]E/CN.4/1994/2 (res. 1993/5). [18]E/1993/23 (res. 1993/79). [19]Ibid. (res. 1993/83). [20]Ibid. (res. 1993/81). [21]E/CN.4/1993/68 & Add.1-3. [22]E/CN.4/Sub.2/1993/33. [23]YUN 1992, p. 816. [24]E/1993/23 (res. 1993/46). [25]E/CN.4/1994/2 (res. 1993/33). [26]E/1993/23 (res. 1993/91). [27]Ibid. (dec. 1993/113). [28]E/CN.4/1990/72. [29]GA res. 45/95, 14 Dec. 1990. [30]E/1993/23 (dec. 1993/114). [31]E/CN.4/Sub.2/1993/7. [32]E/CN.4/1994/2 (res. 1993/32). [33]E/1993/23 (res. 1993/90). [34]A/CONF.157/PC/57. [35]E/1993/23 (res. 1993/29). [36]YUN 1982, p. 980. [37]E/CN.4/1994/2 (res. 1993/22). [38]YUN 1991, p. 627.

Chapter XI

Health, food and nutrition

The global epidemic of acquired immunodeficiency syndrome (AIDS), added to the ills of malaria, diarrhoeal diseases, hunger, nutritional deficiencies and disabilities, continued to challenge the efforts of the United Nations in 1993.

Several United Nations programmes and agencies participated in the fight against the human immunodeficiency virus (HIV), which causes AIDS. The World Health Organization (WHO) continued its Global Programme on AIDS, and the United Nations Development Programme reported on assessments of its HIV and Development Programme.

The Economic and Social Council, in July, supported several recommendations for improved coordination both within and outside the United Nations system in the fight against malaria, cholera and diarrhoeal diseases—diseases that affect several hundred million people and kill some four million of them each year.

In December, the General Assembly adopted Standard Rules on the Equalization of Opportunities for Persons with Disabilities (resolution 48/96). The United Nations Voluntary Fund on Disability came into operation at the beginning of 1993, replacing the fund for the United Nations Decade of Disabled Persons, which ended in 1992.

The World Food Programme (WFP)—a joint undertaking of the United Nations and the Food and Agriculture Organization of the United Nations (FAO)—provided food to 47 million people. Most disasters during the year were the result of acts of man, and 83 per cent of new WFP commitments were in emergency relief.

Health

Primary health care

The United Nations Children's Fund/World Health Organization (UNICEF/WHO) Joint Committee on Health Policy held its twenty-ninth session at Geneva on 1 and 2 February,[1] with the main purpose of recommending collaborative action to help countries achieve the goals of the 1990 World Summit for Children.

The Committee recommended that the Executive Boards of UNICEF and WHO reinforce complementary action to strengthen primary health

care programmes; intensify research; support training, capacity-building, intersectoral cooperation and integrated approaches; focus on those most in need; and mobilize resources to augment national efforts in those areas. It recommended that every effort be made to follow up on the goals of the World Summit for Children, giving special attention to HIV/AIDS in children. The Committee endorsed intermediate goals to help achieve the longer-term targets of the Summit (see PART THREE, Chapter XIV).

The Committee also recommended support for: the management of district health systems in developing countries; the Bamako Initiative (see below); implementation of the ''baby-friendly'' hospital initiative; the prevention and control of AIDS in women and children; healthy life-styles for youth; health education in schools; hygiene education and community water supply and sanitation; and malaria control.

The UNICEF Executive Board, in May,[2] welcomed the Joint Committee's report and endorsed its recommendations.

Bamako Initiative

At its 1993 session, the Executive Board of UNICEF considered a February interim progress report[3] on the Bamako Initiative,[4] adopted by African Ministers of Health in 1987 to improve the quality of primary health care in sub-Saharan Africa through community participation in financing and managing local health services. The report discussed key aspects of the Initiative in Africa, emphasizing the role of the household in changing health behaviour and status. It focused on countries that had taken up the Initiative in the previous year and concluded, on the basis of experience so far, that its implementation could be accelerated if there were a much broader mobilization of financial resources, either directly or through UNICEF.

AIDS prevention and control

In response to a 1992 General Assembly request,[5] the Secretary-General, in a May 1993 note,[6] submitted to the Economic and Social Council the report of the Director-General of WHO on implementation of the global strategy for the prevention and control of AIDS, endorsed by the Assembly in 1987.[7]

The Director-General reviewed the global AIDS situation, the evolution of the global strategy, and the activities of WHO's Global Programme on AIDS in 1992. He also outlined activities by United Nations organizations and specialized agencies and described the coordination of HIV/AIDS activities within the United Nations system.

On 21 December, in **decision 48/452**, the General Assembly took note of the Secretary-General's note.

UNDP action. In a report to the Governing Council of the United Nations Development Programme (UNDP),[8] the UNDP Administrator commented on the analysis and recommendations of an external and independent assessment, undertaken by UNDP's Central Evaluation Office, of country-level activities to address the HIV epidemic. The report also discussed assessments of UNDP's HIV and Development Programme, established in 1992.[9]

The Administrator stated that UNDP had a significant body of knowledge about effective approaches to the epidemic and that the challenge for UNDP and other institutions was to find ways to put those lessons and insights into practice quickly.

The Governing Council, on 18 June,[10] took note of the report and encouraged the Administrator to adopt a community-based and multisectoral approach to HIV and AIDS at the country level. It supported the 1993 World Health Assembly request that the WHO Director-General study, in close consultation with all organizations and bodies concerned, the feasibility of establishing a joint, co-sponsored United Nations Programme on HIV and AIDS. The Governing Council requested the UNDP Administrator to cooperate fully in the consultative process established by the World Health Assembly for that study.

ECONOMIC AND SOCIAL COUNCIL ACTION

On 29 July, on the recommendation of its Economic Committee, the Economic and Social Council adopted **resolution 1993/51** without vote.

Coordination of United Nations activities related to the human immunodeficiency virus/acquired immunodeficiency syndrome (HIV/AIDS)

The Economic and Social Council,

Taking note with appreciation of the report of the Director-General of the World Health Organization on the implementation of the global strategy for the prevention and control of AIDS and on the coordination of HIV/AIDS activities at the global and country levels,

Welcoming the establishment of the Task Force on HIV/AIDS Coordination by the Management Committee of the Global Programme on AIDS, with a two-year mandate,

Taking note of decisions 93/14 and 93/27 A of 18 June 1993 adopted by the Governing Council of the United Nations Development Programme at its fortieth session,

1. *Welcomes* the report of the Director-General of the World Health Organization and invites the World Health Organization and other relevant organizations and bodies of the United Nations system to continue their efforts in fighting, at all levels, the HIV/AIDS pandemic, giving due attention to its multisectoral aspects;

2. *Supports fully* World Health Assembly resolution WHA46.37 of 14 May 1993, in which the Director-General of the World Health Organization is requested to study, in close collaboration with all organizations and bodies of the United Nations system concerned, the feasibility and practicability of establishing a joint and co-sponsored United Nations programme on HIV and AIDS and to develop options for such a programme;

3. *Calls upon* the heads of the United Nations Development Programme, the United Nations Population Fund and the United Nations Children's Fund, and invites the heads of the United Nations Educational, Scientific and Cultural Organization and the World Bank, to cooperate fully in the consultative process established in World Health Assembly resolution WHA46.37 to carry out the study and calls upon the Task Force on HIV/AIDS Coordination, established by the Management Committee of the Global Programme on AIDS, to participate actively in this consultative process;

4. *Requests* the Secretary-General to invite the Director-General of the World Health Organization to include the outcome of the above-mentioned study in the next biennial report on progress in the implementation of the global strategy for the prevention and control of AIDS, to be submitted to the General Assembly through the Economic and Social Council.

Economic and Social Council resolution 1993/51

29 July 1993   Meeting 45   Adopted without vote

Approved by Economic Committee (E/1993/113) without vote, 26 July (meeting 15); 19-nation draft (E/1993/C.1/L.5), orally amended based on informal consultations; agenda item 15 *(m)*.

Sponsors: Algeria, Australia, Austria, Canada, Colombia, Denmark, Finland, Morocco, Netherlands, Romania, Senegal, Sweden, Switzerland, Tunisia, Ukraine, United States, Uruguay, Venezuela, Zimbabwe.

Malaria and diarrhoeal diseases

At its organizational session in February 1993, the Economic and Social Council, by **decision 1993/205**, decided that one of two themes for the coordination segment of the Council's substantive session should be the coordination of United Nations activities in the struggle against malaria and diarrhoeal diseases, cholera in particular.

The Secretary-General submitted a June report[11] on coordinated United Nations activities, noting that several hundred million cases of malaria and diarrhoeal diseases resulted in about four million deaths each year and were a major impediment to social and economic development.

The Secretary-General made a number of recommendations for improving global and regional cooperation against these diseases. They included: the definition of broad policies for development; the strengthening of technical and managerial leadership within the lead agencies; expanded research and exchanges of information; the strengthening of early-warning systems to prevent and control epidemics; the need for balance between investments in specific disease interventions and general health infrastructure; and the need for more effective monitoring, communication and agency collaboration in the fight against malaria and diarrhoeal diseases. The Secretary-General also recommended, among other things, the formation of country-level coordinating groups, convened by the host Government and composed of concerned United Nations and non-governmental organizations and other relevant bodies.

At the coordination segment of its substantive session in July, the Economic and Social Council welcomed the Secretary-General's report and supported its recommendations. It suggested, however, that greater specificity was needed in the plans, targets, resource allocations and implementation schedules of United Nations and Bretton Woods institutions to ensure improved coordination and implementation of programmes in developing countries.

The Council stated that malaria and diarrhoeal diseases could be prevented and controlled with currently available tools, but better instruments and coordination were needed to ensure the effective use of resources. Continued investments were also needed for development and research activities.

The Council requested that the Secretary-General, in collaboration with WHO and other relevant organs, prepare a report on the implementation of these recommendations, specifying goals and workplans, time-frames and resources needed to achieve them.

Disabled persons

Implementation of the Programme of Action

At its 1993 session (Vienna, 8-17 February), the Commission for Social Development considered a note by the Secretary-General,[12] containing the final report of a 1992 expert group meeting convened at Vancouver, Canada,[13] to develop a long-term strategy for implementing the World Programme of Action concerning Disabled Persons to the year 2000 and beyond. The Programme of Action, which provided a policy framework for improving the status of disabled persons, was adopted by the General Assembly in 1982[14] in the context of the United Nations Decade of Disabled Persons (1983-1992).[15]

In October,[16] the Secretary-General submitted a report on the implementation of the World Programme of Action, which discussed international cooperation, related activities of the United Nations and the monitoring of major policy documents in the field of disability. The Secretary-General stated that expectations for the United Nations Decade of Disabled Persons had not been fully realized and that the major challenge of the

post-Decade era would be to adopt activities with direct benefits for people with disabilities.

He noted that the General Assembly encouraged the consideration of disability issues at several major international events between 1993 and 1995, including the 1993 World Conference on Human Rights, the International Year of the Family (1994), the 1994 International Conference on Population and Development, the 1995 Fourth World Conference on Women, and the 1995 World Summit for Social Development.

The Working Group of Ministers, established in 1992 by the International Conference of Ministers Responsible for the Status of Persons with Disabilities,[17] met twice. The first meeting, held in January in Paris, established an international secretariat for the Conference at Montreal, Canada. The second session, at Montreal in April, established two committees on legal, financial and operational issues.

The United Nations Secretariat and the Government of Finland were preparing a manual on the integration of disability issues into national planning and development projects, with a view to their completion and field testing in 1994. Four regional training seminars to strengthen national coordinating committees on disability were scheduled for 1993 and 1994. One was conducted in Nepal in May 1993 for the South Asian Association for Regional Cooperation.

The Secretariat continued to collect and publish statistical data on disability, and the International Disability Statistics Database (DISTAT, version 2) was being prepared by the Statistical Office of the United Nations for dissemination in 1993.

On 20 December, in **decision 48/428**, the General Assembly took note of the Secretary-General's report.

ECONOMIC AND SOCIAL COUNCIL ACTION

On 27 July, on the recommendation of its Social Committee, the Economic and Social Council adopted **resolution 1993/21** without vote.

Positive and full inclusion of persons with disabilities in all aspects of society and the leadership role of the United Nations in the process
The Economic and Social Council
Recommends to the General Assembly the adoption of the following draft resolution:
[For text, see General Assembly resolution 48/95 below.]

Economic and Social Council resolution 1993/21
27 July 1993   Meeting 43   Adopted without vote

Approved by Social Committee (E/1993/106) without vote, 14 July (meeting 10); draft by Commission for Social Development (E/1993/24); agenda item 20.

GENERAL ASSEMBLY ACTION

On 20 December, on the recommendation of the Third (Social, Humanitarian and Cultural) Committee, the General Assembly adopted **resolution 48/95** without vote.

Positive and full inclusion of persons with disabilities in all aspects of society and the leadership role of the United Nations therein

The General Assembly,

Mindful of the pledge made by States, under the Charter of the United Nations, to take action jointly and separately, in cooperation with the United Nations, to promote higher standards of living, full employment, and conditions of economic and social progress and development,

Reaffirming the commitment to human rights and fundamental freedoms, social justice and the dignity and worth of the human person proclaimed in the Charter,

Recalling in particular the international standards of human rights laid down in the Universal Declaration of Human Rights,

Underlining that the rights proclaimed in those instruments should be ensured equally to all individuals without discrimination,

Recalling the provisions safeguarding the rights of women with disabilities in the Convention on the Elimination of All Forms of Discrimination against Women,

Having regard to the Declaration on the Rights of Disabled Persons, the Declaration on the Rights of Mentally Retarded Persons, the Declaration on Social Progress and Development, the Principles for the Protection of Persons with Mental Illness and for the Improvement of Mental Health Care and other relevant instruments adopted by the General Assembly,

Also having regard to the relevant conventions and recommendations adopted by the International Labour Organisation, with particular reference to participation in employment without discrimination for persons with disabilities,

Mindful of the relevant recommendations and work of the United Nations Educational, Scientific and Cultural Organization, in particular the World Declaration on Education for All, and of the work of the World Health Organization, the United Nations Children's Fund and other concerned organizations,

Recognizing that the World Programme of Action concerning Disabled Persons, adopted by the General Assembly in its resolution 37/52 of 3 December 1982, and the definition therein of equalization of opportunities reflect the determination of the international community to ensure that the various international instruments and recommendations will be put to practical, concrete and effective use in improving the quality of life of persons with disabilities and their families and communities,

Acknowledging that the objective of the United Nations Decade of Disabled Persons (1983-1992) to implement the World Programme of Action is still valid and requires urgent and continued action,

Recalling that the World Programme of Action is based on concepts that are equally valid in developed and developing countries,

Convinced that intensified efforts are needed to achieve the full and equal enjoyment of human rights and full participation and inclusion in society of persons with disabilities,

Recognizing that persons with disabilities, their families and representatives and organizations concerned with the needs of persons with disabilities must be ac-

tive partners with States in the planning and implementation of all measures affecting their civil, political, economic, social and cultural rights,

Recalling Economic and Social Council resolution 1990/26 of 24 May 1990, and reaffirming the specific measures required for the attainment of full equality by persons with disabilities, enumerated in detail in the World Programme of Action,

Reaffirming the commitment of the Commission for Social Development to the provisions and rules set out in the ongoing process of elaborating standard rules on the equalization of opportunities for persons with disabilities,

Recognizing also the essential role of the United Nations and the Commission for Social Development in providing leadership and positive guidance to encourage worldwide change by equalizing opportunities, promoting independence and ensuring the full inclusion and participation in society of all persons with disabilities,

Seeking to ensure effective implementation of measures to promote the full inclusion of persons with disabilities in all aspects of society and to affirm the leadership role of the United Nations in that process,

1. *Calls upon* the Secretary-General to maintain the integrity and the identity of the United Nations programme on disabled persons, including the United Nations Voluntary Fund on Disability, in order to promote the equalization of opportunities and full inclusion in society of persons with disabilities;

2. *Urges* the Secretary-General to strengthen, through redeployment of resources, the United Nations programme on disabled persons in order to enable it:

(*a*) To represent the needs of persons with disabilities and their families and communities throughout the United Nations system;

(*b*) To ensure effective coordination and streamlining of efforts to respond to the needs of persons with disabilities, through policy formulation, advocacy and liaison, among all bodies within the United Nations system, particularly the International Labour Organisation, the World Health Organization, the United Nations Educational, Scientific and Cultural Organization, the United Nations Development Programme and the United Nations Children's Fund;

(*c*) To promote equal opportunities and full participation of persons with disabilities and their families and representatives within the United Nations system itself;

(*d*) In cooperation with Member States, bodies within the United Nations system, non-governmental organizations and other appropriate agencies, to extend technical assistance and disseminate information in order to enhance the capacity of Member States to develop, implement and evaluate their efforts to equalize opportunities and provide for the full inclusion in society of persons with disabilities;

3. *Requests* the Secretary-General to report biennially to the General Assembly on the progress of efforts to ensure the equalization of opportunities and full inclusion of persons with disabilities in the various bodies of the United Nations system;

4. *Also requests* the Secretary-General to consider, in view of the importance of ensuring that the needs of persons with disabilities and their families and communities are represented in an equitable manner, strengthening and upgrading the status of the Disabled Persons Unit of the Secretariat through redeployment of resources;

5. *Reaffirms* that the issues of equalization of opportunities and full inclusion in society for persons with disabilities will be an important part of the preparatory process and the agenda of the World Summit for Social Development to be held at Copenhagen on 11 and 12 March 1995;

6. *Welcomes with satisfaction* the commitment of the Commission for Social Development to ensuring that the needs of persons with disabilities and their families and communities will continue to be addressed in all of its work.

General Assembly resolution 48/95

20 December 1993   Meeting 85   Adopted without vote

Approved by Third Committee (A/48/627) without vote, 28 October (meeting 18); draft by ESC (A/C.3/48/L.2); agenda item 109.
Meeting numbers. GA 48th session: 3rd Committee 11-19, 21, 32; plenary 85.

International Day of Disabled Persons

In 1993, the General Assembly recalled with satisfaction the first International Day of Disabled Persons, held on 3 December 1992.[18] It appealed to Governments to observe the Day and reiterated the need to involve disabled persons and their organizations in decisions regarding its celebration.

ECONOMIC AND SOCIAL COUNCIL ACTION

On 27 July, on the recommendation of its Social Committee, the Economic and Social Council adopted **resolution 1993/18** without vote.

International Day of Disabled Persons

The Economic and Social Council

Recommends to the General Assembly the adoption of the following draft resolution:

[For text, see General Assembly resolution 48/97 below.]

Economic and Social Council resolution 1993/18

27 July 1993   Meeting 43   Adopted without vote

Approved by Social Committee (E/1993/106) without vote, 14 July (meeting 10); draft by Commission for Social Development (E/1993/24); agenda item 20.

GENERAL ASSEMBLY ACTION

On 20 December, on the recommendation of the Third Committee, the General Assembly adopted **resolution 48/97** without vote.

International Day of Disabled Persons

The General Assembly,

Recalling all its relevant resolutions, including resolutions 37/52 of 3 December 1982, by which it adopted the World Programme of Action concerning Disabled Persons, and 37/53 of 3 December 1982, in which, *inter alia,* it proclaimed the period 1983-1992 the United Nations Decade of Disabled Persons as a long-term plan of action,

Recalling also its request to the Secretary-General, made in its resolution 45/91 of 14 December 1990, to shift the focus of the United Nations programme on disabled persons from awareness-raising to action, with the aim of achieving a society for all by the year 2010,

Recalling further its resolution 47/3 of 14 October 1992 proclaiming 3 December as the International Day of Disabled Persons,

Noting that, despite an appreciable increase in activities designed to enhance public awareness of the needs and circumstances of people with disabilities and of related issues, there continues to be a need for sustained efforts to overcome physical and social barriers to the full equality and participation of disabled persons,

Aware of the need for broader and more vigorous action and measures at all levels to fulfil the objectives of the Decade and the World Programme of Action,

Bearing in mind that the purpose of the World Programme of Action is to promote effective measures for the prevention of disability, for rehabilitation and for the realization of the goals of full participation of disabled persons in social life and development and of equality, which means opportunities equal to those of the entire population and an equal share in the improvement in living conditions resulting from social and economic development,

1. *Notes with satisfaction* the number of Member States that celebrated the first International Day of Disabled Persons on 3 December 1992;

2. *Appeals* to all Governments to observe the International Day of Disabled Persons, using this opportunity to take the lead in awakening the consciousness of populations regarding the gains to be derived by individuals and society from the integration of disabled persons into every area of social, economic and political life;

3. *Reiterates* the need to involve disabled persons and their organizations in decisions on all matters of concern to them, including the celebration of the International Day of Disabled Persons;

4. *Invites* Member States to consider a way of linking, each year, the observance of the International Day of Disabled Persons with important United Nations events such as the World Conference on Human Rights, held at Vienna from 14 to 25 June 1993, the International Year of the Family, to be observed in 1994, the International Conference on Population and Development, to be held at Cairo in September 1994, the World Summit for Social Development, to be held at Copenhagen in March 1995, and the Fourth World Conference on Women: Action for Equality, Development and Peace, to be held at Beijing in September 1995;

5. *Requests* the Secretary-General to report to the Commission for Social Development at its thirty-fourth session on measures taken by Member States to observe the International Day of Disabled Persons.

General Assembly resolution 48/97

20 December 1993   Meeting 85   Adopted without vote

Approved by Third Committee (A/48/627) without vote, 28 October (meeting 18); draft by ESC (A/C.3/48/L.4); agenda item 109.
Meeting numbers. GA 48th session: 3rd Committee 11-19, 21, 32; plenary 85.

UN Voluntary Fund

In accordance with a 1992 Economic and Social Council decision,[19] the Voluntary Fund for the United Nations Decade of Disabled Persons was renamed the United Nations Voluntary Fund on Disability, effective 1 January 1993.

The Fund, under its new name and mandate, was to be used to strengthen technical cooperation activities through the co-financing of field-based projects, with special emphasis on least developed countries and disadvantaged groups.

From 1980 to 1992, the Fund provided more than $3.2 million in co-financing grants to 187 disability-related projects. The majority of projects supported training for disabled persons in developing countries, closely followed by support for technical exchange programmes, support for organizations of and for disabled persons, and data collection and applied research.

ECONOMIC AND SOCIAL COUNCIL ACTION

On 27 July, on the recommendation of its Social Committee, the Economic and Social Council adopted **resolution 1993/20** without vote.

Development of a plan of action to implement the long-term strategy to further the implementation of the World Programme of Action concerning Disabled Persons

The Economic and Social Council,

Recalling General Assembly resolution 45/91 of 14 December 1990, in which the Assembly invited Member States, specialized agencies and other organizations and bodies of the United Nations system and intergovernmental and non-governmental organizations to implement the agenda for action until the end of the United Nations Decade of Disabled Persons and beyond and the preliminary outline of a long-term strategy to the year 2000 and beyond: a society for all,

Taking note of the deliberations of the General Assembly at its forty-seventh session and of the Commission for Social Development at its thirty-third session on the subject of the long-term strategy,

Emphasizing the need to take rapid action in this connection,

Recalling its resolution 1991/9 of 30 May 1991, in which it recommended that a meeting of experts, to be funded by voluntary contributions, should be held in conjunction with the conference entitled "Independence 1992", to be organized in Canada, with the primary objective of drawing up a long-term strategy to implement the World Programme of Action concerning Disabled Persons to the year 2000 and beyond,

Taking note with appreciation of the report of the United Nations Expert Group Meeting on a Long-Term Strategy to Further the Implementation of the World Programme of Action concerning Disabled Persons to the Year 2000 and Beyond, held at Vancouver, Canada, from 25 to 29 April 1992, and of the important input of non-governmental organizations of persons with disabilities,

Recognizing that the report represents a significant step forward in the development of a plan of action to implement the long-term strategy,

1. *Requests* the Secretary-General to seek the views of Member States on the strategy outlined in the report of the United Nations Expert Group Meeting on a Long-Term Strategy to Further the Implementation of the World Programme of Action concerning Disabled Persons to the Year 2000 and Beyond;

2. *Also requests* the Secretary-General to develop a draft plan of action based on those views, the World Programme of Action concerning Disabled Persons, the report of the Expert Group Meeting, the report of the ad hoc open-ended working group to elaborate standard rules on the equalization of opportunities for disabled persons and other recent developments, as appropriate;

3. *Recommends* that the draft plan of action include priorities and a time-frame for implementation and that it be submitted to the General Assembly for consideration at its forty-eighth session and for approval at its forty-ninth session;

4. *Requests* that the draft plan of action be developed in consultation with the international non-governmental organizations of persons with disabilities having consultative status with the Economic and Social Council.

Economic and Social Council resolution 1993/20

27 July 1993   Meeting 43   Adopted without vote

Approved by Social Committee (E/1993/106) without vote, 14 July (meeting 10); draft by Commission for Social Development (E/1993/106), orally amended; agenda item 20.

GENERAL ASSEMBLY ACTION

On 20 December, on the recommendation of the Third Committee, the General Assembly adopted **resolution 48/99** without vote.

Towards full integration of persons with disabilities into society: a continuing world programme of action

The General Assembly,

Recalling all its relevant resolutions, including resolutions 37/52 and 37/53 of 3 December 1982, 46/96 of 16 December 1991 and 47/88 of 16 December 1992, and recalling also Economic and Social Council decision 1992/276 of 30 July 1992 and Commission on Human Rights resolution 1992/48 of 3 March 1992,

Noting the importance of developing and carrying out concrete long-term strategies for the full implementation of the World Programme of Action concerning Disabled Persons beyond the United Nations Decade of Disabled Persons, with the aim of achieving a society for all by the year 2010,

Welcoming the unreserved reaffirmation in the Vienna Declaration and Programme of Action of the human rights and fundamental freedoms of persons with disabilities,

Reaffirming that the efforts of both the developing and the developed countries are indispensable in mobilizing the world's attention and resources to address the problems of persons with disabilities,

Aware of the major obstacles to the implementation of the World Programme of Action concerning Disabled Persons, foremost among them an inadequate allocation of resources,

1. *Reaffirms* the continuing validity and value of the World Programme of Action concerning Disabled Persons, which provides a firm and innovative framework for disability-related issues;

2. *Reiterates* the responsibility of Governments for removing or facilitating the removal of barriers and obstacles to the full integration of persons with disabilities into society, and supports their efforts in developing national policies to reach specific objectives;

3. *Requests* the Secretary-General to continue to give higher priority and visibility to disability issues within the programme of work of the United Nations system by:

(a) Integrating disability issues into the policies, programmes and projects of the specialized agencies on a broader scale and with higher priority, and asking all the specialized agencies to report on their engagement in the disability field;

(b) Asking the United Nations Development Programme to review how a disability component can be incorporated into all its reconstruction programmes on a continuing basis;

(c) Urging the finalization of the ongoing work on the creation of a disability index based on the Standard Rules on the Equalization of Opportunities for Persons with Disabilities;

(d) Encouraging the activities of the United Nations Children's Fund in promoting prevention and early detection, public awareness and community-based rehabilitation in respect of childhood disabilities;

(e) Publishing a manual on the integration of disability issues into national planning and development projects;

(f) Continuing the work of collecting statistical data about disability matters and finalizing the development of a global disability indicator;

(g) Pursuing his efforts to establish a panel of persons with wide experience in the field of disability, including persons with disabilities, and with due regard to equitable geographical representation, to advise him on disability matters;

(h) Urging Governments to integrate, where possible, disability components into technical assistance and technical cooperation programmes, including the exchange of experience in the disability field under the auspices of the competent specialized agencies;

4. *Encourages* the consideration during major forthcoming events, including the International Conference on Population and Development, to be held in 1994, the International Year of the Family, to be observed in 1994, the Fourth World Conference on Women: Action for Equality, Development and Peace, to be held in 1995, and the World Summit for Social Development, to be held in 1995, of disability issues relevant to their themes;

5. *Recommends* that the regional commissions and other competent regional organizations be fully utilized to explore the best ways and means to improve the specific situation of persons with disabilities in each region;

6. *Invites* Member States and the private sector, including competent non-governmental organizations, to contribute to the United Nations Voluntary Fund on Disability;

7. *Invites* Member States and other donors to pay close attention to the increasing number of persons with disabilities as a consequence of poverty and disease, wars and civil strife and demographic and environmental factors, including natural disasters and catastrophic accidents;

8. *Commends* the launching of the Asian and Pacific Decade of Disabled Persons, 1993-2002, and the adoption of the Proclamation on the Full Participation and Equality of People with Disabilities in the Asian and Pacific Region by the intergovernmental meeting to launch the Decade, convened by the Economic and Social Commission for Asia and the Pacific at Beijing from 1 to 5 December 1992;

9. *Requests* the Secretary-General to report to the General Assembly at its forty-ninth session on relevant developments concerning the present resolution, in the context of his report on the development of a plan of action to implement the long-term strategy to further the implementation of the World Programme of Action concerning Disabled Persons.

General Assembly resolution 48/99

20 December 1993   Meeting 85   Adopted without a vote

Approved by Third Committee (A/48/627) without vote, 12 November (meeting 32); 32-nation draft (A/C.3/48/L.7/Rev.1), orally revised; agenda item 109.

Sponsors: Afghanistan, Armenia, Azerbaijan, Bangladesh, Belarus, Belgium, China, Costa Rica, Côte d'Ivoire, Cyprus, Denmark, Egypt, Finland, Iceland, Indonesia, Iran, Ireland, Italy, Kuwait, Libyan Arab Jamahiriya, Mongolia, Morocco, Myanmar, Nicaragua, Norway, Philippines, Republic of Korea, Romania, Russian Federation, Sweden, Turkey, United Kingdom.

Meeting numbers. GA 48th session: 3rd Committee 11-19, 21, 32; plenary 85.

Standard rules

The Commission for Social Development, at its February session, considered a note by the Secretary-General,[20] which contained the report of the ad hoc open-ended working group to elaborate standard rules on the equalization of opportunities for disabled persons. The draft standard rules were requested by the Economic and Social Council in 1990,[21] and in 1992[22] the General Assembly urged the Commission to expedite them.

ECONOMIC AND SOCIAL COUNCIL ACTION

On 27 July, on the recommendation of its Social Committee, the Economic and Social Council adopted **resolution 1993/19** without vote.

Standard Rules on the Equalization of Opportunities for Persons with Disabilities

The Economic and Social Council

Recommends to the General Assembly the adoption of the following draft resolution:

[For text, see General Assembly resolution 48/96 below.]

Economic and Social Council resolution 1993/19

27 July 1993   Meeting 43   Adopted without vote

Approved by Social Committee (E/1993/106) without vote, 14 July (meeting 10); draft by Commission for Social Development (E/1993/24); agenda item 20.

GENERAL ASSEMBLY ACTION

On 20 December, on the recommendation of the Third Committee, the General Assembly adopted **resolution 48/96** without vote.

Standard Rules on the Equalization of Opportunities for Persons with Disabilities

The General Assembly,

Recalling Economic and Social Council resolution 1990/26 of 24 May 1990, in which the Council authorized the Commission for Social Development to consider, at its thirty-second session, the establishment of an ad hoc open-ended working group of government experts, funded by voluntary contributions, to elaborate standard rules on the equalization of opportunities for disabled children, youth and adults, in close collaboration with the specialized agencies, other intergovernmental bodies and non-governmental organizations, especially organizations of disabled persons, and requested the Commission, should it establish such a working group, to finalize the text of those rules for consideration by the Council in 1993 and for submission to the General Assembly at its forty-eighth session,

Also recalling that the Commission for Social Development, in its resolution 32/2 of 20 February 1991, decided to establish an ad hoc open-ended working group of government experts in accordance with Economic and Social Council resolution 1990/26,

Noting with appreciation the participation of many States, specialized agencies, intergovernmental bodies and non-governmental organizations, especially organizations of disabled persons, in the deliberations of the working group,

Also noting with appreciation the generous financial contributions of Member States to the working group,

Welcoming the fact that the working group was able to fulfil its mandate within three sessions of five working days each,

Acknowledging with appreciation the report of the ad hoc open-ended working group to elaborate standard rules on the equalization of opportunities for persons with disabilities,

Noting the discussion in the Commission for Social Development at its thirty-third session on the draft standard rules contained in the report of the working group,

1. *Adopts* the Standard Rules on the Equalization of Opportunities for Persons with Disabilities, set forth in the annex to the present resolution;

2. *Requests* Member States to apply the Rules in developing national disability programmes;

3. *Urges* Member States to meet the requests of the Special Rapporteur for information on the implementation of the Rules;

4. *Requests* the Secretary-General to promote the implementation of the Rules and to report thereon to the General Assembly at its fiftieth session;

5. *Urges* Member States to support, financially and otherwise, the implementation of the Standard Rules.

ANNEX
Standard Rules on the Equalization of Opportunities for Persons with Disabilities

Introduction

    Background and current needs

    Previous international action

    Towards standard rules

    Purpose and content of the Standard Rules on the Equalization of Opportunities for Persons with Disabilities

    Fundamental concepts in disability policy

Preamble

I.   Preconditions for Equal Participation

    Rule 1. Awareness-raising

    Rule 2. Medical care

    Rule 3. Rehabilitation

    Rule 4. Support services

II. Target Areas for Equal Participation

    Rule 5. Accessibility

    Rule 6. Education

    Rule 7. Employment

    Rule 8. Income maintenance and social security

    Rule 9. Family life and personal integrity

    Rule 10. Culture

    Rule 11. Recreation and sports

    Rule 12. Religion

III. Implementation Measures

    Rule 13. Information and research

    Rule 14. Policy-making and planning

    Rule 15. Legislation

    Rule 16. Economic policies

    Rule 17. Coordination of work

    Rule 18. Organizations of persons with disabilities

    Rule 19. Personnel training

    Rule 20. National monitoring and evaluation of disability programmes in the implementation of the Standard Rules

    Rule 21. Technical and economic cooperation

    Rule 22. International cooperation

IV. Monitoring Mechanism

Introduction

Background and current needs

1.   There are persons with disabilities in all parts of the world and at all levels in every society. The number of persons with disabilities in the world is large and is growing.

2.   Both the causes and the consequences of disability vary throughout the world. Those variations are the result of different socio-economic circumstances and of the different provisions that States make for the well-being of their citizens.

3.   Present disability policy is the result of developments over the past 200 years. In many ways it reflects the general living conditions and social and economic policies of different times. In the disability field, however, there are also many specific circumstances that have influenced the living conditions of persons with disabilities. Ignorance, neglect, superstition and fear are social factors that throughout the history of disability have isolated persons with disabilities and delayed their development.

4.   Over the years disability policy developed from elementary care at institutions to education for children with disabilities and rehabilitation for persons who became disabled during adult life. Through education and rehabilitation, persons with disabilities became more active and a driving force in the further development of disability policy. Organizations of persons with disabilities, their families and advocates were formed, which advocated better conditions for persons with disabilities. After the Second World War the concepts of integration and normalization were introduced, which reflected a growing awareness of the capabilities of persons with disabilities.

5.   Towards the end of the 1960s organizations of persons with disabilities in some countries started to formulate a new concept of disability. That new concept indicated the close connection between the limitation experienced by individuals with disabilities, the design and structure of their environments and the attitude of the general population. At the same time the problems of disability in developing countries were more and more highlighted. In some of those countries the percentage of the population with disabilities was estimated to be very high and, for the most part, persons with disabilities were extremely poor.

Previous international action

6.   The rights of persons with disabilities have been
the subject of much attention in the United Nations and
other international organizations over a long period of
time. The most important outcome of the International
Year of Disabled Persons, 1981, was the World Programme of Action concerning Disabled Persons, adopted
by the General Assembly by its resolution 37/52 of 3
December 1982. The Year and the World Programme
of Action provided a strong impetus for progress in the
field. They both emphasized the right of persons with
disabilities to the same opportunities as other citizens
and to an equal share in the improvements in living conditions resulting from economic and social development.
There also, for the first time, handicap was defined as
a function of the relationship between persons with disabilities and their environment.

7.   The Global Meeting of Experts to Review the Implementation of the World Programme of Action concerning Disabled Persons at the Mid-Point of the United
Nations Decade of Disabled Persons was held at Stockholm in 1987. It was suggested at the Meeting that a
guiding philosophy should be developed to indicate the
priorities for action in the years ahead. The basis of that
philosophy should be the recognition of the rights of persons with disabilities.

8.   Consequently, the Meeting recommended that
the General Assembly convene a special conference to
draft an international convention on the elimination of
all forms of discrimination against persons with disabilities, to be ratified by States by the end of the Decade.

9.   A draft outline of the convention was prepared
by Italy and presented to the General Assembly at its
forty-second session. Further presentations concerning
a draft convention were made by Sweden at the forty-
fourth session of the Assembly. However, on both occasions, no consensus could be reached on the suitability
of such a convention. In the opinion of many representatives, existing human rights documents seemed to
guarantee persons with disabilities the same rights as
other persons.

Towards standard rules

10.   Guided by the deliberations in the General Assembly, the Economic and Social Council, at its first
regular session of 1990, finally agreed to concentrate on
the elaboration of an international instrument of a different kind. By its resolution 1990/26 of 24 May 1990, the
Council authorized the Commission for Social Development to consider, at its thirty-second session, the establishment of an ad hoc open-ended working group of
government experts, funded by voluntary contributions,
to elaborate standard rules on the equalization of opportunities for disabled children, youth and adults, in
close collaboration with the specialized agencies, other
intergovernmental bodies and non-governmental organizations, especially organizations of disabled persons. The
Council also requested the Commission to finalize the
text of those rules for consideration in 1993 and for submission to the General Assembly at its forty-eighth
session.

11.   The subsequent discussions in the Third Committee of the General Assembly at the forty-fifth session showed that there was wide support for the new
initiative to elaborate standard rules on the equalization of opportunities for persons with disabilities.

12.   At the thirty-second session of the Commission
for Social Development, the initiative for standard rules
received the support of a large number of representatives and discussions led to the adoption of resolution
32/2 of 20 February 1991, in which the Commission
decided to establish an ad hoc open-ended working
group in accordance with Economic and Social Council resolution 1990/26.

*Purpose and content of the Standard Rules on the Equalization
of Opportunities for Persons with Disabilities*

13.   The Standard Rules on the Equalization of Opportunities for Persons with Disabilities have been developed on the basis of the experience gained during
the United Nations Decade of Disabled Persons (1983-
1992). The International Bill of Human Rights, comprising the Universal Declaration of Human Rights, the
International Covenant on Economic, Social and Cultural Rights and the International Covenant on Civil
and Political Rights, the Convention on the Rights of
the Child and the Convention on the Elimination of All
Forms of Discrimination against Women, as well as the
World Programme of Action concerning Disabled Persons, constitute the political and moral foundation for
the Rules.

14.   Although the Rules are not compulsory, they can
become international customary rules when they are applied by a great number of States with the intention of
respecting a rule in international law. They imply a
strong moral and political commitment on behalf of
States to take action for the equalization of opportunities for persons with disabilities. Important principles
for responsibility, action and cooperation are indicated.
Areas of decisive importance for the quality of life and
for the achievement of full participation and equality
are pointed out. The Rules offer an instrument for
policy-making and action to persons with disabilities and
their organizations. They provide a basis for technical
and economic cooperation among States, the United Nations and other international organizations.

15.   The purpose of the Rules is to ensure that girls,
boys, women and men with disabilities, as members of
their societies, may exercise the same rights and obligations as others. In all societies of the world there are still
obstacles preventing persons with disabilities from exercising their rights and freedoms and making it difficult for them to participate fully in the activities of their
societies. It is the responsibility of States to take appropriate
action to remove such obstacles. Persons with disabilities and their organizations should play an active role
as partners in this process. The equalization of opportunities for persons with disabilities is an essential contribution in the general and worldwide effort to mobilize human resources. Special attention may need to be
directed towards groups such as women, children, the
elderly, the poor, migrant workers, persons with dual or
multiple disabilities, indigenous people and ethnic minorities. In addition, there are a large number of refugees
with disabilities who have special needs requiring attention.

Fundamental concepts in disability policy

16.   The concepts set out below appear throughout
the Rules. They are essentially built on the concepts in
the World Programme of Action concerning Disabled
Persons. In some cases they reflect the development that
has taken place during the United Nations Decade of
Disabled Persons.

Disability and handicap

17.   The term "disability" summarizes a great number of different functional limitations occurring in any population in any country of the world. People may be disabled by physical, intellectual or sensory impairment, medical conditions or mental illness. Such impairments, conditions or illnesses may be permanent or transitory in nature.

18.   The term "handicap" means the loss or limitation of opportunities to take part in the life of the community on an equal level with others. It describes the encounter between the person with a disability and the environment. The purpose of this term is to emphasize the focus on the shortcomings in the environment and in many organized activities in society, for example, information, communication and education, which prevent persons with disabilities from participating on equal terms.

19.   The use of the two terms "disability" and "handicap", as defined in paragraphs 17 and 18 above, should be seen in the light of modern disability history. During the 1970s there was a strong reaction among representatives of organizations of persons with disabilities and professionals in the field of disability against the terminology of the time. The terms "disability" and "handicap" were often used in an unclear and confusing way, which gave poor guidance for policy-making and for political action. The terminology reflected a medical and diagnostic approach, which ignored the imperfections and deficiencies of the surrounding society.

20.   In 1980, the World Health Organization adopted an international classification of impairments, disabilities and handicaps, which suggested a more precise and at the same time relativistic approach. The International Classification of Impairments, Disabilities and Handicaps makes a clear distinction between "impairment," "disability" and "handicap". It has been extensively used in areas such as rehabilitation, education, statistics, policy, legislation, demography, sociology, economics and anthropology. Some users have expressed concern that the Classification, in its definition of the term "handicap", may still be considered too medical and too centred on the individual, and may not adequately clarify the interaction between societal conditions or expectations and the abilities of the individual. Those concerns, and others expressed by users during the 12 years since its publication, will be addressed in forthcoming revisions of the Classification.

21.   As a result of experience gained in the implementation of the World Programme of Action and of the general discussion that took place during the United Nations Decade of Disabled Persons, there was a deepening of knowledge and extension of understanding concerning disability issues and the terminology used. Current terminology recognizes the necessity of addressing both the individual needs (such as rehabilitation and technical aids) and the shortcomings of the society (various obstacles for participation).

Prevention

22.   The term "prevention" means action aimed at preventing the occurrence of physical, intellectual, psychiatric or sensory impairments (primary prevention) or at preventing impairments from causing a permanent functional limitation or disability (secondary prevention). Prevention may include many different types of action, such as primary health care, prenatal and postnatal care, education in nutrition, immunization campaigns against communicable diseases, measures to control endemic diseases, safety regulations, programmes for the prevention of accidents in different environments, including adaptation of workplaces to prevent occupational disabilities and diseases, and prevention of disability resulting from pollution of the environment or armed conflict.

Rehabilitation

23.   The term "rehabilitation" refers to a process aimed at enabling persons with disabilities to reach and maintain their optimal physical, sensory, intellectual, psychiatric and/or social functional levels, thus providing them with the tools to change their lives towards a higher level of independence. Rehabilitation may include measures to provide and/or restore functions, or compensate for the loss or absence of a function or for a functional limitation. The rehabilitation process does not involve initial medical care. It includes a wide range of measures and activities from more basic and general rehabilitation to goal-oriented activities, for instance vocational rehabilitation.

Equalization of opportunities

24.   The term "equalization of opportunities" means the process through which the various systems of society and the environment, such as services, activities, information and documentation, are made available to all, particularly to persons with disabilities.

25.   The principle of equal rights implies that the needs of each and every individual are of equal importance, that those needs must be made the basis for the planning of societies and that all resources must be employed in such a way as to ensure that every individual has equal opportunity for participation.

26.   Persons with disabilities are members of society and have the right to remain within their local communities. They should receive the support they need within the ordinary structures of education, health, employment and social services.

27.   As persons with disabilities achieve equal rights, they should also have equal obligations. As those rights are being achieved, societies should raise their expectations of persons with disabilities. As part of the process of equal opportunities, provision should be made to assist persons with disabilities to assume their full responsibility as members of society.

Preamble

States,

Mindful of the pledge made, under the Charter of the United Nations, to take joint and separate action in cooperation with the Organization to promote higher standards of living, full employment, and conditions of economic and social progress and development,

Reaffirming the commitment to human rights and fundamental freedoms, social justice and the dignity and worth of the human person proclaimed in the Charter,

Recalling in particular the international standards on human rights, which have been laid down in the Universal Declaration of Human Rights, the International Covenant on Economic, Social and Cultural Rights and the International Covenant on Civil and Political Rights,

Underlining that those instruments proclaim that the rights recognized therein should be ensured equally to all individuals without discrimination,

Recalling the Convention on the Rights of the Child, which prohibits discrimination on the basis of disability and requires special measures to ensure the rights of children with disabilities, and the International Convention on the Protection of the Rights of All Migrant Workers and Members of Their Families, which provides for some protective measures against disability,

Recalling also the provisions in the Convention on the Elimination of All Forms of Discrimination against Women to ensure the rights of girls and women with disabilities,

Having regard to the Declaration on the Rights of Disabled Persons, the Declaration on the Rights of Mentally Retarded Persons, the Declaration on Social Progress and Development, the Principles for the Protection of Persons with Mental Illness and for the Improvement of Mental Health Care and other relevant instruments adopted by the General Assembly,

Also having regard to the relevant conventions and recommendations adopted by the International Labour Organisation, with particular reference to participation in employment without discrimination for persons with disabilities,

Mindful of the relevant recommendations and work of the United Nations Educational, Scientific and Cultural Organization, in particular the World Declaration on Education for All, the World Health Organization, the United Nations Children's Fund and other concerned organizations,

Having regard to the commitment made by States concerning the protection of the environment,

Mindful of the devastation caused by armed conflict and deploring the use of scarce resources in the production of weapons,

Recognizing that the World Programme of Action concerning Disabled Persons and the definition therein of equalization of opportunities represent earnest ambitions on the part of the international community to render those various international instruments and recommendations of practical and concrete significance,

Acknowledging that the objective of the United Nations Decade of Disabled Persons (1983-1992) to implement the World Programme of Action is still valid and requires urgent and continued action,

Recalling that the World Programme of Action is based on concepts that are equally valid in developing and industrialized countries,

Convinced that intensified efforts are needed to achieve the full and equal enjoyment of human rights and participation in society by persons with disabilities,

Re-emphasizing that persons with disabilities, and their parents, guardians, advocates and organizations, must be active partners with States in the planning and implementation of all measures affecting their civil, political, economic, social and cultural rights,

In pursuance of Economic and Social Council resolution 1990/26, and basing themselves on the specific measures required for the attainment by persons with disabilities of equality with others, enumerated in detail in the World Programme of Action,

Have adopted the Standard Rules on the Equalization of Opportunities for Persons with Disabilities outlined below, in order:

(a) To stress that all action in the field of disability presupposes adequate knowledge and experience of the conditions and special needs of persons with disabilities;

(b) To emphasize that the process through which every aspect of societal organization is made accessible to all is a basic objective of socio-economic development;

(c) To outline crucial aspects of social policies in the field of disability, including, as appropriate, the active encouragement of technical and economic cooperation;

(d) To provide models for the political decision-making process required for the attainment of equal opportunities, bearing in mind the widely differing technical and economic levels, the fact that the process must reflect keen understanding of the cultural context within which it takes place and the crucial role of persons with disabilities in it;

(e) To propose national mechanisms for close collaboration among States, the organs of the United Nations system, other intergovernmental bodies and organizations of persons with disabilities;

(f) To propose an effective machinery for monitoring the process by which States seek to attain the equalization of opportunities for persons with disabilities.

I. Preconditions for Equal Participation

Rule 1. Awareness-raising

States should take action to raise awareness in society about persons with disabilities, their rights, their needs, their potential and their contribution.

1. States should ensure that responsible authorities distribute up-to-date information on available programmes and services to persons with disabilities, their families, professionals in the field and the general public. Information to persons with disabilities should be presented in accessible form.

2. States should initiate and support information campaigns concerning persons with disabilities and disability policies, conveying the message that persons with disabilities are citizens with the same rights and obligations as others, thus justifying measures to remove all obstacles to full participation.

3. States should encourage the portrayal of persons with disabilities by the mass media in a positive way; organizations of persons with disabilities should be consulted on this matter.

4. States should ensure that public education programmes reflect in all their aspects the principle of full participation and equality.

5. States should invite persons with disabilities and their families and organizations to participate in public education programmes concerning disability matters.

6. States should encourage enterprises in the private sector to include disability issues in all aspects of their activity.

7. States should initiate and promote programmes aimed at raising the level of awareness of persons with disabilities concerning their rights and potential. Increased self-reliance and empowerment will assist persons with disabilities to take advantage of the opportunities available to them.

8. Awareness-raising should be an important part of the education of children with disabilities and in rehabilitation programmes. Persons with disabilities could also assist one another in awareness-raising through the activities of their own organizations.

9. Awareness-raising should be part of the education of all children and should be a component of teacher-training courses and training of all professionals.

Rule 2. *Medical care*

States should ensure the provision of effective medical care to persons with disabilities.

1. States should work towards the provision of programmes run by multidisciplinary teams of professionals for early detection, assessment and treatment of impairment. This could prevent, reduce or eliminate disabling effects. Such programmes should ensure the full participation of persons with disabilities and their families at the individual level, and of organizations of persons with disabilities at the planning and evaluation level.

2. Local community workers should be trained to participate in areas such as early detection of impairments, the provision of primary assistance and referral to appropriate services.

3. States should ensure that persons with disabilities, particularly infants and children, are provided with the same level of medical care within the same system as other members of society.

4. States should ensure that all medical and paramedical personnel are adequately trained and equipped to give medical care to persons with disabilities and that they have access to relevant treatment methods and technology.

5. States should ensure that medical, paramedical and related personnel are adequately trained so that they do not give inappropriate advice to parents, thus restricting options for their children. This training should be an ongoing process and should be based on the latest information available.

6. States should ensure that persons with disabilities are provided with any regular treatment and medicines they may need to preserve or improve their level of functioning.

Rule 3. *Rehabilitation*[a]

States should ensure the provision of rehabilitation services to persons with disabilities in order for them to reach and sustain their optimum level of independence and functioning.

1. States should develop national rehabilitation programmes for all groups of persons with disabilities. Such programmes should be based on the actual individual needs of persons with disabilities and on the principles of full participation and equality.

2. Such programmes should include a wide range of activities, such as basic skills training to improve or compensate for an affected function, counselling of persons with disabilities and their families, developing self-reliance, and occasional services such as assessment and guidance.

3. All persons with disabilities, including persons with severe and/or multiple disabilities, who require rehabilitation should have access to it.

4. Persons with disabilities and their families should be able to participate in the design and organization of rehabilitation services concerning themselves.

5. All rehabilitation services should be available in the local community where the person with disabilities lives. However, in some instances, in order to attain a certain training objective, special time-limited rehabilitation courses may be organized, where appropriate, in residential form.

6. Persons with disabilities and their families should be encouraged to involve themselves in rehabilitation, for instance as trained teachers, instructors or counsellors.

7. States should draw upon the expertise of organizations of persons with disabilities when formulating or evaluating rehabilitation programmes.

Rule 4. *Support services*

States should ensure the development and supply of support services, including assistive devices for persons with disabilities, to assist them to increase their level of independence in their daily living and to exercise their rights.

1. States should ensure the provision of assistive devices and equipment, personal assistance and interpreter services, according to the needs of persons with disabilities, as important measures to achieve the equalization of opportunities.

2. States should support the development, production, distribution and servicing of assistive devices and equipment and the dissemination of knowledge about them.

3. To achieve this, generally available technical know-how should be utilized. In States where high-technology industry is available, it should be fully utilized to improve the standard and effectiveness of assistive devices and equipment. It is important to stimulate the development and production of simple and inexpensive devices, using local material and local production facilities when possible. Persons with disabilities themselves could be involved in the production of those devices.

4. States should recognize that all persons with disabilities who need assistive devices should have access to them as appropriate, including financial accessibility. This may mean that assistive devices and equipment should be provided free of charge or at such a low price that persons with disabilities or their families can afford to buy them.

5. In rehabilitation programmes for the provision of assistive devices and equipment, States should consider the special requirements of girls and boys with disabilities concerning the design, durability and age-appropriateness of assistive devices and equipment.

6. States should support the development and provision of personal assistance programmes and interpretation services, especially for persons with severe and/or multiple disabilities. Such programmes would increase the level of participation of persons with disabilities in everyday life at home, at work, in school and during leisure-time activities.

7. Personal assistance programmes should be designed in such a way that the persons with disabilities using the programmes have a decisive influence on the way in which the programmes are delivered.

II. Target Areas for Equal Participation

Rule 5. *Accessibility*

States should recognize the overall importance of accessibility in the process of the equalization of opportunities in all spheres of society. For persons with disabilities of any kind, States should *(a)* introduce programmes of action to make the physical environment accessible; and *(b)* undertake measures to provide access to information and communication.

---

[a]Rehabilitation is a fundamental concept in disability policy and is defined above in paragraph 23 of the introduction.

(a) Access to the physical environment

1.   States should initiate measures to remove the obstacles to participation in the physical environment. Such measures should be to develop standards and guidelines and to consider enacting legislation to ensure accessibility to various areas in society, such as housing, buildings, public transport services and other means of transportation, streets and other outdoor environments.

2.   States should ensure that architects, construction engineers and others who are professionally involved in the design and construction of the physical environment have access to adequate information on disability policy and measures to achieve accessibility.

3.   Accessibility requirements should be included in the design and construction of the physical environment from the beginning of the designing process.

4.   Organizations of persons with disabilities should be consulted when standards and norms for accessibility are being developed. They should also be involved locally from the initial planning stage when public construction projects are being designed, thus ensuring maximum accessibility.

(b) Access to information and communication

5.   Persons with disabilities and, where appropriate, their families and advocates should have access to full information on diagnosis, rights and available services and programmes, at all stages. Such information should be presented in forms accessible to people with disabilities.

6.   States should develop strategies to make information services and documentation accessible for different groups of persons with disabilities. Braille, tape services, large print and other appropriate technologies should be used to provide access to written information and documentation for persons with visual impairments. Similarly, appropriate technologies should be used to provide access to spoken information for persons with auditory impairments or comprehension difficulties.

7.   Consideration should be given to the use of sign language in the education of deaf children, in their families and communities. Sign language interpretation services should also be provided to facilitate the communication between deaf persons and others.

8.   Consideration should also be given to the needs of people with other communication disabilities.

9.   States should encourage the media, especially television, radio and newspapers, to make their services accessible.

10.   States should ensure that new computerized information and service systems offered to the general public are either made initially accessible or are adapted to be made accessible to persons with disabilities.

11.   Organizations of persons with disabilities should be consulted when measures to make information services accessible are being developed.

Rule 6.   Education

States should recognize the principle of equal primary, secondary and tertiary educational opportunities for children, youth and adults with disabilities, in integrated settings. They should ensure that the education of persons with disabilities is an integral part of the educational system.

1.   General educational authorities are responsible for the education of persons with disabilities in integrated settings. Education for persons with disabilities should form an integral part of national educational planning, curriculum development and school organization.

2.   Education in mainstream schools presupposes the provision of interpreter and other appropriate support services. Adequate accessibility and support services, designed to meet the needs of persons with different disabilities, should be provided.

3.   Parent groups and organizations of persons with disabilities should be involved in the education process at all levels.

4.   In States where education is compulsory it should be provided to girls and boys with all kinds and all levels of disabilities, including the most severe.

5.   Special attention should be given in the following areas:

(a)   Very young children with disabilities;

(b)   Pre-school children with disabilities;

(c)   Adults with disabilities, particularly women.

6.   To accommodate educational provisions for persons with disabilities in the mainstream, States should:

(a)   Have a clearly stated policy, understood and accepted at the school level and by the wider community;

(b)   Allow for curriculum flexibility, addition and adaptation;

(c)   Provide for quality materials, ongoing teacher training and support teachers.

7.   Integrated education and community-based programmes should be seen as complementary approaches in providing cost-effective education and training for persons with disabilities. National community-based programmes should encourage communities to use and develop their resources to provide local education to persons with disabilities.

8.   In situations where the general school system does not yet adequately meet the needs of all persons with disabilities, special education may be considered. It should be aimed at preparing students for education in the general school system. The quality of such education should reflect the same standards and ambitions as general education and should be closely linked to it. At a minimum, students with disabilities should be afforded the same portion of educational resources as students without disabilities. States should aim for the gradual integration of special education services into mainstream education. It is acknowledged that in some instances special education may currently be considered to be the most appropriate form of education for some students with disabilities.

9.   Owing to the particular communication needs of deaf and deaf/blind persons, their education may be more suitably provided in schools for such persons or special classes and units in mainstream schools. At the initial stage, in particular, special attention needs to be focused on culturally sensitive instruction that will result in effective communication skills and maximum independence for people who are deaf or deaf/blind.

Rule 7.   Employment

States should recognize the principle that persons with disabilities must be empowered to exercise their human rights, particularly in the field of employment. In both rural and urban areas they must have equal opportunities for productive and gainful employment in the labour market.

1.   Laws and regulations in the employment field must not discriminate against persons with disabilities and must not raise obstacles to their employment.

2.   States should actively support the integration of persons with disabilities into open employment. This active support could occur through a variety of measures, such as vocational training, incentive-oriented quota schemes, reserved or designated employment, loans or grants for small business, exclusive contracts or priority production rights, tax concessions, contract compliance or other technical or financial assistance to enterprises employing workers with disabilities. States should also encourage employers to make reasonable adjustments to accommodate persons with disabilities.

3.   States' action programmes should include:

(*a*)   Measures to design and adapt workplaces and work premises in such a way that they become accessible to persons with different disabilities;

(*b*)   Support for the use of new technologies and the development and production of assistive devices, tools and equipment and measures to facilitate access to such devices and equipment for persons with disabilities to enable them to gain and maintain employment;

(*c*)   Provision of appropriate training and placement and ongoing support such as personal assistance and interpreter services.

4.   States should initiate and support public awareness-raising campaigns designed to overcome negative attitudes and prejudices concerning workers with disabilities.

5.   In their capacity as employers, States should create favourable conditions for the employment of persons with disabilities in the public sector.

6.   States, workers' organizations and employers should cooperate to ensure equitable recruitment and promotion policies, employment conditions, rates of pay, measures to improve the work environment in order to prevent injuries and impairments and measures for the rehabilitation of employees who have sustained employment-related injuries.

7.   The aim should always be for persons with disabilities to obtain employment in the open labour market. For persons with disabilities whose needs cannot be met in open employment, small units of sheltered or supported employment may be an alternative. It is important that the quality of such programmes be assessed in terms of their relevance and sufficiency in providing opportunities for persons with disabilities to gain employment in the labour market.

8.   Measures should be taken to include persons with disabilities in training and employment programmes in the private and informal sectors.

9.   States, workers' organizations and employers should cooperate with organizations of persons with disabilities concerning all measures to create training and employment opportunities, including flexible hours, part-time work, job-sharing, self-employment and attendant care for persons with disabilities.

Rule 8.   Income maintenance and social security
States are responsible for the provision of social security and income maintenance for persons with disabilities.

1.   States should ensure the provision of adequate income support to persons with disabilities who, owing to disability or disability-related factors, have temporarily lost or received a reduction in their income or have been denied employment opportunities. States should ensure that the provision of support takes into account the costs frequently incurred by persons with disabilities and their families as a result of the disability.

2.   In countries where social security, social insurance or other social welfare schemes exist or are being developed for the general population, States should ensure that such systems do not exclude or discriminate against persons with disabilities.

3.   States should also ensure the provision of income support and social security protection to individuals who undertake the care of a person with a disability.

4.   Social security systems should include incentives to restore the income-earning capacity of persons with disabilities. Such systems should provide or contribute to the organization, development and financing of vocational training. They should also assist with placement services.

5.   Social security programmes should also provide incentives for persons with disabilities to seek employment in order to establish or re-establish their income-earning capacity.

6.   Income support should be maintained as long as the disabling conditions remain in a manner that does not discourage persons with disabilities from seeking employment. It should only be reduced or terminated when persons with disabilities achieve adequate and secure income.

7.   States, in countries where social security is to a large extent provided by the private sector, should encourage local communities, welfare organizations and families to develop self-help measures and incentives for employment or employment-related activities for persons with disabilities.

Rule 9.   Family life and personal integrity
States should promote the full participation of persons with disabilities in family life. They should promote their right to personal integrity and ensure that laws do not discriminate against persons with disabilities with respect to sexual relationships, marriage and parenthood.

1.   Persons with disabilities should be enabled to live with their families. States should encourage the inclusion in family counselling of appropriate modules regarding disability and its effects on family life. Respite-care and attendant-care services should be made available to families which include a person with disabilities. States should remove all unnecessary obstacles to persons who want to foster or adopt a child or adult with disabilities.

2.   Persons with disabilities must not be denied the opportunity to experience their sexuality, have sexual relationships and experience parenthood. Taking into account that persons with disabilities may experience difficulties in getting married and setting up a family, States should encourage the availability of appropriate counselling. Persons with disabilities must have the same access as others to family-planning methods, as well as to information in accessible form on the sexual functioning of their bodies.

3.   States should promote measures to change negative attitudes towards marriage, sexuality and parenthood of persons with disabilities, especially of girls and women with disabilities, which still prevail in society. The media should be encouraged to play an important role in removing such negative attitudes.

4.   Persons with disabilities and their families need to be fully informed about taking precautions against

sexual and other forms of abuse. Persons with disabilities are particularly vulnerable to abuse in the family, community or institutions and need to be educated on how to avoid the occurrence of abuse, recognize when abuse has occurred and report on such acts.

Rule 10. *Culture*

States will ensure that persons with disabilities are integrated into and can participate in cultural activities on an equal basis.

1. States should ensure that persons with disabilities have the opportunity to utilize their creative, artistic and intellectual potential, not only for their own benefit, but also for the enrichment of their community, be they in urban or rural areas. Examples of such activities are dance, music, literature, theatre, plastic arts, painting and sculpture. Particularly in developing countries, emphasis should be placed on traditional and contemporary art forms, such as puppetry, recitation and story-telling.

2. States should promote the accessibility to and availability of places for cultural performances and services, such as theatres, museums, cinemas and libraries, to persons with disabilities.

3. States should initiate the development and use of special technical arrangements to make literature, films and theatre accessible to persons with disabilities.

Rule 11. *Recreation and sports*

States will take measures to ensure that persons with disabilities have equal opportunities for recreation and sports.

1. States should initiate measures to make places for recreation and sports, hotels, beaches, sports arenas, gym halls etc. accessible to persons with disabilities. Such measures should encompass support for staff in recreation and sports programmes, including projects to develop methods of accessibility, and participation, information and training programmes.

2. Tourist authorities, travel agencies, hotels, voluntary organizations and others involved in organizing recreational activities or travel opportunities should offer their services to all, taking into account the special needs of persons with disabilities. Suitable training should be provided to assist that process.

3. Sports organizations should be encouraged to develop opportunities for participation by persons with disabilities in sports activities. In some cases, accessibility measures could be enough to open up opportunities for participation. In other cases, special arrangements or special games would be needed. States should support the participation of persons with disabilities in national and international events.

4. Persons with disabilities participating in sports activities should have access to instruction and training of the same quality as other participants.

5. Organizers of sports and recreation should consult with organizations of persons with disabilities when developing their services for persons with disabilities.

Rule 12. *Religion*

States will encourage measures for equal participation by persons with disabilities in the religious life of their communities.

1. States should encourage, in consultation with religious authorities, measures to eliminate discrimination and make religious activities accessible to persons with disabilities.

2. States should encourage the distribution of information on disability matters to religious institutions and organizations. States should also encourage religious authorities to include information on disability policies in the training for religious professions, as well as in religious education programmes.

3. They should also encourage the accessibility of religious literature to persons with sensory impairments.

4. States and/or religious organizations should consult with organizations of persons with disabilities when developing measures for equal participation in religious activities.

III. Implementation Measures

Rule 13. *Information and research*

States assume the ultimate responsibility for the collection and dissemination of information on the living conditions of persons with disabilities and promote comprehensive research on all aspects, including obstacles that affect the lives of persons with disabilities.

1. States should, at regular intervals, collect gender-specific statistics and other information concerning the living conditions of persons with disabilities. Such data collection could be conducted in conjunction with national censuses and household surveys and could be undertaken in close collaboration, *inter alia*, with universities, research institutes and organizations of persons with disabilities. The data collection should include questions on programmes and services and their use.

2. States should consider establishing a data bank on disability, which would include statistics on available services and programmes as well as on the different groups of persons with disabilities. They should bear in mind the need to protect individual privacy and personal integrity.

3. States should initiate and support programmes of research on social, economic and participation issues that affect the lives of persons with disabilities and their families. Such research should include studies on the causes, types and frequencies of disabilities, the availability and efficacy of existing programmes and the need for development and evaluation of services and support measures.

4. States should develop and adopt terminology and criteria for the conduct of national surveys, in cooperation with organizations of persons with disabilities.

5. States should facilitate the participation of persons with disabilities in data collection and research. To undertake such research, States should particularly encourage the recruitment of qualified persons with disabilities.

6. States should support the exchange of research findings and experiences.

7. States should take measures to disseminate information and knowledge on disability to all political and administration levels within national, regional and local spheres.

Rule 14. *Policy-making and planning*

States will ensure that disability aspects are included in all relevant policy-making and national planning.

1. States should initiate and plan adequate policies for persons with disabilities at the national level, and stimulate and support action at regional and local levels.

2. States should involve organizations of persons with disabilities in all decision-making relating to plans

and programmes concerning persons with disabilities or affecting their economic and social status.

3. The needs and concerns of persons with disabilities should be incorporated into general development plans and not be treated separately.

4. The ultimate responsibility of States for the situation of persons with disabilities does not relieve others of their responsibility. Anyone in charge of services, activities or the provision of information in society should be encouraged to accept responsibility for making such programmes available to persons with disabilities.

5. States should facilitate the development by local communities of programmes and measures for persons with disabilities. One way of doing this could be to develop manuals or check-lists and provide training programmes for local staff.

Rule 15. *Legislation*

States have a responsibility to create the legal bases for measures to achieve the objectives of full participation and equality for persons with disabilities.

1. National legislation, embodying the rights and obligations of citizens, should include the rights and obligations of persons with disabilities. States are under an obligation to enable persons with disabilities to exercise their rights, including their human, civil and political rights, on an equal basis with other citizens. States must ensure that organizations of persons with disabilities are involved in the development of national legislation concerning the rights of persons with disabilities, as well as in the ongoing evaluation of that legislation.

2. Legislative action may be needed to remove conditions that may adversely affect the lives of persons with disabilities, including harassment and victimization. Any discriminatory provisions against persons with disabilities must be eliminated. National legislation should provide for appropriate sanctions in case of violations of the principles of non-discrimination.

3. National legislation concerning persons with disabilities may appear in two different forms. The rights and obligations may be incorporated in general legislation or contained in special legislation. Special legislation for persons with disabilities may be established in several ways:

(a) By enacting separate legislation, dealing exclusively with disability matters;

(b) By including disability matters within legislation on particular topics;

(c) By mentioning persons with disabilities specifically in the texts that serve to interpret existing legislation.

A combination of those different approaches might be desirable. Affirmative action provisions may also be considered.

4. States may consider establishing formal statutory complaints mechanisms in order to protect the interests of persons with disabilities.

Rule 16. *Economic policies*

States have the financial responsibility for national programmes and measures to create equal opportunities for persons with disabilities.

1. States should include disability matters in the regular budgets of all national, regional and local government bodies.

2. States, non-governmental organizations and other interested bodies should interact to determine the most effective ways of supporting projects and measures relevant to persons with disabilities.

3. States should consider the use of economic measures (loans, tax exemptions, earmarked grants, special funds, and so on) to stimulate and support equal participation by persons with disabilities in society.

4. In many States it may be advisable to establish a disability development fund, which could support various pilot projects and self-help programmes at the grass-roots level.

Rule 17. *Coordination of work*

States are responsible for the establishment and strengthening of national coordinating committees, or similar bodies, to serve as a national focal point on disability matters.

1. The national coordinating committee or similar bodies should be permanent and based on legal as well as appropriate administrative regulation.

2. A combination of representatives of private and public organizations is most likely to achieve an intersectoral and multidisciplinary composition. Representatives could be drawn from concerned government ministries, organizations of persons with disabilities and non-governmental organizations.

3. Organizations of persons with disabilities should have considerable influence in the national coordinating committee in order to ensure proper feedback of their concerns.

4. The national coordinating committee should be provided with sufficient autonomy and resources to fulfil its responsibilities in relation to its decision-making capacities. It should report to the highest governmental level.

Rule 18. *Organizations of persons with disabilities*

States should recognize the right of the organizations of persons with disabilities to represent persons with disabilities at national, regional and local levels. States should also recognize the advisory role of organizations of persons with disabilities in decision-making on disability matters.

1. States should encourage and support economically and in other ways the formation and strengthening of organizations of persons with disabilities, family members and/or advocates. States should recognize that those organizations have a role to play in the development of disability policy.

2. States should establish ongoing communication with organizations of persons with disabilities and ensure their participation in the development of government policies.

3. The role of organizations of persons with disabilities could be to identify needs and priorities, to participate in the planning, implementation and evaluation of services and measures concerning the lives of persons with disabilities, and to contribute to public awareness and to advocate change.

4. As instruments of self-help, organizations of persons with disabilities provide and promote opportunities for the development of skills in various fields, mutual support among members and information sharing.

5. Organizations of persons with disabilities could perform their advisory role in many different ways such as having permanent representation on boards of government-funded agencies, serving on public commis-

sions and providing expert knowledge on different projects.

6. The advisory role of organizations of persons with disabilities should be ongoing in order to develop and deepen the exchange of views and information between the State and the organizations.

7. Organizations should be permanently represented on the national coordinating committee or similar bodies.

8. The role of local organizations of persons with disabilities should be developed and strengthened to ensure that they influence matters at the community level.

Rule 19. *Personnel training*

States are responsible for ensuring the adequate training of personnel, at all levels, involved in the planning and provision of programmes and services concerning persons with disabilities.

1. States should ensure that all authorities providing services in the disability field give adequate training to their personnel.

2. In the training of professionals in the disability field, as well as in the provision of information on disability in general training programmes, the principle of full participation and equality should be appropriately reflected.

3. States should develop training programmes in consultation with organizations of persons with disabilities, and persons with disabilities should be involved as teachers, instructors or advisers in staff training programmes.

4. The training of community workers is of great strategic importance, particularly in developing countries. It should involve persons with disabilities and include the development of appropriate values, competence and technologies as well as skills which can be practised by persons with disabilities, their parents, families and members of the community.

Rule 20. *National monitoring and evaluation of disability programmes in the implementation of the Rules*

States are responsible for the continuous monitoring and evaluation of the implementation of national programmes and services concerning the equalization of opportunities for persons with disabilities.

1. States should periodically and systematically evaluate national disability programmes and disseminate both the bases and the results of the evaluations.

2. States should develop and adopt terminology and criteria for the evaluation of disability-related programmes and services.

3. Such criteria and terminology should be developed in close cooperation with organizations of persons with disabilities from the earliest conceptual and planning stages.

4. States should participate in international cooperation in order to develop common standards for national evaluation in the disability field. States should encourage national coordinating committees to participate also.

5. The evaluation of various programmes in the disability field should be built in at the planning stage, so that the overall efficacy in fulfilling their policy objectives can be evaluated.

Rule 21. *Technical and economic cooperation*

States, both industrialized and developing, have the responsibility to cooperate in and take measures for the improvement of the living conditions of persons with disabilities in developing countries.

1. Measures to achieve the equalization of opportunities of persons with disabilities, including refugees with disabilities, should be integrated into general development programmes.

2. Such measures must be integrated into all forms of technical and economic cooperation, bilateral and multilateral, governmental and non-governmental. States should bring up disability issues in discussions on such cooperation with their counterparts.

3. When planning and reviewing programmes of technical and economic cooperation, special attention should be given to the effects of such programmes on the situation of persons with disabilities. It is of the utmost importance that persons with disabilities and their organizations are consulted on any development projects designed for persons with disabilities. They should be directly involved in the development, implementation and evaluation of such projects.

4. Priority areas for technical and economic cooperation should include:

(*a*) The development of human resources through the development of skills, abilities and potentials of persons with disabilities and the initiation of employment-generating activities for and of persons with disabilities;

(*b*) The development and dissemination of appropriate disability-related technologies and know-how.

5. States are also encouraged to support the formation and strengthening of organizations of persons with disabilities.

6. States should take measures to improve the knowledge of disability issues among staff involved at all levels in the administration of technical and economic cooperation programmes.

Rule 22. *International cooperation*

States will participate actively in international cooperation concerning policies for the equalization of opportunities for persons with disabilities.

1. Within the United Nations, the specialized agencies and other concerned intergovernmental organizations, States should participate in the development of disability policy.

2. Whenever appropriate, States should introduce disability aspects in general negotiations concerning standards, information exchange, development programmes, etc.

3. States should encourage and support the exchange of knowledge and experience among:

(*a*) Non-governmental organizations concerned with disability issues;

(*b*) Research institutions and individual researchers involved in disability issues;

(*c*) Representatives of field programmes and of professional groups in the disability field;

(*d*) Organizations of persons with disabilities;

(*e*) National coordinating committees.

4. States should ensure that the United Nations and the specialized agencies, as well as all intergovernmental and interparliamentary bodies, at global and regional levels, include in their work the global and regional organizations of persons with disabilities.

IV. Monitoring Mechanism

1. The purpose of a monitoring mechanism is to further the effective implementation of the Rules. It will

assist each State in assessing its level of implementation of the Rules and in measuring its progress. The monitoring should identify obstacles and suggest suitable measures that would contribute to the successful implementation of the Rules. The monitoring mechanism will recognize the economic, social and cultural features existing in individual States. An important element should also be the provision of advisory services and the exchange of experience and information between States.

2. The Rules shall be monitored within the framework of the sessions of the Commission for Social Development. A Special Rapporteur with relevant and extensive experience in disability issues and international organizations shall be appointed, if necessary, funded by extrabudgetary resources, for three years to monitor the implementation of the Rules.

3. International organizations of persons with disabilities having consultative status with the Economic and Social Council and organizations representing persons with disabilities who have not yet formed their own organizations should be invited to create among themselves a panel of experts, on which organizations of persons with disabilities shall have a majority, taking into account the different kinds of disabilities and necessary equitable geographical distribution, to be consulted by the Special Rapporteur and, when appropriate, by the Secretariat.

4. The panel of experts will be encouraged by the Special Rapporteur to review, advise and provide feedback and suggestions on the promotion, implementation and monitoring of the Rules.

5. The Special Rapporteur shall send a set of questions to States, entities within the United Nations system, and intergovernmental and non-governmental organizations, including organizations of persons with disabilities. The set of questions should address implementation plans for the Rules in States. The questions should be selective in nature and cover a number of specific rules for in-depth evaluation. In preparing the questions the Special Rapporteur should consult with the panel of experts and the Secretariat.

6. The Special Rapporteur shall seek to establish a direct dialogue not only with States but also with local non-governmental organizations, seeking their views and comments on any information intended to be included in the reports. The Special Rapporteur shall provide advisory services on the implementation and monitoring of the Rules and assistance in the preparation of replies to the sets of questions.

7. The Department for Policy Coordination and Sustainable Development of the Secretariat, as the United Nations focal point on disability issues, the United Nations Development Programme and other entities and mechanisms within the United Nations system, such as the regional commissions and specialized agencies and inter-agency meetings, shall cooperate with the Special Rapporteur in the implementation and monitoring of the Rules at the national level.

8. The Special Rapporteur, assisted by the Secretariat, shall prepare reports for submission to the Commission for Social Development at its thirty-fourth and thirty-fifth sessions. In preparing such reports, the Rapporteur should consult with the panel of experts.

9. States should encourage national coordinating committees or similar bodies to participate in implementation and monitoring. As the focal points on disability matters at the national level, they should be encouraged to establish procedures to coordinate the monitoring of the Rules. Organizations of persons with disabilities should be encouraged to be actively involved in the monitoring of the process at all levels.

10. Should extrabudgetary resources be identified, one or more positions of interregional adviser on the Rules should be created to provide direct services to States, including:

(a) The organization of national and regional training seminars on the content of the Rules;

(b) The development of guidelines to assist in strategies for implementation of the Rules;

(c) Dissemination of information about best practices concerning implementation of the Rules.

11. At its thirty-fourth session, the Commission for Social Development should establish an open-ended working group to examine the Special Rapporteur's report and make recommendations on how to improve the application of the Rules. In examining the Special Rapporteur's report, the Commission, through its open-ended working group, shall consult international organizations of persons with disabilities and specialized agencies, in accordance with rules 71 and 76 of the rules of procedure of the functional commissions of the Economic and Social Council.

12. At its session following the end of the Special Rapporteur's mandate, the Commission should examine the possibility of either renewing that mandate, appointing a new Special Rapporteur or considering another monitoring mechanism, and should make appropriate recommendations to the Economic and Social Council.

13. States should be encouraged to contribute to the United Nations Voluntary Fund on Disability in order to further the implementation of the Rules.

General Assembly resolution 48/96

20 December 1993   Meeting 85   Adopted without vote

Approved by Third Committee (A/48/627) without vote, 28 October (meeting 18); draft by ESC (A/C.3/48/L.3); agenda item 109.
Meeting numbers. GA 48th session: 3rd Committee 11-19, 21, 32; plenary 85.

Tobacco or health

The Economic and Social Council had before it, in January, a 29 June 1992 note[23] by the WHO Director-General transmitting a 1992 World Health Assembly resolution and requesting that the subject "tobacco or health" be put on the agenda of the Economic and Social Council's 1993 session for discussion and follow-up in the General Assembly and organizations of the United Nations system.

At its February organizational session, the Council, by **decision 1993/212**, decided to include the subject as a sub-item for consideration under coordination questions. A report of WHO's Director-General on "tobacco or health" was annexed to a May note by the Secretary-General.[24] The document introduced essential elements on tobacco production, commercialization and consumption, giving an overview of the impact on health, and summarized related policy decisions by the World Health Assembly and proposed multisectoral collaboration for the future.

The WHO Director-General stated that tobacco consumption was a major avoidable cause of death and that the United Nations system should do its utmost to prevent that risk from spreading further, particularly to developing countries.

ECONOMIC AND SOCIAL COUNCIL ACTION

On 30 July, the Economic and Social Council adopted **resolution 1993/79** without vote.

Multisectoral collaboration on "Tobacco or health"
The Economic and Social Council,
Recalling World Health Assembly resolution WHA45.20 of 13 May 1992, in which the Assembly requested multisectoral collaboration within the United Nations system on tobacco or health issues,
Acknowledging the established leadership of the World Health Organization in alerting all Member States to the seriousness of the tobacco pandemic by providing estimates that tobacco use causes 3 million deaths a year and that, based on current smoking patterns, that figure is expected to increase to 10 million a year within the next few decades,
Concerned that, in countries where estimates have been made, more than one third of smokers who begin to smoke during adolescence and continue to smoke throughout their lives will die prematurely as a result of their habit and that, despite long-standing and widespread knowledge of the serious health consequences of tobacco use, worldwide tobacco production exceeds 7 million tons and is still increasing,
Concerned about the economic effects of reduced production in the tobacco-producing countries, which are still unable to develop a viable economic alternative to tobacco,
Recalling that the World Health Assembly, by its resolutions WHA39.14 of 15 May 1986 and WHA43.16 of 17 May 1990, has urged Member States to adopt comprehensive strategies of tobacco control,
Stressing that the serious health consequences of tobacco use cannot be tackled effectively without appropriate strategies for demand reduction,
Noting that the World Bank has adopted a policy of providing no new loans for tobacco growing or manufacturing projects,
Acknowledging the socio-economic context of tobacco production and the concerns of the tobacco-producing countries, particularly those that depend heavily on tobacco production, and acknowledging also that the implementation of comprehensive strategies as recommended by the World Health Organization will involve matters of tobacco agriculture, commerce, trade, taxation and marketing,
Acknowledging also that many international agencies, including the Food and Agriculture Organization of the United Nations, the General Agreement on Tariffs and Trade, the International Labour Organisation, the United Nations Conference on Trade and Development, the United Nations Development Programme, the United Nations Industrial Development Organization, the World Health Organization and the World Bank, must collaborate closely in developing multisectoral approaches to the tobacco or health issue, particularly with respect to the concerns of tobacco-producing developing countries,

Acknowledging further that cultural practices and customs relating to the use of tobacco should be duly taken into account in developing multisectoral approaches to the tobacco or health issue,
1. *Takes note* of the report of the Director-General of the World Health Organization on the need for multisectoral collaboration on tobacco or health;
2. *Urges* Governments to intensify their commitment and efforts designed to reduce tobacco consumption and the demand for tobacco products, including the implementation of comprehensive multisectoral plans at the country level;
3. *Requests* the Secretary-General to seek the full collaboration of the World Bank, the Food and Agriculture Organization of the United Nations, the General Agreement on Tariffs and Trade, the International Labour Organisation, the United Nations Conference on Trade and Development, the United Nations Development Programme, the United Nations Industrial Development Organization, the World Health Organization, other United Nations organizations and other international organizations, as appropriate, in contributing to the successful implementation of effective comprehensive strategies through multisectoral collaboration among international agencies;
4. *Also requests* the Secretary-General to establish, under the auspices of the World Health Organization and within existing resources, a focal point among existing institutions of the United Nations system on the subject of multisectoral collaboration on the economic and social aspects of tobacco production and consumption, taking into particular account the serious health consequences of tobacco use;
5. *Suggests* that the multisectoral collaboration coordinated through the United Nations system focal point seek to offer practical advice and assistance to Member States, at their request, on how they can implement or strengthen comprehensive national tobacco control strategies;
6. *Suggests also* that a review of and recommendations concerning the impact of tobacco production on the economy of tobacco-producing countries, in particular those that depend on tobacco as a major source of income, as well as the impact of tobacco consumption on health, be included in the multisectoral collaboration work coordinated by the focal point;
7. *Invites* Member States and organizations of the United Nations system to develop a range of options, including bilateral and effective multilateral collaboration on agricultural diversification or development of other economic alternatives to tobacco agriculture, as appropriate, to assist economies for which tobacco is a major export, where demand for their tobacco products has decreased as a result of successful strategies for tobacco control;
8. *Requests* the Secretary-General to ensure that the work of the United Nations system focal point begins as soon as possible and that each contributing agency, in consultation with Member States concerned, together with the focal point, develops, before 31 December 1993, individual plans of work, setting out deadlines and achievement milestones, for their agency's contribution to multisectoral collaboration on tobacco or health that will lead to a rapid reduction in the burden of disease and death caused by the pandemic use of tobacco, while giving due consideration to any economic adjustments

that may arise from a reduction in the demand for tobacco products;

9. *Requests* the Secretary-General to report to the Economic and Social Council at its substantive session of 1994 on progress made by the United Nations system focal point in the implementation of multisectoral collaboration on tobacco or health.

Economic and Social Council resolution 1993/79

30 July 1993   Meeting 46   Adopted without vote

3-nation draft (E/1993/L.32), orally revised based on informal consultations; agenda item 4 *(e)*.
Sponsors: Australia, Canada, United States.
Meeting numbers. ESC 31, 32, 40, 46.

REFERENCES

[1]E/ICEF/1993/L.11.   [2]E/1993/34   (dec. 1993/16). [3]E/ICEF/1993/L.6. [4]YUN 1987, p. 859. [5]YUN 1992, p. 821, GA res. 47/40, 1 Dec. 1992. [6]A/48/159-E/1993/59. [7]YUN 1987, p. 645, GA res. 42/8, 26 Oct. 1987. [8]DP/1993/12. [9]YUN 1992, p. 820. [10]E/1993/35 (dec. 93/14). [11]E/1993/68. [12]E/CN.5/1993/4. [13]YUN 1992, p. 821. [14]YUN 1982, p. 981, GA res. 37/52, 3 Dec. 1982. [15]Ibid., p. 983, GA res. 37/53, 3 Dec. 1982. [16]A/48/462. [17]YUN 1992, p. 822. [18]Ibid., GA res. 47/3, 14 Oct. 1992. [19]Ibid., p. 823, ESC dec. 1992/276, 26 July 1992. [20]E/CN.5/1993/5. [21]ESC res. 1990/26, 24 May, 1990. [22]YUN 1992, p. 823, GA res. 47/88, 16 Dec. 1992. [23]E/1993/8. [24]E/1993/56.

Food and agriculture

World food situation

WFC activities. At the 1992 ministerial session[1] of the World Food Council (WFC), the United Nations coordination body on food issues, member States set in motion a review of WFC's future role in the context of the restructuring of the United Nations system. That action effectively suspended WFC's programmed activities, pending completion of the review. The WFC secretariat in Rome was closed and most of its staff reassigned.

On 12 February, the Economic and Social Council decided to undertake an in-depth review of WFC and to submit recommendations to the Assembly for consideration (**decision 1993/208 B**).

In May,[2] the Secretary-General submitted a WFC report, pursuant to a 1992 Assembly resolution on strengthening the United Nations response to world food and hunger problems.[3] Council members agreed on principles to guide United Nations response to those problems, but disagreements concerning the institutional response to those principles remained.

Food aid

CFA activities

In 1993, the Committee on Food Aid Policies and Programmes (CFA), the governing body of WFP, held two sessions at Rome, Italy.

At its thirty-fifth session (31 May-4 June),[4] CFA approved 12 projects recommended by its Sub-Committee on Projects (SCP) at its tenth session (Rome, 24-27 May). Projects included food for schoolchildren, watershed management, small-scale irrigation and food assistance for refugees and displaced persons.

CFA also endorsed the WFP pledging target of $1.5 billion for the 1995-1996 biennium and recognized the importance of one third of the pledges to the regular resources being made in cash. It did not reach consensus on the subject of global food aid resources and the review of food aid policies and programmes. Delegations agreed, however, that the Secretariat should monitor discussions and decisions in other fora and report to the Committee as appropriate. The Committee also agreed that the Secretariat should present its proposals for project criteria to the thirty-eighth session of CFA.

At its thirty-sixth session (25-28 October),[5] CFA approved 11 projects recommended by SCP at its eleventh session.

The Committee took note of reports on the implementation of a 1992 General Assembly request[6] for enhanced coordination of United Nations operational activities[7] and on criteria for project approval.[8]

WFP activities

In 1993, the year of its 30th anniversary, WFP's assistance was of direct benefit to 47 million people who were either disaster victims or beneficiaries of Programme-assisted development projects. The Programme shipped 3.2 million tons of food to poor people during the year, and the total value of relief and development assistance was more than $1.4 billion. Relief assistance accounted for 83 per cent of total new commitments in 1993.

Relief activities

Some 29 million disaster victims, most of them women and children, received WFC assistance in 1993. This was the largest number of people to benefit from WFP relief assistance in any one year. New commitments amounted to some 2.5 million tons of relief food, valued at $1.2 billion.

WFP was the principal source of food assistance for 27 million refugees and displaced people, compared with 14 million in 1992.

This all-time high demand for food for refugees and displaced people was accompanied by a sharp fall in commitments for victims of drought and other natural disasters, with the phasing out of the successful southern Africa drought relief operation. New commitments for victims of natural disasters decreased from 1.2 million tons in 1992 to less than 100,000 tons in 1993.

WFP's relief assistance reached 17.8 million people in Africa and 7.6 million people in the former Yugoslavia, the former Soviet republics and the Middle East. Relief activities were also targeted on some 3.1 million people in south and east Asia and some 200,000 people in the Latin America and Caribbean region.

With substantial deliveries of relief food to areas affected by civil war and strife, WFP strengthened its interaction with United Nations peace-keeping operations. There was a close working relationship with the United Nations Protection Force (UNPROFOR) in the former Yugoslavia, with the United Nations Guard Contingent in Iraq, with the United Nations Operation in Somalia (UNOSOM) and with peace-keeping forces in Mozambique. In Angola, 15,000 tons of food a month were being delivered at the end of 1993 to some 1.4 million victims of war and drought, despite the mining of roads and railways, destruction of bridges and attacks on planes and trucks. In Angola, the flight engineer of a WFP-contracted aircraft lost his life, two WFP employees were severely injured and one staff member disappeared. In Somalia, one employee was shot dead and another was shot and paralysed.

During the year, WFP gave greater attention to disaster mitigation activities, including the identification and design of appropriate projects, vulnerability mapping and emergency training.

Development assistance

At the end of 1993, about 18 million poor people in 83 countries were benefiting from WFP development food aid through 237 operational projects, with a total commitment of $2.8 billion. Of these projects, 107 were in Africa, 70 in Asia and 60 in the Americas.

New development commitments during 1993 totalled $253 million, representing 680,000 tons of food commodities and budget increases for ongoing WFP-assisted development projects. This was the lowest level of commitments in almost two decades. Land development and improvement projects were the largest single category assisted by the Programme.

Resources

During 1993, WFP transferred about $1.6 billion in resources worldwide to the poor and hungry through its regular programme and other expenditure. A target of $1.5 billion was set for donor pledges towards WFP's regular resources for the 1993-1994 biennium .

In its annual report[9] to the Economic and Social Council, FAO and WFC, CFA endorsed a proposed target of $1.5 billion for the 1995-1996 biennium. It expressed concern, however, that only 77 per cent of the target for the previous biennium was achieved. It encouraged donors to try to ensure that current and future biennial targets were met.

ECONOMIC AND SOCIAL COUNCIL ACTION

On 30 July, the Economic and Social Council adopted **resolution 1993/77** without vote.

Target for World Food Programme pledges for the period 1995-1996

The Economic and Social Council,

Taking note of the comments of the Committee on Food Aid Policies and Programmes of the World Food Programme concerning the minimum target for voluntary contributions to the Programme for the period 1995-1996,

Recalling General Assembly resolutions 2462(XXIII) of 20 December 1968 and 2682(XXV) of 11 December 1970, in which the Assembly recognized the experience gained by the World Food Programme in the field of multilateral food aid,

1. *Recommends* to the General Assembly the adoption of the draft resolution annexed to the present resolution;

2. *Urges* States Members of the United Nations and members and associate members of the Food and Agriculture Organization of the United Nations to undertake the preparations necessary for the announcement of pledges at the Sixteenth Pledging Conference for the World Food Programme.

ANNEX
Target for World Food Programme Pledges for the Period 1995-1996

The General Assembly,

Recalling the provisions of its resolution 2095(XX) of 20 December 1965 to the effect that the World Food Programme was to be reviewed before each pledging conference,

Noting that the Programme was reviewed by the Committee on Food Aid Policies and Programmes of the World Food Programme at its thirty-fifth session and by the Economic and Social Council at its substantive session of 1993,

Having considered Economic and Social Council resolution 1993/77 of 30 July 1993 and the recommendation of the Committee on Food Aid Policies and Programmes,

Recognizing the value of and continuing need for multilateral food aid as provided by the World Food Programme since its inception, both as a form of capital investment and for meeting emergency food needs,

1. *Establishes* for the period 1995-1996 a target for voluntary contributions to the World Food Programme of $1.5 billion, of which not less than one third should be in cash and/or services;

2. *Urges* States Members of the United Nations, members and associate members of the Food and Agriculture Organization of the United Nations and appropriate donor organizations to make every effort to ensure that the target is fully attained;

3. *Requests* the Secretary-General, in cooperation with the Director-General of the Food and Agriculture Organization of the United Nations, to convene a pledging conference for this purpose at United Nations Headquarters in 1994.

Economic and Social Council resolution 1993/77

30 July 1993   Meeting 46   Adopted without vote

Draft by Committee on Food Aid Policies and Programmes (E/1993/91); agenda item 3.

Meeting numbers. ESC 24-29, 35, 38, 40, 45, 46.

Food and agricultural development

Fourth replenishment of IFAD

The International Fund for Agricultural Development (IFAD) (see PART SIX, Chapter XVI) continued to provide concessional assistance for financing agricultural projects in developing countries. It became a specialized agency of the United Nations in 1977.[10]

ECONOMIC AND SOCIAL COUNCIL ACTION

On 29 July, the Economic and Social Council adopted **resolution 1993/53** without vote.

Fourth replenishment of the International Fund for Agricultural Development

The Economic and Social Council,

Recalling its resolution 1988/73 of 29 July 1988 on the third replenishment of the International Fund for Agricultural Development,

Bearing in mind General Assembly resolution 47/149 of 18 December 1992 on food and agricultural development, in which the Assembly expressed concern about the increase in hunger and malnutrition and reaffirmed that the right to food was a universal human right,

Taking note of General Assembly resolution 47/197 of 22 December 1992 on international cooperation for the eradication of poverty in developing countries, in which the Assembly, *inter alia*, urged all donors to contribute generously to the fourth replenishment of the International Fund for Agricultural Development,

Bearing in mind resolution CM/Res.1471(LVIII) on the fourth replenishment of the International Fund for Agricultural Development, adopted by the Council of Ministers of the Organization of African Unity at its fifty-eighth ordinary session, held at Cairo from 21 to 26 June 1993,

Reiterating its deep concern about the increasing number of human beings, especially women, who, as a result of acute poverty, continue to suffer from hunger and chronic undernutrition,

Stressing the need further to strengthen international cooperation to overcome poverty and hunger and the urgent requirement to ensure adequate financing for this purpose,

Noting with appreciation the contribution made by the International Fund for Agricultural Development in addressing the needs of the rural poor, particularly small-holding farmers, the landless, rural women and other marginalized groups,

Stressing the necessity of ensuring that the International Fund for Agricultural Development has sufficient resources to consolidate in the years to come the breakthroughs in the fight against hunger and poverty made in its operations over the past fifteen years,

1. *Calls upon* all countries to demonstrate the political will and flexibility to strengthen multilateral support for addressing the problems of hunger and poverty;

2. *Appeals* to all States members of the International Fund for Agricultural Development, the Organisation for Economic Cooperation and Development and the Organization of Petroleum Exporting Countries, and other developing countries, to continue to make every possible effort in the negotiating process in order to complete expeditiously the fourth replenishment of the International Fund for Agricultural Development, at the highest possible level, before the end of 1993.

Economic and Social Council resolution 1993/53

29 July 1993   Meeting 45   Adopted without vote

Draft by Benin on behalf of African States, Chile, and Netherlands (E/1993/L.27), orally revised by Vice-President based on informal consultations; agenda item 3.
Meeting numbers. ESC 24-29, 35, 38, 40, 45.

REFERENCES

[1]YUN 1992, p. 825. [2]A/47/951. [3]YUN 1992, p. 826, GA res. 47/150, 18 Dec. 1992. [4]CFA: 35/17. [5]CFA: 36/13. [6]YUN 1992, p. 552, GA res. 47/199, 22 Dec. 1992. [7]CFA: 36/P/7. [8]CFA: 36/P/8. [9]E/1993/91. [10]YUN 1977, p. 1161.

Nutrition

International Conference on Nutrition

In follow-up to the 1992 International Conference on Nutrition,[1] the WHO Executive Board, at its January 1993 meeting,[2] endorsed the Conference's World Declaration and Plan of Action for Nutrition. It urged member States to strive to eliminate famine and famine-related deaths and nutritional deficiencies by the year 2000 and to incorporate nutrition objectives into national development plans.

The World Declaration and Plan of Action for Nutrition was also brought to the attention of CFA at its October session.[3] In an information note,[4] CFA discussed WFP's contribution to the Plan of Action.

ACC activities

The twentieth session of the Administrative Committee on Coordination (ACC) Subcommittee on Nutrition was held at Geneva from 15 to 19 February 1993.[5] The ACC Organizational Committee stated in April, however, that it could not take note of the Subcommittee's report because it had not been formally adopted.

UNU activities

During 1993, the United Nations University (UNU) completed specialized guidelines for its rapid assessment procedures (RAP) methodology. The specialized guidelines covered such areas as AIDS-related beliefs, attitudes and behaviours and improved household management of diarrhoea.

Working with WHO, UNU developed a master protocol for comparing the effectiveness of weekly versus daily iron supplements for anaemic pregnant women, adolescent girls and preschool children. UNU participated in the ACC Subcommittee on Nutrition, and the UNU-sponsored Group for the Control of Iron Deficiency which was to be redeployed for advocacy purposes as the International Commission for the Prevention of Iron Deficiency.

UNU efforts to establish regional or subregional food composition databases under its International Network of Food Data Systems (INFOODS) continued in 1993. Efforts were proceeding with Arab and south Asian regional groups for the completion of the INFOODS network, while computer facilities were established in New Caledonia. A separate INFOODS regional database for francophone African countries was also under consideration. A companion UNU project continued to help developing countries summarize dietary intake data for the past 30 years and make hard copies of the data available. Data sets for Mexico were completed in 1993, and those for Argentina, the Caribbean and Oceania were awaiting final completion.

A UNU study, *Nutrition and Poverty,* focused on different perceptions of poverty assessment and nutritional status. It attempted to define a standard of nutritional status for comparative assessment purposes and also considered the question of gender bias in nutritional deprivation. Although the evidence suggested a bias against females, the study cautioned that further research was necessary.

REFERENCES

[1]YUN 1992, p. 830. [2]WHO document EB91/1993/REC/1. [3]CFA: 36/13. [4]CFA: 36/P/INF/1. [5]ACC/1993/5.

Chapter XII

Human resources, social and cultural development

During 1993, the United Nations continued to promote human resources, social and cultural development and to implement its crime prevention and criminal justice programme.

Preparations began for the 1995 World Summit for Social Development and proposals were put forward on ways to contribute to its three core issues—greater social integration, poverty reduction and employment generation. Preparatory measures were underway and events were being planned for the observance in 1994 of the International Year of the Family, proclaimed by the General Assembly in 1989.

In 1993, the Assembly proclaimed 1995 the United Nations Year for Tolerance (resolution 48/126).

Concerning crime, the Economic and Social Council, in July, called on the Secretary-General to organize in 1994 a World Ministerial Conference on Organized Transnational Crime (resolution 1993/29). Preparations continued for the Ninth (1995) United Nations Congress on the Prevention of Crime and the Treatment of Offenders.

The United Nations Educational, Scientific and Cultural Organization continued to promote the return or restitution of cultural property to countries of origin.

In October, the Assembly proclaimed 1994 as the International Year of Sport and the Olympic Ideal (48/10) and urged Member States to observe the Olympic Truce (48/11).

In September, the Social Development Division, apart from its Crime Prevention and Criminal Justice Branch, was moved from the Centre for Social Development and Humanitarian Affairs at Vienna and incorporated into the Department for Policy Coordination and Sustainable Development in New York.

Human resources

Human resources development

In response to a 1991 General Assembly request,[1] the Secretary-General submitted a September report on developing human resources for development.[2] He presented an overview of human resources development and discussed official development assistance and efforts to improve cooperation, coordination and monitoring of the human resources development activities of the United Nations system.

The Secretary-General suggested national actions to offset the adverse effects of structural adjustment and stabilization programmes in some developing countries, including: government efforts to improve targeting the most needy while reducing unproductive expenditures, such as military expenditures; allocating at least one fifth of additional aid to human resources development; undertaking an integrated approach when drawing up sectoral policies for human resources development; and removing the structural causes of poverty. He proposed that the United Nations, together with the developing and donor countries, should emphasize betterment of the human condition, including environmental sustainability and participation by all groups and countries in the process.

GENERAL ASSEMBLY ACTION

On 21 December, the General Assembly, on the recommendation of the Second (Economic and Financial) Committee, adopted **resolution 48/205** without vote.

Developing human resources for development
The General Assembly,

Reaffirming its resolutions 44/213 of 22 December 1989, 45/191 of 21 December 1990 and 46/143 of 17 December 1991 on developing human resources for development, as well as its resolutions S-18/3 of 1 May 1990 and 45/199 of 21 December 1990,

Recalling its resolutions 40/179 of 17 December 1985 and 44/234 of 22 December 1989,

Reaffirming that people are central to all developmental activities and that human resources development is an essential means of achieving sustainable development goals,

Recognizing that the concept of human resources development specifically refers to the human component of economic, social and development activities,

Emphasizing that human resources development should contribute to total human development and that there is therefore a need to integrate human resources development into comprehensive strategies for human development which are sensitive to gender considerations, taking into account the needs of all people, in particular the needs of women,

Stressing the need for adequate resources to enhance the capacity of Governments of developing countries to promote human resources development in pursuit of their national programmes, plans and strategies for development,

Stressing also that Governments of developing countries have the primary responsibility for defining and implementing appropriate policies for human resources development,

Recognizing that, while stabilization and structural adjustment programmes are intended to promote economic growth and development, elements of such programmes may have a possibly adverse impact on human resources development, and also that there is a need to take action, in the formulation and implementation of these programmes, to mitigate their negative effects,

Stressing further that a favourable international economic environment is crucial to enhancing human resources development for the promotion of economic growth and development in developing countries,

Emphasizing the importance of international cooperation in supporting national efforts in human resources development in developing countries and the vital roles of North-South and South-South cooperation in this regard,

Emphasizing also the need for organs, organizations and bodies of the United Nations system to give priority to human resources development and to approach the relevant activities in a coordinated and integrated manner,

1. *Takes note* of the report of the Secretary-General;

2. *Emphasizes* that, in the development of human resources, an overall, well-conceived and integrated approach which is sensitive to gender considerations should be adopted, incorporating such vital areas as population, health, nutrition, water, sanitation, housing, communications, education and training and science and technology, as well as taking into account the need to create more opportunities for employment, in an environment that guarantees opportunities for political freedom, popular participation, respect for human rights, justice and equity, all of which are essential for enhancing human capacities to meet the challenge of development;

3. *Also emphasizes* the need to ensure the full mobilization and integration of women in the formulation and implementation of appropriate national policies to promote human resources development;

4. *Reaffirms* the importance of women and youth in human resources development, and in this context welcomes the Fourth World Conference on Women: Action for Equality, Development and Peace, to be held at Beijing from 4 to 15 September 1995, and the proposal noted at the Meeting of the Heads of Government of the Countries of the Commonwealth, held at Limassol, Cyprus, from 21 to 25 October 1993, to convene a global summit on youth at an agreed date;[a]

5. *Stresses* the importance of international support for national efforts and regional programmes for human resources development in developing countries, particularly in the area of national capacity-building, and the need to increase the flow of resources to developing countries for such activities, through, *inter alia*, the improvement of the international economic environment;

6. *Calls upon* the organs, organizations and bodies of the United Nations system, at the request of develop-ing countries, to take appropriate steps to strengthen the support provided by their operational activities to national and regional action and targets for human resources development, in particular by improving coordination and by developing a multisectoral, integrated approach;

7. *Calls upon* the relevant bodies to bear in mind the need to mitigate the possible negative impact and to include appropriate social safety nets in the formulation and implementation of stabilization and structural adjustment programmes in developing countries, taking into account the needs of all people, including the needs of women;

8. *Notes* the important role that non-governmental organizations can play in human resources development;

9. *Requests* the Secretary-General to continue to monitor the activities of the United Nations system in human resources development and, in this regard, to submit to the General Assembly at its fiftieth session a report on the implementation of the present resolution, including further action taken to enhance inter-agency coordination within the United Nations system with regard to human resources development and bearing in mind the definition of human resources development presented in General Assembly resolutions 44/213, 45/191 and 46/143;

10. *Invites* the United Nations system to assist developing countries, at their request, in developing their capacity to assess, *inter alia*, through appropriate indicators, progress made in satisfying, in the pursuit of human resources development, the fundamental economic, social and cultural needs of their populations, and requests the Secretary-General to include in the report requested in paragraph 9 above information on the steps taken towards that end;

11. *Also requests* the Secretary-General to take into account the important role of human resources development in the elaboration of an agenda for development;

12. *Decides* to include in the provisional agenda of its fiftieth session the item entitled "Human resources development".

---

[a]A/48/564.

General Assembly resolution 48/205

21 December 1993   Meeting 86   Adopted without vote

Approved by Second Committee (A/48/730) without vote, 6 December (meeting 45); draft by Vice-Chairman (A/C.2/48/L.56), based on informal consultations on A/C.2/48/L.9, orally revised; agenda item 104.

Meeting numbers. GA 48th session: 2nd Committee 15, 17, 21, 45; plenary 86.

UNDP activities

Human Development Report

The *Human Development Report 1993*, prepared by the United Nations Development Programme (UNDP), focused on participation in development through markets, government and community organizations. The report discussed free and open markets as a form of participation for producers and consumers, people's participation in governance, and people's participation in civil society, particularly the role of non-governmental organizations (NGOs).

The report stated that building societies around people's genuine needs called for new concepts of human security that stressed the security of people, not only of nations; new models of sustainable human development that invested in human potential and created an enabling environment for the full use of human capabilities; new partnerships between the state and the market to combine market efficiency with social compassion; new patterns of national and global governance to accommodate the rise of people's aspirations and the decline of the nation-state; and new forms of international cooperation that focused directly on the needs of people.

UN research and training institutes

UN Institute for Training and Research

UNITAR activities

During 1993, the United Nations Institute for Training and Research (UNITAR) continued to focus on training activities, organizing 66 courses involving some 2,749 participants.

Training programmes covered multilateral diplomacy and international affairs management, including institution building, dispute resolution, peace-keeping and peacemaking; environmental and natural resource management; debt and financial management; and disaster relief management.

In 1993, UNITAR launched its fellowship programme in peacemaking and preventive diplomacy, the first training course of that kind to be held within the United Nations system, for 24 participants (Burg Schlaining, Austria, 6-24 September). Due to newly established links with UNDP, the United Nations Environment Programme (UNEP) and other United Nations institutions and organs, as well as development agencies and training institutes, UNITAR was able to provide training for an increasing number of participants.

GENERAL ASSEMBLY ACTION

On 8 April, the General Assembly, on the recommendation of the Second Committee, adopted **resolution 47/227** without vote.

United Nations Institute for Training and Research
The General Assembly,

Recalling its resolution 46/180 of 19 December 1991,

Having considered the reports of the Secretary-General and of the Acting Executive Director of the United Nations Institute for Training and Research, and taking into account the statements made before the Second Committee of the General Assembly on the Institute,

Noting the steps taken by the Secretary-General to restructure the Institute,

Recognizing the continuing importance and relevance of the interdisciplinary training functions within the United Nations system and the need to respond to the new challenges facing the United Nations and to meet the growing training requirements of Member States and staff in the United Nations system,

Recognizing that, in the context of the ongoing restructuring of the United Nations, the overall capacity of the United Nations in research and data-gathering should be enhanced,

Acknowledging that a restructured Institute should continue to develop a more structured relationship with relevant national and international institutions,

Reaffirming that the Institute should focus on providing training programmes and research activities related to training,

1. *Decides* that, in accordance with the recommendations of the Secretary-General, the building of the United Nations Institute for Training and Research shall be immediately transferred to the United Nations in return for the cancellation of the debt of the Institute and coverage of its financial obligations for 1992;

2. *Also decides* that, in accordance with the recommendations of the high-level consultant, as approved by the Board of Trustees of the United Nations Institute for Training and Research and by the Secretary-General in his report, the headquarters of the Institute shall be transferred to Geneva, and requests the Secretary-General to designate a liaison officer to organize and coordinate the existing training programmes and research activities relating to training in New York, within existing resources, drawing as appropriate on the services of senior fellows who shall be funded from voluntary contributions to the Institute;

3. *Further decides* that, as at 1 January 1993, the funding of all the administrative budget and the training programmes of the Institute shall be covered from voluntary contributions, donations, special-purpose grants and executing agency overheads;

4. *Invites* the international community to make voluntary contributions to the restructured Institute, in particular to its General Fund, so as to assure its viability;

5. *Decides* that the funding of training programmes held at the specific request of Member States of the United Nations and members of other United Nations system organs and specialized agencies should be arranged by the requesting parties;

6. *Requests* the Secretary-General to explore further closer cooperation between the Institute and other qualified national and international institutions, including, *inter alia*, the International Training Centre of the International Labour Organisation, at Turin, Italy, in order to enable the United Nations system to respond to the increasing training needs at both the international and the national level in the most cost-effective manner and in the best interests of the participating Member States;

7. *Invites* the Secretary-General, in the context of the ongoing restructuring process of the United Nations, to continue his work on a comprehensive review of the research capacity of the United Nations system and to make proposals for the enhancement of that capacity, including the possibility of transferring the non-training related research functions of the Institute to other appropriate United Nations bodies, such as the United Nations University, and the possibility of promoting cooperation mechanisms with other relevant national and international research institutes;

8. *Invites* the Institute to improve its cooperation with relevant national, regional and international institutions that can contribute to fulfilling its training and related

research needs in the field of international relations and in response to the new challenges facing the United Nations;

9. *Urges* the Institute to improve its collaboration with the United Nations and its funds and programmes;

10. *Requests* the Secretary-General to submit to the General Assembly at its forty-eighth session a report on the arrangements mentioned above.

General Assembly resolution 47/227

8 April 1993   Meeting 98   Adopted without vote

Approved by Committee (A/47/729) without vote, 16 December (meeting 51); draft by Vice-Chairman of Committee (A/C.2/47/L.91), based on informal consultations on draft A/C.2/47/L.60/Rev.1, orally revised; agenda item 89 *(a)*.

Financial implications. 5th Committee, A/47/914; S-G, A/C.2/47/L.94, A/C.5/47/82.

Meeting numbers. GA 47th session: 2nd Committee 41, 42, 47, 51; 5th Committee 58; plenary 98.

On 21 December, the Assembly, also on the recommendation of the Second Committee, adopted **resolution 48/207** without vote.

United Nations Institute for Training and Research

The General Assembly,

Recalling its resolution 47/227 of 8 April 1993,

Taking note of the report of the Secretary-General,

Noting with appreciation the steps taken to complete the process of restructuring the United Nations Institute for Training and Research, including the write-off of the debt through the disposition of the building of the Institute in New York, the transfer of its headquarters from New York to Geneva, the designing of programmes with a focus on providing training programmes and on research activities related to training and, finally, the introduction of strict administrative and financial management criteria,

Recognizing the importance and relevance of the interdisciplinary training functions within the United Nations system, the research activities and research relating to training aimed at enhancing the effectiveness of the work of the United Nations,

1. *Invites* the international community to make voluntary contributions to the restructured United Nations Institute for Training and Research so as to assure its viability and the future development of its training programmes;

2. *Requests* the Secretary-General to examine, in accordance with paragraph 2 of General Assembly resolution 47/227, the measures taken in 1993 with a view to improving further the organization and coordination of the training programmes and research activities relating to training in New York, and to provide appropriate logistical and administrative support, within existing resources;

3. *Recommends* that, as an interim measure and without budgetary implications, the full-time senior fellows should continue in their functions and status until a final decision is taken in this regard on the basis of the recommendations of the Board of Trustees of the Institute during its June session, but no later than 1 July 1994;

4. *Also requests* the Secretary-General, in the context of his report on the implementation of the present resolution and in pursuance of General Assembly resolution 47/227, to submit to the Assembly at its forty-ninth session:

(a) Proposals for the enhancement of the research capacity of the United Nations system, including the possibility of transferring the non-training-related research functions of the Institute to other appropriate United Nations bodies, such as the United Nations University, and the possibility of promoting cooperation mechanisms with other relevant national and international research institutes;

(b) Information on the possibility of closer cooperation between the Institute and other qualified national and international institutions, including the International Training Centre of the International Labour Organisation at Turin, Italy.

General Assembly resolution 48/207

21 December 1993   Meeting 86   Adopted without vote

Approved by Second Committee (A/48/732) without vote, 13 December (meeting 48); draft by Vice-Chairman (A/C.2/48/L.88), based on informal consultations on A/C.2/48/L.71; agenda item 106.

Financial implications. 5th Committee, A/48/794; S-G, A/C.2/48/L.84, A/C.5/48/57.

Meeting numbers. GA 48th session: 2nd Committee 42, 46, 48; 5th Committee 43; plenary 86.

Financial situation and restructuring of UNITAR

As requested by the General Assembly in April, the Secretary-General reported in November[3] that the UNITAR building in New York had been transferred to the United Nations in exchange for cancellation of its debt and coverage of its 1992 financial obligations. As at 31 December 1992, the building was valued at $10.6 million in the accounts of the United Nations. Effective 1 July 1993, UNITAR headquarters was transferred to Geneva. However, arrangements were made to continue the multilateral diplomacy programmes in New York under United Nations auspices because of the widely expressed view that they had served a useful purpose for a large number of Member States.

In the nine months ending 30 September 1993, UNITAR received government contributions totalling $262,800. Miscellaneous income amounted to $166,400, resulting in total available resources of $429,200. Expenditures amounted to $417,200 as at the end of September. The Secretary-General stated that UNITAR's financial situation remained very tight and fragile and, unless UNITAR mobilized significant contributions and other income during the 1994-1995 biennium, there was serious danger of further financial difficulty.

UN University

UNU activities

In 1993,[4] the United Nations University (UNU), an autonomous academic institution within the United Nations system, continued to carry out research, advanced training and the dissemination of knowledge on subjects of concern to the United Nations and its agencies. Research was carried out on universal human values and global responsibilities; new directions in the world economy; sustaining global life-support systems;

advances in science and technology; and population dynamics and human welfare.

During the year, 63 UNU fellows completed their studies and 82 new fellows started their training. They included 13 fellows in geothermal energy at the National Energy Authority (Iceland); 5 in remote sensing technology at the Instituto de Pesquisas Espaciais (Brazil) and 1 at the University of Leicester (United Kingdom); 16 in biotechnology at various institutions in Argentina, Brazil, Chile, Mexico and Venezuela; 5 in microinformatics at various institutions in Ireland and 9 at the UNU International Institute for Software Technology (Macau); 8 in renewable energy systems at the Indian Institute of Technology (Delhi, India); 9 in limnology and management of inland waters at the University of São Paulo (Brazil); 14 in food science and technology and nutrition at the University of Ghana, the Instituto de Nutrición de Centro America y Panamá (Guatemala), the National Food Research Institute (Japan), the Central Food Technological Research Institute (India), the Universities of Nottingham and Reading (United Kingdom) and the University of Nairobi (Kenya); 1 in science and technology policy at the University of Sussex (United Kingdom); and 1 in economics at the University of Warwick (United Kingdom).

In addition, over 230 individuals attended short-term training courses and workshops in natural hazard reduction, biotechnology, genetic engineering techniques and the application of microcomputers for teaching mathematics and sciences.

Among the 26 titles published by the UNU Press in 1993 were: *Environmental Change and International Law: New Challenges and Dimensions; The Global Greenhouse Regime: Who Pays?; Latin America Today; Peace and Security in the Asia Pacific Region: Post-Cold War Problems and Prospects*; and *Who Will Save the Forests? Knowledge, Power and Environmental Destruction.*

UNU Council

The UNU Council held two sessions in 1993, both in Tokyo—its thirty-ninth (15-20 February), held in conjunction with the inauguration of the UNU permanent headquarters building, and its fortieth (13-17 December). In December, the Council adopted the budget and academic programme for 1994-1995, approved a new statute on dissemination and endorsed a policy on scholarly publishing. Several proposals for new UNU academic initiatives were also approved and an internal assessment group was set up to examine the University's performance under its second Medium-Term Perspective for 1990-1995.

On 30 July, by **decision 1993/332**, the Economic and Social Council took note of the Council's 1992 report.[5]

In November,[3] the Secretary-General stated that the UNU programme budget for the 1994-1995

biennium emphasized strengthening the academic contributions of the University to policy questions that needed to be addressed by the United Nations. Plans were also under way to intensify research activities directly benefiting the United Nations system.

University for Peace

In accordance with a 1991 resolution,[6] the General Assembly considered at its 1993 session the item entitled "University of Peace".

GENERAL ASSEMBLY ACTION

On 25 October, the General Assembly adopted **resolution 48/9** without vote.

University for Peace
The General Assembly,

Recalling that in its resolution 34/111 of 14 December 1979 it approved the idea of establishing a University for Peace as a specialized international centre for postgraduate studies, research and the dissemination of knowledge specifically aimed at training for peace within the system of the United Nations University,

Recalling also that in its resolution 35/55 of 5 December 1980 it approved the establishment of the University for Peace in conformity with the International Agreement for the Establishment of the University for Peace,

Recalling further its resolutions 45/8 of 24 October 1990 and 46/11 of 24 October 1991 on the tenth anniversary of the University, as well as the report of the Secretary-General on that anniversary,

Recognizing that the University has suffered from financial limitations which have impeded the development of the activities and programmes necessary for carrying out its important mandate,

Recognizing also the various activities carried out by the University during the period 1991-1993 largely thanks to the financial contributions made by Costa Rica, Italy and Spain, as well as by the Commission of the European Communities, and other contributions by foundations and non-governmental organizations,

Noting that in 1991 the Secretary-General, with the assistance of the United Nations Development Programme, established a Trust Fund for Peace consisting of voluntary contributions in order to provide the University with the means necessary to extend its sphere of activity to the rest of the world and to take full advantage of its potential capacity for education, research and support of the United Nations, and to carry out its mandate of working to promote peace in the world, with emphasis on specific research and training activities in the context of the report of the Secretary-General entitled "An Agenda for Peace" in the areas of the prevention of conflict, the maintenance and consolidation of peace and the peaceful settlement of disputes,

Recalling that Slovenia acceded to the International Agreement for the Establishment of the University for Peace on 6 June 1992,

Recalling also that in its resolution 46/11 it decided to include in the agenda of its forty-eighth session and biennially thereafter an item entitled "University for Peace",

1. *Reiterates its appreciation* to the Secretary-General for the establishment of the Trust Fund for Peace, consist-

ing of voluntary contributions for the purpose of assisting the University for Peace to develop its activities for the promotion of peace and to ensure that it has the increasing and essential resources to pursue its future activities;

2. *Invites* Member States, non-governmental organizations and intergovernmental bodies as well as interested individuals and organizations to contribute directly to the Trust Fund for Peace and to the budget of the University;

3. *Also invites* Member States to accede to the International Agreement for the Establishment of the University for Peace, thus demonstrating their support of a global institution for peace studies whose mandate is the promotion of world peace;

4. *Decides* to include in the agenda of its fiftieth session the item entitled "University for Peace".

General Assembly resolution 48/9

25 October 1993   Meeting 36   Adopted without vote

40-nation draft (A/48/L.11 and Add.1); agenda item 22.

Sponsors: Afghanistan, Antigua and Barbuda, Argentina, Barbados, Belarus, Bolivia, Cambodia, Cape Verde, Chile, Colombia, Congo, Costa Rica, Cuba, Cyprus, Dominican Republic, Ecuador, El Salvador, Guatemala, Honduras, Italy, Kyrgyzstan, Mongolia, Morocco, Myanmar, Nicaragua, Pakistan, Panama, Paraguay, Peru, Romania, Saint Lucia, Singapore, Spain, Sri Lanka, Suriname, Thailand, Togo, Ukraine, Uruguay, Venezuela.

REFERENCES

[1]YUN 1991, p. 644, GA res. 46/143, 17 Dec. 1991.
[2]A/48/364. [3]A/48/574. [4]A/49/31. [5]YUN 1992, p. 833.
[6]YUN 1991, p. 650, GA res. 46/11, 24 Oct. 1991.

Social and cultural development

Social aspects of development

World social situation

In response to a 1992 Economic and Social Council request,[1] the Secretary-General submitted in January the *Report on the World Social Situation 1993*,[2] which highlighted major improvements in social conditions, drew attention to problems faced in improving social conditions in the difficult economic circumstances of the 1980s, described emerging situations and discussed policies adopted by Governments in response to those situations. It reviewed social development issues in the areas of population growth, urbanization, migration and the situation of refugees; hunger, malnutrition and food supplies; health; education and literacy; housing and sanitation; unemployment; and income distribution and poverty. It examined government expenditure on social services and social and economic indicators that reflect the quality of life. Problem areas in social development were considered, including changes in economic and social institutions; financial crisis and social security reform; ethnic conflicts and national disintegration; production and consumption patterns and the environment; social consequences of tech-

nological advances; and narcotic drug, tobacco and alcohol abuse.

Poverty was the outstanding economic and social problem in the world, afflicting about one fifth of the world's people, almost all of them in developing countries. Objectives expected to be achieved at the 1995 World Summit for Social Development included highlighting the importance of social development issues to policy makers and the public; considering those issues in the light of the new economic and political realities of the world; assessing priorities for social development in policy formulation; evaluating the efficiency of alternative policy instruments; and bringing forth the relative strengths of various organizations and seeking ways to pool their strengths.

A separate section, prepared in accordance with a 1989 General Assembly request,[3] discussed activities carried out to implement the 1969 Declaration on Social Progress and Development.[4]

On 27 July, by **decision 1993/244**, the Economic and Social Council took note of the *Report*.

Social situation in Africa

In response to a 1989 Economic and Social Council request,[5] the Secretary-General submitted, in January, a report[6] describing the critical social situation in Africa and the obstacles which had hindered implementation of the United Nations Programme of Action for African Economic Recovery and Development (1986-1990).[7] It addressed such issues as the state of health, nutrition, education, employment, poverty, population and the environment and the situation of women, youth and refugees.

The report concluded that the continued decline in the African economies, made worse by conventional structural adjustment programmes and unprecedented population growth rates, had left the African family and household in a crisis of unparalleled dimensions. To mitigate the crisis, coherent social development policies were needed that paid attention to all dimensions of human development, including population and the environment and democratization.

Social development

World Summit for Social Development (1995)

In accordance with a 1992 General Assembly resolution,[8] the Preparatory Committee for the World Summit for Social Development held its organizational session in New York from 12 to 16 April 1993,[9] at which it elected officers and adopted its agenda. The Committee decided to hold the World Summit on 11 and 12 March 1995 at Copenhagen, Denmark, preceded by a meeting of personal representatives of heads of State or Government or other high-level representatives from 6 to 10 March 1995. Other decisions adopted by the Committee concerned NGO participation in the World Summit; national contributions; mobilization of voluntary resources of the Trust Fund for the World Summit for Social Development, established in response to a 1992 Assembly resolution;[8] public information; organization of work; the holding of expert meetings in preparation for the Summit; and the provisional agenda for the Committee's first session in 1994. The Committee had before it an April note of the Secretary-General on mobilizing contributions to the Trust Fund[10] and an April note by the Secretariat suggesting guidelines for contributions to the preparatory process of the Summit.[11]

Expert meetings were held on two of the three core issues of the World Summit, one on social integration (The Hague, Netherlands, 27 September–1 October)[12] and the other on the expansion of productive employment (Saltsjöbaden, Sweden, 4-8 October).[13] The third core issue was poverty reduction.

In response to a 1992 Assembly request,[8] the Secretary-General, by an October note,[14] transmitted a report of the regional commissions on activities planned or undertaken in preparation for the World Summit.

By **resolution 1993/64** of 30 July, the Economic and Social Council urged members of the Economic Commission for Africa (ECA) to participate in the preparatory activities for the World Summit and stressed the need for ECA members to adopt a common position on issues to be discussed.

On 20 December, the General Assembly, by **decision 48/428**, took note of the Secretary-General's note transmitting the report of the regional commissions.

Report of the Secretary-General. As decided on 12 February (**decision 1993/204**), the Economic and Social Council, at its high-level segment (28-30 June) focused on the World Summit, including the role of the United Nations system in promoting social development. It asked the Secretary-General to prepare a report on ways of attaining the objectives of the Summit and to examine its core issues. United Nations bodies, including the specialized agencies, were asked to contribute.

As requested, the Secretary-General submitted a June report[15] examining the three core issues of the World Summit—greater social integration, poverty reduction and employment generation—and proposed ways for the United Nations to contribute to social development. He noted that the core issues involved common areas of policy actions, such as the revival of the growth process, affirmative action for the poor, empowerment of marginal and disadvantaged groups, targeted employment generation, human resource develop-

ment, labour market reforms, social security and democratization. They also required a common set of reorientations in international cooperation, including the role of the United Nations system.

In July,[16] the Council's President summarized the debate at the high-level segment, noting that there was wide convergence on the analysis of and prognosis for the world social situation and on the preparation of the World Summit.

GENERAL ASSEMBLY ACTION

On 20 December, on the recommendation of the Third Committee (Social, Humanitarian and Cultural), the General Assembly adopted **resolution 48/100** without vote.

World Summit for Social Development
The General Assembly,

Recalling its resolution 47/92 of 16 December 1992, by which it decided to convene the World Summit for Social Development, agreed on the objectives and core issues of the Summit and, *inter alia*, established a preparatory committee,

Recalling also the deliberations of the Economic and Social Council during the high-level segment of its substantive session of 1993 on the question of the Summit and the deliberations of the Commission for Social Development at its thirty-third session,

Recalling further the decision taken by the Preparatory Committee for the World Summit for Social Development at its organizational session to convene the Summit at Copenhagen on 11 and 12 March 1995, preceded by a meeting of personal representatives of heads of State or Government or other appropriate high-level representatives specifically designated by Governments, from 6 to 10 March 1995,

Considering that the Summit and its preparatory process should strengthen efforts by all countries to promote policies for the enhancement of social integration in all societies, the alleviation and reduction of poverty and the expansion of productive employment,

Considering also the contributions of non-governmental organizations,

Taking into account the need to facilitate the work of the substantive sessions of the Preparatory Committee,

1. *Takes note with appreciation* of the summary prepared by the President of the Economic and Social Council on the deliberations of the Council during the high-level segment of its substantive session of 1993 and of Commission for Social Development resolution 33/1 of 17 February 1993;

2. *Also takes note with appreciation* of the report of the Preparatory Committee for the World Summit for Social Development on its organizational session;

3. *Calls upon* all States, in accordance with paragraph 8 of General Assembly resolution 47/92, to appoint personal representatives of the heads of State or Government or other appropriate high-level representatives to participate in the first session of the Preparatory Committee;

4. *Invites* all States to contribute generously to the voluntary Trust Fund established in accordance with General Assembly resolution 47/92 for the additional activities required for the preparation and holding of

the Summit, particularly the participation of the least developed countries in the Summit and its preparatory process;

5. *Also invites* all States to set up national committees or other arrangements for the Summit and to hold meetings for public debate on the core issues to be addressed by the Summit;

6. *Requests* the Secretary-General to make the necessary provisions, within existing resources, so that the Preparatory Committee may, if it so decides:

(a) Establish, during its first session, a working group of the whole to meet in parallel with the plenary for a duration of one week;

(b) Establish, during its second session, a working group of the whole to meet in parallel with the plenary for a duration of two weeks;

(c) Establish, during its third session, two working groups to meet in parallel with the plenary for a duration of two weeks;

7. *Calls upon* the Secretary-General to report to the Preparatory Committee at its first session on the implementation of the programme of public information for the Summit;

8. *Invites* the organs, organizations and programmes of the United Nations system and other intergovernmental organizations, in particular the United Nations Children's Fund, the United Nations Development Programme, the United Nations Population Fund, the regional commissions and competent regional organizations, the United Nations Centre for Human Settlements (Habitat), the International Labour Organisation, the Food and Agriculture Organization of the United Nations, the United Nations Educational, Scientific and Cultural Organization, the World Health Organization, the World Bank and the International Monetary Fund to inform the Preparatory Committee at its first session about their contributions to the Summit and its preparatory process;

9. *Calls upon* the non-governmental organizations in consultative status with the United Nations and those accredited to the Summit and its preparatory process to contribute fully to the work of the Preparatory Committee and to the Summit;

10. *Requests* the Preparatory Committee to report to the General Assembly at its forty-ninth session on the progress of work of the Committee and the preparations for the Summit.

General Assembly resolution 48/100

20 December 1993   Meeting 85   Adopted without vote

Approved by Third Committee (A/48/627) without vote, 12 November (meeting 32); 100-nation draft (A/C.3/48/L.11/Rev.1), orally revised; agenda item 109.

Sponsors: Afghanistan, Algeria, Angola, Argentina, Armenia, Australia, Austria, Azerbaijan, Bahamas, Bangladesh, Belarus, Belgium, Benin, Burkina Faso, Cameroon, Canada, Cape Verde, Central African Republic, Chad, Chile, China, Costa Rica, Côte d'Ivoire, Cyprus, Democratic People's Republic of Korea, Denmark, Djibouti, Ecuador, Egypt, El Salvador, Ethiopia, Finland, France, Gabon, Germany, Ghana, Greece, Guatemala, Guinea, Guinea-Bissau, Honduras, Iceland, India, Indonesia, Iran, Iraq, Ireland, Italy, Jamaica, Kenya, Kuwait, Latvia, Libyan Arab Jamahiriya, Luxembourg, Madagascar, Malawi, Mexico, Mongolia, Morocco, Myanmar, Namibia, Nepal, Netherlands, Nicaragua, Niger, Nigeria, Norway, Pakistan, Panama, Papua New Guinea, Peru, Philippines, Poland, Portugal, Romania, Russian Federation, Rwanda, Senegal, Sierra Leone, Slovakia, Spain, Sri Lanka, Sudan, Suriname, Swaziland, Sweden, Tajikistan, Thailand, the former Yugoslav Republic of Macedonia, Togo, Trinidad and Tobago, Tunisia, Turkey, Uganda, Ukraine, Uruguay, Venezuela, Viet Nam, Yemen, Zimbabwe.

Meeting numbers. GA 48th session: 3rd Committee 11 to 19, 21, 32; plenary 85.

Monitoring social development plans and programmes

In February,[17] the Commission for Social Development[17] considered a report of the Secretary-General on monitoring international plans and programmes of action relating to social development.[18] It summarized the activities of the United Nations Centre for Social Development and Humanitarian Affairs and the regional commissions in the areas of social development and welfare, youth, ageing, disabled persons and the family.

In response to a 1991 General Assembly request,[19] the Secretary-General, in January,[20] discussed progress achieved in implementing the Guiding Principles for Developmental Social Welfare Policies and Programmes in the Near Future, adopted at a 1987 interregional consultation[21] and endorsed by the Assembly later that year.[22] The report was based on information provided by Governments and the United Nations system and on conclusions drawn from expert meetings. The Secretary-General proposed activities that the Assembly might recommend to Governments, including: participation in international discussions on social development, including preparations for the 1995 World Summit; organizing regional conferences to promote implementation of the Guiding Principles; developing a comprehensive national social policy; establishing national councils for social development; using the observance of the International Year of the Family in 1994 (see below) as an opportunity to draw up an integrated national family strategy; and promoting and facilitating mutual interaction between efforts to implement the Guiding Principles and those to implement Agenda 21, adopted by the 1992 United Nations Conference on Environment and Development.[23]

On 27 July, the Economic and Social Council, by **decision 1993/244**, took note of the Secretary-General's report.

On 20 December, the Assembly, by **decision 48/428**, also took note of it.

Social development cooperation

As requested by the Economic and Social Council in 1991,[24] the Secretary-General submitted a report[25] on progress achieved and obstacles encountered in implementing the social development goals and objectives of the International Development Strategy for the Fourth United Nations Development Decade (the 1990s), adopted by the General Assembly in 1990,[26] and on progress made in carrying out the suggestions and recommendations made in 1990 at an expert group meeting on the social impact of the critical economic environment on developing countries.[27] The Secretary-General described recent thinking on the nature of social development and the scope for social policy in the context of the International Development Strategy and proposed several areas in which existing activities for development and international cooperation might be revised or expanded, based on the recommendations of the expert group.

On 27 July, by **decision 1993/244**, the Economic and Social Council took note of the Secretary-General's report.

International year for tolerance

Pursuant to a 1992 General Assembly request,[28] the Secretary-General, by a June note,[29] transmitted the report of the Director-General of the United Nations Educational, Scientific and Cultural Organization (UNESCO) containing his suggestions on the observance of a United Nations year for tolerance, which UNESCO sought to have proclaimed for 1995. The Director-General described possible UNESCO activities in observance of the year and summarized the Economic and Social Council's criteria and procedures concerning proposals for international years, adopted in 1980.[30] The report contained a draft declaration on tolerance adopted by a meeting of experts (Istanbul, Turkey, 16 and 17 April 1993) and the text of a UNESCO Executive Board decision, adopted in May, on the proclamation of a United Nations year for tolerance and declaration of tolerance.

ECONOMIC AND SOCIAL COUNCIL ACTION

On 29 July, the Economic and Social Council adopted **resolution 1993/57** without vote.

Question of a United Nations year for tolerance

The Economic and Social Council,

Recalling its decision 1992/267 of 30 July 1992,

Taking note of General Assembly resolution 47/124 of 18 December 1992 on the United Nations year for tolerance,

Referring to decision 5.4.3 of 28 May 1993, adopted by the Executive Board of the United Nations Educational, Scientific and Cultural Organization at its one hundred forty-first session,

Bearing in mind its resolution 1980/67 of 25 July 1980 and General Assembly decision 35/424 of 5 December 1980 on guidelines for international years and anniversaries,

1. *Stresses* the importance of national and international efforts to promote tolerance;

2. *Takes note with appreciation* of the report of the Director-General of the United Nations Educational, Scientific and Cultural Organization containing his suggestions on the observance of the United Nations year for tolerance;

3. *Encourages* the United Nations Educational, Scientific and Cultural Organization to continue its work on the preparation of a declaration on tolerance;

4. *Recommends* that the General Assembly, at its forty-eighth session, proclaim 1995 the United Nations year for tolerance.

Economic and Social Council resolution 1993/57

29 July 1993　　　Meeting 45　　　Adopted without vote

21-nation draft (E/1993/L.31); agenda item 4 *(d)*.
Sponsors: Afghanistan, Algeria, Austria, Belarus, Chile, Czech Republic, Guinea, India, Indonesia, Mauritius, Mexico, Morocco, Pakistan, Peru, Romania, Senegal, Slovakia, Togo, Tunisia, Turkey, Ukraine.
Meeting numbers. ESC 31, 32, 40, 45.

GENERAL ASSEMBLY ACTION

On 20 December, on the recommendation of the Third Committee, the General Assembly adopted **resolution 48/126** without vote.

United Nations Year for Tolerance

The General Assembly,

Recalling that the Charter of the United Nations affirms in its preamble that to practise tolerance is one of the principles to be applied to attain the ends pursued by the United Nations of preventing war and maintaining peace,

Recalling also that one of the purposes of the United Nations as set forth in the Charter is the achievement of international cooperation in solving international problems of an economic, social, cultural or humanitarian character and in promoting and encouraging respect for human rights and for fundamental freedoms for all without distinction as to race, sex, language or religion,

Mindful of the Universal Declaration of Human Rights and of the International Covenants on Human Rights,

Bearing in mind the Vienna Declaration and Programme of Action, adopted by the World Conference on Human Rights, held at Vienna from 14 to 25 June 1993,

Convinced that tolerance—the recognition and appreciation of others, the ability to live together with and to listen to others—is the sound foundation of any civil society and of peace,

Recalling its resolution 47/124 of 18 December 1992, in which, *inter alia*, it invited the Economic and Social Council to consider at its substantive session of 1993 the question of proclaiming 1995 the United Nations year for tolerance and to transmit a recommendation to the General Assembly at its forty-eighth session,

Recalling also resolution 5.6 of the General Conference of the United Nations Educational, Scientific and Cultural Organization, concerning the proclamation of 1995 as the United Nations year for tolerance,

Taking note of Economic and Social Council resolution 1993/57 of 29 July 1993, in which the Council recommended that the General Assembly, at its forty-eighth session, proclaim 1995 the United Nations year for tolerance,

Taking into account the note by the Secretary-General, transmitting the report of the Director-General of the United Nations Educational, Scientific and Cultural Organization,

Bearing in mind its decision 35/424 of 5 December 1980 and Economic and Social Council resolution 1980/67 of 25 July 1980 concerning guidelines for international years and anniversaries,

Noting that the preparations for the United Nations year for tolerance will not involve any financial implications for the United Nations,

1. *Proclaims* 1995 the United Nations Year for Tolerance;

2. *Recommends* that the specialized agencies, regional commissions and other organizations of the United Nations system consider in their respective forums the contributions they could make to the success of the Year;

3. *Invites* the United Nations Educational, Scientific and Cultural Organization to assume the role of lead organization for the Year;

4. *Calls upon* all Member States to cooperate with the United Nations Educational, Scientific and Cultural Organization in the preparation of the national and international programmes for the Year and to participate actively in the implementation of the activities to be organized within the framework of the Year;

5. *Invites* interested intergovernmental and non-governmental organizations to exert efforts in their respective fields to contribute adequately to the preparation of programmes for the Year;

6. *Requests* the United Nations Educational, Scientific and Cultural Organization to prepare, in accordance with its General Conference resolution 5.6, a declaration on tolerance;

7. *Decides* to include in the provisional agenda of its forty-ninth session an item entitled "Preparation for and organization of the United Nations Year for Tolerance".

General Assembly resolution 48/126

20 December 1993   Meeting 85   Adopted without vote

Approved by Third Committee (A/48/632/Add.2) without vote, 6 December (meeting 52); 33-nation draft (A/C.3/48/L.46); agenda item 114 *(b)*.

Sponsors: Afghanistan, Albania, Algeria, Argentina, Austria, Azerbaijan, Belarus, Chile, Comoros, Costa Rica, Czech Republic, Dominican Republic, Egypt, Guinea, India, Indonesia, Kyrgyzstan, Lebanon, Mauritania, Mauritius, Morocco, Pakistan, Peru, Philippines, Republic of Korea, Romania, Russian Federation, Senegal, the former Yugoslav Republic of Macedonia, Togo, Tunisia, Turkey, Ukraine.

Meeting numbers. GA 48th session: 3rd Committee 36-52; plenary 85.

The family

International Year of the Family

In response to a 1991 General Assembly request,[31] the Secretary-General submitted an August report[32] updating information presented in his 1992 report[33] on preparations for the 1994 International Year of the Family, proclaimed by the Assembly in 1989.[34] The report contained recommendations made by preparatory and coordinating bodies and other intergovernmental bodies, including: the Commission for Social Development, the Economic and Social Council, the Commission on the Status of Women, the Committee on the Elimination of Discrimination against Women and the World Health Organization. It also outlined preparatory measures for the Year at the national, regional and international levels, as well as events planned for its observance and follow-up.

At least 102 countries had established national coordinating committees or similar mechanisms for the Year and more than 90 countries had initiated national programmes for its preparation and observance or designated national focal points to liaise with the secretariat. Within the United Nations system, 34 offices, bodies and specialized agencies, including the regional commissions, were involved in the preparation for and observance of the Year. In 1993, four regional and interregional preparatory meetings were held to review the situation of families, identify regional priorities and formulate specific recommendations regarding policies concerning families and the observance of the Year for Africa and Western Asia (Tunis, Tunisia, 29 March–2 April); Asia and the Pacific (Beijing, China, 24-28 May); Europe and North America (Valletta, Malta, 26-30 April); and Latin America and the Caribbean (Cartagena, Colombia, 9-14 August).

As at 20 July, contributions to the Voluntary Fund for the International Year of the Family totalled $1,444,540, of which Governments contributed $234,060 and organizations and individuals $1,182,533; some $28,000 was received from other sources.

Annexed to the report was a statement on the Year, jointly issued by concerned organizations and specialized agencies of the United Nations system.

On 20 December, the General Assembly, by **decision 48/428**, took note of the Secretary-General's report.

ECONOMIC AND SOCIAL COUNCIL ACTION

On 27 July, on the recommendation of its Social Committee, the Economic and Social Council adopted **resolution 1993/23** without vote.

International Year of the Family
The Economic and Social Council

Recommends to the General Assembly the adoption of the following draft resolution:
[For text, see General Assembly resolution 47/237 below.]

Economic and Social Council resolution 1993/23

27 July 1993   Meeting 43   Adopted without vote

Approved by Social Committee (E/1993/106) without vote, 14 July (meeting 10); draft by Commission for Social Development (E/1993/24); agenda item 20.

GENERAL ASSEMBLY ACTION

On 20 September, the General Assembly adopted **resolution 47/237** without vote.

International Year of the Family
The General Assembly,

Reaffirming its resolutions 44/82 of 8 December 1989, 45/133 of 14 December 1990 and 46/92 of 16 December 1991 concerning the International Year of the Family, as expressions of the determination of the peoples of the United Nations to promote social progress and better standards of life in larger freedom,

Recalling that major United Nations instruments on human rights and social policy, as well as relevant global plans and programmes of action, call for the widest possible protection and assistance to be accorded to the family,

Convinced that equality between the sexes, women's equal participation in employment and shared parental responsibility are essential elements of modern family policy,

Conscious of the existence of various concepts of the family in different social, cultural and political systems,

Aware, at the same time, that families are the fullest reflection, at the grass-roots level, of the strengths and weaknesses of the social and developmental welfare environment, and as such offer a uniquely comprehensive and synthesizing approach to social issues,

Realizing that families, as basic units of social life, are major agents of sustainable development at all levels of society and that their contribution to that process is crucial for its success,

Stressing that the observance of the Year in 1994 will immediately precede the celebration by the family of nations of the historic fiftieth anniversary of the Charter of the United Nations,

Having considered the report of the Secretary-General, submitted to the Commission for Social Development at its thirty-third session, on the state of preparations for the Year,

1. *Takes note with appreciation* of the report of the Secretary-General on the state of preparations for the International Year of the Family;

2. *Expresses its appreciation* to the Secretary-General for a well-coordinated and impressive effort in the preliminary and preparatory phases to the Year, despite resource constraints, and for the considerable progress made towards its observance;

3. *Notes with satisfaction* that the Year has gained increasing support at all levels and that the preparatory process has enhanced and strengthened the substantive orientation of the Year;

4. *Commends* all Governments, specialized agencies, regional commissions and intergovernmental and non-governmental organizations which have undertaken special efforts to prepare for the observance of the Year;

5. *Urges* Governments, specialized agencies and intergovernmental and non-governmental organizations, especially those which have not yet done so, to intensify the efforts undertaken, *inter alia*, by the identification of national coordinating mechanisms and the elaboration of national programmes of action, in the preparations for and observance of the Year;

6. *Welcomes* the holding in 1993 of four regional and interregional preparatory meetings for the Year, organized by the secretariat for the Year in the Department for Policy Coordination and Sustainable Development of the Secretariat, in close cooperation with the regional commissions, and hosted by the Governments of China, Colombia, Malta and Tunisia;

7. *Takes note with interest* of the proposal by the Government of Slovakia that the Bratislava International Centre of Family Studies be affiliated with the United Nations;

8. *Also takes notes with interest* of the results of the Expert Group Meeting on the Social Consequences of Population Growth and Changing Social Conditions, with Particular Emphasis on the Family, co-sponsored by the Government of Germany and held at Vienna from 21 to 25 September 1992;

9. *Also welcomes* the active involvement of non-governmental organizations in the preparatory process for the Year, including the major global initiative to convene a world non-governmental organization forum entitled "Launching the International Year of the Family, 1994: Strengthening Families for the Well-being of Individuals and Societies", to be held at Valletta from 28 November to 2 December 1993, and calls upon all those concerned to support the event in every possible manner;

10. *Expresses its special gratitude* to Governments and other donors, especially those in the private sector, which have generously responded to earlier appeals to contribute resources to the Voluntary Fund for the International Year of the Family;

11. *Appeals* to all Governments concerned and all other prospective donors to pledge their contributions to the Voluntary Fund, notably during the pledging segments of the regional and interregional preparatory meetings in 1993, with a view to releasing new funds for specific family-oriented projects, particularly in developing countries, during both the Year and the follow-up thereto;

12. *Invites* policy-making organs of specialized agencies and other bodies in the United Nations system to consider, in the context of their substantive mandates, the principles and objectives of the Year and follow-up action to the Year for the benefit of the families of the world;

13. *Also invites* organizations and specialized agencies of the United Nations system to include in their programme budgets for 1994 and 1995, as appropriate, programme elements for the observance of and follow-up to the Year;

14. *Decides* to devote one of its plenary meetings at its forty-eighth session, in early December 1993, to launching the International Year of the Family;

15. *Also decides* that, beginning in 1994, 15 May of every year shall be observed as the International Day of Families;

16. *Requests* the Commission on Human Rights, the Population Commission and the Commission on the Status of Women to include in the agendas of their sessions in 1993 or 1994 consideration of the principles and objectives of the Year in the context of their major areas of concern, and to propose specific follow-up measures regarding human rights, population issues and the advancement of women as each affects or is affected by families, including family-oriented components of the World Conference on Human Rights, held at Vienna from 14 to 25 June 1993, the International Conference on Population and Development, to be held at Cairo from 5 to 13 September 1994, the World Summit for Social Development, to be held at Copenhagen on 11 and 12 March 1995, and the Fourth World Conference on Women: Action for Equality, Development and Peace, to be held at Beijing from 4 to 15 September 1995;

17. *Further decides* to devote two plenary meetings at its forty-ninth session, in 1994, to the implementation of the follow-up to the Year, and to designate those meetings as an international conference on families, which should take place at an appropriate global policy-making level and in keeping with the procedures and practices of the General Assembly;

18. *Appeals* to Member States as well as to all other participants in the observance of the Year to highlight 1994 as a special occasion to benefit families of the world in their quest for a better life for all, based on the principle of subsidiarity, which seeks solutions to problems at the lowest level of the societal structure;

19. *Calls for* a concerted promotional and information campaign on behalf of the Year at the national,

regional and international levels, with the strong participation of the mass media;

20. *Requests* the Secretary-General:

(a) To seek the views of States members of the Commission for Social Development on the desirability of working out a declaration on the role, responsibilities and rights of families on the occasion of the Year;

(b) To plan adequate resources, including staff, through redeployment in the proposed programme budget for the biennium 1994-1995, with a view to ensuring effective observance of and follow-up to the Year, commensurate with its important principles and objectives;

(c) To continue taking specific measures, through all the communication media at his disposal, particularly within the mandates of the Department of Public Information of the Secretariat, to give widespread publicity to the preparations for and observance of the Year, and to increase the dissemination of information on the subject;

(d) To report on the observance of the Year at the national, regional and international levels, and to submit specific proposals on the follow-up to the Year, including a draft plan of action, if deemed appropriate, to the Assembly at its fiftieth session;

21. *Decides* to consider the question of the International Year of the Family at its fiftieth session, on the basis of a report of the Secretary-General under the item entitled "Social Development".

General Assembly resolution 47/237

20 September 1993   Meeting 112   Adopted without vote

Draft by ESC (A/47/1011) in resolution 1993/23; agenda items 12 and 93 *(a)*.

Institutional machinery

Commission for Social Development

At its thirty-third session (Vienna, 8-17 February),[17] the Commission for Social Development recommended to the Economic and Social Council for adoption eight draft resolutions and three draft decisions. It also adopted one resolution and two decisions that called for Council action.

The draft resolutions covered the International Day of Disabled Persons (3 December); the Standard Rules on the Equalization of Opportunities for Persons with Disabilities; development of a plan of action to implement the long-term strategy to further the implementation of the World Programme of Action concerning Disabled Persons; inclusion of persons with disabilities in all aspects of society and the leadership role of the United Nations therein (see previous chapter for action on these four texts); the International Year of the Family (see above); implementation of the International Plan of Action on Ageing; the tenth anniversary of International Youth Year and draft world programme of action for youth towards the year 2000 and beyond (see PART THREE, Chapter XIV for action on these two texts); and the United Nations Research Institute for Social Development (see below).

On 27 July, the Council, by **decision 1993/237**, took note of the Commission's report, endorsed its resolutions and decisions and approved the provisional agenda and documentation for its thirty-fourth (1995) session.

On the same date, by **decision 1993/239**, the Council took note of the Commission's 1993 draft decision entitled "Contribution of comprehensive national social policies to societal management and to the solving of economic, environmental, demographic, cultural and political problems" and asked the Commission to reconsider the draft in 1995.

UN Research Institute for Social Development

In 1993, the United Nations Research Institute for Social Development (UNRISD), an autonomous institution within the United Nations system established to promote research on the social dimensions of development, carried out research on crisis, adjustment and social change; socio-economic and political consequences of the international trade in illicit drugs; environment, sustainable development and social change; ethnic conflict and development; integrating gender into development policy; participation and changes in property relations in communist and post-communist societies; refugees, returnees and local society; and political violence and social movement. UNRISD research projects that focused on the 1995 World Summit for Social Development included rethinking social development in the 1990s; economic restructuring and new social policies; ethnic diversity and public policies; and the challenge of rebuilding war-torn societies.

The Commission on Social Development[17] considered a report of the Board of UNRISD covering the Institute's activities in 1991 and 1992.[35]

ECONOMIC AND SOCIAL COUNCIL ACTION

On 27 July, on the recommendation of its Social Committee, the Economic and Social Council adopted **resolution 1993/25** without vote.

United Nations Research Institute for Social Development

The Economic and Social Council,

Recognizing the importance of research on social issues for the formulation and implementation of development policies and, in this context, the functions and important contribution of the United Nations Research Institute for Social Development,

Emphasizing the important role the Institute can play in the preparations for the World Summit for Social Development, to be held at Copenhagen on 11 and 12 March 1995,

Stressing the need to provide the necessary financial and administrative resources to enable the Institute to play its role and to further enhance its capacity to undertake research on critical problems of social development,

Having considered the report of the Board of the Institute on its activities during the period 1 November 1991 to 31 October 1992,

1. *Expresses its appreciation* to Governments providing financial support to the United Nations Research Institute for Social Development;

2. *Invites* those Governments that have not yet done so to make financial contributions to the Institute according to their capabilities, and those Governments that already support the Institute to consider the possibility of increasing their contributions, in both cases preferably on a regular basis;

3. *Requests* the Secretary-General to continue to provide, within existing resources, financial and administrative services to the Institute in order to give it the capacity to carry out its research on critical social development problems.

Economic and Social Council resolution 1993/25

27 July 1993   Meeting 43   Adopted without vote

Approved by Social Committee (E/1993/106) without vote, 14 July (meeting 10); draft by Commission for Social Development (E/1993/24); agenda item 20.

Crime prevention and criminal justice

Commission on crime prevention and criminal justice

The Commission on Crime Prevention and Criminal Justice, established by the Economic and Social Council in 1992,[36] held its second session at Vienna from 13 to 23 April 1993.[37]

The Commission reviewed its priority themes as set out in a 1992 Council resolution,[38] and discussed, among other things, technical cooperation issues, United Nations standards and norms in crime prevention and criminal justice and cooperation with other United Nations bodies.

The Commission recommended nine draft resolutions for adoption by the Council concerning violence against women (see next chapter); proposed guidelines for the prevention of urban crime; the role of criminal law in the protection of the environment; the 1994 World Ministerial Conference on Organized Transnational Crime; control of the proceeds of crime; strengthening the United Nations crime prevention and criminal justice programme; implementation of General Assembly and Council resolutions concerning crime prevention and criminal justice; preparations for the Ninth (1995) United Nations Congress on the Prevention of Crime and the Treatment of Offenders; and the United Nations African Institute for the Prevention of Crime and the Treatment of Offenders (see below for action on these texts).

It also recommended three draft decisions for adoption by the Council on the organization of future sessions of the Commission; the provisional agenda for its third (1994) session (see below); and the reappointment of two members of the Board of Trustees of the United Nations Interregional Crime and Justice Research Institute (see APPENDIX III).

ECONOMIC AND SOCIAL COUNCIL ACTION

On 27 July, by **decision 1993/243**, the Economic and Social Council took note of the Commission's report on its second session and endorsed its adopted resolutions and decisions. The Council also approved the provisional agenda and documentation for the third (1994) session of the Commission. On the same date, by **decision 1993/242**, the Council decided that the Commission, at its third session, in addition to plenary meetings, should be provided with full interpretation services for eight meetings of the Committee of the Whole, and that future sessions of the Commission should be held for a period of eight days.

Operational activities and coordination

Reports of the Secretary-General. In response to a 1992 Economic and Social Council request,[38] the Secretary-General submitted a January report describing the results of a survey of crime prevention and criminal justice activities carried out within the United Nations system and by intergovernmental organizations and NGOs.[39] The survey focused on three priority themes: organized crime; urban, juvenile and violent criminality; and the administration of justice. The survey showed that organized crime was of concern to the international community, as evidenced by the number of activities undertaken. Of the three priority themes, that of urban, juvenile and violent criminality had the fewest reported activities. A great deal of activity was reported in the area of the administration of justice but was concentrated in more developed regions. An annex to the report listed the 17 United Nations organizations or entities, 41 intergovernmental organizations and 59 NGOs that had responded to the survey questionnaire.

Also in response to a 1992 Council request,[38] the Secretary-General submitted a February report[40] on progress made in establishing a subprogramme on operational activities, planning and coordination in crime prevention and criminal justice; operational activities in the priority areas of organized crime, urban juvenile and violent crime and the administration of justice; criminal justice statistics and information; the possible establishment of a world foundation on crime control and assistance to victims; a convention or other instrument on international cooperation; and the Ninth (1995) United Nations Congress on the Prevention of Crime and the Treatment of Offenders. He also discussed General Assembly and Council action taken since 1991 in crime prevention and criminal justice. The Secretary-General concluded that too short a time had elapsed since the Commission's first (1992) session to assess the United Nations crime prevention and criminal justice programme.

ECONOMIC AND SOCIAL COUNCIL ACTION

On 27 July, on the recommendation of its Social Committee, the Economic and Social Council adopted **resolution 1993/31** without vote.

Strengthening of the United Nations crime prevention and criminal justice programme

The Economic and Social Council,

Recalling General Assembly resolution 46/152 of 18 December 1991, in which the Assembly requested the Secretary-General to give a high level of priority to the activities of the United Nations crime prevention and criminal justice programme,

Taking note of General Assembly resolution 47/91 of 16 December 1992,

Recalling its resolution 1992/22 of 30 July 1992, in section VI of which it accorded high priority to the United Nations crime prevention and criminal justice programme and requested an appropriate share of the overall resources of the United Nations for the programme,

Convinced that the Crime Prevention and Criminal Justice Branch of the Secretariat can only be effective if it is provided with resources that are commensurate with its requirements and that allow it to implement its mandates and to respond in a timely and efficient manner to the increasing requests of Member States for its services,

Taking note of the report of the Secretary-General on the progress made in the implementation of Economic and Social Council resolution 1992/22,

Deeply concerned about the delay in the implementation of General Assembly resolutions 46/152 and 47/91 and Council resolution 1992/22, with respect to strengthening, as resources permit, the United Nations crime prevention and criminal justice programme and upgrading the Crime Prevention and Criminal Justice Branch into a division,

1. *Reaffirms* the importance of the United Nations crime prevention and criminal justice programme and the crucial role it has to play in promoting international cooperation in crime prevention and criminal justice, in responding to the needs of the international community in the face of both national and transnational criminality, and in enabling Member States to achieve the goals of preventing crime within and among States and of improving the response to crime;

2. *Reaffirms also* the importance of the role of the Commission on Crime Prevention and Criminal Justice as the principal policy-making body for the activities of the United Nations in the field of crime prevention and criminal justice;

3. *Reaffirms further* its decision, contained in its resolution 1992/22, section VI, to accord high priority to the United Nations crime prevention and criminal justice programme, in accordance with General Assembly resolution 46/152, and to request an appropriate share of the overall resources of the United Nations for the programme;

4. *Requests* the Secretary-General, as a matter of urgency, to give effect to General Assembly resolutions 46/152 and 47/91 and to Council resolution 1992/22 by strengthening the Crime Prevention and Criminal Justice Branch, by providing it with the resources required for the full implementation of its mandates and by upgrading it into a division, headed by a Director, if necessary by reallocating existing resources;

5. *Takes note* of the proposed programme of work in crime prevention and criminal justice for the biennium 1994-1995, submitted to the Commission on Crime Prevention and Criminal Justice at its second session, and requests the Secretary-General to reflect it, as modified in accordance with decisions of the Commission, in the proposed programme budget for the biennium 1994-1995;

6. *Invites* the Committee for Programme and Coordination, the Advisory Committee on Administrative and Budgetary Questions and the General Assembly to ensure proper follow-up to the proposals of the Secretary-General, pursuant to the present resolution;

7. *Requests* the Secretary-General to report to the Economic and Social Council at its substantive session of 1994, through the Commission on Crime Prevention and Criminal Justice, on progress made in the implementation of Council resolution 1992/22 and the present resolution.

Economic and Social Council resolution 1993/31

27 July 1993   Meeting 43   Adopted without vote

Approved by Social Committee (E/1993/106) without vote, 14 July (meeting 10); draft by Commission on Crime Prevention and Criminal Justice (E/1993/32); agenda item 20.

Also on that date, on the recommendation of its Social Committee, the Council adopted without vote **resolution 1993/34.**

Implementation of General Assembly resolutions 46/152 and 47/91 and Economic and Social Council resolution 1992/22, concerning crime prevention and criminal justice

The Economic and Social Council,

Bearing in mind General Assembly resolution 46/152 of 18 December 1991 on the creation of an effective United Nations crime prevention and criminal justice programme,

Recalling General Assembly resolution 45/109 of 14 December 1990 on computerization of criminal justice,

Bearing in mind General Assembly resolution 46/120 of 17 December 1991 on human rights in the administration of justice,

Bearing in mind also General Assembly resolution 47/91 of 16 December 1992 on crime prevention and criminal justice,

Bearing in mind further section VI of its resolution 1992/22 of 30 July 1992, in which it determined the three priority themes that should guide the work of the Commission on Crime Prevention and Criminal Justice in the development of a detailed programme,

Recalling that in section VII of its resolution 1992/22, it decided, *inter alia,* that the Commission should include in its agenda, beginning with its second session, a standing item on the existing United Nations standards and norms in the field of crime prevention and criminal justice,

Recalling also its resolution 1990/21 of 24 May 1990 on the implementation of United Nations standards and norms in crime prevention and criminal justice,

Taking note of the report of the Pre-sessional Working Group on the Implementation of United Nations Standards and Norms in Crime Prevention and Criminal Justice of the former Committee on Crime Prevention and Control,

Also taking note of the recommendations of the Meeting of Experts for the Evaluation of Implementation of United Nations Norms and Guidelines in Crime Prevention and Criminal Justice,

Recalling section I of its resolution 1992/22, entitled "Strengthening the operational capacity of the United Nations crime prevention and criminal justice programme, especially operational activities and advisory services",

Conscious that preventing and controlling crime is a growing challenge for most Member States and the international community as a whole,

Convinced that developing crime prevention and criminal justice skills is necessary to strengthen the rule of law and to promote democracy,

Alarmed by the negative impact of criminal activities on the development process in many countries, particularly in developing countries and countries in transition,

Bearing in mind the urgent need of the least developed countries for assistance, particularly in training crime prevention and criminal justice officials and practitioners,

Conscious of the relationship between national crime and more sophisticated forms of transnational criminal activities,

Convinced that effective action against crime requires increased technical cooperation activities at the international level, in order to provide appropriate assistance to Member States whose capacity to deal with crime-related issues is insufficient, and to tackle serious forms of international criminal activity, such as organized transnational crime,

Recalling that the General Assembly, in its resolution 46/152, emphasized the practical orientation of the United Nations crime prevention and criminal justice programme and decided that the programme should provide States with practical assistance, such as data collection, information and experience-sharing and training, in order to achieve the goals of preventing crime and improving the response to it,

Concerned about the disparity between the need for technical assistance and the resources available for the United Nations crime prevention and criminal justice programme,

Recalling that in section VI of its resolution 1992/22, it determined that the majority of programme resources should be concentrated on the provision of training, advisory services and technical cooperation in a limited number of areas of recognized need, taking into account the need for technical assistance to developing countries, and that, in implementing special operational activities and advisory services in situations of urgent need, the Secretariat should place major emphasis on serving as a broker and clearing-house,

Convinced that the United Nations crime prevention and criminal justice programme should provide the necessary operational perspective to Member States, thus assisting them in modernizing their criminal justice systems,

Aware that the introduction of modern criminal justice techniques requires education and training of criminal justice personnel,

Mindful that computer-assisted collection, management and distribution of crime prevention and criminal justice information are of growing importance to the effective and humane administration of criminal justice systems,

Expressing its appreciation to the Bureau of Justice Statistics of the United States Department of Justice and the State University of New York at Albany, United States of America, for their strong support in the development of the United Nations Criminal Justice Information Network,

Welcoming the contributions to technical cooperation made on a multilateral or bilateral basis by a number of Governments and institutions and noting in this regard that the United Nations Crime Prevention and Criminal Justice Fund has received contributions from the Governments of France, Italy and Tunisia and from the Helsinki Institute for Crime Prevention and Control, affiliated with the United Nations, and the Asia Crime Prevention Foundation,

Recalling resolution 1/2 of 29 April 1992 of the Commission on Crime Prevention and Criminal Justice, resolutions 1(XXXV), 4(XXXV) and 11(XXXV) of 15 April 1992 of the Commission on Narcotic Drugs and Commission on Human Rights resolution 1992/31 of 18 February 1992,

Reaffirming that the prevention and control of crime require effective, concerted and multidisciplinary action at the national, regional and international levels,

Convinced that the scope of international cooperation in all fields of crime prevention and criminal justice should be extended and increased as a matter of the utmost importance and that technical assistance programmes in crime prevention and criminal justice should be expanded and strengthened as a matter of urgency,

Alarmed by the fact that large financial profits derived from criminal activity may enable transnational criminal organizations to penetrate, infect and corrupt the structure of Governments, legitimate commercial activities and society at large, thereby impeding economic and social development, hampering law and order, undermining the foundation of States and preventing good governance,

Noting, with respect to priority themes, the need to pay particular attention to such issues as organized crime in all its manifestations, money-laundering, the role of criminal law in the protection of the environment, the protection of cultural property from theft and smuggling, domestic violence, the computerization of the administration of criminal justice, juvenile delinquency and street crime,

I. Review of priority themes

1. *Reaffirms* the priority themes formulated by the Commission on Crime Prevention and Criminal Justice at its first session and contained in Economic and Social Council resolution 1992/22, section VI;

2. *Invites* Member States to prepare and circulate in advance of each session proposals on specific objectives and activities, as recommended in Commission resolution 1/1 of 29 April 1992 entitled "Strategic management by the Commission on Crime Prevention and Criminal Justice of the United Nations crime prevention and criminal justice programme", underlining the importance for the third and subsequent sessions of the Commission of implementing the mechanisms, referred

to in paragraphs 32 to 35 of the annex to that resolution, for determining the objectives and the specific activities of the programme;

II. Operational activities of the United Nations Crime Prevention and Criminal Justice Programme

1. *Welcomes with appreciation* the efforts undertaken by the Secretariat to carry out operational activities, notably setting up projects to be implemented in developing countries and countries in transition;

2. *Notes with appreciation* the cooperation between the Crime Prevention and Criminal Justice Branch and other United Nations entities, such as the United Nations International Drug Control Programme, the Division for the Advancement of Women and the Centre for Human Rights of the Secretariat, and recommends that such cooperation be expanded and intensified;

3. *Also notes with appreciation* the support provided by some Member States in the organization of training seminars, *inter alia*, by providing funding and in-kind expertise;

4. *Requests* the Secretary-General to continue elaborating, in accordance with the programme priorities, training curricula that could be implemented in Member States upon request and adapted to particular national or regional conditions and requirements, using new and existing materials such as manuals and other publications, United Nations guidelines, minimum rules and model treaties on crime prevention and criminal justice;

5. *Welcomes with appreciation* the Secretariat's participation in, and contribution to, the work of peace-keeping operations such as those of the United Nations Transitional Authority in Cambodia and the United Nations Protection Force, in accordance with resolution 1992/22;

6. *Requests* the Secretary-General to develop basic courses on United Nations norms and guidelines in the field of crime prevention and criminal justice which can be used, as necessary, for training peace-keeping and emergency mission personnel and their national counterparts;

7. *Also requests* the Secretary-General to ensure the involvement of the Crime Prevention and Criminal Justice Branch in the planning of such missions;

8. *Further requests* the Secretary-General to report to the Commission on Crime Prevention and Criminal Justice, at its third session, on technical cooperation and advisory services of the United Nations crime prevention and criminal justice programme, including appropriate mechanisms for the mobilization of resources;

9. *Requests* the Secretary-General to strengthen the institutional capacity of the United Nations crime prevention and criminal justice programme by providing the Secretariat with adequate human and financial resources, if necessary by reallocating existing resources, as well as by means of voluntary contributions, to enable it to elaborate, execute and evaluate operational activities and advisory services at the request of Member States;

10. *Also requests* the Secretary-General to consider making available the necessary resources for the participation of the least developed countries in the sessions of the Commission on Crime Prevention and Criminal Justice;

11. *Invites* Member States and intergovernmental and non-governmental organizations to contribute to the United Nations Crime Prevention and Criminal Justice Fund in order to augment the implementation of technical assistance projects;

12. *Recommends* to Member States that they integrate, where appropriate, crime prevention and criminal justice components into their priority areas for development, so as to better address crime-related issues in the context of national development;

13. *Reaffirms* the importance of technical cooperation, including that among developing countries;

14. *Recognizes* the relevance of close cooperation between the interregional, regional and associate institutes cooperating with the United Nations in the field of crime prevention and criminal justice and the Crime Prevention and Criminal Justice Branch to the development of technical assistance and research projects at the regional and interregional levels, taking into account regional characteristics and traditions of the various criminal justice systems;

III. United Nations standards and norms in crime prevention and criminal justice

1. *Reaffirms* the importance of United Nations standards, norms and guidelines in crime prevention and criminal justice;

2. *Stresses* the need for further cooperation and concerted action in translating those standards into practice;

3. *Invites* the Commission on Crime Prevention and Criminal Justice to focus on the promotion of the use and application of United Nations standards, norms and guidelines in crime prevention and criminal justice, while recognizing the social, cultural and economic conditions of Member States;

4. *Invites* Governments to pay due attention to United Nations standards, norms and guidelines in crime prevention and criminal justice and to enhance their widest possible dissemination;

5. *Requests* the Secretary-General to ensure the widest possible dissemination of the texts of the standards contained in the *Compendium of United Nations Standards and Norms in Crime Prevention and Criminal Justice*, which has been published only in English, and calls for the reprint of the compendium in English and for its publication in the other five official languages of the United Nations;

6. *Recognizes* the important role that the United Nations Interregional Crime and Justice Research Institute and the institutes associated or affiliated with the United Nations and non-governmental organizations play in promoting the use and application of the United Nations standards and norms in the administration of justice;

7. *Requests* the Secretary-General:

(a) To assist Member States, at their request, in implementing existing United Nations standards in crime prevention and criminal justice;

(b) To strengthen and coordinate activities in this field, including advisory services, training programmes and fellowships, with a view to undertaking joint programmes and developing collaborative mechanisms;

(c) To commence without delay a process of information-gathering to be undertaken by means of surveys, such as reporting systems, and contributions from other sources, initially paying attention to the United Nations standards, norms and guidelines listed in paragraph 8 *(a)* below; the surveys should be conducted over a two-year period in order to enable Member States to have sufficient time to provide replies; the results of the first surveys should be considered at the earliest possible session of the Commission;

8. *Requests* the Commission to establish, at its third session, an open-ended in-sessional working group, in accordance with the rules of procedure of the functional commissions of the Economic and Social Council and subject to the consideration of financial implications, in order to discuss, *inter alia*, the following issues:

(a)   The role of the United Nations in promoting the use and application of the following standards, norms and guidelines, on the understanding that this selection does not imply any priority over other standards, norms and guidelines and is subject to review at future sessions of the Commission:

(i)   The Standard Minimum Rules for the Treatment of Prisoners;

(ii)   The Code of Conduct for Law Enforcement Officials, together with the Basic Principles on the Use of Force and Firearms by Law Enforcement Officials;

(iii)   The Declaration of Basic Principles of Justice for Victims of Crime and Abuse of Power;

(iv)   The Basic Principles on the Independence of the Judiciary;

(b)   The evaluation of the reporting system and other sources of information;

(c)   Measures to improve the dissemination of information, education and technical assistance to enhance their use and application;

9. *Commends* the World Conference on Human Rights and its Preparatory Committee for bearing in mind the existence of important United Nations standards and norms in the administration of justice;

10. *Calls upon* the Commission, at its third session, to pay due attention to the results of the World Conference on Human Rights, held at Vienna from 14 to 25 June 1993, as far as crime prevention and criminal justice issues are concerned;

IV.   Crime prevention and criminal justice information management

A.   *Collection of information*

1. *Takes note* of the report of the Secretary-General on the survey of activities carried out in the field of crime prevention and criminal justice within the United Nations system and by relevant intergovernmental and non-governmental organizations and on coordination of activities with other United Nations bodies, the ongoing activities of the Secretariat concerning the Fourth United Nations Survey of Crime Trends, Operations of Criminal Justice Systems and Crime Prevention Strategies and other initiatives under way to acquire, process and distribute crime prevention and criminal justice data for the benefit of Member States and criminal justice professionals;

2. *Reaffirms* the usefulness of these information activities in crime prevention and criminal justice policy development and programme planning;

3. *Requests* the Secretary-General to report to the Commission on Crime Prevention and Criminal Justice, at its third session, on progress made on the Fourth and Fifth United Nations Surveys of Crime Trends and Operations of Criminal Justice Systems and Crime Prevention Strategies, and other initiatives under way to acquire, process and distribute crime prevention and criminal justice data;

4. *Strongly encourages* Governments to continue to reply promptly to requests of the Secretary-General for crime prevention and criminal justice data in order to ensure that those data can be processed and provided to all Member States and other interested parties in a timely and efficient manner;

B.   *Management of information*

1. *Requests* the Secretary-General to continue and to intensify efforts directed at the modernization of criminal justice techniques and administration, with the needs of developing countries being given special attention, introducing, *inter alia,* compatible information technology to facilitate the administration of criminal justice and to strengthen practical cooperation on crime control between Member States;

2. *Encourages* Member States, the private sector and criminal justice professionals to exchange proposals, information on projects and innovations enhancing criminal justice operations through the Crime Prevention and Criminal Justice Branch;

C.   *Distribution of information*

1. *Requests* the Secretary-General to allocate the necessary services for the transfer of the management and daily operations of the United Nations Criminal Justice Information Network to the Crime Prevention and Criminal Justice Branch;

2. *Invites* Member States to consider the provision of extrabudgetary resources, including but not restricted to the secondment of computer-programming professionals with criminal justice experience, to the Secretariat in order to assist in the orderly transfer of the United Nations Criminal Justice Information Network, and to provide support for its further logistical and substantive development;

3. *Requests* the Secretary-General, as resources permit:

(a)   To strengthen and expand the clearing-house functions of the Crime Prevention and Criminal Justice Branch;

(b)   To organize training courses that would enable criminal justice professionals, in particular those in developing countries, to acquaint themselves with the services of the United Nations Criminal Justice Information Network;

(c)   To establish a support system for developing countries that would, among other things, ensure that basic costs connected with the provision of the necessary modalities, including the costs of membership in the United Nations Criminal Justice Information Network and transmission costs, are covered;

(d)   To report to the Commission on Crime Prevention and Criminal Justice, at its third session, on progress made in the improvement of computerization in criminal justice management, with emphasis on strengthening national capacities for the collection, collation, analysis and utilization of the data;

V.   Cooperation between the Crime Prevention and Criminal Justice Branch and other relevant entities

1. *Welcomes with appreciation* Commission on Narcotic Drugs resolution 10(XXXVI) of 7 April 1993 and Commission on Human Rights resolution 1993/41 of 5 March 1993;

2. *Invites* the various relevant entities of the United Nations system, including but not limited to the Office of Legal Affairs, the Department for Policy Coordination and Sustainable Development, the Department for Development Support and Management Services, the Department for Economic and Social Information and Policy Analysis, the United Nations International Drug Control Programme, the Division for the Advancement of Women, the regional commissions, the Centre for Human Rights, the United Nations Environment Programme, the United Nations Children's Fund, the United Nations Development Programme, the World Health Organization and the United Nations Industrial Development Organization, to cooperate with the Crime Prevention and Criminal Justice Branch and to extend to it their support and assistance in implementation of its mandates;

3. *Decides* to continue its close cooperation in this field with the Commission on Human Rights, the Commission for Social Development, the Commission on Narcotic Drugs, the Commission on the Status of Women and the specialized agencies in order to increase the efficiency and effectiveness of United Nations activities in areas of mutual interest and concern and to ensure coordination and avoidance of duplication;

4. *Recommends* that the Secretary-General consider resorting, where appropriate, to the expertise available in the Crime Prevention and Criminal Justice Branch in matters relating to the work of the International Law Commission on the preparation of a draft statute for the international criminal court and the draft Code of Crimes against the Peace and Security of Mankind;

5. *Invites* Member States to ensure that their efforts and arrangements aimed at cooperation and coordination at the bilateral and regional levels take into account the relevant activities and work of the United Nations crime prevention and criminal justice programme;

6. *Requests* the Secretary-General to encourage and facilitate cooperation and coordination in accordance with the present resolution and to report on the subject to the Commission on Crime Prevention and Criminal Justice at its third session.

Economic and Social Council resolution 1993/34

27 July 1993   Meeting 43   Adopted without vote

Approved by Social Committee (E/1993/106/Add.1) without vote, 14 July (meeting 10); draft by Commission on Crime Prevention and Criminal Justice (E/1993/32), orally amended; agenda item 20.

GENERAL ASSEMBLY ACTION

On 20 December, on the recommendation of the Third Committee, the General Assembly adopted **resolution 48/103** without vote.

Crime prevention and criminal justice

The General Assembly,

Alarmed by high costs of crime, particularly in its new and transnational forms, and the danger posed to the individual as such and to societies and to the welfare of all nations by the rising incidence of crime,

Reaffirming the responsibility assumed by the United Nations in crime prevention and criminal justice,

Emphasizing the need for strengthened regional and international cooperation to combat crime in all its forms and to improve the effectiveness and efficiency of criminal justice systems,

Bearing in mind the goals of the United Nations in the field of crime prevention and criminal justice, specifically the reduction of criminality, more efficient and effective law enforcement and administration of justice, respect for human rights and the promotion of the highest standards of fairness, humanity and professional conduct,

Recognizing that many States suffer from an extreme shortage of human and financial resources, which impedes them from responding adequately to problems related to crime,

Recalling its relevant resolutions as well as the decisions of the Economic and Social Council, in which a high level of priority was accorded to the activities of the United Nations crime prevention and criminal justice programme and an appropriate share of the overall resources of the United Nations requested for the programme,

Recalling also its resolution 47/91 of 16 December 1992, in which it requested the Secretary-General to strengthen the crime prevention and criminal justice programme and to upgrade, as a matter of urgency, the Crime Prevention and Criminal Justice Branch of the Centre for Social Development and Humanitarian Affairs of the Secretariat to a Division,

Taking note of Economic and Social Council resolution 1993/34 of 27 July 1993, in which the Council requested the Secretary-General to strengthen the institutional capacity of the programme to enable it to plan, execute and evaluate operational activities and advisory services in its area of competence, upon request from Member States,

Convinced that the United Nations Crime Prevention and Criminal Justice Branch can be effective only if it is provided with resources commensurate with its requirements and adequate to allow it to implement its mandates and to respond in a timely and efficient manner to the increasing requests of Member States for its services,

Concerned about the delay in the implementation of its resolutions 46/152 of 18 December 1991 and 47/91 and Economic and Social Council resolutions 1992/22 of 30 July 1992 and 1993/31 and 1993/34 of 27 July 1993, with respect to the strengthening of the United Nations crime prevention and criminal justice programme and the upgrading of the Crime Prevention and Criminal Justice Branch to a Division,

1. *Welcomes with appreciation* Economic and Social Council resolutions 1993/27, 1993/28, 1993/29, 1993/30, 1993/31, 1993/32, 1993/33 and 1993/34 of 27 July 1993;

2. *Reaffirms* the importance of the United Nations crime prevention and criminal justice programme and the crucial role it has to play in promoting international cooperation in crime prevention and criminal justice, in responding to the needs of the international community in the face of both national and transnational criminality and in assisting Member States to achieve the goals of preventing crime within and among States and improving the response to crime;

3. *Also reaffirms* the priority attached to the United Nations crime prevention and criminal justice programme, in accordance with General Assembly resolutions 46/152 and 47/91, and the need for an appropriate share of the existing resources of the United Nations for the programme;

4. *Requests* the Secretary-General, as a matter of urgency, to give effect to its resolutions 46/152 and 47/91

and to Economic and Social Council resolutions 1992/22, 1993/31 and 1993/34 by providing the United Nations crime prevention and criminal justice programme with sufficient resources for the full implementation of its mandates, in conformity with the high priority attached to the programme;

5. *Reiterates its request* to the Secretary-General to upgrade the Crime Prevention and Criminal Justice Branch to a Division, as recommended in and in accordance with resolution 47/91;

6. *Also requests* the Secretary-General to provide from existing resources adequate funds to build and maintain the institutional capacity of the United Nations crime prevention and criminal justice programme to respond to requests of Member States for assistance in the field of crime prevention and criminal justice, if necessary through the reallocation of resources;

7. *Further requests* the Secretary-General to take all necessary measures to assist the Commission on Crime Prevention and Criminal Justice, as the principal policy-making body in the field of crime prevention and criminal justice, to perform its functions and to ensure the proper coordination of all relevant activities in the field, in particular with the Commission on Human Rights and the Commission on Narcotic Drugs;

8. *Invites* the Committee for Programme and Coordination and the Advisory Committee on Administrative and Budgetary Questions to ensure proper follow-up to the proposals of the Secretary-General in the implementation of the present resolution;

9. *Requests* the Secretary-General to undertake all steps necessary to ensure the adequate organization of the Ninth United Nations Congress on the Prevention of Crime and the Treatment of Offenders, in accordance with Economic and Social Council resolution 1993/32;

10. *Expresses its support* for the World Ministerial Conference on Organized Transnational Crime, to be held in Italy in the last quarter of 1994, and calls upon Member States to be represented at the Conference at the highest possible level;

11. *Also requests* the Secretary-General to take all measures, within existing resources, to ensure the appropriate organization of the Conference and to submit its conclusions and recommendations to the General Assembly at its forty-ninth session;

12. *Welcomes* the initiative to hold in Italy in June 1994, under the auspices of the Crime Prevention and Criminal Justice Branch, the International Conference on "Laundering and Controlling Proceeds of Crime: a Global Approach", to be organized by the Government of Italy and the International Scientific and Professional Advisory Council;

13. *Invites* the relevant funding agencies of the United Nations to consider including crime prevention and criminal justice activities in their funding programmes, from within their existing resources, taking into account the increasing needs of Member States in the field, and to cooperate closely with the United Nations crime prevention and criminal justice programme in planning and implementing these activities;

14. *Invites* Governments to lend their full support to the United Nations crime prevention and criminal justice programme and to increase financial contributions to the Crime Prevention and Criminal Justice Fund;

15. *Requests* the Secretary-General to report to the General Assembly at its forty-ninth session on the implementation of the present resolution and of resolutions 46/152 and 47/91.

General Assembly resolution 48/103

20 December 1993   Meeting 85   Adopted without vote

Approved by Third Committee (A/48/628) without vote, 12 November (meeting 32); 28-nation draft (A/C.3/48/L.10/Rev.1)); agenda item 110.
Sponsors: Austria, Bahamas, Belgium, Costa Rica, Denmark, Egypt, Finland, France, Germany, Greece, Guatemala, Honduras, Hungary, Iceland, Italy, Luxembourg, Morocco, Netherlands, Nicaragua, Norway, Peru, Philippines, Portugal, Russian Federation, Spain, Sweden, the former Yugoslav Republic of Macedonia, United Kingdom.
Meeting numbers. GA 48th session: 3rd Committee 18-21, 25, 30, 32; plenary 85.

Organized crime

As requested by the Economic and Social Council in 1992,[41] the Secretary-General submitted to the Commission on Crime Prevention and Criminal Justice a January report[42] which discussed the nature and extent of organized crime, its impact on society and future trends.

In April,[37] at the Commission's second session, the Minister of Justice of Italy called on the United Nations to organize and convene, in the second half of 1994, a world ministerial conference on organized transnational crime, for which his Government would act as host.

ECONOMIC AND SOCIAL COUNCIL ACTION

On 27 July, on the recommendation of its Social Committee, the Economic and Social Council adopted **resolution 1993/29** without vote.

World Ministerial Conference on Organized Transnational Crime

The Economic and Social Council,

Alarmed by the increasing dimensions and sophistication of organized transnational crime,

Recognizing the danger posed by organized transnational crime to all countries of the world,

Reaffirming the need for more intensified international cooperation to prevent and control organized transnational crime,

Convinced that effective and concerted action at all levels to prevent and control the activities of organized transnational criminal groups represents an investment in the future for all societies,

Recognizing the need to intensify and coordinate efforts against organized transnational crime at the national and regional levels in order to ensure concerted and efficient global action,

Convinced that the regular exchange and dissemination of information can assist Governments in establishing adequate criminal justice systems and in devising effective strategies and policies against crime,

Convinced also that technical assistance in this field is indispensable,

Convinced further of the need to develop means of cooperating at the investigative and judicial levels,

Considering that the Crime Prevention and Criminal Justice Branch of the Secretariat has at its disposal the knowledge and expertise required to assist Member

States in their efforts against organized transnational crime,

Recalling General Assembly resolutions 45/107, 45/121 and 45/123 of 14 December 1990, 46/152 of 18 December 1991 and 47/87 and 47/91 of 16 December 1992,

Recalling that, in section IV of its resolution 1992/22 of 30 July 1992, the Council recognized the Commission on Crime Prevention and Criminal Justice as the principal policy-making body of the United Nations in the field of crime prevention and criminal justice,

1. *Requests* the Secretary-General to organize, without real growth implications for the overall regular budget of the United Nations for the biennium 1994-1995, a World Ministerial Conference on Organized Transnational Crime, to be held in the third quarter of 1994, which should have the following objectives:

(*a*) To examine the problems and dangers posed by organized transnational crime in the various regions of the world;

(*b*) To consider national legislation and to evaluate its adequacy to deal with the various forms of organized transnational crime and to identify appropriate guidelines for legislative and other measures to be taken at the national level;

(*c*) To identify the most effective forms of international cooperation for the prevention and control of organized transnational crime at the investigative, prosecutorial and judicial levels;

(*d*) To consider appropriate modalities and guidelines for the prevention and control of organized transnational crime at the regional and international levels;

(*e*) To consider whether it would be feasible to elaborate international instruments, including conventions, against organized transnational crime;

2. *Accepts with appreciation* the offer of the Government of Italy to act as host for the Conference;

3. *Invites* all Member States to be represented at the Conference at the highest possible level;

4. *Requests* the Secretary-General to report to the Commission on Crime Prevention and Criminal Justice at its third session on the status of the preparations for the Conference.

Economic and Social Council resolution 1993/29

27 July 1993   Meeting 43   Adopted without vote

Approved by Social Committee (E/1993/106) without vote, 14 July (meeting 10); draft by Commission on Crime Prevention and Criminal Justice (E/1993/32); agenda item 20.

Money laundering

In January,[43] the Secretary-General presented to the Commission on Crime Prevention and Criminal Justice a report on global efforts to prevent and control the use and laundering of the proceeds of crime. He discussed problems confronting Governments and their criminal justice systems and financial institutions. Measures against money laundering included legislative initiatives, regulatory mechanisms ensuring flexibility and adaptability and infrastructure building. The Secretary-General stressed the need for strengthening international cooperation to combat the problem.

ECONOMIC AND SOCIAL COUNCIL ACTION

On 27 July, on the recommendation of its Social Committee, the Economic and Social Council adopted **resolution 1993/30** without vote.

Control of the proceeds of crime

The Economic and Social Council,

Recalling its resolution 1992/22 of 30 July 1992, on the implementation of General Assembly resolution 46/152 of 18 December 1991 concerning operational activities and coordination in the field of crime prevention and criminal justice, in section VI of which the Council determined the work of the Commission on Crime Prevention and Criminal Justice should be guided by three priority themes, one of which included money-laundering,

Recalling also resolution 1/2 of 29 April 1992 of the Commission on Crime Prevention and Criminal Justice on control of the proceeds of crime,

Aware that control of the proceeds of crime is an essential element in the struggle against organized transnational crime,

Convinced that international action against organized and transnational crime requires, in addition to intensified law enforcement, concerted efforts to prevent and control the laundering of the proceeds of crime as an essential means of destroying criminal organizations,

Convinced also that effective control of the proceeds of crime requires concerted global action to curb the capacity of criminal organizations to transfer the proceeds of their illegal activities across national frontiers by taking advantage of gaps in international cooperation,

Convinced further that criminal organizations engage in a multitude of criminal activities generating illicit profits and that international action aimed at controlling the proceeds of crime can therefore only be effective if it takes into account all aspects of the problem,

Noting the efforts already undertaken by the Financial Action Task Force established by the heads of State or Government of the seven major industrialized countries and the President of the Commission of the European Communities, as well as the efforts of the Council of Europe, the European Community and the Inter-American Drug Abuse Control Commission of the Organization of American States,

Recalling the recommendations contained in the Global Programme of Action, adopted by the General Assembly at its seventeenth special session, on measures to be taken against the effects of money derived from, used in or intended for use in illicit drug trafficking, illegal financial flows and illegal use of the banking system,

Welcoming Commission on Narcotic Drugs resolution 5(XXXVI) of 7 April 1993,

1. *Requests* the Crime Prevention and Criminal Justice Branch of the Secretariat:

(*a*) To continue studying the problem of controlling the proceeds of crime;

(*b*) To continue collecting relevant information on national legislation and its implementation;

(*c*) To consider identifying areas of interest to criminal organizations, with a view to evaluating the efficiency and effectiveness of measures taken to control the proceeds derived from criminal activities;

(*d*) To consider, in cooperation with the United Nations bodies concerned and other relevant entities, such as the Financial Action Task Force, the possibility of assisting Governments, at their request, in developing guidelines for the detection, investigation and prosecution of the laundering of the proceeds of crime and in providing information to assist financial institutions in detecting, monitoring and controlling suspicious transactions and in preventing the infiltration of the legitimate economy by the proceeds of crime;

(e) To elaborate appropriate training material for use in providing practical assistance to Member States at their request;

(f) To provide technical assistance to Member States, upon request, in drafting, revising and implementing relevant legislation, in organizing special investigation teams and in training law enforcement, investigative, prosecutorial and judicial personnel;

2. *Invites* the Crime Prevention and Criminal Justice Branch to cooperate closely with the United Nations International Drug Control Programme in matters related to the control of the proceeds of crime;

3. *Welcomes with appreciation* the initiative of the Government of Italy and the International Scientific and Professional Advisory Council in organizing, in cooperation with financial institutions—at the international and national levels—of the various countries that have dealt with the problem of controlling the proceeds of crime, and under the auspices of the Crime Prevention and Criminal Justice Branch, the International Conference on Laundering and Controlling Proceeds of Crime: a Global Approach, to be held in Italy in June 1994.

Economic and Social Council resolution 1993/30

27 July 1993   Meeting 43   Adopted without vote

Approved by Social Committee (E/1993/106) without vote, 14 July (meeting 10); draft by Commission on Crime Prevention and Criminal Justice (E/1993/32); agenda item 20.

Urban crime

In April,[37] the Commission on Crime Prevention and Criminal Justice considered the question of crime prevention in urban areas—established by the Economic and Social Council in 1992[38] as one of the priority themes guiding the Commission's work. The Commission recommended to the Council for adoption a series of guidelines for cooperation and technical assistance in urban crime prevention.

ECONOMIC AND SOCIAL COUNCIL ACTION

On 27 July, on the recommendation of its Social Committee, the Economic and Social Council adopted **resolution 1993/27** without vote.

Proposed guidelines for the prevention of urban crime

The Economic and Social Council,

Recalling its resolutions 1979/20 of 9 May 1979, 1984/48 of 25 May 1984 and 1990/24 of 24 May 1990 and General Assembly resolutions 45/121 of 14 December 1990 and 46/152 of 18 December 1991,

Recalling also its resolution 1992/22 of 30 July 1992,

Recalling further the Milan Plan of Action,[a] the United Nations Standard Minimum Rules for the Administration of Juvenile Justice (The Beijing Rules), the United Nations Guidelines for the Prevention of Juvenile Delinquency (The Riyadh Guidelines),[b] the United Nations

Standard Minimum Rules for Non-custodial Measures (The Tokyo Rules),[c] the Declaration of Basic Principles of Justice for Victims of Crime and Abuse of Power and the resolution entitled "Prevention of urban crime" adopted by the Eighth United Nations Congress on the Prevention of Crime and the Treatment of Offenders,[d]

Aware of the universal character of urban crime,

Recognizing the usefulness of establishing guidelines to facilitate action on preventing urban crime,

Anxious to respond to the call by many States for technical cooperation programmes adapted to local conditions and needs,

1. *Takes note* of the proposed guidelines for cooperation and technical assistance in the field of urban crime prevention, contained in the annex to the present resolution, which are aimed at making urban crime prevention more effective;

2. *Requests* the Secretary-General to disseminate the proposed guidelines as widely as possible, with a view to having them examined by the Commission on Crime Prevention and Criminal Justice at its third session for inclusion in the discussion under item 6 of the provisional agenda for the Ninth United Nations Congress on the Prevention of Crime and the Treatment of Offenders, to be held in 1995, and then published in the most appropriate form, for example in the *Compendium of United Nations Standards and Norms in Crime Prevention and Criminal Justice*;

3. *Encourages* Member States to report on their experiences in elaborating urban crime prevention projects on the basis of the proposed guidelines;

4. *Calls upon* the interregional, regional and associate institutes cooperating with the United Nations in the field of crime prevention and criminal justice and non-governmental organizations to report on their experiences in the field of urban crime prevention and to express their observations;

5. *Requests* the Secretary-General to examine, taking into account the United Nations crime prevention and criminal justice programme, the possibility of coordinating measures for urban crime prevention that may be included in the assistance programmes carried out by other United Nations entities;

6. *Also requests* the Secretary-General to examine, together with international financial institutions, the possibility of including urban crime prevention measures in their assistance programmes.

ANNEX

Proposed guidelines for cooperation and technical assistance in the field of urban crime prevention

A.   Modalities for the design and implementation of cooperation and assistance activities

1.   All cooperation projects for urban crime prevention should comply with the principles set out below.

Local approach to problems

2.   Urban crime is characterized by a multiplicity of factors and forms. For each case a local approach to the problems to be addressed must be adopted. This involves:

(a) A local diagnostic survey of the crime phenomena, their characteristics, factors leading to them, the form they take and their scope;

(b) The identification of all the relevant actors that could take part in compiling this diagnostic survey and in crime prevention: public institutions (national or

local), local elected officials, the private sector (associations, enterprises etc.), community representatives etc.;

(c)   The setting up, from the outset, of consultation mechanisms promoting closer liaison, the exchange of information, joint work and the design of a coherent strategy.

Concerted design of a global crime prevention action plan

3.   The global crime prevention action plan:

(a)   Shall define:

(i)   The nature of the phenomena to be tackled (poverty, unemployment, housing, health and education problems, cultural or inter-ethnic conflicts, drugs etc.);

(ii)   The objectives being pursued and the time-limits fixed for them to be attained;

(iii)   The modalities of action envisaged and the respective responsibilities of those involved *vis-à-vis* the implementation of the plan (national and local resources to be mobilized and resources available through international cooperation);

(b)   Shall involve a wide range of fields:

(i)   Family, young people and adults, relationship between the generations or between social groups etc.;

(ii)   Education, civic values, culture etc.;

(iii)   Employment, training, measures for combating unemployment;

(iv)   Housing;

(v)   Health, drug and alcohol abuse;

(vi)   Government and community welfare aid for the least fortunate members of society;

(vii)   Combating the culture of violence;

(c)   Shall involve a range of actors representing:

(i)   The police, the courts, education, housing, health, social workers etc.;

(ii)   The community: elected officials, associations, volunteers, parents etc.;

(iii)   The economic sector: enterprises, banks, business, public transport etc.;

(d)   Shall provide for action on various levels:

(i)   Primary prevention:

a.   By promoting welfare and health development and progress and by combating all forms of social deprivation;

b.   By promoting communal values and respect for fundamental human rights;

c.   By promoting civic responsibility and social mediation procedures;

d.   By adapting the working methods of the police and the courts (community police and courts);

(ii)   Prevention of recidivism:

a.   Through modified police intervention (rapid response, within the local community etc.);

b.   By modifying methods of judicial intervention:

i.   Diversification of modalities of treatment and of measures taken according to the nature and seriousness of the cases (special system for minors);

ii.   Systematic research on the reintegration of offenders involved in urban crime;

iii.   Socio-educational support within the framework of the sentence, in prison and as preparation for release from prison;

(iii)   After the sentence has been served: aid and socio-educational support, family support etc.;

(iv)   Protection of victims by practical improvements in the treatment of victims by means of the following:

a.   Raising awareness of rights and how to exercise them effectively;

b.   Reinforcing rights (in particular the right to compensation);

c.   Introducing systems of victim reception, assistance and follow-up.

B.   Implementation of the action plan

The national authorities

4.   The national authorities:

(a)   Should provide active encouragement to local actors (information, technical and financial aid etc.);

(b)   Should coordinate national policy and strategies with local strategies and needs (possibly by means of contracts between national and local authorities);

(c)   Should organize interministerial consultation and cooperation mechanisms.

The national and local authorities

5.   The national and local authorities:

(a)   Should be constantly mindful of respect for the fundamental principles of human rights in promoting these activities;

(b)   Should implement training programmes (national and local) to inform and support all the professionals involved in crime prevention (initial training as well as in-service training to accommodate changes in working methods);

(c)   Should compare experiences and organize exchanges of know-how;

(d)   Should provide for means of evaluating regularly the effectiveness of the strategy implemented and the possible revision of it.

---

aA/CONF/121/22.

bGA res. 45/112, annex, 14 Dec. 1990.

cGA res. 45/110, annex, 14 Dec. 1990.

dA/CONF/144/28/Rev.1.

Economic and Social Council resolution 1993/27

27 July 1993   Meeting 43   Adopted without vote

Approved by Social Committee (E/1993/106) without vote, 14 July (meeting 10); draft by Commission on Crime Prevention and Criminal Justice (E/1993/32); agenda item 20.

Criminal law and the environment

In April,[37] the Commission on Crime Prevention and Criminal Justice considered the role of criminal law in the protection of the environment—established by the Economic and Social Council in 1992[38] as one of the priority themes guiding the Commission's work.

The Commission recommended to the Council for adoption a draft resolution on the subject.

ECONOMIC AND SOCIAL COUNCIL ACTION

On 27 July, on the recommendation of its Social Committee, the Economic and Social Council adopted **resolution 1993/28** without vote.

The role of criminal law in the protection of the environment

The Economic and Social Council,

Recalling its resolution 1992/22 of 30 July 1992, in section VI of which it determined that the work of the Commission on Crime Prevention and Criminal Justice should be guided by three priority themes, one of which included the role of criminal law in the protection of the environment, and in section III of which it invited Member States to establish reliable and effective channels of communication among themselves and with the United Nations crime prevention and criminal justice programme, including the regional institutes affiliated with the United Nations,

Recalling also General Assembly resolution 45/121 of 14 December 1990 on the Eighth United Nations Congress on the Prevention of Crime and the Treatment of Offenders, in which the Assembly welcomed the instruments and resolutions adopted by the Congress, *inter alia,* the resolution on the role of criminal law in the protection of nature and the environment,

Recalling further General Assembly resolution 46/152 of 18 December 1991, in which the Assembly called for strengthening regional and international cooperation in combating transnational crime,

Noting with appreciation the collaboration of the Helsinki Institute for Crime Prevention and Control, affiliated with the United Nations, and the Max Planck Institute for Foreign and International Criminal Law, in organizing the Seminar on the Policy of Criminal Law in the Protection of Nature and the Environment in a European Perspective, held at Lauchhammer, Germany, from 25 to 29 April 1992,

Noting also with appreciation the ongoing study on environmental crime, sanctioning strategies and sustainable development, undertaken jointly by the United Nations Interregional Crime and Justice Research Institute and the Australian Institute of Criminology,

1.   *Takes note* of the conclusions of the Seminar on the Policy of Criminal Law in the Protection of Nature and the Environment in a European Perspective, contained in the annex to the present resolution;

2.   *Requests* the Secretary-General to consider the possibility of undertaking activities in the field of environmental crime in the United Nations crime prevention and criminal justice programme, in particular to include environmental crime as an issue for technical cooperation and, for that purpose, to establish, with input from Member States, a roster of experts from all regions in the field of environmental crime;

3.   *Requests* the United Nations Interregional Crime and Justice Research Institute and the regional or associate institutes cooperating with the United Nations in the field of crime prevention and criminal justice to assist the Secretary-General in this endeavour by sharing their expertise;

4.   *Calls upon* Member States and the bodies concerned to continue their efforts to protect nature and the environment using, in addition to measures provided by administrative law and liability under civil law, measures in the field of national criminal law, and to provide requesting Member States with technical cooperation in the field of environmental crime.

ANNEX
Conclusions of the Seminar on the Policy of Criminal Law in the Protection of Nature and the Environment in a European Perspective, held at Lauchhammer, Germany, from 25 to 29 April 1992

1.   The existing state of the environment is serious and calls for efficient countermeasures throughout Europe at the national, supranational and international levels. The environment as a whole and its component elements must be protected in such a way that:

(*a*)   Existing damage will be eliminated or at least reduced (including restoration);

(*b*)   Harm will be prevented;

(*c*)   Risk will be minimized.

2.   There should be enhanced recognition of environmental interests as special or particular legal interests. The necessity of using water, air, the soil and other natural elements to a certain extent, however, precludes a prohibition on every action affecting those environmental interests.

3.   Environmental protection requires an integrated approach employing a variety of instruments for influencing conduct and reducing burdens on the environment, ranging from public participation to the use of sanctions. Regulatory environmental administrative law still remains at the heart of state instruments for the protection of the environment. Other methods of environmental protection, for example, economic incentives or the use of civil sanctions, will be important for many aspects of environmental protection. In addition, criminal law should play a flanking and supporting and, where appropriate, independent role.

4.   The goal in using the threat of sanctions is not only to back up the enforcement of administrative rules, but also to protect environmental interests as such (qualifying them as penally protected interests). Here, too, criminal law can have a general and special preventive effect and may, by its moral stigma, heighten environmental awareness.

5.   Substantive criminal law can play an autonomous and independent role in cases of serious attacks on the environment, including the endangerment of public health or of life or of serious bodily harm. Above and beyond this, the legislator cannot develop behavioural criteria under criminal law which are more stringent than those under administrative law. In that respect, environmental criminal law is closely linked to and dependent upon administrative law, which limits the effect of the former; nevertheless, this does not provide any reason for it not to be used in this context. That limitation is also dependent upon what differences exist in the approach and the means of the administration and the judiciary in the role which they play in protecting the environment. To reduce the risk of non-uniform application, emphasis should be placed on links with administrative regulations by comparison with links with administrative decisions.

6.   Environmental criminal law should encompass all areas of the environment. It is up to the national legislators whether in this respect offences are developed which refer to the environment as a whole or the specific components thereof. The legislator should develop at least a common or similar offence in relation to water, air and soil pollution.

7.   Offences should be differentiated according to their seriousness (with, as a consequence, a different

range of sanctions). One factor is the division according to the state of *mens rea* between intentional and reckless or negligent acts. Another emerging possibility is the use of the concept of endangerment in addition to the traditional use of so-called result crimes in continental legislation.

8. It is not sufficient to use criminal law only to combat damage to other violations of environmental entities. Serious infringements of safety regulations, of other operator duties or of the administrator's preventive control interests can vastly increase the risk that hazards or damage will incur. Therefore it is justifiable to invoke criminal law to deal with the inappropriate handling of hazardous substances, goods and plants or the possible impairment of control interests. A distinction may be drawn between offences which require that the act:

(*a*) Create a concrete or actual danger to environmental objects (so-called concrete endangerment offence);

(*b*) Occur in a situation with a likelihood of danger (see the penal provision in the Convention on the Physical Protection of Nuclear Material, so-called potential endangerment offence);

(*c*) Cover a mode of behaviour which is typically dangerous for the environment (e.g., operation without the necessary permit of a plant classified in a list as typically dangerous; violation of an order prohibiting the running of a plant; illegal disposal or export of dangerous waste; so-called abstract endangerment offence).

9. Minor offences (especially non-severe violations of administrative rules) could, without a loss of efficiency, be sanctioned only by fines or, in countries where a distinction exists between criminal and administrative punitive sanctions, be classified as administrative violations (punishable by a non-criminal fine). In that respect the scope of criminal law could even be restricted.

10. In the context of moves towards the introduction of alternative or additional measures under criminal law in general, in comparison with the traditional use of fines and imprisonment, consideration should also be given to the possibility of using other measures (such as restoration of the status quo; imposition of obligations to improve the state of the environment; confiscation of proceeds from crime). The decision on such a variety of measures may be dependent on the use of those instruments by the administration and on their effect.

11. Support should be given to the extension of the idea of imposing (criminal or non-criminal) fines on corporations (or possibly even other measures) in Europe.

12. When using criminal law and creating new offences in the area of environmental protection, consideration should be given to the need for enforcement resources. In countries where prosecution is not undertaken by the administrative agencies themselves, the application (and effect) of environmental criminal law by the prosecuting authority and judiciary is to a great extent dependent on the use of the knowledge and experience of those agencies and upon their cooperation. In order to reduce conflicts of interests and to enhance the possibility of clearing up cases, legal rules or administrative guidelines for reporting offences by administrative agencies should be developed. Cooperation and coordination between the administrative and criminal agencies is essential. Special training and sufficient staff-

ing should be provided. Further studies on improved measures for enforcement of existing environmental protection legislation should be undertaken.

13. The environment must be protected not only at the national but also at the international level. In this respect criminal law for the protection of the environment should also be developed at the international level.

14. Improvements should be made in the options available for prosecuting extraterritorial or transboundary criminal offences. In that respect:

(*a*) It should be possible to take jurisdiction in all countries over offences of a transboundary nature. Positive conflicts of jurisdiction should be solved. The problem of dealing under the criminal law with acts permitted in one State, and which produce harmful effects in another State where such acts are prohibited, should be examined in the light of the development of international and/or supranational law, including the use of bilateral and multilateral conventions or European Community regulations to develop common environmental standards;

(*b*) The extension of extraterritorial jurisdiction or the possible use or expansion of extradition should be considered.

15. European standards of environmental substantive criminal law should be developed. Following the encouragement for the harmonization of regional legislation given by the adoption of the resolution entitled "The role of criminal law in the protection of nature and environment" by the Eighth United Nations Congress on the Prevention of Crime and the Treatment of Offenders, which was welcomed by the General Assembly at its forty-fifth session, the efforts of the Council of Europe in elaborating a convention and a recommendation on environmental offences should be supported. Such instruments should reflect the basic ideas expressed in paragraphs 6, 8 and 10 above. This will improve international cooperation and reduce the danger of dislocation through the evasion of stricter enforcement in one country by moving to another country.

16. European conventions applicable to international cooperation in the prosecution of offences (e.g., by extradition, mutual assistance, transfer of proceedings) should be adhered to and utilized.

Economic and Social Council resolution 1993/28

27 July 1993   Meeting 43   Adopted without vote

Approved by Social Committee (E/1993/106) without vote, 14 July (meeting 10); draft by Commission on Crime Prevention and Criminal Justice (E/1993/32); agenda item 20.

Alien smuggling

GENERAL ASSEMBLY ACTION

On 20 December, on the recommendation of the Third Committee, the General Assembly adopted **resolution 48/102** without vote.

Prevention of the smuggling of aliens

The General Assembly,

Concerned that the activities of criminal organizations that profit illicitly by smuggling human beings and preying on the dignity and lives of migrants contribute to the complexity of the phenomenon of increasing international migration,

Recognizing that international criminal groups often convince individuals to migrate illegally by various means for enormous profits and use the proceeds from smuggling human beings to finance other criminal activities, thus bringing great harm to the States concerned,

Aware that such activities endanger the lives of those individuals and impose severe costs on the international community, particularly upon certain States that have been called upon to rescue and to provide medical care, food, housing and transportation for these individuals,

Recognizing that socio-economic factors influence the problem of the smuggling of aliens and also contribute to the complexity of current international migration,

Noting that smugglers, particularly in the State of destination of the smuggling of aliens, often force migrants into forms of debt, bondage or servitude, often involving criminal activities, in order to pay for their passage,

Convinced of the need to provide humane treatment and protect the full human rights of migrants,

Recognizing that this illegal smuggling activity has high social and economic costs, contributes to corruption and burdens law enforcement agencies in all States where illegal aliens transit or are found,

Recalling relevant international agreements and conventions, including the International Convention for the Safety of Life at Sea, 1960, the International Convention for the Safety of Life at Sea, 1974, and the Protocol relating thereto of 1978, by which specific safety standards are established for certain passenger ships, each State party is required to take the necessary steps to ensure that no vessel covered by the Conventions and flying its flag is permitted to carry passengers on international voyages unless it meets the standards established by the Conventions, and each port State party is required to prevent a foreign flag passenger vessel from sailing from its port when the condition of the ship or of its equipment is not in compliance with the Conventions,

Recalling also the undertaking of States parties to the Supplementary Convention on the Abolition of Slavery, the Slave Trade, and Institutions and Practices Similar to Slavery, done at Geneva on 7 September 1956, to take all practicable and necessary legislative and other measures to bring about progressively and as soon as possible the complete abolition or abandonment of the practice of debt bondage,

Reaffirming that the sovereignty and territorial integrity of all States must be respected, including their right to control their own borders,

Concerned that the smuggling of aliens undermines public confidence in policies and procedures for immigration and for the protection of refugees,

Noting that the smuggling of aliens can involve criminal elements in many States, including the State or States where the smuggling scheme was planned, the State of nationality of the aliens, the State where the means of transport was prepared, the flag State of any vessels or aircraft that transport the aliens, States through which the aliens transit to their destination or in order to be repatriated and the State of destination,

Taking into account the efforts of the Office of the United Nations High Commissioner for Refugees, the International Organization for Migration, the International Civil Aviation Organization and the International Maritime Organization in responding to requests from States for assistance in dealing with the smuggling of aliens,

Emphasizing the need for States to cooperate urgently at the bilateral and multilateral levels, as appropriate, to thwart these activities,

1. *Condemns* the practice of smuggling aliens in violation of international and national law and without regard for the safety, well-being and human rights of the migrants;

2. *Commends* those States which have cooperated to combat the smuggling of aliens and to address specific incidents where smuggled aliens have needed to be processed in accordance with international standards and the domestic laws and procedures of the State concerned and returned safely to appropriate destinations;

3. *Urges* States to take appropriate steps to frustrate the objectives and activities of smugglers of aliens and thus to protect would-be migrants from exploitation and loss of life, *inter alia*, by amending criminal laws, if necessary, to encompass the smuggling of aliens and by establishing or improving procedures to permit the ready discovery of false travel documents supplied by smugglers;

4. *Requests* States to cooperate in order to prevent the illegal transport by smugglers of third country nationals through their territory;

5. *Requests* States that have not done so to make special efforts to prevent their airports, means of ground transportation and air carriers from being used by smugglers of aliens;

6. *Also requests* States to cooperate in the interest of safety of life at sea, to increase their efforts to prevent the smuggling of aliens on ships and to ensure that prompt and effective action is taken against the smuggling of aliens by ship;

7. *Calls upon* Member States and relevant specialized agencies and international organizations to take into account socio-economic factors and to cooperate at the bilateral and multilateral levels in addressing all aspects of the problem of the smuggling of aliens;

8. *Reaffirms* the importance of existing international conventions in preventing the economic exploitation and loss of life that can result from smuggling aliens, and calls upon all States to exchange information and to consider ratifying or acceding to such conventions where they have not done so and fully to implement and enforce them;

9. *Emphasizes* that international efforts to prevent the smuggling of aliens should not inhibit legal migration or freedom of travel or undercut the protection provided by international law to refugees;

10. *Reaffirms also* the need to observe fully international and national law in dealing with the smuggling of aliens, including the provision of humane treatment and strict observance of all the human rights of migrants;

11. *Requests* the relevant specialized agencies and intergovernmental organizations, in particular the International Organization for Migration, the International Maritime Organization, the International Criminal Police Organization and the International Civil Aviation Organization, to consider ways and means, within their respective spheres of competence, to enhance international cooperation to combat the smuggling of aliens;

12. *Requests* the Commission on Crime Prevention and Criminal Justice to consider giving special attention to the question of the smuggling of aliens at its third session, to be held in 1994, in order to encourage international cooperation to address this problem within the framework of its mandate;

13. *Requests* the Secretary-General to transmit the text of the present resolution to all Member States and to relevant specialized agencies and intergovernmental organizations;

14. *Invites* Member States and relevant specialized agencies and intergovernmental organizations to report to the Secretary-General on the measures they have taken to combat the smuggling of aliens;

15. *Also requests* the Secretary-General to report to the General Assembly on the measures taken by States, specialized agencies and intergovernmental organizations to combat the smuggling of aliens, and decides to consider this question at its forty-ninth session under the item entitled "Crime prevention and criminal justice".

General Assembly resolution 48/102

20 December 1993   Meeting 85   Adopted without vote

Approved by Third Committee (A/48/628) without vote, 19 November (meeting 38); 15-nation draft (A/C.3/48/L.9/Rev.2)); agenda item 110.
Sponsors: Armenia, Australia, Costa Rica, Cyprus, El Salvador, Greece, Guatemala, Guyana, Israel, Mexico, Paraguay, Philippines, Romania, Turkey, United States.
Meeting numbers. GA 48th session: 3rd Committee 18-21, 25, 30, 32, 36, 38; plenary 85.

UN crime prevention and criminal justice programme

Technical assistance

As requested by the Economic and Social Council in 1992,[38] the Secretary-General, in February,[44] outlined steps to operationalize fully the United Nations crime prevention and criminal justice programme and enable it to respond to the needs of Governments and the international community.

The Secretary-General's recommendations for the Commission's consideration included: placing high priority on operationalizing the crime prevention and criminal justice programme, subject to requests arising in emergency situations; inviting United Nations interregional and regional institutes and affiliated and associated institutes to participate in operational activities; developing model training and advisory services projects; expanding and updating the roster of experts to assist in delivering operational activities; holding courses on United Nations norms and guidelines designed to upgrade criminal justice practices; holding training programmes; conducting United Nations surveys of crime trends and criminal justice operations; disseminating information; and undertaking fund-raising.

UN standards and norms

In response to a 1992 Economic and Social Council request,[38] the Secretary-General, in January,[45] provided a description of achievements and difficulties in applying United Nations standards and norms in crime prevention and criminal justice. He proposed a series of recommendations for consideration by the Commission, including: asking Governments to promote the widest possible dissemination of United Nations norms, standards and guidelines; suggesting ways of assisting Member States in implementing existing United Nations norms, standards, guidelines and model treaties; specifying ways to strengthen crime prevention and criminal justice activities; considering ways of monitoring implementation through reporting; and proposing ways of promoting the widest possible dissemination of the texts of standards contained in the *Compendium of United Nations Standards and Norms in Crime Prevention and Criminal Justice*.[46] The Secretary-General also suggested that the Commission consider establishing an open-ended working group to suggest to Member States measures on applying existing United Nations standards and norms in crime prevention and criminal justice.

The United Nations standards could serve as a basis both for domestic legislation and for bilateral or multilateral cooperation against national and transnational forms of crime, the Secretary-General said. United Nations model treaties could facilitate the harmonization of legislation and adoption of common strategies and could be used in joint training administered to criminal justice personnel.

Crime prevention institutes

In January,[47] the Secretary-General provided an overview of the 1992 activities of the United Nations Interregional Crime and Justice Research Institute and the regional institutes affiliated with the United Nations—the African Institute for the Prevention of Crime and the Treatment of Offenders, the Asia and Far East Institute for the Prevention of Crime and the Treatment of Offenders, the Latin American Institute for the Prevention of Crime and the Treatment of Offenders and the Helsinki Institute for Crime Prevention and Control—as well as other institutes cooperating closely with the United Nations, such as the Arab Security Studies and Training Centre, the Australian Institute of Criminology, the International Centre for Criminal Law Reform and Criminal Justice Policy and the International Institute of Higher Studies in Criminal Sciences.

The Secretary-General noted that the joint annual coordination meetings of the United Nations crime prevention and criminal justice programme network were the primary coordination mechanism. However, activities needed to be launched to meet the increasing needs of the developing countries, including clearing-house functions to identify viable policy options, the development, application and evaluation of programmes and strategies, and personnel exchanges among institutes and between the Secretariat and the institutes.

UNAFRI

In response to a 1992 General Assembly request,[48] the Secretary-General submitted a September report[49] on the activities and financial situation of the United Nations African Institute for the Prevention of Crime and the Treatment of Offenders (UNAFRI).

UNAFRI, established in 1987 and located in Uganda, conducted training activities for criminal justice personnel of States of the African region; carried out research; continued efforts to establish a specialized reference library; and provided advisory services to Governments.

The Secretary-General reported that, for the four years up to December 1992, full or partial payment of assessed contributions to UNAFRI had only been received from 8 out of 26 participating members. The financial situation of UNAFRI had become a serious crisis, constraining the Institute's activities, he stated. Morever, its survival after 1993 was uncertain.

ECONOMIC AND SOCIAL COUNCIL ACTION

On 27 July, on the recommendation of its Social Committee, the Economic and Social Council adopted **resolution 1993/33** without vote.

United Nations African Institute for the Prevention of Crime and the Treatment of Offenders

The Economic and Social Council,

Recalling General Assembly resolution 46/152 of 18 December 1991, in the annex to which it is stated that the contributions of the regional institutes for the prevention of crime and the treatment of offenders to policy development and implementation, and their resource requirements, especially those of the United Nations African Institute for the Prevention of Crime and the Treatment of Offenders, should be fully integrated into the United Nations crime prevention and criminal justice programme,

Taking note of General Assembly resolution 47/89 of 16 December 1992,

Bearing in mind section IV, paragraph 2, of its resolution 1992/22 of 30 July 1992,

1. *Expresses its appreciation* to the Government of Uganda for providing host facilities to the United Nations African Institute for the Prevention of Crime and the Treatment of Offenders;

2. *Encourages* Governments and intergovernmental and non-governmental organizations to provide financial and technical support to the Institute to enable it to fulfil its objectives, particularly those concerning training, technical assistance, policy guidance, research and data collection;

3. *Requests* the Secretary-General and the United Nations Development Programme to continue providing assistance and support to the Institute.

Economic and Social Council resolution 1993/33

27 July 1993   Meeting 43   Adopted without vote

Approved by Social Committee (E/1993/106) without vote, 14 July (meeting 10); draft by Commission on Crime Prevention and Criminal Justice (E/1993/32); agenda item 20.

GENERAL ASSEMBLY ACTION

On 20 December, on the recommendation of the Third Committee, the General Assembly adopted **resolution 48/101** by recorded vote.

United Nations African Institute for the Prevention of Crime and the Treatment of Offenders

The General Assembly,

Recalling its resolution 47/89 of 16 December 1992 and taking note of Economic and Social Council resolution 1993/33 of 27 July 1993,

Recalling also its resolution 46/152 of 18 December 1991, in the annex to which it is stated that the contributions of the regional institutes for the prevention of crime and the treatment of offenders to policy development and implementation, and their resource requirements, especially those of the United Nations African Institute for the Prevention of Crime and the Treatment of Offenders, should be fully integrated into the United Nations crime prevention and criminal justice programme,

Aware of the financial difficulties that the Institute continues to face as a result of the fact that many States of the African region are in the category of least developed countries and therefore lack the necessary resources with which to support the Institute,

Conscious of the efforts made thus far by the Institute in fulfilling its mandate through, *inter alia*, the organization of training programmes and regional seminars, as well as the provision of advisory services,

Having considered the report of the Secretary-General,

1. *Expresses its appreciation* to those Governments and intergovernmental bodies that have supported the United Nations African Institute for the Prevention of Crime and the Treatment of Offenders in the discharge of its responsibilities;

2. *Calls upon* Governments and intergovernmental and non-governmental organizations to provide financial and technical support to the Institute to enable it to fulfil its objectives, particularly those concerning training, technical assistance, policy guidance, research and data collection;

3. *Requests* the Secretary-General to ensure that sufficient resources are provided to the Institute, within the overall appropriation of the programme budget, to enable it to carry out, in full and on time, all its obligations;

4. *Requests* the United Nations Development Programme to continue providing programme support to the Institute;

5. *Also requests* the Secretary-General to report to the General Assembly at its forty-ninth session on the implementation of the present resolution.

General Assembly resolution 48/101

20 December 1993   Meeting 85   119-1-49 (recorded vote)

Approved by Third Committee (A/48/628) by recorded vote (102-1-43), 12 November (meeting 32); draft by Zimbabwe for the Group of African States (A/C.3/48/L.8); agenda item 110.
Meeting numbers. GA 48th session: 3rd Committee 18-21, 25, 30, 32; plenary 85.

Recorded vote in Assembly as follows:

In favour: Afghanistan, Algeria, Angola, Antigua and Barbuda, Argentina, Armenia, Bahamas, Bahrain, Bangladesh, Barbados, Belize, Benin, Bhutan, Bolivia, Bosnia and Herzegovina, Botswana, Brazil, Brunei Darussalam, Burkina Faso, Burundi, Cambodia, Cameroon, Cape Verde, Central African Republic, Chad, Chile, China, Colombia, Comoros, Congo, Costa Rica, Côte d'Ivoire, Cuba, Cyprus, Democratic People's Republic of Korea, Djibouti, Dominica, Dominican Republic, Ecuador, Egypt, El Salvador, Ethiopia, Fiji, Gabon, Gambia, Ghana, Grenada, Guatemala, Guinea, Guinea-Bissau, Guyana, Haiti, Honduras, India, Indonesia, Iran, Iraq, Jamaica, Jordan, Kenya, Kuwait, Lao People's Democratic Republic, Lebanon, Lesotho, Libyan Arab Jamahiriya, Madagascar, Malawi, Malaysia, Maldives, Mali, Marshall Islands, Mauritania, Mauritius, Mexico, Mongolia, Morocco, Mozambique, Myanmar, Namibia, Nepal, Nicaragua, Niger,

Nigeria, Oman, Pakistan, Panama, Papua New Guinea, Paraguay, Peru, Philippines, Qatar, Republic of Korea, Rwanda, Saint Lucia, Saint Vincent and the Grenadines, Saudi Arabia, Senegal, Sierra Leone, Singapore, Sri Lanka, Sudan, Suriname, Swaziland, Syrian Arab Republic, Thailand, Togo, Trinidad and Tobago, Tunisia, Uganda, Ukraine, United Arab Emirates, United Republic of Tanzania, Uruguay, Venezuela, Viet Nam, Yemen, Zaire, Zambia, Zimbabwe.

Against: United States.

Abstaining: Albania, Australia, Austria, Azerbaijan, Belarus, Belgium, Bulgaria, Canada, Croatia, Czech Republic, Denmark, Estonia, Finland, France, Georgia, Germany, Greece, Hungary, Iceland, Ireland, Israel, Italy, Japan, Kazakhstan, Kyrgyzstan, Latvia, Liechtenstein, Lithuania, Luxembourg, Malta, Micronesia, Monaco, Netherlands, New Zealand, Norway, Poland, Portugal, Republic of Moldova, Romania, Russian Federation, San Marino, Slovakia, Slovenia, Solomon Islands, Spain, Sweden, the former Yugoslav Republic of Macedonia, Turkey, United Kingdom.

Preparations for the Ninth (1995) Congress

In January,[50] the Secretary-General reviewed preparations for the Ninth (1995) United Nations Congress on the Prevention of Crime and the Treatment of Offenders. He discussed the dates and sites of five regional preparatory meetings to be held in 1994, the provisional agenda of the Congress, as prepared by the Economic and Social Council in 1992,[51] the format of the Congress and topical proposals for workshops. Annexed to the report was the programme of work for the Congress and a summary of proposals for its workshops.

ECONOMIC AND SOCIAL COUNCIL ACTION

On 27 July, on the recommendation of its Social Committee, the Economic and Social Council adopted **resolution 1993/32** without vote.

Preparations for the Ninth United Nations Congress on the Prevention of Crime and the Treatment of Offenders

The Economic and Social Council,

Considering that, pursuant to General Assembly resolutions 415(V) of 1 December 1950 and 46/152 of 18 December 1991, the Ninth United Nations Congress on the Prevention of Crime and the Treatment of Offenders is to be convened in 1995,

Bearing in mind General Assembly resolutions 32/59 and 32/60 of 8 December 1977, 35/171 of 15 December 1980 and 45/121 of 14 December 1990, in which the Assembly noted the importance of the United Nations congresses in the field of crime prevention and criminal justice,

Acknowledging the new role of the congresses stipulated in paragraph 29 of the statement of principles and programme of action of the United Nations crime prevention and criminal justice programme, contained in the annex to General Assembly resolution 46/152,

Emphasizing the importance of undertaking all the preparatory activities for the Ninth Congress in a timely and concerted manner,

Recalling its resolution 1992/24 of 30 July 1992, in which it requested the Secretary-General to prepare a discussion guide for the regional preparatory meetings for the Ninth Congress, to be considered by the Commission on Crime Prevention and Criminal Justice at its second session, incorporating proposals for action-oriented research and demonstration workshops related to the topics selected for the Ninth Congress,

Recalling that, in the same resolution, it requested the Secretary-General to prepare draft rules of procedure for the Ninth Congress, taking into account, *inter alia,* the need for all draft resolutions on the selected topics to be submitted well in advance of the Ninth Congress,

Aware of the role played in crime prevention and criminal justice by the dissemination to the public of relevant information and of the impact on society at large of the mass media, at both the national and international levels,

Considering that, in view of the internationalization of new forms of criminality, the criminal justice community should work hand-in-hand with the mass media to attain an optimal level of dissemination of reliable and timely information on crime prevention,

Aware of the important work to be accomplished by the regional preparatory meetings for the Ninth Congress,

Having considered the report of the Secretary-General on progress made in the preparations for the Ninth Congress,

1. *Notes with appreciation* the invitation of the Government of Uganda to act as host for the African Regional Preparatory Meeting for the Ninth Congress on the Prevention of Crime and the Treatment of Offenders;

2. *Approves* the following provisional agenda for the Ninth Congress, finalized by the Commission on Crime Prevention and Criminal Justice at its second session:

1. Opening of the Congress.
2. Organizational matters.
3. International cooperation and practical technical assistance for strengthening the rule of law: promoting the United Nations crime prevention and criminal justice programme.
4. Action against national and transnational economic and organized crime, and the role of criminal law in the protection of the environment: national experiences and international cooperation.
5. Criminal justice and police systems: management and improvement of police and other law enforcement agencies, prosecution, courts, corrections; and the role of lawyers.
6. Crime prevention strategies, in particular as related to crimes in urban areas and juvenile and violent criminality, including the question of victims: assessment and new perspectives.
7. Adoption of the report of the Congress.

3. *Also approves* the rules of procedure for United Nations congresses on the prevention of crime and the treatment of offenders, as recommended by the Commission at its second session and contained in the annex to the present resolution;

4. *Notes* that the Commission, at its second session, approved a discussion guide for the regional preparatory meetings for the Ninth Congress;

5. *Endorses* the programme of work for the Ninth Congress, including the holding of six workshops on the following topics:

(a) Extradition and international cooperation: exchange of national experience and implementation of relevant principles in national legislation (one day);

(b) Mass media and crime prevention (one day);

(c) Urban policy and crime prevention (one day);

(d) Prevention of violent crime (one day);

(e) Environmental protection at the national and international levels: potentials and limits of criminal justice (two days);

(*f*) International cooperation and assistance in the management of the criminal justice system: computerization of criminal justice operations and the development, analysis and policy use of criminal justice information (two days);

6. *Notes* that all organizational work for the workshops mentioned in paragraph 5 above will be coordinated by the Crime Prevention and Criminal Justice Branch of the Secretariat;

7. *Accepts with appreciation* the initiatives taken by the interregional, regional and associate institutes cooperating with the United Nations in the field of crime prevention and criminal justice to assist the Secretariat in convening the workshops, as well as the initiatives taken by States to participate actively in the organization of and follow-up to such workshops;

8. *Invites* donor countries to cooperate with developing countries to ensure the full participation of the latter in the workshops;

9. *Decides* to include in the programme of work of the Ninth Congress a one-day discussion in plenary meeting on experiences in and practical measures aimed at combating corruption involving public officials;

10. *Invites* Member States, non-governmental organizations and other relevant entities to support financially, organizationally and technically the preparations for the workshops;

11. *Takes note* of the timetable for the five regional preparatory meetings for the Ninth Congress contained in the report of the Secretary-General;

12. *Recommends* that adequate provision be made for the attendance of representatives of the relevant regional commissions at the third and fourth sessions of the Commission and at the Ninth Congress;

13. *Requests* the Secretary-General:

(*a*) To undertake the necessary logistic steps, in collaboration with Member States and the network of crime prevention institutes, to mobilize the participation of relevant parties in the preparations for all six workshops;

(*b*) To allocate, in the context of the proposed programme budget for the biennium 1994-1995, the necessary resources for the organization of the five regional preparatory meetings for the Ninth Congress and of the Congress itself;

(*c*) To make available the necessary resources for the participation of the least developed countries in the regional preparatory meetings for the Ninth Congress and in the Congress itself;

(*d*) To provide the necessary additional resources, including temporary assistance, to the United Nations Office at Vienna, in order to enable the Crime Prevention and Criminal Justice Branch to undertake, in an effective and timely manner, all preparatory and follow-up activities for the Ninth Congress;

(*e*) To provide resources, as required, to ensure a wide and effective programme of public information related to the preparations for the Ninth Congress and the Congress itself;

(*f*) To invite twenty expert consultants to participate in the Ninth Congress, at the expense of the United Nations, as was done for the previous three United Nations congresses on the prevention of crime and the treatment of offenders, thus ensuring that adequate expertise is provided to the Congress by each region for each substantive topic;

(*g*) To appoint, in accordance with the established practice for the congresses, a Secretary-General of the Ninth Congress;

14. *Decides* that the Ninth Congress should be held early in 1995 for a period of ten working days and two days of pre-Congress consultations;

15. *Encourages* Governments to undertake preparations for the Ninth Congress by all appropriate means, with a view to formulating national position papers;

16. *Invites* the Commission to accord high priority, at its third session, to the preparations for the Ninth Congress and to ensure that all necessary organizations and substantive arrangements are made in good time.

ANNEX
Draft rules of procedure for United Nations congresses on the prevention of crime and the treatment of offenders

I. Representation and credentials

Composition of delegations

Rule 1

The delegation of each State participating in the Congress shall consist of a head of delegation and such other representatives, alternate representatives and advisers as may be required.

Designated representatives

Rule 2

An alternate representative or an adviser may act as a representative upon designation by the head of delegation.

Submission of credentials

Rule 3

1. The credentials of representatives shall be issued either by the Head of State or Government or by the Minister for Foreign Affairs.

2. The credentials of representatives and the names of alternate representatives and advisers shall be submitted to the Secretary of the Congress, if possible not later than one week before the opening of the Congress. Any later change in the composition of delegations shall also be submitted to the Secretary of the Congress.

Credentials Committee

Rule 4

1. There shall be a Credentials Committee of nine members appointed by the Congress on the proposal of the President. Its membership shall, as far as possible, be the same as that of the Credentials Committee of the General Assembly of the United Nations at its preceding session.

2. The Credentials Committee shall itself elect from among the representatives of participating States a Chairman and such other officers as it considers necessary.

3. The Credentials Committee shall examine the credentials of representatives and report to the Congress.

Provisional participation in the Congress

Rule 5

Pending a decision of the Congress upon their credentials, representatives shall be entitled to participate provisionally in the Congress.

II. Officers

Elections

Rule 6

The Congress shall elect from among the representatives of participating States a President, 24 Vice-Presidents and a Rapporteur-General, as well as a Chairman for each of the committees provided for in rule 45. These officers shall constitute the General Committee and shall be elected on the basis of equitable geographical distribution.

Acting President

Rule 7

1. If the President finds it necessary to be absent from a meeting or any part thereof, he or she shall designate one of the Vice-Presidents as acting President.

2. A Vice-President acting as President shall have the same power and duties as the President.

Replacement of the President

Rule 8

If the President is unable to perform his or her functions, a new President shall be elected.

Voting rights of the President

Rule 9

The President, or a Vice-President acting as President, shall not vote, but shall designate another member of his or her delegation to exercise that function.

III. General Committee

Chairman

Rule 10

The President or, in his or her absence, one of the Vice-Presidents designated by the President shall serve as Chairman of the General Committee.

Substitute members

Rule 11

1. If the President or a Vice-President or the Rapporteur-General is absent from a meeting of the General Committee, he or she may designate a member of his or her delegation to act as substitute.

2. In case of absence, the Chairman of a committee shall designate another officer of the committee or, if none is available, a member thereof, as a substitute. However, such a substitute shall not have the right to vote if he or she is of the same delegation as another member of the General Committee.

Functions

Rule 12

1. In addition to carrying out other functions provided in these rules, the General Committee shall assist the President in the general conduct of the business of the Congress and, subject to decisions of the Congress, shall ensure the coordination of its work.

2. At the request of the Chairman of a committee, the General Committee may adjust the allocation of work to the committees.

IV. Secretariat

Duties of the Secretary-General

Rule 13

1. The Secretary-General of the United Nations shall appoint a Secretary-General and a Secretary of the Congress and shall provide the staff required by the Congress and its subsidiary organs.

2. The Secretary-General of the Congress or his or her representative shall act in that capacity in all meetings of the Congress and its subsidiary organs. He or she shall direct the staff assigned to perform services in connection with the Congress.

Duties of the secretariat

Rule 14

The secretariat of the Congress shall, in accordance with these rules:

(a) Interpret speeches made at meetings;

(b) Receive, translate, reproduce and distribute the documents of the Congress;

(c) Publish and circulate the report and the official documents of the Congress;

(d) Make and arrange for the keeping of sound recordings of meetings;

(e) Arrange for the custody and preservation of the records of the Congress in the archives of the United Nations;

(f) Generally perform all other work that the Congress may require.

Statements by the secretariat

Rule 15

The Secretary-General of the Congress or any member of the secretariat designated for that purpose may at any time make either oral or written statements concerning any question under consideration.

V. Conduct of business

Quorum

Rule 16

The President may declare a meeting open and permit the debate to proceed when representatives of at least one third of the States participating in the Congress are present. The presence of representatives of a majority of the States so participating shall be required for any decision to be taken.

General powers of the President

Rule 17

1. In addition to exercising the powers conferred upon him or her elsewhere by these rules, the President shall preside at the plenary meetings of the Congress, declare the opening and closing of each such meeting, direct the discussions, accord the right to speak, put questions to the vote and announce decisions. He or she shall rule on points of order and, subject to these rules, have complete control of the proceedings and over the maintenance of order. The President may propose to the Congress the closure of the list of speakers, a limitation on the time to be allowed to speakers and on the number of times participants may speak on a question, the adjournment or closure of the debate, and the suspension or the adjournment of a meeting.

2. The President, in the exercise of his or her functions, remains under the authority of the Congress.

Points of order

Rule 18

Subject to rule 38, a representative may at any time raise a point of order, which shall be immediately decided by the President in accordance with these rules. A representative may appeal against the ruling of the President. The appeal shall be immediately put to the vote, and the ruling of the President shall stand unless overruled by a majority of the representatives present and voting. A representative may not, in raising a point of order, speak on the substance of the matter under discussion.

Speeches

Rule 19

1. No one may address the Congress without having previously obtained the permission of the President, who shall, subject to rules 17 and 22 to 25, call upon speakers in the order in which they signify their desire to speak. The Secretary of the Congress shall be in charge of drawing up a list of such speakers.

2. Debate shall be confined to the question before the Congress and the President may call a speaker to order if his or her remarks are not relevant to the subject under discussion.

3. The Congress may limit the time allowed to speakers and the number of times participants may speak on a question; a motion to set such limits shall be immediately put to the vote. In any event, the President shall limit interventions on procedural questions to a maximum of five minutes. When the debate is limited and a speaker exceeds the allotted time, the President shall call him or her to order without delay.

Precedence

Rule 20

The Chairman or another representative of a subsidiary organ may be accorded precedence for the purpose of explaining the conclusions arrived at by that organ.

Closing of the list of speakers

Rule 21

During the course of a debate the President may announce the list of speakers and, with the consent of the Congress, declare the list closed. When there are no more speakers on the list, the President shall declare the debate closed. Such closure shall have the same effect as closure pursuant to rule 25.

Right of reply

Rule 22

The right of reply shall be accorded by the President to a representative of a State participating in the Congress who requests it. Any other representative may be granted the opportunity to make a reply. Such replies should be as brief as possible.

Suspension or adjournment of the meeting

Rule 23

Subject to rule 38, a representative may at any time move the suspension or the adjournment of the meeting. Such motions shall not be debated, but shall be immediately put to the vote.

Adjournment of debate

Rule 24

A representative may at any time move the adjournment of the debate on the question under discussion. In addition to the proposer of the motion, two representatives may speak in favour of and two against the motion, after which the motion shall be immediately put to the vote.

Closure of debate

Rule 25

A representative may at any time move the closure of the debate on the question under discussion, whether or not any other representative has signified his or her wish to speak. Permission to speak on the closure of the debate shall be accorded only to two speakers opposing the closure, after which the motion shall be immediately put to the vote.

Order of motions

Rule 26

Subject to rule 18, the following motions shall have precedence in the following order over all other proposals or motions before the meeting:

(a) To suspend the meeting;

(b) To adjourn the meeting;

(c) To adjourn the debate;

(d) To close the debate.

Items for consideration

Rule 27

The Economic and Social Council, on the recommendation of the Commission on Crime Prevention and Criminal Justice, shall approve the provisional agenda for the Congress. The Congress shall adopt the provisional agenda and consider the items therein.

Draft resolutions on topics selected for consideration by the Congress

Rule 28

1. Draft resolutions on items of the provisional agenda for the Congress shall be submitted to the Secretary-General of the Congress four months prior to the Congress, and distributed to all Member States not later than two months prior to the Congress.

2. Draft resolutions are proposals requiring the adoption of a decision on the substantive items of the agenda.

Other proposals and amendments

Rule 29

Substantive amendments shall be introduced in writing and handed to the Secretary of the Congress, who shall circulate copies to all delegations in the official languages of the Congress. Unless the Congress decides otherwise, substantive amendments shall be discussed or put to the vote no earlier than twenty-four hours after copies in the official languages of the Congress have been circulated to the delegations.

Rule 30

1. On a written proposal of one or several representatives of Member States submitted at the time of the consideration of the agenda, the Congress may decide, by a two-thirds majority of the representatives present and voting, on the inclusion of other items in its agenda on urgent and important matters.

2. Draft resolutions pertaining to items on the agenda, as defined in paragraph 1 above, shall be submitted to the Secretary of the Congress for distribution in the official languages to the representatives not later than forty-eight hours prior to their consideration.

Withdrawal of proposals and motions

Rule 31

A proposal or motion may be withdrawn by its sponsor at any time before voting on it has commenced, provided that it has not been amended. A proposal or motion thus withdrawn may be reintroduced by any representative.

Decisions on competence

Rule 32

Subject to rule 18, any motion calling for a decision on the competence of the Congress to discuss any matter or to adopt a proposal submitted to it shall be put to the vote before the matter is discussed or a vote is taken on the proposal in question.

Reconsideration

Rule 33

When a proposal or motion has been adopted or rejected, it may not be reconsidered unless the Congress, by a two-thirds majority of the representatives present and voting, so decides. Permission to speak on a motion to reconsider shall be accorded only to two speakers opposing reconsideration, after which the matter shall be immediately put to the vote.

VI. Voting

Voting rights

Rule 34

Each State represented at the Congress shall have one vote.

Majority required

Rule 35

1. Unless the Congress decides otherwise, decisions of the Congress on all matters of substance shall require a two-thirds majority of the representatives present and voting.

2. Unless the Congress decides otherwise, and except as otherwise provided in these rules, decisions of the Congress on all other matters shall be taken by a simple majority of the representatives present and voting. If a vote is equally divided, the proposal or motion shall be regarded as rejected.

3. For the purpose of these rules, the phrase "representatives present and voting" means representatives present and casting an affirmative or negative vote. Representatives who abstain from voting shall be considered as not voting.

Methods of voting

Rule 36

Except as provided in rule 43, the Congress shall normally vote by show of hands, but any representative may request a roll-call vote, which shall then be taken in the English alphabetical order of the names of the States participating in the Congress, beginning with the one whose name is drawn by lot by the President. The name of each participating State shall be called in all roll-call votes, and its representative shall reply "yes", "no" or "abstention".

Explanation of vote

Rule 37

Representatives may make brief statements consisting solely of an explanation of their votes, either before the voting has commenced or after it has been completed. The representative of a State sponsoring a proposal or motion shall not speak in explanation of vote thereon unless it has been amended. The President may limit the time to be allowed for such explanations.

Conduct during voting

Rule 38

The President shall announce the commencement of voting, after which no representative shall be permitted to intervene until the result of the vote has been announced, except on a point of order in connection with the process of voting.

Division of proposals

Rule 39

A representative may move that parts of a proposal shall be voted on separately. If objection is made to the request for division, the motion for division shall be voted upon. If the motion for division is adopted, those parts of the proposal that are approved shall be put to the vote as a whole. If all operative parts of the proposal have been rejected, the proposal shall be considered to have been rejected as a whole.

Amendments

Rule 40

An amendment is a proposal that does no more than add to, delete from or revise part of another proposal. Unless specified otherwise, the word "proposal" in these rules shall be considered as including amendments.

Order of voting on amendments

Rule 41

When an amendment is moved to a proposal, the amendment shall be voted on first. When two or more amendments are moved to a proposal, the Congress shall vote first on the amendment furthest removed in substance from the original proposal, and then on the amendment next furthest removed therefrom, and so on until all the amendments have been put to the vote. Where, however, the adoption of one amendment necessarily implies the rejection of another amendment, the latter shall not be put to the vote. If one or more amendments are adopted, the amended proposal shall then be voted upon.

Order of voting on proposals

Rule 42

If two or more proposals, other than amendments, relate to the same question, they shall, unless the Congress decides otherwise, be voted on in the order in which they were submitted. The Congress may, after each vote on a proposal, decide whether to vote on the next proposal.

Elections

Rule 43

All elections shall be held by secret ballot, unless the Congress decides otherwise in an election where the number of candidates does not exceed the number of elective places to be filled.

Rule 44

1. When one or more elective places are to be filled at one time under the same conditions, those candidates,

in a number not exceeding the number of such places, obtaining in the first ballot a majority of the votes cast and the largest number of votes shall be elected.

2. If the number of candidates obtaining such majority is less than the number of places to be filled, additional ballots shall be held to fill the remaining places.

VII. Subsidiary organs

Committees, subcommittees and working groups

Rule 45

There shall be as many committees of the whole as may be approved from time to time by the Economic and Social Council on the recommendation of the Commission on Crime Prevention and Criminal Justice. Each committee may set up subcommittees and working groups, to the extent permitted by available facilities.

Officers

Rule 46

1. In addition to a Chairman elected by the Congress pursuant to rule 6, each committee shall itself elect a Vice-Chairman and a Rapporteur from among the representatives of participating States.

2. Subcommittees and working groups shall each elect a Chairman and no more than two Vice-Chairmen from among the representatives of participating States.

Applicable rules

Rule 47

The rules contained in sections II and IV to VI above shall be applicable, *mutatis mutandis*, to the proceedings of subsidiary organs, except that:

(*a*) The Chairmen of subsidiary organs other than the committees referred to in rule 45 may exercise the right to vote;

(*b*) A majority of the representatives participating in any subsidiary organs of limited membership shall constitute a quorum;

(*c*) Decisions of subsidiary organs shall be taken by a majority of the representatives present and voting, except that reconsideration of any such decision shall require the majority established by rule 33.

VIII. Languages and documents

Official languages

Rule 48

Arabic, Chinese, English, French, Russian and Spanish shall be the official languages of the Congress.

Interpretation

Rule 49

1. Speeches made in an official language of the Congress shall be interpreted into the other such languages.

2. Statements may be made in a language other than an official language of the Congress if the speaker provides for interpretation into one of the official languages. Interpretation into the other official languages of the Congress by interpreters of the secretariat may be based on the interpretation given in the first such language.

Languages of official documents

Rule 50

Official documents shall be made available in the official languages of the Congress.

Sound recordings of meetings

Rule 51

The secretariat shall make sound recordings of meetings of the Congress and of the committees. Such recordings shall be made of meetings of other subsidiary organs when the body concerned so decides.

IX. Report of the Congress

Rule 52

1. The Congress shall adopt a report, the draft of which shall be prepared by the Rapporteur-General.

2. The report shall be distributed as soon as practicable and not later than six months after the closing of the Congress to all States and to other participants in the Congress.

X. Public and private meetings

General principles

Rule 53

1. The plenary meetings of the Congress and meetings of its subsidiary organs other than the General Committee and the Credentials Committee shall be held in public unless the body concerned decides otherwise.

2. Meetings of the General Committee and the Credentials Committee shall be held in private unless the body concerned decides otherwise.

XI. Other participants and observers

Representatives of organizations that have received a standing invitation from the General Assembly to participate as observers in the sessions and work of all international conferences convened under the auspices of the General Assembly

Rule 54

Representatives designated by organizations that have received a standing invitation from the General Assembly to participate in the sessions and work of all international conferences convened under the auspices of the General Assembly may participate as observers, without the right to vote, in the deliberations of the Congress, its committees, subcommittees and working groups and, as appropriate, in its other subsidiary organs.

Representatives of national liberation movements

Rule 55

Representatives designated by national liberation movements invited to the Congress may participate as observers, without the right to vote, in the deliberations of the Congress, its committees, subcommittees and working groups and, as appropriate, in its other subsidiary organs.

Representatives of United Nations organs and related agencies

Rule 56

Representatives designated by organs of the United Nations, the specialized agencies or the International Atomic Energy Agency may participate as observers, without the right to vote, in the deliberations of the Congress, its committees, subcommittees and working groups and, as appropriate, in its other subsidiary organs.

Observers for other intergovernmental organizations

Rule 57

Observers designated by other intergovernmental organizations invited to the Congress may participate, without the right to vote, in the deliberations of the Congress, its committees, subcommittees and working groups and, as appropriate, in its other subsidiary organs.

Observers for non-governmental organizations

Rule 58

Observers designated by non-governmental organizations invited to the Congress may participate, without the right to vote, in the deliberations of the Congress, its committees, subcommittees and working groups.

Individual experts and consultants

Rule 59

1. Individual experts in the field of crime prevention and the treatment of offenders may be invited to the Congress by the Secretary-General in their individual capacity and may participate, without the right to vote, in the deliberations of the Congress, its committees, subcommittees and working groups.

2. The Secretary-General may invite a small number of expert consultants to participate in the Congress at the expense of the United Nations. In inviting such expert consultants, the Secretary-General shall pay due regard to the principle of equitable geographical representation. Expert consultants thus invited may, as appropriate, initiate and assist in debates in the committees, subcommittees and working groups of the Congress.

Written statements

Rule 60

Written statements related to the work of the Congress submitted by the designated representatives, individual experts or observers referred to in rules 54 to 59 shall be distributed by the secretariat to all delegations in the quantities and in the languages in which the statements are made available to the secretariat for distribution, provided that a statement submitted on behalf of a non-governmental organization shall be on a subject in which it has a special competence.

XII. Amendment or suspension of the rules of procedure

Method of amendment

Rule 61

The present rules may be amended by a decision of the Congress taken by a two-thirds majority of the representatives present and voting upon a recommendation of the General Committee.

Method of suspension

Rule 62

1. Any of the present rules may be suspended by a decision of the Congress, provided that twenty-four hours' notice of the proposal for the suspension has been given, which may be waived if no representative objects; subsidiary organs may by unanimous consent waive rules pertaining to them. Any suspension shall be limited to a specific and stated purpose and to the period required to achieve it.

2. This rule shall not apply to rule 30.

Periodic review of rules

Rule 63

After the completion of each Congress, the Commission on Crime Prevention and Criminal Justice shall make appropriate recommendations to the Economic and Social Council for such amendments to these rules as it may deem necessary.

Economic and Social Council resolution 1993/32

27 July 1993   Meeting 43   Adopted without vote

Approved by Social Committee (E/1993/106) without vote, 14 July (meeting 10); draft by Commission on Crime Prevention and Criminal Justice (E/1993/32), orally amended; agenda item 20.

By **resolution 48/230, section III**, of 23 December, the General Assembly approved, on an exceptional basis, the travel expenses of the representatives of the least developed countries attending the regional preparatory meetings for the Congress and the Congress itself. Those expenses would amount to $141,000, according to a November report of the Secretary-General.[52]

Cultural development

World Decade for Cultural Development

On 12 February, the Economic and Social Council, by **decision 1993/209**, postponed consideration of the biennial progress report on the World Decade for Cultural Development (1988-1991), requested by the General Assembly in 1986,[53] and decided to combine the report with the global mid-term review of the Decade requested by the Assembly in 1991.[54]

Restitution of cultural property

As requested by the General Assembly in 1991,[55] the Secretary-General submitted an October report of the Director-General of UNESCO[56] describing measures taken to promote the return or restitution of cultural property to the countries of origin since the last (1991) meeting of the Intergovernmental Committee for Promoting the Return of Cultural Property to its Countries of Origin or its Restitution in Case of Illicit Appropriation.[57] Developments were outlined regarding bilateral negotiations for the return or restitution of cultural property, international cooperation and steps to curb illicit traffic in cultural property.

The eighth (1993) session of the Intergovernmental Committee was to take place in Guatemala from 7 to 10 June, but owing to the situation in the country at the time, it was postponed until early 1994.

GENERAL ASSEMBLY ACTION

On 2 November, the General Assembly adopted **resolution 48/15** by recorded vote.

**Return or restitution of cultural property
to the countries of origin**

The General Assembly,

Recalling its resolutions 3026 A(XXVII) of 18 December 1972, 3148(XXVIII) of 14 December 1973,

3187(XXVIII) of 18 December 1973, 3391(XXX) of
19 November 1975, 31/40 of 30 November 1976, 32/18
of 11 November 1977, 33/50 of 14 December 1978,
34/64 of 29 November 1979, 35/127 and 35/128 of
11 December 1980, 36/64 of 27 November 1981, 38/34
of 25 November 1983, 40/19 of 21 November 1985,
42/7 of 22 October 1987, 44/18 of 6 November 1989
and 46/10 of 22 October 1991,

Recalling also the Convention on the Means of Prohibiting and Preventing the Illicit Import, Export and Transfer of Ownership of Cultural Property adopted on
14 November 1970 by the General Conference of the
United Nations Educational, Scientific and Cultural Organization,

Taking note with satisfaction of the report of the Secretary-
General submitted in cooperation with the Director-
General of the United Nations Educational, Scientific
and Cultural Organization,

Noting with satisfaction that, following its appeal, other
Member States have become parties to the Convention,

Aware of the importance attached by the countries of
origin to the return of cultural property which is of fundamental spiritual and cultural value to them, so that
they may constitute collections representative of their
cultural heritage,

Reaffirming the importance of inventories as an essential tool for the understanding and protection of cultural
property and for the identification of dispersed heritage
and as a contribution to the advancement of scientific
and artistic knowledge and intercultural communication,

Deeply concerned at the clandestine excavations and the
illicit traffic in cultural property that continue to im-
poverish the cultural heritage of all peoples,

Again supporting the solemn appeal made on 7 June
1978 by the Director-General of the United Nations
Educational, Scientific and Cultural Organization for
the return of irreplaceable cultural heritage to those who
created it,

1. *Commends* the United Nations Educational, Scientific and Cultural Organization and the Intergovernmental Committee for Promoting the Return of Cultural
Property to Its Countries of Origin or Its Restitution
in Case of Illicit Appropriation on the work they have
accomplished, in particular through the promotion of
bilateral negotiations, for the return or restitution of cultural property, the preparation of inventories of mova-
ble cultural property, the reduction of illicit traffic in
cultural property and the dissemination of information
to the public;

2. *Reaffirms* that the restitution to a country of its
objets d'art, monuments, museum pieces, archives,
manuscripts, documents and any other cultural or artistic treasures contributes to the strengthening of international cooperation and to the preservation and
flowering of universal cultural values through fruitful
cooperation between developed and developing
countries;

3. *Recommends* that Member States adopt or
strengthen the necessary protective legislation with regard to their own heritage and that of other peoples;

4. *Requests* Member States to study the possibility of
including in permits for excavations a clause requiring
archaeologists and palaeontologists to provide the national authorities with photographic documentation of
each object brought to light during the excavations immediately after its discovery;

5. *Invites* Member States to continue drawing up, in
cooperation with the United Nations Educational, Scientific and Cultural Organization, systematic inventories
of cultural property existing in their territory and of their
cultural property abroad;

6. *Also recommends* that Member States should ensure
that inventories of museum collections include not only
the items on display but also those in storage, and that
they comprise all necessary documentation, particularly
photographs of each item;

7. *Also invites* Member States engaged in seeking the
recovery of cultural and artistic treasures from the
seabed, in accordance with international law, to facilitate by mutually acceptable conditions the participation
of States having a historical and cultural link with those
treasures;

8. *Appeals* to Member States to cooperate closely with
the Intergovernmental Committee for Promoting the
Return of Cultural Property to Its Countries of Origin
or Its Restitution in Case of Illicit Appropriation and
to conclude bilateral agreements for this purpose;

9. *Also appeals* to Member States to encourage the
mass information media and educational and cultural
institutions to strive to arouse a greater and more general
awareness with regard to the return or restitution of cultural property to its country of origin;

10. *Requests* States parties to the Convention on the
Means of Prohibiting and Preventing the Illicit Import,
Export and Transfer of Ownership of Cultural Property to keep the Secretary-General of the United Nations and the Director-General of the United Nations
Educational, Scientific and Cultural Organization fully
informed of the measures taken to ensure implementation of the Convention at the national level;

11. *Requests* the Secretary-General, in collaboration
with the United Nations Educational, Scientific and Cultural Organization, to continue to develop all possibilities for bringing about the attainment of the aforementioned objectives;

12. *Welcomes* the steady increase in the number of
States parties to the Convention;

13. *Invites once again* those Member States that have
not yet done so to sign and ratify the Convention;

14. *Requests* the Secretary-General of the United Nations, in cooperation with the Director-General of the
United Nations Educational, Scientific and Cultural Organization, to submit to the General Assembly at its fiftieth session a report on the implementation of the present resolution;

15. *Decides* to include in the provisional agenda of its
fiftieth session the item entitled "Return or restitution
of cultural property to the countries of origin".

General Assembly resolution 48/15

2 November 1993   Meeting 47   106-0-25 (recorded vote)

21-nation draft (A/48/L.15 and Add.1); agenda item 21.
Sponsors: Bolivia, Cameroon, Costa Rica, Côte d'Ivoire, Cyprus, Egypt, El Sal-
vador, Ghana, Greece, Guatemala, Mali, Mexico, Mongolia, Morocco,
Nepal, Nicaragua, Niger, Peru, Rwanda, Ukraine, Zaire.

Recorded vote in Assembly as follows:

In favour: Afghanistan, Algeria, Angola, Argentina, Australia, Bahamas,
Bahrain, Barbados, Belarus, Benin, Bhutan, Bolivia, Bosnia and Herzego-
vina, Botswana, Brunei Darussalam, Burkina Faso, Burundi, Cambodia,
Cameroon, Canada, Cape Verde, Central African Republic, Chad, Chile,
China, Colombia, Congo, Costa Rica, Côte d'Ivoire, Croatia, Cuba, Cyprus,
Ecuador, Egypt, Ethiopia, Finland, Ghana, Greece, Guatemala, Guinea,
Guinea-Bissau, Guyana, Haiti, Honduras, Iceland, India, Indonesia, Iran,
Iraq, Jamaica, Kenya, Kuwait, Lao People's Democratic Republic, Leba-

non, Lesotho, Libyan Arab Jamahiriya, Madagascar, Malaysia, Maldives, Mali, Malta, Mauritania, Mauritius, Mexico, Mongolia, Morocco, Mozambique, Myanmar, Namibia, Nepal, New Zealand, Nicaragua, Niger, Norway, Oman, Pakistan, Panama, Papua New Guinea, Peru, Philippines, Qatar, Republic of Korea, Rwanda, Samoa, Saudi Arabia, Seychelles, Sierra Leone, Singapore, Sri Lanka, Sudan, Suriname, Swaziland, Syrian Arab Republic, Thailand, the former Yugoslav Republic of Macedonia, Togo, Tunisia, Turkey, Ukraine, United Arab Emirates, United Republic of Tanzania, Venezuela, Yemen, Zaire, Zambia, Zimbabwe.
Against: none.
Abstaining: Albania, Austria, Belgium, Bulgaria, Czech Republic, Denmark, France, Germany, Hungary, Ireland, Israel, Italy, Japan, Liechtenstein, Luxembourg, Netherlands, Poland, Portugal, Romania, Russian Federation, Slovakia, Spain, Sweden, United Kingdom, United States.

International Year of Sport and the Olympic Ideal and Observance of the Olympic Truce

By a 10 August letter,[58] the United Republic of Tanzania transmitted to the Secretary-General the documents of the 1993 meeting of the Council of Ministers of the Organization of African Unity (Cairo, Egypt, 21-26 June). One resolution adopted by the Council of Ministers dealt with an appeal by the International Olympic Committee to build a peaceful and better world through sport and was the basis of two General Assembly resolutions on the subject.

GENERAL ASSEMBLY ACTION

On 25 October, the General Assembly adopted **resolution 48/10** without vote.

International Year of Sport and the Olympic Ideal
The General Assembly,
Recalling that the International Olympic Committee, founded on the initiative of a Frenchman, Pierre de Coubertin, will be celebrating the centenary of its founding in 1994,
Taking into account its decision 35/424 of 5 December 1980 concerning guidelines for international years and anniversaries,
Noting that the organization of the celebration for the International Year of Sport and the Olympic Ideal at the national and international level will be coordinated by the International Olympic Committee, with the collaboration of the International Sports Federations and the national Olympic committees,
Recognizing that the goal of the Olympic Movement is to build a peaceful and better world by educating the youth of the world through sport and culture,
Recognizing also that the Olympic ideal is to promote international understanding among the youth of the world through sport and culture and is therefore relevant to the International Year of the Family, which will be commemorated in 1994, in accordance with General Assembly resolution 44/82 of 8 December 1989,
Noting also that the preparation for the International Year of Sport and the Olympic Ideal will not involve any financial implications for the United Nations or its Member States, nor will it require the setting up of any administrative structure,
1. *Proclaims* 1994 as International Year of Sport and the Olympic Ideal;
2. *Commends* the Olympic Movement for its ideal to promote international understanding among the youth of the world through sport and culture;

3. *Endorses* the appeal launched by the International Olympic Committee to build a peaceful and better world through sport, supported by resolution CM/Res.1472 (LVIII), adopted by the Council of Ministers of the Organization of African Unity at its fifty-eighth ordinary session, held at Cairo from 21 to 26 June 1993;
4. *Invites* all States, organizations of the United Nations system and interested non-governmental organizations to participate in the observance of the Year and to cooperate with the Secretary-General in achieving the objectives of the Year;
5. *Requests* the Secretary-General to cooperate with the International Olympic Committee in its endeavours to promote the observance of the Year.

General Assembly resolution 48/10

25 October 1993   Meeting 36   Adopted without vote

123-nation draft (A/48/L.8/Rev.1 & Rev.1/Add.1); agenda item 167.
Sponsors: Afghanistan, Albania, Algeria, Andorra, Antigua and Barbuda, Argentina, Armenia, Australia, Austria, Bahamas, Barbados, Belarus, Belgium, Benin, Bhutan, Bolivia, Bosnia and Herzegovina, Botswana, Brunei Darussalam, Bulgaria, Burkina Faso, Burundi, Cambodia, Cameroon, Canada, Cape Verde, Chad, China, Colombia, Comoros, Congo, Costa Rica, Côte d'Ivoire, Croatia, Cuba, Cyprus, Djibouti, Dominica, Dominican Republic, Egypt, El Salvador, Eritrea, Ethiopia, Fiji, France, Gabon, Gambia, Georgia, Germany, Greece, Grenada, Guatemala, Guinea, Guinea-Bissau, Guyana, Honduras, Hungary, Indonesia, Iran, Italy, Japan, Kenya, Kyrgyzstan, Latvia, Lesotho, Libyan Arab Jamahiriya, Liechtenstein, Lithuania, Luxembourg, Madagascar, Mali, Malta, Mauritania, Mauritius, Micronesia, Monaco, Mongolia, Morocco, Mozambique, Namibia, Nepal, New Zealand, Niger, Nigeria, Norway, Oman, Pakistan, Panama, Paraguay, Peru, Poland, Republic of Korea, Romania, Russian Federation, Rwanda, Saint Kitts and Nevis, Saint Vincent and the Grenadines, Samoa, San Marino, Sao Tome and Principe, Senegal, Seychelles, Sierra Leone, Slovakia, Slovenia, Spain, Sudan, Suriname, Swaziland, Togo, Tunisia, Turkey, Uganda, United Arab Emirates, United Republic of Tanzania, United States, Uruguay, Uzbekistan, Vanuatu, Yemen, Zaire, Zambia, Zimbabwe.

On the same date, the Assembly adopted **resolution 48/11** without vote.

Observance of the Olympic Truce
The General Assembly,
Considering the appeal launched by the International Olympic Committee for an Olympic Truce, which was endorsed by one hundred eighty-four Olympic committees and presented to the Secretary-General,
Recognizing that the goal of the Olympic Movement is to build a peaceful and better world by educating the youth of the world through sport, practised without discrimination of any kind and in the Olympic spirit, which requires mutual understanding, promoted by friendship, solidarity and fair play,
Recognizing also the efforts of the International Olympic Committee to restore the ancient Greek tradition of the *ekecheria*, or ''Olympic Truce'', in the interest of contributing to international understanding and the maintenance of peace,
Recalling resolution CM/Res.1472(LVIII), which supports the appeal for an Olympic Truce, adopted by the Council of Ministers of the Organization of African Unity at its fifty-eighth ordinary session, held at Cairo from 21 to 26 June 1993, and endorsed by the Assembly of Heads of State and Government of that organization,
Recognizing further the valuable contribution that the appeal launched by the International Olympic Committee for an Olympic Truce could make towards advancing the purposes and principles of the Charter of the United Nations,

1. *Commends* the International Olympic Committee, the international sports federations and the national Olympic committees for their efforts to mobilize the youth of the world in the cause of peace;

2. *Urges* Member States to observe the Olympic Truce from the seventh day before the opening and the seventh day following the closing of each of the Olympic Games, in accordance with the appeal launched by the International Olympic Committee;

3. *Notes* the idea of the "Olympic Truce", as dedicated in ancient Greece to the spirit of fraternity and understanding between peoples, and urges Member States to take the initiative to abide by the Truce, individually and collectively, and to pursue in conformity with the purposes and principles of the Charter of the United Nations the peaceful settlement of all international conflicts;

4. *Calls upon* all Member States to cooperate with the International Olympic Committee in its efforts to promote the Olympic Truce;

5. *Requests* the Secretary-General to promote the observance of the Olympic Truce among Member States, drawing the attention of world public opinion to the contribution such a truce would make to the promotion of international understanding and the maintenance of peace and goodwill, and to cooperate with the International Olympic Committee in the realization of this objective.

General Assembly resolution 48/11

25 October 1993   Meeting 36   Adopted without vote

122-nation draft (A/48/L.9/Rev.1 and Rev.1/Add.1); agenda item 167.

Sponsors: Afghanistan, Albania, Algeria, Andorra, Angola, Antigua and Barbuda, Argentina, Armenia, Australia, Austria, Bahamas, Barbados, Belarus, Belgium, Benin, Bhutan, Bolivia, Bosnia and Herzegovina, Botswana, Brunei Darussalam, Bulgaria, Burkina Faso, Burundi, Cambodia, Cameroon, Canada, Cape Verde, Chad, China, Colombia, Comoros, Congo, Costa Rica, Côte d'Ivoire, Croatia, Cuba, Cyprus, Djibouti, Dominica, Dominican Republic, El Salvador, Egypt, Eritrea, Ethiopia, Fiji, France, Gabon, Gambia, Georgia, Germany, Greece, Grenada, Guatemala, Guinea, Guinea-Bissau, Guyana, Honduras, Hungary, Indonesia, Iran, Italy, Japan, Kenya, Kyrgystan, Lesotho, Libyan Arab Jamahiriya, Liechtenstein, Luxembourg, Madagascar, Mali, Malta, Mauritania, Mauritius, Micronesia, Monaco, Mongolia, Morocco, Mozambique, Namibia, Nepal, New Zealand, Niger, Nigeria, Norway, Oman, Pakistan, Panama, Paraguay, Peru, Poland, Romania, Republic of Korea, Russian Federation, Rwanda, Saint Kitts and Nevis, Saint Vincent and the Grenadines, Samoa, San Marino, Sao Tome and Principe, Senegal, Seychelles, Sierra Leone, Slovakia, Slovenia, Spain, Sudan, Suriname, Swaziland, Togo, Tunisia, Turkey, Uganda, United Arab Emirates, United Republic of Tanzania, United States, Uruguay, Uzbekistan, Vanuatu, Yemen, Zaire, Zambia, Zimbabwe.

REFERENCES

[1]YUN 1992, p. 835, ESC res. 1992/26, 30 July 1992. [2]*Report on the World Social Situation 1993* (E/1993/50 & Add.1), Sales No. E.93.IV.2. [3]GA res. 44/57, 8 Dec. 1989. [4]YUN 1969, p. 422. [5]ESC res. 1989/46, 24 May 1989. [6]E/CN.5/1993/11. [7]YUN 1986, p. 446, GA res. S-13/2, annex, 1 June 1986. [8]YUN 1992, p. 836, GA res. 47/92, 16 Dec. 1992. [9]A/48/24. [10]A/CONF.166/PC/4. [11]A/CONF.166/PC/3. [12]A/CONF.166/PC/8. [13]A/CONF.166/PC/9. [14]A/48/476. [15]E/1993/77. [16]E/1993/102. [17]E/1993/24. [18]E/CN.5/1993/2 & Add.1. [19]YUN 1991, p. 655, GA res. 46/90, 16 Dec. 1991. [20]A/48/56-E/1993/6. [21]YUN 1987, p. 616. [22]Ibid., GA res. 42/125, 7 Dec. 1987. [23]YUN 1992, p. 672. [24]YUN 1991, p. 656, ESC res. 1991/12, 30 May 1991. [25]E/1993/5. [26]GA res. 45/199, annex, 21 Dec. 1990. [27]YUN 1991, p. 656. [28]YUN 1992, p. 838, GA res. 47/124, 18 Dec. 1992. [29]A/48/210-E/1993/89. [30]YUN 1980, p. 1029, ESC res. 1980/67, annex, 25 July 1980. [31]YUN 1991, p. 657, GA res. 46/92, 16 Dec. 1991. [32]A/48/293. [33]YUN 1992, p. 839. [34]GA res. 44/82, 8 Dec. 1989. [35]E/CN.5/1993/8 & Corr.1. [36]YUN 1992, p. 842, ESC res. 1992/1, 6 Feb. 1992. [37]E/1993/32. [38]YUN 1992, p. 842, ESC res. 1992/22, 30 July 1992. [39]E/CN.15/1993/2. [40]E/1993/10. [41]YUN 1992, p. 849, ESC res. 1992/23, 30 July 1992. [42]E/CN.15/1993/3. [43]E/CN.15/1993/4. [44]E/CN.15/1993/5. [45]E/CN.15/1993/6. [46]*Compendium of United Nations Standards and Norms in Crime Prevention and Criminal Justice,* Sales No. E.92.IV.1. [47]E/CN.15/1993/8 & Add.1. [48]YUN 1992, p. 860, GA res. 47/89, 16 Dec. 1992. [49]A/48/332. [50]E/CN.15/1993/7 & Corr.1. [51]YUN 1992, p. 861, ESC res. 1992/24, 30 July 1992. [52]A/C.5/48/19 & Corr.1. [53]YUN 1986, p. 624, GA res. 41/187, 8 Dec. 1986. [54]YUN 1991, p. 669, GA res. 46/157, 19 Dec. 1991. [55]YUN 1991, p. 670, GA res. 46/10, 22 Oct. 1991. [56]A/48/466. [57]YUN 1991, p. 670. [58]A/48/322.

Chapter XIII

Women

During 1993, preparations were under way for the Fourth World Conference on Women, to be held in 1995 to review and appraise progress in implementing the Nairobi Forward-looking Strategies for the Advancement of Women to the year 2000, adopted at the 1985 World Conference. Work continued throughout the United Nations system on implementing the Strategies—a set of measures to overcome obstacles to the goals and objectives of the United Nations Decade for Women (1976-1985).

The Economic and Social Council, acting on the recommendations of the Commission on the Status of Women, adopted resolutions on a draft declaration on the elimination of violence against women (1993/10); women, environment and development (1993/12); communications on the status of women (1993/11); the 1979 Convention on the Elimination of Discrimination against Women (1993/14); improving the status of women in the United Nations (see PART FIVE, Chapter II) (1993/9); the situation of Palestinian women (see PART TWO, Chapter V) (1993/15); and women and children under apartheid (see PART TWO, Chapter I) (1993/13).

In December, the General Assembly adopted the Declaration on the Elimination of Violence against Women (resolution 48/104), which set forth a definition of violence against women, stated the rights to be applied to eliminate such violence and outlined measures for action by States and the international community.

The Committee on the Elimination of Discrimination against Women considered reports of States parties to the 1979 Convention on the Elimination of Discrimination against Women. At the end of the year, the Convention had 96 signatories and 130 States parties.

During 1993, the Secretary-General proposed the merger of the International Research and Training Institute for the Advancement of Women and the United Nations Development Fund for Women, with a view to strengthening the programmes for the advancement of women and enhancing the efficiency of the work of those organizations.

In September, the United Nations Division for the Advancement of Women was moved from Vienna and incorporated into the newly established Department for Policy Coordination and Sustainable Development in New York.

Advancement of women

Implementation of the Nairobi Strategies

As requested by the General Assembly in 1992,[1] the Secretary-General in September 1993[2] reviewed the implementation of the Nairobi Forward-looking Strategies for the Advancement of Women, adopted in 1985 by the World Conference to Review and Appraise the Achievements of the United Nations Decade for Women.[3] He assessed developments with regard to the priority themes of the Strategies (equality, development, peace), which were to be considered by the Commission on the Status of Women at its thirty-eighth (1994) session, and described preparations for the Fourth (1995) World Conference on Women: Action for Equality, Development and Peace (see below).

The Secretary-General discussed cooperation between the organizations of the United Nations system and the Commission on the Status of Women on the implementation of the Strategies; contributions to forthcoming major international conferences; methods of data collection and compilation; women in vulnerable situations, including migrant women workers; women in development, particularly rural women; women in public life and international decision-making; the system-wide medium-term plan for the advancement of women; and women in the United Nations Secretariat.

In an earlier report,[4] submitted to the Commission on the Status of Women,[5] the Secretary-General presented the proposed programme of work of the United Nations Division for the Advancement of Women for the 1994-1995 biennium, which was based on the implementation of the Nairobi Strategies. In March,[6] the Commission called on the Secretary-General to strengthen the institutional structure and work programme for the advancement of women.

In **resolution 48/108**, the General Assembly called on the Commission to continue to promote the implementation of the Nairobi Strategies (see below).

Monitoring, review and appraisal

1995 World Conference on Women

In 1993, preparations for the Fourth World Conference on Women: Action for Equality, Development and Peace, to be held in Beijing, China, in 1995, accelerated within the United Nations system and at national, regional and international levels.[2] The aim of the Conference was to review and appraise progress achieved in implementing the Nairobi Strategies and to identify measures to ensure the achievement of their objectives during the last five years of the twentieth century. The Secretary-General appointed Gertrude Mongella of the United Republic of Tanzania as Secretary-General of the 1995 Conference, and a Trust Fund for Conference preparatory activities was established, to which 10 Governments had contributed or pledged their support by September 1993.

At its 1993 session,[5] the Commission on the Status of Women, which acted as the preparatory body for the Conference, had before it a series of reports by the Secretary-General. One described preparations for the Conference at the national, regional and international levels, including action taken by non-governmental organizations (NGOs),[7] and another proposed activities and national guidelines for the information campaign for the Conference.[8] In 1992,[9] the Commission had decided that the Conference's agenda should include the second review and appraisal of the implementation of the Nairobi Strategies and the Platform of Action—the final document that would emerge from the Conference. The Secretary-General submitted to the Commission[10] information on data needed for the second review and presented an outline for it, which he stated should emphasize the recommendations and conclusions arising from the first (1990) review and appraisal of the implementation of the Nairobi Strategies.[11] He also submitted a report containing the first draft of the Platform for Action,[12] which comprised sections dealing with a statement of purpose; a diagnosis of the current situation of the world's women; an analytical statement of the most significant obstacles to the advancement of women identified in the diagnosis; key issues and basic needs, linking the status of women to global changes; specific action to be taken to reach obtainable goals in key areas; and a statement about implementation mechanisms.

In March,[13] the Commission took note of the Secretary-General's reports and expressed concern that only a few Governments had established national committees or designated focal points to promote the Conference.

Ad hoc inter-agency meeting. The seventeenth ad hoc inter-agency meeting on women (Vienna, 15 and 16 March) focused on preparations for the 1995 World Conference.[14] It discussed the second review and appraisal and the Platform for Action and reviewed the proposed information programme for the Conference. Annexed to the report was a joint statement of the representatives of 28

United Nations organizations comprising the inter-agency meeting addressed to the 1993 session of the Commission on the Status of Women.

The Economic and Social Council, by **decision 1993/234** of 27 July, decided that an intersessional working group of the Commission should be convened for five working days during the first two weeks of 1994 to develop further the structure of the Platform for Action, as recommended by the Commission.[13]

In **resolution 48/105** of 20 December, the General Assembly requested the International Research and Training Institute for the Advancement of Women (INSTRAW) to assist with preparations for the Conference (see below).

On 20 December, the General Assembly, on the recommendation of the Third (Social, Humanitarian and Cultural) Committee, adopted **resolution 48/108** without vote.

Implementation of the Nairobi Forward-looking Strategies for the Advancement of Women

The General Assembly,

Recalling all its relevant resolutions, in particular resolution 44/77 of 8 December 1989, in which, *inter alia,* it endorsed and reaffirmed the importance of the Nairobi Forward-looking Strategies for the Advancement of Women for the period up to the year 2000 and set out measures for their immediate implementation and for the overall achievement of the interrelated goals and objectives of the United Nations Decade for Women: Equality, Development and Peace,

Recalling also its resolutions 46/98 of 16 December 1991 and 47/95 of 16 December 1992,

Taking into consideration the resolutions adopted by the Economic and Social Council on issues relating to women since the adoption of its resolution 1987/18 of 26 May 1987,

Reaffirming its determination to encourage the full participation of women in economic, social, cultural, civil and political affairs and to promote development, cooperation and international peace,

Conscious of the important and constructive contribution to the improvement of the status of women made by the Commission on the Status of Women, the specialized agencies, the regional commissions and other organizations and bodies of the United Nations system and non-governmental organizations concerned,

Concerned that the resources available in the Secretariat to the programme on the advancement of women are insufficient to ensure adequate support to the Committee on the Elimination of Discrimination against Women and effective implementation of other aspects of the programme, especially the preparations for the Fourth World Conference on Women: Action for Equality, Development and Peace, to be held in 1995,

Taking into account Commission on the Status of Women resolutions 36/8 of 20 March 1992 and 37/7 of 25 March 1993 on the preparations for the Fourth World Conference on Women,

Bearing in mind the important role non-governmental organizations play in all activities for the advancement of women and the fact that some of them, especially those from developing countries, do not enjoy consultative status with the Economic and Social Council,

Noting with satisfaction that the preparations for the Fourth World Conference on Women have entered a substantive stage, that the relevant United Nations bodies, China, as the host country, and other countries all attach great importance to the preparation of the Conference and that the various preparatory activities are being conducted in an in-depth and comprehensive manner,

Considering that 1994 will be a year of crucial importance to the preparations for the Fourth World Conference on Women, that the Commission on the Status of Women will convene an inter-sessional working group to deliberate the content of the Platform for Action and that the five regional commissions will convene their respective regional preparatory meetings for the Conference,

1. *Takes note* of the report of the Secretary-General;

2. *Reaffirms* section I, paragraph 2, of the recommendations and conclusions arising from the first review and appraisal of the implementation of the Nairobi Forward-looking Strategies for the Advancement of Women, contained in the annex to Economic and Social Council resolution 1990/15 of 24 May 1990, which called for an improved pace in the implementation of the Forward-looking Strategies in the crucial last decade of the twentieth century, since the cost to societies of failing to implement them would be high in terms of slowed economic and social development, misuse of human resources and reduced progress for society as a whole;

3. *Urges* Governments, international organizations and non-governmental organizations to implement the recommendations;

4. *Calls again upon* Member States to give priority to policies and programmes relating to the subtheme "Employment, health and education", in particular to literacy, for self-reliance of women and the mobilization of indigenous resources, as well as to issues relating to the role of women in economic and political decision-making, population, the environment, information and science and technology;

5. *Reaffirms* the central role of the Commission on the Status of Women in matters related to the advancement of women and calls upon it to continue promoting the implementation of the Forward-looking Strategies to the year 2000, based on the goals of the United Nations Decade for Women: Equality, Development and Peace and the subtheme "Employment, health and education", and urges all relevant bodies of the United Nations system to cooperate effectively with the Commission in this task;

6. *Requests* the Commission, when considering the priority theme relating to development during its thirty-eighth and subsequent sessions, to ensure its early contribution to the preparatory work for forthcoming major international conferences such as the International Conference on Population and Development, to be held in 1994, the Fourth World Conference on Women: Action for Equality, Development and Peace, to be held in 1995, and the World Summit for Social Development, to be held in 1995, and to address the impact of technologies on women;

7. *Also requests* the Commission to give special attention to women in developing countries, particularly in Africa and the least developed countries, who suffer disproportionately from the effects of the global economic crisis and the heavy external debt burden, and to recommend further measures for the equalization of opportunity and for the integration of the roles and perspective of women, as well as their needs, concerns and aspirations, into the entire development process when considering the priority theme of development;

8. *Emphasizes*, in the framework of the Forward-looking Strategies, the importance of the total integration of women of all ages in the development process, bearing in mind the specific and urgent needs of the developing countries, and calls upon Member States to establish specific targets at each level in order to increase the participation of women in professional, management and decision-making positions in their countries;

9. *Emphasizes once again* the need to give urgent attention to redressing socio-economic inequities at the national and international levels as a necessary step towards the full realization of the goals and objectives of the Forward-looking Strategies through meeting the practical and strategic needs of women;

10. *Strongly urges* that particular attention be given by the competent United Nations organizations and Governments to the special needs of women with disabilities, elderly women and also women in vulnerable situations such as migrant and refugee women and children;

11. *Takes note* of the report of the Secretary-General on the improvement of the situation of women in rural areas, and urges the international community and the competent United Nations bodies and organs to place more emphasis on the sharp increase in the incidence of poverty among rural women;

12. *Welcomes* the recommendations adopted at the United Nations Conference on Environment and Development on women, environment and development in all programme areas, in particular those set out in chapter 24 of Agenda 21, entitled "Global action for women towards sustainable and equitable development";

13. *Urges* organs, organizations and bodies of the United Nations to ensure active participation of women in the planning and implementation of programmes for sustainable development, and requests Governments, in the context of General Assembly resolution 47/191 of 22 December 1992, to consider nominating women as representatives to the Commission on Sustainable Development;

14. *Requests* the Secretary-General, in formulating the system-wide medium-term plan for the advancement of women for the period 1996-2001 and in integrating the Forward-looking Strategies into activities mandated by the General Assembly, to pay particular attention to specific sectoral themes that cut across the three objectives, equality, development and peace, and include, in particular, literacy, education, health, population, the impact of technology on the environment and its effect on women and the full participation of women in decision-making, and to continue to assist Governments in strengthening their national machineries for the advancement of women;

15. *Also requests* the Secretary-General to continue updating the *World Survey on the Role of Women in Development*,

bearing in mind its importance, placing particular emphasis on the adverse impact of the difficult economic situation affecting the majority of developing countries, particularly on the condition of women, giving special attention to worsening conditions for the incorporation of women into the labour force, as well as the impact of reduced expenditures for social services on opportunities available to women for education, health and child care, and to submit a final version of the preliminary version of the updated *World Survey on the Role of Women in Development* to the Economic and Social Council, through the Commission on the Status of Women, in 1994;

16. *Requests* Governments, when presenting candidatures for vacancies in the Secretariat, in particular at the decision-making level, to give priority to candidatures of women, and requests the Secretary-General in reviewing those candidatures to give special consideration to female candidates from underrepresented and unrepresented developing countries;

17. *Requests* the Secretary-General to invite Governments, organizations of the United Nations system, including the regional commissions and the specialized agencies, and intergovernmental and non-governmental organizations to report periodically to the Economic and Social Council, through the Commission, on activities undertaken at all levels to implement the Forward-looking Strategies;

18. *Also requests* the Secretary-General to continue to provide for the existing weekly radio programmes on women in the regular budget of the United Nations, making adequate provisions for broadcasts in different languages, and to develop the focal point for issues relating to women in the Department of Public Information of the Secretariat, which, in concert with the Department for Policy Coordination and Sustainable Development, should provide a more effective public information programme relating to the advancement of women;

19. *Further requests* the Secretary-General to include in his report on the implementation of the Forward-looking Strategies, to be submitted to the General Assembly at its forty-ninth session, an assessment of recent developments that are relevant to the priority themes to be considered at the subsequent session of the Commission and to transmit to the Commission a summary of relevant views expressed by delegations during the debate in the Assembly;

20. *Requests* the Commission to examine the implications of the World Conference on Human Rights and the Vienna Declaration and Programme of Action adopted by the Conference for its central role in matters related to the rights of women within the United Nations system and to report to the Economic and Social Council at its substantive session of 1994;

21. *Requests* the Secretary-General to prepare a report for the Commission, for consideration at its thirty-eighth session, on steps to be taken by the Division for the Advancement of Women, in cooperation with other United Nations bodies, specifically the Centre for Human Rights of the Secretariat, to ensure that relevant human rights mechanisms of the United Nations, such as treaty-monitoring bodies, rapporteurs and working groups, regularly address violations of the rights of women, including gender-specific abuses;

22. *Recognizes* that the Declaration on the Elimination of Violence against Women, proclaimed in General Assembly resolution 48/104 of 20 December 1993, is essential to the attainment of full respect for the rights of women and is an important contribution to efforts aimed at achieving the objectives of the Nairobi Forward-looking Strategies by the year 2000;

23. *Requests* the Secretary-General to lend support to the convening of the regional preparatory meetings so as to lay a good foundation for the Fourth World Conference on Women;

24. *Also requests* the Secretary-General to give more support, from within existing resources, to the Division for the Advancement of Women, acting as secretariat of the Fourth World Conference on Women, by providing sufficient financial and human resources and giving wide publicity to the Conference and its preparatory activities;

25. *Appeals* to countries to compile their national reports in earnest and to forward them in time, both to their respective regional commissions and to the secretariat of the Conference;

26. *Invites* the Secretary-General to play a more active role in appealing to countries to contribute to the Trust Fund for the Fourth World Conference on Women, in order to finance additional activities of the preparatory process and the Conference itself, in particular the participation of least developed countries in the Conference and its preparatory meetings;

27. *Recommends* the further development of methods of compilation and data collection in areas of concern identified by the Commission on the Status of Women, and urges Member States to improve and broaden collection of gender-desegregated statistical information and make it available to the relevant bodies of the United Nations system with a view to preparing, in all official languages, as a background document for the Fourth World Conference on Women, an updated edition of *The World's Women 1970-1990: Trends and Statistics*;

28. *Endorses* the recommendation contained in Commission on the Status of Women resolution 36/8 that regional preparatory conferences should include in their agendas the issue of women in public life, as well as the request for the Secretary-General to include information on the decision-making position of women in public life and in the fields of science and technology in the preparation of the priority theme on peace: "Women in international decision-making", for the Commission at its thirty-ninth session, in 1995;

29. *Requests* the Secretary-General to make available for the Fourth World Conference on Women reports and decisions of the World Conference on Human Rights, the International Conference on Population and Development and the World Summit for Social Development;

30. *Decides*, taking into account Commission on the Status of Women resolution 37/7, to adopt the modalities for the participation in and contribution to the Fourth World Conference on Women and its preparatory process by the non-governmental organizations, particularly those from the developing countries, set out in the annex to the present resolution;

31. *Also requests* the Secretary-General to prepare a report for the Fourth World Conference on Women, to be held in Beijing in 1995, on the extent to which gender concerns have been included in the activities of the relevant human rights mechanisms of the United Na-

tions, such as treaty-monitoring bodies, rapporteurs and working groups;

32. *Further requests* the Secretary-General to report to the General Assembly at its forty-ninth session on measures taken to implement the present resolution.

ANNEX
Participation of non-governmental organizations in the Fourth World Conference on Women and its preparatory body

Non-governmental organizations in consultative status with the Economic and Social Council that express the wish to attend the Conference and the meetings of the Commission on the Status of Women, acting as its preparatory body, will be accredited for participation. Others wishing to be accredited may apply to the Conference secretariat for that purpose in accordance with the following requirements:

(a) The secretariat of the Fourth World Conference on Women will be responsible for the receipt and preliminary evaluation, in accordance with the provisions set out below, of requests from non-governmental organizations for accreditation to the Conference and the Commission on the Status of Women acting as preparatory body;

(b) All such applications must be accompanied by information on the competence of the organization and on its relevance to the work of the preparatory body, indicating the particular areas of the preparations for the Conference to which such competence and relevance pertain, and should include the following:

(i) The purposes of the organization;

(ii) Information on its programmes and activities in areas relevant to the Conference and on the country or countries in which those programmes and activities are carried out;

(iii) Confirmation of its activities at the national and/or the international level;

(iv) Copies of its annual reports, with financial statements and a list of members of the governing body and their country of nationality;

(v) A description of its membership, indicating the total number of members of the governing body and their country of nationality;

(c) Non-governmental organizations seeking accreditation will be asked to confirm their interest in the goals and objectives of the Conference;

(d) In cases where the Conference secretariat believes, on the basis of the information provided in accordance with the present document, that an organization has established its competence and relevance to the work of the Commission on the Status of Women acting as preparatory body, it will recommend to the Commission that the organization be accredited. In cases where the Conference secretariat does not recommend the granting of accreditation, it will make such information available to members of the Commission at least one week prior to the start of each session;

(e) The Commission on the Status of Women will decide on all proposals for accreditation within twenty-four hours of the recommendations of the Conference secretariat having been taken up by the Commission in plenary session. Should a decision not be taken within that period, interim accreditation will be accorded until such time as a decision is taken;

(f) A non-governmental organization that has been granted accreditation to attend one session of the Commission on the Status of Women acting as preparatory body may attend all future sessions and the Conference;

(g) In recognition of the intergovernmental nature of the Fourth World Conference on Women, non-governmental organizations will have no negotiating role in the work of the Conference and its preparatory process;

(h) Relevant non-governmental organizations in consultative status with the Economic and Social Council may be given the opportunity briefly to address the Commission on the Status of Women acting as preparatory body in plenary meeting and its subsidiary bodies. Other relevant non-governmental organizations may also ask to speak briefly at such meetings. If the number of requests is too large, the Commission will request that non-governmental organizations form themselves into constituencies, with each constituency speaking through one spokesperson. Any oral intervention by a non-governmental organization should, in accordance with usual United Nations practice, be made at the discretion of the Chairman and with the consent of the Commission;

(i) Relevant non-governmental organizations may, at their own expense, make written presentations in the official languages of the United Nations during the preparatory process, as they deem appropriate. Those written presentations will not be issued as official documents unless they are in accordance with the rules of procedure of the Conference.

General Assembly resolution 48/108

20 December 1993   Meeting 85   Adopted without vote

Approved by Third Committee (A/48/629) without vote, 1 December (meeting 48); draft by Colombia (for Group of 77 and China) (A/C.3/48/L.33), orally revised; agenda item 111.
Meeting numbers. GA 48th session: 3rd Committee 29-37, 41, 48; plenary 85.

Medium-term plan

By an April note,[15] the Secretariat transmitted to the Economic and Social Council the proposed system-wide medium-term plan for the advancement of women covering the period 1996 to 2001, the last five years of the period designated for the implementation of the Nairobi Strategies. The proposed plan was organized into seven programmes and consisted of three parts: part one described strategies in terms of substantive areas such as discrimination, human resource development, peace and conflict resolution and decision-making; part two focused on improving international action through the development of statistics and technical cooperation; and part three covered actions that synthesized and coordinated the specific activities in parts one and two, including women in development and strengthening national machineries for the advancement of women.

The Commission on the Status of Women, in March, had considered preliminary proposals for the plan.[16] It adopted a resolution,[17] in which it recommended that the plan be revised after the 1995 World Conference on Women. It also made a series of comments on the plan that were incorporated into the version considered by the Council.

ECONOMIC AND SOCIAL COUNCIL ACTION

On 27 July, on the recommendation of its Social Committee, the Economic and Social Council adopted **resolution 1993/16** without vote.

System-wide medium-term plan
for the advancement of women

The Economic and Social Council,

Recalling its resolution 1988/59 of 27 July 1988, by
which it requested the Secretary-General, in his capacity as Chairman of the Administrative Committee on
Coordination, to initiate the formulation of a system-
wide medium-term plan for the advancement of women
for the period 1996-2001,

Having considered the note by the Secretariat containing the proposed system-wide medium-term plan for the
advancement of women for the period 1996-2001,

Convinced that a system-wide medium-term plan for
the advancement of women can enhance coordination
among the organizations of the United Nations system
by providing a framework for including advancement
of women in individual medium-term plans and programme statements,

Bearing in mind the fact that the United Nations planning cycle to which the system-wide medium-term plan
for the advancement of women was matched has
changed, and that there has been a general shift to a
more strategic form of planning,

Recognizing that the Platform for Action to emerge from
the Fourth World Conference on Women: Action for
Equality, Development and Peace, to be held at Beijing
from 4 to 15 September 1995, cannot be reflected in the
system-wide medium-term plan for the advancement of
women for the period 1996-2001, which must be approved in 1993,

1. *Endorses* the system-wide medium-term plan for
the advancement of women for the period 1996-2001 as
a general framework for the coordination of system-wide
efforts, as revised in the light of the comments set out
in the annex to resolution 37/1 of 24 March 1993 of the
Commission on the Status of Women;

2. *Requests* the organizations of the United Nations
system that are preparing medium-term plans for the
period 1996-2001 to incorporate relevant aspects of the
system-wide medium-term plan for the advancement of
women in formulating their individual plans in terms
of advancement of women;

3. *Also requests* the organizations of the United Nations system, when implementing the system-wide
medium-term plan for the advancement of women, to
take account of the importance of ensuring that humanitarian relief, rehabilitation and refugee programmes
provide for the health needs of women and for their protection from violence and sexual abuse, especially in
emergency and conflict situations;

4. *Requests* the Secretary-General, in his capacity as
Chairman of the Administrative Committee on Coordination, to arrange for a revision of the system-wide
medium-term plan after the Platform for Action and the
results of the second review and appraisal of the implementation of the Nairobi Forward-looking Strategies
for the Advancement of Women have been adopted by
the Fourth World Conference on Women: Action for
Equality, Development and Peace;

5. *Also requests* the Secretary-General to ensure that
any revised system-wide medium-term plan for the advancement of women is more concise, takes account of
the changes in the United Nations planning cycle, takes
a more strategic approach, highlighting policy implications, and includes more substantial strategies, time-
frames, concrete measures, resources and allocation of
responsibility for implementation;

6. *Decides* that the Commission on the Status of
Women, together with the Committee for Programme
and Coordination, should be given the responsibility for
monitoring progress on the system-wide medium-term
plan for the advancement of women and that all United
Nations entities should be held accountable for the components of the system-wide medium-term plan for the
advancement of women that fall within their areas of
responsibility.

Economic and Social Council resolution 1993/16

27 July 1993   Meeting 43   Adopted without vote

Approved by Social Committee (E/1993/105) without vote, 13 July (meeting 7); 11-nation draft (E/1993/C.2/L.2); agenda item 19.
Sponsors: Argentina, Australia, Bahamas, Belarus, Belgium, Canada, Denmark, Finland, New Zealand, Norway, Sweden.

Research and Training Institute for
the Advancement of Women

The Board of Trustees of the International Research and Training Institute for the Advancement
of Women (INSTRAW) held its thirteenth session
at Santo Domingo, Dominican Republic, from 15
to 19 February 1993.[18]

The Board discussed the possible merger of IN-
STRAW with the United Nations Development
Fund for Women (UNIFEM), a proposal put forth
by the Secretary-General as part of an effort to
streamline and coordinate the economic and social sectors of the United Nations. The Board
recommended that the Secretary-General establish a task force to study the available options (see
below).

It reviewed INSTRAW's activities to mainstream
gender issues in development strategies and give
visibility to women's contributions to socio-
economic development. It recognized the crucial
role of networking to strengthen the position of
women, particularly with the regional commissions. The Board reviewed its policy on focal points
and approved the nomination of new focal points
in the Netherlands and Zimbabwe. It agreed that
INSTRAW should participate in the observance of
the International Year of the Family (1994) (see
PART THREE, Chapter XII) and in preparations
for the International Conference on Population
and Development (1994) (see PART THREE, Chapter IX) and the Fourth (1995) World Conference
on Women.

INSTRAW activities

Pursuant to a 1991 General Assembly request,[19] the Secretary-General transmitted an

August report[20] on the results of INSTRAW's 1992-1993 work programme.

During 1993, in the area of research, INSTRAW carried out a study on female migration, internal and international, and its consequences for family and society; its purpose was to provide guidelines for compiling more adequate data on female migration. The first phase of a long-term research project on methods for valuating the contribution of women to development was completed.

INSTRAW developed gender training materials and computer models—*"Urban Women in Development Model"* and *"Rural Women in Development Model"*—to assist policy makers. It also began assessing the training needs of women farmers in Eastern European countries in transition.

The first phase of a project to develop communications materials for women and development, consisting of country profiles, national seminars and country-specific strategies in Argentina, Colombia and the Dominican Republic was completed. Material was prepared to sensitize the media and opinion makers to gender issues.

INSTRAW continued its efforts to make women visible through gender disaggregated data by providing technical assistance to Turkey, conducting a sub-regional workshop on statistics and indicators on women for the francophone African countries (Rabat, Morocco, 13-17 December) and preparing a study entitled *"The Situation of Elderly Women: Available Statistics and Indicators".*

In 1993, INSTRAW recorded contributions from Member States in the amount of $3,568,389. At the United Nations Pledging Conference for Development Activities (November 1993), INSTRAW received pledges of contributions for 1994 totalling $582,142.

ECONOMIC AND SOCIAL COUNCIL ACTION

On 27 July, on the recommendation of its Social Committee, the Economic and Social Council adopted **resolution 1993/17** without vote.

International Research and Training Institute for the Advancement of Women

The Economic and Social Council,

Recalling its resolution 1992/21 of 30 July 1992, in which it took note of the report of the Board of Trustees of the International Research and Training Institute for the Advancement of Women on its twelfth session,

Having considered the report of the Board of Trustees of the Institute on its thirteenth session,

Recognizing the important role that the Institute could play in the substantive preparations for the Fourth World Conference on Women: Action for Equality, Development and Peace, to be held at Beijing from 4 to 15 September 1995,

Also recognizing the equally important contributions that the Institute could make in its area of expertise to activities related to the International Year of the Family,

the International Conference on Population and Development and the World Summit for Social Development,

Reaffirming the continuing need for independent research and related training activities for the advancement of women and the role of the Institute therein,

1. *Takes note with satisfaction* of the report of the Board of Trustees of the International Research and Training Institute for the Advancement of Women on its thirteenth session and the decisions contained therein;

2. *Commends* the Institute for activities carried out that contribute to mainstreaming women's issues in development strategies and the appraisal of the contribution of women to social and economic development, particularly in relation to the informal sector;

3. *Expresses its appreciation* of the fact that the Institute maintains and seeks ways to strengthen its mode of operation, for example, by networking, particularly with the regional commissions and the focal points of the Institute, thereby ensuring effective outreach and coordination in order to empower women and strengthen their position at the national and regional levels;

4. *Requests* the Institute to assist in the substantive preparations for the Fourth World Conference on Women: Action for Equality, Development and Peace, given its essential role in research, training and statistics related to women;

5. *Also requests* the Institute to contribute, within its area of expertise, to the activities relevant to the International Year of the Family, to be observed in 1994, the International Conference on Population and Development, to be held at Cairo in 1994, and the World Summit for Social Development, to be held at Copenhagen in 1995;

6. *Reiterates* the importance of maintaining the level of resources devoted to independent research and related training activities, which are crucial for the situation of women;

7. *Calls upon* States and intergovernmental and non-governmental organizations to contribute, through voluntary contributions and pledges, to the United Nations Trust Fund for the International Research and Training Institute for the Advancement of Women, thus enabling the Institute to continue to respond effectively to its mandate.

Economic and Social Council resolution 1993/17

27 July 1993   Meeting 43   Adopted without vote

Approved by Social Committee (E/1993/105) without vote, 13 July (meeting 8); 16-nation draft (E/1993/C.2/L.3); agenda item 19.

Sponsors: Angola, Argentina, Australia, Bahamas, Brazil, Chile, Cuba, Dominican Republic, Mexico, New Zealand, Norway, Peru, Romania, Spain, Uruguay, Venezuela.

GENERAL ASSEMBLY ACTION

On 20 December, on the recommendation of the Third Committee, the General Assembly adopted **resolution 48/105** without vote.

International Research and Training Institute for the Advancement of Women

The General Assembly,

Recalling its resolution 46/99 of 16 December 1991 and taking note of Economic and Social Council resolution 1993/17 of 27 July 1993,

Taking note of the report of the International Research and Training Institute for the Advancement of Women on its activities,

Stressing the need for independent research to ensure that policy-making and project implementation address issues and emerging areas of concern to women, and the role of the Institute therein,

Reaffirming the unique and specific role of the Institute in the areas of research and training that can facilitate the systematic inclusion of women as partners in development programmes and projects,

Recognizing the important role that the Institute could play in the substantive preparations for the Fourth World Conference on Women: Action for Equality, Development and Peace, to be held in 1995,

Convinced that sustainable development cannot be achieved without the full participation of women,

1. *Expresses its satisfaction* with the report of the International Research and Training Institute for the Advancement of Women on its activities;

2. *Commends* the Institute for its efforts to focus on problems that constitute barriers to improving the status of women and thus impede overall development and progress;

3. *Urges* the Institute to continue to strengthen its activities in the areas of research, training and information aimed at mainstreaming gender in development strategies and giving women greater visibility by valuating their contribution to social and economic development as important means of empowering women and improving their status;

4. *Requests* the Institute to assist with the substantive preparations for the Fourth World Conference on Women: Action for Equality, Development and Peace, given its key role in the areas of research and training and its expertise in gender statistics;

5. *Emphasizes* the unique function of the Institute as the only entity within the United Nations system devoted exclusively to research and training for the integration of women in development, and stresses the importance of making its research findings available for policy purposes and for operational activities;

6. *Expresses its appreciation* for the continuing efforts of the Institute to strengthen its programmatic linkages with other United Nations organizations, including the regional commissions, governmental and non-governmental organizations, research institutes and other organizations and groups, thereby broadening the scope of its operations, making optimum use of its limited financial resources and attaining a greater outreach and impact of its work;

7. *Expresses its appreciation also* to those Governments and organizations which have contributed to or supported the activities of the Institute;

8. *Invites* States and intergovernmental and non-governmental organizations to contribute to the United Nations Trust Fund for the International Research and Training Institute for the Advancement of Women so that the Institute can fulfil its mandate and ensure the full participation and proper recognition of women in society;

9. *Requests* the Secretary-General to submit to the General Assembly at its fiftieth session a report on the activities of the International Research and Training Institute for the Advancement of Women, including a detailed description of its administrative and institutional status, under the item entitled "Advancement of women".

General Assembly resolution 48/105

20 December 1993   Meeting 85   Adopted without vote

Approved by Third Committee (A/48/629) without vote, 1 December (meeting 48); 23-nation draft (A/C.3/48/L.30), orally revised; agenda item 111.

Sponsors: Afghanistan, Argentina, Brazil, China, Colombia, Costa Rica, Cuba, Cyprus, Dominican Republic, Ecuador, El Salvador, Indonesia, Kenya, Mexico, Morocco, Myanmar, New Zealand, Peru, Senegal, Spain, Turkey, Uruguay, Venezuela.

Meeting numbers. GA 48th session: 3rd Committee 29-37, 41, 48; plenary 85.

Merger of INSTRAW and UNIFEM

By a June note,[21] the Secretary-General transmitted to the Economic and Social Council a report on the activities of the Task Force on the proposed merger of INSTRAW and UNIFEM, which met from 24 to 26 May. After examining the mandates of the two organizations, the Task Force concluded that they complemented each other very well. The Task Force endorsed the proposed merger and urged that the interactions of the merged organizations with the Commission on the Status of Women be reviewed and rationalized.

By **decision 1993/235** of 27 July, the Council took note of the Secretary-General's report and agreed to the merger, subject to an analysis of the legal, financial and administrative implications, and consideration by the General Assembly.

In November,[22] the Secretary-General presented the proposed legal, financial and administrative arrangements for the merger of INSTRAW and UNIFEM.

Also in November,[23] the Dominican Republic, the host country of INSTRAW, expressed concern over its possible relocation.

In a November note,[24] the Secretariat, replying to the concerns raised by the Dominican Republic, stated that ultimate decisions on the matter were the prerogative of the relevant principal organs of the Organization.

GENERAL ASSEMBLY ACTION

On 20 December, the General Assembly, on the recommendation of the Third Committee, adopted **resolution 48/111** without vote.

Merger of the International Research and Training Institute for the Advancement of Women and the United Nations Development Fund for Women

The General Assembly,

Recalling its resolution 31/135 of 16 December 1976, in which it endorsed the establishment of an International Research and Training Institute for the Advancement of Women, and Economic and Social Council resolution 1998(LX) of 12 May 1976, containing guidelines regarding the activities of the Institute,

Taking note of Economic and Social Council decision 1993/235 of 27 July 1993, in which the Council agreed to the recommendation of the Secretary-General to merge the International Research and Training Institute for the Advancement of Women and the United Nations Development Fund for Women, subject to a proper analysis of the legal, financial and administrative implications of the merger, and subject to consideration by the General Assembly at its forty-eighth session,

Taking note also of the report of the Secretary-General prepared pursuant to Economic and Social Council decision 1993/235,

Emphasizing that the ultimate goal of restructuring should be to strengthen the programmes for the advancement of women and to enhance the efficiency of the work of those organizations, in function, structure and cost-effectiveness,

Recognizing the importance of adequate preparation for the Fourth World Conference on Women: Action for Equality, Development and Peace, to be held in 1995, under the guidance of the Conference secretariat, and the role therein of the International Research and Training Institute for the Advancement of Women,

1. *Affirms* that both the International Research and Training Institute for the Advancement of Women and the United Nations Development Fund for Women should retain their comparative advantages in activities relating to the advancement of women;

2. *Urges* that the interaction between the International Research and Training Institute for the Advancement of Women, the United Nations Development Fund for Women, the Division for the Advancement of Women of the Secretariat, the Commission on the Status of Women and the Committee on the Elimination of Discrimination against Women be reviewed and rationalized within the context of ongoing efforts to revitalize the Economic and Social Council in pursuance of a stronger, more unified programme for the advancement of women;

3. *Requests* the Secretary-General, through the Advisory Committee on Administrative and Budgetary Questions in accordance with rule 157 of the rules of procedure of the General Assembly, to submit to the Economic and Social Council at its substantive session of 1994 a report on the proposed merger of the International Research and Training Institute for the Advancement of Women and the United Nations Development Fund for Women and to include therein:

   (a) A clear analysis of the financial benefits resulting from the merger;

   (b) An estimate of the one-time non-recurrent costs of the merger, including costs of transitional measures, as well as an estimate of the recurrent costs of the merger;

   (c) Details of the current staffing structure of the United Nations Development Fund for Women and the International Research and Training Institute for the Advancement of Women, together with details of the proposed structure, including reporting arrangements;

   (d) Staffing implications;

   (e) A report on consultations with the host Government of the International Research and Training Institute for the Advancement of Women;

4. *Also requests* the Secretary-General to include in his report consideration of potential duplication of training activities of the International Research and Training Institute for the Advancement of Women and the United Nations Development Fund for Women;

5. *Requests* the Economic and Social Council to submit its final recommendations to the General Assembly at its forty-ninth session for its consideration and action before 31 December 1994.

General Assembly resolution 48/111

20 December 1993   Meeting 85   Adopted without vote

Approved by Third Committee (A/48/629) without vote, 1 December (meeting 48); 17-nation draft (A/C.3/48/L.41/Rev.1); agenda item 111.

Sponsors: Angola, Argentina, Bolivia, Costa Rica, Cuba, Cyprus, Dominican Republic, Guatemala, Kenya, Malawi, Morocco, Namibia, Nicaragua, Nigeria, Panama, Sudan, Togo.

Meeting numbers. GA 48th session: 3rd Committee 29-37, 41, 48; plenary 85.

REFERENCES

[1]YUN 1992, p. 863, GA res. 47/95, 16 Dec. 1992. [2]A/48/413. [3]YUN 1985, p. 937. [4]E/CN.6/1993/16. [5]E/1993/27 & Corr.1. [6]Ibid. (res. 37/9). [7]E/CN.6/1993/5. [8]E/CN.6/1993/8. [9]YUN 1992, p. 866. [10]E/CN.6/1993/7. [11]ESC res. 1990/15, annex, 24 May 1990. [12]E/CN.6/1993/6. [13]E/1993/27 (res. 37/7). [14]ACC/1993/9. [15]E/1993/43. [16]E/CN.6/1993/9. [17]E/1993/27 (res. 37/1). [18]E/1993/44. [19]YUN 1991, p. 679, GA res. 46/99, 16 Dec. 1991. [20]A/48/301. [21]E/1993/82. [22]A/48/591. [23]A/C.3/48/6. [24]A/C.3/48/10.

Women and development

In March,[1] the Commission made a series of recommendations to Governments and Member States on improving the integration of women in development and requested the Secretary-General to ensure that the subject of women in development was an integral part of the International Development Strategy for the Fourth United Nations Development Decade (the 1990s), adopted by the General Assembly in 1990.[2]

Integration of women in economic development

By a June note,[3] the Secretary-General submitted to the Economic and Social Council an outline of a report on the effective mobilization and integration of women in development. The outline was submitted in lieu of the actual report, which was requested by the General Assembly in 1991,[4] in order for the final report to be able to take into account developments from the first (1993) session of the Commission on Sustainable Development (see PART THREE, Chapter I), the preparatory process for the International Conference on Population and Development (1994) (see PART THREE, Chapter IX) and the 1993 World Conference on Human Rights (see PART THREE, Chapter X).

By **decision 1993/308** of 29 July, the Council took note of the Secretary-General's June note.

In September, the Secretary-General submitted to the Assembly his report on the effective mobilization and integration of women in development.[5] He described the role of gender in environment and sustainable development and suggested ways in which gender analysis could be included in monitoring Agenda 21, an action programme for the twenty-first century adopted by the United Nations Conference on Environment and Development in 1992.[6] The Secretary-General discussed the gender dimension of poverty, urbanization and population growth and concluded that a condition for achieving sustainable development was the advancement of women.

The General Assembly, by **decision 48/443** of 21 December, took note of the Secretary-General's report. On the same date, by **decision 48/444**, the Assembly took note of a report of the Second (Economic and Financial) Committee,[7] which stated that, following a Committee debate on the effective mobilization and integration of women in development, no action was taken on the subject.

Women in extreme poverty

The Commission on the Status of Women considered a January report by the Secretary-General on women in extreme poverty.[8] He examined factors leading to a relatively higher incidence of poverty among women and discussed gender and household entitlements, female headed households, and the roles of the State, the economy and the community in combating poverty.

By a March resolution,[9] the Commission urged Governments, international organizations, intergovernmental and non-governmental organizations and community-based organizations to examine more closely the structural causes of poverty and ways to overcome it, and to evaluate, from a gender perspective, the effects of current socio-economic policies. It called on Governments to adopt or strengthen measures to facilitate women's access to education, training, health, family planning, productive resources and income-generating employment and to ensure their full participation in the decision-making process. Governments were requested to share national experiences relating to their efforts to deal with extreme poverty, particularly the effects of those efforts on women.

1994 world survey

As requested by the General Assembly in 1989,[10,11] the Secretary-General submitted in February a preliminary version of the *1994 World Survey on the Role of Women in Development*.[12] The *World Survey*, a joint effort of the Secretariat and the United Nations specialized agencies, analysed policy issues and concepts related to the advancement of women and was last updated in 1989.[13]

The preliminary version contained an expanded outline of the *Survey* covering problems including poverty, urbanization, the informal sector, the international economy and the impact on women of the reform of centrally planned economies; and solutions such as human resources development, access to economic instruments and empowerment, and women in decision-making, participation and democratization.

By **decision 1993/308** of 29 July, the Economic and Social Council took note of the preliminary version of the *World Survey*, as did the General Assembly by **decision 48/443** of 21 December.

ECONOMIC AND SOCIAL COUNCIL ACTION

On 27 July, the Economic and Social Council, on the recommendation of its Social Committee, adopted **resolution 1993/12** without vote.

Women, environment and development
The Economic and Social Council,
Taking into account General Assembly resolution 46/167 of 19 December 1991 on women, environment, population and sustainable development, in which the Assembly requested the Secretary-General to include in the report on the effective mobilization and integration of women in development, to be submitted to the General Assembly at its forty-eighth session, a section on the role of women in environment and sustainable development,

Recalling Commission on the Status of Women resolution 36/6 of 20 March 1992, in which the Commission, *inter alia*, urged Governments to adopt laws, policies and programmes to promote women's participation in the preservation of the environment, and invited the Governments of donor countries, international organizations and relevant non-governmental organizations to ensure that greater attention was given to women's contributions to environmental protection and management in their cooperation with and assistance to developing countries,

Welcoming General Assembly resolution 47/191 of 22 December 1992, in which the Assembly took note of the decision of the Secretary-General to establish a new Department for Policy Coordination and Sustainable Development, headed at the Under-Secretary-General level, and called upon the Secretary-General to establish a clearly identifiable, highly qualified and competent secretariat support structure for the Commission on Sustainable Development, the Inter-Agency Committee on Sustainable Development and the High-level Advisory Board, taking into account gender balance at all levels,

Welcoming the inclusion of principle 20 in the Rio Declaration on Environment and Development, adopted by the United Nations Conference on Environment and Development, according to which women have a vital role in environmental management and development and their full participation is therefore essential to achieving sustainable development, and the integration of gender issues into Agenda 21, including the special focus on women in chapter 24 thereof,

Noting that in Agenda 21, paragraph 24.9, it is recommended that the Secretary-General review the adequacy of all United Nations institutions in meeting development and environment objectives, consider how the environment and development programmes of each body of the United Nations system could be strengthened to implement Agenda 21, consider how to incorporate the role of women in programmes and decisions related to sustainable development, and, in particular, make recommendations to strengthen the capacities of United Nations entities with a special focus on women, such as the Division for the Advancement of Women of the Centre for Social Development and Humanitarian Affairs of the Secretariat, the United Nations Development Fund for Women and the International Research and Training Institute for the Advancement of Women,

Noting also the recommendations and objectives proposed for Governments in Agenda 21, chapter 24, including the objective, contained in paragraph 24.2 *(d)*, to establish by 1995 mechanisms at the national, regional and international levels to assess the implementation and impact of development and environment policies and programmes on women and to ensure their contributions and benefits,

Recognizing that the Fourth World Conference on Women: Action for Equality, Development and Peace, to be held at Beijing from 4 to 15 September 1995, will provide significant opportunities for reviewing the current status of women and for establishing priorities for future action, including action in relation to environment and development,

1. *Urges* the Commission on Sustainable Development, the Inter-Agency Committee on Sustainable Development and the High-level Advisory Board to develop appropriate mechanisms to ensure that the objectives and activities in Agenda 21, relating to the role of women in sustainable development, both as agents and as beneficiaries, are supported, that the objectives are met and the activities and other recommended actions are implemented and that Governments and all relevant United Nations entities monitor and report on the subject;

2. *Requests* the Secretary-General to include information on the subject in the section on the role of women in environment and sustainable development in his report on the effective mobilization and integration of women in development, to be submitted to the General Assembly at its forty-eighth session, in accordance with General Assembly resolution 46/167;

3. *Urges* Governments to take into account and to implement the recommendations contained in Agenda 21 in order to ensure the participation of women in developing, and making decisions on, policies and programmes relating to environmental management and sustainable development;

4. *Requests* Governments to include in their reports for the Fourth World Conference on Women: Action for Equality, Development and Peace information on the extent to which the objectives for Governments proposed in Agenda 21, chapter 24, relating to women, have been met and the activities recommended in that chapter have been implemented;

5. *Agrees* to review the current and planned activities of the Commission on the Status of Women in order to determine which recommendations in Agenda 21 relating to women are already being included in those activities and to consider how the others might be incorporated in future activities of the Commission, including the preparations for the Fourth World Conference on Women;

6. *Requests* the Commission on the Status of Women to examine, in its discussion on the preparations for the Fourth World Conference on Women at its thirty-eighth session, the recommendations in Agenda 21 relating to women, with a view to:

(a) Identifying ways of facilitating implementation of the recommendations, including consideration of the role of Governments, intergovernmental organizations and non-governmental organizations;

(b) Considering ways in which the Commission on the Status of Women might cooperate with and provide support for the Commission on Sustainable Development in ensuring the effective integration of issues on the status of women in its programme of work.

Economic and Social Council resolution 1993/12

27 July 1993   Meeting 43   Adopted without vote

Approved by Social Committee (E/1993/105) without vote, 12 July (meeting 6); draft by Commission on Status of Women (E/1993/27); agenda item 19.

Medium-term plan for women and development

In response to a 1989 Economic and Social Council request,[14] the Secretary-General submitted in April a report on the extent to which the system-wide medium-term plan for the period 1990-1995 for women and development had been incorporated into the programmes and programme budgets of the United Nations system.[15] The report was based on information received from organizations and presented an overview of trends in incorporating the plan into their programmes. The Secretary-General concluded that there was an increased awareness and recognition of the issue of the integration of women in economic development. However, further efforts were needed to reflect the full significance and contribution of women to the development process.

By **decision 1993/236** of 27 July, the Council took note of the Secretary-General's report.

Rural women

In response to a 1989 General Assembly request,[16] the Secretary-General submitted a report on the situation of women in rural areas.[17] The Secretary-General presented an analysis of recent trends in rural development policies based on an examination of institutional support, human resources development and implementation of measures that would give rural women broader access to and control of productive resources. He noted a sharp increase in poverty among rural women and growing awareness that poverty had a significant gender dimension. The Secretary-General recommended integrating concerns of rural women into development goals; eliminating gender-based social structures; developing legal literacy programmes for women; and recognizing the economic importance of rural women's activities.

By **decision 1993/236** of 27 July, the Economic and Social Council took note of the Secretary-General's report.

GENERAL ASSEMBLY ACTION

On 20 December, on the recommendation of the Third Committee, the General Assembly adopted **resolution 48/109** without vote.

Improvement of the situation of women in rural areas

The General Assembly,

Recalling its resolutions 34/14 of 9 November 1979, in which it endorsed the Declaration of Principles and the Programme of Action as adopted by the World Conference on Agrarian Reform and Rural Development, and 44/78 of 8 December 1989,

Recalling also the importance attached to the problems of rural women in the Nairobi Forward-looking Strategies for the Advancement of Women,

Recalling further its resolution 47/174 of 22 December 1992, in which it welcomed the adoption of the Geneva Declaration for Rural Women by the Summit on the Economic Advancement of Rural Women, held at Geneva in February 1992, and urged all States to work for the achievement of the goals endorsed in that Declaration,

Welcoming the growing awareness of Governments of the need for strategies and programmes to improve the situation of women in rural areas,

Recognizing that the economic and financial crises in many developing countries have severely affected the socio-economic status of women, especially in rural areas, and noting with deep concern the continuing rise in the number of rural women living in poverty,

Also recognizing the urgent need to take appropriate measures aimed at further improving the situation of women in rural areas,

1. *Takes note* of the report of the Secretary-General;

2. *Invites* Member States to attach greater importance in their national development strategies to the improvement of the situation of rural women, paying special attention to both their practical and strategic needs, by, *inter alia:*

(a) Integrating the concerns of rural women into national development policies and programmes, in particular by placing a higher priority on budgetary allocations related to the interests of rural women;

(b) Strengthening national machineries and establishing institutional linkages among governmental bodies in various sectors and non-governmental organizations concerned with rural development;

(c) Increasing the participation of rural women in the decision-making process;

(d) Improving accessibility of rural women to productive resources;

(e) Investing in the human resources of rural women, particularly through health and literacy programmes;

3. *Requests* the international community, competent United Nations bodies and non-governmental organizations to promote the realization of programmes and projects aimed at the improvement of the situation of rural women;

4. *Invites* the International Conference on Population and Development, to be held in 1994, the World Summit for Social Development and the Fourth World Conference on Women: Action for Equality, Development and Peace, both to be held in 1995, to give due consideration, in formulating respective strategies and actions, to the issue of improving the situation of rural women;

5. *Requests* the Secretary-General to prepare, in consultation with Member States and competent United Nations organizations, a report on the implementation of the present resolution and to submit it, through the Economic and Social Council, to the General Assembly at its fiftieth session.

General Assembly resolution 48/109

20 December 1993   Meeting 85   Adopted without vote

Approved by Third Committee (A/48/629) without vote, 1 December (meeting 48); 61-nation draft (A/C.3/48/L.34), orally revised; agenda item 111.

Sponsors: Afghanistan, Bangladesh, Belarus, Belgium, Bolivia, Burkina Faso, Cameroon, China, Costa Rica, Côte d'Ivoire, Cyprus, Denmark, Dominican Republic, Ecuador, Egypt, Eritrea, Ethiopia, Finland, France, Ghana, Greece, Guatemala, Guinea, Guinea-Bissau, Guyana, Haiti, Iceland, India, Indonesia, Iraq, Jamaica, Kenya, Kyrgyzstan, Lao People's Democratic Republic, Lesotho, Madagascar, Malawi, Malaysia, Mali, Mongolia, Morocco, Myanmar, Nepal, Nicaragua, Niger, Nigeria, Norway, Pakistan, Panama, Philippines, Portugal, Russian Federation, Senegal, Sierra Leone, Suriname, Swaziland, Sweden, Turkey, Uganda, Vanuatu, Viet Nam.

Meeting numbers. GA 48th session: 3rd Committee 29-37, 41, 48; plenary 85.

UN Development Fund for Women

The Consultative Committee on UNIFEM held two sessions in New York in 1993, the thirty-second on 25 and 26 January and the thirty-third from 7 to 9 September. In January, the Committee considered a progress report on UNIFEM's work and endorsed UNIFEM's budget for 1994-1995.

In September, it recommended the replenishment of UNIFEM's 1994-1995 regional programme budgets of $2,418,500 for the Africa Investment Plan; $2,250,000 for the Asia Pacific Development Strategy; and $2,443,000 for the Participatory Action Programme for Latin America and the Caribbean. It recommended approval of $1.5 million to support UNIFEM's initiatives for the Fourth World Conference on Women; $361,443 for the project, statistics on gender issues in Indonesia; and $300,000 for a project in Asia and the Pacific on monitoring the impact of new technologies on women's industrial work. It also recommended the replenishment of UNIFEM's mainstreaming development initiatives facility ($400,000), the small projects facility ($500,000), the monitoring and evaluation facility ($400,000) and the advocacy facility ($1,498,000).

During 1993, UNIFEM continued to work in three key programme areas—agriculture, trade and industry, and macro policy and national planning. They were complemented by technical support for credit, technology transfer, small business development and training.

In Africa, UNIFEM had 64 ongoing projects and programmes, 46 of them national and 18 regional. It developed a commodity-based food security strategy to elevate food crop production to the level of importance accorded cash crops in most national agriculture policies. UNIFEM launched a long-term programme to strengthen the training capacity of 17 women's organizations in South Africa, completed the preparatory phase of its regional internship programme for young African women and assisted women refugees in Eritrea and Liberian women refugees in Ghana and Côte d'Ivoire.

In Asia and the Pacific, UNIFEM supported 51 ongoing projects. It organized gender awareness seminars and a three-day women's summit (Phnom Penh, Cambodia, 5-8 March), with Khemara, an NGO devoted to women's issues. In late June, UNIFEM organized in Cambodia a workshop on women's rights and the Constitution. In Western Asia, UNIFEM started a project to strengthen governmental and NGO support for enterprise development for women.

One of UNIFEM's main programmes in Latin America and the Caribbean was its Andean Women's Food Technology initiative, combining public education on women's role in agriculture with networking assistance for individual production groups and rural cooperatives in Bolivia, Colombia, Ecuador, Peru and Venezuela. To improve women's access to credit, UNIFEM acted as a guarantor of micro-loans for institutions in Bolivia, Brazil, Colombia and Guatemala. In several countries, UNIFEM supported legislative and administrative reform to guarantee women's rights. There were 51 ongoing projects in the region in 1993.

At the global level, UNIFEM strengthened its programmes relating to women, environment and development; women's rights as human rights; women refugees and displaced citizens; and women's changing roles in finance, science and technology, and political decision-making.

In August, the Secretary-General transmitted the report of the Administrator of the United Nations Development Programme (UNDP) on the 1992 activities of the Fund.[18]

UNDP action. On 18 June,[19] the UNDP Governing Council called on UNIFEM to continue to support UNDP in gender-related programme areas and renewed its appeal for increased voluntary financial support to the Fund.

GENERAL ASSEMBLY ACTION

On 20 December, the General Assembly, on the recommendation of the Third Committee, adopted **resolution 48/107** without vote.

United Nations Development Fund for Women

The General Assembly,

Recalling its resolution 39/125 of 14 December 1984, by which it decided to establish the United Nations Development Fund for Women as a separate and identifiable entity in autonomous association with the United Nations Development Programme,

Reaffirming the catalytic role of the Fund in increasing opportunities and options for women in developing countries to participate more effectively in the development of their countries, in line with national priorities,

Recognizing the important contribution the Fund continues to make in galvanizing efforts of the organizations of the United Nations system, as well as other intergovernmental and non-governmental organizations, to formulate and support innovative activities that directly benefit and empower women,

Recognizing also the initiatives of the Fund to provide technical assistance to national machineries for issues related to women and to other relevant line ministries in development planning with sensitivity to gender considerations, and to facilitate national preparatory activities for the Fourth World Conference on Women: Action for Equality, Development and Peace, to be held in 1995,

Emphasizing the position of the Fund as a specialized resource base for development cooperation linking the needs and aspirations of women with resources, programmes and policies for their economic development,

Noting the focused and responsive interventions of the Fund within its regional priority framework and its overall strategic approach to women in development,

1. *Takes note* of the note by the Secretary-General transmitting the annual report of the Administrator of the United Nations Development Programme on the activities of the United Nations Development Fund for Women;

2. *Commends* the Fund for its support of catalytic and innovative projects that strengthen national capacity to improve the situation of women;

3. *Encourages* the Fund to continue to promote initiatives that incorporate the dimension of women in the agendas of the mainstream development efforts of Governments, United Nations organizations, non-governmental organizations and the private sector;

4. *Also encourages* the Fund to continue its support of initiatives regarding women in politics, especially within the democratization process in developing countries;

5. *Welcomes* the advocacy initiatives of the Fund, including its contribution to and participation in the follow-up to Agenda 21, adopted by the United Nations Conference on Environment and Development, and of the Vienna Declaration and Programme of Action, adopted by the World Conference on Human Rights, in particular with respect to efforts to combat violence against women;

6. *Also welcomes* the appointment of an adviser from the United Nations Development Fund for Women to the Department of Humanitarian Affairs of the Secretariat;

7. *Commends* the Fund for its recent signing of a memorandum of understanding with the Office of the United Nations High Commissioner for Refugees, which should contribute to the development of meaningful and lasting solutions to the problem of refugee women and children;

8. *Endorses* the role of the Fund in promoting the strategic importance of the empowerment of women;

9. *Commends* the Fund's initiative to assist developing countries in their preparations for the Fourth World Conference on Women: Action for Equality, Development and Peace, including the preparation of national reports;

10. *Stresses* the importance of the role of the Fund in the preparations for the International Conference on Population and Development and the World Summit for Social Development, the results of which should constitute a major contribution to the Fourth World Conference on Women;

11. *Notes with satisfaction* the steady increase in contributions to the Fund, and urges Governments and public and private donors to continue to extend their support to the Fund through voluntary contributions and pledges to its programmes;

12. *Welcomes* the establishment of new national committees for the Fund in Canada, Liechtenstein and Switzerland, and urges other developed countries to encourage the establishment of national committees;

13. *Stresses* the importance of the work of the Consultative Committee on the United Nations Development Fund for Women in policy and programme directions related to the activities of the Fund;

14. *Requests* the Secretary-General to transmit to the General Assembly at its forty-ninth session a report on the activities of the United Nations Development Fund for Women, to be submitted in accordance with its resolution 39/125.

General Assembly resolution 48/107

20 December 1993   Meeting 85   Adopted without vote

Approved by Third Committee (A/48/629) without vote, 1 December (meeting 48); 11-nation draft (A/C.3/48/L.32); agenda item 111.
Sponsors: Afghanistan, Bahamas, Cameroon, Canada, China, Denmark, Indonesia, Philippines, Poland, Uganda, United Republic of Tanzania.
Meeting numbers. GA 48th session: 3rd Committee 29-37, 41, 48; plenary 85.

REFERENCES
(1)E/1993/27 (res. 37/6). (2)GA res. 45/199, annex, 21 Dec. 1990. (3)E/1993/75. (4)YUN 1991, p. 681, GA res. 46/167, 19 Dec. 1991. (5)A/48/393. (6)YUN 1992, p. 672. (7)A/48/717/Add.4. (8)E/CN.6/1993/3. (9)E/1993/27 (res. 37/8). (10)GA res. 44/77, 8 Dec. 1989. (11)GA res. 44/171, 19 Dec. 1989. (12)A/48/70-E/1993/16. (13)*World Survey on the Role of Women in Development*, Sales No. E.89.IV.2. (14)ESC res. 1989/105, 27 July 1989. (15)E/1993/51. (16)GA res. 44/78, 8 Dec. 1989. (17)A/48/187-E/1993/76. (18)A/48/279. (19)E/1993/35 (res. 93/31).

Status of Women

Commission on the Status of Women

The Commission on the Status of Women, at its thirty-seventh session (Vienna, 17-26 March 1993),(1) recommended seven draft resolutions and two draft decisions for adoption by the Economic and Social Council. The resolutions dealt with a draft declaration on the elimination of violence against women; communications on the status of women; women, environment and development; women and children under apartheid (see PART TWO, Chapter I); the 1979 Convention on the Elimination of All Forms of Discrimination against Women;(2) Palestinian women (see PART TWO, Chapter V); and improving the status of women in the Secretariat (see PART FIVE, Chapter II). The decisions dealt with the report of the Commission's thirty-seventh session and agenda for its thirty-eighth (1994) session; and an inter-sessional working group of the Commission on the Platform for Action for the 1995 World Conference on Women.

1994 session

On 27 July 1993, the Economic and Social Council, by **decision 1993/233**, took note of the Commission's report and approved the provisional agenda and documentation for its thirty-eighth (1994) session.

Violence against women

An expert group meeting on measures to eradicate violence against women (New Brunswick, New Jersey, United States, 4-8 October),(3) organized by the Division for the Advancement of Women in collaboration with the Center for Women's Global Leadership at Douglass College, Rutgers University (New Brunswick), discussed the prevention and punishment of violence against women and made recommendations concerning human rights; law and justice; development; health and education; and peace, peace-keeping, emergencies and armed conflict. The deliberations of the group were based on the draft declaration on the elimination of violence against women, which was subsequently adopted by the General Assembly (see below).

The question of violence against women was also discussed by the Commission on Crime Prevention and Criminal Justice (13-23 April) (see preceding chapter), which recommended a draft resolution on the subject to the Economic and Social Council for adoption.

ECONOMIC AND SOCIAL COUNCIL ACTION

On 27 July, on the recommendation of its Social Committee, the Economic and Social Council adopted **resolution 1993/26** without vote.

Violence against women in all its forms
The Economic and Social Council,
Recalling the report of the Secretary-General on domestic violence,[a]
Recalling also General Assembly resolutions 45/114 of 14 December 1990 on domestic violence and 47/96 of 16 December 1992 on violence against migrant women workers,
Taking note of Commission on Human Rights resolution 1993/46 of 8 March 1993, in which the Commission, *inter alia*, condemned all acts of violence and violations of human rights directed specifically against women,
Referring to the recommendations of the Expert Group Meeting on Violence against Women, held at Vienna from 11 to 15 November 1991,
Reaffirming its resolution 1992/18 of 30 July 1992,
Fully supporting the draft declaration on the elimination of violence against women, elaborated at the Expert Group Meeting on Violence against Women and at the Meeting of the Working Group on Violence against Women of the Commission on the Status of Women, held at Vienna from 31 August to 4 September 1992,
Expressing deep concern about the continuing and endemic violence against women,
Convinced of the necessity of substantially improving the situation of victims of violence,

---
[a]A/CONF.144/17.

Calling attention to the fact that it is important for perpetrators of domestic violence to receive appropriate punishment,

Noting that, unlike rape within the family or in the community, systematic rape used as a political strategy is not mentioned in the documents referred to above,

Strongly condemning systematic rape during armed conflict,

Recognizing the increased public attention that is being given to the issue of violence against women, and how women can be victimized by virtue of their gender,

Recognizing also the work being done by non-governmental organizations in eliminating violence against women, in drawing attention to the nature, severity and magnitude of violence against women and in assisting women who are victims of violence,

Appreciating international cooperation in efforts to combat violence against women,

1. *Urges* Governments, the specialized agencies of the United Nations and the non-governmental organizations concerned:

(a) To take all possible steps to prevent violence against women;

(b) To intensify their efforts to use criminal law to prohibit violent acts against women;

(c) To promote police and penal systems that combine the protection of society with the prosecution and appropriate punishment of perpetrators;

(d) To offer full assistance, including provision of safe shelter, access to the legal system and, where necessary, counselling, medical, financial and other support, to women who are victims of violence;

(e) To improve police training to ensure that all incidents of violence against women are thoroughly investigated and that adequate help and support are given to victims in countries where it is necessary;

(f) To respond quickly to every case that calls for assistance to be provided to the victim;

(g) To take measures to combat violence against women occurring within the community, such as rape, sexual abuse, traditional practices harmful to women, trafficking in women and forced prostitution;

(h) To guarantee appropriate punishment and treatment of offenders, including sentencing strategies that deter perpetrators from repeating offences;

(i) To include the issue of violence against women in all its forms in the preparations for and observance of the International Year of the Family, in 1994, under the question of crime prevention and criminal justice;

(j) To include the issue of violence against women in all its forms under the appropriate item of the provisional agenda for the Ninth United Nations Congress on the Prevention of Crime and the Treatment of Offenders, to be held in 1995;

2. *Requests* the Commission on Crime Prevention and Criminal Justice to include the issue of violence against women in all its forms in the provisional agenda of its third session;

3. *Urges* Governments to give their full support to the adoption by the General Assembly at its forty-eighth session of the draft declaration on the elimination of violence against women, recommended by the Commission on the Status of Women at its thirty-seventh session;

4. *Welcomes* the extrabudgetary funds provided by the Helsinki Institute for Crime Prevention and Control, affiliated with the United Nations, for the publication,

in English, of the document entitled "Strategies for confronting domestic violence: a resource manual", prepared in collaboration with the Government of Canada, the Crime Prevention and Criminal Justice Branch of the Secretariat and the Helsinki Institute and reviewed at an expert group meeting hosted by the International Centre for Criminal Law Reform and Criminal Justice Policy, and requests the Secretary-General to publish it as soon as possible in the other official languages of the United Nations, subject to the availability of regular budgetary or extrabudgetary funds.

Economic and Social Council resolution 1993/26

27 July 1993   Meeting 43   Adopted without vote

Approved by Social Committee (E/1993/106) without vote, 14 July (meeting 10); draft by Commission on Crime Prevention and Criminal Justice (E/1993/32); agenda item 20.

Declaration on the elimination of violence against women

The draft declaration on the elimination of violence against women, prepared by the expert group meeting on violence against women in 1991[4] and by the Commission on the Status of Women's inter-sessional working group on violence against women,[5] was adopted by the Commission and forwarded to the Economic and Social Council.

ECONOMIC AND SOCIAL COUNCIL ACTION

On 27 July, the Economic and Social Council, on the recommendation of its Social Committee, adopted **resolution 1993/10** without vote.

Draft declaration on the elimination of violence against women

The Economic and Social Council,

Recalling its previous resolutions on the elimination of violence against women, especially its resolutions 1991/18 of 30 May 1991 and 1992/18 of 30 July 1992 related to the elaboration of a United Nations declaration on the subject,

Bearing in mind that the Nairobi Forward-looking Strategies for the Advancement of Women identify violence as a major obstacle to the achievement of the objectives of the United Nations Decade for Women: Equality, Development and Peace,

Recognizing that the elimination of violence against women is essential to the achievement of equality for women and is a requirement for the full respect of human rights,

Convinced that a United Nations declaration on the elimination of violence against women would make a positive contribution to the achievement of full equality for women,

Recognizing that the effective implementation of the Convention on the Elimination of All Forms of Discrimination against Women would contribute to the elimination of violence against women and that the declaration would strengthen and complement that process,

1. *Expresses its appreciation* to the experts, Member States and United Nations organizations that contributed to the elaboration of the draft declaration on the elimination of violence against women at the Expert Group Meeting on Violence against Women, held

at Vienna from 11 to 15 November 1991, and at the Meeting of the Working Group on Violence against Women, held at Vienna from 31 August to 4 September 1992;

2.   *Urges* the General Assembly to adopt the draft resolution on the declaration on the elimination of violence against women contained in the annex to the present resolution;

3.   *Urges* Member States to adopt, strengthen and enforce legislation prohibiting violence against women and to take all appropriate administrative, social and educational measures to protect women from all forms of physical, sexual and psychological violence, whether occurring in public or private life, in accordance with the measures contained in the draft declaration;

4.   *Calls upon* States parties to the Convention on the Elimination of All Forms of Discrimination against Women to continue to prepare their reports in accordance with general recommendation 19 on violence against women, adopted by the Committee on the Elimination of Discrimination against Women at its eleventh session;

5.   *Invites* United Nations entities, as well as intergovernmental and non-governmental organizations, to take all possible steps to implement the declaration, once adopted, to disseminate information on it and to promote its understanding;

6.   *Requests* the Secretary-General to provide all facilities and assistance necessary, within existing resources, for the dissemination of information on the declaration, once adopted;

7.   *Also requests* the Secretary-General to report, in consultation with Member States, to the Commission on the Status of Women at its thirty-ninth session, in 1995, and to the Commission on Human Rights at its fifty-second session, in 1996, on the implementation of the declaration, once adopted;

8.   *Urges* Governments to include an evaluation of the impact of the declaration, once adopted, in their preparatory activities for the Fourth World Conference on Women: Action for Equality, Development and Peace, to be held at Beijing from 4 to 15 September 1995.

ANNEX
[For text, see General Assembly resolution 48/104 below.]

Economic and Social Council resolution 1993/10

27 July 1993   Meeting 43   Adopted without vote

Approved by Social Committee (E/1993/105) without vote, 12 July (meeting 6); draft by Commission on Status of Women (E/1993/27); agenda item 19.

GENERAL ASSEMBLY ACTION

On 20 December, the General Assembly, on the recommendation of the Third Committee, adopted **resolution 48/104** without vote.

Declaration on the Elimination of Violence against Women

The General Assembly,

Recognizing the urgent need for the universal application to women of the rights and principles with regard to equality, security, liberty, integrity and dignity of all human beings,

Noting that those rights and principles are enshrined in international instruments, including the Universal Declaration of Human Rights, the International Covenant on Civil and Political Rights, the International Covenant on Economic, Social and Cultural Rights, the Convention on the Elimination of All Forms of Discrimination against Women and the Convention against Torture and Other Cruel, Inhuman or Degrading Treatment or Punishment,

Recognizing that effective implementation of the Convention on the Elimination of All Forms of Discrimination against Women would contribute to the elimination of violence against women and that the Declaration on the Elimination of Violence against Women, set forth in the present resolution, will strengthen and complement that process,

Concerned that violence against women is an obstacle to the achievement of equality, development and peace, as recognized in the Nairobi Forward-looking Strategies for the Advancement of Women, in which a set of measures to combat violence against women was recommended, and to the full implementation of the Convention on the Elimination of All Forms of Discrimination against Women,

Affirming that violence against women constitutes a violation of the rights and fundamental freedoms of women and impairs or nullifies their enjoyment of those rights and freedoms, and concerned about the long-standing failure to protect and promote those rights and freedoms in the case of violence against women,

Recognizing that violence against women is a manifestation of historically unequal power relations between men and women, which have led to domination over and discrimination against women by men and to the prevention of the full advancement of women, and that violence against women is one of the crucial social mechanisms by which women are forced into a subordinate position compared with men,

Concerned that some groups of women, such as women belonging to minority groups, indigenous women, refugee women, migrant women, women living in rural or remote communities, destitute women, women in institutions or in detention, female children, women with disabilities, elderly women and women in situations of armed conflict, are especially vulnerable to violence,

Recalling the conclusion in paragraph 23 of the annex to Economic and Social Council resolution 1990/15 of 24 May 1990 that recognition that violence against women in the family and society was pervasive and cut across lines of income, class and culture had to be matched by urgent and effective steps to eliminate its incidence,

Recalling also Economic and Social Council resolution 1991/18 of 30 May 1991, in which the Council recommended the development of a framework for an international instrument that would address explicitly the issue of violence against women,

Welcoming the role that women's movements are playing in drawing increasing attention to the nature, severity and magnitude of the problem of violence against women,

Alarmed that opportunities for women to achieve legal, social, political and economic equality in society are limited, *inter alia*, by continuing and endemic violence,

Convinced that in the light of the above there is a need for a clear and comprehensive definition of violence against women, a clear statement of the rights to be applied to ensure the elimination of violence against women in all its forms, a commitment by States in respect of their responsibilities, and a commitment by the international community at large to the elimination of violence against women,

Solemnly proclaims the following Declaration on the Elimination of Violence against Women and urges that every effort be made so that it becomes generally known and respected:

Article 1

For the purposes of this Declaration, the term ''violence against women'' means any act of gender-based violence that results in, or is likely to result in, physical, sexual or psychological harm or suffering to women, including threats of such acts, coercion or arbitrary deprivation of liberty, whether occurring in public or in private life.

Article 2

Violence against women shall be understood to encompass, but not be limited to, the following:

(a) Physical, sexual and psychological violence occurring in the family, including battering, sexual abuse of female children in the household, dowry-related violence, marital rape, female genital mutilation and other traditional practices harmful to women, non-spousal violence and violence related to exploitation;

(b) Physical, sexual and psychological violence occurring within the general community, including rape, sexual abuse, sexual harassment and intimidation at work, in educational institutions and elsewhere, trafficking in women and forced prostitution;

(c) Physical, sexual and psychological violence perpetrated or condoned by the State, wherever it occurs.

Article 3

Women are entitled to the equal enjoyment and protection of all human rights and fundamental freedoms in the political, economic, social, cultural, civil or any other field. These rights include, *inter alia*:

(a) The right to life;

(b) The right to equality;

(c) The right to liberty and security of person;

(d) The right to equal protection under the law;

(e) The right to be free from all forms of discrimination;

(f) The right to the highest standard attainable of physical and mental health;

(g) The right to just and favourable conditions of work;

(h) The right not to be subjected to torture, or other cruel, inhuman or degrading treatment or punishment.

Article 4

States should condemn violence against women and should not invoke any custom, tradition or religious consideration to avoid their obligations with respect to its elimination. States should pursue by all appropriate means and without delay a policy of eliminating violence against women and, to this end, should:

(a) Consider, where they have not yet done so, ratifying or acceding to the Convention on the Elimination of All Forms of Discrimination against Women or withdrawing reservations to that Convention;

(b) Refrain from engaging in violence against women;

(c) Exercise due diligence to prevent, investigate and, in accordance with national legislation, punish acts of violence against women, whether those acts are perpetrated by the State or by private persons;

(d) Develop penal, civil, labour and administrative sanctions in domestic legislation to punish and redress the wrongs caused to women who are subjected to violence; women who are subjected to violence should be provided with access to the mechanisms of justice and, as provided for by national legislation, to just and effective remedies for the harm that they have suffered; States should also inform women of their rights in seeking redress through such mechanisms;

(e) Consider the possibility of developing national plans of action to promote the protection of women against any form of violence, or to include provisions for that purpose in plans already existing, taking into account, as appropriate, such cooperation as can be provided by non-governmental organizations, particularly those concerned with the issue of violence against women;

(f) Develop, in a comprehensive way, preventive approaches and all those measures of a legal, political, administrative and cultural nature that promote the protection of women against any form of violence, and ensure that the re-victimization of women does not occur because of laws insensitive to gender considerations, enforcement practices or other interventions;

(g) Work to ensure, to the maximum extent feasible in the light of their available resources and, where needed, within the framework of international cooperation, that women subjected to violence and, where appropriate, their children have specialized assistance, such as rehabilitation, assistance in child care and maintenance, treatment, counselling, and health and social services, facilities and programmes, as well as support structures, and should take all other appropriate measures to promote their safety and physical and psychological rehabilitation;

(h) Include in government budgets adequate resources for their activities related to the elimination of violence against women;

(i) Take measures to ensure that law enforcement officers and public officials responsible for implementing policies to prevent, investigate and punish violence against women receive training to sensitize them to the needs of women;

(j) Adopt all appropriate measures, especially in the field of education, to modify the social and cultural patterns of conduct of men and women and to eliminate prejudices, customary practices and all other practices based on the idea of the inferiority or superiority of either of the sexes and on stereotyped roles for men and women;

(k) Promote research, collect data and compile statistics, especially concerning domestic violence, relating to the prevalence of different forms of violence against women and encourage research on the causes, nature, seriousness and consequences of violence against women and on the effectiveness of measures implemented to prevent and redress violence against women; those statistics and findings of the research will be made public;

(l) Adopt measures directed towards the elimination of violence against women who are especially vulnerable to violence;

(m) Include, in submitting reports as required under relevant human rights instruments of the United Nations, information pertaining to violence against women and measures taken to implement the present Declaration;

(n) Encourage the development of appropriate guidelines to assist in the implementation of the principles set forth in the present Declaration;

(o) Recognize the important role of the women's movement and non-governmental organizations world wide in raising awareness and alleviating the problem of violence against women;

(p) Facilitate and enhance the work of the women's movement and non-governmental organizations and cooperate with them at local, national and regional levels;

(q) Encourage intergovernmental regional organizations of which they are members to include the elimination of violence against women in their programmes, as appropriate.

Article 5

The organs and specialized agencies of the United Nations system should, within their respective fields of competence, contribute to the recognition and realization of the rights and the principles set forth in the present Declaration and, to this end, should, *inter alia*:

(a) Foster international and regional cooperation with a view to defining regional strategies for combating violence, exchanging experiences and financing programmes relating to the elimination of violence against women;

(b) Promote meetings and seminars with the aim of creating and raising awareness among all persons of the issue of the elimination of violence against women;

(c) Foster coordination and exchange within the United Nations system between human rights treaty bodies to address the issue of violence against women effectively;

(d) Include in analyses prepared by organizations and bodies of the United Nations system of social trends and problems, such as the periodic reports on the world social situation, examination of trends in violence against women;

(e) Encourage coordination between organizations and bodies of the United Nations system to incorporate the issue of violence against women into ongoing programmes, especially with reference to groups of women particularly vulnerable to violence;

(f) Promote the formulation of guidelines or manuals relating to violence against women, taking into account the measures referred to in the present Declaration;

(g) Consider the issue of the elimination of violence against women, as appropriate, in fulfilling their mandates with respect to the implementation of human rights instruments;

(h) Cooperate with non-governmental organizations in addressing the issue of violence against women.

Article 6

Nothing in the present Declaration shall affect any provision that is more conducive to the elimination of violence against women that may be contained in the legislation of a State or in any international convention, treaty or other instrument in force in a State.

General Assembly resolution 48/104

20 December 1993   Meeting 85   Adopted without vote

Approved by Third Committee (A/48/629) without vote, 1 December (meeting 48); draft by ESC (A/C.3/48/L.5); agenda item 111.
Meeting numbers. GA 48th session: 3rd Committee 29-37, 48; plenary 85.

Violence against women migrant workers

On 20 December, the General Assembly, on the recommendation of the Third Committee, adopted **resolution 48/110** without vote.

Violence against women migrant workers

The General Assembly,

Recalling that the Charter of the United Nations reaffirms faith in human rights and fundamental freedoms, in the dignity and worth of the human person and in the equal rights of men and women,

Reaffirming the principles set forth in the Convention on the Elimination of All Forms of Discrimination against Women, adopted by the General Assembly in its resolution 34/180 of 18 December 1979 and annexed thereto,

Welcoming the reaffirmation made in the Vienna Declaration and Programme of Action, adopted by the World Conference on Human Rights, that gender-based violence and all forms of sexual harassment and exploitation are incompatible with the dignity and worth of the human person and must be eliminated by legal measures and through national and international cooperation,

Noting that large numbers of women from developing countries continue to venture forth to more affluent countries in search of a living for themselves and their families, as a consequence of poverty, unemployment and other socio-economic situations in their home countries, while acknowledging the primary duty of States to work for conditions that provide employment to their citizens,

Recognizing that it is the duty of sending countries to protect and promote the interests of their citizens who seek or receive employment in other countries, to provide them with appropriate training/education and to apprise them of their rights and obligations in the countries of employment,

Aware of the moral obligation of receiving or host countries to ensure the human rights and fundamental freedoms of all persons within their boundaries, including migrant workers, in particular women migrant workers, who are doubly vulnerable because of their gender and because they are foreigners,

Noting with concern the continuing reports of grave abuses and acts of violence committed against the persons of women migrant workers by some of their employers in some host countries,

Stressing that acts of violence directed against women impair or nullify the enjoyment by women of their human rights and fundamental freedoms,

Convinced of the need to eliminate all forms of discrimination against women and to protect them from gender-based violence,

1. *Expresses grave concern* at the plight of women migrant workers who become victims of physical, mental and sexual harassment and abuse;

2. *Recognizes with appreciation* the efforts exerted by some receiving countries to alleviate the negative situation of women migrant workers;

3. *Welcomes* the recommendation to the General Assembly by the Economic and Social Council in its reso-

lution 1993/10 of 27 July 1993 of the draft Declaration on the Elimination of Violence against Women;

4. *Reaffirms* the provision in the Vienna Declaration and Programme of Action that the rights of women should form an integral part of United Nations human rights activities, including the promotion of all human rights instruments specifically relating to women;

5. *Calls upon* all countries, particularly the sending and receiving States, to cooperate in taking appropriate steps to ensure that the rights of women migrant workers are protected;

6. *Calls upon* the countries concerned to take appropriate measures to ensure that law-enforcement officials and the judiciary assist in guaranteeing the full protection of the rights of women migrant workers;

7. *Urges* both sending and host countries to help ensure that women migrant workers are protected from unscrupulous recruitment practices, if needed, by the adoption of legal measures;

8. *Encourages* Member States to consider signing and ratifying or acceding to the International Convention on the Protection of the Rights of All Migrant Workers and Members of Their Families;

9. *Invites* trade unions to support the realization of the rights of women migrant workers by assisting them in organizing themselves so as to enable them better to assert their rights;

10. *Requests* treaty-monitoring bodies and calls upon non-governmental organizations concerned with violence against women to include, where appropriate, the situation of women migrant workers in their deliberations and findings and to supply relevant information to United Nations bodies and Governments;

11. *Calls upon* non-governmental organizations concerned to conduct, in cooperation with both the sending and the host countries, seminars and training programmes on human rights instruments, particularly those pertaining to migrant workers;

12. *Urges* all States, with the support of relevant non-governmental organizations, to adopt appropriate measures to provide support services to women migrant workers who have become traumatized as a consequence of violations of their rights by, *inter alia*, unscrupulous employers and/or recruiters, and to provide resources for their physical and psychological rehabilitation;

13. *Also urges* that the subject of violence against women migrant workers be included in the agenda of the Fourth World Conference on Women: Action for Equality, Development and Peace, to be held in Beijing in 1995;

14. *Calls upon* competent bodies and specialized agencies of the United Nations system, intergovernmental organizations and non-governmental organizations to inform the Secretary-General of the extent of the problem and to recommend further measures to implement the purposes of the present resolution;

15. *Requests* the Secretary-General to report to the General Assembly at its forty-ninth session on the implementation of the present resolution, taking into account the relevant views of the Commission on the Status of Women in its discussion of the subject of violence against women at its thirty-eighth session, in March 1994.

General Assembly resolution 48/110

20 December 1993   Meeting 85   Adopted without vote

Approved by Third Committee (A/48/629) without vote, 1 December (meeting 48); 24-nation draft (A/C.3/48/L.35), orally revised; agenda item 111.

Sponsors: Australia, Belarus, Belgium, China, Colombia, Costa Rica, Cyprus, Ecuador, Ghana, Guinea-Bissau, Indonesia, Ireland, Mexico, Myanmar, Namibia, Nicaragua, Peru, Philippines, Portugal, Russian Federation, Senegal, Spain, Thailand, Uganda.
Meeting numbers. GA 48th session: 3rd Committee 29-37, 41, 48; plenary 85.

Rape and abuse of women in the former Yugoslavia

In March,[6] the Commission on the Status of Women condemned the rape and abuse of women and children in the former Yugoslavia and urged States and the relevant intergovernmental organizations and NGOs to consider long-term action-oriented plans and programmes and the provision of adequate financial resources to rehabilitate those women and children. It also urged them to ensure that counselling and other support formed an integral part of health and welfare services. It requested the Secretary-General to make available to the Commission, in 1994, the reports of the Commission on Human Rights Special Rapporteur on the situation of human rights in the former Yugoslavia.

The Committee on the Elimination of Discrimination against Women (CEDAW)[7] requested its Chairperson to send a letter to the Special Rapporteur, expressing the Committee's concern over alleged human rights violations against women in the former Yugoslavia. The letter to the Special Rapporteur and his reply were annexed to the Committee's report. CEDAW decided to request, on an exceptional basis and if warranted, reports from the States of the territory of the former Yugoslavia.

The General Assembly, by **resolution 48/143**, strongly condemned the systematic rape and abuse of women in areas of armed conflict in the former Yugoslavia (see also PARTS TWO and THREE, Chapters IV and X, respectively).

Palestinian women

By a January note,[8] the Secretary-General submitted to the Commission a report describing the situation of Palestinian women, as requested by the Economic and Social Council in 1992.[9] The Secretary-General discussed their living conditions, economic situation and employment, education, health and psychological well-being, and gender relations in the Palestinian family (see also PART TWO, Chapter V).

On 27 July, the Economic and Social Council, by **resolution 1993/15**, asked the Secretary-General to assist in the review of the situation of Palestinian women and to submit to the Commission on the Status of Women in 1994 a report containing recommendations and a programme of action aimed at improving their situation.

Women and children under apartheid

In accordance with a 1992 Economic and Social Council request,[10] the Secretary-General submitted to the Commission on the Status of Women a

January report[11] describing the legal, economic and social conditions affecting women and children living under apartheid, and action taken by United Nations organizations and the international community to provide assistance to them (see also PART TWO, Chapter I).

On 27 July, the Council, by **resolution 1993/13**, appealed to the international community to increase its support for women and children under apartheid and asked the Secretary-General to report to the Commission in 1994.

Communications on the status of women

On 19 March,[1] the Commission on the Status of Women appointed a Working Group on Communications concerning the Status of Women to consider ways of making the communications procedure more transparent and efficient. The communications mechanism identified communications received by the Division for the Advancement of Women that revealed a consistent pattern of injustice and discriminatory practices against women. The Working Group was guided by a mandate set out in a 1983 Economic and Social Council resolution.[12] In its report to the Commission, the Working Group stated that it considered communications, confidential and non-confidential, received directly by the Division for the Advancement of Women and by the Centre for Human Rights, the International Labour Organisation and other United Nations bodies and agencies that had been forwarded to the Division. It noted that the most prevalent issues dealt with were cases of sexual violence and equal remuneration. The Working Group proposed that the Commission give attention to the trends emerging from the communications procedure, that it urge Governments to supply more substantive replies and that further publicity be given to the existing procedure.

ECONOMIC AND SOCIAL COUNCIL ACTION

On 27 July, on the recommendation of its Social Committee, the Economic and Social Council adopted **resolution 1993/11** without vote.

Communications on the status of women
The Economic and Social Council,

Recalling its resolutions 76(V) of 5 August 1947 and 304 I (XI) of 14 and 17 July 1950, which form the basis for the mandate of the Commission on the Status of Women to receive at each of its regular sessions a list of confidential and non-confidential communications relating to the status of women,

Taking into consideration its resolution 1983/27 of 26 May 1983, in which it reaffirmed the mandate of the Commission to consider confidential and non-confidential communications on the status of women and authorized the Commission to appoint a working group to consider communications, with a view to bringing to the attention of the Commission those communications, including the replies of Governments, which appeared to reveal a consistent pattern of reliably attested injustice and discriminatory practices against women,

Reaffirming that discrimination against women is incompatible with human dignity and that women and men should participate on the basis of equality, irrespective of race or creed, in the social, economic and political processes of their countries,

Recalling its resolution 1990/8 of 24 May 1990, by which it requested the Secretary-General to examine, in consultation with Governments, the existing mechanisms for communications on the status of women, in order to ensure that such communications received effective and appropriately coordinated consideration in view of the role of communications in the work of the Commission, and to report thereon to the Commission at its thirty-fifth session,

Recalling also its resolution 1992/19 of 30 July 1992, in which it requested the Secretary-General to publicize widely the existence and scope of the communications mechanism of the Commission and to ensure proper coordination of the activities of the Commission in this area with those of the other bodies of the Council, and requested the Commission to consider ways of making the procedure for receiving and considering communications, including the standard of admissibility, more transparent and efficient,

Bearing in mind the conclusion of the Working Group on Communications on the Status of Women, in its report to the Commission at its thirty-fifth session that, while the communications procedure provided a valuable source of information on the effects of discrimination on the lives of women, it should be improved to make it more efficient and useful, and that clear criteria for receiving communications should be given,

1. *Reaffirms* that the Commission on the Status of Women is empowered to make recommendations to the Economic and Social Council on what action should be taken on emerging trends and patterns of discrimination against women revealed by communications on the status of women;

2. *Requests* the Secretary-General to continue to publicize widely the existence and scope of the communications mechanism of the Commission, using all available media;

3. *Also requests* the Secretary-General to continue to support the activities of the Commission with regard to its consideration of communications and to ensure proper coordination of the activities of the Commission in this area with those of the other bodies of the Council;

4. *Invites* the Commission to take into account the report of the Secretary-General on examining mechanisms for communications on the status of women, submitted to the Commission at its thirty-fifth session, when considering ways of making the existing procedure for receiving and considering communications more effective;

5. *Invites* each regional group to appoint, one week before each session of the Commission, a member of the Working Group on Communications on the Status of Women;

6. *Requests* the Secretary-General to report to the Commission at its thirty-eighth session on the ways in which the communications mechanism of the Commission has been publicized;

7. *Also requests* the Secretary-General to ensure that any costs resulting from the activities set out in the pres-

ent resolution are kept to a minimum and that the activities are carried out within existing resources.

Economic and Social Council resolution 1993/11

27 July 1993   Meeting 43   Adopted without vote

Approved by Social Committee (E/1993/105) without vote, 12 July (meeting 6); draft by Commission on Status of Women (E/1993/27); agenda item 19.

Women's rights and legal literacy

In March,[1] the Commission on the Status of Women considered a report of the Secretary-General that examined obstacles to the exercise by women of their legal rights.[13] Those obstacles were identified as a lack of awareness of the rights; illiteracy and a lower level of education; the absence of legislation to implement equal rights; the insensitivity of judicial personnel to gender factors; and family and community resistance to women using the legal system. An expert group meeting (Bratislava, Slovakia, 18-22 May 1992) on increased awareness by women of their rights, including legal literacy—defined as having an awareness of rights and the law, the ability to assert rights and the capacity to mobilize for legal and societal change—recommended that Governments form partnerships with NGOs to mobilize women to act for the enjoyment of their rights; ensure that their legal systems were accessible and gender-neutral; include an understanding of women's rights in school curricula; and adopt measures to make the development of legal literacy a more effective and general process. It also recommended that the relevant United Nations organizations support legal literacy programmes and activities for women and see that support as part of a general effort to promote international standards and norms, especially the 1979 Convention on the Elimination of All Forms of Discrimination against Women.[2] Annexed to the report were extracts from the expert group meeting's report.

Women and drugs

In February,[14] the Secretary-General described action taken or planned by United Nations organizations on women and drug abuse and the role of women in drug control in the context of the United Nations Decade against Drug Abuse (1991-2000). Activities centred on the human immunodeficiency virus (HIV)/acquired immunodeficiency syndrome (AIDS) and intravenous drug abusers; treatment for HIV-infected and drug-dependent prisoners; the social impact of drug trafficking and abuse in low-income urban areas of Latin America and the Caribbean; drug abuse prevention education in Mediterranean countries; and rehabilitation and after-care. A joint position paper on women, drug abuse and HIV/AIDS was being prepared by the World Health Organization, in collaboration with the United Nations Drug Control Programme and the Division for the Advancement of Women, for submission to the Commission on the Status of Women in 1994.

Women and peace

In March,[1] the Commission on the Status of Women considered a report by the Secretary-General on women's participation in the peace process.[15] He noted that, while women's participation in non-governmental activities, such as demonstrations, peace movements, peace education and peace research, had been strong and visible, their participation in the military had been limited. The Secretary-General reviewed the potential role of women in United Nations peace-keeping and suggested studying gender aspects of recent peace-keeping and humanitarian operations and collecting statistics on the participation of women in those operations.

REFERENCES

[1]E/1993/27 & Corr.1. [2]YUN 1979, p. 895, GA res. 34/180, annex, 18 Dec. 1979. [3]E/CN.6/1994/4. [4]YUN 1992, p. 874. [5]Ibid., p. 875. [6]E/1993/27 (res. 37/3). [7]A/48/38. [8]E/CN.6/1993/10. [9]YUN 1992, p. 875, ESC res. 1992/16, 30 July 1992. [10]Ibid., p. 165, ESC res. 1992/15, 30 July 1992. [11]E/CN.6/1993/11. [12]YUN 1983, p. 923, ESC res. 1983/27, 26 May 1983. [13]E/CN.6/1993/2. [14]E/CN.6/1993/13. [15]E/CN.6/1993/4.

Elimination of discrimination against women

Convention on discrimination against women

The Committee on the Elimination of Discrimination against Women (CEDAW), established in 1982[1] under the Convention on the Elimination of All Forms of Discrimination against Women,[2] held its twelfth session at Vienna from 18 January to 5 February 1993.[3]

The Committee considered the reports of 11 States parties (Bangladesh, France, Iraq, Kenya, Nicaragua, Republic of Korea, Romania, Rwanda, Sweden, United Kingdom and Yemen) on legislative, judicial, administrative and other measures they had adopted to give effect to the Convention.

On 4 February, the Committee adopted a suggestion on the World Conference on Human Rights (see PART THREE, Chapter X) containing recommendations on women and human rights issues. It considered ways of contributing to the International Year of the Family (1994); the International Conference on Population and Development (1994); the Fourth World Conference on Women (1995); and the World Summit for Social Development (1995). CEDAW discussed the report of the fourth (1992) meeting of persons chairing the human rights treaty bodies[4] and examined ways of expediting its work. The Committee decided that it should take steps, in common with other human rights treaty bodies, to seek an advisory opinion from the International Court of Justice that would clarify the validity and legal effect of reservations to the Convention in order to assist Governments to reconsider their reservations with a view to withdrawing them.

In March,[5] the Commission on the Status of Women considered the report of CEDAW on its 1993 session and discussed the status of the Convention.

A draft general recommendation and draft general comments were adopted on articles 9 (equality with men regarding nationality), 15 (equality with men regarding legal matters) and 16 (elimination of discrimination against women in matters relating to marriage and family relations) of the Convention, with the agreement that three additions in the draft recommendation would be included in the final draft. The additions referred to the unequal power held by men and women within the family; the impact of the non-recognition of women's unpaid work at home; and the status of a minority of infertile women, who, in many African countries, had no inheritance rights after the death of their husbands. Final approval of the draft was expected at the Committee's 1994 session. Draft general comments and recommendations on other articles of the Convention were being prepared by a working group.

Annexed to the Committee's report were lists of States parties to the Convention as at 1 March 1993 and CEDAW members, and a chart giving the status of submission of reports by States parties under article 18 of the Convention as at the same date.

ECONOMIC AND SOCIAL COUNCIL ACTION

On 27 July, the Economic and Social Council, on the recommendation of its Social Committee, adopted **resolution 1993/14** without vote.

Convention on the Elimination of All Forms of Discrimination against Women

The Economic and Social Council,

Bearing in mind that the Convention on the Elimination of All Forms of Discrimination against Women is the most important international human rights instrument for the promotion of equality between women and men,

Welcoming the growing number of States parties to the Convention, which now stands at one hundred and twenty,

Noting with concern that the Convention is still the human rights instrument with the most reservations, despite the fact that some States parties have withdrawn their reservations to it,

Noting the importance of the monitoring function of the Committee on the Elimination of Discrimination against Women, as demonstrated most recently by the Committee at its twelfth session, at which it adopted suggestion 4 on the World Conference on Human Rights and also adopted, in substance, and decided to place on the provisional agenda of its thirteenth session for final approval without discussion, a draft general recommendation on article 16 and related articles 9 and 15 of the Convention, which would be its contribution to the International Year of the Family,

Taking note of General Assembly resolution 47/94 of 16 December 1992,

Recalling its resolution 1991/25 of 30 May 1991 and other General Assembly and Economic and Social Council resolutions relating to support for the Committee,

Noting that the annual session of the Committee is the shortest of all the annual sessions of the human rights treaty bodies,

Welcoming the expressed intention of the Committee to strengthen the analysis of country reports provided to it,

1. *Supports* the request of the Committee on the Elimination of Discrimination against Women for additional meeting time for its future sessions, as granted for its twelfth and thirteenth sessions;

2. *Welcomes* suggestion 4 on the World Conference on Human Rights, adopted by the Committee at its twelfth session, and the draft general recommendation on article 16 and related articles 9 and 15 of the Convention, adopted, in substance, by the Committee at that session, both of which were submitted to the Commission on the Status of Women at its thirty-seventh session, and encourages the Committee to continue its work in developing detailed general recommendations;

3. *Requests* States parties to the Convention on the Elimination of All Forms of Discrimination against Women to review regularly their reservations and make efforts to withdraw them in order to enable the full implementation of the Convention;

4. *Urges* the Secretary-General to continue to widely publicize the decisions and recommendations of the Committee.

Economic and Social Council resolution 1993/14

27 July 1993   Meeting 43   Adopted without vote

Approved by Social Committee (E/1993/105) without vote, 12 July (meeting 6); draft by Commission on Status of Women (E/1993/27); agenda item 19.

Ratifications, accessions and signatures

As at 31 December 1993,[6] the Convention on the Elimination of All Forms of Discrimination against Women had received 96 signatures and 130 States had become parties to it. During the year, South Africa signed the Convention and Armenia, the Bahamas, Bosnia and Herzegovina, the Czech Republic, the Gambia, India, Maldives, Morocco, Slovakia, Suriname and Tajikistan became parties to it.

In September,[7] the Secretary-General submitted his annual report on the status of the Convention, which contained information on signatures, ratifications, successions and accessions as at 1 August 1993 and on reservations and objections made to specific reservations between 1 August 1992 and 1 August 1993.

REFERENCES

[1]YUN 1982, p. 1149. [2]YUN 1979, p. 895, GA res. 34/180, annex, 18 Dec. 1979. [3]A/48/38. [4]YUN 1992, p. 769. [5]E/1993/27 & Corr.1. [6]*Multilateral Treaties Deposited with the Secretary-General: Status as at 31 December 1993* (ST/LEG/SER.E/12), Sales No. E.94.V.11. [7]A/48/354.

Chapter XIV

Children, youth and ageing persons

In 1993, activities of the United Nations Children's Fund were geared towards achieving intermediate goals for 1995 as a follow-up to the 1990 World Summit for Children. Most of the Fund's allocations went to emergency operations in 64 countries. It provided assistance in the areas of immunization, maternal and child health, control of diarrhoeal diseases and acute respiratory infections, nutrition and household food security, breast-feeding, water supply and sanitation, basic education, urban services, and children in especially difficult circumstances.

In July, the Economic and Social Council adopted a calendar of activities prepared by the Commission for Social Development to mark the tenth anniversary of International Youth Year in 1995. The Commission also made recommendations for further development of a draft world youth programme of action to the year 2000 and beyond.

In December, the General Assembly endorsed recommendations from the third review and appraisal of the International Plan of Action on Ageing along with global and national targets on ageing for the year 2001. It also redesignated the International Year of Older Persons, to be observed in 1999, as the International Year of the Elderly.

Children

UN Children's Fund

During 1993,[1] the United Nations Children's Fund (UNICEF) cooperated in programmes in more than 130 countries, the greatest number of which were in Africa (46), followed by Latin America and the Caribbean (35), Asia (34) and the Middle East and North Africa (14). The Fund expanded its programme to nine Central and Eastern European countries and newly independent States. Programme expenditures totalled $804 million, of which $223 million (28 per cent) was spent on emergency operations; $210 million (26 per cent) on child health; $127 million (16 per cent) on programme planning, advocacy and support; $84 million (10 per cent) on water supply and sanitation; $72 million (9 per cent) on education; $31 million (4 per cent) on nutrition and household

food security; and $57 million (7 per cent) on other programme areas.

Major strategic components of UNICEF activities were aimed at achieving and monitoring the goals for children in the 1990s and promoting the 1989 Convention on the Rights of the Child (see below), advocacy and social mobilization, economic policies linked with social development, common strategies of the United Nations operational activities for development, action to reach the poorest, national capacity-building and empowerment and the environment and sustainable development.

The UNICEF Executive Board held its regular session from 26 April to 7 May[2] and a special session on 6 and 7 October 1993,[3] both in New York. On 7 June,[4] the Board elected officers for the period 1 August 1993 to 31 July 1994. The Programme Committee convened from 28 April to 3 May and on 7 May, while the Committee on Administration and Finance met from 3 to 5 and on 7 May and on 6 and 7 October. (For dates of organizational sessions, see APPENDIX III.)

Programme policy decisions

The Executive Board approved a number of recommendations by its Programme Committee concerning programme policies.

The Board[5] requested the Executive Director to ensure that country programme evaluations became an integral part of the country programming exercise, refine the evaluation information system and report on its status in 1994, and to continue collaboration with other United Nations bodies in developing similar evaluation reporting systems. The Executive Director was also requested to report biennially, starting in 1994, on the results of UNICEF programme and project evaluations and achievements in service delivery, capacity-building and empowerment. The Board noted[6] the findings and recommendations of the multi-donor evaluation of UNICEF initiated by Australia, Canada, Denmark and Switzerland[7] and asked the Executive Director to suggest further use of the evaluation results. The Fund and other interested parties were invited to identify evaluation issues for future consideration and to report on the subject in 1994.

In a separate action, the Executive Director was requested[8] to include in future country programmes plans for UNICEF support of national capacity-building measures and to support the development of indicators for monitoring institutional development plans.

Follow-up to 1990 World Summit for Children

Having reviewed the Executive Director's report[9] on the follow-up to the 1990 World Summit for Children and the implementation of the Summit's World Declaration on the Survival, Protection and Development of Children and Plan of Action,[10] the Executive Board[11] urged heads of State or Government to maintain and strengthen their involvement in the commitments of the Summit and encouraged countries to identify feasible mid-decade targets in their national programmes of action (NPAs). Countries were also encouraged to incorporate NPA activities into the national budget process and make NPAs operational at provincial, municipal and district levels. The Executive Board requested that NPAs be taken into account in the course of poverty reduction, lending and adjustment processes and invited UNICEF, international donors and non-governmental organizations (NGOs) to strengthen the delivery of social services, capacity-building and empowerment as components of NPAs and UNICEF-supported country programmes. The Board called for an increase in official development assistance and national budgetary allocations to priority social sectors. It requested the Executive Director to coordinate the Fund's follow-up activities with those of other United Nations bodies and ensure the integration of NPAs into action for sustainable development.

In response to a 1992 General Assembly request,[12] the Secretary-General submitted to the Assembly in September 1993 a report[13] on action by the international community in response to the World Summit. The report reviewed progress in the preparation of NPAs and their contents, the status of the 1989 Convention on the Rights of the Child,[14] regional and global developments, and responses of the United Nations system, NGOs and the private sector. As at 15 July 1993, NPAs were finalized or under preparation in 143 countries. The Secretary-General noted that, despite the excellent progress made since the World Summit, achievement of the goals for children in the 1990s remained a challenge, requiring greater integration of NPA strategies and implementation of the 1989 Convention with all aspects of national development, mobilization of adequate resources, reinforcement of monitoring systems and promotion of the Summit's pledges through advocacy and social mobilization. In the meantime, implementation of those pledges focused on mid-decade targets identified by regional meetings of heads of State or Government and by UNICEF and the World Health Organization (WHO).

On 21 December, the General Assembly took note of the Secretary-General's report and requested him to submit an updated report to it in 1994 (**decision 48/446**).

Intermediate goals for 1995

The UNICEF/WHO Joint Committee on Health Policy, at its twenty-ninth session (Geneva, 1 and 2 February),[15] recommended intermediate goals for children for 1995, derived from the mid-decade targets adopted in 1992 by the International Conference on Assistance to African Children, the Second Conference on Children, organized by the South Asian Association for Regional Cooperation, and the League of Arab States.

The goals were: 80 per cent immunization coverage of six antigens in all countries, virtual elimination of neonatal tetanus and vitamin A deficiency, the reduction of measles mortality by 95 per cent and measles cases by 90 per cent compared to pre-immunization levels, universal salt iodization in countries affected by iodine deficiency disorders, the elimination of poliomyelitis in selected countries and regions, 80 per cent use of oral rehydration therapy and continued feeding to control diarrhoeal diseases, "baby-friendly" status for all hospitals and an end to the distribution of free and low-cost supplies of breast-milk substitutes in all hospitals and maternity facilities, the interruption of guinea worm disease transmission in all affected villages, a 20 per cent reduction in severe and moderate malnutrition levels compared to 1990, universal ratification of the Convention on the Rights of the Child, an increase of the primary school enrolment/retention rate and a reduction of the 1990 gender gap by one third, and an increase in water supply and sanitation rates so as to narrow the gap between 1990 levels and universal access by 25 and 10 per cent, respectively.

The Executive Board endorsed the goals recommended by the UNICEF/WHO Joint Committee on Health Policy.[16]

Convention on the Rights of the Child

The Executive Board[17] called on all States to ratify or accede to the Convention on the Rights of the Child and to implement it. The Board endorsed the year 1995 as a target date for every State to become a party to the Convention. It requested the Executive Director to assist States to become parties to the Convention, to implement it, and to report on child rights annually until the Convention was universally ratified.

In his report to the General Assembly,[13] the Secretary-General noted that the Convention's implementation was explicit in many NPAs, most notably those of Canada, the Netherlands and the Nordic countries. NPAs were among the few instruments available for setting a time-frame for

Governments to achieve their minimum obligations under the Convention.

The Committee on the Rights of the Child met three times during 1993. Its third[18] and fourth[19] sessions were held at Geneva (11-29 January and 20 September–8 October), and an informal meeting was held at Bangkok, Thailand (23-29 May). It considered reports submitted by Member States and reviewed, among other matters, cooperation with United Nations bodies and other organizations, procedures for urgent action, public information activities, technical advice or assistance, future studies, and reservations to the Convention. The Committee adopted a draft optional Protocol on the involvement of children in armed conflicts, made a statement on the economic exploitation of children and submitted its conclusions and recommendations to the General Assembly for consideration.

In December, the Assembly requested the Secretary-General to undertake a comprehensive study of the situation of children affected by armed conflicts (**resolution 48/157**). It also called on the international community to support efforts to improve the situation of street children (**resolution 48/136**) and emphasized the need for measures to prevent the sale of children, child prostitution and child pornography (**resolution 48/156**). (For further details, see PART THREE, Chapter X.)

Children, environment and sustainable development

In March, the Executive Director submitted a report[20] on UNICEF's response to Agenda 21, adopted by the 1992 United Nations Conference on Environment and Development.[21] As a follow-up to the Conference, the Fund advocated "primary environmental care"—a community-based approach to meet basic needs while ensuring the protection and optimal use of natural resources. The implementation of primary environmental care (PEC) focused especially on the needs of children, women and the very poor, who were most threatened by urban poverty and environmental degradation. The Fund also promoted environmental education for children and women, advocacy and social mobilization.

The Executive Board[22] called on the Executive Director, in cooperation with the Commission on Sustainable Development and other United Nations bodies, to incorporate the PEC perspective and suitable environmental indicators into UNICEF-assisted programmes; assist Governments to include PEC elements in their NPAs; provide seed funds for innovative PEC activities; encourage children and their parents to be focal points for increasing environmental awareness in communities; and support the inclusion of children's and women's concerns into relevant local, national and regional policies and strategies. UNICEF field offices were asked to intensify efforts to reach families living under environmentally stressed and vulnerable conditions, particularly the poorest, and to promote environmental education and cooperation with NGOs. The Board also called for an increase in financial assistance to child-related PEC activities and asked the Executive Director to transmit the goals and strategies for children in the 1990s to the Commission on Sustainable Development for its deliberations on the multi-year thematic programme of work (see PART THREE, Chapter I).

Maurice Pate Memorial Award

In 1993, the Maurice Pate Award, established in 1966[23] in memory of UNICEF's first Executive Director, was presented to the people and State of Ceará, Brazil, for significant contributions to the well-being of children.[24] The $25,000 award recognized the State's efforts to improve and expand health-care services for children and women.

Emergency operations

In 1993, major emergency operations were carried out in Afghanistan, Angola, Ethiopia, Iraq, Kenya, Liberia, Mozambique, Somalia, Sudan and former Yugoslavia.[25] UNICEF provided emergency assistance to 64 countries affected by armed conflicts, health emergencies and natural disasters. Emergencies included an earthquake in India; floods and landslides in Ecuador, Nepal and the Philippines; tropical storms in Cuba and Honduras; a continuing political crisis in Haiti; and insurgencies in Peru. Emergencies in Africa received the largest share (38 per cent) of total allocations from the UNICEF Emergency Programme Fund (EPF), followed by countries in Central and Eastern Europe and the Commonwealth of Independent States (30 per cent), the Americas and the Caribbean (16 per cent), Asia (9 per cent) and the Middle East and North Africa (7 per cent). During the year, the Executive Director authorized releases from EPF totalling some $4.6 million, while advances from the United Nations Central Emergency Revolving Fund (CERF) amounted to $10 million.

UNICEF also provided support for emergencies in the Congo, Côte d'Ivoire, Eritrea, Ghana, Togo and Zaire and assisted Cambodia in strengthening its emergency response capacities. In Lebanon, the Fund moved from immediate relief assistance to a reconstruction and development programme. It concentrated its interventions in Algeria on emergency planning and preparedness and on enhancing emergency communications, security and training. Relief and survival equipment, as well as essential medical supplies, drugs, vaccines and clothing were provided to Armenia, Azerbaijan, Georgia and Tajikistan.

At its April/May session, the Executive Board[26] requested UNICEF to continue to respond to the needs of children in emergency situations, concentrate its efforts on non-food assistance, and report in 1994 on measures to improve its emergency response capacity and the use of EPF. The Fund was encouraged to support emergency programmes with built-in development dimensions for women and children giving due regard to empowerment and capacity-building. The Board urged that UNICEF country programmes link rehabilitation with sustainable development programmes, and give increased attention to disaster prevention and preparedness and vulnerability analysis. It suggested that the Fund increase evaluation of its emergency programmes and its participation in the United Nations system-wide evaluations of those activities. It stressed the need for additional protection for UNICEF staff in emergency situations. The Board confirmed that EPF funds should be used only for rapid responses to emergencies not covered by the Secretariat's Department of Humanitarian Affairs and CERF. It recommended $14 million for EPF for 1994-1995, subject to review after the deliberations on the coordination of United Nations humanitarian assistance by the Economic and Social Council and the General Assembly. (For more details on emergency assistance, see PART THREE, Chapter III.)

UNICEF programmes by region

Africa

Programme expenditures in Africa increased to $299 million in 1993—37.2 per cent of UNICEF total programme expenditures. The Fund's strategy for child survival, protection and development in Africa[27] focused on the maintenance of a high level of resource allocations to the region, strong international advocacy for the needs of African children, programme support for Africa's NPAs, the achievement of Africa's mid-decade goals, advocacy of capacity-building for sustainable development, the promotion of debt relief for the benefit of children and increased social investment, and the development of the United Nations common country strategy in African countries.

During the year, UNICEF continued its support to 23 countries in West and Central Africa,[28] 18 of which were affected by emergencies or political instability, social tension or ethnic violence. The region's infant, under-five and maternal mortality rates were among the highest in the world, caused mainly by malaria, acute respiratory infections (ARI) and diarrhoea, as well as complications during pregnancy or birth. The death toll from measles and neonatal tetanus also remained

significant, and the number of deaths from acquired immunodeficiency syndrome (AIDS) was rising rapidly. The 1991 immunization coverage rate of 50 per cent for three antigens had slipped in several countries, and only seven countries had achieved universal child immunization. The oral rehydration therapy (ORT) use rate exceeded 60 per cent. In most countries, more than 90 per cent of infants were breast-fed at birth and some 70 per cent were breast-fed until 24 months of age. Many States had developed regulations to stop the free or low-cost distribution of breast-milk substitutes at hospitals and health facilities. Some 30 hospitals in the region were declared baby-friendly, and another 170 were in the process of becoming so. Research results in Ghana suggested that a 20 per cent reduction in the under-five mortality rate was attributable to vitamin A supplementation. Among the 12 countries affected by iodine deficiency disorders (IDD), Cameroon and Nigeria took steps to increase salt iodization. Moderate to severe malnutrition rates ranged from 20 to 40 per cent in most countries, aggravated by the inadequacy of child health services. A number of countries took steps to eradicate dracunculiasis (guinea worm disease) through strengthened primary health care, safe water supply and health education. Regional illiteracy rates ranged from 29 per cent in Cape Verde to 89 per cent in the Niger, and student drop-out rates before completion of the fifth grade stood at 70 per cent, however, enrolment rates increased in the Congo, Ghana, Nigeria and Senegal. The unit cost of education was reduced in Ghana and Nigeria, and policies to produce and distribute teaching materials were implemented in Burkina Faso and Ghana.

By the end of the year, almost all countries in eastern and southern Africa[29] had produced final or substantive draft NPAs for children, and Botswana, Namibia, Uganda and the United Republic of Tanzania had begun to decentralize their NPAs to municipal, regional and district levels. A number of Governments restructured national budgets to give higher priority to social and human development sectors. Ongoing conflicts in some countries, however, fueled disease and malnutrition, causing numerous child deaths. There were growing fears of drought in parts of East Africa, including Kenya and Ethiopia. In addition, the human immunodeficiency virus/acquired immunodeficiency syndrome (HIV/AIDS) epidemic had a growing impact on the health and productive capacity of the region. It contributed to infant and maternal mortality and created problems for the breast-feeding of children born to HIV-infected mothers. It was reported that HIV transmission rates from infected mothers to their infants through breast-feeding were as high as 50 per cent. AIDS prevention and control measures were given greater prominence in UNICEF country programming and were linked to family planning issues. Studies were conducted on integrating family planning with the expanded programme on immunization (EPI) in Rwanda and on appropriate combinations of activities for different target groups in Lesotho. Some countries, however, lacked funding for immunization, and coverage rates fell as low as 13 per cent in Ethiopia. Innovative school-based programmes to promote healthy lifestyles and family health education were started in Botswana, Kenya, Uganda and Zimbabwe.

UNICEF undertook multicountry studies on household food security, drought management and nutritional intervention in emergencies and initiated studies on the impact of structural adjustment on access to basic education and on the scope for budgetary restructuring in favour of human development. It organized two inter-country workshops on the implementation of NPAs and provided training in information resource management, emergency management and the psychosocial needs of children. The Fund helped to provide consulting services in water supply and sanitation to Eritrea, Ethiopia, Madagascar and Uganda and continued to promote stronger community health-care systems through the Bamako Initiative (see PART THREE, Chapter XI). Major national, regional and global activities were organized for the Day of the African Child on 16 June.

At its April/May session, the Executive Board[30] reaffirmed UNICEF's commitment to Africa as the region of highest priority. It called on African Governments to accelerate implementation of the Plan of Action adopted by the World Summit for Children and to incorporate their NPAs in national development plans and structural adjustment programmes. The Board urged United Nations agencies and NGOs to help African countries achieve the goals of the World Summit and NPAs, and that UNICEF's country programme strategy for sustainable development involve recipient country nationals in the development, management and implementation of UNICEF policies and programmes. It also called on donor countries and institutions to reduce Africa's debt burden and for the allocation of 20 per cent of official development assistance and national budget allocations to social sector priorities by 1995.

Americas and the Caribbean

In 1993, UNICEF programme expenditures in the Americas and the Caribbean amounted to $80 million, or 10 per cent of total programme expenditures.

An estimated 192 million people were living in absolute poverty in Latin America and the Caribbean,[31] representing 46 per cent of the region's population. Some 176 million people were without safe drinking water supplies and 221 million lacked basic sanitation services. Children, more than any other group, suffered the impact of poverty. Seven million children under five years of age were malnourished, 13 million had low height for their age and about 20 million repeated grades in school. Some 1.3 million children were born annually with low weight, and protein-energy undernutrition was related to an estimated 68 per cent of deaths among children under five years of age. High-to-moderate infant and under-five mortality rates caused by the cumulative effects of malnutrition, poverty, poor quality education and poor access to health services, safe drinking water and sanitation, persisted in Bolivia, Brazil, Guatemala, Haiti, Nicaragua and Panama.

Health systems were modernized in Argentina, Chile, Colombia and the Dominican Republic, and all but six countries of the region conducted measles vaccination campaigns for children between nine months and 14 years of age. Vitamin A deficiency decreased in El Salvador, Guatemala, Honduras, Mexico and Panama, while Argentina, Chile, Costa Rica, Jamaica and Uruguay virtually eliminated commerce in non-iodized salt and six more countries were expected to do so by 1994. Programmes to eliminate iodine deficiency disorders were successfully implemented in the Andean subregion. Good ORT coverage was achieved in Chile, Costa Rica, Cuba, Jamaica, Mexico, Uruguay and Venezuela, and local production of oral rehydration salts was increasing. In Mexico, the ORT use rate stood at 84 per cent and was expected to reach 90 per cent by 1995. The fatality rate from diarrhoeal diseases fell below 1 per cent in Colombia, Ecuador, El Salvador and Peru. The Central American countries and eight others in the region were expected to end the free distribution of breast-milk substitutes at all maternity hospitals and service centres in the near future, with others to follow by 1995.

UNICEF country programmes provided a sharper focus on primary education in the region, allocating more than $1.5 million from its global funds. Increased attention was given to repeat students and drop-out rates and to improving the design of textbooks and self-instructional materials. Bilingual education was being instituted in Bolivia and Ecuador, and initiation school centres operated successfully in Honduras. The Fund expanded its support for water supply and sanitation projects in 10 countries during 1993 to include new projects in Argentina, Chile, Colombia and Cuba. The Fund assisted the Latin American Conference of Catholic Bishops with a module and several radio scripts for family education in child development.

The Executive Board[32] recommended the allocation of an additional $7 million in supplementary funds for the Special Adjustment Facility for Latin America and the Caribbean for 1994-1995 and encouraged donor countries and organizations to support the development efforts of Latin American and Caribbean countries.

Asia

UNICEF programme expenditures in Asia totalled $236 million in 1993, or 29.4 per cent of total programme expenditures. In South Asia,[33] a general increase in poverty as a result of economic reforms was aggravated by heavy floods in Nepal and Pakistan, a major outbreak of a cholera-like disease in Bangladesh, drought and a massive earthquake in India, civil strife in Sri Lanka and instability in Afghanistan. The subregion's 420 million children received less basic support in nutrition and education than any other regional group. At the same time, public policies and organized efforts were better geared in 1993 towards meeting children's needs than at any previous time. Country reports indicated that the distribution of vitamin A was moving ahead, and the guinea worm disease was under control in India and Pakistan. The gap in universal access to safe drinking water was narrowing, but the lowering of the water table due to low rainfall and extraction for irrigation posed technological and environmental challenges. In the area of family planning, it was hoped to increase contraceptive prevalence levels by 50 per cent and raise the minimum age of marriage for females to 18 years.

UNICEF-supported strategies for social development in East Asia and the Pacific[34] focused on poverty reduction, popular participation and improved access to preventive health care, basic education, water supply and sanitation. Life expectancy, infant mortality and school enrolment improved in 1993 in almost all East Asian countries, where increasing prosperity lifted many people out of absolute poverty. Nine countries—China, Democratic People's Republic of Korea, Indonesia, Malaysia, Mongolia, Philippines, Republic of Korea, Thailand, Viet Nam—with more than 90 per cent of the subregion's child population, were expected to lead in the achievement of most of the mid-decade goals. In September, 17 countries pledged support for those goals in the Manila Consensus adopted at a ministerial consultation in the Philippines.

In 1993, inadequate immunization coverage levels ranged from 33 per cent in Cambodia and the Lao People's Democratic Republic to 69 per cent in Myanmar. Universal child immunization, achieved in China, the Democratic People's Republic of Korea, Indonesia, Malaysia, the Philippines, the Republic of Korea, Singapore, Thailand and Viet Nam, was sustained. The incidence of neonatal tetanus, measles and poliomye-litis declined in many countries, and China, Indonesia, Malaysia and Thailand were close to eliminating vitamin A deficiency. Safe drinking water was accessible for more than 80 per cent of the population in the Democratic People's Republic of Korea, the Philippines, the Republic of Korea, Singapore and Thailand; and with the exception of the Philippines, all provided basic sanitation to more than 90 per cent of people. In primary education, the subregion had an average enrolment rate of 60 to 70 per cent, and completion rates were almost universal in the Democratic People's Republic of Korea, Malaysia, the Republic of Korea and Singapore. Other countries, however, continued to face drop-out and retention problems. Some 400 million people in the subregion were at risk of developing IDD, and many countries legalized salt iodization. ORT use rates were still below 40 per cent in some countries, and the complete cessation of free or low-cost supplies of breast-milk substitutes to hospitals and maternity facilities remained a challenge. AIDS remained a major problem for the Asian region as a whole, with an estimated 1 million people infected with HIV, and all countries included HIV/AIDS prevention and control measures in their medium-term plans. The main regional strategy focused on reducing high-risk behaviour through intensive information, education and communication and social mobilization.

Middle East and North Africa

In 1993, UNICEF programme expenditures in the Middle East and North Africa amounted to $119 million, which represented 14.8 per cent of total programme expenditures.

Despite a climate of uncertainty in much of the region, advocacy for children continued to advance.[35] A regional fund-raising strategy was developed to mobilize resources for NPAs, and a regional system to monitor progress towards the mid-decade goals was to become operational in early 1994. The main emphasis of social mobilization and regional networking during the year was on promoting child rights and putting children issues first on national development agendas. Regional meetings were organized to consider the refocusing of medical teaching and training on preventive medicine and on maternal and child health, and to analyse the changing functions and structure of the Arab family. A three-year initiative in early childhood development continued in Iraq, Jordan, Lebanon, Morocco, Tunisia and Turkey, and a study was conducted on the promotion of girls' education in the region. Under its regional Communication for Learning Initiative, UNICEF supported the production and dissemination of television programmes for and about children as well as training in improved production techniques, child rights and mid-decade goals for directors, producers and scriptwriters. The first meeting of a new regional network was held to develop a plan of action to meet the psycho-social needs of children affected by armed conflicts. The Fund continued to support major emergency operations in Iraq and the Sudan. It assisted flood victims in Yemen and participated in an inter-agency emergency programme in southern Lebanon, providing resources to restore health services, water supply and sanitation in public schools.

Most countries sustained universal child immunization achievements and made progress towards the elimination of neonatal tetanus and measles. Poliomyelitis-free zones were identified in the Persian Gulf and Maghreb subregions. Control of diarrhoeal diseases remained a central focus of national health activities, and control of IDD was advanced throughout the region with the adoption of a universal salt iodization strategy. Many countries initiated ARI control programmes, 10 of which were operational in 1993. National commitments were developed to end micronutrient deficiencies by 1995 and to reduce iron deficiency anaemia by the end of the decade. Most countries banned the distribution of free and low-cost infant formula and were integrating the importance of breast-feeding into the curricula of medical schools. Almost every country had hospitals that were "baby-friendly".

Central and Eastern Europe

UNICEF programme expenditures in Central and Eastern Europe and newly independent States totalled $32 million in 1993, or 4 per cent of total programme expenditure. Emergency assistance to children accounted for the majority, with $19.4 million going to emergency operations in the republics of the former Yugoslavia. Programmes of cooperation were established in Albania, Armenia, Azerbaijan, Kazakhstan, Kyrgyzstan, Romania, Tajikistan, Turkmenistan and Uzbekistan.

The transition to market-oriented economies caused profound economic and social disruptions and had severe effects on women and children.[36] Access to and the availability of health care, education, child care and other social services declined as they were restructured along market lines. There was minimal investment in the transformation of health and welfare services, which were often of low quality and lacked well-trained personnel and appropriate equipment. Infectious diseases were on the rise and outbreaks of tuberculosis, diphtheria and cholera were reported in a number of countries. The changing social order brought about a decrease in school attendance and a rise in the number of street children, as well as the frequency and gravity of juvenile crime. In addition, the region saw a dramatic increase in emer-

gencies caused by natural disasters, civil strife and ethnic, religious and political conflicts.

During 1993, UNICEF gradually established its presence in the region. Assessment missions were sent to plan activities and determine programme priorities in Armenia and Azerbaijan. National immunization plans were being developed in Turkmenistan and Uzbekistan, and supplies of vaccines and syringes were delivered to Kazakhstan, Kyrgyzstan and Uzbekistan. Three regional meetings were held to accelerate the preparation of NPAs in nine countries. Strategies to meet mid-decade goals for children were outlined for Albania, Armenia, Azerbaijan, Kazakhstan, Kyrgyzstan, Romania, Tajikistan, Turkmenistan and Uzbekistan, and a two-year project was under way in selected countries to eliminate IDD by 1995. The Fund provided an emergency delivery of vaccines, cold-chain equipment, essential drugs and other medical supplies to Belarus, the Russian Federation and Ukraine and supported the establishment of four community rehabilitation centres in those countries for children and families affected by the Chernobyl disaster. A three-year country programme was launched in Albania, focusing on the provision and promotion of basic services for women and children in health, nutrition and education; support for the implementation of the Convention on the Rights of the Child and the development of a national programme of action; and the establishment of a database of social indicators. A two-year programme in Romania emphasized family and community education for a better response to children's needs and included several projects for the training of social workers, the modernization of approaches to juvenile justice, and the integration of handicapped children into mainstream and preschool education.

UNICEF supported and participated in subregional meetings on health-care management and financing (Alma Ata, Kazakhstan), vaccine planning in Central Asia (Bishkek, Kyrgyzstan), an international training seminar on the international code of marketing of breast-milk substitutes and its implementation (Prague, Czech Republic), three international training workshops on lactation management and the Baby-Friendly Hospital Initiative (St. Petersburg, Russian Federation) and a seminar on children with disabilities in the Baltic States (Vilnius, Lithuania).

UNICEF programmes by sector

Immunization

During 1993, immunization coverage was maintained at about 80 per cent globally. One third of the developing countries showed improved performance and another third a decrease in coverage. UNICEF supported the development of infrastructure and institutions to extend routine services to all children, and encouraged countries to reduce their immunization drop-out rates. Countries with high coverage levels held national immunization days as a means of eradicating polio, eliminating neonatal tetanus and controlling measles. Immunization days were especially successful in China, the Philippines and Viet Nam. The Fund continued its close collaboration with WHO and other partners to strengthen the capacity of several countries for timely and effective disease surveillance.

The provision of adequate vaccines to meet programme needs was a special priority during the year, following a significant increase in vaccine prices. An analysis of the global vaccine situation was prepared under the Children's Vaccine Initiative, which was launched in 1991 by WHO, UNICEF, the United Nations Development Programme (UNDP), the World Bank and the Rockefeller Foundation. Expert teams assessed vaccine quality control and production capacity in Bangladesh, China, Egypt, India, Indonesia, Mexico, Pakistan, the Philippines and Viet Nam. The Vaccine Independence Initiative to help countries procure vaccines through UNICEF began in Morocco and the Philippines, and discussions were under way in 10 other countries. The strategic plan for vaccine research, finalized in 1993, gave priority to the development of multi-antigen vaccines.

Maternal and child health and family planning

UNICEF strengthened its efforts in the areas of maternal and child health, safe motherhood, child spacing and family planning, and continued to support the Safe Motherhood Initiative organized jointly with WHO, UNDP, the World Bank and the Population Council. UNICEF also co-sponsored the Sexual and Reproductive Health Technical Support Group, an interregional effort to provide technical support for strategic programming countries in each region. At the country level, it continued to advocate improved prenatal care and was the largest supplier of iron and folic acid for pregnant women. It provided material and training support to develop referral strategies and improved access to emergency obstetric care in India, prepared programming guidelines for safe motherhood and expanded its efforts to reduce maternal mortality by 50 per cent by the year 2000.

The Executive Board urged[37] the Executive Director to promote sexual and reproductive health as part of UNICEF support for maternal and child health and family planning, paying particular attention to the needs of young people and education in responsible sexual behaviour. It urged him to include support for family planning in collaboration with the Fund's partners and invited United Nations agencies to collaborate with UNICEF child-survival and development efforts as part of their family planning activities. The Executive Director was requested to monitor collaboration in that field and to prepare the relevant operational guidelines.

Control of diarrhoeal diseases

As 3 million children continued to die every year from diarrhoea and dehydration, UNICEF focused its efforts on increasing the use of ORT in combination with continued feeding of the child. In October, a 15-month global programme for increased use of ORT was launched in Mexico, where the mortality rate from diarrhoea had been successfully reduced by 50 per cent in 11 states over a period of 18 months. Other preventive activities promoted with ORT included breast-feeding and hand-washing. Several countries developed comprehensive plans to strengthen case management at district health facilities and involve the commercial sector in the production and promotion of oral rehydration salts. Immunization coverage surveys were modified to include questions on diarrhoeal diseases and facilitate their monitoring.

Acute respiratory infections

ARI, especially pneumonia, remained the single most important cause of child mortality in the world, causing the deaths of 3.6 million children under five years of age every year. Some 19 countries accounted for 80 per cent of under-five mortality cases from pneumonia. While more than two thirds of developing countries had operational plans to control ARI, only 12 per cent carried out national activities to control pneumonia. The strategy to reduce deaths from pneumonia focused on the expansion of services and public information on correct case management. Most countries initiated or strengthened operational strategies to promote the involvement of NGOs, increase training, and make drugs for pneumonia management more widely available. Drug cooperatives were expanded in Indonesia and Thailand, and ethnographic surveys conducted in several countries with a view to adapting programmes to local conditions.

Following efforts to decentralize health care and planning in many countries, guidelines were developed to implement ARI control programmes at the district level. A questionnaire on ARI treatment and referral services was designed for use in household surveys, and questions on maternal knowledge related to ARI and pneumonia were included in immunization coverage surveys. Treatment charts were finalized under the UNICEF/WHO "sick child initiative" for the integrated treatment of diarrhoea, measles, malnutrition, pneumonia and malaria.

Nutrition

A review of NPAs of 79 developing countries indicated that almost all had targets to reduce the incidence of malnutrition, low birth weight and micronutrient deficiencies in accordance with goals set by the World Summit for Children. Key components of national nutrition strategies included the promotion of improved feeding practices and primary health care, micronutrient supplementation or fortification, community participation and nutrition education and surveillance. In 1993, the International Conference on Nutrition identified household food security, access to basic health services and adequate care of children and women as necessary conditions for nutritional well-being.

By 1993, a number of countries had adopted basic elements of UNICEF's new, development-oriented nutrition strategy, and many others were reorienting their nutrition strategies in the same direction. However, 184 million children in the world were malnourished, including 101 million in South Asia alone. The Fund supported country case studies in Brazil, India, Indonesia, Thailand, the United Republic of Tanzania and Zimbabwe to identify critical success factors in improving nutrition, and provided assistance to implement the new strategy in Bangladesh, Bolivia, Ghana, India, Pakistan, the United Republic of Tanzania and Viet Nam. UNICEF also supported activities to improve women's access to resources in situations of food insecurity. It participated in credit and education programmes which made significant gains for women in West Africa. A World Alliance for Nutrition and Human Rights, created in 1992 by UNICEF and the Norwegian Institute of Human Rights, held a special workshop on nutrition, ethics and human rights (New York, January, 1993) and set up task forces to monitor children's nutrition rights and the use of food as a weapon of war or for political reasons.

Representatives from 23 countries with major IDD problems meeting in New York in September, reviewed UNICEF strategy for IDD elimination and endorsed the goal of universal salt iodization. During 1993, the UNICEF consultants made 37 country visits to identify IDD problems and provide technical support for salt iodization. Additional assistance was extended through the International Consultative Council on IDD and the Programme against Micronutrient Malnutrition. In October, Central American countries made a commitment to reintroduce salt iodization and formed a Central American Federation of Salt Producers. Commitments for universal salt iodization were also made by China, Bangladesh, India and the Philippines. Most salt was adequately iodized in South America and Eastern Europe, and rapid progress in salt iodization was reported in several African countries. UNICEF continued to develop its strategy for the elimination of vitamin A deficiency, focusing on children under 24 months of age and linking vitamin A supplementation with food fortification or dietary diversification. UNICEF supported meetings to review the implementation of national strategies in Brazil and Ghana, participated in a study on ways to improve the effectiveness of iron supplementation programmes and organized a consultation on the nutritional importance of zinc in developing countries (Brisbane, Australia). The consultation concluded that zinc deficiency compounded poor growth in children and hindered the absorption of vitamin A.

Breast-feeding

The Baby-Friendly Hospital Initiative (BFHI) remained the major UNICEF strategy to attain, by the year 2000, exclusive breast-feeding of all infants from birth until four to six months of age. In 1993, only 25 per cent of the world's infants were breast-fed exclusively for the first four months but the number of countries implementing the Initiative increased from 90 to 171, and the number of target hospitals and maternity facilities in developing countries grew to 24,000. Of these, 924 were designated as "baby-friendly". Action was taken in 70 countries to end the free or low-cost supply of breast-milk substitutes. However, the practice continued despite government bans in 20 countries. Breast-milk substitutes and bottle-feeding were also widespread in industrialized countries, especially in North America and Japan, where government commitments to end their distribution to all hospitals and maternity facilities by 1994 were lacking.

National breast-feeding training and resource centres were identified and supported in each region. UNICEF participated in a project to review medical textbooks worldwide and replace outdated information on infant feeding, and it co-sponsored four meetings to mobilize the support of international NGOs and organizations of health professionals to develop a common approach to the implementation of BFHI. It helped to prepare a number of exhibits to promote breast-feeding and the Initiative and supported the *BFHI News* monthly newsletter.

The Executive Board[38] called on all manufacturers and distributors of milk substitutes to comply with all government prohibitions on the free and low-cost distribution of their products and urged Governments in industrialized countries to take appropriate action to end such distribution by June 1994. It requested the Executive Director to support Member States in implementing the Initiative.

Dracunculiasis (guinea worm disease) eradication

In 1993, dracunculiasis was endemic in 18 countries of Africa and Asia, with nine of them—Benin,

Burkina Faso, Côte d'Ivoire, Ghana, Mali, Niger, Nigeria, Sudan and Uganda—accounting for more than 90 per cent of some 170,000 known cases in 21,000 affected villages. Other seriously affected countries included Chad, Ethiopia, Kenya, Mauritania, Senegal and Togo, while Cameroon, India and Pakistan had nearly eliminated the disease. Programmes established under UNICEF's interregional programme for dracunculiasis eradication had helped reduce the number of new cases by about 50 per cent a year through surveillance and control activities in almost all affected countries. The programme also covered a village-based reporting system in six countries, research in health education, safe water supply for small and remote villages, the mapping of endemic areas, monitoring of specific interventions, and support for decision-making.

Water supply and sanitation

During the year, the Fund helped more than 90 developing countries to achieve water supply and sanitation goals for the mid-decade and the year 2000. While most countries in Asia and Latin America were expected to attain the targets for water supply coverage, efforts were needed to boost environmental sanitation and hygiene education in Asia and especially in Bangladesh, China, India, Indonesia, Nepal, Pakistan, the Philippines and Viet Nam. In Africa, UNICEF assisted eight countries with better performance rates (Botswana, Burkina Faso, Comoros, Côte d'Ivoire, Gabon, the Gambia, Swaziland and Zimbabwe) to achieve universal coverage, and mobilized additional financial resources for countries with unserved populations in excess of 10 million.

Changes in global and country programme strategies in 1993 shifted the emphasis from service delivery to the health and socio-economic benefits of water supply and sanitation programmes, and stronger links to environmental protection. A UNICEF-sponsored workshop of international experts concluded that increased attention should be given to sector plans and strategies for all programmes, capacity-building for hygiene education at district and community levels, service delivery, the empowerment of communities, and linkages with other strategic sectors such as health, education and the environment. UNICEF supported innovative approaches to community management of rural and urban water supply and sanitation services in Bangladesh, Benin, Guinea, Honduras, India, Uganda and Viet Nam.

Basic education

In 1993, some 130 million children globally had no access to schools and nearly 1 billion adults were illiterate. Substantial additional external resources were needed, especially for low-income countries in sub-Saharan Africa and South Asia, to achieve the goal of universal primary education. UNICEF concentrated its efforts on analysing the primary education situation in individual countries, formulating action plans for enrolment and retention, upgrading the planning capacities of education ministries, reviewing school curricula, producing textbooks and teaching aids, training school principals and teachers, and strengthening the participation of parents and communities in school management and monitoring. UNICEF co-sponsored an Education-For-All Summit of nine highly populated countries (Bangladesh, Brazil, China, Egypt, India, Indonesia, Mexico, Nigeria, Pakistan) in New Delhi, India, from 12 to 16 December. The Summit adopted the Delhi Declaration and Framework for Action which pledged to find a place, teachers and learning materials for every child, to give higher priority in resource allocation to basic education, and to systematically monitor enrolment, attendance, completion and learning achievement. The Fund supported a review of primary education in Bhutan, initiated community-managed village schools in Egypt and promoted village education committees in India. Its assistance to multi-grade schools in Bhutan, Colombia and Viet Nam helped to improve enrolment and reduce the drop-out rate of ethnic minority children. Steps were taken in Nicaragua to reduce drop-out rates in the first two grades.

In Africa, UNICEF organized primary education policy seminars for West and Central Africa (Burkina Faso) and for eastern and southern Africa (Uganda), as well as a regional workshop on comprehensive education analysis for eastern and southern Africa (Nairobi, Kenya). It encouraged Governments to re-examine their budgetary allocations to basic education and find ways to reduce unit cost while improving access and quality. Education cost studies were being prepared in Bhutan, Burkina Faso, Myanmar, Uganda and Viet Nam. UNICEF provided financial support to a research and capacity-building initiative for female education in Africa, the Pan-African Conference on the Education of Girls and education projects for girls in Algeria, Bangladesh, Benin, Burkina Faso, Cameroon, the Central African Republic, the Gambia, the Niger, Senegal and Zambia. As part of the Fund's support for non-formal education, technical and financial assistance for literacy programmes was extended to Bolivia, Botswana, Egypt, Guinea-Bissau, Indonesia, Mozambique, Senegal and South Africa.

UNICEF efforts in early childhood development centred on an integrated approach to the growth and development needs of young children, and included support for health care, nutrition, basic education and women's programmes. A policy review of early child development in 1993 served as a reference for five training workshops and several international forums. Child development initiatives were launched in Bolivia, Costa Rica, Mali, Niger, the Philippines and Thailand, while six countries in the Middle East and North Africa began work on parenting skills and learning through innovative media approaches. To help countries develop tools to assess learning achievement, UNICEF worked with the United Nations Educational, Scientific and Cultural Organization (UNESCO) to implement monitoring projects in China, Jordan, Mali, Mauritius and Morocco and embarked on a project to compile and analyse monitoring indicators in five African countries. A regional seminar was held in February (Dhaka, Bangladesh) on the adaptation of a basic competence assessment methodology.

Urban services

During the year, the Fund responded to some 150 requests for information, distributed about 700 publications and produced several case-studies on experiences with urban services programmes.

The Executive Board[39] endorsed a two-pronged approach to problems of the urban poor, combining an urban focus in all sectoral programmes with a revitalized strategy to deliver urban social services and promote employment. This approach had four main thrusts: the achievement of national decade goals for children and a balanced approach to rural and urban poverty reduction; action on primary environmental care; attention to children in especially difficult circumstances; and application of the concept of "urban development with a human face". The Board urged UNICEF to continue to address the needs of poor urban children and to ensure more effective action on behalf of street children. It called on concerned partners to consider the views of children and adolescents in decision-making and in the evaluation of programmes designed to reach them, and requested the Executive Director to report on the subject biennially.

Children in especially difficult circumstances

UNICEF continued to work closely with the Committee on the Rights of the Child on the issue of child labour and studied the situation in several countries, including Algeria, Bolivia, Niger and Pakistan (for more details on child labour, see PART THREE, Chapter X). The Fund supported children affected by armed conflicts, including unaccompanied children in Eritrea where 50 per cent of returnees were children. In Chad, where 40 per cent of households were separated from children because of conflicts, UNICEF provided treatment and training and

held an assessment workshop in November. Street children were another cause of concern in many countries. They were the subject of surveys in four Ethiopian towns, a seminar on street and working children in Florence, Italy, and meetings on street children in Rio de Janeiro, Brazil. The Fund also completed global reviews of education and health issues affecting working children and of education and adolescent health.

UNICEF finances

In 1993, UNICEF income totalled $866 million, $72 million less than in 1992. Some $539 million was from Government contributions, $160 million from non-governmental sources, $95 million from greeting card and related operations, $49 million from the United Nations system and $45 million from other sources, less $22 million for translation adjustment. Of the total, $509 million went to general resources, $187 million to supplementary funds and $170 million to emergency supplementary funds.

Expenditures totalled $997 million, $65 million more than in 1992. Of the total, $804 million was for programme expenditures, $180 million for administrative expenditures and $13 million for write-offs and other charges.

Budget appropriations

At its April/May session, the Executive Board approved[40] a total of $270,920,000 for general resources funding and $371,167,000 for supplementary funding for programme cooperation. For each region, the respective amounts were: Africa, $82,634,000 and $97,981,000; the Americas and the Caribbean, $13,246,000 and $103,225,000; Asia, $121,540,000 and $107,491,000; Central and Eastern Europe and newly independent States, $18,500,000 and $29,345,000; the Middle East and North Africa, $35,000,000 and $33,125,000; and $179,198 to cover overexpenditure.

The Board approved[41] the general resources and supplementary funds programme budget estimates for 1992-1993 in the respective amounts of $142.6 million and $181.3 million, and for 1994-1995 in the amounts of $140.6 million and $164 million. It also approved the supplementary funds programme plan estimates for 1996-1997, totalling $160.7 million. The Executive Director was authorized to enter into additional commitments to finance existing or new activities within each fund in an amount not exceeding 10 per cent from each activity.

The Board further approved[42] the administrative and programme support budget and related income for 1992-1993 in the respective amounts of $386,954,307 and $35,000,000, and for 1994-1995 in the amounts of $431,363,380 and $26,000,000. Also approved[43] was the medium-term plan[44] as a framework of projections for 1993-1996, including the preparation of up to $330 million in programme expenditures from general resources to be submitted to the Board in 1994.

In other action, the Board approved[45] the level of the reserve for procurement services at $2 million and noted the financial reports for 1992 and the 1990-1991 biennium, as well as related reports of the United Nations Board of Auditors and the Advisory Committee on Administrative and Budgetary Questions (ACABQ) and a review of expenditures and commitments for completed projects financed by supplementary funds.

It authorized[46] the Executive Director to close the two special accounts for the World Summit for Children and transfer the remaining balance of $122,534 to general resources.

Organizational questions

To improve its procedures and rationalize the use of time at its regular sessions, the Executive Board[47] adopted recommendations concerning its documentation, agenda, resolutions and consideration of country programme recommendations. The Board decided[48] that an independent review of the administrative and management structures at UNICEF headquarters should be carried out by the end of 1994.

Greeting Card Operation

During its 1992-1993 season,[49] the contribution of the Greeting Card Operation (GCO) to UNICEF general resources was estimated at $91 million, a decrease against the previous year due to unfavourable exchange rates. The total number of cards sold, however, was projected at 156.5 million, 6.4 million more than the year before. In February 1993, the first global greeting card workshop for UNICEF national committees was held at Geneva.

The Executive Board approved[50] the greeting card and related operations work plan for the fiscal year 1 May 1993 to 30 April 1994, including budgeted expenditures of $69.2 million, and noted that GCO net proceeds for that season were budgeted at $169.8 million. It also noted[51] the GCO financial report and accounts for the year ended 30 April 1992 and the GCO provisional report for the period 1 May 1992–30 April 1993.

Headquarters office accommodation

The Executive Board requested[52] the Executive Director to obtain from the United Nations Development Corporation, New York City and from the City of New Rochelle by 30 June 1993 firm offers for guaranteed space availability for a minimum of 40,000 square feet starting 1 August 1995, and to analyse and submit them to ACABQ by 31 July. It also decided to consider the matter at a special two-day session later in the year.

At its special session, held in October, the Board approved[53] the offer made by the New York City Economic Development Corporation/United Nations Development Corporation and authorized the Executive Director to negotiate and execute a lease/purchase agreement in respect of UNICEF headquarters and to continue negotiations concerning additional space required by the Fund. It decided to review future levels of UNICEF headquarters staff by 15 October 1994 and requested the Executive Director to review the location of the greeting card and related operations in New York.

Inter-agency cooperation

At its twenty-ninth session,[15] the UNICEF/WHO Joint Committee on Health Policy reviewed WHO health policies and UNICEF decisions; district health systems; implementation of the "baby-friendly" hospital initiative; follow-up to the World Summit for Children, including progress made in the areas of health indicators and monitoring methods; maternal health and newborn care; vaccine needs; and control of diarrhoeal diseases and ARI. The Committee also considered reports on collaborative activities in the prevention and control of AIDS in women and children, healthy lifestyles for youth, malaria control and health education, including hygiene education with reference to community water supply and sanitation.

The Executive Board endorsed[16] the Committee's recommendations for further cooperation in those areas.

REFERENCES

[1]E/ICEF/1994/2 (Part II & Part II/Add.1). [2]E/1993/34. [3]E/ICEF/1993/17. [4]E/ICEF/1993/15. [5]E/1993/34 (dec. 1993/5). [6]Ibid. (dec. 1993/6). [7]E/ICEF/1993/CRP.7. [8]E/1993/34 (dec. 1993/3). [9]E/ICEF/1993/12. [10]A/45/625. [11]E/1993/34 (dec. 1993/12). [12]YUN 1992, p. 881, GA dec. 47/447, 22 Dec. 1992. [13]A/48/321. [14]GA res. 44/25, annex, 20 Nov. 1989. [15]E/ICEF/1993/L.11. [16]E/1993/34 (dec. 1993/16). [17]E/1993/34 (dec. 1993/13). [18]CRC/C/16. [19]CRC/C/20. [20]E/ICEF/1993/L.2. [21]YUN 1992, p. 670. [22]E/1993/34 (dec. 1993/14). [23]YUN 1966, p. 385. [24]E/1993/34 (dec. 1993/1). [25]E/ICEF/1994/11. [26]E/1993/34 (dec. 1993/7). [27]E/ICEF/1993/L.4. [28]E/ICEF/1994/6. [29]E/ICEF/1994/5. [30]E/1993/34 (dec. 1993/4). [31]E/ICEF/1994/7. [32]E/1993/34 (dec. 1993/10). [33]E/ICEF/1994/9. [34]E/ICEF/1994/8. [35]E/ICEF/1994/10. [36]E/ICEF/1994/4. [37]E/1993/34 (dec. 1993/11). [38]Ibid. (dec. 1993/15). [39]Ibid. (dec. 1993/8). [40]Ibid. (dec. 1993/9). [41]Ibid. (dec. 1993/21). [42]Ibid. (dec. 1993/20). [43]Ibid. (dec. 1993/17). [44]E/ICEF/1993/3. [45]E/1993/34 (dec. 1993/19). [46]Ibid. (dec. 1993/18). [47]Ibid. (dec. 1993/2). [48]Ibid. (dec. 1993/23). [49]E/ICEF/1994/AB/L.4. [50]E/1993/34 (dec. 1993/24). [51]Ibid. (dec. 1993/25). [52]Ibid. (dec. 1993/22). [53]E/ICEF/1993/17 (dec. 1993/26).

Youth

Programme planning, implementation and follow-up in the field of youth, in accordance with the guidelines adopted during the International Youth Year (IYY) in 1985,[1] were considered in 1993 by the Commission for Social Development at its thirty-third session (Vienna, 8-17 February).[2] Pursuant to a 1991 Economic and Social Council resolution,[3] the Commission established an open-ended ad hoc working group to prepare a draft calendar of activities marking the tenth anniversary of IYY and a draft world youth programme of action towards the year 2000 and beyond.

The working group had before it a report on the subject, submitted by the Secretary-General.[4] The report suggested dividing anniversary activities into a preparatory phase, covering the period 1993-1994 and aimed at raising awareness and initiating substantive action in the field of youth, and an observance phase during 1995, geared towards developing capacities for youth policy programming and implementation. It also provided a tentative framework for the world youth programme in six priority areas—education, employment, hunger, health, environment, drug abuse—and proposed means for implementing the programme.

The working group[5] pointed out that 1995 was an appropriate time to evaluate the objectives of IYY and to elaborate relevant youth policies, programmes and strategies for adoption by the General Assembly, and it suggested linking anniversary activities with other major international events. It amended the draft world youth programme of action to include juvenile delinquency and leisure-time activities among themes covered. It recommended that the focus on hunger should also include poverty, and that the programme should cover all other themes in the field of youth identified by the Assembly in 1990,[6] such as communication, housing, culture and illiteracy.

The group also decided to include a United Nations statement of intent on youth, affirming Member States' commitment to work together to solve the problems facing youth and their belief that every State should provide its young people with opportunities to participate fully in society and its decision-making processes. States should provide gainful employment, protect young people from harmful drugs and the effects of addiction, integrate youth work into national development plans, ensure that youth policies were consistent with international human rights instruments, foster mutual respect and understanding among youth of different racial and religious backgrounds, promote education and youth exchanges, actively engage young people in environmental education and action, better focus population activities on youth, foster equal access for girls and young women to education and employment and ensure public access to data on the situation and needs of young people.

The amended calendar of IYY anniversary activities was annexed to the resolution recommended by the Commission for Social Development to the Economic and Social Council for adoption.

ECONOMIC AND SOCIAL COUNCIL ACTION

On 27 July, the Economic and Social Council, on the recommendation of its Social Committee, adopted **resolution 1993/24** without vote.

Tenth anniversary of International Youth Year and draft world programme of action for youth towards the year 2000 and beyond

The Economic and Social Council,

Considering all relevant General Assembly resolutions, particularly resolutions 40/14 of 18 November 1985, 45/103 of 14 December 1990 and 47/85 of 16 December 1992,

Recognizing the need to improve the situation of youth through concerted action aimed at more effective programming of youth activities and the implementation and evaluation of those programmes at all levels within the framework of the tenth anniversary of International Youth Year: Participation, Development, Peace, in 1995,

Noting the interlinkages between the fiftieth anniversary of the Charter of the United Nations, the World Summit for Social Development, to be held at Copenhagen on 11 and 12 March 1995, and the tenth anniversary of International Youth Year,

Having considered the report of the Secretary-General containing the draft calendar of activities to mark the tenth anniversary of International Youth Year and the draft world programme of action for youth to the year 2000 and beyond,

1. *Endorses* the calendar of activities to mark the tenth anniversary of International Youth Year: Participation, Development, Peace, as set out in the annex to the present resolution;

2. *Requests* the Secretary-General to continue refining the draft world programme of action for youth to the year 2000 and beyond in accordance with proposals to be submitted by Member States, specialized agencies and other bodies within the United Nations system, and concerned intergovernmental and non-governmental organizations, including non-governmental youth organizations, particularly in the light of the deliberations and suggestions of the Commission for Social Development;

3. *Also requests* the Secretary-General to seek the views of Member States on the United Nations statement of intent on youth: problems and potentials, which could become an integral part of the world programme of action for youth;

4. *Urges* Member States, national coordinating committees and non-governmental organizations to prepare national programmes of action for the period 1993-1995 in the context of the preparations for the tenth anniversary of International Youth Year, encompassing provisions for substantive, promotional and informational activities directed towards youth, the authorities and the community at all levels, and to inform the Secretary-General of the progress achieved;

5. *Urges* all specialized agencies and United Nations bodies concerned, including the regional commissions,

to incorporate appropriate activities within their work programmes for the period 1993-1995 in commemoration of the tenth anniversary of International Youth Year;

6. *Invites* the Department of Public Information of the Secretariat to develop and implement a specific international programme of informational activities to be carried out mainly at the national level to ensure that the potential value of the observance of the tenth anniversary of International Youth Year is fully understood;

7. *Urges* the Secretary-General to undertake the necessary measures to ensure that the United Nations Youth Fund remains an important operational mechanism of the subprogramme of the medium-term plan for the period 1992-1997, entitled "Integration of youth in development";

8. *Stresses* the importance of considering the issues of integration and participation of youth in society as part of the preparatory process and final agenda for the World Summit for Social Development, to be held at Copenhagen in 1995;

9. *Calls upon* the Secretary-General to give all possible support, through the redeployment of existing resources, as well as through extrabudgetary resources, to the subprogramme of the medium-term plan for the period 1992-1997, entitled "Integration of youth in development";

10. *Calls upon* the Commission for Social Development to give priority attention at its thirty-fourth session to the refinement of the draft world programme of action for youth towards the year 2000 and beyond, and to establish an ad hoc informal open-ended working group on youth for this purpose, with a view to formulating a final draft to be submitted to the Economic and Social Council in 1995 and to the General Assembly at its fiftieth session.

ANNEX
Calendar of activities to mark the tenth anniversary of International Youth Year: Participation, Development, Peace

I. Preparatory phase (1993-1994)

A. *Activities at the national level*

Preparations could be facilitated by the establishment of a coordinating or preparatory committee at the highest level of government, which would include youth representatives in its membership. Such a body would undertake some or all of the following tasks:

(a) To develop a detailed programme based on an appropriate analysis of the situation of youth;

(b) To review existing youth-related national legislation, policies, plans and programmes, including administrative structures and services for youth;

(c) To collate and disseminate existing data and research on youth-related issues;

(d) To promote action-oriented research and studies by academic institutions, research institutes and youth organizations;

(e) To launch public information campaigns, using the mass media and other information networks, to promote awareness of youth issues and reinforce a positive attitude towards young people;

(f) To raise awareness of particular youth issues by promoting "creative" events, such as drawing, photographic, art and essay competitions, the results of which could be published in 1995;

(g) To promote communication between government and youth groups, and between generations in different formal and informal settings, thereby encouraging the active involvement of young people in the preparation and commemoration of the tenth anniversary and in the shaping of youth policies.

B. *Activities at the international and regional levels*

Non-governmental organizations

1. International and regional non-governmental organizations will clearly have an important role and might thus wish to consider how best they could reorient some of their activities to mark the tenth anniversary. Some of the possibilities for action are:

(a) To carry out or support independent surveys on the situation of young people, support research and facilitate publication or dissemination of research findings, especially where other channels of distribution are difficult to access;

(b) To conduct independent surveys and assessments of existing youth policies, plans and programmes, identifying current and emerging youth issues;

(c) To facilitate the publishing and exchange of information on youth activities, using their publications and information networks;

(d) To promote cultural and educational exhibits and radio and television programmes, highlighting international cooperation on youth issues and concerns;

(e) To encourage their regional and national offices to assist Governments in activities related to the anniversary of International Youth Year.

United Nations agencies and bodies

2. United Nations agencies and bodies may be expected to provide appropriate support to the activities marking the tenth anniversary of International Youth Year, at the level and in a manner corresponding to their respective mandates. In planning their programmes for the period 1993-1994, they might wish to give special consideration to how these could be made to support the activities marking the anniversary. Various possibilities might be considered, as listed below:

(a) To link to the preparations for the tenth anniversary activities pertaining to other major international events, such as the International Year of the Family (1994), the International Conference on Population and Development (1994), the Fourth World Conference on Women: Action for Equality, Development and Peace (1995), the celebration of the fiftieth anniversary of the Charter of the United Nations (1995), the World Summit for Social Development (1995) and the World Conference on Human Rights (1993);

(b) To support Governments in the strengthening of their national youth policies, programmes and strategies;

(c) To organize meetings, seminars, conferences and workshops on specific topics of particular relevance to youth;

(d) To give special attention to youth issues in 1995 in their regular bulletins, journals and newsletters;

(e) To mobilize the substantive resources of their regional and national offices with a view to assisting non-governmental organizations in their preparatory activities.

II. Observance phase (1995)

A. *Activities at the national level*

It is not yet possible to decide the most appropriate manner in which the tenth anniversary of International

Youth Year might be marked in different countries, at different levels of Government and by the different non-governmental entities concerned. The type of activities that should be suggested for implementation in 1995 will depend on the extent to which plans drawn up for the preparatory phase in 1993 and 1994 are finalized and implemented. At this stage, Governments, in cooperation with national youth organizations, might be requested to plan ahead, so that the tenth anniversary could provide an opportunity to initiate substantive measures in favour of youth, taking advantage of the publicity generated by the anniversary and by events such as the following:

(a) Conferences, workshops and debates on youth-related issues, in which prominent persons in the community would take part, for instance, political leaders and scholars, and especially youth leaders;

(b) Statements and appearances by prominent political personalities including, where possible, heads of Government, highlighting the positive contributions young people make to society;

(c) Issuance of commemorative stamps, posters and other souvenir materials;

(d) Designation of a national youth day, week or month during which youth issues could be highlighted in a variety of national events, by means of a special focus on youth, for example, in book fairs and other cultural events or sports competitions;

(e) Special events organized by young people to draw attention to days designated for commemoration by the United Nations and other events widely observed, for example, International Women's Day (8 March), World Health Day (7 April), World Environment Day (5 June), International Day against Drug Abuse and Illicit Trafficking (26 June), World Population Day (11 July), International Day of Peace (third Tuesday in September), United Nations Day (24 October), World AIDS Day (1 December), International Day of Disabled Persons (3 December) and Human Rights Day (10 December).

B. *Activities at the international level*

The General Assembly decided, in its resolution 45/103 of 14 December 1990, to devote a plenary meeting at its fiftieth session to youth questions, as 1995 would mark the tenth anniversary of International Youth Year, which will also be the fiftieth anniversary of the Charter of the United Nations. The Assembly may wish to mark these events in some special manner, for example:

(a) By agreeing to a United Nations statement of intent on youth in conjunction with the adoption in 1995 of a world youth programme of action for youth;

(b) By designating, in 1995, an international youth day.

Economic and Social Council resolution 1993/24

27 July 1993   Meeting 43   Adopted without vote

Approved by Social Committee (E/1993/106) without vote, 14 July (meeting 10); draft by Commission for Social Development (E/1993/24); agenda item 20.

REFERENCES
[1]YUN 1985, p. 978. [2]E/1993/24. [3]YUN 1991, p. 696, ESC res. 1991/11, 30 May 1991. [4]E/CN.5/1993/10. [5]E/CN.5/1993/L.11. [6]GA res. 45/103, 14 Dec. 1990.

Ageing persons

In response to a 1992 General Assembly request,[1] the Commission for Social Development, at its February 1993 session,[2] established an ad hoc informal working group for the third review and appraisal of the implementation of the 1982 International Plan of Action on Ageing.[3]

The working group had before it a report on the Plan, submitted by the Secretary-General.[4] The report stated that the third review was taking place in the midst of a demographic revolution, characterized by unprecedented growth in the numbers and proportions of elderly people in society. It noted that the world's elderly population had grown by 100 million since 1982 and was expected to increase by another 125 million by 2001, with some 70 per cent of that increase in developing countries. The Secretary-General reviewed global initiatives to meet the challenges of ageing as well as national and international activities to implement the Plan of Action in the areas of infrastructure, ageing and development, health and nutrition, housing and environment, family, social welfare, income security and employment and education. The report identified the priorities for international cooperation in ageing as: the exchange of knowledge and experience, research and policy analysis on the implications of ageing for development, training of health-care providers for the elderly, data collection and processing, the establishment of income-generating projects for the elderly, health-care services, formulation and evaluation of policies and programmes on ageing, training of indigenous scholars on ageing, and the establishment of volunteer programmes and educational and training projects for the elderly.

In conclusion, the Secretary-General summarized global targets on ageing for the year 2001, adopted by the Assembly in 1992,[1] and provided a set of corresponding national targets in the priority areas developed in consultation with Governments, United Nations bodies and NGOs.

Acting on the report, the Commission for Social Development recommended a resolution for adoption by the Economic and Social Council.

Coordination in the UN system

The fifth Inter-agency Meeting on Ageing (Vienna, 18-19 February)[5] reviewed United Nations activities in that area, examined implications of the third review of the Plan of Action, discussed system-wide programmes of cooperation for reaching selected targets on ageing by 2001 and identified mechanisms for strengthening the Trust Fund for Ageing. The meeting recommended that United Nations bodies and agencies identify areas for future international cooperation on ageing in the areas set out in the Secretary-General's report (see above), publicize the targets on ageing and incorporate them into their work programmes, and establish a monitoring and evaluation mechanism. It also recommended that the regional commissions assist Member States in setting regional targets and urged UNDP and the United Nations Population Fund (UNFPA) to include a component on ageing in their country-programming exercises. United Nations bodies were invited to cooperate in organizing an expert group meeting to propose indicators for measuring progress in reaching the global targets on ageing, called for by the Assembly in 1992.[1] Other recommendations dealt with maintaining and strengthening the inter-agency consultative mechanism during the United Nations restructuring process, preparations for the International Year of Older Persons (1999), the mobilization of funds for programmes on ageing, and electronic mail as a cost-effective means of inter-agency communication.

ECONOMIC AND SOCIAL COUNCIL ACTION

On 27 July, the Economic and Social Council, on the recommendation of its Social Committee, adopted **resolution 1993/22** without vote.

Implementation of the International Plan of Action on Ageing

The Economic and Social Council,

Mindful that the ageing of populations presents all countries with the major challenge of identifying and supporting new opportunities for older persons and their potential benefits for society,

Convinced that the United Nations remains the intergovernmental organization best equipped to provide leadership to the international community in dealing with the challenges presented by the ageing of individuals and populations,

Noting with satisfaction the deliberations of the International Conference on Ageing convened on 15 and 16 October 1992 by the General Assembly at its forty-seventh session, on the occasion of the tenth anniversary of the adoption of the International Plan of Action on Ageing by the World Assembly on Ageing,

Recalling General Assembly resolution 46/91 of 16 December 1991, by which the Assembly adopted the United Nations Principles for Older Persons, based on the Plan of Action,

Recalling that the States gathered in the World Assembly on Ageing reaffirmed their belief that the fundamental and inalienable rights enshrined in the Universal Declaration of Human Rights should apply fully and undiminishedly to the ageing,

Taking note of General Assembly resolution 47/5 of 16 October 1992, by which the Assembly adopted the Proclamation on Ageing and decided to observe the year 1999 as the International Year of Older Persons,

Taking note also of General Assembly resolution 47/86 of 16 December 1992, in which the Assembly adopted the global targets on ageing for the year 2001, as a prac-

tical strategy on ageing, and urged Member States to support that strategy and to consult the guide for setting national targets on ageing,

Aware of the expanded activities and initiatives of the United Nations programme on ageing,

Noting that, in General Assembly resolution 47/86, the Assembly requested the Commission for Social Development to convene an ad hoc informal working group at its thirty-third session for the third review and appraisal of the implementation of the International Plan of Action on Ageing and for proposing measures in support of setting national targets on ageing in the decade ahead,

Acknowledging with satisfaction the active participation of Member States, specialized agencies and bodies of the United Nations system and interested non-governmental organizations in the third review and appraisal of the implementation of the Plan of Action,

Taking note of the conclusions of the third review and appraisal of the implementation of the Plan of Action, which indicate that although some progress has been made in implementing the Plan of Action, much remains to be done to implement its recommendations fully, particularly in developing countries,

1. *Notes with appreciation* the innovative and forward-looking approach employed in the preparation of the report of the Secretary-General on the third review and appraisal of the implementation of the International Plan of Action on Ageing;

2. *Endorses* the recommendations contained in the report of the Secretary-General, in the form of global and national targets on ageing for the year 2001, which provide a pragmatic focus for the broad and ideal goals of the Plan of Action and accelerate its implementation into the next millennium;

3. *Welcomes* the new conceptual framework and operational nature of the United Nations programme on ageing, provided by the United Nations Principles for Older Persons, the Proclamation on Ageing and the global targets on ageing for the year 2001, to further the implementation of the Plan of Action in the current decade;

4. *Reaffirms* the recommendation made in the Plan of Action and reiterated in numerous General Assembly resolutions, in which the Secretary-General was requested, within the existing regular budget and extra-budgetary resources of the United Nations, to give due consideration to the provision of appropriate increased resources for the implementation of the Plan of Action, particularly in the light of recent and projected developments within the field of ageing;

5. *Calls upon* the Secretary-General to maintain the integrity and the identity of the United Nations programme on ageing, as well as the United Nations Trust Fund for Ageing, in order to assist Member States in fully implementing the recommendations of the Plan of Action;

6. *Urges* Governments, specialized agencies and bodies of the United Nations system and interested non-governmental organizations to explore new approaches to supporting, through partnerships, the activities of the United Nations programme on ageing in the current decade, aimed at assisting Member States in selecting and reaching national targets and implementing the United Nations Principles for Older Persons;

7. *Takes note with interest* of the preliminary findings of the United Nations research project on developmen-

tal implications of population ageing, presented at the Expert Group Meeting on Population Growth and Demographic Structure, held in Paris from 16 to 20 November 1992, expresses its appreciation to the Government of Sweden for supporting this project, and invites the United Nations Population Fund to continue its support for it;

8. *Invites* interested Member States, non-governmental organizations and research centres to support the activities of the United Nations programme on ageing, particularly research activities aimed at suggesting policy options to enhance contributions of the elderly to development;

9. *Urges* the Secretary-General to strengthen, within existing resources, the research component of the United Nations programme on ageing in order to enable it, on the basis of approaches of the third review and appraisal of the implementation of the Plan of Action and the project on developmental implications of population ageing, to develop policy and programme options for assisting Member States in achieving their national targets on ageing for the year 2001 and in implementing the United Nations Principles for Older Persons;

10. *Commends* the United Nations Postal Administration for issuing, on 5 February 1993, a set of six commemorative stamps on the theme "Ageing: Dignity and Participation";

11. *Reiterates* the appeal made by the General Assembly, in the Proclamation on Ageing in the annex to resolution 47/5, to the international community to highlight ageing at major forthcoming events, including the World Conference on Human Rights, held at Vienna from 14 to 25 June 1993, the International Year of the Family to be observed in 1994, the International Conference on Population and Development, to be held at Cairo from 5 to 13 September 1994, the Fourth World Conference on Women: Action for Equality, Development and Peace, to be held at Beijing from 4 to 15 September 1995, the tenth anniversary of International Youth Year, to be observed in 1995, and the World Summit for Social Development, to be held at Copenhagen on 11 and 12 March 1995;

12. *Welcomes* the decision of the General Assembly, in its resolution 47/5, to observe 1999 as the International Year of Older Persons;

13. *Invites* Member States to strengthen their national mechanisms on ageing, *inter alia*, to enable them to serve as national focal points for the preparations for and observance of the Year;

14. *Appeals* to Governments and non-governmental organizations to make known to the Secretary-General their views on the preparations for and observance of the Year in order to ensure an adequate basis for formulating the programme for the Year;

15. *Invites* the regional commissions to take an active part in the preparations for and observance of the Year, focusing on the specific needs and requirements of each region;

16. *Requests* the Secretary-General to draft a conceptual framework of a programme, at the national, regional and international levels, for the preparations for and observance of the Year, and to submit it for consideration by the Commission for Social Development at its thirty-fourth session in 1995, and by the General Assembly at its fiftieth session, in 1995.

Economic and Social Council resolution 1993/22
27 July 1993   Meeting 43   Adopted without vote

Approved by Social Committee (E/1993/106) without vote, 14 July (meeting 10); draft by Commission for Social Development (E/1993/24); agenda item 20.

In other action, the Council, by **decision 1993/238** of 27 July, on the recommendation of the Commission for Social Development, requested the General Assembly to redesignate the International Year of Older Persons as the International Year of the Elderly.

GENERAL ASSEMBLY ACTION

On 20 December, the General Assembly, on the recommendation of its Third Committee, adopted **resolution 48/98** without vote.

Implementation of the International Plan of Action on Ageing

The General Assembly,

Mindful of the growing concern of the international community with the issues related to population and individual ageing,

Noting with satisfaction the clear conceptual framework of the United Nations programme on ageing, revealed in the United Nations Principles for Older Persons, the global targets on ageing for the year 2001 and the Proclamation on Ageing, to further the implementation of the International Plan of Action on Ageing,

Recalling that, in the Proclamation on Ageing, it decided to observe the year 1999 as the International Year of Older Persons,

Taking note of Economic and Social Council resolution 1993/22 of 27 July 1993, in which the Council invited Member States to strengthen their national mechanisms on ageing, *inter alia*, to enable them to serve as national focal points for the preparation for and observance of the International Year of Older Persons,

Noting the recent measures aimed at consolidating the social and economic activities of the United Nations,

1. *Takes note with appreciation* of the report of the Secretary-General on the third review and appraisal of the implementation of the International Plan of Action on Ageing;

2. *Endorses* the recommendations contained in the report of the Secretary-General, in the form of global and national targets on ageing for the year 2001, aimed at streamlining the implementation of the Plan of Action in its second decade;

3. *Calls upon* the Secretary-General to maintain the integrity and the identity of the United Nations programme on ageing;

4. *Commends* the International Institute on Ageing on its training programme and related activities, and invites national, regional and international organizations to cooperate closely with the Institute;

5. *Urges* the United Nations, Member States and non-governmental organizations to support the African Society of Gerontology in developing and implementing a regional programme of activities on ageing;

6. *Invites* interested Member States, non-governmental organizations and research centres to support

the activities of the United Nations programme on ageing, particularly research activities aimed at suggesting policy options to enhance contributions by the elderly to development;

7. *Invites* Governments, non-governmental organizations and United Nations organizations and bodies concerned with ageing to submit to the Secretary-General their proposals for the preparation for and observance of the International Year of Older Persons;

8. *Calls upon* the Secretary-General to draft a conceptual framework of a programme for the preparation for and observance of the International Year of Older Persons and to submit it, through the Commission for Social Development at its thirty-fourth session in 1995, to the General Assembly for consideration at its fiftieth session, in 1995.

General Assembly resolution 48/98

20 December 1993   Meeting 85   Adopted without vote

Approved by Third Committee (A/48/627) without vote, 12 November (meeting 32); 3-nation draft (A/C.3/48/L.6), orally revised; agenda item 109.
Sponsors: Austria, Dominican Republic, Malta.
Meeting numbers. GA 48th session: 3rd Committee 11-19, 21, 32; plenary 85.

By **decision 48/433** of 20 December, the Assembly redesignated the International Year of Older Persons as the International Year of the Elderly.

REFERENCES

[1]YUN 1992, p. 890, GA res. 47/86, 16 Dec. 1992. [2]E/1993/24. [3]YUN 1982, p. 1184. [4]E/CN.5/1993/7. [5]ACC/1993/4.

Chapter XV

Refugees and displaced persons

During 1993, the world's refugee population, including internally displaced persons, increased from 18.9 million to 23 million, severely taxing the capacity of the international community to respond.

The United Nations High Commissioner for Refugees (UNHCR) continued to deal with complex and protracted refugee crises through assistance and protection while pursuing a strategy aimed at prevention, preparedness and voluntary repatriation. Although heavily burdened by new refugee populations, UNHCR assisted some 1.8 million refugees to return home voluntarily in 1993, at a total cost of $191 million. It endeavoured to secure asylum for those compelled to flee and to respond rapidly to their emergency needs, complementing these efforts with prevention and solution-oriented activities in their countries of origin.

Some 469,000 Afghan refugees were repatriated from Iran and Pakistan during 1993, with UNHCR assistance, and an additional 400,000 returned spontaneously. Approximately 155,000 persons returned to Cambodia during the year, completing the repatriation operation there. For some 250,000 refugees from Myanmar in Bangladesh, the signing of two Memoranda of Understanding paved the way for large-scale voluntary repatriation. UNHCR commenced the complex operation of repatriating some 1.5 million refugees to Mozambique from six neighbouring countries. It provided protection and assistance to internally displaced populations in Bosnia and Herzegovina, the Caucasus and parts of Africa and Central Asia. In the former Yugoslavia, UNHCR addressed the largest single group of persons in need of international protection.

In October, the UNHCR Executive Committee considered the international protection of refugees, the question of internally displaced persons, the implementation of its Policy on Refugee Women, refugee situations in Afghanistan and the former Yugoslavia, the follow-up to the 1989 International Conference on Central American Refugees, the Comprehensive Plan of Action for Indo-Chinese Refugees, and increased coordination between UNHCR and non-governmental organizations.

The General Assembly expressed its deep concern at serious threats to the security of refugees and called on States to ensure respect for the principles of refugee protection as well as the humane treatment of asylum-seekers, to uphold asylum as an indispensable instrument for the international protection of refugees, and to respect scrupulously the fundamental principle of non-refoulement (resolution 48/116).

Programme and finances of UNHCR

Programme policy

Executive Committee action. At its forty-fourth session (Geneva, 4-8 October 1993),[1] the Executive Committee of the UNHCR Programme expressed concern at the inadequacy of international protection for various groups of refugees. It noted the size and complexity of the refugee problem, the risk of new refugee situations developing and challenges to refugee protection, including the denial of UNHCR access to people in need of assistance, expulsion, refoulement and unjustified detention. The Committee called on States to uphold asylum as an indispensable instrument for international refugee protection and to respect the fundamental principle of non-refoulement. It stressed the importance of international burden-sharing and supported further exploration by the High Commissioner and States of various asylum strategies, including temporary protection for persons compelled to flee their countries in large numbers and who were in need of international protection.

The Executive Committee expressed concern at the alarming frequency of incidents in which refugees and asylum-seekers, including women and children, were subjected to violence and mistreatment, including killing, torture, military or armed attacks, rape, beatings, intimidation, forced military recruitment and arbitrary or inhumane conditions of detention. It deplored all violations of the right of refugees and asylum-seekers to personal security and condemned persecution through sexual violence. The Committee called on the High Commissioner to pursue the protection of refugee women and girls and supported refugee status for persons whose claim was based on a well-founded fear of persecution, through sexual violence, for reasons of race, religion, nationality, membership of a particular social group or political opinion. It called on the High Commissioner to make every effort to ensure that the needs of refugee children, particularly unaccompanied minors, were covered by UNHCR's activities in cooperation with Governments, non-governmental organizations (NGOs) and intergovernmental organizations, and with the United Nations Children's Fund (UNICEF) in particular. It asked the High Commissioner for a concerted effort to implement UNHCR's Policy on Refugee Women and to reinforce the role of the Senior Coordinator for Refugee Women.

The Committee welcomed increased consultation between UNHCR and NGOs through the Partnership in Action (PARINAC) process, which was jointly launched by the High Commissioner and the International Council on Voluntary Agencies, with a view to establishing a common agenda for field activities.

In her opening statement to the Committee, the High Commissioner stated that humanitarian assistance could make an important contribution to the peace-keeping and peacemaking efforts of the United Nations. However, the situation in the former Yugoslavia had clearly demonstrated that humanitarian endeavours were not a substitute for peace settlements or political negotiations.

ECONOMIC AND SOCIAL COUNCIL ACTION

On 30 July, by **decision 1993/333**, the Economic and Social Council took note of the High Commissioner's report for 1992/93.[2]

GENERAL ASSEMBLY ACTION

On 20 December, the General Assembly, on the recommendation of the Third (Social, Humanitarian and Cultural) Committee, adopted **resolution 48/116** without vote.

Office of the United Nations High Commissioner for Refugees

The General Assembly,

Having considered the report of the United Nations High Commissioner for Refugees on the activities of her Office, as well as the report of the Executive Committee of the Programme of the High Commissioner on the work of its forty-fourth session, and taking note of the statement made by the High Commissioner on 4 November 1993,

Recalling its resolution 47/105 of 16 December 1992,

Reaffirming the purely humanitarian and non-political character of the activities of the Office of the High Commissioner, as well as the crucial importance of the High Commissioner's functions of providing international protection to refugees and seeking solutions to refugee problems,

Welcoming the Vienna Declaration and Programme of Action of the World Conference on Human Rights, particularly as it reaffirms the right to seek and enjoy asylum and the right to return to one's country,

Commending the High Commissioner and her staff for the dedicated manner in which they discharge their responsibilities, and paying special tribute to those staff members who have lost their lives in the course of their duties,

Noting with satisfaction that one hundred and twenty-three States are now parties to the 1951 Convention and/or the 1967 Protocol relating to the Status of Refugees,

Also noting with satisfaction the participation of the High Commissioner in the commemoration of the anniversaries of the Cartagena Declaration on Refugees of 1984 and the Organization of African Unity Convention Governing the Specific Aspects of Refugee Problems in Africa, concluded at Addis Ababa on 10 September 1969,

Welcoming the continuing strong commitment of States to provide protection and assistance to refugees and the valuable support extended by Governments to the High Commissioner in carrying out her humanitarian tasks,

Commending those States, particularly the least developed and those serving as host to millions of refugees, that, despite severe economic and development challenges of their own, continue to admit large numbers of refugees into their territories, and emphasizing the need to share the burden of those States to the maximum extent possible through international assistance, including development-oriented assistance,

Noting with concern that the number of refugees and other persons to whom the Office of the High Commissioner is called upon to provide assistance and protection has continued to increase and that their protection continues to be seriously jeopardized in many situations as a result of denial of admission, unlawful expulsion, refoulement, unjustified detention, other threats to their physical security, dignity and well-being and failure to respect and ensure their fundamental freedoms and human rights,

Recognizing that, in certain regions, the misuse by individuals of asylum procedures jeopardizes the institution of asylum and adversely affects the prompt and effective protection of refugees,

Emphasizing the need for States to assist the High Commissioner in seeking durable and timely solutions to the problems of refugees, as well as to take part in efforts to prevent conditions that might give rise to the flight of refugees, and to address the root causes of refugee outflows, and underlining, in this connection, State responsibility, particularly as it relates to countries of origin,

Welcoming the continuing efforts of the High Commissioner to meet the protection and assistance needs of refugee women and refugee children, who constitute the majority of the world's refugee population and who are often exposed to serious threats to their safety and well-being,

Recognizing the increased demands faced by the Office of the High Commissioner worldwide and the need for all available resources to be fully and effectively mobilized to meet those demands,

1. *Strongly reaffirms* the fundamental importance of the function of the United Nations High Commissioner for Refugees of providing international protection to refugees and the need for States to cooperate fully with her Office in order to facilitate the effective exercise of this function;

2. *Calls upon* all States that have not yet done so, including Governments of newly independent States, to accede to or to declare succession to and to implement fully the 1951 Convention and the 1967 Protocol relating to the Status of Refugees and relevant regional instruments for the protection of refugees;

3. *Calls upon* all States to uphold asylum as an indispensable instrument for the international protection of refugees and to respect scrupulously the fundamental principle of non-refoulement;

4. *Urges* States to ensure access, consistent with relevant international and regional instruments, for all asylum-seekers to fair and efficient procedures for the determination of refugee status and the granting of asylum to eligible persons;

5. *Expresses deep concern* regarding serious threats to the security or the well-being of refugees, including incidents of refoulement, unlawful expulsion, physical attacks and detention under unacceptable conditions, and calls upon States to take all measures necessary to ensure respect for the principles of refugee protection as well as the humane treatment of asylum-seekers in accordance with internationally recognized human rights norms;

6. *Endorses*, in this connection, the conclusions on the personal security of refugees and on refugee protection and sexual violence adopted by the Executive Committee of the Programme of the High Commissioner at its forty-fourth session;

7. *Welcomes* the High Commissioner's policy on refugee children and the activities undertaken to ensure its implementation, aimed at ensuring that the specific needs of refugee children, including in particular unaccompanied minors, are fully met within the overall protection and assistance activities of the Office, in cooperation with Governments and other relevant organizations;

8. *Acknowledges with appreciation* the further progress made in the implementation of measures within the framework of the High Commissioner's programme to ensure the protection and to meet the assistance needs of refugee women and girls, in accordance with the High Commissioner's policy on refugee women;

9. *Stresses* the importance of international solidarity and burden-sharing in reinforcing the international protection of refugees, and urges all States, as well as non-governmental organizations, in conjunction with the Office of the High Commissioner, to cooperate in efforts to lighten the burden borne by States that have received large numbers of asylum-seekers and refugees;

10. *Urges* all States and relevant organizations to support the High Commissioner's search for durable solutions to refugee problems, including voluntary repatriation, integration in the country of asylum and resettlement in a third country, as appropriate, and welcomes in particular the ongoing efforts of her Office to pursue wherever possible opportunities to promote conditions conducive to the preferred solution of voluntary repatriation;

11. *Encourages* the High Commissioner, on the basis of her broad humanitarian experience and expertise, to continue to explore and to undertake protection and assistance activities aimed at preventing conditions that give rise to refugee outflows, bearing in mind fundamental protection principles, in close coordination with the Governments concerned, and within an inter-agency, intergovernmental and non-governmental framework, as appropriate;

12. *Reaffirms its support* for the High Commissioner's efforts, on the basis of specific requests from the Secretary-General or the competent principal organs of the United Nations and with the consent of the concerned State, and taking into account the complementarities of the mandates and expertise of other relevant organizations, to provide humanitarian assistance and protection to persons displaced within their own country in specific situations calling for the particular expertise of the Office, especially where such efforts could contribute to the prevention or solution of refugee problems;

13. *Reaffirms* the importance of incorporating environmental considerations into the programmes of the Office of the High Commissioner, especially in the least developed countries, in view of the impact on the environment of the large numbers of refugees and displaced persons of concern to the High Commissioner;

14. *Recognizes* the need for the international community to explore methods and means better to address within the United Nations system the protection and assistance needs of internally displaced persons, and calls upon the High Commissioner to engage actively in further consultations on this priority issue with the Department of Humanitarian Affairs of the Secretariat and the representative of the Secretary-General on internally displaced persons, and with other appropriate international organizations and bodies, including the International Committee of the Red Cross;

15. *Also recognizes* the value of addressing prevention, protection and solutions on a comprehensive regional basis, and encourages the High Commissioner to consult with States, other relevant United Nations bodies and governmental, intergovernmental and non-governmental organizations, concerning possibilities for additional measures and initiatives in areas affected by complex humanitarian problems involving coerced population movements;

16. *Reaffirms* the importance of promoting and disseminating refugee law and principles for the protection of refugees as well as of facilitating the prevention of and solutions to refugee problems, and encourages the High Commissioner to continue to strengthen the promotion and training activities of her Office, *inter alia*, through increased cooperation with bodies and organizations concerned with human rights and humanitarian law;

17. *Urges* States, the Office of the High Commissioner and non-governmental organizations to pursue their efforts to foster greater public understanding and acceptance of people of different backgrounds and cultures, with a view to dispelling hostile, racist or xenophobic attitudes and other forms of intolerance towards foreigners, including refugees and asylum-seekers, displaced people and persons belonging to minorities;

18. *Notes* the relationship between safeguarding human rights and preventing refugee problems, and reiterates its support for the High Commissioner's efforts to increase cooperation between her Office and the Commission on Human Rights, the Centre for Human Rights of the Secretariat and other relevant international bodies and organizations;

19. *Welcomes* the further progress made by the High Commissioner in enhancing the capacity of her Office to respond to humanitarian emergencies, and encourages her to provide full support to the coordination role of the Emergency Relief Coordinator, especially in major and complex emergencies;

20. *Encourages* the High Commissioner to continue to cooperate fully, including within the framework of the Inter-Agency Standing Committee, with United Nations agencies, intergovernmental organizations and non-governmental organizations, in order to ensure an effective response to complex emergency situations;

21. *Welcomes* the establishment by the High Commissioner of the Partnership in Action Process in conjunction with the International Council of Voluntary Agencies as a means of strengthening and improving collaboration between the Office of the High Commissioner and non-governmental organizations in meeting greatly increased demands, expresses its support for the process of consultations through regional preparatory meetings as well as for the global conference at Oslo in June 1994 and invites Governments to provide financial support to this important initiative;

22. *Expresses deep concern* at conditions in a number of countries and regions that seriously endanger the delivery of humanitarian assistance and the security of the staff of the High Commissioner and other relief workers, deplores the recent loss of lives among personnel involved in humanitarian operations, urges support for initiatives taken by the High Commissioner and within the General Assembly and the Security Council concerning the safety of United Nations and associated personnel, in particular the consideration of new measures to enhance the safety of such personnel, and calls upon States and all parties to conflicts to take all necessary measures to ensure safe and timely access for humanitarian assistance and the security of international and local staff undertaking humanitarian work in the countries concerned;

23. *Calls upon* all Governments and other donors to contribute to the programmes of the High Commissioner and, taking into account the need to achieve greater burden-sharing among donors, to assist the High Commissioner in securing additional and timely income from traditional governmental sources, other Governments and the private sector in order to ensure that the needs of refugees, returnees and displaced persons of concern to the Office of the High Commissioner are met.

General Assembly resolution 48/116

20 December 1993   Meeting 85   Adopted without vote

Approved by Third Committee (A/48/631) without vote, 19 November (meeting 38); 80-nation draft (A/C.3/48/L.26), orally revised; agenda item 113.

Sponsors: Afghanistan, Albania, Angola, Argentina, Armenia, Australia, Austria, Azerbaijan, Belarus, Belgium, Brazil, Bulgaria, Cameroon, Canada, Chile, Costa Rica, Côte d'Ivoire, Croatia, Cyprus, Czech Republic, Denmark, Egypt, El Salvador, Estonia, Ethiopia, Finland, France, Gabon, Germany, Ghana, Greece, Guatemala, Guinea-Bissau, Guyana, Haiti, Hungary, Iceland, Ireland, Israel, Italy, Japan, Kenya, Latvia, Liberia, Liechtenstein, Lithuania, Luxembourg, Malawi, Morocco, Mozambique, Namibia, Netherlands, New Zealand, Nicaragua, Niger, Norway, Pakistan, Panama, Philippines, Poland, Portugal, Republic of Korea, Romania, Russian Federation, Rwanda, San Marino, Senegal, Slovenia, Solomon Islands, Spain, Sudan, Sweden, the former Yugoslav Republic of Macedonia, Turkey, United Kingdom, United Republic of Tanzania, United States, Uruguay, Venezuela, Yemen.

Meeting numbers. GA 48th session: 3rd Committee 23-28, 33, 34, 38; plenary 85.

Programme policy evaluation

The Secretary-General, in March,[3] submitted to the Committee on Programme and Coordination (CPC) an in-depth evaluation of the UNHCR progamme on international protection of and assistance to refugees. The report presented findings and recommendations on: protection, durable solutions, assistance, early warning, contingency planning, training, dissemination, publicity, finance, management and human resources, with the aim of strengthening protection and the search for durable solutions and further delegating operational responsibility for assistance.

In May,[4] CPC endorsed the evaluation and its recommendations and decided that the evaluation, along with the section of CPC's report containing observations by delegations on it, should be transmitted to the UNHCR Executive Committee.

The Executive Committee, in October,[1] requested the High Commissioner to keep the Subcommittee of the Whole on International Protection informed of progress and constraints in implementing the evaluation's protection-related recommendations. It asked UNHCR to present to the Subcommittee on Administrative and Financial Matters its views on the evaluation's recommendations and CPC's comments, paying particular attention to the definition of a proper accountability framework for UNHCR, strategic planning and result-based management.

In April, the High Commissioner established the Working Group on Programme Management and Operational Capacity, which met during May and June and analysed UNHCR's programme management system and procedures, identified problems and suggested ways to improve programme delivery by simplifying procedures, delegating authority to the field and ensuring accountability for activities undertaken by programme managers. The High Commissioner endorsed the Working Group's recommendations in July, and a follow-up group composed of Headquarters staff was charged with their implementation.

UNHCR's evaluation activities during 1992/93 were outlined in a July report[5] to its Executive Committee. UNHCR initiated a number of studies relating to durable solutions to refugee problems, including reviews of the repatriation and reintegration programmes for Cambodian and Nicaraguan refugees and studies on the follow-up to the 1989 International Conference on Central American Refugees and UNHCR's role in formulating and implementing returnee aid and development programmes. In addition, UNHCR commenced a review of its operations in the former Yugoslavia in order to identify the principal lessons learned and examine the broader impact of the emergency on UNHCR activities. Other evaluations covered UNHCR's policy on refugee women, its role in protecting and assisting internally displaced persons, and its policy and practice with regard to refugee enumeration and statistics.

The evaluation strategy introduced at the beginning of 1993 consisted of four principal elements: contracting a greater amount of work to professional evaluation consultants; developing working relationships with research and policy institutes; identifying and training UNHCR staff members with demonstrated aptitude in the evaluation function; and establishing arrangements for seconding experienced staff from governmental evaluation agencies.

Enlargement of UNHCR Executive Committee

By a 3 June note verbale,[6] Spain, noting the growing wave of refugees and displaced persons, particularly in Africa and Europe, and Spain's growing participation in UNHCR's operations and programmes, expressed the view that it should be included in the Executive Committee. It requested the Economic and Social Council to consider the question.

ECONOMIC AND SOCIAL COUNCIL ACTION

On 29 July, the Economic and Social Council by **decision 1993/315**, took note of Spain's request[6] and recommended that the General Assembly take a decision at its forty-eighth (1993) session on the question of increasing the membership of the Committee from 46 to 47 States.

GENERAL ASSEMBLY ACTION

On the recommendation of the Third Committee, the General Assembly on 20 December adopted **resolution 48/115** without vote.

Enlargement of the Executive Committee of the Programme of the United Nations High Commissioner for Refugees

The General Assembly,

Taking note of Economic and Social Council decision 1993/315 of 29 July 1993 concerning the enlargement of the Executive Committee of the Programme of the United Nations High Commissioner for Refugees,

Taking note also of the note verbale dated 3 June 1993 from the Permanent Representative of Spain to the United Nations addressed to the Secretary-General relating to the enlargement of the Executive Committee,

1. *Decides* to increase the number of members of the Executive Committee of the Programme of the United

Nations High Commissioner for Refugees from forty-six to forty-seven States;

2. *Requests* the Economic and Social Council to elect an additional member at its resumed organizational session in 1994.

General Assembly resolution 48/115

20 December 1993   Meeting 85   Adopted without vote

Approved by Third Committee (A/48/631) without vote, 19 November (meeting 38); 6-nation draft (A/C.3/48/L.24); agenda item 113.
Sponsors: Argentina, Belgium, Hungary, Japan, Philippines, Tunisia.
Meeting numbers. GA 48th session: 3rd Committee 23-28, 33, 34, 38; plenary 85.

Financial and administrative questions

Contributions to UNHCR declined slightly in 1993 as funding needs swelled to unprecedented levels. Donors provided $1.13 billion in cash and kind, compared with $1.18 billion in 1992.[7] The United Nations regular budget contribution to UNHCR was also down slightly from $21.2 million in 1992[8] to $20.5 million.

UNHCR struggled during the year to meet a target of $413 million for General Programmes, which represented core activities for refugees and provided flexibility to deal with emergencies and voluntary repatriations. At 31 December, the Office had received $311 million for General Programmes compared with $354 million the previous year. The shortfall was partially offset, however, by a carry-over of $55 million from secondary income in the form of cancelled obligations from previous years, interest earnings and various transfers.

UNHCR's expenditures for 1993 amounted to $1.3 billion; disbursements under the General Programme totalled $392 million and those under Special Programmes $915 million. Regional apportionments were as follows: Europe, $585 million; Africa, $325 million; Asia and Oceania, $144 million; South-West Asia, North Africa and the Middle East, $115 million; and the Americas and Caribbean, $38 million.

Special operations accounted for almost two thirds of UNHCR's activities in 1993. Appeals were launched in conjunction with the United Nations Department of Humanitarian Affairs (DHA) for operations in the former Yugoslavia, the Afghan and Liberian repatriation programmes, and programmes in the Horn of Africa and the republics of the former USSR (for DHA activities, see PART THREE, Chapter III). The humanitarian relief operation in the former Yugoslavia accounted for some 40 per cent ($533 million) of UNHCR's total assistance budget.

UNHCR issued its own appeals for Central America, the Mozambican repatriation, the Myanmar repatriation from Bangladesh (in conjunction with WFP), and a number of other emergency operations. By the end of 1993, the refugee crisis in Burundi had stretched the Office's emergency capacities to the limit. UNHCR was able to mobilize a $13 million three-country emergency response for life-saving operations in Rwanda, the United Republic of Tanzania and Zaire in a matter of days, and in the course of the year it mobilized more than $800 million for special operations, repatriations and emergencies, in addition to sums raised under General Programmes.

In October,[1] the Executive Committee approved country and area programmes and overall allocations for 1994 General Programmes amounting to $418.5 million (including $25 million for the Emergency Fund and $20 million for the General Allocation for Voluntary Repatriation). It recognized that overall estimated financial requirements for Special Programme activities during 1994, subject to the availability of funds, would amount to some $1.2 billion. It requested the Subcommittee on Administrative and Financial Matters to review the financial and programmatic implications of current UNHCR activities, including information related to internally displaced persons.

A General Programmes budget target of $418.5 million was set for 1994, with Special Programmes requirements conservatively estimated at $780 million—a figure that covered only six-months of requirements for the former Yugoslavia.[7]

Accounts

1992 accounts

The audited financial statements on funds administered by UNHCR for the year ended 31 December 1992 showed total expenditures of $1,072 million and total income of $1,158 million, with a reserve balance of $299,283.[9]

(For the Board of Auditors' recommendations, see PART FIVE, Chapter I.)

In **resolution 48/216 D** of 23 December, the General Assembly accepted the financial report of the Board of Auditors on UNHCR and a summary of its principal findings, conclusions and recommendations for remedial action,[10] and approved the Board's recommendations and conclusions. It requested the Office of UNHCR to implement better financial management systems that would permit an effective and economic delivery of its programme and reduce a persistent over-obligation of funds.

Subcommittee on Administrative and Financial Matters

The Executive Committee's Subcommittee on Administrative and Financial Matters (Geneva, 1 October)[11] considered a broad range of issues,

including an update on UNHCR programmes and funding; voluntary repatriation; specific programme-related issues, including the summary report of the Working Group on Programme Management and Operational Capacity, UNHCR's emergency response capacity; the environmental management of refugee sites; UNHCR/World Food Programme (WFP) cooperation; evaluation activities; financial and management questions, including a proposal to create a position of Inspector of Operational Activities; and matters related to human resources.

REFERENCES

[1]A/48/12/Add.1. [2]A/48/12. [3]E/AC.51/1993/2. [4]A/48/16. [5]A/AC.96/809. [6]E/1993/88. [7]E/1994/41. [8]YUN 1992, p. 895. [9]A/48/5/Add.5. [10]A/48/230. [11]A/AC.96/820.

Refugee assistance and protection

Proposed conference on refugees

On 20 December, the General Assembly, on the recommendation of the Third Committee, adopted **resolution 48/113** without vote.

Convening of a United Nations conference for the comprehensive consideration and review of the problems of refugees, returnees, displaced persons and migrants

The General Assembly,

Recalling the 1951 Convention and the 1967 Protocol relating to the Status of Refugees,

Taking into consideration the complexity and urgency of the global refugee crisis and the need for the international community to adopt a comprehensive approach for the coordination of action with regard to refugees, returnees, displaced persons and migrants,

Noting that the International Conference on Population and Development, to be held at Cairo from 5 to 13 September 1994, will address matters related to refugees, displaced persons and migrants,

Welcoming the continued work of the representative of the Secretary-General on internally displaced persons,

Recognizing the need to develop innovative strategies, mechanisms and decisions in this field,

1. *Takes note* of the proposal to convene a United Nations conference for the comprehensive consideration and review of the problems of refugees, returnees, displaced persons and migrants;

2. *Invites* all Member States, the specialized agencies, other international organizations, concerned United Nations bodies, regional organizations and non-governmental organizations concerned to undertake reviews and submit recommendations to the Secretary-General with regard to the appropriateness of convening such a conference, taking into consideration, *inter alia*, the deliberations of the Cairo Conference, as well as the work of the representative of the Secretary-General;

3. *Requests* the Secretary-General to submit to the General Assembly at its forty-ninth session a report on the recommendations received pursuant to paragraph 2 above.

General Assembly resolution 48/113

20 December 1993   Meeting 85   Adopted without vote

Approved by Third Committee (A/48/631) without vote, 22 November (meeting 39); 7-nation draft (A/C.3/48/L.21/Rev.1); agenda item 113.
Sponsors: Azerbaijan, Belarus, Chile, Guyana, Philippines, Russian Federation, Tajikistan.
Meeting numbers. GA 48th session: 3rd Committee 23-28, 33, 34, 38, 39; plenary 85.

Assistance

During 1993, UNHCR's pursuit of a preventive and solution-oriented strategy resulted in its direct engagement in acute crisis or open conflict situations, with attendant risks to its staff and implementing partners. The sheer magnitude of these operations also stretched the capacity of the High Commissioner's Office to the limit, said a report to the General Assembly covering UNHCR activities in 1992/93.[1] It was noted that the ultimate success of the High Commissioner's three-pronged strategy of prevention, preparedness and solutions to refugee problems would depend on the United Nations' ability to develop comprehensive and integrated responses that linked humanitarian action and the protection of human rights with peacemaking, peace-keeping and peace building through governmental, intergovernmental and non-governmental partnerships.

While responding to refugee situations in countries of asylum during the year, UNHCR also focused on activities in countries of origin, seeking to prevent and contain refugee movements.

UNHCR began to provide assistance not only to refugees, returnees and displaced persons, but also, in the case of the former Yugoslavia, to people under direct threat of expulsion or persecution in the form of "ethnic cleansing". The Office addressed the needs of entire communities rather than focusing on individuals. Invoking the human right to remain in one's country of origin, it sought to ensure that people were not forced to flee in the first place.

A major lesson learned during this period of activity was the importance of political initiatives to resolve the causes of refugee problems and the link between refugees and international peace and stability. It was noted that humanitarian assistance could make an important contribution to reducing tensions and promoting reconciliation, but could not be a substitute for political solutions.

UNHCR's activities comprised emergency assistance, care and maintenance, voluntary repatriation, local settlement and resettlement.

The Office's emergency measures facilitated a timely response to an unprecedented number of new, and often concurrent, refugee emergencies around the globe. Emergency activities were financed from UNHCR's Emergency Fund and by special appeals. During 1993, expenditures under the Emergency Fund amounted to $24.9 million, and Special Appeals were issued to cover emergency situations in Armenia, Azerbaijan, Benin, Burundi, Ghana and Tajikistan. In certain instances, UNHCR initially made recourse to the Central Emergency Revolving Fund (CERF), administered by the Under-Secretary-General for Humanitarian Affairs on behalf of the Secretary-General, in anticipation of funding from its own Special Appeals. Recourse was made to CERF for $5 million to cover initial expenditures for the emergency in Tajikistan, $2 million for Georgia and $5 million for the Burundi emergency.

Following the emergency phase of an operation, the basic needs of refugees were met through care and maintenance assistance. Expenditures on such assistance in 1993 amounted to $850.5 million, of which $215.7 million came from General Programmes and $634.9 million from Special Programmes. Large-scale care and maintenance programmes were administered in the former Yugoslavia and neighbouring countries ($551 million); Ethiopia ($12.4 million); Guinea ($16.4 million); Kenya ($54.7 million); and Malawi ($26.3 million). In South-East Asia, a major programme for refugees from Myanmar was implemented in Bangladesh ($17.8 million). Other care and maintenance programmes continued for Vietnamese refugees in Hong Kong ($14.7 million) and for refugees from the Lao People's Democratic Republic and Myanmar in Thailand ($13 million). Expenditures for a programme established in 1993 for Afghan refugees in Pakistan totalled $18.5 million.

UNHCR continued its efforts to provide durable solutions for refugees through voluntary repatriation, local integration and resettlement. In 1993, $190.6 million was spent on voluntary repatriation, with more than 800,000 persons returning to their countries of origin under UNHCR-assisted programmes, most notably to Afghanistan, Cambodia, Ethiopia, Myanmar and Somalia. Repatriations included 747,600 persons returning to Afghanistan from India, Iran and Pakistan (479,600 of them assisted by UNHCR), 431,600 persons from Malawi, the United Republic of Tanzania and other countries of asylum to Mozambique (18,000 assisted) and 239,800 persons from Iran and Turkey to Iraq (1,800 assisted). Expenditures on voluntary repatriation under both General and Special Programmes totalled $190.6 million.

The Office supported the local settlement of refugees within host countries, either with a view to promoting local integration or self-sufficiency pending eventual repatriation. Some $97.7 million was obligated for these purposes under General and Special Programmes combined. Organized settlements were supported in Benin, the Central African Republic, China, the Congo, Côte d'Ivoire, Ethiopia, Ghana, Guinea, Mexico, Papua New Guinea, Senegal, Swaziland, Uganda, the United Republic of Tanzania, Zaire and Zambia. Assistance included the promotion of agricultural activities, small-enterprise development, employment in public works projects, legal advice, counselling, education, vocational training and job placement.

More than 43,700 persons were registered by UNHCR for resettlement in third countries during the year. The main focus of resettlement activity was South-East Asia, where more than 19,000 people, mainly Vietnamese and Lao, were resettled under the Comprehensive Plan of Action, in Australia, Canada and the United States in particular. A number of refugees from the Middle East/South-West Asia (9,734) and Africa (9,406) were also resettled in third countries. A total of 13,375 citizens of Bosnia and Herzegovina departed for resettlement or temporary protection. The United States received the highest number (21,137) of resettlement cases, followed by Canada (6,271) and Australia (3,648). Global expenditures on resettlement were estimated at $11.5 million.

To address the environmental dimensions of refugee programmes in a systematic manner, the High Commissioner appointed a Senior Environmental Coordinator in 1993.

The High Commissioner was a member of the United Nations Inter-Agency Standing Committee, established to ensure greater coordination of humanitarian assistance in the face of complex and protracted emergencies, as well as a stronger link between emergency relief, rehabilitation and development (see PART THREE, Chapter III).

Refugee/returnee aid and development

In 1993, UNHCR endeavoured to increase its cooperation with multilateral and bilateral development agencies and financial institutions. The High Commissioner observed[2] that UNHCR's activities in support of local settlement and reintegration in particular, could only achieve sustainable results if they were integrated with, or complementary to, development activities.

A joint UNHCR/African Development Bank (AfDB) project, resulting from project identification missions in Mozambique in 1992,[3] was expected to commence in 1995, and UNHCR continued to support the AfDB-financed South East Rangeland Rehabilitation Project in Ethiopia, for Ethiopian returnees from Somalia. The joint

UNHCR/International Fund for Agricultural Development (IFAD) South Khorasan Rangeland Rehabilitation and Refugee Income-generating Project in Iran was in its final year and the third phase of the UNHCR/World Bank Income-generating Project for Refugee Areas in Pakistan continued to emphasize training relevant to repatriation.

A significant aspect of UNHCR's attempt to link its assistance to longer-term development activities was its use of Quick Impact Projects (QIPs) to consolidate voluntary repatriation in returnee-impacted areas. They were also used to support the local integration of refugees in asylum countries when possible, to prevent or ease tensions between refugees and the local population. In 1993, QIPs were implemented in Belize, Cambodia, Ethiopia, the Lao People's Democratic Republic, Mozambique, Myanmar, Nepal, Somalia and Sri Lanka.

Refugee women

An external evaluation of UNHCR's Policy on Refugee Women confirmed that progress had been made in different field offices. The evaluation stressed the importance of additional resources for refugee women, the integration of refugee women's issues into emergency response procedures, the development of a gender-based needs assessment, an increased focus on physical protection and expanded gender training.

A gender training course, "People Oriented Planning", was offered to UNHCR staff and implementing partners in various countries. NGO staff trained by UNHCR conducted their own training, thereby increasing course coverage. Some 500 people attended 22 training sessions during the year and a new programme handbook was made available to help staff use the gender analytic framework in their daily duties.

An extensive network was developed among Headquarters and field personnel to coordinate preparations for the 1995 World Conference on Women. Staff were asked to contribute information on refugee women for national reports and to ensure that relevant issues were raised in the preparatory conferences and in discussion of the Platform for Action.

Refugee children

Since about half the world's refugees were children in 1993, UNHCR was concerned that their special needs were met through appropriate protection and assistance. The importance of the 1989 United Nations Convention on the Rights of the Child[4] was stressed as a framework for protecting their best interests. In all actions concerning refugee children, UNHCR continued to give primary consideration to the preservation or restoration of family unity. The approach had three elements: direct services to the child; help for the child through help for the family; and community services for families and children. The UNHCR *Guidelines on Refugee Children*, introduced in 1988,[5] were reviewed in 1993 and a new version was scheduled for distribution in 1994.

Two areas of particular concern to UNHCR remained the nutritional well-being of refugee children and their access to education. A new Memorandum of Understanding between UNHCR and WFP aimed to improve their health and nutritional status and UNHCR's education budget for the year stood at $45 million, including $12 million funded through Special Appeals and the Emergency Fund. UNHCR collaborated with UNICEF, the United Nations Educational, Scientific and Cultural Organization (UNESCO) and other organizations in support of primary and secondary schooling for displaced and refugee children in the former Yugoslavia. Teaching materials developed for UNESCO's *Education for Peace* initiative were used for Somali refugees in countries of asylum, as well as in UNHCR's cross border operations. UNHCR had established special stand-by arrangements with the NGO Radda Barnen whereby, with the assistance of trained community service workers, the needs of refugee children, especially the unaccompanied, were being addressed. In 1993, community workers participated in emergencies in Liberia, Rwanda, Uganda and the United Republic of Tanzania.

Regional assistance

Africa

During 1993, successive emergencies affected millions of drought victims, refugees, returnees and internally displaced persons in the Horn of Africa, Angola, Benin and Ghana, Guinea, Kenya, Liberia, Malawi, Mozambique, Sierra Leone and the Sudan. According to a report on UNHCR activities in Africa, submitted by the High Commissioner in August,[6] the vast majority of refugees being protected and assisted by UNHCR were, as in previous years, destitute women and children, mainly of rural background. Among the reasons for increasing numbers of refugees in Africa were human rights violations, internal conflict and ethnic strife, extreme poverty caused by political and economic instability, famine, drought and environmental degradation.

The refugee situation in sub-Saharan Africa was characterized by conflict-induced displacements, many of which were exacerbated by adverse environmental conditions. As at 31 December, some 5.9 million Africans were refugees and another 15 million were internally displaced. Principal countries of asylum included the Sudan, which hosted some 745,200 refugees, mainly from Ethiopia and

Eritrea; Malawi, with some 713,600, mainly Mozambican, refugees; Guinea, with 656,700, mainly Liberian, refugees; and the United Republic of Tanzania, which had refugees from Burundi, Mozambique, Rwanda and Zaire.

Upheavals in Burundi provoked the most dramatic exodus of the year, with some 580,000 people driven to seek refuge in Rwanda, the United Republic of Tanzania and Zaire. UNHCR administered refugee assistance programmes in all three countries, as well as in Burundi for a limited number of returnees from the United Republic of Tanzania and Rwanda. Elsewhere in eastern Africa, Sudanese continued to flow into Uganda, while Ethiopians and Somalis repatriated from Kenya. Some 3,000 new Sudanese refugees entered northern Uganda during the first quarter of 1993, and 18,000 Chadian refugees fled to the Central African Republic. There was however, encouraging progress as some 50,000 refugees were repatriated from Kenya to Ethiopia in the first quarter of the year, and a tripartite agreement was signed in February concerning the voluntary repatriation of Ethiopian refugees from the Sudan. Preparations for the voluntary repatriation of some 10,000 Ethiopians from camps in Djibouti were completed in December, but the repatriation of Ethiopians and Eritreans from the Sudan met with limited success and only 15,000 out of 50,000 Ethiopians returned.

The political crisis that affected Togo in 1992 resulted in the flight of some 250,000 refugees to Benin and Ghana during 1993 and, in May, UNHCR launched an appeal for $9.9 million for an emergency relief programme. In the Upper Lofa area of Liberia where UNHCR operated an assistance programme for some 175,000 Sierra Leonean refugees and internally displaced persons, all activities were suspended in mid-December 1993 after a major assault by rebel forces. However, the Peace Agreement between the warring Liberian factions (Cotonou, Benin, 25 July)[7] improved prospects for the eventual return of 700,000 refugees (see PART TWO, Chapter I). Although conditions in Liberia and Sierra Leone were not yet conducive to the promotion of a large-scale voluntary repatriation exercise, UNHCR assisted in the repatriation of 6,413 Sierra Leoneans and 19,098 Liberians between October 1992 and January 1993 and provided emergency relief assistance to Sierra Leoneans in the country's interior.

Spontaneous, as well as organized, repatriation to Mozambique continued. At the end of 1993, some 500,000 Mozambicans had returned home following the General Peace Agreement of October 1992.[8] Most returned from Malawi. A basic agreement with South Africa permitted UNHCR assistance to Mozambicans and the repatriation operation was expected to be completed in 1995.

In May, UNHCR launched a $203.4 million appeal for the repatriation and reintegration of Mozambican refugees, of which $55 million was needed for 1993.

In Angola, where continuing insecurity bedevilled efforts to deliver humanitarian assistance, UNHCR managed to assist 112,000 returnees and internally displaced persons. United Nations agencies were granted access for assistance purposes throughout Angola as of September, following efforts by the Secretary-General's Special Envoy. The UNHCR South African Repatriation Operation was concluded successfully in 1993, with more than 17,000 people having returned with UNHCR assistance.

Total 1993 expenditures in Africa amounted to $325.1 million, of which $188.5 million was spent under General Programmes and $136.6 million under Special Programmes.

Report of the Secretary-General. In response to a 1992 General Assembly request,[9] the Secretary-General presented an October report[10] describing assistance by six bodies of the United Nations system—the Department of Humanitarian Affairs, WFP, the United Nations Centre for Human Settlements (Habitat), UNHCR, the Food and Agriculture Organization of the United Nations and IFAD—for African refugees, returnees and displaced persons.

GENERAL ASSEMBLY ACTION

On 20 December, the General Assembly, on the recommendation of the Third Committee, adopted **resolution 48/118** without vote.

Assistance to refugees, returnees and displaced persons in Africa

The General Assembly,

Recalling its resolution 47/107 of 16 December 1992,

Having considered the report of the Secretary-General and that of the United Nations High Commissioner for Refugees,

Bearing in mind that most of the affected countries are least developed countries,

Convinced of the necessity of strengthening the capacity within the United Nations system for the implementation and overall coordination of relief programmes for refugees, returnees and displaced persons,

Welcoming the prospects for voluntary repatriation and durable solutions across the continent,

Recognizing the need for States to create conditions conducive to the prevention of flows of refugees and displaced persons and to voluntary repatriation,

Bearing in mind that the majority of refugees and displaced persons are women and children,

Noting with appreciation the commitment of the countries concerned to do their utmost to facilitate the provision of assistance to the affected populations and to take the necessary measures in this regard,

Realizing the importance of assisting the host countries, in particular those countries that have been hosting refugees for a long time, in remedying environmental deterioration and the negative impact on public services and the development process,

Recognizing the mandate of the High Commissioner to protect and assist refugees and returnees and the catalytic role she plays, together with the international community and development agencies, in addressing the broader issues of development relating to refugees, returnees and displaced persons,

Bearing in mind the necessity of facilitating the work of humanitarian organizations, in particular the supply of food, medicine and health care to refugees, returnees and displaced persons, deploring acts of aggression against personnel of humanitarian organizations, particularly those acts that have led to the loss of life, and stressing the need to guarantee the safety of the personnel of those organizations,

Deeply concerned about the continuing critical humanitarian situation in African countries, in particular in the Horn of Africa, caused by persistent drought, conflict and population movements,

Conscious of the situation of the refugees, returnees and displaced persons in East and Central Africa,

Welcoming regional efforts, such as the mechanism for conflict prevention, management and resolution adopted by the Assembly of Heads of State and Government of the Organization of African Unity at its twenty-ninth ordinary session, held at Cairo from 28 to 30 June 1993,

Taking into account resolution CM/Res.1448(LVIII) on refugees, returnees and displaced persons in Africa, adopted by the Council of Ministers of the Organization of African Unity at its fifty-eighth ordinary session, held at Cairo from 21 to 26 June 1993,

Deeply concerned by the massive presence of refugees and externally displaced persons in Djibouti, which represents 25 per cent of the total population of the country, and by their uninterrupted influx due to the tragic situation in Somalia,

Deeply concerned also by the serious consequences of the presence of refugees and externally displaced persons for the already difficult economic and social situation in Djibouti, which is suffering from prolonged drought and the negative impact of the critical situation in the Horn of Africa,

Recognizing that more than half of the refugees and externally displaced persons in Djibouti are located in Djibouti City in most serious difficulties and without direct international assistance, exerting intolerable pressure on the limited resources of the country and the social infrastructure and causing, in particular, serious problems of security,

Also recognizing the need for cooperation between the Government of Djibouti and the High Commissioner and relevant organizations to find alternative solutions for the problem of refugees in Djibouti City and to be able to mobilize the necessary external assistance to meet their specific needs,

Aware that the refugee population in the refugee camps throughout Djibouti is in a precarious situation, facing the threat of famine, malnutrition and disease, and that it needs adequate external assistance for the provision of foodstuff, medical assistance and the necessary infrastructure for shelter,

Aware also that Eritrea has been devastated by a thirty-year war, which ended in May 1991, and repeated droughts over the years, that its economy and resources have been destroyed and that it is starting anew,

Recognizing the massive task facing Eritrea of repatriating over half a million refugees, particularly from the Sudan, through its Programme for Refugee Reintegration and Rehabilitation of Resettlement Areas in Eritrea, and resettling voluntary returnees already in the country, internally displaced persons and demobilized former combatants, and the enormous burden that this has placed on the Government of Eritrea,

Recognizing also the need for cooperation between the Government of Eritrea and the Department of Humanitarian Affairs of the Secretariat and relevant organizations to enable the mobilization of the necessary international assistance to put the programmes of human resettlement into action in Eritrea,

Deeply concerned about the massive presence of refugees, voluntary returnees, displaced persons and demobilized soldiers in Ethiopia and the enormous burden that this has placed on the country's infrastructure and meagre resources of the country,

Deeply concerned also about the grave consequences this has entailed for Ethiopia's capability to grapple with the effects of the prolonged drought and rebuild the country's economy,

Aware of the heavy burden placed on the Government of Ethiopia and of the need for immediate and adequate assistance to refugees, voluntary returnees, displaced persons, demobilized soldiers and victims of natural disasters,

Deeply concerned about the burden that has been placed on the Government and people of Kenya because of the influx of refugees fleeing the strife and famine that have stricken neighbouring countries and the infiltration of armed bandits and highly dangerous and illegal weapons from the situation obtaining in Somalia,

Aware of the need to improve the security situation in the region, particularly in the border areas, for the safety of the refugees, local community and personnel involved in humanitarian activities,

Recognizing the great contribution and sacrifices that the Government of Kenya has made and continues to make in dealing with this situation, while facing deteriorating conditions caused by the impact of the persistent drought that has affected and continues to affect its own population,

Emphasizing the importance and necessity of continuing assistance to the refugees and displaced persons in Kenya, until such time as this situation has changed,

Deeply concerned about the tragic impact that the civil war in Somalia continues to have on the lives of its people, affecting four to five million people who are either refugees in neighbouring countries or internally displaced and are in need of urgent humanitarian assistance,

Aware that the voluntary repatriation of large numbers of Somali refugees in neighbouring countries and elsewhere, as well as the return of internally displaced persons to their original homes, will still require a planned and integrated international assistance programme designed to cover their basic needs, ensure adequate reception arrangements and facilitate their smooth integration into their respective communities,

Convinced that it is necessary that humanitarian assistance to Somali refugees, returnees and displaced persons be mobilized urgently and delivered without delay in view of the deteriorating situation of the displaced persons and returnees and the mounting pressure the refugees continue to place on the host countries,

Appealing to the Somalis to implement the Addis Ababa Agreement concerning national reconciliation which the Somali leaders signed on 27 March 1993 in order to create an environment conducive to the repatriation of Somali refugees from the neighbouring countries,

Recognizing that the Sudan has been hosting large numbers of refugees over an extended period of time,

Aware of the economic difficulties facing the Government of the Sudan and the need for adequate assistance for the refugees and displaced persons in the Sudan and the rehabilitation of the areas in which they are located,

Commending the Government of the Sudan and the Office of the United Nations High Commissioner for Refugees for the efforts they have undertaken for the voluntary repatriation of the large numbers of refugees to their homelands,

Deeply concerned about the plight of Sudanese refugee children, particularly the problem of unaccompanied minors, and emphasizing the need for their protection, well-being and reunification with their families,

Considering that the repatriation and reintegration of returnees and the relocation of displaced persons are aggravated by natural disasters and that the process poses serious humanitarian, social and economic problems for the Government of Chad,

Cognizant of the appeal to Member States and intergovernmental and non-governmental organizations to continue to provide the necessary assistance to the Government of Chad to alleviate its problems and improve its abilities to implement the programme of repatriation, reintegration and relocation of voluntary returnees and displaced persons,

Noting with appreciation the continuing efforts of the Economic Community of West African States and the Organization of African Unity to restore peace, security and stability in Liberia, and the signing at Cotonou, Benin, on 25 July 1993, of the peace agreement between the Interim Government of National Unity of Liberia, the National Patriotic Front of Liberia and the United Liberation Movement of Liberia for Democracy, as well as the establishment of the United Nations Observer Mission in Liberia, aimed at bringing an end to the conflict,

Deeply concerned about the influx of internally displaced persons, returnees and refugees to Monrovia and the enormous burden this has placed on the infrastructure and fragile economy of the country,

Also deeply concerned that, despite the efforts made to provide the necessary material and financial assistance for the refugees, returnees and displaced persons, the situation remains unsettled and has serious implications for the long-term national development of Liberia, as well as for those West African countries hosting Liberian refugees,

Bearing in mind the continuing need to provide emergency humanitarian assistance to Liberian refugees, returnees and displaced persons, since the security situation is not yet propitious for the conduct of large-scale voluntary repatriation and reintegration,

Recognizing the heavy burden placed on the people and Government of Malawi and the sacrifices they are making in caring for refugees, given the country's limited social services and infrastructure, and the need for adequate international assistance to Malawi to enable it to continue its efforts to provide assistance to the refugees,

Gravely concerned about the continuing serious social, economic and environmental impact of the massive presence of refugees in Malawi, as well as its far-reaching consequences for the long-term development process and environmental effects,

Bearing in mind the findings and recommendations of the 1991 inter-agency mission to Malawi, particularly on the need to strengthen the country's socio-economic infrastructure in order to enable it to provide for the immediate humanitarian relief requirements of the refugees as well as on the long-term national development needs of the country,

Convinced that, because of the serious economic situation and, in particular, because of the effect of devastating drought in southern Africa, there is continued need for the international community to extend maximum and concerted assistance to southern African countries sheltering refugees, returnees and displaced persons,

Welcoming with appreciation the ongoing activities of the High Commissioner for the voluntary repatriation and reintegration of South African returnees, and hoping that the obstacles to the return of all refugees and exiles in conditions of safety and dignity will be removed without delay,

Recognizing the need to integrate refugee-related development projects in local and national development plans,

1. *Takes note* of the report of the Secretary-General and that of the High Commissioner for Refugees;

2. *Commends* the Governments concerned for their sacrifices, for providing assistance to refugees, returnees and displaced persons and for their efforts to promote voluntary repatriation and other measures taken in order to find appropriate and lasting solutions;

3. *Expresses deep concern* at the serious and far-reaching consequences of the presence of large numbers of refugees and displaced persons in the countries concerned and the implications for the security environment and their long-term socio-economic development;

4. *Expresses its appreciation* to the Secretary-General, the High Commissioner, the specialized agencies, the International Committee of the Red Cross, donor countries and intergovernmental and non-governmental organizations for their assistance in mitigating the plight of the large number of refugees, returnees and displaced persons;

5. *Expresses the hope* that additional resources will be made available for general refugee programmes to keep pace with refugee needs;

6. *Appeals* to Member States, international organizations and non-governmental organizations to provide adequate and sufficient financial, material and technical assistance for relief and rehabilitation programmes for the large number of refugees, voluntary returnees and displaced persons and victims of natural disasters and to the affected countries;

7. *Requests* all Governments and intergovernmental and non-governmental organizations to pay particular attention to the protection of special needs of refugee women and children;

8. *Calls upon* the Secretary-General, the High Commissioner, the Department of Humanitarian Affairs of the Secretariat and United Nations humanitarian agencies to continue their efforts to mobilize humanitarian assistance for the relief, repatriation, rehabilitation and resettlement of refugees, returnees and displaced persons, including those refugees in urban areas;

9. *Requests* the Secretary-General to continue his efforts to mobilize adequate financial and material assistance for the full implementation of ongoing projects in rural and urban areas affected by the presence of refugees, returnees and displaced persons;

10. *Requests* the High Commissioner to continue her efforts with the appropriate United Nations agencies, the Organization of African Unity and intergovernmental, governmental and non-governmental organizations in order to consolidate and increase essential services to refugees, returnees and displaced persons;

11. *Also requests* the Secretary-General to submit a comprehensive and consolidated report on the situation of refugees, returnees and displaced persons in Africa to the General Assembly at its forty-ninth session, under the item entitled ''Report of the United Nations High Commissioner for Refugees, questions relating to refugees, returnees and displaced persons, and humanitarian questions'', and an oral report to the Economic and Social Council at its substantive session of 1994.

General Assembly resolution 48/118

20 December 1993   Meeting 85   Adopted without vote

Approved by Third Committee (A/48/631) without vote, 19 November (meeting 38); draft by Algeria on behalf of the African States (A/C.3/48/L.28), orally revised; agenda item 113.
Meeting numbers. GA 48th session: 3rd Committee 23-28, 33, 34, 38; plenary 85.

The Americas and the Caribbean

The High Commmissioner reported[11] continued improvements in the refugee situation in the Americas during 1993, due to the success of regional peace initiatives and the follow-up process to the 1989 International Conference on Central American Refugees (CIREFCA). The consolidation of durable solutions for Central American refugees included the first organized return of several thousand Guatemalan refugees from Mexico; a decline in the number of Haitian refugee-seekers; and steady progress with the voluntary repatriation of Chilean and Surinamese refugees. UNHCR was, however, increasingly concerned at the arrival of asylum-seekers from outside the region, particularly from Africa and China.

In Canada, the introduction of a Bill in February 1993 laid the foundation for significant changes in refugee determination procedures, while in the United States, intense efforts were made to amend the Asylum Act, including measures to expedite exclusion procedures.

UNHCR expanded its activities in Brazil following an accelerated influx of asylum-seekers from Africa, mainly from Angola and Zaire. Democratic reforms in Chile continued to inspire the repatriation of refugees. UNHCR assisted the return of some 1,945 Chileans in 1993.

Despite ongoing problems, UNHCR assisted in the repatriation of 1,796 Haitians from the

Bahamas and Cuba. In February, 208 Haitians repatriated with the assistance of the Cuban Red Cross. Cuban authorities provided asylum to all Haitians who opted to remain in the country and a local integration programme for 46 Haitians in Isla de la Juventud was implemented by the Government. In the same period, 177 Chileans and 281 Salvadorians repatriated from Cuba. Also in February, the United States began in-country processing in Haiti for those who considered that their life or liberty was jeopardized by the country's political situation, but UNHCR did not consider this to be an alternative to the right to seek asylum and was monitoring the situation closely.

In Central America, UNHCR implemented QIP's in Belize, El Salvador and Guatemala and the first collective repatriation of 2,466 Guatemalan refugees was accomplished in January. UNHCR also supported the revision of CIREFCA projects to enhance their impact on refugee, returnee and displaced women in Central America and the implementation of an executive decree by Costa Rica that allowed 10,200 refugees to obtain residence status in the country. UNHCR's direct involvement in a $12 million QIP programme in Nicaragua ended on 30 June.

Arrangements for the United Nations Development Programme (UNDP) to assume the lead-agency role in CIREFCA on 1 July were confirmed at a high-level meeting between UNHCR, UNDP and the Office of the Secretary-General. UNHCR's component of the overall CIREFCA package for 1993/1994 was budgeted at some $40 million.

In 1993, total UNHCR expenditure in the Americas and the Caribbean amounted to $38.1 million, of which $21.1 million was under General Programmes and $16.9 million under Special Programmes.

Follow-up to the International Conference on Central American Refugees

In response to a 1992 General Assembly request,[12] the Secretary-General submitted a September report on the CIREFCA follow-up process.[13] He stated that, as a result of the Central American peace agreements and the CIREFCA process, almost 100,000 persons had been repatriated to El Salvador, Guatemala and Nicaragua and the number of Central American refugees receiving international assistance had decreased by 50 per cent since 1989 to some 75,000.

Through CIREFCA programmes in the first quarter of 1993, UNHCR supported the local integration of Nicaraguans and Salvadorians in their countries of asylum (Belize and Costa Rica) as well as reintegration programmes in their countries of origin. The largest of those programmes was a $12 million QIP which was concluded in Nicaragua in June. It directly benefited 70,000 returnees, demobilized combatants and local populations.

Since the QIP's inception in 1991, a total of 350 micro-projects had been implemented.

The Ninth Ministerial Conference between the European Community (EC) and Central American States (San Salvador, El Salvador, 22 and 23 February), issued a final communiqué that voiced support for CIREFCA by calling for increased resources for refugee and sustainable development programmes in the region.

A total of 153 projects, with total external funding requirements of $335.7 million, had been recorded in seven countries since CIREFCA's inception in 1989. As at January 1993, $240.1 million had been mobilized, of which 38 per cent was contributed through NGOs, 32 per cent through Governments of the region, 24 per cent through UNHCR and 6 per cent through other channels.

In October,[14] the UNHCR Executive Committee reaffirmed its support for the efforts of Belize and Mexico in favour of uprooted populations, especially in the area of human rights. It urged the international community to develop innovative approaches that emphasized social programmes to combat extreme poverty in the transition from repatriation assistance to development cooperation. It reiterated its support for UNDP's lead-agency role, since July, and emphasized the importance of incorporating the needs of refugees, returnees and displaced populations into UNDP's post-CIREFCA strategy. It requested UNHCR and UNDP to convene jointly an informal technical meeting with this objective.

GENERAL ASSEMBLY ACTION

On 20 December, the General Assembly, on the recommendation of the Third Committee, adopted **resolution 48/117** without vote.

International Conference on Central American Refugees

The General Assembly,

Recalling its resolutions 42/1 of 7 October 1987, 42/110 of 7 December 1987, 42/204 of 11 December 1987, 42/231 of 12 May 1988, 43/118 of 8 December 1988, 44/139 of 15 December 1989, 45/141 of 14 December 1990, 46/107 of 16 December 1991 and 47/103 of 16 December 1992,

Bearing in mind that the International Conference on Central American Refugees is related to the initiative of the Central American Presidents expressed in the procedures for the establishment of a firm and lasting peace in Central America, signed at the Esquipulas II summit meeting on 7 August 1987,

Also bearing in mind that the Central American Presidents, at the fourteenth summit meeting, held at Guatemala City from 27 to 29 October 1993, expressing the need to continue the transition from humanitarian assistance to development cooperation, decided to call upon the international community, especially the International Conference on Central American Refugees, which has carried out valuable work in that area, to continue its support for humanitarian and development programmes benefiting uprooted populations,

Recognizing the importance and validity of the Declaration and the Concerted Plan of Action in favour of Central American Refugees, Returnees and Displaced Persons, adopted at the International Conference on Central American Refugees held at Guatemala City in May 1989, and the Declarations of the First and Second International Meetings of the Follow-Up Committee of the Conference,

Recalling of the outcome of the meetings of the Follow-Up Committee of the International Conference on Central American Refugees, held at San José in April 1991, at San Pedro Sula, Honduras, in June 1991, at Tegucigalpa in August 1991, at Managua in October 1991, at San Salvador in April 1992 and at Managua in September and October 1992,

Taking note of the report of the Follow-Up Committee of the Conference, submitted to the Executive Committee of the Programme of the United Nations High Commissioner for Refugees at its forty-fourth session, concerning the implementation of the Concerted Plan of Action,

Noting with satisfaction the efforts being made by the Central American countries, Belize and Mexico to find lasting solutions to the problems of the refugees, returnees and displaced persons in implementing the aims and objectives of the Concerted Plan of Action as an integral part of efforts to achieve a firm and lasting peace and democratization of the region,

Welcoming with satisfaction the progress made in El Salvador in achieving the consolidation of peace in that country, in accordance with the peace agreements and the National Reconstruction Plan, the efforts to achieve peace and reconciliation in Guatemala and the efforts made in Nicaragua to achieve the objectives of national reconciliation and to assist the uprooted populations, all of which continue to encourage movements of voluntary repatriation and settlement of internally displaced persons,

Bearing in mind the joint political and economic communiqué adopted at the ninth Ministerial Conference by the States members of the European Community and Central America, the San José IX Summit held at San Salvador on 22 and 23 February 1993, and the joint declaration of the fourteenth summit meeting of Central American Presidents, held at Guatemala City from 27 to 29 October 1993, in which the need for international support for the programmes carried out within the framework of the International Conference on Central American Refugees was reaffirmed,

Recognizing the substantial support that, *inter alia*, the Secretary-General, the Office of the United Nations High Commissioner for Refugees, the United Nations Development Programme, the donor community and national and international non-governmental organizations have given the Conference since its inception,

Also recognizing that the extension of the duration of the Concerted Plan of Action until May 1994 has enabled substantial progress to be made in the efforts to achieve the proposed objectives and aims,

Taking note of the transfer, on 10 July 1993, of the lead-agency role from the Office of the High Commissioner to the United Nations Development Programme in order to strengthen the Concerted Plan of Action,

Convinced that peace, development and democracy are essential in order to solve the problems of uprooted populations in the region,

1. *Takes note* of the report of the Secretary-General and that of the United Nations High Commissioner for Refugees;

2. *Notes with satisfaction* the progress achieved in the implementation of programmes and projects within the framework of the International Conference on Central American Refugees, and expresses its appreciation to the Office of the United Nations High Commissioner for Refugees and the United Nations Development Programme for their substantial support to the process, and for the invaluable contribution of non-governmental organizations;

3. *Urges* the Central American countries, Belize and Mexico to continue to implement and follow up the programmes benefiting refugees, returnees and displaced persons in accordance with their national development plans;

4. *Reaffirms its conviction* that the voluntary repatriation of refugees and the return of displaced persons to their countries or communities of origin continue to be a positive sign of the progress of peace in the region;

5. *Also reaffirms its conviction* that the processes of return to and reintegration in the countries and communities of origin should continue to take place in conditions of dignity and security and with the necessary guarantees to ensure that the affected populations are included in the respective national development plans;

6. *Supports* the special attention that the Central American countries, Belize and Mexico are giving to the particular needs of refugee, repatriated and displaced women and children and to the measures being adopted to protect and improve the environment and to preserve ethnic and cultural values;

7. *Requests* the Secretary-General, the Office of the High Commissioner, the United Nations Development Programme and other organs of the United Nations system to continue their support for and involvement in the follow-up, implementation and evaluation of the humanitarian programmes developed within the framework of the Conference process;

8. *Emphasizes* the importance of ensuring, upon the conclusion of the Conference process in May 1994, that the needs of refugees, returnees and displaced persons are specifically reflected in a comprehensive and sustained concept of human development and that the United Nations Development Programme, with the collaboration of the High Commissioner, continues to support this approach in the post-Conference strategy;

9. *Expresses its conviction* that the work carried out through the integrated Conference process could serve as a valuable lesson to be applied in other regions of the world;

10. *Calls upon* the international community, particularly the donor countries, to continue to strengthen their generous support for the Conference so as to consolidate the aims and objectives set at the Conference, and to continue to provide their valuable cooperation in the financing and implementation of the social and humanitarian programmes proposed for the period of transition to development, their own development programmes and those programmes relating to environmental protection which are designed to meet the needs of the uprooted populations;

11. *Requests* the Secretary-General to submit to the General Assembly at its forty-ninth session a report on

the process of the International Conference on Central American Refugees, including an analysis of achievements, obstacles and pending tasks.

General Assembly resolution 48/117

20 December 1993   Meeting 85   Adopted without vote

Approved by Third Committee (A/48/631) without vote, 19 November (meeting 38); 30-nation draft (A/C.3/48/L.27); agenda item 113.
Sponsors: Argentina, Belize, Bolivia, Chile, Colombia, Costa Rica, Croatia, Cuba, Ecuador, Egypt, El Salvador, Finland, France, Greece, Guatemala, Guyana, Honduras, Italy, Jamaica, Mexico, Morocco, Nicaragua, Norway, Panama, Peru, Spain, Suriname, Sweden, Uruguay, Venezuela.
Meeting numbers. GA 48th session: 3rd Committee 23-28, 33, 34, 38; plenary 85.

East and South Asia and Oceania

Significant progress was made in repatriating refugees in the Asian subregions during 1993.

In South Asia, the signing of two Memoranda of Understanding between Bangladesh and Myanmar, at Dhaka on 12 May and at Yangon on 5 November, paved the way for the voluntary repatriation of some 250,000 refugees from Myanmar who had sought refuge in Bangladesh in 1991-1992. More than 50,000 had already returned spontaneously and preparations for a large-scale organized return movement of the remainder were at an advanced stage. The unsettled situation in northern Sri Lanka prevented UNHCR from actively promoting repatriation from India; however, it facilitated the return of those refugees who expressed a desire to go back and a total of 6,927 Sri Lankan refugees were repatriated during the year. The influx into Nepal of ethnic Nepalese from Bhutan had risen to 82,219 asylum-seekers in six camps in the south-eastern part of the country by 20 March, but scant progress was made towards a solution.

In South-East Asia, 132,000 Cambodians repatriated between January and April, bringing the number who had returned from Thailand and other countries since the start of the operation in March 1992 to some 387,000. Another 1,000 were repatriated from Indonesia. The reintegration effort was generally successful although problems were encountered with land-mines, the acquisition of land, and the attainment of self-sufficiency. As a result of renewed conflict between the Government and Khmer Rouge forces, thousands of Cambodian nationals were displaced within the country. Some 35,000 ethnic Vietnamese Cambodians escaping ethnic persecution were granted refuge in Viet Nam in early 1993, but some 6,000 persons remained stranded along the Cambodian/Vietnamese border despite negotiations to resolve the issue.

The implementation of the Comprehensive Plan of Action for Indo-Chinese Refugees (CPA) continued with considerable success. Under CPA resettlement operations for Vietnamese and Lao refugees, 5,691 persons resettled during the first quarter of 1993. An understanding was reached on 2 October between Indonesia, Viet Nam and UNHCR regarding the return, without the use of force, of all Vietnamese non-refugees from Indonesia. Following the successful completion of refugee status determinations for some 20,000 UNHCR-assisted Lao refugees in Thailand in October, efforts to voluntarily repatriate and resettle the remaining caseload were promoted vigorously. The Sixth Tripartite Meeting between the Lao People's Democratic Republic, Thailand and UNHCR (Savannakhet, Lao People's Democratic Republic, July) reviewed progress and obstacles towards repatriation, including a shortage of suitable rural sites to absorb repatriation volunteers. According to information provided by the High Commissioner in August,[15] all CPA parties agreed during the first half of 1993 to the repatriation of unaccompanied minors from Indonesia and Hong Kong to Viet Nam. The first of these children left Indonesia and Hong Kong under this family reunion operation in April and June, respectively.

In October,[14] the Executive Committee expressed support for the continued voluntary repatriation programme to Viet Nam and urged all the parties concerned to reinforce their efforts for the return and reintegration of Lao refugees and asylum-seekers from Thailand and neighbouring countries. It called on the international community to continue to contribute generously to CPA until all its objectives had been achieved.

During 1993, total expenditures in Asia and Oceania amounted to $144.4 million, of which $58.4 million came under General Programmes and $85.9 million under Special Programmes.

Europe

In Western Europe, the number of new asylum-seekers declined for the first time since 1987. The estimated number of new requests in 1993 was close to 550,000, compared with 680,000 in 1992. Refugee status was granted to some 50,000 asylum-seekers, while more than 400,000 applicants were rejected. Some 60,000 individual claimants were allowed to stay on humanitarian grounds. Member States of the European Union (formerly EC) persevered in their efforts to harmonize their asylum laws and policies. UNHCR continued to provide advice on the implementation of the 1951 Convention relating to the Status of Refugees[16] and its 1967 Protocol,[17] and expressed concern whenever new legislative and administrative measures inclined towards a departure from Western Europe's liberal asylum traditions. While States increasingly relied on measures such as stricter border controls, visa obligations, air carrier sanctions and safe country of origin and first asylum concepts, UNHCR emphasized that such measures did not offer solutions to the refugee problem, but made it increasingly difficult for persons in need of international protection to gain admission to safety and access to asylum procedures.

By April, seminars to promote refugee law and institution-building had been held in 11 countries for officials of the Ministries of Justice, Interior, Labour and Social Affairs, as well as for NGO representatives. The seminars were organized in cooperation with the International Organization for Migration and included representatives of the United Nations Human Rights Centre, the Council of Europe, the International Committee of the Red Cross and the International Federation of Red Cross and Red Crescent Societies, as well as national experts from Western European refugee and immigration offices.

In Central and Eastern Europe, UNHCR continued to focus its activities on protection, the promotion of refugee law and institution-building, and the operation of limited assistance programmes. National Officer posts were created in cooperation with concerned Governments to pursue in-country legal and training activities, to counter xenophobic trends and to encourage a more positive approach to refugees. Meanwhile, Governments of the region sought to control migratory flows in transit through their territories. Most were seriously affected by events in the former Yugoslavia and provided temporary protection to substantial numbers of persons fleeing conflict areas.

UNHCR extended life-sustaining assistance in Armenia to some 140,000 ethnic Armenians fleeing Nagorny Karabakh, Sumgait and Baku. In Azerbaijan, more than 900,000 persons were displaced by the Nagorny Karabakh conflict. UNHCR's target population in Azerbaijan increased in less than a year from 53,000 to 300,000, including 185,000 Azeri refugees from Armenia. In Georgia, with a displaced population of some 300,000, UNHCR provided limited care and assistance programmes to internally displaced persons from Abkhazia and South Ossetia, as well as to a small number of returnees from North to South Ossetia.

According to an August report of the High Commissioner,[18] the total affected population in the former Yugoslavia was more than 3.6 million at the end of June. In Bosnia and Herzegovina, UNHCR provided assistance to 2.74 million people, about 65 per cent of the total population. During 1993, 11 staff and staff associated with UNHCR lost their lives assisting victims of the conflict. The scope and magnitude of the emergency operation in Bosnia and Herzegovina reached unprecedented levels during the year. UNHCR launched appeals on 9 March for $767.1 million to benefit an estimated 3.8 million people, and on 8 October for $696.5 million to benefit 4.3 mil-

lion people. Airlifts to Gorazde, Maglaj, Sarajevo, Srebrenica and Zepa delivered thousands of metric tonnes of humanitarian relief supplies, food and medicine, and the medical evacuation programme from Sarajevo was a lifeline for serious cases. UNHCR's financial obligations for the Special Operation in the former Yugoslavia totalled $284.6 million in 1993.

Expressing grave concern at the magnitude of the emergency in the former Yugoslavia, particularly in Bosnia and Herzegovina (see PART TWO, Chapter IV), the UNHCR Executive Committee, in October,[14] urged all Governments and concerned parties to ensure implementation of the Comprehensive Response to the Humanitarian Crisis in the former Yugoslavia and to continue to contribute generously to the United Nations Consolidated Inter-Agency Programme of Action.

During 1993, UNHCR's total expenditure in Europe amounted to $585.5 million, of which $25 million was under General Programmes and $560.4 million was under Special Programmes.

Azerbaijan refugee situation

In two communications dated 15 November,[19] Azerbaijan informed the Secretary-General that, as a result of an intensified offensive by Armenia in the south-west of Azerbaijan, more than 37,000 persons had fled their homes since 1 November, in addition to the one million people already displaced from territory occupied by Armenian armed forces. Many refugees had been forced to cross the Araks river into Iran, while others had settled in an overcrowded refugee camp in the Imisli district of Azerbaijan. Azerbaijan noted that snow had fallen throughout the country and temperatures had reached freezing point, creating a desperate need for shelter and food so that the refugees could survive the winter. The Azerbaijani authorities appealed for foreign aid to avoid a catastrophe.

GENERAL ASSEMBLY ACTION

On 20 December, the General Assembly, on the recommendation of the Third Committee, adopted **resolution 48/114** without vote.

Emergency international assistance to refugees and displaced persons in Azerbaijan

The General Assembly,

Recalling its relevant resolutions regarding humanitarian assistance to refugees and displaced persons,

Having considered the report of the United Nations High Commissioner for Refugees,

Recognizing the catalytic role that the High Commissioner plays, together with the international community and development agencies, in the promotion of humanitarian aid and development with a view to finding durable and lasting solutions for refugees and displaced persons,

Expressing its grave concern at the continuing deterioration of the humanitarian situation in Azerbaijan owing to the displacement of large numbers of civilians,

Welcoming the efforts made by the United Nations interim office and the Office of the United Nations High Commissioner for Refugees in Azerbaijan to coordinate the needs assessment and the provision of humanitarian assistance,

Welcoming also the consolidated United Nations interagency humanitarian programme for Azerbaijan for the period 1 July 1993 to 31 March 1994,

Expressing its appreciation to the States and intergovernmental and non-governmental organizations that have responded positively and continue to respond to the humanitarian needs of Azerbaijan, and to the Secretary-General and United Nations bodies for mobilizing and coordinating the delivery of appropriate humanitarian assistance,

Also expressing its appreciation to the Governments of the neighbouring States that provide the necessary humanitarian assistance, including the provision of accommodation and transit routes through their territories for the displaced persons from Azerbaijan,

Noting with alarm that the humanitarian situation in Azerbaijan has continued to deteriorate seriously since the adoption of the programme in June 1993 and that the number of refugees and displaced persons in Azerbaijan has recently exceeded one million,

Aware that the refugees and displaced persons are in a precarious situation, facing the threat of malnutrition and disease, and that appropriate external assistance is needed for the provision of foodstuffs, medical aid and the necessary shelter for the winter,

Deeply concerned about the enormous burden that the massive presence of refugees and displaced persons has placed on the country's infrastructure,

Affirming the urgent need to continue international action to assist Azerbaijan in providing shelter, medication and food to the refugees and displaced persons, especially to the most vulnerable groups,

1. *Welcomes with appreciation* the efforts undertaken by the Secretary-General in drawing the attention of the international community to the acute problems of the Azerbaijani refugees and displaced persons and in mobilizing assistance for them;

2. *Urgently appeals* to all States, organizations and programmes of the United Nations, specialized agencies and other intergovernmental and non-governmental organizations to provide adequate and sufficient financial, medical and material assistance to the Azerbaijani refugees and displaced persons;

3. *Invites* the international financial institutions and the specialized agencies, organizations and programmes of the United Nations system, where appropriate, to bring the special needs of the Azerbaijani refugees and displaced persons to the attention of their respective governing bodies for their consideration and to report on the decisions of those bodies to the Secretary-General;

4. *Invites* the Secretary-General to continue to monitor the overall situation of refugees and displaced persons in Azerbaijan and to make available his good offices as required;

5. *Requests* the United Nations High Commissioner for Refugees to continue her efforts with the appropriate United Nations agencies and intergovernmental,

governmental and non-governmental organizations, in order to consolidate and increase essential services to refugees and displaced persons in Azerbaijan;

6. *Requests* the Secretary-General to report to the General Assembly at its forty-ninth session on the progress made in the implementation of the present resolution.

General Assembly resolution 48/114

20 December 1993   Meeting 85   Adopted without vote

Approved by Third Committee (A/48/631) without vote, 22 November (meeting 39); 24-nation draft (A/C.3/48/L.23/Rev.1); agenda item 113.
Sponsors: Afghanistan, Azerbaijan, Bangladesh, Bosnia and Herzegovina, Costa Rica, Cuba, Egypt, Ethiopia, Guinea-Bissau, Iran, Jordan, Kazakhstan, Kuwait, Kyrgyzstan, Malaysia, Morocco, Pakistan, Republic of Moldova, Saudi Arabia, Sierra Leone, Tajikistan, Turkey, Ukraine, Yemen.
Meeting numbers. GA 48th session: 3rd Committee 23-28, 33, 34, 38, 39; plenary 85.

South-West Asia, North Africa and the Middle East

In South-West Asia, over 4 million Afghans remained in exile (2.5 million in Iran and 1.5 million in Pakistan) at the beginning of 1993 as internecine conflict in Afghanistan continued to undermine efforts to form a broad-based central Government and clouded prospects for a full-scale repatriation. The return of Afghan refugees from Iran and Pakistan slowed during the year, with 468,894 individuals repatriating with UNHCR assistance and an additional 400,000 returning spontaneously. The Afghan refugee population in Iran declined from 2.7 million to 1.8 million between December 1992 and the end of 1993. UNHCR was the lead agency in northern Afghanistan, coordinating assistance to 15,000 displaced persons from the capital who resided in five camps and numerous public locations. Some 23,000 Afghan repatriates who returned from Pakistan during January and February benefited from a UNHCR assistance package consisting of a cash grant and wheat provided by WFP. The number of camp administration units operating in Pakistan was more than halved from 347 before the 1992 mass repatriation[20] to 145. UNHCR expenditure in 1993 for voluntary repatriation of Afghan refugees came to $31.7 million.

The UNHCR Executive Committee, in October,[14] urged the international community to contribute generously to humanitarian programmes in Afghanistan and to the ongoing repatriation operation from Pakistan and Iran.

The easing of the civil war in Tajikistan, which in 1992 had led to the displacement of some 500,000 persons (over 60,000 of whom fled to Afghanistan), enabled about half of the refugees and 80 per cent of the displaced persons to return home. The spontaneous and assisted repatriation of Tajik refugees began shortly after an amnesty agreement and the first meeting of the Quadripartite Commission on Repatriation comprising Afghanistan, Tajikistan, Uzbekistan and UNHCR. Some 13,000 refugees returned spontaneously to Tajikistan and an additional 17,000 returned with UNHCR assistance, primarily to Piandj and Gorno-Badakhshan.

In an 11 January letter,[21] Afghanistan advised the Secretary-General of an exodus of people from Tajiskistan to Afghanistan where they were living under very difficult circumstances. Faced with an extremely difficult financial situation after 14 years of war, the Government of Afghanistan sought emergency United Nations assistance for the Tajik refugees in the form of food, clothing, medicines and shelter. The High Commissioner reported[22] that, following a November 1992 United Nations assessment mission, a joint appeal was launched in January 1993 for $7.8 million—a figure that was later increased to $19.5 million. UNHCR dispatched its first emergency teams to Tajikistan and Uzbekistan in January and launched an emergency operation aimed at preventing further population movements and at assisting the return of internally displaced persons and refugees to their places of origin. The first phase of the emergency assistance programme, involving the transportation of relief supplies by air from Pakistan and Turkey, was completed by June. The second phase involved the regional procurement of building materials for the repair and reconstruction of some 17,000 houses and the provision of supplementary food, fuel and other non-food items. In 1993, expenditures for Tajik refugees in Afghanistan came to $3.9 million. Total UNHCR obligations for Central Asia amounted to $8.7 million.

In January, Iraqi authorities formally requested UNHCR to increase its assistance to 22,500 Iranian refugees at the Al-Tash camp to hasten the voluntary repatriation of approximately 13,000 persons and to provide resettlement opportunities for those unable or unwilling to return to their homeland. UNHCR also continued its assistance programme for some 67,000 Iraqi Kurds and 42,000 Iraqi Shiites. Some 7,000 Iraqis from the southern marshes had sought asylum in Iran since June. When fighting erupted in Azerbaijan in August, Iran helped to transport some 50,000 Azerbaijanis, who crossed into its northern border areas, to take refuge in the safer eastern part of Azerbaijan where seven camps were established. UNHCR provided limited assistance to the group during transportation. In September, the Office initiated a pilot project that covered food, shelter and economic integration for the return of up to 10,200 Iraqi Kurds from neighbouring countries. Some 7,000 individuals were repatriated under the project. UNHCR continued to assist 3,800 Iranian refugees in Iraq's three northern governorates; 20,690 Iranian refugees in the Al-Tash camp in the Al Anbar governorate; 20,000 Iranian Ahwazi refugees in the Wasit and Misan governorates and some 1,200 urban refugees of various nationalities. Saudi Arabia hosted and provided a range of assistance to 24,025 Iraqi refugees located in Rafha camp and, at year's end, the Syrian Arab Republic was hosting a refugee population of 37,100 persons, comprising 35,250 Iraqis, 1,250 Somalis, 300 Eritreans and 300 nationals of other countries. Since the influx to Syria from Iraq began, some 3,000 persons had repatriated voluntarily. UNHCR assisted 3,850 persons in the El Hol refugee camp and to needy urban refugees in Damascus through the Syrian Red Crescent Society.

In Yemen, some 11,300 Somali refugees were moved with UNHCR assistance in May from the Madinat Al Shaab camp (Aden) to the newly constructed Al Khoud camp in the Abyan governorate. Another 1,500 Somalis, who received monthly WFP food rations, were located in the Shihir and Sacar camps at Mukallah. While 512 Somalis from areas other than Mogadishu registered for repatriation, the prevailing insecurity in Somalia prevented their return. Among the 1,025 Ethiopian refugees in Yemen, 262 civilian and ex-navy personnel repatriated in 1993. Total UNHCR obligations in 1993 for Yemen amounted to $3.5 million.

At the request of the Algerian Government, UNHCR began an assistance programme on 1 January for the neediest 9,000 of some 50,000 refugees from Mali and Niger in the southern Algerian provinces of Adrar, Illizi and Tamanrasset. Total 1993 obligations for Algeria, including assistance to Sahraoui refugees, amounted to $4.3 million.

During the first six months of the year, the caseload of Malian refugees entering Mauritania reached 42,000 people. Within the framework of the "Pacte national", signed in April 1992 between Mali and the Mouvements et Fronts unifiés de l'AZAWAD, the Office commenced work in March on a comprehensive plan for the repatriation of Malians willing to return to their homeland. A first group of 6,500 refugees was registered for repatriation at year's end. Allocations for some 38,000 Malian refugees in Mauritania totalled $4.3 million.

Total expenditure in 1993 in South West Asia, North Africa and the Middle East amounted to $115.4 million, of which $57.6 million were disbursed under General Programmes and $57.8 million under Special Programmes.

Refugee protection

UNHCR's main functions on behalf of refugees were to provide international protection and promote durable solutions to their plight. In cases where direct or indirect obstacles were placed in the way of refugee safety and recognition, UNHCR intervened with the authorities to secure the immediate safety of the refugee or asylum-seeker and to interpret certain doctrines enshrined in the 1951 Convention relating to the Status of Refugees[16] and other instruments. The Office's promotional activities sought to strengthen knowledge and understanding of refugee issues, as well as to foster the effective implementation of international legal standards on behalf of refugees, returnees and other persons. The development of model legislation on refugees was at the core of a cooperation project between UNHCR, the Organization of African Unity (OAU) and the Asian-African Legal Consultative Committee. UNHCR participated actively in the World Conference on Human Rights in June (see PART THREE, Chapter X) to ensure that the Vienna Declaration noted the close link between human rights and refugee protection.

In an August note on international protection,[23] the High Commissioner presented a detailed review and analysis of current issues relating to refugee protection, including principles and other aspects of asylum and non-refoulement; respect for human rights; protection of the internally displaced; protection in situations of conflict; and voluntary repatriation. It concluded that the international protection of refugees would be impossible without the cooperation of States in a spirit of international solidarity and burden-sharing, both in providing asylum to those in need and in fostering solutions to refugee problems.

The UNHCR Executive Committee noted with appreciation the continued observance of international protection principles, and commended, in particular, developing countries with limited resources, which hosted the majority of the world's refugees. The Committee[14] underlined the importance of establishing and ensuring access for all asylum-seekers to fair and efficient procedures for the determination of their refugee status and stressed the importance of adopting common criteria, in consultation with UNHCR, to determine responsibility for considering an application for asylum.

The Committee adopted a general conclusion on the personal security of refugees which deplored violence, intimidation, military or armed attacks, forced recruitment and arbitrary or inhumane conditions of detention. It called on States to adopt measures to prevent or remove such threats. In addition to the need to site refugee settlements securely and to ensure unhindered access by UNHCR and other organizations, States were called on to investigate abuses.

The UNHCR Centre for Documentation on Refugees, which provided authoritative and relevant refugee literature and legal and country information, expanded its services and responded to more than 1,700 information requests. All databases were updated and transferred to the UNHCR local area network for easy access. A pilot project was initiated to test the possibilities for granting external access in the near future. Publication of the quarterly *Refugee Abstracts* was suspended temporarily for revision. Collaboration continued with the *International Journal of Refugee Law*, published by Oxford University Press.

International instruments

As at 31 December 1993, the 1951 Convention relating to the Status of Refugees[16] had 121 States parties. Armenia, Azerbaijan, the Bahamas, Bulgaria, Bosnia and Herzegovina, the Russian Federation, Saint Vincent and the Grenadines, Slovakia and Tajikistan became parties in 1993. The 1967 Protocol[17] to the Convention also had 121 States parties, with the same States, with the exception of Saint Vincent and the Grenadines, becoming parties in 1993.[24]

Other intergovernmental legal instruments of benefit to refugees included the 1969 OAU Convention governing the Specific Aspects of Refugee Problems in Africa, the 1957 Agreement relating to Refugee Seamen and its 1973 Protocol, the 1959 European Agreement on the Abolition of Visas to Refugees, the 1980 European Agreement on Transfer of Responsibility for Refugees, and the 1969 American Convention on Human Rights, Pact of San José, Costa Rica.

As at 31 December 1993,[24] there were 40 States parties to the 1954 Convention relating to the Status of Stateless Persons[25] and 16 States parties to the 1961 Convention on the Reduction of Statelessness.[26]

Nansen Medal

The Nansen Medal for 1993—presented since 1954 in honour of Fridtjof Nansen, the first League of Nations High Commissioner for Refugees—was awarded to the NGO, Médecins sans Frontières, in recognition of its exceptional service to refugees.

REFERENCES

[1]A/48/12. [2]E/1994/41. [3]YUN 1992, p. 897. [4]GA res. 44/25, 20 Nov. 1989. [5]YUN 1988, p. 663. [6]A/AC.96/808(Part I). [7]S/26272. [8]YUN 1992, p. 193. [9]YUN 1992, p. 898, GA res. 47/107, 16 Dec. 1992. [10]A/48/444. [11]A/AC.96/808(Part IV). [12]YUN 1992, p. 901, GA res. 47/103, 16 Dec. 1992. [13]A/48/391. [14]A/48/12/Add.1. [15]A/AC.96/808(Part II). [16]YUN 1951, p. 520. [17]YUN 1967, p. 769. [18]A/AC.96/808(Part III). [19]A/48/604-S/26762, A/48/605-S/26763. [20]YUN 1992, p. 904. [21]A/48/64. [22]A/AC.96/808(Parts V & VI). [23]A/AC.96/815. [24]*Multilateral Treaties Deposited with the Secretary-General: Status as at 31 December 1993* (ST/LEG/SER.E/12), Sales No. E.94.V.11. [25]YUN 1954, p. 416. [26]YUN 1961, p. 533.

Chapter XVI

International drug control

The globalization of drug abuse remained a major problem for Governments and United Nations drug control bodies in 1993. With the rising economic and political influence of drug cartels, more and more Governments realized the urgent need for international cooperation in drug control, not only as an expression of solidarity but also as a matter of self defence. Drug trafficking syndicates were becoming increasingly involved in other forms of organized and violent crime.

The International Narcotics Control Board continued to supervise the implementation of drug control treaties and to survey the drug control situation worldwide, while the United Nations International Drug Control Programme provided leadership and coordination for United Nations drug control activities. The Commission on Narcotic Drugs—the main policy-making body of the United Nations on drug control questions—made recommendations on issues ranging from the treatment of drug abusers to cooperation among States against drug trafficking. The Economic and Social Council adopted nine resolutions based on the Commission's recommendations.

The General Assembly called for international action against drug abuse and illicit trafficking within the framework of the United Nations System-Wide Action Plan on Drug Abuse Control (resolution 48/112). It stressed the importance of national and international action to implement existing drug control treaties and called on States to adopt adequate laws, strengthen judicial systems and carry out effective drug control activities in cooperation with other States (48/12).

Drug abuse and international control

UN International Drug Control Programme

During 1993, its second full year of operation, the United Nations Drug Control Programme (UNDCP) carried out its activities on the basis of a three-tiered strategy.[1] At all three levels— national, regional or subregional and global— UNDCP, established in 1991,[2] sought to act as a catalyst for and to coordinate international efforts within the framework of the international drug control instruments. Ensuring a balance between efforts to reduce illicit drug demand and supply was another prominent goal.

As at June 1993, UNDCP was funding more than 150 projects. At the country level, it assisted Governments in formulating and adopting drug control master plans. Major emphasis was placed on strengthening institutional and legislative frameworks for planning and effective implementation of drug control initiatives. At the regional or subregional level, UNDCP concentrated on developing and reinforcing intercountry arrangements with a view to enhancing joint planning and implementation of drug control interventions. It also expanded its working ties with regional organizations. At the global level, UNDCP promoted legal activities aimed at universal adherence and application of the international drug control treaties; intensified its role in demand reduction efforts; adopted measures to enhance inter-agency cooperation; and strengthened its research capabilities, including the expansion of its links with major research institutes.

During the course of the year, UNDCP evaluation policy and procedures underwent a process of fine-tuning in order to, *inter alia*, differentiate between project evaluations and thematic evaluations. Fund-raising and public information activities took on added significance.

UNDCP continued to provide support and services to the International Narcotics Control Board (INCB), supplying substantive and analytical input for its report and assisting it in the publication of three annual technical reports. It organized and funded two regional INCB seminars for drug control administrators (Beijing, China, June; Warsaw, Poland, September).

UNDCP's 1992 activities were described in a February 1993 report of the Programme's Executive Director,[3] which also outlined UNDCP's policy framework, strategic direction and coordination with other bodies.

Action by the Commission on Narcotic Drugs. In April,[4] the Commission invited UNDCP to coordinate all drug-related activities by entities and agencies within the United Nations system. It decided, in particular, to maintain active cooperation with the Commission on Crime Prevention and Criminal Justice and coordination with the Commission for Social Development, the Commission on Transnational Corporations and other intergovernmental bodies.

The Commission requested the Executive Director to coordinate the activities of UNDCP and those of the United Nations Crime Prevention and Criminal Justice Branch, and to report to the Commission in 1994 on the most appropriate ways to achieve effective and efficient coordination and cooperation.

In other action,[5] the Commission requested the Executive Director to propose in 1994 ways for the Commission to cooperate effectively with the Preparatory Committee for the 1995 World Summit for Social Development.

Fund of UNDCP

In a January report on the Fund of UNDCP,[6] the Executive Director presented a revised programme budget for the 1992-1993 biennium and a proposed outline for 1994-1995.

The Fund was established on 1 January 1992, under a 1991 General Assembly resolution,[7] under the direct responsibility of the Executive Director, to finance operational activities mainly in developing countries, helping them comply with their treaty obligations and cope with illicit drug production, trafficking and abuse. The financial resources of the former United Nations Fund for Drug Abuse Control were transferred to the Fund. Its programme budget, based on the Executive Director's proposals, was approved by the Commission on Narcotic Drugs, which reported to the Assembly through the Economic and Social Council.

Activities supported under the Fund were implemented by UNDCP within a network of cooperating organizations, including the United Nations Development Programme (UNDP), other United Nations entities, specialized agencies and non-governmental organizations (NGOs).

For 1992-1993, UNDCP's total requirements were estimated at $186,662,000, i.e., $7,221,500 over the amount of $179,440,500 initially approved, to cover requirements for policy-making organs, executive direction and management, the programme of work and programme support. Total requirements for 1994-1995 were estimated at $197 million.

The Executive Director outlined three options for synchronization of the UNDCP budget cycle with the rest of the United Nations system and presented a financial report on operational activities in 1992.

The Advisory Committee on Administrative and Budgetary Questions (ACABQ), in a March 1993 report,[8] said, with regard to the budget estimates for 1992-1993, that it did not believe that at the present time additional posts, especially at Headquarters, should be created on a permanent basis. Welcoming the Executive Director's initiative in presenting the proposed outline for 1994-1995, it noted that it should reflect current and projected income and expenditure and a broad al-location of resources in terms of programme priorities. Overall, ACABQ believed that a better defined link as to relationship and interaction between regular budget resources, Fund resources and related activities should be reflected in the budget document.

Action by the Commission on Narcotic Drugs. In April,[9] the Commission approved revised budget estimates totalling $186,662,000 for 1992-1993 for the Fund of UNDCP and took note of the proposed outline for 1994-1995, including total requirements estimated at $197 million.

In other action,[10] the Commission noted the new programme budget presentation and approved, as a temporary procedure starting in 1993, a revised budget cycle, including the holding of a reconvened biennial session of the Commission in December to approve the programme budget, as recommended by ACABQ.

At is resumed session (Vienna, 16 and 17 December), the Commission adopted a resolution[11] in which it approved the final budget estimates for 1992-1993, totalling $158,876,900, and the performance report for 1992-1993, totalling $149,012,500, for the Fund. It also approved the initial programme budget for 1994-1995, totalling $187,889,300 for the Fund. The Executive Director was asked, in view of the potential difficulties in fully financing the proposed programme in 1994-1995, to report to the Commission in 1994 on how he intended to balance the financial situation by the end of the 1994-1995 biennium within the resources available.

Illicit traffic

Responding to a 1992 General Assembly request,[12] the Secretary-General submitted an August 1993 report[13] on international action to combat drug abuse and illicit trafficking. The report discussed the involvement of children in drug-related criminal activities; cooperation between UNDCP and the United Nations Crime Prevention and Criminal Justice Branch; global trends in illicit drug traffic and transit; the implementation of the 1988 United Nations Convention against Illicit Traffic in Narcotic Drugs and Psychotropic Substances;[14] and the development of the international drug abuse assessment system (IDAAS), the collection of data on illicit traffic, and technical cooperation with developing countries.

The Secretary-General noted that the Commission on Narcotic Drugs had, in 1992 and 1993, considered trends in illicit drug traffic through reports from subsidiary bodies, namely, the Meetings of Heads of National Drug Law Enforcement Agencies (HONLEAs) in each region and the Subcommission on Illicit Drug Traffic and Related Matters in the Near and Middle East. He said that the development of IDAAS had encountered difficulties related to definitional inconsistencies and insufficient data from countries, but a long-term programme was being prepared to improve the quality and quantity of information entering the IDAAS data bank. Another development was the launching of a Rapid Abuse Assessment System, designed to provide developing countries with a reasonably inexpensive means of determining the nature and extent of their drug abuse problems.

ECONOMIC AND SOCIAL COUNCIL ACTION

On 27 July, the Economic and Social Council, on the recommendation of its Social Committee, adopted **resolution 1993/36** without vote.

Frequency of and arrangements for meetings of Heads of National Drug Law Enforcement Agencies, Europe

The Economic and Social Council,

Taking note of the conclusions of the report of the Second Meeting of Heads of National Drug Law Enforcement Agencies, Europe, held at Vienna from 22 to 26 February 1993,[a]

Convinced that it is essential for the heads of all national drug law enforcement agencies in Europe to meet annually to discuss trends in the illicit traffic in narcotic drugs and psychotropic substances and the action they may take to combat it,

1. *Invites* the Executive Director of the United Nations International Drug Control Programme to convene the Third Meeting of Heads of National Drug Law Enforcement Agencies, Europe, in 1995, and thereafter to convene such meetings every three years under the auspices of the Programme;

2. *Also invites* the Executive Director of the Programme to continue to develop cooperation between the Programme, the Customs Cooperation Council and the International Criminal Police Organization, in order to determine how they might cooperate to organize future annual meetings, and how each meeting might consider progress made in the implementation of recommendations adopted by previous meetings, and to report to the Commission on Narcotic Drugs at its thirty-seventh session, in 1994;

3. *Encourages* Governments to send representatives of law enforcement agencies involved in the investigations of drug trafficking to the annual meetings.

------
[a]E/CN.7/1993/CRP.10.

Economic and Social Council resolution 1993/36

27 July 1993   Meeting 43   Adopted without vote

Approved by Social Committee (E/1993/107) without vote, 16 July (meeting 12); draft by Commission on Narcotic Drugs (E/1993/29/Rev.1), agenda item 21.

Tehran Declaration

In January,[15] the Subcommission on Illicit Drug Traffic and Related Matters in the Near and Middle East reported to the Commission on Narcotic Drugs on its twenty-ninth session (Tehran, Iran, 24-28 October 1992), including the Ministerial-level Conference held at that session. Annexed to the report was the Tehran Declara-

tion adopted at the Conference, which committed member States of the Subcommission to draft comprehensive national and regional drug control strategies. The Declaration outlined policies and action to eliminate illicit cultivation; suppress drug trafficking; confiscate the proceeds of drug trafficking; prevent the diversion of precursors and essential chemicals used in illicit drug manufacture; and to reduce illicit demand.

On 27 July, by **decision 1993/246**, the Economic and Social Council noted the Subcommission's report on its twenty-ninth session, including the Ministerial-level Conference. It also approved the applications by Azerbaijan and Uzbekistan for membership in the Subcommission.

Action by the Commission on Narcotic Drugs. In April,[16] the Commission on Narcotic Drugs encouraged States, by entering into arrangements similar to the Tehran Declaration, to take action to combat the abuse of, and illicit trafficking in, narcotic drugs and psychotropic substances. It invited more States to associate themselves with the Declaration and requested the Secretary-General to bring it to the notice of all Governments.

Implementation of the 1988 UN Convention

In 1993, implementation of the 1988 United Nations Convention against Illicit Traffic in Narcotic Drugs and Psychotropic Substances[14] was considered by several bodies reporting to the Commission on Narcotic Drugs.

Efforts to curb maritime trafficking in narcotic drugs were discussed, among other matters, at the Second Meeting of HONLEA, Europe (Vienna, 22-26 February) and at the International Meeting on Preventive Activities against Illicit Drug Trafficking at Sea (Tokyo, 8-13 February). Discussions focused on how to implement article 17 of the 1988 Convention, dealing with illicit traffic on the high seas.

An Expert Working Group on Mutual Legal Assistance and Related International Confiscation (Vienna, 15-19 February)[17] discussed the implementation of article 7 (on mutual legal assistance in investigations, prosecutions and judicial proceedings in relation to a criminal offence) and relevant parts of article 5 of the Convention, and recommended ways to overcome legal and operational problems.

Action by the Commission on Narcotic Drugs. In April,[18] the Commission requested the UNDCP Executive Director to convene a group of experts to examine the possible mandate, activities and funding of a working group on maritime cooperation to promote universal implementation of the relevant provisions of the 1988 Convention. Among other things, the working group was to develop a comprehensive set of principles for consideration by States adopting laws and policies to implement those provisions and to prepare recommendations, tailored to the needs of especially vulnerable regions, to promote information-sharing and law enforcement against illicit traffic by sea. The Executive Director was requested to prepare for submission to the Commission in 1994 a report based on the conclusions of the group of experts and containing specific recommendations for the establishment of the working group.

In other action,[19] the Commission urged States to consider how, in accordance with article 5 of the Convention, proceeds confiscated from convicted drug traffickers might be shared with their countries of origin or domicile if they had provided assistance leading to the conviction and confiscation. The Commission once more invited Member States to consider contributing confiscated property or proceeds to the Fund of UNDCP to help the Programme fulfil its mandate and invited UNDCP to report to it in 1994 on the confiscation issue.

In related action,[20] the Commission requested UNDCP to help the United Nations Crime Prevention and Criminal Justice Branch to coordinate efforts against the laundering of drug money and to continue developing technical cooperation programmes that included assistance in drafting or revising legislation, training for investigative and financial personnel, intercountry collaboration, and advice on strategies and techniques. Member States were invited to review national legislation and bring it into conformity with the 1988 Convention, and the Executive Director of UNDCP was invited to report on follow-up to the resolution.

Also in April,[21] the Commission requested the Executive Director of UNDCP to report on the implementation of a 1992 Commission request[22] that States adopt legislation to facilitate mutual legal assistance and establish internal mechanisms for the transfer of evidence used in investigations, prosecutions, and judicial proceedings connected with illicit drug trafficking. States were requested to respond promptly to requests for mutual legal assistance and, where appropriate, to supply technical assistance for such purposes.

Taking note of article 3 of the Convention, the Commission, in a resolution on the relationship between illicit traffic in arms and explosives and illicit drug trafficking,[23] recommended that States that had not already done so consider establishing or improving controls on transfers of explosives, munitions and armaments.

ECONOMIC AND SOCIAL COUNCIL ACTION

On 27 July, the Economic and Social Council, on the recommendation of its Social Committee, adopted **resolution 1993/42** without vote.

Measures to assist in the implementation of the United Nations Convention against Illicit Traffic in Narcotic Drugs and Psychotropic Substances of 1988

The Economic and Social Council,

Recalling that the *Commentary on the Single Convention on Narcotic Drugs of 1961*, the *Commentary on the Protocol Amending the Single Convention on Narcotic Drugs, 1961* and the *Commentary on the Convention on Psychotropic Substances* were of considerable value to a number of Governments as a guide in framing legislative and administrative measures for the application of those Conventions in their territories,

Bearing in mind that the United Nations Convention against Illicit Traffic in Narcotic Drugs and Psychotropic Substances of 1988 is a comprehensive document embracing many and varied aspects of combating illicit trafficking in and demand for narcotic drugs and psychotropic substances,

Noting the continuing calls on States that have not already done so to ratify or accede to the 1988 Convention and, to the widest possible extent, to apply its provisions on an interim basis, pending its entry into force for each of them,

Convinced of the great need for and value of a uniform interpretation and application of the 1988 Convention,

Requests the Secretary-General, within existing regular budgetary resources, to prepare a commentary on the United Nations Convention against Illicit Traffic in Narcotic Drugs and Psychotropic Substances of 1988, drawing upon the official records of the Conference for the adoption of the Convention and other relevant materials that may be of assistance to States in their interpretation and effective implementation of the Convention.

Economic and Social Council resolution 1993/42

27 July 1993   Meeting 43   Adopted without vote

Approved by Social Committee (E/1993/107) without vote, 16 July (meeting 12); draft by Commission on Narcotic Drugs (E/1993/29/Rev.1), agenda item 21.

Also on that date, the Council, again on the recommendation of its Social Committee, adopted **resolution 1993/41** without vote.

Promoting the use of memoranda of understanding to facilitate cooperation between customs authorities and other competent administrations and the international trading community, including commercial carriers

The Economic and Social Council,

Deeply concerned about the unlawful use of commercial carriers for the illicit traffic in narcotic drugs and psychotropic substances and in precursor and essential chemicals, as specified in Tables I and II of the United Nations Convention against Illicit Traffic in Narcotic Drugs and Psychotropic Substances of 1988, as well as other substances frequently used in the illicit manufacture of drugs,

Recalling that article 15 of the Convention provides that parties to the Convention shall take appropriate measures to ensure that means of transport operated by commercial carriers are not used for illicit trafficking, and that each Party shall require commercial carriers to take reasonable precautions to prevent the use of their means of transport for the purpose of illicit trafficking,

Recognizing the need constantly to improve the capacity of law enforcement agencies to target and intercept illicit drug trafficking, without hindering the free movement of innocent persons and legitimate international trade,

Welcoming the Declaration on the Further National Development of Memoranda of Understanding between Customs and the Trading Community aimed at Cooperation to prevent Drug Smuggling, which was adopted by the Customs Cooperation Council at Brussels in June 1992, and which recognizes and supports the principle of achieving cooperation between customs and other competent authorities and the international trading community, including commercial carriers, through memoranda of understanding,

Recognizing the significance of the use of memoranda of understanding concluded between the Customs Cooperation Council and international trade and transport organizations for the improvement of cooperation to combat illicit trafficking,

Convinced that such an international initiative needs to be enhanced by agreements at the national level, where the joint development and implementation of cooperative agreements can be most effective,

Believing that manufacturers, traders, shippers, carriers, port and airport authorities and others involved in the international supply chain can significantly cooperate with customs and other competent authorities in the gathering of information for risk assessment and targeting purposes,

Believing also that such a partnership should lead to the improvement of physical security, the streamlined clearance of persons and goods and the specialized training of both official and trade personnel,

Recognizing that the cooperation arising from memoranda of understanding may facilitate the use of controlled delivery, to the extent permitted by the basic principles and legal systems of the parties concerned,

Noting that a number of States have already implemented memoranda of understanding at national and local levels,

Convinced of the urgent need to accelerate the process of concluding memoranda of understanding,

1. *Urges* all States which have not already done so to implement fully article 15 of the United Nations Convention against Illicit Traffic in Narcotic Drugs and Psychotropic Substances of 1988, by taking appropriate measures to prevent the use of commercial means of transport for illicit traffic;

2. *Commends* the Customs Cooperation Council for the progress that it has made in developing the programme of memoranda of understanding, and for the memoranda that it has already concluded with major transport and trading organizations;

3. *Commends also* those Governments which have introduced national programmes of memoranda of understanding, and invites them to share their experiences with other Governments within regional drug cooperation groups and with the Customs Cooperation Council, the United Nations International Drug Control Programme and other appropriate international bodies;

4. *Invites* the Programme, in consultation with the Customs Cooperation Council and other appropriate international bodies, to monitor the effectiveness of programmes of memoranda of understanding developed at the national, regional and international levels in combating illicit traffic;

5. *Also invites* the Programme to promulgate details of memoranda of understanding or measures which have been taken at the international or regional level to implement article 15 of the Convention, and which have been particularly effective;

6. *Requests* the Secretary-General to draw up model texts to assist those countries which require legislation in order to cooperate in controlled deliveries;

7. *Also requests* the Secretary-General to transmit the present resolution to all Governments for consideration and implementation as appropriate;

8. *Further requests* the Secretary-General to report to the Commission on Narcotic Drugs, at its thirty-eighth session, on the progress made in the implementation of the present resolution.

Economic and Social Council resolution 1993/41

27 July 1993   Meeting 43   Adopted without vote

Approved by Social Committee (E/1993/107) without vote, 16 July (meeting 12); draft by Commission on Narcotic Drugs (E/1993/29/Rev.1), agenda item 21.

Implementation of the Global Programme of Action

In response to a 1992 General Assembly request,[24] the Secretary-General submitted to the Commission on Narcotic Drugs in February 1993 an interim report[25] on the implementation by Member States of the Global Programme of Action on international cooperation against illicit production, supply, demand, trafficking and distribution of narcotic drugs and psychotropic substances, adopted by the Assembly at its seventeenth special session in 1990.[26]

In September 1993,[27] the Secretary-General submitted to the Assembly a more elaborate and updated report on the same issue, taking into account new information from 29 Governments and the discussion of the subject in the Commission. The report discussed each of the main topics dealt with in the Global Programme of Action, including the prevention and reduction of drug abuse; treatment, rehabilitation and social reintegration of drug abusers; control of the narcotic drug supply; suppression of illicit drug trafficking; measures against the effects of drug money associated with illicit drug trafficking, illegal financial flows and illegal use of the banking system; strengthening of judicial and legal systems, including law enforcement; measures against the diversion of arms and explosives and illicit traffic by vessels, aircraft and vehicles; the United Nations Decade against Drug Abuse, 1991-2000; and the structure of and resources necessary for UNDCP.

The Secretary-General mentioned concrete examples of measures pursued by Governments and brought to the Assembly's attention recommendations for improving national approaches and international cooperation.

Action by the Commission on Narcotic Drugs. In April,[28] the Commission took note of the Secretary-General's interim report[25] and recommended that the General Assembly pay particular attention to the recommendations in his final report, as well as to reviewing the implementation of the United Nations System-Wide Action Plan on Drug Abuse Control (see below); strengthening coordination between regional and international priority themes; drug demand reduction, including the prevention and reduction of drug abuse, and treatment, rehabilitation and social integration of drug addicts; the effectiveness of international efforts to eradicate illicit cultivation; and the leadership and coordinating role of UNDCP.

United Nations Decade against Drug Abuse

In his September report on the implementation of the Global Programme of Action,[27] the Secretary-General urged Member States to fulfil the Programme's recommendations within the time-frame of the United Nations Decade against Drug Abuse (1991-2000) by enlisting the support of national organizations, personalities and the media to publicize the Decade's objectives; establishing national focal points or coordinating committees to ensure effective promotion of the Decade; and by allocating adequate resources to the Fund of UNDCP.

At its seventeenth special session in 1990,[26] the General Assembly proclaimed 1991-2000 as the United Nations Decade against Drug Abuse to highlight the need for sustained national, regional and global action to implement the Global Programme of Action.

GENERAL ASSEMBLY ACTION

On 28 October, at the end of its five high-level plenary meetings to examine the status of international cooperation against drug abuse and illicit trafficking, the General Assembly adopted **resolution 48/12** without vote.

Measures to strengthen international cooperation against the illicit production, sale, demand, traffic and distribution of narcotic drugs and psychotropic substances and related activities
The General Assembly,

Profoundly alarmed by the magnitude of the rising trend in drug abuse, illicit production of and trafficking in narcotic drugs and psychotropic substances that threaten the health and well-being of millions of persons, in particular the youth, in all the countries of the world,

Deeply concerned by the growth of the drug problem which entails increasing economic costs for those Governments which seek to combat it, causes irreparable loss of human lives and threatens the economic, social and political structures of the countries affected by acts of violence,

Deeply alarmed by the growing violence and economic power of the criminal organizations that engage in the production, trafficking and distribution of drugs, arms and precursors and essential chemicals, which at times place them beyond the reach of the law,

Bearing in mind the provisions of its resolution 47/99 of 16 December 1992, in which it decided to hold four high-level plenary meetings to improve international cooperation in the fight against drugs, in accordance with the international treaties on drug control, the Comprehensive and Multidisciplinary Outline of Future Activities in Drug Abuse Control adopted by the International Conference on Drug Abuse and Illicit Trafficking, the Global Programme of Action adopted at its seventeenth special session, on 23 February 1990, and other relevant documents,

Reaffirming that action against drug abuse and illicit production of and trafficking in narcotic drugs and psychotropic substances should be accorded a higher priority by Governments, the United Nations and all other relevant national, regional and international organizations,

Taking note of the existing drug conventions, the Global Programme of Action and the United Nations System-Wide Action Plan on Drug Abuse Control, which contain a sound and comprehensive framework for drug control activities by States and all relevant international organizations, and stressing the need for consistency in efforts to implement these instruments,

Welcoming the efforts of the international community and the unflinching commitment assumed at the highest level by heads of State and/or Government to increase substantially efforts to achieve coordinated action and set priorities in the international fight against abuse, illicit production and trafficking in drugs,

Convinced that, given the magnitude and the global nature of the drug problem, it is indispensable for Governments to increase efforts in order to intensify concerted action and international cooperation based on the principle of shared responsibility,

Acknowledging that there are obvious links, under certain circumstances, between poverty and the increase in the illicit production of and trafficking in narcotic drugs and psychotropic substances and that the promotion of the economic development of countries affected by the illicit drug trade requires appropriate measures, including strengthened international cooperation in support for alternative development activities in the affected areas in those countries,

Acknowledging also the responsibility of Governments in alleviating poverty, reducing the dependency of their citizens on narcotics and narcotics production and enforcing legal measures against narcotics,

Recognizing that the magnitude of the drug menace requires the formulation of new strategies, approaches, objectives and enhanced international cooperation that, respectful of the sovereignty of States, deal more effectively with the international operations of those who get rich through the illegal traffic in drugs, arms and precursors and essential chemicals, threatening the stability of many societies in the world,

1. *Renews its commitment* further to strengthen international cooperation and increase substantially efforts against the illicit production, sale, demand, trafficking and distribution of narcotic drugs and psychotropic substances, based on the principle of shared responsibility and taking into account experience gained;

2. *Calls upon* States that have not yet done so to ratify and to implement fully all provisions of the Single Convention on Narcotic Drugs of 1961, and that Convention as amended by the 1972 Protocol, the Convention

on Psychotropic Substances of 1971, and the United Nations Convention against Illicit Traffic in Narcotic Drugs and Psychotropic Substances of 1988;

3. *Calls upon* all States to adopt adequate national laws and regulations, to strengthen national judicial systems and to carry out effective drug control activities in cooperation with other States in compliance with those international instruments;

4. *Underlines* the role of the Commission on Narcotic Drugs as the principal United Nations policy-making body on drug control issues;

5. *Reaffirms* the leadership role of the United Nations International Drug Control Programme as the main focus for concerted international action for drug abuse control and as international coordinator of drug control activities, especially within the United Nations system;

6. *Calls upon* States to take all necessary steps to implement the recommendations contained in the Global Programme of Action at the national, regional and international levels;

7. *Reaffirms* that the contribution of United Nations programmes and agencies to the implementation of the Global Programme of Action should continue to be coordinated in accordance with the United Nations System-Wide Action Plan on Drug Abuse Control, and that States represented in the governing bodies of the programmes and agencies concerned should ensure that their agendas consistently reflect and accord adequate priority to drug control activities;

8. *Requests* the Economic and Social Council at its coordination segment in 1994 to examine the status of international cooperation within the United Nations system against the illicit production, sale, demand, trafficking and distribution of narcotic drugs and psychotropic substances in order to recommend ways and means to improve such cooperation, and to report thereon to the General Assembly at its forty-ninth session;

9. *Requests* the Commission on Narcotic Drugs, with the support of the United Nations International Drug Control Programme and in cooperation with the International Narcotics Control Board, to monitor and evaluate action at the national and international level in implementing the international drug control instruments, with a view to identifying areas of satisfactory progress and weakness, and to recommend to the high-level segment of the Economic and Social Council in 1995 appropriate adjustments of drug control activities whenever required;

10. *Requests* the Commission on Narcotic Drugs and the Economic and Social Council, with the assistance of the United Nations International Drug Control Programme and the International Narcotics Control Board, to consider and make recommendations on the following issues, on the basis of the principle of shared responsibility and a balanced, comprehensive and multidisciplinary approach, and without excluding any other aspects that could be addressed:

(a) Reinforcement of policies and strategies for the prevention, reduction and elimination of illicit demand, with particular emphasis on the need for each Government to place a higher priority on treatment, rehabilitation, information and educational campaigns to reduce demand;

(b) Consideration of ways to strengthen and enhance international anti-drug cooperation in programmes of alternative development in order to eliminate illicit drug production and trafficking within the framework of sustainable development, with a view to improving living conditions and contributing to the eradication of extreme poverty;

(c) Careful review of the different aspects of the problem and recommendation to Governments of those areas in which updating and harmonizing national laws and regulations may be appropriate;

(d) Strengthening of the international fight against international criminal drug organizations, which pose serious threats to the efforts to build and strengthen democracy, maintain sustainable economic growth and protect the environment;

(e) Taking into account the situation of transit and producing countries and the crucial role they play in this struggle, with a view to assisting their efforts;

(f) Strengthening of international cooperation to eradicate the growing and dangerous links between terrorist groups, drug traffickers and their paramilitary gangs and other armed criminal groups, which have resorted to all types of violence, thus undermining the democratic institutions of States and violating basic human rights;

(g) Examinination of the question of penalties for offences related to drug trafficking, including money-laundering and traffic in arms, and making recommendations thereon;

(h) Increasing attention to implementing all provisions of the United Nations Convention against Illicit Traffic in Narcotic Drugs and Psychotropic Substances, with special emphasis on targeting the profits and money-laundering operations of drug traffickers, strengthening interdiction procedures by land, sea and air and enforcing the control of precursors and essential chemicals;

(i) Promotion and intensification of human resources development, including the implementation of training programmes to deal with illicit demand, supply and trafficking;

(j) Promotion and encouragement of the active involvement of non-governmental organizations and the private sector in the various aspects of the drug problem;

(k) Taking into consideration, in the course of their work, the recommendations contained in the final report of the Secretary-General on the implementation by Member States of the Global Programme of Action;

11. *Invites* the Commission on Narcotic Drugs at its next session to take the necessary measures to implement the present resolution, including consideration of the convening of an ad hoc expert group to contribute to the examination of the issues above and to the identification of concrete action-oriented recommendations, and to report on its findings to the General Assembly at its fiftieth session, through the Economic and Social Council.

General Assembly resolution 48/12

28 October 1993   Meeting 42   Adopted without vote

Draft by Assembly President (A/48/L.12); agenda item 112.
Meeting numbers. GA 48th session: plenary 37-40, 42.

On 20 December, on the recommendation of the Third Committee, the Assembly adopted **resolution 48/112** without vote.

International action to combat drug abuse and illicit production and trafficking

The General Assembly,

Recalling its resolutions 47/98, 47/100, 47/101 and 47/102 of 16 December 1992 and 48/12 of 28 October 1993,

Gravely concerned that the illicit demand for, production of and traffic in narcotic drugs and psychotropic substances continue to threaten seriously the socio-economic and political systems and the stability, national security and sovereignty of an increasing number of States,

Fully aware that the international community is confronted with the dramatic problem of drug abuse and the illicit cultivation, production, demand, processing, distribution and trafficking of narcotic drugs and psychotropic substances and that States need to work at the international and national levels to deal with this scourge, which has a strong potential to undermine development, economic and political stability and democratic institutions,

Emphasizing that the problem of drug abuse and illicit trafficking has to be considered within the broader economic and social context,

Emphasizing also the need for an analysis of transit routes used by drug traffickers, which are constantly changing and expanding to include a growing number of countries and regions in all parts of the world,

Alarmed by the growing connection between drug trafficking and terrorism in various parts of the world,

Recognizing the efforts of countries that produce narcotic drugs for scientific, medicinal and therapeutic uses to prevent the channelling of such substances to illicit markets and to maintain production at a level consistent with licit demand,

Reaffirming that a comprehensive framework for international cooperation in drug control is provided by the Declaration and the Comprehensive Multidisciplinary Outline of Future Activities in Drug Abuse Control, adopted by the International Conference on Drug Abuse and Illicit Trafficking, the Political Declaration and Global Programme of Action adopted on 23 February 1990, at the seventeenth special session of the General Assembly, and the Declaration adopted by the World Ministerial Summit to Reduce the Demand for Drugs and to Combat the Cocaine Threat, held in London in April 1990, together with the international drug control treaties,

Stressing the important role of the United Nations and its specialized agencies in supporting concerted action in the fight against drug abuse at the national, regional and international levels,

Underlining the role of the Commission on Narcotic Drugs as the principal United Nations policy-making body on drug control issues,

Reaffirming the importance of the role of the United Nations International Drug Control Programme as the main focus for concerted international action for drug abuse control and commending its performance of the functions entrusted to it,

Affirming the proposals set out in the United Nations System-Wide Action Plan on Drug Abuse Control, and recognizing that further efforts are needed to implement and update it,

Inviting the relevant agencies of the United Nations system to make greater progress in incorporating within their programmes and activities action aimed at dealing with drug-related problems,

I

Respect for the principles enshrined in the Charter of the United Nations and international law in the fight against drug abuse and illicit trafficking

1. *Reaffirms* that the fight against drug abuse and illicit trafficking should continue to be based on strict respect for the principles enshrined in the Charter of the United Nations and international law, particularly respect for the sovereignty and territorial integrity of States and non-use of force or the threat of force in international relations;

2. *Calls upon* all States to intensify their actions to promote effective cooperation in the efforts to combat drug abuse and illicit trafficking, so as to contribute to a climate conducive to achieving this end, and to refrain from using the issue for political purposes;

3. *Reaffirms* that the international fight against drug trafficking should not in any way justify violation of the principles enshrined in the Charter of the United Nations and international law;

II

International action to combat drug abuse and illicit trafficking

1. *Reiterates its condemnation* of the crime of drug trafficking in all its forms, and urges continued and effective international action to combat it, in keeping with the principle of shared responsibility;

2. *Supports* the focus on national and regional strategies for drug abuse control, particularly the master-plan approach, and urges the United Nations International Drug Control Programme to keep in mind that these should be complemented with effective interregional strategies;

3. *Requests* the Secretary-General to report on the arrangements made by the Programme to promote and monitor the United Nations Decade Against Drug Abuse, 1991-2000, under the theme, "A global response to a global challenge", and on the progress made in attaining the objectives of the Decade by Member States, the Programme and the United Nations system;

4. *Welcomes* the trend towards ratification and implementation of the Single Convention on Narcotic Drugs of 1961, as amended by the 1972 Protocol, the Convention on Psychotropic Substances of 1971 and the United Nations Convention against Illicit Traffic in Narcotic Drugs and Psychotropic Substances of 1988;

5. *Requests* the Programme to include in its report to the Commission on Narcotic Drugs on the implementation of the United Nations Convention against Illicit Traffic in Narcotic Drugs and Psychotropic Substances a section on experience gained to date in implementing the Convention, which should contain recommendations and strategies for its further implementation, and invites Member States to cooperate with the Programme in this regard;

6. *Encourages* all countries to take action to prevent the illicit arms trade by which weapons are provided to drug traffickers;

7. *Expresses its satisfaction* with the efforts of the Commission on Narcotic Drugs to improve the functioning and impact of the meetings of heads of national drug law enforcement agencies;

8. *Requests* the Programme in its report on illicit traffic in drugs to analyse world-wide trends in illicit traf-

fic and transit in narcotic drugs and psychotropic substances, including methods and routes used, and to recommend ways and means for improving the capacity of States along those routes to deal with all aspects of the drug problem;

9. _Emphasizes_ the link between the illicit production of, demand for and traffic in narcotic drugs and psychotropic substances and the economic and social conditions in the affected countries and the differences and diversity of the problems in each country;

10. _Calls upon_ the international community to provide increased economic and technical support to Governments that request it in support of programmes of alternative development that take fully into account the cultural traditions of peoples;

11. _Takes note_ of the initiative of the Programme to study the concept of swapping debt for alternative development in the area of international drug abuse control, and requests the Executive Director of the Programme to inform the Commission on Narcotic Drugs of any progress made in this area;

12. _Encourages_ Governments to nominate experts for the roster maintained by the Programme, to ensure that the Programme and the Commission on Narcotic Drugs may draw from the widest pool of expertise and experience in implementing its policies and programmes;

13. _Stresses_ the need for effective action to prevent the diversion for illicit purposes of precursors and essential chemicals, materials and equipment frequently used in the illicit manufacture of narcotic drugs and psychotropic substances;

14. _Commends_ the International Narcotics Control Board for its valuable work in monitoring production and distribution of narcotic drugs and psychotropic substances so as to limit their use to medical and scientific purposes, and for the effective manner in which it has implemented its additional responsibilities, under article 12 of the United Nations Convention against Illicit Traffic in Narcotic Drugs and Psychotropic Substances, concerning the control of precursors and essential chemicals;

15. _Expresses its satisfaction_ with efforts being made by the Programme and other United Nations bodies to obtain reliable data on drug abuse and illicit trafficking, including the development of the International Drug Abuse Assessment System;

16. _Recommends_ to the Commission on Narcotic Drugs that it consider, at its thirty-seventh session, the worldwide research study on the economic and social consequences of drug abuse and illicit trafficking prepared by the United Nations Research Institute for Social Development in conjunction with the report of the Executive Director of the Programme on the economic and social consequences of drug abuse and illicit trafficking, and that it consider including this issue as an item on its agenda;

III

Global Programme of Action

1. _Reaffirms_ the importance of the Global Programme of Action as a framework for national, regional and international action to combat the illicit production of, demand for and trafficking in narcotic drugs and psychotropic substances, and its commitment to implementing the mandates and recommendations contained therein;

2. _Calls upon_ States individually and in cooperation with other States to promote the Global Programme of Action and to implement its mandates and recommendations, with a view to translating it into practical action for drug abuse control;

3. _Calls upon_ the relevant bodies of the United Nations, the specialized agencies, the international financial institutions and other concerned intergovernmental and non-governmental organizations to cooperate with and assist States in their efforts to promote and implement the Global Programme of Action;

4. _Requests_ the Commission on Narcotic Drugs, in discharging its mandate to monitor the Global Programme of Action, to take into account the recommendations contained in the report of the Secretary-General on the implementation by Member States of the Global Programme of Action;

5. _Requests_ the Commission on Narcotic Drugs and the United Nations International Drug Control Programme to consider ways and means to facilitate reporting by Governments on the implementation of the Global Programme of Action, so as to increase the level of responses;

IV

Implementation of the United Nations System-Wide Action Plan on Drug Abuse Control: action by agencies of the United Nations system

1. _Reaffirms_ the role of the Executive Director of the United Nations International Drug Control Programme to coordinate and provide effective leadership for all United Nations drug control activities, in order to ensure coherence of actions within the Programme as well as coordination, complementarity and non-duplication of such activities across the United Nations system;

2. _Calls_ for completion of the updated United Nations System-Wide Action Plan on Drug Abuse Control, as was requested in resolution 47/100, in full cooperation with the Administrative Committee on Coordination, in time for the review and recommendation of the Commission on Narcotic Drugs at its thirty-seventh session and for the consideration of the Economic and Social Council at its substantive session of 1994 and of the General Assembly at its forty-ninth session;

3. _Reiterates_ that the following should be included in the updated System-Wide Action Plan:

(_a_) An annex containing agency-specific implementing plans;

(_b_) A reference to the important role of the international financial institutions, as noted in chapter II of the Comprehensive Multidisciplinary Outline of Future Activities in Drug Abuse Control, and the ability of such institutions to promote economic stability and undermine the drug industry;

4. _Calls upon_ all relevant United Nations agencies to complete their agency-specific implementation plans for inclusion in the updated System-Wide Action Plan and to incorporate fully into their programmes all the mandates and activities contained in the Action Plan and its annex;

5. _Requests_ the Commission on Narcotic Drugs to pay particular attention to reviewing the agency-specific implementing plans of the System-Wide Action Plan for consideration by the Economic and Social Council at its coordination segment in 1994;

6. *Requests* the Economic and Social Council, at its coordination segment, to pay due attention to the role of the international financial institutions in supporting international drug control efforts, particularly in the field of alternative development;

7. *Calls upon* the governing bodies of all United Nations agencies associated with the System-Wide Action Plan to include the issue of drug control in their agendas with a view to examining the need for a mandate on drug control, assessing the activities taken to comply with the Action Plan and, as appropriate, reporting on how the issue of drug control is taken into account in the relevant programmes;

8. *Requests* the United Nations International Drug Control Programme, in cooperation with the relevant agencies, particularly the United Nations Children's Fund, to report on the efforts to study the impact of drug abuse and related crime on children and to recommend measures that may be taken to address this problem;

9. *Recommends* that the United Nations International Drug Control Programme cooperate and coordinate with the Crime Prevention and Criminal Justice Branch of the Centre for Social Development and Humanitarian Affairs of the Secretariat on activities to counter drug-related criminality, including money-laundering, to ensure complementary and non-duplication of efforts;

10. *Requests* that the System-Wide Action Plan be reviewed and updated on a biennial basis;

V

United Nations International Drug Control Programme

1. *Welcomes* the efforts of the United Nations International Drug Control Programme to implement its mandates within the framework of the international drug control treaties, the Comprehensive Multidisciplinary Outline of Future Activities in Drug Abuse Control, the Global Programme of Action and relevant consensus documents;

2. *Urges* all Governments to provide the fullest possible financial and political support to the United Nations International Drug Control Programme, in particular by increasing voluntary contributions to the Programme, to enable it to expand and strengthen its operational and technical cooperation activities;

3. *Welcomes also* the work of the Commission on Narcotic Drugs on the consideration of the programme budget of the Fund of the United Nations International Drug Control Programme, in accordance with the mandate contained in section XVI, paragraph 2, of the General Assembly resolution 46/185 C of 20 December 1991;

4. *Takes note* of the note of the Secretary-General on the administrative and financial arrangements of the United Nations Drug Control Programme submitted pursuant to section XVI of resolution 46/185 C;

5. *Notes with appreciation* the efforts made by the United Nations International Drug Control Programme to comply with the approved format and methodology of the programme budget of the Fund of the United Nations International Drug Control Programme, in particular with the relevant resolutions of the Commission on Narcotic Drugs;

6. *Encourages* the Executive Director of the United Nations International Drug Control Programme to continue his efforts to improve the presentation of the budget of the Fund;

VI

1. *Takes note* of the reports of the Secretary-General presented under the item entitled "International drug control";

2. *Requests* the Secretary-General to report to the General Assembly at its forty-ninth session on the implementation of the present resolution.

General Assembly resolution 48/112

20 December 1993   Meeting 85   Adopted without vote

Approved by Third Committee (A/48/630) without vote, 12 November (meeting 32); 24-nation draft (A/C.3/48/L.18); agenda item 112.

Sponsors: Albania, Bahamas, Bangladesh, Belarus, Bolivia, Costa Rica, Côte d'Ivoire, Cuba, Egypt, El Salvador, Guatemala, Guyana, Honduras, Kyrgyzstan, Madagascar, Mexico, Morocco, Myanmar, Pakistan, Philippines, Russian Federation, Turkey, Ukraine, United States.

Meeting numbers. GA 48th session: 3rd Committee 21, 25, 32; plenary 85.

Implementation of the System-Wide Action Plan

The review and updating of the United Nations System-Wide Action Plan on Drug Abuse Control, requested by the General Assembly in 1992,[29] was discussed at two meetings in 1993 by a subsidiary body of the Administrative Committee on Coordination (ACC). That body, the Inter-Agency Meeting on Coordination in Matters of International Drug Abuse Control, met at Vienna (7 and 8 April)[30] and again—renamed the ACC Subcommittee on Drug Control—in Paris (6-8 September).[31] ACC was to review and update the Plan with a view to simplifying and streamlining its presentation for consideration by the Economic and Social Council and the Assembly in 1993.

An update of the Plan was presented to the Council and the Assembly by the Secretary-General, as Chairman of ACC, in June.[32] The Council took note of it on 27 July, by **decision 1993/251**.

At its September meeting, the Subcommittee reviewed a draft of the Secretary-General's report[33] on implementation of the Plan, which outlined action during 1992 by legislative bodies in the United Nations system and described the activities of UNDCP, specialized agencies, regional commissions and other United Nations organs with regard to: drug demand reduction; treatment and rehabilitation of drug abusers; control of narcotic drug supply including licit production, manufacture and supply and prevention of the diversion of precursors; suppression of illicit trafficking; strengthening of judicial and legal systems, including law enforcement; money-laundering and measures to be taken against the diversion of arms and explosives; and illicit traffic by vessels, aircraft and vehicles. Finally, the report discussed cooperation and coordination of those activities. It was agreed that the 1994 report should be consolidated to include the Plan's update and to encompass a system-wide strategy, summary reports of implementation of the strategy by individual agencies and organizations, and agency-specific plans.

ECONOMIC AND SOCIAL COUNCIL ACTION

On 27 July, the Economic and Social Council, on the recommendation of its Social Committee, adopted **resolution 1993/43** without vote.

Implementation of the United Nations System-Wide Action Plan on Drug Abuse Control

The Economic and Social Council,

Recalling the relevant provisions of General Assembly resolutions 44/141 of 15 December 1989, 45/179 of 21 December 1990 and 47/100 of 16 December 1992 concerning the establishment, adjustment and updating of the United Nations System-Wide Action Plan on Drug Abuse Control,

Recalling in particular that the General Assembly, in its resolution 47/100, expressed concern at the limited progress made by the agencies and organizations of the United Nations system towards the implementation of the System-Wide Action Plan, and called on them to incorporate fully into their programmes all the mandates and activities contained in the System-Wide Action Plan,

Bearing in mind that, in accordance with General Assembly resolution 45/179, the Executive Director of the United Nations International Drug Control Programme has the exclusive responsibility for coordinating and providing effective leadership for all United Nations drug control activities, and the Commission on Narcotic Drugs is the principal United Nations policy-making body on drug control issues,

Convinced that the efficiency and effectiveness of international cooperation in the field of drug abuse control depends on the full implementation of all the mandates and activities contained in the System-Wide Action Plan,

1. *Reaffirms* the necessity, in view of the limited resources at the disposal of the United Nations International Drug Control Programme, for all relevant agencies of the United Nations system, as well as other international institutions, to actively contribute, each in its own field of activity, to the effective implementation of the Global Programme of Action adopted by the General Assembly at its seventeenth special session, devoted to the question of international cooperation against illicit production, supply, demand, trafficking and distribution of narcotic drugs and psychotropic substances, and to fully cooperate with the United Nations International Drug Control Programme to that effect;

2. *Calls upon* all entities and agencies of the United Nations system associated with the United Nations System-Wide Action Plan on Drug Abuse Control, including the United Nations Children's Fund, the United Nations Development Programme, the United Nations Population Fund, the World Food Programme, the United Nations Environment Programme, the International Labour Organisation, the Food and Agriculture Organization of the United Nations, the United Nations Educational, Scientific and Cultural Organization, the World Health Organization, the International Fund for Agricultural Development, the United Nations Industrial Development Organization and the Office of the United Nations High Commissioner for Refugees, to establish agency-specific implementation plans for their activities related to drug abuse control, and to fully incorporate the implementation of the System-Wide Action Plan into their planning instruments;

3. *Calls upon* Member States represented in the entities and agencies concerned to consistently emphasize the importance of drug abuse control within the broader context of development, and to ensure that activities and concerns relating to drug abuse control are appropriately reflected, as matters of priority, in their agendas;

4. *Calls upon* the governing bodies of the entities and agencies concerned to facilitate the implementation of the System-Wide Action Plan by designating an agenda item under which it may be considered at their next regular meeting;

5. *Notes* that, in accordance with General Assembly resolution 47/100, the Administrative Committee on Coordination gave due attention, under the direction of the Executive Director of the United Nations International Drug Control Programme, to the updating of the System-Wide Action Plan for the consideration of the Economic and Social Council at its substantive session of 1993 and of the Assembly at its forty-eighth session;

6. *Requests* the United Nations International Drug Control Programme, through its network of field offices, to ensure coordination of all operational activities relating to drug abuse control at the field level, in collaboration with field representatives of other bodies within the United Nations system;

7. *Invites* the Joint Consultative Group on Policies, consisting of the United Nations Development Programme, the United Nations Children's Fund, the United Nations Population Fund, the World Food Programme and the International Fund for Agricultural Development, to further develop its cooperation with the United Nations International Drug Control Programme in order to improve the coordination of activities relating to drug abuse control within the United Nations system;

8. *Requests* the Commission to promote and monitor the implementation of the updated System-Wide Action Plan, and requests the Programme to submit an annual report thereon to the Commission, starting with its thirty-seventh session.

Economic and Social Council resolution 1993/43

27 July 1993   Meeting 43   Adopted without vote

Approved by Social Committee (E/1993/107) without vote, 16 July (meeting 12); draft by Commission on Narcotic Drugs (E/1993/29/Rev.1), agenda item 21.

GENERAL ASSEMBLY ACTION

In **resolution 48/112**, the General Assembly called for completion of the updated Plan, in full cooperation with ACC, in time for review by the Commission on Narcotic Drugs and consideration by the Economic and Social Council and the Assembly in 1994.

Supply and demand

Demand reduction

In 1993,[1] UNDCP carried out various initiatives aimed at reinforcing the conceptual, statistical and operational foundations for concerted demand reduction efforts. Many of its activities in the second half of the year were in pursuance of Economic and Social Council resolution 1993/35 of 27 July (see below), such as meetings and training courses to assist government officials in assessing the extent and patterns of domestic and regionally shared drug abuse problems. As the first in a series of regional initiatives, UNDCP organized an expert forum on demand reduction in eastern and southern Africa (Nairobi, Kenya, 1-5 November).

Considerable progress was made in 1993 in making the International Drug Abuse Assessment System fully operational and over 100 country profiles were prepared. UNDCP financed numerous demand reduction projects at the country level, promoting community involvement and the development of approaches tailored to target group and project location. It worked particularly closely with the World Health Organization (WHO) in a number of country projects, in addition to working on a 13-city investigation of the linkage between intravenous drug use and human immunodeficiency virus (HIV) infection. A new project was launched to examine worldwide knowledge on the effects of drug abuse on fetuses. In collaboration with WHO, UNDCP completed a project on prevention of the abuse of performance-enhancing drugs in sports, to be followed up by a project to develop practical guidelines on drug abuse prevention for use by sports clubs.

Among other activities, UNDCP assisted the international NGO community in organizing the World Forum on the Role of NGOs in Drug Demand Reduction, to be held at Bangkok, Thailand, in December 1994. In preparation for the Forum, four regional consultations were held. In close cooperation with two Governments, UNDCP organized the First International Private Sector Conference on Drugs in the Workplace and the Community (Seville, Spain, 13-15 October), attended by 120 representatives of companies, trade unions, NGOs, educational institutions and international organizations.

Aware of growing substance abuse among children and youth in many developing countries, UNDCP cooperated in the field with the United Nations Children's Fund in defining preventive programmes. UNDCP favoured integrated projects providing immediate assistance to youth at risk from drug abuse and emphasizing education and training.

The International Narcotics Control Board (INCB), in its report for 1993,[34] cited examples of successful demand reduction activities, often at relatively low cost; countries carrying out those activities included Bolivia, Colombia, India, Myanmar, Pakistan and Sri Lanka. The Board noted that community-based detoxification and treatment in Myanmar had led to a considerable reduction in drug-related crime and that Bolivia had achieved good results with strategies to protect street children through education, counselling, the creation of employment and the promotion of alternative lifestyles. The Board noted, however, that demand reduction could not succeed without substantially reducing illicit drug supply. It noted with satisfaction UNDCP's balanced approach in that regard, by assisting in the development of national legal instruments, strengthening law enforcement services, supporting alternative economic development, and assisting in the improvement of social, educational and health conditions. It stated that at the national level, however, the reduction of supply and demand could not be separated and that demand reduction could not be codified or standardized by international legal documents.

Action by the Commission on Narcotic Drugs. In April,[35] the Commission invited Governments to promote treatment and social rehabilitation programmes for drug abusers and to enhance the exchange of information and experience in that field. It requested UNDCP to cooperate closely with the United Nations Crime Prevention and Criminal Justice Branch and other relevant entities and organizations in implementing the resolution.

ECONOMIC AND SOCIAL COUNCIL ACTION

On 27 July, the Economic and Social Council, on the recommendation of its Social Committee, adopted **resolution 1993/35** without vote.

Demand reduction as part of balanced national strategic plans to combat drug abuse

The Economic and Social Council,

Reaffirming the Political Declaration and Global Programme of Action adopted by the General Assembly at its seventeenth special session, in which Member States proclaimed their intention to strengthen policies aimed at the prevention, reduction and elimination of illicit demand for narcotic drugs and psychotropic substances,

Recalling the Comprehensive Multidisciplinary Outline of Future Activities in Drug Abuse Control, adopted by the International Conference on Drug Abuse and Illicit Trafficking, and its previous resolutions on reduction of the demand for narcotic drugs and psychotropic substances, particularly resolution 1991/46 of 21 June 1991,

Acknowledging the work that has been and is being undertaken in demand reduction by a variety of organizations and bodies, including the United Nations International Drug Control Programme, specialized agencies of the United Nations system, in particular the World Health Organization, through the establishment of its Programme on Substance Abuse, and other regional intergovernmental and non-governmental organizations,

Noting the rising trend in and the vast scale of illicit demand for and trafficking in narcotic drugs and psychotropic substances, and the illicit supply, production and distribution of such products,

Deeply concerned about the continuing threat posed by the abuse of narcotic drugs and psychotropic substances to the health and welfare of mankind, to the political, economic, social and cultural structure of communities, and to the stability of States and nations,

Noting the important role that programmes to control supply have been playing, and will continue to play, in the effort to reduce the illicit availability of drugs,

Stressing the importance of the development, by States, of comprehensive strategic plans to combat drug abuse and provide a focus for controlling the supply of, demand for and trafficking in narcotic drugs and psychotropic substances,

Noting the role that Governments play in facilitating the development of demand reduction programmes which can be implemented by either governmental or non-governmental organizations,

Believing that in seeking to combat drug abuse, the effectiveness of programmes to control supplies would be enhanced by complementing and integrating them with appropriate demand reduction strategies,

Noting the importance of developing demand reduction strategies which are specifically targeted and culturally appropriate, and which recognize the social context of the target groups,

Noting that voluntary and non-governmental organizations can play a very important role in the development and implementation of demand reduction strategies,

Recognizing that, as drug abusers are often polydrug abusers, national responses need to be comprehensive, addressing a range of drugs,

Also recognizing that there is no single measure sufficient to address the problem of substance abuse, and that a multidisciplinary and integrated strategy involving the application of measures to counter drug abuse would constitute a more relevant and balanced response,

Noting the links between drug abuse and a wide range of adverse health consequences, including the transmission of the hepatitis viruses and the human immunodeficiency virus,

Acknowledging the importance and benefits of regular evaluation of demand reduction strategies and programmes, and of sharing experiences and information on their evaluation and effectiveness,

1. *Urges* all Governments and competent regional organizations, particularly Governments of countries where serious problems of substance abuse exist or are likely to emerge, to develop a balanced approach within the framework of comprehensive demand reduction activities, giving adequate priority to prevention, treatment, research, social reintegration and training of professional staff in the context of national strategic plans to combat drug abuse;

2. *Calls for* the involvement by governmental and non-governmental organizations, including those concerned with health, education, law enforcement, the private sector and the community, in developing a range of demand reduction strategies;

3. *Emphasizes* the importance of collaborative arrangements between international organizations working in the field of drug abuse control, such as the proposed memoranda of understanding to be drawn up between the United Nations International Drug Control Programme and such organizations as the Inter-national Labour Organisation and the World Health Organization, which will enhance effective cooperation between the bodies concerned, while fully reflecting their respective mandates;

4. *Encourages* the Programme to continue developing demand reduction strategies within the context of national strategic plans to combat drug abuse, taking into account regional and local needs, particularly in countries where more dangerous forms of consumption are appearing;

5. *Requests* the Programme to give priority to assisting countries in the development and implementation of national strategic plans to combat drug abuse, fully integrating efforts to reduce supply and demand;

6. *Encourages* countries which have expertise in demand reduction to make their experiences and knowledge available to countries wishing to develop a demand reduction strategy;

7. *Encourages* the establishment of a regional and international system for the regular exchange of information, experiences, training programmes and new ideas on demand reduction programmes and policies;

8. *Urges* Governments to promote national, subregional, regional and international cooperation in order to facilitate improved coordination, at the policy and operational levels, of personnel dealing with the reduction of both demand and supply;

9. *Stresses* the importance of targeting potential and actual groups of drug abusers and developing programmes designed to reduce demand and tailored to their needs, including prevention, treatment, rehabilitation and social integration;

10. *Requests* the Programme to assist non-governmental organizations in preparing for the World Forum on Drug Demand Reduction, to be held in 1994;

11. *Emphasizes* the necessity of taking into account the existing social and cultural environments when developing strategies to control drug abuse or reduce demand;

12. *Urges* all Governments to provide and support programmes of prevention, treatment and rehabilitation, particularly for youth and those most at risk from substance abuse;

13. *Recognizes* that the use of illicit products may be linked to the abuse of licit substances, and encourages all Governments to give due attention to programmes designed to reduce the abuse of licit substances;

14. *Encourages* the development of strategies of early intervention, especially by primary health-care workers, to prevent and discourage substance abuse;

15. *Reaffirms* the need for Governments to take all appropriate measures to give substance abusers, particularly those who use injections, access to the care of treatment services and agencies;

16. *Urges* all Governments to address the problems raised by hepatitis, the human immunodeficiency virus and acquired immunodeficiency syndrome, and, where appropriate, to take steps, including increased accessibility to treatment and other approaches, to reduce their harmful effects;

17. *Stresses* the importance of collecting appropriate statistical data that could be used in the development of demand reduction strategies, and that should be, as far as possible, reliable, valid and comparable, and encourages the Programme to further elaborate guidelines for collecting statistical data and, in particular, data on drug-related deaths;

18. *Urges* the Programme to facilitate access to and disseminate information received from Governments regarding the development, implementation and evaluation of national strategies and programmes to control substance abuse;

19. *Encourages* the Programme to integrate its annual reports questionnaire into a single simplified document, which should be coordinated, when appropriate, with other international bodies in order to facilitate timely and complete replies by all Member States;

20. *Reaffirms* the request to the Programme to disseminate, through the database of the International Drug Abuse Assessment System, the information on demand reduction received from Governments, specialized agencies of the United Nations system and other intergovernmental and non-governmental organizations, in such a way as to assist Governments and the organizations concerned in developing their policies to reduce demand, in providing technical support to Member States in the submission of data, and in implementing quality-control measures;

21. *Invites* the Executive Director of the Programme to place special emphasis on demand reduction strategies and initiatives in his report to the Commission on Narcotic Drugs at its thirty-seventh session;

22. *Requests* the Secretary-General to transmit the present resolution to all Governments for consideration and implementation.

Economic and Social Council resolution 1993/35

27 July 1993   Meeting 43   Adopted without vote

Approved by Social Committee (E/1993/107) without vote, 16 July (meeting 12); draft by Commission on Narcotic Drugs (E/1993/29/Rev.1), agenda item 21.

Legalization of drugs of abuse

In its 1993 report,[34] INCB reiterated its strong position against the legalization of drugs of abuse. It expressed appreciation for the overall support of Governments for that position at the 1993 sessions of the Economic and Social Council and the Commission on Narcotic Drugs. It noted that the legalization option was rejected by all those who spoke on the subject at the 1993 General Assembly session. The Board expressed the hope that Italy would reverse a decree issued in June repealing the prohibition of the non-medical use of drugs, a step not in the spirit of international drug control treaties. It expressed appreciation that both Portugal and Spain had recently enacted legislation to strengthen measures against the non-medical use of drugs.

ECONOMIC AND SOCIAL COUNCIL ACTION

On 27 July, the Economic and Social Council, on the recommendation of its Social Committee, adopted **resolution 1993/39** without vote.

Control of narcotic drugs and psychotropic substances
The Economic and Social Council,
Recalling the history of the international drug control treaties and the reasons for their development and adoption, in particular the experience of States confronted with an alarming increase in the abuse of narcotic drugs and psychotropic substances,

Mindful of the factors which have led individual States and the international community to rely increasingly on prohibition of the illicit use of narcotic drugs and psychotropic substances as an important element in drug abuse control,

Seriously concerned about the adverse implications for international drug abuse control if such prohibitions were abandoned,

1. *Endorses* the view of the International Narcotics Control Board on the question of legalization of the non-medical use of drugs as expressed in paragraphs 13 to 24 of the report of the International Narcotics Control Board for 1992 and, in particular, the conclusions contained in paragraph 23 of the report;

2. *Urges* all Governments not to derogate from full implementation of the international drug control treaties;

3. *Also urges* all Governments to continue strictly to limit the use of narcotic drugs and psychotropic substances to medical and scientific purposes and other special purposes permitted under the Single Convention on Narcotic Drugs of 1961, that Convention as amended by the 1972 Protocol, the Convention on Psychotropic Substances of 1971 and the United Nations Convention against Illicit Traffic in Narcotic Drugs and Psychotropic Substances of 1988.

Economic and Social Council resolution 1993/39

27 July 1993   Meeting 43   Adopted without vote

Approved by Social Committee (E/1993/107) without vote, 16 July (meeting 12); draft by Commission on Narcotic Drugs (E/1993/29/Rev.1), agenda item 21.

Control of illicit supply

Action by Commission on Narcotic Drugs. In April,[36] the Commission urged its States members and UNDCP to support the development of crop survey systems in areas vulnerable to illicit cultivation, using technologies such as satellite imagery for monitoring. The Programme was requested to call on States to promote the necessary research and scientific and technological cooperation to that end.

Diversion of chemicals for illicit drug production

In a report to the Commission on Narcotic Drugs,[37] INCB discussed the implementation of article 12 of the 1988 United Nations Convention against Illicit Traffic in Narcotic Drugs and Psychotropic Substances.[14] The report outlined action by Governments and competent international bodies to prevent the diversion of chemical precursors used in the manufacture of narcotic drugs or psychotropic substances. As at 1 November 1992, a total of 82 Governments out of 193 countries and territories had submitted information to INCB on their implementation of article 12 and, for 1991, 18 countries and territories had reported seizures of substances listed in the Convention.

INCB proposed that the international community consider providing technical assistance for the enactment of basic legislation and the establishment of administrative and enforcement mechanisms to prevent the diversion of precursors, particularly in Asian countries where chemicals for the illicit manufacture of heroin were produced and trafficked. The Board noted that Africa also merited attention before there was any serious diversion of precursors in the region. Different types of assistance were needed to establish drug control administrations.

ECONOMIC AND SOCIAL COUNCIL ACTION

On 27 July, the Economic and Social Council, on the recommendation of its Social Committee, adopted **resolution 1993/40** without vote.

Implementation of measures to prevent the diversion of precursor and essential chemicals to illicit manufacture of narcotic drugs and psychotropic substances

The Economic and Social Council,

Concerned about the diversion of precursor and essential chemicals, as specified in Tables I and II of the United Nations Convention against Illicit Traffic in Narcotic Drugs and Psychotropic Substances of 1988, as well as other substances frequently used in the illicit manufacture of drugs, from commercial channels to the illicit manufacture of narcotic drugs and psychotropic substances,

Recalling its resolution 1992/29 of 30 July 1992, in which it invited all Governments that had not already done so to establish effective legislative, procedural and cooperative measures to implement the provisions of article 12 of the Convention in order to prevent the diversion of precursor and essential chemicals to the illicit manufacture of narcotic drugs and psychotropic substances,

Noting the effective work of the Chemical Action Task Force, established by the heads of State or Government of the seven major industrialized countries and the President of the Commission of the European Communities, with the participation of representatives of concerned developing countries and other countries, and its practical recommendations for preventing the diversion of precursor and essential chemicals, which build upon the provisions of the Convention,

Noting also the need for the provision of financial, technical and material assistance, including training, to assist Governments in implementing chemical control regimes,

Commending the international cooperation which has resulted from the work of the various international, regional and subregional groups and organizations dealing with issues relating to the control of precursors and essential chemicals,

Noting with approval the dissemination by the United Nations International Drug Control Programme of guidelines for use by national authorities in verifying the authenticity of applications for the export and import of precursor and essential chemicals, identifying suspicious transactions and preventing their diversion to the illicit manufacture of narcotic drugs and psychotropic substances,

Noting the good progress made by the Programme, the International Criminal Police Organization and the Customs Cooperation Council in the establishment of

mechanisms for sharing information held in their databases,

Noting that in the report of the International Narcotics Control Board for 1992, it was stressed that the effectiveness of an international network of databases would depend entirely on the data provided to them by Governments,

Commending the effective work of the Programme in developing and deploying a field testing kit incorporating safe methods of testing and identifying designated chemicals,

Acknowledging the central role of the International Narcotics Control Board and the Programme in the implementation of international chemical control regimes, as well as the intention expressed by the Board and the Programme to strengthen their efforts to promote implementation of articles 12, 13 and 22 of the Convention,

1. *Calls upon* all Governments, which were invited by the Economic and Social Council, in its resolution 1992/29, to establish effective measures to implement article 12 of the United Nations Convention against Illicit Traffic in Narcotic Drugs and Psychotropic Substances of 1988, to take fully into consideration the recommendations contained in the final report of the Chemical Action Task Force;

2. *Requests* the International Narcotics Control Board, in the course of monitoring the implementation of articles 12 and 13 of the Convention, to assist in identifying new diversion techniques, new chemicals that should be regulated and changes that may be required to counter new illicit methods of using chemicals;

3. *Calls upon* Governments to submit promptly to the Board all information required under article 12, paragraph 12, of the Convention;

4. *Urges* Governments that have not already done so to contribute the information necessary for the Board to prepare a directory of administrative and law enforcement authorities and a summary of regulatory controls, in accordance with Council resolution 1992/29;

5. *Requests* the United Nations International Drug Control Programme, drawing on voluntary contributions, to provide financial, technical and material assistance, including training, and to coordinate assistance that international and regional organizations or Governments may provide, in the implementation of chemical control regimes;

6. *Urges* Governments to support training and assistance activities by the Programme, and to coordinate bilateral assistance through the Programme in order to prevent duplication;

7. *Calls upon* Governments to contribute fully to and utilize the databases that are being established to prevent the diversion of chemicals, subject to their domestic law;

8. *Requests* the Customs Cooperation Council, the International Criminal Police Organization, the International Narcotics Control Board and appropriate regional organizations to prepare a memorandum of understanding regarding the exchange of information between their databases;

9. *Urges* Governments to consider fully and, where appropriate, to apply the guidelines disseminated by the Programme, which have been prepared for use by national authorities in preventing the diversion of precursor and essential chemicals;

10. *Requests* the Secretary-General to allocate adequate funds, within existing resources, to enable the Board to discharge its functions under articles 12, 13 and 22 of the Convention, and in accordance with Council resolution 1992/29 and the present resolution;

11. *Calls upon* Governments to provide voluntary resources to enable the Programme to increase technical cooperation and assistance in implementing chemical control measures.

Economic and Social Council resolution 1993/40

27 July 1993   Meeting 43   Adopted without vote

Approved by Social Committee (E/1993/107) without vote, 16 July (meeting 12); draft by Commission on Narcotic Drugs (E/1993/29/Rev.1), agenda item 21.

Diversion of psychotropic drugs for illicit use

In its 1993 report,[34] INCB welcomed the fact that, in response to its request, worldwide stocks of psychotropic substances listed in Schedule II of the 1971 Convention on Psychotropic Substances,[38] including methaqualone and fenetylline, had been reduced in keeping with declining medical requirements.

The Board stated that it had also repeatedly drawn the attention of Governments to large diversions of stimulants, sedative-hypnotics and tranquillizers, included in Schedules III and IV of the 1971 Convention, for illicit use in developing countries. It suggested that Governments apply additional control measures to international trade in those substances and that they report annually to INCB on their import and export.

ECONOMIC AND SOCIAL COUNCIL ACTION

On 27 July, the Economic and Social Council, on the recommendation of its Social Committee, adopted **resolution 1993/38** without vote.

Measures to prevent substances listed in Schedules III and IV of the Convention on Psychotropic Substances of 1971 from being diverted from international trade into illicit channels

The Economic and Social Council,

Alarmed by the continuing diversion of large quantities of substances listed in Schedules III and IV of the Convention on Psychotropic Substances of 1971 from licit manufacture and trade into illicit channels,

Recalling targets 8 and 10 of the Comprehensive Multidisciplinary Outline of Future Activities in Drug Abuse Control,

Recognizing that action to prevent such diversion requires a global response by exporting, transit and importing States,

Bearing in mind the Political Declaration and Global Programme of Action adopted by the General Assembly at its seventeenth special session, particularly the paragraphs on control of supply of narcotic drugs and psychotropic substances,

Reiterating its request, contained in its resolutions 1985/15 of 28 May 1985 and 1987/30 of 26 May 1987, to all Governments, to the extent possible, voluntarily to extend the system of import and export authorizations provided for in article 12, paragraph 1, of the Convention to cover international trade in substances listed in Schedules III and IV,

Reiterating its invitation, contained in its resolution 1991/44 of 21 June 1991, to all Governments to extend the system of voluntary assessments of annual medical and scientific requirements for substances listed in Schedule II to include also substances listed in Schedules III and IV of the Convention,

Taking note with satisfaction of the recommendations of the Conference on Control of International Trade in Psychotropic Substances, held at Strasbourg, France, from 3 to 5 March 1993, which was organized jointly by the International Narcotics Control Board and the Pompidou Group of the Council of Europe,

Having considered the report of the International Narcotics Control Board for 1992, in particular paragraph 59, concerning the successful operation of the system of import and export authorizations and the simplified estimate system with regard to substances listed in Schedule II of the Convention,

Noting with satisfaction that more than ninety Governments have already communicated to the International Narcotics Control Board their assessments of annual medical and scientific requirements for substances listed in Schedules III and IV of the Convention, and that those assessments have been published by the Board with a view to providing guidance for manufacture and export,

1. *Invites* all Governments that have not yet done so to accede to the Convention on Psychotropic Substances of 1971;

2. *Also invites* all Governments that have not yet done so to communicate to the International Narcotics Control Board their assessments of annual medical and scientific requirements for substances listed in Schedules III and IV of the Convention;

3. *Invites* importing States to take more frequent advantage of the provisions of article 13 of the Convention to prohibit the import of psychotropic substances not needed for legitimate use but frequently diverted into illicit channels;

4. *Calls upon* all Governments that do not yet control exports of all substances listed in Schedules III and IV of the Convention by using the system of export authorizations to urgently consider the establishment of such a system;

5. *Calls upon* all Governments for which the control of exports of substances listed in Schedules III and IV of the Convention using the system of export authorizations is not immediately feasible to utilize, in the meantime, other mechanisms, such as the system of pre-export declarations, to ensure that exports of psychotropic substances are in line with the assessments of importing States and that other control requirements in importing States such as import prohibitions under article 13 of the Convention and import authorization requirements are respected;

6. *Invites* all Governments to exercise continuing vigilance to ensure that operations of brokers and transit operators are not used for the diversion of psychotropic substances into illicit channels;

7. *Calls upon* Governments of States with experienced national drug control administrations and the United Nations International Drug Control Programme to provide support such as training and information systems to States that require assistance in establishing effective

control mechanisms for international trade in psychotropic substances;

8. *Requests* the Secretary-General to transmit the present resolution to all Governments and to invite them to bring it to the attention of their competent authorities in order to ensure the implementation of its provisions.

Economic and Social Council resolution 1993/38

27 July 1993   Meeting 43   Adopted without vote

Approved by Social Committee (E/1993/107) without vote, 16 July (meeting 12); draft by Commission on Narcotic Drugs (E/1993/29/Rev.1), agenda item 21.

Narcotic raw material for licit use

Global production of opiate raw materials decreased to about 183 tonnes in morphine equivalent in 1993. INCB, which monitored the global supply and demand of opiates for medical and scientific needs, reported[34] that this fluctuation from the 200 tonne range was due to reductions in the areas harvested and amounts produced in Australia, India and Turkey. Australia, which until 1993 had steadily increased its production of opiate raw materials, accepted a Board recommendation to reduce its area under opium cultivation from 8,030 hectares in 1992 to 6,500 in 1993 and to maintain that level in the coming years. Based on estimates from the five main producer countries—Australia, France, India, Spain and Turkey—INCB projected an increase in global production in 1994 to about 192 tonnes in morphine equivalent.

ECONOMIC AND SOCIAL COUNCIL ACTION

On 27 July, the Economic and Social Council, on the recommendation of its Social Committee, adopted **resolution 1993/37** without vote.

Demand for and supply of opiates for medical and scientific needs

The Economic and Social Council,

Recalling its resolutions 1979/8 of 9 May 1979, 1980/20 of 30 April 1980, 1981/8 of 6 May 1981, 1982/12 of 30 April 1982, 1983/3 of 24 May 1983, 1984/21 of 24 May 1984, 1985/16 of 28 May 1985, 1986/9 of 21 May 1986, 1987/31 of 26 May 1987, 1988/10 of 25 May 1988, 1989/15 of 22 May 1989, 1990/31 of 24 May 1990, 1991/43 of 21 June 1991 and 1992/30 of 30 July 1992,

Emphasizing that the need to balance the global licit supply of opiates against the legitimate demand for opiates for medical and scientific purposes is central to the international strategy and policy of drug abuse control,

Noting the fundamental need for international cooperation and solidarity with the traditional supplier countries in drug abuse control in general and in the universal application of the provisions of the Single Convention on Narcotic Drugs of 1961, in particular,

Having considered the report of the International Narcotics Control Board for 1992, in particular paragraphs 44 to 52 on the demand for and supply of opiates for medical and scientific needs,

Having also considered the valuable recommendations made by the International Narcotics Control Board in

its special report for 1989 on the demand for and supply of opiates for medical and scientific needs,

1. *Urges* all Governments to contribute to the establishment and maintenance of a balance between the licit supply of and demand for opiates for medical and scientific needs, keeping in mind the efforts to solve the problems involved, in particular the problem of excess stocks of opiate raw materials held by the traditional supplier States, and the relevant Economic and Social Council resolutions;

2. *Commends* the International Narcotics Control Board for its efforts in monitoring the implementation of the relevant Economic and Social Council resolutions and, in particular:

(a) In urging the Governments concerned to restrict global production of opiate raw materials to a level corresponding to the actual licit needs and to avoid any proliferation of production;

(b) In convening meetings, during sessions of the Commission on Narcotic Drugs, with the main States importing and producing opiate raw materials;

3. *Requests* the Secretary-General to transmit the present resolution to all Governments for consideration and implementation.

Economic and Social Council resolution 1993/37

27 July 1993   Meeting 43   Adopted without vote

Approved by Social Committee (E/1993/107) without vote, 16 July (meeting 12); draft by Commission on Narcotic Drugs (E/1993/29/Rev.1), agenda item 21.

Regional issues

Africa

According to INCB,[34] cannabis remained the most abused drug in Africa, where its abuse had become endemic in some countries. Illicit cannabis markets were supplied mainly from local and regional sources. Illicit poppy cultivation was reported only in Egypt and Kenya, but illicit trafficking and abuse of opiates, mainly heroin, had increased in several parts of the region. Although the amount of cocaine seized in Africa had decreased, more and more countries were reporting illegal transactions in their territories, and African transit routes and couriers from western Africa were increasingly used by international criminal organizations to transport cocaine from South America to Europe. Cocaine abuse was reported to have spread in Côte d'Ivoire, Ghana, Lesotho, Nigeria and Senegal. The abuse of methaqualone continued to be a major problem in southern and eastern Africa.

INCB suggested that the time was ripe for international consultations on trafficking in khat, following reported links between trade in this stimulant drug and the procurement of weapons in the Horn of Africa.

Technical missions of UNDCP and INCB visited Cameroon and Ethiopia in May to study their systems for controlling licit narcotic drugs and psychotropic substances.

The Sixth Meeting of HONLEA, Africa, was held at Abidjan, Côte d'Ivoire (24-28 May).

Asia

East and South-East Asia

South-East Asia remained a major producer of illicit opium,[34] most of which was grown in the border areas of Myanmar. A yield study in February 1993 attempted to assess the magnitude of poppy cultivation. Other producers included the Lao People's Democratic Republic, Thailand and Viet Nam. Illicit heroin laboratories continued to operate in the so-called Golden Triangle of South-East Asia where, in the opinion of Thai authorities, about 10 tonnes of heroin were produced annually in some 25 clandestine laboratories along the Myanmar and Thai borders. Illicit opium poppy cultivation was reported to be increasing in the Republic of Korea where about 50,000 opium poppy plants were eradicated in the first half of 1993 compared with about 13,000 plants in the same period of 1992. China (mainland and Taiwan Province), Hong Kong, Japan, Malaysia, the Philippines, the Republic of Korea, Thailand and Viet Nam were increasingly used as transit points for illicit consignments of heroin destined for Australia, Canada and the United States, as well as to countries in Europe.

There was a significant increase in cocaine seizures in Hong Kong, Japan, the Philippines and the Republic of Korea, which, according to INCB, could indicate that South American cartels had targeted the region. The illicit manufacture of, traffic in and abuse of amphetamines was identified as a major problem in several countries, including Japan and the Republic of Korea. Illicit traffic in cannabis and the size of cannabis consignments were also on the rise since 1992. Large-scale plantations were detected in the Lao People's Democratic Republic, Myanmar and Thailand. Cannabis was the most abused drug in countries such as Indonesia, Malaysia and the Philippines, and an increase in its abuse was observed in Japan and the Republic of Korea.

South Asia

During 1993,[34] all the South Asian countries were improving their national narcotics legislation and strengthening their drug control administration, law enforcement, treatment programmes and preventive education, with UNDCP assistance.

Transit traffic in heroin from South-West and South-East Asia was reported to be a big and growing problem. Heroin seizures almost doubled in India between 1991 and 1992, a trend that continued in 1993. Heroin abuse was reported to be increasing in Bangladesh, Maldives and Sri Lanka, and remained a major problem in Nepal and in India.

In March, an INCB mission reviewed controls on India's licit cultivation of opium poppy and the production and processing of raw opium and its alkaloids, which it found to be in conformity with the 1961 Single Convention on Narcotic Drugs,[39] although some opium was being diverted into illicit channels. INCB noted that India was a major source of illicit methaqualone, most of which was smuggled to South Africa. In January 1993, Indian authorities seized 3,200 kilograms of methaqualone bound for South Africa.

The Eighteenth Meeting of HONLEA, Asia and the Pacific, was held at Seoul, Republic of Korea (13-17 September).

Western Asia

The cultivation of and illicit traffic in cannabis remained a major problem in the region in 1993.[34] Systematic eradication of cannabis and illicit poppy plantations continued in Lebanon in 1993, but there was considerable illicit traffic in cannabis resin from Afghanistan through Pakistan to Europe, and from newly independent States in Central Asia to other parts of the Commonwealth of Independent States. Afghanistan also remained one of the largest producers of illicit opium and a rise in illicit poppy cultivation was observed in Pakistan. The eradication of a number of small poppy fields was reported in Kazakhstan, Kyrgyzstan and Turkmenistan, but many plots, especially those cultivated in inaccessible mountain areas, went undetected. Illicit traffic in opium, morphine and heroin within the region and the smuggling of heroin, mainly to Europe, remained major problems. Illicit traffic in fenetylline from Europe to large markets in the Arabian Peninsula continued.

The thirtieth session of the Subcommission on Illicit Drug Traffic and Related Matters in the Near and Middle East was rescheduled for budgetary reasons.

Europe

The abolition of border controls within the European Union (formerly the European Community), the opening of borders between East and West, and turmoil in the former republics of Yugoslavia presented major challenges to drug control and law enforcement during the year.[34]

In the former USSR, international trade by road, rail and air was growing steadily with virtually no control mechanisms in place and a rise in crime in Belarus, the Russian Federation and Ukraine was associated with drug trafficking. Controls on licit drug manufacture, trade and distribution were complicated in eastern European countries by a large number of new companies that manufactured and dealt in narcotic drugs, psychotropic substances and precursors.

UNDCP assisted central and eastern European countries in updating or developing new legal instruments related to drug control. In 1993, proposals for new legislation were made in Belarus, Estonia, Latvia, Lithuania, the Russian Federation and Ukraine. National drug control systems were strengthened in several countries, including the Czech Republic, Norway and Slovakia, by creating coordinating bodies.

UNDCP organized the First International Private Sector Conference on Drugs in the Workplace and the Community (Seville, Spain, 13-15 October), and INCB sent missions to Bulgaria and Poland. The Second Meeting of HONLEA, Europe, was held at Vienna (22-26 February).

Latin America and the Caribbean

Drug traffickers continued to take advantage of the strategic position of the Caribbean subregion to transship considerable quantities of cannabis and cocaine, and even heroin, to North America and Europe.[34] Transit traffic in cocaine continued to be the biggest drug-related problem in the region, but cannabis smoking and the inhalation of organic solvents remained the most common forms of drug abuse.

Peru remained the world's largest producer of coca leaf and although interdiction operations intensified, drug law enforcement was complicated by terrorist activity. Authorities were forced to fight not only illicit crop growers but also guerilla forces, which drew a large portion of their income from "war taxes" on illicit plantations and trafficking routes.

Colombia remained the world's largest supplier of cocaine hydrochloride, manufactured from coca paste smuggled from Bolivia and Peru. Some 224 clandestine laboratories were dismantled in Colombia in 1992 and 109 in the first four months of 1993. INCB noted that Venezuela had become a major transit country for Colombian drug cartels. Argentina, Brazil and Chile were identified as increasingly important transit countries for consignments to Asia and Africa, as well as to North America and Europe. Cocaine abuse was reported in most countries of the region. In the Andean subregion, poppy plantations were reported to have expanded on Colombian territory and were detected in Ecuador and Peru. Governments in the eastern Caribbean were planning to establish a regional drug intelligence centre based in Saint Lucia. Also under consideration was a Caribbean Community drug intelligence centre.

During 1993, INCB sent missions to Bolivia, Colombia, Costa Rica, Nicaragua, Peru and Uruguay.

The Sixth Meeting of HONLEA, Latin America and the Caribbean, was rescheduled for budgetary reasons.

On 27 July, by **decision 1993/247**, the Economic and Social Council decided that the Sixth Meeting of HONLEA, Latin America and the Caribbean, should be held in the Dominican Republic.

North America

With drug policy under review by the new Administration of the United States, INCB noted that there appeared to have been a change whereby anti-drug resources were shifted from foreign intervention to domestic education, treatment and law enforcement programmes.[34] Canada's drug control strategy had been renewed in 1992 with an 18 per cent funding increase, and Mexico also continued to pursue a vigorous anti-drug policy.

Cannabis remained the most commonly abused drug. Although it was increasingly grown indoors in the United States, substantial amounts were smuggled into the country from Colombia, Jamaica and Mexico. In Mexico, a crop control programme had reduced illicit poppy cultivation to its lowest level in 10 years and opium production had declined. Mexican heroin was produced almost exclusively for smuggling into the United States, where it accounted for approximately 23 per cent of the illicit market in 1992, down from over 33 per cent in 1988.

Heroin and cocaine abuse remained a significant cause for concern. Cocaine, particularly crack, was the main challenge to drug law enforcement in the United States, where hard-core drug abuse remained a serious problem, particularly among youth in lower-income, inner-city areas.

Applying a comprehensive control system to international trade in precursors, the United States routinely advised INCB of shipments that were stopped or suspended because of suspicious circumstances. Most cases involved the export to Latin America of solvents used for manufacturing cocaine.

Oceania

Although Oceania had not yet become a focus of major international concern, INCB reported[34] increasing cannabis abuse in Australia, Fiji, New Zealand, Samoa and especially Papua New Guinea, where severe health problems were attributed to a potent locally grown hybrid variety. The Board noted that the Pacific Islands were increasingly used as transit points for drug traffic and that a number of countries had made themselves vulnerable to money-laundering by developing off-shore banking operations. The capacity of police and customs services was also inadequate to control the increasing illicit drug trade. INCB welcomed intensified cooperation with the 15 member States and Territories of the South Pacific Forum and with the 27-member South Pacific Commission, which, it said, played an important role in developing legislation and cooperation between police and customs services. It noted that legal instruments were being drafted on extradition and mutual assistance in legal matters, and on the confiscation of proceeds of crime.

Conventions

As at 31 December 1993,[40] 122 States were parties to the 1961 Single Convention on Narcotic Drugs,[39] as amended by the 1972 Protocol,[41] and an additional 23 were parties to the Convention only. During the year, 13 States—Antigua and Barbuda, Armenia, Bosnia and Herzegovina, Burundi, Croatia, the Czech Republic, Dominica, the Dominican Republic, Latvia, Poland, Slovakia, the former Yugoslav Republic of Macedonia and Zimbabwe—became parties. This brought the number of parties to the Convention in its original or amended form to 145.

The number of States parties to the 1971 Convention on Psychotropic Substances[38] stood at 127 as at 31 December.[40] Eighteen States became parties in 1993: Antigua and Barbuda, Armenia, Bosnia and Herzegovina, Burundi, Croatia, Czech Republic, Dominica, Fiji, Israel, Latvia, the Netherlands, Romania, Slovakia, Sri Lanka, the Sudan, the former Yugoslav Republic of Macedonia, Zambia and Zimbabwe. While most parties to the Convention regularly submitted their mandatory annual statistical reports, INCB noted with concern that several countries had failed for over three years to provide annual statistics on psychotropic substances.[34]

As at 31 December, 94 States and the European Union were parties to the 1988 United Nations Convention against Illicit Traffic in Narcotic Drugs and Psychotropic Substances,[14] which entered into force in 1990. Antigua and Barbuda, Argentina, Armenia, Azerbaijan, Bosnia and Herzegovina, Brunei Darussalam, Burundi, Croatia, the Czech Republic, Dominica, the Dominican Republic El Salvador, Fiji, Germany, Guyana, Malaysia, Mauritania, the Netherlands, Romania, Slovakia, the Sudan, the former Yugoslav Republic of Macedonia, Zambia and Zimbabwe ratified or acceded to the Convention during the year. INCB noted with concern that only about 50 per cent of the parties had reported to it for 1993.

To encourage ratification and the establishment of effective drug control structures, UNDCP and other relevant international bodies continued to provide States with legal assistance.

Organizational questions

Commission on Narcotic Drugs

The Commission on Narcotic Drugs held its thirty-sixth session at Vienna from 29 March to 7 April 1993.[42]

On 27 July, the Economic and Social Council, by **decision 1993/250**, took note of the Commission's report on that session and, by **decision 1993/245**, approved the provisional agenda and documentation for the Commission's thirty-seventh (1994) session. By **decision 1993/248** of the same date, the Council decided that a reconvened session of the Commission should take place in December to approve the programme budget for 1994-1995 and the second and final revision of the programme budget for 1992-1993 for the Fund of UNDCP.

The Commission's reconvened thirty-sixth session took place at Vienna on 16 and 17 December.

International Narcotics Control Board

In 1993, INCB held its fifty-fourth and fifty-fifth sessions (Vienna, 4-14 May and 1-18 November).

On 27 July, the Economic and Social Council, by **decision 1993/249**, took note of the 1992 report of INCB.[43] Also on that date, by **decision 1993/252**, the Council took note of the summary of the report,[44] as well as of a note by the Executive Director of UNDCP[45] on administrative arrangements to ensure INCB's full technical independence.

REFERENCES

[1]E/CN.7/1994/2. [2]YUN 1991, p. 721. [3]E/CN.7/1993/3. [4]E/1993/29/Rev.1 (res. 10(XXXVI)). [5]Ibid. (res. 11 (XXXVI)). [6]E/CN.7/1993/5 & Add.1,2. [7]YUN 1991, p. 873, GA res. 46/185 C, 20 Dec. 1991. [8]E/CN.7/1993/11. [9]E/1993/29/Rev.1 (res. 12(XXXVI)). [10]Ibid. (res. 13 (XXXVI)). [11]Ibid. (res. 14(XXXVI)). [12]YUN 1992, p. 913, GA res. 47/102, 16 Dec. 1992. [13]A/48/327. [14]YUN 1988, p. 690. [15]E/CN.7/1993/CRP.5. [16]E/1993/29/Rev.1 (res. 2(XXXVI)). [17]E/CN.7/1993/CRP.13. [18]E/1993/29/Rev.1 (res. 3(XXXVI)). [19]Ibid. (res. 1(XXXVI)). [20]Ibid. (res. 5(XXXVI)). [21]Ibid. (res. 8(XXXVI)). [22]YUN 1992, p. 910. [23]E/1993/29/Rev.1 (res. 9(XXXVI)). [24]YUN 1992, p. 916, GA res. 47/99, 16 Dec. 1992. [25]E/CN.7/1993/7. [26]GA res. S-17/2, annex, 23 Feb. 1990. [27]A/48/286. [28]E/1993/29/Rev.1 (res. 7(XXXVI)). [29]YUN 1992, p. 917, GA res. 47/100, 16 Dec. 1992. [30]ACC/1993/12. [31]ACC/1993/18. [32]A/48/178-E/1993/70. [33]A/48/329 & Corr.1. [34]*Report of the International Narcotics Control Board for 1993* (E/INCB/1993/1), Sales No. E.94.XI.2. [35]E/1993/29/Rev.1 (res. 4(XXXVI)). [36]Ibid. (res. 6(XXXVI)). [37]E/CN.7/1993/6. [38]YUN 1971, p. 380. [39]YUN 1961, p. 382. [40]*Multilateral Treaties Deposited with the Secretary-General: Status as at 31 December 1993* (ST/LEG/SER.E/12), Sales No. E.94.V.II. [41]YUN 1972, p. 397. [42]E/1993/29/Rev.1. [43]*Report of the International Narcotics Control Board for 1992* (E/INCB/1992/1), Sales No. E.93.XI.1. [44]E/1993/45. [45]E/1993/94.

Chapter XVII

Statistics

In 1993, the statistical work of the United Nations was marked by the completion by the Statistical Commission of the revised System of National Accounts (SNA). The revised SNA was the culmination of a 10-year effort—in which 50 experts in national accounting from 40 countries, as well as international and non-governmental organizations, participated—to improve the basis of national accounts, to extend the scope of the national accounting framework and to harmonize different statistical systems. When adopting SNA in July (resolution 1993/5), the Economic and Social Council recommended that it be widely used in compiling national accounts statistics and in comparing national accounting data.

On the basis of a two-year review carried out by an independent review group and the Working Group on International Statistical Programmes and Coordination, the Commission adopted an action plan to strengthen international statistical cooperation and statistical development.

UN statistical bodies

Statistical Commission

The Statistical Commission held its twenty-seventh session in New York from 22 February to 3 March 1993.[1] Its major action was the recommendation to the Economic and Social Council that it adopt the revised SNA. It also made recommendations with respect to SNA's implementation and publication. Other action was taken on strengthening international statistical cooperation; international economic classifications; industrial, service and price statistics; demographic and social statistics; and environment and tourism statistics. Other matters considered were the general development and integration of methodological work, including development indicators; technical cooperation; coordination and integration of international statistical programmes; programme questions; and the fundamental principles of official statistics.

The Commission recommended that it meet in special session in 1994.

ECONOMIC AND SOCIAL COUNCIL ACTION

On 12 July, the Economic and Social Council adopted **resolution 1993/6** without vote.

Special session of the Statistical Commission
The Economic and Social Council,

Noting that the Statistical Commission has completed a fundamental review of the structure and operation of the international statistical system and, as a result, has made recommendations and decisions for strengthening the international statistical system, including the following:

(a) A more active Working Group on International Statistical Programmes and Coordination to monitor progress in coordination and cooperation within the international statistical system between sessions of the Statistical Commission;

(b) Strengthened statistical divisions of the United Nations regional commissions and strengthened regional conferences of national chief statisticians in all five regions in terms of their responsibilities for statistical development in their regions;

(c) More effective working relationships between the Subcommittee on Statistical Activities of the Administrative Committee on Coordination and the Statistical Commission and the Working Group;

(d) The establishment of six task forces as mechanisms for developing a more integrated work programme among international organizations in the following subject areas: national accounts, industrial and construction statistics, international trade statistics, finance statistics, price statistics and environment statistics,

Noting also that the Statistical Commission, at its twenty-seventh session, held from 22 February to 3 March 1993, stressed the importance of implementing the revised System of National Accounts in all parts of the world and unanimously recommended that it be adopted, and endorsing the intention to pursue research into the unresolved issues and to work on future aspects of the accounts,

Aware that the twenty-eighth session of the Commission is scheduled to be held in 1995,

1. *Decides* that a special session of the Commission, of four or five days' duration, shall be held in 1994 for the following purposes:

(a) To review progress made in the implementation of the recommendations and decisions for strengthening the international statistical system in general;

(b) To monitor progress made in implementing the revised System of National Accounts and review plans for the further essential research work already identified;

2. *Also decides* that the provisions of the present resolution should be implemented within the approved budget limit set by the General Assembly for the biennium 1994-1995.

Economic and Social Council resolution 1993/6
12 July 1993   Meeting 30   Adopted without vote
Draft by Statistical Commission (E/1993/26); agenda item 12 *(b)*.

Also on 12 July, by **decision 1993/223**, the Council approved the provisional agenda and documentation for the Commission's 1994 special session and, by **decision 1993/222**, it took note of the report of the Commission on its 1993 session[1] and approved the provisional agenda and documentation for its 1995 session.

Working Group on International Statistical Programmes and Coordination

The Working Group on International Statistical Programmes and Coordination of the Statistical Commission held its sixteenth session at Geneva from 13 to 16 September 1993,[2] as decided by the Economic and Social Council on 16 July (**decision 1993/229**).

The Working Group discussed implementation of the 1993 SNA and plans for further research for updating international standards on national accounts and related statistics; the work of the inter-agency task forces (dealing with national accounts, industrial and construction statistics, international trade statistics, pricing statistics, environment statistics and finance statistics); its methods of work and those of the Commission; aspects of the Commission's recommendations on strengthening international statistical cooperation; fundamental principles of official statistics; coordination of the statistical data-collection activities of international organizations; the medium-term plan of the United Nations Statistical Division; and the provisional agenda and documentation for the Commission's 1994 and 1995 sessions.

The Working Group recommended that its next session be held in New York in early September 1994.

By **decision 1993/224** of 12 July, the Economic and Social Council, bearing in mind the fact that, at its 1993 session, the Commission had discussed strengthening international statistical cooperation (see below), decided that the Working Group should hold four-day sessions in both 1994 and 1995.

ACC Subcommittee

The Subcommittee on Statistical Activities of the Administrative Committee on Coordination (ACC) held its twenty-seventh session at Geneva from 6 to 8 September.[3] It discussed its own future role and functioning; coordination of data-collection activities; issues related to the work of the Statistical Commission's task forces; its own Technical Working Group on Statistical Databases; directories, inventories and other tools and reporting mechanisms for promoting coordination of international statistical work; resources available for statistical work in international organizations; and coordination of statistical programmes.

With regard to its role and functioning, the Subcommittee noted that many changes had occurred in recent years which had an impact on international statistical work and which called for im-

provements in its own functioning. It made a number of recommendations in that regard.

The Subcommittee established parameters for the functioning of the Commission's six task forces and requested specific actions, including the setting of priorities and timetables for their tasks to be completed. It established guidelines for establishing new task forces and agreed to the establishment of task forces for services statistics and the measurement of poverty. The work of the Technical Working Group on Statistical Databases was suspended.

As to tools and reporting mechanisms for promoting statistical coordination, the Subcommittee decided that a number of products, including a new edition of the *Directory of International Statistics*, would be issued during 1994-1995. Suggestions were made to raise awareness at the regional and government levels of the coordination measures being implemented.

International statistical cooperation and coordination

In February/March 1993,[1] the Statistical Commission adopted a plan identifying 19 actions for strengthening international statistical cooperation and statistical development. The action plan was the result of a two-year review carried out by an independent review group and the Working Group on International Statistical Programmes and Coordination. The Commission had before it the Working Group's recommendations and decisions on the subject, adopted at its 1992 session.[4] Also before the Commission was a January report of the Secretary-General[5] containing the Secretariat's comments on those recommendations and decisions and a summary of work done and additional action required to implement them. The Commission further considered a report of the Secretary-General[6] on the proposed programme of work of the Statistical Division for the 1994-1995 biennium and revisions to the medium-term plan for 1992-1997.

Following a review of the Working Group's recommendations and decisions, the Commission revised and adopted 10 recommendations and revised and took note of nine decisions. The recommendations dealt with: the Commission's institutional arrangements, including the possibility of more frequent meetings; the Working Group's institutional arrangements, including that it meet annually; increased emphasis on coordination matters; adherence to United Nations classifications; future topics for discussion by the Commission; and the work of the Statistical Division, the ACC Subcommittee on Statistical Activities and its own task forces.

The Commission recommended that it hold a special session in 1994, with a possible consequent reduction of its regular session scheduled for 1995 (see above).

In September,[2] the Working Group reviewed progress achieved in relation to the Commission's plan of action. It considered that the mandate of the regional commissions in respect of their statistical activities should be specified in operational terms to enable them to play a role in strengthening international statistical coordination; decided that there was a need for wider dissemination of its report, particularly to regional statistical conferences; and adopted decisions on its own functioning, agenda and documentation and on new documentation for the Commission on plans for methodological development in statistics.

Economic statistics

National accounts and balances

In February/March 1993,[1] the Statistical Commission had before it the final draft of the revised SNA.[7] The new draft SNA—revision of which had taken 10 years—was intended to extend the scope of the national accounting framework and harmonize different statistical systems. It was flexible enough to be applied in different circumstances and to be extended to alternative analyses, such as social accounting matrices and environmental accounting. Also before the Commission was a report on work done on the revision by the Intersecretariat Working Group on National Accounts (ISWGNA) in 1992[8] and a note by the International Labour Office concerning statistics of employment in the informal sector.[9]

The Commission unanimously recommended the adoption of the revised SNA and urged ISWGNA to ensure its publication in English before the end of 1993 and to expedite the publication of other language versions. It agreed that the United Nations regional commissions should play a major role in implementing the revised SNA in their respective regions.

ISWGNA submitted to the Commission in January a report on implementation of SNA.[10] It outlined areas where a coordinated international effort was critical: basic data development; handbooks, guidelines, manuals and special studies; training; and technical assistance. It also discussed its own role in the implementation process.

ECONOMIC AND SOCIAL COUNCIL ACTION

On 12 July, the Economic and Social Council adopted **resolution 1993/5** without vote.

1993 System of National Accounts

The Economic and Social Council,

Recognizing that the 1993 System of National Accounts updates, clarifies and simplifies the previous System of National Accounts and is more completely harmonized with other international standards in statistics,

Affirming that the 1993 System of National Accounts is a conceptual and accounting framework that is applicable to all countries,

Recognizing also that the 1993 System of National Accounts emphasizes flexibility, so as to encourage its use in economies that differ widely and to facilitate international comparisons,

Noting that the 1993 System of National Accounts completes the integration of balance sheets, thus providing a fuller picture of the resources at an economy's disposal, consolidates hitherto separate presentations of important elements of an economy, lays the groundwork for dealing with interaction between the economy and the environment, and elaborates an analytical approach to the assessment of poverty through the application of the Social Accounting Matrices,

1. *Expresses its deep appreciation* to the members of the Intersecretariat Working Group on National Accounts—the Statistical Division of the Secretariat, the United Nations regional commissions, the World Bank, the International Monetary Fund, the Organisation for Economic Cooperation and Development and the Statistical Office of the European Communities—and to non-governmental organizations, a number of Member States and many individual experts in national accounting for contributing human and financial resources, for more than ten years, to the development of the 1993 System of National Accounts;

2. *Recommends* that Member States consider using the 1993 System of National Accounts as the international standard for the compilation of their national accounts statistics, in order to promote the integration of economic and related statistics, and as an analytical tool;

3. *Recommends also* that Member States use the 1993 System of National Accounts in the international reporting of comparable national accounting data;

4. *Recommends further* that international organizations consider the 1993 System of National Accounts and the concepts therein when they review standards for particular fields of economic statistics and endeavour to achieve consistency with the 1993 System of National Accounts and, when differences remain, explain the rationale for those differences and provide a full reconciliation with the 1993 System of National Accounts to the extent possible;

5. *Requests* the Secretary-General and the members of the Intersecretariat Working Group on National Accounts to proceed with publication of the 1993 System of National Accounts in all six languages of the United Nations as rapidly as possible and to promote its wide dissemination;

6. *Requests* the members of the Intersecretariat Working Group to continue to be involved in coordinating the implementation of the 1993 System of National Accounts;

7. *Requests* Member States and regional and international organizations to support all aspects of the implementation of the 1993 System of National Accounts, namely, basic data development, the issuance of handbooks, guidelines, manuals and special studies, training activities among both users and producers and technical cooperation activities;

8. *Further requests* Member States and regional and international organizations to provide assistance and support in refining and updating the 1993 System of National Accounts in areas identified in the research agenda, including further developmental work on

methodologies, research on conceptual enhancements and emerging or unresolved issues, and refinement of current recommendations in the light of experience gained in implementation;

9. *Agrees* that the United Nations regional commissions should play a major role in the implementation of the 1993 System of National Accounts in their respective regions and urges the Secretary-General to coordinate, at a high level, the mobilization of bilateral and multilateral resources for the implementation of the 1993 System of National Accounts, including the necessary support for countries and the regional commissions.

Economic and Social Council resolution 1993/5

| 12 July 1993 | Meeting 30 | Adopted without vote |

Draft by Statistical Commission (E/1993/26); agenda item 12 *(b)*.

Tourism statistics

In a report prepared by the World Tourism Organization (WTO) in collaboration with the United Nations Statistical Division,[11] a number of draft recommendations on tourism statistics were presented to the Statistical Commission. The issue had been discussed at the 1991 International Conference on Travel and Tourism Statistics, jointly organized by WTO and Canada. The report outlined the development of and need for tourism statistics, described the concepts and forms of tourism, defined basic tourism units and proposed possible classifications of tourism demand and supply. It also addressed the subject of statistics on tourism expenditure, noting that they were important indicators required by policy makers, planning officials, marketers and researchers. The report described further work to be carried out by WTO in cooperation with other organizations and proposed that the Commission might wish to: consider developments and statistical requirements related to the growing role of tourism in the national economy; consider WTO's draft recommendations on concepts, definitions and classifications of tourism statistics; and consider the Standard International Classification of Tourism Activities (SICTA)[12] and adopt it as a provisional classification.

At its February/March session,[1] the Statistical Commission adopted both WTO's recommendations and SICTA as a provisional classification, and requested that they be published and widely distributed. It emphasized the need for technical cooperation to assist countries to implement WTO's recommendations on tourism statistics.

Price statistics

In a February report on the work of the Statistical Division,[13] the Secretary-General stated that an expert group meeting was held on the methodology of the International Comparison Programme (ICP) and implementation of the 1993 comparison programme (Philadelphia, United States, 27-29 January 1993). The expert group agreed on a plan of future activities: a new direction for the programme would depart from the costly practice of launching benchmark year comparisons every five years and move towards integration with work on national accounts and consumer price indexes.

Also before the Commission was a report of the Secretary-General concerning developments in ICP through 1992.[14]

The Commission took note of the increasing number of countries participating in ICP, stressed its importance and endorsed its continuation. It endorsed the results of the Philadelphia meeting and suggested that priority be given to activities agreed on at the meeting, particularly the preparation and dissemination of harmonized technical documents. The Commission requested the Secretary-General to submit to it in 1995 a progress report on developments in ICP.

Service statistics

At its February/March session,[1] the Statistical Commission discussed work done by national and international agencies and by the Statistical Division in the field of service statistics during 1992.[15]

The Commission welcomed the work of the Voorburg Group on Service Statistics (a cooperative effort by volunteer statistical agencies to address problems associated with data gaps and conceptual issues) and requested the Statistical Division to facilitate dissemination of technical materials, including those of the Voorburg Group. It welcomed the initiatives of the United Nations Conference on Trade and Development, the General Agreement on Tariffs and Trade (GATT) and the Statistical Division, in cooperation with the International Monetary Fund, to carry out further methodological development work with respect to international trade in services. The Commission stressed the need to enhance technical cooperation related to service statistics through advisory services and regional seminars.

International economic classifications

The Secretary-General, in a January report,[16] reviewed progress in implementing revision 3 of the International Standard Industrial Classification of All Economic Activities (ISIC, Rev. 3) and the provisional Central Product Classification (CPC), including the preparation of computerized correspondence tables between ISIC, Rev. 3, CPC, revision 3 of the Standard International Trade Classification (SITC, Rev. 3) and the Harmonized Commodity Description and Coding System (HS). Some problematic areas in preparing the indexes to ISIC were discussed. The report also summarized the results of a survey conducted among national statistical offices regarding the uses of ISIC,

CPC and SITC. Further work on classifications that could be carried out in various international agencies was proposed.

In February/March,[1] the Commission requested the Statistical Division, in cooperation with organizations and countries concerned, to finalize work on the provisional CPC, taking into account the fact that a revised version could not be submitted to the Commission before 1997. The Division was asked to: compile information on country practices regarding the implementation of ISIC, Rev. 3; continue work on computerized correspondence tables, resulting in the linking of a large number of national and international classifications; undertake work on the functional classifications of expenditures, in cooperation with other organizations and countries; and report on those issues and submit drafts of the revised Classification of the Functions of Government and the Classification of Individual Consumption to the Commission in 1995.

For its consideration of international economic classifications, the Commission also had before it a report of the International Labour Office on the revision of the International Classification of Status in Employment (ICSE).[17] The report provided a historical background on ICSE and described its current structure and the need for revision. It also contained proposals for the revision, including a draft resolution on the subject that was adopted by the Fifteenth International Conference of Labour Statisticians (Geneva, 19-28 January 1993).

The Statistical Commission endorsed the revised ICSE adopted by the Conference, welcomed future work called for in the Conference's resolution, and noted that major new technical cooperation in implementing the revised ICSE was not currently required.

Industrial statistics

Following consideration of the Secretary-General's report on preparatory work carried out in 1992 relating to the 1993 World Programme of Industrial Statistics,[8] the Statistical Commission, at its February/March 1993 session,[1] welcomed steps taken to re-orient the Statistical Division's industrial statistics programme. It stressed the importance of measures to contribute to the change-over from ISIC, Rev. 2 to Rev. 3 (see above) and the need to identify and address impediments to the change-over. The Division was asked to carry out further studies of national experiences in the use of ISIC, Rev. 3, and the provisional CPC to understand better how countries were using those classifications, the problems they were encountering in their use and their experiences in relating such classifications to existing national or regional classifications. The Com-

mission emphasized the importance of maintaining continuity in collecting and disseminating general industrial statistics at the international level regardless of institutional arrangements for that activity, and requested that the question of industrial statistics be included in its 1995 agenda.

Environment statistics

In 1993,[1] the Statistical Commission, having considered a report of the Secretary-General covering 1992 activities in environment statistics,[15] welcomed the preparation of an interim *SNA Handbook on Integrated Environmental and Economic Accounting*, which, in accordance with a request of the 1992 United Nations Conference on Environment and Development,[15] should be widely distributed and further developed by the Statistical Division, in cooperation with other international organizations and national experts. The Commission stressed the need to build national capacities in developing countries in all areas of environment statistics, by means of handbooks, training seminars, workshops and country projects, and requested that the Intergovernmental Working Group on the Advancement of Environment Statistics continue its work, incorporating the development of environment and sustainable development indicators and relevant aspects of environmental accounting.

Social and demographic statistics

Population and housing censuses

In February/March 1993,[1] the Statistical Commission, having considered a report of the Secretary-General on work undertaken during 1992 in connection with the 1990 World Population and Housing Census Programme,[18] requested the Statistical Division, in collaboration with the regional commissions, to prepare for the 2000 round of population and housing censuses. The Commission emphasized the importance of census methodological studies on issues such as census cartography, the improved measurement of economic activity, including the revised economic classifications, the use of modern technology, sampling, census pre-testing and quality control, as well as the publication of subject-matter handbooks and technical reports. The Secretary-General was requested to report in 1995 on preparations for the 2000 round of censuses and the Division was asked to review the current recommendations on international migration statistics, in cooperation with the regional commissions, EUROSTAT (the Statistical Office of the European Communities) and other organizations.

In 1993, two subregional workshops were held on strategies for accelerating the improvement of civil registration and vital statistics systems, at

Damascus, Syrian Arab Republic (20-24 June) and Beijing (29 November–3 December).

Statistics on women

The Statistical Commission in 1993[1] had before it a report containing information on the Statistical Division's work during 1991-1992 on statistics on the advancement of women.[18] The Commission expressed its appreciation of the Division's work on gender statistics and strongly supported its continuation. It called on the Division to act as a focal point to ensure continued coordination and integration of international work in that field and called on international statistical services to provide maximum support to preparations for the Fourth World Conference on Women, to be held in 1995.

Other statistical activities

Development and integration of methodological work

The Secretary-General submitted to the 1993 session of the Statistical Commission[1] a report on the general development and integration of methodological work in certain areas,[19] particularly energy statistics and international trade and transport statistics. In an addendum,[20] he and GATT presented their views on the future relationship between SITC and HS (see above).

The Commission asked the Statistical Division to revise the existing United Nations concepts and definitions on international trade statistics to ensure their adequacy and clarity in relation to current circumstances and to ensure their harmonization with the revised SNA and balance of payments. The Division was also asked to publish the results of the research into country practices for international trade statistics, carried out by various international organizations, and make them available to countries, and to revise SITC, Rev. 3, in full correlation with the revised HS and to issue the revision to be effective 1 January 1996, the date of introduction of the revised HS. The Commission recommended that countries adopt HS for compilation and dissemination of their international trade statistics, should they intend to change their commodity classification for their own purposes, and that the Customs Cooperation Council take fully into account the statistical implications of any changes proposed for HS and the statistical needs and capacities of developing countries. It decided to consider the use of CPC in place of SITC, Rev. 3, for analytical purposes as soon as the provisional CPC was revised and evaluated.

Also before the Commission was a report by the United Nations Research Institute for Social Development (UNRISD) on patterns of consumption and qualitative aspects of development.[21] The report focused mainly on developments and experience in monitoring the achievement of social goals and objectives and related human development concerns by means of qualitative indicators. It described UNRISD activities under the Patterns of Consumption project since it reported to the Commission in 1991,[22] reviewed the major lessons and findings of a 1991 expert meeting on qualitative indicators of development and listed the recommendations of that meeting, including action and activities to be undertaken by United Nations organizations.

The Commission agreed that indicator programmes should aim at limited, practical objectives and be closely linked to user needs and asked the Statistical Division to act as focal point to promote full collaboration and coordination at the international level in work on development indicators. The Commission recommended the intensive continuation of planned research work on sound statistical methodology for derived indicators on complex social topics such as poverty and cautioned against the use of complex indicators and indices without a clear understanding and statement of their limitations. It agreed that priority should be assigned to selecting and compiling appropriate indicators to support preparations for the 1995 World Summit for Social Development (see PART THREE, Chapter XII) and agreed to consider the question of development indicators at its 1995 session.

In other action, the Commission emphasized the utmost need for inter-agency collaboration in further development of social-goal monitoring and measurement work and urged that the work of the Economic Commission for Latin America and the Caribbean (ECLAC) be reflected in future development of the programme at the global level. ECLAC was invited to submit in 1995 a paper on its work in developing poverty profiles.

Programme questions

Having considered reports of the Secretary-General in which he reviewed the statistical work of international organizations and the Statistical Division for the period January 1990 to December 1991,[23] and provided updated information on the work of the Division during 1992,[13] the Statistical Commission, in 1993,[1] endorsed the new format of the report on the work of international organizations. It requested its Working Group on International Statistical Programmes and Coordination to consider further improvements in the report as an overall reference tool and asked the ACC Subcommittee on Statistical Activities also to consider those improvements and others, including the classification of the subject areas and functional areas used. The Statistical Division was asked to prepare, in cooperation with international and regional organizations, a similar report for the Commission's 1995 session.

The Commission also considered a report of the Secretary-General on the proposed programme of work of the Statistical Division for 1994-1995 and revisions to the medium-term plan for 1992-1997.[6] It approved both the proposed work programme and the following elements as priority items for 1994-1995: work on coordination of the global statistical system and services to national statistical offices; implementation of the revised SNA; environment statistics, indicators and accounting; strengthening computer processing systems and support; preparations for the 1995 World Conference on Women and other work related to improving gender statistics; preparations for the 1995 World Summit for Social Development; and preparations and support for the 1995-2004 Population and Housing Census Decade.

Technical cooperation

The Statistical Commission considered a report of the Secretary-General on technical cooperation in statistics during 1989-1992.[24] At its February/March 1993 session,[1] it stressed the importance of technical cooperation programmes and

endorsed the activities carried out by the Statistical Division and other international and regional organizations. It emphasized the importance of technical cooperation related to national accounts and other types of economic statistics and urged that resources allocated to that component be increased. The Secretary-General was asked to report in 1995 on technical cooperation in statistics.

During 1993,[25] the United Nations spent some \$14.9 million on technical cooperation projects in the area of statistics. Of that amount, \$7.1 million was provided by UNFPA, \$5.2 million by UNDP, \$482,000 by the United Nations regular programme of technical cooperation, and the remainder came from trust funds.

REFERENCES

[1]E/1993/26. [2]E/CN.3/1994/2. [3]ACC/1993/1. [4]YUN 1992, p. 927. [5]E/CN.3/1993/3 & Add.1. [6]E/CN.3/1993/25. [7]*System of National Accounts 1993* (ST/ESA/STAT/SER.F/2/Rev.4), Sales No. E.94.XVII.4. [8]YUN 1992, p. 928. [9]E/CN.3/1993/5. [10]E/CN.3/1993/6. [11]E/CN.3/1993/14. [12]*Recommendations on Tourism Statistics* (ST/ESA/STAT/SER.M/83), Sales No. E.94.XVII.6. [13]E/CN.3/1993/24. [14]E/CN.3/1993/11. [15]YUN 1992, p. 929. [16]E/CN.3/1993/7. [17]E/CN.3/1993/8. [18]YUN 1992, p. 930. [19]E/CN.3/1993/15. [20]E/CN.3/1993/15/Add.1. [21]E/CN.3/1993/16. [22]YUN 1991, p. 746. [23]E/CN.3/1993/22. [24]YUN 1992, p. 931. [25]DP/1994/26/Add.2.

Chapter XVIII

Institutional arrangements

In 1993, the General Assembly continued to adopt measures for the restructuring and revitalization of the United Nations in the economic and social fields. In view of the enlarged role of the Economic and Social Council, the Assembly requested the Secretary-General to strengthen the secretariat of the Council (resolution 48/162).

The Council established a new subsidiary body, the Commission on Sustainable Development, and created a working group to review the arrangements for consultations with non-governmental organizations.

The Administrative Committee on Coordination and the Committee for Programme and Coordination continued to harmonize system-wide work programmes and activities. Their twenty-seventh series of Joint Meetings was held in October to discuss the results of the 1992 United Nations Conference on Environment and Development and their implications for the United Nations.

Restructuring questions

In the continuing process of the restructuring and revitalization of the United Nations in the economic, social and related fields, the General Assembly had before it in June, at its resumed forty-seventh session, a draft resolution[1] prepared by a working group on the topic, proposing further measures for adoption by the Assembly. Also before the Assembly were draft resolutions on the programme of work for the Second (Economic and Financial) Committee for 1993-1994[2] and on world food security.[3] The chairman of the working group, in an oral report to the Assembly, said that the proposed restructuring and revitalization measures related to the strengthening of the coordination functions and authority of the Economic and Social Council, rationalizing work among the Assembly, the Council and subsidiary bodies, and rationalizing and harmonizing their agendas. If adopted, the proposed measures would enter into force on 1 January 1994. The chairman orally revised the draft resolution to take into account the concerns of some Member States. He also indicated that, due to a lack of time, the working group was unable to consider the other draft resolutions, but he suggested that the Secretariat review the

Second Committee's programme of work for 1993-1994 and that the draft on world food security be considered during the forty-eighth session of the Assembly.

On 25 June, by a recorded vote of 70 to 37, with 14 abstentions, the Assembly postponed action on the draft resolution on the restructuring and revitalization of the United Nations, as orally revised.

In a July letter to the Assembly President,[4] the President of the Economic and Social Council expressed the disappointment of the Council membership over the Assembly's action and urged that a decision be taken before the forty-eighth session of the Assembly so as to expedite further the revitalization and restructuring process.

In September, the Assembly agreed to continue negotiations, with a view to finalizing the revised draft resolution[5] and to defer consideration of the item to its forty-eighth session.

On 20 September, by **decision 47/478**, the Assembly included the item "Restructuring and revitalization of the United Nations in the economic, social and related fields" in the draft agenda of its forty-eighth session.

Report of the Secretary-General. The Secretary-General, in response to a 1991 Assembly request,[6] submitted in November 1993 a second progress report[7] on the implementation of the results of the restructuring and revitalization of the United Nations in the economic, social and related fields. The report discussed issues relating to the coordination and operational activities segments of the Economic and Social Council and the Joint Meetings of the Committee for Programme and Coordination (CPC) and the Administrative Committee on Coordination (ACC). The Secretary-General suggested that the Assembly postpone its proposed review of the reforms so far agreed upon until the outcome of the ongoing negotiations on measures to clarify the functional responsibilities of the Assembly and the Council, to streamline their agendas and to enhance the authority of the Council in respect of operational activities for development. He also suggested that the Council should, during its substantive session, determine the themes for its coordination segment and that the institution of Joint Meetings of CPC and ACC, if maintained, should be organized along the lines of the twenty-seventh series of Joint Meetings, held on 27 October.

On 20 December, by **decision 48/439**, the Assembly took note of the Secretary-General's report.

On 20 December, the General Assembly adopted without vote **resolution 48/162**.

Further measures for the restructuring and revitalization of the United Nations in the economic, social and related fields

The General Assembly,

Reaffirming its resolutions 45/264 of 13 May 1991 and 46/235 of 13 April 1992,

Recalling its resolutions 57(I) of 11 December 1946, 304(IV) of 16 November 1949, 417(V) of 1 December 1950, 1240(XIII) of 14 October 1958, 1714(XVI) of 19 December 1961, 2029(XX) of 22 November 1965, 2211(XXI) of 17 December 1966, 2688(XXV) of 11 December 1970, 2813(XXVI) and 2815(XXVI) of 14 December 1971, 3019(XXVII) of 18 December 1972, 3404(XXX) of 28 November 1975, 31/170 of 21 December 1976, 34/104 of 14 December 1979 and 36/244 of 28 April 1982, and Economic and Social Council resolutions 1084(XXXIX) of 30 July 1965, 1763(LIV) of 18 May 1973 and 1986/7 of 21 May 1986, and other relevant resolutions,

1. *Adopts* the texts contained in the annexes to the present resolution;

2. *Requests* the Secretary-General to implement the further measures for restructuring and revitalization of the United Nations in the economic, social and related fields, as set out in annex I to the present resolution, starting in 1994;

3. *Also requests* the Secretary-General to report to the General Assembly at its forty-ninth session, through the Economic and Social Council at its substantive session of 1994, on the implementation of the present resolution;

4. *Calls upon* the Secretary-General, in view of the decision to enlarge the role of the Economic and Social Council, to strengthen the Council secretariat in order to enable it to provide the necessary support to the Council;

5. *Invites* the specialized agencies, organizations and other bodies of the United Nations system to implement the measures for restructuring within their respective areas of competence, as appropriate;

6. *Decides* to include in the provisional agenda of its forty-ninth session the item entitled "Restructuring and revitalization of the United Nations in the economic, social and related fields".

ANNEX I
Further measures for the restructuring and revitalization of the United Nations in the economic, social and related fields

I. Introduction

1. The United Nations has a unique and paramount role in the promotion of international cooperation for development. In the present historical context—the end of the cold war, the increasing interdependence of nations, the increasing globalization of the world economy and the growing linkages between economic, social and related issues—the need for an enhanced role for the United Nations in international cooperation for devel-

opment has multiplied manifoldly. This entails, on one hand, strengthening the role of the United Nations in promoting international economic cooperation for development as envisaged in the provisions of the Charter of the United Nations and, on the other, restructuring and revitalization of the United Nations in the economic, social and related fields.

2. The United Nations has established goals, targets and programmes for action in the economic, social and related fields. Important milestones of global consensus to promote international economic cooperation include the Declaration on International Economic Cooperation, in particular the Revitalization of Economic Growth and Development of the Developing Countries, adopted by the General Assembly at the eighteenth special session, held in April and May 1990, the International Development Strategy for the Fourth United Nations Development Decade, the final documents adopted by the United Nations Conference on Trade and Development at its eighth session, held at Cartagena de Indias, Colombia, in February 1992, in particular the Declaration and the document entitled "A New Partnership for Development: the Cartagena Commitment", the United Nations New Agenda for the Development of Africa in the 1990s, and the Programme of Action for the Least Developed Countries for the 1990s, adopted at the Second United Nations Conference on the Least Developed Countries, held in Paris in September 1990. The various conventions and consensus agreements, especially Agenda 21, which were adopted at the level of heads of State and Government at the United Nations Conference on Environment and Development, held at Rio de Janeiro in June 1992, mark the beginning of a new global partnership for sustainable development. All these landmarks together provide the overall framework of international cooperation for development.

3. Each country is responsible for its own economic policies for development, in accordance with its specific situation and conditions. Reactivation of economic growth and development in all countries requires concerted efforts by the international community. In this context, particular attention should be given to the growth and development needs of developing countries. Concerns of countries with economies in transition should also be addressed. The policies and actions of the major industrialized countries profoundly influence world economic growth and the international economic environment. Those countries should continue to make efforts to promote sustained and sustainable growth and to narrow imbalances in a manner that should benefit other countries, particularly the developing countries.

4. The coordination of macroeconomic policies should take full account of the interests and concerns of all countries. In this context, efforts should be made to enhance the effectiveness of multilateral surveillance aimed at correcting external and fiscal imbalances, promoting non-inflationary sustained and sustainable growth, lowering real rates of interest and making exchange rates more stable and markets more accessible.

5. The United Nations is a unique forum where, based on the principle of sovereign equality of all States and the universality of its membership, the community of nations can address all issues in an integrated manner. The organs, organizations and bodies of the United Nations system have a vital role to play in furthering the analytical work of relevance to the implementation of global

consensus on international economic cooperation, in promoting and securing the international cooperation needed and in providing technical assistance. The international development system should be given greater coherence by closer inter-agency cooperation and coordination and by organizational measures, including guidelines on reporting, that strengthen the contribution of the system to development. There is also an urgent need to discuss ways of enabling the specialized agencies, which make an indispensable contribution to development, to perform better their mandated functions on the basis of enhanced coordination guidance from the Economic and Social Council. Efforts should be made to promote greater coordination and cooperation among the various components of the United Nations system.

6. The United Nations has also a substantial programme of operational activities through which it provides technical and other assistance for development. There is a continuing need to improve the quality and impact of these activities of the United Nations.

II. Principles for restructuring and revitalization

7. The basic principles and guidelines for restructuring and revitalization of the United Nations in the economic, social and related fields were established by the General Assembly in resolution 45/264 of 13 May 1991 and reaffirmed in resolution 46/235 of 13 April 1992. This effort should also take into account the thrust and principles of the Declaration on International Economic Cooperation, in particular the Revitalization of Economic Growth and Development of the Developing Countries, and Assembly resolution 45/199 of 21 December 1990, and other relevant resolutions. The current reform and all future efforts at reform should respect and build upon those resolutions and should be in conformity with the principles enshrined in the Charter of the United Nations, which is based upon the sovereign equality of all its Members.

III. Institutional Reforms

A. *Complementarity between the work of the General Assembly, the Economic and Social Council and their subsidiary bodies*

8. The objective is to enhance the complementarity between the work of the Economic and Social Council and the work of the General Assembly, in accordance with Article 60 of the Charter, in order to avoid the present overlapping and unnecessary duplication of work, debates and items between these two organs and their subsidiary bodies.

9. Both principal organs should carry out their respective responsibilities, as entrusted to them in the Charter, in the formulation of policies and the provision of guidance to and coordination of United Nations activities in the economic, social and related fields.

10. In order to ensure that the operational activities of the United Nations system effectively assist the recipient countries in their development efforts, improvements are needed at both the policy-making and the operational levels.

1. *The role of the General Assembly*

11. The General Assembly is the highest intergovernmental mechanism for the formulation and appraisal of policy on matters relating to the economic, social and related fields, in accordance with Chapter IX of the Charter. It is the main forum where Governments pursue the development dialogue, which includes all these issues, in its political context. The purpose of the dialogue is to take an integrated view of matters relating to the economic, social and related fields in order to build and deepen the political understanding required for enhanced international development cooperation, to generate impulses for action and to launch initiatives.

2. *The role of the Economic and Social Council*

12. The functions and powers of the Economic and Social Council are provided for in Chapters IX and X of the Charter and elaborated in the relevant resolutions of the General Assembly. With the adoption and implementation of Assembly resolutions 45/264 and 46/235, the Council has been significantly revitalized. The following additional measures will further strengthen the Council:

(a) *High-level segment*

13. As established by the General Assembly in its resolution 45/264, the high-level segment of the Council's substantive session shall continue to consider one or more major economic and/or social policy themes, with ministerial participation. It should also carry out a one-day policy dialogue and discussion with the heads of financial and trade institutions. In this connection, these institutions are invited to furnish relevant special reports and studies on the selected themes, within their respective mandates and areas of expertise, as well as on important developments in the world economy and in international economic cooperation, in accordance with the agreements signed between them and the United Nations.

(b) *Coordination segment*

14. The coordination segment shall continue to deal with one or more themes selected at the organizational session of the Council, as established in Assembly resolution 45/264, and will take up coordination matters arising from subsidiary bodies, principal organs and specialized agencies in the economic, social and related fields. Following the coordination segment there should be agreed conclusions containing specific recommendations to the various parts of the United Nations system for their implementation, in accordance with resolution 45/264. In accordance with the present resolution and resolution 45/264, the Secretary-General should arrange to inform the Council at its following substantive session of steps taken by the United Nations system to give effect to these recommendations.

(c) *Operational activities of the United Nations for the international development cooperation segment*

15. In order to improve the quality and impact of the operational activities of the United Nations and to promote an integrated approach in this field, this segment shall provide coordination and guidance so as to ensure that the policies formulated by the General Assembly, particularly during the triennial policy review of operational activities, are appropriately implemented on a system-wide basis. The work of the operational activities segment would include a high-level meeting, open to all Member States in accordance with Article 69 of the Charter, including ministerial participation, to provide an opportunity for policy makers to engage in broad consultations on international development cooperation. Specific arrangements will be decided upon by the Council at its organizational session. The outcome of

this segment shall be reflected, *inter alia*, in the adoption of decisions and resolutions.

16. This segment will have the following functions:

(a) To provide the United Nations system with cross-sectoral coordination and overall guidance on a system-wide basis, including objectives, priorities and strategies, in the implementation of the policies formulated by the General Assembly in the field of operational activities;

(b) To monitor the division of labour between and cooperation within the bodies of the United Nations system, in particular the development funds and programmes, to include the conduct of field-level coordination, and make appropriate recommendations to the Assembly, as well as to provide guidance, where appropriate, to the system;

(c) To review and evaluate the reports on the work of the development funds and programmes, including the assessment of their overall impact, with a view to enhancing the operational activities of the United Nations on a system-wide basis;

(d) To undertake preparatory work for the triennial policy review of operational activities by the Assembly;

(e) To review the operationally relevant recommendations of the subsidiary bodies of the Council and other relevant bodies in the light of policies established by the Assembly, in order to incorporate them, as appropriate, into the operational activities of the United Nations;

(f) To provide orientation and recommendations to the relevant inter-agency coordination mechanisms and to support and enhance their role.

(d) General segment

17. The Economic and Social Committees of the Council shall be subsumed into the plenary as of 1994. Thus, the Council shall supervise the activities of its subsidiary bodies by considering and taking appropriate action on their reports and recommendations in the general segment.

18. The general segment shall be so organized as to recognize the distinction between economic and social issues as reflected in the draft agenda. In its consideration of the reports of its subsidiary bodies the Council shall concentrate on the conclusions and the adoption of recommendations and shall refrain from duplicating the substantive debate already held. However, further substantive discussions on specific issues shall be undertaken at the request of one or more Member States.

19. The various segments of the Council's substantive session, particularly the operational activities segment, shall be organized in such a way as to ensure that there is adequate time available for proper discussion of any item on the agenda, including those currently dealt with by the Economic and Social Committees, on the basis of the practice of the Council.

20. Ministerial attendance is encouraged throughout sessions of the Council, particularly in the high-level and operational activities segments of its substantive session.

3. *Governing bodies of the United Nations development funds and programmes*

21. The current governing bodies of the United Nations Development Programme/the United Nations Population Fund and the United Nations Children's Fund shall be transformed into Executive Boards. These Boards shall be responsible for providing inter-governmental support to and supervision of the activi-

ties of each fund or programme in accordance with the overall policy guidance of the General Assembly and the Economic and Social Council, in accordance with their respective responsibility as set out in the Charter, and for ensuring that they are responsive to the needs and priorities of recipient countries. The Boards will be subject to the authority of the Council. The need for a separate Executive Board for the United Nations Population Fund shall be further considered in the light of the outcome of the International Conference on Population and Development to be held in 1994.

22. The functions of each Executive Board shall be the following:

(a) To implement the policies formulated by the Assembly and the coordination and guidance received from the Council;

(b) To receive information from and give guidance to the head of each fund or programme on the work of each organization;

(c) To ensure that the activities and operational strategies of each fund or programme are consistent with the overall policy guidance set forth by the Assembly and the Council, in accordance with their respective responsibility as set out in the Charter;

(d) To monitor the performance of the fund or programme;

(e) To approve programmes, including country programmes, and projects with respect to the World Food Programme, as appropriate;

(f) To decide on administrative and financial plans and budgets;

(g) To recommend new initiatives to the Council and, through the Council, to the Assembly as necessary;

(h) To encourage and examine new programme initiatives;

(i) To submit annual reports to the Council at its substantive session, which could include recommendations, where appropriate, for improvement of field-level coordination.

23. The agendas and deliberations of the Executive Boards shall reflect the functions set forth in paragraph 22 above.

24. Membership of each Executive Board shall be with due regard to equitable geographical representation and other relevant factors, with a view to ensuring the broadest and most effective participation. The number of seats on each Board shall take into account the need for the effective conduct of the work of each Board.

25. The Executive Boards of the United Nations Development Programme/the United Nations Population Fund, the United Nations Children's Fund and, subject to the provisions of paragraph 30 below, the World Food Programme, shall have 36 members each, as follows: 8 from African States, 7 from Asian States, 4 from Eastern European States, 5 from Latin American and Caribbean States and 12 from Western European and other States.

26. Each Executive Board shall meet in an annual session at such time as it determines.

27. The regular meetings of the Boards, which shall be held between the annual sessions, shall be held at the premises of the headquarters of the respective organization as of the date when such premises are rendered possible to accommodate such meetings. The Executive Boards of the funds and programmes are encouraged to make the necessary facilities available as

soon as possible without prejudice to the resources of existing programmes and projects. Right of participation in the deliberations of the Board meetings, without the right to vote, shall also be reserved to a member State when its country programme is under consideration. The Executive Board may also invite member States of the respective funds and programmes and participants who manifest a special interest in the item or items under consideration to participate in the deliberations without the right to vote. Decision-making shall continue to be according to existing rules, and the practice of striving for consensus should be encouraged.

28. In order to secure transparency of the system, improved modalities should be developed by the funds and programmes for regular informal briefings and improved information for all member States of the respective funds and programmes.

29. In order to ensure an effective and efficient interaction between the Assembly, the Council and the individual Executive Boards, each Board will submit an annual report on its programmes and activities to the Council at its substantive session. This report will include a section which follows a common structure on the basis of specific areas designated by the Council or the Assembly.

30. The same arrangements should apply to the Committee on Food Aid Policies and Programmes of the World Food Programme, and consultations between the United Nations and the Food and Agriculture Organization of the United Nations should be undertaken as soon as possible for this purpose, in view of the fact that the World Food Programme is an autonomous joint organ of both. This process should lead to the adoption of parallel resolutions by the General Assembly and the Conference of the Food and Agriculture Organization.

B. *Resources for operational activities*

31. The fundamental characteristics of operational activities, especially those relating to their financing, as set forth in the relevant resolutions of the General Assembly, especially resolution 47/199, are reaffirmed.

32. As part of the overall reform process, there is a need for a substantial increase in resources for operational activities for development on a predictable, continuous and assured basis, commensurate with the increasing needs of developing countries, as stated in resolution 47/199. Any new funding system should include mechanisms for all participating countries to demonstrate their responsibility and commitment to the programmes and funds. Such mechanisms should distinguish between the financing arrangements for contributions by developed countries and others in a position to do so, as against the capacity for voluntary contributions from developing countries.

33. To facilitate the development of such a system, the Secretary-General is requested to review and analyse possible changes and improvements in the present funding system, including, but not limited to, multi-year negotiated pledges, and to submit a report with his recommendations in April 1994. The report could include, if possible, an assessment of the likely impact of each option on the overall level of funding and on the level of contributions.

34. The process would include consultations to be held in New York in May 1994 for a period of no more than five days and negotiations on prospective new modalities for financing in a resumed session of the General Assembly in 1994.

C. *Secretariat: the enhanced role and capability of the United Nations Secretariat*

35. The Secretariat administrative reforms should take into account the intergovernmental agreements on the restructuring of the United Nations in the economic, social and related fields with a view better to serve the activities of Member States in the Second and Third Committees of the General Assembly and in the Economic and Social Council and its subsidiary bodies.

36. The ongoing Secretariat reform process is noted. It has the potential to enhance the role of the United Nations in the economic, social and related fields, particularly in the area of research and analysis of global development trends. There is, however, a need to further examine ways and means to enhance the modalities of reporting in the economic, social and related fields. The Secretary-General is requested to make recommendations to the Economic and Social Council at its 1994 session to this effect, including recommendations on the advantages of establishing a system of integrated reports in the economic, social and related fields.

D. *Review*

37. Additional efforts shall be made to improve further the functioning of the United Nations in the field of operational activities. Appropriate arrangements shall be made for a comprehensive review of the implementation of the present resolution as well as of decisions on financing, including the possibility of considering those matters at a high-level meeting of the Economic and Social Council in 1995 and at the fiftieth session of the General Assembly.

38. That review will include consideration of the effectiveness of the measures taken to improve the working methods of the Executive Boards, the possible need for a further modification in the size of the Boards and options for further improving the effectiveness of and representation on these Boards, taking into account the need to combine universality with efficiency and to ensure transparency in decision-making.

ANNEX II
Division of labour between the General Assembly and the Economic and Social Council

A. *Guidelines*

1. The following guidelines shall be applicable to the division of labour between the General Assembly and the Economic and Social Council as of 1994:

(a) The inclusion or deletion of issues and items from the agendas of the Assembly and the Council, as well as the periodicity of their consideration, shall continue to be in accordance with the existing rules of procedure of the Assembly and the Council;

(b) Unnecessary duplication of debates and consideration of items and reports in the Assembly and the Council shall be avoided, according to the division of labour between both principal organs;

(c) Work overload in the Second and Third Committees of the Assembly and in the Council shall be avoided through agreed periodicity, such as biennialization and triennialization;

(d) Clustering of consideration of major economic, social and related issues should not preclude the discussion of any specific issue that a delegation may wish to bring up in accordance with the relevant rules of procedure;

(e) Documentation requirements for each session of the Assembly and the Council should be streamlined, and all documents should be made available according to the six-week rule;

(f) Consideration in the Assembly or the Council of reports of their subsidiary bodies should not repeat the substantive debate already held in the subsidiary body, but should concentrate on the adoption of recommendations. Substantive discussion of the report of a subsidiary body should be undertaken only upon the request of a Member State.

B. *Reports*
2.   The preparation of all reports shall take into consideration the division of labour outlined in paragraph 1 above. To that end, reports from subsidiary organs, the specialized agencies and other bodies of the United Nations system must contain sections referring to one or all of the following, as appropriate: (i) monitoring of the implementation of all previous decisions; (ii) policy recommendations; and (iii) coordination recommendations. The pertinent sections of each report should be discussed in the Assembly or the Council according to the responsibilities of each as set out in the Charter of the United Nations.
3.   The total number of reports requested for each year should be reduced. When a biennial programme of work is adopted, the Secretariat should indicate whether it is in a position to provide the documentation in accordance with the six-week rule. If that is not the case, arrangements must be made to ensure that the Secretariat can comply with the six-week rule in regard to all documentation for the economic, social and related fields.

C. *Methodology of work of the Second Committee*
4.   The draft programme of work of the Second Committee should be considered in informal consultations, with the assistance of the bureau of the Council, during the previous session of the Assembly before August. Once that programme of work has been approved by the Committee at its second meeting, the programme of debates should be changed only in extreme circumstances.
5.   The same criteria should apply to the Council, whose programme of work should be considered in consultation with the Chairman of the Second Committee.
6.   The debates in the Second Committee should be centred around the items listed in section E below.

D. *Agenda for the substantive session of the Economic and Social Council*
7.   The following items are to be considered by the Council at its annual substantive session:
    1.   Adoption of the agenda and other organizational matters.
High-level segment
    2.   Theme or themes to be decided upon at the organizational session of the Council.
Coordination segment
    3.   Coordination of the policies and activities of the specialized agencies and other bodies of the United Nations system related to the following themes:

Theme or themes to be decided upon at the organizational session of the Council.
Operational activities of the United Nations for the international development cooperation segment
    4.   Operational activities of the United Nations for international development cooperation.
General segment
    5.   Social, humanitarian and human rights questions: reports of subsidiary bodies, conferences and related questions.
    6.   Economic and environmental questions: reports of subsidiary bodies, conferences and related questions.
    7.   Regional cooperation in the economic, social and related fields.
    8.   Permanent sovereignty over national resources in the occupied Palestinian and other Arab territories.
    9.   Programme and related questions in the economic, social and related fields.

E. *Agenda for the Second Committee*
8.   The following items are to be considered by the Second Committee:
    1.   Report of the Economic and Social Council.
    2.   Macroeconomic policy questions:
    (a)   Implementation of the commitments and policies agreed upon in the Declaration on International Economic Cooperation, in particular the Revitalization of the Economic Growth and Development of the Developing Countries;
    (b)   Implementation of the International Development Strategy for the Fourth United Nations Development Decade;
    (c)   External debt crisis and development;
    (d)   International conference on the financing of development;
    (e)   Net transfer of resources between developing and developed countries.
    3.   Sustainable development and international economic cooperation:
    (a)   Trade and development;
    (b)   Food and agricultural development;
    (c)   Development of the energy resources of developing countries;
    (d)   International Conference on Population and Development;
    (e)   Human settlements;
    (f)   Science and technology for development;
    (g)   Business and development;
    (h)   International cooperation for the eradication of poverty in developing countries;
    (i)   Implementation of the Programme of Action for the Least Developed Countries for the 1990s;
    (j)   Industrial development cooperation;
    (k)   Integration of the economies in transition into the world economy;
    (l)   Women in development;
    (m)   Cultural development;
    (n)   Human resources development.
    4.   Environment and sustainable development:
    (a)   Implementation of the decisions and recommendations of the United Nations Conference on Environment and Development;
    (b)   Protection of the global climate for present and future generations of mankind;

(c) Desertification and drought.
5. Operational activities for development:
(a) Triennial policy review of operational activities for development of the United Nations system;
(b) Economic and technical cooperation among developing countries.
6. Training and research:
(a) United Nations Institute for Training and Research;
(b) United Nations University.

F. *Strengthening of the coordination of humanitarian and disaster relief assistance of the United Nations, including special economic assistance*
9. The following questions are to be considered in the plenary of the Assembly as sub-items of an item entitled "Strengthening of the coordination of humanitarian and disaster relief assistance of the United Nations, including special economic assistance":
(a) Strengthening of the coordination of emergency humanitarian assistance of the United Nations;
(b) Special economic assistance to individual countries or regions;
(c) Strengthening of international cooperation and coordination of efforts to study, mitigate and minimize the consequences of the Chernobyl disaster;
(d) International cooperation to mitigate the environmental consequences on Kuwait and other countries in the region resulting from the situation between Iraq and Kuwait.
10. Under the above-mentioned item, the following reports will be discussed:
(a) All reports currently submitted under the item entitled "Strengthening of the coordination of humanitarian emergency assistance of the United Nations";
(b) Reports of the Secretary-General on special economic and disaster relief assistance to all individual countries and regions;
(c) The report of the Secretary-General on assistance to the Palestinian people;
(d) Reports of the Secretary-General on the activities of the International Decade for Natural Disaster Reduction;
(e) The reports of the Secretary-General on sub-items *(c)* and *(d)* listed in paragraph 9 above.
11. This cluster of questions shall be discussed in the plenary of the General Assembly in a consolidated debate. A debate in plenary on humanitarian and special economic and disaster relief assistance shall be held every year to consider the implementation of resolutions and the pertinent reports of the Secretary-General on individual countries and regions, including the report on assistance to the Palestinian people. Separate and appropriate arrangements, with interpretation services, should be made available in order to organize informal consultations for discussions on new initiatives or follow-up resolutions on this cluster of questions under the chairmanship of one of the Vice-Presidents of the Assembly or another issue coordinator to be designated each year for the task. The negotiating mechanisms of the Second Committee may be used if necessary, as appropriate. Efforts should be made to avoid overlapping of meetings of the Second and Third Committees and the plenary meetings at which this cluster of questions is considered.

General Assembly resolution 48/162
20 December 1993   Meeting 85   Adopted without vote

Draft by Benin (A/48/L.33); agenda item 56.
Financial implications. 5th Committee, A/48/790; S-G, A/C.5/48/54.
Meeting numbers. GA 48th session: 5th Committee 43; plenary 85.

Establishment of new subsidiary bodies

On 12 February, in accordance with a 1992 General Assembly request,[8] the Economic and Social Council, by **decision 1993/207**, established the Commission on Sustainable Development as a functional commission of the Council (see PART THREE, Chapter I). The Council also decided on the composition of the Commission and the periodicity of its meetings and approved the agenda for its organizational session.

On the same date, by **decision 1993/215**, the Council decided on supplementary arrangements to the rules of procedure for its functional commissions to apply to the Commission on Sustainable Development.

REFERENCES
[1]A/47/L.58. [2]A/47/L.59. [3]A/47/L.60. [4]A/47/991. [5]A/47/L.58/Rev.1 & Corr.1. [6]YUN 1991, p. 749, GA res. 45/264, 13 May 1991. [7]A/48/639. [8]YUN 1992, p. 676, GA res. 47/191, 22 Dec. 1992.

Economic and Social Council

1993 sessions

Agendas

On 2 February, the Economic and Social Council adopted a six-item agenda for its organizational and resumed organizational sessions.[1]

On 12 February, the Council, by **decision 1993/206**, approved the provisional agenda for its 1993 substantive session, including the high-level, operational activities and coordination segments. It also adopted the agenda of items for consideration by its Economic and Social Committees.

On 28 June, by **decision 1993/221**, the Council adopted the agenda for the high-level segment of its substantive session of 1993[2] and approved the organization of work of the segment. On 1 July, by the same decision, it adopted the agenda for its substantive session[2] and approved the organization of work of the session. It also approved the requests made by non-governmental organizations to be heard by the Council at that session.[3] On 16 July, the Council included an item entitled "Elections" in the agenda of its substantive session.

(For agenda lists, see APPENDIX IV.)

Substantive session

Segments of the substantive session

In accordance with a 1991 General Assembly resolution,[4] the Council, as part of its substantive session, held a high-level segment; a segment on coordination of the activities of United Nations agencies, organizations and bodies; an operational activities segment; and a committee segment.

High-level segment

The Council, by **decision 1993/204** of 12 February, decided that the high-level segment of its substantive session should be devoted to consideration of the following major theme: "World Summit for Social Development, including the role of the United Nations system in promoting social development"; and that, without prejudice to the 1991 Assembly resolution on the restructuring and revitalization of the United Nations in the economic, social and related fields,[4] the high-level segment with ministerial participation would be held from 28 to 30 June. It invited the Secretary-General, in preparing a report for the segment, to pay attention to ways of attaining the objectives of the Summit and to examine the core issues and the role of the United Nations (see PART THREE, Chapter XII).

Coordination segment

On 12 February, by **decision 1993/205**, the Economic and Social Council decided that its coordination segment in 1993 should be devoted to the consideration of the following themes: coordination of humanitarian assistance: emergency relief and the continuum to rehabilitation and development; and coordination of the activities of the United Nations system in the fields of preventive action and intensification of the struggle against malaria and diarrhoeal diseases, in particular cholera. The Council further decided that the segment would make specific recommendations on matters related to coordination for implementation by the United Nations system. It requested the Secretary-General to apprise it at its 1994 substantive session of the steps taken by the United Nations to give effect to those recommendations.

In accordance with the 1991 Assembly resolution on restructuring and revitalizing the United Nations,[4] the Secretary-General presented to the Council reports on each of the two themes[5] selected for the 1993 coordination segment. On 9 and 14 July, the Council approved draft agreed conclusions on the two themes.[6]

In his November report on the restructuring and revitalization process,[7] the Secretary-General discussed the arrangements for the selection of themes for the Council's coordination segment. He believed that the Council itself should deter-

mine the themes, and preferably well in advance of its organizational sessions. He stated that the agreed conclusions reached by the Council on its 1993 themes represented progress towards ensuring that the outcome of the coordination segment was fully authoritative.

Operational activities segment

The Council considered the question of operational activities for development at its substantive session in 1993. Discussions during the segment led to policy recommendations, which were adopted on 22 July by **resolution 1993/7**.

In his November report on the restructuring and revitalization process,[7] the Secretary-General stated that proposals being considered by the General Assembly for strengthening the Council's institutional capacity to deal with the issue of operational activities for development of the United Nations system had considerable potential for meeting that objective.

Report for 1993

The work of the Economic and Social Council at its organizational and substantive sessions in 1993 was summarized in its report to the General Assembly.[6]

On 20 December, on the recommendation of the Third (Social, Humanitarian and Cultural) Committee, the Assembly adopted **decision 48/434**, by which it took note of chapters I, II, V (sections A, C and J), VII and IX of the Council's report. On 21 December, on the recommendation of the Second Committee, the Assembly adopted **decision 48/452**, by which it took note of relevant chapters of the report. By two decisions of 23 December, the Assembly took note of the chapters of the report as follows: chapters I, V (sections A and B) and IX, on the recommendation of the Fifth (Administrative and Budgetary) Committee (**decision 48/482**), and chapters I, III, V (section C), VIII and IX (**decision 48/483**).

Cooperation with other organizations

Non-governmental organizations

Review of consultation arrangements

On 12 February, by **decision 1993/214**, the Economic and Social Council decided to conduct, with the assistance of the Committee on Non-Governmental Organizations (NGOs), a general review of the 1968 arrangements for consultation with NGOs,[8] to be completed by 1995. The Committee was requested to consider the modalities for such a review and to submit its proposals to the Council at its 1993 substantive session.

The Committee, at its 1993 session (see below), recommended that the Council establish an open-ended working group to conduct the review.

ECONOMIC AND SOCIAL COUNCIL ACTION

On 30 July, the Council adopted without vote **resolution 1993/80**.

Review of the arrangements for consultation with non-governmental organizations

The Economic and Social Council,

Recalling Article 71 of the Charter of the United Nations,

Recalling also its resolution 1296(XLIV) of 23 May 1968, in particular paragraph 40 *(e)* thereof, which provides that the Committee on Non-Governmental Organizations shall consider matters concerning non-governmental organizations which may be referred to it by the Council or by commissions,

Recognizing the continued validity of its resolution 1296(XLIV) as a useful framework for consultations with non-governmental organizations,

Recalling its decision 1993/214 of 12 February 1993,

Taking note with appreciation of the report of the Committee on Non-Governmental Organizations on its session held in 1993,

1. *Decides* to establish an open-ended working group consisting of representatives of all interested States;

2. *Requests* the open-ended working group to undertake the general review called for by the Economic and Social Council in its decision 1993/214, with a view to updating, if necessary, Council resolution 1296(XLIV), as well as introducing coherence in the rules governing the participation of non-governmental organizations in international conferences convened by the United Nations;

3. *Also requests* the open-ended working group to include in its review an examination of ways and means of improving practical arrangements for the work of the Committee on Non-Governmental Organizations and the Non-Governmental Organizations Unit .of the Secretariat;

4. *Invites* the open-ended working group to submit a progress report for consideration by the Economic and Social Council at its substantive session of 1994 and by the General Assembly at its forty-ninth session;

5. *Requests* the Committee on Non-Governmental Organizations at an inter-sessional meeting in 1994 to review the progress report and to transmit its comments to the Economic and Social Council at its substantive session of 1994;

6. *Invites* United Nations organs, bodies, programmes and specialized agencies to participate in the work of the open-ended working group, in accordance with established practice;

7. *Further invites* the non-governmental organizations in consultative status with the Economic and Social Council to participate in the work of the open-ended working group, in accordance with the provisions of Council resolution 1296(XLIV);

8. *Requests* the open-ended working group to enable other relevant non-governmental organizations, in particular those from developing countries, to contribute their views, in accordance with established practice, as set out in the annex to the present resolution;

9. *Requests* the Secretary-General to provide, within existing resources, the assistance necessary, including documentation, for the implementation of the present resolution;

10. *Decides* to consider this question at its substantive session of 1994 and to make recommendations to the General Assembly with a view to finalizing the general review by 1995, as called for in its decision 1993/214.

ANNEX
Participation of non-governmental organizations in the open-ended working group on the review of consultative arrangements with non-governmental organizations

1. Pursuant to paragraph 7 of the present resolution, non-governmental organizations in consultative status with the Economic and Social Council will participate in the open-ended working group in accordance with the provisions of Council resolution 1296(XLIV) of 23 May 1968.

2. Non-governmental organizations which fall under the following three categories will be accredited upon submission to the Non-Governmental Organizations Unit of the Secretariat a notification of their desire to participate in the review process:

(a) Non-governmental organizations in consultative status with a specialized agency of the United Nations system;

(b) Non-governmental organizations on the roster of the Commission on Sustainable Development;

(c) Other non-governmental organizations accredited for participation in conferences convened under the auspices of the United Nations and/or their preparatory process.

3. Other non-governmental organizations wishing to be accredited may apply to the Non-Governmental Organizations Unit of the Secretariat for that purpose, in accordance with the following requirements:

(a) The Non-Governmental Organizations Unit of the Secretariat shall be responsible for the receipt and preliminary evaluation of requests for accreditation received from non-governmental organizations;

(b) All such applications must be accompanied by the following information:

(i) The aims and purposes of the organization, which should be in conformity with the spirit, purposes and principles of the Charter of the United Nations;

(ii) The date of establishment of the organization, the location of its headquarters and proof of its non-profit nature;

(iii) Information on the programmes and activities of the organization and the country or countries in which they are carried out;

(iv) A copy of the latest annual report and of the most recent budget;

(v) A copy of the constitution and/or by-laws and a list of members of the governing body and their country of nationality;

(vi) A description of the membership of the organization, indicating the total number of members and their geographical distribution.

The requests of organizations that fail to provide the above information will not be considered by the Secretariat.

4. In cases where the Non-Governmental Organizations Unit of the Secretariat believes, on the basis of the information provided in accordance with paragraph 3 above, that an organization has established its relevance to the work of the working group, it will recommend to the working group that the organization be accredited. In cases where the Non-Governmental Organizations Unit of the Secretariat does not recommend the granting of accreditation, it will make available to the working group its reasons for not doing so. The Non-Governmental Organizations Unit of the Secretariat should ensure that its recommendations are available to the working group at least one week prior to the start of each session.

5. The working group will decide on the recommendations of the Non-Governmental Organizations Unit of the Secretariat for accreditation within twenty-four hours of the recommendations having been considered by the working group. In the event of a decision not being taken within this period, interim accreditation shall be accorded until such time as a decision is taken.

6. A non-governmental organization that has been granted accreditation to attend a session of the working group may attend all its future sessions.

7. In recognition of the intergovernmental nature of the working group, non-governmental organizations shall have no negotiating role in the work of the group.

8. Pursuant to paragraph 7 of the present resolution, non-governmental organizations in consultative status with the Economic and Social Council will have the opportunity to address the working group, in accordance with the provisions of paragraphs 31 and 33 of Council resolution 1296(XLIV).

9. Other relevant non-governmental organizations may also ask to speak briefly at such meetings. If the number of requests is too large, the working group shall request the non-governmental organizations to form themselves into constituencies, each constituency speaking through one spokesperson. Any such oral intervention will be made at the discretion of the Chairman and with the consent of the working group, in accordance with normal United Nations practice.

10. Pursuant to paragraph 7 of the present resolution, non-governmental organizations in consultative status with the Economic and Social Council may submit written statements, in accordance with the provisions of paragraphs 29, 30 and 33 of Council resolution 1296(XLIV).

11. Other relevant non-governmental organizations may, at their own expense, make written presentations in any of the official languages of the United Nations. Those written presentations will not be issued as official documents.

Economic and Social Council resolution 1993/80

30 July 1993   Meeting 46   Adopted without vote

Draft by Vice-President (E/1993/63/Corr.2); agenda item 10.
Financial implications. S-G, E/1993/L.44.
Meeting numbers. ESC 33, 34, 42, 46.

Committee on NGOs

The Committee on Non-Governmental Organizations met in New York from 22 March to 2 April and on 4 May 1993.[9] It considered applications for consultative status and requests for reclassification received from NGOs; and reviewed the

quadrennial reports submitted by NGOs in categories I and II consultative status with the Council, as well as future activities and the provisional agenda for its 1995 session. The Committee recommended one draft resolution and three draft decisions for adoption by the Council.

The Committee recommended that consultative status be granted to 43 NGOs which had applied; that 10 NGOs be reclassified; and that the Council withdraw the consultative status of eight organizations that had failed to report on their activities for the period 1986-1989, and reclassify the consultative status of six organizations from category II to Roster.

On 30 July, by **decision 1993/331**, the Council approved the provisional agenda and documentation for the 1995 session of the Committee.

Requests from NGOs for hearings

The Committee on NGOs met again in New York on 11 June[3] to hear requests from NGOs in category I consultative status to address the Council or its sessional committees in connection with items on the Council's agenda. The Committee recommended that 20 NGOs be heard. The Council approved their requests on 1 July by **decision 1993/221**.

ECONOMIC AND SOCIAL COUNCIL ACTION

In July, the Council adopted without vote **decision 1993/329**.

Applications for consultative status and requests for reclassification received from non-governmental organizations

At its 46th plenary meeting, on 30 July 1993, the Economic and Social Council decided:

(a) To grant the following non-governmental organizations consultative status:

Category II

Agence Internationale pour le Développement
American Society of International Law
Association for Counselling, Organization, Research and Development
Association of Development Financing Institutions in Asia and the Pacific
Dhaka Ahsania Mission
Emmaus International Association
Environmental Defense Fund
Human Rights Watch
Indian Institute for Non-Aligned Studies
International Scientific and Educational "Znanie" Association
Institute for International Economic Cooperation and Development
Inter-African Committee on Traditional Practices Affecting the Health of Women and Children (IAC)
International Architects Designers Planners for Social Responsibility (ARC-PEACE)
International Centre for the Legal Protection of Human Rights
International Miners' Organisation

International Society for Traumatic Stress Studies
Islamic Relief
Médecins sans frontières (International)
Mediterranean Water Institute (IME)
Oxfam America
Penal Reform International
Project Concern International, Incorporated
Reporters without Borders—International
Retired and Senior Volunteer Program International
Robert F. Kennedy Memorial
Sisterhood is Global Institute
Society for Threatened Peoples
Union of Luso-Afri-America-Asiatic Capital Cities
World Federation of the Ukrainian Women's Organizations
World Union of Professions (UMPL)

Roster

Asbestos International Association
Chartered Association of Certified Accountants (ACCA)
Christian Solidarity International
European Electronic Mail Association
Federation for Peace and Conciliation
Friedrich Naumann Foundation
Global Forum of Spiritual and Parliamentary Leaders
International Centre for Trade Union Rights
International Federation of Consular Corps and Associations (FICAC)
International Human Rights Association of American Minorities (IHRAAM)
International Lesbian and Gay Association
International Movement against All Forms of Discrimination and Racism
Uranium Institute

(b) To reclassify two organizations from category II to category I and eight organizations from the Roster to category II, as follows:

Category I

International Save the Children Alliance
Rotary International

Category II

Commonwealth Medical Association
Habitat International Coalition
International Association of University Presidents
International Press Institute
International Romani Union
International Society for Prosthetics and Orthotics
International Union of Building Centres (UIBC)
International Union of Socialist Youth

Economic and Social Council decision 1993/329

Adopted without vote

Draft by Committee on NGOs (E/1993/63), agenda item 10.
Meeting numbers. ESC 33, 34, 42, 46.

Before the Council adopted the draft decision as a whole, it adopted the recommendation to grant Human Rights Watch consultative status by a roll-call vote of 31 to 3, with 12 abstentions, and the recommendation to grant Roster status to the International Lesbian and Gay Association by a roll-call vote of 22 to 4, with 17 abstentions.

Also in July, the Council adopted without vote **decision 1993/330**.

Review of quadrennial reports submitted by non-governmental organizations in consultative status with the Economic and Social Council, categories I and II

At its 46th plenary meeting, on 30 July 1993, the Economic and Social Council decided that:

(a) The consultative status of the following eight organizations, which failed to submit a detailed report on their activities for the period 1986-1989 as requested by the Committee on Non-Governmental Organizations in 1991, be withdrawn:
Democratic Youth Community of Europe
European Association of National Productivity Centres
Institute of Social Studies
Inter-African Union of Lawyers
International Cargo Handling Coordination Association
International Centre of Social Gerontology
International Union for Inland Navigation
Third World Foundation

(b) The following six organizations be reclassified from category II to the Roster:
European Organization for Quality Control
Inter-American Planning Society
International Association of Educators for World Peace
International Federation of Senior Police Officers
International Organization of Supreme Audit Institutions
Inter-University European Institute on Social Welfare

Economic and Social Council decision 1993/330

Adopted without vote

Draft by Committee on NGOs (E/1993/63), agenda item 10.
Meeting numbers. ESC 33, 34, 42, 46.

Other organizational matters

1994 work programme

On 12 February 1993, the Economic and Social Council considered its proposed basic programme of work for 1993 and 1994 submitted by the Secretary-General.[(10)] It adopted without vote **decision 1993/210**.

Basic programme of work of the Economic and Social Council for 1994

At its 3rd plenary meeting, on 12 February 1993, the Economic and Social Council took note of the following list of questions for inclusion in the programme of work for 1994:

A.   *High-level segment*
Technology and industrialization in the development process of the developing countries (Council decision 1990/205)
International cooperation against illicit production, supply, demand, trafficking and distribution of narcotic drugs (Council decision 1990/205)

B.   *Other segments*
Coordination of the activities of the specialized agencies, organs, organizations and bodies of the United Nations system in the economic, social and related fields (General Assembly resolution 45/264)
Operational activities for development
    Report of the Secretary-General on the operational activities for development of the United Nations system (General Assembly resolution 47/199)

Report of the Governing Council of the United Nations Development Programme on its forty-first session (General Assembly resolution 2029(XX))

Technical cooperation activities of the United Nations (General Assembly resolution 2029(XX))

United Nations Population Fund (General Assembly resolution 3019(XXVII))

Report of the Committee on Food Aid Policies and Programmes (General Assembly resolution 3404(XXX))

Report of the Executive Board of the United Nations Children's Fund (General Assembly resolution 802(VIII))

Coordination questions

(a) *Reports of coordination bodies*

Report of the Committee for Programme and Coordination on its thirty-fourth session (Council resolution 2008(LX))

Report of the Administrative Committee on Coordination for 1994 (Council resolution 13(III))

(b) *Implementation of the Declaration on the Granting of Independence to Colonial Countries and Peoples by the specialized agencies and the international institutions associated with the United Nations*

Report of the Secretary-General on assistance to the Palestinian people (Council resolution 2100 (LXIII))

Assistance to the oppressed people of South Africa and their national liberation movement provided by the agencies and institutions within the United Nations system (General Assembly resolution 33/183 K)

Programme and related questions

Relevant chapters of the proposed revisions to the medium-term plan for the period 1992-1997

Report of the Committee for Programme and Coordination on its thirty-fourth session

Special economic, humanitarian and disaster relief assistance

Oral reports on special programmes of economic and humanitarian assistance

Oral report on assistance to the drought-stricken areas of Djibouti, Ethiopia, Kenya, Somalia, the Sudan and Uganda (Council resolution 1983/46)

International Decade for Natural Disaster Reduction

Mid-term review of the implementation of the International Framework of Action for the International Decade for Natural Disaster Reduction (General Assembly resolution 44/236, annex)

Sustainable development

Report of the Commission on Sustainable Development on its second session

Report of the High-level Advisory Board

World Decade for Cultural Development

Note by the Secretary-General transmitting the summary evaluation report of the Director-General of the United Nations Educational, Scientific and Cultural Organization (General Assembly resolution 46/157 and Council decision 1993/209)

Cartography

Report of the Secretary-General on the Thirteenth United Nations Regional Cartographic Conference for Asia and the Pacific (Council decision 1991/222)

Report of the United Nations High Commissioner for Refugees

Regional cooperation

Report of the Secretary-General on regional cooperation (Council decision 1979/1), including the

report of the Secretary-General on a subject relating to interregional cooperation of common interest to all regions (Council resolution 1982/50 and decision 1982/174)

Report of the Secretary-General on phase II of the Transport and Communications Decade for Asia and the Pacific, 1985-1994 (General Assembly resolution 39/227 and Council resolutions 1984/78 and 1991/75)

Summaries of the surveys of economic conditions in the five regions prepared by the regional commissions (Council resolution 1724(LIII))

Development and international economic cooperation

World Economic Survey 1994

Report of the High-level Advisory Board on the situation of Namibia (General Assembly resolution 46/204)

Report of the Secretary-General on the main research findings of the system on major global economic and social trends, policies and emerging issues (Council resolution 1986/51, sect. VI)

Final version of the *World Survey on the Role of Women in Development* (General Assembly resolutions 44/77, 44/171, 46/98 and 47/95)

Report of the Secretary-General on his assessment of the implementation of Council resolution 1992/41 on technical cooperation among developing countries

Implementation of the International Development Strategy for the Fourth United Nations Development Decade

Report of the Secretary-General on the review and appraisal of the International Development Strategy for the Fourth United Nations Development Decade (General Assembly resolution 45/199)

Trade and development

Report of the Trade and Development Board (General Assembly resolution 1995(XIX))

Food and agricultural development

Report of the World Food Council on its twentieth session (General Assembly resolution 3348(XXIX))

Note by the Secretary-General transmitting the report of the Director-General of the Food and Agriculture Organization of the United Nations on the progress achieved in the implementation of Council resolution 1992/54 on cooperation in fisheries in Africa

Charter of Economic Rights and Duties of States

Report of the Secretary-General on the progress achieved in compliance with the Charter of Economic Rights and Duties of States (General Assembly resolution 44/170)

International cooperation in tax matters

Report of the Secretary-General on the progress of the work of the Ad Hoc Group of Experts on International Cooperation in Tax Matters (Council resolution 1980/13)

Transnational corporations

Report of the Commission on Transnational Corporations on its twentieth session (Council resolution 1913(LVII)), including the follow-up to the recommendations of the Panel of Eminent Persons on the activities of transnational corporations in South Africa (Council resolution 1986/1)

International Conference on Population and Development

Report of the Secretary-General of the International Conference on Population and Development on the progress made in all aspects of the preparatory activities for the Conference (Council resolution 1991/93)

Development and utilization of new and renewable sources of energy
Report of the Committee on New and Renewable Sources of Energy and on Energy for Development on its first session (Council decision 1992/218)
Development of the energy resources of developing countries
Report of the Secretary-General on the role of the United Nations in the development of ways and means of accelerating the exploration and development of energy resources in developing countries (Council resolution 1992/56)
International cooperation to mitigate the environmental consequences on Kuwait and other countries in the region resulting from the situation between Iraq and Kuwait
Report of the Secretary-General on the implementation of General Assembly resolution 47/151
Public administration and finance
Report of the Secretary-General on the Eleventh Meeting of Experts on the United Nations Programme in Public Administration and Finance (Council decision 1992/287)
Human rights questions
Report of the Human Rights Committee (article 45 of the International Covenant on Civil and Political Rights)
Report of the Committee on Economic, Social and Cultural Rights (Council resolutions 1988(LX) and 1985/17)
Report of the Committee on the Rights of the Child (article 43 of the Convention on the Rights of the Child)
Report of the Commission on Human Rights on its fiftieth session (Council resolutions 5(I) and 9(II))
Documentation for information
Reports submitted by States parties to the International Covenant on Economic, Social and Cultural Rights and by the specialized agencies
Advancement of women
Report of the Committee on the Elimination of Discrimination against Women on its thirteenth session (article 21 of the Convention on the Elimination of All Forms of Discrimination against Women)
Report of the Commission on the Status of Women on its thirty-eighth session (Council resolutions 11(II) and 1147(LXI))
Implementation of the Nairobi Forward-looking Strategies for the Advancement of Women (Council resolution 1988/22)
Report of the Board of Trustees of the International Research and Training Institute for the Advancement of Women (Council resolution 1998(LX))
Social development
Crime prevention and criminal justice
Report of the Commission on Crime Prevention and Criminal Justice on its third session (Council resolution 1992/1)
Question of strengthening international cooperation in combating organized crime (General Assembly resolution 47/87)
Narcotic drugs
Report of the Commission on Narcotic Drugs on its thirty-seventh session (Council resolution 9(I))
Summary of the report of the International Narcotics Control Board (article 15 of the Single Convention on Narcotic Drugs of 1961, article 18 of the Convention on Psychotropic Substances of 1971 and article

23 of the United Nations Convention against Illicit Traffic in Narcotic Drugs and Psychotropic Substances of 1988)
United Nations University
Report of the Council of the United Nations University for 1993

* * *

Reports brought to the attention of the Council
Reports of the Joint Inspection Unit

Economic and Social Council decision 1993/210
Adopted without vote
Draft by President and Bureau based on informal consultations (E/1993/L.9); agenda items 2 & 3.

Calendar of meetings

On 16 July 1993, by **decision 1993/231**, the Economic and Social Council approved the calendar of conferences and meetings for 1994 and 1995 in the economic, social and related fields.[11]

Participation of Yugoslavia (Serbia and Montenegro)

On 28 April, by **resolution 821(1993)**, the Security Council reaffirmed that the Federal Republic of Yugoslavia (Serbia and Montenegro) could not continue automatically the membership of the former Socialist Federal Republic of Yugoslavia in the United Nations. It recommended to the General Assembly that it decide that the Federal Republic of Yugoslavia should not participate in the work of the Economic and Social Council.

On 29 April, the Assembly approved that recommendation by **resolution 47/229**.

REFERENCES
[1]E/1993/2 & Add.1. [2]E/1993/100. [3]E/1993/87. [4]YUN 1991, p. 749, GA res. 45/264, 13 May 1991. [5]E/1993/90 & E/1993/68. [6]A/48/3/Rev.1. [7]A/48/639. [8]YUN 1968, p. 647, ESC res. 1296(XLIV), 23 May 1968. [9]E/1993/63. [10]E/1993/1 & Add.1. [11]E/1993/L.20/Rev.1 & Add.1.

Coordination in the UN system

Inter-agency coordination

ACC activities

In 1993, the Administrative Committee on Coordination, in the follow-up to the 1992 review of its functioning and of the structure of its subsidiary machinery,[1] implemented measures to improve its working methods and established procedures for consultation among executive heads of United Nations organizations on major initiatives.[2] With regard to its subsidiary machinery, ACC established a Senior-level Task Force to review and make policy recommendations on information-sharing. In the light of the Task

Force's recommendations, ACC decided to discontinue its Advisory Committee for the Coordination of Information Systems and to establish an Information Systems Coordination Committee (ISCC), which would report through ACC's Organizational Committee. ISCC was requested to finalize draft terms of reference and establish a work programme with budget proposals.

ACC discussed policy issues related to resource flows and financing for development, the World Summit for Social Development and the Agenda for Development. It agreed to examine further in 1994 the issues relating to the division of labour within the United Nations and the system's access to resources.

ACC also considered progress achieved in the follow-up to the 1992 United Nations Conference on Environment and Development (UNCED) and, on the recommendation of the Inter-Agency Committee on Sustainable Development, decided to establish an ACC Subcommittee on Oceans and Coastal Areas to meet the coordination needs defined in chapter 17 of Agenda 21 adopted by UNCED.[3]

Through its Consultative Committee on Programme and Operational Questions, ACC gave priority attention to enhancing the coherence and effectiveness of the system's operational activities for development, with particular reference to the Assembly's 1992[4] comprehensive triennial policy review of operational activities (see PART THREE, Chapter II).

Among other issues discussed by ACC were actions undertaken by the organizations of the United Nations to assist countries invoking Article 50 of the Charter of the United Nations, dealing with States experiencing economic problems resulting from preventive or enforcement measures taken by the Security Council against another State.

In June, ACC submitted to the Economic and Social Council a report[5] on programmes and resources of the United Nations system for the biennium 1992-1993, with the aim of relating the objectives of United Nations organizations to the corresponding allocations of financial resources. On 30 July, by **decision 1993/326**, the Council took note of the report.

During the year, ACC held two regular sessions (Rome, Italy, 19 and 20 April; New York, 28 and 29 October). Its principal subsidiary bodies met as follows:

Organizational Committee (New York, 8-12 February; Rome, 5-8 and 21-23 April; New York, 18-21, 29 and 30 October); Consultative Committee on Administrative Questions (Personnel and General Administrative Questions) (New York, 1-8 March; Vienna, 12-16 July); Consultative Committee on Administrative Questions (Financial and Budgetary Questions) (Vienna, 8-12 March; Montreal, Canada, 30 August-3 September); Consultative Committee on Substantive Questions (Geneva, 16-19 March); Consultative Committee on Programme and Operational Questions (New York, 3 and 4 June and 20-24 September).

Bodies on specific subjects met as follows:

Subcommittee on Nutrition, twentieth session (Geneva, 15-19 February); fifth Inter-Agency Meeting on Ageing (Vienna, 18 and 19 February); third Ad Hoc Inter-Agency Meeting on the International Year of the Family (Vienna, 10-12 March); seventeenth Ad Hoc Inter-Agency Meeting on Women (Vienna, 15 and 16 March); Inter-Agency Committee on Sustainable Development, first and second meetings (New York, 23-25 March and 8-10 September); Inter-Agency Meeting on Coordination in Matters of International Drug Abuse Control (Vienna, 7 and 8 April, and— after it changed its name to the ACC Subcommittee on Drug Control—Paris, 6-8 September); Subcommittee on Rural Development, twenty-first meeting (Washington, D.C., 5-7 May); Ad Hoc Inter-Agency Consultation on Jointly Funded Secretariats of ACC Standing Committees (Geneva, 6 July); second Ad Hoc Inter-Agency Meeting for the International Conference on Population and Development (Geneva, 13 July); Joint United Nations Information Committee, nineteenth session (London, 20-22 July); Inter-Agency Meeting on Ocean Affairs (Paris, 23 and 24 August); Subcommittee on Statistical Activities, twenty-seventh session (Geneva, 6-8 September); Advisory Committee for the Coordination of Information Systems, seventh session (Geneva, 27-29 September); Subcommittee on Water Resources, fourteenth session (Santo Domingo, Dominican Republic, 6-8 October).

Report for 1992

Parts two and three of the ACC annual overview report for 1992[6] were considered on 10, 12 and 13 May 1993 by CPC,[7] which regretted the late submission of the documentation and its inadequacy. CPC requested ACC to ensure that it was provided in future with up-to-date, appropriate and timely documentation.

Cooperation with financial institutions

In February 1993,[8] the Secretary-General transmitted to the Economic and Social Council a 1992 report of the Joint Inspection Unit (JIU) on United Nations system cooperation with multilateral financial institutions: performance and innovation challenges and examples of fresh approaches. The report recommended that United Nations organizations, in order to enhance cooperative relationships with the multilateral financial institutions, should commit themselves to increasing the competitiveness of their programmes. It suggested ways to foster creativity, responsiveness, sustained performance improvement, and other elements of a competitive posture, as well as topics to be included in the deliberations of executive heads and governing bodies on technical cooperation activities.

Commenting on the report,[9] ACC accepted its recommendations in principle. However, in the view of some ACC members, the recommendations did not present new ideas, and many of the approaches suggested had been overtaken by events.

On 13 July, in **decision 1993/227**, the Economic and Social Council took note of the JIU report and ACC's comments thereon.

UN programme coordination

CPC activities

During 1993, the Committee for Programme and Coordination met in New York for an organizational session on 8 April and 5 May, for the first part of its thirty-third session from 10 to 14 May and for the second part from 6 to 22 October.[7]

The Committee reviewed the efficiency of the administrative and financial functioning of the United Nations. It discussed the proposed programme budget for the biennium 1994-1995; the prototype of a new format of the medium-term plan; establishment of a system of responsibility and accountability of programme managers of the United Nations; and evaluation (see PART FIVE, Chapter I). It also examined the annual report of ACC for 1992,[6] preparations for the Joint Meetings of ACC and CPC, and reports of JIU.

ECONOMIC AND SOCIAL COUNCIL ACTION

On 29 July, by **decision 1993/313**, the Economic and Social Council took note of the report of CPC on the first part of its thirty-third session[7] and endorsed its recommendations. The Council also took note of the updated annual overview report of ACC for 1992,[10] and welcomed the action taken by ACC to enhance the effectiveness of its functioning and to streamline its subsidiary machinery. It requested the Secretary-General to report on his efforts to mobilize and coordinate assistance to countries invoking Article 50 of the Charter. The Council stressed that all system-wide activities undertaken by subsidiary bodies of ACC that had been abolished, particularly those relating to science and technology for development, new and renewable sources of energy and the least developed countries, should continue to be coordinated by the new subsidiary machinery.

GENERAL ASSEMBLY ACTION

By **resolution 48/218**, the General Assembly noted CPC's recommendation that consideration

be given to replacing the current medium-term plan by a new format as outlined in its report.[7] It also endorsed CPC's recommendations on the establishment of a transparent and effective system of accountability and responsibility by 1 January 1995.

Joint Meetings of CPC and ACC

The twenty-seventh Joint Meetings of CPC and ACC were held in New York on 27 October[11] to discuss the results of UNCED and their implications for the United Nations. The Meetings had before them a background paper on the subject,[12] which drew attention to issues addressed by ACC and its Inter-Agency Committee on Sustainable Development and by the Commission on Sustainable Development which were of relevance to CPC.

The Joint Meetings stated that the multidisciplinary nature of UNCED follow-up required an integrated approach to coordination at the policy-making and programme implementation levels. It was therefore crucial to ensure harmonization of policy guidance on sustainable development issues given by the various governing bodies of the United Nations system. It was also suggested that the United Nations assist in coordinating international support for national follow-up activities and support the elaboration of national sustainable development strategies. The Joint Meetings recommended to the Economic and Social Council that it consider science and technology as one of the themes for the coordination segment of its 1994 substantive session.

REFERENCES
[1]YUN 1992, p. 941. [2]E/1994/19. [3]YUN 1992, p. 672. [4]Ibid., p. 552, GA res. 47/199, 22 Dec. 1992. [5]E/1993/84. [6]E/1993/47/Add.1,2. [7]A/48/16. [8]E/1993/18 & Add.1. [9]E/1993/18/Add.2. [10]E/1993/81. [11]E/1994/4. [12]E/1993/121.

Other institutional questions

Work programmes of the Second and Third Committees of the General Assembly

On 20 December, by **decision 48/431**, the General Assembly approved the organization of work of the Third Committee and its biennial programme of work for 1994-1995.

On 21 December, by **decision 48/457**, the Assembly approved the biennial programme of work of the Second Committee for 1994-1995.

PART FOUR

Legal questions

Chapter I

International Court of Justice

In 1993, the International Court of Justice (ICJ) continued to deal with nine contentious cases. Two new disputes and a request for an advisory opinion were referred to the Court, and one case was removed from its list. The Court delivered one Judgment and 10 Orders.

In May, the General Assembly and the Security Council, independently, held elections to fill a vacancy created by the death of one Judge and, in November, they elected five Judges to fill vacancies caused by the expiration of terms (see APPENDIX III).

In September, the Assembly adopted a number of recommendations regarding the use of the Court by States (resolution 47/120 B). On 15 October, the President of the Court addressed the Assembly on the work and role of the Court, emphasizing ICJ's important position as the principal judicial organ of the United Nations and the need to protect it strenuously.

Judicial work of the Court

In 1993, the President made an Order recording the discontinuance of proceedings in the case concerning *Certain Phosphate Lands in Nauru (Nauru v. Australia)*, directing its removal from the Court's list. The Court also made two Orders on two separate requests by Bosnia and Herzegovina against Yugoslavia (Serbia and Montenegro) for an indication of provisional measures and on a similar request by Yugoslavia (Serbia and Montenegro) in the case concerning *Application of the Convention on the Prevention and Punishment of the Crime of Genocide (Bosnia and Herzegovina v. Yugoslavia (Serbia and Montenegro))*. It gave a Judgment in the case concerning *Maritime Delimitation in the Area between Greenland and Jan Mayen (Denmark v. Norway)*. The Court, its President and Vice-President made several Orders on the conduct of proceedings in pending cases.

In July, the Court, in view of developments in environmental law and protection in the past few years and considering that it should be fully prepared to deal with any environmental case within its jurisdiction, established a seven-member Chamber for Environmental Matters as of 6 August 1993. The members of the Chamber were to serve for an initial period of six months.

The 1993 activities of ICJ were covered in two reports to the General Assembly, for the periods 1 August 1992 to 31 July 1993[1] and 1 August 1993 to 31 July 1994.[2] By **decision 48/404** of 15 October 1993, the Assembly took note of the 1992/93 report.

Maritime delimitation in the area between Greenland and Jan Mayen (Denmark v. Norway)

Denmark, in 1988,[3] instituted proceedings against Norway, requesting the Court to decide where a single line of delimitation should be drawn between Denmark's and Norway's fishing zones and continental shelf areas in the waters between the east coast of Greenland and the Norwegian island of Jan Mayen. In 1991, the Reply of Denmark and the Rejoinder of Norway were filed to their respective 1989 Memorial and 1990 Counter-Memorial within the time-limits fixed by a 1990 Court Order.

Having heard oral arguments in the case from 11 to 27 January 1993, the Court, at a public sitting of 14 June, delivered its Judgment,[4] the operative paragraph of which read as follows:

> *The Court,*
> By fourteen votes to one,
> *Decides* that, within the limits defined
> (1) to the north by the intersection of the line of equidistance between the coasts of eastern Greenland and the western coasts of Jan Mayen with the 200-mile limit calculated as from the said coasts of Greenland, indicated on sketch-map No. 2[a] as point A, and
> (2) to the south, by the 200-mile limit around Iceland, as claimed by Iceland, between the points of intersection of that limit with the two said lines, indicated on sketch map No. 2 as points B and D, the delimitation line that divides the continental shelf and fishery zones of the Kingdom of Denmark and the Kingdom of Norway is to be drawn as set out in paragraphs 91 and 92 of the present Judgment.
> *In favour:* President Sir Robert Jennings; Vice-President Oda; Judges Ago, Schwebel, Bedjaoui, Ni, Evensen, Tarassov, Guillaume, Shahabuddeen, Aguilar Mawdsley, Weeramantry, Ranjeva, Ajibola;
> *Against:* Judge ad hoc Fischer.

Vice-President Oda and Judges Evensen, Aguilar Mawdsley and Ranjeva appended declarations to the Judgment. Vice-President Oda and Judges

---

[a]For the sketch-map referred to above, see *Maritime Delimitation in the Area between Greenland and Jan Mayen (Denmark v. Norway), Judgment of 14 June 1993*, I.C.J. Sales No. 635.

Schwebel, Shahabuddeen, Weeramantry and Ajibola appended separate opinions. Judge ad hoc
Fischer appended a dissenting opinion.

Aerial incident of 3 July
1988 (Iran v. United States)

Iran, in 1989, instituted proceedings against the
United States, referring to the destruction of an Iranian
aircraft on 3 July 1988 and the killing of its 290 passengers and crew by missiles launched in Iranian
airspace from the United States guided-missile cruiser
the USS *Vincennes*. The time-limits for written proceedings, fixed in a December 1989 Court Order, were
extended by an Order in June 1990. The Memorial
of Iran was filed within the prescribed time-limit.

In March 1991, within the time-limit fixed for
its Counter-Memorial, the United States filed certain
preliminary objections to the Court's jurisdiction.
By an April 1991 Order,[5] the Court fixed 9 December as the time-limit within which Iran might
present a written statement of its observations and
submissions on those objections. As requested by
Iran, and after the views of the United States were
ascertained, the President of the Court, by Orders
of 18 December 1991[5] and 5 June 1992,[6] extended
that time-limit to 9 June and 9 September 1992,
respectively. Iran's written statement was filed within
the prescribed time-limit and was communicated
to the Secretary-General of the International Civil
Aviation Organization (ICAO) together with the
written pleadings previously filed. Following the
submission of written observations by the ICAO
Council within the time-limit of 9 December 1992,
fixed by the President of the Court, the Court fixed
12 September 1994 as the date for the opening of
hearings in the case.

Certain phosphate lands
in Nauru (Nauru v. Australia)

In 1989, Nauru instituted proceedings against
Australia in a dispute concerning the rehabilitation of certain phosphate lands mined under Australian administration before Nauruan independence.

Within the time-limits fixed by the Court in July
1989, Nauru filed its Memorial in 1990, and Australia filed, in 1991, certain preliminary objections
to the Court's jurisdiction and on the admissibility of the case. Within the time-limit of 19 July 1991,
fixed by an Order of 8 February 1991,[5] Nauru filed
its observations and submissions on those objections. In a Judgment on the Preliminary Objections of 26 June 1992,[6] the Court rejected, with
one exception, Australia's objections and found that
it had jurisdiction to entertain the Application and
that the Application was admissible. In an Order
of 29 June 1992,[7] the President of the Court fixed
29 March 1993 as the time-limit for filing the
Counter-Memorial of Australia, which was filed
within that time-limit.

By an Order of 25 June 1993,[8] the Court fixed
22 December 1993 as the time-limit for filing the
Reply by Nauru and 14 September 1994 for the Rejoinder by Australia. In September, the Parties notified the Court that, having reached a settlement,
they agreed to discontinue the proceedings. On 13
September, the Court made an Order[9] recording
the discontinuance and removing the case from the
Court's list.

Territorial dispute
(Libyan Arab Jamahiriya/Chad)

In 1990, the Libyan Arab Jamahiriya filed a notification of an agreement between it and Chad concerning the peaceful settlement of their territorial
dispute. Each Party duly filed a Memorial in 1991
within the prescribed time-limit and a Reply and
a Counter-Memorial in 1992 within the time-limits
fixed by Orders of August 1991[10] and April 1992,[7]
respectively. The Libyan Arab Jamahiriya chose
José Sette-Camara, and Chad chose Georges M.
Abi-Saab, to sit as Judges ad hoc in the case.

Following the hearings held between 14 June and
14 July 1993, the Court began deliberations on its
Judgment.

East Timor (Portugal v. Australia)

In 1991,[10] Portugal instituted proceedings
against Australia in a dispute concerning certain
activities of Australia with respect to East Timor.
Portugal claimed that Australia, by negotiating with
Indonesia an agreement, signed on 11 December
1989, relating to the exploration and exploitation
of the continental shelf in the area of the Timor
Gap, had caused legal and moral damage to the
people of East Timor and Portugal, which would
become material if the exploitation of hydrocarbon
resources began there.

Within the time-limits fixed by a May 1991
Order,[10] the Portuguese Memorial and the Australian Counter-Memorial were filed in 1991 and
1992, respectively. By an Order of 19 June 1992,[7]
the Court fixed 1 December 1992 and 1 June 1993
as the time-limits for the filing of a Reply by Portugal and a Rejoinder by Australia, respectively.
The Reply by Portugal was filed within the prescribed
time-limit. However, an Order of 19 May 1993[11]
extended to 1 July 1993 the time-limit for the Australian Rejoinder, which was filed accordingly.

Portugal chose Antonio de Arruda Ferrer-Correia,
and Australia chose Sir Ninian Stephen, to sit as
Judges ad hoc in the case.

Maritime delimitation (Guinea-Bissau v. Senegal)

In 1991, Guinea-Bissau instituted proceedings
against Senegal in a dispute concerning the delimitation of all the maritime territories between the
two States. At the same time, previous proceedings

instituted by Guinea-Bissau against Senegal in 1989 concerning the *Arbitral Award of 31 July 1989 (Guinea-Bissau v. Senegal)*[5] were still in progress.

Guinea-Bissau claimed that the result of that Arbitration did not make it possible to establish a definitive delimitation of all the maritime areas over which the Parties had rights, and asked the Court to adjudge and declare what should be the line delimiting all the maritime territories appertaining to Guinea-Bissau and Senegal.

Following the November 1991 Judgment in the case concerning the *Arbitral Award of 31 July 1989 (Guinea-Bissau v. Senegal)*,[5] the President of the Court met with the two Parties in February and October 1992[7] and agreed to their request that no time-limit be fixed for the initial pleadings of the case, pending the outcome of the continuing negotiations on the question of maritime delimitation.

Maritime delimitation and territorial questions between Qatar and Bahrain (Qatar v. Bahrain)

Qatar instituted proceedings in 1991 against Bahrain in respect of disputes relating to sovereignty over the Hawar islands, sovereign rights over the shoals of Dibal and Qit'at Jaradah and the delimitation of the maritime areas of the two States.[12]

In August 1991, Bahrain contested the basis of jurisdiction invoked by Qatar. By an October 1991 Order,[12] the President of the Court decided that written proceedings should first be addressed to the questions of the jurisdiction of the Court to entertain the dispute and of the admissibility of the Application, and fixed the time-limits for the filing of a Memorial by Qatar and a Counter-Memorial by Bahrain, which were filed accordingly in 1992. Also in 1992, Qatar and Bahrain filed their respective Reply and Rejoinder within the time-limits fixed by an Order of June 1992.[13] The Court then fixed 28 February 1994 as the date for the opening of hearings in the case.

Qatar chose José Maria Ruda, and Bahrain chose Nicolas Valticos, to sit as Judges ad hoc in the case.

Questions of interpretation and application of the 1971 Montreal Convention arising from the aerial incident at Lockerbie (Libyan Arab Jamahiriya v. United Kingdom) and (Libyan Arab Jamahiriya v. United States)

In 1992,[13] the Libyan Arab Jamahiriya instituted separate proceedings against the United Kingdom and the United States in respect of a dispute over the interpretation and application of the 1971 Montreal Convention for the Suppression of Unlawful Acts Against the Safety of Civil Aviation,[14] which arose from its alleged involvement

in the crash of Pan Am flight 103 over Lockerbie, Scotland, on 21 December 1988.

In its Applications, the Libyan Arab Jamahiriya referred to the charging and indictment of two of its nationals by the Lord Advocate of Scotland and by a United States Grand Jury, with having caused a bomb to be placed aboard Pan Am flight 103. The bomb subsequently exploded, causing the aircraft to crash, killing all persons aboard. The Libyan Arab Jamahiriya requested the Court to adjudge and declare that the Libyan Arab Jamahiriya had complied fully with all of its obligations under the Montreal Convention, which it claimed to be the only appropriate Convention in force between the Parties, and which required it to establish its own jurisdiction over alleged offenders present in its territory and submit the case to its authorities for prosecution, as there was no extradition treaty between it and the other parties; that the United Kingdom and the United States were in breach of the Convention by rejecting the Libyan Arab Jamahiriya's efforts to resolve the matter within the framework of international law and placing pressure upon it to surrender the two Libyan nationals for trial; and that the United Kingdom and the United States were under a legal obligation to cease and desist from such breaches and from the use of force or threats against the Libyan Arab Jamahiriya and from all violations of its sovereignty, territorial integrity and political independence.

It also made two separate requests for an indication of provisional measures in each case. By two April 1992 Orders,[13] the Court found that the circumstances of the case were not such as to require the exercise of its power to indicate provisional measures. By Orders of 19 June 1992,[13] the Court fixed 20 December 1993 as the time-limit for the filing of a Memorial by the Libyan Arab Jamahiriya and 20 June 1995 for Counter-Memorials by the United Kingdom and United States. The Memorial by the Libyan Arab Jamahiriya was filed within the prescribed time-limit and it chose Ahmed S. El-Koshevi to sit as Judge ad hoc in the case.

Oil platforms (Iran v. United States)

Iran, in 1992,[15] instituted proceedings against the United States regarding a dispute in which Iran alleged that the destruction by United States warships, on 19 October 1987 and 18 April 1988, of three offshore oil production complexes owned and operated by the National Iranian Oil Company constituted a breach of international law and the 1955 Iran/United States Treaty of Amity, Economic Relations and Consular Rights. Iran requested the Court to rule on the matter.

By an Order of December 1992,[15] the time-limits were fixed as 31 May 1993 for the filing of a Memorial by Iran and 30 November 1993 for a Counter-Memorial by the United States. As requested by Iran and after the United States indicated that it had no objection, the President of the Court, by an Order of 3 June 1993,[16] extended those time-limits to 8 June and 16 December 1993, respectively. Iran duly filed its Memorial within the prescribed time-limits, while the United States filed certain preliminary objections to the jurisdiction of the Court.

Application of the Convention on the Prevention and Punishment of the Crime of Genocide (Bosnia and Herzegovina v. Yugoslavia (Serbia and Montenegro))

On 20 March 1993, Bosnia and Herzegovina instituted proceedings against Yugoslavia (Serbia and Montenegro) for alleged violations of the 1948 Convention on the Prevention and Punishment of the Crime of Genocide.[17]

Bosnia and Herzegovina requested the Court to adjudge and declare that Yugoslavia (Serbia and Montenegro) had violated and was continuing to violate several provisions of the Genocide Convention as well as of the Charter of the United Nations, the 1949 Geneva Conventions for the protection of war victims and their 1977 Additional Protocol I,[18] the 1907 Hague Regulations on Land Warfare and the Universal Declaration of Human Rights;[19] that Yugoslavia (Serbia and Montenegro) was using force and the threat of force against Bosnia and Herzegovina, violating its sovereignty and intervening in its internal affairs, as well as encouraging and supporting military and paramilitary actions in and against Bosnia and Herzegovina; that Bosnia and Herzegovina had the sovereign right under the Charter of the United Nations and customary international law to defend itself and to request assistance of any State in doing so, which was not to be impaired by Security Council resolution 713(1991)[20] and subsequent resolutions imposing and reaffirming an arms embargo upon the former Yugoslavia; that those consequent resolutions should not be construed as imposing an arms embargo upon Bosnia and Herzegovina; and that, pursuant to the right to collective self-defence, other States had the right to come to the immediate defence of Bosnia and Herzegovina at its request; that Yugoslavia (Serbia and Montenegro) should cease and desist immediately from its breaches of the foregoing legal obligations; and that Yugoslavia (Serbia and Montenegro) should pay reparations for damages sustained by Bosnia and Herzegovina.

On the same day, Bosnia and Herzegovina requested the Court to indicate provisional measures to the effect that Yugoslavia (Serbia and Montenegro) should cease and desist immediately from all acts of genocide against the people and State of Bosnia and Herzegovina, from military or paramilitary actions and support for such actions in or against Bosnia and Herzegovina and from any other use or threat of force against it; that Bosnia and Herzegovina had the right to seek support and assistance from other States in defending itself; and that other States had the right to come to its immediate defence.

Hearings on the request for an indication of provisional measures were held on 1 and 2 April 1993. On 8 April, at a public sitting, the Court delivered an Order,[21] the operative paragraph of which read as follows:

The Court,

Indicates, pending its final decision on the proceedings instituted on 20 March 1993 by the Republic of Bosnia and Herzegovina against the Federal Republic of Yugoslavia (Serbia and Montenegro), the following provisional measures:

A. (1) Unanimously,

The Government of the Federal Republic of Yugoslavia (Serbia and Montenegro) should immediately, in pursuance of its undertaking in the Convention on the Prevention and Punishment of the Crime of Genocide of 9 December 1948, take all measures within its power to prevent commission of the crime of genocide;

(2) By 13 votes to 1,

The Government of the Federal Republic of Yugoslavia (Serbia and Montenegro) should in particular ensure that any military, paramilitary or irregular armed units which may be directed or supported by it, as well as any organizations and persons which may be subject to its control, direction or influence, do not commit any acts of genocide, of conspiracy to commit genocide, of direct and public incitement to commit genocide, or of complicity in genocide, whether directed against the Muslim population of Bosnia and Herzegovina or against any other national, ethnical, racial or religious group;

In favour: President Sir Robert Jennings; Vice-President Oda; Judges Ago, Schwebel, Bedjaoui, Ni, Evensen, Guillaume, Shahabuddeen, Aguilar Mawdsley, Weeramantry, Ranjeva, Ajibola;

Against: Judge Tarassov.

B. Unanimously,

The Government of the Federal Republic of Yugoslavia (Serbia and Montenegro) and the Government of the Republic of Bosnia and Herzegovina should not take any action and should ensure that no action is taken which may aggravate or extend the existing dispute over the prevention or punishment of the crime of genocide, or render it more difficult of solution.

Judge Tarassov appended a declaration to the Order.

By a letter of 27 April,[22] the Secretary-General communicated the Order to the Security Council.

By an Order of 16 April,[23] the President of the Court fixed 15 October 1993 and 15 April 1994 as the time-limits for the filing of a Memorial by

Bosnia and Herzegovina and a Counter-Memorial by Yugoslavia (Serbia and Montenegro), respectively.

On 27 July, Bosnia and Herzegovina made a second request for the indication of provisional measures to the effect that Yugoslavia (Serbia and Montenegro) should cease and desist from any type of support to any group or individual in Bosnia and Herzegovina and from any efforts, proposals or negotiations to partition, annex or incorporate the sovereign territory of Bosnia and Herzegovina; that such annexation or incorporation should be deemed illegal, null and void; and that all Contracting Parties to the Genocide Convention were obliged, and the Government of Bosnia and Herzegovina should have the means to prevent acts of genocide and defend its people and State from such acts and from partition by means of genocide, including the ability to obtain weapons, equipment and supplies.

In a similar action, Yugoslavia (Serbia and Montenegro), on 10 August, requested the Court to indicate provisional measures requiring Bosnia and Herzegovina to take all measures within its power to prevent acts of genocide against the Bosnian Serbs. Following hearings on those requests on 25 and 26 August, the Court, by an Order of 13 September,[24] held that the present situation demanded the immediate implementation of provisional measures indicated in the April Court Order rather than an indication of additional measures. In declining Bosnia and Herzegovina's requests related to the partition and annexation of its territory and the means of preventing acts of genocide and partition, the Court pointed out that such claims were beyond the scope of its jurisdiction in that case, conferred on it by the Genocide Convention. At the same time, the Court recorded that great suffering and loss of life had been sustained by the population of Bosnia and Herzegovina since and despite its Order of 8 April,[21] and reminded the Parties that they were obliged to take the Court's provisional measures into account seriously.

Following a request by Bosnia and Herzegovina and after the views of Yugoslavia (Serbia and Montenegro) had been ascertained, the Vice-President of the Court, by an Order of 7 October,[25] extended the time-limits for a Memorial by Bosnia and Herzegovina and a Counter-Memorial by Yugoslavia (Serbia and Montenegro) to 15 April 1994 and 15 April 1995, respectively.

Bosnia and Herzegovina chose Elihu Lauterpacht, and Yugoslavia (Serbia and Montenegro) chose Milenko Kreca, to sit as Judges ad hoc in the case.

Gabcíkovo-Nagymaros Project (Hungary/Slovakia)

In 1992, Hungary applied to the Court in a dispute with the Czech and Slovak Federal Republic concerning the projected diversion of the Danube, inviting the Republic to accept the Court's jurisdiction.

Following negotiations between Hungary and the Czech and Slovak Federal Republic, which dissolved into two States on 1 January 1993, Hungary and Slovakia, on 2 July 1993, submitted to the Court certain issues arising out of differences which had existed between Hungary and the Czech and Slovak Federal Republic regarding the implementation and termination of the 1977 Budapest Treaty on the Construction and Operation of the Gabcíkovo-Nagymaros Barrage System and on the construction and operation of the "provisional solution"—a system damming up the Danube on Czechoslovak territory, with resulting consequences on water and the navigation course. A Special Agreement for the submission of those issues to the Court, signed by the Parties on 7 April, recorded that Slovakia was, in that respect, the sole successor State of the Czech and Slovak Federal Republic.

The Court was requested to decide whether Hungary had been entitled to suspend and subsequently abandon, in 1989, the work on the Nagymaros Project and on the part of the Gabcíkovo Project for which it was responsible, and whether the Czech and Slovak Federal Republic had been entitled to execute, in 1991-1992, the "provisional solution". The Court was also requested to determine the legal effects of the termination of the Treaty by Hungary in 1992 and the legal consequences of the Court's Judgment in that case.

By an Order of 14 July 1993,[26] the Court decided that each Party should file a Memorial and a Counter-Memorial within the time-limits of 2 May 1994 and 5 December 1994, respectively.

Legality of the use by a State of nuclear weapons in armed conflict

By a letter of 27 August 1993, the Director-General of the World Health Organization (WHO), pursuant to a 14 May resolution of the World Health Assembly, requested an advisory opinion from the Court on whether the use of nuclear weapons by a State in war or other armed conflict would be a breach of its obligations under international law, in view of the health and environmental effects.

By an Order of 13 September,[27] the Court fixed 10 June 1994 as the time-limit within which WHO and its member States entitled to appear before the Court might submit written statements on the question.

Other questions

Role of the Court

Acting on the Secretary-General's 1992 recommendations concerning the role of ICJ,[28] the General Assembly, by **resolution 47/120 B** of 20 September 1993, encouraged States to make greater use of the Court for the peaceful settlement of disputes and recommended that they accept the Court's jurisdiction, including through the dispute settlement clauses of multilateral treaties. The Assembly requested States to make contributions to the Secretary-General's Trust Fund to Assist States in the Settlement of Disputes through ICJ, established in 1989, and asked the Secretary-General to report periodically on the financial status and use of the Fund.

It decided to continue to examine the Secretary-General's recommendations, including those related to the use of the advisory competence of the Court.

Elections to the Court

The Secretary-General, on 1 February 1993,[29] informed the Security Council of the death, on 14 January, of Judge Lachs, and thus of the occurrence of a vacancy in the Court. The procedure in the General Assembly and in the Security Council for filling the vacancy was outlined in the Secretary-General's 23 April memorandum.[30] On 5 May, the Secretary-General, in accordance with the Statute of the Court, submitted to the Assembly and to the Council a list of candidates[31] for the vacancy, nominated by national groups, and their respective curricula vitae.[32]

On 4 February 1993, the Security Council adopted unanimously **resolution 805(1993)**.

The Security Council,

Noting with regret the death of Judge Manfred Lachs on 14 January 1993,

Noting further that a vacancy in the International Court of Justice for the remainder of the term of office of the deceased Judge has thus occurred and must be filled in accordance with the terms of the Statute of the Court,

Noting that, in accordance with Article 14 of the Statute, the date of the election to fill the vacancy shall be fixed by the Security Council,

Decides that the election to fill the vacancy shall take place on 10 May 1993 at a meeting of the Security Council and at a meeting of the General Assembly at its forty-seventh session.

Security Council resolution 805(1993)
4 February 1993   Meeting 3170   Adopted unanimously
Draft prepared in consultations with Council members (S/25226).

(For results of the elections, see APPENDIX III).

Request for an advisory opinion

In accordance with its 1992 decision,[33] the General Assembly continued in 1993 consideration of its agenda item on the request by the Ibero-American Summit of Heads of State and Government (Madrid, Spain, July 1992) for an advisory opinion from ICJ on the conformity with international law of certain acts involving the extraterritorial exercise of the coercive power of a State and the subsequent exercise of its criminal jurisdiction.

On 9 December, on the recommendation of the Sixth (Legal) Committee,[34] the Assembly decided to continue consideration of the item and include it in the provisional agenda of its 1994 session (**decision 48/414**).

REFERENCES

[1]A/48/4. [2]A/49/4. [3]YUN 1988, p. 795. [4]*Maritime Delimitation in the Area between Greenland and Jan Mayen (Denmark v. Norway), Judgment of 14 June 1993,* I.C.J. Sales No. 635. [5]YUN 1991, p. 818. [6]YUN 1992, p. 980. [7]Ibid., p. 981. [8]*Certain Phosphate Lands in Nauru (Nauru v. Australia), Order of 25 June 1993,* I.C.J. Sales No. 636. [9]*Ibid., Order of 13 September 1993,* I.C.J. Sales No. 639. [10]YUN 1991, p. 819. [11]*East Timor (Portugal v. Australia), Order of 19 May 1993,* I.C.J. Sales No. 633. [12]YUN 1991, p. 820. [13]YUN 1992, p. 982. [14]YUN 1971, p. 739. [15]YUN 1992, p. 983. [16]*Oil platforms (Islamic Republic of Iran v. United States of America), Order of 3 June 1993,* I.C.J. Sales No. 634. [17]YUN 1948-49, p. 959, GA res. 260 A (III), annex, 9 Dec. 1948. [18]YUN 1977, p. 706. [19]YUN 1948-49, p. 535, GA res. 217 A (III), 10 Dec. 1948. [20]YUN 1991, p. 215, SC res. 713(1991), 25 Sep. 1991. [21]*Application of the Convention on the Prevention and Punishment of the Crime of Genocide (Bosnia and Herzegovina v. Yugoslavia (Serbia and Montenegro)), Order of 8 April 1993,* I.C.J. Sales No. 631. [22]S/25686. [23]*Application of the Convention on the Prevention and Punishment of the Crime of Genocide (Bosnia and Herzegovina v. Yugoslavia (Serbia and Montenegro)), Order of 16 April 1993,* I.C.J. Sales No. 632. [24]*Ibid., Order of 13 September 1993,* I.C.J. Sales No. 640. [25]*Ibid., Order of 7 October 1993,* I.C.J. Sales No. 642. [26]*Gabcíkovo-Nagymaros Project (Hungary/Slovakia), Order of 14 July 1993,* I.C.J. Sales No. 638. [27]*Legality of the Use by a State of Nuclear Weapons in Armed Conflict, Order of 13 September 1993,* I.C.J. Sales No. 641. [28]YUN 1992, p. 986. [29]S/25224. [30]A/47/931-S/25657. [31]A/47/940-S/25726. [32]A/47/941-S/25727. [33]YUN 1992, p. 986, GA res. 47/416, 25 Nov. 1992. [34]A/48/617.

Chapter II

Legal aspects of international political relations

In 1993, the General Assembly, its Sixth (Legal) Committee and the International Law Commission (ILC) continued to consider legal aspects of international political and state relations.

ILC again took up the question of an international criminal jurisdiction, including a draft statute of an international criminal court, in the context of the draft Code of Crimes against the Peace and Security of Mankind. It also considered international liability for injurious consequences arising out of acts not prohibited by international law and State responsibility and the law of non-navigational uses of international watercourses. The Assembly, in December, requested the Commission to continue to elaborate a draft statute for an international criminal court as a matter of priority and endorsed its decision to include in its agenda the law and practice relating to reservations to treaties, and State succession and its impact on the nationality of natural and legal persons (resolution 48/31).

The Assembly established an Ad Hoc Committee to elaborate an international convention on the safety and security of United Nations and associated personnel, with particular reference to responsibility for attacks on such personnel (48/37), and decided to continue in 1994 consideration of a convention on jurisdictional immunities of States and their property (decision 48/413).

International Law Commission

The International Law Commission (ILC), at its forty-fifth session (Geneva, 3 May–23 July 1993),[1] continued work on the progressive development and codification of international law; it held 33 public meetings.

At its 1993 session, ILC considered an international criminal jurisdiction, including a draft statute of an international criminal court, in the context of the draft Code of Crimes Against the Peace and Security of Mankind; international liability for injurious consequences arising out of acts not prohibited by international law; State responsibility for wrongful acts; and the law of non-navigational uses of international watercourses. ILC continued to cooperate with the Asian-African Legal Consultative Committee, the European Committee on Legal Cooperation and the Inter-American Juridical Committee.

Members of the Commission prepared outlines on selected topics of international law[2] for ILC's subsequent consideration. ILC's Working Group on the long-term programme of work recommended that topics on the law and practice relating to reservations to treaties and State succession and its impact on the nationality of natural and legal persons be included in the Commission's future agenda.

In accordance with a General Assembly request (resolution 48/31), the Secretariat prepared for ILC's attention a topical summary of the Assembly's Sixth (Legal) Committee discussion in 1993[3] on ILC's report for that year.

The twenty-ninth session of the International Law Seminar—for postgraduate students and young professors or government officials dealing with international law—was held during the ILC session (Geneva, 1-18 June), with one United Nations Institute for Training and Research fellow and 24 other participants of different nationalities, mostly from developing countries. The participants also attended ILC meetings and lectures specifically organized for them. Austria, Cyprus, Denmark, Germany, Ireland, Mexico, Norway, Sweden, Switzerland and the United Kingdom made voluntary financial contributions, thus making it possible to award 15 full and 3 partial fellowships. Since the first seminar in 1964, fellowships had been awarded to 342 of the 643 participants representing 150 nationalities.

International criminal jurisdiction

In response to a 1992 General Assembly request,[4] ILC considered in 1993[1] the question of an international criminal jurisdiction in the framework of the draft Code of Crimes against the Peace and Security of Mankind. The draft Code, originally prepared by ILC in 1954,[5] defined offences that were crimes under international law and for which the responsible individual was to be punished. In accordance with a 1991 Assembly resolution,[6] the Commission received in 1993 the comments and observations of 24 Governments[7] on the draft Code as adopted by ILC on first reading in 1991.[8]

The Commission had before it the eleventh report[9] on the draft Code, submitted by its Special Rapporteur, Doudou Thiam (Senegal), containing a draft statute of an international criminal court consisting of 37 articles divided into three titles. Title I dealt with the creation of the Court, Title II, its organization and functioning, and Title III, its procedure. The Commission also received comments by 13 Governments[10] on the 1992 report of the Working Group[11] on a draft statute for an international criminal jurisdiction.

The Commission considered the report of the Working Group[12] on its 1993 meetings (17 May–16 July) and its revised version[13] containing a draft statute for an international criminal tribunal consisting of 67 articles, which were annexed to the Commission's 1993 report.[1] Those draft articles dealt with the establishment and composition of the court (articles 1-21); jurisdiction and applicable law (22-28); investigation and commencement of prosecution (29-35); trial (36-54); appeal and review (55-57); international cooperation and judicial assistance (58-64); and enforcement of sentences (65-67).

On 21 July, the Commission requested Governments to submit their comments on the proposed draft articles by 15 February 1994, with a view to completing the elaboration of the draft statute at ILC's 1994 session.

International liability

Draft articles on international liability for injurious consequences arising out of acts not prohibited by international law continued to be considered by ILC in 1993 on the basis of the ninth report[14] of its Special Rapporteur on the subject, Julio Barboza (Argentina). The Rapporteur examined the issue of prevention in respect to activities having a risk of causing transboundary harm. He also commented on the obligation of prevention and pointed out the financial and technological inequality between developing and developed countries to monitor those activities involving risk. The Rapporteur presented 11 draft articles dealing with prior authorization (article 11); transboundary impact assessment (12); pre-existing activities (13); performance of activities (14); notification and information (15); exchange of information (16); national security and industrial secrets (17); prior consultation (18); rights of the State presumed to be affected (19); factors involved in a balance of interests (20); and non-transference of risk or harm (20 *bis*).

The Commission referred articles 11 to 20 *bis*, together with article 10 (non-discrimination), which it had examined in 1990,[15] to the Drafting Committee for further examination. The Committee, in a July report,[16] set forth the draft articles it had adopted on first reading, dealing with the scope of the articles (article 1); use of terms (2); prior authorization (11); risk assessment

(12); and measures to minimize the risk (14). In line with its policy of not adopting articles not accompanied by commentaries, ILC took note of the report and decided to defer action on it until its 1994 session.

State responsibility for wrongful acts

In 1993, ILC again considered State responsibility for wrongful acts on the basis of the fifth report on the topic[17] by its Special Rapporteur, Gaetano Arangio-Ruiz (Italy). The report dealt with Part Three of the draft articles on State responsibility (implementation) and contained six draft articles on: conciliation (article 1); task of the conciliation commission (2); arbitration (3); terms of reference of the arbitral tribunal (4); judicial settlement (5); *excès de pouvoir* or violation of fundamental principles of arbitral procedures (6). An annex to the report dealt with the settlement of disputes. The report also addressed the consequences of the so-called "crimes" of States (article 19 of Part One of the draft articles). The Commission referred articles 1 to 6, as well as the annex thereto, to the Drafting Committee but, due to a lack of time, it did not consider article 19 of Part One.

ILC also dealt with articles adopted at the 1992 session by its Drafting Committee,[18] on which it had deferred action pending the submission of commentaries. It adopted a new paragraph 2 to be included in article 1 of Part Two of the draft, as well as articles relating to the cessation of wrongful conduct (article 6); reparation (6 *bis*); restitution in kind (7); compensation (8); satisfaction (10); and assurances and guarantees of non-repetition (10 *bis*).

The Commission also received from the Drafting Committee articles adopted by it in 1993 on first reading[19] pertaining to countermeasures by an injured State (article 11); conditions relating to resort to countermeasures (12); proportionality (13); and prohibited countermeasures (14). It noted the recommendations of the Drafting Committee and deferred action on them until its 1994 session.

In August,[20] the Secretary-General transmitted to the Assembly the draft articles on state responsibility, provisionally adopted by the Commission.

Non-navigational uses of international watercourses

Regarding the law of the non-navigational uses of international watercourses, ILC considered in 1993 the preliminary report on the topic[21] by its Special Rapporteur, Robert Rosenstock (United States). The Special Rapporteur suggested that, before further drafting was undertaken, the issue of whether the outcome of the exercise should take the form of a framework convention or model rules should be discussed. He agreed with the view that ILC recommend provisions on fact-finding and dispute settlement regardless of the final form of its work. The Special Rapporteur presented an examination of the first 10 of a set of draft articles adopted by the Commission in 1991.[22] Twenty Member States and one non-member State presented to the Secretary-General their comments and observations on the draft articles,[23] as requested by the General Assembly in 1991.[6] The Commission referred the 10 articles to its Drafting Committee for examination. In July, it received from the Committee the texts of articles it had adopted[24] pertaining to the scope of the present articles (article 1); use of terms (2); watercourse agreements (3); parties to watercourse agreements (4); equitable and reasonable utilization and participation (5); factors relevant to equitable and reasonable utilization (6); general obligation to cooperate (8); regular exchange of data and information (9); and relationship between different kinds of uses (10). Taking note of the Drafting Committee's recommendations, the Commission deferred action on them until its 1994 session.

GENERAL ASSEMBLY ACTION

On 9 December, the General Assembly, on the recommendation of the Sixth (Legal) Committee, adopted **resolution 48/31** without vote.

Report of the International Law Commission on the work of its forty-fifth session

The General Assembly,

Having considered the report of the International Law Commission on the work of its forty-fifth session,

Emphasizing the need for the progressive development of international law and its codification in order to make it a more effective means of implementing the purposes and principles set forth in the Charter of the United Nations and in the Declaration on Principles of International Law concerning Friendly Relations and Cooperation among States in accordance with the Charter of the United Nations and to give increased importance to its role in relations among States,

Recognizing the importance of referring legal and drafting questions to the Sixth Committee, including topics that might be submitted to the International Law Commission, and of enabling the Sixth Committee and the Commission further to enhance their contribution to the progressive development of international law and its codification,

Recalling the need to keep under review those topics of international law which, given their new or renewed interest for the international community, may be suitable for the progressive development and codification of international law and therefore may be included in the future programme of work of the International Law Commission,

Recognizing also the role of the International Law Commission in the fulfilment of the objectives of the United Nations Decade of International Law,

Expressing its appreciation for the progress achieved by the International Law Commission in its elaboration of a draft statute for an international criminal court, and noting the constructive debate in the Sixth Committee pertaining to this question,

Considering that experience has demonstrated the usefulness of structuring the debate on the report of the International Law Commission in the Sixth Committee in such a manner that conditions are provided for concentrated attention on each of the main topics dealt with in the report, and that this process is facilitated when the Commission indicates specific issues on which expressions of views by Governments are of particular interest for the continuation of its work,

1. *Takes note* of the report of the International Law Commission on the work of its forty-fifth session;

2. *Expresses its appreciation* to the International Law Commission for the work accomplished at that session;

3. *Recommends* that, taking into account the comments of Governments, whether in writing or expressed orally in debates in the General Assembly, the International Law Commission should continue its work on the topics in its current programme;

4. *Takes note with appreciation* of chapter II of the report of the International Law Commission, entitled "Draft Code of Crimes against the Peace and Security of Mankind", which was devoted to the question of a draft statute for an international criminal court;

5. *Invites* States to submit to the Secretary-General by 15 February 1994, as requested by the International Law Commission, written comments on the draft articles proposed by the Working Group on a draft statute for an international criminal court;

6. *Requests* the International Law Commission to continue its work as a matter of priority on this question with a view to elaborating a draft statute, if possible at its forty-sixth session in 1994, taking into account the views expressed during the debate in the Sixth Committee as well as any written comments received from States;

7. *Endorses* the decision of the International Law Commission to include in its agenda the topics "The law and practice relating to reservations to treaties" and "State succession and its impact on the nationality of natural and legal persons", on the understanding that the final form to be given to the work on these topics shall be decided after a preliminary study is presented to the General Assembly;

8. *Notes* the intentions of the International Law Commission for the programme of work for the remainder of the current term of office of its members, and in this connection requests the Commission to resume at its forty-sixth session the consideration of the draft Code of Crimes against the Peace and Security of Mankind and welcomes the Commission's decision to endeavour to complete in 1994 the second reading of the draft articles on the law of the non-navigational uses of international watercourses;

9. *Expresses its appreciation* for the efforts of the International Law Commission to improve its procedures and methods of work;

10. *Requests* the International Law Commission:

(a) To consider thoroughly:

(i) The planning of its activities and programme for the term of office of its members, bearing in mind the desirability of achieving as much progress as possible in the preparation of draft articles on specific topics;

(ii) Its methods of work in all their aspects, bearing in mind that the staggering of the consideration of some topics might contribute, *inter alia*, to a more effective consideration of its report in the Sixth Committee;

(b) To continue to pay special attention to indicating in its annual report, for each topic, those specific issues on which expressions of views by Governments, either in the Sixth Committee or in written form, would be of particular interest for the continuation of its work;

11. *Takes note* of the comments of the International Law Commission on the question of the duration of its session, as presented in its report, and expresses the view that the requirements of the work for the progressive development of international law and its codification and the magnitude and complexity of the subjects on the agenda of the Commission make it desirable that the usual duration of its sessions be maintained;

12. *Reaffirms* its previous decisions concerning the role of the Codification Division of the Office of Legal Affairs of the Secretariat and those concerning the summary records and other documentation of the International Law Commission;

13. *Once again expresses the wish* that seminars will continue to be held in conjunction with the sessions of the International Law Commission and that an increasing number of participants from developing countries will be given the opportunity to attend those seminars, appeals to States that can do so to make the voluntary contributions that are urgently needed for the holding of the seminars, and expresses the hope that the Secretary-General will continue to make every effort, within existing resources, to provide the seminars with adequate services, including interpretation, as required;

14. *Requests* the Secretary-General to forward to the International Law Commission, for its attention, the records of the debate on the report of the Commission at the forty-eighth session of the General Assembly, together with such written statements as delegations may circulate in conjunction with their oral statements, and to prepare and distribute a topical summary of the debate;

15. *Recommends* the continuation of efforts to improve the ways in which the report of the International Law Commission is considered in the Sixth Committee, with a view to providing effective guidance for the Commission in its work;

16. *Also recommends* that the debate on the report of the International Law Commission at the forty-ninth session of the General Assembly commence on 24 October 1994.

General Assembly resolution 48/31

9 December 1993　　　Meeting 73　　　Adopted without vote

Approved by Sixth Committee (A/48/612) without vote, 29 November (meeting 38); 41-nation draft (A/C.6/48/L.11); agenda item 143.

Sponsors: Argentina, Australia, Austria, Brazil, Belarus, Bulgaria, Canada, Chile, Costa Rica, Czech Republic, Denmark, Ecuador, El Salvador, Finland, France, Germany, Hungary, Indonesia, Ireland, Italy, Japan, Morocco, Netherlands, New Zealand, Norway, Poland, Portugal, Republic of Moldova, Romania, Russian Federation, Rwanda, Senegal, Slovakia, Sweden, Thailand, Trinidad and Tobago, Turkey, Ukraine, United Kingdom, Uruguay, Venezuela.

Meeting numbers. GA 48th session: 6th Committee 17-28, 37-38; plenary 73.

REFERENCES

(1)A/48/10. (2)A/CN.4/454. (3)A/CN.4/457. (4)YUN 1992, p. 989, GA res. 47/33, 25 Nov. 1992. (5)YUN 1954, p. 408. (6)YUN 1991, p. 848, GA res. 46/54, 9 Dec. 1991. (7)A/CN.4/L.448 & Add.1. (8)YUN 1991, p. 823. (9)A/CN.4/L.449 & Corr.1. (10)A/CN.4/452 & Add.1-3. (11)YUN 1992, p. 988. (12)A/CN.4/L.488 & Add.1-4 & Corr.1,2. (13)A/CN.4/L.490 & Add.1. (14)A/CN.4/450. (15)A/45/10. (16)A/CN.4/L.487 & Corr.1. (17)A/CN.4/453 & Add.1 & Add.1/Corr.1,2 & Add.2,3. (18)YUN 1992, p. 989. (19)A/CN.4/L.480 & Add.1. (20)A/48/303. (21)A/CN.4/451. (22)YUN 1991, p. 825. (23)A/CN.4/447 & Add.1-3. (24)A/CN.4/L.489.

International State relations and international law

Judicial responsibility for attacks on United Nations personnel

In 1993, several United Nations bodies addressed the question of the judicial responsibility for attacks on United Nations personnel, a subject of growing concern to the Organization (see PART ONE, Chapter I). In March, the President of the Security Council issued a statement[1] on behalf of Council Members demanding that States act promptly to deter, prosecute and punish those responsible for attacks on and other acts of violence against United Nations forces and personnel. He also requested the Secretary-General to report on existing arrangements for their protection, taking into account relevant multilateral instruments and status of forces agreements concluded between the United Nations and host countries. The Special Committee on Peacekeeping Operations, in its May report,[2] agreed that a comprehensive, systematic and practical approach was needed to address the issue and indicated that it would consider, in the light of the Secretary-General's report, what further steps might be taken, including a legally binding international instrument to reinforce existing arrangements.

In response to the Council's request, the Secretary-General, in an August report,[3] outlined the various international legal instruments under which United Nations personnel and forces were protected and suggested that, in the long term, a new international instrument be elaborated to codify and develop further international law relating to their security. The Security Council, by **resolution 868(1993)**, noted the Secretary-General's proposal.

At the request of New Zealand,[4] the General Assembly considered the issue. The Assembly's

Sixth Committee established a working group to examine the question, including proposals by New Zealand[5] and Ukraine[6] outlining the framework for a draft convention on responsibility for attacks on United Nations personnel.

In his oral report to the Committee on 15 November, the Chairman of the Working Group stated that the Group had considered several possibilities for meeting the new challenges and agreed with the Secretary-General's proposal that a new binding legal instrument be elaborated.

GENERAL ASSEMBLY ACTION

On 9 December, the General Assembly, on the recommendation of the Sixth Committee, adopted **resolution 48/37** without vote.

Question of responsibility for attacks on United Nations and associated personnel and measures to ensure that those responsible for such attacks are brought to justice

The General Assembly,

Recalling the report of the Secretary-General entitled "An Agenda for Peace" and General Assembly resolution 47/120 B of 20 September 1993,

Recalling also its resolution 47/72 of 14 December 1992,

Gravely concerned at the increasing number of attacks on United Nations personnel that have caused death or serious injury,

Recalling further the statement made by the President of the Security Council, on behalf of the Council, on 31 March 1993, in which the Security Council, *inter alia*, recognized the need for all relevant bodies of the Organization to take concerted action to enhance the safety and security of United Nations forces and personnel,

Recalling the report of the Special Committee on Peacekeeping Operations,

Having considered the report of the Secretary-General of 27 August 1993 on the security of United Nations operations,

Recalling also Security Council resolution 868(1993) of 29 September 1993,

Noting with appreciation the draft proposals submitted by the delegations of New Zealand and Ukraine under this item,

Welcoming the oral report of the Chairman of the Working Group established under the item,

1. *Decides* to establish an Ad Hoc Committee open to all Member States to elaborate an international convention dealing with the safety and security of United Nations and associated personnel, with particular reference to responsibility for attacks on such personnel;

2. *Decides also* that the Ad Hoc Committee shall be authorized to hold a session from 28 March to 8 April 1994 and, if the Committee itself so decides, to hold a further session from 1 to 12 August 1994, to prepare the text of a draft convention, taking into account any suggestions and proposals from States, as well as comments and suggestions that the Secretary-General may wish to provide on this subject, and bearing in mind views expressed during the debate on this item at the forty-eighth session of the General Assembly;

3. *Requests* the Secretary-General to provide the Ad Hoc Committee with the necessary facilities for the performance of its work;

4. *Requests* the Ad Hoc Committee to report to the General Assembly at its forty-ninth session on progress made towards the elaboration of the draft convention;

5. *Recommends* that at its forty-ninth session a working group be re-established in the framework of the Sixth Committee in the event that further work is required for the elaboration of the draft convention;

6. *Decides* to include in the provisional agenda of its forty-ninth session the item entitled "Question of responsibility for attacks on United Nations and associated personnel and measures to ensure that those responsible for such attacks are brought to justice".

General Assembly resolution 48/37

9 December 1993   Meeting 73   Adopted without vote

Approved by Sixth Committee (A/48/618) without vote, 24 November (meeting 37); 41-nation draft (A/C.6/48/L.12); agenda item 152.
Sponsors: Afghanistan, Argentina, Australia, Austria, Belgium, Brazil, Bulgaria, Canada, Cambodia, Chile, Czech Republic, Denmark, Ecuador, Fiji, Finland, France, Germany, Greece, Hungary, Italy, Malaysia, Nepal, Netherlands, New Zealand, Nigeria, Norway, Peru, Poland, Portugal, Republic of Moldova, Romania, Singapore, Spain, Sweden, Trinidad and Tobago, Tunisia, Ukraine, United Kingdom, United States, Uruguay, Venezuela.
Financial implications. S-G, A/C.6/48/L.14.
Meeting numbers. GA 48th session: 6th Committee 13-16, 29, 35, 37; plenary 73.

International tribunal for the prosecution of violations of humanitarian law in the former Yugoslavia

By **resolution 808(1993)**, the Security Council decided to establish an international tribunal for the prosecution of persons responsible for serious violations of international humanitarian law committed in the territory of the former Yugoslavia since 1991. Acting under Chapter VII of the Charter, the Council, in May, established the Tribunal and adopted its statute (**resolution 827(1993)**); in August, it established a list of 23 candidates to serve as judges (**resolution 857(1993)**). In September, the General Assembly elected 12 judges for the Tribunal (**decision 47/328**) and, in October, the Council appointed Ramón Escovar-Salom (Venezuela) as Prosecutor (**resolution 877(1993)**). (For details see PART TWO, Chapter IV.)

Prevention of terrorism

Report of the Secretary-General. The Secretary-General submitted to the General Assembly an August report with a later addendum[7] containing replies from 14 Member States and 4 United Nations organizations on measures to eliminate international terrorism, as requested by the Assembly in 1991.[8] Annexed to the report was information on the state, as at 22 June 1993, of signatures, ratifications, or accessions to a number of international conventions and protocols relating to terrorism, including those for which the Secretary-General performed depository functions: the 1973 Convention on the Prevention and Punishment of Crimes against Internationally Protected Persons, including Diplomatic Agents,[9] and the 1979 International Convention against the Taking of Hostages.[10]

On 9 December, the Assembly, by **decision 48/411**, requested the Secretary-General to seek the views of Member States on the proposals submitted by Governments[7] or made during the 1993 debate on the item in the Sixth Committee, or as contained in its 1991 resolution[8] on combating international terrorism.

Other action. The Security Council, in November, intensified sanctions under the air and arms embargo imposed against the Libyan Arab Jamahiriya in March 1992[11] to ensure compliance with its January 1992 resolution[12] requesting the surrender for trial of two Libyan nationals suspected in the 1988 bombing of Pan Am flight 103 over Lockerbie, Scotland, as well as cooperation with French authorities investigating the attack in 1989 on Union de transports aériens (UTA) flight 772 in the Niger (**resolution 883(1993)**) (for details, see PART ONE, Chapter I).

Jurisdictional immunities of States and their property

Report of the Secretary-General. In 1993, the Secretary-General submitted comments received from Belgium,[13] Bulgaria,[14] and Japan,[15] on draft articles on jurisdictional immunities of States and their property, which were adopted by ILC in 1991.[16]

Working Group report. In 1992,[17] the General Assembly decided to establish in 1993 a Working Group on jurisdictional immunities of States and their property, to continue consideration of issues relating to the draft articles on that subject and to facilitate the conclusion of a convention through the promotion of general agreement.

The Working Group held 13 meetings between 27 September and 8 October, and a final meeting on 11 November. It discussed the main issues concerning the draft articles, namely: the definition of the terms ''State'' and ''commercial transaction'', including the question of the criterion to be applied in determining whether a contract or transaction was commercial (article 2); the question of the legal distinction between a State and certain of its entities in the matter of State immunity from foreign jurisdiction (5 and 10); the exception of contracts of employment; and immunity from measures of constraint in connection with proceedings before a court. Other issues raised concerned the retroactivity of

the present articles and the possible inclusion of provisions on aircraft and space objects and on the settlement of disputes.

In its report,[18] the Group concluded that although progress had been made on a number of substantive issues, remaining areas of disagreement needed to be narrowed down to arrive at a generally acceptable basis for the elaboration of a convention.

GENERAL ASSEMBLY ACTION

On 9 December, by **decision 48/413**, the General Assembly, on the recommendation of the Sixth Committee, took note of the report of the Working Group and decided that consideration of the substantive issues should continue in the Sixth Committee during 1994 towards the conclusion of a convention on jurisdictional immunities of States and their property through general agreement. The Assembly also decided that it would consider in 1994 ILC's recommendation that an international conference of plenipotentiaries be convened to examine the draft articles and to conclude a convention on the subject. It further decided to include the item in the provisional agenda of that session.

REFERENCES
[1]S/25493. [2]A/48/173. [3]A/48/349-S/26358. [4]A/48/144. [5]A/C.6/48/L.2. [6]A/C.6/48/L.3. [7]A/48/267 Add.1 & Add.1/Corr.1. [8]YUN 1991, p. 823, GA res. 46/51, 9 Dec. 1991. [9]YUN 1973, p. 775, GA res. 3166(XXVIII), annex, 14 Dec. 1973. [10]YUN 1979, p. 1144, GA res. 34/146, annex, 17 Dec. 1979. [11]YUN 1992, p. 55, SC res. 748(1992), 31 Mar. 1992. [12]YUN 1992, p. 53, SC res. 731(1992), 21 Jan. 1992. [13]A/48/313. [14]A/C.6/48/3. [15]A/48/464. [16]YUN 1991, p.830. [17]YUN 1992, p. 992, GA dec. 47/414, 25 Nov. 1992. [18]A/C.6/48/L.4 & Corr.2.

Diplomatic relations

Protection of diplomats

As at 31 December 1993,[1] the number of parties to the various international instruments relating to the protection of diplomats and diplomatic and consular relations was as follows: 172 States were parties to the 1961 Vienna Convention on Diplomatic Relations,[2] with Georgia, Guinea Bissau and the Republic of Moldova acceding, and Bosnia and Herzegovina, the Czech Republic, Slovakia and the former Yugoslav Republic of Macedonia succeeding in 1993; 47 States were parties to the Optional Protocol concerning the acquisition of nationality,[3] with the former Yugoslav Republic of Macedonia succeeding in 1993; and 61 States were parties to the Optional Protocol concerning the compulsory settlement of disputes,[3] with Bosnia and Herzegovina and the former Yugoslav Republic of Macedonia succeeding during the year.

The 1963 Vienna Convention on Consular Relations[4] had 150 parties, with Armenia, Georgia and the Republic of Moldova acceding and Bosnia and Herzegovina, the Czech Republic, Slovakia and the former Yugoslav Republic of Macedonia succeeding in 1993; 36 States were parties to the Optional Protocol concerning the acquisition of nationality;[5] and 44 States were parties to the Optional Protocol concerning the compulsory settlement of disputes.[5]

The 1973 Convention on the Prevention and Punishment of Crimes against Internationally Protected Persons, including Diplomatic Agents,[6] had 86 States parties, with Antigua and Barbuda acceding and Bosnia and Herzegovina, the Czech Republic and Slovakia succeeding in 1993.

Report of the Secretary-General. In accordance with General Assembly resolutions of 1987,[7] 1990[8] and 1992,[9] the Secretary-General, in January 1993, requested States to provide information on serious violations of the protection, security and safety of diplomatic and consular missions and representatives, and on action taken to bring offenders to justice. In August, he submitted to the Assembly a report[10] containing an analytical summary and the texts of the information received. A total of 11 new cases of violations, as well as additional information on previous cases, were reported by States during the period 19 September 1992 to 1 August 1993. In connection with 16 reported cases in respect of which no information had been received within a reasonable period of time, the Secretary-General addressed reminders to the States concerned. Nine follow-up reports were received in response to those reminders. No views were received with respect to enhancing diplomatic protection.

REFERENCES

[1]*Multilateral Treaties Deposited with the Secretary-General: Status as at 31 December 1993* (ST/LEG/SER.E/12), Sales No. E.94.V.11. [2]YUN 1961, p. 512. [3]Ibid., p. 516. [4]YUN 1963, p. 510. [5]Ibid., p. 512. [6]YUN 1973, p. 775, GA res. 3166(XXVIII), annex, 14 Dec. 1973. [7]YUN 1987, p. 1068, GA res. 42/154, 7 Dec. 1987. [8]GA res. 45/39, 28 Nov. 1990. [9]YUN 1992, p. 993, GA res. 47/31, 25 Nov. 1992. [10]A/INF/48/4.

Treaties and agreements

Treaties involving international organizations

The 1986 Vienna Convention on the Law of Treaties between States and International Organizations or between International Organizations[1] was acceded to in 1993 by Australia and the Republic of Moldova. The Czech Republic and Slovakia succeeded Czechoslovakia with respect to the Convention.[2] As at 31 December, 20 States had ratified or acceded to the Convention, which had not yet entered into force.

Registration and publication of treaties by the United Nations

During 1993, some 1,200 international agreements and 1,006 subsequent actions were received by the Secretariat for registration or filing and recording. In addition, there were 377 registrations of formalities concerning agreements for which the Secretary-General performed depositary functions.

The texts of international agreements registered or filed and recorded are published in the United Nations *Treaty Series* in the original languages, with translations into English and French where necessary. In 1993, the following volumes of the *Treaty Series* covering treaties registered or filed in 1978, 1980, 1981, 1982, 1983, 1984, 1985 and 1986 were issued:

1001, 1208, 1270, 1273, 1275, 1308, 1315, 1324, 1326, 1327, 1337, 1338, 1342, 1349, 1358, 1361, 1362, 1363, 1364, 1366, 1370, 1379, 1380, 1386, 1387, 1388, 1392, 1401, 1404, 1417, 1418.

Multilateral treaties

New multilateral treaties concluded under United Nations auspices

The following treaties, concluded under United Nations auspices, were deposited with the Secretary-General during 1993:[2]

International Cocoa Agreement, 1993, concluded at Geneva on 16 July 1993

Amendments to articles 16, 17 and 19(b) of the Convention on the International Maritime Organization, adopted on 4 November 1993

Protocol amending Article 1(a), Article 14(1) and Article 14(3)(b) of the European Agreement of 30 September 1957 concerning the International Carriage of Dangerous Goods by Road (ADR), adopted at Geneva on 28 October 1993

International Convention on Maritime Liens and Mortgages, 1993, done at Geneva on 6 May 1993

International Agreement on Olive Oil and Table Olives, 1986, as amended and extended, 1993, done at Geneva on 10 March 1993

Convention on the Prohibition of the Development, Production, Stockpiling and Use of Chemical Weapons and on their Destruction, opened for signature at Paris on 13 January 1993

Multilateral treaties deposited with the Secretary-General

The number of multilateral treaties for which the Secretary-General performed depositary functions stood at 438 at the end of 1993. During the year, 225 signatures were affixed to treaties for which he performed depositary functions and 968 instruments of ratification, accession, acceptance and approval or notification were transmitted to him. In addition, he received 245 communications from States expressing observations or declarations and reservations made at the time of signature, ratification or accession.

The following multilateral treaties in respect of which the Secretary-General acts as depositary came into force during 1993:[2]

Agreement establishing the Fund for the Development of the Indigenous Peoples of Latin America and the Caribbean, concluded at Madrid, Spain, on 24 July 1992

Agreement concerning the Adoption of Uniform Conditions of Approval and Reciprocal Recognition of Approval for Motor Vehicle Equipment and Parts, done at Geneva on 20 March 1958

Regulation No. 91: Uniform provisions concerning the approval of side-marker lamps for motor vehicles and their trailers

Regulation No. 92: Uniform provisions concerning the approval of replacement exhaust silencing systems (RESS) for motorcycles

European Agreement on Important International Combined Transport Lines and Related Installations (AGTC), concluded at Geneva on 1 February 1991

Fourth Extension of the International Coffee Agreement, 1983, adopted by the International Coffee Council under Resolution No. 363 of 4 June 1993

International Coffee Agreement, 1983 adopted by the International Coffee Council on 16 September 1982, as further extended by resolution 363(E) of 7 June 1993

Convention on Biological Diversity, opened for signature at Rio de Janeiro, Brazil, on 5 June 1992

REFERENCES

[1]YUN 1986, p. 1006. [2]*Multilateral Treaties Deposited with the Secretary-General: Status as at 31 December 1993* (ST/LEG/SER.E/12), Sales No. E.94.V.11.

Chapter III

Law of the sea

In 1993, United Nations efforts to promote the universal acceptance of the 1982 Convention on the Law of the Sea took on an added urgency as the required number of ratifications were deposited for the Convention to enter into force.

The General Assembly, in December, invited States to increase their efforts to achieve universal participation in the Convention and called on all States that had not done so to consider ratifying or acceding to the Convention at the earliest possible date (resolution 48/28).

UN Convention on the Law of the Sea

Signatures and ratifications

The number of ratifications of, or accessions to, the United Nations Convention on the Law of the Sea increased to 60 during 1993 (58 ratifications, 2 accessions) with the receipt of instruments of ratification from Barbados, Guyana, Honduras, Malta, Saint Kitts and Nevis, Saint Vincent and the Grenadines and Zimbabwe.[1]

The Convention, which was adopted by the Third United Nations Conference on the Law of the Sea in 1982,[2] was to enter into force 12 months after receipt of the sixtieth instrument of ratification. On 16 November 1993, Guyana became the sixtieth country to ratify the Convention, establishing the date of the Convention's entry into force as 16 November 1994.

The Convention was closed for signature in 1984, having received 159 signatures.[3]

Impact of entry into force

The entry into force of the Convention on the Law of the Sea would have a marked impact on the practice of States and the activities of a number of international organizations competent in ocean affairs, the Secretary-General stated in November.[4]

He noted that the Convention's entry into force would consolidate and strengthen the provisions that had received general acceptance and would make operative the Convention's unique system for the settlement of disputes. Several outstanding issues dealing with the deep seabed regime were the subject of ongoing consultations.

The date of the Convention's entry into force would affect the work programmes of the Preparatory Commission for the International Seabed Authority and for the International Tribunal for the Law of the Sea. The Commission was to convene the Group of Technical Experts within three months from 16 November 1993 to review the state of deep seabed mining and to establish when commercial production might begin. The Expert Group would report on all matters within its mandate to the Assembly of the International Seabed Authority at its first session, which was to be held on the date the Convention entered into force. The Group would also report on practical arrangements for the establishment of the International Tribunal for the Law of the Sea to the meeting of States parties to the Convention, which was to be convened within six months from 16 November 1994. Finally, the Preparatory Commission was to transfer its property and records to the International Seabed Authority and dissolve itself at the conclusion of the first session of the Assembly.

The Secretary-General stated that his work would be affected by the Convention's entry into force, as would the work of the Division for Ocean Affairs and the Law of the Sea of the United Nations Office of Legal Affairs, which was required to adjust its activities, especially in 1994 and beyond. Those activities related to: the Secretary-General's assumption of various functions, as specified in article 319 of the Convention, including that as the depositary of the Convention; arrangements for the first election of members of the International Tribunal for the Law of the Sea and the meeting of States parties; arrangements for the initial election of the members of the Commission on the Limits of the Continental Shelf; and arrangements for drawing up the lists of conciliators and arbitrators in accordance with annexes V and VII to the Convention, as well as for drawing up the list of experts by the relevant organizations, in accordance with annex VIII to the Convention.

Other developments related to the Convention

Pursuant to a 1992 General Assembly request,[5] the Secretary-General submitted in November a report describing developments relating to the United Nations Convention on the Law of the Sea.[6] The report was divided into two parts. The first part reviewed the status of the Convention in terms of its impact on State practice and national policy, the settlement of conflicts and disputes, maritime safety and environmental protection, waste management, the conservation of living marine resources, and the work of the Preparatory Commission for the International Seabed Authority and for the International Tribunal for the Law of the Sea. The second part outlined the activities of the Secretariat's Division for Ocean Affairs and the Law of the Sea (see below).

States continued to adopt or modify legislation in accordance with the Convention and, as new States came into existence, the number of coastal States as at 15 October 1993 totalled 150. Also as at mid-October, the number of States claiming a 12-mile territorial sea, measured from baselines, had increased to 120 from 114 at the end of 1992, and the number of States claiming a 24-mile contiguous zone had increased from 38 to 44. Eighty-four States claimed a 200-mile exclusive economic zone, while seven based their zones on a line of delimitation, by determination of coordinates or without limits. Forty States based their continental shelf on a depth of 200 metres plus the exploitability criterion, 23 established theirs at the outer edge of the continental margin or 200 miles, and six worked on 200 miles. Another 16 States claimed archipelagic status, although not all had specified archipelagic baselines.

In order to remove problems with aspects of the Convention's deep-sea mining provisions that inhibited industrialized States in particular from ratifying or acceding to it, the Secretary-General had convened informal consultations on those issues with some 30 States. Those consultations in 1993 focused on nine problem areas relating to the deep seabed mining regime, as contained in the Convention: costs to States parties; the Enterprise (see below); decision-making; the Review Conference; technology transfer; production limitation; the compensation fund; the financial terms of contracts; and environmental issues.

The Convention's imminent entry into force gave a sense of urgency to the Secretary-General's efforts, and in April he presented four possible procedural approaches resulting from the consultations. After in-depth discussions in August, however, he concluded that it was not possible at that stage to narrow the discussion to agreed provisions and specific procedures for their adoption.

States involved in disputes over maritime delimitation and related issues continued to pursue settlement through negotiations and the International Court of Justice (ICJ). Croatia and Slovenia, having successfully settled most of their land boundaries, pursued negotiations over the boundary at the mouth of the Dragonja river to the sea, which would generate a maritime boundary in the Bay of Piran. Namibia and South Africa reached agreement on 8 September that South Africa would transfer sovereignty over the enclave of Walvis Bay in 1994.

On 14 June, ICJ delivered its Judgment in the case concerning the maritime delimitation in the area between Greenland and Jan Mayen, fixing a delimitation line for the continental shelf and the fishery zones in that area between Denmark and Norway. The Court divided the area of overlapping claims into three zones, and then divided each of those zones between the two parties, expressing its view that they should enjoy equitable access to the fishing resources. The maritime delimitation case between Guinea-Bissau and Senegal was pending with ICJ. In the case concerning maritime delimitation and territorial questions between Bahrain and Qatar, oral proceedings confined to the issues of jurisdiction and admissibility were scheduled to open in February 1994. (For details on the ICJ cases, see PART FOUR, Chapter I.)

The year saw some new international agreements, rules and standards that were intended to complement the Convention in such areas as maritime safety, waste management, conservation of living marine resources, and other issues related to marine environmental protection.

As follow-up to Agenda 21, adopted in 1992 by the United Nations Conference on Environment and Development,[7] the Inter-Agency Committee on Sustainable Development of the Administrative Committee on Coordination (ACC) agreed to establish an ACC Subcommittee on Oceans and Coastal Areas.

At the regional level, there was a marked acceleration in the establishment of common policies and cooperation, particularly on environmental problems, and decisions were increasingly taken at the ministerial level. Effective marine environmental law and policy, however, generally awaited solutions to problems of land-based sources of pollution. Expectations in that area focused on the preparations of the United Nations Environment Programme for the 1995 intergovernmental meeting called for in Agenda 21.

The issue of conservation and management of living marine resources was addressed in 1993 by the Food and Agriculture Organization of the United Nations (FAO) and by government representatives during the United Nations Conference on Straddling Fish Stocks and Highly Migratory Fish Stocks (see PART THREE, Chapter VIII). FAO started to prepare an International Code of Conduct for Responsible Fishing in consultation with relevant international organizations. The Code was to be formulated within the framework of the Convention on the Law of the Sea and other appropriate international instruments. An outline of the Code was submitted by FAO to the Committee on Fisheries in March 1993. It followed six thematic areas: fishing operations, fishery management practices, fair trade practices, aquaculture development, the integration of coastal fishing in coastal area management and fishery research.

Preparatory Commission

During 1993, the Preparatory Commission for the International Seabed Authority and for the International Tribunal for the Law of the Sea held its eleventh session at Kingston, Jamaica, from 22 March to 2 April.[6] Among the matters considered were the implementation of resolution II adopted by the Third United Nations Conference on the Law of the Sea in 1982,[8] which embodied the regime for the protection of pioneer investment in the development of seabed mining technology, and the preparation of draft rules and agreements.[9]

The General Committee, acting as the Preparatory Commission's executive organ for implementing resolution II, considered and took note of periodic reports submitted by the certifying States (China, France, India, Japan and the Russian Federation) on behalf of pioneer investors. It approved the recommendations of the fourth meeting of the Training Panel and designated five candidates selected by the Panel for training programmes offered by India and the Russian Federation. The Committee also took note of traineeships offered by China and the Interoceanmetal Joint Organization and its certifying States and one in chemical engineering offered by India. It reaffirmed its decision to invite any State member of or observer in the Preparatory Commission to submit candidates for the training programme.

The plenary of the Preparatory Commission held two readings of the draft rules of procedure of the organs of the International Seabed Authority and finalized their texts, except for the so-called ''hard-core'' issues relating to financial and budgetary matters, decision-making on questions of substance, elections and the participation of observers and subsidiary organs.[9]

A draft agreement between the International Seabed Authority and the Government of Jamaica regarding the headquarters of the Authority was approved with some clarifications.

Special Commissions

The Preparatory Commission's four Special Commissions[9] continued to work in accordance with their respective mandates.

Developing land-based producer States

Special Commission 1, which focused on the potential impact of future seabed mining on land-based minerals production in developing countries, completed consideration of all items in its programme of work. Most delegations felt that

draft provisional recommendations drawn up by the Commission Chairman had bridged the various positions of delegations and could be submitted to the International Seabed Authority.

The Enterprise

Special Commission 2 continued its preparations for the Enterprise—the operational arm of the International Seabed Authority. It continued to focus on the development of a training programme, the organizational structure and operational options of the Enterprise and the initial operation of the Enterprise.

The Special Commission also considered the draft final report of the Chairman's Advisory Group of Assumptions. The Group felt that there was a need for continuity in its work and suggested that its successors concentrate on, among other things: the periodic analysis of world markets and metal prices; the evaluation of technological developments; and the state of knowledge of deep sea environments and the possible impact of mining activities.

Seabed mining code

Special Commission 3 continued to prepare the seabed mining code and rules for the exploration and exploitation of polymetallic nodules on the deep seabed. Although some issues remained to be resolved, a number of the draft mining code provisions had in effect met the approval of delegations.

International Tribunal

Special Commission 4 continued to draft practical arrangements to establish the International Tribunal for the Law of the Sea. With the adoption of its draft report by the Preparatory Commission, preparations began for the first Meeting of States Parties to the Convention prior to the Tribunal's inauguration. Agreement had not been reached on the number of official working languages of the Tribunal and how to apply the plan for phasing in the Tribunal.

GENERAL ASSEMBLY ACTION

On 9 December, the General Assembly adopted **resolution 48/28** by recorded vote.

Law of the sea

The General Assembly,

Recalling its previous resolutions, including resolution 47/65 of 11 December 1992, on the law of the sea,

Recognizing that, as stated in the third preambular paragraph of the United Nations Convention on the Law of the Sea, the problems of ocean space are closely interrelated and need to be considered as a whole,

Convinced that it is important to safeguard the unified character of the Convention and related resolutions adopted therewith and to apply them in a manner consistent with that character and with their object and purpose,

Emphasizing the need for States to ensure consistent application of the Convention, as well as the need for harmonization of national legislation with the provisions of the Convention,

Considering that, in its resolution 2749(XXV) of 17 December 1970, it proclaimed that the seabed and ocean floor, and the subsoil thereof, beyond the limits of national jurisdiction (hereinafter referred to as "the Area"), as well as the resources of the Area, are the common heritage of mankind,

Recalling that the Convention provides the regime to be applied to the Area and its resources,

Recalling with satisfaction the expressions of willingness to explore all possibilities of addressing issues of concern to some States in order to secure universal participation in the Convention,

Noting that the sixtieth instrument of ratification of, or accession to the Convention was deposited on 16 November 1993 and that as a consequence the Convention shall enter into force twelve months after the date of deposit of that instrument,

Recognizing the need for cooperation in the early and effective implementation by the Preparatory Commission of resolution II of the Third United Nations Conference on the Law of the Sea,

Noting with satisfaction the progress made in the Preparatory Commission since its inception, including the registration of six pioneer investors and the designation by the Preparatory Commission of reserved areas for the International Seabed Authority from the application areas submitted by the pioneer investors pursuant to resolution II, bearing in mind that such registration entails both rights and obligations for pioneer investors,

Noting also the increasing needs of countries, especially developing countries, for information, advice and assistance in the implementation of the Convention and in their developmental process for the full realization of the benefits of the comprehensive legal regime established by the Convention,

Concerned that the developing countries are as yet unable to take effective measures for the full realization of these benefits owing to the lack of resources and of the necessary scientific and technological capabilities,

Recognizing the need to enhance and supplement the efforts of States and competent international organizations aimed at enabling developing countries to acquire such capabilities,

Recognizing also that the Convention encompasses all uses and resources of the sea and that all related activities within the United Nations system need to be implemented in a manner consistent with it,

Deeply concerned at the current state of the marine environment,

Mindful of the importance of the Convention for the protection of the marine environment,

Noting with concern the use of fishing methods and practices, including those aimed at evading regulations and controls, which can have an adverse impact on the conservation and management of living marine resources,

Considering the need for effective and balanced conservation and management of living marine resources, giving full effect to the relevant provisions in the Convention,

Noting activities carried out in 1993 under programme 10 (Law of the sea and ocean affairs) in the medium-

term plan for the period 1992-1997, as revised, taking into account the restructuring of the Secretariat of the Organization, and of the report of the Secretary-General prepared pursuant to paragraph 21 of General Assembly resolution 47/65,

1. *Recalls* the historic significance of the United Nations Convention on the Law of the Sea as an important contribution to the maintenance of peace, justice and progress for all peoples of the world;

2. *Expresses its satisfaction* at the increasing and overwhelming support for the Convention, as evidenced, *inter alia*, by the one hundred and fifty-nine signatures and sixty ratifications or accessions, and notes that as a consequence the Convention will enter into force on 16 November 1994;

3. *Invites* all States to make renewed efforts to facilitate universal participation in the Convention;

4. *Notes with appreciation* the new developments and the active participation of States in the consultations under the auspices of the Secretary-General aimed at promoting dialogue and at addressing issues of concern to some States in order to achieve universal participation in the Convention;

5. *Also invites* all States to participate in the consultations held under the auspices of the Secretary-General and to increase efforts to achieve universal participation in the Convention as early as possible;

6. *Recognizes* that political and economic changes, including particularly a growing reliance on market principles, underscore the need to re-evaluate, in the light of the issues of concern to some States, matters in the regime to be applied to the Area and its resources, and that a productive dialogue on such issues involving all interested parties would facilitate the prospect of universal participation in the Convention, for the benefit of mankind as a whole;

7. *Calls upon* all States that have not done so to consider ratifying or acceding to the Convention at the earliest possible date, and also calls upon all States to take appropriate steps to promote universal participation in the Convention, including through dialogue aimed at addressing the issues of concern to some States;

8. *Also calls upon* all States to safeguard the unified character of the Convention and related resolutions adopted therewith and to apply them in a manner consistent with that character and with their object and purpose;

9. *Calls upon* States to observe the provisions of the Convention when enacting their national legislation;

10. *Notes* the progress made by the Preparatory Commission for the International Seabed Authority and for the International Tribunal for the Law of the Sea in all areas of its work, including the completion of its draft provisional final report at its eleventh session;

11. *Recalls* the Understanding on the Fulfilment of Obligations by the Registered Pioneer Investors and their Certifying States adopted by the Preparatory Commission on 30 August 1990, as well as the understandings adopted on 12 March 1992 and 18 August 1992;

12. *Expresses its appreciation* to the Secretary-General for his efforts in support of the Convention and for the effective execution of programme 10 (Law of the sea and ocean affairs) in the medium-term plan for the period 1992-1997, and requests him, in the execution of programme 10, to continue to provide an effective response

to the increased needs of States for assistance in the implementation of the Convention;

13. *Also expresses its appreciation* to the Secretary-General for the report prepared pursuant to paragraph 21 of General Assembly resolution 47/65 and requests him to carry out the activities outlined therein, as well as those aimed at the strengthening of the legal regime of the sea;

14. *Calls upon* the Secretary-General to continue to assist States in the implementation of the Convention and in the development of a consistent and uniform approach to the legal regime thereunder, as well as in their national, subregional and regional efforts towards the full realization of the benefits therefrom, and invites the organs and organizations of the United Nations system to cooperate and enhance assistance in these endeavours;

15. *Urges* interested Member States, in particular States with advanced marine capabilities, to review relevant policies and programmes in the context of the integration of the marine sector in national development strategies, and to explore prospects for intensifying cooperation with developing countries, including those of regions active in this field;

16. *Requests* the competent international organizations, the United Nations Development Programme, the World Bank and other multilateral funding agencies, in accordance with their respective policies, to intensify financial, technological, organizational and managerial assistance to the developing countries in their efforts to realize the benefits of the comprehensive legal regime established by the Convention and to strengthen cooperation among themselves and with donor States in the provision of such assistance;

17. *Requests* the Secretary-General to keep under review, in cooperation with States and the competent international organizations, the measures being undertaken and any necessary follow-up action, in order to facilitate the realization by States of the benefits of the comprehensive legal regime established by the Convention, and to report thereon periodically to the General Assembly;

18. *Recognizes* that the protection of the marine environment will be significantly enhanced by the implementation of applicable provisions of the Convention;

19. *Reiterates its call* to States and other members of the international community to strengthen their cooperation and to take measures with a view to giving full effect to the provisions in the Convention on the conservation and management of living marine resources, including the prevention of fishing methods and practices which can have an adverse impact on the conservation and management of living marine resources and, in particular, to comply with bilateral and regional measures applicable to them aimed at effective monitoring and enforcement;

20. *Requests* the Secretary-General to continue and to accelerate the consultations in order to achieve universal participation in the Convention as early as possible and to provide the necessary services for these consultations, the next meeting of which will take place from 31 January to 4 February 1994;

21. *Also requests* the Secretary-General to provide for the convening of the twelfth regular session of the Preparatory Commission at Kingston from 7 to 11 February 1994, during which arrangements will be made for meetings of the Training Panel, and, if necessary, provide for a further meeting of up to two weeks during the summer in New York;

22. *Takes note* of the decision of the Preparatory Commission to convene a meeting of the Group of Technical Experts to review the state of deep seabed mining and to make an assessment of the time when commercial production may be expected to commence;

23. *Notes* the need to make arrangements for the first session of the Assembly of the International Seabed Authority and a meeting of States parties to the Convention, if required, including arrangements for the participation of observers;

24. *Further requests* the Secretary-General to report to the General Assembly at its forty-ninth session, and earlier if appropriate, on developments pertaining to the Convention and all related activities and on the implementation of the present resolution;

25. *Decides* to include in the provisional agenda of its forty-ninth session the item entitled ''Law of the sea''.

General Assembly resolution 48/28

9 December 1993   Meeting 73   144-1-11 (recorded vote)

29-nation draft (A/48/L.40 & Add.1); agenda item 36.

Sponsors: Australia, Brazil, Cameroon, Canada, Cape Verde, Chile, Denmark, Djibouti, Fiji, Guyana, Iceland, Indonesia, Jamaica, Malta, Mauritania, Mexico, Myanmar, New Zealand, Norway, Philippines, Portugal, Senegal, Sierra Leone, Sri Lanka, Sudan, Sweden, Trinidad and Tobago, Ukraine, Uruguay.

Recorded vote in Assembly as follows:

In favour: Afghanistan, Algeria, Andorra, Angola, Antigua and Barbuda, Argentina, Armenia, Australia, Austria, Bahamas, Bahrain, Bangladesh, Barbados, Belarus, Belgium, Belize, Benin, Bhutan, Bolivia, Botswana, Brazil, Brunei Darussalam, Bulgaria, Burkina Faso, Cambodia, Cameroon, Canada, Cape Verde, Central African Republic, Chad, Chile, China, Colombia, Comoros, Congo, Costa Rica, Côte d'Ivoire, Croatia, Cuba, Cyprus, Czech Republic, Denmark, Djibouti, Dominica, Dominican Republic, Egypt, Ethiopia, Fiji, Finland, France, Gabon, Gambia, Ghana, Greece, Grenada, Guatemala, Guinea, Guinea-Bissau, Guyana, Haiti, Honduras, Hungary, Iceland, Indonesia, Iran, Ireland, Italy, Jamaica, Japan, Jordan, Kenya, Kuwait, Lao People's Democratic Republic, Lesotho, Libyan Arab Jamahiriya, Liechtenstein, Lithuania, Luxembourg, Madagascar, Malawi, Malaysia, Maldives, Mali, Malta, Marshall Islands, Mauritania, Mauritius, Mexico, Micronesia, Monaco, Mongolia, Morocco, Mozambique, Myanmar, Namibia, Nepal, Netherlands, New Zealand, Nicaragua, Niger, Nigeria, Norway, Oman, Pakistan, Papua New Guinea, Paraguay, Philippines, Poland, Portugal, Qatar, Republic of Korea, Republic of Moldova, Romania, Russian Federation, Rwanda, Saint Vincent and the Grenadines, Samoa, Saudi Arabia, Senegal, Seychelles, Sierra Leone, Singapore, Slovakia, Slovenia, Solomon Islands, Sri Lanka, Suriname, Swaziland, Sweden, Thailand, the former Yugoslav Republic of Macedonia, Togo, Trinidad and Tobago, Tunisia, Turkmenistan, Uganda, Ukraine, United Arab Emirates, United Republic of Tanzania, Uruguay, Viet Nam, Yemen, Zambia, Zimbabwe.

Against: Turkey.

Abstaining: Azerbaijan, Ecuador, Eritrea, Germany, Israel, Kazakhstan, Panama, Peru, United Kingdom, United States, Venezuela.

On 21 December, the Assembly, in **resolution 48/194**, reaffirmed that the United Nations Conference on Straddling Fish Stocks and Highly Migratory Fish Stocks should complete its work before the forty-ninth (1994) session of the General Assembly, and approved the convening of two further sessions of the Conference in New York in 1994. The Secretary-General was asked to submit the final report on the work of the Conference to the Assembly at its forty-ninth session.

Division for Ocean Affairs and the Law of the Sea

The Division for Ocean Affairs and the Law of the Sea of the Office of Legal Affairs continued its preparations in 1993 for the final ratification of the Convention on the Law of the Sea and its entry into force.[6] Programme 10 of the 1992-1997 medium-term plan[10] on the law of the sea and ocean affairs continued to be implemented, following the existing subprogramme structure and maintaining the same priorities.

The Division continued to assist Governments and regional organizations to implement the Convention and to develop a consistent and uniform approach to its legal regime. Advisory services included: examination of the implications of the Convention for States or intergovernmental organizations; the formulation and harmonization of national maritime legislation; the development and elaboration of marine and coastal zone policies and plans; and the building of national and regional institutional frameworks to help realize benefits under the Convention. The Division assisted Jamaica with the preparation of a pilot project for implementation under the World Bank/International Maritime Organization wider Caribbean initiative for ship-generated wastes project.

A Consultative Meeting on Training in Integrated Management of Coastal and Marine Areas for Sustainable Development (Sassari, Sardinia, Italy, 21-23 June) was held in cooperation with the United Nations Development Programme. The Division provided technical assistance to the International Ocean Institute for the design of an advanced course on the integrated management of coastal and ocean areas, to be implemented at its new regional centres in Colombia, Fiji, India and Senegal.

Several publications on developments in ocean and coastal affairs were completed or in progress in 1993. Among those published were: a compilation of national legislation on the exclusive economic zone;[11] volume II of a compilation of documents of the Preparatory Commission for the International Seabed Authority and for the International Tribunal for the Law of the Sea; a volume of the *Annual Review of Ocean Affairs: Law and Policy, Main Documents*;[12] the eighth volume of *The Law of the Sea: A Select Bibliography—1992*;[13] and *Bibliography on the Law of the Sea (1968-1988): Two Decades of Law-making, State Practice and Doctrine (Multilingual Supplement)*.[14] Three issues of the *Law of the Sea Bulletin*[15] were published in 1993, as well as a *Reference Guide to Law of the Sea Bulletins*, Nos. 1 to 22 (1983-1992).

The computerized Law of the Sea Information System was revised and updated. Extensive revisions were made to the Country Marine Profile Database and the National Marine Legislation Database, and a Polymetallic Nodule Deposits Database was being established. The Library Bibliographic Information System was expanded to include holdings at the Division's reference library at Kingston and the Division's specialized Law of the Sea Library and Reference Collection continued to serve Member States and others. The Division maintained close cooperation with United Nations agencies and bodies.

The Hamilton Shirley Amerasinghe Fellowship on the Law of the Sea—established in 1981[16] and presented annually in honour of the first President of the Third United Nations Conference on the Law of the Sea—was awarded to Poungthong Onoora of the Ministry for Agriculture and Cooperatives of Thailand.

REFERENCES

[1]*Multilateral Treaties Deposited with the Secretary-General: Status as at 31 December 1993* (ST/LEG/SER.E/12), Sales No. E.94.V.11. [2]YUN 1982, p. 178. [3]YUN 1984, p. 108. [4]A/48/527/Add.1. [5]YUN 1992, p. 1000, GA res. 47/65, 11 Dec. 1992. [6]A/48/527. [7]YUN 1992, p. 672. [8]YUN 1982, p. 216. [9]LOS/PCN/130. [10]A/45/6/Rev.1. [11]*Law of the Sea; National Legislation on the Exclusive Economic Zone*, Sales No. E.93.V.10. [12]*Annual Review of Ocean Affairs: Law and Policy, Main Documents*, Sales No. E.93.V.5. [13]*The Law of the Sea: A Select Bibliography— 1992*, Sales No. E.93.V.12. [14]*Bibliography on the Law of the Sea (1968-1988): Two Decades of Law-making, State Practice and Doctrine (Multilingual Supplement)*, Sales No. E.93.V.15. [15]*Law of the Sea Bulletin*, No. 22, January; No. 23, June; No. 24, December. [16]YUN 1981, p. 139.

Chapter IV

Other legal questions

In 1993, the United Nations continued to work on various aspects of international law and international economic law.

The Special Committee on the Charter of the United Nations and on the Strengthening of the Role of the Organization met in March and discussed, among other questions, the economic problems of third States affected by sanctions under Chapter VII of the Charter. In December, the General Assembly asked the Special Committee to give priority consideration to that question in 1994 (resolution 48/36).

Various aspects of relations between the United Nations diplomatic community and the United States were addressed by the Committee on Relations with the Host Country at four meetings held during the year. Voicing concern that the financial indebtedness of certain missions accredited to the Organization had risen to alarming proportions, the Assembly reminded missions, their personnel and Secretariat personnel of their obligations (48/35).

With regard to the United Nations Decade of International Law (1990-1999), the Assembly appealed for contributions to implement the programme for the Decade's second term (1993-1994) (48/30). Within the framework of the Decade, the Assembly approved guidelines and recommendations put forward by the Secretary-General on the United Nations Programme of Assistance in the Teaching, Study, Dissemination and Wider Appreciation of International Law (48/29).

The United Nations Commission on International Trade Law adopted the Model Law on Procurement of Goods and Construction and the Assembly took note of its completion and adoption in December (48/33).

International organizations and international law

Strengthening the role of the United Nations

The Secretary-General, in his annual report to the General Assembly on the work of the Organization,[1] noted that, with the cold war over, the United Nations could play the pivotal role in establishing world order and progress that had been assigned to it by the Charter.

Referring to his 1992 "Agenda for Peace",[2] the Secretary-General added to peace-keeping and preventive diplomacy the concept of peace enforcement, as foreseen in Chapter VII of the Charter for peace-keeping operations that did not necessarily have the consent of all parties concerned. The combined efforts of preventive diplomacy, peace-keeping, peace-building and sometimes peace enforcement, he said, strengthened the opportunity for post-conflict peace-building to prevent the recurrence of violence among nations and peoples.

Special Committee on the Charter

The Special Committee on the Charter of the United Nations and on the Strengthening of the Role of the Organization[3] (New York, 1-19 March 1993) continued to discuss proposals for the maintenance of international peace and security and to examine the peaceful settlement of disputes between States, as requested by the General Assembly in 1992.[4]

The Committee had before it two updated working papers, submitted by the Russian Federation, concerning the maintenance of international peace and security. They proposed new issues for consideration by the Committee,[5] and a draft declaration on the improvement of cooperation between the United Nations and regional organizations.[6] An amendment to the draft declaration was proposed by Mexico. The Committee also examined a proposal by 19 States on the implementation of Charter provisions concerning assistance to third States affected by sanctions under Chapter VII;[7] a working paper on the same subject submitted by India and Nepal;[8] a revision of a 1992 proposal by the Libyan Arab Jamahiriya on the effectiveness of the Security Council in the maintenance of international peace and security;[9] and a revised working paper by Cuba, also on the role of the United Nations in the maintenance of international peace and security.

In considering the peaceful settlement of disputes between States, the Committee had before it draft United Nations conciliation rules, proposed by Guatemala.[10]

Application of sanctions under Chapter VII of the Charter

In response to an invitation contained in a December 1992 statement[11] by the President of the Security Council, the Secretary-General submitted a November report to the Council and the General Assembly on the special economic problems of third States resulting from the application of sanctions under Chapter VII of the Charter.

In March, the issue was taken up by the Special Committee on the Charter[3] (see above) and by an informal open-ended Working Group of the Assembly. Matters discussed included proposals for: the establishment of a fund to assist third States affected by the imposition of sanctions; a study on the effectiveness and management of various types of sanctions and on verification of compliance with sanctions regimes; and for an "economic impact statement" to be considered before the adoption of sanctions. In a May statement to the Working Group, the Secretary-General noted that, as sanctions became more common, more permanent structures might be needed to study and deal with ensuing economic problems, as might consultations between the Security Council, the Secretary-General, international financial institutions, and Member States.

On 20 September, the Assembly, by **resolution 47/120 B, section IV**, decided to continue to examine ways to implement Article 50 of the Charter (see APPENDIX II) and requested the Secretary-General to report annually on its implementation.

Report of the Secretary-General. In his November report on the special economic problems of States as a result of sanctions imposed under Chapter VII,[12] the Secretary-General outlined the practice and experience of the Security Council in applying Article 50 including the procedure for considering applications by States and mechanisms and instruments for following up on the Council's recommendations.

The Secretary-General noted that there was no United Nations mechanism to address the spirit of Article 50 effectively and systematically and recommended the establishment of more orderly and systemic arrangements. In particular, he proposed that the Security Council address the issue of requests for assistance under Article 50 when adopting preventive or enforcement measures; this would provide, at the outset, a clear legal basis for the treatment of such requests. A sanction committee or specially established ad hoc committee could be entrusted with a mandate to consider such requests and to make recommendations to the President of the Council. The Secretary-General also noted that the Economic and Social Council, in accordance with functions and powers

vested in it under Articles 63 and 64 of the Charter, could play an important role in coordinating United Nations efforts to assist in the context of Article 50, giving practical meaning to cooperation between the Security Council and the Economic and Social Council, as provided under Article 65. Other recommendations dealt with appeals for assistance, financial arrangements for resource mobilization, and coordination issues. (For information on special economic assistance to States affected by sanctions against Yugoslavia (Serbia and Montenegro), see PART THREE, Chapter III.)

GENERAL ASSEMBLY ACTION

On 9 December, the General Assembly, on the recommendation of the Sixth (Legal) Committee, adopted **resolution 48/36** without vote.

Report of the Special Committee on the Charter of the United Nations and on the Strengthening of the Role of the Organization

The General Assembly,

Recalling its resolution 3499(XXX) of 15 December 1975, by which it established the Special Committee on the Charter of the United Nations and on the Strengthening of the Role of the Organization, and its relevant resolutions adopted at subsequent sessions,

Recalling also its resolution 47/233 of 17 August 1993 on the revitalization of the work of the General Assembly,

Recalling further its resolution 47/62 of 11 December 1992 on the question of equitable representation on and increase in the membership of the Security Council,

Bearing in mind the reports of the Secretary-General on the work of the Organization submitted to the General Assembly at its thirty-seventh, thirty-ninth, fortieth, forty-first, forty-second, forty-third, forty-fourth, forty-fifth, forty-sixth, forty-seventh and forty-eighth sessions, as well as the views and comments expressed on them by Member States,

Welcoming the report of the Secretary-General of 8 November 1993,

Recalling the elements relevant to the work of the Special Committee on the Charter of the United Nations and on the Strengthening of the Role of the Organization contained in its resolution 47/120 B of 20 September 1993,

Noting the discussions in the Security Council towards strengthening the consultative process in accordance with Article 50 of the Charter with a view to minimizing special economic problems of countries adversely affected as a result of their implementation of preventive or enforcement measures under Chapter VII of the Charter,

Mindful of the desirability for further work being done by the Special Committee in the fields of the maintenance of international peace and security and the peaceful settlement of disputes between States,

Bearing in mind various proposals submitted to the General Assembly at its forty-eighth session aimed at strengthening the role of the Organization and enhancing its effectiveness,

Having considered the report of the Special Committee on the work of its session held in 1993,

1. *Takes note* of the report of the Special Committee on the Charter of the United Nations and on the Strengthening of the Role of the Organization;

2. *Decides* that the Special Committee will hold its next session from 7 to 25 March 1994;

3. *Requests* the Special Committee, at its session in 1994, in accordance with the provisions of paragraph 4 below:

(a) To accord appropriate time for the consideration of all proposals concerning the question of the maintenance of international peace and security in all its aspects in order to strengthen the role of the United Nations and, in this context:

(i) To consider on a priority basis proposals on the implementation of the provisions of the Charter of the United Nations related to assistance to third States affected by the application of sanctions under Chapter VII of the Charter;

(ii) To continue its consideration, also on a priority basis, of the proposal on the enhancement of cooperation between the United Nations and regional organizations;

(iii) To consider other specific proposals relating to the maintenance of international peace and security already submitted to the Special Committee or which might be submitted to the Special Committee at its session in 1994, including the proposal on the strengthening of the role of the Organization and enhancement of its efficiency and the revised proposal submitted with a view to enhancing the effectiveness of the Security Council with regard to the maintenance of international peace and security;

(b) To continue its work on the question of the peaceful settlement of disputes between States and in this context:

(i) To continue its consideration of the proposal on United Nations rules for the conciliation of disputes between States;

(ii) To continue its consideration of other specific proposals relating to the peaceful settlement of disputes between States, in particular those relating to the enhancement of the role of the International Court of Justice;

4. *Also requests* the Special Committee to be mindful of the importance of reaching general agreement whenever that has significance for the outcome of its work;

5. *Decides* that the Special Committee shall continue to accept the participation of observers of Member States in its meetings, including those of its working group, and also decides that the Special Committee shall be authorized to invite other States or intergovernmental organizations to participate in the debate in its plenary meetings on specific items where it considers that such participation would assist its work;

6. *Invites* the Special Committee at its session in 1994 to initiate a review of its membership and to consider various proposals regarding this membership;

7. *Requests* the Special Committee to submit a report on its work to the General Assembly at its forty-ninth session;

8. *Decides* to include in the provisional agenda of its forty-ninth session the item entitled "Report of the Special Committee on the Charter of the United Nations and on the Strengthening of the Role of the Organization".

General Assembly resolution 48/36

9 December 1993   Meeting 73   Adopted without vote

Approved by Sixth Committee (A/48/615) without vote, 29 November (meeting 38); 25-nation draft (A/C.6/48/L.18); agenda item 146.
Sponsors: Australia, Brazil, Bulgaria, Canada, Colombia, Ecuador, Egypt, El Salvador, Ethiopia, Finland, Guatemala, Hungary, Indonesia, Italy, Morocco, New Zealand, Nigeria, Philippines, Romania, Slovakia, Spain, the former Yugoslav Republic of Macedonia, Tunisia, Ukraine, Uruguay.
Meeting numbers. GA 48th session: 6th Committee 5-11, 38; plenary 73.

Host country relations

Pursuant to a 1992 General Assembly request,[13] the Committee on Relations with the Host Country continued to consider various aspects of relations between the United Nations diplomatic community and the United States, its host country.[14] At four meetings between 10 February and 9 November 1993, the Committee considered: the security of missions and the safety of their personnel; issues arising from implementation of the 1947 Headquarters Agreement between the United Nations and the United States,[15] including host country travel regulations; the acceleration of immigration and customs procedures and security arrangements for the Headquarters district; the responsibilities of permanent missions to the United Nations and their personnel, particularly in relation to financial indebtedness; matters related to the use of motor vehicles and parking; and rationalization of the Committee's work.

With regard to security, the Committee was informed of responses to several incidents, including the robbery of a Chinese delegate to the Assembly's 1992 session, the 1992 attack on the mission of Iran, and a case of car-jacking involving an official of the German mission. It was also informed of a seminar on survival in New York, organized at the United Nations on 13 May by the United States mission and the New York City Commission for the United Nations, the Consular Corps and International Business.

The Committee also considered an allegation by Cuba that demonstrations held regularly in the proximity of its mission constituted a deliberate campaign of harassment against mission personnel, and concerns raised by the Russian Federation regarding the security of the Russian mission housing complex. Costa Rica, Cyprus and the Russian Federation drew the Committee's attention to recent security measures related to access to United Nations premises, which, in their view, had inconvenienced their missions. In response, the United States noted that the measures had an impact on the host country as well, and described steps taken to alleviate the problems.

The Committee was informed that all travel restrictions imposed on United Nations staff members of Afghan nationality, and their dependents, were removed by the host country on 11 January 1993, and that an informal meeting was arranged by the Secretariat and the host country mission on the subject of United States customs procedures. In that regard, the Russian Federation reiterated its request that special lines be designated for diplomatic personnel at all terminals at Kennedy Airport in New York. Addressing transportation arrangements, Mali, Sierra Leone and Zimbabwe stated that their mission vehicles were receiving parking tickets in areas traditionally reserved for their vehicles. The United States replied that alternative parking space was being sought for Zimbabwe's mission.

Iraq reminded the Committee of the continuing freeze on its liquid assets in the United States, which had been used by its mission to pay staff salaries, rents and other expenses, and of travel restrictions imposed on mission personnel. The United States responded that rent securities and other funds of Iraq came under the sanctions imposed by the Security Council and came under the jurisdiction of the Council's Sanctions Committee.

The United States reported that the chronic indebtedness of missions and individuals had risen to more than $5 million in 1993 and remained a very serious problem for the host country. It had become difficult to persuade creditors not to seek relief in the civil court system and, although the United States continued to intervene on behalf of missions and individuals with diplomatic privileges and immunities, it also had an obligation to protect the interests of its citizens and creditors who were unable to obtain legal relief. It was noted that when a diplomat, a diplomatic mission or a staff member of the Secretariat failed to pay just debts, this reflected poorly on the entire United Nations community. During the year, the Committee's Working Group on Indebtedness continued its efforts to solve the problem.

In recommendations and conclusions adopted on 9 November, the Committee expressed its anticipation that the host country would continue to take all measures necessary to prevent interference with the functioning of missions and that problems of host country relations raised at its meetings would be duly settled. It stressed the importance and urgency of its Working Group's efforts concerning financial indebtedness and reminded permanent missions, their personnel and Secretariat personnel of their obligations.

On 9 December, the General Assembly, on the recommendation of the Sixth Committee, adopted **resolution 48/35** without vote.

Report of the Committee on Relations with the Host Country

The General Assembly,

Having considered the report of the Committee on Relations with the Host Country,

Recalling Article 105 of the Charter of the United Nations, the Convention on the Privileges and Immunities of the United Nations and the Agreement between the United Nations and the United States of America regarding the Headquarters of the United Nations and the responsibilities of the host country,

Recognizing that effective measures should continue to be taken by the competent authorities of the host country, in particular to prevent any acts violating the security of missions and the safety of their personnel,

Noting the spirit of cooperation and mutual understanding that has guided the deliberations of the Committee on issues affecting the United Nations community and the host country,

Welcoming the increased interest shown by Member States in participating in the work of the Committee,

Welcoming also the efforts to explore ways to rationalize the work of the Committee, and in particular its agenda,

1. *Endorses* the recommendations and conclusions of the Committee on Relations with the Host Country contained in paragraph 58 of its report;

2. *Considers* that the maintenance of appropriate conditions for the normal work of the delegations and the missions accredited to the United Nations is in the interests of the United Nations and all Member States, and expresses the hope that the host country will continue to take all measures necessary to prevent any interference with the functioning of missions;

3. *Expresses its appreciation* for the efforts made by the host country, and hopes that problems raised at the meetings of the Committee will continue to be resolved in a spirit of cooperation and in accordance with international law;

4. *Voices its concern* that the amount of financial indebtedness resulting from non-compliance with contractual obligations of certain missions accredited to the United Nations has increased to alarming proportions, reminds all permanent missions to the United Nations, their personnel and Secretariat personnel of their responsibilities to meet such obligations, and expresses the hope that the efforts undertaken by the Committee, in consultation with all concerned, will lead to a solution of this problem;

5. *Welcomes* the lifting of travel controls by the host country with regard to certain missions and staff members of the Secretariat of certain nationalities, and expresses the hope that the remaining travel restrictions will be removed by the host country as soon as possible, and in this regard notes the positions of the affected States, of the Secretary-General and of the host country;

6. *Supports* the efforts of the Chairman of the Committee, Member States and the Secretariat to explore ways to rationalize the work of the Committee and its agenda, permitting it to remain efficient and responsive, and in keeping with the overall spirit of its mandate;

7. *Requests* the Secretary-General to remain actively engaged in all aspects of the relations of the United Nations with the host country;

8. *Requests* the Committee to continue its work, in conformity with General Assembly resolution 2819(XXVI) of 15 December 1971;

9. *Decides* to include in the provisional agenda of its forty-ninth session the item entitled "Report of the Committee on Relations with the Host Country".

General Assembly resolution 48/35

9 December 1993   Meeting 73   Adopted without vote

Approved by Sixth Committee (A/48/614) without vote, 24 November (meeting 37); 6-nation draft (A/C.6/48/L.10); agenda item 145.
Sponsors: Bulgaria, Canada, Costa Rica, Côte d'Ivoire, Cyprus, Russian Federation.
Meeting numbers. GA 48th session: 6th Committee 35, 37; plenary 73.

United Nations Decade of International Law

In response to requests contained in a 1992 General Assembly resolution,[16] the Secretary-General submitted two 1993 reports on the United Nations Decade of International Law (1990-1999), which the Assembly had declared in 1989.[17] The Decade's aims were to promote acceptance of and respect for the principles of international law; to promote the peaceful settlement of disputes between States, including resort to, and full respect for, the International Court of Justice (ICJ); to encourage the progressive development of international law and its codification, and to encourage its teaching, study, dissemination and wider appreciation. The Assembly adopted the programme of activities for the Decade's second term (1993-1994) in 1992.[16]

In August,[18] the Secretary-General summarized replies from States and international organizations on steps taken to implement the programme of activities for the second term, and views on possible activities for the next term. He also described recent activities of various United Nations bodies related to the progressive development of international law and its codification in such fields such as human rights, disarmament, outer space, economic development, international trade, international drug control and crime prevention and criminal justice, the environment, and the law of the sea.

In September,[19] the Secretary-General submitted a preliminary operational plan for a possible United Nations congress on public international law, including its purpose, timing, organization of work, and issues regarding participation and financing.

Sixth Committee action. The Sixth Committee's Working Group on the Decade, established in 1990 pursuant to a 1989 Assembly resolution[17] with a view to preparing recommendations on the programme of activities for the Decade, held six meetings between 6 October and 16 November 1993.[20] The Working Group discussed the implementation of the programme of activities for the second term (1993-1994) of the Decade and a draft programme for a United Nations congress on public international law. It recommended that the congress be held in 1995 and that the Secretariat proceed with its preparation. It also considered the Secretary-General's report on the protection of the environment in times of armed conflict and commented on specific sections.

Protection of the environment in times of armed conflict

In response to a 1992 General Assembly request,[21] the Secretary-General, in July 1993,[22] presented information received from the International Committee of the Red Cross (ICRC) on the protection of the environment in times of armed conflict. ICRC reviewed existing law on the subject and described related work being carried out under its auspices. In 1993, ICRC convened two meetings of experts (Geneva, January and June) to define the content of existing law, identify problems with implementation and any gaps it might have, determine what action needed to be taken, and draft model guidelines for military manuals. The experts reaffirmed the importance and relevance of the currently applicable rules and recognized the need to look for ways to protect the environment in times of non-international armed conflict. A proposal to protect nature reserves, which could be likened to demilitarized zones or other protected areas, received considerable support. The experts encouraged ICRC to clarify and, where necessary, develop rules to protect the natural environment in times of armed conflict. ICRC raised a number of questions for examination by the Sixth Committee and stated its readiness to clarify rules governing the conduct of hostilities, including those relevant to protection of the environment, and to continue drafting pertinent rules for inclusion in military manuals. Annexed to the report were guidelines for military manuals and instructions on the protection of the environment in times of armed conflict.

GENERAL ASSEMBLY ACTION

On 9 December, the General Assembly, on the recommendation of the Sixth Committee, adopted **resolution 48/30** without vote.

United Nations Decade of International Law

The General Assembly,

Recalling its resolution 44/23 of 17 November 1989, by which it declared the period 1990-1999 the United Nations Decade of International Law,

Recalling also that the main purposes of the Decade, according to resolution 44/23, should be, *inter alia*:

(a) To promote acceptance of and respect for the principles of international law;

(b) To promote means and methods for the peaceful settlement of disputes between States, including resort to and full respect for the International Court of Justice;

(c) To encourage the progressive development of international law and its codification;

(d) To encourage the teaching, study, dissemination and wider appreciation of international law,

Recalling further its resolution 47/32 of 25 November 1992, to which was annexed the programme for the activities for the second term (1993-1994) of the Decade,

Expressing its appreciation to the Secretary-General for his reports submitted pursuant to resolution 47/32,

Recalling that at its forty-fifth session the Sixth Committee established the Working Group on the United Nations Decade of International Law with a view to preparing generally acceptable recommendations on the programme of activities for the Decade,

Noting that at its forty-sixth, forty-seventh and forty-eighth sessions the Sixth Committee reconvened the Working Group to continue its work in accordance with resolutions 45/40 of 28 November 1990, 46/53 of 9 December 1991 and 47/32,

Having considered the report of the Secretary-General containing information received from the International Committee of the Red Cross on the work of the group of experts on the protection of the environment in times of armed conflict, conducted under the auspices of the International Committee, and the draft guidelines for military manuals and instructions on the protection of the environment in times of armed conflict, annexed thereto,

1. *Expresses its appreciation* to the Sixth Committee and its Working Group on the United Nations Decade of International Law for their work at the current session, and requests the Working Group to continue its work at the forty-ninth session in accordance with its mandate and methods of work;

2. *Also expresses its appreciation* to States and international organizations and institutions that have undertaken activities in implementation of the programme for the activities for the second term (1993-1994) of the Decade, including sponsoring conferences on various subjects of international law;

3. *Invites* all States and international organizations and institutions referred to in the programme to provide, update or supplement information on activities they have undertaken in implementation of the programme, as appropriate, to the Secretary-General, as well as to submit their views on possible activities for the next term of the Decade;

4. *Takes note with appreciation*, in this respect, of the International Conference on the Protection of War Victims, held at Geneva from 30 August to 1 September 1993, and its Final Declaration adopted on 1 September 1993,[a] as an important means for reaffirming, strengthening and promoting international humanitarian law, and reminds all States of their responsibility to respect and ensure respect for international humanitarian law in order to protect the victims of war;

5. *Requests* the Secretary-General to submit, on the basis of information received under paragraph 3 above a report to the General Assembly at its forty-ninth session on the implementation of the programme, together with views on possible activities for the next term of the Decade;

6. *Also requests* the Secretary-General to supplement his report, as appropriate, with new information on the activities of the United Nations relevant to the progressive development of international law and its codification, and to submit it to the General Assembly on an annual basis;

7. *Encourages* States to disseminate at the national level, as appropriate, information contained in the report of the Secretary-General;

8. *Appeals* to States, international organizations and non-governmental organizations working in this field and to the private sector to make financial contributions or contributions in kind for the purpose of facilitating the implementation of the programme;

9. *Once again requests* the Secretary-General to bring to the attention of States and international organizations and institutions working in the field of international law the programme annexed to resolution 47/32;

10. *Decides* that a United Nations congress on public international law should be held in 1995, as proposed in part III of the report of the Working Group, and requests the Secretary-General to proceed with the preparations for the congress and keep the Member States informed of the status of the preparations;

11. *Expresses its appreciation* of the work of the group of experts on the protection of the environment in times of armed conflict, conducted under the auspices of the International Committee of the Red Cross, and of the report prepared by the International Committee;

12. *Invites* all States to review the draft guidelines for military manuals and instructions on the protection of the environment in times of armed conflict annexed to the report of the International Committee of the Red Cross and to provide their comments thereon to the International Committee, either directly or through the Secretary-General, no later than 31 March 1994;

13. *Welcomes* the intention of the International Committee of the Red Cross to draw up a new version of the guidelines for military manuals, taking into account the comments made by States on the report of the Secretary-General containing information received from the International Committee, and notes that the International Committee is ready to convene, if need be, a meeting of government experts for that purpose;

14. *Requests* the Secretary-General to invite the International Committee of the Red Cross to report on activities undertaken by it and other relevant bodies with regard to the protection of the environment in times of armed conflict, and to submit the information received in the report to be prepared under paragraph 5 above to the General Assembly at its forty-ninth session;

15. *Decides* to include in the provisional agenda of its forty-ninth session the item entitled "United Nations Decade of International Law".

General Assembly resolution 48/30

9 December 1993   Meeting 73   Adopted without vote

Approved by Sixth Committee (A/48/611) without vote, 29 November (meeting 38); 71-nation draft (A/C.6/48/L.16); agenda item 142.

Sponsors: Algeria, Argentina, Australia, Austria, Belgium, Benin, Bolivia, Brazil, Bulgaria, Chile, Colombia, Costa Rica, Cuba, Czech Republic, Denmark,

[a]A/48/742.

Ecuador, Egypt, El Salvador, Ethiopia, Finland, Germany, Ghana, Greece, Guatemala, Guyana, Hungary, India, Indonesia, Iran, Ireland, Italy, Japan, Jordan, Kenya, Libyan Arab Jamahiriya, Madagascar, Malaysia, Mali, Mexico, Mongolia, Morocco, Myanmar, Nepal, New Zealand, Nigeria, Peru, Philippines, Poland, Portugal, Qatar, Republic of Korea, Republic of Moldova, Romania, Russian Federation, Senegal, Sierra Leone, Slovakia, Spain, Sudan, Thailand, Trinidad and Tobago, Tunisia, Uganda, Ukraine, United Arab Emirates, United Republic of Tanzania, Uruguay, Viet Nam, Zaire, Zambia, Zimbabwe.

Financial implications. Secretary-General, A/C.6/48/L.20.
Meeting numbers. GA 48th session: 6th Committee 31, 32, 38; plenary 73.

UN Programme for the teaching and study of international law

In response to a 1991 General Assembly request,[23] the Secretary-General submitted a November 1993 report[24] on the implementation of the United Nations Programme of Assistance in the Teaching, Study, Dissemination and Wider Appreciation of International Law in 1992-1993, within the framework of the United Nations Decade of International Law.

During the period under review, the United Nations Office of Legal Affairs (OLA) carried out activities in the fields of public international law, international trade law and the law of the sea and ocean affairs. Two sessions of the Geneva International Law Seminar were held during the biennium (see below).

Activities of the United Nations Commission on International Trade Law (UNCITRAL) included a national seminar on international commercial arbitration (Mexico City, 20 and 21 February 1992), the UNCITRAL Congress on the theme of uniform commercial law in the twenty-first century (New York, 18-22 May 1992), a fifth UNCITRAL symposium on international trade law (Vienna, 12-16 July 1993), and national seminars on international trade law in Bangladesh, Indonesia, Pakistan, Poland, Slovenia, Sri Lanka, Thailand and Ukraine. Seminars were also planned for Argentina, Azerbaijan, Belarus, Brazil, Georgia, Kyrgyzstan, Mongolia, the Republic of Moldova and Uzbekistan (see also below, under "International economic law").

The United Nations Institute for Training and Research (UNITAR) provided training on procedures for the settlement of commercial disputes, legal aspects of debt management, and the promotion of cooperation in environment-development negotiations. It also continued to issue publications and disseminate information on various aspects of international law.

A number of publications on international law were issued by the United Nations Educational, Scientific and Cultural Organization, which also created several chairs of international law, with a view to strengthening teaching, training and research in developing countries through inter-university cooperation. Under the United Nations/UNITAR international law fellowship programme, 19 fellowships were awarded in 1992 and 20 in 1993 for courses and seminars at The Hague Academy of International Law (Netherlands). The fellowships were for six weeks and were followed by either three months of training in legal departments of the various United Nations bodies or participation in the International Law Seminar or other special seminars organized by UNITAR. As of April 1993, all aspects of the fellowship programme were financed by OLA. Financing of the Programme of Assistance in general continued to come from appropriations from the regular budget and from voluntary contributions to the Programme's trust fund.

Subject to the availability of new funds, the Secretary-General recommended the continuation of the International Law Seminar, the Hamilton Shirley Amerasinghe Memorial Fellowship programme on the law of the sea, the dissemination of legal documents, and steps to promote training and assistance in international trade law. He also recommended that the number of fellowships awarded under the fellowship programme in international law be evaluated, that consideration be given to providing advisory services and lectures through sending experts to various regions, and that States and international organizations be encouraged to expand their activities under the Programme of Assistance.

The Advisory Committee on the Programme of Assistance held its twenty-seventh session on 10 December 1992 and its twenty-eighth session on 29 October 1993. In 1993, the Committee approved the Secretary-General's recommendations for further implementation of the Programme.

International Law Seminar

Pursuant to a 1991 General Assembly resolution,[25] the twenty-eighth session of the International Law Seminar for postgraduate students of international law and young professors or government officials dealing with international law, was held at Geneva from 1 to 19 June 1992.[24] There were 21 participants, mostly from developing countries, and four United Nations/UNITAR fellows. The twenty-ninth session (Geneva, 1-18 June 1993), held pursuant to a 1992 Assembly resolution,[26] was attended by 24 of the selected candidates and one fellowship holder.

The participants of both sessions attended meetings of the International Law Commission (ILC). Four working groups were established at the 1992 Seminar to deal with the relationship between the International Criminal Court (ICC) and the Security Council, sources of law to be applied by ICC, the initiation of proceedings before ICC and the conferment of jurisdiction on ICC. In 1992, Argentina, Austria, Cyprus, Denmark, Finland,

France, Hungary, Jamaica, Morocco, Sweden, Switzerland and the United Kingdom had awarded, through voluntary contributions, 15 full fellowships and one partial fellowship to participants from developing countries. In 1993, 15 full fellowships and 3 partial fellowships were made available by Austria, Cyprus, Denmark, Germany, Ireland, Mexico, Norway, Sweden, Switzerland and the United Kingdom. Since the Seminar's inception in 1964, fellowships had been awarded to 342 of the 643 participants, representing 150 nationalities.

In 1993, the General Assembly appealed for voluntary contributions to the Seminar in its resolutions on the work of ILC (see PART FOUR, Chapter II) and on the Programme of Assistance.

GENERAL ASSEMBLY ACTION

On 9 December, the General Assembly, on the recommendation of the Sixth Committee, adopted **resolution 48/29** without vote.

United Nations Programme of Assistance in the Teaching, Study, Dissemination and Wider Appreciation of International Law

The General Assembly,

Recalling paragraph 17 of its resolution 46/50 of 9 December 1991, paragraph 1 of section IV of the annex to its resolution 45/40 of 28 November 1990 and paragraph 1 of section IV of the annex to its resolution 47/32 of 25 November 1992,

Taking note with appreciation of the report of the Secretary-General on the implementation of the United Nations Programme of Assistance in the Teaching, Study, Dissemination and Wider Appreciation of International Law and the guidelines and recommendations on future implementation of the Programme within the framework of the United Nations Decade of International Law, which were adopted by the Advisory Committee on the Programme and are contained in section III of that report,

Bearing in mind that the encouragement of the teaching, study, dissemination and wider appreciation of international law is one of the main objectives of the United Nations Decade of International Law, as declared in its resolution 44/23 of 17 November 1989 and further expanded in section IV of the programme for the activities to be commenced during the first term (1990-1992) of the Decade, which is contained in the annex to resolution 45/40, and in section IV of the programme for the activities for the second term (1993-1994) of the Decade, contained in the annex to resolution 47/32,

Considering that international law should occupy an appropriate place in the teaching of legal disciplines at all universities,

Noting with appreciation the efforts made by States at the bilateral level to provide assistance in the teaching and study of international law,

Convinced, nevertheless, that States and international organizations and institutions should be encouraged to give further support to the Programme and increase their activities to promote the teaching, study, dissemination and wider appreciation of international law, in particular those activities which are of special benefit to persons from developing countries,

Reaffirming its resolutions 2464(XXIII) of 20 December 1968, 2550(XXIV) of 12 December 1969, 2838(XXVI) of 18 December 1971, 3106(XXVIII) of 12 December 1973, 3502(XXX) of 15 December 1975, 32/146 of 16 December 1977, 36/108 of 10 December 1981 and 38/129 of 19 December 1983, in which it stated or recalled that in the conduct of the Programme it was desirable to use as far as possible the resources and facilities made available by Member States, international organizations and others, as well as its resolutions 34/144 of 17 December 1979, 40/66 of 11 December 1985, 42/148 of 7 December 1987, 44/28 of 4 December 1989 and 46/50, in which, in addition, it expressed or reaffirmed the hope that, in appointing lecturers for the seminars to be held within the framework of the fellowship programme in international law, account would be taken of the need to secure representation of major legal systems and balance among various geographical regions,

1. *Approves* the guidelines and recommendations contained in section III of the report of the Secretary-General and adopted by the Advisory Committee on the United Nations Programme of Assistance in the Teaching, Study, Dissemination and Wider Appreciation of International Law, in particular those designed to achieve the best possible results in the administration of the Programme within a policy of maximum financial restraint;

2. *Authorizes* the Secretary-General to carry out in 1994 and 1995 the activities specified in his report, including the provision of:

(*a*) A number of international law fellowships in both 1994 and 1995, to be determined in the light of the overall resources for the Programme and to be awarded at the request of Governments of developing countries;

(*b*) A minimum of one scholarship in both 1994 and 1995 under the Hamilton Shirley Amerasinghe Memorial Fellowship on the Law of the Sea, subject to the availability of new voluntary contributions made specifically to the fellowship fund;

(*c*) Subject to the overall resources for the Programme, assistance in the form of a travel grant for one participant from each developing country, who would be invited to possible regional courses to be organized in 1994 and 1995;

and to finance the above activities from provisions in the regular budget, when appropriate, as well as from voluntary financial contributions earmarked for each of the activities concerned, which would be received as a result of the requests set out in paragraphs 14, 15, and 16 below;

3. *Expresses its appreciation* to the Secretary-General for his constructive efforts to promote training and assistance in international law within the framework of the Programme in 1992 and 1993, in particular for the organization of the twenty-eighth and twenty-ninth sessions of the International Law Seminar, held at Geneva from 1 to 19 June 1992 and 1 to 18 June 1993, respectively, and for the activities of the Office of Legal Affairs of the Secretariat related to the fellowship programme in international law and to the

Hamilton Shirley Amerasinghe Memorial Fellowship on the Law of the Sea, carried out, respectively, through its Codification Division and its Division for Ocean Affairs and the Law of the Sea;

4. *Requests* the Secretary-General to consider the possibility of admitting, for participation in the various components of the Programme of Assistance, candidates from countries willing to bear the entire cost of such participation;

5. *Also requests* the Secretary-General to consider the relative advantages of using available resources and voluntary contributions for regional, subregional or national courses, as against courses organized within the United Nations system;

6. *Welcomes*, in particular, the publication, in a single volume and in all official languages of the Organization, of the *Summaries of the Judgments, Advisory Opinions and Orders of the International Court of Justice (1948-1991)*, carried out through the joint efforts of the Codification Division of the Office of Legal Affairs and its secretariat for the Programme of Assistance and of the Registry of the International Court of Justice;

7. *Invites* interested States to consider the option of financing the translation and publication of the Judgments of the International Court of Justice;

8. *Welcomes* the efforts undertaken by the Office of Legal Affairs to bring up to date the United Nations *Treaty Series* and the *United Nations Juridical Yearbook*;

9. *Expresses its appreciation* to the United Nations Institute for Training and Research for its participation in the Programme through the activities described in the report of the Secretary-General;

10. *Also expresses its appreciation* to the United Nations Educational, Scientific and Cultural Organization for its participation in the Programme through the activities described in the report of the Secretary-General;

11. *Further expresses its appreciation* to the Hague Academy of International Law for the valuable contributions it has made to the Programme by enabling selected candidates under the international law fellowship programme to attend its annual international law courses and by providing facilities for seminars organized under the fellowship programme in international law in conjunction with the Academy courses and for its constructive efforts in organizing the regional training and refresher course held at Harare in 1993;

12. *Notes with appreciation* the contributions made by the Hague Academy of International Law to the teaching, study, dissemination and wider appreciation of international law, and calls upon Member States and interested organizations to give favourable consideration to the appeal of the Academy for a continuation of and, if possible, an increase in their financial contributions in order to enable it to carry on with the above-mentioned activities, in particular the summer courses, regional courses and programmes of the Centre for Studies and Research in International Law and International Relations;

13. *Urges* all States and relevant international organizations, whether regional or universal, to make all possible efforts to implement the goals and carry out the activities contemplated in section IV of the programme of activities for the second term (1993-1994) of the United Nations Decade of International Law, dealing with the encouragement of the teaching, study, dissemination and

wider appreciation of international law and contained in the annex to its resolution 47/32;

14. *Requests* the Secretary-General to continue to publicize the Programme and periodically to invite Member States, universities, philanthropic foundations and other interested national and international institutions and organizations, as well as individuals, to make voluntary contributions towards the financing of the Programme or otherwise to assist in its implementation and possible expansion;

15. *Reiterates its request* to Member States and to interested organizations and individuals to make voluntary contributions, *inter alia*, for the International Law Seminar, for the fellowship programme in international law and for the Hamilton Shirley Amerasinghe Memorial Fellowship on the Law of the Sea, and expresses its appreciation to those Member States, institutions and individuals which have made voluntary contributions for this purpose;

16. *Urges* in particular all Governments to make voluntary contributions for the organization of regional refresher courses in international law by the United Nations Institute for Training and Research, especially with a view to covering the amount needed for the financing of the daily subsistence allowance for up to twenty-five participants in each regional course, thus alleviating the burden on prospective host countries and making it possible for the Institute to continue to organize the regional courses;

17. *Also requests* the Secretary-General to report to the General Assembly at its fiftieth session on the implementation of the Programme during 1994 and 1995 and, following consultations with the Advisory Committee on the United Nations Programme of Assistance in the Teaching, Study, Dissemination and Wider Appreciation of International Law, to submit recommendations regarding the execution of the Programme in subsequent years;

18. *Decides* to include in the provisional agenda of its fiftieth session the item entitled "United Nations Programme of Assistance in the Teaching, Study, Dissemination and Wider Appreciation of International Law."

General Assembly resolution 48/29

9 December 1993   Meeting 73   Adopted without vote

Approved by Sixth Committee (A/48/608) without vote, 29 November (meeting 38); 19-nation draft (A/C.6/48/L.17); agenda item 139.
Sponsors: Bangladesh, Cuba, Cyprus, Ethiopia, Ghana, India, Iran, Kenya, Malaysia, Mexico, Netherlands, Nigeria, Rwanda, Senegal, Sudan, Trinidad and Tobago, United Republic of Tanzania, Zambia, Uruguay.
Meeting numbers. GA 48th session: 6th Committee 33, 38; plenary 73.

REFERENCES

(1)A/48/1. (2)YUN 1992, p. 35. (3)A/48/33 & Corr.1. (4)YUN 1992, p. 1005, GA res. 47/38, 25 Nov. 1992. (5)A/AC.182/L.65/Rev.1. (6)A/AC.182/L.72/Rev.1. (7)A/AC.182/L.76/Rev.1. (8)A/AC.182/L.77. (9)YUN 1992, p. 1005. (10)A/AC.182/L.75. (11)YUN 1992, p. 38. (12)A/48/573-S/26705. (13)YUN 1992, p. 1007, GA res. 47/35, 25 Nov. 1992. (14)A/48/26. (15)YUN 1947-48, p. 199, GA res. 169(II), 31 Oct. 1947. (16)YUN 1992, p. 1008, GA res. 47/32, annex, 25 Nov. 1992. (17)GA res. 44/23, 17 Nov. 1989. (18)A/48/312. (19)A/48/435. (20)A/C.6/48/L.9. (21)YUN 1992, p. 991, GA res. 47/37, 25 Nov. 1992. (22)A/48/269. (23)YUN 1991, p. 850, GA res. 46/50, 9 Dec. 1991. (24)A/48/580. (25)YUN 1991, p. 848, GA res. 46/54, 9 Dec. 1991. (26)YUN 1992, p. 989, GA res. 47/33, 25 Nov. 1992.

International economic law

In 1993, legal aspects of international economic law continued to be considered by UNCITRAL and by the Sixth Committee of the General Assembly.

International trade law

Report of UNCITRAL

At its twenty-sixth session (Vienna, 5-23 July 1993), UNCITRAL adopted the Model Law on Procurement of Goods and Construction, which it annexed to its report,[1] and a draft Guide to Enactment of the Model Law. The Commission also examined legal issues in electronic data interchange; guarantees and stand-by letters of credit; case law on UNCITRAL texts (CLOUT); UNCITRAL's future programme of work; the coordination of work on trade law; the status of legal texts as at 13 July 1993;[2] training and assistance; and relevant General Assembly resolutions. The Commission noted the publication of a bibliography[3] of recent writings related to its work as well as the user guide for CLOUT—the system of collecting and disseminating information on court decisions and arbitral awards relating to conventions and model laws emanating from UNCITRAL's work—and the first CLOUT compilation of abstracts summarizing such decisions and awards.

As in previous years, UNCITRAL's annual report was forwarded to the United Nations Conference on Trade and Development (UNCTAD) for comments.

Report of the Secretary-General. In response to a 1992 General Assembly request,[4] the Secretary-General submitted an August 1993 report[5] on travel assistance to enable Commission members from least developed countries (LDCs) to attend meetings of UNCITRAL and its working groups, and on the feasibility of holding consecutive meetings of those working groups to lessen travel expenses. The Secretary-General drew attention to UNCITRAL's discussion on the rationalization of its work at its 1993 session. It was observed that the holding of consecutive working group meetings was impracticable and would not result in savings on travel costs since delegations were usually composed of different experts, according to the nature of the work assigned to each working group, and different members of the UNCITRAL secretariat were normally assigned to service each working group. It was also noted that, if working groups met consecutively, experts might be away from their duty stations for too long. The Secretary-General also

observed that the expert representation of developing countries in the Commission's meetings and working groups remained very low. He said that barely one third of the Commission members from the developing world had been able to attend all working group meetings and he suggested that the General Assembly finalize consideration of the matter in 1993.

GENERAL ASSEMBLY ACTION

On 14 September, the General Assembly, by **decision 47/473**, deferred consideration of granting travel assistance to LDCs and other developing countries that were members of UNCITRAL until its forty-eighth session. On 9 December, in **resolution 48/32**, the Assembly requested the Secretary-General to establish a trust fund for the Commission to grant travel assistance to members from developing countries and decided to continue considering the question of granting travel assistance to members from LDCs at their request and in consultation with the Secretary-General.

Unification of trade law

Procurement

In 1993, UNCITRAL considered the draft Model Law on Procurement of Goods and Construction, adopted by its Working Group on the New International Economic Order (NIEO) in 1992,[6] as well as Secretariat notes containing pertinent comments by Governments,[7] proposed amendments to the draft,[8] and a draft Guide to Enactment of the Model Law.[9]

By a 16 July decision,[1] the Commission adopted the UNCITRAL Model Law on Procurement of Goods and Construction and annexed it to its 1993 report. UNCITRAL requested the Secretary-General to transmit the text of the Model Law, together with the Guide to Enactment of the Model Law, to Governments and other interested bodies. It recommended that all States give favourable consideration to the Model Law when enacting or revising their laws, in view of the need for improvements and uniformity in procurement laws and practice. The Commission further discussed and adopted the Guide to Enactment, subject to implementation of proposed changes.

UNCITRAL also considered a Secretariat note on the proposed elaboration of model statutory provisions on the procurement of services.[10] It agreed that its Working Group on NIEO should proceed with their preparation and that they should be presented in a manner suitable both for States that had adopted the Model Law and for those considering simultaneous adoption of provisions for goods, construction and services.

At its sixteenth session (Vienna, 6-17 December),[11] the Working Group on NIEO considered the draft model legislative provisions on procurement of services and identified pertinent changes to the Model Law, including the addition of an article on special procedures for procurement of services. It decided to complete a final draft text at its March 1994 session.

GENERAL ASSEMBLY ACTION

On 9 December, the General Assembly, on the recommendation of the Sixth Committee, adopted **resolution 48/33** without vote.

Model Law on Procurement of Goods and Construction of the United Nations Commission on International Trade Law

The General Assembly,

Recalling its resolution 2205(XXI) of 17 December 1966, by which it created the United Nations Commission on International Trade Law with a mandate to further the progressive harmonization and unification of the law of international trade and in that respect to bear in mind the interests of all peoples, in particular those of developing countries, in the extensive development of international trade,

Noting that procurement constitutes a large portion of public expenditure of most States,

Noting also that a model law on procurement establishing procedures designed to foster integrity, confidence, fairness and transparency in the procurement process will also promote economy, efficiency and competition in procurement and thus lead to increased economic development,

Being of the opinion that the establishment of a model law on procurement that is acceptable to States with different legal, social and economic systems contributes to the development of harmonious international economic relations,

Being convinced that the Model Law on Procurement of Goods and Construction of the United Nation Commission on International Trade Law will significantly assist all States, including developing countries and States whose economies are in transition, in enhancing their existing procurement laws and formulating procurement laws where none presently exist,

1. *Takes note with satisfaction* of the completion and adoption by the United Nations Commission on International Trade Law of the Model Law on Procurement of Goods and Construction together with the Guide to Enactment of the Model Law;

2. *Recommends* that, in view of the desirability of improvement and uniformity of the laws of procurement, States give favourable consideration to the Model Law when they enact or revise their procurement laws;

3. *Recommends also* that all efforts be made to ensure that the Model Law together with the Guide become generally known and available.

General Assembly resolution 48/33

9 December 1993   Meeting 73   Adopted without vote

Approved by Sixth Committee (A/48/613) without vote, 19 November (meeting 33); 20-nation draft (A/C.6/48/L.7); agenda item 144.

Sponsors: Argentina, Australia, Austria, Belarus, Canada, Cyprus, Denmark, France, Germany, Hungary, Italy, Kenya, Kyrgyzstan, Nigeria, Poland, Russian Federation, Spain, Thailand, Ukraine, United States.

Meeting numbers. GA 48th session: 6th Committee 3, 4, 33; plenary 73.

Carriage of goods by sea

In July,[1] UNCITRAL noted that the liability regime of the 1978 United Nations Convention on the Carriage of Goods by Sea (Hamburg Rules),[12] which entered into force on 1 November 1992, coexisted with liability regimes based on the 1924 International Convention for the Unification of Certain Rules relating to Bills of Lading (Hague Rules) and recommended promotion of the unification of regimes on the basis of the Hamburg Rules.

GENERAL ASSEMBLY ACTION

On 9 December, the General Assembly, on the recommendation of the Sixth Committee, adopted **resolution 48/34** without vote.

United Nations Convention on the Carriage of Goods by Sea, 1978 (Hamburg Rules)

The General Assembly,

Reaffirming its conviction that the progressive harmonization and unification of international trade law, in reducing or removing legal obstacles to the flow of international trade, would significantly contribute to universal economic cooperation among all States on a basis of equality, equity and common interest, and to the elimination of discrimination in international trade and, thereby, to the well-being of all peoples,

Recalling the entry into force, on 1 November 1992, of the United Nations Convention on the Carriage of Goods by Sea, 1978 (Hamburg Rules),

1. *Invites* all States to consider becoming parties to the United Nations Convention on the Carriage of Goods by Sea, 1978 (Hamburg Rules);

2. *Requests* the Secretary-General to continue to make increased efforts to promote wider adherence to the Convention.

General Assembly resolution 48/34

9 December 1993   Meeting 73   Adopted without vote

Approved by Sixth Committee (A/48/613) without vote, 19 November (meeting 33); 9-nation draft (A/C.6/48/L.8); agenda item 144.

Sponsors: Australia, Austria, Cyprus, Hungary, Kyrgyzstan, Morocco, Nigeria, Sweden, Thailand.

Meeting numbers. GA 48th session: 6th Committee 3, 4, 33; plenary 73.

Electronic data interchange

In July,[1] UNCITRAL had before it the report of the Working Group on Electronic Data Interchange on its twenty-fifth session (New York, 4-15 January).[13] The Working Group discussed the legal aspects of electronic data interchange (EDI), including the scope and form of uniform rules on EDI, definitions and general provisions, form requirements, the obligations of parties, the formation of contracts, and liability and risk.

The Commission expressed hope that the Working Group would proceed expeditiously with the preparation of statutory provisions on EDI and decided that the Secretariat should continue to monitor pertinent legal developments in other organizations.

The Working Group continued its consideration of draft provisions for uniform rules on the legal aspects of EDI and related means of trade data communication at its twenty-sixth session (Vienna, 11-22 October).[14]

Guarantees and stand-by letters of credit

In July,[1] UNCITRAL considered the reports of its Working Group on International Contract Practices at its eighteenth (Vienna, 30 November–11 December 1992)[15] and nineteenth (New York, 24 May–4 June 1993)[16] sessions, at which it examined articles 1 to 8 and 9 to 17 of a draft Convention on International Guaranty Letters. UNCITRAL noted that the Working Group had requested the Secretariat to prepare a revised draft of articles 1 to 17 and had agreed to consider whether independent guarantees and stand-by letters of credit should be dealt with in separate parts of the Convention after determining which provisions were applicable exclusively to those issues. The Working Group was requested to complete its work before UNCITRAL's 1995 session.

At its twentieth session (Vienna, 22 November–3 December 1993),[17] the Working Group examined articles 18 to 27 of the draft Convention and completed a final reading of articles 1 and 2(1).

Future programme of work

In July, UNCITRAL considered proposals for its possible future work,[18] made at the UNCITRAL Congress on International Trade Law in 1992.[19] Acting on those proposals, the Commission requested the Secretariat to prepare for its 1994 session draft guidelines for pre-hearing conferences on arbitral proceedings. The Secretariat was also asked to prepare feasibility studies on unification work in the field of assignment of claims and on harmonized rules to deal with cross-border insolvencies. UNCITRAL emphasized the relevance of the Build, Operate and Transfer (BOT) project financing concept to its work, and noted the Secretariat's efforts to monitor the preparation by the United Nations Industrial Development Organization of guidelines for the development, negotiation and contracting of BOT projects.

Coordination of work

In July, UNCITRAL had before it a report of the Secretary-General describing the activities of international organizations related to the harmonization and unification of international trade law.[20] Noting slow progress in the drafting of an international code of conduct on the transfer of technology (see PART THREE, Chapter VII), the Commission sug-

gested cooperation with UNCTAD to expedite completion of that project. It was also suggested that UNCITRAL monitor UNCTAD's work on restrictive business practices (see PART THREE, Chapter IV), since the issues pertinent to that topic were of a legal rather than trade policy nature. The Commission noted with satisfaction its close cooperation with the Asian-African Legal Consultative Committee and the International Institute for the Unification of Private Law.

Training and assistance

UNCITRAL had before it, in July, a Secretariat note on training and technical assistance,[21] describing seminars and symposia on international trade law that had taken place since the Commission's 1992 session. In addition to national seminars in eight countries, the Fifth UNCITRAL Symposium on International Trade Law was held in Vienna (12-16 July 1993). The UNCITRAL secretariat provided regional organizations with technical assistance to review the laws of member States with a view to their harmonization and unification and participated in a workshop on public procurement systems and consultations on international commercial arbitration (Singapore, 16 November) and a postgraduate course in international trade law (Turin, Italy, 10-11 May). It also participated in a number of conferences and meetings held by other organizations (see also above, under "UN Programme for the teaching and study of international law").

In considering the note, the Commission emphasized the need for contributions from States to the UNCITRAL Trust Fund for Symposia, to meet increasing demands for training and technical assistance, especially in developing countries and newly independent States. The need for increased cooperation and coordination with development assistance agencies, particularly those within the United Nations system was also noted.

GENERAL ASSEMBLY ACTION

On 9 December, the General Assembly, on the recommendation of the Sixth Committee, adopted **resolution 48/32** without vote.

Report of the United Nations Commission on International Trade Law on the work of its twenty-sixth session

The General Assembly,

Recalling its resolution 2205(XXI) of 17 December 1966, by which it created the United Nations Commission on International Trade Law with a mandate to further the progressive harmonization and unification of the law of international trade and in that respect to bear in mind the interests of all peoples, in particular those of developing countries, in the extensive development of international trade,

Reaffirming its conviction that the progressive harmonization and unification of international trade law, in reducing or removing legal obstacles to the flow of international trade, especially those affecting the developing countries, would significantly contribute to universal economic cooperation among all States on a basis of equality, equity and common interest and to the elimination of discrimination in international trade and, thereby, to the well-being of all peoples,

Stressing the value of participation by States at all levels of economic development and from different legal systems in the process of harmonizing and unifying international trade law,

Having considered the report of the United Nations Commission on International Trade Law on the work of its twenty-sixth session,

Mindful of the valuable contribution being rendered by the United Nations Commission within the framework of the United Nations Decade of International Law,

Having considered also the report of the Secretary-General,

Concerned about the continuing relatively low incidence of expert representation from developing countries at sessions of the Commission and particularly of its working groups during recent years, due in part to inadequate resources to finance the travel of such experts,

1. *Takes note with appreciation* of the report of the United Nations Commission on International Trade Law on the work of its twenty-sixth session;

2. *Welcomes* the ongoing work of the Commission and appreciates the many proposals on possible future work made during the Congress on International Trade Law of the United Nations Commission on International Trade Law, held in New York from 18 to 22 May 1992, and, in this connection:

(a) Welcomes the decision of the Commission to request its secretariat to commence work in preparation of guidelines for pre-hearing conferences in arbitral proceedings;

(b) Also welcomes the decision of the Commission to continue considering the other proposals made during the Congress as part of its future programme of work;

3. *Reaffirms* the mandate of the Commission, as the core legal body within the United Nations system in the field of international trade law, to coordinate legal activities in this field in order to avoid duplication of effort and to promote efficiency, consistency and coherence in the unification and harmonization of international trade law and, in this connection recommends that the Commission, through its secretariat, continue to maintain close cooperation with the other intergovernmental and non-governmental organizations, including regional organizations, active in the field of international trade law;

4. *Also reaffirms* the importance, in particular for developing countries, of the work of the Commission concerned with training and assistance in the field of international trade law and the desirability of seminars and symposia sponsored by the Commission to provide such training and assistance, and in this connection:

(a) Expresses its appreciation to the Commission for organizing seminars at Bangkok; Jakarta; Lahore, Pakistan; Colombo; Dhaka; Kiev; Warsaw; and Rogaska Slatina, Slovenia, and for assisting the Pacific Economic Cooperation Council with its initiative to promote harmonization of international trade law in the Asia-Pacific region, and to the Governments whose contributions enabled the seminars to take place;

(b) Urges Governments, the relevant United Nations organs, organizations, institutions and individuals to make voluntary contributions to the trust fund for the United Nations Commission on International Trade Law symposia and, where appropriate, to the financing of special projects, and otherwise to assist the secretariat of the Commission in financing and organizing seminars and symposia, in particular in developing countries, and in the award of fellowships to candidates from developing countries to enable them to participate in such seminars and symposia;

(c) Appeals to the United Nations Development Programme and other United Nations bodies responsible for development assistance to support the training and technical assistance programme of the Commission and to cooperate and coordinate their activities with those of the Commission;

5. *Requests* the Secretary-General, in order to ensure full participation by all Member States in the sessions of the Commission and its working groups, to establish a separate trust fund for the Commission to grant travel assistance to developing countries that are members of the Commission, at their request and in consultation with the Secretary-General;

6. *Decides*, in order to ensure full participation by all Member States in the sessions of the Commission and its working groups, to continue its consideration in the competent Main Committee during the forty-eighth session of the General Assembly on granting travel assistance, within existing resources, to the least developed countries that are members of the Commission, at their request and in consultation with the Secretary-General;

7. *Expresses its appreciation* to the Commission for organizing the Fifth Symposium on International Trade Law of the United Nations Commission on International Trade Law at Vienna from 12 to 16 July 1993 during its twenty-sixth session;

8. *Stresses* the importance of bringing into effect the conventions emanating from the work of the Commission for the global unification and harmonization of international trade law, and to this end invites States that have not yet done so to consider signing, ratifying or acceding to these conventions;

9. *Requests* the Secretary-General to submit a report on the implementation of paragraphs 5 and 6 above to the General Assembly at its forty-ninth session.

General Assembly resolution 48/32

9 December 1993   Meeting 73   Adopted without vote

Approved by Sixth Committee (A/48/613) without vote, 19 November (meeting 33); 32-nation draft (A/C.6/48/L.6); agenda item 144.

Sponsors: Argentina, Australia, Austria, Azerbaijan, Belarus, Brazil, Bulgaria, Canada, Cyprus, Czech Republic, Denmark, Finland, France, Germany, Greece, Hungary, Italy, Kenya, Kyrgyzstan, Morocco, Myanmar, Nigeria, Norway, Poland, Russian Federation, Singapore, Spain, Sweden, Thailand, Turkey, Ukraine, Venezuela.

Meeting numbers. GA 48th session: 6th Committee 3, 4, 33; plenary 73.

Legal aspects of the new international economic order

In a July report,[22] the Secretary-General submitted the views and comments of three Member States and four international organizations on the principles and norms of international law relating to the new international economic order to be given priority attention by the Working Group established by the General Assembly in 1991[23] to consider the issue. UNITAR had issued a study on the codification and progressive development of such principles and norms.[24]

On 23 November,[25] the Sixth Committee was informed that the Working Group had considered the Secretary-General's report at its 17 November meeting and proposed that consideration of the item be deferred so that Governments and international organizations could reflect on a new document, possibly based on a re-examination of the UNITAR study. The Working Group had agreed that, if the item could be reformulated to address the principles of international economic relations in the context of international economic cooperation and development, it might be possible to retain it on the Assembly's agenda.

On 9 December, the General Assembly decided to resume consideration of the legal aspects of international economic relations at its fifty-first (1996) session and to include the item on progressive development of the principles and norms of international law relating to the new international economic order in the provisional agenda of that session (**decision 48/412**).

REFERENCES

[1]A/48/17. [2]A/CN.9/381. [3]A/CN.9/382. [4]YUN 1992, p. 1015, GA res. 47/34, 25 Nov. 1992. [5]A/48/296. [6]YUN 1992, p. 1014. [7]A/CN.9/376 & Add.1,2. [8]A/CN.9/377. [9]A/CN.9/375. [10]A/CN.9/378/Add.1. [11]A/CN.9/389. [12]YUN 1978, p. 955. [13]A/CN.9/373. [14]A/CN.9/387. [15]A/CN.9/372. [16]A/CN.9/374 & Corr.1. [17]A/CN.9/388. [18]A/CN.9/378 & Add.1-5. [19]YUN 1992, p. 1012. [20]A/CN.9/380. [21]A/CN.9/379. [22]A/48/268. [23]YUN 1991, p. 854, GA res. 46/52, 9 Dec. 1991. [24]YUN 1984, p. 1115. [25]A/C.6/48/SR.35.

PART FIVE

Administrative and budgetary questions

Chapter I

United Nations financing and programming

In 1993, the United Nations continued to operate under difficult financial conditions brought about by the non-payment of assessed contributions by a number of Member States. The problem was exacerbated by the rapid increase of peace-keeping activities throughout the world.

The General Assembly authorized the Secretary-General to cover costs for peace-keeping operations from the support account, in an amount not to exceed $16,376,250 for the period 1 January to 30 June 1994 (resolution 48/226).

The Assembly approved appropriations for 1994-1995 totalling $2.6 billion. Appropriations for 1994 alone were $1.2 billion. Income estimates for the biennium amounted to $477 million (48/231 A-C).

On the basis of recommendations of the Committee on Contributions, the Assembly determined the assessed contributions of six new Member States. It requested the Committee to take certain criteria into account when determining the scale of assessments for 1995-1997, and requested it to review thoroughly all aspects of the scale methodology (48/223 A-C).

The Assembly accepted the financial reports and audited financial statements for the year ended 31 December 1992 of funds administered by the United Nations High Commissioner for Refugees and of the United Nations Institute for Training and Research, and approved the recommendations of the Board of Auditors. It urged a number of United Nations bodies to implement the Board's 1992 recommendations and again requested them to report on their implementation. The Assembly took note of the United Nations system accounting standards, adopted by the Administrative Committee on Coordination, and invited the Board of Auditors to report on the implications of a possible extension of the term of office of Board members from three to four or six years (48/216 A-D).

UN financing

Financial situation

The precarious financial plight of the United Nations, brought on by the non-payment of dues by a number of Member States, was the subject of several reports of the Secretary-General in 1993. They restated earlier warnings that, unless timely and adequate payments were made by Member States, the financial outlook was bleak. The United Nations regular budget had ended the year 1992 with cash depletion, and had depended on borrowing from other funds and on advance payments of 1993 assessments to provide a small cash balance. A number of peace-keeping missions had experienced shortfalls in collections, forcing them to borrow from the newly established Peace-keeping Reserve Fund, although that was not the Fund's primary purpose, the Secretary General reported in June 1993[1] in response to a 1992 General Assembly resolution.[2] His report gave a broad financial picture of the Organization at the end of May 1993 and projected results for the rest of the year if the trends continued.

By 31 May, only 10 Member States had paid their peace-keeping dues in full and only 8 of them had also paid their regular budget assessments in full. At that time, unpaid contributions totalled $2,235.7 million, almost two thirds of which was owed by permanent Security Council members.

At the end of 1992, unpaid dues to the regular budget were $500.4 million, $61 million over the unpaid balance a year earlier. In January 1993, following adoption in December 1992 of the revised appropriations for 1992-1993,[3] $1,070 million was assessed for the regular budget. Unpaid contributions totalled $938.7 million, of which $366.2 million was outstanding for 1992 and prior years and $572.5 million related to 1993. The balance due was equivalent to 88 per cent of the regular budget assessment for 1993. At the end of May, 47 Member States had fully paid their regular budget assessments for 1993 and prior years.

The cash-flow situation of peace-keeping operations continued to be one of the most serious problems confronting the Organization. Unpaid dues to peace-keeping missions were $1,297 million as at 31 May 1993—double the amount in September 1992.

Ten peace-keeping operations were funded from assessed contributions: United Nations Disengagement Observer Force (UNDOF), United Nations Interim Force in Lebanon (UNIFIL), United Nations Angola Verification Mission (UNAVEM/UNAVEM II), United Nations Iraq-Kuwait Observation Mission (UNIKOM),

United Nations Mission for the Referendum in Western Sahara (MINURSO), United Nations Observer Mission in El Salvador (ONUSAL), United Nations Transitional Authority in Cambodia (UNTAC), United Nations Protection Force (UNPROFOR), United Nations Operation in Somalia (UNOSOM) and United Nations Operation in Mozambique (ONUMOZ). Two completed peace-keeping operations—United Nations Advance Mission in Cambodia (UNAMIC) and United Nations Observer Group in Central America (ONUCA)—had contributions outstanding; those balances had been consolidated into UNTAC and ONUSAL. For two other completed missions— United Nations Iran-Iraq Military Observer Group (UNIIMOG) and United Nations Transition Assistance Group (UNTAG)—accounts were still open and outstanding contributions being sought. The United Nations Peace-keeping Force in Cyprus (UNFICYP), financed from voluntary contributions since its inception in 1964,[4] was to be financed in part from assessments as from 15 June 1993 according to Security Council **resolution 831(1993)**.

Non-payments caused several missions to experience severe cash shortages, with UNIFIL, UNPROFOR, UNTAC, UNAVEM, ONUSAL and UNIKOM being the most affected. In response to their needs, temporary advances were made from the Peace-keeping Reserve Fund (see below). The lending capacity of the Fund being exhausted at one point in 1993, UNTAC had to borrow from the regular budget; this loan was repaid as soon as contributions to UNTAC permitted. The regular budget had lent $17.3 million to the operations by mid-year: $15.3 million to UNAVEM and $2 million to ONUSAL.

One of the consequences of the Organization's recurrent cash-flow problems was the delay in payments to countries which contributed troops and equipment to various missions. Based on troop-strength reports for the period ending 30 April 1993, the United Nations owed them about $284.3 million: $101.4 million in respect of UNIFIL; $118.8 million for UNPROFOR; and $64.1 million for UNTAC.

With large amounts of dues unpaid as at 31 May and in view of the uncertainties about the scope and scale of peace-keeping activities, it was difficult to make cash projections for the rest of the year. At the end of May, usable cash balances on hand, including the Peace-keeping Reserve Fund, were about $725 million, of which $550 million was linked to peace-keeping and $175 million to the regular budget. According to projections, the regular budget would receive between $400 million and $450 million in the remaining seven months. With expenditures for that time projected at $650 million to $700 million within the approved regular budget, it appeared that the regular budget would fall short of cash by the end of 1993.

The Secretary-General therefore urged Member States to improve their payment pattern to cover the shortfalls; otherwise, the regular budget would have to borrow from other funds at the beginning of August and continue to do so thereafter. Severe cash difficulties were also expected for most, if not all, of the newer and larger peace-keeping operations by the end of the year. If the operations continued at projected levels, expenditures for the rest of the year might exceed $1,600 million, notably for UNOSOM and UNPROFOR. With payments projected to fall far below that sum, the resulting negative cash flow would raise the financial crisis of the United Nations to unprecedented levels.

In October,[5] the Secretary-General submitted a report containing an analysis of the Organization's financial situation, according to which there was no change in the pattern of payments and a slightly improved, though still below average, collection pattern as at 30 September. With three months left in 1993, unpaid dues to the regular budget were $783.8 million, of which $304.2 million was due for 1992 and prior years and $479.6 million related to 1993. The total amount outstanding was the equivalent of 72 per cent of the 1993 regular budget assessment.

With the recent increase in United Nations membership, a larger number of Member States were assessed in 1993. Eighteen Members— Australia, Botswana, Canada, Denmark, Finland, France, Iceland, Ireland, Kuwait, Liechtenstein, Luxembourg, Micronesia, Namibia, Netherlands, New Zealand, Norway, Singapore and Sweden— paid their 1993 assessments in full within 30 days. By 30 September, only 62 Members had paid in full, while an unprecedented 116 still had outstanding contributions. Fifty-nine Members had made no contribution at all in 1993, a much larger number than before.

Assessments levied for peace-keeping missions since September 1992 were two-and-one-half times the 1993 assessment for the regular budget. The unpaid balance also doubled, with $1,502.4 million outstanding for peace-keeping as at 30 September 1993. Outstanding assessments to the regular budget and peace-keeping combined were $2,286.2 million. A factor contributing to the magnitude of unpaid dues was that assessments for eight operations, totalling $708.4 million, were issued only in September 1993.

Contributions received during the first two weeks of October totalled $593.7 million, of which $235.8 million was for the regular budget and $357.9 million for peace-keeping. As at 14 October, the amount unpaid was $1,692.5 million: $548 million for the regular budget and $1,144.5 million for peace-keeping.

The cash flow of the Organization remained critical, the Secretary-General noted. After cash balances declined further in July and August, certain Member States made larger than expected payments in September. In 1993, cash was depleted in January and again in August/September. Borrowing from peace-keeping funds had been required for a total of 46 days during those months, with a maximum of $15 million. Cash balances were minimal in March and September and were expected to be so again in December. During only four months of the year was there enough cash on hand to meet the requirements of the next month in full.

With the collection of peace-keeping contributions falling far short of requirements, cash management was dominated by the need to maintain sufficient funds on hand for immediate operational requirements. As a result, payments to troop-contributing countries were inevitably delayed. However, even after delaying such payments, not every peace-keeping operation was fully solvent throughout the year. Five operations—UNAVEM, ONUSAL, UNIKOM, UNTAC and UNPROFOR—had to borrow funds at one time or another. As at 30 September, $80.7 million was owed by UNAVEM, ONUSAL and UNTAC to the Peace-keeping Reserve Fund, UNTAG and UNIIMOG.

The Secretary-General reported an increasing trend in recent months, whereby he was authorized to incur peace-keeping costs without a corresponding authority to assess Member States; the result put an increased strain on the Organization's reserves and rendered its financial situation even more difficult.

According to the Secretary-General, the financial reserves at the disposal of the Organization amounted to $672.6 million, consisting mainly of the Working Capital Fund, the Special Account and the Peace-keeping Reserve Fund. Unpaid assessments of over $2,200 million as at 30 September far surpassed available reserves. Together, the Working Capital Fund, at a level of $100 million unchanged since 1982, and the Peace-keeping Reserve Fund, set at $150 million (see below), provided a funding equivalent of 4.3 per cent of combined regular budget and peace-keeping appropriations, which corresponded to just over two weeks of expenditures.

The low level of available reserves and the delays in the assessment and collection of contributions from Member States for peace-keeping operations resulted in certain operations being unable to meet their obligations. As at 30 September, the United Nations owed troop-contributing States some $605 million, considerably more than in previous years.

Concluding, the Secretary-General remarked that the financial situation, which might have a crippling effect on the Organization's capacity to continue its operations, had caused him to intervene personally at high levels to seek timely payments from Member States. He also addressed the General Assembly, warning of the dire consequences of the Organization's running out of money. The volume and complexity of United Nations operations, in respect of both the regular budget and peace-keeping, were so great that there were few if any contingency measures that could be taken to substitute for the single operational imperative of United Nations financing, namely, that Member States paid their assessed contributions in full and on time.

According to an addendum issued in November,[6] outstanding contributions to the regular budget and peace-keeping totalled $1,574.8 million as at 31 October 1993.

The Secretary-General transmitted to the Assembly an April report on financing an effective United Nations,[7] prepared by an Independent Advisory Group on United Nations Financing, under the co-chairmanship of Shijuro Ogata and Paul Volcker and sponsored by the Ford Foundation. Among the report's recommendations for alleviating the financial condition of the Organization were: requiring Member States to pay dues in four quarterly instalments; charging interest on dues not paid on time; not authorizing the Organization to borrow commercially; stopping the borrowing of funds from peace-keeping accounts to cover regular budget costs, after a reliable means to pay its bills was set up; and increasing the Working Capital Fund from $100 million to $200 million. The Group proposed that the regular budget assessment scale be based on a 3- rather than a 10-year average of Member States' gross domestic product (GDP). It recommended that the United Nations create a revolving reserve fund for peace-keeping set at $400 million and consider the merits of a unified peace-keeping budget, financed from a single annual assessment, and that the Secretary-General be permitted to obligate up to 20 per cent of the estimated cost of a peace-keeping mission once it was approved by the Security Council.

In a November report,[8] the Secretary-General addressed broad policy issues concerning the question of establishing a secure financial base for the Organization in order for it to fulfil its responsibilities effectively and in a timely fashion. He also responded in detail to the recommendations of the Independent Advisory Group, which, he said, merited thorough review by the Assembly.

With regard to the recommendation to divide United Nations expenditures into three categories—with the regular budget financed by assessed contributions, peace-keeping by a separate assessment, and humanitarian and development activities financed largely by voluntary contributions—the Secretary-General agreed that the categorization of current expenditures under those three headings remained broadly valid. At the same time, he noted that the regular budget included resource provisions which partially covered the cost of back-stopping for peace-keeping operations, and that one such operation—UNFICYP—was currently assessed for a cost that exceeded the voluntary contributions received. Also, support-cost income emanating from peace-keeping and voluntary contributions was funding a number of programme support posts and activities. On the financing of peace-keeping operations by separate assessment, he noted that the Assembly since 1973 had authorized an ad hoc scale which recognized the special responsibilities of the permanent members of the Security Council.[9] Concerning humanitarian activities, the Secretary-General stated that in recent years, while not moving away completely from the position that they should be financed through voluntary contributions, Member States had included some amounts related to those activities in peace-keeping operations' budgets, UNOSOM being the first of them. In accordance with a 1991 Assembly resolution,[10] a Central Emergency Revolving Fund, financed by voluntary contributions, was established. As at 30 September 1993, 27 countries and one non-governmental organization had contributed $48.8 million to the Fund, while seven United Nations organizations had obtained advances from it in the amount of $52.7 million. Some $22.4 million had been reimbursed to the Fund, leaving a cash balance of $19.5 million.

The Secretary-General expressed full support for the recommendations that the consensus procedure for approving the regular budget should be continued and that all countries must pay their assessed dues on time and in full. With regard to possible quarterly payment by Member States, instead of an annual lump sum, he said it was feasible only if adopted as part of other changes agreed to by Member States that would ensure that the Organization had adequate cash reserves at all times; if adopted in isolation, that recommendation was not likely to improve cash flow, but could result in collection of less money at the beginning of the year.

Concerning the charging of interest on late payments and depositing such interest income in the Working Capital Fund, the Secretary-General recalled that he had made similar proposals in the past. The recommendation that countries that appropriated their United Nations contribution late in the year should do so earlier would help improve the Organization's financial situation, the Secretary-General said. He also agreed with the recommendations that the United Nations should stop borrowing from peace-keeping accounts to cover regular budget expenditures, once a reliable way to pay its bills was established, and that

the level of the Working Capital Fund should be raised from $100 million to $200 million; in his view, the Fund should be set at $300 million in 1994, representing 25 per cent of the annual regular budget. He considered generally useful the recommendation that the United Nations should deposit budgetary surpluses owed to Member States with regular budget arrears into the Working Capital Fund, but added that a further analysis of its implications would be necessary.

As to the recommendation that he not be given authority to borrow commercially, the Secretary-General maintained his position that he should be allowed to do so, but only when no funds were available under any of the assessed activities. If the proposal were approved, any interest on commercial loans to be paid by the United Nations could be matched by the interest charged to those Member States that did not pay their contribution in full and on time, making such borrowing necessary. The recommendation to base the regular budget assessment rate on a 3-year rather than 10-year average of Member States' GDP should be referred to the Committee on Contributions.

The Secretary-General noted that the recommendations that the international community should accept significantly increased peace-keeping costs and that Governments should consider financing those costs from their national defence budgets were addressed to Member States. He supported the recommendation that a much larger revolving fund, set at $400 million, should be established, as well as the recommendations for a unified peace-keeping budget, financed by a single annual assessment, and for a regular appropriation for peace-keeping training. He concurred with the thrust of the recommendation that he should be permitted to obligate up to 20 per cent of the initial estimated cost of a peace-keeping operation once it was approved by the Security Council; in his view, however, he should be permitted to obligate up to one third of the initial estimated cost, which amount should be assessed on Member States. Regarding the recommendation that all Member States with above average per capita incomes, except for the permanent Security Council members, be included in the B group of developed nations, which paid the same rate of assessment for peace-keeping and the regular budget, he stated that such placement rested with the Assembly.

He would draw the attention of the concerned agencies and programmes to the recommendation that all United Nations programmes funded by voluntary contributions should have their administrative expenditures financed by assessed contributions and that the voluntarily funded agencies should seek a larger portion of their funding from multi-year, negotiated pledges.

Concerning additional financing through non-governmental sources, which the Group regarded as neither practical nor desirable, the Secretary-General remarked that he did not see any inconsistency in attempting to raise funds from such sources through the trust fund mechanism, as long as the activities to be financed were consistent with the Organization's objectives and mandates.

GENERAL ASSEMBLY ACTION

On the recommendation of the Fifth (Administrative and Budgetary) Committee, the General Assembly adopted **resolution 48/220** on 23 December without vote.

Improving the financial situation of the United Nations

The General Assembly,

Recalling its resolution 47/215 of 23 December 1992,

Taking note of the reports of the Secretary-General and the relevant recommendations contained in his report A/48/565 and Corr.1,

Recognizing the need for a continuing dialogue at the intergovernmental level to analyse possible solutions for the improvement of the financial situation of the Organization,

1. *Reaffirms* the obligation of Member States to pay assessed contributions promptly and in full;

2. *Recognizes* that non-payment of assessed contributions in full and on time has damaged and continues to damage the ability of the Organization to implement its activities effectively;

3. *Decides* to continue consideration of this item and, *inter alia*, the above-mentioned reports, at its resumed forty-eighth session.

General Assembly resolution 48/220

23 December 1993   Meeting 87   Adopted without vote

Approved by Fifth Committee (A/48/756) without vote, 11 December (meeting 37); draft by Vice-Chairman (A/C.5/48/L.9); agenda item 124.
Meeting numbers. GA 48th session: 5th Committee 20, 22-25, 37; plenary 87.

Financing of peace-keeping operations

Following consideration of 1992 reports by the Secretary-General on several peace-keeping operations, the Advisory Committee on Administrative and Budgetary Questions (ACABQ), at its special 1993 summer session (New York, 3 May–29 June), made a number of general observations and recommendations.[11] It believed that the presentation of the reports needed to be improved and that the time had come for a different type of report providing for more evaluation and analysis in terms of major expenditure items. Performance reports should contain the proposed and actual staffing tables, indicating the numbers of troops, military observers, police monitors, international contractual personnel and proposed deployment schedules, as well as related savings and overexpenditures. Proposals for new posts should be well justified, as should requests for all additional requirements, with clear rationales for establishing posts at the Assistant Secretary-General (ASG) and Under-Secretary-General (USG) levels. The Committee pointed to the need to limit the volume of documentation, revamp reports and make them more concise, with less narrative, but more tables and graphics, substantiating financial performance and estimates, and with an improved presentation of voluntary contributions and a clear definition of the role of assessed budgets and requirements for humanitarian and development activities, specifying short- and long-term needs.

To help reduce peace-keeping costs, ACABQ reiterated its recommendation that the Secretary-General should request Member States to provide additional civilian personnel for non-core functions. It requested a review of entitlements of mission personnel and suggested a number of cost-saving measures. It called for urgent measures to enhance cost-effectiveness and efficiency of procurement procedures. It saw a need for standard guidelines for financial arrangements and for the disposition of assets following liquidation of an operation. It called for strengthening the internal audit function both in the mission area and at Headquarters and for timely submission of reports. The procedure for requesting commitment authority also needed to be addressed.

In view of the lack of a clear response to a number of its observations and recommendations, ACABQ recommended that the Secretary-General submit a comprehensive report on all issues affecting the successful operation and administration of peace-keeping missions, together with proposals to enhance cost-effectiveness and efficiency and recommendations regarding non-payment or late payment of contributions. It requested him also to make recommendations regarding possible 12-month financial periods and a standardization of performance periods to help simplify the task of the budgetary organs.

GENERAL ASSEMBLY ACTION (September)

On 14 September 1993, the General Assembly, on the recommendation of the Fifth Committee, adopted **resolution 47/218 B** without vote.

Administrative and budgetary aspects of the financing of the United Nations peace-keeping operations

The General Assembly,

Reaffirming the role of the General Assembly in accordance with Article 17 of the Charter of the United Nations,

Having considered the report of the Advisory Committee on Administrative and Budgetary Questions, as well as the introductory statement by its Chairman, on the administrative and budgetary aspects of the financing of the United Nations peace-keeping operations,

1. *Decides* that the administrative, budgetary and management aspects of the financing of the peace-keeping operations shall be reviewed urgently and thoroughly with a view to improving the efficiency and cost-effectiveness of the peace-keeping operations, as well as to providing enhanced budgetary control by Member States;

2. *Endorses* the report of the Advisory Committee on Administrative and Budgetary Questions;

3. *Requests* the Secretary-General to submit a comprehensive report to the General Assembly at its forty-eighth session on all issues which affect the successful operation and administration of the peace-keeping operations, including steps taken to comply with the report of the Advisory Committee and taking into account the views expressed by Member States during the resumed forty-seventh session of the Assembly;

4. *Also requests* the Secretary-General, in this context, to provide an overview of the administrative guidelines applicable to the management of peace-keeping operations;

5. *Further requests* the Secretary-General, in this connection, to report to the General Assembly at its forty-eighth session on arrangements relating to the reimbursement to troop-contributing countries for death, injury, disability and illness resulting from service in the peace-keeping operations, as well as to submit recommendations on arrangements for standardization of compensation, including direct payment to the beneficiaries.

General Assembly resolution 47/218 B

14 September 1993   Meeting 110   Adopted without vote

Approved by Fifth Committee (A/47/832/Add.1) without vote, 3 September (meeting 74); draft by Netherlands (A/C.5/47/L.46); agenda item 124.
Meeting numbers. GA 47th session: 5th Committee 4-10, 34, 42, 45, 50, 52, 68, 69, 70, 72, 74; plenary 110.

Report of the Secretary-General. Pending a full review by the Assembly at its resumed forty-eighth session of separate reports on the financing of peace-keeping operations, the Secretary-General presented in December 1993 a consolidated report on the following operations, requesting financial authority for maintaining them until 30 April 1994: UNDOF, UNIFIL, UNAVEM II, UNIKOM, MINURSO, ONUSAL, UNTAC, UNPROFOR, UNOSOM II, ONUMOZ, UNFICYP, United Nations Observer Mission in Georgia, United Nations Observer Mission Uganda-Rwanda (UNOMUR), United Nations Mission in Haiti, United Nations Observer Mission in Liberia, United Nations Assistance Mission for Rwanda and United Nations Military Liaison Team in Cambodia.[(12)]

ACABQ report. In December,[(13)] ACABQ noted that its comments with regard to each operation were contained in separate reports. In its understanding, the Secretary-General's report represented a consolidation for ease of reference only and did not imply an attempt to submit a consolidated budget for peace-keeping operations. It expressed regret at the late submission of documentation and believed that all reports on peace-keeping should be submitted in a more timely manner. ACABQ therefore requested the Secretary-General to take corrective measures to prevent a recurrence of such a situation and to submit all outstanding reports by 15 January 1994.

The Committee pointed out that in a number of instances its recommendations on certain operations were only up to 31 March rather than 30 April and were for commitment authority rather than appropriation in view of the fact that the relevant budgets had not been considered and approved. In a number of cases, the amount recommended for assessment was less than that recommended for commitment in view of available cash balances or the unencumbered balances of appropriations. Also, the amounts recommended in future would take into account performance during the initial months.

ACABQ stressed that its agreement to consider the Secretary-General's report and make recommendations derived solely from the need to provide for continuation of the operations in question and should not be viewed as a precedent.

GENERAL ASSEMBLY ACTION (December)

On 23 December 1993, the General Assembly, on the recommendation of the Fifth Committee, adopted **resolution 48/227** without vote.

Administrative and budgetary aspects of the financing of the
United Nations peace-keeping operations
The General Assembly,

Having considered the report of the Secretary-General and the related reports of the Advisory Committee on Administrative and Budgetary Questions on the financing of seventeen peace-keeping operations—United Nations Disengagement Observer Force, United Nations Interim Force in Lebanon, United Nations Angola Verification Mission, United Nations Iraq-Kuwait Observation Mission, United Nations Mission for the Referendum in Western Sahara, United Nations Observer Mission in El Salvador, United Nations Transitional Authority in Cambodia, United Nations Protection Force, United Nations Operation in Somalia II, United Nations Operation in Mozambique, United Nations Peace-keeping Force in Cyprus, United Nations Observer Mission in Georgia, United Nations Observer Mission Uganda-Rwanda, United Nations Mission in Haiti, United Nations Observer Mission in Liberia, United Nations Assistance Mission for Rwanda, and United Nations Military Liaison Team in Cambodia— as well as the report of the Advisory Committee on the question under consideration,

Recalling the report of the Advisory Committee on Administrative and Budgetary Questions, which, *inter alia*, addressed the timely submission of reports to the General Assembly,

Expressing its concern that the Secretariat has until now not given the desirable level of attention to the views of the General Assembly in this matter,

Mindful of the fact that peace-keeping requires a reliable and assured funding base for the success of operations and that troop contributors need to be reimbursed on a more regular basis, and that the continuation of irregular budgetary practices may further complicate this situation,

1. *Endorses* the observations and recommendations contained in the report of the Advisory Committee on Administrative and Budgetary Questions;

2. *Notes with concern* that the approach based on the compilation of the abbreviated statements of requirements of peace-keeping operations in a series of separate subsections in the report of the Secretary-General does not allow for proper budgetary scrutiny by the General Assembly;

3. *Notes* that such a compilation of the requirements of the operations represents an exceptional measure in order to expedite the approval of resources necessary for the maintenance of the operations and does not constitute a precedent for the future;

4. *Decides*, therefore, that peace-keeping submissions will continue to be considered on an individual basis until such time as the General Assembly decides otherwise;

5. *Expresses regret* at the worsening trend of the late submission of full cost estimates for the peace-keeping operations despite the deadlines set for the submission of such cost estimates by the General Assembly and assurances by the Secretariat, and notes that none of the cost estimates has been submitted on time at the current session;

6. *Reaffirms its concern* expressed in its resolutions 47/41 C, 47/208 B and 47/210 B of 14 September 1993 about the delays in the submission of budget documents until well into the financing period of the peace-keeping operations, which have contributed to the financial difficulties of the operations;

7. *Takes note* of the reasons advanced by the Secretary-General for the delays in submission, in paragraphs 1 and 2 of his report, and considers that the circumstances related to the regular budget are not related to the timely submission of the cost estimates for peace-keeping operations;

8. *Expresses its concern* about the apparent lack of adequate financial planning relating to peace-keeping;

9. *Emphasizes* that the General Assembly can appropriate resources only on the basis of a detailed consideration and approval of the cost estimates submitted to it by the Secretary-General;

10. *Expresses its concern also* about the insufficient provisions for external audit, and reiterates its request to the Board of Auditors to review its need for resources to perform its functions adequately;

11. *Decides* to consider, on an exceptional basis, the report of the Secretary-General and to take action thereon solely in order to provide for the continuation of the operations in question, without it constituting a precedent, on the understanding that the measures under paragraphs 13 to 15 below will be duly implemented;

12. *Decides also* to take action on each operation within the framework of the present resolution in a separate decision at its current session;

13. *Requests* the Secretary-General to take prompt and definitive corrective measures to prevent the recurrence of delays in the submission of full cost estimates and to report to the General Assembly at its current session, through the Advisory Committee on Administrative and Budgetary Questions, on the implementation of those measures;

14. *Decides further* that all performance and financial reports shall be submitted by 31 January 1994 to Member States, notwithstanding paragraph 10 of resolution 47/41 C, paragraph 10 of resolution 47/208 B, paragraph 15 of resolution 47/234 of 14 September 1993 and paragraph 7 of resolution 47/224 C of 14 September 1993, so that the Assembly will be able to consider appropriating the required resources no later than 31 March 1994 for each operation, well in advance of the commencement of its financial period;

15. *Requests* the Secretary-General to improve the presentation and type of information contained in performance and financial reports, in accordance with recommendations of the Advisory Committee on Administrative and Budgetary Questions in its report;

16. *Decides* to review the matter at its resumed forty-eighth session.

General Assembly resolution 48/227

23 December 1993   Meeting 87   Adopted without vote

Approved by Fifth Committee (A/48/807) without vote, 22 December (meeting 46); draft by Japan (A/C.5/48/L.14), orally revised; agenda item 138 *(a)*. *Meeting numbers.* GA 48th session: 5th Committee 42, 44, 45, 46; plenary 87.

Apportionment of costs

In 1993, the General Assembly again considered the question of placement of Member States into the groups for the apportionment of peace-keeping expenses. First specified in 1973[9] and again in March 1989,[14] the groups were subsequently adjusted by the Assembly in December 1989[15] and in 1991.[16] The original four groups consisted of (1) permanent members of the Security Council; (2) specifically named economically developed Member States not permanent members of the Council; (3) economically less developed Member States; and (4) economically less developed Member States that were specifically named.

By **decision 47/472** of 14 September 1993, the General Assembly deferred to its forty-eighth session further consideration of the issue of placing Member States into groups. On 24 September, it decided to include the item under administrative and bugetary aspects of the financing of the United Nations and to consider the relocation of Belarus and Ukraine from the group of economically developed to less developed Member States. Member States which joined the Organization in 1993 also had to be assigned to the appropriate group.

Belarus and Ukraine requested that they be moved in communications dated 12 August[17] and 16 August,[18] respectively, citing economic hardship since the breakup of the Soviet Union. By a letter of 18 October,[19] Madagascar requested that it be reclassified under the fourth group instead of the third.

GENERAL ASSEMBLY ACTION

In December, the General Assembly adopted **decision 48/472** without vote.

**Administrative and budgetary aspects of the
financing of the
United Nations peace-keeping operations**

At its 87th plenary meeting, on 23 December 1993, the General Assembly, on the recommendation of the Fifth Committee, decided:

(a) To continue during its current session the mandate of the open-ended working group of the Fifth Committee established pursuant to Assembly resolution 47/218 of 23 December 1992;

(b) As an ad hoc arrangement, in respect of the apportionment of peace-keeping expenses, that:

(i) Andorra and Monaco should be included in the group of Member States set out in paragraph 3 (b) of Assembly resolution 43/232 of 1 March 1989, and that their contributions to the financing of peace-keeping operations should be calculated in accordance with the relevant resolution to be adopted by the Assembly regarding the scale of assessments;

(ii) The former Yugoslav Republic of Macedonia should be included in the group of Member States set out in paragraph 3 (c) of resolution 43/232, and that its contributions to the financing of peace-keeping operations should be calculated in accordance with the relevant resolution to be adopted by the Assembly regarding the scale of assessments;

(iii) Eritrea and Madagascar should be included in the group of Member States set out in paragraph 3 (d) of resolution 43/232, and that their contributions to the financing of peace-keeping operations should be calculated in accordance with the relevant resolution to be adopted by the Assembly regarding the scale of assessments;

(c) To consider and decide during its current session the placement of the Czech Republic and Slovakia in the appropriate group as set out in resolution 43/232 for the apportionment of peace-keeping expenses;

(d) To consider, as an exceptional measure, any arrears of Belarus and Ukraine arisen in 1992 and 1993 and for 1994 in the financing of peace-keeping operations as being due to conditions beyond their control, and, accordingly, that the question of the applicability of Article 19 of the Charter of the United Nations related to the loss of voting rights in the General Assembly in this respect would not arise.

General Assembly decision 48/472

Adopted without vote

Approved by Fifth Committee (A/48/807/Add.1) without vote, 21 December (meeting 45); draft by Rapporteur (A/C.5/48/L.12), based on informal consultations; agenda item 138 (b).
Meeting numbers. GA 48th session: 5th Committee 27, 28, 45; plenary 87.

Support account for peace-keeping operations

In an October 1993 report,[20] the Secretary-General discussed the support account for peace-keeping operations, established in 1990 and financed through the inclusion in the respective budgets of an amount equalling 8.5 per cent—a rate derived from the aggregate standard cost of the then existing overload posts—of the cost of the mission's civilian staff component. Introduction of the provision based on a percentage rate eliminated the disproportionate distribution of the costs for overload posts among peace-keeping opera-

tions. The account was intended to meet the needs at Headquarters for the support of ongoing missions, as well as some of the additional workload associated with the pre-implementation phase of prospective ones. As at 1 May 1993, there were 194 posts financed from the support account, of which 91 were at the Professional levels and above and 103 in the General Service category. The equivalent of 50 additional posts (15 Professional and 35 General Service) was provided under general temporary assistance.

The report addressed the feasibility of annualized budget estimates for supporting peace-keeping operations, as well as the methodology for distributing support costs and for their funding, and set forth resource requirements for 1993 and 1994. In view of the transparency of the existing arrangements, the Secretary-General suggested that the current methodology be maintained subject to certain refinements and adjustments, such as the introduction of an annualized budget estimate.

For the remainder of 1993, the Secretary-General sought approval for an additional 199—93 Professional and 106 General Service—posts, 72 of which were authorized by ACABQ. The total cost of the 393 positions in 1994 was estimated at $29.9 million.

For 1993, total projected expenditure under the support account amounted to some $24.5 million, against recorded income of $22.7 million, including an unencumbered 1992 balance of some $2.9 million. Additional estimated income of $4.7 million was projected for 1993. Expenditure for 1994 was estimated at $35.4 million, including an anticipated credit of some $450,000 for relocation and renovation cost, reimbursed to the account from the regular budget.

ACABQ, in December 1993,[21] recommended authorization of $16,376,250 to cover costs borne by the account for the six months from 1 January to June 1994. That amount included provisions for general temporary assistance, overtime, travel and common services, in addition to the cost of the 194 posts approved prior to May 1993 and the 148 posts recommended by ACABQ (instead of the 199 proposed), pending submission of another report by the Secretary-General in early 1994.

GENERAL ASSEMBLY ACTION

On 23 December 1993, the General Assembly, on the recommendation of the Fifth Committee, adopted **resolution 48/226** without vote.

Support account for peace-keeping operations
The General Assembly,

Recalling its resolutions 45/258 of 3 May 1991 and 47/218 A of 23 December 1992,

Having considered the report of the Secretary-General on the support account for peace-keeping operations and the related report of the Advisory Committee on Administrative and Budgetary Questions,

Reaffirming the need to continue to improve the administrative and financial management of peace-keeping operations,

1. *Endorses*, on a provisional basis, the observations and recommendations contained in the report of the Advisory Committee on Administrative and Budgetary Questions relating to the funding from the support account of the posts in the Department of Peace-keeping Operations, the Field Operations Division, the Internal Audit Division and, within the Department of Administration and Management, the Peace-keeping Financing Division and the Purchase and Transportation Service (excluding the six General Service posts proposed), subject to the policy decisions to be taken during the current session of the General Assembly after consideration of the report of the Secretary-General requested in paragraph 6 of the report of the Advisory Committee;

2. *Authorizes* the Secretary-General to enter into commitments to cover costs borne by the support account in an amount not to exceed 16,376,250 United States dollars for the period from 1 January to 30 June 1994, as recommended by the Advisory Committee in paragraph 34 of its report;

3. *Requests* the Secretary-General to submit a report to the General Assembly at its resumed forty-eighth session in accordance with the recommendations contained in paragraph 6 of the report of the Advisory Committee;

4. *Decides* to include in the provisional agenda of its forty-ninth session the item entitled "Administrative and budgetary aspects of the financing of the United Nations peace-keeping operations".

General Assembly resolution 48/226

23 December 1993   Meeting 87   Adopted without vote

Approved by Fifth Committee (A/48/807) without vote, 21 December (meeting 45); draft by Vice-Chairman (A/C.5/48/L.32); agenda item 138 *(a)*.
Meeting numbers. GA 48th session: 5th Committee 42, 44, 45; plenary 87.

Peace-keeping Reserve Fund

On 1 January 1993, a Peace-keeping Reserve Fund was set up under the authority of the Secretary-General, in accordance with a 1992 General Assembly decision,[22] as a cash-flow mechanism to ensure the Organization's rapid response to the needs for peace-keeping operations. The level of the Fund was set at $150 million.

In February 1993,[23] the Secretary-General informed the Assembly of the establishment of the Fund and that an initial sum of $59 million—$42 million from the special account of UNTAG and $17 million from UNIIMOG—had been transferred to it. The remaining $91 million was to be financed from the amount retained under a 1987 Assembly resolution on the Organization's financial emergency, under which the provisions of certain financial regulations were suspended in respect of surpluses.[24]

A total of $32.9 million had been loaned from the Fund to peace-keeping missions that had temporary cash shortages: $15.9 million to UNAVEM,

$12 million to UNIKOM and $5 million to ONUSAL, leaving an available balance of $16.6 million.

In November 1993,[25] the Secretary-General reported that $47 million had been transferred to the Fund from the account of UNTAG and $17.2 million from that of UNIIMOG upon their closure on 31 December 1992. The Fund also received a voluntary contribution of $400,000 from Switzerland and interest income of another $400,000. The balance of $85.5 million required for full funding was to be derived from the payment of arrears to the regular budget. Most of the $64.2 million transferred to the Fund between 1 January and 31 October had been used to meet the cash-flow needs of existing missions rather than for the start-up of new ones. In addition to ONUSAL, UNAVEM and UNIKOM, a loan was made to UNTAC which also experienced cash depletion, and some $0.1 million was loaned to UNOMUR for start-up costs. As at 31 October 1993, the balance in the Fund was $269,634, a balance which, the Secretary-General said, was hardly sufficient to meet needs; even if the Fund were fully funded to its established level of $150 million, it would not be sufficient to meet peace-keeping expenses for one month, which totalled some $215 million. In that context, the Secretary-General pointed to his support for the recommendation of the Independent Advisory Group on United Nations Financing (see above) that a much larger revolving fund be established at the level of $400 million.

By **decision 48/459** of 23 December, the Assembly deferred consideration of the report to its resumed forty-eighth session.

REFERENCES

[1]A/C.5/47/13/Add.1. [2]YUN 1992, p. 1021, GA res. 47/215, 23 Dec. 1992. [3]Ibid., p. 1030, GA res. 47/220 A, 23 Dec. 1992. [4]YUN 1964, p. 165, SC res. 186(1964), 4 Mar. 1964. [5]A/48/503. [6]A/48/503/Add.1. [7]A/48/460 & Corr.1. [8]A/48/565 & Corr.1. [9]YUN 1973, p. 222, GA res. 3101(XXVIII), 11 Dec. 1973. [10]YUN 1991, p. 421, GA res. 46/182, 19 Dec. 1991. [11]A/47/990. [12]A/C.5/48/40. [13]A/48/778. [14]GA res. 43/232, 1 Mar. 1989. [15]GA res. 44/192 B, 21 Dec. 1989. [16]YUN 1991, p. 129, GA res. 45/269, 27 Aug. 1991; ibid., p. 159, GA res. 46/198 A, 20 Dec. 1991. [17]A/48/315. [18]A/48/192. [19]A/C.5/48/13. [20]A/48/470. [21]A/48/757. [22]YUN 1992, p. 1022, GA res. 47/217, 23 Dec. 1992. [23]A/47/898. [24]YUN 1987, p. 1095, GA res. 42/216 A, 21 Dec. 1987. [25]A/48/622.

Efficiency review

Programme planning

In a July 1993 report,[1] the Secretary-General outlined a possible new approach to programme planning, presenting a modified planning, budgeting, monitoring and evaluation cycle, on the basis of recommendations by the Committee for Programme and Coordination (CPC) and ACABQ.[2] In 1992, CPC had recommended that in 1993 a prototype of a possible new format of the medium-term plan be presented, which would address in particular issues concerning the manageability of the drafting and revision process, including the questions of preparation and submission of documentation and the review of programme planning documents by subsidiary intergovernmental machinery. CPC's recommendations were endorsed by the General Assembly,[3] which also reaffirmed the medium-term plan as the principal policy directive of the United Nations, serving as a framework for the formulation of the biennial programme budgets.

The Secretary-General's report reflected the outcome of an ad hoc technical seminar of 23 experts (Mohonk, New York, 22-28 April 1993), all of whom were either current or past members of CPC and ACABQ, including the Chairmen. In its review of the medium-term plan, the seminar identified the following shortcomings: the plan tended to be a bottom-up aggregation of sectoral plans and strategies, rather than providing through a substantive introduction an overarching statement of purpose and direction for the Organization in a specific time-frame; little priority was given to formulation of the plan by programme managers or many Member States and, once adopted, the plan was little used or had little real impact; the link between plan and programme budget was often fairly formalistic and there were frequent repetitions between both; monitoring needed to be considerably refined; the plan's objectives were not precise enough; and much more time was spent on reviewing plans and budgets than on implementation and evaluation. The seminar also noted that peace-keeping activities had largely been excluded from the plan, a lacuna which needed correction.

It was proposed to replace the current introduction to the plan by a policy-level "Perspective" on the direction of the Organization's work, offering an overview of trends and problems, new challenges and solutions. The "Perspective" could be reviewed directly by the Assembly plenary through a working group, with a review by relevant bodies, such as the Commission on Sustainable Development, then CPC, the Economic and Social Council and the Assembly's Main Committees as an alternative. It could be prepared for an 8- to 10-year time-frame, to be amended if need arose.

The Secretary-General said the medium-term plan was used to provide a programmatic structure for the biennial budget and was a general reference to ensure that proposed activities accorded with legislative intent. However, there was a failure in the Secretariat to internalize planning as a management tool, and programme managers rarely referred to the plan once it was adopted. The medium-term programme, an intermediate-level document, should be consistent with the "Perspective" and based on approved mandates. Between the "Perspective" and the budget, duplication had to be avoided. The new planning document should set out the programme for four years instead of the current six. The specialized and regional intergovernmental bodies should play a central role in preparing the document.

The medium-term programme either could be adopted for a fixed period or could "roll", with its duration extended every two years by two years. To provide a linkage with the budget outline and the programme budget, the programme should be divided into two time-frames of two years each. It would thus be prepared, revised or extended every two years and reviewed at the same time as the budget outline. With the new approach to medium-term planning, the current system of biennial programme budgets could be retained or the presentation of annual budgets be considered.

Concluding, the Secretary-General said the Assembly might wish to make recommendations on the nature of and period to be covered by the "Perspective" document; on the medium-term programme of work; and on biennial or annual budgets and their relationship with the medium-term programme and the budget outline. He added that, subject to the Assembly's decision on those proposals, a prototype of a new format for a medium-term programme would be prepared for 1994.

Following discussion of the Secretary-General's report, CPC in October[4] reaffirmed the need for a programmatic planning tool beyond the biennial programme budget. It recommended that consideration be given to replacing the current medium-term plan by a composite document containing a perspective and a programme framework, which listed only major programmes and subprogrammes and provided guidelines against which the preparation and implementation of the programme budget would be assessed.

Contingency fund and programme budget implications

The Secretary-General, in a July 1993 report,[5] reviewed the procedures for providing statements of programme budget implications and for using and operating the contingency fund. The fund was created by the General Assembly in 1986[6] to accommodate additional mandated expenditures not provided for in the proposed programme budget. In 1987, the Assembly adopted criteria for using the fund,[7] which was set at 0.75 per cent of the overall budget. For 1990-1991, the level was the equivalent of $15 million, about $3.2 million of which remained unused at the end of the biennium. For 1992-1993, the fund was set at $18 million, about $11.7 million of which remained unused at the end of 1992. The level was maintained at 0.75 per cent for 1994-1995. The Secretary-General concluded that no changes were necessary in the procedures regarding the contingency fund and that its funding level and general operation appeared satisfactory.

Closely related to the issue of the contingency fund were, in the Secretary-General's view, the treatment of programme budget implications and revised estimates relating to the maintenance of peace and security. He recommended that statements of programme budget implications be extended to include new intergovernmental bodies and all major conferences. A contingency provision for preventive diplomacy and peacemaking activities included in the budget would make the budget more comprehensive and transparent, but would not preclude the possibility of additional requirements.

Secretariat restructuring

In connection with the restructuring of the Secretariat begun in February 1992,[8] the Secretary-General presented in March 1993 revisions to the 1992-1993 programme budget.[9] He stated that the translation into budgetary and programmatic terms of the restructuring involved the creation of new departments as well as the redeployment of posts and redistribution of resources. Accordingly, he requested, among other things, approval by the General Assembly for transfers of resources among sections of the programme budget as detailed in his report and for a revised appropriation of $2,467,775,800, i.e., $263,400 less than the amount approved by the Assembly in 1992.[10]

ACABQ, in March 1993,[11] said that a major difficulty in considering the Secretary-General's report was that it lacked context, a long-term concept or framework for the whole process of restructuring and where the restructuring of the Secretariat fit into that process. The Committee saw a need for a clear statement of an overall restructuring plan and a time-frame for its implementation. It believed that the report should have demonstrated how the proposed changes would better enable the Secretariat to respond to the relevant intergovernmental decisions, particularly to the Assembly's 1986 resolution on the review of the efficiency of the administrative and financial functioning of the United Nations,[12] and to the programme mandates entrusted to it by the Member States, and how the restructuring would achieve the management aim, as stated by

the Secretary-General, of a more responsive, cost-effective and streamlined Secretariat.

By a letter of 29 March to the Chairman of the Fifth Committee,[13] the Chairman of the Committee on Conferences noted that the purpose of the restructuring was to enhance the efficiency and functioning of the Secretariat and that it should be undertaken in a comprehensive and integrated manner and within a specified time period. He also noted that the proposed restructuring within the Department of Administration and Management would result in a gap beween the head of the Department at the USG level and heads of offices at the D-2 level. The Committee sought reassurance that the redistribution of publishing functions among three organizational units—the Office of Conference Services, the Office of General Services and the Department of Public Information (DPI)—would not result in increased costs or delays or inefficiencies in processing documentation. It also drew attention to its mandate to monitor the Organization's policy on publications and requested the Secretariat to ensure that appropriate services were provided to the Committee on Conferences through close coordination between the Office of Conference Services and DPI.

On 6 May 1993, the General Assembly, on the recommendation of the Fifth Committee, adopted **resolution 47/212 B** without vote.

Review of the efficiency of the administrative and financial functioning of the United Nations and programme budget for the biennium 1992-1993

The General Assembly,

Recalling its resolutions 41/213 of 19 December 1986, 42/211 of 21 December 1987, 43/213 of 21 December 1988, 44/200 A to C and 44/201 A and B of 21 December 1989, S-18/3 of 1 May 1990, 45/199, 45/248 A and B, 45/253 and 45/254 A to C of 21 December 1990, 45/264 of 13 May 1991, 46/232 of 2 March 1992, 46/235 of 13 April 1992, 47/199 of 22 December 1992 and 47/212 A and 47/213 of 23 December 1992,

Reaffirming its functions and powers in considering and approving the budgets of the Organization, and, in this context, its role with regard to the structure of the Secretariat and the creation, suppression and redeployment of posts financed from the regular budget of the Organization,

Reaffirming also the responsibilities of the Secretary-General as chief administrative officer of the Organization,

Recalling the Financial Regulations and Rules of the United Nations and the Regulations and Rules Governing Programme Planning, the Programme Aspects of the Budget, the Monitoring of Implementation and the Methods of Evaluation,

Reaffirming the priorities set out in the medium-term plan for the period 1992-1997 as revised and approved under the terms of its resolution 47/214 of 23 December 1992,

Noting that New York is the Headquarters and a centre of the United Nations and that there are currently three additional United Nations centres, at Geneva, Nairobi and Vienna,

Having considered the report of the Secretary-General on the revised estimates as requested by the General Assembly in resolution 47/212 A,

Having also considered the report of the Advisory Committee on Administrative and Budgetary Questions,

Having further considered the letter from the Chairman of the Committee on Conferences addressed to the Chairman of the Fifth Committee,

Taking into account the views expressed by Member States,

I

1. *Approves* a revised appropriation of 2,467,458,200 United States dollars for the biennium 1992-1993 as a result of the restructuring;

2. *Also approves*, subject to the provisions contained in the present section and in sections II and III of the present resolution, the proposals for transfers of resources among sections, as reflected in the annex to the present resolution, and concurs with the recommendations and observations of the Advisory Committee on Administrative and Budgetary Questions;

3. *Further approves* the proposals of the Secretary-General with regard to high-level posts, subject to the following modifications:

(a) Decides to defer action on the proposal of the Secretary-General to abolish the four high-level posts in the Department of Administration and Management and, in this regard, requests him to reconsider his proposals relating to these posts with a view to ensuring that the most senior officials of that Department have a degree of authority that is equivalent to that of the most senior officials in other areas of the United Nations, taking into account the observations and recommendation of the Advisory Committee and the views expressed by Member States;

(b) Requests the Secretary-General to pursue as a matter of urgency his efforts to agree with the Director-General of the General Agreement on Tariffs and Trade on a prompt appointment to the post of Executive Director of the International Trade Centre UNCTAD/GATT at its present level;

(c) Decides to defer action on the proposal of the Secretary-General to abolish the post of Under-Secretary-General of the United Nations Centre for Human Settlements (Habitat) and requests him to reconsider his proposal and to report in the context of the proposed programme budget for the biennium 1994-1995 on future secretariat support arrangements for the United Nations Environment Programme and Habitat, including the question of separate senior management arrangements for Habitat, taking into account the views and recommendations of the Commission on Human Settlements, the Governing Council of the United Nations Environment Programme and the Economic and Social Council and the views expressed by Member States;

II

1. *Stresses again* the need for a timely dialogue between Member States and the Secretary-General on the process of the restructuring of the Secretariat;

2. *Emphasizes* that the restructuring of the Secretariat should be carried out in accordance with the guidance given by the General Assembly, and with the Regulations and Rules Governing Programme Planning, the Programme Aspects of the Budget, the Monitoring of Implementation and the Methods of Evaluation and the Financial Regulations and Rules of the United Nations;

3. *Stresses* the importance of effective coordination of the activities of the departments and units responsible for economic and social issues, and notes the intention of the Secretary-General to devote his personal attention to this task and to establish appropriate internal coordination mechanisms for this purpose, with special attention to the promotion of greater coordination and complementarity in the respective activities of the United Nations, including Headquarters departments, the United Nations Conference on Trade and Development and the United Nations Development Programme, in particular in support of the programmes on Africa and the least developed countries;

4. *Reiterates* the need for the full and effective implementation of all programmes and subprogrammes as set out in the medium-term plan for the period 1992-1997, the revisions thereto, the programme budget and other relevant mandates of the General Assembly, in accordance with the Regulations and Rules Governing Programme Planning, the Programme Aspects of the Budget, the Monitoring of Implementation and the Methods of Evaluation;

5. *Notes* the indication by the Secretary-General that the further restructuring of the Secretariat in the economic and social sectors would entail the decentralization of activities to the field and to the regional commissions and stresses that his proposal relating to decentralization to the field should be in accordance with General Assembly resolution 47/199 and those proposals relating to decentralization to the regional commissions in accordance with the criteria agreed by the Assembly and the Economic and Social Council within their respective mandates and on the basis of clearly identified relative advantages;

6. *Also notes* that the modalities for the proposed integration of the Office for Project Services into the Department for Development Support and Management Services will first be considered by the Governing Council of the United Nations Development Programme and subsequently by the General Assembly in the light of a report of the Secretary-General on the work of the task force mentioned in paragraph 103 of his report, which will include the relevant financial aspects;

7. *Invites* the relevant intergovernmental bodies to report as soon as possible to the General Assembly, through the Committee on Conferences, on the overall implications of applying General Assembly resolution 40/243 of 18 December 1985 to the venues of intergovernmental bodies whose secretariats are affected by the current restructuring;

8. *Requests* the Secretary-General, in the context of the current overall restructuring process and taking into account the need to improve the effectiveness and efficiency of the Organization in accordance with the principles contained in General Assembly resolution 46/232, to review the role of the United Nations Headquarters, centres, the regional commissions and entities in the field, in particular the centres at Vienna and Nairobi,

with a view to improving the distribution of responsibilities among them, on the basis of their relative advantages;

9. *Welcomes*, in this connection, the intention of the Secretary-General, as expressed in paragraph 19 of his report, to consider the relocation of activities in order to provide a clearer purpose for each of the United Nations programmes and sharpen the substantive focus of each of the centres, and requests him to submit, in accordance with the principles and guidelines contained in General Assembly resolution 46/232, adequate proposals in the context of the proposed programme budget for the biennium 1994-1995 to reflect the status of the centre at Nairobi;

10. *Also welcomes,* in this connection, the intention of the Secretary-General, as expressed in paragraph 67 of his report, to identify, on the basis of the approaches underlying the current restructuring exercise, activities that would, in accordance with the principles and guidelines contained in General Assembly resolution 46/232, benefit from a relocation to Vienna and requests him to submit adequate proposals in the context of the proposed programme budget for the biennium 1994-1995;

11. *Requests* the Secretary-General to ensure that any future proposals relating to major changes in the organization of the Secretariat include a timetable for their implementation and, to the extent possible, are submitted in the context of the biennial proposed programme budgets;

12. *Reiterates,* in this context, its request to the Secretary-General contained in its resolution 47/212 A, section II, paragraph 6, to provide the Committee for Programme and Coordination and other concerned intergovernmental bodies with all relevant information which will enable them to identify and analyse the programmatic aspects and consequences of the restructuring of the Secretariat in their areas of competence;

III

1. *Endorses* the commitment of the Secretary-General to strengthen the role of the United Nations in international economic and social cooperation through, *inter alia,* the restructuring of the Secretariat;

2. *Notes* the commitment of the Secretary-General to ensure that the integration of activities resulting from his restructuring proposals, including the creation of the Department for Policy Coordination and Sustainable Development, the Department for Economic and Social Information and Policy Analysis and the Department for Development Support and Management Services, will lead to improved programme delivery as well as economies of scale;

3. *Requests* the Secretary-General to provide to the General Assembly at its forty-eighth session detailed and clearly identifiable information on all costs incurred and savings achieved during the biennium 1992-1993 as a result of the first and second phases of the restructuring of the Secretariat;

4. *Also requests* the Secretary-General, in implementing the restructuring of the Secretariat and in preparing the proposed programme budget for the biennium 1994-1995 on the basis, *inter alia,* of General Assembly resolution 47/213:

(*a*) To take fully into account the results of the intergovernmental review called for in General Assembly resolution 47/212 A, section II, paragraph 6, and the

implementation of the revisions to the programme budget for the biennium 1992-1993 associated with the restructuring process;

(*b*) To provide adequate resources and to identify clearly units, at appropriate levels, for the implementation of all programmes and activities, including those involved in the current phase of restructuring, in particular the programmes on the development of Africa, the least developed countries, transnational corporations, science and technology for development and social development, the newly mandated activities on the protection of global climate and the elaboration of an international convention to combat desertification, particularly in Africa;

(*c*) To strengthen the coordination of the activities on science and technology with the United Nations Development Programme for better management of the United Nations Fund for Science and Technology for Development;

(*d*) To ensure that all activities related to transnational corporations are kept integrated;

(*e*) To review the proposed activities of the new organizational entities in order to ensure that they meet the concerns expressed in paragraphs 9 and 24 of the report of the Advisory Committee on Administrative and Budgetary Questions and to reflect the outcome of this review in the proposed programme budget for the biennium 1994-1995, taking into account the fact that the presence, representation and functions of the United Nations in the field are defined in the relevant resolutions of the General Assembly;

(*f*) To propose improvements in programme delivery and the termination of activities considered obsolete or redundant for the consideration of the relevant intergovernmental bodies, in accordance with regulation 4.6 of the Regulations and Rules Governing Programme Planning, the Programme Aspects of the Budget, the Monitoring of Implementation and the Methods of Evaluation;

(*g*) To elaborate further his proposals with respect to the Department of Administration and Management and the Department of Public Information, taking fully into account the comments expressed in paragraph 33 of the report of the Advisory Committee and of the relevant decisions of the General Assembly, including resolution 47/202 C of 22 December 1992;

(*h*) To reflect all savings to be achieved and all additional costs to be incurred as a result of the restructuring, in accordance with the second paragraph of the introduction to the report of the Secretary-General and paragraphs 25 to 27 of the report of the Advisory Committee;

5. *Notes* that the resources allocated to the departments involved in the restructuring will be reviewed in the context of established procedures for the preparation of the proposed programme budget for the biennium 1994-1995 with a view to ensuring effective programme delivery, taking into account the ongoing elaboration of workload standards and other management techniques as requested in General Assembly resolution 47/212 A, section I;

6. *Invites* the Secretary-General, in the context of the implementation of the current phase of the restructuring of the Secretariat, to consider activities related to the economies in transition in accordance with the relevant mandates contained in resolutions of the General

Assembly and the observations of the Advisory Committee as expressed in paragraph 9 of its report;

7. *Also invites* the Secretary-General to ensure, in the context of the search for improved efficiency, the rationalization of the working arrangements within each department of the Secretariat in order to ensure that resources are used in the most effective way and that the programme managers are fully responsible and accountable;

8. *Requests* the Secretary-General to include in his report to the General Assembly at its forty-eighth session under the agenda item on the review of the efficiency of the administrative and financial functioning of the United Nations information on his efforts to improve the efficiency of the United Nations;

9. *Reaffirms* its request made in its resolution 47/214, section V, that the Secretary-General establish a system of responsibility and accountability of programme managers and report thereon to the General Assembly at its forty-eighth session;

10. *Concurs* with the observations of the Advisory Committee contained in paragraph 34 of its report and urges the Secretary-General to take the necessary measures to strengthen and make more effective the planning, management and administrative support within and between the departments responsible for peace-keeping operations, including the Field Operations Division, and also within the Department for Humanitarian Affairs;

11. *Also concurs* with the observations of the Advisory Committee contained in paragraphs 35 and 36 of its report and reiterates that transfers of resources between sections of the programme budget should be made in accordance with financial regulation 4.5 and financial rule 104.4;

12. *Notes* the intention of the Secretary-General to study the possible establishment of a D-3 level and requests him to take fully into account the observations and recommendations of the Advisory Committee as contained in its report and, in that context, concurs with the specific observation contained in paragraph 48 thereof;

13. *Endorses* the view of the Committee on Conferences as contained in the letter from its Chairman addressed to the Chairman of the Fifth Committee;

14. *Invites* the Secretary-General, particularly with regard to the publication policy of the Organization, to ensure the provision of appropriate support to the Committee on Conferences through, *inter alia*, close coordination among the departments and units concerned.

ANNEX
Restructuring of the Secretariat

Revised appropriation broken down by section

(United States dollars)

Section	Appropriation approved by resolution 47/220 A	Revised appropriation	Increase or (decrease)
1. Overall policy-making, direction and coordination	34,621,700	34,290,900	(330,800)
2. Peace-keeping operations and special missions	109,088,400	109,088,400	—
3. Political and Security Council affairs	4,001,200	4,001,200	—
4. Political and General Assembly affairs and Secretariat services	3,261,700	2,971,100	(290,600)
5. Disarmament	4,577,500	3,964,100	(613,400)
6. Special political questions, regional cooperation, trusteeship and decolonization	2,851,500	2,851,500	—
7. Elimination of apartheid	2,130,900	1,861,300	(269,600)
8. International Court of Justice	18,485,000	18,485,000	—
9. Legal activities	5,342,600	5,342,600	—
10. Law of the sea and ocean affairs	2,312,900	2,022,300	(290,600)
11. Development and international economic cooperation	14,499,100	11,360,200	(3,138,900)
12. Regular programme of technical cooperation	40,146,200	40,146,200	—
13. Department of International Economic and Social Affairs	13,737,600	13,177,400	(560,200)
14. Department of Technical Cooperation for Development	6,786,300	6,786,300	—
15. United Nations Conference on Trade and Development	92,514,000	96,927,200	4,413,200
16. International Trade Centre	18,489,800	18,489,800	—
17. United Nations Environment Programme	12,832,100	12,332,300	(499,800)
18. Centre for Science and Technology for Development	1,402,700	1,133,100	(269,600)
19. United Nations Centre for Human Settlements (Habitat)	12,029,900	12,029,900	—
20. United Nations Centre on Transnational Corporations	3,748,300	3,478,700	(269,600)
21. Social development and humanitarian affairs	14,700,300	10,492,900	(4,207,400)
22. International drug control	13,383,800	13,383,800	—
23. Economic Commission for Africa	72,049,300	72,049,300	—
24. Economic and Social Commission for Asia and the Pacific	55,301,900	55,301,900	—
25. Economic Commission for Europe	42,509,800	42,509,800	—
26. Economic Commission for Latin America and the Caribbean	67,350,700	67,350,700	—
27. Economic and Social Commission for Western Asia	45,333,900	45,333,900	—
28. Human rights	25,007,500	25,158,600	151,100
29. Protection of and assistance to refugees	63,611,700	63,611,700	—
30. Disaster relief operations	2,010,600	2,010,600	—
31. Public information	103,006,000	111,842,000	8,836,000
32. Conference services	106,441,400	106,150,800	(290,600)
33. Administration and management	103,110,200	103,110,200	—
34. Special expenses	47,661,700	47,661,700	—
35. Construction, alteration, improvement and major maintenance	98,850,200	98,850,200	—
36. Staff assessment	402,034,500	401,130,600	(903,900)
37. A. Department of Political Affairs	41,011,000	41,399,800	388,800
B. Outer space affairs	2,074,300	2,367,100	292,800

Section	Appropriation approved by resolution 47/220 A	Revised appropriation	Increase or (decrease)
38. Legal activities	24,155,600	24,155,600	–
39. A. Policy coordination and sustainable development	–	16,966,500	16,966,500
B. Economic and social information and policy analysis	–	16,664,700	16,664,700
C. Development support and management services	–	10,843,500	10,843,500
D. Policy-making organs	–	2,002,100	2,002,100
E. Department of Economic and Social Development	82,116,600	41,587,000	(40,529,600)
40. Department for Humanitarian Affairs	9,870,700	10,216,400	345,700
41. Administration and management	643,588,100	634,567,300	(9,020,800)
TOTAL	2,468,039,200	2,467,458,200	(581,000)

General Assembly resolution 47/212 B

6 May 1993   Meeting 102   Adopted without vote

Approved by Fifth Committee (A/47/932) without vote, 21 April (meeting 66); draft by Vice-Chairman (A/C.5/47/L.36), based on informal consultations, orally revised; agenda items 103 & 104.
Meeting numbers. GA 47th session: 5th Committee 59-62, 66; plenary 102.

Reports of the Secretary-General. In a September 1993 report,[14] the Secretary-General stated as the main objective of the restructuring exercise the consolidation and streamlining of activities into well-defined functional categories aimed at ensuring effective implementation of mandates entrusted to the Secretariat by policy-making organs. During the first phase of the reform, initiated in February 1992,[8] a number of offices were regrouped, related functions consolidated and resources redeployed. As a result, unnecessary bureaucratic layers had been reduced and certain peripheral activities eliminated. Lines of responsibility had been more clearly defined by concentrating the decision-making process in key departments at Headquarters.

The following structural arrangements were put in place: a new Department of Political Affairs was created, incorporating the functions of the Department of Political and Security Council Affairs, the Centre against Apartheid, the Office for Political and General Assembly Affairs, the Department for Special Political Questions, Regional Cooperation, Decolonization and Trusteeship, the Department for Disarmament Affairs and part of the Offices for Research and Collection of Information. The new Department was placed under two Under-Secretaries-General.

Also created was a Department of Peace-keeping Operations, incorporating the former Office of Special Political Affairs, which included the Office of the Military Adviser. The Office for Ocean Affairs and Law of the Sea was integrated into the

Office of Legal Affairs. A new Department for Economic and Social Development was formed, which comprised the Office of the Director-General, the Department for International Economic and Social Affairs, the Department for Technical Cooperation and Development, the Centre on Transnational Corporations and the Centre for Science and Technology for Development. A Department of Humanitarian Affairs was established following adoption of a 1991 Assembly resolution on strengthening the coordination of humanitarian emergency assistance.[15] The new Department absorbed the functions performed by the United Nations Disaster Relief Office, the Unit for Special Emergency Programmes and various offices and units dealing with emergencies and humanitarian assistance. The Department of Conference Services was made an Office and placed within the Department of Administration and Management.

Together, the restructured and consolidated entities represented some 48.1 per cent of the total budget resources approved for 1992-1993.

In order to provide a comprehensive internal audit and ensure compliance with Assembly resolutions and United Nations rules and regulations, as well as to investigate mismanagement and to prevent waste and abuse, an Office for Inspections and Investigations (OII) was created effective 1 September 1993. The Office, headed by an ASG reporting directly to the Secretary-General, was a first step towards setting up a broader audit, inspection and investigation authority. The function of OII, its reporting responsibilities, relation with the Board of Auditors and resource basis were further described in a November note of the Secretary-General.[16]

Concerning further reform, the Secretary-General said that the creation of new linkages and synergies should be key components. Linkages could be improved among agencies and at the field level, between research and operational activities, and among the global activities of the United Nations, sectoral agencies and the Bretton Woods institutions. New policy and programme linkages should effectively address the continuum from humanitarian assistance to rehabilitation and development. During the years to come, high priority would continue to be given to strengthening the Organization's ability to deal with the increased demands for peace-keeping and peacemaking and related field operations. That would be done through greater coordination within a unified and integrated structure, as well as improved budgetary planning and enhanced management control, audit and programme evaluation. In carrying out the reforms at a number of duty stations, a key concern would be improved coordination between

Headquarters and activities at regional and country levels.

In a November report,[17] the Secretary-General proposed further changes in the senior structure of the Secretariat as well as the transfer of certain functions from the Department of Political Affairs to the Department of Administration and Management, leading to a net reduction of $437,200 in the 1994-1995 budget. The purpose of his streamlining efforts, he explained, was not merely to achieve economies, but rather to ensure clear lines of responsibility and reporting, greater managerial accountability and a better understanding that the various mandates of the Organization were parts of a greater whole.

Management improvement

Pursuant to a 1992 Assembly resolution,[3] the Secretary-General submitted a report in October 1993 assessing the system of accountability and responsibility of programme managers in the United Nations.[18]

He stated that vastly increased and more challenging demands had an obvious impact on traditional concepts of responsibility and accountability and on budgeting and programme management. The shorter response time for urgent mandates made it necessary to resort to ad hoc arrangements which might not fit within existing descriptions of programmes and the resources provided for them. The wider range of expertise required for multifaceted mandates, often at short notice, might be scarce or fully occupied in the Secretariat and might therefore have to be procured from outside. The more complicated and increased demands by Member States, coupled with greater managerial discretion, might require adjustments of the rules and regulations that had guided the work of the Secretariat. Procedures and practices of intergovernmental bodies would need to be reviewed in the context of the new realities.

Procedures and practices, including those of intergovernmental bodies, had to be reviewed in the context of the new realities and the balance between centralized controls, and the legitimate concerns for a more decentralized style of management had to be rethought.

Suggestions for improvements would be further examined. They included: more management training at all levels; greater attention to managerial skills in choosing programme managers; and a clearer system of rewards and sanctions for staff, including performance-related pay schemes and more flexible termination provisions. However, there was still a need to address the central problem of finding the balance between the need for greater managerial discretion for senior staff and the ultimate responsibility to Member States. A thorough review of the regulations, procedures and rules of accountability was to be undertaken in the following year aimed at providing programme managers with enough discretion to implement mandates in an effective and efficient manner, while preserving adequate central control and oversight to meet the concerns of Member States. Necessary adjustments to the existing systems of accountability and responsibility would be made.

Alleged misconduct and mismanagement, as well as abuses or violations of United Nations regulations, were to be investigated by the newly established OII, which incorporated functions of the existing main oversight units. Among other tasks of OII were the monitoring and evaluation of programme implementation; assessment of the Organization's management and control systems; and issuing recommendations for policies and measures to promote economy and efficiency, based on its audits, inspections and investigations.

In an October report,[19] the Joint Inspection Unit (JIU) welcomed the creation of OII as a significant step towards improvement. However, it recognized the new Office as only the first step towards the establishment of a higher-level post with broader oversight authority. To ensure more effective oversight, all the serious deficiencies in the current oversight, accountability, internal control and management improvement processes had to be addressed and the key factors required to construct an effective mandate for OII identified, in order to make it an important part of a transparent management system.

Responding in November,[20] the Secretary-General noted that the establishment of OII was a first step towards setting up a broader and higher-level authority for audit, evaluation and investigation. In that regard, he would also be guided by the experience gained by OII. He emphasized that it had been borne in mind that measures taken by the Secretariat could not focus exclusively on the strengthening of an independent oversight mechanism, but that considerable efforts and adequate resources were required at the same time for an integrated system of accountability and responsibility. The latter required that the role and accountability of programme managers be more clearly defined and that the functions of the Department of Administration and Management be strengthened. Also, the plans for a broader authority for audit, evaluation and investigation had to be carefully reviewed to avoid duplication with existing external oversight mechanisms, particularly those of the Panel of External Auditors and JIU itself. Taking those considerations into account, the Secretary-General had some reservations regarding JIU's assumption that a very large oversight office with a $60 million budget and a staff of 220 to 800 might be required. However, he supported the proposal for sufficient resources for the oversight office in order for it to play a significant role in increasing the effectiveness and accountability of the Secretariat.

In December 1993,[(21)] the Secretary-General submitted revised estimates under sections 25 and 31, proposing the redeployment of resources amounting to $11,941,700 from administration and management to OII in the proposed budget for 1994-1995.

ACABQ, in an oral report on 18 December before the Fifth Committee, endorsed the redeployment of resources in the amount proposed by the Secretary-General. It noted, however, that that amount did not include $320,300 in respect of the post of the ASG for Inspections and Investigations. It was ACABQ's understanding that the Assembly had yet to take a decision on establishing OII, in view of which it was drawing attention to the fact that, should the proposal be adopted, a post at the ASG level would need to be provided for.

The Assembly, in **resolution 48/230, section II**, of 23 December, took note of the Secretary-General's reports containing revised estimates[(17), (21)] and ACABQ's recommendations. It approved his proposals for redeployment of resources and decided to continue the current arrangements as contained in his report,[(17)] pending a review of the issue at its resumed session.

GENERAL ASSEMBLY ACTION (December)

On 23 December 1993, the General Assembly, on the recommendation of the Fifth Committee, adopted **resolution 48/218** without vote.

Review of the efficiency of the administrative and financial functioning of the United Nations
The General Assembly,

I

Having considered the relevant documents on the review of the efficiency of the administrative and financial functioning of the United Nations,

Mindful of the need for sustained efforts to improve the efficiency of the administrative and financial functioning of the United Nations,

Stressing that the late issuance of documentation has hampered consideration by the General Assembly of important issues, and that the Secretary-General should ensure that all future reports are issued on time,

A
Mandates and prerogatives

1. *Expresses concern* at the inadequate implementation of General Assembly mandates in some cases and the undertaking of non-mandated measures in other cases;

2. *Stresses again* the importance of sustained, timely and substantive dialogue and consultations between Member States and the Secretary-General;

B
Programme planning

1. *Takes note* of the report of the Secretary-General;

2. *Reaffirms* that the medium-term plan for the period 1992-1997, originally adopted by the General Assembly

in its resolution 45/253 of 21 December 1990 and revised under the terms of Assembly resolution 47/214 of 23 December 1992, constitutes the principal policy directive of the United Nations, as set out in regulation 3.3 of the Regulations Governing Programme Planning, the Programme Aspects of the Budget, and Monitoring of Implementation and the Methods of Evaluation contained in the annex to Assembly resolution 37/234 of 21 December 1982;

3. *Notes* that in its present format the medium-term plan has a limited impact on the work of the Organization;

4. *Regrets* that a prototype of a new format of the medium-term plan has not been provided as requested by the General Assembly in its resolution 47/214;

5. *Notes with appreciation* the recommendation by the Committee for Programme and Coordination that consideration be given to the possibility of replacing the current medium-term plan by a document prepared along a different format as outlined in paragraph 233 of its report, reiterates its request to the Secretary-General to submit to the General Assembly at its forty-ninth session, through the Committee for Programme and Coordination and the Advisory Committee on Administrative and Budgetary Questions, a prototype of a new format of the medium-term plan, taking into account the present resolution and the views expressed by Member States in the Fifth Committee, and decides to give this issue in-depth consideration at its forty-ninth session on the basis of the relevant documentation;

6. *Requests* the Secretary-General to prepare the proposed revisions to the medium-term plan, to be submitted to the General Assembly at its forty-ninth session, in accordance with regulation 3.11 of the Regulations Governing Programme Planning, the Programme Aspects of the Budget, the Monitoring of Implementation and the Methods of Evaluation, and taking into account the relevant conclusions and recommendations of the Committee for Programme and Coordination at its thirty-third session;

C
Restructuring of the Secretariat

1. *Takes note* of the report of the Secretary-General on the restructuring and efficiency of the Secretariat;

2. *Also takes note* of the indication by the Secretary-General in his statement to the Fifth Committee that the Secretariat can now enter into a phase of consolidation;

3. *Regrets* that the report of the Secretary-General does not provide an analysis of the effects of the restructuring on programmes as requested by the General Assembly in its resolutions 46/232 of 2 March 1992 and 47/212 A and B of 23 December 1992 and 6 May 1993 respectively and does not include proposals on decentralization measures;

4. *Requests* the Secretary-General to submit to the General Assembly at its forty-ninth session, through the Committee for Programme and Coordination and the Advisory Committee on Administrative and Budgetary Questions, an analytical report on all aspects of the restructuring of the Secretariat and its effects on the programmes, including those relating to the United Nations Conference on Trade and Development and transnational corporations;

5. *Reaffirms* section II, paragraph 8, of its resolution 47/212 B and requests the Secretary-General to take that

paragraph into account in formulating his forthcoming proposals on decentralization measures;

6. *Reiterates its requests* relating to the International Trade Centre and the United Nations Centre for Human Settlements (Habitat), in section I, paragraphs 3 *(b)* and *(c)*, of its resolution 47/212 B, and stresses the need for the Secretary-General to implement fully and promptly the decisions of the General Assembly contained therein;

7. *Recalls* section VIII of its resolution 44/201 A of 21 December 1989 on the desirability of the establishment of unified conference services at Vienna;

8. *Stresses* the need for the establishment of unified conference services at Vienna as soon as possible and requests the Secretary-General to report on their establishment no later than at its forty-ninth session;

D
High-level posts

1. *Stresses* that, once approved by the General Assembly, high-level posts should be filled promptly in order to enable the relevant entities to function properly and undertake the implementation of their mandates without undue delays;

2. *Decides* to keep under review the number and distribution of high-level posts, including those financed from extrabudgetary resources, and requests the Secretary-General to provide a clear rationale for the establishment of such posts in the context of future proposals he may make;

3. *Also decides*, in the context of section I.C, paragraph 6, of the present resolution, to maintain the current approved senior management arrangement for the United Nations Centre for Human Settlements (Habitat);

E
Improvement of the Management of the United Nations

1. *Takes note* of the note by the Secretary-General on procedures and norms for the creation, suppression, reclassification, conversion and redeployment of posts, regrets that the Secretary-General did not provide a report on those issues and further requests that such a report be submitted, through the Committee for Programme and Coordination and the Advisory Committee on Administrative and Budgetary Questions, to the General Assembly at its forty-ninth session;

2. *Also takes note* of the report of the Secretary-General on accountability and responsibility of programme managers in the United Nations, and regrets that the report does not provide an adequate response to the requests of the General Assembly in its resolutions 46/185 B and 46/189 of 20 December 1991, 47/212 B and 47/214, section V, paragraph 2;

3. *Takes note with appreciation* of the report of the Joint Inspection Unit on accountability and oversight in the United Nations Secretariat and of the comments of the Secretary-General thereon;

4. *Endorses* the recommendations of the Committee for Programme and Coordination on the establishment of a transparent and effective system of accountability and responsibility no later than 1 January 1995, as contained in paragraphs 243 to 245 of its report;

5. *Requests* the Secretary-General to include in the system of accountability and responsibility the following elements, taking into account relevant experiences within and outside the United Nations system:

(a) The establishment of clear responsibility for programme delivery, including performance indicators as a measure of quality control;

(b) A mechanism ensuring that programme managers are accountable for the effective management of the personnel and financial resources allocated to them;

(c) Performance evaluation for all officials, including senior officials, with objectives and performance indicators;

(d) Effective training of staff in financial and management responsibilities;

6. *Also requests* the Secretary-General to submit a report on the establishment of the system to the General Assembly at its forty-ninth session, through the Committee for Programme and Coordination and the Advisory Committee on Administrative and Budgetary Questions;

II

Recalling its responsibility under Article 17 of the Charter of the United Nations with regard to financial and budgetary matters,

Recalling also Article 97 of the Charter concerning the responsibility of the Secretary-General as chief administrative officer,

Recognizing the increased importance, cost and complexity of United Nations activities,

Recognizing also the need for an enhanced oversight function to ensure the effective implementation of these activities in the most cost-effective manner possible,

Recognizing further the need for adequate intergovernmental programme evaluation with full respect for existing legislative mandates,

1. *Recalls* the need for the establishment of a system of responsibility and accountability for United Nations officials, as called for in section I.E of the present resolution;

2. *Reaffirms* the role of the Board of Auditors as an external control mechanism pursuant to General Assembly resolution 74(I) of 7 December 1946, other relevant resolutions of the Assembly and the Financial Regulations and Rules of the United Nations, for oversight, monitoring and control by the Assembly of the administrative and financial functioning of the United Nations;

3. *Recognizes* the role of the Joint Inspection Unit in accordance with its mandate, contained in General Assembly resolution 31/192 of 22 December 1976;

4. *Reaffirms* the existing mandates of relevant intergovernmental and expert bodies of the General Assembly in the field of administration, budgetary and management matters;

5. *Also reaffirms* its decision 47/454 of 23 December 1992;

6. *Emphasizes* the need to ensure respect for the separate and distinct roles and functions of external and internal oversight mechanisms and also to strengthen the external oversight control mechanisms;

7. *Stresses* that oversight mechanisms should guarantee full respect for the individual rights of staff members and due process of law;

8. *Requests* the Panel of External Auditors and the Board of Auditors to provide their views on how oversight functions could be improved, according to current

reporting procedures, and in this regard decides to consider the relevant report of the Joint Inspection Unit;

9. *Resolves* that the decision to establish an additional independent entity, taking into account Article 97 of the Charter, to enhance oversight functions, in particular with regard to evaluation, audit, investigation and compliance, be taken subject to the definition of its modalities, including its relationship with existing control mechanisms;

10. *Stresses*, in this regard, that any administrative structure should be aimed at ensuring efficiency and cost-effectiveness, especially with regard to programme delivery;

11. *Decides*, in this regard, to continue consideration of this issue at the earliest possible opportunity during its current session;

III

Stressing the necessity for the proper management of resources and funds of the United Nations,

Determined to address alleged cases of fraud in the United Nations in an impartial manner, in accordance with due process of law and full respect for the rights of each individual concerned, especially the rights of defence,

Taking note of the views expressed by Member States during its forty-eighth session,

1. *Decides* to study the possibility of the establishment of a new jurisdictional and procedural mechanism or of the extension of mandates and improvement of the functioning of existing jurisdictional and procedural mechanisms;

2. *Also decides* to this end to establish an ad hoc intergovernmental working group of experts in the legal and financial fields which shall work in consultation with the relevant existing bodies and shall submit a report to the General Assembly with specific recommendations no later than at its forty-ninth session;

3. *Further decides* that the working group shall consist of twenty-five members and invites the President of the General Assembly to define the composition of the working group, with due regard for equitable geographical representation, and to convene it as soon as possible but no later than 31 March 1994;

4. *Requests* the Secretary-General to provide the working group with the necessary services;

5. *Also requests* the Secretary-General to seek the views of Member States on the issue identified in paragraph 1 above, and to bring these views to the attention of the working group, as well as to the attention of the General Assembly;

6. *Invites* Member States to make voluntary contributions to fund the activities of the working group;

7. *Decides* to defer consideration of the report of the Secretary-General on the recovery of misappropriated funds to its resumed forty-eighth session, and requests the Advisory Committee on Administrative and Budgetary Questions to comment on it.

General Assembly resolution 48/218

23 December 1993   Meeting 87   Adopted without vote

Approved by Fifth Committee (A/48/801) without vote, 17 December (meeting 42); draft by Chairman (A/C.5/48/L.6), based on informal consultations, orally revised; agenda item 121.
Meeting numbers. GA 48th session: 5th Committee 7-14, 18, 19, 22, 23, 25, 26, 42; plenary 87.

REFERENCES
[1]A/48/277. [2]YUN 1992, p. 1044. [3]Ibid., p. 1046, GA res. 47/214, 23 Dec. 1992. [4]A/48/16. [5]A/48/281. [6]YUN 1986, p. 1025, GA res. 41/213, annex I, 19 Dec. 1986. [7]YUN 1987, p. 1099, GA res. 42/211, annex, 21 Dec. 1987. [8]YUN 1992, p. 1053. [9]A/C.5/47/88. [10]YUN 1992, p. 1030, GA res. 47/220 A, 23 Dec. 1992. [11]A/47/7/Add.15. [12]YUN 1986, p. 1024, GA res. 41/213, 19 Dec. 1986. [13]A/C.5/47/92. [14]A/48/428. [15]YUN 1991, p. 421, GA res. 46/182, 19 Dec. 1991. [16]A/48/640. [17]A/C.5/48/9 & Corr.1 & Add.1. [18]A/48/452. [19]A/48/420. [20]A/48/420/Add.1. [21]A/C.5/48/42.

Programme evaluation

Joint Inspection Unit

In its annual report to the General Assembly,[1] the Joint Inspection Unit—a subsidiary organ of the bodies within the United Nations system—gave an overview of its activities between 1 July 1992 and 30 June 1993. The work programme of JIU for 1993 and beyond was transmitted to the Assembly in April by the Secretary-General,[2] who stated that JIU had been working to develop a more comprehensive work-programming framework and strategy. It had been greatly assisted by the advent of five new Inspectors in January, who contributed fresh insights and new ideas. Recently, JIU changed its focus in the direction of in-depth studies of management systems in operation and programme performance and results, a direction which was followed in the current work programme. Under active consideration for future years were peace-keeping, humanitarian issues, management, budgetary and administrative matters, and coordination and cooperation, especially in the field of development.

In its report, JIU summarized its recent reports on an integrated library network of the United Nations system; decentralization of organizations in the system; managing works of art in the Organization; proposals for improving peace-keeping operations; a more unitary approach to field representation of United Nations organizations; buildings management; working with non-governmental organizations; financing in relation to "An Agenda for Peace"; relationship agreements between the United Nations and its specialized agencies; and the responsiveness of the United Nations to specific development needs of small Member States.

JIU noted that, through its work programme, it had implemented a number of 1992 ACABQ recommendations on action to be taken to enhance the Unit's effectiveness and relevance to Member States and participating organizations.[3] It noted, however, that there was equally a need for the participating organizations to make further efforts to supplement JIU action, through timely issuance of their comments and proper consideration by their governing bodies.

As a means of contributing to improved action, JIU further proposed that: the Assembly review JIU's proposed work programme and decide on the activities to be inspected, investigated and evaluated in order of priority; JIU be invited to present its reports with financial implications to ACABQ for subsequent review and decision by the Assembly and to the legislative organs concerned, with the Inspectors participating in the deliberations on their reports; JIU be invited to meetings when its budget estimates and/or other financial requirements were being discussed; the Assembly authorize a study on using national experts to assist JIU in fields such as peace-keeping and humanitarian assistance; and the Assembly request the Secretary-General to examine the possibility of JIU's having access to extrabudgetary resources for specific projects relating to the operational activities of some participating bodies. It proposed annual meetings between all review and advisory bodies, including ACABQ, CPC, the International Civil Service Commission (ICSC) and the Board of Auditors, to promote better coordination. During the period under review, JIU maintained contact with a number of management and financial bodies having similar responsibilities, such as CPC, the Board of Auditors, the Panel of External Auditors, ACABQ, the Inter-Agency Meeting on Language Arrangements, Documentation and Publications, and other management, evaluation and audit services of participating organizations.

JIU also made observations on follow-up to four of its reports on: management of interpretation services (1986);[4] autonomous United Nations research institutes (1987);[5] human resources development through technical cooperation (1990); and the coordination of activities related to early warning of possible refugee flows (1990).

In October 1993,[6] the Secretary-General reported to the Assembly on the implementation of the recommendations contained in those reports.

GENERAL ASSEMBLY ACTION

The General Assembly, on the recommendation of the Fifth Committee, adopted **resolution 48/221** on 23 December without vote.

Joint Inspection Unit

The General Assembly,

Recalling its previous resolutions, in particular resolution 47/201 of 22 December 1992, and decision 46/446 of 20 December 1991,

Having considered the annual reports of the Joint Inspection Unit for the periods 1 July 1990 to 30 June 1991, 1 July 1991 to 30 June 1992, and 1 July 1992 to 30 June 1993, and its work programmes for the related periods, as well as the reports of the Secretary-General on the

implementation of the recommendations of the Unit and the report of the Advisory Committee on Administrative and Budgetary Questions,

Expressing its appreciation to the Joint Inspection Unit for the measures taken with regard to improving its programming methods, increasing its productivity and enhancing its performance,

Stressing the importance of timely substantive consideration of the reports of the Joint Inspection Unit by Member States and the participating organizations, especially those organizations which have been inspected,

Emphasizing the need for greater management efficiency, transparency and coordination on the part of the participating organizations within the United Nations system,

Reaffirming the statute of the Joint Inspection Unit, the only independent system-wide inspection, evaluation and investigation body,

Recognizing the need to give adequate means to the Joint Inspection Unit in order to enable it to carry out its functions,

1. *Takes note with appreciation* of the report of the Joint Inspection Unit on its activities during the period 1 July 1992 to 30 June 1993, of its work programme for 1993, and of the report of the Secretary-General on the implementation of the recommendations of the Unit;

2. *Requests* the Joint Inspection Unit to study carefully all problems arising during the start-up phase of peace-keeping operations;

3. *Notes with appreciation* the efforts of the Joint Inspection Unit aimed at improving its programming methods, output and quality of work, and requests it to continue its efforts to comply with the recommendations contained in the report of the Advisory Committee on Administrative and Budgetary Questions and that it report thereon to the General Assembly;

4. *Invites* the Joint Inspection Unit, in its future work programmes, to put more emphasis on inspection and evaluation to ensure optimum use of funds in order to enhance the efficiency of the administrative and financial functioning of the United Nations system;

5. *Requests* the Joint Inspection Unit, when appropriate, to provide in its reports information on estimated financial implications or possible cost-savings resulting from implementation of the recommendations formulated therein;

6. *Calls upon* the Joint Inspection Unit to follow up on the implementation of its recommendations and to include the relevant information regularly in its annual reports;

7. *Also invites* the Joint Inspection Unit to maintain a close relationship with the Committee for Programme and Coordination, the International Civil Service Commission, the Advisory Committee on Administrative and Budgetary Questions, the Board of Auditors, the Panel of External Auditors and organizations and bodies within the United Nations system in order to ensure greater and more cost-effective coordination of their respective activities for the promotion of management efficiency, greater accountability and transparency of the United Nations and other participating organizations;

8. *Requests* the executive heads of the participating organizations to increase their efforts to make detailed and timely comments on Joint Inspection Unit reports and to ensure that their governing bodies consider these reports;

9. *Calls upon* the executive heads of the participating organizations concerned to ensure that Joint Inspection Unit recommendations approved by their governing bodies are implemented and to report thereon;

10. *Recognizes* the need to enhance the contribution of the Joint Inspection Unit to the management efficiency and transparency of the organizations within the United Nations system;

11. *Requests* the Secretary-General, taking into account the report of the Advisory Committee on Administrative and Budgetary Questions, to include in the report called for in its decision 47/454 of 23 December 1992 and to be submitted to the General Assembly at its forty-ninth session proposals regarding the procedures for selecting Inspectors, with a view to improving the selection process, with due regard to the principle of equitable geographical distribution;

12. *Requests* the Secretary-General and the executive heads of the participating organizations, without prejudice to article 20 of the statute of the Joint Inspection Unit, to consider providing the Unit with extrabudgetary resources and programme support funds for specific activities of inspection, evaluation and investigation in those areas which are linked to those resources;

13. *Requests* the Secretary-General and the Joint Inspection Unit to study and to report to the General Assembly at its forty-ninth session on means by which the Unit could enhance its inspection and evaluation of specific fields of activities, such as peace-keeping operations, humanitarian assistance, operational activities for development and technical and financial matters;

14. *Requests* the governing bodies of all the participating organizations and programmes, when considering reports of the Joint Inspection Unit, particularly those having financial implications, to keep the Unit informed;

15. *Decides* to keep under review some of the proposals of the Joint Inspection Unit contained in paragraph 40 of its annual report;

16. *Notes* the preliminary work programme of the Joint Inspection Unit for 1994-1995 and beyond.

General Assembly resolution 48/221

23 December 1993   Meeting 87   Adopted without vote

Approved by Fifth Committee (A/48/740) without vote, 4 December (meeting 29); draft by Vice-Chairman (A/C.5/48/L.3), orally revised; agenda item 125.
Meeting numbers. GA 48th session: 5th Committee 11, 15, 16, 18, 29; plenary 87.

REFERENCES
(1)A/48/34. (2)A/48/129. (3)YUN 1992, p. 1051. (4)YUN 1986, p. 1087. (5)YUN 1987, p. 654. (6)A/48/383.

UN budget

Budget for 1992-1993

Revised appropriations

In March 1993,[1] the Secretary-General presented revisions to the programme budget for the 1992-1993 biennium, proposed in connection with the second phase of the Secretariat restructuring initiated in December 1992.[2] The Assembly had provided directives for those revised estimates in a 1992 resolution.[3]

The translation into budgetary and programmatic terms of the second phase of the restructuring involved the creation of new departments, redeployment of posts and redistribution of resources among various sections of the programme budget. A total of 35 high-level posts financed from the regular budget—20 at USG and 15 at ASG level—were proposed, compared to 48 such posts in the budget as adopted by the General Assembly in 1991,[4] leading to savings of $4,516,100.

Through those revised estimates, the Secretary-General sought the Assembly's approval for a revised appropriation of $2,467,775,800, reflecting a reduction of $263,400 from the amount approved in 1992.[5] He also sought approval for changes in the number and distribution of high-level posts for the remainder of the biennium.

ACABQ, also in March,[6] noted that the revised estimates were not submitted in a complete budget format and that various categories of costs related to differing periods within the biennium; there was no indication of the biennialized costs of the resulting structure that could be compared to the structure reflected in the initial appropriation. The lack of such information as well as a clear presentation of the new structure by budget section hindered an evaluation of the financial effects of the restructuring.

The Assembly, in **resolution 47/212 B**, approved a revised appropriation of $2,467,458,200 for 1992-1993 as a result of the restructuring, $290,600 less than requested by the Secretary-General.

Revised estimates for disarmament centres

In 1991, the General Assembly had decided that the administrative costs of the United Nations regional centres for peace and disarmament in Africa (Lomé, Togo), in Asia and the Pacific (Kathmandu, Nepal) and in Latin America and the Caribbean (Lima, Peru) should be financed from the regular United Nations budget, to ensure their continued financial viability.[7] As requested by the Assembly, the Secretary-General submitted to the Fifth Committee a detailed account of the centres' activities in 1992 and those proposed for 1993, together with estimates of 1993 requirements, functional breakdown of staff and the financial positions of the centres.[8] He stated that, owing to the lack of sufficient resources from voluntary contributions, not all activities projected for 1992 had been implemented; part of the difficulty in raising funds was that potential donors wanted to see an infrastructure already in place before committing themselves to contributing to any project.

The Secretary-General noted that the Assembly had authorized under the 1992-1993 budget an appropriation of $506,900 relating to salaries and common staff costs of three P-5 posts for the Directors of the three centres. In order to cover other administrative costs, an additional $300,000 net was required under budget section 37. If those resources could not be found in the contingency fund, implementation of the 1991 resolution would have to be postponed, in accordance with guidelines for using the fund adopted in 1987.[9]

According to a March 1993 report of ACABQ,[10] the 1993 costs of Directors, already appropriated for 1992-1993, should be added to the $300,000 requested by the Secretary-General; total administrative costs under the regular budget in 1993 would amount to about $553,000. To provide administrative support for the three centres combined, ACABQ recommended commitment authority of $150,000 under section 37 of the 1992-1993 budget. In apportioning that amount, the Secretary-General should take into account all relevant factors, including each centre's current financial status and work programme.

ACABQ also recommended that the Secretary-General submit, in the context of the proposed budget for 1994-1995, his long-term proposals for those centres regarding their financial viability. It added that a determination had to be made as to which activities should be carried out by Headquarters on behalf of the centres and those to be entrusted to the centres themselves. In ACABQ's opinion, there was also a need to have a coherent and integrated programme for the centres, bearing in mind related activities funded under the regular budget.

GENERAL ASSEMBLY ACTION

By **resolution 47/219 B** of 6 May 1993, the General Assembly took note of the Secretary-General's revised estimates and ACABQ's recommendations. It approved a commitment authority of $150,000 under section 37 of the 1992-1993 budget in order to provide for the administrative support of the regional centres; that amount would be a first call on the contingency fund in 1993 as it related to a proposal carried over from 1992.

In **resolution 48/228**, the Assembly accepted the Secretary-General's proposal for conversion of the Director's post of the centre at Kathmandu, from the date the Director was permanently located in the centre there.

Final appropriations

In December 1993,[11] the Secretary-General requested final appropriations of $2,411,404,000 for expenditure and $443,320,100 for income. That represented a decrease in expenditure of $56,054,200 (2.3 per cent) from the $2,467,458,200

appropriated by General Assembly **resolution 47/212 B** of May 1993, and a decrease of $27,696,300 (5.9 per cent) in income, resulting in a reduction of $28,357,900 in net requirements. The changes in the levels of resources were due to fluctuations in exchange rates, inflation, decisions of policy-making organs that could not be deferred, unforeseen and extraordinary expenses, and other changes, including further adjustments relating to the restructuring of the Secretariat.

GENERAL ASSEMBLY ACTION

On 23 December 1993, the General Assembly, on the recommendation of the Fifth Committee, adopted **resolution 48/219 A** without vote.

Final budget appropriations for the biennium 1992-1993

The General Assembly

Resolves that for the biennium 1992-1993:

1. The amount of 2,467,458,200 United States dollars appropriated by its resolution 47/212 B of 6 May 1993 shall be decreased by 56,054,200 dollars as follows:

Section	Amount appropriated by resolution 47/212 B	Increase or (decrease)	Final appropriation
	(United States dollars)		
PART I. *Overall policy-making, direction and coordination*			
1. Overall policy-making, direction and coordination	34,290,900	2,565,900	36,856,800
Total, PART I	34,290,900	2,565,900	36,856,800
PART II. *Political affairs*			
2. Peace-keeping operations and special missions	109,088,400	6,778,400	115,866,800
3. Political and Security Council affairs	4,001,200	—	4,001,200
4. Political and General Assembly affairs and Secretariat services	2,971,100	(14,100)	2,957,000
5. Disarmament	3,964,100	103,700	4,067,800
6. Special political questions; regional cooperation; trusteeship and decolonization	2,851,500	128,500	2,980,000
7. Elimination of apartheid	1,861,300	(71,900)	1,789,400
37. Department of Political Affairs	43,766,900	(1,498,800)	42,268,100
Total, PART II	168,504,500	5,425,800	173,930,300
PART III. *International justice and law*			
8. International Court of Justice	18,485,000	1,230,300	19,715,300
9. Legal activities	5,342,600	(18,800)	5,323,800
10. Law of the sea and ocean affairs	2,022,300	(19,600)	2,002,700
38. Legal activities	24,155,600	(2,344,100)	21,811,500
Total, PART III	50,005,500	(1,152,200)	48,853,300

Section	Amount appropriated by resolution 47/212 B	Increase or (decrease)	Final appropriation
	(United States dollars)		
PART IV. *International cooperation for development*			
11. Development and international economic cooperation	11,360,200	1,340,000	12,700,200
12. Regular programme of technical cooperation	40,146,200	(6,042,500)	34,103,700
13. Department of International Economic and Social Affairs	13,177,400	(162,100)	13,015,300
14. Department of Technical Cooperation for Development	6,786,300	(26,900)	6,759,400
15. United Nations Conference on Trade and Development	96,927,200	(4,026,600)	92,900,600
16. International Trade Centre	18,489,800	(1,024,600)	17,465,200
17. United Nations Environment Programme	12,332,300	314,200	12,646,500
18. Centre for Science and Technology for Development	1,133,100	(21,600)	1,111,500
19. United Nations Centre for Human Settlements (Habitat)	12,029,900	(1,974,000)	10,055,900
20. United Nations Centre on Transnational Corporations	3,478,700	(213,900)	3,264,800
21. Social development and humanitarian affairs	10,492,900	396,800	10,889,700
22. International drug control	13,383,800	(214,600)	13,169,200
39A. Policy coordination and sustainable development	16,966,500	(1,254,700)	15,711,800
39B. Economic and social information and policy analysis	16,664,700	(843,900)	15,820,800
39C. Development support and management services	10,843,500	(822,300)	10,021,200
39D. Policy-making organs	2,002,100	(1,036,200)	965,900
39E. Department of Economic and Social Development	41,587,000	(315,800)	41,271,200
Total, PART IV	327,801,600	(15,928,700)	311,872,900
PART V. *Regional cooperation for development*			
23. Economic Commission for Africa	72,049,300	(3,323,300)	68,726,000
24. Economic and Social Commission for Asia and the Pacific	55,301,900	(3,019,700)	52,282,200
25. Economic Commission for Europe	42,509,800	(2,488,300)	40,021,500
26. Economic Commission for Latin America and the Caribbean	67,350,700	(1,138,900)	66,211,800
27. Economic and Social Commission for Western Asia	45,333,900	(12,968,000)	32,365,900
Total, PART V	282,545,600	(22,938,200)	259,607,400
PART VI. *Human rights and humanitarian affairs*			
28. Human rights	25,158,600	(155,400)	25,003,200

Section	Amount appropriated by resolution 47/212 B	Increase or (decrease)	Final appropriation
	(United States dollars)		
29. Protection of and assistance to refugees	63,611,700	(284,400)	63,327,300
30. Disaster relief operations	2,010,600	(59,400)	1,951,200
40. Department of Humanitarian Affairs	10,216,400	393,400	10,609,800
Total, PART VI	100,997,300	(105,800)	100,891,500
PART VII. *Public information*			
31. Public information	111,842,000	2,921,800	114,763,800
Total, PART VII	111,842,000	2,921,800	114,763,800
PART VIII. *Common support services*			
32. Conference services	106,150,800	1,210,300	107,361,100
33. Administration and management	103,110,200	(3,645,700)	99,464,500
41. Administration and management	634,567,300	707,200	635,274,500
Total, PART VIII	843,828,300	(1,728,200)	842,100,100
PART IX. *Special expenses*			
34. Special expenses	47,661,700	3,771,200	51,432,900
Total, PART IX	47,661,700	3,771,200	51,432,900
PART X. *Capital expenditures*			
35. Construction, alteration, improvement and major maintenance	98,850,200	(486,400)	98,363,800
Total, PART X	98,850,200	(486,400)	98,363,800
PART XI. *Staff assessment*			
36. Staff assessment	401,130,600	(28,399,400)	372,731,200
Total, PART XI	401,130,600	(28,399,400)	372,731,200
GRAND TOTAL	2,467,458,200	(56,054,200)	2,411,404,000

2. The Secretary-General shall be authorized to transfer credits between sections of the budget, with the concurrence of the Advisory Committee on Administrative and Budgetary Questions;

3. The total net provision made under the various sections of the budget for contractual printing shall be administered as a unit under the direction of the United Nations Publications Board;

4. The appropriations for the regular programme of technical cooperation under part IV, section 12, shall be administered in accordance with the Financial Regulations of the United Nations, except that the definition of obligations and the period of validity of obligations shall be subject to the following procedures:

(a) Obligations for personal services established in the current biennium shall be valid for the succeeding biennium, provided that appointments of the experts concerned are effected by the end of the current biennium and that the total period to be covered by obligations established for these purposes against the resources of the current biennium does not exceed twenty-four months;

(b) Obligations established in the current biennium for fellowships shall remain valid until liquidated, provided that the fellow has been nominated by the requesting Government and accepted by the Organization and that a formal letter of award has been issued to the requesting Government;

(c) Obligations in respect of contracts or purchase orders for supplies or equipment recorded in the current biennium shall remain valid until payment is effected to the contractor or vendor, unless they are cancelled;

5. In addition to the appropriations approved under paragraph 1 above, an amount of 51,000 dollars is appropriated for each year of the biennium 1992-1993 from the accumulated income of the Library Endowment Fund for the purchase of books, periodicals, maps and library equipment and for such other expenses of the Library at the Palais des Nations as are in accordance with the objects and provisions of the endowment.

General Assembly resolution 48/219 A

23 December 1993   Meeting 87   Adopted without vote

Approved by Fifth Committee (A/48/804) without vote, 19 November (meeting 44); draft by S-G (A/C.5/48/48); agenda item 122.
Meeting numbers. GA 48th session: 5th Committee 39, 40, 44; plenary 87.

On the same date, the Assembly adopted **resolution 48/219 B**, also on the Fifth Committee's recommendation and without vote.

Final income estimates for the biennium 1992-1993

The General Assembly

Resolves that for the biennium 1992-1993:

1. The estimates of income in the amount of 471,016,400 United States dollars approved by its resolution 47/220 B of 23 December 1992 shall be decreased by 27,696,300 dollars as follows:

Income section	Amount approved by resolution 47/220 B	Increase or (decrease)	Final income estimates
	(United States dollars)		
1. Income from staff assessment	408,003,900	(29,820,900)	378,183,000
Total, INCOME SECTION 1	408,003,900	(29,820,900)	378,183,000
2. General income	59,295,200	(1,802,400)	57,492,800
3. Services to the public	3,717,300	3,927,000	7,644,300
Total, INCOME SECTIONS 2 AND 3	63,012,500	2,124,600	65,137,000
GRAND TOTAL	471,016,400	(27,696,300)	443,320,100

2. The income from staff assessment shall be credited to the Tax Equalization Fund in accordance with the provisions of General Assembly resolution 973(X) of 15 December 1955;

3. Direct expenses of the United Nations Postal Administration, services to visitors, catering and related services, garage operations, television services and the sale of publications, not provided for under the budget appropriations, shall be charged against the income derived from those activities.

General Assembly resolution 48/219 B

23 December 1993   Meeting 87   Adopted without vote

Approved by Fifth Committee (A/48/804) without vote, 19 November (meeting 44); draft by S-G (A/C.5/48/48); agenda item 122.
Meeting numbers. GA 48th session: 5th Committee 39, 40, 44; plenary 87.

Second performance report

In December 1993, the Secretary-General presented to the Fifth Committee his second performance report for 1992-1993,[11] with revised estimates of expenditure and income (see above).

ACABQ recommended that the Fifth Committee accept on a provisional basis the reductions proposed by the Secretary-General. It would examine in detail the second performance report in early 1994, at which time it would issue its report on the factors used in preparing the performance report, namely, inflation, currency exchange rates and standard costs, with particular reference to common staff costs. The General Assembly would thus have another opportunity to examine the performance report in the light of ACABQ's detailed comments.

On the recommendation of the Fifth Committee, the Assembly, by **decision 48/460** of 23 December, approved provisionally those revised estimates, which it decided to review in detail at its resumed forty-eighth session. It noted that the performance report did not comply with its 1992 resolution[12] requesting the Secretary-General to improve the budget performance report and make its presentation more timely and more transparent, and requested his compliance.

Budget for 1990-1991

Final appropriations

In March 1993,[13] the Secretary-General presented to the Fifth Committee updated information on the financial results of the 1990-1991 biennium as at 31 December 1992. The General Assembly, in December 1992,[14] had decided to revert to the question of the final appropriations at its resumed forty-seventh session. At the closure of the accounts in March 1992, expenditure and income both exceeded the appropriations approved in 1991,[15] by a net excess of $11,971,200, which was within the net commitment authority of $13,867,100 granted by the Assembly. Included in the expenditures reported at the end of 1991 was an amount of $55,813,200 in unliquidated obligations, which under financial regulation 4.3 remained available for disbursement until 31 December 1992.

As at that date, certain savings had been achieved in the liquidation of obligations, reducing net requirements to $8,382,100. Final expenditure excluded approximately $1.5 million in obligations, representing contractual commitments charged originally against the 1990-1991 budget, in respect of which payments could not be completed prior to 31 December 1992; in accordance with the financial regulations, those valid obligations were transferred as a charge against current appropriations.

Accordingly, the Secretary-General proposed that the Assembly approve an increase in expenditure for 1990-1991 in the amount of $17,662,100 and that it assess Member States in 1994 for that increase, offset by an income of $9,280,000.

The Assembly, by **decision 47/453 B** of 14 September 1993, postponed a decision on the item to its forty-eighth session. It requested the Secretary-General to provide full information on all aspects of supernumeraries and consultants in the final budget performance report for 1992-1993, and to report on their status in the proposed budget for 1994-1995.

Budget for 1994-1995

In December 1993, the General Assembly approved appropriations for the 1994-1995 biennium totalling $2,580,200,200 gross ($2,112,798,500 net). Income estimates of $477,401,700 from sources other than assessed contributions from Member States were also approved. Member States were to be assessed $1,198,902,550 for 1994.

The Secretary-General had proposed a programme budget of $2,749,064,000, i.e., 1.7 per cent higher than the preliminary level of resources included in the budget outline aproved by the Assembly in 1992.[16] The proposed budget was presented to the Assembly through CPC and ACABQ, which made their recommendations following an item-by-item examination of the programme budget proposals. ACABQ recommended a reduction of $186,473,800 in expenditures, of which $10,394,900 was provisional. The Fifth Committee reduced ACABQ's estimates further.

Appropriations

In August 1993,[17] the Secretary-General proposed a programme budget for 1994-1995 at a level of $2,749,064,000, representing a net growth of $25,324,200, or 1 per cent, over the revised appropriation approved by the General Assembly in May 1993, by **resolution 47/212 B**, for the 1992-1993 biennium. Income for 1994-1995 was estimated at $520,278,000, leading to a net proposed appropriation of $2,228,786,000, and resulting in a net increase of $232,344,200.

Proposed increases in expenditure were primarily directed to the three areas of overall policy-making, direction and coordination; political affairs; and human rights and humanitarian affairs. On the other hand, the rationalization of structures and elimination of duplication resulting from the reorganization of the economic and social sectors of the Secretariat introduced economies of scale and released resources, enabling the Secretariat to meet additional demands, such as follow-up to and preparations for major conferences, without budget growth. It also allowed for redirection of some resources to the area of regional cooperation for development.

Resources were to be distributed to substantive activities as follows: common support services (33.7 per cent); staff assessment (16.3 per cent); regional cooperation for development (13.6 per cent); international cooperation for development (11.4 per cent); political affairs (6 per cent); public information (4.9 per cent); human rights and humanitarian affairs (4.7 per cent); capital expenditures (3.3 per cent); jointly financed activities and special expenses (2.4 per cent); international justice and law (2 per cent); and overall policy-making and coordination (1.7 per cent).

About 55.4 per cent of the proposed budget was for costs associated with the 10,171 staff members who constituted the core of the Secretariat. In view of the additional tasks entrusted to the Organization in a variety of domains, the Secretary-General proposed an increase of staff by 68 posts—41 at the Professional and 27 at the General Service level. A significant expansion was devoted to strengthening the Organization's capacities for preventive diplomacy, peaceful settlement of disputes, peace-keeping and peace-building.

The budget was presented in two parts, in accordance with the new budget format approved by the Assembly in 1992.[3] Part one provided the proposed distribution of resources by section, addressed the question of policies, objectives and priorities for the budget period, and described the budget methodology applied; it was supported by annexes. Part two comprised a detailed section-by-section analysis of the programme budget, with information in the form of tables, programme narratives and description of resource requirements.

As stated by the Secretary-General in his introduction to the proposed budget, it included a number of innovations, such as regrouping in a specific part estimates for capital expenditures, including major maintenance and technological innovations. Also, an attempt was being made to present more clearly the resources which had a strong bearing on activities financed from the regular budget, notably voluntary contributions and the support account for peace-keeping operations.

The Fifth Committee approved the budget item by item, in first and second readings.

GENERAL ASSEMBLY ACTION

On 23 December 1993, on the recommendation of the Fifth Committee, the General Assembly adopted **resolution 48/231 A** without vote.

Budget appropriations for the biennium 1994-1995
The General Assembly
Resolves that for the biennium 1994-1995:
1. Appropriations totalling 2,580,200,200 United States dollars are hereby approved for the following purposes:

Section	US dollars
PART I. *Overall policy-making, direction and coordination*	
1. Overall policy-making, direction and coordination	37,049,800
Total, PART I	37,049,800
PART II. *Political affairs*	
3. Political affairs	67,923,600
4. Peace-keeping operations and special missions	101,573,200
Total, PART II	169,496,800
PART III. *International justice and law*	
5. International Court of Justice	18,329,400
7. Legal activities	32,490,000
Total, PART III	50,819,400
PART IV. *International cooperation for development*	
8. Department for Policy Coordination and Sustainable Development	50,355,600
9. Department for Economic and Social Information and Policy Analysis	46,815,700
10. Department for Development Support and Management Services	29,385,800
11A. United Nations Conference on Trade and Development	108,296,400
11B. International Trade Centre UNCTAD/GATT	19,982,200
12A. United Nations Environment Programme	11,384,500
12B. United Nations Centre for Human Settlements (Habitat)	11,854,300
13. Crime control	4,638,200
14. International drug control	13,998,700
Total, PART IV	296,711,400
PART V. *Regional cooperation for development*	
15. Economic Commission for Africa	78,020,100
16. Economic and Social Commission for Asia and the Pacific	59,846,200
17. Economic Commission for Europe	44,684,500
18. Economic Commission for Latin America and the Caribbean	79,992,600
19. Economic and Social Commission for Western Asia	38,226,600
20. Regular programme of technical cooperation	42,910,000
Total, PART V	343,680,000
PART VI. *Human rights and humanitarian affairs*	
21. Human rights	36,063,300
22A. Office of the United Nations High Commissioner for Refugees	45,329,400
22B. United Nations Relief and Works Agency for Palestine Refugees in the Near East	21,007,900
23. Department of Humanitarian Affairs	18,541,200
Total, PART VI	120,941,800
PART VII. *Public information*	
24. Public information	133,145,300
Total, PART VII	133,145,300
PART VIII. *Common support services*	
25. Administration and management	876,856,000
Total, PART VIII	876,856,000
PART IX. *Jointly financed activities and special expenses*	
26. Jointly financed administrative activities	26,192,800
27. Special expenses	31,780,400
Total, PART IX	57,973,200
PART X. *Staff assessment*	
28. Staff assessment	404,949,000
Total, PART X	404,949,000

Section	US dollars
PART XI. *Capital expenditures*	
29. Technological innovations	18,841,500
30. Construction, alteration, improvement and major maintenance	58,306,900
Total, PART XI	77,148,400
PART XII. *Office for Inspections and Investigations*	
31. Office for Inspections and Investigations	11,429,100
Total, PART XII	11,429,100
GRAND TOTAL	2,580,200,200

2. The Secretary-General shall be authorized to transfer credits between sections of the budget, with the concurrence of the Advisory Committee on Administrative and Budgetary Questions;

3. The total net provision made under the various sections of the budget for contractual printing shall be administered as a unit under the direction of the United Nations Publications Board;

4. The appropriations for the regular programme of technical cooperation under part V, section 20, shall be administered in accordance with the Financial Regulations of the United Nations, except that the definition of obligations and the period of validity of obligations shall be subject to the following procedures:

(*a*) Obligations for personal services established in the current biennium shall be valid for the succeeding biennium, provided that appointments of the experts concerned are effected by the end of the current biennium and that the total period to be covered by obligations established for these purposes against the resources of the current biennium does not exceed twenty-four months;

(*b*) Obligations established in the current biennium for fellowships shall remain valid until liquidated, provided that the fellow has been nominated by the requesting Government and accepted by the Organization and that a formal letter of award has been issued to the requesting Government;

(*c*) Obligations in respect of contracts or purchase orders for supplies or equipment recorded in the current biennium shall remain valid until payment is effected to the contractor or vendor, unless they are cancelled;

5. In addition to the appropriations approved under paragraph 1 above, an amount of 51,000 dollars is appropriated for each year of the biennium 1994-1995 from the accumulated income of the Library Endowment Fund for the purchase of books, periodicals, maps and library equipment and for such other expenses of the Library at the Palais des Nations as are in accordance with the objects and provisions of the endowment.

General Assembly resolution 48/231 A

23 December 1994   Meeting 87   Adopted without vote

Approved by Fifth Committee (A/48/811) without vote, 22 December (meeting 46); agenda item 123.
Meeting numbers. GA 48th session: 5th Committee 24, 26-28, 30-46; plenary 87.

Together with the budget appropriations and on the Fifth Committee's recommendation, the Assembly, on 23 December, adopted **resolution 48/231 B** without vote.

Income estimates for the biennium 1994-1995

The General Assembly

Resolves that for the biennium 1994-1995:

1. Estimates of income other than assessments on Member States totalling 477,401,700 United States dollars are approved as follows:

Income section	US dollars
1. Income from staff assessment	411,364,200
2. General income	59,258,800
3. Services to the public	6,778,700
Total	477,401,700

2. The income from staff assessment shall be credited to the Tax Equalization Fund in accordance with the provisions of General Assembly resolution 973(X) of 15 December 1955;

3. Direct expenses of the United Nations Postal Administration, services to visitors, catering and related services, garage operations, television services and the sale of publications, not provided for under the budget appropriations, shall be charged against the income derived from those activities.

General Assembly resolution 48/231 B

23 December 1994   Meeting 87   Adopted without vote

Approved by Fifth Committee (A/48/811) without vote, 22 December (meeting 46); agenda item 123.

Meeting numbers. GA 48th session: 5th Committee 24, 26-28, 30-46; plenary 87.

Also on 23 December and on the Fifth Committee's recommendation, the Assembly adopted **resolution 48/231 C** without vote.

Financing of appropriations for the year 1994

The General Assembly

Resolves that for the year 1994:

1. Budget appropriations in a total amount of 1,234,045,900 United States dollars, consisting of 1,290,100,100 dollars, being half of the appropriations approved for the biennium 1994-1995 by the General Assembly under paragraph 1 of resolution A above, less 56,054,200 dollars, being the decrease in revised appropriations for the biennium 1992-1993 approved by the Assembly in its resolution 48/219 A of 23 December 1993, shall be financed in accordance with regulations 5.1 and 5.2 of the Financial Regulations of the United Nations as follows:

(a) 33,018,750 dollars, being half of the estimated income other than staff assessment approved for the biennium 1994-1995 under resolution B above, increased by 2,124,600 dollars, being the increase in estimated income other than staff assessment for the biennium 1992-1993 approved by the General Assembly in its resolution 48/219 B of 23 December 1993;

(b) 1,198,902,550 dollars, being the assessment on Member States in accordance with General Assembly resolutions 46/221 A and 48/223 A of 20 December 1991 and 23 December 1993 and Assembly decision 47/456 of 23 December 1992 on the scale of assessments for the year 1994;

2. There shall be set off against the assessment on Member States, in accordance with the provisions of General Assembly resolution 973(X) of 15 December

1955, their respective share in the Tax Equalization Fund in the total amount of 175,860,700 dollars, consisting of:

(a) 205,681,600 dollars, being half of the estimated staff assessment income approved for the biennium 1994-1995 under resolution B above;

(b) Less 29,820,900 dollars, being the decrease in the revised income from staff assessment for the biennium 1992-1993 approved by the General Assembly in its resolution 48/219 B of 23 December 1993.

General Assembly resolution 48/231 C

23 December 1994   Meeting 87   Adopted without vote

Approved by Fifth Committee (A/48/811) without vote, 22 December (meeting 46); agenda item 123.

Meeting numbers. GA 48th session: 5th Committee 24, 26-28, 30-46; plenary 87.

Questions relating to the 1994-1995 budget

On 23 December 1993, on the recommendation of the Fifth Committee, the General Assembly adopted **resolution 48/228** without vote.

Questions relating to the proposed programme budget for the biennium 1994-1995

The General Assembly,

I

Reaffirming its resolution 41/213 of 19 December 1986 and subsequent relevant resolutions,

Recalling section VI, paragraph 1, of its resolution 45/248 B of 21 December 1990, in which it reaffirmed that the Fifth Committee is the appropriate Main Committee of the General Assembly entrusted with responsibilities for administrative and budgetary matters,

Recalling also its resolutions 45/253 of 21 December 1990 on programme planning and 47/213 of 23 December 1992 on the proposed programme budget outline for the biennium 1994-1995,

1. *Endorses* the conclusions and recommendations of the Committee for Programme and Coordination on the proposed programme budget for the biennium 1994-1995 contained in the report on the work of the second part of its thirty-third session,[a] without prejudice to the priorities established by the General Assembly;

2. *Deplores* the extraordinary and unacceptable delay in the submission of the proposed programme budget for the biennium 1994-1995 by the Secretary-General, which compelled the General Assembly and its subsidiary organs to conduct a review on the basis of incomplete and inadequately transparent proposals;

3. *Stresses* that the activities included in the proposed programme budget must be derived from the medium-term plan for the period 1992-1997, as adopted by the General Assembly in its resolutions 45/253 and 47/214 of 23 December 1992, and other relevant intergovernmental decisions, and should be aimed at the full implementation of the mandates, policies and priorities previously established;

4. *Reaffirms* its resolution 47/213;

5. *Requests* the Secretary-General, taking into account paragraph 69 of the first report of the Advisory Committee on Administrative and Budgetary Questions on the proposed programme budget for the biennium 1994-1995,[b] to present extrabudgetary resources, including

---

[a]A/48/16.

[b]A/48/7.

backstopping activities, in the proposed programme budget for 1996-1997 so as to show, to the extent possible, objects of expenditure, as is done in respect of the regular budget;

6. *Regrets* that the provisions of section III of its resolution 47/212 B of 6 May 1993 have not been applied to the sections of the proposed programme budget for the biennium 1994-1995;

7. *Stresses* the need for full and comprehensive information regarding the costing parameters applied in the programme budget, including instructions to programme managers on the preparation of the budget, and requests the Secretary-General to ensure that the proposed programme budget for the biennium 1996-1997 contains a clear indication of all the cost elements, including inflation, exchange-rate fluctuations and others;

8. *Requests* the Board of Auditors, as part of its audit of financial systems during the audit of regular budget accounts, to review the development of assumptions used in the presentation of the programme budget and performance reports, with a view to suggesting improvements;

9. *Requests* the Secretary-General to present in future budget documents the actual regular budget and extrabudgetary expenditure by object of expenditure by section for the prior and current bienniums, with appropriate forecasts to the end of the current biennium, to enable comparison with the request contained in the proposed programme budget;

10. *Also requests* the Secretary-General to include every three months in his report on the status of contributions a summary financial statement;

11. *Regrets* that the Secretary-General has not responded to the requests contained in section II, paragraphs 8 to 10, of its resolution 47/212 B;

12. *Reiterates its request* that the Secretary-General review the role of United Nations Headquarters, centres, the regional commissions and entities in the field, in particular the centres at Vienna and Nairobi, with a view to improving the distribution of responsibilities among them on the basis of their relative advantages, submit proposals to reflect the status of the centre at Nairobi and identify activities that would benefit from relocation to Vienna;

13. *Urges* the Secretary-General to submit adequate proposals in response to these requests at the earliest possible time, but no later than at the forty-ninth session of the General Assembly;

14. *Reiterates its request* that the Secretary-General review and develop procedures and norms, including workload analyses, to justify the creation, suppression, reclassification, conversion and redeployment of posts, as contained in section II, paragraph 2, of its resolution 46/185 B of 20 December 1991, and requests the Secretary-General to report thereon to the Assembly at its forty-ninth session;

15. *Stresses* that, whenever a post becomes vacant, a proper programmatic/workload justification will be needed for its retention, abolition or redeployment;

16. *Requests* the Secretary-General to submit proposals relating to activities that may have become obsolete with a view to reallocating resources to priority areas;

17. *Reaffirms* the need for a comprehensive, substantive and timely dialogue between Member States and the Secretary-General on administrative and budgetary matters;

18. *Recalls* its resolution 47/211 of 23 December 1992, in which it approved, *inter alia*, the recommendations of the Board of Auditors with regard to payment to supernumerary staff contained in its report, and requests the Secretary-General to comply no later than 1 July 1994 and to report to the Assembly at its forty-ninth session on its implementation in the context of the agenda item entitled "Personnel questions";

19. *Endorses* the recommendations and observations regarding the vacancy management system and "vacancy pool" contained in paragraphs 17 to 20 of the report of the Advisory Committee on Administrative and Budgetary Questions, and, in this regard, reiterates the obligation of the Secretary-General to comply with financial regulation 4.5 and rule 104.4 relative to transfers of resources between appropriation sections;

20. *Requests* the Secretary-General to consider the desirability and practicability of creating a new budget section relating to resources for the Advisory Committee on Administrative and Budgetary Questions and external oversight mechanisms, including the Board of Auditors and the Joint Inspection Unit, without prejudice to their existing mandates or their autonomy, bearing in mind paragraph *(b)* of General Assembly decision 47/454 of 23 December 1992, and to report thereon to the Assembly at its forty-ninth session;

21. *Also requests* the Secretary-General to respect fully the rules and regulations governing programme planning in the presentation of future proposed programme budgets;

22. *Decides* to make the following changes in the programmatic narrative in the final published version of the proposed programme budget for the biennium 1994-1995:

(a) To replace the references to the report entitled "An Agenda for Peace" as a mandate with references to General Assembly resolutions 47/120 A and B of 18 December 1992 and 20 September 1993, respectively;

(b) In section 3C (Department of Political Affairs II):

(i) To include, in paragraph 3C.36, after the words "resolution 46/137 of 17 December 1991", a reference to paragraph 4.37 of the medium-term plan, as amended in the annex to Assembly resolution 47/214;

(ii) To reformulate paragraph 3C.37 to ensure that references to procedures for electoral assistance duly reflect the provisions adopted by the General Assembly and properly respect the agreed specific functions of the resident coordinators;

(c) To delete the reference to preventive diplomacy under section 3B (Department of Political Affairs I), programme 3, subprogramme 4;

(d) In section 21 (Human rights):

(i) To include reference to the Working Group on the Right to Development;

(ii) To insert the word "mandated" before each reference to fact-finding missions;

23. *Requests* the Secretary-General:

(a) To identify appropriate activities under section 9 (Department for Economic and Social Information and Policy Analysis) of the proposed programme budget, with a view to implementing General Assembly resolutions 44/215 of 22 December 1989 and 46/210 of 20 December 1991;

(b) To reformulate activities under section 9, programme 1, subprogramme 5, in order to reflect all the

aspects of the pertinent resolutions, as well as the relevant mandates of programme 21 (Public administration and finance) of the medium-term plan, and to report thereon to the General Assembly at its forty-ninth session;

(c) To reformulate activities under section 10 (Department for Development Support and Management Services), programme 2, in accordance with the relevant mandates of programme 21 of the medium-term plan, and to report thereon to the General Assembly at its forty-ninth session;

(d) To transfer the responsibility related to the preparation of the reports on the new international humanitarian order from section 21 to section 23 (Department of Humanitarian Affairs);

24. *Also requests* the Secretary-General to strengthen the coordination between the Crime Prevention and Criminal Justice Branch of the Centre for Social Development and Humanitarian Affairs of the Secretariat and the United Nations International Drug Control Programme, taking into account the role of the Director-General of the United Nations Office at Vienna and the observations contained in paragraph IV.51 of the report of the Advisory Committee on Administrative and Budgetary Questions;

II

1. *Approves* the comments and recommendations of the Advisory Committee on Administrative and Budgetary Questions as expressed in chapter I of its first report on the proposed programme budget for the biennium 1994-1995, and requests the Secretary-General to take the necessary measures;

2. *Takes note* of the statement made by the Secretary-General to the Fifth Committee on 24 November 1993 regarding the temporary suspension of recruitment of Professional staff introduced in 1992 and of paragraph 57 of the first report of the Advisory Committee;

3. *Requests* the Secretary-General to submit proposals to the General Assembly at its current session on the provision of and related arrangements for travel services and allowances, with a view to making more effective use of resources, taking into account the practices of Member States;

4. *Decides* that, until such time as posts have been reclassified according to prescribed internal procedures and approved by the General Assembly, no staff member encumbering a post under reclassification review shall be paid at the higher grade level;

5. *Decides also* that the total allocation for consultants and ad hoc experts shall be maintained at its total revised appropriation amount for the biennium 1992-1993, and requests the Secretary-General to take action to make the best use of those resources, taking into account the relevant recommendations of the Board of Auditors and paragraph 74 of the first report of the Advisory Committee;

6. *Decides further* to set the vacancy factor in respect of General Service staff at 0.8 per cent;

7. *Approves*, subject to the modifications below, the recommendations and observations of the Advisory Committee as expressed in chapter II of its first report on the proposed programme budget for the biennium 1994-1995, and requests the Secretary-General to take the necessary measures;

Section 1. Overall policy-making, direction and coordination

8. *Accepts*, in addition to the recommendations of the Advisory Committee on this section, the establishment of one D-1, two P-3 and two General Service posts on a temporary basis for the Executive Office of the Secretary-General, decides to review the staffing of this Office, and requests the Secretary-General to ensure that there is no duplication with the work of other Secretariat units;

9. *Invites* Member States to make voluntary contributions for the financing of activities related to the fiftieth anniversary of the United Nations;

10. *Requests* the Secretary-General to clarify and review the distribution of responsibilities and liaison functions between the United Nations centres in Europe *vis-à-vis* organizations in Europe, taking into account all pertinent considerations and views expressed in the Fifth Committee;

11. *Accepts* the Secretary-General's proposals for an additional P-5 and an additional P-3 post for the Office of the Director-General of the United Nations Office at Geneva on a temporary basis, and decides to keep under review the staffing of the Office of the Director-General on the basis of a report to be submitted to the General Assembly at its forty-ninth session;

Section 3. Political affairs

12. *Notes* that the proposal of the Secretary-General for the merger of sections 3B and 3C of the programme budget should release resources for redeployment within this section;

13. *Accepts* the proposal of the Secretary-General for the conversion of the post of Director of the United Nations Regional Centre for Peace and Disarmament in Asia and the Pacific from the date the Director is permanently located in the Centre at Kathmandu;

14. *Also accepts* the proposals of the Secretary-General for consultants and ad hoc expert groups for the Office of Disarmament Affairs;

Section 4. Peace-keeping operations and special missions

15. *Takes note* of the recommendation of the Advisory Committee in its report and the report of the Secretary-General on the support account for peace-keeping operations, and decides to consider the criteria for the scope and use of the support account for peace-keeping operations for headquarters support for peace-keeping operations at the earliest opportunity during its current session, and, pending the outcome of that review, authorizes the Secretary-General to continue current administrative arrangements concerning the Situation Room;

16. *Decides* to review, at its fiftieth session, the impact of the merger of the Field Operations Division into the Department of Peace-keeping Operations on the overall effectiveness of the Headquarters support system for peace-keeping operations and other field activities, on the basis of a report to be submitted on this matter;

Section 8. Department for Policy Coordination and Sustainable Development

17. *Accepts* the proposals of the Secretary-General for full funding for the ad hoc secretariat on desertification for 1994-1995, subject to any expenditure in 1995 being mandated by the appropriate intergovernmental body;

18. *Endorses* provisional financing for the Non-Governmental Liaison Service through the United Nations regular budget in the amount proposed by the Secretary-General, on the understanding that such fi-

nancing should not be used for salaries, travel and representation activities of the staffs of non-governmental organizations; in this regard, the Secretary-General shall require a report from the Non-Governmental Liaison Service on the use of this amount, which will be subject to audit by appropriate bodies;

19. *Takes note* of the proposal of the Secretary-General regarding the United Nations New Agenda for the Development of Africa in the 1990s, and requests the Secretary-General to consider the creation of a new budget section relating to the New Agenda with recommendations for additional resources and to report thereon to the General Assembly at its resumed forty-eighth session;

20. *Accepts* the proposals of the Secretary-General for the World Summit for Social Development, the Fourth World Conference on Women and the Global Conference on Sustainable Development of Small Island Developing States in the light of the recommendation of the Committee for Programme and Coordination in paragraph 90 of its report, and requests the Secretary-General to ensure that adequate services and resources are provided for those events;

Section 9. Department for Economic and Social Information and Policy Analysis

21. *Accepts* the proposals of the Secretary-General for resources for the preparation and servicing of the International Conference on Population and Development;

22. *Also accepts* the level of resources recommended by the Advisory Committee and requests the Secretary-General to provide adequate posts for activities dealing with micro-economic issues through redeployment;

Section 10. Department for Development Support and Management Services

23. *Accepts*, on a provisional basis, the proposal of the Secretary-General for section 10 related to regular budget funding, and requests a review of his proposals in the light of relevant recommendations and decisions of the Governing Council of the United Nations Development Programme and the recommendations of the Advisory Committee;

24. *Requests* the Secretary-General, in the context of paragraph 33 of the report of the Committee for Programme and Coordination, to review the activities, resources and institutional and organizational arrangements of the Department for Development Support and Management Services, including those related to natural resources, and to report thereon to the General Assembly at its forty-ninth session with proposals aimed at the most effective delivery of technical cooperation to developing countries;

Section 11A. United Nations Conference on Trade and Development

25. *Calls upon* the Secretary-General to ensure that the distribution of resources among the subprogrammes of section 11A properly reflects the priorities agreed at the eighth session of the United Nations Conference on Trade and Development held at Cartagena de Indias, Colombia, taking into account the views of the Trade and Development Board, as well as the restructuring in the economic and social sectors;

26. *Requests* the Secretary-General to submit proposals for the implementation of section III, paragraph 4 *(b)*, of its resolution 47/212 B in the context of his revised estimates for the biennium 1994-1995, and decides in the meantime to redeploy for activities relat-

ing to transnational corporations the temporary D-2 post proposed for abolition in paragraph 11A.57;

27. *Accepts* the proposal of the Secretary-General for resources for consultants and ad hoc expert groups as contained in paragraph 11A.159;

Section 11B. International Trade Centre UNCTAD/GATT

28. *Reiterates its request* in section I, paragraph 3 *(b)*, of its resolution 47/212 B, for the prompt appointment of the Executive Director of the International Trade Centre UNCTAD/GATT;

Section 12B. United Nations Centre for Human Settlements (Habitat)

29. *Reiterates its request* in section I, paragraph 3 *(c)*, of its resolution 47/212 B, and stresses the need for the Secretary-General to implement fully and promptly the decisions of the General Assembly contained therein;

30. *Accepts* the proposal of the Secretary-General for the staffing level for this budget section, as shown in the staffing table 12B.3;

31. *Requests* the Secretary-General to assure the allocation of adequate resources for the preparatory activities for the United Nations Conference on Human Settlements (Habitat), to be held in 1996;

Section 15. Economic Commission for Africa

32. *Requests* the Secretary-General to keep the financial situation of the United Nations African Institute for the Prevention of Crime and the Treatment of Offenders under active review and to submit proposals for any necessary additional funding for the Institute;

Section 21. Human rights

33. *Accepts* the proposals of the Secretary-General for the staffing resources for human rights activities;

34. *Requests* the Secretary-General to review the allocation of resources among the approved programmes in section 21 so as to ensure the most effective delivery of all mandated activities;

35. *Takes note* of the comments of the Advisory Committee on Administrative and Budgetary Questions in paragraph VI.2 of its report on section 21 of the proposed programme budget, in particular the issue of workload justification, and requests the Secretary-General to provide the information requested by the Advisory Committee for review by the General Assembly at its resumed forty-eighth session;

Section 22A. Office of the United Nations High Commissioner for Refugees

36. *Requests* the Secretary-General and the High Commissioner for Refugees to review the existing arrangements for regular budget and extrabudgetary funding for the Office of the United Nations High Commissioner for Refugees, taking fully into account the increased demand upon the Office since 1989, and, if necessary, to submit proposals to the General Assembly at its forty-ninth session through the appropriate intergovernmental bodies;

Section 23. Department of Humanitarian Affairs

37. *Accepts* one additional D-1 post located at Geneva and one additional P-2 post located in New York, decides to increase the reduction proposed by the Advisory Committee in its report from three to five General Service posts, and requests the Secretary-General to keep the staffing needs of this section under review;

Section 24. Public information

38. *Requests* the Secretary-General to review the requirements of the Department of Public Information, taking into account its role, functioning and activities,

with a view to making it more effective, more relevant and more cost-effective and enhancing its ability to respond to the mandates entrusted to it;

39. *Also requests* the Secretary-General to review the resources devoted to public information activities currently proposed outside section 24, to assess their use and to examine the viability and implications of their possible consolidation within that section;

Section 25. Administration and management

40. *Requests* the Secretary-General to study the management and organizational structure of the Department of Administration and Management, in particular the senior posts structure, and the possible consolidation of administrative functions in various units of the Secretariat, and to report thereon to the General Assembly at its forty-ninth session;

41. *Also requests* the Secretary-General, in the light of paragraph VIII.23 of the report of the Advisory Committee, to submit a report to the General Assembly at its resumed forty-eighth session giving justification for his proposals to abolish nineteen posts in the Office of Conference Services, describing carefully the impact of such proposals on activities of the Office and programme delivery, and to submit proposals in this regard;

42. *Further requests* the Secretary-General to submit to the General Assembly at its forty-ninth session a comprehensive study on the organization, management and human resources requirements for the provision of adequate conference services as a basis for the consideration of his proposals for the regular budget for the biennium 1996-1997, and to provide Member States with previous studies on this matter that were carried out during the biennium 1992-1993;

43. *Notes* that the proposed increase in the section for the Department of Administration and Management is not fully justified;

44. *Also notes* the growing imbalance between proposed expenditures for administrative matters and those for substantive issues;

45. *Further notes* the observation of the Committee for Programme and Coordination in paragraph 35 of its report that preference should be given to the redeployment of the proposed increase to the extent possible to priority areas;

Section 27. Special expenses

46. *Expresses concern* about the high costs of after-service health insurance and requests the Secretary-General to seek ways and means to reduce the increases in these costs;

Section 30. Construction, alteration, improvement and major maintenance

47. *Accepts* the recommendations of the Advisory Committee, and decides to reduce further, by 6 million United States dollars, the proposed estimates of the Secretary-General for alterations, improvements and major maintenance at major headquarters locations.

General Assembly resolution 48/228

23 December 1993   Meeting 87   Adopted without vote

Approved by Fifth Committee (A/48/811) without vote, 21 December (meeting 45); draft by Vice-Chairman following informal consultations (A/C.5/48/L.34), orally revised; agenda item 123.

Meeting numbers. GA 48th session: 5th Committee 24, 26-28, 30-45; plenary 87.

Introducing the text, the Fifth Committee Vice-Chairman said it had been drawn up by consensus and represented a delicate political balance. Thanks to the political will of all Member States, it had been possible to analyse properly each budget section and arrive at the decisions set forth in the resolution.

Unforeseen and extraordinary expenses

In a December 1993 report,[18] the Secretary-General requested authorization from the General Assembly to enter into commitments to meet unforeseen and extraordinary expenses arising in the 1994-1995 biennium. He recalled that in 1991 the Assembly had authorized him to enter into such commitments for 1992-1993 or subsequently.[19] It had also authorized commitments not exceeding a total of $3 million a year as he certified related to the maintenance of peace and security, or certain commitments certified by the President of the International Court of Justice (ICJ); or commitments of up to $500,000 as the Secretary-General certified were needed for interorganizational security measures pursuant to a 1981 Assembly resolution.[20] The 1991 resolution also provided for the Secretary-General to report on such commitments and seek related appropriations, and for the Assembly to be convened if a decision of the Security Council created a need for commitments for maintaining peace and security that exceeded $10 million. The challenging circumstances facing the Organization and the increasingly fluid international situation which demanded rapid response made such a procedure in 1994-1995 even more necessary, the Secretary-General believed. However, he considered that the current annual limit of $3 million related to the maintenance of peace and security proved to be restrictive and should be raised to $6 million.

With regard to the commitments certified by the President of ICJ, the Court proposed that the text applied prior to the 1988-1989 biennium be used again. That would involve reinsertion of certain items in respect of maintenance in office of judges not re-elected and the payment of pension, travel and removal expenses of such judges, as well as travel, removal and installation grants for newly elected judges.

ACABQ, in an oral report before the Fifth Committee, agreed with those changes. It recommended approval of a $5 million limit, instead of the $6 million proposed, for maintenance of peace and security.

GENERAL ASSEMBLY ACTION

On 23 December 1993, on the recommendation of the Fifth Committee, the General Assembly adopted **resolution 48/229** without vote.

Unforeseen and extraordinary expenses for the biennium 1994-1995

The General Assembly

1. *Authorizes* the Secretary-General, with the prior concurrence of the Advisory Committee on Administrative and Budgetary Questions and subject to the Financial Regulations of the United Nations and the provisions

of paragraph 3 below, to enter into commitments in the biennium 1994-1995 to meet unforeseen and extraordinary expenses arising either during or subsequent to that biennium, provided that the concurrence of the Advisory Committee shall not be necessary for:

(a) Such commitments, not exceeding a total of 5 million United States dollars in any one year of the biennium 1994-1995, as the Secretary-General certifies relate to the maintenance of peace and security;

(b) Such commitments as the President of the International Court of Justice certifies relate to expenses occasioned by:

(i) The designation of ad hoc judges (Statute of the International Court of Justice, Article 31), not exceeding a total of 300,000 dollars;

(ii) The appointment of assessors (Statute, Article 30), or the calling of witnesses and the appointment of experts (Statute, Article 50), not exceeding a total of 50,000 dollars;

(iii) The maintenance in office for completion of the cases of judges who have not been re-elected (Statute, Article 13, paragraph 3), not exceeding a total of 40,000 dollars;

(iv) The payment of pensions and travel and removal expenses of retiring judges, and travel and removal expenses and installation grant of members of the Court (Statute, Article 32, paragraph 7), not exceeding a total of 180,000 dollars;

(v) The holding of sessions of the Court away from The Hague (Statute, Article 22), not exceeding a total of 50,000 dollars;

(c) Such commitments, in an amount not exceeding 500,000 dollars, in the biennium 1994-1995, as the Secretary-General certifies are required for interorganizational security measures pursuant to section IV of General Assembly resolution 36/235 of 18 December 1981;

2. *Resolves* that the Secretary-General shall report to the Advisory Committee on Administrative and Budgetary Questions and to the General Assembly at its forty-ninth and fiftieth sessions all commitments made under the provisions of the present resolution, together with the circumstances relating thereto, and shall submit supplementary estimates to the Assembly in respect of such commitments;

3. *Decides* that, for the biennium 1994-1995, if a decision of the Security Council results in the need for the Secretary-General to enter into commitments relating to the maintenance of peace and security in an amount exceeding 10 million dollars in respect of the decision, that matter shall be brought to the General Assembly, or, if the Assembly is suspended or not in session, a resumed or special session of the Assembly shall be convened by the Secretary-General to consider the matter.

General Assembly resolution 48/229

23 December 1993   Meeting 87   Adopted without vote

Approved by Fifth Committee (A/48/811) without vote, 21 December (meeting 45); draft by S-G (A/C.5/48/52), orally revised; agenda item 123.
Meeting numbers. GA 48th session: 5th Committee 24, 26-28, 30-45; plenary 87.

Working Capital Fund

The General Assembly in December 1993 established the Working Capital Fund for the 1994-1995 biennium at the level of $100 million. The

provisions of the authorizing resolution (see below) corresponded to those approved in 1991 for the previous biennium.[21] As in the past, the Fund was to be used to finance appropriations pending receipt of assessed contributions and to pay unforeseen and extraordinary expenses.

The Independent Advisory Group on United Nations Financing (see above, under "Financial situation") recommended that the Fund's level be raised to $200 million, with the difference to be financed by a one-time assessment of $100 million. The Secretary-General proposed that the Fund's level be increased to an amount corresponding to 25 per cent of the net annual budget; on that basis, the Fund should be set in 1994 at $300 million.

GENERAL ASSEMBLY ACTION

On 23 December 1993, on the recommendation of the Fifth Committee, the General Assembly adopted **resolution 48/232** without vote.

Working Capital Fund for the biennium 1994-1995
The General Assembly
Resolves that:

1. The Working Capital Fund shall be established for the biennium 1994-1995 in the amount of 100 million United States dollars;

2. Member States shall make advances to the Working Capital Fund in accordance with the scale adopted by the General Assembly for contributions of Member States to the budget for the year 1994;

3. There shall be set off against this allocation of advances:

(a) Credits to Member States resulting from transfers made in 1959 and 1960 from the surplus account to the Working Capital Fund in an adjusted amount of 1,025,092 dollars;

(b) Cash advances paid by Member States to the Working Capital Fund for the biennium 1992-1993 in accordance with General Assembly resolution 46/188 of 20 December 1991;

4. Should the credits and advances paid by any Member State to the Working Capital Fund for the biennium 1992-1993 exceed the amount of that Member State's advance under the provisions of paragraph 2 above, the excess shall be set off against the amount of the contributions payable by the Member State in respect of the biennium 1994-1995;

5. The Secretary-General is authorized to advance from the Working Capital Fund:

(a) Such sums as may be necessary to finance budgetary appropriations pending the receipt of contributions; sums so advanced shall be reimbursed as soon as receipts from contributions are available for the purpose;

(b) Such sums as may be necessary to finance commitments that may be duly authorized under the provisions of the resolutions adopted by the General Assembly, in particular resolution 48/229 of 23 December 1993 relating to unforeseen and extraordinary expenses; the Secretary-General shall make provision in the budget estimates for reimbursing the Working Capital Fund;

(c) Such sums as may be necessary to continue the revolving fund to finance miscellaneous self-liquidating purchases and activities which, together with net sums outstanding for the same purpose, do not exceed 200,000 dollars; advances in excess of the total of 200,000 dollars may be made with the prior concurrence of the Advisory Committee on Administrative and Budgetary Questions;

(d) With the prior concurrence of the Advisory Committee on Administrative and Budgetary Questions, such sums as may be required to finance payments of advance insurance premiums where the period of insurance extends beyond the end of the biennium in which payment is made; the Secretary-General shall make provision in the budget estimates of each biennium, during the life of the related policies, to cover the charges applicable to each biennium;

(e) Such sums as may be necessary to enable the Tax Equalization Fund to meet current commitments pending the accumulation of credits; such advances shall be repaid as soon as credits are available in the Tax Equalization Fund;

6. Should the provision in paragraph 1 above prove inadequate to meet the purposes normally related to the Working Capital Fund, the Secretary-General is authorized to utilize, in the biennium 1994-1995, cash from special funds and accounts in his custody, under the conditions approved in General Assembly resolution 1341(XIII) of 13 December 1958, or the proceeds of loans authorized by the Assembly.

General Assembly resolution 48/232

23 December 1994   Meeting 87   Adopted without vote

Approved by Fifth Committee (A/48/811) without vote, 22 December (meeting 46); agenda item 123.
Meeting numbers. GA 48th session: 5th Committee 24, 26-28, 30-46; plenary 87.

Contingency fund

The contingency fund, created to accommodate additional expenditures relating to each biennium which were derived from legislative mandates not provided for in the proposed programme budget, was established by the General Assembly in 1986.[22]

The level of the fund for 1994-1995 was set at $20 million by the Assembly in 1992.[16] The consolidated amount of $3,803,400 was within the fund's available balance, as noted in a December 1993 report of the Secretary-General.[23] The Secretary-General suggested that the Fifth Committee recommend to the Assembly, under a 1987 resolution setting out criteria for the use of the fund,[9] appropriation of the required amounts under the relevant sections of the programme budget, totalling $3,803,400.

ACABQ, in an oral report to the Fifth Committee, noted that the Secretary-General's report did not include programme budget implications of $152,500 of a resolution on the United Nations New Agenda for the Development of Africa in the 1990s (see PART THREE, Chapter III); the total amount to be drawn from the contingency fund was $3,955,900, rather than the amount proposed

by the Secretary-General. Accordingly, the balance in the fund would be $20 million, less $3,955,900.

By **resolution 48/230, section IX**, of 23 December, the Assembly noted that a balance of $16,044,100 remained in the fund.

REFERENCES

[1]A/C.5/47/88. [2]YUN 1992, p. 1053. [3]Ibid., p. 1028, GA res. 47/212 A, 23 Dec. 1992. [4]YUN 1991, p. 867, GA res. 46/186 A, 20 Dec. 1991. [5]YUN 1992, p. 1030, GA res. 47/220 A, 23 Dec. 1992. [6]A/47/7/Add.15. [7]YUN 1991, p. 68, GA res. 46/37 F, 9 Dec. 1991. [8]A/C.5/47/62. [9]YUN 1987, p. 1099, GA res. 42/211, annex, 21 Dec. 1987. [10]A/47/7/Add.13. [11]A/C.5/48/48. [12]YUN 1992, p. 1032, GA res. 47/219 A, sect. XXVI, 23 Dec. 1992. [13]A/C.5/47/77/Add.1 & Corr.1. [14]YUN 1992, p. 1038, GA dec. 47/453 A, 22 Dec. 1992. [15]YUN 1991, pp. 864 & 866, GA res. 46/184 A & B, 20 Dec. 1991. [16]YUN 1992, p. 1039, GA res. 47/213, 23 Dec. 1992. [17]A/48/6 & Corr.1. [18]A/C.5/48/52. [19]YUN 1991, p. 869, GA res. 46/187, 20 Dec. 1991. [20]YUN 1981, p. 1384, GA res. 36/235, sect. IV, 18 Dec. 1981. [21]YUN 1991, p. 878, GA res. 46/188, 20 Dec. 1991. [22]YUN 1986, p. 1024, GA res. 41/213, 19 Dec. 1986. [23]A/C.5/48/63.

Contributions

Scale of assessments

Assessment rates of new Member States

The Committee on Contributions (fifty-third session, New York, 14 June-2 July 1993)[1] recommended the rates at which six new Member States, which joined the Organization in 1993 (see PART ONE, Chapter V), were to be assessed for contributions to the regular budget of the United Nations.

The recommended rates of assessment were 0.42 per cent for the Czech Republic, 0.13 per cent for Slovakia, 0.02 per cent for the former Yugoslav Republic of Macedonia and 0.01 per cent each for Eritrea and Monaco. For 1993, the former Yugoslav Republic of Macedonia was asked to pay eight twelfths of the suggested rate, and Eritrea and Monaco seven twelfths. The Committee was unable to decide on a similar recommendation for the Czech Republic and Slovakia.

In considering the rates of the two successor States to the former Czechoslovakia and the former Yugoslav Republic of Macedonia, the Committee followed the approach used in 1992 in dividing up the rates of the former Soviet Union and the former Yugoslavia. As a result, the previously approved rate of Yugoslavia was recommended to be reduced by that suggested for the former Yugoslav Republic of Macedonia. For Andorra, subsequently admitted to United Nations membership on 28 July, a rate of 0.01 per cent for 1993 and 1994 was recommended. For 1993, its proportional rate was set at five twelfths of the suggested rate.

The Committee received written and oral representations from several States which used to be part of Czechoslovakia, the Soviet Union and Yugoslavia. They drew attention to the complex political, legal, economic and technical issues underlying the concerns of those States about the level of assessment of the former consolidated States, the manner in which the rates were distributed among them and the perceived discrepancies between their individual rates of assessment and their ability to pay. In sympathy with many of those concerns, the Committee concluded that a determination of assessment rates for those States which better reflected their current ability to pay could be achieved only in the context of a new scale of assessments.

GENERAL ASSEMBLY ACTION

On the recommendation of the Fifth Committee, the General Assembly adopted **resolution 48/223 A** on 23 December 1993 without vote.

The General Assembly,

Taking into account the views expressed in the Fifth Committee during the forty-seventh session of the General Assembly,

Resolves that:

1. The rates of assessment of the following States, admitted to membership in the United Nations in 1993, shall be as follows:

Member State	Date of admission	Per cent
Czech Republic	19 January	0.42
Slovakia	19 January	0.13
The former Yugoslav Republic of Macedonia	8 April	0.02
Eritrea	28 May	0.01
Monaco	28 May	0.01
Andorra	28 July	0.01

2. For the year of their admission, these Member States shall contribute at the rate of one twelfth of these percentages for each full month of membership. Their contributions for 1993 and 1994 shall be applied to the same basis of assessment as for other Member States, except that, in the case of appropriations or apportionments approved by the General Assembly for the financing of peace-keeping operations, the contributions of these States, as determined by the group of contributors to which they may be assigned by the Assembly, shall be calculated in proportion of the calendar year;

3. The 1993 assessments of the Czech Republic and Slovakia shall be credited to Member States; the advance of the former Czechoslovakia to the Working Capital Fund shall be transferred to the two new States in accordance with their rates of assessment;

4. The 1993 assessments of the former Yugoslav Republic of Macedonia shall be deducted from those of Yugoslavia for that year; the rate of assessment of the former Yugoslav Republic of Macedonia shall be deducted from that of Yugoslavia for 1994; the advance of the former Yugoslav Republic of Macedonia to the Working Capital Fund shall be transferred from that of Yugoslavia in accordance with its rate of assessment;

5. The 1993 assessments of Eritrea, Monaco and Andorra shall be taken into account as miscellaneous income in accordance with regulation 5.2 *(c)* of the Financial Regulations of the United Nations; Monaco's 1993 assessment shall be adjusted by seven twelfths of the flat fee paid for its participation in United Nations activities as a non-member State in that year;

6. The advances of Eritrea, Monaco and Andorra to the Working Capital Fund shall be added to the Fund pending the incorporation of their rates of assessment in a 100 per cent scale.

General Assembly resolution 48/223 A

23 December 1993   Meeting 87   Adopted without vote

Approved by Fifth Committee (A/48/806) without vote, 21 December (meeting 45); draft by Chairman following informal consultations (A/C.5/48/L.13); agenda item 127.
Meeting numbers. GA 48th session: 5th Committee 5-9, 12, 41, 42, 45; plenary 87.

Assessments for 1995-1997

On 23 December 1993, on the recommendation of the Fifth Committee, the General Assembly adopted **resolution 48/223 B** without vote.

The General Assembly,

Recalling all its previous resolutions on the scale of assessments, in particular resolution 46/221 B of 20 December 1991,

Having considered the report of the Committee on Contributions,

Reaffirming that the capacity to pay of Member States is the fundamental criterion for determining the scale of assessments,

1. *Requests* the Committee on Contributions to recommend to the General Assembly at its forty-ninth session a scale of assessments for the period 1995-1997 on the basis of the average of two separate machine scales and the following elements and criteria:

   (a) Statistical base periods of seven and eight years;

   (b) Uniform exchange rates in accordance with the criteria contained in paragraph 3 *(b)* of resolution 46/221 B;

   (c) The debt adjustment approach used in the preparation of the scale of assessments for the period 1992-1994;

   (d) A low per capita income allowance formula with a per capita income limit of the average world per capita income for the statistical base period and a gradient of 85 per cent;

   (e) A floor rate of 0.01 per cent and a ceiling rate of 25 per cent;

   (f) A scheme of limits whose effects would be phased out by 50 per cent with a view to its complete phasing out in the scale for the period 1998-2000;

2. *Decides* that in phasing out the scheme of limits, the allocation of additional points resulting therefrom to developing countries benefiting from its application shall be limited to 15 per cent of the effect of the phase-out;

3. *Concurs* with the observations contained in paragraph 70 of the report of the Committee on Contributions on its fifty-second session and paragraph 29 of its report on its fifty-third session and requests the Committee on Contributions to make recommendations to

the General Assembly at its forty-ninth session that address the problems noted in the above-mentioned paragraphs, taking into account the specific circumstances of Belarus and Ukraine and on the basis of non-discriminatory application of the scale methodology;

4. *Decides also* that individual rates for the least developed countries should not exceed their current level, namely, 0.01 per cent.

General Assembly resolution 48/223 B

23 December 1993   Meeting 87   Adopted without vote

Approved by Fifth Committee (A/48/806) without vote, 21 December (meeting 45); draft by Chairman following informal consultations (A/C.5/48/L.13); agenda item 127.
Meeting numbers. GA 48th session: 5th Committee 5-9, 12, 41, 42, 45; plenary 87.

Introducing the draft resolution, Barbados stated that, although there had been major differences of opinion during the consultations on the elements to be incorporated in the preparation of the scale of assessments for 1995-1997, the need to adopt a coherent and transparent methodological criterion on the preparation of future scales had been unanimously recognized. Some elements of the guidelines, based on which the Committee on Contributions was requested to prepare the scale, required clarification. Agreement on a single statistical base period had been reached only by resorting to a new procedure, requesting the Committee to calculate the next scale on the basis of the average of two separate machine scales based on statistical base periods of seven and eight years, respectively. It was envisaged that the Committee would make an average of the two separate scales before applying such adjustments as might be necessary. The elements relating to uniform exchange rates and the debt-adjustment approach would apply in the same way as in the preparation of the current scale.

Scale methodology

In the absence of a new mandate from the General Assembly, the Committee on Contributions, at its 1993 session,[1] reviewed all components of the current scale methodology in preparation for calculating the next scale of assessments. It also considered the possibility of preparing the next scale on the basis of a new approach and provided an illustrative table showing its effect on the rates of Member States. In doing so, the Committee considered the need to address the special problems of the Member States formerly part of Czechoslovakia, the Soviet Union and Yugoslavia. For the review of the current scale methodology, its components were divided into income concepts; conversion of national income to United States dollars; and other elements such as statistical base period, low per capita income allowance and scheme of limits. The Committee followed that approach in order to draw a clearer distinction between components based on technical concepts

and those largely based on non-technical considerations that were deemed important in the United Nations context.

From a technical point of view, the Committee still considered the national income concept to be more sound than other income concepts for the purposes of the scale of assessments, notwithstanding the use of debt-adjusted income in past or future scales. For application in the near future, the Committee further believed that it would be most appropriate to continue using market exchange rates despite the temporary problems connected with countries whose economies were in transition and the periodic problems with exchange rates that were fixed, controlled or existed under circumstances of high inflation.

GENERAL ASSEMBLY ACTION

On 23 December, on the Fifth Committee's recommendation, the General Assembly adopted **resolution 48/223 C** without vote.

The General Assembly

1. *Requests* the Committee on Contributions to undertake a thorough and comprehensive review of all aspects of the scale methodology with a view to making it stable, simpler and more transparent while continuing to base it on reliable, verifiable and comparable data, and to report thereon to the General Assembly at its fiftieth session;

2. *Reaffirms* the principle of capacity to pay as the fundamental criterion for determining the scale of assessments, and agrees, in principle, to establish an ad hoc body to study the implementation of this principle in determining the scale of assessments and to consider its mandates and modalities at a later stage in the forty-eighth session.

General Assembly resolution 48/223 C

23 December 1993   Meeting 87   Adopted without vote

Approved by Fifth Committee (A/48/806) without vote, 21 December (meeting 45); draft by Chairman following informal consultations (A/C.5/48/L.13); agenda item 127.
Meeting numbers. GA 48th session: 5th Committee 5-9, 12, 41, 42, 45; plenary 87.

Budget contributions in 1993

Of the $1,555,011,392 in contributions due to the United Nations regular budget as at 1 January 1993, $1,077,008,024 had been collected from Member States by 31 December, leaving $478,003,368 outstanding. Of the total, $400,823,795 was due for 1993 alone, while $77,179,573 was outstanding from previous years. In addition, non-member States owed $3,931,297 for taking part in United Nations activities. Of that sum—comprising $3,554,231 for 1993 and $377,066 for past years—$350,260 was outstanding as at 31 December 1993.

On 19 January 1993,[2] the Secretary-General informed the President of the General Assembly that 20 Member States—Burkina Faso, Cambodia, Central African Republic, Chad, Comoros,

Dominican Republic, Equatorial Guinea, Gambia, Guatemala, Guinea-Bissau, Haiti, Liberia, Mali, Mauritania, Niger, Sao Tome and Principe, Sierra Leone, Somalia, South Africa and Yemen—were over two years in arrears in paying their contributions to the regular budget and for peace-keeping. By five more letters, dated 15 April,[3] 7 May,[4] 2[5] and 15 June,[6] and 15 September,[7] the Secretary-General stated that the necessary payments had been made by Haiti, Guatemala, Mauritania, Yemen and Sierra Leone, respectively. On 21 September,[8] he stated that, at that time, 14 Member States were in arrears— Cambodia, Central African Republic, Chad, Comoros, Dominican Republic, Equatorial Guinea, Gambia, Guinea-Bissau, Liberia, Mali, Niger, Sao Tome and Principe, Somalia and South Africa. In subsequent letters of 24,[9] 27[10] and 29 September,[11] 4,[12] 6,[13] 11[14] and 14 October[15] and 3 November,[16] he said the necessary payments had been made by Cambodia and the Niger, Guinea-Bissau, Mali, the Central African Republic, the Gambia, Chad, the Dominican Republic and the Comoros, respectively. Those 14 States had thus cut their arrears below the requirement under Article 19 of the Charter, regaining their voting privileges in the Assembly.

REFERENCES

[1]A/48/11. [2]A/47/870. [3]A/47/870/Add.1. [4]A/47/870/Add.2. [5]A/47/870/Add.3. [6]A/47/870/Add.4. [7]A/47/870/Add.5. [8]A/48/414. [9]A/48/414/Add.2. [10]A/48/414/Add.3. [12]A/48/414/Add.4. [13]A/48/414/Add.5. [14]A/48/414/Add.6. [15]A/48/414/Add.7. [16]A/48/414/Add.8.

Accounts and auditing

Accounts of UNHCR and UNITAR

In 1993, the General Assembly accepted the accounts and financial statements for the year ended 31 December 1992 of the United Nations Institute for Training and Research (UNITAR)[1] and the voluntary funds administered by the United Nations High Commissioner for Refugees (UNHCR),[2] as well as the summary of principal findings, conclusions and recommendations for remedial action of the Board of Auditors.

The Board's principal findings and recommendations for remedial action were transmitted to the Assembly by the Secretary-General in July 1993.[3]

With regard to UNITAR, the Board stated that it was unable to satisfy itself that all the transactions included in the financial statements were in accordance with financial regulations and the requisite legislative authority. Expenditures in excess of contributions and other available resources were made in contravention of appropriate statutes. The Board recommended that in view of the Assembly's decision to streamline and restructure the Institute, the UNITAR administration should ensure that its budget was based on realizable income and that programmes or projects did not exceed available voluntary contributions. A liaison officer responsible for the restructuring should be designated and specific guidelines formulated for transferring its accounts and financial services from New York to Geneva, to where UNITAR had been moved.

Concerning UNHCR, the Board recommended that the Internal Audit Division prioritize the strengthening of internal controls on cash resources in field offices in 1994. Administrative lapses and lack of coordination should be assessed and acted on. UNHCR should review its system of allocation of funds to ensure a more efficient distribution of resources and should continue reviewing and cancelling long-outstanding unliquidated obligations, including those raised against contributions in kind amounting to $33.8 million as at 31 December 1992. Field offices should be instructed to comply with reporting requirements, and accounting for contributions in kind should conform to common accounting standards being developed for the United Nations system.

On 23 December 1993, on the recommendation of the Fifth Committee, the General Assembly adopted **resolution 48/216 A** without vote.

The General Assembly,

Having considered, for the year ended 31 December 1992, the financial reports and audited financial statements of the United Nations Institute for Training and Research and the audited financial statements of the voluntary funds administered by the United Nations High Commissioner for Refugees, the reports and audited opinions of the Board of Auditors, as well as the summary of the principal findings, conclusions and recommendations for remedial action of the Board of Auditors,

Noting the steps taken by the executive heads and governing bodies of the United Nations Institute for Training and Research and the Office of the United Nations High Commissioner for Refugees to give appropriate consideration and attention to the recommendations in earlier audit reports, as commented upon by the Board of Auditors in the annexes to its current reports,

1.   *Recognizes* that the Board of Auditors conducts its reviews in a comprehensive manner, as stipulated in regulation 12.5 of the Financial Regulations of the United Nations, and expresses its appreciation to the Board for the action-oriented and concrete recommendations contained in its reports;

2.   *Accepts* the financial report and audited financial statements and the audit opinions and reports of the Board of Auditors regarding the aforementioned organizations;

3.   *Also accepts* the concise summary of principal findings, conclusions and recommendations for remedial action of the Board of Auditors;

4. *Notes with concern* that the Board of Auditors issued a qualified audit opinion on the financial statements of the United Nations Institute for Training and Research, and in this connection reaffirms the importance of compliance with the Financial Regulations of the United Nations, especially regulations 4.1 and 13.2;

5. *Approves* all the recommendations and conclusions of the Board of Auditors;

6. *Requests* the Office of the United Nations High Commissioner for Refugees to implement better financial management systems that will permit an effective and economic delivery of its programme and reduce persistent over-obligation of funds.

General Assembly resolution 48/216 A

23 December 1993   Meeting 87   Adopted without vote

Approved by Fifth Committee (A/48/752) without vote, 4 December (meeting 29); draft by Vice-Chairman (A/C.5/48/L.7, part A), based on informal consultations; agenda item 120.
Meeting numbers. GA 48th session: 5th Committee 19, 20, 22, 23, 29; plenary 87.

Implementation of 1992 recommendations

In October 1993,[4] the Secretary-General reported on the implementation of the recommendations that the Board of Auditors had made in 1992[5] regarding strengthening of budgetary control to avoid over-expenditure of approved budgets; more cost-effective and transparent purchasing policy by reducing the number of exceptions to competitive bidding; more effective managing and controlling of allowances and benefits for staff; compliance with the Board's recommendations on the hiring, remuneration and performance evaluation of experts, consultants and short-term personnel; and improved control over non-expendable property in all locations, including peace-keeping operations. The comments of ACABQ were taken into account in the preparation of the report.

The Secretary-General stated that measures were being taken to ensure compliance with the Board's recommendation that expenditures be incurred only within the approved appropriations. Procedures were being designed under the Integrated Management Information System to ensure that obligations were not accepted if funds were not available. An administrative instruction of January 1992 addressed the establishment of standards for controlling non-expendable property, and property records were being kept by respective departments and offices.

On property accountability in field missions, he stated that 23 of 27 missions had provided inventory reports of non-expendable property; the others were expected to do so by the end of the year.

GENERAL ASSEMBLY ACTION

On 23 December, on the Fifth Committee's recommendation, the General Assembly adopted **resolution 48/216 B** without vote.

The General Assembly,

Recalling its resolution 47/211 of 23 December 1992, and especially paragraphs 9 and 10 thereof,

Having considered the report of the Secretary-General on the implementation of the recommendations of the Board of Auditors in its report for the period ended 31 December 1991,

1. *Recognizes* the role of the Board of Auditors in carrying out comprehensive and financial audits of the United Nations and its organizations and programmes;

2. *Takes note* of the report of the Secretary-General on the implementation of the recommendations of the Board of Auditors, and requests the Board to consider the report when it follows up on its recommendations in its report to the General Assembly at its forty-ninth session;

3. *Notes with deep concern* that, with a few commendable exceptions, most United Nations organizations and programmes have taken no steps to address the requests contained in paragraphs 9 and 10 of its resolution 47/211;

4. *Urges* the executive heads of the International Trade Centre, the United Nations University, the United Nations Relief and Works Agency for Palestine Refugees in the Near East, the United Nations Institute for Training and Research, the United Nations Environment Programme, the United Nations Population Fund and the United Nations Habitat and Human Settlements Foundation to comply fully with paragraphs 9 and 10 of its resolution 47/211;

5. *Reiterates its request* to the executive heads of the United Nations organizations and programmes to submit reports on measures taken or to be taken in response to the recommendations of the Board of Auditors, including timetables for their implementation, to the General Assembly at its resumed forty-eighth session, through the Advisory Committee on Administrative and Budgetary Questions;

6. *Requests* the executive heads of the United Nations organizations and programmes, in preparing the above-mentioned reports, to give particular attention to the recommendations of the Board of Auditors regarding procurement, the employment of consultants and property accountability in field missions, and in this connection requests the Board, in its audits for the biennium 1992-1993, to give particular attention to those matters;

7. *Requests* the Secretary-General and the executive heads of the United Nations organizations and programmes, at the same time as the recommendations of the Board of Auditors are submitted to the General Assembly, through the Advisory Committee on Administrative and Budgetary Questions, to provide the Assembly with their responses and to indicate measures that would be taken to implement these recommendations, with appropriate timetables;

8. *Also requests* the Secretary-General and the executive heads of the United Nations organizations and programmes to draw attention in such reports to the recommendations of the Board of Auditors, the implementation of which would require action by the General Assembly.

General Assembly resolution 48/216 B

23 December 1993   Meeting 87   Adopted without vote

Approved by Fifth Committee (A/48/752) without vote, 4 December (meeting 29); draft by Vice-Chairman (A/C.5/48/L.7, part B), based on informal consultations; agenda item 120.
Meeting numbers. GA 48th session: 5th Committee 19, 20, 22, 23, 29; plenary 87.

Accounting standards

In October 1993,[6] the Secretary-General presented a report on common inter-organization accounting standards, in response to a 1992 General Assembly decision.[7] Since his previous report of September 1992,[8] the Working Party on Accounting Standards, established by the Consultative Committee on Administrative Questions (Financial and Budgetary Questions), had held two meetings, in December 1992 and June 1993, in order to add new provisions to the draft standards and review existing ones. The text of the standards, as adopted by the Administrative Committee on Coordination, was annexed to the Secretary-General's report.

The standards were intended to provide a framework for accounting and financial reporting in the United Nations system which reflected generally accepted accounting principles, while taking into consideration specific characteristics and needs. They were also to promote consistent accounting and financial reporting practice among the organizations. The standards were based essentially on those promulgated by the International Accounting Standards Committee. In developing them, other authoritative sources, including the recommendations of professional bodies concerned with accounting standards in the public sector, were consulted. The Secretary-General concluded that the standards represented an important advance, having been drawn up in a cooperative spirit by the organizations of the United Nations system. He noted the constructive interest of the Panel of External Auditors, whose suggestions had contributed to the attainment of the standards, and invited the Assembly to take note of the standards and the organizations' plans for their application and development.

GENERAL ASSEMBLY ACTION

On 23 December, on the recommendation of the Fifth Committee, the General Assembly adopted **resolution 48/216 C** without vote.

The General Assembly,

Recalling its decisions 46/445 of 20 December 1991 and 47/449 of 22 December 1992,

Having considered the report of the Secretary-General on accounting standards,

1. *Takes note with appreciation* of the report of the Secretary-General;

2. *Takes note* of the United Nations system accounting standards contained in the annex to the report of the Secretary-General, and requests the Secretary-General and the executive heads of the United Nations organizations and programmes to take those standards into account in the preparation of their financial statements for the period ending 31 December 1993;

3. *Also takes note* of the plans of the organization for the application and development of the United Nations system accounting standards, as reflected in paragraphs 9 and 11 of the report of the Secretary-General, and requests the Secretary-General to report thereon to the General Assembly, through the Advisory Committee on Administrative and Budgetary Questions, at its fifty-first session.

General Assembly resolution 48/216 C

23 December 1993   Meeting 87   Adopted without vote

Approved by Fifth Committee (A/48/752) without vote, 4 December (meeting 29); draft by Vice-Chairman (A/C.5/48/L.7, part C), based on informal consultations; agenda item 120.
Meeting numbers. GA 48th session: 5th Committee 19, 20, 22, 23, 29; plenary 87.

Term of office of Board members

On 23 December 1993, on the recommendation of the Fifth Committee, the General Assembly adopted **resolution 48/216 D** without vote.

The General Assembly,

Noting that the United Nations and most of its organizations and programmes have a two-year financial period, but that members of the Board of Auditors have a three-year term of office,

Invites the Board of Auditors, in consultation with the Secretary-General, to report to the General Assembly at its forty-ninth session, through the Advisory Committee on Administrative and Budgetary Questions, on the implications of extending the term of office of members of the Board of Auditors to four or six years.

General Assembly resolution 48/216 D

23 December 1993   Meeting 87   Adopted without vote

Approved by Fifth Committee (A/48/752) without vote, 4 December (meeting 29); draft by Vice-Chairman (A/C.5/48/L.7, part D), based on informal consultations; agenda item 120.
Meeting numbers. GA 48th session: 5th Committee 19, 20, 22, 23, 29; plenary 87.

REFERENCES

[1]A/48/5/Add.4. [2]A/48/5/Add.5. [3]A/48/230. [4]A/48/516.
[5]YUN 1992, p. 1042. [6]A/48/530. [7]YUN 1992, p. 1052, GA dec. 47/449, 22 Dec. 1992. [8]Ibid., p. 1052.

Chapter II

United Nations officials

In 1993, the Secretary-General continued the restructuring of the Secretariat, with the creation of new departments, redeployment of posts and the redistribution of resources among various sections of the programme budget for the remainder of the 1992-1993 biennium and for the proposed 1994-1995 budget.

Matters related to personnel management, the administration of justice in the Secretariat, and amendments to the Staff Rules and Regulations remained on the agenda of the General Assembly, which acted on those issues in resolution 47/226. The Assembly urged the Secretary-General to implement the plan of action for improving the status of women in the Secretariat by 1995, to give greater priority to the recruitment and promotion of women, and to increase the number of women from developing countries (48/106).

The International Civil Service Commission made several recommendations to the Assembly, including changes in the methodology for determining the pensionable remuneration of staff in the General Service and related categories. The Assembly acted on those recommendations in resolution 48/224 and endorsed those concerning the United Nations pension system in resolution 48/225.

Restructuring of the Secretariat

High-level posts for 1992-1993

In response to a 1992 General Assembly request,[1] the Secretary-General submitted a March 1993 report[2] dealing with, *inter alia*, proposed changes in the number and distribution of high-level posts in the United Nations Secretariat for the remainder of the biennium 1992-1993.

In connection with the restructuring of the economic and social sectors of the Secretariat, begun in February 1992, he reiterated his 1992 proposal[3] to establish three new departments headed by Under-Secretaries-General (USGs): the Department for Policy Coordination and Sustainable Development, which would provide support for central coordinating and policy-making functions vested in the Economic and Social Council and its subsidiary bodies, as well as the Assembly's Second and Third Committees; the Department of Economic and Social Information

and Policy Analysis, which would focus on the compilation and dissemination of economic and social statistics, the analysis of long-term trends, the assessment of economic and social policies, the elaboration of projections and the identification of new and emerging issues; and the Department of Development Support and Management Services (DDSMS), which would act as an executing agency for programmes and projects in selected cross-sectoral areas in institution-building and human resources development and serve as a focal point for management services and technical cooperation. The Secretary-General proposed that the latter Department incorporate the Office for Project Services (OPS) of the United Nations Development Programme (UNDP), and that functions and posts be transferred between departments and duty stations.

The Secretary-General further proposed the following: to abolish the USG post in the Department of Economic and Social Development, the USG post of the Executive Director of the United Nations Centre for Human Settlements (UNCHS), following his decision to place the Centre and the United Nations Environment Programme (UNEP) under common direction, and four Assistant Secretary-General (ASG) posts in the Department of Administration and Management (DAM), one each in the Department of Political Affairs (DPA) and the United Nations Conference on Trade and Development; to downgrade the USG post of the head of the Department of Public Information to the ASG level and the ASG post of the head of the International Trade Centre (ITC) to the D-2 level; and to create an ASG post to head the Centre on Human Rights and a temporary ASG post for the Secretary-General of the Fourth (1995) World Conference on Women. He announced his intention to study the possibility of introducing a D-3 senior career level for selected managerial responsibilities, equivalent to an ASG in terms of emoluments. He concluded that the restructuring would thus lead to a reduction of 13 high-level posts, with 3 additional posts remaining vacant pending further proposals.

Acting on the Secretary-General's report, the Advisory Committee on Administrative and Budgetary Questions (ACABQ), also in March,[4] requested a more detailed explanation of the various components, structure and operation of the three proposed departments in the economic and social sectors. It expressed the view that more justification was needed in relation to the transfer of functions and posts beween duty stations as well as to the creation and abolition of high-level posts, and it recommended the development of classification criteria for such posts. Noting that DAM was the largest department in the Secretariat, ACABQ observed that its senior officials should have a degree of authority equivalent to senior officials in other areas of the United Nations and recommended the deferral of action on the proposed abolition of the four ASG posts, pending a further review and explanation of such action. It cautioned that the proposed establishment of a D-3 level would defeat the objective of rationalizing the number of high-echelon posts and requested the Secretary-General to submit a detailed report on the modalities for integrating OPS in DDSMS. In addition, ACABQ made recommendations concerning vacancy management and the transfer of functions within the Secretariat, especially in the public information and common support service sector.

In a March letter to the Chairman of the General Assembly's Fifth (Administrative and Budgetary) Committee,[5] the Chairman of the Committee on Conferences noted that the proposed restructuring within DAM would create a gap between the head of the Department at the USG level and heads of offices at the D-2 level.

GENERAL ASSEMBLY ACTION

On 6 May, at its resumed forty-seventh session, the General Assembly, by **resolution 47/212 B**, approved the Secretary-General's proposals with regard to high-level posts but deferred action on the proposed abolition of the four ASG posts in DAM and the USG post in UNCHS, and requested him to reconsider those proposals. The Secretary-General was also requested to pursue an agreement with the Director-General of the General Agreement on Tariffs and Trade on the prompt appointment of an Executive Director of ITC at its current level. The Assembly concurred with ACABQ's observations regarding the establishment of a D-3 level and endorsed the view of the Committee on Conferences expressed in its Chairman's letter to the Fifth Committee.

High-level posts for 1994-1995

In November, the Secretary-General presented proposed requirements for high-level posts for the biennium 1994-1995.[6] He stated that, despite a dramatic expansion in United Nations activities, there would be no increase in the number of such posts and that the location of most of them would remain unchanged. He also concluded that there was no need to introduce a new D-3 category of senior permanent appointments. He proposed to allocate two ASGs to DAM, one as Controller and the other to oversee conference and general serv-

ices, and to redeploy two ASG posts from that Department: one to head the new Office of Inspections and Investigations, reporting to the Secretary-General, and the other to DPA. In the latter Department, which was to be headed by a USG with the support of two ASGs, changes included the abolition of one USG post. An additional ASG post for the Department of Peace-keeping Operations (DPKO) was to be redeployed from the Protocol and Liaison Service of the Secretary-General's Executive Office. In addition, the Secretary-General proposed to replace the current USG post in UNCHS with an ASG position.

In December,[7] ACABQ expressed the view that institutional arrangements for UNCHS required an intergovernmental decision and requested the Secretary-General to keep his proposal regarding joint direction for UNEP and UNCHS under review. It recommended accommodating the additional ASG post in DPA by downgrading the USG post proposed for abolition. It observed that the decision to retain two ASG posts in DAM instead of four was not fully explained and that the functions of the ASG overseeing conference and general services were not clear. The Committee requested the Secretary-General to resubmit his proposals for the senior structure of DAM and to explain further his proposal to transfer secretariat services to it.

On 23 December, the General Assembly, by **resolution 48/230, section VI**, endorsed ACABQ's observations and recommendations. By **resolution 48/228** of the same date, the Assembly reiterated its requests for the prompt appointment of the Executive Secretary of ITC and for a report on senior management arrangements for UNCHS, and requested the Secretary-General to report in 1994 on the management and organizational structure of DAM. (For further information on the restructuring of the Secretariat and resources required for it, see previous chapter.)

Integration of UNDP/OPS in the Secretariat

In an October report with subsequent addenda,[8] the Secretary-General outlined the modalities for integrating OPS from UNDP into DDSMS, as elaborated by the OPS task force and its working groups on personnel, finance, procurement and governance. The report described, *inter alia*, common and specific personnel arrangements for Professional and General Service staff, as well as those related to project personnel, and estimated the overall staffing requirements of the Office for 1994-1995 at 296 posts, including 58 posts which could be redeployed from the former staffing table of DDSMS (see also PART THREE, Chapter II).

By **decision 48/459** of 23 December, the General Assembly deferred consideration of the Secretary-General's report until its resumed forty-eighth session in 1994.

REFERENCES
[1]YUN 1992, p. 1028, GA res. 47/212 A, 23 Dec. 1992. [2]A/C.5/47/88. [3]YUN 1992, p. 1053. [4]A/47/7/Add.15. [5]A/C.5/47/92. [6]A/C.5/48/9 & Corr.1 & Add.1. [7]A/48/7/Add.2. [8]A/48/502 & Add.1,2.

International Civil Service Commission

The International Civil Service Commission (ICSC) held two sessions in 1993, its thirty-seventh from 8 to 26 March in New York and its thirty-eighth from 15 July to 3 August at Vienna. The Commission examined issues that derived from resolutions and decisions of the General Assembly and governing bodies of other organizations participating in the United Nations common system of salaries and allowances, as well as from its own statute. It considered matters related to pensionable remuneration and pension entitlements, conditions of service of the Professional and higher categories, remuneration of the General Service and related categories, and conditions of service applicable to both categories. A summary of its deliberations and decisions was provided in its nineteenth annual report,[1] on which the General Assembly acted in December (see below).

In a November statement,[2] the Secretary-General indicated that cost reductions resulting from the Commission's 1993 decisions and recommendations amounted to $14,361,800 for 1994 and $18,686,300 for 1995, with an additional reduction of $65,700 estimated for 1993. At the same time, income from staff assessment was estimated to decline by $13,371,900 in 1994 and $17,729,700 in 1995, bringing the net reduction of costs in 1994 and 1995 to $989,900 and $956,600, respectively. He further noted that reductions relating to expenditures for staff assessment and to income from staff assessment, in the amount of $31,101,600 each, would be made in the process of recosting the proposed programme budget 1994-1995.

GENERAL ASSEMBLY ACTION

On 23 December, the General Assembly, on the recommendation of the Fifth Committee, adopted **resolution 48/224** without vote.

United Nations common system: report of the International Civil Service Commission
The General Assembly,
Having considered the nineteenth annual report of the International Civil Service Commission and other related reports,
Reaffirming its commitment to a single unified United Nations common system,
Strongly supporting the work of the International Civil Service Commission as an independent expert body towards regulation and coordination of the conditions of service of the United Nations common system,

I
Staff participation in the work of the Commission
Recalling section II, paragraph 2, of its resolution 45/241 of 21 December 1990, section I, paragraph 5, of its resolution 46/191 A of 20 December 1991 and section I.B of its resolution 47/216 of 23 December 1992,
Noting the changes introduced by the International Civil Service Commission in its working methods that resulted in the full participation of the Coordinating Committee for Independent Staff Unions and Associations of the United Nations System in the work of the Commission,
Regrets the continued suspension of participation by the Federation of International Civil Servants' Associations in the work of the International Civil Service Commission, and again urges that the Commission and the Federation work towards the re-starting of the dialogue between them;

II
Conditions of service of the Professional and higher categories

A. *Comparator*
Recalling section VI of its resolution 46/191 A and section II.C of its resolution 47/216,
Takes note of the programme of work of the International Civil Service Commission outlined in its annual report relating to specific issues regarding the application of the Noblemaire principle, and in this regard stresses the universal character of the United Nations;

B. *Margin considerations*
Recalling section II.A of its resolution 47/216, in which the General Assembly took note of the study by the International Civil Service Commission of the methodology for determining the cost-of-living differential between New York and Washington, D.C., in the context of net remuneration margin calculations, and requested the Commission to submit a report on the application of the methodology to it,
1. *Takes note* of the decisions of the International Civil Service Commission with regard to the introduction of the new methodology;
2. *Notes* the net remuneration margin of 114.2 for the calendar year 1993;
3. *Also notes* from annex VIII to the report of the Commission that the United Nations/United States remuneration ratios range from 186.0 at the P-1 level to 116.5 at the D-2 level, considers that this imbalance should be addressed in the context of the overall margin considerations established by the General Assembly, and reiterates its request to the Commission, contained in section II.G of its resolution 47/216, to make proposals in this regard to it at its forty-ninth session;

C. *Base/floor salary scale*
Recalling section I.H, paragraph 1, of its resolution 44/198 of 21 December 1989, by which it approved the establishment of a floor net salary scale by reference to the corresponding base net salary levels of officials in comparable positions serving at the base city of the comparator civil service, as well as section V of its resolution 47/216,
1. *Approves*, with effect from 1 March 1994, the revised scale of gross and net salaries for staff in the Professional and higher categories contained in annex I to the present resolution;
2. *Requests* the International Civil Service Commission to review and, if necessary, recommend revised rates

of staff assessment consequential upon changes in the base/floor salary scale;

D. *Expatriate entitlements*

Recalling section I.G, paragraph 3, of its resolution 44/198, in which it requested the International Civil Service Commission to collect the necessary information on the practices of the organizations of the United Nations common system regarding the granting of expatriate entitlements to staff members living in their home country while stationed at duty stations located in another country, in order to assess the feasibility of harmonizing practices among organizations,

1. *Notes* the conclusion of the International Civil Service Commission that the practices followed by the organizations of the United Nations common system were consistent with the provisions of the staff regulations and rules as adopted by the governing bodies of the organizations concerned;

2. *Requests* the Commission to study the matter further, with a view to harmonizing the practices of organizations with those of the United Nations and to make recommendations thereon to the General Assembly at its fifty-first session;

E. *Language incentive*

Recalling its resolution 2480 B(XXIII) of 21 December 1968, section III, paragraph 2, of its resolution 38/232 of 20 December 1983 and section I.A of its resolution 47/216,

1. *Decides* that organizations wishing to introduce the language incentive scheme to promote linguistic balance should do so within the parameters set out in the report of the International Civil Service Commission and in this regard requests all United Nations organizations to pay particular attention to the situation of staff members whose mother tongue is not an official language of the United Nations;

2. *Decides also* that the organizations that already have a language incentive scheme should ensure that the scheme is in line with the parameters set out in the report of the Commission;

3. *Requests* the Commission to report on the introduction of the language incentive scheme by the organizations, to review the scheme after taking into account the views expressed in the General Assembly and to report thereon to the Assembly at its fifty-third session;

F. *Relationship between hours of work and remuneration*

Recalling section I.A of its resolution 47/216,

1. *Concurs fully* with the views expressed by the International Civil Service Commission regarding the relationship between hours of work and remuneration as set out in its annual report;

2. *Endorses* the decision of the Commission to maintain the current common system practice with regard to working hours;

G. *Post adjustment issues*

Taking note of paragraph 142 of the report of the International Civil Service Commission,

Requests the International Civil Service Commission to ensure that place-to-place surveys conducted for all headquarters duty stations are fully representative of the cost of living of all staff working in the duty station;

III
General Service salary survey methodology

Recalling section XIII, paragraph 4, of its resolution 45/241 and section X of its resolution 46/191 A, in which, *inter alia*, it requested the International Civil Service Commission to report on its review of the methodology for the conduct of salary surveys of the General Service and related categories at headquarters duty stations,

Recalling its request to the Secretary-General in section XIII, paragraph 3, of its resolution 45/241 and section III of its resolution 47/216 to submit a report on procedures whereby the Secretary-General and other executive heads could take measures regarding salary scales of the General Service category at variance with recommendations of the Commission only after consultations with the appropriate intergovernmental bodies and the Commission,

Taking note of the note of the Secretary-General, in which he proposes that consultation with the Advisory Committee on Administrative and Budgetary Questions be conducted prior to making a decision on the establishment of General Service salaries following a survey carried out by the Commission,

1. *Takes note* of the decisions of the International Civil Service Commission in respect of its review of the general methodology for surveys of best prevailing conditions of employment at non-headquarters duty stations;

2. *Urges* organizations to implement the recommendations of the Commission with regard to salary scales for staff in the General Service and related categories, and requests that, in cases where decisions at variance with the recommendations of the Commission are envisaged, the matter be referred to the governing body of the organization(s) concerned;

IV
Staff assessment and Tax Equalization Fund

Recalling section XXVI, paragraph 4, of its resolution 47/219 A of 23 December 1992, concerning the first performance report on the programme budget for the biennium 1992-1993, in which it urged the International Civil Service Commission to review the rates of staff assessment during 1993,

Recalling also its decision 47/459 of 23 December 1992, in which it requested the Secretary-General to review all aspects of the question of staff assessment as they affected the budgets of the United Nations organizations and programmes, taking into account the views of the Commission and the experience of other organizations of the common system, and to present proposals to the General Assembly at its forty-eighth session, through the Commission,

1. *Adopts*, with effect from 1 March 1994, the revised staff assessment scale and consequential amendments to the Staff Regulations of the United Nations, as contained in annex II to the present resolution, for use in conjunction with gross base salaries for staff in the Professional and higher categories;

2. *Regrets* that it has not received the review of all aspects of the question of staff assessment as requested in its decision 47/459, and requests the Secretary-General to provide the report no later than at its forty-ninth session;

V
Personnel policy considerations

Recalling its request in section XII, paragraph 1, of its resolution 45/241 and section VIII of its resolution 46/191 A that, as a matter of priority, the International Civil Service Commission resume active consideration of the substantive areas covered under articles 13 and 14 of its statute,

Recalling section VII of its resolution 47/216, by which it urged the Commission to give attention in its work programme to measures designed to promote sound personnel management in the international public service,

1. *Notes with appreciation* the action taken by the International Civil Service Commission under articles 13 and 14 of its statute with regard to job classification and human resource management, training in the context of human resource development and the status of women in the United Nations common system;

2. *Urges* the Commission, in this context, to devote further attention to personnel management issues;

3. *Takes note* of the report of the Commission on the implementation of its decisions and recommendations, submitted under article 17 of its statute, and welcomes the action taken by the World Health Assembly and the Governing Body of the International Labour Organisation regarding the extra steps beyond the common system salary scales;

VI

Decisions of Administrative Tribunals

Recalling its resolution 3357(XXIX) of 18 December 1974, by which it established the International Civil Service Commission for the regulation and coordination of the conditions of service of the United Nations common system,

Noting that judgements regarding the conditions of service of staff, including, *inter alia*, salary scales for the General Service and related categories and post adjustment for the Professional and higher categories, by either the United Nations Administrative Tribunal or the Administrative Tribunal of the International Labour Organisation, may have a consequential impact for the United Nations Joint Staff Pension Fund,

Noting also that—while under article 20 of the rules of procedure of the United Nations Administrative Tribunal and under article 17, paragraph 1, of the Rules of Court of the Administrative Tribunal of the International Labour Organisation the Chairman of the Pension Board may, on giving previous notice to the President of the Tribunal concerned, intervene in a case if it is considered that the judgement to be given by the Tribunal could affect the administration of the United Nations Joint Staff Pension Fund—there are no established mechanisms to ensure that the Pension Fund receives timely notice of such cases and that, furthermore, such opportunity is not provided to the Commission by either Tribunal,

1. *Notes* the administrative and financial implications for the organizations of the United Nations common system of judgements Nos. 1265 and 1266 of the Administrative Tribunal of the International Labour Organisation regarding the salary scale resulting from the General Service salary survey for Geneva conducted by the International Civil Service Commission in 1990;

2. *Regrets* in this regard that the Commission and the common system organizations, other than the respondent, did not have an opportunity to have their views presented to the Administrative Tribunal of the International Labour Organisation;

3. *Requests* the Secretary-General to consult fully with the Commission regarding the methodologies, procedures and rationale used in arriving at its decisions or recommendations that are the subject of appeals before the United Nations Administrative Tribunal and to ensure that the views of the Commission are fully reflected in his submissions to the Tribunal;

4. *Also requests* the Secretary-General to consult with the United Nations Joint Staff Pension Board in the event that the outcome of the appeals mentioned in paragraph 3 above have an impact on the United Nations Joint Staff Pension Fund;

5. *Requests* the executive heads of the other organizations of the common system to consult with the Commission and the United Nations Joint Staff Pension Board as set out in paragraphs 3 and 4 above, respectively, in similar cases before the United Nations Administrative Tribunal or the Administrative Tribunal of the International Labour Organisation where they are the respondents;

6. *Urges* the governing bodies of the organizations of the common system to ensure that the executive heads of their organizations consult the Commission and the United Nations Joint Staff Pension Board on all such cases before either Tribunal;

7. *Further requests* the Secretary-General, in consultation with the executive heads of the organizations of the common system, to examine the feasibility of:

(*a*) Amending the statute of the International Civil Service Commission and/or the relationship agreements between the United Nations and the other organizations of the common system with a view to ensuring a coordinated response in all appeals involving the conditions of service of staff of the common system;

(*b*) Introducing arrangements similar to those under article 20 of the rules of procedure of the United Nations Administrative Tribunal and article 17, paragraph 1, of the Rules of Court of the Administrative Tribunal of the International Labour Organisation, with established mechanisms for providing timely notice of such cases to the International Civil Service Commission, to enable the Commission to intervene in appeals before those Tribunals involving decisions or recommendations of the Commission or any other common system issues;

and to report thereon to the General Assembly at its forty-ninth session.

[See following page for Annex I.]

ANNEX II
Amendment to the Staff Regulations of the United Nations

Regulation 3.3

Replace the second table in paragraph (*b*) (i) by the following table:

Total assessable payments (United States dollars)	Staff assessment rates used in conjuction with gross base salaries	
	Staff member with a dependent spouse or dependent child	Staff member with neither a dependent spouse nor a dependent child
First $15,000 per year	9.0	12.4
Next $5,000 per year	21.0	26.9
Next $5,000 per year	25.0	30.4
Next $5,000 per year	29.0	34.7
Next $5,000 per year	32.0	37.0
Next $10,000 per year	35.0	40.7
Next $10,000 per year	37.0	42.8
Next $10,000 per year	39.0	44.5
Next $10,000 per year	40.0	45.4
Next $15,000 per year	41.0	46.4
Next $20,000 per year	42.0	50.5
Remaining assessable payments	43.0	52.6

ANNEX I

*Salary scale for the Professional and higher categories showing annual gross salaries and net equivalents after application of staff assessment**

(United States dollars)

(Effective 1 March 1994)

Level	I	II	III	IV	V	VI	VII	VIII	IX	X	XI	XII	XIII	XIV	XV
Under-Secretary-General															
USG Gross	138,759														
Net D	90,043														
Net S	80,922														
Assistant Secretary-General															
ASG Gross	125,677														
Net D	82,586														
Net S	74,721														
Director															
D-2 Gross	102,177	104,501	106,825	109,147	111,496	113,861									
Net D	69,113	70,460	71,808	73,155	74,503	75,851									
Net S	63,418	64,568	65,718	66,868	67,999	69,120									
Principal Officer															
D-1 Gross	89,918	91,906	93,896	95,882	97,872	99,862	101,852	103,842	105,830						
Net D	62,001	63,156	64,310	65,462	66,616	67,770	68,924	70,078	71,231						
Net S	57,346	58,334	59,319	60,302	61,287	62,272	63,257	64,242	65,226						
Senior Officer															
P-5 Gross	78,948	80,718	82,488	84,258	86,028	87,797	89,567	91,360	93,158	94,959	96,759	98,558	100,359		
Net D	55,530	56,574	57,618	58,662	59,707	60,750	61,794	62,839	63,882	64,926	65,970	67,014	68,058		
Net S	51,466	52,415	53,364	54,313	55,261	56,209	57,158	58,063	58,953	59,845	60,736	61,626	62,517		
First Officer															
P-4 Gross	64,509	66,200	67,896	69,591	71,291	72,986	74,683	76,404	78,130	79,855	81,579	83,308	85,033	86,759	88,485
Net D	46,901	47,920	48,938	49,955	50,974	51,992	53,010	54,028	55,047	56,064	57,082	58,102	59,119	60,138	61,156
Net S	43,618	44,545	45,471	46,397	47,325	48,250	49,177	50,103	51,028	51,952	52,876	53,803	54,728	55,653	56,578
Second Officer															
P-3 Gross	52,274	53,792	55,321	56,887	58,456	60,024	61,592	63,161	64,729	66,319	67,913	69,507	71,101	72,694	74,290
Net D	39,383	40,339	41,296	42,251	43,208	44,165	45,121	46,078	47,034	47,992	48,948	49,904	50,860	51,817	52,774
Net S	36,781	37,649	38,518	39,387	40,258	41,128	41,998	42,869	43,739	44,610	45,481	46,351	47,221	48,091	48,962
Associate Officer															
P-2 Gross	41,695	43,013	44,328	45,665	47,021	48,380	49,738	51,095	52,455	53,811	55,174	56,578			
Net D	32,652	33,508	34,363	35,219	36,074	36,929	37,785	38,640	39,496	40,351	41,206	42,063			
Net S	30,660	31,442	32,221	33,000	33,776	34,553	35,330	36,106	36,884	37,660	38,436	39,216			
Assistant Officer															
P-1 Gross	31,393	32,604	33,812	35,023	36,287	37,551	38,818	40,082	41,346	42,611					
Net D	25,847	26,671	27,492	28,315	29,136	29,958	30,782	31,603	32,425	33,247					
Net S	24,418	25,181	25,942	26,704	27,453	28,203	28,954	29,704	30,453	31,203					

(The header spans *Steps* over columns I–XV.)

D = Rate applicable to staff members with a dependent spouse or child.
S = Rate applicable to staff members with no dependent spouse or child.

*This scale represents the result of a consolidation of 3.6 multiplier points of post adjustment into net base salary. There will be consequential adjustments in the post adjustment indices and multipliers at all duty stations effective 1 March 1994. Thereafter, changes in post adjustment classifications will be effected on the basis of the movements of the newly consolidated post adjustment indices.

General Assembly resolution 48/224

23 December 1993   Meeting 87   Adopted without vote

Approved by Fifth Committee (A/48/737) without vote, 4 December (meeting 29); draft by Australia following informal consultations (A/C.5/48/L.5), orally revised; agenda item 128.
Meeting numbers. GA 48th session: 5th Committee 11, 13, 14, 16, 18, 29; plenary 87.

REFERENCES

(1)A/48/30 & Corr.1. (2)A/C.5/48/18 & Corr.1.

Personnel management

In April, at its resumed forty-seventh session, the General Assembly acted on the Secretary-General's reports on personnel questions, consider-
ation of which it had deferred in 1992.[1] In October 1993, the Secretary-General requested[2] the Assembly to include in the agenda of its forty-eighth session an item on personnel questions in order to consider a report on the equitable geographical representation of Member States in the Secretariat, prepared pursuant to Assembly **resolution 47/226** of 8 April.

In December, ACABQ, in the first report on the proposed programme budget for 1994-1995[3] (see previous chapter), noted that the temporary suspension of external recruitment for posts in the Professional category, introduced in February 1992, had placed a strain on existing staff resources and necessitated numerous exceptions. The Advisory Committee was of the opinion that, given the Organization's expanding responsibilities, the suspension should end. It also noted confusion connected with the redeployment of vacant posts to and from a "vacancy pool" and within and between budget sections. ACABQ underscored the importance of distinguishing between changes in the staffing table resulting from the restructuring, the treatment of vacancies, and proposals for the creation of new posts. It recommended that its prior concurrence be sought when the movement of a post represented a transfer of resources between budget sections.

In a statement before the Fifth Committee on 24 November, the Secretary-General said that, once the budget for 1994-1995 was approved, it might be possible to lift the freeze on recruitment and offer longer-term contracts to senior staff.

By **resolution 48/228** of 23 December, the General Assembly took note of ACABQ's opinion regarding the suspension of recruitment, endorsed its recommendations regarding the vacancy management system, and decided to set the vacancy factor for General Service staff at 0.8 per cent.

GENERAL ASSEMBLY ACTION

On 8 April, the General Assembly, on the recommendation of the Fifth Committee, adopted **resolution 47/226** without vote.

Personnel questions

The General Assembly,

Recalling Articles 8, 97, 100 and 101 of the Charter of the United Nations,

Reaffirming its resolutions 45/239 A to C of 21 December 1990 and 46/232 of 2 March 1992,

Bearing in mind the views expressed by Member States on personnel questions in the Fifth Committee during its forty-seventh session,

Noting with appreciation the statement on personnel questions made by the Secretary-General to the Fifth Committee on 6 November 1992,

Having considered the documents on personnel questions submitted by the Secretary-General to the General Assembly,

Aware of the views expressed by the recognized staff representatives in the Fifth Committee in accordance with its resolution 35/213 of 17 December 1980,

Recognizing that the staff of the Organization is an invaluable asset of the United Nations, and commending its contribution to furthering the purposes and principles of the United Nations,

1. *Reiterates* its full support for the Secretary-General as the chief administrative officer of the Organization, and underlines its full respect for his prerogatives and responsibilities under the Charter of the United Nations;

2. *Stresses* the importance of ensuring that personnel management is conducive to the recruitment and retention of staff of the highest quality;

3. *Urges* the Secretary-General to review and improve, where necessary, all personnel policies and procedures with a view to making them more simple, trans-

parent and relevant to the new demands placed upon the Secretariat, while promoting the full development of staff potential;

4. *Takes note* of the comments in the report submitted by the Secretary-General on the respect for the privileges and immunities of officials of the United Nations and the specialized agencies and related organizations on how best to assist and rehabilitate staff members in dealing with the after-effects of traumatic and stressful security-related experiences, and looks forward to receiving further information thereon at its forty-ninth session;

5. *Reaffirms* the need for the Secretary-General to use to the fullest extent the staff-management consultative mechanisms set out in staff rule 108.2;

6. *Requests* the Secretary-General to implement appropriate measures to ensure that no restriction or discrimination exists in the United Nations for the recruitment, appointment and promotion of men and women;

I. Personnel management planning

Welcoming the integrated approach adopted by the Secretary-General to personnel management planning,

A. *Recruitment*

Reaffirming, in accordance with the Charter of the United Nations, that the paramount consideration in the appointment, promotion, granting or reviewing of permanent contracts and career development of the staff and in the determination of the conditions of service shall be the necessity of securing the highest standards of efficiency, competence and integrity, and with respect to recruitment, that due regard shall be paid to the importance of recruiting the staff on as wide a geographical basis as possible,

Noting the positive results of national competitive examinations for posts at junior Professional levels as a useful tool for recruitment of highly qualified staff,

1. *Requests* the Secretary-General to expedite the national competitive examination process at the P-1 and P-2 levels;

2. *Also requests* the Secretary-General to further his efforts to introduce the competitive examination process at the P-3 level, with due regard to the promotion prospects of staff members at the P-2 level and with a maximum of efficiency and economy;

3. *Further requests* the Secretary-General to take all necessary measures to speed up the examination process and to ensure that successful candidates are offered positions without delay;

4. *Requests* the Secretary-General:

(a) To continue to recruit external candidates in a manner consistent with staff regulation 4.4;

(b) To ensure that the vacancy announcement bulletins are given the widest possible circulation, *inter alia,* by distributing them without delay to the Permanent Missions to the United Nations;

(c) To ensure that the recruitment process is completed as quickly as possible while allowing sufficient time for applications to be received;

5. *Expresses the hope* that the Secretary-General would end the temporary suspension of recruitment as soon as possible;

1. *Composition of the Secretariat*

Noting that the temporary suspension of recruitment, together with a growing number of new Member States, has affected the representation of Member States in the Secretariat,

1. *Reaffirms* that no post should be considered the exclusive preserve of any Member State or group of States;

2. *Recognizes* that the system of desirable ranges has been established as one of the guiding principles to provide in the recruitment of staff for geographical representation of Member States in posts subject to geographical distribution in accordance with Article 101, paragraph 3, of the Charter of the United Nations;

3. *Urges* the Secretary-General, whenever making appointments at all levels to posts subject to geographical distribution, to continue his efforts to ensure that all Member States, in particular the unrepresented and underrepresented Member States, are adequately represented in the Secretariat, bearing in mind the need to increase the number of staff recruited from Member States below the mid-point of their desirable ranges;

4. *Decides* to establish an open-ended Working Group of the Fifth Committee of the General Assembly, and requests its Chairman to convene a meeting of the Working Group for one week at Headquarters, in the spring of 1993, to consider the formula for the determination of equitable geographical representation of Member States in the Secretariat, on the basis of Article 101, paragraph 3, of the Charter, as set out in Assembly resolution 41/206 C of 11 December 1986 and further outlined in Assembly resolutions 42/220 A of 21 December 1987, 45/239 A, 46/232 and other relevant resolutions, and requests the Chairman of the Fifth Committee to report thereon to the Assembly at its forty-eighth session, as an exceptional measure and without prejudice to the full implementation of Assembly resolution 46/220 of 20 December 1991;

5. *Requests* the Secretary-General to exercise flexibility in the application of desirable ranges in individual recruitment cases, keeping in view all parts of the present resolution;

2. *Secondment*

Reaffirming that there are differences inherent in the secondment of staff from government service to the United Nations and secondment between agencies of the United Nations common system,

1. *Reaffirms* that secondment from government service is consistent with Articles 100 and 101 of the Charter of the United Nations and that it can be beneficial to both the Organization and Member States;

2. *Decides* that secondment from government service should, irrespective of the length of its period, be based on a tripartite agreement among the Organization, the Member State and the staff member concerned;

3. *Also decides* that the renewal of a fixed-term appointment that extends the secondment status of a staff member seconded from government service shall be subject to agreement by the Organization, the Government and the staff member concerned;

4. *Calls upon* the Secretary-General, in consultation with the International Civil Service Commission, to develop a standardized contracting procedure to be used for secondments into and out of the Organization that would take into account the legitimate interests of all the three parties mentioned in paragraph 3, while assuring that the conditions set out in Articles 100 and 101 of the Charter and in the Staff Rules are respected;

5. *Amends* staff regulation 4.1 and annex II to the Staff Regulations to read:

"*Regulation 4.1*: As stated in Article 101 of the Charter, the power of appointment of staff members rests with the Secretary-General. Upon appointment, each staff member, including a staff member on secondment from government service, shall receive a letter of appointment in accordance with the provisions of annex II to the present Regulations and signed by the Secretary-General or by an official in the name of the Secretary-General."

"ANNEX II
"LETTERS OF APPOINTMENT

"*(a)* The letter of appointment shall state:

"(i) That the appointment is subject to the provisions of the Staff Regulations and the Staff Rules applicable to the category of appointment in question and to changes which may be duly made in such regulations and rules from time to time;

"(ii) The nature of the appointment;

"(iii) The date at which the staff member is required to enter upon his or her duties;

"(iv) The period of appointment, the notice required to terminate it and period of probation, if any;

"(v) The category, level, commencing rate of salary and, if increments are allowable, the scale of increments and the maximum attainable;

"(vi) Any special conditions which may be applicable;

"*(b)* A copy of the Staff Regulations and the Staff Rules shall be transmitted to the staff member with the letter of appointment. In accepting appointment the staff member shall state that he or she has been acquainted with and accepts the conditions laid down in the Staff Regulations and in the Staff Rules.

"*(c)* The letter of appointment of a staff member on secondment from government service signed by the staff member and by or on behalf of the Secretary-General, and relevant supporting documentation of the terms and conditions of secondment agreed to by the Member State and the staff member, shall be evidence of the existence and validity of secondment from government service to the Organization for the period stated in the letter of appointment.";

3. *Employment of spouses*

Considering that employment possibilities for spouses accompanying staff members contribute to attracting and retaining the most qualified staff,

Noting that the absence of these possibilities may be an obstacle to the mobility of staff,

1. *Invites* the Secretary-General to pursue actively the possibilities of employment of spouses accompanying staff members;

2. *Also invites* the Secretary-General, in his capacity as Chairman of the Administrative Committee on Coordination, to review with his colleagues in the Committee ways to improve coordination and reduce impediments to the employment of qualified spouses accompanying staff members of the United Nations common system organizations, and to report thereon to the General Assembly at its forty-ninth session;

3. *Invites* Governments in host countries to consider granting work permits for or otherwise enabling the employment of spouses accompanying staff members of international organizations;

B. *Career development*

Recognizing that career development is an indispensable part of an effective management of personnel,

Believing that exchange of staff between national Governments and United Nations organizations can enhance their effectiveness and career development,

1. *Endorses* the underlying principles contained in the reports of the Secretary-General on career development at the United Nations and the training programme in the Secretariat;

2. *Recognizes* that the implementation of the career development system as proposed by the Secretary-General in his report on career development at the United Nations requires enhancement of and respect for the authority of the Office of Human Resources Management in accordance with the pertinent recommendations of the Group of High-level Intergovernmental Experts to Review the Efficiency of the Administrative and Financial Functioning of the United Nations;

3. *Urges* the Secretary-General to undertake without delay a complete review of the performance evaluation system currently in use in the Secretariat, in consultation with the International Civil Service Commission as appropriate, with a view to developing it into an effective system that accurately assesses staff performance and improves staff accountability as part of the career development system;

4. *Requests* the Secretary-General to accord priority to the career development needs of staff through appropriate training and rotation of assignments, as appropriate;

5. *Endorses* the proposals of the Secretary-General to improve the training programme, stresses the need to focus training on priority areas of the Organization and concurs with the Secretary-General that appropriate resourcing for training is important;

6. *Urges* the Secretary-General to ensure that under the responsibility of the Office of Human Resources Management effective career counselling is provided to staff in order adequately to assist them in their career planning;

7. *Requests* the Secretary-General to ensure that for those staff members whose performance evaluations consistently show poor levels of performance, procedures outlined in staff regulation 9.1 *(a)* are effectively applied;

8. *Also requests* the Secretary-General to explore ways and means to encourage exchange of staff between the United Nations and national Governments and international organizations and to report thereon to the General Assembly at its forty-ninth session;

9. *Further requests* the Secretary-General to examine or review the possibility and desirability of achieving an appropriate flexibility between career and fixed-term appointments, taking into account the functional and structural needs of the Organization as well as the requirements of a career international civil service, and to report thereon to the General Assembly at its forty-ninth session;

10. *Notes* the implementation of the mobility pilot project in the occupational group of administrative staff, as outlined in the report of the Secretary-General on career development at the United Nations;

11. *Requests* the Secretary-General to incorporate in the programme of activities for the Office of Human Resources Management, within the existing level of the budget provision for that Office, an equal employment opportunity programme, taking due account of the existence of the Focal Point for Women, and entailing procedures to ensure that opportunities for staff selection and advancement are extended on the basis of merit, efficiency, competence and integrity and do not discriminate against staff of either gender, and also requests that these principles be applied by the Secretariat in its pursuit of the benchmarks set out in General Assembly resolution 45/239 C for the participation of women in Professional posts in the Secretariat and in pursuing the goal of the Secretary-General announced in the Fifth Committee on 6 November 1992;

12. *Encourages* the Secretary-General to take into account the knowledge of a second official language of the United Nations in the promotion of all Professional staff, in accordance with relevant General Assembly resolutions;

13. *Urges* the Secretary-General to introduce appropriate measures in conjunction with the International Civil Service Commission to enhance the motivation of the staff in order to increase creativity and productivity;

C. *Improvement of the status of women
in the Secretariat*

Recalling Articles 8 and 101 of the Charter of the United Nations,

Recalling also the goals set in its resolution 45/239 C,

Reaffirming that the Fifth Committee is the appropriate Main Committee of the General Assembly entrusted with responsibility for administrative, budgetary and personnel matters, including, *inter alia*, the issue of representation of women in the Secretariat,

Recognizing that the advancement of women in the Secretariat requires commitment,

Noting the intention of the Secretary-General to bring the gender balance in policy-level positions as close as possible to 50:50 by the fiftieth anniversary of the United Nations,

1. *Urges* the Secretary-General to implement the action programme contained in his report on improvement of the status of women in the Secretariat designed to overcome the obstacles to the improvement of the status of women in the Secretariat;

2. *Requests* the Secretary-General to accord high priority to the recruitment and promotion of women to posts subject to geographical distribution, particularly at the senior policy and decision-making levels, in order to achieve the goals set in its resolution 45/239 C;

3. *Encourages* the Secretary-General to improve the role of the Focal Point for Women so as to reach the benchmarks set out in its resolution 45/239 C;

4. *Appeals* to all Member States to support the efforts of the United Nations, the specialized agencies and related organizations to increase the participation of women in posts in the Professional category and above, by identifying and nominating more women candidates, especially for senior policy-level and decision-making posts, encouraging more women to apply for vacant posts and to sit for the national competitive examinations where applicable and creating and maintaining national rosters of women candidates to be shared with the United Nations, the specialized agencies and related organizations;

II. Administration of justice in the Secretariat

1. *Regrets* that the report on the administration of justice in the Secretariat called for in its resolution

45/239 B has not been submitted to the General Assembly at its forty-seventh session;

2. *Stresses* the importance of a just, transparent, simple, impartial and efficient system of internal justice in the Secretariat;

3. *Requests* the Secretary-General to undertake a comprehensive review of the system of administration of justice, in response to the request contained in its resolution 45/239 B, taking into account the concrete suggestions for improvement of the system proposed by Member States during the forty-fifth session of the General Assembly, in consultation with the staff representatives as appropriate, and to submit a report thereon, including, *inter alia*, information on costs arising to Member States from the system, to the Assembly not later than at its forty-ninth session;

4. *Takes note with satisfaction* of the policies, guidelines and procedures issued by the Secretary-General on 29 October 1992 regarding the equal treatment of men and women in the Secretariat, including those seeking to eliminate sexual harassment from working relationships in the United Nations;

5. *Encourages* the Secretary-General to implement fully these policies, guidelines and procedures and improve them as necessary;

III. Reporting

1. *Requests* the Secretary-General to submit to the General Assembly at its forty-ninth session a comprehensive report on the implementation of all matters covered in the present resolution;

2. *Also requests* the Secretary-General to resume the annual publication of the list of staff of the Secretariat as of 30 June 1993;

IV. Amendments to the Staff Regulations

Taking note of the reports of the Secretary-General on amendments to the Staff Regulations of the United Nations,

Approves the amendments to the Staff Regulations of the United Nations as set forth in the annex to the present resolution.

ANNEX
Amendments to the Staff Regulations of the United Nations

Regulation 3.2, paragraph (a), (b) *and* (d)
For the existing texts, substitute:

"*(a)* The Secretary-General shall establish terms and conditions under which an education grant shall be available to a staff member serving outside his or her recognized home country whose dependent child is in full-time attendance at a school, university or similar educational institution of a type that will, in the opinion of the Secretary-General, facilitate the child's reassimilation in the staff member's recognized home country. The grant shall be payable in respect of the child up to the end of the fourth year of post-secondary studies or the award of the first recognized degree, whichever is the earlier. The amount of the grant per scholastic year for each child shall be 75 per cent of the admissible educational expenses actually incurred, subject to a maximum grant as approved by the General Assembly. Travel costs of the child may also be paid for an outward and return journey once in each scholastic year between the educational institution and the duty station, except that in the case of staff members serving at designated duty stations where schools do not exist

that provide schooling in the language or in the cultural tradition desired by staff members for their children, such travel costs may be paid twice in the year in which the staff member is not entitled to home leave. Such travel shall be by a route approved by the Secretary-General, but not in an amount exceeding the cost of such a journey between the home country and the duty station.

"*(b)* The Secretary-General shall also establish terms and conditions under which, at designated duty stations, an additional amount of 100 per cent of boarding costs subject to a maximum amount per year as approved by the General Assembly may be paid in respect of children in school attendance at the primary and secondary levels.

"*(d)* The Secretary-General shall also establish terms and conditions under which an education grant shall be available to a staff member whose child is unable, by reason of physical or mental disability, to attend a normal educational institution and therefore requires special teaching or training to prepare him or her for full integration into society or, while attending a normal educational institution, requires special teaching or training to assist him or her in overcoming the disability. The amount of this grant per year for each disabled child shall be equal to 100 per cent of the educational expenses actually incurred, up to a maximum amount approved by the General Assembly."

Regulation 3.3, subparagraph (b) *(iii)*
For the existing text, substitute:

"(iii) The Secretary-General shall determine which of the scales of assessment set out in subparagraphs (i) and (ii) above shall apply to each of the groups of personnel whose salary rates are established under paragraph 5 of annex I to the present Regulations;".

Regulation 3.4, paragraphs (a) *and* (d)
For the existing texts, substitute:

"*(a)* Staff members whose salary rates are set forth in paragraphs 1 and 3 of annex I to the present Regulations shall be entitled to receive dependency allowances for a dependent child, for a disabled child and for a secondary dependant at rates approved by the General Assembly as follows:

"(i) The staff member shall receive an allowance for each dependent child, except that the allowance shall not be paid in respect of the first dependent child if the staff member has no dependent spouse, in which case the staff member shall be entitled to the dependency rate of staff assessment under subparagraph *(b)* (i) of regulation 3.3;

"(ii) The staff member shall receive a special allowance for each disabled child. However, if the staff member has no dependent spouse and is entitled to the dependency rate of staff assessment under subparagraph *(b)* (i) of regulation 3.3 in respect of a disabled child, the allowance shall be the same as the allowance for a dependent child in (i) above;

"(iii) Where there is no dependent spouse, a single annual allowance shall be paid for a secondary dependant in respect of either a dependent parent, a dependent brother or a dependent sister.

"*(d)* Staff members whose salary rates are set by the Secretary-General under paragraph 5 or paragraph

6 of annex I to the present Regulations shall be entitled to receive dependency allowances at rates and under conditions determined by the Secretary-General, due regard being given to the circumstances in the locality in which the office is located.''

Annex I to the Staff Regulations
For the existing text of paragraphs 1 to 10, substitute:

''1. The Secretary-General shall establish the salary of the Administrator of the United Nations Development Programme and the salaries of United Nations officials in the Director category and above, in accordance with amounts determined by the General Assembly, subject to the staff assessment plan provided in staff regulation 3.3 and to post adjustments wherever applied. If otherwise eligible, they shall receive the allowances that are available to staff members generally.

''2. The Secretary-General is authorized, on the basis of appropriate justification and/or reporting, to make additional payments to United Nations officials in the Director category and above to compensate for such special costs as may be reasonably incurred, in the interests of the Organization, in the performance of duties assigned to them by the Secretary-General. Similar additional payments in similar circumstances may be made to heads of offices away from Headquarters. The maximum total amount of such payments is to be determined in the programme budget by the General Assembly.

''3. Except as provided in paragraph 5 of the present annex, the salary scales and the scales of post adjustments for staff members in the Professional and higher categories shall be as shown in the present annex.

''4. Subject to satisfactory service, salary increments within the levels set forth in paragraph 3 of the present annex shall be awarded annually, except that any increments above step XI of the Associate Officer level, step XIII of the Second Officer level, step XII of the First Officer level, step X of the Senior Officer level and step IV of the Principal Officer level shall be preceded by two years at the previous step. The Secretary-General is authorized to reduce the interval between salary increments to ten months and twenty months, respectively, in the case of staff subject to geographical distribution who have an adequate and confirmed knowledge of a second official language of the United Nations.

''5. The Secretary-General shall determine the salary rates to be paid to personnel specifically engaged for short-term missions, conferences and other short-term service, to consultants, to Field Service personnel and to technical assistance experts.

''6. The Secretary-General shall fix the salary scales for staff members in the General Service and related categories, normally on the basis of the best prevailing conditions of employment in the locality of the United Nations office concerned, provided that the Secretary-General may, where he deems it appropriate, establish rules and salary limits for payment of a non-resident allowance to General Service staff members recruited from outside the local area.

''7. The Secretary-General shall establish rules under which a language allowance may be paid to staff members in the General Service category who pass an appropriate test and demonstrate continued proficiency in the use of two or more official languages.

''8. In order to preserve equivalent standards of living at different offices, the Secretary-General may adjust the basic salaries set forth in paragraphs 1 and 3 of the present annex by the application of non-pensionable post adjustments based on relative costs of living, standards of living and related factors at the office concerned as compared to New York. Such post adjustments shall not be subject to staff assessment.

''9. No salary shall be paid to staff members in respect of periods of unauthorized absence from work unless such absence was caused by reasons beyond their control or duly certified medical reasons.''

General Assembly resolution 47/226

8 April 1993   Meeting 98   Adopted without vote

Approved by Fifth Committee (A/47/708/Add.2) without vote, 19 March (meeting 57); draft by Vice-Chairman following informal consultations (A/C.5/47/L.21); agenda item 112.
Meeting numbers. GA 47th session: 5th Committee 13, 15-17, 19-22, 25, 28, 50, 57; plenary 98.

Staff composition

In November, the Secretary-General submitted to the General Assembly his annual report[4] on the composition of the United Nations Secretariat by nationality, gender, grade and type of appointment. The total number of Secretariat staff as at 30 June 1993 was 14,558, of whom 10,192 were paid from the regular budget and 4,396 from extrabudgetary resources. There were 4,010 staff in the Professional category and above, 9,682 in the General Service and related categories, and 896 project personnel.

Staff in posts subject to geographical distribution numbered 2,573. As at 30 June, there were 29 unrepresented Member States, the same as the year before, and 25 underrepresented Member States, compared with 21 on 30 June 1992. Changes in representation resulted not only from staff appointments and separations from service, but also from adjustments in the desirable range of posts subject to geographical distribution, changes in the number of Member States, variations in the assessed contribution of individual States or in their population, as well as from changes in the status of some staff members. The report also provided information on groupings of Member States, their desirable ranges and representation at senior levels.

As at 30 June 1993, the number of women in posts subject to geographical distribution was 804, or 31.2 per cent, including three USGs, one ASG, nine at the D-2 level and 31 at the D-1 level. There were also 308 women, or 35 per cent, in posts with special language requirements.

Representation of Member States

In December, the Vice-Chairman of the Fifth Committee submitted a report[5] of the Working Group on the equitable geographical representation of Member States in the Secretariat. The

Working Group, established under General Assembly **resolution 47/226**, held five meetings in New York between 19 and 23 July to consider formulas used for geographical distribution in the United Nations system. Matters addressed during the discussions included the number of posts subject to geographical distribution, types of appointment, posts in bodies and categories excluded from distribution, the system of desirable ranges, and methods used by other international organizations to gauge the geographical representation of their membership. However, the Working Group found itself unable to agree on specific conclusions and recommendations.

On 23 December, by **decision 48/459**, the Assembly deferred consideration of the report until its resumed forty-eighth session in 1994.

Status of women in the Secretariat

During 1993, the Secretary-General submitted two reports on improving the status of women in the United Nations Secretariat.

In a March report to the Commission on the Status of Women,[6] submitted in response to a 1992 General Assembly resolution,[7] he provided a statistical update and summarized implementation of the action programme for improving the status of women[8] as well as the 1992 recommendations of the Steering Committee for the Improvement of the Status of Women in the Secretariat.[9]

The Secretary-General pointed to his March 1993 administrative instruction containing the Steering Committee's recommendations on the appointment and promotion of women and stipulating, *inter alia*, that qualified women in the service of the Organization under any type of appointment, who had a good performance record and at least one year's experience, would be regarded as internal candidates for available professional vacancies. He also indicated his intention to give priority to the promotion and recruitment of qualified women candidates in departments with less than 35 per cent women overall and less than 25 per cent women at levels P-5 and above. To bring the balance in policy-level positions as close to parity as possible by 1995, he had requested the Office of Human Resources Management (OHRM) to prepare a plan of action for 1993 and 1994, which included measures for attracting qualified women to fill vacancies and to increase the number of posts available for successful candidates from competitive examinations.

Acting on the report, the Commission on the Status of Women[10] expressed concern at the slow progress made in improving the situation of women in the Secretariat, and recommended a resolution for adoption by the Economic and Social Council (see below).

In an October report on the improvement of the status of women in the Secretariat,[11] submitted in response to a 1992 Assembly request,[7] the Secretary-General described the situation as at 30 June 1993 and developments between July 1992 and June 1993. He noted that the number of women at the ASG and D-2 levels remained comparable to the previous year. Women at the D-1 level numbered 31, an increase from 26 the year before. Women represented 21.1 per cent of staff promoted from P-5 to D-1. The Senior Review Group, appointed in 1990 to review promotions to the Director level, recommended two more women for D-2 posts in July 1993, bringing the number of women at that level to 11. There were 103 women at the P-5 level, up from 94 a year earlier, and women promoted from the P-4 to P-5 level during the reporting period numbered 39, out of a total of 94 promotions. Of staff promoted from P-3 to P-4 and from P-2 to P-3, 46.9 per cent and 52.7 per cent respectively were women. During the 12-month period ending 30 June 1993, 44 of the 119 staff members recruited in the Secretariat (37 per cent) were women. The report noted that 76 Member States, including 23 new Members of the United Nations, had no women nationals in posts subject to geographical distribution as at June 1993.

In October,[12] the Administrative Committee on Coordination (ACC) approved a policy statement on the prevention of sexual harassment, recommended by its Consultative Committee on Administrative Questions (Personnel and General Administrative Questions) (CCAQ(PER)).[13] Statistical data on the status of women in the United Nations common system were considered in 1993 by ICSC[14] as a follow-up to the recommendations of its working group on the subject, which were endorsed by the Commission in 1992.[8] The data covered the distribution and recruitment of staff by gender and level, the distribution of women by occupation, and the time in grade by gender and level.

ECONOMIC AND SOCIAL COUNCIL ACTION

On 27 July, the Economic and Social Council, on the recommendation of its Social Committee, adopted **resolution 1993/9** without vote.

Improvement of the status of women in the Secretariat

The Economic and Social Council,

Recalling Articles 1 and 101 of the Charter of the United Nations,

Recalling also Article 8 of the Charter, which provides that the United Nations shall place no restrictions on the eligibility of men and women to participate in any capacity and under conditions of equality in its principal and subsidiary organs,

Recalling further the relevant paragraphs of the Nairobi Forward-looking Strategies for the Advancement of

Women, especially paragraphs 79, 306, 315, 356 and 358,

Recalling the relevant resolutions and decisions of the General Assembly, the Economic and Social Council and other bodies that have continued to focus on this question since the adoption of Assembly resolution 2715(XXV) of 15 December 1970, in which the question of the employment of women in the Professional category was first addressed,

Noting with concern that the goal of a 30 per cent participation rate of women in posts subject to geographical distribution by the end of 1990 was not achieved,

Noting also with concern that the participation rate of women in posts at the D-1 level and above remains unreasonably low, although some welcome improvements have been made in the form of recent appointments by the Secretary-General,

Aware that a comprehensive policy aimed at preventing and combating sexual harassment should be an integral part of personnel policy,

Commending the Secretary-General for his administrative instruction on procedures for dealing with cases of sexual harassment,

Recalling the goal set by the General Assembly in resolutions 45/125 of 14 December 1990, 45/239 C of 21 December 1990, 46/100 of 16 December 1991 and 47/93 of 16 December 1992 of a 35 per cent overall participation rate of women in posts subject to geographical distribution by 1995,

Recalling also the goal set by the General Assembly in resolution 45/239 C of a 25 per cent participation rate of women in posts at the D-1 level and above by 1995,

Bearing in mind that a visible commitment by the Secretary-General, especially during the continuing restructuring phase, is essential to the achievement of the targets set by the General Assembly,

Welcoming the commitment of the Secretary-General, expressed in his statement to the Fifth Committee of the General Assembly on 6 November 1992 to bringing the gender balance in policy-level positions as close to fifty-fifty as possible, and his commitment, expressed in his message on the occasion of International Women's Day, to ensuring that the number of women in Professional posts in the Secretariat reflected the world population as a whole by the fiftieth anniversary of the United Nations in 1995,

Welcoming also the evaluation and analysis of the main obstacles to the improvement of the status of women in the Secretariat contained in the report of the Secretary-General,

Welcoming further the action programme outlined in the report of the Secretary-General, designed to remove the obstacles to the improvement of the status of women in the Secretariat,

Welcoming the development by the Secretary-General of a plan of action for 1993 and 1994 to improve the status of women in the Secretariat by 1995,

1. *Urges* the Secretary-General to implement fully the action programme designed to remove the obstacles to the improvement of the status of women in the Secretariat, and notes that his visible commitment is essential to the achievement of the targets set by the General Assembly;

2. *Also urges* the Secretary-General to further examine existing work practices within the United Nations system with a view to increasing flexibility so as to re-

move direct or indirect discrimination against staff members with family responsibilities, further considering such issues as job-sharing, flexible working hours, child-care arrangements, career-break schemes and access to training;

3. *Further urges* the Secretary-General, in accordance with the Charter of the United Nations, to accord greater priority to the recruitment and promotion of women in posts subject to geographical distribution, particularly in senior policy-level and decision-making posts, in order to achieve the goals set in General Assembly resolutions 45/125, 45/239 C, 46/100 and 47/93 of an overall participation rate of 35 per cent by 1995 and 25 per cent in posts at the D-1 level and above by 1995;

4. *Strongly urges* the Secretary-General to make further use of the opportunity offered by the United Nations reorganization process to promote more women into senior-level positions;

5. *Urges* the Secretary-General, in accordance with the Charter, to increase the number of women employed in the Secretariat from developing countries, particularly those which are unrepresented or underrepresented, and from other countries that have a low representation of women;

6. *Strongly encourages* Member States to support the efforts of the United Nations and the specialized agencies to increase the percentage of women in Professional posts, especially at the D-1 level and above, by identifying and submitting more women candidates, encouraging women to apply for vacant posts and creating national rosters of women candidates;

7. *Requests* the Secretary-General, within existing resources, to ensure that adequate machinery, with the authority of enforcement and the responsibility of accountability, including a senior-level official devoted to the implementation of the action programme and the recommendations in the report on obstacles to the improvement of the status of women in the Secretariat, is maintained and strengthened during the course of the programme for the period 1991-1995;

8. *Also requests* the Secretary-General further to develop comprehensive policy measures aimed at the prevention of sexual harassment in the Secretariat;

9. *Further requests* the Secretary-General to ensure that a progress report containing, *inter alia*, policy measures aimed at the prevention of sexual harassment in the Secretariat is submitted to the Commission on the Status of Women at its thirty-eighth session and to the General Assembly at its forty-ninth session and to ensure that it is issued in accordance with the six-week rule for the circulation of documentation.

Economic and Social Council resolution 1993/9

27 July 1993   Meeting 43   Adopted without vote

Approved by Social Committee (E/1993/105) without vote, 12 July (meeting 6); draft by Commission on the Status of Women (E/1993/27); agenda item 19.

GENERAL ASSEMBLY ACTION

On 20 December, the General Assembly, on the recommendation of the Third (Social, Humanitarian and Cultural) Committee, adopted **resolution 48/106** without vote.

Improvement of the status of women in the Secretariat

The General Assembly,

Recalling Articles 1 and 101 of the Charter of the United Nations,

Recalling also Article 8 of the Charter, which provides that the United Nations shall place no restrictions on the eligibility of men and women to participate in any capacity and under conditions of equality in its principal and subsidiary organs,

Recalling further the relevant paragraphs of the Nairobi Forward-looking Strategies for the Advancement of Women, especially paragraphs 79, 315, 356 and 358,

Recalling the relevant resolutions and decisions of the General Assembly, the Economic and Social Council and other bodies that have continued to focus on this area since the adoption of Assembly resolution 2715(XXV) of 15 December 1970, in which the question of the employment of women in the Professional category was first addressed,

Taking note of the progress report of the Secretary-General,

Recalling also the goal set in its resolutions 45/125 of 14 December 1990, 45/239 C of 21 December 1990, 46/100 of 16 December 1991 and 47/93 of 16 December 1992 of a 35 per cent overall participation rate of women in posts subject to geographical distribution by 1995,

Noting with concern that the current rate of increase in the appointment of women is insufficient to achieve the objective of a 35 per cent participation rate of women in posts subject to geographical distribution by 1995,

Recalling further the goal set in its resolution 45/239 C of a 25 per cent participation rate of women in posts at the D-1 level and above by 1995,

Also noting with concern that the participation rate of women in posts at the D-1 level and above remains unreasonably low, although some welcome improvements have been made,

Aware that a comprehensive policy aimed at preventing sexual harassment should be an integral part of personnel policy,

Commending the Secretary-General for his administrative instruction on procedures for dealing with cases of sexual harassment,

Bearing in mind that a visible commitment by the Secretary-General is essential to the achievement of the targets set by the General Assembly,

Welcoming the commitment of the Secretary-General, expressed in his statement to the Fifth Committee of the General Assembly on 6 November 1992, to bringing the balance in policy-level positions as close to fifty-fifty as possible, and his commitment, expressed in his message on the occasion of International Women's Day, 1993, to see that the number of women in Professional posts in the Secretariat reflects the world population as a whole by the fiftieth anniversary of the United Nations in 1995,

Welcoming also the development by the Secretary-General of a plan of action for 1993 and 1994 to improve the status of women in the Secretariat by 1995,

1. *Urges* the Secretary-General to implement fully the plan of action to improve the status of women in the Secretariat by 1995, noting that his visible commitment is essential to the achievement of the targets set by the General Assembly;

2. *Also urges* the Secretary-General to examine further existing work practices within the United Nations system with a view to increasing flexibility so as to remove direct or indirect discrimination against staff members with family responsibilities, including consideration of such issues as job-sharing, flexible working hours, child-care arrangements, career break schemes and access to training;

3. *Further urges* the Secretary-General, in accordance with the Charter of the United Nations, to accord greater priority to the recruitment and promotion of women in posts subject to geographical distribution, particularly in senior policy-level and decision-making posts and within those parts of the United Nations system and its specialized agencies where representation of women is considerably below the average, in order to achieve the goals set in its resolutions 45/125, 45/239 C, 46/100 and 47/93 of an overall participation rate of 35 per cent by 1995 and 25 per cent in posts at the D-1 level and above by 1995;

4. *Strongly urges* the Secretary-General to make further use of the opportunity offered by the United Nations reorganization process to promote more women into senior-level positions;

5. *Calls on* the Secretary-General to strengthen, from within existing resources, the focal point for women within the Secretariat to ensure authority of enforcement and responsibility of accountability and to enable it more effectively to monitor and facilitate progress in the 1995 action programme;

6. *Urges* the Secretary-General to increase the number of women employed in the Secretariat from developing countries, particularly those which are unrepresented or underrepresented, and from other countries that have a low representation of women, including countries in transition;

7. *Strongly encourages* Member States to support the efforts of the United Nations and the specialized agencies to increase the percentage of women in Professional posts, especially at the D-1 level and above, by identifying and submitting more women candidates, encouraging women to apply for vacant posts and creating national rosters of women candidates to be shared with the Secretariat, specialized agencies and regional commissions;

8. *Requests* the Secretary-General further to develop comprehensive policy measures aimed at the prevention of sexual harassment in the Secretariat;

9. *Also requests* the Secretary-General to ensure that a progress report on the status of women in the Secretariat containing, *inter alia*, policy measures aimed at the prevention of sexual harassment in the Secretariat, is presented to the Commission on the Status of Women at its thirty-eighth session, in accordance with the relevant rules on the delivery timetable for documentation, and to the General Assembly at its forty-ninth session.

General Assembly resolution 48/106

20 December 1993   Meeting 85   Adopted without vote

Approved by Third Committee (A/48/629) without vote, 1 December (meeting 48); 63-nation draft (A/C.3/48/L.31); agenda item 111.

Sponsors: Afghanistan, Albania, Angola, Australia, Austria, Bahamas, Bangladesh, Belarus, Bolivia, Burkina Faso, Burundi, Cameroon, Canada, Central African Republic, Costa Rica, Côte d'Ivoire, Cyprus, Czech Republic, Denmark, Dominican Republic, Estonia, Ethiopia, Finland, Germany, Ghana, Greece, Guatemala, Guinea-Bissau, Guyana, Haiti, Iceland, Indonesia, Ireland, Israel, Italy, Jamaica, Libyan Arab Jamahiriya, Liechtenstein, Mongolia, Morocco, Myanmar, Netherlands, New Zealand, Nica-

ragua, Nigeria, Norway, Pakistan, Philippines, Poland, Portugal, Republic of Korea, Romania, Senegal, Singapore, Slovenia, Spain, Sweden, Turkey, Ukraine, United Kingdom, United States, Yemen, Zambia.
Meeting numbers. GA 48th session: 3rd Committee 29-37, 41, 48, plenary 85.

Staffing of UN missions

In October,[15] the Secretary-General transmitted to the General Assembly a report of the Joint Inspection Unit (JIU) on staffing of the United Nations peace-keeping and related missions (civilian component). JIU made recommendations on the planning and management of peace-keeping operations at Headquarters and in the field, on recruitment, briefing and training, and on the conditions of service of civilian personnel. It recommended ensuring better delineation of authority between DPKO and other Secretariat entities dealing with such operations, strengthening DPKO by recruiting experienced and competent civilian and military personnel, merging the Field Operations Division (FOD) into DPKO, establishing a core team responsible for peace-keeping operations and a post of Police Commissioner within DPKO, strengthening the recently established 24-hour situation room and designating focal points to deal with queries of Member States. With regard to the functioning of field structures, JIU recommended establishing clear lines of authority and interrelationship between major officials in missions, creating or strengthening joint operation centres to function on a 24-hour basis, and delegating more administrative and financial authority to the field.

Recommendations concerning recruitment provided for the creation of a "pre-certified" roster and a roster of selected retirees for recruitment; the more active use of outside recruitment and of United Nations Volunteers; the secondment of staff from specialized agencies and regional organizations; the use of stand-by personnel from Member States; the encouragement of local staff recruitment and suitable contractual instruments; and the formulation of new policies and procedures with a better field orientation. Other recommendations dealt with the creation of a pool of trained personnel at different management levels, provision for special training programmes and on-the-job training, and the security of personnel.

Submitting his comments in December,[16] the Secretary-General said that the integration of FOD into DPKO had been carried out and the post of Police Advisor was established in the Department. He further pointed to his proposal to redeploy a number of posts for the creation of a focal point unit within DPKO and noted that the concept of a joint operations centre was already in effect in the field missions in Somalia and the former Yugoslavia and was being introduced into other large multidimensional missions. The Secretary-General also stated that both a pre-certified roster of personnel and a roster of retirees had been established and

described steps taken to implement other recommendations.

In response to a 1992 General Assembly request,[17] the Secretary-General presented a December 1993 report[18] on the use of civilian personnel in peace-keeping operations. He examined arrangements for the use of personnel provided by Governments, staff assigned from the Secretariat and other organizations of the United Nations system, civilians recruited individually from outside the system, the use of United Nations Volunteers, and personnel contracted internationally and locally. The Secretary-General concluded that no single source could provide the civilian personnel required for field missions and that a mix was usually necessary for missions to function effectively and at minimum cost.

On 23 December, by **decision 48/459**, the Assembly deferred consideration of the Secretary-General's note[16] with comments on JIU's report until its resumed forty-eighth session in 1994.

Post classification system

In August, ACC's CCAQ(PER)[13] considered alternative arrangements for the Director category, including its de-linking from the Professional grades, an increase in D-level remuneration, and the introduction of a pay-for-performance scheme and time-limited assignments. The Committee also examined two alternative adjustments to the introduction of a P-6 grade. Under the first, a P-6 would be equal in all respects to D-1, but classified to account for technical rather than directorial complexity. Under the second arrangement, P-6 would be a separate level between P-5 and D-1. In December,[12] ACC requested CCAQ(PER) to complete and report on its studies of these matters in 1994.

In 1993,[14] ICSC considered a status report on job classification and human resources development in the United Nations common system. It noted progress achieved in developing job classification standards and the need to maintain their accuracy and relevance. It decided to pursue the development of practical solutions to problems identified in the administration of the job classification system. Lastly, it reaffirmed that job classification was compatible with effective career planning, and indeed a prerequisite for it.

In **resolution 48/228**, the General Assembly decided that, until posts were reclassified according to prescribed internal procedures and approved by it, no staff member encumbering a post under reclassification review should be paid at the higher grade level.

Career development and training

In 1993, the promotion system in the Secretariat changed from the Vacancy Management and

Redeployment System, in force from 1988 to 1992, to one involving a grade-by-grade promotion review of eligible staff once a year. A new Placement and Promotion System was to be introduced in the near future, which would provide for a review of candidates as vacancies occurred.

In its 1993 report,[14] ICSC reiterated the importance of training to organizational efficiency and to enhancing the career objectives of staff. It approved guidelines for the evaluation of training proposed by CCAQ(PER),[13] and recommended their application in organizations of the United Nations common system.

In **resolution 47/226** on personnel questions, the General Assembly endorsed the principles contained in the Secretary-General's 1992 reports[19] on career development at the United Nations and the training programme in the Secretariat and made a number of requests for action to improve the career development system and the training programme in respect of staff accountability and performance evaluation, rotation of assignments, career counselling, equal employment opportunities, language requirements and staff motivation.

Staff rules and regulations

On 8 April, the General Assembly, by **decision 47/457 B**, took note of the Secretary-General's 1991[20] and 1992[21] reports on amendments to the Staff Rules of the United Nations. In **resolution 47/226** of the same date (see above), the Assembly approved amendments to the Staff Regulations of the United Nations, proposed by the Secretary-General in 1991[20] and 1992.[21]

In November 1993, the Secretary-General submitted his annual report[22] containing the texts of provisional rules and amendments to the Staff Regulations. The changes applicable to all staff, except technical cooperation project personnel and staff specifically engaged for conference and other short-term service, concerned the function of the Appointment and Promotion Board to make recommendations to the Secretary-General on proposed probationary and other appointments of a probable duration of one year or more, excluding the appointment of persons for service with a mission; the selection of staff members qualified for promotion; minimum periods of service in grade as a normal requirement for consideration for promotion; and lateral transfers or reassignments of a probable duration of one year or more. The changes applicable to staff specifically engaged for short-term service and assignments of limited duration concerned two types of non-career appointments: the traditional short-term appointment of up to six months, intended for language and other conference services, and an appointment of limited duration, expected to last between three months and three to four years in such activities as peace-keeping and peacemaking, technical cooperation, and humanitarian and emergency operations. The provisions on travel arrangements were also revised.

By **decision 48/459** of 23 December, the Assembly deferred consideration of the report until its resumed forty-eighth session in 1994.

Staff representation

On 23 December, by **decision 48/459**, the General Assembly again deferred consideration of the Secretary-General's 1992 report on the cost of staff representation activities,[21] reviewing the nature and level of regular budget funding for those activities, until its resumed forty-eighth session.

Privileges and immunities

In response to a March 1993 Security Council request,[23] the Secretary-General submitted an August report on the security of United Nations operations[24] and arrangements to protect United Nations forces and personnel. On 20 September, in **resolution 47/120 B, section VII**, the General Assembly welcomed the report and decided to consider further steps to enhance the status and safety of personnel involved in United Nations operations. (For more information on the security of United Nations operations, see PART ONE, Chapter I, and PART FOUR, Chapter II.)

On 8 April, the Assembly, by **decision 47/457 C**, requested the Secretary-General to submit updated information on respect for the privileges and immunities of officials of the United Nations and the specialized agencies and related organizations, pursuant to its 1990[25] and 1992[26] resolutions.

In September 1993, the Secretary-General, on behalf of and with the approval of ACC, submitted a note[27] with updated information on the subject. He said that developments of the last year had pushed the acceptable safety threshold for personnel of the United Nations system to a level inconceivable in the past. The banner of the Organization no longer provided staff with safe passage and an unwritten guarantee of protection, and staff were often at risk simply by virtue of their employment with organizations of the system. Although the primary responsibility for the security of staff rested with host Governments or other governmental authorities, the United Nations was increasingly called on to operate in areas where there was no Government or where the Government was unable to fulfil its commitments under the Charter.

Since 1 July 1992, there had been 19 fatalities among staff members belonging to different organizations, bringing the number of fatalities since the beginning of 1992 to 30. As at 30 June 1993, there were 45 officials under detention or missing, including 28 staff members of the United Nations Relief and Works Agency for Palestine Refugees in the Near East (UNRWA) who were arrested during the period 1 July 1992 to 30 June 1993. Of 70 UNRWA staff members arrested during that period, 40 were subsequently released without charge or trial, and two were charged, tried and sentenced.

The note also discussed the taxation of United Nations officials by host countries and restrictions on their official and private travel. On 1 February, the Secretary-General received from Switzerland a note verbale stating that tax liability would no longer be applied to officials of international organizations residing in its Canton of Vaud. However, Israel continued to levy an exit tax on personnel of UNRWA and the United Nations Truce Supervision Organization, and problems related to the taxation of officials were experienced by the International Labour Organisation (ILO) and the United Nations Industrial Development Organization. The Secretary-General also reported that, on 24 September 1992,[28] he had received from the United States a note verbale stating that the United Nations staff members who were nationals of Georgia could enjoy unrestricted travel in the United States. The United States took similar action with regard to nationals of Afghanistan on 11 January 1993 (see PART FOUR, Chapter IV). UNRWA, however, continued to report travel restrictions imposed by Israel on its staff.

On 8 November, a representative of the United Nations Security Coordinator reported to the Fifth Committee that nine UNRWA staff members had been released from detention since 30 June.

Also in November, the Secretary-General submitted to the General Assembly comments by the Coordinating Committee for Independent Staff Unions and Associations of the United Nations System (CCISUA) on the issues of security and independence of the international civil service.[29] The Committee called for adequate pressure on Member States that ignored their responsibility under the Charter for the security of United Nations personnel and urged closer monitoring of Charter violations. It stressed the need for strategies for the safety of staff on peace-keeping and humanitarian missions, a quicker response to the needs of staff members injured on duty, and more humanitarian treatment of staff returning from detention or suffering from undue pressure exerted by their Governments. CCISUA said that a medical team to visit illegally detained staff should be on line before the end of 1993 and it recommended reactivation of the Secretary-General's Task Force

on the Security and Independence of the International Civil Service.

On 23 December, by **decision 48/462**, the Assembly took note of the Secretary-General's note[27] and of the Security Coordinator's statement to the Fifth Committee.

REFERENCES

[1]YUN 1992, p. 1059, GA dec. 47/457 A, 23 Dec. 1992. [2]A/48/238. [3]A/48/7. [4]A/48/559. [5]A/C.5/48/45. [6]E/CN.6/1993/15. [7]YUN 1992, p. 1062, GA res. 47/93, 16 Dec. 1992. [8]Ibid., p. 1061. [9]Ibid., p. 1060. [10]E/1993/27. [11]A/48/513. [12]ACC/1993/28. [13]ACC/1993/22. [14]A/48/30 & Corr.1. [15]A/48/421. [16]A/48/421/Add.1. [17]YUN 1992, p. 1025, GA res. 47/218 A, 23 Dec. 1992. [18]A/48/707. [19]YUN 1992, p. 1063. [20]YUN 1991, p. 896. [21]YUN 1992, p. 1064. [22]A/C.5/48/37. [23]S/25493. [24]A/48/349-S/26358. [25]GA res. 45/240, 21 Dec. 1990. [26]YUN 1992, p. 1065, GA res. 47/28, 25 Nov. 1992. [27]A/C.5/48/5. [28]YUN 1992, p. 1006. [29]A/C.5/48/17.

Staff costs

In its 1993 report,[1] ICSC continued to advise the General Assembly on staff salaries and allowances and made recommendations regarding pensionable remuneration and pension entitlements. The Commission continued to monitor the net remuneration margin between officials in comparable positions of the United States Federal Civil Service and the United Nations system. It reaffirmed its 1992 decision[2] that a new methodology for determining the cost-of-living differential between New York and Washington, D.C., should be used in net margin calculations and decided to implement the new methodology in calculations for 1993, along with the margin calculation methodology endorsed by the Assembly in 1989.[3] The application of those methodologies resulted in a margin for the 1993 calendar year of 114.2.

ICSC recommended a 3.6 per cent increase in the current base/floor salary scale, through the consolidation of post adjustment, and a revised staff assessment scale, both with effect from 1 March 1994, as well as a new procedure for determining a common staff assessment scale and the introduction of a common staff assessment scale for determining the pensionable remuneration of all categories of staff in 1997. It further recommended the income replacement approach using 66.25 per cent of the net pensionable salary for determining the net pensionable remuneration of the General Service and related categories, to be implemented with the first adjustment of the salary scale on or after 1 April 1994, and decided that subsequent adjustments of pensionable remuneration should be made on the basis of a 1-to-1 interim adjustment procedure.

The Commission proposed parameters for a language incentive scheme for staff in the Professional and higher categories, examined criteria and modalities for payment of special occupational rates, and decided that the use of post adjustment classes should be eliminated as of 1 January 1994. In response to a 1989 Assembly request,[3] ICSC reviewed the expatriate entitlements of staff living in the home country and stationed elsewhere, with a view to harmonizing existing practices. It also reviewed the general methodology for surveys of best prevailing conditions of employment at non-headquarters duty stations (see below), decided to maintain the current practices with regard to working hours and remuneration, and requested ILO to bring its practices concerning extra steps beyond the salary scale into line with that of the common system.

The Assembly acted on ICSC's recommendations in **resolution 48/224** (see above, under "International Civil Service Commission").

Emoluments of top-echelon officials

On 6 May, the General Assembly, by **decision 47/460 B**, again deferred consideration of the Secretary-General's two 1991 reports on remuneration for JIU inspectors[4] and his 1991[5] and 1992[6] reports on the question of honoraria payable to members of organs and subsidiary organs of the United Nations.

Special representatives, envoys and related positions

In August,[7] ACABQ noted that the Secretary-General had recently appointed a number of representatives and envoys at the ASG and USG levels. It requested him to explain the rationale for establishing such high-level posts and to develop criteria for determining related emoluments. The General Assembly, by **decision 47/474** of 14 September, requested the Secretary-General to report on the issues raised by ACABQ with regard to the establishment of special representatives, envoys and related positions.

In a November report,[8] the Secretary-General said that most of the positions in question were in peace-keeping or observer missions approved by the Security Council, and normally corresponded to the USG or ASG level, depending on the size and complexity of the mission. As at 30 September, there were 22 officials in that category (6 at the USG level and 16 at the ASG level), who were remunerated from the budgets approved for their missions. Another category comprised envoys appointed by the Secretary-General to assist him in the exercise of his good offices and related functions. Their rank was determined by the level of responsibilities and the scope and complexity of activities supervised. There were 13 officials in that category (10 at the USG level and 3 at the ASG level), 3 of whom assisted the Secretary-General for a $1 a year honorarium or reimbursement of travel expenses. Others were remunerated on a "when actually employed" basis or on time-limited assignments, and were funded as unforeseen and extraordinary expenses. In addition, 4 officials assisted the Secretary-General in various capacities, including one for a $1 a year honorarium. The report noted that emoluments for all three categories were determined in accordance with the Staff Rules and Regulations and, in cases of limited-duration assignments, were prorated for the length of employment.

By **decision 48/459** of 23 December, the Assembly deferred consideration of the report until its resumed forty-eighth session in 1994.

Remuneration of International Tribunal members

In July,[9] ACABQ considered the question of financing the International Tribunal for the Prosecution of Persons Responsible for Serious Violations of International Humanitarian Law Committed in the Territory of the Former Yugoslavia since 1991, established by the Security Council in May (see PART TWO, Chapter IV). It requested the Secretary-General to provide detailed justification for the number of posts in the Tribunal and their grade level, as well as the allowances of its judges.

In a December report,[10] the Secretary-General noted that, according to the statute of the Tribunal, the remuneration of its judges was the same as that for judges of the International Court of Justice (ICJ). Pending a further review, scheduled for the Assembly's forty-eighth session, that remuneration, as revised by the General Assembly in 1990,[11] included an annual salary of $145,000, a special allowance to the President and Vice-President of the Tribunal and the reimbursement of education costs for children. Should the Tribunal be established at The Hague, Netherlands, the floor/ceiling salary scale would also be applicable. Judges were to give up all other remunerated occupations for the duration of their judgeship.

The Secretary-General further proposed a pension entitlement of $20,000 for a member of the Tribunal who served a full four-year term, to be increased in case of re-election by an additional $150 per month, up to a maximum of $30,000 a year. In case of death, the survivors' entitlement should equal one month's base salary for each year of service, subject to a minimum of one month and a maximum of four months. The relocation allowance upon completion of service should amount to 12 weeks of net salary, while an entitlement after four continuous years or more of eligibility should total 16 weeks of annual net base salary.

On 23 December, by **decision 48/459**, the General Assembly deferred consideration of the report until its resumed forty-eighth session in 1994. By the same decision, it deferred consideration of a report on remuneration for members of ICJ, requested in 1990.[11] The report was not issued at the time of the decision.

Salaries and allowances

By **decision 47/468** of 6 May, the General Assembly, further to its 1990 resolution on the same issue,[12] noted that remuneration for Secretariat officials should be separate and distinct from that for other officials serving the Assembly and that the Staff Rules and Regulations were not necessarily applicable to the latter. The Secretary-General was requested to submit background information on the subject.

In **resolution 48/228**, the Assembly expressed concern at the high costs of after-service health insurance and requested the Secretary-General to seek ways to reduce increases in those costs. On 23 December, it noted a significant increase in the common staff costs of salaries and overtime payments, particularly with respect to security officers, and requested the Board of Auditors to pay special attention to that matter in its audit of the United Nations accounts for 1992-1993 (**decision 48/481**). It also invited the Board to consider the issue of vacancies resulting from the deployment of staff to peace-keeping operations and their impact on salaries and common staff costs (**decision 48/460**).

On the same date, by **decision 48/459**, the General Assembly deferred consideration of a report on the question of staff assessment, requested in 1992.[13] The report was not issued at the time of the decision.

Supernumerary staff

On 23 December, the General Assembly, by **decision 48/460**, reiterated its 1992 endorsement[14] of the Board of Auditors' 1992 recommendation[15] that payments to supernumerary staff should not have been effected without prior approval of the Assembly. It noted that such payments were not authorized by the Assembly and requested the Secretary-General to report at its resumed forty-eighth session in 1994 on all aspects of the use of supernumerary staff during 1990-1991 and 1992-1993. It also invited the Board of Auditors to consider the matter in its audit of the United Nations accounts for 1992-1993.

The Board had noted, in 1992, that maintaining supernumerary staff at the United Nations Office at Vienna by-passed the objectives of retrench-

ment mandated by the General Assembly in 1986,[16] and that no termination indemnity should be paid to a staff member on a temporary appointment already completed.

Relationship agreements

On 12 February, the Economic and Social Council decided to initiate a discussion of the relationship agreements between the United Nations and the member organizations of the common system, taking into account the views of JIU, ICSC and background information by the Secretary-General (**decision 1993/211**). A review of those agreements was called for by the General Assembly in 1992,[17] in view of the 1991 decision of the International Telecommunication Union (ITU)[18] to grant a special post allowance to its staff of the Professional and higher categories to compensate for temporary additional work required to implement changes in ITU's functioning.

In March, CCAQ(PER)[19] considered the issue and concluded that it could not identify any problems at the working level which would justify a review of the agreements. In April,[20] ACC took note of that conclusion.

In a June note,[21] the Secretary-General reviewed pertinent provisions of the Charter of the United Nations and the statute of ICSC, which was established in 1974[22] for the regulation and coordination of the United Nations common system. He noted that, in 1991, the Commission had considered ITU's unilateral action incompatible with the common system and that, in 1992, the ITU Administrative Council had accepted the Commission's position, endorsed by the Assembly,[23] but concluded that there was a legal commitment to grant the special post allowance to the staff who had already performed additional work. Subsequently, ICSC had reiterated its view on the matter. Pertinent extracts from ICSC's 1991[18] and 1992[24] reports were transmitted to the Council by another June 1993 note.[25]

In September,[26] the Secretary-General transmitted to the Council JIU's report on relationship agreements and ACC's comments. The report reviewed specific sections of the 17 agreements concluded between the United Nations and specialized agencies and the International Atomic Energy Agency, relating to personnel matters or to a unified international civil service. It noted that the agreements had never been revised and could not reflect all the developments that took place after their conclusion. To consolidate the common system further, JIU recommended an evaluation of the agreements' implementation and assessment of the application of particular provisions; a more active and specific application of existing coordinating measures; an enhanced role for ICSC in regulating and coordinating conditions of service in the common system; the establishment of a procedure for approving interpretations and understandings of relevant provisions by the General Assembly and the governing bodies of member organizations; supplementary arrangements with executive heads on modalities of practical cooperation; and more active involvement of Member States in the maintenance of coherent positions regarding staff salaries and conditions of service in different organizations. JIU also recommended that the Committee for Programme and Coordination (CPC) be entrusted with formulating draft resolutions and decisions on coordination questions or that an inter-sessional committee on coordination matters be created within the Economic and Social Council; that a portion of the Council's sessions be devoted to system-wide coordination; and that periodic joint meetings between CPC and ACC be devoted to the same objective.

Commenting on the report, ACC noted that JIU had undertaken a broader review than envisaged by the Assembly and the Council, and that a number of the recommended actions were already being undertaken. ACC was of the view that the review of agreements as well as understanding on their interpretation would evolve in the course of restructuring the inter-agency machinery. At the same time, a fuller application of coordination measures would depend significantly on the initiative of Member States. ACC agreed with the proposal to enhance ICSC's exposure to various organizations but believed that the Commission's participation in their meetings would not be beneficial. Noting existing agreements on inter-agency cooperation in the context of peace-keeping, ACC stated that the need for further arrangements would have to be clearly identified before entering into any new inter-agency agreement. It welcomed the recommendation for the greater involvement of Member States in coordination matters, noting that some complications might be avoided if their representatives maintained consistent positions in the governing bodies of different organizations. Lastly, it underscored the fact that coordination questions were already the main subject of CPC/ACC joint meetings.

By **decision 1993/337** of 8 December, the Economic and Social Council took note of the documents transmitted to it for discussion of the relationship agreements.

General Service salaries

In a September note to the Fifth Committe,[27] submitted in response to a 1990 General Assembly request,[28] the Secretary-General reviewed procedures whereby he and other executive heads could take measures on salary scales of the General Service category at variance with ICSC's recom-

mendations only after consultations with the appropriate intergovernmental bodies and the Commission. The Secretary-General proposed that, in addition to the existing consultation mechanism, there should also be consultations with ACABQ prior to a decision on General Service salaries.

ICSC, in 1993,[1] reviewed the general methodology for surveys of the best prevailing conditions of employment at non-headquarters duty stations. Its review was based on the findings of an informal working group composed of representatives of the ICSC secretariat, United Nations organizations, the Federation of International Civil Servants' Associations and CCISUA and followed a 1992 review of the methodology for surveying the best prevailing conditions at headquarters duty stations.[29] The Commission noted that while the methodologies used for both headquarters and non-headquarters duty stations were based on the Flemming principle, they measured conditions of service in very different labour markets and office structures; the headquarters methodology operated in largely homogenous office structures in well-established economies, while the non-headquarters methodology was applied to offices with an extremely diverse composition located in countries with widely varying economies.

In the context of its review, ICSC addressed questions such as salaries, selection of jobs, selection of employers, job classification standards, pensionable remuneration and its own role in the two review processes. As a result, it approved certain changes to the methodology which became effective 1 July 1993. The Commission decided to maintain existing provisions with regard to the treatment of the non-pensionable component of remuneration, pending a further review of the issue in 1996.

The Assembly, in **resolution 48/224, section III**, noted ICSC's decisions with respect to its review of the general methodology for surveys of best conditions at non-headquarters duty stations. It urged organizations to implement the Commission's recommendations with regard to salary scales for staff in the General Service and related categories and requested that, in cases where decisions at variance with those recommendations were envisaged, the matter be referred to the governing body of the organization(s) concerned.

Pensions

During 1993, the number of participants in the United Nations Joint Staff Pension Fund increased from 61,968 to 63,329, or by 2.2 percent; the number of periodic benefits in award increased from 33,923 to 35,435, or by 4.5 per cent. On 31 December, the breakdown of the periodic benefits in award was as follows: 11,688 retirement benefits,

6,427 early retirement benefits, 5,736 deferred retirement benefits, 4,963 widows' and widowers' benefits, 5,896 children's benefits, 669 disability benefits and 56 secondary dependants' benefits. In the course of the year, 4,186 lump-sum withdrawal and other settlements were paid.

During the same period, the principal of the Fund increased from \$10,246,849,744 to \$11,160,603,611, or by 8.9 per cent.

The investment income of the Fund during the year amounted to \$893,907,978, comprising \$567,664,880 in interest and dividends and \$326,243,098 in net profit on sales of investments. After deduction of investment management costs amounting to \$13,827,607, net investment income was \$880,080,371.

The Fund was administered by the 33-member United Nations Joint Staff Pension Board, which held its forty-fifth session (special) in New York from 24 to 30 June 1993.[30] In accordance with the General Assembly's 1991 decision to biennialize the Fifth Committee's work,[31] the Fund's forty-fifth session was scheduled to take place in 1994. However, in 1992,[32] the Assembly asked ICSC, in cooperation with the Board, to finalize in 1993 the review of the pensionable remuneration and pensions of the General Service staff and related categories. The special session was held to deal with that issue.

The Board also considered: amendments to the Fund's Regulations governing the methodology for determining pensionable remuneration, as requested by the Assembly in 1992;[33] a study of the "income inversion" anomaly and its possible reduction, requested by the Assembly in the same resolution; the Fund's administrative expenses; and methodology and actuarial assumptions to be used in the next actuarial valuation of the Fund. The Board also decided to provide the Assembly with a status report on problems related to the interpretation and application of the three transfer agreements between the Fund and the former USSR, Byelorussian SSR and Ukrainian SSR, which the Board had started to discuss in 1991 and 1992.

The Board also examined the management of the Fund's investments, financial statements and schedules for the year ending 31 December 1992, the investment return during the year ending 31 March 1993, and amendments to the Fund's Administrative Rules and Rules of Procedure, adopted by its Standing Committee. In accordance with articles 9 and 20 of the Fund's Regulations, the Board dealt with the membership of its Committee of Actuaries and its Investments Committee.

ACABQ submitted its comments on the Board's report in October,[34] and the Assembly acted on the Board's recommendations in December (see below).

Pension Fund investments

The market value of the Fund's assets as at 31 March 1993 was \$11,407 million, an increase of \$1,296 million over the previous year. Total investment return for the year ended 31 March 1993 was 11.6 per cent, which, after adjusting for inflation, represented a "real" rate of return of 8.2 per cent. Investment income from interest and dividends amounted to \$568 million in 1993. New funds, which became available for investment (contributions plus investment income, less benefit payments and investment expenses), totalled \$588.5 million, while realized capital gains amounted to \$326.2 million.

The Fund remained one of the most diversified pension funds in the world, as the proportion of its assets exposed to currencies other than the United States dollar, which was the Fund's unit of account, as well as the ratio of equities to total assets continued to increase. In order to preserve the Fund's principal, the defensive policy adopted in the mid-1980s was continued but slightly changed. It consisted of increasing holdings in selected equities which appeared undervalued and with potential for future appreciation.

The book value of development-related investments also increased. Investments in development institutions amounted to \$1,139.7 million in June 1993, compared with \$1,050 million a year earlier, while direct investments in specific developing countries totalled \$506.4 million, up from \$487.6 million in 1992. Close contacts were maintained with international organizations, regional development institutions, Governments and private sources to ensure full awareness of investment opportunities in developing countries, and follow-up missions were undertaken to Africa, Asia, Latin America and the Middle East.

The implementation of new custodial arrangements for the Fund's assets, aimed at their diversification, through the introduction of parallel accounting and reporting systems and establishment of regional custodians, began in early 1993. The purpose of the new arrangements was to ensure effective risk management and greater control and flexibility, and reduce costs such as custody fees, which exceeded \$5.8 million in 1993.

GENERAL ASSEMBLY ACTION

On 23 December, the General Assembly, on the recommendation of the Fifth Committee, adopted **resolution 48/225** without vote.

United Nations pension system

The General Assembly,

Recalling its resolutions 45/242 of 21 December 1990, 46/191 A and 46/192 of 20 December 1991 and 47/203 of 22 December 1992,

Having considered the report of the United Nations Joint Staff Pension Board for 1993 to the General Assembly and to the member organizations of the United Nations Joint Staff Pension Fund, chapter III of the report of the International Civil Service Commission, and the related report of the Advisory Committee on Administrative and Budgetary Questions,

I
Pensionable remuneration of staff in the General Service
and related categories

Recalling that, in section III of its resolution 45/242, the General Assembly requested the International Civil Service Commission, in full cooperation with the United Nations Joint Staff Pension Board, to submit recommendations to it at its forty-sixth session in respect of the comprehensive review of the methodology for determining the pensionable remuneration and consequent pensions of staff in the General Service and related categories,

Also recalling section III of its resolution 46/191 A, section II of its resolution 46/192 and section III of its resolution 47/203,

Noting with satisfaction that close cooperation between the Commission and the Board has enabled the two bodies to complete the comprehensive review in 1993 and to reach agreement on the methodology for determining the levels of pensionable remuneration of staff in the General Service and related categories,

1. *Approves* the recommendations made by the International Civil Service Commission that the income replacement approach, applying 66.25 per cent of the net pensionable salary, should be used to determine the pensionable remuneration for staff in the General Service and related categories, and that the revised methodology should be implemented on the occasion of the first adjustment of the salary scale, on or after 1 April 1994, subject to the transitional measures applied on the occasion of the introduction of the 1992 staff assessment scale;

2. *Notes* that the recommendations of the Commission in paragraph 85 of its report do not eliminate the income inversion anomaly and that further attention will need to be given to its elimination;

3. *Approves* the recommendation that subsequent adjustments of pensionable remuneration, until the introduction of the common staff assessment scale in 1997, should be made on the basis of a 1:1 interim adjustment procedure;

4. *Approves also* the procedure outlined in paragraph 44 of the report of the Commission for determining the common staff assessment scale, with two separate sets of rates (single and dependent);

5. *Requests* the Commission, in close cooperation with the United Nations Joint Staff Pension Board, as part of the comprehensive review in 1996 of the methodology to determine the pensionable remuneration and consequent pensions of staff in the Professional and higher categories, to develop a common staff assessment scale for the determination of the pensionable remuneration of all categories of staff using the procedure approved in paragraph 4 above and reflecting the latest available tax rates;

6. *Also requests* the Commission to recommend to the General Assembly at its fifty-first session a common staff assessment scale, together with the effective date and

modalities for its implementation, including appropriate transitional measures as required;

7. *Decides* that, following the introduction of the common staff assessment scale in 1997, the income replacement approach should be used to determine the pensionable remuneration of staff in the General Service and related categories on the occasion of comprehensive salary surveys, with subsequent adjustment of pensionable remuneration between comprehensive surveys to be made on the basis of a 1:1 interim adjustment procedure;

8. *Notes* that the Commission, in close cooperation with the Board, will continue to keep under review the matter of the pensionable remuneration and consequent pensions of staff in the General Service and related categories;

9. *Amends*, with effect from 1 April 1994, article 54 (*a*) of the Regulations of the United Nations Joint Staff Pension Fund, as set out in annex I to the present resolution;

10. *Amends also*, with effect from 1 April 1994, paragraph 6 of annex I to the Staff Regulations of the United Nations, as set out in annex II to the present resolution, and urges the other member organizations of the United Nations Joint Staff Pension Fund to take similar action to amend their Staff Regulations or Staff Rules as appropriate;

II
Actuarial matters

1. *Takes note* of the observations of the United Nations Joint Staff Pension Board in section III.C of its report on the methodology and assumptions to be used in the actuarial valuation of the United Nations Joint Staff Pension Fund as at 31 December 1993, in particular the changes in the rates of mortality for pensioners and the rates of incidence of disability as set out in paragraphs 108 and 109, respectively, of the report of the Board;

2. *Takes note also* of the observations of the Panel of External Auditors, the Pension Board and the Committee of Actuaries, as well as the views of Member States, on the request made by the General Assembly in resolution 47/203 that the Board consider the form in which it presents the results of the actuarial valuations, and of the intention of the Board to report on this matter, following discussion with the Board of Auditors, to the Assembly at its forty-ninth session;

3. *Takes note further* of the observations of the Board in section III.C of its report on matters related to the operation and application of the transfer agreements that had been concluded, effective 1 January 1981, between the United Nations Joint Staff Pension Fund and the former Union of Soviet Socialist Republics, Ukrainian Soviet Socialist Republic and Byelorussian Soviet Socialist Republic;

III
Administrative expenses

1. *Approves* expenses chargeable directly to the United Nations Joint Staff Pension Fund, totalling 39,291,900 United States dollars net for the biennium 1994-1995, and an increase in expenses of 365,400 dollars net for the biennium 1992-1993, for the administration of the Fund;

2. *Authorizes* the United Nations Joint Staff Pension Board to supplement the voluntary contributions to the

Emergency Fund, for the biennium 1994-1995, by an amount not exceeding 200,000 dollars.

IV
Other matters

Takes note of the other matters dealt with in the report of the United Nations Joint Staff Pension Board.

ANNEX I
Amendments to the Regulations of the United Nations Joint Staff Pension Fund

Article 54
Pensionable remuneration

Replace paragraph *(a)* and subparagraph (i) thereof with the following texts:

"*(a)*   In the case of participants in the General Service and related categories, pensionable remuneration shall be the equivalent in dollars of the sum of:

"(i)   The participant's gross pensionable salary, as determined on the occasion of comprehensive salary surveys and subsequently adjusted between such salary surveys, in accordance with the methodology approved by the General Assembly and set out in appendix A to these Regulations,".

Subparagraphs (ii) and (iii) remain unchanged; the reference in paragraph *(b)* to "the appendix hereto" shall be changed to "Appendix B hereto".

Add the following appendix to the Regulations of the Fund:

"Appendix A

"1.   *Methodology for determining the gross pensionable salary for participants in the General Service and related categories*

"(a)   Effective 1 April 1994, and subject to paragraph *(b)* below, the methodology for determining the gross pensionable salary for participants in the General Service and related categories on the occasion of comprehensive salary surveys shall be as follows:

"(i)   66.25 per cent of the net pensionable salary, determined in accordance with the procedure approved by the International Civil Service Commission, is calculated at each grade and step;

"(ii)   The amounts in subparagraph (i) above are grossed up, using the applicable staff assessment rates;

"(iii)   The amounts in subparagraph (ii) above, divided by 0.6625 and expressed in local currency, constitute the gross pensionable salary.

"*(b)*   The methodology in paragraph *(a)* above shall be applied on the occasion of the first adjustment due to the application of the interim adjustment procedure for net salaries on or after 1 April 1994, should such adjustment take place before a comprehensive salary survey.

"2.   *Adjustment of the gross pensionable salary between comprehensive salary surveys*

"The gross pensionable salary shall be adjusted on the same date and by the same percentages as the net pensionable salary of participants in the General Service and related categories is adjusted."

The existing appendix shall become "Appendix B".

ANNEX II
Amendment to the Staff Regulations of the United Nations

Add the following sentence at the end of paragraph 6 of annex I to the Staff Regulations:

"The gross pensionable salaries of such staff shall be determined in accordance with the methodology specified in article 54 *(a)* of the Regulations of the United

Nations Joint Staff Pension Fund and are shown in the salary scales applicable to such staff."

General Assembly resolution 48/225

23 December 1993   Meeting 87   Adopted without vote

Approved by Fifth Committee (A/48/738) without vote, 4 December (meeting 29); draft by Australia following informal consultations (A/C.5/48/L.4); agenda item 129.
Meeting numbers. GA 48th session: 5th Committee 11, 13, 14, 16, 18, 29; plenary 87.

REFERENCES
[1]A/48/30 & Corr.1. [2]YUN 1992, p. 1066. [3]GA res. 44/198, 21 Dec. 1989. [4]YUN 1991, p. 905 & A/C.5/46/17. [5]YUN 1991, p. 905. [6]YUN 1992, p. 1067. [7]A/47/1004. [8]A/C.5/48/26. [9]A/47/980. [10]A/C.5/48/36. [11]GA res. 45/250 A, 21 Dec. 1990. [12]GA res. 45/249, 21 Dec. 1990. [13]YUN 1992, p. 1068, GA dec. 47/459, 23 Dec. 1992. [14]Ibid., p. 1042, GA res. 47/211, 23 Dec. 1992. [15]A/47/5 (vol. I). [16]YUN 1986, p. 1024, GA res. 41/213, 19 Dec. 1986. [17]YUN 1992, p. 1068, GA res. 46/191 B, 31 July 1992. [18]YUN 1991, p. 910. [19]ACC/1993/6. [20]ACC/1993/14. [21]E/1993/66. [22]YUN 1974, p. 875, GA res. 3357(XXIX), 18 Dec. 1974. [23]YUN 1991, p. 900, GA res. 46/191 A, 20 Dec. 1991. [24]YUN 1992, p. 1068. [25]E/1993/83. [26]E/1993/119 & Add.1. [27]A/C.5/48/4. [28]GA res. 45/241, sect. XIII, 21 Dec. 1990. [29]YUN 1992, p. 1069. [30]A/48/9 & Corr.1. [31]YUN 1991, p. 888, GA res. 46/220, 20 Dec. 1991. [32]YUN 1992, p. 1072, GA res. 47/203, sect. I, 22 Dec. 1992. [33]Ibid., GA res. 47/203, sect. III, 22 Dec. 1992. [34]A/48/517.

Travel

Standards of accommodation for air travel

Responding to a 1991 General Assembly request,[1] the Secretary-General submitted an August 1993 report[2] on standards of accommodation for air travel covering the period from 1 July 1992 to 30 June 1993. With regard to delegation travel, 32 journeys in first-class air accommodation for one representative of each Member State designated as a least developed country (LDC) attending regular, special or emergency sessions of the General Assembly were paid for at a cost of $168,511. With regard to exceptions to the standards of accommodation of staff and others travelling on behalf of the Organization, which the Secretary-General was authorized to make on a case-by-case basis, 66 cases of first-class travel and 69 cases of business-class travel were authorized at a total additional cost of $149,553, compared with $201,373 for the previous reporting period. The latter figure was adjusted to include 2 cases of first-class travel and 3 cases of business-class travel approved *ex post facto* and unreported in 1992, at a total additional cost of $1,698.

Annexed to the report were lists of exceptions granted by categories which covered: arduous journeys; medical conditions or advanced age; the unavailability of regular standards of accommodation; and travel for eminent persons or prominent persons who donated their services free of charge to the Organization.

On 23 December, by **decision 48/459**, the General Assembly deferred consideration of the report until its resumed forty-eighth session in 1994. By **resolution 48/228** of the same date, the Assembly requested the Secretary-General to submit proposals on the provision of, and related arrangements for, travel services and allowances.

Review of travel and related entitlements

In October, the Secretary-General submitted an updated review of travel and related entitlements for members of organs and subsidiary organs and staff members of the United Nations,[3] pursuant to a 1992 Assembly decision[4] to defer consideration of his report on the subject until the forty-eighth session. The Secretary-General noted that two new subsidiary bodies which were entitled to payment of travel expenses had been established since his 1992 report: the High-level Advisory Board on Sustainable Development and the Commission on Sustainable Development (see PART THREE, Chapter I). He reiterated his proposals to limit the payment of travel expenses for representatives in subsidiary organs of the Assembly and the Economic and Social Council to those from LDCs, with estimated savings of $754,000 per annum, and to reconsider the previously authorized exceptional travel entitlements for representatives in functional commissions of the Council nominated directly by their Governments. The Secretary-General requested the Assembly to decide on the travel entitlements for representatives in the Commission on Sustainable Development beyond 1993 and to address the issue of exceptional travel assistance to representatives from LDCs and other developing countries. Annexed to the report were updated lists of subsidiary bodies whose members were entitled to travel expenses or both travel and subsistence expenses for attending meetings.

On 23 December, by **decision 48/459**, the Assembly deferred consideration of the report until its resumed forty-eighth session in 1994.

REFERENCES
[1]YUN 1991, p. 913, GA dec. 46/450, 20 Dec. 1991.
[2]A/C.5/48/3. [3]A/C.5/48/14. [4]YUN 1992, p. 1075, GA dec. 47/460 A, 23 Dec. 1992.

Administration of justice

In its annual note to the General Assembly,[1] the United Nations Administrative Tribunal reported that it had delivered 47 judgements during the year. They related to cases brought by staff members against the Secretary-General or the executive heads of other United Nations bodies to resolve disputes involving terms of appointment and related rules and regulations.

The Tribunal met in annual plenary session in New York on 17 November 1993 and held two panel sessions (Geneva, 1 June–2 July; New York, 18 October–19 November).

In a 16 September letter[2] requesting the inclusion of an additional item in the agenda of the Assembly's forty-eighth session, Australia, Benin, France and Ireland asked for a review of the procedure under article 11 of the Tribunal's statute governing the review of its judgements. In the explanatory memorandum annexed to the letter, they pointed to criticism that the existing procedure was not adequate. In the opinion of some delegations, the procedure should be abolished and replaced with a practical mechanism for resolving staff employment problems.

By **decision 48/415** of 9 December, the Assembly, on the recommendation of the Sixth (Legal) Committee, requested the Secretary-General to review the procedure and report on the subject in 1994 and included the item in the provisional agenda of its forty-ninth session.

REFERENCES
[1]A/INF/48/7. [2]A/48/232.

Chapter III

Other administrative and management questions

In 1993, the Committee on Conferences considered measures to improve the utilization of conference-servicing within the United Nations system and reviewed the work of the Office of Conference Services. It recommended measures to control and limit documentation and reviewed the United Nations publications policy. The Committee examined changes to the approved calendar of conferences and meetings for 1993 and reviewed the draft calendar of conferences and meetings for 1994-1995, which was approved by the General Assembly in December (resolution 48/222 A).

Other administrative and management questions under review in 1993 included the issues of works of art at the United Nations, information systems and the introduction of new technologies.

Conferences and meetings

In 1993, the Committee on Conferences reviewed the draft calendar of conferences and meetings for the 1994-1995 biennium and examined requests for additions and changes to the approved calendar of conferences and meetings for 1993.[1]

The Committee discussed issues related to the calendar, including measures to improve the utilization of conference-servicing resources, the organization of work and coordination of all organizational aspects of conference servicing. It also dealt with the need to control and limit the amount of documentation. The Committee reviewed the United Nations publications policy, the work of the Office of Conference Services (OCS) and the organization of work of the Committee on Conferences.

Other matters dealt with in the Committee's October report[2] included the restructuring of the OCS and the consequences for conference servicing of the economy measures announced by the Secretary-General in August in the light of the financial crisis of the Organization (see PART FIVE, Chapter I).

The Committee held an organizational session in New York on 2 March. The first part of its substantive session was held from 17 to 21 May and the second part from 14 to 17 September and on 2 and 3 November, also in New York.

Calendar of meetings

Calendar for 1993

In March, the Committee on Conferences agreed that proposed changes to the calendar which did not have budget implications could be dealt with by the Secretariat in consultation with the Bureau of the Committee. The Committee was advised of a number of such changes in 1993.

The Committee approved a request from the Intergovernmental Negotiating Committee for a Framework Convention on Climate Change to convene its seventh session in New York from 15 to 19 or 20 March 1993 to prepare for the first session of the Conference of the Parties to the Convention.

A meeting of the Special High-level Council for the International Decade for Natural Disaster Reduction (1990-1999),[3] originally scheduled for Geneva in 1992, was rescheduled to take place in New York on 25 January 1993 to enable the Secretary-General to meet with the Special High-level Council.

A meeting of Governmental Experts from Landlocked and Transit Developing Countries and Representatives of Donor Countries and Financial and Development Institutions, scheduled to be held at Geneva, was convened—with the Committee's approval—in New York from 17 to 19 May to ensure maximum attendance by representatives of the land-locked developing countries.

The International Civil Service Commission received approval to hold its thirty-eighth (1993) session at Vienna from 15 July to 3 August rather than in New York.

The fourth session of the Preparatory Committee for the World Conference on Human Rights was extended until 7 May to enable it to conclude examination of the draft final document for the World Conference.

The Committee approved the rescheduling of the first session of the Preparatory Committee for the Global Conference on the Sustainable Development of Small Island Developing States from 2-13 August to 30 August–10 September.

The Committee considered requests from subsidiary bodies for exceptions to be made to a 1985 General Assembly resolution[4] which stated that no subsidiary organ of the Assembly should meet at Headquarters during a regular session of the

Assembly unless authorized by the Assembly. In September,[5] the Committee informed the Assembly that it did not object to requests to meet in New York during the Assembly's forty-eighth (1993) session made by the Executive Board of the United Nations Children's Fund, the Committee on Relations with the Host Country, the Committee on the Exercise of the Inalienable Rights of the Palestinian People, the Working Group on the Financing of the United Nations Relief and Works Agency for Palestine Refugees in the Near East, the Preparatory Committee for the Fiftieth Anniversary of the United Nations, the Advisory Committee on the United Nations Educational and Training Programme for Southern Africa, the Committee of Trustees of the United Nations Trust Fund for South Africa, the Special Committee against Apartheid, the Intergovernmental Group to Monitor the Supply and Shipping of Oil and Petroleum Products to South Africa, the Special Committee to Select the Winners of the United Nations Human Rights Prize and the Committee itself. In November,[6] the Committee informed the Assembly that it did not object to a similar request by the Governing Council of the United Nations Development Programme (UNDP).

1994-1995 draft calendar

On 15 and 16 September, the Committee on Conferences reviewed the draft calendar of conferences and meetings for the 1994-1995 biennium. In May, it reviewed the consolidated statement of scheduled special conferences for 1994[7] and considered the draft calendar of conferences and meetings of subsidiary organs of the Economic and Social Council for 1994-1995, in accordance with a 1988 Council decision.[8] In November, the Committee reviewed the section of the proposed programme budget for 1994-1995 relating to conference servicing.[9]

The Committee recommended that the General Assembly adopt the draft calendar of conferences and meetings as amended and authorize the Committee to make the necessary adjustments arising from actions taken by the Assembly in 1993. Concerning a proposal to the Assembly that the Advisory Committee on Administrative and Budgetary Questions (ACABQ) meet outside its headquarters (New York), the Committee on Conferences drew the Assembly's attention to the fact that ACABQ was not listed among the United Nations bodies exempt from meeting outside established headquarters, as set out in a 1985 Assembly resolution.[4] The Committee recommended that the Assembly take into account the possible adverse effects of such departures from the 1985 "headquarters rule" on the schedule and work of the Assembly's Fifth (Administrative and Budget-

ary) Committee. The Secretariat was asked to report on the legal reasons and experience of those subsidiary bodies which met away from their established headquarters.

The Committee recommended the adoption of the 1994-1995 draft calendar of conferences and meetings of the subsidiary organs of the Economic and Social Council. It expressed concern at the increasing number of requests made by intergovernmental bodies for exceptions to the biennialization of their sessions.

Conference and meeting services

As requested by the General Assembly in 1992,[10] the Secretary-General submitted in April a report on the improved utilization of conference-servicing resources at the United Nations.[11] The report contained statistics for 1992 on the planned and actual utilization of conference resources allocated to a limited sample of bodies that had been meeting for several years in New York, Geneva and Vienna. The total number of sessions held in 1992 by those bodies was 42 and the total utilization factor was 3,259, resulting in an average utilization factor of 78 per cent, unchanged from 1991. In 1993, the Committee on Conferences recommended to the Assembly that it invite those bodies whose utilization factor was below the benchmark figure—utilization of less than 80 per cent of their allocated resources for three sessions—to review and revise, if necessary, the amount of conference-servicing resources requested.

Also in April, the Secretary-General submitted information on existing conference services, resources and facilities system-wide which could lead to a more effective organization of work and use of conference services.[12] The information was based on replies received from secretariats at headquarters locations, including the regional commissions and the specialized agencies. The Committee on Conferences requested the Secretariat to provide data on the level of staff posts, the nature of the meetings convened, the capacity utilization at each of the headquarters locations, regional commissions and other organizations and on comparative costs of meetings in New York, Geneva and Vienna.

The Committee was informed that agreement in principle had been reached with the United Nations Industrial Development Organization on the establishment of unified conference services at Vienna to be administered by the United Nations. The Committee urged the Secretary-General to conclude negotiations on the transition as soon as possible.

The Committee recommended that the Assembly request the Secretary-General, as Chairman of the Administrative Committee on Coordination (ACC), to enhance system-wide coordination of conference activities, including coordination of meetings schedules, with a view to optimizing the use of available conference services, resources and facilities.

In accordance with a 1992 Assembly request,[(10)] the Secretary-General, by an August note,[(13)] brought to the attention of all United Nations organs the Assembly's resolutions and guidelines on the use of conference-servicing resources and information on the notional costs per hour of meeting time.

By **resolution 48/228** of 23 December, the Assembly requested the Secretary-General to submit in 1994 a study on the organization, management and human resources requirements for the provision of adequate conference services as a basis for consideration of his 1996-1997 regular budget proposals. It also requested him to provide Member States with studies on the subject that were carried out in the 1992-1993 biennium.

GENERAL ASSEMBLY ACTION

On 23 December, the General Assembly, on the recommendation of the Fifth Committee, adopted **resolution 48/222 A** without vote.

Pattern of conferences

The General Assembly,

Having considered the report of the Committee on Conferences,

Recalling its relevant resolutions, including resolutions 43/222 B of 21 December 1988, 46/190 of 20 December 1991 and 47/202 A to C of 22 December 1992,

1. *Approves* the draft calendar of conferences and meetings of the United Nations for the biennium 1994-1995 as submitted and amended by the Committee on Conferences;

2. *Authorizes* the Committee on Conferences to make adjustments in the calendar of conferences and meetings for 1994 that may become necessary as a result of action and decisions taken by the General Assembly at its forty-eighth session;

3. *Invites* the Executive Board of the United Nations Children's Fund and the Governing Council of the United Nations Development Programme to increase their efforts to rationalize their meeting and documentation requirements with a view to reducing them to the maximum extent possible;

4. *Also invites* the Executive Board of the United Nations Children's Fund and the Governing Council of the United Nations Development Programme to consider dispensing with summary records;

5. *Welcomes* the decision of the Committee on Conferences to continue to monitor the conference services provided to organs and programmes not funded from the regular budget of the United Nations with a view to identifying cost savings;

6. *Endorses* the efforts of the Committee on Conferences to improve the utilization of conference-servicing resources, and takes note of the Committee's decision in paragraph 23 of its report to raise the benchmark fig-

ure to 80 per cent, pending further analysis of the expanded methodology;

7. *Welcomes* the decision of the Committee on Conferences to continue the experimental methodology in respect of the utilization of conference-servicing resources, and requests the Secretariat to expand the information presented to include analyses of trends and figures on the utilization of conference-servicing capacity;

8. *Endorses* the decision of the Committee on Conferences to request its Chairman to consult on its behalf with the chairmen of organs concerned, where the utilization factor is lower than the established benchmark figure applicable for the last three sessions, and requests the Committee to report the results of the consultations to the General Assembly at its forty-ninth session;

9. *Urges* those bodies whose utilization factor is below the applicable benchmark figure for the last three sessions to review and consider reducing the amount of conference-servicing resources requested;

10. *Recommends* that the measures to ensure optimum utilization of conference services contained in annex II to the report of the Committee on Conferences be implemented, as applicable, by all subsidiary organs in order to achieve the most efficient and effective use of conference-servicing resources;

11. *Requests* the chairmen of the relevant organs and subsidiary bodies of the General Assembly to propose to Member States, at the beginning of each session, the adoption of time-limits for speakers;

12. *Welcomes* the decision of the Committee on Conferences to play an informational role *vis-à-vis* subsidiary organs, providing clear directives to the Secretariat, to set standards and to heighten awareness;

13. *Renews its requests* to the Secretariat, contained in paragraph 5 of its resolution 47/202 A and paragraph 10 of its resolution 47/202 B, to bring to the attention of all organs information on the notional costs per hour of meeting time and on the notional cost per page of documentation;

14. *Reiterates its view*, expressed in section VIII of its resolution 44/201 A of 21 December 1989, on the desirability of the establishment of unified conference services at Vienna, stresses, in this context, that the combined financial burden for providing conference services to the United Nations Office at Vienna and the United Nations Industrial Development Organization should, in the long run, benefit from the unification agreement, and urges the Secretary-General to conclude the negotiations with the United Nations Industrial Development Organization in that regard as quickly as possible and to report thereon to the General Assembly no later than at its forty-ninth session;

15. *Notes with appreciation* the system-wide coordination of conference activities and the agreement reached with regard to establishing a systematic exchange of information and language staff to promote effective utilization of conference staff;

16. *Requests* the Secretary-General, as Chairman of the Administrative Committee on Coordination, through the established mechanism of the Inter-Agency Meeting on Language Arrangements, Documentation and Publications, to enhance that coordination, including coordination of meeting schedules, with a view to optimizing the use of available conference services,

resources and facilities, with due regard to quality, and making possible the effective participation of Member States, and to report on the results achieved to the General Assembly at its fiftieth session through the Committee on Conferences;

17. *Emphasizes* that any decisions to convene world conferences should take into account the impact of such conferences on the capacity of the United Nations system to provide conference services and the capacity of Member States to participate in them;

18. *Welcomes* the benefits from the application of technological innovations to conference servicing, including gains in productivity and reductions in costs, and emphasizes that the primary goal of the introduction of new technology should be to enhance the quality of conference services and ensure their timely provision;

19. *Reaffirms* the general principle that, in drawing up the schedule of conferences and meetings, United Nations bodies shall plan to meet at their respective established headquarters;

20. *Requests* the Secretary-General to review the legal basis and experience of all subsidiary bodies that meet away from their established headquarters, thus constituting a departure from General Assembly resolution 40/243 of 18 December 1985, and to report thereon to the Assembly at its forty-ninth session through the Committee on Conferences;

21. *Requests* the Advisory Committee on Administrative and Budgetary Questions, when deciding upon its meeting schedule, including meetings away from Headquarters, to take into account the programme of work of the Fifth Committee;

22. *Endorses* the decision of the Committee on Conferences that in future its review of the proposed programme budget for conference services should be expanded to include conference services at the United Nations Office at Nairobi and at the regional commissions.

General Assembly resolution 48/222 A

23 December 1993   Meeting 87   Adopted without vote

Approved by Fifth Committee (A/48/753) without vote, 10 December (meeting 35); draft by Rapporteur following informal consultations (A/C.5/48/L.8); agenda item 126.
Meeting numbers. GA 48th session: 5th Committee 19, 21-23, 35; plenary 87.

Workload standards for conference-servicing staff

On 23 December, the General Assembly, by **decision 48/459**, deferred consideration of a 1992 report on unified workload standards for conference-servicing staff within the United Nations system[16] until its resumed forty-eighth session.

REFERENCES

(1)YUN 1992, p. 1079, GA res. 47/202 A, 22 Dec. 1992. (2)A/48/32/Rev.1. (3)GA res. 44/236, 22 Dec. 1989. (4)YUN 1985, p. 1256, GA res. 40/243, 18 Dec. 1985. (5)A/48/417. (6)A/48/417/Add.1. (7)A/C.5/48/1. (8)YUN 1988, p. 897, ESC. dec. 1988/103, 5 Feb. 1988. (9)A/48/32/Rev.1/Add.1. (10)YUN 1992, p. 1079, GA res. 47/202 A, 22 Dec. 1992. (11)A/AC.172/88/Add.11. (12)A/AC.172/152 & Add.1 & Corr.1. (13)A/AC.172/INF/15. (14)YUN 1992, p. 1081.

Documents and publications

Documentation control and limitation

By a June note,[1] the Secretary-General updated the policies laid down by the General Assembly regarding the control and limitation of documentation, as requested by the Assembly in 1969.[2] The note, which enumerated policy decisions adopted by the Assembly, most recently in 1992,[3] was distributed to all Member States. The policy decisions applied, for the most part, to documentation for the Assembly and its subsidiary bodies. The Assembly had invited other United Nations organs, in particular the Economic and Social Council and its subsidiary bodies, to apply the same policies to their documentation. The note summarized Assembly recommendations to limit and control general documents, meeting records, statements, reports and studies, annexes and supplements to the Official Records, documentation for treaty bodies and special conferences, and statements of programme budget implications. Annexed to the note were a list of meeting record entitlements and revised guidelines for the format and contents of reports of the subsidiary organs of the Assembly, as well as guidelines for the control and limitation of documentation for special conferences.

In May,[4] the Committee on Conferences reviewed the criteria for, status of and guidelines on the provision of written meeting records and on the possibility of issuing the verbatim records of the Security Council in final form only. It also discussed the problems faced by OCS owing to the increase in the volume of documentation and the late submission of documents by author departments.

The Committee recommended that the Assembly instruct all bodies entitled to written meeting records to review the need for such records and to decide whether they should be discontinued or maintained for some or all of their meetings.

The Committee requested OCS to identify incentives to ensure compliance on the part of substantive departments with the 10-week rule for the submission of pre-session documents to the Office. It also recommended to the Assembly to invite intergovernmental bodies to review their agendas for the purpose of combining agenda items and limiting requests for pre-session documentation.

Economy measures

Regarding the economy measures announced by the Secretary-General in August in the light of the financial crisis of the Organization, the Committee on Conferences expressed concern that the measures departed from General Assembly resolutions of 1987[5] concerning the equal treatment of all official languages and of 1981[6] on the simultaneous distribution of documents in those languages. The Committee informed the Assembly that the measures would affect the ability of the Assembly and its Main Committees to complete their work in 1993, leading to resumed sessions in 1994 and additional expenditure. In addition, the Committee considered the Secretary-General's decision to limit the distribution of documents to missions to only two official copies to be too restrictive.

Security Council documentation

By notes of 27 July[7] and 31 August,[8] the President of the Security Council stated that the Council members had agreed on a series of proposals to streamline the Council's documentation, including issuing verbatim records only in final form beginning 1 January 1994.

GENERAL ASSEMBLY ACTION

On 23 December, the General Assembly, on the recommendation of the Fifth Committee, adopted **resolution 48/222 B** without vote.

The General Assembly,

Recalling its resolutions on the control and limitation of documentation, including resolutions 33/56 of 14 December 1978, 36/117 B of 10 December 1981, 37/14 C of 16 November 1982, 45/238 B of 21 December 1990 and 47/202 B of 22 December 1992,

Reaffirming the need for and desirability of written meeting records for some bodies of a political or legal nature,

Considering, on the one hand, the effects of the introduction of technological innovations and, on the other, the increase in the workload and the reduced staffing in the Office of Conference Services,

1. *Expresses concern* about the late issuance and distribution of documentation, including summary and verbatim records of United Nations bodies;

2. *Requests* the Secretary-General to submit to the General Assembly at its forty-ninth session, through the Committee on Conferences, an analytical report on the factors that contribute to this situation, including the increase in the workload of the Office of Conference Services, the level of staffing, workload standards, the late submission of documents by author departments and the effects of the introduction of technological innovations in the Office;

3. *Encourages* all bodies currently entitled to written meeting records to review the need for such records, particularly verbatim records, and to communicate their recommendations to the General Assembly at its forty-ninth session;

4. *Calls upon* the Secretariat to strengthen planning and forecasting of parliamentary documentation in both author departments and the Office of Conference Services, and the training of those responsible for the preparation of parliamentary documentation in author departments;

5. *Also requests* the Secretary-General to take all necessary measures to ensure that documents are submitted by author departments in compliance with the ten-week rule in order to permit processing on time in all official languages, and to include information on the impact of those measures in the report on compliance with the six-week rule requested in paragraph 9 of resolution 47/202 B;

6. *Invites* intergovernmental bodies and their members to review, as appropriate, their agendas with a view, *inter alia*, to combining agenda items and limiting requests for pre-session documentation;

7. *Calls upon* the Secretariat to provide the Office of Conference Services with adequate resources, especially technological resources, to enable it to respond to its increased workload and maintain a high standard of services, with due respect to the principle of equal treatment of the official languages of the United Nations as laid down in General Assembly resolution 42/207 C of 11 December 1987;

8. *Expresses its deep concern* regarding the economy measures announced by the Secretary-General on 26 August 1993 in the context of the financial crisis without prior consultation with Member States, those measures being in contradiction with the principle of equal treatment of the official languages of the United Nations as laid down in resolution 42/207 C;

9. *Concurs* with the recommendation of the Committee on Conferences, contained in paragraph 140 of its report, that cuts in conference servicing introduced by the Secretary-General on 26 August 1993, and subsequently lifted in New York, be lifted also at Geneva and Vienna;

10. *Endorses* the letter from the Chairman of the Committee on Conferences to the President of the General Assembly, contained in paragraph 136 of the report of the Committee, which reflects the opinions of the Committee on the economy measures announced by the Secretary-General.

General Assembly resolution 48/222 B

23 December 1993   Meeting 87   Adopted without vote

Approved by Fifth Committee (A/48/753) without vote, 10 December (meeting 35); draft by Rapporteur following informal consultations (A/C.5/48/L.8); agenda item 126.

Meeting numbers. GA 48th session: 5th Committee 19, 21-23, 35; plenary 87.

Publications policy

In October,[9] the Secretary-General submitted a report outlining the findings and recommendations of a review of the United Nations publications policy, pursuant to a 1991 request of the General Assembly.[10] The report examined the publications policy, including the definition of publications and their mandate, and discussed its implementation by the Publications Board and its working committee and working groups; the Department of Public Information; the Programme Planning and Budget Division; author departments; OCS; and the Office of General Services. The report also discussed coordination with other United Nations duty stations and organizations and preparation and dissemination of publications, including their free distribution and sales, external publishing activities and copyright.

In his conclusions, the Secretary-General stated that the restructuring of the publishing activities at Headquarters was expected to provide a new focus to the planning and implementation of the United Nations publications programme and to integrate it more closely with the other public information activities of the Organization. The reconstituted Publications Board in its review of the publications programme for 1994-1995 was applying the modified criteria for publications set out in the report and sought to take fully into account the concerns expressed in the Committee on Information and in the General Assembly.

The Assembly, by **decision 48/459** of 23 December, deferred consideration of the Secretary-General's report until its resumed forty-eighth session.

REFERENCES

[1]A/INF/48/1. [2]YUN 1969, p. 830, GA res. 2538(XXIV), 11 Dec. 1969. [3]YUN 1992, p. 1083, GA res. 47/202 B, 22 Dec. 1992. [4]A/48/32/Rev.1. [5]YUN 1987, p. 1173, GA res. 42/207 C, 11 Dec. 1987. [6]YUN 1981, p. 1376, GA res. 36/117 B, 10 Dec. 1981. [7]S/26176. [8]S/26389. [9]A/C.5/48/10. [10]YUN 1991, p. 921, GA res. 46/185 B, sect. VI, 20 Dec. 1991.

UN premises and property

Addis Ababa and Bangkok conference facilities

In November,[1] the Secretary-General submitted to the Fifth Committee a progress report on the construction of additional conference facilities at Addis Ababa and Bangkok, projects which were approved by the General Assembly in 1984.[2]

The Secretary-General reported that the pace of work at Addis Ababa continued at the 1992 level, as the contractor was unable to achieve the higher production rates anticipated by his revised timetable. Consultants and the administration considered the contractor's latest timetable projecting the completion of construction and commissioning by the end of 1994 as too optimistic and considered the first half of 1995 more realistic. The total project cost, estimated at $107,576,900, was not expected to increase.

The conference facilities at Bangkok were completed in the first quarter of 1993, followed by an inauguration ceremony on 9 April. The building was used for a number of major conferences and smaller meetings during the year. It was expected that the total project cost would not exceed the authorized $48,540,000.

The General Assembly, by **decision 48/459** of 23 December, deferred consideration of the Secretary-General's report until its resumed forty-eighth session.

Office accommodation at Geneva

In December,[3] the Secretary-General submitted a report to the Fifth Committee describing the problem of office accommodation at the United Nations Office at Geneva. He stated that the issue of space allocation had become critical, owing to the increased activities of some departments and offices and the transfer of others to Geneva. Proposals were presented to cover the immediate requirements, including the provision of rent-free and concessional office space by the Swiss authorities and renovation of existing facilities. He also made projections for additional long-term requirements.

In his conclusions, the Secretary-General stated that the General Assembly might wish to approve his proposal to accept an offer by the Swiss authorities of 13,504 square metres of rent-free and concessional office space at the Geneva Executive Centre.

The Assembly, by **decision 48/459** of 23 December, deferred consideration of the report of the Secretary-General until its resumed forty-eighth session.

Works of art in the United Nations

By a February note,[4] the Secretary-General transmitted to the General Assembly a report of the Joint Inspection Unit (JIU) containing recommendations for managing and maintaining works of art in the United Nations. JIU recommended that the Secretary-General submit proposals for an arts policy for adoption by the Assembly; reorganize and strengthen the Arts Committee of the United Nations; inform Member States of measures planned to develop, preserve and safeguard the arts collection of the United Nations; and engage a part-time curator to assure the relevance, coherence and value of the collection.

In June,[5] the Secretary-General stated that JIU's basic premise of comparing the collection of art in the United Nations to national collections in major museums did not appear appropriate, as the Organization was not involved in a programme of acquisition, but was a repository of donations. He agreed with the recommendations to strengthen the Arts Committee and to develop a comprehensive registry of the works of art, but was of the view that a curator was not needed; a periodic review by the Buildings Management Service of the United Nations Department of Administration and Management should suffice to identify physical deterioration of the works of art.

On 23 December, the General Assembly, on the recommendation of the Fifth Committee, adopted **resolution 48/217** without vote.

Managing works of art in the United Nations: report of the Joint Inspection Unit

The General Assembly,

Having considered the report of the Joint Inspection Unit entitled ''Managing works of art in the United Nations'' and the comments of the Secretary-General thereon,

Aware of the further comments and explanations provided by the representative of the Secretary-General,

1. *Takes note with appreciation* of the report of the Joint Inspection Unit entitled ''Managing works of art in the United Nations'' and the comments of the Secretary-General thereon;

2. *Requests* the Secretary-General to continue to improve the management of works of art in such a manner as to avoid additional costs to the regular budget of the United Nations, with due regard to the quality of services being provided;

3. *Recommends* the strengthening of the Arts Committee of the United Nations by the advice of local experts in honorary capacities;

4. *Also requests* the Secretary-General to report on the subject to the General Assembly at its fiftieth session.

General Assembly resolution 48/217

23 December 1993   Meeting 87   Adopted without vote

Approved by Fifth Committee (A/48/801) without vote, 8 November (meeting 13); draft by Vice-Chairman (A/C.5/48/L.2); agenda item 121.
Meeting numbers. GA 48th session: 5th Committee 7-13; plenary 87.

REFERENCES

[1]A/C.5/48/30. [2]YUN 1984, p. 620, GA res. 39/236, 18 Dec. 1984. [3]A/C.5/48/29. [4]A/48/72. [5]A/48/72/Add.1.

Information systems and computers

Technological innovations

During 1993, efforts continued towards upgrading the technological infrastructure of the United Nations in the areas of desktop and larger computers and in communications technology to enhance connectivity among major duty stations.

The total number of personal computers at Headquarters had increased by 44 per cent from 3,450 in 1992 to 5,000 in 1993. At offices away from Headquarters, the number had increased by 23 per cent from 5,600 in 1992 to 6,950 in 1993. The capacity to share information among users was increased through local area networks (LANs).

Additional LAN servers were acquired to house large organizational databases for the integrated management information system (IMIS), the optical disk system and for Internet gopher service.

Efforts continued at Headquarters to improve network services. The LAN wiring project, to install Ethernet cables and fiber optic cables, was more than halfway completed by December. It enabled the successful implementation of the first version of IMIS in its user offices at Headquarters.

As a direct result of the progress made in LAN wiring, the user base of electronic mail at Headquarters grew from 200 to 2,400. Electronic mail was also installed in field service missions.

In the area of LAN management, modern network management tools and techniques were adopted to ensure the smooth flow of data.

Several new technological applications were either tested or introduced, including packet switching equipment, a news-wire service for clients in political areas, and a public-access server through the Internet service.

The Committee on Conferences continued to monitor the applications of new technologies in the area of conference servicing and requested the Secretariat to report in 1994 on the long-range plan and the time-frame for introducing each new application of new technology at each United Nations duty station.

Telecommunications

During 1993, work continued on upgrading and developing the United Nations global telecommunications network. Digital private automatic branch exchange switches were installed in United Nations Offices at Geneva and Vienna, and those in the Economic and Social Commission for Asia and the Pacific at Bangkok, the Economic Commission for Africa at Addis Ababa and the United Nations Office at Nairobi were modernized.

A new voice-mail system was installed at Headquarters and a facsimile switch introduced in the central telegraph operations to lower transmission costs and reduce the level of manual work.

In order to improve telecommunications between Headquarters and peace-keeping missions, communications circuits were upgraded to digital mode via satellite to Cambodia, Mozambique, Somalia and the former Yugoslavia.

In November, the Secretary-General submitted a report[1] on the United Nations telecommunication system, containing updated information on a proposed satellite backbone network to meet urgent requirements of the United Nations. It discussed the engineering of the proposed satellite network, as well as its organizational and management structure, project budget and implementation timetable and costs, benefits and financing. The proposals related to the installation of seven Earth stations: one at the United Nations Office at Nairobi, two at the United Nations Office at Geneva and one each at the seat of the regional commissions at Addis Ababa, Amman, Bangkok and Santiago. The network was designed to meet the United Nations' own requirements and enhance connectivity between Headquarters and the regional commissions, field offices and specialized agencies. It would be expanded and configured to meet peace-keeping and humanitarian requirements. Based on an implementation schedule of approximately three and a half years starting in 1993, the total project cost was estimated at $18,212,700. Annexed to the report was a comparison of telephone rates—published commercial rates, special United Nations volume discounts and United Nations network rate—for calls originating in New York; a comparison of sample telex rates; a proposed organizational structure model for a telecommunications section at regional commissions and Nairobi; and a table of United Nations leased circuits and proposed configurations.

The General Assembly, by **decision 48/459** of 23 December, deferred consideration of the Secretary-General's report until its resumed forty-eighth session.

Integrated management information system

The fifth progress report on the IMIS project was submitted to the Fifth Committee by the Secretary-General in October 1993.[2] The project, approved by the General Assembly in 1988,[3] was to develop an integrated system for the processing of and reporting on administrative actions at all major duty stations, to replace numerous independent systems which were no longer capable of providing the support needed by management. A first series of applications related mainly to human resources was successfully implemented at Headquarters in September.

The Assembly, by **decision 48/459** of 23 December, deferred consideration of the Secretary-General's progress report until its resumed forty-eighth session.

UN informatics system

As requested by the Economic and Social Council in 1992,[4] the Secretary-General submitted in June a report on international cooperation in the field of informatics.[5] The report described United Nations efforts to make electronic information readily available to Member States and discussed the creation by the Advisory Committee for the Coordination of Information System (ACCIS) of a prototype information module, UN-EARTH, a snapshot of general information on United Nations organizations and agencies disseminated on diskette and made available on IN-TERNET by UNDP. It also discussed the computer and information systems training activities conducted by the United Nations Institute for Training and Research (UNITAR), the United Nations Conference on Trade and Development, the Dag Hammarskjöld Library in New York and the

United Nations library at Geneva. The report concluded that United Nations informatics activities were limited and uncoordinated, owing to the lack of an appropriate coordinating mechanism. At its seventh session (Geneva, 27-29 September),[6] ACCIS discussed, among other things, activities carried out by its secretariat in the 1992-1993 biennium and its 1994-1995 work programme.

In November, ACC created the Senior-Level Task Force on United Nations Information Systems to identify policy issues relating to coordination and to propose mandates, structures and secretariat arrangements for ACCIS and the International Computing Centre (ICC), a Geneva-based United Nations institution.

In December,[7] ACC, having considered the recommendations of the Task Force, decided to discontinue ACCIS and to establish an Information Systems Coordination Committee. ACC requested the Management Committee of ICC to study the Task Force recommendation concerning the transformation of ICC into an information management service centre with a broader role to provide information-based services on a full cost-recovery basis.

In November,[8] the 1994-1995 budget estimates for ICC were submitted by the Secretary-General. The Centre, authorized by the General Assembly in 1970[9] and operating since 1971,[10] offered a comprehensive range of data and text processing and related telecommunication services to organizations of the United Nations system. Its 1994-1995 budget estimates amounted to $25,099,000. Special focus was placed during the biennium on the standardization of the Centre's software operating environment to conform to international and industrial standards. The United Nations share for the use of ICC during 1994-1995 was estimated at $5,639,100.

On 23 December, by **resolution 48/230, section VII**, adopted on the recommendation of the Fifth Committee, the General Assembly approved the ICC 1994-1995 budget estimates, amounting to $25,099,000.

ECONOMIC AND SOCIAL COUNCIL ACTION

On 29 July, the Economic and Social Council adopted **resolution 1993/56** without vote.

The need to harmonize and improve United Nations informatics systems for optimal utilization and accessibility by all States

The Economic and Social Council,

Recalling its resolutions 1991/70 of 26 July 1991 and 1992/60 of 31 July 1992 on the need to harmonize and improve United Nations informatics systems for optimal utilization and accessibility by all States,

Taking note of the report of the Secretary-General concerning the follow-up action taken, in particular the examination of the Advisory Committee for the Coordination of Information Systems and of the International Computing Centre, initiated by the Administrative Committee on Coordination in the context of the review of their functioning, as well as other measures taken so far,

1. *Reiterates* the high priority that it attaches to easy, economical, uncomplicated and unhindered access for States Members of the United Nations and for observers through, *inter alia*, their permanent missions, to the growing number of computerized databases and information systems and services of the United Nations;

2. *Expresses concern* at the limited progress achieved thus far and reiterates its call for the urgent implementation of measures to achieve these objectives;

3. *Stresses once again* the urgent need for representatives of States to be closely consulted and actively associated with the respective executive and governing bodies of the relevant United Nations institutions dealing with informatics within the United Nations system, so that the specific needs of States as internal end-users can be given due priority;

4. *Calls on* Member States to pursue similar action in the governing bodies of the specialized agencies in which they are represented;

5. *Urges* the Administrative Committee on Coordination to ensure full and effective consultations between the senior-level task force that it has established and the representatives of States, so that their views and requirements are duly incorporated in the report of the senior-level task force;

6. *Requests* that the initial phases of the action programme to harmonize and improve United Nations informatics systems for optimal utilization and accessibility by all States be implemented from within existing resources and in full consultation with the representatives of States;

7. *Requests* the Secretary-General to report to the Economic and Social Council at its substantive session of 1994 on the follow-up action taken on the present resolution.

Economic and Social Council resolution 1993/56

29 July 1993   Meeting 45   Adopted without vote

91-nation draft (E/1993/L.33); agenda item 4 *(c)*.

Sponsors: Afghanistan, Algeria, Angola, Argentina, Australia, Austria, Bahamas, Bangladesh, Belarus, Belgium, Benin, Bhutan, Brazil, Cameroon, Canada, Chile, China, Colombia, Cuba, Cyprus, Czech Republic, Democratic People's Republic of Korea, Denmark, Dominican Republic, Egypt, El Salvador, Estonia, Ethiopia, Finland, France, Gabon, Germany, Ghana, Greece, Guinea, Hungary, Indonesia, Iran, Ireland, Italy, Kenya, Kuwait, Latvia, Libyan Arab Jamahiriya, Madagascar, Malawi, Malaysia, Mauritius, Mexico, Morocco, Myanmar, Nepal, Netherlands, New Zealand, Nigeria, Norway, Pakistan, Panama, Peru, Philippines, Poland, Portugal, Qatar, Republic of Korea, Romania, Russian Federation, Senegal, Singapore, Slovakia, Spain, Sri Lanka, Sudan, Suriname, Swaziland, Sweden, Switzerland, Syrian Arab Republic, Thailand, Togo, Trinidad and Tobago, Tunisia, Turkey, Ukraine, United Kingdom, United Republic of Tanzania, United States, Uruguay, Venezuela, Viet Nam, Yemen, Zaire.

Integrated library network

In March,[11] the Secretary-General submitted his comments on a JIU report setting forth proposals for an integrated library network of the United Nations system.[12] The Secretary-General made a series of recommendations supporting the creation of an effective and integrated library network.

The comments of ACC on the JIU report were submitted by the Secretary-General in May.[13]

By **decision 1993/227** of 13 July, the Economic and Social Council took note of the JIU report and the comments of the Secretary-General and of ACC thereon.

REFERENCES

[1]A/C.5/48/11. [2]A/C.5/48/12. [3]YUN 1988, p. 901, GA res. 43/217, sect. XII, 21 Dec. 1988. [4]YUN 1992, p. 1087, ESC res. 1992/60, 31 July 1992. [5]E/1993/86. [6]ACC/1993/26. [7]ACC/1993/28. [8]A/C.5/48/8. [9]YUN 1970, p. 872, GA res. 2741(XXV), 17 Dec. 1970. [10]YUN 1971, p. 674. [11]A/48/83. [12]A/47/669. [13]A/48/83/Add.1.

Other administrative and budgetary arrangements

Fiftieth anniversary of the United Nations (1995)

In its report to the General Assembly,[1] the Preparatory Committee for the Fiftieth Anniversary of the United Nations reviewed activities of the United Nations system, Member States and non-governmental organizations in preparation for commemoration of the anniversary (see PART ONE, Chapter V).

The Committee was informed that the financial situation of the Organization precluded making funds from the regular United Nations budget available for financing commemorative programmes and events. The Secretary-General therefore established a Trust Fund for the Fiftieth Anniversary Celebrations and urged Member States to support it.

The Committee agreed that it was essential that its secretariat be assured of adequate staff and related resources. It requested its Chairman to raise that concern with the Secretary-General.

GENERAL ASSEMBLY ACTION

On 23 December 1993, on the recommendation of the Preparatory Committee for the Fiftieth Anniversary of the United Nations, the General Assembly adopted **resolution 48/215** without vote.

Commemoration of the fiftieth anniversary of the United Nations in 1995

The General Assembly,

Recalling that on 19 October 1993 it considered and took note of the report of the Preparatory Committee for the Fiftieth Anniversary of the United Nations and adopted the draft decision proposed in paragraph 16 of that report,

Noting that, in paragraph 14 of the report of the Preparatory Committee, it was stated that anniversary and commemorative programmes and events in connection with the fiftieth anniversary of the United Nations could not be financed from the regular budget, but would be financed from a Trust Fund for the Fiftieth Anniversary Celebrations established by the Secretary-General for that purpose,

Noting also that, in paragraph 15 of the report of the Preparatory Committee, it is recorded that "the Committee agreed that it was essential to the effective functioning and proper management of the fiftieth anniversary that its secretariat be assured of adequate staff and related resources",

1. *Approves*, on an exceptional basis, the creation of the post of Special Adviser, at the Under-Secretary-General level, against general temporary assistance resources for organizing and coordinating activities related to the commemoration of the fiftieth anniversary of the United Nations;

2. *Requests* the Secretary-General to provide adequate secretariat support for the Preparatory Committee for the Fiftieth Anniversary of the United Nations.

General Assembly resolution 48/215

23 December 1993   Meeting 87   Adopted without vote

Draft by Australia (A/48/L.51); agenda item 47.

UNITAR

The Secretary-General reported in November[2] that the UNITAR building, valued at $10.6 million, had been transferred to the United Nations in exchange for the cancellation of the debt and coverage of UNITAR's 1992 financial obligations. The headquarters of UNITAR were transferred to Geneva, effective 1 July (see PART THREE, Chapter XII).

Fifth Committee work programme

By **decision 48/458** of 23 December, the General Assembly, on the recommendation of the Fifth Committee, approved the Committee's biennial work programme for 1994-1995, as annexed to the decision.

REFERENCES

[1]A/48/48. [2]A/48/574.

UN Postal Administration

In 1993, the gross revenue of the United Nations Postal Administration (UNPA) from its sale of philatelic items both at Headquarters and at overseas offices totalled more than $16 million. Revenue from the sale of stamps for philatelic pur-

poses was retained by the United Nations. Under the terms of an agreement between the Organization and the United States, revenue from the sale of United States dollar-denominated stamps used for postage from Headquarters was reimbursed to the United States Postal Service. Similarly, postal agreements between the United Nations and the Governments of Switzerland and Austria required that revenue derived from the sale of Swiss franc-denominated stamps and Austrian schilling-denominated stamps for postage be reimbursed to the Swiss and Austrian postal authorities, respectively.

During the year, UNPA released six commemorative stamp issues, two definitive stamps, two souvenir cards, six maximum cards and three postcards.

The first set of six commemorative stamps, entitled "Ageing: Dignity and Participation", was released on 5 February to call global attention to the ageing of populations and challenges facing older persons.

On 3 March, UNPA launched a multi-year stamp series on "Endangered Species". Each year, 12 endangered species would be featured on stamps to highlight the need for the protection of endangered species throughout the world. Three maximum cards accompanied the issue.

On 7 May, the United Nations issued six stamps with the theme "Healthy Environment" to commemorate the forty-fifth anniversary of the World Health Organization. A souvenir card was also released. Two definitive stamps and three postal cards were issued on the same day.

The fifth and final set of stamps in the Human Rights Series was issued on 11 June to illustrate articles 25 to 30 of the Universal Declaration of Human Rights.[1]

To observe the International Day of Peace, UNPA on 21 September issued three stamps and a souvenir card on the theme of peace.

On 29 October, a set of three stamps and three maximum cards were issued on the theme of environment-climate.

The General Assembly, by **resolution 48/219 B**, resolved that direct expenses of UNPA, which were not provided for under the budget appropriations, should be charged against the income derived from its activities.

REFERENCE

[1]YUN 1948-49, p. 535, GA res. 217 A (III), 10 Dec. 1948.

PART SIX

Intergovernmental organizations related to the United Nations

Chapter I

International Atomic Energy Agency (IAEA)

In 1993, the International Atomic Energy Agency (IAEA) continued to foster peaceful uses of nuclear energy, establish and administer safeguards, provide technical assistance to member States and establish health and safety standards.

The thirty-seventh session of the IAEA General Conference (Vienna, 27 September–1 October 1993) adopted resolutions relating to measures to resolve international radioactive waste management issues; the early conclusion of a nuclear safety convention; piratical utilization of food irradiation; producing potable water economically; strengthening the effectiveness and improving the efficiency of the safeguards system; and a nuclear-weapon-free zone in Africa.

Armenia, Croatia, the Czech Republic, Lithuania and Slovakia became IAEA members, bringing the total number of member States to 118 at the end of 1993 (see Annex I).

Nuclear safety and radiation protection

In 1993, a group of experts continued to develop a nuclear safety convention. Consensus was achieved on the fundamental principles of nuclear safety which should be adopted as binding international legal obligations of parties to the convention.

Six Operational Safety Review Team missions (China, France, Romania, Russian Federation, Slovakia, Slovenia) and five follow-up visits (Bulgaria, Germany, Japan, Russian Federation, South Africa) were made to nuclear powerplants. In addition, 12 Assessment of Safety Significant Events Team missions (Bulgaria, Czech Republic, France, Lithuania, Netherlands, Russian Federation (4), Slovakia, Ukraine (2)) were carried out to review the operational safety performance of installations, and an International Regulatory Review Team visited Bulgaria to assist in strengthening the country's nuclear regulatory body.

In May, a joint United Nations Development Programme (UNDP)/IAEA initiative was launched to strengthen radiation and nuclear safety infrastructures in the successor States of the former USSR. Fact-finding missions to Armenia, Estonia, Kazakhstan, Kyrgyzstan, Latvia, Lithuania and Uzbekistan formed the basis for country-specific programmes. In addition, IAEA assisted the successor States of the former USSR and Eastern European countries in implementing consistent international safety assessments and made recommendations regarding improvements in the safety of nuclear installations.

A safety guide was completed on criteria for intervention after a nuclear or radiation emergency. Work continued on improving the capabilities of the Emergency Response Unit and the overall effectiveness of IAEA to respond to a nuclear accident or radiological emergency.

During 1993, there were five Radiation Protection Advisory Team missions (Croatia, Kuwait, Lebanon, Mauritius, Myanmar). Through individual monitoring services to member States, some 9,000 dosimeters and 1,000 finger dosimeters were distributed.

The International Nuclear Event Scale information system continued to be operational for nuclear powerplants and, on a trial basis, for all other nuclear facilities except medical and military facilities. In 1993, 65 events were reported to the system.

A new programme was initiated to collect and review environmental monitoring data with the collaboration of the United Nations Scientific Committee on the Effects of Atomic Radiation and the World Health Organization (WHO). It aimed at setting up a database to include external radiation levels and radioactive concentrations in atmospheric aerosols, precipitation, drinking-water, groundwater, surface water, sea water, selected bio-indicators and food items under normal conditions.

Nuclear power

Assistance to IAEA member States for nuclear power programme planning and development included support to China, Colombia and Peru, for carrying out studies to assess the nuclear option; Romania, for energy demand forecasting, electricity expansion planning and nuclear programme implementation; the Philippines, for the comparative economic assessment of nuclear and fossil powerplants in the overall power development programme; the Czech Republic and Slovakia, to evaluate and select sites for spent-fuel storage and disposal; Indonesia, for a feasibility study for its first nuclear powerplant on the Muria Peninsula (Java) and for training; Thailand, to examine the introduction of nuclear power into electricity grids; and Iran, for a training course in nuclear power engineering.

IAEA activities in non-electrical applications of advanced reactors focused on coupling nuclear reactors with desalination processes and on feasibility studies of sea-water desalination using nuclear energy for potable water production.

At the end of 1993, the Power Reactor Information System (PRIS) database included information on the status and operating experience of 430 nuclear powerplants. There were 69 users in 29 countries and four international organizations. A subset of the databank, MicroPRIS, for users of personal computers, had 179 subscribers in 53 member States.

Nuclear fuel cycle

World uranium production in 1993 declined further by some 2,000 tonnes to 34,000 tonnes, which met only about 60 per cent of the world-wide reactor-related requirements. Six countries produced nearly 67 per cent of the total.

In the area of reactor-fuel technology and performance, technical committee meetings were held on the influence of water chemistry on fuel cladding behaviour (Rez, Czech Republic, October); advances in control materials for water reactors; and the safe handling, transportation and storage of separated plutonium in civilian nuclear-power programmes.

A mission to Hungary advised on the safety of spent-fuel storage.

Radioactive waste management

IAEA's radioactive waste management programme focused on developing and promulgating its Radioactive Waste Safety Standards, building and strengthening waste management infrastructures, developing radiological and safety criteria for waste disposal, and coordinating international radiological/environmental assessment projects. Other areas emphasized were advisory service missions, guidance on the safety and technical aspects of decommissioning nuclear facilities, quality assurance management for waste packaging and disposal systems, safety assessment in near-surface disposal facilities and the environmental restoration of contaminated land masses.

Under the Radioactive Waste Management Advisory Programme, two regular missions and one follow-up mission were organized. In cooperation with UNDP, projects to enhance safety and provide sound environmental management of radioactive wastes were developed for four pilot countries. Reviews of the national waste management programmes of the Czech Republic and Finland were conducted as part of IAEA's Waste Management Assessment and Technical Review Programme.

During the year, IAEA began implementing the International Arctic Seas Assessment Project to evaluate the health and environmental risks posed by the wastes that had been dumped into the Arctic seas and to assess the feasibility of possible remedial actions. The IAEA Marine Environment Laboratory (Monaco) participated in the Russian-Norwegian expedition to the Arctic dump sites to sample and analyse water, sediment and biota in the region.

Food and agriculture

Under a joint IAEA/Food and Agriculture Organization of the United Nations (FAO) programme, member States were assisted in using nuclear techniques in their agricultural research and development to improve food production, reduce food losses, improve soil fertility and water availability and protect the environment.

Significant advances were made in restoring damaged soils and improving the efficiency of water use and phosphorus uptake by crops. Progress was made in the genetic improvement of crops through the combined use of induced mutations and other techniques such as *in vitro* propagation and cloning, doubled haploids, deoxyribonucleic acid (DNA)-based marker mutations, electrophoresis of proteins and flow cell cytometry for measuring ploidy.

The first phase of a Latin American regional project on the genetic improvement of seed-propagated crops focused on mutation breeding and *in vitro* techniques such as the use of doubled haploids. Major crop improvements were achieved in wheat, rice, barley and common bean, resulting in the production of promising mutant lines and the release of mutant varieties. A research coordination meeting was held on improving basic food crops in Africa through plant breeding, including the use of induced mutations (Nairobi, Kenya, September). The major objective of the project was the breeding of improved varieties of staple food crops, emphasizing indigenous species. Another research coordination meeting on the application of DNA-based marker mutations for improving cereals and other sexually reproduced crop species was combined with another meeting on the use of novel DNA finger-printing techniques for detecting and characterizing genetic variation in vegetatively propagated crops.

Research and development at the Agency's Laboratory at Seibersdorf, Austria, focused mainly on the genetic improvement of vegetatively propagated and tropical crops of major importance, through *in vitro* mutation breeding in association with advanced methods of molecular biology. A radiation treatment service was provided at no cost to FAO and IAEA member States to foster the application of nuclear techniques in national crop-improvement programmes. In 1993, more than 600 radiation service treatments for 48 member States were provided by the Seibersdorf Laboratory. Most of these were seed samples which were irradiated. In August, a joint FAO/IAEA Central Laboratory was established within the Laboratory at Seibersdorf to develop and distribute immunoassay-based disease diagnostic kits for veterinary services in developing countries.

Prospects for increasing the application of the sterile-insect technique to combat the Mediterranean fruit fly were enhanced by the development at the Laboratory, using nuclear techniques, of "Vienna 42", a strain which allowed the release of sterile males alone. The production of sterile males was important because sterile females persisted in stinging the fruit, allowing the entry of micro-organisms which caused the fruit to rot. A model project was developed using the sterile-insect technique against tsetse flies to eradicate the vector of African animal trypanosomiasis from Zanzibar, United Republic of Tanzania.

Human health

The human health programme emphasized creating mechanisms to promote quality in nuclear medicine and radiotherapy processes in developing countries. IAEA collaborated with the Latin American Association of Societies of Nuclear Medicine and Biology in founding the Ibero-American Board for the Certification of Nuclear Physicians in Latin America, Spain and Portugal.

Projects in nuclear medicine and applied radiation biology and radiotherapy continued to enhance indigenous capabilities, including the production of radioactive reagents and radiopharmaceuticals and the use of computer-assisted radiotherapy planning for various types of cancer.

The IAEA/WHO Network of Secondary Standard Dosimetry Laboratories included 67 laboratories and six national organizations in 54 member States, as well as 14 affiliated members. Services continued in the areas of calibration and dose intercomparison and support for technology transfer. The Seibersdorf Laboratory took over the technical activities of the International Dose Assurance Service for radiation-processing dosimetry.

Nutritional and health-related environment studies focused on micronutrient malnutrition and the use of nuclear analytical techniques for studying non-radioactive pollutants in environmental samples and human tissues.

Physical and earth sciences

IAEA's activities in the area of industrial applications of radiation and radioisotopes focused on methods for minimizing industry-related environmental pollution, non-destructive testing and nucleonic control systems for on-line mineral analysis. Work continued on nuclear methods for evaluating healing pathways of pollutant damage in the environment and for removing toxic flue gases from coal-fired power stations.

Water resources development projects dealt with water resources assessment, geothermal resource assessment, studies of sediment transport and related problem, environmental investigations in the hydrosphere and atmosphere, analytical and intercalibration services, and training scientists from developing countries.

Five national/regional nuclear data libraries were incorporated into the Agency's database. IAEA continued to develop the atomic and molecular/plasma-material interaction database system. In 1993, it fulfilled some 700 requests from scientists in 75 member States for experimental and evaluated data and related documentation, data-processing codes and publications.

Some 4,600 scientists participated in activities of the International Centre for Theoretical Physics (Trieste, Italy). Over 50 per cent of them came from developing countries.

Technical cooperation

The most significant development in 1993 in IAEA's technical cooperation activities was the approval by the Board of Governors of the first 12 model projects for the 1994 programme. The projects were formulated in close cooperation with the recipient Governments, which committed substantial resources to them. The model project concept, responding to real needs and designed to have a socio-economic impact on end-users, introduced a new approach to the technical cooperation programme.

Under the programme, a total of 1,373 projects were operational, including 860 continued from 1992 and 412 newly approved projects. Activities covered the provision of training to more than 2,500 scientists, the assignment of 2,978 experts and lecturers, and the completion of 172 training courses. Total new resources available for technical cooperation amounted to $52.9 million, the largest amount ever recorded. The Technical Assistance and Cooperation Fund accounted for 81.1 per cent of those resources, with extrabudgetary funds accounting for 14.8 per cent, and UNDP for 2 per cent. The programme emphasized food and agriculture, which accounted for 20.2 per cent of all disbursements, followed by safety-related activities (19.7 per cent), such as radioactive waste management, radiation protection and the safety of nuclear installations, physical and chemical sciences (18.1 per cent), industry and earth sciences (14.5 per cent) and human health (14.4 per cent).

Agency safeguards responsibilities

During 1993, 2,042 safeguards inspections were performed. IAEA carried out six inspections in

Iraq, bringing the total number of inspections to 22 since May 1991, and implemented the essential elements of the plan for the destruction, removal and rendering harmless of items indicated in a 1991 Security Council resolution.[a] Inspections were also carried out in the Democratic People's Republic of Korea and South Africa (for details of IAEA activities in South Africa, see PART TWO, Chapter I; for details of its activities in the Democratic People's Republic of Korea and Iraq, see PART TWO, Chapter III).

At the end of December 1993, 194 safeguards agreements were in force with 116 States (and Taiwan). In 1993, safeguards agreements pursuant to the 1968 Treaty on the Non-Proliferation of Nuclear Weapons (NPT)[b] entered into force with Latvia, Solomon Islands and Tonga. The 1972 safeguards agreement with Czechoslovakia continued to be applied in the Czech Republic and Slovakia to the extent relevant to the territory of each State. In addition, the 1973 safeguards agreement with the former Yugoslavia continued to be applied in Croatia, Slovenia and the Federal Republic of Yugoslavia (Serbia and Montenegro) to the extent relevant to the territory of each of those States.

During 1993, safeguards were applied in 46 States under agreements pursuant to NPT or to NPT and the 1967 Treaty for the Prohibition of Nuclear Weapons in Latin America and the Caribbean (Treaty of Tlatelolco), in one State under an agreement pursuant to the Treaty of Tlatelolco and in nine States under bi- or trilateral agreements. Safeguards activities pursuant to NPT in Iraq continued and IAEA applied safeguards to nuclear installations in Taiwan.

As at 31 December 1993, safeguards agreements were in force with 100 States pursuant to NPT. For 57 non-nuclear-weapon States party to NPT, there was still no safeguards agreement in force in accordance with the Treaty. As far as IAEA was aware, five of those States had significant nuclear activities.

NPT safeguards agreements were in force with all 11 signatories of the South Pacific Nuclear Free Zone Treaty (Rarotonga Treaty) and safeguards were applied in one of those States pursuant to such an agreement.

Twenty of the 24 Latin American States party to the Treaty of Tlatelolco had concluded safeguards agreements with IAEA pursuant to that Treaty and 17 of them were in force. Safeguards agreements pursuant to Additional Protocol I of the Treaty were in force with two States with territories in the zone of application of the Treaty.

Nuclear information

The International Nuclear Information System (INIS), with 86 States and 17 international organizations participating, had a bibliographic database on nuclear literature totalling 1,700,078 records by year's end.

The INIS Clearing-house distributed about 440,000 microfiches, representing 24 million printed pages of documents. By the end of 1993, the number of documents available on microfiche was almost 278,000.

Secretariat

At the end of 1993, the IAEA secretariat staff totalled 2,188, with 833 in the Professional and higher categories and 1,355 in the General Service category. Among the 601 staff members in posts subject to geographical distribution, 85 nationalities were represented.

Budget

The regular budget for 1993 amounted to $206,922,000, of which $198,259,000 was to be financed by member States on the basis of the 1993 scale of assessment; $5,419,000 from income from reimbursable work for others; and $3,244,000 from other miscellaneous income. However, because of a shortfall in expected receipts, steps were taken to reduce the budget by 12 per cent to $177,364,100. Actual expenditures from the regular budget amounted to $175,323,802; the authority to spend an amount of $16,628,800 was reserved for deferred programme activities to be carried out in 1994 if arrears of contributions were received in time. An allocation of $1,685,000 to the Equipment Replacement Fund was also approved. As a result, the unused budget amounted to $7,865,398.

The target for voluntary contributions to the Technical Assistance and Cooperation Fund in 1993 was established at $55.5 million, of which $43 million was pledged by member States.

NOTE: For further information, see *The Annual Report for 1993*, published by IAEA.

[a]YUN 1991, p. 172, SC res. 687(1991), 3 Apr. 1991.
[b]YUN 1968, p. 17, GA res. 2373(XXII), annex, 12 June 1968.

Annex I.   MEMBERSHIP OF THE INTERNATIONAL ATOMIC ENERGY AGENCY
(As at 31 December 1993)

Afghanistan, Albania, Algeria, Argentina, Armenia, Australia, Austria, Bangladesh, Belarus, Belgium, Bolivia, Brazil, Bulgaria, Cambodia, Cameroon, Canada, Chile, China, Colombia, Costa Rica, Côte d'Ivoire, Croatia, Cuba, Cyprus, Czech Republic, Democratic People's Republic of Korea, Denmark, Dominican Republic, Ecuador, Egypt, El Salvador, Estonia, Ethiopia, Finland, France, Gabon, Germany, Ghana, Greece, Guatemala, Haiti, Holy See, Hungary, Iceland, India, Indonesia, Iran, Iraq, Ireland, Israel, Italy, Jamaica, Japan, Jordan, Kenya, Kuwait, Lebanon, Liberia, Libyan Arab Jamahiriya, Liechtenstein, Lithuania, Luxembourg, Madagascar, Malaysia, Mali, Mauritius, Mexico, Monaco, Mongolia,

Morocco, Myanmar, Namibia, Netherlands, New Zealand, Nicaragua, Niger, Nigeria, Norway, Pakistan, Panama, Paraguay, Peru, Philippines, Poland, Portugal, Qatar, Republic of Korea, Romania, Russian Federation, Saudi Arabia, Senegal, Sierra Leone, Singapore, Slovakia, Slovenia, South Africa, Spain, Sri Lanka, Sudan, Sweden, Switzerland, Syrian Arab Republic, Thailand, Tunisia, Turkey, Uganda, Ukraine, United Arab Emirates, United Kingdom, United Republic of Tanzania, United States, Uruguay, Venezuela, Viet Nam, Yugoslavia,* Zaire, Zambia, Zimbabwe.

*Refers to the former Socialist Federal Republic of Yugoslavia. The IAEA General Conference, in 1992, decided that Yugoslavia (Serbia and Montenegro) could not continue automatically the membership of the former Yugoslavia and that, therefore, it should apply for membership and should not take further part in the work of the Board and the General Conference.

Annex II.   OFFICERS AND OFFICES OF THE INTERNATIONAL ATOMIC ENERGY AGENCY

BOARD OF GOVERNORS
(For the period October 1993–September 1994)

OFFICERS

Chairman: Ronald Walker (Australia).
Vice-Chairmen: Agus Tarmidzi (Indonesia), József Vigassy (Hungary).

MEMBERS

Argentina, Australia, Brazil, Canada, Chile, China, Colombia, Cuba, Egypt, Ethiopia, Finland, France, Germany, Hungary, India, Indonesia, Ireland, Italy, Japan, Lebanon, Libyan Arab Jamahiriya, Malaysia, Nigeria, Paraguay, Philippines, Poland, Russian Federation, Saudi Arabia, Sweden, Switzerland, Syrian Arab Republic, Tunisia, Ukraine, United Kingdom, United States.

SENIOR SECRETARIAT OFFICERS

Director General: Hans Blix.
Special Assistants to the Director General: Nina Alonso, John Tilemann, Pierre Villaros.
Secretary, Secretariat of the Policy-making Organs: Muttusamy Sanmuganathan.
Deputy Director General for Safeguards: Bruno Pellaud.

Deputy Director General for Nuclear Energy and Safety: Boris Semenov.
Deputy Director General for Administration: David B. Waller.
Deputy Director General for Technical Cooperation: Jihui Qian.
Deputy Director General for Research and Isotopes: Suoo Machii.

HEADQUARTERS AND OTHER OFFICES

HEADQUARTERS
International Atomic Energy Agency
Wagramerstrasse 5
(P.O. Box 100, Vienna International Centre)
A-1400 Vienna, Austria
  Cable address: INATOM VIENNA
  Telephone: (43) (1) 23600
  Telex: 1-12645 ATOM A
  Facsimile: (43) (1) 234564

LIAISON OFFICE
International Atomic Energy Agency Liaison Office at the United Nations
1 United Nations Plaza, Room 1155
New York, N.Y. 10017, United States
  Telephone: (1) (212) 963-6010, 6011, 6012
  Telex: 42 05 44 UNH
  Facsimile: (1) (212) 751-4117

The Agency also maintained offices at Geneva; Tokyo; and Toronto, Canada.

Chapter II

International Labour Organisation (ILO)

In 1993, the International Labour Organisation (ILO) continued activities in its six major programme areas: promotion of policies to create employment and satisfy basic human needs; development of human resources; improvement of working and living conditions and environment; promotion of social security; strengthening of industrial relations and tripartite (government/employer/worker) cooperation; and the advancement of human rights in social and labour matters. The main instruments of action continued to be standard-setting, technical cooperation activities, research and publishing.

Membership in ILO rose to 169 in 1993, with the admission of Bosnia and Herzegovina, the Czech Republic, Eritrea, Georgia, Kazakhstan, Slovakia, Tajikistan, the former Yugoslav Republic of Macedonia and Turkmenistan (see Annex I).

On 27 May, the 56-member Governing Body of ILO re-elected Michel Hansenne (Belgium) for a second five-year term as Director-General of the International Labour Office beginning 4 March 1994.

Meetings

The eightieth session of the International Labour Conference (Geneva, 2-22 June) had before it the annual report of the ILO Governing Body, the report of the Director-General concerning social protection and the thirtieth special report on the effect of apartheid on labour and employment in South Africa.

The Conference adopted a new Convention and Recommendation on the Prevention of Major Industrial Accidents and discussed the protection of part-time workers with a view to adopting standards in 1994.

A general discussion focused on the complementarity between ILO technical cooperation and international labour standards. A special sitting discussed the Director-General's report on the situation of workers of the occupied Arab territories.

A tripartite Conference committee again examined the application of ILO Conventions and Recommendations by member States and reviewed the application of ILO standards on workers with family responsibilities.

Among industrial meetings held during the year were: the Tripartite Meeting on Safety and Related

Issues pertaining to Work on Offshore Petroleum Installations (Geneva, 20-28 April); tenth session of the Committee on Salaried Employees and Professional Workers (Geneva, 5-13 May); Tripartite Meeting on the Effects of Technological Changes in the Clothing Industry (Geneva, 14-22 September); fifth session of the Joint Committee on the Public Service (Geneva, 20-28 October); Tripartite Meeting on the Social Effects of Structural Change in Banking (Geneva, 23 November–1 December); and the thirteenth session of the Metal Trades Committee (Geneva, 8-15 December).

The Fifteenth International Conference of Labour Statisticians (Geneva, 19-28 January) focused on international standards concerning informal sector employment statistics; statistics of various forms of industrial action; and revision of the International Classification of Status in Employment.

International standards

During 1993, ILO activities concerning Conventions and Recommendations consisted of standard-setting and supervision of the application of standards.

Standard-setting

In 1993, the International Labour Conference adopted the Prevention of Major Industrial Accidents Convention (No. 174) and Recommendation (No. 181), 1993. The Chemicals Convention, 1990 (No. 170) entered into force on 4 November 1993, having received the requisite number of ratifications.

During the year, 398 ratifications of ILO Conventions by 38 member States were registered, bringing the total number of ratifications as at 31 December 1993 to 6,050. There was one denunciation by Portugal of the Night Work (Women) Convention, 1919 (No. 4).

Supervision of standards

In March, the Committee of Experts on the Application of Conventions and Recommendations was able to note 42 instances in 1993 in which Governments had changed their law and practice to come into closer conformity with ratified Conventions, following the Committee's earlier comments. In addition, it dealt with 251 instances in which employers' or workers' organizations exercised their right to make observations on the application of Conventions ratified by Governments.

The Committee carried out a general survey of the application by member States of selected international labour standards, whether or not they had been ratified by all countries. The 1993 survey dealt with the application of the Workers with Family Responsibilities Convention (No. 156) and Recommendation (No. 165), 1981.[a]

The Governing Body's Committee on Freedom of Association, which examined complaints of violations of freedom of association received from employers' and workers' organizations, met three times in 1993 to deal with complaints alleging violations of trade union rights.

A number of special procedures were pursued to examine complaints and representations under various articles of the ILO Constitution. Complaints under article 26 were examined concerning the application of ratified Conventions by Côte d'Ivoire and Sweden, and representations under article 24 were examined concerning Brazil, Myanmar, Poland, Sweden and Venezuela.

Employment and development

Active labour-market policies

The active labour-market policies programme assisted member States to formulate and implement effective labour-market policies to improve access to employment and income, with the aim of reducing the impoverishment of vulnerable groups and stimulating labour productivity in order to create favourable conditions for economic growth with employment security.

ILO focused on employment problems associated with the transition from centralized planning to a more market-oriented economy in Central and Eastern Europe and the countries of the former USSR, carrying out a programme of labour-market research analysis and policy advisory services in the Central Asian republics. Analytical work also extended to developing economies in transition, with initial attention placed on Viet Nam, Nicaragua and Mozambique.

With a view to improving labour-market information systems in member States, new methodologies were developed for monitoring poverty and new approaches were identified for measuring female labour force participation. Assistance to member States was provided through several technical cooperation projects, including a project to develop labour-market information systems in support of employment policies in Portuguese-speaking countries in Africa.

ILO obtained insights into the practices of businesses by conducting labour surveys in Bulgaria, Chile, Hungary, Malaysia, Mexico, the Philippines and the Russian Federation. For example, the survey in Mexico showed how different employers reacted to structural adjustment and the expected signing of the North American Free Trade Agreement. While some enterprises modernized and developed the skills of their employees, others, particularly smaller establishments, reacted more defensively and economized by increasing the proportion of workers who were employed under flexible labour contracts.

In November, at the request of the ILO Governing Body's Committee on Employment and Social Policy, a comprehensive paper was produced on active labour-market policies. The paper defined the concept and objectives underlying an ILO framework for active labour-market policies, described their implementation and set out new directions for future work.

Working environment

The International Programme for the Improvement of Working Conditions and Environment continued to assist countries in promoting occupational safety and health and improving working conditions.

Several activities and publications aimed to promote the adoption and strengthening of the implementation of international labour standards on occupational safety and health. National projects, training workshops and seminars in Africa, Asia and the Pacific and Latin America were held to enhance national action on prevention of major industrial and other accidents in hazardous activities such as construction and the use of chemicals. ILO carried out two regional projects in the English-speaking countries of Africa and 20 countries in Asia to assist in drawing up and implementing national policies on safety and health and to enhance training and information capabilities.

As a follow-up to the 1992 United Nations Conference on Environment and Development,[b] ILO provided support to Governments and workers' and employers' organizations to deal with environmental and sustainable development matters. The Coordinating Group for the Harmonization of Chemical Classification Systems, established within the framework of the International Programme on Chemical Safety, proposed harmonized classification criteria for acute toxicity and danger to the environment. Through inter-agency cooperation, International Basic Safety Standards for Protection against Ionizing Radiation and for the Safety of Radiation Sources were prepared. Guidance notes on practical measures to be taken at enterprise level were issued on several safety and health subjects. Six issues

[a]YUN 1981, p. 1396.
[b]YUN 1992, p. 670.

of the bulletin *Safety and Health at Work* were published, compact discs (CD-ROMs) with 100 occupational safety and health databases were distributed, and an Asian-Pacific network and several national networks on safety and health were set up.

Activities to improve working conditions and quality of working life included technical cooperation, standard-setting, research and publications. Technical cooperation activities aimed to improve working conditions and productivity in small- and medium-sized enterprises and to prevent and reduce alcohol and drug problems in the workplace. ILO continued to focus on the protection of working children and the gradual elimination of child labour. Under the International Programme on the Elimination of Child Labour, which was launched with the support of Germany, more than 120 projects with government institutions, trade unions, employers' organizations and non-governmental organizations were being implemented in six countries. A two-year interdepartmental project on child labour was also completed. To address problems of workers with family responsibilities, a survey of major problems related to the care of the elderly was carried out. Standard-setting on part-time work and the preparation for standard-setting to protect homeworkers were also undertaken. Issues of the *Conditions of Work Digest* were published on monitoring and surveillance and testing in the workplace.

Field activities

In 1993, total expenditure on operational activities from all sources of funds stood at nearly $149 million, almost a 9 per cent decrease from 1992. Trust funds and multi-bilateral sources provided close to $63.3 million, representing some 43 per cent of overall expenditure. As in the past, the United Nations Development Programme remained the largest single source of external funding, providing some $59 million—close to 40 per cent of overall ILO expenditure on operational activities. The ILO regular budget provided about $18.4 million, representing 12.4 per cent, and the United Nations Population Fund some $8.3 million, representing 5.6 per cent.

The three leading programmes in terms of annual expenditure were the employment and development programme ($39 million), comprising primarily projects in support of rural development, migration and population and employment strategies; the enterprise and cooperative development programme ($34.8 million); and the programme on vocational training systems, rehabilitation and training policies ($22.2 million). Other significant technical programmes focused on industrial relations and labour administration ($6.7 million), working conditions and environment ($10 million)

and sectoral activities ($7.7 million). ILO spent $1.7 million and $8 million, respectively, for activities in support of employers' and workers' organizations. Africa remained in the forefront of ILO operational activities ($60 million, representing 40 per cent of the total expenditure), followed by Asia and the Pacific ($41.4 million), the Americas ($22 million), interregional and global ($16.8 million), Europe ($6.1 million) and the Arab States ($2.2 million).

Educational activities

In 1993, priority was given to assisting member States in raising national capacity-building to formulate training policies and effectively manage national vocational training systems. ILO emphasized facilitating effective responses by Governments, employers and workers to the rapid changes occurring in the training environment and to structural adjustment measures, particularly in the countries undergoing transition from a centrally planned to a market economy; improving skills and incomes at the local community level in developing countries; and promoting training opportunities for women and youth. Increased efforts were made to integrate people with disabilities into the mainstream of vocational training. Throughout the year, a sustained effort was made to increase the capacities of the non-governmental sectors engaged in social development to collaborate with Governments in formulating and implementing national training strategies. Applied research resulted in practical guidelines for decision-makers and trainers.

ILO's International Institute for Labour Studies stressed links between labour institutions, industrial organizations and economic development in order to define social policies which combined growth with equity. The relationships between labour institutions and economic development were examined through case-studies covering Africa, Asia and Latin America. In November, a symposium on poverty explored aspects of anti-poverty policies, including macroeconomic and sectoral policies, labour markets, social integration, and the organization and representation of the poor.

The impact of globalization on industrial organization was examined in the context of changing patterns of trade, capital and the international division of labour. The Institute's Forum on Labour in a Changing World Economy examined the importance of labour costs for investment location relative to other factors such as social infrastructures, skill endowments and access to markets.

Tripartite participants from 22 countries attended the 1993 international internship course on active labour policy development. The course was designed to enhance the capacity of social policy makers to develop and manage national programmes in a changing global setting.

Secretariat

As at 31 December 1993, the total number of full-time staff under permanent, fixed- and short-term appointments at ILO headquarters and elsewhere was 3,311. Of these, 1,330 were in the Professional and higher categories and 1,981 were in the General Service or Maintenance categories. Of the Professional staff, 387 were assigned to technical cooperation projects.

Budget

The International Labour Conference in June 1993 adopted a budget of $466.51 million for the 1994-1995 biennium, which, at the exchange rate of 1.45 Swiss francs to the United States dollar, amounted to 676,439,500 Swiss francs.

NOTE: For further information on ILO, see *Report of the Director-General, Activities of the ILO, 1993.*

Annex I. MEMBERSHIP OF THE INTERNATIONAL LABOUR ORGANISATION
(As at 31 December 1993)

Afghanistan, Albania, Algeria, Angola, Antigua and Barbuda, Argentina, Armenia, Australia, Austria, Azerbaijan, Bahamas, Bahrain, Bangladesh, Barbados, Belarus, Belgium, Belize, Benin, Bolivia, Bosnia and Herzegovina, Botswana, Brazil, Bulgaria, Burkina Faso, Burundi, Cambodia, Cameroon, Canada, Cape Verde, Central African Republic, Chad, Chile, China, Colombia, Comoros, Congo, Costa Rica, Côte d'Ivoire, Croatia, Cuba, Cyprus, Czech Republic, Denmark, Djibouti, Dominica, Dominican Republic, Ecuador, Egypt, El Salvador, Equatorial Guinea, Eritrea, Estonia, Ethiopia, Fiji, Finland, France, Gabon, Georgia, Germany, Ghana, Greece, Grenada, Guatemala, Guinea, Guinea-Bissau, Guyana, Haiti, Honduras, Hungary, Iceland, India, Indonesia, Iran, Iraq, Ireland, Israel, Italy, Jamaica, Japan, Jordan, Kazakhstan, Kenya, Kuwait, Kyrgyzstan, Lao People's Democratic Repubic, Latvia, Lebanon, Lesotho, Liberia, Libyan Arab Jamahiriya, Lithuania, Luxembourg, Madagascar, Malawi, Malaysia, Mali, Malta, Mauritania, Mauritius, Mexico, Mongolia, Morocco, Mozambique, Myanmar, Namibia, Nepal, Netherlands, New Zealand, Nicaragua, Niger, Nigeria, Norway, Pakistan, Panama, Papua New Guinea, Paraguay, Peru, Philippines, Poland, Portugal, Qatar, Republic of Korea, Republic of Moldova, Romania, Russian Federation, Rwanda, Saint Lucia, San Marino, Sao Tome and Principe, Saudi Arabia, Senegal, Seychelles, Sierra Leone, Singapore, Slovakia, Slovenia, Solomon Islands, Somalia, Spain, Sri Lanka, Sudan, Suriname, Swaziland, Sweden, Switzerland, Syrian Arab Republic, Tajikistan, Thailand, the former Yugoslav Republic of Macedonia, Togo, Trinidad and Tobago, Tunisia, Turkey, Turkmenistan, Uganda, Ukraine, United Arab Emirates, United Kingdom, United Republic of Tanzania, United States, Uruguay, Uzbekistan, Venezuela, Viet Nam, Yemen, Yugoslavia,* Zaire, Zambia, Zimbabwe.

*Refers to the former Socialist Federal Republic of Yugoslavia. In March 1993, the ILO Governing Body decided to instruct the Director-General not to invite the Federal Republic of Yugoslavia (Serbia and Montenegro) to ILO meetings or to recognize credentials submitted on its behalf as long as that State had not been recognized by the United Nations as the continuation of the former Yugoslavia or admitted to ILO as a new member.

Annex II. OFFICERS AND OFFICES OF THE INTERNATIONAL LABOUR ORGANISATION
(As at 31 December 1993)

MEMBERSHIP OF THE GOVERNING BODY OF THE INTERNATIONAL LABOUR OFFICE

Chairman: John Nkomo (Zimbabwe), Government Group.
Vice-Chairmen: Jean-Jacques Oechslin (France), Employers' Group; William Brett (United Kingdom), Workers' Group.

REGULAR MEMBERS

Government members

Argentina, Australia, Brazil,* Chile, China,* Congo, Czech Republic, France,* Germany,* Ghana, India,* Indonesia, Iran, Italy,* Japan,* Kenya, Mexico, Nicaragua, Niger, Norway, Qatar, Romania, Russian Federation,* Tunisia, United Kingdom,* United States,* Venezuela, Zimbabwe.

Employers' members

J. Aka Angui (Côte d'Ivoire), M. Eurnekian (Argentina), A. Gazarin (Egypt), G. Hultin (Finland), A. Katz (United States), A. M. Mackie (United Kingdom), M. Nasr (Lebanon), J. S. Neves Filho (Brazil), B. Noakes (Australia), J.-J. Oechslin (France), T. D. Owuor (Kenya), A. Tabani (Pakistan), R. Thüsing (Germany), H. Tsujino (Japan).

Workers' members

M. Ben Seddik (Morocco), W. Brett (United Kingdom), I. Doucouré (Mali), U. Engelen-Kefer (Germany), R. Falbr (Czech Republic), M. Ferguson (Australia), C. Graz (United States), S. Itoh (Japan), J. Mugalla (Kenya), H. Naik (India), J. Parrot (Canada), A. Sanchez Madariaga (Mexico), K. Tapiola (Finland), G. Vera (Venezuela).

DEPUTY MEMBERS

Government deputy members

Canada, Cuba, Egypt, Gabon, Hungary, Mali, Mauritius, Netherlands, New Zealand, Pakistan, Panama, Philippines, Poland, Portugal, Spain, Sudan, Swaziland, Uruguay.

Employers' deputy members

J. Aboghe Obame (Gabon), I. P. Anand (India), F. Diaz Garaycoa (Ecuador), C. Hak (Netherlands), J. C. Halliwell (Canada), I. C. Imoisili (Nigeria), J. M. Lacasa Aso (Spain), T. Makeka (Lesotho), E. Millette (Trinidad and Tobago), A. R. D. Mokhzani (Malaysia), M. A. Ould Sidi Mohamed (Mauritania), J. de Regil Gomez (Mexico), L. Sasso-Mazzufferi (Italy), O. Touré (Mali).

Workers' deputy members

C. Egyei (Ghana), K. Ahmed (Pakistan), R. Briesch (France), Y. Kara (Israel), I. Klochkov (Russian Federation), O. Martines Bargas (Brazil), I. Mayaki (Niger), D. T. Mendoza (Philippines), Z. Rampak (Malaysia), J. Sandos (Central African Republic), G. Sibanda (Zimbabwe), L. Trotman (Barbados), R. Vanni (Italy), T. Wojcik (Poland).

*Member holding a non-elective seat as a State of chief industrial importance.

SENIOR OFFICIALS OF THE INTERNATIONAL LABOUR OFFICE

Director-General: Michel Hansenne.
Deputy Directors-General: David Taylor, Heribert Maier, Mary Chinery-Hesse.
Assistant Directors-General: Faisal Abdel-Rahman, Jorge Capriata d'Auro, Tadashi Nakamura, Anees Ahmad, Shukri Dajani.

Director of the International Centre for Advanced Technical and Vocational Training: Jean-François Trémeaud.
Director of the International Institute for Labour Studies: Padmanabh Gopinath.

HEADQUARTERS, LIAISON AND OTHER OFFICES

HEADQUARTERS
International Labour Office
4 Route des Morillons
CH-1211 Geneva 22, Switzerland
  Cable address: INTERLAB GENEVE
  Telephone: (41) (22) 799-6111
  Telex: 415647 ILO CH
  Facsimile: (41) (22) 798-8686

LIAISON OFFICE
International Labour Organisation Liaison Office with the United Nations
220 East 42nd Street
Suite 3101
New York, N.Y. 10017
  Telephone: (1) (212) 697-0150
  Telex: 422716
  Facsimile: (1) (212) 883-0844

ILO also maintained regional offices at Abidjan, Côte d'Ivoire; Bangkok, Thailand; Geneva; and Lima, Peru; as well as other liaison offices with the European Community at Brussels, Belgium; and with the Economic Commission for Latin America and the Caribbean at Santiago, Chile.

Chapter III

Food and Agriculture Organization of the United Nations (FAO)

The twenty-seventh biennial session of the Conference of the Food and Agriculture Organization of the United Nations (FAO) (Rome, Italy, 6-24 November 1993) approved FAO's programme of work and budget for 1994-1995 and adopted resolutions on food, agriculture and administrative and financial matters. With regard to the 1994-1999 medium-term plan, it endorsed the following priorities: environment and sustainable development; policy advice; people in development; poverty alleviation, nutrition and food security; and technical and economic cooperation among developing countries.

The Conference expressed concern over the reduction in world agricultural production in 1993 and the unevenness of progress among countries and regions, in particular the deterioration of food security in sub-Saharan Africa and in large parts of Central and Eastern Europe. In the area of environment and sustainable development, it decided to revise the International Undertaking on Plant Genetic Resources to be in harmony with the Convention on Biological Diversity,[a] signed at the 1992 United Nations Conference on Environment and Development.[b] It also adopted the Voluntary International Code of Conduct for Plant Germplasm Collecting and Transfer to contribute to the conservation and rational use of plant genetic resources for sustainable development. The Conference reviewed the implementation of the Plan of Action for the Integration of Women into Agricultural and Rural Development, which called for women's increased access to income, credit, education and decision-making.

The Conference appointed Jacques Diouf of Senegal to the office of Director-General for a period of six years beginning on 1 January 1994. It readmitted South Africa as a member of FAO and also admitted nine new members (Armenia, Bosnia and Herzegovina, Croatia, the Czech Republic, Eritrea, Kyrgyzstan, Slovakia, Slovenia, the former Yugoslav Republic of Macedonia), bringing total membership to 169, one associate member and one member organization as at 31 December 1993 (see Annex I).

World food situation

In 1993, a sharp drop in global food production combined with a draw-down of stocks brought supplies close to the minimum necessary to safeguard world food security. In general, a large proportion of the developing countries experienced a decline in food security. Global production of staple foods fell almost 4 per cent below 1992 production. It was almost entirely accounted for by reduced maize output in the United States. Developing countries and low-income food-deficit (LIFD) countries increased estimated production by 2 million and 3 million tonnes, respectively. None the less, per caput cereal production in the majority of LIFD countries continued to fall in 1993.

World cereal production was estimated at 1,875 million tonnes, 5 per cent below the previous year. Wheat supplies showed a gain, reaching 709 million tonnes. Coarse grains production dropped some 80 million tonnes, 9 per cent less than in 1992, and rice (paddy) production fell by 8 million tonnes to 520 million tonnes. For roots and tubers, the second most important group of staple foods, production was up by 2 per cent in 1993, reaching 150 million tonnes in grain equivalent. The growth was particularly pronounced in developing countries, especially in LIFD countries, which accounted for over three quarters of world production. Cassava production rose by 7 per cent and the world output of pulses rose by 4 per cent over the previous year. Milk production decreased by 1 per cent to 581 million tonnes.

Activities in 1993

Emergency assistance

Estimates of the total volume of food aid in cereals to be made available in 1993/94 stood at 11.4 million tonnes, nearly 23 per cent less than the 15.2 million tonnes provided in 1992/93, reflecting a reduced level of budgetary allocations from all major donors except Australia. Total shipments of food aid to developing countries were estimated at 7.8 million tonnes, well below the levels provided during previous years. In particular, cereal food-aid shipments to LIFD countries fell to 7 million tonnes, nearly one third less than in 1992/93 and substantially less than in previous years. Sub-Saharan Africa continued to be the major recipient of food aid, as much as 60 per cent of which was earmarked to meet emergency needs

[a]YUN 1992, p. 683.
[b]ibid., p. 670.

of refugees, displaced persons and drought-affected households. The successor States of the USSR and Eastern European countries received around 4 million tonnes. Food aid played an important role in establishing food supplies in countries that lacked the necessary resources to import needed cereals. In addition to cereal food aid, donors provided approximately 1.7 million tonnes of aid in non-cereal commodities, mainly vegetable oil, pulses, dairy products, meat and fish.

FAO applied its food security assistance scheme to assist Benin, Bhutan, Viet Nam and 10 Latin American and Caribbean countries in formulating comprehensive food security programmes. Using teams of experts, it aimed at accurate diagnosis of problems, realistic formulation of solutions and capacity-building at the national level.

In January, FAO appealed to the international community to increase food aid to those countries in Africa torn by civil strife and faced with the results of prolonged drought. A special report on Africa issued by FAO's Global Information and Early Warning System listed 20 countries as facing exceptional food emergencies: Angola, Botswana, Ethiopia, Kenya, Lesotho, Liberia, Madagascar, Malawi, Mauritania, Mozambique, Namibia, Rwanda, Sierra Leone, Somalia, Sudan, Swaziland, United Republic of Tanzania, Zaire, Zambia, Zimbabwe.

FAO deployed 1.5 million doses of live vaccine to Egypt to help control the outbreak of Rift Valley fever, a highly contagious viral disease causing high rates of abortion and neonatal mortality in animals.

FAO's Emergency Centre for Locust Operations—reactivated following an outbreak of the desert locust in the Red Sea coastal areas in late 1992—acted as a clearing-house for information, analysing locust reports and weather and habitat data derived from ground and satellite sources, and issued early warnings to neighbouring countries as locusts migrated. The Centre channelled aid from the donor community to affected zones in the form of technical assistance, sprayers, pesticides, flying hours, communications equipment, spare parts, and training and operating expenses. More than 3.9 million hectares were treated in affected countries since the beginning of the outbreak.

During the year, FAO's Office of Special Relief Operations provided agricultural inputs to Somalia, at the same time rehabilitating abattoirs and veterinary clinics and distributing income-generating supplies such as chickens and fishing gear. In addition, through 15 emergency relief projects, FAO channelled almost $7 million to Somalia to help farmers and fishermen combat drought, famine and the effects of civil war. By rebuilding agricultural infrastructure in the rural areas, FAO also helped the urban poor, whose numbers increased because of people fleeing rural areas (see PART THREE, Chapter III).

Field programmes

FAO provided technical advice and support through its field programme in all areas of food and agriculture, fisheries, forestry and rural development. In 1993, 1,951 field projects were under way at an expenditure of $309 million. They were funded through trust funds provided by donor countries and other international funding sources ($163.8 million), the United Nations Development Programme ($110.3 million) and the technical cooperation programme from FAO's regular budget ($34.9 million).

During the year, international financing institutions approved some $1,469 million in funding for 32 agricultural and rural development projects, prepared with the assistance of FAO's Investment Centre. Total investments in those projects, including contributions from recipient Governments, amounted to $2,476 million.

Rural development

In the context of the United Nations Year of Indigenous People (1993), FAO conducted case-studies on indigenous groups in Bolivia, India and Mexico, focusing on the particular needs and constraints to development of rural native communities. They assessed issues such as access to land and employment, common resources management and the role of women in the communities.

FAO conducted projects aimed at reassessing and reorienting its development efforts in African countries. One of the projects, centred in drought-prone southern Africa, would develop indicators for measuring poverty and establish a database for continuous poverty monitoring.

FAO examined methods in land management applied by Sahelian communities and by local administrations, among them awareness-building, diagnosis, programming and establishment of committees. In 15 case-studies, the need to incorporate long-term considerations for protection and replenishment of the environment was stressed.

Crops

In 1993, FAO's Fertilizer Programme was renamed the Plant Nutrition Programme to reflect important changes in FAO's approach to plant nutrition. The Programme promoted activities for nutrient management based on a comprehensive vision of the cropping cycle.

During the year, FAO continued to promote integrated pest management (IPM), a system to reduce reliance on pesticides by encouraging farmers to use biological control methods and natural predators, such as spiders and wasps, to avert pests. On a study tour organized by FAO in August, plant protection specialists from 22 countries visited Bangladesh, Indonesia, the Philippines and Viet Nam to see IPM practices that had helped over half a million rice growers minimize pesticide use and raise profits.

As part of a global programme to implement the 1985 International Code of Conduct on the Distribution and Use of Pesticides,[c] 13 Caribbean countries were assisted in establishing national pesticide regulation and control schemes. In South America, five countries (Argentina, Brazil, Chile, Paraguay, Uruguay) were assisted in setting up intercountry standards and requirements to harmonize regulatory procedures for registering and controlling pesticides.

Efforts continued to promote hybrid rice technology in Asia. From 1991 to 1993, FAO assisted Viet Nam to expand its original 100 hectares of experimental hybrid rice production to almost 1,000 hectares. By 1993, producers in the northern provinces were planting close to 40,000 hectares of the rice, accounting for a 17.5 per cent increase in output.

FAO began preparing the first global report on the state of the world's plant genetic resources and a concrete plan of action for approval and adoption at a major conference, to be held in 1996.

Livestock

In 1993, FAO supported a wide range of livestock-related activities, from feeding systems and meat and dairy production to animal health and the conservation and management of animal genetic resources.

FAO and the United Nations Environment Programme published the *World Watch List for Domestic Animal Diversity*, the first attempt to document the state of global livestock and genetic diversity.

FAO joined with animal welfare organizations to initiate joint activities in Africa and Asia to promote humane treatment of slaughter animals while heightening the quality of meat products. In Malawi, FAO introduced captive bolt pistols (stun guns) that would protect animals from unnecessary suffering at the time of slaughter.

FAO coordinated an inter-agency study to expand the information base on interactions between livestock production systems and the environment. Issues to be dealt with were methane emissions from stomach fermentation in ruminants, improvement in feed, animal manure management, animal waste disposal, domestic animal genetic diversity, wildlife diversity, and the integration of cropping and livestock systems.

Fisheries

In 1993, the FAO Conference adopted the Agreement to Promote Compliance with International Measures by Fishing Vessels on the High Seas, the first step towards developing an international code of conduct for responsible fishing, being formulated FAO. Reports on the status of high-seas marine resources and of migrating and straddling fish stocks crossing the boundaries between exclusive economic zones and the high seas were presented to the United Nations Conference on Straddling Fish Stocks and Highly Migratory Fish Stocks (see PART THREE, Chapter VIII).

In November, the FAO Council established an Indian Ocean Tuna Fish Commission. The Commission would join a network of other regional fishery bodies to foster international cooperation, covering almost 50 per cent of the total area of the world's oceans and inland waters.

At the East-West Fisheries Conference (St. Petersburg, Russian Federation, May), 300 participants, including 120 from East and Central Europe and the Russian Federation, discussed cooperation in developing trade links and joint ventures, utilization of pelagic species, quality assurance and privatization of the fisheries sectors.

Forestry

Under the FAO Tropical Forest Action Programme, involving 90 partners, a Mediterranean Forestry Action Programme was finalized.

FAO joined with several international partners to establish a programme to improve neem seed viability and genetic variability outside the species' natural range. Neem foliage and seeds held valuable insecticidal and medicinal properties and protected crops from wind erosion in arid areas.

The Forests, Trees and People Programme of FAO continued to improve the livelihoods of rural people of developing countries through sustainable management of forest resources. As a result of a workshop on dispute resolution in forest management (Costa Rica, September), Bolivia, Ecuador, Mali and Thailand began to institutionalize training programmes for environmental dispute resolution.

Nuclear techniques

During the year, FAO and the International Atomic Energy Agency (IAEA) jointly conducted research on a variety of topics in plant improvement, crop varieties and atmospheric nitrogen fixation.

Using the mutation breeding technique, which induced inheritable changes in the genetic background of a plant and then selected offspring with the desirable characteristics, scientists raised the yields of sesame and improved oil quality. To date, 19 mutant varieties had been officially released. In addition, 30 promising sesame mutant lines were obtained in Bangladesh, Egypt, Pakistan and Sri Lanka.

[c]YUN 1985, p. 1287.

A research programme in Africa used neutron moisture meters to measure water use by crops and crop varieties and identified some varieties of cereals that were more efficient in water use than others. Another research programme used a gene-marker technique to track down soil micro-organisms that could help leguminous species fix atmospheric nitrogen and produce higher yields.

FAO and IAEA established a laboratory within IAEA at Seibersdorf, Austria, to promote nuclear-based methods and related molecular techniques to diagnose livestock diseases. Priority was given to the diseases of greatest importance, such as rinderpest, trypanosomiasis and foot-and-mouth disease.

Information

FAO produced *Agriculture: Towards 2010*, a revised and updated version of a study originally published in 1979 and last updated in 1987. Designed to address how the future might unfold, it analysed trends in food security, nutrition and agricultural development and projected the most likely outcomes by the year 2010.

In 1993, FAO produced 251 publications, nine periodicals and seven yearbooks, many of them published in Arabic, Chinese, English, French and Spanish. FAO distributed supplemental diskettes with important publications, which contained statistical information and programmes that allowed the user to read, display and manipulate the data provided.

Advances were made in the development of the World Agricultural Information Centre (Rome) to provide its users easy and economical access to information from over 40 FAO databases. In addition, a pilot phase of the AQUASTAT database on water use in rural development and the Scheme Irrigation Management Information System software were completed.

Nutrition

In 1993, FAO's activities in nutrition focused on food security at the household level versus overall food availability. An aggregate household food-security index was being developed to serve as a tool for monitoring food security trends worldwide.

FAO produced nutrition profiles for 100 developing countries to provide a concise view of food and nutrition status, agricultural production and economic and demographic data, and assisted over 40 countries in preparing their national plans of action for nutrition.

In Viet Nam, a project to increase knowledge of nutrition within households, in particular among women and mothers, resulted in a significant reduction in children's undernutrition and an increase in production of food from home gardens. The project emphasized vitamin-A deficiency.

Secretariat

At the end of 1993, the number of staff employed at FAO headquarters was 3,262, of whom 1,224 were in the Professional and higher categories and 1,975 in the General Service category. Field project personnel and those in regional and country offices numbered 2,687: 839 in the Professional and higher categories and 1,637 in the General Service category. Of the 274 Associate Professional Officers working with FAO, 63 were at headquarters and 211 were in the field or in regional or country offices.

Budget

The FAO Conference in 1993 approved a working budget for the 1994-1995 biennium of $673.1 million. The largest sum of $319 million was appropriated to technical and economic programmes, followed by $101 million to development support programmes.

NOTE: For further information on FAO, see *FAO Annual Review: A Summary of the Organization's Activities During 1993*, issued by FAO.

Annex I.   MEMBERSHIP OF THE FOOD AND AGRICULTURE ORGANIZATION
(As at 31 December 1993)

Afghanistan, Albania, Algeria, Angola, Antigua and Barbuda, Argentina, Armenia, Australia, Austria, Bahamas, Bahrain, Bangladesh, Barbados, Belgium, Belize, Benin, Bhutan, Bolivia, Bosnia and Herzegovina, Botswana, Brazil, Bulgaria, Burkina Faso, Burundi, Cambodia, Cameroon, Canada, Cape Verde, Central African Republic, Chad, Chile, China, Colombia, Comoros, Congo, Cook Islands, Costa Rica, Côte d'Ivoire, Croatia, Cuba, Cyprus, Czech Republic, Democratic People's Republic of Korea, Denmark, Djibouti, Dominica, Dominican Republic, Ecuador, Egypt, El Salvador, Equatorial Guinea, Eritrea, Estonia, Ethiopia, Fiji, Finland, France, Gabon, Gambia, Germany, Ghana, Greece, Grenada, Guatemala, Guinea, Guinea-Bissau, Guyana, Haiti, Honduras, Hungary, Iceland, India, Indonesia, Iran, Iraq, Ireland, Israel, Italy, Jamaica, Japan, Jordan, Kenya, Kuwait, Kyrgyzstan, Lao People's Democratic Republic, Latvia, Lebanon, Lesotho, Liberia, Libyan Arab Jamahiriya, Lithuania, Luxembourg, Madagascar, Malawi, Malaysia, Maldives, Mali, Malta, Mauritania, Mauritius, Mexico, Mongolia, Morocco, Mozambique, Myanmar, Namibia, Nepal, Netherlands, New Zealand, Nicaragua, Niger, Nigeria, Norway, Oman, Pakistan, Panama, Papua New Guinea, Paraguay, Peru, Philippines, Poland, Portugal, Qatar, Republic of Korea, Romania, Rwanda, Saint Kitts and Nevis, Saint Lucia, Saint Vincent and the Grenadines, Samoa, Sao Tome and Principe, Saudi Arabia, Senegal, Seychelles, Sierra Leone, Slovakia, Slovenia, Solomon Islands, Somalia, South Africa, Spain, Sri Lanka, Sudan, Suriname, Swaziland, Sweden, Switzerland, Syrian Arab Republic, Thailand, the former Yugoslav Republic of Macedonia, Togo, Tonga, Trinidad and Tobago, Tunisia, Turkey, Uganda, United Arab Emirates, United Kingdom, United Republic of Tanzania, United States, Uruguay, Vanuatu, Venezuela, Viet Nam, Yemen, Yugoslavia,* Zaire, Zambia, Zimbabwe; *Associate member:* Puerto Rico; *Member organization:* European Economic Community.

*Refers to the former Socialist Federal Republic of Yugoslavia. In 1992, the FAO Council decided that the Federal Republic of Yugoslavia (Serbia and Montenegro) should not participate in the work of the Council or its subsidiary bodies.

Annex II. MEMBERS OF THE COUNCIL OF THE FOOD AND AGRICULTURE ORGANIZATION
(As at 31 December 1993)

Independent Chairman: José Ramón López Portillo.
Angola, Argentina, Australia, Bangladesh, Belgium, Brazil, Burkina Faso, Canada, Cape Verde, Chile, China, Colombia, Congo, Cuba, Cyprus, Egypt, France, Germany, Honduras, Hungary, India, Indonesia, Iran, Italy, Japan, Lebanon, Libyan Arab Jamahiriya, Madagascar, Malaysia, Mexico, Nigeria, Norway, Republic of Korea, Rwanda, Saudi Arabia, Slovakia, Spain, Sri Lanka, Swaziland, Syrian Arab Republic, Thailand, Trinidad and Tobago, Tunisia, Uganda, United Kingdom, United Republic of Tanzania, United States, Venezuela, Zaire.

Annex III. OFFICERS AND OFFICES OF THE FOOD AND AGRICULTURE ORGANIZATION
(As at 31 December 1993)

SENIOR OFFICERS

Director-General: Edouard Saouma.
Deputy Director-General: H. W. Hjort.
Deputy Director-General, Office of Programme, Budget and Evaluation: V. J. Shah.
Director, Office of Internal Audit, Inspection and Management Control: G. Peter Wilson.
Special Adviser to the Director-General/Assistant Director-General for Environment and Sustainable Development: P. J. Mahler.
Assistant Director-General, Administration and Finance Department: K. Mehboob.
Assistant Director-General, Agriculture Department: H. de Haen.
Assistant Director-General, Development Department: André G. Regnier.
Assistant Director-General, Economic and Social Policy Department: H. W. Hjort (Officer-in-Charge).

Assistant Director-General, Fisheries Department: W. Krone (acting).
Assistant Director-General, Forestry Department: C. H. Murray.
Assistant Director-General, Department of General Affairs and Information: M. Alessi.
Assistant Director-General and Regional Representative for Africa: R. T. N'Daw.
Assistant Director-General and Regional Representative for Asia and the Pacific: A. Z. M. Obaidullah Khan.
Assistant Director-General and Regional Representative for Europe: M. Zjalic.
Assistant Director-General and Regional Representative for Latin America and the Caribbean: R. Moreno.
Assistant Director-General and Regional Representative for the Near East: Atif Yehya Bukhari.

HEADQUARTERS AND OTHER OFFICES

HEADQUARTERS
Food and Agriculture Organizaton
Viale delle Terme di Caracalla
00100 Rome, Italy
  Cable address: FOODAGRI ROME
  Telephone: (39) (6) 52251
  Telex: 610181 FAO I
  Facsimile: (39) (6) 5225-3152

LIAISON OFFICE
Food and Agriculture Organization Liaison Office with the United Nations
1 United Nations Plaza, Room 1125
New York, N.Y. 10017, United States
  Cable address: FOODAGRI NEWYORK
  Telephone: (1) (212) 963-6036
  Facsimile: (1) (212) 888-6188

FAO also maintained liaison offices in Washington, D.C., and at Geneva, and regional offices at Accra, Ghana; Bangkok, Thailand; Cairo, Egypt; and Santiago, Chile.

Chapter IV

United Nations Educational,
Scientific and Cultural Organization (UNESCO)

During 1993, the United Nations Educational, Scientific and Cultural Organization (UNESCO) continued to promote cooperation among nations through its education, science and technology, social and human sciences, culture and communication, information and informatics activities.

The twenty-seventh session of the General Conference of UNESCO, held in Paris from 25 October to 16 November, approved a budget of $455,490,000 for the 1994-1995 biennium and reconfirmed the agency's priority activities. It re-elected Federico Mayor as UNESCO Director-General for a second six-year term.

In 1993, UNESCO's membership increased to 181 with the admission of Andorra, Bosnia and Herzegovina, the Czech Republic, Eritrea, Niue, Slovakia, the Solomon Islands, Tajikistan, the former Yugoslav Republic of Macedonia, Turkmenistan and Uzbekistan (see Annex I).

Education

UNESCO's major education activities focused on basic education for all (EFA), the renewal of educational systems and educational advancement and policy.

As a follow-up to the World Conference on Education for All held in Jomtien, Thailand, in 1990, UNESCO assisted member States to diagnose basic learning needs, set national EFA goals and devise effective strategies to achieve those goals. Also as follow-up to the Jomtien Conference, the second meeting of the International Consultative Forum on Education for All was held at New Delhi, India (8-10 September). In 1993, the first Jomtien progress report on EFA status and trends was released and an EFA videobank containing innovative projects was created. The Education-for-All Summit of Nine High-Population Countries (New Delhi, 13-16 December), sponsored by UNESCO, the United Nations Children's Fund (UNICEF) and the United Nations Population Fund (UNFPA), adopted a declaration and a plan of action in which Governments pledged to universalize primary education and reduce illiteracy. A new training programme for national professionals in evaluating and following up non-formal basic education was started with the support of the German Development Foundation and the UNESCO Institute for

Education (Hamburg, Germany). The Scheme of Humanitarian Assistance for Refugee Education (SHARE) was launched to train refugee teachers, construct buildings and provide educational materials for refugees. The Pan-African Conference on the Education of Girls (Ouagadougou, Burkina Faso, 28 March-1 April), organized jointly with UNICEF, discussed attracting and retaining girls in the education system and set up counselling programmes in 14 African countries.

Under the renewal of educational systems, the newly established International Commission on Education for the Twenty-First Century held two sessions (Paris, 2-4 March; Dakar, Senegal, 18-21 September). In 1993, UNESCO launched Project 2000+ on Science Education for All and in July, the International Forum on Science and Technology Literacy for All adopted a declaration endorsing further development of that project. Activities under the International Project on Technical and Vocational Education (UNEVOC), launched during the year, included an international consultation on the role of technical and vocational education in education systems (Turin, Italy, 14-18 June) and an international workshop on curriculum development in technical and vocational education (Turin, 30 August-2 September). UNESCO published jointly with the World Health Organization, a guide to plan, implement and evaluate school-based acquired immunodeficiency syndrome (AIDS) education and UNESCO produced an advocacy film for school-based AIDS education. Under an initiative launched in 1991 to foster inter-university cooperation (UNITWIN), 45 UNESCO Chairs had been set up in 25 countries by the end of the year. In addition, 27 university networks were established and 75 projects from 53 countries were processed.

In 1993, UNESCO continued to promote the advancement of education through participation in emergency assistance programmes and reconstruction operations pertaining to education in Albania, Armenia, Bosnia and Herzegovina, Cambodia, Croatia, Iraq, Slovenia and Somalia, and initiated activities for rebuilding Palestinian educational and cultural institutions, including an international symposium (Granada, Spain, 9 and 10 December), a workshop on developing a Palestinian secondary school curriculum (East Jerusalem, 27-31 November) and the granting of 57 international fellowships. The sixth regional conference of Ministers of Education of the Asia and the Pacific region (Kuala Lumpur, Malaysia, 21-24 June) adopted recommendations and a declaration focusing on education for all, education for women and girls, the quality and relevance of education and international and regional cooperation. The UNESCO Institute for Educational Planning (Paris) continued to implement its annual training programme and its training-of-trainers programme and introduced new intensive training courses. UNESCO continued to disseminate information on education through periodicals and publications such as the *World Education Report*. Among other activities were a regional technical meeting on training strategies of primary head-teachers (Paris, 29-31 March), a meeting of experts on the education of information specialists in the Arab region (Rabat, Morocco, 10-13 May) and a technical consultation on a comparative study of private secondary education (Quezon City, Philippines, 5-7 July).

Natural sciences

Activities under the programme on science for progress and the environment focused on science and technology for development, the environment and natural resources management and science, technology and society.

Advanced postgraduate training in research was provided to mathematicians, physicists, chemists and specialists in cell and molecular biology, neurobiology, virology and related sciences, and researchers were awarded fellowships and research grants. UNESCO extended emergency assistance to the Russian Academy of Science to implement a project to limit the brain drain from the country. The third International Congress of Engineering Deans and Industry Leaders took place (Paris, 23-26 June) as did an international meeting on scientific cooperation in physics (Paris, 24 and 25 June). Activities in energy research included a high-level expert meeting of the World Solar Summit Process (Paris, 5-9 July); a summer school session on solar electricity for rural and remote areas (Paris, 5-30 July); a symposium on strategic issues for the reform of energy systems in Central and Eastern Europe and a round table on organization and regulation of electricity systems (Paris, 22-26 November); and an international symposium on energy and society (Paris, 13-17 December). One regional and three national seminars were held on industrial and hazardous wastes and treatment technology in South-East Asia, and the first *World Science Report* was prepared for publication.

UNESCO's Programme on Man and the Biosphere (MAB), the International Hydrological Programme (IHP) and the Intergovernmental

Oceanographic Commission (IOC) adopted new strategies and action plans as a follow-up to the 1992 United Nations Conference on Environment and Development (UNCED).[a]

The MAB Programme was adjusted to focus on the implementation of Agenda 21, an action programme adopted by UNCED, and the 1992 Convention on Biological Diversity.[b] It continued to monitor the international network of 324 biosphere reserves in 83 member States and provided assistance in carrying out national assessments and action plans for upgrading and developing biosphere reserves, and consolidation and reinforcement of the landscape dimension in biosphere reserves.

Among activities of IHP were an international symposium on limnology, climatology and palaeoclimatology of the East African lakes (Jinja, Uganda, February); the International Conference on Hydrology (Paris, 22-27 March), co-sponsored by the World Meteorological Organization (WMO) and the International Council of Scientific Unions (ICSU); and the inception of the Latin American and Caribbean Hydrological Cycle, Water Resources Activities and Observation/Information System.

In cooperation with WMO and ICSU, IOC co-sponsored the World Climate Research Programme and promoted programmes on coastal marine research and on training and education in marine sciences. IOC provided information on events in the oceans and seas adjacent to coastal and island States through its quarterly *Products Bulletin of the Integrated Global Ocean Services System*, and continued to improve the efficiency of the International Tsunami Warning System in the Pacific Ocean. A symposium on bridging the gap between science and decision-making in global climate change mitigation (Venice, Italy, 6 and 7 May) took place, as did a meeting of experts on oceanography, ecology and environmental aspects of the Persian Gulf and the Sea of Oman (Tehran, Iran, 29 November–3 December). Other activities dealt with studies of coastal marine productivity, mangrove management in Africa and environmental studies and training in the Baltic Sea.

Activities under the International Geological Correlation Programme aimed at improving the use and collection of geological information and strengthening seismological networks and volcano observatories as well as training and research centres. The Programme conducted studies on the integration of environmental and development aspects in disaster reduction and on the establishment of a regional disaster monitoring system. It developed training modules on reducing earth-

[a]YUN 1992, p. 670.
[b]Ibid., p. 683.

quake and flood disasters, provided training to scientists and undertook post-earthquake reconnaissance missions as well as missions of the International Mobile Early-Warning System for Volcanic Eruptions.

The Global Terrestrial Observing System carried out research in agro-silvo-pastoral development, rural land use dynamics, land-inland water ecotones, tropical soil biology and fertility, and forest-atmosphere interactions, and provided training in ecology and natural resources management. UNESCO also continued its activities relating to arid zones and the problems of desertification, particularly under a regional project for the Sahel countries of Africa, and organized a training course in radio-ecology, attended by participants from Belarus, the Russian Federation and Ukraine.

UNESCO's project on the environment and population education and information for human development aimed at developing an integrated approach to achieve people-centred, equitable and sustainable development. Activities to promote environmental education included disseminating information, developing national strategies and action plans, training educators and preparing environmental education curriculum prototypes for primary and secondary schools and teacher education.

In cooperation with UNFPA, UNESCO organized the International Congress on Population Education and Development (Istanbul, Turkey, 14-17 April), which adopted the Istanbul Declaration and an action framework for population education on the eve of the twenty-first century, which was endorsed by the UNESCO General Conference later in the year.

Social and human sciences

In 1993, UNESCO continued to promote the international development of the social and human sciences and to study their contribution to social change.

Among activities concerning women as agents of social change were a meeting on the legal and social rights of women in the Balkan countries (Ankara, Turkey, 8-12 June) and a meeting on the impact of socio-economic changes on women in the period of transition to market-oriented economies (Sofia, Bulgaria, 14-18 June). Studies were undertaken on the participation of women in the democratic process in Africa and on the economic, political, social and cultural obstacles to women's rights in Africa. Activities related to youth continued to be promoted through the International Youth Clearing House and Information Service (INFOYOUTH). A workshop was held to develop a literacy training programme for peri-urban South African youth (Gaborone, Botswana, 20-24 March). In addition, UNESCO published volumes in anthropology, economics, political science and

sociology of *The International Bibliography of the Social Sciences*, and a book entitled *Women in developing economies: Making Visible the Invisible*.

Under activities related to the promotion of peace, human rights and the elimination of all forms of discrimination, the International Congress on Education for Human Rights and Democracy (Montreal, Canada, 8-11 March) adopted a plan of action, which constituted UNESCO's contribution to the World Conference on Human Rights (see PART THREE, Chapter X). UNESCO chairs for human rights education were established at the Comenius University (Bratislava, Slovakia) and the Nicolas Copernicus University (Torun, Poland), studies were undertaken on the cultural rights of minorities in Africa, Asia and Europe, and an international network was set up to identify new international standards for combating sexual exploitation, particularly prostitution of women. UNESCO launched a programme to promote a culture of peace in El Salvador and was developing similar programmes for Guatemala and Mozambique.

In response to a 1991 UNESCO General Conference proposal, welcomed by the United Nations General Assembly in 1992,[c] the UNESCO secretariat submitted to the 1993 General Conference a study and a plan of action with a view to proclaiming 1995 the United Nations year for tolerance. A meeting of experts (Istanbul, 16 and 17 April) prepared a draft Declaration on Tolerance and forwarded it to the General Assembly for adoption (see PART THREE, Chapter XII).

The 1993 Félix Houphouët-Boigny Peace Prize was awarded jointly to Yasser Arafat, Chairman of the Palestinian Liberation Organization, Yitzhak Rabin, Prime Minister of Israel and Shimon Peres, Foreign Minister of Israel.

Culture

Cultural activities in 1993 emphasized the promotion of international cultural cooperation and culture for development, and the preservation and enrichment of the cultural heritage and cultural identities. Those activities took place in the context of the World Decade for Cultural Development (1988-1997), proclaimed by the General Assembly in 1986.[d] By the end of 1993, 839 projects were being undertaken under the Decade around the world, of which 197 were receiving financial assistance from UNESCO (see PART THREE, Chapter XII). Several projects for sustained development in the Maya region began under the Maya World programme, a data bank for the production of audio-visual aids was created under the Baroque World programme, and a study

[c]YUN 1992, p. 838, GA res. 47/124, 18 Dec. 1992.
[d]YUN 1986, p. 624, GA res. 41/187, 8 Dec. 1986.

of the cultural needs of the Palestinian people was carried out under UNESCO's Arabia Plan. UNESCO also continued an integral study of the Silk Roads in Central Asia and launched, in cooperation with the World Tourism Organization, a programme for cultural tourism on the Silk Roads.

The World Commission on Culture and Development, established in 1992, received pledges of some $2 million and decided on its initial lines of inquiry.

The seventeenth session of the World Heritage Committee (Cartagena, Colombia, 4-11 December) placed 35 additional sites on the World Heritage list, bringing the total to 411. The Committee also revised the criteria for the list to include cultural landscapes and geological sites and adopted strategic orientations and recommendations for the implementation of the 1972 Convention for the Protection of the World Cultural and Natural Heritage. During the year, activities were carried out to safeguard the cultural heritage of the Old City of Jerusalem, Hué City in Viet Nam and the Angkor monuments in Cambodia. The Intergovernmental Conference for the Safeguarding and Development of the Historic Area of Angkor (Tokyo, Japan, 12 and 13 October) was held; an international meeting of experts (Paris, 16 and 17 June) considered new directions for the Programme to Safeguard the Intangible Cultural Heritage; and an international congress was convened (Paris, 29 June-1 July) to discuss issues related to the conservation of stone and other materials. In addition, two meetings were organized in cooperation with the Government of Mexico to consider issues related to education, work and cultural pluralism (Oaxaca, May) and to the rights of indigenous populations (Campeche, June).

Communication

UNESCO's communication programme continued to encourage the free flow of information, support communication for development and promote new communication technologies (see also PART ONE, Chapter V).

UNESCO provided financial assistance to the International Freedom of Expression Exchange Network, a collaborative effort of 40 media organizations from 20 countries, and supported a round table on the rights of journalists and media organizations (Ljubljana, Slovenia, 3-6 February). In October, the Intergovernmental Council of the International Programme for the Development of Communication (IPDC) approved 59 communication projects. A project on communication for basic education in the least developed countries was launched in Benin, Burkina Faso, Guinea, Mali and the Niger. Media technology seminars were held and technical support services were granted.

New projects approved in 1993 under the Intergovernmental Informatics Programme (IIP) brought the number of projects funded in the 1992-1993 biennium to 38, for a total of $3.4 million. Through its 111 national focal points, IIP continued to develop the INFORMAFRICA programme, which was introducing informatics into education systems in Africa; strengthen regional informatics networks in Africa, the Arab States, the Baltic States and Eastern Europe; and harmonize and coordinate activities between the two regional informatics networks in Asia and the Pacific.

Secretariat

As at 31 December 1993, UNESCO had a full-time staff of 2,401, comprising 941 in the Professional and higher categories, drawn from 143 nationalities, and 1,460 in the General Service category.

Budget

The General Conference of UNESCO, at its 1991 session, approved a budget of $444,704,000 for the 1992-1993 biennium, which was subsequently increased to $446,736,565. The level of the Working Capital Fund was fixed at $17,200,000 and the total assessment placed on member States (after deducting miscellaneous income) was $432,216,000.

NOTE: For further information on UNESCO's activities in 1993, see *Report of the Director-General 1992-1993*, published by UNESCO.

Annex I.   MEMBERS OF THE UNITED NATIONS EDUCATIONAL, SCIENTIFIC AND CULTURAL ORGANIZATION
(As at 31 December 1993)

Afghanistan, Albania, Algeria, Andorra, Angola, Antigua and Barbuda, Argentina, Armenia, Australia, Austria, Azerbaijan, Bahamas, Bahrain, Bangladesh, Barbados, Belarus, Belgium, Belize, Benin, Bhutan, Bolivia, Bosnia and Herzegovina, Botswana, Brazil, Bulgaria, Burkina Faso, Burundi, Cambodia, Cameroon, Canada, Cape Verde, Central African Republic, Chad, Chile, China, Colombia, Comoros, Congo, Cook Islands, Costa Rica, Côte d'Ivoire, Croatia, Cuba, Cyprus, Czech Republic, Democratic People's Republic of Korea, Denmark, Djibouti, Dominica, Dominican Republic, Ecuador, Egypt, El Salvador, Equatorial Guinea, Eritrea, Estonia, Ethiopia, Fiji, Finland, France, Gabon, Gambia, Georgia, Germany, Ghana, Greece, Grenada, Guatemala, Guinea, Guinea-Bissau, Guyana, Haiti, Honduras, Hungary, Iceland, India, Indonesia, Iran, Iraq, Ireland, Israel, Italy, Jamaica, Japan, Jordan, Kazakhstan, Kenya, Kiribati, Kuwait, Kyrgyzstan, Lao People's Democratic Republic, Latvia, Lebanon, Lesotho, Liberia, Libyan Arab Jamahiriya, Lithuania, Luxembourg, Madagascar, Malawi, Malaysia, Maldives, Mali, Malta, Mauritania, Mauritius, Mexico, Monaco, Mongolia, Morocco, Mozambique, Myanmar, Namibia, Nepal, Netherlands, New Zealand, Nicaragua, Niger, Nigeria, Niue, Norway, Oman, Pakistan, Panama, Papua New Guinea, Paraguay, Peru, Philippines, Poland, Portugal, Qatar, Republic

of Korea, Republic of Moldova, Romania, Russian Federation, Rwanda, Saint Kitts and Nevis, Saint Lucia, Saint Vincent and the Grena-
dines, Samoa, San Marino, Sao Tome and Principe, Saudi Arabia, Senegal, Seychelles, Sierra Leone, Slovakia, Slovenia, Solomon Islands,
Somalia, Spain, Sri Lanka, Sudan, Suriname, Swaziland, Sweden, Switzerland, Syrian Arab Republic, Tajikistan, Thailand, the former Yugoslav
Republic of Macedonia, Togo, Tonga, Trinidad and Tobago, Tunisia, Turkey, Turkmenistan, Tuvalu, Uganda, Ukraine, United Arab Emirates,
United Republic of Tanzania, Uruguay, Uzbekistan, Venezuela, Viet Nam, Yemen, Yugoslavia,* Zaire, Zambia, Zimbabwe.

Associate members
Aruba, British Virgin Islands, Netherlands Antilles.

*On 25 October 1993, the UNESCO General Conference decided that the representatives of the Federal Republic of Yugoslavia (Serbia
and Montenegro) should not participate in the work of its 1993 session.

Annex II.   OFFICERS AND OFFICES OF THE UNITED NATIONS EDUCATIONAL, SCIENTIFIC AND CULTURAL ORGANIZATION
(As at 31 December 1993)

*MEMBERS OF THE EXECUTIVE BOARD**

Algeria, Angola, Australia, Bahrain, Benin, Botswana, Brazil, Bulgaria, Chile, China, Colombia, Costa Rica, Côte d'Ivore, Denmark, Egypt, El Salvador, Ethiopia, France, Germany, Ghana, Guyana, India, Italy, Jamaica, Japan, Jordan, Madagascar, Malaysia, Mali, Mexico, Morocco, Namibia, Netherlands, Niger, Nigeria, Oman, Pakistan, Philippines, Poland, Portugal, Republic of Korea, Romania, Russian Federation, Seychelles, Spain, Switzerland, Tonga, Trinidad and Tobago, Tunisia, Turkey, Zambia.

*According to a constitutional amendment passed by the UNESCO General Conference in 1992, Executive Board Members would no longer serve in their individual capacity, but would be considered member States.

PRINCIPAL OFFICERS OF THE SECRETARIAT

Director-General: Federico Mayor.
Acting Deputy Director-General: Adnan Badran.

Assistant Directors-General: Thomas Keller, Khamliène Nhouyvanisvong *(acting)*, Colin Power, Adnan Badran, Francine Fournier, Henri Lopes, Henrikas Iouchkiavitchious.

HEADQUARTERS AND OTHER OFFICES

HEADQUARTERS
UNESCO House
7 place de Fontenoy
75352 Paris 07-SP, France
  Cable address: UNESCO PARIS
  Telephone: (33)(1) 45-68-10-00
  Telex: 204461
  Facsimile: (33)(1) 45-67-16-90

UNESCO also maintained liaison offices at Geneva and Vienna.

NEW YORK LIAISON OFFICE
United Nations Educational, Scientific and Cultural Organization
2 United Nations Plaza, Room 900
New York, N.Y., 10017, United States
  Cable address: UNESCORG NEWYORK
  Telephone: (1) 212-963-5995
  Facsimile: (1) 212-355-5627

Chapter V

World Health Organization (WHO)

The World Health Assembly, the governing body of the World Health Organization (WHO), at its forty-sixth annual session (Geneva, 3-14 May 1993), approved an effective working budget of $822.1 million for the 1994-1995 biennium. In doing so, the Assembly endorsed five priority areas for the Organization's work: health in a changing environment; proper food and nutrition for a healthy life; integrated disease control as part of overall health care and human development; dissemination of information for advocacy and for educational, managerial and scientific purposes; and intensified health development action in support of countries most in need.

The Assembly adopted a resolution calling for a study on the feasibility of establishing, with other involved United Nations bodies, a joint co-sponsored United Nations programme on the human immunodeficiency virus (HIV) and acquired immunodeficiency syndrome (AIDS). In other action, the Assembly confirmed WHO's commitment to the eradication of poliomyelitis and urged member States to strengthen their programmes against tuberculosis. It requested the Director-General to reinforce WHO leadership in pursuing efforts to improve and strengthen national capacity for malaria control.

Dr. Hiroshi Nakajima was reappointed WHO Director-General for a second five-year term beginning July 1993.

During 1993, the membership of WHO increased to 187, with the admission of the Czech Republic, Eritrea, Estonia, Slovakia, the former Yugoslav Republic of Macedonia and Tuvalu; Puerto Rico and Tokelau were associate members (see Annex I).

Health system infrastructure

Health systems development and research

An interregional consultation on programming of technical cooperation among developing countries (TCDC) in health (Jakarta, Indonesia, February) considered strategies for promotion and advocacy, recommended establishing national focal points for TCDC in health and considered monitoring, evaluation and financing of activities.

In the area of health systems research, WHO promoted research in 15 medical schools in different regions. A global working group (Lilongwe, Malawi, November) set long-term priorities to strengthen research institutions and consolidate knowledge in areas of concern to many countries. Innovative approaches for further institutionalizing health systems research were developed through regional task forces and meetings (Copenhagen, Denmark, October; Yangon, Myanmar, October).

The priority WHO initiative for intensified cooperation with peoples in greatest need was being implemented in 25 countries at the end of 1993. A major thrust of the initiative was to coordinate national resources and programmes while mobilizing international support to meet health and development needs.

The cornerstone of WHO's work in global information transfer was the quarterly *International Digest of Health Legislation*. A December meeting (Cairo, Egypt) provided an opportunity to exchange information and experience on and promote the concept of health legislation as a tool for strengthening health policies and strategies.

Primary health care systems

In 1993, a WHO study group reviewed recent changes in the methods used in different countries to finance health services. A network was established to provide expert advice on the financing and economics of health services in central and eastern Europe. An intercountry consultation of ministers of health (Windhoek, Namibia, October) reviewed experience with user fees and insurance systems, and an international master's degree programme in health economics, co-sponsored by WHO and the World Bank, began at Chulalongkorn University (Bangkok, Thailand, June). Infrastructure development was the subject of the technical discussions during the 1993 World Health Assembly.

An intercountry workshop on primary health care development (Cairo, April) devised approaches for strengthening local and district planning. A regional meeting (Harare, Zimbabwe, November–December) discussed approaches to urban health development. Policies to improve the health of the urban poor were discussed at an interregional meeting (Manila, Philippines, August).

Public information and education for health

In addition to arranging regular briefings, press conferences and interviews, and producing press releases, features and fact sheets, WHO produced press kits and documentation for special days and observances, such as World Health Day (7 April), which had as its theme ''Handle life with care: prevent violence and negligence''; World No-Tobacco Day (31 May) on the theme of ''Health services: our window to a tobacco-free world''; World Diabetes Day (14 November); and World AIDS Day (1 December) on the theme ''AIDS: time to act''.

WHO and the United Nations Environment Programme (UNEP) organized meetings on supportive environments for health (Nairobi, Kenya, June; Bangkok, November) for countries in Africa, South-East Asia and the Western Pacific. A November meeting (San José, Costa Rica) issued guidelines for comprehensive approaches to school health education in the Americas. An international AIDS conference (Berlin, June) organized a working group on strengthening the role of schools in preventing HIV infection.

Health science and technology

Health protection and promotion

World Health Day (7 April) on the theme of accident and injury prevention, drew particular attention to violence against girls and women, including physical and mental abuse and hidden violence of discrimination or denial of food, medical care, education and a safe environment. The World Health Assembly highlighted the importance of eliminating female genital mutilation and other social and behavioural obstacles affecting the health of women and children. A preparatory meeting (Copenhagen, March) on investing in women's health drew up a plan for a European women's health forum. A regional commission for Arab women was being established and the WHO Regional Committee for the Eastern Mediterranean held technical discussions on the role of women in support of health for all.

In May, the Director-General established a new division responsible for all WHO activities relating to food aid, food safety and nutrition. An Asian conference on street food (Beijing, China, October), convened by WHO and the International Life Sciences Institute (Washington, D.C.), considered the risk of transmission of cholera and other food-borne diseases by street-vended foods.

WHO provided technical support in translating the International Code of Marketing of Breast-milk Substitutes into appropriate national measures in Guatemala, Iraq, Morocco, the Syrian Arab Republic, the United Republic of Tanzania and Viet Nam. Ninety developing and 14 industrialized countries joined the WHO/United Nations Children's Fund (UNICEF) Baby-friendly Hospital Initiative, whereby hospital procedures were adapted, and staff trained, to encourage breast-feeding of newborn infants.

In November, a WHO expert committee discussed reference data and guidelines for accurately assessing body mass and growth as indicators of physical welfare. WHO and the Food and Agriculture Organization of the United Nations (FAO) joined in organizing a consultation (Rome, Italy, October) on the role of fats and oils in human nutrition, particularly in relation to chronic noncommunicable diseases.

World Health Day, which focused on accident and injury prevention, was followed by consultations intended to build up a pool of technical expertise and establish a network of public health experts concerned with the prevention of intentional injury. At the Second World Conference on Injury Control (Atlanta, United States, May), organized by a WHO collaborating centre with the support of others, aimed at strengthening technical cooperation between research institutes, furthering the adoption of common standards of analytical methodology for injury control and arousing interest in the WHO programme for community safety. In December, WHO convened a symposium (Brussels, Belgium) on neurotrauma prevention and management. WHO co-sponsored an all-Africa conference on tobacco control (Harare, November), at which tobacco-producing countries took initial steps to harmonize their control programmes and considered ways to reduce their economic dependence on tobacco. On World No-Tobacco Day (31 May), WHO issued information and recommendations on the role of health services and health personnel in attaining a tobacco-free society.

Health of specific population groups

In December, a WHO expert committee considered maternal and child health and family planning in the 1990s and reviewed trends and technical advances and their applicability to national programmes. WHO worked with FAO, the United Nations Educational, Scientific and Cultural Organization, the International Labour Organisation (ILO) and the United Nations Population Fund (UNFPA) to provide support to national family planning and population programmes through eight regional teams. At an interregional meeting (Bangkok, May), national programme managers, policy makers and representatives of nongovernmental organizations (NGOs) and United Nations bodies agreed on strategies to increase the choice of contraceptive methods available and ensure a high quality of care in family planning programmes.

WHO and the United Nations Development Programme (UNDP) launched a project to strengthen the capacity of countries to reduce maternal mortality. In collaboration with the International Confederation of Midwives and UNICEF, WHO convened an international workshop (Vancouver, Canada, May) to examine ways to improve the quality of maternal health care. The Organization launched a regional support project on accelerated action for safe motherhood in the African region and held a workshop (Brazzaville, Congo, February) to brief participants on topics such as the regional family health data bank.

An intercountry consultation (Beirut, Lebanon, June) prepared a social profile of adolescent girls, including factors that could affect their reproductive health, and suggested action to provide special services for that group.

In May, the ILO/WHO Committee on the Health of Seafarers reviewed the occupational health problems of seafarers and made recommendations on injury prevention, prevention of blood-borne and sexually transmitted diseases, education to prevent drug and alcohol abuse, as well as mental diseases and psychosocial disturbances. An international directory of occupational health databases was issued in collaboration with the International Commission on Occupational Health.

Protection and promotion of mental health

In 1993, WHO organized three meetings on neurology and public health (Venice, Italy, May; Limoges, France, October; Berlin, December) to increase awareness of the burden of neurological disorders.

A WHO expert committee issued a report dealing with the prevention of alcohol and drug abuse in the workplace, which recommended combining comprehensive prevention policies and health promotion programmes. A consultation organized jointly with the United Nations International Drug Control Programme (UNDCP) (Vienna, June) reviewed the difficult task of small regulatory agencies trying to control unofficial drug distribution systems and outlined guidelines for import control and inspection. As part of efforts to rationalize prescribing psychotropic drugs in the Americas, a seminar was organized (Montevideo, Uruguay, October) to make government officials, prescribers and journalists more aware of the problem of inappropriate drug use.

Environmental health

In May 1993, the World Health Assembly endorsed a new global strategy for health and environment, based on the recommendations of the WHO Commission on Health and Environment. The Assembly asked WHO to carry out studies on potential environmental hazards to human health and to establish alliances with financial and other organizations to ensure that health goals were incorporated into their programmes on environment and development. Education, training and research in environmental health were promoted through the WHO global environmental epidemiology network, whose membership included some 2,000 institutions and individuals in all regions. Training workshops were held in several countries and a textbook on basic epidemiology was published.

During the year, a conference on sustainability of rural and urban water supplies took place (Accra, Ghana, April) and the WHO Regional Committee for Africa endorsed the establishment of a programme to accelerate water-supply and sanitation development.

A workshop on urban health was held (Manila, August); a second meeting for French-speaking African countries in the Healthy Cities project was convened (Tunis, Tunisia, September); a regional workshop on urban health was held (Harare, November); and a global Healthy Cities conference took place (San Francisco, United States, December). Regional workshops on the promotion of health-supportive environments were held (Nairobi, July; Bangkok, November).

Diagnostic, therapeutic and rehabilitative technology

A consultation on the design of a new type of high voltage X-ray machine for use in providing radiotherapy in developing countries was organized jointly with the International Atomic Energy Agency (IAEA) and the United Nations Industrial Development Organization (UNIDO) (Washington, D.C., December).

An international meeting on the role of the pharmacist drew up recommendations to improve the quality of pharmaceutical services and discussed pharmaceutical care (Tokyo, August–September). WHO participated in a UNIDO consultation on the industrial use of medicinal and aromatic plants in Asia and the Pacific (Vienna, July), which highlighted the need for coherent national policies and effective regulation to control the quality and use of such products. WHO continued to publish the quarterly periodical *WHO drug information* and the monthly *WHO pharmaceuticals newsletter*.

During the year, training activities were carried out to promote community-based rehabilitation. WHO, in collaboration with the International Leprosy Association, provided training in the United States for professional staff of leprosy programmes. In November, WHO hosted two meetings with representatives of 32 NGOs supporting rehabilitation programmes in developing countries.

Disease prevention and control

Although the goal of immunizing 80 per cent of the world's children was achieved in 1991, about 6,000 children a day died in 1993 because they were not vaccinated. WHO's Expanded Programme on

Immunization reported little progress in extending immunization coverage to hard-to-reach populations. In addition, there was a decline in coverage in the growing number of countries affected by war and severe economic conditions. Computer software was developed to improve the forecasting of needs for vaccines and equipment and global policies on safe injections were updated.

In May, the World Health Assembly stressed the gravity of the malaria situation and urged WHO and its member States to initiate effective and sustainable control programmes. A WHO meeting on malaria control in September considered the managerial and budgetary aspects of the plan of work for 1993-1999 and analysed resource needs from donor countries. Meetings in Brazzaville (March), New Delhi, India (March) and Kunming, China (November) worked out plans for malaria control and evaluation guidelines in Africa, South-East Asia and the Western Pacific, respectively.

In 1993, the WHO expert committee on schistosomiasis focused on the increasing problem posed by the disease in urban centres of Africa and Brazil and among refugees, especially in Cambodia. The importance of an intersectoral approach to water resource development schemes to control schistosomiasis and other parasitic diseases was the subject of a WHO publication, *Parasitic diseases in water resources development*. In its review of the current status of the epidemiology and control of foodborne trematode infections (Manila, October), a WHO study group found that some 40 million people were infected and that a coordinated control strategy was needed.

Dengue and dengue haemorrhagic fever epidemics threatened about 2,000 million people living in 100 countries in Africa, the Americas and Asia and the Pacific. In May, the World Health Assembly called on member States to strengthen prevention and control programmes, concentrating on vector control, expanded diagnostic capabilities, strengthened surveillance and increased community awareness, and asked WHO to focus on research in dengue surveillance, epidemiology, vaccine development and vector control.

From 1985 to the end of 1993, the incidence of leprosy was reduced by 40 per cent, a decrease of estimated cases from 5.5 to 3.1 million. Some 4.3 million patients were cured through multidrug therapy. To attain the objective of eliminating leprosy as a public health problem by the year 2000, a strategy of targeting high-priority countries was adopted. India had 52 per cent of all estimated cases of leprosy and five other countries (Bangladesh, Brazil, Indonesia, Myanmar and Nigeria) had a further 27 per cent. To promote the prevention and management of disabilities due to leprosy, a manual for health workers was published

and training modules for managers of leprosy control programmes were revised.

The WHO/UNDP/World Bank special programme for research and training in tropical diseases continued its twofold approach of developing better tools against six groups of tropical diseases (malaria, schistosomiasis, lymphatic filariasis/onchocerciasis, leprosy, African trypanosomiasis/Chagas disease and leishmaniasis) and promoting research capacity in endemic countries, with special attention to women and tropical diseases. A joint initiative was launched by the ministers of health of Argentina, Bolivia, Brazil, Chile, Paraguay and Uruguay to eliminate Chagas disease by the year 2000 by controlling vectors and screening blood products.

Preventing the estimated 3 million annual deaths of children under five years old from diarrhoea remained a high priority objective for WHO. Training activities emphasized case management and better programme management. A manual on diarrhoea for use in medical schools was published and four guides were issued, including one for health workers to be used in counselling mothers. The Organization's global task force on cholera control continued to coordinate WHO support to countries. In addition to publishing guidelines, WHO pursued control efforts in all the countries concerned, particularly in Africa, where there were many more deaths than in South America. There was a resurgence of the disease in the Eastern Mediterranean and in South-East Asia a new strain of cholera emerged.

By the end of the year, 192 acute respiratory infection training units had been established in 28 countries in an effort to reduce the deaths associated with pneumonia of some 4 million children annually. As part of providing direct technical support to countries, WHO organized one workshop for African ethnographers for adaptation of terminology for use at the local level, and another, in planning, evaluation and problem-solving (Cotonou, Benin, November), for African consultants. A meeting of principal investigators was held to analyse the results of a multicentre study on the clinical signs and etiological agents of pneumonia, sepsis and meningitis in infants under three months old (Beijing, November).

Tuberculosis was the world's leading cause of death from a single infectious agent, accounting for over a quarter of avoidable deaths among adults. The epidemic was becoming more difficult to control because of the emergence of multidrug-resistant strains of the bacillus and because of the HIV pandemic. In April, WHO declared tuberculosis a global emergency, warning that the disease would claim 30 million lives in the next decade unless urgent steps were taken to curb its spread. In view of the gravity of the situation, the World

Health Assembly, in 1993, urged WHO members to strengthen national programmes by detecting smear-positive cases through microscopic examination, introducing standardized short-course chemotherapy, case registries and evaluation of treatment results, providing reliable antituberculosis drugs and promoting public awareness of prevention. A vigorous publicity campaign was launched to bring the crisis to public attention, an information package for non-scientists was widely disseminated and an issue of *World Health* magazine was devoted to tuberculosis.

By the end of the year, an estimated 15 million HIV infections and 3 million AIDS cases had occurred since the beginning of the pandemic. In May, the World Health Assembly requested the Director-General to study the feasibility and practicability of establishing a joint and cosponsored United Nations programme on HIV and AIDS, in close consultation with the executive heads of UNDP, UNICEF, UNFPA, the United Nations Educational, Scientific and Cultural Organization and the World Bank. In July, the Economic and Social Council expressed its support for the study. WHO continued to strengthen national AIDS programmes by providing technical assistance through its regional offices and developed a computerized database to facilitate monitoring of country programmes. The theme of World AIDS Day (1 December)—"AIDS: time to act"—highlighted the need for urgent action and served as a call for a global multisectoral approach to the HIV/AIDS threat.

WHO cooperated with a consortium of six NGOs in treating some 2.5 million people for onchocerciasis (river blindness). A consultation on the effects of solar ultraviolet radiation on the eye (September) led to a call for a major international study on the subject. Training of personnel in Africa in blindness prevention continued to be a priority. WHO organized a workshop for African Portuguese-speaking countries (Maputo, Mozambique, October) where it planned strategies for national blindness prevention. An intercountry meeting on national blindness prevention programmes (Cairo, April) called for fuller programme evaluation.

Around the world, about 7 million new cases of cancer occurred annually, about half of them in developing countries. Two-thirds of all cancers were attributable to lifestyle and the environment. To maximize the impact of limited resources in cancer control and palliative care, WHO continued to support prevention through promotion of healthy lifestyles, early detection of breast, mouth and cervical cancer, use of a model list of 22 essential drugs for chemotherapy and training in radiotherapy. A WHO working group (Banff, Canada, September) approved a manual on palliative care for those providing home care. Meetings organized jointly by WHO and the International Association for the Study of Pain (Arezzo, Italy, June; Paris, August) prepared guidelines on cancer pain relief and supportive care for children.

The WHO project for multinational monitoring of trends and determinants of cardiovascular diseases continued in 25 countries and entered the final stage of data collection. The third and final population survey was prepared and a special training workshop was organized (Gargano, Italy, March). An international conference on preventive cardiology (Oslo, Norway, June–July) held workshops on preventing cardiovascular diseases in countries of the Eastern Mediterranean, cardiovascular diseases in developing countries and the establishment of a global database. A WHO study group (October) reviewed global demographic changes in relation to the epidemiology of cardiovascular diseases in the elderly.

Secretariat

As at 31 December 1993, the total number of full-time staff employed by WHO was 4,456 on permanent and fixed-term contracts. Of these, 1,589 staff members, drawn from 144 nationalities, were in the Professional and higher categories, and 2,867 were in the General Service category. Of the total number, 54 were in posts financed by UNDP, UNEP, UNDCP and UNFPA.

Budget

The forty-sixth (1993) World Health Assembly approved an effective working budget of $822,101,000 for the 1994-1995 biennium.

NOTE: For further information on WHO activities, see *The Work of WHO, 1992-1993, Biennial Report of the Director-General.*

Annex I.   MEMBERSHIP OF THE WORLD HEALTH ORGANIZATION
(As at 31 December 1993)

Afghanistan, Albania, Algeria, Angola, Antigua and Barbuda, Argentina, Armenia, Australia, Austria, Azerbaijan, Bahamas, Bahrain, Bangladesh, Barbados, Belarus, Belgium, Belize, Benin, Bhutan, Bolivia, Bosnia and Herzegovina, Botswana, Brazil, Brunei Darussalam, Bulgaria, Burkina Faso, Burundi, Cambodia, Cameroon, Canada, Cape Verde, Central African Republic, Chad, Chile, China, Colombia, Comoros, Congo, Cook Islands, Costa Rica, Côte d'Ivoire, Croatia, Cuba, Cyprus, Czech Republic, Democratic People's Republic of Korea, Denmark, Djibouti, Dominica, Dominican Republic, Ecuador, Egypt, El Salvador, Equatorial Guinea, Eritrea, Estonia, Ethiopia, Fiji, Finland, France, Gabon, Gambia, Georgia, Germany, Ghana, Greece, Grenada, Guatemala, Guinea, Guinea-Bissau, Guyana, Haiti, Honduras, Hungary, Iceland, India, Indonesia, Iran, Iraq, Ireland, Israel, Italy, Jamaica, Japan, Jordan, Kazakhstan, Kenya, Kiribati, Kuwait, Kyrgyzstan, Lao

People's Democratic Republic, Latvia, Lebanon, Lesotho, Liberia, Libyan Arab Jamahiriya, Lithuania, Luxembourg, Madagascar, Malawi, Malaysia, Maldives, Mali, Malta, Marshall Islands, Mauritania, Mauritius, Mexico, Micronesia, Monaco, Mongolia, Morocco, Mozambique, Myanmar, Namibia, Nepal, Netherlands, New Zealand, Nicaragua, Niger, Nigeria, Norway, Oman, Pakistan, Panama, Papua New Guinea, Paraguay, Peru, Philippines, Poland, Portugal, Qatar, Republic of Korea, Republic of Moldova, Romania, Russian Federation, Rwanda, Saint Kitts and Nevis, Saint Lucia, Saint Vincent and the Grenadines, Samoa, San Marino, Sao Tome and Principe, Saudi Arabia, Senegal, Seychelles, Sierra Leone, Singapore, Slovakia, Slovenia, Solomon Islands, Somalia, South Africa, Spain, Sri Lanka, Sudan, Suriname, Swaziland, Sweden, Switzerland, Syrian Arab Republic, Tajikistan, Thailand, the former Yugoslav Republic of Macedonia, Togo, Tonga, Trinidad and Tobago, Tunisia, Turkey, Turkmenistan, Tuvalu, Uganda, Ukraine, United Arab Emirates, United Kingdom, United Republic of Tanzania, United States, Uruguay, Uzbekistan, Vanuatu, Venezuela, Viet Nam, Yemen, Yugoslavia,* Zaire, Zambia, Zimbabwe.

Associate members

Puerto Rico, Tokelau.

*Refers to the former Socialist Federal Republic of Yugoslavia. In May, the World Health Assembly considered that the Federal Republic of Yugoslavia (Serbia and Montenegro) could not continue automatically the membership of the former Socialist Federal Republic of Yugoslavia. It decided that the Federal Republic of Yugoslavia should apply for membership in WHO and, in the meantime, could not participate in the work of WHO's principal and subsidiary organs.

Annex II.   OFFICERS AND OFFICES OF THE WORLD HEALTH ORGANIZATION
(As at 31 December 1993)

OFFICERS OF THE FORTY-SIXTH WORLD HEALTH ASSEMBLY

President: C. Örtendahl (Sweden).
Vice-Presidents: Dr. R. Pereira (Honduras), H. Lini (Vanuatu), Dr. A. Sattar Yoosuf (Maldives), Dr. B. M. Kawimbe (Zambia), Dr. S. Dallal (Lebanon).
Chairman, Committee A: Dr. M. Sidhom (Tunisia).
Chairman, Committee B: B. N. Taitt (Barbados).

MEMBERS OF THE EXECUTIVE BOARD*

Chairman: J. F. Girard (France).
Vice-Chairmen: Dr. L. C. Sarr (Senegal), B. A. Grillo (Uruguay), Dr. M. Sidhom (Tunisia).
Rapporteurs: J. Mbede (Cameroon), J. F. Varder (Denmark).

Members were designated by: Afghanistan, Bolivia, Bulgaria, Cameroon, Canada, China, Denmark, France, Greece, Iraq, Jamaica, Japan, Maldives, Mexico, Mongolia, Myanmar, Philippines, Portugal, Qatar, Russian Federation, Rwanda, Sao Tome and Principe, Senegal, Seychelles, Sierra Leone, Swaziland, Syrian Arab Republic, Tunisia, United Kingdom, United States, Uruguay.

*The Executive Board consists of 31 persons designated by member States elected by the World Health Assembly.

SENIOR OFFICERS OF THE SECRETARIAT

Director-General: Dr. Hiroshi Nakajima.
Assistant Directors-General: D. G. Aitken, Dr. F. S. Antezana, Dr. R. H. Henderson, Dr. Hu Ching-Li, Dr. J. P. Jardel, Dr. N. P. Napalkov.
Director, Regional Office for Africa: Dr. G. L. Monekosso.

Director, Regional Office for the Americas: (Pan American Sanitary Bureau): Dr. C. Guerra de Macedo.
Director, Regional Office for South-East Asia: Dr. U Ko Ko.
Director, Regional Office for Europe: Dr. J. E. Asvall.
Director, Regional Office for the Eastern Mediterranean: Dr. H. A. Gezairy.
Director, Regional Office for the Western Pacific: Dr. S. T. Han.

HEADQUARTERS AND OTHER OFFICES

HEADQUARTERS
World Health Organization
20 Avenue Appia
CH-1211 Geneva 27, Switzerland
  Cable address: UNISANTE GENEVA
  Telephone: (41) (22) 791-21-11
  Telex: 415416
  Facsimile: (41) (22) 791-07-46

WHO OFFICE AT THE UNITED NATIONS
2 United Nations Plaza
New York, NY 10017, United States
  Cable address: UNSANTE NEW YORK
  Telephone: (1) (212) 963-6001
  Telex: 234292
  Facsimile: (1) (212) 223-2920

WHO also maintained regional offices at Alexandria, Egypt; Brazzaville, Congo; Copenhagen, Denmark; Manila, Philippines; New Delhi, India; and Washington, D.C.

Chapter VI

International Bank for
Reconstruction and Development (World Bank)

During the fiscal year 1993 (1 July 1992 to 30 June 1993), the International Bank for Reconstruction and Development (World Bank) and its affiliate, the International Development Association (IDA), continued to provide economic assistance to developing countries, emphasizing poverty reduction and expanded access to health, education and other social services. Efforts to encourage borrowers to capitalize on the positive links between poverty alleviation and sound environmental policies—while redressing the environmental damage arising from poorly conceived growth strategies—were among the Bank's priorities. The Bank elaborated environmental strategies for several key regions and countries, expanded its research on a broad range of environmental topics, continued to integrate environmental concerns into its country-policy dialogues and undertook a series of internal reviews to improve its capacity to take account of social, cultural, resettlement and rehabilitation issues in project design and implementation.

During fiscal 1993, the Bank committed $27,632 million as follows: $16,945 million for its loans; $6,751 million for IDA credits; and $3,936 million for gross investments made by the Bank's second affiliate, the International Finance Corporation.

As at 31 December 1993, 177 States were members of the World Bank. New members in 1993 were Croatia, the Czech Republic, Micronesia, Slovakia, Slovenia, Tajikistan and the former Yugoslav Republic of Macedonia (see Annex I).

Lending operations

In fiscal 1993, the Bank made 122 loans to 45 countries amounting to $16,945 million, a 12 per cent increase over fiscal 1992. This brought its cumulative total of loan commitments to $235,154 million since its inception in 1946.

Agriculture and rural development

The Bank approved lending to 15 countries for 17 agricultural projects in fiscal 1993, totalling $1,918.8 million. China received $425 million, of which $325 million went to improve the grain market and $100 million to help with flood control and land drainage in the Taihu basin. Poland was extended a loan of $300 million to assist the Government's medium-term agriculture sector adjust-

ment programme. A loan of $250 million to Colombia was intended to assist the Government in introducing and sustaining financial and trade policy changes, and a loan of $215 million to Morocco was approved for making large-scale irrigation more efficient, cost-effective and sustainable.

Development finance companies

Four countries received $582 million to assist their development finance companies in fiscal 1993. Indonesia received $307 million to support governmental regulatory and institutional reforms in the financial sector, aimed at helping to lower the risk of financial instability, improve the efficiency of resource allocation and transform the State commercial banks. China was granted $150 million to assist the Tianjin municipal government to restructure its industrial sector by modernizing businesses in the machine-tool, construction-equipment, electronic-components, automotive-parts and electric-motors subsectors. A loan of $75 million to Ecuador was to provide funds for term financing in the private sector, improve the performance of the finance sector and promote trade liberalization. Colombia was extended a loan of $50 million to assist the export development process.

Education

In fiscal 1993, 11 education projects in nine countries were approved for a total of $968 million. Malaysia received loans amounting to $248 million, of which $141 million was to create some 250,000 new student places, expand equitable access to primary and secondary education and increase the quality of pre-service training for the country's higher-level skilled workers and technicians. Brazil was granted $212 million to improve the quality of education for some 3 million children in the first four grades of primary school in four north-eastern states. In Mexico, an $80 million loan supported the expansion of early childhood development services to the country's poorest states. In Algeria, a $40 million Bank project supported the introduction of a pilot system designed to assess learning outcomes and quality in basic and secondary education; it also supported teacher training. A $32 million project in Jamaica aimed at improving the quality, efficiency and equity of lower secondary education, emphasizing schools serving the poorest students.

Energy

Sixteen energy projects—in oil, gas, coal and power—were assisted in 12 countries in fiscal 1993 at a cost of $3,021 million. India received $845 million, of which $400 million helped to finance a five-year investment programme of new coal- and gas-based power stations of the National Thermal Power Corporation, and $350 million to improve the efficiency in power transmission and system operations. A $610 million loan was extended to the Russian Federation to finance the purchase of essential inputs for existing oil-production operations in western Siberia. Of the $400 million granted to China, $300 million was for the construction of its largest pumped-storage hydroelectric plant in Zhejiang province, while $100 million went into the completion of a hydroelectric power facility to meet increased electricity demands in Fujian province. A loan of $300 million to Argentina served to complete the permanent structures of the Yacyretá hydroelectric project, install its first six units, connect them to the national grid and implement environmental protection and resettlement measures.

Industry

In fiscal 1993, loans for the industrial sector totalling $685 million were granted to four countries. China received $250 million to control industrial water pollution cost effectively in the Jiangsu region. Peru also received a $250 million loan to support its privatization programme and related sectoral policy, legal and regulatory reforms. A loan of $130 million was granted to Egypt to implement strategies to develop the tourism industry while controlling environmental degradation in tourist areas. Bulgaria secured a loan of $55 million to make available investment and export credits, aimed at encouraging a strong supply response to ongoing governmental reforms.

Non-project

In fiscal 1993, the Bank granted non-project loans totalling $2,980 million to 12 countries. Argentina received $850 million, of which $450 million was a debt and debt-service reduction loan that would finance interest and principal collateral for the par bonds to be issued in exchange for eligible debt and support the implementation of a debt agreement between the country and its commercial-bank creditors. The other loan, of $400 million, to Argentina was a financial-sector adjustment loan to assist in reducing the role of the State in the financial sector, strengthen the banking sector and its supervisory framework and

provide resources for the country's debt and debt-service reduction arrangements. A $600 million loan was made to the Russian Federation for foreign exchange to finance imports needed in support of its stabilization and economic reform programme. Poland received $450 million to support its enterprise and bank restructuring and privatization programme. A loan of $300 million was made to India to support measures taken by the Government to liberalize further the external sector and investment regime. Peru was granted $150 million as supplemental funds for the Government's macroeconomic stabilization programme and broad-based structural reforms in the fiscal and social sectors, privatization, agriculture and labour policy.

Population, health and nutrition

In fiscal 1993, Bank lending for population, health and nutrition amounted to $706.8 million for 11 projects. Iran received a $141.4 million loan to expand its primary health-care system in rural areas and its family-planning programme. Venezuela was granted $94 million for a project that sought to control both vector and waterborne endemic diseases (malaria, in particular) in poor rural and peri-urban areas. A loan of $93.5 million was extended to Indonesia for a project to improve infant, child and maternal health. Hungary received $91 million to finance the rehabilitation of selected institutional-care facilities, the introduction of management-information systems in hospitals and training in public-health management. A loan of $90 million went to Chile to support policy and institutional reform and priority health facility investments.

Public sector management

In fiscal 1993, the Bank approved $576 million in loans to support public sector management reforms in five countries. Argentina received $300 million to support the second phase of its public enterprise reform programme. Hungary was granted a loan totalling $132 million to support reforms in its social insurance system. The Russian Federation received a $70 million loan to increase the capacity of its Federal Employment Service to process the anticipated upsurge of benefit claims from the growing numbers of unemployed following economic restructuring and privatization. The Philippines received $63 million to computerize its tax administration system.

Technical assistance

The Bank approved seven loans to six countries for technical assistance in fiscal 1993, totalling $212.3 million. The Russian Federation received $90 million to assist in implementing its privatization programme. Peru was granted $41.8 million, of which $30 million was to assist in preparing and implementing its privatization programme and related sectoral policy, legal and regulatory reforms. A $30 million loan extended to Venezuela supported judicial reforms aimed at improving its enabling environment for private sector development.

Telecommunications

During fiscal 1993, three loans were made by the Bank in telecommunications for a total of $264 million. The Philippines received $134 million to finance the 1992-1996 investment programme of the Philippine Long Distance Company, aimed at extending and improving telephone facilities in provincial areas. In Morocco, a loan of $100 million went to expand the country's telecommunications network and to finance a time slice of the 1992-1994 investment programme of the National Post and Telecommunications Authority.

Transportation

The Bank made 15 loans to 11 countries, totalling $2,584.6 million for transportation projects. China received $930 million, of which $420 million supported the efforts of the Ministry of Railways in preparing the railway system to serve a future market-oriented economy. A $480 million loan was made to Mexico to protect and enhance past investments in the federal highway network. A loan of $340 million was extended to Argentina to finance a four-year time slice of the maintenance programme of the National Highway Directorate and its road construction needs. Indonesia received $197.1 million, of which $155 million was to improve the road network in selected rural areas of eastern Indonesia.

Urban development

The Bank made 10 loans to eight countries in the amount of $1,687.5 million for urban development projects. It approved two loans totalling $420 million to Mexico, of which $220 million went to a government programme to reduce air pollution in Mexico City and $200 million supported a project to improve the quality and efficiency of urban transport systems in medium-sized cities. Morocco received $234 million, of which $130 million was for a project to benefit resettled squatter and low-income households by providing serviced lots at affordable prices. Turkey was extended $285 million to reconstruct essential housing, infrastructure and other facilities damaged by an earthquake in 1992 and to restore economic activity in the affected area. Algeria was granted $200 million to accelerate the completion of a public-housing programme and private unfinished stock through the supply of construction materials and the provision of technical

assistance. Brazil received $128.5 million to consolidate financial, institutional and organizational policy changes required to achieve sustainable, integrated multimodal transport in Rio de Janeiro.

Water supply and sanitation

In fiscal 1993, seven loans to six countries totalling $758.5 million were approved for water supply and sanitation. Of the two loans totalling $390 million made to Brazil, $245 million supported the creation of two urban water-basin authorities for the Guarapiranga River near São Paulo and for the upper Iguacu River in Curtiba, and $145 million supported a project to restore water quality in the system of rivers and reservoirs in the metropolitan area of Belo Horizonte. Turkey was granted a $129.5 million loan to provide water supply, sewerage, flood protection and solid waste services in Greater Bursa. The Republic of Korea received $110 million to expand waste-water treatment plants in Kwangju and Seoul. A loan of $80 million to Indonesia supported a project that would provide safe, adequate and easily accessible water supply and sanitation services, as well as a programme of health and hygiene education.

Economic Development Institute

In fiscal 1993, the Economic Development Institute (EDI) continued to impart knowledge and experience accumulated in the World Bank and elsewhere, with the strategic objective of strengthening development decision-making in the Bank's member countries. To further its objective, EDI relied on training activities, institution-building programmes and its publications programme. Of the 152 training programmes organized by EDI, 17 of them dealt with agriculture, 31 with development management, 37 with finance and industry, 24 with human resources, 17 with infrastructure and urban development, and 26 with macroeconomics.

EDI carried out 38 training programmes in Africa, 25 in Asia, 43 in Europe and Central Asia, 19 in Latin America and the Caribbean, and 16 in the Middle East and North Africa. Some 40 EDI training activities in the former USSR emphasized the training of instructors in enterprise management and banking and of senior officials involved in restructuring enterprises, privatization and the management of commercial banks. A quarter of EDI's training activities in 1993 took place in sub-Saharan Africa. To help in South Africa's transition from apartheid to democracy, EDI was engaged in a training programme to prepare those who would be entering government service to perform better their responsibilities. EDI collaborated with Viet Nam to carry out a United Nations Development Programme project that supported the country's efforts to move from a command-driven economy to a market-oriented one. In the Middle East and North Africa, 16 training and institutional assistance activities were completed, covering public sector management, environmental assessments, higher education and water resources management.

EDI was involved in three institution-building programmes in Latin America aimed at strengthening the abilities of local institutions to improve living conditions in low-income settlements. It also helped organize national and regional workshops in cooperation with Governments and non-governmental organizations to improve development programmes. In October 1992, the Joint Vienna Institute began to provide training to officials from Central and Eastern Europe and the republics of the former USSR.

EDI prepared and published training materials on policy analysis and reform. Sixty-five new titles were published in fiscal 1993 and a total of 20,000 items were sent out in response to 4,000 requests. Although EDI's highest priority remained its training programmes in Africa, it placed increasingly more emphasis on its activities in Central and Eastern Europe and the former USSR. The shift was reflected in the publication of over a dozen titles in Russian.

Co-financing

The volume of co-financing anticipated in support of Bank-assisted operations in fiscal 1993 was $11,230 million. About 48 per cent of all Bank-assisted projects and programmes were co-financed. The largest source of co-financing continued to be official bilateral and multilateral development institutions, which together accounted for $7,759 million or 69 per cent of the total.

Other major co-financing activities in fiscal 1993 included those under the Special Programme of Assistance (SPA) for sub-Saharan Africa. In the second phase of SPA, covering 1991-1993, donors pledged $7 billion of co-financing and coordinated financing for quick-disbursing balance-of-payments assistance in support of adjustment programmes in 27 countries. As at 31 December 1992, SPA donors had allocated some $5.3 billion, or nearly 80 per cent of the pledged amount, and had disbursed some 50 per cent, or more than $2.5 billion, of those allocations in the eligible countries.

Financing activities

During fiscal 1993, the Bank raised $12,700 million through medium- and long-term borrowings in 12 currencies and currency units, including $11,200 million of fixed-rate borrowings and $1,500 million of variable-rate borrowings. Borrowings were made up of $4,187 million in United States dollars, $3,842 million in Japanese yen, $708 million in deutsche mark, $771 million in Swiss francs and $3,168 million in Canadian dollars, European currency units, French francs, Irish pounds, Italian lire, Netherlands guilders, pounds sterling and Spanish pesetas.

After $3,600 million of currency swaps and a notional par volume of $3,800 million of interest-rate swaps, all of the year's borrowings were fixed-rate liabilities denominated in United States dollars, yen, mark, Swiss francs and guilders.

As at 30 June 1993, short-term borrowings outstanding were $3,789 million equivalent, comprising $2,483 million from official sources through the Bank's central bank facility and $1,306 million from market borrowings in United States dollars.

Capitalization

The total subscribed capital of the Bank as at 30 June 1993 was $165,589 million or 90 per cent of authorized capital of $184,048 million. The permissible increase of net disbursements ("headroom") was $78,861 million, or 43 per cent of the Bank's lending limit.

Secretariat

As at 30 June 1993, the staff of the World Bank numbered 6,197, of whom 4,005 were in the Professional or higher categories, drawn from 121 nationalities.

Income, expenditures and reserves

The Bank's gross revenues, generated mainly from loans and investments, totalled $9,451 million in fiscal 1993, a decline of $223 million from fiscal 1992. Net income was $1,130 million, down $515 million from the previous year. Expenses rose by about $253 million to $8,215 million, $679 million of which covered administrative costs that had increased by $67 million over fiscal 1992.

On 30 June 1993, reserves amounted to $12,000 million, and the reserves-to-loan ratio stood at 11.4 per cent, excluding prefunding of interest waivers.

NOTE: For further details regarding the Bank's activities, see *The World Bank: Annual Report 1993.*

Annex I.   MEMBERSHIP OF THE WORLD BANK
(As at 31 December 1993)

Afghanistan, Albania, Algeria, Angola, Antigua and Barbuda, Argentina, Armenia, Australia, Austria, Azerbaijan, Bahamas, Bahrain, Bangladesh, Barbados, Belarus, Belgium, Belize, Benin, Bhutan, Bolivia, Botswana, Brazil, Bulgaria, Burkina Faso, Burundi, Cambodia, Cameroon, Canada, Cape Verde, Central African Republic, Chad, Chile, China, Colombia, Comoros, Congo, Costa Rica, Côte d'Ivoire, Croatia,* Cyprus, Czech Republic, Denmark, Djibouti, Dominica, Dominican Republic, Ecuador, Egypt, El Salvador, Equatorial Guinea, Estonia, Ethiopia, Fiji, Finland, France, Gabon, Gambia, Georgia, Germany, Ghana, Greece, Grenada, Guatemala, Guinea, Guinea-Bissau, Guyana, Haiti, Honduras, Hungary, Iceland, India, Indonesia, Iran, Iraq, Ireland, Israel, Italy, Jamaica, Japan, Jordan, Kazakhstan, Kenya, Kiribati,

Kuwait, Kyrgyzstan, Lao People's Democratic Republic, Latvia, Lebanon, Lesotho, Liberia, Libyan Arab Jamahiriya, Lithuania, Luxembourg, Madagascar, Malawi, Malaysia, Maldives, Mali, Malta, Marshall Islands, Mauritania, Mauritius, Mexico, Micronesia, Mongolia, Morocco, Mozambique, Myanmar, Namibia, Nepal, Netherlands, New Zealand, Nicaragua, Niger, Nigeria, Norway, Oman, Pakistan, Panama, Papua New Guinea, Paraguay, Peru, Philippines, Poland, Portugal, Qatar, Republic of Korea, Republic of Moldova, Romania, Russian Federation, Rwanda, Saint Kitts and Nevis, Saint Lucia, Saint Vincent and the Grenadines, Samoa, Sao Tome and Principe, Saudi Arabia, Senegal, Seychelles, Sierra Leone, Singapore, Slovakia, Slovenia,* Solomon Islands, Somalia, South Africa, Spain, Sri Lanka, Sudan, Suriname, Swaziland, Sweden, Switzerland, Syrian Arab Republic, Tajikistan, Thailand, the former Yugoslav Republic of Macedonia,* Togo, Tonga, Trinidad and Tobago, Tunisia, Turkey, Turkmenistan, Uganda, Ukraine, United Arab Emirates, United Kingdom, United Republic of Tanzania, United States, Uruguay, Uzbekistan, Vanuatu, Venezuela, Viet Nam, Yemen, Zaire, Zambia, Zimbabwe.

*Yugoslavia ceased to be a member of the World Bank effective 25 February 1993 and was succeeded by Croatia, Slovenia and the former Yugoslav Republic of Macedonia.

Annex II. EXECUTIVE DIRECTORS AND ALTERNATES, PRINCIPAL OFFICERS AND OFFICES OF THE WORLD BANK
(As at 30 June 1993)

EXECUTIVE DIRECTORS AND ALTERNATES

Appointed Director	Appointed Alternate	Casting the vote of
E. Patrick Coady	Mark M. Collins, Jr.	United States
Yasuyuki Kawahara	Kiyoshi Kodera	Japan
Fritz Fischer	Harald Rehm	Germany
Jean-Pierre Landau	Jérôme Haas	France
David Peretz	David Stanton	United Kingdom

Elected Director	Elected Alternate	Casting the votes of
Bernard Snoy (Belgium)	Nurcan Akturk (Turkey)	Austria, Belarus, Belgium, Czech Republic, Hungary, Kazakhstan, Luxembourg, Slovakia, Turkey
Eveline Herfkens (Netherlands)	Ileana Ionescu (Romania)	Armenia, Bulgaria, Cyprus, Georgia, Israel, Netherlands, Republic of Moldova, Romania, Ukraine
Frank Potter (Canada)	Hubert Dean (Bahamas)	Antigua and Barbuda, Bahamas, Barbados, Belize, Canada, Dominica, Grenada, Guyana, Ireland, Jamaica, Saint Kitts and Nevis, Saint Lucia, Saint Vincent and the Grenadines
Bimal Jalan (India)	M. A. Syed (Bangladesh)	Bangladesh, Bhutan, India, Sri Lanka
Enzo Grilli (Italy)	Fernando S. Carneiro (Portugal)	Albania, Greece, Italy, Malta, Portugal
Angel Torres (Venezuela)	Gabriel Castellanos (Guatemala)	Costa Rica, El Salvador, Guatemala, Honduras, Mexico, Nicaragua, Panama, Spain, Venezuela
Jorunn Maehlum (Norway)	Helga Jonsdottir (Iceland)	Denmark, Estonia, Finland, Iceland, Latvia, Lithuania, Norway, Sweden
Wang Liansheng (China)	Zhang Shengman (China)	China
Ibrahim A. Al-Assaf (Saudi Arabia)	Ahmen M. Al-Ghannam (Saudi Arabia)	Saudi Arabia
Mohamed Benhocine (Algeria)	Arshad Farooq (Pakistan)	Afghanistan, Algeria, Ghana, Iran, Morocco, Pakistan, Tunisia
John H. Cosgrove (Australia)	Bong-Hee Won (Republic of Korea)	Australia, Kiribati, Marshall Islands, Mongolia, New Zealand, Papua New Guinea, Republic of Korea, Samoa, Solomon Islands, Vanuatu
Pedro Malan (Brazil)	(vacant)	Brazil, Colombia, Dominican Republic, Ecuador, Haiti, Philippines, Suriname, Trinidad and Tobago
Faisal A. Al-Khaled (Kuwait)	Mohamed W. Hosny (Egypt)	Bahrain, Egypt, Jordan, Kuwait, Lebanon, Libyan Arab Jamahiriya, Maldives, Oman, Qatar, Syrian Arab Republic, United Arab Emirates, Yemen
Jean-Daniel Gerber (Switzerland)	Jan Sulmicki (Poland)	Azerbaijan, Kyrgyzstan, Poland, Switzerland, Turkmenistan, Uzbekistan
Aris Othman (Malaysia)	Jannes Hutagalung (Indonesia)	Fiji, Indonesia, Lao People's Democratic Republic, Malaysia, Myanmar, Nepal, Singapore, Thailand, Tonga, Viet Nam
O. K. Matambo (Botswana)	Harry M. Mapondo (Malawi)	Angola, Botswana, Burundi, Ethiopia, Gambia, Guinea, Kenya, Lesotho, Liberia, Malawi, Mozambique, Namibia, Nigeria, Seychelles, Sierra Leone, Sudan, Swaziland, Uganda, United Republic of Tanzania, Zambia, Zimbabwe

Elected Director	Elected Alternate	Casting the votes of
Boris G. Fedorov (Russian Federation)	Alexander N. Doumnov (Russian Federation)	Russian Federation
Nicolás Flaño (Chile)	Julio Nogues (Argentina)	Argentina, Bolivia, Chile, Paraguay, Peru, Uruguay
Jean-Pierre Le Bouder (Central African Republic)	Ali Bourhane (Comoros)	Benin, Burkina Faso, Cameroon, Cape Verde, Central African Republic, Chad, Comoros, Congo, Côte d'Ivoire, Djibouti, Equatorial Guinea, Gabon, Guinea-Bissau, Madagascar, Mali, Mauritania, Mauritius, Niger, Rwanda, Sao Tome and Principe, Senegal, Togo, Zaire

NOTE: Cambodia, Iraq, Somalia and South Africa did not participate in the 1992 regular election of Executive Directors. Croatia, Micronesia, Slovenia and Tajikistan became members after that election.

PRINCIPAL OFFICERS*

President: Lewis T. Preston.
Managing Directors: Attila Karaosmanoglu, Sven Sandstrom, Ernest Stern.
Vice President and Controller: Stephen D. Eccles.
Vice President, Financial Policy and Risk Management: Johannes F. Linn.
Vice President and Treasurer: Jessica P. Einhorn.
Vice President, Latin America and Caribbean Regional Office: S. Shahid Husain.
Vice President, Africa Regional Office: Edward V. K. Jaycox.
Vice President, East Asia and Pacific Regional Office: Gautam S. Kaji.
Vice President, Middle East and North Africa Regional Office: Caio K. Koch-Weser.

Vice President, Europe and Central Asia Regional Office: Wilfried P. Thalwitz.
Vice President, South Asia Regional Office: Joseph D. Wood.
Vice President, Co-financing and Financial Advisory Services: Koji Kashiwaya.
Vice President, Development Economics, and Chief Economist: D. C. Rao (acting).
Vice President and Special Adviser: Visvanathan Rajagopalan.
Director-General, Operations Evaluation: Robert Picciotto.
Vice President and General Counsel: Ibrahim F. I. Shihata.
Vice President and Secretary: Timothy T. Thahane.
Vice President, Personnel and Administration: Bilsel H. Alisbah.

*The World Bank and IDA had the same officers and staff.

HEADQUARTERS AND OTHER OFFICES

HEADQUARTERS
The World Bank
1818 H Street, N.W.
Washington, D.C. 20433, United States
  Cable address: INTBAFRAD WASHINGTONDC
  Telephone: (1) (202) 477-1234
  Telex: MCI 248423 WORLDBANK
      MCI 64145 WORLDBANK
      TRT 82987 WORLDBANK
      TRT 197688 WORLDBANK
  Facsimile: (1) (202) 477-6391

NEW YORK OFFICE
The World Bank Mission to the United Nations
809 UN Plaza, Suite 900
New York, N.Y. 10017, United States
  Cable address: INTBAFRAD NEWYORK
  Telephone: (1) (212) 963-6008
  Facsimile: (1) (212) 697-7020

The Bank also maintained major regional offices at Abidjan, Côte d'Ivoire; Bangkok, Thailand; Nairobi, Kenya; Paris; Riga, Latvia; Tallinn, Estonia; Tokyo; and Vilnius, Lithuania.

Chapter VII

International Finance Corporation (IFC)

The International Finance Corporation (IFC) is an affiliate of the International Bank for Reconstruction and Development (World Bank). It was established in 1956 to further economic growth in developing member countries by promoting private-sector investment. During the 1993 fiscal year (1 July 1992 to 30 June 1993), IFC provided direct loans and equity financing in international capital markets as well as an array of advisory services to businesses and Governments on issues related to private investment.

As at 30 June 1993, IFC had a total membership of 155, following the admission of Belarus, the Comoros, Micronesia, Kyrgyzstan, Lithuania, the Marshall Islands and the Russian Federation. Czechoslovakia ceased to be a member and was succeeded by the Czech Republic and Slovakia. Two of the five successor States of the former Yugoslavia—Croatia and Slovenia—also joined IFC (see Annex I).

Financial and advisory services

As many countries accelerated the move to a market economy, demand for IFC's financial and advisory services increased sharply. IFC expanded its presence worldwide, opening several new offices or missions in areas of increased activities, notably in the former Soviet Union and in Latin America. It resumed its activities in Lebanon and stepped up its investment programme in China.

During fiscal 1993, IFC approved $2.1 billion in financing for 185 projects, including its Africa Enterprise Fund (AEF) projects. Helping companies in developing countries achieve a proper balance between debt and equity financing was a key IFC objective. Equity and quasi-equity investments approved during the year came to $519 million, 24 per cent of total approvals. The Corporation also mobilized considerable cofinancing, approving $1.8 billion in financing from other investors and lenders through loan syndications and the underwriting of securities issues. The total costs of the projects approved were estimated to be $17 billion. Thus, for every $1 of financing approved by IFC for its own account, other investors and lenders would provide $7.

The environment was an urgent priority for IFC, which was trying to increase awareness for environmentally sound projects in developing countries. During fiscal 1993, IFC strengthened its environmental review process, expanded its collaboration with other institutions on environmental issues, and intensified its efforts to channel private-sector resources into the environmental goods and services sector in developing countries.

During project appraisal, IFC reviewed the environmental analysis done by the project sponsor to ensure that the project was environmentally sound and sustainable and that it complied with the World Bank's environmental policies and guidelines, as well as with the requirements of the host country.

IFC actively encouraged investments in environmental projects in such areas as water supply and wastewater treatment, solid and hazardous waste management, manufacture of clean production technology and pollution-control equipment, recycling and ecotourism.

At the beginning of fiscal 1993, IFC was reorganized, which increased its responsiveness, enabling it to develop regional strategies more closely attuned to the specific needs of different regions and to deepen its in-house expertise in several critical sectors—infrastructure, chemicals and petrochemicals, agribusiness, oil and gas, and mining. Continued strong growth was projected in IFC's operations for the remainder of the 1990s. IFC's Board of Directors approved a three-year plan for fiscal years 1994-1996 that envisaged annual growth in nominal terms of around 13 per cent.

Regional projects

In fiscal 1993, IFC extended its operations to a broader range of member countries, reflecting the impact of changes in the investment environment in a number of countries as the emphasis on market-driven economic development accelerated. Investments were approved in 54 countries, compared with 51 countries in fiscal 1992, contributing to the Corporation's long-term objective of achieving a regionally balanced and diversified portfolio. The amount of financing approved for IFC's own account increased for most regions, with the biggest percentage increase in Europe.

Loans and investments totalling $473 million were approved for 54 projects in countries with per capita incomes of $400 or less. Approvals in the poorest countries accounted for 29 per cent of the projects and 22 per cent of the financing approved for IFC's own account.

Sub-Saharan Africa

IFC approved 45 projects in 18 countries in sub-Saharan Africa during fiscal 1993, including AEF projects. As at 30 June 1993, its committed portfolio included loans and investments for 166 companies in 32 countries.

In dollar terms, natural resource–based projects dominated IFC's approvals. A $108 million loan was approved, of which up to $68 million would be syndicated, for a $334 million gas project in Nigeria. IFC also approved $11.4 million in equity investment for an oil- and gas-development project in Côte d'Ivoire and a $10 million loan for the expansion of a bauxite mining project in Sierra Leone. A loan of $10 million was also approved for Zimbabwe to support the expansion of a coal mine.

Several agribusiness projects were approved during fiscal 1993, including loans totalling $21 million for the rehabilitation of two sugar plantations in Zimbabwe that had been affected by drought. IFC also approved a loan of $2 million for the creation of a shrimp farm in Madagascar.

In the tourism sector, IFC approved four hotel projects in Guinea, Nigeria, the United Republic of Tanzania and Zimbabwe, and in manufacturing, loans and equity of $4.8 million were approved for the expansion of a soap and edible-oil producer in Côte d'Ivoire.

In the financial sector, besides approving debt and equity financing for several merchant and investment banks and leasing and insurance companies, IFC helped to establish three investment funds: the Mauritius Fund Limited, the first closed-end fund to invest in Mauritius ($5 million in equity); the Emerging Markets Gold Fund, a global fund that would invest in gold-mining companies in a number of developing countries, including Ghana; and the Africa Fund, which would invest in stock markets in North Africa and sub-Saharan Africa ($7.5 million in equity).

Through AEF, IFC approved total financing of $11 million—$10 million in loans and $1 million in equity—for 20 projects in 13 countries. The projects approved were in a broad range of industries, including light manufacturing, fishing, agriculture and tourism.

IFC provided technical assistance and advisory services to enterprises of all sizes, including to larger companies in such areas as debt mobilization for large projects, feasibility studies, project appraisals and privatization. It also advised Governments on capital-market development, privatization and foreign direct investment. Over the past seven years, the Corporation's Foreign Investment Advisory Service (FIAS) provided advisory assistance on foreign direct investment to more than two thirds of the countries in sub-Saharan Africa. In fiscal 1993, FIAS began to work in eight countries where it had not worked before and completed policy advisory projects in 10 countries.

Asia

In fiscal 1993, IFC approved 39 projects in nine countries in the Asia region. As at 30 June 1993, its committed portfolio included loans and investments for 183 companies in 11 countries.

IFC approved financing totalling $43 million for two cement companies and a commercial bank in China. In the Philippines, it approved $148 million in financing for two powerprojects, playing a crucial role in the construction of a 700-megawatt coal-fired powerplant in Pagbilao by providing debt and equity financing for its own account and bringing United States and Japanese export-import banks into the project, while serving as the sponsor's financial adviser. In Sri Lanka, IFC approved financing for a telecommunications project in the private sector ($1.4 million in equity). In response to Thailand's growing shortages of domestically refined petroleum products, IFC approved a $350 million loan—$75 million for its own account and $275 million to be syndicated with international financial institutions—to help finance a $1.9 billion, 5-million-ton-per-year oil refinery. IFC was also financing the construction of Thailand's first facility to produce purified terephthalic acid to supply producers of polyester chips and fibres. Thailand and other countries in the region were net importers of purified terephthalic acid. IFC approved loans and equity of $24 million, while a future $125 million would come from syndications.

New investment in general manufacturing was dampened by both the world-wide economic slow-down and by infrastructural bottlenecks in some countries, particularly in power. Several manufacturing companies in the region increased their share capital, however, through rights issues to which IFC subscribed as a shareholder. IFC also approved financing for projects in the textiles, paper, automotive and cement industries.

In the tourism and service sectors, IFC approved financing for such ventures as a shipping company in Indonesia ($17 million in loans and equity and $10 million in syndications), two hotels and a hospital in Thailand ($57.9 million in loans and equity and $35 million in syndications) and the construction of a conference centre for a large hotel in Nepal (a $0.8 million loan).

In the financial sector, IFC approved investments in a number of capital-markets projects, including the establishment of a venture-capital fund in the Philippines ($2.5 million in equity) and a joint-venture bank in China ($7.5 million in equity and stand-by). It also approved loan financing for leasing companies in India and Indonesia, while participating in increasing the capital of a number of financial institutions in which it was already a shareholder, to support continued development.

In fiscal 1993, IFC continued to provide wide-ranging technical assistance to both businesses and Governments, structuring and mobilizing, for instance, funds for constructing a hotel in Indonesia and advising Sri Lanka on the financial restructuring of Air Lanka, the national airline. It also undertook a comprehensive review of the Indian stock markets and recommended changes to modernize and internationalize them. In China, IFC began to provide technical assistance to the new securities regulatory commission, focusing on regulations for the country's rapidly expanding stock markets. IFC also prepared a study for Tonga on the feasibility of introducing a second commercial bank.

FIAS provided advice on strengthening the investment environment to six countries in the region: Bangladesh, India, Mongolia, Nepal, Sri Lanka and Viet Nam. Two meetings organized by FIAS attracted several countries to discuss ways to create a more favourable environment for foreign direct investment.

Europe

In fiscal 1993, IFC approved 20 projects in four European countries. As at 30 June, its committed portfolio included loans and investments for 105 companies in 11 countries.

IFC approved its first projects in Russia soon after it joined the Corporation. They included a credit line of $15 million to the International Moscow Bank and loans and equity totalling $71.5 million for two oil-development projects. IFC approved its largest investments to date in Central and Eastern Europe. One of them, a $371 million loan to SKODA Automobilova A.S., the Czech Republic's recently privatized producer of motor vehicles, would help to finance a $4.3 billion five-year investment programme to build a new engine plant, introduce new models and increase manufacturing capacity.

Financing through loans, equity and syndications totalling $67.2 million was approved for Poland's first float-glass plant, a joint venture formed by Pilkington (United Kingdom) and Poland's biggest sheet-glass manufacturer. Another large project in Poland, for which loans and equity totalling $46.2 million were approved, involved the modernization of a newly privatized manufacturer of specialty and alloy steel near Warsaw.

To encourage investment in Central and Eastern Europe, IFC helped to establish several investment funds, including the New Europe East Investment Fund to support foreign investment in and technology transfer to reforming economies of Europe, including the former Soviet Union. The Private Equity Fund—Europe would make venture capital available to local private enterprises.

IFC approved financing for nine projects in Turkey, including four capital-market projects as well as projects in the hotel and manufacturing industries.

Demand for IFC advisory services was great in the European countries in transition. Advice and technical assistance on a wide range of issues was provided to Governments and businesses in more than 10 countries. The most noteworthy advisory assignment involved preparing and implementing, with backing from the United States Agency for International Development and the United Kingdom Know-How Fund, the privatizations of hundreds of large companies and thousands of small enterprises in Russia, as well as scores of small firms in Ukraine. IFC designed privatizations that were being used as models in both countries. In Poland, IFC was helping to implement the restructuring and privatization strategy it had designed for the country's cement and lime industries. In the Czech Republic, it advised Etibank, a state mining and mineral-processing company, on a joint venture to manufacture soda ash. Russia received technical assistance from IFC in setting up securities markets such as stock exchanges, developing the regulatory framework, training staff and selecting equipment. IFC also provided advice on capital-market development in Hungary, Poland, Romania and Slovenia, mostly in connection with establishing and regulating securities markets.

FIAS provided advice on foreign direct investment to a number of Governments in the region.

Latin America and the Caribbean

In fiscal 1993, IFC approved 52 projects in 16 countries in Latin America and the Caribbean. As at 30 June, its committed portfolio included loans and investments for 261 companies in 23 countries.

Although economic liberalization in Latin America had gained the attention of foreign investors, they often remained reluctant to invest in the region because of the political instability of many countries. Consequently, IFC continued to play a catalytic role for investments in the region. In fiscal 1993, the Corporation accomplished several of its objectives by helping various companies gain access to international capital markets. For example, IFC, through loans, syndications and underwriting costing $61.8 million, underwrote a bond issue by a Mexican cement producer in the European bond markets, arranged a currency swap of Deutsche mark into United States dollars, and syndicated a loan for the company. It also underwrote, in the amount of $14.4 million, part of the international equity issue by Corporación Financiera del Valle, a Colombian company, and approved a $15 million investment in the Latin American Corporate Bond Fund, the first fund to enable institutional investors to invest in debt issues of private-sector Latin American companies.

To support the development of domestic capital markets, IFC approved $25 million towards the establishment of the Scudder Latin American Trust for Independent Power to provide equity capital for private-sector power projects in the region. Playing a catalytic role, IFC led the management of the fund, made an investment in the fund for its own account, helped to attract institutional portfolio investors, and promoted equity issues in the domestic markets. Similarly, IFC approved equity of $10 million for a new private equity fund and a new investment-management company in Mexico.

IFC gave increasing importance to financing private-sector infrastructure projects in Latin America. It approved financing totalling $167.7 million for two telecommunications projects in Argentina and $27 million for one such project in Mexico, while providing an interest-rate hedging facility of $13.8 million to Chile's largest telecommunications operator. Other infrastructure projects for which IFC approved financing included the modernization of two privatized railroads in Argentina; power projects in Argentina, Belize, Chile and Guatemala; and a private port in Mexico.

IFC approved credit lines for medium-sized companies in Panama and Costa Rica and was also involved in the restructuring, conversion or expansion of a number of industrial companies in Argentina, Brazil, Guatemala, Jamaica and Mexico.

Because of the slow-down in the petrochemicals industry worldwide, many Latin American companies concentrated on consolidating and strengthening existing operations. Mexico's petrochemicals industry continued to expand, however, because of the country's improved investment climate and because downstream petrochemical industries had been opened up to the private sector. IFC approved financing totalling $73 million for modernizing and relocating glycol and ethanol amine plants of Grupo Idesa S.A. de C.V.

A wide range of technical assistance and advisory services was provided in the region by IFC, which advised small- and medium-sized enterprises and assisted Governments with capital-market development. It provided advice on privatization issues as well as on foreign direct investment. FIAS assisted the Governments of Argentina, the Bahamas, El Salvador and Paraguay on foreign direct-investment policies and institutions and was involved in foreign-investment promotion in Bolivia and Venezuela.

Central Asia, the Middle East and North Africa

As part of its reorganization at the beginning of fiscal 1993, IFC's Central Asia, Middle East and North Africa Department assumed responsibility for operations in Pakistan and the new Central Asian republics.

In fiscal 1993, IFC approved 28 projects in seven countries in the region. As at 30 June 1993, its committed portfolio included loans and investments for 74 companies in nine countries.

In support of Morocco's privatization efforts, IFC approved a syndicated line of credit of $70 million for a group of leasing companies and an equity investment of $4.3 million in a privatization investment fund. It continued to finance projects in the tourism sector. In Tunisia, IFC approved financing of $65 million in loans and syndications for an oil-development joint venture, sponsored by British Gas, as well as $3.9 million in financing for a producer of sanitary ware.

In Egypt, IFC approved an equity investment of $16.5 million in the first privatized Egyptian bank, which would serve as a model for future privatizations. Investments in a number of sectors in Pakistan were approved, including in the textiles industry ($7.5 million), hotel construction ($15 million), cement production ($38.9 million) and banking ($25 million). IFC also approved financing for Pakistan's first securities depository, for Oman's first leasing company, and for the expansion of a successful pharmaceutical group in Jordan. In Lebanon, IFC approved its first project since 1978: a syndicated line of credit of $45 million to five leading Lebanese banks and a loan for a ceramic floor-tile producer ($6 million).

IFC continued to provide technical assistance and advisory services to businesses and Governments in the region. In Algeria, Egypt, Iran, Kyrgyzstan and Pakistan, it advised Governments on various aspects of capital-market development, in particular providing assistance in developing the legal and structural framework required for securities markets, a leasing industry and the banking sector. In Iran and Jordan, IFC helped negotiate and structure joint ventures to make better use of the countries' natural resources.

FIAS provided advice on foreign direct investment to a number of Governments in the region. It completed projects in Algeria, Jordan, Morocco, Pakistan and the United Arab Emirates and began a study of ways to facilitate linkages between foreign and local firms in Egypt.

Financial operations

IFC's net income for fiscal 1993 was $142 million, representing a return of 5.6 per cent on its net worth. Net income was down from the $180 million posted in fiscal 1992 because of the low interest-rate environment and a decrease in loan-portfolio income. However, the equity portfolio continued to perform strongly. Equity income reached $155 million, up from $149 million in the

previous year. Dividends totalled $38 million, compared to $35 million in fiscal 1992, and capital gains, at $117 million, were slightly higher than the previous year.

Capital and retained earnings

At the end of fiscal 1993, IFC's net worth, the total of paid-in capital and retained earnings, came to $2.7 billion, up from $2.4 billion at the end of fiscal 1992.

Secretariat

As at 30 June 1993, IFC's regular staff numbered 831, recruited from 99 countries.

NOTE: For further details of IFC's activities, see *International Finance Corporation Annual Report 1993*, published by the Corporation.

Annex I.   MEMBERSHIP OF THE INTERNATIONAL FINANCE CORPORATION
(As at 30 June 1993)

Afghanistan, Albania, Algeria, Angola, Antigua and Barbuda, Argentina, Australia, Austria, Bahamas, Bangladesh, Barbados, Belarus, Belgium, Belize, Benin, Bolivia, Botswana, Brazil, Bulgaria, Burkino Faso, Burundi, Cameroon, Canada, Cape Verde, Central African Republic, Chile, China, Colombia, Comoros, Congo, Costa Rica, Côte d'Ivoire, Croatia, Cyprus, Czech Republic, Denmark, Djibouti, Dominica, Dominican Republic, Ecuador, Egypt, El Salvador, Equatorial Guinea, Ethiopia, Fiji, Finland, France, Gabon, Gambia, Germany, Ghana, Greece, Grenada, Guatemala, Guinea, Guinea-Bissau, Guyana, Haiti, Honduras, Hungary, Iceland, India, Indonesia, Iran, Iraq, Ireland, Israel, Italy, Jamaica, Japan, Jordan, Kenya, Kiribati, Kuwait, Kyrgyzstan, Lao People's Democratic Republic, Lebanon, Lesotho, Liberia, Libyan Arab Jamahiriya, Lithuania, Luxembourg, Madagascar, Malawi, Malaysia, Maldives, Mali, Marshall Islands, Mauritania, Mauritius, Mexico, Micronesia, Mongolia, Morocco, Mozambique, Myanmar, Namibia, Nepal, Netherlands, New Zealand, Nicaragua, Niger, Nigeria, Norway, Oman, Pakistan, Panama, Papua New Guinea, Paraguay, Peru, Philippines, Poland, Portugal, Republic of Korea, Romania, Russian Federation, Rwanda, Saint Lucia, Samoa, Saudi Arabia, Senegal, Seychelles, Sierra Leone, Singapore, Slovakia, Slovenia, Solomon Islands, Somalia, South Africa, Spain, Sri Lanka, Sudan, Swaziland, Sweden, Switzerland, Syrian Arab Republic, Thailand, Togo, Tonga, Trinidad and Tobago, Tunisia, Turkey, Uganda, United Arab Emirates, United Kingdom, United Republic of Tanzania, United States, Uruguay, Vanuatu, Venezuela, Viet Nam, Yemen, Zaire, Zambia, Zimbabwe.

Annex II.   EXECUTIVE DIRECTORS AND ALTERNATES, OFFICERS AND OFFICES OF THE INTERNATIONAL FINANCE CORPORATION
(As at 30 June 1993)

Appointed Director	*Appointed Alternate*	*Casting the vote of*
E. Patrick Coady	Mark M. Collins, Jr.	United States
Yasuyuki Kawahara	Kiyoshi Kodera	Japan
Fritz Fischer	Harald Rehm	Germany
Jean-Pierre Landau	Jerome Haas	France
David Peretz	David Stanton	United Kingdom

Elected Director	*Elected Alternate*	*Casting the votes of*
Bernard Snoy (Belgium)	Nurcan Akturk (Turkey)	Austria, Belarus, Belgium, Czech Republic, Hungary, Luxembourg, Slovakia, Turkey
Enzo Grilli (Italy)	Fernando S. Carneiro (Portugal)	Albania, Greece, Italy, Portugal
Bimal Jalan (India)	M. A. Syed (Bangladesh)	Bangladesh, India, Sri Lanka
Angel Torres (Spain)	Gabriel Castellanos (Guatemala)	Costa Rica, El Salvador, Guatemala, Honduras, Mexico, Nicaragua, Panama, Spain, Venezuela
Frank Potter (Canada)	Hubert Dean (Bahamas)	Antigua and Barbuda, Bahamas, Barbados, Belize, Canada, Dominica, Grenada, Guyana, Ireland, Jamaica, St. Lucia
Jorunn Maehlum (Norway)	Helga Jonsdottir (Iceland)	Denmark, Finland, Iceland, Lithuania, Norway, Sweden
Eveline Herfkens (Netherlands)	Ileana Ionescu (Romania)	Bulgaria, Cyprus, Israel, Netherlands, Romania

Elected Director	Elected Alternate	Casting the votes of
John H. Cosgrove (Australia)	Bong-Hee Won (Republic of Korea)	Australia, Kiribati, Marshall Islands, Mongolia, New Zealand, Papua New Guinea, Republic of Korea, Samoa, Solomon Islands, Vanuatu
Pedro Malan (Brazil)	(vacant)	Brazil, Colombia, Dominican Republic, Ecuador, Haiti, Philippines, Trinidad and Tobago
Aris Othman (Malaysia)	Jannes Hutagalung (Indonesia)	Fiji, Indonesia, Lao People's Democratic Republic, Malaysia, Myanmar, Nepal, Singapore, Thailand, Tonga, Viet Nam
Nicolas Flaño (Chile)	Julio Nogues (Argentina)	Argentina, Bolivia, Chile, Paraguay, Peru, Uruguay
Faisal A. Al-Khaled (Kuwait)	Mohamed W. Hosny (Egypt)	Egypt, Jordan, Kuwait, Lebanon, Libyan Arab Jamahiriya, Maldives, Oman, Syrian Arab Republic, United Arab Emirates, Yemen
O. K. Matambo (Botswana)	Harry M. Mapondo (Malawi)	Angola, Botswana, Burundi, Ethiopia, Gambia, Guinea, Kenya, Lesotho, Liberia, Malawi, Mozambique, Namibia, Nigeria, Seychelles, Sierra Leone, Sudan, Swaziland, Uganda, United Republic of Tanzania, Zambia, Zimbabwe
Jean-Pierre Le Bouder (Central African Republic)	Ali Bourhane (Comoros)	Benin, Burkina Faso, Cameroon, Cape Verde, Central African Republic, Comoros, Congo, Côte d'Ivoire, Djibouti, Equatorial Guinea, Gabon, Guinea-Bissau, Madagascar, Mali, Mauritania, Mauritius, Niger, Rwanda, Senegal, Togo, Zaire
Mohamed Benhocine (Algeria)	Arshad Farooq (Pakistan)	Afghanistan, Algeria, Ghana, Iran, Morocco, Pakistan, Tunisia
Ibrahim A. Al-Assaf (Saudi Arabia)	Ahmed M. Al-Ghannam (Saudi Arabia)	Saudi Arabia
Boris G. Fedorov (Russian Federation)	Alexander N. Doumnov (Russian Federation)	Russian Federation
Jean-Daniel Gerber (Switzerland)	Jan Sulmicki (Poland)	Kyrgyzstan, Poland, Switzerland
Wang Liansheng (China)	Zhang Shengman (China)	China

PRINCIPAL OFFICERS

President: Lewis T. Preston.*
Executive Vice President: William S. Ryrie.
Vice President, Capital Markets: Daniel F. Adams.
Vice President, Corporate Business Development: Makarand V. Dehejia.
Vice President, Finance and Planning: Richard H. Frank.
Vice Presidents, Operations: Wilfried E. Kaffenberger, Jemal-ud-din Kassum.
Vice President and General Counsel: José E. Camacho.
Secretary: Timothy T. Thahane.*

Director, Asia Department: Varel Freeman.
Director, Central Asia, Middle East and North Africa Department: André G. Hovaguimian.
Director, Europe Department: Edward A. Nassim.
Director, Latin America and the Caribbean Department: Helmut Paul.
Director, Sub-Saharan Africa Department: Tei Mante.

Director, Agribusiness Department: Karl Voltaire.
Director, Central Capital Markets Department: Farida Khambata.
Director, Chemicals, Petrochemicals and Fertilizers Department: Jean-Philippe F. Halphen.
Director, Corporate Finance Services Department: Philippe Liétard.
Director, Infrastructure Department: Everett J. Santos.
Director, Oil, Gas, and Mining Department: M. Azam K. Alizai.
Director, Controller's and Budgeting Department: R. Michael Barth.
Director, Corporate Planning Department: Nissim Ezekiel.
Director, Economics Department and Chief Economic Adviser: Guy Pierre Pfeffermann.
Deputy General Counsel, Legal Department: Daoud L. Khairallah.
Director, Personnel and Administration: Christopher Bam.
Director, Technical and Environmental Department: Andreas M. Raczynski.
Director, Treasury and Financial Policy Department: Robert D. Graffam.

*Held the same position in the World Bank.

HEADQUARTERS AND OTHER OFFICE

HEADQUARTERS
International Finance Corporation
1850 I Street, N.W.
Washington, D.C. 20433, United States
Cable address: CORINTFIN WASHINGTONDC
Telephone: (1) (202) 477-1234
Telex: FTCC 82987, RCA 248423, WU 64145
Facsimile: (1) (202) 477-6391

NEW YORK OFFICE
International Finance Corporation
809 UN Plaza, Suite 900
New York, N.Y. 10017, United States
Cable address: CORINTFIN NEWYORK
Telephone: (1) (212) 963-6008
Facsimile: (1) (212) 697-7020

Chapter VIII

International Development Association (IDA)

The International Development Association (IDA), established in 1960 as an affiliate of the International Bank for Reconstruction and Development (World Bank), provides assistance for the same purposes as the Bank, but primarily to poorer developing countries and on easier terms. Though legally and financially distinct from the Bank, IDA shares the same staff.

The funds used by IDA—called credits to distinguish them from World Bank loans—come mostly as subscriptions in convertible currencies from members, general replenishments from its more industrialized and developed members and transfers from the Bank's net earnings. Credits are made only to Governments, have 10-year grace periods and 35- or 40-year maturities and are interest-free.

During the fiscal year 1993 (1 July 1992 to 30 June 1993), IDA continued to promote economic development, concentrating on countries with annual per capita gross national product of $635 or less (in 1991 dollars). In fiscal 1993, IDA's 123 approved credits in the amount of $6,745.3 million were distributed among 44 countries. In addition, Samoa received $6.1 million as supplementary financing to a previous loan.

The majority of IDA funds for lending were provided by its Part I (industrialized) member countries and several Part II (developing) countries under a series of replenishment agreements. Fiscal year 1993 was the third and the last year of the ninth replenishment of IDA resources (IDA-9), which provided funds to finance commitments to IDA borrowers in fiscal years 1991-1993. During the year, one formal notification to participate in IDA-9 was received from Greece. As at 30 June 1993, at the close of the IDA-9 commitment period, donor contributions totalled 11,121 million special drawing rights (SDRs). IDA's commitment authority for fiscal 1993 amounted to SDR 4,538 million and was derived mainly from the release of the third tranche of donors' contributions to IDA-9. The commitment authority from reflows approved by the Executive Directors for the fiscal 1991-1993 period and other resouces amounted to SDR 3,304 million. Therefore, total available IDA resources for the IDA-9 period amounted to SDR 14,425 million. Against those resources, IDA made IDA-9 credit commitments of SDR 13,728 million.

In December 1992, the representatives of donor Governments reached an agreement on a tenth replenishment of IDA resources (IDA-10) of SDR 13 billion to provide funds to cover credit commitments in fiscal years 1994 to 1996.

During 1993, IDA membership rose to 155 with the admission of Armenia, Croatia, the Czech Republic, Georgia, the Marshall Islands, Micronesia, Slovakia, Slovenia, Tajikistan and the former Yugoslav Republic of Macedonia (see Annex I).

Lending operations (credits)

By 30 June 1993, IDA had made cumulative commitments totalling $77,816.4 million. In fiscal 1993, lending commitments amounted to $6,751.4 million, of which $2,770.3 million went to 27 countries in Africa; $1,165 million to four countries in East Asia and the Pacific; $2,271.2 million to five countries in South Asia; $104.4 million to two countries in Europe and Central Asia; $316.7 million to four countries in Latin America and the Caribbean; and $123.8 million to two countries in the Middle East and North Africa. India was the largest borrower with 10 credits totalling $1,532.7 million, followed by China with eight credits totalling $1,017 million.

Agriculture and rural development

In fiscal 1993, IDA approved agriculture and rural development projects in 18 countries, totalling $1,347.9 million. China received $527 million, of which $165 million went to strengthen grain marketing and $147 million to address constraints limiting agricultural productivity in Sichuan province. India received $369.7 million, of which $117 million went to increase rural incomes among tribal people in Bihar State and $106 million to accelerate growth through rural development in Rajasthan State. Pakistan was granted $83 million, of which $54.2 million was to improve productivity on waterlogged lands in Punjab province. Of $70.8 million extended to Malawi, $45.8 million supported agricultural research and extension activities on improved seeds and fertilizers.

Education

During the fiscal year, 19 countries received $1,038.2 million for education projects. India was granted $165 million to improve basic education in Uttar Pradesh and upgrade the quality of schools and access to them. Ghana received $110.1 million, of which $65.1 million was to improve primary schools by constructing classrooms and housing for teachers, lengthening school hours and providing teacher training. A $106 million credit went to Pakistan to improve access, equity and efficiency in Baluchistan's primary-education system, particularly for girls. China received $100 million for civil works, equipment, materials, specialist services and training to support lower-middle-school teacher training. Bolivia was granted $90.7 million, of which $50.7 million supported the delivery of integrated child development services to poor children between six months and six years of age.

Energy

Ten countries received credits totalling $520 million for energy-related projects in fiscal 1993. The United Republic of Tanzania received $200 million to meet the growing demand for electricity through the construction of the Lower Kihansi hydroelectric scheme. Ghana was granted $80 million to finance the country's electricity-investment programme. A $50 million credit was extended to Guinea to cover transitional costs associated with privatization of the national power utility and to improve the regulatory framework of the energy sector.

Industry

IDA granted $401.6 million for 11 industrial projects in nine countries in fiscal 1993. Of $120.9 million extended to Zambia, $100 million supported the country's parastatal-reform and privatization programme, a key component in the country's ongoing structural adjustment programme. A $100 million credit granted to Uganda supported policy and institutional reforms in the financial system. Of $65.8 million extended to Sri Lanka, $60 million supported policy and regulatory reforms in the financial sector. Ghana received $41 million to establish a revolving export-credit refinance and guarantee facility for private exporters.

Non-project credits

In fiscal 1993, 12 countries received credits amounting to $600.8 million to finance non-project areas. Ethiopia received $275 million, of which $250 million supported its structural adjustment programme designed to transform economic management and raise investment, particularly by the private sector. Zimbabwe received $125 million for the second phase of its structural adjustment programme. Bangladesh received $103.5 million, of which $100 million was for a second industrial-sector adjustment credit aimed at extending import liberalization, promoting exports and developing the private sector. A $60 million

credit extended to Kyrgyzstan supported reform efforts by providing foreign exchange for imports critical to production and for technical assistance.

Population, health and nutrition

Twelve countries received IDA credits totalling $1,104.8 million for 14 projects. India received $779 million, of which $500 million was to assist primary education, primary health care, disease control, nutrition, and compensation, redeployment and retraining of surplus workers; $194 million to improve the nutrition and health of preschool children and pregnant and nursing women; and $85 million for the country's National Leprosy Eradication Programme. A $70 million credit was extended to the Philippines to strengthen local health departments and non-governmental organizations providing health and nutrition services to the urban poor. A credit of $64.5 million was granted to Zimbabwe to finance a programme for sexually transmitted disease prevention and care.

Public-sector management

In fiscal 1993, IDA approved credits amounting to $32.6 million for five public-sector management projects in five countries. Guyana received a credit of $12 million to establish a public-sector salary structure providing longer-term employment and a related recruitment programme. In Sierra Leone, a credit of $10 million was granted to finance a technical assistance programme aimed at increasing the effectiveness of budgeting and expenditure control and accountability, standards of public administration and the efficiency of public enterprise. A $7 million credit was extended to Burkina Faso for consultants and equipment to support private-sector growth through institutional reforms.

Technical assistance

In fiscal 1993, IDA credits totalling $300.6 million were extended to nine countries for technical assistance projects. China received $160 million, of which $60 million was for technical assistance, training and equipment to strengthen the central bank and the Ministry of Finance; $50 million to provide technical assistance to strengthen the Chinese Academy of Sciences and the National Environmental Protection Agency; and an additional $50 million to help finance activities related to the country's economic reform programme. The United Republic of Tanzania received two IDA credits totalling $54.9 million, of which $34.9 million was to implement the Government's parastatal-reform and civil service–reform programme and $20 million was to improve accounting and auditing standards, the legal system and the administration of justice. A credit of $29 million was extended to Uganda to introduce new systems and equipment aimed at increasing and improving financial data at the Ministry of Finance and Economic Planning, the Uganda Revenue Authority and the Bank of Uganda.

Telecommunications

IDA credits totalling $89.1 million were extended to Guinea and the United Republic of Tanzania during fiscal 1993. The United Republic of Tanzania received a credit of $74.5 million to establish a market-oriented regulatory and policy framework for the telecommunications sector and rehabilitate and expand the local and long-distance network. Guinea received $14.6 million to support the newly created Société des télécommunications and the Office de la poste guinéenne.

Transportation

During fiscal 1993, credits totalling $584.1 million were granted to 12 countries for transportation projects. Nigeria received $153 million to improve the condition of its road networks, of which $85 million was for Oyo and Osun States and $68 million was to support a sustainable improvement programme for high-priority roads in Jigawa and Kano States. A $96 million credit was granted to Ethiopia to finance urgent rehabilitation of its main roads, particularly between Addis Ababa and Assab. A $65 million credit was extended to Honduras for institutional and regulatory reform of the country's transportation system and for improving transport infrastructure to promote export growth.

Urban development

IDA granted credits amounting to $291.2 million to six countries for urban development projects. A $110 million credit to China went to strengthen urban services in four major cities in Zhejiang province. Pakistan received $100 million to implement its national programme aimed at restoring vital infrastructure, which had been destroyed by floods in September 1992.

Water supply and sewerage

In fiscal 1993, IDA granted credits to six countries totalling $395.4 million for water-supply and sewerage projects. China received $120 million to improve Changchun Municipality's water supply and to reduce water pollution. A $92 million credit was granted to India to improve access to potable rural water-supply systems and environmental-sanitation facilities in some 1,200 villages in Karnataka State.

Secretariat

The principal officers, staff, headquarters and other offices of IDA are the same as those of the World Bank (see PART SIX, Chapter VI).

Annex I. MEMBERSHIP OF THE INTERNATIONAL DEVELOPMENT ASSOCIATION
(As at 31 December 1993)

Part I members*

Australia, Austria, Belgium, Canada, Denmark, Finland, France, Germany, Iceland, Ireland, Italy, Japan, Kuwait, Luxembourg, Netherlands, New Zealand, Norway, Russian Federation, South Africa, Sweden, Switzerland, United Arab Emirates, United Kingdom, United States.

Part II members*

Afghanistan, Albania, Algeria, Angola, Argentina, Armenia, Bangladesh, Belize, Benin, Bhutan, Bolivia, Botswana, Brazil, Burkina Faso, Burundi, Cambodia, Cameroon, Cape Verde, Central African Republic, Chad, Chile, China, Colombia, Comoros, Congo, Costa Rica, Côte d'Ivoire, Croatia,† Cyprus, Czech Republic, Djibouti, Dominica, Dominican Republic, Ecuador, Egypt, El Salvador, Equatorial Guinea, Ethiopia, Fiji, Gabon, Gambia, Georgia, Ghana, Greece, Grenada, Guatemala, Guinea, Guinea-Bissau, Guyana, Haiti, Honduras, Hungary, India, Indonesia, Iran, Iraq, Israel, Jordan, Kazakhstan, Kenya, Kiribati, Kyrgyzstan, Lao People's Democratic Republic, Latvia, Lebanon, Lesotho, Liberia, Libyan Arab Jamahiriya, Madagascar, Malawi, Malaysia, Maldives, Mali, Marshall Islands, Mauritania, Mauritius, Mexico, Micronesia, Mongolia, Morocco, Mozambique, Myanmar, Nepal, Nicaragua, Niger, Nigeria, Oman, Pakistan, Panama, Papua New Guinea, Paraguay, Peru, Philippines, Poland, Portugal, Republic of Korea, Rwanda, Saint Kitts and Nevis, Saint Lucia, Saint Vincent and the Grenadines, Samoa, Sao Tome and Principe, Saudi Arabia, Senegal, Sierra Leone, Slovakia, Slovenia,† Solomon Islands, Somalia, Spain, Sri Lanka, Sudan, Swaziland, Syrian Arab Republic, Tajikistan, Thailand, the former Yugoslav Republic of Macedonia,† Togo, Tonga, Trinidad and Tobago, Tunisia, Turkey, Uganda, United Republic of Tanzania, Uzbekistan, Vanuatu, Viet Nam, Yemen, Zaire, Zambia, Zimbabwe.

*Members of IDA are classified in two parts on the basis of the level of their contributions and voting power.

†Yugoslavia ceased to be a member of IDA effective 25 February 1993 and was succeeded by Croatia, Slovenia and the former Yugoslav Republic of Macedonia.

Annex II. EXECUTIVE DIRECTORS AND ALTERNATES AND OFFICES OF THE INTERNATIONAL DEVELOPMENT ASSOCIATION
(As at 30 June 1993)

Appointed Director	Appointed Alternate	Casting the vote of
E. Patrick Coady	Mark M. Collins, Jr.	United States
Yasuyuki Kawahara	Kiyoshi Kodera	Japan
Fritz Fischer	Harald Rehm	Germany
Jean-Pierre Landau	Jérôme Haas	France
David Peretz	David Stanton	United Kingdom

Elected Director	Elected Alternate	Casting the votes of
Bernard Snoy (Belgium)	Nurcan Akturk (Turkey)	Austria, Belgium, Czech Republic, Hungary, Kazakhstan, Luxembourg, Slovakia, Turkey
Eveline Herfkens (Netherlands)	Ileana Ionescu (Romania)	Cyprus, Israel, Netherlands
Frank Potter (Canada)	Hubert Dean (Bahamas)	Belize, Canada, Dominica, Grenada, Guyana, Ireland, Saint Kitts and Nevis, Saint Lucia, Saint Vincent and the Grenadines
Bimal Jalan (India)	M. A. Syed (Bangladesh)	Bangladesh, Bhutan, India, Sri Lanka
Enzo Grilli (Italy)	Fernando S. Carneiro (Portugal)	Albania, Greece, Italy, Portugal
Angel Torres (Spain)	Gabriel Castellanos (Guatemala)	Costa Rica, El Salvador, Guatemala, Honduras, Mexico, Nicaragua, Panama, Spain
Jorunn Maehlum (Norway)	Helga Jonsdottir (Iceland)	Denmark, Finland, Iceland, Latvia, Norway, Sweden
Wang Liansheng (China)	Zhang Shengman (China)	China
Ibrahim A. Al-Assaf (Saudi Arabia)	Ahmed M. Al-Ghannam (Saudi Arabia)	Saudi Arabia
Mohamed Benhocine (Algeria)	Arshad Farooq (Pakistan)	Afghanistan, Algeria, Ghana, Iran, Morocco, Pakistan, Tunisia
John H. Cosgrove (Australia)	Bong-Hee Won (Republic of Korea)	Australia, Kiribati, Marshall Islands, Mongolia, New Zealand, Papua New Guinea, Republic of Korea, Samoa, Solomon Islands, Vanuatu
Pedro Malan (Brazil)	(Vacant)	Brazil, Colombia, Dominican Republic, Ecuador, Haiti, Philippines, Trinidad and Tobago
Faisal A. Al-Khaled (Kuwait)	Mohamed W. Hosny (Egypt)	Egypt, Jordan, Kuwait, Lebanon, Libyan Arab Jamahiriya, Maldives, Oman, Syrian Arab Republic, United Arab Emirates, Yemen
Jean-Daniel Gerber (Switzerland)	Jan Sulmicki (Poland)	Kyrgyzstan, Poland, Switzerland, Uzbekistan
Aris Othman (Malaysia)	Jannes Hutagalung (Indonesia)	Fiji, Indonesia, Lao People's Democratic Republic, Malaysia, Myanmar, Nepal, Thailand, Tonga, Viet Nam
O. K. Matambo (Botswana)	Harry M. Mapondo (Malawi)	Angola, Botswana, Burundi, Ethiopia, Gambia, Guinea, Kenya, Lesotho, Liberia, Malawi, Mozambique, Nigeria, Sierra Leone, Sudan, Swaziland, Uganda, United Republic of Tanzania, Zambia, Zimbabwe
Boris G. Fedorov (Russian Federation)	Alexander N. Doumnov (Russian Federation)	Russian Federation
Nicolás Flaño (Chile)	Julio Nogues (Argentina)	Argentina, Bolivia, Chile, Paraguay, Peru
Jean-Pierre Le Bouder (Central African Republic)	Ali Bourhane (Comoros)	Benin, Burkina Faso, Cameroon, Cape Verde, Central African Republic, Chad, Comoros, Congo, Côte d'Ivoire, Djibouti, Equatorial Guinea, Gabon, Guinea-Bissau, Madagascar, Mali, Mauritania, Mauritius, Niger, Rwanda, Sao Tome and Principe, Senegal, Togo, Zaire

NOTE: Cambodia, Iraq, Somalia and South Africa did not participate in the 1992 regular election of Executive Directors. Croatia, Micronesia, Slovenia and Tajikistan became members after the election.

HEADQUARTERS AND OTHER OFFICES

HEADQUARTERS
International Development Association
1818 H Street, N.W.
Washington, D.C. 20433, United States
Cable address: INDEVAS WASHINGTONDC
Telephone: (1) (202) 477-1234
Telex: MCI 248423 INDEVAS
MCI 64145 INDEVAS
TRT 197688 INDEVAS
TRT 82987 INDEVAS
Facsimile: (1) (202) 477-6391

IDA also maintained offices in Paris and Tokyo.

NEW YORK OFFICE
International Development Association
809 United Nations Plaza (9th floor)
New York, N.Y. 10017, United States
Cable address: INDEVAS NEWYORK
Telephone: (1) (212) 963-6008
Facsimile: (1) (212) 697-7020

Chapter IX

International Monetary Fund (IMF)

The International Monetary Fund (IMF) intensi-fied its efforts to provide policy advice as well as financial and technical assistance to its increasingly diverse membership. During its fiscal year 1993 (1 May 1992 to 30 April 1993), IMF played a cen-tral role in supporting the transformation of the former centrally planned economies into market-based systems. Arrangements were approved for the Russian Federation, each of the Baltic States, and many of the members in Central and East-ern Europe whose economies were in transition. Both the scope and extent of the Fund's opera-tions expanded significantly, and for the first time IMF was close to achieving the universality of membership that was a goal since its founding al-most 50 years earlier.

As at 31 December 1993, IMF had a total mem-bership of 178 countries. The Czech Republic and Slovakia succeeded to the membership of former Czechoslovakia, and Tajikistan and Micronesia were admitted as new members of the Fund (see Annex I).

IMF facilities and policies

IMF provided financial assistance to its mem-bers under a variety of facilities and policies to ena-ble them to regain a viable balance of payments, economic growth and exchange-rate stability.

Stand-by arrangements, focusing on specific macroeconomic policies such as exchange-rate and interest-rate policies and designed to help coun-tries overcome short-term balance-of-payments difficulties, typically covered 12 to 18 months but could extend to three years. Extended arrange-ments were available to support medium-term pro-grammes of three years, during which time more intractable balance-of-payments difficulties, at-tributable to structural as well as macroeconomic problems, were addressed.

The structural adjustment facility (SAF), launched in 1986,[a] provided balance-of-payments assistance on concessional terms to low-income de-veloping countries to support medium-term macroeconomic and structural adjustment pro-grammes. In December 1987, the Executive Board established the enhanced structural adjustment fa-cility (ESAF),[b] which was similar to SAF in objec-tive, eligibility and programme features, but differed in scope, terms of access and funding sources. After extending ESAF for one additional

year, the Executive Board agreed in April 1993 that the experience of low-income countries under ESAF had been favourable and that the facility should be renewed and extended. The terms and conditions of the enlarged ESAF would be the same as those of its predecessor, with increased empha-sis on protecting programmes through social safety nets and contingency mechanisms; providing timely technical assistance, in cooperation with other institutions, to those groups most in need of it; and strengthening countries' administrative ability to implement reforms. During 1993, dis-bursements under SAF amounted to 21.2 million special drawing rights (SDRs) (about $29.1 million) and those under ESAF to SDR 227.3 million (about $312.2 million).

The compensatory and contingency financing facility (CCFF) assisted members to meet shortfalls in their export receipts and/or excesses in the cost of their cereal imports. Through a combination of additional financing and adjustment, contin-gency financing enabled these countries to main-tain the momentum of their adjustment pro-grammes in the face of adverse external shocks, such as declines in export earnings, increase in im-port prices and interest-rate fluctuations. During 1993, Moldova and Romania made drawings under CCFF for a total of SDR 90.3 million (about $126.1 million). IMF provided resources under the buffer-stock financing facility to assist members in financing contributions to approved interna-tional buffer stocks of commodities.

Financial assistance

IMF disbursements to its members in 1993 to-talled SDR 5.3 billion (about $7.3 billion), the same level as 1992. Disbursements under shorter-term stand-by arrangements declined substan-tially, from SDR 3.32 billion in 1992 to SDR 1.05 billion in 1993. Those under extended arrange-ments more than doubled, from SDR 0.91 billion to SDR 1.85 billion, underscoring the members' increased need for medium-term IMF resources to help them overcome structural balance-of-payments problems. Thus, in recognition of the special needs of its members and as a result of the shift to market-oriented economic systems, IMF

[a]YUN 1986, p. 1159.
[b]YUN 1987, p. 1252.

established the systematic transformation facility (STF) in April 1993 to operate through 1994. In 1993, IMF disbursed SDR 1.4 billion (about $1.9 billion) under STF to 11 countries (Belarus, Cambodia, Estonia, Kazakhstan, Kyrgyzstan, Latvia, Lithuania, Moldova, Russian Federation, Slovakia and Viet Nam).

As at 31 December 1993, IMF had 44 various arrangements in effect with member countries, with total commitments of SDR 7.7 billion (about $10.6 billion), down from 51 in effect at the end of December 1992. There were 16 stand-by arrangements (Costa Rica, Czech Republic, Dominican Republic, El Salvador, Estonia, Guatemala, Hungary, Jordan, Kyrgyzstan, Latvia, Lithuania, Moldova, Pakistan, Panama, Poland and Viet Nam); 5 extended arrangements (Argentina, Egypt, Jamaica, Peru and Zimbabwe); 3 SAF arrangements (Comoros, Ethiopia and Rwanda); and 20 ESAF arrangements (Albania, Benin, Bolivia, Burkina Faso, Burundi, Equatorial Guinea, Guinea, Honduras, Kenya, Lao People's Democratic Republic, Lesotho, Malawi, Mali, Mauritania, Mongolia, Nepal, Sri Lanka, Uganda, United Republic of Tanzania and Zimbabwe).

Liquidity

IMF's liquidity position improved considerably with the payments of the quota increases after the Ninth General Review of Quotas entered into force in November 1992. By the end of April 1993, these increases, together with the quotas of new members, raised total IMF quotas to SDR 144.6 billion, compared with SDR 91.2 billion at the end of April 1992. The quota increases enabled IMF to make more credit available to its members. (The enlarged access policy, which had enabled IMF to provide additional financing from borrowed resources to members whose payments imbalances were large in relation to their quotas, was terminated in November 1992 when the Ninth General Review of Quotas became effective.)

As at 30 April 1993, IMF liquid resources amounted to SDR 68 billion (about $95.5 billion), compared with SDR 37.4 billion (about $52.5 billion) a year earlier. Total usable resources received by IMF from payments for the increases in quotas amounted to SDR 31.1 billion, of which SDR 9.1 billion was received in SDRs (payments for the reserve asset portion of the increases, net of reserve tranche purchases in SDRs) and SDR 22 billion was received in currencies considered to be sufficiently strong to be used in IMF transactions. IMF's adjusted and uncommitted usable resources totalled SDR 52.2 billion, compared with SDR 20.9 billion a year earlier.

The Fund's liquid liabilities increased substantially from SDR 25.6 billion as at 30 April 1992 to SDR 33.7 billion as at 30 April 1993, representing primarily an increase in reserve tranche positions from SDR 21.9 billion to SDR 30.3 billion. However, outstanding borrowing by IMF decreased from SDR 3.7 billion to SDR 3.4 billion. The ratio of IMF's adjusted and uncommitted usable resources to its liquid liabilities—the liquidity ratio—nearly doubled from 81.6 per cent to 154.9 per cent over the same period.

SDR activity

During fiscal 1993, total gross transfers of SDRs reached the record level of SDR 34.2 billion, substantially higher than the previous peak of SDR 22.6 billion reached in fiscal 1984, when reserve asset payments for quota increases under the Eighth General Review took place. Transfers of SDRs among participants and prescribed holders nearly doubled to SDR 11.1 billion, mainly as a result of the substantial increase in prescribed operations associated with the use of the same-day SDR loan/repayment mechanism by members paying the reserve asset portion of their quota subscriptions and increases. Members sought more SDRs (generally to discharge obligations to IMF) than other members were prepared to sell, and IMF was unable to arrange for all the requested acquisitions. Fewer members indebted to IMF were thus able to effect repurchases in SDRs, which declined from SDR 1.8 billion in fiscal 1992 to SDR 0.6 billion in fiscal 1993. More members drew on the IMF General Resources Account (GRA) to make payments for their quota increases. As a result, IMF's holdings of SDRs in GRA increased sharply to SDR 7.93 billion from SDR 0.68 billion at the end of the previous fiscal year.

Policy on arrears

The amount of overdue financial obligations to IMF remained high during fiscal year 1993. However, as a result of the sustained implementation of IMF's strengthened cooperative strategy, the level of arrears declined for the first time in a decade from SDR 3.5 billion (about $4.9 billion) at the end of fiscal year 1992 to SDR 3 billion (about $4.2 billion) at the end of fiscal year 1993. The strengthened cooperative strategy consisted of: preventing new arrears; intensifying collaboration among the members concerned, IMF and other multilateral and official bilateral financial institutions to resolve existing protracted arrears; and implementing, as necessary, remedial and deterrent measures to prevent any new arrears from becoming protracted.

Most cases of short-term arrears were resolved during fiscal year 1993; almost all of the amount that remained outstanding was owed by members in arrears to IMF by six months or more. By the end of April 1993, seven members remained ineligible to use IMF's resources because of overdue obligations. Effective 9 August 1993, IMF suspended the voting rights of the Sudan (in arrears to the Fund since July 1984) in accordance with the Third Amendment of the Articles of Agreement, which empowers IMF to suspend the voting and related rights of a member that persists in its failure to settle overdue financial obligations to IMF.

Technical assistance and training

The demand for IMF's technical assistance and training continued to rise during fiscal 1993, primarily as a result of the shift towards market-oriented economies in the newly independent countries of the former Soviet Union as well as in Central and Eastern Europe. The increase in the number of countries with IMF-supported programmes and the acceleration of structural reforms in many member States also created a higher demand for technical assistance.

The reform of consumer subsidies figured prominently in Fund-supported programmes for a number of developing countries, as well as in policy advice provided to countries in transition to market economies. Adjustments needed to reduce budgetary outlays and provide appropriate producer incentives were accompanied by a variety of social safety-net measures, including limited transfers in cash and kind to vulnerable countries such as Central and Eastern European States, States of the former Soviet Union and developing countries like Guyana and Ethiopia.

IMF technical assistance concerning social safety nets frequently helped to clarify the options available, and therefore to shape a Government's sustainable adjustment effort. In several transition economies such as Belarus, Kyrgyzstan and Ukraine, IMF helped in subsidy reduction and restructuring of the public sector. Greece, Indonesia, States of the former Soviet Union, Brazil, Bolivia and other Latin American States—all of them countries facing severe budgetary imbalances as a result of major social-security programmes—were given assistance in the area of pensions.

The IMF Institute provided training for officials from member countries through residential and generally longer-term courses at its headquarters and at the Joint Vienna Institute. The Institute also conducted shorter courses and seminars in the field at either the national or the regional level. Moreover, it offered lecturing assistance for other training institutions and briefings for visiting groups in Washington, D.C.

The Institute offered 13 courses and three seminars for officials at IMF headquarters and eight courses and one seminar at the Joint Vienna Institute, training a total of 816 persons in a wide range of subjects. These programmes were complemented by 21 external training courses, 12 seminars for senior officials, and lecturing assistance for six other training institutions. Six training courses were organized within the former USSR and Central and Eastern Europe, and more than half the external seminars were held in the same group of countries. IMF offered similar training activities in other parts of the world, including Africa.

IMF–World Bank collaboration

Both IMF and the World Bank continued to focus on global economic issues and worked at strengthening the economies of their member States. However, the Bank remained primarily a development institution, whereas the Fund was a cooperative institution that sought to maintain an orderly system of payments and receipts between countries.

IMF's greater emphasis on structural aspects of its programmes made close collaboration between the two institutions important, particularly in the development of programmes supporting members' requests for resources assistance under IMF's structural adjustment and enhanced structural adjustment facilities.

Secretariat

As at 31 December 1993, the total full-time staff of IMF—including fixed-term and permanent employees—was 2,326, recruited from 122 countries.

NOTE: For details of IMF activities in fiscal year 1993, see *International Monetary Fund, Annual Report of the Executive Board for the Financial Year Ended April 30, 1993.*

Annex I. MEMBERSHIP OF THE INTERNATIONAL MONETARY FUND
(As at 31 December 1993)

Afghanistan, Albania, Algeria, Angola, Antigua and Barbuda, Argentina, Armenia, Australia, Austria, Azerbaijan, Bahamas, Bahrain, Bangladesh, Barbados, Belarus, Belgium, Belize, Benin, Bhutan, Bolivia, Botswana, Brazil, Bulgaria, Burkina Faso, Burundi, Cambodia, Cameroon, Canada, Cape Verde, Central African Republic, Chad, Chile, China, Colombia, Comoros, Congo, Costa Rica, Côte d'Ivoire, Croatia, Cyprus, Czech Republic, Denmark, Djibouti, Dominica, Dominican Republic, Ecuador, Egypt, El Salvador, Equatorial Guinea, Estonia, Ethiopia, Fiji, Finland, France, Gabon, Gambia, Georgia, Germany, Ghana, Greece, Grenada, Guatemala, Guinea, Guinea-Bissau, Guyana, Haiti, Honduras, Hungary, Iceland, India, Indonesia, Iran, Iraq, Ireland, Israel, Italy, Jamaica, Japan, Jordan, Kazakhstan, Kenya, Kiribati, Kuwait, Kyrgyzstan, Lao People's Democratic Republic, Latvia, Lebanon, Lesotho, Liberia, Libyan Arab Jamahiriya, Lithuania, Luxembourg, Madagascar, Malawi, Malaysia, Maldives, Mali, Malta, Marshall Islands, Mauritania, Mauritius, Mexico, Micronesia, Mongolia, Morocco, Mozambique, Myanmar, Namibia, Nepal, Netherlands, New Zealand, Nicaragua, Niger, Nigeria, Norway, Oman, Pakistan, Panama, Papua New Guinea,

Paraguay, Peru, Philippines, Poland, Portugal, Qatar, Republic of Korea, Republic of Moldova, Romania, Russian Federation, Rwanda, Saint Kitts and Nevis, Saint Lucia, Saint Vincent and the Grenadines, Samoa, San Marino, Sao Tome and Principe, Saudi Arabia, Senegal, Seychelles, Sierra Leone, Singapore, Slovakia, Slovenia, Solomon Islands, Somalia, South Africa, Spain, Sri Lanka, Sudan, Suriname, Swaziland, Sweden, Switzerland, Syrian Arab Republic, Tajikistan, Thailand, the former Yugoslav Republic of Macedonia, Togo, Tonga, Trinidad and Tobago, Tunisia, Turkey, Turkmenistan, Uganda, Ukraine, United Arab Emirates, United Kingdom, United Republic of Tanzania, United States, Uruguay, Uzbekistan, Vanuatu, Venezuela, Viet Nam, Yemen, Zaire, Zambia, Zimbabwe.

Annex II.   EXECUTIVE DIRECTORS AND ALTERNATES, OFFICERS AND OFFICES OF THE INTERNATIONAL MONETARY FUND
(As at 31 December 1993)

Appointed Director	*Appointed Alternate*	*Casting the vote of*
Karin Lissakers	vacant	United States
Stefan Schoenberg	Erika Wagenhoefer	Germany
Marc-Antoine Autheman	Michel Sirat	France
Hiroo Fukui	Naoki Tabata	Japan
David Peretz	John Dorrington	United Kingdom

Elected Director	*Elected Alternate*	*Casting the votes of*
Jacques de Groote (Belgium)	Johann Prader (Austria)	Austria, Belarus, Belgium, Czechoslovakia, Hungary, Kazakhstan, Luxembourg, Turkey
Godert A. Posthumus (Netherlands)	Oleh Havrylyshyn (Ukraine)	Armenia, Bulgaria, Cyprus, Georgia, Israel, Netherlands, Republic of Moldova, Romania, Ukraine
Roberto Marino (Mexico)	Gerver Torres (Venezuela)	Costa Rica, El Salvador, Guatemala, Honduras, Mexico, Nicaragua, Spain, Venezuela
Giulio Lanciotti (Italy)	Ioannis Papadakis (Greece)	Albania, Greece, Italy, Malta, Portugal, San Marino
Douglas E. Smee (Canada)	Garrett F. Murphy (Ireland)	Antigua and Barbuda, Bahamas, Barbados, Belize, Canada, Dominica, Grenada, Ireland, Jamaica, Saint Kitts and Nevis, Saint Lucia, Saint Vincent and the Grenadines
Jarle Bergo (Norway)	Eva Srejber (Sweden)	Denmark, Estonia, Finland, Iceland, Latvia, Lithuania, Norway, Sweden
Ewen Waterman (Australia)	Amando M. Tetangco, Jr. (Philippines)	Australia, Kiribati, Marshall Islands, Mongolia, New Zealand, Papua New Guinea, Philippines, Republic of Korea, Samoa, Seychelles, Solomon Islands, Vanuatu
A. Shakour Shaalan (Egypt)	Yacoob Yousef Mohammed (Bahrain)	Bahrain, Egypt, Iraq, Jordan, Kuwait, Lebanon, Libyan Arab Jamahiriya, Maldives, Oman, Qatar, Syrian Arab Republic, United Arab Emirates, Yemen
Muhammad Al-Jasser (Saudi Arabia)	Abdulrahman A. Al-Tuwaijri (Saudi Arabia)	Saudi Arabia
L. J. Mwananshiku (Zambia)	Barnabas S. Dlamini (Swaziland)	Angola, Botswana, Burundi, Ethiopia, Gambia, Kenya, Lesotho, Liberia, Malawi, Mozambique, Namibia, Nigeria, Sierra Leone, Sudan, Swaziland, Uganda, United Republic of Tanzania, Zambia, Zimbabwe
Konstantin G. Kagalovsky (Russian Federation)	Aleksei V. Mozhin (Russian Federation)	Russian Federation
K. P. Geethakrishnan (India)	L. Eustace N. Fernando (Sri Lanka)	Bangladesh, Bhutan, India, Sri Lanka
Daniel Kaeser (Switzerland)	Krysztof Link (Poland)	Azerbaijan, Kyrgyzstan, Poland, Switzerland, Turkmenistan, Uzbekistan
Alexandre Kafka (Brazil)	Juan Carlos Jaramillo (Colombia)	Brazil, Colombia, Dominican Republic, Ecuador, Guyana, Haiti, Panama, Suriname, Trinidad and Tobago
Abbas Mirakhor (Iran)	Omar Kabbaj (Morocco)	Afghanistan, Algeria, Ghana, Iran, Morocco, Pakistan, Tunisia
J. E. Ismael (Indonesia)	Kleo-Thong Hetrakul (Thailand)	Fiji, Indonesia, Lao People's Democratic Republic, Malaysia, Myanmar, Nepal, Singapore, Thailand, Tonga, Viet Nam
Zhang Ming (China)	Wei Benhua (China)	China
A. Guillermo Zoccali (Argentina)	Alberto F. Jiménez de Lucio (Peru)	Argentina, Bolivia, Chile, Paraguay, Peru, Uruguay
Corentino V. Santos (Cape Verde)	Yves-Marie T. Koissy (Côte d'Ivoire)	Benin, Burkina Faso, Cameroon, Cape Verde, Central African Republic, Chad, Comoros, Congo, Côte d'Ivoire, Djibouti, Equatorial Guinea, Gabon, Guinea, Guinea-Bissau, Madagascar, Mali, Mauritania, Mauritius, Niger, Rwanda, Sao Tome and Principe, Senegal, Togo, Zaire

SENIOR OFFICERS

Managing Director: Michel Camdessus.
Deputy Managing Director: Richard D. Erb.
Economic Counsellor: Michael Mussa.
Counsellor: Sterie T. Beza.
Counsellor: Leo Van Houtven.
Counsellor: Mamoudou Touré.
Director, Administration Department: Graeme F. Rea.
Director, African Department: Mamoudou Touré.
Director, Central Asian Department: Hubert Neiss.
Director, European I Department: Massimo Russo.
Director, European II Department: John Odling-Smee.
Director, External Relations Department: Shailendra J. Anjaria.
Director, Fiscal Affairs Department: Vito Tanzi.
Director, IMF Institute: Patrick B. de Fontenay.
General Counsel, Legal Department: François P. Gianviti.

Director, Middle Eastern Department: Paul Chabrier.
Director, Monetary and Exchange Affairs Department: J. B. Zulu.
Director, Policy Development and Review Department: John T. Boorman.
Director, Research Department: Michael Mussa.
Secretary, Secretary's Department: Leo Van Houtven.
Director, South-East Asia and Pacific Department: Kunio Saito.
Director, Statistics Department: John B. McLenaghan.
Treasurer, Treasurer's Department: David Williams.
Director, Western Hemisphere Department: Sterie T. Beza.
Director, Bureau of Computing Services: Warren N. Minami.
Director, Bureau of Language Services: Patrick Delannoy.
Director, Office in Europe (Paris): Joaquín Ferrán.
Director and Special Trade Representative, Office in Geneva: Helen B. Junz.
Director, Office of Budget and Planning: Lindsay A. Wolfe.
Director, Office of Internal Audit and Review: Marcello Caiola.

HEADQUARTERS AND OTHER OFFICES

HEADQUARTERS
International Monetary Fund
700 19th Street N.W.
Washington, D.C. 20431, United States
  Cable address: INTERFUND WASHINGTONDC
  Telephone: (1) (202) 623-7000
  Telex: (RCA) 248331 IMF UR, (MCI) 64111 IMF UW,
    (TRT) 197677 FUND UT
  Facsimile: (1) (202) 623-4661

    IMF also maintained offices at Geneva and in Paris.

IMF OFFICE, UNITED NATIONS, NEW YORK
International Monetary Fund
1 United Nations Plaza, Room 1140
New York, N.Y. 10017, United States
  Cable address: INTERFUND NEW YORK
  Telephone: (1) (212) 963-6009
  Facsimile: (1) (212) 319-9040

Chapter X

International Civil Aviation Organization (ICAO)

The International Civil Aviation Organization (ICAO) promotes the efficiency and safety of civil air transport. Its objectives were set forth in annexes to the Convention on International Civil Aviation (Chicago, United States, 1944) which prescribe standards, recommended practices and procedures for facilitating civil aviation operations.

In 1993, scheduled traffic of the world's airlines increased to some 250 billion tonne-kilometres. The airlines carried about 1.17 billion passengers and 18 million tonnes of freight. The passenger load factor and the weight load factor on total scheduled services (domestic and international) remained unchanged at 66 per cent and 58 per cent, respectively. Air freight rose by 8 per cent to 67.7 billion tonne-kilometres, and airmail traffic increased by 3 per cent. Overall passenger/freight/mail tonne-kilometres were up by 4 per cent compared to the previous year and international tonne-kilometres increased by 8 per cent.

The ICAO Assembly held its thirtieth (extraordinary) session (Montreal, Canada, 25-26 May 1993) and elected the Czech Republic to fill a vacancy on the Council created as a result of the dissolution of Czechoslovakia on 31 December 1992.

During the year, the ICAO Council held three regular sessions. In June, the Council decided that the fact-finding investigation which ICAO initiated in 1983 regarding the shooting down of Korean Air Lines flight KAL-007 on 31 August 1983 had been completed, but stopped short of endorsing its conclusions. The Council urged States to take measures to ensure the safety of air navigation of civil aircraft. In December, the Council decided to suspend action taken in 1989 by the ICAO Assembly urging Contracting States to ban air links and suspend or terminate bilateral air transport agreements with South Africa because of its apartheid policies. The Council's decision was made in the light of the General Assembly's October 1993 move to lift its sanctions against South Africa (**resolution 48/1**).

In 1993, membership of ICAO rose to 182 with the admission of Belarus, Bosnia and Herzegovina, the Czech Republic, Eritrea, Kyrgyzstan, Slovakia, Tajikistan, the former Yugoslav Republic of Macedonia and Turkmenistan.

Activities in 1993

Air navigation

In the area of air navigation, ICAO continued to update and implement its specifications and regional plans. The specifications consisted of International Standards and Recommended Practices contained in 18 technical annexes to the Chicago Convention and Procedures for Air Navigation Services. To promote their uniform application, ICAO made available guidance material consisting of new and revised technical manuals and circulars. The ICAO regional offices continued to be the principal means of assisting States in implementing regional plans, which covered air navigation facilities and services required for international air navigation in the nine ICAO regions. ICAO's efforts were supplemented by experts who advised States on installing new facilities and services and operating existing ones.

Six air navigation meetings recommended changes to ICAO specifications—among them, the Third Asia/Pacific (ASIA/PAC) Regional Air Navigation Meeting (Bangkok, Thailand, 19 April-6 May), which discussed the new ICAO communications, navigation, surveillance and air traffic management (CNS/ATM) systems and made important decisions governing the transition plan from the existing aviation infrastructure in the ASIA/PAC region to the modern space-age environment. The Fourth Meeting of the Special Committee for the Monitoring and Coordination of Development and Transition Planning for the Future Air Navigation System (Montreal, 15 September-1 October) completed its final version of the global coordinated plan for the transition to the ICAO CNS/ATM systems.

Other project areas that received special attention in 1993 included accident and incident investigation and reporting, aerodromes, airport and airspace congestion, audiovisual training aids, aviation environmental matters, aviation medicine, bird strikes to aircraft, common geodetic reference, aircraft airworthiness, controlled flight into terrain, flight safety and accident prevention, flight safety and human factors, meteorology, telecommunications and search and rescue.

Air transport

ICAO continued in 1993 to collect and publish data on traffic, finances, fleet and personnel of commercial air carriers; traffic and finances of international airports and route facilities; aircraft accidents; civil aircraft on register; general aviation activities and civilian pilot licences.

A meeting of the statistics panel (Montreal, 29 November-3 December) reviewed the status of statistics reporting to ICAO and provided advice on possible measures for improvement. The Technical Advisory Group on Machine Readable Travel Documents (Montreal, 6-9 July) finalized specifications for machine readable official travel documents and for a machine readable crew member certificate. A Facilitation Area Meeting (New Delhi, India, 30 August-3 September) discussed a wide range of facilitation problems in Asia and the Pacific. The Pacific Area Traffic Forecasting Group (Tokyo, 12-23 April) developed traffic forecasts for Asia and the Pacific to assist in developing air navigation systems planning. Workshops and seminars were held on forecasting and economic planning (Cairo, Egypt, 29 March-2 April); statistics (Beijing, China, 29 March-2 April); air transport regulatory policy (Quito, Ecuador, 19-23 April; Budapest, Hungary, 24-28 May; Cairo, 18-22 October); and airport and route facility management (Nairobi, Kenya, 4-8 October; Vienna, 13-17 December).

ICAO continued to cooperate closely with other international organizations such as the International Air Transport Association, the Airports Council International, the Customs Cooperation Council, the World Tourism Organization, the International Organization for Standardization, the International Maritime Organization and the Universal Postal Union. It also continued to provide secretariat services to three independent regional civil aviation bodies—the African Civil Aviation Commission, the European Civil Aviation Conference and the Latin American Civil Aviation Commission.

ICAO maintained its responsibilities for the administration of the Danish and the Icelandic joint financing agreements for air navigation services, to which 22 Governments were contracting parties in 1993. The two agreements, signed in 1956 and amended in 1982, concern the provision of certain air navigation services for Greenland and the Faeroe Islands and in Iceland.

Legal matters

In March, the ICAO Council considered the general work programme of the Legal Committee, approved by the Council in 1992,[a] and agreed that a rapporteur should be appointed for the establishment of a legal framework for global navigation satellite systems. A rapporteur was appointed in July.

A regional seminar, attended by 30 delegates from 17 States of East and West Africa, was held (Mauritius, 1-3 December) to discuss major issues and challenges in the legal field.

The following ratifications, adherences or successions to the 1944 Convention on International Civil Aviation, ICAO's constituent instrument, and to certain conventions and protocols on international air law were registered in 1993:

Convention on International Civil Aviation (Chicago, 1944)
Belarus, Bosnia and Herzegovina, Czech Republic, Eritrea, Kyrgyzstan, Slovakia, Tajikistan, the former Yugoslav Republic of Macedonia, Turkmenistan
Convention for the Unification of Certain Rules Relating to International Carriage by Air (Warsaw, 1929)
Croatia, Yugoslavia (Serbia and Montenegro)
Convention on the International Recognition of Rights in Aircraft (Geneva, 1948)
Belgium, Croatia, Estonia, Hungary, Morocco, Turkmenistan
Protocol to Amend the Convention for the Unification of Certain Rules Relating to International Carriage by Air Signed at Warsaw on 12 October 1929 (The Hague, 1955)
Croatia, United Arab Emirates, Yugoslavia (Serbia and Montenegro)
Convention, Supplementary to the Warsaw Convention, for the Unification of Certain Rules Relating to International Carriage by Air Performed by a Person other than the Contracting Carrier (Guadalajara, 1961)
Croatia
Convention on Offences and Certain other Acts Committed on Board Aircraft (Tokyo, 1963)
Croatia, Czech Republic, Estonia
Convention for the Suppression of Unlawful Seizure of Aircraft (The Hague, 1970)
Estonia
Convention for the Suppression of Unlawful Acts against the Safety of Civil Aviation (Montreal, 1971)
Estonia
Additional Protocol No. 1 to Amend the Convention for the Unification of Certain Rules Relating to International Carriage by Air Signed at Warsaw on 12 October 1929 (Montreal, 1975)
Croatia, Cyprus, Yugoslavia (Serbia and Montenegro)
Additional Protocol No. 2 to Amend the Convention for the Unification of Certain Rules Relating to International Carriage by Air Signed at Warsaw on 12 October 1929 as Amended by the Protocol Done at The Hague on 28 September 1955 (Montreal, 1975)
Croatia, Cyprus, Yugoslavia (Serbia and Montenegro)
Additional Protocol No. 3 to Amend the Convention for the Unification of Certain Rules Relating to International Carriage by Air Signed at Warsaw on 12 October 1929 as Amended by the Protocols Done at The Hague on 28 September 1955 and at Guatemala City on 8 March 1971 (Montreal, 1975)
Cyprus, Turkey
Montreal Protocol No. 4 to Amend the Convention for the Unification of Certain Rules Relating to Interna-

[a]YUN 1992, p.1146.

*tional Carriage by Air Signed at Warsaw on 12 Oc-
tober 1929 as Amended by the Protocol Done at The
Hague on 28 September 1955* (Montreal, 1975)
Croatia, Cyprus, Turkey, Yugoslavia (Serbia
and Montenegro)

*Protocol for the Suppression of Unlawful Acts of Violence
at Airports Serving International Civil Aviation, Supplementary to the Convention for the Suppression of Unlawful Acts against the Safety of Civil Aviation, done
at Montreal on 23 September 1971* (Montreal, 1988)
Canada, Czech Republic, Estonia, Israel,
Monaco

*Convention on the Marking of Plastic Explosives for the
Purpose of Detection* (Montreal, 1991) (not in force)
Czech Republic, Egypt

Technical cooperation

During 1993, ICAO's technical cooperation programmes were financed by the United Nations Development Programme (UNDP), trust funds and the
associate experts programme. Total 1993 expenditures for all technical cooperation programmes came
to $39.9 million, 9.9 per cent below the amount of
$44.3 million in 1992.

ICAO had resident missions in 33 countries during all or part of 1993. It gave assistance to 82 countries in the form of fellowships; visits from experts
assigned to intercountry projects; and subcontractual
arrangements. It engaged 367 experts from 43 countries during all or part of the year, 249 on assignment under UNDP and 121 on trust fund projects
(including 7 under the associate experts programme).
The number of experts in the field at the end of
1993 was 111. A total of 675 fellowships were awarded
in 1993, 650 of which were implemented.

Equipment purchases and subcontracts continued
to represent a substantial portion of the technical
cooperation programme. In addition to UNDP and
trust fund projects, 67 Governments or organizations were registered with ICAO under its Civil Aviation Purchasing Services at the end of 1993. The
total for equipment and subcontracts committed
during 1993 amounted to $12.8 million, compared
with $13.73 million in 1992.

The following were recipients of UNDP country
projects executed by ICAO, costing a total of $21.48
million:

Africa: Botswana, Burkina Faso, Burundi, Cam-
eroon, Central African Republic, Chad, Ethiopia,
Gambia, Guinea, Kenya, Madagascar, Malawi,
Mali, Mauritania, Mozambique, Namibia, Niger,
Nigeria, Rwanda, Sierra Leone, Swaziland, Togo,
Uganda, United Republic of Tanzania, Zaire, Zam-
bia.

Americas: Argentina, Brazil, Chile, Colombia,
Dominican Republic, Ecuador, Guyana, Honduras,
Panama, Peru, Suriname, Uruguay.

Arab States: Egypt, Jordan, Kuwait, Lebanon,
Oman, Saudi Arabia, Somalia, Sudan, Syrian Arab
Republic, United Arab Emirates, Yemen.

Asia/Pacific: Bangladesh, Bhutan, Cambodia,
China, Democratic People's Republic of Korea,
India, Indonesia, Kiribati, Lao People's Democratic
Republic, Maldives, Mongolia, Myanmar, Nepal,
Pakistan, Sri Lanka.

Europe: Romania.

ICAO also executed UNDP intercountry and interregional projects in Africa, the Americas, the Arab
States, and Asia and the Pacific for some $1.5 mil-
lion.

Trust fund projects totalling $7.3 million were
executed by ICAO in Argentina, Bahamas, Bolivia,
Brunei Darussalam, Cameroon, Côte d'Ivoire, Fiji,
Guinea-Bissau, Indonesia, Iraq, Jordan, Lesotho,
Libyan Arab Jamahiriya, Morocco, Oman, Papua
New Guinea, Peru, Republic of Korea, Sao Tome
and Principe, Saudi Arabia, Sierra Leone, Trinidad
and Tobago, Viet Nam, Yemen and Zambia.

Secretariat

As at 31 December 1993, the total number of staff
members in the ICAO secretariat stood at 763: 302
employees recruited from 80 countries in the Professional and higher categories and 461 in the General
Service and related categories. Of the total, 199 persons were employed in regional offices.

Budget

Appropriations for the 1993 financial year totalled
$47,958,000.

Appropriations for 1994 were $51,317,000.

NOTE: For further details on the activities of ICAO
in 1993, see *Annual Report of the Council—1993.*

Annex I.   MEMBERSHIP OF THE INTERNATIONAL CIVIL AVIATION ORGANIZATION
(As at 31 December 1993)

Afghanistan, Albania, Algeria, Angola, Antigua and Barbuda, Argentina, Armenia, Australia, Austria, Azerbaijan, Bahamas, Bahrain, Bangladesh, Barbados, Belarus, Belgium, Belize, Benin, Bhutan, Bolivia, Bosnia and Herzegovina, Botswana, Brazil, Brunei Darussalam, Bulgaria, Burkina Faso, Burundi, Cambodia, Cameroon, Canada, Cape Verde, Central African Republic, Chad, Chile, China, Colombia, Comoros,
Congo, Cook Islands, Costa Rica, Côte d'Ivoire, Croatia, Cuba, Cyprus, Czech Republic, Democratic People's Republic of Korea, Denmark,
Djibouti, Dominican Republic, Ecuador, Egypt, El Salvador, Equatorial Guinea, Eritrea, Estonia, Ethiopia, Fiji, Finland, France, Gabon, Gam-
bia, Germany, Ghana, Greece, Grenada, Guatemala, Guinea, Guinea-Bissau, Guyana, Haiti, Honduras, Hungary, Iceland, India, Indonesia,
Iran, Iraq, Ireland, Israel, Italy, Jamaica, Japan, Jordan, Kazakhstan, Kenya, Kiribati, Kuwait, Kyrgyzstan, Lao People's Democratic Republic,
Latvia, Lebanon, Lesotho, Liberia, Libyan Arab Jamahiriya, Lithuania, Luxembourg, Madagascar, Malawi, Malaysia, Maldives, Mali, Malta,

Marshall Islands, Mauritania, Mauritius, Mexico, Micronesia, Monaco, Mongolia, Morocco, Mozambique, Myanmar, Namibia, Nauru, Nepal, Netherlands, New Zealand, Nicaragua, Niger, Nigeria, Norway, Oman, Pakistan, Panama, Papua New Guinea, Paraguay, Peru, Philippines, Poland, Portugal, Qatar, Republic of Korea, Republic of Moldova, Romania, Russian Federation, Rwanda, Saint Lucia, Saint Vincent and the Grenadines, San Marino, Sao Tome and Principe, Saudi Arabia, Senegal, Seychelles, Sierra Leone, Singapore, Slovakia, Slovenia, Solomon Islands, Somalia, South Africa, Spain, Sri Lanka, Sudan, Suriname, Swaziland, Sweden, Switzerland, Syrian Arab Republic, Tajikistan, Thailand, the former Yugoslav Republic of Macedonia, Togo, Tonga, Trinidad and Tobago, Tunisia, Turkey, Turkmenistan, Uganda, Ukraine, United Arab Emirates, United Kingdom, United Republic of Tanzania, United States, Uruguay, Uzbekistan, Vanuatu, Venezuela, Viet Nam, Yemen, Zaire, Zambia, Zimbabwe.

Annex II. OFFICERS AND OFFICES OF THE INTERNATIONAL CIVIL AVIATION ORGANIZATION
(As at 31 December 1993)

ICAO COUNCIL

OFFICERS

President: Assad Kotaite (Lebanon).
First Vice-President: S. Al-Ghamdi (Saudi Arabia).
Second Vice-President: A. de L. Gil (Brazil).
Third Vice-President: M. El Amiri (Morocco).
Secretary: Philippe Rochat (Switzerland).

MEMBER STATES

Argentina, Australia, Belgium, Brazil, Cameroon, Canada, China, Colombia, Czech Republic, Ecuador, Egypt, France, Germany, Iceland, India, Indonesia, Italy, Japan, Kenya, Lebanon, Mexico, Morocco, Nicaragua, Nigeria, Pakistan, Russian Federation, Saudi Arabia, Senegal, Spain, Trinidad and Tobago, United Kingdom, United Republic of Tanzania, United States.

PRINCIPAL OFFICERS OF THE SECRETARIAT

Secretary General: Philippe Rochat.
Director, Bureau of Administration and Services: V. Pattanayak.
Director, Air Transport Bureau: V.D. Zubkov.
Director, Air Navigation Bureau: W. Fromme.

Director, Technical Cooperation Bureau: A.R. El Hicheri.
Director, Legal Bureau: M. Pourcelet.
Chief, External Relations Office: E. Faller.
Chief, Public Information Office: Hutton G. Archer.

HEADQUARTERS AND OTHER OFFICES

HEADQUARTERS
International Civil Aviation Organization
1000 Sherbrooke Street West, Suite 400
Montreal, Quebec, Canada H3A 2R2
Cable address: ICAO MONTREAL
Telephone: (1) (514) 285-8219
Telex: 05-24513
Facsimile: (1) (514) 288-4772

ICAO also maintained regional offices at Bangkok, Thailand; Cairo, Egypt; Dakar, Senegal; Lima, Peru; Mexico City; Nairobi, Kenya; and Neuilly-sur-Seine, France.

Chapter XI

Universal Postal Union (UPU)

The Universal Postal Union (UPU), established in 1874 at Berne, Switzerland, continued in 1993 to exchange postal services among nations. It promoted the organization and improvement of postal services and the development of international collaboration in this area. At the request of its members, it participated in various forms of postal technical assistance.

In 1993, UPU membership rose to 185, with the admission of Azerbaijan, Bosnia and Herzegovina, the Czech Republic, Eritrea, Georgia, Kyrgyzstan, Slovakia, the former Yugoslav Republic of Macedonia and Turkmenistan. (See Annex I for complete membership.)

Activities of UPU organs

Universal Postal Congress

The Universal Postal Congress, the supreme legislative authority of UPU, composed of all member States, normally meets every five years. The most recent Congress, the twentieth, took place in Washington, D.C., in 1989, and the twenty-first was scheduled to meet at Seoul, Republic of Korea, in 1994.

The work of the Congress consisted mainly of examining and revising the acts of UPU based on proposals submitted by member States, the Executive Council or the Consultative Council for Postal Studies (CCPS), and of making administrative arrangements for UPU activities. The acts in force since 1 January 1991 were those of the 1989 Congress.

Executive Council

At its 1993 session (Berne, 26 April–14 May), the Executive Council—which carries out the work of UPU between Congresses—considered administrative matters and examined studies concerning international mail referred to it by the 1989 Congress.

The Council held a general discussion on monopoly and competition and reviewed general matters and the structure of UPU; regulatory aspects, pricing and remuneration of letter post; air conveyance and quality control; parcel post; postal financial services; technical cooperation; human resource management; and finance.

Consultative Council for Postal Studies

The annual session of CCPS (Berne, 11-26 October) reviewed progress achieved in implementing the Washington General Action Plan, adopted at the 1989 UPU Congress to serve as a master plan for the bodies of UPU and for postal administrations during 1990-1994. Other issues considered were the post and its markets; development of rapid services; operations and quality of service; modernization; management; human resources; technical cooperation; UPU relations with the International Organization for Standardization; multilingual vocabulary of the international postal service; and follow-up to CCPS studies.

The Electronic Transmission Standards Group, aimed at establishing a world-wide postal electronic data interchange (EDI) system adapted to postal operational needs and accessible to all UPU members, focused on standardizing EDI codes, messages and bar codes in order to provide reference tools for all administrations wishing to participate in EDI activities.

Postal security matters continued to be dealt with by the Postal Security Action Group, which focused on establishing a postal security network. Three manuals and an operational binder on postal security were made available to postal administrations. Two 2-week postal security training courses were held: one for Central and Eastern Europe (Helsinki, Finland, May) and another for Asia and the Pacific (Beijing, China, August).

During the year, symposia were held on sales programmes in the postal environment (11 and 12 October); express mail service (EMS) (13 and 14 October); and the post and the environment (12 October).

International Bureau

Under the general supervision of the Executive Council, the International Bureau—the UPU secretariat—served the postal administrations of member States as an organ for liaison, information and consultation.

During 1993, the Bureau collected, coordinated, published and disseminated international postal service information. At the request of postal administrations, it also conducted inquiries and acted as a clearing-house for settling certain accounts between them. It continued its programme of studying the operation of the international postal network and monitoring the quality of international mail circulation, and carried out six service-quality tests, two for EMS and four for ordinary mail. An update to the *Compendium of Delivery Standards*, containing information from some 90 postal administrations, and the *Manual of Quality of Service Standards—International Network* were distributed. The Bureau fielded 12 missions to 32 postal administrations to examine the state of regional postal services. Work on developing a database to facilitate the quality of service analysis started in 1993.

As at 31 December 1993, the number of permanent and temporary staff members employed by the Bureau was 155, of whom 64 were in the Professional and higher categories (drawn from 42 countries) and 91 in the General Service category. As French remained the sole official UPU language, 15 officials were employed in the Arabic, English, Portuguese, Russian and Spanish translation services.

Technical cooperation

In 1993, technical cooperation provided by UPU was financed for the most part by the United Nations Development Programme (UNDP), with UNDP/UPU project expenditures amounting to $1.9 million. Assistance was also provided through the UPU Special Fund (voluntary contributions in cash and in kind from member States) and the regular budget for a total of $1.7 million. Multiyear projects financed by UPU and in execution numbered 71; 116 experts and consultants undertook missions during the year, and 236 fellowships were awarded.

In addition, UPU provided bilateral and multilateral assistance to national postal administrations and participated in special programmes in such areas as the second United Nations Transport and Communications Decade in Africa (1991-2000),[a] the Transport and Communications Decade for Asia and the Pacific, phase II (1992-1996),[b] technical cooperation among developing countries, the action programme for the least developed countries and combating the illicit transmission of narcotic drugs by post. Fellowships and training courses were also offered by a number of countries.

The six UPU regional advisers appointed in 1991 (two in Africa, one in Latin America and the Caribbean, two in Asia and the Pacific and one in the Arab countries), monitored and assessed the progress achieved in implementing the Washington General Action Plan. Twenty-two technical assistance country projects were proposed, revised or approved for financing. UNDP approved a regional project entitled "Transformation of postal services into enterprises, modernization of administrative and operational structures" and a support project for African, Arab, Asian, European and Latin American countries.

Budget

Under UPU's self-financing system, contributions are payable in advance by member States based on the following year's budget. At its 1992 session, the Executive Council approved the 1993 budget of 29,087,690 Swiss francs, to be financed by contributions from member States. In 1993, the Council approved the 1994 budget at a total of 30,548,630 francs, also to be financed by member States.

NOTE: For details of UPU activities, see *Report on the Work of the Union, 1993*, published by UPU.

[a]YUN 1991, p. 301, ESC res. 1991/83, 26 July 1991.
[b]Ibid., p. 312, ESC res. 1991/75, 26 July 1991.

Annex I.   MEMBERSHIP OF THE UNIVERSAL POSTAL UNION
(As at 31 December 1993)

Afghanistan, Albania, Algeria, Angola, Argentina, Armenia, Australia, Austria, Azerbaijan, Bahamas, Bahrain, Bangladesh, Barbados, Belarus, Belgium, Belize, Benin, Bhutan, Bolivia, Bosnia and Herzegovina, Botswana, Brazil, Brunei Darussalam, Bulgaria, Burkina Faso, Burundi, Cambodia, Cameroon, Canada, Cape Verde, Central African Republic, Chad, Chile, China, Colombia, Comoros, Congo, Costa Rica, Côte d'Ivoire, Croatia, Cuba, Cyprus, Czech Republic, Democratic People's Republic of Korea, Denmark, Djibouti, Dominica, Dominican Republic, Ecuador, Egypt, El Salvador, Equatorial Guinea, Eritrea, Estonia, Ethiopia, Fiji, Finland, France, Gabon, Gambia, Georgia, Germany, Ghana, Greece, Grenada, Guatemala, Guinea, Guinea-Bissau, Guyana, Haiti, Honduras, Hungary, Iceland, India, Indonesia, Iran, Iraq, Ireland, Israel, Italy, Jamaica, Japan, Jordan, Kazakhstan, Kenya, Kiribati, Kuwait, Kyrgyzstan, Lao People's Democratic Republic, Latvia, Lebanon, Lesotho, Liberia, Libyan Arab Jamahiriya, Liechtenstein, Lithuania, Luxembourg, Madagascar, Malawi, Malaysia, Maldives, Mali, Malta, Mauritania, Mauritius, Mexico, Monaco, Mongolia, Morocco, Mozambique, Myanmar, Namibia, Nauru, Nepal, Netherlands, Netherlands Antilles and Aruba, New Zealand, Nicaragua, Niger, Nigeria, Norway, Oman, Pakistan, Panama, Papua New Guinea, Paraguay, Peru, Philippines, Poland, Portugal, Qatar, Republic of Korea, Republic of Moldova, Romania, Russian Federation, Rwanda, Saint Kitts and Nevis, Saint Lucia, Saint Vincent and the Grenadines, Samoa, San Marino, Sao Tome and Principe, Saudi Arabia, Senegal, Seychelles, Sierra Leone, Singapore, Slovakia, Slovenia, Solomon Islands, Somalia, Spain, Sri Lanka, Sudan, Suriname, Swaziland, Sweden, Switzerland, Syrian Arab Republic, Thailand, the former Yugoslav Republic of Macedonia, Togo, Tonga, Trinidad and Tobago, Tunisia, Turkey, Turkmenistan, Tuvalu, Uganda, Ukraine, United Arab Emirates, United Kingdom, United Kingdom Overseas Territories, United Republic of Tanzania, United States, Uruguay, Vanuatu, Vatican City, Venezuela, Viet Nam, Yemen, Yugoslavia (Serbia and Montenegro), Zaire, Zambia, Zimbabwe.

Annex II.   ORGANS, OFFICERS AND OFFICE OF THE UNIVERSAL POSTAL UNION
(As at 31 December 1993)

EXECUTIVE COUNCIL
(Elected to hold office until the twenty-first (1994) Universal Postal Congress)

Chairman: United States.
Vice-Chairmen: Cameroon, China, Hungary, Italy.
Secretary-General: Adwaldo Cardoso Botto de Barros, Director-General of the International Bureau.
Members: Argentina, Australia, Bahamas, Belgium, Benin, Brazil, Cameroon, Canada, China, Colombia, Costa Rica, Cuba, Ethiopia, Germany, Hungary, Indonesia, Italy, Japan, Kenya, Kuwait, Lebanon, Mongolia, Morocco, New Zealand, Nigeria, Pakistan, Poland, Republic of Korea, Sweden, Switzerland, Togo, Tunisia, United Arab Emirates, United Kingdom, United Republic of Tanzania, United States, Venezuela, Yugoslavia (Serbia and Montenegro), Zambia, Zimbabwe.

CONSULTATIVE COUNCIL FOR POSTAL STUDIES
(Elected to hold office until the twenty-first (1994) Universal Postal Congress)

Chairman: Russian Federation.
Vice-Chairman: Canada.
Secretary-General: Adwaldo Cardoso Botto de Barros, Director-General of the International Bureau.
Members: Algeria, Argentina, Australia, Austria, Belgium, Brazil, Canada, China, Cuba, Denmark, Egypt, France, Germany, Greece, India, Indonesia, Iraq, Ireland, Italy, Japan, Jordan, Kenya, Mexico, Morocco, Netherlands, New Zealand, Pakistan, Russian Federation, Saudi Arabia, Spain, Switzerland, Thailand, Tunisia, United Kingdom, United States.

INTERNATIONAL BUREAU

SENIOR OFFICERS
Director-General: Adwaldo Cardoso Botto de Barros.
Deputy Director-General: Jaime Ascandoni.
Assistant Directors-General: El Mostafa Gharbi, Musarapakkam S. Raman, Moussibahou Mazou.

HEADQUARTERS
Universal Postal Union
Weltpoststrasse 4
Berne, Switzerland
  Postal address: Union postale universelle
                    Case postale
                    3000 Berne 15, Switzerland
  Cable address: UPU BERNE
  Telephone: (41) (31) 350 31 11
  Telex: 912761 UPU CH
  Facsimile: (41) (31) 350 31 10

Chapter XII

International Telecommunication Union (ITU)

In 1993, the 42-member Administrative Council of the International Telecommunication Union (ITU), at its forty-eighth session (Geneva, 21 June–1 July), reviewed financial and administrative matters and decided to convene a World Telecommunication Development Conference in 1994 at Buenos Aires, Argentina.

ITU membership rose to 182 in 1993 with the admission of Andorra, the Czech Republic, Eritrea, Georgia, Kazakhstan, Micronesia, Slovakia, the former Yugoslav Republic of Macedonia and Turkmenistan (see Annex I).

Conferences

The World Telecommunication Standardization Conference (WTSC-93) (Helsinki, Finland, 1-12 March) focused on further streamlining the ITU Telecommunication Standardization Sector to increase its competitiveness in global standardization. WTSC-93 set up 15 study groups and adopted 458 new or revised recommendations submitted by them. The first World Radiocommunication Conference (WRC) was organized at Geneva (15-19 November), as was the associated first Radiocommunication Assembly (8-16 November). Among other things, the Conference set the agenda for the 1995 WRC and the preliminary agenda for the 1997 WRC. The Assembly reviewed the work achieved by the ITU Radiocommunication Sector study groups which supported the work of Conferences and issued recommendations on technical and operational questions for radiocommunication systems and services.

Radiocommunication Sector

On 1 March 1993, the Radiocommunication Sector became functional. The Radiocommunication Bureau, which supported all Sector activities, replaced the specialized secretariats of the International Radio Consultative Committee, the International Frequency Regulation Board and the former General Secretariat staff engaged in radiocommunication matters. The Bureau provided services to administrations and users in application of the ITU radio regulations, in coordination and registration of radio frequency assignments and satellite orbits, and assisted to resolve cases of harmful interference. It assigned call sign series, provided maritime mobile information services and conducted seminars and training sessions

for national frequency management requirements, in close cooperation with the Bureau for Telecommunication Development. The Bureau provided the specialized technical secretariat for the Radiocommunication Assembly and its study groups in developing recommendations for spectrum utilization and radio system characteristics. The part-time Radio Regulations Board reviewed and approved procedures for application of the radio regulations, and was consulted by the Bureau on issues of application of the radio regulations when required.

Study groups focused on spectrum management techniques, fixed satellite service, radiowave propagation in non-ionized and ionized media, science services, mobile radiodetermination, amateur and related satellite services, fixed service, broadcasting service (sound), broadcasting service (television) and inter-service sharing and compatibility.

The Bureau examined and recorded in the Master International Frequency Register 89,687 frequency assignment notices received from member countries. At the end of 1993, the Register contained particulars of 1,185,776 assignments representing 5,564,593 records.

Telecommunication Standardization Sector

During 1993, the Telecommunication Standardization Bureau's main activities included organizing the work of study groups and their working parties and completing recommendations. Excluding WTSC-93, 36 meetings were held in 1993. Twenty-four new recommendations and 21 revised recommendations were approved by members after WTSC-93, bringing the total for 1993 to 201 new recommendations and 302 revised recommendations. Thirteen recognized operating agencies and eight scientific or industrial organizations were admitted to participate in the work of the Telecommunication Standardization Sector in 1993, increasing the total number to 89 recognized operating agencies, 142 scientific or industrial organizations and 38 international organizations.

Technical cooperation

United Nations Development Programme (UNDP) assistance for ITU technical projects decreased in 1993. The Field Operations Department, however, continued to assist developing countries, especially least developed countries

(LDCs), by providing specialists from headquarters, outside experts, technical cooperation among developing countries (TCDC) missions and fellowships. It also organized workshops, study groups and seminars. In 1993, the Department handled 139 projects costing approximately $17 million. Of the 827 missions undertaken in 1993, 260 were to LDCs. In addition to organizing 65 TCDC missions and granting 410 fellowships, ITU field offices undertook 99 missions.

In Africa, 20 technical assistance projects were implemented by the Telecommunication Development Bureau (BDT) costing $3.7 million. Human resources development activities included courses on digital satellite communications technology (Lusaka, Zambia, September; Abidjan, Côte d'Ivoire, November), in English and French, respectively; study of administrative, managerial and operational aspects of the Staff Training College at Ndola (Zambia, January); a training development workshop at the Staff Training College of Zambia Posts and Telecommunications Corporation (July); telecommunication training managers meeting (Maputo, Mozambique, October); a high-level management seminar for English-speaking LDCs in Africa (Maputo, October); a training workshop for French- and Lusophone-speaking countries (Dakar, Senegal, April); and a seminar on human resources management and training for French speaking countries (Dakar, November).

In the Americas, BDT developed a regional programme on rural and low-income strata telecommunication. It provided assistance to the telecommunications training centres in the region and prepared books on telecommunication policies and on training for the Americas region. Projects, mostly financed by trust funds, provided assistance to Brazil, to research and develop the design of telecommunication equipment and modernize its telecommunication system; Colombia, to implement an advanced training programme; Costa Rica, to modernize the tariff structure of the telegraph system; Chile, to train personnel; Ecuador, to set up an information system; El Salvador, to strengthen organizations; Honduras, to improve institutional management, supply equipment and assist in maintenance; the Netherlands Antilles, to analyse optical fibre systems and evaluate tenders; Nicaragua, to strengthen the Post and Telecommunications Institute and the tariff structure for the telephone service; Panama, for tariff structures for the telephone service; Paraguay, for its telecommunications system; and Peru, to strengthen technologies and to assist in training. Advisory services were provided to Suriname. In addition, 45 missions were carried out, 14 new projects were prepared and 21 projects already undertaken were supervised. In addition to the above

projects, ITU organized 25 TCDC missions and nine seminars and meetings in the region and granted 67 fellowships.

In Asia and the Pacific, ITU focused on applying new technologies and using computer-aided management techniques. Projects were implemented to strengthen national telecommunication technical and administrative services in Afghanistan, to rehabilitate the telecommunication sector; Bangladesh, to provide experts to examine tender documents for a new earth station and prepare specifications for digital multi-access radio, examine specifications for switching systems and install a computer-aided system to acquire and analyse traffic data; Bhutan, to assist in implementing the telecommunication development plan and provide fellowship training; Cambodia, to support telecommunication development, monitor a new communications network and train personnel; China, to implement a telecommunication modernization programme; India, to upgrade All India Radio sound archives, refurbish stored material and introduce optical disc storage facilities; Iran, to establish a rural telecommunication network; the Lao People's Democratic Republic, to prepare a proposal for financing the expansion of telecommunication facilities; Nepal, to establish quality control management and to set up a repair centre; Sri Lanka, to develop telecommunication management; Tuvalu, to assist in converting the telecom billing system; and Viet Nam, to develop a telecommunications master plan and train personnel. The services of experts were provided to the Maldives and Mongolia.

The third regional telecommunication exhibition organized by ITU, "Asia TELECOM 93", was held (Singapore, 17-22 May). Human resources development activities were carried out in India, Indonesia, the Lao People's Democratic Republic and Pakistan. During 1993, ITU aimed at rebuilding a South Pacific telecommunication support programme. Among the main activities undertaken in West and South Asia were monitoring and providing support for ongoing projects and sectoral support to identify areas of assistance. Twenty-four missions were carried out, 12 projects were supervised and 14 new project proposals were prepared. Eleven missions were carried out in South-East Asia and three project proposals were prepared. The participants at the Asia and Pacific Regional Telecommunication Coordination Meeting (Bali, Indonesia, 1 and 2 December) agreed to inform ITU of all ongoing and follow-up telecommunication activities and to exchange information among all parties. A working group (Bali, 3 December) discussed telecommunication policies and strategies.

Support for developing regional telecommunication in the Arab States continued to be provided under the modern Arab telecommunication development (MODARABTEL) project financed by UNDP. The Fourth Steering Committee Meeting (Rabat, Morocco, October) assessed and approved all implemented and future activities of the project. Among them were a network on data communication, a network on management information systems in training, a network on applied research in telecommunications, a sub-network on digital cellular mobile radio systems and a network for a statistical database in telecommunications. The lead countries for those networks were Egypt, Morocco, Tunisia, Saudi Arabia and the Syrian Arab Republic, respectively. In cooperation with UNDP, technical and administrative assistance was provided to develop national telecommunication services in the Libyan Arab Jamahiriya, Saudi Arabia, the Sudan, Tunisia and Yemen. Human resources development projects relating to telecommunications were carried out in Algeria, Djibouti, Lebanon and Morocco.

Activities carried out by ITU and the Commonwealth of Independent States included rebuilding and strengthening existing networks. Funding came mostly as loans from the World Bank and the European Bank for Reconstruction and Development. The second phase of a human resources management project in Hungary was being prepared. In Europe in 1993, ITU carried out 59 missions, conducted 24 workshops and trained 474 persons, in addition to improving and updating five databases.

Activities under the special programme for LDCs included workshops on optical fibre technology (Bangladesh, October), financial management in telecommunications for Asia and the Pacific (Singapore, December) and outside plant maintenance for the Arab region (Yemen, November), and a training course on outside plant installation and maintenance for Africa (Malta, November). In addition to sending advisory missions, fellowships were granted to LDCs.

Secretariat

As at 31 December 1993, 719 officials (excluding staff on short-term contracts and project personnel) were employed by ITU either at headquarters or in the field. Of these, 10 were elected officials, 568 had permanent contracts and 141 had fixed-term contracts; 74 nationalities were represented in posts subject to geographical distribution.

Budget

The adjusted budget for 1993 totalled 137,270,950 Swiss francs or $95,327,048 (based on an exchange rate as at 31 December 1993 of $1.00 = SwF 1.44). In addition, SwF 5,301,500 ($3,681,597) was programmed for the technical cooperation special accounts budget, and SwF 8,577,400 ($5,956,527) for the supplementary publications budget.

In 1993, the Administrative Council adopted a budget for 1994 amounting to SwF 139,975,000, SwF 5,213,000 for technical cooperation and SwF 9,580,000 for the supplementary publications budget.

NOTE: For further information on ITU activities, see *Report on the Activities of the International Telecommunication Union in 1993*, published by ITU.

Annex I.   MEMBERSHIP OF THE INTERNATIONAL TELECOMMUNICATION UNION
            (As at 31 December 1993)

Afghanistan, Albania, Algeria, Andorra, Angola, Antigua and Barbuda, Argentina, Armenia, Australia, Austria, Azerbaijan, Bahamas, Bahrain, Bangladesh, Barbados, Belarus, Belgium, Belize, Benin, Bhutan, Bolivia, Bosnia and Herzegovina, Botswana, Brazil, Brunei Darussalam, Bulgaria, Burkina Faso, Burundi, Cambodia, Cameroon, Canada, Cape Verde, Central African Republic, Chad, Chile, China, Colombia, Comoros, Congo, Costa Rica, Côte d'Ivoire, Croatia, Cuba, Cyprus, Czech Republic, Democratic People's Republic of Korea, Denmark, Djibouti, Dominican Republic, Ecuador, Egypt, El Salvador, Equatorial Guinea, Eritrea, Estonia, Ethiopia, Fiji, Finland, France, Gabon, Gambia, Georgia, Germany, Ghana, Greece, Grenada, Guatemala, Guinea, Guinea Bissau, Guyana, Haiti, Honduras, Hungary, Iceland, India, Indonesia, Iran, Iraq, Ireland, Israel, Italy, Jamaica, Japan, Jordan, Kazakhstan, Kenya, Kiribati, Kuwait, Lao People's Democratic Republic, Latvia, Lebanon, Lesotho, Liberia, Libyan Arab Jamahiriya, Liechtenstein, Lithuania, Luxembourg, Madagascar, Malawi, Malaysia, Maldives, Mali, Malta, Mauritania, Mauritius, Mexico, Micronesia, Monaco, Mongolia, Morocco, Mozambique, Myanmar, Namibia, Nauru, Nepal, Netherlands, New Zealand, Nicaragua, Niger, Nigeria, Norway, Oman, Pakistan, Panama, Papua New Guinea, Paraguay, Peru, Philippines, Poland, Portugal, Qatar, Republic of Korea, Republic of Moldova, Romania, Russian Federation, Rwanda, Saint Vincent and the Grenadines, Samoa, San Marino, Sao Tome and Principe, Saudi Arabia, Senegal, Sierra Leone, Singapore, Slovakia, Slovenia, Solomon Islands, Somalia, South Africa, Spain, Sri Lanka, Sudan, Surinam, Swaziland, Sweden, Switzerland, Syrian Arab Republic, Thailand, the former Yugoslav Republic of Macedonia, Togo, Tonga, Trinidad and Tobago, Tunisia, Turkey, Turkmenistan, Uganda, Ukraine, United Arab Emirates, United Kingdom, United Republic of Tanzania, United States, Uruguay, Uzbekistan, Vanuatu, Vatican City State, Venezuela, Viet Nam, Yemen, Yugoslavia,* Zaire, Zambia, Zimbabwe.

*Refers to the former Socialist Federal Republic of Yugoslavia. No ruling was made by the policy-making bodies of the Union on the position of the former Yugoslavia in ITU bodies.

Annex II.   OFFICERS AND OFFICE OF THE INTERNATIONAL TELECOMMUNICATION UNION

ADMINISTRATIVE COUNCIL AND PRINCIPAL OFFICERS

PRINCIPAL OFFICERS OF THE UNION
Secretary-General: Pekka Tarjanne (Finland).
Deputy Secretary-General: Jean Jipguep (Cameroon).

ITU ADMINISTRATIVE COUNCIL
Algeria, Argentina, Australia, Benin, Brazil, Bulgaria, Burkina Faso, Cameroon, Canada, Cape Verde, China, Colombia, Cuba, Egypt, France, Germany, Greece, India, Indonesia, Italy, Jamaica, Japan, Kenya, Kuwait, Malaysia, Mali, Mexico, Morocco, Nigeria, Pakistan, Philippines, Republic of Korea, Romania, Russian Federation, Saudi Arabia, Senegal, Spain, Sweden, Switzerland, Thailand, United Republic of Tanzania, United States.

RADIO COMMUNICATION BUREAU
Director: Richard C. Kirby (United States).

TELECOMMUNICATION STANDARDIZATION BUREAU
Director: Theodor Imer (Germany).

TELECOMMUNICATION DEVELOPMENT BUREAU
Director: A. Ph. Djiwatampu (Indonesia).

RADIO REGULATIONS BOARD
Chairman: M. Miura (Japan).
Vice-Chairman: Mohamed Harbi (Algeria).
Members: William H. Bellchambers (United Kingdom), Gary C. Brooks (Canada), Vladimir V. Kozlov (Russian Federation).

HEADQUARTERS

International Telecommunication Union
Place des Nations
CH-1211 Geneva 20, Switzerland
Cable address: BURINTERNA GENEVA
Telephone: (41) (22) 730-5111
Telex: 421000 UIT.CH
Facsimile: (41) (22) 733-7256 (Group 2/3)
E-Mail addresses: X.400   C=CH, A=ARCOM,
                                         P=ITU, S=ITUMAIL
Internet address: ITUMAIL at ITU.CH

Chapter XIII

World Meteorological Organization (WMO)

In 1993, the World Meteorological Organization (WMO) continued its activities in accordance with the programmes and budget adopted in 1991 by the World Meteorological Congress for the period 1992-1995. The Congress meets once every four years, but the 36-member Executive Council meets annually to supervise the implementation of WMO's programmes and regulations. At its forty-fifth session (Geneva, 8-18 June 1993), the Council adopted policy and strategy principles for the fourth WMO long-term plan (1996-2005) to ensure that meteorology and operational hydrology contributed to sustainable development, the implementation of Agenda 21 of the 1992 United Nations Conference on Environment and Development (UNCED),[a] the 1992 United Nations Framework Convention on Climate Change[b] and the proposed international convention to combat desertification.[c] The Council approved the *Guidelines on the Role of National Meteorological and Hydrological Services in the Implementation of Agenda 21 and the Framework Convention on Climate Change.*

During the year, WMO continued to contribute to the International Decade for Natural Disaster Reduction (1990-2000) (IDNDR)[d] with activities focused on risk assessment and technology.

Nine States—the Czech Republic, Eritrea, Georgia, Kazakhstan, Slovakia, Tajikistan, the former Yugoslav Republic of Macedonia, Turkmenistan and Uzbekistan—acceded to the WMO Convention in 1993, bringing WMO's membership to 169 States and 5 Territories (see Annex I).

World Weather Watch

The World Weather Watch Programme (WWW), the core programme of WMO, continued to provide global observational data and processed information required by members for operational and research purposes. Its essential elements were the Global Observing System (GOS), which provided observational data for weather analysis, forecasts and warnings; the Global Telecommunication System (GTS), which offered telecommunication facilities for the rapid collection, exchange and distribution of observational data and processed information; and the Global Data-Processing System (GDPS), which provided for the processing, storage and retrieval of observational data and made processed information available.

World Weather Watch implementation

GOS, the main source of observational data needed to prepare weather analysis, forecasts and warnings, included 9,800 land stations, 7,360 Voluntary Observing Ships, 620 active drifting buoys at sea, 3,000 aircraft, and a system of at least four polar-orbiting and five geo-stationary satellites. The space-based sub-system of GOS provided valuable and continuous operational satellite data. During the year, WMO extended its cooperative agreements with satellite projects in China, the European Community, India, Japan, the Russian Federation and the United States. The Commission for Basic Systems (CBS) Working Group on Observations, at its sixth session (Geneva, 17-21 May 1993) considered the introduction of new observing technologies such as the Automated Shipboard Aerological Programme, automated aircraft observing and reporting systems and wind-profilers, into GOS.

Satellite-based telecommunications played a central role at all levels of GTS. The data-collection and dissemination missions of meteorological satellites were of utmost importance in areas where commercial telecommunications could not provide member States with cost-effective services, such as those delivered by METEOSAT satellites over Africa. The new Regional Meteorological Telecommunication Network in Region IV (North and Central America) entered its implementation phase during the year and GDPS continued to expand its information processing services. The quality of warnings, forecasts and predictions improved through the introduction of more powerful computers and/or higher-resolution analysis and forecasting systems at GDPS centres. Efforts were made to enhance the parameterization of physical phenomena in numerical models and to define needs and specifications. Activities included the design of data-processing facilities for national meteorological centres to bridge the technology gap between GDPS centres in developing countries and those in more developed countries. WMO members were invited to state their requirements for numerical weather prediction (NWP) products at

[a]YUN 1992, p. 672.

[b]Ibid., p. 681.

[c]Ibid., p. 686.

[d]GA res. 44/236, 22 Dec. 1989.

the International Workshop on Users' Requirements (Montreal, Canada, 14-17 September) with the aim of improving the quality of warnings, forecasts and predictions. The CBS Working Group on Data Processing reviewed those requirements during its eighth session (Geneva, 15-19 November) with a view to establishing procedures for experimental distribution of those products. A training seminar on the use of NWP products from advanced GDPS centres was held at Toulouse, France (20-25 September).

Instruments and methods of observation

Data quality, the development of composite observing systems and long-term data homogeneity were major objectives of the Instruments and Methods of Observation Programme. Several instrument intercomparisons were started or completed in 1993. Among those completed were the seven-year WMO Solid Precipitation Measurement Intercomparison made in 13 countries, and the WMO Wind Instrument Intercomparison in France. Canada and France started the WMO Intercomparison of Present Weather Sensors/System during the year to provide better performance characteristics and to enhance the use of automatic weather stations.

Meetings held under the Programme included sessions of the Working Group on Surface Measurements (Reading, United Kingdom, 19-23 April) and the Working Group on Upper-air Measurements (Geneva, 10-14 May).

The WMO Radiosonde Intercomparisons which started in 1984 was completed in 1993. Reports of all trials and comparisons were published in the *Instruments and Observing Methods Report* series.

Tropical cyclones

In 1993, the Tropical Cyclone Programme focused mainly on the transfer of technology to developing countries. As follow-up to the 1990 Special Experiment Concerning Typhoon Recurvature and Unusual Movement (SPECTRUM), China, in cooperation with WMO, organized the Third Technical Conference on SPECTRUM (Shanghai, 25-29 October). Like its predecessors, the conference was designed to transfer research findings from SPECTRUM to meteorologists in the typhoon region. The *Global Guide to Tropical Cyclone Forecasting* was released during the third international workshop on tropical cyclones (Santa Cruz, Mexico, November/December). The publication provided meteorologists and training institutions with the most up-to-date technique for forecasting tropical cyclones.

World Climate Programme

The World Climate Programme (WCP) consisted of the World Climate Data and Monitoring Programme (WCDMP), the World Climate Applications and Services Programme (WCASP), the World Climate Impact Assessment and Response Strategies Programme (WCIRP) and the World Climate Research Programme (WCRP).

The Intergovernmental Meeting on WCP (Geneva, 14-16 April), convened by WMO and co-sponsored by the United Nations Environment Programme (UNEP), the United Nations Educational, Scientific and Cultural Organization (UNESCO), the Intergovernmental Oceanographic Commission (IOC), the Food and Agriculture Organization of the United Nations (FAO), the United Nations Development Programme (UNDP) and the International Council of Scientific Unions (ICSU), adopted guidelines for national and international climatological activities.

The Commission for Climatology (CCl) had the lead role in implementing the WCDMP and WCASP. The eleventh session of CCl (Havana, Cuba, 15-26 February) emphasized members' responsibility for processing climate data and for submitting it to international centres and archives. WCDMP continued to expand its capacity to help member States and to improve the availability of timely climate data for research, climate change detection, impact assessment and other applications. New Climate Computing (CLICOM) software and manuals were distributed to more than 80 members and international organizations during the year. New CLICOM training tutorials were near completion and CLICOM training seminars were organized in a number of countries.

The Data Rescue in Regional Association I (Africa) (DARE) project was operational in 28 African countries in 1993. UNEP provided funding for equipment and the International Data Rescue Coordination Centre (IDCC) (Brussels), operated by the Royal Meteorological Institute of Belgium, provided training in data management. There were more than 1,300 DARE I microfilms in the IDCC inventory at the end of the year. An expert meeting on Data Rescue in Regional Association IV (North and Central America) (DARE IV) (Barbados, August) developed plans to rescue climate data in the Caribbean.

The WMO Technical Conference on Tropical Urban Climates (Dhaka, Bangladesh, 28 March–2 April) was held in cooperation with the International Council for Building Research, Studies and Documentation, the International Federation for Housing and Planning, the International Geographical Union, UNEP and the World Health Organization. The conference recommended activities to reinforce the Tropical Urban Climate Experiment, and follow-up to the Second World Climate Conference and the sustainable development agenda of UNCED.

WMO continued its collaboration with other organizations, especially in assessing the impact of energy production and use on climate. Activities included the International Atomic Energy Agency-initiated joint project on databases and methodologies for the comparative assessment of energy sources for electricity generation, the energy efficiency 2000 project coordinated by the United Nations Economic Commission for Europe and the global energy efficiency 21 project.

World Climate Research Programme

WCRP, undertaken jointly by WMO, IOC/UNESCO and ICSU, continued to organize research into the basic physical processes that determine the Earth's climate, including the refinement of models to quantify changes related to the buildup of greenhouse gases in the atmosphere.

The Global Energy and Water Cycle Experiment (GEWEX) Scientific Steering Group held its sixth session at San Diego, United States, from 1 to 5 February. Its first major field experiment was the GEWEX Continental-Scale International Project to study the energy budget and hydrological cycle of the Mississippi river basin. Proposals for similar large-scale studies were also under consideration for the catchments of rivers flowing into the Baltic Sea, the Amazon basin, several Arctic river basins, and the region influenced by the Asian monsoon.

The highlight of the Tropical Ocean and Global Atmosphere Programme during 1993 was the successful completion in February of the intensive observing period of the Coupled Ocean-Atmosphere Response Experiment (COARE) above the warm water pool in the western tropical Pacific. COARE, the largest atmospheric and oceanic field study carried out in the tropical zone since 1974, involved some 11,000 atmospheric soundings, 700 days of ship observations, 45 aircraft missions, continuous profiles of wind and temperature from four sites, and the measurement of oceanic temperature, salinity and currents from 20 moorings. A broad spectrum of atmospheric weather conditions was observed, including the behaviour of convective systems and their interaction with the ocean.

The World Ocean Circulation Experiment (WOCE), to observe global oceanic circulation at all depths during the period 1990-1997, peaked during 1993. Of the 62 hydrographic sections planned, almost half had been surveyed at least partially and 10 were completed. The successful launching of the United States-French TOPEX/POSEIDON satellite was a milestone for WOCE. The satellite's altimeter instruments provided the most accurate measurements to date of changes in global sea level.

Progress was made during the year with the Arctic Climate System Study (ACSYS) to investigate Arctic Ocean circulation and its impact on global climate. The second session of the ACSYS Scientific Steering Group was held at Hamburg, Germany (4-8 October). In the Antarctic, WCRP initiatives led to the launching of the International Programme for Antarctic Buoys, an activity to measure surface air pressure, air temperature and buoy position over an area of the southern ocean and Antarctic marginal seas.

The Atmospheric Model Intercomparison Project was conducted under WCRP auspices by the United States Department of Energy's Programme for Climate Model Diagnosis and Intercomparison. By the end of 1993, 30 groups from around the world had completed simulations of the ten-year period (1979-1988) under specified standard conditions. A range of diagnostic projects examined the ability of the current generation of atmospheric models to represent mean climate and a wide variety of climate statistics on global and regional scales.

Other meetings under the WCRP included the fifth session of the Working Group on Radiative Fluxes (San Diego, 8-12 February) and the fourteenth session of the Joint Scientific Committee for WCRP (Hamilton, Bermuda, 15-20 March).

Atmospheric research and environment

A total of 33 meetings and training courses were organized under WMO's Atmospheric Research and Environment Programme in 1993. They included the Fourth International Conference on Southern Hemisphere Meteorolgy and Oceanography (Hobart, Australia, 29 March–2 April); the WMO consultation of experts to complete the assessment of world-wide atmospheric acid deposition (Egbert, Canada, 1-5 June); the fifth meeting of the Steering Committee for Long-term Asian/African Monsoon Studies (Yokohama, Japan, 20 and 21 July); the WMO Meeting of Experts on CO_2 Measurements (Rome, Italy, 7-10 September); the International Conference on CO_2 Measurements and Analysis (Carqueiranne, France, 13-17 September); a training course on weather forecasting (Nanjing, China, 20 September–15 October); a training workshop on background atmospheric composition monitoring for the Global Atmospheric Watch (GAW) (Halkidiki, Greece, 11-15 October); and a training course on background atmospheric composition measurements (Budapest, Hungary, 1-27 November).

During the year, new GAW global observatories were established in Algeria, Argentina, Brazil, China, Indonesia and Kenya, and stations in the Global Ozone Observing System continued to provide near-real time data for WMO's periodic bulletins on the state of the Antarctic Layer during the austral spring period.

Several member States focused on the development or improvement of monthly, seasonal, and other long-period weather forecasts. The western Pacific workshop on seasonal to interannual climate variability (Melbourne, Australia, June) noted promising preliminary experiments for tropical regions that suggested the potential for improved coupled ocean-atmosphere models to capture phenomena such as the El Niño/Southern Oscillation (ENSO), which could lead to useful seasonal or even longer-term forecasts.

The *Register of National Weather Modification Projects for 1991*, the *Proceedings of the WMO Workshop on Cloud Microphysics and Applications to Global Change* and the *Report of the Third International Cloud Modelling Workshop* were published in 1993.

Applications of meteorology

Agricultural meteorology

The Advisory Working Group of the Commission for Agricultural Meteorology (CAgM) (Geneva, 6-10 September) reviewed the draft text of the Fourth Long-term Plan, approved the agenda for the eleventh session of CAgM and made recommendations on scientific lectures to be organized for the session. Scientists from meteorological, agricultural and water resources services attended workshops jointly organized by WMO and FAO on the use of agrometeorological data for effective irrigated crop production, and training in the use of the Interactive Statistics Package was provided to participants from 18 countries in Central and North America.

A joint meeting of Regional Associations III (South America) and IV (North and Central America) Working Groups on Agricultural Meteorology (Guatemala, 8-12 February) discussed the preparation of reports on the agrometeorology of sweet potatoes, oil palm, cocoa beans, date palm, coconut palms and forage maize. Among other items covered were the protection of crops from frost, pests and diseases; the requirements for biological data and the establishment of databanks; crop water requirements for rain-fed and irrigated crops; meteorological inputs to an early warning system on agricultural production; and the effects of meteorological phenomena such as *El Niño* and global warming on agricultural productivity. A meeting of the Regional Association V (South-West Pacific) Working Group on Agrometeorology (Quezon City, Philippines, 16-19 March) considered problems identified by members, and the impact of ENSO. Subjects recommended for further study included the organization of national services; studies on the agrometeorology of avocado, pineapple, mango and grapefruit; crop protection and production; the impact of tropical cyclones; agrometeorological data management; national drought plans; early warning systems; and training.

An illustrated manual on locusts and codes for transmitting pest data was published in Arabic, English and French and sent to observing stations in all countries affected by locusts.

Aeronautical meteorology

The worldwide implementation of new aeronautical meteorological codes began on 1 July, bringing to fruition years of cooperation between WMO, the International Civil Aviation Organization (ICAO) and user organizations. The new codes followed far-reaching amendments to standards and recommended practices for meteorological reports and forecasts for aviation.

Implementation of the codes required extensive training and WMO organized several training events, including regional training seminars for English-speaking countries in Central America and the Caribbean (Barbados, 4-7 May); for Spanish-speaking countries in Latin America (Bogotá, Colombia, 10-13 May); and for personnel in 15 French-speaking countries in Africa (Niamey, Niger). WMO personnel participated in ICAO regional seminars on the new codes in Nairobi, Kenya, and Cairo, Egypt, in June.

The planned satellite broadcasting of data from Washington and London over the World Area Forecast System (WAFS) also progressed in 1993. Satellite distribution of WAFS data from both cities was expected to begin in 1994.

Marine meteorology

At its eleventh session (Lisbon, Portugal, 19-30 April), the Commission for Marine Meteorology reviewed the main achievements of its programme, including implementation of the new WMO marine broadcast system under the International Maritime Organization (IMO) Global Maritime Distress and Safety System. The Commission also discussed a restructuring of the WMO Marine Climatological Summaries Scheme.

A WMO/IOC Technical Conference on Space-based Ocean Observation (Bergen, Norway, 6-10 September) provided a forum for users and potential users of data and the agencies designing and operating the satellites to exchange information.

Data from *in-situ* platforms and Voluntary Observing Ships (VOS) in particular, continued to provide essential ground-truthing for satellite observations and real-time reports for immediate use.

The key link between national meteorological services and VOS was provided by the international network of Port Meteorological Officers (PMOs). WMO organized an international seminar/workshop (London, 20-25 September) for about 50 PMOs from 30 countries, to enhance international coordination among the officers and educate them in current shipping practices, observing requirements and facilities and communications.

Public weather services

A team of experts from five countries was enlisted to prepare initial public weather services programme plans embracing: the content of forecasts and warnings; presentation and dissemination techniques, public information and education; and the exchange and coordination of hazardous weather information between neighbouring countries.

Hydrology and water resources

The first World Water Day was celebrated on 22 March to increase awareness of the need for better management of the world's water resources. Among the problems identified were: increasing water scarcity, water-borne diseases, pollution, flooding, droughts and conflicts in international river basins. The event coincided with the fourth joint UNESCO/WMO/ICSU International Conference on Hydrology Towards the 21st Century: Research and Operational Needs (Paris, 22-26 March). The Conference, which made recommendations in the areas of hydrological research, operational hydrology, interdisciplinary studies and capacity building, followed up on discussions at the ninth session of the Commission of Hydrology (Geneva, 5-15 January). The Geneva session reviewed the Hydrology and Water Resources Programme, planned activities for the next four years and made proposals for the WMO Fourth Long-term Plan. On the Commission's recommendation, WMO intensified its activities in water quality monitoring. It placed more emphasis on technical assistance in water quality assessment and management and initiated regional training workshops on water quality monitoring. A workshop on water quality on small islands was organized for Caribbean countries at St. Joseph, Trinidad and Tobago, in July.

WMO completed a UNDP-funded project to strengthen the overall capacity of the Water Resources Bureau of Papua New Guinea. The project trained personnel, set up computerized databases for water quantity and quality, undertook watershed management studies to evaluate land use and the impact of pollution from mining, and installed a pilot satellite-based telemetry station.

Meetings held under the Hydrology and Water Resources Programme included an international workshop on sea-level changes and their consequences for hydrology and water resources (Noordwijkerhout, Netherlands, 19-23 April); a workshop on global environmental change and land surface processes in hydrology, which discussed modelling and measuring problems (Tucson, United States, 17-21 May); a conference on water and environment issues (Delft, Netherlands, 3 and 4 June); and an international symposium on precipitation and evaporation (Bratislava, Slovakia, 20-24 September).

Education and training

During the year, instructors under WMO's Education and Training Programme participated in the second meeting of the Working Group on Distance and Computer-aided Learning (Boulder, United States, 10 July); the third meeting of the Standing Conference of Heads of Training Institutions of National Meteorological Services (Boulder, 11 and 12 July); and the First International Conference on Computer-aided Learning and Distance Learning in Meteorology, Hydrology and Oceanography (Boulder, 5-9 July). The Korean Meteorological Administration hosted a regional training seminar for national instructors (Seoul, 6-17 December) and the Third International Conference on School and Popular Meteorological and Oceanographic Education was held at Toronto, Canada, from 14 to 18 July.

Some 536 persons participated in 24 training events organized by WMO in 22 countries during 1993. The Organization also co-sponsored or supported 30 training events organized by members or by national institutions. The number of the WMO Regional Meteorological Training Centres (RMTCs) increased to 19 with the addition of the Nanjing Institute of Meteorology for Class I Training in Chinese and English and the Advanced Meteorological Sciences Training Centre of the Iran Meteorological Organization in Tehran for Class I, II, III and IV Training in Farsi and English. The RMTC global network trained more than 3,000 students during the 1992-1993 biennium.

Drawing on funds from various sources, WMO awarded 32 long-term and 147 short-term fellowships. The WMO Training Library continued to strengthen and expand its holdings of audiovisual training and computer-assisted learning materials to meet the increasing needs of WMO members.

Technical cooperation

In 1993, countries received technical assistance valued at $26.3 million, financed by UNDP (27.8 per cent), the WMO Voluntary Cooperation Programme (VCP) (29.2 per cent), trust funds (38.3 per cent) and the WMO regular budget (4.7 per cent). Donors contributed some $7 million to VCP, while member States provided equipment, expert services and fellowships. Some 80 countries received support for 141 VCP projects, 69 of which were completed in 1993. Eighty-one countries received assistance totalling $1.23 million from the regular budget.

The resource mobilization unit of the WMO secretariat became operational on 1 March. It initiated negotiations with major financial institutions, transnational companies, large consulting engineering firms and others, for financial support for technical cooperation projects.

Secretariat

As at 31 December 1993, the total number of full-time staff employed by WMO (excluding 26 professionals on technical assistance projects) on permanent and fixed-term contracts stood at 289. Of these, 134 were in the Professional and higher categories (drawn from 52 nationalities) and 155 in the General Service and related categories.

Budget

The year 1993 was the second year of the eleventh financial period (1992-1995), for which the 1991 WMO Congress had established a maximum expenditure of 236,100,000 Swiss francs (SwF). The budget was based on zero real growth in programmes, but for the first time, the Congress made provision for cost increases due to inflation. This afforded more stable purchasing power for programmes. Of the assessed contributions totalling SwF 55,943,762 for the year, SwF 12,069,882 remained unpaid. Total unpaid contributions due from members stood at SwF 17,634,766.

The approved regular budget for the 1992-1993 biennium was SwF 112,010,000. The accumulated cash surplus for the biennium was SwF 3.3 million. In addition to regular budget expenditure, there were extra-budgetary activities in technical cooperation projects. WMO also administered several trust funds and special accounts financed by various members and international organizations.

NOTE: For further details on WMO activities, see the *World Meteorological Organization Annual Report, 1993*, published by the agency.

Annex I.   MEMBERSHIP OF THE WORLD METEOROLOGICAL ORGANIZATION
          (As at 31 December 1993)

Afghanistan, Albania, Algeria, Angola, Antigua and Barbuda, Argentina, Armenia, Australia, Austria, Bahamas, Bahrain, Bangladesh, Barbados, Belarus, Belgium, Belize, Benin, Bolivia, Botswana, Brazil, Brunei Darussalam, Bulgaria, Burkina Faso, Burundi, Cambodia, Cameroon, Canada, Cape Verde, Central African Republic, Chad, Chile, China, Colombia, Comoros, Congo, Costa Rica, Côte d'Ivoire, Croatia, Cuba, Cyprus, Czech Republic, Democratic People's Republic of Korea, Denmark, Djibouti, Dominica, Dominican Republic, Ecuador, Egypt, El Salvador, Eritrea, Estonia, Ethiopia, Fiji, Finland, France, Gabon, Gambia, Georgia, Germany, Ghana, Greece, Guatemala, Guinea, Guinea-Bissau, Guyana, Haiti, Honduras, Hungary, Iceland, India, Indonesia, Iran, Iraq, Ireland, Israel, Italy, Jamaica, Japan, Jordan, Kazakhstan, Kenya, Kuwait, Lao People's Democratic Republic, Latvia, Lebanon, Lesotho, Liberia, Libyan Arab Jamahiriya, Lithuania, Luxembourg, Madagascar, Malawi, Malaysia, Maldives, Mali, Malta, Mauritania, Mauritius, Mexico, Mongolia, Morocco, Mozambique, Myanmar, Namibia, Nepal, Netherlands, New Zealand, Nicaragua, Niger, Nigeria, Norway, Oman, Pakistan, Panama, Papua New Guinea, Paraguay, Peru, Philippines, Poland, Portugal, Qatar, Republic of Korea, Romania, Russian Federation, Rwanda, Saint Lucia, Sao Tome and Principe, Saudi Arabia, Senegal, Seychelles, Sierra Leone, Singapore, Slovakia, Slovenia, Solomon Islands, Somalia, South Africa,* Spain, Sri Lanka, Sudan, Suriname, Swaziland, Sweden, Switzerland, Syrian Arab Republic, Tajikistan, Thailand, the former Yugoslav Republic of Macedonia, Togo, Trinidad and Tobago, Tunisia, Turkey, Turkmenistan, Uganda, Ukraine, United Arab Emirates, United Kingdom, United Republic of Tanzania, United States, Uruguay, Uzbekistan, Vanuatu, Venezuela, Viet Nam, Yemen, Yugoslavia,† Zaire, Zambia, Zimbabwe.

Territories:
British Caribbean Territories, French Polynesia, Hong Kong, Netherlands Antilles, New Caledonia.

   *Suspended by the Seventh (1975) Congress from exercising the rights and privileges of a member.

   †Refers to the former Socialist Federal Republic of Yugoslavia. The WMO governing body took no legislative action in 1993 on the membership status of the former Yugoslavia.

Annex II.   OFFICERS AND OFFICE OF THE WORLD METEOROLOGICAL ORGANIZATION

MEMBERS OF THE WMO EXECUTIVE COUNCIL

President: Zou Jingmeng (China).
First Vice-President: J. W. Zillman (Australia).
Second Vice-President: S. Alaimo (Argentina).
Third Vice-President: A. Lebeau (France).

Members: M. E. Abdalla (Sudan), A. A. Algain (Saudi Arabia), I. H. Al-Majed (Qatar) *(acting)*, M. Bautista Pérez (Spain), A. Bedritsky (Russian Federation) *(acting)*, A. Cissoko (Côte d'Ivoire), A. J. Dania (Netherlands Antilles), D.K. Dawson (Canada) *(acting)*, E. Ekoko-Etoumann (Cameroon), G. Faraco (Italy) *(acting)*, H. M. Fijnaut (Netherlands), E. W. Friday (United States), J. Hunt (United Kingdom) *(acting)*, R. L. Kintanar (Philippines), J. C. de Jesus Marques (Brazil), B. Mlenga (Malawi), T. Mohr (Germany) *(acting)*, E. A. Mukolwe (Kenya), L. Ndorimana (Burundi) *(acting)*, K. Ninomiya (Japan) *(acting)*, N. Sen Roy (India) *(acting)*, H. Trabelsi (Tunisia), J. Zielinski (Poland).

NOTE: The Executive Council is composed of four elected officers, the six Presidents of the regional associations (see below), who are *ex-officio* members, and 26 elected members. Members serve in their personal capacities, not as representatives of Governments. As at 31 December 1993, three seats in the Executive Council were vacant.

SENIOR MEMBERS OF THE WMO SECRETARIAT

Secretary-General: G. O. P. Obasi.
Deputy Secretary-General: D. N. Axford.
Assistant Secretary-General: A. S. Zaitsev.
Director, World Weather Watch Department: J Rasmussen.
Director, Basic Systems: D. C. Schiessl.
Director, World Climate Programme Department: V. Boldirev.
Director, Joint Planning Staff for the World Climate Research Programme: P. Morel.
Director, Joint Planning Staff for the Global Climate Observing System: T. W. Spence.
Director, Atmospheric Research and Environment Programme Department: F. Delsol.
Director, Hydrology and Water Resources Department: J. Rodda.

Director, Technical Cooperation Department: R. A. de Guzman.
Director, Education and Training Department: G. Necco.
Director, Administration Department: J. K. Murithi.
Director, Languages, Publications and Conferences Department: A. W. Kabakibo.
Regional Director for Africa: W. Degefu.
Regional Director for the Americas: G. Lizano.
Regional Director for Asia and the South-West Pacific: T. Y. Ho.
Special Assistant to the Secretary-General: S. Chacowry.
Secretary, Intergovernmental Panel on Climate Change: N. Sundararaman.
Acting Director, Intergovernmental Negotiating Committee for a Framework Convention on Climate Change: J. L. Breslin.

PRESIDENTS OF REGIONAL ASSOCIATIONS AND TECHNICAL COMMISSIONS

REGIONAL ASSOCIATIONS

I. Africa: K. Konaré (Mali).
II. Asia: H. A. Taravat (Iran).
III. South America: W. Castro Wrede (Paraguay)
IV. North and Central America: N. Kawas (Honduras).
V. South-West Pacific: S. Karjoto (Indonesia) *(acting)*.
VI. Europe: A. Grammeltvedt (Norway).

TECHNICAL COMMISSIONS

Aeronautical Meteorology: C. H. Sprinkle (United States).
Agricultural Meteorology: C. J. Stigter (Netherlands).
Atmospheric Sciences: D. J. Gauntlett (Australia).
Basic Systems: A. A. Vasiliev (Russian Federation).
Climatology: W. J. Maunder (New Zealand).
Hydrology: K. Hofius (Germany).
Instruments and Methods of Observation: J. Kruus (Canada).
Marine Meteorology: R. J. Shearman (United Kingdom).

HEADQUARTERS

World Meteorological Organization
41, Avenue Giuseppe-Motta
(Case postale No. 2300)
CH-1211, Geneva 2, Switzerland
Cable address: METEOMOND GENEVA
Telephone: (41) (22) 730-81-11
Telex: 414199A OMM CH
Facsimile: (41) (22) 734-23-26
E-Mail: Omnet-WMO,ETR

Chapter XIV

International Maritime Organization (IMO)

In 1993, the International Maritime Organization (IMO) held the eighteenth session of its biennial Assembly (London, 25 October–5 November), at which it considered and approved its work during the previous two years. The Assembly adopted amendments to the annex of the International Regulations for Preventing Collisions at Sea, 1972, regarding changes to signals and lights, and to the annex of the International Convention for Safe Containers, 1972, to introduce the units of the International Organization for Standardization. Also adopted were 36 technical resolutions, some of which dealt with procedures for operational control; life-saving and search and rescue; fire safety; radio communications; tonnage measurement; fatigue factors in manning and safety; survey and inspection of tankers and bulk carriers; standards for ship manoeuvrability; piracy; guidelines to assist flag States; the Code for the Safe Carriage of Irradiated Nuclear Fuel, Plutonium and High-Level Radioactive Wastes in Flasks on Board Ships; and the International Safety Management Code. The Assembly adopted the 1994-1995 IMO budget and elected 32 member States to serve during the 1994-1995 biennium on the IMO Council—IMO's governing body between Assembly sessions. It also adopted amendments to the IMO Convention which would increase the Council's membership from 32 to 40. The amendments were to enter into force 12 months after being accepted by two thirds of IMO member States.

During the year, IMO membership rose to 147 with the acceptance of the IMO Convention by Albania, Bosnia and Herzegovina, the Czech Republic, Eritrea, Georgia, Latvia, Paraguay, Slovakia, Slovenia, the former Yugoslav Republic of Macedonia and Turkmenistan (see Annex I for complete membership).

In May, the Joint United Nations/IMO Conference of Plenipotentiaries adopted the Convention on Maritime Liens and Mortgages. The Convention would improve conditions for ship financing and the development of national merchant fleets and promote international uniformity in maritime liens and mortgages. The Convention opened for signature on 1 September and was to enter into force six months following the date on which 10 States had expressed their consent to be bound by it.

Activities in 1993

In November, the International Maritime Prize for 1992 was presented to Yoshio Sasamura (Japan), who had served IMO from 1964 to 1989 in various capacities, including as Secretary of IMO's Maritime Safety Committee and as Assistant Secretary-General. The prize is awarded annually to the individual or organization judged to have done the most to promote the objectives of IMO.

The theme for World Maritime Day, which was observed at IMO headquarters in London on 29 September, was "Implementation of IMO standards—the key to success".

World Maritime University

In December, 95 students representing 55 countries graduated from the World Maritime University at Malmö, Sweden. The University was founded by IMO in 1983 to provide advanced postgraduate training in maritime administration, environmental protection, port and shipping management, maritime education and training and maritime safety administration.

In 1993, the University received a grant of $1 million from the Seafarers Trust of the International Transport Workers Federation (ITF), part of which would be used to endow an ITF chair in the human factor in maritime safety.

Prevention of pollution

Amendments adopted in 1991 to annex I (oil pollution) and annex V (garbage pollution) of the International Convention for the Prevention of Pollution from Ships, 1973, as modified by the Protocol of 1978 relating thereto (MARPOL 73/78), entered into force on 4 April. The amendments to annex I required oil tankers of 150 gross tons (gt) and above and ships other than tankers of 400 gt and above to carry a shipboard oil pollution emergency plan approved by the Administration of the country whose flag the ship flew. The amendments to annex V designated the Wider Caribbean area (the Caribbean, the Gulf of Mexico and other seas and bays extending as far south as French Guiana) as one of the special areas where garbage dumping would be strictly controlled. In October, IMO launched a $5.5 million Wider Caribbean Initiative on Ship-Generated Waste to reduce the discharge of all forms of such wastes in the region.

In addition, 1992 amendments to MARPOL 73/78 entered into force on 6 July,[a] requiring tankers to be fitted with double hulls to protect against oil pollution in the event of collision or stranding. Alternative methods providing the same level of protection for the cargo were acceptable. The amendments also reduced the amount of oil tankers are permitted to discharge into the sea from 60 litres to 30 litres per nautical mile.

In November, the contracting parties to the 1972 Convention on the Prevention of Marine Pollution by Dumping of Wastes and Other Matter (the London Convention) agreed to ban the dumping into the sea of low-level radioactive wastes such as those from nuclear power production and from the industrial, medical and research uses of radioisotopes. They also adopted amendments to the Convention banning the incineration at sea of industrial wastes and phasing out the dumping of industrial wastes by 31 December 1995. The amendments were to enter into force on 19 February 1994, 100 days after their adoption.

Regarding the prevention of air pollution from ships, IMO's Marine Environment Protection Committee began preparing a new annex to MARPOL 73/78 to reduce pollution by nitrogen oxides, sulphur oxides and volatile organic compounds and to control incineration and fuel oil quality. The annex was expected to be completed in 1994.

Ship security and safety of life at sea

A protocol to the 1977 Torremolinos International Convention for the Safety of Fishing Vessels was adopted on 2 April at an international conference at Torremolinos, Spain, to amend the parent Convention, which had never entered into force and had become outdated. Taking into account recent developments in fishing and fishing vessel technology, the Protocol addressed safety provisions such as automatically controlled machinery spaces, improved life-saving appliances, immersion suits and thermal protective aids, satellite communication systems and other components of the Global Maritime Distress and Safety System.

On 1 August, new regulations intended to improve shipping safety and aid search and rescue operations came into force. The regulations, contained in amendments to the 1974 International Convention for the Safety of Life at Sea (SOLAS), made it mandatory for all ships of 300 gt and above to be fitted with the NAVTEX system—which transmits printed maritime safety information telegraphically—and with emergency position-indicating radio beacons.

In 1993, the IMO Assembly adopted the International Safety Management Code, which was designed to provide an international standard for the safe management and operation of ships and for pollution prevention. It was expected to be used as the basis for a new chapter in the 1974 SOLAS Convention. The Assembly adopted resolutions dealing with life-saving and search and rescue operations concerning marking inflatable life-rafts; training requirements for crews of fast rescue boats; conditions for the approval of servicing stations for inflatable life-rafts; symbols related to life-saving appliances and arrangements; and minimum training requirements for personnel nominated to assist passengers in emergency situations on passenger ships. In addition, four resolutions were adopted on fire safety, dealing with fire-resistant materials, sprinkler systems, fire safety information and lighting to indicate escape routes.

Unlawful acts at sea

In February and March, a working group on piracy and armed robbery visited three States in the Strait of Malacca region—Indonesia, Malaysia and Singapore—where some 200 attacks on shipping had been reported in 1991. A series of measures designed to combat incidents of piracy and armed robbery were adopted by the IMO Assembly based on the recommendations of the working group.

Secretariat

As at 31 December 1993, the IMO secretariat employed 297 staff members. Of these, 115 were in the Professional and higher categories and 182 were in the General Service and related categories.

Budget

In 1993, the IMO Assembly approved a work programme and budget of 34,328,800 pounds sterling for 1994-1995: 16,724,200 pounds for 1994 and 17,604,600 pounds for 1995.

[a] YUN 1992, p. 1162.

Annex I.   MEMBERSHIP OF THE INTERNATIONAL MARITIME ORGANIZATION
(As at 31 December 1993)

Albania, Algeria, Angola, Antigua and Barbuda, Argentina, Australia, Austria, Bahamas, Bahrain, Bangladesh, Barbados, Belgium, Belize, Benin, Bolivia, Bosnia and Herzegovina, Brazil, Brunei Darussalam, Bulgaria, Cambodia, Cameroon, Canada, Cape Verde, Chile, China, Colombia, Congo, Costa Rica, Côte d'Ivoire, Croatia, Cuba, Cyprus, Czech Republic, Democratic People's Republic of Korea, Denmark, Djibouti, Dominica, Dominican Republic, Ecuador, Egypt, El Salvador, Equatorial Guinea, Eritrea, Estonia, Ethiopia, Fiji, Finland, France, Gabon, Gambia, Georgia, Germany, Ghana, Greece, Guatemala, Guinea, Guinea-Bissau, Guyana, Haiti, Honduras, Hungary, Iceland, India, Indonesia, Iran, Iraq, Ireland, Israel, Italy, Jamaica, Japan, Jordan, Kenya, Kuwait, Latvia, Lebanon, Liberia, Libyan Arab Jamahiriya, Luxembourg, Madagascar, Malawi, Malaysia, Maldives, Malta, Mauritania, Mauritius, Mexico, Monaco, Morocco, Mozambique, Myanmar, Nepal, Netherlands, New

Zealand, Nicaragua, Nigeria, Norway, Oman, Pakistan, Panama, Papua New Guinea, Paraguay, Peru, Philippines, Poland, Portugal, Qatar, Republic of Korea, Romania, Russian Federation, Saint Lucia, Saint Vincent and the Grenadines, Sao Tome and Principe, Saudi Arabia, Senegal, Seychelles, Sierra Leone, Singapore, Slovakia, Slovenia, Solomon Islands, Somalia, Spain, Sri Lanka, Sudan, Suriname, Sweden, Switzerland, Syrian Arab Republic, Thailand, the former Yugoslav Republic of Macedonia, Togo, Trinidad and Tobago, Tunisia, Turkey, Turkmenistan, United Arab Emirates, United Kingdom, United Republic of Tanzania, United States, Uruguay, Vanuatu, Venezuela, Viet Nam, Yemen, Yugoslavia*, Zaire.

Associate members

Hong Kong, Macau.

   *Refers to the former Socialist Federal Republic of Yugoslavia. The IMO Assembly took no legislative action in 1993 on the membership status of the former Yugoslavia.

Annex II.   OFFICERS AND OFFICE OF THE INTERNATIONAL MARITIME ORGANIZATION
(As at 31 December 1993)

IMO COUNCIL AND MARITIME SAFETY COMMITTEE

IMO COUNCIL
Chairman: M.S.Tighilt (Algeria).
Members: Algeria, Argentina, Australia, Bahamas, Brazil, Canada, China, Cyprus, Egypt, France, Germany, Greece, India, Indonesia, Iran, Italy, Japan, Kuwait, Mexico, Morocco, Netherlands, Nigeria, Norway, Poland, Republic of Korea, Russian Federation, Saudi Arabia, Singapore, Spain, Sweden, United Kingdom, United States.

MARITIME SAFETY COMMITTEE
Chairman: T. Funder (Denmark).
Membership in the Maritime Safety Committee is open to all IMO member States.

OFFICER AND OFFICE

PRINCIPAL OFFICER OF IMO SECRETARIAT
Secretary-General: W.A. O'Neil.

HEADQUARTERS
International Maritime Organization
4 Albert Embankment
London, SE1 7SR, England
   Cable address: INTERMAR LONDON SE1
   Telephone: (44) (71) 735-7611
   Telex: 23588 IMOLDN G
   Facsimile: (44) (71) 587-3210

Chapter XV

World Intellectual Property Organization (WIPO)

During 1993, the World Intellectual Property Organization (WIPO) continued to promote respect for the protection and use of intellectual property through cooperation among States and ensuring administrative cooperation among the intellectual property "Unions." WIPO's three governing bodies, namely, the General Assembly, the Conference and the Coordination Committee, held their twenty-fourth series of meetings (Geneva, 20-29 September) and approved a draft programme and budget covering the period 1994-1995 in the amount of 230 million Swiss francs. They decided to apply as from 1 January 1994, for a four-year trial period covering the bienniums 1994-1995 and 1996-1997, a unitary contribution system, under which each member State would pay one contribution only, regardless of the number of contribution-financed Unions of which it was a member.

In 1993, WIPO's membership increased to 143, with Armenia, Bhutan, Bolivia, Estonia, Latvia and Saint Lucia acceding to the Convention establishing WIPO, and Bosnia and Herzegovina, the Czech Republic, the Republic of Moldova, Slovakia, the former Yugoslav Republic of Macedonia and Uzbekistan declaring continued application or succession to prior membership in the Convention (see Annex I).

Membership in the treaties administered by WIPO increased with the adherences or declarations of continued application as follows: The number of members of the Paris Convention for the Protection of Industrial Property rose to 117 with the accession of Belarus, Bolivia, Bosnia and Herzegovina, the Czech Republic, El Salvador, Latvia, the Republic of Moldova, Slovakia, the former Yugoslav Republic of Macedonia and Uzbekistan. Membership to the Berne Convention for the Protection of Literary and Artistic Works increased to 105 with the addition of Albania, Bolivia, Bosnia and Herzegovina, the Czech Republic, El Salvador, Gambia, Jamaica, Kenya, Namibia, Nigeria, Saint Lucia, Slovakia and the former Yugoslav Republic of Macedonia. The Czech Republic and Slovakia succeeded to Czechoslovakia's membership in the Madrid Agreement for the Repression of False or Deceptive Indications of Source on Goods, the Strasbourg Agreement Concerning the International Patent Classification and the Lisbon Agreement for the Protection of Appellations of Origin and

their International Registration, thus changing the memberships to 31, 27 and 17 respectively. Cuba, the Czech Republic, Greece, Poland, Slovakia, Trinidad and Tobago, and Yugoslavia (Serbia and Montenegro) acceded to the Budapest Treaty on the International Recognition of the Deposit of Microorganisms for the Purposes of Patent Procedure, bringing the number of States parties to 29. Bolivia, the Czech Republic, Greece, Jamaica, the Netherlands, Nigeria, Slovakia and Switzerland acceded to the Rome Convention for the Protection of Performers, Producers of Phonograms and Broadcasting Organizations, bringing the number of member States to 45. China, Cyprus, the Czech Republic, Greece, Jamaica, the Netherlands, Slovakia and Switzerland became parties to the Geneva Convention for the Protection of Producers of Phonograms Against Unauthorized Duplication of Their Phonograms, raising membership to 50. With the accession of Armenia, Croatia and Switzerland to the Brussels Convention Relating to the Distribution of Programme-Carrying Signals Transmitted by Satellite, this instrument's membership rose to 18. With the signatures of Belarus and Morocco, the number of adherents to the Nairobi Treaty on the Protection of the Olympic Symbol increased to 34. Bosnia and Herzegovina, the Czech Republic, Slovakia and the former Yugoslav Republic of Macedonia signed the Nice Agreement Concerning the International Classification of Goods and Services for the Purposes of the Registration of Marks as well as the Locarno Agreement Establishing an International Classification for Industrial Design, bringing the number of member States to 38 and 21, respectively. The number of States parties to the Patent Cooperation Treaty (PCT) rose to 63 with the accession of Belarus, China, the Czech Republic, Latvia, the Niger, Slovakia, Slovenia, Trinidad and Tobago, Uzbekistan and Viet Nam. Belarus, Bosnia and Herzegovina, the Czech Republic, Kazakhstan, Slovakia, the former Yugoslav Republic of Macedonia and Uzbekistan joined the Madrid (International Registration of Marks) Agreement, bringing the number of States parties to 38. With the adherence of Côte d'Ivoire and Yugoslavia (Serbia and Montenegro) to the Hague (International Deposit of Industrial Designs) Agreement, membership increased to 23. Brazil, Chile, the Czech Republic and Slovakia became parties to the Treaty on the International

Registration of Audiovisual Works, bringing the number of member States to 9.

The 17 treaties in the two main fields of intellectual property administered by WIPO in 1993 were as follows, listed in order of the year of adoption:

Industrial property: Paris Convention for the Protection of Industrial Property; Madrid Agreement for the Repression of False or Deceptive Indications of Source on Goods; Madrid Agreement Concerning the International Registration of Marks; The Hague Agreement Concerning the International Deposit of Industrial Designs; Nice Agreement Concerning the International Classification of Goods and Services for the Purpose of the Registration of Marks; Lisbon Agreement for the Protection of Appellations of Origin and their International Registration; Locarno Agreement Establishing an International Classification for Industrial Designs; PCT; Strasbourg Agreement Concerning the International Patent Classification; Budapest Treaty on the International Recognition of the Deposit of Microorganisms for the Purposes of Patent Procedure; Nairobi Treaty on the Protection of the Olympic Symbol; Vienna Agreement Establishing an International Classification of the Figurative Elements of Marks.

Copyright and neighbouring rights: Berne Convention for the Protection of Literary and Artistic Works; Rome Convention for the Protection of Performers, Producers of Phonograms and Broadcasting Organizations; Geneva Convention for the Protection of Producers of Phonograms Against Unauthorized Duplication of Their Phonograms; Brussels Convention Relating to the Distribution of Programme-Carrying Signals Transmitted by Satellite; Treaty on the International Registration of Audiovisual Works.

Activities in 1993

Development cooperation

During 1993, technical, legal, industrial and commercial training was given to government officials and personnel through courses, study visits, workshops, seminars, training attachments abroad and on-the-job training by WIPO officials or consultants. Some 90 such events were organized mainly in developing countries. In addition, 80 study visits to both industrialized and developing countries were organized for officials of developing countries to provide basic instruction on industrial property or copyright, or specialized information in areas such as: computerization of industrial property office administration, the use of computerized patent information databases (including the use of CD-ROM technology), legal and economic aspects of industrial property, the administration of the collection and distribution of copyright royalties and the use of trademarks for marketing products and services. In all, 39 developing countries, 10 industrialized countries and 9 intergovernmental organizations hosted the courses and meetings or organized them jointly with WIPO for about 6,000 people from some 118 developing countries. Besides WIPO officials, some 165 outside experts were invited as speakers, about 40 per cent of whom were nationals of developing countries.

In 1993, the WIPO Academy was created with the aim of conducting encounter sessions on current intellectual property issues, at the policy level, for middle to senior government officials from developing countries. Three sessions, one each conducted in English, French and Spanish, were held for 35 officials from 33 developing countries. WIPO also awarded the first three long-term scholarships to three developing-country nationals for intellectual property law studies in an industrialized country.

WIPO officials and outside consultants undertook 202 missions to 76 developing countries to advise government authorities on upgrading administrative procedures, computerization, the provision of patent information services and setting up organizations for the collective administration of rights under copyright law.

WIPO continued to promote the use by developing countries of the vast resources of technological information contained in patent documents through its state-of-the-art search service, supplying some 450 search reports and copies of 2,550 patent documents to 20 Governments and institutions during 1993.

In January, WIPO hosted a meeting with the member States of the Association of South East Asian Nations and in October with the member States of the Common Market of the Southern Cone, to discuss cooperation in harnessing their respective intellectual property systems to achieve common economic and trade goals.

Setting of norms and standards

In May, the fifth session of the Committee of Experts on the Settlement of Intellectual Property Disputes Between States concluded that a sixth session was necessary to examine further proposals, which was subsequently approved by the WIPO General Assembly in September. The Preparatory Meeting for the Diplomatic Conference for the Conclusion of a Treaty on the Settlement of Intellectual Property Disputes Between States, which also met in May, was to be reconvened for a second part in conjunction with the Committee of Experts' sixth session in 1994.

Regarding the Draft Patent Law Treaty, the Assembly of the Paris Union, which met in April and September, asked the WIPO Director-General to convene an extraordinary session of the Assembly, when appropriate, to fix a date for continuing the Diplomatic Conference for the Conclusion of a Treaty Supplementing the Paris Convention as far as Patents are Concerned (Patent Law Treaty). The first part of the Conference took place in 1991.[a]

A draft of the Trademark Law Treaty and Regulations was discussed by the Committee of Experts on the Harmonization of Laws for the Protection of Marks at its fifth (June) and sixth (November–December) sessions. At the latter session, the Committee of Experts reviewed the draft and agreed on various amendments. The Preparatory Meeting for the Diplomatic Conference for the Conclusion of the Trademark Law Treaty decided that the Director-General should convene the Conference from 10 to 28 October 1994.

In June, the third session of the Committee of Experts on a Possible Protocol to the Berne Convention for the Protection of Literary and Artistic Works considered the norms the Protocol might contain to clarify or widen the rights of authors and other owners of copyright.

At its first session in June, the Committee of Experts on a Possible Instrument on the Protection of the Rights of Performers and Producers of Phonograms discussed the norms a possible future multilateral treaty should contain to ensure better international protection of the rights of performers and producers of sound recordings. At its second session in November, it completed the first examination of a proposal for a new instrument and identified a number of issues for further examination.

In September, the WIPO General Assembly approved the establishment of a WIPO Arbitration Center for the resolution of intellectual property disputes between private parties as from 1 July 1994. Four dispute-settlement procedures would be available to enterprises and individuals: mediation, arbitration, expedited arbitration (designed particularly for small-scale disputes) and a combined procedure, providing for mediation and, in default of settlement through mediation, arbitration.

International registration activities

Patent Cooperation Treaty (PCT). A proposal by the International Bureau for the Bureau to become an alternative receiving office under the PCT as at 1 January 1994, was approved by the Assembly of the PCT Union in September. The Assembly appointed the Spanish Patent and Trademark Office as an International Searching Authority and designated Chinese as a language in which an official text of the PCT was to be established.

In 1993, the number of record copies of international applications received by the International Bureau amounted to 28,577, an increase of 10.26 per cent over 1992. The average number of PCT contracting States designated per international application was 31.46. International applications thus replaced some 900,000 national applications.

During the year, the International Bureau organized some 50 information and training seminars for over 3,200 persons (government officials, lawyers and representatives of private circles) to promote the PCT. In addition, briefings were given at WIPO headquarters on the PCT and its operations.

At its fifteenth session in June, the PCT Committee for Technical Cooperation approved a new list of periodicals under the PCT minimum documentation and discussed the use of optical discs as data carriers for the exchange of patent documents forming part of the PCT minimum documentation between patent offices.

A June meeting of the International Searching and International Preliminary Examining Authorities under the PCT agreed on the modification to certain sections of the Administrative Instructions and to certain forms and PCT Search Guidelines.

The International Bureau continued to cooperate with the European Patent Office (EPO) and the United States Patent and Trademark Office in developing a system to enable applicants to prepare European, United States and international (PCT) applications in machine-readable form. The system, called EASY (Electronic Application System), would allow applicants to input the various data to be given in the request; to do automatic validity checks of such data; to prepare the remainder of the international application (description, claims and abstract) using a word processor; and submit the drawings as facsimile images. The International Bureau also concluded an agreement with EPO for the inclusion of the PCT data in ESPACE-ACCESS discs (a searchable index produced by the EPO) and explored further cooperation in the use of CD-ROM technology.

The first set of some 140 CD-ROMs containing the PCT international applications published in 1989 was issued in 1993 as part of a project to issue the whole backfile (1978 to 1989) of the 66,700 published PCT applications by the end of 1994.

Madrid Agreement. In 1993, 16,498 international trademark registrations were made by the International Bureau, 5 per cent more than in 1992. As the average number of countries covered by each international registration was 10, the international registrations in 1993 had the equivalent effect of some 165,000 national registrations. There were 4,264 renewals in 1993, 21 per cent less than in 1992.

[a]YUN 1991, p. 1003.

The computerization of the International Trademark Register was completed in 1993. The entry and validation of data relating to some 280,000 international registrations in force in the System of Electronic Marks' Interrogation, Registration and Administration (SEMIRA) database were completed in May. Work continued on the Madrid Agreement and Madrid Protocol System (MAPS) and the MAPS Assisted Translation and Classification Help for Examiners System (MATCHES) computerized systems intended to facilitate the automatic classification and translation (English to French and French to English) of terms appearing in the list of goods and services under the Nice Classification. The MAPS system was designed to replace the existing SEMIRA system.

The Marks Information Optically Stored archiving and publishing system was upgraded in 1993. It was originally set up to rationalize documentation management and improve and facilitate access to the files of international registrations and their publication. Scanning of the backlog of more than 160,000 international registration files was completed.

The Read-Only Memory of Madrid Actualized Registry Information CD-ROM "biblio discs" (text only) were produced, compiling the relevant data of each international mark registered in the International Trademark Register. Digitalizing of the backlog image database (amounting to some 105,000 images) was completed and the first "image disc" (containing figurative elements of marks only) was issued, together with the monthly "biblio disc."

Hague Agreement. In 1993, the number of industrial design deposits, renewals and prolongations received by the International Bureau was 5,191, an increase of 8.53 per cent over the 1992 figure.

At its third session in April, the Committee of Experts on the Development of the Hague Agreement Concerning the International Deposit of Industrial Designs discussed a draft new act of the Hague Agreement Concerning the International Deposit of Industrial Designs prepared by the International Bureau on the basis of the outcome of the Committee's previous sessions. In November, the International Bureau published a revised version of the draft new act to be discussed by the Committee of Experts in 1994.

Countries in transition to market economies

WIPO invited officials of countries in transition to market economies for discussions at its headquarters and organized study visits to various countries. The International Bureau assisted those countries to prepare laws dealing with intellectual property and to establish administrative structures to implement those laws. Assistance and training were also offered in relation to accession to WIPO-administered treaties. The International Bureau, through seminars and special training courses, promoted awareness of the importance of intellectual property in those countries.

It also assisted the Interstate Council on the Protection of Industrial Property (which groups nine States of the former USSR, namely, Armenia, Belarus, Kazakhstan, Kyrgyzstan, the Republic of Moldova, the Russian Federation, Tajikistan, Ukraine and Uzbekistan) in setting up a regional patent system under the proposed Eurasian Patent Convention.

Secretariat

As at 31 December 1993, WIPO employed 426 staff members, drawn from 57 nationalities. Of these, 144 were in the Professional and higher categories, and 282 were in the General Service category.

Budget

WIPO's principle income was derived from ordinary and special contributions from member States and from international registration services (primarily under the PCT and the Madrid Agreement). Contributions were paid on the basis of a class-and-unit system by members of the Paris, Berne, International Patent Classification, Nice, Locarno and Vienna Unions and by WIPO member States not belonging to any of the Unions. Income in 1993 amounted to $93.5 million; expenditures totalled $73.5 million, of which $39.7 million was staff costs.

NOTE: For further information on the agency, see *Governing Bodies of WIPO and the Unions Administered by WIPO*, published by WIPO.

Annex I.   MEMBERSHIP OF THE WORLD INTELLECTUAL
PROPERTY ORGANIZATION AND UNIONS ADMINISTERED BY WIPO
(As at 31 December 1993)

Albania, Algeria, Angola, Argentina, Armenia, Australia, Austria, Bahamas, Bangladesh, Barbados, Belarus, Belgium, Benin, Bhutan, Bolivia, Bosnia and Herzegovina, Brazil, Bulgaria, Burkina Faso, Burundi, Cameroon, Canada, Central African Republic, Chad, Chile, China, Colombia, Congo, Costa Rica, Côte d'Ivoire, Croatia, Cuba, Cyprus, Czech Republic, Democratic People's Republic of Korea, Denmark, Ecuador, Egypt, El Salvador, Estonia, Fiji, Finland, France, Gabon, Gambia, Germany, Ghana, Greece, Guatemala, Guinea, Guinea-Bissau, Haiti, Holy See, Honduras, Hungary, Iceland, India, Indonesia, Iraq, Ireland, Israel, Italy, Jamaica, Japan, Jordan, Kazakhstan, Kenya, Latvia, Lebanon,

Lesotho, Liberia, Libyan Arab Jamahiriya, Liechtenstein, Lithuania, Luxembourg, Madagascar, Malawi, Malaysia, Mali, Malta, Mauritania, Mauritius, Mexico, Monaco, Mongolia, Morocco, Namibia, Netherlands, New Zealand, Nicaragua, Niger, Norway, Pakistan, Panama, Paraguay, Peru, Philippines, Poland, Portugal, Qatar, Republic of Korea, Republic of Moldova, Romania, Russian Federation, Rwanda, Saint Lucia, San Marino, Saudi Arabia, Senegal, Sierra Leone, Singapore, Slovakia, Slovenia, Somalia, South Africa, Spain, Sri Lanka, Sudan, Suriname, Swaziland, Sweden, Switzerland, Thailand, the former Yugoslav Republic of Macedonia, Togo, Trinidad and Tobago, Tunisia, Turkey, Uganda, Ukraine, United Arab Emirates, United Kingdom, United Republic of Tanzania, United States, Uruguay, Uzbekistan, Venezuela, Viet Nam, Yemen, Yugoslavia (Serbia and Montenegro),* Zaire, Zambia, Zimbabwe.

Annex II.　OFFICERS AND OFFICES OF THE WORLD INTELLECTUAL PROPERTY ORGANIZATION
(As at 31 December 1993)

GENERAL ASSEMBLY

OFFICERS
Chairman: Jean Claude Combaldieu (France).
Vice-Chairmen: Dominic M. Mills (Ghana), Valery L. Petrov (Ukraine).

MEMBERS
Albania, Algeria, Argentina, Armenia, Australia, Austria, Bahamas, Bangladesh, Barbados, Belarus, Belgium, Benin, Bolivia, Bosnia and Herzegovina, Brazil, Bulgaria, Burkina Faso, Burundi, Cameroon, Canada, Central African Republic, Chad, Chile, China, Colombia, Congo, Costa Rica, Côte d'Ivoire, Croatia, Cuba, Cyprus, Czech Republic, Democratic People's Republic of Korea, Denmark, Ecuador, Egypt, El Salvador, Fiji, Finland, France, Gabon, Gambia, Germany, Ghana, Greece, Guinea, Guinea-Bissau, Haiti, Holy See, Honduras, Hungary, Iceland, India, Indonesia, Iraq, Ireland, Israel, Italy, Jamaica, Japan, Jordan, Kazakhstan, Kenya, Latvia, Lebanon, Lesotho, Liberia, Libyan Arab Jamahiriya, Liechtenstein, Lithuania, Luxembourg, Madagascar, Malawi, Malaysia, Mali, Malta, Mauritania, Mauritius, Mexico, Monaco, Mongolia, Morocco, Namibia, Netherlands, New Zealand, Niger, Norway, Pakistan, Paraguay, Peru, Philippines, Poland, Portugal, Republic of Korea, Republic of Moldova, Romania, Russian Federation, Rwanda, Saint Lucia, San Marino, Senegal, Slovakia, Slovenia, South Africa, Spain, Sri Lanka, Sudan, Suriname, Swaziland, Sweden, Switzerland, Thailand, Togo, Trinidad and Tobago, Tunisia, Turkey, Uganda, Ukraine, United Kingdom, United Republic of Tanzania, United States, Uruguay, Uzbekistan, Venezuela, Viet Nam, Yugoslavia (Serbia and Montenegro),* Zaire, Zambia, Zimbabwe.

*In September, the Governing Bodies of WIPO decided to extend to their 1993 session their 1992 decision that Yugoslavia (Serbia and Montenegro) should not participate in any meeting of WIPO's Governing Bodies.

COORDINATION COMMITTEE

OFFICERS
Chairman: Fernándo Zapata Lopez (Colombia).
Vice-Chairmen: Roland Grossenbacher (Switzerland), S. V. Giri (India).

MEMBERS
Angola, Argentina, Australia, Austria, Belgium, Brazil, Cameroon, Canada, Central African Republic, Chile, China, Colombia, Cuba, Czech Republic, Democratic People's Republic of Korea, Denmark, Egypt, El Salvador, Finland, France, Germany, Greece, Hungary, India, Indonesia, Ireland, Italy, Japan, Kenya, Lebanon, Malawi, Mexico, Morocco, Namibia, Netherlands, Nigeria, Pakistan, Panama, Paraguay, Peru, Portugal, Republic of Korea, Romania, Russian Federation, Singapore, Slovenia, Spain, Sri Lanka, Sudan, Sweden, Switzerland, Syrian Arab Republic, Togo, Ukraine, United Kingdom, United States, Uruguay, Venezuela.

INTERNATIONAL BUREAU

Director-General: Arpad Bogsch.
Deputy Directors-General: François Curchod.
Assistant Directors-General: Gust Ledakis, Carlos Fernandez Ballesteros, Mihály Ficsor.
Legal Counsel: Gust Ledakis.
Director, Bureau for Relations with International Organizations: Khamis Suedi.
Director, Industrial Property Law Department: Ludwig Baeumer.
Director, Developing Countries (Industrial Property Law) Division: James Quashie-Idun.
Director, International Classifications Division: Bo Hansson.
Director, Industrial Property Information Division: Akihiro Nakamura.
Director, Developing Countries Industrial Property Information Division: Raymond Andary.

Director, Patent Cooperation Treaty Administration Department: Daniel Bouchez.
Director, Patent Cooperation Treaty Legal Division: Busso Bartels.
Director, Developing Countries Patent Cooperation Treaty Division: Zhengfa Wang.
Director, International Registrations Division: Bruno Machado.
Directors, Development Cooperation and External Relations Bureaux: Ibrahima Thiam (Africa); Kamil Idris (Arab Countries); Narendra Kumar Sabharwal (Asia and the Pacific); Ernesto Rubio (Latin America and the Caribbean).
Director, General Administrative Services/Computerization Division: Phillip Higham.
Director, General Administrative Services/Languages Division: Bernard Dondenne.

HEADQUARTERS AND OTHER OFFICE

HEADQUARTERS
World Intellectual Property Organization
34 chemin des Colombettes
1211 Geneva 20, Switzerland
　Cable address; WIPO Geneva or OMPI Genève
　Telephone: (41) (22) 730-91-11
　Telex: 412 912 OMPI CH
　Facsimile: (41) (22) 733-5428

WIPO OFFICE AT THE UNITED NATIONS
2 United Nations Plaza, Room 560
New York, N.Y. 10017, United States
　Telephone: (1) (212) 963-6813
　Telex: 420544 UNH UI
　Facsimile: (1) (212) 963-4801

Chapter XVI

International Fund for Agricultural Development (IFAD)

The International Fund for Agricultural Development (IFAD), continued to provide concessional assistance for financing agricultural projects in developing countries. It was established in 1977 to achieve food security through increased agricultural production, and improved nutrition and income for the poorest rural populations, including the landless, marginal farmers, pastoralists, fisherfolk, indigenous peoples and poor women.

IFAD's membership rose to 150 during 1993 with the admission of Armenia, the Cook Islands and Kyrgyzstan. Of its member countries, 22 were in Category I (developed countries), 12 in Category II (oil-exporting developing countries) and 116 in Category III (other developing countries) (see Annex I).

The sixteenth session of the Governing Council of IFAD (Rome, Italy, 20-22 January) approved a 1993 budget of $50.4 million plus a contingency of $650,000. It appointed Fawzi Hamad Al-Sultan of Kuwait as its new President for a four-year term.

The Council endorsed the report and recommendations of the consultation on the fourth replenishment of the Fund's resources,[a] established in 1992 to cover the period 1995-1997, and requested a final report and any recommendations thereon no later than at its seventeenth (1994) session.

The IFAD Executive Board held three regular sessions in 1993 (April, September and December), approving loans for 32 new projects, including seven loans under the Special Programme for Sub-Saharan African Countries Affected by Drought and Desertification (SPA) and one funded both from the Regular Programme and SPA resources. It also approved four technical assistance grants and a grant of $3 million for the Gaza Strip and Jericho Relief and Development Programme. At each session, the Board reviewed a number of policy and operational matters, including the Fund's liquidity, its lending terms and conditions, and a strategy for improving nutrition through its rural investment projects. The Board reviewed reports on the management of IFAD's Investment Portfolio and approved a transfer of $5 million to the General Reserve for 1993, bringing the total Reserve to $90 million as at 31 December.

The Board approved a programme of work at a level of special drawing rights (SDRs) 230 million for loans and grants under the 1994 Regular Programme, and endorsed a budget of $50.9 mil-

lion, including a contingency of $350,000. Also approved were the programme of work and estimated administrative expenditures of SPA for 1994 of SDR 22 million and $5.15 million respectively, including a contingency of $75,000.

Resources

Member States pledged $567.4 million in the third replenishment of resources for the period 1990 to 1994. In October, a consultation on the fourth replenishment of the Fund's resources (Rome, 23-24 October) agreed, subject to agreement between countries in Categories I and II with respect to burden-sharing, that $600 million would be an appropriate target for the fourth replenishment covering the period 1995-1997.

Contributions to the second and final phase of SPA (SPA-II), initiated in 1992, amounted to $91 million at the end of 1993. Total commitments made to SPA since its inception in 1986 amounted to $364 million, of which $342 million was in loans.

Activities in 1993

Loans and technical assistance grants approved in 1993 under the Regular Programme and SPA totalled SDR 276.5 million ($383.1 million), 16 per cent above the 1992 level in terms of SDRs. The amount allocated covered 33 projects worth SDR 264.6 million ($366.5 million) and 58 technical assistance grants worth SDR 11.9 million ($16.5 million). Twenty-seven loans amounting to SDR 221.15 million ($306.2 million) were financed from the Fund's Regular Programme and seven loans totalling SDR 43.45 million ($60.3 million) from SPA, including one loan financed from both Programmes. Of 58 grants, 44 amounting to SDR 9.8 million ($13.67 million) were financed from the Fund's Regular Programme. An additional 14 grants were funded by IFAD for SDR 2 million ($2.85 million). The average size of lending per project in 1993 was SDR 8.3 million ($11.5 million).

Under the Regular Programme, twenty-five projects were initiated by IFAD, with 69 per cent of them co-financed with other donors.

During the year, 14 projects in 14 African countries were approved for a total of SDR 111.6 million ($154.6 million) under the Regular Programme and SPA combined. The countries of

[a]YUN 1992, p. 1169.

Sub-Saharan Africa received 45 per cent of that amount. The projects dealt with rural resources management in Burundi; restructuring of national agricultural services in Côte d'Ivoire; cooperative development in Ethiopia; rural enterprises in Ghana; horticulture and traditional food crops in Kenya; rural finance and enterprise support in Lesotho; agricultural services and rural financial services in Malawi; artisanal fisheries in Mozambique; agricultural support in Nigeria; national smallholders support in Sao Tome and Principe; smallholder agricultural development in Swaziland; extension and rural financial services in the United Republic of Tanzania; and smallholder dry areas resources development in Zimbabwe.

Six projects in the Asia and the Pacific region, involving SDR 66 million ($91.1 million), focused on integrated agricultural production and water management in Bangladesh; agricultural development in areas inhabited by minorities in Yunnan Province, China; financial services for the rural poor in India; rural development in Papua New Guinea; financial services for small-scale crop and livestock producers on the outer islands in Tonga; and participatory resource management in Viet Nam.

In Latin America and the Caribbean, seven projects received loans of SDR 47.8 million ($66.2 million) to deal with low-income family support in Brazil; agricultural production efficiency in the Dominican Republic; self-sustained agricultural development in Honduras; the capitalization of small farmers in Nicaragua; rural development in Panama; support for smallholders in Suriname; and smallholder support through diversification of farm production in Uruguay.

The Near East and North Africa region, which also covered Albania, Somalia and the Sudan, received SDR 39.3 million ($54.6 million) in 1993 under the Regular and Special Programmes combined. The projects dealt with rural development in Albania; assistance to poor rural families in the Gaza Strip and Jericho; income diversification in Jordan; agricultural services in the Sudan; integrated agricultural development in Tunisia; and environmental protection in Yemen.

Workshops on rural development project implementation were held in Gabon (Libreville, 3-8 May) and Morocco (Marrakech, 26 October–4

November), and the Agricultural Management Training Programme for Africa, initiated in 1984 in cooperation with the World Bank, continued to enhance the management capacity of government and project staff involved in agricultural development. As a follow-up to the Geneva Declaration for Rural Women adopted by the Summit on the Economic Advancement of Rural Women in 1992,[b] IFAD prepared strategy papers and guidelines for project gender analysis and completed case studies on women in development in IFAD projects in Bolivia, Dominica, Egypt, Lesotho, Nepal and Papua New Guinea. Among projects approved in 1993, 15 targeted women as major beneficiaries.

Secretariat

As at 31 December 1993, the IFAD secretariat had a total of 259 staff, of whom 105 were in the Professional and higher categories and 154 in the General Service category.

Income and expenditure

Total revenue under the Regular Programme for 1993 was $176 million, consisting of $139.9 million of investment income, including gains of $6.9 million resulting from active portfolio management and $35.9 million from interest and service charges on loans. Total operational and administrative expenses for the year amounted to $44 million (including an exchange gain on operations of $.7 million), compared with a budget, before contingency, of $49.3 million. The excess of revenue over expenses for the year was $131 million.

Total revenue under SPA for 1993 was $14.9 million, consisting of $14 million of investment income, including gains from active portfolio management of $200,000 and $900,000 from interest and service charges on loans. Total expenses for the year amounted to $3.5 million, compared with a budget, before contingency, of $5.9 million. The excess of revenue over expenses for the year was $11.5 million.

NOTE: For further details on IFAD activities in 1993, see *Annual Report 1993*, published by the Fund.

[b]YUN 1992, p. 869.

Annex I.   MEMBERS OF THE INTERNATIONAL FUND FOR AGRICULTURAL DEVELOPMENT
            (As at 31 December 1993)

Category I members
Australia, Austria, Belgium, Canada, Denmark, Finland, France, Germany, Greece, Ireland, Italy, Japan, Luxembourg, Netherlands, New Zealand, Norway, Portugal, Spain, Sweden, Switzerland, United Kingdom, United States.

Category II members
Algeria, Gabon, Indonesia, Iran, Iraq, Kuwait, Libyan Arab Jamahiriya, Nigeria, Qatar, Saudi Arabia, United Arab Emirates, Venezuela.

Category III members
Afghanistan, Albania, Angola, Antigua and Barbuda, Argentina, Armenia, Bangladesh, Barbados, Belize, Benin, Bhutan, Bolivia, Botswana, Brazil, Burkina Faso, Burundi, Cambodia, Cameroon, Cape Verde, Central African Republic, Chad, Chile, China, Colombia, Comoros, Congo, Cook Islands, Costa Rica, Côte d'Ivoire, Cuba, Cyprus, Democratic People's Republic of Korea, Djibouti, Dominica, Dominican Republic, Ecuador, Egypt, El Salvador, Equatorial Guinea, Ethiopia, Fiji, Gambia, Ghana, Grenada, Guatemala, Guinea, Guinea-Bissau, Guyana, Haiti, Honduras, India, Israel, Jamaica, Jordan, Kenya, Kyrgyzstan, Lao People's Democratic Republic, Lebanon, Lesotho, Liberia, Madagascar, Malawi, Malaysia, Maldives, Mali, Malta, Mauritania, Mauritius, Mexico, Morocco, Mozambique, Myanmar, Namibia, Nepal, Nicaragua, Niger, Oman, Pakistan, Panama, Papua New Guinea, Paraguay, Peru, Philippines, Republic of Korea, Romania, Rwanda, Saint Kitts and Nevis, Saint Lucia, Saint Vincent and the Grenadines, Samoa, Sao Tome and Principe, Senegal, Seychelles, Sierra Leone, Solomon Islands, Somalia, Sri Lanka, Sudan, Suriname, Swaziland, Syrian Arab Republic, Thailand, Togo, Tonga, Trinidad and Tobago, Tunisia, Turkey, Uganda, United Republic of Tanzania, Uruguay, Viet Nam, Yemen, Yugoslavia,* Zaire, Zambia, Zimbabwe.

*Refers to the former Socialist Federal Republic of Yugoslavia. In 1992, the IFAD Executive Board decided that the Federal Republic of Yugoslavia (Serbia and Montenegro) could not continue automatically the membership of the former Yugoslavia and that, therefore, it should apply for membership.

Annex II.   OFFICERS AND OFFICES OF THE INTERNATIONAL FUND FOR AGRICULTURAL DEVELOPMENT
(As at 31 December 1993)

EXECUTIVE BOARD

Chairman: Fawzi Hamad Al-Sultan.

MEMBERS
Category I: Belgium, France, Germany, Japan, Sweden, United States.
Alternates: Canada, Denmark, Italy, Netherlands, United Kingdom.

Category II: Iraq, Kuwait, Libyan Arab Jamahiriya, Nigeria, Saudi Arabia, Venezuela.
Alternates: Algeria, Gabon, Indonesia, Iran, Qatar, United Arab Emirates.

Category III: Argentina, Brazil, China, Côte d'Ivoire, Ghana, Turkey.
Alternates: Ethiopia, Mexico, Morocco, Pakistan, Panama, Sri Lanka.

SENIOR SECRETARIAT OFFICERS

President: Fawzi Hamad Al-Sultan.
Chef de Cabinet: Uday Abhyankar.
Internal Auditor: John McGhie.
Vice-President: Donald S. Brown.
Controller: Vernon G. Jorssen.
Treasurer: Tor Myrvang.

Director, Personnel Division: Alan Prien.
Assistant President, Project Management Department: (Vacant)
Assistant President, Economic Policy and Resource Strategy Department: (Vacant)
Assistant President, General Affairs Department: Abdou Ciss.
Director, Legal Services Division: Mohammad Nawaz.

HEADQUARTERS AND OTHER OFFICES

HEADQUARTERS
International Fund for Agricultural Development
Via del Serafico 107
00142 Rome, Italy
Cable address: IFAD ROME
Telephone: (39) (6) 54591
Telex: 620330
Facsimile: 5043463

LIAISON OFFICES
IFAD Liaison Office
1 United Nations Plaza, Room 1208
New York, N.Y. 10017, United States
Telephone: (1) (212) 963-0546
Facsimile: (1) (212) 963-2787

IFAD Liaison Office
1775 K Street, N.W., Suite 410
Washington, D.C. 20006, United States
Telephone: (1) (202) 331-9099
Facsimile: (1) (202) 331-9366

Chapter XVII

United Nations Industrial Development Organization (UNIDO)

In 1993, the United Nations Industrial Development Organization (UNIDO) continued its activities in the areas of industrial operations, strategies and promotion. Its special programmes supported industrial growth and restructuring and included the Industrial Development Decade for Africa, assistance to least developed countries, industrial cooperation among developing countries, integration of women in industrial development, cooperation with industrial enterprises and non-governmental organizations, environment and private sector development.

The fifth session of the UNIDO General Conference, held at Yaoundé, Cameroon, from 6 to 10 December, focused on policy reform emphasizing advisory and technical services for private sector development and mobilizing investment and other resources. It approved a new organizational structure and readjustment of the work programme and budgets for the biennium 1994-1995.

The Industrial Development Board held its fifth special (January), resumed tenth (March), and eleventh sessions (June/July, October and November). The Board dealt with UNIDO policies within the current 1992-1997 medium-term plan; future policies in accordance with the priorities in the 1994-1999 medium-term plan; cooperation in industrial development; guidelines for special trust funds; the 1994-1995 work programme and budget; and organizational and staff structure of UNIDO. The Programme and Budget Committee held its ninth regular and first additional sessions in April, June and November.

During the year, Azerbaijan, the Czech Republic, Kyrgyzstan, the Republic of Moldova, Slovakia, Tajikistan and the former Yugoslav Republic of Macedonia joined UNIDO, bringing its membership to 166 as at 31 December 1993. Canada withdrew its membership effective 31 December (see Annex I).

Policy issues

In 1993, UNIDO established a policy framework and a corresponding reconfiguration of its organizational structure. The reform was made in the light of recent global economic, industrial and technological developments and comprised five objectives: industrial and technological growth and competitiveness; development of human resources for industry; equitable development through industrial

development; environmentally sustainable industrial development; and international cooperation in industrial investment and technology.

Industrial strategies and operations

A total of 1,713 technical assistance projects valued at $118.8 million were implemented or under implementation in 1993. Africa (including the African Arab States) received 34.2 per cent; the Arab States, 2.8 per cent; Asia and the Pacific, 26.2 per cent; Latin America and the Caribbean, 9.2 per cent; and Europe, 3.3 per cent. Interregional and global projects accounted for 24.2 per cent.

Implementation of industrial operations

Agro-based industries. Technical cooperation expenditures for agro-based industries amounted to $13 million, of which some 14 per cent was financed by the United Nations Development Programme (UNDP). A total of 165 projects were implemented or under implementation. The projects focused on introducing cleaner technologies and pollution abatement in the food, leather and textile subsectors; developing and adapting suitable technologies for small- and medium-scale industries; rehabilitating industries through improved technology and management, better trained personnel and quality control; and developing and implementing large-scale programmes in the leather and footwear industry.

Chemical industries. Expenditures for technical cooperation in the chemical industry sector totalled $22.9 million, with 27 per cent financed by UNDP. A total of 280 projects were either implemented or under implementation in 1993. Reducing environmental impact of industrial operations remained central to the activities of the UNIDO Chemical Industries Branch. The transfer of cleaner production technologies, recycling technologies, treatment of industrial waste and the dissemination of those technologies constituted a major part of its work. As an implementing agency of the 1987 Montreal Protocol on Substances that Deplete the Ozone Layer,[a] UNIDO initiated projects in Brazil and Egypt to phase out chlorofluorocarbons in polymerfoam manufacturing. Other activities were carried out in the petroleum refining and petrochemical industries, industrial

[a]YUN 1987, p. 686.

utilization of medicinal and aromatic plants, pharmaceuticals, the pulp and paper industries and safety in the development and use of pesticides.

Engineering industries. Expenditures in engineering industry projects amounted to $10.7 million, with approximately 71 per cent financed from UNDP resources. A total of 162 projects were implemented or under implementation in such areas as computer applications to industrial design; manufacturing; industrial maintenance and spare parts manufacture; electronic components and equipment; transportation; telecommunications equipment and systems; environmental protection and energy generation and consumption; and metalworking and machine tools.

Industrial human resource development. Expenditure for fellowship and other training components in all technical cooperation projects amounted to $14.3 million, as compared with $16.4 million in 1992. Of that total, $9.7 million was spent on fellowships and study tours and $4.6 million on group training activities and meetings. Expenditure for training that received substantive back-stopping from the Industrial Human Resource Development Branch amounted to $2 million, with some 3 per cent financed by UNDP. A total of 104 projects were implemented with emphasis on managerial training and development of human resources in advanced technologies, quality control and productivity techniques.

Industrial management and rehabilitation. Technical cooperation expenditures amounted to $3.3 million, with some 58 per cent financed by UNDP. A total of 63 projects were either implemented or under implementation. The industrial management programme emphasized the transfer of knowledge and technical know-how through training, seminars and workshops and enterprise restructuring projects. In the rehabilitation programme, a pilot project initiated in 1992 assisted 15 enterprises in Poland in 1993.

Industrial strategies and policies. Technical cooperation expenditures amounted to $5.2 million, with some 69 per cent financed by UNDP. Seventy-nine projects were implemented or under implementation. Technical cooperation focused on advice for industrial strategy and policy formulation and on capacity-building, including human resource development, networking for strengthened competitiveness, institutions and decision support systems. In the strategic management of industrial development, UNIDO continued 11 projects to upgrade competitiveness and productivity and to promote small-scale industries.

Institutional infrastructure. A total of 211 projects were implemented or under implementation, with expenditures amounting to $13.8 million, some 71 per cent of which was financed from UNDP resources. Technical cooperation activities focused

on small- and medium-scale industries and institutional support for industrial development.

Metallurgical industries. Technical cooperation expenditures in metallurgical industries amounted to $4.6 million, with some 65 per cent financed by UNDP. A total of 81 projects were implemented or under implementation. Environment management and cleaner production in the iron and steel sector were addressed through programmes in Africa, South-East Asia, Eastern Europe and Latin America and the Caribbean. In the foundry and metal transformation sector, projects in Colombia, Indonesia and Sri Lanka focused on private sector foundries and provided technical and administrative assistance and investment advice.

Industrial promotion

Industrial promotion activities focused on reinforcing links in the areas of industrial investment, consultations and industrial technology development and promotion.

Industrial investment programme. A total of 171 investment promotion projects were concluded in 1993 amounting to $954.4 million. The total value of technical cooperation activities implemented was $19.6 million. Identification missions led to 12 new project proposals on industrial cooperation in Asia, Eastern Europe and Latin America. Of the 171 projects concluded, 21 projects, representing $22.3 million, were in Africa; 62 valued at $239.6 million were in Asia and the Pacific; 39 amounting to $204.2 million were in Latin America and the Caribbean; and 49 costing $488.3 million were in the Arab countries, Europe and the Mediterranean.

Technical cooperation for feasibility studies amounted to $8.3 million, with 8 interregional/global, 10 intercountry and 60 country projects in 40 countries under implementation. The Industrial Development Fund was the major source of financing, followed by UNDP, trust funds and the UNIDO Regular Programme of Technical Cooperation.

Industrial technology development and promotion. Under a new UNIDO programme, guidelines on the revitalization of industrial technology research institutes were finalized in cooperation with the International Development Research Centre (Canada) and the Third World Academy of Sciences (Italy).

An outcome of the new programme was a technical cooperation project between institutes in Thailand and Chile for the commercialization of research and development and for the development of policies and strategies for applied research. A project was approved to establish a network of institutions and organizations for monitoring and assessing selected technologies. Under the programme, activities continued in the areas of industrial and technological information; technology promotion; and technology policy, acquisition and negotiation.

System of Consultations. The UNIDO System of Consultations, a mechanism for achieving the goals of the 1975 Lima Declaration and Plan of Action on Industrial Development and Cooperation,[b] principally to restructure world industry and increase the share of developing countries in world production, held four consultations during 1993: the First Consultation on the Construction Industry (Tunis, Tunisia, 3-7 May); the Regional Consultation on the Industrial Utilization of Medicinal and Aromatic Plants in Asia and the Pacific (Vienna, 5-8 July); the Regional Consultation on Animal Feed and Related Industries in Africa (Vienna, 5-8 October); and the Consultation on Downstream Petrochemical Industries in Developing Countries (Tehran, Iran, 7-11 November).

Other activities included a workshop on developing the fisheries industry of the islands in the Western Indian Ocean (Antananarivo, Madagascar, June); a regional expert group meeting on software technology and cooperation initiatives (Curitiba, Brazil, December); a workshop on improving the performance of industrial plants for English-speaking African countries (Kampala, Uganda, November); a workshop on rehabilitation and privatization of industries (Dar es Salaam, United Republic of Tanzania, September); and a workshop on measures to improve the competitiveness of the sugar cane industry in Africa (Port Louis, Mauritius, December).

Area programmes

UNIDO developed, implemented and monitored operational programmes at country, subregional and regional levels. Project approvals from UNDP indicative planning figure resources, cost-sharing, cash-counterpart and special measures in 1993 amounted to $9.3 million. Of the 59 technical support services at the programme level (TSS-1) projects approved by the UNDP Governing Council for the 1992-1993 biennium for implementation by UNIDO,[c] 56 were implemented at a value of $3.2 million. During the year, 150 country programme and five regional programme reviews were undertaken. A total of 1,369 project ideas and concepts were identified, among which 380 projects were developed for appraisal and approval.

Second Industrial Development Decade for Africa (1993-2002)

Under the programme for the Second Industrial Development Decade for Africa (IDDA),[d] $4.5 million was allocated in 1993 for technical cooperation, of which $4.02 million was delivered. Regarding country projects, high priority was given to agricultural machinery, investment promotion, engineering, food processing, textiles, chemicals, in particular pharmaceuticals, management and rehabilitation and human resources development. Regional projects emphasized the agro-industries, particularly leather and food, technology transfer, feasibility studies, energy and environment and human resources development. Nearly $900,000 worth of projects were implemented under co-financing arrangements. Projects for the least developed countries (LDCs) accounted for the bulk of activities.

Under the supplementary activity component, $1,862,100 was allocated for 1993. Delivery totalled $2,301,563 (including carry-over funds from 1992) and covered activities related to financial resources mobilization, investment promotion, support for technology acquisition and negotiation, human resources development emphasizing local entrepreneurship and integration of women in industrial development.

Assistance to LDCs

UNIDO assistance to LDCs focused on the follow-up activities related to the implementation of the Programme of Action for the Least Developed Countries for the 1990s.[e] Activities focused on human resources development; industrial development in rural areas; macroeconomic conditions and mobilization of financial resources for industrial development; development of the industrial service, scientific and technological base; and integration of women in industrial development. Development of ''seed'' programmes for LDCs continued to be an important initiative of UNIDO.

New approvals generated for LDCs amounted to $8.4 million, representing 67 projects, while net approvals amounted to $7.4 million with delivery level reaching $20 million.

A ministerial-level symposium on financing the industrial action programme was held in Cameroon.

Industrial cooperation among developing countries

UNIDO continued to support economic and technical cooperation among developing countries. In 1993, special attention was given to promoting cooperation among business enterprises in the South. Some 30 projects were implemented, among them one between China and Viet Nam in the machine tool industry; and a workshop on Brazil's achievements in computer applications in the textile and apparel industries.

[b]YUN 1975, p. 473.
[c]YUN 1992, p. 1174.
[d]Ibid., p. 468.
[e]GA res. 45/206, 21 Dec. 1990.

In addition to an expert group meeting on patents, licensing and know-how in the petrochemical industries (Manama, Bahrain, November), five technical workshops/expert group meetings were held in industrial processing of medicinal plants (Panajachel, Guatemala); research and development of mineral resources (Hyderabad, India); direct reduction process of iron ore (Cairo, Egypt); processing of lead and zinc sulphide ores (Guangzhou, China); and cooperation in small- and medium-scale industries (Manama).

Integration of women in industrial development

The UNIDO programme and plan of action for the integration of women in industrial development (1990-1995) featured activities to mainstream women within UNIDO technical cooperation, study and research activities and projects specifically targeting women. Women-in-development experts were attached to country programming missions (Burundi, Mozambique, Niger and Sierra Leone) and to programming missions for the development of the small- and medium-scale industrial sectors (Cameroon, Ghana and Zambia). Projects for the development and transfer of appropriate technologies continued to be implemented in the area of food processing with the introduction of energy-saving and environmentally sound technology. A database containing information notes on women in industry for 102 developing countries was further strengthened.

Secretariat

As at 31 December 1993, 1,238 staff members served at headquarters, of whom 405 were in the Professional and higher categories and 833 in the General Service and related categories.

Technical cooperation

UNIDO continued to focus its technical cooperation activities mainly on developing countries, with the net value of project approvals totalling $79.2 million, as compared to $113.6 million in 1992. Of that amount, $56.9 million represented non-UNDP-funded activities. Total technical cooperation delivery in 1993 amounted to $118.8 million.

Budget

The UNIDO General Conference in 1991 approved the regular budget for the 1992-1993 biennium at a level of $181,013,400, to be financed from assessed contributions from member States, in both United States dollars and Austrian schillings (AS). On the basis of an exchange rate of $1.00 = AS 12.90, member States were assessed $179,262,600, consisting of $19,718,900 plus the equivalent in dollars of AS 2,058,116,310. For the Regular Programme of Technical Cooperation, including IDDA, the sum of $10,755,700, which had been appropriated by the General Conference in 1991 at the same exchange rate, was adjusted in 1993 to $12,149,800 at the biennial average rate of exchange of $1.00 = AS 11.26. That comprised $4,580,100 for the technical cooperation component of IDDA and $7,569,700 for the other components.

To deal with the situation caused by UNIDO's continuing cash-flow difficulties, the General Conference, in 1993, decided to allow the temporary allocation of the unutilized balances of the 1990-1991 appropriation in the amount of $8,746,822.

NOTE: For further information on UNIDO, see *Annual Report of UNIDO 1993*, published by UNIDO.

Annex I. MEMBERSHIP OF THE UNITED NATIONS INDUSTRIAL DEVELOPMENT ORGANIZATION
(As at 31 December 1993)

Afghanistan, Albania, Algeria, Angola, Argentina, Armenia, Australia, Austria, Azerbaijan, Bahamas, Bahrain, Bangladesh, Barbados, Belarus, Belgium, Belize, Benin, Bhutan, Bolivia, Bosnia and Herzegovina, Botswana, Brazil, Bulgaria, Burkina Faso, Burundi, Cameroon, Canada,* Cape Verde, Central African Republic, Chad, Chile, China, Colombia, Comoros, Congo, Costa Rica, Côte d'Ivoire, Croatia, Cuba, Cyprus, Czech Republic, Democratic People's Republic of Korea, Denmark, Djibouti, Dominica, Dominican Republic, Ecuador, Egypt, El Salvador, Equatorial Guinea, Ethiopia, Fiji, Finland, France, Gabon, Gambia, Georgia, Germany, Ghana, Greece, Grenada, Guatemala, Guinea, Guinea-Bissau, Guyana, Haiti, Honduras, Hungary, India, Indonesia, Iran, Iraq, Ireland, Israel, Italy, Jamaica, Japan, Jordan, Kenya, Kuwait, Kyrgyzstan, Lao People's Democratic Republic, Lebanon, Lesotho, Liberia, Libyan Arab Jamahiriya, Lithuania, Luxembourg, Madagascar, Malawi, Malaysia, Maldives, Mali, Malta, Mauritania, Mauritius, Mexico, Mongolia, Morocco, Mozambique, Myanmar, Namibia, Nepal, Netherlands, New Zealand, Nicaragua, Niger, Nigeria, Norway, Oman, Pakistan, Panama, Papua New Guinea, Paraguay, Peru, Philippines, Poland, Portugal, Qatar, Republic of Korea, Republic of Moldova, Romania, Russian Federation, Rwanda, Saint Kitts and Nevis, Saint Lucia, Saint Vincent and the Grenadines, Sao Tome and Principe, Saudi Arabia, Senegal, Seychelles, Sierra Leone, Slovakia, Slovenia, Somalia, Spain, Sri Lanka, Sudan, Suriname, Swaziland, Sweden, Switzerland, Syrian Arab Republic, Tajikistan, Thailand, the former Yugoslav Republic of Macedonia, Togo, Tonga, Trinidad and Tobago, Tunisia, Turkey, Uganda, Ukraine, United Arab Emirates, United Kingdom, United Republic of Tanzania, United States, Uruguay, Vanuatu, Venezuela, Viet Nam, Yemen, Yugoslavia,† Zaire, Zambia, Zimbabwe.

*Canada withdrew its membership from UNIDO effective 31 December 1993.

†Refers to the former Socialist Federal Republic of Yugoslavia. On 30 March, the General Conference of UNIDO adopted a resolution stating that the Federal Republic of Yugoslavia (Serbia and Montenegro) could not automatically continue to hold the membership of the former Socialist Federal Republic of Yugoslavia. The Conference decided that the Federal Republic of Yugoslavia (Serbia and Montenegro) would have to apply for membership in UNIDO and that it should not participate in the work of the Programme and Budget Committee, the Industrial Development Board or the Conference itself.

Annex II. OFFICERS AND OFFICES OF THE
UNITED NATIONS INDUSTRIAL DEVELOPMENT ORGANIZATION
(As at 31 December 1993)

INDUSTRIAL DEVELOPMENT BOARD

OFFICERS
President: Thereza Maria Machado Quintella (Brazil).
Vice-Presidents: Vicomte Georges Vilain XIII (Belgium), Fisseha Yimer (Ethiopia), Kamal Naim Bakshi (India).
Rapporteur: Nikolai V. Tchoulkov (Russian Federation).

MEMBERS
Austria, Belarus, Belgium, Bolivia, Brazil, Cameroon, Chile, China, Costa Rica, Cuba, Egypt, Ethiopia, Finland, France, Germany, Ghana, Greece, Guinea, Hungary, India, Indonesia, Iran, Iraq, Italy, Japan, Kuwait, Mexico, Morocco, Netherlands, Nigeria, Norway, Pakistan, Peru, Republic of Korea, Romania, Russian Federation, Saudi Arabia, Senegal, Slovakia, Spain, Sudan, Switzerland, Syrian Arab Republic, Thailand, Trinidad and Tobago, Tunisia, Turkey, Uganda, United Kingdom, United States, Venezuela, Zaire, Zimbabwe.

PROGRAMME AND BUDGET COMMITTEE

OFFICERS
Chairman: Jasim Y. Yamal (Qatar).
Vice-Chairmen: Yuri V. Zaitsev (Russian Federation), Christopher Hulse (United Kingdom), L. Carillo (Cuba).
Rapporteur: T. M. El Kouny (Egypt).

MEMBERS
Algeria, Austria, Brazil, Bulgaria, China, Colombia, Cuba, Egypt, France, Germany, India, Italy, Japan, Kenya, Malawi, Mexico, Netherlands, Nigeria, Philippines, Poland, Qatar, Russian Federation, Rwanda, Sweden, United Kingdom, United States, Yugoslavia.

HEADQUARTERS AND OTHER OFFICES

HEADQUARTERS
United Nations Industrial Development Organization
Vienna International Centre
P.O. Box 300
A-1400 Vienna, Austria
  Cable address: UNIDO Vienna
  Telephone: (43) (1) 211310
  Telex: 135612
  Facsimile: (43) (1) 232156

  UNIDO also maintained an office at Geneva.

LIAISON OFFICE
UNIDO Liaison Office
1 United Nations Plaza, Room 1110
New York, N.Y. 10017, United States
  Telephone: (1) (212) 963-6882

Chapter XVIII

Interim Commission for the International Trade Organization (ICITO) and the General Agreement on Tariffs and Trade (GATT)

During 1993, the General Agreement on Tariffs and Trade (GATT) continued to serve as a multilateral instrument with the principal objective of liberalizing international trade to facilitate economic growth and development. It provided agreed rules for international trade and served as a forum in which countries could discuss trade problems and negotiate the reduction of various restrictive and distortive measures.

The United Nations Conference on Trade and Employment (Havana, Cuba, November 1947–March 1948) drew up a charter for an International Trade Organization (ITO) and established an Interim Commission for the International Trade Organization (ICITO). The charter of ITO was never accepted, but the Conference's Preparatory Committee members negotiated tariffs among themselves and drew up GATT, which entered into force on 1 January 1948. Since then, ICITO has served as the GATT secretariat.

The most authoritative body of GATT, the Session of Contracting Parties, postponed to January 1994 its forty-ninth (1993) regular session because of intense activities in the Uruguay Round of multilateral trade negotiations.

In 1993, the number of Contracting Parties to GATT rose to 114 with the addition of Bahrain, Brunei Darussalam, the Czech Republic, Dominica, Fiji, Mali, Saint Lucia, Saint Vincent and the Grenadines, Slovakia and Swaziland (see Annex I).

Multilateral trade negotiations

Uruguay Round

The Uruguay Round of Multilateral Trade Negotiations, launched in September 1986[a] at Punta del Este, Uruguay, was concluded by 15 December 1993 at Geneva. The Uruguay Round, which would expand world trade by $755 billion annually by the year 2002, produced the most comprehensive trade agreement ever, with new multilateral rules for liberalizing trade in goods and services, intellectual property rights and investment measures.

The Uruguay Round package consisted of a Final Act comprising some 28 new agreements and national schedules on tariff concessions and ini-

tial commitments for liberalizing trade in services. The Trade Negotiations Committee—the most senior body of the Uruguay Round—approved a work programme for the post-Round period, including recommendations on the subject of trade and environment for adoption at a Ministerial meeting to sign the Final Act in April 1994 in Marrakesh, Morocco.

The Uruguay Round package, intended to improve market-access, was estimated to produce world income gains of $235 billion and trade gains of $755 billion annually by the year 2002. Developed countries' tariffs on industrial products were reduced by 38 per cent, lowering average duties from 6.3 to 3.9 per cent. Tariff bindings (maximum duties) would cover 99 per cent of industrial products entering developed countries and 72 per cent for developing countries. The General Agreement on Trade in Services had three major elements: the Framework Agreement containing basic obligations (such as most-favoured-nation and national treatment); the annexes addressing the special situations of individual services sectors (financial services, telecommunications, air transport, movement of labour); and market-opening commitments submitted by participants that would be the subject of further liberalization in future rounds of negotiations.

The Uruguay Round produced the most extensive agreement on intellectual property ever negotiated, covering patents, copyrights, the rights of performers and producers of sound recordings, trademarks, geographical indications including appelations of origin, industrial design, layout designs of integrated circuits and trade secrets. Other agreements provided for the progressive integration of textiles and clothing products into the GATT rules over a ten-year period; greater liberalization of trade in agriculture; and bringing all measures affecting import and export competition under more effective GATT rules and disciplines. They also strengthened disciplines and clarified current rules on antidumping, subsidies and countervailing measures, safeguards, customs valuation, import licensing and technical barriers to trade. New rules would cover trade-related investments, rules of origin and

[a]YUN 1986, p. 1211.

preshipment inspection. The rules and procedures relating to settlement of disputes would also improve.

GATT, which existed on a provisional basis, would become a permanent world trade body through the establishment of the World Trade Organization (WTO) on 1 January 1995 to implement the results of the Round. (See also PART THREE, Chapter IV.)

Implementation of the Tokyo Round agreements

The agreements of the Tokyo Round (1973-1979), the seventh round of multilateral trade negotiations, concluded with a major package of tariff concessions, agreements on non-tariff measures and an improved legal framework for GATT. Various committees established at the conclusion of the Tokyo Round continued to supervise tariff schedules, administer the new agreements and provide a forum for discussing related issues.

Reports received by the Committee on Anti-Dumping Practices covering the period 1 July 1992 to 30 June 1993 indicated that among the 26 parties to the Agreement on Anti-Dumping Practices, 68 investigations had been initiated by the United States, 61 by Australia, 37 by Canada, 33 by the European Community (EC), 24 by Mexico, 7 by the Republic of Korea, 4 each by Austria, Brazil and New Zealand and 3 by India. Complete data for outstanding final actions (definitive duties or price undertakings) were not available for all signatories. For those signatories notifying such data, measures in force stood at 662 as at 30 June. Most of the measures were accounted for by the United States (279), EC (185), Canada (81) and Australia (64). Dumped products were defined as those sold to an importer at a price lower than that charged by the producer in his domestic market.

Six of the 24 signatories to the Subsidies and Countervailing Measures Agreement initiated countervailing duty investigations during the period 1 July 1992 to 30 June 1993: the United States had initiated 42, Australia, 12; Austria, 4; Chile, 2; Brazil, 1; and EC, 1. Two dispute settlement panels were established, one to examine the imposition by Brazil of provisional and countervailing duties on certain types of milk from EC and another to examine the imposition by the United States of countervailing duties on certain steel products originating in several EC member States. A panel report was adopted on United States measures affecting the export of softwood lumber from Canada.

In December, an informal Working Group established by the Government Procurement Committee adopted the text of a new agreement on Government Procurement to replace the current Government Procurement Code in 1996. The new Agreement covered services, including construc-

tion services; procurement at the sub-central level (states, provinces, departments and prefectures); and procurement by public utilities. Although the Agreement, which would apply to contracts above certain thresholds in value, was considered a balanced package, participants intended to expand the coverage further, prior to its signature in April 1994.

In 1993, the Czech Republic, Indonesia, Malaysia, Morocco, Slovakia and Thailand signed the Agreement on Technical Barriers to Trade, bringing the total number of signatories to 45. Observer status was granted to Saudi Arabia and Taipei. In May and November, the Committee on Technical Barriers to Trade dealt with the implementation and administration of the Agreement and its annual review. The Committee on Customs Valuation examined national legislation of Argentina, Mexico and Romania relating to the implementation and administration of the Customs Valuation Agreement. At the end of 1993, there were 29 signatories to the Agreement on Import Licensing Procedures. The Committee on Import Licensing examined replies from 12 signatories to a GATT questionnaire on the subject.

Other GATT activities

Special session of Contracting Parties

The Contracting Parties held a special session on 9 June and appointed Peter Sutherland (Ireland) Director-General of GATT with effect from 1 July 1993. Because of the intense Uruguay Round activities, the forty-ninth regular session of the Contracting Parties was postponed to January 1994.

Council of Representatives

In 1993, the Council of Representatives, GATT's highest body between sessions of the Contracting Parties, oversaw a large number of requests for accession to GATT as well as for observer status. During the year, it established working parties to examine requests for accession.

Trade and development

The Committee on Trade and Development continued to review, discuss and negotiate trade issues of interest to developing countries. In 1993, the Committee considered follow-up activities to the 1992 United Nations Conference on Environment and Development (UNCED),[b] regional trade arrangements between developing countries and the extension of the Generalized System of Preferences (GSP) to economies in transition. The Committee resolved a procedural debate in GATT regarding the Southern Common Market

[b]YUN 1992, p. 670.

Agreement between Argentina, Brazil, Paraguay and Uruguay. During the year, Australia, Austria, Finland, Japan, New Zealand, Norway, Sweden and the United States notified the Committee of their respective GSP schemes.

Trade and environment

At the conclusion of the Uruguay Round of multilateral trade negotiations, the Trade Negotiations Committee decided to draw up a comprehensive work programme on trade, environment and sustainable development for adoption at the ministerial meeting scheduled for April 1994. The Group on Environmental Measures and International Trade and the Committee on Trade and Development examined connections between trade and environment as a follow-up to UNCED, in particular, the trade provisions of existing multilateral environmental agreements, the transparency of trade-related environmental measures and the trade effects of packaging and labelling requirements.

Textile arrangement

On 9 December, the Textile Committee decided to maintain in force the Multifibre Arrangement (MFA), as extended by the 1986 Protocol for a further period of 12 months from 1 January to 31 December 1994, since the Uruguay Round had not been completed at that time. MFA had governed much of the world's trade in textiles and clothing since 1974.

Technical cooperation

The GATT secretariat's Technical Cooperation Division conducted some 47 technical cooperation missions to developing countries in 1993 to assist officials in preparing draft schedules of concessions and commitments on market access and offers of initial commitments on services. Particular attention was paid to helping least-developed and smaller developing countries in Africa. It also organized several general seminars on GATT and the Uruguay Round in countries in Africa, Asia and Latin America. Technical missions were sent to Bolivia and Peru to assist with preparations for trade policy review. In November, the Committee on Trade and Development stressed the importance of strengthening the effectiveness of the Division's work to better assist developing countries in the implementation of the results of the Uruguay Round.

Training programme

From the programme's inception in 1955 to the end of 1993, a total of 1,341 trade officials from 123 countries and 10 regional organizations attended GATT trade policy courses. In 1993, two regular 14-week courses were held, one in English and one in French. Switzerland provided financial assistance for a workshop on negotiating techniques as part of the course.

To facilitate the integration of Central and Eastern European countries into the multilateral trading system, the GATT secretariat held another nine-week special trade policy course (Geneva, May) attended by officials from Albania, Armenia, Azerbaijan, Belarus, Bulgaria, the Czech Republic, Estonia, Georgia, Hungary, Kazakhstan, Kyrgyzstan, Latvia, Lithuania, Poland, the Republic of Moldova, Romania, the Russian Federation, Slovakia, Ukraine and Uzbekistan.

International Trade Centre

The International Trade Centre (ITC), established by GATT in 1964 and operated jointly with the United Nations Conference on Trade and Development since 1968, implemented various technical cooperation activities with GATT in 1993. GATT and the United Nations contributed equally to the ITC regular budget, which totalled $18.3 million in 1993. The Centre's technical cooperation activities with developing countries in trade promotion amounted to $24.6 million, with some 96 national, 49 regional and 88 interregional projects under implementation. During the year, ITC focused on trade and environment, women in trade development and export-based rural development.

Secretariat

As at 31 December 1993, the GATT secretariat employed 446 staff members (including temporary posts connected with the Uruguay Round negotiations)—195 in the Professional and higher categories and 251 in the General Service category.

Budget

Member countries of GATT contributed to the budget in accordance with a scale assessed on the basis of each country's share in the total trade of the Contracting Parties and associated Governments. The total budget for 1993 was 89,040,000 Swiss francs, or approximately $59.9 million. (The United Nations rate of exchange as at 31 December 1993 was SwF 1.49 = US$1.)

NOTE: For further information on GATT, see *GATT Activities 1993: An Annual Review of the Work of the GATT*, published by GATT.

Annex I. CONTRACTING PARTIES TO THE GENERAL AGREEMENT ON TARIFFS AND TRADE
(As at 31 December 1993)

Antigua and Barbuda, Argentina, Australia, Austria, Bahrain, Bangladesh, Barbados, Belgium, Belize, Benin, Bolivia, Botswana, Brazil, Brunei Darussalam, Burkino Faso, Burundi, Cameroon, Canada, Central African Republic, Chad, Chile, Colombia, Congo, Costa Rica, Côte d'Ivoire, Cuba, Cyprus, Czech Republic, Denmark, Dominica, Dominican Republic, Egypt, El Salvador, Fiji, Finland, France, Gabon, Gambia, Germany, Ghana, Greece, Guatemala, Guyana, Haiti, Hong Kong, Hungary, Iceland, India, Indonesia, Ireland, Israel, Italy, Jamaica, Japan, Kenya, Kuwait, Lesotho, Luxembourg, Macau, Madagascar, Malawi, Malaysia, Maldives, Mali, Malta, Mauritania, Mauritius, Mexico, Morocco, Mozambique, Myanmar, Namibia, Netherlands, New Zealand, Nicaragua, Niger, Nigeria, Norway, Pakistan, Peru, Philippines, Poland, Portugal, Republic of Korea, Romania, Rwanda, Saint Lucia, Saint Vincent and the Grenadines, Senegal, Sierra Leone, Singapore, Slovakia, South Africa, Spain, Sri Lanka, Suriname, Swaziland, Sweden, Switzerland, Thailand, Togo, Trinidad and Tobago, Tunisia, Turkey, Uganda, United Kingdom, United Republic of Tanzania, United States, Uruguay, Venezuela, Yugoslavia,* Zaire, Zambia, Zimbabwe.

*Refers to the former Socialist Federal Republic of Yugoslavia. The GATT Council decided, on 19 June 1993, that the Federal Republic of Yugoslavia (Serbia and Montenegro) could not continue automatically the contracting party status of the former Yugoslavia in GATT. The Council agreed that the Federal Republic of Yugoslavia should apply for accession to GATT and that it should not participate in the work of the Council and its subsidiary bodies.

ANNEX II. OFFICERS AND OFFICE OF THE GENERAL AGREEMENT ON TARIFFS AND TRADE
(As at 31 December 1993)

OFFICERS

OFFICERS OF THE CONTRACTING PARTIES*
Chairman of the Contracting Parties: B. K. Zutshi (India).
Vice-Chairmen of the Contracting Parties: Alastair Bisley (New Zealand), Jakob Esper Larsen (Denmark), Jesús Seade (Mexico).
Chairman of the Council of Representatives: András Szepesi (Hungary).
Chairman of the Committee on Trade and Development: Mohammed Zahran (Egypt).

SENIOR OFFICERS OF THE SECRETARIAT
Director-General: Peter Sutherland.
Deputy Directors-General: Warren A. Lavorel, Anwarul Hoda, Jesús Seade.

SENIOR OFFICER OF THE INTERNATIONAL TRADE CENTRE UNCTAD/GATT
Officer-in-Charge: Raju Makil.

*Elected at the December 1992 session of the Contracting Parties to hold office until the end of the next session scheduled for January 1994.

HEADQUARTERS

GATT Secretariat
Centre William Rappard
154, rue de Lausanne
1211 Geneva 21, Switzerland
Cable address: GATT GENEVA
Telephone: (41) (22) 739-51-11
Telex: 412 324 GATT CH
Facsimile: (41) (22) 731-42-06

Appendices

Appendix I

Roster of the United Nations

(As at 31 December 1993)

MEMBER	DATE OF ADMISSION	MEMBER	DATE OF ADMISSION	MEMBER	DATE OF ADMISSION
Afghanistan	19 Nov. 1946	Estonia	17 Sep. 1991	Monaco	28 May 1993
Albania	14 Dec. 1955	Ethiopia	13 Nov. 1945	Mongolia	27 Oct. 1961
Algeria	8 Oct. 1962	Fiji	13 Oct. 1970	Morocco	12 Nov. 1956
Andorra	28 July 1993	Finland	14 Dec. 1955	Mozambique	16 Sep. 1975
Angola	1 Dec. 1976	France	24 Oct. 1945	Myanmar	19 Apr. 1948
Antigua and Barbuda	11 Nov. 1981	Gabon	20 Sep. 1960	Namibia	23 Apr. 1990
Argentina	24 Oct. 1945	Gambia	21 Sep. 1965	Nepal	14 Dec. 1955
Armenia	2 Mar. 1992	Georgia	31 July 1992	Netherlands	10 Dec. 1945
Australia	1 Nov. 1945	Germany[3]	18 Sep. 1973	New Zealand	24 Oct. 1945
Austria	14 Dec. 1955	Ghana	8 Mar. 1957	Nicaragua	24 Oct. 1945
Azerbaijan	2 Mar. 1992	Greece	25 Oct. 1945	Niger	20 Sep. 1960
Bahamas	18 Sep. 1973	Grenada	17 Sep. 1974	Nigeria	7 Oct. 1960
Bahrain	21 Sep. 1971	Guatemala	21 Nov. 1945	Norway	27 Nov. 1945
Bangladesh	17 Sep. 1974	Guinea	12 Dec. 1958	Oman	7 Oct. 1971
Barbados	9 Dec. 1966	Guinea-Bissau	17 Sep. 1974	Pakistan	30 Sep. 1947
Belarus	24 Oct. 1945	Guyana	20 Sep. 1966	Panama	13 Nov. 1945
Belgium	27 Dec. 1945	Haiti	24 Oct. 1945	Papua New Guinea	10 Oct. 1975
Belize	25 Sep. 1981	Honduras	17 Dec. 1945	Paraguay	24 Oct. 1945
Benin	20 Sep. 1960	Hungary	14 Dec. 1955	Peru	31 Oct. 1945
Bhutan	21 Sep. 1971	Iceland	19 Nov. 1946	Philippines	24 Oct. 1945
Bolivia	14 Nov. 1945	India	30 Oct. 1945	Poland	24 Oct. 1945
Bosnia and Herzegovina	22 May 1992	Indonesia[4]	28 Sep. 1950	Portugal	14 Dec. 1955
Botswana	17 Oct. 1966	Iran (Islamic Republic of)	24 Oct. 1945	Qatar	21 Sep. 1971
Brazil	24 Oct. 1945	Iraq	21 Dec. 1945	Republic of Korea	17 Sep. 1991
Brunei Darussalam	21 Sep. 1984	Ireland	14 Dec. 1955	Republic of Moldova	2 Mar. 1992
Bulgaria	14 Dec. 1955	Israel	11 May 1949	Romania	14 Dec. 1955
Burkina Faso	20 Sep. 1960	Italy	14 Dec. 1955	Russian Federation[6]	24 Oct. 1945
Burundi	18 Sep. 1962	Jamaica	18 Sep. 1962	Rwanda	18 Sep. 1962
Cambodia	14 Dec. 1955	Japan	18 Dec. 1956	Saint Kitts and Nevis	23 Sep. 1983
Cameroon	20 Sep. 1960	Jordan	14 Dec. 1955	Saint Lucia	18 Sep. 1979
Canada	9 Nov. 1945	Kazakhstan	2 Mar. 1992	Saint Vincent and the Grenadines	16 Sep. 1980
Cape Verde	16 Sep. 1975	Kenya	16 Dec. 1963	Samoa	15 Dec. 1976
Central African Republic	20 Sep. 1960	Kuwait	14 May 1963	San Marino	2 Mar. 1992
Chad	20 Sep. 1960	Kyrgyzstan	2 Mar. 1992	Sao Tome and Principe	16 Sep. 1975
Chile	24 Oct. 1945	Lao People's Democratic Republic	14 Dec. 1955	Saudi Arabia	24 Oct. 1945
China	24 Oct. 1945	Latvia	17 Sep. 1991	Senegal	28 Sep. 1960
Colombia	5 Nov. 1945	Lebanon	24 Oct. 1945	Seychelles	21 Sep. 1976
Comoros	12 Nov. 1975	Lesotho	17 Oct. 1966	Sierra Leone	27 Sep. 1961
Congo	20 Sep. 1960	Liberia	2 Nov. 1945	Singapore[5]	21 Sep. 1965
Costa Rica	2 Nov. 1945	Libyan Arab Jamahiriya	14 Dec. 1955	Slovakia[1]	19 Jan. 1993
Côte d'Ivoire	20 Sep. 1960	Liechtenstein	18 Sep. 1990	Slovenia	22 May 1992
Croatia	22 May 1992	Lithuania	17 Sep. 1991	Solomon Islands	19 Sep. 1978
Cuba	24 Oct. 1945	Luxembourg	24 Oct. 1945	Somalia	20 Sep. 1960
Cyprus	20 Sep. 1960	Madagascar	20 Sep. 1960	South Africa	7 Nov. 1945
Czech Republic[1]	19 Jan. 1993	Malawi	1 Dec. 1964	Spain	14 Dec. 1955
Democratic People's Republic of Korea	17 Sep. 1991	Malaysia[5]	17 Sep. 1957	Sri Lanka	14 Dec. 1955
Denmark	24 Oct. 1945	Maldives	21 Sep. 1965	Sudan	12 Nov. 1956
Djibouti	20 Sep. 1977	Mali	28 Sep. 1960	Suriname	4 Dec. 1975
Dominica	18 Dec. 1978	Malta	1 Dec. 1964	Swaziland	24 Sep. 1968
Dominican Republic	24 Oct. 1945	Marshall Islands	17 Sep. 1991	Sweden	19 Nov. 1946
Ecuador	21 Dec. 1945	Mauritania	27 Oct. 1961	Syrian Arab Republic[2]	24 Oct. 1945
Egypt[2]	24 Oct. 1945	Mauritius	24 Apr. 1968	Tajikistan	2 Mar. 1992
El Salvador	24 Oct. 1945	Mexico	7 Nov. 1945	Thailand	16 Dec. 1946
Equatorial Guinea	12 Nov. 1968	Micronesia (Federated States of)	17 Sep. 1991	The former Yugoslav Republic of Macedonia	8 Apr. 1993
Eritrea	28 May 1993				

MEMBER	DATE OF ADMISSION	MEMBER	DATE OF ADMISSION	MEMBER	DATE OF ADMISSION
Togo	20 Sep. 1960	United Kingdom of Great Britain and Northern Ireland	24 Oct. 1945	Vanuatu	15 Sep. 1981
Trinidad and Tobago	18 Sep. 1962			Venezuela	15 Nov. 1945
Tunisia	12 Nov. 1956			Viet Nam	20 Sep. 1977
Turkey	24 Oct. 1945	United Republic of Tanzania[7]	14 Dec. 1961	Yemen[8]	30 Sep. 1947
Turkmenistan	2 Mar. 1992	United States of America	24 Oct. 1945	Yugoslavia[9]	24 Oct. 1945
Uganda	25 Oct. 1962			Zaire	20 Sep. 1960
Ukraine	24 Oct. 1945	Uruguay	18 Dec. 1945	Zambia	1 Dec. 1964
United Arab Emirates	9 Dec. 1971	Uzbekistan	2 Mar. 1992	Zimbabwe	25 Aug. 1980

[1]Czechoslovakia, which was an original Member of the United Nations from 24 October 1945, split up on 1 January 1993 and was succeeded by the Czech Republic and Slovakia.

[2]Egypt and Syria, both of which became Members of the United Nations on 24 October 1945, joined together—following a plebiscite held in those countries on 21 February 1958—to form the United Arab Republic. On 13 October 1961, Syria, having resumed its status as an independent State, also resumed its separate membership in the United Nations; it changed its name to the Syrian Arab Republic on 14 September 1971. The United Arab Republic continued as a Member of the United Nations and reverted to the name of Egypt on 2 September 1971.

[3]Through accession of the German Democratic Republic to the Federal Republic of Germany on 3 October 1990, the two German States (both of which became United Nations Members on 18 September 1973) united to form one sovereign State. As from that date, the Federal Republic of Germany has acted in the United Nations under the designation Germany.

[4]On 20 January 1965, Indonesia informed the Secretary-General that it had decided to withdraw from the United Nations. By a telegram of 19 September 1966, it notified the Secretary-General of its decision to resume participation in the activities of the United Nations. On 28 September 1966, the General Assembly took note of that decision and the President invited the representatives of Indonesia to take their seats in the Assembly.

[5]On 16 September 1963, Sabah (North Borneo), Sarawak and Singapore joined with the Federation of Malaya (which became a United Nations Member on 17 September 1957) to form Malaysia. On 9 August 1965, Singapore became an independent State and on 21 September 1965 it became a Member of the United Nations.

[6]The Union of Soviet Socialist Republics was an original Member of the United Nations from 24 October 1945. On 24 December 1991, the President of the Russian Federation informed the Secretary-General that the membership of the USSR in all United Nations organs was being continued by the Russian Federation.

[7]Tanganyika was admitted to the United Nations on 14 December 1961, and Zanzibar, on 16 December 1963. Following ratification, on 26 April 1964, of the Articles of Union between Tanganyika and Zanzibar, the two States became represented as a single Member: the United Republic of Tanganyika and Zanzibar; it changed its name to the United Republic of Tanzania on 1 November 1964.

[8]Yemen was admitted to the United Nations on 30 September 1947 and Democratic Yemen on 14 December 1967. On 22 May 1990, the two countries merged and have since been represented as one Member.

[9]Refers to the former Socialist Federal Republic of Yugoslavia.

Appendix II

Charter of the United Nations and Statute of the International Court of Justice

Charter of the United Nations

NOTE: The Charter of the United Nations was signed on 26 June 1945, in San Francisco, at the conclusion of the United Nations Conference on International Organization, and came into force on 24 October 1945. The Statute of the International Court of Justice is an integral part of the Charter.

Amendments to Articles 23, 27 and 61 of the Charter were adopted by the General Assembly on 17 December 1963 and came into force on 31 August 1965. A further amendment to Article 61 was adopted by the General Assembly on 20 December 1971, and came into force on 24 September 1973. An amendment to Article 109, adopted by the General Assembly on 20 December 1965, came into force on 12 June 1968.

The amendment to Article 23 enlarges the membership of the Security Council from 11 to 15. The amended Article 27 provides that decisions of the Security Council on procedural matters shall be made by an affirmative vote of nine members (formerly seven) and on all other matters by an affirmative vote of nine members (formerly seven), including the concurring votes of the five permanent members of the Security Council.

The amendment to Article 61, which entered into force on 31 August 1965, enlarged the membership of the Economic and Social Council from 18 to 27. The subsequent amendment to that Article, which entered into force on 24 September 1973, further increased the membership of the Council from 27 to 54.

The amendment to Article 109, which relates to the first paragraph of that Article, provides that a General Conference of Member States for the purpose of reviewing the Charter may be held at a date and place to be fixed by a two-thirds vote of the members of the General Assembly and by a vote of any nine members (formerly seven) of the Security Council. Paragraph 3 of Article 109, which deals with the consideration of a possible review conference during the tenth regular session of the General Assembly, has been retained in its original form in its reference to a "vote of any seven members of the Security Council", the paragraph having been acted upon in 1955 by the General Assembly, at its tenth regular session, and by the Security Council.

WE THE PEOPLES
OF THE UNITED NATIONS
DETERMINED
to save succeeding generations from the scourge of war, which twice in our lifetime has brought untold sorrow to mankind, and
to reaffirm faith in fundamental human rights, in the dignity and worth of the human person, in the equal rights of men and women and of nations large and small, and
to establish conditions under which justice and respect for the obligations arising from treaties and other sources of international law can be maintained, and
to promote social progress and better standards of life in larger freedom,

AND FOR THESE ENDS
to practice tolerance and live together in peace with one another as good neighbours, and
to unite our strength to maintain international peace and security, and
to ensure, by the acceptance of principles and the institution of methods, that armed force shall not be used, save in the common interest, and
to employ international machinery for the promotion of the economic and social advancement of all peoples,

HAVE RESOLVED TO
COMBINE OUR EFFORTS TO
ACCOMPLISH THESE AIMS
Accordingly, our respective Governments, through representatives assembled in the city of San Francisco, who have exhibited their full powers found to be in good and due form, have agreed to the present Charter of the United Nations and do hereby establish an international organization to be known as the United Nations.

Chapter I
PURPOSES AND PRINCIPLES

Article 1
The Purposes of the United Nations are:

1. To maintain international peace and security, and to that end: to take effective collective measures for the prevention and removal of threats to the peace, and for the suppression of acts of aggression or other breaches of the peace, and to bring about by peaceful means, and in conformity with the principles of justice and international law, adjustment or settlement of international disputes or situations which might lead to a breach of the peace;

2. To develop friendly relations among nations based on respect for the principle of equal rights and self-determination of peoples, and to take other appropriate measures to strengthen universal peace;

3. To achieve international co-operation in solving international problems of an economic, social, cultural, or humanitarian character, and in promoting and encouraging respect for human rights and for fundamental freedoms for all without distinction as to race, sex, language, or religion; and

4. To be a centre for harmonizing the actions of nations in the attainment of these common ends.

Article 2
The Organization and its Members, in pursuit of the Purposes stated in Article 1, shall act in accordance with the following Principles.

1. The Organization is based on the principle of the sovereign equality of all its Members.

2. All Members, in order to ensure to all of them the rights and benefits resulting from membership, shall fulfil in good faith the obligations assumed by them in accordance with the present Charter.

3. All Members shall settle their international disputes by peaceful means in such a manner that international peace and security, and justice, are not endangered.

4. All Members shall refrain in their international relations from the threat or use of force against the territorial integrity or political independence of any state, or in any other manner inconsistent with the Purposes of the United Nations.

5. All Members shall give the United Nations every assistance in any action it takes in accordance with the present Charter, and shall refrain from giving assistance to any state against which the United Nations is taking preventive or enforcement action.

6. The Organization shall ensure that states which are not Members of the United Nations act in accordance with these Principles so far as may be necessary for the maintenance of international peace and security.

7. Nothing contained in the present Charter shall authorize the United Nations to intervene in matters which are essentially within the domestic jurisdiction of any state or shall require the Members to submit such matters to settlement under the present Charter; but this principle shall not prejudice the application of enforcement measures under Chapter VII.

Chapter II
MEMBERSHIP

Article 3

The original Members of the United Nations shall be the states which, having participated in the United Nations Conference on International Organization at San Francisco, or having previously signed the Declaration by United Nations of 1 January 1942, sign the present Charter and ratify it in accordance with Article 110.

Article 4

1. Membership in the United Nations is open to all other peace-loving states which accept the obligations contained in the present Charter and, in the judgment of the Organization, are able and willing to carry out these obligations.

2. The admission of any such state to membership in the United Nations will be effected by a decision of the General Assembly upon the recommendation of the Security Council.

Article 5

A Member of the United Nations against which preventive or enforcement action has been taken by the Security Council may be suspended from the exercise of the rights and privileges of membership by the General Assembly upon the recommendation of the Security Council. The exercise of these rights and privileges may be restored by the Security Council.

Article 6

A Member of the United Nations which has persistently violated the Principles contained in the present Charter may be expelled from the Organization by the General Assembly upon the recommendation of the Security Council.

Chapter III
ORGANS

Article 7

1. There are established as the principal organs of the United Nations: a General Assembly, a Security Council, an Economic and Social Council, a Trusteeship Council, an International Court of Justice, and a Secretariat.

2. Such subsidiary organs as may be found necessary may be established in accordance with the present Charter.

Article 8

The United Nations shall place no restrictions on the eligibility of men and women to participate in any capacity and under conditions of equality in its principal and subsidiary organs.

Chapter IV
THE GENERAL ASSEMBLY

Composition

Article 9

1. The General Assembly shall consist of all the Members of the United Nations.

2. Each Member shall have not more than five representatives in the General Assembly.

Functions and powers

Article 10

The General Assembly may discuss any questions or any matters within the scope of the present Charter or relating to the powers and functions of any organs provided for in the present Charter, and, except as provided in Article 12, may make recommendations to the Members of the United Nations or to the Security Council or to both on any such questions or matters.

Article 11

1. The General Assembly may consider the general principles of co-operation in the maintenance of international peace and security, including the principles governing disarmament and the regulation of armaments, and may make recommendations with regard to such principles to the Members or to the Security Council or to both.

2. The General Assembly may discuss any questions relating to the maintenance of international peace and security brought before it by any Member of the United Nations, or by the Security Council, or by a state which is not a Member of the United Nations in accordance with Article 35, paragraph 2, and, except as provided in Article 12, may make recommendations with regard to any such questions to the state or states concerned or to the Security Council or to both. Any such question on which action is necessary shall be referred to the Security Council by the General Assembly either before or after discussion.

3. The General Assembly may call the attention of the Security Council to situations which are likely to endanger international peace and security.

4. The powers of the General Assembly set forth in this Article shall not limit the general scope of Article 10.

Article 12

1. While the Security Council is exercising in respect of any dispute or situation the functions assigned to it in the present Charter, the General Assembly shall not make any recommendation with regard to that dispute or situation unless the Security Council so requests.

2. The Secretary-General, with the consent of the Security Council, shall notify the General Assembly at each session of any matters relative to the maintenance of international peace and security which are being dealt with by the Security Council and shall similarly notify the General Assembly, or the Members of the United Nations if the General Assembly is not in session, immediately the Security Council ceases to deal with such matters.

Article 13

1. The General Assembly shall initiate studies and make recommendations for the purpose of:

   a. promoting international co-operation in the political field and encouraging the progressive development of international law and its codification;

   b. promoting international co-operation in the economic, social, cultural, educational, and health fields, and assisting in the realization of human rights and fundamental freedoms for all without distinction as to race, sex, language, or religion.

2. The further responsibilities, functions and powers of the General Assembly with respect to matters mentioned in paragraph 1(b) above are set forth in Chapters IX and X.

Article 14

Subject to the provisions of Article 12, the General Assembly may recommend measures for the peaceful adjustment of any situation, regardless of origin, which it deems likely to impair the general welfare or friendly relations among nations, including situations resulting from a violation of the provisions of the present Charter setting forth the Purposes and Principles of the United Nations.

Article 15

1. The General Assembly shall receive and consider annual and special reports from the Security Council; these reports shall include an account of the measures that the Security Council has decided upon or taken to maintain international peace and security.

2. The General Assembly shall receive and consider reports from the other organs of the United Nations.

Article 16

The General Assembly shall perform such functions with respect to the international trusteeship system as are assigned to it under Chapters XII and XIII, including the approval of the trusteeship agreements for areas not designated as strategic.

Article 17

1. The General Assembly shall consider and approve the budget of the Organization.

2. The expenses of the Organization shall be borne by the Members as apportioned by the General Assembly.

3. The General Assembly shall consider and approve any financial and budgetary arrangements with specialized agencies referred to in Article 57 and shall examine the administrative budgets of such specialized agencies with a view to making recommendations to the agencies concerned.

Voting

Article 18

1. Each member of the General Assembly shall have one vote.

2. Decisions of the General Assembly on important questions shall be made by a two-thirds majority of the members present and voting. These questions shall include: recommendations with respect to the maintenance of international peace and security, the election of the non-permanent members of the Security Council, the election of the members of the Economic and Social Council, the election of members of the Trusteeship Council in accordance with paragraph 1(c) of Article 86, the admission of new Members to the United Nations, the suspension of the rights and privileges of membership, the expulsion of Members, questions relating to the operation of the trusteeship system, and budgetary questions.

3. Decisions on other questions, including the determination of additional categories of questions to be decided by a two-thirds majority, shall be made by a majority of the members present and voting.

Article 19

A Member of the United Nations which is in arrears in the payment of its financial contributions to the Organization shall have no vote in the General Assembly if the amount of its arrears equals or exceeds the amount of the contributions due from it for the preceding two full years. The General Assembly may, nevertheless, permit such a Member to vote if it is satisfied that the failure to pay is due to conditions beyond the control of the Member.

Procedure

Article 20

The General Assembly shall meet in regular annual sessions and in such special sessions as occasion may require. Special sessions shall be convoked by the Secretary-General at the request of the Security Council or of a majority of the Members of the United Nations.

Article 21

The General Assembly shall adopt its own rules of procedure. It shall elect its President for each session.

Article 22

The General Assembly may establish such subsidiary organs as it deems necessary for the performance of its functions.

Chapter V
THE SECURITY COUNCIL

Composition

Article 23[1]

1. The Security Council shall consist of fifteen Members of the United Nations. The Republic of China, France, the Union of Soviet Socialist Republics, the United Kingdom of Great Britain and Northern Ireland, and the United States of America shall be permanent members of the Security Council. The General Assembly shall elect ten other Members of the United Nations to be non-permanent members of the Security Council, due regard being specially paid, in the first instance to the contribution of Members of the United Nations to the maintenance of international peace and security and to the other purposes of the Organization, and also to equitable geographical distribution.

2. The non-permanent members of the Security Council shall be elected for a term of two years. In the first election of the non-permanent members after the increase of the membership of the Security Council from eleven to fifteen, two of the four additional members shall be chosen for a term of one year. A retiring member shall not be eligible for immediate re-election.

3. Each member of the Security Council shall have one representative.

Functions and powers

Article 24

1. In order to ensure prompt and effective action by the United Nations, its Members confer on the Security Council primary responsibility for the maintenance of international peace and security, and agree that in carrying out its duties under this responsibility the Security Council acts on their behalf.

2. In discharging these duties the Security Council shall act in accordance with the Purposes and Principles of the United Nations. The specific powers granted to the Security Council for the discharge of these duties are laid down in Chapters VI, VII, VIII, and XII.

3. The Security Council shall submit annual and, when necessary, special reports to the General Assembly for its consideration.

Article 25

The Members of the United Nations agree to accept and carry out the decisions of the Security Council in accordance with the present Charter.

Article 26

In order to promote the establishment and maintenance of international peace and security with the least diversion for armaments of the world's human and economic resources, the Security Council shall be responsible for formulating, with the

---

[1]Amended text of Article 23, which came into force on 31 August 1965. (The text of Article 23 before it was amended read as follows:

1. The Security Council shall consist of eleven Members of the United Nations. The Republic of China, France, the Union of Soviet Socialist Republics, the United Kingdom of Great Britain and Northern Ireland, and the United States of America shall be permanent members of the Security Council. The General Assembly shall elect six other Members of the United Nations to be non-permanent members of the Security Council, due regard being specially paid, in the first instance to the contribution of Members of the United Nations to the maintenance of international peace and security and to the other purposes of the Organization, and also to equitable geographical distribution.

2. The non-permanent members of the Security Council shall be elected for a term of two years. In the first election of non-permanent members, however, three shall be chosen for a term of one year. A retiring member shall not be eligible for immediate re-election.

3. Each member of the Security Council shall have one representative.)

assistance of the Military Staff Committee referred to in Article 47, plans to be submitted to the Members of the United Nations for the establishment of a system for the regulation of armaments.

Voting

Article 27 [2]

1. Each member of the Security Council shall have one vote.

2. Decisions of the Security Council on procedural matters shall be made by an affirmative vote of nine members.

3. Decisions of the Security Council on all other matters shall be made by an affirmative vote of nine members including the concurring votes of the permanent members; provided that, in decisions under Chapter VI, and under paragraph 3 of Article 52, a party to a dispute shall abstain from voting.

Procedure

Article 28

1. The Security Council shall be so organized as to be able to function continuously. Each member of the Security Council shall for this purpose be represented at all times at the seat of the Organization.

2. The Security Council shall hold periodic meetings at which each of its members may, if it so desires, be represented by a member of the government or by some other specially designated representative.

3. The Security Council may hold meetings at such places other than the seat of the Organization as in its judgment will best facilitate its work.

Article 29

The Security Council may establish such subsidiary organs as it deems necessary for the performance of its functions.

Article 30

The Security Council shall adopt its own rules of procedure, including the method of selecting its President.

Article 31

Any Member of the United Nations which is not a member of the Security Council may participate, without vote, in the discussion of any question brought before the Security Council whenever the latter considers that the interests of that Member are specially affected.

Article 32

Any Member of the United Nations which is not a member of the Security Council or any state which is not a Member of the United Nations, if it is a party to a dispute under consideration by the Security Council, shall be invited to participate, without vote, in the discussion relating to the dispute. The Security Council shall lay down such conditions as it deems just for the participation of a state which is not a Member of the United Nations.

Chapter VI
PACIFIC SETTLEMENT OF DISPUTES

Article 33

1. The parties to any dispute, the continuance of which is likely to endanger the maintenance of international peace and security, shall, first of all, seek a solution by negotiation, enquiry, mediation, conciliation, arbitration, judicial settlement, resort to regional agencies or arrangements, or other peaceful means of their own choice.

2. The Security Council shall, when it deems necessary, call upon the parties to settle their dispute by such means.

Article 34

The Security Council may investigate any dispute or any situation which might lead to international friction or give rise to a dispute, in order to determine whether the continuance of the dispute or situation is likely to endanger the maintenance of international peace and security.

Article 35

1. Any Member of the United Nations may bring any dispute, or any situation of the nature referred to in Article 34, to the attention of the Security Council or of the General Assembly.

2. A state which is not a Member of the United Nations may bring to the attention of the Security Council or of the General Assembly any dispute to which it is a party if it accepts in advance, for the purposes of the dispute, the obligations of pacific settlement provided in the present Charter.

3. The proceedings of the General Assembly in respect of matters brought to its attention under this Article will be subject to the provisions of Articles 11 and 12.

Article 36

1. The Security Council may, at any stage of a dispute of the nature referred to in Article 33 or of a situation of like nature, recommend appropriate procedures or methods of adjustment.

2. The Security Council should take into consideration any procedures for the settlement of the dispute which have already been adopted by the parties.

3. In making recommendations under this Article the Security Council should also take into consideration that legal disputes should as a general rule be referred by the parties to the International Court of Justice in accordance with the provisions of the Statute of the Court.

Article 37

1. Should the parties to a dispute of the nature referred to in Article 33 fail to settle it by the means indicated in that Article, they shall refer it to the Security Council.

2. If the Security Council deems that the continuance of the dispute is in fact likely to endanger the maintenance of international peace and security, it shall decide whether to take action under Article 36 or to recommend such terms of settlement as it may consider appropriate.

Article 38

Without prejudice to the provisions of Articles 33 to 37, the Security Council may, if all the parties to any dispute so request, make recommendations to the parties with a view to a pacific settlement of the dispute.

Chapter VII
ACTION WITH RESPECT TO THREATS TO THE PEACE, BREACHES OF THE PEACE, AND ACTS OF AGGRESSION

Article 39

The Security Council shall determine the existence of any threat to the peace, breach of the peace, or act of aggression and shall make recommendations, or decide what measures shall be taken in accordance with Articles 41 and 42, to maintain or restore international peace and security.

Article 40

In order to prevent an aggravation of the situation, the Security Council may, before making the recommendations or deciding upon the measures provided for in Article 39, call upon the parties concerned to comply with such provisional measures as it deems necessary or desirable. Such provisional measures shall be without prejudice to the rights, claims, or position of the parties concerned. The Security Council shall duly take account of failure to comply with such provisional measures.

---

[2]Amended text of Article 27, which came into force on 31 August 1965. (The text of Article 27 before it was amended read as follows:

1. Each member of the Security Council shall have one vote.

2. Decisions of the Security Council on procedural matters shall be made by an affirmative vote of seven members.

3. Decisions of the Security Council on all other matters shall be made by an affirmative vote of seven members including the concurring votes of the permanent members; provided that, in decisions under Chapter VI, and under paragraph 3 of Article 52, a party to a dispute shall abstain from voting.)

Article 41

The Security Council may decide what measures not involving the use of armed force are to be employed to give effect to its decisions, and it may call upon the Members of the United Nations to apply such measures. These may include complete or partial interruption of economic relations and of rail, sea, air, postal, telegraphic, radio, and other means of communication, and the severance of diplomatic relations.

Article 42

Should the Security Council consider that measures provided for in Article 41 would be inadequate or have proved to be inadequate, it may take such action by air, sea, or land forces as may be necessary to maintain or restore international peace and security. Such action may include demonstrations, blockade, and other operations by air, sea, or land forces of Members of the United Nations.

Article 43

1. All Members of the United Nations, in order to contribute to the maintenance of international peace and security, undertake to make available to the Security Council, on its call and in accordance with a special agreement or agreements, armed forces, assistance, and facilities, including rights of passage, necessary for the purpose of maintaining international peace and security.

2. Such agreement or agreements shall govern the numbers and types of forces, their degree of readiness and general location, and the nature of the facilities and assistance to be provided.

3. The agreement or agreements shall be negotiated as soon as possible on the initiative of the Security Council. They shall be concluded between the Security Council and Members or between the Security Council and groups of Members and shall be subject to ratification by the signatory states in accordance with their respective constitutional processes.

Article 44

When the Security Council has decided to use force it shall, before calling upon a Member not represented on it to provide armed forces in fulfilment of the obligations assumed under Article 43, invite that Member, if the Member so desires, to participate in the decisions of the Security Council concerning the employment of contingents of that Member's armed forces.

Article 45

In order to enable the United Nations to take urgent military measures, Members shall hold immediately available national airforce contingents for combined international enforcement action. The strength and degree of readiness of these contingents and plans for their combined action shall be determined, within the limits laid down in the special agreement or agreements referred to in Article 43, by the Security Council with the assistance of the Military Staff Committee.

Article 46

Plans for the application of armed force shall be made by the Security Council with the assistance of the Military Staff Committee.

Article 47

1. There shall be established a Military Staff Committee to advise and assist the Security Council on all questions relating to the Security Council's military requirements for the maintenance of international peace and security, the employment and command of forces placed at its disposal, the regulation of armaments, and possible disarmament.

2. The Military Staff Committee shall consist of the Chiefs of Staff of the permanent members of the Security Council or their representatives. Any Member of the United Nations not permanently represented on the Committee shall be invited by the Committee to be associated with it when the efficient discharge of the Committee's responsibilities requires the participation of that Member in its work.

3. The Military Staff Committee shall be responsible under the Security Council for the strategic direction of any armed forces placed at the disposal of the Security Council. Questions relating to the command of such forces shall be worked out subsequently.

4. The Military Staff Committee, with the authorization of the Security Council and after consultation with appropriate regional agencies, may establish regional sub-committees.

Article 48

1. The action required to carry out the decisions of the Security Council for the maintenance of international peace and security shall be taken by all the Members of the United Nations or by some of them, as the Security Council may determine.

2. Such decisions shall be carried out by the Members of the United Nations directly and through their action in the appropriate international agencies of which they are members.

Article 49

The Members of the United Nations shall join in affording mutual assistance in carrying out the measures decided upon by the Security Council.

Article 50

If preventive or enforcement measures against any state are taken by the Security Council, any other state, whether a Member of the United Nations or not, which finds itself confronted with special economic problems arising from the carrying out of those measures shall have the right to consult the Security Council with regard to a solution of those problems.

Article 51

Nothing in the present Charter shall impair the inherent right of individual or collective self-defence if an armed attack occurs against a Member of the United Nations, until the Security Council has taken measures necessary to maintain international peace and security. Measures taken by Members in the exercise of this right of self-defence shall be immediately reported to the Security Council and shall not in any way affect the authority and responsibility of the Security Council under the present Charter to take at any time such action as it deems necessary in order to maintain or restore international peace and security.

Chapter VIII
REGIONAL ARRANGEMENTS

Article 52

1. Nothing in the present Charter precludes the existence of regional arrangements or agencies for dealing with such matters relating to the maintenance of international peace and security as are appropriate for regional action, provided that such arrangements or agencies and their activities are consistent with the Purposes and Principles of the United Nations.

2. The Members of the United Nations entering into such arrangements or constituting such agencies shall make every effort to achieve pacific settlement of local disputes through such regional arrangements or by such regional agencies before referring them to the Security Council.

3. The Security Council shall encourage the development of pacific settlement of local disputes through such regional arrangements or by such regional agencies either on the initiative of the states concerned or by reference from the Security Council.

4. This Article in no way impairs the application of Articles 34 and 35.

Article 53

1. The Security Council shall, where appropriate, utilize such regional arrangements or agencies for enforcement action under its authority. But no enforcement action shall be taken under regional arrangements or by regional agencies without the authorization of the Security Council, with the exception of measures against any enemy state, as defined in paragraph 2 of this Article, provided for pursuant to Article 107 or in regional arrangements directed against renewal of aggressive policy on the part of any such state, until such time as the Organization may, on request of the Governments concerned, be charged with the responsibility for preventing further aggression by such a state.

2.   The term enemy state as used in paragraph 1 of this Article applies to any state which during the Second World War has been an enemy of any signatory of the present Charter.

Article 54

The Security Council shall at all times be kept fully informed of activities undertaken or in contemplation under regional arrangements or by regional agencies for the maintenance of international peace and security.

Chapter IX
INTERNATIONAL ECONOMIC
AND SOCIAL CO-OPERATION

Article 55

With a view to the creation of conditions of stability and well-being which are necessary for peaceful and friendly relations among nations based on respect for the principle of equal rights and self-determination of peoples, the United Nations shall promote:
  a.   higher standards of living, full employment, and conditions of economic and social progress and development;
  b.   solutions of international economic, social, health, and related problems; and international cultural and educational co-operation; and
  c.   universal respect for, and observance of, human rights and fundamental freedoms for all without distinction as to race, sex, language, or religion.

Article 56

All Members pledge themselves to take joint and separate action in co-operation with the Organization for the achievement of the purposes set forth in Article 55.

Article 57

1.   The various specialized agencies, established by intergovernmental agreement and having wide international responsibilities, as defined in their basic instruments, in economic, social, cultural, educational, health, and related fields, shall be brought into relationship with the United Nations in accordance with the provisions of Article 63.

2.   Such agencies thus brought into relationship with the United Nations are hereinafter referred to as specialized agencies.

Article 58

The Organization shall make recommendations for the co-ordination of the policies and activities of the specialized agencies.

Article 59

The Organization shall, where appropriate, initiate negotiations among the states concerned for the creation of any new specialized agencies required for the accomplishment of the purposes set forth in Article 55.

Article 60

Responsibility for the discharge of the functions of the Organization set forth in this Chapter shall be vested in the General Assembly and, under the authority of the General Assembly, in the Economic and Social Council, which shall have for this purpose the powers set forth in Chapter X.

Chapter X
THE ECONOMIC AND SOCIAL COUNCIL

Composition

Article 61[3]

1.   The Economic and Social Council shall consist of fifty-four Members of the United Nations elected by the General Assembly.

2.   Subject to the provisions of paragraph 3, eighteen members of the Economic and Social Council shall be elected each year for a term of three years. A retiring member shall be eligible for immediate re-election.

3.   At the first election after the increase in the membership of the Economic and Social Council from twenty-seven to fifty-

four members, in addition to the members elected in place of the nine members whose term of office expires at the end of that year, twenty-seven additional members shall be elected. Of these twenty-seven additional members, the term of office of nine members so elected shall expire at the end of one year, and of nine other members at the end of two years, in accordance with arrangements made by the General Assembly.

4.   Each member of the Economic and Social Council shall have one representative.

Functions and powers

Article 62

1.   The Economic and Social Council may make or initiate studies and reports with respect to international economic, social, cultural, educational, health, and related matters and may make recommendations with respect to any such matters to the General Assembly, to the Members of the United Nations, and to the specialized agencies concerned.

2.   It may make recommendations for the purpose of promoting respect for, and observance of, human rights and fundamental freedoms for all.

3.   It may prepare draft conventions for submission to the General Assembly, with respect to matters falling within its competence.

4.   It may call, in accordance with the rules prescribed by the United Nations, international conferences on matters falling within its competence.

Article 63

1.   The Economic and Social Council may enter into agreements with any of the agencies referred to in Article 57, defining the terms on which the agency concerned shall be brought into relationship with the United Nations. Such agreements shall be subject to approval by the General Assembly.

2.   It may co-ordinate the activities of the specialized agencies through consultation with and recommendations to such agencies and through recommendations to the General Assembly and to the Members of the United Nations.

Article 64

1.   The Economic and Social Council may take appropriate steps to obtain regular reports from the specialized agencies. It may make arrangements with the Members of the United Nations and with the specialized agencies to obtain reports on the steps taken to give effect to its own recommendations and to recommendations on matters falling within its competence made by the General Assembly.

2.   It may communicate its observations on these reports to the General Assembly.

Article 65

The Economic and Social Council may furnish information to the Security Council and shall assist the Security Council upon its request.

Article 66

1.   The Economic and Social Council shall perform such functions as fall within its competence in connexion with the carrying out of the recommendations of the General Assembly.

---

[3]Amended text of Article 61, which came into force on 24 September 1973. (The text of Article 61 as previously amended on 31 August 1965 read as follows:
  1.   The Economic and Social Council shall consist of twenty-seven Members of the United Nations elected by the General Assembly.
  2.   Subject to the provisions of paragraph 3, nine members of the Economic and Social Council shall be elected each year for a term of three years. A retiring member shall be eligible for immediate re-election.
  3.   At the first election after the increase in the membership of the Economic and Social Council from eighteen to twenty-seven members, in addition to the members elected in place of the six members whose term of office expires at the end of that year, nine additional members shall be elected. Of these nine additional members, the term of office of three members so elected shall expire at the end of one year, and of three other members at the end of two years, in accordance with arrangements made by the General Assembly.
  4.   Each member of the Economic and Social Council shall have one representative.)

2. It may, with the approval of the General Assembly, perform services at the request of Members of the United Nations and at the request of specialized agencies.

3. It shall perform such other functions as are specified elsewhere in the present Charter or as may be assigned to it by the General Assembly.

Voting

Article 67

1. Each member of the Economic and Social Council shall have one vote.

2. Decisions of the Economic and Social Council shall be made by a majority of the members present and voting.

Procedure

Article 68

The Economic and Social Council shall set up commissions in economic and social fields and for the promotion of human rights, and such other commissions as may be required for the performance of its functions.

Article 69

The Economic and Social Council shall invite any Member of the United Nations to participate, without vote, in its deliberations on any matter of particular concern to that Member.

Article 70

The Economic and Social Council may make arrangements for representatives of the specialized agencies to participate, without vote, in its deliberations and in those of the commissions established by it, and for its representatives to participate in the deliberations of the specialized agencies.

Article 71

The Economic and Social Council may make suitable arrangements for consultation with non-governmental organizations which are concerned with matters within its competence. Such arrangements may be made with international organizations and, where appropriate, with national organizations after consultation with the Member of the United Nations concerned.

Article 72

1. The Economic and Social Council shall adopt its own rules of procedure, including the method of selecting its President.

2. The Economic and Social Council shall meet as required in accordance with its rules, which shall include provision for the convening of meetings on the request of a majority of its members.

Chapter XI
DECLARATION REGARDING NON-SELF-GOVERNING TERRITORIES

Article 73

Members of the United Nations which have or assume responsibilities for the administration of territories whose peoples have not yet attained a full measure of self-government recognize the principle that the interests of the inhabitants of these territories are paramount, and accept as a sacred trust the obligation to promote to the utmost, within the system of international peace and security established by the present Charter, the well-being of the inhabitants of these territories, and, to this end:

a. to ensure, with due respect for the culture of the peoples concerned, their political, economic, social, and educational advancement, their just treatment, and their protection against abuses;

b. to develop self-government, to take due account of the political aspirations of the peoples, and to assist them in the progressive development of their free political institutions, according to the particular circumstances of each territory and its peoples and their varying stages of advancement;

c. to further international peace and security;

d. to promote constructive measures of development, to encourage research, and to co-operate with one another and,

when and where appropriate, with specialized international bodies with a view to the practical achievement of the social, economic, and scientific purposes set forth in this Article; and

e. to transmit regularly to the Secretary-General for information purposes, subject to such limitation as security and constitutional considerations may require, statistical and other information of a technical nature relating to economic, social, and educational conditions in the territories for which they are respectively responsible other than those territories to which Chapters XII and XIII apply.

Article 74

Members of the United Nations also agree that their policy in respect of the territories to which this Chapter applies, no less than in respect of their metropolitan areas, must be based on the general principle of good-neighbourliness, due account being taken of the interests and well-being of the rest of the world, in social, economic, and commercial matters.

Chapter XII
INTERNATIONAL TRUSTEESHIP SYSTEM

Article 75

The United Nations shall establish under its authority an international trusteeship system for the administration and supervision of such territories as may be placed thereunder by subsequent individual agreements. These territories are hereinafter referred to as trust territories.

Article 76

The basic objectives of the trusteeship system, in accordance with the Purposes of the United Nations laid down in Article 1 of the present Charter, shall be:

a. to further international peace and security;

b. to promote the political, economic, social, and educational advancement of the inhabitants of the trust territories, and their progressive development towards self-government or independence as may be appropriate to the particular circumstances of each territory and its peoples and the freely expressed wishes of the peoples concerned, and as may be provided by the terms of each trusteeship agreement;

c. to encourage respect for human rights and for fundamental freedoms for all without distinction as to race, sex, language, or religion, and to encourage recognition of the interdependence of the peoples of the world; and

d. to ensure equal treatment in social, economic, and commercial matters for all Members of the United Nations and their nationals, and also equal treatment for the latter in the administration of justice, without prejudice to the attainment of the foregoing objectives and subject to the provisions of Article 80.

Article 77

1. The trusteeship system shall apply to such territories in the following categories as may be placed thereunder by means of trusteeship agreements:

a. territories now held under mandate;

b. territories which may be detached from enemy states as a result of the Second World War; and

c. territories voluntarily placed under the system by states responsible for their administration.

2. It will be a matter for subsequent agreement as to which territories in the foregoing categories will be brought under the trusteeship system and upon what terms.

Article 78

The trusteeship system shall not apply to territories which have become Members of the United Nations, relationship among which shall be based on respect for the principle of sovereign equality.

Article 79

The terms of trusteeship for each territory to be placed under the trusteeship system, including any alteration or amendment, shall be agreed upon by the states directly concerned, including the mandatory power in the case of territories held under mandate by a Member of the United Nations, and shall be approved as provided for in Articles 83 and 85.

Article 80

1. Except as may be agreed upon in individual trusteeship agreements, made under Articles 77, 79, and 81, placing each territory under the trusteeship system, and until such agreements have been concluded, nothing in this Chapter shall be construed in or of itself to alter in any manner the rights whatsoever of any states or any peoples or the terms of existing international instruments to which Members of the United Nations may respectively be parties.

2. Paragraph 1 of this Article shall not be interpreted as giving grounds for delay or postponement of the negotiation and conclusion of agreements for placing mandated and other territories under the trusteeship system as provided for in Article 77.

Article 81

The trusteeship agreement shall in each case include the terms under which the trust territory will be administered and designate the authority which will exercise the administration of the trust territory. Such authority, hereinafter called the administering authority, may be one or more states or the Organization itself.

Article 82

There may be designated, in any trusteeship agreement, a strategic area or areas which may include part or all of the trust territory to which the agreement applies, without prejudice to any special agreement or agreements made under Article 43.

Article 83

1. All functions of the United Nations relating to strategic areas, including the approval of the terms of the trusteeship agreements and of their alteration or amendments, shall be exercised by the Security Council.

2. The basic objectives set forth in Article 76 shall be applicable to the people of each strategic area.

3. The Security Council shall, subject to the provisions of the trusteeship agreements and without prejudice to security considerations, avail itself of the assistance of the Trusteeship Council to perform those functions of the United Nations under the trusteeship system relating to political, economic, social, and educational matters in the strategic areas.

Article 84

It shall be the duty of the administering authority to ensure that the trust territory shall play its part in the maintenance of international peace and security. To this end the administering authority may make use of volunteer forces, facilities, and assistance from the trust territory in carrying out the obligations towards the Security Council undertaken in this regard by the administering authority, as well as for local defence and the maintenance of law and order within the trust territory.

Article 85

1. The functions of the United Nations with regard to trusteeship agreements for all areas not designated as strategic, including the approval of the terms of the trusteeship agreements and of their alteration or amendment, shall be exercised by the General Assembly.

2. The Trusteeship Council, operating under the authority of the General Assembly, shall assist the General Assembly in carrying out these functions.

Chapter XIII
THE TRUSTEESHIP COUNCIL

Composition

Article 86

1. The Trusteeship Council shall consist of the following Members of the United Nations:

a. those Members administering trust territories;
b. such of those Members mentioned by name in Article 23 as are not administering trust territories; and
c. as many other Members elected for three-year terms by the General Assembly as may be necessary to ensure that the total number of members of the Trusteeship Council is equally divided between those Members of the United Nations which administer trust territories and those which do not.

2. Each member of the Trusteeship Council shall designate one specially qualified person to represent it therein.

Functions and powers

Article 87

The General Assembly and, under its authority, the Trusteeship Council, in carrying out their functions, may:
a. consider reports submitted by the administering authority;
b. accept petitions and examine them in consultation with the administering authority;
c. provide for periodic visits to the respective trust territories at times agreed upon with the administering authority; and
d. take these and other actions in conformity with the terms of the trusteeship agreements.

Article 88

The Trusteeship Council shall formulate a questionnaire on the political, economic, social, and educational advancement of the inhabitants of each trust territory, and the administering authority for each trust territory within the competence of the General Assembly shall make an annual report to the General Assembly upon the basis of such questionnaire.

Voting

Article 89

1. Each member of the Trusteeship Council shall have one vote.
2. Decisions of the Trusteeship Council shall be made by a majority of the members present and voting.

Procedure

Article 90

1. The Trusteeship Council shall adopt its own rules of procedure, including the method of selecting its President.
2. The Trusteeship Council shall meet as required in accordance with its rules, which shall include provision for the convening of meetings on the request of a majority of its members.

Article 91

The Trusteeship Council shall, when appropriate, avail itself of the assistance of the Economic and Social Council and of the specialized agencies in regard to matters with which they are respectively concerned.

Chapter XIV
THE INTERNATIONAL COURT OF JUSTICE

Article 92

The International Court of Justice shall be the principal judicial organ of the United Nations. It shall function in accordance with the annexed Statute, which is based upon the Statute of the Permanent Court of International Justice and forms an integral part of the present Charter.

Article 93

1. All Members of the United Nations are *ipso facto* parties to the Statute of the International Court of Justice.

2. A state which is not a Member of the United Nations may become a party to the Statute of the International Court of Justice on conditions to be determined in each case by the General Assembly upon the recommendation of the Security Council.

Article 94

1. Each Member of the United Nations undertakes to comply with the decision of the International Court of Justice in any case to which it is a party.

2. If any party to a case fails to perform the obligations incumbent upon it under a judgment rendered by the Court, the other party may have recourse to the Security Council, which may, if it deems necessary, make recommendations or decide upon measures to be taken to give effect to the judgment.

Article 95

Nothing in the present Charter shall prevent Members of the United Nations from entrusting the solution of their differences to other tribunals by virtue of agreements already in existence or which may be concluded in the future.

Article 96

1. The General Assembly or the Security Council may request the International Court of Justice to give an advisory opinion on any legal question.

2. Other organs of the United Nations and specialized agencies, which may at any time be so authorized by the General Assembly, may also request advisory opinions of the Court on legal questions arising within the scope of their activities.

Chapter XV
THE SECRETARIAT

Article 97

The Secretariat shall comprise a Secretary-General and such staff as the Organization may require. The Secretary-General shall be appointed by the General Assembly upon the recommendation of the Security Council. He shall be the chief administrative officer of the Organization.

Article 98

The Secretary-General shall act in that capacity in all meetings of the General Assembly, of the Security Council, of the Economic and Social Council, and of the Trusteeship Council, and shall perform such other functions as are entrusted to him by these organs. The Secretary-General shall make an annual report to the General Assembly on the work of the Organization.

Article 99

The Secretary-General may bring to the attention of the Security Council any matter which in his opinion may threaten the maintenance of international peace and security.

Article 100

1. In the performance of their duties the Secretary-General and the staff shall not seek or receive instructions from any government or from any other authority external to the Organization. They shall refrain from any action which might reflect on their position as international officials responsible only to the Organization.

2. Each Member of the United Nations undertakes to respect the exclusively international character of the responsibilities of the Secretary-General and the staff and not to seek to influence them in the discharge of their responsibilities.

Article 101

1. The staff shall be appointed by the Secretary-General under regulations established by the General Assembly.

2. Appropriate staffs shall be permanently assigned to the Economic and Social Council, the Trusteeship Council, and, as required, to other organs of the United Nations. These staffs shall form a part of the Secretariat.

3. The paramount consideration in the employment of the staff and in the determination of the conditions of service shall be the necessity of securing the highest standards of efficiency, competence, and integrity. Due regard shall be paid to the importance of recruiting the staff on as wide a geographical basis as possible.

Chapter XVI
MISCELLANEOUS PROVISIONS

Article 102

1. Every treaty and every international agreement entered into by any Member of the United Nations after the present Charter comes into force shall as soon as possible be registered with the Secretariat and published by it.

2. No party to any such treaty or international agreement which has not been registered in accordance with the provisions of paragraph 1 of this Article may invoke that treaty or agreement before any organ of the United Nations.

Article 103

In the event of a conflict between the obligations of the Members of the United Nations under the present Charter and their obligations under any other international agreement, their obligations under the present Charter shall prevail.

Article 104

The Organization shall enjoy in the territory of each of its Members such legal capacity as may be necessary for the exercise of its functions and the fulfilment of its purposes.

Article 105

1. The Organization shall enjoy in the territory of each of its Members such privileges and immunities as are necessary for the fulfilment of its purposes.

2. Representatives of the Members of the United Nations and officials of the Organization shall similarly enjoy such privileges and immunities as are necessary for the independent exercise of their functions in connexion with the Organization.

3. The General Assembly may make recommendations with a view to determining the details of the application of paragraphs 1 and 2 of this Article or may propose conventions to the Members of the United Nations for this purpose.

Chapter XVII
TRANSITIONAL SECURITY ARRANGEMENTS

Article 106

Pending the coming into force of such special agreements referred to in Article 43 as in the opinion of the Security Council enable it to begin the exercise of its responsibilities under Article 42, the parties to the Four-Nation Declaration, signed at Moscow, 30 October 1943, and France, shall, in accordance with the provisions of paragraph 5 of that Declaration, consult with one another and as occasion requires with other Members of the United Nations with a view to such joint action on behalf of the Organization as may be necessary for the purpose of maintaining international peace and security.

Article 107

Nothing in the present Charter shall invalidate or preclude action, in relation to any state which during the Second World War has been an enemy of any signatory to the present Charter, taken or authorized as a result of that war by the Governments having responsibility for such action.

Chapter XVIII
AMENDMENTS

Article 108

Amendments to the present Charter shall come into force for all Members of the United Nations when they have been adopted by a vote of two thirds of the members of the General Assembly and ratified in accordance with their respective constitutional processes by two thirds of the Members of the United Nations, including all the permanent members of the Security Council.

Article 109 [4]

1. A General Conference of the Members of the United Nations for the purpose of reviewing the present Charter may be held at a date and place to be fixed by a two-thirds vote of the members of the General Assembly and by a vote of any nine members of the Security Council. Each Member of the United Nations shall have one vote in the conference.

2. Any alteration of the present Charter recommended by a two-thirds vote of the conference shall take effect when ratified in accordance with their respective constitutional processes by two thirds of the Members of the United Nations including all the permanent members of the Security Council.

3. If such a conference has not been held before the tenth annual session of the General Assembly following the coming into force of the present Charter, the proposal to call such a conference shall be placed on the agenda of that session of the General Assembly, and the conference shall be held if so decided by a majority vote of the members of the General Assembly and by a vote of any seven members of the Security Council.

Chapter XIX
RATIFICATION AND SIGNATURE

Article 110

1. The present Charter shall be ratified by the signatory states in accordance with their respective constitutional processes.

2. The ratifications shall be deposited with the Government of the United States of America, which shall notify all the signatory states of each deposit as well as the Secretary-General of the Organization when he has been appointed.

3. The present Charter shall come into force upon the deposit of ratifications by the Republic of China, France, the Union of Soviet Socialist Republics, the United Kingdom of Great Britain and Northern Ireland, and the United States of America, and by a majority of the other signatory states. A protocol of the ratifications deposited shall thereupon be drawn up by the Government of the United States

of America which shall communicate copies thereof to all the signatory states.

4. The states signatory to the present Charter which ratify it after it has come into force will become original Members of the United Nations on the date of the deposit of their respective ratifications.

Article 111

The present Charter, of which the Chinese, French, Russian, English, and Spanish texts are equally authentic, shall remain deposited in the archives of the Government of the United States of America. Duly certified copies thereof shall be transmitted by that Government to the Governments of the other signatory states.

IN FAITH WHEREOF the representatives of the Governments of the United Nations have signed the present Charter.

DONE at the city of San Francisco the twenty-sixth day of June, one thousand nine hundred and forty-five.

---

[4] Amended text of Article 109, which came into force on 12 June 1968. (The text of Article 109 before it was amended read as follows:

1. A General Conference of the Members of the United Nations for the purpose of reviewing the present Charter may be held at a date and place to be fixed by a two-thirds vote of the members of the General Assembly and by a vote of any seven members of the Security Council. Each Member of the United Nations shall have one vote in the conference.

2. Any alteration of the present Charter recommended by a two-thirds vote of the conference shall take effect when ratified in accordance with their respective constitutional processes by two thirds of the Members of the United Nations including all the permanent members of the Security Council.

3. If such a conference has not been held before the tenth annual session of the General Assembly following the coming into force of the present Charter, the proposal to call such a conference shall be placed on the agenda of that session of the General Assembly, and the conference shall be held if so decided by a majority vote of the members of the General Assembly and by a vote of any seven members of the Security Council.)

Statute of the International Court of Justice

Article 1

THE INTERNATIONAL COURT OF JUSTICE established by the Charter of the United Nations as the principal judicial organ of the United Nations shall be constituted and shall function in accordance with the provisions of the present Statute.

Chapter I
ORGANIZATION OF THE COURT

Article 2

The Court shall be composed of a body of independent judges, elected regardless of their nationality from among persons of high moral character, who possess the qualifications required in their respective countries for appointment to the highest judicial offices, or are jurisconsults of recognized competence in international law.

Article 3

1. The Court shall consist of fifteen members, no two of whom may be nationals of the same state.

2. A person who for the purposes of membership in the Court could be regarded as a national of more than one state shall be deemed to be a national of the one in which he ordinarily exercises civil and political rights.

Article 4

1. The members of the Court shall be elected by the General Assembly and by the Security Council from a list of persons nominated by the national groups in the Permanent Court of Arbitration, in accordance with the following provisions.

2. In the case of Members of the United Nations not represented in the Permanent Court of Arbitration, candidates shall be nominated by national groups appointed for this purpose by their governments under the same conditions as those prescribed for mem-

bers of the Permanent Court of Arbitration by Article 44 of the Convention of The Hague of 1907 for the pacific settlement of international disputes.

3. The conditions under which a state which is a party to the present Statute but is not a Member of the United Nations may participate in electing the members of the Court shall, in the absence of a special agreement, be laid down by the General Assembly upon recommendation of the Security Council.

Article 5

1. At least three months before the date of the election, the Secretary-General of the United Nations shall address a written request to the members of the Permanent Court of Arbitration belonging to the states which are parties to the present Statute, and to the members of the national groups appointed under Article 4, paragraph 2, inviting them to undertake, within a given time, by national groups, the nomination of persons in a position to accept the duties of a member of the Court.

2. No group may nominate more than four persons, not more than two of whom shall be of their own nationality. In no case may the number of candidates nominated by a group be more than double the number of seats to be filled.

Article 6

Before making these nominations, each national group is recommended to consult its highest court of justice, its legal faculties and schools of law, and its national academies and national sections of international academies devoted to the study of law.

Article 7

1. The Secretary-General shall prepare a list in alphabetical order of all the persons thus nominated. Save as provided in Article 12, paragraph 2, these shall be the only persons eligible.

2. The Secretary-General shall submit this list to the General Assembly and to the Security Council.

Article 8
The General Assembly and the Security Council shall proceed independently of one another to elect the members of the Court.

Article 9
At every election, the electors shall bear in mind not only that the persons to be elected should individually possess the qualifications required, but also that in the body as a whole the representation of the main forms of civilization and of the principal legal systems of the world should be assured.

Article 10
1. Those candidates who obtain an absolute majority of votes in the General Assembly and in the Security Council shall be considered as elected.
2. Any vote of the Security Council, whether for the election of judges or for the appointment of members of the conference envisaged in Article 12, shall be taken without any distinction between permanent and non-permanent members of the Security Council.
3. In the event of more than one national of the same state obtaining an absolute majority of the votes both of the General Assembly and of the Security Council, the eldest of these only shall be considered as elected.

Article 11
If, after the first meeting held for the purpose of the election, one or more seats remain to be filled, a second and, if necessary, a third meeting shall take place.

Article 12
1. If, after the third meeting, one or more seats still remain unfilled, a joint conference consisting of six members, three appointed by the General Assembly and three by the Security Council, may be formed at any time at the request of either the General Assembly or the Security Council, for the purpose of choosing by the vote of an absolute majority one name for each seat still vacant, to submit to the General Assembly and the Security Council for their respective acceptance.
2. If the joint conference is unanimously agreed upon any person who fulfils the required conditions, he may be included in its list, even though he was not included in the list of nominations referred to in Article 7.
3. If the joint conference is satisfied that it will not be successful in procuring an election, those members of the Court who have already been elected shall, within a period to be fixed by the Security Council, proceed to fill the vacant seats by selection from among those candidates who have obtained votes either in the General Assembly or in the Security Council.
4. In the event of an equality of votes among the judges, the eldest judge shall have a casting vote.

Article 13
1. The members of the Court shall be elected for nine years and may be re-elected; provided, however, that of the judges elected at the first election, the terms of five judges shall expire at the end of three years and the terms of five more judges shall expire at the end of six years.
2. The judges whose terms are to expire at the end of the above-mentioned initial periods of three and six years shall be chosen by lot to be drawn by the Secretary-General immediately after the first election has been completed.
3. The members of the Court shall continue to discharge their duties until their places have been filled. Though replaced, they shall finish any cases which they may have begun.
4. In the case of the resignation of a member of the Court, the resignation shall be addressed to the President of the Court for transmission to the Secretary-General. This last notification makes the place vacant.

Article 14
Vacancies shall be filled by the same method as that laid down for the first election, subject to the following provision: the Secretary-

General shall, within one month of the occurrence of the vacancy, proceed to issue the invitations provided for in Article 5, and the date of the election shall be fixed by the Security Council.

Article 15
A member of the Court elected to replace a member whose term of office has not expired shall hold office for the remainder of his predecessor's term.

Article 16
1. No member of the Court may exercise any political or administrative function, or engage in any other occupation of a professional nature.
2. Any doubt on this point shall be settled by the decision of the Court.

Article 17
1. No member of the Court may act as agent, counsel, or advocate in any case.
2. No member may participate in the decision of any case in which he has previously taken part as agent, counsel, or advocate for one of the parties, or as a member of a national or international court, or of a commission of enquiry, or in any other capacity.
3. Any doubt on this point shall be settled by the decision of the Court.

Article 18
1. No member of the Court can be dismissed unless, in the unanimous opinion of the other members, he has ceased to fulfil the required conditions.
2. Formal notification thereof shall be made to the Secretary-General by the Registrar.
3. This notification makes the place vacant.

Article 19
The members of the Court, when engaged on the business of the Court, shall enjoy diplomatic privileges and immunities.

Article 20
Every member of the Court shall, before taking up his duties, make a solemn declaration in open court that he will exercise his powers impartially and conscientiously.

Article 21
1. The Court shall elect its President and Vice-President for three years; they may be re-elected.
2. The Court shall appoint its Registrar and may provide for the appointment of such other officers as may be necessary.

Article 22
1. The seat of the Court shall be established at The Hague. This, however, shall not prevent the Court from sitting and exercising its functions elsewhere whenever the Court considers it desirable.
2. The President and the Registrar shall reside at the seat of the Court.

Article 23
1. The Court shall remain permanently in session, except during the judicial vacations, the dates and duration of which shall be fixed by the Court.
2. Members of the Court are entitled to periodic leave, the dates and duration of which shall be fixed by the Court, having in mind the distance between The Hague and the home of each judge.
3. Members of the Court shall be bound, unless they are on leave or prevented from attending by illness or other serious reasons duly explained to the President, to hold themselves permanently at the disposal of the Court.

Article 24
1. If, for some special reason, a member of the Court considers that he should not take part in the decision of a particular case, he shall so inform the President.
2. If the President considers that for some special reason one of the members of the Court should not sit in a particular case, he shall give him notice accordingly.

3. If in any such case the member of the Court and the President disagree, the matter shall be settled by the decision of the Court.

Article 25

1. The full Court shall sit except when it is expressly provided otherwise in the present Statute.

2. Subject to the condition that the number of judges available to constitute the Court is not thereby reduced below eleven, the Rules of the Court may provide for allowing one or more judges, according to circumstances and in rotation, to be dispensed from sitting.

3. A quorum of nine judges shall suffice to constitute the Court.

Article 26

1. The Court may from time to time form one or more chambers, composed of three or more judges as the Court may determine, for dealing with particular categories of cases; for example, labour cases and cases relating to transit and communications.

2. The Court may at any time form a chamber for dealing with a particular case. The number of judges to constitute such a chamber shall be determined by the Court with the approval of the parties.

3. Cases shall be heard and determined by the chambers provided for in this Article if the parties so request.

Article 27

A judgment given by any of the chambers provided for in Articles 26 and 29 shall be considered as rendered by the Court.

Article 28

The chambers provided for in Articles 26 and 29 may, with the consent of the parties, sit and exercise their functions elsewhere than at The Hague.

Article 29

With a view to the speedy dispatch of business, the Court shall form annually a chamber composed of five judges which, at the request of the parties, may hear and determine cases by summary procedure. In addition, two judges shall be selected for the purpose of replacing judges who find it impossible to sit.

Article 30

1. The Court shall frame rules for carrying out its functions. In particular, it shall lay down rules of procedure.

2. The Rules of the Court may provide for assessors to sit with the Court or with any of its chambers, without the right to vote.

Article 31

1. Judges of the nationality of each of the parties shall retain their right to sit in the case before the Court.

2. If the Court includes upon the Bench a judge of the nationality of one of the parties, any other party may choose a person to sit as judge. Such person shall be chosen preferably from among those persons who have been nominated as candidates as provided in Articles 4 and 5.

3. If the Court includes upon the Bench no judge of the nationality of the parties, each of these parties may proceed to choose a judge as provided in paragraph 2 of this Article.

4. The provisions of this Article shall apply to the case of Articles 26 and 29. In such cases, the President shall request one or, if necessary, two of the members of the Court forming the chamber to give place to the members of the Court of the nationality of the parties concerned, and, failing such, or if they are unable to be present, to the judges specially chosen by the parties.

5. Should there be several parties in the same interest, they shall, for the purpose of the preceding provisions, be reckoned as one party only. Any doubt upon this point shall be settled by the decision of the Court.

6. Judges chosen as laid down in paragraphs 2, 3 and 4 of this Article shall fulfil the conditions required by Articles 2, 17 (paragraph 2), 20, and 24 of the present Statute. They shall take part in the decision on terms of complete equality with their colleagues.

Article 32

1. Each member of the Court shall receive an annual salary.

2. The President shall receive a special annual allowance.

3. The Vice-President shall receive a special allowance for every day on which he acts as President.

4. The judges chosen under Article 31, other than members of the Court, shall receive compensation for each day on which they exercise their functions.

5. These salaries, allowances, and compensation shall be fixed by the General Assembly. They may not be decreased during the term of office.

6. The salary of the Registrar shall be fixed by the General Assembly on the proposal of the Court.

7. Regulations made by the General Assembly shall fix the conditions under which retirement pensions may be given to members of the Court and to the Registrar, and the conditions under which members of the Court and the Registrar shall have their travelling expenses refunded.

8. The above salaries, allowances, and compensation shall be free of all taxation.

Article 33

The expenses of the Court shall be borne by the United Nations in such a manner as shall be decided by the General Assembly.

Chapter II
COMPETENCE OF THE COURT

Article 34

1. Only states may be parties in cases before the Court.

2. The Court, subject to and in conformity with its Rules, may request of public international organizations information relevant to cases before it, and shall receive such information presented by such organizations on their own initiative.

3. Whenever the construction of the constituent instrument of a public international organization or of an international convention adopted thereunder is in question in a case before the Court, the Registrar shall so notify the public international organization concerned and shall communicate to it copies of all the written proceedings.

Article 35

1. The Court shall be open to the states parties to the present Statute.

2. The conditions under which the Court shall be open to other states shall, subject to the special provisions contained in treaties in force, be laid down by the Security Council, but in no case shall such conditions place the parties in a position of inequality before the Court.

3. When a state which is not a Member of the United Nations is a party to a case, the Court shall fix the amount which that party is to contribute towards the expenses of the Court. This provision shall not apply if such state is bearing a share of the expenses of the Court.

Article 36

1. The jurisdiction of the Court comprises all cases which the parties refer to it and all matters specially provided for in the Charter of the United Nations or in treaties and conventions in force.

2. The states parties to the present Statute may at any time declare that they recognize as compulsory *ipso facto* and without special agreement, in relation to any other state accepting the same obligation, the jurisdiction of the Court in all legal disputes concerning:

a. the interpretation of a treaty;

b. any question of international law;

c. the existence of any fact which, if established, would constitute a breach of an international obligation;

d. the nature or extent of the reparation to be made for the breach of an international obligation.

3. The declarations referred to above may be made unconditionally or on condition of reciprocity on the part of several or certain states, or for a certain time.

4. Such declarations shall be deposited with the Secretary-General of the United Nations, who shall transmit copies thereof to the parties to the Statute and to the Registrar of the Court.

5. Declarations made under Article 36 of the Statute of the Permanent Court of International Justice and which are still in force shall be deemed, as between the parties to the present Statute, to be acceptances of the compulsory jurisdiction of the International Court of Justice for the period which they still have to run and in accordance with their terms.

6. In the event of a dispute as to whether the Court has jurisdiction, the matter shall be settled by the decision of the Court.

Article 37

Whenever a treaty or convention in force provides for reference of a matter to a tribunal to have been instituted by the League of Nations, or to the Permanent Court of International Justice, the matter shall, as between the parties to the present Statute, be referred to the International Court of Justice.

Article 38

1. The Court, whose function is to decide in accordance with international law such disputes as are submitted to it, shall apply:
   a. international conventions, whether general or particular, establishing rules expressly recognized by the contesting states;
   b. international custom, as evidence of a general practice accepted as law;
   c. the general principles of law recognized by civilized nations;
   d. subject to the provisions of Article 59, judicial decisions and the teachings of the most highly qualified publicists of the various nations, as subsidiary means for the determination of rules of law.

2. This provision shall not prejudice the power of the Court to decide a case *ex aequo et bono*, if the parties agree thereto.

Chapter III
PROCEDURE

Article 39

1. The official languages of the Court shall be French and English. If the parties agree that the case shall be conducted in French, the judgment shall be delivered in French. If the parties agree that the case shall be conducted in English, the judgment shall be delivered in English.

2. In the absence of an agreement as to which language shall be employed, each party may, in the pleadings, use the language which it prefers; the decision of the Court shall be given in French and English. In this case the Court shall at the same time determine which of the two texts shall be considered as authoritative.

3. The Court shall, at the request of any party, authorize a language other than French or English to be used by that party.

Article 40

1. Cases are brought before the Court, as the case may be, either by the notification of the special agreement or by a written application addressed to the Registrar. In either case the subject of the dispute and the parties shall be indicated.

2. The Registrar shall forthwith communicate the application to all concerned.

3. He shall also notify the Members of the United Nations through the Secretary-General, and also any other states entitled to appear before the Court.

Article 41

1. The Court shall have the power to indicate, if it considers that circumstances so require, any provisional measures which ought to be taken to preserve the respective rights of either party.

2. Pending the final decision, notice of the measures suggested shall forthwith be given to the parties and to the Security Council.

Article 42

1. The parties shall be represented by agents.

2. They may have the assistance of counsel or advocates before the Court.

3. The agents, counsel, and advocates of parties before the Court shall enjoy the privileges and immunities necessary to the independent exercise of their duties.

Article 43

1. The procedure shall consist of two parts: written and oral.

2. The written proceedings shall consist of the communication to the Court and to the parties of memorials, counter-memorials and, if necessary, replies; also all papers and documents in support.

3. These communications shall be made through the Registrar, in the order and within the time fixed by the Court.

4. A certified copy of every document produced by one party shall be communicated to the other party.

5. The oral proceedings shall consist of the hearing by the Court of witnesses, experts, agents, counsel, and advocates.

Article 44

1. For the service of all notices upon persons other than the agents, counsel, and advocates, the Court shall apply direct to the government of the state upon whose territory the notice has to be served.

2. The same provision shall apply whenever steps are to be taken to procure evidence on the spot.

Article 45

The hearing shall be under the control of the President or, if he is unable to preside, of the Vice-President; if neither is able to preside, the senior judge present shall preside.

Article 46

The hearing in Court shall be public, unless the Court shall decide otherwise, or unless the parties demand that the public be not admitted.

Article 47

1. Minutes shall be made at each hearing and signed by the Registrar and the President.

2. These minutes alone shall be authentic.

Article 48

The Court shall make orders for the conduct of the case, shall decide the form and time in which each party must conclude its arguments, and make all arrangements connected with the taking of evidence.

Article 49

The Court may, even before the hearing begins, call upon the agents to produce any document or to supply any explanations. Formal note shall be taken of any refusal.

Article 50

The Court may, at any time, entrust any individual, body, bureau, commission, or other organization that it may select, with the task of carrying out an enquiry or giving an expert opinion.

Article 51

During the hearing any relevant questions are to be put to the witnesses and experts under the conditions laid down by the Court in the rules of procedure referred to in Article 30.

Article 52

After the Court has received the proofs and evidence within the time specified for the purpose, it may refuse to accept any further oral or written evidence that one party may desire to present unless the other side consents.

Article 53

1. Whenever one of the parties does not appear before the Court, or fails to defend its case, the other party may call upon the Court to decide in favour of its claim.

2. The Court must, before doing so, satisfy itself, not only that it has jurisdiction in accordance with Articles 36 and 37, but also that the claim is well founded in fact and law.

Article 54
1. When, subject to the control of the Court, the agents, counsel, and advocates have completed their presentation of the case, the President shall declare the hearing closed.
2. The Court shall withdraw to consider the judgment.
3. The deliberations of the Court shall take place in private and remain secret.

Article 55
1. All questions shall be decided by a majority of the judges present.
2. In the event of an equality of votes, the President or the judge who acts in his place shall have a casting vote.

Article 56
1. The judgment shall state the reasons on which it is based.
2. It shall contain the names of the judges who have taken part in the decision.

Article 57
If the judgment does not represent in whole or in part the unanimous opinion of the judges, any judge shall be entitled to deliver a separate opinion.

Article 58
The judgment shall be signed by the President and by the Registrar. It shall be read in open court, due notice having been given to the agents.

Article 59
The decision of the Court has no binding force except between the parties and in respect of that particular case.

Article 60
The judgment is final and without appeal. In the event of dispute as to the meaning or scope of the judgment, the Court shall construe it upon the request of any party.

Article 61
1. An application for revision of a judgment may be made only when it is based upon the discovery of some fact of such a nature as to be a decisive factor, which fact was, when the judgment was given, unknown to the Court and also to the party claiming revision, always provided that such ignorance was not due to negligence.
2. The proceedings for revision shall be opened by a judgment of the Court expressly recording the existence of the new fact, recognizing that it has such a character as to lay the case open to revision, and declaring the application admissible on this ground.
3. The Court may require previous compliance with the terms of the judgment before it admits proceedings in revision.
4. The application for revision must be made at latest within six months of the discovery of the new fact.
5. No application for revision may be made after the lapse of ten years from the date of the judgment.

Article 62
1. Should a state consider that it has an interest of a legal nature which may be affected by the decision in the case, it may submit a request to the Court to be permitted to intervene.
2. It shall be for the Court to decide upon this request.

Article 63
1. Whenever the construction of a convention to which states other than those concerned in the case are parties is in question, the Registrar shall notify all such states forthwith.
2. Every state so notified has the right to intervene in the proceedings; but if it uses this right, the construction given by the judgment will be equally binding upon it.

Article 64
Unless otherwise decided by the Court, each party shall bear its own costs.

Chapter IV
ADVISORY OPINIONS

Article 65
1. The Court may give an advisory opinion on any legal question at the request of whatever body may be authorized by or in accordance with the Charter of the United Nations to make such a request.
2. Questions upon which the advisory opinion of the Court is asked shall be laid before the Court by means of a written request containing an exact statement of the question upon which an opinion is required, and accompanied by all documents likely to throw light upon the question.

Article 66
1. The Registrar shall forthwith give notice of the request for an advisory opinion to all states entitled to appear before the Court.
2. The Registrar shall also, by means of a special and direct communication, notify any state entitled to appear before the Court or international organization considered by the Court, or, should it not be sitting, by the President, as likely to be able to furnish information on the question, that the Court will be prepared to receive, within a time limit to be fixed by the President, written statements, or to hear, at a public sitting to be held for the purpose, oral statements relating to the question.
3. Should any such state entitled to appear before the Court have failed to receive the special communication referred to in paragraph 2 of this Article, such state may express a desire to submit a written statement or to be heard; and the Court will decide.
4. States and organizations having presented written or oral statements or both shall be permitted to comment on the statements made by other states or organizations in the form, to the extent, and within the time limits which the Court, or, should it not be sitting, the President, shall decide in each particular case. Accordingly, the Registrar shall in due time communicate any such written statements to states and organizations having submitted similar statements.

Article 67
The Court shall deliver its advisory opinions in open court, notice having been given to the Secretary-General and to the representatives of Members of the United Nations, of other states and of international organizations immediately concerned.

Article 68
In the exercise of its advisory functions the Court shall further be guided by the provisions of the present Statute which apply in contentious cases to the extent to which it recognizes them to be applicable.

Chapter V
AMENDMENT

Article 69
Amendments to the present Statute shall be effected by the same procedure as is provided by the Charter of the United Nations for amendments to that Charter, subject however to any provisions which the General Assembly upon recommendation of the Security Council may adopt concerning the participation of states which are parties to the present Statute but are not Members of the United Nations.

Article 70
The Court shall have power to propose such amendments to the present Statute as it may deem necessary, through written communications to the Secretary-General, for consideration in conformity with the provisions of Article 69.

Appendix III

Structure of the United Nations

General Assembly

The General Assembly is composed of all the Members of the United Nations.

SESSIONS
Resumed forty-seventh session: 19 January, 11 February, 16 March, 8, 15, 20 and 29 April, 6, 10 and 28 May, 15, 22 and 25 June, 28 July, 17 August and 14, 15 and 20 September 1993.
Forty-eighth session: 21 September–23 December 1993 (suspended).

OFFICERS
Resumed forty-seventh session
President: Stoyan Ganev (Bulgaria).
Vice-Presidents: Afghanistan, Belize, Benin, Cape Verde, China, Comoros, France, Gabon, Ireland, Kuwait, Lesotho, Libyan Arab Jamahiriya, Nicaragua, Philippines, Russian Federation, Sri Lanka, Suriname, Turkey, United Kingdom, United States, Yemen.

Forty-eighth session
President: Samuel Insanally (Guyana).[a]
Vice-Presidents:[b] Bangladesh, Burkina Faso, Canada, China, Egypt, France, Grenada, Guatemala, India, Iran, Liberia, Liechtenstein, Pakistan, Poland, Republic of Korea, Russian Federation, United Kingdom, United Republic of Tanzania, United States, Zaire, Zambia.

[a]Elected on 21 September 1993 (dec. 48/302).
[b]Elected on 21 September 1993 (dec. 48/304).

The Assembly has four types of committees: (1) Main Committees; (2) procedural committees; (3) standing committees; (4) subsidiary and ad hoc bodies. In addition, it convenes conferences to deal with specific subjects.

Main Committees
On 17 August 1993 (res. 47/233), the Assembly decided that, beginning with its forty-eighth session, the Main Committees were to be as follows:

Disarmament and International Security Committee (First Committee)
Special Political and Decolonization Committee (Fourth Committee)
Economic and Financial Committee (Second Committee)
Social, Humanitarian and Cultural Committee (Third Committee)
Administrative and Budgetary Committee (Fifth Committee)
Legal Committee (Sixth Committee)

The above six Committees replaced the following seven of previous sessions:

Political and Security Committee (disarmament and related international security questions) (First Committee)
Special Political Committee
Economic and Financial Committee (Second Committee)
Social, Humanitarian and Cultural Committee (Third Committee)
Trusteeship Committee (including Non-Self-Governing Territories) (Fourth Committee)
Administrative and Budgetary Committee (Fifth Committee)
Legal Committee (Sixth Committee)

The General Assembly may constitute other committees, on which all Members of the United Nations have the right to be represented.

OFFICERS OF THE MAIN COMMITTEES
Resumed forty-seventh session

First Committee[a]
Chairman: Nabil A. Elaraby (Egypt).
Vice-Chairmen: Pasi Patokallio (Finland), Dae Won Suh (Republic of Korea).
Rapporteur: Jerzy Zaleski (Poland).

Fifth Committee[a]
Chairman: Marian-George Dinu (Romania).
Vice-Chairmen: Maria Rotheiser (Austria), El Hassane Zahid (Morocco).
Rapporteur: Jorge Osella (Argentina).

[a]The only Main Committees to meet at the resumed session.

Forty-eighth session[a]

[a]Chairmen elected by the Main Committees; announced by the Assembly President on 21 September 1993 (dec. 48/303).

First Committee
Chairman: Adolf Ritter von Wagner (Germany).
Vice-Chairmen: Behrouz Moradi (Iran), Javier Ponce (Ecuador).
Rapporteur: Macaire Kabore (Burkina Faso).

Fourth Committee
Chairman: Stanley Kalpagé (Sri Lanka).
Vice-Chairmen: Gheorghe Chirila (Romania), Ngoni Sengwe (Zimbabwe).
Rapporteur: Anuson Chinvanno (Thailand).

Second Committee
Chairman: René Valéry Mongbe (Benin).
Vice-Chairmen: Leandro Arellano Resendiz (Mexico), Ryszard Rysinski (Poland).
Rapporteur: Irene Freudenschuss (Austria).

Third Committee
Chairman: Eduard Kukan (Slovakia).
Vice-Chairmen: Noria Abdullah Ali Al-Hamami (Yemen), Barend C. A. F. van der Heijden (Netherlands).
Rapporteur: Rosa Carmina Recinos de Maldonado (Guatemala).

Fifth Committee
Chairman: Rabah Hadid (Algeria).
Vice-Chairmen: Jorge A. Osella (Argentina), Maria Regina Serrao Emerson (Portugal).
Rapporteur: Mahbub Kabir (Bangladesh).

Sixth Committee
Chairman: María del Luján Flores (Uruguay).
Vice-Chairmen: Ali Thani Al-Suwaidi (United Arab Emirates), Matthew Neuhaus (Australia).
Rapporteur: Oleksandr F. Motsyk (Ukraine).

Procedural committees

General Committee
The General Committee consists of the President of the General Assembly, as Chairman, the 21 Vice-Presidents and the Chairmen of the seven (six from the forty-eighth session) Main Committees.

Credentials Committee
The Credentials Committee consists of nine members appointed by the General Assembly on the proposal of the President.

Forty-eighth session
Austria, Bahamas, China, Côte d'Ivoire, Ecuador, Mauritius, Russian Federation, Thailand, United States.[a]

[a]Appointed on 21 September 1993 (dec. 48/301).

Standing committees
The two standing committees consist of experts appointed in their individual capacity for three-year terms.

Advisory Committee on Administrative and Budgetary Questions
Members:
To serve until 31 December 1993: Leonid E. Bidnyi (Russian Federation); Even Fontaine-Ortiz (Cuba); M'hand Ladjouzi (Algeria); Linda S. Shenwick (United States); Clive Stitt (United Kingdom).[a]
To serve until 31 December 1994: Ahmad Fathi Al-Masri (Syrian Arab Republic); Kwaku Dua Dankwa (Ghana); Zoran Lazarevic (Yugoslavia); Ernest Besley Maycock (Barbados); C. S. M. Mselle, *Chairman* (United Republic of Tanzania).
To serve until 31 December 1995: Gérard Biraud (France); Jorge José Duhalt (Mexico); Tadanori Inomata (Japan); Wolfgang Münch, *Vice-Chairman* (Germany); Ranjit Rae (India); Yu Mengjia (China).

[a]Appointed on 19 January 1993 (dec. 47/305 C) to replace Richard Kinchen (United Kingdom), who had resigned.

On 3 December 1993 (dec. 48/313), the General Assembly appointed the following five members for a three-year term beginning on 1 January 1994 to fill the vacancies occurring on 31 December 1993: Leonid E. Bidnyi (Russian Federation), Simon Khoam Chuinkam (Cameroon), Inga Eriksson Fogh (Sweden), Even Fontaine-Ortiz (Cuba), Linda S. Shenwick (United States).

Committee on Contributions
Members:
To serve until 31 December 1993: Syed Amjad Ali, *Chairman* (Pakistan); Henrik Amneus (Sweden); Yuri A. Chulkov (Russian Federation); Atilio Norberto Molteni (Argentina);[a] Ugo Sessi (Italy); Wang Liansheng (China).
To serve until 31 December 1994: Kenshiroh Akimoto (Japan); David Etuket (Uganda); John D. Fox (United States); Ion Goritza (Romania); Imre Karbuczky (Hungary); Vanu Gopala Menon (Singapore).
To serve until 31 December 1995: Tarak Ben Hamida (Tunisia); Sergio Chaparro Ruíz (Chile); Norma Goicochea Estenoz (Cuba); Peter Gregg, *Vice-Chairman* (Australia);[b] Mohamed Mahmoud Ould El Ghaouth (Mauritania); Dimitri Rallis (Greece).

[a]Resigned in June 1993; Jorge Alberto Osella (Argentina) was appointed on 15 June (dec. 47/313 B) to fill the resultant vacancy.
[b]Resigned in October 1993; Neil Hewitt Francis (Australia) was appointed on 3 December (dec. 48/314 A) to fill the resultant vacancy.

On 3 December 1993 (dec. 48/314 A), the General Assembly appointed the following six members for a three-year term beginning on 1 January 1994 to fill the vacancies occurring on 31 December 1993: Yuri A. Chulkov (Russian Federation), Alvaro Gurgel de Alencar (Brazil), Li Yong (China), Ugo Sessi (Italy), Agha Shahi (Pakistan), Adrien Teirlinck (Belgium).
On 23 December (dec. 48/314 B), the Assembly appointed Syed Amjad Ali (Pakistan) as a member emeritus of the Committee, in recognition of his service as its Chairman for 27 consecutive years.

Subsidiary and ad hoc bodies
The following subsidiary and ad hoc bodies were functioning in 1993, or were established during the General Assembly's resumed forty-seventh session or forty-eighth session. (For other related bodies, see p. 1370.)

Ad Hoc Committee on the Indian Ocean
The 44-member Ad Hoc Committee on the Indian Ocean met at United Nations Headquarters from 21 June to 2 July 1993.

Members: Australia *(Vice-Chairman)*, Bangladesh, Bulgaria, Canada, China, Djibouti, Egypt, Ethiopia, Germany, Greece, India, Indonesia *(Vice-Chairman)*, Iran, Iraq, Italy, Japan, Kenya, Liberia, Madagascar *(Rapporteur)*, Malaysia, Maldives, Mauritius, Mozambique *(Vice-Chairman)*, Netherlands, Norway, Oman, Pakistan, Panama, Poland, Romania, Russian Federation, Seychelles, Singapore, Somalia, Sri Lanka *(Chairman)*, Sudan, Thailand, Uganda, United Arab Emirates, United Republic of Tanzania, Yemen, Yugoslavia, Zambia, Zimbabwe.

Sweden, a major maritime user of the Indian Ocean, participates as an observer.

Advisory Committee on the United Nations Educational and Training Programme for Southern Africa
Members: Belarus, Canada, Denmark, India, Japan, Liberia, Nigeria, Norway *(Chairman)*, United Republic of Tanzania, United States, Venezuela, Zaire, Zambia *(Vice-Chairman)*.

Advisory Committee on the United Nations Programme of Assistance in the Teaching, Study, Dissemination and Wider Appreciation of International Law
The Advisory Committee on the United Nations Programme of Assistance in the Teaching, Study, Dissemination and Wider Appreciation of International Law held its twenty-eighth session at United Nations Headquarters on 29 October 1993.

Members (until 31 December 1995): Bangladesh, Colombia, Cuba, Cyprus, Ethiopia, France, Germany, Ghana *(Chairman)*, India, Iran, Italy, Kenya, Malaysia, Mexico, Netherlands, Nigeria, Romania, Russian Federation, Sudan, Trinidad and Tobago, Ukraine, United Kingdom, United Republic of Tanzania, United States, Uruguay.

Board of Auditors
The Board of Auditors consists of three members appointed by the General Assembly for three-year terms.

Members:
To serve until 30 June 1994: Auditor-General of Ghana.
To serve until 30 June 1995: Comptroller and Auditor-General of the United Kingdom.
To serve until 30 June 1996: Comptroller and Auditor-General of India.

On 3 December 1993 (dec. 48/315), the General Assembly appointed the Auditor-General of Ghana for a three-year term beginning on 1 July 1994.

Committee for the United Nations Population Award
The Committee for the United Nations Population Award is composed of: *(a)* 10 representatives of United Nations Member States elected by the Economic and Social Council for a three-year period, with due regard for equitable geographical representation and the need to include Member States that had made contributions for the Award; *(b)* the Secretary-General and the UNFPA Executive Director, to serve ex officio; and *(c)* five individuals eminent for their significant contributions to population-related activities, selected by the Committee, to serve as honorary members in an advisory capacity for a renewable three-year term.
The Committee met at United Nations Headquarters on 26 January and 17 February 1993.

Members (until 31 December 1994): Belarus, Burundi, Cameroon, Ecuador, El Salvador, India, Japan, Mexico, Netherlands *(Chairman)*, Rwanda.
Ex-officio members: The Secretary-General and the UNFPA Executive Director.
Honorary members (until 31 December 1994): Robin Chandler Duke, Takeo Fukuda, Miguel de la Madrid Hurtado, F. Bradford Morse, Victoria Sekitoleko.

Committee of Trustees of the United Nations Trust Fund for South Africa
Members: Chile, Morocco, Nigeria *(Vice-Chairman)*, Pakistan, Sweden *(Chairman)*.

Committee on Applications for Review of Administrative Tribunal Judgements
The Committee on Applications for Review of Administrative Tribunal Judgements held, at United Nations Headquarters, its fortieth session on 18 and 20 January and its forty-first session on 15 and 16 July 1993.

Members (until 20 September 1993) (based on the composition of the General Committee at the General Assembly's forty-seventh session): Afghanistan, Austria, Belize, Benin, Bulgaria, Cape Verde, China, Comoros, Egypt, El Salvador, France, Gabon, Iran *(Chairman)*, Ireland, Kuwait, Lesotho, Libyan Arab Jamahiriya, Nicaragua, Philippines, Romania, Russian Federation, Sri Lanka, Suriname, Tunisia, Turkey, United Kingdom *(Rapporteur)*, United States, Uruguay, Yemen.

Members (from 21 September 1993) (based on the composition of the General Committee at the General Assembly's forty-eighth session): Algeria, Bangladesh, Benin, Burkina Faso, Canada, China, Egypt, France, Germany, Grenada, Guatemala, Guyana, India, Iran, Liberia, Liechtenstein, Pakistan, Poland, Republic of Korea, Russian Federation, Slovakia, Sri Lanka, United Kingdom, United Republic of Tanzania, United States, Uruguay, Zaire, Zambia.

Committee on Conferences
The Committee on Conferences consists of 21 Member States appointed by the President of the General Assembly according to a specific pattern of equitable geographical distribution, to serve for a three-year term.

Members:
To serve until 31 December 1993: Chile *(Vice-Chairman)*, Cyprus, France, Gabon, Japan, Kenya, Russian Federation.
To serve until 31 December 1994: Honduras, Hungary *(Rapporteur)*, Iran *(Chairman)*, Jamaica, Mozambique, Senegal, Turkey *(Vice-Chairman)*.
To serve until 31 December 1995: Austria, Fiji, Grenada, Jordan, Morocco *(Vice-Chairman)*,[a] Niger,[a] United States.

[a]Appointed on 17 February 1993; the Assembly took note of their appointment on 8 April (dec. 47/311 B).

On 11 November 1993 (dec. 48/312), the General Assembly took note of the appointment by its President of the following members for a three-year term beginning on 1 January 1994 to fill the vacancies occurring on 31 December 1993: Chile, Egypt, France, Gabon, Japan, Pakistan, Russian Federation.

Committee on Information
The 81-member Committee on Information held its fifteenth session at United Nations Headquarters from 10 to 28 May 1993.

Members: Algeria, Argentina *(Vice-Chairman)*, Bangladesh, Belarus, Belgium, Benin, Brazil, Bulgaria, Burkina Faso, Burundi, Chile, China, Colombia, Congo, Costa Rica, Côte d'Ivoire, Cuba, Cyprus, Denmark, Ecuador, Egypt, El Salvador, Ethiopia, Finland, France, Germany, Ghana, Greece, Guatemala, Guinea, Guyana, Hungary, India, Indonesia, Iran, Ireland *(Rapporteur)*, Italy, Jamaica, Japan, Jordan, Kenya *(Vice-Chairman)*, Lebanon,

Malta, Mexico, Mongolia, Morocco, Nepal, Netherlands, Niger, Nigeria, Pakistan *(Chairman)*, Peru, Philippines, Poland *(Vice-Chairman)*, Portugal, Republic of Korea, Romania, Russian Federation, Senegal, Singapore, Slovakia,[a] Somalia, Spain, Sri Lanka, Sudan, Syrian Arab Republic, Togo, Trinidad and Tobago, Tunisia, Turkey, Ukraine, United Kingdom, United Republic of Tanzania, United States, Uruguay, Venezuela, Viet Nam, Yemen, Yugoslavia, Zaire, Zimbabwe.

[a]On 19 January 1993 (dec. 47/322), the General Assembly took note of its President's appointment of Slovakia to fill, with immediate effect, the seat vacated by the former Czechoslovakia.

On 10 December 1993 (dec. 48/318), the General Assembly appointed Gabon and Israel members.

Committee on Relations with the Host Country
Members: Bulgaria *(Vice-Chairman)*, Canada *(Vice-Chairman)*, China, Costa Rica *(Rapporteur)*, Côte d'Ivoire *(Vice-Chairman)*, Cyprus *(Chairman)*, France, Honduras, Iraq, Mali, Russian Federation, Senegal, Spain, United Kingdom, United States (host country).

Committee on the Exercise of the Inalienable Rights of the Palestinian People
Members: Afghanistan *(Vice-Chairman)*, Belarus, Cuba *(Vice-Chairman)*, Cyprus, Guinea, Guyana, Hungary, India, Indonesia, Lao People's Democratic Republic, Madagascar, Malaysia, Mali, Malta *(Rapporteur)*, Nigeria, Pakistan, Romania, Senegal *(Chairman)*, Sierra Leone, Tunisia, Turkey, Ukraine, Yugoslavia.

Committee on the Peaceful Uses of Outer Space
The 53-member Committee on the Peaceful Uses of Outer Space held its thirty-sixth session at United Nations Headquarters from 7 to 18 June 1993.

Members: Albania, Argentina, Australia, Austria *(Chairman)*, Belgium, Benin, Brazil *(Rapporteur)*, Bulgaria, Burkina Faso, Cameroon, Canada, Chad, Chile, China, Colombia, Czech Republic,[a] Ecuador, Egypt, France, Germany, Greece,[b] Hungary, India, Indonesia, Iran, Iraq, Italy, Japan, Kenya, Lebanon, Mexico, Mongolia, Morocco, Netherlands, Niger, Nigeria, Pakistan, Philippines, Poland, Romania *(Vice-Chairman)*, Russian Federation, Sierra Leone, Spain,[b] Sudan, Sweden, Syrian Arab Republic, Ukraine, United Kingdom, United States, Uruguay, Venezuela, Viet Nam, Yugoslavia.

[a]Appointed by the General Assembly on 19 January 1993 (dec. 47/321) to fill the seat vacated by the former Czechoslovakia.

[b]Replaced Turkey and Portugal, respectively, in accordance with a three-year system of rotation agreed on by the Group of Western European and Other States.

Disarmament Commission
The Disarmament Commission, composed of all the Members of the United Nations, met at United Nations Headquarters on 23 March, 14 April and between 19 April and 10 May 1993.

Chairman: Brazil.
Vice-Chairmen: Benin, Bulgaria, Canada, Ecuador, Ireland, Mauritius, Mongolia, Republic of Korea.
Rapporteur: Czech Republic.

High-level Committee on the Review of Technical Cooperation among Developing Countries
The High-level Committee on the Review of Technical Cooperation among Developing Countries, composed of all States participating in UNDP, held its eighth session at United Nations Headquarters from 25 to 28 May and on 4 June 1993.

President: Uruguay.
Vice-Presidents: Bangladesh, Latvia.
Rapporteur: Mali.

Intergovernmental Group to Monitor the Supply and Shipping of Oil and Petroleum Products to South Africa

The Intergovernmental Group to Monitor the Supply and Shipping of Oil and Petroleum Products to South Africa was composed of 10 Member States appointed by the Assembly President, in consultation with the regional groups and the Chairman of the Special Committee against Apartheid, on the basis of equitable geographical distribution and ensuring representation of oil-exporting and -shipping States.

Members: Algeria, Cuba *(Rapporteur)*, Indonesia, Kuwait *(Vice-Chairman)*, New Zealand, Nicaragua, Nigeria, Norway,[a] Ukraine, United Republic of Tanzania *(Chairman)*.

[a]Withdrew from membership on 16 March 1993.

On 20 December 1993 (res. 48/159 C), the General Assembly terminated the mandate of the Group.

Intergovernmental Negotiating Committee for a Framework Convention on Climate Change

The Intergovernmental Negotiating Committee for a Framework Convention on Climate Change, open to all States Members of the United Nations or members of the specialized agencies, held two sessions in 1993: its seventh at United Nations Headquarters from 15 to 20 March and its eighth at Geneva from 16 to 27 August.

Chairman: Argentina.
Vice-Chairmen: Algeria, Australia, India.
Vice-Chairman/Rapporteur: Poland.

Intergovernmental Negotiating Committee for the Elaboration of an International Convention to Combat Desertification in those Countries Experiencing Serious Drought and/or Desertification, particularly in Africa

In 1993, the Intergovernmental Negotiating Committee for the Elaboration of an International Convention to Combat Desertification in those Countries Experiencing Serious Drought and/or Desertification, particularly in Africa, open to all States Members of the United Nations or members of the specialized agencies, held an organizational session at United Nations Headquarters from 26 to 29 January, its first session at Nairobi, Kenya, from 24 May to 3 June and its second session at Geneva from 13 to 24 September.

Chairman: Sweden.
Vice-Chairmen: Benin, India, Peru.
Rapporteur: Russian Federation.

International Civil Service Commission

The International Civil Service Commission consists of 15 members who serve in their personal capacity as individuals of recognized competence in public administration or related fields, particularly in personnel management. They are appointed by the General Assembly, with due regard for equitable geographical distribution, for four-year terms.

The Commission held two sessions in 1993: its thirty-seventh at United Nations Headquarters from 8 to 26 March, and its thirty-eighth at Vienna from 15 July to 3 August.

Members:
To serve until 31 December 1993: Mario Bettati (France); Lucretia Myers (United States); Antônio Fonseca Pimentel (Brazil); Alexis Stephanou (Greece); Ku Tashiro (Japan).
To serve until 31 December 1994: Mohsen Bel Hadj Amor, *Chairman* (Tunisia); Turkia Daddah (Mauritania); André Xavier Pirson (Belgium); Jaroslav Riha (Czech Republic); Carlos S. Vegega, *Vice-Chairman* (Argentina).
To serve until 31 December 1996: Humayun Kabir (Bangladesh); Valery Fiodorovich Keniaykin (Russian Federation); Ernest Rusita (Uganda); Missoum Sbih (Algeria); Mario Yango (Philippines).

On 23 December 1993 (dec. 48/319), the General Assembly reappointed the following for a four-year term beginning on 1 January 1994 to fill the vacancies occurring on 31 December 1993: Mario Bettati (France), Lucretia Myers (United States), Antônio Fonseca Pimentel (Brazil), Alexis Stephanou (Greece), Ku Tashiro (Japan).

ADVISORY COMMITTEE ON POST ADJUSTMENT QUESTIONS

The Advisory Committee on Post Adjustment Questions consists of six members, of whom five are chosen from the geographical regions of Africa, Asia, Latin America, Eastern Europe, and Western Europe and other States; and one, from ICSC, who serves ex officio as Chairman. Members are appointed by the ICSC Chairman to serve for four-year terms.

The Advisory Committee held its seventeenth session at United Nations Headquarters from 4 to 10 May 1993.

Members: Emmanuel Oti Boateng (Ghana); Yuki Miura (Japan); Hugues Picard (France); Andrei Filippovich Revenko (Russian Federation); Rafael Trigueros Mejía (Costa Rica); Carlos S. Vegega, *Chairman* (Argentina).

International Law Commission

The International Law Commission consists of 34 persons of recognized competence in international law, elected by the General Assembly to serve in their individual capacity for a five-year term. Vacancies occurring within the five-year period are filled by the Commission.

The Commission held its forty-fifth session at Geneva from 3 May to 23 July 1993.

Members (until 31 December 1996): Husain M. Al-Baharna (Bahrain); Awn S. Al-Khasawneh (Jordan); Gaetano Arangio-Ruiz (Italy); Julio Barboza, *Chairman* (Argentina); Mohamed Bennouna (Morocco); Derek William Bowett (United Kingdom); Carlos Calero Rodrigues (Brazil); James R. Crawford (Australia); John De Saram, *Rapporteur* (Sri Lanka); Gudmundur Eiriksson, *First Vice-Chairman* (Iceland); Salifou Fomba (Mali); Mehmet Güney (Turkey); Kamil E. Idris, *Second Vice-Chairman* (Sudan); Andreas J. Jacovides (Cyprus); Peter C. R. Kabatsi (Uganda); Abdul G. Koroma (Sierra Leone); Mochtar Kusuma-Atmadja (Indonesia); Ahmed Mahiou (Algeria); Vaclav Mikulka (Czech Republic); Guillaume Pambou-Tchivounda (Gabon); Alain Pellet (France); Pemmaraju Sreenivasa Rao (India); Edilbert Razafindralambo (Madagascar); Patrick Lipton Robinson (Jamaica); Robert B. Rosenstock (United States); Shi Jiuyong (China); Alberto Szekely (Mexico); Doudou Thiam (Senegal); Christian Tomuschat (Germany); Edmundo Vargas Carreño (Chile); Vladlen Vereshetin (Russian Federation); Francisco Villagran Kramer (Guatemala); Chusei Yamada (Japan); Alexander Yankov (Bulgaria).

Investments Committee

The Investments Committee consists of nine members appointed by the Secretary-General, after consultation with the United Nations Joint Staff Pension Board and ACABQ, subject to confirmation by the General Assembly. Members serve for three-year terms.

Members:
To serve until 31 December 1993: Francine J. Bovich (United States); Jean Guyot, *Chairman* (France); Michiya Matsukawa (Japan).
To serve until 31 December 1994: Ahmed Abdullatif (Saudi Arabia); Aloysio de Andrade Faria (Brazil); Stanislaw Raczkowski (Poland).
To serve until 31 December 1995: Yves Oltramare (Switzerland); Emmanuel Noi Omaboe (Ghana); Juergen Reimnitz (Germany).

On 3 December 1993 (dec. 48/316), the General Assembly confirmed the appointment by the Secretary-General of Francine J. Bovich (United States), Jean Guyot (France) and Michiya Matsukawa (Japan) as members for a three-year term beginning on 1 January 1994 to fill the vacancies occurring on 31 December 1993.

Joint Advisory Group on the International Trade Centre UNCTAD/GATT

The Joint Advisory Group was established in accordance with an agreement between UNCTAD and GATT with effect from 1 January 1968, the date on which their joint sponsorship of the International Trade Centre commenced.

Participation in the Group is open to all States members of UNCTAD and to all contracting parties to GATT.

The Group held its twenty-sixth session at Geneva from 8 to 11 November 1993.

Chairman: Netherlands.
Vice-Chairmen: Ghana, Peru.
Rapporteur: Japan.

Joint Inspection Unit

The Joint Inspection Unit consists of not more than 11 Inspectors appointed by the General Assembly from candidates nominated by Member States following appropriate consultations, including consultations with the President of the Economic and Social Council and with the Chairman of ACC. The Inspectors, chosen for their special experience in national or international administrative and financial matters, with due regard for equitable geographical distribution and reasonable rotation, serve in their personal capacity for five-year terms.

Members:
To serve until 31 December 1993: Raúl Quijano (Argentina).
To serve until 31 December 1994: Kahono Martohadinegoro (Indonesia).
To serve until 31 December 1995: Andrzej Abraszewski, *Vice-Chairman* (Poland); Erica-Irene A. Daes, *Chairman* (Greece); Richard Vognild Hennes (United States); Kabongo Tunsala (Zaire).
To serve until 31 December 1997: Fatih Bouayad-Agha (Algeria); Homero Luis Hernández-Sánchez (Dominican Republic); Boris Petrovitch Krasulin (Russian Federation); Francesco Mezzalama (Italy); Khalil Issa Othman (Jordan).

On 20 September 1993 (dec. 47/329), the General Assembly reappointed Raúl Quijano (Argentina) for a five-year term beginning on 1 January 1994.

Office of the United Nations High Commissioner for Refugees (UNHCR)

The United Nations High Commissioner for Refugees reports to the General Assembly through the Economic and Social Council.

EXECUTIVE COMMITTEE OF THE HIGH COMMISSIONER'S PROGRAMME

The Executive Committee held its forty-fourth session at Geneva from 4 to 8 October 1993.

Members: Algeria, Argentina, Australia, Austria, Belgium, Brazil, Canada, China, Colombia, Denmark, Ethiopia, Finland, France, Germany, Greece, Holy See, Hungary, Iran, Israel, Italy, Japan, Lebanon, Lesotho, Madagascar, Morocco, Namibia, Netherlands *(Chairman)*, Nicaragua *(Rapporteur)*, Nigeria, Norway, Pakistan *(Vice-Chairman)*, Philippines, Somalia, Sudan, Sweden, Switzerland, Thailand, Tunisia, Turkey, Uganda, United Kingdom, United Republic of Tanzania, United States, Venezuela, Yugoslavia, Zaire.

On 20 December 1993 (res. 48/115), the General Assembly increased the number of members from 46 to 47 and requested the Economic and Social Council to elect the additional member at its resumed organizational session in 1994.

United Nations High Commissioner for Refugees: Sadako Ogata.[a]
Deputy High Commissioner: Martin Douglas Stafford (until 31 July), Gerald Walzer (Acting) (1 August to 30 November), Gerald Walzer (from 1 December).

---

[a]On 4 November 1993 (dec. 48/307), the General Assembly extended her term of office for five years beginning on 1 January 1994.

Panel of External Auditors

The Panel of External Auditors consists of the members of the United Nations Board of Auditors and the appointed external auditors of the specialized agencies and IAEA.

Preparatory Committee for the Fiftieth Anniversary of the United Nations

The Preparatory Committee for the Fiftieth Anniversary of the United Nations, consisting of the members of the General Committee and open to the participation of all Member States, met at United Nations Headquarters on 22 February, 16 March, 23 April, 20 May, 8 June and 10 September 1993.

Chairman: Australia.
Vice-Chairmen: Botswana, Chile, Finland, Malaysia, Mauritania, Oman, Poland.
Rapporteur: Jamaica.

Preparatory Committee for the Global Conference on the Sustainable Development of Small Island Developing States

In 1993, the Preparatory Committee for the Global Conference on the Sustainable Development of Small Island Developing States (scheduled for 1994), open to all invited to participate in the 1992 United Nations Conference on Environment and Development,[1] held, at United Nations Headquarters, an organizational session on 15 and 16 April and the first part of its first session from 30 August to 10 September.

Chairman: Australia.
Vice-Chairmen: Antigua and Barbuda, Cape Verde, Romania.
Vice-Chairman/Rapporteur: Japan.

Preparatory Committee for the United Nations Conference on Human Settlements (Habitat II)

The Preparatory Committee for the United Nations Conference on Human Settlements (Habitat II) (scheduled for 1996), open to all States Members of the United Nations or members of the specialized agencies, held an organizational session at United Nations Headquarters from 3 to 5 March 1993.

Chairman: Canada.
Vice-Chairmen: Azerbaijan, Kenya, Sri Lanka.
Rapporteur: Ecuador.
Ex-officio member of the Bureau: Turkey.

Preparatory Committee for the World Conference on Human Rights

The Preparatory Committee for the World Conference on Human Rights (held in June 1993), open to all States Members of the United Nations or members of the specialized agencies, held its fourth (final) session at Geneva from 19 April to 7 May 1993.

Chairman: Morocco.
Vice-Chairmen: Ireland, Venezuela, Yemen.
Rapporteur: Poland.

Preparatory Committee for the World Conference on Natural Disaster Reduction

On 21 December 1993 (res. 48/188), the General Assembly established a Preparatory Committee for the World Conference on Natural Disaster Reduction (to be held in 1994), which was to meet at Geneva no later than March 1994.

Preparatory Committee for the World Summit for Social Development

The Preparatory Committee for the World Summit for Social Development (scheduled for 1995), open to all States Members of the United Nations or members of the specialized agencies, held an organizational session at United Nations Headquarters from 12 to 16 April 1993.

---

[1]YUN 1991, p. 489, GA res. 46/168, 19 Dec. 1991.

Chairman: Chile.
Vice-Chairmen: Australia, Cameroon, Denmark (ex officio), India, Indonesia, Latvia, Mexico, Netherlands, Poland, Zimbabwe.
Rapporteur: (One of the Vice-Chairmen).

Scientific and Technical Committee on the International Decade for Natural Desaster Reduction

The Scientific and Technical Committee on the International Decade for Natural Disaster Reduction, composed of scientific and technical experts appointed by the Secretary-General in consultation with their Governments, held its fourth session at New Delhi, India, from 1 to 5 February 1993.

Members: Alexandra Amoako-Mensah (Ghana); Anand S. Arya (India); Mohammed Benblidia (Algeria); Driss Ben Sari (Morocco); James Bruce, *Chairman* (Canada); Claudia Candanedo (Panama); Barbara Carby (Jamaica); Umberto G. Cordani (Brazil); Alberto Giesecke (Peru); Ailsa Holloway (Zimbabwe); Vaino Kelha (Finland); Roman L. Kintanar (Philippines); Michel Lechat (Belgium); C. J. Littleton (Australia); Giuseppe Luongo (Italy); Philippe Masure (France); Dallas Peck (United States); Erich Plate (Germany); Mariló Ruiz de Elvira (Spain); Atsushi Takeda (Japan); Albert Tevoedjre (Benin); Yuri Vorobiev (Russian Federation); J. J. Wagner (Switzerland); Xie Li-Li (China).

Special Committee against Apartheid

Members: Algeria, Ghana, Guinea, Haiti, India *(Rapporteur)*, Indonesia, Malaysia, Nepal *(Vice-Chairman)*, Nigeria *(Chairman)*, Peru, Philippines, Somalia, Sudan, Syrian Arab Republic, Trinidad and Tobago *(Vice-Chairman)*, Ukraine *(Vice-Chairman)*, Zimbabwe.

SUBCOMMITTEE ON DEVELOPMENTS IN SOUTH AFRICA
Members: Algeria, Haiti, India, Indonesia, Malaysia, Peru, Trinidad and Tobago, Ukraine, Zimbabwe *(Chairman)*.

SUBCOMMITTEE ON THE IMPLEMENTATION
OF UNITED NATIONS RESOLUTIONS ON SOUTH AFRICA
Members: Ghana *(Chairman)*, Guinea, Nepal, Nigeria, Philippines, Somalia, Sudan, Syrian Arab Republic.

Special Committee on Peace-keeping Operations

The 34-member Special Committee on Peace-keeping Operations met at United Nations Headquarters on 5 and 19 April, from 21 to 23 April and on 19 May 1993.

Members: Afghanistan, Algeria, Argentina *(Vice-Chairman)*, Australia, Austria, Canada *(Vice-Chairman)*, China, Denmark, Egypt *(Rapporteur)*, El Salvador, Ethiopia, France, Germany, Guatemala, Hungary, India, Iraq, Italy, Japan *(Vice-Chairman)*, Mauritania, Mexico, Netherlands, Nigeria *(Chairman)*, Pakistan, Poland *(Vice-Chairman)*, Romania, Russian Federation, Sierra Leone, Spain, Thailand, United Kingdom, United States, Venezuela, Yugoslavia.

Special Committee on the Charter of the United Nations and on the Strengthening of the Role of the Organization

The 47-member Special Committee on the Charter of the United Nations and on the Strengthening of the Role of the Organization met at United Nations Headquarters from 1 to 19 March 1993.

Members: Algeria, Argentina, Barbados, Belgium, Brazil, China, Colombia, Congo, Cyprus, Czech Republic,[a] Ecuador *(Vice-Chairman)*, Egypt, El Salvador, Finland *(Chairman)*, France, Germany, Ghana, Greece, Guyana, Hungary *(Vice-Chairman)*, India, Indonesia, Iran, Iraq, Italy, Japan, Kenya, Liberia, Mexico, Nepal, New Zealand, Nigeria, Pakistan *(Vice-Chairman)*, Philippines, Poland, Romania, Russian Federation, Rwanda, Sierra Leone, Spain, Tunisia *(Rapporteur)*, Turkey, United Kingdom, United States, Venezuela, Yugoslavia, Zambia.

[a]On 19 January 1993 (dec. 47/323), the General Assembly took note of its President's appointment of the Czech Republic as a member to fill, with immediate effect, the seat vacated by the former Czechoslovakia.

Special Committee on the Situation with regard to the Implementation of the Declaration on the Granting of Independence to Colonial Countries and Peoples

Members: Afghanistan, Bulgaria, Chile, China, Congo, Côte d'Ivoire, Cuba *(Vice-Chairman)*, Czech Republic[a] *(Vice-Chairman)*, Ethiopia, Fiji, Grenada, India, Indonesia, Iran, Iraq, Mali, Papua New Guinea *(Chairman)*, Russian Federation, Sierra Leone *(Vice-Chairman)*, Syrian Arab Republic *(Rapporteur)*, Trinidad and Tobago, Tunisia, United Republic of Tanzania, Venezuela, Yugoslavia.

[a]On 19 January 1993 (dec. 47/312 B), the General Assembly confirmed its President's nomination of the Czech Republic as a member to fill, with immediate effect, the seat vacated by the former Czechoslovakia.

SUBCOMMITTEE ON SMALL TERRITORIES,
PETITIONS, INFORMATION AND ASSISTANCE
The Subcommittee is composed of all the members of the Committee.

Chairman: Tunisia.
Rapporteur: Iran.

Special Committee to Investigate Israeli Practices Affecting the Human Rights of the Palestinian People and Other Arabs of the Occupied Territories

Members: Malaysia,[a] Senegal, Sri Lanka *(Chairman)*.

[a]Accepted its nomination as a member on 17 September 1993; replaced the former Socialist Federal Republic of Yugoslavia.

Special Committee to Select the Winners of the United Nations Human Rights Prize

The Special Committee to Select the Winners of the United Nations Human Rights Prize was established pursuant to a 1966 General Assembly resolution[2] recommending that a prize or prizes in the field of human rights be awarded not more often than at five-year intervals.

On 10 December 1993 (dec. 48/410 B), the Assembly awarded prizes to the following individuals and organizations: Hassib Ben Ammar (Tunisia), Erica Daes (Greece), James Grant (United States), International Commission of Jurists, medical personnel of the Central Hospital of Sarajevo (Bosnia and Herzegovina), Sonia Picado Sotela (Costa Rica), Ganesh Man Singh (Nepal), Sudanese Women's Union (Sudan), Father Julio Tumiri Javier (Bolivia).

Members: The Presidents of the General Assembly and the Economic and Social Council, and the Chairmen of the Commission on Human Rights, the Commission on the Status of Women and the Subcommission on Prevention of Discrimination and Protection of Minorities.

United Nations Administrative Tribunal

Members:
To serve until 31 December 1993: Luis M. de Posadas Montero, *Second Vice President* (Uruguay); Ioan Voicu (Romania).
To serve until 31 December 1994: Balanda Mikuin Leliel (Zaire); Samarendranath Sen, *President* (India); Hubert Thierry (France).
To serve until 31 December 1995: Jerome Ackerman, *First Vice-President* (United States); Francis R. Spain (Ireland).

On 3 December 1993 (dec. 48/317), the General Assembly appointed Mayer Gabay (Israel) and Luis M. de Posadas Montero (Uruguay) for a three-year term beginning on 1 January 1994 to fill the vacancies occurring on 31 December 1993.

United Nations Capital Development Fund

The United Nations Capital Development Fund was set up as an organ of the General Assembly to function as an autonomous organization within the United Nations framework. The chief executive officer of the Fund, the Managing Director, exercises his functions under the general direction of the Executive Board, which reports to the Assembly through the Economic and Social Council.

EXECUTIVE BOARD
The UNDP Governing Council acts as the Executive Board of the Fund and the UNDP Administrator as its Managing Director;

[2]YUN 1966, p. 458, GA res. 2217 A (XXI), annex, 19 Dec. 1966.

UNDP provides the Fund with, among other things, all headquarters administrative support services.

Managing Director: William H. Draper III (until 15 July 1993), James Gustave Speth (from 16 July) (UNDP Administrator).

United Nations Commission on International Trade Law (UNCITRAL)

The United Nations Commission on International Trade Law consists of 36 members elected by the General Assembly, in accordance with a formula providing equitable geographical representation and adequate representation of the principal economic and legal systems of the world. Members serve for six-year terms.

The Commission held its twenty-sixth session at Vienna from 5 to 23 July 1993.

Members:

To serve until the day preceding the Commission's regular annual session in 1995: Bulgaria *(Vice-Chairman)*, Cameroon, Canada, China, Costa Rica, Denmark, Egypt, France, Germany, Japan, Mexico, Morocco, Nigeria *(Chairman)*, Russian Federation, Singapore, Togo, United Kingdom.

To serve until the day preceding the Commission's regular annual session in 1998: Argentina *(Vice-Chairman)*, Austria, Chile, Ecuador, Hungary, India, Iran, Italy, Kenya, Poland, Saudi Arabia, Slovakia,[a] Spain *(Vice-Chairman)*, Sudan, Thailand *(Rapporteur)*, Uganda, United Republic of Tanzania, United States, Uruguay.

[a]Elected on 19 January 1993 (dec. 47/319) to fill the seat vacated by the former Czechoslovakia.

United Nations Conciliation Commission for Palestine

Members: France, Turkey, United States.

United Nations Conference on Trade and Development (UNCTAD)

Members of UNCTAD are Members of the United Nations or members of the specialized agencies or of IAEA.

Members: Afghanistan, Albania, Algeria, Andorra,[a] Angola, Antigua and Barbuda, Argentina, Armenia, Australia, Austria, Azerbaijan, Bahamas, Bahrain, Bangladesh, Barbados, Belarus, Belgium, Belize, Benin, Bhutan, Bolivia, Bosnia and Herzegovina, Botswana, Brazil, Brunei Darussalam, Bulgaria, Burkina Faso, Burundi, Cambodia, Cameroon, Canada, Cape Verde, Central African Republic, Chad, Chile, China, Colombia, Comoros, Congo, Costa Rica, Côte d'Ivoire, Croatia, Cuba, Cyprus, Czech Republic,[b] Democratic People's Republic of Korea, Denmark, Djibouti, Dominica, Dominican Republic, Ecuador, Egypt, El Salvador, Equatorial Guinea, Eritrea,[c] Estonia, Ethiopia, Fiji, Finland, France, Gabon, Gambia, Georgia, Germany, Ghana, Greece, Grenada, Guatemala, Guinea, Guinea-Bissau, Guyana, Haiti, Holy See, Honduras, Hungary, Iceland, India, Indonesia, Iran, Iraq, Ireland, Israel, Italy, Jamaica, Japan, Jordan, Kazakhstan, Kenya, Kuwait, Kyrgyzstan, Lao People's Democratic Republic, Latvia, Lebanon, Lesotho, Liberia, Libyan Arab Jamahiriya, Liechtenstein, Lithuania, Luxembourg, Madagascar, Malawi, Malaysia, Maldives, Mali, Malta, Marshall Islands, Mauritania, Mauritius, Mexico, Micronesia, Monaco,[c] Mongolia, Morocco, Mozambique, Myanmar, Namibia, Nepal, Netherlands, New Zealand, Nicaragua, Niger, Nigeria, Norway, Oman, Pakistan, Panama, Papua New Guinea, Paraguay, Peru, Philippines, Poland, Portugal, Qatar, Republic of Korea, Republic of Moldova, Romania, Russian Federation, Rwanda, Saint Kitts and Nevis, Saint Lucia, Saint Vincent and the Grenadines, Samoa, San Marino, Sao Tome and Principe, Saudi Arabia, Senegal, Seychelles, Sierra Leone, Singapore, Slovakia,[b] Slovenia, Solomon Islands, Somalia, South Africa, Spain, Sri Lanka, Sudan, Suriname, Swaziland, Sweden, Switzerland, Syrian Arab Republic, Tajikistan, Thailand, the former Yugoslav Republic of Macedonia,[d] Togo, Tonga, Trinidad and Tobago, Tunisia, Turkey, Turkmenistan, Uganda, Ukraine, United Arab Emirates, United Kingdom, United Republic of Tanzania, United States, Uruguay,

Uzbekistan, Vanuatu, Venezuela, Viet Nam, Yemen, Yugoslavia,[e] Zaire, Zambia, Zimbabwe.

[a]Became a Member of the United Nations and, *ipso facto*, of UNCTAD on 28 July 1993.
[b]Became a Member of the United Nations and, *ipso facto*, of UNCTAD on 19 January 1993.
[c]Became a Member of the United Nations and, *ipso facto*, of UNCTAD on 28 May 1993.
[d]Became a Member of the United Nations and, *ipso facto*, of UNCTAD on 8 April 1993.
[e]Refers to the former Socialist Federal Republic of Yugoslavia.

Secretary-General of UNCTAD: Kenneth K. S. Dadzie.[a]

[a]Appointment extended by the General Assembly on 16 March 1993 (dec. 47/324) for one year, to 31 March 1994.

TRADE AND DEVELOPMENT BOARD

The Trade and Development Board is a permanent organ of UNCTAD. It reports to UNCTAD as well as annually to the General Assembly through the Economic and Social Council.

BOARD MEMBERS AND SESSIONS

The membership of the Board is open to all UNCTAD members. Those wishing to become members of the Board communicate their intention to the Secretary-General of UNCTAD for transmittal to the Board President, who announces the membership on the basis of such notifications.

The Board held the following sessions in 1993, at Geneva: its second (pre-sessional) executive session on 5 March, the second part of its thirty-ninth session from 15 to 26 March, its third executive session on 27 April, its fourth (pre-sessional) executive session on 13 September and the first part of its fortieth session from 20 September to 1 October.

Members: Afghanistan, Albania, Algeria, Angola, Argentina, Armenia, Australia, Austria, Azerbaijan,[a] Bahrain, Bangladesh, Barbados, Belarus, Belgium, Benin, Bhutan, Bolivia, Brazil, Bulgaria, Burkina Faso, Burundi, Cameroon, Canada, Central African Republic, Chad, Chile, China, Colombia, Congo, Costa Rica, Côte d'Ivoire, Cuba, Cyprus, Czech Republic,[b] Democratic People's Republic of Korea, Denmark, Dominica, Dominican Republic, Ecuador, Egypt, El Salvador, Equatorial Guinea, Ethiopia, Finland, France, Gabon, Georgia, Germany, Ghana, Greece, Grenada, Guatemala, Guinea, Guyana, Haiti, Honduras, Hungary, India, Indonesia, Iran, Iraq, Ireland, Israel, Italy, Jamaica, Japan, Jordan, Kenya, Kuwait, Lebanon, Liberia, Libyan Arab Jamahiriya, Liechtenstein, Luxembourg, Madagascar, Malaysia, Mali, Malta, Mauritania, Mauritius, Mexico, Mongolia, Morocco, Myanmar, Namibia, Nepal, Netherlands, New Zealand, Nicaragua, Nigeria, Norway, Oman, Pakistan, Panama, Papua New Guinea, Paraguay, Peru, Philippines, Poland, Portugal, Qatar, Republic of Korea, Romania, Russian Federation, Sao Tome and Principe, Saudi Arabia, Senegal, Sierra Leone, Singapore, Slovakia,[b] Somalia, Spain, Sri Lanka, Sudan, Suriname, Sweden, Switzerland, Syrian Arab Republic, Thailand, the former Yugoslav Republic of Macedonia,[c] Togo, Trinidad and Tobago, Tunisia, Turkey, Uganda, Ukraine, United Arab Emirates, United Kingdom, United Republic of Tanzania, United States, Uruguay, Venezuela, Viet Nam, Yemen, Yugoslavia, Zaire, Zambia, Zimbabwe.

[a]Became a member on 27 April 1993.
[b]Became a member on 5 March 1993.
[c]Became a member on 13 September 1993.

OFFICERS (BUREAU) OF THE BOARD

Second (pre-sessional) executive, second part of the thirty-ninth, third executive and fourth (pre-sessional) executive sessions
President: Turkey.
Vice-Presidents: Bolivia, Democratic People's Republic of Korea, Denmark (second part of thirty-ninth, third and fourth executive sessions), Honduras, Japan (second executive session), Mauritius, Morocco, Netherlands (second part of thirty-ninth,

third and fourth executive sessions), Poland, Russian Federation, United Kingdom (second executive session), United States.
Rapporteur: Nepal.

Fortieth session (first part)
President: Jordan.
Vice-Presidents: Belgium, Czech Republic, Ecuador, India, Jamaica, Japan, Russian Federation, Sudan, Tunisia, United States.
Rapporteur: Netherlands.

SUBSIDIARY ORGANS OF THE TRADE AND DEVELOPMENT BOARD

The main committees of the Board are open to the participation of all interested UNCTAD members, on the understanding that those wishing to attend a particular session of one or more of the committees communicate their intention to the Secretary-General of UNCTAD during the preceding regular session of the Board. On the basis of such notifications, the Board determines the membership of the main committees.

INTERGOVERNMENTAL GROUP OF EXPERTS ON RESTRICTIVE BUSINESS PRACTICES

The Intergovernmental Group of Experts on Restrictive Business Practices, which is open to the participation of all UNCTAD members, held its twelfth session at Geneva from 18 to 22 October 1993.

Chairman: Argentina.
Vice-Chairmen: Germany, Indonesia, Peru, Russian Federation, United States.
Rapporteur: Morocco.

SPECIAL COMMITTEE ON PREFERENCES

The Special Committee on Preferences, which is open to the participation of all UNCTAD members, held its twentieth session at Geneva from 10 to 14 May 1993.

Chairman: Indonesia.
Vice-Chairmen: Benin, Chile, Denmark, Sri Lanka, United States.
Rapporteur: Russian Federation.

STANDING COMMITTEE ON COMMODITIES

The Standing Committee on Commodities did not meet in 1993.

Members: Afghanistan, Algeria, Argentina, Armenia, Australia, Austria, Bangladesh, Belgium, Bolivia, Brazil, Bulgaria, Canada, China, Colombia, Côte d'Ivoire, Cuba, Czech Republic, Democratic People's Republic of Korea, Denmark, Ecuador, Egypt, El Salvador, Equatorial Guinea, Ethiopia, Finland, France, Germany, Ghana, Greece, Honduras, Hungary, India, Indonesia, Iran, Iraq, Ireland, Israel, Italy, Jamaica, Japan, Jordan, Kenya, Lebanon, Libyan Arab Jamahiriya, Madagascar, Malaysia, Mali, Mexico, Morocco, Myanmar, Nepal, Netherlands, New Zealand, Nigeria, Norway, Pakistan, Panama, Paraguay, Peru, Philippines, Poland, Portugal, Republic of Korea, Romania, Russian Federation, Saudi Arabia, Senegal, Singapore, Slovakia, Spain, Sri Lanka, Sudan, Sweden, Switzerland, Thailand, Togo, Trinidad and Tobago, Tunisia, Turkey, United Kingdom, United Republic of Tanzania, United States, Uruguay, Venezuela, Viet Nam, Yugoslavia, Zambia, Zimbabwe.

STANDING COMMITTEE ON DEVELOPING SERVICES SECTORS: FOSTERING COMPETITIVE SERVICES SECTORS IN DEVELOPING COUNTRIES--INSURANCE

The Standing Committee on Developing Services Sectors: Fostering Competitive Services Sectors in Developing Countries addresses various problem areas of developing economies. In 1992, its focus was on shipping; in 1993, it held its first session on insurance (Geneva, 1 to 5 February).

Members: Afghanistan, Algeria, Argentina, Armenia, Australia, Austria, Bangladesh, Belgium, Bolivia, Brazil, Bulgaria, Cameroon, Canada (shipping), Chile, China, Colombia, Costa Rica,

Côte d'Ivoire, Croatia, Cuba, Cyprus, Czech Republic, Democratic People's Republic of Korea, Denmark, Ecuador, Egypt, El Salvador, Ethiopia, Finland, France, Gabon (shipping), Germany, Ghana, Greece *(Vice-Chairman)*, Honduras, Hungary, India *(Chairman)*, Indonesia, Iran, Iraq, Ireland, Israel, Italy, Jamaica, Japan *(Rapporteur)*, Jordan, Kenya, Lebanon, Lesotho, Liberia, Libyan Arab Jamahiriya, Madagascar (shipping), Malaysia, Mali, Malta, Mauritius, Mexico *(Vice-Chairman)*, Mongolia, Morocco, Myanmar, Nepal, Netherlands, New Zealand, Niger, Nigeria *(Vice-Chairman)*, Norway, Pakistan, Paraguay, Peru, Philippines *(Vice-Chairman)*, Poland, Republic of Korea, Romania, Russian Federation *(Vice-Chairman)*, Saudi Arabia, Senegal, Seychelles, Slovakia, Spain, Sri Lanka, Sudan, Sweden, Switzerland, Thailand, Trinidad and Tobago, Tunisia, Turkey, United Kingdom, United Republic of Tanzania, United States, Uruguay, Venezuela, Viet Nam, Yugoslavia, Zambia, Zimbabwe.

STANDING COMMITTEE ON ECONOMIC COOPERATION AMONG DEVELOPING COUNTRIES

The Standing Committee on Economic Cooperation among Developing Countries held its first session at Geneva from 11 to 15 January 1993.

Members: Afghanistan, Algeria, Argentina, Armenia, Austria, Bangladesh *(Vice-Chairman)*, Bolivia, Brazil *(Vice-Chairman)*, China, Colombia, Côte d'Ivoire, Cuba, Democratic People's Republic of Korea, Denmark *(Vice-Chairman)*, Egypt, El Salvador, Ethiopia, France, Georgia, Germany, Ghana, Greece, Honduras, India, Indonesia, Iran, Iraq, Israel, Jamaica, Japan, Jordan, Kenya *(Chairman)*, Lebanon, Libyan Arab Jamahiriya, Madagascar, Malaysia, Mali, Mauritius, Mexico, Mongolia, Morocco, Myanmar, Nepal, Netherlands, Niger, Nigeria, Norway, Pakistan, Panama, Peru, Philippines, Republic of Korea, Romania, Russian Federation *(Rapporteur)*, Saudi Arabia, Senegal, Spain, Sri Lanka, Sudan, Sweden, Switzerland, Syrian Arab Republic, Thailand, Togo, Trinidad and Tobago, Tunisia *(Vice-Chairman)*, Turkey, United Kingdom, United Republic of Tanzania, United States *(Vice-Chairman)*, Uruguay, Venezuela, Viet Nam, Yugoslavia, Zambia, Zimbabwe.

STANDING COMMITTEE ON POVERTY ALLEVIATION

The Standing Committee on Poverty Alleviation held its first session at Geneva from 18 to 22 January 1993.

Members: Afghanistan, Algeria, Angola, Argentina, Armenia, Australia, Austria, Bangladesh, Belgium, Bolivia, Brazil, Cameroon, Canada, Chile *(Chairman)*, China, Colombia, Côte d'Ivoire, Cuba, Czech Republic, Democratic People's Republic of Korea, Denmark, Dominican Republic, Egypt, El Salvador *(Vice-Chairman)*, Ethiopia, Finland, France, Germany, Ghana, Greece, Honduras, India, Indonesia, Iran, Iraq, Ireland, Israel, Italy, Jamaica, Japan, Jordan, Kenya, Lebanon, Libyan Arab Jamahiriya, Madagascar, Malaysia, Mali, Mexico, Morocco, Myanmar, Nepal, Netherlands, Nigeria, Norway, Pakistan, Panama, Paraguay, Peru, Philippines, Poland, Portugal *(Vice-Chairman)*, Republic of Korea, Romania, Russian Federation *(Vice-Chairman)*, Saudi Arabia, Senegal, Slovakia, Spain, Sri Lanka *(Vice-Chairman)*, Sudan, Sweden, Switzerland, Thailand, Togo, Trinidad and Tobago, Tunisia *(Vice-Chairman)*, Turkey, United Kingdom, United States *(Rapporteur)*, Uruguay, Viet Nam, Yugoslavia, Zambia, Zimbabwe.

United Nations Development Fund for Women (UNIFEM)

The United Nations Development Fund for Women is a separate entity in autonomous association with UNDP. The Director of the Fund, appointed by the UNDP Administrator, conducts all matters related to its mandate and the Administrator is accountable for its management and operations.

CONSULTATIVE COMMITTEE

The Consultative Committee on UNIFEM to advise the UNDP Administrator on all policy matters affecting the Fund's activities is composed of five Member States designated by the General

Assembly President with due regard for the financing of the Fund from voluntary contributions and to equitable geographical distribution. Each State member of the Committee serves for a three-year term and designates a person with expertise in development cooperation activities, including those benefiting women.

The Committee held its thirty-second and thirty-third sessions at United Nations Headquarters on 25 and 26 January and from 7 to 9 September 1993, respectively.

Members (until 31 December 1994): Bahamas *(Chairman)*, Denmark, Indonesia, Poland, Uganda.

Director of UNIFEM: Sharon Capeling-Alakija.

United Nations Environment Programme (UNEP)

GOVERNING COUNCIL

The Governing Council of UNEP consists of 58 members elected by the General Assembly according to a specific pattern of equitable geographical representation.

The Governing Council, which reports to the Assembly through the Economic and Social Council, held its seventeenth session at Nairobi, Kenya, from 10 to 21 May 1993.

Members:
To serve until 31 December 1993: Argentina, Austria, Barbados, Brazil, Burundi, China, France, Gabon, Gambia, Germany, Indonesia *(Vice-President)*, Japan, Kuwait, Lesotho, Mauritius, New Zealand, Norway, Peru, Philippines *(Vice-President)*, Russian Federation, Spain, Thailand, Tunisia, Ukraine, United States, Venezuela *(Vice-President)*, Yugoslavia, Zaire, Zimbabwe.
To serve until 31 December 1995: Australia, Bangladesh, Bhutan, Botswana, Cameroon, Chile, Colombia, Congo, Côte d'Ivoire, Denmark *(Vice-President)*, Guyana, India, Iran, Italy, Kenya, Malaysia, Mexico, Netherlands, Nigeria *(President)*, Pakistan, Poland *(Rapporteur)*, Portugal, Romania, Rwanda, Senegal, Slovakia,[a] Sri Lanka, United Kingdom, Uruguay.

[a]Elected on 19 January 1993 (dec. 47/318) to fill the seat vacated by the former Czechoslovakia.

On 11 November 1993 (dec. 48/309), the General Assembly elected the following for a four-year term beginning on 1 January 1994 to fill the vacancies occurring on 31 December 1993: Argentina, Brazil, Bulgaria, Burundi, Canada, China, Costa Rica, Democratic People's Republic of Korea, France, Gabon, Gambia, Germany, Guinea-Bissau, Hungary, Indonesia, Japan, Nicaragua, Republic of Korea, Russian Federation, Spain, Sudan, Sweden, Switzerland, Syrian Arab Republic, United States, Venezuela, Zaire, Zambia, Zimbabwe.

Executive Director of UNEP: Elizabeth Dowdeswell.

United Nations Institute for Disarmament Research (UNIDIR)

BOARD OF TRUSTEES

The Secretary-General's Advisory Board on Disarmament Matters, composed in 1993 of 19 eminent persons selected on the basis of their personal expertise and taking into account the principle of equitable geographical representation, functions as the Board of Trustees of UNIDIR; the Director of UNIDIR reports to the General Assembly and is an ex-officio member of the Advisory Board when it acts as the Board of Trustees.

Members: Ednan T. Agaev (Russian Federation); A. Bolaji Akinyemi (Nigeria); Martin Chungong Ayafor (Cameroon); Marcos Castrioto de Azambuja, *Chairman* (Brazil); Mitsuro Donowaki (Japan); Muchkund Dubey (India); Emmanuel A. Erskine (Ghana); Curt Gasteyger (Switzerland); Henny J. van der Graaf (Netherlands); Josef Holik (Germany); François de la Gorce (France); James F. Leonard (United States); Peggy Mason (Canada); Rogelio Pfirtner (Argentina); Mohamed I. Shaker (Egypt); John Simpson (United Kingdom); Siti Azizah Abod (Malaysia); J. Soedjati Djiwandono (Indonesia); Klaus Törnudd (Finland).

Director of UNIDIR: Sverre Lodgaard.

United Nations Institute for Training and Research (UNITAR)

The Executive Director of UNITAR, in consultation with the Board of Trustees of the Institute, reports through the Secretary-General to the General Assembly and, as appropriate, to the Economic and Social Council and other United Nations bodies.

BOARD OF TRUSTEES

The Board of Trustees of UNITAR is composed of: *(a)* not less than 11 and not more than 30 members, which may include one or more officials of the United Nations Secretariat, appointed on a broad geographical basis by the Secretary-General, in consultation with the Presidents of the General Assembly and the Economic and Social Council; and *(b)* four ex-officio members.

The Board did not meet in 1993.

Members: Giuseppe Baldocci (Italy), Jorge Berguno (Chile), Michel de Bonnecorse (France), Ibrahim A. Gambari (Nigeria), Ahmad Kamal (Pakistan), Shunji Kobayashi (Japan), Winfried Lang (Austria), Juan Carlos Sanchez Arnau (Argentina), Mohammed Ahmed Sherif (Libyan Arab Jamahiriya), Gleb Smirnov (Russian Federation), Wang Guangya (China), Penelope Anne Wensley (Australia).
Ex-officio members: The Secretary-General, the President of the General Assembly, the President of the Economic and Social Council and the Executive Director of UNITAR.

Executive Director of UNITAR: Marcel Boisard (acting).

United Nations Joint Staff Pension Board

The United Nations Joint Staff Pension Board is composed of 33 members, as follows:

Twelve appointed by the United Nations Staff Pension Committee (four from members elected by the General Assembly, four from those appointed by the Secretary-General, four from those elected by participants);
Twenty-one appointed by staff pension committees of other member organizations of the United Nations Joint Staff Pension Fund (seven from those chosen by the bodies corresponding to the General Assembly, seven from those appointed by the chief administrative officers, seven from those chosen by the participants).

The Board held its forty-fifth session (special) at United Nations Headquarters from 24 to 30 June 1993.

Members:
United Nations
  Representing the General Assembly: Members: J. J. Duhalt (Mexico); T. Inomata, *Second Vice-Chairman* (Japan); M. G. Okeyo (Kenya); S. Shearouse (United States). Alternates: L. E. Bidnyi (Russian Federation); T. B. Hamida (Tunisia); C. Stitt (United Kingdom); R. Rae (India).
  Representing the Secretary-General: Members: M. Wells (United States); C. Dodson (United States); K. Walton (United Kingdom); A. Miller (Australia). Alternate: D. Bull (United Kingdom).
  Representing the Participants: Members: B. Hillis (Canada); V. Baeza (Chile); N. Kakar (India); S. Johnston (United States). Alternates: A. Kruiderink (Netherlands); O. Lugo (Colombia).
Food and Agriculture Organization of the United Nations
  Representing the Governing Body: Member: C. Bonaparte (Haiti). Alternate: S. Abdallah (Syrian Arab Republic).
  Representing the Executive Head: Member: A. T. Slater (United States). Alternate: G. Zorn (United States).
  Representing the Participants: Member: A. Marcucci, *First Vice-Chairman* (Italy). Alternate: M. Arrigo (Italy).
World Health Organization
  Representing the Executive Head: Member: D. G. Aitken, *Chairman* (United Kingdom). Alternate: D. Sanvicenti (Italy).
  Representing the Participants: Member: M. Dam (United States). Alternate: V. Paterson (United States).

International Labour Organisation
  Representing the Governing Body: Member: Y. Chotard (France). Alternate: W. M. Yoffee (United States).
  Representing the Executive Head: Member: R. Smith (United Kingdom). Alternate: A. Busca (Italy).
United Nations Educational, Scientific and Cultural Organization
  Representing the Governing Body: Member: G. V. Rao (India).
  Representing the Participants: Member: A. McLurg (United Kingdom). Alternate: J. Taillefer (France).
United Nations Industrial Development Organization
  Representing the Governing Body: Member: E. Zador (Hungary).
  Representing the Executive Head: Member: A. Ingram (Australia).
International Civil Aviation Organization
  Representing the Executive Head: Member: D. J. Goossen, *Rapporteur* (Netherlands).
  Representing the Participants: Member: C. Gallagher-Croxen (Canada).
International Atomic Energy Agency
  Representing the Participants: Member: W. Scherzer (Austria).
International Telecommunication Union
  Representing the Participants: Member: J. Desbiolles (France). Alternate: H. de Groot (Sweden).
International Maritime Organization
  Representing the Participants: Member: D. Bertaud (France).
Interim Commission for the International Trade Organization/ General Agreement on Tariffs and Trade
  Representing the Governing Body: Member: P. Cheung (Hong Kong).
World Meteorological Organization
  Representing the Executive Head: Member: E. Renlund (Sweden).
World Intellectual Property Organization
  Representing the Executive Head: Member: B. Machado (France).
International Fund for Agricultural Development
  Representing the Governing Body: Member: D. Ertle (Germany).

STANDING COMMITTEE OF THE PENSION BOARD

  The Standing Committee met at United Nations Headquarters on 29 and 30 June 1993.

Members (elected at the Board's forty-fourth session):
United Nations (Group I)
  Representing the General Assembly: Members: T. Inomata, J. Duhalt. Alternates: R. Rae, S. Shearouse.
  Representing the Secretary-General: Members: C. Dodson, A. Miller. Alternates: K. Walton, D. Bull.
  Representing the Participants: Members: B. Hillis, V. Baeza. Alternates: N. Kakar, S. Johnston.
Specialized agencies (Group II)
  Representing the Governing Body: Member: C. Bonaparte (FAO).
  Representing the Executive Head: Member: D. G. Aitken (WHO). Alternate: D. Sanvicenti (WHO).
  Representing the Participants: Member: M. Dam (WHO). Alternate: A. Marcucci (FAO).
Specialized agencies (Group III)
  Representing the Governing Body: Member: W. M. Yoffee (ILO). Alternate: Y. Chotard (ILO).
  Representing the Executive Head: Member: D. Daly (UNESCO). Alternate: C. Kerlouegan (UNESCO).
Specialized agencies (Group IV)
  Representing the Executive Head: Member: D. Goethel (IAEA). Alternate: U. Peer (UNIDO).
  Representing the Participants: Member: J. Desbiolles (ITU). Alternate: C. Gallagher-Croxen (ICAO).
Specialized agencies (Group V)
  Representing the Governing Body: Member: R. G. Lewis (IMO). Alternate: P. Cheung (ICITO/GATT).
  Representing the Participants: Member: S. Mbele-Mbong (WMO). Alternate: V. Yossifov (WIPO).

COMMITTEE OF ACTUARIES

  The Committee of Actuaries consists of five members, each representing one of the five geographical regions of the United Nations.

Members: A. O. Ogunshola (Nigeria), *Region I* (African States); K. Takeuchi (Japan), *Region II* (Asian States); E. M. Chetyrkin (Russian Federation), *Region III* (Eastern European States); H. Pérez Montas (Dominican Republic), *Region IV* (Latin American States); L. J. Martin (United Kingdom), *Region V* (Western European and other States).

United Nations Population Fund (UNFPA)

  The United Nations Population Fund, a subsidiary organ of the General Assembly, plays a leading role in the United Nations system in promoting population programmes and assists developing countries at their request in dealing with their population problems. It operates under the overall policy guidance of the Economic and Social Council and under the financial and administrative policy guidance of the Governing Council of UNDP.

Executive Director: Dr. Nafis I. Sadik.
Deputy Executive Director (Policy and Administration): Katsuhide Kitatani (until 28 February 1993), Hirofumi Ando (from 1 May).
Deputy Executive Director (Programme): Joseph Van Arendonk.

United Nations Relief and Works Agency for Palestine Refugees in the Near East (UNRWA)

ADVISORY COMMISSION OF UNRWA

  The Advisory Commission of UNRWA met at Vienna on 6 October 1993.

Members: Belgium, Egypt, France, Japan, Jordan, Lebanon, Syrian Arab Republic, Turkey *(Chairman)*, United Kingdom, United States.

WORKING GROUP ON THE FINANCING OF UNRWA

  The Working Group met twice in 1993, on 9 September and 22 October.

Members: France, Ghana, Japan, Lebanon, Norway *(Rapporteur)*, Trinidad and Tobago, Turkey *(Chairman)*, United Kingdom, United States.

Commissioner-General of UNRWA: Ilter Türkmen.
Deputy Commissioner-General: William L. Eagleton.

United Nations Scientific Committee on the Effects of Atomic Radiation

  The 21-member United Nations Scientific Committee on the Effects of Atomic Radiation held its forty-second session at Vienna from 17 to 28 May 1993.

Members: Argentina, Australia, Belgium, Brazil, Canada *(Chairman)*, China, Egypt, France, Germany, India, Indonesia, Japan, Mexico, Peru *(Vice-Chairman)*, Poland, Russian Federation, Slovakia,[a] Sudan, Sweden *(Rapporteur)*, United Kingdom, United States.

[a]Appointed on 19 January 1993 (dec. 47/320) to fill the seat vacated by the former Czechoslovakia.

United Nations Staff Pension Committee

  The United Nations Staff Pension Committee consists of four members and four alternates elected by the General Assembly, four members and two alternates appointed by the Secretary-General, and four members and two alternates elected by the participants in the United Nations Joint Staff Pension Fund. The term of office of the elected members is three years, or until the election of their successors.

Members:
Elected by Assembly (to serve until 31 December 1994): *Members:* Jorge José Duhalt Villar (Mexico), Tadanori Inomata

(Japan), Michael G. Okeyo (Kenya), Susan Shearouse (United States). *Alternates:* Tarak Ben Hamida (Tunisia),[a] Leonid E. Bidnyi (Russian Federation), Richard Kinchen (United Kingdom),[b] Ranjit Rae (India).

Appointed by Secretary-General (until June 1993): *Members:* Armando Duque, Anthony J. Miller. *Alternates:* Dulcie Bull, Alexander Barabanov; (from June 1993): *Members:* Melissa Wells, Christine Dodson, Anthony J. Miller, Keith Walton. *Alternate:* Dulcie Bull.

Elected by Participants (to serve until 31 December 1995): *Members:* Bruce C. Hillis, Viviana Baeza, Susanna H. Johnston, Narinder Kakar. *Alternates:* Anton Kruiderink, Orlando Lugo.

[a]Appointed on 20 April 1993 (dec. 47/325 A) to replace Mohamed Ferid Belhaj (Tunisia), who resigned earlier that month.

[b]Resigned on 1 June 1993; Clive Stitt (United Kingdom) was appointed on 15 June (dec. 47/325 B) to fill the resultant vacancy.

United Nations Trust Committee for the United Nations Fund for Namibia

Members: Australia, Finland, India, Nigeria, Romania, Senegal, Turkey, Venezuela *(Vice-Chairman/Rapporteur),* Yugoslavia, Zambia *(Chairman).*

United Nations University

COUNCIL OF THE UNITED NATIONS UNIVERSITY

The Council of the United Nations University, the governing board of the University, reports annually to the General Assembly, to the Economic and Social Council and to the UNESCO Executive Board through the Secretary-General and the UNESCO Director-General. It consists of: *(a)* 24 members appointed jointly by the Secretary-General and the Director-General of UNESCO, in consultation with the agencies and programmes concerned including UNITAR, who serve in their personal capacity for six-year terms; *(b)* the Secretary-General, the Director-General of UNESCO and the Executive Director of UNITAR, who are ex-officio members; and *(c)* the Rector of the University, who is normally appointed for a five-year term.

In 1993, the Council held two sessions, in Tokyo: its thirty-ninth from 15 to 20 February and its fortieth from 13 to 17 December.

Members:

To serve until 2 May 1995: Claude Frejacques (France); Josephine Guidy-Wandja (Côte d'Ivoire); Sippanondha Ketudat (Thailand); Felipe E. MacGregor (Peru); Lucille Mair, *Chairman* (Jamaica); Abdel Salam Majali (Jordan); Lydia Makhubu (Swaziland); Vladlen A. Martynov (Russian Federation); Fatima Mernissi (Morocco);[a] Rafael Portaencasa (Spain); Wang Shaoqi (China); Mihaly Simai (Hungary); Raimo Vayrynen (Finland).

To serve until 2 May 1998: Vladimir Dlouhy (Czech Republic); Hideo Kagami (Japan); Sang Soo Lee (Republic of Korea); Edson Machado de Sousa (Brazil); Madina Ly-Tall (Mali); Lucien F. Michaud (Canada); A. P. Mitra (India); Jacob L. Ngu (Cameroon); Luis Manuel Peñalver (Venezuela); Victor Rabinowitch (United States); Frances Stewart (United Kingdom); J. A. van Ginkel (Netherlands).

Ex-officio members: The Secretary-General, the Director-General of UNESCO and the Executive Director of UNITAR.

[a]Resigned in June 1993; no replacement was appointed in 1993.

Rector of the United Nations University: Heitor Gurgulino de Souza.

The Council maintained four standing committees during 1993: Committee on Finance and Budget; Committee on Institutional and Programmatic Development; Committee on Statutes, Rules and Guidelines; Committee on the Report of the Council.

United Nations Voluntary Fund for Indigenous Populations

BOARD OF TRUSTEES

The Board of Trustees to advise the Secretary-General in his administration of the United Nations Voluntary Fund for Indigenous Populations consists of five members with relevant experience in issues affecting indigenous populations, appointed in their personal capacity by the Secretary-General for a three-year term. At least one member is a representative of a widely recognized organization of indigenous people.

The Board held its sixth session at Geneva from 25 to 29 April 1993.

Members: Leif Dunfjeld (Norway); Ole Ntimama (Kenya); Lois O'Donoghue (Australia); Victoria Tauli-Corpuz (Philippines); Augusto Willemsen-Díaz, *Chairman* (Guatemala).

United Nations Voluntary Fund for Victims of Torture

BOARD OF TRUSTEES

The Board of Trustees to advise the Secretary-General in his administration of the United Nations Voluntary Fund for Victims of Torture consists of five members with wide experience in the field of human rights, appointed in their personal capacity by the Secretary-General with due regard for equitable geographical distribution and in consultation with their Governments.

The Board held its twelfth session at Geneva from 19 to 28 April 1993.

Members: Elizabeth Odio Benito (Costa Rica); Ribot Hatano (Japan); Ivan Tosevski (Yugoslavia); Amos Wako (Kenya); Jaap Walkate, *Chairman* (Netherlands).

United Nations Voluntary Trust Fund on Contemporary Forms of Slavery

The United Nations Voluntary Trust Fund on Contemporary Forms of Slavery provides financial assistance to representatives of non-governmental organizations dealing with the matter to participate in the deliberations of the Working Group on Contemporary Forms of Slavery of the Subcommission on Prevention of Discrimination and Protection of Minorities, and extends humanitarian, legal and financial aid to individuals whose human rights have been severely violated as a result of contemporary forms of slavery.

BOARD OF TRUSTEES

The Board of Trustees to advise the Secretary-General in his administration of the Fund consists of five persons with relevant experience in the field of human rights and contemporary forms of slavery in particular, appointed in their personal capacity by the Secretary-General for a three-year renewable term, in consultation with the Chairman of the Subcommission and with due regard to equitable geographical distribution.

The Board held its first session at Geneva from 22 to 26 March 1993.

Members (until 31 December 1995): Swami Agnivesh, *Chairman* (India); Michel Bonnet (France); Tatiana Matveeva (Russian Federation); Cheikh Saad-Bouh Kamara (Mauritania); Eugenia Zamora Chavarria (Uruguay).

World Food Council

The World Food Council, at the ministerial or plenipotentiary level, functions as an organ of the United Nations and reports to the General Assembly through the Economic and Social Council. It consists of 36 members nominated by the Economic and Social Council and elected by the Assembly according to a specific pattern of equitable geographical distribution. Members serve for three-year terms.

The Council did not meet in 1993.

Members:

To serve until 31 December 1993: Bangladesh, Bulgaria, Canada, China, Colombia, Gambia, Kenya, Lesotho, Mexico, Nepal, Turkey, United States.

To serve until 31 December 1994: Albania, Australia, Central African Republic, Germany, Guatemala, Honduras, Indonesia, Nicaragua, Russian Federation, Swaziland, Thailand, Uganda.

To serve until 31 December 1995: Ecuador, France, Guinea-Bissau, Hungary, India,[a] Iran, Italy, Japan, Nigeria, Norway, Peru and Tunisia.

[a]Nominated by the Economic and Social Council on 12 February 1993 (dec. 1993/201) and elected by the General Assembly on 6 May (dec. 47/306 B).

Executive Director: vacant.

On 29 April 1993 (dec. 1993/218), the Economic and Social Council nominated the following States for election by the General Assembly for a three-year term beginning on 1 January 1994 to fill 10 of the 12 vacancies occurring on 31 December 1993: Bangladesh, Brazil, China, Liberia, Malawi, Mexico, Pakistan, Sudan, Turkey, United States. The Assembly elected them on 11 November 1993 (dec. 48/310). No further elections were held in 1993 to fill the remaining seats, allocated to one member each from Eastern European and Western European and other States.

Conferences

United Nations Conference on Straddling Fish Stocks and Highly Migratory Fish Stocks

In 1993, the United Nations Conference on Straddling Fish Stocks and Highly Migratory Fish Stocks held, at United Nations Headquarters, its first (organizational) session from 19 to 23 April and its second session from 12 to 30 July 1993. Participating were the following 109 States and Territories:

Algeria, Antigua and Barbuda, Argentina, Australia, Austria, Barbados, Belgium, Benin, Brazil, Bulgaria, Burundi, Cameroon, Canada, Cape Verde, Chile *(Vice-Chairman)*, China, Colombia, Cook Islands, Costa Rica, Côte d'Ivoire, Cuba, Cyprus, Denmark, Djibouti, Ecuador, Egypt, Fiji *(Chairman)*, Finland, France, Gabon, Gambia, Germany, Ghana, Greece, Guinea, Guinea-Bissau, Guyana, Hungary, Iceland, India, Indonesia, Iran, Ireland, Israel, Italy *(Vice-Chairman)*, Jamaica, Japan, Kenya, Kiribati, Latvia, Lesotho, Libyan Arab Jamahiriya, Liechtenstein, Lithuania, Madagascar, Malaysia, Maldives, Mali, Malta, Marshall Islands, Mauritania *(Vice-Chairman)*, Mauritius, Mexico, Micronesia, Morocco, Myanmar, Namibia, Netherlands, New Zealand, Nigeria, Norway, Panama, Papua New Guinea, Peru, Philippines, Poland, Portugal, Republic of Korea, Romania, Russian Federation, Saint Lucia, Samoa, Senegal, Seychelles, Sierra Leone, Singapore, Solomon Islands, Spain, Sri Lanka, Sweden, Switzerland, Syrian Arab Republic, Thailand, Togo, Tonga, Trinidad and Tobago, Tunisia, Turkey, Uganda, Ukraine, United Arab Emirates, United Kingdom, United Republic of Tanzania, United States, Uruguay, Vanuatu, Venezuela, Zambia, Zimbabwe.

World Conference on Human Rights

The World Conference on Human Rights was held at Vienna from 14 to 25 June 1993; 171 States participated.

President: Austria.

Vice-Presidents: Australia, Bangladesh, Bhutan, Burundi, Cameroon, Canada, Chile, China, Costa Rica, Croatia, Cuba, Denmark, El Salvador, Ethiopia, France, Gambia, India, Ireland, Jamaica, Japan, Kenya, Kuwait, Latvia, Mauritania, Mauritius, Mexico, Namibia, Nigeria, Pakistan, Peru, Philippines, Romania, Russian Federation, Senegal, Spain, Syrian Arab Republic, Thailand, the former Yugoslav Republic of Macedonia, Tunisia, United Kingdom, United States, Venezuela, Yemen, Zimbabwe.

Rapporteur-General: Poland.

Security Council

The Security Council consists of 15 Member States of the United Nations, in accordance with the provisions of Article 23 of the United Nations Charter as amended in 1965.

MEMBERS
Permanent members: China, France, Russian Federation, United Kingdom, United States.
Non-permanent members: Brazil, Cape Verde, Djibouti, Hungary, Japan, Morocco, New Zealand, Pakistan, Spain, Venezuela.

On 29 October 1993 (dec. 48/306), the General Assembly elected Argentina, the Czech Republic, Nigeria, Oman and Rwanda for a two-year term beginning on 1 January 1994, to replace Cape Verde, Hungary, Japan, Morocco and Venezuela, whose terms of office were to expire on 31 December 1993.

PRESIDENTS
The presidency of the Council rotates monthly, according to the English alphabetical listing of its member States. The following served as Presidents during 1993:

Month	Member	Representative
January	Japan	Yoshio Hatano
February	Morocco	Ahmed Snoussi
March	New Zealand	Terence Christopher O'Brien
April	Pakistan	Jamsheed K. A. Marker
May	Russian Federation	Yuliy M. Vorontsov
June	Spain	Juan Antonio Yañez-Barnuevo
July	United Kingdom	Sir David Hannay
August	United States	Madeleine Korbel Albright
September	Venezuela	Adolfo R. Taylhardat
October	Brazil	Ronaldo Mota Sardenberg
November	Cape Verde	José Luis Jesus
December	China	Li Zhaoxing

Military Staff Committee

The Military Staff Committee consists of the chiefs of staff of the permanent members of the Security Council or their representatives. It meets fortnightly.

Standing committees

Each of the three standing committees of the Security Council is composed of representatives of all Council members:

Committee of Experts (to examine the provisional rules of procedure of the Council and any other matters entrusted to it by the Council)
Committee on the Admission of New Members
Committee on Council Meetings Away from Headquarters

Peace-keeping operations and special missions

United Nations Truce Supervision Organization (UNTSO)
Chief of Staff: Major-General Krishna Narayan Singh Thapa (until 30 November).

United Nations Military Observer Group in India and Pakistan (UNMOGIP)
Chief Military Observer: Brigadier-General Ricardo Jorge Galarza-Chans.

United Nations Peace-keeping Force in Cyprus (UNFICYP)
Special Representative of the Secretary-General in Cyprus: Oscar Hector Camilión (until 19 March), Joe Clark (from 21 May).
Deputy Special Representative (resident in Cyprus): Gustave Feissel (from 1 April).
Force Commander: Major-General Michael F. Minehane.

United Nations Disengagement Observer Force (UNDOF)
Force Commander: Major-General Roman Misztal.

United Nations Interim Force in Lebanon (UNIFIL)
Force Commander: Lieutenant-General Lars-Eric Wahlgren (until 22 February), Major-General Trond Furuhovde (from 23 February).

United Nations Iraq-Kuwait Observation Mission (UNIKOM)
Chief Military Observer: Major-General Timothy K. Dibuama (until 20 August), Brigadier-General Vigar Aabrek (acting) (21 August to 30 November), Major-General Krishna Narayan Singh Thapa (from 1 December).

United Nations Angola Verification Mission (UNAVEM II)
Special Representative of the Secretary-General: Margaret Joan Anstee (until 27 June), Alioune Blondin Beye (from 28 June).
Chief Military Observer: Brigadier-General Michael Nyambuya (acting) (until 8 July), Major-General Chris Abutu Garuba (from 9 July).

**United Nations Mission for the Referendum
in Western Sahara (MINURSO)**
Special Representative of the Secretary-General: Sahabzada Yaqub-Khan.
Force Commander: Colonel André Van Baelen.

United Nations Observer Mission in El Salvador (ONUSAL)
Special Representative and Chief of Mission: Iqbal Syed Riza (until 6 March), Augusto Ramírez-Ocampo (from 1 April).
Chief Military Observer: Brigadier-General Víctor Suanzes Pardo (until 31 May).

United Nations Protection Force (UNPROFOR)
Personal Envoy of the Secretary-General: Cyrus R. Vance.
Special Representative: Thorvald Stoltenberg (from 14 May to 30 November), Yasushi Akashi (from 1 December).
Force Commander: Lieutenant-General Satish Nambiar (until 2 March), Lieutenant-General Lars-Eric Wahlgren (3 March to 30 June), General Jean Cot (from 1 July).

United Nations Transitional Authority in Cambodia (UNTAC)
The mandate entrusted to UNTAC was successfully concluded on 24 September 1993.

Special Representative of the Secretary-General: Yasushi Akashi.
Force Commander: Lieutenant-General John M. Sanderson.

United Nations Operation in Somalia (UNOSOM II)
On 26 March 1993 (res. 814(1993)), the Security Council expanded the size and mandate of the United Nations Operation in Somalia. UNOSOM II took over responsibilities of the Unified Task Force led by the United States.

Special Representative of the Secretary-General: Ismat T. Kittani (until 5 March), Admiral Jonathan Trumbull Howe (from 9 March).
Deputy Special Representative of the Secretary-General: Lansana Kouyate (from 1 July).
Force Commander: Cevic Bir (from 16 February).
Chief Military Observer: Brigadier-General Imtíaz Shaheen (until 14 May).

United Nations Observer Mission in South Africa (UNOMSA)
Special Representative of the Secretary-General: Lakhdar Brahimi (from 16 October).
Chief of Mission: Angela King.

United Nations Operation in Mozambique (ONUMOZ)
Special Representative of the Secretary-General: Aldo Ajello.
Force Commander: Major-General Lélio Gonçalves Rodrigues da Silva (from 14 February).

United Nations Observer Mission Uganda-Rwanda (UNOMUR)
On 22 June 1993 (res. 846(1993)), the Security Council established the United Nations Observer Mission Uganda-Rwanda to verify that no military assistance reached Rwanda. UNOMUR was integrated within UNAMIR upon the latter's establishment (see below).

Chief Military Observer: Brigadier-General Romeo A. Dallaire.

United Nations Observer Mission in Georgia (UNOMIG)
On 24 August 1993 (res. 858(1993)), the Security Council established the United Nations Observer Mission in Georgia to assist in making progress towards a political settlement of the conflict in Abkhazia.

Special Envoy of the Secretary-General for Georgia: Edouard Brunner.
Chief Military Observer: Brigadier-General John Hvidegaard.

United Nations Observer Mission in Liberia (UNOMIL)
On 22 September 1993 (res. 866(1993)), the Security Council established the United Nations Observer Mission in Liberia to monitor implementation of the Cotonou Peace Agreement and cease-fire violations.

Special Representative of the Secretary-General: Trevor Gordon-Somers.
Chief Military Observer: Major-General Daniel Ishmael Opande.

United Nations Mission in Haiti (UNMIH)
On 23 September 1993 (res. 867(1993)), the Security Council authorized the establishment and immediate dispatch of the United Nations Mission in Haiti to monitor implementation of the Governors Island Agreement and the political accords contained in the New York Pact.

Special Representative of the Secretary-General: Dante Caputo.
Commander of the military unit: Colonel Gregg Pulley.
Commander of the police unit: Superintendent Jean-Jacques Lemay.

United Nations Assistance Mission for Rwanda (UNAMIR)
On 5 October 1993 (res. 872(1993)), the Security Council established the United Nations Assistance Mission for Rwanda to monitor observance of the cease-fire agreement and assist in coordination of humanitarian assistance.

Special Representative of the Secretary-General: Jacques-Roger Booh-Booh.
Force Commander: Brigadier-General Romeo A. Dallaire.

United Nations Military Liaison Team in Cambodia
On 4 November 1993 (res. 880(1993)), the Security Council established a team of 20 military liaison officers for a single period of six months with a mandate to report on matters affecting security in Cambodia.

Chief Military Liaison Officer: Colonel A. N. M. Muniruzzaman.

Economic and Social Council

The Economic and Social Council consists of 54 Member States of the United Nations, elected by the General Assembly, each for a three-year term, in accordance with the provisions of Article 61 of the United Nations Charter as amended in 1965 and 1973.

MEMBERS

To serve until 31 December 1993: Argentina, Austria, Botswana, Chile, France, Germany, Guinea, Japan, Malaysia, Morocco, Peru,

Somalia, Spain, Syrian Arab Republic, Trinidad and Tobago, Togo, Turkey, Yugoslavia.[a]
To serve until 31 December 1994: Angola, Australia, Bangladesh, Belarus, Belgium, Benin, Brazil, Colombia, Ethiopia, India, Italy, Kuwait, Madagascar, Philippines, Poland, Suriname, Swaziland, United States.
To serve until 31 December 1995: Bahamas, Bhutan, Canada, China, Cuba, Denmark, Gabon, Libyan Arab Jamahiriya, Mexico, Nigeria, Norway, Republic of Korea, Romania, Russian Federation, Sri Lanka, Ukraine, United Kingdom, Zaire.

[a]On 29 April 1993 (res. 47/229), the General Assembly decided that the Federal Republic of Yugoslavia (Serbia and Montenegro) should not participate in the work of the Economic and Social Council.

On 21 October 1993 (dec. 48/305), the General Assembly elected the following for a three-year term beginning on 1 January 1994 to fill the vacancies occurring on 31 December 1993: Bulgaria, Chile, Costa Rica, Egypt, France, Germany, Ghana, Greece, Indonesia, Ireland, Japan, Pakistan, Paraguay, Portugal, Senegal, United Republic of Tanzania, Venezuela, Zimbabwe.

SESSIONS
Organizational session for 1993: United Nations Headquarters, 26 January and 2-5, 12 and 16 February.
Resumed organizational session for 1993: United Nations Headquarters, 6, 29 and 30 April and 26 May.
Substantive session of 1993: Geneva, 28 June–30 July (high-level segment, 28-30 June).
Resumed substantive session of 1993: United Nations Headquarters, 21 October and 8 December.

OFFICERS
President: Juan Somavía (Chile).
Vice-Presidents: Martin Huslid (Norway), Lansana Kouyate (Guinea), Oleksandr Slipchenko (Ukraine), Byung Yong Soh (Republic of Korea).

Subsidiary and other related organs

SUBSIDIARY ORGANS
In addition to two regular sessional committees, the Economic and Social Council may, at each session, set up other committees or working groups, of the whole or of limited membership, and refer to them any items on the agenda for study and report.
Other subsidiary organs reporting to the Council consist of functional commissions, regional commissions, standing committees, expert bodies and ad hoc bodies.
The inter-agency Administrative Committee on Coordination also reports to the Council.

Sessional bodies

SESSIONAL COMMITTEES
Each of the sessional committees of the Economic and Social Council consists of the 54 members of the Council.

Economic Committee. Chairman: Martin Huslid (Norway). *Vice-Chairmen:* René Valéry Mongbe (Benin), Mohammad Sinon Mudzakir (Malaysia).
Social Committee. Chairman: Byung Yong Soh (Republic of Korea). *Vice-Chairmen:* Tudor Mircea (Romania), A. Missouri Sherman-Peter (Bahamas).

Functional commissions

Commission for Social Development
The Commission for Social Development consists of 32 members, elected for four-year terms by the Economic and Social Council according to a specific pattern of equitable geographical distribution.
The Commission held its thirty-third session at Vienna from 8 to 17 February 1993.

Members:
To serve until 31 December 1994: Argentina *(Chairman)*, Austria, Cyprus *(Vice-Chairman)*, Dominican Republic, Ghana, Guinea, Iran, Madagascar, Nigeria, Sweden, Ukraine.
To serve until 31 December 1995: Belarus, Côte d'Ivoire, France, Germany, Haiti, Indonesia, Mexico, Pakistan, Russian Federation *(Rapporteur)*, Sudan *(Vice-Chairman)*, United States.
To serve until 31 December 1996: Bolivia, Cameroon, Chile, China, Denmark, Malta, Netherlands *(Vice-Chairman)*, Philippines, Yugoslavia, Zimbabwe.

Commission on Crime Prevention and Criminal Justice
The Commission on Crime Prevention and Criminal Justice consists of 40 Member States, elected by the Economic and Social Council for three-year terms according to a specific pattern of equitable geographical distribution.

The Commission held its second session at Vienna from 13 to 23 April 1993.

Members:
To serve until 31 December 1993: Austria, Burkina Faso, Costa Rica, Cuba, Dominican Republic, Finland, Gabon, Germany, Guinea-Bissau, Hungary, Japan, Libyan Arab Jamahiriya, Malawi, Malaysia, Russian Federation, Saudi Arabia, Sri Lanka *(Vice-Chairman)*, Tunisia *(Rapporteur)*, Uganda, Zaire.
To serve until 31 December 1994: Australia, Bolivia, Bulgaria, China, France, Ghana, Indonesia, Iran, Italy *(Vice-Chairman)*, Madagascar, Nicaragua, Nigeria, Paraguay, Peru, Philippines, Poland *(Chairman)*, Republic of Korea, Sierra Leone, Uruguay *(Vice-Chairman)*, United States.

On 29 April 1993 (dec. 1993/218), the Economic and Social Council elected the following for a three-year term beginning on 1 January 1994 to fill the vacancies occurring on 31 December 1993: Austria, Brazil, Colombia, Congo, Cuba, Finland, Germany, Hungary, Japan, Malawi, Malaysia, Morocco, Pakistan, Russian Federation, Sri Lanka, Sudan, Tunisia, Uganda, United Republic of Tanzania, Zaire.

Commission on Human Rights
The Commission on Human Rights consists of 53 members, elected for three-year terms by the Economic and Social Council according to a specific pattern of equitable geographical distribution.
The Commission held its forty-ninth session at Geneva from 1 February to 12 March 1993.

Members:
To serve until 31 December 1993: Argentina, Australia, Austria, Burundi, China, Czech Republic,[a] Gambia, Germany, Indonesia *(Vice-Chairman)*, Japan, Mauritania, Peru, Portugal, Venezuela, Zambia.
To serve until 31 December 1994: Angola, Bangladesh, Barbados, Bulgaria, Canada, Chile *(Vice-Chairman)*, Colombia, Costa Rica, Cuba, Cyprus, Gabon, India, Iran, Kenya, Lesotho, Libyan Arab Jamahiriya, Netherlands *(Vice-Chairman)*, Nigeria, Russian Federation, Sri Lanka, Syrian Arab Republic, Tunisia *(Chairman)*, United Kingdom, Uruguay.
To serve until 31 December 1995: Brazil, Finland, France, Guinea-Bissau, Malaysia, Mauritius, Mexico, Pakistan, Poland *(Rapporteur)*, Republic of Korea, Romania, Sudan, Togo, United States.

[a]Elected on 2 February 1993 (dec. 1993/201).

On 29 April 1993 (dec. 1993/218), the Economic and Social Council elected the following for a three-year term beginning on 1 January 1994 to fill the vacancies occurring on 31 December 1993: Australia, Austria, Cameroon, China, Côte d'Ivoire, Ecuador, Germany, Hungary, Indonesia, Italy, Japan, Malawi, Mauritania, Peru, Venezuela.

SUBCOMMISSION ON PREVENTION OF
DISCRIMINATION AND PROTECTION OF MINORITIES
The Subcommission consists of 26 members elected by the Commission on Human Rights from candidates nominated by Mem-

ber States of the United Nations, in accordance with a scheme to ensure equitable geographical distribution. Members serve in their individual capacity as experts, each for a four-year term.

The Subcommission held its forty-fifth session at Geneva from 2 to 27 August 1993.

Members:

To serve until February 1994: Awn Shawkat Al-Khasawneh, *Chairman* (Jordan); Judith Sefi Attah (Nigeria); Stanislav V. Chernichenko (Russian Federation); Erica-Irene A. Daes (Greece); Leandro Despouy (Argentina); El Hadji Guissé (Senegal); Claude Heller (Mexico); Louis Joinet (France); Fatma Zohra Ksentini (Algeria); Claire Palley (United Kingdom); Gilberto Bergne Saboia (Brazil); Rajindar Sachar (India); Tian Jin (China).

To serve until February 1996: Miguel Alfonso Martínez (Cuba); Marc Bossuyt (Belgium); Volodymyr Boutkevitch (Ukraine); Linda Chavez (United States); Asbjorn Eide, *Vice-Chairman* (Norway); Clemencia Forero Ucros, *Vice-Chairman* (Colombia); Ribot Hatano (Japan); Ahmed Mohamed Khalifa (Egypt); Ioan Maxim, *Rapporteur* (Romania); Muksum-Ul-Hakim (Bangladesh); Said Naceur Ramadhane (Tunisia); Halima Embarek Warzazi (Morocco); Fisseha Yimer, *Vice-Chairman* (Ethiopia).

Commission on Narcotic Drugs

The Commission on Narcotic Drugs consists of 53 members, elected for four-year terms by the Economic and Social Council from among the Members of the United Nations and members of the specialized agencies and the parties to the Single Convention on Narcotic Drugs, 1961, with due regard for the adequate representation of *(a)* countries which are important producers of opium or coca leaves, *(b)* countries which are important in the manufacture of narcotic drugs, and *(c)* countries in which drug addiction or the illicit traffic in narcotic drugs constitutes an important problem, as well as taking into account the principle of equitable geographical distribution.

The Commission held its thirty-sixth session at Vienna from 29 March to 7 April and on 16 and 17 December 1993.

Members:

To serve until 31 December 1993: Australia, Bahamas, Belgium, Bulgaria, China, Colombia, Ecuador, Gambia, Ghana, Hungary, Indonesia, Japan, Libyan Arab Jamahiriya, Malaysia, Mexico *(Chairman)*, Russian Federation, Senegal, Spain, Sweden, United Kingdom.

To serve until 31 December 1995: Bolivia *(Rapporteur)*, Canada, Chile, Czech Republic,[a] Egypt, France, Gabon, Germany, India, Iran *(Vice-Chairman)*, Italy, Jamaica, Lesotho, Madagascar, Morocco, Netherlands, Nicaragua, Nigeria, Norway, Pakistan, Peru, Philippines, Poland *(Vice-Chairman)*, Republic of Korea, Switzerland, Syrian Arab Republic, Thailand, Tunisia, Turkey *(Vice-Chairman)*, United States, Uruguay, Venezuela, Yugoslavia.

[a]Elected on 2 February 1993 (dec. 1993/201).

On 29 April 1993 (dec. 1993/218), the Economic and Social Council elected the following for a four-year term beginning on 1 January 1994 to fill the vacancies occurring on 31 December 1993: Australia, Bahamas, Belgium, China, Colombia, Côte d'Ivoire, Finland, Ghana, Guinea, Japan, Lebanon, Liberia, Mexico, Paraguay, Romania, Russian Federation, Spain, Sri Lanka, Ukraine, United Kingdom.

Commission on Science and Technology for Development

The Commission on Science and Technology for Development consists of 53 members, elected for four-year terms by the Economic and Social Council according to a specific pattern of equitable geographical representation.

The Commission held its first session at United Nations Headquarters from 12 to 23 April 1993.

Members (to serve until 31 December 1996):[a] Antigua and Barbuda, Austria, Azerbaijan,[b] Belarus, Belgium *(Vice-Chairman)*, Bolivia, Brazil, Bulgaria, Burundi,[b] Canada,[c] Cape Verde,[d] Chile,

China, Colombia, Congo,[d] Costa Rica, Denmark,[d] Egypt, Ethiopia *(Rapporteur)*, Germany, Guatemala, India, Ireland,[e] Jamaica, Japan *(Chairman)*, Jordan, Kuwait, Libyan Arab Jamahiriya, Malawi,[d] Malaysia,[b] Malta,[d] Marshall Islands, Mexico, Morocco, Netherlands, Niger,[b] Nigeria,[d] Pakistan, Philippines, Romania, Russian Federation, Saudi Arabia, Spain, Togo,[b] Uganda, Ukraine, United Kingdom, United Republic of Tanzania,[b] United States, Uruguay *(Vice-Chairman)*, Viet Nam.[b]

[a]Two seats allocated to members from Western European and other States remained vacant in 1993.
[b]Elected on 12 February 1993 (dec. 1993/201).
[c]Elected on 16 July 1993 (dec. 1993/230).
[d]Elected on 6 April 1993 (dec. 1993/218).
[e]Elected on 29 April 1993 (dec. 1993/218).

Commission on Sustainable Development

On 12 February 1993 (dec. 1993/207), the Economic and Social Council established the Commission on Sustainable Development as a functional commission of the Council. The Commission was to be composed of 53 Member States of the United Nations and members of the specialized agencies, elected for three-year terms according to the following allocation of seats: 13 for African States; 11 for Asian States; 6 for Eastern European States; 10 for Latin American and Carribean States; and 13 for Western European and other States.

The Commission held an organizational session from 24 to 26 February and its first session from 14 to 25 June 1993, both at United Nations Headquarters.

Members:[a]

To serve until 31 December 1993: Angola, Barbados, Belarus, Bulgaria, Canada *(Vice-Chairman)*, Guinea, India, Italy, Japan, Madagascar, Malaysia *(Chairman)*, Mexico, Morocco, United Kingdom, United States, Venezuela.

To serve until 31 December 1994: Algeria, Australia, Austria, Benin, Brazil, Colombia, Cuba, Czech Republic *(Vice-Chairman)*, Egypt, France, Hungary, Nigeria, Norway, Philippines, Singapore, Sri Lanka, Vanuatu.

To serve until 31 December 1995: Antigua and Barbuda *(Vice-Chairman)*, Belgium, Bolivia, Burkina Faso, Chile, China, Gabon, Germany, Iceland, Indonesia, Malawi, Namibia, Netherlands, Pakistan, Poland, Republic of Korea, Russian Federation, Tunisia *(Vice-Chairman)*, Turkey, Uruguay.

[a]Elected on 16 February 1993 (dec. 1993/201).

On 29 April 1993 (dec. 1993/218), the Economic and Social Council elected the following for a three-year term beginning on 1 January 1994 to fill the vacancies occurring on 31 December 1993: Barbados, Belarus, Bulgaria, Canada, Guinea, India, Italy, Japan, Malaysia, Mexico, Morocco, Uganda, United Kingdom, United Republic of Tanzania, United States, Venezuela.

Commission on the Status of Women

The Commission on the Status of Women consists of 45 members, elected for four-year terms by the Economic and Social Council according to a specific pattern of equitable geographical distribution. In 1993, it also acted as the preparatory body for the Fourth World Conference on Women: Action for Equality, Development and Peace (scheduled for Beijing, China, 4-15 September 1995).

The Commission held its thirty-seventh session at Vienna from 17 to 26 March 1993.

Members:

To serve until 31 December 1993: Bahamas, Cyprus, Ecuador, Egypt *(Chairman)*, Ghana, India, Indonesia *(Vice-Chairman)*, Iran, Jamaica, Malaysia, Nigeria, Uganda, Zimbabwe.

To serve until 31 December 1994: Bangladesh, Bulgaria, Côte d'Ivoire, Italy, Mexico *(Vice-Chairman)*, Netherlands *(Vice-Chairman)*, Philippines, Russian Federation *(Rapporteur)*, Rwanda, United States, Zaire.

To serve until 31 December 1995: Chile, China, Finland, Madagascar, Pakistan, Peru, Slovakia,[a] Spain, Venezuela, Zambia.

To serve until 31 December 1996: Algeria, Australia, Belarus, Colombia, Cuba, France, Guinea-Bissau, Japan, Sudan, Thailand.

[a]Elected on 2 February 1993 (dec. 1993/201).

On 29 April and 29 July 1993 (dec. 1993/218 and 1993/230), the Economic and Social Council elected the following for a four-year term beginning on 1 January 1994 to fill the vacancies occurring on 31 December 1993: Bahamas, Costa Rica, Cyprus, Ecuador, Guinea, India, Iran, Kenya, Libyan Arab Jamahiriya, Malaysia, Namibia, Republic of Korea, Tunisia.

Population Commission

The Population Commission consists of 27 members elected for four-year terms by the Economic and Social Council according to a specific pattern of equitable geographical distribution. The Commission did not meet in 1993.

Members:
To serve until 31 December 1993: Botswana, China, Iran, Mexico, Panama, Russian Federation, United Kingdom, United States, Zambia.
To serve until 31 December 1995: France, Honduras, Japan, Madagascar, Netherlands, Pakistan, Poland, Rwanda, Sudan.
To serve until 31 December 1996: Bangladesh, Belgium, Cameroon, Canada, Colombia, Germany, Hungary, Nicaragua, United Republic of Tanzania.

On 29 April 1993 (dec. 1993/218), the Economic and Social Council elected the following for a four-year term beginning on 1 January 1994 to fill 8 of the 9 vacancies occurring on 31 December 1993: China, India, Jamaica, Mexico, Russian Federation, Tunisia, United Kingdom, United States. No further elections were held in 1993 to fill the remaining seat, allocated to a member from African States.

Statistical Commission

The Statistical Commission consists of 24 members elected for four-year terms by the Economic and Social Council according to a specific pattern of equitable geographical distribution. The Commission held its twenty-seventh session at United Nations Headquarters from 22 February to 3 March 1993.

Members:
To serve until 31 December 1993: Argentina, France, Germany, Kenya *(Rapporteur),* Netherlands *(Chairman),* Russian Federation, Togo, Zambia.
To serve until 31 December 1995: China, Czech Republic,[a] Ghana, Jamaica, Morocco, Pakistan, Poland *(Vice-Chairman),* United States.
To serve until 31 December 1996: Australia, Brazil, India, Japan *(Vice-Chairman),* Mexico *(Vice-Chairman),* Sweden, Ukraine, United Kingdom.

[a]Elected on 2 February 1993 (dec. 1993/201).

On 29 April 1993 (dec. 1993/218), the Council elected the following for a four-year term beginning on 1 January 1994 to fill the vacancies occurring on 31 December 1993: Argentina, Botswana, France, Germany, Kenya, Russian Federation, Spain, Zambia.

Regional commissions

Economic and Social Commission for
Asia and the Pacific (ESCAP)

The Economic and Social Commission for Asia and the Pacific held its forty-ninth session at Bangkok, Thailand, from 21 to 29 April 1993.

Members: Afghanistan *(Vice-Chairman),* Australia *(Vice-Chairman),* Azerbaijan, Bangladesh *(Vice-Chairman),* Bhutan, Brunei Darussalam *(Vice-Chairman),* Cambodia, China *(Vice-Chairman),* Democratic People's Republic of Korea, Fiji, France,

India *(Vice-Chairman),* Indonesia *(Vice-Chairman),* Iran *(Vice-Chairman),* Japan *(Vice-Chairman),* Kazakhstan *(Vice-Chairman),* Kiribati *(Vice-Chairman),* Kyrgyzstan *(Rapporteur),* Lao People's Democratic Republic *(Vice-Chairman),* Malaysia *(Vice-Chairman),* Maldives *(Vice-Chairman),* Marshall Islands, Micronesia, Mongolia, Myanmar, Nauru, Nepal *(Vice-Chairman),* Netherlands, New Zealand, Pakistan, Papua New Guinea, Philippines *(Vice-Chairman),* Republic of Korea *(Vice-Chairman),* Russian Federation *(Vice-Chairman),* Samoa, Singapore *(Vice-Chairman),* Solomon Islands *(Vice-Chairman),* Sri Lanka, Tajikistan, Thailand *(Chairman and Vice-Chairman),* Tonga *(Vice-Chairman),* Turkmenistan, Tuvalu *(Vice-Chairman),* United Kingdom, United States, Uzbekistan, Vanuatu *(Vice-Chairman),* Viet Nam *(Vice-Chairman).*
Associate members: American Samoa, Cook Islands, French Polynesia, Guam, Hong Kong, Macau, New Caledonia, Niue, Northern Mariana Islands, Palau.

Switzerland, not a Member of the United Nations, participates in a consultative capacity in the work of the Commission.

Economic and Social Commission for Western Asia (ESCWA)

The Economic and Social Commission for Western Asia did not meet in 1993.

Members: Bahrain, Egypt, Iraq, Jordan, Kuwait, Lebanon, Oman, Palestine, Qatar, Saudi Arabia, Syrian Arab Republic, United Arab Emirates, Yemen.

Economic Commission for Africa (ECA)

The Economic Commission for Africa meets in annual session at the ministerial level known as the Conference of Ministers. The Commission held its twenty-eighth session (nineteenth meeting of the Conference of Ministers) at Addis Ababa, Ethiopia, from 3 to 6 May 1993.

Members: Algeria, Angola, Benin, Botswana, Burkina Faso, Burundi, Cameroon *(Chairman),* Cape Verde, Central African Republic, Chad, Comoros, Congo, Côte d'Ivoire, Djibouti, Egypt, Equatorial Guinea, Ethiopia, Gabon, Gambia *(Second Vice-Chairman),* Ghana, Guinea, Guinea-Bissau, Kenya, Lesotho, Liberia, Libyan Arab Jamahiriya, Madagascar, Malawi, Mali, Mauritania, Mauritius, Morocco, Mozambique, Namibia, Niger, Nigeria, Rwanda, Sao Tome and Principe, Senegal, Seychelles, Sierra Leone, Somalia, South Africa,[a] Sudan, Swaziland, Togo, Tunisia *(Rapporteur),* Uganda *(First Vice-Chairman),* United Republic of Tanzania, Zaire, Zambia, Zimbabwe.

[a]On 30 July 1963, the Economic and Social Council decided that South Africa should not take part in the work of ECA until conditions for constructive cooperation had been restored by a change in South Africa's racial policy (YUN 1963, p. 274, ESC res. 974 D IV (XXXVI)).

Switzerland, not a Member of the United Nations, participates in a consultative capacity in the work of the Commission.

Economic Commission for Europe (ECE)

The Economic Commission for Europe held its forty-eighth session at Geneva from 19 to 27 April 1993.

Members: Albania, Andorra,[a] Armenia,[a] Austria, Azerbaijan,[a] Belarus, Belgium, Bosnia and Herzegovina, Bulgaria, Canada, Croatia, Cyprus, Czech Republic,[a] Denmark, Estonia, Finland, France *(Vice-Chairman),* Georgia,[a] Germany, Greece, Hungary, Iceland, Ireland, Israel, Italy, Kazakhstan,[a] Kyrgyzstan,[a] Latvia, Liechtenstein, Lithuania, Luxembourg, Malta, Monaco,[a] Netherlands, Norway, Poland, Portugal, Republic of Moldova, Romania, Russian Federation, San Marino, Slovakia,[a] Slovenia, Spain, Sweden, Switzerland *(Chairman),* the former Yugoslav Republic of Macedonia,[a] Turkey, Turkmenistan,[a] Ukraine, United Kingdom, United States, Uzbekistan,[a] Yugoslavia.[b]

[a]Became a member in 1993, after the forty-eighth session.
[b]On 30 July 1993 (dec. 1993/316), the Economic and Social Council decided that the Federal Republic of Yugoslavia (Serbia and Montenegro)

should not participate in the work of ECE as long as the Federal Republic did not participate in the work of the General Assembly.

The Holy See, which is not a Member of the United Nations, participates in a consultative capacity in the work of the Commission.

Economic Commission for Latin America and the Caribbean (ECLAC)
The Economic Commission for Latin America and the Carribbean did not meet in 1993.

Members: Antigua and Barbuda, Argentina, Bahamas, Barbados, Belize, Bolivia, Brazil, Canada, Chile, Colombia, Costa Rica, Cuba, Dominica, Dominican Republic, Ecuador, El Salvador, France, Grenada, Guatemala, Guyana, Haiti, Honduras, Italy, Jamaica, Mexico, Netherlands, Nicaragua, Panama, Paraguay, Peru, Portugal, Saint Kitts and Nevis, Saint Lucia, Saint Vincent and the Grenadines, Spain, Suriname, Trinidad and Tobago, United Kingdom, United States, Uruguay, Venezuela.
Associate members: Aruba, British Virgin Islands, Montserrat, Netherlands Antilles, Puerto Rico, United States Virgin Islands.

Germany and Switzerland participate in a consultative capacity in the work of the Commission.

Standing committees

Commission on Human Settlements
The Commission on Human Settlements consists of 58 members elected by the Economic and Social Council for four-year terms according to a specific pattern of equitable geographical distribution; it reports to the General Assembly through the Council.
The Commission held its fourteenth session at Nairobi, Kenya, from 26 April to 5 May 1993.

Members:
To serve until 31 December 1994: Antigua and Barbuda, Bangladesh, Brazil, Cameroon, Chile *(Rapporteur)*, Colombia, Egypt, Finland *(Chairman)*, Iran, Japan, Nigeria, Pakistan, Romania *(Vice-Chairman)*, Russian Federation, Sierra Leone, Turkey, Uganda *(Vice-Chairman)*, United Kingdom, United States, Zimbabwe.
To serve until 31 December 1995: Austria, Barbados, Belarus, Botswana, Bulgaria, Germany, Ghana, Greece, Haiti, India, Jordan, Kenya, Malaysia, Mexico, Norway, Philippines *(Vice-Chairman)*, Sri Lanka, Sudan, United Republic of Tanzania.
To serve until 31 December 1996: Azerbaijan,[a] Bahamas, Canada, China, France, Hungary, Indonesia, Italy, Jamaica, Lesotho,[a] Libyan Arab Jamahiriya, Madagascar,[a] Malawi, Netherlands, Papua New Guinea, Somalia, Sweden, United Arab Emirates, Venezuela.

[a]Elected on 12 February 1993 (dec. 1993/201).

Commission on Transnational Corporations
The Commission on Transnational Corporations consists of 48 members, elected from all States for three-year terms by the Economic and Social Council according to a specific pattern of geographical distribution.
The Commission held its nineteenth session at United Nations Headquarters from 5 to 15 April 1993.

Members:
To serve until 31 December 1993:[a] Bahamas, Bangladesh, Belgium *(Vice-Chairman)*, Bulgaria, Burundi, Chile, Colombia, Ghana, India, Iraq, Italy, Kenya, Poland, Republic of Korea, Zambia.
To serve until 31 December 1994: Congo, Costa Rica, Gabon, Guatemala *(Rapporteur)*, Indonesia, Jamaica, Mexico, Netherlands, Pakistan *(Vice-Chairman)*, Russian Federation, Sudan, Swaziland, Sweden, Thailand, United Kingdom, United States.
To serve until 31 December 1995:[b] Algeria, Argentina, Belarus, Benin *(Chairman)*, China, France, Germany, Japan, Malaysia,[c] Peru, Romania *(Vice-Chairman)*, Switzerland, Tunisia, Uruguay, Zimbabwe.

Expert advisers: Antonio Colombo (Italy), Peter Hansen (Denmark), Ivan Ivanov (Russian Federation), Samuel Esson Kwesi Jonah (Ghana), Gösta Karlsson (Sweden), Sanjaya Lall (India), Jacques Leflon (France), Lim Kee-Ming (Singapore), Sylvia Ostry (Canada), Rudolf A. Oswald (United States), Edward J. Saperstein (United States), Osvaldo Sunkel (Chile).

[a]One seat allocated to a member from Western European and other States remained unfilled in 1993.
[b]One seat allocated to a member from Asian States remained unfilled in 1993.
[c]Elected on 12 February 1993 (dec. 1993/201).

On 29 April 1993 (dec. 1993/218), the Economic and Social Council elected the following for a three-year term beginning on 1 January 1994 to fill 10 of the 16 vacancies occurring on 31 December 1993: Bangladesh, Belgium, Bulgaria, Czech Republic, Democratic People's Republic of Korea, Italy, Panama, Paraguay, Venezuela, Zambia. No further elections were held in 1993 to fill the remaining seats, allocated to three members from African States, two members from Asian States and one member from Western European and other States.

Committee for Programme and Coordination
The Committee for Programme and Coordination is the main subsidiary organ of the Economic and Social Council and of the General Assembly for planning, programming and coordination and reports directly to both. It consists of 34 members nominated by the Council and elected by the Assembly for three-year terms according to a specific pattern of equitable geographical distribution.
During 1993, the Committee held, at United Nations Headquarters, an organizational session on 8 April and 5 May, and its thirty-third session from 10 to 14 May and from 6 to 22 October.

Members:
To serve until 31 December 1993: Brazil, Bulgaria, Burundi, Chile, Colombia, Congo, Germany *(Rapporteur)*, India *(Chairman)*, Indonesia, Iraq, Italy, Netherlands, Nigeria, Norway, Pakistan, Poland *(Vice-Chairman)*, Trinidad and Tobago *(Vice-Chairman)*, Uganda, Ukraine, United Kingdom.
To serve until 31 December 1994: Bahamas, France, Ghana *(Vice-Chairman)*, Russian Federation, United States, Uruguay, Zambia.
To serve until 31 December 1995: China, Egypt, Japan, Kenya, Nicaragua, Republic of Korea, Togo.

On 29 April 1993 (dec. 1993/218), the Economic and Social Council nominated the following Member States for a three-year term beginning on 1 January 1994 to fill the vacancies occurring on 31 December 1993: Argentina, Belarus, Brazil, Bulgaria, Cameroon, Canada, Comoros, Congo, Cuba, Germany, India, Indonesia, Iran, Netherlands, Norway, Pakistan, Romania, Senegal, Trinidad and Tobago, Ukraine, United Kingdom. All but Bulgaria were elected by the Assembly on 11 November (dec. 48/311).

Committee on Non-Governmental Organizations
The Committee on Non-Governmental Organizations consists of 19 members elected by the Economic and Social Council for a four-year term according to a specific pattern of equitable geographical representation.
The Committee met at United Nations Headquarters from 22 March to 2 April and on 4 May 1993.

Members (until 31 December 1994): Bulgaria *(Vice-Chairman)*, Burundi, Chile *(Vice-Chairman)*, Costa Rica, Cuba, Cyprus, Ethiopia, France, Greece, Iraq, Ireland *(Rapporteur)*, Lesotho, Libyan Arab Jamahiriya, Nicaragua, Oman, Philippines *(Chairman)*, Russian Federation, Sudan *(Vice-Chairman)*, Sweden.

Expert bodies

Ad Hoc Group of Experts on International Cooperation in Tax Matters
The membership of the Ad Hoc Group of Experts on International Cooperation in Tax Matters—to consist of 25 members,

from 15 developing and 10 developed countries, appointed by the Secretary-General to serve in their individual capacity—remained at 24 in 1993, with one member from a developing country still to be appointed.

The Ad Hoc Group did not meet in 1993.

Members:[a] Julius Olasoji Akinmola (Nigeria), E. Bunders (Netherlands), Mohamed Chkounda (Morocco), Imad El-ish (Syrian Arab Republic), Mordecai S. Feinberg (United States), D. José Ramón Fernández-Pérez (Spain), Antonio H. Figueroa (Argentina), Mayer Gabay (Israel), Hugo Hanisch-Ovalle (Chile), Jose Rodolfo Hülse (Brazil), Nemi Chand Jain (India), Daniel Lüthi (Switzerland), Reksoprajitno Mansury (Indonesia), Thomas Menck (Germany), Canute R. Miller (Jamaica), Naoti Oka (Japan), Alfred Philipp (Austria), Alain Ruellan (France), Aaron Schwartzman (Mexico), J. B. Shepherd (United Kingdom), Rainer Söderholm (Finland), Mohammed Taraq (Pakistan), André Titty (Cameroon).

[a]The seat held by an expert from Egypt was vacant in 1993.

Committee for Development Planning

The Committee for Development Planning is composed of 24 experts representing different planning systems. They are appointed by the Economic and Social Council, on nomination by the Secretary-General, to serve in their personal capacity for a term of three years.

The Committee did not meet in 1993.

Members:[a] Abdlatif Y. Al-Hamad (Kuwait), Gerassimos D. Arsenis (Greece), Edmar Bacha (Brazil), Prithvi Nath Dhar (India), Karel Dyba (Czech Republic), Just Faaland (Norway), Ricardo Ffrench-Davis (Chile), Tchabouré Aymé Gogue (Togo), Keith Broadwell Griffin (United Kingdom), Patrick Guillaumont (France), Ryokichi Hirono (Japan), Helen Hughes (Australia), Nicolai N. Liventsev (Russian Federation), Solita C. Monsod (Philippines), Henry Nau (United States), Maureen O'Neil (Canada), T. Ademola Oyejide (Nigeria), Pu Shan (China), Akilagpa Sawyerr (Ghana), Udo Ernst Simonis (Germany), George Suranyi (Hungary), Mahbub ul Haq (Pakistan), Miguel Urrutia (Colombia), Ferdinand van Dam (Netherlands).

[a]The Economic and Social Council, on the proposal of the Secretary-General, decided that the Committee should hold its twenty-ninth session in January 1994 with the same membership as that of its twenty-eighth (1992) session.

Committee of Experts on the Transport of Dangerous Goods

The Committee of Experts on the Transport of Dangerous Goods is composed of experts from countries interested in the international transport of dangerous goods. The experts are made available by their Governments at the request of the Secretary-General. The membership, to be increased to 15 in accordance with a 1975 resolution of the Economic and Social Council,[3] was 14 in 1993.

The Committee did not meet in 1993.

Members: Canada, China, France, Germany, India, Italy, Japan, Netherlands, Norway, Poland, Russian Federation, Sweden, United Kingdom, United States.

Committee on Economic, Social and Cultural Rights

The Committee on Economic, Social and Cultural Rights consists of 18 experts serving in their personal capacity, elected by the Economic and Social Council from among persons nominated by States parties to the International Covenant on Economic, Social and Cultural Rights. The experts have recognized competence in the field of human rights, with due consideration given to equitable geographical distribution and to the representation of different forms of social and legal systems. Members serve for four-year terms.

The Committee held two sessions in 1993, at Geneva: its eighth from 10 to 28 May and its ninth from 22 November to 10 December.

Members:
To serve until 31 December 1994: Philip Alston, *Chairman* (Australia); Abdel Halim Badawi (Egypt); Virginia Bonoan-Dandan, *Rapporteur* (Philippines); Luvsandanzangiin Ider (Mongolia); Valeri

I. Kouznetsov (Russian Federation); Jaime Alberto Marchan Romero (Ecuador); Alexandre Muterahejuru, *Vice-Chairman* (Rwanda); Bruno Simma (Germany); Javier Wimer Zambrano (Mexico).
To serve until 31 December 1996: Madoe Virginie Ahodikope (Togo); Juan Alvarez Vita, *Vice-Chairman* (Peru); Dumitru Ceausu (Romania); Abdessatar Grissa (Tunisia); María de los Angeles Jimenez Butragueño (Spain); Kenneth Osborne Rattray (Jamaica); Chikako Taya (Japan); Philippe Texier (France); Margerita Vysokajova, *Vice-Chairman* (Czech Republic).

Committee on Natural Resources

The Committee on Natural Resources consists of 24 government-nominated experts from different Member States, who possess the necessary qualifications and professional or scientific knowledge and who act in their personal capacity. They are elected by the Economic and Social Council for four-year terms, according to the following regional allocation of seats: African States (6), Asian States (5), Latin American and Caribbean States (4), Eastern European States (3), Western European and other States (6).

The Committee held its first session at United Nations Headquarters from 29 March to 8 April 1993.

Members (until 31 December 1996):[a] Regis Percy Arslanian (Brazil); Guillermo Jorge Cano, *Vice-Chairman* (Argentina);[b] Denis A. Davis, *Rapporteur* (Canada); Vladislav M. Dolgopolov (Russian Federation); Malin Falkenmark (Sweden); Ugo Farinelli (Italy); Marek Hoffmann, *Vice-Chairman* (Poland);[b] Sheik Ibrahim bin Sheik Ali (Malaysia);[b] Patricio Jerez (Nicaragua); Mohammad Nawaz Khan (Pakistan);[b] Godfrey L. S. Leshange (United Republic of Tanzania);[b] Patrick Maselino (Zambia);[b] José Manuel Mejía Angel (Colombia); Thomas P. Z. Mpofu, *Chairman* (Zimbabwe);[b] Erastus Kabutu Mwongera (Kenya);[b] Lukabu Khabouji N'Zaji (Zaire); Dossou Barthélémy Otchoun (Benin);[b] Hendrik Martinus Oudshoorn (Netherlands); Neculai Pavlovschi (Romania); Karlheinz Rieck (Germany); R. W. Roye Rutland (Australia); Luiz Fernando Soares de Assis (Brazil);[b] Natarayan Suryanarayanan (India);[b] Aldo Truccio (Argentina); Zhang Hai-Lun, *Vice-Chairman* (China).

[a]One seat allocated to a member from Asian States remained unfilled in 1993.
[b]Elected on 12 February 1993 (dec. 1993/201).

Committee on New and Renewable Sources of Energy and on Energy for Development

The Committee on New and Renewable Sources of Energy and on Energy for Development consists of 24 government-nominated experts from different Member States, who possess the necessary qualifications and professional or scientific knowledge and who act in their personal capacity. They are elected by the Economic and Social Council for four-year terms according to the following regional allocation of seats: African States (6), Asian States (5), Latin American and Caribbean States (4), Eastern European States (3), Western European and other States (6).

The Committee did not meet in 1993.

Members (until 31 December 1996):[a] Marcelino K. Actouka (Micronesia), Mohammad Al Ramadhan (Kuwait), Mohammed Salem Sarur Al-Sabban (Saudi Arabia), Messaoud Boumaour (Algeria), José Luis Bozzo (Uruguay), Bernard Devin (France), Ronaldo Costa Filho (Brazil), Paul-Georg Gutermuth (Germany), Wolfgang Hein (Austria), Christian Atoki Ileka (Zaire), Thomas B. Johansson (Sweden), Virgil Musatescu (Romania), Alexander A. Penchev (Bulgaria), Giovanni Carlo Pinchera (Italy), Juan Camilo Restrepo Salazar (Colombia), Zoilo Rodas Rodas (Paraguay), E. V. R. Sastry (India), Wilhelmus C. Turkenburg (Netherlands), Dmitri B. Volfberg (Russian Federation), Zhang Guocheng (China).

[a]Four seats allocated to members from African States remained unfilled in 1993.

---

[3]YUN 1975, p. 734, ESC res. 1973(LIX), 30 July 1975.

**Intergovernmental Working Group of Experts on International
Standards of Accounting and Reporting**

The Intergovernmental Working Group of Experts on International Standards of Accounting and Reporting, which reports to the Commission on Transnational Corporations, consists of 34 members, elected for three-year terms by the Economic and Social Council according to a specific pattern of equitable geographical distribution. Each State elected appoints an expert with appropriate experience in accounting and reporting.

The Group held its eleventh session at United Nations Headquarters from 4 to 12 March 1993.

Members:

To serve until 31 December 1993: Brazil *(Vice-Chairman)*, China, Egypt, France, Gabon, Kenya, Lebanon,[a] Mauritius, Mexico, Morocco, Panama, Russian Federation, Spain, Sweden, Switzerland, Thailand, Turkey.

To serve until 31 December 1994: Bulgaria, Chile, Costa Rica, Cyprus, Germany *(Vice-Chairman)*, Hungary, India *(Vice-Chairman)*, Italy, Jordan *(Chairman)*, Malawi, Netherlands *(Rapporteur)*, Nigeria, Pakistan, Sudan, Swaziland, United Kingdom, Uruguay.

[a]Elected on 12 February 1993 (dec. 1993/201).

On 29 April 1993 (dec. 1993/218), the Economic and Social Council elected the following for a three-year term beginning on 1 January 1994 to fill the vacancies occurring on 31 December 1993: Brazil, China, France, Gabon, Germany, Kenya, Lebanon, Mexico, Morocco, Russian Federation, Senegal, Spain, Sweden, Switzerland, Thailand, Tunisia, Turkey.

United Nations Group of Experts on Geographical Names

The United Nations Group of Experts on Geographical Names represents various geographical/linguistic divisions, of which there were 21 in 1993, as follows: Africa Central; Africa East; Africa South; Africa West; Arabic; Asia East (other than China); Asia South-East and Pacific South-West; Asia South-West (other than Arabic); Baltic; Celtic; China; Dutch- and German-speaking; East Central and South-East Europe; East Mediterranean (other than Arabic); Eastern Europe, Northern and Central Asia; India; Latin America; Norden; Romano-Hellenic; United Kingdom; United States of America/Canada.

The Group of Experts did not meet in 1993.

Ad hoc body

**Population Commission acting as the Preparatory Committee for
the International Conference on Population and Development**

The Population Commission, acting as the Preparatory Committee for the International Conference on Population and Development (scheduled for Cairo, Egypt, 5-13 September 1994), open to the participation of all States, held its second session at United Nations Headquarters from 10 to 21 May 1993.

Chairman: Ghana.
Vice-Chairmen: Antigua and Barbuda, Brazil, Finland, Hungary, India, Indonesia, Netherlands, Senegal.
Vice-Chairman/Rapporteur: Poland.
Ex officio member of the Bureau: Egypt.

Administrative Committee on Coordination

The Administrative Committee on Coordination held two sessions in 1993: the first at Rome, Italy, on 19 and 20 April, and the second at United Nations Headquarters on 28 and 29 October.

The membership of ACC, under the chairmanship of the Secretary-General of the United Nations, includes the executive heads of ILO, FAO, UNESCO, ICAO, WHO, the World Bank, IMF, UPU, ITU, WMO, IMO, WIPO, IFAD, UNIDO, IAEA and the secretariat of the Contracting Parties to GATT.

ACC also invites to take part in the work of its sessions senior officers of the United Nations and the executive heads of UNCTAD, UNDP, UNEP, UNFPA, UNHCR, UNICEF, UNITAR, UNRWA, WFP and the United Nations International Drug Control Programme.

ACC has established subsidiary bodies on organizational, administrative and substantive questions.

Other related bodies

**International Research and Training Institute for
the Advancement of Women (INSTRAW)**

The International Research and Training Institute for the Advancement of Women, a body of the United Nations financed through voluntary contributions, functions under the authority of a Board of Trustees.

BOARD OF TRUSTEES

The Board of Trustees is composed of 11 members serving in their individual capacity, appointed by the Economic and Social Council on the nomination of States; and ex-officio members. Members serve for three-year terms, with a maximum of two terms.

The Board, which reports to the Council and where appropriate to the General Assembly, held its thirteenth session at Santo Domingo, Dominican Republic, from 15 to 19 February 1993.

Members (until 30 June 1993):

To serve until 30 June 1993: Gertrude Ibengwe Mongella (United Republic of Tanzania); Amara Pongsapich (Thailand); Pilar Escario Rodriguez-Spiteri (Spain).

To serve until 30 June 1994: Fatima Benslimane Hassat, *Vice-President* (Morocco); Gule Afruz Mahbub (Bangladesh); D. Gail Saunders, *Rapporteur* (Bahamas); Renata Siemienska-Zochowska, *President* (Poland); Kristin Tornes (Norway).

To serve until 30 June 1995: Ihsan Abdalla Algabshawi (Sudan); Aida González Martínez (Mexico); Els Postel-Coster (Netherlands).

On 29 April 1993 (dec. 1993/218), the Economic and Social Council appointed the following for a three-year term beginning on 1 July 1993 to fill the vacancies occurring on 30 June: Noëlie Kangoye (Burkina Faso), Amara Pongsapich (Thailand), Pilar Escario Rodríguez-Spiteri (Spain).

Members (from 1 July 1993):

To serve until 30 June 1994: Fatima Benslimane Hassat (Morocco), Gule Afruz Mahbub (Bangladesh), D. Gail Saunders (Bahamas), Renata Siemienska-Zochowska (Poland), Kristin Tornes (Norway).

To serve until 30 June 1995: Ihsan Abdalla Algabshawi (Sudan), Aida González Martínez (Mexico), Els Postel-Coster (Netherlands).

To serve until 30 June 1996: Noëlie Kangoye (Burkina Faso), Amara Pongsapich (Thailand), Pilar Escario Rodríguez-Spiteri (Spain).

Ex-officio members: The Director of the Institute, and a representative of the Secretary-General, each of the regional commissions and the Institute's host country (Dominican Republic).

Director of the Institute: Margaret Shields.

United Nations Children's Fund (UNICEF)

EXECUTIVE BOARD

The UNICEF Executive Board, which reports to the Economic and Social Council and, as appropriate, to the General Assembly, consists of 41 members elected by the Council from Member States of the United Nations or members of the specialized agencies or of IAEA, for three-year terms.

In 1993, the Board held, at United Nations Headquarters, an organizational session on 9 and 10 February, its regular session from 26 April to 7 May, an organizational session on 7 June (with its composition as at 1 August) and a special session on 6 and 7 October.

Members (until 31 July 1993):

To serve until 31 July 1993: Czech Republic[a] *(Second Vice-Chairman)*, Denmark, India, Indonesia, Liberia, Sierra Leone, Spain, Sri Lanka, Switzerland, Uruguay.

To serve until 31 July 1994: Angola, Australia, Brazil, Central African Republic, Congo, Ethiopia, France, Italy, Jamaica *(Fourth Vice-Chairman)*, Japan, Nicaragua, Norway, Pakistan, Republic of Korea, Russian Federation, Senegal *(First Vice-Chairman)*, United Kingdom, United Republic of Tanzania, United States, Yemen, Yugoslavia.

To serve until 31 July 1995: Bulgaria, Canada *(Chairman)*, China, Colombia, Costa Rica, Germany, Mozambique, Netherlands, Nepal *(Third Vice-Chairman)*, Sweden.

[a]Elected on 2 February 1993 (dec. 1993/201).

On 30 April and 26 May 1993 (dec. 1993/218), the Economic and Social Council elected the following for a three-year term beginning on 1 August 1993 to fill the vacancies occurring on 31 July: Burkina Faso, Finland, Ghana, India, Indonesia, Lebanon, Romania, Suriname, Switzerland, Turkey.

Members (from 1 August 1993):

To serve until 31 July 1994: Angola, Australia, Brazil, Central African Republic, Congo, Ethiopia, France, Italy, Jamaica, Japan, Nicaragua *(Fourth Vice-Chairman)*, Norway, Pakistan, Republic of Korea, Russian Federation, Senegal, United Kingdom, United Republic of Tanzania *(Chairman)*, United States, Yemen, Yugoslavia.

To serve until 31 July 1995: Bulgaria *(Second Vice-Chairman)*, Canada, China, Colombia, Costa Rica, Germany, Mozambique, Netherlands, Nepal, Sweden.

To serve until 31 July 1996: Burkina Faso, Finland *(First Vice-Chairman)*, Ghana, India, Indonesia, Lebanon *(Third Vice-Chairman)*, Romania, Suriname, Switzerland, Turkey.

Executive Director of UNICEF: James P. Grant.

United Nations Development Programme (UNDP)

GOVERNING COUNCIL

The Governing Council of UNDP, which reports to the Economic and Social Council and through it to the General Assembly, consists of 48 members, elected by the Council from Member States of the United Nations or members of the specialized agencies or of IAEA. Twenty-seven seats are allocated to developing countries and 21 to economically more advanced countries; members serve three-year terms.

In 1993, the Governing Council held, at United Nations Headquarters, an organizational session and a special session from 16 to 19 February, its fortieth session from 1 to 18 June and a special session on 16 December.

Members:

To serve until the day preceding the February 1994 organizational session: Algeria, Austria, China, Cuba, Finland, Ghana, Indonesia, Italy, Japan, Kuwait, Nicaragua, Russian Federation, Saint Lucia, United Kingdom, United States, Zimbabwe.

To serve until the day preceding the February 1995 organizational session: Belgium, Bolivia *(Vice-President)*, Cameroon, Canada, Congo *(President)*, Fiji, France, Gambia, Lesotho, New Zealand, Norway, Pakistan, Romania, Somalia, Spain, Yemen.

To serve until the day preceding the February 1996 organizational session: Benin, Côte d'Ivoire, Ecuador, Germany, India, Iran *(Vice-President)*, Jamaica, Netherlands *(Vice-President)*, Peru, Poland *(Vice-President)*, Portugal, Republic of Korea, Slovakia,[a] Sudan, Sweden, Switzerland.

[a]Elected on 2 February 1993 (dec. 1993/201).

On 30 April 1993 (dec. 1993/218), the Economic and Social Council elected the following for a three-year term beginning on the first day of the February 1994 organizational session to fill the vacancies occurring the preceding day: Austria, Botswana, China, Cuba, Denmark, Italy, Japan, Morocco, Papua New Guinea, Philippines, Russian Federation, Sierra Leone, Trinidad and Tobago, United Kingdom, United States, Uruguay.

Administrator of UNDP:[a] William H. Draper III (until 15 July), James Gustave Speth (from 16 July).
Associate Administrator: Luis Maria Gomez.

[a]On 15 June 1993 (dec. 47/327), the General Assembly confirmed the appointment of James Gustave Speth for a four-year term beginning on 16 July.

United Nations Interregional Crime and Justice Research Institute (UNICRI)

Established by the Economic and Social Council in 1989, the United Nations Interregional Crime and Justice Research Institute contributes, through research, training, field activities and the collection, exchange and dissemination of information, to the formulation and implementation of improved policies in the field of crime prevention and control.

BOARD OF TRUSTEES

To serve until 26 November 1993: Moustafa El-Augi (Lebanon), José A. Rios Alves da Cruz (Brazil).

To serve until 26 November 1994: Régis de Gouttes (France), Sushil Swarup Varma (India).

To serve until 26 November 1995: Tolani Asuni (Nigeria), Pierre-Henri Bölle (Switzerland), Dusan Cotic (Yugoslavia).

On 27 July 1993 (dec. 1993/241), the Economic and Social Council endorsed the reappointment, by the Commission on Crime Prevention and Criminal Justice, of Moustafa El-Augi and José A. Rios Alves da Cruz to the Board of Trustees for a term expiring on 26 November 1998.

United Nations Research Institute for Social Development (UNRISD)

BOARD OF DIRECTORS

The Board of Directors of UNRISD reports to the Economic and Social Council through the Commission for Social Development. The Board consists of:

The Chairman, appointed by the Secretary-General: Keith Griffin (United Kingdom);

Ten members, nominated by the Commission for Social Development and confirmed by the Economic and Social Council (to serve until 30 June 1995): Lars Anell (Sweden),[a] Fahima Charaf-Eddine (Lebanon), Georgina Dufoix (France), Ingrid Eide (Norway),[a] Tatyana Koryagina (Russian Federation),[a] Kinhide Mushakoji (Japan), Guillermo O'Donnell (Argentina), Maureen O'Neil (Canada),[a] Akilagpa Sawyerr (Ghana),[a] Rehman Sobhan (Bangladesh).

Nine other members, as follows: a representative of the Secretary-General, a representative of the United Nations Office at Vienna/Centre for Social Development and Humanitarian Affairs, the Director of the Latin American Institute for Economic and Social Planning, the Director of the Asian and Pacific Development Institute, the Director of the African Institute for Economic Development and Planning, the Executive Secretary of ESCWA, the Director of UNRISD (ex officio), and the representatives of two of the following specialized agencies, appointed in rotation: ILO, FAO, UNESCO, WHO.

[a]Membership for an additional two years, beginning on 1 July 1993, confirmed by the Economic and Social Council on 27 July (dec. 1993/240).

Director of the Institute: Dharam Ghai.

World Food Programme

COMMITTEE ON FOOD AID POLICIES AND PROGRAMMES

The Committee on Food Aid Policies and Programmes, the governing body of WFP, reports annually to the Economic and Social Council, the FAO Council and the World Food Council. It consists of 42 members (27 from developing countries and 15 from more economically developed ones), of which 21 are elected by the Economic and Social Council and 21 by the FAO Council, from Member States of the United Nations or from members of FAO. Members serve for three-year terms.

In 1993, the Committee held two sessions at Rome, Italy: its thirty-fifth from 31 May to 4 June and its thirty-sixth from 25 to 28 October.

Members:
To serve until 31 December 1993:
  Elected by Economic and Social Council: Belgium, Egypt, El Salvador, Indonesia, Japan, Pakistan, Sweden.
  Elected by FAO Council: Argentina, Brazil *(Rapporteur, thirty-fifth session)*, Burundi, China, Netherlands, Saudi Arabia, United Republic of Tanzania.
To serve until 31 December 1994:
  Elected by Economic and Social Council: Colombia, Cuba, Ethiopia, Ghana, Norway, Syrian Arab Republic, United Kingdom *(Rapporteur, thirty-sixth session)*.
  Elected by FAO Council: Angola, Cameroon, Democratic People's Republic of Korea, France, Germany, Mexico, Romania.
To serve until 31 December 1995:
  Elected by Economic and Social Council: Denmark, Dominican Republic, Hungary, India, Italy, Niger, Nigeria.
  Elected by FAO Council: Australia *(Second Vice-Chairman)*, Bangladesh *(First Vice-Chairman)*, Burkina Faso, Canada *(Chairman)*, Senegal, Sri Lanka, United States.

On 30 April 1993 (dec. 1993/218), the Economic and Social Council elected Belgium, El Salvador, Finland, Indonesia, Japan, Libyan Arab Jamahiriya and Pakistan and, on 25 November, the FAO Council elected Argentina, Brazil, Chad, China, Netherlands, Saudi Arabia and Zimbabwe, all for a three-year term beginning on 1 January 1994 to fill the vacancies occurring on 31 December 1993.

Executive Director of WFP: Catherine Bertini.
Deputy Executive Director: Salahuddin Ahmed.

Conference

Fifth United Nations Regional Cartographic Conference for the Americas

The Fifth United Nations Regional Cartographic Conference for the Americas was held at United Nations Headquarters from 11 to 15 January 1993. Participating were the following 34 States:

Algeria, Argentina, Bahamas, Bahrain, Brazil, Brunei Darussalam, Canada *(Rapporteur)*, Chile, China, Colombia *(President)*, Cuba, Ecuador, El Salvador, Finland, France, Germany, Guatemala, Honduras, Japan, Libyan Arab Jamahiriya, Malawi, Mexico *(First Vice-President)*, Oman, Panama, Paraguay, Peru, Romania, Russian Federation, Spain, Trinidad and Tobago, Ukraine, United Kingdom, United States *(Second Vice-President)*, Uruguay.

Trusteeship Council

Article 86 of the United Nations Charter lays down that the Trusteeship Council shall consist of the following:

Members of the United Nations administering Trust Territories;
Permanent members of the Security Council which do not administer Trust Territories;
As many other members elected for a three-year term by the General Assembly as will ensure that the membership of the Council is equally divided between United Nations Members which administer Trust Territories and those which do not.[a]

[a]During 1993, only one Member of the United Nations was an administering member of the Trusteeship Council, while four permanent members of the Security Council continued as non-administering members.

MEMBERS
Member administering a Trust Territory: United States.
Non-administering members: China, France, Russian Federation, United Kingdom.

SESSION
Sixtieth session (first part): United Nations Headquarters, 12-17 May and 1 November 1993.

OFFICERS
President: Thomas L. Richardson (United Kingdom).
Vice-President: Jean Félix-Paganon (France).

International Court of Justice

Judges of the Court
The International Court of Justice consists of 15 Judges elected for nine-year terms by the General Assembly and the Security Council.

The following were the Judges of the Court serving in 1993, listed in the order of precedence:

Judge	Country of nationality	End of term[a]
Sir Robert Y. Jennings, *President*	United Kingdom	2000
Shigeru Oda, *Vice-President*	Japan	1994
Roberto Ago	Italy	1997
Stephen M. Schwebel	United States	1997
Mohammed Bedjaoui	Algeria	1997
Ni Zhengyu	China	1994
Jens Evensen	Norway	1994
Nikolai K. Tarassov	Russian Federation	1997
Gilbert Guillaume	France	2000
Mohamed Shahabuddeen	Guyana	1997
Andrés Aguilar Mawdsley	Venezuela	2000

Judge	Country of nationality	End of term[a]
Christopher G. Weeramantry	Sri Lanka	2000
Raymond Ranjeva	Madagascar	2000
Bola A. Ajibola	Nigeria	1994
Géza Herczegh[b]	Hungary	1994

[a]Term expires on 5 February of the year indicated.
[b]Elected by the General Assembly (dec. 47/326) and the Security Council on 10 May 1993 to fill a vacancy resulting from the death of Manfred Lachs (Poland) on 14 January.

On 10 November 1993, elections were held in both the General Assembly (dec. 48/308) and the Security Council to fill the vacancies occurring on 6 February 1994 with the expiration of the terms of office of the following Judges: Shigeru Oda (Japan), Ni Zhengyu (China), Jens Evensen (Norway), Bola A. Ajibola (Nigeria), Géza Herczegh (Hungary).

The following Judges were elected for a term of office ending on 5 February 2003: Carl-August Fleischhauer (Germany), Géza Herczegh (Hungary), Abdul Koroma (Sierra Leone), Shigeru Oda (Japan), Shi Jiuyong (China).

Registrar: Eduardo Valencia-Ospina.
Deputy Registrar: Bernard Noble.

Chamber formed in the case concerning the *Land, Island and Maritime Frontier Dispute (El Salvador/Honduras)*

Members: José Sette Câmara *(President)*, Sir Robert Y. Jennings, Shigeru Oda.
Ad hoc members: Nicolas Valticos, Santiago Torres Bernárdez.

Chamber of Summary Procedure

Members: Sir Robert Y. Jennings (ex officio), Shigeru Oda (ex officio), Stephen M. Schwebel, Ni Zhengyu, Jens Evensen.
Substitute members: Nikolai K. Tarassov, Andrés Aguilar Mawdsley.

Chamber for Environmental Matters

In order to be prepared to the fullest possible extent to deal with any environmental case falling within its jurisdiction, the Court established, effective 6 August 1993, a seven-member Chamber for Environmental Matters.

Members: Stephen M. Schwebel, Mohammed Bedjaoui, Jens Evensen, Mohamed Shahabuddeen, Christopher G. Weeramantry, Raymond Ranjeva, Géza Herczegh.

Parties to the Court's Statute

All Members of the United Nations are *ipso facto* parties to the Statute of the International Court of Justice. Also parties to it are the following non-members: Nauru, Switzerland.

States accepting the compulsory jurisdiction of the Court

Declarations made by the following States, a number with reservations, accepting the Court's compulsory jurisdiction (or made under the Statute of the Permanent Court of International Justice and deemed to be an acceptance of the jurisdiction of the International Court) were in force at the end of 1993:

Australia, Austria, Barbados, Belgium, Botswana, Bulgaria, Cambodia, Canada, Colombia, Costa Rica, Cyprus, Denmark, Dominican Republic, Egypt, Estonia, Finland, Gambia, Guinea-Bissau, Haiti, Honduras, Hungary, India, Japan, Kenya, Liberia,

Liechtenstein, Luxembourg, Madagascar, Malawi, Malta, Mauritius, Mexico, Nauru, Netherlands, New Zealand, Nicaragua, Nigeria, Norway, Pakistan, Panama, Philippines, Poland, Portugal, Senegal, Somalia, Spain, Sudan, Suriname, Swaziland, Sweden, Switzerland, Togo, Uganda, United Kingdom, Uruguay, Zaire.

United Nations organs and specialized and related agencies authorized to request advisory opinions from the Court

Authorized by the United Nations Charter to request opinions on any legal question: General Assembly, Security Council.
Authorized by the General Assembly in accordance with the Charter to request opinions on legal questions arising within the scope of their activities: Economic and Social Council, Trusteeship Council, Interim Committee of the General Assembly, Committee on Applications for Review of Administrative Tribunal Judgements, ILO, FAO, UNESCO, ICAO, WHO, World Bank, IFC, IDA, IMF, ITU, WMO, IMO, WIPO, IFAD, UNIDO, IAEA.

Committees of the Court

BUDGETARY AND ADMINISTRATIVE COMMITTEE

Members: Sir Robert Y. Jennings (ex officio), Shigeru Oda (ex officio), Stephen M. Schwebel, Mohammed Bedjaoui, Nikolai K. Tarassov, Gilbert Guillaume, Mohamed Shahabuddeen.

COMMITTEE ON RELATIONS

Members: Mohammed Bedjaoui, Ni Zhengyu, Andrés Aguilar Mawdsley.

LIBRARY COMMITTEE

Members: Roberto Ago, Christopher G. Weeramantry, Raymond Ranjeva.

RULES COMMITTEE

Members: Roberto Ago, Mohammed Bedjaoui, Ni Zhengyu, Jens Evensen, Nikolai K. Tarassov.

Other United Nations–related bodies

The following bodies are not subsidiary to any principal organ of the United Nations but were established by an international treaty instrument or arrangement sponsored by the United Nations and are thus related to the Organization and its work. These bodies, often referred to as "treaty organs", are serviced by the United Nations Secretariat and may be financed in part or wholly from the Organization's regular budget, as authorized by the General Assembly, to which most of them report annually.

Commission against Apartheid in Sports

The Commission against Apartheid in Sports was established under the International Convention against Apartheid in Sports.[4] It consists of 15 members elected for four-year terms by the States parties to the Convention to serve in their personal capacity, with due regard for equitable geographical distribution and representation of the principal legal systems, particular attention being paid to participation of persons having experience in sports administration.

The Commission, which normally reports annually to the General Assembly through the Secretary-General, did not meet in 1993.

Members:
To serve until 2 March 1993:[a] Tesfay Fichala (Ethiopia), Raul González Rodriguez (Mexico), Lionel A. Hurst (Antigua and Barbuda), Sedfrey Ordoñez (Philippines), Allan Rae (Jamaica), Boris Topornin (Russian Federation).

To serve until 24 June 1995: Gbedevi Zikpi Aguigah (Togo), Abdul Karim Al-Ethawy (Iraq), James Victor Gbeho (Ghana), Joseph Lagu (Sudan), Francis Malambugi (United Republic of Tanzania), Ernest Besley Maycock (Barbados), Vladimir Platonov (Ukraine), Jai Pratap Rana (Nepal), Zoumana Traoré (Burkina Faso).

[a]No elections were held to fill the vacancies occurring on 2 March 1993.

Committee against Torture

The Committee against Torture was established under the Convention against Torture and Other Cruel, Inhuman or Degrading Treatment or Punishment.[5] It consists of 10 experts elected for four-year terms by the States parties to the Convention to serve in their personal capacity, with due regard for equitable geographical distribution and for the usefulness of the participation of some persons having legal experience.

In 1993, the Committee, which reports annually to the General Assembly, held, at Geneva, its tenth session from 19 to 30 April and its eleventh session from 8 to 19 November.

Members:
To serve until 31 December 1993: Alexis Dipanda Mouelle, *Vice-Chairman* (Cameroon); Yuri A. Khitrin (Russian Federation);

---

[4]YUN 1985, p. 166, GA res. 40/64 G, annex, 10 Dec. 1985.
[5]YUN 1984, p. 815, GA res. 39/46, annex, article 17, 10 Dec. 1984.

Dimitar Nikolov Mikhailov, _Vice-Chairman_ (Bulgaria); Bent Sorensen (Denmark); Joseph Voyame, _Chairman_ (Switzerland). _To serve until 31 December 1995:_ Hassib Ben Ammar (Tunisia); Peter Thomas Burns, _Rapporteur_ (Canada); Fawzi El Ibrashi (Egypt); Ricardo Gil Lavedra, _Vice-Chairman_ (Argentina); Hugo Lorenzo (Uruguay).

Committee on the Elimination of Discrimination against Women

The Committee on the Elimination of Discrimination against Women was established under the Convention on the Elimination of All Forms of Discrimination against Women.[6] It consists of 23 experts elected for four-year terms by the States parties to the Convention to serve in their personal capacity, with due regard for equitable geographical distribution and for representation of the different forms of civilization and principal legal systems.

The Committee, which reports annually to the General Assembly through the Economic and Social Council, held its twelfth session at Vienna from 18 January to 5 February 1993.

Members:
To serve until 15 April 1994: Charlotte Abaka (Ghana); Ryoko Akamatsu (Japan); Emna Aouij (Tunisia); Dora Gladys Nancy Bravo Nuñez de Ramsey (Ecuador); Ivanka Corti, _Chairman_ (Italy); Norma Monica Forde (Barbados); Zagorka Ilic (Yugoslavia); Tatiana Nikolaeva, _Vice-Chairman_ (Russian Federation); Teresita Quintos-Deles, _Rapporteur_ (Philippines); Lin Shangzhen (China); Mervat Tallawy (Egypt); Rose N. Ukeje, _Vice-Chairman_ (Nigeria).
To serve until 15 April 1996: Gül Aykor (Turkey); Carlota Bustelo García del Real (Spain); Silvia Rose Cartwright (New Zealand); Evangelina García-Prince, _Vice-Chairman_ (Venezuela); Liliana Gurdulich de Correa (Argentina); Salma Khan (Bangladesh); Pirkko Anneli Mäkinen (Finland); Elsa Victoria Muñoz-Gómez (Colombia); Ahoua Ouedraogo (Burkina Faso); Hanna Beate Schöpp-Schilling (Germany); Kongit Sinegiorgis (Ethiopia).

Committee on the Elimination of Racial Discrimination

The Committee on the Elimination of Racial Discrimination was established under the International Convention on the Elimination of All Forms of Racial Discrimination.[7] It consists of 18 experts elected for four-year terms by the States parties to the Convention to serve in their personal capacity, with due regard for equitable geographical distribution and for representation of the different forms of civilization and principal legal systems.

The Committee, which reports annually to the General Assembly through the Secretary-General, held two sessions in 1993, at Geneva: its forty-second from 1 to 19 March and its forty-third from 2 to 20 August.

Members:
To serve until 19 January 1994: Mahmoud Aboul-Nasr (Egypt); Hamzat Ahmadu, _Vice-Chairman_ (Nigeria); Michael Parker Banton, _Rapporteur_ (United Kingdom); Régis de Gouttes (France); George O. Lamptey (Ghana); Carlos Lechuga Hevia (Cuba); Agha Shahi (Pakistan); Michael E. Sherifis (Cyprus); Rüdiger Wolfrum (Germany).
To serve until 19 January 1996: Theodoor van Boven (Netherlands); Ion Diaconu, _Vice-Chairman_ (Romania); Eduardo Ferrero Costa (Peru); Ivan Garvalov (Bulgaria); Yuri A. Rechetov (Russian Federation); Shanti Sadiq Ali, _Vice-Chairman_ (India); Song Shuhua (China); Luis Valencia Rodriguez, _Chairman_ (Ecuador); Mario Jorge Yutzis (Argentina).

Committee on the Rights of the Child

The Committee on the Rights of the Child was established under the Convention on the Rights of the Child.[8] It consists of 10 experts elected for four-year terms by the States parties to the Convention to serve in their personal capacity, with due regard for equitable geographical distribution and for representation of the principal legal systems.

The Committee, which reports biennially to the General Assembly through the Economic and Social Council, held its third and fourth sessions at Geneva from 11 to 29 January and from 20 September to 8 October 1993.

Members (until 28 February 1993):
To serve until 28 February 1993: Hoda Badran, _Chairman_ (Egypt); Flora C. Eufemio, _Vice-Chairman_ (Philippines); Antônio Carlos Gomes da Costa (Brazil); Swithun Tachiona Mombeshora (Zimbabwe); Marta Santos País, _Rapporteur_ (Portugal).
To serve until 28 February 1995: Luis A. Bambaren Gastelumendi, _Vice-Chairman_ (Peru); Akila Belembaogo (Burkina Faso); Thomas Hammarberg (Sweden); Youri Kolosov, _Vice-Chairman_ (Russian Federation); Sandra Prunella Mason (Barbados).

The States parties to the Convention, on 23 February 1993, elected the following for a four-year term beginning on 1 March 1993: Hoda Badran (Egypt), Flora C. Eufemio (Philippines), Swithun Tachiona Mombeshora (Zimbabwe), Marta Santos País (Portugal), Marilia Sardenberg Zelner Gonçalves (Brazil).

Members (from 1 March 1993):
To serve until 28 February 1995: Luis A. Bambaren Gastelumendi (Peru); Akila Belembaogo, _Vice-Chairman_ (Burkina Faso); Thomas Hammarberg, _Vice-Chairman_ (Sweden); Youri Kolosov (Russian Federation); Sandra Prunella Mason, _Vice-Chairman_ (Barbados).
To serve until 28 February 1997: Hoda Badran, _Chairman_ (Egypt); Flora C. Eufemio (Philippines); Swithun Tachiona Mombeshora (Zimbabwe); Marta Santos País, _Rapporteur_ (Portugal); Marilia Sardenberg Zelner Gonçalves (Brazil).

Conference on Disarmament

The Conference on Disarmament, the multilateral negotiating forum on disarmament, reports annually to the General Assembly and is serviced by the United Nations Secretariat.

The Conference met at Geneva from 19 January to 26 March, 10 May to 25 June and 26 July to 3 September 1993.

Members: Algeria, Argentina, Australia, Belgium, Brazil, Bulgaria, Canada, China, Cuba, Egypt, Ethiopia, France, Germany, Hungary, India, Indonesia, Iran, Italy, Japan, Kenya, Mexico, Mongolia, Morocco, Myanmar, Netherlands, Nigeria, Pakistan, Peru, Poland, Romania, Russian Federation, Sri Lanka, Sweden, United Kingdom, United States, Venezuela, Yugoslavia,[a] Zaire.

[a]Refers to the former Socialist Federal Republic of Yugoslavia.

The presidency, which rotates in English alphabetical order among the members, was held by the following in 1993: Brazil, Bulgaria, Canada, China, Cuba, Egypt, the last also for the recess until the 1994 session.

Human Rights Committee

The Human Rights Committee was established under the International Covenant on Civil and Political Rights.[9] It consists of 18 experts elected by the States parties to the Covenant to serve in their personal capacity for four-year terms.

In 1993, the Committee, which reports annually to the General Assembly through the Economic and Social Council, held three sessions: its forty-seventh at United Nations Headquarters from 22 March to 8 April, its forty-eighth at Geneva from 12 to 30 July and its forty-ninth at Geneva from 18 October to 5 November.

Members:
To serve until 31 December 1994: Nisuke Ando, _Chairman_ (Japan); Christine Chanet (France); Vojin Dimitrijevic, _Vice-_

---

[6]YUN 1979, p. 898, GA res. 34/180, annex, article 17, 18 Dec. 1979.
[7]YUN 1965, p. 443, GA res. 2106 A (XX), annex, article 8, 21 Dec. 1965.
[8]GA res. 44/25, annex, 20 Nov. 1989.
[9]YUN 1966, p. 427, GA res. 2200 A (XXI), annex, part IV, 16 Dec. 1966.

Chairman (Yugoslavia); Omran El-Shafei, *Vice-Chairman* (Egypt); Kurt Herndl (Austria); Birame Ndiaye (Senegal); Julio Prado Vallejo (Ecuador); Waleed Sadi (Jordan); Bertil Wennergren, *Vice-Chairman* (Sweden).
To serve until 31 December 1996: Francisco José Aguilar Urbina *Rapporteur* (Costa Rica); Marco Tulio Bruni Celli (Venezuela); Elizabeth Evatt (Australia); János Fodor (Hungary); Laurel B. Francis (Jamaica); Rosalyn Higgins (United Kingdom); Rajsoomer Lallah (Mauritius); Andreas V. Mavrommatis (Cyprus); Fausto Pocar (Italy).

International Narcotics Control Board (INCB)

The International Narcotics Control Board, established under the Single Convention on Narcotic Drugs, 1961, as amended by the 1972 Protocol, consists of 13 members, elected by the Economic and Social Council for five-year terms, three from candidates nominated by WHO and 10 from candidates nominated by Members of the United Nations and parties to the Single Convention.

The Board held two sessions in 1993, at Vienna: its fifty-fourth from 4 to 14 May and its fifty-fifth from 1 to 18 November.

Members:
To serve until 1 March 1995: Dr. Cai Zhi-ji (China);[a] Huáscar Cajías Kauffmann (Bolivia); Mohsen Kchouk, *Second Vice-President* (Tunisia); Mohamed Mansour, *Rapporteur* (Egypt); Maruthi Vasudev Narayan Rao (India); Oskar Schröder (Germany).
To serve until 1 March 1997: Sirad Atmodjo (Indonesia);[a] Abdol-Hamid Ghodse, *President* (Iran);[a] Gottfried Machata (Austria); Bunsom Martin (Thailand); Herbert S. Okun (United States); Manuel Quijano, *First Vice-President* (Mexico); Sahibzada Raoof Ali Khan (Pakistan).

[a]Elected from candidates nominated by WHO.

Preparatory Commission for the International Seabed Authority and for the International Tribunal for the Law of the Sea

The Preparatory Commission for the International Seabed Authority and for the International Tribunal for the Law of the Sea was established by the Third United Nations Conference on the Law of the Sea. It consists of States, self-governing associated States, territories enjoying full internal self-government and international organizations which have signed or acceded to the United Nations Convention on the Law of the Sea. As at 31 December 1993, the Commission had 160 members.

In 1993, the Commission held its eleventh session at Kingston, Jamaica, from 22 March to 2 April.

Members: Afghanistan, Algeria *(Vice-Chairman)*, Angola, Antigua and Barbuda, Argentina, Australia, Austria, Bahamas, Bahrain, Bangladesh, Barbados, Belarus, Belgium, Belize, Benin, Bhutan, Bolivia, Botswana, Brazil *(Vice-Chairman)*, Brunei Darussalam, Bulgaria, Burkina Faso, Burundi, Cambodia, Cameroon *(Vice-Chairman)*, Canada, Cape Verde *(Chairman)*, Central African Republic, Chad, Chile *(Vice-Chairman)*, China *(Vice-Chairman)*, Colombia, Comoros, Congo, Cook Islands, Costa Rica, Côte d'Ivoire, Cuba, Cyprus, Czech Republic,[a] Democratic People's Republic of Korea, Denmark, Djibouti, Dominica, Dominican Republic, Egypt, El Salvador, Equatorial Guinea, Ethiopia, European Economic Community, Fiji, Finland, France *(Vice-Chairman)*, Gabon, Gambia, Ghana, Greece, Grenada, Guatemala, Guinea, Guinea-Bissau, Guyana, Haiti, Honduras, Hungary, Iceland, India *(Vice-Chairman)*, Indonesia, Iran, Iraq *(Vice-Chairman)*, Ireland, Italy, Jamaica *(Rapporteur-General)*, Japan *(Vice-Chairman)*, Kenya, Kuwait, Lao People's Democratic Republic, Lebanon, Lesotho, Liberia *(Vice-Chairman)*, Libyan Arab Jamahiriya, Liechtenstein, Luxembourg, Madagascar, Malawi, Malaysia, Maldives, Mali, Malta, Marshall Islands, Mauritania, Mauritius, Mexico, Micronesia, Monaco, Mongolia, Morocco, Mozambique, Myanmar, Namibia, Nauru, Nepal, Netherlands *(Vice-Chairman)*, New Zealand, Nicaragua, Niger, Nigeria *(Vice-Chairman)*, Niue, Norway, Oman, Pakistan, Panama, Papua New Guinea, Paraguay, Philippines, Poland, Portugal, Qatar, Republic of Korea, Romania, Russian Federation *(Vice-Chairman)*, Rwanda, Saint Kitts and Nevis, Saint Lucia, Saint Vincent and the Grenadines, Samoa, Sao Tome and Principe, Saudi Arabia, Senegal, Seychelles, Sierra Leone, Singapore, Slovakia,[a] Solomon Islands, Somalia, South Africa, Spain, Sri Lanka *(Vice-Chairman)*, Sudan, Suriname, Swaziland, Sweden, Switzerland, Thailand, Togo, Trinidad and Tobago, Tunisia, Tuvalu, Uganda, Ukraine, United Arab Emirates, United Republic of Tanzania, Uruguay, Vanuatu, Viet Nam, Yemen, Yugoslavia, Zaire, Zambia, Zimbabwe.

[a]Succeeded to the membership of the former Czechoslovakia.

Principal members of the United Nations Secretariat

(as at 31 December 1993)

Secretariat

The Secretary-General: Boutros Boutros-Ghali

Executive Office of the Secretary-General

Assistant Secretary-General, Chief of Staff: Jean-Claude Aimé
Under-Secretary-General, Special Adviser to the Secretary-General: Chinmaya R. Gharekhan
Assistant Secretary-General, Special Adviser to the Secretary-General: Alvaro de Soto

Protocol and Liaison Service

Assistant Secretary-General, Chief of Protocol: Aly I. Teymour

Office of Legal Affairs

Under-Secretary-General, Legal Counsel: Carl-August Fleischhauer

Department of Political Affairs

Under-Secretaries-General: Marrack Goulding, James O. C. Jonah
Assistant Secretary-General: Benon V. Sevan

Department of Peace-keeping Operations

Under-Secretary-General: Kofi Annan
Assistant Secretary-General: Iqbal Syed Riza

Department for Development Support and Management Services

Under-Secretary-General: Ji Chaozhu

Department for Policy Coordination and Sustainable Development

Under-Secretary-General: Nitin Desai

Department for Economic and Social Information and Policy Analysis

Under-Secretary-General: Jean-Claude Milleron

Economic and Social Commission for Asia and the Pacific

Under-Secretary-General, Executive Secretary: Rafeeuddin Ahmed

Economic and Social Commission for Western Asia

Under-Secretary-General, Executive Secretary: Sabah Eddin Shukri Bakjaji

Economic Commission for Africa
Under-Secretary-General, Executive Secretary: Layashi Yaker

Economic Commission for Europe
Under-Secretary-General, Executive Secretary: Yves Berthelot

Economic Commission for Latin America and the Caribbean
Under-Secretary-General, Executive Secretary: Gert Rosenthal

United Nations Centre for Human Settlements
Under-Secretary-General, Officer-in-Charge: Elizabeth Dowdeswell
Officer-in-Charge, United Nations Habitat and Human Settlements Foundation: Elizabeth Dowdeswell

Department of Humanitarian Affairs
Under-Secretary-General, Emergency Relief Coordinator: Jan K. Eliasson

Department of Administration and Management
Under-Secretary-General: Melissa Wells
Deputy to the Under-Secretary-General, Controller: Yukio Takasu

OFFICE FOR INSPECTIONS AND INVESTIGATIONS
Assistant Secretary-General: Mohamed Aly Niazi

OFFICE OF GENERAL SERVICES
Director: Carole R. Thompson

OFFICE OF HUMAN RESOURCES MANAGEMENT
Director: Christine Dodson

OFFICE OF CONFERENCE SERVICES
Director: Françoise P. Cestac

Department of Public Information
Assistant Secretary-General: Marco Vianello-Chiodo

Secretariat of the United Nations Fiftieth Anniversary
Under-Secretary-General, Special Adviser to the Secretary-General for Public Policy: Gillian Sorensen

United Nations Office at Geneva
Under-Secretary-General, Director-General of the United Nations Office at Geneva: Vladimir Petrovsky
Assistant Secretary-General, Personal Representative of the Secretary-General: Sotirios G. Mousouris

Centre for Human Rights
Assistant Secretary-General: Ibrahima Doc Fall

United Nations Office at Vienna
Under-Secretary-General, Director-General of the United Nations Office at Vienna: Giorgio Giacomelli

International Court of Justice Registry
Assistant Secretary-General, Registrar: Eduardo Valencia-Ospina

Secretariats of subsidiary organs, special representatives and other related bodies

International Trade Centre UNCTAD/GATT
Officer-in-Charge: Raju Makil

Office of the Special Envoy of the Secretary-General for Haiti
Under-Secretary-General, Special Envoy: Dante Mario Caputo

Special Representative of the Secretary-General for the controversy between Guyana and Venezuela
Under-Secretary-General, Personal Representative: Alister McIntyre

Office of the United Nations High Commissioner for Refugees
Under-Secretary-General, High Commissioner: Sadako Ogata
Assistant Secretary-General, Deputy High Commissioner: Gerald Walzer

United Nations Angola Verification Mission
Under-Secretary-General, Special Representative of the Secretary-General: Alioune Blondin Beye
Chief Military Observer: Major-General Chris Abutu Garuba

United Nations Assistance for the Reconstruction and Development of Lebanon
Coordinator: Hans van der Kloet

United Nations Children's Fund
Under-Secretary-General, Executive Director: James P. Grant
Assistant Secretary-General, Deputy Executive Director, Programmes: Richard Jolly
Assistant Secretary-General, Deputy Executive Director, Operations: Karin Sham Poo
Assistant Secretary-General, Deputy Executive Director, External Relations: Guido Bertolaco

United Nations Compensation Commission
Assistant Secretary-General, Executive Secretary: Carlos Alzamora Traverso

United Nations Conference on Population and Development
Under-Secretary-General, Secretary-General of the Conference: Dr. Nafis I. Sadik

Fourth World Conference on Women
Assistant Secretary-General, Secretary-General of the Conference: Gertrude Mongella

United Nations Conference on Trade and Development
Under-Secretary-General, Secretary-General of the Conference: Kenneth K. S. Dadzie
Assistant Secretary-General, Deputy Secretary-General of the Conference: Carlos Fortin

United Nations Development Programme
Administrator: James Gustave Speth
Associate Administrator: Luis Maria Gomez
Assistant Administrator and Director, Bureau for Finance and Administration: Toshiyuki Niwa
Assistant Administrator and Director, Bureau for Special Activities: Jean-Jacques Graisse
Assistant Administrator and Director, Bureau for Programme Policy and Evaluation: Gustaf Edgren
Assistant Administrator and Director, Office for Project Services: Reinhart Helmke
Executive Director, United Nations Population Fund: Dr. Nafis I. Sadik
Deputy Executive Director, United Nations Population Fund, Policy and Administration: Hirofumi Ando
Deputy Executive Director, United Nations Population Fund, Programme: Joseph Van Arendonk
Assistant Administrator and Regional Director, Regional Bureau for Africa: Ellen Johnson Sirleaf
Assistant Administrator and Regional Director, Regional Bureau for Arab States: Ali Ahmed Attiga
Assistant Administrator and Regional Director, Regional Bureau for Asia and the Pacific: vacant
Assistant Administrator and Regional Director, Regional Bureau for Latin America and the Caribbean: Fernando Zumbado

United Nations Disengagement Observer Force
Assistant Secretary-General, Force Commander: Major-General Misztal

United Nations Environment Programme
Under-Secretary-General, Executive Director: Elizabeth Dowdeswell

United Nations Fund for Drug Abuse Control
Assistant Secretary-General, Executive Director: Giorgio Giacomelli

United Nations Institute for Training and Research
Acting Executive Director: Marcel Boisard

United Nations Interim Force in Lebanon
Assistant Secretary-General, Force Commander: Major-General Trond Furuhovde

United Nations International Drug Control Programme
Under-Secretary-General, Executive Director: Giorgio Giacomelli

United Nations Iraq-Kuwait Observation Mission
Assistant Secretary-General, Chief Military Observer: Major-General Krishna N. S. Thapa

United Nations Military Observer Group in India and Pakistan
Chief Military Observer: Brigadier-General Ricardo Jorge Galarza Chans

United Nations Mission for the Organization of a Referendum in Western Sahara
Under-Secretary-General, Special Representative of the Secretary-General: Sahabzada Yaqub-Khan

United Nations Observer Mission in El Salvador
Under-Secretary-General, Special Representative of the Secretary-General and Chief of Mission: Augusto Ramírez Ocampo

United Nations Operation in Somalia
Under-Secretary-General, Special Representative of the Secretary-General: Jonathan Trumbull Howe

United Nations Peace-keeping Force in Cyprus
Under-Secretary-General, Special Representative of the Secretary-General: Joe Clark
Assistant Secretary-General, Force Commander: Major-General Michael F. Minehane

United Nations Protection Force
Under-Secretary-General, Special Representative of the Secretary-General: Yasushi Akashi
Assistant Secretary-General, Force Commander: General Jean Cot

United Nations Relief and Works Agency for Palestine Refugees in the Near East
Under-Secretary-General, Commissioner-General: Ilter Türkmen
Assistant Secretary-General, Deputy Commissioner-General: William L. Eagleton

United Nations Truce Supervision Organization
Assistant Secretary-General, Chief of Staff: vacant

United Nations University
Under-Secretary-General, Rector: Heitor Gurgulino de Souza
Assistant Secretary-General, Director, World Institute for Development Economics Research: Mihaly Simai

---

On 31 December 1993, the total number of staff of the United Nations holding permanent, probationary and fixed-term appointments with service or expected service of a year or more was 15,649. Of these, 5,764 were in the Professional and higher categories and 9,885 were in the General Service, Manual Worker and Field Service categories. Of the same total, 13,978 were regular staff serving at Headquarters or other established offices and 1,671 were assigned as project personnel to technical cooperation projects. In addition, at the end of December 1993, UNRWA had some 19,891 local area staff, including temporary assistance.

Appendix IV

Agendas of United Nations principal organs in 1993

This appendix lists the items on the agendas of the General Assembly, the Security Council, the Economic and Social Council and the Trusteeship Council during 1993. For the Assembly and the Economic and Social Council, the column headed "Allocation" indicates the assignment of each item to plenary meetings or committees.

Agenda item titles have been shortened by omitting mention of reports, if any, following the subject of the item. Where the subject-matter of an item is not apparent from its title, the subject is identified in square brackets; this is not part of the title.

General Assembly

Agenda items considered at the resumed forty-seventh session
(19 January — 20 September 1993)

Item No.	Title	Allocation
8.	Adoption of the agenda and organization of work.	Plenary
10.	Report of the Secretary-General on the work of the Organization.	Plenary
11.	Report of the Security Council.	Plenary
12.	Report of the Economic and Social Council.	Plenary, 2nd, 3rd, 4th, 5th
15.	Elections to fill vacancies in principal organs:	
	(c) Election of a member of the International Court of Justice.[1]	Plenary
16.	Elections to fill vacancies in subsidiary organs and other elections:	
	(a) Election of twelve members of the World Food Council;	Plenary
	(d) Election of a member of the Governing Council of the United Nations Environment Programme;[1]	Plenary
	(e) Election of a member of the United Nations Commission on International Trade Law.[1]	Plenary
17.	Appointments to fill vacancies in subsidiary organs and other appointments:	
	(a) Appointment of members of the Advisory Committee on Administrative and Budgetary Questions;	[2]
	(b) Appointment of members of the Committee on Contributions;	5th
	(g) Appointment of members of the Committee on Conferences;	Plenary
	(h) Appointment of a member of the Joint Inspection Unit;	Plenary
	(i) Confirmation of the appointment of the Secretary-General of the United Nations Conference on Trade and Development;	Plenary
	(j) Appointment of members and alternate members of the United Nations Staff Pension Committee;[1]	Plenary
	(k) Confirmation of the appointment of the Administrator of the United Nations Development Programme.[1]	Plenary
18.	Implementation of the Declaration on the Granting of Independence to Colonial Countries and Peoples.	[3]
19.	Admission of new Members to the United Nations.	Plenary
22.	The situation of democracy and human rights in Haiti.	Plenary
28.	The situation in Afghanistan and its implications for international peace and security.	Plenary
30.	Question of Palestine.	Plenary
31.	Revitalization of the work of the General Assembly.	Plenary
35.	The situation in the Middle East.	Plenary
36.	The situation in Central America: procedures for the establishment of a firm and lasting peace and progress in fashioning a region of peace, freedom, democracy and development.	Plenary
40.	Question of equitable representation on and increase in the membership of the Security Council.	Plenary
42.	Armed Israeli aggression against the Iraqi nuclear installations and its grave consequences for the established international system concerning the peaceful uses of nuclear energy, the non-proliferation of nuclear weapons and international peace and security.	Plenary
45.	Question of Cyprus.	[4]
46.	Consequences of the Iraqi occupation of and aggression against Kuwait.	Plenary
47.	Restructuring and revitalization of the United Nations in the economic, social and related fields.	Plenary

---

[1]Sub-item added at the resumed session.
[2]Allocated to the Fifth Committee at the first part of the session in 1992 but considered only in plenary meeting at the resumed session.
[3]Allocated to the Fourth Committee at the first part of the session in 1992 but considered only in plenary meeting at the resumed session.
[4]Not allocated; consideration deferred to the forty-eighth session.

Item No.	Title	Allocation
63.	Review of the implementation of the recommendations and decisions adopted by the General Assembly at its tenth special session.	1st
71.	Effects of atomic radiation.	5
72.	International cooperation in the peaceful uses of outer space.	5
76.	Questions relating to information.	5
79.	Report of the United Nations Conference on Environment and Development.	6
89.	Training and research:	
	(a) United Nations Institute for Training and Research.	2nd
93.	Social development:	
	(a) Questions relating to the world social situation and to youth, ageing, disabled persons and the family.	7
103.	Review of the efficiency of the administrative and financial functioning of the United Nations.	5th
104.	Programme budget for the biennium 1992-1993.	5th
106.	Current financial crisis of the United Nations.	5th
107.	Financial emergency of the United Nations.	5th
111.	Scale of assessments for the apportionment of the expenses of the United Nations.	5th
112.	Personnel questions.	5th
115.	Financing of the United Nations peace-keeping forces in the Middle East.	2
116.	Financing of the United Nations Iran-Iraq Military Observer Group.	2
117.	Financing of the United Nations Angola Verification Mission.	5th
118.	Financing of the United Nations Transition Assistance Group.	2
119.	Financing of the United Nations Observer Group in Central America.	5th
120.	Financing of the activities arising from Security Council resolution 687(1991):	
	(a) United Nations Iraq-Kuwait Observation Mission;	5th
	(b) Other activities.	5th
121.	Financing of the United Nations Mission for the Referendum in Western Sahara.	5th
122.	Financing of the United Nations Observer Mission in El Salvador.	5th
123.	Financing of the United Nations Transitional Authority in Cambodia.	5th
124.	Administrative and budgetary aspects of the financing of the United Nations peace-keeping operations.	5th
133.	Report of the Special Committee on the Charter of the United Nations and on the Strengthening of the Role of the Organization.	8
137.	Financing of the United Nations Protection Force.	5th
143.	The situation in Bosnia and Herzegovina.	Plenary
145.	Financing of the United Nations Operation in Somalia.	5th
147.	Programme budget for the biennium 1990-1991.	5th
152.	Convening of an international conference on Somalia.	Plenary
153.	Financing of the United Nations Operation in Mozambique.[9]	5th
154.	Emergency assistance to Cuba.[9]	Plenary
155.	Financing of the International Tribunal for the Prosecution of Persons Responsible for Serious Violations of International Humanitarian Law Committed in the Territory of the Former Yugoslavia since 1991.[9]	5th
156.	Election of judges of the International Tribunal for the Prosecution of Persons Responsible for Serious Violations of International Humanitarian Law Committed in the Territory of the Former Yugoslavia since 1991.[9]	Plenary
157.	Financing of the United Nations Peace-keeping Force in Cyprus.[9]	5th

Agenda of the forty-eighth session
(first part, 21 September — 23 December 1993)

Item No.	Title	Allocation
1.	Opening of the session by the Chairman of the delegation of Bulgaria.	Plenary
2.	Minute of silent prayer or meditation.	Plenary

---

[5]Allocated to the Special Political Committee at the first part of the session in 1992 but considered only in plenary meeting at the resumed session.
[6]Allocated to the Second Committee at the first part of the session in 1992 but considered only in plenary meeting at the resumed session.
[7]Allocated to the Third Committee at the first part of the session in 1992 but considered only in plenary meeting at the resumed session.
[8]Allocated to the Sixth Committee at the first part of the session in 1992 but considered only in plenary meeting at the resumed session.
[9]Item added at the resumed session.

Item No.	Title	Allocation
3.	Credentials of representatives to the forty-eighth session of the General Assembly:	
	(a) Appointment of the members of the Credentials Committee;	Plenary
	(b) Report of the Credentials Committee.	Plenary
4.	Election of the President of the General Assembly.	Plenary
5.	Election of the officers of the Main Committees.	Plenary
6.	Election of the Vice-Presidents of the General Assembly.	Plenary
7.	Notification by the Secretary-General under Article 12, paragraph 2, of the Charter of the United Nations.	Plenary
8.	Adoption of the agenda and organization of work.	Plenary
9.	General debate.	Plenary
10.	Report of the Secretary-General on the work of the Organization.	Plenary
11.	Report of the Security Council.	Plenary
12.	Report of the Economic and Social Council.	Plenary, 2nd, 3rd, 4th, 5th
13.	Report of the International Court of Justice.	Plenary
14.	Report of the International Atomic Energy Agency.	Plenary
15.	Elections to fill vacancies in principal organs:	
	(a) Election of five non-permanent members of the Security Council;	Plenary
	(b) Election of eighteen members of the Economic and Social Council;	Plenary
	(c) Election of five members of the International Court of Justice.	Plenary
16.	Elections to fill vacancies in subsidiary organs and other elections:	
	(a) Election of twenty-nine members of the Governing Council of the United Nations Environment Programme;	Plenary
	(b) Election of twelve members of the World Food Council;	Plenary
	(c) Election of twenty members of the Committee for Programme and Coordination;	Plenary
	(d) Election of the United Nations High Commissioner for Refugees.	Plenary
17.	Appointments to fill vacancies in subsidiary organs and other appointments:	
	(a) Appointment of members of the Advisory Committee on Administrative and Budgetary Questions;	5th
	(b) Appointment of members of the Committee on Contributions;	5th
	(c) Appointment of a member of the Board of Auditors;	5th
	(d) Confirmation of the appointment of members of the Investments Committee;	5th
	(e) Appointment of members of the United Nations Administrative Tribunal;	5th
	(f) Appointment of members of the International Civil Service Commission;	5th
	(g) Appointment of members of the Committee on Conferences;	Plenary
	(h) Appointment of a member of the Joint Inspection Unit;	Plenary
	(i) Confirmation of the appointment of the Secretary-General of the United Nations Conference on Trade and Development.	Plenary
18.	Implementation of the Declaration on the Granting of Independence to Colonial Countries and Peoples.	Plenary, 4th[10]
19.	Admission of new Members to the United Nations.	Plenary
20.	Forty-fifth anniversary of the Universal Declaration of Human Rights.	Plenary
21.	Return or restitution of cultural property to the countries of origin.	Plenary
22.	University for Peace.	Plenary
23.	Programmes and activities to promote peace in the world.	Plenary
24.	United Nations New Agenda for the Development of Africa in the 1990s.	Plenary
25.	Question of the Comorian island of Mayotte.	Plenary
26.	Cooperation between the United Nations and the Conference on Security and Cooperation in Europe.	Plenary
27.	Cooperation between the United Nations and the League of Arab States.	Plenary
28.	Cooperation between the United Nations and the Latin American Economic System.	Plenary
29.	Cooperation between the United Nations and the Organization of the Islamic Conference.	Plenary
30.	Necessity of ending the economic, commercial and financial embargo imposed by the United States of America against Cuba.	Plenary
31.	The situation of democracy and human rights in Haiti.	Plenary
32.	Complete withdrawal of foreign military forces from the territories of the Baltic States.	Plenary
33.	Question of equitable representation on and increase in the membership of the Security Council.	Plenary
34.	The situation in the Middle East.	Plenary

---

[10]Chapters of the report of the Special Committee on the Situation with regard to the Implementation of the Declaration on the Granting of Independence to Colonial Countries and Peoples relating to specific Territories.

Item No.	Title	Allocation
35.	Question of Palestine.	Plenary
36.	Law of the sea.	Plenary
37.	Zone of peace and cooperation of the South Atlantic.	Plenary
38.	Elimination of apartheid and establishment of a united, democratic and non-racial South Africa.	Plenary, 4th[11]
39.	United Nations Educational and Training Programme for Southern Africa.	Plenary
40.	The situation in Central America: procedures for the establishment of a firm and lasting peace and progress in fashioning a region of peace, freedom, democracy and development.	Plenary
41.	Emergency international assistance for peace, normalcy and reconstruction of war-stricken Afghanistan.	2nd
42.	The situation in Bosnia and Herzegovina.	Plenary
43.	Cooperation between the United Nations and the Organization of African Unity.	Plenary
44.	Strengthening of the coordination of humanitarian emergency assistance of the United Nations.	Plenary
45.	International assistance for the rehabilitation and reconstruction of Nicaragua: aftermath of the war and natural disasters.	Plenary
46.	Question of the Falkland Islands (Malvinas).	Plenary, 4th[11]
47.	Commemoration of the fiftieth anniversary of the United Nations in 1995.	Plenary
48.	Declaration of the Assembly of Heads of State and Government of the Organization of African Unity on the aerial and naval military attack against the Socialist People's Libyan Arab Jamahiriya by the present United States Administration in April 1986.	Plenary
49.	Armed Israeli aggression against the Iraqi nuclear installations and its grave consequences for the established international system concerning the peaceful uses of nuclear energy, the non-proliferation of nuclear weapons and international peace and security.	Plenary
50.	Launching of global negotiations on international economic cooperation for development.	Plenary
51.	Implementation of the resolutions of the United Nations.	Plenary
52.	The situation in Afghanistan and its implications for international peace and security.	Plenary
53.	Revitalization of the work of the General Assembly.	Plenary
54.	Question of Cyprus.	12
55.	Consequences of the Iraqi occupation of and aggression against Kuwait.	Plenary
56.	Restructuring and revitalization of the United Nations in the economic, social and related fields.	Plenary
57.	Prohibition of the development and manufacture of new types of weapons of mass destruction and new systems of such weapons.	1st
58.	Reduction of military budgets:	
	(a) Reduction of military budgets;	1st
	(b) Transparency of military expenditures.	1st
59.	Compliance with arms limitation and disarmament agreements.	1st
60.	Education and information for disarmament.	1st
61.	Chemical and bacteriological (biological) weapons.	1st
62.	Scientific and technological developments and their impact on international security.	1st
63.	The role of science and technology in the context of international security, disarmament and other related fields.	1st
64.	Verification in all its aspects, including the role of the United Nations in the field of verification.	1st
65.	Amendment of the Treaty Banning Nuclear Weapon Tests in the Atmosphere, in Outer Space and under Water.	1st
66.	Comprehensive nuclear-test-ban treaty.	1st
67.	Establishment of a nuclear-weapon-free zone in the region of the Middle East.	1st
68.	Establishment of a nuclear-weapon-free zone in South Asia.	1st
69.	Conclusion of effective international arrangements to assure non-nuclear-weapon States against the use or threat of use of nuclear weapons.	1st
70.	Prevention of an arms race in outer space.	1st
71.	General and complete disarmament:	
	(a) Notification of nuclear tests;	1st
	(b) Prohibition of the development, production, stockpiling and use of radiological weapons;	1st
	(c) Prohibition of the production of fissionable material for weapons purposes;	1st
	(d) Prohibition of the dumping of radioactive wastes;	1st
	(e) Relationship between disarmament and development;	1st

[11]Hearings of organizations and individuals having an interest in the question.
[12]On 24 September 1993, the General Assembly adopted the General Committee's recommendation that the item be allocated at an appropriate time during the session.

Item No.	*Title*	*Allocation*
	(f) Regional disarmament;	1st
	(g) Transparency in armaments;	1st
	(h) International arms transfers;	1st
	(i) Conventional disarmament on a regional scale.	1st
72.	Review and implementation of the Concluding Document of the Twelfth Special Session of the General Assembly:	
	(a) United Nations disarmament fellowship, training and advisory services programme;	1st
	(b) Convention on the Prohibition of the Use of Nuclear Weapons;	1st
	(c) United Nations Disarmament Information Programme;	1st
	(d) Nuclear-arms freeze;	1st
	(e) Regional confidence-building measures;	1st
	(f) United Nations Regional Centre for Peace and Disarmament in Africa, United Nations Regional Centre for Peace and Disarmament in Asia and the Pacific and United Nations Regional Centre for Peace, Disarmament and Development in Latin America and the Caribbean.	1st
73.	Review of the implementation of the recommendations and decisions adopted by the General Assembly at its tenth special session:	
	(a) Report of the Disarmament Commission;	1st
	(b) Report of the Conference on Disarmament;	1st
	(c) Status of multilateral disarmament agreements;	1st
	(d) Advisory Board on Disarmament Matters;	1st
	(e) United Nations Institute for Disarmament Research.	1st
74.	Israeli nuclear armament.	1st
75.	Convention on Prohibitions or Restrictions on the Use of Certain Conventional Weapons Which May Be Deemed to Be Excessively Injurious or to Have Indiscriminate Effects.	1st
76.	Question of Antarctica.	1st
77.	Strengthening of security and cooperation in the Mediterranean region.	1st
78.	Implementation of the Declaration of the Indian Ocean as a Zone of Peace.	1st
79.	Review of the implementation of the Declaration on the Strengthening of International Security.	1st
80.	Maintenance of international security.	1st
81.	Consolidation of the regime established by the Treaty for the Prohibition of Nuclear Weapons in Latin America and the Caribbean (Treaty of Tlatelolco).	1st
82.	Implementation of the Declaration on the Denuclearization of Africa.	1st
83.	Effects of atomic radiation.	4th
84.	International cooperation in the peaceful uses of outer space.	4th
85.	United Nations Relief and Works Agency for Palestine Refugees in the Near East.	4th
86.	Report of the Special Committee to Investigate Israeli Practices Affecting the Human Rights of the Palestinian People and Other Arabs of the Occupied Territories.	4th
87.	Comprehensive review of the whole question of peace-keeping operations in all their aspects.	4th
88.	Questions relating to information.	4th
89.	Science and peace.	4th
90.	Question of the composition of the relevant organs of the United Nations.	4th
91.	Development and international economic cooperation:	
	(a) Trade and development;	2nd
	(b) Implementation of the Programme of Action for the Least Developed Countries for the 1990s;	2nd
	(c) Effective mobilization and integration of women in development;	2nd
	(d) Economic and technical cooperation among developing countries;	2nd
	(e) Environment;	2nd
	(f) Desertification and drought;	2nd
	(g) Human settlements;	2nd
	(h) Science and technology for development;	2nd
	(i) Entrepreneurship;	2nd
	(j) Integration of the economies in transition into the world economy.	2nd
92.	External debt crisis and development.	2nd
93.	International cooperation for the eradication of poverty in developing countries.	2nd
94.	Operational activities for development:	
	(a) United Nations Development Programme;	2nd
	(b) United Nations Capital Development Fund;	2nd
	(c) United Nations technical cooperation activities;	2nd
	(d) United Nations Volunteers programme.	2nd
95.	International cooperation for economic growth and development:	
	(a) Implementation of the commitments and policies agreed upon in the Declaration on International Economic Cooperation, in particular the Revitalization of Economic Growth and Development of the Developing Countries;	2nd
	(b) Implementation of the International Development Strategy for the Fourth United Nations Development Decade.	2nd

Item No.	*Title*	*Allocation*
96.	International Conference on Population and Development.	2nd
97.	International conference on the financing of development.	2nd
98.	International Decade for Natural Disaster Reduction.	2nd
99.	Implementation of decisions and recommendations of the United Nations Conference on Environment and Development:	
	(a) Elaboration of an international convention to combat desertification in those countries experiencing serious drought and/or desertification, particularly in Africa;	2nd
	(b) Global Conference on the Sustainable Development of Small Island Developing States;	2nd
	(c) Sustainable use and conservation of the marine living resources of the high seas: United Nations Conference on Straddling Fish Stocks and Highly Migratory Fish Stocks.	2nd
100.	Special programmes of economic assistance.	2nd
101.	International assistance for the economic rehabilitation of Angola.	2nd
102.	Assistance for the reconstruction and development of El Salvador.	2nd
103.	International cooperation and assistance to alleviate the consequences of war in Croatia and to facilitate its recovery.	2nd
104.	Human resources development.	2nd
105.	Strengthening of international cooperation and coordination of efforts to study, mitigate and minimize the consequences of the Chernobyl disaster.	2nd
106.	Training and research: United Nations Institute for Training and Research.	2nd
107.	Elimination of racism and racial discrimination.	3rd
108.	Right of peoples to self-determination:	
	(a) Right of peoples to self-determination;	3rd
	(b) Effective realization of the right of self-determination through autonomy.	3rd
109.	Social development, including questions relating to the world social situation and to youth, ageing, disabled persons and the family.	3rd
110.	Crime prevention and criminal justice.	3rd
111.	Advancement of women.	3rd
112.	International drug control.	3rd
113.	Report of the United Nations High Commissioner for Refugees, questions relating to refugees, returnees and displaced persons and humanitarian questions.	3rd
114.	Human rights questions:	
	(a) Implementation of human rights instruments;	3rd
	(b) Human rights questions, including alternative approaches for improving the effective enjoyment of human rights and fundamental freedoms;	3rd
	(c) Human rights situations and reports of special rapporteurs and representatives.	3rd
115.	Situation of human rights in Estonia and Latvia.	3rd
116.	Information from Non-Self-Governing Territories transmitted under Article 73 *e* of the Charter of the United Nations.	4th
117.	Activities of those foreign economic and other interests which impede the implementation of the Declaration on the Granting of Independence to Colonial Countries and Peoples in Territories under colonial domination and efforts to eliminate colonialism, apartheid and racial discrimination in southern Africa.	4th
118.	Implementation of the Declaration on the Granting of Independence to Colonial Countries and Peoples by the specialized agencies and the international institutions associated with the United Nations.	4th
119.	Offers by Member States of study and training facilities for inhabitants of Non-Self-Governing Territories.	4th
120.	Financial reports and audited financial statements, and reports of the Board of Auditors:	
	(a) United Nations Institute for Training and Research;	5th
	(b) Voluntary funds administered by the United Nations High Commissioner for Refugees.	5th
121.	Review of the efficiency of the administrative and financial functioning of the United Nations.	5th
122.	Programme budget for the biennium 1992-1993.	5th
123.	Proposed programme budget for the biennium 1994-1995.	5th
124.	Improving the financial situation of the United Nations.	5th
125.	Joint Inspection Unit.	5th
126.	Pattern of conferences.	5th
127.	Scale of assessments for the apportionment of the expenses of the United Nations.	5th
128.	United Nations common system.	5th
129.	United Nations pension system.	5th
130.	Financing of the United Nations peace-keeping forces in the Middle East:	
	(a) United Nations Disengagement Observer Force;	5th
	(b) United Nations Interim Force in Lebanon.	5th
131.	Financing of the United Nations Angola Verification Mission.	5th

Item No.	*Title*	*Allocation*
132.	Financing of the activities arising from Security Council resolution 687(1991):	
	(a) United Nations Iraq-Kuwait Observation Mission;	5th
	(b) Other activities.	5th
133.	Financing of the United Nations Mission for the Referendum in Western Sahara.	5th
134.	Financing of the United Nations Observer Mission in El Salvador.	5th
135.	Financing of the United Nations Transitional Authority in Cambodia.	5th
136.	Financing of the United Nations Protection Force.	5th
137.	Financing of the United Nations Operation in Somalia II.	5th
138.	Administrative and budgetary aspects of the financing of the United Nations peace-keeping operations:	
	(a) Financing of the United Nations peace-keeping operations;	5th
	(b) Relocation of Belarus and Ukraine to the group of Member States set out in paragraph 3 *(c)* of General Assembly resolution 43/232.	5th
139.	United Nations Programme of Assistance in the Teaching, Study, Dissemination and Wider Appreciation of International Law.	6th
140.	Measures to eliminate international terrorism.	6th
141.	Progressive development of the principles and norms of international law relating to the new international economic order.	6th
142.	United Nations Decade of International Law.	6th
143.	Report of the International Law Commission on the work of its forty-fifth session.	6th
144.	Report of the United Nations Commission on International Trade Law on the work of its twenty-sixth session.	6th
145.	Report of the Committee on Relations with the Host Country.	6th
146.	Report of the Special Committee on the Charter of the United Nations and on the Strengthening of the Role of the Organization.	6th
147.	Convention on jurisdictional immunities of States and their property.	6th
148.	Request for an advisory opinion from the International Court of Justice.	6th
149.	Financing of the United Nations Operation in Mozambique.	5th
150.	Observer status for the Economic Cooperation Organization in the General Assembly.	Plenary
151.	United Nations initiative on opportunity and participation.	Plenary
152.	Question of responsibility for attacks on United Nations and associated personnel and measures to ensure that those responsible for such attacks are brought to justice.	6th
153.	Observer status for the Permanent Court of Arbitration in the General Assembly.	Plenary
154.	United Nations interim offices.	2nd
155.	Assistance in mine clearance.	Plenary
156.	Rationalization of the work and reform of the agenda of the First Committee.	1st
157.	Observer status for the Latin American Parliament in the General Assembly.	Plenary
158.	Observer status for the Conference on Security and Cooperation in Europe in the General Assembly.	Plenary
159.	Financing of the International Tribunal for the Prosecution of Persons Responsible for Serious Violations of International Humanitarian Law Committed in the Territory of the Former Yugoslavia since 1991	5th
160.	Financing of the United Nations Peace-keeping Force in Cyprus.	5th
161.	Review of the procedure provided for under article 11 of the statute of the Administrative Tribunal of the United Nations.	6th
162.	Financing of the United Nations Observer Mission in Georgia.	5th
163.	Programme budget for the biennium 1990-1991.	5th
164.	Financing of the United Nations Observer Mission Uganda-Rwanda.	5th
165.	Financing of the United Nations Mission in Haiti.	5th
166.	Financing of the United Nations Observer Mission in Liberia.	5th
167.	Building a peaceful and better world through sport.	Plenary
168.	Personnel questions.	5th
169.	Economic assistance to States affected by the implementation of the Security Council resolutions imposing sanctions against the Federal Republic of Yugoslavia (Serbia and Montenegro).	2nd
170.	The situation in Burundi.	Plenary
171.	Emergency assistance for the socio-economic rehabilitation of Rwanda.	2nd
172.	Necessity of adopting effective measures for the promotion and protection of the rights of children throughout the world who are victims of especially difficult circumstances, including armed conflicts.	3rd
173.	Financing of the United Nations Assistance Mission for Rwanda.	5th
174.	Financing of the United Nations Military Liaison Team in Cambodia.	5th
175.	Emergency action to combat locust infestation in Africa.	Plenary

Security Council

Agenda items considered during 1993

*Item
No.* [13]   *Title*

1. Admission of new Members.
2. The situation in Bosnia and Herzegovina.
3. The situation between Iraq and Kuwait.
4. The situation prevailing in and adjacent to the United Nations Protected Areas in Croatia.
5. An agenda for peace: preventive diplomacy, peacemaking and peace-keeping.
6. The situation in the Middle East.
7. The situation in Angola.
8. The situation in Georgia.
9. Date of an election to fill a vacancy in the International Court of Justice.
10. Central America: efforts towards peace.
11. Further report of the Secretary-General pursuant to Security Council resolution 743(1992) (situation in the former Yugoslavia).
12. Establishment of an international tribunal for the prosecution of persons responsible for serious violations of international humanitarian law committed in the territory of the former Yugoslavia.
13. The situation concerning Western Sahara.
14. The situation in Cambodia.
15. The situation relating to Rwanda.
16. The situation in Liberia.
17. The situation in Somalia.
18. Report of the Secretary-General pursuant to Security Council resolution 807(1993) (situation in the former Yugoslavia).
19. The situation relating to Nagorny Karabakh.
20. The question of South Africa.
21. The situation in Mozambique.
22. The situation in the Republic of Bosnia and Herzegovina.
23. Participation of the Federal Republic of Yugoslavia (Serbia and Montenegro) in the work of the Economic and Social Council.
24. Election of a member of the International Court of Justice.
25. The situation in Cyprus.
26. Letter dated 12 March 1993 from the Permanent Representative of the Democratic People's Republic of Korea to the United Nations addressed to the President of the Security Council; letter dated 19 March 1993 from the Secretary-General addressed to the President of the Security Council; note by the Secretary-General (situation between the International Atomic Energy Agency and the Democratic People's Republic of Korea on the question of safeguards).
27. Consideration of the draft report of the Security Council to the General Assembly.
28. The question concerning Haiti.
29. The situation in the former Yugoslav Republic of Macedonia.
30. Applications made under Article 50 of the Charter of the United Nations as a consequence of the implementation of measures imposed against the former Yugoslavia.
31. Follow-up to resolution 817(1993) (question of the name of "the former Yugoslav Republic of Macedonia").
32. United States notification of 26 June 1993 measures against Iraq.
33. United Nations Protection Force.
34. Complaint by Ukraine regarding the Decree of the Supreme Soviet of the Russian Federation concerning Sevastopol.
35. Conference on Security and Cooperation in Europe missions in Kosovo, Sandjak and Vojvodina, the Federal Republic of Yugoslavia (Serbia and Montenegro).
36. The situation in Tajikistan and along the Tajik-Afghan border.
37. The situation in Croatia.
38. Security of United Nations operations.
39. Navigation on the Danube river in the Federal Republic of Yugoslavia (Serbia and Montenegro).
40. The situation in Burundi.
41. Election of five members of the International Court of Justice.
42. Letters dated 20 and 23 December 1991, from France, the United Kingdom of Great Britain and Northern Ireland and the United States of America (France, United Kingdom and United States v. Libyan Arab Jamahiriya, in connection with legal procedures related to the attacks against Pan Am flight 103 and UTA flight 772).

---

[13]Numbers indicate the order in which items were taken up in 1993.

Economic and Social Council

Agenda of the organizational session for 1993
(26 January and 2-5, 12 and 16 February 1993)
and of the resumed organizational session for 1993
(6, 29 and 30 April and 26 May 1993)

Item No.	Title	Allocation
1.	Election of the Bureau.	Plenary
2.	Adoption of the agenda and other organizational matters.	Plenary
3.	Basic programme of work of the Council.	Plenary
4.	International Conference on Population and Development and its preparatory process.	Plenary
5.	Institutional arrangements to follow up the United Nations Conference on Environment and Development.	Plenary
6.	Elections and appointments to subsidiary and related bodies of the Council and confirmation of representatives on the functional commissions.	Plenary

Agenda of the substantive session of 1993
(28 June—30 July 1993)
and of the resumed substantive session of 1993
(21 October and 8 December 1993)

Item No.	Title	Allocation
	High-level segment (28-30 June)	
1.	Adoption of the agenda.	Plenary
2.	World Summit for Social Development, including the role of the United Nations system in promoting social development.	Plenary
3.	Policy dialogue and discussion on important developments in the world economy and international economic cooperation with heads of multilateral financial and trade institutions of the United Nations system.	Plenary
4.	Conclusion of the high-level segment.	Plenary
	Other segments	
1.	Adoption of the agenda and other organizational matters.	Plenary
2.	Coordination of the policies and activities of the specialized agencies and other bodies of the United Nations system related to the following themes:	
	(a) Coordination of humanitarian assistance: emergency relief and the continuum to rehabilitation and development;	Plenary
	(b) Coordination of the activities of the United Nations system in the fields of preventive action and intensification of the struggle against malaria and diarrhoeal diseases, in particular cholera.	Plenary
3.	Operational activities for development.	Plenary
4.	Coordination questions:	
	(a) Reports of the coordination bodies;	Plenary
	(b) Implementation of the Declaration on the Granting of Independence to Colonial Countries and Peoples by the specialized agencies and the international institutions associated with the United Nations;	Plenary
	(c) International cooperation in the field of informatics;	Plenary
	(d) Question of a United Nations year for tolerance;	Plenary
	(e) Multisectoral collaboration on tobacco or health.	Plenary
5.	Programme and related questions.	Plenary
6.	Special economic, humanitarian and disaster-relief assistance:	
	(a) Special programmes of economic assistance;	Plenary
	(b) Humanitarian assistance.	Plenary
7.	International Decade for Natural Disaster Reduction.	Plenary
8.	Strengthening of international cooperation and coordination of efforts to study, mitigate and minimize the consequences of the Chernobyl disaster.	Plenary
9.	Sustainable development.	Plenary
10.	Non-governmental organizations.	Plenary
11.	United Nations University.	Plenary

Item No.	Title	Allocation
12.	Statistical and cartographic questions:	
	(a) Statistics;	Plenary
	(b) Cartography.	Plenary
13.	Report of the United Nations High Commissioner for Refugees.	Plenary
14.	Regional cooperation.	Economic
15.	Development and international economic cooperation:	
	(a) Trade and development;	Economic
	(b) Food and agricultural development;	Economic
	(c) Science and technology for development;	Economic
	(d) Transnational corporations;	Economic
	(e) Natural resources;	Economic
	(f) Population questions;	Economic
	(g) Human settlements;	Economic
	(h) Environment;	Economic
	(i) Desertification and drought;	Economic
	(j) Transport of dangerous goods;	Economic
	(k) Effective mobilization and integration of women in development;	Economic
	(l) Economic and technical cooperation among developing countries;	Economic
	(m) Prevention and control of acquired immunodeficiency syndrome (AIDS).	Economic
16.	Permanent sovereignty over national resources in the occupied Palestinian and other Arab territories.	Economic
17.	Implementation of the Programme of Action for the Second Decade to Combat Racism and Racial Discrimination.	Social
18.	Human rights questions.	Social
19.	Advancement of women.	Social
20.	Social development.	Social
21.	Narcotic drugs.	Social
22.	Elections.	Plenary
23.	Committee for Development Planning.[14]	Plenary

Trusteeship Council

Agenda of the first part of the sixtieth session
(12-17 May and 1 November 1993)

Item No.   *Title*

1. Adoption of the agenda.
2. Report of the Secretary-General on credentials.
3. Election of the President and the Vice-President.
4. Examination of the annual report of the Administering Authority for the year ended 30 September 1992: Trust Territory of the Pacific Islands.
5. Examination of petitions.
6. Offers by Member States of study and training facilities for inhabitants of Trust Territories.
7. Dissemination of information on the United Nations and the International Trusteeship System in Trust Territories.
8. Cooperation with the Committee on the Elimination of Racial Discrimination.
9. Second Decade to Combat Racism and Racial Discrimination.
10. Attainment of self-government or independence by the Trust Territories and the situation in Trust Territories with regard to the implementation of the Declaration on the Granting of Independence to Colonial Countries and Peoples.
11. Cooperation with the Special Committee on the Situation with regard to the Implementation of the Declaration on the Granting of Independence to Colonial Countries and Peoples.
12. Adoption of the report of the Trusteeship Council to the Security Council.
13. Letter dated 13 May 1993 from the Deputy Permanent Representative of the United States of America to the United Nations addressed to the President of the Trusteeship Council, informing the Council of the intention of the Government of Palau to hold a plebiscite regarding the Compact of Free Association and inviting the Trusteeship Council to consider the dispatch of a mission to observe this plebiscite.
14. Letter dated 9 September 1993 from the Deputy Permanent Representative of the United States of America to the United Nations addressed to the President of the Trusteeship Council, informing the Council of the intention of the Government of Palau to hold a plebiscite regarding the Compact of Free Association and inviting the Trusteeship Council to consider the dispatch of a mission to observe this plebiscite.

---

[14]Item considered at the resumed substantive session only.

Appendix V

United Nations Information Centres and Services

ACCRA. United Nations Information Centre
Gamel Abdul Nassar/Liberia Roads
(P.O. Box 2339)
Accra, Ghana
Serving: Ghana, Sierra Leone

ADDIS ABABA. United Nations Information
Service, Economic Commission for Africa
Africa Hall
(P.O. Box 3001)
Addis Ababa, Ethiopia
Serving: Ethiopia

ALGIERS. United Nations Information Centre
19 Avenue Chahid El Ouali, Mustapha Sayed
(Boîte Postale 823, Alger-Gare, Algeria)
Algiers, Algeria
Serving: Algeria

AMMAN (relocated from Baghdad). United
Nations Information Service, Economic and
Social Commission for Western Asia
28 Abdul Hameed Sharaf Street
(P.O. Box 927115)
Amman, Jordan
Serving: Iraq

ANKARA. United Nations Information Centre
197 Atatürk Bulvari
(P.K. 407)
Ankara, Turkey
Serving: Turkey

ANTANANARIVO. United Nations Information
Centre
22 Rue Rainitovo, Antasahavola
(Boîte Postale 1348)
Antananarivo, Madagascar
Serving: Madagascar

ASUNCION. United Nations Information
Centre
Estrella 345, Edificio City (3er piso)
(Casilla de Correo 1107)
Asunción, Paraguay
Serving: Paraguay

ATHENS. United Nations Information Centre
36 Amalia Avenue
GR-10558 Athens, Greece
Serving: Cyprus, Greece, Israel

BANGKOK. United Nations Information Serv-
ice, Economic and Social Commission for
Asia and the Pacific
United Nations Building
Rajdamnern Avenue
Bangkok 10200, Thailand
Serving: Cambodia, Hong Kong, Lao
People's Democratic Republic, Malaysia,
Singapore, Thailand, Viet Nam

BEIRUT. United Nations Information Centre
Apt. No. 1, Fakhoury Building
Montée Bain Militaire, Ardati Street
(P.O. Box 4656)
Beirut, Lebanon
Serving: Jordan, Kuwait, Lebanon,
Syrian Arab Republic

BRAZZAVILLE. United Nations Information
Centre
Avenue Foch, Case Ortf 15
(P.O. Box 13210 or 1018)
Brazzaville, Congo
Serving: Congo

BRUSSELS. United Nations Information Centre
Avenue de Broqueville 40
1200 Brussels, Belgium
Serving: Belgium, Luxembourg,
Netherlands; liaison with EEC

BUCHAREST. United Nations Information
Centre
16 Aurel Vlaicu
(P.O. Box 1-701)
Bucharest, Romania
Serving: Romania

BUENOS AIRES. United Nations Information Centre
Junín 1940 (1er piso)
1113 Buenos Aires, Argentina
Serving: Argentina, Uruguay

BUJUMBURA. United Nations Information
Centre
117 Avenue de la Poste
(Boîte Postale 2160)
Bujumbura, Burundi
Serving: Burundi

CAIRO. United Nations Information Centre
1191 Corniche El Nile
World Trade Centre, P.O. Box 982
(Boîte Postale 262)
Cairo, Egypt
Serving: Egypt

COLOMBO. United Nations Information Centre
202-204 Bauddhaloka Mawatha
(P.O. Box 1505, Colombo)
Colombo 7, Sri Lanka
Serving: Sri Lanka

COPENHAGEN. United Nations Information
Centre
37 H.C. Andersens Boulevard
DK-1553 Copenhagen V, Denmark
Serving: Denmark, Finland, Iceland,
Norway, Sweden

DAKAR. United Nations Information Centre
12 Avenue Roume, Immeuble UNESCO
(Boîte Postale 154)
Dakar, Senegal
Serving: Cape Verde, Côte d'Ivoire,
Gambia, Guinea, Guinea-Bissau, Maurita-
nia, Senegal

DAR ES SALAAM. United Nations Information
Centre
Samora Machel Avenue
Matasalamat Building (1st floor)
(P.O. Box 9224)
Dar es Salaam, United Republic of Tanzania
Serving: United Republic of Tanzania

DHAKA. United Nations Information Centre
House 25, Road 11
Dhanmandi
(G.P.O. Box 3658, Dhaka 1000)
Dhaka 1209, Bangladesh
Serving: Bangladesh

GENEVA. United Nations Information Service, United Nations Office at Geneva
Palais des Nations
1211 Geneva 10, Switzerland
Serving: Bulgaria, Poland, Switzerland

HARARE. United Nations Information Centre
Dolphin House (ground floor)
123 L. Takawira Street/Union Avenue
(P.O. Box 4408)
Harare, Zimbabwe
Serving: Zimbabwe

ISLAMABAD. United Nations Information
Centre
House No. 26
88th Street, G-6/3
(P.O. Box 1107)
Islamabad, Pakistan
Serving: Pakistan

JAKARTA. United Nations Information Centre
Gedung Dewan Pers (5th floor)
32-34 Jalan Kebon Sirih
Jakarta, Indonesia
Serving: Indonesia

KABUL. United Nations Information Centre
Shah Mahmoud Ghazi Watt
(P.O. Box 5)
Kabul, Afghanistan
Serving: Afghanistan

KATHMANDU. United Nations Information
Centre
Pulchowk, Patan
(P.O. Box 107, Pulchowk)
Kathmandu, Nepal
Serving: Nepal

KHARTOUM. United Nations Information Centre
United Nations Compound
University Avenue
(P.O. Box 1992)
Khartoum, Sudan
  Serving: Somalia, Sudan

KINSHASA. United Nations Information Centre
Bâtiment Deuxième République
Boulevard du 30 Juin
(Boîte Postale 7248)
Kinshasa, Zaire
  Serving: Zaire

LAGOS. United Nations Information Centre
17 Kingsway Road, Ikoyi
(P.O. Box 1068)
Lagos, Nigeria
  Serving: Nigeria

LA PAZ. United Nations Information Centre
Av. Mariscal
Santa Cruz No. 1350
(Apartado Postal 9072)
La Paz, Bolivia
  Serving: Bolivia

LIMA. United Nations Information Centre
320/326 Genera Jacinto Lara
San Isidro
(P.O. Box 14-0199)
Lima, Peru
  Serving: Peru

LISBON. United Nations Information Centre
Rua Latino Coelho, 1
Ed. Aviz, Bloco A-1, 10º
1000 Lisbon, Portugal
  Serving: Portugal

LOME. United Nations Information Centre
107 Boulevard du 13 Janvier
(Boîte Postale 911)
Lomé, Togo
  Serving: Benin, Togo

LONDON. United Nations Information Centre
18 Buckingham Gate
London SW1E 6LB, England
  Serving: Ireland, United Kingdom

LUSAKA. United Nations Information Centre
P.O. Box 32905
Lusaka 10101, Zambia
  Serving: Botswana, Malawi, Swaziland, Zambia

MADRID. United Nations Information Centre
Avenida General Perón, 32-1
(P.O. Box 3400, 28080 Madrid)
28020 Madrid, Spain
  Serving: Spain

MANAGUA. United Nations Information Centre
Reparto Bolonia
Porton Hospital Militar IC Lago
IC Abajo
Managua, Nicaragua
  Serving: Nicaragua

MANAMA. United Nations Information Centre
Villa 131, Road 2803
Segaya
(P.O. Box 26004, Manama)
Manama 328, Bahrain
  Serving: Bahrain, Qatar, United Arab Emirates

MANILA. United Nations Information Centre
NEDA Building
106 Amorsolo Street
Legaspi Village, Makati
(P.O. Box 7285 (DAPO), 1300 Domestic Road, Pasay City)
Metro Manila, Philippines
  Serving: Papua New Guinea, Philippines, Solomon Islands

MASERU. United Nations Information Centre
Corner Kingsway and Hilton Hill Road
opposite Sanlam Centre
(P.O. Box 301, Maseru 100)
Maseru, Lesotho
  Serving: Lesotho

MEXICO CITY. United Nations Information Centre
Presidente Masaryk 29 (7º piso)
11570 México, D.F., Mexico
  Serving: Cuba, Dominican Republic, Mexico

MOSCOW. United Nations Information Centre
4/16 Ulitsa Lunacharskogo
Moscow 121002, Russian Federation
  Serving: Russian Federation

NAIROBI. United Nations Information Centre
United Nations Office
Gigiri
(P.O. Box 34135)
Nairobi, Kenya
  Serving: Kenya, Seychelles, Uganda

NEW DELHI. United Nations Information Centre
55 Lodi Estate
New Delhi 110003, India
  Serving: Bhutan, India

OUAGADOUGOU. United Nations Information Centre
Avenue Georges Konseiga
Secteur No. 4
(Boîte Postale 135)
Ouagadougou 01, Burkina Faso
  Serving: Burkina Faso, Chad, Mali, Niger

PANAMA CITY. United Nations Information Centre
Street 53 and Via Ricardo Arango
Mitsui Bank Building (1st floor)
(P.O. Box 6-9083 El Dorado)
Panama City, Panama
  Serving: Panama

PARIS. United Nations Information Centre
1 Rue Miollis
75732, Paris Cedex 15, France
  Serving: France

PORT OF SPAIN. United Nations Information Centre
2nd floor, Bretton Hall
16 Victoria Avenue
(P.O. Box 130)
Port of Spain, Trinidad, W.I.
  Serving: Antigua and Barbuda, Bahamas, Barbados, Belize, Dominica, Grenada, Guyana, Jamaica, Netherlands Antilles, Saint Kitts and Nevis, Saint Lucia, Saint Vincent and the Grenadines, Suriname, Trinidad and Tobago

PRAGUE. United Nations Information Centre
Panska 5
11000 Prague 1, Czech Republic
  Serving: Czech Republic, Slovakia

RABAT. United Nations Information Centre
Angle Charia Ibnouzaid
Et Zankat Roundanat, No. 6
(Boîte Postale 601)
Rabat, Morocco
  Serving: Morocco

RIO DE JANEIRO. United Nations Information Centre
Palácio Itamaraty
Av. Marechal Floriano 196
20080 Rio de Janeiro, RJ Brazil
  Serving: Brazil

ROME. United Nations Information Centre
Palazzetto Venezia
Piazza San Marco 50
00186 Rome, Italy
  Serving: Holy See, Italy, Malta

SANA'A. United Nations Information Centre
Al-Khorashi Building
opposite Awqaf Housing Complex
Sharaa Al-Siteen
(P.O. Box 551)
Sana'a, Yemen
  Serving: Yemen.

SAN SALVADOR. United Nations Information Centre
Edificio Escalón (2º piso)
Paseo General Escalón y 87 Avenida Norte
Colonia Escalón
(Apartado Postal 2157)
San Salvador, El Salvador
  Serving: El Salvador

SANTA FE DE BOGOTA. United Nations Information Centre
Calle 100 No. 8A-55, Of. 815
(Apartado Aéreo 058964)
Santa Fé de Bogotá 2, Colombia
  Serving: Colombia, Ecuador, Venezuela

SANTIAGO. United Nations Information Service, Economic Commission for Latin America and the Caribbean
Edificio Naciones Unidas
Avenida Dag Hammarskjöld
(Avenida Dag Hammarskjöld s/n, Casilla 179-D)
Santiago, Chile
  Serving: Chile

SYDNEY. United Nations Information Centre
Suite 1 (2nd floor), 125 York Street
(P.O. Box 4045, Sydney N.S.W. 2001)
Sydney N.S.W. 2000, Australia
  Serving: Australia, Fiji, Kiribati, Nauru,
New Zealand, Samoa, Tonga, Tuvalu,
Vanuatu

TEHRAN. United Nations Information Centre
185 Ghaem Magham Farahani Avenue
(P.O. Box 15875-4557, Tehran)
Tehran, 15868 Iran
  Serving: Iran

TOKYO. United Nations Information Centre
UNU Building (8th floor)
53-70 Jingumae 5-chome, Shibuya-ku
Tokyo 150, Japan
  Serving: Japan, Trust Territory of the
Pacific Islands

TRIPOLI. United Nations Information Centre
Muzzafar Al Aftas Street
Hay El-Andalous (2)
(P.O. Box 286)
Tripoli, Libyan Arab Jamahiriya
  Serving: Libyan Arab Jamahiriya

TUNIS. United Nations Information Centre
61 Boulevard Bab-Benat
(Boîte Postale 863)
Tunis, Tunisia
  Serving: Tunisia

VIENNA. United Nations Information Serv-
  ice, United Nations Office at Vienna
Vienna International Centre
Wagramer Strasse 5
(P.O. Box 500, A-1400 Vienna)
A-1220 Vienna, Austria
  Serving: Austria, Germany, Hungary

WASHINGTON, D.C. United Nations Information Centre
1775 K Street, N.W., Suite 400
Washington, D.C. 20006, United States
  Serving: United States

WINDHOEK. United Nations Information
Centre
134 Robert Mugabe Avenue
(Private Bag 13351)
Windhoek, Namibia
  Serving: Namibia

YANGON. United Nations Information Centre
6 Natmauk Road
(P.O. Box 230)
Yangon, Myanmar
  Serving: Myanmar

YAOUNDE. United Nations Information Centre
Immeuble Kamdem, Rue Joseph Clère
(Boîte Postale 836)
Yaoundé, Cameroon
  Serving: Cameroon, Central African
Republic, Gabon

Indexes

Using the subject index

The index contains two types of entries:

Subject terms, including geographical names, are in most cases based on the subject descriptors used in the United Nations Bibliographical Information System (UNBIS), published in the *UNBIS Thesaurus* (United Nations Publication: Sales No. E.85.I.20). In order to minimize subentries, the index lists broad and narrow terms in their separate alphabetical positions; for example, "human rights", "racial discrimination" and "right to development". Subjects pertaining to the United Nations or the system as a whole, such as "contributions (UN)", "finances (UN)" and "staff (UN/UN system)", are indexed separately, with cross-references under "United Nations".

Names of organizations and subsidiary bodies, conferences, United Nations Secretariat departments and offices, programmes, and special decades and observances are indexed under their key word: Apartheid, Spec. Ct. against; Development Decade, 4th UN; Law of the Sea, 3rd UN Cf. on the; Maritime Day, World; Peace-keeping Operations, Department of. Names of specialized agencies and of non–United Nations organizations are alphabetized under the first word of their title: Inter-American Cs. on Human Rights; World Meteorological Organization.

Bodies/subjects/topics are listed only when substantive information is given.

Abbreviations

In addition to the abbreviations listed on p. xv, the subject index uses the following:

ASG	Assistant Secretary-General
CD	Conference on Disarmament
cf(s).	conference(s)
cl(s).	council(s)
cs(s).	commission(s)
ct(s).	committee(s)
DC	Disarmament Commission
DG	Director-General
LOS	Law of the Sea
mtg(s).	meeting(s)
sess.	session
SCPDPM	Subcommission on Prevention of Discrimination and Protection of Minorities of the Commission on Human Rights
spec.	special
UNCLS	United Nations Conference on the Law of the Sea
UNJSPB	United Nations Joint Staff Pension Board
USG	Under-Secretary-General

Subject index

Page numbers in bold-face type indicate resolutions and decisions

Accountants, International Federation of, 773

Accounting and Reporting, Intergovernmental Working Group of Experts on International Standards of (TNCs Cs.), 773, **774** (SG/ESC); 11th sess., 1367; membership increase, proposal deferred, 773; members/officers, 1367

accounting/auditing (UN) (1992), 1206, **1206-1207** (SG/GA); standards of, 1208, **1208** (SG/GA); state of, global review, 773 (SG); strengthening, implementation of 1992 recommendations, 1207, **1207** (SG/ACABQ/GA)

Accounting Standards, Working Party on: mtgs., 1208

acquired immunodeficiency syndrome/human immunodeficiency virus (AIDS/HIV), 304 (OAU), 605 (ECA), 689, 690, 691, 693, 699 (UNDP), 1059 (UNICEF), 1269 (WHO/ESC)

attitudes/beliefs towards, 992 (UNU)

cases of, estimated, 1269 (WHO)

contraceptives and, 834 (UNFPA)

coordination in UN: Task Force on, 972, **972** (SG/ESC)

& discrimination, 869-70 (Human Rights Cs./ESC/Spec. Rapporteur/SCPDPM)

education, 1260 (UNESCO/WHO)

information/education activities, 834 (UNFPA), 1266 (WHO cf.)

national programmes, technical assistance, 1269 (WHO)

prevention/control, 22 (SG), 827-28 (ESC), 971-72, **972** (WHO DG/GA/UNDP/ESC), 1057 (UNICEF)

WHO Global Programme on, 972

see also under children; maternal and child health care; youth

acute respiratory infections, 1061 (UNICEF), 1268 (WHO); "sick child initiative", 1061 (UNICEF/WHO)

Ad Hoc Committee . . . for specific ct., see key word(s) of title

Administration and Management, Department of (Secretariat), 11; USG named UN Security Coordinator, 96 (SG); ASG posts, proposed abolition of, 1209, 1210 (SG/ACABQ); offices (Inspections/Investigations; General Services; Human Resources; Cf. Services), 1373; USG/Deputy (Controller), 1373

administrative and budgetary questions, 1171-1242; see also budget (UN); financial situation (UN); staff (UN/UN system)

Administrative and Budgetary Questions, Advisory Ct. on (ACABQ): report, 1176, **1177**

administrative and management questions (UN/UN system), 11 (SG), 1209-23, 1241-42; Inspections and Investigations, ASG for, 11 (SG); integrated information system, 11 (SG); see also conferences/mtgs. (UN); documentation (UN); Secretariat

(UN); staff (UN/UN system); and under United Nations main heading

Administrative Ct. on Coordination, see Coordination, Administrative Ct. on (ACC)

Administrative Tribunal, ILO: judgements, **1213** (GA)

Administrative Tribunal, UN, **1213** (GA); judgements, 1223 (GA); members/officers, 1354

Administrative Tribunal Judgements, Ct. on Applications for Review of (GA): sess./members/officers, 1351

aeronautical meteorology: new codes, 1306 (WMO/ICAO)

Afghanistan: cholera epidemic, 383, 734; refugee situation, 60 (SG), 734, 738, 1071, 1087; see also Tajikistan

Afghanistan, UN Office for the Coordination of Humanitarian and Economic Assistance Relating to, 734-35, 738

Afghanistan and Pakistan, Office of the SG in, 37 (SG), 383; financing, 383 (SG/GA)

Afghanistan situation, 36-37 (SG), 381-83 (SG/GA/OSGAP); consideration deferred, 382 (GA)

cease-fire, 382 (SG); Joint Cs. (Islamic Cf./Afghan parties), 382

emergency humanitarian assistance/relief, 382 (SG), 731-32, **732-33** (SG/GA); draft action rehabilitation plan, 731

human rights, 929-32 (Spec. Rapporteur, 929, 930; Human Rights Cs., 929-30; GA, **930-31**); of refugees, 731 (Tripartite Cs.), 736, 929-30; Spec. Rapporteur, mandate renewed, 930 (ESC)

mine clearance, 54 (SG), 734

peace accords (March), 381, 382; (May) 382

Africa, 26 (SG), 225-306, 587-608 (ECA), 690 (UNDP), 1042 (UNIFEM), 1056-57 (UNICEF), 1265, 1267 (WHO), 1278 (IFC), 1293 (ITU), 1304 (WMO), 1318-19 (IFAD)

agriculture, 590 (ECA)

civil aviation, technical assistance, 1294 (ICAO)

commodities, diversification fund: FAO feasibility study, 712, **713** (SG/GA)

communications, mtg. of African experts, 195 (IPDC)

conflicts in, prevention/management/resolution, OAU-UN cooperation, 304, **305** (SG/GA)

debt crisis/resources, 26 (SG), 590 (ECA), 711 (UNDP), 711-29 (SG), **713** (GA)

development policy, 592-95 (ECA); & indigenous NGOs, role of, 26 (SG/ECA); information for, 594, **594-95** (PADIS/ESC/GA); see also Africa in the 1990s, UN New Agenda for the Development of

drug abuse/trafficking, 1106 (HON-LEA/INCB/UNDCP)

economic cooperation, 589, 592 (ECA/MULPOCs)

economic/social trends, 589-91 (ECA), 592-93 (ECA survey), 673 (1993 World Economic Survey); subregional performance, 591

education, 1063 (UNICEF)

energy development, 602

environment, 603, 711

fisheries, 602-603

food/agriculture, 602 (ECA); food aid, 990-91 (WFP), 1256 (FAO)

human settlements, 605 (ECA); urban management workshop, 847

industrial development, 596-98 (ECA/IDDA); see also Africa, 2nd Industrial Development Decade for (1993-2002)

international trade, 710-11 (UNCTAD); implications of Uruguay Round, 588, 596; export/import trends, 590-91

least developed countries in, 26 (SG), 357 (UNDP), 591 (ECA), 711, **713** (UNDP/GA)

locust/grasshopper infestation, emergency action, 745, **745-46** (FAO/GA)

marine affairs, 601 (ECA)

mass communication: expert mtg., 195 (IPDC); & education informatics, 195 (UNESCO); & press freedom, 196 (IPDC)

Multinational Programming and Operational Centres (MULPOCS): strengthening, 588, 589, 592 (ECA)

natural resources development, 601-602 (ECA)

population, 605 (ECA); Dakar/Ngor Declaration, 605; UNFPA allocations, 836

public administration, 595 (ECA); & fiscal affairs, 595-96

refugee assistance, 1079-80, **1080-82** (UNHCR/SG/GA); expenditures, 1080; protection of refugees, 1969 OAU Convention on, 1089; see also country names and regional entries

science/technology, 800 (UNFSTD), 1286 (Intergovernmental Experts Ct./ECA)

social development/humanitarian affairs, 28 (SG), 603-605; Human Development Agenda, 603 (ECA); social situation, 999 (SG)

space applications, 184 (UN Programme/ESA), 185 (UN Programme/UNDP); proposed centre, 183

technical cooperation, 690 (UNDP)

tourism development, 600-601 (ECA)

735; delivery of, 451, 482 (UNHCR/ICRC); & refugees, **448**, 451 (GA/UNHCR)

military flights, ban on: violations, 463-65 (communications, 463; SC, 463, **463-64**; SG, 463, 464, 465)

safe areas: situation (March/April), 451-55 (communications, 451, 452, 455; SC, 451-52, **452-53**, 453-54; SC mission, 454-55); (May/June), 455-59 (communications, 455, 456; SC, **455-56, 457-58**, 458, **459**; SG, 458-59); (July-Dec.), 459-60 (communications/SC); fact-finding mission, **453** (SC), 453 (composition), 454-55 (report)

Vance-Owen peace plan: negotiations, 467-68, 468-75 (SC, 468, 469-70, 470, 471, **471-74**, 474; SG, 468, 468-69, 470, 470-71, 474-75); confederation proposals, 475-77, **477-78** (ICFY/SC); deliberations, 478 (ICFY); Dec. summary, 478

Botswana: LDC list, 675; & South Africa, **873** (GA)

Brazil: economic trends, 636 (ECLAC); education, 1271 (World Bank); fellowships, remote sensing, 184; refugees in, 1082 (UNHCR); UNDP project, 693; urban development/water supply, 1273 (World Bank)

breast-feeding, 1054, 1061 (UNICEF); Baby-friendly Hospital Initiative, 1061, 1266 (UNICEF/WHO)

Breast Milk Substitutes, International Code of Marketing of, 1266 (WHO)

British Virgin Islands, 170, **170-72, 173-74** (Colonial Countries Ct./GA); NSGT information to UN, 164; scholarships to, 163

Brunei: admission to GATT, 1326

budget (UN) (1990-1991): appropriations, final, 1194-95, **1195** (SG/GA)

budget (UN) (1992-1993), 1191-94 appropriations, revised, 1191-92 (SG/ACABQ/GA); final, 1192-94 (SG/GA); 2nd performance report, 1194 (SG/ACABQ/GA)

budget (UN) (1994-1995), 1195-1203 appropriations, 1195, **1195-96** (SG/GA); financing for 1994, **1197** (GA); income estimates, **1197** (GA)

contingency fund, 1203 (SG/ACABQ/GA)

questions relating to, **1197-1201** (GA) unforeseen/extraordinary expenses, 1201, **1201-1202** (SG/ACABQ/GA)

Working Capital Fund, 1202, **1202-1203** (Advisory Group/GA)

see also contributions (UN); financial situation (UN); programmes (UN)

Buenos Aires Plan of Action for Promoting and Implementing TCDC, see under technical cooperation among developing countries (TCDC)

building materials, see construction/building materials

Bulgaria: industry loan, 1272 (World Bank); impact of SC sanctions against Yugoslavia (Serbia and Montenegro), 717

Burkina Faso, 690 (UNDP), 1284 (IDA)

Burundi: elections in, 262; military coup, 262-64 (SC, 262, 263-64; Spec. Envoy, 262; SG, 262-63; GA **263**), 724; emer-

gency aid/refugees, 724-25, 1079 (GA/SC/UNHCR); Regional Summit, 263; SG Spec. Representative, appointment, 263

business practices, restrictive, see restrictive business practices

Cambodia: declared constitutional monarchy, 374, 375, **380** (SG/SC); telecommunications, 1300 (ITU); UNDP activities, 689, 691; UNFPA missions to, 837

Cambodia, UN Advance Mission in (UNAMIC): financing, 375-76, **376** (SG/ACABQ/GA), 377, 378 (SG)

Cambodia, UN Military Liaison Team in: Chief Officer, 379, 380, 1361; establishment, 378-79, **380** (SG/SC); financing, 380 (SG/SC), 380-81, **381** (SG/ACABQ/GA)

Cambodia, UN Transitional Authority in (UNTAC), 49, 50 (SG), 360, 361-63, **363-65** (SG/SC), 365 (communications), 365-67, **367** (SG/SC); Commander/Spec. Representative, 1361; financing, 375-76, **376-77** (SG/GA), 377-78, **378** (SG/ACABQ/GA); personnel, safety of, **367**, 367-70 (SG/SC); SG progress reports, 361-63, 365-67, 368-69; termination/completion of mandate, 372, 373, **374** (SG/SC), 374, 375 (SG/SC)

Cambodia Mine Action Centre, **380** (SC); future status, 373

Cambodia situation, 49-50 (SG), 360-81

cease-fire: implementation/violations, 361-62, **364** (SC), 365, 372

civil administration/civil police, 362, 363

Constituent Assembly, inaugural mtg./cts. established/officers, 371

elections in, 49-50 (SG), 361-63, **363-65** (SG/SNC/SC), 366-67, **367** (SG/SC), 370, **370** (Spec. Representative/SC); official results, 370-71, **371** (SG/SC); post-election period, 726-30 (communications, 372; SC, **373-74**, 374; SG, 371-72, 372-73)

& human rights, 361 (UNTAC/SG), 365, 373, 374 (SG), 874 (Human Rights Cs.), 932, **932-33** (Human Rights Cs./GA); Spec. Representative, appointment, 874, **932-33** (GA)

Interim Joint Administration (Provisional National Government): establishment, Co-Chairmen, 371-72 (SG); financial aid to, 372, 375, 377 (SG)

mine clearance programme, 54 (SG), 373, **380** (SG/SC); Trust Fund for, 378; UNTAC unit, deployment extended, 374, **380** (SG/SC)

natural resources, export moratorium, 363; Declaration, SNC mtg., 363, **364** (SG/SC); UNTAC draft plan, 366

Paris Agreements (1991), 360-61; implementation, 362, **364**, **367** (SG/SC)

reconstruction/rehabilitation, 363, 366; International Ct. on, 373 (SG)

refugee repatriation, 49 (SG), 362, 365 (SG), 1071, 1085 (UNHCR); Cambodia-Viet Nam situation, 1085

Supreme National Cl. (SNC), 361, 363, **364**, 373 (SG/SC); & natural resources protection, 363, **364** (SG/SC)

UN integrated office, proposed establishment, 373; & Military Liaison Team, 379 (SG)

Cameroon: press ethics seminar, 195 (IPDC)

Canada: drug control, 1108; refugee situation, 1082; withdrawal from UNIDO, 1321

cancer, 1269 (WHO)

cannabis, 1106, 1107, 1108

Capital Development Fund, UN, see Development Fund, UN Capital (UNCDF)

capital punishment, see death penalty, abolition of

cardiovascular diseases, 1269 (WHO)

Caribbean Community (CARICOM): 14th Heads of State Cf., documents circulation, 221

Caribbean Cl. for Science and Technology, 642

Caribbean Development and Cooperation Ct., 642

Caribbean Documentation Centre, 642

Caribbean Mtg. of Experts for a Regional Plan of Action on Population and Development, 831

Caribbean region, 642 (ECLAC), 1057-58 (UNICEF); natural resources exploitation, **159** (GA); population activities, 642; refugees, 1082-83; seminar, 152 (Colonial Countries Ct.); & ship waste project, 1154 (World Bank/IMO); water-quality training, 1307 (WMO); see also Americas; Economic Cs. for Latin America and the Caribbean; and country names and subject entries

Caribbean States, Organization of Eastern, 642

Cartagena Commitment (1992): & technology transfer, 800

Cartographic Cf. for Asia and the Pacific, 13th UN Regional, see Asia and the Pacific, 13th UN Regional Cartographic Cf. for

Cartographic Cf. for the Americas, 5th UN Regional, see Americas, 5th UN Regional Cartographic Cf. for the

cartography, 601, 602 (ECA), 790-91; see also geographical names

cassava production, 1255 (FAO)

Cayman Islands, 170, **170-72**, 174 (Colonial Countries Ct./GA)

Censuses, Intersecretariat Working Group on (ECE), 635

Central Africa: economic trends, 591; security issues, 133-34, **134** (Standing Ct./GA)

Central Africa, Standing Advisory Ct. on Security Questions in: mtgs., 133, **134** (GA), 147

Central African States, Economic Community for: non-aggression pact, 133-34, **134** (SG/GA)

Central America: economic cooperation, 308-309; peace/security issues, 307-12; refugee assistance, 1082, 1083; social/economic trends, 643 (ECLAC); technical cooperation, 309; see also Americas; Caribbean region; country names

World, 1304; Climate Data and Monitoring Programme, World, 1304; Climate Impact Assessment and Response Strategies Programme, World, 813, 1304; Climate Research Programme, World, 1304, 1305; Intergovernmental Mtg., 1304; marine research/training, 1261 (UNESCO/WMO/ICSU)

Climatology, Cs. for: 11th sess., 1304

coal: clean technology promotion, 631 (ECE), 788

Coal, Working Party on (ECE): 3rd sess., 631

coarse grains, roots, tubers: production, 590 (ECA), 620 (ESCAP), 1255 (FAO); Regional Coordination Centre for Research and Development, 620 (ESCAP)

cocaine abuse, 1106, 1107, 1108

Cocoa Agreement, International, 760

Coffee Agreement, 1983 International: extensions/suspensions, 760; new agreement, negotiations, 760

Colombia, 693 (UNDP), 1271 (World Bank), 1280 (IFC); & Central America cooperation (Group of 3), 309 (SG); drug cartels/manufacturing, 1108

colonial countries, 152-79
  human rights violations in, **873** (GA)
  information dissemination, 161, **161-62** (Colonial Countries Ct./DPI/GA); publications, **161** (GA)
  military activities in, 160, **160-61** (Colonial Countries Ct./GA)
  see also International Trusteeship System; Non-Self-Governing Territories; self-determination of peoples; and under names of Territories

Colonial Countries and Peoples, 1960 Declaration on the Granting of Independence to: implementation, **153-54** (GA); & foreign interests impeding, 158-59, **159-60** (Colonial Countries Ct./GA); by international organizations, 154, **154-56**, 156-**58** (Colonial Countries Ct./SG/ESC/GA); technical cooperation/assistance to, report, 154, **155** (ESC President/ESC)

Colonial Countries and Peoples, Spec. Ct. on the Situation with regard to the Implementation of the Declaration on the Granting of Independence to (Colonial Countries Ct.), 152; members/officers, 1354; rationalization of work, 152 (working group); report, **153** (GA); Subct. on Small Territories, Petitions, Information and Assistance, 152, 1354; Working Group, 152

Colonialism, Decade for the Eradication of (1990-2000): Action Plan, implementation, 71, **153** (Colonial Countries Ct./GA)

Colonial Territories, Week of Solidarity with the Peoples of All, as well as Those in South Africa, 161

Committee ... for specific ct., see key word(s) of title

commodities, 759-61; Coding System, 1113; Common Fund for, 759; prices decline in, 759; supply and export earnings, 759; see also agricultural products; metals; minerals; and names of individual commodities

Commodities, 1980 Agreement Establishing the Common Fund for: & ITC role, 757; signatures/ratifications, 759

Commodities, Standing Ct. on (TDB): ad hoc mtgs., bauxite, 760; Intergovernmental

Expert Groups, on Iron Ore, 761, on Tungsten, 761; members, 1356

Commodity Description and Coding System, Harmonized (Customs Cooperation Cl.), 641 (ECLAC), 1113, 1115 (SG/Statistical Cs.)

Commonwealth, mtg. of heads of Government: documents circulation, 221; & Mediterranean security, 85, **86** (GA)

Commonwealth of Independent States (CIS): economic trends, 627-28; & GSP, 756 (TDB); nuclear safety, 692 (UNDP/IAEA); security/disarmament, symposium, 145; & Tajikistan, 515, 516; telecommunications, 1300 (ITU); UNDP projects, 692, 697

communication, see information; mass communication; public information (UN); telecommunications

Communication, International Programme for the Development of (IPDC), 194-95, 1263; Intergovernmental Cl./Bureau, 195, 1263; projects, 195

communications satellites, 183, 184 (UNISPACE-82), 185 (UN Space Programme); role in medical advice, 188; see also geostationary orbit; remote sensing; satellites; telecommunications

Comorian island of Mayotte, 264, **265-66** (SG/GA), **873** (GA)

Comoros, Islamic Federal Republic of the, 264; admission to IFC, 1277

Comparison Programme, International (ICP), 1113 (SG); see also price statistics

Conferences, Ct. on: sess., 1233; members/officers, 1351

conferences/meetings (UN), 1233-36
  calendar of: (1993), 1233-34; (1994-1995), 1234, **1235** (Ct. on Cfs./GA)
  services, 11-12 (SG), 1234-35, **1235-36** (SG/Ct. on Cfs./GA); coordination, 1235, **1235**; economy measures, effect of, 1233; staff workload, 1236 (GA); Bangkok Centre inaugurated, 28; Vienna Centre, UNIDO-UN agreement, 1234, **1235**
  see also documents (UN); geographic and subject entries

Conference Services, Office of: Director, 1373; restructuring, 1233

conservation: wildlife, 818 (UNEP)

construction/building materials: 1st global consultation, 846 (UNCHS/UNIDO)

Consular Relations, 1963 Vienna Convention on/Optional Protocols: States parties, 1147

container transport, see multimodal transport

continental shelf, 1150; see also Greenland; East Timor

Continental Shelf, Cs. on Limits of the: election of members, 1149

Contraceptive Requirements and Logistic Management Needs in Developing Countries, Global Initiative on (UNFPA), 834, 836 (UNDP Ct.)

contraceptives: & AIDS prevention, 834 (UNFPA/WHO); see also family planning

Contract Practices, Working Group on International (UNCITRAL), 1166

Contract Practices in Industry, Working Party on International (ECE), 629

contributions (UN): assessments, new members, 1203-1204, **1204** (Contributions

Ct./GA); for 1995-1997, **1204-1205**, 1205 (GA); methodology, 1205, **1205** (Contributions Ct./GA); to UN regular budget, 1205-1206 (SG)

Contributions, Ct. on (GA): 53rd sess., 1203

Cook Islands: admission to IFAD, 1318

Coordination, Administrative Ct. on (ACC), 1129-30 (ESC); Joint Mtgs. with CPC, 1131; members, 1367; 1992 overview report, 1130; review, 13-14 (SG); subsidiary bodies, 1130, 1367

Coordination, Ct. for Programme and (CPC), 1131 (ESC/GA); members/officers, 1365; 33rd sess., 1131, 1365

coordination in UN system: inter-agency, 1129-30; with financial systems, 1130-31 (JIU/ESC); humanitarian affairs, Inter-Agency Standing Ct., 720; Joint Mtgs. CPC/ACC, 1131 (ESC); UN programmes, 1131 (CPC/ESC/GA); see also Economic and Social Cl. (ESC); Joint Inspection Unit (JIU); programmes (UN)

copyright/neighbouring rights: conventions, 1314 (WIPO); see also industrial property; intellectual property; patents

Costa Rica, 1280 (IFC); & refugee situation, 1083; see also Central America situation

Côte d'Ivoire, 1278 (IFC)

Cotopaxi space station, see under space

Crime and Justice Research Institute, UN Interregional, **1009** (ESC); Board of Trustees, members, 1006, 1368

Crime and the Treatment of Offenders, 9th UN Congress on the Prevention of (1995): preparations, 1006, 1021, **1021-27** (Cs./SG/ESC)

crime prevention and criminal justice, 1006-1007, **1007**, 1007-11, **1011-12** (SG/ESC/GA); information activities, **1010** (ESC); money laundering, 1013, **1013-14** (SG/ESC); operational activities/coordination, 1006, **1009** (SG/ESC); organized crime, Cf. on, 1012, **1012-13** (SG/ESC); regional institutes, 1019 (SG); standards/norms, **1011-12**, 1019 (ESC/SG); survey on UN activities, 996 (SG); technical assistance, 1019 (SG); urban crime, proposed guidelines, 1014, **1014-15** (Cs./ESC); see also death penalty; drugs of abuse; human rights: judicial system; juveniles; torture

Crime Prevention and Criminal Justice, Cs. on: 2nd sess., 1006 (ESC); members/officers, 1362

Crime Prevention and Criminal Justice Branch, UN: & UN entities, **1010-11** (ESC); & drug money laundering, 1093, **1099**, 1101 (UNDCP/GA); & illicit drug traffic, 1091; technical assistance, 1019 (SG)

Crime Prevention and Criminal Justice Programme, UN: implementation, 1006-12 (SG, 1006-1007; ESC, **1007-11**, **1011-12**); strengthening, **1007** (ESC)

Criminal Police Organization, International (Interpol), **1092** (ESC)

Croatia: admission to FAO, 1255; to IAEA, 1245; to IDA, 1283; to IFC, 1277; to ILO, 1250; to World Bank, 1271; assistance to, 27, 493 (SG), 734-35, **735** (SG/UNDP/GA); see also Slovenia: maritime boundary dispute

Croatia: UN protected areas/pink zones, situation in, 482-93

400-401, 401, 402); Agreed Minutes, 400, 402 (SC)

cease-fire (1991): compliance, 398-99 (UN Spec. Cs./IAEA); financing of, consideration deferred, 399 (GA)

chemical/biological weapons/ballistic missiles, 423-24 (UNSCOM); see also nuclear issues: high-level talks (below)

compensation claims, 426-27 (communications/UN Cs.)

& DMZ, 403-406 (Cs., 403; SC, 404-405, **406**; SG, 403-404, 405-406)

environmental consequences, 820 (UNEP)

humanitarian assistance, 428 (SG/inter-agency programme); escrow account (oil product sales), 430 (SG); 1992 Memorandum of Understanding, implementation, 399, 428

Kurds/minority populations, 428-29

Kuwaiti property, return of, 403 (UN Coordinator), 425-26

nuclear issues: high-level talks, 420-23, 423-25 (Spec. Cs.); monitoring/verification, 425 (UNSCOM); on-site inspections, 411-20; spec. mission, 419-20 (UNSCOM)

repatriation, 428 (communications)

sanctions, 1991 guidelines, 427, 427-28 (SC Sanctions Ct./communications/SC)

UN Compensation Cs./Fund: finances, 426, 430; Governing Cl., 426

UN Spec. Cs. on Monitoring (UNSCOM): finances/privileges/immunities, 414

War Crimes Report (US), 429-30

Iron Deficiency, International Cs. for the Prevention of (UNU Group for Control of), 992-93

Iron Ore, Intergovernmental Group of Experts on (Commodities Standing Ct.): 2nd sess., 761

irradiated nuclear fuel, see under radioactive wastes

Irrigation and Drainage, International Programme for Technology Research for, 786

Irrigation Management Information System, Scheme, 1258 (FAO)

Islamic Cf., Organization of the, see Organization of the Islamic Cf.

island developing countries, 170, **170-71** (Colonial Countries Ct./GA); regional technical mtgs., 679; sustainable development of, cf. on, 679, **679-80** (SG/GA); see also country names

Island Developing Countries and Donor Countries and Organizations, 1990 Governmental Experts Mtg. of: report, **155**, **157**, **172** (GA)

Island Developing States, Global Cf. (1994) on the Sustainable Development of Small, 197, 199 (DPI/JUNIC); pre-Cf. consultation, 679, **680**; Preparatory Ct., 679, **680** (GA), 1353 (members/officers); see also Pacific Island Developing Countries, Spec. Body on

Island States, Alliance of Small, 679

Israel: & GA credentials, 212-13; & nuclear armament, 122, **122** (SG/GA); see also Iraq; Lebanon situation; Middle East peace process; Palestine question; Syrian Arab Republic; territories occupied by Israel

Israeli Practices Affecting the Human Rights of the Palestinian People and Other Arabs of the Occupied Territories, Spec. Ct. to Investigate, see Territories, Spec. Ct. to Investigate Israeli Practices Affecting the Human Rights of the Palestinian People and Other Arabs of the Occupied (Ct. on Israeli practices)

Israel-Syria Mixed Armistice Cs.: & UNTSO/UNDOF, 549

Jamaica: communications project, 195 (IPDC); education loan, 1271-72 (World Bank)

Japan: economic trends, 610

Jerusalem, status of, see under Palestine question

Joint Inspection Unit (JIU), 1189-90, **1190-91** (GA); members/officers, 1352; remuneration for, 1226 (SG/GA); see also subject entries

Joint Staff Pension Board, UN, see Pension Board, UN Joint Staff

Jordan & Palestine refugees (UNRWA): education, 569-70; health services, 570-71; refugee camp, total registered in, 568; see also Middle East peace process; Palestine refugees: assistance to

journalists/broadcasters: & Middle East, 532 (DPI); science & technology referral services, 800; training programme, 198 (DPI)

judicial system, independence of: Basic Principles, **1010** (ESC); see also human rights

jute/jute products, 692 (UNDP)

juveniles: & crime, 1006 (SG); see also Child, Convention on the Rights of the; youth

Kampuchea, Party of Democratic, 361; see also Cambodia situation

Kampuchea, People's Revolutionary Party of, renamed, 361; see also Cambodia situation

Kazakhstan: admission to ILO, 1250; to ITU, 1299; to WMO, 1303; press freedom, UNESCO mission, 196; see also strategic arms treaties

Kenya: humanitarian relief efforts, 58-59 (SG), 723; refugee situation, 59 (SG)

Kiribati: solar power project, 592

Korea, Democratic People's Republic of (DPRK): economic trends, 610

Korea, Republic of: economic trends, 610; 1983 air incident, 1292 (ICAO); satellite communications workshop (1994), 185 (UN Programme); water supply loan, 1273 (World Bank)

Korean question, 355-60

Armistice Agreement (1953), violations, 355-56

Denuclearization, North-South Joint Declaration on, 357 (SC)

exercise "Team Spirit", resumption, 356, 357

IAEA safeguards, DPRK non-compliance, 110, 355, 356-60 (communications, 357-58; IAEA, 356-57, 359-60; SC 357, **358**, 359; GA, 360)

Non-Proliferation Treaty (1968), DPRK withdrawal, 109, 356, 357 (SC), 358, **358**, 359 (SC); suspension of withdrawal, 359

UN Command: Military Armistice Cs., composition/Joint Duty Office, 355; Neutral Nations Supervisory Cs., composition/duties, 355; report, 355-56

war remains, return of, 356

Kuwait: refugees in, 571 (UNRWA); see also Iraq-Kuwait situation

KwaZulu, 229, 230, 236; & South Africa political violence, 232

Kyrgyzstan: admission to FAO, 1255; to ICAO, 1292; to IFAD, 1318; to IFC, 1277; to UNIDO, 1321; to UPU, 1296; non-project credit, 1284 (IDA)

labour, 1250-53; conventions, denunciation/in force/ratifications, 1250; educational activities, 1252-54 (ILO); freedom of association, violations, 1251; international standards, 1250-51; mtgs., 1250; see also apartheid; employment; industry; International Labour Organisation (ILO); technical/vocational training; trade unions; working conditions

Labour in a Changing World Economy, Forum on, 1252

Labour Policy Development, International Leadership Course on Active, 1252-53

Labour Statisticians, 15th International Cf. of, 1114, 1250

Labour Studies, International Institute for (ILO), 1252-53

Lagos Plan of Action, see Monrovia Strategy for the Economic Development of Africa, 1980 Lagos Plan of Action

Land-locked and Transit Developing Countries and Representatives of Donor Countries and Financial and Development Institutions, Mtg. of Governmental Experts from, 680-81, **681** (TDB/GA)

land-locked developing countries, 680-81, **681-82**, 682 (SG/TDB/GA); in Central Asia, 613, **614** (Governmental Experts Mtg./GA); symposium (1994), **682** (GA)

Land-locked Developing Countries, Spec. Body on Least Developed and: lst sess., 613

land management, 846 (UNCHS), 1256 (FAO)

Lao People's Democratic Republic: asylum-seekers, repatriation, 1085; economic trends, 611; telecommunications, 1300 (ITU); see also under Mekong River Basin Ct.

Latin America: crop improvement, 1246 (IAEA); foreign investment flows, **774** (GA); mineral exploration, training, 782; see also Latin America and the Caribbean, Economic Cs. for; and country names and subject entries

Latin America, Agency for the Prohibition of Nuclear Weapons in (OPANAL), General Cf., 13th sess., **119** (GA)

Latin America, 2nd Annual Mtg. of Ministers for Housing and Urban Development in, 640, 843 (UNCHS)

Latin America and the Caribbean, 635-44 (ECLAC), 693 (UNDP), 1279-80 (IFC); de-

Index of resolutions and decisions

Numbers in italics indicate that the text is summarized rather than reprinted in full. (For dates of sessions, refer to Appendix III.)

How to obtain volumes of the *Yearbook*

The 1985 to 1988 and 1991 to 1993 volumes of the *Yearbook of the United Nations* are sold and distributed in the United States, Canada and Mexico by Kluwer Academic Publishers, 101 Philip Drive, Norwell, Massachusetts 02061; in all other countries by Kluwer Academic Publishers Group, P.O. Box 322, 3300 AH Dordrecht, Netherlands.

Other recent volumes of the *Yearbook* may be obtained in many bookstores throughout the world and also from United Nations Publications, Sales Section, Room DC2-853, United Nations, New York, N.Y. 10017, or from United Nations Publications, Palais des Nations, Office C-115, 1211 Geneva 10, Switzerland.

Older editions are available in microfiche.

Yearbook of the United Nations, 1992 Vol. 46. Sales No. E.93.I.1 $150.	**Yearbook of the United Nations, 1984** Vol. 38. Sales No. E.87.I.1 $90.
Yearbook of the United Nations, 1991 Vol. 45. Sales No. E.92.I.1 $115.	**Yearbook of the United Nations, 1983** Vol. 37. Sales No. E.86.I.1 $85.
Yearbook of the United Nations, 1988 Vol. 42. Sales No. E.93.I.100 $150.	**Yearbook of the United Nations, 1982** Vol. 36. Sales No. E.85.I.1 $75.
Yearbook of the United Nations, 1987 Vol. 41. Sales No. E.91.I.1 $105.	**Yearbook of the United Nations, 1981** Vol. 35. Sales No. E.84.I.1 $75.
Yearbook of the United Nations, 1986 Vol. 40. Sales No. E.90.I.1 $95.	**Yearbook of the United Nations, 1980** Vol. 34. Sales No. E.83.I.1 $72.
Yearbook of the United Nations, 1985 Vol. 39. Sales No. E.88.I.1 $95.	**Yearbook of the United Nations, 1979** Vol. 33. Sales No. E.82.I.1 $72.

The Yearbook *in microfiche*

Yearbook Volumes 1-41 (1946-1987) are now available in microfiche. Individual volumes are also available, and prices can be obtained by contacting the following: United Nations Publications, Sales Section, Room DC2-853, United Nations, New York, N.Y. 10017, or United Nations Publications, Palais des Nations, Office C-115, 1211 Geneva 10, Switzerland.

NOTES

NOTES

NOTES

NOTES

NOTES

NOTES

NOTES

NOTES

NOTES

NOTES

NOTES

NOTES